Guide to the Literature of Art History 2

Guide to the Literature of Art History 2

Max Marmor
Alex Ross

AMERICAN LIBRARY ASSOCIATION
Chicago
2005

While extensive effort has gone into ensuring the reliability of information appearing in this book, the publisher makes no warranty, express or implied, on the accuracy or reliability of the information, and does not assume and hereby disclaims any liability to any person for any loss or damage caused by errors or omissions in this publication.

The paper used in this publication meets the minimum requirements of American National Standard for Information Sciences—Permanence of Paper for Printed Library Materials, ANSI Z39.48-1992. ∞

Library of Congress Cataloging-in-Publication Data
Marmor, Max
Guide to the literature of art history 2 / Max Marmor, Alex Ross.
p. cm.
Continues Guide to the literature of art history.
Includes index.
ISBN 0-8389-0878-0
1. Art—Historiography—Bibliography. I. Ross, Alex. II. Title: Guide to the literature of art history. III. Title.
Z5931.M374 2004
[N380]
016.7'09—dc22 2004016170

Printed in the United States of America

09 08 07 06 05 5 4 3 2 1

Contents

Preface

This bibliography supplements the greatest of modern art bibliographies, Etta Arntzen and Robert Rainwater's *Guide to the Literature of Art History* (ALA, 1980). Much as Arntzen and Rainwater's effort represented a twenty-year update of Mary Chamberlin's venerable *Guide to Art Reference Books* (ALA, 1959), so our own brings what we have come to call GLAH 1 up-to-date after twenty years.

Since 1977 (GLAH 1's cutoff date) the literature of art has flourished remarkably. An anecdote underscores the contrast: halfway through work on this book, the director of a distinguished university library, about to deliver a paper on the demise of the scholarly monograph, expressed surprise that we were engaged on a major annotated reference bibliography, and still more that the literature of art *warranted* this expansive effort. We hope the reader will agree that it did and does.

Unlike GLAH 1, GLAH 2 did not begin as an effort to revise a standard work; it has been conceived as a supplement from the beginning. The only GLAH 1 titles repeated here have been notably reprinted, undergone some significant revision (new edition, English translation, etc.), or, in the case of monographic series and sets, evolved since 1977 through the appearance of new volumes, new series, or title changes. A handful of important titles published prior to 1977 and omitted from GLAH 1, the importance of which has only become clear recently, has been included.

Like GLAH 1, GLAH 2 "is addressed primarily"—in Arntzen's words—"to persons doing serious subject research in the field of art history. It is intended for graduate students laying the groundwork for research efforts and for art historians, in particular those who seek background and specific information outside their areas of specialization. It will also be valuable to librarians who are concerned with the acquisition and use of art literature." Like Arntzen and Rainwater, we have "kept in mind … collectors, scholars in the related humanistic disciplines, bibliographers, writers, editors, booksellers and reprint publishers." Also like them, and indeed to a perhaps greater degree, we have sought to represent the literature of art in its international scope, while still focusing upon our primary Anglophone audience.

The organization adheres strictly to that of GLAH 1, facilitating consultation of the two volumes in tandem as well as cross-references. Like GLAH 1, GLAH 2 omits monographs on individual artists, and with a better conscience since the appearance of Wolfgang Freitag's standard *Art Books* (2nd ed., Garland, 1997). Most titles, though by no means all, are again in Western European languages, even in the sections on "non-western" art, on the assumption that the bibliographies listed here will lead the student to vernacular literature on these subjects. Meanwhile, we have consciously expanded those sections in response to the growing diversification of the literature of art and art historical practice. In response to the same disciplinary evolution, we have added two new chapters not present in GLAH 1. One is on Patronage and Collecting (Chapter S); another, on Cultural Heritage (Chapter T), treats in some depth art conservation and preservation as well as relevant ethical and legal issues in the domain of cultural property. Chapter J (Architecture) now includes a much fuller treatment of landscape architecture.

Once again, the selection of titles reflects a critical examination of virtually all the literature of art history published since 1977. If this volume's gestation period was half that of GLAH 1, this may be attributed to the fact that it is very much the product of the team of scholar/librarians who produced it. The choices embodied in the selection of titles reflect the backgrounds, experience, and expertise of these colleagues as art librarians who have, collectively, devoted hundreds of years to helping art historians, students, and other readers explore the literature of art—and many of whom are themselves art historians of no small accomplishment.

Our technical cutoff date is 1998, though numerous key works published since have been included as well; the temptation to examine the new book shelf in the latter stages of the project was difficult to resist!

A final note: GLAH 2 embodies the efforts of our contributors. But in the interest of coherence, consistency, uniformity of format, style, and even "voice," the editors have reshaped the work of the entire team in subtle and less subtle ways. Final responsibility for the authority and reliability of *Guide to the Literature of Art History* rests with them alone; final credit is due to our contributors.

MAX MARMOR
ALEX ROSS

Acknowledgments

We are most grateful to Etta Arntzen and Robert Rainwater, matchless editors of volume 1 of this *Guide* (GLAH 1, as we call it throughout this volume), for graciously blessing this enterprise; we hope GLAH 2 meets their expectations.

This bibliography might never have seen the light of day without the financial support at a critical juncture of the Samuel H. Kress Foundation, which unblinkingly intervened to support the final production stages of our work (final edits, sgml conversion, indexing). Max Marmor is also indebted to the Yale University Library for a three-month research leave early on. Both editors are indebted to their colleagues at Yale, Stanford, and, most recently in Marmor's case the Andrew W. Mellon Foundation, for bearing with them during several years of work on this project, and still more for picking up the inevitable slack in their daily performance as librarians and library administrators.

GLAH 2 was a bi-coastal editorial enterprise, spanning Palo Alto and New Haven. But the book itself is also national in scope, being the product of twenty-four art librarians from all across America. The names of these contributors are listed elsewhere in this book, but we wish to acknowledge them—their efforts, generosity, and patience—here: Mary Clare Altenhofen (Harvard), David Austin (U. Illinois), Peter Blank (Art Institute of Chicago), Amanda Bowen (Harvard), Christine Bunting (U.C. Santa Cruz), Elizabeth Byrne (U.C. Berkeley), Kate Chipman (formerly Columbia), Russ Clement (Northwestern), Susan Craig (University of Kansas), Ross Day (Goldwater Library, Metropolitan Museum of Art), Alexandra de Luise (Queens College, CUNY), Paula Gabbard (Columbia), Laura Gutierrez-Witt (U. Texas, Austin), Clare Hills-Nova (NYU), B. J. Irvine (Indiana U.), Katie Keller (Stanford), Sheila Klos (Dumbarton Oaks), Tom McNulty (NYU), Julie Mellby (Toledo Museum of Art), Lee Robinson (New York Public Library), Kathleen Salomon (Getty Research Institute), Eleanor Thompson (Winterthur). We also wish to acknowledge those colleagues who were initially part of the GLAH 2 team, but had, for reasons personal or professional, to withdraw from the project: Wolfgang Freitag (formerly Harvard), Katherine Haskins (Yale), Susan Moon (UC Santa Barbara), Minoti Pakrasi (Stanford), Doralynn Pines (Metropolitan Museum of Art), Barbara Polowy (Smith), Jack Robertson (Monticello). Thanks to all.

Thanks are also due the several distinguished art historians and art librarians—too many to list individually here—who reviewed various sections of the book or functioned more informally as consultants. They will recognize their contributions throughout, as will the many colleagues who facilitated access to their collections, sometimes even looking up crucial bibliographic data for us on inexcusably short notice, at the eleventh hour.

The GLAH 2 project has throughout been an experiment in the application of new technologies to the production of what is, finally, a quite traditional reference book. We had a project website from the outset, as well as a "listserv" for the team, though it was used mostly for editorial pronouncements (often ex cathedra) from the editors. What we did not anticipate going in was that our eventual typesetter would not only accept but positively prefer the use of sgml (standard generalized markup language) as a production format. Happily, as noted above, the Kress Foundation stepped forward with financial support permitting the editors to incorporate conversion to sgml as a key element in the final editing of the book. Here, too, we have debts of gratitude to repay with words. Doug Black, of West Rock Visions in New Haven, was patience itself in working with Max Marmor to devise a project-specific "document type definition" (glah.dtd) for the book (compliant with standards of the Text Encoding Initiative or TEI), in creating a conversion script, in overseeing (well beyond the call of contractual duty) the hand-markup of the individual chapters, and in pioneering the use of xml cascading style sheets to test formatting and design options. The manual markup itself was performed by the dynamic duo of Barbara Rockenbach and Kirsten Jensen, then colleagues at Yale.

Our editors and friends at ALA Editions (Art Plotnik, initially our project editor, succeeded by Marlene Chamberlain, and Troy Linker and Dianne Rooney) have been helpful and patient partners throughout. The book benefited immensely from the excellent text editing of ALA's Mary Huchting and Ellie Barta-Moran.

We would like to express our gratitude—and apologies—to the Art Libraries Society of North America. For the better part of a decade, GLAH 2 occupied much of the professional time and energy of a score of excellent art librarians who, were it not for this engagement, would surely have filled numerous essential posts in ARLIS/NA and filled its publications with significant contributions.

Finally, thanks to the friends and families of the editors and the entire GLAH 2 team. Life did not cease for any of us during our long labor on *Guide to the Literature of Art History,* volume 2. Children were born, parents passed away, the world turned.

Contributors

Mary Clare Altenhofen
Chapter C: Sales Records
Chapter I: Histories and Handbooks (Western Countries)
Chapter S: Patronage and Collecting

David Austin
Chapter K: Sculpture (General Works; Techniques; Histories and Handbooks)

Peter Blank
Chapter O: Photography

Amanda Bowen
Chapter B: Directories
Chapter M: Painting (Collections and Inventories; Painters; Techniques; Histories and Handbooks)

Christine Bunting
Chapter D: Visual Resources

Elizabeth Byrne
Chapter J: Architecture (Bibliography; Dictionaries and Encyclopedias)

Kathe Chipman
Chapter J: Architecture (Histories and Handbooks)

Russ Clement
Chapter A: Bibliography (Bibliographies of Individual Artists)
Chapter M: Painting (Western Countries, Australia-Greece)

Susan Craig
Sections throughout on Asia

Ross Day
Sections throughout on The Americas

Alexandra de Luise
Chapters Q (Periodicals) and R (Series)

Paula Gabbard
Chapter A: Bibliography (Current Serials; Retrospective; Catalogs of Art Libraries; Prehistoric; Ancient-Medieval; Renaissance-Modern)

Laura Gutierrez-Witt
Sections throughout on Latin America

Clare Hills-Nova
Chapter P: Decorative Arts (Costume; Textiles)
Chapter T: Cultural Heritage

B. J. Irvine
Sections throughout on Africa and Oceania

Katharine Keller
Chapter A: Bibliography (Western Countries)

Sheila Klos
Chapter J: Architecture (Western Countries; Landscape Design)

Max Marmor
Chapter G: Historiography, Methodology, and Theory
Chapter H: Sources and Documents
Chapter I: Histories and Handbooks (Collections and Inventories; General Works; Techniques; Prehistoric; Ancient; Celtic and Germanic; Early Christian-Byzantine; Islamic; Carolingian-Gothic; Renaissance-Baroque; Neoclassical-Modern)
Chapter L: Drawings (with Alex Ross)
Chapter N: Prints (with Alex Ross)

Tom McNulty

Chapter K: Sculpture (Western Countries) (with Lee Robinson)

Julie Mellby

Chapter M: Painting (Western Countries, Italy-United States)

Lee Robinson

Chapter K: Sculpture (Western Countries) (with Tom McNulty)

Alex Ross

Chapter E: Dictionaries and Encyclopedias
Chapter L: Drawings (with Max Marmor)
Chapter N: Prints (with Max Marmor)

Kathleen Salomon

Chapter F: Iconography

Eleanor Thompson

Chapter P: Decorative and Applied Arts (Basketry; Ornament; Furniture; Clocks and Watches; Pottery and Porcelain; Glass; Enamels; Metalwork; Medals; Gems and Jewelry; Rugs and Carpets; Tapestries; Embroidery and Needlework; Ivory and Scrimshaw; Jade; Lacquer; Wallpaper)

Guide to the Literature of Art History 2

A. Bibliography

The art bibliographies listed in this chapter are general in nature inasmuch as they include entries for more than one art medium. Those dealing exclusively with specific media, e.g., architecture, sculpture, painting, prints, photography, or the decorative arts, are listed in the appropriate chapters. The same applies to bibliographies devoted to specific subjects such as iconography.

CURRENT SERIALS

A1 Annual register of book values. The arts and architecture. [v.1, 1992–]. York, Eng., Clique, 1993– . Series ed.: Michael Cole.

Formerly known as International rare book prices. Arts & architecture, v.1–6, 1986–91. York, Eng., Picaflow, 1987–92.

"ARBV provides annual record of the pricing levels of . . . selected English language . . . out-of-print, used or antiquarian books within a number of specialty subject areas and gives likely sources and suppliers for such books in Britain and the United States of America. It is intended to be used by both the experienced book man and the newcomer to book-collecting. . . . Emphasis is placed . . . on books falling within the lower to middle range of the pricing scale of 30,000 or so separate titles recorded in the annual volumes."—*Introd.*

Citations selected from catalogs of more than 150 dealers from Great Britain and the United States are alphabetically arranged by author. A directory of dealers appears at end.

A2 Art and archaeology technical abstracts [computer file], v.1, 1955– . Santa Monica, Calif., Getty Center. Updated semiannually.

See GLAH 1:A1 for original annotation and paper ed.

Also available on 35mm microfilm: Wooster, Ohio, Bell & Howell.

Also available through a direct internet connection from the Conservation Information Network (BCIN), a joint project of the Getty Conservation Institute and the Department of Canadian Heritage, Canada. See GLAH 2:A8 for Conservation Information Network.

A3 Art book biannual, no.1, Feb. 1991–no.1, 1997. Ithaca, N.Y., Worldwide Books, 1992–1997.

Bibliography of exhibition catalogs and selected books about art compiled from Worldwide Books New Titles lists (Feb. 1991 to the present). Arranged by Worldwide Books' item numbers. Brief annotations often follow bibliographic citations.

Related title which ceased with v.23, 1987: Worldwide art catalogue bulletin (GLAH 1:A17), subsequently consolidated into a three-volume bibliography, Worldwide bibliography of art exhibition catalogues, 1963–1987 (GLAH 2:A62). Nothing currently available from Worldwide Books fills the gap between 1987 and 1991.

Indexes at end: title, artist, geographic (chronological arrangement within European art), special topic, and medium.

A4 Art index [computer file], Oct. 1984– . N.Y., Wilson, [1987–]. Art abstracts [computer file], Spring, 1994– . N.Y., Wilson, 1995– . Art full text [computer file], Jan. 1997– . N.Y., Wilson, [1997–].

See GLAH 1:A3 for original annotation and paper ed. See also GLAH 2:A17 for Art index retrospective.

Art index and Art abstracts are available both in a CD-ROM version and through the internet from various vendors. Art full text is only available through the internet.

Online version of Art index; a cumulative author and subject index to a selected list of fine arts periodicals and museum bulletins (GLAH 1:A3), begun in Sept. 1984. Art abstracts incorporates the online version of Art index, and includes abstracts beginning Spring 1994. Art full text incorporates both indexes, and includes full text of selected journals beginning Jan. 1997.

A5 Arts & humanities citation index, v.1, 1975– . Philadelphia, Institute for Scientific Information, 1976– . Issued semiannually.

Coverage from 1975 to date also available on CD-ROM and from 1988 to date through the internet from various vendors.

Indexes articles and book reviews from more than 1,000 fully indexed and 5,100 selectively indexed journals. In addition, all of the references cited and the individual works of art addressed in these articles, as well as book reviews, can be searched by cited authors (or artists).

Arrangement of paper ed.: Source Index (alphabetically arranged by authors of articles); Citation Index (alphabetically arranged by authors cited); Miscellaneous Citation Index (alphabetically arranged by corporate bodies cited); "Permuterm" Subject Index (alphabetically arranged by keywords in title or, if title does not describe the subject, by terms supplied by indexer); and Corporate Index (first, geographic with subheadings for institutions; second, directly by institution).

A6 Bibliography of the history of art: BHA. Bibliographie d'histoire de l'art, v.1, [1989–]. Santa Monica, Calif., Getty Center, 1991– . Issued quarterly with annual cumulative indexes.

English and French.

Also available as an annually updated CD-ROM, and through the internet from vendors. (See also FRANCIS at GLAH 2:A10.)

As a merger of RILA: Répertoire international de la littérature de l'art (1975–89) (GLAH 1:A15 and GLAH 2:A53) and Répertoire d'art et d'archéologie (1910–89) (GLAH 1:A14 and GLAH 2:A52), BHA is a classed, abstracted index to "books, periodical articles from more than 3,000 titles, conference proceedings, festschriften and other collected essays, exhibition catalogues, selected art dealers' catalogues, doctoral dissertations, and microform publications. [It includes] visual arts in all media, not only the traditional Fine Arts (architecture, sculpture, painting, drawing and prints) but also the decorative and applied arts including popular art, folk art, and all objects of material culture that are of interest to the art historian. BHA covers current literature of European art from late Antiquity [4th c. AD] to the present and American art from the European discoveries to the present. [It] covers art anywhere in the world that reflects contact with the Western tradition. Christian art in Asia Minor and Africa, European colonial art in India, Africa, the Far East and Australia, and non-western art insofar as it has influenced the art of Europe and the Americas are covered even though they fall outside the geographic limits of BHA."—*Introd.*

Each issue has a list of periodicals analyzed and indexes of authors and subjects. Annual cumulative indexes in English and French.

A7 Bibliography on the relations of literature and other arts. Published annually in Yearbook of comparative and general literature, v.34, 1985– .

Annual classified bibliography of current books and articles. Recent issues include author and subject indexes.

In v.32, 1983, a related bibliography appeared: Dolders, Arno, "Ut Pictura Poesis: a selective, annotated bibliography of books and articles, published between 1900 and 1980, on the interrelation of literature and painting from 1400 to 1800."

Prior to its appearance in the Yearbook, "Bibliography on the relations of literature and other arts," ed. by Stephen Sher, was separately published by the Department of German, Dartmouth College, from 1968–84.

A8 Conservation information network (BCIN) [computer file]. Hull, Quebec, CHIN-RCIP. Electronic data and programs. 1997– .

Searchable database of more than 172,000 bibliographic records on conservation and restoration of cultural property, this site also offers a forum for exchange of such information. Incorporates Art and archaeology technical abstracts, additional technical reports, conference proceedings, journal articles, books, audiovisual materials, unpublished sources, as well as sources from a worldwide network of contributors including the Canadian Conservation Institute, Smithsonian Center for Materials Research and Education, Getty Conservation Institute, International Centre for the Study of the Preservation and the Restoration of Cultural Property, International Council of Museums, and the International Council on Monuments and Sites.

A9 Dissertation topics. Published in each June issue of Art bulletin, v.63, no.2, 1981– .

Title varies.

Lists authors, titles, and directors of dissertations completed and in progress in the United States and Canada. Completed dissertations are listed first, dissertations in progress follow, both in a classified arrangement. Each year's list covers submissions from the previous year.

Prior to 1981, list appeared annually in Art journal from v.31, 1971 to v.40, 1980.

A10 FRANCIS [computer file], 1984/90– . Vandoeuvre-lès-Nancy, CNRS, INIST, 1991– .

Available on CD-ROM and through the internet from various vendors. After 1994, FRANCIS indexes appear only in computerized formats.

FRANCIS is a multilingual, multidisciplinary bibliographic database that merges 20 databases in the humanities and social sciences from 1972 to the present, including: Répertoire d'art et d'archéologie (GLAH 1:A14 and GLAH 2:A52); Bulletin signalétique. Série 525: Préhistoire (GLAH 1:A76 and GLAH 2:A85); Bulletin signalétique 526: Art et archéologie. Proche-Orient, Asie, Amérique (GLAH 1:A80 and GLAH 2:A122); and Bibliography of the history of art (GLAH 2:A6).

A11 Hochschulen und Forschungsinstitute. Published annually in Kunstchronik, Jahrg. 1, 1948– .

Lists authors, titles, and directors of German dissertations (completed and in progress) and master's theses. Also selectively lists dissertations from Austria, Switzerland, the Netherlands, Great Britain, Scandinavia, and the United States. Arranged by country, with subheadings for cities and institutions.

A12 Liste des travaux soutenus ou préparés en histoire de l'art et archéologie, 1987– . Published annually in Histoire de l'art: bulletin d'information de l'Institut national d'histoire de l'art, v.1, 1988– .

Lists authors, titles, and directors of French art history and archeology dissertations (completed and in progress) and master's theses. Each year's list covers submissions from previous year. Broadly classified arrangement.

A13 Visual resources bibliography . . . , 1984– . Published annually in Visual resources, v.3, 1986– .

Alphabetically arranged by author, this bibliography lists books and articles of interest to art historians, especially visual resource curators, archivists, or librarians. Bibliography covers items published two years prior to publication of journal.

Index at end by broad subject headings.

RETROSPECTIVE

A14 Art books, 1876–1949: including an international index of current serial publications. N.Y., Bowker, 1981. xviii, 780p.

See also the following entries: Art books, 1950–1979 and Art books, 1980–1984.

Bibliography of 21,000 books published in the United States (and a few from England and Canada), compiled from American book publishing record cumulative 1876–1949, drawn from A catalog of books represented by Library of Congress printed cards (1898–1942) and its Supplement (1942–47) and from the Library of Congress author catalog (1948–52). Entries are standard catalog records arranged by Library of Congress subject headings and followed by author and title indexes. The book sections are followed by an alphabetical subject arrangement of a selection, international in scope, of about 3,000 current art serials.

Title index to the serials is at end.

A15 Art books, 1950–1979: including an international index of current serial publications. N.Y., Bowker, 1979. li, 1500p.

Bibliography of 37,000 books (primarily published in the United States), arranged by Library of Congress subject headings (p.1–1134), and followed by author (p.1135–86) and title (p.1187–1282) indexes.

Includes a geographic guide to museums (p.1347–1446), a guide to museum permanent collection catalogs (p.1447–75), and a publishers and distributors directory (p.1476–1500).

See also adjacent entries for Art books, 1876–1949 and Art books, 1980–1984.

A16 Art books, 1980–1984: including an international index of current serial publications. N.Y., Bowker, 1985. xx, 571p.

Bibliography of approximately 9,600 books (primarily published in the United States), arranged by Library of Congress subject headings (p.1–400). Citations drawn from Bowker's American book publishing record cumulative 1980–1984. Author (p.401–16) and title (p.417–46) indexes follow.

The next section is an international list of about 3,000 serials. A bibliography of active serials arranged by subject (p.447–524) is followed by a list of serials that have ceased (p.525–32) and a title index (p.533–50) to both current and ceased serials. At the end is a publishers' and distributors' directory (551–71), with U.S. addresses.

See also adjacent entries for Art books, 1876–1949, and Art books, 1950–1979.

A17 Art index retrospective [computer file]. N.Y., Wilson, 1998–2000.

See GLAH 1:A3 for original annotation and paper ed. (called Art index). See also GLAH 2:A4 for computer database eds. of Art index, Art abstracts, and Art full text.

Available on CD-ROM and through the internet from various vendors.

Retrospective online conversion of Art index providing author and subject indexing from 420 art periodicals published between 1924 and 1984.

A18 Art Institute of Chicago. Ryerson Library. Index to art periodicals [microform]. N.Y., Hall, [1962]. 22 microfilm reels.

See GLAH 1:A19 for original annotation, paper ed., and supplement.

——— [microform]. 1st supplement. N.Y., Hall, [1975]. 1 microfilm reel.

A19 Art Libraries Society. ARLIS union list of microforms on art, design & related subjects. Comp. by Chris Nichols. [England], [ARLIS/UK and Eire], 1988. 40p.

Now updated and available through the internet with the same title. Ed. by Douglas Dodds and Aileen Cook. A union list of microform sets held in 56 U.K. and Irish libraries. Microforms of single works, whether monographs or serials, are not included unless the works were only published in micro format. The initial list was compiled from the catalogs of the various microform publishers and formed the basis of a survey sent to libraries. The survey, forming the basis of this union list, indicates which (if any) libraries own each cited item. Each entry gives a full bibliographic citation along with the cost of the set.

The union list is followed by a directory of microform publishers, a directory of contributing libraries, and a general subject index.

A20 Art Libraries Society. ARLIS union list of periodicals on art, design & related subjects [microform]. 3d ed. [Manchester, England], Art Libraries Society, 1984. 2 microfiches + guide (8p.)

Ed. by John Kirby. 1st ed., A union list of periodicals on art and related subject fields, comp. by Graham R. Bullock, 1978; 2d ed., ARLIS union list of periodicals on art design & related subjects [microform], ed. by John Kirby, 1982.

Union list of 83 U.K. libraries' holdings of periodicals. Editor warns that information on holdings may be incomplete. The accompanying paper guide offers a list of participating libraries and their addresses.

A21 Art Libraries Society of North America. Historical bibliography of art museum serials from the United States and Canada. Ed. by Sheila M. Klos and Christine M. Smith. Tucson, Ariz., Art Libraries Society of North America, 1987. 58p. (Occasional papers, no.5)

Provides "a reference source for the bibliographic verification of art museum serials titles, including their exact publishing history. [It includes] periodicals published by public museums and galleries primarily devoted to art which maintain permanent collections."—*Introd.*

Citations are arranged alphabetically by name of museum or gallery followed by appendix of institutions that have apparently never published serials within the scope of this project. Serials title index at the end excludes such generic titles as Annual, Annual Bulletin, Annual Report, Bulletin, Calendar, Calendar of Events, Journal, Newsletter, Quarterly, Quarterly Bulletin.

A22 ______. Central Plains Chapter. Central Plains union list of serial exhibition catalogs: a project of the Central Plains Chapter, Art Libraries Society of North America. Coordinated by Marianne L. Cavanaugh. St. Louis, [The Chapter], 1994. xi, 141p.

Now available through the internet with the same title. Ed. by Marianne L. Cavanaugh. A union list of exhibition catalogs, produced in numbered series and held in 17 libraries located in the Central Plains area of the United States (Arkansas, Kansas, Missouri, Nebraska, and Oklahoma). All the catalogs represent exhibits held in this same geographic area. The list is preceded by a directory of participating libraries. Corporate author/title index at end.

A23 Art serials in Edinburgh libraries: a union list. 2d ed. Edinburgh, National Library of Scotland, 1987. vii, 215p.

1st ed., Union list of art periodicals in Edinburgh libraries, 1979.

Union list of approximately 3,600 serials held at 15 libraries in Edinburgh. In addition to serials, monographic series have been included. The list is preceded by a directory of participating libraries.

A24 Art serials: union list of art periodicals and serials in research libraries in the Washington DC metropolitan area. Ed. by Carolyn S. Larson. Washington, D.C., Washington Art Library Resources Committee, 1981. xxxiii, 161p.

Includes approximately 5,300 periodical titles and holdings (to Aug. 1, 1980) of 34 libraries in 19 institutions in the Washington, D.C. area. The alphabetically arranged list is preceded by a directory of participating libraries with their addresses, phone numbers, hours, directors' names, interlibrary loan policies, and subject specialties.

A25 Baxter, Paula. International bibliography of art librarianship: an annotated compilation. München, Saur, 1987. v, 94p. (IFLA publications, 37)

Classified bibliography covering English-language books and articles on all matters of concern to art librarians published between 1908 and 1986.

Author index, p.91–94.

A26 Bibliographie bildende Kunst: deutschsprachige Hochschulschriften und Veröffentlichungen ausserhalb des Buchhandels, 1966–1980 = Bibliography of the fine arts: bibliography of German-language university dissertations and publications outside the book trade, 1966–1980. München, Saur, 1992. 6v.

Lists nearly 30,000 works, arranged alphabetically by title, of "grey literature" on the fine arts from German-speaking countries. "Grey literature" includes dissertations and theses and publications of institutes as well as privately printed or privately financed publications in German-speaking countries. These titles were compiled from "Deutsche Bibliographie, Deutsche Nationalbibliographie, Österreichische Bibliographie, Das Schweizer Buch, . . . directories of university papers in German-speaking countries, . . . Deutsche Forschungsberichte, as well as special directories of university papers written in German but in non-German-speaking countries."—*Introd.*

A27 Bibliography of museum and art gallery publications and audio-visual aids in Great Britain and Ireland. Somerset House, Teaneck, 1978–1980. 2v. V.1, (1977), comp. by Jean Lambert; v.2, (1978/79), comp. by Michael Roulstone.

Arranged alphabetically by institution, this work lists materials published and distributed by 811 museums, art galleries, and related institutions in Great Britain and Ireland.

Author, title, and subject indexes at end of each volume.

A28 Böllmann, Elisabeth. Verzeichnis von Ausstellungskatalogen in den Beständen der Universitätsbibliothek Graz. Graz, Die Universitätsbibliothek, 1986. 191p. (Bibliographische Information, 41)

List of approximately 1,700 exhibition catalogs (primarily art) held in the library at the University of Graz. Arranged alphabetically by title.

Indexes: keyword, p.117–57; geographic by place of exhibition, p.158–91.

A29 Bonafede, Cecilie Wiborg. Kunstvitenskap: veiledning til referanselitteratur i Universitetsbiblioteket i Oslo, Fagseksjon for kunsthistorie, Universitetet i Oslo, biblioteket, og Nasjonalgalleriets bibliotek. Oslo, [Universitetsbiblioteket], 1991. 180p. (UBO veiledninger, 17)

Annotated classified bibliography of reference sources in art, aesthetics, iconography, architecture, decorative arts, and conservation.

Index of authors, editors, and corporate bodies, p.169–80.

A30 Burt, Eugene C. Erotic art: an annotated bibliography with essays. Boston, Hall, 1989. xix, 396p.

"A major goal of this bibliography has been to provide comprehensive coverage of the subject," resulting in a decision to include publications from the popular press when they contribute significantly to "an understanding of the history of erotic art."—*Introd.*

Contents: (1) General background; (2) General surveys; (3) The ancient world; (4) Asia; (5) Ethno-art—Africa, Oceania, and the Native Americas; (6) The western world (to the end of the 19th century); (7) The modern world.

Author index, p.377–96.

A31 Cataloghi di collezioni d'arte nelle biblioteche fiorentine (1840–1940). A cura di Giovanna De Lorenzi. Pisa, Scuola Normale Superiore, 1988. xxiv, 692p.

(Quaderni del Seminario di Storia della Critica D'Arte, 3)
Union catalog of private collection and public auction catalogs of single European art collections published between 1840 and 1940. Arranged by art collector, if known, and if not, by place of sale. The ten contributing libraries: Biblioteca Marucelliana; Biblioteca Nazionale di Firenze; Biblioteca degli Uffizi; Fondazione Berenson; Fondazione Longhi; Istituto Nazionale di Studi sul Rinascimento; Kunsthistorisches Institut in Florenz; Istituto Olandese Universitario di Storia dell'Arte; Museo Nazionale del Bargello; Museo Stibbert.

Indexes: Authors, Art collectors, and a concordance between this work and F. Lugt, Répertoire des catalogues de ventes publiques intéressant d'art ou la curiosité (GLAH 1:C17).

A32 Catalogo collettivo dei periodici di archeologia e storia dell'arte: Biblioteca dell'istituto nazionale di archeologia e storia dell'arte, Bibliotheca Hertziana, Deutsches Archäologisches Institut, École Française. [A cura di Rosalba Grosso e Antonella Aquilina.] Roma, Biblioteca di archeologia e storia dell'arte, 1992. xv, 198p.
Alphabetically arranged union list of 6,748 periodical titles held in four major Italian art and archeology libraries (Biblioteca dell'Istituto Nazionale di Archeologia e Storia dell'Arte, Bibliotheca Hertziana, Deutsches Archäologisches Institut, and École Française). Lists holdings of each periodical in the four libraries.

A33 Catalogue collectif des periodiques des écoles d'art. Paris, L'École Nationale Superieure des Beaux-Arts, Mars, 1984. 8 leaves of introductory matter, 72 leaves.
Modeled on the Bibliothèque Nationale's Catalogue collectif des périodiques du début du 17ème s. à 1939, Paris, Bibliothèque Nationale, 1977–82, 5v., this catalog lists art periodicals in 37 national, regional, and municipal schools of art in France. Main section is alphabetically arranged by periodical title listing ranges of years held at each institution. Introduction includes a list of contributing institutions with addresses, telephone numbers, and directors current as of Jan. 1983.

A34 Cicognara, Leopoldo, conte. Catalogo ragionato dei libri d'arte e d'antichità posseduti dal conte Cicognara. [Reprint.] Bologna, Forni, 1987. 2v.
Reprint of GLAH 1:A28. A new ed. with scholarly apparatus is included as part of the full-text microfiche version of Cicognara's library (the Fondo Cicognara, Vatican Library). See Cicognara library: literary sources in the history of art and kindred subjects (Urbana, Ill., published by the Leopoldo Cicognara Program at the Univ. of Illinois Library in assoc. with the Vatican Library, 1989–). Includes titles not listed in the original ed. but present in the Fondo Cicognara.

A35 Collins, Judith. Bibliography of Arts Council exhibition catalogues, 1942–1980. London, Arts Council of Great Britain, 1982. 83p.
Includes every exhibition catalog published by the Arts Council of Great Britain from 1942 through Dec. 1980. Arranged by year of publication, and within each year, alphabetically by title.

Index of authors, p.70–73. Index of titles, p.74–83.

A36 The Concordia University art index to nineteenth century Canadian periodicals. Ed. by George Hardy. [Montreal], Concordia Univ., 1981. xiii, 304p.
Alphabetically arranged unannotated author and subject index to articles about the visual arts published in 31 Canadian periodicals. Subject coverage is not restricted to 19th century nor to Canadian art. The bulk of the periodicals indexed were published between 1830 and 1900, but there is sporadic coverage from the final years of the eighteenth century.

The index is preceded by an annotated alphabetical list of the periodicals indexed (p.vii–xiii). These annotations can include the periodical's founder, owner, publisher, editor, publication history, subjects covered, and point of view.

A37 Courtauld Institute of Art, London University. The Courtauld Institute of Art periodicals index [microform]. Bath, England, Mindata, 1989. 277 microfiches.
Classified abstracted index to nearly 200 art periodicals. Begun in the 1930s and maintained by the staff of the Courtauld Institute until 1983.

Author index at end, fiche 208–77.

A38 Ehresmann, Donald L. Fine arts: a bibliographic guide to basic reference works, histories, and handbooks. 3d ed. Englewood, Colo., Libraries Unlimited, 1990. xvii, 373p.
See GLAH 1:A35 for 1st ed., 1975; 2d ed., 1979.

"For the third edition of Fine Arts [which has 2,051 entries], books published in the decade since the appearance of the second edition have been surveyed, and 258 titles have been added. The literature published before September 1, 1978 (cut-off date for the second edition) has been reviewed afresh with the result that 72 titles have been added. . . . To increase the usefulness of the bibliography a new chapter—chapter 7—on the historiography of art history has been added."—*Pref.*

Companion volume to the author's Applied and decorative arts: a bibliographic guide to basic reference works, histories, and handbooks (1993) (GLAH 2:P6), and his Architecture: A bibliographic guide to basic reference works, histories, and handbooks (1984) (GLAH 2:J17).

Author/title index, p.313–53. Subject index, p.355–73.

A39 Freitag, Wolfgang M. Art books: a basic bibliography of monographs on artists. 2d ed. N.Y., Garland, 1997. xxvi, 542p. (Garland reference library of the humanities, v.1264)
1st ed. 1985. Bibliography of "monographs and works of a monographic character on 1,870 artists from all historical periods and from all countries."—*Introd.*

Almost 14,000 titles cover artists in painting, drawing, sculpture, architecture, graphic arts, photography, and decorative and applied arts. Most artists listed are Western European or North American. Titles include treatises, published dissertations, biographies, catalogues raisonnés, bibliographies, artists' writings of a biographical or theoretical nature, and some published artists' letters. Essays on a single artist within periodicals or collections (e.g., festschriften, yearbooks, and general museum catalogs) are not included. Catalogues raisonnés are marked with the abbreviation (CR).

"Selection of biographical dictionaries and other reference works containing information on artists," p.xix–xxvi. Author index, p.461–542.

A40 Frick Art Reference Library. Original index to art periodicals. Boston, Hall, 1983. 12v.

Also available in a microfilm ed., 12 reels. Boston, Hall, 1983.

Alphabetically arranged index to 27 art periodicals published in the United States and Europe from the mid-19th century to 1959. Citations are listed by author and artist or subject.

A41 Index to nineteenth-century American art periodicals. Ed. by Mary M. Schmidt. Madison, Conn., Sound View, 1999. 2v.

Also available through the internet. Author, title, and subject indexing of 42 art periodicals published in the United States between 1840 and 1907. Articles, poems, illustrations, notes, stories, and even advertisements are indexed.

A42 Jones, Lois Swan. Art information and the internet: how to find it, how to use it. Phoenix, Oryx, 1998. xv, 279p.

Both an abbreviated update of the author's Art information (see following title) and a guide to a large number of internet sites of use to art historians. Jones offers a methodological approach to finding, evaluating, and using these internet resources.

Contents: Pt.1. Basic information formats: (I) Electronic data and the internet; (II) Other information formats and their publishers' web sites; Pt.2. Types of web sites and how to find them: (III) Web sites of museums; (IV) Web sites of academic institutions, corporate sponsors, and individuals; (V) Cultural, civic, and professional organizations; national trusts; and foundations; (VI) Web presence of libraries: overviews, search strategies, and services; (VII) Web sites of serials and indexes to art and literature; (VIII) Buying and selling art; Pt.3. How to use and supplement web information; (IX) Basic research methodology: finding and supplementing web data; (X) Art historical styles and periods; (XI) Documenting the lives of artists and art collectors; (XII) Studying works of art; (XIII) Resources for architecture, decorative arts, fashion, graphic arts, photography, and sculpture; (XIV) North American (U.S.), Canadian, and Native American studies; (XV) Non-European cultures; (XVI) Additional art information; Appendix One: Artists' past competitive exhibitions; Appendix Two: Professional associations: web sites and journals.

Index, p.247–79.

A43 ———. Art information: research methods and resources. 3d ed. Dubuque, Kendall/Hunt, 1990. xxiv, 373p.

See GLAH 1:A41 for 1st ed., 1978; 2d ed., Art research: methods and resources: a guide to finding art information, 1984.

Numerous bibliographic citations, many of them annotated. The first two sections make up the body of the work: Section A focuses on research methodology, and Section B is a systematically arranged bibliography. New to this ed. are a chapter on database searches and citations to 275 serials within appropriate subject areas.

Contents: Sec.A: Methodology: Pt.1. Before research begins: (1) Planning a research project; (2) Utilizing the library; Pt.2. Basic research methodology: (3) Tools for compiling bibliographies and chronologies; (4) Database searches; Pt.3. Methodology beyond the basics: (5) Specialized art research resources; (6) Research on individual works of art; (7) Subjects and symbols: methodology and literature; (8) Research on people: special reference tools; (9) Architectural research. Sec.B: A bibliography of research sources: Pt.4. General art research tools: (10) Art encyclopedias and dictionaries; (11) Artistic styles, periods, and cultures: prehistoric through gothic; (12) Artistic styles, and historic periods: renaissance to contemporary; (13) North American studies; (14) Other geographic locations; (15) Museum collection and exhibition information; (16) Indexing and abstracting resources and databases; (17) Bibliographies for art research; (18) Sales information; (19) Visual resources and subject indexing projects; (20) Other resources; Pt.5. Specialized resources for various media and disciplines: (21) Architecture; (22) Prints and the art of the book; (23) Photography; (24) Decorative arts and crafts; (25) Fashion, costumes, and jewelry; (26) Film and video; (27) Commercial design; (28) Museum studies and art/museum education; Pt.6. Iconographic resources: (29) References on subjects and symbols in art. Sec.C: Research centers: (30) North American and European art research centers. Appendixes: (A)-(D) English-foreign language dictionaries; (E) Terminology; (F) Databases; their primary subjects, and vendors.

Index to publications, subjects, and professions, p.337–73.

A44 Kleinbauer, W. Eugene, and Slavens, Thomas P. Research guide to the history of Western art. Chicago, ALA, 1982. x, 229p. (Sources of information in the humanities, no.2)

Designed to assist the researcher in the use of resources in art history. "Each volume [in the series] is divided into two parts. The first features a survey of the field . . . , and the second is an annotated list of major reference works."—*Pref.*

Contents: Pt.I. The field of art history: (1) Art history and its related disciplines; (2) Determinants of writing art history; (3) Studying the art object; (4) Perspectives on change; (5) Psychological approaches; (6) Art and society; Pt.II. Reference works: General works; Ancient; Byzantine and medieval; Renaissance and baroque; Modern; United States and Canadian art.

Author/title index, p.193–219. Subject index, p.221–29.

A45 Lincoln, Betty Woelk. Festschriften in art history, 1960–1975: bibliography and index. N.Y., Garland, 1988. xiv, 220p. (Garland reference library of the humanities, v.745)

Fills the gap between Paul Rave's Kunstgeschichte in Festschriften (GLAH 1:A48) and the indexing of festschriften offered first by RILA: Répertoire international de la littérature de l'art (1975–89) (GLAH 1:A15), and subsequently by Bibliography of the history of art (GLAH 2:A6). Includes "a bibliography and an analytical index of festschriften in art history and related fields in the humanities and social sciences . . . [covering subjects that range] from the beginning of the Christian era to the present."—*Pref.*

The main bibliography of 344 entries is alphabetically arranged by name of person or institution honored.

Subject index, p.107–96. Author index, p.199–216. Index of dedicatees, p.219–20.

A46 London. Victoria and Albert Museum. The Victoria and Albert Museum: a bibliography and exhibition chronology, 1852–1996. Comp. by Elizabeth James. London, Fitzroy Dearborn, 1998. xxvii, 804p.

This unannotated bibliography was published as part of the celebration of the Victoria and Albert Museum's 150th anniversary. Chronologically arranged within four sections: monographic publications, periodicals (some of which include tables of contents), related publications, and exhibition catalogs.

Name index, p.615–85. Title index, p.687–741. Series index, p.743–54. Subject index, p.755–804.

A47 Musée d'Art et d'Histoire de Genève. Bibliothèque d'Art et d'Archéologie. Répertoire des périodiques de la Bibliothèque d'Art et d'Archéologie du Musée d'Art et d'Histoire de Genève: état au 30 juin 1983. Réd. par Marie-Françoise Guillermin. Genève, Le Musée, 1984. vi, 176p. (Publications de la Bibliothèque d'Art et d'Archéologie, 1)

Catalog of the holdings of approximately 3,000 periodical titles held in the Art and Archeology Library of the Museum of Art and History of Geneva. No indexes.

A48 National Library of Canada. Public Services Branch. Union Catalogue of Serials Division. Union list of serials in fine arts in Canadian libraries. Inventaire des publications en série dans le domaine des Beaux-Arts dans les bibliothèques Canadiennes. Ottawa, National Library, 1978. vii, 236p.

Non-comprehensive union catalog of fine arts serials held in individual Canadian libraries. This catalog is alphabetically arranged by title, unless the title is non-distinctive (e.g., Bulletin of, Journal of, etc.), in which case the title is listed by the corporate body responsible for the publication. Holdings "are taken from the Union Catalogue of Serials at the National Library [of Canada] in which nearly 200 libraries are represented, from the two checklists of periodicals (323 titles) completed by over 80 libraries . . . , and from serials lists and individual reports provided by 20 libraries particularly for this list. An attempt has been made to achieve a balanced geographic representation of holding libraries, but for widely held titles it was impossible to include the holdings of every library."—*Introd.*

A49 New York. Metropolitan Museum of Art. Catalog of the Metropolitan Museum of Art publications. Boston, Hall, 1990. 172p.

Produced by the cataloging department of the museum's Thomas J. Watson Library, this dictionary catalog represents a bibliography of publications by and about the Metropolitan Museum of Art published between 1870 and 1986. Intended for use in conjunction with Publications of the Metropolitan Museum of Art on microfiche, 1870 to the present (1990), it stands alone as a bibliography and even includes entries not represented in the microfiche set, for example, periodical titles, periodical articles, and books about the museum published elsewhere.

A50 Periodicals contents index: PCI [computer file]. Alexandria, Va., Chadwyck-Healey, 1993– .

Available on CD-ROM and through the internet.

Table of contents index to periodicals published since 1770 in the social sciences and the humanities. "For bibliographic control of an extremely vast and formidable frontier of early periodical literature before 1975 . . . the PCI cannot be surpassed."—*Review* by K. Salomon, Art libraries journal, v.20, no.3, 1995, p.33.

A51 Reference publication in art history. N.Y., Hall, 1982–1996. 30v.

An unnumbered series of bibliographies in all fields of art history. Sometimes listed as "Reference publications in . . ."

Contents: Carl F. Barnes, Villard de Honnecourt, the artist and his drawings: a critical bibliography, 1982; Madeline Harrison Caviness, Stained glass before 1540: an annotated bibliography, 1983; Walter S. Gibson, Hieronymus Bosch: an annotated bibliography, 1983; Dorothy F. Glass, Italian Romanesque sculpture: an annotated bibliography, 1983; James H. Stubblebine, Dugento painting: an annotated bibliography, 1983; Slobodan Ćurčić, Art and architecture in the Balkans: an annotated bibliography, 1984; Robert Deshman, Anglo-Saxon and Anglo-Scandinavian art: an annotated bibliography, 1984; Louise Hanson, The art of Oceania: a bibliography, 1984; Martin Werner, Insular art: an annotated bibliography, 1984; Janet Catherine Berlo, The art of pre-Hispanic Mesoamerica: an annotated bibliography, 1985; Carla Lord, Royal French patronage of art in the fourteenth century: an annotated bibliography, 1985; E. James Mundy, Painting in Bruges, 1470–1550: an annotated bibliography, 1985; Lawrence Nees, From Justinian to Charlemagne: European art, 565–787: an annotated bibliography, 1985; Martha Levine Dunkelman, Central Italian painting, 1400–1465: an annotated bibliography, 1986; Barbara G. Lane, Flemish painting outside Bruges, 1400–1500: an annotated bibliography, 1986; Linda B. Parshall, Art and the Reformation: an annotated bibliography, 1986; Charles M. Rosenberg, Fifteenth-century North Italian painting and drawing: an annotated bibliography, 1986; Daniel P. Biebuyck, The arts of Central Africa: an annotated bibliography, 1987; Caroline Karpinski, Italian printmaking, fifteenth and sixteenth centuries: an annotated bibliography, 1987; Thomas W. Lyman, French Romanesque sculpture: an annotated bibliography, 1987; Gretel Chapman, Mosan art: an annotated bibliography, 1988; Patrick M. De Winter, European decorative arts, 1400–1600: an annotated bibliography, 1988; Thomas DaCosta Kaufmann, Art and architecture in Central Europe, 1550–1620: an annotated bibliography, 1988; Eugene C. Burt, Erotic art: an annotated bibliography with essays, 1989; Jan van der Meulen, Chartres: sources and literary interpretation: a critical bibliography, 1989; Paula Chiarmonte, Women artists in the United States: a selective bibliography and resource guide on the fine and decorative arts, 1750–1986, 1990; Eugene W. Kleinbauer, Early Christian and Byzantine architecture: an annotated bibliography and historiography, 1992; Martin Davies, Romanesque architecture: a bibliography, 1993; Cassandra L. Langer, Feminist art criticism: an annotated bibliography, 1993; Helaine Silverman, Ancient Peruvian art: an annotated bibliography, 1996.

A52 Répertoire d'art et d'archéologie [computer file], 1st ser. 1973–1989. Santa Monica, Calif., Getty, 1996.

See GLAH 1:A14 for paper version.

On CD-ROM and available through the internet from various vendors.

Merged with RILA (below) to form BHA (GLAH 2:A6) in 1991.

A53 RILA: Répertoire international de la littérature de l'art. International repertory of the literature of art [computer file], 1975–1989. Santa Monica, Calif., Getty, 1996.

See GLAH 1:A15 for original annotation and paper ed.

On CD-ROM and available through the internet from various vendors.

Merged with Répertoire d'art et d'archéologie (above) to form BHA (GLAH 2:A6) in 1991.

A54 Robinson, Doris. Fine arts periodicals: an international directory of the visual arts. Voorheesville, N.Y., Peri, 1991. xviii, 570p.

Classified annotated list of periodicals, newsletters, and newspapers published once a year or more frequently about the visual arts. Foreign-language publications are included if they are indexed or abstracted by at least one of the 38 indexing or abstracting services listed in the introductory matter, or if the periodical includes English-language summaries. Along with standard bibliographic data, citations include publisher address, phone number, editor, and language of publication. Also includes information on the presence of reviews, bibliographies, biographies, interviews, obituaries, job lists, and circulation figures, as well as whether the periodical indexes itself, what major indexing or abstracting service indexes it, and other information provided by the publisher.

Title index, p.501–26. Publisher & organization index, p.527–45. ISSN index, p.547–53. Country of publication index, p.555–57. Subject index, p.559–70.

A55 Schettini Piazza, Enrica. La banca e il libro: catalogo delle pubblicazioni delle aziende e degli istituti di credito italiani. Con la collab. di Vanni Scheiwiller. Pres. di Piero Barucci. Pref. di Umberto Eco. Roma, Bancaria editrice, 1991. 2v. il. (part col.)

Bibliography of books privately published by or for Italian banks. Bank names arranged alphabetically within which books are listed by date of publication.

Indice degli autori, v.2, p.[755]–832. Indice delle voci e soggetti, v.2, p.[833]–988. Indice delle Aziende e degli Istituti di Credito, p.[990]–1007.

A56 Schlosser, Julius von. La littérature artistique; manuel des sources de l'histoire de l'art moderne. Trad. de l'allemand par Jacques Chavy. Mise à jour d'Otto Kurz. Trad. de l'italien par Marc Le Cannu. Ed. française mise à jour par Paola Di Paolo Stathopoulos . . . [et al.] Pref. par André Chastel. Paris, Flammarion, 1984. 741p.

See GLAH 1:A49 for original annotation.

Translation of: Die Kunstliteratur, with the 3d corrected and updated Italian ed.: La letturatura artistica. (See GLAH 1:A49.) 1st German ed. 1924; reprinted, 1985; 1st Italian ed. Florence, 1935 (with bibliography supplied by Otto Kurz, 1937); 2d Italian ed. Florence (with additional bibliography by Kurz), 1956; 3d Italian ed. Florence (again updated by Kurz), 1964; reprinted Florence, La Nuova Italia, 1977; 1st Spanish ed. Madrid, 1976.

Classic survey on the literature of art, now translated into French, with a French translation of Otto Kurz's memoir. Updated, but with new and old errors, to June 1, 1983 (see review by Max Marmor in Burlington magazine, v.130, Oct. 1988, p.783–84).

A57 Stampfli, Sabine, comp. Katalog älterer Kunstbücher auf der Universitätsbibliothek Basel (1495–1847). Basel, Die Bibliothek, 1978. 151 leaves.

Catalog of art books held at the University of Basel Library by established authors who were actively publishing prior to 1800. Arranged alphabetically by author, with cross-references from titles and secondary authors; publication dates range from 1495 to 1847.

Indexes: broad subjects, p.131–38; city of publication, p.139–40; chronological by year of publication, p.141–43; engravers' names, p.144–51.

A58 Standortverzeichnis von Zeitschriften und Serien zur bildenden Kunst in Bibliotheken der Deutschen Demokratischen Republik. [Red. Bearb., Helgard Sauer und Sigrid Stein.] Dresden, Die Landesbibliothek, 1984. vii, 495p.

Alphabetically arranged union catalog of 3,100 fine arts periodicals and series held in 53 academic and other East German libraries. Citations list holdings from the mid-18th century to the present and give title, place of publication, and individual libraries' holdings.

No indexes.

A59 United States. National Gallery of Art. Guide to the National Gallery of Art microform holdings. Comp. by Diana Vogelsong. Washington, D.C., National Gallery of Art Library, 1990. 88p.

Well-annotated guide to the microform holdings of the National Gallery of Art as of July 1989. This guide is in several sections: the first is a list of monographic materials arranged alphabetically by main entry, followed by a keyword index; the second section is a list of periodical titles on microform; and the third is a list of photographic archives on microform, again listed alphabetically by main entry, followed by an index under broad medium or subject categories.

A60 University of California, Santa Barbara. Arts Library. Subject index to art exhibition catalog collection of the Arts Library, University of California at Santa Barbara [microform]. Cambridge, England, Chadwyck-Healey, 1977–1990.

Index to 45,000 exhibition catalogs held at the University of California, Santa Barbara, of which ca. 5,000 appear in the same publisher's microfiche set, Art exhibition catalogues republished on microfiche (1975–83[?]). Updated semiannually with periodic cumulations. Index includes listings by subject (including artists' names), author of catalog, title, and organizing body (museum, gallery, etc.).

A61 World museum publications 1982: a directory of art and cultural museums, their publications and audio-visual materials. N.Y., Bowker, 1982. xx, 711p.

The main section (Museum publications and audio-visual materials index), arranged by museum name, separately cites publications (exhibition catalogs, collection catalogs, monographs, serials) and audio-visual materials (slide sets, posters, color reproductions of works of art, audio tapes, video tapes, and films) produced by the museum. Citations for publications include author/title information, notes on illustrations, and prices. Citations for audio-visual materials include author/title information, running time, sound information, titles of individual art works in slide sets, as well as prices.

The main section is preceded by a geographic guide (p.1–172) to the approximately 10,000 museums that contributed to this publication. Museum addresses and often a description of the museum's permanent collections are provided. At the end of the publication is a key to publishers' and distributors' abbreviations (p.689–711) serving as a directory.

Author index—publications, p.411–97. Title index—publications, p.499–634. Title index—audio-visual materials, p.635–87.

A62 Worldwide bibliography of art exhibition catalogues 1963–1987. Millwood, N.Y., Kraus, 1992. 3v.

Compiled from the complete contents of The Worldwide art catalogue bulletin (GLAH 1:A17), this classified bibliography cites "more than 17,500 exhibition catalogues from museums and galleries throughout the world. . . . Most entries appear in more than one section; each citation gives complete bibliographic information, wherever it appears."—*Introd.*

Contents: v.1: Geographical sections: (A) Western art; (B) Non-Western art; v.2: (C) Media section; v.3: (D) Topical section; (E) Monograph section.

Title index at end of v.3, p.2323–2537.

SEE ALSO: Bibliographie zur symbolik, ikonographie und mythologie (GLAH 1:F1).

CATALOGS OF ART LIBRARIES

A63 Biblioteca di Archeologia e Storia dell'Arte (Rome, Italy). Le edizioni del XVII secolo della Biblioteca di Archeologia e Storia dell'Arte: catalogo. A cura di Isotta Scandaliato Ciciani. Roma, La Biblioteca, 1983. 321p. il.

Alphabetically arranged by author, this catalog cites works published between 1601 and 1700 held in the Biblioteca di Archeologia e Storia dell'Arte in Rome.

Indice degli autori e titoli, dei commandatori, tradutori e curatori, p.299–311, Supp. p.53–64. Indice dei tipografi e degli editori, p.313–21, Supp. p.65–73. Indice topografico dei tipografi e degli editori, Supp. p.75–82. Indice cronologico, Supp. p.83–88.

———. Supplemento, 1986. 88p. il.

A64 Bibliotheca Hertziana. Kataloge der Bibliotheca Hertziana in Rom (Max-Planck-Institut). Wiesbaden, Reichert, 1985–1994. 16v. (Systematischer Standortkatalog); 33v. (Alphabetischer Katalog); 8v. (Aufsatzautoren Katalog).

Catalog, in three parts, of one of the major Italian art historical libraries in Rome comprising almost 150,000 volumes. Section I (Systematischer Standortkatalog), the shelf list, shows a system of classification developed in the mid-1960s designed by the staff of the Hertziana that "is wholly tailored to the character of the Hertziana as a specialized library for research in Italian art."—*Introd.*

Section II (Alphabetischer Katalog) cites works in the collection by author and title, and Section III (Aufsatzautoren Katalog) lists authors of journal articles and other miscellaneous contributions (e.g. festschriften and congress proceedings). "The work of cataloguing for this section has not been uniform: fifty-two leading journals and yearbooks as well as all miscellaneous volumes have been regularly indexed . . . but for other periodicals there are unavoidable arrears."—*Introd.*

No future vols. are planned.

A65 Columbia University. Library. Avery Architectural and Fine Arts Library. Catalog of the Avery Memorial Architectural Library of Columbia University. 2d ed., enl. Boston, Hall, 1968. 19v.

1st ed., 1958. See GLAH 1:A58 for earlier supplements.

"Records all books and periodical titles added to the Avery Architectural and Fine Arts Library . . . from May 1979 through December 1981."—*Pref.* of 5th supplement. Microfilm versions of 2d ed. and supplements 2–4 published by Hall from 1968 to 1980.

———. 4th supplement. 2d ed. Boston, Hall, 1980. 3v.

———. 5th supplement. 2d ed. Boston, Hall, 1982. 4v.

A66 Florence. Kunsthistorisches Institut. Katalog des Kunsthistorischen Instituts in Florenz. Catalog of the Institute for the History of Art in Florence. Boston, Hall, 1964. 9v.

See GLAH 1:A61 for original annotation and previous supplement. No microform ed. ever published for original 9-vol. set or 1st supplement.

______. [microform]. 2d supplement. Boston, Hall, 1972. 4 microfilm reels.
______. [microform]. 3d supplement. Boston, Hall, 1976. 4 microfilm reels.

A67 Harvard University. Fine Arts Library. Catalogue of the Harvard University Fine Arts Library, the Fogg Art Museum [microform]. Boston, Hall, 1971. 15 microfilm reels.
See GLAH 1:A63 for original annotation and paper ed.
______. [microform]. 1st supplement. Boston, Hall, 1975. 3v. or 3 microfilm reels.

A68 ______. ______. Card catalogs of the Harvard University Fine Arts Library [microform]. München, Saur, 1984. 520 microfiches and guide (96p.)
Accompanying guide entitled: Guide to the card catalogs of the Harvard University Fine Arts Library, 1895–1981. "The origin of the present Fine Arts Library can be traced to the merger in 1962–63 of the former Fogg Museum Library (then containing 40,000 volumes) and the fine arts collection of Widener Library (60,000 volumes). This union created one of the world's largest university art libraries with collections of books, periodicals, photographs and slides together under one roof. In 1978 the Fine Arts Library also absorbed the book and periodicals collections of the Rübel Asiatic Research Bureau, the curatorial collection of the Fogg's Department of Oriental Art which contains over 12,000 volumes on the visual arts of the Far East, mainly in the Chinese, Japanese and Korean languages."—*Introd.*

This microform set therefore reflects the larger scope of the entire Harvard Library's holdings on the visual arts. Approximately 25,000 auction sales catalogs are listed in a separate section of this microfiche set by dealer and then by date of sale. The Rübel Asiatic Research Collection is also in a separate section. The two other sections of this microfiche collection are the Shelf list catalog of the Fine Arts Library and the main Dictionary catalog. The Dictionary catalog supersedes the G.K. Hall catalogue of 1971 and its 1976 supplement, as it contains entries through February 1981. The other sections are current through December 1983.

A69 ______. ______. Catalog of the Rübel Asiatic Research Collection, Harvard University Fine Arts Library. London, Saur, 1989. 7v.
Also available in a microfilm ed.: Rübel Asiatic Research Collection-Dictionary catalog: titles cataloged through December 1983. Munich, Saur, 1984. 33 fiche.

"Its 12,000 volumes of monographs and periodicals cover the art of East Asia, Central Asia, Southeast Asia and India. Particularly strong are holdings on Chinese ritual bronzes, Buddhist arts, Chinese and Japanese painting, Japanese woodblock prints, and East Asian ceramics. In addition to textual materials, Rübel has extensive holdings of fine scroll reproductions of Chinese and Japanese art, and rubbings of incriptions from stone monuments."—*Pref.*

Catalog entries are filed alphabetically letter by letter, except that personal surnames always precede other entries. All author and title entries for materials in East Asian languages are romanized, but the cards also contain the original characters and an English translation of the title. The library utilizes the Rübel Library Classification System developed in 1974 by Yenshew Lynn Chao.

Following the Dictionary catalog is the Catalog of reproductions of Chinese and Japanese art, and the Mei shu Ts'ung shu and I-shu ts'ung Pien.

The publication represents the cataloged holdings as of December 31, 1985.

Contents: (1) A-B; (2) C-D; (3) E-I; (4) J-MA; (5) ME-PA; (6) PE-S; (7) T-Z.

A70 ______. Villa I Tatti, Florence. Berenson Library. Catalogues of the Berenson Library of the Harvard University Center for Italian Renaissance Studies at Villa I Tatti, Florence, Italy [microform]. Boston, Hall, 1972. 4 microfilm reels.
See GLAH 1:A64 for original annotation and paper ed.

A71 London. Victoria and Albert Museum. National Art Library Catalogue. Author catalogue [microform]. London, Mindata, 1986. 706 microfiches.
See GLAH 1:A73 for paper ed.

Subject catalog provides subject access to one of Britain's major art research libraries with particular strengths in the decorative and applied arts. "The catalogue is divided into four sections: General alphabetical sequence; Fine art and archaeology; Applied and minor arts; Book art. Cross references occur between these categories."—*Pref.*
______. The Victoria and Albert Museum Library. Subject catalogue [microform]. 1983. 879 microfiches.

A72 London University. Warburg Institute. Library. Catalog of the Warburg Institute Library [microform]. [2d ed.] Boston, Hall, 1967. 22 microfilm reels.
See GLAH 1:A66 for original annotation, paper ed., and supplement.
______ [microform]. 1st supplement. Boston, Hall, 1971. 2 microfilm reels.

A73 New York. Metropolitan Museum of Art. Library catalog of the Metropolitan Museum of Art, New York. 2d ed. rev. and enl. Boston, Hall, 1980. 48v.
See GLAH 1:A67 for 1st ed., 1966–1980. 28v. and its supplements.
______. 1st supplement. 2d ed. Boston, Hall, 1982. 1v.
______. 2d supplement. 2d ed. Boston, Hall, 1985. 4v.
______. 3d supplement. 2d ed. Boston, Hall, 1987. 3v.
______. 4th supplement. 2d ed. Boston, Hall, 1990. 3v.
______. 5th supplement. 2d ed. Boston, Hall, 1994. 3v.
Microfilm version of 2d ed. and supplements 2–3 published by Hall from 1980–1987.

A74 ______. ______. Robert Goldwater Library. Catalog of the Robert Goldwater Library, the Metropolitan Museum of Art. Boston, Hall, 1982.
"The Robert Goldwater Library was founded in 1957 as the Museum of Primitive Art Library. In 1975, when the Museum of Primitive Art became the Department of Primitive Art at the Metropolitan Museum of Art, the Library became the departmental library. . . . The arts of the native peoples

of Africa, Oceania, and the Americas are covered with special strengths in West Africa, precolumbian Mexico and Peru, and New Guinea."—*Introd.*

Divided by author/title and subject, with separate indexes for serials and auction catalogs. Analytical entries included for periodical articles and collected works.

A75 New York. Museum of Modern Art. Library. Annual bibliography of modern art, 1986– . Boston, Hall, 1987– .

Dictionary catalog that forms an annual supplement to Catalog of the Library of the Museum of Modern Art, New York City (see following entry). "The museum library became a special member of the Research Libraries Group, Inc., in 1980, and since 1981 has entered all its cataloging records—except those for artist files containing fugitive material—into the Research Libraries Information Network, the RLIN database."—*Introd.*

Each Annual bibliography is compiled from RLIN records of both new and older publications acquired by the library in the year of each volume's coverage.

A76 ———. ———. ———. Catalog of the Library of the Museum of Modern Art, New York City [microform]. Boston, Hall, 1976. 28 microform reels.

Also available on CD-ROM with the title: Bibliography of modern art on disk (1998). See GLAH 1:A68 for original annotation and paper ed.

Supplemented by the Annual bibliography of modern art (see preceding entry).

A77 New York. Whitney Museum of American Art. Catalog of the Library of the Whitney Museum of American Art. Boston, Hall, 1979. 2v.

Catalog of more than 10,000 books and exhibition catalogs covering 20th-century American art, and a core collection of publications about earlier American centuries and international 20th-century art.

——— [microform]. Boston, Hall, 1979. 2 microfilm reels.

A78 Ottawa. National Gallery of Canada. Library. Catalogue of the Library of the National Gallery of Canada. Catalogue de la Bibliothèque de la Galerie Nationale du Canada. Boston, Hall, 1973. 8v.

See GLAH 1:A71 for original annotation.

———. 1st supplement. Boston, Hall, 1981. 6v.

A79 Paris. Université. Bibliothèque d'Art et d'Archéologie (Fondation Jacques Doucet). Catalogue général, périodiques. [2d ed.] Nendeln, Liechtenstein, Kraus-Thomson Organization, 1972. 224p.

See GLAH 1:A72 for original ed.

Second ed. is updated (to January 1, 1970) and expanded ed. of v.14 of the library's Catalogue général . . . , first published in 1937.

A80 Washington, D.C. Freer Gallery of Art, Washington, D.C. Library. Dictionary catalog of the Library of the Freer Gallery of Art, Smithsonian Institution [microform]. 2d enl. ed. on microfiche. Boston, Hall, 1991. 252 microfiche and printed guide (vi, 9p.)

See GLAH 1:A62 for printed 1st ed. (in 6v.) of this catalog of an important library that specializes in the art of the Far East, India, and the Near East.

A81 Washington, D.C. Smithsonian Institution. Libraries. National Museum of African Art Branch. Catalog of the Library of the National Museum of African Art Branch of the Smithsonian Institution Libraries. Boston, Mass., Hall, 1991. 2v. (Smithsonian Institution Libraries Research Guide, 7)

Documents more than 20,000 volumes located in the branch library. Access is provided by main entry, added entries, titles, series titles, and subject headings.

A82 Zentralinstitut für Kunstgeschichte in München. Bibliothek. Kataloge der Bibliothek des Zentralinstituts für Kunstgeschichte in München [microform]. München, Saur, 1982– . (1,025) microfiches in 4 parts + guide (280p.) and ongoing microfiche supplements to each part.

Catalog of one of the most important art history libraries in Europe with holdings of approximately 300,000 volumes including "literature from all branches of European art and literature on art history from the early Middle Ages to the present day."—*Introd.*

Alphabetischer Katalog is the main author and title catalog; Katalog der unselbständigen Schriften is an author catalog of journal articles and book essays (e.g. festschriften, conference reports, etc.) published after 1949; Sachkatalog is a subject catalog of entries within topographic, artist, and portrait sections.

Contents: Alphabetischer Katalog; Katalog der unselbständigen Schriften (Aufsatzkatalog); Sachkatalog; Begleitheft zum Sachkatalog (the guide).

PREHISTORIC

A83 Ausgewählte Bibliographie zur Vorgeschichte von Mitteleuropa. Hrsg. von Rolf Hachmann. Unter Mitarb. von Johannes Boese . . . [et al.] Stuttgart, Steiner, 1984. lxiii, 390p.

Classified bibliography (books and periodical articles) of European prehistory. After a first general chapter with chronological and topical subdivisions, subsequent chapters are divided into regions of Europe, again using chronological and topical subdivisions.

Register, p.357–90.

A84 Bibliographies sur l'âge du fer. Montagnac, Mergoil, 1988. ca. 350p. (Bibliographies thématiques en archéologie, 1–8)

Series director: Michel Feugère.

Eight separate bibliographies (books, articles in periodicals and books, and other published essays), compiled by different authors. Each has its own arrangement (author, subject, or topographic) and many have geographic, site, thematic, and/or chronological indexes. Focus is on French Iron Age archeology, but other geographic areas are included.

Contents: (1) La vie quotidienne en Europe aux ages de métaux; (2) L'Age du fer en Bretagne; (3) L'Age du fer en Languedoc occidental et en Roussillon; (4) L'Age du fer en Languedoc oriental; (5) Les fibules protohistoriques; (6) L'armement au Deuxième age du fer; (7) Les lampes préromaines; (8) Le verre préromain.

A85 Francis bulletin signalétique 525, Préhistoire et protohistoire, v.45–48, 1991–1994. Vandoeuvre-lès-Nancy, CNRS, INIST, Sciences humaines et sociales.

See GLAH 1:A76 for earlier vols., and GLAH 2:A239 for related title: Francis bulletin signalétique 526: Art et archéologie (Proche-orient, Asie, Amérique).

After 1994, available only on CD-ROM or through the internet from various vendors (see FRANCIS at GLAH 2:A10).

A86 Hendrickx, Stan. Analytical bibliography of the prehistory and the early dynastic period of Egypt and northern Sudan. Louvain, Louvain Univ. Pr., 1995. 328p. (Egyptian prehistory monographs)

Alphabetically arranged by author, this bibliography of 7,407 entries includes books, periodical articles, essays (e.g., in festschriften, conference proceedings, etc.), auction and sales catalogs (particularly of 1964+ Christie's and Sotheby's in London) with pertinent illustrations or information regarding the provenance of objects that would interest archeologists. Also includes dissertations available through UMI. Hendrickx made use of Kent R. Weeks' An historical bibliography (GLAH 2:A88), but nearly 450 titles in Weeks are not here because they fall out of the scope of this work; e.g., some titles related to the rock-art of Gebel Uweinat, Libya, and others covering racial and biblical theories on the period. Some works published as late as 1993 are included.

Author index, p.[269]–92. Thematic index, p.[293]–304. Topographical index, p.[305]–29.

A87 Pickin, Frances R. A worldwide archaeological sample. New Haven, Human Relations Area Files, 1983. 2v. (xii, 274 leaves) (HRAFlex books; W6–009. Bibliography series)

Geographically arranged bibliography of general books on a region followed by specific monographs, surveys, and locality reports for more than 500 archeological sites within 29 geographic sections. "The Worldwide archaeological sample is thus a geographically representative worldwide sample of archaeologically defined sequences and/or cultures. Its purpose and design is twofold. Not only does it describe a set of prehistoric data for hologeistic anthropologists seeking non-ethnographically based samples but it introduces anthropological archaeologists to the possibilities of doing worldwide comparison with their data. . . . Deciding upon the actual location for each section was . . . determined by three factors: site density, time depth in the area and the number of site reports in English. . . . Four factors influenced the choice of particular sites: [the site's location within the section, the amount of data published on the site, the language used in the report (English was emphasized), and the availability of reports to the author.]"—*Introd.*

Index, p.267–74.

A88 Weeks, Kent R. An historical bibliography of Egyptian prehistory. With the ed. assistance of Catharine Roehrig . . . [et al.] Winona Lake, Ind., Eisenbrauns, 1985. xxii, 138p. (Published for the American Research Center in Egypt [Columbia University])

Alphabetically arranged by author, this bibliography of 2,515 entries includes books, articles, book reviews, essays, archeological surveys, excavation reports, and travelers' reports. Although there is no subject index to this bibliography, Weeks' 13-page introduction devotes a paragraph to describing and exemplifying each type of publication listed in the bibliography (bibliography, history of Egyptian prehistorical research, geological studies, climatological studies, the river Nile, etc.) and can be regarded as a thematic index.

ANCIENT—MEDIEVAL

Current Serials

A89 L'Année philologique [microform]: bibliographie critique et analytique de l'antiquité gréco-latine, 1924/26– . Chico, Calif., Scholars. Microfiche.

See GLAH 1:A77 for original annotation and paper ed.

See also Database of classical bibliography (GLAH 2:A99) for CD-ROM version.

A90 Archäologische Dissertationen. Published annually since 1970 in Archäologischer Anzeiger. Berlin, de Gruyter, Heft 1, 1963– .

Bibliography of completed archeological dissertations from German, Swiss, and Austrian universities. Arranged alphabetically by author, gives title and institution.

A91 Bibliographie. Published annually in Beiträge zur Sudanforschung. Wien-Mödling, Druckerei St. Gabriel, Bd. 1, 1986– .

Annotated bibliography of current literature (books, festschriften, and periodical articles) on the history and archeology of ancient Sudan. Each bibliography lists materials published several years previously.

A92 Bibliographie. Published annually in Byzantinoslavica, v.2 (1930)– .

Classified bibliography of current literature (books and periodical articles) of which Pt.9, "Art Byzantin, archéologie," covers Byzantine art and archeology from antiquity to the Middle Ages. Includes Roman- and Slavic-language citations.

A93 Bibliographie, 1957– . Published annually in Cahiers de civilisation médiévale Xe-XIIe siècles, t.1, jan./ mars, 1958– .

Unannotated bibliography of current literature (books, articles, conference reports, etc.) on medieval civilization, arranged alphabetically as a subject index, with many cross-references to other entries. Each year's bibliography lists materials published several years previously. Followed by a section of citations to reviews previously published in Cahiers to books listed in earlier Bibliographies.

A94 Bibliographie. Published annually in Revue d'histoire ecclesiastique, v.33, 1937– .

Classified bibliography of current literature (books and periodical articles) on ancient to medieval ecclesiastical matters, including sections on archeology and art history. Each year's bibliography lists materials published several years previously.

A95 Bibliographische Notizen und Mitteilungen. Published annually in Byzantinische Zeitschrift, 1892– . (Reprint. N.Y., Johnson Reprint, 1964– .)

See GLAH 1:A79 for original publication.

Also available on 35mm microfilm: München, Beck, n.d.

A96 Bulletin analytique d'histoire romaine. Strasbourg, Association pour l'étude de la civilisation romaine, t. 1, 1962– .

Bibliography to current periodical literature on ancient Roman history, with numbered citations arranged by author. Citations lack annotations, but do include keyword, geographic, and thematic headings after each entry. Computer-generated indexes follow citations: [current] authors, [ancient] people and gods; [ancient] authors and sources, places and sites, thematic subdivided by keywords, keywords alone.

A97 Byzantinische Zeitschrift. Supplementum bibliographicum. Hrsg. von Peter Schreiner. Stuttgart, Teubner, v.1– , 1994– .

Published as a supplement to "Bibliographische Notizen und Mitteilungen," in Byzantinische Zeitschrift (GLAH 1:A79 and GLAH 2:A95), and like the "Bibliographische" in BZ, Pt.7, "Archäologie und Kunstgeschichte" is a classified bibliography of literature on Byzantine art and the arts of antiquity. Beginning with v.84/85 (1991/92), the editors of BZ realized they no longer had the space to accommodate the ever-growing "Bibliographische Notizen" section, so a separate bibliographic supplement was begun. Future supplements will be smaller than the first and will cover current literature one or two years after it has appeared.

Author index precedes classified bibliography.

A98 Current Swedish archaeology, 1993– . Stockholm, Swedish Archaeological Society, v.1 (1993)– .

Continuation of Swedish archaeology: 1976/80–1981/85, 1983–85, 2v., which is itself a continuation of Swedish archaeological bibliography: 1939/48–1971/75, 1951–1978, 6v. (GLAH 1:A86).

Current ed.: Mats Burström and Anders Carlsson.

When it changed its title from Swedish archaeological bibliography to Swedish archaeology, this publication also changed its scope and format. Essays are smaller, and while they continue to list bibliography, they tend to focus more on scholarly developments of the period rather than on publications. Second, there is no longer a complete bibliographic index at the end of each volume but rather a bibliography at the end of each small article. Finally, fewer essays are published on archeology outside of Sweden. Current Swedish archaeology continues in a similar format as Swedish archaeology.

A99 Database of classical bibliography: DCB [computer file], v.1, 1976/87– . Atlanta, Scholars, 1995– .

Available on CD-ROM (with user's guide, 122p.) and through the internet.

General ed.: Dee L. Clayman.

CD-ROM version of L'Année philologique (see GLAH 1:A77 and GLAH 2:A89), updated annually, incorporating retrospectively 3–5 vols. of L'Année philologique per year.

Based on L'Année philologique, Database of classical bibliography "contains citations of all known scholarly work published in any language anywhere in the world in the areas of ancient Greek and Latin language and linguistics, Greek and Roman history, literature, philosophy, art, archaeology, religion, mythology, music, science, early Christian texts, numismatics, papyrology, and epigraphy. Its coverage begins with the second millennium B.C. with pre-classical archaeology, and ends with the period of transition from late antiquity to the middle ages (roughly 500–800 A.D.)"—*Introd.* to user's guide.

A100 Deutsches Archäologisches Institut. DYABOLA [computer file]: Sachkataloge des Deutschen Archäologischen Instituts. Subject catalogues of the German Archaeological Institut (DAI) on CD-ROM. Ennepetal, Biering und Brinkmann, [1988?]– . CD-ROM with user's guide (38p.)

CD-ROM version of Archäologische Bibliographie (see GLAH 1:A83) with semiannual or annual updates. Internet version in preparation.

Includes the subject catalogs of the German Archeological Institute in Rome (1956 to date), and Bibliographies of Iberian archeology from the German Archeological Institute in Madrid (1991 to date) and the Archeology of Roman provinces from the Römisch-Germanische Kommission, Frankfurt (1992 to date).

A101 Dissertations in progress, or dissertations completed. Published in ICMA newsletter, 1994– .

Preceded by: International census of doctoral dissertations in medieval art, 1982–93. Ed. by Dorothy F. Glass. Assist. eds.: Martha Easton and Margaret Lubel. N.Y., International Center of Medieval Art, 1994. iii, 30p., which was preceded by ICMA census of doctoral dissertations, pt.4, Gesta, v.21, 1982, p.159–62; ICMA census of doctoral dissertations, pt.2–3, [separate single leaves] ICMA newsletter, 1980, n.2–3; and Studies and dissertations in medieval art recently completed or in progress (1963–67), Gesta, v.7, 1968, p.62–64.

Arranged by country, then alphabetically by institution, then by author. Lists works produced in Northern Europe, the United Kingdom, France, Canada, and the United States. Sources used to compile this list were Dissertation abstracts on disc (UMI), Kunstchronik, Histoire de l'art, and v.46, n.1

(1992) of Scriptorium. Information about ordering UMI registered dissertations is included at the end.

A102 Harvard University. Dumbarton Oaks. Center for Byzantine Studies, Washington, D.C. Author index of Byzantine studies [microform]. Ed. by Jelisaveta Stanojevich Allen. [Zug, Switzerland], IDC, 1986–[1991]. Pt.1: 170 microfiches; Pt.2: 267 microfiches + 5 leaves in binder.

See GLAH 1:A79 for Bibliographische Notizen und Mitteilungen in BZ, and GLAH 1:A93 for the Dumbarton Oaks bibliographies Series I: Literature on Byzantine art, 1892–1967.

Cumulative index of all annotated bibliographic entries published in the journal Byzantinische Zeitschrift from 1892–1981 (Part 1) and from 1982–1990 (Part 2). Also including bibliographic references from Krumbacher's Geschichte der Byzantinischen Literatur and a compilation of Slavic authors in the Cyrillic alphabet from 77 journals, most issued before 1917. For "scholars pursuing studies on all aspects of Byzantine civilization; Late Antique and Early Christian studies; Patristic studies; and Slavic, Armenian, and Georgian studies; as well as the relations of the Western mediaeval and Arabic worlds with Byzantium."—*Introd.*, Pt.1.

Primary arrangement of both parts of index is by author, followed by a title index of works by anonymous authors, a festschrift index (arranged under name of honoree), an index to articles about scholars (personalia, bibliographies, and necrologies), and a dissertation index arranged alphabetically by granting institution (only those listed in BZ). In Part 1 only there is a symposium index (listed by location of meetings), and an alphabetical name index to Migne's Patrologiae Graeca. In Part 2 only there is an index of museum, exhibition, private collection, and sales catalogs, and a congress index (listed by best-known names).

A103 Index Islamicus (East Grinstead, England). Index Islamicus: new books, articles and reviews on Islam and the Muslim world, 1994, no.1– . London, Bowker-Saur, 1994– . Quarterly (including a bound annual volume).

Also available on CD-ROM and through the internet.

For earlier versions see GLAH 1:A85.

Current ed.: G. J. Roper and C. H. Bleaney.

The Quarterly Index Islamicus published by Mansell ceased with v.17 (1993). (Also available on microfilm through Mansell.) In 1994, Bowker-Saur published the Index in its current format, with new numbering (no.1–). "Each year's publication will henceforth be recorded in an annual bound volume, which will normally appear at the end of the following year: the first such volume, for 1993, will appear at the end of 1994." [It appeared in 1995.] "More up-to-date information will, however, appear in advance fascicles, of which this is the first. These replace the old Quarterly Index Islamicus."—*Introd.* 1994, no.1.

The full title for the annual bound volume varies from the fascicles above: Index Islamicus: A bibliography of books, articles and reviews on Islam and the Muslim world published in the year, 1993 (1995–).

A new larger classification scheme has been adopted, placing art in section 11, architecture in section 12, and archeology in section 18. In addition to citing books, periodical articles, and essays in collected volumes, this new version of the Index has a substantial section listing reviews of books (and other materials).

Index Islamicus (1165–1905), ed. W. H. Behm, (1858); reprinted (Millersville, Pa., Adiyok, 1989); 5th supplement, 1976–80, ed. by J. D. Pearson (1983); 6th supplement, 1981–85, ed. by G. J. Roper (1991).

A104 International medieval bibliography. Founded by Robert S. Hoyt and Peter H. Sawyer. [v.1], 1967– . Leeds, Univ. of Leeds, 1968– . Currently issued biannually.

Current ed.: Alan V. Murray.

Also available, updated annually, on CD-ROM.

Classified bibliography on all medieval topics including articles, essays within books, festschriften, and colloquium papers, but not book reviews or reprints. Sections on archeology, architecture, and art history.

"Limited to A.D. 500–1500 with some extensions to suit certain topics and areas (e.g. Russia). . . . Works on Africa, the Near East and such oriental topics as the Mongols are only included when they have direct bearing on the study of medieval Europe."—*Introd.*

Indexes of authors and topics.

A105 Istituto Nazionale di Archeologia e Storia dell'Arte, Rome. Biblioteca. Annuario bibliografico di archeologia, n.s. 1, 1982– . Rome, Palombi, 1983– .

Ed.: Enrica Pannozzo.

See GLAH 1:A94 for original series of which no further vols. were published. After an approximately 20-year hiatus, a new series has begun, with citations for literature published between final vol. of old series and first vol. of new. No change from first series in coverage or arrangement.

A106 Nestor, [v.1]– . Bloomington, Ind. Program in Classical Archaeology, Indiana University, Oct. 1958– . Monthly (except July–Sept.).

From 1957 to date, this bibliography is available as an ftp file via the internet and on disk as ASCII files to allow for simple importing to any database program.

Issued 1957–1977 by Institute for Research in the Humanities, University of Wisconsin, 1978–1995 by Program in Classical Archeology, Indiana University, and 1995– by the Department of Classics at the University of Cincinnati. Prior to 1957, published as Mycenaean bibliography, no.1–10, Feb. 1957–June 1958 by E.L. Bennett, New Haven, Conn.

Primarily an unclassed, unannotated current bibliography of Minoan and Mycenaean archeology and inscriptions. Includes non-Roman languages. Frequently gives detailed announcements for past and future international conferences, lectures, and symposia in the field. Author index produced annually.

Retrospective

A107 Beck, Diemut. Verzeichnis der Zeitschriften in der Bibliothek der Römisch-Germanischen Kommission: Bestand am 30. April 1976. Mainz am Rhein, Zabern, 1977. 198p. (Beiheft zum Bericht der Römisch-Germanischen Kommission, 57, 1976)

List of 1,800 journals (with volumes held) in the Bibliothek der Römisch-Germanischen Kommission (DAI). Arranged alphabetically by country of publication, with an index to titles at the end.

A108 Berghe, Louis Vanden. Bibliographie analytique de l'archéologie de l'Iran ancien. Avec la collab. de B. De Wulf et E. Haerinck. Leiden, Brill, 1979. xxv, 329p.

Classified unannotated bibliography of books, articles, essays in books, encyclopedias, and congress reports on the archeology of ancient Iran.

Contents: Pt.I. Généralités; Pt.II. Bibliographie par régions et par sites; Pt.III. Bibliographie par périodes.

Indexes: topographical, p.304–11; author, p.312–29.

______. 1st supplement. (1978–1980) Leiden, Brill, 1981.

______. 2d supplement. (1981–1986) Leiden, Brill, 1987.

______. 3d supplement. (1987–1995) Leiden, Brill, 1996.

A109 Bibliographie de l'art byzantin et postbyzantin: la contribution grecque 1991–1996; pub. à l'occasion du XIXe Congrès international des études byzantines, Copenhagen 1996. Athènes, Centre de recherches de l'art byzantin et postbyzantin, 1996. 183p.

See GLAH 1:A88 for earlier ed., covering the years 1945–1969.

Bibliography of Byzantine and medieval literature from 1991–1996. Compiled by I. Bitha, A. Katsioti, E. Katsa on the occasion of the 19th International Congress of Byzantine Studies in Copenhagen. Contains a list of 2,229 publications (which include not only books, but periodicals, acts of congresses, encyclopedias, etc.), many of which are in Greek (with French translations).

Index: des auteurs, p.163–71, classement géographique, p.172–76, par matière, p.177–83.

A110 Bibliographie der Deutschsprachigen Arabistik und Islamkunde: von den Anfängen bis 1986 nebst Literatur über die arabischen Länder der Gegenwart. Hrsg. von Fuat Sezgin. Frankfurt am Main, Goethe-Univ., 1990–1996. 21v. (Veröffentlichungen des Institutes für Geschichte der Arabisch-Islamischen Wissenschaften, Reihe A: Texte und Studien, Bd. 3, 1–21)

A 21-volume set of classified unannotated bibliographies of German-language literature on the Islamic and Arabic world. Includes materials published up to 1986. v.1: Allgemeines und Hilfsmittel der Forschung, (1990) and v.6: Kulturgeschichte: Gewerbe, Handwerke und Künste, (1991) include sections on art and archeology. V.12–18 repeat all citations of previous volumes arranged by primary author, v.19 is an index to reviewers, v.20 is an index to all names listed in the set, and v.21 is an index of special concepts.

A111 Bibliographie zur Archäologie des Mittelalters in Mitteleuropa, 1981–1985, hrsg. von Marion Tippmann. And Bibliographie zur . . . , 1986–1990, hrsg. von Jürgen Pape und Sven Spiong. Published in Zeitschrift für Archäologie des Mittelalters, v.14–15, 1986, p.187–246; v.20, 1992, p.129–203.

Classified bibliography of current literature (books, essays, periodical articles) on medieval archeology of Germany (East and West), Austria, Switzerland, and the Netherlands. List of journals consulted, arranged by country of publication, is followed by an index of authors cited.

A112 Bibliographies sur l'époque romaine: ouvrage publié avec le concours du Ministère de la Culture (Sous-Direction de l'Archéologie). Montagnac, Mergoil, 1991. vi, 616p., maps. (Bibliographies thématiques en archéologie, 9–22)

Series director: Michel Feugère. Fourteen bibliographies compiled by different authors. Each bibliography has its own arrangement (author or subject or topographic), often with geographic, site, thematic and/or chronological indexes.

Contents: (9) L'Aquitaine gallo-romaine; (10) La Franche-Comté gallo-romaine; (11) L'Indre gallo-romaine; (12) Metz antique; (13) L'Ile-de-France gallo-romaine; (14) Les nécropoles à incinération à l'époque romaine; (15) Les monnaies romaines; (16) Les amphores à l'époque romaine; (17) L'argenterie à l'époque romaine; (18) La vaisselle de bronze à l'époque romaine; (19) Les lampes romaines; (20) Les fibules à l'époque romaine; (21) Les instruments médicaux et chirurgicaux du monde gréco-romaine; (22) L'équipement militaire à l'époque romaine.

A113 Chapman, Gretel. Mosan art: an annotated bibliography. Boston, Hall, 1988. xxv, 363p. (Reference publication in art history)

Annotated classified bibliography covering "the Meuse Valley (located in present-day east Belgium and in part of the southern Netherlands) from the late Carolingian period to the mid-thirteenth century. . . . The purpose of this bibliography is to provide a handbook to the study of Mosan art seen as a cultural manifestation of an area of northern Europe during the central Middle Ages."—*Introd.*

Author index, p.331–44. Subject index, p.345–63.

A114 Contributi editoriali italiani alla ricerca archeologica, 1980–1987: mostra del libro = Italian publishing contributions to archaeological research, 1980–1987: book exhibition. [Catalogo a cura di Luisa Musso.] [Roma], Ministero per i beni culturali e ambientali, 1990. 293p. [16]p. of plates, col. il. (Quaderni di Libri e riviste d'Italia, 21)

This classified bibliography was published as part of an exhibition in Cairo in 1990 celebrating international cooperation in archeological research. Organized by the Italian Ministry for Cultural Heritage with the assistance of the Italian Embassy in Cairo.

Contents: (1) General publications; (2) Prehistory and protohistory; (3) Minoan and Mycenaean civilizations; (4) Civilizations of Greece and Magna Graecia; (5) Phoenician and Punic civilizations; (6) Etruscology; (7) Civilizations of pre-Roman Italy; (8) Roman civilization; (9) Rome; (10) Roman provinces; (11) Christian, early mediaeval and proto-Byzantine civilizations; (12) Egyptology; (13) Oriental studies; (14) African, American and Oceanian civilizations; (15) Periodicals.

List of publishers and printers, p.281–90.

A115 Coulson, William D.E., and Freiert, Patricia N. Greek and Roman art, architecture, and archaeology: an annotated bibliography. 2d ed. N.Y., Garland, 1987. viii, 204p. (Garland reference library of the humanities, v.580)

See GLAH 1:A90 for 1st ed.

Selected bibliography with long annotations that attempts to describe appropriate audience for each book. Author has attempted to include only inexpensive books in print at the time he compiled the bibliography. He has included fewer than half of the titles from the first ed., of which few are still in print, and he has usually written new annotations for these relisted titles.

Contents: General; Archaeology (methods and techniques); Prehistoric; Greek; Etruscan; Roman; Sites of multiple periods; Additional resources (bibliographical sources, series, museum collections and publications, biographies, tradition [history and influence], novels).

Index, p.173–204.

A116 Creswell, Keppel Archibald Cameron. A bibliography of the architecture, arts and crafts of Islam to 1st Jan. 1960. [Cairo], American Univ. at Cairo Pr. (Distr. by Oxford Univ. Pr., 1961). xxiv, 1330, xxvp.

See GLAH 1:A91 for original annotation and first supplement.

———. 2d supplement; Jan. 1972 to Dec. 1980 (with omissions from previous years). By J.D. Pearson, assist. by Michael Meinecke and George T. Scanlon. Cairo, American Univ. in Cairo Pr., 1984. xxi, 575p.

2d supplement contains 11,000 entries covering nine years of publishing, as well as corrections or titles missed (particularly in Arabic, Persian, and Turkish languages) from the original ed. or the first supplement. Given the large number of entries in this supplement, the editorial committee chose to eliminate annotations unless the reader would be misled by the title, and they chose not to include tables of contents.

———. 3d supplement; Jan. 1981–Dec. 1985. Forthcoming.

A117 Crosby, Everett Uberto; Bishko, C. Julian; and Kellogg, Robert L. Medieval studies: a bibliographical guide. N.Y., Garland, 1983. xxv, 1131p. (Garland reference library of the humanities, v.427)

"This [classified] bibliography [of 9,000 entries] is an annotated reference work to the major collections of sources and the secondary literature considered to be of basic importance for the history and the culture of the western European Middle Ages, Byzantium, and medieval Islamic civilization . . . dealing with the period from the third century A.D. to the sixteenth."—*Introd.*

In addition to geographically arranged chapters, linguistically arranged chapters, and still other chapters arranged by subjects, there are chapters on aesthetics (p.863–64), symbolism and iconography (p.865–71), history of art (p.872–96), architecture (p.897–908), sculpture (p.909–14), painting (p.915–21), stained glass, mosaics, enamels (p.922–24), manuscript illumination (p.925–30), and archeology (p.953–59).

Index of authors and editors, p.1058–1127. Index of topics, p.1129–31.

A118 Ćurčić, Slobodan. Art and architecture in the Balkans; an annotated bibliography. Boston, Hall, 1984. xxv, 427p. il. (Reference publication in art history)

Primarily organized by the geographic territories of the modern states of Albania, Bulgaria, and Yugoslavia (following a general chapter on the Balkans), this heavily annotated bibliography of art and architecture chronologically encompasses the Middle Ages. (See the author's definition of the Middle Ages in his preface.) Within each geographically defined chapter, separate sections are arranged by media or special sites, always following a preliminary general section.

Author index, p.385–95. General index, p.397–427.

A119 Deshman, Robert. Anglo-Saxon and Anglo-Scandinavian art: an annotated bibliography. Boston, Hall, 1984. xxii, 125p. (Reference publication in art history)

Classified annotated bibliography of Anglo-Saxon and Anglo-Scandinavian art from approximately the last third of the 9th century to the first quarter of the 12th century. Coins and architecture not included. Within each classification the author has chosen not to arrange citations chronologically or by author. "Instead [he has] opted for a less systematic, more flexible organization that seems better suited to the practical needs of the users. This arrangement has been guided by one or more of the following general principles. Related writings treating the same monument or problem were grouped together. Within each section or subsection writings with a more general, comprehensive scope were placed before those with a more specialized, limited one. More recent or more significant literature was also accorded priority, as were entries that contain essential documentation about a work or art . . . cross-references call attention to related entries included under other headings."—*Pref.*

Index of authors and editors, p.103–07. Index of places and subjects, p.109–25.

A120 Ellis, Linda, comp. Laboratory techniques in archaeology: a guide to the literature, 1920–1980. N.Y., Garland, 1982. xiv, 419p. (Garland reference library of social sciences, v.110)

Classified bibliography of the literature on the applications of science in archeology.

Contents: (1) General works; (2) Remote sensing; (3) Chronometry; (4) Environmental reconstruction; (5) Materials analysis; (6) Data management; (7) Addenda.

Geographical index, p.373–80. Method index, p.381–83. Materials index, p.384–86. Author index, p.387–419.

A121 Feuer, Bryan Avery. Mycenaean civilization: a research guide. N.Y., Garland, 1995. xl, 421p. (Garland reference library of the humanities, v.1525) (Research guides to ancient civilization, v.5)

Solidly annotated bibliography of books and articles for the non-specialist on Mycenaean civilization, particularly material published in English. The material culture section (art, architecture, painting, etc., p.179–268) and regional and site reports section (p.303–80) are of interest to art historians.

Glossary, p.381–86. Indexes: author, p.387–96; place-name, p.397–406; subject, p.407–21.

A122 Francis bulletin signalétique 526: Art et archéologie (Proche-Orient, Asie, Amérique). v.45–48, 1991–1994. Vandoeuvre-lès-Nancy, CNRS, INIST.

See GLAH 1:A80 for earlier vols. and GLAH 2:A85 for related title: Francis bulletin signalétique 525, Préhistoire et protohistoire.

After 1994, available only on CD-ROM or on the internet through various vendors (see FRANCIS at GLAH 2:A10).

A123 Goldman, Bernard. The ancient arts of western and central Asia: a guide to the literature. Ames, Iowa State Univ. Pr., 1991. ix, 303p.

Classified annotated bibliography (books, periodical articles, exhibition catalogs, archeological reports) on the arts of those who lived anywhere from the eastern shores of the Mediterranean to the eastern borders of Chinese Turkestan (Sinkiang province) and from the Ukraine and southern Soviet Asia to Pakistan and the Arabian peninsula. Chronologically the material stretches from neolithic times to the coming of Islam. Tibet, Mongolia, and Egypt are not included. Regardless of their importance, rare items held only in a small number of libraries in the United States have been excluded.

Preceding the bibliography is a reference key functioning as a subject index (of names, topics, periods, geographic areas) to the alphabetically sorted classification scheme organizing the bibliography.

Appendix 1: Chronologies and king lists, p.240–57; Appendix 2: Research and writing for publication, p.258–71. Glossary, p.272–87. Author index, p.288–300. General index (topics not covered in the reference key), p.301–03.

A124 Haerinck, E. Pre-Islamic archaeology of Kuwait, northeastern Arabia, Bahrain, Qatar, United Arab Emirates and Oman: a bibliography. Ed. by E. Haerinck and K.G. Stevens. Gent, [s.n.], 1985. xi, 53p. map.

Bibliography of field reports, excavation reports, books, journal articles, conference articles, and essays in books published between 1879–1984 on the geographic areas described in the title from prehistory to the 7th century A.D. Studies in Arabic, Russian, and Japanese are not included. Citations are arranged by period, and within that by region, and each period begins with a general works section. Author index at end.

______. 1st supplement 1985–1995. Ed. by K.G. Stevens. Leuven, Peeters, 1996. vi, 82p.

A125 Halton, Thomas P., and O'Leary, Stella. Classical scholarship: an annotated bibliography. [3d ed.] White Plains, N.Y., Kraus, 1986. xx, 396p.

[1st ed.], R. P. McGuire, Introduction to classical scholarship: a syllabus and bibliographic guide , 1955; 2d ed., 1961. A basic bibliographic guide to scholarship in classical studies. This ed. covers materials published through 1980. Chapter J: Art and archaeology (p.227–302) provides an annotated classified bibliography of sources important to students of ancient art.

Subject index, p.355–77. Author index, p.379–96.

A126 Hansen, Peter Allan. A bibliography of Danish contributions to classical scholarship from the sixteenth century to 1970. Copenhagen, Royal Library, Department of National Bibliography. ([Distr. by] Rosenkilde and Bagger, 1977.) xviii, 335p. (Danish humanist texts and studies, v.1)

Classified, unannotated bibliography (books, periodical articles, essays in books, conference proceedings) of all classical scholarship from Danish authors. Of interest to art historians are two sections: Topography (p.186–215) and Art and archeology (p.216–66).

List of collective headings and anonymous works in nos.1–1155, p.309. Mythological index, p.309–10. Iconographical index, p.310–11. Index of artists, p.311. Index annorum, p.311–17. Index of Danish and foreign classical scholars, p.318–35.

A127 Dumbarton Oaks. Dumbarton Oaks Research Library. Byzantine Library serials list (September 1990). Washington, D.C., Dumbarton Oaks Research Library, 1990. 277p.

Serials holdings list of approximately 1,670 titles at the Dumbarton Oaks Research Library as of Sept. 1990. "Titles included cover all aspects of Byzantium, as well as the antecedent cultures of Greece and Rome and the contemporary Slavic, Islamic, and Western Latin societies in contact with Byzantium."—*Introd.*

A128 ______. ______. Dictionary catalogue of the Byzantine collection of the Dumbarton Oaks Research Library, Washington, D.C., Boston, Hall, 1975. 12v.

This dictionary catalog offers more than 84,000 volumes of primarily Byzantine art and archeology, but "includ[ing] all aspects of Byzantine civilization and . . . antecedent cultures which exerted an important influence on the development of Byzantium, as well as contemporary cultures which influenced or were influenced by Byzantium and later cultures on which Byzantium was a dominant influence."—*Introd.*

A129 Heizer, Robert Fleming; Hester, Thomas R.; and Graves, Carol. Archaeology, a bibliographical guide to the basic literature. N.Y., Garland, 1980. xi, 434p. (Garland reference library of social science, v.54)

Selective unannotated bibliography (books, articles in periodicals and books and other published essays), arranged by primary author, with a complete author index at the end. "The bibliography is slanted toward New World and English-language publications, although we have made an effort to include reasonable coverage of the Old World, Africa, and Asia."—*Pref.*

A130 Lindenlaub, Marie-Luise. Deutschsprachige Dissertationen zur Archäologie des Mittelmeerraums:

1945–1977. Berlin, Deutsches Archäologisches Institut, 1979. 288p.
Classified compilation of German-language dissertations from Germany (East and West), Austria, and Switzerland primarily about the archeology of Greece and Rome, but also of the Near East and Egypt, excluding Islamic archeology. Chronologically it extends to the 5th century A.D.

In addition to standard bibliographic information, entries list the granting institution, subsequent publication history (if any), and citations to summaries and reviews.

Includes an author index, charts breaking down the number of dissertations produced from the three countries year by year, and a chart showing how many dissertations from each institution are listed in the bibliography.

A131 Makjanic, Rajka. British archaeological reports complete catalogue, 1974–1994. Oxford, Tempus Reparatum Archaeological and Historical Associates Limited, 1994. iii, 48p.
Complete catalog of the British archaeological reports (international and British series) from 1974–1994. All 828 vols. are listed in two sections (International and British), followed by author, subject, geographical, and [chronological] period indexes.

A132 Mathaf al-Misri. Maktabah. Catalogue de la Bibliothèque du Musée Égyptien du Caire, 1927–1958. Par Dia' Abou-Ghazi et Abd El-Mohsen El-Khachab. Le Caire, Organisme Général des Imprimeries Gouvernementales, 1966–1992. 6v.
Published as a supplement to the Catalogue de la Bibliothèque du Musée Égyptien du Caire, ed. by M. Henri Munier. Le Caire, Impr. de l'Institut français d'archéologie orientale (1927–28). This supplement, like its predecessor, is arranged alphabetically by author. It lists publications acquired between 1927 and 1958, both books and periodical articles. No indexes.

A133 Medieval studies: an introduction. 2d ed. Ed. by James M. Powell. Syracuse, N.Y., Syracuse Univ. Pr., 1992. xviii, 438p. il. 1st ed. 1976.
13 bibliographically laden essays on medieval studies, each followed by classified unannotated bibliographies. Chapter 4: Archaeology, by David Whitehouse (bibl. p.176–84); Chapter 12: Tradition and innovation in medieval art, by Wayne Dynes (bibl. p.392–400).

Index of authors and titles cited, p.433–38.

A134 Nachschlagewerke und Quellen zur Kunst = Art reference works and sources [microform]. München, Saur, 1999– .
Microfiche collection of bibliographies, encyclopedias, and source works in art. Teil 1: Internationale Bibliographien zur Kunstliteratur zwischen 1500–1850 = International bibliographies of art literature between 1500–1850 (ed. by Ulrich Schütte) promises to offer bibliographies on graphic art, architecture, painting, sculpture, and landscape gardening from German-speaking countries, England, France, Italy, Spain, and the U.S.A.

A135 Nawabi, Y.M. A bibliography of Iran: a catalogue of books and articles on Iranian subjects, mainly in European languages. [Tehran], Iranian Culture Foundation, 1969–1992. 9v.
Broadly classified bibliography of books, journal articles, and book reviews. Entries listed by author within each broad subject heading. Of particular interest to art historians: v.3: Archeology, architecture and art, incl. numismatics; v.4: Travels and description.

No indexes.

A136 Nees, Lawrence. From Justinian to Charlemagne: European art, 565–787: an annotated bibliography. Boston, Hall, 1985. xvi, 278p. 1 il. (Reference publication in art history)
Classified annotated bibliography (books, articles, and other published essays) of Christian art from A.D. 565 to A.D. 787. Although all Justinianic and Carolingian art is excluded, the bibliography includes a number of studies devoted to later works of art with significant bearing on the period covered. Islamic and Jewish art are almost completely excluded. English language eds. are listed wherever possible, with no attempt to trace foreign versions of the same work.

Contents: General bibliography; Byzantine and other eastern Mediterranean art: from Justinian to iconoclasm; The "Dark Ages" in the west: from the Germanic invasions to Charlemagne; The Migration period; Merovingian Francia; Italy; Visigothic Spain.

Author index, p.267–78.

A137 Pearson, James Douglas, ed. A bibliography of Pre-Islamic Persia. London, Mansell, 1975. xxix, 288p. (Persian studies series, no.2)
Series ed.: E. Yarshater.

Classified bibliography (monographic literature, periodical articles, and essays in festschriften) compiled under the auspices of the Royal Institute of Translation and Publication of Iran. It "represents an attempt to include all the printed literature in western European languages . . . [and] . . . a selection of publications in the Persian language . . . prepared by Dr. Ahmad Tafazzoli of the University of Tehran."—*Introd.*

Section D: Art and archaeology (p.321–70) is of interest to art historians. Author index at end.

A138 Phillips, Jill M. Archaeology of the collective East: Greece, Asia Minor, Egypt, Lebanon, Mesopotamia, Syria, Palestine: an annotated bibliography. N.Y., Gordon, 1977. 151p.
Alphabetically arranged by author, this is an unclassified but extensively annotated bibliography of 47 English-language books on archeology for the general reader. A short essay on archeology and the cinema follows (p.117–21), then an unannotated bibliography of further suggested general reading (p.127–47), and a small section of periodical and newspaper articles (p.148–50).

No indexes.

A139 Pohanka, Reinhard. Bibliographie des Iran: nach den Büchern mit iranistischen Themen in der Österreichischen Nationalbibliothek, der Bibliothek der Universität Wien und der Bibliothek der Österreichischen Akademie der Wissenschaften. Wien, Österreichischen Akademie der Wissenschaften, 1985. 309p. (Sitzungsberichte/Österreichische Akademie der Wissenschaften, Philosophisch-historische Klasse; Bd. 454) (Veröffentlichungen der Iranischen Kommission. Sonderband)

Classified bibliography of books about Iranian subjects held at the three largest libraries in Vienna: the Austrian National Library, the Library of the University of Vienna, and the Library of the Austrian Academy of Sciences. Section 5 is Art (p.100–16), and section 6 is Archeology (p.117–31). Author index at end.

A140 Porter, Bertha, and Moss, Rosalind Louisa Beauford. Topographical bibliography of ancient Egyptian hieroglyphic texts, reliefs, and paintings. 2d ed. rev. and augm. Assisted by Ethel W. Burney. Oxford, Griffith Institute Ashmolean Museum, 1960– . (7)v. maps, diagrs., plans, microfiche.

See GLAH 1:A96 for 1st ed. and GLAH 1:A97 for earlier vols. of 2d ed.

Contents: v.1. Theban necropolis. Pt.1. Private tombs, reprinted 1970, 1985, 1994; Pt.2. Royal tombs and smaller cemeteries, reprinted 1973, 1985, 1994; v.2. The Theban temples, reprinted 1984, 1994; v.3. Memphis. Pt.1. Abu Rawash to Abusir, reprinted 1994; Pt.2. Saqqara to Dahshur, fasc.1, 1978; fasc.2, 1979; fasc.3, 1981; fasc.1–3 in 1, 1981; v.4. Lower and Middle Egypt, (1st ed.) 4 microfiche, 1981; v.5. Upper Egypt, sites (1st ed.), reprinted 1962, 4 microfiches, 1981; v.6. Upper Egypt, chief temples (1st ed.), reprinted 1970, 1991; v.7. Nubia, the deserts, and outside Egypt, (1st ed.) reprinted 1962, 1975, 1995.

A141 Poucet, Jacques, and Hannick, J.M. Aux sources de l'Antiquité gréco-romaine: guide bibliographique. 5th ed., rev., augm. Bruxelles, Artel, 1997. 313p.

1st ed. published as Introduction aux études classiques: guide bibliographique. [Louvain-la Neuve, Belgium], CIACO, 1988; 2d ed., 1989; 4th ed. under the present title, 1995; 6th ed. forthcoming. An occasionally annotated bibliographic guide, divided into three sections. The first cites published secondary sources under chapters by general discipline, within which Chapter 4: Les sources archéologiques (p.81–102) offers sources important to scholars of ancient art. The second section cites reference sources (encyclopedias, dictionaries, journals, dissertation lists, etc.), arranged within chapters by publication type. The third section cites sources on specific disciplines, within which Chapter M: Art (p.264–71) begins with general monographs and articles, followed by sources within specific medium. Under each medium, it is further divided by location (general, Greek, Etruscan and Italian, Roman).

Indexes: modern authors (p.277–90); ancient authors (p.291–98); abbreviations used (p.299); listed sets, series, serials (p.300–02).

A142 Rassegna dei periodici. Published annually in Arte medievale, II Serie, Anno III, n.2-Anno X, n.2, 1989–1993.

Classified annotated bibliography of periodical articles on medieval art. Each year's bibliography covers material published several years previously.

A143 Society of Antiquaries of London, Library. Bibliography of periodical literature: accessions to the library of the Society of Antiquaries of London. No. 1 (Sept. 1989)-no. 2 (Oct. 1989–30 Sept. 1990). London, The Society, Library, 1989–1991. 2v.

Supplement to Antiquaries journal. Subject index to periodical articles from journals received in the society's library between Sept. 1989 and Sept. 1990.

In addition, Antiquaries journal has regularly published two bibliographies of note: (1) "List of accessions to the library," published annually, v.1, 1921– . A classified accessions list, with full bibliographic information and the price of each book acquired; (2) "Periodical literature," published less regularly and not appearing in the journal since 1990. A table of contents list of archeological and historical journals.

Covers art and archeology from antiquity through the Middle Ages from all countries.

A144 Syria and Lebanon in antiquity: bibliography, by Jinan Muddarès, 1968–1973. Published in Berytus: archaeological studies, v.18, 1969; v.20, 1971; v.22, 1973-v.23, 1974.

Classified bibliography of periodical articles published between 1968–1973. Art and archeology is the first section, and an author index is at the end of each bibliography.

A145 Van Keuren, Frances Dodds. Guide to research in classical art and mythology. Chicago, American Library Association, 1991. x, 307p.

Designed as a guide to research in the use of major classification tools in the field of classical art and mythology. Each chapter begins with an extensive discussion of a small number of books and then expands to discuss the literature within the scope of the chapter. Multiple sections, each followed by a bibliography on other references, handbooks, and other supplementary sources, can be found in every chapter.

Contents: Pt.1. General research: (1) Greek art and architecture; (2) Etruscan art and architecture; (3) Roman art and architecture; Pt.2. Mythology: (4) Classical mythology in ancient and later literature; (5) Classical mythology in ancient art; (6) Greek gods and heroes in ancient art; (7) Greek drama in ancient art; (8) Classical antiquity in art after antiquity; Pt.3. Media studies: (9) Greek sculpture; (10) Athenian vases; (11) South Italian and Sicilian vases; (12) Etruscan mirrors; (13) Ancient engraved gems; (14) Greek coins; (15) Roman republican coins; (16) Roman imperial coins; (17) Greek and Roman interior decoration.

Author-title index, p.263–97. Subject index, p.301–07.

A146 Vattuone, Riccardo. Scienze dell'antichità: periodici esistenti nelle Biblioteche bolognesi. Bologna, Cooperativa Libraria Universitaria Editrice, 1975. 166p.

Union list of periodicals on antiquity held in 26 libraries of Bologna. The alphabetically arranged list is preceded by a list of participating libraries with their addresses.

A147 Woodhead, Peter. Keyguide to information sources in archaeology. London, Mansell, 1985. xiv, 219p.
This work "aims to provide an integrated guide to the documentation, reference aids and key organizational sources of information in archaeology worldwide. . . . Part I is a narrative account of the major forms of archaeological literature, together with a brief historical introduction to the subject and a discussion of the scope of modern archaeology and its relationship with other subjects, the various bodies in the field, education and careers, and the origins and utilization of archaeological information. . . . Part II is an annotated bibliography of reference sources. . . . Part III is a list of selected archaeological organizations."—*Introd.*

Bibliographic section (Pt.II) is annotated.

Contents: Pt.I: (1) History and scope of archaeology; (2) Archaeological information: its origins and utilization; (3) Who, what, where?; (4) Keeping up to date with current publications, developments and events; (5) Finding out about the literature of archaeology; (6) The literature of archaeology; (7) Other sources of information; Pt.II: General archaeology: worldwide and multi-regional; Archaeological science; Europe; Africa; America; Asia; Australasia; Arctic; Pt.III: International and multi-regional organizations; Organizations by country.

Index, p.187–219.

RENAISSANCE—MODERN

Current Serials

A148 ABM: ArtBibliographies modern on disc [computer file], v.15, 1984– . Oxford, European Bibliographic Center. (Distr. by ABC-CLIO, 1993– .)
See GLAH 1:A102 for original annotation and paper ed.

Available on CD-ROM and through the internet from various vendors.

A149 Iter: the bibliography of Renaissance Europe (1300–1700) [internet resource]. Toronto, Ont., Centre for Reformation and Renaissance Studies of the University of Toronto, 1996– .
Online index to books, reviews, bibliographies, catalogs, journal articles, etc. A collaborative effort between the Centre for Reformation and Renaissance Studies, the Renaissance Society of America, and the Arizona Center for Medieval and Renaissance Studies. To date, more than 400 journals published since 1859 have been indexed.

Retrospective

A150 Academies of art between Renaissance and Romanticism: bibliography. Published in Leids kunsthistorisch jaarboek, v.5–6, 1986–87, p.561–90.
The bibliography following the theme issue "Academies of art between Renaissance and Romanticism" was based upon N. Pevsner's Academies of art, past and present (GLAH 1:G22). In addition, it drew upon "requests for bibliographical information . . . sent to all academies of which one may suppose that the history goes back to the 18th century or before. Provincial and municipal archives were also approached. . . . Likewise, the authors of this volume were asked to compose a bibliography relating to the academy the history of which they were dealing with. [This was combined with] the results of the bibliographical research of A.R.E. de Heer and the members of the editorial staff . . . [and] Répertoire d'Art, Art Index, and RILA. . . . These have been studied for literature after 1940 (that is, after Pevsner) up to and including the 1987 volumes."—*Pref.* to Bibliography.

Arrangement: After a general section, countries are arranged in alphabetical order, and within each country are general sections, then sections arranged by city. Citations appear chronologically within these sections.

A151 Amsterdam (Netherlands). Stedelijk Museum. International index to art exhibition catalogues, 1895–1991 [microform]. Lisse, MMF, 1993. 867 microfiches in binder with guide (47p.)
Index to exhibition and museum catalogs in the library of the Stedelijk Museum of Modern Art, Amsterdam.

"The microfiches are divided into different categories: by artist, by city, by UDC code, traveling exhibitions (general/countries), museum and private collections, by artists groups/associations/biennials, etc., prizes won by artists, exhibitions in the Stedelijk Museum and Fodor Museum."—*Guide.*

A152 Arntz-Bulletin; Dokumentation der Kunst des 20. Jahrhunderts. Haag/Oberbayern, Arntz-Winter. (Distr. in America by Wittenborn, [1976]–1983.) v.2, no.1–6. il.
See GLAH 1:A100 for v.1, pt.1–11, 1968–[1974], annotations of which still apply to v.2. Ed. by Wilhelm F. Arntz.

"[These] present catalogue[s], published as special edition[s], [are] destined to provide brief but adequate information on all the catalogues raisonnés which appeared from 1945 to the end of 1974 . . . for the first time ever all compilations available in print on written and verbal statements by an artist have also been included in this record." No new sections, supplements, etc. have been published since 1984.

______. Sonderband [1]: Werkkataloge zur Kunst des 20. Jahrhunderts: Catalogues raisonnés. [1975?] (Verzeichnis der seit 1945–[1974] erschienenen)

______. Sonderband 2: Werkkataloge zur Kunst des 20. Jahrhunderts: mit Nachtragen der Jahre 1945–1973. 1984. (Verzeichnis der von 1974–1983 erschienenen)

A153 Bauhaus-Ideen 1919–1994: Bibliographie und Beiträge zur Rezeption des Bauhausgedankens. Berlin, Reimer, 1994. 493p.
After several essays on the reception of Bauhaus ideas throughout the 20th century, there follows an annotated bibliography of books, newspaper and periodical articles, radio broadcasts, films, and assorted advertisements on Bauhaus reception between 1919–1990. The largest section (p.147–361) covers international literature, the second section

(p.361–409) covers East German literature, and the final section (p.410–15) is a small supplement of newly found titles. Following the indexes is a chronological list of exhibitions about the Bauhaus.

Indexes: author, p.419–39; name, p.440–50; place, p.451–52; Bauhaus locations, p.453–60; architectural subject index, p.461–63; keyword index, p.464–72.

A154 Bell, Doris L. Contemporary art trends 1960–1980: a guide to sources. Metuchen, Scarecrow, 1981. x, 171p.

Bibliographic essays that discuss books and articles on contemporary art of the 1960s to the 1980s. Works about single artists are not included.

Contents: General works; Trends (short essays on various art trends, e.g. Air Art, Art Povera, Body Art, Earthworks, Happenings, Op-art, Super-realism, etc.); Group Zero and Fluxus; Countries/areas; Biennales and other international exhibitions; Contemporary art journals (an alphabetically arranged annotated list of journals on contemporary art not indexed by Art index); Bibliography (dividing out books from journal articles, it is arranged by main entry and functions as an index to all the bibliographic material cited in the book).

A155 Belotti, Monica. Le edizioni settecentesche della Biblioteca del conte Giacomo Carrara, conservata presso l'Accademia Carrara e la Biblioteca civica di Bergamo. Published in Libri & documenti (Archivio Storico Civico e Biblioteca Trivulziana), v.16, no.2, p.16–61; v.16, no.3, p.1–46; v.17, no.1, p.1–56; v.17, no.2, p.1–62; v.17, no.3, p.1–28, (1991–92). il.

Annotated catalog of the 18th-century publications of the private library of Count Giacomo Carrara now held at the Accademia Carrara and the Biblioteca Civica A. Mai di Bergamo, the vast majority of which are on art and architecture. The introduction preceding this bibliography gives a thorough history of the collection, describing and illustrating many noteworthy items.

Indexes (v.17, no.3, p.9–28): chronological, geographical (place of publication), name (of editors and of typographers).

A156 Chelap, Patty, comp. Bibliography: symbolist art, 1974–1984. Published in Art journal, v.45, no.2, 1985, p.171–80.

Complements Anderson, David L., Symbolism: a bibliography of symbolism as an international and multidisciplinary movement (GLAH 1:A105). This bibliography of dissertations, books, journal articles, and exhibition catalogs covers sources published since the appearance of Anderson's book, which, unlike Chelap, does not focus exclusively on symbolism in the visual arts.

A157 Chénieux-Gendron, Jacqueline; Le Roux, Françoise; and Vienne, Maïté. Inventaire analytique de revues surréalistes ou apparentées: le surréalisme autour du monde 1929–1947. Paris, CNRS, 1994. 463p.

Thorough description and analysis of 49 single issues of 13 journals with articles or illustrations by surrealist authors or artists. Illustrations, including cover pages, are carefully described. Index of all names cited at end, p.413–63.

A158 Chicago. Art Institute. Surrealism & its affinities: the Mary Reynolds collection. A bibliography compiled by Hugh Edwards. [2d ed.] Chicago, Art Institute, [1973]. 147p. il., 17 plates.

See GLAH 1:A109 for 1st ed.

The entire text of the 1st ed. has been preserved with all additions marked with an asterisk following details of size and pagination. New periodicals are marked with an asterisk, and additional volumes of periodicals listed in the 1st ed. have been marked with a double asterisk.

Indexes: names and titles, p.140–46; periodicals, p.146–47; illustrations, p.147.

A159 Convegno di studi sul surrealismo (1973: Salerno). Studi sul surrealismo: bibliografia in materia d'arte e di teatro quale contributo per la conoscenze di quanto è stato pubblicato in Italia fino alla data del Convegno di studi sul surrealismo (1973). Roma, Officina, 1976. 79p. (Saggi/Documenti, 6:2)

Art historians will be drawn to the first chapter of this bibliography, "Contributo a una bibliografia sul surrealismo," by Arcangelo Cascavilla and Maria Rosaria De Rosa. This is an unannotated bibliography of surrealism in the visual arts, with small sections on surrealism in politics and surrealism in psychoanalysis. Includes 14 sections devoted to citations of books and articles on 14 individual artists.

The final chapter, "Contributo a una bibliografia sul teatro surrealista," by Attilio Mauro Caproni, deals exclusively with surrealism in theater.

No indexes.

A160 Dokumentations-Bibliothek zur Kunst des 20. Jahrhunderts. Bibliography of 20th century art publications. Hans Bolliger für Kornfeld & Klipstein. San Francisco, Wofsy, 1991. 607p. il.

Originally published as six auction catalogs, reprinted here with more than 4,000 titles of rare monographs, illustrated books, pamphlets, manifestos, posters, and other ephemera, as well as artists' books and other original art of the 20th century. The introduction and final pages are numbered as if the six auction catalogs were continuously numbered (but they are not). The auctions were held in Bern, Switzerland, in 1957, 1958, 1968, 1969, 1976, and 1977 by the house of Klipstein & Kornfeld. Entries gives full citation, price, and notes.

Index of names and titles at end of reprint.

A161 Falqui, Enrico. Bibliografia e iconografia del futurismo. [Reprint.] Firenze, Sansoni Antiquariato, 1959. 239p. il. ports. 100 plates. (Contributi alla Biblioteca bibliografica italica, 21) (Repr.: Firenze, Casa Editrice le Lettere, 1988.)

Bibliographic section (p. 29–110) lists books and periodical articles about futurism, beginning with theory/criticism and continuing with sections by discipline (literature, theater, music, and art).

Iconography section (with plates) has portraits, illustrations of posters, broadsides, and other ephemeral publications of the futurists.

Index of authors, titles, subjects, p.231–39.

A162 Ford, Simon. The realization and suppression of the Situationist International: an annotated bibliography, 1972–1992. San Francisco, AK Pr., 1995. 149p.

A well-annotated classified bibliography listing books, essays in books, periodicals (journals and newspapers), exhibition catalogs, manifestos, pamphlets, and other ephemeral material.

Contents: General works; Related movements; Works on or by ex-situationists; American pro-situs & milieu; British pro-situs & milieu; Book reviews; 1989 exhibition & catalogue reviews; Selected addresses; Index.

A163 Gray, John. Action art: a bibliography of artists' performance from futurism to fluxus and beyond. Westport, Conn., Greenwood, 1993. xiv, 343p. (Art reference collection, no.16)

Bibliography of 3,700 briefly annotated entries (of books, dissertations, periodical and newspaper articles, films, videos, and audiotapes) covering action art prior to the 1970s. However, coverage of a few artists whose work extends beyond the end of 1969 are included, when their post-1969 work is seen as an extension of work begun during the 1960s. When artists have a small connection to action art, materials are included only when related to this intersection. Publication dates of items cited range from 1914 to late 1992.

Contents: (1) Action Art 1909–1952: the antecedents: Futurism, Dada, Cubism, Russian Performance, the Bauhaus and Black Mountain College; (2) Action Art 1950s–1970s: Gutai, Happenings, Fluxus, Viennese Actionism, Destruction in art, the Provos, Situationism and beyond: (a) General works; (b) Country studies; (3) Biographical and critical studies; Appendices: (I) Reference works; (II) Libraries and archives; (III) Addenda; (IV) List of artists/artists groups by country; (V) List of artists groups and collectives.

Indexes: artist, p.299–306; subject, p.307–12; title, p.313–16; author, p.317–43.

A164 Havlice, Patricia Pate. Earth scale art: a bibliography, directory of artists, and index to reproductions. Jefferson, N.C., McFarland, 1984. 138p.

Bibliography of books, periodical articles, and exhibition catalogs on earth scale art in general and on the earth scale art of single artists. "This book is arranged in four parts, beginning with a bibliography of general articles [Part I]. The main section, Part II, lists the work of 32 artists who devoted a portion of their careers to earth scale art. [As much biographical information as the author could find is also listed for each artist in Part II.] Part III is an author index to the bibliographical material. Part IV, an index to titles of art works, refers the user to reproductions listed under the separate artist's entries."—*Pref.*

A165 Held, John. Mail art: an annotated bibliography. Metuchen, Scarecrow, 1991. xlviii, 534p.

Heavily annotated bibliography, sorted by type of publication (books, magazines, newspapers, catalog essays).

Included here are "the accumulated accounts of mail art from more than eight hundred authors from thirty-seven countries. The earliest entry is from the inaugural edition of the Village Voice in 1955. The latest is from the official publication of the Soviet Ministry of Culture, Iskusstvo, appearing in the October 1989 issue. . . . This is not only the largest bibliography of mail art ever compiled, but also of rubber stamp art, artist postage stamps, Ray Johnson and the New York Correspondence School, as well as a number of artists who have participated in the medium over the years. Other subjects, like artist publications, art and communication, and Fluxus can also be researched through this volume to great benefit."—*Introd.*

Indexes: author, p.431–44; title, p.445–94; subject, p.495–534.

A166 Heppner, Irene. Bibliography on portraiture: selected writings on portraiture as an art form and as documentation. Boston, Hall, 1990. 2v. ports.

"While emphasis is on American portraits and portraiture as well as on British developments that influenced trends in America, all epochs of civilization are considered. Most entries are from English-language publications, with a few in foreign languages."—*Introd.* Includes books, articles, exhibition catalogs, collection catalogs, theses. Vol.1 lists authors (or museums); vol.2 consists of a classified arrangement, divided into two major parts: general and special media. Entries are reproduced from card catalog format.

Index to topics, p.913–47.

A167 Hesse, Gritta, and Bingel, Marie Agnes, comp. Künstler der jungen Generation: Literaturverzeichnis zur Gegenwartskunst in der Amerika-Gedenkbibliothek, Berliner Zentralbibliothek = Artists of the young generation: literature on contemporary art in the American Memorial Library, Berlin Central Library. München, Saur, 1987. 353p.

See GLAH 1:A112 for original annotation and earlier ed.

Selective bibliography of artists born after 1915, arranged alphabetically by artist's last name. Brief biographical information (year and place of birth) begins each artist's section. Bibliographic entries are arranged under each artist in reverse chronological order.

"This bibliography is the result of twenty years' work collecting and classifying literature in a specialized department of the American Memorial Library. . . . It contains approximately 17,000 entries on material published up through 1985 on the work of about 6,500 artists. . . . This work is a library catalog; it is not a bibliography which strives to be all-encompassing. The exhibition catalogs and books are primarily from German-speaking countries. Nevertheless, the presence of foreign artists is greater than 50%, because the art scene is international."—*Introd.*

No indexes.

A168 Kaufman, Edward, and Irish, Sharon. Medievalism: an annotated bibliography of recent research in the architecture and art of Britain and North America.

N.Y., Garland, 1988. xlvii, 279p. (Garland reference library of the humanities, v.791)

Classified annotated bibliography of the medieval-revivalist traditions primarily in architecture, but including the other arts, within Great Britain and North America. Medievalism is here described beginning in the late 16th century and dying, at least for the purposes of this bibliography, in the mid-20th century. The chronological range of publication dates for included materials is 1960–84, with some earlier notable exceptions.

General index, p.251–79.

A169 Kaufmann, Thomas DaCosta. Art and architecture in Central Europe, 1550–1620: an annotated bibliography. Boston, Hall, 1988. xxxvii, 316p. (Reference publication in art history)

Classified annotated bibliography (of books, periodical articles, and dissertations readily available in America) covering "the area comprising the contemporary states of the German Federal Republic, German Democratic Republic, Austria, Switzerland, the regions of Bohemia and Moravia in Czechoslovakia, Slovenia in Yugoslavia, of Silesia and Pomerania with Gdansk, now in Poland, and also East Prussia, now divided between Poland and the Soviet Union. This region corresponds approximately to the area of the Holy Roman Empire, without the Low Countries, Lorraine, and other French-speaking enclaves, and with the addition of Danzig and East Prussia."—*Introd.*

The bibliographic section begins with chapters on sources and general works (p.1–46), followed by chapters arranged alphabetically by geographic region (p.47–294). The last chapter alphabetically lists traveling artists (p.295–304). Author index, p.305–16.

A170 Kuenzli, Rudolf E. Dada bibliography: 1973–1978; and Dada bibliography: 1978–1983. In Dada/Surrealism, 10–11 (1982), p.161–201; and 13 (1984), p.129–64.

Selective bibliographies of books, exhibition catalogs, dissertations, and periodical articles covering artistic and literary aspects of Dada from its beginnings until 1923. Each bibliography is broken into two parts, the first covering general aspects of Dada, and the second individual Dadaists with subdivisions for each artist as follows: (A) Works by Dadaists, reprints, and translations; (B) Articles and letters by Dadaists and translations; (C) Books and dissertations on individual Dadaists; (D) Exhibition catalogs on individual Dadaists; (E) Articles and parts of books on individual Dadaists.

Preceded by small bibliographies in the early issues of this journal; e.g., "A selected bibliography of works on Dada/Surrealism in North America: 1969–1972." In Dada/Surrealism, 2 (1972), p.81–84. No further bibliographies on Dada were published in this journal after v.13 (1984).

See following entry for related bibliography.

A171 ———, and Ungar, Steven. Bibliography on Surrealism, 1973–1982. Published in Dada/Surrealism, 12 (1983), p.90–126.

Conceived as a companion to the Dada bibliography (above), this is also a selective bibliography of books, exhibition catalogs, dissertations, and periodical articles on artistic and literary aspects of Surrealism. It shares the same organizational structure as the Dada bibliography above. Later bibliographies on Surrealism appear in the journal Mélusine (see GLAH 2:A183).

A172 Lekatsas, Barbara. The Howard L. and Muriel Weingrow collection of avant-garde art and literature at Hofstra University: an annotated bibliography. Westport, Conn., Greenwood, 1985. xxv, 322p. 64 plates, il. (part col.)

This catalog of the Weingrow collection, originally assembled by Philip Kaplan between 1920 and 1970, is arranged by main entry (p.3–242) followed by a list of periodicals held in the collection (p.243–86). It represents entries for "over 4,000 items consisting of illustrated books, secondary works, periodicals, catalogs, manuscripts, pamphlets, posters, photographs, and original prints representing the major avant-garde movements of the twentieth century. The collection also included forty-four books, mostly illustrated editions, from the nineteenth century."—*Introd.*

The focus of this collection is the Surrealist, Expressionist, and Dadaist movements, although limited materials from other early 20th-century movements are also included.

Indexes: authors and illustrators, p.287–306; titles, p.307–22.

A173 Modern art bibliographical series. Oxford, Clio, 1982–1984. 3 vols.

A numbered series of bibliographies on modern art.

Contents: (1) Tribal and ethnic art, 1982; (2) Photography, 1982; (3) Design, 1984.

A174 Nordic art magazines = Nordiske kunst- og kulturtidsskrifter = Pohjoismaiset taide- ja kulttuurilehdet = Norræn list- og menningartímarit = Nordiska konst- och kulturtidskrifter. Norway, Esset Grafisk, [1991?]. 71p. il.

Classified list of 130 periodicals published in Denmark, Finland, Iceland, Norway, and Sweden about contemporary art worldwide. Besides standard bibliographic information, citations list editor, editorial staff, phone and FAX numbers, typical number of pages per issue, frequency, subscription price, scope of periodical, and where indexed.

Contents: General culture magazines; Architecture; Visual art; Design - crafts; Aesthetics - criticism - theory; Photography - film - video; Art history; Musicology.

A175 Pacciani, Riccardo. Per una bibliografia sul manierismo nelle arti figurative (1972–1982). Published in Manierismo e letteratura, atti del congresso internazionale, Torino, 12–15 ottobre 1983. A cura di Gabriella Bosco . . . [et al.] Torino, Maynier, 1986. 631p. il. (Collana di critica, linguistica e poetica)

Classified bibliography (p.47–103) of books, congress reports, and periodical articles written between 1972 and 1982 on mannerism in the pictorial arts. No indexes.

A176 Parshall, Linda B., and Parshall, Peter W. Art and the Reformation: an annotated bibliography. Boston,

Hall, 1986. xlvi, 282p. il. (Reference publication in art history)

Classified annotated bibliography (of books with their reviews, articles in periodicals, and dissertations) on art of the Reformation primarily in Germany, France, Belgium, Holland, and Switzerland. "In our need to draw a reasonable limit to the scope of this project . . . we chose to give serious but somewhat less detailed attention to Austria, Scandinavia, and the eastern European countries. England seemed to us a largely separable problem, and so we have treated it in a general way. Furthermore, the Counter Reformation . . . is included only where it figured importantly as an adversary and stimulus to Reformation controversy in the arts."—*Pref.*

Contents: (1) Standard reference sources; (2) The image controversy; (3) Iconoclasm; (4) The Reformation period and art; (5) Text illustration and printed propaganda; (6) Reformation religious iconography; (7) Artists of the Reformation; (8) Architecture, architectural decoration, and furnishing; (9) Decorative and minor arts; (10) Iconography of the reformers.

Index of authors, editors, and compilers, p.255–67. Index of exhibitions by location, p.269. Index of subjects, p.271–82.

A177 Perneczky, Géza. The magazine network: the trends of alternative art in the light of their periodicals, 1968–1988. [Trans. from Hungarian by Tibor Szendrei.] [Stephen Perkins, assist. ed.] Köln, Edition Soft Geometry, 1993. 285p.

Abridged trans. of A Hálo, 1991.

"This is a scholarly dissertation on the network of artists' magazines, periodicals and communications which are outside the mainstream of periodical literature. Here we have explained, discussed and illustrated a myriad of publications which have been untouched by the academic community, but which are integral to the study of contemporary art."—*Review*, Judith Hoffberg, Umbrella, June 1991.

Collected essays about the history of alternative art publications created from 1968 to 1988 (p.11–204), followed first by a selective bibliography on the subject (p.205–18) and then by a register of alternative art periodicals with coded annotations (p.219–65).

Name and title index, p.267–85.

A178 Prause, Marianne. Bibliographie zur Kunstgeschichte des 19. Jahrhunderts: Publikationen der Jahre 1967–1979 mit Nachträgen zu den Jahren 1940–1966. München, Prestel, 1984. xii, 1019p. (Materialien zur Kunst des neunzehnten Jahrhunderts, Bd.31)

Supplements GLAH 1:A115.

Supplementing the earlier ed., this selective bibliography uses a similar but expanded classification scheme for work published from 1967 to 1979 and newly discovered material published between 1940 and 1966. Material on individual artists forms the largest section of the bibliography (p.369–867). Citations to reviews of materials listed in this bibliography are also incorporated.

Topographisches Register, p.[871]–89. Künstler- und Personenregister, p.[891]–924. Verfasser-Register, p.[925]–1007. Sachregister, p.[1009]–19.

A179 Salaris, Claudia. Bibliografia del futurismo: 1909–1944. Con una lettera inedita di Corrado Govoni a F.T. Marinetti sul libro futurista. [Roma], Biblioteca del Vascello, 1988. 118p. il.

Annotated bibliography of materials about futurism from 1909 to 1944. This work is arranged by type of publication: works by single authors (p.21–73), collective works (p.74–79), manifestos (p.79–92), journals (p.93–103), avant-garde non-futurist journals (p.103–05), parodies and satires (books and leaflets) (p.106–07), satirical journals with theme issues on futurism (p.107), criticism (p.108–13), and name index (p.114–18).

Preceded by an essay on futurism by the author, and a letter from C. Govoni to F.T. Marinetti.

A180 Schäfer, Jörgen. Dada in Köln: ein Repertorium. In verbindung mit Angela Merte. Frankfurt, Lang, 1995. 290p. (Bibliographien zur Literatur- und Mediengeschichte, Bd. 3)

Exhaustive classified annotated bibliography of primary and secondary sources about the Dada movement in Cologne. Name index at end.

A181 Schimmelman, Janice G. A checklist of European treatises on art and essays on aesthetics available in America through 1815. Worcester, Mass., American Antiquarian Society, 1983. 95–195p. (Reprinted from the Proceedings of the American Antiquarian Society, v.93, pt.1, Apr. 1983.)

This small annotated bibliography offers rich insight into what was available to Americans in the 17th and 18th centuries. "Although it is limited by the number of extant American book catalogues from [the] period, it is hoped that students of American culture will find it a useful tool in determining those classical and Romantic concepts that helped to mold the taste of early American society."—*Author's introductory remarks.*

In compiling these 45 treatises and essays, the author scoured book catalogs of about 350 libraries and booksellers as well as a number of indexes and checklists of books published or available in America. The full title of each first ed. is listed, followed by the first English translation when applicable. Original spellings, capitalizations, and abbreviations have been preserved.

A182 Studing, Richard, and Kruz, Elizabeth, comp. Mannerism in art, literature, and music: a bibliography. San Antonio, Trinity Univ. Pr., 1979. xvii, 60p. (Checklists in the humanities and education)

Bibliography of 20th-century criticism on Mannerism in the visual arts, literature, and music, the largest section covering the visual arts.

Contents: (1) Art, p.1–30; (2) Exhibitions and related publications, p.31–36; (3) Literature, p.37–46; (4) Music, p.47–52; (5) Interdisciplinary publications, p.53–56; Addendum, p.57–60.

A183 Le Surréalisme à l'université: inventaire des thèses et bibliographie. Published in Mélusine: cahiers du

Centre de Recherche sur Surréalisme, v.1 (1979)–v.12 (1991).

For related title, see Kuenzli and Ungar, "Bibliography on Surrealism, 1973–1982" (GLAH 2:A171).

The first title ("Inventaire des thèses") is a classified bibliography of French theses and dissertations on Surrealist subjects for the years 1970–91. Each citation lists the author, title, director, granting institution, and date.

The second title is a classified bibliography of books and reprints of books and journals published between 1976–91, frequently listing table of contents. Sometimes these sections are published to showcase certain aspects of Surrealism (see v.4, 1983, p.357–80: "Catalogue de l'exposition: livres surréalistes: vitrines"), or to showcase single Surrealists (see v.9, 1987, p.283–88: "Hans Arp: bibliographie sélective").

A184 Tate Gallery, London. Archive. The Tate Gallery Archive, an index on microfiche, 1986 [microform]. London, Ormonde (Distr. in U.S. by Clearwater), 1986. 122 microfiches + 1 guide (xi leaves) in binder.

"Tate Gallery Archive was set up in the late 1960s, principally to collect material of 20th century British artists and their associates and to be the depository of the Gallery's own records more than thirty years old. However, the contents of this Index will demonstrate that it has a wider range extending to 20th century artists worldwide and British artists working prior to the 20th century. This material comes in many different forms: personal letters, notebooks, diaries, drafts of texts, sketchbooks, drawings, photographs, printers' proofs, press-cuttings, ledgers and official registers, audio-visual records (both tape and transcript), film and microfiche, posters, private view cards, annotated exhibition catalogues and diverse ephemera."—*Introd.*

This index is divided into two sections: Personal records of artists (includes personal papers, microform records, audio-visual records, and posters), and Records of the Tate Gallery (listed and available to view in situ, but not yet fully indexed).

A185 Weisberg, Gabriel P., and Weisberg, Yvonne M.L. Japonisme: an annotated bibliography. N.Y., Garland, 1990. xxviii, 445p. il. (Co-published with the International Center for Japonisme) (Garland reference library of the humanities, v.695)

"Among the goals of this annotated bibliography have been, first, to chronicle the history of Japanese art's impact on the West, and second, to move beyond superficialities by returning to the earliest Western encounters with Japan to see how contacts with the Far East changed over the decades."—*Introd.*

Heavily annotated bibliography arranged by type of publication (books, catalogs, articles, dissertations, reviews, and notes), and within that, by date.

Indexes: author, p.405–13; subject, p.414–45.

SEE ALSO: Bibliography of German expressionism: catalog of the Library of the Robert Gore Rifkind Center for German Expressionist Studies at the Los Angeles County Museum of Art (GLAH 2:A188).

WESTERN COUNTRIES

Baltic Countries

A186 Böckler, Erich, and Fischer, Henrik. Bibliographie zur baltischen Bau- und Kunstgeschichte, 1939–1981. Berlin, Deutscher Verlag für Kunstwissenschaft, 1984. vii, 56p. (Schrifttum zur deutschen Kunst. Sonderheft.)

See GLAH 1:A131 for series entry.

Classified bibliography of books and periodical literature on all aspects of the art and architecture of the Baltic region, including Estonia, Latvia, Lithuania, and the former German provinces of East and West Prussia. Includes coverage of Baltic art abroad. Library locations, where known, are given. Covers the literature published between 1939 and 1981. Includes reviews.

Register: Künstler, p.50. Länder, Landschafter und Orte, p.51–52. Verfasser, p.53–56.

France

A187 Inventaire général des monuments et des richesses artistiques de la France. Répertoire des inventaires. Paris, Impr. Nationale, 1971– . (28) fasc.

See GLAH 1:A120 for earlier fasc.

Contents: (3) pt.1, Ile-de-France (1983); (5) Haute-Normandie (1975); (6) Basse-Normandie (1982); (8) Pays de la Loire (1986); (11) Aquitaine (1978); (13) Champagne-Ardenne (1991); (16) Franche-Comté (1984); (17) Bourgogne (1979); (18) Auvergne (1977); (19) Rhône-Alpes; (20) Languedoc Roussillon; (21) Provence-Côte d'Azur; (22) Corse; (28) Fascicule National.

Germany and Austria

A188 Robert Gore Rifkind Center for German Expressionist Studies. Library. Bibliography of German expressionism: catalog of the Library of the Robert Gore Rifkind Center for German Expressionist Studies at the Los Angeles County Museum of Art. Boston, Hall, 1990. 272p. il.

Catalog of some 4,000 volumes, of which one-third are rare early catalogs and monographs documenting the work of 150 artists. Includes 110 contemporary periodicals, exhibition and oeuvre catalogs, and a large secondary sources collection.

A189 Schroeter, Eva-Maria. Bibliographie zur Kunstgeschichte Heidelbergs. Heidelberg, Kunsthistorisches Institut der Universität Heidelberg, 1993. 229p. (Veröffentlichungen zur Heidelberger Altstadt, Heft 27)

Also available via the internet. Classified bibliography of books, some analyzed, and periodical literature on the art and architecture of this city and surrounding area. Within each category, items are arranged alphabetically by author.

Personen- und Titelregister, p.183–229.

A190 Wichmann, Hans, ed. Bibliographie der Kunst in Bayern. Wiesbaden, Harrassowitz, 1961–83. 5v.

(Bayerische Akademie der Wissenschaften, Munich. Kommission für bayerische Landesgeschichte. Bibliographien, Bd. 1–5.)
See GLAH 1:A135 for earlier vols.
Contents: (5) Namenregister for Bd. 1–4.

Great Britain and Ireland

A191 British archaeological bibliography, v.1, no.1, Apr. 1992– . London, British Archaeological Society, 1992– . Semiannual.
Continues GLAH 1:A136 and GLAH 1:A138. Available online via the internet. Classified annotated bibliography of current books and periodical literature relating to the archeology of Great Britain and Ireland. Includes more general literature on archeology, heritage management, public and political aspects of archeology, and the sciences as applied to archeology. Includes coverage of more than 350 British and Irish periodicals and 150 numbered monographic series. For publications outside Britain and Ireland, a separate list of approximately 360 serials and monographic series are examined. A complete list of serial publications examined for each issue appears at the end of the preface. Each volume includes an Abstracts section-finder and Cross-reference guide for ease of use. Author, subject indexes. Appendixes: Directory of periodicals and monographs; Directory of book publishers; Directory of other abstract publications and serial bibliographies for archaeology and related disciplines; Directory of information on archaeology in the British Parliament.

A192 Dobai, Johannes. Die Kunstliteratur des Klassizismus und der Romantik in England. Bern, Benteli, 1974–[1984?]. 4v.
See GLAH 1:A139 for earlier vols.
Contents: (4) Registerband. Bearb. von Katharina Dobai.

A193 Handbook for British and Irish archaeology: sources and resources. Comp. by Cherry Lavell. Edinburgh, Edinburgh Univ. Pr., 1997. 480p.
"The main aim of this book is to indicate at least some of the rich resources available in Britain and Ireland, many of them grossly underused."—*Introd.* Compiles authoritative information on organizations, national societies, and special interest groups; bibliographies; dictionaries; map lists; record office directories; grant sources; archeological touring guides; etc.
Index of authors and subjects, p.383–421.

A194 King, Anthony. British and Irish archaeology: a bibliographical guide. Manchester, Manchester Univ. Pr., 1994. xii, 324p. (History and related disciplines select bibliographies)
Classified, annotated bibliography of 6,000 books and articles, primarily in English, on British and Irish archeology, covering material published 1960–1990. Arranged chronologically, from the Paleolithic to 19th-century industrial archeology. Each period is subdivided, with standard sections including general surveys, chronology, environment, settlements, religious and industrial sites, economics, artifacts, and arts. The first chapter covers general works and studies of methodology. Index of authors, editors, and organizations, p.301–24.

A195 Werner, Martin. Insular art: an annotated bibliography. Boston, Hall, 1984. xxxiv, 395p. (Reference publication in art history)
Classified bibliography of books and periodical literature (including reviews) on the art of the British from the 5th–9th centuries, and of Ireland up to the 11th century. The introduction surveys the history of research in this area. Topical arrangement beginning with General topics, followed by History; Language, literature, learning, exegesis, liturgy; Manuscripts and manuscript illustration; Art and archeology; Sculpture; Metalwork, textiles, beads; and Ecclesiastical architecture. Material is further divided geographically, as well as by prominent individual works, e.g., Book of Kells. Includes material published until 1979. An appendix lists more recent scholarly literature through 1982. Detailed annotations.
Author index, p.373–95.

Italy

A196 Arte moderna a Firenze: cataloghi di esposizioni 1900–1933. A cura di Artemisia Calcagni Abrami e Lucia Chimirri. Firenze, Centro Di, 1988. 79p. il. (Cataloghi/Gabinetto stampe delle Biblioteca nazionale centrale di Firenze; nuova ser., 2) (Mostre, 26) (Centro Di cat., 222)
Catalog of the exhibition, Biblioteca Nazionale Centrale, Florence (1988), which is in itself a census of exhibition catalogs arranged chronologically. Bibliographic entries include an abbreviation for the holding library, and bibliographic references where available. The lengthy introduction summarizes the exhibition and publishing activities of various Florentine galleries and societies during this period. Includes many illustrations of catalog title pages.
Appendix, p.63–65, lists chronologically catalog citations for which there is no known holding library. Indice dei nomi, p.75–79. Bibliography, p.67–74, arranged chronologically, covers 1863–1986.

A197 Bollettino bibliografico, 1950– . Published quarterly in Commentari: rivista di critica e storia dell'arte, anno 1–27, 1950–1978; n.s., anno 1 (1995)– .
Loosely classified list of books and periodical articles on Italian art and architecture appearing in each quarterly issue of Commentari (GLAH 1:Q134).

A198 Degrassi Maltese, Livia. Repertorio di bibliografia per i beni culturali della Liguria. Genova, SAGEP, 1980. 419p.
International bibliography of books and archival and periodical literature on the art and architecture of this region, published from the 17th century through 1976. Includes iconographic references. Some entries include brief annotations. Bibliographic entries, arranged alphabetically by au-

thor, are followed by two indexes. Continued by Nuti (GLAH 2:A202).

Indice dei luoghi e materie, p.267–343. Indice degli artisti, p.345–410.

A199 Fucinese, Damiano Venanzio. Arte e archeologia in Abruzzo: bibliografia. Rome, Università degli studi, Istituto di fondamenti dell'architettura; Officina, 1978. xxii, 381p.

Bibliography covering five centuries of books and periodical literature on the Abruzzo region. The 4,733 entries are arranged chronologically. The introduction includes an overview about the Abruzzo. Includes a separate list of important manuscripts, p.292–306. Brief annotations.

Indice degli autori, p.317–35. Indice degli artisti, p.336–52. Indice dei nomi propri, p.353–56. Indice delle località, p.357–76. Indice analitico, p.377–81.

A200 Gilbert, Creighton. Tesi di laurea in storia dell'arte italiana dalle Università Austriache, inglesi, olandesi, statunitensi, svizzere e tedesche (1945–1975). Published in Arte lombarda 70/71, no.3–4, 1984, p.5–24.

Classified, unannotated listing. Entries include UMI number where available.

A201 Mitchell, Bonner. Italian civic pageantry in the High Renaissance: a descriptive bibliography of triumphal entries and selected other festivals for state occasions. Firenze, Leo S. Olschki, 1979. 186p. (Biblioteca de bibliografia italiana, 89)

Covers the years 1494–1550. Each festival entry includes a summary of events and an annotated list of published sources and studies. Manuscript sources are excluded. Arranged alphabetically by city and then chronologically. Citations for "festival books" include European library locations. Preface includes valuable bibliographic citations for festival studies.

Indexes: Principal elements of the festivals, p.168–69; Artists, authors of plays and verses, composers and musicians, p.170–72; Titles of plays and poems, first lines of musical compositions, p.173–74; Principal participants in the festivals, and selected personages and personifications from the apparati and dramatic presentations, p.175–78; Authors of sources and studies, scholarly editors, p.179–83.

A202 Nuti, Anna Luisa. Repertorio de bibliografia per i beni culturali della Liguria. Genova, SAGEP, 1984. 127p. il.

Supplement to 1980 ed. by Livia Degrassi Maltese (GLAH 2:A198). Covers material published from 1977–1982. Bibliographic entries, arranged alphabetically by author, are followed by two indexes.

Indice dei luoghi e materie, p.75–98. Indice degli artisti, p.99–124.

A203 Raspi Serra, Joselita. Cataloghi delle mostre di arte italiana dal VI al XVII secolo in Italia e all'estero dal 1930 al 1945. Salerno, Pietro Laveglia, 1980. 156p. (Piccola Biblioteca Laveglia, 18–19. Saggi: arte, 1)

Listing of 93 exhibition catalogs published between 1930 and 1945, arranged chronologically. Entries include all bibliographic information plus the authors of introductory material, a list of exhibiting artists and the number of works shown by each artist. The introduction describes the evolution of the exhibition catalog during this period, as well as the selection criteria for this bibliography.

A204 Rosenberg, Charles M. Fifteenth-century North Italian painting and drawing: an annotated bibliography. Boston, Hall, 1986. xxxi, 224p. (Reference publication in art history)

Within each of its divisions there are three subgroups: general, city, and artists. Within the city section, further subgroups include general, guidebooks, collections and museums, and monuments. Entries arranged chronologically within each section.

Contents: General bibliography; Emilia-Romagna; Liguria; Lombardy; The Piedmont.

Index of artists, p.203–13. Index of authors, p.215–24.

Latin America

A205 Biblioteca Nacional José Martí. Bibliografía de arte cubano. Ciudad de La Habana, Ed. Pueblo y Educación, 1985. 346p.

Systematic bibliography of Cuban art based on the holdings of this important library.

Contents: (A) Libros y folletos; (I) Obras de interés general; (II) Referencias generales; (III) Arte indocubano; (IV) Arquitectura y urbanismo; (V) Monumentos, estatuaria y epigrafía; (VI) Escultura; (VII) Pintura, dibujo y grabado; (VIII) Diseño gráfico; (IX) Artes populares e industriales; (X) Artes escénicas: danza y teatro; (B) Catálogos de exposiciones (1847–1978); (C) Índices.

Índice analítico, p.246–324. Índice de titulos, p.324–46.

A206 Burt, Eugene C. Latin American art: five-year cumulative bibliography: 1985 through 1989. Seattle, Data Arts, [1991?]. 89p. (EthnoArts index. Supplemental publication, no.6)

"This cumulative bibliography brings together all Latin American art related items which appeared in the first five volumes of Ethnoarts Index coverage of Latin America (volumes 3 through 7) . . . [and] includes a variety of categories of publications: books, periodical articles, catalogs, book reviews, exhibition reviews, conference papers, theses and dissertations, and other special types."—*Introd.*

Abbreviations, p.iii. Subject index, p.77–84. Author index, p.84–89.

A207 Contemporary Latin American artists: exhibitions at the Organization of American States 1941–1964. Ed. by Annick Sanjurjo. Lanham, Md., Scarecrow, 1997. viii, 506p.

Lists 750 exhibitions including more than 2,000 artists. "These exhibits were important not only because they included most of the artists that today are regarded as the masters or precursors of modern Latin American or Caribbean art . . . but, moreover, because they documented the . . . birth of modern Latin American art."—*Pref.* Continued by the following title.

Index of artists, p.461–88. Index of exhibitions by country, p.489–506.

A208 Contemporary Latin American artists: exhibitions at the Organization of American States 1965–1985. Ed. by Annick Sanjurjo. Metuchen, N.J., Scarecrow, 1993. xiii, 720p. il., plates.

Lists 380 exhibitions of the work of more than 1,000 artists. Each exhibition entry includes biographical information. Exhibition entries arranged by year. Continues the preceding title.

Index of artists, p.671–99. Index of exhibitions by country, p.700–20.

A209 Findlay, James A. Modern Latin American art: a bibliography. Westport, Conn., Greenwood, 1983. 301p. (Art reference collection, 3)

Covers late 19th- and 20th-century books and exhibition catalogs devoted to 20th-century Latin American art. Excludes monographs on individual artists and periodical articles, although periodical titles are listed. Occasional brief annotations. Entries arranged by country and then by medium.

Index [authors, artists, and periodical titles], p.265–301.

A210 Godoy Llerena, Luis Alberto. Bibliografía del arte peruano: extraido de las Hemerotecas del Museo Nacional de la Cultura Peruana y Biblioteca Nacional. Lima, Peru, Instituto Nacional de Cultura, Centro de Investigación y Restauración de Bienes Monumentales, 1983. 1v.

Ambitious bibliography of the literature on Peruvian art. Discontinued with vol. 1.

Contents: Vol. 1: (A) Generales; (B) Arquitectura, pintura, escultura; (C) Artes menores

A211 Handbook of Latin American art = Manual de arte latinoamericano: a bibliographic compilation. Gen. ed. Joyce Waddell Bailey. Santa Barbara, ABC-Clio, 1984– . (2)v. in 3.

Comprehensive classified bibliography from colonial through contemporary periods for all of Latin America. Covers books, periodical articles, exhibition catalogs, reviews. Subject outline in each volume. Author, artist indexes included.

A212 Handbook of Latin American studies (online) = HLAS online [computer file]. [Washington, D.C.], Hispanic Division of the Library of Congress, 1995– . Annual.

Online version of: Handbook of Latin American studies. See GLAH 1:A147 for print ed. and original annotation. In English and Spanish. Includes citations from v.1– of print version. Also includes unverified, provisional citations from upcoming vols.

Contains records describing books, book chapters, articles, and conference papers published in the field of Latin American studies. Coverage includes relevant books as well as more than 800 social science and 550 humanities journals and volumes of conference proceedings. Most records include abstracts with evaluations.

A213 Neistein, José. A Arte no Brasil: dos primórdios ao século vinte, uma bibliografia seleta, anotada = Art in Brazil: from its beginnings to modern times, a selected, annotated bibliography. Washington, D.C., Brazilian-American Cultural Institute, 1997. v, 535p.

Text in Portuguese and English.

"The annotated bibliography . . . appeared in even-numbered issues 16 to 52 of the Handbook of Latin American Studies, and in some off-numbered issues, between 1953 and 1992."—*Pref.*

Contents: (1) Preface; (2) Reference and theoretical works; (3) Colonial period; (4) 19th century; (5) 20th century; (6) Folk art; (7) Afro-Brazilian and Indian traditions; (8) Cinema; (9) City planning, architecture and landscaping architecture; (10) Photography; (11) Miscellaneous; (12) Cartoons and comic strips; (13) Index of artists and authors (p.511–35).

A214 Puerto, Cecilia. Latin American women artists, Kahlo and look who else: a selective, annotated bibliography. Westport, Conn., Greenwood, 1996. xiv, 237p. il. (Art reference collection, 21)

"My purpose in compiling this bibliography is to raise awareness about the rich and extraordinarily diverse contributions which 20th-century women artists in and from Latin America have made to the world of art."—*Pref.* Includes monographs, exhibition catalogs, dissertations, theses, videorecordings, and periodical literature.

Contents: The bibliography: Individual artists; General works; Appendix I: Collective exhibitions; Appendix II: Artists by country.

Name index, p.221–37.

A215 Rivas Dugarte, Rafael Angel. Bibliografía de las artes plasticas en Venezuela. Caracas, Instituto Universitario Pedagogico de Caracas, 1987. xvi, 382p. (La Cultura en Venezuela, 2)

Substantial, 3,490-entry bibliography. Not annotated, but well-indexed.

Contents: Fuentes generales: bibliografías, diccionarios, historias; Fuentes bibliográficas; Fuentes hemerográficas.

Indice de siglas y abreviaturas, p.xv. Indice sistemático, p.355–82.

A216 Victoria, José Guadalupe. Una bibliografía de arte novohispano. Con la colab. de Pedro Angeles Jiménez . . . [et al.] México, Univ. Nacional Autónoma de México, Instituto de Investigaciones Estéticas, 1995. 364p. (Apoyo a la docencia, 2)

Unannotated bibliography covering all aspects of colonial Mexican art, including painting, architecture, sculpture, applied arts, engraving, city planning, and historic preservation. Includes general works, chapters in books, periodical articles, catalogs, guides, and obituaries.

Siglas de bibliotecas consultadas, p.31. Siglas de elementos o datos catalográficos, p.33. Índice de artistas, p.337–39. Índice de monumentos, p.341–46. Índice de obras, p.347–49. Índice geográfico, p.351–56. Autores citados en la bibliografía, p.357–74.

A217 Weismann, Elizabeth Wilder. The history of art in Latin America, 1500–1800: some trends and challenges in the last decade. Published in Latin American research review, v.10, no.1, 1975, p.7–50.
Overview of the literature from 1963 to 1975 with assessments of specific works. Supplements the Handbook of Latin American studies colonial art section. Includes books and articles, as well as sources of photographic or visual documentation.

Low Countries

A218 Bibliographie de l'histoire de l'art national = Bibliographie van de nationale kunstgeschiedenis. Published in Revue belge d'archéologie et d'histoire de l'art, v.43, 1974– .
Classified, unannotated bibliography of books and articles on Belgian art history appearing in most annual vols. of Revue belge d'archéologie et d'histoire de l'art (GLAH 1:Q293). Each year's bibliography lists materials published in the previous year, sometimes two previous years. Author, geographic, and artist indexes.

A219 Netherlands. Rijksbureau voor Kunsthistorische Documentatie. Bibliography of the Netherlands Institute for Art History. v.1–17, 1943/45–1973/74. The Hague, Rijksbureau, 1943–1974.
See GLAH 1:A152 for earlier vols. Ed. varies. Continued by irregular new acquisitions lists, since ceased.
Contents: (15) pt.1, Painting, old art; pt.2, Sculpture, old art; pt.3, Arts and crafts, old art; pt.4, Personalia; (16) pt.1, Painting, old art; pt.2, Sculpture, old art; pt.3, Arts and crafts, old art; pt.4, Personalia; (17) pt.1, Painting, old art; pt.2, Sculpture, old art; pt.3, Arts and crafts, old art; pt.4, Personalia.

Russia and Eastern Europe

A220 Bleha, Josef, ed. Bibliografie ceské vytvarne umelecké literatury, 1965–1970. Praha, Státni knihovna Csr, 1982. 184p. (Edice Odborné bibliografie SBI).
A supplement to GLAH 1:A24. Lists literature of the graphic and plastic arts published in Czechoslovakia between 1965–70. Author index at end.

A221 Kõks, Endel. A bibliography of Estonian art and artists outside Estonia = Välis-Eesti kunstielu bibliograafia. Stockholm, Välis-Eesti & EMP, 1984. 114p. il.
Alphabetical listing by author of 765 "articles about artists of Estonian origin, their work, and the general art life of Estonians outside Estonia."—*Pref.* The bibliographic entries, dating back to 1935, include book and periodical literature. All titles are given in the original language accompanied by an English translation. When the artist's name does not appear in the title, it is given in parentheses. Preface and table of contents in English as well as Estonian.
Isikunimede register/Index of names, p.107.

A222 Library of Congress. Visual arts in Poland: an annotated bibliography of selected holdings in the Library of Congress. Compiled by Janina W. Hoskins. Washington, D.C., Library of Congress (Distr. by the U.S. Government Printing Office, Supt. of Docs., 1993). xiii, 219p. il. (part col.)
This survey contains 868 entries including books, periodicals, and individual articles, published since the 19th century on all aspects of Polish art and architecture, published either in Poland or in the West. Most of the material is in Polish, but works in English, French, German, and Italian are also included. Book titles in Polish include English translations.
Contents: Historical, multi-media, and thematic surveys; Architecture; Sculpture; Painting; Prints; Decorative arts; Folk art; Photography; Art collections; Periodicals; Bibliography and reference works.
Name index, p.195–220.

A223 Polska bibliografia sztuki 1801–1944. Oracowaly Janina Wiercinska and Maria Liczbinska. Wroclaw, Zaklad Narodowy im. Ossolinskich, 1975– . (4)v.
See GLAH 1:A157 for pre-publication citation. At head of title: Polska Akademia Nauk, Instytut Sztuki. A comprehensive bibliography of Polish art, including all works published in Polish on art, both Polish and foreign; works by Polish historians in all languages, including works published outside Poland; and works on Polish art published abroad.
Contents: (1) Malarstwo polske. cz. 1. Prace ogólne. Historia. Malarze. A-K. cz. 2. Malarze. L-Z. (2) Rysunek, grafika, sztuka ksiazki i druku. (3) Rzezba. (4) Architektura. cz 1. Zródla. Opracowania ogólne. Historia. Architekci i budowniczowie. Continued by articles in Rocznik historii sztukit.4, 1964-t.13: 1981.

Scandinavia

A224 Copenhagen. Kunstakademiets Bibliotek. Bibliografi over dansk kunst [Bibliography of Danish art], v.1, 1971–1980. København, Kunstakademiets Bibliotek, 1972–1983. 10v.
See GLAH 1:A159 for pre-publication citation. Annual bibliography on Danish art and architecture, Danish art abroad, and foreign art with special connections to Danish art. Includes books as well as periodical literature, and a selection of exhibition catalogs. Sales catalogs and newspaper articles are excluded. Arranged by subject. Available as a database at the Kunstakademiets Bibliotek.

A225 Langballe, Anne M. Hasund, and Danbolt, Gunnar. Norsk kunsthistorisk bibliografi: skrifter om norsk kunst utgitt til og med 1970 = Bibliography of Norwegian art history: literature on Norwegian art published up to the end of 1970. Oslo, Universitetsforlaget, 1976. xxxii, 390p. (Norsk bibliografisk bibliotek, v.51)
Comprehensive, classified bibliography of books and periodical literature on all aspects of Norwegian art and architecture from 1000 to 1970. Includes archeology, ethnology, history, and cultural history. Some titles for the years 1971–

75 are also included, especially bibliographies. Preface and table of contents in English as well as Norwegian.

Register over forfattere, kunstnere, arkitekter, kunstsamlere og portretterte, p.356–90. Supplement: Norsk kunsthistorisk bibliografi 1978/1979. Unni Bliksvar . . . [et al.] Oslo, [s.n.], 1985. 2v. in 1.

Spain and Portugal

A226 Alvarez Casado, Ana Isabel. Repertorio bibliográfico en prensa periódica española, 1936–1948. Madrid, Consejo Superior de Investigaciones Científicas, 1994. 172p.

Annotated bibliography of art books and exhibition catalogs which were reviewed in Spanish periodicals between 1936–1948, arranged alphabetically by author. Each entry includes the book review citation/s. Lengthy preface describes the Spanish periodicals cited within.

Indice de autores y materias, p.159–72.

A227 Bibliografía del arte en España; articulos de revistas clasificados por materias. Maria Paz Aguilo . . . [et al.] Madrid, Consejo Superior de Investigaciones Científicas, Instituto Diego Velazquez, 1976. 1008p.

Classified bibliography of periodical literature on all aspects of Spanish art and architecture. List of indexed journals.

A228 Reyes Pacios Lozano, Ana. Bibliografía de arquitectura y techumbres mudéjares, 1857–1991. [Teruel], Instituto de Estudios Turolenses, Excma. Diputacion Provincial de Teruel, [1993]. 450p. (Serie Estudios mudejares)

Classified, annotated bibliography of books and periodical literature on Mudejar art and architecture in Spain.

Índice de autores, p.347–62. Índice de títulos, p.363–94. Índice de materias, p.395–422. Índice onomástico, p.423–26. Índice de topónimos, p.427–36. Índice de obras artísticas, p.437–50.

Switzerland

A229 Bibliographie zur schweizer Kunst, Bibliographie zur Denkmalpflege = Bibliographie de l'art suisse, Bibliographie de la conservation des biens culturels, v.8 (1985/86)– . Zurich, Institut für Denkmalpflege ETH, 1987– . Annual.

Continues Bibliographie zur schweizerischen Kunst und Denkmalpflege = Bibliographie de l'art Suisse et de la conservation des monuments historiques (see next entry). Bibliographic essays on Swiss numismatics by Benedikt Zäch in v.14.

A230 Bibliographie zur schweizerischen Kunst und Denkmalpflege = Bibliographie de l'art suisse et de la conservation des monuments historiques, v.1–7, 1979–84/85. Zurich, Institut für Denkmalpflege ETH, 1980–1986. Annual.

Annual classified bibliography of book and periodical literature on all aspects of Swiss art and architecture, including historic preservation and conservation, archeology, numismatics, and folk art. Entries in German, French, and Italian. Some entries are analyzed or include brief annotations. Index of subjects, places, and personal names. Continued by Bibliographie zur schweizer Kunst, Bibliographie zur Denkmalpflege = Bibliographie de l'art Suisse, Bibliographie de la conservation des biens culturels (see preceding entry).

United States and Canada

A231 Archives of American Art. The card catalog of the manuscript collections of the Archives of American Art. Wilmington, Scholarly Resources, 1980. 10v.

Reproduces more than 40,000 catalog cards covering 5,000 collections. Indexes approximately six million documents collected by the archives since 1954. "Since most of its users conduct their research within the context of individuals, indexing is chiefly by personal names."—*Introd.* Entire database also available online from the Smithsonian Institution.

———. 1st supplement, 1981–1984. Wilmington, Scholarly Resources, 1985.

A232 Arts in America: a bibliography. Ed. by Bernard Karpel. Washington, D.C., published for the Archives of American Art by the Smithsonian Institution Press, 1979. 4v.

See GLAH 1:A164 for pre-publication citation. Comprehensive bibliography of book and periodical literature covering all aspects of art and architecture in America, including photography, film, theater, dance, and music. Includes publications through 1975. Contains almost 25,000 entries by more than 20 contributors. Contributors' names are listed on the table of contents and at the head of each section. Each section begins with a table of contents, and explanatory notes introduce each subsection.

Contents: (1) Art of the Native Americans; Architecture; Decorative arts; Design: nineteenth century; Design: twentieth century; Sculpture; Art of the west; (2) Painting: seventeenth-eighteenth century; Painting: nineteenth century; Painting: twentieth century; Graphic arts: seventeenth-nineteenth century; Graphic arts: twentieth century; Graphic artists: twentieth century; (3) Photography; Film; Theater; Dance; Music; Serials and periodicals on the visual arts; Dissertations and theses on the visual arts; Visual resources; (4) Index.

A233 Bronner, Simon J. American folk art: a guide to sources. New York and London, Garland, 1984. xxxi, 313p. [30] leaves of plates. il. (Garland reference library of the humanities, v.464)

Annotated bibliography of books and periodical literature which attempts to place folk art study in the context of broader cultural studies. Each of the 13 chapters begins with an essay by an expert in the field.

Contents: Background and history, by Simon J. Bronner; Art criticism and aesthetic philosophy, by Michael Owen Jones and Verni Greenfield; Genres, by Kenneth L. Ames; Biographies, by Sara Selene Faulds and Amy Skillman; Region and locality, by C. Kurt Dewhurst and Marsha Mac-

Dowell; Ethnicity and religion, by Robert T. Teske; Afro-Americans, by Eugene W. Metcalf; Workers and trades, by Doris D. Fanelli and Simon J. Bronner; Symbol, image, and theme, by Elaine Eff; Collectors and museums, by Elizabeth Mosby Adler; Educators and classrooms, by Kristin G. Congdon; Films, by William Ferris; and Topics on the horizon, by Simon J. Bronner.

Author index, p.285–98. Subject index, p.299–313.

A234 Grauerholz, Angela. Catalogues canadiens en art contemporain = Canadian catalogues on contemporary art. Montreal, Centre d'information Artexte, 1981–99. (17)v. Annual.

To be continued as a biennial publication beginning in 2001. Annotated bibliography of exhibition catalogs on contemporary Canadian art, including Inuit and Amerindian art. Arranged alphabetically by artist in the case of single artist exhibitions, otherwise by title. Includes an alphabetical listing of museums and galleries by province, and a list of forthcoming catalogs and out-of-print catalogs.

A235 Hayes, Janice E. Bibliography on Canadian feminist art. Montreal, Graduate School of Library and Information Studies, McGill University, 1986. 43p. (Occasional paper, 9)

Annotated bibliography of book and periodical literature in English on Canadian feminist art published from 1960 to December 1984. Entries cover both applied and visual arts. Does not include items on individual artists. Only items dealing with three or more artists were included.

Contents: General; Collective biography; Galleries; Exhibitions: catalogs and criticisms; Visual and applied arts; Journal titles.

Author index, p.39–40. Title index, p.41–43.

A236 Igoe, Lynn, and Igoe, James. 250 years of Afro-American art: an annotated bibliography. New York, Bowker, 1981. xxv, 1266p.

Comprehensive annotated bibliography of approximately 25,000 citations from books and periodical literature that document the life and work of 3,900 artists, covering the fields of fine arts and crafts over three centuries. Work divided into three parts; Basic bibliography, Subject bibliography, and Artist bibliography. The latter includes references to specific artworks reproduced in the literature cited in this work. Entries in the Subject and Artist bibliographies are cross-referenced to the Basic bibliography. Two appendixes: Artwork by anonymous artists; Artwork by groups.

A237 Lerner, Loren R., and Williamson, Mary F. Art and architecture in Canada: a bibliography and guide to the literature to 1981 = Art et architecture au Canada; bibliographie et guide de la documentation jusqu'en 1981. Toronto, Univ. of Toronto Pr., 1991. 2v.

Comprehensive bilingual bibliography of books and periodical literature on the arts and architecture in Canada. Vol. 1 consists of 9,555 entries, listed under a series of subject headings representing a variety of topics, media, historical periods, and geographical areas. Includes writings on Inuit and Native American art. Within each topic and area, the entries appear chronologically according to date of publication. Each citation is followed by an abstract in English or French, or in both languages, depending on the language of the original document. All scholarly apparatus, introductory essays, guides to using vols. 1 and 2, and abbreviations are in both languages. Vol. 2 consists of author and subject indexes. The Subject index uses index terms based on those developed by RILA (GLAH 1:A15).

Contents: (1) Introductory essay, Towards the discovery of Canadian cultural history, by Ramsay Cook, p.xi–xiii; La découverte de l'histoire culturelle du Canada, p.xv–xvii; Art, p.3–482; Artists, p.483–782; Architecture, p.783–986; (2) Author index, p.3–34; Subject index, p.35–300; Index des sujets traités, p.301–570.

A238 Schimmelman, Janice Gayle. American imprints on art through 1865: books and pamphlets on drawing, painting, sculpture, aesthetics, art criticism, and instruction: an annotated bibliography. Boston, Hall, 1990. ix, 419p.

This annotated bibliography identifies 637 titles and covers a broad range of art literature: addresses and essays, biographies of artists, histories of art, descriptions of paintings and sculpture, art journals, trade catalogs of artists' materials, practical handbooks on the preparation and use of materials, and instructional books on the techniques of drawing, painting, and perspective. Entries are arranged alphabetically by either the name of the author, name of the artist in brackets if no author is identified, or title. Each entry includes complete bibliographical information, description of the contents, and modern locations as identified by the National Union Catalog: Pre-1956 Imprints, Checklist of American Imprints, and OCLC.

Contents: (1) American imprints on art through 1865; (2) Books and pamphlets listed by date of publication; (3) Selected bibliography.

Index of names and titles, p.385–419.

ASIAN COUNTRIES

General Works

A239 Francis bulletin signalétique 526: Art et archéologie: Proche-Orient, Asie, Amérique, v.45, no.1 (1991)–v.48, no.4 (1994). Nancy, Centre national de la recherche scientifique, Institut de l'information scientifique et technique, Sciences humaines et sociales, 1991–94.

Ceased with v.48, no.4 (1994). Continues GLAH 1:A80 (ceased with v.44, 1990).

A240 Walravens, Hartmut. Bibliographien zur ostasiatischen Kunstgeschichte in Deutschland. Hamburg, Bell, 1983–84. 4v. il., ports.

Vols. 1–3 contain citations and selected offprints for writings by and about some of the pioneering German scholars of Asian art. Vol. 4 presents a series of offprints of critical reviews of the 1912 East Asian art exhibition at the Königlichen Akademie der Künste, Berlin.

Each volume has name, title, and subject indexes.

Contents: (1) Adolf Fischer, Frieda Fischer, Karl With, Ludwig Bachhofer; (2) Alfred Salmony; (3) Otto Kümmel; (4) Die ostasienausstellung Berlin 1912 und die Presse.

AFRICA, OCEANIA, THE AMERICAS

General Works

A241 Burt, Eugene C. Ethnoart: Africa, Oceania, and the Americas: a bibliography of theses and dissertations. N.Y., Garland, [1988]. xix, 191p. (Garland reference library of the humanities, 840)

Citations of master's degree theses and doctoral dissertations (1,022 entries) dating from the late 19th century through April 1987. Includes selected bachelor degree honors theses from British and Commonwealth universities. No annotations.

Author index, p.131–41. Date index, p.143–49. Institution index, p.151–59. Subject index, p.161–91.

A242 ______. Serials guide to ethnoart: a guide to serial publications on visual arts of Africa, Oceania, and the Americas. N.Y., Greenwood, [1990]. xv, 368p. (Art reference collection, 11)

Directory of 682 serials including the following information (as available): title; subtitle; former title; ISSN number; OCLC number; Faxon number; publisher; frequency; subscription cost; ethnoart focus; editorial focus; first year of publication; language of text; illustrations; editorials; ads; books received list; book reviews; article abstracts; self-indexed; indexes other publications; relevancy rating; and notes. Nine appendixes provide recommendations based on a "rating of the level of relevancy of the publication to ethnoart based on the frequency that ethnoart-oriented articles, reviews, etc. appear."—*Pref.*

Additional appendixes: Serials with indexing, bibliographic, and abstracting services, p.301–03. Ceased serials, p.304–05. Serial titles by country of publication, p.306–25. Rotated title keyword index, p.327–68.

A243 EthnoArts index, v.5, no.1(Jan.–Mar., 1987)– . [Seattle, Data Arts], 1987– . Quarterly; series of five-year cumulations.

Continues Tribal arts review (v.1–4, 1983–86). List of periodicals indexed at the beginning of each issue.

The only up-to-date continuing bibliography for the "visual art, architecture or the artistic aspects of material culture or archaeology of any of the indigenous peoples of Africa, Oceania, or the Americas."—*Introd.* Includes books, periodical literature, exhibition catalogs and reviews, conference papers, book reviews, theses, dissertations, and other types of publications. Descriptive abstracts provided for some entries.

Contents: EAI notes and news; Book reviews; EAI abbreviations; Ethnoart (general); Africa; Latin America; North America; Oceania; Subject index; Author index.

A244 Tribal and ethnic art. Oxford, Clio, [1982]. 99p. (Modern art bibliographical series, 1)

"Tribal and Ethnic Art . . . contains 900 abstracts of books, available dissertations, periodical articles and exhibition catalogues with essays or texts published between 1972 and 1979, relating to the study or exposition of the artifacts and aesthetics of cultural groups who are largely non-European. [The series is] based on the bi-annual ARTbibliographies MODERN [GLAH 1:A102], which covers literature on post-1800 art published since 1972, and thus studies relating to pre-European contact cultures only are excluded, as are those which are anthropological or ethnological."—*Introd.*

Africa

A245 African art: five-year cumulative bibliography; mid-1983 through 1988. Ed. by Eugene C. Burt. Seattle, Data Arts, [1990]. iii, 170p. (EthnoArts index supplemental publication, 3)

Cumulative bibliography of all African art-related items which appeared in EthnoArts index from July 1, 1983, to December 31, 1988.

A246 The arts of Africa: an annotated bibliography. v.1–6, 1986–97. [Atlanta], African Studies Association, 1989–97.

Compiled by Janet L. Stanley, National Museum of African Art Branch Library, Smithsonian Institution Libraries, this bibliography "covers significant publications on the visual arts and architecture of Africa. . . . The bibliography is arranged by broad general topics and by country/geographic regions."—*Introd.* In addition, publications on African material culture, on the image of the Black in the Western world, and on the influence of African art on European art are included. Each volume has author and subject indexes.

A247 Biebuyck, Daniel P. The arts of Central Africa: an annotated bibliography. Boston, Hall, [1987]. xxi, 300p. (Reference publication in art history)

"The bibliography covers ethnic units established in Zaire (formerly called Congo Free State, Belgian Congo, and Democratic Republic of Congo). . . . The primary focus is on their visual arts, particularly on sculpture in diverse media (mostly wood, ivory, bone, soapstone, and clay)."—*Pref.* Covering both book and periodical literature, most works include annotations.

Contents: List of journals; Bibliographies; Classification of languages; General ethnographies; Travelogues; General studies on African art; General studies on Zairian art; Northwestern Zaire; Northeastern Zaire; West central Zaire; East central Zaire; Southwestern Zaire; The Lunda-Cokwe Complex in southern Zaire, northern Angola, and northern Zambia; Southeastern Zaire; South central Zaire.

Author index, p.261–72. Ethnic group index, p.273–83. Subject index, p.285–300.

A248 Burt, Eugene C. An annotated bibliography of the visual arts of East Africa. Bloomington, Indiana Univ. Pr., [1980]. xv, 371p. (Traditional arts of Africa)

Entries for 2,028 books, periodicals, articles, and archival sources on any aspect of material culture are included.

Contents: East Africa: general; Kenya; Tanzania; Makonde group; Uganda.

Culture [ethnic group] index, p.314–31. Author index, p.332–59. Subject index, p.360–71.

A249 Stanley, Janet. African art: a bibliographic guide. N.Y., Africana, [1985]. vii, 55p.

"This bibliography is an introductory guide to the literature of African art and is intended to be a critical 'best books' list."—*Introd.*

Contents: (1) Periodicals; (2) Bibliographies and reference books; (3) General surveys of African art; (4) Regional studies of African art; (5) African crafts and utilitarian arts; (6) African architecture; (7) Rock art, stone sculptures and ancient terracottas; (8) Contemporary art and tourist art; (9) African art market and collecting African art.

Index, p.53–55.

Oceania

A250 Hanson, Louise, and Hanson, F. Allan. The art of Oceania: a bibliography. Boston, Hall, [1984]. xviii, 539p. (Reference publication in art history)

The most comprehensive bibliography (6,650 entries) of the art and architecture of Oceania. Includes monographs, catalogs, theses, dissertations, and periodical literature. "Annotations are provided in cases where titles give incomplete or unclear information about works and their contents."—*Pref.*

Contents: Cross-region [treating data from two or more regions]; Polynesia; Micronesia; Melanesia; Australia; Sale catalogues.

Personal name index, p.403–29. Title index, p.430–511. Subject index, p.512–39.

A251 Oceanic art: five-year cumulative bibliography; mid-1983 through 1988. Ed. by Eugene C. Burt. Seattle, Data Arts, 1990. 55p. (EthnoArts index supplemental publication, 2)

Cumulative bibliography of all Oceanic art-related items which appeared in EthnoArts index from July 1, 1983, to December 31, 1988.

The Americas

A252 Berlo, Janet Catherine. The art of prehispanic Mesoamerica: an annotated bibliography. Boston, Hall, 1985. xiii, 272p. (Reference publication in art history/non-Western arts)

Historiographic essay and 1,533-entry selective bibliography on pre-contact arts from north-central Mexico to the mouth of the Ulua River. Excludes site reports and works on pre-Hispanic manuscripts.

Subject index, p.225–72.

A253 Dept. of Indian and Northern Affairs. Inuit art bibliography. 2d ed. [Ottawa], The Dept., 1992. 733, 69p.

1st ed. 1987.

This bibliography (2,368 entries) represents the "books, pamphlets, journals, newspaper articles, video, films, catalogues and brochures" collected by the Section Library and Documentation Centre of Indian and Northern Affairs Canada since the late 1940s.

Keyword index, [group 2] p.1–69.

A254 Ethnographic bibliography of North America. By George Peter Murdock and Timothy J. O'Leary. 4th ed. New Haven, Human Relations Area File, 1975. 5v. maps. (Behavior science bibliographies)

See GLAH 1:A184 for previous eds.

Extensive expansion on the 3d ed. (approximately 28,000 entries are new to this ed.), covering books and articles from the period 1960–1972 on the ethnography of native North Americans. Arranged by culture region and then by ethnic group. Entries deemed "basic cultural descriptions" are highlighted with asterisks. Includes works on archeology and art.

Contents: (1) General North America; (2) Arctic and Subarctic; (3) Far West and Pacific Coast; (4) Eastern United States; (5) Plains and Southwest.

A255 ———. Supplement, 1973–1987. By M. Marlene Martin and Timothy J. O'Leary. New Haven, Human Relations Area File, 1990. 3v. maps.

Update of preceding title, with approximately 26,000 additional entries on the ethnography of native North Americans, arranged into the same culture regions as the original.

Contents: (1) Indexes; (2–3) Citations.

A256 Parezo, Nancy J.; Perry, Ruth M.; and Allen, Rebecca. Southwest Native American arts and material culture: a guide to research. N.Y., Garland, 1991. 2v. (Studies in ethnic art, 1) (Garland reference library of the humanities, 1337)

More than 8,400 references to works published between 1844 and 1988, including "books, monographs, journals and magazine articles, pamphlets, dissertations and theses, museum exhibition catalogs, directories, and a few government documents. . . . All cited works contain information on tangible objects . . . that have been or are currently being made and utilized by Native Americans of the region."—*Pt.1, Resource guide.* Introductory Resource guide includes "A beginner's guide to Southwest Native American material culture" arranged by material type, bibliographies, indexes, and journal titles.

Culture index, p.1135–1319. Subject index, p.1321–1506.

SEE ALSO: Francis bulletin signalétique 526: Art et archéologie: Proche-Orient, Asie, Amérique (GLAH 2:A122).

BIBLIOGRAPHIES OF INDIVIDUAL ARTISTS

This section is arranged alphabetically by artist's name.

Aalto, Alvar, 1898–1976

A257 Miller, William C. Alvar Aalto: an annotated bibliography. N.Y., Garland, 1984. xxix, 244p. il. (Garland bibliographies in architecture and planning, v.4) (Garland reference library of the humanities, v.390)

Partially annotated bibliography of 1,174 books, catalogs, essays, lectures, and articles by and about Aalto, arranged chronologically by date of publication, 1921–80.

Contents: (1) The published essays, lectures, and conversations of Alvar Aalto; (2) Books, monographs, and catalogues on Alvar Aalto and his architecture; (3) Material on Aalto in books and monographs on Finland, and on Finnish and Scandinavian architecture and art; (4) Material on Aalto found in collected works and general reference sources on architecture; (5) Periodical issues and articles of periodicals on Aalto and his architecture.

Author index, p.191–97. Title index, p.199–229. Building list and project index, p.231–44.

Bosch, Hieronymus, c. 1450–1516

A258 Gibson, Walter S. Hieronymus Bosch: an annotated bibliography. Boston, Hall, 1983. xxxvi, 212p. 1 port. (Reference publication in art history)

Organizes and annotates approximately 1,000 general studies, essays, specialized studies, periodical articles, and exhibitions relating to Hieronymus Bosch. Includes brief, critical annotations and notes variant editions and translations. Introduction: a critical history (p.xix–xxxi) is a historical bibliographic essay on Bosch criticism.

Index of authors, p.191–98. Index of paintings and drawings attributed to Bosch, p.199–207. Index of subjects and symbols, p.209–12.

Braque, Georges, 1882–1963

A259 Clement, Russell T. Georges Braque: a bio-bibliography. Westport, Conn., Greenwood, 1994. xvii, 231p. (Bio-bibliographies in art and architecture, no.3)

Lists 54 items by Georges Braque in the primary bibliography. Secondary bibliography (1,047 citations) includes books and articles categorized by (1) biography, career, and association with Picasso; (2) works; and (3) exhibitions. Introduction consists of a biographical sketch, a chronology of the artist's life, and a bibliographic overview. Notes variant editions and translations. Partially annotated.

Art works index, p.213–14. Personal names index, p.215–17. Subject index, p.229.

Brunelleschi, Filippo, 1377–1446

A260 Bozzoni, Corrado, and Carbonara, Giovanni. Filippo Brunelleschi: saggio di bibliografia. Roma, Istituto di fondamenti dell'architettura dell'Università, 1977–78. 2v.

Detailed, scholarly bibliography of Brunelleschi literature arranged chronologically beginning with 15th-century manuscripts and concluding with publications in 1978.

Contents: (1) Schede, 1436–1976; (2) Schede e indici.

Appendice, v.2, p.167–212. Indici analitico, v.2, p.215–52. Indice degli autori, v.2, p.253–72.

Burchfield, Charles, 1893–1967

A261 Makowski, Colleen Lahan. Charles Burchfield: an annotated bibliography. Lanham, Scarecrow, 1996. x, 210p.

Briefly annotated bibliography of 1,450 numbered items arranged by type of material and then chronologically.

Contents: (1) Exhibition history; (2) Exhibition catalogs; (3) Periodical articles; (4) Books; (5) Museum collections; (6) Non-print media.

Index, p.181–209.

Dürer, Albrecht, 1471–1528

A262 Mende, Matthias. Dürer-Bibliographie. Wiesbaden, Harrassowitz, 1971. xliv, 707p. plates.

Scholarly subject bibliography of literature on the life and works of Albrecht Dürer. Includes 10,271 books and periodical articles dating from the 17th to the 20th centuries.

Contents: (1) Schrifttumsverzeichnisse; (2) Schriftliche Quellen; (3) Dürers Herkunft und Familie; (4) Dürers äussere Erscheinung und Krankheitsbild; (5) Das Dürerhaus; (6) Museen und Sammlungen; (7) Dürers Werk; (8) Monographien und zusammenfassendes Schrifttum; (9) Biographie und künstlerische Entwicklung; (10) Dürer und die geistigen und politischen Strömungen seiner Zeit; (11) Ikonographie und Sachkunde; (12) Dürers Kunsttheorie; (13) Dürer und die Naturwissenschaften; (14) Werkstatt und Schüler; (15) Dürer und seine Zeitgenossen; (16) Dürers Nachleben.

Verfasserregister, p.619–68. Topographisches Register, p.669–76. Personennamen, p.677–93. Dürer-Werk-Register, p.694–707.

Fabergé, Peter Carl, 1846–1920

A263 McCanless, Christel Ludewig. Fabergé and his works: an annotated bibliography of the first century of his art. Metuchen, Scarecrow, 1994. viii, 408p. il.

Includes 1,772 citations to journals, newspapers, advertisements, and other printed and audiovisual materials dating from 1899 to 1992, arranged chronologically by date of publication.

Chronology of the house of Fabergé, p.7–9. Genealogy chart of the Fabergé family, p.11. Glossary of proper names, p.17–21. Index, p.367–408.

Gauguin, Paul, 1848–1903

A264 Clement, Russell T. Paul Gauguin: a bio-bibliography. N.Y., Greenwood, 1991. xxii, 324p. (Bio-bibliographies in art and architecture, no.1)

Identifies 101 items by Paul Gauguin in the primary bibliography. Secondary bibliography (1,274 citations) includes contemporary accounts through 1906, writings about Gauguin's works, and literature from exhibitions relating to Gauguin. Organized by general topic. Notes variant editions and translations. Partially annotated. Introduction includes a biographical sketch and a chronology of the artist.

Index of art works, p.293–96. Index of personal names, p.297–324.

Hans Holbein the Younger, 1497/98–1543

A265 Michael, Erika. Hans Holbein the Younger: a guide to research. N.Y., Garland, 1997. xix, 749p. (Artist resource manuals, v.2) (Garland reference library of the humanities, 1480)

Annotated bibliography of 2,518 entries, organized by genre and format, that includes primary sources and archival documents to 1800, monographs, museum and exhibition catalogs, and sections on drawings, prints, iconography, technique, patronage, influences, and reception.

Introduction (p.3–97) includes biographical and critical subdivisions. Index of authors, p.731–49.

Homer, Winslow, 1836–1910

A266 Davis, Melinda Dempster. Winslow Homer: an annotated bibliography of periodical literature. Metuchen, Scarecrow, 1975. viii, 130p.

Lists exhibition notices and reviews chronologically (1875–1973), critical evaluations, individual works (articles and reproductions of works), portraits, and obituaries from 22 indexing sources and 16 monographs. Entries include a bibliographic citation to the periodical and an annotation.

Sources consulted, p.127–30.

Kahn, Louis, 1901–1974

A267 Brown, Jack Perry. Louis I. Kahn: a bibliography. N.Y., Garland, 1987. xi, 97p. (Garland reference library of the humanities, v.678)

Chronological list of 606 items by and about Kahn dating from 1924–1986.

Contents: Chronology; (1) Writings about Louis I. Kahn; (2) Books, parts of books and theses about Kahn; (3) Articles about Kahn in journals.

Author index, p.91–94. Building and project index, p.95–97.

A268 ———, and Markowitz, Arnold L. Louis Kahn and Paul Zucker: two bibliographies. Ed. by Frederick D. Nichols. N.Y., Garland, 1977. vii, 145p. (American association of architectural bibliographers, papers, v.12) (Garland reference library of the humanities, v.116)

Lists 424 books, articles, speeches, and obituaries for Kahn and 490 for Zucker. Includes chronologies and building indexes for both architects.

A269 Smith, Charles R. Paul Rudolph and Louis Kahn: a bibliography. Metuchen, Scarecrow, 1987. xii, 224p. il.

Two-part bibliographic chronology of citations arranged according to commissions dating from the architects' early careers through part of 1986. Includes biographical and philosophical references as well as critiques, portraits, obituaries, book reviews, and biographical chronologies of each architect.

Contents: (1) Paul M. Rudolph; (2) Louis I. Kahn.

Index to Paul M. Rudolph, p.213–19. Index to Louis I. Kahn, p.220–24.

Le Corbusier (Jeanneret, Charles-Edouard), 1887–1965

A270 Brady, Darlene. Le Corbusier: an annotated bibliography. N.Y., Garland, 1985. xvi, 302p. (Garland reference library of the humanities, v.407)

Comprehensive bibliography of monographs through 1982 and articles and dissertations through 1981 by and about Le Corbusier. Only the entries for monographs are annotated.

Author index, p.239–51. Subject index, p.253–72. Place index, p.273–83. Chronological index, p.285–302.

Leonardo da Vinci, 1452–1519

A271 Guerrini, Mauro. Bibliotheca Leonardiana, 1493–1989. Presentazioni di Augusto Marinoni, Carlo Pedretti. Milano, Editrice Bibliografica, 1990. 3v. (2,216p.)

Detailed, scholarly bibliography of 6,192 printed books and periodical articles published between 1493 and 1989 on Leonardo, arranged by date of publication in vol. 1, thematically in vol. 2, and indexed in vol. 3. Complements Verga (see following title).

Contents: (1) I manoscritti di Leonardo; Opere di Leonardo da Vinci; Opere su Leonardo da Vinci; (2) Indice degli autori; Indice dei titoli; Indice dei seriali; Indice dei luoghi di pubblicazione delle edizioni anteriori al 1821; Subdivisione e indice delle edizioni per lingua del testo; Concordanze; (3) Opere su Leonardo da Vinci; Indice dei soggetti; Indice delle notazioni di classificazione; Ordine tematico; Appendice.

A272 Verga, Ettore. Bibliografia Vinciana, 1493–1930. Bologna, N. Zanichelli, 1931. (Repr.: N.Y., Franklin, 1970.) 2v. (835p.)

Annotated bibliography in Italian of 2,900 books and periodical articles arranged chronologically by publication date.

Contents: (1) Opere di Leonardo da Vinci; I trattati; Manoscritti e disegni di Leonardo da Vinci; (2) Scritti su Leonardo da Vinci.

Indice degli scrittori, p.775–800. Indice delle persone e della cose, p.801–35.

Matisse, Henri, 1869–1954

A273 Bock-Weiss, Catherine C. Henri Matisse: a guide to research. N.Y., Garland, 1996. cii, 690p. (Artist resource manuals, v.1)

Critical, annotated bibliography and research guide to a century of literature on Matisse that identifies 1,408 books and articles and numerous exhibitions and catalogs. "I have gathered, summarized, and evaluated the major literature on the artist primarily from France, the United States, Germany, and the Scandinavian countries, where major Matisse collections bear witness to early and intense interest in the artist's work."—*Foreword.*

Contents: (1) Primary documentation; (2) General studies, catalogues, and collections of essays; (3) Specific media; (4) General articles; (5) Individual works; (6) Fauvism; (7) Collections and collectors; (8) Matisse and other artists; (9) Books on Matisse for children; (10) Exhibitions and catalogues.

Index of authors, p.663–71. Index of subjects and themes, p.673–76. Index of artworks, p.677–90.

A274 Clement, Russell T. Henri Matisse: a bio-bibliography. Westport, Conn., 1993. xvii, 393p. (Bio-bibliographies in art and architecture, no.2)

Identifies 1,858 sources, including 127 items by Henri Matisse in the primary bibliography and an extensive exhibitions section (p.276–363). Organized by general topic. Partially annotated. Notes variants and translations. Includes a biographical sketch, chronology, and bibliographic overview.

Art works index, p.365–67. Personal names index, p.369–89. Subject index, p.391.

Meryon, Charles, 1821–1868

A275 Collins, R.D.J. Charles Meryon: a bibliography. Dunedin, New Zealand, Univ. of Otago Pr., 1986. 237p.

Annotated bibliography of books, sales catalogs, periodical articles, and exhibition catalogs on the 19th-century French printmaker Charles Meryon, arranged chronologically by date of publication.

Index of authors, p.224–30. General index, p.230–37.

Michelangelo Buonarroti, 1475–1564

A276 Dussler, Luitpold. Michelangelo-Bibliographie 1927–1970. Wiesbaden, Harrassowitz, 1974. x, 292p.

Annotated entries for 2,220 books and articles, arranged alphabetically by author. Continuation of Ernst Steinmann and Rudolf Wittkower's Michelangelo Bibliographie 1510–1926, Leipzig, Klinkhardt & Biermann, 1927. (Repr.: Hildesheim, Olms, 1967.) Also supplements Hans Werner Schmidt, "Nachtrag und Fortsetzung der Michelangelo-Bibliographie von Steinmann-Wittkower bis 1930" in Ernst Steinmann's Michelangelo im Spiegel seiner Zeit, Leipzig, Poeschel & Trepte, 1930, p.63–94.

Sachregister, p.[269]–74. Personenregister, p.[275]–83. Ortsregister, p.[284]–92.

Mies van der Rohe, Ludwig, 1886–1969

A277 Spaeth, David A. Ludwig Mies van der Rohe: an annotated bibliography and chronology. With a foreword by George Edson Danforth. N.Y., Garland, 1979. xv, 280p. (American association of architectural bibliographers, papers, v.13) (Garland reference library of the humanities, v.115)

Annotated list of 732 books and articles arranged chronologically by date of publication from 1910 to 1977. A biographical chronology, beginning in 1886, runs concurrently with the citations.

Notes, p.261–68. Index, p.269–80.

Moore, Henry, 1898–1986

A278 Henry Moore bibliography. [Comp. and ed. by Alexander Davis.] Hertfordshire, England, Henry Moore Foundation, 1992–94. 5v. il.

"This is the official Henry Moore bibliography of publications issued throughout the world during his lifetime. Titles published after 31 August 1986 will be documented in future volumes. It includes books, exhibition and sales catalogues, newspaper and periodical articles, films and video cassettes, sound recordings, microforms, print albums, facsimiles, dissertations and other publications in 36 languages. . . The arrangement is chronological from 1920 to 1986 and within each year the grouping is by type of publication."—*Introd.* Includes 14,850 numbered and annotated citations.

Contents: (1) Bibliography 1898–1970; (2) Bibliography 1971–86; (3) Chronology of Moore's life and career; Henry Moore and his critics; Citations and sources; Index 1899–1986; Concordance; (4) Bibliography supplement 1898–1986; Bibliography 1986–1991; (5) Monographs 1934–1993; Henry Moore's library; Index 1898–1991; Concordance.

A279 Teague, Edward H. Henry Moore: bibliography and reproductions index. Jefferson, N.C., McFarland, 1981. v, 165p. il. plates.

Identifies 902 books, exhibition catalogs, periodical articles, and audiovisual materials as well as 2,300 reproductions of works cited in indexes to the literature and in books on Moore.

Contents: Biography; Exhibitions chronology; The bibliography; The reproductions index.

Sources consulted, p.159–60. Index to authors, p.161–65.

Parrish, Maxfield, 1870–1966

A280 Norell, Irene P. Maxfield Parrish, New Hampshire artist, 1870–1966: a contribution toward a bibliography, with notes. Preliminary ed.. San Jose, Calif., I. P. Norell, 1971. iii, 41p. 3-p. addenda.

Briefly annotated, preliminary bibliography on Maxfield Parrish that includes Bibliographies, p.7; Magazines, p.11–20; Newspapers, p.23–24; Illustrations in books and magazines, p.27–31; Books, p.35–38; Miscellanea, p.41

Picasso, Pablo, 1881–1973

A281 Kibbey, Ray Anne. Picasso: a comprehensive bibliography. N.Y., Garland, 1977. xxi, 287p. (Garland reference library of the humanities, v.45)

Identifies and briefly annotates 1,543 books, catalogues raisonnés, exhibition catalogs, dissertations and theses, essays, special issues of periodicals, periodical articles, literary works by Pablo Picasso, livres d'artistes, bibliographies, and archival materials published through 1976. Index includes author names, titles of art works and monographs, galleries, and subjects.

Index, p.249–87.

Pugin, A.W.N., 1812–1852

A282 Belcher, Margaret. A. W. N. Pugin: an annotated bibliography. London, Mansell, 1987. xxiv, 496p. 12 il.

Exhaustive critical bibliography of works by and about Pugin, noted for its extensive research and descriptive commentary. Individual entries include size of publication, notes about plates and illustrations, and criticism.

Contents: (1) Publications by Pugin; (2) Illustrations by Pugin for the works of others; (3) Works sometimes attributed to Pugin; (4) Publications about Pugin; (5) Biographical glossary.

Index, p.479–96.

Rossetti, Dante Gabriel, 1828–1882

A283 Fennell, Francis L. Dante Gabriel Rossetti: an annotated bibliography. N.Y., Garland, 1982. xvi, 282p. (Garland reference library of the humanities, v.286)

Annotated bibliography of 1,195 books and periodical articles about Rossetti's artistic and literary career published from the time of Rossetti's death in April 1882 up to January 1, 1980. Entries 656–979 (p.155–219) include critical assessments of Rossetti as an artist.

Contents: (1) Bibliographies; (2) Source materials for literary works; (3) Source materials for artistic works; (4) Letters; (5) Biographical studies; (6) Studies of Rossetti as a writer; (7) Studies of Rossetti as an artist; (8) Studies of Rossetti as a poet-painter; (9) Dissertations.

A Rossetti chronology, p.xv–xvi. Index, p.261–82.

Rudolph, Paul, 1918–1999

See Kahn, Louis.

Russell, Charles Marion, 1864–1926

A284 Yost, Karl, and Renner, Frederic G. A bibliography of the published works of Charles M. Russell. Lincoln, Univ. of Nebraska Pr., 1971. xii, 317p. plates (part col.)

Identifies, organizes, and extensively annotates approximately 3,500 works, including collations, gallery catalogs, periodicals, newspapers, portfolios and sets, color prints, black-and-white prints, postcards, Christmas cards, ephemera, advertisements, Montana Historical Society, price lists, stationery, related objects, appearances, and references without illustrations. Cutoff date Dec. 31, 1966. Updates and adds four times the number of citations in Karl Yost's Charles M. Russell, the cowboy artist: a bibliography, Pasadena, Calif., Trail's End, 1948.

Index to paintings, drawings, and sculpture, p.277–307. General index, p.309–17.

Sargent, John Singer, 1856–1925

A285 Getscher, Robert H., and Marks, Paul G. James McNeil Whistler and John Singer Sargent: two annotated bibliographies. N.Y., Garland, 1986. vi, 520p. (Garland reference library of the humanities, v.467)

Two annotated bibliographies of books, pamphlets, periodical articles, exhibitions, reviews, illustrations, and designs related to Whistler (p.1–377) and Sargent (p.379–470). Includes primary and secondary materials.

Index, p.473–520.

Shahn, Ben, 1898–1969

A286 Eckstein, Patricia Schlamowitz. Ben Shahn, 1898–1969: an annotated bibliography of books, pamphlets, and exhibition catalogs by, about, and illustrated by the artist. [Los Angeles?], Eckstein, 1978. xxxi, 57 leaves.

Compiled as a master's thesis for the UCLA library and information science program.

Smith, W. Eugene, 1918–1978

A287 Johnson, William. W. Eugene Smith: a chronological bibliography, 1934–1980. Tucson, Center for Creative Photography, Univ. of Arizona, 1980–84. 3v. (Center for Creative Photography bibliography series, no.1)

Partially annotated bibliography of approximately 1,750 books, portfolios, periodical and newspaper articles, exhibition catalogs, and photographs by and about Smith. References are arranged alphabetically by title within each format section for each year.

Contents: (1) 1934–51; (2) Additions to part 1; 1952–80; (3) Addendum: 1938–83.

Chronological index to articles by W. Eugene Smith, v.2, p.249–58. Author index to articles about W. Eugene Smith, v.2, p.259–61.

Villard de Honnecourt, fl. c. 1220–1240

A288 Barnes, Carl F., Jr. Villard de Honnecourt: the artist and his drawings: a critical bibliography. Boston, Hall, 1982. lvii, 121p. il. (Reference publication in art history)

Includes a lengthy, informative introduction about the artist/mason Villard de Honnecourt and his 13th-century architectural manuscript preserved in the Bibliothèque Nationale, Paris; facsimile editions and concordance with the manuscript; writings about Villard and his drawings arranged chronologically, 1666–1981; miscellany regarding exhibitions; and an appendix of churches attributed to Villard. Annotated.

Author index, p.109–12. Subject index, p.113–21.

Whistler, James McNeill, 1834–1903

See Sargent, John Singer.

Wright, Frank Lloyd, 1867–1959

A289 Meehan, Patrick J. Frank Lloyd Wright: a research guide to archival sources. With a foreword by Adolf K. Placzek. N.Y., Garland, 1983. xxxiii, 681p. il. (Garland bibliographies in architecture and planning, v.3) (Garland reference library of the humanities, v.294)

Annotated, descriptive catalog and research aid to archival materials in more than 50 public and private collections. Identifies more than 500 manuscripts by Wright dating from 1894 to 1959.

Contents: (1) The Frank Lloyd Wright archival collections; (2) The Frank Lloyd Wright manuscripts.

Appendix A, undated Frank Lloyd Wright manuscripts, p.579–83. Appendix B, compiled chronology of buildings, designs, and projects of Frank Lloyd Wright, p.585–644. Index of buildings, designs, projects, and places, p.645–56. Index of names, titles, and topics, p.657–73. Index of correspondents, p.675–77. Index of archives and collections, p.679–81.

A290 Sweeney, Robert Lawrence. Frank Lloyd Wright: an annotated bibliography. Foreword by Adolf K. Placzek. Los Angeles, Hennessey & Ingalls, 1978. xliv, 303p. 12 plates.

Annotated list of 2,095 books and articles by or about Wright published between 1886 and 1977, arranged chronologically. The introduction includes biographical and bibliographical overviews.

Appendix A, Taliesen publications, p.246–55. Appendix B, Frank Lloyd Wright buildings recorded by the historic American buildings survey, p.256–59. Building and place index, p.261–84. Name and title index, p.285–303.

Zucker, Paul, 1889–1971

See Kahn, Louis.

B.
Directories

This chapter is divided into two sections. The first lists general art directories; the second lists museum directories. General art directories contain essential information about a variety of art organizations and institutions around the world. Museum directories supply information about art museums' collections, staff, and hours.

Most museums and other art organizations now maintain their own internet sites, containing reliable, current information. These sites should be consulted as a supplement to the information offered in this chapter.

GENERAL DIRECTORIES

B1 American art directory, v.1, 1898– . New Providence, N.J., Bowker, 1898– . Biennial.

See GLAH 1:B1 for original annotation.

Essential reference for American art institutions and organizations. Provides contact information for national and regional organizations in the U.S. and Canada; museums, libraries, and associations in the U.S. and Canada (arranged by geographic location); art schools in the U.S. and Canada (arranged by geographic location); major museums abroad; major art schools abroad; state art councils; state directors and supervisors of education; art magazines; newspaper art editors and critics; scholarships and fellowships; open exhibitions; traveling exhibition booking agencies.

Subject index provides institution name(s); personnel index lists title and institutional affiliation of individuals; organizational index lists geographical location.

B2 Art & design documentation in the UK and Ireland: a directory of resources. Comp. and ed. by Gillian Varley. [N.p.], ARLIS/UK & Ireland, 1993. v, 241p.

Guide to nearly 400 libraries and archives in the United Kingdom and Ireland with collections relating to art and design. Entries include contact person, scope of collection, hours, type of catalog.

Regional index, p.219–24. Subject index, p.225–41.

B3 Art in America annual guide to galleries, museums, artists, 1982– . N.Y., Brant Art Publ., 1982– . Annual.

Guide is the Aug. issue of Art in America. Useful and current guide to museum and gallery activities for the year.

Contents: Museum preview for coming year; preceding year in review; The Guide (U.S. museums, galleries, university galleries, nonprofit exhibition spaces, corporate consultants, private dealers, and print dealers), arranged geographically.

Alphabetical indexes provided for each of the guide categories, to artists represented by one or more of the gallery spaces, and by author or artist to articles published in Art in America for preceding year.

B4 Art Libraries Society of North America handbook and list of members, 1982– . Raleigh, N.C., ARLIS/NA, 1982– . Annual. Title, 1975–1981: Directory of members.

Contents: Executive Board; ARLIS/NA: a history and overview; Strategic plan; Articles of incorporation; Bylaws; Standing committees; Ad hoc committees and appointments; Group moderators; Group statements of purpose; ARLIS/NA guidelines; Chapters and chapter officers; Individual members; Overseas members and subscribers; Institutional members; Business affiliate members; Divisions, sections, and round tables; Index of individuals by institution; Geographical index.

B5 ARTnews international directory of corporate art collections, 1993/94ed. Ed. by Shirley Reiff Howarth. N.Y., ARTnews, [1993]. 573p.

1st ed. 1988. 2d ed. 1990. Supersedes Directory of corporate art collections, v. 1–3, 1982–84, and the 1986 ARTnews directory of corporate art collections. Beginning with the 1996 ed., only available on disk. Issued in cooperation with International Art Alliance.

Lists 1,294 corporate art collections in the U.S. and abroad, including a description of the collection, a contact person if any and selected bibliographical references. Indicates where the collection is displayed and what loan conditions apply. Appendixes include group exhibitions of corporate art collections and important holdings which have been dispersed or absorbed.

Indexes by state and country, p.503–14; type of business, p.515–24; media and type of collection, p. 525–47; and personnel, p.548–73.

B6 Catalog of museum publications and media: a directory and index of publications and audiovisuals available from United States and Canadian institutions. Paul Wasserman, managing ed. Esther Herman, assoc. ed. 2d ed. Detroit, Gale, 1980. xi, 1044p.

See GLAH 1:B12 for 1st ed., Museum media, and original annotation. This ed. "offers updated and current details for 992 institutions compared to the 732 institutions covered in the first edition."—*Pref.*

Contents: (I) Museum publications and media; (II) Title and keyword index; (III) Periodicals index; (IV) Subject index; (V) Geographic index.

B7 Directorio de arte Latinoamericano = Latin American art directory, 1996– . Buenos Aires, Arte al Dia Internacional; Miami Beach, Oficina Comercial in Miami, American Art Corporation, 1996– . Annual.

Directory of museums, galleries, dealers, critics, art magazines, publishers, professional organizations, photographers, schools, and other arts institutions, arranged by country.

B8 Directory of art and design faculties in colleges and universities, U.S. and Canada, 1995–96. [4th ed.] Missoula, Mont., CMS Pub., [1995]. vii, 543p.

1st ed. 1987; 2d ed. 1991; 3d ed. 1995.

Schematic but exceptionally broad listing of art departments at American academic institutions, 1,537 in this ed. Entry for each school provides address, telephone and fax numbers, degrees offered, and the names of teaching faculty. Numerical codes next to each faculty name indicate teaching interests, a key to which is listed inside the front and back covers.

Indexes: Faculty grouped by teaching interest, p.253–445; alphabetical by faculty name, p.449–511; graduate degrees offered, p.515–22; alphabetical by institution name, p.525–43.

B9 Directory of M.A. & Ph.D. programs in art, art history and related areas. N.Y., College Art Association, [1999]. 194p.

1st ed. 1992. Supersedes Directory of Ph.D. programs in art history, 4th rev. ed. 1984.

Primary resource for students investigating graduate programs in the U.S. Listings for more than 160 graduate art history programs include specific degrees offered, admissions requirements, names of faculty and their fields of specialization, statistical breakdown of students, description of curriculum requirements, list of recent dissertation topics, available resources such as slides and library materials, financial information, placement assistance and "major changes anticipated." Briefer listings provided for Canadian programs. Geographic and faculty name indexes.

B10 Directory of historians of Latin American art. San Antonio, Research Center for the Arts, Univ. of Texas, 1981. 47p.

Lists 209 art historians and related scholars arranged alphabetically. Indexed by scholars' areas of interest. Includes guide to graduate schools with Latin American art history programs.

B11 Directory of MFA programs in the visual arts. N.Y., College Art Association, [1999]. 175p.

Previous eds. published in 1976, 1980, 1987, 1992, and 1996.

Guide to more than 200 programs offering the MFA in studio art. Entries include admission requirements, faculty, characteristics of student body, curriculum requirements, resources such as studios and computer hardware, financial support, placement assistance, and comments. The focus is on the U.S.; only addresses provided for Canadian programs. Lists by area of study and by state serve as indexes.

B12 Doling, Tim. Visiting arts regional profile: Asia Pacific arts directory. Paris, UNESCO Publishing and Visiting Arts, [1996]. 3v.

"The directory, a co-operative venture between Visiting Arts and UNESCO, arises out of their joint recognition of the value of cultural networking and of the need for the compilation of detailed cultural databases for hitherto sparsely documented regions of the world."—*Introd.*

Each country or territory listed has a separate chapter with the following subdivisions: (1) Cultural agencies; (2) Performing arts; (3) Visual arts; (4) Arts festivals; (5) Arts training and research; (6) Cultural libraries, archives, and resource centres; (7) Foundations which fund the arts.

Contents: (1) Australia, Fiji, New Caledonia, New Zealand, Papua New Guinea, Solomon Islands, Vanuatu; (2) Brunei Darussalam, Cambodia, Indonesia, Lao People's Democratic Republic, Malaysia, Myanmar, Philippines, Singapore, Thailand, Viet Nam; (3) China, Hong Kong, Japan, Republic of Korea, Macao.

B13 Guide to architecture schools. Ed. John K. Edwards. 6th ed. Washington, D.C., Association of Collegiate Schools of Architecture, [1998]. viii, 338p. il.

1st four eds. titled Guide to architecture schools in North America; 3d ed. 1982; 4th ed. 1989; 5th ed. 1994.

Comparative guide to architecture programs. Entries include application requirements for each degree, statistical data on the make-up of students and faculty, descriptions of facilities, programs, financial aid, and a list of faculty. Less detailed information is available for affiliate institutions, including some foreign programs. An alphabetical list of faculty provides their institutional affiliations. "Schools of architecture worldwide" provides addresses for hundreds of foreign schools.

B14 International directory of arts = Internationales Kunst-Adressbuch = Annuaire international des beaux-arts = Annuario internazionale delle belle arti = Anuario internacional de las artes. 24th ed. München, Saur, 1998. 3v. Biennial.

See GLAH 1:B10 for 1st–14th eds.;15th–21st eds. published: Frankfurt, Art Adress Verlag.

Remains the best single international directory of art institutions. Precise scope has varied. Sections in the current ed. include museums and public galleries; universities, academies, and colleges; associations; antiques and numismatics dealers; galleries; auctioneers; restorers; art publishers; art periodicals; antiquarian and art booksellers. Entries for each organization include address, phone number, sometimes a fax number, and usually the name of one or more staff members. Indexes for persons and institutions.

Index of degree types, p.328–33. Organizations in architecture and related fields, p.334–35. Abbreviations, p.336. Index of schools, p.337–38.

B15 Latin American art, a resource directory. [Chief ed., Belgica Rodriguez. Assist. ed., Jose Bustillos]. Washington, D.C., Museo de Arte de las Americas, OEA, [1994?]. 64p.

Directory of art journals, museums, galleries, cultural centers, art critics, biennials, and art fairs related to Latin American art.

B16 Money for visual artists. Researched by Douglas Oxenhorn. New exp. 2d ed. N.Y., American Council for the Arts; Allworth Pr., [1993]. viii, 317p.

1st ed. 1991.

Lists 221 organizations providing grants and other types of support to visual artists. Each entry includes address, contact person, brief profile of the organization, a summary of direct support programs, and an outline of the application process.

Indexes by name, p.295–97, by geographic area, p.298–303, and by type of support, p.304–12. Selected reading, p.313.

B17 Organizing artists: a document and directory of the National Association of Artists' Organizations. 4th ed. Washington, D.C., National Association of Artists' Organizations, [1998]. 143p. il.

3d ed., 1992.

Resource for information on non-profit gallery and performance spaces. More than a directory, it advocates the value of artists' organizations. The first section includes testimonials by artists, several essays on the state of arts in the United States and a timeline of political and artistic events from 1905 to 1990. The remaining portion lists several types of organizations: NAAO members, service and advocacy organizations, national AIDS/HIV resource organizations, artists' residencies, media centers, regional and national government agencies, and foundations. Entries for member organizations include addresses, phone and fax numbers, a description of activities, gallery space, and often annual budgets. Members are also listed by geographic region; alphabetical index.

B18 Thompson, Marie Claude. Les sources de l'histoire de l'art en France: répertoire des bibliothèques, centres de documentation et ressources documentaires en art, architecture et archéologie. Avec le concours de Catherine Schmitt et Nicole Picot. Paris, Association des bibliothécaires français, [1993]. 310p.

Directory of nearly 600 French libraries open to the public for research in art, design, architecture, theater arts, and archeology. Organized by département, each entry includes address, telephone and fax numbers, access policies, hours, and a brief outline of collections. Indexes include cities, départements, name of institution, type of institution, and key word subjects.

Bibliography, p.309–10.

B19 Werenko, John D. Guide to American art schools. Borgna Brunner, project ed. Boston, Hall, [1987]. xxvi, 281p., maps.

Somewhat dated but detailed guide to 384 undergraduate and graduate art programs in the United States, selected on the basis of curriculum and accreditation by the National Association of Schools of Art and Design. Entries are organized by geographic region and then by state; each includes a brief history of the program, degrees offered, facilities, and admissions requirements. A comparative chart illustrates graphically which of 40 major fields of study are available at each school.

Alphabetical index of institutions, p.279–81.

MUSEUMS DIRECTORIES

B20 American Association of Museums. The official museum directory, 1971– . New Providence, N.J., Bowker, 1971– . Annual.

See GLAH 1:B14 for original annotation.

29th ed. lists more than 8,000 museums, aquariums, botanic gardens, historic houses, nature centers, planetariums, and zoos, accredited by the Association. In addition to museum listings, information about the Association is included as well as contact information for state and regional arts organizations, humanities councils, and international museum associations. A second volume serves as an advertising supplement, listing products and services of interest to the museum profession.

B21 Danilov, Victor J. Corporate museums, galleries, and visitor centers: a directory. N.Y., Greenwood, 1991. 211p. il.

Describes 329 corporate museums, galleries, and visitor centers throughout the world. About two-thirds are located in the United States; the others come from 16 other countries.

Contents: (1) Corporate museums and exhibits; (2) Corporate art museums, galleries, and sculpture gardens; (3) Corporate visitor and information centers.

Selected bibliography, p.197–98. Index, p.199–211.

B22 Directory of museums in Africa. UNESCO-ICOM Documentation Centre. Ed. by Susanne Peters . . . [et al.] = Répertoire des musées en Afrique. Centre de documentation UNESCO-ICOM. Rédigé par Susanne Peters . . . [et al.] London, Kegan Paul, [1990]. 211p. il., maps.

Bilingual guide to museums in 47 African countries; entries include brief description of collections.

Indexes by name of museum, p.185–93; city or town, p.194–201; and by subject, p.202–11.

B23 Edson, Gary. International directory of museum training. N.Y., Routledge, [1995]. xiv, 411p. il., 10 plates.

Supersedes various eds. of Museum studies programs in the United States and abroad and Museum studies international, rev. ed., Washington, D.C., Office of Museum Programs, Smithsonian Institution,1988.

Lists several hundred museum training programs, primarily in institutions in Western countries. Entries include types of degrees offered, areas of specialization, and name of contact person. Directory section is preceded by three chapters: Introduction to museum training; Museum training in a changing world; Museum work today.

Glossary of museum training terms, p.367–75. Selected bibliography organized by discipline, p.379–91. Museum training indices [organized by degree, discipline, type of financial aid, and name of institution], p.403–11.

B24 Flannigan, Thomas, and Flannigan, Ellen. Tokyo museums: a complete guide. Rutland, Charles E. Tuttle, 1993. 245p. il., maps, plates.

Includes one-page descriptions of nearly 200 museums in the Tokyo area with entries organized under broad subject headings, e.g., art, history, science, toys. Each entry includes museum name, transportation directions, a description of the collection, address, phone number, hours, and admission cost.

B25 Handbuch der Museen = Handbook of museums. Bundesrepublik Deutschland, Deutsche Demokratische Republik, Österreich, Schweiz, Liechtenstein. 2. neubearb. Aufl. München, Saur, 1981. 779p.

See GLAH 1:B17 for 1st ed.

Somewhat out-of-date but important for its listings of more than 5,000 museums in four Northern European countries. Collection descriptions included.

Indexed by place name, p.699–740; by museum name, p.741–63; and by subject, p.764–[80].

B26 Hudson, Kenneth, and Nicholls, Ann. The Cambridge guide to the museums of Britain and Ireland. Rev. pbk. ed. Cambridge, Cambridge Univ. Pr., [1989]. x, 16, 452p. il., col. plates, maps.

This guidebook includes more than 2,000 art, history, and science museums and historic houses in Great Britain and Ireland. Brief description of collections provided.

Indexed by institution name, p.433–43; by subject, p.443–51; and by museums associated with individuals, p.452.

B27 ______. The Cambridge guide to the museums of Europe. Cambridge, Cambridge Univ. Pr., [1991]. 509p. il., col. plates, maps.

Similar format to the above, listing more than 2,000 museums in Western Europe.

Indexed by subject, p.475–93; museum name, p.494–506; and museums associated with individuals, p.507–09.

B28 I Mille musei d'Italia. Firenze, Primavera, [1988]. 4v. il. (part col.)

Organized by geographic region, this work lists Italian art, history, and archeology museums. A brief description of collections is included with a summary of the museum's best known works, where appropriate. A supplemental list is provided of noteworthy churches and historic houses in each geographic location.

Each volume indexed by name of museum and by artists mentioned in the annotations.

Contents: (1) Piemonte, Valle d'Aosta, Liguria, Lombardia; (2) Emilia-Romagna, Trentino-Alto Adige, Veneto, Friuli-Venezia Giulia; (3) Toscana, Marche, Umbria; (4) Lazio, Abruzzo, Molise, Campania, Puglia, Basilicata, Calabria, Sicilia, Sardegna.

B29 Museums of the world. [Ed. Michael Zils; asst. ed. Marco Schulze]. 7th rev. and enl. ed. München, Saur, 2000. viii, 817p. (Handbook of international documentation and information, v. 16)

See GLAH 1:B21 for 2d ed.; 3d ed. 1981; 4th ed. 1992; 5th ed. 1995; 6th ed. 1997.

7th ed. provides very brief, basic information on nearly 40,000 museums in 194 countries. All entries have been updated and fax numbers have been added where available.

Alphabetical index, p.585–690. Personality index, p.693–98. Subject index, p.701–815.

B30 Museums yearbook, 1976– . London, Museums Association, 1976?– . Annual.

Supersedes Museums calendar, 1967–75.

Ed. of 2000 vol., Mike Wright.

Directory of more than 2,500 museums and cultural properties in the U.K., arranged alphabetically by city. Entries supply basic information about location, collection, facilities, hours, and staff.

National museum and heritage organisations and government bodies, p.17–22. Area museum councils, p.23–24. Specialist groups, p.25–28. Regional federations, p.29. Related organisations, p.30–43. International museum and heritage organisations, p.44–48. Directory of courses, p.433–44. Directory of consultants, p.445–60. Buyer's guide to suppliers and services, p.461–584. Index, p.585–96.

B31 New York Times traveler's guide to art museum exhibitions 2000. Ed. Fletcher Roberts. Consulting ed. Susan S. Rappaport. N.Y., N.Y. Times [1999-]. Annual.

Originally published as: Traveler's guide to museum exhibitions, Washington, D.C., Museum Guide Publications, 1989–91; Traveler's guide to art museum exhibitions, 1992–99.

Lists major exhibitions to be held at more than 350 art museums in the U.S., Canada, Europe, and Japan. Each entry includes highlights of the permanent collection, hours, and admission fees. Editorial schedule precludes complete entries for all museums. Summary list of important traveling exhibitions and their successive venues with dates.

B32 Roberts, Laurance P. Roberts' guide to Japanese museums of art and archaeology. Rev. and updated. Tokyo, Simul, 1987. iv, 383p. il.

See GLAH 1:B23 for original annotation; 2d ed. with the present title, 1978.

347 entries arranged in alphabetical order by the English name of the museum with indexes providing cross references for the Japanese name, prefecture, and subject. Each entry includes the English name, Japanese name, address, telephone number, collection description with author's personal comment, hours, admission charge, and transportation directions.

Glossary, p.321–43. Indexes [by Japanese names, by branch museums and other collections, by prefectures, and by types of collections], p.344–48.

SEE ALSO: American art directory (GLAH 2:B1); International directory of arts (GLAH 2:B14).

C. Sales Records

The compilation and publication of auction sale results has been transformed during the last decade by electronic database technology. Traditional print publications have changed formats and publishers; increased interest in the purchase and sale of artworks has driven the development of dynamic data available through the internet; auction houses have consolidated. In this chapter we have attempted to update information from GLAH 1 where publications have ceased or changed titles or publishers. Following the convention adopted in Chapter Q, Periodicals, in the case of serials that have changed titles we have provided separate entries only for the most recent version, the annotation giving the full publication history. But in the case of the many titles that merged, we have provided separate entries for each title. When a printed reference also appears as an electronic resource or when electronic replaces print, we have attempted to track the succession of formats and coverage; as throughout this volume, however, we have not cited internet addresses, which are notoriously subject to change. For wholly new electronic publications, we have described current content and availability. The heightened commercial interest in all types of art sales and the fluid nature of digital delivery make this information inherently and unusually subject to revision.

CURRENT SERIALS

C1 Annuaire des cotes international = International art price annual, 1988–97. Paris, ADEC-Production, 1989–97. Annual.

Entries in French and English. The 1988 ed. covered French auctions only. With 1989, expanded to include sales in Western Europe, North America, Japan, and Scandinavia. Merged with Art price index international in 1998 to form Art price annual international & Falk's art price index (see GLAH 2:C3).

Also available in a series of cumulative CD-ROM versions: ADEC: International art prices, [Naples, Florida], Gordon's Print Price Annual, 1994–99. Annual. Title changed in 1999 to ADEC/Art Price Annual International & Falk's Art Price Index, reflecting the merger with Art price index international and covering the years 1987–98. Contains 1,300,000 records from more than 1,200 auction firms, including painting, drawing, miniatures, prints, posters, sculpture, and photography. Searchable by artist, title, medium, price, auction house, and date. With the 2000 ed., the title changed to Artprice.com, Saint-Romain-au-Mont-d'Or, France, Artprice.com, 2000– . Available in two disks, Fine Art or Works on Paper, augmented by access to online updates via internet. The Fine Art database is comprised of more than 2,000,000 auction results covering 172,000 artists with works including painting, sculpture, miniatures, tapestries and ceramics. The Works on Paper database provides access to approximately 900,000 auction results for 70,000 artists in drawing, prints, posters, and photography. Covers January 1987 through March 2001. Also available as an internet database by subscription.

C2 L'annuel des arts, 01– , 1993– . [Paris], A. Israel, 1993– . Annual.

Continues L'officiel des arts; guide semestriel des ventes, 1–6, Mars 1989–Août 1991, Paris, Ed. Van Wilder, 1989–91. Semiannual.

Covers 110 auction houses in Western Europe, U.S.A., Australia, Taiwan, Israel, Singapore, Uruguay, Russia, and Turkey. Indexes international sales of paintings, drawings, prints, and sculpture for 19th- and 20th-century artists. Entries include artist name, birth date, title, dimensions, medium, sale date, auction house, and price in British pounds, French francs, and U.S. dollars. Contains selected artist signatures and monograms, 16th through 18th centuries.

C3 Art price annual international & Falk's art price index, 1998– . Saint-Romain-au-Mont-d'Or, France, ADEC/Art Price Annual, 1998– .

Formed by the merger of International art price annual (GLAH 2:C1) and Art price index international (see following entry).

The 2000 ed. covers 170,000 entries for 59,000 artists works sold at 5,000 auctions. Coverage includes paintings, sculptures, drawings, prints, photographs, miniatures, posters, and tapestries.

For CD-ROM and internet database eds., see the annotation for International art price annual GLAH 2:C1.

C4 Art price index international, '94–97. Madison, Conn., Sound View Press, 1993–98. Annual.

Merged with International art price annual (GLAH 2:C1) in 1998 to form Art price annual international & Falk's art price index (see preceding entry).

Comprehensive index to auction results covering nearly 400 auction houses and including many smaller venues. Detailed introduction and explanation of entries provides a good overview of auction practices and conventions. Covers paintings, drawings, watercolors, miniatures, sculpture, prints, photographs, posters, and animation.

C5 Art prices current: a record of sale prices at the principal London, Continental, and American auction rooms with indexes to the artists, engravers, and collectors. n.s. v.1–59, 1921/22–1972/73. London, Dawson, 1908–73.

See GLAH 1:C4 for original annotation. Ceased with v.59 (1972/73).

C6 Art sales index, 1984/85– . Ed. by Duncan Hislop. Virginia Water, Eng., Art Sales Index, 1985– . Annual.

Continues The annual art sales index (GLAH 1:C1) which ceased in 1984.

Comprehensive index for sales of paintings, drawings, watercolors, prints, miniatures, and sculpture. Includes annual compilations of record prices, turnover, and works sold for more than £1 million and a useful cross-index to artist names. Auction house coverage has expanded over the years and now numbers 460 internationally including many smaller venues.

Also available as a CD-ROM database covering 1989–98. Coverage gives access to approximately 1.65 million auction records for artworks by more than 100,000 artists. Records may be retrieved by 27 different headings and results may be saved, annotated, and exported. Art Sales Index has recently been released as an internet database by subscription containing auction sales records since the 1950s. Images are now being added.

C7 ArtFact complete [computer file]. North Kingstown, Rhode Island, ArtFact, Inc., 1989– .

Since its inception, ArtFact has increased its database to include more than 4 million auction sales results from more than 850 auction houses. Nearly half of the participating auction houses provide full transcriptions of their catalog entries. Also contains approximately 55,000 color images. Includes furniture, antiques, collectibles, and jewelry. Searchable by keyword with features such as proximity searching and implicit truncation. Available as an internet database by subscription.

C8 Artnet.com [computer file]. N.Y., ArtNet Worldwide, 1985– .

One of the earliest databases to provide access to international fine art auction records. Offers sale results for more than 2 million artworks sold through 500 auction houses in 28 countries since 1985. More than 600,000 records contain color images. Sales are searchable by artist name, auction house, title, medium, size, price, execution date, and date of sale. Artnet.com also offers a newly developed database of more than 38,000 African art sales records from 1927 to the present. These records include works in various media sold internationally through more than 90 auction houses. Both databases are available on the internet by subscription.

C9 Australian art sales digest 2001: a survey of Australian and New Zealand sales of art at auction from 1988 to 2000. Victoria, Australia, Acorn Antiques Pty., 2001. 565p. il.

Compilation of more than 100,000 sales results for nearly 5,000 artists who have lived or worked in New Zealand or Australia from the 19th century to the present. Entries include artist name, birth and death dates, title, medium, date of work, size, auction information, and price.

Also available as an internet database with some images by subscription.

C10 Belgian artists in the world's salerooms, 1988–89– . Bruxelles, Arts Antiques Auctions, [1989–]. Annual.

Covers 98 auction houses in Europe, Canada and the U.S. Includes painting, drawings, watercolors, prints, posters, photographs, sculpture, and mixed media. Indexed by medium and artist name. The 1997 and later eds. expanded coverage to artists who lived, worked, or died in Belgium from 1800 to the present day.

C11 Christie's review of the year. London, Christie's, 1996– . Annual.

Continues Christie's review of the season. See GLAH 1:C5 for original annotation.

C12 Contemporary print portfolio, no.1-, Spring 1990– . Shawnee Mission, Kan., Bon A Tirer Pub., 1990– . Semiannual.

"A quick reference auction report from more than 235 sales of contemporary prints held during the past fifteen years."—*Pref.* Includes works produced from 1950 to the present. The 9th ed. of this index covers the work of approximately 300 artists in 6,000 individual prints. Entries are arranged alphabetically by artist and include catalogue raisonné numbers.

C13 Gordon's print price annual, 1978– . Phoenix, Gordon's Art Reference, 1978– . Annual.

See GLAH 1:C6a for original annotation.

CD-ROM and internet database versions: Full-text, searchable, covering the years 1986–2000. Includes the bibliography of monographs, exhibition catalogs, and index to advertisers present in the printed version. Updated annually. Images will be added to the internet database.

C14 Le guidargus de la peinture du XIXe siècle à nos jours, 1980– . Paris, Éd. de l'amateur, 1980– . Annual.

Features well-known artists from a selected number of auction houses. Artist entries include brief biographical and critical remarks, bibliographic references, and a listing of works sold. Emphasizes painting but includes watercolors, drawings, serigraphs, and pochoir. The 2000 ed. contains a short essay on the emergence and importance of electronic resources for auction sales information.

C15 i-on-Art: old master paintings [computer file]. Milan, Global Art Systems, [1999–].

CD-ROM database of auction records for old master paintings sold by Christie's (London, New York, Amsterdam, and Monte Carlo), Dorotheum (Vienna), Phillips (London), and Sotheby's (London, New York, Amsterdam, and Monte Carlo) from 1990 to 2000. A considerably smaller selection of auction records from 1986 to 1990 is also included. All of the more than 70,000 records contain color images. Searchable indexes include artist, title, provenance, literature, auction house, date, and price. Bibliography and exhibition history are included. Pre-1990 sales are being added, and current sales are updated annually.

C16 International art market: current world market prices of art, antiques & objets d'art, v.1–23, Mar., 1961–Nov./Dec. 1983. Woodbury, N.Y., Interart, 1961–83.

See GLAH 1:C6 for original annotation. Ceased with v.23.

C17 Kunstpreis Jahrbuch. München, Kunst und Technik, 1980– . Annual.

Continues Art-price Annual = Kunstpreis Jahrbuch (GLAH 1:C3); the English-language ed. ceased with v.34 (1979). Title and imprint vary. 1999 ed. titled Auktionspreise im Kunstpreis Jahrbuch.

Remains an invaluable source for its extensive coverage of the decorative arts and its detailed categorization of objects. Includes paintings, drawings, prints, icons, medals, sculptures, photographs, furniture, carpets, stoneware, faience, porcelain, glass, silver, jewelry, Judaica, metalware, clocks and watches, scientific and musical instruments, toys, antiquities, Asian and Islamic art, and arms and armor. Now published in three vols. covering international sales from more than 350 auction venues worldwide with particular emphasis on the smaller German houses. Numerous small black-and-white illustrations.

C18 Lawrence's dealer print prices international 2000. Ed. by Lisa Reinhardt. Phoenix, Gordon's Art Reference, 2000. 842p.

Contains more than 30,000 entries from international private print dealer catalogs. Includes contact information for all dealers listed, bibliography, and a listing of catalogues raisonnés. Also available in CD-ROM version covering the years 1992–2000 and as an internet database by subscription.

C19 Leonard's combined price index of art auctions [computer file], 1996– . Newton, Mass., Auctions Index, 1995– . Annual.

CD-ROM database containing combined data from Leonard's annual price index of art auctions (v.1–17, 1980/81–1996/97) and v.1–3 of Leonard's annual price index of prints, posters & photographs (v.4, 1994/95, excluded prints), both now ceased.

Covers paintings, drawings, and sculpture sold at approximately 100 auction houses, with an emphasis on smaller venues in the United States. Also includes selected bibliographies of works on prints, posters, photography, and photographer monographs as well as glossaries of art terminology. Covers print, poster, and photograph auction results from approximately 115 houses worldwide with an emphasis on smaller venues in the United States. Searchable by artist name, title, auction house, medium, and date of sale.

C20 Le livre international des ventes: estampes, dessins, aquarelles, peintures, sculptures. Année 27 (1988)–Année 32 (1994). Zurich, Ed. M.; Lausanne, Acatos, 1989–1994. [Comp.] Enrique Mayer.

Merged with International auction records (GLAH 1:C7) to form MAYER (see following entry).

C21 MAYER. Lausanne, Ed. Acatos, 1995– .

Continues Mayer, Enrique. International auction records (GLAH 1:C7), which ceased with v.28 (1994), merging with Livre international des ventes to form the present title.

The print ed. of MAYER is now complemented by databases covering a decade of sale results. The MAYER international auction records database was recently purchased by icollector.com. Access to the database is now free of charge. "The 1987–1997 database contains more than 1,000,000 auction records of sales to 31.12.1997. More than 800 auction houses in 40 countries contribute information. The important lower and middle markets are fully represented as well as all the major houses. Works from every period are featured and the selection is not restricted to those that achieve high prices. The coverage is truly international and ranges from the works of the great masters to those of lesser known and of younger artists who are appearing in the public sales for the first time. In all there are listings on more than 75,000 artists of more than 100 different nationalities."—*Press release* from icollector.com website, March 2000. The internet database, titled Art price guide, and latest CD-ROM ed. contain results for more than 1,000,000 sales of paintings, watercolors, drawings, prints, posters, and sculpture from 900 auction houses. Allows searching by artist name, title, date of execution, media, date of sale, sale price, and auction house. Currency conversions are calculated. Does not include images.

CD-ROM version: MAYER: International auction records. Lausanne, Éd. Acatos, 1994–1998.

C22 Photographic art market: auction price results and analysis, 1980/81– . N.Y., Falk-Leeds, 1981– . Annual.

Publisher varies.

Indexes auction results for photographs by photographer name and includes date of sale, auction house, dimensions, print type, date of photograph, estimate, and price, including buyer's premium. The 1981 vol. includes "an introduction to fine art photography, an overview of the market, several sections devoted to acquisition strategy, and a grading system for collectible photographs." —*Introd.* Some vols. also contain an auction season overview and other articles excerpted from the Photograph collector.

C23 Print price index, '92– . Madison, Conn., Sound View Pr., 1991– . Annual.

A comprehensive listing of international sale results indexed to provide access by type of prints as well as artist. Categories included are books with prints, botanical, Japanese and Oriental, natural history, portfolios of prints, posters, sporting, and topographical. Good coverage of smaller sale venues, especially in France and the United States. Prices recorded are hammer prices. Includes a directory of print dealers arranged by country and state.

C24 Sotheby's art at auction, 1986–87– . London, Sotheby's Publications, 1987. Annual.
Continues Art at auction: the year at Sotheby Parke Bernet. See GLAH 1:C2 for original annotation.

RETROSPECTIVE

C25 The artronix index: photographs at auction, 1952–1984. Ed. by Bhupendra Karia. N.Y., Artronix Data Corp., 1986. xliii, 1507p.
Outstanding reference for the history of photography. Includes multiple indexes to information compiled from 264 sales of photographic materials held primarily from 1972 through 1984. Individual entries include photographer name, title, dimensions, date, process, descriptions of mounts, notes, inscriptions, estimated values, and prices realized. A detailed chronology of photographic processes accessible both by subject and personal name indexes is of value. Also includes a master index with cross-references to all headings used throughout the publication.

C26 Art sales catalogues, 1600–1881 [microform]. Zug, Switz., IDC, 1986– . 3520+ microfiches, il.
Complements Frits Lugt's indispensable Répertoire des catalogues de ventes publiques intéressant l'art ou la curiosité (see GLAH 1:C17 and GLAH 2:C40). At completion, the project will include all the art sales catalogs from 1600 to 1860 listed in Lugt. This high-quality microfiche collection will also contain titles not found in Lugt, but located subsequently in various libraries. Each catalog is reproduced in its entirety. Multiple examples are included where unique annotations occur. At present, the published microfiche cover more than 31,000 sales catalogues. Printed guides accompany each section. A CD-ROM version is under consideration.

Contents: (Part 1) 1600–1825; (Part 2) 1826–1860; (Supplement 1) 1826–1860; (Part 3) 1861–1881.

Further supplements forthcoming.

C27 Auction prices of old masters, 1970–1980. Ed. by Richard Hislop. Weybridge, Surrey, [Eng.], Art Sales Index, 1982. 13, 678p. il., plates (The ASI decade publication)
Index to auction records for pre-19th-century oil paintings, watercolors, and drawings excerpted from The art sales index (see GLAH 2:C6). Entries are international in scope and arranged by artist. Few illustrations. Several collections of excerpts from this title have been issued by the publisher in the same series: Auction prices of 19th century artists, 1970–1980, ed. by Richard Hislop (2v.; 1982); Auction prices of American artists: auctions, 1970–1978, ed. by Richard Hislop (1979); Auction prices of impressionist and 20th century artists, 1970–1980, ed. by Richard Hislop (2v.; 1981).

C28 Beurdeley, Michel. Trois siècles de ventes publiques. Pref. de Maurice Rheims. [Paris], Tallandier, 1988. 234p. il. (part col.)
Lively descriptions of major international art sales of historic significance from 1650 to 1987. Includes a substantial preface by Maurice Rheims and an introduction by the author outlining the social and economic history and impact of art auctions. The bibliography contains general works on the history of sales as well as selected reviews and published sales catalogs. No index.

Tableaux des prix records, p.229–30. Bibliographie sélective, p.231–32.

C29 Christie's pictorial archive [microform]. London, Mindata, [1980–]. ca. 498 microfiches, il.
Microfiche reproduction of records, including images, for items auctioned by Christie's, London, between ca. 1910–1980. Different media within departments are treated individually. Accompanied by a printed Index to artists. Sale prices and dates of sales are not uniformly included throughout.

Contents: Oriental; Ceramics, Furniture; General decorative and applied art; Dutch and Flemish school; Italian school; British school; French school; German school; Scandinavian schools; Topographical and decorative prints; Old master prints; Painting and graphic arts; Impressionist and modern art; Antiquities; Silver and objects of vertu; Books and manuscripts.

C30 Christie's pictorial archive, New York, 1977–1985 [microform]. Bath, Eng., Mindata, 1986. 595 microfiches, il.
Microfiche reproduction of records, including images, for items auctioned by Christie's, New York. "Works of fine and applied art auctioned by Christie's from the opening of their New York salesrooms in 1977. The items were photographed for catalogue illustration and to provide a unique record for attribution and reference purposes."—*p.1.* Includes date of sale and price realized.

C31 Christie's pictorial sales review [microform]. Bath, England, Mindata, 1986. 341 microfiches, il.
This series, originally intended to be updated by annual supplements, comprises "Works of fine art auctioned by Christie's King Street London sale rooms from the start of the 1980–81 sale season."—*p.1.* The full catalog description, illustration, date, and price realized are arranged by artist name. These good quality microfiche reproductions cover auctions held through 1985.

Contents: (1) Old master, continental 19th century pictures; (2) Old master and continental drawings; (3) English and Victorian pictures and drawings; (4) Impressionist, modern and contemporary paintings, drawings, and sculptures.

C32 Corpus of paintings sold in The Netherlands during the nineteenth century. Ed. by Burton B. Fredericksen. With archival contrib. by Ruud Priem. Assist. by

Julia I. Armstrong. Los Angeles, Provenance Index of the Getty Information Institute, 1998– . (1v.)
The first volume contains results from 182 sales held in Amsterdam, Rotterdam, Leiden, The Hague, Delft, and other cities. Includes the results of substantial research on provenance and private collections. Also available in a CD-ROM version as part of the Getty Provenance Index (GLAH 2:C34) and included in a free internet database through the Getty Research Institute.
Contents: (1) 1801–1810.

C33 Frick Art Reference Library sales catalogue index [microform]. Boston, Hall Micropublications, 1992. 230 microfiches.
Microfiche ed. of the index to the Frick Library's extensive collection of historic and modern auction sales catalogs. The index is arranged by date of sale, auction house, and collection name. Accompanied by A guide to the Frick Art Reference Library sales catalogue index. As of 2000, the retrospective conversion of the Frick Library's sales catalog holdings is complete and all records have been added to the SCIPIO database (GLAH 2:C46).

C34 Getty provenance index: cumulative edition on CD-ROM [computer file]. Los Angeles, J. Paul Getty Trust, 1999. 1 computer disk + 1 users guide (88p. il.)
A series of databases containing information crucial to the study of the collecting practices of past centuries. Two new databases are included in the 1999 release: Public Collections and Provenance of Paintings. Public Collections contains cataloging information on the individual paintings, executed by artists born before 1900, from a selection of American and British museums. The Provenance of Paintings database comprises information on the provenance of paintings from American and British collections found in the Public Collections database. Also includes three inventory databases (Italy, The Netherlands, Spain; see also Documents for the History of Collecting, GLAH 2:S15) and five catalog databases (Belgium 1801–1820, Britain 1801–1820 [see also Index of paintings sold in the British Isles during the nineteenth century, GLAH 2:C37], France 1801–1810 [see also Répertoire des tableaux vendus en France au XIXe siècle, GLAH 2:C45], Germany 1690–1800 [see also Verzeichnis der verkauften Gemälde im deutschsprachigen Raum vor 1800, GLAH 2:C48], The Netherlands 1801–1810 [see also Corpus of paintings sold in The Netherlands during the nineteenth century, GLAH 2:C32]). More than 580,000 records in total. Also available as a free internet service through the Getty Research Institute.

C35 Graves, Algernon. Art sales from early in the eighteenth century to early in the twentieth century. [Reprint.] Bath, Eng., Kingsmead Reprints, 1973. 3v. in 1.
See GLAH 1:C15 for original annotation.

C36 Hoet, Gerard. Catalogus of naamlyst van schilderyen met derzelver pryzen, zedert een langen reeks van jaaren zoo in Holland als op andere plaatzen in het openbaar verkogt, benevens een verzameling van lysten van verscheyden nog in wezen zynde cabinetten. [Reprint.] Soest, Davaco, 1976. 3v.
The original 1752 publication was compiled by Hoet to track fluctuations in the sale prices of Dutch paintings from 1684 to 1752. A third vol. was produced by Pieter Terwesten after Hoet's death bringing the coverage to 1768 and the total number of catalogs abstracted to more than 300. Each vol. contains indexes by artist name and seller name. The Catalogus is arranged by sale date, and individual entries include prices. Many entries contain additional information on medium, subject matter, and dimensions.

C37 Index of paintings sold in the British Isles during the nineteenth century. Ed. by Burton Fredericksen. Assist. by Julia I. Armstrong and Doris A. Mendenhall. Santa Barbara, ABC-Clio [1988–]. (4)v. in 7 (Provenance index of the Getty Art History Information Program).
Four vols. of this scholarly and richly detailed publication have appeared thus far, providing coverage for the years 1801–20. The vols. have increased in size as a result of extensive searching in previously unexamined collections. V.2–3 contain data from approximately 900 catalogs, of which roughly 30% are not recorded by Lugt (see GLAH 1:C17 and GLAH 2:C40). Information is arranged in four indexes by sales catalog, by artist, by owner, and by previous owner. In addition to sale information, this publication contains a wealth of biographical and contextual detail of the early 19th-century art trade in Britain. Also available in a CD-ROM version as part of the Getty Provenance Index (GLAH 2:C34) and included in a free internet database through the Getty Research Institute.
Contents: (1) 1801–1805; (2) 1806–1810 (2 pts.); (3) 1811–1815 (2 pts.); (4) 1816–1820 (2 pts.)

C38 The Knoedler library [microform]. [N.Y.], Knoedler (Distr. by Chadwyck-Healey, 1973). 23,000 microfiches, il.
Collection of approximately 13,000 international sales catalogs reproduced in their entirety. The collection is arranged by country, auction house, and date. Strong in late 19th- and early 20th-century American and French materials. Catalogs included are recorded in SCIPIO record "Notes" fields and include Knoedler fiche number (for SCIPIO see GLAH 2:C46). Sotheby's catalogs are excluded.

C39 Leonard's price index of Latin American art at auction. [Ed. and publ. by Susan Theran.] Newton, Mass., Auction Index, 1999. 537p. il.
Covers 30 years of sale results from all North American auction houses. Objects represent all media and periods. Contains more than 1,000 biographies and brief essays on Latin American art and artists in English. Includes some illustrations.

C40 Lugt, Frits. Répertoire des catalogues de ventes publiques: intéressant l'art ou la curiosité, tableaux, dessins, estampes, miniatures, sculptures, bronzes, émaux, vitraux, tapisseries, céramiques, objets d'art, meubles, antiquités, monnaies, médailles, camées, intailles, armes, instruments, curiosités naturelles, etc. La Haye, M. Nijhoff, 1938–1987. 4v. (Publications du Rijksbureau voor kunsthistorische en ikonografische documentatie)

See GLAH 1:C17 for original annotation and previous vols. Internet version announced by IDC, Leiden.

Contents: (IV) Quatrième periode, 1901–1925 (1987).

C41 Mireur, Hippolyte. Dictionnaire des ventes d'art faites en France et à l'étranger pendant les XVIIIme & XIXme siècles. [Reprint.] Saint-Romain-au-Mont d'Or, Artprice.com, 2001. 7v.

See GLAH 1:C18 for original annotation and previous eds.

C42 Moulin, Raoul Jean. Le marché de la peinture en France. [Nouv. ed.] Paris, Éd. de Minuit, [1989], 1967. 613p. il. (Sens commun)

See GLAH 1:C20 for earlier ed. 2d French ed., Éd. Minuit, 1967. Abridged English trans. of the 1967 ed., The French art market: a sociological view, trans. by Arthur Goldhammer, New Brunswick, N.J., Rutgers Univ. Pr., 1987.

C43 Nader, Gary. Latin American art price guide: auction records May 1977–May 1993: includes paintings, drawings, sculptures and graphics. [Coral Gables, Fla.], G. Nader, 1993. 290p.

Index, arranged by artist name, of works sold at Latin American art auctions held at Christie's and Sotheby's, New York. Covers the years May 1977 through May 1993 and contains more than 14,000 paintings, sculptures, drawings, prints, and photographs from more than 1,300 artists.

C44 Reitlinger, Gerald. The economics of taste: the rise and fall of picture prices 1760–1960. [Reprint.] N.Y., Hacker, 1982. 3v.

See GLAH 1:C24 for original annotation.

C45 Répertoire des tableaux vendus en France au XIXe siècle. Éd. par Benjamin Peronnet, Burton B. Fredericksen. Assisté par Julia I. Armstrong, Sophie Hauser, Armelle Jacquinot. [Los Angeles,] Provenance Index of the Getty Information Institute, 1998– . (1v.in 2)

The first volume contains results from 283 sales. Includes commentary on individual sales and an index of paintings arranged by artist. Additional vols. forthcoming. Also available in a CD-ROM version as part of the Getty Provenance Index (GLAH 2:C34) and included in a free internet database through the Getty Research Institute.

(Vol. 1., pt.1) 1801–1810: A–N; (Vol. 1., pt. 2) 1801–1810: O–Z et anonymes.

C46 SCIPIO: Sales catalog index project input online [computer file]. Mountain View, Calif., Research Libraries Group, Art and Architecture Program, 1980– .

The SCIPIO database is an online union catalog that offers access to cataloging records for art and rare book sales catalogs for auctions held from the late 16th century to the present. Searchable indexes include auction house name and place, seller name, date of sale, and title of sale. Records include the dates and places of sales, the auction houses, sellers, institutional holdings, titles of works, and Lugt, Lancour, and Knoedler numbers. Contributors include institutions with pre-eminent auction sales catalog collections. New records are added daily. Available via the internet by subscription.

An early union catalog of titles from the SCIPIO database was published as Index of art sales catalogs, 1981–1985: a union list from the SCIPIO database. Boston, Hall, 1987, 2v.

C47 Sotheby's pictorial archive [microform]. Bathwick, Bath, Eng., Mindata, [1995?] 235 microfiches.

Contains images and sale information from Sotheby's London archive from 1950 to 1994. Each category is arranged by artist name and includes title, date, physical description, and price.

Contents: British paintings, 1500–1850; British watercolours to 1850; Old master paintings; Victorian paintings; Modern British paintings, drawings and sculpture.

C48 Verzeichnis der verkauften Gemälde im deutschsprachigen Raum vor 1800. [By] Tilman von Stockhausen and Thomas Ketelsen. Ed. by Burton B. Fredericksen and Julia I. Armstrong. Assist. by Michael Müller. [Los Angeles], Provenance Index of the Getty Information Institute, 2001– .

Forthcoming. Index of paintings sold in Germany prior to 1800. Will also available in a CD-ROM version as part of the Getty Provenance Index (GLAH 2:C34) and included in a free internet database through the Getty Research Institute.

D. Visual Resources

The titles listed and described in this chapter include guides for picture searching, organization and management of visual collections, collection directories, sources and indexes of reproductions, and pictorial archives. Reproductive media now include not only traditional cast models, prints, book illustrations, and photographic surrogates, but also CD-ROM image compilations, electronic databases, and online commercial picture exchanges. Imaging initiatives such as ARTstor (a project of The Andrew W. Mellon Foundation) promise to create internet-based digital libraries in support of the history of art. Visual resources professionals are increasingly called upon to acquire, document, organize, maintain, and provide access to images across this wide range of media. Beyond simply locating images, visual resources professionals provide intellectual access to visual archives through subject analysis, indexing, and authority control in describing images. Many general reference sources such as the Art index (GLAH 2:A4), the Bibliography of the history of art (GLAH 2:A6), the Grove dictionary of art (GLAH 2:E4) also guide users to illustration sources. Within this quickly evolving landscape, publications, electronic discussion groups, and activities promoted through organizations such as the Art Libraries Society/North America (ARLIS/NA) and the Visual Resources Association (VRA) remain the best sources for current information on visual resources-related topics, particularly for highly specialized and technical resources not mentioned here.

GUIDES FOR PICTURE SEARCHING, ORGANIZATION, AND MANAGEMENT OF VISUAL COLLECTIONS

D1 Besser, Howard, and Trant, Jennifer. Introduction to imaging: issues in constructing an image database. Santa Monica, Getty Art History Information Program, c1995. 48p. il. (part col.)

Introduction to the vocabulary, technology, and processes of digital imagery. This guide provides direction in creating image databases of works typically represented in museum collections. Chapters review the composition of a digital image, define users and uses of an image database, and discuss methods employed to construct an image database, as well as to integrate images into an existing information infrastructure. Contains information on technical standards, and a selective discussion of active organizations and initiatives in the area of digital imaging. Also available on the internet.

Glossary, p.42–46. Bibliography, p.47–48.

D2 Beyond the book: extending MARC for subject access. Ed. by Toni Petersen and Pat Molholt. Boston, Hall, [1990]. ix, 275p. il.

14 essays selected to provide a sample of current thinking on the use of MARC (MAchine Readable Cataloging), the international standard for coding cataloging data. Intended for catalogers of images, museum objects, archives, and other non-book materials. The authors examine MARC as a vessel to contain data and as a communications format, and how subject access can be enhanced beyond the subject field currently available in the MARC format. Essays range from discussion on the practical steps used to extend or accommodate MARC, descriptions of cataloging projects that make use of the format in new ways, to calls for new advances in the field and use of the format for access to non-traditional materials, including visual image collections.

Contributors, p.259–63. Name index, p.265–71. Subject index, p.273–75.

D3 Bunting, Christine, ed. Reference tools for fine arts visual resources collections. Tucson, Art Libraries Society of North America, 1984. 55p. (Occasional papers of the Art Libraries Society of North America, no. 4)

Annotated bibliography providing information on important sources, of both practical and theoretical nature, directed to the visual resource professional. Part I provides suggestions for a core reference book collection for visual resources collections. Citations for professional literature, sources of reproduction, management guides, collection directories, cataloging manuals, photographic and conservation manuals, and equipment directories are given in Part II. Part III notes useful general art reference works. Part IV provides citations to histories and handbooks for various culture groups and media. Titles with high-quality illustrations are selected to facilitate visual comparisons.

Author-title index, p.51–55.

D4 Evans, Hilary. Picture librarianship. N.Y., Saur, 1980. 136p. (Outlines of modern librarianship)

Simple advice for the professional picture librarian regarding the organization, care, and use of material of all general subject types.

Contents: (1) Nature and function of the picture library; (2) Acquisition; (3) Care and maintenance; (4) Access and retrieval; (5) Classification and cataloguing; (6) Lending and copying; (7) Making a charge for services; (8) Copyright; (9) Administration.

Organizations, p.131–32. Further reading, p.133. Index, p.135–36.

D5 ———. Practical picture research: a guide to current practice, procedure, techniques, and resources. N.Y., Blueprint, 1992. xi, 265p. il., plates.

1st ed., North Pomfret, Vt., David & Charles, 1979, The art of picture research: a guide to current practice, procedures, techniques and resources.

Updates information and guides researchers through the most obvious steps of picture research, gives warnings about common pitfalls, and helps in confronting the most frequently encountered problems. Divided into six sections. The first defines the qualification, training, and career opportunities available to a picture researcher. The second deals with types and varieties of picture sources. Part three provides information on the procedures for accessing and retrieving material, including information on copyright and fees. Section four is on picture selection, with descriptions on reproduction methods and photographic techniques. Part five includes information about taking on researching assignments. The final section on reference information was compiled by Lesley Coleman.

Associations and [other key] picture organizations, p.230–40. Libraries and services, p.241–45. Reference books, p.245–51. Glossary, p.252–62. Index, p.[263]–65.

D6 Computers and the history of art. Ed by Anthony Hamber . . . [et al.] London, Mansell, [1989]. xiii, 213p. il.

Sixteen papers by different authors, mostly taken from previous conferences of the Computers and the History of Art Group (CHArt), established in 1985. Essays range from detailed descriptions of actual research projects in process to debates about the possibilities and problems created by automation, and have been grouped in themes of electronic imaging, databases and data modeling, and application. Processing and databasing, pictorial/visual analysis, museums and curatorial problems, conservation, and referencing and storing works of art are covered. For recent CHArt activities, see the journal Computers and the history of art (GLAH 2:Q152).

Contributors, p.[207]–08. Index, p.[209]–13.

D7 Guidelines for the visual resources profession. Ed. by Kim Kopatz. Florida, ARLIS/NA; Dearborn, VRA, 2000. xii, 154p.

Intended for working or prospective visual resources professionals, this publication provides practical and theoretical information for managing visual collections.

Contents: Introduction, by Margaret Webster. Sections: Criteria for the hiring and retention of visual resources professionals; The education of a visual resources professional; The visual resources position; The institution and the visual resources position; The visual resources collection; technology and the future. Appendixes: Professional organizations; Internet resources; Recommended courses for visual resources professionals; Strategies for continuing professional education and development; Sample job descriptions for a hypothetical visual resources collection; Performance review checklist; University of Arizona, College of Architecture's policy, continuing status and promotion, academic professionals; Selected previous visual resource professional status surveys; VRA/ARLIS professional status survey; Recommended guidelines for use in reviews/accreditation of visual resources collections; Special Libraries Association competencies for special librarians of the 21st century.

Bibliography, p.147–52. Contributors, p.153–54.

D8 Hess, Stanley W. An annotated bibliography of slide library literature. Syracuse, N.Y., School of Information Studies, Syracuse Univ., 1978. 47p. (Bibliographic studies, no. 3)

Bibliography of 250 annotated titles giving information on literature written on the subject of slide libraries. Approximately half of the entries deal with works printed prior to 1960; the rest are 1960 to 1977 imprints. Topics include acquisition and selection of slides, care and preservation, cataloging and classification of both audio-visual and slide material, using slides for instruction, planning physical facilities, and general education. Although some information is dated, this work provides a good historic overview of the literature and beginnings of visual resources collections and organization.

D9 Hourihane, Colum. Subject classification for visual collections: an inventory of some of the principal systems applied to content description in images. Columbus, Visual Resources Association, 1999. x, 49p. (Visual Resources Association special bulletin, no. 12)

International inventory of forty-two general classification systems or systems specific to an individual project for subject analysis and access of images. For each system, directory information and a description of the collection, the system, and the subject index are given. Examples and references when available are provided. List of systems. Appendix of ICONCLASS users.

Selected ICONCLASS bibliography, p.40–41. Bibliography, p.42–49.

D10 Irvine, Betty Jo. Slide libraries: a guide for academic institutions, museums, and special collections. 2d ed. With the assist. of P. Eileen Fry. Littleton, Colo., Libraries Unlimited, 1979. 321p. il.

See GLAH 1:D5 for 1st ed.

The 2d ed. reflects both the increase in professional activity of visual resources professionals and the increase in automation applications. Additional examples of cataloging and classification applications are also given. Information on environmental controls and preservation has been added and bibliographies have been updated. Both eds. give formal recognition to the complex nature of visual resources libraries and the need to establish valid criteria for their effective utilization and development. Chapters outline standard administrative practices, classification systems, production methods, physical facilities, supplies and equipment, and indicate basic guidelines for efficient organization and administration of visual collections.

Bibliographies at the end of each chapter. Selected bibliography, p.241–81. Directory of distributors and manufacturers of equipment and supplies, p.283–91. Directory of slide sources, p.292–303. Directory of slide libraries, p.304–10. Index, p.311–21.

D11 Markey, Karen. Subject access to visual resources collections: a model for computer construction of thematic catalogs. N.Y., Greenwood, [1986]. xx, 189p. il. (New directions in information management, no. 11)

Systematic approach to describing the subject content in visual images, based on Erwin Panofsky's theory of iconography and iconology. The author suggests compiling a searching tool or a thematic catalog of primary and secondary subject matter to aid those involved in image retrieval. This method was tested on 100 works of Northern European painting from the late Medieval period. The author includes a discussion of Panofsky's theoretical framework, a step-by-step approach to the construction of the thematic catalog, the results of compiling a catalog, and a comparison of the thematic catalog with other approaches to describing subject matter. Appendix A: Sources of reproductions and pre-iconographical descriptions for twenty works of art. Appendix B: Clusters in context.

Bibliography, p.179–84.

D12 Picture librarianship. Ed. by Helen P. Harrison. Phoenix, Oryx, 1981. xii, 542p.

Handbook on picture librarianship with a concentration on techniques and practices used in organizing photographs and illustrations. Aimed at librarians rather than picture researchers. Provides information on selection, access to material, processes and operations, preservation and storage, and arrangement and indexing issues encountered in picture libraries. Chapters on education and training and administration. Case studies and descriptions of types of picture libraries contained in the second half of the guide provide accounts of unique collections and present a survey of picture libraries through the 1970s in the U.S. and the United Kingdom.

Bibliography, p.494–517. Index, p.518–42.

D13 Ritzenthaler, Mary Lynn; Munoff, Gerald J.; and Long, Margery S. Archives & manuscripts: administration of photographic collections. Chicago, Society of American Archivists, 1984. 173p. il. (part col.) (SAA basic manual series)

Guide to managing photograph collections directed toward archivists, manuscript curators, librarians, picture specialists, and those who work with historical photographs. Evolved from SAA workshops on administration of photographic collections. Chapters are written by specialists from an archival perspective, stressing the principle of provenance and the development of systems to organize, access, and preserve entire collections.

Contents: (1) Photographs in archival collections, by Margery S. Long; (2) History of photographic processes, by Gerald J. Munoff; (3) Appraisal and collecting policies, by Margery S. Long; (4) Arrangement and description, by Gerald J. Munoff; (5) Preservation of photographic materials, by Mary Lynn Ritzenthaler; (6) Legal issues, Mary Lynn Ritzenthaler; (7) Managing a photographic copy service, by Mary Lynn Ritzenthaler.

Glossary, p.153–55. Bibliography, p.156–59. Supplies for the care and storage of photographic material, p.160–63. Funding resources for photographic collections, p.164. Index, p.165–71.

D14 Robl, Ernest H. Organizing your photographs. N.Y., Amphoto, 1986. 191p. il. (part col.)

Guide to the organization of photographic collections. Designed for those with no professional library experience or with limited knowledge of visual media. Explains how methods derived from library practice can aid in collection management.

Contents: (1) Catalog design and production; (2) Storing and using your collection; (3) Personal computer applications; (4) Strategies for growth; (5) Appendices: A. Organizations in picture librarianship; B. Glossary; C. Annotated bibliography.

Index, p.188–91.

D15 Schuller, Nancy S. Management for visual resources collections. Graphics by F. Terry Arzola. 2d ed. Englewood, Colo., Libraries Unlimited, 1989. xii, 169p. il.

Previous ed., Mid-America College Art Association, 1979.

Present ed. provides a framework and examples for planning and decision making in the management of a visual resources collection whose primary function is to support research, teaching, or historical documentation.

Contents: (1) Planning goals and objectives; (2) Facilities planning; (3) Budgeting; (4) Staffing; (5) Reports and statistics; (6) policies and procedures manuals; (7) Circulation and control; (8) Microcomputer applications; Appendix A: Sample floor plans; Appendix B: Sample job descriptions; Appendix C: Glossary.

Bibliography, p.151–60. Index, p.161–69.

D16 Schultz, John, and Schultz, Barbara. Picture research: a practical guide. N.Y., Van Nostrand Reinhold, [1991]. ix, 326p. il.

Guidebook defining the profession of picture research for the picture professional and for others using visual material in their work. Includes historical background on reproduction processes and business and practical guidance for current researchers.

Contents: (1) Picture research and the visual heritage; (2) Production and reproduction of photographs; (3) Profiles of professionals in photography; (4) Researchers and buyers;

(5) Public sources: museums and archives; (6) Commercial picture agencies; (7) Legal issues; (8) Electronic picture transmission and research; Appendix A: Picture research: a training seminar for the corporation. Appendix B: Handling and storing photographs. Appendix C: Professional organizations worldwide.

Extensive annotated bibliography. Glossary, p.291–98. Bibliography, p.299–318. Index, p.319–26.

D17 Straten, Roelof van. Iconography, indexing, ICONCLASS: a handbook. Leiden, Foleor, 1994. 250p. il.

Personal account of the theory and practice of iconographic indexing as it relates to the ICONCLASS system and its method of facilitating the storage and retrieval of iconographic data. (ICONCLASS is the alphanumerical decimal classification system for the iconography of Western art; see GLAH 1:F18.)

Contents: (1) The theory of iconography [a revision of Panofsky's iconographical theory]; (2) The iconographic indexer and his work; (3) The ICONCLASS system; (4) Indexing Italian prints with ICONCLASS; (5) ICONCLASS: remarks and additions [including specific problems related to the use of ICONCLASS]; Appendix 1: Outline of the ICONCLASS system; Appendix 2: Composition and iconography; Appendix 3: Bibliography [covering publications on ICONCLASS].

Index, p.241–44.

D18 Sutcliffe, Glyn. Slide collection management in libraries and information units. Brookfield, Vt., Gower, 1995. xii, 219p.

Aimed at the practicing slide manager that attempts to provide information and make linkages between disparate fields that use slide material. The appendixes, directed primarily to curators in Great Britain, provide listings on database packages, automated management systems, professional associations, producers and publishers of multimedia and imaging systems, and centers of activity in audio-visual and image management.

Contents: (1) Background and trends in slide collection management; (2) The literature of slide collection management; (3) Slide acquisitions; (4) The technical preparation of slides as stock items; (5) Slide retrieval; (6) Commercially available slide management and retrieval packages; (7) Medical slide collections; (8) Optical disc systems and the slide; (9) Some principles of slide library management.

Bibliography, p.157–78. Appendices I–VI, p.181–204. Index, p.217–19.

D19 Zorich, Diane M. Introduction to managing digital assets: options for cultural and educational organizations. [Los Angeles], Getty Information Institute, 1999. x, 157p.

A Getty Information Institute commissioned report. Discusses options for managing intellectual property, particularly in a networked environment. "The report reviews traditions of rights administration and content distribution across genres, and offers a generic and thematic assessment of issues an institution should consider when developing intellectual property management strategies and selecting partners to assist in these strategies."—*Foreword.*

Contents: Introduction; What are intellectual property rights?; The distribution of intellectual property over electronic networks; Administering intellectual property in cultural organizations; Structure, function, and operations of intellectual property service providers; Managing content and usage; Rightsholder and user issues; Economic considerations; Summary: issues, trends, and challenges; Another perspective; Acronyms; Appendices: A note on methodology; Organizations and projects reviewed; Review questions; Questionnaire for reviewing intellectual property management service providers.

Glossary, p.149–52. Bibliography, p.153–57.

COLLECTION DIRECTORIES

D20 Davidson, Martha; Duarte, Carlota; and Núñez, Raul Solano, eds. Picture collections, Mexico: a guide to picture sources in the United Mexican States. Metuchen, N.J., Scarecrow, 1988. xix, 292p. il., plates, maps, plans.

Guide to 502 sources of 32 million pictures made and preserved in Mexico. Includes collections of photographs, prints, drawings, paintings and other still, two-dimensional images, copy photos, reproductions, as well as original works. All material is basically documentary in character. Collection sources are listed alphabetically within major categories: archives, libraries (general and university), museums, other institutions (government, private institutes, university departments, and institutes), photographers, private collectors, and publishers. Within each entry, information is organized under standard headings: Name of source and address information, director's name, photo request information, collection name, description of material, subjects, dates, collection availability and access, fees, catalog/finding aids, and comments. Introductory comments on picture research, definitions of photographic reproduction techniques, and information on copyright considerations are given.

Glossary, p.232–39. Alphabetical index of picture sources, p.243–52. Location index of picture sources, p.253–61. Artists and photographers index, p.262–66. Geographical index, p.267–71. Personal name index [pictures of individuals identified by name], p.272–73. Topical index, p.274–92.

D21 Evans, Hilary, and Evans, Mary. Picture researcher's handbook: an international guide to picture sources and how to use them. 6th ed. N.Y., Routledge, 1996. 649p. il.

See GLAH 1:D4 for 1st ed.; 2d ed., London, Saturday Ventures, 1979; 3d ed., Wokingham, Berkshire, Van Nostrand Reinhold U.K., 1986; 4th ed., London, Van Nostrand Reinhold International, 1989; 5th ed., N.Y., Van Nostrand Reinhold, 1992.

Directory of international picture sources. Entries include: collection name and address, description of material held, procedures for use, working hours, research information, approximate number of items held.

Contents: (1) General sources includes multiple subject collections, collections relating to more than one country, national collections, large stock agencies; (2) Regional sources includes collections with geographical material covering several countries and emphasizing travel and topographical subjects; (3) National sources includes collections related to a particular country; (4) Specialist sources includes collections with material in a specific subject area, such as art, film, or photography.

Places index, p.483–84. Sources index, p.485–506. Subject index, p.507–16.

D22 Godfrey, Jenny, and McKeown, Roy. Visual resources for design. [Worcestershire, England], ARLIS/UK and Ireland, 1995. 1v. (unpaged), il.

Primarily an international selection of commercial suppliers of visual material (slides, videos, CD-ROMs, films, etc.) in the subject area of design history. Design includes such topics as architecture; textiles; glass; furniture; interior design; industrial history; fashion; graphic, product and environmental design; etc. An essay, "Design history and everyday life: issues of visual resources," by Jeremy Aynsley and a listing of general sources for visual information precede the directory listing. Presented in alphabetical order by individual supplier, entries include name and contact information, subject and format coverage, and information on availability and catalogs published. Indexes to physical formats and subjects are appended.

D23 Guide to rights and reproduction at American art museums. Ed. by Mary M. Lampe. Ann Arbor, Visual Resources Assoc., 1996. 1v. (unpaged). (Visual Resources Association special bulletin, no. 10)

Guide to rights and reproductions for 230 American art museums and galleries. Arranged alphabetically by institution name. Entries include contact information, giving name, address, fax/phone numbers, and contact person. Collections information (availability of catalogs, slide lists, commercial sources); format availability; special services offered; reproduction conditions; scholarly, nonprofit, or commercial fees; credit line requirements; processing and materials fees; and use fees are given for most entries.

Index to institutions (unpaginated). Reproduction services questionnaire (unpaginated).

D24 Guide to Canadian photographic archives = Guide des archives photographiques canadiennes. Christopher Seifried, ed. [New ed.] Ottawa, Public Archives Canada, 1984. xxvi, 727p.

Previous ed., 1979.

Guide to photographic collections in 139 Canadian archival institutions including archives of governmental and educational institutions, private companies and associations, libraries, museums, and other research-oriented organizations that allow public access to their holdings. This ed., which closed in 1982, contains 8,631 entries and provides revised indexing systems from the previous ed. Entries are listed in alphabetical order by title of collection and may be in English and/or French, depending on the language used by the reporting repository. Each entry includes a reference number, title, life date or date a corporate body was founded, geographical location and occupation, collection type and quantity, inclusive dates, collection description, repository name, and control number. A list of participating repositories with address information precedes the entries.

Repository index, p.571–600. Subject index [giving headings for personal, corporate, and geographical names, and for objects, events and activities], p.603–714. Photographer index, p.717–27.

D25 McKeown, Roy. National directory of slide collections. [London], British Library Board [Distr. in the U.S. by American Library Association, 1990]. 310p. (British Library information guide, 12)

Listing of slide collections in the United Kingdom. Covers non-commercial collections, including academic institutions, public library authorities, national and local authority museums and galleries, government libraries and departments, research institutions, professional associations, learned societies, teaching hospitals, postgraduate medical centers, and schools of nursing. Arranged alphabetically by institutional name, directory entries provide address and contact information, statistics on collection size, content coverage, access and loan information, and services and fees. Availability of collection guides is indicated.

Subject index, p.217–90. Regional index [to collections, geographically arranged by regional location with postal code sub-divisions], p.291–310.

D26 Picture sources UK. Ed., Rosemary Eakins. Associate ed., Elizabeth Loving. London, Macdonald, 1985. 474p.

Directory of sources of illustrations in the United Kingdom. Includes only those collections that make material available for reproduction. Library or photographic archives housed in museums or art galleries are treated as picture sources. Chapters arranged by type of library, including anthropology and archeology, fine art and architecture, performing arts, and specialized collections. Alphabetically arranged entries within each chapter provide contact information; information on type, number, and size of collection; dates of coverage; subject listing; and information on access and conditions. Two introductory essays, on pictures and the law, and an introduction to picture research.

How to use the directory, p.6–7. Index of collections and subcollections, p.408–21. Subject index, p.422–74.

D27 Robl, Ernest H., ed. Picture sources 4. [4th ed.] N.Y., Special Libraries Association, 1983. xi, 180p. il., plates.

See GLAH 1:D11 for 3d ed.

Directory of North American commercial and non-commercial picture collections used for searching pictures of all types—from art reproductions and news photographs to maps and cartoons. 980 entries, which contain updated citations from previous eds. (1st ed., 1959; 2d ed., 1964; 3d ed., 1975) and 200 new collection listings are included. The listing is alphabetical by collection or organization name. Each entry gives address and contact name, content holdings, subject coverage, chronological coverage, and access information.

Collections index, p.133–44. Geographic index, p.145–48. Subject index, p.149–80.

D28 The visual resources directory: art slide and photograph collections in the United States and Canada. Ed., Carla Conrad Freeman. Canadian ed., Barbara Stevenson. Englewood, Colo., Libraries Unlimited, 1995. xvii, 174p. (Visual resources series)

Directory of 528 visual resources collections in the U.S. and Canada providing information solicited by questionnaire in 1992 and 1993. Gives information on location, scope, development, and holding strengths of collections listed. Includes slide and photographic collections limited to still images documenting art, architecture, design, and related fields, as established in art and/or art history departments, museums and galleries, or in various types of libraries or historical collections where emphasis is on research and teaching. Entries for U.S. collections are listed first and are arranged alphabetically by state, city, and institution. Canadian collections are alphabetized by province, city, and institution. Individual entries are numbered and provide information on institutional name, address, and name of individual in charge of collection. Appendix A: Brief history of Canadian visual resources collections. Appendix B: Visual resources organizations and journals.

Institutional index, p.155–58. Personnel index, p.159–61. Index by type of collection, p.163–68. Subject index [gathered from holdings and subject concentration data], p.169–74.

D29 Walker, Sandra C., and Beetham, Donald W. Image buyer's guide: an international directory of sources for slides and digital images for art and architecture. 7th ed. Englewood, Colo., Libraries Unlimited, 1999. xxi, 186p. (Visual resources series)

See GLAH 1:D3 for 3d ed., 1976; 4th ed., Mid-America College Art Association, 1980; 5th ed., Libraries Unlimited, 1985; 6th ed., Libraries Unlimited, 1990.

Designed to assist in identifying sources of images depicting art and architecture available from commercial vendors, museums, or other institutions and non-profit organizations. Information provided in the 366 entries was gathered from questionnaires sent to vendors worldwide. Most of the data gathered reflect the image market as it existed at the end of 1997. Running updates on image market news appear in the quarterly VRA bulletin (see GLAH 2:Q340) and the directory is updated on the internet by an Image Providers Directory. Part I lists digital image providers, including consortiums. Part II gives slide providers in North America, and Part III lists providers in Asia, Australia, Britain, Europe, and Ireland.

Appendix 1: Image providers no longer selling images: United States and Canada; Other countries. Appendix 2: Sources of slides coordinated with texts.

Name index, p.161–72. Subject index, p.173–86.

D30 World photography sources. Ed., David N. Bradshaw. Executive ed., Catherine Hahn. N.Y., Directories, 1982. xxvii, (various paginations), il.

Directory providing information on locating international picture sources. Data for this directory was gathered in 1982. Sources have been classified by specialty and type into twelve sections: Agriculture, general (including stock agencies, institutions, photographers), geography and history (for U.S. and foreign sources), industry, military, performing arts, personalities, plants and animals, science, social sciences, sports, and visual arts. Individual entries include name of source and address, contact name, subject description of collection, number of pictures in archive, procedures for contacting sources, fees and service information, archive personnel, and date archive was established. In addition to the listings and indexes, an introductory essay on picture researching is provided.

Alphabetical list of sources and major collections, p.1–15. Numerical list of sources, p.17–32. Geographical list of sources, p.34–50. Subject index, p.53–76. Bibliography, p.77–81. [List of major pictorial source] organizations, p.82–85.

SEE ALSO: International photography: George Eastman House index to photographers, collections, and exhibitions (GLAH 2:O25); La Documentation française. Répertoire des collections photographiques en France, 1990 (GLAH 2:O29).

REPRODUCTIONS—SOURCES AND INDEXES

D31 Appel, Marsha C. Illustration index VIII, 1992–1996. Metuchen, N.J., Scarecrow, 1998. xi, 464p.

Previous vols. of Illustration index, all published by Scarecrow: Illustration index, by Lucile E. Vance, 1957, covers 1950–June 1956; Illustration index, First supplement, by Lucile E. Vance, 1961, covers 1956–1959; Illustration index, 2d ed., by Lucile E. Vance and Esther M. Tracey, 1966, covers 1950–June 1963; Illustration index, 3d ed., by Roger C. Greer, 1973, covers July 1963–December 1971; Illustration index, 4th ed., by Marsha C. Appel, 1980, covers 1972–1976; Illustration index V, by Marsha C. Appel, 1984, covers 1977–1981; Illustration index VI, by Marsha C. Appel, 1988, covers 1982–1986; Illustration index VII, by Marsha C. Appel, 1993, covers 1987–1991.

Current ed. covers the years 1992–1996 and provides indexing to ten major pictorial periodicals in 28,000 individual entries. Most illustrations referenced are photographs, although paintings, drawings, and lithographs are included as well. Advertisements are excluded. This vol. follows the scope and format of previous vols. IV–VII. Subject headings are listed alphabetically with illustrations within journal articles given separate entries. There are 19,000 subject headings encompassing about 28,000 entries, with several key listings, such as art works, architectural structures, festivals, occupations, etc., and an extensive system of cross-references. Individual citations under subject entries include journal title abbreviation, vol. number and pagination, medium, color designation, code indicating size of illustration, month and date of publication. A list of periodicals indexed and address of each publication is provided.

D32 Architecture on screen: films and videos on architecture, landscape architecture, historic preservation, city and regional planning. Comp. and ed. by the Program for Art on Film. Nadine Covert . . . [et al.], eds. [N.Y.], Program for Art on Film; [Hall, 1994]. xl, 238p. il.

Contains references to 940 film and video titles on the subject of architecture, landscape architecture, historic preservation, and city and regional planning. Includes documentaries and some feature films, animated, dramatic, and experimental works that originated in the U.S. and 35 other countries between 1927 and 1992. Titles were selected from the more extensive Art on film database, a critical inventory of films and videos on the visual arts compiled by the Program for Art on Film. Career educational titles have been excluded. Four introductory essays, a short bibliography, and list of organizations and film festivals precede the entries. Annotated listings of films and videos are arranged alphabetically by title, each containing information on series, running time, color, format, date, country, language, edition/version, production agency, and credits. Source information (distributors or archival sources), an evaluation, comments by the Program for Art on Film or Metropolitan Museum of Art staff, and reviews and awards are also given for each title.

Contents: Altered states of vision: film, video, and the teaching of architectural history, by Barry Bergdoll; Backlot America: the impact of film and television on architecture, by Donald Albrecht; Space in time: filming architecture, by Murray Grigor; Reflections on quality: evaluating films on art, by Nadine Covert.

Subject headings, p.179–81. Subject index, p.183–201. Geographic index, p.203–10. Names index, p.211–17. Series index, p.219–22. Sources index [providing names and contact information for distributors and producers], p.223–38.

D33 Art on screen: a directory of films and videos about the visual arts. Comp. and ed. by the Program for Art on Film, Nadine Covert . . . [et al.], eds. [N.Y.], Program for Art on Film; [Hall, 1991]. xiv, 283p. il.

Directory of 914 film and video titles selected from the Program for Art on Film's visual arts inventory, Art on Film Database. Covering productions released from 1975/1976 to 1990, this selected list includes documentaries and shorts distributed in the U.S. and art-related dramatic feature films. Films on photography and, to a large extent, films on architecture or landscape gardens have been excluded. Five essays with an accompanying filmography provide context for the individual annotated documentary/shorts and feature film listings which follow. Arranged in the two sections, entries are listed alphabetically by title. The following elements are included in all entries: title, series title, running time, color/black & white indication, format, date work was produced or copyrighted, country where film was produced, language, edition/version, producing agency, credits, distributor, synopsis, evaluation, comments, citations of reviews, and awards.

Contents: Art on screen: films and television on art—an overview, by Henriette Montgomery and Nadine Covert; Art history and films on art, by Judith Wechsler; Programming films on art in the museum—an introduction, by Susan Delson; Celluloid portraits: feature films on art and artists, by Carrie Rickey; Reflections on quality: evaluating films on art, by Nadine Covert.

Subject headings, p.[227]–29. Subject index [provided separately for Documentaries and Features sections], p.231–53. Directors of feature films index, p.[255]–57. Name index, p.[259]–65. Series title index, p.[267]–69. Source index [providing contact information for distributors], p.[271]–83.

D34 Art on screen on CD-ROM. [computer file]. N.Y., Program for Art on Film, Hall, 1995– . Computer laser optical disks; 4 3/4 in.

Derived from the Program for Art on Film's visual arts inventory, Art on Film Database. Extensive coverage of films and videos from more than 70 countries. 23,000 entries for productions on the visual arts released primarily from 1970 to 1994. Entries include important information such as title, date, language, distribution source, credits, genre, audience level, synopsis and comments, review citations, awards, and other notes. 27 indexed fields including title, subject headings (style, technique, etc.), artist name, synopsis, genre, language, etc. Key word searching is supported.

D35 Besemer, Susan P. From museums, galleries, and studios: a guide to artists on film and tape. Comp. by Susan P. Besemer and Christopher Crosman. Westport, Conn., Greenwood, [1984]. xvi, 199p. (Art reference collection, no. 6)

Listing of more than 600 films, videos, and audio cassettes documenting contemporary visual artists. Derived from primary sources, entries list only productions in which artists are heard or seen with their work and consist primarily of interviews produced by commercial and independent producers, museums, art galleries, universities, or other educational institutions. The first section deals with entries for individual artists, giving name, mediagraphic citation (providing information that is dated to the 1980s), and a narrative annotation. In section two, entries for multiple artists are arranged alphabetically by title.

Directory [of distributors in the United States and sources for purchasing, renting, or borrowing the productions, including four college and university film libraries], p.[158]–67. Index [by subject, title, place, and institution], p.[168]–99.

D36 Films and videos on photography. Comp. by the Program for Art on Film, Direction des musées de France. [N.Y.], Program for Art on Film, 1990. ix, 114p.

Annotated list of films and videos about photography comprising 511 entries that bring together records from the databases of the Program for Art on Film's Critical Inventory of Films on Art and Base Audiart of the audiovisual department of the Direction des Musées de France, Ministry of Culture and Communication, Paris. Both documentary and educational films are listed. Alphabetically arranged by title, each entry includes filmographic data, credits giving director and producers, sources including distribution information, a brief annotation, reviews, and awards.

Subject index, p.85–95. Names index, p.97–103. Source index [gives addresses of distributors or producers], p.105–14.

D37 Garrigan, Kristine Ottesen. Victorian art reproductions in modern sources: a bibliography. N.Y., Garland, 1991. xxxix, 575p. (Garland reference library of the humanities, v. 1225)

Index of 84 book and catalog sources on Victorian art, listing 5,000 works and 950 artists who were actively producing in Britain during the years of Victoria's reign (1837–1901). Reproduction information is drawn from books on art and literature, as well as collection and exhibition catalogs, primarily published from 1966 to 1989. Oil paintings, drawings, and watercolors are included. Except for major Pre-Raphaelites, monographs and catalogs on specific artists are excluded from indexing. Artists are listed alphabetically, with life dates and Royal Academy membership, if applicable. Specific works by title are then listed alphabetically. Medium, date of completion and/or first exhibition venue, current location, and photo sources are provided for each title. Reproduction source information is also given, followed by page or plate number, referring back to an indexed bibliography. Color reproduction and special formats are noted.

Selected title index, p.531–42. Selected subject index, p.543–75.

D38 Havlice, Patricia Pate. World painting index. Metuchen, Scarecrow, 1977. 2v.

Reference work designed to aid users in locating reproductions of paintings by international artists in 1,167 books and catalogs published from 1940 to 1989. Paintings are defined as works in oil, tempera, gouache, acrylic, fresco, pastel, and watercolor. The arrangement is the same in the main set and supplements: v.1 begins with a numbered bibliography of the 1,167 illustrated volumes, followed by a listing of the paintings titles arranged alphabetically under artists' names. Each painting title is followed by one or more numbers that connect it to illustrations in books in the bibliography. (Anonymous paintings are listed alphabetically in a separate sequence.) V.2 presents all of the paintings titles again, rearranged in one continuous alphabetical sequence. Almost all paintings titles are given in English, regardless of the artist's nationality.

———. First supplement, 1973–1980. Metuchen, Scarecrow, 1982. 2v.

———. Second supplement, 1980–1989. Metuchen, Scarecrow, 1995. 2v.

D39 Korwin, Yala H. Index to two-dimensional art works. Metuchen, Scarecrow, 1981. 2v.

Index to art works "produced in color on a flat surface."—*Pref.* Works included here are defined as being "unique originals," including paintings, collages, illustrations, frescoes, murals, stained glass, mosaics, tapestries, and embroideries. Prints and photographs are excluded. Contains 35,000 entries to works reproduced in English language publications between 1960 and 1977. V.I includes an artist index, giving brief biographical information, title and date of work, location of original (institution or private collection), reproduction source, and black and white or color designation. Directions for use, p.viii–x. List of books indexed, p.xi–xxvi. V.II is an alphabetically arranged title/subject index.

Location symbols for institutional and private collections, p.[867]–974. Lost, stolen, or destroyed art works, p.[975]–76.

D40 Kreisel, Martha. Photography books index: a subject guide to photo anthologies. Metuchen, Scarecrow, 1980. xi, 286p.

Provides access by subject and photographer to published photographs. The photographers index gives name, life dates, photograph title and date, and source. A subject index provides photograph title, photographer, and source information. Includes a portrait index that is divided into categories of children, men, and women; the alphabetical arrangement within each category gives the sitter's name, portrait photographer, and source information. Each entry provides individual source reference, page number, and an indication if reproduction is in color. Books indexed represent photo anthologies; technical manuals and works not classified by the Library of Congress as photography books (e.g., travelogs) have been excluded.

List of books indexed, p.x–xi.

D41 ———. Photography books index II: a subject guide to photo anthologies. Metuchen, Scarecrow, 1985. xi, 261p.

Supplements the preceding title, extending coverage to 1982. Photographers' names and dates have been verified and updated so some discrepancy between the entries in the 1980 main vol. and this supplement may occur. There are also slight alterations and refinements of the subject headings.

D42 Laing, Ellen Johnston. An index to reproductions of paintings by twentieth-century Chinese artists. Eugene, Asian Studies Program, Univ. of Oregon, 1984. xx, 530p. (Asian Studies Program publication, 6) (Repr.: Ann Arbor, Center for Chinese Studies, Univ. of Michigan, 1998, with "minimal" corrections)

Covers the period from 1912 to around 1980 and includes the names of approximately 3,500 traditional-style artists along with lists of their works, reproduced in 264 monographs, books, journals, and catalogs. Artists' entries include name, alternate names, dates of birth and death, birthplace, art education, memberships, teachers, subject specialities, and professional affiliation. Biographical information is followed by a listing of paintings by the artist and a source for a reproduction.

D43 New York Graphic Society. Fine art reproductions. Greenwich, Conn., The Society, [1994]. 562p. il. (part col.)

Contains 2,000 art images. Each plate gives the order number, title, artist name, and size in inches and centimeters. A master price list with effective date and ordering information accompanies the catalog. Contents: Ordering information; Groups and figures grouped by subject; Impressionism; Still life florals; Landscape; Seascape; Americana; Hunting/sports; Western/southwestern; Children's and whimsical; Posters; Photography; Abstract; Modern masters; Architecture/decorative; Portraits; Asian; Royal botanicals; Etchings and engravings [some are hand colored European prints]; Religious.

Numerical index, p.551–61. Index [by artist name, then title, order number, page number], p.562–[72].

D44 Parry, Pamela Jeffcott, comp. Contemporary art and artists: an index to reproductions. Westport, Conn., Greenwood, [1978]. xlix, 327p.

All media except architecture and decorative arts are covered; however, works in photography, film, and crafts are listed only if their makers are active in other media. Includes works of art dating from approximately 1940 to the mid-1970s. In general, artists who died prior to the 1950s are excluded. Information has been gathered from more than 60 major English-language books and exhibition catalogs that survey contemporary art or focus on medium, country, or style; monographs on individual artists are excluded. The artist index gives artist's name, nationality, life dates, and full entry for each work, which includes title, date, material, location, and publication in which the illustration of the work appears, along with page/plate reference and a designation as to whether the illustration is in color or black and white. Subject and title index is limited to works with representational or semi-abstract themes.

List of books indexed, p.[xiii]–xv. Keys to symbols for locations of works of art, p.[xvii]–xlix. Abbreviations, p.li.

D45 ______. Photography index: a guide to reproductions. Westport, Conn., Greenwood, [1979]. xviii, 372p.

Reference work used for locating reproductions of photographs, including those of artistic and documentary journalistic intent, by both known and anonymous photographers. Entries are based on illustrations available in 80 major books, photo anthologies, surveys, and exhibition catalogs, the latest published in 1977. Part I is a chronological index to anonymous photographs. Part II is an alphabetically arranged index by photographer, with entries providing some biographical statistics on the artist, title, date of work, type of photographic media used, and the publication in which the reproduction appears. Part III is a subject and title index.

List of subject headings, p. [xiii]–xiv. List of books indexed, p. [xv]–xviii. Abbreviations, p. [xix].

D46 ______, and Chipman, Kathe, comp. Print index: a guide to reproductions. Westport, Conn., Greenwood, [1983]. xxiv, 310p. (Art reference collection, no. 4)

Aids in locating illustrations of prints dating from the 18th century to the mid-1970s. Coverage includes works by more than 2,100 printmakers. The index has compiled data from 100 English-language monographs and catalogs, so printmakers represented are principally Western. Includes an artist index in Part I and a subject and title index in Part II. Artists are listed alphabetically, with alternate names, nationality, and life dates provided, along with a listing of related prints. Prints are dated and their technique identified. At least one reproduction source is noted for each print, along with a page or plate reference for the illustration. Color reproductions are also noted. The subject and title index in Part II is useful for locating particular persons, places, events, or themes. Portraits are listed alphabetically by sitter. References to the artist index are given for reproduction source information.

List of books indexed, p.[xiii]–xx. Abbreviations, p.[xxi]. List of subject headings, p.[xxiii]–xxiv.

D47 Teague, Edward H., comp. Index to Italian architecture: a guide to key monuments and reproduction sources. N.Y., Greenwood, [1992]. xxv, 278p. (Art reference collection, no. 13)

Facilitates access to pictures of 1,800 works of Italian architecture. Provides citations to illustrations of architectural, engineering, and planning works reproduced in 80 books published from the 1950s to 1991. Coverage includes most historical periods and styles. Separate indexes to site, architect, chronological period, type, and work. The site index is the principal index, listing works alphabetically by location. The entry for each work gives name, alternate name, date of work, architect, and citation information organized according to exterior view, interior view, plan, section, or elevation. Coded source information refers the user to the original title and page where the illustration appears. The architect index lists architects, engineers, planners, and others responsible for works given in the site index. Names and alternate names of architects and their life dates are provided, accompanied by a list of each architect's works with execution date and site. The chronological index is arranged broadly by century and then by site, with works listed alphabetically. Within the type index, works are listed by architectural type, then site. A work index provides an alphabetical listing of names and alternate names of works and parts of works, giving sites for each.

List of [building] type headings used, p.[xiii]–xv. List of books indexed, p.[xvii]–xxv. Abbreviations, p.[xxvii].

D48 ______, comp. World architecture index: a guide to illustrations. N.Y., Greenwood, [1991]. xix, 447p. (Art reference collection, no. 12)

A reference source for locating images of approximately 7,200 architectural works. The Index is international in scope and covers most historical periods and styles. Architectural, engineering, and planning works reproduced in more than 100 books are represented. The editor has surveyed and indexed titles in well-known monographic series, standard histories and surveys, the Encyclopedia of world art (GLAH 1:E4), and the MacMillan encyclopedia of architects (GLAH 2:J70). Site, architect, type, and work indexes are provided. The site index is the principal index and is referenced by the other three indexes. Alphabetically arranged by location, the site index gives name and alternate name of works, date of works, architect's name, and citation information organized by exterior, interior views, plan, section, or elevation. Coded source information refers the user to the original title and page where the illustration appears. Indication is given if illustrations appear in color, and if exterior or interior views are photographic or drawing illustrations. The architect index covers architects, engineers, planners, or other persons responsible for design and building; name, alternate name, life dates, and works are listed alphabetically. Within the type index, works can be located by architectural type, country, and then by site. The work index provides names and alternate names of works and parts of works, giving sites for each.

List of [building] type headings used, p.[xi]–xii. List of books indexed, p.[xiii]–xix. Abbreviations, p.[xxi].

D49 Thomison, Dennis, comp. The black artist in America: an index to reproductions. Metuchen, Scarecrow, 1991. lx, 396p.

Black artists have been inadequately represented in traditional collections of reproductions. This index aims to provide access to the published reproductions of fine art by American black artists. Information on artists and their work has been gathered from books, periodicals, and exhibition catalogs primarily of American origin up to 1990. Covers artists born or principally residing in the U.S. Indexes artists working broadly in painting, sculpture, printmaking, drawing, collage, and assemblage. Divided into three sections. The first section provides a list of institutions represented and a key to symbols of bibliographic sources. Section two is the index to the published reproductions arranged by artist. Supplied biographical information includes name, life dates, birth and death places, media in which the artist has worked, other sources of biographical information, and sources of portraits or photographs of the artist. Titles of individual works are then arranged alphabetically for each artist, accompanied by information on medium, date, location of original, where reproduction appears (including page/plate information and color plate designation). When available, further bibliographic information is given for artists.

List of abbreviations, p.[xv]. Bibliography of periodical articles, exhibition catalogs, books, dissertations, and audiovisual materials, p.[320]–80. Subject index, p.[381]–96.

D50 Williams, Lynn Barstis, comp. American printmakers, 1880–1945: an index to reproductions and biocritical information. Metuchen, Scarecrow, 1993. xxxvi, 441p.

Index to prints and their makers, born or active in the United States, particularly those artists of historical importance who have not achieved renown or recognition. Covers the time period from the Etching Revival of the 1880s to American Scene Realism of 1945. Posters and other forms of commercial prints are excluded. Reference dictionaries on American art, and art books and catalogs have been indexed. Sales catalogs, periodical articles, and books on technique are excluded. A list of indexed sources with abbreviations is given in the annotated bibliography, p. [xv]–xxxiii. The printmaker index, arranged alphabetically, provides life dates and title listings of prints which are reproduced. Where available, information on medium, date, source, and format is given for each title entry. A reference to the book or catalog reproducing the print, and the page number on which the reproduction is found is then given.

Abbreviations, p.[xxxv]–xxxvi. Subject index, p.[293]–430. Author-title index, p.[431]–41.

D51 Wright, Christopher, comp. Old master paintings in Britain: an index of continental old master paintings executed before c. 1800 in public collections in the United Kingdom. Totowa, N.J., Sotheby Parke Bernet, [1976]. xvi, 287p. maps.

List of old master paintings produced in Western Europe (excluding the British Isles) and held in public collections in the United Kingdom. Useful for finding out where a particular picture is located and what attribution it has been given by the owner. Public collections are here defined as national museums, municipal museums and collections, university collections, national trusts, and collections and museums which, although private property, are permanently open to the public. All paintings were executed from ca. 1200 to the end of the 18th century, including oil, tempera, fresco, or a combination of these media. Icons, miniatures, watercolors, drawings and other forms of graphic art, and manuscript illustrations are excluded.

Divided into sections. The first is an alphabetically arranged list by artist name. For each artist the city of birth and life dates are provided. The artist's works are then listed by location and institution. Painting titles are given in accordance with the attribution of the owner. Institutional catalog or inventory date and number are given and, if the painting is reproduced, an illustration reference is also provided. The index of locations, alphabetical by site followed by museum, provides a brief history of individual collections. This is followed by a listing, divided by national schools, of all artists represented in the collection. A bibliography, again organized by location and then museum, provides information on relevant catalogs and listings through 1975.

D52 ———. Paintings in Dutch museums: an index of oil paintings in public collections in the Netherlands by artists born before 1870. Totowa, N.J., Sotheby Parke Bernet, [1980]. xxi, 591p. map.

Includes works in oil, tempera, fresco, and some panel painting produced in Western Europe to the end of the 19th century. Icons, miniatures, watercolors, drawings, graphic art, and manuscript illuminations are excluded. Section I is an artist listing, with paintings for each arranged in alphabetical order by collection location and institutional name. Museum catalog or inventory numbers are given. If the painting is reproduced in a bibliographic source, the plate reference is also given in abbreviated form. Section II is an index of locations, p.517–65, arranged alphabetically by city and then by collection. The entry for each collection gives a list, divided by national school, of all the artists represented in it.

Full references are found in Section III's Bibliography, p.569–91, which provides both art historical literature and museum publications.

D53 ———. The world's master paintings: from the early Renaissance to the present day: a comprehensive listing of works by 1,300 painters and a complete guide to their locations worldwide. N.Y., Routledge, [1992]. 2v.

Lists publicly available paintings by a wide selection of European and American painters from the Early Renaissance to the 1990s. Four parts in two vols. The first part provides an alphabetical list of all painters included, with page references. Part two, on the painters and paintings, is organized by national schools and periods. For each artist, a short biographical statement and a bibliography are provided, followed by titles of paintings with dates listed under their institutional locations. Part three is devoted to locations and institutions. Arranged alphabetically by city, with a short general description of each collection's scope, a bibliography (if available), and a mention of key holdings. A complete list of painters represented in the collection then follows. Part four is an index of titles of paintings listed alphabetically under each century, with references back to painter and institution.

General [annotated] bibliography, v.2, p.[1]–3.

PICTORIAL ARCHIVES

D54 The Alinari photo archive: being the Alinari, Anderson, and Brogi photo collections of Italian and other art and architecture reproduced on microfiches [microform]. Ed. by and under the supervision of L. D. Couprie. Zug, IDC, 1982. [1344] microfiches.

Includes approximately 120,000 images of Italian art and architecture in private and public collections. Manuscripts are not included. The images are from the photographic collections of the Alinari brothers' enterprise (Fratelli Alinari Fotografi Editori) and from the firms of James Anderson and Giacomo Brogi, which were acquired by the Alinari. The set is published in a series of 17 parts, produced in eight vols. with the last vol. being the key to the archive. Parts 1–16 are arranged first by photographic collection, then by Italian province, with Rome and the Vatican having separate sections. The listing is further subdivided by place and museum collection. Fiche headings provide a guide to place name, monument, or museum. Series number 17 covers works outside of Italy. V.8 provides consultation information on the archive, including a finding aid (p.9–45), a table of contents of the printed catalogs, a chart for the artist indexes of the printed catalogs, and a chart for the subject indexes of the printed catalogs.

Materials from the Archivi Alinari in Florence also reproduced as: The Villani photo archives: art and architecture [microform]. Leiden, IDC, 1997, 191 fiches reproducing 8,970 glass negatives and 512 positive prints.

A separate booklet, The Alinari photo archive . . . guide to the microform collection, ed. by L. D. Couprie in 1988, provides information on consulting the archive without the finding aids, information on the finding aids, an alphabetical index of Italian place names (p.46–71), and an alphabetical index of Italian provinces (p.73–81.)

D55 American Committee for South Asian Art Archive. A.C.S.A.A. Archive [of South Asian art; photo collection on microfiche. Ed. by Susan L. Huntington and Walter M. Spink] [microform]. Zug, Switzerland, Inter Documentation Co., [1977?] 173 microfiches in 4 boxes il.

Collection of 7,114 photographs of Kushan and Gupta art. Accompanied by a printed guide to the contents.

D56 Caisse nationale des monuments historiques et des sites (France). Archives photographiques. Fine and decorative arts in France [microform]. London, Mindata, 1983. [1014] microfiches.

Series of eight sets documenting photographic records of the French State Archives, covering more than 70,000 principal works of art in more than 200 public and private French collections, and major works from foreign sources exhibited in France. Frames include captioning providing name of artist, title, medium, museum location, a catalog reference, negative number, and format information. A separate printed index of artists and sculptors indicates where a work by a named artist may be found on the fiche. On fiche, there is an Index Thématique, acting as an iconographical reference source to the archives, which includes names of persons, places, buildings, and historical and mythological events. On fiche, there is also an inventory list of several hundred galleries and museums, including foreign collections (excluding national museums) whose work is included on the fiche. A list of works represented is provided for each institution.

Contents: (1) Paintings in the Louvre and national museums and "modern art" [public and private modern art collections in Paris]; [2] Paintings in provincial and other museums; [3] Drawings in the Louvre and national museums; [4] Drawings in provincial [and other] museums and engravings; [5] Decorative art [includes important items from the Louvre, Musée Cluny, and Oriental collections of Musée Guimet, tapestries]; [6] Sculpture, ivories, bronzes, stained glass [includes items from Musée Rodin and the Louvre]; [7] Antiquities [includes works in the Louvre, and series of illustrations from the Egyptian Museum, Cairo]; [8] Manuscripts [includes illuminated and other manuscripts from national and provincial libraries and museums].

D57 The Conway Library: the Courtauld Institute of Art [microform]. Haslemere, Surrey, Emmett, 1987. [7049] microfiches.

The microform version of the Conway Library represents more than one million photographic images, some dating from the 19th century, from a collection originally given to the Courtauld Institute of Art in 1931 by Sir Martin Conway. Information on each image is annotated on the photographic mount, including the Conway negative number. Title strips on fiche provide part number, subject description, country reference. There is a printed contents list that supplies information contained on the fiche header strips.

Contents: (1) Architecture (Part A) [covers France, Italy from medieval period to 20th century; arranged alphabetically by location]; (2) Architecture (Part B) [covers British Isles, Germany, Spain, and the rest of Europe, South America, Africa, Islamic architecture, and Asia, from the medieval period to 20th century; arranged alphabetically by location]; (3) Architectural drawings [covers Italy, Germany, Britain, France, Netherlands, Switzerland, United States, from 14th to 20th centuries; arranged by century]; (4) Sculpture [covers 15th to 20th centuries, also includes other minor arts and non-sculptural works by sculptors; arranged by sculptor]; (5)

Medieval arts [covers classical to medieval period in Europe and the eastern Mediterranean, includes sculpture, metalwork, ivories, wall and panel painting, cameos, stained glass, Byzantine monuments; arranged by type]; (6) Manuscripts [covers western, byzantine, east Christian manuscripts from 4th to 18th centuries; arranged by century and then by country].

D58 ———. 5 year update 1987–1992 [microform]. Haslemere, Surrey, Emmett, 1993. [860] microfiches.

Reflects the growing collection of the Conway Library, comprising new material on architecture, architectural drawings, sculpture, applied arts, medieval arts, and manuscripts. The update basically follows the order of the original microfiche set. All information about each photograph is annotated on the mount and gives the Conway negative number. Information on the title strips guides users, and a printed contents list is also provided. Five original sculptural collections not photographed for the original microform set have been added here. Now included is a new section on applied arts which covers non-sculptural metalwork, ceramics, jewelry, church furniture and plate, furniture and woodwork, glass, textiles, theater design, photographic arts, and video installations. Arrangement is by century. Beginning in 1997, an electronic index to the entire Conway Library was made available, by subscription, at the Emmett Publishing web site.

D59 The early Alinari photographic archive of art & architecture in Italy [microform]. London, Mindata, 1980. [122] microfiches.

More than 7,000 photographs of art and architecture in Italy taken by the brothers Alinari in the 19th century are included. The images represented are from the collection of the Victoria and Albert Museum in London. The 122 fiches are arranged alphabetically by city. There are major sections on Rome and Florence, including works from museums and galleries. Translated captions provide a description and the negative number for each image. Fiche title strips give information on the principal subjects illustrated. An accompanying printed index provides an alphabetical listing of locations with principal works noted, along with the fiche and frame reference.

D60 Fototeca Unione. Ancient Roman architecture: photographic archive on microfiche [microform]. Rome, Fototeca Unione, (Distr. by Univ. of Chicago Pr., 1977–1982). 261 microfiches.

Issued in 2 binders. Includes a 22-page booklet ("3d ed.") ed. by Karin Bull-Simonsen Einaudi.

Reproduction of a photographic and bibliographic archive of Ancient Roman Architecture and Topography of the Fototeca Unione, part of the International Union of Institutes of Archeology, History, and History of Art in Rome, at the American Academy in Rome, begun by Ernest Nash and built over several decades. It was not intended to be a finished set.

List of abbreviations, p.11–13. Rome by monument, index, p.14–16. Italy, by site, index, p.17–19. Empire by modern country, p.20. Empire, by site, p.21–22.

D61 Index der antiken Kunst und Architektur: Denkmaler des griechisch-römischen Altertums in der Photosammlung des Deutschen Archäologischen Instituts Rom = Index of ancient art and architecture: monuments of Greek and Roman cultural heritage in the photographic collection of the German Archaeological Institute in Rome [microform]. Hrsg. . . . unter der Leitung der Bernard Andreae. Bearb. von Lilian Balensiefen . . . [et al.] Red. des Begleitbandes, Jacqueline Prandt. N.Y., Saur, [1988]–91. [2714] microfiches.

Provides representations of monuments of Greek and Roman culture from the collection of 300,000 photographs of the Deutsches Archäologisches Institut, Rome. Arrangement is by subject, including architectural works, figurative architectural sculpture, ideal sculpture, portrait sculpture, vases, terracottas, and paintings. There is a printed index organized by categories including monument type, geographical location, iconography, and historical subject. Fiche reference and content information are also provided. Includes references to negative numbers at the DAI, Rome. A graphical users' interface (GUI), known as "Arachne," available via an internet site at the University of Illinois at Chicago provides a method for searching this set for architecture, architectural fragments, sculpture, and other ancient artifacts.

D62 L'Index photographique de l'art en France [microform]. [Ed. par Bildarchiv Foto Marburg im Forschungsinstitut für Kunstgeschichte der Philipps-Universität Marburg]. N.Y., Saur, [1979–1981]. [976] microfiches.

Based on Richard Hamann's photographic collection begun in 1913. Documents the art of France, covering the last twelve centuries. 95,000 photographs of works of architecture, sculpture, painting, crafts, and archeological artifacts are included. Arrangement of the reproductions is topographical with distant views of locations first, followed by individual views of religious and secular monuments. A similar topographic arrangement of museum objects is presented next including works from public and private collections. The 976 fiches were compiled incrementally; updates start a new topographical alphabetization, although the fiche are numbered consecutively. There is no individual index; however, the Marburger Index (GLAH 2:D63) regularly makes references to this archive set.

D63 Marburger Index: Bilddokumentation zur Kunst in Deutschland [microform]. Bildarchiv Foto Marburg im Forschungsinstitut für Kunstgeschichte der Philipps-Universität, Rheinisches Bildarchiv Köln. München, Verlag Dokumentation, [Distr. by Saur, 1976–].

See GLAH 1:D7 for original entry.

Corpus of reproductions of German art and architecture from the Bildarchiv Foto Marburg, the Deutsche Fotothek der Sächsischen Landesbibliothek in Dresden, and many other photo collections of the departments for the preservation of historical monuments, photo libraries, and archives in Germany, including the former East Germany. Issued in installments, the complete ed. to 1990 reproduces more than one million photographs of works of architecture, painting, sculpture, prints, decorative arts, and crafts from the Middle Ages to the present. Each installment is organized topographically; however, one numerical sequence organizes the entire fiche collection. Works of municipal architecture are arranged before sacred and secular architecture. Individual museums and works held in their collections follow. Iconographical indexing is provided through various indexes which utilize ICONCLASS (GLAH 1:F18) as a classification system. As part of the complete microfiche ed., a Text inventory and index of art in Germany issued in eight installments on fiche provides an object inventory with 100,000 works of art along with index catalogs. The indexes locate the photographs on the entire set of fiche and contain information about the works of art, including artist biographical information, title, date, location, institute, museum inventory number, subject terms, and dimensions of the work. Accompanied by a 129p. user's manual, N.Y., Saur, 1985, written by Lutz Heusinger, which provides background to the history, concept, development, and use of the Marburger Index and its classification schemes. Separate microfiche collections of images on Austrian, Italian, Spanish/Portuguese, and Swiss art and architecture, derived from the Foto Marburg archive, have also been produced by Saur.

D64 [Marburger Index (CD-ROM)]. Marburger Index Datenbank Wegweiser zur Kunst in Deutschland. Bildarchiv Foto Marburg; Computer & Letteren, Universiteit Utrecht. [computer file]. New Providence, Saur, 1995– . 1 computer disk; 4 3/4 in. + 1 manual (6p.) + 1 reference card (10p.)

Annual publication planned as an enhancement to the text and catalog section of the Marburger Index fiche compilation (see preceding entry). As of the 2d ed. of 1996, 21,000 images are included, representing works from German collections. Additionally, the database provides textual access to 150,000 works of art in fields of painting, sculpture, drawing, book illumination, graphic arts, and photography. There are four query options—a search may be conducted by objects, subject matter, artists, or place and time. Many fields may be searched, including artist's name, artist's workshop, artist's patron, country of origin, object name, type and genre, material or artistic technique, time period, photo collection, location of object, and subject matter. Boolean searching is supported. Subject indexing utilizes the classification system ICONCLASS (see also GLAH 1:F18). ICONCLASS Browser and the ICONCLASS Bibliography are both provided on the CD-ROM. Subjects may be searched using proper names and German keywords. The ICONCLASS Browser, which is in English, allows searching the database using assigned classification notations and keywords. Object descriptions and artists' biographical statements are in German. Entries provide illustration concordance numbers back to the Marburger Index fiche collection. Within the entries, references to other bibliographic sources on a particular object may provide the citation page or illustration number and give color or black and white image designation; this can be useful for locating alternative sources of reproductions.

D65 Victoria and Albert Museum, London. Art of India: paintings and drawings in the Victoria and Albert Museum: catalogue and microfiche guide. Haslemere, Surrey, U.K., Emmett Pub., 1992. 221p.

Title from binder cover: Art of India. Issued in a looseleaf binder. Accompanied by a printed text: Art of India. Haslemere, Surrey, U.K., Emmett Pub., 1992. Both the catalog and the microfiche publication organize the paintings and drawings in broad chronological and regional groups and, within each group, by museum number.

Guide to museum numbers, p.5. Concordance of museum numbers, p.199–221.

D66 The Witt Library, Courtauld Institute of Art, London [microform]. Haslemere, Surrey, Emmett, 1990. [14,854] microfiches.

Holds approximately two million images of works of western art from the 13th century to the present, including 1.4 million reproductions of work by more than 50,000 artists from 23 national schools. The contents are divided into four parts separated by national school and alphabetically arranged by artist. Paintings, drawings, and prints are reproduced. Further information on each work is given within the fiche frame, including title, medium, and date. Information varies with each image; documentation may include location, provenance, reproduction citation, exhibition, and sale information. Fiche title-strip information cites national school, box and fiche numbers.

There is no comprehensive index to the set; however, the Marburger Index (GLAH 2:D63) often makes reference to this archive set. For published checklists of artists represented in the Witt Library, see A checklist of painters, c.1200–1994 represented in the Witt Library (GLAH 2:M38) and, for British artists, Checklist of British artists in the Witt Library, compiled by the Witt Computer Index (GLAH 2:M301).

D67 ______. 10 year update, 1981–1991 in the Courtauld Institute of Art [microform]. Haslemere, Surrey, Emmett, 1992. [5719] microfiches.

560,000 reproductions of works of art have been added to the Witt Library between 1981 and 1991. This ed. comprises images and text taken from exhibition and sale catalogs, journal and newspaper clippings, photographic collections of public bodies. The material has been donated by collectors and scholars, or obtained by the Witt Library's survey team.

The update is organized in the same manner as the original microfiche ed. There is a printed contents list. Separate publications on German artists and American artists have been produced by Emmett Publishing, Inc., which are selected and drawn from the original Witt Library microfiche set and the ten year update. The German artist set contains works of 8,000 German and Austrian artists from the 12th to the 20th century, complete in 1,794 black and white fiches with a printed artists index. The American artist set contains 803 fiches and a printed artist index, offering access to 50,000 works of art by 4,000 artists. Based at the Courtauld Institute of Art, the Witt Computer Index provides access to a database of 100,000 reproductions of paintings, drawings, and prints of American and British artists which are in the Institute's Witt Library. The database can be queried via a request to the Witt staff. Information on 4,000 American artists working between the 17th century and the present and 630 18th-century British artists may be searched. Catalog title entries feature date and provenance information, bibliographic citations, excerpts from published sources, and annotations by staff and visiting scholars to the Witt. The ICONCLASS classification scheme is utilized for subject searches.

E. Dictionaries and Encyclopedias

This chapter contains dictionaries and encyclopedias that treat multiple art forms or provide entries on artists, or both. Some useful encyclopedias from closely related humanities areas, such as medieval studies, are also included. Encyclopedias that cover specific media or specialized subjects, such as architecture or iconography, can be found in subsequent chapters.

GENERAL WORKS

E1 Bihalji-Merin, Oto, and Tomaševic, Nebojša-Bato, eds. World encyclopedia of naive art. [Trans., Kordija Kveder . . . (et al.)] Secaucus, N.J., Chartwell, 1984. 735p. il. (part col.), ports.

British ed., London, Muller, 1984.

International biographical dictionary of naïve artists of the 19th and 20th centuries. Signed entries. Small photographic portraits of many of the artists and numerous color illustrations of their works. No bibliographies at the ends of entries.

Contributors, p.[6]–[7]. A hundred years of naive art, by Oto Bihalji-Merin, p.17–84. Historical surveys of naive art in individual countries, p.[637]–98. Important naive art exhibitions, museums, and galleries, p.699–705. Biographies of contributors with key to initials, p.706–10. Bibliography, p.711–16. Artists according to country, p.728–35.

E2 The Bulfinch pocket dictionary of art terms. 3d rev. ed. Rev. and ed. by David G. Diamond. Boston, Little, Brown, 1992. 1v. (unpaged) il.

1st ed., by Mervyn Levy, The pocket dictionary of art terms, Greenwich, Conn., N.Y. Graphic Society, 1961; 2d rev. ed., by Julia M. Ehresmann, 1979.

Brief definitions of media, movements, and technical terms from Western painting, sculpture, printmaking, decorative arts, and architecture.

"Important revisions and additions have been made concerning art trends of the last twenty years. . . . Most importantly, theoretical terms from other disciplines . . . are included for the first time and their relevance to art is explained."—*Pref.*

Bibliography, p.[170]–[85].

E3 The concise Oxford dictionary of art and artists. Ed. by Ian Chilvers. 2d ed. N.Y., Oxford Univ. Pr., 1996. viii, 584p.

1st ed. 1990. Spanish ed., Madrid, Alianza, 1995.

An "abridged version of The Oxford Dictionary of Art [GLAH 2:E20; 1st ed., 1988]. . . . It is about a fifth shorter than the parent work, but the majority of the entries are unchanged or amended only slightly; the reduction in length has been achieved . . . by recasting the longer discursive articles (such as those on printmaking techniques) in much pithier form and by dropping certain marginal classes of entry. These include, for example, all entries on book-printing, unless there is a very close connection with a major artist."—*Pref.*

No bibliographies.

E4 The dictionary of art. Ed., Jane Turner. N.Y., Grove, 1996. 34v. il.

Also referred to as the Grove dictionary of art.

One of the most significant art reference works ever produced—a monumental, and largely successful, attempt to encompass the field of art history. "The objective was clear enough: to produce, in 25 million words, an illustrated reference work that provided comprehensive coverage of the history of all the visual arts worldwide, from prehistory to the present. Like our renowned sister publication, the New Grove Dictionary of Music and Musicians, 20 vols (London, 1980), we aimed to present this comprehensive account using the highest possible standards of scholarship, while at the same time ensuring that entries were accessible to non-specialists."—*Pref.* Almost 7,000 authors contributed some 45,000 signed articles, from a few lines to hundreds of pages in length, accompanied by up-to-date bibliographies and many black-and-white illustrations. Particular attention was given to establishing geographical balance in the work's scope, and the result is a reference set that provides, in addition to its articles on European art, "the most comprehensive coverage of the arts of Asia, Africa, Australasia, and the Americas ever published in one source."—*Pref.* Entries include biographical treatment of artists, dealers, art historians, and other art world figures; coverage of the art history of countries, cities, and archeological sites; and detailed entries on art theory, movements, art forms, building types, and art materials and techniques.

Also available as a CD-ROM and in a more or less continuously revised and corrected internet version, with links to color illustrations from the Bridgeman Art Library. Indexing of the print Dictionary is extremely thorough but cannot compete with the electronic access provided by the online versions.

Spin-off collections of Dictionary entries are also being published in a handy 1v. format (see GLAH 2:E9, GLAH 2:E62, GLAH 2:E107, GLAH 2:E108, GLAH 2:E132, GLAH 2:E137, GLAH 2:E141, GLAH 2:E168).

General abbreviations, v.1, p.xxix–xxxiv. Appendix A, List of locations, v.33, p.750–888. Appendix B, List of periodical titles, v.33, p.889–960. Appendix C, Lists of standard reference books and series, v.33, p.961–69. Appendix D, List of contributors, v.33, p.970–87. Index, v.34, p.1–1075. Appendix [E], Non-western dynasties and peoples, v.34, p.1077–81.

E5 Encyclopedia of aesthetics. Michael Kelly, ed. in chief. N.Y., Oxford Univ. Pr., 1998. 4v. il.

"Includes more than six hundred essays, alphabetically arranged, on approximately four hundred individuals, concepts, periods, theories, issues, and movements in the history of aesthetics. The entries range from the most ancient aesthetic traditions around the world to the Greco-Roman era, the Middle Ages, the Renaissance, the Enlightenment, Romanticism, Modernism, and Postmodernism, up to the present. The central historical focus, however, is the genealogy of Western aesthetics from its inception in the early eighteenth century in Europe to the present. . . . Specifically, how have key aesthetic concepts and issues—such as appropriation, autonomy, beauty, genius, iconology, ideology, metaphor, originality, semiotics, sexuality, taste, and truth—evolved?"—*Pref.*

Lengthy, signed articles, equipped with thorough bibliographies, by more than 500 scholarly contributors from the fields of art history, philosophy, literary theory, psychology, feminist theory, sociology, and anthropology, among others.

Directory of contributors, v.4, p.489–506. Index, v.4, p.507–72.

E6 Encyclopedia of world art. N.Y., McGraw-Hill [1959–1987] 17v. il., maps, plans., plates (part col.)

See GLAH 1:E4 for original annotation. The original 15v. set has been supplemented at intervals by two vols. that attempt an update of art historical knowledge and methodologies established since the publication of the Encyclopedia.

Contents: (16) Supplement: World art in our time [1983], ed. by Bernard S. Myers; (17) Supplement II: New discoveries and perspectives in the world of art [1987], ed. in chief, David Eggenberger.

E7 Glossarium artis: dreisprachiges Wörterbuch der Kunst. München, Saur, 1971– . (10)v. il.

See GLAH 1:E7 for original annotation. Series of dictionaries of terms covering an eclectic group of subjects: medieval and early modern architecture and construction, urban design, liturgical objects, and architectural conservation. Brief definitions in German, with French and, in recent eds., English equivalents of the main term, which is usually in German. Bibliography and indexes in each vol. Sponsored by the Comité International d'Histoire de l'Art. Until 1982 published principally by Niemeyer, Tübingen.

Contents: (1) Burgen und feste Plätze: europäischer Wehrbau vor Einführung der Feuerwaffen (3. neu bearb. u. erw. Aufl., 1996); (2) Kirchengeräte, Kreuze und Reliquarie der christlichen Kirchen (3. vollst. neu bearb. und erw. Aufl., 1992); (3) Bogen und Mauerwerk (3. neu bearb. und erw. Aufl., 1999); (4) Paramente und Bücher der christlichen Kirchen (2. Aufl., 1982); (5) Treppen (2. vollst. neu bearb. und erw. Aufl., 1985); (6) Gewölbe (3. vollst. neu bearb. und erw. Aufl., 1988); (7) Festungen: der Wehrbau nach Einführung der Feuerwaffen (2. vollst. neu bearb. und erw. Aufl., 1990); (8) Das Baudenkmal: Denkmalschutz und Denkmalpflege (2. überarb. und erw. Aufl., 1994); (9) Städte: Stadtpläne, Plätze, Strassen, Brücken (1987); (10) Holzbaukunst: Fachwerk, Dachgerüst, Zimmermannswerkzeug (1997).

E8 Grassi, Luigi, and Pepe, Mario. Dizionario di arte. Torino, UTET, 1995. xi, 986p. col. il., plates.

Original ed., Dizionario della critica d'arte, 1978, 2v. Rev. pocket ed., Dizionario dei termini artistici, Milano, TEA, 1994.

Impressive work that provides relatively brief but probing and substantive entries which examine the intellectual and conceptual histories of terminology from aesthetics, the philosophy of art, and art history, including coverage of art forms, iconographical themes, periods, groups and movements, technique, building types, optics, etc. Most entries supply etymological information and many in-text references to current and antiquarian sources, which are presented in detail in the bibliographic index. No biographical articles.

Indice bibliografico di opere e autori citati in forma abbreviata, p.[951]–86.

E9 The Grove dictionary of art. From renaissance to impressionism: styles and movements in western art 1400–1900. Ed. by Jane Turner. N.Y., St. Martin's, 2000. xii, 377p.

Focused selection of entries from the Dictionary of art (GLAH 2:E4).

List of contributors, p.viii–ix. General abbreviations, p.x–xi. Appendix A, List of locations, p.[368]–74. Appendix B, List of periodical titles, p.[375]–77. Appendix C, List of standard reference books and series, p.[378].

E10 Haggar, Reginald George. A dictionary of art terms: painting, sculpture, architecture, engraving and etching, lithography and other art processes, heraldry. N.Y., Hawthorn, [1962]. 416p. illus. (1 col.) (Repr.: Poole, Dorset, New Orchard; distr. by Sterling, N.Y., 1984)

British ed., London, Oldbourne Pr., [1962].

Standard older dictionary of mainly English-language terms. Coverage of 20th-century art ends with early Abstract Expressionism. Mixture of brief definitions and longer articles on selected topics, e.g., certain art forms, artists' materials. Illustrated with occasional line drawings. Regularly cites related literary works in entries on visual arts movements. No artist biographies. Glossary contains separate lists of French, German, and Italian terms, with English equivalents, useful for students preparing for graduate art history language exams.

Glossary, p.375–408. Bibliography, p.411–16.

E11 Haubenreisser, Wolfgang. Wörterbuch der Kunst. Begründ. von Johannes Jahn. 12. durchgeseh. und erw. Aufl. Stuttgart, Kröner, 1995. ix, 937p. il. (Kröners Taschenausgabe, Bd. 165)

9th ed., von Johannes Jahn, 1979; 10th ed. 1983; 11th ed. 1989.

Latest version of a pocket dictionary continuously published by Kröner since the work's founding by Jahn in 1939. Aims for broad coverage of Western and Asian art from ancient times to the late 20th century. Includes, in brief entries averaging about 200 words in length, artists and architects, periods, styles, art forms, building types, major classical and Biblical iconographical themes, technical terms, principal classical archeological sites, and a few key art works. Up-to-date bibliographical citations appended to entries. Small, sparse illustrations.

Häufiger vorkommende Abkürzungen, p.[x].

E12 International dictionary of art and artists. Foreword by Cecil Gould. Ed., James Vinson. Chicago, St. James Pr., 1990. 2v. il.

Unusual work based partly on the format of St. James's very successful reference series on contemporary artists (e.g., GLAH 2:E56). Instead of conventional artist biographies, "Artists" vol. provides for each artist covered brief biographical data, a thorough bibliography including some journal articles, and an assessment of the artist's significance by one of a group of about 200 art historian-contributors. Covers Western European and U.S. painters and sculptors from the 13th through 20th century. "Art" vol. contains essays of ca. 1,000 words, by the same roster of contributors, on more than 500 key artworks. Useful, detailed review, Art documentation, v.10, no.1, 1991, p.44–45.

Contents: (1) Artists; (2) Art.

E13 Langmuir, Erika, and Lynton, Norbert. Yale dictionary of art and artists. New Haven, Yale Univ. Pr., 2000. viii, 753p.

"The purpose of this dictionary is twofold: to act as a reference book for travelers and gallery visitors, and also to provide at-home information to students of western art history and general readers interested in the subject. . . . Entries include painters, sculptors, printmakers, etc., but not architects, except those who practiced as one or more of the above, and the specialized field of Byzantine art has not been included. . . . The period covered runs from 1300 to the present day."—*Pref.*

In addition to artist biographies, includes entries on terminology related to technique, notable artworks, art forms, and movements. No bibliographies.

E14 Lexikon der Kunst: Malerei, Architektur, Bildhauerkunst. [Gesamtleit., Wolf Stadler. Red., Eckhart Bergmann . . . [et al.] Freiburg, Herder, 1987–90. 12v. il. (part col.)

Comprehensive, heavily illustrated, well-crafted work whose lengthy, unsigned entries cover the usual array of subject matter—artists, architects, technical terms, regional and chronological surveys, building types, significant individual artworks, or related groups of works. Particularly thorough coverage of media and movements, especially those of the 20th century. Entries of several thousand words, with many color illustrations, are not uncommon for major movements. Coverage of Asian and African art includes some entries on individual artists.

Some bias in coverage toward Germanic art and artists is detectable. Many architectural entries have accompanying ground plans and axonometric drawings.

Bibliographies at ends of most articles are current through the mid-1980s. Hinweise für die Benutzung, v.1, p.[5]–[6]. Bildregister, v.12, p.360–73. Korrekturen und Ergänzungen, v.12, p.377. "Verzeichnis der Abkürzungen" at front of each vol.

E15 Lexikon der Kunst: Architektur, bildende Kunst, angewandte Kunst, Industrieformgestaltung, Kunsttheorie. [Begründ. von Gerhard Strauss. Hrsg. von Harald Olbrich . . . [et al.] Neubearb. Leipzig, Seemann, 1987–94. 7v. il. (part col.)

See GLAH 1:E9 for 1st ed.

A major art encyclopedia with special strength in its treatment of East European and Third World countries. Originally a product of the former East Germany, with a very pronounced Marxist-Leninist bias, the Lexikon has been undergoing a gradual softening of its positions throughout the publication of its 2d ed. (German reunification took place in 1990 between the appearance of the second and third vols. of the 2d ed. See review of v.3 and v.4 of the 2d ed., Zeitschrift für Kunstgeschichte, v.56, no.4, 1993, p.582–84, for a discussion of the effect of a changing political climate on the character of the Lexikon.)

Particularly thorough coverage of East European, Asian, and African artists, who are often the subjects of longer articles than some of their very significant Western counterparts. Rivals the much bigger Dictionary of art (GLAH 2:E4) in its detailed treatment of the art and architectural attributes of smaller East European cities, from Brno to Varna. Provides excellent coverage of the archeological sites of European prehistoric cultures as well as the avant-garde movements of the 20th century. Also includes entries on iconographical themes, prominent works of art and architecture, and artforms and building types.

The mostly black-and-white illustrations are small and murky; in general, the frugal production values of the 1st ed. have been carried over to the 2d.

Lengthy bibliographies at ends of most articles. "Abkürzungen" and "Autorenverzeichnis" at front of each vol.

E16 Lucie-Smith, Edward. The Thames and Hudson dictionary of art terms. N.Y., Thames and Hudson, 1984. 208p. il.

Concentrates on technical terms, media, movements, and styles in Western and Asian art and architecture from ancient Egypt to the early 1980s. Brief but pithy, well-written definitions. Many small but useful black-and-white illustrations, which are effectively connected to the entries to which they apply. No artist biographies. No bibliography.

Abbreviations, p.8. Table of dynasties, p.206–07.

E17 Mayer, Ralph. The HarperCollins dictionary of art terms and techniques. Rev. and ed. by Steven Sheehan. 2d ed. N.Y., HarperPerennial, 1991. v, 474p. il.
See GLAH 1:E11 for 1st ed. British ed., Collins dictionary of art terms and techniques, Glasgow, HarperCollins, 1993.

Definitions mainly treat materials and techniques in painting and the graphic arts. Some coverage of movements and media. No artist biographies.

Books for further reading, p.469–74.

E18 Mollett, J. W. Dictionary of art and archaeology. [Reprint.] London, Bracken, 1996. [6], 350p. il.
See GLAH 1:E12 for original annotation.

E19 Murray, Peter, and Murray, Linda. The Penguin dictionary of art and artists. 7th ed. N.Y., Penguin, 1997. xvii, 579p.
See GLAH 1:E13 for 3d, and previous, eds. 4th ed. 1976; 5th ed. 1983; 6th ed. 1989.

"This edition has been prepared by only one of the original compilers; Peter Murray died suddenly in April 1992."—*Pref.*

Brief entries on artists, periods, movements, and terminology in Western painting, sculpture, and the graphic arts from 1300 to the late 20th century. Coverage of contemporary art relatively weak. No illustrations or bibliography in this ed.

Abbreviations, p.vi–vii. List of general (non-biographical) articles, p.viii–xiii.

E20 The Oxford dictionary of art. Ed. by Ian Chilvers and Harold Osborne. Consultant ed., Dennis Farr. New ed. N.Y., Oxford Univ. Pr., 1997. xi, 647p.
1st ed. 1988. Catalan ed., Barcelona, Ediciones 62, 1996.

"The Oxford Dictionary of Art is a descendant of the three Oxford Companions edited by Harold Osborne [GLAH 1:E14, GLAH 1:P22; GLAH 2:E68], but is in effect a new book. A few of the shorter entries have been taken over more or less unchanged from the Companions, but most of the text has been completely rewritten, and there are also over 300 new entries (out of a total of about 3,000) on personalities and topics not covered by the Companions."—*Introd.*

Well-written entries, averaging about 200 words, on artists and other art world figures; groups; art forms and kinds of art; movements; major monuments, museums and events; technical terms; and historiographical concepts. Detailed coverage extends from the art of ancient Greece to the work of contemporary artists, but none born after 1945. Omits articles on architecture, Asian art, and the art of individual countries. For a work of this size, particularly good coverage of art historians and early writers and theorists on art. No bibliographies.

Abbreviations, p.[xii]. Chronology, p.[617]–32. Index of galleries and museums, p.[633]–44. A selection of Christian and classical themes in painting and sculpture, p.[645]–47.

E21 Phaidon encyclopedia of art and artists. Oxford, Phaidon, 1978. 704p. il. (part col.), plates, ports.
One-vol. version of the Pall Mall encyclopedia of art, published in the U.S. as the Praeger encyclopedia of art, N.Y., Praeger, 1971, 5v. (GLAH 1:E15).

"The encyclopedia is composed of three categories of articles. There are biographies documenting the work of painters, sculptors, graphic artists, and architects active in the West from medieval times to the present. These are complemented by articles on periods, styles, schools and movements, and by surveys of the art of civilizations whose individual artists are mainly unknown, at least in the West."—*Pref.*

Condensation of the original 5v. work has been accomplished by reducing the size of selected articles, and by eliminating altogether some entries and illustrations, as well as the bibliographies and contributors' initials at the ends of articles.

E22 Pierce, James Smith. From abacus to Zeus: a handbook of art history. 5th ed. Englewood Cliffs, N.J., Prentice Hall, 1995. viii, 209p. il., maps.
1st ed. 1968; 2d ed. 1977; 3d ed. 1987; 4th ed. 1991.

Several different short dictionaries in one handy vol. intended as an aid for undergraduates or other art history beginners. Data in entries are keyed to illustrations in the most widely used art history surveys. First chapter includes art and architectural technical and critical terminology with some entries as long as 600 words. Following chapters mostly cover iconographical themes. Chronology includes pronunciation help for difficult names.

Contents: (1) Art terms, processes and principles; (2) Gods, heroes, and monsters; (3) Christian subjects: Devotional subjects, Narrative subjects; (4) Saints and their attributes; (5) Christian signs and symbols.

Chronology of painters, photographers, sculptors, and architects, p.169–83. Maps, p.185–86. Index, p.[187]–201. Table of parallel illustrations in Gardner, Janson, and Hartt, p.203–09.

E23 Réau, Louis. Dictionnaire polyglotte des termes d'art et d'archéologie Réimpression de l. éd. de 1953 augm. de tables de renvois en allemand, anglais et italien. Osnabrück, Zeller, 1977. 961p.
See GLAH 1:E17 for 1953 ed.

New material consists of more than 700 camera-ready pages of alphabetically arranged German, English, and Italian terms, with French equivalents, attached to a reprint of the 1953 text, which supplied French terms, occasional brief definitions in French, and the terms' equivalents in several languages.

E24 Sulzer, Johann Georg. Allgemeine Theorie der schönen Künste: in einzeln nach alphabetischer Ordnung der Kunstwörter aufeinanderfolgenden, Artikeln abgehandelt. [Reprint.] Einl. von Giorgio Tonelli. 2., unveränd. Nachdruck. N.Y., Olms, 1994. 5v. il.
See GLAH 1:E23 for previous eds. English trans. of selections, Aesthetics and the art of musical composition in the German Enlightenment, N.Y., Cambridge Univ. Pr., 1995.

E25 The Thames and Hudson dictionary of art and artists. Ed., Nikos Stangos. Consulting ed., Herbert Read. Rev., expanded and updated ed. N.Y., Thames and Hudson, 1994. 384p. il. (World of art)

In entries averaging about 100 words, provides biographies of artists and important art historians, as well as coverage of artists' groups, movements, art forms, periods in art history, and technical terminology. Extends chronologically from ancient Greece to the late 20th century; provides some coverage of Asian and African art. Particularly thorough treatment of contemporary artists and movements to the early 1990s. Architecture excluded. Small but clear illustrations are usually in the same two-page spread as the entry to which they refer.

"The majority of entries on movements and artists active before 1945 were originally written for the Encyclopaedia of the Arts (London, Thames and Hudson, 1966), whose consulting editor was Sir Herbert Read. . . . Many of these entries, however, have been substantially revised and updated, and about 40 per cent more have been added."—*Foreword.*

Abbreviations, p.[6].

E26 Urdang, Laurence. Fine and applied arts terms index. Frank R. Abate, managing ed. Detroit, Gale, 1983. 773p.

"We have selected terms for inclusion in the Index from more than 150 sources; dictionaries and encyclopedias, auction catalogues, periodicals, and other published materials have been culled for words and phrases dealing with every period and style of fine and applied art—paintings, sculpture, carpets, furniture, flatware, jewelry, clocks, barometers—in short, almost every conceivable object that may have yielded to the collector."—*Foreword.*

More than 45,000 terms presented alphabetically in Index section with symbols indicating what sources they were taken from. Prefatory note explains that the terms have not been edited for consistency, "hence, peculiarities of spelling and other typographic details have been reproduced exactly as they appeared originally" in the source publications. No definitions. Sources, some annotated, are listed in the Bibliography.

How to use this book, p.9–10. Bibliography, p.11–33.

SEE ALSO: Mayer, The artist's handbook of materials and techniques (GLAH 2:M44); Artists' pigments: a handbook of their history and characteristics (GLAH 2:T134).

PREHISTORIC

E27 Dictionnaire de la préhistoire. Dir., André Leroi-Gourhan. Secrétaire gén., Dominique Baffier. 2e éd. Paris, Pr. Univ. de France, 1994. 1277p. il.

1st ed. 1988.

Provides coverage of Paleolithic, Neolithic, Bronze and Iron Age cultures worldwide, with extraordinarily comprehensive inclusion of specific sites. Also has entries for hominid fossil finds, and for pottery, tools, weapons, and other artifacts, and even flora and fauna associated with certain sites. Signed articles; average approximately 300 words. Many have brief appended bibliographies, current through the late 1980s. No biographical entries. No index.

Bibliographie générale, p.[1199]–1213. Cartes et tableaux, p.[1214]–63. Liste des articles traités par chacun des auteurs, p.[1265]–77.

ANCIENT

E28 A dictionary of archaeology. Ed. by Ian Shaw and Robert Jameson. Malden, Mass., Blackwell, 1999. xv, 624p. il., maps.

Omits coverage of classical Greece and Rome in order "to make room for a much more comprehensive coverage of previously neglected areas, such as the archaeology of China, Japan and Oceania, as well as longer articles on theory and methodology."—*Pref.*

Entries average about 250 words in length and are signed. Coverage of archeological theory is especially strong. No biographical entries. No index, but cross reference system is effective.

Bibliographies at ends of entries current to the early 1990s. Contributors, p.[xi]. Bibliographical abbreviations, p.[xiv]–xv.

E29 Enciclopedia dell'arte antica, classica e orientale. Roma, Istituto della Enciclopedia italiana, [1958–1966]. 7v. il., col. plates, maps, facsims., plans.

See GLAH 1:E29 for original annotation and earlier supplements.

______. Atlante delle forme ceramiche. Roma, Istituto della Enciclopedia italiana, 1981–1985. 2v. il.

Illustrated survey of pottery, and related clay artifacts, of the Roman Empire.

Contents: (1) Ceramica fine romana nel bacino mediterraneo (medio e tardo impero); (2) Ceramica fine romana nel bacino mediterraneo (tardo ellenismo e primo impero).

______. Indici. Roma, Istituto della Enciclopedia italiana, 1984. xiii, 629p.

Index to v.1–7 and to the first supplement (1973).

______. Pompei, pitture e mosaici. [Dir. di red., Giovanni Pugliese Carratelli. Red., Ida Baldassarre]. Roma, Istituto della enciclopedia italiana, 1990–1999. 10v. il. (part col.)

Pictorial survey of excavated Pompei, arranged topographically, including paintings and drawings by 18th- and 19th-century artists as well as photographs.

______. Secundo Supplemento 1971–1994. Roma, Istituto della Enciclopedia italiana, 1994–1997. 5v. il. (part col.), maps, plans.

Provides a thorough updating of the original set and first supplement with similar scholarly, signed articles, fresh bibliographies, and excellent illustrations. Coverage includes archeological sites, individual artists, significant works, art forms, and iconographical themes, from Roman Britain to the Far East.

"Abbreviazioni dei testi antichi," and "Abbreviazioni bibliografiche," at front of each vol.

E30 Kipfer, Barbara Ann. Encyclopedic dictionary of archaeology. N.Y., Kluwer Academic/Plenum, 2000. xi, 708p.

Brief, well-written entries covering archeological methods, artifact types, art forms, figures from ancient history, notable archeologists, and world archeological sites. Coverage of latter is remarkably inclusive. No index or cross-references. No bibliographies at the ends of individual entries.

Archaeological abbreviations, p.ix–x. Bibliography, p.617–21. Supplementary list of archaeological sites and terms, p.623–77. Writing and archaeology: a timeline, p.679–708.

E31 The Oxford classical dictionary. Ed. by Simon Hornblower and Antony Spawforth. 3d ed. N.Y., Oxford Univ. Pr., 1996. liv, 1640p.

1st ed. 1949; 2d ed. 1970. Shortened version, The Oxford companion to classical civilization, 1998.

Convenient source of reliable, concise information on the history, topography, and culture of the ancient world. Many articles more than 1,000 words in length. This ed., largely rewritten between 1991 and 1994 by 364 contributors, aims to be accessible to specialists and general readers alike. Changes include a greater emphasis on interdisciplinary approaches to classical studies, broader coverage of areas outside Greece and Italy, fuller treatment of the history of women in the ancient world, and more thematic entries (e.g., "Ecology," "Literacy," "Technology").

Bibliographies at ends of most entries. List of new entries, p.xi–xiv. Index to initials of contributors, p.xvii–xxviii. Abbreviations used in the present work, p.xxix–liv.

E32 The Oxford companion to archaeology. Ed. in chief, Brian M. Fagan. Eds., Charlotte Beck . . . [et al.] N.Y., Oxford Univ. Pr., 1996. xx, 844p. il., maps.

An attempt to shape nearly 700 entries by more than 400 contributors into "an overview of archaeology from a global perspective."—*Introd.* Entries are signed and average more than 1,000 words in length. Bibliographies are current through the early 1990s. Many lengthy, survey entries on regions or cultures rely on the index to provide access to data on specific sites. Coverage also includes detailed treatment of archeological methods, biographies of major archeologists, and many entries on collateral topics seen from an archeological perspective—e.g., "Elm decline," "Land transportation," "Waste management." Useful review, American journal of archaeology, v.102, no.1, 1998, p.186–87.

Contributors, p.[xiii]–xx. [Maps, timelines, etc.], p.[776]–[818]. Index, p.820–44.

E33 The Oxford encyclopedia of archaeology in the Near East. Prepared under the auspices of the American Schools of Oriental Research. Eric M. Meyers, ed. in chief. N.Y., Oxford Univ. Pr., 1997. 5v. il., maps.

A major encyclopedia in which the results of "archaeological fieldwork, epigraphy, and literary-historical studies" (*Pref.*) are used to examine the material culture and everyday life of the peoples in a vast area of Semitic influence stretching from Sardinia eastward to Anatolia and Iran and south to Ethiopia, and chronologically from prehistory through the period of the crusades. Covers archeological sites, architectural monuments, building and artifact types, and inscriptions.

Also includes many entries on archeological theory and practice, major archeologists who worked in the Near East, and annotated bibliographies as entries under such headings as "Reference works" and "Periodical literature." More than 1,100 entries, including many of 2,000 or more words, contributed by an international group of 560 scholars.

Bibliographical citations at ends of entries. Appendix 1, Egyptian Aramaic texts, v.5, p.393–410. Appendix 2, Chronologies, v.5, p.411–16. Appendix 3, Maps, v.5, p.417–30. Directory of contributors, v.5, p.431–50. Synoptic outline of contents, v.5, p.451–59. Index, v.5, p.461–553. "Abbreviations and symbols" at front of each vol.

E34 Pauly, August Friedrich von. Paulys Real-Encyclopaedie der classischen Altertumswissenschaft. Supplement. Neue Bearb. unter Mitwirk. zahlreicher Fachgenossen hrsg. von Georg Wissowa. Stuttgart, Metzler, 1903–1978. 15v. illus.

See GLAH 1:E31 for original series.

E35 ———. Der kleine Pauly: Lexikon der Antike auf der Grundlage von Pauly's Realencyclopädie der classischen Altertumswissenschaft unter Mitwirk. zahlreicher Fachgelehrter bearb. und hrsg. von Konrat Ziegler und Walther Sontheimer. [Reprint.] Köln, Ad Libros, 1989. 5v.

See GLAH 1:E31 for original annotation.

E36 Der neue Pauly: Enzyklopädie der Antike: Altertum. Hrsg. von Hubert Cancik und Helmuth Schneider. Stuttgart, Metzler, 1996– . (11)v. il., maps.

Major new dictionary of classical civilization contains signed articles by hundreds of contributors covering peoples; historical and cultural figures; topography; mythology; social, legal, and economic concepts; scientific and technical knowledge; artifact types; important works of art and architecture; and so on. Most entries are relatively brief, although essays of several thousand words, with footnotes and extensive bibliographies, cover the major topics. Entries in the last three vols. of the set, in a separate alphabetical sequence, cover classical influence on subsequent cultures and provide a survey of the history and present state of the academic study of classical antiquity.

Useful review in Reference reviews Europe online, 1998, DA-98–1/2, which explains that the Neue Pauly "does not replace the Kleine Pauly [GLAH 2:E35]—to say nothing of the Realencyclopädie [GLAH 2:E34]—and scholars will presumably have to consult all three."

Heavily cross-referenced; an index vol. will eventually be published. "Abkürzungsverzeichnis" at front of some vols.

EARLY CHRISTIAN—BYZANTINE

E37 The Oxford dictionary of Byzantium. [Ed. by] Alexander P. Kazhdan . . . [et al.] N.Y., Oxford Univ. Pr., 1991. 3v. (li, 2232p.) il., maps.

"Ours is . . . the first attempt to collect within a single work data concerning all fields of Byzantine studies."—*Pref.*

Stresses both a cross-disciplinary approach "in which history, philology, art, and liturgy [are] interwoven and combined," and an emphasis on "the man in the street . . . with special focus on subjects such as the family, diet, emotions, and everyday life."—*Pref.*

Five thousand signed entries by more than 100 contributors; entries average 250–300 words, with up to 1,000 for important topics; each ends with bibliographic citations. Covers all territory ever within the Byzantine empire, as well as external regions that had significant relations with Byzantium. Art and architectural entries include coverage of artists, architects, media, monuments, cities/archeological sites, and iconographical themes.

Directory of contributors, v.1, p.xlvii–li. "General abbreviations," "Abbreviations of manuscript citations," "Bibliographic abbreviations" at front of each vol.

E38 Reallexikon zur byzantinischen Kunst. Unter Mitwirkung von Marcell Restle. Hrsg. von Klaus Wessel. Stuttgart, Hiersemann, 1966– . (6)v. illus., maps, plans.

See GLAH 1:E33 for original annotation. Continues to be issued in five or six fascicles per vol., but the number of articles in a typical vol. has diminished markedly, from 90 in v.1 to only 22 in v.5 (although the average length of articles has increased significantly). Thus, the progress of this reference work from A to Z has slowed noticeably. In a recent fascicle preface, Marcell Restle, editor-in-chief since the death of Klaus Wessel in 1987, blames this phenomenon in part on the burgeoning of Byzantine studies and the resulting excavations and research that have created increasing amounts of data that must be absorbed and integrated into RbK entries.

"Ikonographisches Register," "Topographisches Register," and "Abkürzungen" in each vol.

ISLAMIC

E39 The Encyclopaedia of Islam. Ed. by a commmittee consisting of H. A. R. Gibb . . . [et al.] New ed. Leiden, Brill, 1960– . (11)v. illus., plates, fold. maps (part col.) diagrs., plans.

See GLAH 1:E34 for original annotation.

Issued in fascicles; most recent is no.183–184, 2001, "Yabisa"–"Yildiz."

Available as a CD-ROM, but without the material in the supplement fascicles listed below.

Since the description of the Encyclopedia in GLAH 1, a series of associated publications have also been produced:

______. Supplement, fasc. 1–2. Leiden, Brill, 1980.

______. Supplement, fasc. 3–4. Leiden, Brill, 1981.

______. Supplement, fasc. 5–6. Leiden, Brill, 1982.

Supplements augment entries in main set through "I".

______. Index of proper names to volumes I–IX and to the supplement, fascicules 1–6. Compiled and ed. by E. van Donzel. Leiden, Brill, 1998. 440p.

______. Index of subjects to volumes I–IX and to the supplement, fascicles 1–6. Compiled by P.J. Bearman. Leiden, Brill, 1998. 297p.

______. Glossary and index of terms to volumes I–IX and to the supplement, fascicles 1–6. [Ed. by] P.J. Bearman . . . [et al.] Leiden, Brill, 2000. 427p.

Indexes cumulate and supersede previous index eds.

E40 Isa, Ahmad Muhammad. Islamic art terms: lexicon, explained and illustrated. Illustrated by Mahmoud Al-Toukhy. Istanbul, Research Centre for Islamic History, Art and Culture, 1994. vi, 194, 41p. il. (Islamic arts and crafts series, 8)

Arabic definitions are provided for more than 1,350 Western art and architectural terms, mostly English. Many marginal line drawings keyed to entries.

Follows other "praiseworthy individual attempts" to establish a lexicon of Arabic art terms "such as the books titled The Lexicon of archeological terms, by Yehia El Shihabi (Damascus, 1967), the Lexicon of civilisational words and terms of art, by the Academy of Arabic Language (Cairo, 1980), the Dictionnaire trilingue des termes d'art, by Afif Bahnassi (Dar El Ra'ed, Beirut, 1981), and the Encyclopaedia of Islamic architecture, by Abdurrahim Ghaleb (Beirut, 1988), and other lexica and indexes that were appendixed to a number of books translated into Arabic."—*Pref.*

Several Arabic appendixes are present, along with a 21p. Arabic index to the terms and a bibliography of Western and Arabic sources.

CAROLINGIAN—GOTHIC

E41 Dictionary of the Middle Ages. Joseph R. Strayer, ed. in chief. N.Y., Scribner, 1982–1989. 13v. il.

Extremely useful source of scholarly, detailed information on many aspects of the history, topography, and culture of the medieval world, from Northwest Europe to the farthest Asian reaches of the Caliphate, and including Christian and Muslim North Africa, from 500 to 1500. Contains about 5,000 signed entries by approximately 1,300 contributors, mostly faculty from American and Canadian universities. An effort has been made to keep the entries readable enough to be as accessible to beginning students as to experienced scholars. Includes many entries, of both the focused and survey types, on art and architecture. Manuscript illumination, specific archeological sites, and Islamic tribal art are special strengths. But its chief usefulness to art historians will probably lie in the background information available in its lucid essays of several thousand words on key concepts regarding the medieval world, e.g., "Calendars," "Kingship," "Serfs and serfdom." Provides a nice refuge for readers of English who need an authoritative source approaching the detail of the Lexikon des Mittelalters (GLAH 2:E43).

Useful review in Reference reviews Europe online, 1999, D-99–1/4, which briefly compares this work with the Lexikon des Mittelalters (GLAH 2:E43).

Bibliographies at ends of articles contain as many citations to English-language sources as possible. Excellent subject index in v.13 (p.1–565). Contributors, v.13, p.567–606. Errata, v.13, p.607–13.

E42 Enciclopedia dell'arte medievale. Roma, Istituto della Enciclopedia italiana, 1991–2000. 11v. il. (part col.)

Another major specialist art encyclopedia from the publisher of the Enciclopedia dell'arte antica, classica e orientale (GLAH 2:E29). Reminiscent of the earlier set in terms of scholarly and editorial excellence, breadth of coverage, generous format, and high production standards. Long, signed entries treat the history of art and architecture from the 6th through the 14th centuries in Europe and relevant stretches of the Near East and North Africa. Coverage includes very detailed treatment of cities and larger regions, iconographical subjects, liturgical objects, artists, media, architectural features, building types, monastic orders, and major monuments. Some coverage of Jewish and Islamic art. Extremely full bibliographies at the ends of entries separate primary sources from later, secondary works, with the latter current through at least the early 1990s. Splendid illustrations, most in color. Many ground plans.

Review of v.1, Arte veneta, v.44, 1993, p.68–70.

Each vol. has at front, "Elenco delle abbreviazioni," "Abbreviazioni bibliografiche," and rosters of "Consulenti" and "Collaboratori" for that particular vol.

E43 Lexikon des Mittelalters. München, Artemis, [1977]–1999. 10v.

A monumental encyclopedia of the highest scholarly quality that will be a fundamental reference work in medieval studies for decades to come. Contains more than 30,000 signed entries by about 3,000 contributors. Provides detailed treatment of most aspects of medieval history, topography, and culture, with coverage of Latin and Byzantine Europe, the Middle East, and Muslim and Christian North Africa, from 300 to 1500. Includes much coverage of the visual arts and architecture, including entries on cities and larger regions; fortresses, religious structures, and archeological sites; iconographical themes; building types and architectural features; techniques and materials. Tends to scatter its data among relatively brief, focused entries rather than consolidate it in broader surveys. Outstanding strengths are its detailed coverage of historically significant figures and families, relatively brief entries on aspects of daily life, and its treatment of the texts and liturgies of the three major religions.

Useful review in Reference reviews Europe online, 1999, D-99–1/4, which briefly compares this work with the Dictionary of the Middle Ages (GLAH 2:E41).

Bibliographical citations at ends of entries. Abkürzungsverzeichnis, v.1, p.xvii–lxiii. Registerband, [v.10], contains a classed index, an alphabetical listing of entries in the entire work, and a list of all contributors and their entries. Extensive system of cross-references helps mitigate weakness of index.

E44 List, Claudia, and Blum, Wilhelm. Sachwörterbuch zur Kunst des Mittelalters: Grundlagen und Erscheinungsformen. Stuttgart, Belser, 1996. 381p. il. (Belser Lexikon)

Provides substantive coverage of art in Europe and Byzantium from the early 4th to the late 14th century, with entries on specific artworks and monuments, building types, regional styles, architectural features, liturgical objects, iconographical themes, and so on. Effective system of cross-references improves access to longer survey articles. Achieves some geographic balance in its coverage, although entries devoted to individual works of art and architecture from Germanic countries outnumber those of other countries combined. Brief etymologies supplied for terms. Particularly effective summary treatment of manuscript illumination; appendix "Skriptorien" lists major examples by school. Illustrations negligible. No bibliographies at end of articles but extensive, classified one as appendix.

Skriptorien, p.366–67. Abkürzungen, p.368. Zitierte Literatur und Literatur in Auswahl, p.368–80.

E45 Vogüé, Melchior de, and Neufville, Jean. Glossaire de termes techniques à l'usage des lectures de "La Nuit des temps."4. éd. rev. et corr. par Raymond Oursel. La Pierre-Qui-Vire, Yonne, Zodiaque, 1989. 534p. il. (part col.) (Introductions à la nuit des temps, 1)

1st ed. 1965; 2d ed. 1971; 3d ed. 1983.

Dictionary of terms relating principally to Romanesque church architecture; compiled to aid readers of the Nuit des temps series (GLAH 2:R72). Main alphabetical sequence provides detailed definitions of architectural features, building types, construction methods and tools, sculptural techniques, liturgical objects, etc. Terms and definitions in French, with brief etymologies and the equivalent term in German, English, Spanish, and Italian supplied. An appendix contains alphabetically arranged German, English, and Italian terms, with French equivalents. Heavily illustrated mainly with marginal line drawings and the series' characteristic razor-sharp black-and-white illustrations.

Abbreviations, p.[28]. Index analytique, p.463–73. Équivalences, p.[475]–[535].

RENAISSANCE—BAROQUE

E46 Encyclopedia of the Renaissance. Paul F. Grendler, ed. in chief. N.Y., Scribner's, 1999. 6v. il. (part col.), maps.

Distinguished, well-written work that presents lengthy, signed scholarly entries on a broad variety of historical, cultural, and sociological topics without sacrificing clarity that makes it as useful to beginning students as to experienced scholars. Nearly 1,200 entries by 638 contributors. "Presents a panoramic view of the cultural movement and the period of history called the Renaissance. The chronological coverage begins in Italy in approximately 1350, then broadens geographically to embrace the rest of Europe in the middle to late fifteenth century."—*Introd.* Informed by the results of much recent scholarship, particularly studies of humanism throughout Europe, a focus on the social history of the Renaissance, and the study of women in the Renaissance. Bibliographic citations at the end of entries current through the mid 1990s. Published in assoc. with the Renaissance Society of America.

Contents, v.1, p.ix–xvii. Chronology, v.1, p.xxv–lxiii. Systematic outline of contents, v.6, p.345–54. Directory of contributors, v.6, p.355–72. Index, v.6, p.373–579. "Common abbreviations used in this work," at front of each vol.

E47 The New Century Italian Renaissance encyclopedia. Ed. by Catherine B. Avery. Ed. consultants, Marvin B. Becker [and] Ludovico Borgo. N.Y., Appleton-Century-Crofts [1972]. xiii, 978p. il., map.

Primary coverage on figures of historical, cultural, or religious importance from the late 13th century to around the death of Michelangelo (1564). Entries average 200 words, but 1,000 or more are devoted to the most important names. Entries also for significant families, famous literary works, and art/architectural terms. Coverage included for many important figures from outside Italy. No bibliography.

E48 Rachum, Ilan. The Renaissance: an illustrated encyclopedia. N.Y., Mayflower, 1979. 611p. il. (part col.)

Brief entries on the history, culture, and major figures of the Renaissance throughout Europe. Murky illustrations.

Bibliographic citations at ends of most entries. Maps, p.[590]–97. Tables, p.[598]–601. Select bibliography, p.[602]–05. Index, p.[606]–11.

NEOCLASSICAL—MODERN

E49 L'Art du XIXe siècle: dictionnaire de peinture et de sculpture. Sous la dir. de Jean-Philippe Breuille. Paris, Larousse, 1993. 777p. col. il.

Unsigned entries, averaging about 300 words, on 19th-century European and American artists and other art world figures—critics, collectors, dealers, etc.—along with selective coverage of groups, movements, iconographical themes, and French art journals.

Collaborateurs, p.6–8. Abréviations, p.10. Bibliographie sélective, p.769–77.

E50 L'Art du XXe siècle: dictionnaire de peinture et de sculpture. Sous la dir. de Jean-Philippe Breuille. Paris, Larousse, 1991. 895p. il. (part col.)

Unsigned entries, averaging about 300 words, on 20th-century European and American artists, groups, and movements. No bibliographies.

Collaborateurs, p.10–11. Abréviations, p.13.

E51 Atkins, Robert. Artspeak: a guide to contemporary ideas, movements, and buzzwords, 1945 to the present. 2d ed. N.Y., Abbeville, 1997. 208p. il. (part col.)

1st ed. 1990.

Well-written entries averaging approximately 400 words define movements, groups, concepts, media, and techniques. No bibliographies.

Artchart [chronology of movements], p.8. Timeline, p.9–36. Index, p.187–207.

E52 ______. Artspoke: a guide to modern ideas, movements, and buzzwords, 1848–1944. N.Y., Abbeville, 1993. 224p. il. (part col.)

Movements, media, groups, concepts, and events covered in entries averaging about 400 words. No bibliographies.

Artchart [chronology of movements], p.8. Timeline, p.9–40. Index, p.216–23.

E53 Bosseur, Jean-Yves. Vocabulaire des arts plastiques de XXe siècle. Paris, Minerve, 1998. 236p. il.

Ruminative entries in French on 65 key concepts relating to 20th-century art—e.g., "Anti-art," "Espace," "Gesamtkunstwerk," "Multiples."

Bibliographie, p.221–[24]. Index des termes, p.225–[27]. Index des mouvements, p.229–[30]. Index des noms, p.231–[37].

E54 Busse, Joachim. Internationales Handbuch aller Maler und Bildhauer des 19. Jahrhunderts. Wiesbaden, Busse, 1977. 72, 1403p. col. il., plates. (Busse-Verzeichnis, 19)

Gargantuan biographical index gives bare-bones data, including dates, place of birth and death, artistic occupation, and citations to biographical and auction-price reference works, on more than 80,000 artists who were alive at some point between 1806 and 1880.

Literatur-Hinweise, p.1387. Abkürzungs-Verzeichnis, p.1389–98.

E55 Chilvers, Ian. A dictionary of twentieth-century art. N.Y., Oxford Univ. Pr., 1998. xiv, 670p.

Provides 1,700 entries on artists and other art world personalities, movements, media, techniques, organizations, and serial exhibitions and publications. Begun as a project to revise and abridge The Oxford companion to twentieth-century art (GLAH 2:E68), it evolved into a different and much larger work than was originally planned. No index or bibliographies. Occasionally, sources are quoted and cited in the entries.

Abbreviations, p.[xv].

E56 Contemporary artists. Ed., Joann Cerrito. Advisers, Jean-Christophe Ammann . . . [et al.] 4th ed. Detroit, St. James Pr., 1996. xx, 1340p. il. (Contemporary arts series)

See GLAH 1:E48 for 1st ed. 2d ed., N.Y., St. Martin's Pr., 1983. 3d ed., Chicago, St. James Pr., 1989.

Flagship publication of a series that contains many useful biographical dictionaries of artists. Not a cumulative work since a significant number of artists are deleted from each ed. and new ones added. Internal organization has remained very similar from ed. to ed. "Each entry includes biographical data, a comprehensive list of individual exhibitions, a selection of up to ten important group exhibitions, a list of public collections that include works by the artist, and primary and secondary bibliographies. In this edition, entries also include a list of permanent public installations, such as murals, outdoor sculptures, and environmental works. Many artists have contributed a statement about their work or about art in general, as well as a photograph of a representative work. Finally, critical essays have been contributed by specialists in the field."—*Ed. note.*

Advisers/contributors, p.ix–x. List of entrants, p.xiii–xx. Nationality index, p.[1321]–30. Notes on advisers and contributors, p.[1331]–40.

E57 Contemporary women artists. Eds., Laurie Collier Hillstrom, Kevin Hillstrom. Detroit, St. James Pr., 1999. xx, 760p. il.

Entries, which resemble those in other St. James biographical dictionaries of artists, e.g., Contemporary artists (GLAH 2:E56), provide, in addition to basic biographical data, exhibition history, works in collections, bibliographical references, a sampling of critical reception, and, often, a comment by the artist. "Contemporary women artists provides biographical and career information on more than 350 of the world's most prominent and influential contemporary (20th century) women artists. [It] covers figures who have worked, or are currently working, in the visual arts—including painting, sculpture, drawing, printmaking, collage, photography, ceramics, mixed media, electronic media, performance art, video, design, and graphic arts."—*Ed. note.*

Advisers/contributors, p.xiii–xiv. List of entrants, p.xvii–xx. Bibliography, p.[733]–36. Nationality index, p.[737]–42. Medium index, p.[743]–50. Notes on advisers and contributors, p.[751]–60.

E58 Delarge, Jean-Pierre. Dictionnaire des arts plastiques modernes et contemporains. Paris, Gründ, 2001. 1367p.

Some entries provide rather perfunctory coverage of groups, movements, techniques, and media, but most of this work is devoted to highly opinionated biographical entries on more than 10,000 20th-century artists of all kinds and other art-world figures. Coverage is worldwide but focuses on Western and Southern Europe. Selective list of exhibitions, locations of key works, and brief, significant quotes by or about the artist at the end of many entries.

Principales abréviations utilisées, p.6.

E59 Dictionnaire de l'art moderne et contemporain. Sous la dir. de Gérard Durozoi. Paris, Hazan, 1992. xx, 676p. il. (part col.)

Korean trans., Pusan, Arutte, 1994. Spanish trans., Madrid, Akal, 1997.

Includes 20th-century artists, groups, movements, critics, and influential journals and other key publications. Covers selected Asian artists as well as those of Europe and the Americas. Signed entries average about 200 words in length. Effective positioning of small illustrations, many in color.

Bibliographies at ends of most entries. Liste des collaborateurs, p.xi–xiii.

E60 Dictionary of international contemporary artists: about 400 of the most internationally recognized contemporary artists. [Ed., Giancarlo Politi. Ed. assist., Rachele Ferrario, Paola Gaggiotti.] [Milan?], Flash Art Books, [1995]. 356p. il.

Brief but informative entries cover mostly European and American artists. For each, presents chronology of one-person and group exhibitions and useful bibliography.

E61 Groupes, mouvements, tendances de l'art contemporain depuis 1945. [Sous la dir. de Mathilde Ferrer. Avec Marie-Hélène Colas-Adler]. 2. éd. rev. et augm. Paris, École nationale supérieure des beaux-arts, 1990. 183p.

1st ed. 1989.

Signed entries of 250 to 750 words explain about 70 of the leading movements, groups, and concepts of the late 1940s through 1980s.

Bibliographies at ends of entries current through the 1980s. Liste des auteurs, p.5. Lexique, p.159–73. Index, p.175–83. Table, p.[185]–[86].

E62 The Grove dictionary of art. From expressionism to post-modernism: styles and movements in 20th-century Western art. Ed. by Jane Turner. N.Y., St. Martin's, 2000. xii, 430p. il. (part col.), plates, facsims.

British ed., London, Macmillan Reference, 2000.

Focused selection of entries from the Dictionary of art (GLAH 2:E4).

List of contributors, p.viii–ix. General abbreviations, p.x–xi. Appendix A, List of locations, p.[420]–27. Appendix B, List of periodical titles, p.[428]–30.

E63 Guide to exhibited artists. Santa Barbara, Clio Press, 1985. 5v.

Earlier versions, Dictionary of contemporary artists, 1981; International directory of exhibiting artists, 1982–83.

Recent brief biographical and exhibition data on artists from the files of Clio Press, publisher of ARTbibliographies Modern (GLAH 2:A148). "The information has been obtained from two main sources, exhibition catalogues or announcements and the artists themselves."—*Introd.*

Contents: (1) European painters; (2) North American painters; (3) Printmakers; (4) Sculptors; (5) Craftsmen.

Museum and gallery index at end of each vol.

E64 Le Thorel-Daviot, Pascale. Petit dictionnaire des artistes contemporains. Paris, Bordas, 1996. 287p. col. il.

Brief entries on European, American, and a few Asian artists provide basic biographical information, a paragraph summarizing the artist's work, a brief comment by the artist, and bibliographical references. A small color illustration of one work by each artist is provided.

Index commenté des mouvements, p.275–83. Glossaire, p.284–85. Bibliographie, p.286–87.

E65 Marks, Claude. World artists, 1950–1980: an H.W. Wilson biographical dictionary. N.Y., Wilson, 1984. xvi, 912p. ports.

Well-written entries of 1,000 words or more on 312 artists of Europe and the Americas who were working at some point between 1950 and 1980. At the end of each entry are a selective list of exhibitions, works in collections, and a bibliography. Small portrait photographs of many of the artists.

Artists included, p.vii–x. Key to pronunciation; key to abbreviations, p.xvi.

E66 ______. World artists 1980–1990: an H.W. Wilson biographical dictionary. N.Y., Wilson, 1991. xii, 413p. il.

Well-written 2,000-word entries on more than 100 European and American artists active in the 1980s. At the end of each entry are a selective list of exhibitions, works in collections, and a bibliography. Small portrait photographs of many of the artists.

Artists included, p.vii–viii. Key to pronunciation; key to abbreviations, p.xii.

E67 North American women artists of the twentieth century: a biographical dictionary. Ed. by Jules Heller and Nancy G. Heller. N.Y., Garland, 1995. xxii, 612p. il. (Garland reference library of the humanities, v.1219)

Biographical entries averaging about 300 words on some 1,500 women artists (including photographers) of Canada, Mexico, and the U.S. born before 1960. More than 100 scholarly contributors. Entries contain selective accounts of artists' exhibitions and collections holding their work.

"As researchers, we both have been frustrated many times by being unable to locate basic information about many of the artists included in this volume—especially those working outside the United States. This leads directly to another reason for producing this particular kind of reference book—to try and create a better understanding between and among the artists and art audiences in these three countries."—*Introd.*

Bibliography at end of each entry. Contributors, p.[xiii]–xvii. Index, p.[601]–12.

E68 The Oxford companion to twentieth-century art. Ed. by Harold Osborne. N.Y., Oxford Univ. Pr., 1981. x, 656p. il. (part col.), plates. (Repr. with corrections, 1990).

Spanish trans., Madrid, Alianza, 1990.

Covers artists, movements, terms, and the development of modern art in countries and regions. Entries for important movements or countries can be several pages in length. "It is not a dictionary or an encyclopedia, but is intended as a handbook and a guide for students and others who wish to find their way intelligently through the exuberant jungle of contemporary art. Special attention has been given to the fluctuations of artistic ideas and to . . . changing aesthetic presuppositions."—*Pref.*

Selective bibliography, p.[601]–48.

E69 St. James guide to Black artists. Ed., Thomas Riggs. Detroit, St. James Pr., 1997. xxiv, 625p. il.

Entries, which resemble those in other St. James biographical dictionaries of artists, e.g., Contemporary artists (GLAH 2:E56), provide, in addition to basic biographical data, exhibition history, works in collections, bibliographical references, a sampling of critical reception, and, often, a comment by the artist. Includes nearly 400 painters, sculptors, printmakers, photographers, ceramicists, and textile workers. Published in assoc. with the Schomburg Center for Research in Black Culture. "[This] is a unique compendium of information on artists of African descent. Though focused on the twentieth century, selected nineteenth-century artists are also included. About three-fourths of the entrants are African Americans, and the remainder are from Africa, the Caribbean, and other parts of the diaspora."—*Pref.*

Advisers, p.xv. Contributors, p.xvii. List of entrants, p.xxi–xxiv. A selected bibliography on black artists, p.[593]–97. Nationality index, p.[599]–604. Medium index, p.[605]–13. Index to illustrations, p.[615]–18. Notes on advisers and contributors, p.[619]–25.

E70 Verzeichnis der bildenden Künstler von 1880 bis heute: ein biographisch-bibliographisches Nachschlagewerk zur Kunst der Gegenwart. [Hrsg. und bearb. von] Roger M. Gorenflo. Darmstadt, Brün, 1988. 3v. (989p.)

Index that provides access to biographical data on some 32,000 modern artists worldwide from more than 600 monographs, exhibition catalogs, and biographical dictionaries.

Bibliographischer Schlüssel und bibliographische Hilfsmittel, v.3, p.961–89. "Abkürzungen" and "Abkürzungen der Länder" at front of each vol.

E71 Walker, John Albert. Glossary of art, architecture and design since 1945. Foreword by Clive Phillpot. 3d ed., rev., enl., and illustrated. Boston, Hall, 1992. 1v. (unpaged) il.

See GLAH 1:E36 for 1st ed.; 2d ed., Hamden, Conn., Linnet; London, Bingley, 1977. British ed., London, Library Association, 1992.

An indispensable vade mecum for contemporary art. Brief but substantive, well-written entries, most with an appended multi-item bibliography of books, exhibition catalogs, and articles, current to the early 1990s. Has an excellent, comprehensive index to names and subjects. "For this new edition the vast majority of existing entries have been revised and updated. Some lesser-used and out-of-date terms have been deleted and several of the older ones have been shortened. In most cases, however, expansion has been necessary in respect of both entries and bibliographies in order to take account of artistic developments and publications since 1977. A number of new entries have been added to fill gaps for the period 1945 to 1977 and more than 150 brand-new entries have been included to take account of terms that have appeared in the literature of art and design since the last edition. . . . Unlike previous editions this one is illustrated."—*Introd.*

Bibliography, p.[341]–[49]. Index, p.[351]–[99].

E72 Women artists of color: a bio-critical sourcebook to 20th century artists in the Americas. Ed. by Phoebe Farris. Westport, Conn., Greenwood, 1999. xx, 496p. il.

Approximately 100 artist entries are arranged alphabetically within four ethnic groupings. Entries include basic biographical data, selective lists of exhibitions in which the artist's work has appeared, collections that hold her work, publications by and about her, a statement by the artist, and a biographical essay of approximately 1,000 words, by Farris or one of her contributors, surveying the artist's career.

"This book attempts to provide a representative sample of older and/or deceased artists who helped pave the way for future generations; mature, midcareer mainstream artists with national/international reputations; and younger, emerging artists. The media presented range from traditional painting and sculpture to newer forms such as video, conceptual, and performance art."—*Introd.*

Contents: (1) Native American women artists; (2) Latin American women artists; (3) African American women artists; (4) Asian Pacific American women artists.

Afterword: Parts of a puzzle, by Moira Roth, p.[461]–69. Cultural resources [institutions, groups, journals, etc.], p.[471]–73. Index, p.[475]–93. About the editor and contributors, p.[495]–96.

GENERAL DICTIONARIES OF ARTISTS

E73 Allgemeines Künstlerlexikon bio-bibliographischer Index A–Z = The artists of the world: bio-bibliographical index A–Z. München, Saur, 1999–2000. 10v.

Biographical index intended by Saur to supply some interim coverage of artists while its Allgemeines Künstlerlexikon (AKL; see GLAH 2:E74), an updating of Thieme-Becker and Vollmer (GLAH 1:E50, GLAH 1:E52), appears alphabetically at the rate of several vols. per year. Entries include name(s), artistic occupation(s), date and place of birth and death if known, country code(s) and bibliographical references. "Names and biographical information from over 200 important national and international dictionaries of artists . . . were compiled for the Index. The names and information thus collected were added to the information already contained in full on our database created from the Thieme-Becker and Vollmer biographical dictionaries and the volumes of the AKL so far published. . . . Important bio-bibliographical information available to the editors was also included."—*Pref.*

Each vol. has at front, "Sources," "Professions" [i.e., artistic occupations], and "Countries."

E74 Allgemeines Künstlerlexikon: die bildenden Künstler aller Zeiten und Völker. [Begründ. und Mithrsg. von Günter Meissner.] München, Saur, 1992– . (30)v. + indexes: Bd. 1–10; Bd. 11–20.

Greatly augmented revision and consolidation of Thieme-Becker (T-B) and Vollmer (V), (GLAH 1:E50, E52), incorporating much new information—the result of almost 100 years of additional research—on every significant artist and architect, and entries for figures not covered at all in the earlier sets. New material will make the AKL approximately three times longer than the T-B-V combination by the time it is completed. Entries are signed and written in most cases by established authorities with a prior record of publication on their subjects. Individual entries are more efficiently organized than in T-B and V, with special symbols marking the location in each entry of collections holding the artist's important works (or a chronological list of buildings in the case of an architect), exhibition history, and up-to-date bibliography. Like the combination of T-B and V, the AKL covers all countries, and all periods in which there are artists known by name or oeuvre.

Alphabetization scheme seems more conventional and user-friendly than in T-B and V. "Abkürzungsverzeichnis" sections in each vol. make deciphering abbreviations much easier than in the earlier sets. Names of Asian artists no longer given in Asian characters in addition to transliterated form. Two-vol. indexes appear at 10-vol. intervals: first index vol. arranges the artists in the previous 10 vols. by country, artistic activity (e.g., "Zeichner"), and birth date. Second index vol. reshuffles them by artistic activity, country, and birth date.

Earlier, failed attempt by Seemann, Leipzig (1983–90, 3v.), to establish this project was subsumed by the AKL.

Available as a CD-ROM containing additional biographical entries.

"Internationaler Lexikonbeirat," "Autorenverzeichnis," "Benutzungshinweise," and "Abkürzungsverzeichnis," containing both general and bibliographical abbreviations, at front of most vols.

E75 Artist biographies master index. Barbara McNeil, ed. Detroit, Gale, 1986. xviii, 700p. (Gale biographical index series, no. 9)

"A consolidated index to more than 275,000 biographical sketches of artists living and dead, as they appear in a selection of the principal current and retrospective biographical dictionaries devoted to the fine and applied arts, including painters, sculptors, illustrators, designers, graphic artists, craftsmen, architects, and photographers."—*T.p. note.*

Bibliographic key to source codes [i.e., list of indexed biographical dictionaries], p.xi–xviii.

E76 Bénézit, Emmanuel. Dictionnaire critique et documentaire des peintres, sculpteurs, dessinateurs et graveurs de tous les temps et de tous les pays par un groupe d'écrivains spécialistes français et étrangers. Nouvelle éd., entièrement ref. Sous la dir. de Jacques Busse. Paris, Gründ, 1999. 14v.

See GLAH 1:E37 for original annotation and previous eds.

Second in inclusiveness only to the combination of the much older Thieme-Becker and Vollmer (GLAH 1:E50, GLAH 1:E52). Many more long, signed entries than in the previous ed. For many artists, the sections of bibliographical citations, museum collection information, and auction prices fetched by their work seem greatly expanded. Facsimiles of artists' signatures occasionally illustrated. No coverage of architects, unless they also worked in other media.

Evolution du pouvoir d'achat du franc depuis 1901, v.1, p.8–9. Cours à Paris du dollar américain (USD) et de la livre sterling (GBP) depuis 1901, v.1, p.10–11. Principales abréviations utilisées, v.1, p.12. Bibliographie générale, v.14, p.955–58.

E77 Dictionary of women artists. Ed., Delia Gaze. Picture eds., Maja Mihajlovic, Leanda Shrimpton. Chicago, Fitzroy Dearborn, 1997. 2v. (xlviii, 1512p.) il.

Covers 600 painters, sculptors, printmakers, photographers, and decorative/applied artists, as well as artists working in newer forms of expression. Signed entries by more than 300 scholarly contributors. Entries include basic biographical information; chronological list of principal individual and group exhibitions, selected writings of the artist, bibliography of citations about the artist, and an essay of 1,000 words or more by a specialist on the artist. "The book is the fruit of the extensive scholarly interest in the subject of women artists that has been manifested since the 1970s, as part of a wider reexamination of women's history. While there are already very useful works of reference in the field, no previously published dictionary has covered such a wide-ranging historical and geographical span with such detailed entries. . . . For practical reasons, certain firm parameters were established at the outset: the project would be concerned only with the Western tradition in art, and it would exclude women born after 1945; the emphasis would be historical rather than contemporary, and no attempt would be made to cover architecture, interior or garden design, or fashion."—*Ed. note*.

Contents: (1) Introductory surveys: Women as artists in the Middle Ages, by Annemarie Weyl Carr; Convents, by Marilyn Dunn; Guilds and the open market, by Lynn F. Jacobs and Els Kloek; Court artists, by Valerie Mainz; Academies of art, by Wendy Wassyng Roworth . . . [et al.]; Copyists, by Lisa Heer; Printmakers, by David Alexander; Amateur artists, by Katalijne van der Stighelen and Lisa Heer; Training and professionalism, 19th and 20th centuries, by Pamela Gerish Nunn, et al.; Modernism and women artists, by Bridget Elliott; Feminism and women artists, by Mara D. Witzling; Artists, A–I; (2) Artists, J–Z.

Advisers, v.1, p.xi. Contributors, v.1, p.xi–xiv. General bibliography, v.1, p.xxxi–xlviii. Notes on advisers and contributors, v.2, p.[1487]–1508. "Alphabetical list of artists" and "Chronological list of artists" at front of each vol.

E78 Dunford, Penny. A biographical dictionary of women artists in Europe and America since 1850. Philadelphia, Univ. of Pennsylvania Pr., 1989. xxiv, 340p. il. (part col.)

Covers approximately 800 artists in entries that average about 400 words. Selective lists, at the end of most entries, of the artist's publications, locations of her key works, and citations of writings about her. No index, but there are helpful cross references.

"Because of the impossibility of an exhaustive dictionary, photographers and film/video makers have been excluded. Although there are examples of video artists, they have been principally involved in other media, usually performance art. The number of textile artists is also limited, partly because of the problem of obtaining information. As a result there is a bias towards traditional Fine Art media. While the majority of artists in the dictionary are painters or sculptors, a much wider range of media is represented for the modern period."—*Introd.*

Abbreviations, p.[xv]–xvii. Bibliography, p.[335]–40.

E79 Edelstein, Debra. Pronunciation dictionary of artists' names, Art Institute of Chicago. Rev. and ed. by Debra Edelstein. 3d rev. ed. Boston, Little, Brown, 1993. 1v. (unpaged).

See GLAH 1:E43 for previous eds.

Now includes photographers and printmakers in addition to the original categories: painters, sculptors, draftsmen. "Of the original 1500 artists, approximately half appear in this edition; those deleted either are no longer considered art historically significant or were contemporary artists fashionable in 1935 but unknown today. Added to the volume are approximately 3500 new names reflecting changing art historical assessments, a broader geographical distribution, and a recognition that names native English speakers intuitively pronounce may present difficulties to speakers of other languages."—*Pref.*

E80 Havlice, Patricia Pate. Index to artistic biography. Metuchen, N.J., Scarecrow Pr., 1973. 2v.

See GLAH 1:E42 for original annotation.

"Covers 70 additional titles containing approximately 44,000 names. . . . The format of this volume is identical to the original work."—*Pref.*

———. 1st supplement, 1981.

A second supplement has been announced for 2002.

E81 Künstler: kritisches Lexikon der Gegenwartskunst. [Hrsg. Lothar Romain, Detlef Bluemler]. München, WB Verlag, 1988– . (13)v. (loose-leaf) il. (part col.), ports.

Entries take form of ca. 15p. fascicle devoted to a significant contemporary artist and containing biographical facts; exhibition history; bibliography; a substantive, signed critical assessment of the artist's work; and many illustrations. Each loose-leaf vol. contains several fascicles. Every third vol. a new alphabetical sequence is begun. Coverage is international but Germanic artists predominate.

E82 Mallett, Daniel Trowbridge. Mallett's Index of artists: international-biographical, including painters, sculptors, illustrators, engravers and etchers of the past and the present. [Reprint.] N.Y., Peter Smith, [1999?] xxxiv, 493p.

See GLAH 1:E44 for original annotation.

E83 Petteys, Chris. Dictionary of women artists: an international dictionary of women artists born before 1900. With the assist. of Hazel Gustow . . . [et al.] Boston, Hall, 1985. xviii, 851p. port.

Brief entries provide basic biographical data on more than 21,000 women painters, sculptors, printmakers, and illustrators. "Photographers, architects, craftsworkers, and designers have all been omitted unless their skills were adjunct to painting, sculpture, printmaking, or illustration."—*Pref.* Entries include data about the artist's schooling, exhibition information, and bibliographical references.

Contributors, p.[xv]–xvi. Abbreviations, p.[xvii]–xviii. Bibliography, p.[781]–851.

E84 Thieme-Becker/Vollmer Gesamtregister: Register zum Allgemeinen Lexikon der bildenden Künstler von der Antike bis zur Gegenwart und zum Allgemeinen Lexikon der bildenden Künstler des XX. Jahrhunderts. [Datenverarb., Andreas Klimt, Mathias Wündisch]. München, Saur; Leipzig, Seemann, 1996–97. 6v.

Index to artists and architects included in the biographical dictionaries by Thieme-Becker (GLAH 1:E50) and Vollmer (GLAH 1:E52). The first sequence of 3 vols. arranges the artists by country, artistic activity, and birth date. The second sequence of 3 vols. reshuffles them by artistic activity, country, and birth date.

Contents: (1) Länder: Bd.1. Ägypten-Frankreich; Bd.2. Frankreich-Kanada; Bd.3. Kenia-Vietnam; (2) Künstlerische Berufe: Bd.1. Altarkünstler-Karikaturist; Bd.2. Kartenmacher-Maler; Bd.3. Maler-Zeichner.

E85 Union list of artist names. James M. Bower, project manager. Murtha Baca, senior ed. N.Y., Hall, 1994. 4v. il.

Project of the Getty Art History Information Program (now defunct) to record variant versions of artists' names. Volumes contain about 200,000 names representing approximately 100,000 individual artists and architects. Entries supply artist's preferred name, variant names, sources of information about the artist from among Getty contributor projects, and often some bibliography. "The names of artists and architects in the ULAN have been culled from nine Getty projects spanning a broad spectrum of art documentation types, including abstracting and indexing services, research photographic archives, scholarly databases that document primary source materials, and object collections from archives and museums."—*Foreword.*

Also available in an internet version managed by the Getty Vocabulary Program.

History of the project, v.1, p.3–10. Guide to the use of the ULAN, v.1, p.11–20. Selected ULAN bibliography, v.1, p.23–38.

E86 Weinberg, Robert E. A biographical dictionary of science fiction and fantasy artists. N.Y., Greenwood, 1988. xvi, 346p.

In addition to biographical information, entries include lists of books and magazine spreads illustrated, with dates of publication. Covers more than 250 artists.

How to use this book, p.[xi]–xii. Abbreviations, p.[xiii]–xvi. Science fiction art: a historical overview, p.[1]–31. Science fiction art: what still exists, p.[303]–313. Art awards, p.[315]–17. Bibliography, p.[319]–21. Index of biographical entries, p.[323]–27. Index, p.[329]–46.

ARTISTS' MARKS

E87 Agnellini, Maurizio. Firma d'artista: 2600 firme di pittori dell'Ottocento italiano. Milano, Fenice 2000, 1995. 177p. il. (Le guide della Fenice)

Reproduces signatures of Italian painters and sculptors born in the 19th century.

E88 Castagno, John. American artists: signatures and monograms, 1800–1989. Metuchen, N.J., Scarecrow, 1990. xv, 826p. il.

Reproduces the signatures and monograms of more than 5,000 artists, including Canadians and Latin Americans.

List of abbreviations and sources, p.xi–xv. Alternate name cross-references, p.[767]–73. Indecipherable signatures and symbols, p.[775]–83. Monograms arranged by initials, p.[785]–826.

E89 ______. Latin American artists' signatures and monograms: colonial era to 1996. Lanham, Md., Scarecrow, 1997. xiii, 673p. il.

Presents signatures and monograms of 1,100 artists, along with considerable biographical data.

List of abbreviations and sources, p.13–16. Monograms/initials, p.653–59. Illegible signatures, p.661–67. Symbols, p.669. Alternate name cross-references, p.671–73.

E90 ______. Old Masters: signatures and monograms, 1400–born 1800. Lanham, Md., Scarecrow, 1996. 379p. il.

"Art historians and collectors will find this current vol. of artists' signatures of considerable value in researching the artworks of the Old Masters. Included are signature examples for these artists dating from the 14th century and born no later than 1800. This volume is presently the only such book focusing exclusively on signature examples taken not only from oil paintings but also watercolors, pastels, drawings, prints, and other works."—*Introd.*

List of abbreviations and sources, p.[xi]–[xiii]. Alternate name cross-references, p.[351]–59. Supplemental section with additional initial and monogram information, p.[361]–74. Supplemental section with additional alternate signature names information, p.[375]–79.

E91 Falk, Peter H. Dictionary of signatures and monograms of American artists: from the colonial period to the mid 20th century. Madison, Conn., Sound View (Distr. by Dealer's Choice, Land O'Lakes, Fla., 1988). 556p. il.

Reproduces signatures and monograms of about 4,500 artists.

Monograms, a visual index, p.467–541. Circular shapes, p.543–48. Pictorial marks and odd shapes, p.549–52. Undecipherable monograms, p.553–56.

E92 Goldstein, Franz. Monogrammlexikon 1: Internationales Verzeichnis der Monogramme bildender Künstler seit 1850 = Dictionary of monograms 1: international list of monograms in the visual arts since 1850. Rev. and expanded by Ruth Kähler and Hermann Kähler. 2. Aufl. N.Y., De Gruyter, 1999. xv, 1136p. il.

See GLAH 1:E56 for 1st ed.

Revision of a standard reference work. Supplies facsimiles of the monograms of approximately 14,000 painters, printmakers, illustrators, sculptors, and other artists active after 1850. Artist entries provide useful references to biographical dictionaries. "The most significant change introduced in this edition is that the monogram illustrations precede the text section. A numeration system links the two. The illustrations can now be offered in better quality. . . . Revision has concentrated on amending the biographical data, which have been supplemented where possible. In some cases new monogram variants have been added. Despite the modified outward appearance of this edition, the distinctiveness and achievement of the Goldstein work has been preserved."—*Foreword.*

Sources, p.[xiii]–xv. Index, p.[675]–[877]. Biographical index, p.[879]–1136.

E93 Haslam, Malcolm. Marks and monograms: the decorative arts, 1880–1960. Rev. and enl. ed. London, Collins and Brown, 1995. 448p. il.

1st ed., Marks and monograms of the modern movement 1875–1930: a guide to the marks of artists, designers, retailers, and manufacturers from the period of the Aesthetic Movement to Art Deco and Style Moderne, Guildford [Eng.], Lutterworth, 1977.

Reproduces the marks, monograms, and signatures of artists, workshops, and manufacturers in the applied arts: ceramics, glass, metalwork, jewelry, graphics, furniture, and textiles.

Index, p.411–48.

E94 Jackson, Radway. The visual index of artists' signatures and monograms. Introd. by Andrew Festing. [New and rev. ed.] London, Cromwell, 1991. 239p., il.

1st ed., The shorter dictionary of artists' signatures, London, Foulsham, 1980; U.S. ed., The concise dictionary of artists' signatures, N.Y., Alpine, 1981.

Covers more than 7,000 painters, printmakers, and sculptors from the 15th through late 20th century.

Visual index [particularly obscure monograms and signatures], p.[205]–38. Pictorial marks, p.239.

E95 Monogrammlexikon 2: internationales Verzeichnis der Monogramme bildender Künstler des 19. und 20. Jahrhunderts = Dictionary of monograms 2: international list of monograms in the visual arts of the 19th and 20th centuries. Ed. by Paul Pfisterer. N.Y., De Gruyter, 1995. xviii, 1067p. il.

Provides facsimiles of the monograms of about 13,000 painters, printmakers, illustrators, sculptors, and other artists active after 1800. Intended as a continuation of Goldstein (GLAH 2:E92), it constitutes a valuable complement to that work.

Sources, p.xviii. Key to the classification of scripts used, p.xix–xx. Number index, p.[663]–860. Monogrammist index, p.[861]–1067.

E96 Nahum, Peter. Monograms of Victorian and Edwardian artists. [s.l.], Victoria Square, 1976. 325, [1]p. il.

"This book is designed as a rapid and practical guide to the identification of over 4000 monograms of artists, illustrators, craftsmen and architects working and exhibiting in Great Britain between 1830 and 1930."—*Foreword.*

Some of this material was revised and republished in the author's Victorian painters' monograms . . ., London, Foulsham, 1977.

How to analyse a monogram, p.[vii]. [Artist index], p.293–325. Selected bibliography, p.[326].

E97 Pfisterer, Paul. Signaturenlexikon = Dictionary of signatures. Unter Mitarb. von Claire Pfisterer. N.Y., de Gruyter, 1999. xvi, 993p. il.

"The book is intended to be a collection of nineteenth and especially twentieth century signatures from Europe and the United States."—*Foreword.*

Reproduces 16,103 artists' signatures.

Quellenverzeichnis, p.[xi]–xiii. Arbeitstechniken, p.[xiv]. Hilfstabelle, p.[xv]–xvi. Biographischer Index, p.[745]–993.

E98 Prein, Wolfgang. Handbuch der Monogramme in der europäischen Graphik vom 15. bis zum 18. Jahrhundert = Manual of monograms in European graphic arts from the 15th to the 18th centuries. München, Deutscher Kunstverlag, [1989–91]. 2v. il.

Compiled partly with the aim of updating Nagler's coverage (GLAH 1:E58) of the monograms of printmakers and draftsmen. Reproduces the monograms of nearly 2,500 artists.

Künstlerverzeichnis für Band I und II, v.2, p.281–307. "Verzeichnis der abgekürzt zitierten Literatur" at front of each vol.

E99 Signatures et monogrammes d'artistes des XIXe et XXe siècles. 2e ed. Paris, Van Wilder, 1999. xiv, 484p. il. (part col.)

1st ed. 1998.

Presents more than 8,500 signatures and 1,600 monograms of artists from Europe and the Americas. Most of the data came from art auction catalogs of the 1990s; some were obtained directly from artists.

Monogrammes, p.[407]–84.

WESTERN COUNTRIES

Australia

E100 The dictionary of Australian artists: painters, sketchers, photographers and engravers to 1870. Ed. by Joan Kerr. N.Y., Oxford Univ. Pr., 1992. xxii, 889p. il.

"A grand panorama of Australian cultural life during the first hundred years of European settlement unfolds in this volume. . . . We have covered all six colonies: country towns as well as cities, amateurs as well as professionals, unpretentious residents as well as distinguished visitors. . . . [The] sole criterion for inclusion was that a person must have set foot on Australian soil before 1870 and made a painting, sketch, photograph or pictorial print."—*Introd.* Entries average approximately 300 words, but important figures can get more than 1,000. Longer entries signed; many end with selective lists of the artist's works, collections in which his or her art is represented, and bibliographical citations. More than 200 contributors. Many clear black-and-white illustrations.

Bibliographical note, p.xiii. Contributors, p.xiv–xviii. Major exhibitions to 1870, p.xix–xx. Abbreviations, p.xxi. Institutions, p.xxii.

E101 McCulloch, Alan. The encyclopedia of Australian art. [3d ed.] Rev. and updated by Susan McCulloch. Honolulu, Univ. of Hawaii Pr., 1994. 879p. il. (part col.)

1st ed., Hawthorn, Aus., Hutchinson, 1968; 2d ed., 1984; 3d ed., also St. Leonard's, Aus., Allen and Unwin, 1994; London, Herbert, 1994.

Some of the more than 5,000 entries treat groups, movements, media, and institutions in Australian art, but most provide brief biographies of painters, illustrators, printmakers, sculptors, decorative artists, and photographers from the 18th through 20th century. Most biographical entries supply information about schooling, exhibitions, awards, collections in which the artist's work is represented, and bibliographical citations. Introduction is a brief history of Australian art. Useful illustrations.

"Artists have been chosen for inclusion if their work is represented by purchase in a national, state, or regional gallery or they have won a major prize."—*Pref.*

Abbreviations, p.14–15. Appendix 1, Collections: private and corporate, p.783–86. Appendix 2, Exhibitions, p.787–95. Appendix 3, Festivals, p.796–97. Appendix 4, Funding, p.798. Appendix 5, Galleries, public and private, p.799–834. Appendix 6, Magazines, journals and newsletters, p.835–41. Appendix 7, Prizes, awards and scholarships, p.842–63. Appendix 8, Schools and universities, p.864–73. Appendix 9, Trusts and foundations, p.874–75.

Canada

E102 Contemporary Canadian artists. Toronto, Gale Canada, 1997. iii, 627p. il.

Well-organized, multi-page biographical entries include a critical assessment, selective exhibition and collection history, and some bibliography. "There is still much ground work needed to uncover and give voice to the many women artists who were recognized in their own times but are now forgotten, and also to those artists who contributed to art activity in the Maritimes, Prairie and Western provinces. There is an awareness of such exclusions from this list and amends have been made, but students should be aware that this book is only a starting point."—*Introd.*

Subject index [arranged by medium], p.625–27.

E103 Karel, David. Dictionnaire des artistes de langue française en Amérique du Nord: peintres, sculpteurs, dessinateurs, graveurs, photographes, et orfèvres. [Québec], Musée du Québec; Pr. de l'Université Laval, 1992. lxxx, 962p. 80 plates.

Covers French artists who settled in Canada, the United States, or Mexico. Biographical entries of 1,000 words or more for significant figures.

Bibliographical references at ends of entries. Sigles et abréviations, p.[xxix]. Code de références, p.[841]–60. Bibliographie, p.[861]–89. Appendices: Lieu d'activité, lieu d'origine, p.[893]–912. Contexte, p.[913]–15. Typologie des artistes, p.[916]–62.

E104 MacDonald, Colin S. A dictionary of Canadian artists. 5th ed., rev. and exp. Ottawa, Canadian Paperbacks, 1997– . (1)v.

See GLAH 1:E65 for original annotation and 1st and 2d eds.; 3d ed., 1975 (repr., 1977). 4th ed., 1986.

Brief but fluent, well-written entries with very full bibliographies.

Contents: (1) A–F.

Abbreviations, v.1, p.[vii].

E105 McKendry, Blake. A to Z of Canadian art: artists and art terms. Kingston, Ont., McKendry, 1997. vi, 242p.

Brief biographies of Canadian artists and definitions of terms, with special reference to Canadian art. Bibliographical references at ends of most entries.

Bibliography, p.215–42.

France

E106 Ferment, Claude. Dictionnaire des termes de l'art: anglais/français & français/anglais. Paris, La Maison du Dictionnaire, 1994. [14], 490p. il. (part col.), plates.

Provides an equivalent term, with an occasional line or two of explanation rather than a full definition. Many cross-references.

E107 The Grove dictionary of art. From David to Ingres: early 19th-century French artists. Ed. by Jane Turner. N.Y., St. Martin's, 2000. xii, 414p. il. (part col.), plates, ports.

British ed., London, Macmillan Reference, 2000.

Focused selection of entries from the Dictionary of art (GLAH 2:E4).

List of contributors, p.viii–ix. General abbreviations, p.x–xi. Appendix A, List of locations, p.[404]–11. Appendix B, List of periodical titles, p.[412]–14. Appendix C, Lists of standard reference books and series, p.[415].

E108 The Grove dictionary of art. From Monet to Cézanne: late 19th-century French artists. Ed. by Jane Turner. N.Y., St. Martin's, 2000. xii, 434p. il. (part col.), plates, ports.

British ed., London, Macmillan Reference, 2000.

Focused selection of entries from the Dictionary of art (GLAH 2:E4).

List of contributors, p.viii–ix. General abbreviations, p.x–xi. Appendix A, List of locations, p.[426]–34. Appendix B, List of periodical titles, p.[435]. Appendix C, Lists of standard reference books and series, p.[436].

E109 Monneret, Sophie. L'impressionnisme et son époque: dictionnaire international illustré. Paris, Denoël, 1978–1981. 4v. il. (part col.)

Impressionism interpreted broadly. While such artists as Monet, Renoir, and Morisot have the longest entries, there is also considerable coverage of figures like Fattori, Munch, Sargent, Liebermann, and Turner, and such groups as the Macchiaioli and the Nabis. In addition to artists, entries cover other artworld figures (dealers, critics, collectors), groups, and regions associated with artists or groups. Entries on major artists as long as 20,000 words. Helpful illustrations, many half-page and in color. No bibliographical citations at ends of entries.

Histoire et sens de l'impressionnisme, by René Huyghe, v.1, p.7–33. Noms communs [entries on aspects of 19th-century European art], v.3, p.[121]–278. L'impressionnisme à l'étranger [country-by-country survey], v.3, p.[279]–336. Index des oeuvres d'art citées ou décrites et des sujets traités, v.4, p.[9]–129. Index des noms propres, v.4, p.[131]–215. Exemples de signatures d'artistes répertoriés ou cités dans cet ouvrage, v.4, p.[217]–[32]. Index des oeuvres littéraires et musicales, v.4, p.[233]–51. Index des lieux et des pays, v.4, p.253–80. Cartes de France des hauts lieux de l'impressionnisme, v.4, p.[281]–[88]. Index des musées, v.4, p.289–96. Tableaux chronologiques, v.4, p.297–336. Bibliographie, v.4, p.[369]–409.

E110 Néraudau, Jean-Pierre. Dictionnaire d'histoire de l'art. Paris, Presses universitaires de France, 1985. xi, 521p. il.

Brief but substantive entries on French art and architectural terms, with a strong emphasis on the applied arts and architecture. Most entries begin with a sentence or two on the term's etymology. Numbers at the end of some articles refer to items in the bibliography. Small black-and-white illustrations. No artist biographies.

Bibliographie, p.[491]–508. Index des noms propres, p.[509]–521.

Germany and Austria

E111 Apelt, Mary L. English-German dictionary, art history-archaeology = English-deutsches Wörterbuch für Kunstgeschichte und Archäologie. Berlin, Schmidt, 1987. 253p.

Alphabetical list of approximately 7,500 English terms, mainly concerning art and architectural technique, iconography, and archeology, with their German equivalents. "The list of terms which appears here has been compiled from English and German works within the fields, professional journals, exhibition catalogues and art lexicons and dictionaries. Since this dictionary is mainly intended to be a reader's aid, it is not an exhaustive lexicon."—*Pref.*

E112 ———. German-English dictionary: art history, archaeology = Deutsch-Englisches Wörterbuch für Kunstgeschichte u. Archäologie. 2. überarb. u. erg. Aufl. Berlin, Schmidt, 1990. 277p.

1st ed. 1982.

Alphabetical list of more than 8,000 German terms, mainly from the areas of technique, iconography, and archeology, with their English equivalents. "This second, revised edition includes corrections and some 100 additional words."—*Pref.*

E113 Reallexikon zur deutschen Kunstgeschichte. Stuttgart, Metzler, 1937– . (9)v. il., ports., diagrs., facsims., plans.

See GLAH 1:E87 for original annotation.

Issued in fascicles; most recent is 106, 1997, "Fleuronné"-"Flocktapete." "Nachtrag" section at the end of some vols. contains additional entries. Published since v.6 under the auspices of the Zentralinstitut für Kunstgeschichte, Munich.

"Verzeichnis der Abkürzungen" at front of vols.

E114 Wilhelmi, Christoph. Künstlergruppen in Deutschland, Österreich und der Schweiz seit 1900: ein Handbuch. Stuttgart, Hauswedell, 1996. x, 431p. il.

Entries, arranged alphabetically, devote about half a page to the history of each of 242 artists' groups. Each entry contains a list of a group's members, and most end with at least one bibliographic citation. The author's introduction analyzes the causes, functions, goals, and limits of artists' groups or movements, such as Die Brücke and Novembergruppe, with a 47-item bibliography.

Künstlergruppen in chronologischer Abfolge, p.373–[80]. Namenregister der an Gruppen Beteiligten, p.381–431.

Great Britain and Ireland

E115 Bradshaw, Maurice. Royal Society of British Artists, members exhibiting, 1824–1962. Leigh-on-Sea, Lewis, 1973–77. 5v.

See GLAH 1:E98 for original annotation and previous vols.

Contents: (4) 1931–46; (5) 1947–62.

E116 Buckman, David. Dictionary of artists in Britain since 1945. Bristol (Eng.), Art Dictionaries, 1998. xiv, 1344p. il.

Brief entries "cover painters, sculptors, draughtsmen, teachers, [and] video, film, installation, and performance artists born in the United Kingdom. Foreign artists are included if they have a significant presence. Those who are primarily illustrators or craft workers, such as potters, are usually not included."—*Introd.*

Includes more than 10,000 entries.

Abbreviations, p.47–48. Select bibliography, p.1329–44.

E117 Graves, Algernon. The Society of artists of Great Britain, 1760–1791: the Free Society of Artists, 1761–1783; a complete dictionary of contributors and their work from the foundation of the societies to 1791. London, Bell, 1907. viii, 354p., plates. (Repr.: Bath, Kingsmead, 1969)

Presents the artists alphabetically. Under each name gives a chronological list of works by that artist shown at exhibitions of the societies. For each work provides title, an occasional annotation, catalog number, date of the exhibition, and, often, address of the artist.

An account of the Society of Artists of Great Britain . . . , p.[293]–328. An account of the Free Society of Artists . . . , p.[329]–41. Index to the portraits exhibited at both societies, as well as the owners of buildings, parks, etc., p.[345]–50. Index of horses, dogs, and other animals, whose names are given in the dictionary of exhibitors, as well as of the owners of such animals, p.[353]–54.

E118 Johnson, Jane. Works exhibited at the Royal Society of British Artists, 1824–1893 and at The New English Art Club, 1888–1917: an Antique Collectors' Club research project. [Woodbridge, Eng.], Antique Collectors' Club, 1975. 2v.

Lists the artists alphabetically in two sequences, the first for the Royal Society of British Artists, the second for the New English Art Club. Under each name gives a chronological list of works by the artist shown at exhibitions of that particular society. For each work provides title, and the first few lines of an associated quotation, if any; catalog number; date of the exhibition; and address of the artist. The introduction is a brief history of the early years of the Society.

Abbreviations used in this work, v.1, p.[x]; v.2, p.[v]. Appendix: list of artists whose works were loaned for exhibition [at the Royal Society of British Artists] and who were either deceased or nonregular exhibitors, v.2, p.534–39. New English Art Club: list of members 1888–1917w, v.2, p.541–44.

E119 ———, and Greutzner, A. The dictionary of British artists, 1880–1940: an Antique Collectors' Club research project listing 41,000 artists. [Suffolk, Eng.], Antique Collectors' Club, 1976. 567p. (Dictionary of British art, v.5)

Brief entries for 41,000 artists, mostly painters, who exhibited between 1880 and 1940 at one or more of 49 venues (including public museums, artists' societies, and commercial galleries) in the British Isles. Entries give basic biographical data, if known, and tell how many works an artist exhibited at each venue, but not the date of exhibition. Constitutes an attempt to continue and broaden the coverage provided by Graves's A dictionary of artists who have exhibited works in the principal London exhibitions from 1760 to 1893 (GLAH 1:E92). The introduction is a survey of the exhibition of progressive art in Britain in the late 19th and early 20th century.

List of galleries and societies with their abbreviations, p.3. General abbreviations, p.5. Selected bibliography, p.6.

E120 McEwan, Peter J. M. Dictionary of Scottish art and architecture. Woodbridge, Suffolk, Eng., Antique Collectors' Club, 1994. 626p. ports.

Covers societies, academies, groups, and more than 10,000 artists and architects from the 15th through 20th centuries. Devotes 1,000 words or more to important figures. Selective mention of exhibitions and abbreviated bibliographical citations at the end of many of the biographical entries. "The intention has been to provide the most relevant details of all painters, engravers and etchers who met a comprehensive range of criteria, and all architects, carvers, designers, draughtsmen, embroiderers, illustrators, jewellery designers, masons, photographers and stained glass window designers who met slightly more rigorous criteria."—*Introd.*

Lack of indexes and a key to bibliographical abbreviations diminishes the usefulness of an otherwise excellent work.

E121 Royal Academy of Arts (Great Britain). Royal Academy exhibitors, 1905–1970; a dictionary of artists and their work in the summer exhibitions of the Royal Academy of Arts. Wakefield, EP, [1973]–82. 6v.

See GLAH 1:E97 for original annotation.

Adheres to the usual format for dictionaries of this type. Artists are presented alphabetically in a long sequence through all six vols. Under each artist's name is a chronological list of works shown at R.A. summer exhibitions. The title of each work is given, along with its original number in the show's catalog. The address of the artist, as it was reported at the time of each exhibition, is also supplied.

E122 The Royal Scottish Academy exhibitors, 1826–1990: a dictionary of artists and their work in the Annual Exhibitions of the Royal Scottish Academy. Charles Baile de Laperrière, ed. Compiled by Meta Viles and Joanna Soden, assist. by Pamela Scott. Wiltshire, Eng., Hilmarton Manor, 1991. 4v.

The usual arrangement—artists are presented alphabetically in a continuous sequence through all four vols. Under each artist's name is a chronological list of works shown in the Academy's annual exhibitions. The title of each work is given, along with its original number in the show's catalog. The address of the artist, as it was reported at the time of each exhibition, is usually supplied.

[Roster of] members . . . , v.1, p.xxi–xxxiv.

E123 The Society of Women Artists exhibitors 1855–1996: a dictionary of artists and their works in the annual exhibitions of The Society of Women Artists. Charles Baile de Laperrière, ed. Compiled by Joanna Soden. Wiltshire, Eng., Hilmarton Manor, 1996. 4v.

Artists are presented alphabetically in a continuous sequence through all four vols. Under each artist's name is a chronological list of works shown in the Society's annual exhibitions. The title of each work is given, along with its original number in the show's catalog and its price. The address of the artist, as it was reported at the time of each exhibition, is also supplied.

A history of the Society of Women Artists, by Katy Deepwell, v.1, p.xvii–xxxi. Exhibition venues, v.1, p.xxxvii–xxxviii. [Roster of] members, v.1, p.xlvii–lxvi.

E124 Spalding, Frances. 20th century painters and sculptors. Assist. ed., Judith Collins. Woodbridge, Suffolk, Eng., Antique Collectors' Club, 1990. 482p. il. (part col.) (Dictionary of British art, v.6)

Brief entries on more than 4,000 painters, printmakers, and sculptors (including installation artists), but excluding, in general, illustrators, photographers, and performance artists, unless they also worked in one of the foregoing media. "The tighter focus obtained by concentrating primarily on painters and sculptors can be seen to be less conservative than forward-looking. For despite all that new technology offers the artist, painting and sculpture still today have undiminished vitality and are the means by which artists choose to affirm the intransigence of the British imagination."—*Pref.*

Black-and-white illustrations usually on same page as the

entry for the artist whose work they represent. Introduction is brief history of British 20th-century art.

Abbreviations, p.9.

E125 Stewart, Ann M. Irish art societies and sketching clubs: index of exhibitors, 1870–1980. Dublin, Four Courts Press, 1997. 2v.

Provides information about participants in the exhibitions of 16 societies and clubs. Artists are presented alphabetically in a continuous sequence. Under each artist's name is a chronological list of works shown in the exhibitions of the various societies. The title of each work is given, along with its original number in the show's catalog and its price. The address of the artist, as it was reported at the time of each exhibition, is often supplied.

Note on the societies included in this index, v.1, p.ix–x.

E126 ______. Royal Hibernian Academy of Arts: index of exhibitors and their works, 1826–1979. With a summary history of the R.H.A. by C. de Courcy. Dublin, Manton, 1985–1987. 3v.

Artists are presented alphabetically in a continuous sequence through all three vols. Under each artist's name is a chronological list of works shown in the Academy's annual exhibitions. The title of each work is given, along with its original number in the show's catalog and its price. The address of the artist, as it was reported at the time of each exhibition, is also supplied.

"Notes on the use of text" [i.e., abbreviations] at front of each vol.

E127 The Thames and Hudson encyclopaedia of British art. General ed., David Bindman. Ed. for medieval art, Nigel Morgan. N.Y., Thames and Hudson, 1985. 320p. il.

Brief but substantive and generally well-written entries on artists (including foreigners who worked in England) and other art world figures, groups, institutions, monuments, media, and techniques. Coverage from Anglo-Saxon times to the early 1980s. Particularly good coverage of manuscript illumination. Many small black-and-white illustrations.

Bibliographic citations at ends of most entries. Subject index, p.8–10. List of contributors, p.11–12. Bibliography, p.297–99. World gazetteer of museums and galleries containing British art, by Rosemary Treble, p.300–19.

Italy

E128 A Concise encyclopaedia of the Italian Renaissance. Ed. by J.R. Hale. N.Y., Oxford Univ. Pr., 1981. 360p. il.

British ed., London, Thames and Hudson, 1981.

Brief, well-written, signed entries by more than 30 specialist scholars on subjects concerning the history, politics, culture, and notable figures of the Italian Renaissance. Entries of 1,000 words or more for some major topics.

Bibliographic citations at ends of most entries. Subject index, p.[6]–[13]. List of contributors, p.[14]. Tables of succession, p.[352]–57. Glossary of Italian terms, p.358–59. Bibliographical note, p.360.

E129 Dizionario degli artisti italiani del XX secolo. [Dir., Umberto Allemandi]. Torino, Bolaffi, 1979. 2v. il.

Painters and sculptors covered in v.1 in brief entries that include basic biographical information, collection and exhibition data, and bibliography. Black-and-white thumbnail illustrations scattered throughout the text. V.2 contains 345 full-page plates, mostly in color.

Contents: (1) Voci biografiche e biografico-critiche di 1336 artisti; (2) Appendice iconografica, riproduzioni a colori delle opere di 343 autori.

Indice degli artisti italiani del xx secolo presenti nei Cataloghi Nazionali Bolaffi d'Arte Moderna n.1–14 (1962–1979), v.1, p.[383]–418. Indice delle tavole, v.2, p.[349]–51.

E130 Dizionario dell'arte italiana. [Coord., Giovanni Anzani.] Milano, Electa, [1981]. 410p. il. (part col.)

Substantive, illustrated biographical entries for painters, sculptors, and architects from the 13th through mid-20th century. Covers Italians and foreign artists who worked in Italy. Major figures get 1,000 words, or more, but no bibliographical information is supplied. Biographical section is followed by "Profilo dell'arte italiana," a series of heavily illustrated essays on periods in the history of Italian art, from late antiquity through the mid-20th century.

E131 Fergonzi, Flavio. Lessicalità visiva dell'italiano: la critica dell'arte contemporanea, 1945–1960. Pisa, Scuola normale superiore, [1996]. 2v. (Strumenti e testi, 2)

Historical dictionary of words and phrases extracted from key art texts of the 1945–60 period, including writings by artists and critics, and essays from exhibition catalogs, particularly those of the Venice Biennales and Rome Quadriennales. Indexes in v.2 provide access to the terms via the names of writers who used them and dates of usage.

La lingua dell'arte contemporanea, 1945–1960, v.1, p.vii–xxxiv. Nota del curatore, v.1, p.xxxv–xxxvii. Bibliografia schedata, v.1, p.xxxix–xliv. Elenco delle abbreviazioni bibliografiche, v.1, p.xlv–xlvii. Indice ordinato per autore-anno-lemma, v.2, p.1–59. Indice ordinato per anno-lemma-autore, v.2, p.61–161. Indice dei lemmi, v.2, p.163–351.

E132 The Grove dictionary of Art. Encyclopedia of Italian Renaissance and mannerist art. Ed. by Jane Turner. London, Macmillan Reference; N.Y., Grove's Dictionaries, 2000. 2v. (xxv, 1881p.) il. (part col.)

Focused selection of entries from the Dictionary of art (GLAH 2:E4).

General abbreviations, v.1, p.xix–xxiv. Appendix A, List of locations, v.2, p.1821–32. Appendix B, List of periodical titles, v.2, p.1833–39. Appendix C, Lists of standard reference books and series, v.2, p.1840–41. Appendix D, Contributor list, v.2, p.1842–43.

E133 Masciotta, Michelangelo. Dizionario di termini artistici. Firenze, Le Monnier, 1969. 269p.

Definitions of more than 2,000 Italian words and phrases relating to aspects of art and architecture from ancient times through the early 20th century. Many foreign terms covered that have gained acceptance in Italy through long usage.

Some 17th-century and 18th-century terminology and definitions from the dictionaries of Baldinucci (GLAH 1:H53) and Milizia, respectively, are also included. Brief etymologies supplied at the beginning of most entries. French, English, and German equivalents given. An appendix contains alphabetically arranged French, English, and German terms, with Italian equivalents.

Repertorio: Francese-Italiano, p.[217]–33; Inglese-Italiano, p.[235]–51; Tedesco-Italiano, p.[253]–69.

Latin America

E134 Cavalcanti, Carlos. Dicionário brasileiro de artistas plásticos. Brasília, Instituto Nacional do Livro, 1973–1980. 4v. il. (Coleção Dicionários especializados, 5)

Covers Brazilian artists and foreign artists who worked in Brazil, including painters, printmakers, illustrators, sculptors, decorative and applied artists, and architects. Entries supply basic biographical information, with selective data on schooling, teaching, prizes won, exhibitions in which the artist participated, and collections that own his or her work. Entries average about 100 words, but more than 1,000 words are devoted to some major figures. The hundreds of black-and-white illustrations, though variable in quality, constitute a valuable corpus.

E135 Crespi, Irene, and Ferrario, Jorge. Lexico tecnico de las artes plásticas. 6a. ed. Buenos Aires, Editorial Universitaria, 1995. [8], 139, [2], 113p. il. (Manuales: artes plásticas)

1st ed. 1971., 2d ed. 1977., 3d ed. 1982., 4th ed. 1985., 5th ed. 1990.

Brief but substantive entries cover technical terms, philosophical concepts concerning the visual arts, media, and art historical periods. Treatment of chemical and physical terminology is a particular strength. Focuses primarily on European art and relies heavily on the writings of pillars of early 20th-century art history, such as Wölfflin, Worringer, and Arnheim. No index, but cross-references liberally provided. Helpful use of illustrations, many full-page, to explain difficult concepts.

Autores consultados, p.[7].

E136 Estrada, Leonel. Arte actual: diccionario de términos y tendencias. Colab. de María Isabel de Molina, María Luisa E. de Vélez. Medellín, Colombia, Colina, [1985]. 247p. il. (part col.)

Brief entries on 20th-century groups, movements, and technical terms. Focuses on Europe and the U.S., but there is occasional mention of Latin American developments. Illustrated mainly with art that has appeared in past Bienales de Arte de Medellín.

Cronologia de los movimientos artísticos del siglo xx, p.243–45. Bibliografia, p.246–47.

E137 The Grove dictionary of art. Encyclopedia of Latin American and Caribbean art. Ed., Jane Turner. N.Y., Grove's Dictionaries, 1999. 782p. il. (part col.), plates.

Focused selection of entries from the Dictionary of art (GLAH 2:E4).

General abbreviations, p.xv–xx. Appendix A, List of locations, p.739–47. Appendix B, List of periodical titles, p.748–50. Appendix C, List of contributors, p.751. Index, p.752–82.

E138 Tovar de Teresa, Guillermo. Repertorio de artistas en México: artes plásticas y decorativas. Con la colab. de Gabriel Breña Valle . . . [et al.] Prólogo, Octavio Paz. Diseño, Franco Maria Ricci. [México], Grupo Financiero Bancomer, 1995–1997. 3v. il. (part col.)

Covers artists from the 16th through 20th centuries, including architects and photographers. Entries average more than 400 words; most have endnotes and bibliography. Superb color illustrations, many full-page, take advantage of set's large format. Two to three illustrations per artist.

Low Countries

E139 Dictionnaire biographique illustré des artistes en Belgique depuis 1830. [Réd., Arthur Tommelein et Iris D. Tommelein.] Bruxelles, Arto, 1995. iv, 492p. il. (part col.)

Brief entries on painters, sculptors, and draughtsmen. References from entries to corresponding illustrations. No bibliographies.

Abréviations, p.iv.

E140 Dutch art : an encyclopedia. Ed. by Sheila D. Muller. Advisory board, Walter S. Gibson . . . [et al.] N.Y., Garland, 1997. xxx, 489p. il. (part col.), plates, maps. (Garland reference library of the humanities, v.1021)

Wide-ranging work that presents substantive signed entries by more than 100 scholarly contributors on artists, architects, critics, theorists, media, groups, movements, cities, as well as topics in cultural and intellectual history that relate to the visual arts. Chronological coverage from the middle of the 15th century to the late 20th. Many full-page illustrations.

Bibliographies and cross-references at ends of most entries. A reader's guide and bibliographical note, p.xvii–xxii. Contributors, p.xxiii–xxx. Index, p.463–89.

E141 The Grove dictionary of art. From Rembrandt to Vermeer: 17th-century Dutch artists. Ed. by Jane Turner. N.Y., St. Martin's Pr., 2000. xii, 421p. il. (part col.)

British ed., London, Macmillan Reference, 2000.

Focused selection of entries from the Dictionary of art (GLAH 2:E4).

List of contributors, p.ix. General abbreviations, p.x–xi. Appendix A, List of locations, p.[412]–18. Appendix B, List of periodical titles, p.[419]–21. Appendix C, Lists of standard reference books and series, p.[422].

E142 Piron, Paul-L. De belgische beeldende kunstenaars uit de 19de en 20ste eeuw. Brussels, Art in Belgium, [1999]. 2v. col. il.

Brief entries on painters, sculptors, and draftsmen. Late 20th-century figures receive fullest treatment. Many full-page illustrations. No individual artist bibliographies.

Beknopte toelichting bij gebruikte afkortingen in dit werk, p.1611. Referentie-en naslagwerken, p.1611–13.

Russia and Eastern Europe

E143 Chrzanowska-Pienkos, Jolanta, and Pienkos, Andrzej. Leksykon sztuki polskiej XX wieku: sztuki plastyczne. Poznan, KURPISZ, 1996. 280p., col. il.
Brief entries on 20th-century Polish artists and other art world figures, groups, academies, museums, and journals. Covers painters, printmakers, illustrators, sculptors, and artists working in newer media, such as video and installation. Nicely designed. Small but decent color illustrations show at least one work for the majority of the artists covered, usually on the same page as the artist's entry.

Indeks pojêc i nazw, p.[269]–72. Indeks nazwisk, p.[273]–80.

E144 Milner, John. A dictionary of Russian and Soviet artists, 1420–1970. Woodbridge, Suffolk, Eng., Antique Collectors' Club, 1993. 483p. il. (part col.)
Entries for approximately 2,000 painters, graphic artists, sculptors, decorative artists, and designers of various kinds. No architects unless they also worked in one or more of the foregoing media. Entries of more than 2,000 words for important figures. Introduction is an essay by the author surveying the history of Russian art. Many full-page illustrations.

Selective lists of significant works, bibliographical citations, and locations of major collections at ends of most entries. Conventions [including abbreviations and forms of Russian names], p.30–32. Appendix: the Russian alphabet transliterations, p.481. Bibliography, p.482–83.

E145 Prut, Constantin. Dictionar de arta moderna. Bucuresti, Albatross, 1982. 486, [1]p. il. (part col.)
Entries averaging about 200 words provide a general treatment of modern art in Europe and the Americas, with coverage of the usual major artists, architects, groups, and movements. However, a large proportion of the artists and architects covered in the biographical entries are Romanian, which makes this work potentially valuable to specialists.

Bibliographical citations at ends of entries. Bibliografie generala, p.484–[87].

E146 Sokol, Stanley S. The artists of Poland: a biographical dictionary from the 14th century to the present. Jefferson, N.C., McFarland, 2000. 263p. ports.
Brief entries on almost 1,300 painters, printmakers, sculptors, architects, and other artists, of Polish birth or descent.

Bibliographical citations at ends of entries, including many to Polish sources. Abbreviations, p.5–6. Index, p.253–63.

Scandinavia

E147 Norsk kunstnerleksikon: bildende kunstnere, arkitekter, kunsthandverkere. Red. av Nasjonalgalleriet. Redaksjonskomite, Leif Ostby . . . [et al.] Red. darbeid., Glenny Alfsen, Bodil Sorensen. Oslo, Universitetsforlaget, 1982–1986. 4v. il. (part col.)
Covers Norwegian painters, sculptors, graphic artists, architects, decorative artists, and craftsworkers from about the 17th century. Brief, well-organized, signed entries provide basic biographical information including schooling, prizes and grants won, teaching experience, works in collections, and thorough bibliography. Entries on important figures can amount to several thousand words.

Medarbeidere, v.1, p.[6]. Forkortelser, v.1, p.[10]–12. Rettelser, v.4, p.597–603.

E148 Weilbach: dansk kunstnerleksikon. Hovedred., Sys Hartmann. Kobenhavn, Munksgaard, 1994–2000. 9v.
See GLAH 1:E148 for previous eds.

Entries for Danish painters, sculptors, graphic artists, architects, decorative artists, and artists working in contemporary genres. Covers schooling, prizes and grants won, travels, teaching experience, works in collections, bibliography. Most entries brief, but important figures get 1,000 words or more. V.9 includes supplement of additional artist entries and geographical index of architects.

"Forfattere," "Vejledning," and "Forkortelser" at front of each vol.

Spain and Portugal

E149 Arroyo Fernández, María Dolores. Diccionario de términos artísticos. Madrid, Alderabán, 1997. 293p. il. (DIDO diccionarios)
Brief definitions of technical terms, media, movements, motifs, and styles in Western and Asian art and architecture from antiquity through the late 20th century. Illustrated with occasional line drawings. No artist biographies.

Bibliografía, p.291–93.

E150 Bonet, Juan Manuel. Diccionario de las vanguardias en España, 1907–1936. Madrid, Alianza, 1995. 654p. il.
Entries for poets, musicians, cinematographers, critics, etc., as well as painters, sculptors, architects, and other visual artists. Also includes groups, institutions, and cities and other regions significant to the early 20th-century Spanish avant-garde. Coverage of literary reviews, as well as popular periodicals and scholarly journals in the arts, a special strength. Most entries brief, though substantive, but significant figures or important topics can get extended treatment of 1,000 words or more. Many entries end with a bibliographical citation or two.

Por dónde seguir trabajando, p.645–50. Publicaciones periódicas, p.651–54.

E151 Diccionario de pintores y escultores españoles del siglo XX. [Dir. ed., Mario Antolín Paz.] Madrid, Forum Artis, 1994–2000. 15v. col. il.
Signed entries averaging about 200 words supply basic biographical data and summarize the artist's schooling, exhibitions, prizes, prominent collections holding his or her

work, and sometimes end with a bibliographic citation or two. Covers foreign artists who worked in Spain, as well as natives. Hundreds of small color illustrations.

Prólogo, by Mario Antolín Paz, et al., v.1, p.ix–xxvi, is a brief survey of Spanish 20th-century art.

Relación de autores, v.1, p.v–vii.

E152 Enciclopedia del arte español del siglo XX. Dir. por Francisco Calvo Serraller. Madrid, Mondadori, 1991–1992. 2v.

Thorough, authoritative work that presents in v.1 lengthy, detailed biographical entries on painters, sculptors, graphic artists, and artistas experimentales, including chronological lists of artists' exhibition activity, their works owned by public and private collections, and their writings. V.2 contains biographical entries for prominent Spanish art historians, critics, and collectors, as well as entries for art journals, museums, artists' groups, salons, and commercial galleries. Entries on commercial galleries provide chronological exhibition histories. Individual bibliographies provided for most figures treated in v.2. In sum, a treasure trove of information not easily found elsewhere.

Contents: (1) Artistas; (2) El contexto.

Individual artist bibliographies at ends of most entries. Exposiciones programaticas (indice cronológico), v.2, p.[441]–45. Galerías, v.2, p.[446]–48. Grupos artísticos, v.2, p.[449]–50. Instituciones, v.2, p.[451]–53. Premios, v.2, p.[454]–55. Profesionales, v.2, p.[456]–59. Revistas, v.2, p.[460]–62. Índice, v.2, p.[463].

E153 Enciclopedia vivent de la pintura i l'escultura catalanes. Dir., Rafael Santos Torroella. Barcelona, Ambit Serveis, 1985– . (14)v. il. (part col.), ports.

Biographical entries for 20th-century Catalan artists include portrait of the artist, exhibition history (sometimes selective), awards received, museums that have the artist's work (though titles not specified), but the focus of the work is illustrations—as many as 10p. of illustrations on each artist, some in color. Parallel Catalan/Spanish texts. V.11, 12 not yet published. "Annex" vols., which start with v.13, begin new alphabetical sequence covering additional artists.

E154 Pamplona, Fernando de. Dicionário de pintores e escultores portugueses ou que trabalharam em Portugal. 3a. ed. [Porto, Portugal], Livraria Civilização Editora, 1991– . (2)v. il. (part col.)

See GLAH 1:E158 for 1st ed. 2d ed., 1987–88, 5v.

Covers Portuguese painters, sculptors, graphic artists, and architects (and foreign artists who worked in Portugal) from the 15th through 20th centuries. Brief biographical entries supply exhibition histories, an accounting of works in collections, and bibliography. Signatures of some artists illustrated. Artists judged important have entries more than 500 words in length. Many full-page illustrations.

Illustration index ("Índice das gravuras") at end of each vol.

E155 Spanish artists from the fourth to the twentieth century: a critical dictionary. Frick Art Reference Library. N.Y., Hall, 1993–96. 4v.

More a bibliography than a biographical dictionary, with data from the Frick's Authority File of Artists. For each of about 7,000 artists, entries supply birth and death dates, variant names, art occupation (if not painter), sometimes a line or two of crucial identifying data, and a set of abbreviated bibliographical citations. Full citations are provided in bibliographies in vols. 1, 2, and 4. "Spanish Artists includes sculptors in addition to painters and draftsmen, as well as some architects, printmakers, and applied artists."—*Introd.*

General bibliography, v.4, p.[1]–142. Chronological index, v.4, p.[143]–89. Comprehensive index [of names], v.4, p.[191]–453.

E156 Tannock, Michael. Portuguese 20th century artists: a biographical dictionary. Chichester, Eng., Phillimore, 1978. xv, 188 p. 381 il. (part col.)

Brief entries supply basic information—a line or two of biography and chronology, lists of exhibitions, collections, and prizes. Covers 2150 painters, sculptors, watercolorists, graphic artists, and ceramicists. Significant corpus of illustrations. "The information contained in this Dictionary has been written in a style limited to factual data and avoiding any form of artistic comment. My intention was hopefully to escape the pitfall that besets many reference books on contemporary art which express views and opinions that may diverge from what is later proved by the course of history."—*Introd.*

Historical summary of Portuguese art from 1900 to 1974, by José-Augusto França, p.xvi–xxv. Awards, p.187. Museums, p.188.

Switzerland

E157 Biografisches Lexikon der schweizer Kunst: unter Einschluss des Fürstentums Liechtenstein = Dictionnaire biographique de l'art suisse: principauté du Liechtenstein incluse = Dizionario biografico dell'arte svizzera: principato del Liechtenstein incluso. Hrsg., Schweizerisches Institut für Kunstwissenschaft, Zürich und Lausanne. [Zürich], Neue Zürcher Zeitung, 1998. 2v. (xviii, 1195p.), il. (part col.) + 1 computer disk (4 3/4").

Covers painters, sculptors, and graphic artists from the 15th to the late 20th century. Also includes contemporary artists working in such media as performance, installation, and video. Substantive entries average about a thousand words in length; most include a list of collections that own the artist's work, and a bibliography. Many thumbnail illustrations, some in color. Some 12,000 artists are covered in the Institut's SIKART database, but only about 10% are included with full entries in the present vols. The database is more fully represented on the accompanying CD-ROM, which contains information, including bibliographies, on many artists omitted from the printed vols. Supersedes Lexikon der zeitgenössischen schweizer Künstler (see following entry).

Hinweise zur Benutzung, v.1, p.xv–xvi. Autorinnen, Autoren, v.1, p.xvii–xviii. Abgekürzt zitierte Lexika, v.1, p.xviii. Register der Namensvarianten, v.2, p.1174–91. Fotonachweis, v.2, p.1192–95.

E158 Lexikon der zeitgenössischen schweizer Künstler = Dictionnaire des artistes suisses contemporains. Schweizerisches Institut für Kunstwissenschaft. [Leit., Hans-Jörg Heusser.] Frauenfeld [etc.], Huber, 1981. xxiv, 539p.

Biographical entries for 2,182 living painters, sculptors, graphic and decorative artists, photographers, and artists working in newer media, such as video, conceptual art, and environmental art. (No architects unless also active in one or more of the foregoing media.) Entries are also supplied for a few artists' groups. Artist entries, in German, French, or Italian according to the artist's preference, give basic biographical data and include selective information on locations of the artist's work, exhibitions, and some bibliography. Superseded by the Biographisches Lexikon der schweizer Kunst (see preceding entry).

Verzeichnis der Verstorbenen, p.415–437. Verzeichnis der Künstler nach Wohnorten, p.438–59. Verzeichnis der Künstler nach Bürgerorten, p.460–83. Verzeichnis der Künstler nach Tätigkeiten, p.484–532.

United States

E159 The Annual and biennial exhibition record of the Whitney Museum of American Art, 1918–1989. Peter Hastings Falk, ed. Andrea Ansell Bien, asst. ed. Madison, Conn., Sound View, 1991. 468p. il. (The Exhibition record series)

Presents the artists' names in an alphabetical sequence. Under each name is given a chronological list of works by that artist shown at the Whitney annuals and biennials. For each work, title, catalog number, date of the exhibition, and address of the artist are provided.

The annual and biennial exhibitions at the Whitney Museum of American Art, 1932 to 1989: a history and evaluation of their impact upon American art, by Bruce Lineker, p.9–57. List of catalogues, p.58–61. Index by owner, p.431–42. Index by places and last names, p.445–68.

E160 The Annual exhibition record of the National Academy of Design, 1901–1950: incorporating the annual exhibitions, 1901–1950 and the winter exhibitions, 1906–1932. Peter Hastings Falk, ed. Andrea Ansell Bien, asst. ed. Madison, Conn., Sound View, 1990. 622p. il.

Continues coverage begun by Bartlett Cowdrey (GLAH 1:I484) and Maria Naylor (GLAH 1:I483).

Presents the artists' names in an alphabetical sequence. Under each name is given a chronological list of works by that artist shown at the annual and winter exhibitions of the Academy. For each work, title, catalog number, date of the exhibition, and address of the artist are provided.

Index of jurors, p.18–44. Index by owner, p.563–78. Index by places and last names, p.579–619.

E161 The Annual exhibition record of the Pennsylvania Academy of the Fine Arts. Ed. by Peter Hastings Falk. Madison, Conn., Sound View, 1988–1989. 3v. il.

V.1 is a republication with minor revisions of the 1955 index compiled by Anna Wells Rutledge (GLAH 1:I488).

Each vol. presents the artists' names in an alphabetical sequence. Under each name is given a chronological list of works by that artist shown at the annual exhibitions of the Academy. For each work, title, an occasional annotation, catalog number, date of the exhibition, and address of the artist are provided. Each vol. is equipped with an index of owners' names, and of subjects or places, and each contains an essay by Cheryl Leibold, Academy archivist, on a different aspect of the history of the exhibitions. V.1 has list of catalogs; 2 and 3 contain indexes of jurors' names.

Contents: (1) 1807–1870; (2) 1876–1913; (3) 1914–1968.

E162 The Biennial exhibition record of the Corcoran Gallery of Art, 1907–1967. Peter H. Falk, ed. Andrea Ansell Bien, asst. ed. Madison, Conn., Sound View, 1991. 335p. il. (The Exhibition record series)

Presents the artists' names in an alphabetical sequence. Under each name is given a chronological list of works by that artist shown at the Gallery's biennial exhibitions. For each work, title, catalog number, date of the exhibition, and address of the artist are provided.

The biennial exhibitions of contemporary American paintings at the Corcoran Gallery of Art, 1907–1967, by Linda Crocker Simmons, p.7–28. List of catalogues, p.38–39. Index of jurors, p.[45]–52. Index by owner, p.297–310. Index by places and last names, p.313–35.

E163 The Boston Art Club: exhibition record, 1873–1909. Comp. and ed. by Janice H. Chadbourne, Karl Gabosh, and Charles O. Vogel. Madison, Conn., Sound View, 1991. 479p. il. (The Exhibition record series)

Presents the artists' names in an alphabetical sequence. Under each name is given a chronological list of works by that artist shown at the Club's exhibitions. For each work, title, catalog number, date of the exhibition, and address of the artist are provided.

History of the Boston Art Club, 1854–1950, by Charles O. Vogel, p.11–17. List of exhibition catalogues, p.41–[49]. Owner index, p.419–41. Appendix I, Boston Art Club members . . . , p.443–52. Appendix X, Boston Art Club permanent collection as of February 1915, p.475–76. Appendix XI, Bibliography, p.477–79.

E164 Cummings, Paul. Dictionary of contemporary American artists. 6th ed. N.Y., St. Martin's Pr., 1994. x, 786p. il.

See GLAH 1:E172 for 3d ed.; 4th ed. 1982; 5th ed. 1988.

Entries provide a tightly woven fabric of basic information, including schooling, teaching, awards, exhibitions, collections, and bibliographical citations. "Questionnaires, personal interviews, and intensive research have brought together significant data regarding the careers of these 900 artists, chosen essentially on the basis of the following criteria: representation in museum, public, and private collections; representation in major American and international exhibitions; influence as teachers; recognition received from fellow artists, dealers, critics, and others with a professional interest in the fine arts."—*How to use this book.* Not a cumulative work, since some artists have been deleted from recent eds., beginning with the 4th, 1982. A new feature in the current ed. is the intercalation of the names of deleted artists, along with the edition(s) in which their entry appeared. Annotated bibliography.

Index of artists and pronunciation guide, p.[9]–16. Key to museums and institutions . . . , p.[17]–46. Galleries representing the artists in this book, p.[47]–53. Bibliography, p.[731]–86.

E165 Dawdy, Doris Ostrander. Artists of the American West: a biographical dictionary. Chicago, Sage, [1974]–1985. 3v.

Brief entries on more than 4,000 painters, illustrators, and printmakers born before 1900 who worked in "the seventeen states lying roughly west of the 95th meridien."—*Pref.* Most entries supply basic biographical data, a few bibliographical citations, and a paragraph or two of background information.

Index to volumes I–III, v.3, p.513–68. "Bibliography" at end of each vol.

E166 Falk, Peter H. The annual exhibition record of the Art Institute of Chicago, 1888–1950. Andrea Ansell Bien, asst. ed. Madison, Conn., Sound View, 1990. 1117p. il. (The Exhibition record series)

Presents the artists' names in an alphabetical sequence. Under each name is given a chronological list of works by that artist shown at the annual exhibitions of the Art Institute. For each work, title, catalog number, date of the exhibition, and address of the artist are provided.

A brief history of the annual exhibition of American paintings and sculpture, 1888–1950, by John W. Smith, p.7–16. Index of jurors, p.22–44. Index by owner, p.990–1015. Index by places and last names, p.1016–1115.

E167 Fielding, Mantle. Mantle Fielding's dictionary of American painters, sculptors and engravers. Ed. by Glenn B. Opitz. 2d newly-rev., enl., and updated ed. Poughkeepsie, N.Y., Apollo, 1986. xv, 1081p.

1st ed. by Opitz, 1983. See GLAH 1:E173 for earlier versions.

"Close to 2500 additional artists' biographies are included in this new 1986 edition . . . [which] now totals over 12,000 names, with biographical information drawn from an extensive library of source material, including both readily available and many out-of-print references, as well as resumes submitted from artists in response to our solicitation for information. Biographical information and corrections submitted by readers have also been incorporated."—*Pref.* Entries average about 60 words and include information on subjects' awards, group and solo shows, museums holding their works (the latter sometimes listed by title), association memberships, teaching experience. Concentrates on less well-known figures; does not expend extra space on leading artists about whom information is readily available from many other published sources.

Abbreviations, p.ix–xv. Bibliography, p.1074–81.

E168 The Grove dictionary of art. Encyclopedia of American art before 1914. Ed. by Jane Turner. N.Y., Grove's Dictionaries, 2000. xxiii, 688p. il. (part col.)

Focused selection of entries from the Dictionary of art (GLAH 2:E4).

General abbreviations, p.xvii–xxii. Appendix A, List of locations, p.660–66. Appendix B, List of periodical titles, p.667–69. Appendix C, Lists of standard reference books and series, p.670. Appendix D, Early America contributor list, p.671. Index, p.673–88.

E169 Kovinick, Phil, and Yoshiki-Kovinick, Marian. An encyclopedia of women artists of the American West. Austin, Univ. of Texas Pr., 1998. xxxv, 405p. il. (American studies series)

Entries averaging 300–500 words treat several hundred selected women painters, graphic artists, and sculptors working from the 1840s through the mid-1990s in the "geographical region encompassing the 17 most western contiguous states."—*Pref.*

Bibliographical references at ends of entries; small, clear black-and-white illustrations. Western women artists: an overview, p.[xvii]–xx. Index of names, p.[xxi]–xxxii. List of abbreviations, p.[xxxiii]–xxv. Artists II [brief biographies of additional artists], p.[341]–92. Selected bibliography, p.[393]–405.

E170 Marlor, Clark S. A history of the Brooklyn Art Association with an index of exhibitions. N.Y., Carr, 1970. vii, 421p. il., ports.

Presents the artists' names in an alphabetical sequence. Under each name is given a chronological list of works by that artist shown at the Association's exhibitions. For each work, title, catalog number, date of the exhibition, and, often, address of the artist are provided.

Introductory chapters provide a history of the Association. Appendix B, Catalogues of exhibitions, p.395–402.

E171 ______. The Society of Independent Artists: the exhibition record 1917–1944. Park Ridge, N.J., Noyes, 1984. xiii, 600p.

Presents the artists' names in an alphabetical sequence. Under each name is given a chronological list of works by that artist shown at the Society's exhibitions. For each work, title, catalog number, date of the exhibition, and address of the artist are provided.

Introductory chapters present a decade-by-decade history of the Society.

Catalogs of exhibitions, p.593–96. Index of text, p.597–600.

E172 Perkins, Robert F., and Gavin, William J., III. The Boston Athenaeum art exhibition index, 1827–1874. Mary Margaret Shaughnessy, asst. ed. Boston, Mass., The Library of the Boston Athenaeum (Distr. by MIT Pr., 1980). xv, 325p. il, plates.

Presents the artists' names in an alphabetical sequence. Under each name is given a chronological list of works by that artist shown at the Athenaeum's exhibitions. For each work, title, catalog number, date of the exhibition, address of the artist if known, and name of the owner if available, are provided.

List of exhibition catalogues, p.3–5. Owner index, p.177–230. Subject index, p.233–75.

E173 Samuels, Peggy, and Samuels, Harold. The illustrated biographical encyclopedia of artists of the American West. Garden City, N.Y., Doubleday, 1976. xxvi, 549p. il. (Repr.: Secaucus, N.J., Castle, 1985)

Covers 1,700 U.S. and Canadian artists who portrayed Western themes, from the explorer artists of the early 19th century, such as George Catlin and Karl Bodmer, to Georgia O'Keeffe in the late 20th. Includes painters, sculptors, printmakers, and illustrators. Entries supply basic biographical data, list sources of information about the artist, and mention representative auction prices, if available. A paragraph or two attempts to place the artist's career in context. Small black-and-white illustrations.

Abbreviations, p.xi–xiv. Sources and source abbreviations, p.xv–xxvi. References and reference abbreviations, p.xxvi.

E174 Who was who in American art, 1564–1975: 400 years of artists in America. Peter Hastings Falk, ed.-in-chief. Audrey Lewis, head of research. Madison, Conn., Sound View, 1999. 3v. (3724 p.) il.

1st ed. 1985.

Vastly enlarged version of a standard reference source. Covers more than 50,000 painters, printmakers, sculptors, photographers, decorative and applied artists, and critics and historians who worked in the U.S. Entries contain basic biographical information, including schooling, teaching, selective exhibition history, collections that own the artist's work, a few paragraphs of commentary on important figures, and bibliographical citations.

General abbreviations, v.1, p.16–19. Art institutions: museums, exhibitions, schools, clubs, associations and societies, v.1, p.21–33. European teachers of American artists, v.1, p.35–38. A note on the international exhibitions, v.1, p.39. Sources: key to citations of bibliographical sources, v.3, p.3693–3724.

E175 Yarnall, James L. The National Museum of American Art's index to American art exhibition catalogues: from the beginning through the 1876 centennial year. Comp. by James L. Yarnall and William H. Gerdts with the assist. of Katharine Fox Stewart and Catherine Hoover Voorsanger. Boston, Hall, 1986. 6v. (xxxvii, 4944 p.)

A highly important reference work that supplies a detailed survey of art exhibited in the U.S. and Canada from the late 18th to the mid-19th century.

Indexes more than 118,000 individual entries from 952 U.S. exhibition catalogs published from 1773 through 1876. Individual works of art arranged alphabetically by artist in a sequence that extends through all six vols. For each work, title, medium, price (if for sale), owner, catalog number in original publication, and any original annotation are given.

American art exhibitions and their catalogues: from the beginning through 1876, by William H. Gerdts, v.1, p.xvii–xxxvii. Exhibition title index, by location, v.1, p.1–46. Owner index, v.6, p.4631–4808. Subject index, v.6, p.4809–4944.

ASIAN COUNTRIES

General Works

E176 Auboyer, Jeannine, et al. Oriental art: a handbook of styles and forms.Trans. by Elizabeth Bartlett and Richard Bartlett. N.Y., Rizzoli, 1980. 608p. il.

Trans. of Grammaire des formes et des styles. Fribourg, Office du Livre, 1978.

Attempts to acquaint the reader with the styles, mythologies, religions, and civilizations of Asiatic civilizations including South, South-east, and East Asia. Each civilization (country) is introduced with a brief account of its art and history, followed by classification of the country's art into categories, e.g., temples, sculpture, ceramics. The categories are illustrated to provide visual reference and allow comparisons.

E177 Munsterberg, Hugo. Dictionary of Chinese and Japanese art.N.Y., Hacker, 1981. vii, 354p.

Provides definitions for more than 2,400 terms including artists' names, techniques, places, religious and mythological terms, art objects, and styles. Standard English-language dictionary for the topic with succinct, pragmatic definitions.

Bibliography, p.353–54.

China

E178 Chung-kuo mei shu tz'u tien. (Hsiung shih mei shu tz'u tien ta hsi).[2d ed.] T'ai-pei, Hsiung shih t'u shu ku fen yu hsien kung ssu, 1989. 797p. il (part col.)

1st ed. 1987.

In Chinese. A useful dictionary of Chinese art organized by medium: painting (p.64–303), calligraphy (p.304–83), seals (p.384–407), prints (p.408–439), architecture (p.440–79), minor decorative arts such as lacquer and embroidery (p.480–509), ceramics (p.510–71), bronzes (p.572–615), sculpture (p.616–737). Each section includes terminology, schools, and individuals.

Name index, p.738–49. Term index, p.750–74. [Each organized by stroke count.] Index to the illustrations, p.775–87. Pictorial table of Chinese art, p.788–89. Information on art institutions on the Chinese mainland, p.790–97.

E179 Liu, Charles, ed. Artists of Taiwan. [T'ai-pei], Artists Magazine, [1994]. 305p. col. il.

Biographical dictionary of contemporary Taiwanese artists. Entries include name, address, telephone and fax numbers, specialization, media, year and place of birth, sex, education, awards, exhibitions, and collections. Includes many color reproductions of the artists' work.

Contents: Perspectives in the emergence and development of indigenous art in Taiwan, by Hsing-Yueh Lin; The brief analysis of Taiwanese art history, by Lifa Shaih; The new phase of contemporary art in Taiwan, by Victoria Lu.

Abbreviations, p.14. Chinese index, p.301–05.

E180 The Ming Biographical History Project of the Association for Asian Studies. Dictionary of Ming biography, 1368–1644. Ed. by L. Carrington Goodrich and Chaoying Fang. N.Y., Columbia Univ. Pr., 1976. 2v., plates.

A massive project begun in 1958 with contributions from numerous scholars. A model reference work. The signed entries are often several pages long and include bibliographical references as well as biographical details for all major figures of the Ming period.

Contents: (1) A–L; (2) M–Z.

E181 Seymour, Nancy N. An index-dictionary of Chinese artists, collectors, and connoisseurs: with character identification by modified stroke count. Metuchen, Scarecrow, 1988. xvi, 987p.

Includes more than 5,000 Chinese names and biographies from the T'any Dynasty through the modern period. Entries include full characters, biographical information, alternative names, and types of work. Also includes a chapter on identifying Chinese characters for the non-Chinese scholar, an index of modified stroke count, a list of alternate names, a tool for translating between pinyin and Wade-Giles romanization, and a select bibliography.

Chronology of Chinese Dynasties, p.898–910. Pinyin and Wade-Giles romanization, p.911–27. Selected bibliography, p.923–29. Character index of Chinese names, p.930–87.

E182 Yū, Chien-hua. Chung-kuo mei shu chia jen ming tz'u tien. Shang-hai, Shang-hai jen mei shu ch'u pan she: Hsin hua shu tien Shang-hai fa hsing so fa hsing,1981. 2124 p. (Repr.: 1991)

In Chinese. The most comprehensive dictionary of Chinese artists' biographies. This indispensable work is organized by surname and stroke count. Each entry includes basic biographical information such as dynasty, alternate names, place of origin, and specialties, as well as bibliographic references.

The numbering is not consecutive throughout the volume. In addition to the main dictionary, the work includes an index of artists' surnames, an index of all artists' names, an alternate names index, and an appendix of 20th-century Chinese artists organized by stroke count.

Japan

E183 A dictionary of Japanese art terms = Wa-Ei taisho: Nihon bijutsu yogo jiten: bilingual [Japanese and English].Tokyo, Tokyo Bijutsu, 1990. vi, 793p. il.

In Japanese and English. A standard dictionary of 4,300 Japanese art terms, organized alphabetically by romanized Japanese term followed by the English translation of the term, a short explanation in English and a translation of the explanation into Japanese characters. Includes painting, calligraphy, sculpture, applied arts, architecture, and gardens. Additional features include line drawings of architecture, sculpture, swords, and costume with specific terms for various elements indicated. (p.673–89).

Chronological table of Japanese art, p.690–93. Index of terms in Chinese characters arranged by the number of strokes, p.694–724. Index of romanized Japanese terms, p.725–56. Index of English terms p.757–93.

E184 Fujimori, Koei. Nihon bijutsuka jiten.Tokyo, Oandoemu Rimiteddo, 1994. 1116p. il. (part col.)

Substantial biographical dictionary of Japanese artists, illustrated with many portraits.

Indexes (artists, galleries and collections, associations and suppliers), p.1005–16.

E185 Ishida, Hisatoyo, et al. Nihon bijutsushi jiten.Tokyo, Heibonsha, 1987. 1108 p. il. (part col.), plates.

In Japanese. Dictionary of Japanese art with entries for artists, terminology, schools, etc. organized in alphabetical order. Additional material includes essays on Japanese art.

List of national treasures, p.1046–55. List of Japanese art museums organized by prefecture, p.1056–62. List of contributors, p.1063–64. Index to terms that appear in the entries, p.1065–1108.

E186 Schneider, Philip. The Japanese signature handbook: an invaluable guide in the identification of the artists who were important creators of netsuke, inro, ojime, oki-mono, lacquer, sword blades, tsuba, sword furniture, armor, pottery, ceramics, ukiyo-e prints, paintings. Hollywood, Schneider, [1978]. 146p. il.

Intended for the non-Japanese collector of Japanese art. A small format book with signatures arranged in tables to aid identification. Neither comprehensive nor a substitute for a biographical tool but useful for the intended purpose.

E187 Tazawa, Yutaka, ed. Biographical dictionary of Japanese art. N.Y., Kodansha, 1981. 825p. il., plates, maps.

Published in collaboration with the International Society for Educational Information with contributions from 48 scholars.

The 863 artists' biographical entries are arranged by medium, i.e., painting, prints, calligraphy, photography, graphic design, sculpture, tea ceremony, architecture, gardens, ceramics, swords, metalwork, and textiles. Each topical area has an introductory essay and each biographical entry includes the surname (or school name), personal name, dates, and basic biographical sketch, description of style and major works and accomplishments, and the location of one or two representative works.

Glossary, p.712–17. Bibliography, p.720–84. Index, p.785–824.

AFRICA, OCEANIA, THE AMERICAS

Africa

E188 Berman, Esmé. Art and artists of South Africa: an illustrated biographical dictionary and historical survey of painters, sculptors and graphic artists since 1875. New upd. and enl. ed., 3d ed. [Reprint.] Half-

way House [South Africa], Southern Book Publishers, 1993. xviii, 545p. il. (part col.), plates.
Repr. of the rev. and enl. 1983 ed., Cape Town, Balkema, 1983. 1st ed. 1970. "There are well over 400 biographical entries in this edition, 210 of them in depth. Existing references to living artists have been brought up to date and, where relevant, extra visual material has been introduced . . . "—*Foreword.*

Contents: Historical table; Historical survey; Appendix A: Artists who have participated in major exhibitions; Appendix B: Painters, sculptors and graphic artists who have exhibited professionally since 1900.

Bibliography and reference, p.527–30. Index, p.531–45.

E189 Biebuyck, Daniel P.; Kelliher, Susan; and McRae, Linda. African ethnonyms: index to art-producing peoples of Africa. N.Y., Hall, [1996]. xxviii, 378p.
An invaluable resource which makes African "name identification easier by clustering all the variant names under a single entry-form name. . . . [The] cluster includes the name of the country or countries where people are located, the language affiliation, the preferred name used in the Library of Congress Subject Headings [on-line database, June 1996] and the Art and Architecture Thesaurus [version 2.1, 1996], and a coded list of sources to consult for additional information."—*Intro.*

Contents: African ethnonyms.

Language notes, p.283–88. Toponyms index, p.289–95. Country index, p.297–313. List of abbreviations, p.315–33. Bibliography, p.335–78.

E190 Kelly, Bernice M. Nigerian artists: a who's who and bibliography. Comp. by Bernice M. Kelly. Ed. by Janet L. Stanley. Published for the National Museum of African Art Branch, Smithsonian Institution Libraries, Washington, D.C., London, Hans Zell, 1993. vii, 600p. 16 col. il.
This bibliography "is a milestone for modern Nigerian art, an historical marker which represents a coherent summation of where Nigerian artists are thirty years after independence. It is an impressive record indeed of more than 350 professional artists" active from 1920 to 1990.—*Pref.*

Contents: Chronology of Nigerian art, 1920–1992; Who's who of artists.

Modern Nigerian art, 1920–1991: an annotated bibliography, p.502–81. Subject index to the bibliography, p.582–90. Index of artists by name, p.591–94. Index of artists by media, p.595–600.

E191 Ogilvie, Grania. The dictionary of South African painters and sculptors, including Namibia. Assisted by Carol Graff. [Rosebank, Johannesburg, South Africa], Everard Read, [1988]. xvii, 799p. [84]p. of plates (part col.).
A major reference book on modern southern African art which documents "over 1,800 painters, sculptors and graphic artists who were born, lived in or are presently living in South Africa or Namibia."—*Pref.*

Family trees, p.771. Select bibliography, p.773–81. Useful addresses, p.783–93.

E192 Schaedler, Karl-Ferdinand. Lexikon Afrikanische Kunst und Kultur. [München], Klinkhardt and Biermann, [1994]. 447p. il. (part col.).
With numerous illustrations and detailed entries, this dictionary provides extensive coverage of the art and culture of Africa.

Literatur, p.413–47.

The Americas

E193 Miller, Mary, and Taube, Karl. The gods and symbols of ancient Mexico and the Maya: an illustrated dictionary of Mesoamerican religion. N.Y., Thames and Hudson, 1993. 216p. il., maps.
Dictionary entries "include both discursive commentary and encapsulated identifications, ranging from concepts and ideas, ritual practices and participants, to particular deities, objects, symbols, flora and fauna, natural phenomena, and sacred places."—*Pref.*

Guide to sources and bibliography, p.[194]–214.

E194 Muser, Curt. Facts and artifacts of ancient Middle America: a glossary of terms and words used in the archaeology and art history of pre-Columbian Mexico and Central America. N.Y., Dutton, 1978. 212p. il., maps, col. plates, tables.
A cross-disciplinary dictionary of proper names (mythological and historical entities, placenames) and art historical and archeological concepts. While excavations and scholarship have changed dramatically since 1978, this work still provides ready access to a widely diverse nomenclature.

E195 St. James guide to Native North American artists.Ed. by Roger Matuz. Detroit, St. James Pr., 1998. xxxii, 691p. il., ports.
A selection of more than 350 biographical and critical entries on native North American artists of all media working in the 20th century. Most entries consist of biographical data (including variant names and tribal affiliation where appropriate), exhibitions, publications, collections, an artist's statement, an illustration from the artist's oeuvre, and an essay on the artist.

Bibliography, p.649–51. Name index, p.655–60. Tribe index, p.663–68. Geographic index, p.671–74. Medium index, p.677–82. Index to illustrations, p.685–86.

F. Iconography

Most of the titles listed and described here represent reference literature, that is, bibliographies, indexes, dictionaries, encyclopedias. While a very few monographic treatments have been included, most such studies (e.g., the books of Émile Mâle) may be found in more appropriate chapters through use of the indexes in the back of this volume.

GENERAL WORKS

F1 Becker, Udo. The Continuum encyclopedia of symbols. Trans. by Lance W. Garner. N.Y., Continuum, 1994. 345p. il., col. plates, tables.

Trans. of Lexikon der Symbole. Freiburg im Breisgau, Herder, 1992.

Richly illustrated encyclopedic dictionary of symbols arranged alphabetically by subject. Entries cover a wide range of topics from letters, numbers, plants, and the elements to architectural symbolism, everyday objects such as knives and pitchers, animals, mythological creatures, cults, and ritual practices.

Bibliography, p.344–45.

F2 Bell, Robert E. Dictionary of classical mythology, symbols, attributes, & associations. Santa Barbara, ABC-Clio, 1982. xi, 390p. il.

A dictionary of classical mythology arranged by subject (e.g., bear, charioteer, murder [of nephew], wings, etc.). Each entry provides the names and brief descriptions of the gods or goddesses associated with the subject heading. Entries usually include literary references to the Loeb classical library series. Additional chapters on names and heroic expeditions provide thorough definitions or lists of persons.

Contents: Symbols, attributes, and associations; Surnames, epithets, and patronymics; Heroic expeditions: Argonauts, Calydonian boar hunt, Trojan War; Guide to persona.

F3 Biedermann, Hans. Dictionary of symbolism: cultural icons and the meanings behind them. Trans. by James Hulbert. N.Y., Facts on File, 1992. x, 465p. il.

Trans. of Knaurs Lexikon der Symbole. München, Droemer Knaur, 1989.

"The purpose of this book is to acquaint the reader with the symbols that have been most significant throughout the history of civilization . . . this volume seeks to be as inclusive as possible, primarily through the material that goes beyond 'Eurocentric' concerns. . . . [It] is addressed to the general reader who seeks to know more about how images have been experienced and how their meanings have been extended."—*Pref.* Arranged alphabetically, the long, detailed entries cover a wide range of subjects. Illustrated throughout the text. Unique pictorial index provides access by illustration. Extremely thorough general index.

Bibliography, p.397–400. Pictorial Index, p.401–35. General Index, p.437–65.

F4 Iconography at the crossroads: papers from the colloquium sponsored by the Index of Christian Art, Princeton University, 23–24 March 1990. Ed. by Brendan Cassidy. Princeton, N.J., Index of Christian Art, Dept. of Art and Archaeology, Princeton Univ., 1993. 249p. il., plates. (Index of Christian art occasional papers, II)

This useful compilation of papers covering medieval and Renaissance themes presents "a fairly balanced conspectus of current approaches [to iconography] with contributions by both art historians and representatives from other branches of the humanities."—*Introd.*

Contents: (1) Introduction: iconography, texts, and audiences, by Brendan Cassidy; (2) Unwriting iconology, by Michael Ann Holly; (3) The politics of iconology, by Keith Moxey; (4) Iconography as a humanistic discipline ("Iconography at the crossroads"), by Irving Lavin; (6) Mouths and meanings: towards an anti-iconography of medieval art, by Michael Camille; (7) Medieval art as argument, by Herbert L. Kessler; (8) Disembodiment and corporality in Byzantine images of the saints, by Henry Maguire; (9) Diagrams of the medieval brain: a study in cerebral localization, by Ynez Violé O'Neill; (10) Gendering Jesus crucified, by Richard C. Trexler; (11) Medieval pictorial systems, by Wolfgang Kemp; (12) Piero della Francesco's iconographic innovations at Arezzo, by Marilyn Aronberg Lavin; (13) Miracles happen: image and experience in Jan van Ecyk's Madonna in a church, by Craig Harbison; (14) The Annunciation to Christine: authorial empowerment in The book of the city of ladies, by V. A. Kolve; (15) The "Mystical signature" of Christopher Columbus, by John V. Fleming; (16) Cleriadus et Meliadice:

a fifteenth-century manual for courtly behavior, by Howard Mayer Brown; (17) Images of music in three prints after Maarten van Heemskerck, by H. Colin Slim; (18) Index.

F5 Chevalier, Jean, and Gheerbrant, Alain. A dictionary of symbols. Trans. by John Buchanan-Brown. Cambridge, Mass., Blackwell, 1994. ix, 1174p.

See GLAH 1:F2 for 1st French ed. Trans. of Dictionnaire des symboles: mythes, rêves, coutumes, gestes. Ed. rev. et augm. Paris, R. Laffont/Jupiter, 1982.

Substantially enlarged from 1st French ed. Long scholarly entries on a wide range of symbols. Alphabetical arrangement. No illustrations.

Bibliography, p.[1150]–74.

F6 Cooper, J. C. An illustrated encyclopaedia of traditional symbols. N.Y., Thames and Hudson, 1979. 208p. il.

"The pattern adopted in this Encyclopaedia is first to present the generalized or universal acceptance of the interpretation of a symbol, then to particularize its diverse applications in varying traditions, cultural and geographic."—*Introd.* Valuable for its global approach to each symbol discussed.

Glossary, p.202–03. Bibliography, p.203–07.

F7 Hall, James. Dictionary of subjects and symbols in art. Rev. ed. Introd. by Kenneth Clark. N.Y., Harper and Row, 1979. xxix, 349p. il.

See GLAH 1:F7 for 1st ed.

Revised ed. includes additions and corrections as well as a "Supplementary index" (p. [346]–49) which "is intended to supplement the dictionary by providing references to such matters as religious beliefs, ideas and social customs which are mentioned in the subject articles. The index also includes a number of extra entries for 'identifying objects' omitted from the first edition."—*Pref. to supplementary index.*

F8 ———. Illustrated dictionary of symbols in eastern and western art. Illustrated by Chris Puleston. London, John Murray, 1994. xii, 244p. il., tables.

Uses the symbol as the starting point for discussing narrative references in a global context. Good cross-references. Small hand-drawn illustrations, charts, tables, and useful explanatory chapters and appendices.

Contents: (1) How to use this book; (2) About symbols in art; (3) The Dictionary, 1: Abstract signs; 2: Animals; 3: Artefacts; 4: Earth and sky; 5: Human body and dress; 6: Plants; Collectives

Appendix: the transcription of Chinese, p.216. Notes and references, p.217–21. Bibliography, p.223–24. Chronological tables (Egypt, Mesopotamia, India, China, Japan, Tibet, The West), p.225–33. Index, p.236–44.

F9 Hunger, Herbert. Lexikon der griechischen und römischen Mythologie: mit Hinweisen auf das Fortwirken antiker Stoffe und Motive in der bildenden Kunst, Literatur und Musik des Abendlandes bis zur Gegenwart. 8., erw. Aufl. Wien, Brüder Hollinek, 1988. xi, 557p. il.

1st ed. 1953.

Substantially revised and augmented since the first ed. While not strictly an art resource, this German reference work is important to iconographers trying to find representations of classical themes. Each entry is divided into three sections: a description of the myth, an iconographic explanation of the myth's significance in art and literature, and finally a list of the titles, artists, and locations (where applicable) of works of art, literature, music, opera, and theater that deal with the theme.

Bibliography, p.549–56.

F10 ICONCLASS browser ed. 2.0 [computer file]. Utrecht, ICONCLASS Research & Development Group, 1994. 7 computer disks

1st ed. 1992 was accompanied by User's guide, 110p. and Dutch printer's devices: a pilot project, pictorial information systems in the humanities [computer file]. 1 computer disk + 1 manual. 77p. il.

Electronic ed. of the printed ICONCLASS system, bibliography, and index (GLAH 1:F18). Third ed. forthcoming. Also available on the internet. The internet version lacks some of the features available in the disk version, most notably the ICONCLASS bibliography.

F11 ICONCLASS indexes. Dutch prints. Leiden, Foleor, 1994– . (3)v.

Eight vols. projected. "The series will give detailed iconographic access to the Dutch prints reproduced in the first seven volumes of The illustrated Bartsch [GLAH 1:N12 and GLAH 2:N9] covering the prints described in Adam von Bartsch's Le peintre-graveur [GLAH 1:N13], volumes 1–5 as well as to the supplementary volumes 50–59 of The illustrated Bartsch. The eight volumes will deal with the prints in a more or less chronological order, thus enabling researchers interested in prints from a particular period to only consult the two or three index volumes that apply."—*Introd.*

Contents: (4) Straten, Roelof van. Hendrik Goltzius and his school: an iconographic index to A. Bartsch, Le peintre-graveur, vol. 3 (1994); (7) Straten, Roelof van. Seventeenth century I: an iconographic index to A. Bartsch, Le peintre-graveur, vols. 1 and 2 (1995); (8) Straten, Roelof van. Seventeenth century II: an iconographic index to A. Bartsch, Le peintre-graveur, vols. 4 and 5 (1995).

Includes bibliographical references.

F12 ICONCLASS indexes. Early German prints. Leiden, Foleor, 1995– . (4)v.

Five vols. projected. Designed to give detailed iconographic access via ICONCLASS indexing to the German prints of the later 15th and 16th centuries described by Adam von Bartsch in vols. 6 and 10 of Le peintre-graveur (GLAH 1:N13) and reproduced in vols. 8, 9, and 23 of The illustrated Bartsch (GLAH 1:N12 and GLAH 2:N9).

Contents: (1) Laupichler, Fritz, and Straten, Roelof van. Martin Schongauer and his school: an iconographic index to A. Bartsch, Le peintre-graveur, vols. 6 and 10 (1995); (2) Laupichler, Fritz, and Straten, Roelof van. Albrecht Dürer and his time I: an iconographic index to A. Bartsch, Le peintre-graveur, vol. 7 (1996); (3) Albrecht Dürer and his time II: an iconographic index to A. Bartsch, Le peintre-graveur, vol. 8 (1996); (4) Virgil Solis and his time: an iconographic index to A. Bartsch, Le peintre-graveur, vol. 9 [pt.1] (1999).

Includes bibliographical references.

F13 ICONCLASS indexes. Italian prints. Doornspijk, Davaco, 1987– . (4)v.

Set provides extremely detailed iconographic access via the ICONCLASS system to prints in A. M. Hind's Early Italian engraving (GLAH 1:N115) and The illustrated Bartsch (GLAH 1:N12 and GLAH 2:N9). A fifth vol. covering prints unknown to Bartsch is projected.

Contents: (1) Straten, Roelof van. Early Italian engraving: an iconographic index to A. M. Hind, Early Italian engraving, London 1938–1948 (1987); (2) Straten, Roelof van. Marcantonio Raimondi and his school: an iconographic index to A. Bartsch, Le peintre-graveur, vols. 14, 15 and 16 (1988); (3) Straten, Roelof van with the assistance of Fritz Laupichler. Antonio Tempesta and his time: an iconographic index to A. Bartsch, Le peintre-graveur, vols. 12, 17 and 18 (1987); (4) Straten, Roelof van. The seventeenth century: an iconographic index to A. Bartsch, Le peintre-graveur, vols. 19, 20 and 21 (1990).

Includes bibliographical references.

F14 Index iconologicus [microform]. Sanford, N.C., Microfilming Corp. of America, 1980. [433] microfiches + guide (vi, 18p.).

Microform ed. of the paper index developed by Dr. Karla Langedijk at Duke University beginning in 1969. The Index was designed "to continue where the Princeton Index [of Christian Art] breaks off [at A.D. 1400] and to broaden its scope by focusing on both Christian and secular art. . . . The Index consists of more than 60,000 alphabetically filed entries . . . [which] . . . contain, in addition to photographic reproductions of art works much literary, bibliographic, and historical information. . . . The most important elements in the Index are the photographs of art work published by the Warburg Institute as illustrations to Bartsch's Le peintre-graveur [GLAH 1:N13]. . . . Photographs are indexed by subject themes, content, or artist . . . and each . . . is accompanied by its Bartsch citation and citations from other interpretive sources . . . [as well as] lists of other bibliographic and interpretive aids, bestiaries, cross references, Biblical texts, information cards, etc. . . . [The Index] can be used by scholars and students in two ways. When used alone it provides a systematic iconographic classification of Christian and secular art concentrating on the 16th and 17th centuries. The Index provides access by word, image and artist to many aspects of European cultural history. The combination of visual and verbal data in one place plus the complete citation of inscriptions, texts, quotations, and mottos make Index Iconologicus a self-contained research tool. If the Index is used with Bartsch's Le Peintre Graveur and the other catalogues that are cited on each picture card, the user has access to both the image and the detailed descriptions and histories that these works contain."—*Introd.*

F15 Kämmerling, Ekkehard, ed. Ikonographie und Ikonologie: Theorien, Entwicklung, Probleme. Köln, DuMont, 1987. 521p. (Bildende Kunst als Zeichensystem, 1)

Notable collection of reprints of influential and critical essays in German on iconography and iconology originally published between 1928 and 1977. Includes the complete bibliography of each author.

Contents: Skizze einer Geschichte der beabsichtigten und der interpretierenden Ikonographie (1973), von Jan Bialostocki; Symbolik und Ikonographie der christlichen Kunst: zur Methodologie der christlichen Ikonographie (1928), von Karl Künstle; Die Ikonologie und ihre wichtige Rolle bei der systematischen Auseinandersetzung mit christlicher Kunst (1931), von G. J. Hoogewerff; Die Genesis der Ikonologie (1967), von William S. Heckscher; Warburgs Begriff der Kulturwissenschaft und seine Bedeutung für die Ästhetik (1931), von Edgar Wind; Zum Problem der Beschreibung und Inhaltsdeutung von Werken der bildenden Kunst (1932/1964), von Erwin Panofsky; Ikonographie und Ikonologie (1939/1955), von Erwin Panofsky; Die Interpretation visueller Symbole in der bildenden Kunst (1955), von Rudolf Wittkower; Ikonologie und allgemeine Kunstgeschichte (1966/1979), von Erik Forssman; Ikonologie (1966), von Michael Liebmann; Zur Kritik der kunstwissenschaftlichen Symboltheorie (1967/1978), von Lorenz Dittmann; Kritik der Ikonologie (1977), von Otto Pächt; Ziele und Grenzen der Ikonologie (1972), von Ernst H. Gombrich; Panofsky und die Interpretation von Bildern (1973), von David Mannings; Beiträge zu einem Übergang von der Ikonologie zur kunstgeschichtlichen Hermeneutik (1978), von Oskar Bätschmann.

F16 Liungman, Carl G. Dictionary of symbols. Trans. from the Swedish. N.Y., Norton, 1994. ix, 596p. il.

Trans. of Symboler-västerländska ideogram. Malmö, Merkur, 1974. 1st Eng. ed. Santa Barbara, Calif., ABC-Clio, 1991.

"The intention of this work is that it should function both as a reference work in Western Cultural history and as a tool for those working with ideograms, e.g., logotype and trademark designers, those engaged in advertising, interior designers, researchers in communication, art historians, art and history teachers, etc."—*Introd.* Unique tool that provides access to graphic symbols from both a textual and a visual starting point. Well-designed and illustrated indexes.

Contents: (I) Introduction; (II) Ideographic dictionary; (III) Word index; (IV) Graphic index; (V) Graphic search index.

F17 Lurker, Manfred. Dictionary of gods and goddesses, devils and demons. N.Y., Routledge & Kegan Paul, 1987. x, 451p. il.

Trans. of Lexikon der Götter und Dämonen. Stuttgart, Kröner, 1984.

A general dictionary of gods and goddesses important for its multicultural coverage.

Appendix I: Functions, aspects, spheres of competence, p.394–417. Appendix II: Symbols, attributes, motifs, p.418–46. Bibliography, p.447–51.

F18 Morales y Marin, Jose Luis. Diccionario de iconologia y simbologia. Madrid, Taurus, 1984. 378p. il. plates.

Scholarly dictionary in Spanish. International in scope including non-western subjects. Entries include bibliographic references and are richly illustrated.

Indice de attributos, p.349–62. Bibliografia, p.363–78.

F19 Rager, Catherine. Dictionnaire des sujets mythologiques, bibliques, hagiographiques, et historiques dans l'art. [Turnhout, Belgium], Brepols, 1994. x, 762p.

A substantial French topical dictionary. Includes unique indexes that allow access to subjects by miracle or place of event. Focuses on western art only. Good cross-references.

Quelques lieux d'action militaire, p.744–58. Quelques miracles, p.759–62.

F20 Reid, Jane Davidson, with the assistance of Chris Rohmann. The Oxford guide to classical mythology in the arts, 1300–1990s. N.Y., Oxford Univ. Pr., 1993. 2v.

"An encyclopedic catalog of [more than 30,000] artworks dating from the early Renaissance to the present that treat subjects in Greek and Roman mythology. Organized into entries on mythological figures or themes, listings of artworks delineate the history of artistic interest in classical mythology as presented in the fine arts, music, dance, and literature of the past seven centuries."—*Introd.* Each entry includes a description of the subject, a list of the major classical literary sources for the subject and bibliographic references to additional books on the topic. The listing of artworks comprises the bulk of each entry, and includes pertinent information on titles, dates (of creation, publication, or performance as applicable), locations, versions, revisions, translations, studies, copies, and other works related to the original, and bibliographic source references.

List of sources, p.1073–118. Index of artists, p.1119–310.

F21 Rochelle, Mercedes. Mythological and classical world art index: a locator of paintings, sculptures, frescoes, manuscript illuminations, sketches, woodcuts, and engravings executed 1200 B.C. to 1900 A.D., with a directory of institutions holding them. Jefferson, N.C., McFarland, 1991. viii, 279p.

A locator arranged by subject that covers artworks from the classical period through the 19th century. Each entry includes a brief description of the subject (person, god, goddess, or event) and its historical or mythological significance followed by titles and locations of paintings taken from an extensive international selection of collections, museums, and repositories. An additional index of artists provides access to artworks by artists' names.

Bibliography p.239–47. Artist index, p.247–79.

F22 Straten, Roelof van. Iconography, Indexing, ICONCLASS: a handbook. Leiden, Foleor, 1994. xv, 244p. il. plates.

A handbook that serves as an explanatory guide to the author's interpretation and use of the ICONCLASS system as first exemplified in his ICONCLASS indexes to Italian prints. Includes detailed directions to assist both researchers and indexers.

Contents: List of illustrations; Introduction; (1) The theory of iconography; (2) The iconographic indexer and his work; (3) The ICONCLASS system; (4) Indexing Italian prints with ICONCLASS; (5) ICONCLASS: remarks and additions.

Appendix 1: Outline of the ICONCLASS system. Appendix 2: Composition and iconography. Appendix 3: Bibliography [on] ICONCLASS, p.233–39. Index, p.241–44.

F23 ______. An introduction to iconography. Trans. from the German by Patricia de Man. Rev. Eng. ed. Langhorne, Penn., Gordon and Breach, 1994. 151p. il. plates. (Documenting the image, 1)

Trans. of Einführung in die Ikonographie. Berlin, Reimer, 1989. Original ed., Inleiding in de iconografie. Muiderberg, Coutinho BV, 1985, rev. ed., 1991. Originally presented as the author's doctoral thesis.

Detailed handbook for students and teachers of art history that should fill a gap in methodology courses. The Theoretical section clearly explains and places in historical context basic concepts of iconography and iconology. The Practical section provides extensive annotated references to bibliographic and archival resources for further study.

Contents: Introduction to the series; List of illustrations; Preface; Introduction; (1) Theoretical Section: 1. What is iconography?; 2. Personification; 3. Allegory; 4. Symbols, attributes, and symbolic representations; (2) Practical Section: 5. Literary sources of subjects in art; 6. Iconographic handbooks and photo archives; 7. ICONCLASS: a new method of research in iconography; (3) Appendix: an overview of the ICONCLASS System;

Index p.149–51.

F24 Studies in the fine arts. Iconography. Ann Arbor, UMI Research Press, 1979–84. 10v. il.

Series ed. Linda Seidel. Part of the larger UMI series. Includes dissertations reflecting an iconographical approach.

Contents: (1) Riess, Jonathan B. Political ideals in medieval Italian art: the frescoes in the Palazzo dei Priori, Perugia (1297) (1981); (2) Dixon, Laurinda S. Alchemical imagery in Bosch's "Garden of Delights" (1981); (3) Watters, David H. "With bodilie eyes": eschatological themes in Puritan literature and gravestone art (1981); (4) DeMott, Barbara. Dogon masks: a structural study of form and meaning (1982); (5) Fishman, Jane Susannah. Boerenverdriet: Violence between peasants and soldiers in early modern Netherlands art (1982); (6) Glanz, Dawn. How the West was drawn: American art and the settling of the frontier (1982); (7) Durantini, Mary Frances. The child in seventeenth-century Dutch painting (1983); (8) Smith, David R. Masks of wedlock: seventeenth-century Dutch marriage portraiture (1982); (9) Lalumia, Matthew Paul. Realism and politics in Victorian art of the Crimean War (1984); (9) [sic] Kaplan, Paul H. D. The rise of the black magus in western art (1985).

F25 Tardy. Dictionnaire des arts, de l'histoire, des lettres et des religions. Paris, Tardy, 1987–1990. 3v. il., plates.

Cover title: Dictionnaire des thèmes et décors.

Although this is a broad dictionary covering more than iconography, it is noteworthy for the lists of artworks on specific themes.

Contents: (1) Thèmes de l'Occident classique; (2) Décors de l'Occident classique; (3) Thèmes et decors du XXe siècle.

F26 Thompson, Philip, and Davenport, Peter. The dictionary of graphic images. N.Y., St. Martin's, 1980. 258p. il.

Unique resource that traces iconographic symbols through their use as graphic cliches in modern day advertising, signs, etc. Designed to "fill the gap between the numerous dictionaries of historic symbols and the living visual language that artists and designers had been evolving during the last 50 years or so."—*Authors' note.*

SEE ALSO: Janson, Iconographic index to Stanislas Lami's Dictionnaire des sculpteurs de l'Ecole française aux dix-neuvième siècle (GLAH 2:K180); Marburger Index Datenbank [computer file] (GLAH 2:D64); Schweers, Gemälde in deutschen Museen: Katalog der augestellten und depotgelagerten Werke = Paintings in German museums: catalogue of exhibited works and depository holdings (GLAH 2:M29); Studies in iconography (GLAH 2:Q322).

ANCIENT

F27 Aghion, Irène; Barbillon, Claire; and Lissarague, François. Gods and heroes of classical antiquity. [Trans. by N. Amico.] N.Y., Flammarion, 1996. 317p. il. (part col.) (Flammarion iconographic guides)

Intended to "provide ready access to the narrative content of many works that readers are likely to come across in museums or books. . . . A concise collection of the tales that have inspired artists throughout the centuries."—*Introd.* Alphabetical arrangement, with individual mythological characters and episodes treated separately. Includes a brief account of the historical or mythological tradition, ancient and modern representations, and as appropriate, a list of attributes, cross-references to other entries, sources, and a concise bibliography. Principal iconographic repertories are listed in the general bibliography.

Bibliography, p.311–12. Index of people, authors, places, p.313–17.

F28 Black, Jeremy A., and Green, Anthony. Gods, demons, and symbols of ancient Mesopotamia: an illustrated dictionary. Illustrated by Tessa Rickards. Austin, Univ. of Texas Pr., 1992. 192p. il.

"An introductory guide to the beliefs and practices of the ancient Mesopotamians, as revealed in their art and their writings between about 3000 BC and the advent of the Christian era. Gods, goddesses, demons, monsters, magic, myths, religious symbolism, ritual and the spiritual world are all discussed in alphabetical entries ranging from short accounts to extended essays."—*Dust jacket.* Includes cross-references between Sumerian and Akkadian names.

Bibliography, p.191–92.

F29 Hart, George. A dictionary of Egyptian gods and goddesses. London, Routledge & Kegan Paul, 1986. xv, 229p. il.

Thorough dictionary aimed toward undergraduates and non-specialists. Entries on gods and goddesses are arranged alphabetically and describe their symbolism, origin, and various renderings.

Outline time-chart, p.xiii. Select further reading, p.227–29. Alternative renderings of divine names, p.229.

F30 Leick, Gwendolyn. A dictionary of ancient Near Eastern mythology. N.Y., Routledge, 1991. xiii, 199p. plates.

This dictionary "is intended as a general reference work for students of religious studies, anthropology and oriental studies and attempts to make the subject accessible to a wider academic audience."—*Introd.* An accessible English-language resource for students of art history researching ancient Near Eastern art. Extensive bibliography, excellent illustrations.

Chronological chart, p.xiii. Glossary, p.168–75. Bibliography, p.176–88. Index, p.189–99. Illustrations, p.200–26.

F31 Lexicon iconographicum mythologiae classicae [LIMC]. Zürich, Artemis, 1981–. (8)v. il. plates.

Entries in English, French, German, or Italian. Published by the Fondation pour le Lexicon iconographicum mythologiae classicae (LIMC). Each vol. consists of two parts, text and plates. On-line version forthcoming.

Monumental encyclopedia of Greek, Etruscan, and Roman mythological iconography. Also includes "non-Classical figures [who have been depicted] in Classical style or have points of contact with the Graeco-Roman world: for instance, the Arab Allath, who can appear under the guise of Athena/Minerva."—*Review*, American journal of archaeology, v.86, no. 4, 1982, p.599–600. Entries in the text vols. are arranged alphabetically by mythological figure. Each extremely detailed, signed entry begins with cross-references and references to literary sources, a full bibliography, and a catalog of works of art with references to the plate vols. Long, scholarly commentaries follow. Plate vols. are also arranged alphabetically by personage to foster comparative study of like images, and contain exceptional black and white reproductions and fine details.

Contents: (I) Aara-Aphlad (1981); (II) Aphrodisias-Athena (1984); (III) Atherion-Eros (1986); (IV) Eros-Herakles (1988); (V) Herakles-Kenchrias (1990); (VI) Kentauroi-Oiax (1992); (VII) Oidipous-Theseus (1994); (VIII) forthcoming (1997).

Indices: (1) Museen, Sammlungen, Orte = Museums, collections, sites. (2) Literarische und Epigraphische Quellen zu nicht erhaltenen Werken; mythologische Namen = Literary and epigraphical sources mentioning lost works; mythological names (1999).

F32 Lurker, Manfred. The gods and symbols of ancient Egypt: an illustrated dictionary. [Trans. by Barbara Cumming]. Rev., enl., and picture-ed. by Peter A. Clayton. N.Y., Thames and Hudson, 1980. 142p. il.

Trans. of Götter und Symbole der alten Ägypter. Bern, Scherz, 1974.

Although dated, Lurker's dictionary remains a useful resource. Each entry provides a description of the iconographical significance of the symbol, god, or goddess under discussion.

Contents: Introduction to the world of Egyptian symbolism; The cultural and religious history of Egypt; The dictionary.

Map of Egypt, p.22. Chronological table, p.132–35. Select bibliography, p.136–37. Index to the illustrations, p.139–41.

F33 Wilkinson, Richard H. Reading Egyptian art: a hieroglyphic guide to ancient Egyptian painting and sculpture. London, Thames and Hudson, 1992. 224p. il.

Useful guide for undergraduates and non-specialists, "designed to allow the non-specialist to 'read' the major hieroglyphs found in Egyptian painting and sculpture and to understand much of the symbolic content of Egyptian art which is usually only accessible to the trained Egyptologist."—*Pref.* Well-illustrated, page-length entries are arranged topically by genre.

Contents: History and art of Egypt; Catalog of Hieroglyphs; Gardiner's sign list.

Bibliography, p.220–22. Index, p.223–24.

CHRISTIAN

F34 Apostolos-Cappadona, Diane. Dictionary of Christian Art. N.Y., Continuum, 1994. 376p. il.

A good single-vol. dictionary in English, useful for beginning students learning about Christian art and iconography.

Bibliography, p.351–53. List of illustrations and captions, p.354–68. Index, p.369–76.

F35 Duchet-Suchaux, Gaston, and Pastoureau, Michel. The Bible and the saints. Trans. by David Radzinowicz Howell. N.Y., Flammarion, 1994. 360p. il., plates. (Flammarion iconographic guides)

Trans. of Bible et les saints. Paris, Flammarion, 1990.

This is the first guide in a projected series of iconographical guides published by Flammarion. Each entry provides variant names and titles for subjects, a descriptive paragraph, a list of attributes, cross references to other entries, and a brief bibliography. A more extensive bibliography is included at the end. Well illustrated with many color reproductions.

Index of attributes and their associated figures, p.354–56. Bibliography p.357–59.

F36 Earls, Irene. Baroque art: a topical dictionary. Westport, Conn., Greenwood, 1996. xv, 332p.

"This dictionary is . . . a reference source for identifying and understanding the art of Italy and northern Europe during the 1600s. . . . Also included are a limited number of entries on characteristic schools, media, techniques and other terminology one might find in the art history volumes covering this period."—*Pref.* Arranged in a single alphabetical sequence.

List of popes of the Baroque age, p.[309]. List of artists, p.[311]–15. Bibliography, p.[317]–19. Index, p.[321]–32.

F37 ———. Renaissance art: a topical dictionary. N.Y., Greenwood, 1987. xv, 345p.

"This dictionary is . . . a quick reference source for identifying and understanding Renaissance art of Italy and northern Europe. It contains basic information about topics that were common subjects of painting, sculpture, and decorative arts of the period. Additionally, entries on characteristic schools, techniques, media, and other terminology have been included."—*Pref.* Arranged in a single alphabetical sequence.

List of artists, p.[315]–21. Bibliography, p.[323]–27. Index, p.[329]–45.

F38 Erffa, Hans Martin von. Ikonologie der Genesis: die christlichen Bildthemen aus dem Alten Testament und ihre Quellen. [München], Deutscher Kunstverlag, 1989–95. 2v.

An extremely ambitious and scholarly project that aims to cover in detail all aspects of the iconography of Genesis. Each entry includes a dense description of the topic replete with biblical and bibliographical references, followed by three valuable bibliographical lists. (1) Schriftquellen (QU) includes bibliographic references to the topic made by early Christian, Jewish, classical antique and Arabic authors; (2) Literature (LIT) contains references to non-art historical material on the subject; (3) Ikonographie (IKON) provides bibliographic references to art historical literature on the topic.

Abkürzungsschlüssel, v.1, p.521–29, v.2, p.503–13. Ikonographischer Index, v.1, p.531–42, v.2, p.515–33. Druckfehlerberichtigungen im I. Band, v.2, p.501.

F39 Friedman, John Block, and Wegmann, Jessica M. Medieval iconography: a research guide. N.Y., Garland, 1998. xxiv, 437p. (Garland medieval bibliographies, 20) (Garland reference library of the humanities, 1870)

"The present volume aims to help the researcher locate visual motifs, whether in medieval art or literature, and to understand how they function in yet other medieval literary or artistic works. . . . We envision . . . the advanced undergraduate, the graduate student, or the literary scholar as the primary audience for the book."—*Introd.* 1,896 annotated bibliographical entries.

Contents: Part one [research tools]: (1) Art; (2) Other tools. Part two [iconographic themes]: (3) Learned imagery; (4) The Christian tradition; (5) The natural world; (6) Medieval daily life.

Index, p.[413]–37.

F40 Garnier, François. Le langage de l'image au Môyen Age. Paris, Leopard d'or, 1982–[1989]. 2v., il., plates.

Although more of a thesis than a reference book, this is an extremely ambitious and useful iconographical exploration of various compositions and gestures in medieval art. Illustrated chapters are arranged by type of composition or gesture and then further broken down into sections of even greater detail.

Contents: (1) Signification et symbolique: (I) Le langage iconographique; (II) La documentation et son exploitation; (III) Aspects généraux du langage iconographique: cadres et structures; (IV) Les éléments; (V) Les dimensions; (VI) Les situations; (VII) Les positions du corps; (VIII) Positions et expressions de la tête; (IX) Gestes de la main et du bras; (X) Positions et gestes des jambes et des pieds; (XI) Relations avec les objets. Conclusion. (2) Grammaire des gestes: (Première partie) Quelques aspects essentiels du langage iconographique: (I) Réalisme et symbolisme; (II) Figuration du temps; (III) Figuration actif/passif, en état/en action; (IV) Corrélations et contextes; (Deuxième partie) Comportements corporels: (I) Situation: Double silhouetté; (II) La tête; (III) Gestes et positions de la main; (IV) Gestes et positions des bras; (V) Relations avec le pied/la jambe; (Troisième partie) Relations avec les éléments: (I) La boule; (II) La ceinture; (III) La colonne: (IV) La corde au cou; (V) Le cornet; (VI) L'édifice; (VII) La foudre céleste; (VIII) La fleur de lis; (IX) Le miroir; (X) Le phylactère; (XI) L'offrande du poisson; (XII) Le vêtement; (XIII) Vice ou vertu: le suicide; Conclusion provisoire.

Index des significations, v.1, p.249–50. Index des photograpies et des dessins, v.1, p.251–54; Index des photographies, des dessins et des gravures, v.2, p.[291]–99. Bibliographie, v.1, p.255–56, v.2, p.[301]–02. Index général, v.1, p.283–84, v.2, p.[285]–89.

F41 Grabar, André. Les voies de la création en iconographie chrétienne: antiquité et moyen âge. Paris, Flammarion, 1979. 341p. il. (Idées et recherches)

Includes a French translation of his classic Christian iconography: a study of its origins, 1968 (GLAH 1:I159). Augmented ed. of this scholarly work includes a new, second section on the Middle Ages.

Contents: Avant-propos; Antiquité: Première partie. (I) Les premiers pas; (II) L'assimilation de l'iconographie contemporaine. Deuxième partie. (III) Le portrait; (IV) La scène historique; (V) Dogmes exprimés par une image; (VI) Dogmes représentés par des images juxtaposées. Moyen Age: Introduction; Byzance; L'image chrétienne en occident: principes et réalisations; Le problème de l'iconographie populaire au moyen âge; Conclusion.

Bibliographie sommaire, p.203–14. Illustrations, p.215–33. Index, p.335–39.

F42 Jacobus de Varagine. The golden legend: readings on the saints. Trans. by William Granger Ryan. Princeton, Princeton Univ. Pr., 1993. 2v.

Trans. of Legenda aurea, based on the Latin ed. of Th. Graesse, Leipzig, 1845. See GLAH 1:F35 for earlier partial trans. (repr., Salem, N.H., Ayer, 1994).

The first complete modern English translation. This 2-vol. set supersedes Ryan's earlier partial translation and will be indispensable to the study of iconography.

Index, p.397–400.

F43 Kaftal, George. Iconography of the saints in the painting of north west Italy. Firenze, Le Lettere, 1985. ix–xviii, 818 numb. cols. 958 il., col. plates. (Saints in Italian art, 4)

See GLAH 1:F39, GLAH 1:F40 for earlier vols.

"This volume completes [the author's] study of the Iconography of Saints in Italian Painting from its beginning until the early years of the XVIth century. The present volume deals with the iconography of the saints represented on panels, frescoes, mosaics and exceptionally manuscript illuminations belonging to the Schools of North West Italy. Topographically these schools include Lombardy, Piedmonte, Savoy, and Liguria."—*Introd.*

Contents: (I) Saints and blessed, Unidentified saints and blessed; (II) Index of attributes and distinctive signs; Index of painters; Topographical index of painters; Bibliographical index; Index of saints and blessed.

F44 Marienlexikon. Hrsg. im Auftrag des Institutum Marianum Regensburg e. V. von Remigius Bäumer und Leo Scheffczyk. St. Ottilien, EOS, 1988–94. 6v., il.

Dense encyclopedia covering the topic of the Virgin Mary and her cult that includes many references to works of art. This ambitious set supersedes the abortive Lexikon der Marienkunde project (GLAH 1:F43). Signed scholarly articles include excellent bibliographical notes and literary references.

F45 Ohlgren, Thomas H., ed. Corpus of insular and Anglo-Saxon illuminated manuscripts [computer file]. ed. 1.0. Orem, Utah, Infobusiness, 1991. 2 computer disks; 3 3/4 in.

Accompanied by Infobase user; Infobusiness manual; Reference guide, 19p. il.

"Consists of revised and expanded entries from Ohlgren's Insular and Anglo-Saxon manuscripts, an iconographic catalogue (AD 625–1100) [GLAH 2:F48] for 229 illuminated manuscripts produced or owned in the British Isles. Each entry contains codicology and iconographic descriptions, and the software allows users to approach subjects by a variety of search commands."—*Manual.*

F46 ———. Illuminated manuscripts: an index to selected Bodleian Library color reproductions. N.Y., Garland, 1977. xxxiii, 646p. il. plates. (Garland reference library of the humanities, 89)

"This reference tool provides intellectual access to five hundred of the Bodleian slide sets containing some 20,000 color transparencies from over 1,100 manuscripts and renaissance books in the Bodleian collection. . . . This volume is unique in giving descriptions of the iconography of each illuminated folio or page. Since each descriptor is followed by a frame number, individual slide retrieval is possible."—*General introd.* Although the computer technology utilized to compile this index is dated and therefore the presentation is difficult to read and decipher, this index remains unsurpassed in the quantity of iconographical information it provides, making the effort required to use it worthwhile.

Index to slide set titles, p.243–51. Index to negative references, p.252–61. Index to titles of manuscripts, p.262–76.

Index to shelfmarks, p.277–316. Index to provenance, p.317–28. Index to dates executed, p.329–43. Index to languages of texts, p.344–46. Index to artists or schools of illumination, p.347–48. Index to authors of texts, p.349–55. Index to contents, p.368–646.

F47 ______. Illuminated manuscripts and books in the Bodleian Library: a supplemental index. N.Y., Garland, 1978. xxxii, 583p. il., plates. (Garland reference library of the humanities, 123).

Supplement to the preceding entry. "Comprises an additional 250 abstracts of and indices to the Bodleian Library filmstrips. . . . Altogether, this volume provides access to over ten thousand folios and pages from 672 manuscripts and one hundred printed books . . . dating in the main from the ninth century through the seventeenth century."—*Introd.*

Index to libraries, p.202. Index to slide set titles, p.203–07. Index to negative references, p.208–12. Index to titles of manuscripts, p.213–31. Index to shelfmarks, p.232–313. Index to provenance, p.314–327. Index to dates executed, p.328–50. Index to languages of texts, p.351–57. Index to artists or schools of illumination, p.358–61. Index to authors of texts, p.362–70. Index to scribes, p.371. Index to types of manuscripts, p.372–86. Index to contents, p.387–583.

F48 ______. Insular and Anglo-Saxon illuminated manuscripts: an iconographic catalogue, c. A.D. 625 to 1100. N.Y., Garland, 1986. 480p. il. (Garland reference library of the humanities, 631)

An iconographical catalog of all 229 extant English and Irish illuminated manuscripts and their illustrations. The index to iconographical contents ". . . makes this book . . . an extraordinary reference resource. From Aaron (brother of Moses) to Zodiac, there are approximately 3,750 index terms utilized, many of them see and see also cross-references."—*Review*, Art documentation, v.5, no.4, 1986, p.182. Iconographical descriptions of illustrations are adopted from the Editor's file at the Index of Christian Art at Princeton.

Photo-Bibliography, p. xxi–vii. Index to manuscripts, p.306–14. Index to authors and titles, p.315–18. Index to places of origin and provenance, p.319–21. Index to dates, p.322–24. Index to iconographic contents, p.325–400. Illustrations, p.403–80.

F49 Roberts, Helene E. Iconographic index to Old Testament subjects represented in photographs and slides of paintings in the visual collections, Fine Arts Library, Harvard University. N.Y., Garland, 1987. xi, 197p. il., plates. (Garland reference library of the humanities, 729)

A highly useful index organized according to the ICONCLASS system that should assist any researcher looking for works of art on particular Old Testament themes. Companion vol. to the following entry.

Contents: Introduction; Index of concepts, terms, and proper names; Iconclass classification of Old Testament themes; listing of themes and paintings representing them.

F50 ______, and Hall, Rachel. Iconographic index to New Testament subjects represented in photographs and slides of paintings in the visual collections, Fine Arts Library, Harvard University. Volume I: Narrative paintings of the Italian School. N.Y., Garland, 1992. 254p. il. (Garland reference library of the humanities, 1154)

Companion vol. to the preceding entry, also using the ICONCLASS system to organize New Testament themes depicted in Italian paintings.

Contents: Introduction; (I) Index of concepts, terms, and proper names; (II) Paintings in the collection: (A) John the Baptist and the early life of Mary; (B) Birth and youth of Christ; (C) Public life of Christ from his Baptism until the Passion; (D) Passion of Christ, Entombment, and Descent into Limbo; (E) Resurrection, Appearance, and Ascension of Christ; Pentecost; Later Life and Assumption of the Virgin; (F) Lives and Acts of the Apostles of Christ, and (G) Revelation of John, the Apocalypse.

F51 Rochelle, Mercedes. Post-Biblical saints art index: a locator of paintings, sculptures, mosaics, icons, frescoes, manuscript illuminations, sketches, woodcuts, and engravings, created from the 4th century to 1950, with a directory of the institutions holding them. Jefferson, N.C., McFarland, 1994. ix, 357p.

Unique subject index to more than 4,200 saints including some about whom little is known. Entries contain a description of the saint's title and significance, priestly order, martyrdom, dates of death, and feast days. Also included is a locator of depictions of the saint in art that describes the scenes and provides references to their present locations. A directory provides the location of each artwork mentioned. The lengthy index of attributes and events provides detailed access points for identifying saints. Thorough bibliography.

Index of artists, p.247–96. Index of attributes and events, p.297–318. Directory, p.319–42. Bibliography, p.343–57.

F52 Ross, Leslie. Medieval art: a topical dictionary. Westport, Conn., Greenwood, 1996. xxiv, 292p.

"This dictionary has been designed to provide a quick reference source for identifying and comprehending the subjects, stories, symbols, and themes frequently represented in early Christian, western medieval, and Byzantine art."—*Pref.*

Selected bibliography, p.[273]–78. General index, p.[279]–89. Index of saints, p.[291]–92.

F53 Schenone, Héctor H. Iconografía del arte colonial. [Buenos Aires?], Fundación Tarea, 1992–98. 3v.

Handbook of religious iconography in colonial Latin America. V.1–2 treat the saints, each entry giving brief biography, lists known images at colonial sites, and iconographical attributes. V.3 treats the life of Christ.

Contents: (1–2) Los santos; (3) Jesucristo.

Bibliographies in each vol.

F54 Schiller, Gertrud. Ikonographie der christlichen Kunst. [1. Aufl. Gütersloh] Mohn, [1966–]. (5)v.

See GLAH 1:F51 for earlier vols., which began appearing in 2d ed. in 1969.

Contents: (4/2) Maria (1980); (5/1) Die Apokalypse des Johannes: Textteil (1990); (5/2) Die Apokalypse des Johannes: Bildteil (1991).

Registerbeiheft zu den Bänden 1 bis 4/2, bearb. von Rupert Schreiner (1980), 120p.

F55 Sebastián, Santiago. Iconografía e iconología del arte novohispano. Pres. de José Pascual Buxó. México, D.F., Azabache, 1992. 179p. col. il. (Arte novohispano, 6)

Important study of the iconography of colonial art in Latin America.

Contents: Imagenes de la Iglesia; Iconografia de Maria y de Cristo; Las imagenes hagiograficas de las ordenes religiosas; La imagen de la muerte y el mas alla; Las imagenes del humanismo; El lenguaje emblematico; Iconografia del Indio y de los pueblos europeos.

Bibliografia, p.177–79.

F56 Seibert, Jutta. Lexikon christlicher Kunst: Themen, Gestalten, Symbole. Freiburg im Breisgau, Herder, 1980. 352p. il., plates.

Substantial general iconographical dictionary includes more than 1,000 entries on themes and symbols in Christian art. Richly illustrated with more than 300 line drawings and black and white reproductions. Good cross-references, references to biblical passages, and a very useful index to biblical themes that refers back to the entries in the dictionary.

Literaturhinweise, p.347. Bibelstellen-Register, p.348–52.

F57 Sinding-Larsen, Staale. Iconography and ritual: a study of analytical perspectives. Oslo, Universitetsforlaget [Distr. by Columbia Univ. Pr., 1984]. 210p.

A scholarly study that "analyzes the methodological basis for investigation of the relationship between liturgy and iconography in Medieval and Renaissance art."—*Abstract*, RILA, International repertory of the literature of art, v. 14, 1988, p.395. Includes noteworthy bibliographies of non-art historical resources important for the art historian's study of Christian liturgy, ritual, teachings concerning sacred images, and Church furniture.

Contents: (I) Introduction; (II) Functional context for Christian iconography; (III) Empirical parameters; (IV) Systems in interaction.

Bibliographies, p.196–203. Index, p.204.

F58 Speake, Jennifer. The Dent dictionary of symbols in Christian art. London, Dent, 1994. xi, 178p.

The more than 800 entries emphasize the biographies and attributes of frequently depicted saints. Good cross-references. "Among recent works (e.g. dictionaries of the saints) no other recent publications match the coverage of this one."—*Review*, Choice, July/August 1995.

Select bibliography, p.161–62. Some saints' names, p.163–64. Visual index, p.167–78.

F59 Spitzing, Günter. Lexikon byzantinisch-christlicher Symbole: die Bilderwelt Griechenlands und Kleinasiens. München, Diederichs, 1989. 344p. il., plates.

Important for its focus on the iconography and symbolism of the art of the Byzantine Empire. Detailed entries often include illustrations or tables and charts. Includes bibliographical and cross-references.

Contents: (I) Der Bildkosmos der byzantinishen Kirche; (II) Byzantinisch-christliche Symbole und Bildmotive von ABC bis Zahl; (III) Anhang: Entzifferungshilfen für Bildbeischriften (griechisch-deutsch).

Die Entwicklung des byzantinischen Reiches, p.327–29. Kunstgeschichtliche Epochen von der frühchristlichen Zeit bis zur Gegenwart, p.330–31. Die wichtigsten byzantinischen Monumente, p.332–41. Literaturverzeichnis, p.342–44.

SEE ALSO: Mâle, Religious art in France: the late Middle Ages: a study of medieval iconography and its sources (GLAH 2:I316); Mâle, Religious art in France, the thirteenth century: a study of medieval iconography and its sources (GLAH 2:I317); Mâle, Religious art in France, the twelfth century: a study of the origins of medieval iconography (GLAH 1:I285).

JEWISH

F60 Index of Jewish art: iconographical index to Hebrew illuminated manuscripts. Ed. by Bezalel Narkiss and Gabrielle Sed-Rajna in collab. with Jonathan Benjamin . . . [et al.] Jerusalem, Israel Academy of Sciences and Humanities, 1976– . (10)v. il. facsims.

Distr. by K.G. Saur, 1978–81.

Each vol. consists of index cards measuring 16 x 21 cm., an index guide, and corrected references to the previous vol. In English, French, and Hebrew. V.5 contains a cumulative subject index to v.1–5.

The Index was devised to complement the Princeton index of Christian art as a comprehensive iconographical index to Jewish art, defined as "objects made for the use and appreciation of people living according to the Jewish tradition, in their ritual and everyday life, including artifacts created by non-Jewish artists. The scope of Jewish, as distinct from early Israelite art is confined in this definition to the Hellenistic period onwards."—*Introd.* Published to date are the areas with which the Index began, concentrating solely on Hebrew illuminated manuscripts, because this area is the most heavily illustrated in Jewish art. Each vol. consists of an index pamphlet and a collection of index cards. Earlier vols. included more cards with information that by 1994 was streamlined into two types of cards to describe each object. The General card gives a systematic analytical description of each manuscript, and includes the following fields: Index of Jewish art number, object, origin, date, medium, collection number, name/title of manuscript, contents, codicology, binding colophon, history, decoration programme, bibliography. The Object card includes a facsimile photograph and describes the subjects depicted in the manuscript with the following additional fields: folio number; photographer; artist/maker; subject/reference; description. Very high quality black-and-white reproductions. On-line version announced. "A monumental contribution to the history of Jewish art, costume, and customs, and to comparative iconography."—*Review*, Art bulletin LXI, no.1, March 1979, p.107.

Contents: (1) Birds' Head Haggadah; Erna Michael Haggadah; Chantilly Haggadah; Greek Haggadah (1976?); (2) Index; References (München, K. G. Saur, 1981); II/I: Hileq and Bileq Haggadah, Paris, Bibliothèque Nationale, ms. Hébr. 1933 (1978); II/2: 2nd Nürnberg Haggadah, Jerusalem, Schocken Library, ms. 24087, part 1 (1978); II/3: 2nd Nürnberg Haggadah, Jerusalem, Schocken Library, ms. 24087, part 2 (1981); II/3: Yahuda Haggadah, Jerusalem, Israel Museum, ms. 180/50, parts 1 and 2 (1981); (3) Rothschild Miscellany, Jerusalem, Israel Museum, ms. 180/51; Index, References (1983); (4) Illuminated manuscripts of the Kaufmann Collection at the Library of the Hungarian Academy of Sciences; Index; References (1988); (5) Illuminated manuscripts of the Copenhagen Collection at the Royal Library, Copenhagen; Index; References (1994); (6) Index of ancient Jewish art (1984); (7) Shoshanim Le David: a synagogue and its ritual objects; (8–9) Gross Family Collection: (I) Objects; (II) Manuscripts and printed books (1985); (10) The synagogues of Bar'am; Jerusalem ossuaries (1987).

ASIAN COUNTRIES

China

F61 Eberhard, Wolfram. A dictionary of Chinese symbols: hidden symbols in Chinese life and thought. Trans. by G. L. Campbell. N.Y., Routledge and Kegan Paul, 1986. 332p. il.

Trans. of Lexicon chinesischer symbole. Zürich, Buchclub Ex Libris, 1985.

Includes entries for more than 400 symbols from Chinese culture. Entries are in alphabetical order by the English-language term and include the Chinese term in romanization and character. Definitions frequently make reference to literary or artistic works and occasionally include an illustration.

Bibliography, p.329–32.

F62 Oort, H. A. van. The iconography of Chinese Buddhism in traditional China. Leiden, Brill, 1986. 2v. il., plates. (Iconography of religions. Section 12: East and Central Asia; fasc. 5, 1–2)

A selected bibliography is followed by essays, a catalog of illustrations, and plates. Includes many photographs of sculpture and paintings.

Contents: (1) Han to Liao; (2) Sung to Ch'ing.

Selected bibliography, v.1, p.[ix]–x; v.2, p.[vii]–viii.

EMBLEM BOOKS

F63 AMS studies in the emblem. No. 1– . N.Y., AMS Pr., 1988– .

An irregular monographic series comprised of a variety of scholarly studies of emblem books and emblems.

Contents: (1) Daly, Peter M. The English emblem and the continental tradition (1987); (2) Manning, John, ed. The emblems of Thomas Palmer: two hundred poosees (1988); (3) Young, Alan R. English tournament imprese (1988); (4) Andrea Alciato and the emblem tradition: essays in honor of Virginia Woods Callahan (1989); (6) Daly, Peter M., ed. The Index of Emblem Art symposium (1990); (8) Katz, Wendy R. The emblems of Margaret Gatty: a study of allegory in nineteenth-century children's literature (1993); (9) Tung, Mason. Two concordances to Ripa's Iconologia (1993); (9) [sic] The art of the emblem: essays in honor of Karl Josef Holtgen (1993); (11) Heckscher, William S., and Sherman, Agnes B. Emblematic variants: literary echoes of Alciati's term emblema: a vocabulary drawn from the title pages of emblem books (1992); (13) Deviceful settings: the English Renaissance emblem and its contexts: selected papers from the Third International Emblem Conference, Pittsburgh (1993) (1999).

F64 Black, Hester M. A short title catalogue of the emblem books and related works in the Stirling Maxwell collection of Glasgow University Library (1499–1917). Ed. and rev. by David Weston. Brookfield, Vt., Scolar Pr., 1988. 99p.

Includes entries for 1,777 editions held in the Stirling Maxwell collection, ". . . probably the largest [collection] ever assembled . . . about 1500 of which are for emblem books, device books, emblematic encyclopaedias, works on emblem theory, and iconologies. The remainder relates to fête and ceremonial books."—*Introd.*

Contents: Introduction; Alphabetical short-title list; Appendix of manuscripts in the Stirling Maxwell and other collections.

Chronological index, p.87–99.

F65 Campa, Pedro F. Emblemata Hispanica: an annotated bibliography of Spanish emblem literature to the year 1700. Durham, Duke Univ. Pr., 1990. xii, 248p. il., plates.

"Comprises the production of Spanish emblem literature published from 1540 to 1700. It includes all the editions of Spanish emblem books, emblem books written by Spaniards in other languages, as well as polyglot editions of emblem books in which Spanish is one of the featured languages."—*Introd.* Some sources on Spanish-American emblematics are also included. Entries are arranged chronologically by author within thematic sections, and include imprint, pagination, signatures, number of emblems, and notes identifying dedicatees, artists and/or engravers. Bibliographic information and cross-references to other bibliographies, libraries, and call numbers, and descriptions of modern facsimiles, and composite editions follow each entry. Lengthy thematic bibliographies of secondary sources are included in separate sections. Useful appendixes.

Contents: Introduction; Abbreviations; Key to libraries; Major sources for this bibliography; Primary Sources: (A) Alciato in Spain. Editions and commentaries; (S) Emblem books in Spanish. Authors; (T) Translations into Spanish. Authors; (F) Emblem books written by Spaniards in other languages; (P) Polyglot editions containing Spanish text. Authors. Secondary Sources: (I) Emblem Compendia, library inventories, contemporary definitions of emblem, glossaries, commentaries, poetic treatises and emblem theory not contained in emblem books; (II) Mythographies, iconographies, arts of painting, works on paradoxography, numismatic works, emblematic topoi, visual motifs, proverbs and apothegms, studies on collectors and collecting, works on antiquarianism, studies on word and image, works on natural history, cultural studies, studies in mythology, and studies in art history and architecture of importance to Spanish emblem literature; (III) Overviews of Spanish emblem literature and short mentions of Spanish writers not included under studies of individual authors; (IV) Studies about emblem books and about emblem writers included in the primary sources of this bibliography; (V) Emblem literature: the emblem and literature; (VI) The emblem and the arts; (VII) Studies about fêtes, funerals, and royal entries. Appendix X: Bibliographic ghosts, untraceable or lost emblem books, and related items; Appendix Y: Short-title list of items often included in emblem book bibliographies, manuscripts, iconologies, symbologies, bestiaries, and other miscellaneous entries akin to emblem books; Appendix Z: Short-title bibliography to fêtes, royal entries, and funeral books of the Spanish golden age containing emblematic material.

Index of copies examined, p.219. Index of places of publication, p.220–22. Index of dates of publication, p.223–25. Index of printers, publishers, and booksellers, p.226–27. Index of artists, p.228. Index of dedicatees, p.229–30. Index of names, p.231–41. Index of subjects, p.242–48.

F66 Corpus librorum emblematum. 1– . N.Y., Saur; Montreal, McGill-Queen's University Pr., 1987– .

Editor: Peter M. Daly. Publisher varies.

A series of studies on and bibliographies of emblem books.

Contents: Daly, Peter M., and Silcox, Mary V. The English emblem: bibliography of secondary literature (1990); Daly, Peter M., and Silcox, Mary V. The modern critical reception of the English emblem (1991); Daly, Peter M., and Dimler, G. Richard, eds. The Jesuit series (1997); Sider, Sandra, and Obrist, Barbara, eds. Bibliography of emblematic manuscripts (1997).

F67 Diehl, Huston. An index of icons in English emblem books, 1500–1700. Norman, Univ. of Oklahoma Pr., 1986. xiii, 258p. il.

A comprehensive complement to Henkel and Schöne's Emblemata (GLAH 1:F73). This subject index "makes available for the first time an alphabetical compilation of every icon in every English emblem book (including the polyglot editions of Continental books with English texts) printed in the sixteenth and seventeenth centuries. It indexes the twenty-four extant English emblem books of this period and one manuscript."—*Introd.* Entries are arranged alphabetically by words or phrases that identify the emblematic image and provide references to all extant English emblem books including that image. Provides mottos and descriptions of icons or pictures. Includes cross-references to related images. A separate section on illustrations gives descriptive information about the number, type, format and content of the illustrations in each book, along with a single exemplary image for each title.

Bibliography of sixteenth- and seventeenth-century English emblem books, p.253–54. Index, p.255–58.

F68 Emblem book facsimile series. Brookfield, Vt., Ashgate, 1996– .

A new series created in association with Glasgow University Library and its extensive emblem book holdings. "The general editors decided that the objective initially should be to provide those texts from the late sixteenth and early seventeenth centuries which would be most referred to by the students of the period, or which are too scarce to be easily consulted."—*Introd.* Includes scholarly introductions.

Contents: Vaenius, Otto. Amorum emblemata, 1996.

F69 Emblem books: a microfiche project [microform]. Zug, InterDocumentation, 1981 [?] [ca. 2000] microfiches + 1 catalog. [4], 23p. il.

Reproduces 354 emblem books.

This enormous collection of emblem books on microfiche is an extremely valuable resource for anyone needing ready access to emblem books. The publisher's ambitious project was "to bring together . . . all known emblem books with the exception of identical later editions and reprints . . . through the cooperation of a number of libraries with strong collections."—*Catalog.* Incomplete.

The supplements (below) reproduce, respectively, 135 and 279 emblem books from the National Library of Austria in Vienna. Coverage in the supplements is intentionally broad, and includes titles which are often excluded from strict definitions of emblem books, such as books with Dances of Death, iconologies, royal entries, festivities and funerals, hieroglyphs, and books in the tradition of the Stultifera Navis.

———. Supplement 1: a microfiche project [microform]. Ed. by Wim van Dongen. Zug, Inter Documentation, [198–?]. [ca. 780] microfiches + 1 catalog. 11p. il., plates.

———. Supplement 2: a microfiche project. Ed. by Wim van Dongen. Zug, Inter Documentation, [1985?]. 1303 microfiches + 1 catalog. 23p. il., plates.

F70 Emblem books at the University of Illinois: a bibliographic catalogue. Boston, Hall, 1993. 363p. il.

Thorough bibliography of emblem books and related items held in the Rare Book and Special Collections Library at the University of Illinois at Urbana-Champaign. Part One includes descriptions of 601 original editions and some reissues published in 1800 or earlier. Detailed entries are arranged alphabetically by author or title followed by a transcription of the title page, a bibliographic description of an ideal copy, pagination or foliation, formulae, descriptions of illustrated matter, information unique to the university's copy, and bibliographic references. Part Two is a checklist of short-title descriptions of 408 emblem books in reprint, facsimile, or microform ed.

Contents: Part one: original editions. Comp. by Thomas McGeary; Part two: reprints and microforms. Comp. by N. Frederick Nash; Cross-references.

F71 Emblem books in the Princeton University Library: short-title catalogue. Compiled by William S. Heckscher and Agnes B. Sherman with the assistance of Stephen Ferguson. Princeton, Princeton University Library, 1984. vii, 105p.

Alphabetical checklist of nearly 800 original editions, facsimiles, and microfilm reproductions of emblem books held by Princeton University Library. Approximately sixty percent of the entries are for original editions. Entries include cross-references to related editions. Useful indexes.

Contents: Introduction; Note on the collection; Note on indexes; Short-title catalogue of emblem books; Index of printers, booksellers, and publishers.

Indexes to places of publication, p.59–80. Chronological indexes, p.81–105.

F72 Emblematisches Cabinet. 1– . Hrsg. von Wolfgang Harms und Michael Schilling. N.Y., Olms, 1971– .

Series of reprints of a wide range of editions of emblem books published for the most part in Germany and the Netherlands in the 16th and 17th centuries. Each vol. includes substantial scholarly appendixes. Size varies. Some vols. unnumbered.

Contents: (2) Veen, Otto van. Amorum emblemata, figuris Aeneis incisa (1608), 1970; (4) Rollenhagen, Gabriel. Nucleus emblematum selectissimorum (1611), 1985; (9) Oetinger, Friedrich Christoph. Biblisches und emblematisches Wörterbuch (1776), 1987; (12) Boissard, Jean Jacques. Emblematum liber (1593), 1977; (s.n.) Dilherr, Johannes Michael. Drei-standige Sonn-und Festtag-Emblemata, oder Sinne-bilder. Nürnberg (1660), 1994; (s.n.) Bry, Johann Theodor de. Emblemata secularia (1611), 1994.

F73 Index emblematicus. Toronto, Univ. of Toronto Pr., 1985– .

Series of critical indexes to and reproductions of emblem books.

Contents: Daly, Peter M., and Callahan, Virginia W., eds. Andreas Alciatus (1985); Daly, Peter M., and Duer, Leslie T., eds. The English emblem tradition (1988–). (5)v.

F74 The Jesuit series. Ed. by Peter M. Daly and G. Richard Dimler. Montreal, McGill-Queen's Univ. Pr., 1997– . (2)v. (Corpus librorum emblematum)

"When completed, the Jesuit Series will encompass all extant books of emblems, works illustrated with emblems, and books dealing with the theory and practice of emblematics written by members of The Society of Jesus. Also included are translations and adaptations in all languages of Jesuit works by Catholics and non-Catholics alike. . . . The complete bibliography will probably comprise some 1,700 entries; about 500 first editions and a further 1,200 subsequent editions, issues, and translations. Many books are described here for the first time." This series is "the keystone of the database known as 'The Union Catalogue of Emblem Books' and of this series of reference works, the 'Corpus Librorum Emblematum'."—*Introd.*

Contents: Part one (A–D); Part two (D–E).

Includes cross-reference indexes.

F75 Landwehr, John. Emblem and fable books printed in the low countries, 1542–1813: a bibliography. 3d rev. and augm. ed. Utrecht, HES, 1988. 444p.

See GLAH 1:F74 for previous ed.

Revised ed. includes 918 entries for emblem books published in Belgium and Holland from 1554 to 1813, 150 additional titles, and 40 variants. New to this ed. is a lengthy bibliography of 235 Netherlandish fable books (1542–1913) following the same detailed format as the emblem book section. Unlike previous eds., does not contain entries for facsimiles, reprints, or modern editions.

Contents: Reference works (a choice); Anonyms and pseudonyms; List of libraries; Emblem books printed in the Low Countries 1554–1813: Portraits; Bibliography; Concordances, new editions, variants; Fable books printed in the Low Countries 1542–1813: Illustrators; Bibliography.

Indexes: Publishers (printers-booksellers), p.393. Printers-booksellers unknown or not given, p.395–415. "Selbstverlag," p.419. Book illustrators, p.421–28. Original plates, p.428. Manuscripts or copies with manuscript-notes, p.428. General index, p.429–44.

F76 Montagu, Jennifer. An index of emblems of the Italian academies: based on Michele Maylender's Storie [i.e. Storia] delle accademie d'Italia. [London], Warburg Institute, Univ. of London, 1988. iii, 77p.

Intended to be used in conjunction with Michele Maylander's classic Storia delle Accademie d'Italia (Bologna, L. Cappelli, 1926–30). Unique, specialized index designed to assist in the identification of academic imprese found in works of art. Indexes provide access to the emblems either from an alphabetical listing of the mottoes or from verbal descriptions of the figures included in the image, arranged alphabetically by keyword. No illustrations.

F77 Okayama, Yassu. The Ripa index: personifications and their attributes in five editions of the Iconologia. Doornspijk, Davaco, 1992. xiv, 628p.

Indexed editions of Ripa were determined by their availability in libraries in original or reprint.

Useful index to Cesare Ripa's Iconologia (see GLAH 1:F79) conceived by the ICONCLASS team at the University of Leiden in order to facilitate research on personifications and on symbolism in general. Part one indexes "the personifications in alphabetical order according to their Italian names with short descriptions based upon the texts of the five editions. . . . In the second part, the words used to describe the personifications are arranged in alphabetical order, with entries that include the context in which a term is used, and with reference to the Italian (Dutch or French) names of personifications."—*Introd.* Includes cross-references to ICONCLASS notations (see GLAH 1:F18; GLAH 2:F10).

Contents: Introduction; The personifications; Alphabetical index.

F78 The Renaissance and the Gods: a comprehensive collection of Renaissance mythologies, iconologies and iconographies, with a selection of works from the Enlightenment. Ed. with and introd. by Stephen Orgel. N.Y., Garland, 1976. 53v. il.

A valuable series of reprints that "remains one which no serious college art or literature department can afford to ignore: studies not only in antiquity and the Renaissance, but in the nature of myth and its relation to visual and conceptual schemes will want to draw heavily upon such a resource."—*Review*, Art in America, v.66, no.2, 1978, p.27. Each vol. is reprinted in its entirety with a brief introduction explaining its history. Various editions of the same title are included, for example, four editions of Cesare Ripa's Iconologia (1611, 1644, 1704, 1766).

F79 Symbola et emblemata = Studies in renaissance and baroque symbolism, 1– . Leiden, Brill, 1989– .

Ongoing monographic series comprised of scholarly studies on emblems and some reprints. Vols. contain high quality black-and-white reproductions.

Contents: (1) Maksimovich-Ambodik, Nestor. Emvlemy i simvoly, 1788: the first Russian emblem book (1989); (2) The European emblem: selected papers from the Glasgow conference, 11–14 August 1987 (1990); (3) The emblem in Renaissance and baroque Europe: selected papers of the Glasgow International Emblem Conference, 13–17 August 1990 (1992); (4) Spectacle & image in Renaissance Europe: selected papers of the XXXIInd conference at the Centre d'études superieures de la Renaissance de Tours, 29 June–8 July 1989 (1993); (5) Elders, William. Symbolic scores: studies in the music of the Renaissance (1994); (6) Plett, Heinrich F. English Renaissance rhetoric and poetics: a systematic bibliography of primary and secondary sources (1995); (7) European iconography East and West: selected papers of the Szeged international conference, June 9–12, 1993 (1996).

PORTRAITS

F80 Frazier, Patrick. Portrait index of North American Indians in published collections. 2d ed., rev. and enl. Washington, D.C., Library of Congress, 1996. xx, 200p. ports.

A unique index that "was compiled to provide a means for locating and identifying published portraits of individual Indians within tribes, and to do so by taking into account the several variations by which an Indian may be identified."—*Introd.* The entries, which range chronologically from the colonial period to the 1990s and are arranged alphabetically by tribe and then by individual, include references to the sources and page numbers in which the individuals are illustrated.

Index, p.133–200.

F81 Dictionary of British portraiture. Ed. by Richard Ormond and Malcolm Rogers. N.Y., Oxford Univ. Pr., 1979–81. 4v.

"The aim . . . is to provide a listing of the portraits of famous figures in British history that are either in galleries and institutions, or in collections accessible to the public. It is intended for the general researcher and student who needs a reliable guide to portraits on public view of which illustrations can be obtained relatively easily. . . . The question of selection was a thorny one. We have relied heavily, though not exclusively, on the Dictionary of National Biography."—*Introd.*

Coverage from the 16th to about the mid-20th century. Entries supply name and dates of the subject, a line of biographical data, and then list portraits, giving medium, brief description, location, and, where known, date and artist's name.

Contents: (1) Davies, Adriana. The Middle Ages to the early Georgians: historical figures born before 1700 (1979); (2) Kilmurray, Elaine. Later Georgians and early Victorians: historical figures born between 1700 and 1800 (1979); (3) Kilmurray, Elaine. The Victorians: historical figures born between 1800 and 1860 (1981); (4) Davies, Adriana. The twentieth century: historical figures born before 1900 (1981).

"Abbreviations" at front of all vols. Index [of subjects, i.e., sitters], v.4, p.[125]–76.

F82 National Portrait Gallery, Great Britain. Complete illustrated catalogue 1856–1979. Comp. by K. K. Yung. Ed. by Mary Pettman. London, The Gallery, 1981. x, 749p. il. ports.

"A comprehensive checklist of every painting, drawing, miniature, photograph and work of sculpture in the main collection. All are illustrated, and the catalogue, with some 5,500 entries, now forms the largest and most extensive survey of British portraiture extant."—*Dust jacket.* Portraits are arranged by type and then alphabetically by sitter. Small black-and-white illustrations.

Contents: Introduction; Catalogue: single and double portraits; Groups; Collections; Unknown sitters.

Index of artists, engravers and photographers p.711–49.

THE AMERICAS

F83 The iconography of Middle American sculpture. Texts by Ignacio Bernal . . . [et al.] [N.Y.], The Metropolitan Museum of Art, 1973. 167p. il.

Papers presented at a symposium held at the Metropolitan Museum of Art (1970). In spite of the dated and succinct texts its articles remain benchmarks in the consideration of iconography of Mexico and Central America.

Contents: The iconology of Olmec art, by Michael Coe; Stone reliefs in the Dainzú area, by Ignacio Bernal; Iconographic aspects of architectural profiles at Teotihuacan and in Mesoamerica, by George Kubler; The eastern Gulf coast, by Gordon Ekholm; Maya rulers of the Classic period and the divine right of kings, by J.E.S. Thompson; The late pre-Hispanic Central Mexican (Aztec) iconographic system, by H.B. Nicholson; West Mexican art: secular or sacred?, by Peter Furst; Stone sculpture from southern Central America, by Wolfgang Haberland; Mesoamerican art and iconography and the integrity of the Mesoamerican ideology system, by Gordon Willey; Science and humanism among Americanists, by George Kubler.

SEE ALSO: Miller and Taube, The gods and symbols of ancient Mexico and the Maya: an illustrated dictionary of Mesoamerican religion (GLAH 2:E193).

G. Historiography, Methodology, and Theory

This chapter is limited to general works on the historiography of art and methodologies of art historical research, including research methods. A small selection of titles (including a few anthologies) dealing with contemporary debates concerning art historical methodology are included in response to the prominence of these debates in contemporary art history. Histories of aesthetics are not included, though major studies of the history and theory of art criticism are cited.

G1 Academies of art between Renaissance and Romanticism. Ed. by Anton W.A. Boschloo. 's-Gravenhage, SDU Uitgeverij, 1989. 592p. il. (Leids kunsthistorisch jaarboek, 5–6, 1986–1987)

Essays in Dutch (with English summary), English, French, German, and Italian.

Geographical survey of early art academies through the 18th century. "The aim of this publication is to show how matters stand at present with regard to research into the world of academies some half a century after the appearance of Nikolaus Pevsner's standard work Academies of Art past and Present [GLAH 1:G22]. . . . Our aim has been to present a balanced account of the most important academies."—*Pref.*

Notes at ends of chapters. Bibliography, p.561–90.

G2 Adams, Laurie. The methodologies of art: an introduction. N.Y., IconEditions, 1996. xvii, 236p. il. (part col.)

"In this book I survey some of the methodologies used in reading pictures, sculptures, and architecture, with a view to enriching the viewer's response to works of art. Each chapter is illustrated with examples, primarily of Western art, that appear in the major textbooks used in American colleges and schools."—*Pref.* Readable, general introduction to art historical methodologies.

Contents: (1) What is art?; (2) Formalism and style; (3) Iconography; (4) Contextual approaches I: Marxism; (5) Contextual approaches II: Feminism; (6) Biography and autobiography; (7) Semiotics I: Structuralism and Post-Structuralism; (8) Semiotics II: Deconstruction; (9) Psychoanalysis I: Freud; (10) Psychoanalysis II: Winnicott and Lacan; (11) Aesthetics and psychoanalysis: Roger Fry and Roland Barthes.

Bibliography of works cited, p.221–25. Index, p.227–36.

G3 Altmeister moderner Kunstgeschichte. Hrsg. von Heinrich Dilly. Berlin, Reimer, 1990. 295p. il. (Kunstgeschichte zur Einführung)

Conceived as a supplementary vol. to Kunstgeschichte: Eine Einführung (GLAH 2:G55). Profiles of fifteen 20th-century art historians, modeled upon Wolfgang Waetzoldt's pioneering Deutsche Kunsthistoriker (GLAH 1:G28).

Contents: Einleitung, von Heinrich Dilly; Wilhelm von Bode, von Wofgang Beyrodt; Alois Riegl, von Wolfgang Kemp; Heinrich Woelfflin, von Nikolaus Meuer; Bernard Berenson, von Heinrich Dilly; Julius Meier-Graefe, von Ron Manheim; Aby Warburg, von Martin Warnke; Emile Mâle, von Heinrich Dilly; Julius von Schlosser, von Edwin Lachnit; Erwin Panofsky, von Renate Heidt Heller; Nikolaus Pevsner, von Stefan Muthesius; Hans van de Waal, von Mechthild Beilmann; A.K. Porter, von Bernd Nikolai; Wilhelm Pinder, von Marlite Halbertsma; Roberto Longhi, von Andreas Beyer; Hans Sedlmayr, von Norbert Schneider.

Notes at ends of chapters. Personnenregister, p.[289]–295.

G4 Art history and its methods: a critical anthology. Selection and commentary by Eric Fernie. London, Phaidon, 1995. 384p. il.

Introduces undergraduates to the variety of approaches and methods constituting art historical study. Divided into three sections: an introductory essay, "A History of methods"; selected texts from historical and contemporary writers (e.g., Giorgio Vasari, Joshua Reynolds, Erwin Panofsky, E. H. Gombrich, and T. J. Clark); and a "Glossary of concepts" including "Hegelianism," "Art history," "Style," "Marxism," arranged alphabetically.

Selected bibliography, p.369. Index, p.370–83.

G5 Bakewell, Elizabeth; Beeman, William O.; and Reese, Carol McMichael. Object, image, inquiry: the art historian at work. Marilyn Schmitt, general ed. Santa Monica, Getty Art History Information Program, 1988. xii, 199p. il.

"Report on a collaborative study by the Getty Art History Information Program (AHIP) and the Institute for Research in Information and Scholarship (IRIS), Brown University." — *Title page.* Results of "a nine-month collaborative study of the processes that art historians follow in the conduct of research. . . . The study was intended to serve as a basis for discovering what kinds of automated tools would be of use to art historians."—*Introd.*

Contents: Introduction: Description of the AHIP-IRIS collaborative study; The interviews; The case studies; Appendixes.

G6 Barasch, Moshe. Modern theories of art. N.Y., New York Univ. Pr., 1990. 2v.

Supplements the author's Theories of art (see following entry). Lucid survey of modern theories of art. Thematic arrangement.

Contents: (1) From Winckelmann to Baudelaire; (2) From Impressionism to Kandinsky.

Notes at ends of chapters. Bibliographical essay, v.1, p.391–407, v.2, p.371–82. Name index, v.1, p.409–14, v.2, p.383–85. Subject index, v.1, p.415–20, v.2, p.386–89.

G7 ———. Theories of art: from Plato to Winckelman. N.Y., New York Univ. Pr., 1985. xiv, 394p.

Introductory survey of "the major stages in the development of European art theory" through the early 18th century.—*Introd.*

Contents: Introduction; (1) Antiquity; (2) The Middle Ages; (3) The early Renaissance; (4) The artist and the medium: some facets of the High Renaissance; (5) The late Renaissance; (6) Classicism and the Academy.

Notes at ends of chapters. Name index, p.379–85. Subject index, p.387–94.

G8 Barnet, Sylvan. A short guide to writing about art. 6th ed. N.Y., Longman, 1999.

1st ed., 1981; 2d ed., 1985; 3d ed., 1989; 4th ed., 1992; 5th ed., 1997.

Unusually helpful guide for the art history student, informed and faithfully kept up-to-date.

Contents: (1) Writing about art; (2) Analysis; (3) Writing a comparison; (4) How to write an effective essay; (5) Style in writing.

Index, p.273–80. Symbols commonly used in annotating papers, p.[282]. Frequently asked questions, p.[283].

G9 Bauer, Hermann. Kunsthistorik: eine kritische Einführung in das Studium der Kunstgeschichte. Dritte, durchges. und erg. Aufl. München, Beck, 1989. 213p.

1st ed. 1976.

Systematic introduction to the methodology and terminology of art history. Includes a topical survey of art historical genres; the history of art historical writing; the problematics of art history.

Contents: (1) Das "Kunstwerk" als Gegenstand der Kunstgeschichtsschreibung; (2) Die Geschichte der Kunstgeschichtsschreibung und die Entstehung von Begriffen, Methoden und Problemen; (3) Kunsthistorik; (4) Der Mensch und die Kunstgeschichte; (5) Möglichkeiten und Ziele einer künftigen Kunstgeschichtsschreibung.

Anmerkungen, p.[161]–80. Literaturverzeichnis, p.[181]–207. Register, p.[209]–13.

G10 Baxandall, Michael. Patterns of intention: on the historical explanation of pictures. New Haven, Yale Univ. Pr., 1985. xii, 147p. il., plates.

Revised version of lectures delivered at the University of California, Berkeley (1982). "The lectures addressed a question: If we offer a statement about the causes of a picture, what is the nature and basis of the statement? . . . What this book is primarily concerned with is criticism, which I take in the unclassical sense of thinking and saying about particular pictures things apt to sharpen our legitimate satisfactions in them. And it is concerned with just one element in criticism, the cause-inferring strain inherent in our thinking about pictures as about other things."—*Pref.*

Texts and references, p.[138]–47. Index of subjects, p.[148].

G11 Bazin, Germain. Histoire de l'histoire de l'art: de Vasari à nos jours. Paris, Michel, 1986. 652p.

Wide-ranging, personal overview of European writing on the history of art from the Renaissance to the present, by the former chief conservator of paintings at the Louvre. Informed and scholarly but accessible to the student and general reader.

Contents: Avertissement; (I) Les prolégomènes; (II) De l'histoire de l'art à la science de l'art; (III) Voies et moyens; (IV) Territoires; Au fil des temps.

Notes, p.[573]–[626]. Index, p.[627]–[50].

G12 Belting, Hans. The end of the history of art? Trans. by Christopher S. Wood. Chicago, Univ. of Chicago Pr., 1987. xiii, 120p.

Rev. trans. of: Das Ende der Kunstgeschichte? 2. Aufl. München, Deutscher Kunstverlag, 1984; 1. Aufl. 1983; 3. Aufl., München, Beck, 1995, completely rewritten and with the subtitle: "Eine Revision nach zehn Jahren."

"The following essay is above all else an assessment of the discipline as it is practiced today, and more particularly, an inquiry into its old and new problems in light of our contemporary experience of art. The second essay provides what the first lacks, namely, a retrospective on the earlier tradition of art-historical writing."—*Pref.* "The English version incorporates a number of revisions, clarifications, and altogether new observations, mainly in the sections of the first essay on modern and contemporary art."—*Pref.*

Contents: (1) The end of the history of art? Reflections on contemporary art and contemporary art history; (2) Vasari and his legacy: The history of art as a process.

Notes, p.97–120.

G13 Bialostocki, Jan. Stil und Ikonographie: Studien zur Kunstwissenschaft. [2d ed.] Köln, DuMont, 1981. 327p. 64 il. (DuMont Taschenbücher, 113)

See GLAH 1:G2 for original ed.

Notes at ends of chapters. Personenregister, p.232–[38].

G14 Brush, Kathryn. The shaping of art history: Wilhelm Vöge, Adolph Goldschmidt, and the study of medieval art. N.Y., Cambridge Univ. Pr., 1996. xiii, 263p. il.

"This study examines some of the intellectual and historical circumstances that helped define the study of art history. It does so by tracing and contextualizing the ways in which the first generation of professional interpreters of art in Germany shaped discourse on medieval art."—*Introd.*

Contents: Part I: Mentalités: (1) Art history and cultural history during the 1880s: the discursive range. Part II: "Monumental styles" in medieval art history: (2) Wilhelm Vöge and the beginnings of the monumental style in the middle ages (1894); (3) Thematic and methodological range in the scholarship of Goldschmidt and Vöge to ca. 1905. Part III: Resonances: (4) German and international responses at the turn of the century; (5) Implications for later discourse in medieval art history.

Notes, p.155–229. Bibliography, p.231–53. Index, p.255–63.

G15 Cahn, Walter. Masterpieces: chapters on the history of an idea. Princeton, Princeton Univ. Pr., 1979. xix, 168p. il., plates. (Princeton essays on the arts, 7)
Urbane essay in the history of ideas.

Contents: Preface; Introduction; (I) The artisanal masterpiece; (II) Man, the divine masterpiece; (III) Toward the enduring monument: Nantes, Brou, Margaret of Austria; (IV) Masterpieces of the French renaissance; (V) Chef d'oeuvre and masterpiece; (VI) The classic masterpiece; (VII) The absolute masterpiece.

Bibliographical note, p.[157]–59. Index, p.[161]–68.

G16 Calligram: essays in new art history from France. Ed. by Norman Bryson. N.Y., Cambridge Univ. Pr., 1988. xxix, 183p. il. (Cambridge new art history and criticism)
Collection of essays intended "to stimulate awareness of other ways of thinking about images." "All art history needs to do is to appropriate the advance, take from literary criticism everything of service to itself, make reading and practical criticism regular components of art historical training, and the discipline will be at once more stable, more mature, and more nourishing than before."—*Introd.*

Contents: Introduction, by Norman Bryson; (1) Art as semiological fact, by Jan Mukarofsky; (2) Time and the timeless in Quattrocento painting, by Yves Bonnefoy; (3) Giotto's joy, by Julia Kristeva; (4) The trompe l'oeil, by Jean Baudrillard; (5) Towards a theory of reading in the visual arts: Poussin's The Arcadian Shepherds, by Louis Marin; (6) Las Meninas, by Michel Foucault; (7) The world as object, by Roland Barthes; (8) Ambrosia and gold, by Michel Serres; (9) In black and white, by Jean-Claude Lebensztejn; (10) Turner translates Carnot, by Michel Serres;

Contributors, p.ix–x. Index, p.181–83.

G17 Carrier, David. Artwriting. Amherst, Univ. of Massachusetts Pr., 1987. xii, 161p. il.
"Artwriting is the product of my effort as philosopher and art critic to understand the development of recent American art criticism."—*Ackn.* Thoughtful and influential essay on the rhetoric of contemporary interpretive writing about art, mindful of the history of art literature.

Contents: Overture; (1) Beginning in narrative art histories; (2) Endings in narrative art histories; (3) The presentness of art; (4) The art system; (5) Art fashion; (6) The rhetoric of artwriting.

Notes, p.141–55. Index, p.157–61.

G18 ———. Principles of art history writing. University Park, Pennsylvania State Univ. Pr., 1991. xiii, 249p. il.
Attempts to answer "two simple questions: Why does the argumentation of present-day art historians differ so dramatically from that of earlier artwriters? And since those modern historians often disagree, how is objectivity in art history possible."—*Introd.* Lucid, careful study of the rhetoric and conventions of writing about art.

Contents: Introduction. Part one: Case studies: interpretation in present-day art history. Part two: the history of art history. Part three: toward a revisionist art history. Conclusion.

Index, p.245–49.

G19 Chandra, Pramod. On the study of Indian art. Cambridge, Mass., Published for the Asia Society by Harvard Univ. Pr., 1983. 134p. il., plates. (Polsky lectures in Indian and Southeast Asian art and archaeology)
Thoughtful study of the historiography of Indian art, embracing architecture, sculpture, and painting.

Notes, p.[115]–21. References, p.[122]–29. Index, p.[130]–34.

G20 Critical terms for art history. Ed. by Robert S. Nelson and Richard Shiff. Chicago, Univ. of Chicago Pr., 1996. xvi, 364p. il.
Wide-ranging anthology of "essays about art history in the late twentieth century."—*p.ix.* Essays on 22 themes prominent in contemporary art historical discourse.

Contents: At the place of a foreword: someone looking, reading, and writing, by Robert S. Nelson; Operations: (1) Representation, by David Summers; (2) Sign, by Alex Potts; (3) Simulacrum, by Michael Camille. Communications: (4) Word and image, by W. J. T. Mitchell; (5) Narrative, by Wolfgang Kemp; (6) Context, by Paul Mattick, Jr.; (7) Meaning/interpretation, by Stephen Bann; Histories: (8) Originality, by Richard Shiff; (9) Appropriation, by Robert S. Nelson; (10) Art history, by David Carrier; (11) Modernism, by Charles Harrison; (12) Avant-garde, by Ann Gibson; (13) Primitive, by Mark Antliff and Patricia Leighten; (14) Ritual, by Suzanne Preston Blier; (15) Fetish, by William Pietz; (16) Gaze, by Margaret Olin; (17) Gender, by Whitney Davis; (18) Modes of production, by Terry Smith; (19) Commodity, by Paul Wood; (20) Collecting/museums, by Donald Preziosi; (21) Value, by Joseph Leo Koerner and Lisbet Koerner; (22) Postmodernism/postcolonialism, by Homi K. Bhabha. Afterword: Figuration, by Richard Shiff.

References, p.329–47. Contributors, p.349–51. Index, p.353–64.

G21 Didi-Huberman, Georges. Devant l'image: question posée aux fins d'une histoire de l'art. Paris, Editions de Minuit, 1990. 332p. il. (Collection "Critique")
Thoughtful critique of art historical claims to objectivity in interpretation, informed by a psychoanalytic perspective.

Includes bibliographical references. Index, p.321–26.

G22 Dilly, Heinrich. Deutsche Kunsthistoriker, 1933–1945. [München], Deutscher Kunstverlag, [1988]. 94p. (Kunstgeschichte und Gegenwart)

Brief but important essay on art historical practice in Nazi Germany.

Contents: Einleitung; Probleme der Kunstgeschichte; Quantitative Entwicklung; Selbstbeschränkung und Standardisierung; Aufgaben der Kunstgeschichtsschreibung; Museumsdienst; Akademische Praxis; Kunstgeschichte auf neuen Wegen; Nachwort.

Personenverzeichnis, p.93–4.

G23 ———. Kunstgeschichte als Institution: Studien zur Geschichte eine Disziplin. Frankfurt am Main, Suhrkamp, 1979. 300p.

A revision of the author's thesis, Freie Universität Berlin, 1977. "Deals with problems of academic recognition of the field of art history at German speaking universities. Traces this development on three levels: in the area of presentation of art historical objects, in the area of basic scientific hypotheses, and in the field of the prerequisites of organization of art historical theory and usage. The first study, on institutionalization of this field, treats various forms of legitimation of methodical information, appealing to the history of the discipline. The second study compares the hypotheses of Johann Joachim Winckelmann and Carl Friedrich von Rumohr. In the third study, the diverse institutional combinations of both basic concepts of the writing of art history construct a systematic framework for a fragmented history of the recognition of this discipline through the system represented by the universities."— *Author abstract*, as cited in Bibliography of the history of art, record XRIL41588-G.

Anmerkungen und Quellennachweis, p.259–[65]. Literaturverzeichnis, p.266–[92]. Personenregister, p.293–[301].

G24 Dvořák, Max. The history of art as the history of ideas. Trans. by John Hardy. Boston, Routledge & Kegan Paul, 1984. ix, 114p. il., plates.

Trans. of Kunstgeschichte als Geistesgeschichte, München, Piper, 1928; 1. Aufl. 1924; new ed. with a postscript by Artur Rosenauer, Berlin, Mann, 1995.

One of the great documents of art historiography.

Index, p.109–14.

G25 Dynes, Wayne, and Mermoz, Gérard. "Art History," in Dictionary of Art [GLAH 2:E4], v.2, p.530–40.

Overview, with brief bibliographies.

Contents: (I) Historical development, by Wayne Dynes; (II) Modern institutional practice, by Wayne Dynes; (III) Contemporary issues, by Gérard Mermoz.

G26 The Early years of art history in the United States: notes and essays on departments, teaching, and scholars. Ed. by Craig Hugh Smyth and Peter M. Lukehart. Princeton, Dept. of Art and Archaeology, Princeton Univ., 1993. xxiii, 205p. il., 64p. of plates.

Collection of essays first presented at College Art Association of America annual conferences, 1987–89.

Contents: Preface; Part I: Glimpses of some early departments of History of Art in the United States. Part II: Three decades of art history in the United States (1910–1940): five figures. Part III: Institutionalizing art history: the early discipline in the United States.

Notes on the contributors, p.[xiii]–xvii. List of illustrations, p.[xix]–xxiii. Index, p.[195]–205.

G27 Elkins, James. Our beautiful, dry, and distant texts: art history as writing. University Park, Pennsylvania State Univ. Pr., 1997. xvii, 300p. il.

"This is a book about the vexed relations between art historical writing and attempts to account for that writing. I am interested in what it means to move from studying artists and artworks to considering interpretive methods and historiography. . . . A large portion of this book, and most of its arguments, were prompted by what I take to be limitations of contemporary accounts of art history."—*Pref.*

Includes bibliographical references. Index, p.[298]–300.

G28 The Expanding discourse: feminism and art history. Ed. by Norma Broude and Mary D. Garrard. N.Y., IconEditions, 1992. x, 518p. il.

"The twenty-nine essays in this volume represent what is to our minds some . . . of the best feminist art-historical writing of the last decade."—*Pref.* A sequel to the editors' previous anthology, Feminism and art history (see following entry).

Notes at ends of chapters. Notes on the contributors, p.[503]–05. Index, p.[506]–18.

G29 Feminism and art history: questioning the litany. Ed. by Norma Broude and Mary D. Garrard. N.Y., Harper & Row, 1982. ix, 358p. il. (IconEditions)

Pioneering anthology of essays, inspired by and in part delivered at sessions of the annual College Art Association conferences (1978–79). "As a compendium of important recent ideas on the subject, the book will, we hope, be of use to scholars, students, and general readers unfamiliar with the effect of feminist thinking on art history."—*Pref. and ackn.*

Notes at ends of chapters. Notes on contributors, p.[347]–50. Index, p.[351]–58.

G30 Feminist art criticism: an anthology. Ed. by Arlene Raven . . . [et al.] Ann Arbor, UMI Research Press, 1988. xii, 248p. il. (Studies in the fine arts. Criticism, no. 27)

"The essays fall into two broad categories: accounts of different female artists, and efforts to formulate a female art-criticism."— *Foreword.*

Notes at ends of chapters. Contributors, p.[239]–42. Index, p.[243]–48.

G31 Frankfurter Schule und Kunstgeschichte. Hrsg. von Andreas Berndt . . . [et al.] Berlin, Reimer, 1992. 202p. il.

Contents: Zur Einführung, von Heinrich Dilly; Von der Ideologie—zur Ikonologiekritik, die Warburg-Renaissancen, von Michael Diers; Adorno und die kunsthistorische Diskussion der Avantgarde vor 1968, von Jutta Held; Adornos Theorie des Naturschönen, von Norbert Schneider; Der kunsthistorische Nachthimmel, ein Beitrag zur Kritik kunsthistorischer Praxis, von Heinrich Dilly; Thesen der Kritischen Theorie bei der Analyse der NS-Kunst, von Hans-Ernst Mittig; Der simulierte Benjamin, Mittelalteriche Bemerkungen zu seiner Aktualität, von Horst Bredekamp; Kunstgeschichte zwischen affirmativer Kultur und Kulturindustrie, von Michael Müller; Walter Benjamins Passagenwerk als Modell fur eine kunstgeschichtliche Synthese, von Otto Karl Werckmeister; Kunst und Geschichte nach dem Mauerfall: Marx-zu Hegel—auf den Kopfstellen!, von Berthold Hinz; Kunstgeschichte und Frankfurter Schule—ein Rückblick, von Johann Konrad Eberlein.

Notes at ends of some chapters.

G32 Freedberg, David. The power of images: studies in the history and theory of response. Chicago, Univ. of Chicago Pr., 1989. xxv, 534p. il.

An important historical exploration of the human response to images. "This book is not about the history of art. It is about the relations between images and people in history. It consciously takes within its purview all images, not just those regarded as artistic ones. It is the product of a long-standing commitment to ideas which traditional forms of the history of art—as well as most current ones—seem either to have neglected or to have left inadequately articulated."—*Introd.*

Contents: (1) The power of images: response and repression; (2) The god in the image; (3) The value of the commonplace; (4) The myth of aniconism; (5) Consecration: making images work; (6) Image and pilgrimage; (7) The votive image: invoking favor and giving thanks; (8) Invisibilia per visibilia: meditation and the uses of theory; (9) Verisimilitude and resemblance: from sacred mountain to waxworks; (10) Infamy, justice, and witchcraft: explanation, sympathy, and magic; (11) Live images: the worth of visions and tales; (12) Arousal by image; (13) The sense and censorship; (14) Idolatry and iconoclasm; (15) Representation and reality.

Abbreviations, p.443–44. Notes, p.445–505. Bibliography, p.507–17. Index, p.519–34.

G33 German essays on art history. Ed. by Gert Schiff. N.Y., Continuum, 1988. lxxii, 282p. il., plates (The German library, 79)

"The essays presented in this volume are meant to introduce the interested reader to some of those writers who initiated and shaped the study of art in the German-speaking countries."—*Introd.* Welcome anthology of selected texts by seminal art historians including Winckelmann, Rumohr, Wickhoff, Riegl, Dvořák, Schlosser, Warburg, and Panofsky. Uniformly fine translations, with helpful annotations and a long historiographic introduction by the editor.

G34 Germann, Georg. Vitruve et le vitruvianisme: introduction à l'histoire de la theorie architecturale. Trad. de l'allemand par Michele Zaugg et Jacques Gubler. Lausanne, Presses polytechniques et universitaires romandes, 1991. viii, 264p. il. (Collection architecture)

Trans. of Einführung in die Geschichte der Architekturtheorie, 2d. verb. Aufl., Darmstadt, Wissenschaftliche Buchgesellschaft, 1987; 1. Aufl. 1980.

Brief introductory survey of architectural theory from Vitruvius through 19th-century historicism. Focus on the Vitruvian tradition as reflected in seminal theoretical treatises. Bibliographie, p.[237]–53. Index des noms propres, p.255–64.

G35 Goldstein, Carl. Teaching art: academies and schools from Vasari to Albers. N.Y., Cambridge Univ. Pr., 1996. xvi, 350p. il.

"This is a book about teaching visual art in the Renaissance tradition. . . . It also examines a range of questions raised during the course of the reaction against this teaching tradition beginning in the nineteenth century, with attention to alternative methods, particularly those grounded in the theory and practice of modernism."—*Introd.* An important reexamination of a subject pioneered by Nikolaus Pevsner's Academies of art, past and present (GLAH 1:G22).

Contents: Introduction: academic questions; (1) The problem of the first academy; (2) A tradition in the making; (3) The triumph of the academy leading to the reaction of the Avant-Garde; (4) Doctrine 1: art history; (5) Doctrine 2: theory and practice; (6) The copy; (7) The antique; (8) Life drawing; (9) Art and science; (10) Style; (11) Originality; (12) The revolt of the crafts; (13) Teaching modernism; Epilogue: Postmodernist contingencies.

Notes, p.301–20. Bibliography, p.321–39. Index, p. 341–50.

G36 Greenhalgh, Michael, and Duro, Paul. Essential art history. London, Bloomsbury, 1992. 311p.

Also available on the internet.

Alphabetically arranged dictionary of art-historical terms. Principally devoted to western art, this handy volume focuses upon painting and sculpture to the exclusion of architecture and the decorative arts. Includes artists who have written on art and selected influential art historians. Many entries feature brief bibliographies. Historiographic introduction.

Contents: Introduction: the literature of the discipline; A note on the contents; A note on the references; A–Z section.

G37 Hadjinicolaou, Nicos. Art history and class struggle. Trans. by Louise Asmal. London, Pluto Pr., 1978. 206p. il., plates.

Trans. with revisions of Histoire de l'art et lutte des classes. Paris, Maspero, 1973; Spanish ed., Mexico, Siglo Veintiuno, 1981 (and later eds.).

"This book is devoted to the study of the bourgeois ideology of 'art' and to its variants, which in practice constitute what is usually described as art history."—*Introd.* Famous, polemical Marxist analysis of art historical practice.

Includes bibliographical references. Subject index, p.[198]–200. Name index, p.[201]–06.

G38 Halbertsma, Marlite. Wilhelm Pinder und die deutsche Kunstgeschichte. Worms, Werner, 1992. 246p. il.

Trans. of the author's dissertation, Wilhelm Pinder en de Duitse kunsgeschiedenis, Gröningen, Försten, 1985. Attempts to describe an important phase in the history of German art historical scholarship, from 1900 to 1945, by focusing upon the methodology of one eminent practitioner.

Contents: Einführung; (I) Kunstgeschichte als Geistsgeschichte; (II) Das Problem der Generation; (III) Methoden-streit und Kunstgeographie; (IV) Wilhelm Pinder ergreift Partei; Anlagen; Zusammenfassung.

Anmerkungen, p.186–223. Bibliographie, p.224–40. Register, p.241–[47].

G39 ———, and Zijlmans, Kitty, eds. Gezichtspunten: een inleiding in de methoden van de kunstgeschiedenis. Nijmegen, SUN, 1993. 352p.

A collection of essays by Dutch art historians on the methodologies of art history.

Bibliographies at the end of chapters.

Contents: (1) Het kunstwerk, de context, de tijd en its lovers, van Kitty Zijlmans, Marlite Halbertsma; (2) De geschiedenis van de kunstgeschiedenis in de Duitsprekende landen en Nederland van 1764 tot 1933, van Marlite Halbertsma; (3) Verklaren en ordenen. Over stijlanalytische benaderingen, van Gerrit Willems; (4) Iconologie en historische antropologie: een toenadering, van Reindert Falkenburg; (5) Een bril voor het onschuldige oog. Marxisme, neomarxisme en post-marxisme in de kunstgeschiedenis, van Frans Jozef Witteveen; (6) Vrouwenstudies kunstgeschiedenis, van Marlite Halbertsma; (7) Kunst, geschiedenis en sociologie, van Ton Bevers; (8) Ceci n'est pas une pipe. Kunstgeschiedenis en semiotiek, van Arie Jan Gelderblom; (9) Kunstgeschiedenis als systeemtheorie, van Kitty Zijlmans.

Over de auteurs, p.345–46. Personenregister, p.347–52.

G40 Haskell, Francis. History and its images: art and the interpretation of the past. New Haven, Yale Univ. Pr., 1993. 558p. il. (part col.)

A pioneering study "devoted to the impact of the image on the historical imagination."—*Introd.* The author surveys the ways in which cultural historians from the 14th century (Francesco Petrarch) to the 20th (Johan Huizinga) have availed themselves of the visual arts to understand and visualize the past.

Contents: Introduction; Part 1: The discovery of the image; (1) The early numismatists; (2) Portraits from the past; (3) Historical narrative and reportage; (4) The issue of quality. Part 2: The use of the image; (5) Problems of interpretation; (6) The dialogue between antiquarians and historians; (7) The birth of cultural history; (8) The arts as an index of society; (9) The Musée des Monuments Français; (10) Michelet; (11) Museums, illustrations and the search for authenticity; (12) The historical significance of style; (13) The deceptive evidence of art; (14) Art as prophecy; (15) Huizinga and the "Flemish Renaissance."

Notes, p.[496]–519. Works cited in the text and notes, p.[520]–42. Illustrations, p.[543]–48. Index, p.[549]–58.

G41 Hauser, Arnold. The sociology of art. Trans. by Kenneth J. Northcott. Chicago, Univ. of Chicago Pr., 1982. xxi, 776p.

Trans. of Soziologie der Kunst. München, Beck, 1974; Hungarian ed., Budapest, Gondolat, 1982.

Hauser's monumental, posthumous work which attempts to provide a comprehensive analysis of the "sociological problems" of art production, reception, and interpretation. Hauser bases his methodology largely on neo-, or Western, Marxist principles influenced by the Frankfurt School and other adapters of Marxist critique to the aims of cultural studies.

Bibliographical references.

G42 Histoire de l'histoire de l'art: cycles de conférences organisées au musée du Louvre par le Service culturel. Sous la direction scientifique d'Edouard Pommier. [Paris], Louvre, Klincksieck, 1995– . (1)v. (Louvre conférences et colloques)

In French, with translations from English, German, Italian and Spanish. Reproduces four lecture cycles delivered at the Louvre (October 10–November 14, 1991 and January 25–March 15, 1993).

Contents: (1) De l'antiquité au XVIIe siècle; (II) XVIIIe et XIXe siècles.

Notes at ends of some chapters. Index général, v.1, p.371–86, v.2, p.445–59. Index des notions, p.387–88.

G43 Hüttinger, Eduard. Porträts und Profile: zur Geschichte der Kunstgeschichte. Mit einem Beitrag von Gottfried Boehm. St. Gallen, Erker, 1992. 384p.

Collection of 31 historiographic essays by the author. Most are profiles of individual art historians, published in connection with birthdays or as obituaries between 1961 and 1986.

G44 Isager, Jacob. Pliny on art and society: the Elder Pliny's chapters on the history of art. Odense, Denmark, Odense Univ. Pr., 1991. 263p. (Odense University classical studies, v.17)

Originally presented as the author's thesis, Odense Universitet, 1990.

"The present book aims at being a comprehensive study of the art chapters in books 33 to 37 of the Natural History. This has never been attempted before in spite of the fact that the text by virtue of its status as the sole surviving art history from antiquity has been and always will remain relevant."—*Introd.*

Summary in Danish, p.244–51. Bibliographical references, p.252–63.

G45 Johnson, William McAllister. Art history: its use and abuse. Toronto, Univ. of Toronto Pr., 1988. xvii, 374p. il.

Idiosyncratic, polemical essay on contemporary academic art history.

Contents: Preface; Introduction: Art history in translation; (1) Research; (2) Bibliography; (3) Writing; (4) University and public life; (5) Cataloguing theory; (6) Cataloguing practice.

Notes, p.[327]–49. Index, p.[351]–73.

G46 Kategorien und Methoden der deutschen Kunstgeschichte, 1900–1930. Beiträge von Oskar Bätschmann . . . [et al.] Hrsg. von Lorenz Dittmann. Stuttgart, Steiner, 1985. 364p. il., plates.

"Aus den Arbeitskreisen 'Methoden der Geisteswissenschaften' der Fritz Thyssen Stifung."—*p.[2].* A collection of essays intended to identify the main problems that engaged German art history from the turn of the century through the Weimar Republic, and to bring them into meaningful relationship to contemporary art history.

Contents: Zur Theorie des Neuen Bauens in Deutschland, von Erik Forssman; Kategorien der Plastik in der deutschen Kunstgeschichte der zwanziger Jahre, von Eduard Trier; Der Begriff des Kunstwerks in der deutschen Kunstgeschichte, von Lorenz Dittmann; Logos in der Geschichte: Erwin Panofsky's Ikonologie, von Oskar Bätschmann; Die Krise der Repräsentation: Die Kunstgeschichte und die moderne Kunst, von Gottfried Boehm; Der Epochenbegriff und die Kunstgeschichte, von Götz Pochat; Nationalstil und Nationalismus in der Kunstgeschichte der zwanziger und dreissiger Jahre, von Lars Olaf Larsson; Die Anfänge der Ostasiatischen Kunstgeschichte in Deutschland, von Eleanor von Erdberg; Art history and the concept of art, von Michael Podro; Transzendentale Elemente in der Kunstphilosophie und in der Kunstgeschichte: Zur Geschichte der Kunsttheorie 1900–1930, von Gerd Wolandt; Probleme der allgemeinen Kunstwissenschaft, von Wolfhart Henckmann.

Notes at ends of chapters. Angaben zu den Autoren, p.[335]–44. Namenregister, p.[345]–52. Sachregister, p.[353]–64.

G47 Kauffmann, Georg. Die Entstehung der Kunstgeschichte im 19. Jahrhundert. Opladen, Westdeutscher Verlag, 1993. 56p. il., ports. (Gerda Henkel Vorlesung)

Important lecture on 19th-century art historians. "Der Vortrag wurde am 24. Januar 1992 in Düsseldorf gehalten"—*Verso of t.p.*

Contents: Das Panorama; Der romantische Impuls; Der Aufbruch der Wissenschaft; Das "Fach" in der zweiten Jahrhunderthälfte; Ausblick in das 20. Jahrhundert.

Includes bibliographical references. Der Autor, p.[58]. Gerda Henkel Vorlesungen, p.[59]–[60].

G48 Kleinbauer, W. Eugene. Modern perspectives in Western art history: an anthology of twentieth-century writings on the visual arts. [Reprint.] Buffalo, Univ. of Toronto Pr. in assoc. with the Medieval Academy of America, 1989. xiii, 528p., il. (Medieval Academy reprints for teaching, 25)

Repr. of GLAH 1:G11, commonly used in courses on art historiography and methodology.

G49 Kris, Ernst, and Kurz, Otto. Legend, myth, and magic in the image of the artist: a historical experiment. Pref. by E. H. Gombrich. Trans. by Alastair Lang, rev. by Lottie M. Newman. New Haven, Yale Univ. Pr., 1979. xvi, 159p.

Based on Die Legende vom Kuenstler. Vienna, Krystall, 1934. Additions to the original text by Otto Kurz.

"This book deals with society's attitude to the artist. . . . We hope that this study will constitute the preliminary work for a future sociology of the artist."—*Introd.* Brief, suggestive study of typical, recurring themes in the biographical literature on artists, from antiquity to the present. A classic.

Contents: Preface, by E. H. Gombrich; (1) Introduction; (2) The heroization of the artist in biography; (3) The artist as magician; (4) The special position of the artist in biography.

Bibliography, p.133–47. Index, p.149–59.

G50 Kruft, Hanno-Walter. A history of architectural theory: from Vitruvius to the present. Trans. by Ronald Taylor . . . [et al.] N.Y., Princeton Architectural Pr., 1994. 706p. il., plates.

Trans. of Geschichte der Architekturtheorie: von der Antike bis zur Gegenwart, Munich, Beck, 1985; 2d ed. 1986; 3d rev. "Studienausgabe," 1991; Italian ed., Roma, Laterza, 1988.

Magisterial survey of European and American architectural theory from antiquity to the present. Informed, judicious, authoritative. Will be the standard textbook for the foreseeable future.

Notes [including texts of quotations in the original language], p.447–609. Bibliography, p.[613]–73. Supplement to the bibliography, p.[674]–80. English-language translations of sources, p.[681]–84. Index of names, p.[685]–706.

G51 Kubler, George. Esthetic recognition of ancient Amerindian art. New Haven, Yale Univ. Pr., 1991. xvi, 276p. il. (Yale publications in the history of art)

70 brief biographical essays on individuals (69 men, one woman) who wrote on Amerindian esthetics, from Christopher Columbus to Sir John Eric Sidney Thompson (d. 1975). "The object of this book is to find how ancient American objects of esthetic value in the visual order have been considered since the Discovery by Columbus."—*Author's pref.*

Contents: (1) American antiquity; (2) Salvaging Amerindian antiquity before 1700; (3) Idealist studies of Amerindia from above; (4) Empiric esthetics from below; (5) Americanist historians of art since 1840; (6) Anthropologists and archaeologists after 1875; Epilogue.

Notes, p.200–41. Bibliography, p.243–70. Index, p.271–76.

G52 Kultermann, Udo. The history of art history. N.Y., Abaris Books, 1993. ix, 278p. ports.

Trans. of Geschichte der Kunstgeschichte (GLAH 1:G13); 2. Aufl. Frankfurt, Ullstein, 1981; 3. überarb. und erw. Aufl., München, Prestel, 1990.

Introductory historical survey of European and American literature on the history of art from the Renaissance to the present. Attempts to present "enduring achievements in the literature of art history," to trace the evolution of art history as a scholarly and academic discipline, and "to set the various periods of art historiography within their contemporary artistic context."—*Pref.* Includes many portraits of writers and art historians.

Contents: Introduction; (I) Artists' histories; (II) Poussin and the French Academy; (III) Art in the Enlightenment; (IV) The Laocoön debate; (V) Winckelmann's revolution; (VI) Toward an historical discipline; (VII) Goethe as art historian; (VIII) Art history in Romanticism; (IX) Rumohr and the Berlin School; (X) Jakob Burckhardt and the Renaissance; (XI) Reality and method; (XII) Art history in the Gründerzeit; (XIII) The Dresden Holbein debate; (XIV) Impressionist aesthetics; (XV) The Vienna School; (XVI) The discovery of form; (XVII) Art history at the turn of the century; (XVIII) Art history of Expressionism; (XIX) The founding of iconology; (XX) Foundations of art history today; Epilogue: The image of the art historian.

Notes, p.253–69. Suggestions for further reading, p.270. Index of names, p.271–78.

G53 ———. Kleine Geschichte der Kunsttheorie. Darmstadt, Wissenschaftliche Buchgesellschaft, 1987. xviii, 369p.

Introductory historical survey of art theory from antiquity to the late 20th century. Brief description of non-western developments. Emphasis upon German philosophical aesthetics and 20th-century developments.

Contents: Vorwort; Einleitung: Pygmalion und das Symbol des Kuenstlers; (1) Vorgeschichte und Altertum; (2) Das Mittelalter; (3) Die Renaissance; (4) Manierismus und Barock; (5) Das 18. Jahrhundert; (6) Klassik und Romantik; (7) Kunst als Arbeit—Die Kunsttheorie des Realismus; (8) Form und Symbol; (9) Abstraktion; (10) Neue Grundlagen; (11) Zeitgenössische Tendenzen; (12) Schluss.

Literaturverzeichnis, p.319–56. Register, p.[357]–69.

G54 Kunst und Kunsttheorie: 1400–1900. Hrsg. von Peter Ganz . . . [et al.] Wiesbaden, Harrassowitz, 1991. viii, 462p. il. (Wölfenbütteler Forschungen, 48)

Wide-ranging series of lectures delivered at the 22nd Wölfenbütteler Symposion, December 1–5, 1987 ("Kunstgeschichte von Vasari bis Winckelmann") and at the 24th Wölfenbütteler Symposion, November 27–December 1, 1988 ("Kunstgeschichte seit Winckelmann") in the Herzog August Bibliothek Wölfenbüttel.

Contents: Ghiberti, Alberti und die frühen Italianer, von Gerda S. Panofsky; Giorgio Vasari: Kunstgeschichtliche Perspektiven, von Julian Kliemann; The dispute about Disegno and Colorito in Venice: Paolo Pino, Lodovico Dolce and Titian, by Thomas Puttfarken; Carel van Mander zwischen Vasari und Winckelmann, von Wolfgang Freiherr von Löhneysen; Kunst vor ihrer Geschichte: Zum kunsthistoriographischen Verfahren des Franciscus Junius, von Martin Warnke; "La più bella antichità che sappiate desiderare": History and style in Giovan Pietro Bellori's "Lives," by Elisabeth Cropper; Roger de Piles and the history of art, by Svetlana Alpers; Zur Entwicklung des Stilbegriffs bei Winckelmann, von Lorenz Dittmann; Die Museifizierung der Kunst und die Folgen für die Kunstgeschichte, von Günter Busch; Der letzte Homer: Zum philosophischen Ursprung der Kunstgeschichte im Deutschen Idealismus, von Beat Wyss; ". . . Woran meine ganze Seele gesogen . . .": Das Galerieerlebnis—eine verlorene Dimension der Kunstgeschichte? von Klaus Herding; Spontaneität und Rekonstruktion: Zur Rolle, Organisationsform und Leistung der Kunstkritik im Spannungsfeld von Kunsttheorie und Kunstgeschichte, von Stefan Germer, Hubertus Kohle; Kunstgeschichte als Universitätsfach, von Wolfgang Beyrodt; Kunstbeschreibung und Illustration in Deutschland im 19. Jahrhundert, von Regine Timm; Die Anfänge der historisch-kritischen Kunstgeschichtsschreibung, von Gabriele Bickendorf; National Museum, the art market and Old Master paintings, by Jaynie Anderson; Are works of art provisional or canonical in form? Fiedler, Hildebrand and Woelfflin, by Michael Podro; Kunstgeschichte und Kulturgeschichte oder Kunstgeschichte nach Aufgaben, von Mikolaus Meier; Alois Riegl and the aesthetics of disintegration, by Margaret Iversen.

Includes bibliographical references. Personenregister, p.453–62.

G55 Kunstgeschichte: eine Einführung. Hrsg. von Hans Belting . . . [et al.] 3. durchges. und erw. Aufl. Berlin, Reimer, [1990?]. 377p. il.

1st ed., 1986.

Collection of essays by 15 specialists, intended to provide a comprehensive introduction to the scope of art history as an academic discipline.

Contents: Einleitung, von Heinrich Dilly; Teil 1: Gegenstandsbestimmung; Gegenstandsbereiche der Kunstgeschichte, von Martin Warnke; Teil 2: Gegenstandssicherung; Die Gegenstandssicherung allgemein, von Willibald Sauerländer; Materialle Befundsicherung an Skulptur und Malerei, von Ulrich Schiessl; Befundsicherung an Architektur, von Dethard von Winterfeld; Alterssicherung, Ortssicherung und Individualsicherung, von Willibald Sauerländer; Teil 3: Gegenstandsdeutung; Einleitung, von Hans Belting und Wolfgang Kemp; Form, Struktur, Stil: Die formanalytischen und formgeschichtlichen Methoden, von Hermann Bauer; Inhalt und Gestalt: die ikonographisch-ikonologische Methode, von Johan Konrad Eberlein; Anleitung zur Interpretation: kunstgeschichtliche Hermeneutik, von Oskar Bätschmann; Das Werk im Kontext, Hermann Bauer; Kunstwerk und Betrachter: Der rezeptionsästhetische Ansatz, von Wolfgang Kemp; Kunst als Zeichen: Die semiotisch-[semantische?] Methode, von Rolf Duroy und Guenter Kerner; Dyaden zu dritt: Der (analytisch-) kunstpsychologische Ansatz, von Hartmut Kraft; Kunst und Gesellschaft: Der sozialgeschichtliche Ansatz, von Norbert Schneider; Geschichte und Geschlecht: Der feministische Ansatz, von Ellen Spickernagel; Wechselseitige Erhellung: Die Kunstgeschichte und ihre Nachbardisziplinen.

Notes at ends of chapters. Sachregister, p.367–71. Namenregister, p.372–75.

G56 Kunsthistoriker in eigener Sache: Zehn autobiographische Skizzen. Hrsg. von Martina Sitt. Einl. von Heinrich Dilly. Berlin, D. Reimer, 1990. 330p. il., ports.

Autobiographical sketches by ten prominent contemporary art historians. Intended to explore and elucidate the art historian's choice of vocation.

Portraits of the authors, passim. Notes at ends of chapters.

Contents: Vorwort, von Martina Sitt; Einleitung, von Heinrich Dilly; Am Anfang war das Auge: Otto Pächt, von Martina Sitt; "Wenn's euch Ernst ist, was zu sagen . . ." Wandlungen in der kunstgeschichtliches Betrachtung, von Ernst H. Gombrich; Produktive Konflikte, von Werner Hofmann; Erinnerungen, von Joseph Gantner; Das Kunstwerk als Kraftquelle, von Werner Schmalenbach; Zur Psychologie der Kunst und ihrer Geschichte, von Rudolf Arnheim; Kunst und Wahrheit, von Heinrich Lützeler; Bis an die Grenze des Aussagbaren . . . , von Max Imdahl; Frühe Wege zur Kunstgeschichte, von J. A. Schmoll gen. Eisenwerth; Zersplitterte Erinnerung, von Wilibald Sauerländer.

Personenregister, p.[325]–30.

G57 The language of art history. Ed. by Selim Kemal and Ivan Gaskell. N.Y., Cambridge Univ. Pr., 1991. x, 245p. (Cambridge studies in philosophy and art)

"The purpose of this volume . . . is to offer a range of responses by philosophers and art historians to some crucial issues generated by the relationship between the art object and the language of art history."—*p.1.*

Contents: (1) Art history and language: some issues, by Selim Kemal and Ivan Gaskell; (2) Presence, by Jean-François Lyotard; (3) Writing and painting: the soul as hermeneut, by Stanley Rosen; (4) Correspondence, projective properties, and expression in the arts, by Richard Wollheim; (5) The language of art criticism, by Michael Baxandall; (6) Baxandall and Goodman, by Catherine Lord and José A. Benardete; (7) Figurative language in art history, by Carl R. Hausman; (8) Cézanne's physicality: the politics of touch, by Richard Shiff; (9) Conditions and conventions: on the disanalogy of art and language, by David Summers; (10) A minimal syntax for the pictorial: the pictorial and the linguistic—analogies and disanalogies, by Andrew Harrison.

Notes at ends of chapters. Index, p.240–45.

G58 Lavalleye, Jacques. Introduction à l'archéologie et à l'histoire de l'art. 4. ed. Louvain-La-Neuve, Institut supérieur d'archéologie et d'histoire de l'art, 1979. xxii, 221p. il. (Publications d'histoire de l'art et d'archéologie de l'Université catholique de Louvain, 17)

See GLAH 1:G15 for previous eds.

G59 Lützeler, Heinrich. Kunsterfahrung und Kunstwissenschaft: systematische und entwicklungsgeschichtliche Darstellung und Dokumentation des Umgangs mit der bildenden Kunst. Freiburg, Alber, 1975. 3v. (Orbis academicus, 1/15, 1–3)

Ambitious, thematic anthology documenting mankind's encounter with art in Europe from late antiquity to the 20th century. To a significant extent, a genre-based survey of the literature of art, with an emphasis upon historiography and methodology.

Contents: (1) Einleitung; Erster Teil: Die ausserwissenschaftlichte Kunsterfahrung [includes poetic responses to the visual arts, art criticism, the relationship of art and society, the evaluation of art]; Zweiter Teil: Die vorwissenschaftliche Kunsterfahrung [includes travel guides, biographies of artists, chronicles]; Dritter Teil: Künstler über Kunst [includes instructional manuals, art theory, self-portraiture]; Vierter Teil: Kunsterfahrung in der Wissenschaft: Überblick [includes methodology and historiography]; Fünfter Teil: Grundlagen der Kunstwissenschaft [includes connoisseurship, hermeneutics, style, tradition, epistemology, description of artworks, aesthetic values]. (2) Sechster Teil: Die heteronome Grundlegung der Kunstwissenschaft [includes theology, philosophy, psychology, social history of art, art and science]; Siebter Teil: Die autonome Grundlegung der Kunstwissenschaft [includes iconography, iconology, formalism, the materials of the artist]; Achter Teil: Die Offenheit des Kunstwerkes [includes structuralism, the non finito, Geistesgeschichte, sociology of art, patronage, the art market, the idea of the great artist, biography of artists, geography and nationalism, history of world art, comprehensive surveys, comparative art history. (3) [Notes, bibliography, indexes, plates].

Anmerkungen: Bd.3, p.[1519]–63. Bibliographie, Bd.3, p.[1565]–1706. Personen- und Ortsregister, Bd.3, p.1709–70. Sachregister, Bd.3, p.1771–1849.

G60 Metzler Kunsthistoriker Lexikon: zweihundert Porträts deutschsprachiger Autoren aus vier Jahrhunderten. Von Peter Betthausen, Peter H. Feist und Christiane Fork unter Mitarb. von Karin Rührdanz und Jürgen Zimmer. Stuttgart, Metzler, 1999. xvii, 523p.

200 biographical sketches of Germanophone art historians.

Bibliographie, p.501–10. Namenregister, p.511–23.

G61 Michels, Karen. Transplantierte Kunstwissenschaft: deutschsprachige Kunstgeschichte im amerikanischen Exil. Berlin, Akademie, 1999. xvii, 255p., ports. (Studien aus dem Warburg-Haus, 2)

Revision of the author's Habilitationsschrift, University of Hamburg. Important analysis of the emigration of Germanophone art historians to the United States during the Nazi years, focusing upon institutional settings, pedagogical and research programs.

Verzeichnis der emigrierten deutschsprachigen Kunsthistoriker, p.195–200. Siglenverzeichnis, p.201. Literaturverzeichnis, p.202–30. Personenregister, p.231–37.

G62 Miedema, Hessel. "Kunst" historisch. Maarssen, Gary Schwartz, 1989. 221p. il.

An important, untranslated essay on art historical methodology by an accomplished student of Dutch art history.

Contents: Kunst; Historisch: Iconografie; Kunsttheorie; Stilistiek; Iconology; Het aanzien van het kunstwerk; Het aanzien van de kunstenaar; Het aanzien van de kunst; Besluit.

Includes bibliographical references.

G63 Minor, Vernon Hyde. Art history's history. Englewood Cliffs, N.J., Prentice Hall, 1994. xii, 211p. il.

"It is my intention to attempt to describe in this book what art history is, where it came from, what ideas, institutions and practices form its background, how it achieved its present shape, and what critical methods it uses."—*Introd.* Aimed at "those who are encountering art history for the first time or nearly the first time."—*Introd.*

Contents: Introduction; Part one: The Academy. Part two: What is art? Answers from antiquity to the eighteenth century. Part three: The emergence of method and modernism in art history.

Bibliographies at the end of chapters. Index, p.207–11.

G64 Mitter, Partha. Much maligned monsters: a history of European reactions to Indian art. Chicago, Univ. of Chicago Pr., 1992. xxiii, 351p. il.

1st ed. Oxford, Clarendon Press, 1977. Originally presented as the author's thesis, University of London.

Informed study of the western reception of Indian art, including western historiography.

Contents: (I) Indian art in travellers' tales; (II) Eighteenth century antiquarians and erotic gods; (III) Orientalists, picturesque travellers, and archaeologists; (IV) Historical and philosophical interpretations of Indian art; (V) The Victorian interlude; (VI) Toward the twentieth century: a reassessment of present attitudes. Appendix 1: Outline of early European collections of Indian art; Appendix 2: On Elephanta and Salsette from Castro's Roteiro.

Notes, p.287–320. Bibliography, p.330–43. Index, p.345–51.

G65 Moxey, Keith P. F. The practice of theory: poststructuralism, cultural politics, and art history. Ithaca, Cornell Univ. Pr., 1994. xv, 153p. il.

"This book is intended to promote a theoretical awareness that will enable . . . [previous conventions of art history writing] to locate themselves within the broader intellectual landscape offered by the humanities as a whole" and to challenge the claim that "there is no place in art history for theory and that our discipline's success depends upon its capacity to assume that the theories on which it bases its results cannot be called into question."—*Pref.*

Contents: Preface; Part one: Cultural politics: Theory; Introduction; (1) Representation; (2) Ideology; (3) Authorship: Part two: Cultural politics: practice; (4) Panofsky's Melancolia; (5) The paradox of mimesis; (6) Seeing through; (7) Making "genius."

Index, by Celeste Newbrough, p.[149]–53.

G66 The New art history. Ed. by Frances Borzello and A. L. Rees. London, Camden Pr., 1986. 173p.

An influential anthology that offers "a review of the new developments in art history for the interested but not necessarily specialist reader. . . . All contributors share the conviction that the principles and methods of traditional art history must come under scrutiny."—*Introd.*

Contents: Introduction, by A. L. Rees and Frances Borzello; Reviewing art history, by Dawn Ades; How revolutionary is the new art history? by Stephen Bann; On newness, art and history: reviewing Block, 1979–85, by Jon Bird; "Something about photography theory," by Victor Burgin; Teaching and learning, by Mary F. Gormally and Pamela Gerrish Nunn; New lamps for old, by Tom Gretton; Taste and tendency, by Charles Harrison; Saussure v. Peirce: Models for a semiotics of visual art, by Margaret Iversen; Photography, history and writing, by Ian Jeffrey; The landscape of reaction: Richard Wilson (1713?–1782) and his critics, by Neil McWilliam and Alex Potts; Feminism, art history and cultural politics, by Lynda Nead; Pater, Stokes and art history: the aesthetic sensibility, by Michael O'Pray; The new art history and art criticism, by Paul Overy; History of art and the undergraduate syllabus: is it a discipline and how should we teach it?, by Marcia Pointon; Art's histories, by Adrian Rifkin; Art history and difference, by John Tagg.

Notes at ends of some chapters. Notes on contributors, p.[172]–73.

G67 New feminist criticism: art, identity, action. Ed. by Joanna Frueh . . . [et al.] N.Y., IconEditions, 1994. xxii 345p. il.

"Offers a wide range of feminist criticism, sparked by ideas and events of the 1980s and early 1990s."—*Introd.*

Notes at ends of chapters. Notes on contributors, p.[327]–30. Index, p.[331]–45.

G68 Panichi, Roberto. La teoria dell'arte nell'antichità. Firenze, Alinea, 1997. 141p. il. (Saggi e documenti, 161)

Lucid, scholarly study of art theory in classical antiquity, embracing art criticism, philosophy of art, and esthetics.

Contents: (1) Linee generali; (2) Per la definizione del concetto di critica; (3) Categorie critiche; (4) La storia naturale di Plinio e le sue fonti; (5) Note pliniane su Protegene, Timante, Lisippo, Apelle. La questione dell'ethos in Polignoto e Zeusi secondo la poetica aristotelica; (6) Letteratura periegetica. Pausania; (7) Marco Vitruvio Pollione: la restaurazione del noto; (8) Agatarco di samo e la prospettiva; (9) Il caso di Apaturio di Alabanda; (10) L'architettura nella teoria dell'arte; (11) L'anomino del sublime; (12) Spunti di critica nell'età imperiale; (13) Fondamenti estetici: Platone; (14) L'indirizzo psicologico: Aristotele; (15) La soluzione mistica; Plotino; (16) Il sacro fuoco d'Olimpia; (17) Nel salotto di Diotima.

Bibliografia, p.[139]–41.

G69 Panofsky, Erwin. Perspective as symbolic form. Trans. by Christopher S. Wood. N.Y., Zone Books (Distr. by MIT Pr., 1991). 196p.

Trans. of Die Perspektive als symbolische Form, which first appeared in Vorträge der Bibliothek Warburg 4 (1924–1925), p.[258]–330; French ed. Paris, Éditions de minuit, 1973; Italian ed. Milano, Feltrinelli, 1961; 4a ed. 1979.

Includes bibliographical references.

G70 Pevsner, Nikolaus. Academies of art, past and present. [Reprint.] New pref. by the author. N.Y., Da Capo, 1973. x, xiv, 323p. il.

See GLAH 1:G22 for original ed. (1940). Spanish trans., Academias de arte: pasado y presente. Madrid, Ediciones Catedra, 1982.

G71 Podro, Michael. The critical historians of art. New Haven, Yale Univ. Pr., 1982. xxvi, 257p. il.

"The present book examines a central tradition within the literature of the visual arts. The foundations of that tradition lay in German philosophical aesthetics of the late eighteenth and early nineteenth century and it stretches from roughly 1827 to 1927, from the writings of Hegel and Rumohr to that of Riegl, Woelfflin, Warburg and Panofsky."—*Introd.*

Contents: Introduction; Part one: (I) The project; (II) Hegel; (III) Schnaase's prototype of critical history; (IV) From Semper to Goeller. Part two; Introduction to part two; (V) Riegl; (VI) Woelfflin; (VII) The Principles and its problems; (VIII) From Springer to Warburg; (IX) Panofsky; (X) The tradition reviewed.

Notes, p.[218]–50. A select bibliography, p.[251]–54. Index, p.[255]–57.

G72 ———. The manifold in perception: theories of art from Kant to Hildebrand. Oxford, Clarendon Pr., 1972. xv, 129 il., plates.

A rigorous examination of "German aesthetic theory from Kant through the end of the 19th Century." Examines pertinent texts "in order to re-locate notions in current use, like 'aesthetic detachment,' within the sustained systematic discourse of which they were once part."—*Pref.*

Contents: (I) Introduction: three types of demarcation; (II) Kant; (III) Schiller's conception of morality and its visual image; (IV) The Aesthetic education of mankind; (V) Herbart's vision of the mind; (VI) Visual perception; (VII) Schopenhauer's theories of art; (VIII) Fiedler's analogy of vision and language; (IX) The tradition from Kant in contemporary retrospect.

Bibliography and abbreviations, p.[xiii]–xv. Index, p.[127]–29.

G73 Preziosi, Donald, ed. The Art of art history: a critical anthology. N.Y., Oxford Univ. Pr., 1998. 595p. il. (part col.), facsims., ports. (Oxford history of art)

A "collection of resources for constructing a critical history of art history . . . made up of essays and excerpts from books written on a number of interrelated themes over the past two centuries."—*Introd.*

Contents: Introduction: Art history: making the visible legible, by Donald Preziosi; (1) Art as history; (2) Aesthetics; (3) Style; (4) History as an art; (5) Mechanisms of meaning: iconography and semiology; (6) Modernity and its discontents; (7) The gendered subject; (8) Deconstruction and the limits of interpretation; (9) The Other: art history and/as museology; Afterword.

Notes, p.528–68. List of texts, p.569–70. Biographical notes, p.574–75. Glossary, p.576–83. Index, p.584–95.

G74 ______. Re-thinking art history: meditations on a coy science. New Haven, Yale Univ. Pr., 1989. xvi, 269p. il.

"The six chapters of the book represent several probes into the archaeology of art history—several test trenches beneath the rhetorical surfaces of disciplinary practice . . . [with] the modest aim of foregrounding some of the primary metaphorical substructures of modern art historical practice."—*Pref.*

Notes, p.181–244. Bibliography, p.245–64. Index, p.265–69.

G75 Problemi di metodo: condizioni di esistenza di una storia dell'arte. A cura di Lajos Vayer. Bologna, CLUEB, [1982]. 268p. il., plates. (Atti del XXIV Congresso internazionale di storia dell'arte, v. 10)

Contributions in English, French, German, Italian, and Spanish.

Wide-ranging collection of lectures on the methodologies of art history, presented at the 24th International Congress of the History of Art, Bologna (1979).

Bibliographical references at the end of most lectures.

G76 Riegl, Alois. Problems of style: foundations for a history of ornament. Trans. by Evelyn Kain. Annotations, glossary, and introd. by David Castriota. Pref. by Henri Zerner. Princeton, Princeton Univ. Pr., 1992. xxxiii, 406p. il.

Trans. of Stilfragen: Grundlegungen zu einer Geschichte der Ornamentik. Berlin, Siemens, 1893; repr.: Mittenwald, Maander, 1985 (Kunstwissenschaftliche Studientexte, Bd. 1); Italian ed. Milano, Feltrinelli, 1963.

Well-translated, annotated English version of a classic of the historiography of art; central to subsequent discussions of the evolution of artistic styles, periodization in art history, and the history of ornament.

Annotations, p.307–96. Glossary of terms and concepts used by Riegl, p.397–406.

G77 Roskill, Mark. The interpretation of pictures. Amherst, Univ. of Massachusetts Pr., 1989. xvi, 124p. il.

"This book is a series of essays on the way that pictures are interpreted. Uses examples from the Renaissance to the modern period to bring out the principles and problems that govern the bringing into being of a considered text that, if generally accepted, causes the work of art that is its subject to be viewed in a certain light."—*Pref.*

Contents: (1) The rhetoric of art historical writing: employment, tenor, tropology; (2) The study of imagery and creative processes; (3) Indeterminacy and the institutions of art history; Conclusion: Revisionist interpretation and art history today; Supplements: (1) Iconography; (2) Style as a tool of interpretation.

Notes, p.[103]–20. Index, p.[121]–24.

G78 ______. What is art history? 2d ed. Amherst, Univ. of Massachusetts Pr., 1989. 192p. il.

See GLAH 1:G23 for original ed. Changes in this ed. are limited to corrections of mistakes, updating of captions when locations of works have changed, etc. Includes an Introduction to the second edition.

References and books for further reading, p.183–88. Index, p.189–92.

G79 Sciolla, Gianni Carlo. Materiali per la storia della critica d'arte del Novecento. Torino, Editrice Tirrenia-Stampatori, 1980. 193p.

Studies of major 20th-century art historians, based upon the author's academic lectures on the history of art criticism, University of Turin, delivered since 1972.

Contents: Parte prima: La "scuola" di Vienna e la critica d'arte del primo Novecento; Parte seconda: Orientamenti storiografici e problemi metodologici della critica d'arte fra le due guerre; Parte terza: Orientamenti storiografici e problemi metodologici dal secondo dopoguerra agli anni settanta; Parte quarta: Problemi e prospettive degli anni settanta.

Bio-bibliographies of art historians at the end of chapters.

G80 "State of research in . . ." Published periodically in Art bulletin, v.68, 1986– .

Series of articles on current methodologies in specific areas of the history of art. Title varies.

Contents: Corn, Wanda, "Coming of age: historical scholarship in American art," v.70, June 1988, p.188–207; Cropper, Elizabeth, and Dempsey, Charles, "Italian painting of the seventeenth century," v.69, December 1987, p.494–509; Gouma-Peterson, Thalia, and Mathews, Patricia, "The feminist critique of art history," v.69, September 1987, p.326–

57; Haverkamp-Begemann, Egbert, "Northern baroque art," v.69, December 1987, p.510–19; Hood, William, "Italian renaissance art," v.69, June 1987, p.174–86; Kessler, Herbert L., "On the state of medieval art history," v.70, June 1988, p.166–87; Kuspit, Donald, "Conflicting logic: twentieth century art at the cross roads," v.69, March 1987, p.117–32; Ridgway, Brunhilde Sismondo, "The state of research on ancient art," v.68, March 1986, p.7–23 (response by Hood, William, "In defense of art history: a response to Brunhilde Sismondo Ridgway," v.68, September 1986, p.480–81; reply by Ridgway, p.481–82); Shiff, Richard, "Art history and the nineteenth century: realism and resistance," v.70, March 1988, p.25–49; Silver, Larry, "Northern European art of the renaissance era," v.68, December 1986, p.518–35 (response by Hindman, Sandra, "The illustrated book: an addendum to the state of research in northern renaissance art," v.68, December 1986, p.536–42); Spector, Jack, "The state of psychoanalytic research in art history," v.70, March 1988, p.49–76; Stafford, Barbara Maria, "The eighteenth century: towards an interdisciplinary model," v.70, March 1988, p.6–25; Trachtenberg, Marvin, "Some observations on recent architectural history," v.70, June 1988, p.208–41.

G81 The subjects of art history: historical objects in contemporary perspective. Ed. by Mark A. Cheetham, Michael Ann Holly, Keith Moxey. N.Y., Cambridge Univ. Pr., 1998. xii, 336p. il.

Collection of 16 essays by the editors and 13 other writers, seeking to provide "an introduction to the historiography and theory of the history of art."—*Pub. advertisement.*

Contents: Part one: Philosophy of history and historiography; Part two: The subjects and objects of art history; Part three: Places and spaces for visual studies.

Index, p.329–36.

G82 Theories of the arts in China. Ed. by Susan Bush and Christian Murck. Princeton, Princeton Univ. Pr., 1983. xxvi, 447p. il.

Papers presented at a conference sponsored by the Committee on Studies of Chinese Civilization of the American Council of Learned Societies held June 6–June 12, 1979, at the Breckinridge Public Affairs Center of Bowdoin College, York, Maine.

Notes at ends of chapters. Contributors, p.[425]–26. Glossary for Chinese and Japanese texts in the notes, p.[427]–34. Index-Glossary, p.[435]–47.

G83 Tournikiotis, Panayotis. The historiography of modern architecture. Cambridge, Mass., MIT Pr., 1999. xi, 334p. il., plans.

"A thoughtful, intelligent, and sometimes astute study of a reasonable number (and choice) of historians of the modern movement: Nikolaus Pevsner, Emil Kaufmann, Siegfried Giedion, Bruno Zevi, Leonardo Benevolo, Henry-Russell Hitchcock, Reyner Banham, Peter Collins, and Manfredo Tafuri."—*Review* by Harry Malgrave in CAA reviews (Jan.–June 2000).

Contents: (1) The art historians and the founding genealogies of modern architecture; (2) The critical resurgence of modern architecture; (3) The social confirmation of modern architecture; (4) The objectification of modern architecture; (5) History in search of time present; (6) Architecture, time past, and time future; (7) History as the critique of architecture; (8) Modern architecture and the writing of histories.

Notes, p.269–317. Bibliography, p.319–35. Index of names, p.337–44.

G84 Vanbergen, J. F. H. H. Voorstelling en betekenis: theorie van de kunsthistorische interpretatie. Assen, Van Gorcum, 1986. 208p. il. (Ancorae, v.3)

An introduction to art historical theories and methods of explanation and interpretation.

Contents: (1) Inleiding; (2) De iconologische theorie; (3) Typus; (4) Modus; (5) Stijl; (6) Expressie en intentie; (7) De voorstelling as tekst; (8) Metataal en kritiek; (9) Noten.

Noten, p.168–95. Register, p.207–8.

G85 Vansina, Jan. Art history in Africa: an introduction to method. Drawings by C. Vansina. N.Y., Longman, 1984. xiv, 233p. il.

"The book is an exposé of the approach to art history in general as it relates to Africa. It is an introduction to the questions art historians should ask about the objects of study and to the ways they should follow when seeking answers to such questions. It applies the general epistemology and methods used in the discipline to the specific situation of art in Africa."—*Introd.*

Contents: (1) Introduction; (2) Identification; (3) Society, the mother of art; (4) Media and techniques; (5) Style; (6) The interpretation of icons; (7) Culture and art; (8) The creative process; (9) The creative process: foreign inputs; (10) Wider perspectives; (11) Art in history.

References and further reading, p.214–23. Index, p.225–33.

G86 Visual culture: images and interpretations. Ed. by Norman Bryson . . . [et al.] Hanover, N.H., University Pr. of New England, 1994. xxix, 429p. il.

"Essays originally written for a National Endowment for the Humanities Summer Institute entitled 'Theory and Interpretation in the Visual Arts,' held at the University of Rochester during July and August 1989."—*Pref.* 15 essays intended "to encourage discussion of theoretical perspectives in art history."—*Pref.* A sequel to Visual theory (see following entry).

Contents: Introduction; Feminism/Foucault—Surveillance/sexuality, by Griselda Pollock; Men's work? Masculinity and modernism, by Lisa Tickner; The discontinuous city: picturing and the discursive field, by John Tagg; Hieronymus Bosch and the "World Upside Down": the case of The Garden of Earthly Delights, by Keith Moxey; Observations on style and history in French painting of the male nude, 1785–1794, by Thomas Crow; The renunciation of reaction in Girodet's Sleep of Endymion, by Whitney Davis; The theater of revolution: a new interpretation of Jacques-Louis David's Tennis Court Oath, by Wolfgang Kemp; Géricault and "masculinity," by Norman Bryson; Strategies of identification, by Ernst van Alphen; Fassbinder and Lacan: a reconsideration of gaze, look, and image, by Kaja Silverman; Feminism, psychoanalysis, and the study of popular culture, by Constance Penley; The ecology of images, by Andrew Ross; Wölfflin and the imagining of the Baroque, by Michael Ann Holly; Dead flesh, or the smell of painting, by Mieke Bal; Form and gender, by David Summers.

Notes at ends of chapters. Contributors, p.[413]–15. Index, p.[417]–29. Contributors, p.[413]–15. Index, p.[417]–29.

G87 Visual theory: painting and interpretation. Ed. by Norman Bryson . . . [et al.] N.Y., HarperCollins, 1991. ix, 286p. il.

Lectures delivered at an institute on "Theory and Interpretation in the Visual Arts," held at Hobart and William Smith Colleges in July and August 1987. Selected lectures were chosen for publication with a goal of "locating art history within the context of theoretical debates currently taking place in other fields and . . . examining interpretative models that might generate the basis for future art historical work."—*Pref.*

Contents: Introduction; (1) Women, art and power, by Linda Nochlin; commentaries by Ellen Wiley Todd and Ludmilla Jordanova; (2) Semiology and visual interpretation, by Norman Bryson; commentary by Stephen Melville; (3) Using language to do business as usual, by Rosalind Krauss; commentary by Norman Bryson; (4) What the spectator sees, by Richard Wollheim; commentaries by Flint Schier and Martin Kelly; (5) Depiction and the golden calf, by Michael Podro; commentary by Timothy Erwin; (6) Description and the phenomenology of perception, by Arthur C. Danto; commentaries by Martin Donogho and Garry Hagberg; (7) Real metaphor: towards a redefinition of the "conceptual" image, by David Summers; commentaries by David Radcliffe and Shelly Errington.

Notes at ends of each chapter. Notes on contributors, p.[274]–75. Index, p.[276]–86.

G88 Waetzoldt, Wilhelm. Deutsche Kunsthistoriker. [Reprint]. Berlin, Spiess, 1986. 2v.

Reprint of GLAH 1:G28

G89 Watkin, David. The rise of architectural history. Westfield, N.J., Eastview, 1980. xi, 204p.

"This book is a first attempt to sketch the outline of the study of architectural history from the seventeenth century to the present day, primarily in England, though also taking into account German, French, Italian and American historiography."—*Pref.*

Contents: Preface; (I) The continental background 1700–1914; (II) America; (III) English antiquarians and the Gothic Revival; (IV) The history of the "English Tradition": 1900–1945; (V) The establishment of art history; (VI) Victorian and Neo-Classical studies; (VII) Some recent tendencies.

Select bibliography, p.191–96. Index, p.197–204.

G90 Wendland, Ulrike. Biographisches Handbuch deutschsprachiger Kunsthistoriker im Exil: Leben und Werk der unter dem Nationalsozialismus verfolgten und vertriebenen Wissenschaftler. München, Saur, 1999. 2v.

Biographical dictionary of émigré Germanophone art historians who went into exile during the Nazi era.

Contents: (1) A–K; (2) L–Z.

Abkürzungsverzeichnis, v.1, p.[xxi]–xxii. Abkürzungen der Literatur und Archivalien, p.[xxiv]–xlii.

G91 Wien und die Entwicklung der kunsthistorischen Methode. Leitung der Sektion: Leopold D. Ettlinger. Red.: Stefan Krenn, Martina Pippal. Wien, Böhlau, 1984. 127p. (Akten des XXV. Internationalen Kongresses für Kunstgeschichte, 1)

Contributions in English, French, German, and Italian.

Essays on seminal figures of the Vienna School of art history, presented at the International Congress of the History of Art (Vienna, 1983).

G92 Wolff, Janet. Aesthetics and the sociology of art. 2d ed. Ann Arbor, Univ. of Michigan Pr., 1993. xiv. 130p.

1st ed., Boston, Allen & Unwin, 1983.

"This book deals with what I have called 'the sociological challenge to aesthetics.' It reviews the many ways in which sociological approaches . . . raise uncomfortable and important questions for traditional aesthetics."—*Introd. to the second ed.* Well-known, brief, and accessible text.

References at end of each essay. Bibliography, p.117–26. Index, p.127–30.

G93 ______. The social production of art. 2d ed. Washington Square, New York Univ. Pr., 1993. 207p.

1st ed., N.Y., St. Martin's Press, 1981.

Sociological study of the production, distribution, and reception of art.

Notes and references, p.[144]–65. Bibliography p. [166]–86. Index, p.[187]–96.

G94 Women as interpreters of the visual arts, 1820–1979. Ed. by Claire Richter Sherman and Adele M. Holcomb. Westport, Conn., Greenwood, 1981. xxiv, 487p. il. (Contributions in women's studies, 18)

"This volume attempts to repair the neglect of women's attainments as interpreters of the visual arts. . . . Twelve biographical and critical essays on representative European and American women reveal the range of their contributions to the field. These essays are preceded by three introductory chapters that review the careers of about a hundred other women who, from 1820 until 1979, made important contributions as interpreters of the visual arts."—*Introd. note.*

Selected bibliography, p.[441]–57. Index, p.[459]–83. Notes on contributors, p.[485]–87.

G95 Wrigley, Richard. The origins of French art criticism: from the Ancien Régime to the Restoration. N.Y., Oxford Univ. Pr., 1993. xii, 427p. il., plates.

"This book is a study of the circumstances in which art criticism came to be an established form of commentary on contemporary art in France, and how those specific conditions shaped the nature of the criticism that was produced."—*Introd.* Exemplary study.

Contents: Introduction; (1) The Salon in context; (2) The

Salon; (3) In search of an art public; (4) Between the studio and the Salon; (5) Censorship and diffusion of criticism during the Ancien Régime; (6) The status of criticism; (7) The language of art criticism; (8) The hierarchy of the genres; Conclusion. Appendices: (I) Some independent exhibitions, lotteries, and subscription schemes; (II) Some extensions to Salon exhibitions; (III) Production of Salon pamphlets and press reviews; (IV) A question of attribution: Lefébure or Carmontelle?

Abbreviations, p.[xi]–xii. Bibliography, p.[363]–416. Index, p.[417]–27.

SEE ALSO: Architectural theory and practice from Alberti to Ledoux (GLAH 2:J199); Art in theory, 1815–1900 (GLAH 2:I245); Art in theory, 1900–1990 (GLAH 2:I246); Belting, Likeness and presence (GLAH 2:I211); Chipp, Theories of modern art (GLAH 1:I238); Ehresmann, Fine arts: a bibliographic guide (GLAH 2:A38); Kleinbauer and Slavens, Research guide to the history of western art (GLAH 2:A44); Stiles and Selz, Theories and documents of contemporary art: a sourcebook of artists' writings (GLAH 2:I294); Tafuri, Theories and history of architecture (GLAH 2:J128); Taylor, Nineteenth-century theories of art (GLAH 2:I295).

H. Sources and Documents

This bibliography of sources and documents is highly selective. With the exception of general anthologies and collections, these titles embrace the period from antiquity to the mid-19th century. Late 19th- and 20th-century sources, both individual titles and collections, are listed elsewhere (mostly in Chapter I, Histories and Handbooks) and may be located by title and subject through the index.

GENERAL WORKS

H1 Documents of art and architectural history. N.Y., Broude, 1981–92. (9?)v.

Most vols. published in 1980–81.

"Documents of art and architectural history is a numbered series of facsimile editions of major works relevant to the history of painting, sculpture, and architecture from the Renaissance to the present. Each volume . . . is a full-size reproduction of the original text . . . prefaced by a note dealing with the printing history of the edition reproduced and with matters of textual and bibliographical interest."—*Pub. note.*

Contents: Series 1: Biography and lexicography; Series 2: Theory and practice. Sample titles: Algarotti, Francesco. Saggio sopra la pittura (1763); Baldinucci, Filippo. Vocabolario toscano dell'arte del disegno (1681); Bellori, Giovanni Pietro. Le vite de' pittori, scultori ed architetti moderni: parte prima (1672); Bosse, Abraham. Sentimens sur la distinction des diverses manières de peinture . . . etc. (1649); Cellini, Benvenuto. Due trattati (1568); Gaurico, Pomponio. De sculptura (1504); Mander, Carel van, Het Schilder-Boeck (1604); Orlandi, Pellegrino Antonio. Abecedario pittorico (1704); Piero della Francesca. De prospectiva pingendi (manuscript facs.) (published in 1992); Vasari, Le vite de più eccellenti architetti, pittori, et scultori italiani (1550).

H2 Fonti per la storia dell'arte. Treviso, Canova, 1973– . (13?)v.

Loosely coordinated series of reprints and studies of sources and documents in the history of art; unrelated to following entry.

Selective contents: Carradori, Francesco. Istruzione elementare per gli studiosi della scultura, 1802 (1979); Cozens, Alexander. A new method of assisting the invention in drawing original compositions of landscape, 1785 (1981); Lanzi, Luigi. Viaggio del 1793 pel Genovesato e il Piemontese (1984); Ludovico da Pietralunga. Descrizione della basilica di S. Francesco e di altri santuari di Assisi (manuscript facs., 1982); Marulli, Vincenzo. Su l'architettura e su la nettezza delle città, 1807 (1975); Moreno, Paolo. Testimonianze per la teoria artistica di Lisippo (1973); Orsini, Baldassare. Guida al forestiere per l'augusta città di Perugia, 1784 (1973); Ottonelli, Giovanni Domenico. Trattato della pittura e scultura uso et abuso loro, 1652 (1973); Pascoli, Leone. Vite de' pittori, scultori, ed architetti viventi (manuscript facs., 1981); Ridolfi, Carlo. Le maraviglie dell'arte, 1648 (repr. of 1914–24 ed., Roma, SOMU, 1965); Silos, Giovanni Michele. Pinacotheca, sive Romana pictura et sculptura, 1673 (1979).

H3 Fonti per la storia dell'arte. Firenze, Le Lettere, 1991– . (3)v.

Loosely coordinated series of reprints of sources and documents in the history of art; unrelated to preceding entry.

Contents: (1) Biffi, Giuseppe. Pitture, scolture et ordini d'architettura (1990); (2) Schlosser, Julius. Quellenbuch: repertorio di fonti per la storia dell'arte del medioevo occidentale (1992); (3) Bon Castellotti, Marco. Collezionisti a Milano nel '700 (1991).

H4 Friedenthal, Richard. Letters of the great artists. London, Thames and Hudson, [1963.] 2v. il., plates.

A select, readable anthology of letters, personal documents, and other self-revelatory writings (e.g., poetry), theoretical and programmatic statements. Capsule biographies.

Contents: (1) From Ghiberti to Gainsborough; (2) From Blake to Pollock.

H5 Holt, Elizabeth Gilmore. A Documentary history of art. [Reprint.] Princeton, Princeton Univ. Pr., 1981–1986. 3v.

See GLAH 1:H3 for previous eds.

Continued by The Triumph of art for the public: the emerging role of exhibitions and critics. Garden City, Anchor, 1979 (Repr.: Princeton, Princeton Univ. Pr., 1983); The Art of all nations, 1850–73: the emerging role of exhibitions and critics. Garden City, N.Y., Anchor, 1981 (Repr.: Princeton, Princeton Univ. Pr., 1982); and The expanding world of art, 1874–1902. New Haven, Yale Univ. Pr., 1988 (1)v. No more published.

H6 The printed sources of western art. Portland, Ore., Collegium Graphicum, 1972. 43v.
Series of facsimile reprints of early modern treatises on art and architecture. No modern critical apparatus. Gen. ed. Theodore Besterman.

Selective contents: (7) Alberti, Leon Battista. De pictura praestantissima (1540); (25) Junius, Franciscus. De pictura veterum. Libri III (1637).

H7 Quellen und Schriften zur bildenden Kunst. Berlin, Hessling, 1966–79; Berlin, Spiess, 1979– . (6)v.
See GLAH 1:R54 for previous vols.

Selective contents: (5) Die Kataloge der Dresdner Akademic-Ausstellungen 1801–1850 (1975); (6) C. P. Warnke. Die ornamentale Groteske in Deutschland 1500–1650, 2v. (1979).

H8 Sources and documents in the history of art series. Englewood, N.J., Prentice-Hall, 1965–80.
Series ed.: Horst W. Janson. See GLAH 1:H6 for previous vols.

Contents: Pollitt, Jerry Jordan. The art of ancient Greece, 1400–31 B.C. (rev. ed., Cambridge Univ. Pr., 1990); ______, The art of Rome, c. 753 B.C.–337 A.D. (repr. Cambridge Univ. Pr., 1983); Mango, Cyril. The art of the Byzantine Empire, 312–1452 (repr. Univ. of Toronto Pr., 1986); Frisch, Teresa G. Gothic art, 1140–c. 1540 (repr. Univ. of Toronto Pr., 1987); Klein, Robert, and Henri Zerner. Italian art, 1500–1600 (repr. Northwestern Univ. Pr., 1989); Stechow, Wolfgang. Northern Renaissance art, 1400–1600 (repr. Northwestern Univ. Pr., 1989); Engass, Robert, and Jonathan Brown. Italy and Spain, 1600–1750 (repr. Northwestern Univ. Pr., 1992); Eitner, Lorenz. Neoclassicism and romanticism, 1750–1850: (1) Enlightenment / revolution; (2) Restoration / twilight of humanism (repr. Harper & Row, 1989); Davis-Weyer, Caecilia. Early medieval art, 300–1150 (repr. Univ. of Toronto Pr., 1986); Gilbert, Creighton. Italian art, 1400–1500 (1980; repr. Northwestern Univ. Pr., 1992).

ANCIENT

Single Sources

H9 Pausanias. Guide to Greece. Trans. with an introd. by Peter Levi. Illustrated with drawings from Greek coins by John Newberry. Maps and plans by Jeffery Lacey. [Harmondsworth], Penguin, [1971]. 2v. il., maps, plans.
See GLAH 1:H8 for James Frazer's standard Eng. ed.

Readable, reliable English paperback version of the classic 2d-century A.D. guide to ancient Greece, with a modest running commentary reflecting modern scholarship on the monuments and sites.

Contents: (1) Central Greece; (2) Southern Greece.

Select bibliography, v.1, p.517–[19], v.2, p.503–4. Index, v.1, p.543–[87], v.2, p.505–32.

Vol.1 and 8 of a new bilingual French ed. with the Greek on facing pages have recently appeared: Description de la Grèce. Texte établi par Michel Casevitz, trad. par Jean Pouilloux, commenté par François Chamoux. Paris, Belles Lettres, 1992 (Collection des universités de France). There is also a recent reprint of an important 19th century ed.: Pausaniae Graeciae descriptio. Ediderunt Hermann Hitzig et Hugo Blümner, N.Y., Olms, 1984, 3v., originally published Leipzig, O.R. Reisland, 1896–1910.

H10 Plinius Secundus, C. The Elder Pliny's Chapters on the history of art. Trans. by K. Jex-Blake. With commentary and historical introd. by E. Sellers. Additional notes contributed by Heinrich Ludwig Urlichs. Pref. to the 1st and 2d American ed. and select bibliography by Raymond V. Schoder. [Reprint.] Chicago, Ares, 1977. [A]–Y, c, 252p.
Reprint of GLAH 1:H9, with a new preface and "further bibliography 1960–1975."

H11 Vitruvius, Pollio. Vitruvius, ten books on architecture. Trans. by Ingrid D. Rowland. Commentary and ill. by Thomas Noble Howe. With additional commentary by Ingrid D. Rowland and Michael J. Dewar. N.Y., Cambridge Univ. Pr., 1999. xvi, 333p. il.
Supersedes the previously standard English ed. (GLAH 1:H10).

Index, p.319–33.

Other noteworthy recent Vitruvius editions include: De l'architecture. Texte établi, trad. e commenté par Jean Soubiran. Paris, Société d'édition "Les Belles lettres," 1969–95. 10v. (Collection des universités de France). Includes the Latin text with French transl. Each vol. ed., trans. and with commentary by a different scholar.

Louis Callebat has produced a monumental dictionary of technical Vitruvian vocabulary: Dictionnaire des termes techniques du De architectura de Vitruve. Éd. par Louis Callebat et Philippe Fleury avec la collaboration de Marie-Thérèse Cam . . . [et al.] N.Y., Olms-Weidmann, 1995 (Alpha-Omega. Reihe A, Lexika, Indizes, Konkordanzen zur klassischen Philologie, 123); and an equally ambitious concordance: Vitruve De architectura concordance: documentation bibliographique, lexicale et grammaticale. Ed. L. Callebat, P. Bouet, Ph. Fleury, M. Zuinghedau. N.Y., Olms-Weidmann, 1984. 2v. (Alpha-Omega. Reihe A, Lexika, Indizes, Konkordanzen zur klassischen Philologie, 43)

A handy, small-format Latin ed. has also appeared, ed. by Laura Cherubini. Pisa, Giardini, 1975 (Scriptorum Romanorum quae extant omnia, 218–221).

A scholarly Italian ed. with commentary is Di architectura. A cura di Pierre Gros. Trad. e commento di Antonio Corso e Elisa Romano. 2v. Torino, Einaudi, 1998 (I milleni).

Gustina Scaglia has published an annotated Italian version of Francesco di Giorgio's important 15th-century Italian translation of Vitruvius, based upon the autograph manuscript bound into the Codex Magliabechianus II.1.141 in the Biblioteca Nazionale, Florence: Il "Vitruvio Magliabechiano" di Francesco di Giorgio Martini. Firenze, Edizioni Gonnelli, 1985 (Documenti inediti di cultura toscana, 6).

For recent editions of other early translations see: De architectura libri I-V, tradotto in volgare da Giambattista Caporali e stampato in Perugia da Iano Bigazzini nel 1536 (repr. Perugia, Volumnia, 1985); and L'architettura di Vitruvio nella versione di Carlo Amati (1829–1830), a cura di Gabriele Morolli. Firenze, Alinea, 1988 (Saggi e documenti. Sezione letteratura architettonica, 67) reprinted, with a brief introduction, from the original ed. published in two vols., Milan, G. Pirola, 1829–30.

Collections

H12 Hebert, Bernhard D. Schriftquellen zur hellenistischen Kunst: Plastik, Malerei und Kunsthandwerk der Griechen vom vierten bis zum zweiten Jahrhundert. Horn, F. Berger, 1989. xiv, 300p. (Grazer Beiträge. Supplementband, 4)

Includes numerous excerpts from Greek and Latin sources.

Literaturhinweise und Abkürzungsverzeichnis, p.xi–xii. Konkordanz mit Overbeck, p.283–85. Register, p.286–300.

H13 Reinach, Adolphe Joseph. Recueil Milliet: textes grecs et latins relatifs à l'histoire de la peinture ancienne. Pub., trad. et commentés, sous le patronage de l'Association des études grecques, par Adolphe Reinach. Avant-propos par S. Reinach. [Reprint.] Chicago, Ares, 1981. viii, 429p.

See GLAH 1:H16 for original ed. Also recently reprinted, with an introd. and notes by Agnes Rouveret. Paris, Macula, 1985 (Collection Deucalion)

MEDIEVAL

Single Sources

H14 Cennini, Cennino. Il libro dell'arte. Pref., commento e note di Mario Serchi. Firenze, Le Monnier, 1991. 194p. il. (part col.), plates.

See GLAH 1:H17 for the standard ed. with Eng. trans.

Bibliografia, p.183–6. Index alfabetico della materia, p.177–82.

For a recent French trans. see Le livre de l'art. Trad. critique, commentaires et notes par Colette Deroche. Paris, Berger-Levrault, 1991.

H15 Suger, Abbot of Saint Denis. Abbot Suger on the Abbey Church of St.-Denis and its art treasures. Ed., trans., and annot. by Erwin Panofsky. 2d ed. by Gerda Panofsky-Soergel. Princeton, Princeton Univ. Pr., 1979. xix, 285p. il.

See GLAH 1:H18 for 1st ed.

First published in 1946, this brilliant study, with English translations of the writings of Abbot Suger (1081–1151) on the rebuilding of the abbey church of St. Denis, has been revised for the second ed. by the author's widow with the aid of an advisory panel of distinguished medievalists. It incorporates the corrections and additions left by the author at his death in 1968 and thus reflects the current state of Suger scholarship at that time.

Glossary, p.260–61. Bibliographic abbreviations, p.262–63. Additional bibliography since 1945, p.264–75. Index, p.277–85.

H16 Theophilus, called also Rugerus. The various arts. Ed. and trans. by C. R. Dodwell. [Reprint.] N.Y., Oxford Univ. Pr., 1986. lxxvii, 178p. (Oxford medieval texts)

Reprint of GLAH 1:H19.

H17 Villard de Honnecourt, 13th century. Carnet de Villard de Honnecourt: d'après le manuscrit conservé à la bibliothèque Nationale de Paris (no. 19093). Présenté et commenté par Alain Erlande-Brandenburg, et al. Paris, Stock, 1986. 126p., facsims.

See GLAH 1:H20 for an earlier facsimile ed., with commentary in German.

Full-page black-and-white illustrations of the 33 leaves of the Villard portfolio, accompanied by essays by four scholars.

Contents: Villard de Honnecourt, témoin de son temps, par Régine Pernoud; Villard de Hoonecourt, l'architecture et la sculpture, par Alain Erlande-Brandenburg; Villard de Honnecourt, architecte-ingénieur, par Jean Gimpel; Les dessins techniques du Carnet de Villard de Honnecourt, par Roland Bechmann.

Orientation bibliographique, p.51–[52].

Collections

H18 Knögel-Anrich, Elsmarie. Schriftquellen zur Kunstgeschichte der Merowingerzeit. Mit einem Vorwort von Kurt Böhner. N.Y., Olms,1992. xii, 258p., 1 port.

See GLAH 1:H22 for 1st ed.

The new ed. features a 12-page essay by Böhner, placing the author's achievement in the context of the historiography of medieval art in the 1930s.

H19 Mortet, Victor, and Deschamps, Paul. Recueil de textes relatifs à l'histoire de l'architecture et à la condition des architectes en France, au moyen âge, XIIe-XIIIe siècles. Pref. de Léon Pressouyre. Bibliographies des sources, Olivier Guyotjeannin. Paris, Ed. du Comité des travaux historiques et scientifiques, 1995. 1096p. (CTHS format, 15)

Reprint in one vol. of GLAH 1:H25–26.

H20 Schlosser, Julius, von. Quellenbuch: repertorio di fonti per la storia dell'arte del medioevo (secoli IV-XV). Con un'aggiunta di nuovi testi e aggiornamenti critico-bibliografici a cura di Janos Vegh. Firenze, Le Lettere, 1992. xxx, xxiv, 598p. il. (Fonti per la storia dell'arte, 2)

See GLAH 1:H28 for 1st ed. (Repr.: Hildesheim, Olms, 1976).

Reprints the German text of the 1st ed., adding 190 pages of critical material in Italian, including translations and additional bibliography.

H21 ———. Schriftquellen zur Geschichte der karolingischen Kunst. [Reprint.] 2. Nachdruck der Ausgabe Wien 1892. N.Y., Olms, 1988. xvi, 482p.
Reprint of GLAH 1:H29 and GLAH 1:H5 (n.F. Bd. 4)

RENAISSANCE—NEOCLASSICAL

Single Sources

15th–16th Centuries

H22 Alberti, Leone Battista. On the art of building in ten books. Trans. by Joseph Rykwert with Neil Leach and Robert Tavernor. Cambridge, Mass., MIT Pr., 1988. xxiii, 442p. il.
See GLAH 1:H31 for original annotation. Supersedes Leoni's 17th-century translation.

Abbreviations used in the notes, p.363–65. Notes, p.366–416. Bibliography, p.417–19. Glossary, p.420–28. Index, p.429–42.

Other recent scholarship includes a word concordance and facsimile of the 1st Latin ed. (1485): Lücke, Hans-Karl. Alberti Index: Leon Battista Alberti. De re aedificatoria 1485: Index verborum. München, Prestel, 1975–79. 4v. There is also a lemmatized concordance: Fresnillo Núñez, Javier. Leon Battista Alberti, De re aedificatoria: a lemmatized concordance. N.Y., Olms-Weidmann, 1996. 3v. (Alpha-Omega. Reihe B, Indizes, Konkordanzen, statistische Studien zur mittellateinischen Philologie, 7)

Recent Italian ed.: L'architettura. Trad. di Giovanni Orlandi. Introd. e note di Paolo Portoghesi. Milano, Il Polifilo, 1989. Revised reprint in one vol. of the Italian translation that appeared alongside the original Latin in GLAH 1:H31.

Spanish facsimile ed.: A facsimile reprint of Francisco Locano's 1582 Spanish trans. with an introduction by José María de Azcárate: Los diez libros de architectura. [Valencia], Albatros, 1977. (Collección Juan de Herrera, 3)

A critical ed. of Pellegrino Tibaldi's important commentary on Alberti's treatise is Sandro Orlando ed., L'Architettura di Leon Battista Alberti nel commento di Pellegrino Tibaldi. Roma, De Luca, 1988.

H23 ———. De statua. A cura di Marco Collareta. Livorno, Sillabe, [1998]. 54p. il. (Arte e memoria, 2)
Latin text with Italian trans. and commentary.

Includes bibliographical references, p.53–54.

Another recent Italian ed.: De statua. Introd., trad., e note a cura di Mariarosaria Spinetti. Napoli, Liguori, 1999 (Domini) (Critica e letteratura, 9). Includes Latin text with Italian trans. and commentary.

H24 ———. On painting. Trans. by Cecil Grayson. With an introd. and notes by Martin Kemp. N.Y., Penguin, 1991. 101p. il.
The English text, reprinted from the bilingual GLAH 1:H32.

Explanatory notes, p.97–101.

Lodovico Domenichi's 1547 Italian ed. has been recently reprinted: Sala Bolognese, Forni, 1988.

H25 Armenini, Giovanni Battista. De' veri precetti della pittura. Ed. a cura di Marina Gorreri. Pref. di Enrico Castelnuovo. Torino, Einaudi, 1988. lxv, 292p. il., plates (part col.) (I Millenni)
See GLAH 1:H33 for earlier eds.

The latest and most complete Italian ed. of a notable treatise on the practical aspects of painting. Important for the study of 16th-century art.

English ed.: On the true precepts of the art of painting, ed. and trans. from the Italian with an introductory study, critical and historical notes, and bibliography by Edward J. Olszewski. N.Y., Franklin, 1977.

H26 Cellini, Benvenuto. I trattati dell'oreficeria e della scultura. Novamente messi alle stampe secondo la originale dettatura del codice Marciano per cura di Carlo Milanesi. Si aggiungano i discorsi e i ricordi intorno all'arte, le lettere e le suppliche, le poesie. [Reprint.] Firenze, Le Monnier, 1994. xiv, lviii, 487p., [1] leaf of plates, geneal. table.
See GLAH 1:H36 for original ed. This ed. originally published in 1857. Includes index.

Léopold Laclanché's 1847 French trans. has recently been reprinted: Traités de l'orfèvrerie et de la sculpture. Paris, École nationale supérieure des beaux-arts, 1992. 217p. (Beaux-arts histoire). This features a "Preface, index, glossaire, bibliographie, chronologie d'Adrien Goetz."

H27 Colonna, Francesco. Hypnerotomachia Poliphili. The strife of love in a dream. The entire text translated for the first time into English with an introd. by Joscelyn Godwin. N.Y., Thames and Hudson, 1999. xix, 474p. il.
See GLAH 1:H37 for earliest eds.

The first complete Eng. trans. Includes the original woodcut illustrations.

For a critical ed. of the original text, see Hypnerotomachia Poliphili. Ed. crit. e commento a cura di Giovanni Pozzi e Lucia A. Ciapponi. Ristampa anastatica in formato ridotto con correzioni, una premessa e un aggiornamento bibliografico. Padova, Antenore, 1980. 2v. il. (Medioevo e umanesimo, 38–39).

The 1499 Aldine text has recently been reprinted, with a new Italian translation and commentary, by Marco Ariani and Mino Gabriele (Milano, Adelphi, 1998 [Classici, 66]).

The text has also been reproduced in The dream of Poliphilo: the soul in love. Related and interpreted by L. Fierz-David. Trans. By Mary Hottinger. Dallas, Spring Publications, 1987 (The Jungian classics series, 8); first published N.Y., Pantheon, 1950 (The Bollingen series, 25).

H28 Della prospettiva. [By] Paolo dal Pozzo Toscanelli. A cura di Alessandro Parronchi. Milano, Edizioni Il Polifilo, 1991. liii p., 23 leaves, il. (Testi e documenti, 5)
Includes a slightly reduced facsimile and transcription of the anonymous illustrated text contained in Codex 2110 of the Biblioteca Riccardiana, Florence, Italy, written in the early 1460s, previously believed to be the work of Leon Battista Alberti and now attributed to Toscanelli. Includes an introd. by the ed., with bibliographical references.

H29 Dolce, Lodovico. Dialogo nel quale si ragiona della qualità, diversità e proprietà dei colori. [Bologna], Forni, 1985. 87 [i.e., 174]p.

Facsim. of: Venetia, G.B., M. Sessa, 1565. See GLAH 1:H39 for Dolce's treatise on painting.

H30 Filarete, Antonio Averlino, *known as*, 15th cent. Trattato di architettura.Testo a cura di Anna Maria Finoli e Liliana Grassi. Introd. e note di Liliana Grassi. Milano, Il Polifilo, [1972]. 2v. il., 141p. of facsims. (Classici italiani di scienze tecniche e arti. Trattati di architettura, v.2)

See GLAH 1:H40 for the standard Eng. ed. and facsimile.

This ed. includes facsimile reproductions from the Codex Magliabechiano and Codex Palatino; it is "published with the cooperation of the Consiglio Nazionale delle Ricerche."

Indice dei nomi e delle cose notevoli, p.[705]–29.

A Spanish ed. has also recently appeared, Tratado de arquitectura. Ed. de Pilar Pedraza. Vitoria-Gasteiz: EPHIALTE, Instituto de Estudios Iconograficos, 1990 (Colección fuentes para el estudio de la historia del arte, 1)

H31 Ghiberti, Lorenzo. I commentarii: Biblioteca nazionale centrale di Firenze, II, I, 333. Introd. e cura di Lorenzo Bartoli. Firenze, Giunti, 1998. 316p. il. (Biblioteca della scienza italiana, 17)

Critical ed., based upon the sole surviving manuscript, with a long introduction by the editor.

Includes bibliographical references. Indice delle fonti, p.[309]. Indice dei nomi, p.[311]–16.

For a partial English trans., see The commentaries of Lorenzo Ghiberti. [Extracts, with trans. and notes by members of the staff of the Courtauld Institute of Art]. [London], Courtauld Institute of Art [194–?]. 36 leaves. See also Der dritte Kommentar Lorenzo Ghibertis: Naturwissenschaften und Medizin in der Kunsttheorie der Frührenaissance. Eingel., komment. und übers. von Klaus Bergdolt. Weinheim, VCH, Acta Humaniora, 1988. ci, 584p. il. This includes the text of Book three of Ghiberti's Commentarii, in German and Italian, with an important scholarly commentary on facing pages. Originally the author's doctoral thesis, Universität Heidelberg, 1986.

H32 Gilio, Giovanni Andrea. Due dialogi. [A cura di Paolo Barocchi.] Firenze, Studio per edizioni scelte, 1998. xv, 144p. (Tabulae artium, 1)

Facsimile reprint of the 1564 ed., with a brief preface by the editor.

Notizie biografiche, p.[146]. Dati bibliografici, p.[146–47].

H33 Leonardo da Vinci. Libro di pittura: edizione in facsimile del Codice Urbinate lat. 1270 nella Biblioteca apostolica vaticana. A cura di Carlo Pedretti. Trascrizione critica di Carlo Vecce. Firenze, Giunti, 1995. 2 v. il. (part col.), facsims.

Also available in a paperback trade ed. (Biblioteca della scienza italiana, 9)

Contents: facsimile vol. of Libro di pittura (Codice Urbinate lat.1270) and commentary vol. accompanied by publisher's leaflet ([4]p.).

Includes bibliographical references.

H34 Lomazzo, Giovanni Paolo. Idea del tempio della pittura. Ed. commentata e trad. di Robert Klein. Firenze, Instituto nazionale di studi sul Rinascimento, 1974. 2v. il.

Italian text with French trans. and commentary.

Notes, v.2, p.[647]–745. Notes sur le texte, v.2, p.[747]–68. Les oeuvres peintes, v.2, p.[769]–84.

H35 ______. Scritti sulle arti. A cura di Roberto Paolo Ciardi. Firenze, Marchi & Bertolli, 1973–74. 2v. (Raccolta pisana di saggi e studi, 33–34)

Vol. 2 published by Centro Di.

Scholarly ed. of Lomazzo's principal writings on art, some never before published.

Contents: (1) Introduzione; Appendice bibliografica; nota filologica; Bibliografia; Libro de sogni; Idea del tempio della pittura; (2) Trattato dell'arte della pittura, scoltura et architettura.

Bibliografia, v.1, p.[xciii]–cxii. Appendici bibliografica, v.2, p.633–34. Indice analitico, p.635–719.

H36 ______. A tracte containing the artes of curious paintinge carvinge and buildinge. [Reprint.] Trans. by Richard Haydocke. England, Gregg International, 1970. 11, 9, 218p. il.

Reprint in one vol. of the 1598 ed. (See GLAH 1:H43, annotation.)

H37 Martini, Francesco di Giorgio. "Taccuino": Urb. lat. 1757: seconda metà del xv sec. Milano, Jaca book, 1991. 191 leaves il., facsims. (Codices e Vaticanis selecti, LXXX)

"Il volume, in edizione facsimile, è una copia fedele del codice Urb. lat. 1757. Nella riproduzione si è sempre avuto a disposizione l'originale."

Commentary vol. by Luigi Michelini Tocci. Facsimile and commentary issued together in a box (20 cm.). Commentary vol. includes bibliographical references and index.

H38 ______. Trattato di architettura. Pres. di Luigi Firpo. Introd., trascriz. e note di Pietro C. Marani. Firenze, Giunti Barbèra, 1979–1994. 3v. col. facsims. (Testi e codici rinascimentali. Fondazione Leonardo da Vinci)

See GLAH 1:H44 for earlier ed.

Critical ed. of the Codex Ashburnham 361 (Biblioteca Laurenziana, Florence), one of the principal surviving manuscripts containing Francesco di Giorgio's writings and drawings on architecture, city planning, engineering, and military architecture.

For an account of the surviving manuscripts, see Gustina Scaglia, Francesco di Giorgio: checklist and history of manuscripts. . . . Bethlehem, Lehigh Univ. Pr., 1992. 298p.

Contents: v.1 contains a scholarly introduction, and a transcription of the manuscript with critical apparatus; v.2 is a facsimile of the manuscript, written in 1489 (54 numbered leaves, written on both sides, with colored il.); v.3, an "appendix" published in 1994, contains an introduction, transcription, and facsimile of an eight-page fragment of the

Ashburnham codex discovered in the early 1980s in the Biblioteca Municipale in Reggio Emilia.

H39 Michiel, Marcantonio. Der Anonimo Morelliano: mit Text und Übers. von Theodor Frimmel. 1. Abt. N.Y., Olms, 1974. xxix, 126p.

Reprint of GLAH 1:H5 (Neue Folge, Bd. 1). Bound with Paccioli, Luca. Divina proportione.

See GLAH 1:H45 for an English ed.

H40 Norgate, Edward. Miniatura or the art of limning. Ed., introd. and annot. by Jeffrey M. Muller & Jim Murrell. New Haven, Published for the Paul Mellon Centre for British Art by Yale Univ. Pr., 1997. ix, 297p. il. (part col.), plates.

The first critical ed. of "the most important source for the study of Tudor and Stuart miniature painting."—*Pref.* Supersedes the only previous ed. (1919). Includes a scholarly introduction, historical notes and appendixes.

Bibliography, p.259–77. Index, p.278–97.

H41 Palladio, Andrea. The four books on architecture. Trans. by Robert Tavernor and Richard Schofield. Cambridge, Mass., MIT Pr., 1997. xxxv, 436p. il.

See GLAH 1:H46 for the original 1570 ed. and subsequent eds. This excellent, scholarly trans. supersedes Isaac Ware's 1738 version.

Notes, p.[347]–78. English and Italian glossary, by Richard Schofield, p.379–419. Bibliography, p.421–30.

For a recent, critical Italian ed. see I quattro libri dell'architettura. A cura di Licisco Magagnato e Paola Marini. Introd. di Licisco Magagnato. Milano, Edizioni Il Polifilo, 1980. 4v. in 1 (lxxi, 580 p.), il. plans (Classici italiani di scienze tecniche e arti. Trattati di architettura, v.6)

A recent selection of Palladio's lesser-known writings on art: Scritti sull'architettura (1554–1579). A cura di Lionello Puppi. Vicenza, Neri Pozza, 1988.

H42 Pellegrini, Pellegrino. L'architettura. Ed. critica a cura di Giorgio Panizza. Introd. e note di Adele Buratti Mazzotta. Milano, Il Polifilo, 1990. lxiv, 486p. il. (Classici italiani di scienze tecniche e arti. Trattati di architettura, v.7, pt.1)

Critical ed. of Pellegrini's treatise.

Elenco delle sigle e delle opere citate in forma abbreviata, p.[lxi]–lxiv. Nota sul testo, p.[425]–74. Indice delle note linguistiche e filologiche, p.[477]–79. Indice dei nomi, p.[480]–86.

H43 Serlio, Sebastiano. Architettura civile. Libri sesto, settimo e ottavo nei manoscritti di Monaco e Vienna. A cura di Francesco Paolo Fiore. Premesse e note di Tancredi Carunchio e Francesco Paolo Fiore. Milano, Il Polifilo, 1994. li, 662p. il. (Classici italiani di scienze, tecniche e arti. Trattati di architettura, v.5, pt.1)

Critical ed. of the sixth, seventh, and eighth "books" of Serlio's great treatise, based on surviving manuscripts.

Nota al testo, p.[623]–24. Elenco delle opere citate in forma abbreviata, p.[625]–52. Indice dei nomi e dei luoghi, p.[653]–62.

H44 ______. Sebastiano Serlio on architecture: Books I–V of Tutte l'opere d'architettura et prospetiva. Trans. from the Italian with an introd. and commentary by Vaughan Hart and Peter Hicks. New Haven, Yale Univ. Pr., 1996– . (1)v. il.

See GLAH 1:H47 for original ed.

Superb scholarly English translation of Books I–V of Serlio's great treatise.

Commentary [i.e., Notes], p.[430]–56. Glossary, p.[457]–59. Bibliography, p.[460]–65. Index, p.[475]–84.

H45 Vandelvira, Alonso de. El tratado de arquitectura de Alonso de Vandelvira. Ed. con introd., notas, variantes y glosario hispano-francés de arquitectura. [Por] Geneviève Barbé-Coquelin de Lisle. Madrid, Confederación Española de Cajas de Ahorros, 1977. 2v.

Critical ed. with facsimile of an important 16th-century Spanish architectural treatise.

Contents: (1) Text; (2) Facsimile.

Glosario hispano-francés de arquitectura, t.1, p. [171]–88. Fuentes manuscritas, t.1, p.[189]. Bibliografía, t.1, p.[191]–206.

H46 Vasari, Giorgio. Le vite de' più eccellenti pittori, scultori e architettori: nelle redazioni del 1550 e 1568. Testo a cura di Rosanna Bettarini. Commento secolare a cura di Paola Barocchi. Firenze, Sansoni, 1966– . (14)v.

See GLAH 1:H48a for previous vols. Imprint varies: v.4–5 pub. Firenze, Studio per edizioni scelte.

Each vol. consists of separately bound text and commentary parts with "testo" pt. 1 and "commento" pt. 2. The text vols. offer the text of both the first (1550) ed. and the second (1568) ed.

Includes bibliographical references and indexes, as well as a concordance and philological indexes.

A critical ed. of the original ed. (1550) of Vasari's lives (see GLAH 1:H48) has recently appeared: Le vite de' più eccellenti architetti, pittori, et scultori italiani, da Cimabue insino a' tempi nostri, nell'edizione per i tipi di Lorenzo Torrentino, Firenze 1550. A cura di Luciano Bellosi e Aldo Rossi. Pres. di Giovanni Previtali. Torino, Giulio Einaudi, 1986. lxv, 1,037p. il., plates, ports. (I millenni)

Three recent Eng. eds. have appeared:

The lives of the artists. Trans. with an introd. and notes by Julia Conaway Bondanella and Peter Bondanella. N.Y., Oxford Univ. Pr., 1991. xxiii, 586p. (The World's classics). An accessible, modern English trans. of 36 of Vasari's Lives.

Lives of the artists: a selection. Trans. by George Bull. N.Y., Viking Penguin, 1987. 2v. (Penguin classics). 39 of Vasari's Lives. Vol.1 of this trans. first published in 1965; v.2 first published in 1987.

Lives of the painters, sculptors, and architects. Trans. by Gaston du C. de Vere. With an introd. and notes by David Ekserdjian. N.Y., Knopf (Distr. by Random House, 1996). 2v. (Everyman's library). Reprint in 2 vols. of the only complete English trans. of Vasari's Lives (see GLAH 1:H48a, annotation).

Also noteworthy is a complete French trans.: Le vies des meilleurs peintres, sculpteurs et architectes. Trad. e commentée sous la dir. d'André Chastel. Paris, Berger-Levrault, 1981–89. 12v.

H47 Vignola, Giacomo Barozzi, *known as*. Le due regole della prospettiva practica: a reproduction of the copy in the British Library. Ed. I. Danti. [Reprint.] Alburgh, Archival Facsimiles, 1987. [176]p.

Facsimile of ed. published Rome, Zannetti, 1583.

H48 ______. Regola delli cinque ordini d'architettura. [Reprint.] [Bologna?], Cassa di risparmio di Vignola, 1974. 32, [5] leaves, all il.

Reprint of the 1563 ed. See GLAH 1:H49 for 1562 ed.

17th Century

H49 Baglione, Giovanni. Le vite de' pittori, scultori et architetti: dal pontificato di Gregorio XIII del 1572 in fino à tempi di Papa Urbano Ottavo nel 1642. Ed. comment. a cura di Jacob Hess e Herwarth Rottgen. Città del Vaticano, Biblioteca apostolica vaticana, 1995– . (3)v. (Studi e testi [Biblioteca apostolica vaticana], 367–369)

"In collaborazione con la Bibliotheca Hertziana, Roma (Max-Planck-Institut)." See GLAH 1:H50 for earlier eds.

Facsimile ed., with commentary, of the 1642 copy of Baglione's Lives in the Vatican Library.

Contents: (1) Ristampa anastatica [of the Rome, Andrea Fei, 1642 ed.]; (2) Varianti, postille, commenti: prima e seconda Giornata; (3) Varianti, postille, commenti: terza Giornata.

For an ed. that includes a reprint of the 2d ed., published in Rome by Manelsi in 1649, as well as the index produced in Velletri by Zampetti in 1924, see the 1990 Forni reprint edited by C. Gradara Pesci.

Abbreviazioni bibliografiche, v.3, p.[735]–45. Indice onomastico, p.[749]–87. Indice toponomastico, p.[789]–848.

H50 Baldinucci, Filippo. Notizie dei professori del disegno da Cimabue in qua: per le quali si dimostra come, e per chi le belle arti di pittura, scultura, e architettura lasciata la rozzezza delle maniere greca, e gottica, si siano in questi secoli ridotte all' antica loro perfezione. Opera di Filippo Baldinucci Fiorentino distinta in secoli, e decennali. Firenze, S.P.E.S., 1974–1975. 7v. fold. geneal. tables.

Reprint (with new materials) of GLAH 1:H52

Selective contents: (2)–(5) Con nuove annotazioni e supplementi per cura di F. Ranalli; (6) Appendice con nota critica e supplementi per cura di Paola Barocchi; (7) Appendice per cura di Paola Barocchi; indice per cura di Antonio Boschetto.

H51 Boschini, Marco. Il gioielli pittoreschi: virtuoso ornamento della citta di Vicenza. [Reprint.] Bologna, Forni, 1976.

Reprint of the 1677 ed., Venice, Nicolini.

H52 Caramuel Lobkowitz, Juan. Arquitectura civil recta y oblicua. [Reprint.] Estudio preliminar, Antonio Bonet Correa. Madrid, Ediciones Turner, [1984.] 3v. il., plans.

Reprint, with new introd. Originally published 1678.

Contents: (1–2) Facsimile of text; (3) Plates.

H53 Carducci, Vincenzio. Vincente Carducho: Dialogos de la pintura: su defensa, origen, esencia, definicion, modos y diferencias. Ed., prólogo y notas de Francisco Calvo Serraller. Madrid, Turner, 1979. cxxxiii, 483p. il., facsims.

Text taken from 1633 ed. (GLAH 1:H59). Notes in French, Italian, Latin, or Spanish.

Bibliography, p.cxxxi–cxxxii. Indice onomastico y analitico, p.453–83.

H54 Cropper, Elizabeth. The ideal of painting: Pietro Testa's Düsseldorf notebook. Princeton, Princeton Univ. Pr., 1984. xviii, 288p. il., 72p. of plates.

Publishes for the first time, with transcription and commentary, Pietro Testa's (1611–1650) important notebook in the Kunstmuseum Düsseldorf (Budde 132), described as "neither a treatise nor a sketchbook but a gathering of fragmentary notes on different subjects made at different moments in Testa's life; they were assembled after his death and Testa never intended for them to be published as a whole."—*Introd.* Includes a monographic study of Testa.

Contents: Part One. (1) A Lucchese artist in Rome; (2) Bound theory and blind practice: Il Liceo della Pittura; (3) The garden of letters; (4) Pietro Testa and Roman Classicism. Part Two. Pietro Testa's Notebook in the Kunstmuseum, Düsseldorf; Note to the reader; Editorial symbols; Transcription of the Düsseldorf Notebook and commentary. Appendix One: Sources cited by Testa in the Düsseldorf Notebook; Appendix Two: Mounting, size, and numbering of folios.

Bibliography, p.[275]–282. Index, p.[283]–88.

H55 Félibien, André, Sieur des Avaux et de Javercy. Entretiens sur les vies et sur les ouvrages des plus excellens peintres, anciens et modernes: (entretiens I et II). [Reprint.] Introd., établissement du texte et notes par René Démoris. Paris, Société d'édition "Les Belles Lettres," 1987. 374p. il., plates, facsims. (Nouveaux confluents)

See GLAH 1:H62 for previous eds. The text used is that of the 2d ed., Paris, Mabre-Cramoisy, 1685–88, which is identical with that of 1690, the last seen by Félibien himself.

Wherever possible, the editor has indicated the present location of the works mentioned by Félibien. Variant spellings and terms from the 1666 ed. are indicated in the margins of the text; a listing of them appears on p.359ff. The bibliography chapter consists of a publication history of the Entretiens and of other works by Félibien, and of a critical bibliography.

Contents: Introduction; Note sur cette édition; Épitre; Préface; Premier entretien; Second entretien; Notes de l'éditeur; Table (index fourni par Félibien); Variantes.

Note bibliographique, p.[369]–74.

H56 Guarini, Guarino. Architettura civile. Introd. di Nino Carboneri. Note e appendice a cura di Bianca Tavassi La Greca. Milano, Il Polifilo, 1968. xlviii, 471p. plates (Classici italiani di scienze tecniche e arti. Trattati di architettura, v. 8)

Critical ed. of Guarini's treatise.

Bibliography, p.xl–xlvi.

H57 Junius, Franciscus. De pictura veterum libri tres (Roterodami 1694). Ed., trad. et commentaire du livre I par Colette Nativel. Genève, Droz, 1996. 725p. il. (Travaux du grand siècle, 3)

See GLAH 1:H64 for previous eds. Latin text of Book I with translation and commentary in French.

Bibliographie, p.[593]–689. Index (index locorum, index nominum), p.[691]–719.

H58 ———. The literature of classical art. Ed. by Keith Aldrich, Philipp Fehl, Raina Fehl. Berkeley, Univ. of California Pr., 1987. 2v. il. (California studies in the history of art, 22)

See GLAH 1:H64 for previous eds. Translated from Latin. Vol. 2 also translated by the editors.

Contents: (1) The painting of the ancients; (2) A lexicon of artists & their works.

Bibliography, v.2, p.427–507. Index locorum antiquorum, v.2, p.511–48. General index, v.2, p.549–611.

H59 Mander, Carel van. The foundation of the noble free art of painting. Trans. by J. Bloom . . . [et al.] Ed. by Elizabeth A. Honig. [New Haven, Yale University], 1985. 81 leaves.

Trans. of: Den grondt der edel vry schilder-const, "undertaken by the members of the seminar 'Early Defenses of Netherlandish Art' taught in the Fall of 1984 by Celeste Brusati" at Yale University.

Privately distributed in mimeograph. The only complete if expressly "amateurish" English trans. of this important source.

H60 ———. Karel van Mander, the lives of the illustrious Netherlandish and German painters, from the first edition of the Schilder-boeck (1603–1604): preceded by the lineage, circumstances and place of birth, life and works of Karel van Mander, painter and poet and likewise his death and burial, from the second edition of the Schilder-boeck (1616–1618). With an introd. and trans., ed. by Hessel Miedema. Doornspijk, Davaco, 1994– . (6)v.

See GLAH 1:H69 for previous eds. Supersedes the previous English ed. of C. Van de Wall.

Contents: (1) The text; (2) Commentary on biography and lives, fol.196r01–211r35; (3) Lives, fol.211r36–236v36; (4) Lives / fol.236v37–261v44; (5) Commentary on lives, fol.262r01–291r47; (6) Commentary on lives, 291v01–end.

H61 Pacheco, Francisco. Arte de la pintura. Ed., introd. y notas de Bonaventura Bassegoda i Hugas. Madrid, Catedra, 1990. 782p.

See GLAH 1:H71 for earlier eds. of this important treatise on painting.

Índice, p.751–78.

H62 Passeri, Giovanni Battista. Vite de' pittori, scultori ed architetti che anno lavorato in Roma, morti dal 1641 fino al 1673. [Reprint.] [Bologna], Forni, 1976 (Italica gens, repertori di bio-bibliografia italiana, 84)

Reprint of the 1772 ed. (GLAH 1:H72). Another reprint: Roma, Vivarelli, 1977. The 1934 German critical ed. (See GLAH 1:H72 annotation) has been reprinted recently, Worms, Wernersche Verlagsgesellschaft, 1995.

18th–Early 19th Centuries

H63 Bossi, Giuseppe. Scritti sulle arti. A cura di Roberto Paolo Ciardi. Firenze, Studio per Edizioni Scelte, 1982. 2v.

First scholarly ed. of Bossi's writings on art.

Contents: (1) Nota critica; La teoria artistica; La didattica artistica e la considerazione dell'opera d'arte; (2) Epistolario; Epistolario canoviano; Appunti di viaggio; Poesie. Appendice: Relazione su un disegno dell'Appiani.

Criteri di trascrizione e di edizione, p.845–47; Note, p.849–942; Elenco cronologico delle lettere, p.943–50. Indice onomastico e toponomastico, p.951–1006.

H64 Diderot, Denis. Diderot on art. Ed. and trans. by John Goodman. Introd. by Thomas Crow. New Haven, Yale Univ. Pr., 1995. 2v. il.

See GLAH 1:H91 for a critical French ed. of the Salons.

The first reliable English selection of Diderot's important writings on the art and public exhibitions of his time.

Contents: (1) The Salon of 1765 and Notes on painting; (2) Salon of 1767.

Select bibliography, v.1, p.[241]–42, v.2, p.[333]–34. Index, v.1, p.[243]–50, v.2, p.[335]–44.

H65 Goethe, Johann Wolfgang von. Goethe on art. Sel., ed., and trans. by John Gage. Berkeley, Univ. of California Pr., 1980. xx, 251p. il.

Excellent anthology, authoritatively ed. and trans.

Contents: Introduction; (I) General aesthetics; (II) Classical art; (III) Medieval and Renaissance art; (IV) Baroque and contemporary art.

Further reading, p.[245]–46. Index, p.[247]–51.

H66 Hogarth, William. The analysis of beauty. Ed. with an introd. and notes by Ronald Paulson. New Haven, Published for the Paul Mellon Centre for British Art by Yale Univ. Pr., 1997. lxii, 162p. il., plates (some folded).

Critical ed. of the entire text of Hogarth's great treatise on aesthetics.

Manuscripts of The Analysis of Beauty; supplementary pages, p.[115]–37. Notes to the illustrations, p.[143]–55. Index, p.[157]–62.

H67 Le Brun, Charles. L'expression des passions & autres conférences; Correspondance. Prés. par Julien Philipe. Paris, Éd. Dédale; Maisonneuve et Larose, 1994. 281p. il. (part col.) (Collection "L'art écrit")

Contents: Présentation; Les Conférences; Correspondance.

Chronologie, p.267–[76]. Bibliographie sélective, p.277–[80].

H68 Palomino de Castro y Velasco, Antonio. Lives of the eminent Spanish painters and sculptors. Trans. by Nina Mallory. N.Y., Cambridge Univ. Pr., 1987. xviii, 405p. il.

Scholarly trans. of: Vidas de los pintores y estatuarios eminentes españoles (GLAH 1:H111).

Table of names of the painters and sculptors whose lives are contained in this volume, p.387–88. Bibliography, p.389–397. Index, p.398–405.

H69 Pascoli, Lione. Vite de' pittori, scultori, ed architetti moderni. Ed. critica dedicata a Valentino Martinelli. Introd. di Alessandro Marabottini. Perugia, Electa Editori Umbri, 1992. 1170p. il., plates.

Original ed. in 2v., 1730–1736 (see GLAH 1:H112). Includes updated biographical and archival information as well as critical commentary contributed by forty-six scholars.

Bibliografia, coordinamento di Letizia Lanzetta, p.1041–1105. Indice dei nomi e dei luoghi, a cura di Raffaella Stanzione, p.1106–70.

H70 Reynolds, Joshua, Sir. Discourses on art. [Reprint.] Ed. by Robert R. Wark. New Haven, Published for the Paul Mellon Centre for Studies in British Art by Yale Univ. Pr., 1997. xxxv, 349p. il., plates.

1st ed. San Marino, Henry E. Huntington Library and Art Gallery, 1959; 2d ed. New Haven, Yale Univ. Pr., 1975. Text of the 1797 ed., the last which passed through Reynolds' hands.

Selected bibliography, p.337–41. Index, p.343–49.

H71 Viollet-le-Duc, Eugène-Emmanuel. The foundations of architecture: four essays from the Dictionnaire raisonné of Viollet-le-Duc. Introd. by Barry Bergdoll. Trans. by Kenneth D. Whitehead. N.Y., Braziller, 1990. 272p. il.

Contents: Introduction: The Dictionnaire raisonné: Viollet-le-Duc's encyclopedic structure for architecture; Selections from the Dictionnaire raisonné: Architecture; Construction; Restoration; Style.

Notes, p.265–72.

H72 Zanetti, Antonio Maria. Della pittura veneziana, in cui osservasi l'ordine del Busching, e si conserva la dottrina e le definizioni del Zanetti. [Reprint.] Bologna, Forni, 1978. 2v. in 1, fronts.

Reprint of the 1797 ed., Venice, F. Tosi.

Collections

France

H73 Collection des pièces sur les beaux-arts (1673–1808) [microform]: dite Collection Deloynes. Paris, Bibliothèque Nationale, 1980. 504 microfiches.

Microform of the 63-vol. Deloynes collection in the Département des estampes et de la photographie, Bibliothèque Nationale. Includes pamphlets, manuscripts, exhibition catalogs, etc. See GLAH 1:A33 for Georges Duplessis' well-known catalog of the Deloynes collection.

H74 France. Archives nationales. Archives de l'École nationale supérieure des beaux-arts (AJ52 1 à 1415). Inventaire par Brigitte Labat-Poussin avec la collab. de Caroline Obert. Paris, Centre historique des archives nationales, 1998. 576p.

Important archival inventory which documents the administration of the school, its library and museum collections, and instruction, 1793–present.

Sources complémentaires, p.[17]–20. Table générale des dossiers du personnel et des élèves, p.[237]–515. Index de l'inventaire, p.[517]–76.

H75 Grant, Susan. Paris: a guide to archival sources for American art history. Washington, D.C., Archives of American Art, Smithsonian Institution, 1997. 89p. il.

"Conceived as a tool to help scholars locate archival material germane to the history of the American visual arts in Paris."—*Pref. and ackn.*

Contents: Section I: Paris sources; Section II: Sources outside Paris; Section III: Research aids.

Index of American artists' names, p.81–89.

Germany and Austria

H76 Kunsttheorie und Kunstgeschichte des 19. Jahrhunderts in Deutschland: Texte und Dokumente. Hrsg. von Wolfgang Beyrodt . . . [et al.] Stuttgart, Reclam, 1982– . (3)v. (Universal-Bibliothek, Nr. 7888–[7889 (5), 8043 (4)])

Anthology of literary texts on German art, art historiography, and theory in the 19th century.

Each vol. includes bibliographical references, biographical sketches, and indexes of personal names.

Selective contents: (1) Kunsttheorie und Malerei, hrsg. von Werner Busch; Kunstwissenschaft, hrsg. von Wolfgang Beyrodt; (2) Architektur, hrsg. von Harold Hammer-Schenk; (3) Skulptur und Plastik, hrsg. von Ulrich Bischoff.

Great Britain and Ireland

H77 British Architectural Library. Architecture in manuscript, 1601–1996: a guide to the British Architectural Library manuscripts and archives collection. Comp. by Angela Mace. Herndon, Va., Mansell, 1998. xxiv, 628p. il.

"The RIBA British Architectural Library's collections of manuscripts and archives is, in effect, the national collection of the papers of past and present British architects."—*Introd.*

Name index, p.469–508. Place index, p.509–42. Subject index, p.543–628.

H78 Tate Gallery. Archive. The Tate Gallery Archive, and index on microfiche [microform]. N.Y., Clearwater, 1986. 122 microfiches + guide (ix leaves).
"Contains more than 26,500 entries . . . of the catalogued contents of the Archive."—*Guide.*

Italy

H79 L'arte del Quattrocento nelle testimonianze coeve. [By] Creighton E. Gilbert. Firenze; Vienna, IRSA, 1988. 249p. il. (Biblioteca artibus et historiae)
Italian ed. of the excellent anthology which the author contributed to Prentice-Hall's Sources and documents in the history of art series (GLAH 2:H8). Reproduces the sources in the original languages, mostly Italian and Latin. Some excerpts are more fully reproduced than in the previous ed., and a few other slight changes have been introduced. A very few new texts have been included.
Indice dei nomi citati, p.241–49.

H80 Barocchi, Paola. Pittura e scultura nel Cinquecento. Livorno, Sillabe, 1998. xix, 170p. il., plates. (Arte e memoria, 1)
Critical ed. of a small selection of Cinquecento works.
Contents: Varchi, Benedetto. Lezzione della maggioranza delle arti; Lettere di artisti a Benedetto Varchi; Borghini, Vincenzio. Da una "Selva di notizie."
Tavole delle abbreviazioni, p.[xvii]–xix. Indice, p.[145]–70.

H81 Borghesi Bichi, Scipione, conte. Nuovi documenti per la storia dell' arte senese. Raccolti da S. Borghesi e L. Banchi. Appendice alla raccolta dei documenti pubblicata dal comm. Gaetano Milanesi. [Reprint.] Siena, E. Torrini, 1898. [Soest, Netherlands, DAVACO, 1970] ix, 702p. plates, facsim.
Reprint of GLAH 1:H167.

H82 Classici italiani di scienze tecniche e arti. Trattati di architettura. Milano, Edizioni Il Polifilo, 1966– . (7?)v.
An important series of critical eds. of Italian treatises on architecture.
Contents: (1) Alberti, Leon Battista. L'architettura (De re aedificatoria) (2v., 1966) (see GLAH 1:H31); (2) Filarete, Antonio Averlino. Trattato di architettura (2v., 1972); (3) Martini, Francesco di Giorgio. Trattati di architettura ingegneria e arte militare (2v., 1967) (see GLAH 1:H44); (4) Scritti rinascimentali di architettura (1978); (5, pt. 1) Serlio, Sebastiano. Architettura civile. Libri sesto, settimo e ottavo nei manoscritti di Monaco e Vienna (1994); (5, pt.2) Trattati [di] Pietro Cataneo, Giacomo Barozzi da Vignola . . . [et al.] (1985); (6) Palladio, Andrea. Quattro libri dell'architettura (1980); (7, pt.1) Pellegrini, Pellegrino. L'architettura (1990); (7, pt.2) Borromini, Francesco. Opus architectonicum (1998).

H83 Documenti per la storia dell'arte a Padova. [Raccolti da] Antonio Sartori. A cura di Clemente Fillarini. Con un saggio di Franco Barbieri. Vicenza, N. Pozza, 1976. [xxiv], 666p., port. (Fonti e studi per la storia del Santo a Padova, 4; Fonti, 3)
Documents for the history of art in Padua.
Contents: Artisti: pittori, scultori e architetti; Orefici; Maestranze artistiche.
Sigle e abbreviazioni, p.[xxiv]. Indice dei nomi, p.[625]–66.

H84 Fonti per la storia dell'arte e dell'architettura. Roma, Archivio Guido Izzi, 1989– . (3)v. il. (Also v.1–3 in the series Parole e forme)
New critical eds. of source documents.
Contents: (1) Vasari, Giorgio. Proporzioni. A cura e con introd. di Mario Curti (1989); (2) Baglione, Giovanni. Le nove chiese di Roma (1639). A cura e con introd. di Liliana Barroero (1990); (3) Introduzione alli cinque ordini dell'architettura: trattato anonimo della fine del Seicento. A cura di Mario Curti e Paola Zampa (1995).

H85 Letteratura artistica dell'età barocca: antologia di testi. A cura di Gianni Carlo Sciolla, con la collab. di Tiziano Marghetich. Torino, Giappichelli, 1983. 316p.
Handy, modestly produced anthology of literary sources for 17th-century art history.
Contents: (I) Scritti e trattati teorici; (II) Biografie d'artisti; (III) Diari e autobiografie; (IV) Componimenti in versi; (V) Scritti sulle tecniche; (VI) Periegetica; (VII) Lettere; (VIII) Appendice.
Includes bibliographical references.

H86 Letteratura artistica dell'età dell'umanesimo: antologia di testi, 1400–1520. A cura di Gianni Carlo Sciolla, con la collab. di Antonio Tessari. Torino, Giappichelli, 1982. 232p.
Handy, modestly produced anthology of literary sources for Renaissance art history.
Contents: (I) Trattati teorici; (II) Elogi e vite d'artisti; (III) Ricordi; (IV) Componimenti poetici e letterari; (V) Trattati tecnici; (VI) Periegetica; (VII) Lettere; (VIII) Contratti e dununzie dei beni.
Includes bibliographical references.

H87 Letteratura artistica del Settecento: antologia di testi. A cura di Gianni Carlo Sciolla, con la collab. di Angela Griseri e Tiziano Marghetich. Torino, Giappichelli, 1984. 323p.
Handy, modestly produced anthology of literary sources for 18th-century art history.
Contents: (I) Gli artisti del passato e del presente; (II) Il culto dell'antico; (III) La riscoperta del medioevo; (IV) La teoria sulle arti; (V) Le tecniche artistiche; (VI) Descrizioni di opere d'arte e di collezioni; (VII) Restauro e conservazione delle opere d'arte; (VIII) Il dibattito sull'architettura e la città.
Includes bibliographical references.

H88 Scritti d'arte del Cinquecento. A cura di Paolo Barocchi. Milano-Napoli, Ricciardi, 1971–77. 3v. (La letteratura italiana. Storia e testi, 32). Reprint in 9 vols.: Torino, Einaudi, 1977–79 (Classici Ricciardi, 33, 74, 79, 82, 91, 94, 97–99)

Magisterial anthology of literary sources of 16th-century Italian art history. Includes painting, sculpture, and architecture. Supplements GLAH 1:H156.

Contents: (1) Generalia; Arti e scienze; Le arti; Pittura, scultura, poesia, musica; Pittura e scultura; Pittura; (2) Scultura; L'artista; L'imitazione; Bellezza e grazia; Proporzioni, misure, giudizio; Disegno; Colore; (3) L'invenzione; Le grottesche; I ritratti; Imprese; Collezionismo; Vitruviana; La città; La villa; La fortificazione.

Tavola delle abbreviazione, v.1, p.[xviii]–xxxi; v.2, p.[xi]–xxviii; v.3, p.[xi]–xxx. Nota ai testi, v.1, p.[1051]–1133; v.2, p.[2345]–78; v.3, p.[3541]–91.

H89 Gli Scritti dei Carracci: Ludovico, Annibale, Agostino, Antonio, Giovanni Antonio. A cura di Giovanna Perini. Introd. di Charles Dempsey. Bologna, Nuova Alfa, 1990. 202p. (Villa Spelman colloquia, v.2)

Publishes for the first time all known writings by or attributed to the Carracci, along with a selection of letters, most previously unpublished, pertinent to the texts.

Glossario, p.185. Bibliografia, p.187–92. Indice dei nomi, p.[193]–202.

H90 Scritti rinascimentali di architettura: patente a Luciano Laurana, Luca Pacioli, Francesco Colonna, Leonardo da Vinci, Donato Bramante, Francesco di Giorgio, Cesare Cesariano, Lettera a Leone X. A cura di Arnaldo Bruschi, Corrado Maltese, Manfredo Tafuri . . . [et al.] Milano, Il Polifilo, 1978. lxx, 499p. il., plates (Classici italiani di scienze tecniche e arti. Trattati di architettura, 4)

Contents: Introd., di Arnoldo Bruschi; Federico da Montefeltro, Patente a Luciano Laurana, a cura di Arnaldo Bruschi, trascr. di Domenico De Robertis; Luca Pacioli, De divina proportione, a cura di Arnaldo Bruschi, trascr. di Andrea Masini; Francesco Colonna, Hypnerotomachia Poliphili, a cura di Arnaldo Bruschi; Leonardo da Vinci, Frammenti sull'architettura, a cura di Corrado Maltese; Pareri sul tiburio del Duomo di Milano: Leonardo, Bramante, Francesco di Giorgio, a cura di Arnaldo Bruschi; verbale con il Consiglio di Francesco di Giorgio trascr. Da Domenico De Robertis; Cesare Cesariano et gli studi vitruviani nel Quattrocento, a cura di Manfredo Tafuri; Brani dal Vitruvio del Cesariano, trascr. Di Andrea Masini; Lettera a Leone X, a cura di Renato Bonelli.

Indice dei fogli dei codici di Leonardo, p.[487]–88. Indice dei nomi e delle cose notevoli, p.[489]–99.

Latin America

H91 Archivo General de la Nación (México). Catálogos de documentos de arte en el Archivo General de la Nación, México. México, D.F., Univ. Nacional Autónoma de México, Institute de Investigaciones Esteticas, 1984– . (26)v.

Collection of documents on the art of Mexico; some vols. are catalogs of the holdings of the Archivo General de Notarias.

Contents: (1) Ramo: Matrimonios (pt.1); (2) Ramo: Templos y conventos (pt.1); (3) Ramo: Obras públicas; (4) Ramos: Mercedes; (5) Ramo: Matrimonios (pt.2); (6) Ramo: Real fisco; (7) Notários; (8) Ramo: Indios; (9) Ramo: Templos y conventos (pt.2); (10) Ramo: Reales cédulas duplicados; (11) Colección Abelardo Carillo y Gariel; (12) Ramo: Templos y conventos (pt.2, v.2); (13) Ramo: Ordenanzas; (14) Ramo: Templos y conventos (pt.2, v.3); (15) [Untitled]; (16) Protocolos (pt.1); (17) Ramo: Templos y conventos (pt.2, v.4); (18) Ramo: Matrimonios (pt.3); (19) Colección Manuel Toussaint; (20) Ramo: Historia; (21) Real casa de moneda y apartado; (22) Críticas y noticias en el periódico Excélsior, 1940–1949; (23) Real casa de moneda y apartado (pt.2); (24) Colección Manuel Toussaint (pt.2); (25) Noticias y opiniones sobre música y artes plásticas en el periódico Excélsior durante 1917; (26) Archive Erasto Cortés Juárez.

H92 Fernández, Justino, and Báez Macías, Eduardo. Guía del archivo de la antigua Academia de San Carlos. México, [Univ. Nacional Autónoma de México], 1968–93. 4v. il. (v.1: Anales del Instituto de Investigaciones Estéticas, 37, suplemento 3) (v.2–4: Instituto de Investigaciones Estéticas. Estudios y fuentes del arte en México, 31, 35, 36)

Chronological guide to nearly 10,000 documents useful for the study of colonial and 19th-century Mexican art.

Contents: (1) 1781–1800; (2) 1801–1843; (3) 1844–1867; (4) 1867–1907.

Indexes in each vol.

H93 The papers of Latino & Latin American artists. [Washington, D.C.], Archives of American Art, Smithsonian Institution, 1996. 48p. il. (part col.)

"In this guide, [the] term Latino refers to Americans of Mexican, Puerto Rican, Cuban, Dominican, and Central and South American descent. Latin American refers to Mexicans, Central and South Americans, and peoples of the Caribbean of Spanish and French heritage. . . . Through the accumulation of these separate but interrelated collections, the Archives of American Art gathers together in one place cross-cultural documentation on such subjects as Mexican muralism in the United States, European and Latin American strains of surrealism, New Deal art patronage, and the Chicano art movement."—*Introd.* Describes 148 discrete collections.

Index, p.41–48.

Low Countries

H94 Fontes historiae artis Neerlandicae. Duverger, Erik. Brussel, Koninklijke Academie voor Wetenschappen, Letteren en Schone Kunsten van België, 1984– . (10)v.

Contents: Duverger, Erik. Antwerpse kunstinventarissen uit de zeventiende eeuw (1984– . [9]v.); Schouteet, Albert. De vlaamse primitieven te Brugge: bronnen voor de schilderkunst te Brugge tot de dood van Gerard David (1989– . [1]v.)

Spain and Portugal

H95 Artists' techniques in Golden Age Spain: six treatises in translation. Ed. and trans. by Zahira Veliz. N.Y., Cambridge Univ. Pr., 1986. xix, 224p. il.

Includes texts listed in GLAH 1:H71 (Pacheco) and H111 (Palomino).

Contents: Arts of poetry, and of painting and symmetry, with principles of perspective, by Felipe Núñes; Dialogues on paintings, by Vicente Carducho; The art of painting, by Francisco Pacheco; A tract on the art of painting: Anonymous treatise ca.1656; Principles for studying the sovereign and most noble art of painting, by José García Hidalgo; The pictorial museum and optical scale, by Antonio Palomino y Velasco.

Notes, p.191–216. Selected bibliography, p.217–20. Index, p.221–24.

United States

H96 Archives of American Art. Archives of American Art, Smithsonian Institution: a checklist of the collection, September 1977. 2d ed. rev., ca. 200p.

1st ed. 1975.

"The present revised edition includes a listing of all collections."—*Foreword.*

H97 ———. The card catalog of the manuscript collections of the Archives of American Art. Wilmington, Del., Scholarly Resources, 1980. 10v.

Photographic reproduction of the card catalog of the leading collection of primary sources for American art. The Archives was founded in 1954 and incorporated into the Smithsonian Institution in 1970.

———. 1981–1984 supplement. Wilmington, Scholarly Resources, 1985. vii, 542p.

H98 ———. The card catalog of the oral history collections of the Archives of American Art. Wilmington, Del., Scholarly Resources, 1984. vii, 343p.

Photographic reproduction of the catalog.

"The catalogue of the Archives of American Art oral history collections consists of 2,500 cards describing both transcribed and untranscribed tape recordings. The majority refer to interviews, but they also cover panel discussions, symposia, meetings, lectures, readings, and monologues."—*Pref.*

H99 ———. Government and art: a guide to sources in the Archives of American Art. Washington, D.C., The Archives, 1995. 206p. il.

Focuses upon federal involvement with the arts, but includes "papers relating to state, city, and local government's connections with art as well as papers of international scope. This is not a guide to collection but to those parts of collections . . . that concern this topic."—*Introd.*

Index, p.177–206.

H100 ———. Guide to archival sources for French-American art history in the Archives of American Art. Washington, D.C., The Archives, 1992. iv, 128p. il.

Entries are chronological. The original papers are in the Archives unless otherwise noted. Collections that have been microfilmed are identified and are available at the Archives' several offices around the country or through interlibrary loan.

Index, p.13–28.

H101 ———. Guide to archival sources for Italian-American art history in the Archives of American Art. Washington, D.C., The Archives, [1994?]. xi, 73p. il.

Entries are chronological. The original papers are in the Archives unless otherwise noted. Collections that have been microfilmed are identified and are available at the Archives' several offices around the country or through interlibrary loan.

Index, p.63–73.

H102 ———. Reading records: a researcher's guide to the Archives of American Art. Washington, D.C., The Archives, 1997. 120p. il. (part col.), facsims. (Archives of American art journal, v.35, no.1–4, 1995).

A helpful illustrated overview of the Archives' rich collections.

H103 New York Public Library. The artists file [microform]. Alexandria, Va., Chadwyck-Healey, [1987]–89. 11,281 microfiches il. + index (10 microfiches in looseleaf binder)

Reproduces the Library's valuable clippings file of more than 1.5 million items.

H104 Pacini, Marina. Philadelphia: a guide to art-related archival materials. Washington, D.C., Archives of American Art, 1994. x, 144p. il., ports.

Supersedes the preliminary guide, Art-related archival materials in the Philadelphia region, 1984–1989: survey, published in 1990.

Contents: Section I: Institutional holdings; Section II: Gift and loan materials available at the Archives of American Art.

Index, p.125–44.

SEE ALSO: Art in theory, 1815–1900 (GLAH 2:I245); Art in theory, 1900–1990 (GLAH 2:I246); Chipp, Theories of modern art (GLAH 1:I238); Stiles and Selz, Theories and documents of contemporary art (GLAH 2:I294); Taylor, Nineteenth-century theories of art (GLAH 2:I295).

ASIAN COUNTRIES

Collections

China

H105 Bush, Susan, and Shih, Hsio-yen, eds. Early Chinese texts on painting. Cambridge, Mass., Harvard Univ. Pr., 1985. xii, 391p. il., plates.

An anthology of more than 30 texts about painting presented in chronological chapters from the Han dynasty of 3d century B.C. to the Yüan dynasty of 14th century A.D. Within the chapters, the texts are grouped by subject.

Contents: (1) Pre-T'ang interpretation and criticism; (2) T'ang criticism and art history; (3) Sung art history; (4) The landscape texts; (5) Sung literati theory and connoisseurship; (6) Yüan criticism and writings on special subjects.

Biographies of painters, critics and calligraphers, p.291–351. Glossary of Chinese terms, p.352–54. Glossary of Chinese names and titles, p.355–62. Bibliography, p.[363]–78. Index, p.379–91.

I. Histories and Handbooks

This chapter includes histories, handbooks, manuals, encyclopedic series, and exhibition catalogs that treat more than one medium. General dictionaries of art and archeology may be found in Chapter E, Dictionaries and Encyclopedias. Sources and documents for the period before the late 19th century are in Chapter H, Sources and Documents, and general bibliographies are in Chapter A.

COLLECTIONS AND INVENTORIES

I1 The Frick Collection: an illustrated catalogue. N.Y., The Frick Collection (Distr. by Princeton Univ. Pr., 1968–). (7)v. il. (part col.)

See GLAH 1:I1 for original annotation and previous vols.

Contents: (5) Furniture, Italian and French (1992); (6) Furniture and gilt bronzes, French (1992).

I2 Kupferstichkabinett Berlin. Das Berliner Kupferstichkabinett: ein Handbuch zur Sammlung. Hrsg. von Alexander Duckers. Mit Beitr. von Sigrid Achenbach . . . [et al.] Berlin, Akademie, 1994. 571p. il. (part col.)

Splendid handbook embracing prints and drawings.

Verzeichnis der abgekürzt zitierten Literatur, p.537–56. Literatur zu den Sammlungsbeständen und zur Sammlungsgeschichte, p.557–63. Verzeichnis der in der Sammlung vertretenen und im Handbuch genannten Künstler, p.564–71.

I3 New York. Metropolitan Museum of Art. The Metropolitan Museum of Art at home. N.Y., Metropolitan Museum of Art, 1987. 12v.

Series title used in advertising, not present in each vol. This series of 12 vols. seeks, collectively, to "represent the scope of the Metropolitan Museum's holdings while selectively presenting the very finest objects from each of its curatorial departments."—*Dir. foreword to v.1.* Texts by the museum's curators; well-illustrated in color.

Contents: Greece and Rome; Egypt and the Ancient Near East; Europe in the Middle Ages; The Renaissance in Italy and Spain; The Renaissance in the North; Europe in the age of monarchy; Europe in the age of Enlightenment and Revolution; Modern Europe; The United States of America; Asia; The Islamic world; The Pacific islands, Africa, and the Americas.

I4 ———. The Robert Lehman Collection. N.Y., Metropolitan Museum of Art, 1987– . (10)v. il. (part col.), facsims., ports.

Magnificent, scholarly catalog of this outstanding collection.

Contents: (1) Pope-Hennessy, John. Italian paintings; (2) Sterling, Charles . . . [et al.] Fifteenth to eighteenth century European paintings: France, Central Europe, the Netherlands, Spain, and Great Britain; (4) Hindman, Sandra . . . [et al.] Illuminations; (5) Forlani Tempesti, Anna. Italian fifteenth- to seventeenth-century drawings; (6) Shaw, James Byam, and Knox, George. Italian eighteenth-century drawings; (7) Haverkamp-Begemann, Egbert . . . [et al.] Fifteenth-to eighteenth-century European drawings: Central Europe, The Netherlands, France, England; (8) Clark, Carol. American drawings and watercolors; (10) Rasmussen, Jörg. Italian majolica; (11) Lanmon, Dwight P., with Whitehouse, David B. Glass; (14) Mayer-Thurman, Christa C. European textiles.

Includes bibliographical references and indexes.

GENERAL WORKS

I5 Adams, Laurie Schneider. Art across time. Boston, McGraw-Hill College, 1999. 2v. il. (part col.), maps, plans, ports.

"While comprehensive, Art across Time avoids an encyclopedic approach to art history and attempts instead a more manageable narrative that is suitable for a one-year survey course."—*Pref.* Emphasis upon pedagogical features.

Contents: (1) Prehistory to the fourteenth century; (2) The thirteenth century to the present.

Separately paginated glossary, suggestions for further reading, notes, index, at back of each vol.

I6 ———. A history of Western art. N.Y., Abrams, 1994. 512p. il. (part col.), col. maps.

"The object of this text is to introduce students to the history of western art and of its most important styles. . . . This book differs from most others in its focus on relatively fewer works in greater depth."—*Pref.*

Contents: Part one: Introduction; Part two: The ancient world; Part three: The Christian world; Part four: The Renaissance; Part five: Early modern through the Nineteenth Century; Part six: The Twentieth Century.

Glossary, p.[485]–92. Suggestions for further reading, p.[493]–500. Notes, p.[501]. Index, p.[504]–12.

I7 Art & ideas. London, Phaidon, 1997– . (8)v.

Unnumbered series of monographs on the major regions, periods, and styles of the history of world art. Titles in this series are not cited individually in GLAH 2.

Selective contents: Bloom, Jonathan M. Islamic arts (1997); Dehejia, Vidya. Indian art (1997); Gale, Matthew. Dada & surrealism (1997); Godfrey, Tony. Conceptual art (1998); Irwin, David. Neoclassicism (1997); Lowden, John. Early Christian & Byzantine art (1997); Morphy, Howard. Aboriginal art (1998); Spivey, Nigel Jonathan. Greek art (1997).

I8 L'Art et les grandes civilisations. Paris, Mazenod, 1965– . (29)v.

Lavishly produced monographic survey of world art. Some vols. published by Citadelles or jointly by Citadelles and Mazenod. A few early vols. are recorded in GLAH 1 under their monographic titles. Recent Eng. translations, which do not appear as a series, are cited individually elsewhere in this chapter.

Contents: (1) Leroi-Gourhan, André. Préhistoire de l'art occidental (1965; new ed. 1995; Eng. ed. GLAH 1:I30); (2) Michalowski, Kazimierz. L'art de l'ancienne Égypte (1968; new ed. 1994; Eng. ed. GLAH 1:I43); (3) Papaioannou, Kostas. L'art grec (1972; new ed. 1993; Eng. ed. 1989); (4) Andreae, Bernard. L'art de l'ancienne Rome (1973; new ed. 1998; Eng. ed. 1977); (5) Sivaramamurti, Calambur . . . [et al.] L'art en Indie (1974; new ed. 1999; Eng. ed. 1977); (6) Papadopoulo, Alexandre. L'Islam et l'art musulman (1976; Eng. ed. 1976); (7) Amiet, Pierre. L'art antique du Proche-Orient (1977); (8) Alcina Franch, José. L'art précolumbien (1978; 1996; Eng. ed. 1983); (9) Watson, William. L'art de l'ancienne Chine (1979; new ed. 1997; Eng. ed. 1981); (10) Elisseeff, Danielle. L'art de l'ancien Japon (1980; Eng. ed. 1985); (11) Coche de la Ferté, Étienne. L'art de Byzance (1981); (12) Durliat, Marcel. L'art roman (1982); (13) Erlande-Brandenburg, Alain. L'art gothique (1983; Eng. ed. 1989); (14) Jestaz, Bertrand. L'art de la renaissance (1984; Eng. ed. 1995); (15) Durliat, Marcel. Des barbares à l'an mil (1985); (16) Bottineau, Yves. L'art baroque (1986); (17) Thierry, Jean Michel. Les arts arméniens (1987; Eng. ed. 1989); (18) Kerchache, Jacques. L'art africain (1988; Eng. ed. 1993); (19) Vaughan, William. L'art du XIXe siècle, 1780–1850 (1989; Eng. ed. GLAH 2:I298); (20) Cachin, Françoise. L'art du XIXe siècle, 1850–1905 (1990; Eng. ed. 1999); (21) Allenov, Mikhail Mikhailovich . . . [et al.] L'art russe (1991); (22) Martin, Jennifer. L'art des États-Unis (1992); (23) Kaeppler, Adrienne Lois . . . [et al.] L'art océanien (1993; Eng. ed. 1997); (24) Girard-Geslan, Maud. L'art d'Asie du Sud-Est (1994; Eng. ed. 1998); (25) Sed-Rajna, Gabrielle. Art juif (1995; Eng. ed. 1997); (26) Bouillon, Jean-Paul . . . [et al.] L'art du XXe siècle, 1900–1939 (1996); (27–28) Morel, Philippe . . . [et al.] L'art italien (2v., 1997–98); (29) Chuvin, Pierre. L'art de l'Asie centrale (1999).

I9 Berthoud, Émile. 2000 ans d'art chrétien. Chambray-lès-Tours, CLD, [1997]. 473p. col. il.

Beautifully illustrated survey of Christian art across two millenia, intended for a general audience. Lacks any scholarly apparatus.

I10 Cambridge introduction to the history of art. N.Y., Cambridge Univ. Pr., 1981–85. 8v. il.

Most vols. are brief handbooks on the history of western art.

Contents: (1) Woodford, Susan. The art of Greece and Rome (1982); (2) Shaver-Crandell, Anne. The middle ages (1982); (3) Letts, Rosa Maria. The renaissance (1981); (4) Mainstone, Madeleine, and Mainstone, Rowland. The seventeenth century (1981); (5) Jones, Stephen. The eighteenth century (1985); (6) Reynolds, Donald. The nineteenth century (1985); (7) Lambert, Rosemary. The twentieth century (1981); (8) Woodford, Susan. Looking at pictures (1983).

I11 Cornell, Sara. Art: a history of changing style. Englewood Cliffs, Prentice-Hall, 1983. 455p. il. (part col.)

Introductory survey of western art history intended for secondary school students and others "unfamiliar with the subject."—*Pref.*

Contents: Introduction; Part 1: The ancient world. Part 2: The middle ages. Part 3: The renaissance. Part 4: The romantics. Part 5: The modern world.

Bibliography, p.[437]–41. Sources of quotations, p.441–42. Index, p.[443]–55.

I12 Cossío, Manuel Bartolomé and Pijoán y Soteras, José. Summa artis; historia general del arte. Bilbao, Espasa-Calpe, 1931– . (41)v. il., plates (part col.)

See GLAH 1:I5 for previous vols.

Contents: (24) Camon Aznar, José. La pintura española del siglo XVI (2d ed., 1979); (25) ______. La pintura española del siglo XVII (2d ed., 1989); (26) Hernandez Diaz, José. La escultura y la arquitectura españolas del siglo XVII (1982; 5th ed., 1991); (27) Camon Aznar, José. Arte español del siglo XVIII (1984; 4th ed., 1991); (28/29) Sebastian, Santiago. Arte iberoamericano desde la colonización a la independencia (2v., 1985; 4th ed., 1992); (30) Franca, José Augusto. Arte portugués (1986; 3d ed., 1991); (31/32) Carrete Parrondo, Juan. El Grabado en España (2v.; 4th ed., 1994); (33) Luna, Juan J. Pintura británica (1500–1820) (2d ed., 1990); (34) Buendía, J. Rogelio. Arte europeo y norteamericano del siglo XIX (2d ed., 1991); (35, Pt.1) Gómez-Moreno, María Elena. Pintura y escultura españolas del siglo XIX (1993); (35, Pt.2) Navascúes Palacio, Pedro. Arquitectura española, 1808–1914 (1993); (36/37) Bozal Fernández, Valeriano. Pintura y escultura españolas del siglo XX (1900–1939). (2v., 1993); (38) Marchán Fiz, Simón. Fin de siglo y los primeros "ismos" del XX (1890–1917) (1994); (39) Marchán Fiz, Simón. Las Vanguardias históricas y sus sombras (1917–1930) (1995); (40) Baldellou Santolaria, Miguel Angel and Capitel, Antón. Arquitectura española del siglo XX

(1995); (41) Capitel, Antón. Arquitectura europea y americana después de las vanguardias (1996); (42) Cerámica española (1997); (43) Arte africano (1998); (44) Arte ruso (1998); (45) Artes decorativas I–II (2v., 1999).

I13 Gage, John. Color and culture: practice and meaning from antiquity to abstraction. Boston, Little, Brown, 1993. 335p. il. (part col.)

Pioneering cultural history of color, from the ancient Greeks to the late 20th century. Treats color theory, color perception, and color symbolism. "This is an historical study . . . [which] looks for the origins of the methods and concepts of visual art and treats art as the most vivid surviving manifestation of general attitudes toward colour expressed in visual form."—*Introd.* The author has also published a companion volume, containing further studies in the history and theory of color: Color and meaning: art, science and symbolism (Berkeley, Univ. of California Pr., 1999).

Contents: Introduction; (1) The classical inheritance; (2) The fortunes of Apelles; (3) Light from the east; (4) A Dionysian aesthetic; (5) Colour-language, colour-symbols; (6) Unweaving the rainbow; (7) Disegno versus colore; (8) The peacock's tail; (9) Colour under control; the reign of Newton; (10) The palette: "mother of all colours"; (11) Colours of the mind: Goethe's legacy; (12) The substance of colour; (13) The sound of colour; (14) Colour without theory: the role of abstraction.

Notes to the text, p.271–302. Bibliography, p.303–23. Index, p.328–35.

I14 Gardner, Helen. Art through the ages. 10th ed. Ed. by Richard G. Tansey, Fred S. Kleiner. Fort Worth, Tex., Harcourt Brace Jovanovich, 1996. xvi, 1200p. il. (part col.)

See GLAH 1:I7 for 6th ed. 7th ed. 1980; 8th ed. 1986; 9th ed. 1991.

"The text has been thoroughly revised and in large part rewritten. We have endeavored to update it in accordance with contemporary art-historical and archeological scholarship. Specialists have reviewed each chapter. . . . A great effort has been made to enhance the quality of the photographs. . . . New maps and timelines open each chapter, and more works in North American collections have been included to encourage the careful study of originals. A comprehensive package of teaching and study aids also accompanies the tenth edition."—*Pref.*

Glossary, p.[1158]–68. Bibliography, p.[1169]–79. Index, p.[1182]–1200.

I15 Gombrich, E. H. The story of art. 16th ed., exp. and redesigned. London, Phaidon, 1995. 688p. il. (part col.), maps.

See GLAH 1:I9 for the 12th ed.; 13th ed. 1978; 14th ed. 1984; 15th ed. 1989.

Latest version of a classic introduction to the history of art, by a great practitioner.

"A note on art books," p.638–54. Chronological charts and maps, p.655–69. List of illustrations by location, p.670–73. Index and glossary, p.674–86.

I16 Greenhalgh, Michael. The classical tradition in art. Dallas (Distr. by Southwest Book Services, 1978). 271p. il., plans.

"This book is a survey of the development of the classical tradition in art and architecture from the fall of the Roman Empire to the time of Ingres. . . . What I have attempted to describe is the history of an intellectual attitude toward Antiquity which led certain artists to re-interpret antique ideas and antique models not slavishly but creatively."—*Foreword.*

Contents: Acknowledgements; Foreword; Introduction: What is Classicism?; (1) Classicism from the fall of Rome to Nicola Pisano: survival and revival; (2) Antique art and the Renaissance: a gallery of types; (3) Roma quanta fuit, ipsa ruina docet; (4) Nicola Pisano and Giotto: founders of Renaissance Classicism; (5) The early Renaissance; (6) The high Renaissance; (7) Classicism in Italian architecture; (8) The classical revival in seventeenth-century Italy; (9) Art in seventeenth-century France; (10) Architecture in France: Renaissance to Neoclassicism; (11) Neoclassicism in painting and sculpture; (12) Ingres and the subversion of the classical tradition.

Bibliography, p.235–62. Index, p.263–71.

I17 Harris, Ann Sutherland, and Nochlin, Linda. Women artists 1550–1950. Los Angeles, Los Angeles County Museum of Art, 1976. 368p. il. (part col.)

Catalog of the pioneering exhibition, Los Angeles County Museum of Art (1976–77), and other locations. Includes an introductory overview of the subject.

Artists' bibliographies, collections, exhibitions, literature, p.339–62. General bibliography, p.362–65. Index of artists, p.366–67.

I18 Hartt, Frederick. Art: a history of painting, sculpture, architecture. 4th ed. N.Y., Abrams, 1993. 1127p. il. (part col.), maps.

See GLAH 1:I11 for original ed. 2d ed. 1986; 3d ed. 1989. The 4th ed. of this standard survey features 100 more color illustrations. The number of women artists has been "somewhat" increased.

I19 Heller, Nancy. Women artists: an illustrated history. N.Y., Abbeville, 1987. 224p. il. (part col.), ports.

"The purpose of this book is to provide a richly illustrated overview of some of the most interesting professional women painters and sculptors in the Western world, from the Renaissance to the present."—*Pref.*

Notes, p.210–17. Selected bibliography, p.218–21. Index, p.222–24.

I20 Histoire de l'art. [Par Albert Chatelet, Bernard Philippe Groslier.] Paris, Larousse, 1985. 2v. (Repr., 1995 in one vol.)

Popular reference volume.

Index, p.769–80.

I21 Histoire de l'art Flammarion. Ouvrage dirigé par Françoise Hamon et Philippe Dagen. Paris, Flammarion, 1995– . (4)v. il. (chiefly col.)

Beautifully illustrated history of the world's art to be completed in 6 vols.

Forthcoming: Arts premiers; Asie.

Contents: Préhistoire et antiquité (1997); Moyen Âge: la Chrétienté et l'Islam (1996); Temps Modernes (XVe-XVIIIe siècles) (1996); Époque contemporaine (XIXe-XXe siècles) (1995).

I22 Histoire de l'art 1000–2000. Sous la dir. d'Alain Mérot. [Paris], Hazan, 1995. 542p. color il.

Well-produced survey of western art from Romanesque to the 20th century, with texts provided by a team of specialists.

Bibliographie, p.[509–15]. Lexique, p.516–23. Index, p.524–42.

I23 Honour, Hugh, and Fleming, John. The visual arts: a history. 5th ed. N.Y., Abrams, 1999. 928p. il. (part col.), col. maps

1st ed. 1982; 2d ed. 1986; 3d ed. 1991; 4th ed. 1995. 5th ed. published in the U.K. under the title A world history of art. London, Lawrence King, 1999.

The 4th ed. was substantially revised and expanded throughout. It included a fuller account of art techniques and greater attention to the social role of the arts; a new chapter on the 1980s and 1990s; supplementary sections devoted to sources and documents; and brief descriptions of works "in context." The "substantial additions made to the fourth edition have now been supplemented by a 'Concepts' section" and other features.—*Pref. to the fifth ed.*

Glossary, p.[888]–900. For further reading, p.[901]–09. Index, p.[910]–26.

I24 Hooker, Denise, ed. Art of the western world. London, Boxtree, 1989. 464p. il. (part col.)

"Unlike previous histories of art written from a single viewpoint, this book brings together distinguished scholars whose specialist interests span Western art from Classical antiquity to the present day. . . . They introduce the reader to the diversity of approaches now current within art history, ranging from detailed analyses of different styles and techniques of art and architecture to feminist, Marxist and post-modernist interpretations."—*Pref.* Based on a British television series.

Contents: (1) Greek art, by John Boardman; (2) Roman art, by Richard Brilliant; (3) The early Middle Ages, by Paul Crossley; (4) Gothic, by William Clark; (5) The early Renaissance in Italy, by John White; (6) The early Renaissance in the North, by Catherine Reynolds; (7) The High Renaissance in Rome, by A. Richard Turner; (8) The High Renaissance in Venice, by David Rosand; (9) Italy, France and Austria in the 17th century, by Jeremy Wood; (10) Spain and the Netherlands in the 17th century, by Ivan Gaskell; (11) The age of reason, by Robin Middleton; (12) The age of passion, by Robin Middleton; (13) Realism and Impressionism, by John House; (14) Post-Impressionism, by Griselda Pollock; (15) Alienation and innovation, 1900–1918, by Christopher Green; (16) Between utopia and crisis, 1918–1939, by Christopher Green; (17) The last moderns, by Rosalind Krauss; (18) Post-modernism: within and beyond the frame, by Rosalind Krauss.

Further reading, p.448–50. Glossary, p.451–52. Index, p.461–64.

I25 Janson, H. W. History of art. Rev. and exp. by Anthony F. Janson. N.Y., Abrams, 1997. 1000p. il. (part col.)

See GLAH 1:I15 for 1st and 2d eds. 3d ed. 1986; 4th ed. 1991; 5th ed. 1995.

Remains the standard textbook survey of the history of art. The 5th ed. featured 119 excerpted primary source readings; 111 redrawn line drawings, diagrams, and floor plans; heavily revised sections on Baroque, Rococo, and contemporary art; addition of 18 new artists, many African-American; redesigned timelines; sections on techniques and processes; and a newly updated bibliography. This revision "completes the process of transforming the book into purely a history of western art."—*Pref. and ackn. to the fifth ed. rev.*

Books for further reading, by Max Marmor, p.926–35. Glossary, p.935–42. Index, p.943–59.

I26 Kemp, Martin. The science of art: optical themes in western art from Brunelleschi to Seurat. New Haven, Yale Univ. Pr., 1990. 375p. il. (part col.)

"My intention has been to outline . . . the major profiles of optically minded theory and practice in art, and to set these profiles beside the geometry of vision and the physics of colour in the history of scientific thought."—*Introd.* An original and important study of the formative contribution of science to the visual arts from the Renaissance to the 19th century.

Contents: Introduction; Part I: Lines of sight; Part II: Machine and mind; Part III: The colour of light; Appendix I: Explanation of linear perspective; Appendix II: Brunelleschi's demonstration panels.

Notes, p.346–62. Select bibliography, p.363–64. Index, p.365–74.

I27 Kissick, John. Art, context and criticism. 2d ed. Boston, McGraw-Hill; Madison, Brown & Benchmark, 1996. 512p. il. (part col.)

1st ed., Madison, Brown & Benchmark, 1993.

"My method . . . is to place considerable weight on the idea of art as a socially generated idea, carrying with it the values of its historical situation and telling us, as a modern audience, about our own values and biases."—*Pref.* "The second edition . . . presents the reader with an expanded overview of the social and contextual issues."—*Pref. to second ed.*

Contents: Introduction; (1) The beginnings of art; (2) The art of the classical world; (3) Art and religion: the visual worlds of Judaism, Christianity, Islam, Hinduism, and Buddhism; (4) Issues and ideas in Renaissance art; (5) Arts, issues, and innovations in the Baroque era; (6) Reason and revolution: eighteenth- and early nineteenth-century art in Europe; (7) The modern world and its art; (8) Art in the Americas; (9) Art in the twentieth century; (10) Contemporary art, issues, and ideas.

Glossary, p.[495]–501. Suggested reading, p.[502]–03. Index, p.[505]–12.

I28 Lohneysen, Wolfgang, Freiherr von. Eine neue Kunstgeschichte. N.Y., De Gruyter, 1984. 464p. il.

A thematic, theoretically engaged exploration of the history of art.

Contents: Einleitung; (1) Wirklichkeit; (2) Macht und Glaube; (3) Gesellschaft; (4) Gemeinschaft, Staat und Revolution.

Anhang: Chronologie der abgebildeten Werke, p.444–46. Kleines Lexikon zum Text, p.447–62. Abkürzungsverzeichnis, p.463.

I29 Oxford history of art. N.Y., Oxford Univ. Pr., 1997– . (16)v.

A new series of "up-to-date, fully illustrated introductions to a wide variety of subjects written by leading experts in their field. They will appear regularly, building into an interlocking and comprehensive series."—*Pub. note.* Projected in more than 50 vols. Titles in this series are not cited individually elsewhere in this chapter.

Selective contents: Andrews, Malcolm. Landscape and western art (1999); Berlo, Janet Catherine. Native North American art (1998); Brettell, Richard R. Modern art 1851–1929 (1999); Causey, Andrew. Sculpture since 1945 (1998); Clarke, Graham. The photograph (1997); Clunas, Craig. Art in China (1997); Craske, Matthew. Art in Europe 1700–1830 (1997); Curtis, Penelope. Sculpture 1900–1945: after Rodin (1999); Elsner, Jas. Imperial Rome and Christian triumph (1998); Osborne, Robin. Archaic and classical Greek art (1998); Patton, Sharon F. African-American art (1998); Preziosi, Donald, ed. The art of art history: a critical anthology (1998); Stalley, R. A. Early medieval architecture (1999); Upton, Dell. Architecture in the United States (1998); Welch, Evelyn S. Art and society in Italy, 1350–1500 (1997); Woodham, Jonathan M. Twentieth century design (1997).

I30 Oxford history of western art. Ed. by Martin Kemp. N.Y., Oxford Univ. Pr., 2000. xii, 564p. il.

Important, multi-author survey with more than 50 distinguished contributors.

Contents: (1) The foundations: Greece and Rome c.600 BC–410 AD; (2) Church and state: the establishing of European visual culture 410–1527; (3) The art of nations: European visual regimes 1527–1770; (4) The era of revolutions 1770–1914; (5) Modernism and after 1914–2000; Epilogue.

Chronology, p.528–35. Glossary, p.536–39. Further reading, p.540–47. Index, p.550–64.

I31 Perspectives. N.Y., Abrams, 1995– .

Published in the U.K. as Everyman art library. London, Weidenfeld and Nicolson. Unnumbered series of accessible handbooks for the general reader. Titles in this series are not cited individually elsewhere in this chapter.

Contents: Blier, Suzanne Preston. The royal arts of Africa (1998); Camille, Michael. Gothic art: glorious visions (1996); Clark, Toby. Art and propaganda in the twentieth century (1997); Cole, Alison. Virtue and magnificence: the art of the Italian Renaissance courts (1995); D'Alleva, Ann. Art of the Pacific islands (1998); Flynn, Tom. The body in three dimensions (1998); Fortini Brown, Patricia. Art and life in Renaissance Venice (1997); Green, Miranda J. Celtic art: reading the messages (1997); Guth, Christine. Art of Edo Japan (1996); Harbison, Craig. The mirror of the artist: northern Renaissance art in its historical context (1995); Irwin, Robert. Islamic art in context (1997); Mathews, Thomas F. Byzantium: from antiquity to the Renaissance (1998); Partridge, Loren W. The art of Renaissance Rome, 1400–1600 (1996); Petzold, Andreas. Romanesque art (1995); Pultz, John. The body and the lens: photography 1839 to the present (1995); Smith, Paul. Impressionism: beneath the surface (1995); Taylor, Brandon. Avant-garde and after: rethinking art now (1995); Tomlinson, Janis A. From El Greco to Goya: painting in Spain, 1561–1828 (1997); Turner, A. Richard. Renaissance Florence: the invention of a new art (1997); Westermann, Mariët. A worldly art: the Dutch republic, 1585–1718 (1996).

I32 Pischel-Fraschini, Gina. A world history of art: painting, sculpture, architecture, decorative arts. With an introd. by Luisa Becherucci. Rev. ed. N.Y., Simon and Schuster, 1975. 754p. col. il.

Trans. of GLAH 1:I22, though not obviously related.

I33 Sed-Rajna, Gabrielle. Jewish art. With essays by Ziva Amishai-Maisels . . . [et al.] Trans. from the French by Sara Friedman and Mira Reich. N.Y., Abrams, 1997. 635p. il. (part col.)

First pub. in French trans. as part of the series L'art et le grandes civilisations (GLAH 2:I8). Lavishly illustrated survey of the subject, edited by an authority.

Contents: Oriental sources of Jewish art: sacred spaces; Ancient synagogues: architecture, murals, mosaics; The development of Jewish art in the west: architecture, illumination, ritual objects; Jewish artists: from the eighteenth century to the present day; Documentation.

Chronology, p.611–15. Glossary, p.616–18. Bibliography, p.619–27. Index, p.628–35.

I34 Silver, Lawrence. Art in history. N.Y., Abbeville Press, 1993. 496p. il. (part col.), maps, plans.

"Art in History . . . was written with a specific goal in mind: to present works of art with a greater depth of treatment and a more historical and contextual view of their audiences and cultures than most survey volumes. . . . This volume aims to provide an introduction to the means by which art functions in and for its culture, while providing a visual primer of images saturated in the significance of their distinctive epochs."—*Pref.*

Contents: (1) Introduction: the roles of the artist; (2) Ancient ancestors; (3) Christian culture; (4) Early renaissance; (5) Later renaissance in Italy; (6) Age of Absolutism; (7) Dawn of the modern era; (8) Nature and novelty; (9) In search of modernity; (10) World War II to present.

Glossary, p.474–80. Bibliography, p.482–86. Index, p.487–96.

I35 Steer, John, and White, Antony. Atlas of western art history: artists, sites, and movements from ancient Greece to the modern age. N.Y., Facts on File, 1994. 335p. il., maps (part col.)

A color atlas of western art history from the ancient world (700 B.C.) to 1950. Chronologically arranged entries with maps on facing pages. "The texts relate to the maps and we hope that by using them the purpose and function of the maps will become clear to the reader. But equally they are designed to provide a general introduction to someone approaching each subject for the first time. . . . In principle the virtue of the cartographic approach is to tie the subject quite literally to the ground: to where works of art were produced."—*Introd.*

Contents: Introduction; The ancient world: 700 B.C.–313 A.D.; The medieval world: 4th–15th centuries; The renaissance; Baroque and rococo: 1600–1789; The modern world: 1789–1950.

Consultants and contributors, p.12. Index, p.314–31.

I36 Stokstad, Marilyn. Art history. [By] Marilyn Stokstad with the collab. of Bradford R. Collins and with chapters by Stephen Addiss, Chu-tsing Li, Marilyn M. Rhie . . . [et al.] Rev. ed. N.Y., Abrams, 1999. 2v. il. (part col.), maps, plans.

1st ed., 1995.

An unusually wide-ranging and imaginative survey textbook aimed at the general reader and undergraduate student. "What is needed is a new text for a new generation of teachers and students, a text that balances formalist traditions with the newer interests of contextual art history and also meets the needs of a diverse and fast-changing student population."—*Pref. to the first ed.* Includes a "complete ancillary package, including slide sets, CD-ROM, videodisc, a student Study Guide, and an Instructor's Resource Manual with Test Bank."—*Pref. to the first ed.* The revised ed. includes substantive changes in the treatment of Western art of the Renaissance, Baroque and Rococo, and Modern periods.

Each vol. includes a separately paginated glossary, bibliography, "website directory of museums and sites," and index.

Contents: Vol.1: (1) Prehistory and prehistoric art of Europe; (2) Art of the Ancient Near East; (3) Art of ancient Egypt; (4) Aegean art; (5) Art of ancient Greece; (6) Etruscan art and Roman art; (7) Early Christian, Jewish, and Byzantine art; (8) Islamic art; (9) Art of India before 1100; (10) Chinese art before 1280; (11) Japanese art before 1392; (12) Art of the Americas before 1300; (13) Art of ancient Africa; (14) Early medieval art in Europe; (15) Romanesque art; (16) Gothic art. Vol.2: (17) Early renaissance art in Europe; (18) Renaissance art in sixteenth-century Europe; (19) Baroque, Rococo, and Early American art; (20) Art of India after 1100; (21) Chinese art after 1280; (22) Japanese art after 1392; (23) Art of the Americas after 1300; (24) Art of Pacific cultures; (25) Art of Africa in the modern era; (26) Neoclassicism and Romanticism in Europe and the United States; (27) Realism to Impressionism in Europe and the United States; (28) The rise of modernism in Europe and the United States; (29) Art in the United States and Europe since World War II.

I37 Storia dell'arte europea. Milano, Jaca Book, 1995– . (4)v. il. (part col.), plans, ports.

Multi-vol. survey of European art, medieval and after, by a team of specialists.

Contents: Castelfranchi Vegas, Liana. L'arte del medioevo (rev. ed., 1994); Cassanelli, Roberto . . . [et al]. Cantieri medievali (1995); Castelfranchi Vegas, Liana, and Santoro, Fiorella Sricchia. L'arte del rinascimento (2v., 1996–97; v.1 first published as L'arte del Quattrocento in Italia e in Europa); Béguin, Sylvie. La bottega dell'artista: tra Medioevo e Rinascimento (1998).

I38 Storia universale dell'arte. [Torino], Unione Tipografico-Editrice Torinese, 1953– . il., plates, plans.

Successor series to GLAH 1:I22, with new authors. The unnumbered titles in this series are not cited individually elsewhere in GLAH 2.

Contents: Sezione prima, Civiltà antiche e primitive. Nougier, Louis-René. La Preistoria (1982); Moscati, Sabatino. Il mondo punico, (2v., 1980); Donadoni, Sergio. L'Egitto (1981); Moscati, Sabatino. Le civiltà periferiche del vicino oriente antico: mondo anatolico e mondo siriano (1989); Martin, Roland. La Grecia e il mondo greco, (2v., 1984); Mansuelli, Guido Achille. Roma e il mondo romano, (2v., 1981); Grottanelli, Vinigi L. Le Americhe (1983). Sezione seconda, Civiltà dell'Oriente. Bussagli, Mario. L'Arte del Gandhára (1984); Boisselier, Jean. Il Sud-Est asiatico (1986). Sezione terza, Civiltà dell'Occidente. Skubiszewski, Piotr. L'arte europea dal VI al IX secolo (1995); Cutler, Anthony. L'arte bizantina e il suo pubblico (1986); De Fusco, Renato. Il Quattrocento in Italia (1984); Bialostocki, Jan. Il Quattrocento nell'Europa settentrionale (1989) (trans. of GLAH 1:I396); Collareta, Marco. L'arte in Europa, 1500–1570 (1998); Arbore-Popescu, Grigore. L'arte nell'età delle monarchie assolute (1997); De Seta, Cesare. Il secolo della borghesia (2v., 1999); Gualdoni, Flaminio. Le forme del presente (1997).

I39 Univers des formes. Paris, Gallimard, 1960– .

See GLAH 1:I4 for titles available in the Amer. ed., entitled Arts of mankind, and titles through v.24 not translated into English. Titles in this series are not cited individually elsewhere in this chapter.

Contents: (25) Duval, Paul Marie. Les Celtes (1977); (26) Aldred, Cyril, et al. Les temps des pyramides: de la préhistoire aux Hyksos 1560 av. J.-C. (1978); (27) Aldred, Cyril, et al. L'Empire des conquérants: l'Égypte au Nouvel Empire (1560–1070) (1979); (28) Aldred, Cyril, et al. L'Égypte du crépuscule: de Tanis à Méroé, 1070 av. J-C.-IVè siècle apr. J.-C. (1980); (29) Avril, François, et al. Les temps des Croisades (1982); (30) Avril, François, et al. Les royaumes d'Occident (1983); (31) Baudez, Claude F. et al. Les Mayas (1984); (32) Lavallée, Danièle. Les Andes de la Préhistoire aux Incas (1985); (33) Bernal, Ignacio. Le Mexique des origines aux Aztéques (1986); (34) Erlande-Brandenburg, Alain. Le conquète de l'Europe, 1260–1380 (1987); (35) Recht, Roland. Automne et renouveau: 1380–1500 (1988); (36?) Sauerländer, Willibald. Le siècle des cathédrales, 1140–1260 (1989); (37) Vialou, Denis. La préhistoire (1991); (38) Kruta, Venceslas. L'Europe des origines: la protohistoire 6000–500 avant J.-C. (1992); (39) Schiltz, Véronique. Les Scythes et le nomades des steppes: VIIIe siècle avant J.-C.-Ier siècle après J.-C. (1994); (40) Hofmann, Werner. Une époque en rupture, 1750–1830 (1995); (41) Cutler, Anthony. Byzance médiévale, 700–1204 (1996); (42) Arasse, Daniel. Le Renaissance maniériste (1997).

I40 Yale University Press Pelican history of art. New Haven, Yale Univ. Pr., 1992– . il., plates (part col.)

Revised editions and reissues (sometimes difficult to distinguish) of volumes in the distinguished Pelican history of art series, originally ed. by Nikolaus Pevsner (GLAH 1:I18). Some vols. in the original series have been split into two vols. Many but by no means all of the voluminous titles in the new series are cited individually throughout GLAH 2.

Selective contents: Blair, Sheila S., and Bloom, Jonathan M. The art and architecture of Islam 1250–1800 (1994); Blunt, Anthony. Art and architecture in France, 1500–1700, 5th ed. (1999); Brendel, Otto. Etruscan art, 2d ed. (1995); Brown, Jonathan. Painting in Spain: 1500–1700 (1998); Conant, Kenneth John. Carolingian and Romanesque architecture, 800 to 1200, 2d integrated ed. rev. (1978); Dodwell, C. R. The Pictorial arts of the West 800–1200 (1993); Ettinghausen, Richard, and Grabar, Oleg. The art and architecture of Islam, 650–1250 (1994); Frankfort, Henri. The art and architecture of the ancient Orient, 4th ed. (1996); Freedberg, S. J. Painting in Italy, 1500–1600, 3d ed. (1993); Hamilton, George Heard. The art and architecture of Russia (1993); Heydenreich, Ludwig. Architecture in Italy, 1400–1500 (1996); Hamilton, George Heard. Painting and sculpture in Europe, 1880–1940, 6th ed. (1993); Hitchcock, Henry Russell. Architecture: nineteenth and twentieth centuries, 4th ed. (1992); Hood, Sinclair. The arts in prehistoric Greece (199?); Kalnein, Wend von. Architecture in France in the eighteenth century (1995); Krautheimer, Richard. Early Christian and Byzantine architecture. 4th ed. rev. (1986); Lasko, Peter. Ars sacra, 800–1200, 2d ed. (1994); Lawrence, A. W. Greek architecture, 5th ed. (1996); Levey, Michael. Painting and sculpture in France, 1700–1789 (1993); Lotz, Wolfgang. Architecture in Italy, 1500–1600 (1995); Novotny, Fritz. Painting and sculpture in Europe, 1780–1880 (1992?); Rosenberg, Jakob; Slive, Seymour; and E.H. ter Kuile. Dutch art and architecture, 1600–1800, 3d ed. (1993); Sandars, N. K. Prehistoric art in Europe (1992); Sickman, L. C. S. The art and architecture of China (1992); Slive, Seymour. Dutch painting 1600–1800 (1995); Smith, William Stevenson. The art and architecture of ancient Egypt. Rev. with additions (1998); Strong, Donald Emrys. Roman art, 2d ed. (1988); Summerson, John. Architecture in Britain, 1530 to 1830, 9th ed. (1993); Vlieghe, Hans. Flemish art and architecture, 1585–1700 (1998); Ward Perkins, J.B. Roman imperial architecture, 2d integ. ed. (1981); Watson, William. The arts of China to AD 900 (1995); Waterhouse, Ellis Kirkham. Painting in Britain 1530 to 1790, 5th ed. (1994); White, John. Art and architecture in Italy 1250–1400, 3d ed. (1993); Williamson, Paul. Gothic sculpture 1140–1300 (1995); Wittkower, Rudolf. Art and architecture in Italy, 1600 to 1750 (1999).

I41 Wilkins, David G.; Schultz, Bernard; and Linduff, Katheryn M. Art past/art present. 3d ed. N.Y., Abrams, 1997. 628p. il. (part col.)

1st ed. 1990; 2d ed. 1994.

"We have written Art past/art present especially for the person with a general interest in learning about art and art history, and for the one-semester introductory course in art history or art appreciation."—*Pref. and ackn. to the third ed.* A survey textbook, chronologically arranged.

Glossary, p.604–12. Bibliography, p.613–15. Index, p.616–28.

TECHNIQUES

I42 Ayres, James. The artist's craft: a history of tools, techniques, and materials. Oxford, Phaidon, 1985. 240p. il. (part col.)

Well-illustrated survey. Does not include printmakers' tools.

Contents: (I) Introduction; (II) The studio; (III) Drawing; (IV) Painting; (V) Sculpture; (VI) Postscript; Appendices.

Notes, p.215–28. Select bibliography, p.229–31. Glossary, p.232–34. Index, p.236–40.

PREHISTORIC

I43 L'art des cavernes: atlas des grottes ornées paléolithiques françaises. Avant-propos d'André Leroi-Gourhan. Paris, Ministère de la culture, Direction du patrimoine, Sous-direction de l'archéologie, Impr. nationale, 1984. 673p. il. (part col.), plates. (Atlas archéologiques de la France)

Monumental topographical survey of cave painting in France.

Bibliographie générale, p.635–59. Index des noms d'auteurs, p.661–64. Index des termes scientifiques et techniques définis dans les chapitres d'introduction, p.665–66. Index des noms, p.667–70.

I44 Leroi-Gourhan, André. The dawn of European art: an introduction to Palaeolithic cave painting. Trans. by Sara Champion. N.Y., Cambridge Univ. Pr., 1982. 77p. il., plates (Imprint of man)

Trans. of Più antichi artisti d'Europa.

Popular introduction by an expert.

Contents: Introduction; Technique; Form; Space; Animation and time; The message; The actors; The contents of the message.

Bibliography, p.77. No index.

I45 Sandars, N. K. Prehistoric art in Europe. [New Haven], Yale Univ. Pr., [1992?] 508p. il., maps (Yale University Press pelican history of art)

See GLAH 1:I33 for original ed.

"In the first chapter fresh material discoveries and techniques have brought about an extraordinary lengthening of the time-scale; later . . . new attitudes have led to some radical rethinking on such things as the origins of the western Megalithic tradition in building, and the role of the east Mediterranean and the Middle East in the development and spread of metallurgy."—*Foreword to the second ed.*

I46 Twohig, Elizabeth Shee. The megalithic art of Western Europe. N.Y., Oxford Univ. Pr., 1981. xi, 259p. il. (part col.), plates

"This publication provides a catalogue and study of the megalithic art of western Europe."—*Introd.*

Contents: (I) Introduction; (II) Discussion: (1) General introduction to megalithic monuments and art; (2) Iberian megalithic art; (3) French megalithic art; (4) Irish and British megalithic art; (5) Art possibly related to megalithic art; (6) Origin and function of megalithic tombs; (7) Summary and conclusions; (III) Catalogue: (1) Iberia; (2) France; (3) Ireland and Britain; Appendix 1: Iberian sites claimed as megalithic art; Appendix 2: Ireland and Scotland: miscellaneous sites.

List of decorated sites, p.[ix]–xi. List of discussion figures, maps and tables, p.[xii]. Bibliography, p.[240]–51. Index, p.[252]–59.

ANCIENT

General Works

I47 L'art de l'antiquité. Paris, Gallimard; Réunion des musées nationaux, 1995–97. 2v. il., maps (part col.) (Collection manuels d'histoire de l'art)

Survey of the art of the Mediterranean world from prehistory to the fall of Rome.

Contents: (1) Les origines de l'Europe; (2) L'Egypte et le Proche-Orient.

Glossaire, v.1, p.568–71, v.2, p.446–48. Bibliographie, v.1, p.572–77, v.2, p.450–52. Index, v.1, p.578–89, v.2, p.454–61.

I48 Art in the ancient world: a handbook of styles and forms / Pierre Amiet . . . [et al.] Trans. by Valerie Bynner. N.Y., Rizzoli, 1981. 567p. il., maps, plans.

A handbook produced as part of a series by a team of experts at the Louvre. Intended for "travellers, scholars, art-lovers and dealers, among others." Employs line drawings as its principal vehicle, with accompanying captions.

Contents: The Middle East; Egypt; Greece: Etruria and the Etruscans; Rome.

List of abbreviations, p.8. Glossary, p.565–67.

I49 Glories of the past: ancient art from the Shelby White and Leon Levy collection. Ed. by Dietrich von Bothmer. N.Y., Metropolitan Museum of Art (Distr. by Abrams, 1990). x, 280p. il. (part col.)

Published in conjunction with the exhibition, Metropolitan Museum of Art (1990–91). Beautifully illustrated catalog of an excellent private collection.

Contents: Early Aegean; Ancient Near East and Central Asia; Greek and Etruscan; Roman; Late Antique.

Bibliographical abbreviations, p.268. Glossary, p.269–70. Index, p.271–80.

I50 Handbuch der Archäologie, im Rahmen des Handbuchs der Altertumswissenschaft. Neu hrsg. von Ulrich Hausmann. München, Beck, 1969– . (5)v. il.

See GLAH 1:I36 for previous vols.

Contents: (2) Kuhnen, Hans-Peter. Vorderasien II: Palästina in Griechisch-Römischer Zeit (1990); (3) Zazoff, Peter. Die antiken Gemmen (1983); (4) Koch, Guntram und Sichtermann, Hellmut. Römische Sarkophage (1982); [Unnumbered] Fuchs, Werner und Floren, Josef. Die griechische Plastik, Bd. 1, Die geometrische und archaische Plastik.

I51 Wolf, Walther. The origins of Western art: Egypt, Mesopotamia, the Aegean. N.Y., Universe Books (Distr. by St. Martin's, 1989). 207p. il. (part col.) (Herbert history of art and architecture)

Trans. of Frühe Hochkulturen. Stuttgart, Belser, 1969. Originally published as: The origins of western art. London, Weidenfeld and Nicolson, 1972.

A comparative study of the three artistic traditions, each seen as embodying "vastly different solutions to artistic problems."—*Foreword.*

Bibliography, p.202–03. Index, p.204–07.

Egypt

I52 Ägyptisches Museum. [Hrsg. von] Staatliche Museen zu Berlin, Stiftung Preussischer Kulturbesitz. [Hrsg: Karl-Heinz Priese. Autoren, Caris-Beatrice Arnst . . . et al.] Mainz., Zabern, 1991. xii, 285p. chiefly col. il., maps.

Catalog of the exhibition held at the former East Berlin part of the Ägyptisches Museum at the Museumsinsel Berlin (1991), documenting one of the premier collections of Egyptian art.

Contents: Das vor- und frühstaatliche Ägypten; Das Alte Reich; Das Mittlere Reich; Das frühe Neue Reich; Amarna; Das späte Neue Reich ("Ramessidenzeit"); Die Spätzeit; Die griechisch-römische Zeit; Bestattung und Bestattungsbeigaben; Bronzen, Kunstgewerbe, Schmuck, Skarabäen; Nubien und Nordsudan; Die Papyrussammlung.

Konkordanzliste, p.284–85.

I53 Africa in antiquity: the arts of ancient Nubia and the Sudan. Brooklyn, Brooklyn Museum, 1978. 2v.

Published in conjunction with the exhibition, Brooklyn Museum (1978), and other locations. For the proceedings of a related symposium see Africa in antiquity: the arts of ancient Nubia and the Sudan. Proceedings of the symposium held in conjunction with the exhibition.

Contents: (1) The essays; (2) Wenig, Steffen. The catalogue.

Abbreviations, v.1, p.13, v.2, p.9. Subject bibliography, v.1, p.139–41, v.2, p.333–46. Concordances, v.2, p.347–52. Index, v.2, p.354–63.

I54 Aldred, Cyril. Egyptian art, in the days of the pharaohs, 3100–320 B.C. N.Y., Oxford Univ. Pr., 1980. 252p. il. (part col.) (World of art)

Introductory historical survey by an authority.

Select bibliography, p.241–42. Index and glossary, p.248–52.

I55 Bourriau, Janine. Pharaohs and mortals: Egyptian art in the Middle Kingdom. Catalogue by Janine Bourriau. With a contrib. by Stephen Quirke. N.Y., Cambridge Univ. Pr.; Cambridge, [Eng.], Fitzwilliam Museum, 1988. vi, 167p. il. (part col.), plates.

Catalog of the exhibition, Fitzwilliam Museum (1988), intended "to illustrate the distinctive style of the epoch in all the arts . . . no previous exhibition on this theme has been mounted."—*Foreword.*

Contents: Foreword by Michael Jaffé; Introduction; (1) Royal and private sculpture; (2) Writing and literature; (3) Funerary art; (4) Art and magic; (5) Decorative art.

Abbreviations and concordances, p.6. Index of private names and titles, p.164–66.

I56 Brooklyn Museum. Ancient Egyptian art in the Brooklyn Museum. [By] Richard Fazzini . . . [et al.] N.Y., Thames and Hudson, 1989. xv, 100p. il. (part col.), map.

Accessible introduction to one of the outstanding collections of Egyptian art, beautifully illustrated, with a catalog of 100 objects and a brief history of the collection.

Abbreviations, p.xiv–xv.

I57 D'Auria, Sue; Lacovara, Peter; and Roehrig, Catharine H. Mummies & magic: the funerary arts of ancient Egypt. Boston, Museum of Fine Arts, 1988. 272p. il. (part col.), map, plans.

Catalog of the exhibition, Museum of Fine Arts, Boston (1988), based upon the Museum's collections.

Bibliography, p.248–65. Index, p.266–72.

I58 Davis, Whitney. The canonical tradition in ancient Egyptian art. N.Y., Cambridge Univ. Pr., 1989. xx, 272p. il. (Cambridge new art history and criticism)

Contents: (1) Introduction; (2) The canonical representation of figures and groups; (3) Variability, convention, and laws; (4) The order of iconography; (5) Academic production; (6) The emergence of canonical conventions; (7) The explanation of variance: toward a history of the authority of the canonical image.

Notes, p.225–44. List of abbreviations, p.[245]–46. References, p.247–67. Index, p.269–72.

I59 Egypt's dazzling sun: Amenhotep III and his world. By Arielle P. Kozloff and Betsy M. Bryan with Lawrence M. Berman and an essay by Elisabeth Delange. Cleveland, Cleveland Museum of Art (Distr. by Indiana Univ. Pr., 1992). xxiv, 476p. il. (part col.)

Published in conjunction with the exhibition, Cleveland Museum of Art (1992), and other locations. "Amenhotep III's reign was one of the most artistically productive in Egypt's history. . . . Attempting to define systematically the art production of a single reign is a rare, perhaps unique undertaking in the field of Egyptology."—*Foreword.* Organized by medium and genre.

Includes bibliographical references. Chronology, p.xxi. Key to abbreviations, p.452–60.

I60 Egypt's golden age: the art of living in the New Kingdom 1558–1085 B.C. Boston, Museum of Fine Arts, 1982. 336p. il.

Catalog of the exhibition, Museum of Fine Arts, Boston (1982), and other locations. Based upon the collections of the Museum. The objects in this exhibition, most excavated by the museum personnel, "derive not from royal tombs or temples but from the homes of average Egyptians."—*Foreword.* Arranged by form of domestic object.

Bibliography, p.312–33. Concordance, p.333. Addenda and errata, p.334.

I61 Gaballa, G. A. Narrative in Egyptian art. Mainz am Rhein, Zabern, 1976. 167p. il., plates.

At head of title: Deutsches Archäologisches Institut. Abteilung Kairo. A careful survey of narrative pictorial conventions and techniques in Egyptian two-dimensional art.

Contents: Introduction; Part one: From the Predynastic Period to the end of the Middle Kingdom; Part two: The New Kingdom and Later.

Notes, p.142–58. Index, p.159–67.

I62 Götter, Pharaonen. [Wissenschaftliche Bearb. und Katalog, Dietrich Wildung, Günter Grimm]. [Recklinghausen, Auslieferung, A. Bongers, 1978]. 36, [292]p. chiefly il. (part col.)

Catalog of the exhibition, Villa Hügel, Essen (1978), and other locations. Catalog of 175 objects, derived mostly from the collections of the Egyptian Museum, Cairo and the Greco-Roman Museum, Alexandria.

Empfohlene Literatur, [p.289–90].

I63 Hayes, William Christopher. The scepter of Egypt: a background for the study of the Egyptian antiquities in the Metropolitan Museum of Art. 5th printing, rev. N.Y., The Museum (Distr. by Abrams, 1990). 2v. il., fold. maps.

See GLAH 1:I41 for original ed. This ed. includes a list of accession numbers for all objects illustrated and an up-to-date chronology.

I64 Iversen, Erik. Canon and proportions in Egyptian art. 2d ed., fully revised in collab. with Yoshiaki Shibata. Warminster, Aris and Phillips, 1975. [2], 94p. il.

Contents: Metrology and canon; The Egyptological history of the canonical problem; The structure of the canon; The application of the system of proportion; The origin of the canon; The typology of the canon; The late canon.

Bibliography and list of abbreviations, p.89–91.

I65 Museo archeologico nazionale di Napoli. La Collezione egiziana del Museo archeologico nazionale di Napoli. Napoli, Arte tipografica, [1989]. v, 314p. il. (part col.), map, plans.

Catalog of an important collection derived mostly from distinguished private collections, and thus bearing witness to the history of responses to Egyptian art. Published in conjunction with a reorganization of the collection.

Glossario, p.285–92. Quadro cronologico, p.293. Lista dei nomi egiziani, p.294–98. Bibliografie, p.299–309. Abbreviazioni bibliografiche, p.310. Tavola di concordanza, p.311–14.

I66 Museo civico archeologico di Bologna. La collezione egiziana. [Catalogo a cura di Sergio Pernigotti.] [Milano], Leonardo arte, 1994. 143p. col. ill.

Catalog of the exhibition, Museo civico archeologico di Bologna (1994), documenting an excellent collection of Egyptian art, organized into a new department of the museum in 1993.

Bibliografia essenziale, p.[142]–43.

I67 Museo egizio di Torino. Catalogo del museo egizio di Torino. Serie seconda, Collezioni. Torino, Pozzo, 1972– . (7)v.

Catalog of one of the outstanding Egyptological collections in the world. Supplements Serie 1: Monumenti e testi. 8v.

Contents: (1) Tosi, Mario. Stele e altre epigrafi di Deir el Medina, n.50001–50262; (2) Habachi, Labib. Tavole d'offerta, are a bacili da libagione, n.22001–22067; (3) López, Jesús. Ostraca ieratici, 4v.; (4) Dolzani, Claudia. Vasi canopi, n.19001–19153; (5) Bergamini, Giovanni. Sigilli a cilindro mesopotamici, n.7001–70044; (6) Delorenzi, Enzo. Le mummie del Museo egizio di torino, n.13001–13026; (7) Archi, Alfonso, and Pomponio, Francesco. Testi cuneiformi neo-sumerici da Drehem, n.0001–0412.

I68 Museu Nacional (Brazil). Catálogo da Coleçao do Egito Antigo existente no Museu Nacional, Rio de Janeiro = Catalogue of the Egyptian Collection in the National Museum, Rio de Janeiro. Por Kenneth A. Kitchen. Prep. com a colabor. da Maria da Conceiçao Beltrao. Rio de Janeiro, Museu Nacional, Universidade Federal de Rio de Janeiro; Warminster, England, Aris & Phillips, 1990, 1988. 2v. il.

Catalog of the collection, illustrated with inadequate black-and-white photographs and hieroglyphic transcriptions.

Contents: (I) Texto = Text; (II) Illustraçoes = Plates.

Bibliografia selcionada = select bibliography, v.1, p.262. Índices e concordáncias, v.1, p.263–76.

I69 Paris. Musée National du Louvre. Département des antiquités égyptiennes. Catalogue des stèles, peintures et reliefs égyptiens de l'Ancien Empire et de la Première Période Intermédiaire: vers 2686–2040 avant J.-C. Par Christiane Ziegler. Paris, Réunion des musées nationaux; Ministère de la culture, de la communication, des grands travaux et du Bicentenaire, 1990. 375p. il. (part col.), maps.

Catalogue of the Louvre's major collection of Egyptian antiquities of the Old Empire.

Includes bibliographical references. Abbréviations bibliographiques, p.332–46. Index, p.349–51. Index des traductions conventionnelles, p.352–57. Index des textes hiéroglyphiques, p.358–75.

I70 Robins, Gay. Proportion and style in ancient Egyptian art. Drawings by Ann S. Fowler. Austin, Univ. of Texas Pr., 1994. x, 283p. il.

"This book is a study of a fundamental aspect of ancient Egyptian art, namely, the use of squared grids made by artists in drawing preliminary sketches of scenes and figures."—*Introd.*

Contents: (1) Introduction; (2) Previous work on the grid and proportions; (3) Methods; (4) Proportions in the Old and Middle Kingdom; (5) Proportions in the New Kingdom; (6) Changes in the Amarna period; (7) The Late Period and after; (8) Composition and the grid; (9) Nonhuman elements and the grid; (10) Changing proportions and style.

Abbreviations, p.[261]. Notes, p.[263]–72. Bibliography, p.[273]–78. Index, p.[279]–83.

I71 Saleh, Mohamed. The Egyptian Museum, Cairo: official catalog. [By] Mohamed Saleh and Hourig Sourouzian. Photographs: Jürgen Liepe. [Trans. by Peter Der Manuelian and Helen Jacquet-Gordon.] Mainz, Zabern, 1987. 268p. il. (chiefly col.), 1 map, 2 plans.

Trans. of Hauptwerke im Ägyptischen Museum Kairo. Mainz, Zabern, 1987.

Official catalog of the "largest and most important material source on ancient Egyptian civilization."—*Pref.*

Glossary, p.31–34. Key to the bibliography and selected works, p.35–38.

I72 Scott, Gerry D. Ancient Egyptian art at Yale. New Haven, Yale University Art Galley, 1986. 229p. il. (part col.)

Catalog of the collection of Egyptian artifacts housed in both the Peabody Museum of Natural History and in the Yale University Art Gallery.

Bibliography, p.207–17. Concordance, p.218–19. Indices, p.221–29.

I73 Seipel, Wilfried. Götter, Menschen, Pharaonen: 3500 Jahre ägyptische Kultur: Meisterwerke aus der Ägyptisch-Orientalischen Sammlung des Kunsthistorischen Museums Wien. Hrsg. von Meinrad Maria Grewenig. Stuttgart, Hatje, 1993. 320p. il. (part col.)

Catalog of the exhibition, Historisches Museum der Pfalz (1993), and other locations, documenting works from the outstanding Egyptian collection of the Kunsthistoriches Museum, Vienna.

Literatur, p.317–20.

I74 Il Senso dell'arte nell'antico Egitto. Milano, Electa, 1990. 263p. il. (part col.)

Catalog of the exhibition, Museo Civico Archeologico, Bologna (1990). Catalog of 242 objects, with a focus upon artistic quality and appreciation, preceded by a historical introduduction.

Glossario, p.257–59. Bibliografia, p.260–63.

I75 Smith, William Stevenson. The art and architecture of ancient Egypt. Rev. with additions by William Kelly Simpson. N.Y., Penguin, 1998. xiii, 296p. il. (Yale University Press pelican history of art)

See GLAH 1:I45 for original ed. and annotation; rev. ed. with additions, 1981. The preface to the new ed. outlines recent developments in the field, including major excavations, publication of museum holdings, and new scholarship.

Abbreviations, p.252. Notes, p.253–77. Bibliography, p.278–90. Index, p.291–96.

I76 Studien zur ägyptischen Kunstgeschichte. Hrsg. von Marianne Eaton-Krauss und Erhart Graefe. Hildesheim, Gerstenberg, 1990. x, 112p. il., plates (Hildesheimer ägyptologische Beiträge, 29)
Papers presented at a conference held 1987 in Münster/Westfalen, intended to survey the status of studies in Egyptian art history.
Includes bibliographical references. Abkürzungsverzeichnis, p.ix–x.

I77 Sudan: ancient kingdoms of the Nile. Ed. dir. by Dietrich Wildung. Trans. from the German by Peter Der Manuelian. Trans. from the French by Kathleen Guillaume. N.Y., Flammarion, 1997. xi, 428p. il. (chiefly col.), maps.
German ed. Sudan, Antike Königreiche am Nil. Tübingen, Wasmuth, 1996. Beautifully illustrated, scholarly catalog of the exhibition, Institut du Monde Arabe (1997), and other locations.
Contents: The prehistory of the Sudan; The first kingdoms (2500–1075 B.C.); Napata and the Kushite Dynasty: kings of the sacred mountain (1000–656 B.C.); The kingdom of Napata and Meroe.
Notes, p.418–21. Bibliography, p.422–24.

I78 Vassilika, Eleni. Egyptian art. [By] Eleni Vassilika with contrib. from Janine Bourriau. Photography by Bridget Taylor and Andrew Morris. N.Y., Cambridge Univ. Pr., 1995. viii, 139p. col. il. (Fitzwilliam Museum handbooks)
"This book is an introduction to four thousand years of Egyptian art illustrated by a selection of highlights from the collections of the Fitzwilliam Museum."—*Introd.*
Glossary of Egyptian deities, p.5–9. Selected bibliography and abbreviations, p.138–39.

I79 Wildung, Dietrich. Sesostris und Amenemhet: Ägypten im Mittleren Reich. München, Hirmer, 1984. 255p. il. (part col.), maps.
French ed.: L'âge d'or de l'Egypte: le Moyen Empire. Paris, Presses Univ. de France, 1984.
Survey of the Middle Kingdom by an authority.
Contents: Das Mittlere Reich im Blickfeld der Nachwelt; Theben—Die Wiege des Mittleren Reiches; Memphis—Die Reichshauptstadt; Das Leben in der Provinz; Die Nachbarvölker; Das Bild der Zeit im Spiegel der Kunst; Ausklang.
Chronologie des Mittleren Reiches, p.236. Verzeichnis der Abbildungen, p.237–46. Ausgewählte Bibliographie, p.247–48. Nachweis der zitierten altägyptischen Texte, p.248. Register, p.249–55.

I80 Wilkinson, Richard H. Reading Egyptian art: a hieroglyphic guide to ancient Egyptian painting and sculpture. London, Thames & Hudson, 1992. 224p. il.
"This book has been designed with this goal in mind—to allow the non-specialist to 'read' the major hieroglyphs found in Egyptian painting and sculpture and to understand much of the symbolic content of Egyptian art which is usually only accessible to the trained Egyptologist."—*Pref.*
Contents: Preface; How to use this book; Introduction; Catalog of hieroglyphs.
Glossary, p.218–20. Further reading, p.220–22 (arranged by hieroglyphics). Location of illustrated objects, p.222–23. Index, p.224.

I81 Ziegler, Christiane. The Louvre: Egyptian antiquities. With the collab. of Christophe Barbotin and Marie-Hélène Rutschowscaya. London, Scala, 1990. 95p. col. il.
Brief overview of the Louvre's magnificent collection, with color illustrations and accompanying text.

Western Asia

General Works

I82 Amiet, Pierre. Art of the ancient Near East. Trans. from the French by John Shepley and Claude Choquet. [Ed. by Naomi Noble Richard.] N.Y., Abrams, 1980. 618p. il. (part col.)
Trans. of L'art antique du proche-orient. Paris, Mazenod, 1977 (L'art et les grandes civilizations, 7).
A monumental survey of Ancient Near Eastern art and architecture.
Contents: Part one: The historical perspective; Introduction: The rediscovery of the Ancient Near East; The prehistoric foundations of Eastern civilization; The birth of historical civilizations; The early dynastic period and the beginnings of history; The second millennium: the center shifts; The first millennium: toward the universal empire. Part two: The image as document; Documentary photographs; Identification of the photographs. Part three: The principal sites of Ancient Near Eastern art. Part four: Reconstructions. Part five: A lexicon; Images of gods and goddesses; Lists of gods and goddesses; Kings and sovereigns.
Historical chronology, p.[599–604]. Glossary, p.[605]–06. Bibliography, p.[607]–10. Index, p.[611]–18.

I83 Chronologies in Old World archaeology. Ed. by Robert W. Ehrich. 3d ed. Chicago, Univ. of Chicago Pr., 1992. 2v. il., maps.
See GLAH 1:I51 for previous versions and eds.
"This present edition reflects not only the explosion of archaeological activity in the years since [1961] but also the spate of publication, improved communications between archaeologists and scholars in related fields, and the practice of holding focused symposia of general and specific interest attended by specialists from several countries. . . . It has been necessary to concentrate on four major objectives: (1) sequences, (2) distributions and relationships, (3) calibrated radiocarbon and relative dates, and (4) pertinent bibliographies and sources."—*Introd.*

I84 Collon, Dominique. Ancient Near Eastern art. London, Published for the Trustees of the British Museum by British Museum Pr., 1995. 247p. il. (part col.), maps.
"This survey of Ancient Near Eastern art is based on the collections of the British Museum."—*Ackn.* While "some

periods and areas are poorly represented in the Museum's collections" (*Introd.*)—e.g., Neolithic outside Jericho; Syria, Lebanon, Iran and Turkey—this is an excellent survey of the subject.

Contents: Introduction; (1) From village to town before 3000BC; (2) Temple, cemetery and palace: the 3rd millennium BC; (3) Trade and diplomacy: the 2nd millennium BC; (4) Great empires: the 1st millennium BC; (5) Parthians and Sasanians beyond the Euphrates: c.238BC–AD651; (6) Survival and revival.

General chronology, p.228–29. Mesopotamian chronology, by C. B. F. Walker, p.230–38. Further reading, p.239. Sources of illustrations, p.240–41. Index, p.242–47.

I85 Frankfort, Henri. The art and architecture of the ancient Orient. New Haven, Yale Univ. Pr., 1996. 456p. il. (Yale University Press pelican history of art)

Reissue of this standard work, based upon the fourth (revised) impression; see GLAH 1:I52.

I86 Paris. Musée National du Louvre. The royal city of Susa: ancient Near Eastern treasures in the Louvre. Ed. by Prudence O. Harper, Joan Aruz, and Francoise Tallon. N.Y., Metropolitan Museum of Art (Distr. by Abrams, 1992). xix, 316p. il. (part col.)

Published in conjunction with the exhibition, Metropolitan Museum of Art (1992–93).

A selection from "the antiquities found during French excavations at Susa over the last hundred years, which are now in the Louvre [and] include some of the masterpieces of Ancient Near Eastern art."—*Foreword.*

Contents: Susa in the Ancient Near East, by Pierre Amiet; Prehistoric Susa, by Elizabeth Carter . . . [et al.]; Protoliterate Susa, by Elizabeth Carter . . . [et al.]; The Old Elamite period, by Elizabeth Carter . . . [et al.]; The Middle Elamite period, by Elizabeth Carter . . . [et al.]; The Mespotamian presence, by Prudence O. Harper and Pierre Amiet; Popular art at Susa, by Agnès Spycket; The Neo-Elamite period, by Elizabeth Carter . . . [et al.]; Susa in the Achaemenid period, by Oscar White Muscarella . . . [et al.]; The written record, by Matthew W. Stolper and Béatrice André-Salvini; Technical appendix, by Annie Caubet . . . [et al.]

Contributors to the catalogue, p.288. Concordance, p.289–90. Bibliography, p.291–306. Index, p.307–15.

Anatolia

I87 The Anatolian civilisations. [Ed. by Ferit Edgü.] [Istanbul], Turkish Ministry of Culture and Tourism, [1983]. 3v. il. (part col.) (The Council of Europe, XVIIIth European art exhibition)

Catalog of the exhibition, Topkapi Palace Museum, Istanbul (1983), and other locations.

Contents: (1) Prehistoric/Hittite/Early Iron Age; (2) Greek/Roman/Byzantine; (3) Seljuk/Ottoman.

Abbreviations and bibliography, v.1, p.304–11, v.2, p.201–3, v.3, p.316–23.

Cyprus

I88 Karageorghis, Vassos. Archaia kypriaké techné sto Mouseio tou Hidrymatos Pieridé = Ancient Cypriote art in the Pierides Foundation Museum. Larnaka, Cyprus, Hidryma Pieridé, 1985. 279p. il.

In English and Greek.

"The archaeological collection of the Pierides Foundation Museum is perhaps the richest private collection of Cypriote antiquities in Cyprus."—*p.[13].* Beautifully illustrated, scholarly catalog.

Chronological table, p.7. Bibliography, p.278–79.

I89 Morris, Desmond. The art of ancient Cyprus, with a check-list of the author's collection. Oxford, Phaidon Press in assoc. with Jonathan Cape, 1985. 368p. il. (part col.)

Aims to provide "an overall introduction to the subject" (*Pref.*) while also providing a catalog of the author's distinguished collection of Cypriot antiquities.

Contents: (I) Epochs; (II) Vessels; (III) Representations; (IV) Decorations.

Check-list of the author's collection, p.353–59. Bibliography, p.360–63. Restorations, p.364. Index, p.365–67.

I90 New York. Metropolitan Museum of Art. Ancient art from Cyprus: the Cesnola collection at the Metropolitan Museum of Art. [By] Vassos Karageorghis, in collab. with Joan. R. Mertens and Marice E. Rose. N.Y., The Museum (Distr. by Abrams, 2000). xiii, 305p. il. (chiefly col.), col. maps.

Beautifully illustrated catalog of an important collection, "the first group of Mediterranean antiquities to enter the nascent museum."—*Pref.*

Contents: Introduction; (I) The prehistoric period (ca. 10,000–ca. 1050 B.C.); (II) The Cypro-Geometric and Cypro-Archaic periods (ca. 1050–ca. 480 B.C.); (III) The Cypro-Classical period (ca. 480–ca. 310 B.C.); (IV) The Hellenistic and Roman periods (ca. 310 B.C.–ca. A.D. 330).

Note to the reader, p.xi. Chronology, p.xii-xiii. Bibliography of works cited, p.294–305.

Mesopotamia

I91 Lloyd, Seton. The archaeology of Mesopotamia: from the Old Stone Age to the Persian conquest. Rev. ed. N.Y., Thames and Hudson, 1984. 251p. il.

Standard introduction to the subject, chronologically arranged and principally concerned with "the material remains and with the progress of excavations which have revealed them . . . rather than with the philological contribution."—*Pref. to the first ed.*

Notes on the text, p.233–38. Bibliography, p.239–44. Index, p.246–51.

Persia (Ancient Iran)

I92 The Arts of Persia. Ed. by R. W. Ferrier. New Haven, Yale Univ. Pr., 1989. x, 334p. il.

A major collaborative survey, with chapters by specialists in the principal media.

Contents: (1) Historical introduction, by R. W. Ferrier; (2) Early art, by C. Hill; (3) The art of the Achaemenians, by M. Roaf; (4) The art of the Parthians, by E. Keal; (5) The art of the Sasanians, by G. Hermann; (6) Architecture, by Robert Hillenbrand; (7) Some vernacular buildings of the plateau, by E. Beazley; (8) Carpets, by J. Housego; (9) Textiles, by J. Allgrove McDowell; (10) Metalwork, by J. Allan; (11) Jewellery, by R. W. Ferrier; (12) Coins, by H. Mitchell-Brown; (13) Painting, by Ernst Grube and Eleanor Sims; (14) Painting in the Post-Safavid Period, by B. W. Robinson; (15) The arts of the book, by Barbara Brend; (16) Lacquerwork, by L. Diba; (17) Ceramics, by M. Rogers; (18) Tilework, by J. Scarce; (19) Glass, by R. Charleston; (20) Calligraphy, by A. Schimmel.

Maps, p.[viii]–[ix]. Glossary, p.x. Notes and bibliographies, p.315–31. Index, p.332–34.

I93 Highlights of Persian art. Ed. by Richard Ettinghausen and Ehsan Yarshater. Boulder, Westview, 1979. xviii, 391p. il. (chiefly col.) (Persian art series, 1)

"Brings together within two covers an exploration of the salient features and phases of the whole spectrum of Persian art."—*Foreword.* Essays by authorities.

Contents: Introduction: the immanent features of Persian art, by Richard Ettinghausen; (1) Questions and comments on "Amlash" pottery, by Robert H. Dyson; (2) Ancient bronzework from Luristan, by P. R. S. Moorey; (3) Pursuing Scythian art, by Ann Farkas; (4) Achaemenid art, monumental and minute, by Edith Porada; (5) Court silver of Sasanian Iran, by Prudence O. Harper; (6) Color and design in Persian pottery, by Charles K. Wilkinson; (7) Iranian architecture: the evolution of a tradition, by Priscilla Soucek; (8) The heroic art of the East Iranian world, by Guitty Azarpay; (9) Poetry and calligraphy: thoughts about their interrelation in Persian culture, by Annemarie Schimmel; (10) Isfahan as a mirror of Persian architecture, by Oleg Grabar; (11) World awareness and human relationships in Iranian painting, by Richard Ettinghausen; (12) Safavid textiles and rugs, by M. S. Diamond; (13) The tradition of wall painting in Iran, by Basil Gray; (14) Persian painting in the Qajar period, by B. W. Robinson; (15) Contemporary Persian painting, by Ehsan Yarshater.

Concordance, p.379–85.

Syria and Palestine

I94 The Phoenicians. Under the scientific dir. of Sabatino Moscati. N.Y., Abbeville, 1988. 764p. il. (part col.)

Trans. of I fenici. Milan, Bompiani, 1988.

Monumental catalog of the exhibition, Palazzo Grassi, Venice (1988).

Contents: (I) Phoenician civilization; (II) The great areas; (III) The world of art; (IV) The Phoenicians and the world outside.

General bibliography, p.575–80. Catalogue, p.[583]–749. Catalogue bibliography, p.750–54.

Classical World

General Works

I95 Burn, Lucilla. The British Museum book of Greek and Roman art. N.Y., Thames and Hudson, 1992. 223p. il. (part col.), maps

"This book is written not for the specialist, but for anyone curious about Greek and Roman art. . . . The purpose of the book is to introduce the British Museum's collection of Greek and Roman antiquities . . . and at the same time to provide a general introduction to Greek and Roman art and culture."—*Pref.*

Contents: (1) Greece in the Bronze Age; (2) The emergence of Greece: the Geometric and Orientalizing periods; (3) Archaic Greece; (4) Classical Greece: sculpture in bronze and marble; (5) Classical Greece: the minor arts; (6) The Greeks in Southern Italy and Sicily; (7) Monumental sculpture in Lycia and Caria; (8) The Hellenistic world; (9) Cyprus; (10) Italy before the Romans; (11) The Roman world: sculpture, coinage, and the Emperor; (12) The Roman world: the decorative and minor arts.

Suggestions for further reading, p.212–14. Maps, p.215–17. Glossary, p.218–19. Illustration references, p.220. Index, p.221–23.

I96 The Oxford history of classical art. Ed. by John Boardman. N.Y., Oxford Univ. Pr. 1993. ix, 406p. il. (part col.), 28 pages of plates, maps, plans.

"This volume has been designed . . . to serve a public interested in classical antiquity both for its own sake and for its legacy to the western world. . . . The aim has been less to provide a historical narrative or categorization of the arts with pictures attached than to engage the reader's attention more directly by pictures of objects and monuments."—*Ed. pref.*

Contents: (1) Introduction, by John Boardman; (2) Preclassical Greece, by Alan Johnston; (3) The classical period, by John Boardman; (4) The Hellenistic period, by R. R. R. Smith; (5) Rome: the Republic and early Empire, by J. J. Pollitt; (6) The later Roman Empire, by Janet Huskinson; (7) The diffusion of classical art, by John Boardman.

List of colour plates, p.viii–ix. List of maps, p.ix. Further reading, p.[379]–82. List of illustrations, p.[383]–92. General index, p.[393]–406.

Crete, Mycenae, Greece

I97 Ancient Greek art and iconography. Ed. by Warren G. Moon. Madison, Univ. of Wisconsin Pr., 1983. xviii, 346p. il.

"The essays in this volume were presented as papers in Madison, Wisconsin, 9–11 April 1981."—*Pref.* "The essays in this volume illustrate the changing modes of storytelling and of style in ancient Greek art from the Bronze Age of the fifteenth century BC through the Greco-Roman period. . . . The essays present a selective history of Greek art."—*Introd.*

Contents: Introduction; (1) The iconography of the ship fresco from Thera, by Ellen N. Davis; (2) Symbol and story in Geometric art, by John Boardman; (3) Archaic vase-painting vis-à-vis "free" painting at Corinth, by D. A. Amyx; (4) Stesichoros and the François Vase, by Andrew Stewart; (5) An Exekian puzzle in Portland: further light on the relationship between Exekias and Group E, by Evelyn Elizabeth Bell; (6) Painting, politics, and genealogy: Peisistratos and the Neleids, by H. A. Shapiro; (7) The Priam Painter: some iconographic and stylistic considerations, by Warren G. Moon; (8) Some thoughts on the origins of the Attic Head Vase, by William R. Biers; (9) Achilles Lord of Scythia, by Gloria Ferrari Pinney; (10) Euphronios and his fellows, by Jirí Frel; (11) The Centaur's smile: Pindar and the Archaic aesthetic, by Barbara Hughes Fowler; (12) Paragone: sculpture versus painting, Kaineus and the Kleophrades Painter, by Beth Cohen; (13) Painterly and pictorial in Greek relief sculpture, by Brunilde Sismondo Ridgway; (14) Attic vase-painting and the home textile industry, by Eva C. Keuls; (15) Mythological repertoire of Brauron, by Lilly Kahil; (16) The lettering and the iconography of "Macedonian" coinage, by N. G. L. Hammond; (17) A Dionysiac procession on a monumental Shape 8 oinochoe, by Konrad Schauenburg; (18) Some aspects of the Gospel in the light of Greek iconography, by Karl Schefold.

Notes at end of chapters. Glossary, p.299–300. Selected bibliography, p.301–32. Index of artists, p.333–34. Index of collections, p.335–42. General index, p.343–46.

I98 Arte e artigianato in Magna Grecia. A cura di Enzo Lippolis. Napoli, Electa, 1996. 541p. il. (part col.), maps. (I Greci in Occidente).

Catalog of the exhibition, ex Convento di San Domenico, Taranto (1996), one of a series of four exhibitions devoted to the theme "I Greci in Occidente." Focus upon craftsmen and materials.

Contents: Il reperimento e la lavorazione delle materie prime; La produzione artigianale.

Bibliografia, p.513–39.

I99 Barber, R. L. N. The Cyclades in the Bronze Age. Iowa City, Univ. of Iowa Pr., 1987. xiii, 283p. il., plans.

Careful survey of archeological evidence for Bronze Age civilization.

Notes, p.[247]–62. Bibliography, p.[263]–75. Index, p.[276]–83.

I100 Biers, William R. The archaeology of Greece: an introduction. 2d ed. Ithaca, Cornell Univ. Pr., 1996. 350p. il. (part col.), maps.

1st ed. 1980; rev. ed. 1987.

A solid introductory survey, chronologically arranged.

Suggestions for further reading, p.336–38. Select bibliography, p.339–40. Glossary, p.341–44. Index, p.345–50.

I101 Boardman, John. The diffusion of classical art in antiquity. Princeton, Princeton Univ. Pr., 1994. 352p. il., maps (The A.W. Mellon lectures in the fine arts, 1993) (Bollingen series XXXV, 42)

"This book is about Greek art as a medium of communication to non-Greek cultures and it therefore deals more with the responses to images that are sometimes misunderstood and often reinterpreted than with the communication of shared ideas. . . . We look at Greek art from the outside for a change, as a foreign art, and at styles and subjects sometimes long divorced from their origins."—*Pref.*

Contents: Introduction; (1) Greek art; (2) The Near East and the Persian Empire; (3) The Semitic world and Spain; (4) The East after Alexander the Great; (5) Egypt and North Africa; (6) The countries of the Black Sea; (7) Italy; (8) Europe; (9) Conclusion.

List of maps, p.9. Abbreviations, p.323. Notes, p.323–48. Index, p.349–52.

I102 ______. Greek art. 4th ed. rev. and exp. N.Y., Thames and Hudson, 1996. 304p. il. (part col.), map (World of art)

See GLAH 1:I84 for previous eds. of this authoritative, popular treatment. "The difference in this new edition lies partly in its increased length, in fuller account of various aspects of architecture and decoration, and of the role of art and artists in Greek society."—*Pref.*

I103 Carpenter, Thomas H. Art and myth in ancient Greece: a handbook. London, Thames and Hudson, 1991. 256p. il. (World of art)

"This book is an introductory survey of myth as it appears in surviving ancient Greek visual arts created between about 700 and 323 B.C. . . . The focus is ancient Greek narrative art."—*Introd.*

Contents: (1) Introduction; (2) A demonstration of method: the return of Hephaistos; Troilos and Achilles; (3) Portraits of the gods; (4) The ascendancy of the Olympians; (5) Perseus; Bellerophon; (6) Herakles; (7) Theseus; (8) Argonauts; Calydonian boar hunt; (9) The Trojan War; (10) The aftermath of the war.

Abbreviations, p.246. A selected list of further reading, p.247–49. Index of mythological subjects, p.253–56. Index of common attributes, p.256.

I104 Coldstream, J. N. Geometric Greece. [Maps by Kenneth Clarke.] N.Y., St. Martin's, 1977. 405p. il.

The standard survey of the period. "This book deals with Greek civilization from c.900 to c.700 B.C. . . . The purpose of this book . . . is to provide an archaeological survey of the Geometric period, amplified where possible by information from literary sources."—*Introd.*

Contents: (I) The passing of the Dark Ages, c.900–770 B.C.; (II) The Greek renaissance, c.770–700 B.C.: regional survey; (III) Life in eighth-century Greece.

Abbreviations, p.13–15. Glossary, p.371–72. Bibliography and site index, p.373–91. Index, p.395–405.

I105 Doumas, Christos. Cycladic art: ancient sculpture and ceramics of the Aegean from the N. P. Goulandris Collection. [Trans. by Alexandria Doumas.] Washington, D.C., National Gallery of Art, 1979. 124p. il. (part col.)

Catalog of the exhibition, National Gallery of Art, Washington, D.C. (1979), and other locations. The Goulandris collection is "the largest and most important assemblage of this material in private hands anywhere in the world."—*Foreword.*

I106 Getz-Preziosi, Pat. Early Cycladic art in North American collections. With essays by Jack L. Davis and Elizabeth Oustinoff. Richmond, Virginia Museum of Fine Arts (Distr. by the University of Washington Press, 1987). xx, 345p. il.

Catalog of the exhibition, Virginia Museum of Fine Arts (1987). "Early Cycladic Art in North American Collections is the first exhibition to focus solely on Early Cycladic figures and vessels in the museums and private collections of this continent. It is unusual in that it places nearly equal emphasis on the two types of marble objects, and it treats their development in an integrated manner."—*Pref.*

Contents: Perspectives on the prehistoric Cyclades: an archaeological introduction, by Jack L. Davis; Mastery in marble: the early Cycladic figures and vessels, by Pat Getz-Preziosi; The early Cycladic sculptor: materials and methods, by Elizabeth Oustinoff.

Lenders to the exhibition, p.xii–xiii. Abbreviations, p.xiv–xx. Catalogue of figures and vessels, by Pat Getz-Preziosi, p.122–327. Concordances, p.328–331. Select bibliography, p.332–33. Index of figures and vessels by collection, p.334–41. Index of sculptors, p.342–43.

I107 The Greek world: art and civilization in Magna Graecia and Sicily. Ed. by Giovanni Pugliese Carratelli. [Trans. Andrew Ellis . . . (et al.)]. N.Y., Rizzoli, 1996. 799p. il. (part col.), maps (part col.)

Italian ed. Milano, Bompiani, 1996. Catalog of the exhibition, Palazzo Grassi, Venice (1996), one of a series of four major exhibitions on Greek civilization.

Works on exhibit, p.[659]–758. Bibliography, p.[759]–71. Bibliography of the files, p.772–79. Index of names, p.[781]–95.

I108 Hampe, Roland, and Simon, Erika. The birth of Greek art: from the Mycenaean to the archaic period. Foreword by John Boardman. N.Y., Oxford Univ. Pr., 1981. 316p. il. (part col.), maps, plans.

Trans. of Tausend Jahre frühgriechische Kunst. München, Hirmer, 1980.

A monumental attempt to demonstrate the continuity of Mycenaean and Greek art. "The period to be dealt with extends from about 1600 BC beyond the end of the Mycenaean world (c. 1100 BC) into the so-called Dark Ages, through the Geometric and down to the end of the Orientalizing period (c. 600 BC)."—*Introd.* "Where most accounts of the arts of Greece deal with either the Bronze Age on its own, or the better charted later progress to the Classical, this book concentrates on the exploration of continuity between the two, setting the achievements of the last phase of the Bronze Age of Mycenaean Greece beside those of the later renascent Greece, and continuing the story on into the early Archaic, where new influences from the non-Greek world begin to work their spell, sometimes quickening, sometimes hindering that progress to the Classical."—*Foreword.*

Contents: Introduction; Architecture and planning; Metalwork; Weapons; Stone vessels; Pottery; Engraving; Jewellery and ornament; Ivory, bone and wood; Sculpture; Conclusion.

Bibliography, p.285–309. Glossary, p.310–13. Index, p.314–16.

I109 Havelock, Christine Mitchell. Hellenistic art: the art of the classical world from the death of Alexander the Great to the Battle of Actium. 2d ed. N.Y., Norton, 1981. 283p. il.

See GLAH 1:I95 for previous ed. The 2d ed. incorporates the most significant scholarly contributions made in the decade since the first edition, and includes an updated bibliography.

I110 Higgins, Reynold Alleyne. Minoan and Mycenaean art. New rev. ed. N.Y., Thames and Hudson, 216p. il. (part col.), maps, plans. (World of art)

See GLAH 1:I96 for original ed. Rev. ed. N.Y., Oxford Univ. Pr., 1981. "This edition was prepared with the assistance of Dr Lyvia Morgan. Recent research and discoveries have been incorporated in text and illustrations."—*Note on the new rev. ed.*

I111 Holloway, R. Ross. A view of Greek art. Providence, Brown Univ. Pr., [1973]. xxii, 213p. il.

"This book . . . is concerned with the monumental art of ancient Greece. However, it is not a history of Greek monuments (still less, a history of Greek art) but a discussion of essential elements that affected the nature of Greek creative expression in visual form."—*Pref.*

Contents: (1) Archaic sculptural form; (2) Archaic architectural form; (3) Narration in archaic art; (4) Olympia; (5) The Parthenon; (6) Late Phidian expressionism; (7) Change in the fourth century; (8) The hellenistic epilogue; Appendix A: Greek authors of the fifth century on art; Appendix B: Chronological chart.

List of maps and illustrations, p.[vii]–xx. Bibliographical note, p.[203]. Index, p.[205]–13.

I112 Hood, Sinclair. The arts in prehistoric Greece. N.Y., Penguin, 1978. 311p. il. (Pelican history of art) (Repr.: New Haven, Yale Univ. Pr., 1994)

Authoritative survey. Arranged by medium.

Abbreviations, p.[242]. Notes, p.[243]–75. Bibliography, p.[277]–[89]. Index, p.301–11.

I113 Hurwit, Jeffrey M. The art and culture of early Greece, 1100–480 B.C. Ithaca, Cornell Univ. Pr., 1985. 367p. il.

"This book presents a synthesis of Archaic culture: it seeks to place the art and architecture of early Greece in its literary, historical, and intellectual contexts. . . . I am concerned about origins: the origins of representation, of epic poetry, of the polis, of the stone temple, of mythological narrative art, of lyric poetry, of monumental stone sculpture, of philosophy, of tragedy, of the so-called optical revolution, of democracy, and even of the Classical style."—*Pref.*

Abbreviations, p.11–12. Glossary of Greek words and technical terms, p.357–60. Index, p.361–67.

I114 Martin, Roland. L'art grec. [Paris], Livre de Poche, 1994. 730p. il. (part col.) (Encyclopédies d'aujourd'hui)

Survey by an authority on Greek architecture. First pub. in an Italian trans. in 2 vols., La Grecia e il mondo greco. Torino, UTET, 1984 (Storia universale dell'arte. Sezione prima, Civiltà antiche e primitive).

Bibliographie, p.[683]–97. Chronologie, p.[699]–704. Glossaire, p.[705]–13. Index de noms de lieux, p.[715]–21. Index de noms de personnes, p.[723]–30.

I115 Morris, Sarah. P. Daidalos and the origins of Greek art. Princeton, Princeton Univ. Pr., 1992. xxx, 411p. il., plates.

Speculative, wide-ranging essay on the origins of Greek art.

Abbreviations, p.xxv–xxx. Bibliography, p.[387]–400. Index of ancient sources, p.[401]–6. General index, p.[407]–11.

I116 New perspectives in early Greek art. Ed. by Diana Buitron-Oliver. Washington, D.C., National Gallery of Art (Distr. by the University Press of New England, 1991). 308p. il. (part col.) (Studies in the history of art, 32) (Studies in the history of art. Symposium papers, 16)

Proceedings of a symposium sponsored by the Center for Advanced Studies in the Visual Arts (May 1988) and held in conjunction with the exhibition, "The human figure in early Greek art," National Gallery of Art, Washington, D.C. (1988). Important papers by leading scholars.

Contents: Archaic Greece: an era of discovery, by Alan L. Boegehold; The social function of art in early Greece, by Oswyn Murray; The representation of nature in early Greek art, by Jeffrey M. Hurwit; The alphabetic impact on Archaic Greece, by Mabel L. Lang; Homer's Anthropomorphism: narrative and ritual, by Walter Burkert; The human figure in Homer, by Bernard Knox; Myth and tradition from Mycenae to Homer, by Emily Vermeule; Theseus: aspects of the hero in Archaic Greece, by H. A. Shapiro; Aegean sanctuaries: forms and function, by Bernard C. Dietrich; Early monumental religious architecture at Old Smyrna, by Richard V. Nicholls; The sanctuary of Iria on Naxos and the birth of monumental Greek architecture, by Vassilis Lambrinoudakis; A vase-painter as dedicator on the Athenian Acropolis: a new view of the Painter of Acropolis 606, by Olga Tzahou-Alexandri; The dress of the Archaic Greek korai, by Evelyn B. Harrison; Early bronze sheets with figured scenes from the Acropolis, by Evi Touloupa; The human figure in Archaic Greek coinage, by Mando Oeconomides; The drawing of the human figure on early red-figure vases, by Dyfri Williams.

Notes at ends of chapters. Abbreviations, p.303–6.

I117 Onians, John. Art and thought in the Hellenistic Age: the Greek world view, 350–50 BC. London, Thames and Hudson, 1979. 192p. il., map.

A speculative exploration of the parallels between Hellenistic art, literature, philosophy, and science.

Contents: Prologue: Athens and Atlantis—a myth of style and civilization; (1) Fourth-century attitudes; (2) Art: its classification and criticism; (3) Allegory, images and signs; (4) Measure and scale; (5) Time and space; Greek epilogue-Roman prologue.

Guide to further study, p.182–83. Index, p.189–92.

I118 Papaioannou, Kostas. The art of Greece. Trans. from the French by I. Mark Paris. N.Y., Abrams, 1989. 637p. il. (part col.)

Trans. of L'art grec. Paris, Mazenod, 1972 (L'Art et les grandes civilisations, 3); new, rev. ed. 1993.

A standard survey of Greek art and architecture, authoritative, richly illustrated and documented.

Contents: Part one: The art and civilization of ancient Greece; The Creto-Mycenaean heritage; The Dark Age and Geometric art; Gods and divinity; Pre-classical Greece; The triumph of Freedom; Man and the universe in classical thought; The birth and development of classical forms; The city in crisis; Post-classical art of the fourth century; The legacy of Alexander. Part two: The image as document; Color plates; Documentary photographs; Identification of the photographs. Part three: Principal archaeological sites of the ancient Greek world. Part four: Forms and structures; Architecture; Vases. Part five: A lexicon; Political and military chronology; Catalogues: Gods, heroes and other mythological figures; Architects; Sculptors; Painters of murals and panels; Vase painters; Philosophers; Writers and orators.

Bibliography, p.621–23. Index, p.624–37.

I119 Pedley, John Griffiths. Greek art and archaeology. 2d ed. N.Y., Abrams, 1997. 384p. il. (part col.), maps, plans.

1st ed. 1992.

Excellent survey by period, Bronze Age through Hellenistic. "The main purpose of this book is to introduce beginning students . . . to the major monuments of Greek archaeology . . .. Another purpose is to make the principal documents of Greek art and archaeology more easily accessible."—*Pref.* The 2d ed. features an increased emphasis upon the Hellenistic period.

Glossary, p.[368]–71. Select bibliography, p.[372]–75.

I120 Pollitt, J. J. Art in the Hellenistic age. N.Y., Cambridge Univ. Pr., 1986. [xii], 329p. il., maps.

"The chapters of this book have two aims. One is to explore the ways in which Hellenistic art is an expression of the cultural experience and aspirations of the Hellenistic age. . . . The other is to present a selective history of the formal development of this art around those genres, schools, or styles which seem to me to have been of particular importance."—*Pref.*

Contents: Introduction: Hellenistic art and the temperament of the Hellenistic age; Prologue: the phases of Hellenistic art; (1) Royal iconography; (2) Lysippos and his school; (3) Personality and psychology in portraiture; (4) The sculpture of Pergamon; (5) Hellenistic baroque; (6) Rococo, realism and the exotic; (7) Rome as a center of Hellenistic art; (8) Style and retrospection: neoclassicism and archaism; (9) Pictorial illusion and narration; (10) Hellenistic mosaics; (11) Hellenistic architecture: theatrical and scholarly forms; (12) Alexandria and the Pharaoh; Appendixes: (I) The chronology of Hellenistic sculpture; (II) The ruler cult and its imagery; (III) Aspects of royal patronage; (IV) Bactria and India; (V) The tomb at Belevi.

Abbreviations, p.291–92. Bibliography, p.293–301. Notes, p.303–19. Sources of illustrations, p.321–23. Index, p.325–29.

I121 Richter, Gisela Marie Augusta. A handbook of Greek art. 9th ed. N.Y., Da Capo Press, 1987. 431p. il.

See GLAH 1:I107 for 6th ed. 7th ed. 1974; 8th ed. 1983.

The 9th ed. incorporates corrections listed as corrigenda in the 8th ed. Two recent publications are added to the Addendum to the bibliography. No other changes.

I122 Robertson, Martin. A shorter history of Greek art. N.Y., Cambridge Univ. Pr., 1981. xi, 240p. il.

See GLAH 1:I108 for original 2v. ed.

"This is a shortened version of A History of Greek Art . . .. Since it is less than a quarter the length the scope is very different. . . . The book is meant to be a more or less self-sufficient introduction to the subject."—*Pref.*

Contents: (1) The seeds of Greek art: Geometric and Orientalising; (2) The beginning of monumental Greek art: the early Archaic period; (3) Ripe Archaic art; (4) The great change: Late Archaic and Early Classical; (5) The Classical moment; (6) Developments into the fourth century; (7) The second change: Classical to Hellenistic; (8) Hellenistic art.

Notes, p.209–15. Abbreviations and bibliography, p.217–18. Indexes, p.225–36 (general index), p.236–40 (museums and collections).

I123 Whitley, James. Style and society in dark age Greece: the changing face of a pre-literate society, 1100–700 BC. N.Y., Cambridge Univ. Pr., 1991. xx, 225p. il., plates (New studies in archaeology)

"This book is a study of the connexions between style, burial and society in Athens during the so-called Dark Ages (1100–700 BC). . . . My main proposition is that art historical and historical research, particularly in the absence of written sources, must go hand in hand."—*Pref. and ackn.*

Contents: (1) Introduction; (2) Theoretical perspectives; (3) Athens and Attica: the historical background; (4) Methods and chronology; (5) Athens: the analysis of the burials; (6) The wider Dark Age world; (7) Conclusions.

List of tables, xiv. List of abbreviations, p.xix–xx. Appendix: grave index, p.199–208. Bibliography, p.209–20. Index of sites and regions, p.221–22. General index, p.223–25.

I124 Woodford, Susan. An introduction to Greek art. Ithaca, Cornell Univ. Pr., 1986. xiii, 186p., il. (part col.), plates.

"The purpose of this book is to make the beauty of Greek art more readily accessible and comprehensible."—*Pref.* A slight but informed introduction for the general reader.

Note on terminology, p.xi. Glossary, p.177–80. Further reading, p.181. Index, p.183–86.

Etruria and Rome

I125 Andreae, Bernard. The art of Rome. Trans. from the German by Robert Erich Wolf. N.Y., Abrams, 1977. 655p. il. (part col.)

Trans. of L'art de l'ancienne Rome. Paris, Mazenod, 1973 (L'Art et les grandes civilisations, 4). German ed., Freiburg, Herder, 1973, entitled Römische Kunst (Ars antiqua, 5). The standard survey of Roman art and architecture, authoritative, richly illustrated and documented.

Contents: Introduction. Part one: City to Empire in the world of the Spirit; (I) "These are imperial arts, and worthy thee"; (II) The rise of Rome: toward political hegemony; (III) The Roman revolution: toward artistic hegemony; (IV) The age of Augustus; (V) The Julio-Claudian house; (VI) The Flavian house; (VII) Nerva and Trajan; (VIII) Hadrian and Antoninus Pius; (IX) Marcus Aurelius, Lucius Verus Commodus: the last of the Antonines; (X) The Severan Dynasty; (XI) The soldier-emperors; (XII) The tetrarchy and the triumph of Christianity under Constantine the Great. Part two: The image as document; Documentary photographs; Identification of the photographs. Part three: Description of archaeological sites: architecture and urbanism in the Roman Empire. Part four: Roman architecture: techniques and types. Part five: A lexicon; Events in Roman history; Imperial genealogies; Biographical information; Terms in art and architecture.

Notes to the text, p.629–30. Bibliography, p.[631]–45. Index, p.646–55.

I126 L'art des peuples italiques: 3000 à 300 avant J.-C. [Naples], Electa Napoli, 1993. 406p. il. (part col.), maps.

Catalog of the exhibition, Musée Rath, Geneva (1993–94), and other locations, based upon the Etruscan and Roman collections of the Musée d'art et d'histoire, Geneva and private collections in Switzerland.

Glossaire, p.403–4. Abréviations, p.405. Index de prêts, p.406.

I127 Brendel, Otto. Etruscan art. 2d ed. New Haven, Yale Univ. Pr., 1995. 535p. il., map. (Yale University Press pelican history of art)

A monumental study, published posthumously in 1978, and revised and updated for this second ed. "Otto Brendel's exploration of the art, culture and society of Etruria takes us through the four main periods of creativity: the Villanovan and Orientalizing era, the Archaic era, the Classical era, and culminates in the Hellenistic era when Etruscan art became extinct."—*Pub. note.*

Contents: Editor's foreword. Part one: the Villanovan and Orientalizing periods. Part two: the early and middle Archaic periods. Part three: the late Archaic period. Part four: the Classical era: the fifth century. Part five: the Classical era: the fourth century. Part six: the Hellenistic period: late manifestations and legacy.

List of abbreviations, p.[433]. Notes, p.435–80. Select bibliography, p.[481]–85. Additional bibliography 1978–1994 [by Francesca R. Serra Ridgway], p.[486]–513. List of illustrations, p.[514]–21. Index, p.[522]–35.

I128 Buranelli, Francesco. The Etruscans: legacy of a lost civilization from the Vatican Museums. With an introd. and trans. by Nancy Thomson de Grummond. Memphis, Lithograph Pub. Co., 1992. 207p. il.

Catalog of an exhibition. Well-illustrated introduction for a general audience.

Glossary, p.200–01. Suggestions for further reading on the Etruscans in English, p.202. Bibliography, p.203–07.

I129 Civiltà dei Romani. A cura di Salvatore Settis. Milano, Electa, 1990–1993. 4v. il. (part col.), maps, plans.

Monumental collaborative study of Roman civilization, including the arts, architecture, and material culture. Richly illustrated.

Bibliography and index in each vol.

Contents: (1) La città, il territorio, l'impero; (2) Il potere e l'esercito; (3) Il rito e la vita privata; (4) Un linguaggio comune.

I130 Cristofani, Mauro. L'arte degli etruschi: produzione e consumo. Torino, Einaudi, 1978. xxiii, 227p. il., plates (Saggi, 605)

Important, somewhat polemical study of Etruscan art by an authority, emphasizing culture over material culture.

Contents: L'arte degli Etruschi; Storia di una problema; Il retaggio protostorico e l'influenza dell'arte orientale; Il contatto con il mondo greco e l'organizzazione delle maestranze artistiche; Maestranze greche e maestranze locali; Arte rurale e arte urbana; Il problema della recezione dell'arte classica; L'Ellenismo.

Notes at ends of chapters. Indice dei luoghi e dei nomi, p.[217]–27.

I131 Etruscan life and afterlife: a handbook of Etruscan studies. Ed. by Larissa Bonfante. Detroit, Wayne State Univ. Pr., 1986. xxviii, 289p. il., maps.

A collection of studies "designed to complement more popular works, and to lead students back to the standard texts, as well as to more specialized literature in the field."—*Pref.*

Contents: (I) Rediscovery, by Nancy Thomson de Grummond; (II) History: land and peoples, by Mario Torelli; (III) International contacts: commerce, trade, and foreign affairs, by Jean MacIntosh Turfa; (IV) Art, by Marie-Françoise Briguet; (V) Architecture, by Friedhelm Prayon; (VI) Coinage, by David Enders Tripp; (VII) An archaeological introduction to the Etruscan language, by Emeline Richardson; (VIII) Daily life and afterlife, by Larissa Bonfante.

Abbreviations, p.xvi–xviii. Bibliographies at ends of chapters. Selected readings, p.279–81. Index, p.282–91.

I132 Gli Etruschi: mille anni di civiltà. [Dir. responsabile, Giovanna Magi. Coord. e consulenza, Maurizio Martinelli. Introd. a cura di Giovannangelo Camporeale, Gabriele Morolli]. Firenze, Bonechi, 1990– . (1)v. 640p., col. il., maps, plans.

Regional survey of Etruscan art and civilization. Published to date: v.1.

Glossario, v.1, p.37–40.

I133 Grant, Michael. Art in the Roman Empire. N.Y., Routledge, 1995. xxii, 146p. il., maps

"I have chosen the title Art in the Roman Empire, rather than the more usual one of Roman Art, because I want readers to appreciate that all the art of the Roman empire was not concentrated in Rome. . . . I have avoided attempting yet another general handbook, and have instead tried my best to be selective."—*Introd.* A popular treatment by a well-known classicist.

Contents: Introduction. Part I: Sculpture. Part II: Architecture. Part III: Other arts; Epilogue.

List of Roman Emperors, p.123–24. Notes, p.125–33. Select bibliography, p.134–41. Index, p.142–46.

I134 A handbook of Roman art: a comprehensive survey of all the arts of the Roman world. Ed. by Martin Henig. Ithaca, Cornell Univ. Pr., 1983. 288p. il. (part col.), plates.

Expressly conceived as a companion to Richter's classic Handbook of Greek art (GLAH 2:I121). An informed survey of Roman art arranged according to media, by a group of specialists.

Contents: Introduction; (1) Early Roman art, by Tom Rasmussen; (2) Architecture, by Thomas Blagg; (3) Sculpture, by Anthony Bonanno; (4) Wall painting and stucco, by Joan Liversidge; (5) Mosaics, by David Smith; (6) The luxury arts: decorative metalwork, engraved gems and jewellery, by Martin Henig; (7) Coins and medals, by Richard Reece; (8) Pottery, by Anthony King; (9) Terracotta revetments, figurines and lamps, by Donald Bailey; (10) Glass, by Jennifer Price; (11) Epigraphy, by Robert Ireland; (12) Late antiquity, by Richard Reece.

Abbreviations, p.[249]. Vessel forms, p.[250]. Glossary, p.[251]–54. Notes, p.[256]–70. Select general bibliography, p.[271]–80. Index, p.[281]–88.

I135 Hannestad, Niels. Roman art and imperial policy. Højbjerg, Jutland Archaeological Society (Distr. by Aarhus University Press, 1986). 485p. il. (part col.), maps, plans, ports.

Trans. of Romersk kunst som propaganda. Copenhagen, Berlingske, 1976 (Berlingske leksikonbibliotek, 103).

"Most of what we normally perceive as art during the Roman period may be regarded as more or less direct manifestations of propaganda. Art served primarily . . . to strengthen the power and reputation of the person who paid for or commissioned it. . . . My intention in this study . . . is . . . to elucidate the form and function of state art and propaganda in Rome in the Republican and Imperial periods."—*Introd.*

Contents: Preface; Introduction; (I) The Republic; (II) The Augustan principate; (III) The Julio-Claudians; (IV) The Flavians; (V) The adoptive Emperors; (VI) The Severans; (VII) The Dominate; Conclusion; Epilogue.

Notes, p.351–422. Bibliography, p.423–58. Abbreviations, p.458–60. Index, p.465–73. Dansk resumé, p.475–78. Chronological table of emperors, p.479–83.

I136 Heintze, Helga, Freifrau von. Roman art. [Reprint] N.Y., Universe Books (Distr. to the trade by St. Martin's Press, 1990). 200p. il. (part col.) (The Universe history of art and architecture)

Repr. of 1972 ed. Trans. of Römische Kunst. Stuttgart, Belser, 1969 (Belser Stilgeschichte, 3); repr. München, Deutscher Taschenbuch Verlag, 1978. Respected survey.

Contents: Architecture; Relief sculpture; Painting and mosaics; Statues; Portrait sculpture.

Bibliography, p.193–95. Index, p.196–200.

I137 Ramage, Nancy H., and Ramage, Andrew. The Cambridge illustrated history of Roman art. Cambridge, Cambridge Univ. Pr., 1991. 304p. il. (part col.), ports.

"The book is intended first and foremost for students and readers who are launching into the study of Roman art perhaps for the first time. We . . . have tried to explain what may not be obvious in terms of background, be it linguistic, historical, or religious."—*Pref.* Solid, well-written historical survey.

Glossary, p.290–93. Select bibliography, p.294–96. Index, p.298–304.

I138 ———. Roman art: Romulus to Constantine. 2d ed. Englewood Cliffs, N.J., Prentice Hall, 1996. 320p. il. (part col.)

"This book is intended first and foremost for students and readers who are launching into the study of Roman art perhaps for the first time."—*Pref.*

Contents: Introduction; (1) The Villanovan and Etruscan forerunners, 1000–200 BC; (2) The Roman Republic, 200–27 BC; (3) Augustus and the Imperial idea, 27 BC–AD 14; (4) The Julio-Claudians, AD 14–68; (5) The Flavians, AD 68–98; (6) Trajan, optimus princeps, AD 98–117; (7) Hadrian and the Classical revival, AD 117–138; (8) The Antonines, AD 138–193; (9) The Severans, AD 193–235; (10) The soldier emperors, AD 235–284; (11) The tetrarchs, AD 284–312; (12) Constantine, AD 307–337 and the aftermath.

Roman emperors, p.288. Ancient authors, p.289. Glossary, p.290–93. Select bibliography, p.294–96. Index, p.298–304.

I139 Rasenna: storia e civiltà degli Etruschi. [By] Massimo Pallottino . . . [et al.] Pref. di Giovanni Pugliese Carratelli. Milano, Libri Scheiwiller, 1986. xiv, 729p. il. (part col.) (Antica madre, 9)

Monumental survey of Etruscan history and culture, each chapter by a leading authority.

Contents: Immagini e realtà della civiltà etrusca, di Massimo Pallottino; La storia, di Mario Torelli; Economia e società, di Mauro Cristofani; La religione, di Mario Torelli; Vita privata, di Giovannangelo Camporeale; I documenti scritti e la lingua, di Massimo Pallottino; Urbanistica e architettura, di Giovanni Colona; L'arte, di Francesco Roncalli; Topografia storica della regione etrusca, di Guido A. Mansuelli; Appendice: Gli Etruschi e la Magna Grecia, di Maria Bonghi Jovino; La stele di Lemnos, di Carlo de Simone; Il "liber linteus" di Zagabria, di Francesco Roncalli.

Bibliographies at end of chapters. Abbreviazioni, p.728.

I140 Spivey, Nigel Jonathan. Etruscan art. London, Thames and Hudson, 1997. 216p. il. (part col.), map (World of art)

Contents: Introduction: Etruria and the limits of demystification; (1) The emergence of Etruscan culture; (2) Etruria and the orient; (3) Etruria hellenized; (4) The Etruscan cities as centres of art; (5) From Etruscan Rome to Roman Etruria; (6) The Etruscan legacy.

Timeline, p.200. Chronology, p.201–2. Bibliography and sources, p.203–6. Index, p.213–16.

I141 Sprenger, Maja, and Bartolini, Gilda. The Etruscans: their history, art, and architecture. [Foreword, by Max Hirmer.] Photographs by Max and Albert Hirmer. Trans. from the German and the Italian by Robert Erich Wolf. N.Y., Abrams, 1983. 176, [211]p. il. (part col.)

Trans. of Die Etrusker. München, Hirmer, 1977.

An important and comprehensive re-examination of eight centuries of Etruscan art, richly illustrated with 288 photographs, most made for this publication.

Contents: Outline of Etruscan history, by Maja Sprenger; Development and characteristics of Etruscan art; The artistic creations; Plates; Documentary catalogue of the plates, by Gilda Bartolini.

Appendices: Chronology of Etruscan history, p.161–62. The gods, p.162. The twelve cities of the Etruscan Confederacy, p.162. Concise glossary, p.163–64. Bibliography, p.164–67. List of works and monuments by location, p.168–71. Index, p.172–76.

I142 Strong, Donald Emrys. Roman art. Prepared for press by J. M. C. Toynbee. 2d ed., rev. and annot. under the editorship of Roger Ling. N.Y., Penguin Books, 1988. 408p. il. (Pelican history of art)

See GLAH 1:A135 for previous ed. "The guiding principle of the new edition has been to interfere with the text as little as possible and to concentrate on providing full annotation, absent in the first two [printings]."—*Pref. to the second ed.* See GLAH 1:I135 for the circumstances that caused this lacuna.

List of abbreviations, p.[329]–31. Notes, p.[332]–71. Glossary, p.[372]–74. Bibliography, p.[375]–87. Index, p.[395]–406.

I143 Torelli, Mario. L'arte degli Etruschi. Con un'appendice di Giampiero Pianu. Roma, Laterza, 1985. 356p. il. (part col.) (Grande opere)

"One of the best recent surveys of Etruscan art, expressly focusing upon craftsmanship (produzione artigianale)."—Brendel, Etruscan art (GLAH 2:I127) [bib supp].

Contents: Premessa; (1) La fase formativa; (2) La cultura orientalizzante; (3) L'arcaismo; (4) Il V secolo; (5) La cultura figurativa della koiné; (6) Il tardo ellenismo in Etruria; Postfazione.

Bibliografia, p.[337]–43. Glossario, p.[345]–46. Indice dei nomi, p.[349]–53. Fonti iconografiche, p.[354].

I144 Turcan, Robert. L'art romain dans l'histoire: six siècles d'expressions de la romanité. Paris, Flammarion, 1995. 383p. il. (part col.)

A beautifully illustrated survey of Roman art. Focuses upon the art of Rome and Italy to the exclusion of provincial art.

Contents: Introduction: Problématique d'un art "romain"; (I) L'hommage des images aux morts; (II) La mémoire et la gloire; (III) Ut poesis pictura; les arrière-mondes du décor peint; (IV) Le classicisme augustéen; (V) Mutations d'un long siècle: de Tibère à Nerva; (VI) Quasi reddita jinventute: les années 100; (VII) Hadrien ou l'arbitre des arts; (VIII) La paix antoninienne; (IX) La crise et le tournant du siècle d'or; (X) Rome sévérienne; (XI) Temps d'anarchie militaire; ferments et foisonnements précurseurs; (XII) La brique et la courbe ou l'apogée d'un crépuscule; Epilogue.

Chronologie, p.362–63. Glossaire, p.364–66. Bibliographie, p.367–[75]. Principales abréviations, p.[375]. Index des noms propres, p.[376]–[380]. Index des lieux et monuments, p.381–83.

I145 Virginia Museum of Fine Arts. Art of late Rome and Byzantium in the Virginia Museum of Fine Arts. By Anna Gonosová and Christine Kondoleon. Technical entries by Lawrence Becker . . . [et al.] Richmond, Va., The Museum, 1994. xvii, 451p. il., map.

"The collection of Late Roman and Byzantine art in the Virginia Museum of Fine Arts consists of 136 objects that date between A.D. 250 and 1450 and come from both the eastern and western parts of the Late Roman and Byzantine Empires. All major categories of artistic media are represented."—*Introd.*

Contents: The Catalogue: (1) Jewelry; (2) Domestic art; (3) Coins; (4) Works of doubtful authenticity; Appendices: technical and material studies.

Abbreviations, p.xv. Glossary, p.416–19. Bibliography, p.421–43. Concordance, p.444–45. Index, p.447–51.

I146 Walker, Susan. Roman art. Cambridge, Mass., Harvard Univ. Pr., 1991. 72p. il. (part col.)

"This is a very personal view of Roman art. Rather than attempt in a short book a history of artistic developments at Rome from the early days on the Palatine to the rise of the Christian city, I have chosen to write about four important themes."—*Pref.*

Contents: (1) Learning to love luxury: the Romans and Greek art; (2) Roman portraits; (3) From Bath to Baalbek: public art in the Roman empire; (4) The Romans at home.

Further reading, p.71. Index, p.72.

I147 Die Welt der Etrusker: archäologische Denkmäler aus Museen der sozialistischen Länder. [Katalogred., Max Kunze, Volker Kästner]. Berlin, Henschelverlag, 1988. 436p. il. (part col.)

Catalog of the exhibition, Altes Museum, Berlin (1988), and other locations. Documents the rich Etruscan collections of the DDR, Hungary, Poland, and Russia. See also the proceedings of a related symposium: Die Welt der Etrusker: internationales Kolloquium. Hrsg. von Huberta Heres und Max Kunze. Berlin, Akademie-Verlag, 1990.

Contents: Die Welt der Etrusker: zur Einführung; (A) Die Formierung der etruskischen Kultur im Rahmen der italischen Eisenzeit (10.-7. Jh. v.u.Z.); (B) Die Blütezeit der etruskischen Stadtkulturen in Italian (7. bis Mitte 5. Jh. v.u.Z.); (C) Die Etrusker in Kampanien; (D) Die etruskischen Stadtkulturen von der 2. Hälfte des 5. Jh. v.u.Z. bis zum Hellenismus und der Eingliederung in den römischen Staat; (E) Goldschmiedekunst; (F) Spiegel; (G) Steinschneidekunst; (H) Münzen; (I) Der etruskische Norden und die Auswirkungen der etruskischen Kultur auf Mitteleuropa; (K) Fälschungen etruskischer Kunstwerke; (L) Etruskische Kunst in Berlin.

Verzeichnis der Fachausdrücke, p.425–27. Abkürzungsverzeichnis zur Literatur, p.428–30. Ortsverzeichnis, p.431–32. Verzeichnis der älteren Sammlungen, p.433–34. Mythologisches Register, p.435–36.

I148 Zanker, Paul. The power of images in the Age of Augustus. Trans. by Alan Shapiro. Ann Arbor, Univ. of Michigan Pr., 1988. vii, 385p. il.

"Art and architecture are mirrors of a society. . . . This book tries to illustrate how a fundamental change in the political system led to the creation of a new visual language that both reflects an altered mentality and contributed significantly to the process of change. . . . This book is based upon lectures delivered in Ann Arbor [Michigan] and at the American Academy in Rome in 1983 and 1984 as the Thomas Spencer Jerome Series."—*Introd.* An unusually imaginative and influential study.

Contents: Introduction; (1) Conflict and contradiction in the imagery of the dying Republic; (2) Rival images: Octavian, Antony, and the struggle for sole power; (3) The great turning point: intimations of a new Imperial style; (4) The Augustan program of cultural renewal; (5) The mythical foundations of the new Rome; (6) Form and meaning of the new mythology; (7) The new imagery in the private sphere; (8) The Roman Empire of Augustus: Imperial myth and cult in east and west; Conclusion.

Notes and references for further reading, p.341–70. Illustration sources, p.371–79. Index of sites and museums, p.381–85.

CELTIC AND GERMANIC

I149 Celtic art. Ed. by Barry Raftery with the collab. of Paul-Marie Duval . . . [et al.] [Paris], Unesco; Flammarion, 1990. 171p. il. (part col.), maps (Unesco collection of representative works. Art album series)

Accessible survey.

Contents: Introduction, by Otto-Herman Frey; (1) The rise of Celtic art, by Venceslas Kruta; (2) The climax of Celtic art, by Miklós Szabó; (3) Celtic coins, by Paul-Marie Duval; (4) The end of Celtic art on the continent: later Celtic art in the southern region, by Gilbert Kaenel; (5) Celtic art in Britain and Ireland, by Andrew Sherratt and Barry Raftery; (6) Aftermath: Celtic Christianity, by Michael Ryan; Conclusion: The unity of Celtic art, by Paul-Marie Duval.

Chronology, p.158–59. Glossary, p.161–65. Bibliography, p. 166–67. Index, p.168–70.

I150 The Celts. Ed. by Sabatino Moscati . . . [et al.] N.Y., Rizzoli, 1991. 711p. il. (part col.)

Trans. of: I Celti. Milano, Bompiani, 1991. Published in conjunction with the exhibition, Palazzo Grassi (Venice, 1991).

Monumental survey of Celtic civilization.

Contents: In search of the ancient Celts; The age of the princes, sixth century B.C.; The formation of the La Tène culture, fifth century B.C.; The first historical expansion, fourth century B.C.; The age of the warriors, third century B.C.; The Celts of Iberia; The Era of the Oppida, second–first century B.C.; The island Celts; The Christian Celts; Appendix: the ancient writers, ed. by Luana Kruta Poppi.

General bibliography, p.[691]–700. Index, p.[701]–10.

I151 Das Keltische Jahrtausend. Hrsg. von Hermann Dannheimer und Rupert Gebhard. Mainz am Rhein, Zabern, 1993. xv, 400p. il. (part col.) (Ausstellungskataloge der Prähistorischen Staatssammlung, 23)

At head of title: Prähistorische Staatssammlung München, Museum für Vor- und Frühgeschichte.

Catalog of the exhibition, the Museum (1993), and other locations.

Seeks to provide an archeological overview of 1,000 years of Celtic culture.

Contents: Einführung; Gesellschaft; Besiedlung; Mensch, Natur und Umwelt; Kunst; Kult; Wirtschaft und Handel; Keltisches Geld; Nachbarvölker; Keltisches Tradition; Katalog der Ausstellung.

Glossar, p.369–71. Zeittafel, p.372. Verzeichnisse, p.373. Verzeichnis der abgekürzte zitierten Literatur, p.374–92. Quellenverzeichniss, p.393.

I152 Kruta, Venceslas. The Celts of the West. Photographs by Werner Forman. Trans. by Alan Sheridan. London, Orbis, 1985. 128p. col. il. (Echoes of the ancient world)

Accessible introduction by an authority. Original language undetermined.

Contents: The Celts of the Western Seaboard enter history; Daily life and work; Society; The heroic ideal; Art; The gods; Epilogue.

Bibliography, p.124. Index, p.125–27.

I153 Laing, Lloyd Robert, and Laing, Jennifer. Art of the Celts. London, Thames and Hudson, 1992. 216p. il. (part col.) (World of art)

Readable survey.

Contents: (1) Introduction; (2) The beginnings of Celtic art; (3) La Tène art in Europe; (4) Art in Iron Age Britain and Ireland; (5) The renaissance of Celtic art, c.400–1200; (6) Celtic revivals.

Glossary, p.209–10. Select bibliography, p.211–12. Location of objects, p.212–13. Index, p.214–16.

I154 Lessing, Erich. Les Celtes. Racontés en images par Erich Lessing. Textes écrits par Venceslas Kruta. Préf. Paul-Marie Duval. Pour le chapitre "Les Celtes danubies et l'expansion balkanique," Miklós Szabó. Fribourg, Hatier, 1982. 255p. il. (part col.)

Beautifully illustrated evocation of Celtic art and culture.

Quelques dates marquantes du passé celtique. Index des documents. Bibliographie (all unpaginated).

Contents: La redécouverte du passé celtique; Les Celtes, entre la préhistoire et l'histoire; De la forêt hercynienne aux Apennins; Les Celtes danubies et l'expansion balkanique; Les oppida des Iie et Ier siècles avant notre ère; Celtes païens des Iles britanniques; Les Génie celtique et civilisation européenne; Le monde d'images des Celtes.

I155 Megaw, M. Ruth, and Megaw, Vincent. Celtic art: from its beginnings to the Book of Kells. N.Y., Thames and Hudson, 1989. 288p. il. (part col.), maps.

"Our central theme is the prehistory of the Celts of the continent and basically, this book is as much archaeology as it is art history."—*Pref.*

Contents: Introduction; (1) The antecedents of Celtic Iron Age art; (2) The chieftainly art of the early La Tène Celts; (3) The arts of expansion; (4) The sword bearers: the Celts of the later third and second centuries BC; (5) Cities, centralization and coinage; (6) Insular pre-Roman Celtic art; Epilogue: into the Christian era.

Chronological table, p.[258]. Bibliography, p.259–76. Sources of illustrations, p.276–79. Index, p.280–88.

I156 Musée des antiquités nationales. L'art celtique de la Gaule au Musée des antiquités nationales. Par Alain Duval. Paris, Ministère de la culture, de la communication, du Bicentenaire et des grands travaux; Ed. de la Réunion des musées nationaux, 1989. 135p. il. (part col.), maps (part col.) (Monographies des musées de France)

Contents: (1) Le premier style; (2) Les débuts du style végétal continu; (3) Du style végétal continu au style plastique; (4) Le style plastique; (5) Le style sévère; Conclusion.

Chronologie, p.14. Orientation bibliographique, p.133–35.

EARLY CHRISTIAN—BYZANTINE

I157 Age of spirituality: a symposium. Ed. by Kurt Weitzmann. N.Y., Metropolitan Museum of Art, published in assoc. with Princeton Univ. Pr., 1980. viii, 174p. il.

Proceedings of a symposium held in conjunction with the exhibition of the same title (see following entry).

Contents: Introduction, by Kurt Weitzmann; After Gibbon's decline and fall, by Arnaldo Momigliano; Art and society in Late Antiquity, by Peter R. L. Brown; Constantinople: the rise of a new capital in the East, by Hans-Georg Beck; The Imperial heritage of Early Christian Art, by Beat Brenk; A shadow outline of virtue: the classical heritage of Greek Christian literature (second to seventh century), by Ihor Ševčenko; The continuity of Classical art: culture, myth, and faith, by George M. A. Hanfmann; Christology: a central problem of Early Christian theology and art, by Massey H. Shepherd, Jr.; Success and failure in Late Antique church planning, by Richard Krautheimer; Christian imagery: growth and impact, by Ernst Kitzinger.

Notes at ends of chapters. Index, p.165–74.

I158 Age of spirituality: late antique and early Christian art, third to seventh century. Ed. by Kurt Weitzmann.

N.Y., Metropolitan Museum of Art, published in assoc. with Princeton Univ. Pr., 1979. xxxi, 735p. il., plates.

Monumental catalog of the pioneering exhibition, Metropolitan Museum of Art (1977–78).

Contents: (I) The imperial realm; (II) The classical realm; (III) The secular realm; (IV) The Jewish realm; (V) The Christian realm. Appendix: Chronology.

Glossary, p.674–81. Bibliography, p.682–723. Index, p.724–35.

I159 Art of the Christian world, A.D. 200–1500: a handbook of styles and forms. By Yves Christe . . . [et al.] N.Y., Rizzoli, 1982. 504p. il., maps, plans.

Trans. of Le Monde chrétien. Paris, Bibliothèque des arts, 1982. British ed. has title: Art in the Christian world, 300–1500. A quick-reference handbook. Brief period introductions, followed by maps and line drawings of "carefully selected buildings and monuments, sculptures, and other objets d'art."—*Pref.*

Contents: Christian art from its origins to the beginning of the 11th century; Byzantine art from the 9th to the 15th century; Romanesque art and the origins of Gothic art; Gothic art.

Glossary, p.503–04.

I160 Arte profana e arte sacra a Bisanzio. A cura di Antonio Iacobini, Enrico Zanini. Roma, Argos, 1995. 671p. il. (Milion, 3)

Papers presented to the international conference, "L'arte profana a Bisanzio," Rome (1990), now revised. Texts in Italian, English, French, or German.

Contents: Il Foro di Teodosio I a Costantinopoli, di Claudia Barsanti; Cisterne a Dara, di Italo Furlan; Il restauro giustinianeo delle mura di Palmira, di Enrico Zanini; Il palazzo di Qasr ibn-Wardan dopo gli scavi e i restauri, di Fernanda de' Maffei; Les thèmes iconographiques profanes dans la peinture monumentale byzantine du VIe au XVe siècle, di Jacqueline Lafontaine-Dosogne; Profane art in Byzantium?, di John Lindsay Opie; Archäologie und Denkmalpflege im Bereich des "Grossen Palastes" von Konstantinopel, di Werner Jobst; Nuovi mosaici pavimentali nella regione di Hamā, di Abdurrazzaq Zaqzuq; Il mosaico pavimentale d'epoca umayyade della chiesa di S. Giorgio nel Deir al-Adas (Siria), di Raffaella Farioli Campanati; L'Ascensione di Alessandro in un pluteo del Museo di Mistra, di Patrizia Angiolini Martinelli; I musici dell'affresco detto degli "Skomorochi" nella cattedrale della Santa Sofia a Kiev, di I. F. Točkaja, A. M. Zajaruznyj; Per una lettura musicologica dell'affresco detto degli "Skoromochi" nella cattedrale della Santa Sofia di Kiev, di Francesco Luisi; Sacred and profane: the locus of the political in middle Byzantine art, di Anthony Cutler; La cartografia bizantina, le sue fonti classiche e il suo rapporto con le arti figurative, di Mauro della Valle; L'Epitalamio di Andronico II. Una cronaca di nozze dalla Costantinopoli paleologa, di Antonio Iacobini; Raffigurazioni di strumenti agricoli in un manoscritto di Esiodo nella Biblioteca Ariostea di Ferrara, di Andrea Paribeni; I disegni nei manoscritti delle Opere i giorni di Esiodo; problemi della tradizione iconografica e testuale, di Giovanna Derenzini; Quelque observation sur les fragments du tissu "aux lions passants" de Siegburg: une proposition de reconstruction, di Laura d'Adamo; Le vesti nel "De cerimoniis aulae Byzantinae" di Costantino VII Porfirogenito, di Guido Fauro; I due medaglioni di Adana nel Museo Archeologico di Istanbul, di Asnû Bilban Yalçin; Arte e artigianato artistico profano nel Corpus degli oggetti d'arte bizantina in Italia, di Mara Bonfioli; The Mandylion at Monreale, di Ernst Kitzinger; Reimpiego di marmi bizantini a Torcello, di Alessandra Guiglia Guidobaldi; Il piatto d'argento con Nereide nella Galleria Sabauda di Torino, di Silvia Pasi; Pantaleone d'Amalfi e le porte bizantine in Italia meridionale, di Maria Vittoria Marini Clarelli; Il calamaio argenteo nel Tesoro del Duomo di Padova, di Giulia Grassi.

Notes at ends of chapters.

I161 Bank, A. V. (Alisa Vladimirovna). Byzantine art in the collections of Soviet museums. [Text and sel. by Alice Bank]. [Enl. ed.?] Leningrad, Aurora, 1985. 337, [1]p. chiefly il. (part col.)

Trans. of Vizantiiskoe iskusstvo v sobraniiakh Sovetskogo Soiza. Izd. 3-e, dop.

Well-illustrated survey of the rich Byzantine collections in the former Soviet Union.

Notes on the plates, p.[269]–[328]. Abbreviations, p.330–[35]. Bibliography, p.336–[338].

I162 Beckwith, John. Early Christian and Byzantine art. 2d (integrated) ed. N.Y., Penguin Books, 1979. 405p. il.

See GLAH 1:I149 for original ed.

"For the second edition it has proved necessary to make only one or two changes in the text, but the Notes and Bibliography have been extensively amplified."—*Foreword* [to the 2d ed.].

I163 Byzance et les images. Sous la dir. d'André Guillou et de Jannic Durand. Paris, La Documentation française, 1994. 379p. il. (Louvre conférences et colloques)

Proceedings of the symposium, Musée du Louvre (1992), held on the occasion of the exhibition, Byzance, l'art byzantin dans les collections publiques françaises (see following entry).

Contents: Le monde des images à Byzance, par André Guillou; Images sculptées et propagande impériale du IVe au VIe siècle: recherches récentes sur le colonnes honorifiques et les reliefs politiques à Byzance, par Jean-Pierre Sodini; L'attitude byzantine à l'égard des antiquités gréco-romaines, par Cyril Mango; L'image de culte et le portrait, par Gilbert Dagron; The emancipation of the Crucifixion, par Anna Kartsonis; Les images byzantines et leurs degrés de signification: l'example de l'Hodigitria, par Gordana Babić; The Emperor at St. Sophia: viewer and viewed, par Robin Cormack; Close encounters: contact between holy figures and the faithful as represented in Byzantine works of art, par Nancy Patterson Ševčenko; Uses of luxury: on the functions of consumption and symbolic capital in Byzantine culture, par Anthony Cutler; L'iconoclasme, par Todor Sabev.

Notes at ends of chapters. Index, p.371–77.

I164 Byzance, l'art byzantin dans les collections publiques francaises. [Coord. ed., Marie-Claude Bianchini.] Paris, Bibliothèque nationale; Ed. de la Réunion des musées nationaux, 1992. 528p. il. (part col.), facsims., geneal. tables, maps.

Monumental catalog of the exhibition, Musée du Louvre (1992), and other locations. See previous entry for the symposium held on this occasion.

As noted in the Introduction, French collections are especially rich in examples of the sumptuary arts of Byzantium: illuminated manuscripts, ivories, etc.

Contents: Introduction, par Jannic Durand; (1) Les origines: de Constantin à l'Iconoclasme; (2) L'Empire iconoclaste; (3) L'Empire des Macedoniens et des Comnènes; (4) L'empire latin et l'Empire de Paléologues.

Chronologie, p.502–07. Glossaire, p.508–09. Bibliographie des ouvrages cités, p.510–22. Expositions, p.523. Index, p.524–28.

I165 Byzantine and Post-Byzantine art. [Ed. by Acheimastou-Potamianou . . . (et al.) Trans. by Timothy Cullen, Thetis Xanthaki.] Athens, Ministry of Culture, 1985. 265p. il. (part col.)

Catalog of the exhibition, Old University, Athens, Greece (1985–86).

"The aim of the Exhibition of Byzantine and Post-Byzantine Art was to present works of art produced in the Byzantine period and after the fall of Constantinople . . . with special emphasis on those brought to light in the last twenty years."—*Introd.*

Contents: Sculpture—wood-carvings; Wall-paintings; Icons; Manuscripts; Goldsmith-work, silver, metalwork; Minor sculpture; Church embroideries; Ceramics; Coins.

Bibliography-abbreviations, p.252–62. Index of exhibits [i.e., index of exhibited objects], p.263. Iconographical index, p.264–65.

I166 Effenberger, Arne. Frühchristliche Kunst und Kultur: von den Anfängen bis zum 7. Jahrhundert. München, Beck, 1986. 383p. il. (part col.), [2] folded p. of plates, maps, plans.

Survey of early Christian art and civilization aimed at a popular audience.

Contents: Die Anfänge der christlichen Kunst; Spätantike und frühchristliche Denkmäler des 3. Jahrhunderts; Die Kunst im 4. Jahrhunderts; Die Kunst im 5. und 6. Jahrhunderts.

Literaturhinweise, p.332–51. Register, p.368–83.

I167 The glory of Byzantium: art and culture of the Middle Byzantine era, A.D. 843–1261. Ed. by Helen C. Evans and William D. Wixom. N.Y., Metropolitan Museum of Art (Distr. by Abrams, 1997). xxvii, 574p. il. (chiefly col.), map, plans.

Monumental catalog of the exhibition, Metropolitan Museum of Art (1997). "'The Glory of Byzantium' focuses on the four centuries that embrace the second great era of Byzantine culture (843–1261). . . . The exhibition and the accompanying catalogue explore four interrelated themes: the religious and secular cultures of the Byzantine Empire during its Second Golden Age; the empire's interactions with its Christian neighbors and rivals, its relations with the Islamic East, and its contact with the Latin West."—*Pref.*

Contents: Byzantine society and civilization, by Speros P. Vryonis, Jr.; Religious organization and church architecture, by Thomas. F. Mathews; Manuscripts, by Jeffrey C. Anderson; Popular imagery, by Annemarie Weyl Carr; Images of the court, by Henry Maguire; Secular architecture, by Robert G. Ousterhout; Luxury objects, by Ioli Kalavrezou; Ceramic arts of everyday life, by Eunice Dauterman Maguire; Christian neighbors, by Helen C. Evans; Kievan Rus', by Olenka Z. Pevny; The Bulgarians, by Joseph D. Alchermes; The Georgians, by S. Peter Crowe; The Armenians, by Helen C. Evans; Christians in the Islamic east, by Thelma K. Thomas; Crusader art, by Jaroslav Folda; Byzantium and the Islamic east, by Priscilla Soucek; Byzantine art and the Latin west, by William D. Wixon.

Lenders to the exhibition, p.xxii–xxiv. Contributors to the catalogue, p.xxv–xxvii. Notes to the essays, p.510–21. Bibliography, p.522–59. Glossary, p.560–62. Index, p.563–74.

I168 Gough, Michael. The origins of Christian art. N.Y., Praeger, [1973]. 216p. il. (part col.)

Introductory survey.

Contents: (1) Prologue: the classical world and its heritage; (2) Paganism baptized: Christian art before Constantine; (3) From Constantine to Justinian; (4) Justinian and after.

Bibliography, p.203–04. Index, p.212–16.

I169 Innovation in der Spätantike: Kolloquium Basel 6. und 7. Mai 1994. Hrsg. von Beat Brenk. Wiesbaden, Reichert, 1996. 455p. il., plates (Spätantike, frühes Christentum, Byzanz. Reihe B, Studien und Perspektiven, Bd. 1)

Proceedings of a symposium devoted to innovation in late antique, early Christian and Byzantine art, architecture, and iconography.

Includes bibliographical references.

I170 Kemp, Wolfgang. Christliche Kunst: ihre Anfänge, ihre Strukturen. München, Schirmer/Mosel, 1994. 307p. il. (part col.), 16p. of plates

Attempts to define the nature of Christian art through the interpretation of selected exemplars of early Christian art, mostly from the post-Constantinian period (5th–6th centuries).

Contents: Beziehungssinne; (1) "Multis modis"—"Auf vielerlei Weise"; (2) Bezugssysteme in Vergleich: Pagane und christliche Bildsummen; (3) Der "Grosse Code": Die Bibel und ihre frühchristliche Rezeption; (4) Die illustrierte Bibel als Geschichtsbuch und als visuelle Synthese; (5) "Argumentum Historiae": Die Mosaiken von Santa Maria Maggiore in Rom; (6) Chresis und Diakrisis: Über christliche Diptychen; (7) "Die Fuelle des Sinnes": die Bildertuer von Santa Sabina in Rom; Nachwort: "Spolia multa"—"Reiche Beute"; Nachbemerkung.

Anmerkungen, p.288–306.

I171 Kitzinger, Ernst. Byzantine art in the making: main lines of stylistic development in Mediterranean art, 3rd–7th century. Cambridge, Mass., Harvard Univ. Pr., 1977. xii, 175p. il. (part col.), plates.
A classic volume, based upon the author's lectures as Slade Professor of Fine Art at the University of Cambridge, 1974. "The book is concerned with art in the Mediterranean world from the third through the seventh century. . . . It will extend only to the pictorial arts and will not include architecture. It will be my purpose to trace, on the basis of a representative series of monuments, the main lines in the evolution of artistic forms."—*Introd.*

Contents: Introduction; (1) Ancient art in crisis; (2) Regeneration; (3) Fifth-century conflicts—1; (4) Fifth-century conflicts—2; (5) The Justinian synthesis; (6) Polarization and another synthesis—1; (7) Polarization and another synthesis—2; Epilogue.

Notes, p.129–53. Index of modern authors cited, p.167–69. General index, p.171–75.

I172 Koch, Guntram. Early Christian art and architecture: an introduction. London, SCM Pr., 1996. vii, 184p. il., 32 pages of plates.
"The present volume is an 'introduction' to the architecture and art of the early Christian period, not a 'history of early Christian art'."—*Postscript.*

Contents: (I) General; (II) Architecture; (III) Burials; (IV) Paintings and mosaics; (V) Sculptures; (VI) Small-scale forms of art; (VII) Museums and collections with Early Christian Art; (VIII) Bibliographies on individual chapters; (XI) Abbreviations; (X) Postscript.

Bibliographies on individual chapters, p.[160]–75. Abbreviations, p.[176]–77. Index, p. [180]–84.

I173 Maguire, Henry. Art and eloquence in Byzantium. Princeton, Princeton Univ. Pr., 1981. xxii, 148p. il. plates.
"The essential premise of this book is . . . that the sermons and hymns of the Byzantine church influenced the ways in which Byzantine artists illustrated narrative texts."—*Introd.* A thoughtful exploration.

Contents: (I) Rhetoric in the Byzantine church; (II) Description; (III) Antithesis; (IV) Hyperbole; (V) Lament; Conclusion.

Notes, p.[113]–41. Index, p.[143]–48.

I174 Mathews, Thomas F. The clash of gods: a reinterpretation of early Christian art. Princeton, Princeton Univ. Pr., 1993. x, 223p. il. (part col.)
"This is a study of that critical period of art when a new Christian pantheon replaced the Greco-Roman panoply of pagan gods."—*Ackn.* A radical reinterpretation of early Christian imagery, polemicizing against traditional attempts to interpret the imagery of early Christian art as an adaptation of imperial Roman imagery.

Contents: (1) The mistake of the emperor mystique; (2) The chariot and the donkey; (3) The magician; (4) Larger-than-life; (5) Christ chameleon; (6) Convergence; Epilogue.

List of abbreviations, p.181. Notes, p.183–203. List of figures, p.205–11. Index, p.213–23.

I175 Milburn, R. L. P. Early Christian art and architecture. Aldershot, England, Scolar Press, 1988. xviii, 318p. il., facsims., maps, plans.
"The purpose of this book is to survey the several elements of [the] Christian heritage from its early beginnings to the middle of the sixth century."—*Foreword.* Wide-ranging survey.

Contents: (1) Signs and symbols; (2) House-churches; (3) The catacombs I; (4) The catacombs II; (5) Stone carving; (6) Church buildings; (7) Church buildings in Asia; (8) Egypt: Nubia and Ethiopia: the churches of North Africa; (9) Greece and the Balkans; Spain; (10) Ravenna; (11) The foundations of Justinian; (12) Fonts and baptisteries; (13) Mosaic; (14) Carved ivories; (15) Arts and crafts; (16) Coins and gems; (17) Textiles; (18) Writings and illustrated books; Epilogue.

Bibliography, p.[306]–12. Index, p.[313]–18.

I176 Naissance des arts chrétiens: atlas de monuments paléochrétiens de la France. [Comité de red. Noël Duval . . . et al.] Paris, Imprimerie nationale, 1991. 434p. il. (chiefly col.), plans, ports.
Monumental atlas of Early Christian art in France. Texts by leading authorities.

Contents: Le premiers siècles du christianisme en Gaule; Sources écrites et numismatiques; Édifices de culte, décor architectural et mobilier liturgique; Sarcophages sculptés, mobilier funéraire et arts mineurs; Histoire de l'archéologie chrétienne.

Bibliographies at end of chapters. Références bibliographiques, p.369–86. Glossaire, p.387–404. Index nominum, p.405–20. Index topographique, p.421–34.

I177 Les premiers monuments chrétiens de la France. Sous la dir. scientifique de Noël Duval. Introd. de Jean Guyon. Paris, Picard; Ministère de la culture et de la francophonie, Direction du patrimoine, Sous-direction de l'archéologie, 1995– . (3)v. il., maps, plans. (Atlas archéologiques de la France)
Archeological atlas of Early Christian monuments in France.

Contents: (1) Sud-Est et Corse; (2) Sud-Ouest et Centre; (3) Ouest, Nord et Est.

Includes bibliographical references.

I178 Rodley, Lyn. Byzantine art and architecture: an introduction. N.Y., Cambridge Univ. Pr., 1994. xiv, 380p. il., maps, plans.
"This book is directed towards university students of either art history or Byzantine studies, and others whose interest in Byzantine art and architecture demands more than a popular treatment. . . . My object, then, has been to offer a brief survey of selected examples of Byzantine art and architecture, discussion of the particular difficulties presented by some of this material, and assessment of the issues, controversies and approaches it has generated. I hope thus to equip the student with a critical framework with which to approach the more specialized scholarly literature."—*Pref.*

Contents: Introduction; (1) The early Christian period; (2) The sixth century; (3) The dark ages and iconoclasm; (4) The Macedonian dynasty; (5) The Comnene dynasty;

(6) The Latin occupation of Constantinople; (7) Palaiologan period; (8) Approaches to the study of Byzantine art and architecture; Appendices: (1) Armenian art and architecture; (2) The Copts; (3) Byzantine ceramics; (4) Byzantine coins and seals; (5) Byzantine emperors.

List of abbreviations, p.[xi]. Glossary, p.[355]–60. Select bibliography, p.[361]–63. Sources of plans, p.[364]–67. Index, p.[370]–80.

I179 Schug-Wille, Christa. Art of the Byzantine world. Text by Christa Schug-Wille. [Trans. from the German by E. M. Hatt.] N.Y., Abrams, [1969.] 263p. il. (part. col.), map. (Panorama of world art)

Trans. of Byzanz und seine Welt. Baden-Baden, Holle, 1969. French and Italian eds., 1970.

Solid survey.

Contents: Art of the Early Christian Church; Constantine and Theodosius; Justinian and Ravenna; Justinian and Byzantium; The Macedonian Renaissance and Byzantine Classicism; The spread of Byzantine art in the west; Late Byzantine art; The spread of Byzantine art in the east: Serbia, Macedonia, and Romania; Russian art.

Chronological tables, p.253–55. Bibliography, p.257–59. Index, p.260–62.

I180 Spätantike und frühes Christentum. [Hrsg. des Katalogs und Ausstellungsleitung: H. Beck und P.C. Bol im Auftrag des Dezernats Kultur und Freizeit der Stadt Frankfurt am Main]. Frankfurt am Main, Liebieghaus Museum Alter Plastik, 1983. xiii, 698p. il.

Monumental catalog of the exhibition, Liebieghaus (1983). A major exhibition catalog devoted to the evolution of late antique and early Christian art, with special attention to the historical, philosophical, and religious background.

Contents: Vorwort; (I) Die Christen und der Stadt; (II) Die Religionen im Römischen Reich; (III) THEIOS ANER [GK]; (IV) Die Christen und die Kunst; Katalog.

Leihgeber, p.xi–xiii.

I181 Weitzmann, Kurt, and Kessler, Herbert L. The frescoes of the Dura synagogue and Christian art. Washington, D.C., Dumbarton Oaks Research Library and Collection, 1990. xiv, 202p. il., plates.

Important study of the parallels between the 3d-century fresco panels at the Dura Europas synagogue and early Christian art.

Contents: Part I, by Kurt Weitzmann, devoted to the individual panels and their Christian parallels; Part II, by Herbert L. Kessler, devoted to the program and structure of the frescoes.

Includes bibliographical references. Selected bibliography, p.185–95. Index, p.197–202.

I182 Wharton, Annabel Jane. Art of empire: painting and architecture of the Byzantine periphery: a comparative study of four provinces. University Park, Pennsylvania State Univ. Pr., 1988. 198p. il.

"In this study I hope to show how a context in the hinterlands of the Empire affected the making of all provincial buildings—great and small. Local traditions and distinct patterns of patronage made their marks on even the most cosmopolitan structures. At the same time, I argue that the relative receptivity of the provinces to metropolitan artistic conventions indicates the ideological power of those conventions."—*Chapter I.*

Notes, p.[165]–87. Index of names, p.[190]–95. Iconographic index, p.[197]–98.

ISLAMIC

I183 Atil, Esin. The age of Sultan Süleyman the Magnificent. Washington, D.C., National Gallery of Art; N.Y., Abrams, 1987. 356p. il. (part col.)

Catalog of the exhibition, National Gallery of Art (1987), and other locations. Authoritative survey of the efflorescence of Ottoman art under the patronage of the great sultan (1520–1566). See also the catalogs of the British Museum and Grand Palais exhibitions (GLAH 2:I204, GLAH 2:I206).

List of objects, p.305–23. Concordance, p.325–26. Shortened references, p.327–37. Select bibliography, p.339–45. Glossary, p.347–50. Index, p.351–56.

I184 Blair, Sheila, and Bloom, Jonathan M. The art and architecture of Islam 1250–1800. New Haven, Yale Univ. Pr., 1994. xiii, 348p. il., maps (part col.) (Yale University Press pelican history of art)

A sequel to Ettinghausen and Grabar's volume in the same series on Islamic art and architecture 650–1250 (GLAH 2:I191). "This book surveys the art and architecture of the traditional Islamic lands between the Atlantic and Indian oceans and the Eurasian steppe and the Sahara in the period from the Mongol conquests in the early thirteenth century to the European conquests of the early nineteenth."—*Introd.*

Contents: Part I: 1250–1500; (1) Introduction; (2) Architecture in Iran and Central Asia under the Ilkhanids and their successors; (3) The arts in Iran and Central Asia under the Ilkhanids and their successors; (4) Architecture in Iran and Central Asia under the Timurids and their contemporaries; (5) The arts in Iran and Central Asia under the Timurids and their contemporaries; (6) Architecture in Egypt under the Bahri Mamluks (1260–1389); (7) Architecture in Egypt, Syria, and Arabia under the Circassian Mamluks (1389–1517); (8) The arts in Egypt and Syria under the Mamluks; (9) Architecture and the arts in the Maghrib under the Hafsids, Marinids, and Nasrids; (10) Architecture and the arts in Anatolia under the Beyliks and Early Ottomans; (11) Architecture and the arts in India under the Sultanates. Part II: 1500–1800; (12) The arts in Iran under the Safavids and Zands; (13) Architecture in Iran under the Safavids and Zands; (14) Architecture and the arts in Central Asia under the Uzbeks; (15) Architecture under the Ottomans after the conquest of Constantinople; (16) The arts under the Ottomans after the conquest of Constantinople; (17) Architecture and the arts in Egypt and North Africa; (18) Architecture in India under the Mughals and their contemporaries in the Deccan; (19) The arts in India under the Mughals and their contemporaries in the Deccan; (20) The legacies of later Islamic art.

Notes, p.[315]–32. Bibliography, p.[333]–39. Glossary, p.[340]. Index, p.[341]–48.

I185 Brend, Barbara. Islamic art. Cambridge, Mass., Harvard Univ. Pr., 1991. 240p. il.

Introductory survey.

Contents: Introduction; (1) The legacy of empires: Syria, Iraq and Iran under the caliphs; (2) Lands of the west: Egypt, North Africa and Spain; (3) Renewal from the east: the Seljuks enter Iran and Anatolia; (4) The rule of lords and slaves: Zangids, Ayyubids and Mamluks; (5) The last eastern invaders: the Mongol and Timurid empires; (6) Fervour, opulence and decline: Iran under the Safavids and Qajars; (7) East and west of the Bosphorus: the Ottoman Empire; (8) Emperors in Hindustan: Sultanate and Mughal India; Conclusion.

Select bibliography, p.233–34. Glossary, p.235–37. Index, p.238.

I186 Brentjes, Burchard. Mittelasien, Kunst des Islam. Unter Mitarb. von Karin Rührdanz. 2. Aufl. Leipzig, Seemann, 1982. 399p. il. (part col.), maps.

Study of Islamic art in Central Asia.

Contents: Islam und Kunst; Die mittelalterliche Architektur in Mittelasien; Die bildende Kunst Mittelasiens; Die angewandten und dekorativen Künste Mittelasiens in Tradition und Gegenwart.

Anmerkungen, p.363–70. Begriffserklärungen, p.371–72. Wichtige Dynastien Mittelasiens, p.373–75. Zeittafel, p.[376–78]. Literaturhinweise, p.381–86. Register, p.393–[400].

I187 Derman, M. Ugur. Letters in gold: Ottoman calligraphy from the Sakip Sabanci collection, Istanbul. N.Y., Metropolitian Museum of Art (Distr. by Abrams, 1998). xii, 196p. col. il.

Catalog of the exhibition, Metropolitan Museum of Art, New York (1998), and other locations. Includes "seventy one rare and beautiful calligraphies and illuminated manuscripts from the magnificent collection assembled by the prominent Turkish businessman and philanthropist Sakip Sabanci. . . . Almost every major Ottoman calligrapher working in the fifteenth to the early twentieth century is represented."—*Dir. Foreword.*

Note to the reader, p.xi. The genealogy of Ottoman calligraphers, p.186. The six scripts, p.187–88. Glossary, p.189–91. Selected bibliography, p.192–93. Index, p.194–96.

I188 Dreaming of paradise: Islamic art from the collection of the Museum of Ethnology, Rotterdam. [Rotterdam?], Martial & Snoeck, [1993]. 221p. il. (part col.), maps.

Beautifully illustrated catalog of the exhibition, Museum of Ethnology, Rotterdam (1993–96).

Includes bibliographical references. Bibliography, p.201–05. Spelling, dates and translations, p.211. Chronological chart of Islam, p.[214–15]. MESA transcription system, p.216–17.

I189 Enderlein, Volkmar. Islamische Kunst. Dresden, VEB Verlag der Kunst, 1990. 324p. il. (part col.), plans

Textbook survey.

Contents: Einfuhrung; Die Kunst im Zeitalter des arabischen Kalifats; Die Kunst der Seldschukenzeit; Die Kunst der Mongolenzeit; Die Kunst in den islamischen Grossreichen des Osmanen, der Safawiden und der Moghuln; Die Auflösung der islamischen Kunst im Zeitalter des Kolonialismus und das Entstehen nationaler Kunstäusserungen im 20. Jahrhunderts; Anhang.

Fachwörterverzeichnis, p.262–[65]. Zeittafeln, p.266–[79]. Bibliographie zur islamischen Kunst, berarb. von Regina Hickmann, p.[280]–319. Register, p.321–[25].

I190 Eredità dell'Islam: arte islamica in Italia. A cura di Giovanni Curatola. [Testi di Bianca Maria Alfieri . . . et al.] [Italy], Silvana, 1993. 518p. col. il., map.

Catalog of the exhibition, Palazzo Ducale, Venice (1993–94). A scholarly survey with illustrated catalog entries incorporated alongside the text. Each chapter by an authority.

Bibliographical references at end of chapters. Bibliografia, p.499–518. Cronologia, p.518.

I191 Ettinghausen, Richard, and Grabar, Oleg. The art and architecture of Islam, 650–1250. [Reprint.] New Haven, Yale Univ. Pr., 1994. 448p. il. (Yale University Press pelican history of art)

Reprint of 1987 ed.; previous reprints, 1989, 1991.

The standard treatment by two great authorities. Complemented by Blair and Bloom's vol. in the same series (GLAH 2:I184).

Contents: Part one: The Caliphate; (1) The rise of Islam and the artistic climate of the period; (2) The Umayyads and their art: 650–750; (3) The Abassid tradition: 750–950. Part two: The breakdown of the Caliphate; (4) The Muslim west: 750–1260; (5) The Fatimids in North Africa and Egypt: 910–1171; (6) Iran and Central Asia. Part Three: The Eleventh to Thirteenth Centuries; (7) Architecture; (8) The decorative arts.

List of the principal abbreviations, p.[385]. Notes, p.[387]–414. Bibliography, p.[415]–28. Index, p.439–48.

I192 ______. Islamic art and archaeology: collected papers. Prepared and ed. by Myriam Rosen-Ayalon. With an introd. by Oleg Grabar. Berlin, Mann, 1984. 1320p. il.

58 papers of the great scholar, with an introductory appreciation.

Contents: (A) On the nature of Islamic art; (B) Islamic themes in Islamic art; (C) The interpretation of key pieces; (D) In search of lost meaning or function; (E) Regional aspects of Islamic art; (F) Interactions between Islamic art and that of other arts; (G) The Islamic world as seen by outsiders; (H) The study of Islamic art; (I) Published posthumously.

Sources of Richard Ettinghausen's papers reprinted in this volume, p.1319–20.

I193 Die Gärten des Islam. Hrsg.: Hermann Forkl, Johannes Kalter, Thomas Leisten . . . [et al.] Stuttgart,

Hansjörg Mayer, in Zusammenarb. mit dem Linden-Museum Stuttgart, 1993. 388p. il. (part col.)

Catalog of the exhibition, Linden-Museum, Stuttgart (1993). Attempts to exemplify the multifaceted character of Islamic art and culture from Sub-Saharan Africa to Pakistan, Central and Southeast Asia, employing as a central theme the "Islamic garden."

Literaturverzeichnis, p.382–87.

I194 Grabar, Oleg. The formation of Islamic art. Rev. and enl. ed. New Haven, Yale Univ. Pr., 1987. xix, 232p. il.

See GLAH 1:I176 for original ed.

"Revising the book . . . was not merely a question of updating its information and bibliography . . . ; I also wished to review, modify, and perhaps expand certain conclusions and especially some of the explicit or implicit hypotheses that guided the earlier work."—*Postscriptum: twelve years later* (p.203). The author's revisions to this standard introduction focus upon "history and chronology," "theory and interpretation," and the "contemporary significance" of Islamic art.

List of illustrations, p.ix–xiv. Appendix: chronology of the early Muslim world, p.215. Bibliography, p.217–26. Index, p.227–32.

I195 Hillenbrand, Robert. Islamic art and architecture. N.Y., Thames and Hudson, 1999. 288p. il. (part col.) (World of art)

Readable, chronological survey by an authority.

Select bibliography, p.281–82. Glossary, p.283–84. Index, p.285—88.

I196 L'Islam dans les collections nationales. Paris, Éditions des Musées nationaux, 1977. 301p. il. (part col.)

Catalog of the exhibition, Grand Palais, Paris (1977). Includes more than 700 objects from French collections.

Bibliographie, p.297–301.

I197 Islamic art: common principles, forms and themes. Ed. by Ahmed Mohammed Issa, Tahsin Ömer Tahaoglu. Damascus, Dar Al-Fikr, 1989. 289, 165p. il. (part col.), plans.

Proceedings of the International Symposium held in Istanbul (1983). Wide-ranging collection of papers, many by leading authorities. Text in English, with some contributions in French and Arabic.

Includes bibliographical references.

I198 Lentz, Thomas W., and Lowry, Glenn D. Timur and the princely vision: Persian art and culture in the fifteenth century. Los Angeles, Los Angeles County Museum of Art, 1989. 395p. il. (part col.)

Catalog of the exhibition, the Museum (1989), and other locations. "A first step toward understanding the relationship between Timurid art and its political and historical context."—*Introd.* See also the anthology of related texts published as: A Century of princes: sources on Timurid history and art. Sel. and trans. by W. M. Thackston. Cambridge, Mass., The Aga Khan Program for Islamic Architecture, 1989.

Contents: Introduction; (I) Timur and the image of power; (II) Shahrukh and the princely network; (III) The Kitabkhana and the dissemination of the Timurid vision; (IV) Sultan-Husayn and the restructuring of the Timurid facade; (V) The Timurid resonance; Catalogue; Appendices.

Glossary, p.380–81. Bibliography, p.382–86. Index, p.387–92. Lenders to the exhibition, p.394–95.

I199 The Nasser D. Khalili Collection of Islamic Art. General ed., Julian Raby. N.Y., Nour Foundation in assoc. with Azimuth Eds. and Oxford Univ. Pr., 1992– . (27)v. il. (chiefly col.)

Magnificent scholarly catalog of the great private collection of Islamic art in all media.

Selective contents: (1) Déroche, Françoise. The Abbasid tradition (1992); (2) James, David. The master scribes (1992); (3) James, David. After Timur: Qur'ans of the 15th and 16th centuries (1992); (4, part 1) Bayani, Manijeh; Contadini, Anna; and Stanley, Tim. The decorated word: Qur'ans of the 17th to 19th centuries (1999); (5) Safwat, Nabil F. The art of the pen (1996); (6) Khan, Geoffrey. Bills, letters and deeds: Arabic papyri of the 7th to 11th centuries (1993); (8) Leach, Linda York. Paintings from India (1998); (9) Grube, Ernst J. Cobalt and lustre (1994); (12) Science, tools & magic (2v., 1997); (16) Wenzel, Marian. Ornament and amulet: rings of the Islamic lands (1993); (21) Alexander, David. The arts of war: arms and armour of the 7th to 19th centuries (1992); (22) Lacquer of the Islamic lands (2v., 1996–97); (23) Venoit, Stephen. Occidentalism, Islamic art in the 19th century (1997); (27) Blair, Sheila S. A compendium of chronicles: Rashid al-Din's illustrated history of the world (1995).

I200 New York. Metropolitan Museum of Art. Islamic art in the Metropolitan Museum of Art. Ed. by Richard Ettinghausen. [N.Y.], Metropolitan Museum of Art, 1972. vii, 334p. il.

Published in conjunction with the Museum's centennial (1970–71). Scholarly catalog of the collection, organized by medium, with each section written by a specialist.

Contents: Painting; Pottery; Metal; Wood; Stone; Carpets; Combined media; Islam in Europe.

Bibliographical references at ends of sections.

I201 Papadopoulo, Alexandre. Islam and Muslim art. Trans. from the French by Robert Erich Wolf. N.Y., Abrams, 1976. 631p. il. (part col.)

Trans. of Islam et l'art musulman. Paris, Mazenod, 1976 (L'art et les grandes civilisations, 6). Magnificent survey of Islamic and Muslim art.

Contents: Part one: Islam and Muslim civilization; Part two: The Muslim arts; Part three: Architecture; Part four: The image as document [documentary photographs]; Part five: The principal sites of Muslim art; Part six: Prayer halls and other interiors; Part seven: a lexicon [of historical characters].

Glossary, p.608–11. Notes to the text, p.612–14. Bibliography, p.615–19. Index, p.620–31.

I202 Rogers, J. M. Empire of the Sultans: Ottoman art from the collection of Nasser D. Khalili. [Catalogue

written by J. M. Rogers, devised and arranged by Julian Raby.] Geneva, Musée d'art et d'histoire; [London], Nour Foundation in assoc. with Azimuth Editions, 1995. 285p. col. il., map.
Catalog of the exhibition, Musée Rath, Geneva (1995). Beautifully illustrated scholarly catalog of nearly 200 of the 20,000 objects in the prestigious Khalili collection. See also the multi-vol. catalog of the Khalili collection in course of publication (GLAH 2:I199).

Concordance by catalogue number, p.276. Concordance by accession number, p.277. Bibliography, p.278–85.

I203 ______. Islamic art & design, 1500–1700. London, Published for the Trustees of the British Museum by British Museum Publications, 1983. 167p. il. (part col.), map.
Catalog of the exhibition, British Museum, London (1983). More than 200 examples of Islamic painting, manuscript illumination, calligraphy, paper-cuts, textiles, pottery, metalwork, and jewelery.

Ottoman, Safavid and Mughal rulers, p.159. Glossary, p.160–61. Bibliography of works cited, p.162–67.

I204 ______, and Ward, R. M. Süleyman the Magnificent. London, British Museum, 1988. xiv, 225p. il. (part col.), maps, ports. (part col.)
Catalog of the exhibition, British Museum, London (1988), and other locations. Includes more than 160 objects from the British Museum collection and the Turkish national collections documenting the efflorescence of Ottoman art under the patronage of the great sultan (1520–1566). See also the catalogs of the Grand Palais and National Gallery of Art (U.S.) (GLAH 2:I206, GLAH 2:I183) exhibitions.

Note on transliteration, p.xiii. Abbreviations, p.xiii. Chronology, p.xiv. Glossary, p.216–18. Bibliography, p.219–24. Concordance, p.225.

I205 Schimmel, Annemarie. Calligraphy and Islamic culture. N.Y., New York Univ. Pr., 1984. xiv, 264p., il., plates (part col.)
Based upon the author's Kevorkian lectures, New York University (1981–82). Treats the position and training of the Islamic calligrapher, and the religious significance of calligraphy in Muslim culture.

Contents: (I) Styles of calligraphy; (II) Calligraphers, dervishes, and kings; (III) Calligraphy and mysticism; (IV) Calligraphy and poetry; Appendixes.

The Arabic alphabet, p.xiii–xiv. Abbreviations in notes and bibliography, p.159–60. Notes, p.161–207. Bibliography, p.209–31. Index of proper names, p.233–50. Index of technical terms, p.251–59. Index of Koran and prophetic traditions, p.260–61. Index of book titles, p.262–64.

I206 Soliman le Magnifique. Paris, Ministère des affaires étrangères; Secrétariat d'Etat aux relations culturelles internationales; Association française d'action artistique, 1990. 388p. il. (chiefly col.), map.
Catalog of the exhibition, Grand Palais, Paris (1990) devoted to the efflorescence of Ottoman art under the patronage of the great sultan (1520–1566). See also the catalogs of the British Museum and National Gallery of Art (U.S.) exhibitions (GLAH 2:I204, GLAH 2:I183). Accompanied by a scholarly conference, with the proceedings published as Soliman le Magnifique et son temps. Ed. by Gilles Veinstein. Paris, Documentation française, 1992.

Glossaire, p.317. Bibliographie, p.318–25. Index, p.327–38.

I207 Treasures of Islam. [Ed. by Toby Falk]. London, Sotheby's; Philip Wilson, 1985. 400p. col. il.
Catalog of the important exhibition, Musée Rath, Geneva (1985).

Contents: Introduction, by Oleg Grabar; The aesthetics of Islam, by A. S. Melikian-Chirvani; Private collectors and Islamic arts of the book, by Stuart Cary Welch; The arts of the book; The Arab lands; Iran, Afghanistan and Central Asia; Turkey; India, by Anthony Welch; Lacquer, oil-paintings and later arts of the book, by B. W. Robinson; Ceramics, by Oliver Watson; Metalwork, by James W. Allan; Arms and armour, by David Alexander and Howard Ricketts; Carpets and textiles, by Donald King; Architectural ornament and decorative arts, by Marilyn Jenkins; The art of Islamic coinage, by Michael L. Bates and Robert E. Darley-Doran.

Additional exhibits, p.396. Bibliography, p.396–97. Index, p.398–400.

I208 Welch, Anthony. Calligraphy in the arts of the Muslim world. Austin, Univ. of Texas Pr., published in coop. with The Asia Society, 1979. 216p. il.
Catalog of the loan exhibition, Asia House Gallery, N.Y. (1979), and other locations. Includes more than 90 objects.

The Arabic alphabet, p.212. Bibliography, p.213–16.

CAROLINGIAN—GOTHIC

I209 L'art du Moyen Age: Occident, Byzance, Islam. Sous la dir. de Jean-Pierre Caillet. Paris, Gallimard; Réunion des musées nationaux, 1995. 589p. il. (part col.), col. maps (Collection manuels d'histoire de l'art)
Contents: Occident, par Jean-Pierre Caillet et Fabienne Joubert. (I) Le premier essor de l'art chrétien; (II) Permanences, acculturations et résistances dans l'Europe barbare; (III) La "renaissance carolingienne"; (IV) Mutations autour de l'an mil; (V) L'établissement de l'ordre roman; (VI) L'humanisme gothique; (VII) L'Italie, ou les fondements d'un autre humanisme; (VIII) Vers un art "international"?; (IX) Les derniers feux du Moyen Age occidental: Byzance, par Catherine Jolivet-Lévy. (I) "Siècles obscurs" et iconoclasme: rupture ou continuité?; (II) L'apogée: l'art byzantin sous les Macédoniens et les Comnènes; (III) La domination latine (1204–1261); (IV) La Renaissance des Paléologues, ultime floraison artistique (1261–1453); (V) L'héritage de Byzance: l'art post-byzantin. Islam, par Marianne Barrucand. (I) Le premier art islamique: le Proche-Orient umayyade (660–750); (II) L'art classique abbaside et ses prolongements provinciaux; (III) Turcs et Mongols; (IV) Le

Proche-Orient des Fatimides aux Mamelouks; (V) Al-Andalus et les empires maghrébins; (VI) L'art de l'Islam post-médiéval.

Cartographie, p.544–57. Glossaire, p.560–66. Bibliographie, p.567–72. Index, p.573–89.

I210 Barral i Altet, Xavier. Artistes, artisans et production artistique au Moyen Age. Organisé et éd. par Xavier Barral i Altet. Paris, Picard, 1986–1990. 3v. il., maps, plans.

Proceedings of an important international colloquium on medieval art production, devoted to the definition of the artist and the artisan and their place in society, professional structures, and the role of collaboration and specialization (Rennes, 1983). Texts in French, English, and Spanish.

Contents: (1) Les hommes; (2) Commande et travail; (3) Fabrication et consommation de l'œuvre.

I211 Belting, Hans. Likeness and presence: a history of the image before the era of art. Trans. by Edmund Jephcott. Chicago, Univ. of Chicago Pr., 1994. xxiv, 651p. il. (part col.), plates.

Trans. of Bild und Kult—eine Geschichte des Bildes vor dem Zeitalter der Kunst. München, Beck, 1990.

An important, wide-ranging exploration of the meaning of "holy images" in medieval art and culture. "My book does not 'explain' images nor does it pretend that images explain themselves. Rather, it is based on the conviction that they reveal their meaning best by their use. I therefore deal with people and with their beliefs, superstitions, hopes, and fears in handling images."—*Foreword.*

Appendix: texts on the history and use of images and relics, p.491–556. Notes, p.557–603. Bibliography, p.605–15. Index of persons and places, p.617–32. Index of subjects, p.633–50.

I212 Calkins, Robert G. Monuments of medieval art. N.Y., Dutton, 1979. xx, 299p. il. (part col.), plates.

A study of "representative examples of major art forms."—*Pref.* "The following topical discussions are intended to serve as an introduction to the art and architecture of the Middle Ages. Although they are arranged more or less chronologically . . . they are not intended to present a complete survey of medieval art."—*Pref.*

Contents: Introduction; (I) The early Christian period; (II) The Byzantine era; (III) The period of the barbarian invasions; (IV) The Carolingian and Ottonian empires; (V) The Romanesque period; (VI) The Gothic period; (VII) The medieval illuminated manuscript; (VIII) The secular realm.

Selected bibliography, p.[273]–80. Index, p.[281]–99.

I213 Camille, Michael. The Gothic idol: ideology and image-making in medieval art. N.Y., Cambridge Univ. Pr., 1989. xxxii, 407p. il.

An important study of idolatry in medieval art, which "charts the complex interdependence of scriptural and visual traditions . . . [and] also attempts to uncover realms of intervisual and not just intertextual meanings, where images do not just 'reflect' texts innocently but often subvert or alter their meaning."—*Pref.*

Contents: Part one: The Gothic anti-image; (1) Idols and originals; (2) Idols of the pagans; (3) Idols of the Saracens; (4) Idols of the Jews; Part two: Gothic idols; (5) Idols in the Church; (6) Idols in society; (7) Idols in the mind; Epilogue: Idols as art.

Notes, p.353–98. Index, p.399–407.

I214 Duby, Georges. The age of the cathedrals: art and society, 980–1420. Trans. by Eleanor Levieux and Barbara Thompson. Chicago, Univ. of Chicago Pr., 1981. v, 312p. il., plates.

Trans. of Temps des cathédrales. Paris, Gallimard, 1976. Originally published in 3 vols., Geneva, Skira, 1966–67; German ed. Frankfurt am Main, Suhrkamp, 1980; Hungarian ed. Budapest, Gondolat, 1984.

A suggestive essay on medieval art by a distinguished French medievalist. Attempts to trace in broad strokes the impact of deep societal changes (e.g., the rise of feudalism) on the art of the middle ages.

Contents: Part one: The monastery, 980–1130; Part two: The cathedrals, 1130–1280; Part three: The palace, 1280–1420; Illustrations.

Index, p.307–12.

I215 ———. Medieval art. Switzerland, Brooking International, 1995. 3v. il. (part col.)

First published Geneva, Skira, 1966–67. Repr. in one vol. as History of medieval art, 980–1440. New ed. N.Y., Rizzoli, 1986.

Contents: Making of the Christian west; Europe of the cathedrals; Foundations of a new humanism.

I216 Erlande-Brandenburg, Alain. Gothic art. Trans. from the French by I. Mark Paris. N.Y., Abrams, 1989. 630p. il. (part col.)

Trans. of L'art gothique. Paris, Mazenod, 1983 (L'art et les grandes civilisations, 13). Monumental survey by an authority.

Contents: Part one: The evolution of Gothic art; (I) The Gothic vision; (II) The context of creation; (III) The birth of a style; (IV) The Gothic explosion; (V) The Gothic of invention; (VI) The Gothic of princes and burghers. Part two: The image as document; Color plates; Documentary photographs; Identification of the photographs. Part three: The great monuments of Gothic architecture; Early Gothic art: the birth of a style; High Gothic in Europe; Rayonnant art: the Gothic of invention; Flamboyant art: the Gothic of princes and burghers; Military, domestic, and civil architecture; Rib vaulting: techniques and achievements. Part four: Lexicon; Biographical notes.

Glossary, p.615–6. Bibliography, p.617–21. Index, p.622–30.

I217 Europäische Kunst um 1300. Leitung der Sektion, Gerhard Schmidt. Red., Elisabeth Liskar. Wien, Böhlau, 1986. 409p. il. (International Congress of the History of Art, 25th: 1983: Vienna, Austria. Akten des XXV. Internationalen Kongresses für Kunstgeschichte, Bd. 6)

Selected papers presented at the 25th International Congress of the History of Art, Vienna (1983). Texts in English, French, German, and Italian.

Includes bibliographical references.

I218 Les Fastes du Gothique: le siècle de Charles V. Paris, Éd. de la Réunion des musées nationaux, 1981. 461p. il. (part col.)

Catalog of the important exhibition, Grand Palais, Paris (1981–1982). Encyclopedic overview of Gothic art in France.

Répertoire des artistes, p.429–35. Liste des ouvrages cités en abrégé, p.436–37. Bibliographie, p.438–47. Expositions, p.448–49. Table des manuscrits exposés, p.450–51. Index, p.452–56.

I219 Folda, Jaroslav. The art of the crusaders in the Holy Land, 1098–1187. N.Y., Cambridge Univ. Pr., 1995. xxx, 672p. il. (part col.), plates.

A monumental "attempt to discuss what we know about the art of the Crusades in the Holy land, using art historical method to its fullest potential for synthetic interpretive study," addressing the fact that no previous study "attempts to present [Crusader art] as a coherent chapter in the history of medieval art with adequate photographic documentation."—*Introd.*

Notes, p.481–603. Gazeteer, p.605–11. Bibliography, p.613–37. General index, p.639–59. Personal proper names index, p.660–70. Index of manuscript repositories, p.671–72.

I220 Formes de la nuit. Saint-Léger-Vauban, Zodiaque, 1981– . (12)v. il. (part col.)

Notable series of monographs on medieval art.

Contents: (1) Brozzi, Mario. Les Lombards (1981); (2) Crespi, Gabriele. L'Europe musulmane (1982); (3) Newman, John Henry. L'Europe des monastères (2d ed., 1988); (4) Lévis-Godechot, Nicole. Chartres: révélée par sa sculpture et ses vitraux (1987); (5–6) Oursel, Raymond. France romane (2v., 1989–91); (7) Cirkovic, Sima M. La Serbie au Moyen Age (1992); (8) Durliat, Marcel. L'Espagne romane (1993); (9) Kinder, Terryl Nancy. L'Europe Cistercienne (1997); (9 [sic]) Velmans, Tania, and Novello, Adriano Alpago. Miroir de l'invisible: peintures murales et architecture de la Géorgie (VIe–XVe s.) (1996); (10) Kinder, Terryl Nancy. L'Europe cistercienne (2d ed., 1988); (11) Harbison, Peter. L'art médiéval en Irlande (1998); (12) Christe, Yves. Jugements derner (2000).

I221 Gaignebet, Claude, and Lajoux, Jean-Dominique. Art profane et religion populaire au Moyen Age. Paris, Presses Univ. de France, 1985. 363p. il. (part col.), plates.

Wide-ranging study of medieval secular art and popular piety, including folklore and erotica.

Bibliographie, p.327–36. Index, p.337–63.

I222 Huizinga, Johan. The autumn of the Middle Ages. Trans. by Rodney J. Payton and Ulrich Mammitzsch. Chicago, Univ. of Chicago Pr., 1996. xxii, 467p. il.

Trans. of Herfsttij der Middeleeuwen (see GLAH 1:I193 for the previous, abridged Eng. trans.). Includes a trans. introd. as well as the text of the prefaces to the Dutch and German eds., in trans. Includes documentation missing from the previous trans. as well as revised trans. of citations previously published only in the original languages.

Notes (including translator's notes to this ed.), p.397–440. Bibliography, p.441–49. Index, p.451–67.

I223 Jantzen, Hans. High Gothic: the classic cathedrals of Chartres, Reims, Amiens. [Reprint.] Trans. from the German by James Palmes. Princeton, Princeton Univ. Pr., 1984. xiii, 181p. il., plates.

See GLAH 1:J162 for earlier U.S. eds. and original annotation. Repr. of N.Y., Pantheon, 1962. Trans. of Kunst der Gotik. Hamburg, Rowohlt, 1957; new ed., exp. and rev. and with a new preface, Berlin, Reimer, 1987. Dutch ed., 1959.

I224 Lasko, Peter E. Ars sacra, 800–1200. 2d ed. New Haven, Yale Univ. Pr., 1994. xii, 319p. il. (part col.), maps. (Yale University Press pelican history of art)

See GLAH 1:I198 for previous ed.

"The second edition has been expanded in two ways. First, the virtual explosion of literature in this field . . . has resulted not only in the need to add considerably to the references, but has also resulted in some changes of mind on my part. . . . Second, the editorial decision to incorporate the art and architecture of Britain . . . has meant the inclusion of a new chapter on Anglo-Saxon art and some expansion in Chapters 13 and 21."—*Pref. to the second ed.*

I225 Mellinkoff, Ruth. Outcasts: signs of otherness in northern European art of the late Middle Ages. Berkeley, Univ. of California Pr., 1993. 2v. il. (part col.)

A pioneering study of the iconography of "otherness" in the art of the period, focusing upon marginalized elements of society: heretics, Muslims, Jews, racial and ethnic minorities, and the other stigmatized groups.

Contents: (1) Text; (2) Illustrations.

Abbreviations, v.1, p.235–38. Notes, v.1, p.239–315. Bibliography, v.1, p.317–40. Index, v.1, p.341–60.

I226 Nichols, Stephen G. Romanesque signs: early medieval narrative and iconography. New Haven, Yale Univ. Pr., 1983. xiii, 248p. il.

An important study of narrative techniques and historicizing iconography in Romanesque art.

Contents: (1) The discourse of history; (2) Historia and theosis; (3) Charlemagne redivivus: from history to Historia; (4) Historia and the poetics of the Passion; (5) Roncevaux and the poetics of place/person in the Song of Roland.

Notes, p.205–36. Index, p.237–48.

I227 Ornamenta ecclesiae: Kunst und Künstler der Romanik. Hrsg. von Anton Legner. Köln, Stadt Köln, 1985. 3v. il.

Monumental catalog of the important exhibition of Romanesque church art, Schnütgen-Museum in der Josef-Haubrich-Kunsthalle, Köln (1985).

Contents: (1) (A) Ordo et artes; (B) Fabrica; (C) Liturgica; (2) (D) Coloniensia; (E) Ornamenta ecclesiarum coloniensium; (F) Kölner Kunst der Romanik; (3) (G) Antike und Byzanz; (H) Sacrae reliquiae.

Abgekürtzt ziterte Literatur, v.3, p.204–06.

I228 Scheller, R. W. Exemplum: model-book drawings and the practice of artistic transmission in the Middle Ages (ca. 900–ca. 1470). Trans. by Michael Hoyle. Amsterdam, Amsterdam Univ. Pr., 1995. xi, 434p. il. (part col.)

See GLAH 1:I203 for the author's previous Survey of medieval model books. (Note: the author's name is misspelled in GLAH 1). The present volume is "much more comprehensive." "The accent has now been placed more explicitly on issues for which model books may supply important evidence but which cover a broader terrain, such as the relationship between original and copy, production processes and the various forms of artistic transmission in the Middle Ages."—*Pref.*

Index, p.[413]–34.

I229 Snyder, James. Medieval art: painting-sculpture-architecture, 4th–14th century. N.Y., Abrams, 1989. 511p. il. (part col.)

Standard historical survey of the art of the Middle Ages by a specialist in the art of northern Europe. The treatment of medieval architecture focuses upon decoration and ornament.

Notes, p.[475]–86. Select bibliography, p.[487]–93. Timetables of medieval history and art, p.[494]–97. Index, p.[498]–511.

I230 Stokstad, Marilyn. Medieval art. N.Y., Harper & Row, 1986. xxix, 446p. il. (part col.), plates.

"My purpose in writing Medieval art has always been to introduce the lay reader, the museum visitor, and the student to this period. . . . Medieval art includes the art and building of what is now Western Europe from the second to the fifteenth centuries."—*Pref.* A solid introductory study.

Contents: Preface; (I) Art in the first centuries of the Christian era; (II) The art of the triumphant Christian church; (III) The golden age of Byzantium; (IV) Barbarian art; (V) Carolingian art; (VI) Art outside the Carolingian Empire; (VII) The imperial tradition: Ottonian and Romanesque art in the Holy Roman Empire; (VIII) Romanesque art in Western Europe; (IX) The origins of the Gothic style; (X) High Gothic art in France; (XI) National styles in Gothic art; (XII) Late Gothic art.

Chronological table, p.xxiv–xxvii. Glossary, p.397–411. Suggestions for further reading, p.413–23. Index, p.425–46.

I231 Swaan, Wim. The late Middle Ages: art and architecture from 1350 to the advent of the Renaissance. With photos by the author. Ithaca, N.Y., Cornell Univ. Pr., 1977. 232p. il. (part col.)

"Our subject is the final harvest of the Gothic style, from 1350 to the advent of the Renaissance, in the countries of Northern Europe and the Iberian Peninsula."—*Pref.* Organized by country.

Notes, p.[210]–19. Glossary, p.221–23. Bibliography, p.[224]–27. Index, p.[229]–32.

I232 Zarnecki, George. Romanesque. N.Y., Universe Books (Distr. by St. Martin's Pr., 1989). 196p. il. (part col.) (The Universe history of art and architecture)

Previously published as: Romanesque art. 1971.

RENAISSANCE—BAROQUE

I233 Bauer, Hermann. Barock: Kunst einer Epoche. Berlin, Reimer, 1992. 292p. il. (part col.), plates.

Thoughtful essay by an authority.

Contents: (I) Eine Anekdote anstelle einer Einleitung; (II) Der Begriff "Barock"—Zur Geschichte der Barockforschung; (III) " . . . IAM REGNAT APOLLO"; (IV) Rom, das "neue Theater"; (V) Das barocke Schloss; (VI) Barockkunst und barockes Fest; (VIII) Zeremoniell und Repräsentation; (VIII) Concettismo; (IX) Theater und Theatralik; (X) Illusionismus.

Notes at ends of chapters. Glossary, p.[287]–91.

I234 Boone, Danièle. L'art baroque. Neuchâtel, Ides et Calendes, 1988. 256p. il. (part col.)

Survey addressed to a general audience.

Contents: Rome; Cortone, Bernini, Borromini; Les dernières splendeurs romaines; Le relais piémontais; L'éternelle mouvance vénitienne; Les royaumes du sud; Des lieux et des hommes; Prague la magnifique; Le siècle de Rubens; L'Europe réformée; Le choix français; Pierre Puget; Le baroque ibérique; Annexes.

Bibliographie, p.251–252. Index, p.253–55.

I235 Held, Julius Samuel, and Posner, Donald. 17th and 18th century art: baroque painting, sculpture, architecture. N.Y., Abrams, [1971]. 439p. il. (part col.) (Library of art history)

Standard survey text.

Contents: (1) Italy in the seventeenth century; (2) France in the seventeenth century; (3) Spain in the seventeenth century; (4) Flemish painting in the seventeenth century; (5) Dutch painting in the seventeenth century; (6) Northern European architecture in the seventeenth and eighteenth centuries; (7) France in the eighteenth century; (8) Italy in the eighteenth century; (9) English painting in the eighteenth century; (10) Germany and Austria in the seventeenth and eighteenth centuries.

Notes, p.409–[19]. Chronological chart, p.420–[23]. Selected bibliography, p.424–[27]. Index, p.428–38.

I236 Jestaz, Bertrand. The art of the Renaissance. Trans. from the French by I. Mark Paris. N.Y., Abrams, 1995. 608p. il. (part col.)

Trans. of Art de la renaissance. Paris, Mazenod, 1984 (L'art et les grandes civilisations, 14). Lavishly produced and illustrated survey.

Contents: The recovery period, 1400 to c.1480; The age of classicism, 1480 to c.1520; Classicism's developments and challenges, 1520 to c.1600.

Catalogue: great architecture of the Renaissance, p.[469]–575. Biographies, p.577–90. Bibliography, p.591–97. Index, p.598–607.

I237 Martin, John Rupert. Baroque. N.Y., Harper & Row, 1977. 367p. il.

Thematic survey by an authority, "attempting to define the essential characteristics of Baroque art."—*Introd.*

Contents: (1) The question of style; (2) Naturalism; (3) The passions of the soul; (4) The transcendental view of reality; (5) Space; (6) Time; (7) Light; (8) Attitudes to antiquity; Appendix A: Peter Paul Rubens, On the imitation of statues; Appendix B: Paul Fréart de Chantelou, Bernini in France; Appendix C: Arnold Houbraken, life of Rembrandt; Appendix D: Francisco Pacheco, On the aim of painting; Appendix E: Philippe de Champaigne, On Poussin's Rebecca and Eliezer.

Notes, p.[297]–304. Books for further reading, p.[305]–9. Catalogue of illustrations, p.[311]–57. Index, p.[359]–67.

I238 Snyder, James. Northern Renaissance art: painting, sculpture, the graphic arts from 1350 to 1575. N.Y., Abrams, 1985. 559p. il. (part col.)

Standard survey text.

Contents: Part One: The International style; Part Two: Painting, graphics, and sculpture in the Netherlands, Germany, and France from 1425 to 1500; Part Three: The Renaissance in Germany, the Netherlands, and France from 1500 to 1575.

Notes, p.[524]–33. Select bibliography, p.[534]–37. Genealogy of the House of Valois, p.[538]. Timetable of the arts, history, and science 1300–1575, p.[538]–45. Index, p.[546]–59.

I239 Welt des Barock. Hrsg. von Rupert Feuchtmüller und Elisabeth Kovács. Wien, Herder, 1986. 2v. il. (part col.), facsims., plates, ports.

Catalog of the exhibition, Augustiner Chorherrenstift St. Florian (1986). Substantial, wide-ranging exhibition catalog, with essays, devoted to the culture of the Austrian Baroque.

Contents: (1) Text; (2) Katalog.

Gekürzt zitierte Literatur, v.1, p.18–19. Verwendete Abkürzungen, v.1, p.20.

NEOCLASSICAL—MODERN

I240 Ades, Dawn. Dada and surrealism reviewed. Introd. by David Sylvester and a supplementary essay by Elizabeth Cowling. London, Arts Council of Great Britain, 1978. xi, 475p., il. (part col.), plates.

Catalog of the important exhibition, Hayward Gallery, London (1978). Survey of the movements structured around their critical reception.

Addenda, p.469. Corrigenda, p.470. Indices, p.471–75.

I241 The age of modernism: art in the 20th century. Ed. by Christos M. Joachimides and Norman Rosenthal. Essays by Brooks Adams . . . [et al.] Co-ord. eds., Gerti Fietzek and Henry Meyric Hughes. Stuttgart, Hatje, 1997. 672p. il. (part col.), ports.

Catalog of the exhibition, Martin-Gropius-Bau, Berlin (1997). Portions of text trans. from the German. "This exhibition is not about the whole evolution of twentieth-century art; it is about Modernism in art."—*p.9.* Focuses on "the essential media of painting and sculpture" broadly construed, from 1907 to the present, attempting to offer a retrospective on Modernism from a contemporary perspective. Beautifully illustrated, wide-ranging, provocative.

Biographies of the artists [with portraits], p.574–660. The authors, p.661. Lenders to the exhibition, p.662–63. Index of names, p.666–72.

I242 Archer, Michael. Art since 1960. N.Y., Thames and Hudson, 1997. 224p. il. (World of art)

Brief, accessible survey.

Contents: (1) The real and its objects; (2) The expanded field; (3) Ideology, identity and difference; (4) Postmodernism; (5) Assimilations; Conclusion.

Timeline, p.216–17. Select bibliography, p.218. Index, p.223–24.

I243 Arnason, H. H. History of modern art: painting, sculpture, architecture, photography. [With] Daniel Wheeler, revising author. 4th ed. N.Y., Abrams, 1998. 856p. il. (part col.)

See GLAH 1:I235 for the 1st and 2d eds. 3d ed., 1986 [Marla F. Prather, revising author].

Latest ed. of the standard textbook survey of modern art. Bibliography, p.[806]–28. Index, p.[829]–53.

I244 Art after modernism: rethinking representation. Ed. and with an introd. by Brian Wallis. Foreword by Marcia Tucker. N.Y., New Museum of Contemporary Art; Boston, Godine, 1984. xviii, 461p. il. (Documentary sources in contemporary art)

Important anthology of essays on contemporary art.

Contents: (I) Image/author/critique; (II) Dismantling Modernism; (III) Paroxysms of painting; (IV) Theorizing Postmodernism; (V) The fictions of mass media; (VI) Cultural politics; (VII) Gender/difference/power.

I245 Art in theory, 1815–1900: an anthology of changing ideas. Ed. by Charles Harrison and Paul Wood, with Jason Gaiger. Malden, Mass., Blackwell, 1998. xx, 1097p.

"The aim of this book is to provide students of art, art history and aesthetics as well as the interested general reader with a substantial and representative collection of texts, drawn from a wide variety of nineteenth-century sources."—*Introd.* Supplements the following entry.

Contents: (I) Feeling and nature; (II) The demands of the present; (III) Modernity and bourgeois life; (IV) Temperaments and techniques; (V) Aesthetics and historical awareness; (VI) The idea of modern art.

Bibliography, p.[1067]–80. Index, p.[1084]–97.

I246 Art in theory, 1900–1990: an anthology of changing ideas. Ed. by Charles Harrison and Paul Wood. Cambridge, Mass., Blackwell, 1992. xxv, 1189p.

"The aim of this book is to equip the student of modern art and the interested general reader with a substantial and representative collection of relevant texts, drawn from a wide variety of sources."—*Introd.* Substantial anthology of the literature of modern art, mostly presented as excerpts from longer texts. All excerpts include references to the full text. Brief biographical notes on the authors.

Contents: (I) The legacy of Symbolism; (II) The idea of the modern world; (III) Rationalization and transformation; (IV) Freedom, responsibility and power; (V) The individual and the social; (VI) Modernization and Modernism; (VII) Institutions and objections; (VIII) Ideas of the Postmodern.

Bibliography, p.1129–54. Index, p.1169–89.

I247 Boime, Albert. A social history of modern art. Chicago, Univ. of Chicago Pr., 1987–90. 2v.

Series "devoted to the social history of art in the modern epoch" making "a distinct leap in art history studies by moving beyond stylistic divisions and viewing developments in terms of major historical periods."—*Pref. to v.1.*

Contents: (1) Art in an age of revolution, 1750–1800 (1987); (2) Art in an age of Bonapartism, 1800–1815 (1990).

Notes, v.1, p.491–510, v.2, p.657–88. Index, v.1, p.511–21, v.2, p.691–706.

I248 Busch, Werner. Das sentimentalische Bild: die Krise der Kunst im 18. Jahrhundert und die Geburt der Moderne. München, Beck, 1993. 537p. il.

Wide-ranging study of the roots of "the modern" in late-18th century art.

Contents: (1) Historie; (2) Genre; (3) Landschaft; (4) Porträt; (5) Karikatur.

Anmerkungen, p.483–506. Bibliographie, p.507–30. Register, p.531–36.

I249 Concepts of modern art: from fauvism to postmodernism. 3d ed., exp. and upd. Ed. by Nikos Stangos. London, Thames and Hudson, 1994. 424p. il.

1st ed. Harmondsworth, Penguin, 1974; rev. and enl. ed., N.Y., Harper and Row, 1981.

A useful dictionary of modern art movements, with essays on 18 movements by specialists.

Selected bibliographies, p.410–15. Index, p.416–24.

I250 Dada: l'arte della negazione. [Cura della mostra, Giovanni Lista, Arturo Schwarz, Rosella Siligato.] Roma, De Luca, 1994.

Catalog of the exhibition, Palazzo delle Esposizioni, Rome (1994). Survey of the Dada movement worldwide.

Biografie degli artisti, p.[333]–68. Bibliografie, p.[369]–74.

I251 Documents of twentieth-century art. N.Y., Viking, 1971– .

See GLAH 1:I240 for previous (and anticipated) vols. in series. Various publishers (most Boston, Hall; some Berkeley, Univ. of Calif. Pr.). Originally, N.Y., Viking.

Selective contents: Autobiography of Surrealism (1980); Dada painters and poets: an anthology (1981); Kandinsky, complete writings on art (1982); Marcel Duchamp, notes (1983); Joan Miro, selected writings and interviews (1986); The new art, the new life, the complete writings of Piet Mondrian (1986); Russian art of the avant-garde (1988); Motherwell, Robert. Collected writings (1992); German Expressionism, documents . . . [etc.] (1993); Matisse on art (1995; 1st ed. 1973, 2d ed. 1978); Robert Smithson, the collected writings (1996; first ed. 1979); Flight out of time: a Dada diary by Hugo Ball (1996; first pub. 1974); Pop art: a critical history (1997).

I252 Durozoi, Gérard. Histoire du mouvement surréaliste. Paris, Hazan, 1997. 759p.

Monumental history of the surrealist movement, 1919–69.

Biographies, p.649–712. Bibliographie, p.713–37. Index des noms de personnes, p.738–50. Index des revues, p.751–52.

I253 Einstein, Carl. Die Kunst des 20. Jahrhunderts. Hrsg. und komment. von Uwe Fleckner und Thomas W. Gaehtgens. Berlin, Fannei & Walz, 1996. 363p. il. (part col.) (Werke / Carl Einstein, Bd. 5)

See GLAH 1:I241 for original ed. New. ed. appearing as part of the author's collected writings.

I254 Eisenman, Stephen. Nineteenth century art: a critical history. [With contrib. by] Thomas Crow . . . [et al.] London, Thames and Hudson, 1994. 376p. il. (part col.)

"This is a radical reconsideration of the origins of modern painting and sculpture in Europe and North America. . . . [It] embraces many aspects of the so-called 'new' art history—attention to issues of class and gender, reception and spectatorship, racism and Eurocentrism. . . . The authors insist that there is a profound sympathy between these new methods and the art under examination."—*Dust jacket.*

Contents: Introduction: critical art and history; Classicism and romanticism; New world frontiers; Realism and materialism; Modern art and life.

Chronology, p.351–64. Selected bibliography, p.365–67. Index, p.373–76.

I255 Face à l'histoire, 1933–1996: l'artiste moderne devant l'événement historique. Conception et realis., Jean-Paul Ameline. Paris, Flammarion; Ed. du Centre Pompidou, 1996. 620p. il. (part col.), ports.

Wide-ranging collection of essays on the modern artist's confrontation with historical and political events.

Bibliographie, p.601–04. Liste des oeuvres, p.605–17. Index, p.617–20.

I256 Golding, John. Cubism: a history and an analysis, 1907–1914. 3d ed. Cambridge, Mass., Belknap Press of Harvard Univ. Pr., 1988. xvi, 237p. il., plates.

See GLAH 1:I244 for previous eds. Includes a narrative Preface to the third edition, which discusses the evolution of the author's views.

Bibliography, p.202–18. Index, p.227–37.

I257 Goldwater, Robert John. Primitivism in modern art. Enl. ed. Cambridge, Mass., Belknap Pr. of Harvard Univ. Pr., 1986. xxv, 339p. il.

See GLAH 1:I245 for original ed. "For this new expanded paperback edition . . . two important essays by Robert Goldwater have been added . . . and a bibliography of the author's work is appended. No changes have been made in the text as it appeared in the second, revised edition."—*Pub. note to the enl. ed.*

I258 ______. Symbolism. N.Y., Harper & Row, 1979. [vii], 286p. il.

Wide-ranging, authoritative essay on Symbolism as movement and philosophy, published posthumously.

Contents: (1) Introduction; (2) From Synthetism to Symbolism; (3) Suggestion, mystery, dream; (4) Supernaturalism and Naturalism; (5) Criticism and theory; (6) Idéistes; (7) Correspondences.

Abbreviations used in catalogue of illustrations, p.259–60. Catalogue of illustrations compiled by Kristin Murphy, p.261–81. Index, p.282–86.

I259 Green, Christopher. Cubism and its enemies: modern movements and reaction in French art, 1916–1928. New Haven, Yale Univ. Pr., 1987. 325p. il. (part col.)

Important contextual study of the movement. "I have tried . . . to look at Cubism and art in France between 1916 and 1928 in terms of the meanings available then. It is this concern that has led me to structure the book in terms of oppositions. . . . A major intention is to explore the works, theories and attitudes of the Cubists . . . in contradistinction to other very different works, theories and attitudes in other milieux."—*Introd.*

Contents: (I) Late Cubism in France, 1916–1928: a narrative; (II) Art worlds; (III) Cubism and the conservative opposition; (IV) Radical alternatives.

Abbreviations, p.[300]. Notes, p.[301]–20. Index, p.[321]–25.

I260 Grundberg, Andy, and Gauss, Kathleen McCarthy. Photography and art: interactions since 1946. Fort Lauderdale, Fort Lauderdale Museum of Art; N.Y., Abbeville, 1987. 272p. il. (part col.)

Published in conjunction with the exhibition, Fort Lauderdale Museum of Art (1987), and other locations. Aims to chart "the emergence of photography as a vital force in contemporary art since the end of World War II [and] to show the enormous influence photographic imagery has had on the more traditional . . . visual arts of painting, sculpture, drawing, and printmaking."—*Pref.*

Contents: Introduction, by Andy Grundberg and Kathleen McCarthy Gauss; (1) The enduring Modernist impulse, by Andy Grundberg; (2) Surrealism, Symbolism, and the fictional photograph, by Kathleen McCarthy Gauss; (3) Popular culture, Pop art, by Andy Grundberg; (4) Breaking the mold: experiments in technique and process, by Kathleen McCarthy Gauss; (5) Conceptual art and the photography of ideas; (6) In the studio: construction and invention; (7) Camera culture in a postmodern age, by Andy Grundberg.

Notes to the text, p.232–34. Artists' biographies, p.236–63. Bibliography, p.264–68. Index, p.269–71.

I261 Hamilton, George Heard. Painting and sculpture in Europe, 1880–1940. 6th ed. New Haven, Yale Univ. Pr., 1993. 621p. il. (part col.) ([Yale University Press] pelican history of art)

See GLAH 1:I247 for previous eds. 3d ed. 1979, repr. with corrections 1982. "In this new edition changes of ownership have been recorded wherever possible, and death dates added. For the first time, colour plates replace some of the black and white illustrations and the bibliography has been extensively enlarged and updated by Richard Cork."—*Foreword* [to the 6th ed.].

Bibliography, p.[553]–91. Index, p.[601]–21.

I262 Hillier, Bevis. The style of the century, 1900–1980. New chapter by Kate McIntyre. London, Herbert Pr., 1998. 239p. il. (part col.)

1st ed. 1983.

"This book attempts to convey the pervasiveness of style, and to show its close relation to 'lifestyle'. My canvas is the whole of the twentieth century so far."—*Introd.* Survey, from Edwardiana to "punk."

Index, p.235–39.

I263 Honour, Hugh. Romanticism. N.Y., Harper & Row, 1979. 415p. il.

A sequel to the author's equally important and wide-ranging Neo-Classicism (GLAH 1:I249). Devoted to "Romanticism as an historical phenomenon, not as a state of mind found in all periods and cultures."—*Introd.*

Contents: Introduction; (1) For lack of a better name; (2) The morality of landscape; (3) Frozen music; (4) The last enchantments of the Middle Age; (5) The sense of the past; (6) The cause of liberty; (7) Artist's life; (8) The mysterious way; (9) Epilogue.

Notes, p.325–65. Books for further reading, p.366–71. Catalogue of illustrations, p.372–408. Index, p.[409]–15.

I264 Hulten, Karl Gunnar Pontus. Futurism & futurisms = Futurismo & Futurismi. N.Y., Abbeville Pr., 1986. 639p. il. (part col.)

Trans. of Futurismo e futurismi. Milano, Bompiani, 1986. French ed., Futurisme et futurismes. Paris, Chemin vert, 1986.

Catalog accompanying the exhibition, Palazzo Grassi, Venice (1986), the first major Futurism exhibition in Europe.

Contents: Futurism & Futurisms, by Pontus Hulten; Futurist prophecies, by Pontus Hulten; Toward Futurism 1880–1909; Futurism, 1909–1918; Futurisms 1909–1930; Dictionary of Futurism.

Chronology, p.616–22. Catalog of the works exhibited (not reproduced in color section), p.623–31. Bibliography, p.632–33. Index, p.634–37.

I265 Hunter, Sam, and Jacobus, John. Modern art: painting, sculpture, architecture. 3d rev. ed. N.Y., Abrams, 2000. 448p. il. (part col.)

1st ed., 1976; 2d ed. 1985. "Produced by the Vendome Press/ an Alexis Gregory book"; 3d ed. 1992.

A "history of the ideas, forms, and events that have brought us to the modern and post-modern worlds of art and architecture."—*Pref. and ackn.* Intended for the general reader and undergraduates. Chronological in arrangement, with the focus upon distinct movements in modern art.

Notes, p.441. Bibliography, p.441–44. Index, p.445–48.

I266 Individuals: a selected history of contemporary art, 1945–1986. Essays by Kate Linker, Donald Kuspit, Hal Foster . . . [et al.] Organized by Julia Brown Turrell. Ed. by Howard Singerman. Los Angeles, Museum of Contemporary Art; N.Y., Abbeville, 1986. 371p. il.

Published in conjunction with the exhibition, Museum of Contemporary Art, Los Angeles (1986–88). Important exhibition and catalog on post-war art.

Checklist of the exhibition, p.338–62. Index, p.365–69.

I267 Lucie-Smith, Edward. Art of the 1930s: the age of anxiety. N.Y., Rizzoli, 1985. 264p. il. (part col.)

"This book . . . takes a particularly crucial epoch, and tries to relate the Modernist painting and sculpture of the period to other developments, many of them deeply hostile to everything the artists of the avant-garde stood for."—*Author's note.*

Contents: (1) The end of Weimar and the making of Nazi art; (2) Socialist Realism in Russia; (3) Italy: pluralism under a dictatorship; (4) The Mexican muralists; (5) The middle age of the École de Paris; (6) Parisian fashions: Surrealism and Neo-Classicism; (7) Abstraction, Neo-Romanticism and Social Realism in France; (8) England: the struggle to be modern; (9) English Abstract art; (10) Portugal, Latin America, Holland and Belgium in the 1930s; (11) The fate of the refugees; (12) American Abstract art; (13) Social Realism in America; (14) Patronage of the arts in America.

Chronology, p.255–57. Bibliography, p.258–60. Index, p.261–64.

I268 ______. Art today. London, Phaidon, 1995. 511p. col. il.

"This book is a survey of the . . . period from 1960 to the present."—*Introd.*

Contents: Pop & after; The survival of Abstraction; Minimal & Conceptual; Land art, light and space, Body art; Neo-Dada, Arte Povera & Installation; Neo-Expressionism; Realism in America; Post-Modernism and Neo-Classicism; British figurative painting; New British sculpture; New art in New York; Out of New York; Latin America; Perestroika art; The Far East; African & Afro-Caribbean art; Racial minorities; Feminist & gay.

Notes, p.480. Artists' biographies, p.481–97. Bibliography, p.498–503. Chronology, p.504–05. Index, p.507–10.

I269 ______. Movements in art since 1945. 3d rev. and exp. ed. N.Y., Thames and Hudson, 1995. 304p. il. (part col.) (World of art)

1st published in the U.S. under the title Late Modern: the visual arts since 1945 (N.Y., Praeger, 1969). New, rev. ed. N.Y., Thames and Hudson, 1985.

Introductory survey of post-war art.

Contents: (1) Style into content; (2) Abstract Expressionism; (3) The European scene; (4) Post-painterly Abstraction; (5) Pop, environments and happenings; (6) Abstract sculpture, Minimal Art, Conceptual Art; (7) Arte povera, Post-Minimalism and their heritage; (8) Neo-Expressionist tendencies in the 1980s; (9) America in the 1980s; (10) Questioning the western modernist canon from the "margins"; (11) Issue-based art: African-American, Afro-Caribbean, feminist and gay art.

Text references, p.289–90. Select bibliography, p.290–95. Index, p.301–04.

I270 ______. Visual arts in the twentieth century. London, L. King, 1996. 400p. il. (part col.), ports.

A chronological survey of the arts of the 20th century, by decade, through 1995. Each chapter is divided by medium (architecture, painting, sculpture, photography).

Notes, p.384–86. Bibliography, p.387–91. Index, p.394–400.

I271 Lynton, Norbert. The story of modern art. 2d ed. Englewood Cliffs, Prentice Hall, 1989. 400p. il. (part col.), ports.

1st ed., Ithaca, Cornell Univ. Pr.,1980. "For this edition I have been able to make some amendments in the text, convert some black-and-white illustrations into colour plates, trim the last chapter, add a new chapter for the 1980s, and add to and update the biographies and bibliography."—*Pref. to the second ed.*

Popular survey of modern art for the general reader.

Biographical notes, p.365–91. Bibliography, p.392–95. Index, p.397–400.

I272 Making their mark: women artists move into the mainstream, 1970–85. [By] Randy Rosen, curator [and] Catherine C. Brawer, assoc. curator. N.Y., Abbeville Pr., 1989. 300p. il. (part col.)

Catalog of the exhibition, Cincinnati Art Museum (1989), and other locations. Important treatment of a seminal moment, documenting "the prominent and catalytic role played by so many women in redirecting and redefining the interest of mainstream art."—*p.7.*

Artists' biographies, p.237–65. Selected group exhibitions, p.266–69. Public collections, p.270–74. Selected general bibliography, p.275–77. Checklist of the exhibition, p.284–92. Index, p.293–300.

I273 Martin, Marianne W. Futurist art and theory, 1909–1915. [Reprint.] N.Y., Hacker Art Books, 1978. xxxii, 228p. il., plates.

First pub. Oxford, Clarendon, 1968.

Contents: (I) Painting and sculpture in Italy during the later nineteenth century; (II) New directions: the Florentine movement; (III) F. T. Marinetti: life and work before the launching of Futurism; (IV) The first manifesto and the Futurist aesthetic; (V) Futurist painting theory and its sources; (VI) The artists: their beginnings; (VII) The first Futurist paintings of Boccioni, Carrà and Russolo: 1910 to summer 1911; (VIII) Severini's work, 1910–11; (IX) the Milanese artists and Cubism in 1911; (X) The Paris exhibition and its aftermath: theory 1912–13; (XI) Painting 1912–13: Severini; (XII) Painting 1912–13: The Milanese artists and Soffici;

(XIII) Boccioni's sculpture: 1912–13; (XIV) Giacomo Balla: 1912–13; (XV) The final years: 1914–15; Appendix: On the Futurists' controversies.

Selected bibliography, p.[207]–13. Index, p.215–28.

I274 McShine, Kynaston. An international survey of recent painting and sculpture. [Ed. by Harriet Schoenholz Bee and Jane Fluegel.] N.Y., Museum of Modern Art, 1984. 364p.

Catalog of the exhibition, Museum of Modern Art (1984). "Featuring work of the last decade by an international group of artists, it is the first contemporary survey of painting and sculpture organized by the Museum in some years."—*Introd.*

Documentation [individual and group exhibition histories], p.[342]–59.

I275 Minimal art: a critical anthology. Ed. by Gregory Battcock. Introd. by Anne M. Wagner. Berkeley, Univ. of Calif. Pr., 1995. xv, 454p. il.

1st ed. N.Y., Dutton, 1968. Reprinting of a classic anthology on Minimalism, with a new introduction, "Reading Minimal Art," by Anne M. Wagner.

Bibliography, p.445–47. Supplementary bibliography, p.447–49. Index, p.[451]–54.

I276 Modern art: practices and debate. New Haven, Yale Univ. Pr., in assoc. with the Open University, 1993. 4v.

"A series of four books about art and its interpretation from the mid-nineteenth century to the end of the twentieth. Each of the books is self-sufficient and accessible to the general reader. As a series, they form the main texts of an Open University course. . . . They represent a range of approaches and methods characteristic of contemporary art-historical debate."—*Pref. to v.4.*

Contents: Frascina, Francis. Modernity and modernism: French painting in the nineteenth century; Harrison, Charles; Frascina, Francis; and Perry, Gill. Primitivism, cubism, abstraction: the early twentieth century; Fer, Briony. Realism, rationalism, surrealism: art between the wars; Wood, Paul, et al. Modernism in dispute: art since the Forties.

I277 Movements in modern art. London, Tate Gallery, 1997– . 8v. il. (part col.)

Accessible, brief surveys.

Contents: Batchelor, David. Minimalism (1997); Harrison, Charles. Modernism (1997); Malpas, James. Realism (1997); Cottington, David. Cubism (1998); Behr, Shulamith. Expressionism (1999); Humphreys, David. Futurism (1999); McCarthy, David. Pop art (2000); Heartney, Eleanor. Postmodernism (2001).

I278 Museum of Modern Art (New York, N.Y.) Library. Artists files [microform]. Alexandria, Va., Chadwyck-Healey, 1986. 5,697 microfiches il. + index (300p.)

More than 200,000 items compiled by and located in the MoMA Library, documenting the life and work of more than 20,000 modern artists including painters, sculptors, graphic, installation, mixed media and performance artists, and other figures of the international art world. Materials range from gallery announcements and invitations, clippings, and press releases to posters, reviews, and anthology excerpts. Some files consist of only one or two items, others have hundreds. Arranged alphabetically by artist.

I279 ———. Artists scrapbooks [microform]. Alexandria, Va., Chadwyck-Healey, 1986. 642 microfiches il.

Original scrapbooks compiled by and located in the MoMA Library. Issued in 4 binders, each with contents page at front. Arranged alphabetically by 44 individual artists with three multi-artist collections at the end.

Contents: (1) Albers-Dubuffet; (2) Ensor-Nadelman; (3) Picasso; (4) Richter-Wright. Sidney Janis Gallery. Israeli art. Bauhaus scrapbook.

I280 Needham, Gerald. 19th century realist art. N.Y., Harper & Row, 1988. xvii, 350p. il.

"The purpose of this book is . . . to analyze the issues of Realism in the context of their chronological development, and to provide an outline but not a detailed history of the movement."—*Foreword.*

Contents: (1) The dilemmas of Realism; (2) The origins of Realism, ca 1800–1832; (3) The desire to record the world, 1830–1850; (4) The situation of art in 1848; (5) The first generation of Realist painters; (6) Realism throughout Europe; (7) Changing ideas and the early work of Manet; (8) Impressionism; (9) The end of Realism.

Bibliography, p.334–39. Index, p.340–50.

I281 New York Public Library. Artists file [microform]. Alexandria, Va., Chadwyck-Healey, 1987–89. 11,381 microfiches il. + index (10 microfiches) issued in loose-leaf binder with [4]p. of text.

Valuable source of biographical and other information on artists and craftspeople from all over the world. Reproduces a valuable clippings file of 1.5 million items on more than 80,000 painters, sculptors, architects, craftspeople, jewelers, furniture and interior designers, commercial artists, fashion designers, collectors, connoisseurs, critics and curators, art historians, silversmiths, commercial artists, and couturiers. Covers the period from the 19th century, including major and minor masters as well as popular artists and purveyors of kitsch. Includes newspaper clippings, American and international, including regional newspapers, magazine clippings, popular and specialist American and foreign magazines and journals, press releases, newsletters and other announcements, auction and exhibition catalogs, including lists of exhibitions, invitation cards, book jackets, engravings, museum newsletters, exhibition brochures, and reproductions and original photographs. Arranged alphabetically by artist.

Index.

I282 Novotny, Fritz. Painting and sculpture in Europe, 1780–1880. [Trans. from the German by R. H. Boothroyd.] New Haven, Yale Univ. Pr., 1992[?] 483p. il. (Yale University Press pelican history of art)

See GLAH 1:I255 for first ed. 2d ed. 1970, repr. with minor revisions and updated bibliography, 1978. The present ed. seems to be a reprint of the 1978 ed.

I283 Paris-Berlin, 1900–1933: rapports et contrastes France, Allemagne: art, architecture, graphisme, littérature, objets industriels, cinéma, théâtre, musique. Nouv. éd. Paris, Centre Georges Pompidou; Gallimard, 1992. 757p. il. (part col.)

1st ed. 1978. Originally published to accompany one in a series of four important exhibitions at the Centre Georges Pompidou (see following entries) on international modernism before World War II.

I284 Paris-Moscou, 1900–1930. Arts plastiques, arts appliqués et objets utilitaires, architecture-urbanisme, agitprop, affiche, théâtre-ballet, littérature, musique, cinéma, photo créative. [3d ed.] Paris, Centre Georges Pompidou; Gallimard, 1991. 779p. il. (part col.)

1st and 2d ed. 1979. Originally published to accompany one in a series of four important exhibitions at the Centre Georges Pompidou on international modernism before World War II.

I285 Paris-New York, 1908–1968 . . . Nouv. éd. Paris, Centre Georges Pompidou; Gallimard, 1991. 955p. il. (part col.)

1st ed. 1977. Originally published to accompany one in a series of four important exhibitions at the Centre Georges Pompidou on international modernism before World War II.

I286 Paris-Paris, 1937–1957 . . . Nouv. éd. Paris, Centre Georges Pompidou; Gallimard, 1992. 799p. il. (part col.)

1st ed. 1981. Originally published to accompany one in a series of four important exhibitions at the Centre Georges Pompidou (see previous entries) on international modernism before World War II.

I287 "Primitivism" in 20th century art: affinity of the tribal and the modern. Ed. by William Rubin. N.Y., Museum of Modern Art (Distr. by New York Graphic Society Books, 1984). 2v. il. (part col.)

Published to accompany the exhibition, Museum of Modern Art (1984). A monumental survey of "primitivism—the interest of modern artists in tribal art and culture, as revealed in their thought and work."—*Introd.* Takes up where Goldwater's pioneering essay, Primitivism in modern art (GLAH 2:I257), left off. Includes essays on individual artists and movements by a range of specialists.

Notes at ends of chapters.

I288 Robertson, Jack. Twentieth-century artists on art: an index to writings, statements, and interviews by artists, architects, and designers. 2d enl. ed., N.Y., Hall, 1996. xvi, 834p.

1st ed. 1985.

Intended to provide easy and direct access to twentieth-century artists' words. Covers 14,400 artists (compared to 5,000 in the 1st ed.).

Bibliography of sources indexed, p.1–45.

I289 Rosen, Charles, and Zerner, Henri. Romanticism and realism: the mythology of nineteenth-century art. N.Y., Viking Press, 1984. xi, 244p. il.

"We have tried in this book to redefine both avant-garde and official art."—*Pref.* A collection of important essays.

Contents: The fingerprint: a vignette; (I) Romanticism: the permanent revolution; (II) Caspar David Friedrich and the language of landscape; (III) The romantic vignette and Thomas Bewick; (IV) The reproductive image and photography; (V) The juste milieu and Thomas Couture; (VI) Realism and the avant-garde; (VII) The recovery of the past and the modern tradition; (VIII) The ideology of the licked surface: official art.

Notes on the illustrations, p.233–36. Index, p.237–44.

I290 Rosenblum, Robert, and Janson, H. W. 19th century art. N.Y., Abrams, 1984. 527p. il. (part col.)

An attempt by two leading scholars to "overhaul the history of nineteenth-century art." —*Pref. and ackn.*

Contents: Painting, by Robert Rosenblum; Sculpture, by H. W. Janson.

Bibliography, p.[506]–14. Index, p.[515]–27.

I291 Sandler, Irving. Art of the postmodern era: from the late 1960s to the early 1990s. N.Y., IconEditions, 1996. xxx, 636p. il. (part col.), plates.

Substantial history of art since the Sixties.

Contents: (1) Postminimalism; (2) The impact of 1968 on European art; (3) First-generation feminism; (4) Pattern and decoration painting; (5) Architectural sculpture; (6) New Image painting; (7) The art world of the 1970s; (8) American Neoexpressionism; (9) The Italian Transavantguardia and German Neoexpressionism; (10) Media art; (11) Postmodernist art theory; (12) The consumer society and Deconstruction art; (13) The art world in the first half of the 1980s; (14) East Village art; (15) Commodity art, Neogeo, and the East Village art scene; (16) The "Other": From the marginal into the mainstream; (17) Into the 1990s.

Notes at ends of chapters. Bibliography p.557–616. Index, p.617–36.

I292 Selz, Peter Howard. Art in our times: a pictorial history, 1890–1980. N.Y., Abrams, [1981]. 590p. il. (part col.)

"This book, with its 1,600 illustrations, provides a comprehensive and inclusive visual record of the art of the twentieth century. It contains not only the most significant monuments but also works of art that are now neglected but were important at the time of their creation."—*Pref. and ackn.* Excludes photography. A decade-by-decade presentation covering architecture, painting, sculpture, and related media, 1890s to 1970s.

Selected bibliography, p.559–65. Index, p.567–84.

I293 Stich, Sidra. Anxious visions: surrealist art. With essays by James Clifford . . . [et al.] Berkeley, University Art Museum, University of California at Berkeley; New York, Abbeville Pr., 1990. 295p. il. (part col.)

Catalog of the exhibition, University Art Museum, University of California, Berkeley (1990).

"The following study aims to relate Surrealist art to some of the changing views about human nature and to the disturbing events [of the years between the wars]. It . . . focuses attention on the broad social, cultural, and political climate."—*p.25.*

Biographies, p.233–53. Chronology, p.255–78. Selected bibliography, p.279–83. Checklist of the exhibition, p.284–89. Index, p.290–95.

I294 Stiles, Kristine, and Selz, Peter. Theories and documents of contemporary art: a sourcebook of artists' writings. Berkeley, Univ. of Calif. Pr., 1996. xxii, 1003p. il. (California studies in the history of art, 35)

Continues the series begun with Herschel B. Chipp's Theories of modern art (GLAH 1:I238) and continued by Taylor's Nineteenth-century theories of art (GLAH 2:I295). Substantial, wide-ranging anthology of excerpts from literary sources in translation, arranged chronologically, with brief introductions to each chapter. Some texts translated into English for the first time, others are published for the first time. "We sought to include texts that had a wide impact . . . texts addressed to aesthetic and art historical canons . . . new media and technology . . . gender, race, class, sexuality, and other diversity issues; and methodological strategies ranging from formalist to feminist to postmodernist."—*Pref.*

Contents: (1) Gestural abstraction; (2) Geometric abstraction; (3) Figuration; (4) Material culture and everyday life; (5) Art and technology; (6) Installations, environments, and sites; (7) Process; (8) Performance art; (9) Language and concepts.

Notes, p.897–911. Bibliography, p.913–56. Index, p.983–1003.

I295 Taylor, Joshua C. Nineteenth-century theories of art. Berkeley, Univ. of Calif. Pr., 1987. xii, 563p. il. (California studies in the history of art, 24)

Continues the series begun with Herschel B. Chipp's Theories of modern art (GLAH 1:I238). Substantial, wide-ranging anthology of literary sources in translation, arranged thematically, with brief biographical introductions to each chapter. Most entries are complete essays.

Contents: (I) Beauty and the language of form; (II) Art and the community of souls; (III) Truth to nature and the nature of truth; (IV) Art and society; (V) An art of pure vision; (VI) Art as creation.

Editorial references throughout. Index, p.553–63.

I296 Tisdall, Caroline, and Bozzolla, Angelo. Futurism. N.Y., Oxford University Press, 1978. 216p. il. (part col.), ports. (World of art)

Readable introduction.

Contents: (1) The means of Futurism; (2) The roots of Futurism; (3) Painting and sculpture up to 1913; (4) Literature and theatre; (5) Futurist music; (6) The Futurist city; (7) Photodynamism and Futurist cinema; (8) Futurism and women; (9) Lacerba; (10) Art of the war years and after; (11) Futurism and fascism.

Sources and further reading, p.210. Index, p.214–16.

I297 Varnedoe, Kirk, and Gopnik, Adam. High & low: modern art, popular culture. N.Y., Museum of Modern Art (Distr. by Abrams, 1990). 460p. (part fold.) il. (part col.)

Published in conjunction with the exhibition, Museum of Modern Art (1990–91), and other locations. An important study of "the evolving relationship . . . between modern art and popular culture" in the 20th century.—*Introd.* Accompanied by an anthology of essays entitled: Modern art and popular culture: readings in high & low (N.Y., Museum of Modern Art; Abrams, 1990).

Contents: Introduction; Words; Graffiti; Caricature; Comics; Advertising; Contemporary reflections; Coda.

Notes to the text, p.415–27. Bibliography, p.429–49. Index of illustrations, p.457–60.

I298 Vaughan, William, and Cachin, Françoise. Arts of the 19th century. Introd., captions, and biographical notes trans. from the French by James Underwood. N.Y., Abrams, 1998–. (1)v. il. (part col.)

First pub. in French trans. for the series L'art et les grandes civilisations, 19–20 (GLAH 2:I8). Lavishly illustrated survey of the period.

Contents: (1) 1780–1850; (2) 1850–1905 (forthcoming).

I299 ______. Romanticism and art. [Repr. with rev.] N.Y., Thames and Hudson, 1994. 288p. il. (part col.)

1st ed. 1978. Popular introduction by an authority.

Contents: (1) Attitudes and ambiguities; (2) Hope and fear; (3) The heroic era; (4) The medieval revival; (5) Transcendent landscapes; (6) "Natural painture"; (7) Sensation; (8) "Romanticizing the world."

Sources, p.281. Further reading, p.281–82. Index, p.287–88.

I300 Waller, Susan. Women artists in the modern era: a documentary history. Metuchen, N.J., Scarecrow Pr., 1991. xii, 392p.

"The documents in this volume have been selected to illuminate the historical experience of women artists. They include letters, journals, and memoirs of artists, critics' reviews of women's work at exhibitions and discussions of women's capabilities, and the minutes and reports of artists' societies and schools. They document the lives of individual women artists and the institutional and cultural parameters that conditioned what women attempted and what they accomplished."—*Pref.*

Contents: (I) Women and the Academies; (II) Wives and artists; (III) Lady amateurs; (IV) Strong-minded artists; (V) Women and the decorative arts; (VI) Women in art schools; (VII) Women artists organize; (VIII) Women and the Avant-Garde.

Suggested further readings, p.351–54. References, p.355–73. Index, p.375–92.

I301 Wheeler, Daniel. Art since mid-century: 1945 to the present. N.Y., Vendome Pr., (Distr. by Rizzoli International, 1991). 344p. il. (part col.)

A "comprehensive, one-volume history of late-modern and post-modern art."—*Pref. and ackn.*

Contents: (1) Modernism and its origins; (2) The New York school: Abstract Expressionism: 1945–60; (3) The European school of painting; (4) Sculpture at mid-century; (5) Into the Sixties: Pop Art and New Realism; (6) Assemblage, environments, happenings; (7) Post-painterly abstraction; (8) Minimalism: formalist sculpture in the United States; (9) Op, Kinetic, and Light Art; (10) The Post-Modern reaction: Conceptual, Performance, and Process Art; (11) Earth and site works; (12) Resurgent realism, photo-realist painting, hyper-realist sculpture; (13) Pattern and decoration; (14) New image art; (15) Fin de siècle: from Neo-Expressionism to Neo-Abstraction.

Bibliography, p.337–40. Index, p.341–44.

WESTERN COUNTRIES

Australia

I302 Allen, Christopher. Art in Australia from colonization to Postmodernism. N.Y., Thames and Hudson, 1997. 224p. il. (part col.) (World of art)

A concise survey of non-indigenous Australian art intended for the general reader. Offers a well-illustrated, accessible introduction with good coverage of the contemporary period. "An engaging narrative that offers a point of departure for those wishing to incorporate Australian art into a curriculum or to satisfy cultural curiosity."—*Review*, New art examiner, v.25, fall 1998, p.64.

Contents: (1) Colonization; (2) Settlement; (3) Unsettlement; (4) The uninhabitable; (5) Escape routes; (6) Homeless.

Timeline, p.[216–17]. Bibliography, p.218. Index, p.223–24.

I303 Dreamings, the art of aboriginal Australia. Peter Sutton . . . [et al.] Ed. by Peter Sutton. N.Y., Braziller in assoc. with the Asia Society Galleries, 1988. xiii, 266p. il. (part col.), maps.

Catalog of the exhibition, Asia Society Galleries, N.Y. (1988), and other locations. Examines and illustrates a broad range of Aboriginal art within its cultural context. "This book is unique in its field in at least three ways. It contains the first extended overview of the history of Aboriginal art scholarship (Ch.V). It presents substantial analysis of the Aboriginal aesthetic which shows how it is integrated with the distinctive world view and social values of Aboriginal tradition (Ch. I–III). And it examines the cultural, economic, and political context of the production of Western Desert paintings for an Australian and world art market (Ch. IV)."—*Introd.*

Contents: (I) Dreamings, by Peter Sutton; (II) Responding to aboriginal art, by Peter Sutton; (III) The morphology of feeling, by Peter Sutton; (IV) Dreamings in acrylic: Western Desert art, by Christopher Anderson and Françoise Dussart; (V) Perceptions of aboriginal art: a history, by Philip Jones; (VI) Survival, regeneration and impact, by Peter Sutton, Philip Jones, and Steven Hemming; Postscript, by Peter Sutton.

Biographies of the artists, p.235–42. Notes, p.243–53. References, p.254–61. Index, p.262–64.

I304 Haese, Richard. Rebels and precursors: the revolutionary years of Australian art. [2d ed.] Ringwood, Victoria, Penguin Books, 1988. 323p. il. (part col.), plates.

1st ed., London, Lane, 1981.

A study of modern art in Australia emphasizing the formative decades of the 1920s through 1940s. Focuses on political and social contexts for the development of modernism. Few illustrations.

Selective contents: (1) Reaction and progress; (2) The politics in painting; (3) Democracy and modernism; (4) Liberalism and anarchism; (5) Dissent and division; (6) Communism and culture; (7) The season in hell; (8) Patronage and professionalism; (9) Cultural reconstruction; (10) The radical diaspora.

Notes, p.296–304. Bibliography, p.309–12. Index, p.312–[24].

I305 Moore, William. The story of Australian art from the earliest known art of the continent to the art of today. [Facsimile reprint.] London, Angus & Robertson, 1980. 2v., il. col. front., plates, ports.

See GLAH 1:I264 for original publication and annotation.

I306 Smith, Bernard. European vision and the South Pacific. [3d ed.] South Melbourne, Oxford Univ. Pr., 1989. xiii, 370p. il. (part col.), maps, ports.

See GLAH 1:I265 for original annotation. 2d ed., 1985.

I307 ———. Place, taste, and tradition: a study of Australian art since 1788. [2d ed., rev.] Melbourne, Oxford Univ. Pr., 1979. 304p. il.

1st ed., Sydney, U. Smith Pty. [1945]. "The publication of the second edition of a book that has been out of print for over thirty years calls for a personal explanation since the new edition will be read not so much for the information it contains—most of which is now available elsewhere—as for the light that it may possibly throw upon the emergence of an interest in the history of Australian art and the evaluative processes, both critical and historical, which were involved."—*Pref.* This early work is still of interest for its examination, considered radical at the time, of the relationships between Australian art, economics, and politics. Covers movements and trends from the colonial period to modernism.

Notes, p.282–83. Bibliography, p.284–87. Chronological table, p.[288]–91. Index, p.292–304.

I308 Willis, Anne-Marie. Illusions of identity: the art of a nation. [Sydney], Hale and Iremonger, 1993. 205p. il.

Examines the evolution of Australian art in the context of "national culture" and "new art history." Seeks to "dismantle commonly held assumptions about both the value of and methodologies used in addressing the visual imagery and art of a particular nation."—*Introd.*

Contents: (1) Decentring nation; (2) Art of assimilation; (3) Nation as landscape; (4) Nation and otherness; (5) Making the image of modern Australia; (6) National economy as image.

Notes at ends of chapters. Bibliography, p.[192]–98. Index, p.[199]–205.

Canada

I309 Mellen, Peter. Landmarks of Canadian art. Toronto, McClelland and Stewart, 1978. 260p. il. (part col.)

A very general but well-illustrated survey of Canadian painting and sculpture from pre-history to the early 1970s. Utilizes key works to initiate discussions of different styles and schools.

Contents: (1) This sacred land: art of the native peoples; (2) Art for the glory of God: the early explorers of the French regime; (3) The garrison and the frontier: documenting the new society; (4) Contradictions and change: art in the Victorian era; (5) The Canadian spirit in art: the Group of Seven and their contemporaries; (6) The search within: contemporary art; (7) New ways of seeing.

Bibliography, p.257. Index, p.259–60.

I310 National Gallery of Canada. Canadian art. General eds., Charles C. Hill, Pierre B. Landry. Ottawa, The National Gallery, 1988– . (2)v.

See GLAH 1:I270 for original publication. Also published in French as Art canadien.

Two of the four projected vols. of this new ed. have been published. When complete, the catalog will include the entire collection of Canadian art in the National Gallery consisting of painting, sculpture, drawings, prints, decorative arts, and video works. This ed. covers works collected from 1880 through 1980. Each vol. is arranged alphabetically by artist.

Contents: (1) Painting, A–F; (2) Painting, G–K.

Numerical index, v.1, p.407–15, v.2, p.393–401.

SEE ALSO: Art and architecture in Canada: a bibliography and guide to the literature to 1981 (GLAH 2:A237)

France

I311 Adhémar, Jean. Influences antiques dans l'art du Moyen Age francais. Préf. de Léon Pressouyre. [Reprint.] Paris, Ed. du C.T.H.S., 1996. xxviii, 463p. il.

See GLAH 1:273 for 1st ed.

The reprint ed. contains a lengthy preface describing the historical context for and reaction to the original publication. An extensive bio-bibliography through 1987 is included. Bibliographie des travaux de Jean Adhémar, p.[429]–63.

I312 Blunt, Anthony. Art and architecture in France, 1500–1700. 4th ed., revised by Richard Beresford. New Haven, Yale Univ. Pr., 1999. xi, 319p. il. (part col.) (Yale University Press pelican history of art)

See GLAH 1:I274 for previous eds. Also published as Art et architecture en France, 1500–1700. Trad. de Monique Chatenet. Paris, Macula, 1983.

This posthumous ed. contains a new preface, many additional illustrations, updated bibliography, considerable revision of footnotes including addenda, and corrections based on the French ed.

Notes, p.[275]–99. Bibliography, p.[300]–7. Index, p.[308]–19.

I313 Chastel, André. French art. Trans. by Deke Dusinberre. N.Y., Flammarion, [1994]– . (3)v.

Trans. of L'art français, Paris, Flammarion, 1993– . (4)v.

Superbly illustrated and organized, these volumes comprise Chastel's last work. A lengthy introduction, left unfinished at his death, has been excerpted and interspersed throughout.

Contents: (I) Prehistory to the Middle Ages; (II) The Renaissance, 1430–1620; (III) Art under the Ancien Régime, 1620–1775; (IV) The age of eloquence, 1775–1820 (forthcoming).

Two further vols. are planned for the original French ed., on the 19th and 20th centuries respectively.

Bibliography and index in each vol.

I314 L'inventaire général des monuments et des richesses artistiques de la France. Inventaires topographiques. [Paris] Ministère des affaires culturelles, 1969– . (16)v.

See GLAH 1:I280 for previous vols.

Contents: Morbihan: Canton Belle-Ile-en-Mer (1978); Bas-Rhin: Canton de Saverne (1978); Charente-Maritime: Canton Ile de Ré, 2v. (1979); Haut-Rhin: Canton Thann (1980); Vaucluse: Cantons Cadenet et Pertuis, Pays d'Aigues (1981); Meuse: Canton Gondrecourt-le-Chateau (1981); Sarthe: Canton La Ferté-Bernard (1983); Cantal: Canton Vic-sur-Ceré (1984); Ardeche: Canton de Viviers (1989); Pyrénées-Atlantiques: Vic-Bilh, Morlaàs et Montanerès: Cantons de Garlin, Lembeye, Thèze, Morlaàs, Montaner (1989).

I315 Levey, Michael. Painting and sculpture in France, 1700–1789. New Haven, Yale Univ. Pr., 1993. 318p. il. (part col.) (Yale University Press pelican history of art)

See GLAH 1:I281 for related, previous ed. Portions of this volume first appeared in Levey's Art and architecture in the eighteenth century in France (1972). This new publication, covering only painting and sculpture, has been revised and greatly expanded. Very good quality illustrations, many in color. Bibliography is arranged by artist as well as media.

Notes, p.[299]–306. Select bibliography, p.[307]–10. Index, p.[311]–18.

I316 Mâle, Emile. Religious art in France, the late middle ages: a study of medieval iconography and its sources. Ed. by Harry Bober. Trans. by Marthiel Mathews. [5th ed., rev.] Princeton, Princeton Univ. Pr., 1986. xiii, 597p. il. (Bollingen series, v.90:3) (Studies in religious iconography / by Emile Mâle)

See GLAH 1:I284 for previous eds. Trans. of the 5th ed., rev. and corr., of L'art religieux de la fin du moyen âge en France: étude sur l'iconographie du moyen âge et sur ses sources d'inspiration.

The English translations of this and the following landmark volumes continue the series initiated by GLAH 1:I285.

Additions and corrections assembled through various previous eds. have been incorporated into the footnotes. Recent publications have also been added to the footnotes. All the illustrations in the original eds. have been replaced with better quality ones and some new illustrations have been added.

Notes, p.[451]–548. Bibliography, p.[549]–73. Index, p.[587]–97.

I317 ———. Religious art in France, the thirteenth century: a study of medieval iconography and its sources. Ed. by Harry Bober. Trans. by Marthiel Mathews. Princeton, Princeton Univ. Pr., 1984. 564p. il. (Bollingen series, v.90:2) (Studies in religious iconography / by Emile Mâle)

See GLAH 1:I283 for previous eds. and translations. Trans. of the 9th ed. of L'art religieux du XIIIe siècle en France: étude sur l'iconographie du moyen âge et sur ses sources d'inspiration.

Contains an appendix, "List of principal works illustrating the life of Christ (End of the twelfth century, thirteenth and fourteenth centuries)."

Notes, p.[408]–99. Bibliography, p.[501]–24. Index, p.[537]–64.

I318 Modern art in Paris: two-hundred catalogues of the major exhibitions reproduced in facsimile in forty-seven volumes. Sel. and org. by Theodore Reff. N.Y., Garland, 1981. 47v.

Important series of reprints of key Parisian exhibition catalogs of the late 19th century.

Selective contents: Exhibitions of draftsmen and illustrators; Exhibitions of Impressionist art; Exhibitions of Realist art; Exhibitions of Symbolists and Nabis; Salons of the "Indépendants," 1892–1895; World's fair of 1855; World's fair of 1867; World's fair of 1889; World's fair of 1900.

I319 Vergnolle, Eliane. L'art roman en France. Paris, Flammarion, 1994. 383p. il. (part col.), maps, plans.

In-depth, scholarly survey of architecture, painting, and sculpture from 980–1180. Very fine color illustrations throughout. Useful for the advanced reader. "With . . . profound scholarship and sensitivity, the reader is guided through . . . monumental architectural achievements . . . illuminated wall paintings, stained glass, mosaic pavements and enamels. These various media are not discussed in separate chapters but are treated as phenomena of the same closely related artistic trends. This brilliant work should be in every library and on the shelf of every medievalist."—*Review*, Burlington magazine, v.137, Sept. 1995, p.619.

Contents: (I) Le champ de l'étude; (II) Les conditions de la création; (III) Préfiguration (980–1020); (IV) Création (1020–1060); (V) Vers un nouveau décor monumental (1010–1060); (VI) Explosion (1060–1090); (VII) Maturité (1090–1140); (VIII) L'essor du décor monumental (1090–1140); (IX) Ruptures et mutations (1140–1180).

Notes, p.353–67. Glossaire, p.368–69. Bibliographie, p.370–78. Index, p.379–83.

I320 Zerner, Henri. L'art de la Renaissance en France: l'invention du classicisme. Paris, Flammarion, 1996. 414p. il. (part col.), plans.

Comprehensive analysis of the development of Renaissance art and architecture in France in the 16th century. Examines themes and trends from the major and minor arts, with an emphasis on architecture and painting. Explores the Italian influence on the evolution of style and taste within French cultural context. "Zerner must be congratulated for this stimulating survey of a crucial period. With more than 400 pages and 451 illustrations it constitutes a landmark in the study of French renaissance art."—*Review*, Burlington magazine, v.141, April 1999, p.237.

Contents: (I) Le gothique à la renaissance; (II) Fontainebleau, Rosso et la gallerie François Ier; (III) Le classicisme antiquisant des années 1540: Cellini, Serlio et Primatice; (IV) Les enseignements de Fontainebleau; (V) Lescot, Goujon et le Louvre; (VI) Les Clouet; (VII) Jean Cousin et la peinture; (VIII) Jean Cousin et les métiers d'art; (IX) Paris et les provinces; (X) La sculpture et la mort; (XI) Le sentiment national—Philibert de l'Orme.

Notes, p.390–402. Bibliographie, p.403–9. Index, p.410–14.

Germany and Austria

I321 Belting, Hans. The Germans and their art: a troublesome relationship. Trans. by Scott Kleager. New Haven, Yale Univ. Pr., 1998. vi, 120p. il.

Collection of essays by a thoughtful practitioner.

Contents: (I) New questions, old answers; (II) Searching for the German style; (III) Art historians and the "German question"; (IV) Resistance to the modern movement in Germany; (V) The banning of German expressionism and "degenerate art"; (VI) The escape into "occidental art"; (VII) German art; Epilogue.

Sources, p.112–20.

I322 Berlin und die Antike: Architektur, Kunstgewerbe, Malerei, Skulptur, Theater und Wissenschaft vom 16. Jahrhundert bis heute. Hrsg. von Willmuth Arenhövel. Berlin, Deutsches Archaologisches Institut (Ausl. Wasmuth), 1979. 2v.

Catalog published to accompany the exhibition marking the 150th anniversary of the Deutsches Archäologisches Institut (Schloss Charlottenburg, 1979). Well-organized combination of scholarly essays and an illustrated catalog of more than 1000 detailed entries with references. Explores the influence of antiquity on culture in Berlin from the 16th to the 20th centuries. Covers fine arts, decorative and applied arts, architecture and architectural decoration, printing and graphic arts, and theatrical and film design.

Zeitafel, v.1, p.470–89. Verzeichnis de Fachausdrücke, v.1, p.490–97. Verzeichnis der abgekürtzen Literatur, v.1, p.498–503, v.2, p.571–73. Register, v.1, p.506–25, v.2, p.574–86.

I323 Braunfels, Wolfgang. Die Kunst im Heiligen Römischen Reich Deutscher Nation. München, Beck, 1979–1989. 6v.

Landmark study suitable for the advanced reader or researcher. Originally conceived as a definitive eight vol.

study; six vols. were published before Braunfels death in 1989. Comprehensive, scholarly work with many fine quality black-and-white illustrations and plans. Unpublished vols. are (VII) Das Werk der Bürger und der Höfe, 1250–1648 and (VIII) Vom Barock zur bürgerlichen Bildung, 1648–1870.

Contents: Die Räume: (I) Die weltlichen Fürstentümer; (II) Die geistlichen Fürstentümer; (III) Reichsstädte, Grafschaften, Reichsklöster. Die Grenzen: (IV) Grenzstaaten im Westen und Süden, deutsche und romanische Kultur; (V) Grenzstaaten im Osten und Norden, deutsche und slawische Kultur. Die Zeiten: (VI) Das Werk der Kaiser, Bischöfe, Äbte und ihrer Künstler, 750–1250.

Anmerkungen, v.I, p.381–[403], v.II, p.393–[436], v.III, p.437–[62], v.IV, p.387–[405], v.V, p.349–[74], v.VI, p.309–[24]. Personen- und Ortsregister, v.I, p.407–[24], v.II, p.439–[51], v.III, p.465–[78], v.IV, 407–[16], v.V, p.377–[85], v.VI, p.325–[32].

I324 Davidson, Mortimer G. Kunst in Deutschland, 1933–1945: eine wissenschaftliche Enzyklopädie der Kunst im Dritten Reich. 2. überarb. Aufl. Tübingen, Grabert, 1988– . (3v. in 4)

Unable to verify existence of previous ed.

An exhaustive compilation of art and architecture produced in Germany under the Nazis. "The purpose of this encyclopedia is precisely to give the public the opportunity to form its own judgement. . . . Its sole aim is to present the works themselves and to offer this field, if not an exhaustive documentation, still the world's most comprehensive survey existing to date."—*Foreword*. Texts in English, French, and German. Each entry is accompanied by a photograph and each vol. contains detailed biographical notes.

Contents: (1) Skulpturen; (2:1) Malerei, A–P; (2:2) Malerei, R–Z; (3:1) Architektur.

Bibliographie/Bibliography, v.1, p.[519]–34, v.2/2, p.[475]–87, v.3, p.[579]–621.

I325 Degenerate art: the fate of the avant-garde in Nazi Germany. Los Angeles, Los Angeles County Museum of Art, 1991. 423p. il. (part col.), ports.

Catalog published in conjunction with the exhibition, Los Angeles County Museum of Art and the Art Institute of Chicago (1991). The goal of the exhibition was to reconstruct, as closely as possible, and analyze the far-reaching legacy of the 1937 National Socialist exhibition, Entartete Kunst, which toured Germany and Austria for four years.

Contents: 1937: modern art and politics in prewar Germany, by Stephanie Barron; Beauty without sensuality/the exhibition Entartete Kunst, by George L. Mosse; Three days in Munich, July 1937, by Peter Guenther; Entartete Kunst, Munich 1937: a reconstruction, by Mario-Andreas von Lüttichau; An "educational exhibition": the precursors of Entartete Kunst and its individual venues, by Christoph Zuschlag; The fight for modern art: the Berlin Nationalgalerie after 1933, by Annegret Janda; On the trail of missing masterpieces: modern art from German galleries, by Andreas Hüneke; The Galerie Fischer auction, by Stephanie Barron; A musical facade for the Third Reich, by Michael Meyer; Film censorship during the Nazi era, by William Moritz.

Facsimile of the Entartete Kunst exhibition brochure, p.356–91. Chronology, p.391–401. Exhibition ephemera, p.404. Entartete Kunst: the literature, p.405. Selected bibliography, p.405–11. Index, p.419–23.

I326 Dehio, Georg Gottfried. Geschichte der deutschen Kunst: Kunstgeschichte als Kulturgeschichte. Hrsg. von Eugen Thurnher. Berlin, Nicolai, 1993. 183p. (Deutsche Bibliothek des Ostens)

See GLAH 1:I295 for 1923–34 ed. in 8v.

This compilation of selections, excerpted from vols. I–III (1930–31) includes a substantial essay by Thurnher on the historical context for Dehio's work and its subsequent influence.

Contents: (I) Was heisst "deutsche Kunst?"; (II) Römisches Erbe und romanische Kunst; (III) Staufisches Kaisertum und frühe Gotik; (IV) Universale Kirche und französische Gesellschaftskultur; (V) Deutscher Bürgersinn in der Spätgotik; (VI) Werbau und Wohnbau; (VII) Humanismus, Renaissance, Reformation; (VIII) Die Welt des Barock; (IX) Musik, Dichtung, Kunst Anmerkungen zum Nachwort, p.181–82.

I327 ______. Handbuch der deutschen Kunstdenkmäler. Begründ. vom Tag für Denkmalpflege 1900: Fortgeführt von Ernst Gall. Neubearb. besorgt durch die Dehio-Vereinigung. München, Deutscher Kunstverlag, 1964– .

See GLAH 1:I296 for previous vols. and eds. Some previous vols. were reprinted since the publication of GLAH 1, but have been omitted here. New eds. for Berlin, Brandenburg, Hessen, Mecklenburg-Vorpommern, and Rheinland are in preparation. Supp. vols. (Sonderbände) published in conjunction with the series are Mitteldeutschland (1991), München (1996), and West- und Ostpreussen (1993). Revised vols. are listed here:

Contents: Hessen (1982); Bezirke Berlin, DDR und Potsdam (1983); Rheinland/Pfalz/Saarland (1984); Landes Nordrhein-Westfalen II: Westfalen (1986); Bezirke Cottbus und Frankfurt/Oder (1987); Bayern II: Niederbayern (1988); Bayern III: Schwaben (1989); Bayern IV: München und Oberbayern (1990); Sachsen-Anhalt (1990); Bezirk Halle (1990); Bezirke Neubrandenburg, Rostock, Schwerin, Mecklenburg (1990); Bayern V: Regensburg und die Oberpfalz (1991); Bremen, Niedersachsen (1992); Baden-Wurttemburg I: die Regierungsbezirke Stuttgart und Karlsruhe (1993); West- und Ostpreussen (1993); Regierungsbezirke Stuttgart und Karlsruhe (1993); Berlin (1994); Hamburg, Schleswig-Holstein (1994); München (1996); Sachsen I: Regierungsbezirk Dresden (1996); Baden-Wurttemburg II: die Regierungsbezirke Freiburg und Tübingen (1997); Sachsen II: Regierungsbezirke Leipzig und Chemnitz (1998); Bayern I: Franken (1999); Sachsen-Anahlt II: Regierungsbezirk Dessau und Halle (1999).

I328 Dehio-Handbuch: die Kunstdenkmäler Österreichs. Hrsg. vom Institut fur österreichische Kunstforschung der Bundesdenkmalamtes. Wien, Schroll, 1976– . (9)v.

See GLAH 1:I297 for previous ed.

Later vols. in this ed. are ed. by the Bundesdenkmalamt, Abteilung fur Denkmalforschung.

Contents: Karten (1976); Burgenland (1976); Graz (1979); Tirol (1980); Stiermark (1982); Voralberg (1983); Salzburg (1986); Niederösterreich, nördlich der Donau (1990); Wien, 3v. (1993–96).

I329 Feuchtmüller, Rupert. Kunst in Österreich: vom frühen Mittelalter bis zur Gegenwart. Wien, Forum, [1972–73]. 2v. il. (part col.)

In-depth survey of fine arts, architecture, and decorative arts of Austria illustrated throughout with full size plates in color and black and white. Despite its publication date, this is still a useful overview, especially for its extensive classified bibliography.

Contents: (1) Die Romanik, die Gotik, die Renaissance; (2) Das Barock, das 19. Jahrhundert, das 20. Jahrhundert.

Literaturverzeichnis, v.1, p.265–74, v.2, p.286–96. Erläuterungen der wichtigsten Fachausdrücke, v.1, p.275–78, v.2, p.284. Personen-, Orts- und Sachregister, v.1, p.280–87, v.2, p.273–83.

I330 German art from Beckmann to Richter: images of a divided country. Ed. by Eckhart Gillen. [Trans., Susan Bernofsky . . . (et al.)]. Köln, DuMont Buchverlag; [Berlin,] Berliner Festspiele GmbH and Museumspädagogischer Dienst Berlin (Distr. by Yale Univ. Pr., 1997). 546p. il. (part col.)

Substantial survey published in conjunction with the exhibition, Deutschlandbilder: Kunst aus einem geteilten Land, Martin-Gropius-Bau, Berlin (1997–98). Aims "to present and interpret as objectively as possible" the German cultural landscape of the post-war era.

Artists' biographies, p.500–45. Selected exhibitions and publications on German art after 1945, p.545.

I331 German art in the 20th century: painting and sculpture 1905–1985. Ed. by Christos M. Joachimides . . . [et al.] [Munich], Prestel (Distr. by Te Neues, 1985). 518p. il. (part col.), ports.

Published to accompany the first in an ambitious series of exhibitions coordinated by the Royal Academy to survey major accomplishments in 20th century art. Shown at the Royal Academy, London and at the Staatsgalerie, Stuttgart in 1985–86. Well-illustrated with brief, informative essays on pivotal artists and movements by noted art historians and curators.

Bibliographical references throughout the text. Biographies of the artists, p.[478]–501. Chronology, p.[502]–10. Selected bibliography, p.[511]–12. Index, p.[516]–18.

I332 Geschichte der bildenden Kunst in Österreich. [Hrsg. von Hermann Fillitz im Auftrag der Österreichische Akademie der Wissenschaften Wien.] N.Y., Prestel, 1998– . (3)v. il. (part col.), maps, plans.

Monumental, beautifully produced survey of Austrian art, from the early Middle Ages through the Baroque.

Selective contents: (1) Früh- und Hochmittelalter, hrsg. von Hermann Fillitz (1998); (2) Gotik, hrsg. von Günter Brucher (2000); (4) Barock, hrsg. von Hellmut Lorenz (1999).

Includes bibliographical references. Glossar, v.1, p.[586]–87, v.2, p.[593]–95. Regentenverzeichnis, v.1, p.587. Bibliographie, v.1, p.588–610, v.2, p.[596]–618, v.3, p.[641]–75. Register, v.1, p.[611]–14, v.2, p.[619]–22 [Ortsregister], p.[623] [Personenregister], v.3, p.[677]–80 [Ortsregister], p.680–86 [Personenregister].

I333 Geschichte der deutschen Kunst. Leipzig, Seemann, 1981– . (10)v.

In-depth survey of German arts and architecture by notable scholars. Suitable for the advanced reader. Volumes contain extensive timelines organized by media. Modestly illustrated.

Contents: Geschichte der deutschen Kunst, 1350–1470, hrsg. von Ernst Ullmann (1981); Kunst der DDR, 1945–1959, hrsg. von Ullrich Kuhirt (1982); Ullman, Ernst. Deutsche Architektur und Plastik, 1470–1550: Sonderband (1984); Ullmann, Ernst. Deutsche Malerei, Graphik, Kunsthandwerk, 1470–1550: Sonderband (1985); Feist, Peter H. . . . [et al.] Geschichte der deutschen Kunst, 1848–1890 (1987); Geschichte der deutschen Kunst, 1890–1918, hrsg. von Harald Olbrich (1988); Geschichte der deutschen Kunst, 1200–1350, hrsg. von Friedrich Mobius (1989); Geschichte der deutschen Kunst, 1918–1945, hrsg. von Harald Olbrich (1990).

Each vol. contains notes and index.

I334 Geschichte der deutschen Kunst. München, Beck, 1998–2000. 3v.

The chapters in this well-illustrated and comprehensive survey are divided into concise sections treating individual monuments, media, iconography, architectural elements, artists, and historical trends. The very detailed table of contents allows quick access to specific topics. Covers all media and includes many illustrations, plans, and elevations.

Contents: (1) Klotz, Heinrich. Mittelalter 600–1400; (2) Warnke, Martin. Spätmittelalter unf frühe Neuzeit 1400–1750; (3) Klotz, Heinrich. Aufklärung und Moderne 1750–2000.

Anmerkungen, v.1, p.[434]–37, v.2, p.[456]–72. Fachausdrücke, v.1, p.[438]–42, v.2, p.[473]–76. Bibliographie, v.1, p.[443]–60, v.2, p.[477]–83. Ortsregister, v.1, p.[461]–66, v.2, p.[484]–86. Nameregister, v.1, p.[467]–71, v.2, p.[487]–92.

I335 Gordon, Donald E. Expressionism, art and idea. New Haven, Yale Univ. Pr., 1987. xvii, 263p. il. (part col.), plates.

With original research begun in the early 1970s, this volume is one of the earliest comprehensive studies of German Expressionism to appear in English. Published after Gordon's death in 1984, its goal is to present the reader with a cohesive analysis of the numerous artists and disparate trends now identified as Expressionism. Emphasis on painting and sculpture, with briefer treatments of architecture and the graphic arts. Includes chapters on intellectual context and critical response. Modestly illustrated.

Notes, p.217–43. Bibliography, p.245–57. Index, p.259–63.

I336 Kunst in Berlin, 1648–1987. [Katalogred., Arne Effenberger . . . (et al.)] Berlin, Henschelverlag, 1987. 511p. il. (part col.)

Catalog of the exhibition, Altes Museum, Staatliche Museen zu Berlin (1987) marking the 750th anniversary of Berlin. Though this catalog reflects some technical limitations common to publishing in the former Eastern Bloc, it is useful for the large range of objects included, the detailed catalog entries, and the vast bibliography. Essays are interspersed throughout the catalog.

Contents: (A) Barock in Berlin. Holländische Kultur in Brandenburg, 1648–1694; (B) Barock in Berlin. Schlüter und die Kunst seiner Zeit, 1694–1713; (C) Barock in Berlin. Spartanische Jahre für die Kunst, 1713–1740; (D) Friderizianisches Rokoko und Frühklassizismus. Von Knobelsdorff bis Chodowiecki, 1740–1795; (E) Klassizismus und Romantik. Zwischen Schadow und Schinkel, 1795–1815; (F) Biedermeier und Spätromantik. Zwischen Blechen und Cornelius, 1815–1848; (G) Nachbiedermeier. Menzel und seine Zeitgenossen, 1848–1871; (H) Gründerbarock, Naturalismus, Secession, Expressionismus: Der Sturm - Brücke - Erster Weltkrieg, 1871–1918; (I) Die zwanziger Jahre: Novembergruppe - Konstructivismus - Berlin DADA - Verismus - Neue Sachlichkeit - Proletarisch-revolutionäre und antifaschistische Kunst, 1918–1933; (K) Berliner Künstler in Verfolgung und Widerstand, 1933–1945; (L) Sozialistisch-realistisches Kunstschaffen im neuen Berlin, 1945–1987.

Verzeichnis der abgekürzt zitierten Literatur, p.483–500. Künstlerverzeichnis, p.500–7. Nachträge, p.509–11.

I337 Kunst in der DDR. Köln, Kiepenheuer & Witsch, 1990. 470p. il.

Twenty-one essays on a broad range of art and artists in the former East Germany followed by numerous entries describing artistic activity in five cities and regions, Berlin, Die Norden, Dresden, Chemnitz/Altenburg and Leipzig/Halle. A very useful volume for its overview of modern and contemporary arts in Germany before the removal of the Berlin Wall. Includes author biographies and a list of noteworthy museums and galleries.

Register, p.462–70.

I338 Legner, Anton. Deutsche Kunst der Romanik. München, Hirmer, 1982. 210p. il. (part col.), plates.

Thorough survey of Romanesque art and architecture covering the regions comprised by present-day Germany, Switzerland, and Austria. Includes examples of textiles, stained glass, furniture, seals, metalwork, and book arts. Very well illustrated with full-size plates, many in color. The bibliography is classified and the plates, numbering nearly 500, are followed by annotated entries containing additional bibliographic citations.

Bibliographie, p.124–32, 199–201. Ortsregister, p.202–7. Namenregister, p.207–9.

I339 Lieb, Norbert. München, die Geschichte seiner Kunst. [München], Callwey, [1988] [4., vollig überarb. und erw. Aufl.] 619p. il. (part col.)

1st ed., München, Callwey, 1971. 2d ed., 1977. 3d ed., 1982.

Detailed survey of art and architecture in Munich set against an historical backdrop from the Middle Ages through the post-war period. Includes useful index of buildings and monuments arranged by type.

Künstler-Register, p.608–12. Werk-Register, p.613–17.

I340 Österreichische Kunsttopographie. Wien, Schroll, 1907– . (50)v.

See GLAH 1:I302 for previous vols.

Contents: (42) Die profanen Bau- und Kunstdenkmäler der Stadt Linz. Die Altstadt (1977); (44) Wien, die Profanenbauten des III. IV. und V. Bezirkes (1980); (45) Stadt Innsbruck. II.Teil: Die Profanenbauten (1981); (46) Stadt Graz. Die Profanenbauten des IV. und V. Bezirkes (1984); (47) Stadt Innsbruck. Die Hofbauten (1986); (48) Die Kunstsammlungen des Augustiner-Chorherrenstiftes St. Florian (1988); (49) Die Kunstdenkmäler des politischen Bezirkes Mattersburg (1993); (50) Die Profanen Bau- und Kunstdenkmäler der Stadt Linz. Die Landstrasse. Obere und Untere Vorstadt (1986); (51) Die Profanen Bau- und Kunstdenkmäler der Stadt Friesach (1991); (52) Die Sakralen Kunstdenkmler der Stadt Innsbruck, 2v. (1994); (53) Die Kunstdenkmäler der Stadt Graz (1997).

I341 Papenbrock, Martin. Entartete Kunst, Exilkunst, Widerstandskunst in westdeutschen Austellungen nach 1945: eine kommentierte Bibliographie. Weimar, Verlag und Datenbank für Geisteswissenschaften, 1996. 564p. (Schriften der Guernica-Gesellschaft, 3)

Bibliography seeking to quantify the presence of persecuted and proscribed artists in West German exhibitions after the war, based on more than 1,000 exhibitions and artists.

Ausstellungen, p.71–413. Künstler, p.415–551. Ausgewählte Literatur, p.553–64.

I342 The Romantic spirit in German art, 1790–1990. Ed. by Keith Hartley . . . [et al.] London, Thames and Hudson, 1994. 501p. il. (part col.), maps.

Exhaustive catalog of the exhibition (Royal Scottish Academy, 1994), and other locations. Examines romanticism in 19th- and 20th-century German art and traces its influence on subsequent periods through the post-war and contemporary era. "What we have done . . . is to look at a series of these concepts that go together to make up the movement as a whole. These go under the main rubrics of Nature, Man and History and deal specifically with ideas such as the divine spirit in Nature, the unity of the cosmos, man's (and more specifically the artist's) ultimate loneliness and subsequent longing for fellowship and community with like-minded individuals, the loss of Innocence and consequent longing to regain the wholeness of Paradise, and utopias of the past."—*Introd.* 47 essays by German and British historians and curators, profusely illustrated.

Scholarly notes and references throughout. Biographies, p.[485]–93. Chronology, p.[494]–501.

I343 Suckale, Robert. Kunst in Deutschland: von Karl dem Grossen bis heute. Koln, DuMont, 1998. 688p. il. (part col.)

Beautifully realized survey covering 1200 years of art and architecture produced by the German-speaking peoples of

Europe. Seeks to place artistic production firmly in a political and social context as well as exploring links with other European cultures. Covers all media. Superbly illustrated and formatted.

Contents: (1) Die Kaiserkunst (800–1060); (2) Gregorianische Kirchenreform und ritterliche Hofkultur (1060–1250); (3) Übernahme und Umwandlung der französischen Gotik (1250–1420); (4) Höhepunkte und Krisen der Kunst im Zeitalter der Reformationen (1420–1530); (5) Die Fürstenkunst nach italienischem Vorbild (1530–1650); (6) Die Kunst im Absolutismus - der nachgeholte Barock (1650–1760); (7) Die Freisetzung der Künste in der modernen Gesellschaft (1760–1890); (8) Das 20. Jahrhundert - die Epoche der Avantgarden und ihres Scheiterns.

Literaturempfehlungen, p.637–56. Register, p.658–83.

I344 Varnedoe, Kirk. Vienna 1900: art, architecture & design. N.Y., Museum of Modern Art, 1986. 264p. il. (part col.)

Published on the occasion of the exhibition, the Museum (1986). A landmark exhibition on art and design in fin-de-siècle Vienna.

Notes, p.227–35. Chronology, p.237–44. Bibliography, p.245–56. Index, p.261–64.

I345 Vienna, 1890–1920. Ed. by Robert Waissenberger with contributions by Hans Bisanz . . . [et al.] N.Y., Rizzoli, 1984. 276p. il. (part col.)

Trans. of Wien, 1890–1920. Wien, Ueberreuter, 1984.

The first of Waissenberger's two volumes (see the following title) on Vienna provides a comprehensive introduction to the artistic, political, cultural, intellectual, and social life during this period marked by intense artistic activity. Includes sections on music, opera, literature, and theatre. The English translation is readable and very well illustrated.

Select bibliography, p.263. Guide to persons mentioned in the book, p.265–70. Index, p.272–76.

I346 Vienna in the Biedermeier era, 1815–1848. Ed. by Robert Waissenberger with contributions by Hans Bisanz . . . [et al.] N.Y., Rizzoli, 1986. 280p. il. (part col.), map, music, plans.

Trans. of Wien, 1815–1848: Burgersinn und Aufbegehren, die Zeit des Biedermeier und Vormarz. Wien, Ueberreuter, 1986.

Companion to the preceding title. Uses the same well organized, accessible format to examine the development and influence of the Biedermeier style in Vienna. Covers painting, sculpture, architecture, decorative and graphic arts, fashion, literature, and music.

Guide to persons mentioned in the book, p.272–76. Index, p.277–80.

Great Britain and Ireland

I347 Age of chivalry: art in Plantagenet England, 1200–1400. Ed. by Jonathan Alexander and Paul Binski. London, Royal Academy of Arts in assoc. with Weidenfield and Nicolson, 1987. 575p. il. (part col.), maps, plans.

Published to accompany the third of a trilogy of exhibitions (see also GLAH 2:I352, GLAH 2:I354) intended to make "accessible to the British public nearly five centuries of their art inheritance."—*Foreword.* The catalog of this exhibition (Royal Academy of Art, 1987–88) presents a cohesive view of artistic production in the Middle Ages through in-depth, readable essays covering history, iconography, religion, patronage, style, and technique. The essays are followed by 748 detailed, well-illustrated catalog entries covering all media.

Selective contents: Image and history, by Jeffrey Denton; Attitudes to the visual arts: the evidence from written sources, by T. A. Heslop; The language of images in medieval England, 1200–1400, by Michael Camille; Women and art in England in the 13th and 14th centuries, by Veronica Sekules; Artists, craftsmen, and design in England, 1200–1400, by Nigel Ramsay; Medieval heraldry, by Anne Payne; English gothic architecture, by Paul Crossley; The English response to French gothic architecture, c.1200–1350, by Christopher Wilson; Architecture and liturgy, by Peter Draper; The kingdom of heaven: its architectural setting, by Nicola Coldstream; Sculpture, by Paul Williamson; Gothic ivory carving in England, by Neil Stratford; English seals in the 13th and 14th centuries, by T. A. Heslop; Woodwork, by Charles Tracy; Misericords, by Christa Grössinger; Wall painting, by David Park; Panel painting, by Pamela Tudor-Craig; Stained glass, c.1200–1400, by Richard Marks; Manuscript illumination of the 13th and 14th centuries, by Nigel J. Morgan and Lucy Freeman Sandler; Embroidery and textiles, by Donald King; Metalwork in England, c.1200–1400, by Marian Campbell; Arms and armour by Claude Blair; Monumental brasses by Paul Binski; Decorative wrought iron, by Jane Geddes; Jewellery, pottery, and tiles, by John Cherry; The wheel of fortune: the appreciation of gothic since the middle ages, by Thomas Cooke.

Glossary, p.541–44. Bibliography, p.545–65. Index, p.566–72.

I348 Arnold, Bruce. A concise history of Irish art. [Rev. ed.] N.Y.,Oxford, 1977. 180p. il. (part col.) (World of art) (Repr.: N.Y., Thames and Hudson, 1989)

1st ed.: N.Y., Praeger, 1969.

Brief introduction to the major stylistic phases of Irish art and architecture. Modestly illustrated. "Landscape, topography, portraiture, historical painting, silver, glass, even architecture—a distinctive national style and character, a difference of light, a sense of history evolving and of people being involved in it, are all contributory factors to the overall idea which has been the mainspring of this book."—*Introd.*

Contents: (1) The Celtic era; (2) From the Viking invasion to 1700; (3) The age of Swift; (4) Ireland her own; (5) Landscape into art; (6) The Celtic revival; (7) Jack Yeats and the moderns.

Bibliography, p.175–76. Index, p.177–80.

I349 The arts of Britain. Ed. by Edwin Mullins. Oxford, Phaidon, 1983. 288p. il. (part col.)

Well-illustrated essays survey the fine arts, architecture, decorative, and applied arts. "The theme of this book is the visual arts of Britain in the widest possible sense, embracing whatever the people of these islands have built and shaped, coloured and decorated with a more than utilitarian purpose, from pre-history to the present day."—*Pref.*

Contents: (1) Painting and drawing, by Edwin Mullins; (2) Photography, by John Taylor; (3) Prints and book illustration, by Joyce Irene Whalley; (4) Folk art, by James Ayres; (5) Architecture, by J. M. Richards; (6) Building in the vernacular, by James Ayres; (7) Stained glass, by David O'Connor; (8) Garden design, by Arthur Hellyer; (9) Sculpture, by Paul Williamson and Nicholas Penny; (10) Arms and armour, by G. M. Wilson; (11) Ceramics, by Gaye Blake Roberts; (12) Glass, by Charles Hajdamach; (13) Textiles, by Joan Allgrove McDowell; (14) Jewellery, by Anna Somers Cocks; (15) Silver, by Philippa Granville; (16) Furniture, by Geoffrey Beard; (17) Clocks and watches, by Charles Aked; (18) Musical instruments, by Jeremy Montagu; (19) Modern studio crafts, by Marigold Coleman; (20) Industrial design, by Stephen Bayley; (21) Early Britain, by Barry Cunliffe; (22) North America: the British legacy, by James Ayres.

Public collections, p.275–77. Bibliography, p.278–82. Index, p.283–87.

I350 British art in the 20th century: the modern movement. Munich, Prestel, (Distr. by Te Neues, 1986). 457p., il. (part col.), ports.

Published to accompany the second in a series of exhibitions, Royal Academy of Art (1987) examining modern and contemporary painting and sculpture. Essays are followed by a chronological catalog of 310 objects with additional commentary selected to illustrate major artistic trends and influences. Very well illustrated.

Selective contents: Formalism and the figurative tradition in British painting, by Andrew Causey; The emancipation of modern British sculpture, by Richard Cork; Critical theories and the practice of art, by Charles Harrison; Machine Age, apocalypse and pastoral, by Richard Cork; Figure and place: a context for five post-war artists, by Dawn Ades; Art controversies of the seventies, by Caroline Tisdall; British twentieth century art: a transatlantic view, by Robert Rosenblum.

Biographies of the artists, p.[418]–48. Selected bibliography, p.[449]–52. Index of names, p.[455]–57.

I351 Cambridge guide to the arts in Britain. Ed. by Boris Ford. Cambridge, [Eng.], Cambridge Univ. Pr., 1988–1991. 9v., il. (part col.)

Well-organized, detailed, and readable, these handbooks are arranged chronologically and include discussions of cultural, social and historical context throughout. Covers music, theater, and literature as well as architecture and the fine, applied, and decorative arts. Each vol. contains extensive bibliographies which include monographs, periodical literature, primary sources, references to relevant institutions, biographies, and suggested readings. Separate place name, personal name, and subject indexes. Sparsely illustrated, but valuable for a wide range of reading and research needs.

Contents: (1) Prehistoric, Roman and early medieval; (2) The Middle Ages; (3) Renaissance and Reformation; (4) The seventeenth century; (5) The Augustan age; (6) Romantics to early Victorians; (7) The later Victorian age; (8) The Edwardian age and the inter-war years; (9) Since the Second World War.

Each vol. contains suggested reading and references.

I352 English Romanesque art, 1066–1200. [Ed. by George Zarnecki, Janet Holt, and Tristram Holland.] London, Weidenfield and Nicolson, The Arts Council of Great Britain, 1984. 416p. il. (part col.), map, plans.

Published to accompany the first in a series of three exhibitions on Medieval English art (see also GLAH 2:I347, GLAH 2:I354). This exhibition (Hayward Gallery, 1984) included manuscripts, wall paintings, stained glass, sculpture, ivory, metalwork, seals, coins, book bindings, pottery, and textiles. Substantial introductory essays and catalog entries by noted art historians and curators. The bibliography is arranged by media and contains useful brief essays and annotations. Modestly illustrated.

Selective contents: General introduction, by George Zarnecki; English Romanesque architecture, by Richard Gem; The historical background, by Christopher Brooke; Manuscripts, by Jonathan Alexander and Michael Kauffmann; Wall paintings, by George Zarnecki; Stained glass, by Madeline H. Caviness; Sculpture, by Peter Lasko . . . [et al.]; Metalwork, by Neil Stratford . . . [et al.]; Decorative ironwork, by Jane Geddes; Seals, by T. A. Heslop; Coins, by Marion Archibald; Bindings, by Mirjam Foot; Pottery, by John Cherry; Textiles, by Donald King; Rediscovery of the Romanesque, by Thomas Cocke and C.R. Dodwell.

Bibliography, p.[393]–406. Chronology, p.[407]–11. Map, p.412. Glossary, p.[413]–16.

I353 Fallon, Brian. Irish art, 1830–1990. Belfast, Appletree, 1994. 208p. il. (part col.), plates.

This recent survey, suitable for the general reader, attempts to fill in gaps persistent in the history of visual culture in Ireland and to place Irish artistic accomplishments in social and historical contexts.

Contents: (1) The Irish romantics; (2) Maclise: the Irish Victorian; (3) The French connection; (4) The new century; (5) The gold and silver age; (6) Into the modern movement; (7) Irish sculpture; (8) The crafts revival; (9) The modern epoch.

Bibliography, p.[195]–99. Index, p.[201]–8.

I354 Golden age of Anglo-Saxon art, 966–1066. Ed. by Janet Backhouse, D. H. Turner, Leslie Webster. With contrib. by Marion Archibald . . . [et al.] Bloomington, Univ. of Indiana Pr., 1985. 216p. il. (part col.), plates.

Catalog accompanying the second in a series of three exhibitions (See GLAH 2:I347, GLAH 2:I352) devoted to English medieval art. The catalog of this exhibition (British Museum, 1984–85) follows the format of its companion publications. "This is a reference book of lasting value that should have its place on the shelves of all who are involved with the study of any aspect of late Anglo-Saxon civilization."—*Review*, Antiquity, v.61, no.231, March 1987, p.141.

Selective contents: The legacy of Alfred, by Leslie Webster; Illuminated manuscripts, by D. H. Turner; Metalwork and sculpture, by Leslie Webster; Anglo-Saxon architecture of the 10th and 11th centuries, by Richard Gem; Literature, learning and documentary sources, by Janet Backhouse; Anglo-Saxon coinage, Alfred to the Conquest, by Marion M. Archibald; After the Conquest, by Janet Backhouse.

Bibliography, p.210–15. Further reading, p.216.

I355 Harbison, Peter. Irish art and architecture from prehistory to the present. London, Thames and Hudson, 1978. 272p. il. (part col.), facsims., map, plans, ports. (Repr.: London, Thames and Hudson, 1993)

Still useful, this survey offers a simple, well-organized introduction to artistic activity over a span of 5,000 years. The authors have tried to place the works selected for discussion and analysis "in the context of their time and to relate them to contemporary styles of art and architecture outside Ireland."—*Pref.*

Bibliography, p.265–68. Index, p.269–72.

I356 Henig, Martin. The art of Roman Britain. Ann Arbor, Univ. of Michigan Pr., 1995. 224p. il. (part col.) plates.

In this survey the author re-evaluates the merits of Roman art imported to or produced in Britain. "Although Anglo-Saxon art finds a place in most courses on art in the British Isles, Roman Britain has until now been beneath the notice of professional art historians. . . . I have attempted to present, in seven chapters, how art was practiced and what it meant in Roman Britain."—*Introd.*

Contents: (1) The art of the Celts; (2) Art in the era of conquest; (3) Art and the Roman army; (4) The uses of art in Roman Britain; (5) Natives and strangers in Roman Britain; (6) Artists and their patrons; (7) Art in late Roman Britain; (8) Attitudes to the art of Roman Britain.

Abbreviations, p.190. Notes and references, p.191–203. Bibliography, p.204–12. Glossary, p.213–14. Index, p.215–24.

I357 Kennedy, S. B. Irish art and modernism, 1880–1950. Belfast, Institute of Irish Studies, Queen's Univ. of Belfast, 1991. xii, 397p. il. (part col.)

Published to accompany the exhibition (Hugh Lane Municipal Gallery of Art and the Ulster Museum, 1991–92). Examines the connection between Irish 20th-century artists and external trends of international modernism. Seeks to refute the "popular view of the development of Irish art in the first half of the 20th century [which] is that it was little touched by the theories and ideas of the modern movement."—*Introd.* Contains nine chapters analyzing historical background and artistic trends from the 1920s–1950s as well as illustrated catalog entries for 132 works. Appendix 1: Society of Dublin Painters. Appendix 2: White Stag Group. Appendix 3: Irish Exhibition of Living Art.

Notes, p.345–67. Bibliography, p.376–86. Index, p.387–97.

I358 Laing, Lloyd Robert. Early English art and architecture: archaeology and society. Phoenix Mill, [Eng.], Sutton, 1996. 246p. il. (part col.), plates, maps, plans.

Survey covering the 5th to 12th century. Through archeological and other evidence, artistic production is examined in its social, religious, and economic context. "This book has been written in order to tie together the now huge amount of constantly changing material that has been accumulated on the Anglo-Saxons. . . . It also considers the legacy of Anglo-Saxon England to the Norman world."—*Introd.*

Contents: (1) The first Saxon settlers, 400–c.600 AD; (2) The pagan kingdoms, 600–c.700 AD; (3) The beginnings of Christianity, 600–c.800 AD (The middle Saxons); (4) The late Saxons, c.800–1066 (The Viking era); (5) The Saxo-Norman overlap; (Appendix) Sources for the Anglo-Saxons.

Bibliography, p.218–39. Index, p.240–46.

I359 Macmillan, Duncan. Scottish art in the 20th century. Edinburgh, Mainstream, 1994. 192p. col. il.

Introductory survey of painting and sculpture with many good quality color illustrations. Expanded, updated, and more fully illustrated version of the last six chapters of the author's Scottish art 1460–1990 (GLAH 2:M289).

Contents: (1) The early modernists; (2) Between the wars; (3) Wartime and the post-war world; (4) The 1960s and 1970s; (5) Old themes and new beginnings.

Notes, p.[175]–76. List of plates, p.176–81. Select bibliography, p.[182]–86. Index, p.[187]–92.

I360 The Oxford history of English art. Ed. by T. S. R. Boase, Oxford [Eng.], Clarendon, 1949– . (11)v.

See GLAH 1:I313 for previous vols.

Contents: (11) Farr, Dennis. English art, 1879–1940 (1978).

I361 Scotland creates: 5,000 years of art and design. Ed. by Wendy Kaplan. London, Glasgow Museums & Art Galleries in assoc. with Weidenfeld and Nicolson, 1990. 200p. il. (part col.)

Catalog published to accompany the exhibition, McLellan Galleries, Glasgow (1990–91). Seeks to identify and define a national character in art produced in Scotland from prehistory through the contemporary period. Essays prepared by art historians and curators cover the fine, decorative, and applied arts. Well illustrated, mostly in color. The bibliography is arranged by chapter.

Contents: (1) Art and design, 3000 BC–AD 1000, by John C. Barrett; (2) Art and the Church before the Reformation, by John Higgitt; (3) In search of Scottish art: native traditions and foreign influences, by David H. Caldwell; (4) Scotland's artistic links with Europe, by James Holloway; (5) Scottish design and the art of the book, 1500–1800, by John Morris; (6) The eighteenth-century interior in Scotland, by Ian Gow; (7) Industrial design in Scotland, 1700–1900, by John Hume; (8) Sir Walter Scott and nineteenth century painting in Scotland, by Lindsay Errington; (9) How many swallows make a summer? Art and design in Glasgow in 1900, by Roger Billcliffe; (10) "A gleam of Renaissance hope": Edinburgh at the turn of the century, by Elizabeth Cumming; (11) Scottish modernism and Scottish identity, by Tom Normand.

Bibliography, p.185–187. Index, p.189–92.

I362 Sheehy, Jeanne. The rediscovery of Ireland's past: the Celtic revival, 1830–1930. Photographs by George

Mott. London, Thames and Hudson, 1980. 208p. il. (part col.), facsims. (1 col.), plans, ports.

Introduction to the development and influence of Irish nationalism and historicism on fine arts, architecture and decorative arts. Many illustrations.

Contents: (1) Introduction; (2) The antiquarians; (3) Young Ireland; (4) Painting, sculpture and architecture; (5) Popular and applied arts; (6) The Celtic revival; (7) Hugh Lane and the Gallery of Modern Art; (8) Later developments in architecture; (9) The Arts and Crafts movement; (10) Painting and sculpture after 1900.

Notes, p.194–99. Bibliography, p.200–3. Index, p.205–8.

I363 Walker, Dorothy. Modern art in Ireland. Foreword by Seamus Heaney. Dublin, Lilliput, 1997. 239p. il. (part col.)

Personal account, embracing artists from abroad who lived or worked in Ireland.

Bibliography, p.223–31. Index, p.233–39.

I364 Wilson, David M. Anglo-Saxon art: from the seventh century to the Norman conquest. London, Thames and Hudson, 1984. 224p. il. (part col.)

Well-illustrated survey examines the period through direct observation and analysis of surviving works of art. Covers architecture, sculpture, manuscript illumination, metalwork, and textiles. This "text constitutes the first general survey of the subject in some 40 years."—*Review*, Antiquity, v.61, no.231, March 1987, p.141.

Contents: (1) Taste, personalities and survival; (2) The seventh-century explosion; (3) The eighth and ninth centuries; (4) Influences; (5) From Alfred to the Conquest.

Sources, p.216–20. Index, p.221–24.

Italy

I365 Abbate, Francesco. Storia dell'arte nell'Italia meridionale. Roma, Donzelli, 1997– . (1)v. il. (part col.) (Progetti Donzelli)

Conceived as a 3-vol. history of art in Southern Italy, from the 6th to the end of the 18th century.

Contents: (1) Dai Longobardi agli Svevi (1997).

I366 L'arte a Roma nel secolo XVI. Di Sandro Benedetti e Giuseppe Zander. Bologna, Cappelli, 1990–1992. 2v. il., plans. (Storia di Roma, v.29)

See GLAH 1:I329 for a previous vol. in the series on Rome in the 15th Century.

Architectural projects are arranged by papal reign while painting and sculpture are treated by artist and chronologically. Scholarly work suitable for the advanced reader. Minimally illustrated in black and white.

Contents: (1) L'architettura; (2) La pittura e la scultura.

Vol.1: Appendice: Parte I: Cronologia, p.[613]–80; Parte II: Cenni bibliografici, p.[681]–718. Indice dei nomi, p.[725]–49. Indice dei luoghi e delle opere, p.[750]–77. Vol.2: Appendice: Parte I: Cronologia, p.[435]–72; Parte II: Bibliografici, p.[473]–502. Indice analitico, p.[505]–26.

I367 Bairati, Eleonora, and Finocchi, Anna. Arte in Italia: lineamenti di storia e materiali di studio. 3a ed. Torino, Loescher, 1988. 3v. il. (part col.)

1st ed. 1984. Intended as a handbook for students. The text and bibliography are updated in the 3d ed.

Contents: (1) Dalla preistoria al XIV secolo; (2) L'Italia nel Rinascimento; (3) Dal XVII al XX secolo.

Orientamenti bibliografici, v.1, p.565–69, v.2, p.502–04, v.3, p.768–772. Indice dei nomi, dei luoghi e delle cose notevoli, v.1, p.571–79, v.2, p.507–18, v.3, p.773–95.

I368 Bertaux, Émile. L'art dans l'Italie méridionale. Rome, École française de Rome, 1968–1978. 6v.

See GLAH 1:I322 for previous eds.

Volumes 1–3 are facsimile reprints of the 1903 ed. Volumes 4–6 are supplements to the work of Bertaux compiled under the direction of Adriano Prandi and published as L'art dans l'Italie méridionale, aggiornamento dell'opera di Émile Bertaux by the École française de Rome. These last three vols. consist of critical commentary by multiple authors following the structure of Bertaux's original text with the goal of bringing the scholarship up-to-date. Extensive notes and references appear throughout and large black-and-white illustrations have been added. The index in v.5 has also been published separately.

Indice geografico, v.5, p.1009–1044. Indice dei nomi propri, v.5, p.1045–1075. Indice degli argomenti, v.5, p.1077–1091.

I369 Blunt, Anthony. Artistic theory in Italy, 1450–1600. [Fourth corr. and upd. impr.]. Oxford, Oxford Univ. Pr., [1978]. vii, 170p. il. (Repr.: Oxford, Oxford Univ. Pr., 1989)

See GLAH 1:I323 for previous eds. Numerous previous reprints.

Apart from minor corrections to the text and the removal of some references, the text included here is that of the second ed. "The bibliography has, however, been completely revised and extended to include the large number of new and often well annotated editions of texts which have appeared in the last ten or fifteen years."—*Pref.*

Bibliography, p.[160]–65. Index, p.[168]–70.

I370 Burckhardt, Jakob Christoph. The civilization of the Renaissance in Italy. Trans. by S. G. C. Middlemore. With a new introd. by Peter Burke and notes by Peter Murray. London, Penguin, 1990. vii, 389p. (Repr.: Oxford, Phaidon, 1995)

See GLAH 1:I324 for previous eds. and numerous reprints.

Nearly all the notes from the standard Middlemore trans. have been removed in this new ed. Those remaining have been updated and expanded. Many new notes and references have been added.

Notes, p.[353]–70. Index, p.[371]–89.

I371 Chastel, André. Art et humanisme à Florence au temps de Laurent ler Magnifique: études sur la Renaissance et l'humanisme platonicien. [3e. ed. mise à jour.] Paris, Presses Univ. de France, 1982. xxiii, 580p. il. plates.

See GLAH 1:I325 for previous eds.

Contains a new preface as well as major corrections and additions. The bibliography and extensive footnotes have been updated.

Bibliographie, p.[523]–49. Index, p.[551]–68.

I372 Di Genova, Giorgio. Storia dell'arte italiana del '900. Bologna, Bora, 1986– . (4)v. in 6. il. (part col.)

Vol. 1–2 subtitled: per generazioni. Substantial history of 20th-century Italian art "by generations."

Contents: (1) Generazione maestri storici (3v.); (2) Generazione primo decennio (1986, rev. and upd. ed. 1996); (3) Generazione anni Dieci; (4) Generazione anni Venti.

Bibliographies and indexes in each vol.

I373 Hartt, Frederick. History of Italian Renaissance art: painting, sculpture, architecture. 4th ed., rev. by David G. Wilkins. N.Y., Abrams, 1994. 696p. il. (part col.), maps (part col.)

See GLAH 1:I332 for 1st ed. 2d ed., N.Y., Abrams, 1979; 3d ed., rev. and exp., Englewood Cliffs, N.J., Prentice-Hall, 1987.

The 4th ed. has been revised to maintain "the canon of works selected by Hartt to characterize the development of Italian renaissance art as well as the sequence in which he ordered them . . . new ideas and scholarship have been included where possible."—*Pref.* The bibliography has been extensively updated. Some black-and-white illustrations have been replaced with color, and some new illustrations have been added.

Glossary, p.662–68. Bibliography, p.669–77. Index, p.678–96.

I374 Hersey, George L. High renaissance art in St. Peter's and the Vatican: an interpretive guide. Chicago, Univ. of Chicago Pr., 1993. xiii, 305p. il.

A hybrid of guide and historical survey, this well-organized book examines the Vatican complex and its contents in considerable depth. "The advantage of a more generous volume like this is that group identity of these achievements and their common meanings, both conscious and otherwise, can be brought out."—*Pref.*

Contents: (1) Introduction: "The liberation of Italy"; (2) Personae; (3) The new St. Peter's; (4) The Cortile del Belvedere and museums; (5) The Stanze; (6) The Sistine Chapel and The Last Judgement; (7) The Loggie; (8) The tragedy of the tomb.

Chronology, p.277–79. Further reading, p.281–87. Analytical index, p.289–305.

I375 History of Italian art. Pref. by Peter Burke. Trans. by Ellen Bianchini and Claire Dorey. Cambridge, [Eng.], Polity Pr., 1994. 2v.

Trans. of essays from Storia dell'arte italiana. (GLAH 2:I383), selected to represent the diverse viewpoints and topics present in that twelve vol. series.

Contents: Vol. 1: (1) The Italian artist and his roles, by Peter Burke; (2) Centre and periphery, by Enrico Castelnuovo and Carlo Ginzburg; (3) Italian art and the art of antiquity, by Nicole Dacos; (4) The dispersal and conservation of art-historical property, by Francis Haskell; (5) The public reception of art, by Anna Mura. Vol.2: (1) The periodization of the history of Italian art, by Giovanni Previtali; (2) The iconography of Italian art, 1100–1500: an approach, by Salvatore Settis; (3) The history of art and the forms of religious life, by Bruno Toscano; (4) Renaissance and pseudo-Renaissance, by Federico Zeri; (5) Towards the modern manner: from Mantegna to Raphael, by Giovanni Romano.

Each essay is followed by notes and references.

Index, v.1, p.[325]–37, v.2, p.[489]–99.

I376 Italian art in the 20th century: painting and sculpture, 1900–1988. Ed. by Emily Braun; with contributions by Alberto Asor Rosa . . . [et al.] Munich, Prestel (Distr. by Te Neues, 1989). 465p. il. (part col.), ports.

Chronological survey in the form of essays by noted art historians with emphasis on the impact of historical and social context. Published to accompany the third in the series of national exhibitions sponsored by the Royal Academy of Art (1989). Very well-illustrated. Scholarly footnotes follow each essay.

Biographies of the artists, p.[425]–45. Selected bibliography, p.[454]–57. Index of names, p.[461]–65.

I377 Lavagnino, Emilio. L'arte moderna dai neoclassici ai contemporanei. [Reprint.] [Torino], UTET, [1961]. 2v. (Storia dell'arte classica e italiana, 5)

See GLAH 1:I336 for 1st ed. Essentially a reprint of the text, these vols. contain several new illustrations and color plates and minor additions to the bibliography.

Bibliografia essenziale, p.1503–18. Indice degli artisti, p.1519–36. Indice dei luoghi e dei monumenti, p.1537–89.

I378 Maltese, Corrado. Storia dell'arte in Italia 1785–1943. Bibliographic appendix by Francesca Bertozzi and Rodolfo Profumo. [2d ed.]. Torino, Einaudi, 1992. xxxii, 505p. il., plates, plans. (Einaudi Tascabili, 113)

See GLAH 1:I340 for 1st ed.

The bibliographies, now combined at the end of the text and arranged thematically, have been updated and substantially expanded. Black-and-white illustrations are quite small.

Appendice bibliografica, p.[437]–67. Indice analitico, p.[469]–505.

I379 Memoria dell'antico nell'arte italiana. A cura di Salvatore Settis. Torino, Einaudi, 1984–1986. 3v. (Biblioteca di storia dell'arte, n.s. 1–3)

Essays by various authors examine, in detail, themes of the rediscovery and influence of antiquity on Italian art from the medieval to the modern period. Essays contain footnotes and references and each vol. contains a separate personal and place name index.

Selective contents: (1) L'uso dei classici; (2) I generi e i temi ritrovati; (3) Dalla tradizione all'archeologia.

Indice dei nomi, v.1, p.[447]–65, v.2, p.[443]–63, v.3, p.[489]–518. Indice dei luoghi, v.1, p.[467]–77, v.2, p.[465]–80, v.3, p.[519]–39.

I380 Paoletti, John T., and Radke, Gary M. Art in Renaissance Italy. London, Lawrence King, 1997. 480p. il. (part col.)

Survey covering artistic activity in Rome, Florence, Venice, the Veneto, Assisi, Siena, Milan, Pavia, Padua, Mantua, Verona, Ferrara, Urbino, and Naples with an emphasis on placing works in their historical, social, and political context through the inclusion of Renaissance texts and the study of material culture and patronage.

Artists' biographies, p.439–51. Genealogies, p.452–55. Time chart, p.[456–57]. City plans, p.[458–60]. Glossary, p.461–63. Bibliography, p.464–70. Index, p.472–80.

I381 Partridge, Loren M. The art of Renaissance Rome. N.Y., Abrams, 1996. 184p. il. (part col.), maps. (Perspectives)

Concise, well-illustrated survey of art and architecture in Rome emphasizing urban projects and issues of patronage. The author "approaches his chosen exemplars from the patron's point of view, but also deftly addresses questions of function, iconography, and artistic merit."—*Review*, Burlington magazine, v.139, June 1997, p.409. Numerous useful plans and maps. Written in a lively style suitable for a general audience.

Contents: (Introduction) Patronage and popes: saints or sinners; (1) Urbanism: rotting cadavers and the new Jerusalem; (2) Churches: Harmony of the spheres and construction chaos; (3) Palaces: magnificence and mayhem; (4) Altarpieces: spirit and matter; (5) Chapel decoration: space, time, and eternity; (6) Halls of state: arts of power; (Conclusion) 1600 and beyond.

Timeline, p.[174–75]. Renaissance popes, p.176. Bibliography, p.176–79. Index, p.181–84.

I382 Romanini, Angiola Maria. Il Medioevo. Firenze, Sansoni, 1988. 493p. il. (part col.), plans. (Storia dell'arte classica e italiana, 2)

Substantial survey of medieval Italian art.

Contents: (I) Tardo-antico e Cristianesimo; (II) La "caduta dell'impero"; (III) I Longobardi in Italia; (IV) Dal "sacro romano impero" all'arte ottoniana; (V) Arts romanica; (VI) L'età gotica; (VII) Il "dolce stil novo" del gotico italiano.

Indice delle illustrazioni, p.483–[91].

I383 Storia dell'arte italiana. Torino, Einaudi, 1979?–1983. 12 v. in 14. il.

Selections from this title have been published in English trans. as History of Italian art (GLAH 2:I375). This multivol. three-part history of Italian art forms the second part of an ambitious series published by Einaudi. The first was the general history, Storia d'Italia (1972–76); the third is Storia della letteratura Italiana (1982–91). In the present publication, as in the others, emphasis has been placed on cultural, social, political, and economic contexts in which the arts are produced. Essays have been contributed by an international group of scholars and each contains footnotes and references. Good quality black-and-white illustrations throughout. Each vol. contains separate personal and place name indexes.

Selective contents: Parte prima: Materiali e problemi: (1) Questioni e metodi; (2) L'artista e il pubblico; (3) L'esperienza dell'antico, dell'Europa, della religiositá; (4) Ricerche spaziali e tecnologie. Parte seconda: Dal medioevo al novecento: (5) Dal Medioevo al Quattrocento; (6) Dal Cinquecento all'Ottocento, 2v.; (7) Il Novecento. Parte terza: Situazioni momenti indagini: (8) Inchieste su centri minori; (9) Grafica e immagine, 2v.; (10) Conservazione, falso restauro; (11) Forme e modelli; (12) Momenti di architettura.

I384 Venturi, Adolfo. Nuovi indici generali e note di aggiornamento alla Storia dell'arte italiana di Adolfo Venturi. A cura di Fabrizia Rossetti e Stefania Rossetti. Milano, Hoepli, [1988]. viii, 482p.

See GLAH 1:I356 for previous ed. of this index.

This new version of indexes to Venturi enhances the structure of those prepared for the 1975 edition. The present editors have expanded the index of artists by approximately 500 names and corrected errors to present an accurate accounting of artist references throughout the 25 vols. in the original survey (GLAH 1:I355). Additionally, the location index for works of art has been corrected and updated with approximately 3,000 new notes describing "the actual status of numerous artistic works (location, restoration, transfer, robbery, destruction, fraud, attribution, etc.)."—*Pref.*

Indice generale degli artisti, p.3–219. Appendice, p.220–21. Indice generale delle illustrazioni ordinate secondo i luoghi, p.224–482.

I385 White, John. Art and architecture in Italy 1250–1400. [3d ed.]. New Haven, Yale Univ. Pr., 1993. 684p. il. (part col.) (Yale University Press pelican history of art).

See GLAH 1:I358 for 1st ed. 2d (integrated) ed., N.Y., Viking Penguin, 1987.

The text is the same as in the second ed.; however, the bibliography has been revised and significantly expanded. Some black-and-white illustrations has been replaced with color plates.

Bibliography, p.[639]–61. Index, p.[665]–84.

I386 Wittkower, Rudolf. Art and architecture in Italy, 1600 to 1750. Revised by Jennifer Montagu and Joseph Connors. New Haven, Conn., Yale University Pr., 1999. (Yale University Press pelican history of art) 3v.

See GLAH 1:I359 for previous eds. Also published as 3d rev. ed., repr. with corrections and bibliography. Harmondsworth, [Eng.], Penguin, 1980 and 5th ed., New Haven, Yale Univ. Pr., 1982 (The Yale University Press pelican history of art).

A large format ed. of the landmark study on the Italian Baroque. Changes for this ed. consist of selected corrections of artists' dates, inclusion of new material in the bibliography, the addition of 100 new illustrations, and a substantial critical introduction.

Contents: (1) The early baroque 1600–1625; (2) The high baroque 1625–1675; (3) Late baroque and rococo 1675–1750.

Each vol. contains notes and index. Bibliography, v.3, p.[123]–56.

SEE ALSO: Wackernagel, The world of the Florentine Renaissance artist (GLAH 2:S69).

Latin America

I387 Ades, Dawn. Art in Latin America: the modern era, 1820–1980. With contrib. by Guy Brett . . . [et al.] New Haven, Yale Univ. Pr., 1989. 361p. il. (part col.)
Catalog of the exhibition, Hayward Gallery, London (1989). Seeks "to present a view of 160 years of the art of Latin America."—*Foreword.* Selective focus on key themes, including the relationship with European art and with modernism, the tension between art and politics, indigenism, nationalism, and the search for cultural identity.

Contents: (1) Independence and its heroes; (2) Academies and history painting; (3.i) Traveller-reporter artists and the empirical tradition in Post-Independence Latin America, by Stanton Loomis Catlin; (3.ii) Nature, science and the picturesque; (4) José María Velasco; (5) Posada and the popular graphic tradition; (6) Modernism and the search for roots; (7) The Mexican mural movement; (8) The Taller de Gráfica popular; (9) Indigenism and social realism; (10) Private worlds and public myths; (11) Arte madí / Arte concreto-invención; (12) A radical leap, by Guy Brett; (13) History and identity.

Notes, p.301–05. Manifestos, p.306–37. Biographies, p.338–59. Select bibliography, p.360.

I388 Argentina, 1920–1994: art from Argentina. Ed. by David Elliott. Oxford, Museum of Modern Art, 1994. 144p. il. (part col.)
Catalog of the exhibition, Museum of Modern Art, Oxford (1994). A selection of essays amplifies and contextualizes the work of 27 artists.

Bibliography, p.138–41. Chronology, p.141–42. Index, p.143–44.

I389 Art d'Amérique latine, 1911–1968. Paris, Musée national d'art moderne, Centre Georges Pompidou, 1992. 523p. il. (part col.)
Multi-author catalog of the ambitious exhibition, Musée National d'Art Moderne, Centre Georges Pompidou (1992–93). Emphasizes the Latin American contribution to international modernism.

Contents: (1) Les précurseurs; (2) Le muralisme mexicain; (3) Surréalismes et surréalistes; (4) Du constructivisme au cinétisme; (5) Figurations; (6) Architecture.

Chronologies, p.483–87. Bibliographie, p.497–500. Biographies, p.501–15. Index, p.516–21.

I390 Arte argentina dalla indipendenza ad oggi, 1810–1987. Rome, Istituto italo-latino americano, 1987. 266p. il. (part col.)
Catalog of the exhibition, Istituto Italo-Latino Americano, Rome (1987), based on loans from Argentine museums.

[Bibliografía], p.265.

I391 Arte moderno en América Latina. Aracy A. Amaral . . . [et al.] Damián Bayón, ed. Madrid, Taurus, 1985. 349p. il. (part col.) (Ensayistas, 267. Serie Maior)
Anthology of articles by 24 art historians and critics of different Latin American nationalities covering the architecture, painting, and sculpture of their respective countries.

Bibliographical references throughout.

I392 Arte novohispano. Napoles, Mexico, Azabache, 1991. 7v. il. (part col.)
Contents: (1) Tovar de Teresa, Guillermo, et al. La utopia mexicana del siglo XVI, lo bueno, lo verdadero y lo bello (1992); (2) Sartor, Mario. Arquitectura y urbanismo en nueva España, siglo XVI (1992); (3) Bérchez, Joaquín. Arquitectura mexicana de los siglos XVII y XVIII (1992); (4) Tovar de Teresa, Guillermo. Pintura y escultura en nueva España 1557–1640 (1992); (5) Burke, Marcus B. Pintura y escultura en nueva España, el barroco (1992); (6) Sebastián, Santiago. Iconografía e iconología del arte novohispano (1992); (7) López Guzman, Rafael, et al. Arquitectura y carpinteria mudejar en nueva España (1992).

Includes bibliographies.

I393 Baddeley, Oriana, and Fraser, Valerie. Drawing the line: art and cultural identity in contemporary Latin America. N.Y., Verso, 1989. viii, 164p. il. (part col.) (Critical studies in Latin American culture)
Authors suggest "themes and ideas to provide structure for the study of Latin American art," within the context of broader Latin American cultural studies.—*Introd.*

Contents: (1) Mapping landscapes; (2) Confronting a colonial past; (3) The politics of Latin American art; (4) The surrealist continent; (5) Forms of authenticity; Afterword: drawing the line.

Notes, p.141–47. Select bibliography, p.149–51. Index, p.159–64.

I394 Barocco latino americano. [Roma, Istituto italo-latino americano, 1980]. 227p. il. (part col.)
Published in conjunction with the exhibition "promossa e organizzata dall'Istituto italo-latino americano/IILA sotto gli auspici dell'UNESCO," (1980)—*p.[5].*

Brief essays on the Latin American contribution to the Baroque, by Paolo Portoghesi and other scholars, followed by a catalog of the exhibition.

Nota bibliografica, p.226–27.

I395 Bayón, Damián, and Marx, Murillo. History of South American colonial art and architecture: Spanish South America and Brazil. With contrib. by Myriam Ribeiro de Oliveira . . . [et al.] [Trans. by Jennifer Blankley . . . (et al.)] N.Y., Rizzoli, 1992. 442p. il. (part col.)
1st ed. Historia del arte colonial sudamericano: Sudamérica Hispana y el Brasil. Barcelona, Eds. Poligrafia, 1989.

Ambitious, collaborative study combining a chronological survey of architecture, painting, and sculpture with "an index of the principal monuments."—*Pref.*

Parts one and two cover South America (except Brazil) from the 16th through the early 19th century; part three focuses on Brazil during the same period.

Index of principal monuments, p.257–84. Glossary, p.285–86. Bibliography, p.287–92. Index of main monuments—Brazil, p.407–21. Glossary [for part three], p.422. Bibliography, p.423–24. Index of illustrations, p.427–35. Index of names, p.437–42.

I396 Castedo, Leopoldo. Historia del arte iberoamericano. Madrid, Alianza, 1988. 2v. il. (part col.)

Standard survey of Latin American art from the pre-Columbian era to the 20th century.

Contents: (1) Precolombino; El arte colonial; (2) Siglo XIX; Siglo XX.

Includes bibliographies at ends of sections. Indice onomastico, p.329–38. Indice analitico, p.339–42.

I397 Day, Holliday T., and Sturges, Hollister. Art of the fantastic: Latin America, 1920–1987. With contrib. by Edward Lucie-Smith . . . [et al.] Indianapolis, Indianapolis Museum of Art. (Distr. by Indiana Univ. Pr., 1987). 302p. il. (part col.)

Catalog of the exhibition, Indianapolis Museum of Art (1987), and other locations. Explores "one of the most powerful modes of expression in Latin American culture: the fantastic."—*Prol.* Includes critiques and biographies of 30 artists by major Latin American critics.

Bibliography, p.291–95. General bibliography, p.296–97. Biographies of artists, p.298–302.

I398 Fernández, Justino. Arte moderno y contemporáneo de México. Prologo de Manuel Toussaint. México, Univ. Nacional Autónoma de México, 1993–1994. 2v. il. (part col.)

See GLAH 1:I368 for 1st ed.; GLAH 1:I367 for 2d ed. of v.1; 3d ed., 1983.

Contents: (1) El arte del siglo XIX; (2) El arte del siglo XX.

Bibliografía general, v.2, p.159–68. Índice de nombres, v.2, p.179–85.

I399 Historia del arte ecuatoriano. [Coord. gen. de toda la obra, Hernán Crespo Toral, José Ma. Vargas.] Quito, Salvat Editores Ecuatoriana, 1977–1978. 4v. col. il.

Narrative of Ecuadorian art from prehispanic to contemporary periods. Texts published in these vols. have also been reissued by the publisher as Arte colonial de Ecuador: siglos XVI–XVII (1985) and Arte de Ecuador: siglos XVIII–XIX (1977).

Indice, v.4, p.211–60.

I400 Historia del arte hispanoamericano. Madrid, Alhambra, 1988. 3v. il. (part col.)

Survey of art in Latin America from the pre-Columbian era to the present. Each volume is written by a specialist on the period.

Contents: (1) Alcina Franch, J. Arte precolombino (1987); (2) Bernales Ballesteros, J. Siglos XVI a XVIII (1987); (3) Bayón, Damián. Siglos XIX y XX (1988).

Bibliographies at ends of chapters.

I401 Historia del arte mexicano. Dir. gen., Juan Salvat, José Luis Rosas. [2a ed.] [Mexico City, Mexico], SEP, Salvat, [1986]. 16v. il. (part col.)

See GLAH 1:I371 for previous ed.

Popular survey of Mexican art. Each division of four volumes was edited by a specialist on the period covered and includes essays by well-known scholars. Short bibliographies accompany each essay.

Contents: (1–4) Arte prehispánico; (5–8) Arte colonial; (9–12) Arte del siglo XIX; (13–16) Arte contemporáneo.

Indice general, v.16, p.2416–55.

I402 Historia general del arte en la Argentina. Buenos Aires, Academia Nacional de Bellas Artes, [1982]– . (8)v. il. (part col.)

Comprehensive survey of Argentine art from the pre-Columbian era to the present, comprised of scholarly essays by specialists in many fields.

Contents: (1–2) Desde los comienzos hasta fines del siglo XVIII; (3–4) Siglo XIX hasta 1876; (5–6) Fines del siglo XIX y comienzos del siglo XX; (7–8) Comienzos del siglo XX.

Notes and bibliographies after each chapter.

I403 História geral da arte no Brasil. [Walter Zanini, coord. e dir. ed. Cacilda Teixeira da Costa, pesquisa, assist. ed. e coord. técnica. Marília Saboya de Albuquerque, pesquisa e assist. ed.] São Paulo, Instituto Walther Moreira Salles: Fundação Djalma Guimarães, 1983. 2v. il. (part col.)

Substantial, multi-author survey of Brazilian art from pre-European to contemporary. Includes standard topics plus sections on photography, industrial design, visual communications, Afro-Brazilian art, folk art, and art education. Notes, bibliographies follow each chapter. Indexes of names.

I404 Images of Mexico: the contribution of Mexico to 20th century art. Catalogue of the exhibition ed. by Erika Billeter. With texts by Alicia Azuela . . . [et al.] Dallas, Dallas Museum of Art, 1987. 442p. il. (part col.)

Also published in a Spanish-language ed. Catalog of the exhibition, Dallas Museum of Art (1987). Seeks to "prove that Mexican art is part of an international canon only now being formed."—*Dir. pref.* Includes 17 essays by art historians and critics on painting, graphic arts, photography, and cinema.

Chronology, p.442–[61]. Artists' biographies and list of works, p.[462]–[86].

I405 Latin American art in the twentieth century. Ed. by Edward J. Sullivan. [London, Phaidon, 1996]. 352p. il. (part col.)

Spanish ed., Madrid, Nerea, 1996.

"An overview of artistic activity in Latin America in the twentieth century."—*Pref.* 17 essays, each on a different country, by Latin American art historians. The essays generally trace the history of art of the last 100 years, tending to focus on painting, sculpture, and graphic arts, and excluding architecture, photography, and folk art, with some consideration of social and political influences.

Contents: Mexico, by Teresa del Conde; Central America, by Monica Kupfer; Cuba, by Giulio Blanc and Gerardo Mosquera; Dominican Republic, by Jeannette Miller; Puerto Rico, by Enrique García-Gutiérrez; Venezuela, by Rina Carvajal; Colombia, by Ivonne Pini; Ecuador, by Lenín Oña; Peru, by Natalia Majluf; Brazil, by Ivo Mesquita; Bolivia, by Pedro Querejazu; Paraguay, by Ticio Escobar; Uruguay, by Alicia Haber; Argentina, by Marcelo Pacheco; Chile, by Milan Ivelic; Chicano art, by Victor Zamudio-Taylor.

Selected general bibliography, p.334. Selected bibliographies by country, p.335–40. Index, p.341–51.

I406 Latin American artists of the twentieth century. Ed. by Waldo Rasmussen . . . [et al.] N.Y., The Museum of Modern Art, 1993. 424p. col. il.

Published in conjunction with the exhibition, Museum of Modern Art (1993). "Intended to introduce the vast and complex field represented by the exhibition, elucidating some of the circumstances in which the works of more than four generations of Latin American artists have been created."—*Introd.* 15 essays written by noted art critics and scholars. Includes work (and biographies) of 96 artists of four generations. Introductory essay gives history of advocacy and collection of Latin American art by MOMA. Extensive notes.

Biographies of the artists, p.371–98. Selected bibliography, p.399–412. Index, p.421–24.

I407 Latin American women artists = Artistas latinoamericanas: 1915–1995. [By] Geraldine P. Biller, guest curator. With essays by Bélgica Rodríguez . . . [et al.] Milwaukee, Milwaukee Art Museum, 1995. 198p. il. (part col.)

In English and Spanish. Catalog of the exhibition, Milwaukee Art Museum (1995), and other locations. "One of the first exhibitions to document the important contributions of women artists to the development of twentieth century Latin American art."— *Pref.*

Contents: Latin American women artists, 1915–1995, by Geraldine P. Biller; Latin American art: seeking out a national-international dialogue, by Bélgica Rodríguez; Abstraction in Mexico and beyond, by Edward J. Sullivan; The pen and the paintbrush, by Marina Pérez de Mendiola; Artists of the exhibition: selected plates and biographies.

General bibliography, p.177–84. Artists' bibliographies, p.185–98.

I408 Lemos, Carlos Alberto Cerqueira; Leite, José Roberto Teixeira; and Gismonti, Pedro Manuel. The art of Brazil. With an introd. by Pietro Maria Bardi and an essay by Oscar Niemeyer. [Trans. by Jennifer Clay.] N.Y., Harper & Row, 1983. 318p. il. (part col.) (Icon editions)

Portuguese ed., São Paulo, Abril, 1982.

Survey of art and architecture in Brazil from the arrival of Europeans in 1500 to 1980.

Contents: Early colonial art; The baroque; Neoclassicism and eclecticism in the nineteenth century; The modern revolution; Modern architecture; Contemporary research.

Biographies of the artists, p.295–307. Chronology, p.308–13. Index, p.314–18.

I409 Lombán, Juan Carlos. Historia del arte latinoamericano. Buenos Aires, Asociación Cultural Kilmes, 1994. 410p. il. (part col.)

Broad survey of Latin American art from pre-Columbian to contemporary.

Bibliografia, p.375–84. Indice analitico, p.385–95.

I410 Lucie-Smith, Edward. Latin American art of the 20th century. N.Y., Thames and Hudson, 1993. 216p. il. (part col.) (World of art)

Highly readable survey with thoughtful consideration of movements and their relationships to social and political milieus.

Contents: (1) Forerunners and independents; (2) The first modern movements; (3) Mexican muralism; (4) Muralism beyond Mexico; (5) The exiles; (6) Mexico: four women and one man; (7) A climate of change; (8) Geometric abstraction; (9) Informal abstraction; (10) Expressionist tendencies; (11) Realism, pop art, and surrealism; (12) The present day.

Select bibliography, p.208–10. Index, p.214–16.

I411 Mexico: splendors of thirty centuries. Introd. by Octavio Paz. [Trans. by Edith Grossman . . . et al.] N.Y., Metropolitan Museum of Art; Boston, Little, Brown, 1990. 712p. il. (part col.), maps.

Catalog of the landmark exhibition, Metropolitan Museum of Art (1990–1991), and other locations. Comprehensive survey of Mexican art from the pre-Columbian era to the present, with chapters by specialists devoted to each of the main pre-Columbian sites, to the confrontation with European art in the first centuries after contact, and to modern developments.

Contents: Precolumbian art; Viceregal art; Nineteenth-century art; Twentieth-century art.

Further reading, p.699–700. Index, p.701–12.

I412 Modernidade: vanguardas artísticas na América Latina. Ana Maria de Moraes Belluzzo (org.). Colab.: Aracy Amaral . . . [et al.] São Paulo, UNESP, 1990. 319p. il. (part col.) (Cadernos de cultura, 1)

Bilingual (Portuguese-Spanish) collection of essays by major Latin American art historians on modernism in Latin America.

Manifestos e declarações 1921–1959 [anthology of manifestos], p.239–308. Cronologia 1910–1964, p.309–17. Bibliografia, p.318–[39].

I413 Museo de Bellas Artes, Venezuela. Catálogo general: colección pintura y escultura latinoamericana. Caracas, Museo de Bellas Artes, 1980. 345p. il. (part col.)

Holdings arranged under painting, sculpture, and popular art.

Notas biográficas: pintores latinoamericanos, p.295–324. Notas biográficas: escultores latinoamericanos, p.325–33. Indice de artistas, p.334–35. Citas, p.336. Catálogos consultados, p.337–40. Bibliografía general sobre arte latinoamericano existente en la Biblioteca del Museo de Bellas Artes, p.341–45.

I414 Oettinger, Marion. The folk art of Latin America: visiones del pueblo. N.Y., Dutton, in assoc. with the Museum of American Folk Art, 1992. xix, 107p. col. il., col. map.

Catalog of the exhibition, Museum of American Folk Art, New York (1992), and other locations. Provides an overview of Latin American folk art, its nature, expressions, artists, and forms, focusing on "those objects that are central to Latin American religious and secular life."—*Pref.*

Notes, p.99–100. List of works cited, p.101–02. Annotated bibliography, p.102–05.

I415 Pintura, escultura y fotografia en Iberoamerica: siglos XIX y XX. Coord. de Rodrigo Gutiérrez Viñuales . . . [et al.] Madrid, Catedra, 1997. 547p. il. (Manuales arte Catedra)

Multi-author survey of modern painting, sculpture, and photography in Latin America.

Contents: (1) Introducción; (2) La pintura y la escultura en el siglo XIX; (3) La pintura y la escultura en el siglo XX; (4) La fotografía en Iberoamérica; (5) Políticas culturales y artísticas en Iberoamérica.

Bibliografía, p.485–512. Índice de nombres, p.513–30. Índice de obras, p.531–47.

I416 Pontual, Roberto. Entre dois séculos: arte brasileira do século XX na Coleçao Gilberto Chateaubriand. Rio [i.e., Rio de Janeiro], JB, 1987. 585p. il. (part col.), plates.

Substantial catalog of an important private collection of 20th-century Brazilian art.

Bibliografia, p.546–47. Biografias, p.549–85. Índice onomástico, p.541–45.

I417 Sayer, Chloë. Arts and crafts of Mexico. Special photography by David Lavender. San Francisco, Chronicle Books, 1990. 160p. il. (part col.), map.

Surveys the subject, emphasizing the role of craft within popular culture.

Contents: (I) Introduction; (II) The textile arts; (III) Jewelry and adornment; (IV) Ceramics; (V) An abundance of crafts; (VI) Toys and miniatures; (VII) Ceremonial and ephemeral arts; Collecting Mexican folk art; Mexico's indigenous peoples.

Glossary, p.154. Bibliography, p.155–56. Index, p.157–59.

I418 Scott, John F. Latin American art: ancient to modern. Gainesville, Univ. Pr. of Florida, 1999. xxiv, 240p. il. (part col.), plates, maps.

"Brief overview" of the subject.—*Introd.*

Contents: (1) Earliest native American art; (2) First high cultures; (3) The classic civilizations; (4) Empires and integration; (5) Colonial art of the American viceroyalties; (6) Art after independence.

Bibliography, p.[227]–32. Index, p.233–40.

I419 Sebastián, Santiago. El barroco iberoamericano: mensaje iconográfico. Madrid, Encuentro, 1990. 374p. 230 il. (part col.), map. (Pueblos y culturas)

French trans., Paris, Editions du Seuil, 1991.

Typological study of the Baroque architecture of Latin America.

Contents: Cultura y sociedad; Formas y espacios; La Iglesia de la Contrarreforma; La tradición biblica; Iconografía de Cristo y de María; Las nuevas devociones; Las Postrimerías; Un renovado humanismo: la emblemática; Iconografía de las órdenes religiosas; Epílogo.

Bibliografía, p.354–60. Indice de artistas, p.361–63. Indice temático e iconográfico, p.364–67. Indice de ilustraciones y figuras, p.370–74.

I420 Toussaint, Manuel. Arte colonial en México. 5. ed. México, Univ. Nacional Autónoma de México, Instituto de Investigaciones Estéticas, 1990. xiii, 303p. il., plates. (part col.)

See GLAH 1:I377 for previous eds., including 1967 English trans.; 4th ed., 1983.

Notas de los capítulos, p.253–61. Bibliografía, p.262–63. Índice de ilustraciones, p.264–76. Índice de personas, p.277–90. Índice de lugares, p.291–300.

I421 Traba, Marta. Art of Latin America, 1900–1980. [Washington, D.C.], Inter-American Development Bank. (Distr. by the Johns Hopkins Univ. Pr., 1994). xiv, 178p. col. il.

Spanish trans., Washington, D.C., 1994.

Critical essay on 20th-century Latin American art and its evolution by noted critic. Intended to accompany a 1985 exhibition, but delayed because of Traba's untimely death.

Artist index, p.167–78.

Low Countries

I422 L'art moderne en Belgique, 1900–1945. Sous le réd. de Robert Hoozee . . . [et al.] Anvers, Mercator, 1992. 445p. il. (chiefly col.), facsims., ports.

Survey of painting, sculpture, and graphic arts presented in a very well-illustrated, large-format volume. Unusually detailed chronology includes information about coinciding movements, exhibitions, and influential historical events in Europe.

Contents: Avant la Première Guerre mondiale, by Robert Hoozee; L'art moderne en exil, 1914–1921, by Piet Boyens; Bruxelles et Anvers, centres de l'avant-garde, 1917–1925, by Inge Henneman; Le mouvement Sélection, by Inge Henneman; L'expressionisme après la Première Guerre mondiale, by Monique Tahon-Vanroose; Le néo-réalisme, by Helke Lauwaert; Le surréalisme, by Serge Goyens de Heusch.

Notes, p.326–36. Chronique, 1900–1944, p.338–97. Biographies, p.400–23. Bibliographie, p.433. Expositions, p.434–35. Index, p.437–45.

I423 Dawn of the golden age: northern Netherlandish art, 1580–1620. Ed., Ger Luijten . . . [et al.] Amsterdam, Rijksmuseum (Distr. by Yale Univ. Pr., 1994). 718p. il. (part col.), ports.

Trans. of Dageraad der gouden eeuw: Noordnederlandse kunst, 1580–1620. Amsterdam, Rijksmuseum, 1994.

This beautifully illustrated volume, authored by curators and academic art historians, was published to accompany an exhibition, Rijksmuseum (1993–94). In addition to several essays, it contains 347 detailed catalog entries arranged by media and theme which provide complete coverage of painting, sculpture, drawing, prints and decorative arts. Also contains artist biographies.

Contents: Northern Netherlandish art, 1580–1600, by Wouter Th. Kloek; The turning point in the history of Dutch art, by J. Bruyn; The appreciation of paintings around 1600, by Hessel Miedema; Art lovers and their paintings: Van Mander's Schilder-boeck as a source for the history of the art market in the northern Netherlands, by Martin Jan Bok; Print publishers in the Netherlands, 1580–1620, by Christiaan Schuckman.

Bibliography, p.677–707. Index, p.709–17.

I424 Flemish art from the beginning till now. Under the dir. of Herman Liebaers . . . [et al.] Assist. by Piet Baudouin . . . [et al.] Trans. by John Cairns. Antwerp, Mercatorfonds, 1985. 587p. il. (part col.), plate.

Trans. of Vlaamse kunst van de oorsprong tot heden. Antwerp, Mercatorfonds, 1985.

Massive introductory survey of Flemish fine arts, architecture, decorative arts, stained glass, and manuscript illumination from the Middle Ages to the early 20th century. Essays edited by the curatorial staffs of major museums in Antwerp, Ghent, and Bruges are arranged chronologically. Large format with numerous illustrations primarily in color.

Index, p.575–86.

I425 Gelder, Hendrik Enno van, and Duverger, J. Kunstgeschiedenis der Nederlanden. Zeist [Netherlands], W. de Haan, 1963–1965. 12v. (Phoenix geillustreerde stansaardwerken)

See GLAH 1:I381 for previous ed. This ed. also available in microform. Gravenhage, Netherlands. Koninklijke Bibliotheck Lange Voorhout 34, 1979. 1 microfilm reel.

Contents: (1–3) De middleeeuwen; (4–5) Renaissance; (6) Zeventiende-eeuwse schilderkunst (i.e., Gouden eeuw I); (7) Gouden eeuw II; (8) Archttiende eeuw; (9–12) Negentiende en twintigste eeuw.

Includes bibliographies.

I426 Kunstreisboek voor Nederland. 8. geheel. herziende en verm. druk. Houten [Netherlands], Van Kampen & Zoon, 1985– . (4)v.

See GLAH 1:I384 for previous, 1-vol. ed. Frequently reissued.

Contents: (1) Zeeland; (2) Zuid-Holland; (3) Drenthe; (4) Noord-Holland.

I427 De Nederlandse monumenten van geschiedenis en kunst. Utrecht, Oosthoek, 1912– . (20) v.

See GLAH 1:I386 for previous vols.

Contents: De Provincie Overijsel: Noord en oost Salland (1974); De Provincie Noordholland: Amsterdam Burgerweeshuis (1975); De Provincie Noordholland: Amsterdam het R. C. Maagdenhuis (1980); De Provincie Friesland: Noordelijk oostergo: Ferwerderadeel (1981); De Provincie Gelderland: Rijk van Nijmegen: Westelijk gedeelte (1982); De Provincie Gelderland: Rijk van Nijmegen: Oostelijk gedeelte en de Duffelt (1983); De Provincie Friesland: Noordelijk oostergo: De Dongeradelen (1983); De Provincie Friesland: Noordelijk oostergo: Dantumadeel (1984); Sint Janskathedraals'-Hertogenbosch (1985); De Provincie Gelderland: Land van Maas en Waal (1986); De Provincie Friesland: Noordelijk oostergo: Kollumerland en Nieuw Kruisland (1989); De Provincie Utrecht: Utrecht de huizen binnen de ingels, 2v. (1989); De Provincie Zuid-Holland: Vijfheerenlanden met Asperen, Heukelum en Spijk (1989); De Provincie Limburg: Margraten, Mheer en Noorbeek (1991); De Provincie Zuid-Holland: Voorne putten (1992); De Provincie Zuid-Holland: Alblasserwaard (1992); De Provincie Zuid-Holland: De Krimpenerwaard (1995); De Provincie Utrecht: De Utrechtse Heuvelrug (1999); De Provincie Limburg: Landgoed Sint-Gerlach (1999).

I428 Overy, Paul. De Stijl. N.Y., Thames and Hudson, 1991. 216p. il. (part col.) (World of art)

Detailed, readable survey of the De Stijl movement and its influence on the development of other modern styles. Suitable for the beginning or intermediate reader. Good illustrations.

Contents: (1) Producing De Stijl; (2) De Stijl and modern Holland; (3) Writing De Stijl; (4) Painting; (5) Sculpture and furniture; (6) Colour designs and collaboration; (7) Architecture; (8) Social housing and the International Style; (9) The machine aesthetic and European modernism; (10) De Stijl in France; (11) Reproducing De Stijl.

Select bibliography and sources, p.201–7. Index, p.213–16.

I429 Prevenier, Walter, and Blockmans, Wim. The Burgundian Netherlands. Picture research by An Blockmans-Delva. Foreword by Richard Vaughn. Cambridge, [Eng.], Cambridge Univ. Pr., 1986. 403p. il. (part col.), facsims., geneal. tables, maps, ports.

Trans. of Pay-Bas bourguignons. [Paris,] Albin Michel, [1983]

Focuses on the emergence and development of a single geographic and economic area from 1380–1530. Provides analysis of the fine arts, architecture, and decorative arts grounded in the historical, social, and political identity of the region. Well illustrated throughout. Appendices include a chronology of events, genealogical chart, maps, socio-economic data, and a brief discussion of currencies in use.

Selective bibliography, p.396–97. Index, p.398–403.

I430 Rosenberg, Jakob; Slive, Seymour; and Kuile, E. H. ter. Dutch art and architecture, 1600–1800. 3d ed. [Reprint.] New Haven, Yale Univ. Pr., 1993. 502p. il. (Yale University Press pelican history of art)

Reprint of GLAH 1:I388.

SEE ALSO: Dutch art: an encyclopedia (GLAH 2:E140).

Russia and Eastern Europe

I431 Akademiia nauk SSSR. Institut istorii iskusstv. Geschichte der russischen Kunst. [Red. I. E. Grabar, W.N. Lasarew und W.S. Kemenow. Übersetz. von Kurt Küppers. Hrsg. mit Unterstützung des Kultur-

fonds der Deutschen Demokratischen Republik.] Dresden, Verlag der Kunst, 1957–1976. 6v. il. (part col.), plans.
See GLAH 1:I392 for previous vols.

Contents: (6) Die russische Kunst in der zweiten Hälfte des 18. Jahrhunderts.

I432 Art and culture in nineteenth-century Russia. Ed. by Theofanis George Stavrou. Bloomington, Indiana Univ. Pr., 1983. xix, 268p., il. plates.
"This book is the result of two scholarly projects, a lecture series and a symposium, which were held in the fall of 1978 in connection with the exhibition The art of Russia 1800–1850 organized by the University of Minnesota Gallery with the Committee on Institutional Cooperation and the Ministry of Culture of the U.S.S.R."—*Pref.* Collection of interdisciplinary scholarly essays by recognized experts in the field. Extensive notes and references follow each chapter.

Selective contents: (1) Notes on the emergence and nature of the Russian intelligentsia, by Nicholas Riasanovsky; (2) St. Petersburg and Moscow as cultural symbols, by Sidney Monas; (3) On the Russianess of the Russian nineteenth-century novel, by Donald Fanger; (4) Native song and national consciousness in nineteenth-century Russian music, by Malcolm Hamrick Brown; (5) Russian art and society 1800–1850, by S. Frederick Starr; (6) Russian painting in the nineteenth century, by John E. Bowlt; (7) Russian painters and the pursuit of light, by Joshua Taylor; (8) The intelligentsia and art, by Elizabeth Kridl Valkenier; (9) Architecture in nineteenth-century Russia: the enduring classic, by Albert Smith; (10) The neoclassical ideal in Russian sculpture, by Janet Kennedy; (11) A survey of the trends in Russian decorative arts of the first half of the nineteenth century, by Paul Schaffer; (12) Nineteenth-century Russian caricature, by John E. Bowlt; (13) Russian folk art and "high" art in the early nineteenth century, by Alison Hilton.

Index, p.261–68.

I433 Art in Poland, 1572–1764: land of the winged horsemen by Jan K. Ostrowski . . . [et al.] Trans. by Krystyna Malcharek. Alexandria, Va., Art Services International, in assoc. with Yale Univ. Pr., 1999. 380p. il. (part col.), map.
Catalog of a traveling exhibition organized and circulated by Art Services International, in cooperation with the Walters Art Gallery (Baltimore). Well-illustrated survey of artistic development during the two centuries following the Polish Renaissance. Comprised of essays by well-known scholars. 137 catalog entries include paintings, sculpture, architecture, decorative arts, and arms and armor.

Contents: Definition and self-definition in Polish culture and art, by Thomas DaCosta Kaufmann; History of Poland in the 16th–18th centuries, by Adam Zamoyski; Polish Baroque art in its social and religious context, by Jan K. Ostrowski; Mechanisms of contact between Polish and European Baroque, by Jan K. Ostrowski; The impact of the Orient on the culture of old Poland, by Zdzislaw Zygulski; Architecture in Poland 1572–1764, by Piotr Krasny.

Biographies of artists, p.360–66. Significant political events in Poland, 1550–1770, p.367–68. Glossary, p.369–70. Bibliography, p.371–77. Index, p.378–80.

I434 Balogh, Jolán. Die Anfänge der Renaissance in Ungarn: Matthias Corvinus und die Kunst. [Übers. aus dem Ungarischen, Hildegard Baranyai.] Graz, Akademische Druck- u. Verlagsanstalt, 1975. xviii, 453p. il. (part col.) (Forschungen und Berichte des Instituts für Kunstgeschichte der Karl-Franzens-Universität Graz, 4)
Important study of art and patronage at the court of Matthias Corvinus in the second half of the 15th century.

Contents: (I) Die Mäzene; (II) Bauten; (III) Skulpturen, Kleinplastik; (IV) Malerei, Buchkunst, Graphik; (V) Das Kunsthandwerk; (VI) Ankäufe, Handelsverbindungen.

Nachtrag zur Literatur, p.309. Ortsnamenkonkordanz, p.310–12. Register, p.435–53.

I435 The Baroque in Central Europe: places, architecture and art. Ed. by Manlio Brusatin and Gilberto Pizzamiglio. Photographs by Mark Smith. With essays by Gottfried Biedermann . . . [et al.] N.Y., Marsilio, 1992. xvi, 319p. il. (chiefly col.)
Published in conjunction with the "Year of the Baroque," a series of events held in 1992–93 by the Commission of the Central European Initiative whose members comprise the geographic basis for this volume: Austria, the former Czechoslovakia (now the Czech Republic and Slovakia) Croatia, Hungary, Italy, Poland, and Slovenia. Documents the influence and spread of stylistic features of the Baroque from 1600–1750. Arranged by country, region, and city, this volume contains excellent color illustrations and descriptions of key monuments and works of art with bibliographic references. The internal organization and detailed table of contents minimize the absence of an index.

I436 Gotik in Slowenien. Ljubljana, Narodna Galerija Ljubljana, 1995. 436p. il. (part col.)
A handsome catalog accompanying the exhibition, Narodna Galerija Ljubliana (1995) covering painting, sculpture, architecture, and illuminated manuscripts produced in the territories constituting present-day Slovenia from the middle of the 13th century to the end of the 15th century. Brief introductory essays on the historical period and media accompany 238 detailed, often extensive, catalogue entries. Very well-illustrated, primarily in color.

Einführende Literatur, p.23. Bibliographie, p.403–31.

I437 Gray, Camilla. The Russian experiment in art, 1863–1922. Rev. and enl. ed. by Marian Burleigh-Motley. N.Y., Thames and Hudson, 1986. 324p. il. (part col.) (World of art)
See GLAH 1:I405 for previous eds.

This landmark publication has been reworked after the author's death through the inclusion of a full set of new notes and corrections. Additionally, the illustrations have been annotated with new information and interpretation and the bibliography has been completely updated.

Text references, p.277–79. Bibliography, p.313–19. Notes: text revisions, p.282–95. Index, p.321–24.

I438 Hamilton, George Heard. The art and architecture of Russia. [New Haven], Yale Univ. Pr., [1992] xxiv,

342p. il. plates, map. (The Yale University Press pelican history of art)
See GLAH 1:I406 for previous eds. The bibliography has been updated for this ed.

Abbreviations, p.[416]–17. Notes, p.[418]–48. Bibliography, p.[449]–54. Index, p.[462]–82.

I439 History of art in Poland. Warsaw, Arkady, 1983– . (4)v.
Trans. of Dzieje Sztuki w Polsce. Warszawa, Arkady, 1982– . (4)v.

This series provides a detailed survey of Polish art and architecture from 1038 to the early 19th century with the exclusion of the Gothic period. Includes many good quality black-and-white illustrations of lesser know monuments as well as numerous plans and elevations. Later eds. of Renaissance in Poland volumes have been published in Polish.

Contents: Kozakiewiczowie, Helena, and Kozakiewiczowie, Stefan. Renaissance in Poland. Trans. by Doreen Heaton Rotworowska (1976); Swiechowski, Zygmunt. Romanesque art in Poland. Trans. by Alina Kozinska-Baldyga and Jerzy A. Baldyga (1983); Lorentz, Stanislaw, and Rottermund, Andrzej. Neoclassicism in Poland. Trans. by Jerzy A. Baldyga (1986); Karpowicz, Mariusz. Baroque in Poland. Trans. by Jerzy A. Baldyga (1991).

Each vol. contains bibliography, indexes of localities, monuments, and persons.

I440 The history of Hungarian art in the twentieth century. [By] Gábor Andrási . . . [et al.] Trans. by John Bátki. Budapest, Corvina, 1999. 290p. il. (part col.)
Trans. of Magyar képzomuvészet a 20. században. Budapest. Corvina Kiadó, 1999. Survey of 20th-century art in Hungary, intended to supersede Lajos Németh, Modern magyar müvészet. Budapest, Corvina, 1972. Does not treat architecture and the applied arts.

Contents: 1896–1919; 1919–1945; From 1945 to the seventies; The seventies; The eighties: "The avant-garde is dead"; Contemporary art in the nineties.

Selected bibliography, p.268–71. Index, p.281–90.

I441 Höfler, Janez. Die Kunst Dalmatiens vom Mittelalter bis zur Renaissance (800–1520). Graz, Akademische Druck, 1989. 338p. il. (part col.) (Forschungen und Berichte des Institutes für Kunstgeschichte der Karl-Franzens Universität Graz, 8)
Detailed survey of the region which now forms modern Croatia. Examines both the fine and decorative arts with particular emphasis on religious and secular architecture. Suitable for the advanced reader. Bibliography is arranged by chronological period.

Anmerkungen, p.318–23. Literaturauswahl, p.324–26. Zeitschriftenabkürzungen, p.326. Abbildungsverzeichnis, p.327–32. Künstler- und Ortsverzeichnis, p.333–38.

I442 Introduction to Russian art and architecture. Ed. by Robert Auty and Dimitri Obolensky. With the ed. assist. of Anthony Kingsford. N.Y., Cambridge Univ. Pr., 1980. xxxi, 194p. il. (Companion to Russian studies, v.3)
Introductory survey covering the 10th–20th centuries which aims "to tell in concise fashion what happened when, to trace the development of genres and styles, to give an indication of what seems art-historically important and why, and lastly to contradict a few prevalent myths and locate the chief unresolved problems."—*Introd.*

Selective contents: (1) Art and architecture of old Russia, 988–1700, by Robin Milner-Gulland; (2) Art and architecture in the Petersburg age, 1700–1860, by Robin Milner-Gulland; (3) Art and architecture in the age of revolution, 1860–1917, by John Bowlt; (4) Art and architecture in Soviet Russia, by John Bowlt.

Bibliography, p.173–81. Index, p.183–94.

I443 Ivancevic, Radovan. Art treasures of Croatia. [Trans., Madge Phillips Tomasevic]. [2d. ed., War ed.] Zagreb, ITP Motovun, 1993. 216p. il. (part col.) plans, map.
1st ed., Zagreb, Motovun, 1986. Trans. of Umjetnicko blago Hrvatske.

Richly illustrated in color, this volume is a general survey of art and architecture in the region comprised by modern-day Croatia from the Greco-Roman period to the present day. The Afterword contains a partial enumeration and comments on monuments destroyed in 1991–92.

Selective contents: Traces of prehistoric communities; Greek colonisation of the eastern Adriatic; Roman urbanisation; The first Croatian state; The renewal of towns and raising of monasteries; The age of free cities, nobility, and preaching orders; The divergent paths of the north and south; The Northern revival; From classicism to symbolism; The early twentieth century; Afterword for the war edition.

Bibliography, p.204. Index, p.213–16.

I444 Kaufmann, Thomas DaCosta. Court, cloister, and city: the art and culture of Central Europe, 1450–1800. Chicago, Univ. of Chicago Pr., 1995. 576p. il., maps.
Scholarly analysis of society, culture, history and their relationship to the arts. Emphasis on an understanding of the effect of the political complexities of the region through the early modern era. The author "discounts 19th- and 20th-century notions of nationhood and ethnicity, reviving instead other forms of cultural identity: family, estate, craft, class, city, religion, and reason. In so doing, he demolishes many of the smug certainties of cultural history as perceived from a purely West European standpoint."—*Review*, The spectator, 13 April 1996, p.40. Suitable for the advanced reader or researcher.

Contents: (1) Prologue to the Renaissance: art and architecture of the fifteenth century in Russia and Hungary; (2) Jagellonians and Hapsburgs: art of the courts c.1500; (3) Art of the towns: the role of German-speaking artists, c.1500; (4) The Renaissance in German-speaking lands: Dürer, his contemporaries, and humanism; (5) The problem of the reception of the Renaissance: the Reformation and art; (6) Court, castle, and city in the mid-sixteenth century; (7) Kunst und Kunstkammer: collecting as a phenomenon of the Renaissance in Central Europe; (8) Princely patronage of the later sixteenth and early seventeenth centuries: the example and impact of art at the court of Rudolf II; (9) Art on the eve of the Thirty Years' War: the Catholic Reformation and the arts; (10) Art and the Thirty Years' War; (11) Art and architecture and the Thirty Years' War; (12) Polonia victoriosa; Austria victoriosa; (13) Early eighteenth century architecture, art and collecting at the German courts; Excursus: St. Petersburg and environs in the eighteenth century; (14) Early eighteenth century art and architecture in the Bohemian lands; (15) South German art and architecture of the early eighteenth century in its European context; (16) The transformation of the arts at court from the mid-eighteenth century; (17) Arts and audiences of the later eighteenth century: painterly pyrotechnics and its alternatives; (18) The critical response: collecting, criticism, the Enlightenment and the arts.

Notes, p.465–552. Index, p.553–76.

I445 Mansbach, Steven A. Modern art in Eastern Europe: from the Baltic to the Balkans, ca. 1890–1939. N.Y., Cambridge Univ. Pr., 1999. xvi, 384p. il. (part col.), plates.

"This book offers both the general reader and the specialist access to a world of seldom-considered visual material. The interpretive overview reclaims the essential role played by eastern European artists in the genesis of the modern aesthetics with which we are familiar in the West."—*Pref.*

Contents: (1) The Czech lands; (2) Poland and Lithuania; (3) The Baltic states of Latvia and Estonia; (4) The southern Balkans of the former Yugoslavia: Slovenia, Croatia, Serbia, and Macedonia; (5) Romania; (6) Hungary.

Notes, p.321–55. List of artists, p.356–58. Selected bibliography, p.359–70. Index, p.371–84.

I446 Muthesius, Stefan. Art, architecture and design in Poland, 966–1990: an introduction. Königstein im Taunus, Langewiesche Nachfolger H. Koster, 1994. 107, [1]p. il. (part col.), maps.

A concise, up-to-date survey of Polish art and architectural history with good illustrations. "This book fills a gap that has long existed in the market for an introductory study on Polish art and architecture. It serves, however, a wider purpose; it also offers an overview of the beginnings of Polish art-historical thought and the formation of the concept of Polish art."—*Review*, Art history, v.19, June 1996, p.321.

Selective contents: Art, nation, politics and the art historian; The early periods; Gothic architecture; Church fittings in the late middle ages; The Polish renaissance; Sarmatism; Warsaw town palaces; The last king as patron; 1760–1900: Palladianism, garden architecture, neo-classicism, neo-gothic; Painting and nationalism from the late 18th to the early 20th centuries; The art of the 20th century.

General bibliography, p.104–6. Index, p.107.

I447 Renaissance art in Bohemia. Text by Jiřina Hořejsí . . . [et al.] [Trans. by Pavla Dlouhá with revisions by Hugh Newbury.] London, Hamlyn, 1979. 245p. il. (part col.), maps.

Unable to identify original ed. Also published as Die Kunst der Renaissance und des Manierismus in Böhmen. Hanau/ M. Dausien, 1979.

Introductory survey with many good quality black-and-white photographs provides English language access to 16th-century art, architecture, and decorative arts in the Czech Lands now chiefly comprised by the Czech Republic.

Contents: Arts in Bohemia under the Jagiellos, by Jiřina Hořejsí [and] Jarmila Vacková; Arts in the Renaissance and Mannerist periods: The court of Ferdinand I and Maximilian II at Prague, the Renaissance outside the royal court, the Pernštejn interlude, the palace and the château, the town, the church, the architecture at Rudolph II's court, by Jarmila Krčálová; Artistic crafts in the period of the Renaissance and Mannerism: Decorative art at the court of Rudolph II, by Emanuel Poche; Arts at the court of Rudolph II: The emperor and art, themes and ideas of Rudolphine art, The development and personalities of Rudolphine painting, sculpture at the court of Rudolph II, by Jaromír Neumann;

Notes, p.218–22. Bibliography, p.222–34. Index of names, p.237–40. Index of places, p.241–43. Maps, p.245.

I448 Romanian art. [Eng. trans. eds., Delia Răzdolescu, Alexandra Dobrotă]. Bucharest, Meridiane, 1984. 2v. il. (part col.), plans.

Trans. of Arta romaneasca. Bucureşti, Editura Meridiane, 1982.

Building on Oprescu's Istoria artelor plastice în România (GLAH 1:I412), the authors have developed two independent volumes which aim to be the "first attempt at presenting the general evolution of art on the territory of this country from its origin down to the present days."—*Foreword.* Illustrations are of somewhat inferior quality though many little-known works are reproduced.

Selective contents: (v.1) Prehistory, antiquity, Middle Ages, Renaissance, Baroque, by Vasile Drăguţ; (v.2) Modern and contemporary ages, by Vasile Florea.

Selected bibliography and notes, v.1, p.487–[95], v.2, [436]–38. Index, v.1, p.497–[510], v.2, p.439–[46].

I449 Russian modernism. Introd. by Jean-Louis Cohen. Comp. and annot. by David Woodruff and Ljiljana Grubisic. Santa Monica, Getty Research Institute for the History of Art and the Humanities, 1997. 215p. il. (chiefly col.) (Bibliographies and dossiers: the collections of the Getty Research Institute for the History of Art and the Humanities, 1)

"The aim of the Getty Research Institute's collection . . . is not to compete with the great bibliographic or museological holdings that already exist in older or larger institutions but to allow researchers a direct glimpse of certain extremely fragile documents. . . . At the core of the collection are several hundred books and periodicals acquired by the Parisian collector Marc Martin-Malburet."—*Introd.*

List of cited works, p.182–85. List of Soviet organizations and acronyms, p.186–94. Index, p.195–214.

I450 Sarabianov, Dmitri V. Russian art: from neoclassicism to the avant-garde, 1800–1917: painting, sculpture, architecture. N.Y., Abrams, 1990. 320p. il. (part col.)

Well-organized and readable, this amply illustrated introductory survey of Russian art emphasizes historical and cultural contexts and antecedents. The primary focus is on painting.

Contents: Part I 1800–1860: (1) The end of Russian classicism; (2) Early romanticism; (3) Early realism; (4) The fate of romantic academic art; (5) Alexander Ivanov; (6) The beginnings of critical realism; (7) Sculpture and architecture; Part II 1860–1895: (1) The realists of the 1860s; (2) The Society for Travelling Art Exhibitions ("The Wanderers"); (3) Genre painting and Ilya Repin; (4) History painting; (5) Landscape painting; (6) Sculpture and architecture; Part III 1895–1917: (1) The beginnings of symbolism and Russian art nouveau; (2) From impressionism to Russian art nouveau; (3) The Moscow painters; (4) The "World of Art" group; (5) The "Blue Rose" group; (6) The "Knave of Diamonds," the "Donkey's Tail," and neoprimitivism; (7) The avant-garde; (8) Sculpture and architecture.

Notes, p.[306]. Select bibliography, p.[307]–8. Index, p.[315]–20.

I451 Stanislawski, Ryszard. Europa, Europa: das Jahrhundert der Avantgarde in Mittel- und Osteuropa. [Bonn], Kunst- und Ausstellungshalle der Bundesrepublik Deutschland, 1994. 4v. il.

Catalog produced to accompany the exhibition of the same name, Kunst- und Ausstellungshalle der Bundesrepublik Deutschland, Bonn (1994). Extraordinarily comprehensive examination of the origins and character of avant-garde artistic activity in Eastern Europe and Russia. Beautifully illustrated throughout, it contains the works of many artists little known in the West and numerous short essays by an international group of art historians and curators. Bibliographies are arranged by subject and publication type.

Selective contents: (1) Bildende Kunst, Fotografie, Videokunst; (2) Architektur, Literatur, Theater, Film, Musik; (3) Dokumente; (4) Biografien.

Verzeichnis der Textquellen, v.3, p.232–66. Bibliographische Hinweise, v.4, p.150–53. Personenregister, v.4, p.183–98.

I452 Thierry, Jean Michel. Armenian art. Principal sites by Patrick Donabédian, with the assist. of Jean Michel and Nicole Thierry. Trans. from the French by Celestine Dars. N.Y., Abrams in assoc. with the Prelacy of the Armenian Apostolic Church of America-Catholicosate of Cilicia, 1989. 613p. il. (part col.) geneal. tables, maps, plans.

Richly illustrated text covers art produced in the region comprised by present-day Armenia from the 6th century B.C. through the 18th century. Covers art, architecture, and the decorative arts with an emphasis on architecture. Originality and the cultural identity of the diverse Armenian peoples is stressed throughout. Useful for the general reader.

Contents: Armenian art from the 6th century B.C. to the 7th century A.D.: pagan Armenian art, the early Christian era, the golden age of the early middle ages; The age of the kingdoms (9th–12th century): the art of the Kingdom of Ani, the art of the Kingdom of Vaspurakan; the Palatine Church of the Holy Cross at Atlt'amar, the age of the diaspora in Asia Minor, the art of eastern Siunia; The age of the feudal states (12th–15th century): the art of northern Armenia, the art of southwestern Armenia, the art of the Kingdom of Cilicia, the art of the diaspora; Armenian art in modern times (17th–18th century): architecture and the plastic arts, the minor arts, the art of the diaspora.

Chronology and genealogy, p.605-[11]. Glossary, p.612. Bibliography, p.613. Index of names, p.617–23.

I453 A thousand years of Czech culture: riches from the National Museum in Prague. Winston-Salem, N.C., Old Salem; Prague, The Czech Republic National Museum (Distr. by the University of Washington Pr., 1996). xiii, 166p. il. (part col.), map.

Catalog of an exhibition, Old Salem (1996–97). Substantial essays provide an accessible, up-to-date synthesis of the artistic culture of the Czech Republic (Bohemia, Moravia, and parts of Silesia) in historical context. Covers a wide range of fine and decorative arts including some objects never before exhibited outside the Czech Republic. Contains many fine color illustrations.

Contents: History of Czech lands in the Middle Ages, by Vladimir Brych; Art in the Czech lands from the sixth to the twelfth centuries, by Vladimir Brych; Christianity in the Czech lands, by Jan Royt; The cultural history of the Jews in Czech lands, by Lena Korba-Novotná; Czech history in the early modern period, by Marie Ryantová; Fine art from the thirteenth to the nineteenth centuries, by Martin Mádl; One thousand years of Czech music, by Dagmar Vanišová; Czech theater, by Markéta Trávníčková; Czech folk art and culture, by Jiřina Langhammerová; Modern Czech history, by Stanislav Slavik.

Selected bibliography, p.163–66.

SEE ALSO: Ćurčić, Art and architecture in the Balkans: an annotated bibliography (GLAH 2:A118); Russian art of the avant-garde (GLAH 2:I251).

Scandinavia

I454 The art of Norway, 1750–1914. [Ed. by Louise Lincoln]. Minneapolis, Minneapolis Institute of the Arts, 1978. 223p. il. (part col.), plates, map.

Catalog of the exhibition, Elvehjem Museum of Art, University of Wisconsin, Madison (1979), and other locations. Serves as an introduction for the general reader to painting, sculpture, decorative, and folk arts. Brief essays on individual media and brief catalog entries for 251 objects. Modestly illustrated.

Selected basic references and works in English on Norwegian art and history, 1750–1914, p.220. Index of Norwegian artists, p.221.

I455 A history of Swedish art. By Mereth Lindgren . . . [et al.] Trans. by Roger Tanner. [Lund], Signum, 1987. 277p. il. (part col.)

Abridged trans. of Svensk konsthistoria. [2. uppl.] [Lund], Signum, 1986.

Handsomely illustrated introduction to painting, sculpture, and architecture from pre-history through the 1970s. Integrates discussions of style with analyses of historical events and influences outside Scandinavia.

Index, p.273–77.

I456 Kaalund, Bodil. The art of Greenland: sculpture, crafts, painting. Trans. by Kenneth Tindall. Berkeley, Univ. of California Pr., 1983. 224p. il. (part col.)

Trans. of Grønlands kunst. [København, Denmark, Politikens, 1979]

Introduction to Greenland's art and material culture from pre-history to the 1970s. Particular emphasis is given to the sculpture, crafts, and rituals before 1900. Arranged by media and well-illustrated throughout.

References, p.218–20. Index of names, p.221–24.

I457 Kent, Neil. Triumph of light and nature: Nordic art, 1740–1940. N.Y., Thames and Hudson, 1987. 240p. il. (part col.)

A general introductory survey of painting and sculpture in Sweden, Denmark, Norway, Finland, and Iceland. Readable and well-illustrated, it was conceived to address the increasing interest in Scandinavian art generated by several large international exhibitions held in the early to mid-1980s.

Contents: (1) Art of the royal courts, 1740–1800; (2) Classicism, 1800–1850; (3) The awakening of national art, 1830–1870; (4) Continentalism and revolution, 1830–1875; (5) Skagen, 1830–1910; (6) Nature, light and mood, 1879–1910; (7) Tradition and the birth of modernism, 1900–1940.

Notes on the text, p.219. Biographies, p.220–29. Select bibliography, p.229. Index, p.237–40.

I458 Landscapes from a high latitude: Icelandic art, 1909–1989. Ed. by Julia Freeman . . . [et al.] Foreword by Magnus Magnusson. London, Pub. for the Government of Iceland and the City of Reykjavik by Lund Humphries, 1989. 135p. il. (part col.)

Catalog of the exhibition, Barbican Art Centre, London (1989), and other locations. One of the few publications in English devoted to 20th-century Icelandic art. "The history of art and cultural substructure are broadly and informatively discussed, together with the place of such work, and its aesthetic value, both in Iceland today and in Scandinavia and Northern Europe as a whole."—*Pub. jacket note.* A well-illustrated survey that touches on sculpture, decorative arts, and architecture as well as painting.

Contents: A bird's-eye view of Icelandic culture, by Sigurður A. Magnússon; Reflections on Icelandic art, by Halldór Björn Runólfsson; Symbolism: the constant strain in Icelandic art, by John Russell Taylor; Not the land, but an idea of a land, by Michael Tucker.

Biographies and list of works, p.121–32. Bibliography, p.[133]–135.

I459 Norges kunsthistori. Red., Knut Berg . . . [et al.] Oslo, Gyldendal, 1981–1983. 7v. il.

A scholarly survey by multiple authors covering the arts and architecture of Norway from prehistoric times through the 1970s. Includes industrial design. Very well illustrated throughout.

Contents: (1) Fra Oseberg til Borgund; (2) Høymiddelalder og Hansa-tid; (3) Nedgangstid og ny reisning; (4) Det unge Norge; (5) Nasjonal vekst; (6) Mellomkrigstid; (7) Inn i en ny tid.

Notes at ends of chapters. Person- og sakregister, v.7, p.467–510.

I460 Ny dansk kunsthistorie. [Hovedred., Peter Michael Hornung.] København, Fogtdal, 1993–1996. 10v. il. (part col.)

Beautifully illustrated survey of the fine arts, architecture, and decorative arts arranged thematically and by artistic period. Excellent coverage of modern and contemporary movements.

Contents: (1) Frederiksen, Hans Jørgen and Kolstrup, Inger-Lise. Troens kunst; (2) Johannsen, Birgitte Bøggild and Johannsen, Hugo. Kongens kunst; (3) Bramsen, Henrik. Fra rokoko til guldalder; (4) Hornung, Peter Michael. Realismen; (5) Wivel, Henrik. Symbolisme og impressionisme; (6) Abildgaard, Hanne. Tidlig modernisme; (7) Jørgensen, Henning and Villadsen, Villads. Tradition og surrealisme; (8) Jespersen, Gunnar. Cobra; (9) Bogh, Mikkel. Geometri og bevgelse; (10) Bogh, Mikkel . . . [et al.] Kunsten i mediernes tid.

Bibliographies and indexes in each vol. Cumulative index, v.10, p.242–71.

I461 Okkonen, Onni. Suomen taiteen historia. 2. painos. Porvoo, Soderstrom, [1955]. 869p. il. (part col.) plates.

See GLAH 1:I430 for 1st ed.

I462 Shetelig, Haakon. Scandinavian archaeology. Trans. by E. V. Gordon. [Reprint.] N.Y., AMS, 1978. xix, 458p. il. plates.

See GLAH 1:I433 for original publication.

I463 Smith, John Boulton. The golden age of Finnish art: art nouveau and the national spirit. [2d rev. ed.] Helsinki, Otava, 1985. 237p. il. (part col.)

1st ed., Helsinki, Otava, 1976.

Expanded text drawing on the collections of the new Museum of Applied Arts in Helsinki and other newly available material. This well-illustrated study covers art and architecture and discusses developing Finnish styles in political, social, and intellectual context. Also examines the influence of other European movements in the latter part of the 19th century.

Contents: (I) From 1800–1880; (II) From eighteen-eighty into the nineties; (III) Historical and cultural background, 1890–1910: development of the nation; (IV) The eighteen-nineties: romantic Finnish naturalism and symbolism; (V) Gallen-Kallela, Kalevala, and Finnish national art; (VI) The Sparres, Finch, and the Iris Factory; (VII) National romanticism in architecture, from Karelian cabins to the Paris Pavilion; (VIII) High national romanticism, 1900–1905; (IX) Rationalism: a move towards modern architecture; (X) Design in the new century; (XI) Sculpture, painting, printmaking.

Bibliography, p.231–34.

I464 Valkonen, Markku. Finnish art over the centuries. Trans. by Martha Gaber Abrahamsen. Helsinki, Otava Pub., 1992. 159p. il. (part col.)

Trans. of Kuvien Suomi: Suomen taiteen vuosisadat. Helsingissä, Otava, 1992. French ed., L'art finlandais: au fil des âges. Helsinki, Otava, 1992.

A detailed introductory survey focusing on the late 18th century to the contemporary period. Considerable attention is given to distinguishing Finnish national character in the arts as well as placing these artistic achievements within a European context.

Select bibliography, p.157. Index, p.158–59.

I465 Les Vikings . . . les Scandinaves et l'Europe, 800–1200. Dir. du catalogue, Else Roesdahl, Jean-Pierre Mohen, Francois-Xavier Dillman. Paris, Association française d'action artistique, 1992. 428p. il. (part col.) maps.

Catalog published to accompany the exhibition, Grand Palais, Paris (1992), and other locations. Explores the penetration of Viking culture and artistic activity into Europe. Covers all forms of artistic production and architecture. Contains 41 very well illustrated essays and a catalog of 617 objects.

Tableau chronologique, 800–1200, p.393–99. Glossaire, p.395. Les auteurs des articles, p.396. Bibliographie, p.398–423. Index géographique, p.424–26. Index thématique, p.427–28.

I466 Wilson, David M., and Klindt-Jensen, Ole. Viking art. [2d ed.] Minneapolis, Univ. of Minnesota Pr., 1980. 173p. il. plates. (The Nordic series, v.6)

See GLAH 1:I437 for 1st ed.

The introduction has been slightly revised and a list of 19 new sources has been added to the end of the bibliography.

Bibliography, p.162–66. Index, p.169–73.

Spain and Portugal

I467 al-Andalus: the art of Islamic Spain. Ed. by Jerrilynn D. Dodds. N.Y., Metropolitan Museum of Art (Dist. by Abrams), 1992. xxx, 432p. il. (chiefly col.), maps, plans.

Comprehensive catalog of the exhibition, Metropolitan Museum of Art (1992) including essays by noted scholars for the period. Many good-quality illustrations throughout. The catalog is arranged chronologically and includes ivories, metalwork, jewelry, textiles, ceramics, arms and armor, manuscripts, carpets, architectural elements, coins, and scientific instruments.

Contents: Islamic Spain, the first four centuries: an introduction, by Oleg Grabar; The Great Mosque of Cordoba, by Jerrilynn D. Dodds; Madinat al-Zahra: the triumph of the Islamic state, by Antonio Vallejo Triano; Luxury arts of the Caliphal period, by Renata Holod; Arts of the Taifa kingdoms, by Cynthia Robinson; The fortification of al-Andalus, by Juan Zozaya; The Almoravids and Almohads: an introduction, by Manuel Casamar Perez; The architectural heritage of Islamic Spain in North Africa, by Christian Ewert; The ceramics of al-Andalus, by Guillermo Rossello-Bordoy; Almoravid and Almohad textiles, by Cristina Partearroyo; The arts of the book, by Sabiha Khemir; The Alhambra: an introduction, by Dario Cabanelas Rodriguez; The palaces of the Alhambra, by James Dickie (Yaqub Zaki); The city plan of the Alhambra, by Jesus Bermudez Lopez; The gardens of the Alhambra and the concept of the garden in Islamic Spain, by D. Fairchild Ruggles; The legacy of Islam in Spain, by Juan Vernet.

Glossary, p.393–94. Bibliography, p.395–412. Index, p.413–31.

I468 Ars hispaniae. Historia universal del arte hispanico. Madrid, Editorial Plus-Ultra, 1947– . (22)v.

See GLAH 1:I438 for previous eds. and vols.

Contents: (6) Cook, W. W. S., and Gudiol Ricart, José, Pintura e imagineria romanicas. 2. ed. actualizada. (1980).

I469 Art and architecture of Spain. Ed. by Xavier Barral i Altet . . . [et al.] Trans. by Dominic Currin. 1st North American ed. Boston, Little, Brown, 1998. 575p. il. (part col.), maps.

Trans. of Historia del arte de España. [Barcelona], Lunwerg, 1996. French trans., L'art espagnol. Paris, Bordas, 1996.

This comprehensive full-color survey covers Spanish art and architecture from prehistory to the contemporary period in essays by noted authors. The bibliography and chronology are particularly useful.

Contents: Prehistory and first contacts with Mediterranean antiquity, by Eduardo Ripoll Perelló; Roman art and architecture in Spain, by Javier Arce; From antiquity to the middle ages, Christianity and the Visigothic world, by Pere de Palol; Pre-Romanesque and Romanesque art, by Xavier Barral i Altet; Gothic Spain, by Núria de Dalmases; The presence of Islam and Islamic art, by Christian Ewert and Fernando Valdés Fernández; The art of the Renaissance, by Fernando Checa; The Baroque, by Joan-Ramon Triadó; The art of colonial Spanish America, by Joaquín Bérchez Gomez and Rafael Lopez Guzmán; Francisco de Goya, by Manuela Mena Marqués; The nineteenth century: from Neoclassicism to industrialism, by Carlos Reyero; Spanish art from 1900 to 1939, by Jaime Briheuga Sierra; Pablo Picasso, by Germain Viatte; Contemporary art, architecture and design, by Pilar Parcerisas and Manuel Borja Villel.

Comparative chronology, p.538–55. Maps, p.556–59. Glossary of terms, p.560–63. Bibliography, p.564–67. Index, p.568–73.

I470 The art of medieval Spain, A.D. 500–1200. N.Y., Metropolitan Museum of Art (Distr. by Abrams, 1993). xiv, 358p. il. (part col.), maps.

Catalog of the exhibition, Metropolitan Museum of Art. Planned for 1993–94 but postponed. Complements the Al-Andalus exhibition (GLAH 2:I467). Beautifully illustrated.

Contents: Introduction; Visigothic Spain; Islamic Spain; The Kingdom of Asturias and Mozarabic Spain; Romanesque Spain.

Bibliography, p.330–49. Index, p.350–56.

I471 Bottineau, Yves. L'Art de cour dans l'Espagne des lumières, 1746–1808. Paris, De Boccard, 1986. x, 517p. il., plates, facsims., geneal., table, plans.

Complements Bottineau's pioneering thesis, L'art de cour dans l'Espagne de Philippe V (1700–1746) (GLAH 1:I439).

Provides a thorough historical and political context for royal patronage of Ferdinand VI, Charles III, and Charles IV. Includes numerous extracts from primary source materials. "Both this book and its predecessor are essential works of reference for the student of any aspect of eighteenth century Spain."—*Review*, Burlington magazine, v.130, Oct. 1988, p.778–79. Includes two appendixes containing original source material. Scholarly notes and references throughout. Black-and-white illustrations are of inferior quality.

Selective contents: Pt.I: Les sources de la création: (1) Les conditions de longue durée; (2) Les sources artistiques: héritages dynastiques et nationaux: exemples contemporain; (3) Les contingences humaines; Pt.II: Les permanences: (1) Les structures administratives; (2) Cadeaux et achats: de l'article de mode a l'objet de collection; (3) Les manufactures; Pt.III: Le double mouvement de la création: (1) Le temps de Ferdinand VI 1746–1759: le baroque italo-espagnol et son contexte éclectique; (2) Le temps de Charles III 1759–1788: la mise a jour de l'italianisme et les progrès de la restauration nationale; (3) Le temps de Charles IV 1788–1808: le néoclassicisme: affirmation nationale et ouverture vers l'étranger.

Index, p.[475]–512.

I472 Catálogo monumental de España. [Facsimile reprint.] Madrid, Ministerio de Instrucción Pública y Bellas Artes, 1915–57. 11v.

See GLAH 1:I441 for previous vols. and eds.

Contents: Gómez-Moreno, Manuel, Provincia de León. Ed. facsim., 2a. León, Editorial Nebrija, 1979. 2v.

I473 La España gotica. [Dir., Joan Sureda Pons]. [Madrid], Encuentro, 1987– . (15)v. il., (part col.), plates.

Each vol. contains introductory essays on art and history, architecture, painting, sculpture, and decorative arts followed by brief essays on individual monuments. Well illustrated with many plans. Short bibliographies follow each essay. Vols. contain detailed tables of contents in lieu of indexes.

Contents: (1) La epoca de los monasterios; (2) Cataluña/1; (3) Cataluña/2; (4) Valencia y Murcia; (5) Baleares; (6) Aragon; (7) Navarra; (8) Pais Vasco; (9) Castilla y Leon/1 (10) Castilla y Leon/2, Asturias y Cantabria; (11) Andalucia; (12) Galicia; (13) Castilla-La Mancha; (14) Extremadura; (15) La epoca de las universidades.

I474 Franca, José Augusto. A arte em Portugal no secolo XIX. 3a ed. Lisboa, Bertrand, 1990. 2v.

See GLAH 1:I445 for 2d ed.

Continued by the following title.

I475 ______. A arte em Portugal no secolo XX. 2a ed. Venda Nova, Bertrand, 1984. 660p. il. (part col.) plates.

See GLAH 1:I446 for 1st ed. The 2d ed. contains corrections, revisions, a new introduction, and several additions to the bibliography.

Notas, p.539–605. Quadro cronológico, p.608–29. Indices, p.633–55.

I476 ______. Arte portugues. 3. ed. [Reprint.] Madrid, Espasa-Calpe, 1991. 715p. il. (part col.) (Summa artis, historia general del arte, 30)

Reprint of 1. ed. Madrid, Espasa-Calpe, 1986; "2. ed." 1989.

I477 Historia da arte em Portugal. Lisboa, Publicácoes Alfa, 1986–[1988]. 14v.

This general survey includes many color illustrations of varying quality. The absence of an index limits usefulness but the extensive bibliography, arranged by subject or media, will be helpful to the reader. Bibliographies include references to periodical literature.

Contents: (1) Alarcão, Jorge de. Do paleolítico à arte visigótica; (2) Almeida, Carlos Alberto Ferreira de. Arte da Alta Idade Média; (3) Almeida, Carlos Alberto Ferreira de. O românico; (4) Dias, Pedro. O gótico; (5) Dias, Pedro. O manuelino; (6) Markl, Dagoberto. O renascimento; (7) Serrão, Vítor. O maneirismo; (8) Moura, Carlos. O limiar do barroco; (9) Correia Borges, Nelson. Do barroco ao rococó; (10) Anacleto, Regina. Neoclassicismo e romantismo; (11) Rio-Carvalho, Manuel. Do romantismo ao fim do século; (12) Gonçalves, Rui Mário. Pioneiros da modernidade; (13) Gonçalves, Rui Mário. De 1945 à actualidade; (14) Vieira de Almeida, Pedro and Fernandes, José Manuel. A arquitectura moderna.

Each vol. includes a timeline and bibliography.

I478 História da arte portuguesa. Dir. de Paulo Pereira. [Lisboa], Temas e Debates, 1995. 3v.

Scholarly survey of Portuguese art emphasizing painting, sculpture and architecture. Well-illustrated, primarily in color, with many plans and maps. Good coverage of the contemporary period. Extensive bibliography follows each chapter.

Contents: (1) Da pré-história ao "modo" gótico; (2) Do "modo" gótico ao Maneirismo; (3) Do barroco à contemporaneidade.

Glossário, v.3, p.651–7. Índice onomástico, v.3, p.658–70. Índice toponímico, v.3, p.670–89.

I479 Inventário artístico de Portugal. Lisbon, Academia Nacional de Bellas Artes, 1943– . (13)v.

See GLAH 1:I449 for previous vols.

Contents: (8) Espanca, Túlio, Distrito de Évora (2v., 1975); (9) Espanca,Túlio, Distrito de Évora (zona sul) (2v., 1978); (10) Nogueira Gonçalves, A., Distrito de Aveiro, zona do norte (1981); (11) Nogueira Gonçalves, A., Distrito de Aveiro, zona de Nordeste (1991); (12) Espanca, Túlio, Distrito de Beja (2v., 1992); (13) Carvalho Quaresma, Maria Clementina de, Cidade do Porto (1995).

I480 Tierras de España. Madrid, Fundación Juan March, 1974– . (10)v.

These lavishly illustrated volumes focus on regional architecture and the arts and also contain sections on history, geography, and literature authored by specialists. The series provides access for the advanced reader or researcher to large numbers of lesser known monuments and works of art.

Contents: Baleares (1974); Aragón (1977); Asturias (1978); Extremadura (1979); Andalucía, 2v. (1980); Castilla la Nueva, 2v. (1982); Canarias (1984); Valencia (1985); País Vasco (1987); Navarra (1988).

Each vol. contains notes, bibliography, and an index.

Switzerland

I481 1000 years of Swiss art. Ed. by Heinz Horat. [Trans., BMP Translation Services . . .]. N.Y., Hudson Hills, 1992. 374p. il. (part col.), maps.

21 essays on specialized topics by multiple contributors. Covers art, architecture, and town planning from the middle ages through the 20th century. Very well illustrated.

Contents: The writing tablets of Charlemagne: two ivory diptychs in the Abbey Library of St. Gallen, by Rudolf Schnyder; The fourteenth century Gradual of Wettingen, by Peter Hoegger; Picture and prayer: late medieval passion-centered piety in St. Gallen prayer books, by Peter Ochsenbein; Big form - small form: on interactions of late medieval art in border areas, by Nott Caviezel; The Swiss carnation masters: anonymity and artistic personality: painters between the late Middle Ages and the Renaissance, by Christoph Eggenberger; Konrad Witz and the Council of Basel, by Dorothee Eggenberger; Painting learns to fly: Hans Bock the Elder, The fall of the angels (1582). Fore-words on the subject of floating, flying, falling, by Emil Maurer; Memento mori: art and the cult of the dead in central Switzerland, by Peter Felder; A copybook for stonemasons between the Gothic and the Renaissance, by Adolf Reinle; Santa Croce in Riva San Vitale: an early work, by Carlo Maderno, by Heinz Horat; Art history and art historiography of the Lake Constance region, by Albert Knoepfli; High altar and church floor, by Paul Hofer; Aspects of Genevois architecture from the Reformation to the nineteenth century, by Leila el-Wakil; Lucerne: the simultaneity of urban processes in the nineteenth century, by Beat Wyss; "My true home in this world . . .": John Ruskin and Switzerland, by Georg Luck; A Sunday morning (1908–1909) by Edouard Vallet, by Georg Germann; From Heimatkunst to "degenerate" art: on contemporary reception of Swiss painting, 1890–1914, by Hans A. Lüthy; How Danube and Bosporus made a European out of Le Corbusier, by Adolf Max Vogt; Whistler, Welles, and the "Swiss" cuckoo clock, by Dario Gamboni; Rémy Zaugg and the museum collection of Lucerne, by Jean-Christophe Ammann; On the emergence of a cybernetic mass culture and its implications for the making of art, by Robert Fischer.

Notes and bibliographic references at end of each essay. Bibliography, p.374.

I482 Ars Helvetica: die visuelle Kultur der Schweiz. Hrsg. von Florens Deuchler. Disentis [Switzerland], Pro Helvetia/Desertina Verlag, 1987–1993. 13v. il. (part col.), maps, ports., plans.

Beautifully produced set prepared in honor of the 700th anniversary of the founding of the Swiss Federation. Essays explore the development of Swiss art and architecture in detailed historical context. Volumes are organized by chronological period, media, and narrative themes. The index vol. includes an extensive subject index.

Contents: (I) Kunstgeographie, von Dario Gamboni; (II) Kunstbetrieb, von Florens Deuchler; (III) Sakrale Bauten, von Heinz Horat; (IV) Profane Bauten, von André Meyer; (V) Malerei des Mittelalters, von Christop Eggenberger und Dorothee Eggenberger; (VI) Malerei der Neuzeit, von Oscar Bätschmann; (VII) Skulptur, von Paul-André Jaccard; (VIII) Kunsthandwerk, von Eva-Maria Lösel; (IX) Volkskunst, von Nicolas Bouvier; (X) Nationale Bildthemen, von Hans Christoph von Tavel; (XI) Industrieform und Reklame, von Stanislaus von Moos; (XII)Kunstszenen Heute, von Beat Wyss; (XIII) Register I–XII.

Notes, bibliography, and index in each vol. Cumulative index in v.XIII.

I483 Die Kunstdenkmäler der Schweiz = Les monuments d'art et d'histoire de la Suisse = I monumenti d'arte e di storia dall Svizzera. Basel, Birkhäuser, 1927– . (92)v.

See GLAH 1:I462 for previous vols. and eds.

See v.92, Kanton Aargau:VII, for a complete, detailed listing of all vols. published thus far.

Contents: (65) Kanton Schwyz: I, neu. Ausg. (1978); (66) Kanton Zürich: III (1978); (67) Kanton Wallis: II; (1979); (68) Canton Ticino: II (1979); (69) Canton de Vaud: III (1979); (70) Kanton Appenzeller: II (1980); (71) Canton de Vaud: IV (1981); (72) Kanton Appenzeller: III (1981); (73) Canton Ticino: III (1983); (74) Kantons Appenzell Innerrhoden (1984); (75) Kanton Bern: I (1985); (76) Kanton Zürich: VII (1986); (77) Kanton Basel: III (1986); (78) Kanton Uri (1986); (79) Kantons Zürich: VIII (1986); (80) Kanton Luzern (1987); (81) Canton de Fribourg: IV (1989); (82) Kanton Schwyz: II, neu. Ausg. (1989); (83) Kanton Thurgau: IV (1989); (84) Kanton Wallis: III (1991); (85) Kanton Thurgau: V (1992); (86) Kanton Solothurn (1994); (87) Kanton Aargau:VII (1995); (88) Kanton Zürich: IX (1997); (89) Canton de Genéve: I (1997); (90) Kantons Bern Landband: II (1998); (91) Canton de Vaud:V (1998); (92) Kanton Aargau: VII (1998).

I484 Kunstführer durch die Schweiz. Begr. von Hans Jenny. 6., durchges. Aufl. Hrsg. von der Gesellschaft für Schweizerische Kunstgeschichte. Wabern, Buchler, 1976– . (3)v.

See GLAH 1:I463 for previous eds.

Selective contents: (1) Aargau, Appenzell, Glarus, Graubünden, Luzern, St. Gallen, Schaffhuasen, Schwyz, Thurgau, Unterwalden, Uri, Zug, Zurich; (2) Genf, Neuenburg, Waadt, Wallis, Tessin; (3) Basel-Landschaft, Basel-Stadt, Bern Freiburg, Jura, Solothurn.

Vols. include specialized glossaries and indexes to names and places.

Turkey

I485 The art and architecture of Turkey. Ed. by Ekrem Akurgal . . . [et al.] N.Y., Rizzoli, 1980. 268p. il. (part col.), maps.

Thorough survey of Anatolian Turkish arts and architecture from pre-history through the Ottoman Empire. Chapters are authored by specialists.

Contents: Introduction: the position and role of Anatolia in world history, by Ekrem Akurgal; Anatolia from the neolithic period to the end of the Roman world, by Akrem Ekurgal; Byzantine art in Turkey, by Semavi Eyice; Anatolian-Seljuk architecture, by Aptullah Kuran; Turkish architecture in Asia Minor in the period of the Turkish Emirates, by M. Oluş Arik; Architecture of the Ottoman period, by Dogan Kuban; Architectural decoration and the minor arts, by Gönül Öney; Turkish metalwork, by Ülker Erginsoy; Turkish miniature painting, by Filiz Çaman.

Bibliographical references at ends of chapters. Select bibliographies, p.249–58. Glossary, p.259–61. Index, p.262–68.

I486 Aslanapa, Oktay. Türk sanati. [Istanbul], Remzi Kitabevi, 1984. xv, 454p. il. (part col.), plans.

See GLAH 1:I465 for previous ed.

The author states that this publication contains a great many additions and changes to the 1971 ed. The bibliography has also been updated. A related ed., Türk Sanati. Ankara, Kültür Bakanligi, 1990– . (Kültür Bakanligi Yayinlari, 1196) (Kültür Eserleri, 158), contains portions of the 1984 text as well as new chapters on Azerbijani art and arts of the Karahan period.

Bibliography, p.397–453.

I487 Glassie, Henry H. Turkish traditional art today. Bloomington, Indiana Univ. Pr., 1993. xi, 947p. il. (part col.), maps. (Indiana University Turkish studies, 11)

Comprehensive survey of modern Turkish arts including those areas usually regarded as handicrafts. "Art is a troubled word, and it is my intention to trouble it more by centering my account radically in the Turkish concept so that it can stand to challenge western notions that narrow the word's meaning."—*Introd.* Illustrations are small, but plentiful, and contain a good level of detail. The bibliography contains useful essays introducing each subject area.

A note on Turkish, p.873–80. Bibliography, p.881–923. Index of objects, p.930–31. Index, p.932–47.

I488 Sözen, Metin. The evolution of Turkish art and architecture. Istanbul, Haset Kitabevi, 1987. 336p. il. (part col.), plans. (Aksit culture and tourism publications, 2)

Introductory survey of architecture and the decorative arts presented through discussions of key monuments and works within their cultural and historical context by leading scholars in Turkish art history. Covers the 10th through the 19th centuries. Very well illustrated.

Bibliography, p.323–27. Index, p.328–35.

I489 Turkish art. Ed. by Esin Atil. Washington, D.C., Smithsonian Institution Pr., 1980. 386p. il. (part col.), map, plans.

Published with the student in mind, this volume "was designed as a handbook to be used either in surveys of the history of Islamic art or as supplementary reading in courses in Near Eastern and Turkish studies . . . also conceived to benefit the reader who has little or no background in the field by defining the characteristic features, techniques, and styles of the art and architecture executed between the twelfth and twentieth centuries under the patronage of the Seljuks and the Ottomans."—*Foreword.*

Contents: Introduction, by Oleg Grabar; The Turks in history, by Roderic H. Davison; Architecture, by Ülkü Bates; The art of the book, by Esin Atil; Ceramics, by Walter B. Denny; Rugs and textiles, by Louise W. Mackie.

Notes and references follow each chapter. Turkish dynasties, p.[374]. Selected bibliography, p.[375]–77. Index, p.[379]–86.

United States

I490 American art in the 20th century: painting and sculpture, 1913–1993. Ed. by Christos M. Joachimides and Norman Rosenthal. Coordinating ed. David Anfam. Essays by Brook Adams . . . [et al.] Munich, Prestel (Distr. by Te Neues, 1993). 490p. il. (part col.), ports.

Published to accompany the fourth in a series of exhibitions (Royal Academy of Art, 1993) examining 20th-century art. Essays by well-known art historians.

Bibliographical references at end of each essay. Biographies of the artists, p.439–77. Selected bibliography, p.478–81. The authors, p.482–83. Index of names, p.486–90.

I491 American art: painting, sculpture, architecture, decorative arts, photography. By Milton Brown . . . [et al.] Ed., Theresa C. Brakeley. Designer, Gerald Pryor. N.Y., Abrams; Englewood Cliffs, N.J., Prentice-Hall, [1979]. 616p. il. (part col.)

Basic texts drawn from Milton Brown's American art to 1900 (N.Y., Abrams, 1977) and the 1973 ed. of Hunter and Jacobus's American art of the twentieth century (GLAH 1:I477), with additions, combine to cover the Colonial period to the 1970s. A solid introduction to the subject. Includes a chapter on early photography.

Bibliography, p.590–603. Index, p.604–15.

I492 American art: readings from the Colonial era to the present. Ed. by Harold Spencer. N.Y., Scribner's, 1980. xv, 392p. il.

39 selections from the writings of major artists, architects, critics, and historians on aspects of American art and architecture from the colonial era through the mid-1970s compiled by a well-known art history anthologist.

Bibliography, p.362–73. Index, p.377–92.

I493 Art Institute of Chicago. American arts at the Art Institute of Chicago: from colonial times to World War I. [By] Judith A. Barter, Kimberly Rhodes, and Seth A. Thayer. With contrib. by Andrew Walker. Chicago, Art Institute of Chicago (Distr. by Hudson Hills Pr., 1998). 359p. il.

"This catalogue presents a selection of notable objects from the almost three thousand works in the collections of the Department of American Arts at The Art Institute of Chicago. . . . This volume is the first book devoted specifically to the museum's important American paintings, sculpture, and decorative arts from roughly 1650 . . . to World War I."—*Pref.*

Glossary of decorative arts terms, p.345–51. Index, p.352–59.

I494 Ashton, Dore. American art since 1945. N.Y., Oxford Univ. Pr., 1982. 224p. il. (part col.)
Key work introducing modern art movements, artist, and major works through a sharply focused readable narrative. "There are few critic-historians more astute in discerning the complex reactions and interactions that have shaped recent American painting and sculpture, or more eloquent in giving written form to visual matters."—*Review*, Art journal, XLII, no.4, winter 1982, p.355.
Notes, p.212–14. Index, p.222–24.

I495 Baigell, Matthew. A concise history of American painting and sculpture. Rev. ed. N.Y., IconEditions, 1996. xxvi, 435p. il.
1st ed. 1984.
"In this survey I have concentrated on that part of American art which developed from northern and western European traditions in order to sustain the narrative flow."—*Introd.* A standard survey.
Contents: (1) Colonial art; (2) The new nation; (3) Self-discovery; (4) At home and abroad; (5) Early modernism; (6) Between the world wars; (7) International presence; (8) Contemporary diversity.
Selected bibliography, p.397–406. Index, p.407–20.

I496 Bearden, Romare, and Henderson, Henry. A history of African-American artists, from 1792 to the present. N.Y., Pantheon, 1993. xvii, 541p. il. (part col.)
Arranged as a chronological survey, lengthy bio-historical essays comprise a history of African-American painting, sculpture, and printmaking from the 19th through the 20th century. Covers artists born before 1926. Readable, well-illustrated, and current. "Believing individual histories to be the most revealing, we focused on significant individual artists in each period and how they developed. We sought to examine their work and how it related to that of other American artists, to influential art movements in Europe, to prevailing American social and political conditions, and to the artists' lives and problems."—*Introd.*
Notes, p.479–514. Index, p.515–32.

I497 Chicano art: resistance and affirmation, 1965–1985. Ed. by Richard Griswold del Castillo . . . [et al.] Los Angeles, Wight Art Gallery, Univ. of Calif., 1991. 373p. il. (part col.)
Published in conjunction with the exhibition, Wight Art Gallery, UCLA (1991), and other locations. Emphasizes movements in the western and southwestern regions of the U.S. Includes essays and catalog of works exhibited. Index of artists contains dates and some artists' statements.
Contents: The political and social contexts of Chicano art, by Shifra M. Goldman and Tomás Ybarra Frausto; The pachucho's flayed hide: the museum, identity, and the Buenas Garrasby, Marcos Sanchez-Tranquilino and John Tagg; Mexico in Aztlán, Aztlán in Mexico: the dialectics of Chicano-Mexicano art, by David R. Maciel; In the City of Angels, chameleons, and phantoms: Asco, a case study of Chicano art in urban tones (or Asco was a four-member word), by Harry Gamboa, Jr.; El mundo femenino: Chicana artists of the movement—A commentary on development and production, by Amalia Mesa-Bains; Articulate signs of resistance and affirmation in Chicano public art, by Victor A. Sorell; Rasquachismo: a Chicano sensibility, by Tomás Ybarra-Frausto; Exhibitions of Chicano art, by Jacinto Quirarte; Looking for alternatives: notes on Chicano art, 1960–90, by Philip Brookman; The contexts of Chicano art and culture: a selected chronology, by Holly Barnet-Sanchez and Dana Leibsohn.
Index of artists, p.346–60. Chicano glossary of terms, p.361–66. Selected bibliography, p.367–70.

I498 Craven, Wayne. American art: history and culture. Madison, Wis., Brown & Benchmark (Distr. by Abrams, 1994). 687p. il. (part col.), maps, plans.
In this large and copiously illustrated volume, the author has attempted "the first inclusive look at five centuries of the architecture, painting, sculpture, decorative arts, and photography created by the diverse peoples who have given direction to the arts of America."—*Pub. jacket note.* Organized by broad chronological periods, with divisions for media and sub-divisions for individuals, movements, and types. The extensive bibliography is arranged by movement, medium, and artist name.
Glossary, p.[641]–45. Bibliography p.[646]–64. Notes, p.664–65. Index, p. [672]–87.

I499 Deák, Gloria-Gilda. Picturing America, 1497–1899: prints, maps, and drawings bearing on the New World discoveries and on the development of the territory that is now the United States. Princeton, Princeton Univ. Pr., 1988. 2v. il.
Documentary anthology based on materials in the Stokes Collection and other collections of the New York Public Library.
Bibliography, v.1, p.603–33. Concordance, v.1, p.635–39. Subject index, v.1, p.641–49. Index to artists, engravers, publishers, printers, and sources, v.1, p.650–57.

I500 Fineberg, Jonathan. Art since 1940: strategies of being. 2d ed., N.Y., Abrams, 2000. 528p. il. (part col.)
1st ed.: N.Y., Abrams, 1995.
Essential survey for the modern and contemporary period covers all art forms in a very well-illustrated and stimulating account. The second ed. contains revisions, additions, and expanded bibliography. "A dynamic layout . . . and dramatic juxtapositions keep eye and mind moving and engender a sense of open-endedness quite different from a 'this led to that' survey format. Nor is the art treated as hermetic, a progression of styles existing in a vacuum; events in music and dance as well as in the political area intersect with the artworks in a variety of ways."—*Review* of 1st ed. Art journal, v.55, no.2, summer 1996, p.103.
Contents: (1) Introduction; (2) New York in the forties: (3) A dialog with Europe; (4) Existentialism comes to the fore; (5) The new European masters of the late forties; (6) Some international tendencies of the fifties; (7) The Beat Generation: the fifties in America; (8) The European vanguard of the later fifties; (9) The landscape of signs: American pop art 1960–1965; (10) In the nature of materials: the later sixties; (11) Politics and Postmodernism: the transition

to the seventies; (12) Surviving the corporate culture of the seventies; (13) Painting at the end of the seventies; (14) The eighties; (15) New tendencies of the nineties; (16) To say the things that are one's own.

Bibliography, p.[506]–11. Notes, p.[512]–22. Index, p.[523]–28.

I501 Goetzmann, William H., and Goetzmann, William N. The West of the imagination. N.Y., Norton, 1986. 458p. il. (part col.)

Conceived by a cultural historian as a "sweeping survey of the visual images of the West that included paintings, drawings, cartoons, photographs and films."—*Pref.* Research for this publication spawned the PBS television series of the same name. Scholarly and readable survey which covers the period beginning with the late 18th century through the works of Georgia O'Keeffe. The authors have produced "a rich and remarkable study that surpasses the six-part documentary that shared the same title. . . . In sum, this book has both visual and intellectual rewards for all readers interested in American culture."—*Review*, American historical review, v.93, no.1, Feb. 1988, p.215–16.

Notes, p.435–46. Index, p.447–58.

I502 Goldman, Shifra M., and Ybarra-Frausto, Tomás. Arte Chicano: a comprehensive annotated bibliography of Chicano art, 1965–1981. Berkeley, Chicano Studies Library Publications Unit, Univ. of California, Berkeley, 1985. viii, 350p. (Chicano Studies Library publication series, 11)

Extensive bibliography of Chicano art, indexed by subject, author or artist, and title.

Alphabetical list of Chicano artists, p.765–72. Periodicals cited in bibliography, p.773–78.

I503 Hughes, Robert. American visions: the epic history of art in America. N.Y., Knopf, 1997. ix, 635p. il. (part col.)

Hughes' highly personalized account of American art is a companion publication to the eight-part PBS television series. Coverage begins with the early colonial periods and the inclusion of furniture, folk art, and commercial design is useful. "It is not intended as a scholarly text, still less an exhaustive one. It is meant for that creature who, American academics often profess to believe, no longer exists: the general intelligent reader."—*Introd.*

Contents: (1) O my America, My new founde [sic] land; (2) The republic of virtue; (3) The wilderness of the west; (4) American renaissance; (5) The gritty cities; (6) Early modernism; (7) Streamlines and breadlines; (8) The empire of signs; (9) The age of anxiety.

Index, p.621–33.

I504 In pursuit of beauty: Americans and the Aesthetic Movement. N.Y., Metropolitan Museum of Art, 1986. 511p. il. (part col.)

Comprehensive exhibition catalog published to accompany the exhibition (Metropolitan Museum of Art, 1986–87). Covers late 19th-century fine and decorative arts and architecture produced in America in response to the Arts and Crafts Movement. 11 in-depth essays are readable and richly illustrated. Includes a substantial dictionary of artists, architects, artisans, and manufacturers with additional references for each entry and scholarly notes throughout.

Contents: (1) Artifact as ideology: the aesthetic movement in its American cultural context, by Roger B. Stein; (2) Decorating surfaces: aesthetic delight, theoretical dilemma, by Catherine Lynn; (3) Surface ornament: Wallpapers, carpets, textiles, and embroidery, by Catherine Lynn; (4) The artful interior, by Marilynn Johnson; (5) Art furniture: wedding the beautiful to the useful, by Marilynn Johnson; (6) A new renaissance: stained glass in the aesthetic period, by Alice Cooney Freylinghuysen; (7) Aesthetic forms in ceramics and glass, by Alice Cooney Freylinghuysen; (8) Metalwork: an eclectic aesthetic, by David A. Hanks with Jennifer Toher; (9) Painters and sculptors in a decorative age, by Doreen Bolger Burke; (10) American architecture and the aesthetic movement, by James D. Kornwolf; (11) An aestheticism of our own: American writers and the aesthetic movement, by Jonathan Freedman.

Selected bibliography, p.488–502. Index, p.503–10.

I505 Johnson, Diane. American Art Nouveau. N.Y., Abrams, 1979. 311p. il. (part col.)

Survey offering broad coverage of the emergence and development of art nouveau styles in painting, sculpture, architecture, decorative arts, and graphics. Many good quality color plates and black-and-white illustrations. Bibliography arranged by topic and individual artist.

Contents: (1) The American cultural renaissance, 1876–1893: Oscar Wilde's aesthetic message; The artist-craftsman ideal; The knight errant; Art in the World's Columbian Exposition, Chicago, 1893. (2) Louis Comfort Tiffany and Art Nouveau applied arts in America: Art and industry; New concepts of American interior design, 1876–1904; American glass and Art Nouveau windows; American silver; Glass vases and pottery; (3) Louis H. Sullivan and American Art Nouveau architecture: The Transportation Building, Chicago, 1893; Sullivan's stylistic "sources" and "affinities"; The Auditorium Theater interior, Chicago, 1886–88; The Getty tomb, Chicago, 1890; The Guaranty Building, Buffalo, 1894–95; Sullivan's concept of ornamentation; European and American Art Nouveau architectural design; Sullivan's work as Art Nouveau. (4) Will H. Bradley and the poster and periodical movements, 1893–1897: Development of the poster; the "poster style"; The periodical and poster "craze"; Will H. Bradley and American Art Nouveau graphic design; The decline of the aesthetic; The philistine. (5) Decorative painting and sculpture in America: Photography and Japanese prints: the new classicism; The Symbolist attitude; Decorative painting, graphic illustration and Symbolist theses; Sculpture.

Chronology, p.289–91. Notes, p.292–98. Bibliography, p.299–304. Index, p.305–11.

I506 The Latin American spirit: art and artists in the United States, 1920–1970. Essays by Luis R. Cancel . . . [et al.] N.Y., Bronx Museum of the Arts in assoc. with Abrams. 1988. 343p. il. (part col.)

Published in connection with an exhibition, Bronx Museum of Arts (1989) and four other locations. A survey of influences and development characterizing the work of Latin American artists in the U.S., with particular emphasis on Puerto Rico.

Contents: Mexican and Mexican-American artists: 1920–1970, by Jacinto Quirarte; The special case of Puerto Rico, by Marimar Benítez; Constructivism and geometric abstraction, by Nelly Perazzo; New York Dada and new world Surrealism, by Lowery S. Sims; The United States and socially concerned Latin American art, by Eva Cockcroft; The Latin American presence, Pt.I: The abstract spirit; Pt.II: Reality and figuration, by Félix Angel; "Magnet—New York": conceptual, performance, environmental and installation art, by Carla Stellweg.

Biographies, p.313–26. Notes, p.327–32. Bibliography, p.333–39.

I507 Lewis, Samella. African American art and artists. [Upd. and rev. ed.] Berkeley, Univ. of California Pr., 1994. 302p. il. (part col.)

1st ed. Art: African American. N.Y., Harcourt Brace Jovanovich, 1978; 2d rev. ed. Berkeley, Univ. of California Pr., 1990.

This updated ed. of one of the first surveys of African American art is still a useful entry point to the literature. The chronological arrangement by historical period begins in 1619 and includes 173 more years than Bearden's similarly constructed work (GLAH 2:I496). The modern period includes media-specific sections and the bibliography contains numerous citations to periodical literature.

Selective contents: 1619–1865: Cultural deprivation and slavery; 1865–1920: Emancipation and cultural dilemma; 1920–1940: New Americanism and ethnic identity; 1940–1960: Social and political awareness; 1960–1990: Political and cultural awareness.

Bibliography, p.293–300. Index, p.301–02.

I508 Poesch, Jessie J. The art of the old South: painting, sculpture, architecture, & the products of craftsmen, 1560–1860. N.Y., Knopf, 1983. xii, 384p. il. (part col.)

Amply illustrated, in-depth survey. Emphasizes social, cultural, and economic history and attempts to demonstrate the "consciousness among Southerners themselves of having mind set, value systems and ways of life distinct from the rest of America."—*Introd.* The notes contain extensive scholarly references.

Notes, p.339–59. Select bibliography, p.361–66. Index, p.367–81.

I509 Porter, James A. Modern Negro art. With a new introd. by David C. Driskell. Washington, D.C., Howard Univ. Pr., 1992. xxxvii, 276p. il. (part col.) (Moorland-Spingarn series)

1st ed.: N.Y., Dryden, 1943; [Rev.ed.] N.Y., Arno, 1969.

The 1992 reprint of the classic first study of the art of African Americans contains a new introduction to place this work in current art historical context. Though the bibliography has not been updated, this study remains a key work in the field covering the 18th to the early 20th century. Includes as appendix, Memorabilia of the early negro artist.

Notes, p.165–74. Bibliography, p.175–84. James A. Porter chronology, p.185–88. Select Porter bibliography, p.189–91. Index, p.193–200.

I510 Powell, Richard J. Black art and culture in the 20th century. N.Y., Thames and Hudson, 1997. 256p. il. (part col.)

Significant assessment, focusing on the U.S.

Contents: (1) Art, culture and "the souls of black folk"; (2) Enter and exit the "new negro"; (3) The cult of the people; (4) Pride, assimilation and dreams; (5) "Black is a color"; (6) Culture as currency; Conclusion: through a glass, diasporally.

Biographical notes, p.226–36. Select bibliography and sources, p.237–46. Index, p.253–56.

I511 The power of feminist art: the American movement of the 1970s, history and impact. N.Y., Abrams, 1994. 318p. il. (part col.), ports.

Illustrated survey of the period with essays by well-known artists and art historians. "The power of feminist art is itself a prime example of feminist collaboration, built upon the knowledge, memories, and experiences of its eighteen contributors. The first book on its subject, it reproduces and discusses hundreds of works of feminist art from the 1970s and beyond."—*Pref.* Contains many good quality color and black-and-white illustrations.

Contents: (I) Seeds of change: feminist art and education in the early seventies. The feminist art programs at Fresno and CalArts, 1970–75, by Faith Wilding; Womanhouse, by Arlene Raven; Conversations with Judy Chicago and Miriam Schapiro; (II) Building a network: feminist activism in the arts. Feminist politics: network and organizations, by Mary D. Garrard; Exhibitions, galleries and alternative spaces, by Judith K. Brodsky; Writing (and righting) wrongs: feminist art publications, by Carrie Rickey; Starting from scratch: the beginnings of feminist art history, by Linda Nochlin; (III) Challenging modernism: the facets of feminist art. Social protest: racism and sexism, by Yolanda M. López and Moira Roth; Feminist performance art: performing, discovering, transforming ourselves, by Josephine Withers; Recovering her story: feminist artists reclaim the great goddess, by Gloria Feman Orenstein; The body through women's eyes, by Joanna Frueh; The pattern and decoration movement, by Norma Broude; Collaboration, by Judith E. Stein; (IV) Beyond the seventies: the impact of feminist art. Backlash and appropriation, by Mira Schor; Affinities: thoughts on an incomplete history, by Suzanne Lacy; The feminist continuum: art after 1970, by Laura Cottingham.

Notes, p.289–99. Selected bibliography, p.300–4. Illustrated timeline: A highly selective chronology, p.[305–8]. Index, p.309–18.

I512 Self-taught artists of the 20th century: an American anthology. San Francisco, Chronicle, 1998. 256p. il. (part col.)

Catalog of the exhibition, Museum of American Folk Art (1998), and other locations. Covers 32 American well and lesser known 20th-century artists in essays by individual contributors. Color illustrations throughout. A well-conceived introduction which emphasizes the richness and diversity of American "outsider" art.

Contents: The artworld and its outsiders, by Arthur C. Danto; Critical fictions: race, "outsiders" and the construction of art history, by Maurice Berger; The presence of mind in the production of American folk art, by Gerald L. Davis.

Timeline, p.211–22. Selected readings, p.244–51. Index, p.253–56.

I513 Shipp, Steve. American art colonies, 1850–1930: a historical guide to America's original art colonies and their artists. Westport, Greenwood Press, 1996. xv, 159p. il.

Provides brief historical essays for 16 American art colonies including brief biographies of key members and bibliographic references.

Contents: (1) Carmel-Monterey; (2) Cornish; (3) Cos Cob; (4) Cragsmoor; (5) East Hampton; (6) Gloucester-Rockport; (7) Laguna Beach; (8) Lawrence Park; (9) New Hope; (10) North Conway; (11) Old Lyme; (12) Provincetown; (13) Santa Barbara; (14) Santa Fe; (15) Taos; (16) Woodstock.

Bibliography, p.[129]–38. Index, p.[139]–59.

ASIAN COUNTRIES

General Works

I514 Buddhism: art and faith. Ed. by W. Zwalf. London, British Museum, 1985. 300p. il. (part col.)

Catalog of the exhibition, British Museum (1985), and other locations, based on the collections of the British Museum and British Library.

Contents: (1) Early cult monuments; (2) The Buddha legend; (3) The scriptures and their transmission; (4) The Buddha image; (5) Afghanistan, Pakistan and Kashmir; (6) Eastern India; (7) Nepal and Tibet; (8) The Deccan and south India; (9) Sri Lanka; (10) Burma; (11) Thailand and Cambodia; (12) Indonesia; (13) Central Asia; (14) China; (15) Korea; (16) Japan.

Bibliography, p.294–96. Index, p.297–300.

I515 Clark, John. Modern Asian art. Honolulu, Univ. of Hawaii Pr., 1998. 344p. il. (part col.)

"This book will instance histories, domains, and processes in the discourses of modernity in art as they may be found in a range of Asian countries."—*Introd.* The Introduction spells out the author's methodology in approaching a field that is "empirically rich and ideologically complex."

Contents: (1) Introduction: a disciplinary field; (2) Prehistories; (3) The transfer; (4) Formation of the neotraditional; (5) The aristocrats; (6) The plebians; (7) The professional artist; (8) Exhibition: the salon and the establishment; (9) The avant-garde; (10) Nationalism and allegories of the state; (11) Cycles of integration and autonomy; (12) The contemporary; Postscript.

List of interviews, p.313–16. Bibliography, p.317–37. Index, p.338–44.

I516 Fisher, Robert E. Buddhist art and architecture. N.Y., Thames and Hudson, 1993. 216p. il. (part col.), maps (World of Art)

A useful introduction to Buddhist art in Asia. Chapters on Buddhist art in India and neighboring regions, China, Korea and Japan, and South-East Asia. Well illustrated.

Select bibliography, p.209–11. Glossary, p.211–13. Index, p.214–16.

I517 Hutt, Julia. Understanding Far Eastern art: a complete guide to the arts of China, Japan and Korea—ceramics, sculpture, painting, prints, lacquer, textiles and metalwork. [Foreword by Margaret Medley.] Oxford, Phaidon, 1987. 208p. il. (part col.), map.

Aimed at the non-specialist to promote aesthetic appreciation of Far Eastern art. Describes how artists and craftsmen worked and with what instruments. Chapters focus on media, i.e., painting, prints and printed books, ceramics, metalwork, sculpture and carvings, lacquer, and textiles and dress, and discuss Chinese, Japanese, and Korean traditions together. Illustrated with line drawings that show the methods and tools of the artists.

Select bibliography, p.204. Index, p.206–08.

I518 La Plante, John D. Asian art. 3d ed. Dubuque, Brown, 1992. xv, 287p. il. (part col.)

Introduction to the arts of India, China, and Japan. Presents the major artistic developments in these countries. Representative examples of architecture, sculpture, painting, and decorative arts are included. Chapters are grouped by country and presented historically from early civilizations to contemporary.

Selected bibliography p.279–80. Index, p.281–87.

I519 Lee, Sherman E. A history of Far Eastern art. 5th ed. Ed. by Naomi Noble Richard. N.Y., Abrams, 1994. 576p. il. (part col.), maps.

See GLAH 1:I495 for 3d ed. and original annotation; 4th ed., 1982.

A thorough revision of the standard general survey text, by a distinguished authority.

Contents: (1) Early culture and art: the Stone Age, the Bronze Age, and the Early Iron Age; (2) The international influence of Buddhist art; (3) The rise of national Indian and Indonesian styles; (4) Chinese, Korean, and Japanese national styles and their interplay.

Notes, p.557. Bibliography, p.557–63. Index, p.564–76.

I520 Seckel, Dietrich. Buddhist art of East Asia. Trans. by Ulrich Mammitzsch. Bellingham, Western Washington Univ. Pr., 1989. viii, 411p. il.

Trans. of Buddhistische Kunst Ostasiens. Stuttgart, Kohlhammer, 1957.

"Professor Seckel's work . . . has not only stood the test of time remarkably well, it has also remained the only attempt to date to provide a systematic survey of East Asian Buddhist art."—*Trans. pref.*

Chronological chart, p.251–52. Abbreviations, p.255–56. Notes, p.257–80. Bibliography, p.281–300. Index, p.397–410.

Central Asia

I521 The arts of Central Asia: the Pelliot collection in the Musée Guimet. [Gen. ed. Jacques Giès. Trans. by Hero Friesen in collab. with Roderick Whitfield.] London, Serindia, 1996. 2v. in 1. 235p.

Trans. of Les arts de l'asie centrale: la collection Paul Pelliot du musée national des arts asiatique-Guimet. Paris, Réunion des musées nationaux, 1995–96.

The result of a single expedition, 1906–09.

Notes at end of each "volume."

I522 British Museum. The art of Central Asia: the Stein collection in the British Museum. Tokyo, Kodansha International in coop. with the Trustees of the British Museum (Distr. by Kodansha International/USA through Harper and Row, 1982–85). 3v. il. (part col.), map.

Text in English; captions in English and Japanese.

Magnificently produced catalog of the collection, "made on three lengthy expeditions, in 1900–01, 1906–08 and 1913–16. . . . In these three volumes, the pictorial material from Dunhuang is shown in Volumes 1 and 2, while Volume 3 is devoted to the textiles from Dunhuang and a selection of the finest objects from other sites from all three expeditions."—*Pref.*

Contents: (1–2) Whitfield, Roderick. Paintings from Dunhuang; (3) Whitfield, Roderick. Textiles, sculpture, and other arts.

Bibliographies and other scholarly apparatus conclude each vol.

I523 Crossroads of Asia: transformation in image and symbol in the art of ancient Afghanistan and Pakistan. Ed. by Elizabeth Errington and Joe Cribb with Maggie Claringbull. Cambridge, Ancient India and Iran Trust, 1992. xiv, 306p. il. (part col.), maps.

Catalog of the exhibition, Fitzwilliam Museum, Cambridge (1992).

Seeks "to chart the . . . transmission of motifs and techniques from the Greek world through Afghanistan to Pakistan and north-west India, and to explore changes in both form and meaning. The focus is primarily on metalwork, although other media are included for comparative purposes."—*Pref.*

Catalog entries include long, signed annotations.

Technical analysis, p.241–87. General bibliography, p.288–96. Index and glossary, p.297–306.

I524 Härtel, Herbert. Along the ancient silk routes: Central Asian art from the West Berlin State Museums. The exhibition lent by the Museum für Indische Kunst, Staatliche Museen Preussischer Kulturbesitz, Berlin, Federal Republic of Germany. [Catalog by Herbert Härtel and Marianne Yaldiz, with contrib. by Raoul Birnbaum . . . (et al.)] N.Y., Metropolitan Museum of Art, [1982?] 223p. il. (part col.)

Excellent scholarly catalog, published in conjunction with the exhibition, Metropolitan Museum of Art (1982).

Selected bibliography, p.221–23.

China

I525 Andrews, Julia Frances, and Shen, Kuiyi. A century in crisis: modernity and tradition in the art of twentieth-century China. With essays by Jonathan Spence . . . [et al.] N.Y., Guggenheim Museum (Distr. by Abrams, 1998). [17], 329p. il. (part col.), maps.

Catalog of the exhibition, Guggenheim Museum Soho (1998), and other locations. "The first exhibition held outside China's own borders to tell a comprehensive story of China's modern art."—*Introd.*

Contents: Introduction; Innovations in Chinese painting, 1850–1950; The modernist generations, 1920–1950; Art for new China, 1950–1980; Transformations of tradition, 1980 to the present.

Select bibliography, p.324–27. Index of catalogue reproductions, p.328–29.

I526 The British Museum book of Chinese art. [By] Jessica Rawson, Anne Farrer, Jane Portal . . . [et al.] Ed. by Jessica Rawson. N.Y., Thames and Hudson, 1993. 395p. il. (part col.), maps.

Although prepared for the opening of the Joseph E. Hotung Gallery of Oriental Antiquities at the British Museum in 1992, this book serves as an introductory survey of Chinese art. Includes chapters on "Bronzes and jades for ritual"; "Calligraphy and painting for official life"; "Sculpture for tombs and temples"; "Decorative arts for display"; "Ceramics for use"; and "Luxuries for trade." The chapters are followed by an extensive reference section with chronologies, archeological and Buddhist sites, architecture, tombs, artists and terminology, ceramics, and a glossary of terms.

Select bibliography, p.371–83. Index, p.384–95.

I527 Great bronze age of China: an exhibition from the People's Republic of China. Ed. by Wen Fong. N.Y., Metropolitan Museum of Art; Knopf, [1980]. xv, 386p. il. (part col.), maps.

Catalog of the exhibition, Metropolitan Museum of Art (1980), and other locations. The proceedings of a related symposium were published as The great bronze age of China: a symposium. George Kuwayama, ed. Los Angeles, Los Angeles County Museum of Art (Distr. by Univ. of Washington Pr., 1983).

The bronze and jade objects included in the exhibit and documented in the substantial catalog range from the Shang and Zhou period to the Qin and Han periods and come from museums all over China. Also included are terracotta figures and horses from the recently excavated tumulus of the First Emperor Qin Shihuangdi. The four introductory essays by Ma Chengyuan, Robert Bagley, Kwang-chih Chang, and Robert Thorp provide a valuable introduction to the bronze age of China. The description of individual items in the catalog is accompanied by ten chapters introducing corresponding periods, each prepared by a scholar and providing a valuable and enduring record for the exhibition.

Glossary, p.377–81. Bibliography, p.382–86.

I528 Laing, Ellen Johnston. The winking owl: art in the People's Republic of China. Berkeley, Univ. of California Pr., [1988]. x, 194p. il., col. plates.

Concentrates on the period from 1949, the founding of the PRC, to 1976, the year of Mao's death, with chapters treating selected topics. The work is not intended as an exhaustive history of art in the PRC but tries to approach the art from the vantage point of Chinese concerns.

Brief biographical notices of artists, p.167–73. Bibliography, p.175–88. Index, p.189–94.

I529 Lawton, Thomas. Chinese art of the Warring States period: change and continuity, 480–222 B.C. Washington, D.C., Freer Gallery of Art, Smithsonian Institution (Distr. by Indiana Univ. Pr., 1982). 202p. il. (part col.), maps.

Catalog of the exhibition, Freer Gallery of Art (1982). Documents the rich holdings of the Freer Gallery dating from the Warring States period in China. Following a general introduction, the object entries are organized in broad general categories: bronze vessels, fittings, and weapons; bronze mirrors; bronze garment hooks; jades; and lacquer ware.

Selected bibliography, p.193–98. Index of Chinese and Japanese names and terms, p.199–202.

I530 Li, Chu-tsing, and Watt, James C. Y., eds. The Chinese scholar's studio: artistic life in the late Ming period: an exhibition from the Shanghai Museum. N.Y., Thames and Hudson, [1987]. xii, 218p. il. (part col.)

Catalog of the exhibition, Asia Society Galleries (1987), and other locations.

Focused on the lives of the artists during the late Ming period in the Songjiang, Jiading, and Jiaxing regions, the catalog is prefaced by six major chapters by various authorities on different aspects of the scholar-artist and 78 pages of illustrations of objects in the exhibition. In addition to the works of art by the literati artists, the exhibit included decorative objects of the scholar's studio. Catalog entries are grouped by media: painting and calligraphy; printed books and rubbings; ceramics; decorative arts; scholar's accoutrements; and collected objects.

Bibliography, p.212–15.

I531 Munakata, Kiyohiko. Sacred mountains in Chinese art. Champaign, Krannert Art Museum, Univ. of Illinois at Champaign-Urbana, [1991]. vi, 200p. il. (part col.), map.

Catalog of the exhibition, Krannert Art Museum and the Metropolitan Museum of Art (1991). Includes objects in bronze, ceramic, paint, rubbing, and scupture depicting the revered mountains of China. Illuminates the connections between the objects and Chinese myth, poetry, and vision.

References, p.195–99.

I532 Possessing the past: treasures from the National Palace Museum, Taipei. [By] Wen Fong, James C. Y. Watt. With contrib. by Chang Lin-Sheng . . . [et al.] N.Y., Abrams, 1996. xv, 648p., il. (part col.), maps.

Published in conjunction with the exhibition Splendors of Imperial China: Treasures from the National Palace Museum, Taipei, Metropolitan Museum of Art (1996), and other locations. The exhibition was also accompanied by a supplementary optical disk and a conventional catalog prepared by Maxwell K. Hearn, Splendors of Imperial China; treasures from the National Palace Museum, N.Y., Metropolitan Museum of Art, 1996. Another set of scholarly symposium papers was published under the title: Arts of the Sung and Yüan. Ed. by Maxwell K. Hearn and Judith G. Smith. N.Y., Dept. of Asian Art, Metropolitan Museum of Art, 1996.

A massive work that both documents the wide-ranging exhibition and presents a comprehensive history of Chinese art and culture. The 475 objects in the exhibition are from the National Palace Museum collection and include paintings, calligraphy, textiles, jades, bronzes, porcelains, and other media. Essays by leading scholars.

Contents: (I) Foundations of civilization; (II) The vision of a cosmic order; (III) Cultural efflorescence during the Sung Dynasty; (IV) The Mongol conquest; (V) The Ming Dynasty: empire of restoration; (VI) The Ch'ing Dynasty: a new orthodoxy.

Chronology of Dynastic China, p.xiv. Notes, p.565–609. Bibliography, p.610–24. Index, p.636–46.

I533 Stories from China's past: Han dynasty pictorial tomb reliefs and archaeological objects from Sichuan Province, People's Republic of China. Exhibition organized by Lucy Lim. San Francisco, Chinese Culture Foundation, [1987]. 209p. il., map.

Catalog of the exhibition, Chinese Culture Center of San Francisco (1987), and other locations. Exhibit of funerary reliefs, stone and pottery sculptures, and other artifacts from Sichuan Province dating from the Han dynasty. Includes scholarly essays as well as catalog entries for more than 70 objects. Illustrated with 29 color plates and 189 black-and-white images.

Glossary of Chinese names and terms, p.200–04. Selected bibliography, p.205–09.

I534 Sullivan, Michael. Art and artists of twentieth-century China. Berkeley, Univ. of California Pr., 1996. xxx, 354p., il. (part col.)

"The theme of this book is the rebirth of Chinese art in the twentieth century under the influence of Western art and culture."—*Foreword and ackn.*

Using his own 1959 book, Chinese art of the twentieth century (GLAH 1:I524), as the basis for this work, the author presents a major survey of 90 years of Chinese art. The 25 chapters are grouped in five parts. With 94 color plates and 278 illustrations, the book presents a visual and textual account of 20th-century Chinese art.

Contents: (1) 1900–1937: the impact of the west; (2) 1937–1948: war and civil war; (3) 1949–1976: art in the era of Mao Zedong; (4) Other currents; (5) After Mao: art enters a new era.

Notes, p.283–96. Biographical index, p.297–325. Selected bibliography, p.327–34. Index, p.335–54.

I535 Tregear, Mary. Chinese art. Rev. ed. London, Thames and Hudson, 1997. 216p. il. (part col.), maps, plans. (World of art)

1st ed. 1980.

Accessible introductory survey.

Contents: (1) Neolithic crafts; (2) Hieratic art in the bronze age; (3) Status and decoration; (4) Nationalism and expression; (5) The imprint of Buddhism; (6) Internationalism and showmanship; (7) Space and monumentality; (8) Court and Chan Buddhist arts; (9) Tradition and invention; (10) Eclecticism and innovation; (11) Individualism and eccentricity; (12) Enquiry and dislocation.

Select bibliography, p.201. Index, p.214–16.

I536 Watson, William. The arts of China to AD 900. New Haven, Yale Univ. Pr., 1995. [x], 276p. il. (part col.), maps (Yale University Press pelican history of art)

An important new survey, continued by the following title. Departs from the precedent of Sickman and Soper's previous vol. on Chinese art in this distinguished series (GLAH 1:I520) by including the decorative and applied arts.

Contents: (1) Neolithic art; (2) Shang art; (3) Bronze in the Xizhou Period: 1027–771 B.C.; (4) Bronze in the Chunqiu and Zhanguo Periods: 771–476, 475–221; (5) Jade; (6) Lacquer art; (7) Inner Asia and the Chinese borders; (8) Cultural unity: the Han Empire; (9) Iconography under the western Han; (10) Draughtsmanship and painting under the eastern Han; (11) Architecture in retrospect from the second century A.D.; (12) The period of the Six Dynasties; (13) The age of division: sculpture of the northern Wei first phase; (14) Yungang cave-shrine: northern Wei second phase; (15) Northern Wei third phase: A.D. 495–535; (16) Monumental sculpture of the mid-sixth century; (17) Draughtsmanship and painting of the Six Dynasties in Henan, Hebei and Jiangsu; (18) Pre-Tang mural painting in west China; (19) Architecture from Han to Tang; (20) The Buddhist icon: Tang International Style; (21) Tang secular painting, figures and landscape; (22) Buddhist sculpture under the Tang; (23) Tang non-Buddhist sculpture and decorated objects.

List of bibliographical abbreviations, p.246. Notes, p.247–58. Bibliography, p.259–69. Glossary of Chinese characters, p.270–72. Index, p.273–76.

I537 ———. The arts of China, 900–1620. New Haven, Yale Univ. Pr., 2000. 286p. il. (part col.), map. (Yale University Press pelican history of art)

Successor to Watson's companion vol. in the series, taking the "account to the mid-17th Century, ending with Ming and a brief extension into Qing."—*Pref.*

Contents: (1) Landscape painting under the Northern Song 960–1126; (2) Decorative style under Song: the earlier phase; (3) Decorative style under Song and Jin: the later phase; (4) Painting under Southern Song 1127–1279; (5) Architecture I: towers and the imaginary; (6) Architecture II: the wooden frame, brick building, domestic; (7) Sculpture; (8) Landscape, plants and trees painted under Yuan 1279–1368; (9) Mural painting; (10) Painting under Ming 1368–1643; (11) Decorative themes under Yuan and Ming.

Notes, p.261–71. Works consulted, p.272–78. Glossary, p.279–83. Index, p.284–86.

I538 ———. Arts of dynastic China. N.Y., Abrams, 1981. 633p. il. (part col.)

Trans. of L'art de l'ancienne Chine. Paris, Mazenod, 1979 (L'art et les grandes civilisations, 9)

Magisterial survey in an important series.

Contents: Part one: The evolution of style; (I) Early traditions; (II) The hieratic cycle; (III) Realistic art; (IV) Architecture; (V) Philosophized art; (VI) Decorative art; Part two: The image as document; Photographs; Identification of the photographs; Drawings of architectural details and wall reliefs; Part three: The principal archaeological sites; Part four: Appendices.

The painters, p.607–10. Chronology, p.611–12. Bibliography, p.613–20. Guide to pronunciation, p.621–22. Index, p.623–33.

I539 Weidner, Marsha, ed. Latter days of the law: images of Chinese Buddhism, 850–1850. Lawrence, Spencer Museum of Art, Univ. of Kansas; Honolulu, Univ. of Hawaii Pr., 1994. 481p. il. (part col.)

Catalog of the exhibition, Spencer Museum of Art (1994), and other locations.

Surveys Chinese Buddhist pictorial art, e.g., paintings, woodblock-printed illustrations, pictorial textiles, and ink rubbings, from the late Tang period through the late Qing dynasty. Offers both a general introduction to Chinese Buddhism and its imagery as well as a scholarly investigation of later Buddhist paintings.

Select bibliography, p.453–56. Index, p.457–81.

I540 ———. Views from jade terrace: Chinese women artists, 1300–1912. Indianapolis, Indianapolis Museum of Art; N.Y., Rizzoli, [1988]. 231p. il. (part col.)

Catalog of the exhibition, Indianapolis Museum of Art (1988), and other locations.

First exhibition ever devoted to paintings by Chinese women artists and offering a view of the historical, social, and cultural position of women artists in China. Representative works from the wide variety of women artists through six centuries, ending with the start of the modern era. Includes scholarly essays and catalog entries.

Contents: Women in the history of Chinese painting, by Marsha Weidner; Wives, daughters, and lovers: three Ming Dynasty women painters, by Ellen Johnston Laing; Daughters of the muses of China, by Irving Yucheng Lo; Flowers from the garden: paintings in the exhibition, by Marsha Weidner; Catalogue.

Index of extant and reproduced paintings by women, p.176–87. Selected bibliography, p.188. Index and list of Chinese and Japanese terms, p.189–210. Chronology, p.211.

I541 Whitfield, Roderick, and Farrer, Anne. Caves of the thousand Buddhas: Chinese art from the silk route. Ed. by Anne Farrer. With contrib. by S. J. Vainker and Jessica Rawson. London, British Museum, [1990]. 208p., il. (part col.), maps, ports.

Catalog of the exhibition, British Museum (1990).

Includes 163 objects from the Stein collection at the British Museum organized in three groups: paintings on textiles and paper recovered from Cave 17 at Dunhuang, non-painting textile items from Cave 17, and a wide variety of archeological finds from Stein's Central Asian expeditions. Intended to serve not only as an exhibition catalog but also as a short guide to the Stein collection with many color illustrations.

Selected bibliography, p.204–05. Index, p.206–08.

I542 Wu Hung. Monumentality in early Chinese art and architecture. Stanford, Stanford Univ. Pr., 1995. xviii, p.376. il., maps.
Using the theme of monumentality, this work offers an historical inquiry of early Chinese art history. Decorative, pictorial, and architectural forms are discussed together and related to their ritual and religious context, value systems, political discourse, and other societal concerns.
Notes, p.287–325. Works cited, p.327–49. Character list, p.351–59. Index, p.361–76.

India, Nepal, Pakistan, Tibet

I543 Alamkara: 5000 years of Indian art. Essays by R. C. Sharma . . . [et al.] Ahmedabad, Usmanpura (Distr. by Univ. of Washington Pr., 1994). 143p. il. (part col.)
Catalog of the exhibition, National Museum, Singapore (1994–95), and other locations, offering an overview of Indian art in terms of thematic categories.
Contents: A glimpse of Indian art, by R.C. Sharma; Indian painters as designers of decorative art objects in the Mughal period, by Jagdish Mittal; Some aspects of the decorative repertoire of northern Indian (Nagara) temple architecture, by Ratan Parimoo; Alamkara: defining 5,000 years of Indian art, by Kwa Chong Guan; The catalogue.
Selected glossary, p.132–33. List of exhibits, p.134–43.

I544 The Arts of India. Ed. by Basil Gray. Ithaca, Cornell Univ. Pr., 1981. 224p. il. (part col.), maps.
Multi-authored survey from Prehistory to the 20th century, embracing Buddhist, Hindu, Jain, Islamic, and modern art.
Contents: Buddhist, Hindu and Jain art. Introduction: Prehistory to the classical tradition of wall painting, by Basil Gray; The sculpture and architecture of Northern India, by Pramod Chandra; The sculpture and architecture of Southern India, by Aschwin de Lippe; Western Himalayan Hindu architecture and sculpture, by Penelope Chetwode; Art in the Islamic Period. The architecture and gardens of Islamic India, by Peter Andrews; Painting in Islamic India until the sixteenth century, by Heather Marshall; Later Mughal painting, by Linda York Leach; Painting for the Rajput courts, by Andrew Topsfield; Decorative arts of the Mughal period, by Mark Zebrowski. Modern art. Folk art in India today, by Stephen Huyler; Modern painting since 1935, by Geeta Kapur.
Bibliography, p.217–20. Glossary, p.221. Index, p.222–24.

I545 Arts of India, 1550–1900. Ed. by John Guy and Deborah Swallow. [Contrib. by] Rosemary Crill . . . [et al.] London, Victoria & Albert Museum, 1990. 240p. il. (part col.)
Catalog of the exhibition celebrating the opening of the Nehru Gallery of Indian Art, Victoria and Albert Museum (1990). "This volume aims . . . to show that an understanding of artistic dynamics in India depends not only on the examination of the centres of high culture but also on the analysis of regional solidarities, and the patterns by which relationships between local, regional and central cultures are refined and developed."—*Introd.*
Contents: (1) Introduction, by Deborah Swallow; (2) The arts of pre-Mughal India, by John Guy; (3) The age of the Mughals, by Susan Stronge; (4) The Sultanates of the Deccan, by Susan Stronge; (5) The Rajput courts, by Rosemary Crill; (6) Europeans and the textile trade, by Veronica Murphy; (7) The later provincial courts and British expansion, by Veronica Murphy; (8) The Raj: India 1850–1900, by Deborah Swallow.
Glossary, p.228–29. Bibliography, p.230–37. Index, p.238–40.

I546 Brand, Michael, and Lowry, Glenn D. Akbar's India: art from the Mughal city of victory. N.Y., Asia Society Galleries (Distr. by Sotheby Publications, 1985). 162p. il. (part col.)
Catalog of the exhibition, Asia Society Galleries (1985–86), and other locations, organized in celebration of the Festival of India and intended to explore "the relationship between the architectural and social environment created at Fatehpur-Sikri and the development of new artistic forms and images."—*Introd.*
Notes, p.129–34. Chronology, p.158. Bibliography, p.160–62. Index, p.[163–66].

I547 Chayet, Anne. Art et archéologie du Tibet. Paris, Picard, 1994. 247p. il. (part col.), maps. (Manuels d'archéologie d'Extrème-Orient. Civilisations de l'Himalaya)
Overview of Tibetan art.
Contents: (I) Découverte de l'art Tibétain; (II) Découvertes archéologiques; (III) Savoir, art et oeuvre au Tibet; (IV) L'architecture; (V) Peinture et sculpture; Conclusion; Annexes.
Liste des caractères chinois, p.228–29. Bibliographie, p.230–38. Index, p.239–47.

I548 Craven, Roy C. Indian art: a concise history. [Reprint.] N.Y., Praeger, 1997. 256p. il. (part col.), maps, plans.
Reprint of 1976 ed. entitled A concise history of Indian art.
General introductory survey.
Contents: (1) Harappan culture: beginnings on the Indus; (2) Historical and religious origins; (3) The Mauryan period: the first imperial art; (4) The Shunga dynasty: chaityas, viharas and stupas; (5) The Andhra period: the "world mountains"; (6) The Kushan period: Gandhara and Mathura; (7) The Gupta and Post-Gupta periods; (8) South India: Pallavas, Cholas and Hoysalas; (9) The medieval period in North India; (10) Islamic India: architecture and painting; (11) Jain, Rajasthani and Pahari painting; Epilogue.
Bibliography, p.250–52. Index, p.253–56.

I549 Fisher, Robert E. Art of Tibet. N.Y., Thames and Hudson, 1997. 224p. il. (chiefly col.), map, ports. (World of art)
Introductory survey.

Contents: (1) The Tibetan pantheon; (2) Structures, objects and images; (3) The development of Tibetan styles (11th–14th centuries); (4) The refinement of Tibetan styles (15th–19th centuries).

Glossary, p.216–17. Bibliography, p.218–19. Index, p.221–24.

I550 Ghose, D. C. Bibliography of modern Indian art. New Delhi, Lalit Kala Akademi, 1980. xiv, 290p.

"The first bibliography on contemporary Indian art."—*Foreword.*

Contents: (1) General; (2) Trends and progress in Indian art; (3) Influences; (4) Art and revivalism; (5) Revivalism and its criticism; (6) Progressive artists' movement; (7) Painting; (8) Sculpture; (9) Mural paintings in India; (10) Graphics; (11) Individual artists' list; (12) Art schools; (13) Art education; (14) Conferences and seminars; (15) Art galleries and museums; (16) Art appreciation; Appendixes.

Name index, p.249–90.

I551 Goetz, Hermann. Rajput art and architecture. Ed by Jyotindra Jain and Jutta Jain-Neubauer. Wiesbaden, Steiner, 1978. xxi, 229p. il., plates (Schriftenreihe des Südasien-Instituts der Universität Heidelberg, 26)

Posthumously published collection of the great scholar's articles on this subject, which he intended to turn into a "comprehensive study on Rajput art."—*Pref.*

Bibliography, p.197–206. Index, p.218–29.

I552 Goswamy, B. N. Essence of Indian art. Photographs by Jean-Louis Nou. [San Francisco], Asian Art Museum of San Francisco, 1986. 285p. il. (part col.)

Beautifully produced catalog of the exhibition, Asian Art Museum of San Francisco (1986), and other locations. Thematically structured according to the nine rasas or "sentiments," evoking "the methods Indian artists used to provoke a particular response from their audience."—*Foreword.*

Glossary, p.275–80. Bibliography, p.281–83.

I553 Harle, J. C. The art and architecture of the Indian subcontinent. 2d ed. New Haven, Yale Univ. Pr., 1994. 601p. il. (part col.), maps. (Yale University Press pelican history of art)

1st ed., Harmondsworth, Middlesex, Eng., Penguin Books, 1986; reprinted with corrections, 1987, 1990.

Comprehensive survey from the Indus Valley civilization to the 18th century. Unlike Benjamin Rowland's original Indian volume in this series (GLAH 1:I542), which dealt with Southeast Asia as well as the Indian subcontinent, "the present work oversteps the political boundaries of India only to include Afghanistan, Bangladesh, Nepal, Pakistan, and Sri Lanka, but it adds a section on Indo-Muslim architecture."—*Pref.*

Contents: (1) Early Indian art; (2) The Gupta period; (3) The post-Gupta period; (4) The later Hindu period; (5) South India; (6) Painting; (7) Indo-Islamic architecture; (8) Sri Lanka; (9) Nepal.

Notes, p.[489]–536. Bibliography, p.[537]–65. Index, p.[577]–601.

I554 Huntington, Susan L. The art of ancient India, Buddhist, Hindu, Jain. With contrib. by John C. Huntington. N.Y., Weatherhill, 1985. xxix, 786p. il. (part col.), plates.

"The need for an up-to-date overview of the art of South Asia has been apparent for decades. . . . This volume reflects our efforts to provide such a synthesis."—*Pref.* The standard survey.

Contents: Part one: Foundations of Indic civilization: the prehistoric and protohistoric periods; Part two: Period of the early dynasties; Part three: Dynasties of the middle period; Part four: Later northern schools; Part five: Later schools of the Deccan and the south.

Notes, p.619–58. Select bibliography, p.659–713. Glossary, p.715–32. List of maps, p.733. Illustration index, p.735–46. Index, p.747–86.

I555 ———, and Huntington, John C. Leaves from the Bodhi tree: the art of Pāla India (8th–12th centuries) and its international legacy. [Dayton, Ohio], Dayton Art Institute in assoc. with the Univ. of Washington Pr., 1989. 615p. il. (part col.)

Substantial catalog of the exhibition, Dayton Art Institute (1989–90), and other locations. "This exhibition explores the range of Pāla period art and traces its influences in Southeast Asia . . . in the Himalayan region, mainly Nepal and Tibet; and in China."—*Introd.*

Note on transliteration and pronunciation, p.19. Select bibliography, p.575–86. Glossary, p.587–601. Guide to subjects and themes, p.601–04. Maps and chart of Tibetan painting styles, p.605–15.

I556 In the image of man: the Indian perception of the universe through 2000 years of painting and sculpture. [Catalog ed. by George Michell.] London, Weidenfeld and Nicolson, 1982. 231p. il. (part col.), map.

Catalog of the exhibition, Hayward Gallery, London (1982). "Intended to focus on concepts which were quintessentially Indian . . . to demonstrate the cross-fertilization of cultural beliefs in the Indian sub-continent from ancient times to the nineteenth century."—*Introd.*

Contents: Introduction to Indian sculpture, by George Michell; Introduction to Indian painting, by Linda York Leach; Glossary of sculpture styles, by George Michell; Glossary of painting styles, by Linda York Leach; The catalogue: (1) The natural world; (2) The abundance of life; (3) Man in the cosmos; (4) The four goals of life; (5) Life at court; (6) Devotion; (7) Enlightenment; (8) Mythology of Vishnu; (9) Mythology of Shiva and the Goddess.

Glossary of terms and deities, p.227–28. Select bibliography, p.229. Guide to deities, p.230–31.

I557 Jacques Marchais Museum of Tibetan Art. Treasures of Tibetan Art: collections of the Jacques Marchais Museum of Tibetan Art. [By] Barbara Lipton and Nima Dorjee Ragnubs. Essay on Tibetan Buddhism by Donald S. Lopez, Jr. Photographs by Geoffrey Clements. Foreword by His Holiness the Fourteenth Dalai Lama. Staten Island, N.Y., The Museum; Oxford Univ. Pr., 1996. xix, 295p. il. (part col.)

Scholarly catalog of highlights from the museum's collections.

Tibetan transliterations, p.273–76. Selected bibliography, p.277–81. Tibetan references, p.282–84. Index, p.285–95.

I558 Jagdish Chandra. Bibliography of Indian art, history and archaeology. Delhi, Delhi Printers Prakashan (Distr. Humanities Pr., 1978). [unpaginated] il.

Only volume published of an ambitious general bibliography, arranged by media (art, architecture, sculpture, painting, handicraft) and planned for several vols.

I559 Klimburg-Salter, Deborah E. The silk route and the diamond path: esoteric Buddhist art on the trans-Himalayan trade routes. Essays by Maximilian Klimburg . . . [et al.] Los Angeles, Published under the sponsorship of the UCLA Art Council, 1982. 254p. il. (part col.)

Published on the occasion of the exhibition, Wight Art Gallery, UCLA (1982–83), and other locations.

"It is our intention in this exhibition and catalogue to suggest theoretical perspectives for the study of the Buddhist arts of the western Himalayas and . . . to place the arts within their historical, ideological, and aesthetic contexts. . . . The focus on this study is the monastic art that developed along the trade routes which traversed the Himalayas connecting ancient northwest India and the western Himalayas with Central Asia."—*Pref.*

Glossary of Sanskrit and other names and terms, p.243–44. Bibliography, p.245–54.

I560 Krishna Deva. Images of Nepal. New Delhi, Archaeological Survey of India, 1984. x, 93p. il., plates.

The result of an "iconographical survey of the Nepal Valley" embracing "the icons in the temples and the monasteries as well as the stray images in the Kathmandu Valley. . . . An attempt has been made to classify the rich iconographical wealth of the Nepal Valley and present a summary."—*Pref.* Includes Brahmanical, Buddhist, and Tantric iconography.

Bibliography, p.86–87. Index, p.88–93.

I561 Liu, Li-chung. Buddhist art of the Tibetan Plateau. Comp. and photographed by Liu Lizhong. Ed. and trans. by Ralph Kiggell. San Francisco, China Books and Periodicals, 1988. 362p. col. il.

Trans. of Tsang ch'uan fo chiao i shu. Hong Kong, 1987.

Presents "some of the most splendid examples of Tibet's heritage contained in the famous monasteries."—*Pref.* Mostly color plates.

Contents: Tibetan monasteries: search and discovery; The origins and development of Tibetan Buddhism; Architecture; Sculpture; Painting; Cultural objects; Monastic activities; Tibetan Buddhism in Beijing; The eight temples of Chengde; Appendixes: The major Tibetan monasteries; The Yarlung and Tubo kings; The fourteen Dalai Lamas; The ten Panchen Lamas; The Ganden Phodrang Regency; Afterword.

Index, p.356–60.

I562 Los Angeles County Museum of Art. Art of Nepal: a catalogue of the Los Angeles County Museum of Art collection. By Pratapaditya Pal. Berkeley, Los Angeles County Museum of Art in assoc. with Univ. of California Pr., 1985. 257p. il. (part col.)

Scholarly catalog of one of the most comprehensive collections outside Nepal, based originally on the Heeramaneck collection and consisting primarily of sculptures in several media, paintings, and drawings.

Glossary, p.239–44. Bibliography, p.245–50. Index, p.251–55.

I563 ______. Art of Tibet: a catalogue of the Los Angeles County Museum of Art collection. By Pratapaditya Pal. With an appendix on inscriptions by H. E. Richardson, and additional entries on textiles by Dale Carolyn Gluckman. Exp. ed. Los Angeles, The Museum (Distr. by Abrams, 1990). 343p. il. (part col.), map.

Scholarly catalog of the most important collection outside Tibet, based in the acquisition of the Heeramaneck collection.

Contents: Painting; Sculpture; Ritual objects; Addenda; Appendix.

Bibliography, p.335–38. Index, p.339–43.

I564 Michell, George. Architecture and art of southern India: Vijayanagara and the successor states. N.Y., Cambridge Univ. Pr., 1995. xxii, 302p. il., maps. (The new Cambridge history of India, I, 6)

"The overall aim of this volume is to provide an introduction to the architecture and art of Southern India, under the Vijayanagara empire and the lesser kingdoms that succeeded it."—*Introd.*

Contents: (1) Introduction; (2) Historical framework; (3) Temple architecture: the Kannada and Telugu zones; (4) Temple architecture: the Tamil zone; (5) Palace architecture; (6) Sculpture; (7) Painting; (8) Conclusion.

Bibliographical essay, p.278–82. Bibliography, p.283–94. Index, p.295–300.

I565 ______, and Zebrowski, Mark. Architecture and art of the Deccan Sultanates. N.Y., Cambridge Univ. Pr., 1999. xxi, 297p. il. (part col.), maps, 16p. of plates. (The new Cambridge history of India, I, 7)

"The aim here is to present the broadest possible appreciation of the Deccan in terms of architectural activity and artistic patronage."—*Pref.*

Contents: (1) Historical framework; (2) Forts and palaces; (3) Mosques and tombs; (4) Architectural decoration; (5) Miniature painting: Ahmadnagar and Bijapur; (6) Miniature painting: Golconda and other centres; (7) Textiles, metalwork and stone objects; (8) Temples; (9) Conclusion; Appendix:

Dynastic lists of Deccan rulers.

Bibliographical essay, p.278–81. Bibliography, p.282–88. Index, p.289–97.

I566 Mitter, Partha. Art and nationalism in colonial India: occidental orientations. N.Y., Cambridge Univ. Pr., 1994. xxix, 475p. il. (part col.)

"My purpose is to tell the story of colonial art . . . the vast canvas of Indian colonial culture, with its conflicts of interests and the interactions between colonial hegemony and national self-imaging."—*Pref.*

Contents: Part 1: Prologue: (1) The phenomenon: occidental orientations; Part 2: The age of optimism: (2) Art education and Raj patronage; (3) Salon artists and the rise of the Indian public; (4) The power of the printed image; (5) The artist as charismatic individual: Raja Ravi Varma; Part 3: The great wave of cultural nationalism: (6) Bengali patriots and art for the nation; (7) Ideology of swadeshi art; (8) How the past was salvaged by swadeshi artists; (9) Westernisers and orientalists: public battle of styles; Part 4: Epilogue: (10) The passing of the age of oriental art.

Notes, p.381–435. Bibliography, p.436–50. Index, p.451–75.

I567 Mookerjee, Ajit. Ritual art of India. Rochester, Vt., Inner Traditions, 1998. 176p. il. (part col.)

Originally published, London, Thames and Hudson, 1985.

"This study is an attempt to reveal the inward-seeking quality of Indian art, no matter what its subject-matter, iconography or chronology."—*Pref.*

Contents: (1) Primal form; (2) Nature worship; (3) Fertility rites; (4) Popular cults; (5) Sivaism; (6) Vishnuism; (7) Saktism; (8) Syncretism; (9) Death and rebirth; (10) Bliss-consciousness.

Bibliography, p.166–68. Glossary, p.169–74. Index, p.175–76.

I568 Naqvi, Akbar. Image and identity: fifty years of painting and sculpture in Pakistan. Karachi, Oxford Univ. Pr., 1998. xli, 870p. il. (part col.)

"This book is a narrative, a story . . . as well as . . . a calendar of dates which helps to identify . . . the birth, education, travels, and works of the artists. [It] is also an account of my own involvement with art and artists for over forty years."—*Introd.* Substantial but poorly illustrated, personal account of contemporary art in Pakistan.

Notes at ends of chapters. Glossary, p.851–60. Index, p.861–70.

I569 National Museum of India. Masterpieces from the National Museum collection. Ed. by S. P. Gupta. New Delhi, National Museum, 1985. x, 232p. il. (part col.), plates.

Catalog planned to accompany an exhibition cancelled due to prior commitment of artworks to the Festival of India loan program. Intended as a handbook to the collections. Director's foreword. Includes archeological artifacts, manuscripts, paintings, coins and epigraphy, arms and armor, decorative arts.

I570 Newark Museum. Catalogue of the Newark Museum Tibetan collection. [By] Valrae Reynolds, Amy Heller. 2d ed. Newark, N.J., Newark Museum, 1983– . (2)v. il., map.

Rev. ed. of Catalogue of the Tibetan collection and other Lamaist articles in the Newark Museum. 1st ed. 1950–71 in 5 vols. Vol.3 by Valrae Reynolds, Amy Heller, and Janet Gyatso.

Contents: (1) Introduction; (3) Sculpture and painting.

I571 Pal, Pratapaditya. Art of the Himalayas: treasures from Nepal and Tibet. With contrib. from Ian Alsop . . . [et al.] N.Y., Hudson Hills Press in assoc. with the American Federation of Arts (Distr. by Rizzoli, 1991). 208p. il. (part col.), map.

Catalog of the exhibition organized by the American Federation of Arts, Newark Museum (1992), and other locations. Based on the Zimmerman collection, which is "particularly strong in Nepali bronzes and paintings."—*Pref.*

Contents: Art from Nepal: Introduction; Sculptures and ritual objects; Paintings and drawings; Art from Tibet: Introduction; Sculptures and ritual objects; Paintings; Ritual textiles; Appendixes.

Bibliography, p.200–03. Index, p.204–07.

I572 ———. The peaceful liberators: Jain art from India. With contrib. by Shridhar Andhare . . . [et al.] Los Angeles, Calif., Los Angeles County Museum of Art; N.Y., Thames and Hudson, 1994. 279p. il. (part col.)

Published in conjunction with the exhibition, Los Angeles County Museum of Art (1994–95), and other locations. "The most comprehensive presentation to date of artwork emerging from the Jain religion."—*Foreword.*

Contents: Introduction, by Pratapaditya Pal; Following the Jina, worshiping the Jina: an essay on Jain rituals, by John E. Cort; Are Jains really Hindus? Some parallels and differences between Jain and Hindu philosophies, by Gerald James Larson; Jain pilgrimage: in memory and celebration of the Jinas, by Phyllis Granoff; Jain monumental painting, by Shridhar Andhare; Jain manuscript painting, by John Guy; Catalogue of the exhibition: Architectural pieces; ritual objects and symbols; Images of Jinas; Images of Deities; The art of the book; The cosmic and mortal realms; Appendix.

Bibliography, p.262–69. Sanskrit names and terms with diacritical marks, p.270–71. Index, p.272–76.

I573 ———. Tibet: tradition and change. Essay and catalogue entries by Pratapaditya Pal, with contrib. by Lobsang Lhalungpa . . . [et al.] Trans. of inscriptions . . . by Lobsang Lhalungpa. Photographs . . . by John Bigelow Taylor. Albuquerque, Albuquerque Museum, 1997. xvi, 284p. il. (part col.), map.

Published in conjunction with the exhibition, Albuquerque Museum (1997–98).

Attempts to cover "the long history and rich diversity of Tibetan art with roughly only a hundred objects . . . only from American collections."—*Pref.* Beautiful color plates.

Glossary, p.257–64. Sanskrit words, p.264. Tibetan words, p.265. Bibliography, p.266–75.

I574 Palast der Götter, 1500 Jahre Kunst aus Indien. Hrsg. Haus der Kulturen der Welt, Berlin, Staatliche Museen zu Berlin, Preussischer Kulturbesitz. [Autoren, Shashi P. Asthana . . . [et al.] Red., Marianne Yaldiz. Übers., Martin Pfeiffer. Berlin, Reimer, 1992. 244p. il. (chiefly col.), map.

Catalog of the important exhibition, Grosse Orangerie, Schloss Charlottenburg, Berlin (1992), exploring the religious significance of Indian art across 15 centuries.

Bibliographie, p.239–44.

I575 Plaeschke, Herbert, and Plaeschke, Ingeborg. Hinduistische Kunst: das indische Mittelalter. Wien, Böhlaus, 1978. 177p. il. (part col.), 1 map, plans.

Compact survey of the background and development of Indian art during the "middle ages" (5th–13th century), organized thematically across architecture, the pictorial arts, and the human figure in art, and focusing upon representative monuments.

Literaturhinweise, p.170. Namen- und Sachverzeichnis, p.170–72.

I576 Rhie, Marylin M., and Thurman, Robert A. F. Wisdom and compassion: the sacred art of Tibet. Photographs by John Bigelow Taylor. N.Y., Abrams, 1991. 406p. il. (part col.) (Repr.: 1992).

Catalog of the important exhibition, Asian Art Museum of San Francisco (1991), and other locations, intended to "demonstrate the function of this quintessentially religious art within its sacred context and to present its qualities as a distinctive body of fine art."—*Overview.*

Contents: Wisdom and compassion: the heart of Tibetan culture, by Robert A. F. Thurman; Tibet, its Buddhism, and its art, by Robert A. F. Thurman; Tibetan Buddhist art: aesthetics, chronology, and styles, by Marylin M. Rhie; The sacred art of Tibet: Catalogue: Tibetan sacred history; Tibetan Buddhist orders; Tibetan perfected worlds; Techniques of Tibetan painting and sculpture, by Gilles Béguin.

Glossary, p.389–93. Bibliography, p.394–97. Index, p.398–405.

I577 Tibetan art: towards a new definition of style. London, Laurence King, in assoc. with Alan Marcuson, 1997. 319p. col. il.

Reproduces selected papers delivered at an international symposium on Tibetan art (London, 1994). Aims to provide an introduction to the subject as well as providing a reference book for scholars and students.

Note on foreign terms, p.292. Footnotes, p.292–305. Bibliography, p.306–11. Glossary, p.312–14. Index, p.315–19.

I578 Till, Barry, and Swart, Paula. Art from the roof of the world: Tibet = Sur le toit du monde: l'art du Tibet. Victoria, Art Gallery of Greater Victoria, 1989. 159p. il. (part col.)

Text in English and French. Catalogue of the exhibition, Art Gallery of Greater Victoria (1989), and other locations.

I579 Topsfield, Andrew, and Beach, Milo Cleveland. Indian paintings and drawings from the collection of Howard Hodgkin. N.Y., Thames and Hudson, 1991. 111p. (part fold.) il. (chiefly col.)

Catalog of the exhibition, Arthur M. Sackler Gallery, Washington, D.C. (1992), and other locations.

Contents: Notes on the collection, by Howard Hodgkin; Rajput and Mughal painting in Howard Hodgkin's collection, by Andrew Topsfield; Catalogue, by Milo Cleveland Beach and Andrew Topsfield.

Bibliography, p.110–11.

I580 Welch, Stuart Cary. India, art and culture, 1300–1900. N.Y., Metropolitan Museum of Art; Holt, Rinehart, and Winston, 1985. 478p. il. (part col.)

Catalog of the exhibition, Metropolitan Museum of Art (1985). "Documents six critical centuries of artistic synthesis, change, and survival . . . spanning all parts of the continent."—*p.22.*

Contents: (I) The great tradition; (II) Tribe and village; (III) The Muslim courts; (IV) The Rajput world; (V) The British period.

Chronology, p.450–57. Glossary, p.458–61. Bibliography, p.462–70. Index, p.471–77.

I581 Williams, Joanna Gottfried. The art of Gupta India, empire and province. Princeton, N.J., Princeton Univ. Pr., 1982. xxvi, 209p., il., plates.

"Ultimately, it is the purpose of this book to relate works of art, selected on the basis of their aesthetic character and located on a grid of time, place, and social milieu, to factors outside the realm of art that may explain or correlate with their particular nature."—*Introd.*

Contents: Introduction: issues and methods; (I) The point of departure; (II) The inception of Gupta art, A.D. 370–415; (III) Maturity and crisis, A.D. 415–485; (IV) Gupta art after the Guptas, A.D. 485–550; (V) The beginnings of the medieval, A.D. 550–650; Epilogue; Appendix.

List of Abbreviations, p.xxvii. Bibliography, p.189–200. Index, p.201–9.

I582 Ypma, Herbert J. M. Indiamodern: traditional forms and contemporary design. London, Phaidon, 1994. 239p. il. (chiefly col.)

A beautifully illustrated introduction to contemporary architectural and design culture in India.

Bibliography, p.236.

Japan

I583 Cunningham, Michael R. The triumph of Japanese style: 16th century art in Japan. With contrib. by Suzuki Norio; Miyajima Shin'ichi . . . [et al.] [Cleveland], Cleveland Museum of Art in coop. with Indiana Univ. Pr., [1991]. xiii, 154p. il. (part col.)

Catalog of the exhibition, Cleveland Museum of Art (1991).

Spanning the Muromachi and the Momoyama periods, the 16th century was a time when a bold national style of art emerged in Japan. This exhibition includes ceramics, lacquerware, paintings, and textiles from a number of museums in Japan and the United States gathered to commemorate the 75th anniversary of the Cleveland Museum of Art.

Suggested reading, p.150–51.

I584 Elisseeff, Danielle, and Elisseeff, Vadime. Art of Japan. Trans. by I. Mark Paris. N.Y., Abrams, 1985. 622p. il. (part col.), map.

Trans. of L'art de l'ancien Japon. Paris, Mazenod, 1980. (L'art et les grandes civilisations, X)

Following a thematic rather than chronological sequence, this work is lavishly illustrated with many full-page, full-color reproductions of Japanese art and architecture. After a historical chapter, the book begins with architecture and closes with the Japanese love of life's pleasures.

Contents: (1) Paths to Japanese art; (2) Documentation.

Concise biographies, p.[591]–600. Chronological table, p.[601–06]. Bibliography, p.608–14. Index, p.615–22.

I585 The Great Eastern Temple: treasures of Japanese Buddhist art from Todai-ji. Organized by Yutaka Mino. Chicago, Art Institute of Chicago; Bloomington, Indiana Univ. Pr., [1986]. 180p. il. (part col.)

Catalog of the exhibition, Art Institute of Chicago (1986).

Tōdai-ji, a Buddhist monastery of several buildings located in Nara, is one of the most precious of Japan's cultural assets. This exhibition displayed 150 cultural treasures from this important Buddhist monument including sculpture, painting, decorative arts, and calligraphy spanning 1,200 years.

Bibliography, p.173–75.

I586 Hempel, Rose. The golden age of Japan, 794–1192. Trans. by Katherine Watson. N.Y., Rizzoli, 1983. 252p. il. (part col.)

Trans. of Japan zur Heian-Zeit: Kunst und Kultur. Fribourg, Office du Livre, 1983.

Standard work on Japanese art of the Heian period. Intended for a scholarly audience, this work presents a comprehensive outline of Heian Japan religion, sculpture, politics, architectural and city planning, Chinese and Japanese literature and calligraphy, and related topics.

Glossary, p.232–38. Bibliography, p.239–41. Index, p.243–51.

I587 Hizo nihon bijutsu taikan. [Japanese art: the great European collections.] Supervised by Tadashi Kobayashi. N.Y., Kodansha, 1992–94. 12v. il. (part col.)

Contents: (1) British Museum I; (2) British Museum II; (3) British Museum III; (4) British Museum IV, Ashmolean Museum, Victoria and Albert Museum; (5) Chester Beatty Library; (6) Musée Guimet; (7) Museum für Ostasiatische Kunst; (8) Museum für Ostasiatische Kunst der Stadt Köln; (9) Rijksmuseum voor Volkenkunde; (10) National Museum, Krakow; (11) Österreichisches Museum für Angewandte Kunst, Viena; Náprstek Muzeum and National Gallery, Prague; The Museum of Applied Arts, Budapest; (12) Selected Japanese arts in Europe.

I588 Ichiko, Teiji; Masaru, Sekino; and Yoshiho, Yonezawa. Nihon gakujutsu shiryo somokuroku. Tokyo, Hatsubai Asahi Shuppansha, 1988-Nendoban. 2v.

1st ed. 1982. Cover title: The general catalogue of learned materials in Japan.

Directory of national treasures and important cultural properties. Vol.1 includes sections on paintings (p.3–470), sculpture (p.473–566), architecture (p.569–618), crafts (p.621–66), swords and weapons (p.669–713), lacquer (p.717–35), textiles, (p.739–58), ceramics (p.761–870), calligraphy (p.873–74), archeological items (p.877–98), and other media (p.901–36). Each of these sections is organized by title of the work and includes information on the dimensions, the owning institution, and the artist. Most of the sections are subdivided between Japanese work and foreign work in Japan. Indexes to the entries by artists' names (p.3–183) and owning institutions (p.187–390) are in separately numbered section of the volume. Vol.2 covers calligraphy (p.3–117), books (p.121–582), ancient documents (p.585–876), and other paper documents (p.879–92). These sections are also listed in title order with the author index (p.3–141) and institution index (p.145–72) in a separately numbered section of the volume.

I589 International Research Center for Japanese Studies. Kaigai Nihon Bijutsu Chosa Purijekuto hokoku = Report of Japanese Art Abroad Research Project. Kyoto, Kokusai Nihon Bunka Kenkyu Senta, 1993– . (6)v. il. (part col.)

In Japanese and English.

Begun in 1991 by the International Research Center for Japanese Studies, this project intends to construct a database with textual and pictorial information related to Japanese art located outside of Japan. The catalogs provide basic information on the collections, data on the pieces, and small, color reproductions. The volumes consist primarily of photographs taken for the project on site.

Contents: (1) Catalogue of Japanese Art in the Pushkin State Museum of Fine Arts (1993); (2) Catalogue of Japanese Art in the State Hermitage Museum (1993); (3) Catalogue of Japanese Art in the Náprstek Museum (1994); (4) Catalogue of Japanese Art in the National Gallery, Prague (1994); (5) Ferenc Hopp Museum of Eastern Asiatic Arts, Budapest (1995); (6) Index of ukiyo-e in western collections (1996).

Indexes of included artists appear at end of each vol.

I590 Japan: the shaping of Daimyo culture, 1185–1868. Ed. by Yoshiaki Shimizu. Washington, D.C., National Gallery of Art, 1988. xi, 402p. col. il., ports.

"The first attempt anywhere, including Japan, to explore the artistic legacy of the daimyo," that is, feudal lords who controlled the provinces of Japan for much of the medieval and early modern periods.—*Foreword.*

Contents: Daimyo and daimyo culture, by Martin Collcutt; Daimyo and art, by Yoshiaki Shimizu; Catalogue: Portraiture; Calligraphy; Religious sculpture; Painting; Arms and armor; Lacquer; Ceramics; Textiles; Tea ceremony utensils; Nō-related works.

Literature, p.391–93. Bibliography, p.394–402.

I591 Japanese Arts Library. Rosenfield, John, general ed. Tokyo, Kodansha (Distr. by Harrassowitz, [1977–1987]). 15v. il., plates.

Volumes originally appeared in the Japanese-language series, Nihon no bijutsu.

An important series because it provides for the first time adequate college-level, English-language resources for many of the important topics of Japanese art. Each vol. provides numerous illustrations, some in color, of significant objects as well as a glossary of terms and bibliography.

Contents: (1) Fujioka, Ryōichi. Shino and Oribe ceramics (1977); (2) Mōri, Hisashi. Japanese portrait sculpture

(1977); (3) Takeda, Tsuneo. Kanō Eitoku (1977); (4) Okazaki, Jōji. Pure land Buddhist painting (1977); (5) Nishikawa, Kyotaro. Bugaku masks (1978); (6) Hosono, Masanobu. Nagasaki prints and early copperplates (1978); (7) Nakagawa, Sensaku. Kutani ware (1979); (8) Kanazawa, Hiroshi. Japanese ink paintings: early Zen masterpieces (1979); (9) Suzuki, Kakichi. Early Buddhist architecture in Japan (1980); (10) Hashimoto, Fumio, ed. Architecture in the shoin style: Japanese feudal residences (1981); (11) Sugiyama, Jirō. Classic Buddhist sculpture: the Tempyō period (1982); (12) Satō, Kanzan. The Japanese sword (1983); (13) Kawahara, Masahiko. The ceramic art of Ogata Kenzan (1985); (14) Hinago, Motoo. Japanese castles (1986); (15) Ishida, Hisatoyo. Esoteric Buddhist paintings (1987).

I592 Japan's golden age: Momoyama. [By] Money L. Hickman . . . [et al.] New Haven, Yale Univ. Pr. in assoc. with Sun and Star 1996 and Dallas Museum of Art, 1996. 320p. il. (chiefly col.), maps.

Catalog of the exhibition, Dallas Museum of Art (1996).

Important presentation of Momoyama (16th-century) art and culture. Introductions to each catalog section by specialists.

Contents: Catalogue: Portraiture; Sculpture; Painting; Calligraphy; Tea ceremony utensils and ceramics; Lacquer and metalwork.

I593 Kidder, J. Edward, Jr. The art of Japan. London, Century, 1985. 319p. col. il. map.

Trans. of Arte del Giappone. Milan, Mondadori, 1985.

Extensively illustrated with colorful, often full-page, photographs. Chapters are organized in chronological order and provide a very accessible text for the beginning student.

Bibliography, p.315. Index, p.316–19.

I594 ______. Early Buddhist Japan. N.Y., Praeger, [1972]. 212p. il., maps (Ancient peoples and places, 78)

A standard history of the archeology of the early centuries of Buddhism in Japan.

Bibliography, p. 162–64.

I595 Mason, Penelope. History of Japanese art. N.Y., Abrams, 1993. 431p. il., plates (part col.), map.

The standard introductory text for the topic. Intended for the beginning student of Japanese art and culture. Nicely illustrated with numerous colored plates and plans.

Contents: (1) The birth of Japan: the Jomon and Yayoi periods and the Kofun era; (2) Encounter with China and Buddhism: the Asuka, Hakuho, and Nara periods; (3) New beginnings and the formulation of court culture: the Heian period; (4) Samurai culture and the coming of Pure Land and Zen Buddhism: the early feudal period; (5) A turbulent transition: the Momoyama period; (6) Peace and stability in later feudal times: the Tokugawa, or Edo, period; (7) After feudalism: the modern period.

Glossary, p.388–92. A reader's guide to the arts of Japan, by Sylvan Barnet and William Burto, p.393–404. Index, p.405–30.

I596 Munroe, Alexandra. Japanese art after 1945: scream against the sky. N.Y., Abrams, 1994. 416p. il. (part col.)

Catalog of the exhibition, Yokohama Museum of Art (1994), and other locations.

An interpretive survey of 50 years of Japanese avant-garde art with 200 works, including painting, sculpture, photography and performance, video, film, and installation art, by more than 100 artists. Chapter 15 is an anthology of 39 statements, texts, and interviews with artists and critics on postwar Japanese art.

Glossary, p.393–98. Bibliography, p.399–411. Index, p.412–16.

I597 Paine, Robert Treat, and Soper, Alexander Coburn. The art and architecture of Japan. 3d ed. with rev. and upd. notes and bibliography to pt.1 by D. B. Waterhouse. Harmondsworth, Penguin, 1981. 524p. il. (Pelican history of art)

See GLAH 1:I559 for original annotation. Waterhouse's revisions to Paine's contribution are to the bibliography, which has been expanded to the same scale as that for Part Two. No revisions have been made to Part Two, with two minor exceptions. —*Pref. to Part One (third ed.)*

I598 Pearson, Richard. Ancient Japan. N.Y., Braziller; Washington, D.C., Arthur M. Sackler Gallery, Smithsonian Institution, [1992]. 324p. il. (part col.), maps.

Catalog of the exhibition, Sackler Gallery (1992). "This volume and the accompanying exhibition of more than 250 objects, most recovered in excavations conducted over the past two decades, survey the archaeology of ancient Japan from the first evidence of human activity during the Paleolithic period through the establishment of a central state in the seventh and eighth centuries A.D."—*Introd.*

A comprehensive survey of Japanese prehistory from the Paleolithic period to the establishment of a central Buddhist state through period chapters followed by specific site and artifact descriptions. All 258 objects in the exhibition are reproduced with extended captions.

References, p.312–17. Index, p.318–24.

I599 Self, James, and Hirose, Nobuko. Japanese art signatures: a handbook and practical guide. London, Bamboo, 1987. 399p., il.

"The aim of the present book is to make it feasible, even for those with no formal training in the Japanese language, to be able to decipher and correctly read the names, and common adjuncts to signatures, like dates and the age of the artist."—*Foreword.*

Includes a dictionary of more than 1,600 characters, a catalog of more than 11,000 names used by artists and craftsmen, and a lexicon of character variations.

Bibliography, p.365–75.

I600 Shimizu, Christine. L'art japonais. Paris, Flammarion, 1997. 495p. col. il., maps.

Survey of Japanese art history from the beginnings through the modern era. Pays close attention to the social and historical setting.

Repères chronologiques, p.448–49. Bibliographie, p.475–79. Table d'équivalence des termes bouddhiques japonais/sanskrit, p.480. Index des termes techniques, p.481–85. Index des ouvrages cités, p.486–87. Index des sites, p.488–90. Index des noms de personnes, p.491–95.

I601 Smith, Lawrence; Harris, Victor; and Clark, Timothy. Japanese art: masterpieces in the British Museum. N.Y., Oxford Univ. Pr., 1990. 256p. col. il.
Published on the occasion of the opening of a new suite of Japanese galleries in the British Museum. Documents the most comprehensive Japanese art collection in Europe. Chapters include introductory essays as well as catalog entries.

Chronology, p.248. Glossary, p.248–50. Bibliography, p.251–53. Index, p.253–56.

I602 Stanley-Baker, Joan. Japanese art. N.Y., Thames and Hudson, 1984. 216p. il. (part col.) map (World of art)
A survey intended to introduce the most significant art in Japan and to identify "aspects of the Japanese spirit which were developed in art forms."—*Introd.*

Select bibliography, p.203–05. Index, p.214–15.

I603 Swindon, Elizabeth de Sabato, et al. The women of the pleasure quarter: Japanese paintings and prints of the Floating World. Lanham, Md., Hudson Hills Pr., 1996. 195p. il. (part col.)
Catalog of the exhibition, the Worcester Art Museum (1996), and other locations. With examples drawn primarily from the John Chandler Bancroft collection of Japanese woodblock prints and paintings, the catalog intends to increase understanding of traditional Japanese popular culture. Images from the Edo period of the courtesans who became cultural icons.

Selected bibliography, p.191–92.

I604 Tokugawa, Bijutsukan. The Shogun age exhibition from the Tokugawa Art Museum, Japan. Tokyo, the Shogun Age Exhibition Executive Committee, 1983. 279p. il. (part col.), map.
Catalog of the exhibition, Los Angeles County Museum of Art (1983), and other locations.

Owned by the Tokugawa shoguns who ruled Japan during the Edo period, the 300 art works in the exhibit range from painted screens and scrolls to swords and armor, from tea ceremony utensils to Nō theater costumes and masks. "This catalog is not simply a list of the exhibits, but is intended to transmit a sense of the history, culture, and life of the great daimyo (feudal lords) of the Edo period through articles that once constituted their possessions."—*Ed. notes.*

I605 Twelve centuries of Japanese art from the Imperial collection. [Ed. by Lynne Shaner.] Introd. by Ann Yonemura. Contrib. by Hirabayashi Moritoku . . . [et al.] Washington, D.C., Smithsonian Institution, 1997. 224p. col. il., col. map.
Catalog of the exhibition, Arthur M. Sackler Gallery (1997–98), celebrating "the consistently influential and occasionally revolutionary role of the imperial household in the development of Japanese art through the centuries."—*Foreword*, by Milo Cleveland Beach.

Bibliography, p.222–24.

I606 Yamasaki, Shigehisa. Chronological table of Japanese art. Tokyo, Geishinsha, [1981]. 885p.
In English and Japanese.

Covers various genres of the arts (cultural properties) dating from the 6th century to the present. Includes all works designated National Treasures and many of the Important Cultural Properties for a total of about 6,000 entries. Entries are in both Japanese and English.

Index of art works, p.[305]–28. List of owners and collectors, p.[529]–786. Index of personal names, p.[787]–867.

Korea

I607 Arts of Korea. Contrib. Chung Yang-mo . . . [et al.] Coord. ed. Judith G. Smith. N.Y., Metropolitan Museum of Art (Distr. by Abrams, 1998). 511p. il. (part col.), maps.
Published in conjunction with the exhibition celebrating the opening of the Arts of Korea Gallery, Metropolitan Museum of Art (1998). The exhibition incorporated 100 masterworks of Korean art in a range of media.

Contents: The art of the Korean potter: from the neolithic period to the Chosŏn Dynasty, by Chung Yang-mo; Tradition and transformation in Korean Buddhist sculpture, by Kim Lena; The origin and development of landscape painting in Korea, by Ahn Hwi-joon; Artistic tradition and the depiction of reality: true-view landscape painting of the Chosŏn Dynasty, by Yi Sŏng-mi; An Kyŏn and the Eight Views tradition, by Kim Hongnam; The Korean art collection in the Metropolitan Museum of Art, by Pak Youngsook.

Endnotes, p.451–79. Bibliography, p.481–83. Index, p.485–507.

Southeast Asia

I608 Art of Southeast Asia. By Maud Girard-Geslan . . . [et al.] Pref. by Albert le Bonheur. Trans. from the French by J. A. Underwood. N.Y., Abrams, 1998. 635p. il. (part col.), maps.
Trans. of Art de l'Asie du Sud-Est. Paris, Citadelles et Mazenod, 1994. (L'art et les grandes civilisations, 24)

Substantial survey in a distinguished series.

Contents: Protohistory, by Maud Girard-Geslan; The art of Burma, by Donald M. Stadtner; The art of Thailand and Laos, by Valérie Zaleski; Khmer art, by Thierry Zéphir; The art of Champa, by Albert Le Bonheur; Vietnamese art, by Maud Girard-Geslan; Indonesian art, by Marijke J. Klokke; Traditional arts, by Maud Girard-Geslan.

Documentation for the illustrations, p.437–615. Bibliography, p.616–21. Glossary, p.622–26. Index, p.627–35.

I609 Lowry, John. Burmese art. London, H.M. Stationery Off. (Distr. by Pendragon House, 1974). vii, [107]p. il.

Brief, introductory discussion, "almost entirely concerned with the Buddha image," with a catalog of 50 objects from the Victoria and Albert Museum.

Index [unpaginated].

I610 An ocean apart, contemporary Vietnamese art from the United States and Vietnam. With an essay by Jeffrey Hantover. Trans. by Nguyen Ngoc Bich. Washington, D.C., Smithsonian Institution Traveling Exhibition Service; Boulder, Colo., Roberts Rinehart Publishers (Distr. by Publishers Group West, 1995). 112p. col. il., map.

Introduction to "the relatively little known world of contemporary painting, sculpture, and mixed media works by Vietnamese and Vietnamese American artists."—*Foreword.*

Index of artists, p.112.

I611 Ozhegova, N. I., and Oshegow, Sergij. Kunst in Burma: 2000 Jahre Archiktektur [sic], Malerei und Plastik im Zeichen des Buddhismus und Animismus. [Übers. aus dem Russischen von Christian Heidmann.] Leipzig, Seemann, 1988. 337p. il. (part col.), maps, plans.

Trans. from the manuscript entitled Iskusstvo Birmy.

Survey of the art and architecture of Burma.

Contents: Ideologische Grundlagen der klassischen Kunst Burmas; Die Kunst Pagans—das Goldene Zeitalter; Die Zeit der feudalen Zersplitterung; Die Kunst Burmas seit dem Ende des 18. Jahrhunderts.

Anmerkungen, p.304–08. Glossar, p.309–21. Zeittafel, p.322–26. Register, p.327–37.

I612 Phillips, Herbert P. The integrative art of modern Thailand. Berkeley, Lowe Museum of Anthropology, University of California, 1992. x, 138p. il. (chiefly col.), plates.

Catalog of the exhibition, Lowe Museum of Anthropology (1992), the first travelling exhibition of contemporary Thai art in the U.S.

Contents: Historical and cultural context: (1) The emergence of contemporary Thai art; (2) Other artistic genres; (3) The art community; (4) International influences; Exhibition artwork: Celebrations of Buddhism; Impressions of daily life; At one with nature; In search of identity.

Artists' profiles, p.129–35. Bibliography, p.136–37.

I613 Poshyananda, Apinan. Modern art in Thailand: nineteenth and twentieth centuries. N.Y., Oxford Univ. Pr., 1992. xxiv, 259p. il. (part col.)

"Thai modernism is treated here as a broad social and cultural field in which the plastic arts are embedded and to which they give visibility."—*Foreword.*

Contents: (1) The threshold of modern art in Siam; (2) Modern Thai painting and sculpture at a crossroads; (3) Progressive trends in modern Thai art; (4) The art scene of the 1960s; (5) Abstract and non-figurative art; (6) Thematic art; (7) Taste, value, and commodity; (8) From modern to (post?): modern art in Thailand; (9) Conclusion; Appendices.

Bibliography, p.238–52. Index, p.253–59.

I614 Strachan, Paul. Pagan: art and architecture of old Burma. Whiting Bay, Arran [Scotland], Kiscadale, 1989. vii, 159p. il. (part col.), plates.

"This work is in all senses an introduction to the art and architecture of the Pagan Dynasty . . . built upon over a century of Pagan studies."—*Introd.*

Contents: (1) The rise of a dynasty at Pagan; (2) The Pagan temple and stupa; (3) Images: style and iconography; (4) The early period c.850–1120; (5) The middle period c.1100–1170; (6) The late period c.1170–1300, I: Inner circle monuments; (7) The late period c.1170–1300, II: Outer circle monuments.

Glossary, p.140–42. Notes, p.144–51. Bibliography, p.152–5. Index, p.156–59.

I615 Stratton, Carol, and Scott, Miriam McNair. The art of Sukhothai: Thailand's golden age from the mid-thirteenth to the mid-fifteenth centuries: a cooperative study. Photographs by Robert Stratton, Robert McNair Scott. Drawings by Tirachai Kambhu na Ayudhaya. N.Y., Oxford Univ. Pr., 1981. xxxiv, 163p. il. (part col.), maps, plates.

Devoted to the "pivotal Sukhothai period during which the Thais created their first expressions in architecture, sculpture, painting and ceramics."—*Pref.*

Contents: (1) Sukhothai history; (2) Sukhothai architecture; (3) Sukhothai sculpture; (4) Sukhothai painting and drawing; (5) Ceramics of the Sukhothai period.

Glossary, p.[141]–52. Bibliography, p.[153]–58. Index, p.[159]–63.

I616 Van Beek, Steve, and Invernizzi Tettoni, Luca. The arts of Thailand. Rev. and upd. ed. N.Y., Thames and Hudson, 1991. 248p. il. (part col.)

1st ed., An introduction to the arts of Thailand. Hong Kong, Travel Pub. Asia, [1985].

Accessible introduction for the general reader.

Glossary, p.241–43. Index, p.246–47. Selected bibliography, p.248.

AFRICA, OCEANIA, THE AMERICAS

General Works

I617 Affinities of form. The Raymond and Laura Wielgus Collection of the arts of Africa, Oceania, and the Americas. [By] Diane M. Pelrine. With an introd. by Roy Sieber. Photographs by Michael Cavanagh and Kevin Montague. Munich, Prestel, [1996]. 231p., 100 col. plates, col. maps.

Catalog of the exhibition, Portland Museum of Art (1996–97), and other locations. Organized by the Indiana University Art Museum, Bloomington, this exhibition documents a collection "widely regarded by scholars as one of the finest of its kind in the world."—*Foreword.*

Contents: Collectors, museums, and ethnographic arts in the United States; Africa; Oceania; The Americas; Ex-Collection objects.

Bibliography, p.225–30. Index of peoples and places, p.231.

I618 Die anderen Modernen: zeitgenössische Kunst aus Afrika, Asien und Lateinamerika. [Katalogred., Ute Hermanns, Maria Ferreira Morais (Assistenz). Übers., Mary Carroll . . . [et al.] Hrsg., Haus der Kulturen der Welt. Heidelberg, Braus, 1997. 162p. il. (part col.)

In German and English. Catalog of the exhibition, Haus der Kulturen der Welt, Berlin (1997). Seeks to provide a corrective to Eurocentric perspectives on modern art.

Biographien, p.122–37.

I619 Corbin, George A. Native arts of North America, Africa, and the South Pacific: an introduction. N.Y., Harper and Row, 1988. xxvii, 313p. il., maps, col. plates. (Icon editions)

"The purpose of this book is to provide [an] introduction to the art of the indigenous peoples of North America, West and Central Africa, and the South Pacific. It is written from the point of view of an art historian using traditional art historical techniques and points of view."—*Introd.* A significant introduction that seeks to take into account recent scholarship as well as the growing interest of the art market in these traditional arts.

Contents: (1) Introduction; (2) Alaskan Eskimo art and art of the Northwest Coast; (3) Art of the Southwestern United States; (4) Art of the Woodlands Period and of the Mississippian Period, and art of the Great Lakes and Plains; (5) West African art of Mali, the Ivory Coast, and Ghana; (6) Art of Nigeria; (7) Art of Central Africa; (8) Australian aboriginal and Island New Guinea art; (9) Art of Island Melanesia; (10) Art of Polynesia.

Glossary, p.285–87. Notes, p.288–93. Bibliography, p.294–305. Index, p.307–13.

SEE ALSO: The Metropolitan Museum of Art at home (GLAH 2:I3).

Africa

I620 Africa: the art of a continent. Ed. by Tom Phillips. Munich, Prestel, [1995]. 613p. il. (part col.), maps.

Catalog of the exhibition, Royal Academy of Arts, London (1996), and other locations. This monumental art exhibition and catalog includes beautiful colored plates of the whole of Africa, from Egypt to Ife to Great Zimbabwe.

Contents: Why Africa? Why art?, by Kwame Anthony Appiah; Europe, African art, and the uncanny, by Henry Louis Gates, Jr[.]; The African past, by Peter Garlake; Ancient Egypt and Nubia, by Edna R. Russman and László Török; Eastern Africa, by John Mack; Southern Africa, by Patricia Davison; Central Africa, by Daniel Biebuyck and Frank Herreman; West Africa and the Guinea coast, by John Picton; Sahel and Savanna, by René A. Bravmann; Northern Africa, by Timothy A. Insoll, M. Rachel MacLean, Nadia Erzini, Rachel Ward.

Bibliography, p.597–613.

I621 Africa: the art of a continent: 100 works of power and beauty. [N.Y.], Guggenheim Museum, [1996]. 191p. il., 100 col. plates, map.

U.S. ed. of the preceding title, with fewer plates and different texts. "The first major art exhibition ever to present Africa as an entity unbroken by the Sahara."—*Pref.*

Contents: Why Africa? Why art?, by Kwame Anthony Appiah; Putting northern Africa back into Africa, by Ekpo Eyo; Historical contacts and cultural interaction, Sub-Saharan Africa, northern Africa, the Muslim world, and southern Europe, tenth–nineteenth century A.D., by Peter Mark; Europe, African art, and the uncanny, by Henry Louis Gates, Jr.; Enduring myths of African art, by Suzanne Preston Blier; Ancient Egypt and Nubia; Eastern Africa; Southern Africa; Central Africa; Western Africa and the Guinea Coast; Sahel and Savanna; Northern Africa.

Selected bibliography, p.187–90.

I622 African aesthetics. The Carlo Monzino Collection. [By] Susan Mullin Vogel. Photographs by Mario Carrieri. [N.Y., Center for African Art, 1986]. xxiii, 224p. 179 il. (part col.), map.

Catalog of the exhibition, Center for African Art (1986). A handsomely illustrated handbook of a significant collection.

Contents: African aesthetics; Catalogue; Technical data.

Bibliography, 221–24. Index, p.[227].

I623 African art in Southern Africa: from tradition to township. Ed. by Anitra Nettleton and David Hammond-Tooke. [Johannesburg], Ad. Donker, [1989]. 252p. il. (part col.), maps.

The editors present a history of aspects of black South African art in which form and technique are emphasized ranging from traditional to modern art.

Contents: (1) Introduction by Anitra Nettleton and David Hammond-Tooke; (2) Reflections on African art, by David Hammond-Tooke; (3) " . . . In what degree . . . (they) are possessed of ornamental taste": a history of the writing on black art in South Africa, by Anitra Nettleton; (4) San rock art, by J. D. Lewis-Williams; (5) Carvers, kings and thrones in nineteenth-century Zululand, by Sandra Klopper; (6) The crocodile does not leave the pool: Venda court arts, by Anitra Nettleton; (7) The art of the Lobedu, by Patricia Davison; (8) Art and communication: Ndzundza Ndebele wall decorations in the Transvaal, by Elizabeth Ann Schneider; (9) Ways of seeing, ways of buying; images of tourist art and culture expression in contemporary beadwork, by Eleanor Preston-Whyte and Jo Thorpe; (10) Township art: context, form and meaning, by Frances Verstraete; (11) A change of regime: art and ideology in Rhodesia and Zimbabwe, by Marion Arnold; (12) "Garden of Eden or political landscape?": street art in Mamelodi and other townships, by Steven Sack; (13) The Polly Street art scene, by David Koloane.

Notes and references, p.231–52.

I624 African art studies: the state of the discipline. Washington, D.C., National Museum of African Art, [1990]. 143p. il.

A symposium held in conjunction with the opening of the National Museum of African Art (1987) representing papers by American, European, and African scholars.

Contents: Introduction, by Roy Sieber; The history of African art studies, by Adrian A. Gerbrands; African art studies today, by Henry John Drewal; The future of African art studies: an African perspective, by Rowland Abíodun; African art studies at the crossroads: an American perspective, by Suzanne Preston Blier; Discussion of papers: response by Ekpo Eyo, Mikelle Smith Omari, Simon Ottenberg, John Pemberton III.

Includes bibliographies.

I625 African masterpieces and selected works from Munich: the Staatliches Museum für Völkerkunde. By Maria Kecskési. N.Y., Center for African Art, [1987]. vii, 425p. il. (part col.), maps.

Catalog of the exhibition, Center for African Art, New York (1987), and other locations. The Staatliches Museum für Völkerkunde has one of the major African art collections in the world including more than 20,000 objects from which 450 are illustrated in this catalog.

Contents: Foreword, by Susan Vogel; Western Sudan; The Guinea Coast; Yoruba art and culture; Ancient Benin: history and art of a kingdom; Cameroon, Gabon; Cameroon Grasslands and coast; Art of the western Cameroon forest; Art of the southern Cameroon forest; Central Africa; The kingdoms of lower Zaire; The Kuba empire and its neighbors; The Luba empire and borderland; Eastern and southern Africa.

Bibliography, p.418–25.

I626 African material culture. Ed. by Mary Jo Arnoldi, Christraud M. Geary, and Kris L. Hardin. Bloomington, Indiana Univ. Pr., [1996]. 369p. il. maps.

Papers from an international, interdisciplinary conference and workshop held at the Rockefeller Study and Conference Center, Bellagio, Italy. Assessment of and new approaches to the study of African material culture.

Contents: (1) Technological style and the making of culture: three Kono contexts of production, by Kris L. Hardin; (2) Magical iron technology in the Cameroon grassfields, by Michael Rowlands and Jean-Pierre Warnier; (3) When nomads settle: changing technologies of building and transport and the production of architectural form among the Gabra, the Rendille, and the Somalis, by Labelle Prussin; (4) Ceramics from the Upemba Depression: a diachronic study, by Kanimba Misago; (5) Objects and people: relationships and transformations in the culture of the Bambala, by Kazadi Ntole; (6) Sticks, self, and society in Booran Oromo: a symbolic interpretation, by Aneesa Kassam and Gemetchu Megerssa; (7) Material narratives and the negotiation of identities through objects in Malian theatre, by Mary Jo Arnoldi; (8) The consumption of an African modernity, by Michael Rowlands; (9) Household objects and the philosophy of Igbo social space, by Chike Aniakor; (10) Hoes and clothes in a Luo household: changing consumption in a colonial economy, 1906–1936, by Margaret Jean Jay; (11) The passive object and the tribal paradigm: colonial museography in French West Africa, by Philip L. Ravenhill; (12) Art, politics, and the transformation of meaning: Bamum art in the twentieth century, by Christraud M. Geary; (13) Mami Wata shrines: exotica and the construction of self, by Henry John Drewal; (14) Zaïrian popular painting as commodity and as communication, by Bogumil Jewsiewicki.

Index, p.359–69.

I627 Afrika. [Bearb. des Katalogs, Renate Wente-Lukas.] [Offenbach am Main, Deutsches Ledermuseum, 1988]. 227p. il. (part col.), maps. (Kataloge, 3)

Catalog of the exhibition, Deutsches Ledermuseum (1988).

Devoted to the collection and exhibition of leather goods from around the world, this museum has featured its African collection in this catalog including some non-leather objects, such as woven and carved wooden objects. Leather technology, tools and processes, aesthetics and decoration, and functions of objects are covered.

Contents: Herkunft und datierung der Objekte; Definitionen; Die Savannenregion Westafrikas; Eisen und Schmied; Der Markt; Die Tuareg in der zentralen Sahara; Die Mauren in der westlichen Sahara; Bergbauern in Nordkamerun; Lederkunst im Maghreb—Marokko, Algerien, Tunesien; Christliches Äthiopien; Viehzüchter Nordost-, Ost- und Südafrikas; Geheimbundwesen im südnigerianischen Urwald; Musikinstrumente.

Ausgewählte Literatur, p.222–25.

I628 Akan transformations: problems in Ghanaian art history. Ed. by Doran H. Ross and Timothy F. Garrard. [Los Angeles], Museum of Cultural History, UCLA, [1983]. 111p. 139 il., map. (Monograph Series, Museum of Cultural History, UCLA, no. 21)

Catalog of the exhibition, Museum of Cultural History Gallery, UCLA (1983). "This anthology is partially designed as a supplement to the Museum of Cultural History's publication, The Arts of Ghana [GLAH 2:I649]."—*Introd.*

Contents: Akan Kuduo: form and function, by Raymond A. Silverman; A corpus of 15th to 17th century Akan brasscastings, by Timothy F. Garrard; Four unusual Forowa from the Museum of Cultural History, by Doran H. Ross; The Akan double-bladed sword: a case of Islamic origins, by Doran H. Ross; Akan Pseudo-weights of European origin, by Timothy F. Garrard; Modern antiquities: a study of a Kumase workshop, by Doran H. Ross and Raphael X. Reichert; Three unconventional objects from Ghana, by E. Nii Quarcoopome; Catalogue, by Betsy D. Quick and Doran H. Ross.

Bibliography, p.108–10.

I629 Arnoldi, Mary Jo. Playing with time: art and performance in central Mali. Bloomington, Indiana Univ. Pr., [1995]. xx, 227p. il. (part col.)

A scholarly study of a significantly large group of objects used in the puppet masquerade.

Contents: (1) A Bamana Tonko festival, Kirango, June 1979; (2) The definition and history of the Segou puppet masquerade theatre; (3) The Sego bò's expressive forms; (4) Time, timing, and the performance process; (5) Bringing the past into the present in masquerade theatre; (6) The production of meaning and the play of interpretations; Conclusion: Kuma man nyi; Kumabaliya fana man nyi.

Glossary, p.205–08. Masquerade list [Bamana name and English name], p.209–11. Bibliography, p.213–20. Index, p.221–27.

I630 ———, and Kreamer, Christine Mullen. Crowning achievements: African arts of dressing the head. With contrib. by Michael Oládèjo Afoláyan . . . [et al.] Los Angeles, Fowler Museum of Cultural History, UCLA, [1995]. 192p. il. (part col.)

Catalog of the exhibition, Fowler Museum of Cultural History, UCLA (1995).

Contents: (1) Introduction, by Mary Jo Arnoldi; (2) Focus on twelve African hats, by Mary Jo Arnoldi and Christine Mullen Kreamer; (3) Crowning glories: the head and hair, by Mary Jo Arnoldi; Coiffure moderne: a gallery of African hair styles, 1970–1990; (4) Practical beauty: headgear for daily wear, by Christine Mullen Kreamer; (5) Spectacular hats for special occasions, by Christine Mullen Kreamer; (6) Wrapping the head, by Mary Jo Arnoldi; (7) Yoruba headties, by Michael Oládèjo Afoláyan and Betty Wass; (8) Lega hats: hierarchy and status, by Elisabeth L. Cameron; (9) Headdresses and the titleholding among the Kuba, by Patricia Darish and David A. Binkley; (10) Transatlantic influences in headwear, by Christine Mullen Kreamer.

Bibliography, p.185–91.

I631 Art and ambiguity: perspectives on the Brenthurst Collection of Southern African art. [Johannesburg], Johannesburg Art Gallery, 1991. 197p. il. (part col.)

Catalog of the exhibition, Johannesburg Art Gallery (1991).

Contents: Ambiguity, style and meaning, by Patricia Davison; Looking from the outside: the historical context of the Brenthurst Collection of Southern African art, by Johan van Schalkwyk; Tradition, authenticity and tourist sculpture in 19th and 20th century South Africa, by Anitra Nettleton; Headrests: Tsonga types and variations, by Rayda Becker; "Zulu" headrests and figurative carvings: the Brenthurst Collection and the art of South-east Africa, by Sandra Klopper; Southern African beadwork: issues of classification and collecting, by Diane Levy; Public pleasures: smoking and snuff-taking in Southern Africa, by Ann Wanless; Map of Southern Africa showing language and political groupings (c.1900–1950), by W. D. Hammond-Tooke.

I632 Art and healing of the Bakongo. Commented by themselves: minkisi from the Laman collection. Kikongo texts trans. and ed. by Wyatt MacGaffey. Stockholm, Folkens Museum—Etnografiska, [Distr. in North America by Indiana Univ. Pr., 1991]. viii, 184p. map. (Monograph series, Folkens museum etnografiska, no.16)

"The forty-five Kongo minkisi described . . . were selected . . . because for each of them a text has been found, written in KiKongo, that describes either the identical object or one of the same name and appearance, from the same region in Lower Congo (Lower Zaire)." —*Introd.*

Contents: Divination; Healing; Wealth and warfare; Attack.

Indexes: Minkisi by station of origin, p.155–64; Minkisi by acquisition number, p.165–74; Master list of Minkisi, p.175–84.

I633 Art/artifact: African art in anthropology collections. With essays by Arthur Danto . . . [et al.] Introd. by Susan Vogel. Photographs by Jerry L. Thompson. N.Y., Center for African Art, [1988]. 195p. il. (part col.), map.

Catalog of the exhibition, Center for African Art (1988), and other locations. This book is "an invaluable new resource on anthropology, museums, art history, and African material culture."—*Review*, African arts, v.22, no.1, Nov., 1988, p.14.

Contents: Artifact and art, by Arthur C. Danto; Art and anthropology on a sliding scale, by Richard M. Gramly; The Buffalo Museum of Science collection; "Things African prove to be a favorite theme": the African collection at Hampton University, by Jeanne Zeidler and Mary Lou Hultgren; Hampton University collection; Art as evidence: a brief history of the American Museum of Natural History African collection, by Enid Schildkrout; American Museum of Natural History collection.

Index, p.194.

I634 Art of Côte d'Ivoire from the collections of the Barbier-Mueller Museum. Ed. by Jean Paul Barbier. Authors, Jean-Noël Loucou . . . [et al.] [Geneva], Barbier-Mueller Museum, 1993. 2v. il. (part col.), maps.

Scholarly essays and catalog of a significant collection of West African art.

Contents: (1) Peoples and cultures of Côte d'Ivoire, by Jean-Noël Loucou; The Senufo, by Anita Glaze; The Poro of the Senufo, by Gilbert Bochet; Face masks from the Senufo region, by Timothy F. Garrard; A speculative journey in the Senufo lands, by Jean Paul Barbier; Bondoukou: the artistry of a city and countryside, by René Bravmann; The peoples of Western Côte d'Ivoire, by Marie-Noël Verger-Fèvre; Masks in the Dan area of Côte d'Ivoire, by Marie-Noël Verger-Fèvre; We masks, by Pierre Harter; The art of metal in Western Côte d'Ivoire, by Elze Bruyninx; The Guro, by Ariane Deluz; Art of the Yohure, by Alain-Michel Boyer; The Baule: an introduction, by Timothy F. Garrard; Art of the Baule, by Alain-Michel Boyer; The Lagoons Peoples, by Monica Blackmun Visonà; The arts of metal in Côte d'Ivoire, by Timothy F. Garrard; Concluding remarks, by Jean Paul Barbier. (2) Catalogue.

Vernacular glossary, v.2, p.193–210. Bibliography, v.2, p.211–18. Index [for both volumes], v.2, p.219–29.

I635 Bacquart, Jean-Baptiste. The tribal arts of Africa. N.Y., Thames and Hudson, 1998. 240p. il. (chiefly col.)

"This selection ranges widely and aims to create a work that is both accessible and at the same time useful to professionals. It includes objects that are representative and characteristic of traditional artistic production throughout Africa south of the Sahara."—*Introd.* Includes 865 illustrations, 195 in color.

Bibliography, p.232. Major museums, p.233–35. Major dealers, p.236. Glossary, p.237. Index, p.239–40.

I636 Barley, Nigel. Foreheads of the dead: an anthropological view of Kalabari ancestral screens. Washington, D.C., Published for the National Museum of African Art by the Smithsonian Institution Pr., [1988]. 88p. il. (part col.)

Catalog of the exhibition, National Museum of African Art (1988–89). This catalog is a "well illustrated, comprehensive, and definitive monograph."—*Review*, International journal of African historical studies, v.22, no.3, 1989, p. 521.

Contents: Foreheads of the dead: an anthropological view of Kalabari ancestral screens; Catalogue raisonné of Kalabari ancestral screens in museum collections.

Bibliography, p.86–88.

I637 Ben-Amos, Paula Girshick. The art of Benin. [London], British Museum Pr., [1995]. 2d ed. 128p. 100 il. (part col.), maps.

The standard work on the art of the Benin in its historical, religious, and social context.

Contents: Art, history, and politics; Art, belief and ritual.

Bibliography, p.123–26. Index, p.127–28.

I638 Biebuyck, Daniel P. The arts of Zaire. Berkeley, Univ. of California Pr., [1985–86]. 2v. il., col. plates.

The first in a series of volumes "that will deal with several large regions of Zaire; it also includes an introduction on the history of Central African art studies."—*Pref. to v.1.*

Contents: (1) Southwestern Zaire; (2) Eastern Zaire.

Bibliography, v.1, p.[255]–99, v.2, p.285–301. Index, v.1, p.[301]–13, v.2, p.[303]–14.

I639 ______. Lega culture: art, initiation, and moral philosophy among a central African people. Berkeley, Univ. of California Pr., [1973]. xxiii, 268p., 110 plates, map.

The standard work on the art and culture of the Lega.

Contents: (1) The Lega; (2) Lega culture; (3) The Bwami association; (4) The art of Bwami; Appendix I: Lineages of Banasalu Clan; Appendix II: Initiations into Lutumbo Lwa Kindi in Banasalu Clan.

Bibliography, p.241–51. Index, p.253–68.

I640 Bildende Kunst der Gegenwart in Senegal = Anthologie des arts plastiques contemporains au Sénégal = Anthology of contemporary fine arts in Senegal. Ed. by Friedrich Axt and El Hadji Moussa Babacar Sy. Introd. by Léopold Sédar Senghor. Frankfurt am Main, Museum für Völkerkunde, 1989. 278p. il. (part col.)

This trilingual anthology of modern Sénégalese art and artists is a major contribution to documenting the post-Independence period in Sénégal.

Contents: The School of Fine Arts of Senegal, by Kalidou Sy; The Ecole Normale Supérieure d'Education Artistique, by Kalidou Sy; The Musée Dynamique, by Ousmane Sow Huchard; The Galerie Nationale d'Art, by El Hadji M.B.Sy; The workshop of Senegalese decorative art, by Anne Jean-Bart; The salons of the Senegalese artists, by Ousmane Sow Huchard; The exhibitions of Senegalese contemporary art abroad, by Djibril Tamsir Niane; Independent exhibitions of Senegalese contemporary art at home and abroad, by Friedrich Axt; Artists' associations in Senegal, by Ben Mouhamed Diop; The "Cité of the Artists" and the "Village of Arts," by El Hadji M.B.Sy; The social and economic situation of the artists of the "Ecole de Dakar," by Issa Samb; Criticism of representation, by Issa Samb; Painting, by Pierre Lods; Sculpture, by Anne Jean-Bart; Engraving, by Kalidou Sy; Ceramics, by El Hadji M.B.Sy; Batik, by Aïssa Djionne; Glass painting, by Serigne NDiaye; Forty artists from Senegal; Appendix: The Senegal, by Friedrich Axt; The collection of contemporary Senegalese art of the Museum of Ethnology in Frankfort/Main, FRG.

I641 Blier, Suzanne Preston. Royal arts of Africa: the majesty of form. London, Laurence King, 1998. 272p. il. (part col.), maps.

Seeks to provide a "meta-narrative" for Africa's kingdoms, while taking into account the "complexity (and variability) of its underlying fabric."—*Introd.*

Contents: Introduction: paradoxes of rule; (1) The Benin Kingdom: politics, religion, and natural order; (2) Yoruba and Dahomey: divine authority and the arts of royal history; (3) The Asante Kingdom: the golden age of Ghana; (4) Cameroon grasslands: royal art patronage in contexts of change; (5) Kongo and Kuba: the art of rulership display; Conclusion: the continuing vitality of Africa's courtly arts.

Timeline, p.252–59. Glossary, p.260. Bibliography, p.261–65. Index, p.268–72.

I642 Boone, Sylvia Ardyn. Radiance from the waters: ideals of feminine beauty in Mende art. Photographs by Sylvia Ardyn Boone and Rebecca Busselle. New Haven, Yale Univ. Pr., [1986]. xxii, 281p. il. map. (Yale publications in the history of art, 34)

"This work will stand as a major contribution to the study of African art and the Sowo mask in particular. It is recommended for collections not only of African art but also women's art and aesthetics."—*Review*, Art documentation, v.6, no.1, spring 1987, p.45.

Contents: Prologue: Conducting research into Mende art; (1) Mende history and culture: a brief overview; (2) The Sande society; (3) Kpanguima: the world of beauty that Sande makes; (4) Physical and metaphysical aspects of Mende feminine beauty; (5) Sowo: the good made visible.

Glossary, p.249–51. Selected bibliography, p.253–70. Index, p.273–81.

I643 Bourgeois, Arthur P. Art of the Yaka and Suku. Traduction et adaptation en français, J. B. Donne. Meudon, France, Alain et Françoise Chaffin, [1984]. 271p. il. (part col.), map.

Text in English and French. Devoted to the art and society of a major Southern Savanna society, this book "should become the definitive work of the decade on Yaka and Suku art."—*Review*, African arts, v.18, no.4, Aug. 1985, p.21.

Contents: Geography, anthropology, history; Political and social life; Material culture; Style areas; Related styles and influences.

Glossary, p.268–69. Bibliography, p.270–71.

I644 Bravmann, René A. African Islam. [Washington, D.C.], Smithsonian Institution Pr., [1983]. 120p. 91 il. [2] leaves of col. plates, map.

Catalog of the exhibition, National Museum of African Art (1983).

One of the most comprehensive volumes on the complex artistic interactions of Islam and the cultures of Black Africa. A wide variety of Islamic-influenced artforms and decorated utilitarian objects are illustrated.

Contents: (1) A passion for the words of God; (2) God's secrets—shaped in silence; (3) Victory from Allah, battles waged with words and weapons; (4) Ramadan, Islamic holy days and an African sensibility; (5) al-Buraq, African variations on an ancient Islamic theme; (6) Islamic patterns, a penchant for beauty and privacy; (7) The Swahili coast, a bazaar of forms and styles.

Bibliography, p.118–20.

I645 Catalogue: ten years of collecting (1979–1989). Standard Bank Foundation Collection of African Art, University Art Galleries Collection of African Art, and selected works from the University Ethnological Museum Collection. Ed. by David Hammond-Tooke and Anitra Nettleton. [Catalogue compiled by Rayda Becker]. Johannesburg, Univ. of the Witwatersrand, Johannesburg Art Galleries, 1989. 139p. il. (part col.), map.

Catalog of the exhibition, Gertrude Posel Gallery and Studio Gallery, Senate House (Johannesburg) (1989), and other locations. Amply illustrated, this catalog documents a major South African collection which includes a great variety of artforms.

Contents: Part 1: (1) Venda art, by Anitra Nettleton; (2) Tsonga-Shangana beadwork and figures, by Rayda Becker, Anitra Nettleton; (3) Art of the Pedi and Ntwane, by Anitra Nettleton, David Hammond-Tooke; (4) Ndebele beadwork, by Diane Levy; (5) The art of traditionalists in Zululand-Natal, by Sandra Klopper; (6) The beadwork of the Cape Nguni, by Anitra Nettleton, Sipho Ndabambi, David Hammond-Tooke; (7) Transitional sculpture, by Elizabeth Dell; (8) From country to city: the development of an urban art, by Steven Sack. Part 2: (1) Catalogue of holdings of Southern African material, by Diana L. Newman, Fiona Rankin-Smith, Rayda Becker.

I646 Collection Barbier-Mueller. African art from the Barbier-Mueller Collection, Geneva. Ed. by Werner Schmalenbach. With essays by Enrico Castelli . . . [et al.] Photographs by Roger Asselberghs. Trans. from the French, Jeffrey Haight. Trans. from the German, Russell Stockman. [München], Prestel, [1988]. 314p. 200 il. (part col.), maps.

Originally published in German as the catalog for the exhibition, Kunstsammlung Nordrhein-Westfalen, Düsseldorf (1988), and other locations.

A beautifully illustrated catalog of a major African art collection with essays and catalog documentation by noted scholars.

Contents: Toward an aesthetic in Black African art, by Werner Schmalenbach; Toward an anthropology of Black African art, by Louis Perrois. Catalogue: The Sudanese Savanna, by Christopher Roy; North and West Guinea Coast, by William Siegmann; East Guinea Coast, by William Siegmann; Atlantic Equatorial Africa, by Louis Perrois; The Zaire Basin, by François Neyt; East Africa, by Enrico Castelli and Gaetano Speranza.

Bibliography, p.309–12. Index of tribes and cultures, p.313–[15].

I647 Cole, Herbert M. Icons: ideals and power in the art of Africa. Washington, D.C., Published for the National Museum of African Art by the Smithsonian Institution Pr., [1989]. 207p. 206 il. (part col.), maps.

Catalog of the exhibition, National Museum of African Art (1989–1990). Provides "the combination of a simple memorable thesis, a careful reliance on recent interpretive research, and accessible level of exposition, and numerous, richly varied illustrations."—*Review*, International journal of African historical studies, v.24, 1991, p.678.

Contents: (1) Introduction: icons, ideals, and powers; (2) Useful images: the life of art in Africa; (3) Iconic conventions: the ideology of form; (4) Two as one: the male and female couple; (5) Maternity and abundance: the woman and child; (6) Hunters, warriors, and heroes: the forceful male; (7) Riders of power: the mounted leader; (8) Ambiguous aliens: the stranger in African art history; (9) Change and continuity: the icons in twentieth-century art.

Bibliography, p.196–207.

I648 ———. Mbari: art and life among the Owerri Igbo. Bloomington, Indiana Univ. Pr., [1982]. xx, 261p. il. (part col.) (Traditional arts of Africa)

The summation of field work and extensive research, this definitive study shows Mbari art to be a highly distinctive and very localized artform.

Contents: (1) Introduction: the setting; (2) The gods and the people; (3) The people and processes of Mbari; (4) Form; (5) Inspiration, individuality, and aesthetics; (6) Meaning; (7) Conclusions. Glossary, p.221–24; Appendix A: Tree altars; Appendix B: Ndimgbe names; Appendix C: Master list of Mbari subjects in sculpture; Appendix D: Mbari house at Obaku, Oratta clan, Owerri.

Bibliography, p.237–42. Index, p.259–61.

I649 ———, and Ross, Doran H. The arts of Ghana. Los Angeles, Museum of Cultural History, UCLA, 1977. xv, 230p. 401 il. (part col.), maps.

Catalog of the exhibition, Frederick S. Wight Gallery, UCLA (1977), and other locations. "This is the first comprehensive exhibition dealing with Ghanaian art to be organized. Over 500 pieces from 102 museums, galleries, and private collections" were included.—*Foreword.* The catalog is abundantly illustrated and thoroughly documented.

Contents: (1) Introduction to Ghana; (2) History; (3) Akan arts; (4) Personal adornment; (5) Domestic and utilitarian arts; (6) Architecture; (7) Cult arts; (8) State arts; (9) Secular arts of voluntary organizations; (10) Festivals; (11) Art and history in Ghana.

Bibliography, p.222–27.

I650 Contemporary art of Africa. Ed. by André Magnin with Jacques Soulillou. [N.Y.], Abrams, 1996. 192p. il. (part col.), maps.

This book provides biographical sketches, illustrations, and brief essays about the painting and sculpture of sixty sub-Saharan artists.

Contents: Territory; Frontier; World.

Additional artists of sub-Saharan Africa, p.180–82. Glossary, p.183–84. Selected bibliography, p.185–86. Index, p.188–91.

I651 Cornet, Joseph. Art Royal Kuba. Milano, Edizioni Sipiel, [1982]. 343p. 353 il. (part col.), maps.

Extensively illustrated, this comprehensive study covers Kuba masks and masquerades, regalia, royal burial ceremonies, and architecture of the capital city.

Contents: (1) Géographie et histoire; (2) La personne du roi; (3) La statuaire royale; (4) La capitale royale; (5) Le système décoratif; (6) Les costumes; (7) Masques et danses; (8) Le muyuum ou la dynastie en attente; (9) Les regalia; (10) Mort et funérailles du roi; (11) Conclusion.

Bibliographie, by Bushabu Piema Kwete, p.321–29. Index des noms, p.331–39.

I652 Corps sculptés, corps parés, corps masqués: chefs-d'oeuvre de Côte-d'Ivoire. Paris, Ministére de la Coopération et du Développement, 1989. 249p. il. (part col.), map.

Catalog of the exhibition, Galeries Nationales du Grand Palais (1989). This comprehensive exhibition of the arts of Côte d'Ivoire was a major cooperative undertaking between the French and Ivoirien governments. Ivoirien masks, figures, regalia, and textiles from all regions of the country are represented.

Contents: (1) Filiations, identités (quand le corps des dieux, des génies ou des ancêtres reproduit celui des hommes vivants); (2) Puissances incarnées (quand le corps se masque et l'identité se dédouble); (3) Pouvoirs signifiés (quand le corps se pare et signifie l'authorité, la beauté, la richesse ou l'influence).

Bibliographie, p.246–[50].

I653 Dowson, Thomas A. Rock engravings of Southern Africa. Foreword by David Lewis-Williams. [Johannesburg], Witwatersrand Univ. Pr., [1992]. xii, 124p. il. (part col.), maps.

"This is certainly a major book, a landmark because of the lack of other books on engravings."—*Review*, African arts, v.27, no.3, July 1994, p.20.

Contents: Recording rock engravings; Contacting the spirit world; Capturing the rain; Visions of the spirit world; Sensations of the spirit world; Animals; Working with the rock; The individual engraver; A Damaraland Valley.

Bibliography, p.123–24.

I654 Drewal, Henry John, and Pemberton, John, III. Yoruba: nine centuries of African art and thought. With Rowland Abiodun. Ed. by Allen Wardwell. N.Y., The Center for African Art in assoc. with Abrams, [1989]. 256p. 275 il. (part col.), maps.

Catalog of the exhibition, The Center for African Art (1989), and other locations. Written by eminent scholars, this book is an authoritative and comprehensive survey of Yoruba art.

Contents: (1) The Yoruba world, by Henry John Drewal, John Pemberton III, and Rowland Abiodun; (2) Ife: origins of art and civilization, by Henry John Drewal; (3) The stone images of Esie, by John Pemberton III; (4) The kingdom of Owo, by Rowland Abiodun; (5) Art and ethos of the Ijebu, by Henry John Drewal; (6) The Oyo empire, by John Pemberton III; (7) The carvers of the northeast, by John Pemberton III; (8) The artists of the western kingdoms, by Henry John Drewal; (9) The river that never rests, by Henry John Drewal, John Pemberton III, and Rowland Abiodun.

Glossary of Yoruba words, p.248–49. Bibliography, p.250–55. Index, p.256.

I655 Duchâteau, Armand. Benin. Royal art of Africa from the Museum für Völkerkunde, Vienna. [München], Prestel, 1994. 136p. 128 il. (part col.), maps.

Catalog of the exhibition, Museum of Fine Arts, Houston (1994), and other locations. "Among the oldest and finest African collections in Europe, the Benin holdings of the Museum für Völkerkunde" are beautifully illustrated and documented "in this comprehensive and detailed volume."—*Foreword.* This catalog is substantially the same as Duchâteau's Benin, Art royal d'Afrique, Brussels, Crédit Communal, 1990.

Contents: The history of the kingdom of Benin; The court hierarchy; The art of brasscasting; The art of Benin and its symbolism; The history of the Benin collection in Vienna.

Glossary, p.121–22. Bibliography, p.133–36.

I656 Elephant: the animal and its ivory in African culture. Ed. by Doran H. Ross. Los Angeles, Fowler Museum of Cultural History, UCLA, [1992]. xxi, 415p. il. (part col.), maps.

Catalog of the exhibition, Fowler Museum of Cultural History, UCLA (1992). Lavishly illustrated and complemented by the essays of noted scholars, this monumental study spans the depiction of the elephant from the prehistoric period to the twentieth century.

Contents: (1) Imagining elephants: an overview, by Doran H. Ross; (2) The African elephant in its environment, by Jeheskel Shoshani; (3) Proboscideans, hominids, and prehistory, by John A. Van Couvering; (4) Talking (gray) heads: elephant as metaphor in African myth and folklore, by Donald J. Cosentino; (5) Sama Ba: the elephant in Bamana art, by Mary Jo Arnoldi and Kate Ezra; (6) Of pachyderms and power: ivory and the elephant in the art of Central Côte d'Ivoire, by Philip L. Ravenhill; (7) More than meets the eye: elephant memories among the Akan, by Doran H. Ross; (8) The elephant and its ivory in Benin, by Barbara Winston Blackmun; (9) Image and indeterminacy: elephants and ivory, by Henry John Drewal; (10) The Igbo: prestige ivory and elephant spirit power, by Herbert M. Cole; (11) Elephants, ivory, and chiefs: the elephant and the arts of the Cameroon grassfields, by Christaud M. Geary; (12) Elephants, ivory and art: Duala objects of persuasion, by Rosalinde G. Wilcox; (13) The teeth of Nyim: the elephant and ivory in Kuba art, by David A. Binkley; (14) The stampeding of elephants: elephant imprints on Lega thought, by Elisabeth Cameron; (15) Ivory from Zariba country to the land of the Zinj, by Sidney Littlefield Kasfir; (16) Under the sun:

elephants in Ethiopian painting, by Girma Fisseha; (17) The ivory trade in Africa: an historical overview, by Edward A. Alpers; (18) The material culture of ivory outside Africa, by David A. Shayt; (19) Epilogue: the future of elephants, real and imagined, by Doran H. Ross.
References cited, p.397–413.

I657 Eyo, Ekpo, and Willett, Frank. Treasures of ancient Nigeria. [Ed. by Rollyn O. Krichbaum. Photographer, Dirk Bakker. Designer, Betty Binns.] N.Y., Knopf in assoc. with The Detroit Institute of Arts, 1980. xiii, [162]p. il. (part col.), map.
Catalog of the exhibition, The Detroit Institute of Arts (1980), and other locations. The standard work on the antiquities of Nigeria.
Contents: Preface, by Michael Kan; Introduction, by Ekpo Eyo; Nigerian art: an overview, by Frank Willett.
Selected bibliography, p.159–[62].

I658 Felix, Marc Leo. Mwana hiti: life and art of the matrilineal Bantu of Tanzania: Leben und Kunst der matrilinearen Bantu von Tansania. [München, Fred Jahn, 1990]. 504p. il. maps.
An extensive treatment of the art of the matrilineal peoples of east-central Tanzania. The most comprehensive resource on the traditional arts of any East African people to date. Text in English and German.
Contents: A short history of the Bantu; The etymology of Mwana hiti; Linguistics; Ethnography of the Zaramo and Kwere peoples of Eastern Tanzania, by Kathryn Weinrich; Mwana hiti in Zaramoland, by Kathryn Weinrich; An idea's journey, by Kathryn Weinrich; Who made what?; A stylistic and morphological analysis of trunk figures, by Niangi Batuwkisi; Stylistic zones of the Tanzanian hinterland, by Niangi Batuwkisi; Stylistic subdivision of African art, by Niangi Batuwkisi; "Masters of style", by Niangi Batuwkisi; Stylistic diagnoses, by Niangi Batuwkisi; Typology and taxonomy; Typology table; Multivariate analysis of typological data, by Bernard Tursch; Post analysis observations, by Bernard Tursch; Typological inventory of the Tanzanian hinterland, by Bernard Tursch; The search for the source, by Bernard Tursch; Youth; Initiation; Maturity; Death; Symbols; Icons; The man on the stool.
Bibliography, p.502–03.

I659 Fischer, Eberhard, and Himmelheber, Hans. The arts of the Dan in West Africa. Fieldwork in collab. with George Wowoa W. Tahmen, Saniquellie, Liberia; and Tiemoko Gba, Man, Ivory Coast. Photographs of objects by Isabelle Wettstein and Brigitte Kauf. Zürich, Museum Rietberg, 1984. 192p. 248 il. map.
This book is an enlarged ed. of the catalog that was published in German to accompany the exhibition "Die Kunst der Dan" organized by the Rietberg Museum at the Helmhaus in Zürich. It is a major scholarly work on the art of the Dan people of Liberia (including the culturally related Kran and Gere).
Contents: (1) The Dan: habitat and community; (2) Cosmology; (3) The masquerades of the Dan: an introduction; (4) The masquerades of the Dan: a classification; (5) The masquerades of the Dan: epilogue; (6) Other artifacts made of wood; (7) Dan brass-casting; (8) Pottery of the Dan; (9) Murals of the Dan; (10) Artistic tradition among the Dan; (11) Literature (p.191–92).

I660 ———, and Homberger, Lorenz. Die Kunst der Guro, Elfenbeinküste. Zürich, Museum Rietberg, 1985. 312p. 289 il. map.
Catalog of the exhibition, Museum Rietberg, Zürich (1985). Enhanced by numerous field photographs, this work is a valuable survey of the art and culture of the Guro who live in an area of central Côte d'Ivoire.
Contents: (1) Vorwort; (2) Einleitung: zur Dokumentation der Guro-Kultur; (3) Habitat und Gesellschaft; (4) Zur Kunst der Guro; (5) Heute lebende Bildhauer; (6) Werkverfahren der Bildhauer; (7) Masken; (8) Figuren; (9) Webrollenhalter; (10) Löffel; (11) Stühle; (12) Weberei; (13) Töpferei; (14) Schlussbemerkungen; (15) Literaturverzeichnis (p.311–12).

I661 Förster, Till. Die Kunst der Senufo. Museum Rietberg Zürich, aus Schweizer Sammlungen. Texte: Till Förster. Katalog: Lorenz Homberger. Objektfotos: Wettstein + Kauf. Zürich, Museum Rietberg, 1988. 126p. il. map.
Catalog of the exhibition, Museum Rietberg, Zürich (1988). The inclusion of numerous field photographs makes this an especially valuable survey of the art of the Senufo of West Africa.
Contents: (1) Einleitung; (2) Brücken zwischen den Lebensstufen; (3) Die Auseinanderstetzung mit der Wildnis; (4) Haushaltgegenstände; (5) Anmerkungen; (6) Bibliographie (p.122–23); (7) Glossar der Senar-Begriffe (p.124–26).

I662 Gallois Duquette, Danielle. Dynamique de l'art Bidjogo (Guinée-Bissau): contribution à une anthropologie de l'art des sociétés africaines. [Lisboa], Instituto de investigação Científica Tropical, [1983]. 261p., plates (part col.), maps.
Including numerous field photographs, this book is a valuable survey of the art and culture of Bidjogo, Guinea Bissau.
Contents: (1) Vecteurs de la création en architecture et culture matérielle; (2) Les symboles du pouvoir; (3) Histoire et actualité dans l'expression de l'initiation des hommes; (4) Contexte visuel et dialectique de l'initiation des femmes; (5) Sculpteur, sculpture et sacrifice; (6) Les sculptures sacrées, formes et fonctions; (7) Artisanat et aliénation.
Lexique Bidjogo, p.237–39. Lexique Creole, p.241–42. Bibliographie, p.251–61.

I663 Garlake, Peter S. Great Zimbabwe. [N.Y.], Thames and Hudson, [1973]. 224p. il., 17 col. plates, maps. (New aspects of antiquity)
One of the standard works on the civilization of Great Zimbabwe and its archaeological ruins
Contents: (1) The architecture of the ruins; (2) Early exploration; (3) The first investigations; (4) Archaeological excavations; (5) Crafts, symbols and trade at Great Zimbabwe; (6) The archaeological background; (7) Traditions and history; (8) Towards a history of Great Zimbabwe.
Bibliography, p.211–14. Index, p.220–24.

I664 Geary, Christraud M. Images from Bamum: German colonial photography at the court of King Njoya, Cameroon, West Africa, 1902–1915. Washington, D.C., Published for the National Museum of African Art by the Smithsonian Institution Pr., [1988]. 151p. 88 il. map.

Catalog of the exhibition, National Museum of African Art (1988). "A systematic study of a corpus of images taken in one place over a sustained period of time" and documents "the flourishing visual traditions and imposing architectural structures of Bamum."—*Foreword.*

Contents: Bamum before 1900: the history of a kingdom; (2) Photography in Cameroon: applying a new technology; (3) Prestigious images: the acceptance of photography in Bamum; (4) A myth comes to life: King Njoya in photographs; (5) Glimpses of reality: the palace and its inhabitants; (6) Art and ritual recorded: using photographs in research; (7) Through a woman's eyes: the images of Anna Wuhrmann.

Bibliography, p.146–51.

I665 Gebauer, Paul. Art of Cameroon: with a catalog of the Gebauer Collection of Cameroon Art at the Portland Art Museum and the Metropolitan Museum of Art. Portland, Oregon, Portland Art Museum in assoc. with the Metropolitan Museum of Art, 1979. xx, 375p. il., maps.

Together with numerous field photographs, this book richly documents two collections which are major sources for the understanding of Cameroon art.

Contents: Introduction, by Roy Sieber; (1) The Republic of Cameroon; (2) The Cameroonians; (3) Art in traditional society; (4) The major arts; (5) Royal art; (6) The minor arts; (7) The artist in society; (8) Tradition and change; (9) The Cameroon Collection.

Bibliography, p.369–73.

I666 Gillon, Werner. Collecting African art. With an introd. by William Fagg and photographs by Werner Forman, Jo Furman, and the late Eliot Elisofon. N.Y., Rizzoli in assoc. with Christie's, [1980]. x, 183p. 216 il., col. plates, maps.

Amply illustrated, this work provides a regional approach to African art that highlights particular kinds of artifacts which are produced in given areas.

Contents: African art—an introduction; The regions and tribes of Africa and their styles.

Bibliography, p.175–79. Index, p.180–83.

I667 ______. A short history of African art. N.Y., Facts on File, [1984]. 405p. 257 il. 14 maps.

An introductory text covering a broad range of Africa's artistic heritage.

Contents: Preface, by Roy Sieber; (1) Introduction: an approach to the history of Africa's visual arts; (2) The rock art of Africa; (3) The ancient Nubians; (4) The Nok culture; (5) The kingdoms of the Western Sudan; (6) The art of the Sherbro, Bulom and Kissi; (7) Kanem-Borno and the "Sao" culture; (8) "Kororofa"—the Jukun and related peoples; (9) The art of the Akan; (10) Igbo-Ukwu, the Niger Delta and the Cross River; (11) The Yoruba and their neighbors; (12) Benin—the art of the Edo City State; (13) The art of the southern Savanna; (14) Eastern Africa; (15) Arts of southern Africa.

Bibliography, p.375–94. Index, p.395–405.

I668 Glaze, Anita J. Art and death in Senufo village. Bloomington, Indiana Univ. Pr., [1981]. xvi, 267p. 90 il., col. plates, map. (Traditional arts of Africa)

"This text is essentially a study of meaning, of the nature and purpose of art in the life rhythms of a typical Senufo village."—*Pref.*

Contents: (1) Senufo farmer and artisan groups of the Kufulo region; (2) Art and the women's sphere; (3) Art and the men's sphere; (4) The funeral as synthesis; (5) Conclusion.

Bibliography, p.246–54. Glossary, p.255–60. Index, p.261–67.

I669 Jones, G. I. The art of Eastern Nigeria. N.Y., Cambridge Univ. Pr., 1984. x, 230p. 120 il., map.

Illustrated primarily with field photographs from the 1930s, this is a major study of the styles and forms of West African art, specifically Eastern Nigeria.

Contents: (1) The social and historical background; (2) Domestic arts and crafts; (3) Costume and dress; (4) Religion and magic; (5) Secret societies and their masquerades; (6) Mud sculpture and its derivatives; (7) Architecture; (8) Carving in stone, ivory and wood; (9) Sculpture in wood: the main forms and styles; (10) The Lower Niger and the Delta major styles; (11) The Anang (Ibibio) and Cross River major styles and the Ogoni area; (12) The anomalous and unclassified areas.

Bibliography, p.220–22. Index, p.223–30.

I670 Kennedy, Jean. New currents, ancient rivers: contemporary African artists in a generation of change. Washington, D.C., Smithsonian Institution Pr., [1992]. 204p. il. (part col.)

This survey focuses on nearly 150 sub-Saharan African artists representing diverse media and styles and includes paintings, graphics, tapestries, and sculptures.

Contents: (1) Defining the spirit; (2) Responding to the challenge; (3) Crescent in the hand; (4) Wax and gold: Ethiopia; (5) Creators of myth; (6) Testament.

Bibliography, p.194–99. Index, p.201–04.

I671 Kerchache, Jacques; Paudrat, Jean-Louis; and Stéphan, Lucien. Art of Africa: the principal ethnic groups of African art by Françoise Stoullig-Marin. Trans. from the French by Marjolijn de Jager. [N.Y.], Abrams, [1993]. 619p. 1,069 il. (part col.), maps.

Lavishly illustrated, this is a monumental book which includes a major treatise on African sculpture by Lucien Stéphan. Concentrates on the major sculpture-producing traditions of Western and Central Africa.

Contents: (1) Comparative aesthetics and African sculpture, by Lucien Stéphan; (2) African art: the golden age, An initiatory passage by Jacques Kerchache; (3) The principal ethnic groups, by Françoise Stoullig-Marin.

Glossary, p.596–97. Bibliography, p.598–603. Index, p.604–17.

I672 Kings of Africa. Art and authority in Central Africa: collection Museum für Völkerkunde Berlin. [Ed. by] Erna Beumers, Hans-Joachim Koloss. Utrecht, The Netherlands, Foundation Kings of Africa, [1992?]. 327p. il. (part col.), 190 col. plates, maps.

Catalog of the exhibition, MECC, Maastricht (1992). Lavishly illustrated with extensive notes on each plate, this catalog documents works from a major collection of Central African art and includes essays by eminent scholars in the field.

Contents: History of Central African civilization, by Jan Vansina; Kings in tropical Africa, by Jan Vansina; Central African religion, by Daniel P. Biebuyck; The conditions of appreciation, contemplating a collection of Fang (and Kota) mobiliary art, by James W. Fernandez; Kwifon and Fon in Oku, on kingships in the Cameroon Grasslands, by Hans-Joachim Koloss; The kingdom of Bamum, by Claude Tardits; The regalia of the kingdom of Kongo, 1491–1895, by John Thornton; The Mwanangana Chokwe chief and art (Angola), by Marie-Louise Bastin; The Kuba kingdom (Zaire), by Jan Vansina; Fragments of forsaken glory: Luba royal culture invented and represented (1883–1992) (Zaire), by Mary H. Nooter.

I673 Lawal, Babatunde. The Gẹ̀lẹ̀dé spectacle: art, gender, and social harmony in an African culture. Seattle, Univ. of Washington Pr., [1996]. xxiv, 327p. il., 21 col. plates, maps.

Illustrated with numerous field and museum photographs, this study explores the use of the visual and performing arts to promote social harmony in sub-Saharan Africa, focusing on the Gẹ̀lẹ̀dé, a community festival of masquerade, dance, and song. Systematic coverage of the spectacle's cultural background, historical origins, aesthetics, and iconography are provided.

Contents: (1) African art and social order; (2) Iwà, the dialectics of Yoruba existence; (3) Ipilẹ̀sẹ̀, The roots of Gẹ̀lẹ̀dé; (4) Irépọ̀, gender and social harmony through Gẹ̀lẹ̀dé; (5) Iran, the Gẹ̀lẹ̀dé spectacle; (6) Idira, costume aesthetics and iconography; (7) Igi Gẹ̀lẹ̀dé, sculpted messages on headdresses; (8) Ojú Inú, critical perspectives on Gẹ̀lẹ̀dé; (9) Conclusion.

Glossary of Yoruba terms, p.291–96. Bibliography, p.297–310. Index, p.313–27.

I674 Lewis-Williams, David, and Dowson, Thomas. Images of power: understanding Bushman rock art. Johannesburg, Southern Book Publishers, 1989. 196p. il. (part col.), maps.

The standard introduction to the Bushman rock art of southern Africa.

Contents: (1) The Bushmen and their art; (2) Detailed explanations; (3) Artistic splendor; (4) Viewing the art.

Sites open to the public, p.184–87. Museums with rock art collections, p.188. Suggestions for further reading, p.189. Some other works cited in this book, p.190–91. Index, p.192–96.

I675 Mack, John. Madagascar. Island of the ancestors. [London], Published for the Trustees of the British Museum by British Museum Publications, [1986]. 96p. il. (part col.), maps.

Catalog of the exhibition, British Museum (1986). Landmark book on the history and material culture of Madagascar.

Contents: Part (1): The ancestors of the Malagasy: Early settlers; Islam and astrology; The rise of the kingdoms; The European legacy. Part (2): The living and the dead: The concept of "the ancestors"; Burial, reburial and famadihana; Tombs and cenotaphs; Funerary sculpture.

Chronology, p.93. Bibliography, p.94–5. Index, p.96.

I676 Maurer, Evan M., and Roberts, Allen F. Tabwa: the rising of a new moon: a century of Tabwa art. Ann Arbor, University of Michigan Museum of Art, [1985]. xvi, 288p. il., 15 col. plates, maps.

Catalog of the exhibition, National Museum of African Art (1986), and other locations. Illustrated with more than 400 field and museum photographs and including essays by eminent scholars, this catalog provides significant documentation of Tabwa arts and culture.

Contents: Social and historical contexts of Tabwa, by Allen F. Roberts; Tabwa sculpture and the great traditions of East Central Africa, by François Neyt, translated by Samuel G. Ferraro; A note on "Prime objects" and variation in Tabwa figural sculpture, by Bernard de Grunne; Catalogue of the exhibition, by Evan M. Maurer and Allen F. Roberts; A catalogue raisonné of Tabwa art, by Evan M. Maurer.

Glossary, by Allen F. Roberts, p.279–83. Additional reading, p.285.

I677 Memory: Luba art and the making of history. Ed. by Mary Nooter Roberts and Allen F. Roberts. With contrib. by S. Terry Childs . . . [et al.] N.Y., Museum for African Art, [1996]. 259p. il. (part col.), maps.

Catalog of the exhibition, Museum for African Art (1996), and other locations. Beautifully illustrated, this book provides scholarly essays on "the broad themes of memory and the construction of history manifest in Luba social, religious, and artistic practices."—*Pref.*

Contents: Foreword, From memory to history: processes of Luba historical consciousness, by Jan Vansina; Introduction, Audacities of memory, by Mary Nooter Roberts and Allen F. Roberts; (1) Re/constructing Luba pasts, by S. Terry Childs and Pierre de Maret; (2) Forging memory, by William J. Dewey and S. Terry Childs; (3) Body memory, by Mary Nooter Roberts and Allen F. Roberts, with an essay by Jeanette Kawende Fina Nkindi and Guy De Plaen; (4) Luba memory theater, by Mary Nooter Roberts; (5) Mapping memory, by Mary Nooter Roberts and Allen F. Roberts; (6) Memory in motion, by Mary Nooter Roberts and Allen F. Roberts; (7) Peripheral vision, by Allen F. Roberts, with a contribution from Pierre Petit; Afterword, The idea of Luba, by V. Y. Mudimbe.

Bibliography, p.248–52. Glossary, p.253. Index, p.254–55.

I678 Meyer, Piet. Kunst und religion der Lobi. Fotos der Kunstwerke von Isabelle Wettstein und Brigitte Kauf. Zürich, Museum Rietberg, 1981. 184p. il. (part col.), maps. (Publikationsstiftung für das Museum Rietberg Zürich, Bd. 3)

Extensively illustrated, this volume surveys the art and culture of the Lobi who inhabit south-western Burkina Faso and north-eastern Côte d'Ivoire.

Contents: (1) Die Lobi; (2) Die thila; (3) Kommunikation zwischen thila und Menschen; (4) Die Holzskulptur; (5) Lehmgegenstände für die thila; (6) Eisengegenstände für die thila; (7) Gelbgussgegenstände; (8) Elfenbeinschmuck.

Glossar, p.179–82. Bibliographie, p.183–84.

I679 Miller, Judith von D. Art in East Africa: a guide to contemporary art. London, F. Muller, [1975]. Imprint covered by label which reads: Africana Publishing Company, New York. 125p. il. (part col.)

This basic guide covers art in Kenya, Tanzania, and Uganda and includes information about artists, art movements, art galleries, museums, craft workshops, art schools, art societies, and art competitions.

Contents: (1) Artists in East Africa; (2) Art movements in East Africa; (3) Art institutions in East Africa.

Directory of art institutions in East Africa, p.81–82. Biographies of artists in East Africa, p.83–110. Bibliography, p.111–13. Index, p.115–25.

I680 Mount, Marshall Ward. African art: the years since 1920. New introd. by the author. [Reprint.] N.Y., Da Capo Pr., 1989. xviii, 236p. 97 il. (part col.), map.

Originally published by Indiana University Press, Bloomington, 1973, this paperback ed. includes corrections and a new introduction by the author.

A broadly based survey of the state of contemporary African art from the colonial period to the early 1970s.

Contents: Foreword, by Paul S. Wingert; (1) Survivals of traditional styles; (2) Mission-inspired art; (3) Souvenir art; (4) The emergence of a new art: introduction; (5) Art schools in French-speaking Africa; (6) Art schools in English-speaking East and Central Africa; (7) Art schools in English-speaking West Africa; (8) Artists independent of African art schools; (9) Summary; Appendix: Autobiographies of two African artists.

Glossary of names, p.199–203. Bibliography, p.204–10. Index, p.231–36.

I681 Musée royal de l'Afrique centrale. Masterpieces from central Africa. The Tervuren Museum. Ed. by Gustaaf Verswijver . . . [et al.] Photography by Roger Asselberghs. [Ed. by Gustaaf Verswijver, Els De Palmenaer, Viviane Baeke, and Anne-Marie Bouttiaux-Ndiaye.] N.Y., Prestel, [1996]. 200p. il., 126 col. plates, map.

Catalog of the exhibition, Canadian Museum of Civilization, Ottawa/Hull (1996–1997), and other locations. Devoted to acquiring Central African artifacts since 1897, the Tervuren Museum's collections represent great diversity and extensive ethnographic documentation which is summarized for each piece that is illustrated in this handsome catalog.

Contents: Masterpieces from Central Africa: the Tervuren Museum, by Alain Nicolas. Bibliography, p.196–200.

I682 Museum für Völkerkunde, Frankfurt am Main. Wegzeichen: Kunst aus Ostafrika 1974–89 = Signs: art from East Africa 1974–89. [By] Johanna Agthe. Frankfurt am Main, Museum für Völkerkunde, 1990. 541p. 82 il. (part col.), 198 col. plates, map. (Afrika-Sammlung, 5)

In German and English. This collection covers a collection of contemporary East African art acquired by the museum between 1974 and 1989 and represents artists from Kenya, Uganda, Tanzania, and (in a few cases) Mozambique.

Contents: (1) Traditional art in East Africa; (2) Contemporary art in East Africa; (3) Cultural policies in Kenya and contemporary art; (4) Art education as a subject at school; (5) Directions in East African art; (6) Ways of becoming an artist; (7) Life as an artist; (8) Campaigns and slogans; (9) Artistic subjects; (10) Tradition from the artist's point of view; (11) Rural life as an artistic subject; (12) The town as artistic subject; (13) Narrative pictures; (14) Caricature (15) Other subjects; Etale Sukuro: art to the people.

Appendix: List of the artists, p.513. List of the subjects, p.516–18. Supplementary explanations for some of the works, p.519–28. Glossary, p.533–34. Bibliography, p.535–540.

I683 The neglected tradition: towards a new history of South African art (1930–1988). Johannesburg Art Gallery. Guest curator: Steven Sack. Johannesburg, Johannesburg Art Gallery, [1988]. 155p. il. (part col.)

Catalog of the exhibition, Johannesburg Art Gallery (1988–1989).

This scholarly catalog has historic importance "by tracing the development and influence of black South African artists, and for the first time documenting this development and influence through an exhibition and research catalogue."—*Foreword.* Extensive bibliography has 1,255 citations.

Contents: The pioneers; The Polly Street era; Rorke's drift art and craft centre; The new generation; New generation sculpture.

Biographies, p.97–134. Bibliography, p.135–53.

I684 Neyt, François. The arts of the Benue: to the roots of tradition: Nigeria. Assist. by Andrée Désirant. [S.l.] Editions Hawaiian Agronomics, [1985]. 215p. il. (part col.), maps.

A survey of the art and culture of the peoples living on the lands along the Benue River between the Cameroon Mountains and the Niger River.

Contents: Preface, by Ekpo Eyo; (1) The Benue State; (2) The Igala. Art at the service of kingship?; (3) The Idoma. Art at the service of the sacred; (4) The Tiv. Art and the cultural mutations.

Bibliography, p.212–14.

I685 Nunley, John W. Moving with the face of the devil: art and politics in urban West Africa. Urbana, Univ. of Illinois Pr., 1987. xxiv, 281p. 75 il., 8 col. plates, maps.

Illustrated with fieldwork photographs, this book is a major exposition and contribution to the knowledge of contemporary West African masquerades.

Contents: (1) The great experiment; (2) Freetown; (3) Ode-lay organization; (4) The Ode-lay societies; (5) Ode-lay aesthetics; (6) The Ode-lay artist; (7) Music of the Freetown societies; (8) A theory of art and performance; (9) Conflict as a factor of society life; (10) The politicization of urban secret societies; (11) Unity and control; (12) Tea kettles and the cooling effects of art; Appendix 1: Freetown masking societies in 1978 by Ward; Appendix 2: permission for masked devil procession; Appendix 3; Police public notice—masked devils; Appendix 4: Minutes of meeting between Paddle, Firestone, and Bloody Mary Societies.

Glossary, p.256–60. Bibliography, p.261–67. Index, p.269–81.

I686 Perrois, Louis, and Delage, Marta Sierra. The art of equatorial Guinea: the Fang tribes. N.Y., Rizzoli, 1990. 177p. il. (part col.), maps.

An in-depth study of the art and material culture of the Fang in Cameroon.

Contents: Fang art among the arts of Africa; Rites and beliefs: Fang objects and symbols; The Fang migrations; The ethnic history of the Fang of equatorial Guinea.

Bibliography, p.171–77.

I687 Powell, Ivor. Ndebele: a people and their art. Photographer, Mark Lewis. Ndebele advisor and project coord., Mark Hurwitz. N.Y., Cross River Pr., Division of Abbeville Publishing Group, [1995]. 160p. il. (part col.), map.

Lavishly illustrated primarily in color, this book provides a valuable overview of the art and culture of the Ndebele of southern Africa.

Contents: (1) History; (2) Beliefs and practices; (3) Mural art; (4) Homesteads; (5) Beads and adornments; (6) Contemporary trends.

Glossary, p.154–57. Index, p.158–60.

I688 Robbins, Warren M., and Nancy Ingram Nooter. African art in American collections: survey 1989. Washington, D.C., Smithsonian Institution Pr., [1989]. vii, 607p. 1,596 il., maps.

This book is a significant visual record of primarily masks and figures from sub-Saharan Africa owned mainly by private collectors and some public collections in the United States and Canada. Appendixes include a complete list of collections and a comprehensive inventory of sculptural styles.

Contents: Foreword, African art: where the hand has ears, by Amadou Hampate Ba; The two worlds of African art, by Warren M. Robbins; Illustrations, introductory notes and captions, by Nancy Ingram Nooter.

African art in American collections, p.571–73. Bibliography, p.575–89. Style index, p.591–92.

I689 Roy, Christopher D. Art and life in Africa: selections from the Stanley Collection, exhibitions of 1985 and 1992. [Iowa City], University of Iowa Museum of Art (Distr. by the Univ. of Washington Pr., [1992]). x, 265p. il. (part col.), maps.

A revised and expanded version of the 1985 exhibition catalog. Includes field photographs and extensive notes for each illustrated work from the Western Sudan, Guinea Coast, the Equatorial Forest, the Southern Savanna, and East Africa.

Contents: Catalogue of the 1985 exhibition; Catalogue of the 1992 exhibition.

Selected bibliography, p.257–61. Index, p.263–65.

I690 ———. Art of the Upper Volta rivers. Trad. et adaptation en français F. Chaffin. Meudon, France, Alain et Françoise Chaffin, [1987]. 384p. 325 il., col. plates, maps.

Text in English and French. A major contribution on the masking traditions of the Red and Black Volta rivers region of Burkina Faso, with extensive field photographs.

Contents: Introduction; Mossi; Kurumba; Gurunsi (Nuna, Winiama, Lela); Bwa; Marka Dafing; Bobo; Bolô; Tusyâ.

Style map, p.368–75. Glossary, p.376–78. Bibliography, p.379–81.

I691 Schildkrout, Enid, and Keim, Curtis A. African reflections: art from northeastern Zaire. With contrib. by Didier Demolin . . . [et al.] [Color photographs by Lynton Gardiner]. Seattle, Univ. of Washington Pr., [1990]. 271p. il. (part col.), maps.

Catalog of the exhibition, American Museum of Natural History, New York (1990), and other locations.

A major treatise on the art of the Mangbetu, the Zande, and neighboring peoples in northeastern Zaire. This book also documents the American Museum of Natural History's Congo Expedition (1909–1915).

Contents: (1) Art, ethnography, and history in northeastern Zaire; (2) Through western eyes: the making of the Mangbetu myth; (3) Collecting in the Congo: the American Museum of Natural History Congo Expedition, 1909–1915; (4) Reconstructing the past, by Jan Vansina; (5) Mangbetu social organization in the early colonial period; (6) The art and technology of daily life; (7) The art of adornment; (8) The craft of power and the art of kings; (9) Dealing with destiny: aspects of Mangbetu thought; (10) Music and dance in northeastern Zaire, Part 1: The social organization of Mangbetu music, by Didier Demolin; Part 2: Collecting culture: musical instruments and musical change, by Thomas Ross Miller; (11) Art, culture, and tribute among the Azande, by John Mack; (12) Reflections on Mangbetu art.

Bibliography, p.263–66. Index, p.267–71.

I692 Seven stories about modern art in Africa: an exhibition organized by the Whitechapel Art Gallery. Concept and general editor, Clémentine Deliss. Paris, Flammarion, 1995. 319p. il. (part col.), map.

Catalog of the exhibition, Whitechapel Art Gallery, London (1995), and other locations. This landmark catalog presents the history of modern African art through the painting, sculpture and theatrical installations of more than sixty artists. The seven sections of the exhibition cover works from Nigeria, Senegal, Sudan, Ethiopia, South Africa, Kenya, and Uganda.

Contents: 7 + 7 = 1: Seven stories, seven stages, one exhibition, by Clémentine Deliss; Inside, outside, by Everlyn Nicodemus; The quest: from Zaria to Nsukka, a story from Nigeria, by Chika Okeke; Objects of performance, a story from Senegal, by El Hadji Sy; The Khartoum and Addis connections, two stories from Sudan and Ethiopia, by Salah M. Hassan; Moments in art, a story from South Africa, by David Koloane; Concrete narratives and visual prose, two stories from Kenya and Uganda, by Wanjiku Nyachae; Recollections, a collection of interviews, reminiscences, articles and manifestoes from Nigeria, from Senegal, from Sudan and Ethiopia, from South Africa, from Kenya and Uganda.

Art colleges, universities and schools, p.291–96. International workshops, by Elsbeth Court, p.296–97. Movements, centres, workshops and collectives, by Elsbeth Court, p.297–301. African art in Africa, by Elsbeth Court, p.302–06. International events, by Elsbeth Court, p.306–08. Further reading, p.308–11. References, p.314–18.

I693 Sieber, Roy, and Walker, Roslyn Adele. African art in the cycle of life. Washington, D.C., Published for the National Museum of African Art by the Smithsonian Institution Pr., [1987]. 155p. il. (part col.), map.

Catalog of the exhibition, National Museum of African Art (1987–1988). A major exhibition catalog illustrated with significant objects from European, North American, and private collections as well as field photographs. Text by Roy Sieber. Catalog and bibliography by Roslyn Adele Walker.

Contents: (1) Continuity; (2) Transition; (3) Toward a secure world; (4) Governance; (5) Status and display; (6) Imports; (7) Departure.

Bibliography, p.149–55.

I694 Somalia in word and image. Ed. by Katheryne S. Loughran . . . [et al.] Washington, D.C., Published by the Foundation for Cross Cultural Understanding, in coop. with Indiana University Pr., Bloomington, [1986]. 175p. il. (part col.), maps.

Catalog of the exhibition, Mathers Museum, Indiana University (1986), and other locations. The first major exhibition and catalog to treat the art and culture of Somalia. "The catalog is an excellent demonstration of the importance of historic illustrations to document African art."—*Review*, Art documentation, v.5, no.4, winter 1986, p.187.

Contents: Introduction: Word and image on the Horn of Africa, by John William Johnson; The artistic heritage of Somalia, by Mary Jo Arnoldi; Somali verbal and material arts, by Said Sheikh Samatar; The literary culture of the Somali people, by B. W. Andrzejewski; Society and culture in the Riverine region of southern Somalia, by Lee V. Cassanelli; Somali wood engravings, by Vinigi L. Grottanelli; Islam in Somalia, by I. M. Lewis.

Selected bibliography, p.175.

I695 Steiner, Christopher B. African art in transit. N.Y., Cambridge Univ. Pr., [1994]. xv, 220p. 42 il., maps.

Based on extensive fieldwork, this book surveys the commodification and circulation of African art objects in the international art market.

Contents: Introduction: The anthropology of African art in a transnational market; (1) Commodity outlets and the classification of goods; (2) The division of labor and the management of capital; (3) An economy of words: bargaining and the social production of value; (4) The political economy of ethnicity in a plural market; (5) The quest for authenticity and the invention of African art; (6) Cultural brokerage and the mediation of knowledge; Conclusion: African art and the discourses of value.

References, p.195–210. Index, p.211–20.

I696 University of Fort Hare. Images of man: contemporary South African Black art and artists. A pictorial and historical guide to the collection of the University of Fort Hare housed in the De Beers Centenary Art Gallery. [By] E. J. De Jager. [Alice], Fort Hare Univ. Pr. in assoc. with the Fort Hare Foundation, [Distr. Saayman and Weber (Pty), 1992]. 220p. il. (part col.), [2] leaves of col. plates.

The University of Fort Hare has one of the finest and most comprehensive collections of its kind within or outside of South Africa. All major artists are represented as well as some less well-known ones.

Contents: (1) Art and society; (2) The Black artists: past and present; (3) Contemporary Black (African) art in Southern Africa: A social historical perspective; (4) Five pioneer painters: Sekoto, Pemba, Bhengu, Mvusi and Mohl; (5) Transition to the 1960s: Eric Ngcobo and Gladys Mugundlandlu; (6) Establishment and realization: the 1960s and 1970s; (7) The township art movement; (8) The Rorke's drift tradition: Azaria Mbatha and John Muafangejo; (9) Three mystics: Cyprian Shilakoe, Dan Rakgoathe and Harry Moyaga; (10) The sculptors; (11) Personal imagery and African heritage; (12) The post 1970s.

Index of Black artists referred to and/or illustrated, p.217–18. Bibliography, p.219–20.

I697 Vallées du Niger. [Paris, Éd. de la Réunion des musées nationaux, 1993]. 573p. il. (part col.), maps.

Catalog of the exhibition, Musée national des Arts d'Afrique et d'Océanie, Paris (1993–1994), and other locations. Monumental catalog with abundant illustrations of the art and cultural traditions of the civilizations of the Niger.

I698 Vogel, Susan. Africa explores: 20th century African art. Assisted by Ima Ebong. Contrib. by Walter E. A. van Beek . . . [et al.] N.Y., Center for African Art, [1991]. 294p. il. (part col.)

Catalog of the exhibition, Center for African Art (1991), and other locations. Lavishly illustrated, this major survey of contemporary African art emphasizes Western and Central Africa.

Contents: (1) Traditional art: elastic continuum, by Susan Vogel; Enter the bush: a Dogon mask festival, by Walter E. A. van Beek; (2) New functional art: future traditions, by Susan Vogel; (3) Urban art: art of the here and now, by Susan Vogel; Painting in Zaire: from the invention of the West to the representation of social self, by Bogumil Jewsiewicki; (4) International art: the official story, by Susan Vogel; Negritude: between mask and flag—Senegalese cultural ideology and the "École de Dakar," by Ima Ebong; (5) Extinct art: inspiration and burden, by Susan Vogel; Afrokitsch, by Donald John Cosentino; The selfhood of the other: reflections of a Westerner on the occasion of an exhibition of contemporary art from Africa, by Thomas McEvilley; "Reprendre": enunciations and strategies in contempoary African arts, by V. Y. Mudimbe.

Bibliography, p.288–94. Index, p.294-[95].

I699 Wilcox, A. R. The rock art of Africa. N.Y., Holmes and Meier Publishers, [1984]. xvi, 287p. il., 67 col. plates, maps.

The first major state-of-the-art survey of African rock art which provides an encyclopedic review of the literature.

Contents: (1) Historical introduction; (2) The study of rock art—aims and problems; (3) Terms and techniques; (4) Africa—the background, physical and climatic; (5) The peopling of the art regions; (6) The Maghreb and Sahara; (7) Bovidean outliers: the Horn of Africa, Kenya, Southern Sudan and West Africa; (8) The Central African art zone; (9) The Central Tanzanian Sub-Region; (10) The Southern African art zone; (11) Art Sub-Region 1: Zimbabwe and North-East Transvaal; (12) The Tsodilo Hills; (13) Art Sub-Region 2: South-West Africa/Namibia; (14) Art Sub-Region 3: Southern and South-Western Cape; (15) Art Sub-Region 4: Drakensberg-Maluti Massif and surrounding areas; (16) Art Sub-Region 5: the Northern Cape; (17) Art Sub-Region 6: South-West Transvaal and adjoining areas; (18) The mobiliary art; (19) The non-representational art; (20) The handprints; (21) The overall picture; (22) Problems and possibilities; (23) The raisons d'être.

Select bibliography and references, p.267–79. Index, p.281–87.

I700 The Yoruba artist: new theoretical perspectives on African arts. Ed. by Rowland Abiodun, Henry J. Drewal, and John Pemberton III. Washington, D.C., Smithsonian Institution Pr., [1994]. ix, 275p. il. (part col.), map.

Essays by eminent scholars based on a symposium on Yoruba art held at the Museum Rietberg, Zürich (1992).

Contents: (1) Art, identity, and identification: a commentary on Yoruba art historical studies, by John Picton; (2) Introduction: An African(?) art history: promising theoretical approaches in Yoruba art studies, by Rowland Abiodun; (3) Stylistic analysis and the identification of artists' workshops in Ancient Ife, by Frank Willett; (4) Ifa trays from the Osogbo and Ijebu regions, by Hans Witte; (5) The Ulm Opón Ifá (ca. 1650): a model for later iconography, by Ezio Bassani; (6) Anonymous has a name: Olowe of Ise, by Roslyn Adele Walker; (7) In praise of metonymy: the concepts of "tradition" and "creativity" in the transmission of Yoruba artistry over time and space, by Olabiyi Babalola Yai; (8) Introduction: in praise of artistry, by John Pemberton III; (9) Lagbayi: the itinerant wood carver of Ojowon, by Wande Abimbola; (10) The role of Oríkì Oríle and Ìtàn in the reconstruction of the architectural history of the palace of Gbongan, by Oba Solomon Babayemi, the Olufi of Gbongan; (11) Polyvocality and the individual talent: three women Oríkì singers in Okuku, by Karin Barber; (12) Drumming for the Egungun: the poet-musician in Yoruba masquerade theater, by Akin Euba; (13) Embodied practice/embodied history: mastery of metaphor in the performances of diviner Kolawole Ositola, by Margaret Thompson Drewal; (14) Introduction: Yoruba art and life as journeys, by Henry John Drewal; (15) Beyond aesthetics: visual activism in Ile-Ife, by Michael D. Harris; (16) The transformation of Ogun power: the art of Rufus Ogundele, by Jutta Ströter-Bender; (17) The three warriors: Atlantic altars of Esu, Ogun, and Osoosi, by Robert Farris Thompson; (18) Yoruba-American art: new rivers to explore, by John Mason.

Bibliography, p.251–66. Glossary of Yoruba terms, p.267–73.

I701 Zahan, Dominique. Antilopes du soleil: arts et rites agraires d'Afrique noire. Avec 50 figures, 538 dessins, 1 carte. Wien, Édition A. Schendl, 1980. 195p. il. 101p. of plates, map.

The definitive study on the chi-wara, or antelope headdress of the Bambara masking society associated with agricultural rituals. Profusely illustrated with drawings of the complete range of iconographic varieties of male and female chi-wara.

Contents: (1) Généralités; (2) Le savoir et ses dimensions; (3) Les alentours du nom; (4) La manière d'être de l'objet; (5) L'épiphanie cosmique; (6) Aliment et venin; (7) Le sacre de l'histoire; (8) Choisir les hommes.

Bibliographie, p.163–65. Répartition géographique du Tyiwara, p.166–69. Index des auteurs cités, p.170. Index analytique des matières, p.171–75.

SEE ALSO: Vansina, Art history in Africa: an introduction to method (GLAH 2:G85).

Oceania

I702 Art and artists of Oceania. Ed. by Sidney M. Mead and Bernie Kernot. [Palmerston North, N.Z.], Dunmore Pr., 1983. 308p. il., maps.

Eighteen papers from the Second International Symposium on the Arts of Oceania. During the conference, the Pacific Arts Association was established. This book is the first major publication sponsored by the association.

Contents: [1] General section; Attitudes to the study of Oceanic art, by Sidney Mead; Among the Kilenge "Art is something which is well done," by Philip Dark; The role of women artists in Polynesia and Melanesia, by Jehanne Teilhet; Changing Western attitudes to Oceanic art, by Jean Guiart; Art, ethno-aesthetics and the contemporary scene, by Nelson Graburn; Negative and positive influences, by Katarina Mataira; [2] Melanesia and Micronesia; Inspiration and convention in Lakalai paintings, by Ann Chowning; Pots, power and progress in the Trans-Gogol, by Colin De'Ath; Shell-inlaid shields from the Solomon Islands, by Deborah Waite; Kominimung shields, by Dirk Smidt; The decorative motifs of Palauan clubhouses, by David Robinson; [3] Polynesia; The meeting house in contemporary New Zealand, by Bernie Kernot; Contemporary arts in Oceania, by Albert Wendt; Art and Maori construction of reality, by Allan Hanson; Moko, by Dave Simmons; The Veil of Orthodoxy, by Roger Neich; Tokelau cuisine, by Judith Huntsman; The cave of images, by Roger Rose.

I703 The art of the Pacific Islands. [By] Peter Gathercole, Adrienne L. Kaeppler, Douglas Newton. Washington,

D.C., National Gallery of Art, 1979. 365p. il. (part col.), maps.
Catalog of the exhibition, National Gallery of Art (1979).
A beautifully illustrated volume, "one of the standard reference books on the subject. It is a catalogue of . . . one of the largest and most comprehensive such exhibitions ever attempted, for which objects from Pacific collections all over the world had been borrowed."—*Review*, Apollo, v.120, no.273, Nov. 1984, p.360.
Contents: Foreword, by J. Carter Brown; Continuities and changes in western Pacific art, by Douglas Newton; Polynesian cultural history, by Peter Gathercole; Aspects of Polynesian aesthetic traditions, by Adrienne L. Kaeppler; New Zealand Maori, by Peter Gathercole.
Bibliography, p.359–65.

I704 Arts of the south seas: island Southeast Asia, Melanesia, Polynesia, Micronesia: the collections of the Musée Barbier-Mueller. Ed. by Douglas Newton. N.Y., Prestel, 1999. 368p. il. (part col.)
Trans. of Arts des mers du Sud: Insulinde, Melanesie, Polynesie, Micronesie: collections du Musée Barbier-Mueller. Paris, Biro, 1998.
Seeks "to present the islands of the Philippines and Indonesia on an equal footing with those of Melanesia, and more abundantly than those of Micronesia and Polynesia."—*Foreword.* Multi-author survey, arranged by region.
Notes and bibliographies, p.363–68.

I705 Barrow, Terence. Art and life in Polynesia. Rutland, Vt., Charles E. Tuttle, 1973. 191p. 323 il. (part col.), map.
Written by a noted scholar in the field, this older, standard work is "an important contribution to furthering our knowledge of Polynesian art."—*Foreword.*
Contents: (1) Introduction; (2) Art areas of Polynesia.
Bibliography, p.181–84. Glossary of artifact names, p.188. Index, p.189–90.

I706 ______. The art of Tahiti and the neighbouring Society, Austral and Cook Islands. [London], Thames and Hudson, [1979]. 93p. 102 il. (part col.), maps.
A generously illustrated history of the wooden sculpture, ceremonial costumes and weapons of the Tahitians, including contemporary engravings from Captain Cook's expedition.
Contents: The Society islands; The Austral islands; The Cook islands.
Bibliography, p.[94]. Index, p.[96].

I707 Bodrogi, Tibor. Oceanian art. Budapest, Corvina, [1959]. 41p. 170 il. (part col.)
Primarily composed of plates illustrating objects in the Ethnographical Museum of Budapest.
Contents: Primitive art as seen through European eyes; Oceania, Melanesia, Polynesia, Micronesia; Indonesia.
Bibliography, p.39–40. Principal collectors and collections, p.41.

I708 Brake, Brian. Art of the Pacific. Photographs by Brian Brake. Conversations by James McNeish. With commentary by D. R. Simmons. N.Y., Abrams, 1979. 239p. chiefly il. (part col.)
Photographic appreciation, followed by a series of "conversations" ("with living people . . . from tape recordings").
Index, p.240.

I709 Buck, Peter Henry. Arts and crafts of Hawaii, by Te Rangi Hiroa. [Reprint.] [Honolulu], Bishop Museum, 1964. 606p. il. (Bernice P. Bishop Museum special publication, 45)
See GLAH 1:I634 for original publication. Reprint in 14 parts.
Contents: Food; Houses; Plaiting; Twined baskets; Clothing; Canoes; Fishing; Games and recreation; Musical instruments; War and weapons; Religion; Ornaments and personal adornment; Death and burial; Index.

I710 ______. Arts and crafts of the Cook Islands. [Reprint.] N.Y., Kraus Reprint, 1971. i, 533p. 275 il. 16 leaves of plates, maps. (Bernice P. Bishop Museum bulletin, 179)
An early classic, this work is extensively illustrated with diagrams and field and museum photographs.
Contents: Material culture; Cultural differentiation; Cultural processes.
Literature cited, p.527–29. Index, p.530–33.

I711 Buehler, Alfred; Barrow, Terry; and Mountford, Charles P. The art of the South Sea Islands, including Australia and New Zealand. [Rev. ed.] N.Y., Greystone, [1968]. 255p. il. (part col.), maps. (Art of the world)
See GLAH 1:I635 for original ed. Substantially the same as the previous ed.

I712 Cook voyage artifacts in Leningrad, Berne, and Florence museums. Ed. by Adrienne L. Kaeppler. With contrib. by L. G. Rozina, Karl Henking, Enrico H. Giglioli. Trans. by Ella Wiswell, Denzel Carr, Mildred M. Knowlton. Honolulu, Bishop Museum Pr., [1978]. x, 186p. 260 il. (part col.) (Bernice P. Bishop Museum special publication, 66)
Scholarly descriptions of three major collections of ethnographic objects attributed to the voyages of Captain James Cook.
Contents: The Cook Voyage Collection in Leningrad, introduction, by Adrienne L. Kaeppler; The James Cook Collection in the Museum of Anthropology and Ethnography, Leningrad, by L. G. Rozina; The James Cook Collection in Berne, introduction, by Adrienne L. Kaeppler; A description of the Webber Collection, based on the monograph, by Karl H. Henking; The Cook Collection in Florence, introduction by Adrienne L. Kaeppler; Notes on an ethnographic collection made during the third voyage of Cook and preserved until the end of the last century in the Royal Museum of Physics and Natural History in Florence, by Enrico Hillyer Giglioli; A document concerning the collection acquired during the third voyage of Captain Cook in the National Museum of Anthropology and Ethnology in Florence, by A. Mordini; On the origin of the collection preserved in the

National Museum of Anthropology and Ethnology held to be gathered by Cook, by Adelaide Fabiani.
Literature cited, p.181–84. Index, p.185–86.

I713 Dreamings: the art of Aboriginal Australia. Ed. by Peter Sutton. N.Y., Braziller, [1988]. xiii, 266p. il. (part col.), maps.
Catalog of the exhibition, Asia Society, New York (1988), and other locations.
"Unique in its field in at least three ways. It contains the first extended overview of the history of Aboriginal art scholarship. . . . It presents a substantial analysis of the Aboriginal aesthetic. . . . And it examines the cultural, economic, and political context of the production of Western Desert paintings for an Australian and world art market."—*Introd.* "One of the most significant books on the Aboriginal art of Australia published so far."—*Review*, African arts, v.23, no.3, July 1990, p.91.
Contents: (I) Dreamings, by Peter Sutton; (II) Responding to Aboriginal art, by Peter Sutton; (III) The morphology of feeling, by Peter Sutton; (IV) Dreamings in acrylic: western desert art, by Christopher Anderson and Françoise Dussart; (V) Perceptions of Aboriginal art: a history, by Philip Jones; (VI) Survival, regeneration, and impact, by Peter Sutton, Philip Jones, Steven Hemming; Postscript, by Peter Sutton.
Biographies of artists, p.235–42. Notes, p.243–53. References, p.254–61. Index, p.262–64.

I714 Edge-Partington, James. Ethnographical album of the Pacific Islands. Originally published as An album of the weapons, tools, ornaments, articles of dress of natives of the Pacific Islands. Second ed. exp. and ed. by Bruce L. Miller. With additional maps and portraits of Pacific Island natives. [Bangkok, Thailand], SDI, 1996. 391p., 238p., 237p., il., 31 leaves of plates, maps.
A monumental work originally published from 1890–98. This volume provides historically significant drawings of the art and culture of Australia and the Pacific Islands and is primarily composed of illustrations and descriptive annotations for more than 6,000 objects which were extant in museums, societies, and private collections at the turn of the century. The new ed. includes the typesetting of the original hand-written commentary, enlarged plates, a complete subject index, and additional appendixes.
Contents: Series I; Series II; Series III [list of plates by geographical area].
Appendix I: notes on the history of contact and brief descriptions of the islands noted by Edge-Partington, p.226–28; Appendix II: portraits of natives of the Pacific Islands, pl.1–21; Appendix III: maps, pl.22–31. Bibliography, p.229–31. Index, Series I, II, III, p.232–237.

I715 The eloquent dead: ancestral sculpture of Indonesia and Southeast Asia. Ed. by Jerome Feldman. [Los Angeles], Museum of Cultural History, UCLA [1985]. 204p. 270 il. (part col.), map.
Catalog of the exhibition, Wight Art Gallery, UCLA (1985).
Contents: Ancestors in the art of Indonesia and Southeast Asia, by Jerome Feldman; Ancestral manifestations in the art of Nias Island, by Jerome Feldman; Ancestors and living men among the Batak, by Elisabeth L. Cameron; The significance of ancestors in the arts of the Dayak of Borneo, by Eugenia Sumnik-Dekovich; The soul that is seen: the Tau Tau as shadow of death, reflection of life in Toraja tradition, by Eric Crystal; Korwar of the Biak, by Wilhelm G. Solheim II; Ancestor motifs of the Paiwan, by Elisabeth L. Cameron; Magamaog: benevolent ancestor of the Yami, by Elisabeth L. Cameron and Eugenia Sumnik-Dekovich; Catalogue: Lesser Dundas and Moluccas; Philippines; Madagascar; Appendix: a Toraja house from Tondon, by Eric Crystal.
Bibliography, p.199–204.

I716 Exploring the visual art of Oceania: Australia, Melanesia, Micronesia, and Polynesia. Ed. by Sidney M. Mead, assisted by Isabelle Brymer and Susan Martich. Honolulu, Univ. Pr. of Hawaii, [1979]. xviii, 455p. il., maps.
Papers from Symposium 1: The Art of Oceania held at McMaster University, Hamilton, Ontario (1974) which marked "the first attempt to bring together, from different parts of the world, the people who are concerned with the study of the art and material culture of the Pacific area."—*Introd.*
Contents: (1) Early Lapita art from Polynesia and Island Melanesia: continuities in ceramic, barkcloth, and tattoo decorations, by Roger C. Green; (2) Prehistoric and recent art styles in Papua New Guinea, by Douglas Newton; (3) Rock art in the western Pacific, by Jim Specht; (4) The archaeology of Australian Aboriginal Art, by Lesley Maynard; (5) The art of Irian Jaya: a survey, by Adrian A. Gerbrands; (6) The art of the peoples of Western New Britain and their neighbors, by Philip J. C. Dark; (7) The art of the Baining: New Britain, by George A. Corbin; (8) A survey of Polynesian art, by Adrienne L. Kaeppler; (9) The equivocal nature of a masking tradition in Polynesia, by Jehanne H. Teilhet; (10) On the origin and diversity of "Tahitian" Janiform fly whisks, by Roger G. Rose; (11) Changing attitudes to the study of Maori carving, by Peter Gathercole; (12) Admiralty Island "ancestor" figures? by Mino Badner; (13) Aspects of style and symbolism in the art of the Solomon Islands, by Deborah B. Waite; (14) Style provinces and trading areas in North and Northeast New Guinea, by Tibor Bodrogi; (15) The problem of meaning in art, by Anthony Forge; (16) Aesthetics of the Aika, by Erik Schwimmer; (17) Artmanship in the Star Harbour Region, by Sidney M. Mead; (18) Art and artists in the context of Kwoma Society, by Christian Kaufmann; (19) Adam Smith in the garden: supply, demand, and art production in New Britain, by David R. Counts; (20) Where does art begin on Puluwat? by Peter W. Steager; (21) New directions in contemporary arts, by Nelson H. H. Graburn; (22) Traditional handicraft in a changing society: manufacture and function of stenciled Tapa on Moce Island, by Simon Kooijman; (23) Art in changing New Ireland, by Phillip Lewis; (24) Establishing museums in developing countries: the case of Papua New Guinea, by Dirk Smidt; (25) Toward the scientific study of art in Melanesia, by Jean Guiart; Conclusion: themes in the study of Oceanic art, by Roy L. Carlson; Appendix: recommendations and resolutions.

The contributors, p.417. References, p.419–50. Index, p.451–55.

I717 Firth, Raymond William. Art and life in New Guinea. London, Studio, 1936. 126p. il., maps.
An early work composed primarily of black-and-white field and museum photographs accompanied by descriptive explanations.

Contents: The shape of the land; Physical and cultural types; Forms of settlement; Canoes in the native culture; Art and recreation; Art and ritual; Qualities of New Guinea art; The primitive artist; Method and design; The critique of primitive art.

Select bibliography, p.126.

I718 Force, Roland W., and Force, Maryanne. The Fuller Collection of Pacific artifacts. London, Lund Humphries, [1971]. xvi, 360p. il., map.
Chiefly illustrations, this volume provides visual and descriptive documentation of the A. W. F. Fuller Collection of ethnological and archaeological Pacific artifacts in the Field Museum of Natural History, Chicago, Illinois.

Contents: The man and his collection; Polynesia; Melanesia; Australia.

Bibliography, p.352–56. Index, p.357–60.

I719 Hamilton, Augustus. The art workmanship of the Maori race in New Zealand: a series of illustrations from specially taken photographs, with descriptive notes and essays on the canoes, habitations, weapons, ornaments, and dress of the Maoris, together with lists of the words in the Maori language used in relation to the subjects. Dunedin, N.Z., Printed and published for the Board of Governors [of the New Zealand Institute] by Fergusson & Mitchell, 1896. 438p. [vi]. il., 6 col. plates.
Extensively illustrated with field and museum photographs, diagrams, and plans, this monumental study is an early classic on Maori art and culture.

Contents: Part 1: On the canoes of the Maoris; List of canoe words; On the historical canoes of the Maori migrations to New Zealand, with the names of canoes mentioned in Maori traditions and myths. Part 2: The habitations of the Maoris; List of words relating to houses and pas. Part 3: The weapons of the Maoris; The implements of agriculture and handicraft; The snares and implements used in hunting rats and birds for food; List of words used in connection with the subjects. Part 4: The dress of the Maori; Personal ornaments; List of words connected with these subjects. Part 5: The social institutions of the Maori people; Games and amusements; Musical instruments; List of words connected with social intercourse.

Index, p.i–[vi].

I720 Hersey, Irwin. Indonesian primitive art. Singapore, Oxford Univ. Pr., 1991. 112p. 64 il. (part col.) (The Asia collection)
The standard introduction to the history of Indonesian primitive art from its origins in the Dong-son culture of northern Vietnam to the present day.

Contents: (1) Introduction; (2) Adat, ancestors, and "the ancient people"; (3) Origins and inputs; (4) The Batak of Sumatra; (5) The cultures of Nias, Enggano, Mentawei, and Nicobar; (6) Borneo's indigenous cultures; (7) The Toraja of Sulawesi; (8) The art of Nusa Tenggara; (9) Leti and the Lower Moluccas; (10) The Korwar style of Irian Jaya; (11) The further shores; (12) Primitive Indonesian art today; Appendix: collecting the primitive art of Indonesia.

Select bibliography, p.107–8. Index, p.109–12.

I721 Joppien, Rüdiger, and Smith, Bernard. The art of Captain Cook's voyages. New Haven, Yale Univ. Pr., 1985–88. 3v. in 4. il. (part col.)
These volumes include a "Descriptive catalogue of all the known original drawings of peoples, places, artefacts and events and the original engravings associated with them."—*T.p.*

Contents: (1) The voyage of the Endeavour 1768–1771 with a descriptive catalogue; (2) The voyage of the Resolution and Adventure 1772–1775 with a descriptive catalogue; (3) Text. The voyage of the Resolution and Discovery 1776–1780 with a descriptive catalogue.

I722 Kaeppler, Adrienne Lois. "Artificial curiosities": being an exposition of native manufactures collected on the three Pacific voyages of Captain James Cook, R.N. at the Bernice Pauahi Bishop Museum, January 18, 1978–August 31, 1978, on the occasion of the Bicentennial of the European Discovery of the Hawaiian Islands by Captain Cook—January 18, 1778. Honolulu, Bishop Museum Pr., [1978]. xvi, 293p. 622 il. (part col.), maps. (Bernice P. Bishop Museum special publication, 65)
Contents: Realization of the exhibition; Introductory exhibition in the Kahili Room; Ethnography and the voyages of Captain Cook; Exposition of the native manufactures collected on the three Pacific voyages of Captain Cook; Appendix I: The Cook Collection exhibited at the Colonial and Indian Exhibition; Appendix II: The Worden Hall Collection; Appendix III: Cook voyage objects in Glasgow, Greenwich, and Wellington.

References cited, p.289–92.

I723 ———. Oceanic art. N.Y., Abrams, 1997. 633p. il. (chiefly col.)
First pub. as v.23 of the series L'art et le grandes civilisations (GLAH 2:I8). The first major survey in more than 30 years, bringing together the results of recent discoveries and research. Monumental overview.

Contents: Introduction, by Douglas Newton; Polynesia and Micronesia, by Adrienne Kaeppler; Melanesia, by Christian Kaufmann; Documentation; Principal Oceanic cultural groups.

Bibliography, p.[615]–25. Index, p.[627]–33.

I724 Kelm, Heinz. Kunst vom Sepik. Berlin, Museum für Völkerkunde, [1966–68]. 3v. (Veröffentlichungen des Museums für Völkerkunde, neue folge 10, 11, 15. Abteilung Südsee, V, VI, VII)

Composed of more than 1,200 illustrations with extensive descriptions, this set is a catalog of the folk art holdings of the Sepik River Valley (Indonesia and Papua New Guinea) in the Abteilung Südsee of the Museum für Völkerkunde, Berlin.

I725 Kirker, Anne. New Zealand women artists. A survey of 150 years. [Rev. ed.] East Roseville, NWS, Australia, Craftsman House, [1993]. 255p. 66 il., 64 col. plates.

Extensively illustrated, this volume is the first comprehensive study of the subject.

Contents: (1) The pioneers; (2) Towards a professional status; (3) The achievement of Frances Hodgkins; (4) In search of modernism; (5) The other expatriate painters; (6) Rita Angus and the assertion of a national identity; (7) Figures as the expressive concern; (8) Towards abstraction; (9) The development of sculpture; (10) A new way of seeing; (11) Approaching the '90s.

Further reading, p.[247]–48. Index, p.[250]–55.

I726 Krämer, Augustin Friedrich. Die Málanggane von Tombára, München, Georg Müller, 1925. 91p., 100 leaves of pl.

The only work on the malanggan art of New Ireland.

Contents: Das Land Tombára; Das Leben der Eingeborenen; Totenkult; Málangganfeste des Mittelgebiets; Die Málanggane.

Wichtigste Literatur von 1870 an, p.90–91.

I727 Layton, Robert. Australian rock art: a new synthesis. N.Y., Cambridge Univ. Pr., [1992]. xi, 284p., il. maps.

"The purpose of this book is to bring together the work of anthropologists and archaeologists and show how each can illuminate the other."—*p.2.* As a "major work . . . [it] synthesizes the basic (and in some cases very detailed) data for the continent . . . This is . . . the most important book in this field."—*Review*, Antiquity, v.68, March 1994, p.161.

Contents: (1) Anthropological and archaeological approaches to Australian rock art; (2) Rock art and indigenous religion; (3) Rock art as an expression of secular and subversive themes; (4) Rock art and the colonial impact; (5) Putting statements in their cultural context; (6) Figure and motif; (7) Stylistic variations in time and space; (8) Rock art and human adaptation in Australia. Appendix one: sources for samples used in distribution analysis; Appendix two: results of computer analysis of sites and regions.

Glossary, p.259–60. References, p.261–72. Index, p.273–84.

I728 Linton, Ralph, and Wingert, Paul S. Arts of the South Seas. In collab. with Rene d'Harnoncourt. Color il. by Miguel Covarrubias. [Reprint.] [N.Y.], Museum of Modern Art, 1972. 199p. il. (part col.)

Reprint of a work published in conjunction with the exhibition held at the Museum of Modern Art (1946).

Contents: Arts of the South Seas; Polynesia; Micronesia; Melanesia; Australia.

Bibliography, p.196–99.

I729 Maori: art and culture. Ed. by D. C. Starzecka. Contrib. by Janet Davidson . . . [et al.] London, British Museum Pr., 1998. 180p. il. (part col.), maps.

"The subject of this book is Maori culture in general . . . with emphasis on the two greatest achievements of Maori artistic creativity, wood-carving and fibre arts."—*Ed. foreword.* Based on the British Museum collections.

Glossary of Maori terms, p.161–62. References, p.163–65. Index, p.166–68.

I730 Melanesien, schwarze Inseln der Südsee: eine Ausstellung des Rautenstrauch-Joest-Museums für Völkerkunde der Stadt Köln. [Köln], Kunsthalle Köln, 1972. 223p. il. (part col.), maps.

Catalog of the exhibition, Rautenstrauch-Joest-Museum für Völkerkunde der Stadt Köln (1972). The text and catalog of works were prepared by Waldemar Stöhr.

Contents: Die Inseln und ihre Entdecker; Die Melanesier—Gestern und Heute; Religion und Gesellschaft; Kunst und Künstler; Kultur- und Stilregionen Melanesiens.

Literatur, p.217–23.

I731 Meyer, Anthony J. P. Oceanic art. Photographs [by] Olaf Wipperfürth. [Edison, N.J.], Knickerbocker Pr., [1996]. 2v. il. (part col.), maps.

With English, French, and German texts and plate documentation, this large and lavishly illustrated set provides encyclopedic coverage of Oceanic art, history, and culture.

Contents: (1) Pre-contact Oceania: geography, history and culture; European explorations of Oceania; Melanesia; (2) Polynesia; Micronesia; Oceanic art: is it art?

Glossary, v.2, p.636–38. Suggested reading, v.2, p.640.

I732 Moore, David R. Arts and crafts of the Torres Strait. [Aylesbury], Shire Ethnography, [1989]. 64p. 50 il. maps. (Shire ethnography, 10)

This study includes information about the utilitarian, religious, recreational, personal, commercial, and military products of the island craftsmen.

Contents: (1) Introduction; (2) The search for food; (3) Religion and magic; (4) Recreations; (5) Personal adornment; (6) Trade; (7) Warfare; (8) Post-contact developments; (9) Museums; (10) Further reading (p.61).

Index, p.62–64.

I733 Reports of the Cambridge Anthropological Expedition to Torres Straits. Volume IV: Arts and Crafts. Cambridge, Eng., Cambridge Univ. Pr., 1912. [By A. C. Haddon et al.] xxiii, 393p. 390 il., 40 leaves of plates, map. (Repr.: N.Y., Johnson Reprints, 1971)

"The present volume deals with the arts of life in Torres Straits, including those actions and objects which are connected with its material and aesthetic aspects."—*Pref.*

Contents: Introduction and daily life, by A. C. Haddon; (1) Decoration of the person and toilet, by A. C. Haddon; (2) Personal ornaments and clothing, by A. C. Haddon; (3) Textiles, by A. Hingston Quiggin; (4) Houses, by A. Wilkin and A. C. Haddon; (5) Domestic utensils and tools, by A. C. Haddon; (6) Food and its preparation, and narcotics, by A. C. Haddon; (7) Horticulture, by A. C. Haddon; (8) Hunting and fishing, by A. C. Haddon; (9) Weapons and objects employed in warfare, by A. C. Haddon; (10) Transport and canoes, by A. C. Haddon; (11) Science, by A. C. Haddon, including Astronomy, by W. H. R. Rivers, and a Calendar, by S. H. Ray; (12) Music, by C. S. Myers; (13) Sound-producing instruments, by A. C. Haddon; (14) Songs, by A. C. Haddon; (15) Dances and dance paraphernalia, by A. C. Haddon; (16) Greetings, salutations, and various social customs, by S. H. Ray, A. C. Haddon, and J. Bruce; (17) Games and toys, by A. C. Haddon; (18) Decorative, pictorial and glyptic art, by A. C. Haddon.

I734 Schneebaum, Tobias. Embodied spirits. Ritual carvings of the Asmat. Salem, Peabody Museum of Salem, 1990. 104p. il. (part col.), maps.

Catalog of the exhibition, Peabody Museum of Salem (1990), and other locations. This exhibition "brings together a group of carvings from two of the most important collections of Asmat art in the United States: that of the Peabody Museum of Salem and that of the Crosier Asmat Museum" of Hastings, Nebraska.—*Pref.*

Contents: (1) Asmat and the world; (2) Creating embodied spirits; (3) Managing the power of bodies and spirits; (4) Interpreting Asmat culture; (5) The exhibition: embodied spirits. All chapters are by Schneebaum except Chapter (4) which includes the following essays: Primary Asmat religious and Philosophical concepts, by Bishop Alphonse A. Sowada, O.S.C.; Spirit children, by Reverend Gerard A. Zegwaard, M.S.C.; Ethnographic collecting and ethnographic studies in the context of medical research, by D. Carleton Gajdusek, M.D.

Selected bibliography, p.101. Gajdusek bibliography, p.102–04.

I735 Stöhr, Waldemar. Kunst und Kultur aus der Südsee. Sammlung Clausmeyer Melanesien. Köln, Rautenstrauch-Joest-Museum, 1987. 389p. il. (part col.), 32 leaves of plates. (Ethnologica, Neue Folge, Band 6)

A well-illustrated and documented catalog of a major collection of Oceanic art.

Contents: Stilregionen Melanesiens; Mittlerer Sepik und Randgebiete; Unterer Sepik und Nordküste Neuguineas; Maprik-Gebiet und Waschkuk-Berge; Nordostküste Neuguineas (Astrolabe-Bay und Huon-Golf); Südost-Neuguinea; Irian Jaya (West-Neuguinea); Binnenland von Neuguinea; Nord-Melanesien (Bismarckarchipel); Neu-Britannien; Neu-Irland; Inselgruppen im Nordwesten des Bismarck-Archipels; Ost-Melanesien (Salomonen und Santa-Cruz-Inseln); Südost-Salomonen; Zentral-Salomonen; Nordwest-Salomonen; Santa-Cruz-Inseln; Vanuatu (Neue Hebriden); Neu-Kaledonien; Katalog—Sammlung Clausmeyer: Melanesien.

Literaturverzeichnis, p.379–89.

I736 Te Maori. Maori art from New Zealand collections. Ed. by Sidney Moko Mead. Text by Sidney Moko Mead . . . [et al.] Photographs by Athol McCredie. N.Y., Abrams, [1984]. 244p. il. (part col.), maps.

Catalog of the exhibition, Metropolitan Museum of Art (1984), and other locations. The first "international exhibition devoted exclusively to Maori Art"—*Ackn.* "Undoubtedly the most important exhibition of Maori art yet assembled, and this catalogue does it full justice."—*Review*, Archaeology, v.40, no.2, March–April 1987, p.72.

Contents: The ebb and flow of Mana Maori and the changing context of Maori art, by Sidney Moko Mead; The roots of Maori culture, by Agnes Sullivan; Becoming Maori art, by Sidney Moko Mead; Tribal art styles, by David R. Simmons; Pathways in the Maori world, by Anne Salmond; Maori artists of time before, by Bernie Kernot; As the old net piles up on shore, the new net goes fishing, by Piri Sciascia; Maps; Contributors; Catalogue, by David R. Simmons.

Glossary, p.236–39. Bibliography, p.240–43.

I737 Thomas, Nicholas. Oceanic art. [N.Y.], Thames and Hudson, [1995]. 216p. 181 il. (part col.), maps. (World of art)

A basic survey of the history of Oceanic art and culture.

Contents: (1) Revelations: Sepik art; (2) Ancestors and architecture: Maori art; (3) The art of war; (4) The art of the body; (5) Maternal symbolism and male cults; (6) Barkcloth, exchange and sanctity; (7) Feathers, divinity and chiefly power; (8) Narrative art and tourism; (9) National independence, indigenous minorities and migrants.

Bibliography, p.209–10. Index, p.215–16.

I738 University of California, Los Angeles. Museum of Cultural History. The people and art of the Philippines. [By] Father Gabriel Casal . . . [et al.] Los Angeles, Museum of Cultural History, UCLA, [1981]. 270p. 263 il., 20 col. plates, maps.

Catalog of the exhibition, Museum of Cultural History, UCLA (1981–82), and other locations. This catalog documents the first comprehensive exhibition of the arts of the Philippines in the U.S. and is the only book on this subject.

Contents: Philippine prehistory, by Wilhelm G. Solheim II; Colonial artistic expressions in the Philippines (1565–1989), by Father Gabriel Casal and Regalado Trota Jose, Jr.; Arts and peoples of the southern Philippines, by Eric S. Casino; Arts and peoples of the northern Philippines, by George R. Ellis.

References cited, p.264–68.

I739 Wardwell, Allen. Island ancestors: Oceanic art from the Masco Collection. Photographs by Dirk Bakker. [Seattle], Univ. of Washington Pr. in assoc. with the Detroit Institute of Arts, [1994]. xiii, 282p. col. il., maps.

Catalog of the exhibition, Kimbell Museum, Fort Worth (1994–96), and other locations. Organized by the Detroit Institute of Arts, this catalog is lavishly illustrated with color plates and documents a major private collection of Oceanic art.

Contents: The Oceanic cultures; The Masco Collection.

Bibliography, p.273–77. Index, p.279–82.

I740 ———. The art of the Sepik River. [Chicago, Art Institute of Chicago, 1971]. 100p. 215 il. (part col.), maps.

Catalog of the exhibition, Art Institute of Chicago (1971). A well-illustrated introduction to the arts of the Sepik River (New Guinea).

Contents: Coastal zone, Murik and Adjoria groups; The lower Sepik area; The middle Sepik; Upper Sepik, Hunstein Mountains, Bahinemo group.

Bibliography, p.98–99.

I741 Wingert, Paul S. Art of the South Pacific Islands. N.Y., Beechhurst Pr., [1953]. 64p. 102 il. (1 col.), maps.

Published in conjunction with the exhibition, M. H. de Young Memorial Museum, San Franciso (1953). Some references and a complete catalog are retained to document one of the earliest and most comprehensive exhibits of South Pacific Island artists.

Contents: Art of the South Pacific Islands.

Bibliography, p.46.

SEE ALSO: Smith, European vision and the South Pacific (GLAH 2:I306).

The Americas

I742 Alcina Franch, José. Pre-Columbian art. Trans. from the French by I. Mark Paris. N.Y., Abrams, 1983. 614p. il. (part col.), maps, plans.

Trans. of L'art précolombien. Paris, Mazenod, 1978 (Art et les grandes civilisations, 8)

An encyclopedic attempt to encompass the pre-Columbian art and architecture of Latin America in one vol. 177p. of col. plates, 771 black-and-white illustrations (of varying quality), supplemented by brief overviews of the principal cultures. Part 3 includes 63 essays on the principal archeological sites, with photographs, plans, and elevation drawings; culture maps; chronological tables; and an illustrated essay on the major deities. Most of the titles cited in the bibliography were published before 1970, many before 1960.

Contents: (1) Pre-Columbian art; (2) The image as document; (3) Principal archaeological sites.

Bibliography, p.593–605. Index, p.607–14.

I743 The ancient Americas: art from sacred landscapes. Richard F. Townsend, general ed. With essays by Anthony F. Aveni . . . [et al.] Chicago, Art Institute, 1992. 397p. il. (part col.), maps.

Spanish ed., La antigua América: el arte de los parajes sagrados. México, Grupo Azabache, 1993.

Catalog of the exhibition, Art Institute of Chicago (1992), and other locations. Divided into five chapters, the first thematic and the remainder geocultural. Within each chapter are 3–8 essays, 24 in all, by leading authors in each field on selected styles/periods or media, condensed versions of the authors' more extensive publications on the topic.

Notes at ends of each chapter. Bibliography, p.383–92.

I744 Ancient West Mexico: art and archaeology of the unknown past. Gen. ed., Richard F. Towensend. With essays by Patricia Rieff Anawalt . . . [et al.] Chicago, Art Institute (Distr. by Thames & Hudson, 1998). 308p. il. (part col.), maps.

Catalog of the exhibition, Art Institute of Chicago (1998), and other locations. Comprehensive overview of the role of sculptural production in West Mexico. Fourteen authored essays.

Contents: (1) The Teuchitlan tradition: an archaeological prospect; (2) Interpreting the tomb sculptures of ancient West Mexico; (3) Comparative views; (4) A modernist perspective.

Bibliography, p.298–305.

I745 Arts of the Amazon. Ed. by Barbara Braun. Text by Peter G. Roe. Pref. by Adam Meckler. N.Y., Thames & Hudson, 1995. 128p. il. (part col.), map.

A concise but welcome overview of the traditional arts of the Indians of the Amazon Basin. Its breadth of coverage helps to overcome its lack of depth. Illustrated chiefly from a private U.S. collection.

Contents: The Amazon today, by Barbara Braun; Arts of the Amazon, by Peter G. Roe; (1) Pottery; (2) Basketry; (3) Textiles; (4) Hard carvings; (5) Featherwork; (6) Body decoration; (7) Art as performance.

Notes, p.122–24. Bibliography, p.124–25. Index, p.126–28.

I746 Between continents, between seas: Precolumbian art of Costa Rica. Text by Susan Abel-Vidor . . . [et al.] N.Y., Abrams, 1981. 240p. il. (part col.)

Published in conjunction with the exhibition, Detroit Institute of Arts (1981), and other locations. Essentially a catalog of 293 objects (not all illustrated), supplemented by scholarly articles summarizing archeological regions and periods and the principal art media.

Contents: The archaeology of Costa Rica, by Michael Snarskis; Ethnohistorical approaches to the archaeology of Greater Nicoya, by Suzanne Abel-Vidor; Ethnohistory and ethnography in the Central Highlands-Atlantic Watershed and Diquís, by Luis Ferrero A.; Guayabo de Turrialba and its significance, by Oscar Fonseca Zamora; Traditions of Costa Rican stone sculptures, by Mark Graham; Jade, by Elizabeth Easby; Gold work, by Warwick Bray; Technical appendix: perspectives on Costa Rican jade, by Frederick Lange, Ronald Bishop, and Lambertus van Zelst; Catalogue, by Michael Snarskis.

Bibliography, p.229–40.

I747 Bruhns, Karen Olsen. Ancient South America. N.Y., Cambridge Univ. Pr., 1994. xxiii, 424p. il., maps. (Cambridge world archaeology)

An overview of the prehistory of the continent, with an emphasis on the Andean region. Individual chapters on ceramics, textiles, metallurgy, and iconography. Provides an archeological and historical background to art history research in the region.

Glossary of technical and specialist terms used in South American archaeology, p.[385]–400. Bibliography of general works and by chapter, p.[401]–17. Index, [418]–24.

I748 Chiefly feasts: the enduring Kwakiutl potlatch. Ed. by Aldona Jonaitis. With essays by Douglas Cole . . . [et al.] N.Y., American Museum of Natural History (Distr. by University of Washington Press, 1991). 300p. il. (part col.), col. map.

Published in conjunction with the exhibition, American Museum of Natural History (1991). Profiles the Kwakwaka'wakw collection of the American Museum of Natural History, the traditions which gave rise to it, and the historical circumstances of its appropriation by museums. A case study in both collection history and conscientious reinterpretation.

Contents: (1) Chiefly feasts: the creation of an exhibition, by Aldona Jonaitis; (2) Streams of property, armor of wealth: the traditional Kwakiutl potlatch, by Wayne Suttles; (3) The history of the Kwakiutl potlatch; (4) George Hunt, collector of Indian specimens, by Ira Jacknis; (5) The contemporary potlatch, by Gloria Cranmer Webster; (6) Postscript: the treasures of Siwidi, by Judith Ostrowitz and Aldona Jonaitis.

Bibliography, p.289–95. Index, p.297–300.

I749 Colección Arte y tesoros del Perú. Lima, Banco de Crédito del Perú, 1973– .

An unnumbered series of richly illustrated studies, chiefly on individual pre-contact cultures of the Andes, but also covering colonial and contemporary Peruvian art. Some volumes include extensive essays by noted scholars.

Contents: Arte precolombino: Museo Nacional de Antropología y Arqueología, Peru (3v., 1977–); Chavín formativo (1981); Chancay (1982); Paracas (1983); Huari (1984); Moche (1985); Nazca (1986); Chimú (1988); Lambayeque (1989); Vicús (1994); and Tucumé (1996).

I750 Crossroads of continents: cultures of Siberia and Alaska. [Ed. by] William W. Fitzhugh and Aron Crowell. Washington, D.C., Smithsonian Institution Pr., 1988. 360p. il., maps.

Catalog of the exhibition, National Museum of Natural History (1988), and other locations. 37 essays divided into five sections: "Peoples of Siberia and Alaska"; "Strangers arrive," five essays on Russian and American exploration of the region; "Crosscurrents of time," four essays on the prehistoric population of the region; "Thematic views," 14 essays on ethnology, art and material culture; and "New lives for ancient people," a trend analysis of contemporary culture patterns.

Bibliography, p.354–59.

I751 Hail, Barbara A., and Duncan, Kate C. Out of the north: the Subarctic collection of the Haffenreffer Museum of Anthropology. Bristol, R.I., The Museum, 1989. 301p. il. (part col.), maps. (Studies in anthropology and material culture, 5)

Uses the museum's holdings "as a jumping-off point for discussion and analysis of historic and contemporary Subarctic collections."—*Foreword.*

Contents: (1) The Subarctic region: people, history and art; (2) Emma Shaw Colcleugh: Victorian collector; (3) Styles and style change; (4) Subarctic arts today; Epilogue: women's work, women's art; Catalogue.

Bibliography, p.294–301.

I752 Handbook of Middle American Indians. Supplement. Victoria Reifler Bricker, general ed. Austin, Univ. of Texas Pr., 1981– . (5)v. il., maps, plans.

Update and supplement to the Handbook (1964–76; see GLAH 1:I611) to be produced as new scholarship warrants.

Contents: (1) Archaeology (1981), ed. by Jeremy A. Sabloff, includes a general overview of archaeology in the region between 1960 and 1980, and ten authored articles on developments at specific sites; (5) Epigraphy (1992), ed. by Victoria Reifler Bricker, contains ten articles on writing systems and their decipherment, and on the historical and linguistic analysis of manuscripts and sculptural inscriptions.

I753 Handbook of North American Indians. William C. Sturtevant, gen. ed. Washington, D.C., Smithsonian Institution Pr., 1978– . (11)v. il., maps.

A projected "20-volume set planned to give an encyclopedic summary of what is known about the prehistory, history, and cultures of the aboriginal peoples of North America who lived to the north of the urban civilizations of central Mexico."—*Pref, v.8.* Each volume includes articles on the prehistoric and historic development of the culture region; its linguistics and demography; and a comprehensive bibliography and index. Individual authored articles on each cultural group within the region feature the topics of language and territory, population, material culture, social culture, archeology and history, and a critical synonymy of the terms used for the culture group.

Contents: (4) History of Indian-White relations; (5) Arctic; (6) Subarctic; (7) Northwest coast; (8) California; (9) Southwest [Pueblo peoples]; (10) Southwest [non-Pueblo peoples and regional topics]; (11) Great Basin; (12) Plateau; (15) Northeast; (17) Languages.

I754 Holm, Bill. Northwest Coast Indian art: an analysis of form. Seattle, Univ. of Washington Pr., 1965. ix, 115p. il., map. (Thomas Burke Memorial Washington State Museum monograph, no. 1) (Repr.: Vancouver, Douglas & McIntyre, 1988.)

A seminal effort to synthesize Northwest Coast Indian design elements from diverse object types.

Contents: Historical background; Symbolism and realism; Uses of two-dimensional art; Elements of the arts; Principles of form and organization; Conclusions.

Bibliography, p.105–08. Index, p.109–15.

I755 Inca, Perú: 3000 ans d'histoire. Coordination et réd., Sergio Purin. Gent, Belgium, Imschoot, 1990. 2v. il. (part col.), facsims., maps, plans, ports.

Catalog of the exhibition, Musées royaux d'art et d'histoire, Brussels (1990). Through signed and illustrated essays of 10–20p. each provides extensive coverage of Peruvian civilizations and their major arts. Lacks table of contents.

Contents: (1) Civilisations précolombiennes du Pérou; Archéologie du Pérou [17 essays]; Arts et techniques du Pérou ancien [9 essays]; L'empire Inca [5 essays]. (2) Catalogue [378 entries].

Bibliography, v.1, p.490–501.

I756 Kubler, George. The art and architecture of ancient America: the Mexican, Maya and Andean peoples. [3d (integrated) ed.] New Haven, Yale Univ. Pr., 1993. 576p. il., maps, plans. (Yale University Press pelican history of art)

See GLAH 1:I618 for previous eds. This paperback-only ed. includes new textual material, but the reduction in format and integration of the plates with text has caused the quality of illustration to suffer. "As to the framework and method of the book . . .. [I]n effect, the principal changes in Americanist thought do not contradict the positions taken here when the original text was delivered to the publishers in 1959."—*Foreword.*

I757 Lapiner, Alan. Pre-Columbian art of South America. N.Y., Abrams, 1976. 460p. il. (part col., part mounted), maps.

An older work, the text of which has been superseded, but with illustrations of objects then in private hands which are not often reproduced elsewhere. Remains the most current overview of the arts of the entire continent.

Contents: Peru; Ecuador; Colombia-Venezuela; Bolivia-Argentina-Chile; Brazil.

Visual glossary, p.453–54. Bibliography, p.455–59.

I758 Maya. Ed. by Peter Schmidt, Mercedes de la Garza, Enrique Nalda. [Milan], Bompiani, 1998. 695p. col. il. (part folded), col. maps.

Catalog of the exhibition, Palazzo Grassi, Venice (1998–99). The most exhaustive treatment of the Maya to date. Signed and illustrated catalog entries for 514 objects; 29 signed essays cover the history, cosmology, and major arts of the Maya (architecture, epigraphy, portable objects and ceramics); and the archeological sites of Copán, Tikal, Chichén Itzá, Uxmal, and Calakmul.

Timeline, p.[651–59]. Glossary, p.[661]–70. Maya gods, p.671. Bibliography, p.672–82. Index of names, 683–94.

I759 Morley, Sylvanus Griswold, and Brainerd, George W. The ancient Maya. 5th ed. rev. by Robert J. Sharer. Stanford, Stanford Univ. Pr., 1994. xx, 892p. il., maps, plans.

See GLAH 1:I622 for original annotation and previous eds.; 4th ed. 1983.

I760 The Olmec world: ritual and leadership. With essays by Michael D. Coe . . . [et al.] Principal photographers, John Bigelow Taylor, Justin Kerr, and Bruce M. White. Princeton, Princeton Univ. Art Museum (Distr. by Abrams, 1995). xi, 344p. il. (part col.), maps.

Catalog of the exhibition, Princeton University Art Museum (1995), and other locations. Eight essays focus on the ritual use of the small-scale Olmec stone carvings. Catalog is divided into eight thematic categories and contains 252 entries with extensive descriptive notes and bibliographical references.

Contents: Preparing the way, by David A. Friedel; Olmec archaeology, by Richard A. Diehl and Michael D. Coe; Art, ritual, and rulership in the Olmec world, by F. Kent Reilly III; Art in Olmec culture, by Carolyn E. Tate; Shamanism, transformation, and Olmec art, by Peter T. Furst; The rainmakers: the Olmec and their contribution to Mesoamerican belief and ritual, by Karl A. Taube; The Olmec mountain and Tree of Creation in Mesoamerican cosmology, by Linda Schele; Rocks and minerals employed by the Olmec as carvings, by George E. Harlow.

Glossary, p.120–22. Bibliography, p.331–37. Index, 338–44.

I761 Pasztory, Esther. Aztec art. N.Y., Abrams, 1983. 335p. il. (part col.), maps.

"A great asset of this book is the author's intention to include every known major work of Aztec art and as many of the minor pieces as possible. . . . But there are also many relatively unknown objects . . . which have all been brought together and made available in a single volume."—*Review*, Archaeology, v.37, Nov.–Dec. 1984, p.6.

Contents: (1) Historical and cultural background; (2) A definition of Aztec art; (3) Aztec architecture and cliff sculpture; (4) The major monuments of Tenochtitlán; (5) Codices; (6) Stone sculpture; (7) Lapidary arts; (8) Wood sculpture and turquoise mosaic; (9) Featherwork; (10) Terracotta sculpture; (11) Ceramics.

Glossary, p.300–21. Bibliography, p.[312]–22. Index, p.323–34.

I762 Schele, Linda, and Miller, Mary Ellen. The blood of kings: dynasty and ritual in Maya art. Photographs by Justin Kerr. Fort Worth, Kimbell Art Museum; N.Y., Braziller, 1986. xii, 335p. il. (part col.)

Catalog of the exhibition, Kimbell Art Museum (1986), and other locations. Controversial at the time of publication for de-romanticizing the Maya (for some scholars unflatteringly). The benchmark for modern Maya scholarship. "A combination of exhibition catalog and polemic, the book argues for a pervasive use of blood-sacrifice and blood iconography in the classic period."—*Review*, Handbook of Latin American studies, v.49, 1989.

Contents: Introduction; (1) The royal person; (2) Kingship and the rites of accession; (3) Courtly life; (4) Bloodletting and the vision quest; (5) Warfare and captive sacrifice; (6) The ballgame; (7) Death and the journey to Xibalba; (8) Kingship and the Maya cosmos; The Maya calendar; The hieroglyphic writing system.

Suggestions for further reading, p.329. Index, p.330–35.

I763 Taíno: Pre-Columbian art and culture from the Caribbean. Ed. by Fatima Bercht . . . [et al.] With contrib. by Ricardo E. Alegría . . . [et al.] N.Y., Monacelli Pr. and El Museo del Barrio, 1997. 189p. il. (part col.), maps.

Catalog of the exhibition, Museo del Barrio (1997–98), the U.S. venue for an exhibition originally held in Paris at the Musée du Petit Palais, 1994. A more lavish but less scholarly treatment appears in its Paris counterpart, L'art des sculpteurs taïnos: chefs d'œuvre des Grands Antilles précolombiennes. Sous la dir. de Jacques Kerchache. Paris, Paris-Musées, 1994.

Contents: The Caribbean before European Conquest: a chronology, by Samuel M. Wilson; An introduction to Taíno culture and history, by Ricardo E. Alegría; The daily life of the Taíno people, by Marcio Veloz Maggiolo; The Taíno social and political order, by Samuel M. Wilson; To be seated with "great courtesy and veneration": contextual aspects of the Taíno duho, by Joanna M. Ostapkowicz; The creation myths of the Taíno, by José Juan Arrom; Taíno stone collars, elbow stones, and three-pointers, by Jeffery B. Walker; Zemi three-pointer stones, by Shirley McGinnis; Ancestor worship and cosmology among the Taíno, by Peter E. Siegel; The bat and the owl: nocturnal images of death, by Manuel A. García Arévalo; Just wasting away: Taíno shamanism and concepts of fertility, by Peter G. Roe; Epilogue: The beaded Zemi in the Pigorini Museum, by Dicey Taylor, Marco Biscione, and Peter G. Roe; Appendices, trans. by Susan C. Griswold: Diario del primer viaje, by Christopher Columbus and others; De Orbe Novo Decades, by Pietro Martire d'Anghiera; Apologética historica de las Indias, by Bartolomé de las Casas.

Bibliography, p.181–89.

I764 Teotihuacan: art from the city of the gods. Ed. by Kathleen Berrin and Esther Pasztory. N.Y., Thames and Hudson, 1993. 288p. il. (part col.)

Catalog of the exhibition, Fine Arts Museums of San Francisco (1993). Eleven signed essays contextualize the archeological historiography and the objects uncovered at Teotihuacán. The first section, "Envisioning a city," includes essays on the place of Teotihuacán in the art and archeology of Mexico; the second, "Uncovering the past," includes four essays on the archeological program at Teotihuacán and the conclusions drawn from it; "Beyond Teotihuacán" explores the influence of the culture on subsequent cultures.

Bibliography, p.279–84. Index, p.285–87.

I765 Trésors du nouveau monde. [Coord. du catalogue, Lin et Emile Deletaille.] Brussels, Musées royaux d'art et d'histoire, 1992. 484p. col. il., maps.

Dutch ed., Schatten uit de nieuwe wereld.

Catalog of the exhibition, Musées royaux d'art et d'histoire (1992). Essentially a "great treasures" book, with 11 brief essays (4–9p. each); nevertheless illustrates more than 500 objects from both continents. Includes illustrated maps and timelines.

I766 Wardwell, Allen. Tangible visions: Northwest Coast Indian shamanism and its art. N.Y., Monacelli Pr., 1996. vii, 336p. il. (part col.), col. maps.

A sumptuous study of the masks and other ritual carvings associated with shamanistic practice among the Northwest Coast Indians, particularly the Tlingit. "I cannot praise highly enough Wardwell's impeccable scholarship in this book. . . . He has researched the materials on shamanism among the Northwest Coast people superbly, thoroughly scrutinizing virtually every published work on the topic and carefully referencing all sources of information."—*Review*, American Indian art magazine, v.23, no.1, winter 1997, p.85.

Contents: (1) Problems and parameters; (2) The oldest religion; (3) Visions and spirit quests; (4) Objects of power; (5) Spirit helpers; (6) A collection of shamanistic objects.

Bibliography, p.330–34. Synonymy, p.335.

J. Architecture

This chapter is intended primarily as a general resource for the architectural historian rather than the practicing architect or professional student of architecture. Textbooks and technical manuals are omitted. However, selected bibliographical guides, dictionaries, and directories of importance to the architect are included. Monographic series are generally clustered under the series title. While the coverage of city planning is not deep, landscape architecture is treated more fully than in GLAH 1. Materials on historic preservation may be found in Chapter T, Cultural Heritage. Specialized studies of the history of architectural theory are in Chapter G, Historiography, Methodology, and Theory, early sources and documents in Chapter H, Sources and Documents. Materials on interior design and furniture will be found in Chapter P, Decorative Arts. General dictionaries and encyclopedias of architecture are clustered together, but those addressing specific periods or regions are distributed appropriately among histories and handbooks of those periods and regions. Similarly, directories and biographical dictionaries of architects will be found under the appropriate subject or specialization.

BIBLIOGRAPHY

J1 American architectural books [microform]: based on the Henry-Russell Hitchcock bibliography of the same title and "A list of architectural books available in America before the revolution," by Helen Park. New Haven, Research Publications, [1973]. 128 microfilm reels.

A collection of reprints, in bibliographic sequence, of all the "meaningfully non-duplicatory items in the Henry Russell Hitchcock [GLAH 1:J11] and Helen Park [GLAH 1:J17] bibliographies. Other-than-first editions were included where the later edition was a meaningful variant."—*Introd.* 854 of the total 1,431 original Hitchcock entries, and all 87 of the original Park entries are included.

Accompanied by Index to the microfilm edition of American architectural books, comp. by Julie K. Ellison. New Haven, Research Publications, 1973. Index entries follow the original Hitchcock entry numbers, provide reel number, and where a volume or edition was omitted, includes explanatory symbols. Park items are listed by Park number, author, short title, and imprint date, with reel number. An errata list alerts the user to discrepancies and corrections to some reels which were reissued after initial publication.

J2 Architecture reading lists and course outlines. Ed. by Georgia Bizios. Chapel Hill, Eno River Pr., 1991– . (4)v.

Series of thematic compilations of undergraduate and graduate architectural teaching materials, including course syllabi and reading lists, from 28 universities. Later volumes update and revise some previous versions.

Contents: (1) Architectural theory and criticism, urban design theory, architectural history; (2) Architectural design, human behavior, special topics; (3) Architectural design, architectural theory and criticism, environmental issues, human behavior, professional practice, special topics, urban design theory and history; (4) Architectural design, architectural theory, history, criticism, human behavior, professional practice, special topics, urban design theory and history.

J3 Architecture series: bibliography. Ed. by Judith Vance. Monticello, Ill., Vance Bibliographies. No.1–2386, June, 1978–Dec. 1990.

A wide and impressive array of brief bibliographies (ca. 10–30p.) on all aspects of architecture compiled by hundreds of different authors. Although quality of individual bibliographies varies considerably, most are good starting points for undergraduates or laymen.

Cumulative indexes for: no. 1–1000, June 1978–July 1983, in no. 999 (authors), no. 997 (titles), no. 998 (subjects); no. 1001–2000, July 1983–March 1988, in no. 2001 (authors), no. 2002 (titles), no. 2003 (subjects); no. 2001–2386, March 1988–Dec. 1990, in no. 2384 (authors), no. 2385 (titles), no. 2386 (subjects).

J4 Art Institute of Chicago. Ryerson and Burnham Libraries. Burnham index to architectural literature. N.Y., Garland, 1989. 10v.

Alphabetical index to 213 U.S. and foreign journals and more than 600 monographs from 1919 to mid-1960s. Emphasis on American Midwest. Includes 160 journals not indexed elsewhere, and retrospective indexing of selected journals to their beginnings prior to 1919. Less than 3%

overlap with Avery Index (GLAH 2:J14) for serial titles prior to 1934, and 30% of titles afterward (*Pref.*). Includes lists of periodicals and monographs indexed.

Access is primarily geographic with cross-references to names of architects.

J5 Avery's choice: five centuries of great architectural books: one hundred years of an architectural library, 1890–1990. Adolf K. Placzek, general editor. [Foreword by] Angela Giral. N.Y., Hall, [1997]. xxvii, 292p. il. (part col.), plates.

"A record of the most important books on architecture published from 1485 to 1985, selected and described in celebration of the 100th anniversary of [the Avery Architectural and Fine Arts Library of Columbia University]."—*Introd.*

Eleven scholarly essays by the editor, a former Avery Librarian, and six other architectural historians provide an overview of architectural literature, organized chronologically and by country. Following each essay are signed, extensive, and annotated entries, arranged by country, for the 427 titles included in the beautifully illustrated book.

Contents: Preface, a brief history of the Avery Architectural and Fine Arts Library; Introduction, Avery's choice and the literature of architecture; (1) The rise of the Renaissance; (2) The Renaissance spreads; (3) Classicism and Baroque in the seventeenth and eighteenth centuries; (4) North America before 1800; (5) Revivalism, eclecticism and innovation in the nineteenth century; (6) The twentieth century; (7) Introduction to the future.

Author index, p.273–75. Title index, p.277–81. Date index, p.283–92.

J6 Bamford, Lawrence Von. Design resources: a guide to architecture and industrial design information. Jefferson, N.C., McFarland, 1984. 319p.

Guide to information sources on architectural and industrial design with emphasis on needs of practitioners.

Contents: (1) Printed resources [by form and subject]; (2) Non-print resources [by form]; (3) Special resources and research services.

Subject index, p.265–82. Author and title index, p.283–319.

J7 Bibliografia di base: storia, teoria e critica dell'architettura. A cura di Giovanni Denti. Firenze, Alinea, 1985. 91p. il. (Saggi e documenti, 47)

Guide to approximately 1,000 Italian language basic books on the history, theory, and criticism of architecture. International coverage, but emphasis on Italy.

Contents: Introduzione e indicazioni per la consultazione; Storia dell'architettura; Testi riguardanti la vita e l'opera di singoli personaggi; Testi riguardanti singole costruzioni e progetti; Testi riguardanti singole città; Fonti e documenti; Teoria e critica dell'architettura; Dizionari.

J8 British Architectural Library. Architectural publications index, periodicals indexed and books catalogued by the British Architectural Library. v.23, 1995– . London, RIBA, 1995– . Quarterly. The 4th issue is an annual cumulation.

Combines and expands the RIBA Library review of periodicals, 1933–46; the RIBA Library bulletin, 1946–72; the RIBA annual review of periodical articles, 1965–72. Supersedes Architectural periodicals index, 1973–94 (GLAH 1:J20).

An alphabetically arranged subject index to articles in more than 400 worldwide periodicals received in the British Architectural Library (formerly the Royal Institute of British Architects Sir Banister Fletcher Library). Headings are derived from Architectural keywords, London, RIBA, 1982). Subjects covered include both current and historical aspects of architecture and allied arts, construction, design and environmental studies, landscape, and planning, with an emphasis on Great Britain. Generally excludes book reviews, letters, and news items.

Each issue includes a Names index, Subject headings, Topographical and building names index, Periodicals indexed, and since 1989, a list of books cataloged. Cumulative issues also include Major series and special issues indexed.

In addition to print, available on CD-ROM as Architectural publications index on disc, which is updated quarterly and includes more than 200,000 records from 1978– , with 10,000 records added annually. Accompanied by a user manual and quick reference summary.

Also available from online vendor(s).

J9 ______. British Architectural Library unpublished manuscripts [microform]. London, World Microfilms, 1978. 16 microfilm reels.

"This selection of the R.I.B.A.'s manuscripts is based on the Index prepared by the Royal Historical Commission on Manuscripts." Included are papers, correspondence, account books, etc. of more than 30 prominent 17th- to 20th-century British architects, artisans, and builders, which also provide detailed descriptions of many famous buildings.

Accompanied by British Architectural Library unpublished manuscripts: list of contents and index of reels, 9p., which provides a reference to the National Register of Archives identification code and finding aid and a brief description of each collection.

J10 ______. Early imprints collection. Early printed books, 1478–1840: catalogue of the British Architectural Library early imprints collection. Comp. by Nicholas Savage . . . [et al.] London, Bowker-Saur, 1994– . (3)v. il.

Contents: (1) A–D (1994); (2) E–L (1995); (3) M–R (1996). 5 vols. projected, including comprehensive index (v.5).

Illustrated catalog of approximately 4,000 titles from one of the world's greatest collections of early architectural incunables, books, and printed ephemera. Several important books are thoroughly cataloged here for the first time. Each entry has a complete, detailed bibliographic description, including contents, copy of the title page, collation, details on the printing and illustrations, other editions, copies in other collections, and physical description. Includes related subjects, such as carpentry, interior design, ornament, perspective, and landscape architecture.

Arranged alphabetically by author. Uniform titles used for translations. Each vol. includes a Guide to the catalogue;

Bibliographical references; Abbreviations; List of illustrations; Illustrations, and Catalogue.

The fifth vol. "will be a fully cross-referenced names index, including all authors, publishers, artists and others associated with the publication of each work, and a separate provenance index."—*Guide to the catalogue.*

J11 ———. Royal Institute of British Architects rare books collection [microform]. London, World Microfilms, [1975–77]. 35 microfilm reels il., plans.

Microfilm reproductions of 157 16th- to 18th-century rare books from the British Architectural Library.

Contents: (1) English pattern books, 5 reels, 48 vols.; (2) Cottage architecture, 2 reels, 15 vols.; (3) Country houses and palaces, 4 reels, 21 vols.; (4) Ancient civilisation, 4 reels, 18 vols.; (5) Architectural treatises and works on perspective, 20 reels, 55 vols. Accompanied by 5p. list of titles by part and reel.

J12 Campbell, Cindy. Architects: a guide to biographical sources. In collab. with Jewel Lowenstein. Chicago, Council of Planning Librarians, 1989. 15p. (CPL bibliography, no.233)

Annotated guide to biographical works in architecture located in the Blackader-Lauterman Library of Architecture and Art, McGill University. Excludes works devoted solely to one architect. Includes international sources, and sources by country. Canadian emphasis.

J13 Columbia University. Libraries. Avery Architectural Library. Architectural trade catalogs from the Avery Library, Columbia University, on microfiche [microform]. N.Y., Clearwater [Distr. by Congressional Information Service, Inc., 1988]. [3,477] microfiches.

Reprints more than 2,000 American architecture and building arts trade catalogs, invaluable documentary sources on the history, technology, and marketing of architecture and building. Catalogs are organized into 16 subject categories using the Sweet's Catalog outline. Within each section, catalogs are organized alphabetically by manufacturer.

Contents: (1) General and miscellaneous; (2) Sitework; (3) Concrete; (4) Masonry; (5) Metals; (6) Wood and plastics; (7) Thermal and moisture protection; (8) Doors and windows; (9) Finishes; (10) Specialties; (11) Equipment; (12) Furnishings; (13) Special construction; (14) Conveying systems; (15) Mechanical; (16) Electrical.

Two printed guides accompany the microfiche: a 1988 loose-leaf accession list and shelf list arranged by Sweet's Catalog categories, and a 236p. Guide to architectural trade catalogs from Avery Library, Columbia University, ed. by Norman A. Ross (Frederick, Md., UPA Academic Editions, 1989), which includes introductory and explanatory information, as well as a guide to the microfiche by Sweet's (building materials) Catalog category, and alphabetical, geographical, chronological, and subject indexes.

J14 ———. Avery index to architectural periodicals. 2d ed., rev. and enl. Boston, Hall, 1973. 15v.

See GLAH 1:J5 for 1st ed. and previous supplements to the 2d ed.; 3d supplement, 1977–78; 4th supplement, 1979–1982; 5th supplement, 1983–1984; 6th supplement, 1985– . Annual. Continues without break the seven supplements (1963–72) to the original ed. of the Avery Index. Since 4th supplement, 1984, co-published with the Getty Information Institute.

Index to more than 400 current and approximately 1,000 retrospective periodicals in all areas of architecture and building with additional coverage of archeology, interior design, landscape architecture, and city planning. List of periodicals indexed in front of 1st vol. of each supplement.

A CD-ROM version, Avery index on disc, which is updated annually and cumulative since 1977, has been co-published by G.K. Hall and the Getty Information Institute. Contains approximately 179,000 records; approximately 17,000 added annually.

Also available from online vendor(s).

J15 ———. Avery obituary index of architects, Columbia University. 2d ed. Boston, Hall, 1980. iii, 530p.

Revises and expands 1st ed. (GLAH 1:J4) through mid-1979, but after 1960 excludes artists. Obituaries after 1979 are incorporated into the Avery index to architectural periodicals (see preceding title).

J16 Construction index, an annotated annual index of articles in the fields of building design and construction, v.1– , 1987– . Ed., Susan Greenwald. Chicago, ArchiText, 1987– . Annual.

Quarterly, with annual cumulations through v.6; annual, v.7– .

Annotated, selective index to 68 professional and trade journals, including 48 current titles. Emphasis on information of use to practicing professionals in building design and construction.

Arranged by an augmented CSI Masterformat classification, which is explained in Subject headings alphabetical cross reference, special issue, 1989.

Also available online through Iconda (GLAH 2:J20).

J17 Ehresmann, Donald L. Architecture: a bibliographic guide to basic reference works, histories, and handbooks. Littleton, Colo., Libraries Unlimited, 1984. xvi, 338p.

Annotated bibliography of English- and Western European-language books published between 1875 and 1980 on architectural history available in U.S. libraries. Complements author's Fine arts: a bibliographic guide (GLAH 2:A38) and Applied and decorative arts: a bibliographic guide (GLAH 1:P2).

Contents: (1) Reference works; (2) General histories and handbooks; (3) Primitive and prehistoric; (4) Ancient; (5) Early Christian; (6) Byzantine; (7) Medieval; (8) Renaissance; (9) Baroque and rococo; (10) Modern (19th and 20th cent.); (11) European [by country]; (12) Oriental; (13) New world; (14) Africa and Oceania (with Australia).

Author-title index, p.281–310. Subject index, p.311–38.

J18 Gretes, Frances C. Directory of international periodicals and newsletters on the built environment. 2d ed. N.Y., Van Nostrand Reinhold, [1992]. xx, 442p.

Updates 1st ed., 1986.

Mostly annotated listing of more than 1,600 titles from 57 countries. Intended to "guide the specialized audience through the maze of international publications," titles selected had substantial number of relevant articles; for foreign titles, had substantial circulation, English summaries, or were indexed in a published or online source; were currently published; and had sufficient bibliographic data available at the time the directory was published (*Introd.*).

Brief annotations include regular features, where indexed, scope of coverage, language, and type and quality of illustrations. Arranged by broad topics, chapters have subdivisions, where appropriate, to facilitate quick access.

Contents: Introduction; User's guide; (1) Architecture; (2) Office practice; (3) Building types; (4) Historic preservation and architectural history; (5) Interior design; (6) Lighting and signage; (7) Fine arts, decorative arts, and antiques; (8) Planning, urban design, housing, transportation, and the environment; (9) Landscape design and gardening; (10) Building and construction; (11) Building services and systems; (12) Engineering; (13) Real estate development and facility management; (14) Job leads/doing business abroad; Indexes, abstracts, and on-line services.

Alphabetical index, p.357–94. Geographical index, p.395–434. Subject index, p.435–42.

J19 Harris, Eileen. British architectural books and writers, 1556–1785. Assist. by Nicholas Savage. N.Y., Cambridge Univ. Pr., [1990]. 571p. il.

See GLAH 1:J9 for a provisional notice of this publication. Thorough, scholarly catalog, dictionary, and overview of British architectural literature, including non-British writers known through translations, 1556–1785. Following eight essays on the types of books included, publishers and booksellers, and architectural engraving, is the main catalog in dictionary form. "Each writer on architecture is critically discussed in terms of total output, and this assessment is followed by a comprehensive and fully annotated catalogue of editions and works. . . . Serve[s] not only as the most reliable source of facts and further[s] bibliography but also the major, freestanding scholarly essay on [these] subjects."—*Review*, Journal of the Society of Architectural Historians, v.52, March 1993, p.103. The location of each publication in one or more of 136 key collections is also noted.

Contents: Introductory essays: (1) Books on the orders; (2) Books of designs and pattern-books; (3) Carpenters' manuals; (4) Measuring and price books; (5) Books on bridges; (6) Archaeological books; (7) Publishers and booksellers; (8) Architectural engraving; Writers and their books.

Key to the bibliographical format, p.14–15. Abbreviations, p.16–17. Key to the symbols of locations, p.18–21. Notes to the introductory essays, p.64–68. Chronological index of titles and editions 1556 to 1800, p.513–32. Index, p.533–71.

J20 ICONDA [computer database]. Stuttgart, IRB and [Norwood, Mass.], SilverPlatter, [1991?– .]

CD-ROM. International construction database of the International Council for Building Research Studies and Documentation in collaboration with the Informationszentrum Raum und Bau of the Fraunhofer-Gesellschaft. Covers world literature of all fields of architectural design, building construction, civil engineering, and city planning from 1976. Emphasis on building research and practice. Includes abstracts and indexing for more than 600 journals (more than 140 of them published in the English language), including Construction index (GLAH 2:J16), plus books, reports, theses, and conference proceedings from more than 48 countries. German emphasis. Approximately 30,000 records and 25,000 abstracts added annually. More than 460,000 records in the database. Citations in English.

Accompanied by thesaurus, FINDEX: facet-oriented indexing system for architecture and construction engineering (Stuttgart, IRB, 1985). Online help and database guides, plus printed manuals available.

Also available from online vendor(s).

J21 Information sources in architecture and construction. Ed. by Valerie J. Nurcombe. 2d ed. London, Bowker-Saur, [1996]. 489p. (Guides to information sources)

Upd. and exp. ed. of Information sources in architecture, ed. by Valerie J. Bradfield (London, Butterworths, 1983). 2d ed. is international in scope, with strong British emphasis. Evaluates the most helpful and accessible information sources for architecture, construction, and design in all forms, including periodicals, databases, trade literature, standards, maps, and drawings. Acknowledging the built-in obsolescence of such a guidebook, contributors also provide methodologies for information-gathering and keeping up with new publications in their fields of expertise, and provide bibliographies.

Selective contents: (2) Associations, organizations and libraries, by Jeanne M. Brown; (3) Periodicals, by Katharine R. Chibnik; (24) Buildings, people, places: architectural history, by Margaret Culbertson and Mary Nixon; Appendix A [Organizations and associations]; Appendix B [Acronyms and abbreviations].

Index, p.465–89.

J22 IRB-Literaturdokumentation: LIDO. Stuttgart, IRB Verlag, Spring, 1998– .

Title varies: IRB-Literaturauslese, 1988?–98 ; IRB-Literaturauslese plus, 199?–1998.

Irregular series of specialized, annotated bibliographies focusing on important architects, the science, history, and practice of architecture, structural engineering, building, and planning. Each bibliography is produced on demand, often updated and reissued with a different number, and is created from the several databases, including ICONDA (GLAH 2:J20). Subject coverage is international in scope, but German and European in emphasis. Annotations are in German.

J23 Johns Hopkins University. John Work Garrett Library. The Fowler collection of early architectural books [microform]. New Haven, Research Publications, [1978?]. 86 microfilm reels.

A collection of reprints of 448 rare architectural volumes donated to Johns Hopkins in 1945, plus 36 other important early works added afterward. Although a few influential 19th-century works are included, the majority of the titles date from the 18th, 17th, and 16th centuries. They represent various editions of exemplary works by the great masters of the Renaissance, particularly Vitruvius, Serlio, Vignola, Palladio, and Scamozzi.

Texts are organized alphabetically by author, and within author, chronologically. Accompanied by The Fowler architectural collection of the Johns Hopkins University: catalogue: guide to the microfilm collection comp. by Laurence Hall Fowler and Elizabeth Baer (Woodbridge, Conn., Research Publications, 1982). The guide, a significant contribution to architectural bibliography, provides complete bibliographic information for each title and an index to the original 448 volumes in the collection, plus updates the 1961 ed. of the catalog (GLAH 1:J13; Repr.: San Francisco, Wofsy, 1991) by providing microfilm reel numbers for each title.

J24 Johnson, Donald Leslie, and Langmead, Donald. Makers of 20th century modern architecture: a bio-critical sourcebook. Westport, Conn., Greenwood Press, [1997]. lxiii, 387p. il., plates.

Biographical dictionary of architects and engineers who "initiated, developed, or advanced" modern (mostly Western) architecture in the 20th century. Includes a substantial introductory essay and overview of 20th-century architecture. Plates with descriptive captions are inserted in the middle of the book.

Each entry provides a brief chronology and biography and a footnoted critical essay, with bibliography. A "coda" contains intriguing quotes.

Contents: Reader's guide [includes a bibliography]; Whither we went [introductory essay]; Abbreviations; Bio-critical studies; Coda; Chronology and founders.

Name index, p.365–75. Place index, p.[377]–87.

J25 Kaufman, Peter, [and] Gabbard, Paula. American doctoral dissertations in architectural and planning history, 1898–1972. In Studies in the history of art, v.35, 1990, p. 288–313.

Published as appendix to the volume of Studies titled "The Architectural historian in America." "Lists 370 doctoral dissertations completed at 42 American universities up to 1972 in the fields of architectural and planning history."—*p.288.* Brief essay provides overview of the development of architectural history in America and shifts in academic taste and ideology.

Citations are listed chronologically in separate lists for architectural history (p.291–304) and planning history (p.311–12). Entries provide author, title, university, and where applicable cite abstract in Dissertation abstracts international and order number from University Microfilms International.

University index for architectural history, p.305–08. Author index for architectural history, p.308–10. University index for planning history, p.313. Author index for planning, p.313.

J26 O'Neal, William B., ed., The American Association of Architectural Bibliographers. Papers. Charlottesville, Univ. of Virginia Pr., v.1–11, 1965–74; v.12–13, N.Y., Garland, 1977–79. Annual. (Garland reference library of the humanities, v.116–115 [sic])

See GLAH 1:J16 for original annotation and previous vols. Ed., v.12–13, Frederick D. Nichols.

Selective contents: (12) Louis Kahn and Paul Zucker: two bibliographies (1978); (13) Spaeth, David A. Ludwig Mies van der Rohe: an annotated bibliography and chronology (1979).

J27 Paris. Bibliothèque Forney. L'architecture dans les collections de périodiques de la Bibliothèque Forney. Par Laure Lagardère. Paris, Mairie de Paris, Direction des affaires culturelles, Bibliothèque Forney, [1990]. 179p. il.

Detailed bibliography of the complete collection of architecture, public works, building science and engineering, urbanism, and landscape periodical titles in the Bibliothèque Forney. Excludes contemporary reprints (except for De Stijl) and includes many titles unique to this rich, international (mostly French) collection. Details of dates, format, frequency, language, contents, indexes, and holdings are provided for each title. Chronological arrangement by decade for "revues anciennes," and broad subject arrangement for "revues contemporaines," which are also divided into "française" and "étrangère."

Liste chronologique, p.145–59. Tableau synoptique, p.161–63. Index alphabetique général, p.167–79.

J28 Russell, Terence. The built environment, a subject index 1800–1960. [Surrey, U.K.], Gregg [Distr. by Gower, Brookfield, Vt., 1989]. 4v.

Bibliographic survey of all aspects of the built environment. More than 70,000 entries, international in scope, but British in emphasis. Includes books, conference proceedings, pamphlets, significant periodical titles. Within each subject category entries are arranged chronologically.

Contents: (1) Town planning and urbanism: architecture; gardens and landscape design; (2) Environmental technology; constructional engineering; building and materials; (3) Aesthetics; decorative art and industrial design; international exhibitions and collections; recreational and performing arts; (4) Public health; municipal services; community welfare.

J29 Saggi e documenti. Sezione bibliografie di architettura e urbanistica, n. 1– , 1986/87(?)– . Firenze, Alinea, 1986/87(?)– . Irregular. Ed. by Giovanni Denti.

Continues: Bibiblioteca di architettura, saggi e documenti, 1–25, 1975–1986(?), Firenze, Uniedit.

Italian-language in-depth bibliographies on subjects as diverse as Frank Lloyd Wright, architectural technology, industrialized building, and Le Corbusier, each compiled by an expert in that field. Scope of literature varies with subject and volume, although heavy emphasis on Italian sources.

J30 Schimmelman, Janice Gayle. Architectural books in early America: architectural treatises and building handbooks available in American libraries and bookstores through 1800. New Castle, Del., Oak Knoll Pr., 1999. ix, 221p.

1st ed. (Worcester, Mass., American Antiquarian Society, 1986) bore present subtitle only. Appeared originally in Proceedings of the American Antiquarian Society, v.95 pt.2, Oct., 1985, p.317–500.

A list of 147 "European architectural books available in America through 1800" and of " . . . all eighteenth-century libraries and bookstores that either circulated or sold architectural books."—*Introd.* Expands and "clarifies" Helen Park's List of architectural books available in America before the Revolution (GLAH 1:J17) by adding 65 titles.

Arranged alphabetically by author and treatise, with English translations and variant titles, as well as references for each title to other important bibliographies of publications available in early America.

Contents: Checklist; Appendix A, Publication dates and imprints of books cited, in order of number of references, p.163–76; Appendix B, Treatises listed by date of earliest American catalogue reference, p.177–83; Appendix C, Treatises listed alphabetically by individual library or firm, p.184–205; Appendix D, Libraries and booksellers listed in order of the size of their collections, p.206–10.

Bibliography, p.211–12. Index to checklist, p.213–21.

J31 Stiverson, Cynthia Zignego. Architecture and the decorative arts: the A. Lawrence Kocher Collection of Books at the Colonial Williamsburg Foundation. Introd. by Lawrence Wodehouse. Foreword by Albert Frey. West Cornwall, Conn., Locust Hill Pr., 1989. xli, 245p.

Catalog of the 462 books Kocher, architect, educator, and one-time editor of Architectural record, amassed for research on colonial American architecture. It includes early and rare practical architectural design books, influential treatises and pattern books, and books known to have been in the libraries of colonists, but also books on the social life and aesthetics of English and American life from 1607 through the early 20th century.

Entries are alphabetical by author, with complete citations, physical and binding details, collation, provenance, and information on the first edition. References to other architectural bibliographies are noted.

Contents: Key to abbreviations; Sources consulted for Virginia associations; Bibliography of additional sources; Publications by and about A. Lawrence Kocher; Catalogue of the Kocher collection.

Index, p.227–45.

J32 Twentieth century building materials, 1900–1950: an annotated bibliography. Comp. by George M. Bleekman III . . . [et al.] Washington, D.C., U.S. Dept. of the Interior, National Park Service, Preservation Assistance Division. For sale by the U.S. G.P.O., Supt. of Docs., 1993. iv, 52p. il. (NPS reading list)

Annotated bibliography of information on building materials introduced or significantly developed during the first half of the 20th century. Includes books, periodical articles, government publications, professional reports, and product information.

Contents: General building materials: background information; Classifications of materials; Construction systems; Additional resources.

J33 United States. National Gallery of Art. The Mark J. Millard architectural collection. Washington, D.C., National Gallery of Art; N.Y., Braziller, [1993–]. (3)v. il.

Scholarly, well-illustrated catalog of the National Gallery's Mark J. Millard collection, one of the "finest collections of rare illustrated books and bound series of prints on Western European architecture, design, and topography. The collection, approximately 560 titles in more than 750 volumes, focuses on the most beautiful and influential prints and books published between the end of the fifteenth century and the beginning of the nineteenth century."—*Pref.*

Entries are listed alphabetically by author, then chronologically, and contain a complete bibliographic description and a catalog text, plus details on publishing history, binding, and provenance.

Contents: (1) French books, sixteenth through nineteenth centuries. Introduction and catalogue, Dora Wiebenson; bibliographic description, Claire Baines (1993); (2) British books, seventeenth through nineteenth centuries. Catalogue entries, Robin Middleton . . . [et al.]; bibliographic descriptions, Claire Baines, Gerald Beasley (1998); (3) Northern European books, sixteenth to early nineteenth centuries. Introd. essay, Harry Mallgrave; bibliographic descriptions, Gerald Beasley . . . [et al.] (1998); (4) Italian and Spanish books, fifteenth through nineteenth centuries. Essays and introd., Martha Pollak; bibliographic descriptions, Claire Baines . . . [et al.] (2000).

J34 Viaro, Alain M., and Ziegler, Arlette. Architectures traditionnelles dans le monde: repérages bibliographiques. [Paris], UNESCO, [1984?] ix, 118p. (Établissements humains et environnement socio-culturel)

Partially annotated bibliography of worldwide vernacular architecture from mostly French, British, and American articles and books, including many social science sources, up to ca. 1983. Emphasis on Africa and Asia. Includes several thousand citations, all of which provide publication source.

Arranged by continent, then country. Large section of general sources on vernacular architecture, environment, ethnology, geography, religion, and urbanism.

J35 Ward, Jack W. Construction information source and reference guide: books, manuals, handbooks, reports, studies, associations, societies, institutes, labor unions, trade journals, newsletters, periodicals, computerized information retrieval, publishing houses & book sources. 4th ed. Phoenix, Construction Publications, 1981. ix, 474p.

1st ed., 1966; 2d ed., 1970; 3d ed., 1973.

Extensive guide to practical information sources on building and construction.

Contents: (1) Books, manuals, handbooks, reports, studies (divided by topic); (2) Associations, societies, institutes; (3) Labor unions; (4) Trade journals, newsletters, periodicals; (5) Computerized information retrieval; (6) Publishing houses and book sources.

J36 Wayne, Kathryn M. Architecture sourcebook: a guide to resources on the practice of architecture. Detroit,

Omnigraphics, [1997]. 417p. (Design reference series, 2)

Thorough guide to the literature for practicing American architects, plus methods for researching newer material on the subject.

Part one, Building types has 14 chapters on different building types. Each chapter includes Library of Congress subject headings, introductory reference sources, names and addresses of relevant associations, bibliographies, books and periodical titles, and selected articles on that topic. Part two, Additional reference sources, has a chapter each on core collections of Dictionaries and encyclopedias; Indexes, Handbooks and manuals, and Periodicals. Appendix I, Architecture collections in the United States. Appendix II, Publication sources.

Author/title index, p.363–403. Subject index, p.405–17.

J37 Wodehouse, Lawrence. Indigenous architecture worldwide: a guide to information sources. Detroit, Gale Research, [1980]. x, 392p. (Art and architecture information guide series, 12) (Gale information guide library)

Partially annotated bibliography of English-language literature published through 1977 on worldwide vernacular architecture, including hundreds of books, the Encyclopedia of world art (GLAH 1:E4), Architectural review (GLAH 1:Q42), Journal of the Society of Architectural Historians (GLAH 1:Q322), and National geographic. Citations note presence of illustrative materials.

Contents: (1) Indigenous architecture worldwide [with introductory bibliographic essay, and bibliographies for general material, and for continent, divided by country]; (2) The vernacular as a nineteenth-century revival style and an influence in twentieth-century architecture [essay, with introduction, selection of general reference works, and bibliographies on architects]. Appendix: The use of the National geographic magazine as a research tool.

Author indexes, p.305–20. Title index, p.321–40. Geographic and building location index, p.341–55. Subject index, p.357–92.

SEE ALSO: Architecture in manuscript, 1601–1996: guide to the British Architectural Library manuscripts and archives collection (GLAH 2:H77); Architecture on screen: films and videos on architecture, landscape architecture, historic preservation, city and regional planning (GLAH 2:D32); Doumato, Architecture and women: a bibliography (GLAH 2:J439); Goode's bibliography: doctoral dissertations relating to American architectural history, 1897–1995 (GLAH 2:J440); Institut français d'architecture. Archives d'architecture du XXe siècle (GLAH 2:J271); Sharp, Sources of modern architecture (GLAH 2:J206).

DICTIONARIES AND ENCYCLOPEDIAS

J38 Architektur: Hochbau—Stadtplanung und Städtebau: Bildfachwörterbuch englisch-deutsch-ungarisch-polnisch-russisch-slowakisch = Architecture: building construction—urban planning and design: pictorial thesaurus and dictionary English-German-Hungarian-Polish-Russian-Slovakian [Hrsg. Eduard Führ. Autoren, Subhash Anand . . . [et. al.] Düsseldorf, Werner-Verlag, 1996. 502p. il.

Pictorial thesaurus in six languages is the result of a four-year research project with participants from the United States, Germany, Hungary, Poland, the Ukraine, and the Slovak Republic. Terms, many illustrated, are systematically arranged according to subject area in the thesaurus. Separate alphabetical index for each language.

J39 Ballast, David Kent. The Encyclopedia of associations and information sources for architects, designers, and engineers. [Armonk, N.Y.], Sharpe Professional, [1998]. 814p. + CD-ROM.

Broad array of information sources for professionals, covering architectural history, building, preservation, and practice. Entries for organizations include full address, e-mail, and internet addresses, as well as description of each organization. A separate section describes publications and services of the organizations. Chapters on journals and newsletters include description of each, subscription information, where indexed, and whether document delivery is available.

Contents: (1) Associations and organizations; (2) Resources of associations and organizations; (3) Journals; (4) Newsletters; (5) Online databases; (6) CD-ROMs; (7) Research organizations and testing laboratories; (8) Directories; (9) Indexes to periodicals; (10) Federal government information sources; (11) World Wide Web sites; (12) Indexes:

Keywords, p.655–73; Name index, p.675–702; Index of titles of association resources, p.703–97; Acronym index, p.799–812; MasterFormat index, p.813–14. CD-ROM provides full-text and Boolean searches.

J40 Bianchina, Paul. Illustrated dictionary of building materials and techniques, an invaluable sourcebook of the tools, terms, materials, and techniques used by building professionals. N.Y., Wiley, [1993]. xi, 238p. il.

1st. ed. Blue Ridge Summit, Penn., TAB Books, 1986.

4,500 definitions and cross-references arranged alphabetically, with grouping of like terms under a single heading, e.g., "window" is divided into 24 sub-parts (bay window, bow window, etc.), each with its own definition.

Contents: Dictionary; Appendixes: Common abbreviations; Conversions, tables, weights; Building and framing information; Lumber and plywood information; Hardware information; Electrical information.

Bibliography of sources, p.237–38.

J41 Ching, Frank. A visual dictionary of architecture. N.Y., Van Nostrand Reinhold, [1995]. 319p. il.

Organized by broad clusters that reflect basic aspects of architecture, which are detailed in the table of contents. Encourages browsing but also permits instant access through a comprehensive alphabetical index of terms (p.285–318). Important and interesting quotes about architecture (p.319). Thousands of clear illustrations are an integral part of the dictionary.

J42 Construction dictionary. 9th ed. [Phoenix, Ariz.], Greater Phoenix Arizona Chapter #98 of the National Association of Women in Construction, [1996]. viii, 634p. il.

[1st ed.], 1966; rev. ed., 1968; [3d ed.], 1973; 4th ed., 1978; 5th. ed., 1981; 6th. ed., 1985; 7th ed., 1989; 8th ed., 1991.

More than 15,000 terms and 16,000 definitions of specialized, slang, and obscure construction terms. Contents: Dictionary of construction terms and abbreviations; Construction associations and government agencies; Facts and figures; Architectural and engineering symbols.

J43 Contemporary architects. Ed. by Muriel Emanuel. 3d ed. N.Y., St. James, 1994. xix, 1,125p. il. (Contemporary arts series).

[1st] ed., 1980; 2d ed., 1987.

Includes 585 architects, engineers, theorists, and landscape architects worldwide who worked in the last 50 years or who influenced 20th-century architecture. Each entry has a brief biography, chronological list of works, selected list of exhibitions and publications by and about, statement by the architect when provided, and an evaluative essay. Many entries accompanied by photographs or illustrations of major works.

Index of 1,000 major public buildings by designers included in the book is arranged by country, then city, p.1089–1116. Notes on advisers and contributors, p.1119–24.

J44 Cowan, Henry J., and Smith, Peter R. Dictionary of architectural and building technology. With contrib. by José Carlos Damski . . . [et al.] N.Y., Spon, [1998]. ix, 263p. il.

[1st ed.] based on Cowan's Dictionary of architectural science, London, Applied Science, 1973; [Rev. and exp. ed.], Dictionary of architectural and building technology, N.Y., Elsevier, 1986.

Comprehensive dictionary of architectural and building technology, including measurements, building materials, construction, facility management, solar energy, and computer terms. It excludes timber-related terminology. Includes 3,500 terms, 2,000 newly added, with appropriate cross references. Emphasis on British, Australian, and American terms.

J45 Curl, James Stevens. Encyclopaedia of architectural terms, with illustrations by the author and John J. Sambrook. London, Donhead, [1997]. xii, 352p. il.

"Introduction to the vocabulary used to describe our built heritage so that the basic architectural elements can be identified."—*Pref.* British emphasis. Includes historical terms and many illustrations.

Bibliography, p.349–52.

J46 Dictionary of building preservation. Ed. by Ward Bucher. Christine Madrid, illustration ed. N.Y., Preservation Press; Wiley, 1996. x, 560p. il.

"Intended to serve two main purposes: first, to clarify the specialized terms used in the preservation field in the United States and Canada; and second, to allow a recorder to fully describe a historic resource."—*Introd.*

Bibliography, p.555–60.

J47 Dictionnaire de l'architecture du XXe siècle. Sous la dir. de Jean-Paul Midant. [Paris], Hazan; Institut français d'architecture, [1996]. 987p. il. (part col.)

Well-illustrated, pithy, and signed entries on architects, movements, terms, and subjects concerning 20th-century architecture. International in scope. Covers 1,800 architects. Each entry includes bibliographic reference.

Les Auteurs, p.xii–xiii. Liste des entrées, p.xiv–xx, arranged by country.

J48 Elsevier's dictionary of architecture in five languages: English, French, Spanish, German, and Dutch. Comp. by J.-P. Vandenberghe. Amsterdam, Elsevier, 1988. x, 519p. il.

Significant architectural terms used in European practice. No definitions.

"Basic table" gives English/American terms with their French, Spanish, German, and Dutch equivalents. Separate sections for French, Spanish, German, and Dutch terms with reference to their entries in the Basic table.

Bibliography, p.ix–x. Illustrations, p.507–19.

J49 Enciclopedia dell'architettura Garzanti. Milan, Garzanti, 1996. 1036p. il., plans, plates.

Italian encyclopedia of architecture and architects, compiled by Italian scholars, but with an international focus. Emphasis on 20th century.

The bulk of the publication is the well-illustrated dictionary with entries ranging from very brief to rather long. Forty pages of photographic plates illustrating 16 major building types are inserted in the middle of the dictionary. Following the encyclopedia and called "Appendici" are two additional sections, the first a chronologically arranged essay by Enrico Morteo, "Storia dell'architettura,"(p.[965]–1024), with 72 pages of photographic plates. The last section is the "Bibliografia" (p.[1025]–1036), a bibliographic essay by Luciano Patetta, organized into "Trattati, manuali, teorie di architettura" and "Storia e critica dell'architettura."

Indice, p.[1037].

J50 Encyclopedia of architectural technology. Ed. by Pedro Guedes. N.Y., McGraw-Hill, [1979]. 313p. il.

British ed. Macmillan encyclopedia of architecture and technological change. London, Macmillan, 1979.

Covers in non-technical language "architectural technology, architectural sociology, and architectural development" for a "new perspective" and understanding of architecture.—*Introd.* 30 authors contributed to the publication, which has more than 800 illustrations. Entries, organized into six topical sections, provide concise historical overviews.

Contents: (1) Stylistic periods and geographical adaptations; (2) Built forms and building types; (3) Structures—ideas, elements, structural systems, and the processes of erecting buildings; (4) Services, mechanical and environmental systems; (5) Building materials; (6) Tools, techniques, and fixings.

Index, p.[314–20].

J51 Encyclopedia of architecture, design, engineering & construction. Joseph A. Wilkes, ed.-in-chief. Robert T. Packard, assoc. ed. N.Y., Wiley, [1988–90]. 5v. il. (Wiley-Interscience publication)

Published in conjunction with the American Institute of Architects. Multi-purpose source for architectural history, design, practice, and construction with selective and uneven coverage by more than 500 contributors.

Most entries have bibliographies. Alphabetical arrangement, with Supplement in vol.5 for articles that missed initial deadline and new topics (p.442–659).

Index, v.5, p.661–808.

J52 Encyclopedia of building technology. Ed. by Henry J. Cowan. Englewood Cliffs, N.J., Prentice Hall, [1988]. xxii, 322p. il.

210 alphabetical articles in non-technical language by 161 international architectural, construction, and building experts. Each entry has a bibliography and cross-references to related articles. Includes list of contributors.

Abbreviations, p.xx. Index to contributors, p.311. General index, p.313–22.

J53 Fantastici, Agostino. Vocabolario di architettura: prima edizione completa dal manoscritto autografo di Agostino Fantastici. A cura e con un saggio di Gianni Mazzoni. Fiesole (Firenze), Cadmo, [1994]. 429p. il, col. plates. (Esedra, 6)

1,357 architectural, building, and civil engineering terms in use in Tuscany in the first half of the 18th century. Definitions compiled by architect-designer Fantastici (1782–1845) from the many early and classical treatises he used in his own work, and published together for the first time from the original manuscripts now in the Biblioteca Comunale degli Intronati di Siena.

Contents: Vocabolario di architettura; L'architetto Agostino Fantastici nella cultura del suo tempo di Gianni Mazzoni.

Note [bibliography], p.397–412. Indice analitico, p.415–29.

J54 Fleming, John; Honour, Hugh; and Pevsner, Nikolaus. The Penguin dictionary of architecture and landscape architecture. 5th ed. [London], Penguin, [1998]. vii, 643, [1]p. il., plans.

See GLAH 1:J26 for 2d ed.; 3d ed., 1980; 4th ed., [1991].

Revises and expands previous ed. to include "contemporary architects who have recently become prominent internationally" (*Foreword*), and for the first time landscape architecture. Bibliographies included in most entries. Occasional line drawings or plans.

Bibliographic abbreviations, p.639–43.

J55 Forbes, J. R. Dictionnaire d'architecture et de construction = Dictionary of architecture and construction. Pref. de M. Brackenbury. 3e éd. rev. et augm. N.Y., Lavoisier, [1995]. 439, [3]p.

Expands 1st ed. 1984, 2d ed., 1988, with 5,000 additional terms.

French-English and English-French dictionary of historical and contemporary terms useful in architectural practice, restoration, landscape, environment, building, and construction. Where appropriate, distinguishes between American and British English usage.

Includes list of abbreviations.

J56 Gelbrich, Uli. Dictionary of architecture and building, English-German. N.Y., Elsevier, 1989. 418p.

30,000 English-language terms commonly used in architecture and construction with their German equivalents.

Abkürzungen und Kurzwörter, p.413–18.

J57 Glossary of urban form. Ed. by Peter J. Larkham and Andrew N. Jones. [Birmingham, Ala.], Urban Morphology Research Group, School of Geography, University of Birmingham, [1991]. 98p. il. (Historical geography research series, no. 26)

Recent terms, international and interdisciplinary, used in all aspects of urban morphology, including the environmental aspects of architecture, urbanization, city planning, and land use. Bibliographic references for most entries, with explanation of origins and country of primary use. Scholarly bibliographic introduction provides history and evolution of urban morphology research and terminology.

Selective contents: Introduction: Urban form, urban morphology and urban historical geography, by Peter J. Larkham, p.1–8; Index: Glossary terms indexed by main headings; Glossary.

References, p.86–98.

J58 González Licón, Héctor Javier, and Julio César Márquez Díaz. Glosario de terminos tecnico arquitectonicos. [Morelia, Michoacán, Universidad Michoacana de San Nicolás de Hidalgo, Escuela de Arquitectura,] Secretaría de Difusión Cultural, Ed. Universitaria, [1994]. 194p.

Glossary of technical architectural terms in Mexican usage.

Bibliografía, p.193–94.

J59 Greene, Fayal. The anatomy of a house: a picture dictionary of architectural and design elements. Illustrations by Bonita Bavetta. N.Y., Doubleday, [1991]. 108p. il.

Layman's pictorial dictionary of hundreds of the parts of a house arranged by element, e.g., roof, window, floors, etc.

Extensive table of contents, but no index. Includes directory of sources and resources (p.95–105).

Bibliography of helpful books and magazines, p.107–08.

J60 Hardwick, Benjamin [und] Manfred Markus. Bauen und Architektur = Building and architecture: 4000 words thematically arranged. Essen, Verlag Die Blaue Eule, [1994]. 174p. il. + 1 computer disk. (English for specific purposes, Bd. 1)

English-German vocabulary of wide-ranging architecture and building terms concentrating on contemporary practice. Includes IBM-compatible computer diskette containing the word lists and indexes.

Footnotes provide etymology, and phonetic symbols aid in pronunciation of English terms. A list of abbreviations and phonetic symbols is included. Arranged into 3 major themes, and several subdivisions under each, with English and German equivalents for each term: (I) General aspects of building and architecture; (II) Small conventional houses; (III) Other buildings and structures.

German-English index, p.119–46. English-German index, p.147–74.

J61 Harris, Cyril M., ed. Dictionary of architecture & construction. 3d ed., N.Y., McGraw-Hill, 2000. ix, 1028p. il.

See GLAH 1:J27 for 1st ed.; 2d ed. 1993.

Revised, updated, and comprehensive source for authoritative definitions of more than 24,500 terms compiled from numerous professional, standards, and trade associations related to architecture and building. Includes 2,200 line drawings.

J62 ______, ed. Historic architecture sourcebook. N.Y., McGraw-Hill, [1977]. viii, 581p. il. (Repr.: N.Y., Dover, 1983.)

Definitions of 5,000 terms relating to historic architecture, including ancient [i.e., ancient Near Eastern, Egyptian], Greek and Hellenistic, Roman, Early Christian, Chinese, Japanese, Indian, Islamic, Mesoamerican, Romanesque, Gothic, Renaissance, and modern. Includes 2,100 line drawings.

J63 The Illustrated encyclopedia of architects and architecture. Ed. by Dennis Sharp. N.Y., Whitney Library of Design, [1991]. 256p. il. (part. col.)

Section 1 is an international biographical dictionary of well-known architects, historic and contemporary, with brief bibliographic references and lists of their major buildings. Section 2, "Architecture and the history of ideas," consists of 8 brief, well-illustrated essays that place architects in their context. Cross references refer the reader to biographical entries.

Glossary of terms, p.246–49. Index of names, major buildings, and projects, p.250–56.

J64 International dictionary of architects and architecture. Ed. by Randall J. Van Vynckt. European consultant, Doreen Yarwood. Photo and graphic researcher, Suhail Butt. Detroit, St. James Press, [1993]. 2v., il., plans.

"Features 523 architects and 467 buildings and sites that have figured prominently in Western architectural history."—*Introd.* (1) Architects is a biographical dictionary with a chronology of major works, brief bibliography of works by and about the architect, and a signed critical essay for each entry. (2) Architecture consists of geographically arranged signed essays with bibliographies, organized by continent, and then country, except for the first section, "Classical sites and monuments."

Each vol. has indexes by architect name, building or site name, and geographic location, as well as notes on contributors.

J65 Jones, Frederic H. The concise dictionary of architectural and design history. Los Altos, Calif., Crisp, [1992]. 344p.

All-purpose dictionary of approximately 2,000 names and terms in two parts: first, a dictionary of terms, and second, a dictionary of architects and designers.

J66 Kadatz, Hans-Joachim. Seemanns Lexikon der Architektur. [Leipzig], Seemann, [1994]. 262, [2]p. il.

Updated ed. of Wörterbuch der Architektur (1980). More than 2,000 terms, including names. Includes cross references to other entries, and for historical terms, gives origins and period of usage. Well illustrated.

Literaturhinweise, p.[263].

J67 Koepf, Hans. Bildwörterbuch der Architektur. Dritte Aufl. überarb. von Günther Binding. Mit eng., franz. und ital. Fachglossar. Stuttgart, Kröner, 1999. 634p. il.

1st ed. 1968; 2d ed. 1974.

Terminological dictionary followed by an illustrated appendix of architectural forms, historically arranged, and a glossary of English, French, and Italian technical terms.

Abbildungen von Prototypen der Baukunst, p.511–35. Literaturverzeichnis, p.[536]–54. Fremdsprachiges Fachglossar, p.[555]–634.

J68 Leva Pistoi, Mila. Il nomenclatore di architettura. [Progetto e realizzazione del testo, Mila Leva Pistoi, Marina Molino e Maria Maddalena Piovesana. Voci di urbanistica e pianificazione territoriale, Riccardo Bedrone]. Torino, Rosenberg & Sellier, [1993]. 318p. il.

Well-illustrated Italian dictionary of more than 2,200 terms for the history and practice of architecture, building, and urban design, with phonetic pronunciations.

Includes list of abbreviations, p.6.

J69 Lever, Jill, and Harris, John. Illustrated dictionary of architecture, 800–1914. [2d ed.] London, Faber and Faber, [1993]. 218p. il., 317 plates.

Exp. and rev. ed. of GLAH 1:J28.

J70 Macmillan encyclopedia of architects. Adolf K. Placzek, ed. in chief. N.Y., Free Pr., [1982]. 4v. il.

Essential dictionary of more than 2,400 critical biographies by recognized scholars. Each entry includes a chronology of major works and bibliography by and about each architect. Covers architects (and landscape architects, planners and a few critics) born before 31 December 1930, or deceased at the date of publication.

In addition to an introductory essay, there is a list of biographies, directory of contributors, chronological table of contents, general bibliography, glossary, index of names, and index of works.

J71 Maliszewski-Pickart, Margaret. Architecture and ornament: an illustrated dictionary. Jefferson, N.C., McFarland, [1998]. x, 198p. il.

A dictionary and an overview of architectural ornament and detailing, with an appendix on how to describe architecture. The first part, 131 clearly labeled plates of illustrations arranged by building part, e.g., windows and doors, walls, stairs, etc., allows readers to visually identify a building element in a series of illustrations. Once the building element is identified, it can be located in the dictionary part.

Contents: How to use this book; Illustrations; Dictionary; Appendix: Describing architecture.

Selected bibliography, p.197–98.

J72 Means illustrated construction dictionary. Ed. by Kornelis Smit & Howard M. Chandler. Illustrations by Carl W. Linde. New unabridged ed. Kingston, Mass., R.S. Means, 1991. vii, 691p. il.

Terms in everyday usage in current U.S. construction trades and professions. Illustrated throughout. Abbreviations beginning with each letter of the alphabet precede the definitions for that section.

J73 Müller, Werner. DTV-Atlas zur Baukunst: Tafeln und Texte. Tafeln, Entwurf, Gunther Vogel. Ausführung, Inge und István Szász. Originalausg., 9. Aufl. München, Deutscher Taschenbuch, 1992. 2v. il. chiefly col., maps, plans, elev.

1. Aufl. Bd. 1, 1974, Bd. 2, 1981. French-ed.

J74 Atlas d'architecture mondiale: Mésopotamie, Egypte, Egée, Grèce, Rome, Byzance. [Paris], Stock, 1978. 2v.

Profusely illustrated pictorial encyclopedia of the history of world architecture. Chronological arrangement and detailed index for each vol.

Contents: (1) Allgemeiner Teil, Baugeschichte von Mesopotamien biz Byzanz: Verzeichnis der Abkürzungen und Fachsausdrücke, Einleitung, Architektur als autonomer Prozess, Bauelemente, Bauwerk als Organismus, Architektur als geschichtsbedingte Form, Mesopotamien, Ägypten, Ägäis, Hellas, Rom, Frühes Christentum; Rom und Byzanz/Neuorientierung der antiken Kunst; (2) Baugeschichte von der Romanik bis zur Gegenwart: Einleitung, Mittelalter, Neuzeit I, Neuzeit II , 20. Jahrhundert/Drei Generationen der modernen Architektur, Gegenwart: Strömungen und Tendenzen.

Literatur- und Quellenverzeichnis, v.1, p.274–77, v.2, p.565–73. Register, v.1, p.278–88, v.2, p.574–600.

J75 Multilingual dictionary of architecture and building terms. Ed. by Chris Grech. N.Y., Spon, [1998]. xxi, 453p.

2,644 key terms used in building design and construction in English, French, German, Spanish, and Italian. Emphasis on terms used in the design office and on routine building work. European emphasis.

Part I, Translations, is a numerical list of English-language terms with their French, German, Italian, and Spanish equivalents across each 2-page spread. Part II, Word indexes, consists of 4 separate alphabetical word lists in French, German, Italian, and Spanish with references to the entry number of the English listing in Part I.

J76 Oudin, Bernard. Dictionnaire des architectes. Nouv. éd., rev. et augm. [3d ed.] [Paris], Seghers, [1994]. 664p. il.

1st ed., 1970; 2d ed., 1982.

Worldwide coverage of more than 1,000 architects from all periods. Brief biographical entries with summaries of major buildings and contribution to field.

Illustrated glossary, p.561–77. Geographic index to buildings, alphabetical by country, then state and city, p.579–64.

J77 Paniagua Soto, José Ramón. Vocabulario básico de arquitectura. 8a ed. [Madrid], Cátedra, [1996]. 339 [69]p. il., plates. (Cuadernos Arte Cátedra, 4)

Spanish language dictionary of more than 3,500 Castillian terms used in the history and practice of architecture. Etymology is given for each word, along with synonyms, most commonly accepted usage, and cross references to related terms and plates, where appropriate.

Bibliografía para el estudio de las voces castellanas referentes al campo de la arquitectura, p.17–23.

J78 Perspectives: an anthology of 1001 architectural quotations. Ed. by Charles Knevitt. Illus. by Louis Hellman. Foreword by Sir Hugh Casson. Alantic Highlands, N.J. (Distr. in the U.S.A. and Canada by Humanities Press, [1986]). 159p. il.

"Dictionary" of architectural quotations from a wide range of architects, critics and surprising other people, such as Pasternak, Orwell, and John Milton.

Arranged in 14 categories (e.g., Architecture is . . . ; Theory; Critics; Town, City, Suburb; etc.).

Index of sources, p.155–58. Index of themes, p.159.

J79 Plazola Cisneros, Alfredo. Enciclopedia de arquitectura Plazola. Coautores, Alfredo Plazola Anguiano y Guillermo Plazola Anguiano. [Estado de Mexico], Plazola Editores, 1994– . (8)v. il., plans, plates (part col.)

Expanded, corrected and retitled ed. of vols. II and III of Arquitectura habitacional, 2a ed, Mexico, Editorial Limusa, 1990. 10v. projected.

Spanish-language encyclopedia of worldwide architecture and architects, including biographies of important architects and the development and history of the architecture of the major cultures of the world. Mexican and Latin American emphasis. Entries provide etymology of terms.

Contents: (1) A; (2) A–B; (3) C; (4) D–E; (5) F–G; (6) H; (7) I–M; (8) Mes–O; (9) P–R; and (10) S–Z forthcoming.

Bibliographical references in each vol.

J80 Practically speaking: a dictionary of quotations on engineering, technology and architecture. Sel. and arranged by Carl C. Gaither and Alma E. Cavazos-Gaither. Illus. by Andrew Slocombe. Philadelphia, Institute of Physics Pub., 1999. xv, 367p. il.

"Designed as an aid for the general reader who has an interest in these topics as well as for the experienced engineer, architect or technician."—*Pref.*

Subject by author index, p.303–44. Author by subject index, p.345–67.

J81 Stein, J. Stewart. Construction glossary: an encyclopedic reference and manual. 2d ed. N.Y., Wiley, 1993. xx, 1137p.

Terms used by U.S. construction industry and related trades. "Definitions include multiple meanings, historical references, specification language, reference standards, manufacturers' recommended descriptions, and scientific and engineering analysis."—*Pref.*

Arranged into 16 divisions following the organization of Masterformat (Alexandria, Va., Construction Specifications Institute, 1988) plus sections for Professional services; Construction categories; Technical-scientific and related data; Reference data sources; and appendixes with abbreviations, weights and measures, carpentry abbreviations.

Overall index, p.1111–37.

J82 Stierlin, Henri. Encyclopaedia of world architecture. [2d ed. London, Macmillan, 1979.] 2v. il., plans, plates (part col.)

Concise introductory essays in French, German, and English on historical periods of architecture through 1960s. Illustrated with scaled elevations and plans, and occasional color photos. Brief informative descriptions and captions for each illustration are provided in French, German, and English.

Contents: (1) Egypt; From Middle East to megaliths; Greece; The Roman Empire; Byzantium; The early Middle Ages; The Romanesque period; Gothic; Renaissance; Baroque (Italy and Central Europe); Iberian and Colonial Baroque; The dawn of modern times; (2) India; South-east Asia; China; Japan; Persia; Seljuk and Ottoman Turkey; Moslem India; Ancient Mexico; The Mayas; Peru; The modern period.

Index, v.2 [French], p.479–84, [German], p.485–90, [English], p.491–96. Table of contents, v.2, p.497–99.

J83 Traister, John E. Illustrated dictionary for building construction. Liburn, Ga., Fairmont (Dist. by PTR Prentice-Hall, 1993). 465p. il.

Clear definitions of more than 1,000 technical terms which "engineers, architects, contractors, consultants" use daily in the U.S. and Canada. 15 appendixes provide detailed charts, diagrams, formulas, abbreviations, trade organizations, etc.

Table of contents of appendixes, p.347–48.

J84 The visual dictionary of buildings. N.Y., Dorling Kindersley, 1992. 64p., col. il. (Eyewitness visual dictionaries)

Labeled, full-color illustrations with explanatory text depict representative historical and contemporary structures, architectural elements, and building components from ancient times to the present.

Index, p.60–64.

J85 White, Antony, and Robertson, Bruce. Architecture & ornament, a visual guide. [N.Y.], Design Press [TAB], [1990]. 112p. il., plates, maps.

A pictorial, encyclopedia-style guide to Western architecture and architectural ornament from classical to modern times. Detailed plates in 3 sections (Buildings, Structures, and Ornament) illustrate specific terms and elements.

Contents: Plates; Glossary of terms; Style timechart; Architects' lifelines; Major architectural sites (maps arranged by style or period).

J86 Yarwood, Doreen. Encyclopaedia of architecture. N.Y., Facts on File, [1986]. 446p. il.

Compact, heavily illustrated general encyclopedia of architecture, architects, and building methods and materials.

Index, p.433–46. Bibliography, p.430–32.

J87 Who's who in architecture: from 1400 to the present. Ed. by J. M. Richards, American consultant, Adolph K. Placzek. N.Y., Holt, Rinehart and Winston, [1977]. 368p. il. (part col.)

Brief biographies of more than 600 architects, landscape architects, and planners active between 1400 and the mid-1970s in Western Europe, the Americas, modern Israel, the British Commonwealth and Japan. Includes cross references to names cited elsewhere in the text, and occasional bibliographic sources.

List of contributors, p.11–12. Further reading, p.360–61. Select index of buildings, p.363–68.

SEE ALSO: Glossarium artis (GLAH 2:E7); Gottfried, American vernacular design, 1870–1940: an illustrated glossary (GLAH 2:J459).

HISTORIES AND HANDBOOKS

General Works

J88 Ackerman, James S. The villa: form and ideology of country houses. Princeton, Princeton Univ. Pr., 1990. 304p. il. (Bollingen series, XXXV, 34) (The A.W. Mellon lectures in the fine arts, 1985)

An expansion of the six lectures delivered in 1985, "composed of a general introductory chapter treating the typology of the villa in the western world since antiquity, and ten chapters that focus on moments of innovation and change in the history of villa building."—*Foreword.*

Prominent figures are the Medici, Palladio, Thomas Jefferson, A. J. Downing, Wright, and Le Corbusier. Ackerman notes in his postscript that villas are distinguished from farmhouses or country cottages by "the intense, programmatic investment of ideological goals."—*p.286.*

Notes, p.287–99. Index, p.301–04.

J89 The Architect: chapters in the history of the profession. Ed. by Spiro Kostof. N.Y., Oxford Univ. Pr., 1977. x, 371p. il., maps, ports.

An essential source that complements and updates M. S. Briggs' The Architect in history (Oxford, Clarendon, 1927, repr. 1974).

Contents: (1) The practice of architecture in the ancient world: Egypt and Greece, by Spiro Kostof; (2) Roman architects, by William L. MacDonald; (3) The architect in the Middle Ages, East and West, by Spiro Kostof; (4) The emergence of the Italian architect during the fifteenth century, by Leopold D. Ettlinger; (5) The new professionalism in the Renaissance, by Catherine Wilkinson; (6) The Royal Building Administration in France from Charles V to Louis XIV, by Myra Nan Rosenfeld; (7) The rise of the professional architect in England, by John Wilton-Ely; (8) The École des Beaux-Arts and the architectural profession in the United States: the case of John Galen Howard, by Joan Draper; (9) Architectural education in the thirties and seventies: a personal view, by Joseph Esherick; (10) On the fringe of the profession: women in American architecture, by Gwendolyn Wright; (11) Architectural practice in America, 1865–1965—ideal and reality, by Bernard Michael Boyle.

Notes at ends of chapters. Index, p.351–71.

J90 Architectural History Foundation books. N.Y., Architectural History Foundation; Cambridge, Mass., MIT Pr., 1978– . (35)v. il., maps, plans.

Selective contents: (1) Serlio, Sebastiano. Sebstiano Serlio on domestic architecture (1978); (2) Otto, Christian F. Space into light: the churches of Balthasar Neumann (1979); (3) Connors, Joseph. Borromini and the Roman oratory, style and society (1980); (4) Le Corbusier sketchbooks: v.1–2, 1914–1948, 1950–1954 (1981), v.3–4, 1954–1957, 1957–1964 (1982); (5) Hanna, Paul R., and Jean S. Frank Lloyd Wright's Hanna house, 2v. (1981 and 1987, 1982); (6) Searing, Helen, ed. In search of modern architecture: a tribute to Henry-Russell Hitchcock (1982); (7) Turner, Paul Venable. Campus, an American planning tradition (1984); (8) Brownlee, David Bruce. The Law Courts: the architecture of George Edmund Street (1984); (9) Krinsky, Carol Herselle. Synagogues of Europe: architecture, history, meaning (1985); (10) Upton, Dell. Holy things and profane: Anglican parish churches in colonial Virginia (1986); (11) Quinan, Jack. Frank Lloyd Wright's Larkin building: myth and fact (1987); (12) Friedman, David. Florentine new towns (1988); (13) Branner, Robert. The cathedral of Bourges and its place in Gothic architecture (1989). [After these titles, vols. (some 22) were unnumbered, and a few still are forthcoming.]

Vols. include notes, bibliography, and index.

J91 Architectural technology up to the scientific revolution: the art and structure of large-scale buildings. Ed. by Robert Mark. Cambridge, Mass., MIT Pr., 1993. xvi, 252p. il. (New liberal arts series)

A well-illustrated explication of historic building technology that includes engineers as well as architectural historians among its 12 contributors.

Selective contents: (1) Interpreting large-scale building technology; (2) Soils and foundations; (3) Walls and other vertical elements; (4) Vaults and domes; (5) Timber roofs and spires; Conclusion: artisans, architects, and the scientific revolution.

Bibliographies at end of each chapter. Glossary, p.[236]–42. Index, p.[244]–52.

J92 Arnheim, Rudolf. The dynamics of architectural form. Based on the 1975 Mary Duke Biddle lectures at the Cooper Union. Berkeley, Univ. of California Pr., 1977. vi, 289p. il.

Trans. of Dynamique de la forme architecturale. Bruxelles, Mardaga, 1986. "When I decided to write about architecture, I thought at first of simply applying to this new subject the principles I had developed in [Art and visual perception: a psychology of the creative eye, rev. ed., Berkeley, Univ. of Calif. Pr., 1974]. . . . [In part] because the broader experiential range of architecture invited a different treatment, the present book is more an explorer's report on high-spots of the man-made environment than the outcome of a professional analysis."—*p.7.*

Contents: (I) Elements of space; (II) Vertical and horizontal; (III) Solids and hollows; (IV) As it looks and as it is; (V) Mobility; (VI) Order and disorder; (VII) Symbols through dynamics; (VIII) Expression and function.

Notes, p.275–77. Bibliography, p.279–83. Index, p.285–89.

J93 Benevolo, Leonardo. The history of the city. Trans. by Geoffrey Culverwell. Cambridge, Mass., MIT Pr., 1980. 1011p. il.

Trans. of Storia della città. Roma, Laterza, 1975; 2d ed. [1976]; new ed. in 4 vols., 1993. "Provides a basic history of the man-made environment . . . in the form of a short written text combined with a large number of illustrations."—*Introd.* In 14 chapters covering from prehistoric times to the 1970s.

Index of names, p.1009

J94 Boyer, M. Christine. The city of collective memory: its historical imagery and architectural entertainments. Cambridge, Mass., MIT Pr., 1994. x, 560p. il.

Began "as a critique of the practices of historic preservation, urban design, and postmodern architecture" and evolved "to explore the larger issue of how images from the nineteenth century have been translated into contemporary views of the city, how the restoration of former architectural and neighborhood traces forged a hybrid layering of architectural sites and a constant migration from one time period to another."—*Ackn.*

Contents: (1) The place of history and memory in the contemporary city; (2) City images and representational forms; (3) The city and the theater; (4) The art of collective memory; (5) Topographical travelogues and city views; (6) Invented traditions and cityscapes; (7) The instruments of memory; (8) Manhattan montage; (9) The city as radical artifice.

Notes, p.[495]–548. Index, p.[549]–58.

J95 Braunfels, Wolfgang. Monasteries of Western Europe: the architecture of the orders. Trans. by Alastair Laing. [Reprint.] N.Y., Thames and Hudson, 1993. 263p. il.

See GLAH 1:J34 for the original ed. (1972). Trans. of Abendländische Klosterbaukunst. Köln, DuMont Schauberg, [1969]. The English ed. is considerably expanded. Includes "Selections from documentary sources" with parallel Latin text and English translation.

Notes, p.[249]–50. Bibliography, p.251–54. Index, p.[260]–63.

J96 ———. Urban design in Western Europe: regime and architecture, 900–1900. Trans. by Kenneth J. Northcott. Chicago, Univ. of Chicago Pr., 1988. xiii, 407p. il., plans.

Trans. of Abendländische Stadtbaukunst: Herrschaftsform und Baugestalt. Köln, DuMont Schauberg, 1976. Described as "the counterpart to the author's Monasteries of Western Europe [see preceding entry] . . . which involved roughly the same geographic area."—*Pref.* "This book grew out of a sense of uneasiness [which], in turn, arose out of the state of cities in the 20th century."—*Introd.*

Contents: Cathedral cities; City states; Sea powers; Imperial cities; Ideal cities; Seats of a princely court; Capital cities; The second and third Rome.

Bibliography, p.373–91. Index, p.393–407.

J97 Cambridge studies in the history of architecture. Ed. by Robin Middleton, Joseph Rykwert, and David Watkin. Cambridge, Eng., Cambridge Univ. Pr., 1992–1996. 5v. il.

Self-described as "a new series of historical studies intended to embrace a wide chronological range, from antiquity to the twentieth century, and to become a natural counterpart to Cambridge studies in the history of art [GLAH 2:R26] . . . intended primarily for professional historians of architecture and their students." In selected instances, titles in this series are listed individually elsewhere in this chapter.

Contents: Picon, Antoine. French architects and engineers in the Age of Enlightenment (1992); Tyack, Geoffrey. Sir James Pennethorne and the making of Victorian London (1992); Tait, A. A. Robert Adam: drawings and imagination (1993); Erlande-Brandenburg, Alain. The cathedral: the social and architectural dynamics of construction (1994); Watkin, David. Sir John Soane: enlightenment thought and the Royal Academy lectures (1996).

Vols. include bibliography and index.

J98 Centre canadien d'architecture. Architecture and its image: four centuries of architectural representation: works from the collection of the Canadian Centre for Architecture. Ed. by Eve Blau and Edward Kaufman. Montreal, Centre Canadien d'Architecture/Canadian Centre for Architecture (Distr. by MIT Pr., 1989). 369p. il. (part col.)

Published in conjunction with the exhibition that marked the opening of the CCA and the tenth anniversary of its founding. Intended "to suggest ways in which the relationships among images can convey new understanding of the larger relationship between architecture and representation."—*Introd.*

In addition to the editors, contributors include Robin Evans, William Alexander McClung, Hélène Lipstadt, and Robert Bruegmann.

Bibliographical references. Index of names, p.365–69.

J99 ———. Photography and architecture, 1839–1939. [Ed. by] Richard Pare. Introd. by Phyllis Lambert. Catalog by Catherine Evans Inbusch and Marjorie Munsterberg. Montreal, Centre canadien d'architecture/Canadian Centre for Architecture; N.Y., Callaway, 1982. 282p. il.

Catalog of the exhibition of photographs from the CCA collection, Galerie Lempertz Contempora, Cologne (1982), and other locations. The 147 plates are followed by catalog entries for 80 photographers, including biographical information and a reference for each.

Bibliography, p.273–77. Index, p.278–82.

J100 Colvin, Howard Montagu. Architecture and the afterlife. New Haven, Yale Univ. Pr., 1991. xi, 418p. il. (part col.), map.

"Rather than attempt to write a comprehensive history of funerary architecture in all its aspects, I have preferred to explore in each chapter one or two important themes. The result is a series of interconnected essays, which . . . provide the reader with a continuous but by no means exhaustive history of funerary architecture in western Europe."—*Pref.*

Contents: (I) Megalith and tumulus; (II) From tumulus to mausoleum; (III) The mausoleum of Halicarnassus; (IV) The mausolea of the Roman emperors; (V) The Romans and their monuments; (VI) From mausoleum to martyrium; (VII) Christian burial and medieval church architecture; (VIII) The revival of the architectural tomb; (IX) Chantries and funerary churches in medieval Europe; (X) The family chapel in Renaissance Italy; (XI) Triumphal tombs and the Counter-Reformation; (XII) The princely burial church in Catholic Europe; (XIII) The family chapel in Protestant England and Sweden; (XIV) The return of the mausoleum; (XV) Funerary architecture in the eighteenth and early nineteenth centuries; (XVI) The triumph of the cemetery.

Bibliography, p.375–402. Index, p.403–18.

J101 Curl, James Stevens. A celebration of death: an introduction to some of the buildings, monuments, and settings of funerary architecture in the Western European tradition. Rev. ed. London, Batsford, 1993. xxiv, 408p. il., plans.

1st ed., 1980.

"An introduction to funerary architecture, to cemetery design, and to memorials and monuments in the Western European tradition."—*Introd.*

Notes, p.368–77. Bibliography, p.378–90. Index, p.391–404.

J102 Evans, Robin. The projective cast: architecture and its three geometries. Cambridge, Mass., MIT Pr., 1995. xxxvii, 413p. il.

Seeks "to pin down the elusive relationship that exists between buildings and their representations."—*Ackn.*

Contents: Introduction: Composition and projection; (1) Perturbed circles; (2) Persistent breakage; (3) Seeing through paper; (4) Piero's heads; (5) Drawn stone; (6) The trouble with numbers; (7) Comic lines; (8) Forms lost and found again; (9) Rumors at the extremities.

Notes, p.[372]–401. Index, p.[404]–13.

J103 Fitchen, John. Building construction before mechanization. Cambridge, Mass., MIT Pr., 1986. xvii, 326p. il.

"An attempt to identify the problems of building construction and to recover reasonable and likely answers to what procedures were adopted, here and there, through the ages." This intriguing text covers to the "pre-present."—*Pref.*

Contents: (1) The role of the builder; (2) The nature of building construction and sources of information about its former practices; (3) Physical and cultural forces affecting building construction; (4) Jerry-building and the unending quest for standards of safety; (5) Prior planning and the order and sequence of building operations; (6) Stresses in buildings and the problems they raise; (7) Falsework and lifting devices; (8) Rope and ladders: the builder's habitual implements; (9) The role of wood in building construction; (10) Oversized blocks and projecting stones as aids in masonry construction; (11) Transportation in building construction; (12) The problem of ventilation; (13) Native house building; (14) Building Cheops' pyramid.

Bibliography, p.297–314. General index, p.317–22. Index of authors quoted, p.323–24. Index of references to illustrations, p.325–26.

J104 Fletcher, Banister, Sir. Sir Banister Fletcher's a history of architecture. 20th ed. Ed. by Dan Cruickshank. Consultant eds., Andrew Saint, Peter Blundell Jones, Kenneth Frampton. Assistant ed., Fleur Richards. Boston, Architectural Pr., 1996. xxxviii, 1794p. il.

See GLAH 1:J37 for previous eds. of this standard work; 19th ed. London, Butterworths, 1987.

"The nineteenth edition [of the book] was, in effect, a rethink of the Banister Fletcher structure . . . the twentieth edition is, necessarily, an extensive revision and extension of the nineteenth rather than a major overhaul or exercise in restructuring. Nevertheless, about 35 per cent of the text is new, the book is nearly 200 pages longer, and a significant series of chapters have been recast, extended or introduced."—*Pref.*

Bibliography, p.1671–1712. Glossary, p.1713–30. Index, p.1731–94.

J105 Frankl, Paul. Principles of architectural history; the four phases of architectural style, 1420–1900. Trans. and ed. by James F. O'Gorman. With a foreword by James S. Ackerman. [Cambridge, Mass., MIT Pr., 1968]. xxi, 215p. il., plans.

Trans. of Die Entwicklungsphasen der neueren Baukunst. Leipzig, Teubner, 1914. Begun in 1912 as the author's Habilitationsschrift in Munich for Heinrich Wölfflin.

The foreword by Ackerman explains the context of Frankl's work and its relationship to Heinrich Wölfflin's Renaissance und Barock and Kunstgeschichtliche Grundbegriffe or Principles of art history (GLAH 1:I233), which influenced the translator's choice of title for this book. Ackerman further explains Frankl's use of two interlocking systems—critical and historical—for the analysis of post-medieval architectural monuments.

Bibliographical notes, p.[196]–206. Index, p.[207]–15.

J106 Gloag, John. The architectural interpretation of history. London, A. & C. Black, 1975. xvii, 348p. il., plates.

An older history with a traditional, non-North American focus, by the historian of furniture and ornament.

Contents: (1) The interpretative quality of architecture; (2) The tyranny of eternal repetition; (3) Lost empires; (4) The classical phase: Persia and Greece; (5) The classical phase: Roman power; (6) The death of the gods and the age of faith; (7) The successor states and the Muslim world; (8) Prelude to Gothic; (9) Mediaeval civilisation; (10) Renaissance and revolution; (11) The golden age of taste and reason; (12) Looking backwards; (13) Shadows of the future.

List of references, p.319–37. Index, p.341–48.

J107 Hegemann, Werner. City planning, housing. Pref. by R. M. MacIver. N.Y., Architectural Book Publishing Co., [1936]–38. 3v. fronts. (v.2–3; v.2, port.), il. (incl. maps, plans).

"To supplement and—within a small compass—to bring up to date a previous and much larger volume entitled 'The American Vitruvius, an architect's handbook of civic art' [see following entry]."—*Introd.*

Vol.3 ed. by William W. Forster and Robert C. Weinberg.

Contents: (1) Historical and sociological; (2) Political economy and civic art; (3) A graphic review of civic art, 1922–1937.

J108 ———, and Peets, Elbert. The American Vitruvius: an architects' handbook of civic art. Ed. with an introd. by Alan J. Plattus. Pref. by Leon Krier. Introd. essay by Christiane Crasemann Collins. [Reprint, with new prefatory matter.] N.Y., Princeton Architectural Pr., 1988. xxii, 298p. il.

See GLAH 1:J46 for original ed. and previous repr. Publ. in Catalan as El Vitrubio americano: manual de arte civil para el arquitecto. Barcelona, Caja de arquitectos fundacion, [1993].

Bibliography, p.[294]. Index, p.[295]–98.

J109 Kostof, Spiro. The City assembled: the elements of urban form through history. With the collaboration of Greg Castillo. Original drawings by Richard Tobias. Boston, Little, Brown, 1992. 320p. il. (part col.).

A companion to the author's previous The city shaped (see following entry). This work "focus[es] on the constituent elements of city building common to all settlement patterns, independent of the modes of classification distinguished in The city shaped."—*Introd.*

As with the companion work, Kostof organizes his material within five categories: (1) The city edge; (2) Urban divisions; (3) Public places; (4) The street; (5) Urban process.

Notes, p.306–10. Bibliography, p.311–13. Index, p.315–20.

J110 ———. The City shaped: urban patterns and meanings through history. Original drawings by Richard Tobias. Boston, Little, Brown, 1991. 352p. il. (part col.), maps.

"This book is an architectural historian's attempt to make accessible, to architects, urban designers, and the general public, the universal experience of making cities."—*Introd.* Includes a broad range of geographical and cultural examples, and wide variety of illustrations, plans, and aerial photographs. Complements The city assembled (see preceding entry).

Takes five approaches to urban form.

Contents: (1) Organic patterns; (2) The grid; (3) The city as diagram; (4) The grand manner; (5) The urban skyline.

Notes, p.337–40. Bibliography, p.341–42. Index, p.344–52.

J111 ———. A History of architecture: settings and rituals. Original drawings by Richard Tobias. 2d ed., rev. by Greg Castillo. N.Y., Oxford Univ. Pr., 1995. 792p. il. (part col.), plates, maps.

1st ed., 1985. Revised after Kostof's death in Dec. 1991, using typescripts and videotapes from his lectures "to establish the narrative and basic text for the final chapters of this edition."—*Pref.* "This book is something of a compromise. It is a general survey of architectural history that tries to reconcile the traditional grand canon of monuments with a broader, more embracing view of the built environment."—*Pref.* to the first ed.

In three parts: A place on earth; Measuring up; The search for self.

Bibliographies ("Further reading") at the ends of the 29 chapters. Glossary, p.767–75. Index, p.776–92.

J112 Krinsky, Carol Herselle. Synagogues of Europe: architecture, history, meaning. N.Y., Architectural History Foundation; Cambridge, Mass., MIT Pr., 1985. x, 457p. il. (Architectural History Foundation books, 9)

Pioneering study, divided into two parts. "The first gives a general picture of the conditions under which European synagogues were designed" (nature, furnishings, changes through the centuries, and messages conveyed by the buildings). "The second part . . . offers short and specific accounts of individual synagogues in many European countries . . . chosen to exemplify all architectural types and styles."—*Pref.*

Notes, p.105–36. Appendix I: List of selected architects. Appendix II: List of extant Polish synagogues. Glossary, p.432–33. Notes for the visitor, p.434–35. Bibliography, p.436–44. Index, p.445–55.

J113 Mark, Robert. Light, wind, and structure: the mystery of the master builders. Cambridge, Mass., MIT Pr., 1990. xvii, 209p. il. (New liberal arts series)

"Deals mainly with three historic eras that witnessed the development of new large-scale building types that retain great influence in architectural planning up to the present day."—*Pref.* Uses modern engineering tools to clarify the technological underpinning of these developments and to obtain new knowledge of early design techniques. Aimed for the general reader as well as architecture and architectural history students.

Contents: (1) Problems of technological interpretation in historic architecture; (2) The technology of light, wind and structure; (3) Reinterpreting ancient Roman structure; (4) Structural experimentation in High Gothic architecture; (5) Christopher Wren, seventeenth-century science, and great Renaissance domes; (6) The technological legacy of historic architecture.

Notes, p.[183]–200. Glossary, p.[201]–04. Index, p.[205]–09.

J114 Nervi, Pier Luigi, ed. History of world architecture. N.Y., Abrams, 1971–1980. 15v.

See GLAH 1:J52 for previous vols., which also were first publ. in the Italian series Storia universale dell'architettura.

Contents: Martin, Roland. Greek architecture: architecture of Crete, Greece, and the Greek world (1974); Guidoni, Enrico. Primitive architecture (1978); Tafuri, Manfredo; and Dal Co, Francesco. Modern architecture (1979); Middleton, Robin; and Watkin, David. Neoclassical and 19th century architecture (1980).

These vols. were reissued in 1988, 1987, 1986, and 1987, N.Y., Electa/Rizzoli.

J115 Norberg-Schulz, Christian. Genius loci: towards a phenomenology of architecture. N.Y., Rizzoli, 1980. 213p. il.

Trans. of Genius loci - paesaggio, ambiente, architettura. Milano, Electa, 1979.

This book forms the culmination to a series begun with the author's Intentions in architecture (1963) and Existence, space and architecture (1971) and is also related to his historical study, Meaning in Western architecture (GLAH 2:J116). His primary aim here is "to investigate the psychic implications of architecture rather than its practical side."—*Pref.*

Contents: Place? Natural place; Man-made place; Prague; Khartoum; Rome; Place; Place today.

Notes, p.203–07. Index of names and places, p.209–12.

J116 ———. Meaning in Western architecture. Rev. ed. London, Studio Vista, 1980. 236p. il.

See GLAH 1:J53 for original ed. Publ. in French as La signification dans l'architecture occidentale. 2d ed., Bruxelles, Mardaga, [1977].

This revision of the 1975 history is redesigned, incorporating footnotes within the chapters. Text appears unchanged.

Selected bibliography, p.228–30. Index, p.230–36.

J117 Nuttgens, Patrick. The story of architecture. 2d ed. London, Phaidon, 1997. 351p. il. (part col.), col. maps, plans.

1st ed. Englewood Cliffs, Prentice-Hall, 1983.

Beautifully illustrated survey of western architecture from prehistory to contemporary.

Chronological charts, p.308–16. Glossary, p.317–20. Bibliography, p.321–24. Biographies of architects, p.325–34. Index, p.335–50.

J118 Planning and cities. General ed., George R. Collins. N.Y., Braziller, [1968–75]. 14v. il.

See GLAH 1:J56 for previous vols. The following errata should be noted: Choay, Françoise. The modern city: planning in the 19th century [title correction]; Ward-Perkins, J. B. The cities of ancient Greece and Italy [publ. in 1974, not 1973]. Vols. are indexed.

Contents: Ferguson, Francis. Architecture, cities and the systems approach (1975); Galantay, Ervin Y. New towns: antiquity to the present (1975).

J119 Risebero, Bill. The story of Western architecture. Rev. ed. Cambridge, Mass., MIT Pr., 1997. 304p. il.
1st ed. N.Y., Scribner, 1979.

Readable survey, prehistory to the modern world, for the general reader, with line drawings as illustrations.

Bibliography, p.296. Index, p.297–304.

J120 Roisecco, Giulio. L'architettura del ferro. Roma, Bulzoni, 1972– . (7)v. il.
See GLAH 1:J57 for previous vols. The original plan of the work was revised in the 1980s, and the present plan is to complete the series in 17 vols. Recent vols. by Romano Jodice. Publisher varies.

Contents: L'Italia (1796–1914); La Russia (1815–1914).

J121 Rosenau, Helen. The ideal city: its architectural evolution in Europe. 3d ed., [rev.], London, Methuen, 1983. x, 195p. il.
See GLAH 1:J58 for previous eds.

This ed. was occasioned in part, by "a changed intellectual situation . . . based on the fact that an attitude of pessimism now prevails. It is therefore important to remember the role of the idea of planning in the past, the fuller realization of social values during European history and the theoretical as well as the practical values in studying historical regulative models."—*Pref.*

The three parts are now named: Introductory survey, Phases of progress, and Ambivalent tendencies in the nineteenth centuries; some of the eight chapters are renamed.

Appendix, p.[186]–87. Concise bibliography, p.[188]–90. Index, p.[191]–95.

J122 Roth, Leland M. Understanding architecture: its elements, history, and meaning. N.Y., IconEditions, 1993. xxxi, 542p. il. (part col.), plates, maps.
An unusual introductory text, in that the first part (The elements of architecture) "begins with a definition of what architecture is and continues with chapters that explore function, structural principles, and elements of design."—*Pref.* It reflects the author's interest in our perception and understanding of the man-made environment. Part Two is a conventional survey by period.

Notes and Suggested readings, at end of each of the 21 chapters. Chronological table, p.138. Glossary, p.519–30. Index, p.531–42.

J123 Rowe, Colin, and Koetter, Fred. Collage city. Cambridge, Mass., MIT Pr., [1978]. 185p. il.
Also publ. in French and German under the same title (Paris, Centre George Pompidou, 1993, in Supplémentaires series; Basel, Birkhäuser, 1984, as no.27 in the series Geschichte und Theorie der Architektur).

A theoretical book on society and architecture. Profusely illustrated with city views, plans, early maps, and photographs.

Contents: Utopia: decline and fall? After the millennium; Crisis of the object: predicament of texture; Collision city and the politics of "bricolage"; Collage city and the reconquest of time; Excursus.

Notes, p.182–83. Index, p.184–[86].

J124 Rykwert, Joseph. On Adam's house in Paradise: the idea of the primitive hut in architectural history. 2d ed. Cambridge, Mass., MIT Pr., 1981. 250p. il.
1st ed. 1972, in the series Museum of Modern Art papers on architecture, 2. This ed. incorporates new material, in four appendixes.

Contents: (1) Thinking and doing; (2) Necessity and convention; (3) Positive and arbitrary; (4) Nature and reason; Gothic excursus; (5) Reason and grace; (6) The rites; (7) A house for the soul.

Notes, p.195–[205]. Appendixes, p.209–21. Bibliography, p.225–39. Index, p.245–50.

J125 Scruton, Roger. The aesthetics of architecture. Princeton, Princeton Univ. Pr., 1979. x, 302p. il. (Princeton essays on the arts, 8)
"The book . . . is designed first to introduce the subject of aesthetics to those who have an interest in architecture, second, to explain the nature and value of aesthetic taste."—*Pref.*

Contents: (1) Introduction: The problem of architecture; (2) Architecture and design; (3) Has architecture an essence?; (4) Experiencing architecture; (5) Judging architecture; (6) Freud, Marx and meaning; (7) The language of architecture; (8) Expression and abstraction; (9) The sense of detail; (10) Conclusion: Architecture and morality.

Notes, p.265–90. Bibliography, p.291–92. Indexes, p.293–302.

J126 Scully, Vincent Joseph. Architecture: the natural and the manmade. N.Y., St. Martin's, 1991. xiii, 388p. il. (part col.), maps.
An outgrowth of some 45 years of research and teaching, this work was conceived visually, to depict the relationship of manmade structures to the natural world, which the author suggests "has been most neglected by Western architectural critics and historians."—*Pref.*

Contents: (1) America: the sacred mountain; (2) The sacred mountain in Mesopotamia, Egypt, and the Aegean; (3) The Greek temple; (4) Olympia and the Acropolis of Athens; (5) Hellenistic and Roman: the ideal world of interior space; (6) The Gothic cathedral: structure; (7) The Gothic cathedral: experience; (8) Italian urbanism: the town and the garden; (9) The French classic garden: the art of Pourtraiture; (10) The shape of France: gardens, fortifications, and modern urbanism; (11) Palladio, the English garden, and the modern age.

Index, p.381–88.

J127 Summerson, Sir John Newenham. The classical language of architecture. Rev. and enl. London, Thames and Hudson, 1980. 144p. il. (World of art library)
Publ. in German as Die Klassische Sprache der Architektur. Braunschweig, Vieweg, 1983 (Bauwelt Fundamente, 63). "Originated in a series of six talks broadcast by the BBC in 1963." 1st ed., 1963 ([London], British Broadcasting Corporation); reissued in 1966 (Cambridge, Mass., MIT Pr.). In his preface to the 1980 ed., the author notes changes in attitudes toward the Modern Movement and the trend of architectural development, which caused him to revise portions of the final chapter.

Contents: (1) The essentials of classicism; (2) The grammar of antiquity; (3) Sixteenth-century linguistics; (4) The rhetoric of the Baroque; (5) The light of reason—and archaeology; (6) Classical into modern.

Glossary, p.122–35. Notes on the literature of classical architecture, p.135–39. Index, p.141–44.

J128 Tafuri, Manfredo. Theories and history of architecture. [Trans. by Giorgio Verrecchia]. N.Y., Harper & Row, 1980. 324p. il. (IconEditions)

First publ. in Italian as Teorie e storia dell'architettura. Bari, Laterza, 1968. The English ed. is a trans. of the 4th ed. (1976) in which Tafuri strove to preserve the book's "topicality" and to address the theme of crisis in architecture. French ed., Théories et histoire de l'architecture. Paris, Editions SADG, 1976.

Contents: (1) Modern architecture and the eclipse of history; (2) Architecture as "indifferent object" and the crisis of critical attention; (3) Architecture as metalanguage: the critical value of the image; (4) Operative criticism; (5) Instruments of criticism; (6) The tasks of criticism.

Index of names, p.[315]–24.

J129 Taschen's world architecture. Köln, Taschen, 1997– . (12)v. col. il.

Splendid series of monographs on a range of periods. Also published in German.

Contents: Wildung, Dietrich. Egypt from prehistory to the Romans (1997); Stierlin, Henri. Greece: from Mycenae to the Parthenon (1997); ______. The Roman empire (1996– [1]v.); ______. Islam (1996– [1]v.); ______. Turkey, from the Selcuks to the Ottomans (1998); ______. Hindu India: from Khajuraho to the temple city of Madurai (1998); ______. The Maya: palaces and pyramids of the rainforest (1997); Barral i Altet, Xavier. The early middle ages: from late antiquity to A.D. 1000 (1997); ______. The Romanesque: towns, cathedrals and monasteries (1998); Binding, Gunther. High gothic: the age of the great cathedrals (1999); Khan, Hasan-Uddin. International style: modernist architecture from 1925 to1965 (1998); Jodidio, Philip. New forms: architecture of the 1990s (1997).

J130 Trachtenberg, Marvin, and Hyman, Isabelle. Architecture, from prehistory to post-modernism: the Western tradition. N.Y., Abrams, 1986. 606p. il. (part col.).

A standard, chronological survey with a large number of illustrations (including 74 color plates), that "centers on monumental architecture that is the most sensitive, powerful touchstone of the cultural process."—*Introd.* Excludes the history of the profession and building trades.

Glossary, p.581–87. Bibliography, p.589–93. Index, p.594–605.

J131 Watkin, David. A history of Western architecture. N.Y., Thames and Hudson, 1986. 591p. il. (part col.), plans. (Repr.: London, King, 1992)

Intended as the first architectural history to take into account "the change of mood in the architectural scene since the 1970s."—*Pref.* Emphasis is on the 18th–20th centuries.

Glossary, p.[577]–78. For further reading, p.[579]–84. Index, p.[586]–91.

J132 Zevi, Bruno. Architecture as space: how to look at architecture. Ed. by Joseph A. Barry. Trans. by Milton Gendel. Rev. ed. N.Y., Horizon, [1974]. 310p. il. (Repr.: N.Y., Da Capo, 1993)

1st ed., 1957. Trans. of Saper vedere l'architettura. Torino, Einaudi, [1948]. The reprint has "author emendations and updatings in the bibliography and notes."

Contents: (1) Architecture—the unknown; (2) Space—protagonist of architecture; (3) The representation of space; (4) Space through the ages; (5) Interpretations of architecture; (6) Toward a modern history of architecture.

Bibliography [with commentary], p.245–87. Notes, p.289–303. Index of names, p.305–07. Index of places and structures, p.309–10.

J133 ______. The modern language of architecture. Seattle, Univ. of Washington Pr., 1978. xiv, 241p. il.

Part one, "A guide to the Anticlassical Code," was first publ. as p.1–84 of Il linguaggio moderno dell'architettura (Torino, Einaudi, 1973). Part two,"Architecture versus architectural history," was first publ. in Architettura e storiografia (Milano, Tamburini, [1951]). The two parts formed the basis of two Walker-Ames lectures delivered at the University of Washington, Seattle (1977).

Topics include design methodology, antiperspective, shell and membrane structures, Le Corbusier, medieval through baroque terminology, and newer aspects of architectural culture.

Index, p.234–41.

SEE ALSO: Architecture on screen (GLAH 2:D32); Kruft, A history of architectural theory: from Vitruvius to the present (GLAH 2:G50); Teague, Edward. World architecture index: a guide to illustrations (GLAH 2:D48); Watkin, David. The rise of architectural history (GLAH 2:G89).

Ancient

Dictionaries and Encyclopedias

J134 Ginouvès, René, and Martin, Roland. Dictionnaire méthodique de l'architecture grecque et romaine. Avec la collaboration de Filippo Coarelli . . . [et al.] Dessins de Jean-Pierre Adam . . . [et al.] [Athens], École française d'Athènes, 1985– . (3)v. il. (part col.) (Collection de l'École française de Rome, 84)

V.2 by René Ginouvès and others.

An ongoing and impressive scholarly dictionary. Arrangement is topical.

Contents: (1) Matériaux, techniques de construction, techniques et formes du décor (1985); (2) Eléments constructifs—supports, couvertures, aménagements intérieurs (1992); (3) Espaces architectureaux, bâtiments et ensembles.

Each vol. includes indexes in seven languages (French, German, English, Italian, modern Greek, ancient Greek, and Latin), and bibliography (abbreviations).

J135 Leick, Gwendolyn. A dictionary of ancient Near Eastern architecture. With illustrations by Francis J. Kirk. N.Y., Routledge, 1988. xix, 261p. il.

Entries range in length from one line ("curtine wall") to several pages ("temple", "Saqqara") and may conclude with brief bibliographical references. Includes five simple but useful maps. Lacks introduction or explanation of intent.
Index, p.253–61.

J136 Nash, Ernest. Pictorial dictionary of ancient Rome. [Reprint.] N.Y., Hacker, 1981. 2v. il., plans.
Reprint of GLAH 1:J90.

J137 Richardson, Lawrence. A new topographical dictionary of ancient Rome. Baltimore, Johns Hopkins Univ. Pr., 1992. xxxiv, 458p. il., maps.
An essential source. Complements Ernest Nash's Pictorial dictionary of ancient Rome (GLAH 2:J136) and serves as a replacement for S. B. Platner and T. Ashby's A topographical dictionary of ancient Rome (GLAH 1:J91; repr., Roma, L'Erma di Bretschneider, 1965). Illustrations are limited to plans (which are not common in Nash), some fragments of the Marble Plan, and a few line drawings.
Bibliographical notes and abbreviations, p.xxvii–xxxiv. Glossary, p.435–44. Chronological list of dated monuments, p.445–58.

J138 Travlos, John. Bildlexikon zur Topographie des antiken Attika. Tübingen, Wasmuth, 1988. xvi, 487p. il., maps, photos, plans, site plans.
Complements the author's standard topographical dictionary of ancient Athens (see GLAH 1:J77 for German original ed. and English trans.). Continues the previous format of excellent visual and scholarly documentation for 30 classical archeological sites in Attica.
Bibliographical references within entries. Register, p.481–86. Inschriften, p.[487].

Histories and Handbooks

Egypt and Western Asia

J139 Clarke, Somers, and Engelbach, Reginald. Ancient Egyptian construction and architecture. [Reprint.] N.Y., Dover, 1990. xviii, 242p., map. (Dover books on architecture)
See GLAH 1:J64 for original ed., entitled Ancient Egyptian masonry: the building craft.

J140 Edwards, I. E. S. The pyramids of Egypt. Rev. ed., with new material. N.Y., Penguin, 1993. xxii, 324p. il., plates, maps, plans.
1st ed., 1947; rev. ed., 1961; "new" ed., repr. with rev. bibliography, 1985; rev. ed., 1991.
Remains a basic source.
Contents: (1) Mastabas and early burial customs; (2) Step pyramids; (3) The transition to the true pyramid; (4) The Giza group; (5) Pyramids of the Vth and VIth dynasties; (6) Middle Kingdom pyramids; (7) Later pyramids; (8) Construction and purpose.
Table of major pyramids of the Old and Middle Kingdoms, p.295–96. Bibliography, p.297–[314]. Index, p.315–[25].

J141 Murnane, William J. The Penguin guide to ancient Egypt. 2d ed. N.Y., Penguin, 1996. 526p. il., maps.
1st ed. 1983.
A practical guide, amply illustrated with plans of important buildings. Part One provides background on the land, traditions, and history. Part Two covers the sites, from North to South.
Appendix: Capsule king list and history of ancient Egypt, p.[351]–56. Further reading, p.[513]–14. General index, p.[515]–22. Index of localities, p.[523]–[30].

Classical World

General Works

J142 Curl, James Stevens. Classical architecture: an introduction to its vocabulary and essentials, with a select glossary of terms. London, Batsford, 1992. 231p. il., plans.
"This book is an attempt to explain what Classical Architecture is, and to show various permutations, combinations, and types of Classicism in Architecture. It is restricted to being an introduction to the subject."—*Pref.*
Contents: (I) Introduction; (II) The Graeco-Roman roots of classical architecture; (III) The Renaissance period; (IV) Baroque, Rococo, and Palladianism; (V) Neoclassicism and after; (VI) Epilogue.
Glossary, p.171–222. Select bibliography, p.223–25. Index, p.226–31.

J143 Giuliani, Cairoli Fulvio. L'edilizia nell'antichità. Roma, La nuova Italia scientifica, 1990. 226p. il. (Studi superiori NIS. Architettura)
An essay on structural engineering in antiquity, by an archeologist, arguing the importance of the subject for classical studies.
Abbreviazioni bibliografiche, p.[221]–23. Riferimenti bibliografici, p.[225]–26.

J144 Hersey, George L. The lost meaning of classical architecture: speculations on ornament from Vitruvius to Venturi. Cambridge, Mass., MIT Pr., 1988. 201p. il.
The author attempts to answer the question "why do we still use the classical orders" and reflects on "the actual content of this architecture and . . . on the names of its ornamental components."—*p.1.*
Contents: Troping ornament; Architecture and sacrifice; Images of temple founders; The caryatid and Persian porticoes; Francesco di Giorgio, Michelangelo, and Raphael; Caesariano, the Vitruvius Teutsch, and Sambin.
Notes, p.[157]–81. Bibliography, p.[183]–91. Index, p.193–201.

J145 Onians, John. Bearers of meaning: the classical orders in antiquity, the Middle Ages, and the Renaissance. Princeton, Princeton University Pr., 1988. xvi, 351p. il.
Concentrates "on a limited series of buildings and a limited series of treatises," but nonetheless a pioneering study. The

21 chapters are equally divided between individuals—Vitruvius, Alberti, Filarete, Francesco di Giorgio Martini, Francesco Colonna, Luca Pacioli, Bramante, Raphael, and Serlio—and chronological treatment of the orders.

Notes, p.331–35. Bibliography, p.337–42. Index, p.343–51.

J146 Rykwert, Joseph. Dancing column: on order in architecture. Cambridge, Mass., MIT Pr., 1996. xviii, 598p. il., plans.

Sets out to fulfill at least two conditions: "To provide the context, an anthropological rather than a historical one, within which the columns were formed . . . [and] to be historical and . . . provide a genealogy of this idea [the timelessness of their configurations], show how the columns were constituted and altered in time, how they were worked and perceived by their makers, and what accounts had been offered of their transformations."—*Pref.* Extensive documentation is provided in notes.

Contents: (I) Order in building; (II) Order in the body; (III) The body and the world; (IV) Gender and column; (V) The literary commonplace; (VI) The rule and the song; (VII) The hero as a column; (VIII) The known and the seen; (IX) The mask, the horns, and the eyes; (X) The Corinthian virgin; (XI) A native column?; (XII) Order or intercourse.

Notes, p.[392]–521. Abbreviations and ancient texts, p.[522]–31. Bibliography, p.[532]–77. Index, p.[578]–98.

J147 Tomlinson, R. A. Greek and Roman architecture. London, British Museum Pr., 1995. 128p. il. (part col.), maps. (Classical bookshelf)

Readable introduction for the general reader.

Contents: (1) The origins of classical architecture; (2) Greek temples; (3) Greek cities: houses, theatres and halls; (4) The Hellenistic world; (5) Hellenistic continuity under Rome; (6) The Romans in Italy; (7) The Roman Empire in the east; (8) The Roman Empire in the west.

Glossary, p.[124]–25. Further reading, p.125. Index, p.[126]–27.

J148 Tzonis, Alexander, and Lefaivre, Liane. Classical architecture: the poetics of order. Cambridge, Mass., MIT Pr., 1986. x, 306p. il., maps.

"This book investigates the poetics of classical architecture. It studies the canon, that is, how classical buildings are put together as formal structures, and it studies how such structures produce a tragic discourse and become pieces of public art with critical, moral, and philosophical meaning. . . . The book originates in part from De Taal van de Klassicistiese Architektuur (Nijmegen, SUN, 1983), a much shorter publication."—*Pref. and ackn.*

References, p.289–95. Illustration sources, p.297–99. Index of terms, p.301–03. Index of names and buildings, p.305–06.

Crete, Mycenae, Greece

J149 Graham, James Walter. The palaces of Crete. Rev. ed. Princeton, Princeton Univ. Pr., 1987. xvii, 293p. il., plates.

See GLAH 1:J73 for original ed. The 1987 ed. includes a 1968 "Addendum to the preface," while an additional preface discusses changes in the literature.

Contents: (I) The land, the people, and the history of Minoan Crete; (II) The major palaces; (III) Minor palaces, villas, and houses; (IV) The central court and the bull games; (V) The residential quarters of the royal family; (VI) Public apartments; (VII) Other rooms; (VIII) Building materials and forms; (IX) Windows and doors; (X) Stairs and storeys; (XI) Decorative features; (XII) Furnishings and equipment; (XIII) Procedures and principles; Addenda.

Bibliography, p.270–74. Abbreviations, p.275–76. Index, p.283–93.

J150 Coulton, J. J. Greek architects at work: problems of structure and design. London, Elek, 1977. 196p. il., pl. (Elek archaeology and anthropology)

A practical, building-oriented approach to Greek architecture that employs numerous line drawings to explain details.

Contents: (1) Architect, patron and project; (2) The problem of beginning; (3) The problem of design; (4) The problem of scale; (5) Form, mass and space; (6) Some later problems with the orders; (7) Aspects of structure and technique.

Notes, p.161–81. Bibliography, p.182–88. Glossary, p.[189]–91. Index, p.[193]–96.

J151 Knell, Heiner. Architektur der Griechen: Grundzüge. 2, verb. Aufl. Darmstadt, Wissenschaftliche Buchgesellschaft, 1988. ix, 326p. il., plates, plans. 1st ed. 1980 entitled Grundzüge der griechischen Architektur (Grundzüge, 38)

Introductory survey.

Bibliographie, p.285–318. Register, p.319–26.

J152 Lawrence, Arnold Walter. Greek architecture. Rev. by R. A. Tomlinson. 5th ed. New Haven, Yale University Pr., 1996. viii, 243p. il., plans, photos, sections (Yale University Press Pelican history of art)

See GLAH 1:J74 for 2d ed. and original annotation, 1962. 3d ed., 1967; 4th ed., 1983.

Etruria and Rome

J153 Adam, Jean Pierre. Roman building: materials and techniques. Trans. by Anthony Mathews. Bloomington, Indiana Univ. Pr., 1994. 360p. il.

Trans. of Construction romaine. 2d ed. Paris, Picard, 1989.

Contents: (1) Surveying; (2) Materials; (3) Construction using large stone blocks; (4) Structures of mixed construction; (5) Masonry construction; (6) Arches and vaults; (7) Carpentry; (8) Wall covering; (9) Floors; (10) Civil engineering; (11) Domestic and commercial architecture.

Illustrated lexicon of mouldings, p.328–32. Notes, p.333–50. Bibliography, p.351–57. Index, p.358–60.

J154 Anderson, James C., Jr. Roman architecture and society. Baltimore, Johns Hopkins Univ. Pr., 1997. xxiii, 442p. il. (Ancient society and history)

"Offered as a useful synthesis of [the] evidence for the realia—the people and organizations, planning and topography—of building in the world of ancient Rome. . . . Designed for anyone who would like to know more about how architecture was done, who did it, who paid for it, and how it affected the daily lives of those who lived and worked within it."—*Introd.*

Contents: (1) How the Romans organized building; (2) How the Romans organized space.

Notes, p.337–401. Bibliography, p.403–32. Index, p.433–42.

J155 Architecture and architectural sculpture in the Roman Empire. Ed. by Martin Henig. Oxford, Oxford Univ. Committee for Archaeology, 1990. 163p. il., maps, plans. (Oxford University Committee for Archaeology, 29)

Anthology of papers on Roman architecture and architectural sculpture, by leading scholars and intended for specialists and the general reader. Several of the papers were first presented at a symposium at Oxford University (1987).

Contents: (1) Quintillian and the idea of Roman art, by John Onians; (2) The architecture of Nero's Golden House, by David Hemsoll; (3) The architecture and construction scenes on Trajan's Column, by J. C. N. Coulston; (4) Street plaques at Pompeii, by Roger Ling; (5) Roman architecture in a Greek world: the example of Sicily, by R. J. A. Wilson; (6) Sculpture in Nabataean Petra, and the question of Roman influence, by Margaret Lyttleton and Thomas Blagg; (7) The architectural impact of Rome in the east, by Hazel Dodge; (8) Classical architecture in Roman Egypt, by Donald M. Bailey; (9) Dignam congruentemque splendori patriae: aspects of urban renewal under the Severi, by Susan Walker; (10) Caryatids and other supporters, by G. Lloyd-Morgan; (11) A house for Minerva; temples, aedicula shrines, and signet-rings, by Martin Henig.

Notes and bibliographies at ends of chapters. Index, p.163–[64].

J156 Castagnoli, Ferdinando. Topografia antica: un metodo di studio. Roma, Istituto poligrafico e Zecca dello Stato, Libreria dello Stato, 1993. 2v. il.

A publication of the Università degli studi di Roma "La Sapienza," Dipartimento di scienze storiche, archeologiche e antropologiche dell'antichità, Sezione di topografia antica. Provides impressive documentation, including a history of topographical studies of ancient Rome and a survey of documentary sources.

Contents: Roma: Storia degli studi; Fonti; Storia della città; La zona archeologica. Italia: Architettura, urbanistica, centuriazione; Lavinio.

Bibliographical references throughout. Bibliografia, v.1, p.[ix]–xvi. Indice, v.2: Cose notevoli, p.[1055]–84. Fonti letterarie classiche, medioevali, rinascimentali, p.[1085]–1104. Iscrizioni, p.[1105]–08. Monete, p.[1109]–10. Manoscritti, p.[1111]–12.

J157 ———. Topografia di Roma antica. Torino, Società editrice internazionale, 1980. viii, 119p. il., plates, maps, plans. (Manuali universitari. 1, Per lo studio delle scienze dell'antichità)

"Nuova edizione interamente rifatta dell'opera Topografia di Roma antica pubblicata nella Enciclopedia classica [GLAH 1:E29]."—*T.p. verso. Introduction to the subject.*

Contents: Parte prima. (I) Fonti scritte; (II) Fonti archeologiche; (III) Strumenti di lavoro. Parte seconda. (I) Geografia; (II) Storia della città; (III) Organizzazione e amministrazione della città; (IV) Descrizione topografica.

Bibliographical references at ends of chapters. Abbreviazioni, p.vii– viii. Addenda, p.119.

J158 Gros, Pierre. L'architecture romaine: du début du IIIe siècle av. J.-C. à la fin du Haut-Empire. Paris, Picard, 1996– . (1)v. il. (part col.), maps. (Manuels d'art et d'archéologie antiques)

Monumental new history of Roman architecture, scholarly, lavishly produced and illustrated.

Contents: (1) Le monuments publics (1996).

J159 MacDonald, William Lloyd. The architecture of the Roman Empire: an introductory study. New Haven, Yale Univ. Pr., 1982–1986. 2v. il., maps (Yale publications in the history of art, 17, 35).

See GLAH 1:J88 for original ed. of v.1. The rev. ed. corrects errors, updates the bibliography, and adds a chapter to incorporate recent studies.

Contents: Vol.2: An urban appraisal: (I) Introduction; (II) Urban armatures; (III) Connective architecture; (IV) Passage architecture; (V) Public buildings; (VI) Classicism fulfilled; (VII–VIII) Empire imagery: cardinal themes [and] Baroque modes; (IX) Form and meaning.

Both vols. include list of abbreviations, notes, bibliography, list of illustrations, and index. Vol.2 also has List of principal emperors, p.[302].

J160 ———. The Pantheon: design, meaning, and progeny. Cambridge, Mass., Harvard Univ. Pr., 1976. 160p. il.

History and analysis, accompanied by a typological study of domed round buildings and those with temple-front porches.

Contents: (1) In the temple of the whole world; (2) The building proper; (3) Background and principles of design; (4) The problem of meaning; (5) "The most celebrated edifice."

Bibliography, p.135–37. Notes, p.138–46. Index, p.157–60.

J161 ———, and Pinto, John A. Hadrian's villa and its legacy. New Haven, Yale Univ. Pr., [1995]. x, 392p. il., maps, photos. (part col.), plans, site plans.

Solid scholarship complemented by impressive book design.

Contents: (I) Introduction; (II) The site; (III) Familiar architecture; (IV) Unfamiliar architecture; (V) The high ground; (VI) Art; (VII) The villa in use; (VIII) Survival and rediscovery; (IX) The draftsman's vision; (X) The landscape of allusion; (XI) Art dispersed; (XII) After 1800.

Piranesi's Pianta commentary, p.[331]–39. Abbreviations, p.[341]–42. Notes, p.[343]–74. Bibliography, p.[375]–80. Index, p.[383]–92.

J162 Rykwert, Joseph. The idea of a town: the anthropology of urban form in Rome, Italy and the ancient world. Cambridge, Mass., MIT Pr., 1988. 242p. il.

1st ed., Princeton, Princeton Univ. Pr., 1976. An added preface to the 1988 ed. addresses the question of change of context over 30 years—archeology, history, and views of the urban situation.

Contents: (1) Town and rite: Rome and Romulus; (2) City and site; (3) Square and cross; (4) Guardians of centre, guardians of boundaries; (5) The parallels; (6) The city as curable disease: ritual and hysteria.

Abbreviations, p.[19]–21. Notes, p.[204]–31. Index, p.[233]–42.

J163 Sear, Frank. Roman architecture. Rev. ed. London, Batsford, 1989. 288p. il., maps, plans.

1st ed., 1982.

Introductory, readable survey, chronologically arranged. "I have aimed to be clear rather than comprehensive. I have selected what I regard as the most significant buildings of each era or province, and have in each case attempted to put them into their historical or cultural context."—*Foreword.*

Glossary, p.277–79. Bibliography, p.280–85. Index, p.285–88.

J164 Ward Perkins, J. B. Roman imperial architecture. 2d (integrated) ed. N.Y., Penguin, 1981. 532p. il. (Pelican history of art)

First publ. as parts 2–4 of Etruscan and Roman architecture, 1970 (GLAH 1:I18, no.32).

Contents: Part One: Architecture in Rome and Italy from Augustus to the mid third century. Part Two: The architecture of the Roman provinces. Part Three: Late pagan architecture in Rome and the provinces.

Select glossary, p.[491]–97. Bibliography, p.[498]–510. Index, p.[518]–32.

Early Christian—Byzantine

Bibliography

J165 Kleinbauer, W. Eugene. Early Christian and Byzantine architecture: an annotated bibliography and historiography. Boston, Hall, 1992. cxxiii, 779p. (Reference publication in art history)

Covers monographs, catalogs, dissertations, and journal articles published to 1991. Tries "to assemble the most representative examples of studies dealing with a single topic regardless of their date of publication rather than to list only the most recent."—*Pref.*

Annotations vary greatly in length and indicate both subject matter and methodology. Generally, does not repeat Literature on Byzantine Art, 1892–1967 (GLAH 1:A93) and Slobodan Ćurčić's Art and architecture in the Balkans (GLAH 2:A118).

Contents: Prolegomena to a historiography of Early Christian and Byzantine architecture; General [divided into eight subjects and forms]; Topics [150, arranged alphabetically]. Appendix: Nineteenth-century photography of Early Christian and Byzantine architecture (with five-page bibliography).

Author index, p.671–95. Subject index, p.697–779.

Histories and Handbooks

J166 Krautheimer, Richard. Corpus basilicarum christianarum Romae = The early Christian basilicas of Rome (IV–IX cent.) Città del Vaticano, Pontificio istituto di archeologia cristiana, 1937–1977. 5v. il. (some folded), facsims., plans (some folded). (Monumenti di antichità cristiana, ser.2, v.II)

See GLAH 1:J93 for v.1–4. Vol.5 by Richard Krautheimer, Spencer Corbett, and Alfred K. Frazer. Text in English. For each of the three churches discussed, assembles bibliography, ancient descriptions and illustrations, dates, general description, analysis (archeological evidence, graphic evidence, literary evidence), reconstruction, and chronology. "Corrigenda et addenda," 1 leaf inserted in v.5.

Selective contents: Vol.5: S. Giovanni in Laterno; S. Paolo fuori le Mura; S. Pietro; Historical position [for the three churches]; Comparative dimensions.

Abbreviations, p.[v]–ix.

J167 ———. Early Christian and Byzantine architecture. 4th ed., rev. by Richard Krautheimer and Slobodan Ćurčić. N.Y., Viking, 1986. 556p. il. (Pelican history of art)

See GLAH 1:J94 for 2d ed. 3d ed., 1979, reissued with revisions, 1981. In addition to incorporating corrections and revisions based on new research, the 4th ed. brings footnotes up to date and eliminates some obsolete bibliography.

Bibliography, p.[523]–25. Index, p.537–53.

Islamic

Dictionaries and Encyclopedias

J168 Petersen, Andrew. Dictionary of Islamic architecture. N.Y., Routledge Reference, 1996. ix, 342p. il., maps.

An encyclopedic dictionary that aims to include the less well-known Muslim cultures of Southeast Asia, India, East and West Africa along with the Middle East and North Africa. Includes vernacular architecture, viewing it as providing a context for the more famous monuments. Entries cover particular dynasties or historic styles, sites and buildings, regions, and building types. The larger entries conclude with brief, fairly scholarly "further reading" suggestions.

Index, p.323–42.

Histories and Handbooks

J169 Architecture of the Islamic cultural sphere. Zurich, Muslim Architecture Research Program, 1986– . (6)v. il.

An important series, with many further vols. announced.

(1a) Introduction to Islamic architecture (1986); (1b) Determinants of Islamic architecture (1998); (2a) Mosques

(1986); (3a) Khawarizm (1990); (3b) Bukhara (1993); (4a) Islamic arches.

J170 Architecture of the Islamic world: its history and social meaning: with a complete survey of key monuments and 758 illustrations, 112 in color. By Ernst J. Grube . . . [et al.] Ed. by George Michell. N.Y., Morrow, 1978. 288p. il. (part col.) (Repr.: N.Y., Thames and Hudson, 1984)

Excellent multiauthor survey placing the subject in its cultural setting.

Contents: Architecture and society. Introduction: What is Islamic architecture?, by Ernst J. Grube; (1) Allah and eternity: mosques, madrasas and tombs, by James Dickie (Yaqub Zaki); (2) The architecture of power: palaces, citadels and fortifications, by Oleg Grabar; (3) Trade and travel: markets and caravanserais, by Eleanor Sims; (4) Architects, craftsmen and builders: materials and techniques, by Ronald Lewcock; (5) The elements of decoration: surface, pattern and light, by Dalu Jones; (6) Vernacular architecture: the house and society, by Guy T. Petherbridge. Key monuments of Islamic architecture [arranged by country, with various authors].

Glossary, p.281–82. Select bibliography, p.282–84. Index, p.284–88.

J171 Barrucand, Marianne, and Bednorz, Achim. Moorish architecture in Andalusia. Köln, Taschen, 1992. 235p. il. (part col.), maps.

Contents: Introduction; Events up to the end of the 9th century; The architecture of the 8th century and 9th centuries; A golden age: the Caliphate; The architecture of the 10th century; The age of the petty kings; The architecture of the Taifa period; The period of Berber domination; Almoravid and Almohad architecture; The rule of the Nasrids; The architecture of the Nasrids; Conclusion.

Notes, p.221–27. Glossary, p.228–30. Bibliography, p.231–34.

J172 Çelik, Zeynep. Displaying the Orient: architecture of Islam at nineteenth-century world's fairs. Berkeley, Univ. of California Pr., 1992. xv, 245p. il. (Comparative studies on Muslim societies, 12).

Focuses on those expositions where the architectural representation of Islam was significant.

Contents: (1) Muslim visitors to world's fairs; (2) Islamic quarters in Western cities; (3) Search for identity: architecture of national pavilions; (4) Exposition fever carried East; (5) The impact.

Notes, p.200–25. Selected bibliography, p.226–34. Index, p.235–45.

J173 Creswell, Keppel Archibald Cameron. A short account of early Muslim architecture. Rev. and suppl. by James W. Allan. Rev. and enl. ed. Aldershot, Scolar, 1989. xx, 435p. il.

First published 1958 as a reduced format of the author's monumental study of Early Muslim architecture (GLAH 1:J97). Also published in Arabic in 1984.

Includes bibliographical references. Bibliography, p.[420]–23. Index, p.[424]–35.

J174 Franz, Heinrich Gerhard. Palast, Moschee und Wüstenschloss: das Werden der islamischen Kunst, 7.-9. Jahrhundert. Graz, Akademische Druck- u. Verlagsanstalt, 1984. 166p. il., plates, plans.

An authoritative, concise survey of Islamic architecture and associated arts, continued by the same author's Von Baghdad bis Cordoba (see following entry).

J175 ______. Von Baghdad bis Cordoba: Ausbreitung und Entfaltung der Islamischen Kunst 850–1050. Graz, Akademische Druck- u. Verlagsanstalt, 1984. 211p. il., plates, plans. (Forschungen und Berichte des Instituts für Kunstgeschichte der Karl-Franzens-Universität Graz, 6)

Continuation of the same author's Palast, Moschee und Wüstenschloss (see preceding entry).

Schrifttum, p.167–81. Glossar, p.183–96. Index, p.207–11.

J176 Golombek, Lisa, and Wilber, Donald Newton. The Timurid architecture of Iran and Turan. Princeton, Princeton Univ. Pr., 1988. 2v. il. (part col.), maps, plans (Princeton monographs in art and archaeology, 46)

Contributors: Terry Allen, Leonid S. Bretanitskii, Robert Hillenbrand, Renata Holod, Antony Hutt, L. Iu. Man'kovskaia, H. M. Nasirly, and Bernard O'Kane.

The 10 chapters cover topics such as concept design, materials and methods of construction, decoration, and design theory.

Contents: (I) The Timurid world; (II) Timurid architecture; (III) Timurid architecture defined; (IV) Catalogue of monuments.

List of monuments, v.1, p.ix–xiv. Appendixes: Supplementary catalog of monuments, Timurid builders and craftsmen, Patrons known from standing monuments, Genealogical table for Timur, v.1, p.445–68. Glossary, v.1, p.469–71. Abbreviations, v.1, p.472. Bibliography: primary sources, secondary sources, v.1, p.473–95. Index, v.1, p.497–510.

J177 Golvin, Lucien. Essais sur l'architecture religieuse musulmane. [Paris], Klincksieck, 1970–79. 4v. il., map, plates (Archéologie méditerranéenne, 5)

Monumental study of Islamic religious architecture.

Contents: (1) Généralités; (2) L'art relgieux des Umayyades de Syrie; (3) L'architecture religieuse des "grands Abbâsides", la Mosquée de Ibn T'ûlûn, l'architecture religieuse des Aghalbides; (4) L'architecture religieuse hispano-mauresque.

J178 Hillenbrand, Robert. Islamic architecture: form, function and meaning. N.Y., Columbia Univ. Pr., 1994. 645p. il. (part col.), plans, plates.

An impressive history, thorough and detailed, incorporating vast numbers of plans and line drawings along with photographs.

Contents: The scope of the enquiry: problems and approaches; The mosque; The minaret; The madrasa; The mausoleum; The caravansari; The palace.

Glossary of Islamic terms, p.598–600. Select bibliography, p.601–07. Index of individual monuments, p.613–25.

Index of terms in foreign (principally Islamic) languages, p.626–28. Index of proper names, p.629–34. Subject index, p.635–45.

J179 Holod, Renata, and Khan, Hasan-Uddin. The contemporary mosque: architects, clients, and designs since the 1950s. N.Y., Thames and Hudson, 1997. 288p. il. (part col.), plans.

UK ed. entitled The mosque and the modern world: architects, patrons and designs since the 1950s.

Wide-ranging, beautifully illustrated survey of contemporary mosque architecture, with an emphasis upon patronage structures.

Contents: (1) Personal patronage; (2) The State as client; (3) Commissions by local government bodies; (4) Mosques for public and commercial institutions; (5) Local community projects worldwide; (6) Islamic centres in the west.

Notes on the text, p.254–73. Key mosques and Islamic centres, p.274–79. Select bibliography, p.280–84. Glossary, p.285. Sources of illustrations, p.286. Index, p.287–88.

J180 Korbendau, Yves. L'architecture sacrée de l'Islam. Courbevoie, ACR, 1997. 479p. col. il., col. maps.

Monumental, beautifully illustrated atlas of Islamic sacred architecture.

Contents: Les éléments religieux; Les éléments d'architecture; Répertoire des monuments.

Tableau chronologique, p.[10–11]. Bibliographie, p.478. Glossaire, p.479.

J181 Lehrman, Jonas Benzion. Earthly paradise: garden and courtyard in Islam. Berkeley, Univ. of California Pr., 1980. 240p. il. (part col.), map, plans.

"Aims to present a picture of the gardens and courtyards . . . as they exist today [and] to serve as a general introduction to the subject."—*Pref.* Well-illustrated, with some color photographs.

Contents: Setting the scene; Characteristics; Moorish Spain; Safavid Iran; Mughal India; Other regions. Also includes proposals for restoration and preservation, a horticultural note, glossary, lists of dynasties and emperors, and a chronology.

Bibliography, p.233–34. Index, p.237–40.

J182 The mosque: history, architectural development & regional diversity. Ed. by Martin Frishman and Hasan-Uddin Khan. Texts by Mohammad Al-Asad . . . [et al.] N.Y., Thames and Hudson, 1994. 288p. il. (part col.), maps, plans.

A comprehensive overview of the history of the mosque as an architectural building type, with special attention to regional variations.

Notes on the text, p.273–78. Bibliography, p.279–82. Glossary, p.282. Chronological table, p.283. Sources of illustrations, p.284. Index, p.285–88.

J183 Pereira, José. Islamic sacred architecture: a stylistic history. New Delhi, Books & Books, 1994. ix, 379p. il. (part col.), plates.

Contents: Basic concepts; History; Idiomatics; Axiomorphics; Aesthetics. Appendix: a comprehensive classification of Muslim sacred structures.

Selected bibliography, p.[349]–51. Index, p.[362]–79.

SEE ALSO: Blair and Bloom, The art and architecture of Islam 1250–1800 (GLAH 2:I184); Ettinghausen and Grabar, The art and architecture of Islam 650–1250 (GLAH 2:I191).

Carolingian—Gothic

Bibliography

J184 Davies, Martin. Romanesque architecture: a bibliography. N.Y., Hall, 1993. xxv, 306p. maps. (Reference publication in art history)

Lists 1,662 works, including translations, in nearly all European languages. No annotations. Brief introductions to chapters and their sections.

Contents: (1) Romanesque architecture: General surveys, etc.; (2) Series on Romanesque art and architecture; (3) Medieval architecture: General surveys, etc.; (4) France; (5) Germany; Austria, and Switzerland; (6) Italy; (7) Spain and Portugal; (8) British Isles; (9) The Low Countries; (10) Scandinavia; (11) Eastern Europe; Appendixes: Audiovisual material, Unpublished theses (emphasis on materials available in England and France), Addenda (all divided geographically).

Author index, p.275–95. Subject index, p.297–306.

Histories and Handbooks

J185 Les Bâtisseurs des cathédrales gothiques. Publié sous la direction de Roland Recht. Avec les contrib. de: Jacques Le Goff . . . [et al.] Strasbourg, Éd. les Musées de la Ville de Strasbourg, [1989]. 498p. il. (part col.), plans.

Published in connection with the exhibition, Ancienne Douane, Strasbourg (1989). Imposing study of the Gothic cathedral, emphasizing the role of drawings in the design process and in the shaping of architectural conventions.

Bibliographical notes at ends of chapters.

Contents: (I) La cathédrale gothique; (II) Le chantier en activité; (III) Quelques chantiers; (IV) L'architecte; (V) Le dessin d'architecture et ses applications; (VI) Les battisseurs vus par le XIXe siècle; Catalogue des oeuvres exposées.

J186 Bizzarro, Tina Waldeier. Romanesque architectural criticism: a pre-history. Cambridge, Cambridge Univ. Pr., 1992. vii, 253, [20]p. il.

Covers the Romanesque churches of France, Catalonia, and Norman England, from ca.1000 to ca.1140. Has as one of its theses that a language of architectural history shapes subsequent histories.

Contents: (1) Seventeenth century French criticism: birth of a distinction; (2) England, 1538–1730: from the Tudor chorographers through the Restoration; (3) English criticism, 1740–1818; (4) French Enlightenment criticism,

1700–1818; (5) Gunn's "Romanesque," de Gerville's "romane," and their critical legacy. Appendix: An introduction to latter-day criticism: Proles Ignara Parentis.

Notes, p.161–212. Bibliography, p.213–46. Index of names, p.247–50. General index, p.251–53.

J187 Calkins, Robert G. Medieval architecture in Western Europe: from A.D. 300 to 1500. N.Y., Oxford Univ. Pr., 1998. x, 342p. il. + 1 computer laser optical disk.

Significant introductory survey, aiming "to fill a gap between the very selective and cursory mention of major medieval buildings in general surveys of art or architectural history and the in-depth books on particular periods or regions."—*Pref.*

Contents: (1) Classical antecedents; (2) Early Christian buildings to A.D. 500; (3) Justinian's buildings; (4) Later Byzantine variations; (5) Early monasticism and northern traditions; (6) Carolingian assimilations and innovations; (7) Ottonian continuations; (8) Visigothic, Asturian, Muslim, and Mozarabic beginnings in Spain; (9) Early Romanesque solutions; (10) Romanesque styles in France; (11) Other Romanesque variations: Germany and Italy; (12) Anglo-Saxon, Norman, and Anglo-Norman Romanesque; (13) Early Gothic in France; (14) Thirteenth-century Gothic in France; (15) Regional Gothic styles; (16) The rayonnant style in France and European imitations; (17) Late Gothic elaborations and innovations; (18) Secular architecture in the middle ages; (19) Medieval builders and building practices.

Notes, p.313–17. Bibliography, p.319–35. Index, p.337–42.

J188 Conant, Kenneth John. Carolingian and Romanesque architecture, 800 to 1200. 2d integrated ed., rev.; repr. with corr. Harmondsworth, Penguin, 1978. 522p. il., col. maps, plans. (The Pelican history of art, PZ13)

See GLAH 1:J108 for 1st ed. 2d ed., 1966; "3d rev. ed.," 1973; "4th ed." is a repr. (New Haven, Yale Univ. Pr., 1993).

This ed. commences with a fine section of maps (p.14–27) of different areas of Europe at various times, including Scandinavia and the Holy Land.

Index, p.[509]–22. Bibliography, p.[493]–500.

J189 Erlande-Brandenburg, Alain. The cathedral: the social and architectural dynamics of construction. N.Y., Cambridge Univ. Pr., 1994. xxii, 378p. il., maps. (Cambridge studies in the history of architecture)

Trans. of La cathédrale. Paris, Fayard, 1989.

The author has tried "to transcend piecemeal description and thus to achieve a global perspective" using newly discovered sources and a new concept of history that clarify the interaction "between holy town and town, cathedral and palace, and between canonial precinct and hôtel-Dieu."—*Pref.*

Contents: The bishop in the city; The imperial dream; The Gregorian reform; Gothic construction; Men, finance and administration; The churches and the cathedral; The Gothic palace; The canonial precinct; The hôtel Dieu.

Selective bibliography by chapter, and bibliographical references, p.358–62. Index, p.363–78.

J190 Heitz, Carol. L'architecture religieuse carolingienne: les formes et leurs fonctions. Paris, Picard, 1980. 288p. il., map, plans.

Scholarly survey of Carolingian architecture.

Notes, p.[234]–52. Plan de Saint-Gall, p.254–60. Bibliographie, p.[261–81]. Index des noms, p.[281]–85.

J191 Horn, Walter William, and Born, Ernest. The plan of St. Gall: a study of the architecture & economy of, & life in a paradigmatic Carolingian monastery. With a foreword by Wolfgang Braunfels; a translation into English by Charles W. Jones of the Directives of Adalhard, 753–826, the Ninth Abbot of Corbie, and with a note by A. Hunter Dupree on the significance of the plan of St. Gall to the history of measurement. Berkeley, Univ. of California Pr., 1979. 3v. il. (part. col.), plans, maps. (California studies in the history of art, 19)

Corrigenda and errata addendum for v.3 inserted. Abridged version published as: Price, Lorna. The plan of St. Gall in brief: an overview based on the 3-volume work by Walter Horn and Ernest Born. Berkeley, Univ. of California Pr., 1982.

Monumental study of this "paradigmatic Carolingian monastery."

Bibliography, v.3, p.167–200.

J192 Lavedan, Pierre. L'urbanisme au Moyen Age. Genève, Droz, 1974. 184p. il., plates. (Bibliothèque de la Société française d'archéologie, 5)

Index, p.[165]–72.

Contents: Origines et formes de la ville medievale; (I) Les anciennes villes romaines; (II) Villes d'accession; (III) La création urbaine en France; (IV) La création urbaine hors de France; (V) Le cadre de la vie urbaine à la fin du moyen age.

J193 Müller, Werner. Grundlagen gotischer Bautechnik: ars sine scientia nihil. München, Deutscher Kunstverlag, [1990]. 318p. il., plans.

In German, with summary in English. A technical study of Gothic architecture.

Sachverzeichnis, p.311–18.

J194 Munich. Zentralinstitut für Kunstgeschichte. Vorromanische Kirchenbauten. Katalog der Denkmäler bis zum Ausgang der Ottonen. München, Prestel, 1990–1991. 2v. il., maps, plans. (Veröffentlichungen des Zentralinstituts für Kunstgeschichte in München, III/1–2)

See GLAH 1:J118 for previous ed. (3v., 1966–1971). Bd.1 is a reprint. Bd.2, Nachtragsband, is a supplement compiled by Werner Jacobsen, Leo Schaefer, and Hans Rudolf Sennhauser, with the assistance of Matthias Exner, Jozef Mertens, and Henk Stoepker.

The supplement has the same format and definitive documentation as the original three vols., and includes an abbreviations list (p.8–11) and an appendix listing those buildings not treated in the main text (p.476–90).

J195 Radding, Charles, and Clark, William W. Medieval architecture, medieval learning: builders and masters in the age of romanesque and gothic. New Haven, Yale Univ. Pr., 1992. xiii, 166p. il.

Italian ed.: Architettura e sapere nel medioevo. Milano, Vita e Pensiero, 1997.

Important exploration of the relationship between medieval architecture and medieval scholarship, focusing upon the role of specialization in shaping the evolution of both architecture and scholarship.

Bibliography, p.151–64. Index, p.165–66.

J196 Simson, Otto Georg von. The Gothic cathedral: origins of Gothic architecture and the medieval concept of order. 3d ed., with additions. Princeton, Princeton Univ. Pr., 1988. xxiii, 282p. il., 51p. of plates. (Bollingen series, 48)

1st ed., 1956 [N.Y., Pantheon]; 2d ed., 1962; 2d ed., rev., 1964. Trans. of Die gotische Kathedrale. Darmstadt, Wissenschaftliche Buchgesellschaft, 1968. Previous English eds. included an appendix by Ernst Levy, On the proportion of the South Tower of Chartres Cathedral. The 3d ed. adds a new section on the rose window of Chartres and is updated within the preface and postscript (1961), p.238–41. Also publ. in Spanish as La catedral gótica, Madrid, Alianza, 1982.

"This essay seeks to understand Gothic architecture as an image, more precisely, as the representation of supernatural reality."—*Introd.*

Contents: (I) Gothic design and the medieval concept of order (Gothic form; Measure and light); (II) The birth of the Gothic (Suger of St.-Denis; The new church; Sens and Chartres West); (III) The consummation (The palace of the Virgin; The cathedral of Chartres).

Abbreviations, p.[247]–48. List of works cited, p.[249]–68. Index, p.[269]–82.

J197 Ullmann, Ernst. Die Welt der gotischen Kathedrale. Mit Fotos von Werner Neumeister. Wien, Edition Tusch, 1981. 291p. il. (part col.), plans.

Accessible survey of Gothic architecture by a wide-ranging scholar.

Contents: Die Kathedrale im Urteil der Zeiten; Die Gestalt der Kathedrale; Funktion und Baugeschehen; Das Weltbild; Ausbildung und Verbreitung der Kathedralgotik; Die Gotische Kathedrale.

Literaturauswahl, p.268–69. Erläuterung der Fachausdrücke, p.269–72. Zeittafel, p.272–77. Übersichtstafeln, p.278–90. Ortsregister, p.291–[92].

J198 Wilson, Christopher. The Gothic cathedral: the architecture of the great church, 1130–1530, with 220 illustrations. N.Y., Thames and Hudson, 1990. 304p. il.

A basic survey, well-illustrated.

Contents: (I) Early Gothic; (II) Thirteenth-century Gothic; (III) Late Gothic.

Glossary, p.[291]–94. Select bibliography, p.295–98. Index of persons and works, p.299–303.

Renaissance—Baroque

J199 Architectural theory and practice from Alberti to Ledoux. Ed. by Dora Wiebenson. Foreword by Adolf Placzek. Contrib. by James S. Ackerman . . . [et al.] 2d ed., rev. [Chicago], Architectural Publications (Distr. by the Univ. of Chicago Pr., 1983). Unpaginated [ca.100p.] il.

1st ed., 1982. The only change is the correction of errors. Published in association with exhibition, Yale University (1982), and other locations.

"This book is intended to be both an ideal catalog, supplementing [the three exhibitions], and as a survey and guide for those interested in the history of architectural theory. . . . Some areas of architectural theory and practice are represented by only a few examples, other more peripheral areas such as garden structures and fortifications reluctantly have been omitted."—*Pref.*

In three sections:

Contents: (I) The publications; (II) Architects and amateurs; (III) The elements of architecture.

Entries are by 49 contributors.

Bibliography (4p.). Index (2p.).

J200 De architectura. Paris, Picard, 1983– . (7)v. il., plans. Proceedings of a series of colloquia held in Tours, 1977–1990. Papers are in English, French, German, Italian, and Spanish. Vols. include French summaries and bibliographic notes.

Contents: (1) La maison de ville à la Renaissance; recherches sur l'habitat urbain en Europe aux XVe et XVIe siècles (1983); (2) L'escalier dans l'architecture de la Renaissance (1985); (3) Les traités d'architecture de la Renaissance (1988); (4) Les chantiers de la Renaissance (1991); (5) L'emploi des ordres dans l'architecture de la Renaissance (1992); (6) Architecture et vie sociale: l'organisation interiéure des grandes demeures à la fin du Moyen Age et à la Renaissance (1994); (7) L'église dans l'architecture de la Renaissance (1995).

In addition to the Colloques vols., there is a related series of Études:

Contents: Boudon, Françoise, and Blécon, Jean. Philibert Delorme et le château royal de Saint-Léger-en-Yvelines (1985); Chatenet, Monique. Le château de Madrid au bois de Boulogne (1987); Boudon, Françoise; Blécon, Jean; and Grodecki, Catherine. Le château de Fontainebleau de François Ier à Henri IV: les bâtiments et leurs fonctions (1998).

J201 Lavedan, Pierre; Hugueney, Jeanne; and Henrat, Philippe. L'urbanisme à l'époque moderne: XVIe–XVIIIe siècles. Genève, Droz, 1982. 310, cclxxxiiip. il., plates (Bibliothèque de la Société française d'archéologie, 13)

A massive study, equally divided between text and plates, based on three types of documents: maps and plans, ancient views (prints), and travel accounts. It follows the authors' Urbanisme au Moyen Age (GLAH 2:J192) in the same collection.

Contents: (I): Le XVIe siècle; (II): XVIIe–XVIIIe siècles; (III) Urbanisme hors d'Europe.

Includes bibliographic notes.

J202 Lemerle, Frédéric, and Yves Pauwels. L'architecture à la renaissance. Paris, Flammarion, 1998. 254p. il. (part col.), plans.

Informed survey of Italian Renaissance architecture and its European legacy.

Contents: La naissance de "l'architecture": du moderne à l'antique; (I) Prélude: le gothique de la renaissance; (II) La renaissance florentine; (III) L'Italie face à la nouvelle architecture; (IV) Les débuts de l'italianisme en France; (V) L'italianisme en Europe; (VI) L'architecture savante à Rome; (VII) La diffusion de la nouvelle architecture en Italie; (VIII) L'architecture savante dans la péninsule iberique; (IX) La renaissance classique en France; (X) La diffusion de l'architecture savante en Europe; Conclusion: La renaissance après la renaissance.

Glossaire des termes d'architecture, p.249–50. Bibliographie, p.251–[55].

J203 Scott, Geoffrey. The architecture of humanism: a study in the history of taste. London, Architectural Pr., [1980]. xxix, 266p.

Based on the rev. ed. of 1924. 1st ed., 1914, London, Constable; 2d ed., 1924, repr. N.Y., Norton, 1954, 1974; Gloucester, Mass., P. Smith, 1965.

This ed. is unique in that it has a foreword by David Watkin, which provides a biography of Scott and analyzes the impact and significance of this work, noting that it is important "as an expression of that vanished world of cultivated Anglo-American connoisseurship."

Contents: (I) Renaissance architecture; (II) The Romantic fallacy; (III) The Romantic fallacy: naturalism and the picturesque; (IV) The mechanical fallacy; (V) The ethical fallacy; (VI) The biological fallacy; (VII) The academic tradition; (VIII) Humanist values; (IX) Conclusion. An "analytic summary" serves as a detailed table of contents. Epilogue, 1924.

Bibliography, p.266.

J204 Smith, Gil R. Architectural diplomacy: Rome and Paris in the late Baroque. N.Y., Architectural History Foundation; Cambridge, Mass., MIT Pr., 1993. x, 367p. il.

"The scope . . . is largely confined to the exchanges between French and Roman architectural traditions in the last quarter of the seventeenth century."—*Pref.*

Contents: (I) Aggregation of the Roman and French academies: union of convenience or strategic alliance; (II) Concorso of 1677; (III) The interim years: 1678 to 1692.

Notes, p.317–58. Selected bibliography, p.359–60. Selected glossary, p.361. Index, p.363–67.

J205 Triumph of the Baroque: architecture in Europe 1600–1750. Ed. by Henry A. Millon. N.Y., Rizzoli, 1999. 621p. il. (part col.), facsims., maps, plans.

Published to accompany the exhibition, Palazzina di Caccia di Stupinigi (1999).

Contents: Introduction, by Henry Millon; Birth of the Baroque in Rome, by Paolo Portoghesi; The Baroque and its buildings, by Christian Norberg-Schulz; Architecture in the seventeenth century in Europe, by Hilary Ballon; The age of the Late Baroque and Rococo, by Christian Norberg-Schulz; The architecture of the Russian state: between east and west, 1600–1760, by Dmitry Shwidkovsky; "Mostrar l'invenzione"—the role of Roman architects in the Baroque period, by Elizabeth Kieven; Architectura est scientia aedificandi: reflection on the scope of architectural and architectural-theoretical literature, by Werner Oechslin; From the "Ideal City" to real cities: perspectives, chorographies, models, vedute, by Fernando Marías; Architectural painting: fantasy and caprice, by Jörg Garms; Garden displays of majestic will, by Michel Conan; Urban transformations, by Claude Mignot; Military architecture in Baroque Europe, by Simon Pepper; Turin: an example for the town planning and architectural models of European capitals in the seventeenth and eighteenth centuries, by Vera Comoli Mandracci; The Royal Palace of Caserta by Luigi Vanvitelli: the genesis and development of the project, by Cesare de Seta; The architectural model in the sphere of influence of the Imperial Court in Vienna, by Michael Krapf; Appendix.

Chronology, p.600–601. Bibliography, p.602–14. Index of names, p.615–17. Index of works, 618–21.

Neoclassical—Modern

Bibliography

J206 Sharp, Dennis. Sources of modern architecture: a critical bibliography. 2d ed., rev. and enl. London, Granada, 1981. 192p. il., facsims., ports.

See GLAH 1:J126 for 1st ed. This ed. includes references to new eds. and new areas of research, expanding by about 40 percent.

Index of architects and authors, p.183–91.

Dictionaries and Encyclopedias

J207 Encyclopedia of 20th century architecture. General ed., Vittorio Magnago Lampugnani. Rev. and enl. ed. N.Y., Abrams, 1986. 384p. il.

See GLAH 1:J134 for previous eds. Trans. of Hatje-Lexikon der Architektur des 20. Jahrhunderts, trans. and ed. by Barry Bergdoll. Originally published in English in 1964 as Encyclopedia of modern architecture, trans. and adapted from Knaurs Lexikon der modernen Architektur, ed. by Gerd Hatje and Wolfgang Pehnt. Publ. in French as Dictionnaire encyclopédique de l'architecture moderne & contemporaine (Paris, P. Sers, 1987) and in Spanish as Enciclopedia GG de la arquitectura del siglo XX (Barcelona, G. Gili, 1989). Signed entries by some 60 architectural historians and critics. Many include bibliographical references. They cover architects, schools, styles, associations, countries, construction terms, and materials.

Index, p.373–84.

Histories and Handbooks

J208 Architectural documents. N.Y., Rizzoli, 1982–1988. 5v. il., plans.

Contents: Tafuri, Manfredo. Vittorio Gregotti, buildings and projects (1982); Dini, Massimo. Renzo Piano, progetti e architetture, 1964–1983 (1983); Nicolin, Pierluigi. Mario Botta: buildings and projects 1961–1982 (1984); Rykwert, Joseph. Robert and James Adam: the men and the style (1985); Norberg-Schulz, Christian. The concept of dwelling: on the way to figurative architecture (1985); ———. Architecture, meaning and place: selected essays (1988).

J209 Architecture culture, 1943–1968: a documentary anthology. Comp. by Joan Ockman with the collaboration of Edward Eigen. [N.Y.], Columbia Univ. Graduate School of Architecture, Planning, and Preservation; Rizzoli, 1993. 464p. il. (Columbia books of architecture. Studio work)

"Aims to examine the relationship between historical documents and the culture in which they were first introduced [and] to relate these texts with an ongoing and very contemporary discourse that calls into question the boundaries between theory and practice."—*Foreword.*

73 texts presented chronologically. Each is preceded by a brief one-page analysis. Authors range from F. L. Wright to J. J. P. Oud, the German Democratic Republic, Jane Jacobs, Christopher Alexander, Michel Foucault, and Hans Hollein.

Selected bibliography, p.463. Index of authors, p.464.

J210 The architecture of the École des beaux-arts. Ed. by Arthur Drexler. Essays by Richard Chafee . . . [et al.] N.Y., Museum of Modern Art (Distr. by MIT Pr., 1977). 525p. il. (part col.)

Based on the exhibition, Museum of Modern Art (1975–76), presenting 200 drawings for architectural projects.

Contents: Engineer's architecture: truth and its consequences, by Arthur Drexler; The teaching of architecture at the École des Beaux-Arts, by Richard Chafee; Architectural composition at the École des Beaux-Arts from Charles Percier to Charles Garnier, by David Van Zanten; The romantic idea of architectural legibility: Henri Labrouste and the neogrec, by Neil Levine; Beaux-arts buildings in France and America.

Notes to the essays, p.[495]–517. Lists of architects and their works, p.[519]–23.

J211 Architecture theory since 1968. Ed. by K. Michael Hays. Cambridge, Mass., MIT Pr., 1998. xv, 807p. il. (Columbia books of architecture)

A substantial and wide-ranging anthology of contemporary writings on architectural theory, chronologically arranged.

Notes at ends of essays. Index, p.[802–08].

J212 At the end of the century: one hundred years of architecture. Los Angeles, Museum of Contemporary Art; Abrams, 1998. 336p. il. (part col.)

Beautifully illustrated catalog of the exhibition, Museum of Contemporary Art, Los Angeles (1998). Survey's "the global terrain of 20th-century architecture and urbanism."—*Foreword.*

Contents: Re-examining architecture and its history at the end of the century, by Elizabeth A. T. Smith; Space, time, and movement, by Anthony Vidler; The exhibitionist house, by Beatriz Colomina; Internationalism versus regionalism, by Hajime Yatsuka; Cultural intersections: re-visioning architecture and the city in the twentieth century, by Zeynep Çelik; Urban architecture and the crisis of the modern metropolis, by Jean-Louis Cohen; Latin America: the places of the "Other," by Jorge Francisco Liernur.

Bibliography, p.321–31. Index, p.332–36.

J213 Banham, Reyner. The architecture of the well-tempered environment. 2d ed. Chicago, Univ. of Chicago Pr., 1984. 319p. il.

1st ed., [1969]. Practical aspects of building.

Contents: (1) Unwarranted apology; (2) Environmental management; (3) A dark satanic century; (4) The kit of parts: heat and light; (5) Environments of large buildings; (6) The well-tempered home; (7) The environment of the machine aesthetic; (8) Machines à habiter; (9) Towards full control; (10) Concealed power; (11) Exposed power; (12) A range of methods; (13) A breath of intelligence.

"Readings in environmental technology," p.313. Index, p.315–19.

J214 ———. Theory and design in the first machine age. [Reprint.] Cambridge, Mass., MIT Pr., 1980. 338p. il.

1st ed., London, Architectural Press, 1960. This paperback ed. differs "in the addition to the bibliographies of a few substantial works of scholarship that have come to my notice since the original text was completed."—*p.13.* Published in German as Die Revolution der Architektur: Theorie und Gestaltung im ersten Maschinenzeitalter. Braunschweig, Vieweg, 1990.

Twenty-two chapters in four sections: (1) Predisposing causes: academic and rationalist writers, 1900–1914; (2) Italy: Futurist manifestos and projects, 1909–1914; (3) Holland: The legacy of Berlage: De Stijl, 1917–1925; (4) Paris: The world of art and Le Corbusier; (5) Germany: Berlin, the Bauhaus, the victory of the new style.

Index to proper names and buildings, p.331–34. Index to topics, publications, and organizations, p.335–38.

J215 Benevolo, Leonardo. The origins of modern town planning. Trans. by Judith Landry. Cambridge, Mass., MIT Pr., [1967]. xiv, 154p. il., facsims., maps, plans.

Trans. of Le origini dell'urbanistica moderna. Bari, Laterza, 1963; 2d ed., 1964; 3d ed. rev. 1968.

Complements the author's previous History of modern architecture (GLAH 1:J129) by addressing "a new relationship between town-planning and politics" (meaning social and economic planning) and "the avant-garde movements from Morris onwards."—*Pref.*

Contents: The growth of the industrial town; Great expectations (1815–48); Nineteenth century utopias [Owen, Saint-Simon, Fourier, Godin, and Cabet]; The beginnings of town-planning legislation in England and France; 1848 and its consequences.

Bibliographic footnotes within chapters. Index, p.148–54.

J216 ———. Storia dell'architettura moderna. 17th ed., rev. Roma, Laterza, 1993. 1058p. il. (Grandi opere)

Eng. ed., 1971 (GLAH 1:J129) has index. Publ. in French as Histoire de l'architecture moderne (Paris, Dunod, 1978–1988) and in German as Geschichte der Architektur des 19. und 20. Jahrhunderts, ([München], Callwey, [1964]).

Bibliography, p.[1021]–29. Name index, p.[1033]–51.

J217 Colomina, Beatriz. Privacy and publicity: modern architecture as mass media. Cambridge, Mass., MIT Pr., 1994. xi, 389p. il.

A theoretical study of Adolf Loos and others.

Contents: Archive; City; Photography; Museum; Interior; Window.

Notes, p.[336]–79. Index, p.[384]–89.

J218 Companion to contemporary architectural thought. Ed. by Ben Farmer and Hentie Louw. Consultant ed., Adrian Napper. N.Y., Routledge, 1993. x, 673p. il., maps.

A substantial, ambitious anthology of writings aimed at providing "an appreciation of the general state of the architectural world as it appears at the close of the twentieth century."—*Pref.*

Contents: (1) Introduction; (2) Responses [to people, places]; (3) Influences [of society, function, precedent, technology]; (4) Elements and attributes [form, space, architectural elements]; (5) Approaches and appreciation; (6) Case studies.

Contributors, p.[621]–35. Index, p.[636]–73.

J219 Conrads, Ulrich, and Sperlich, Hans G. The architecture of fantasy: utopian building and planning in modern times. Trans., ed., and exp. by Christine Crasemann Collins and George R. Collins. N.Y., Praeger, 1962. 187p. il., plans (Books that matter)

Trans. of Phantastische Architektur. Stuttgart, Hatje, [1960]. A heavily-illustrated survey of 15 types of futuristic, spontaneous, and grotesque designs that were selected "to pay tribute to human imagination."—*Pref.*

Includes section of documents and excerpts, p.129–56: Paul Scheerbart; Adolf Behne; Arbeitsrat für Kunst; Aus dem Ütopischen Briefwechsel; Einzelne Werke und Architekten.

Notes, p.155–74. Name index, p.175–[76].

J220 Curtis, William J. R. Modern architecture since 1900. 3d ed. London, Phaidon, 1996. 736p. il. (part col.).

1st ed., 1982; 2d ed., 1987.

A standard survey that concentrates "on buildings of high visual and intellectual quality."—*Pref.* "With the third edition the aim has been to integrate new knowledge and experience . . . and to accentuate themes that were left undeveloped" in previous eds.—*Pref. to the third ed.*

Contents: Part 1: The formative strands of modern architecture; Part 2: The crystallization of modern architecture between the wars; Part 3: Transformation and dissemination after 1940; Part 4: Continuity and change in the late twentieth century.

Bibliographical note, p.690–92. Books referred to in shortened form in notes, p.693. Notes, p.694–719. Index, p.720–36.

J221 De Benedetti, Mara. Antologia dell'architettura moderna: testi, manifesti, utopie. Bologna, Zanichelli, 1988. xvii. 840p. il.

Important, substantial anthology of documents presenting modern architectural theory and ideologies.

Contents: (1) Art nouveau, Jugendstil, Secession; (2) Berlage; (3) La "Scuola di Chicago"; (4) Garden City e Cité industrielle; (5) Vecchie città ed edilizia nuova: il problema del centri storici; (6) Loos; (7) Il Deutscher Werkbund; (8) La stagione delle avanguardie; (9) Le Corbusier e "L'esprit nouveau"; (10) Internationale Architektur; (11) I CIAM; (12) Il costruttivismo sovietico; (13) Hof e Siedlung; (14) La costruzione del "Movimento moderno"; (15) L'Italia; (16) Il neoempirismo scandinavo.

Bibliografia, p.795–828. Indice degli autori, p.829–33. Indice dei nomi, p.834–40.

J222 De Fusco, Renato. Storia dell'architettura contemporanea. 6th ed. Roma, Laterza, 1997. viii, 642p. il., plans, ports. (Grandi opere)

1st ed. 1974. Standard handbook, frequently revised and/or reissued as a "new" ed.

Includes bibliographical references and index.

J223 The Experimental tradition: essays on competitions in architecture. Ed. by Hélène Lipstadt. N.Y., Princeton Architectural Pr., 1989. 186p. il.

Catalog of an exhibition organized by the Architectural League of New York entitled "The Experimental tradition: twenty-five years of American architecture competitions, 1960–1985" and shown at six other American cities. "This volume places twenty-five years of American architecture competitions . . . in a wider historical context and recalls these debates."—*Foreword.*

Contents: (I) The experimental tradition, by Hélène Lipstadt; (II) Competing in the academy and the marketplace: European architecture competitions, 1401–1927, by Barry Bergdoll; (III) Coming to terms: architecture competitions in America and the emerging profession, 1789–1922, by Sarah Bradford Landau; (IV) In the shadow of the Tribune tower: American architecture competitions, 1922–1960, by Hélène Lipstadt; (V) Transforming the tradition: American architecture competitions, 1960 to the present, by Hélène Lipstadt; (VI) The battle for the monument: the Vietnam Veterans Memorial, by Mary McLeod; (VII) The promise and perils of art museum competitions: the New Orleans Museum of Art, by Helen Searing; (VIII) Ten competitions.

Index, p.184–86.

J224 Fanelli, Giovanni. Storia dell'architettura contemporanea: spazio, struttura, involucro. Roma, Laterza, 1998. 532p. il. (Grandi opere)

Substantial thematic survey of formal solutions in 20th-century architecture.

Contents: (I) Chicago: dall'architettura del grattacielo al mito wrightiano dello spazio; (II) Vienna, o del sublime della superficie; (III) Berlage, Plečnik, Garnier: parete e telaio a confronto; (IV) Da Gaudí a Behrens, la struttura tra espressione logica e monumentalismo; (V) Futurismo, costruttivismo, De Stijl: la struttura a traliccio tra collage e congegno dinamico; (VI) Perret, Le Corbusier, Mies van der Rohe: nuovi ordini architettonici; (VII) "International Style" e "New Traditionalism"; (VIII) La lezione di Kahn: oltre il contemporaneo.

Note, p.[489]–512. Indice dei nomi e delle opere, p.[515]–29.

J225 Ford, Edward R. The details of modern architecture. Cambridge, Mass., MIT Pr., 1990–1996. 2v. il.

Vol.2 has subtitle: 1928–1988.

An important technical study of detailing in architectural Modernism, based upon construction documents. Episodic but valuable.

Notes, v.1, p.357–60, v.2, p.[431]–35. Bibliography, v.1, p.361–63, v.2, p.[437]–[40]. Index, v.1, p.364–71, v.2, p.[441]–[48].

J226 Frampton, Kenneth. Modern architecture: a critical history. 3d ed., rev. and enl. N.Y., Thames and Hudson, 1992. 376p. il. (World of art)

1st ed., 1980; 2d ed., rev. and enl., 1985. This ed. has an expanded bibliography intended to indicate the range of works that the author "would have included had more space been available" and revisions in Part II "in order to register the latest activities of the neo-avant-garde and to record the more specific recent achievements of the high-tech architects."—*Pref.*

Contents: (I) Cultural developments and predisposing techniques, 1750–1939; (II) A critical history, 1836–1967; (III) Critical assessment and extension into the present, 1925–91.

Bibliography, p.345–66. Index, p.366–76.

J227 ______. Studies in tectonic culture: the poetics of construction in nineteenth and twentieth century architecture. Ed. by John Cava. Cambridge, Mass., MIT Pr., 1995. [xiii], 430p. il., photos, plans, drawings, elevations, sections.

First publ. in German as Grundlagen der Architektur: Studien zur Kultur des Tektonischen. München, Oktagon, 1993. Benefits from the vast number and various types of illustrations.

Of the ten chapters, four are devoted to the development of tectonic culture: Introduction: Reflections on the scope of the tectonic; Greco-Gothic and Neo-Gothic: the Anglo-French origins of tectonic form; The rise of the tectonic: core form and art form in the German Enlightenment, 1750–1870; Postscriptum: the tectonic trajectory, 1903–1994. Six chapters focus on the accomplishments and influence of individual architects (Frank Lloyd Wright, Auguste Perret, Ludwig Mies van der Rohe, Louis Kahn, Jørn Utzon, and Carlo Scarpa).

Notes, p.[389]–411. Bibliography, p.[413]–21. Index, p.[425]–30.

J228 Functional architecture: the international style, 1925–1940 = Funktionale Architektur, 1925–1940. [Gestalt. und Red., Gabriele Leuthäuser, Peter Gössel. English trans., John Bannister, Karen Williams. Trad. française, Françoise Laugier-Morun.] Köln, Taschen, 1990. 399p. chiefly il.

In German, English, and French. A collection of photographs from 1929–1937 publications, arranged by country (29 of them) preceded by an introduction (p.[9]–30) outlining the three principles of functionalism: architecture as volume, concerning regularity, the avoidance of applied decoration.

Lacks index and bibliography.

J229 Glancey, Jonathan. C20th architecture: the structures that shaped the century. Woodstock, N.Y., Overlook, 1998. 400p. il. (part col.)

"An introduction to twentieth-century architecture."—*Foreword.* Profiles of 370 buildings, arranged by type, with color photographs.

Contents: Arts and crafts; Classicism; Organic; Modernism; Postmodernism; Robotic; Cities; Futures.

Index, p.396–99.

J230 Haan, Hilde de, and Haagsma, Ids. Architects in competition: international architectural competi[ti]ons of the last 200 years. London, Thames and Hudson, 1988. 219p. il. (part col.)

Trans. of Architecten als rivalen. [Amsterdam], Meulenhoff/ Landshoff, 1988.

Examines 15 important competitions from the past 200 years, in Europe, Washington, Sydney and Kyoto, followed by essays by Dennis Sharp and Kenneth Frampton. Extensively illustrated.

Bibliography, p.208–12. Index, p.214–17.

J231 Hitchcock, Henry-Russell. Architecture, nineteenth and twentieth centuries. 4th ed., repr. with additions to the bibliography. Harmondsworth, Penguin, 1987, 1977. 696p. il., plans (The Pelican history of art, PZ15) (Repr.: New Haven, Yale Univ. Pr., 1992)

See GLAH 1:J135 for previous eds.

The 1987 reprint "incorporates one or two emendations to the text, and considerable additional bibliography, covering the years from 1976 to spring 1986."—*Pref.*

Index, p.[665]–96.

J232 ______, and Johnson, Philip. The international style. N.Y., Norton, 1996. 269p. il.

First publ. 1932 under title The international style: architecture since 1922 in conjunction with the most important architectural exhibition of the century. A 1966 ed. (N.Y., Norton) included a new foreword by Hitchcock (p.vii–xiii) and an appendix (p.237–255) that reprinted an article from the August 1951 issue of Architectural record in which Hitchcock commented on a series of quotations from the original 1932 text. Also publ. in German as Der Internationale Stil, 1932 (Braunschweig, Vieweg, 1985; Bauwelt Fundamente, 70). The 1996 ed. includes a new foreword by Philip Johnson.

Contents: (I) Introduction: the idea of style; (II) History; (III) Functionalism; (IV) A first principle: architecture as volume; (V) Surfacing material; (VI) A second principle: concerning regularity; (VII) A third principle: the avoidance of applied decoration; (VIII) Architecture and building; (IX) Plans; (X) The "Siedlung."

Indexes: architects, countries, p.257–60.

J233 ———. Modern architecture: romanticism and reintegration. [Reprint, with a foreword by Vincent Scully.] N.Y., Da Capo Pr., 1993. xxiii, 252p. il.
1st ed., 1929, N.Y., Payson & Clarke Ltd.; repr. 1970, N.Y., Hacker.
Contents: (One) The age of romanticism; (Two) the new tradition; (Three) The new pioneers.
Appendix [analysis of the experimentation in architecture between 1250 and 1750], p.223–36. Bibliographical note, p.[239]–41. Index, p.[245]–52.

J234 Jencks, Charles. The language of post-modern architecture. 6th ed. N.Y., Rizzoli, 1991. 204p. il. (part col.).
First publ. 1977 as an Architectural design monograph (London, Academy Editions); rev., enl. ed., 1978; 3d ed., 1981; 4th ed., 1984. Superb color photographs. Jencks, the author of numerous books on post-modernism, has added a chapter to each ed. of this work.
Contents: Introduction: death for rebirth; (I) The death of modern architecture; (II) The modes of architectural communication; (III) Post-modern architecture.
Notes, p.196–200. Index, p.201–04.

J235 ———. Modern movements in architecture. 2d ed. Harmondsworth, Penguin, 1985. 448p. il., plans.
See GLAH 1:J136 for 1st ed.
This ed. has a new introduction and postscript (changed from "Architecture and revolution" to "Late-Modernism and Post-Modernism").
Notes, p.391–409. Bibliography, p.411–12. Index, p.420–48.

J236 Johnson, Philip, and Wigley, Mark. Deconstructivist architecture. N.Y., Museum of Modern Art (Distr. by New York Graphic Society Books, Little, Brown, 1988). 104p. il.
Published on the occasion of the exhibition, Museum of Modern Art (1988). This is the first exhibition curated by Philip Johnson since 1954. Its impact has been similar to that of the 1932 Modern architecture exhibit that prophesied the International style (see GLAH 2:J232).
The catalog features an introductory essay by Wigley followed by projects by seven architects, with commentaries by Wigley: Frank O. Gehry, Daniel Libeskind, Rem Koolhaas, Peter Eisenman, Zaha M. Hadid, Coop Himmelblau, and Bernard Tschumi.

J237 Klotz, Heinrich. The history of postmodern architecture. Trans. by Radka Donnell. Cambridge, Mass., MIT Pr., 1988. 461p. il. (part col.).
Trans. of Moderne und Postmoderne: Architektur der Gegenwart, 1960–1980. Braunschweig, Vieweg, 1984.
Surveys "the manifold movements and trends of present-day architecture [in order] to illustrate the thesis that post-modern architecture needs to be seen as a revision of modernism."—*p.[xiv]*. Excellent illustrations.
Contents: Modernism; Subterfuges and reorientations; Preconditions for postmodern architecture; Postmodern architecture; Epilogue; Postscript: since 1980.
Notes, p.[439]–46. Bibliography, p.[447]–49. Index, p.[453]–61.

J238 ———. Postmodern visions: drawings, paintings, and models by postmodern architects. Contrib. writers, Volker Fischer . . . [et al.] N.Y., Abbeville, 1985. 357p. il. (part col.)
Trans. of Revision der Moderne. München, Prestel, 1984. Catalog of the exhibition, Deutsches Architekturmuseum, Frankfurt am Main (1984). An anthology of works by 35 contemporary architects.
Bibliography, p.353–54. Index, p.355–57.

J239 ———. 20th century architecture: drawings, models, furniture from the exhibition of the Deutsches Architekturmuseum, Frankfurt am Main. N.Y., Rizzoli, 1989. 349p. il. (part col.).
Trans. of Architektur des 20. Jahrhunderts: Zeichnungen, Modelle, Mobel. Frankfurt am Main, 1989. Published in conjunction with the exhibition, Deutsches Architekturmuseum (1989).
Features 73 topics, illustrated by designs by a wide variety of the major architects of the century.
Short biographies of architects, p.339–45. Index, p.347–50.

J240 Kultermann, Udo. Architecture in the 20th century. N.Y., Van Nostrand Reinhold, 1993. viii, 306p. il.
Trans. of Die Architektur im 20. Jahrhundert. 3d ed., Köln, DuMont, 1982; first publ. in 1977; 2., erw. Aufl. 1980.
A text that evolved from 25 years teaching at an architecture school, with a focus on practical usefulness and an attempt to be impartial.
Contents: (I) Puristic tendencies: architecture, science, and industry and the attitude towards the machine; (II) Empiristic tendencies: organic architecture and technology serving man and nature; (III) Syncretic tendencies: urbanistic architecture and building within a context; (IV) Autonomous architecture since 1970: regional identity and the regaining of tradition.
Notes, p.251–76. Critical bibliography, p.277–85. Index of names, p.289–99. Index of places, p.301–06.

J241 Loyer, François. Architecture of the industrial age, 1789–1914. Trans. by R. F. M. Dexter. Geneva, Skira, 1983. 319p. il. (part col.)
Trans. of Le siècle de l'industrie. Geneva, Skira, 1983.
A heavily illustrated survey covering Europe, Britain, and, to a lesser extent, the U.S.
Contents: (I) Academicism (Planning the landscape, 1789–1830; The mechanical revolution, 1830–1850); (II) Eclecticism (Industry in its splendour, 1850–1870; The debate on architecture; Industrial architecture); (III) Art nouveau (Past and present, 1870–1914; The "Belle epoque," 1890–1914; Modern times).
Notes and bibliographical references, p.295–302. List of illustrations [by medium, with buildings listed by city], p.303–15. Index of names, p.317–19.

J242 Norberg-Schulz, Christian. Roots of modern architecture. Ed. and photographed by Yukio Futagawa. Tokyo, A.D.A. Edita, 1988. 214p. il.

A well-illustrated theoretical study, in English and Japanese, that is "organized according to the problems which were taken up by the modern movement, and follows the line of development which Giedion called the 'new tradition.'"—*Pref.* The implicit chronology is indicated by "pre-modern," "modern," and "post-modern" designations.

Contents: The New World and the new architecture; The free plan; The open form; The natural house; The democratic institution; The healthy city; The new regionalism; The new monumentality; The new place.

Footnotes, p.198–200. Select bibliography, p.201–03 (in Japanese, p.203–11). Index, p.212–14.

J243 Oppositions books. Cambridge, Mass., MIT Pr., published for the Graham Foundation for Advanced Studies in the Fine Arts, Chicago, Ill., and the Institute for Architecture and Urban Studies, N.Y., 1981–1982. 5v. il, maps, plans.

A short-lived, but widely used, series.

Contents: Colquhoun, Alan. Essays in architectural criticism: modern architecture and historical change (1981); Rossi, Aldo. A scientific autobiography (1981); Rossi, Aldo. The architecture of the city (1982); Loos, Adolf. Spoken into the void: collected essays, 1897–1900 (1982); Ginzburg, Moisei Iakovlevich. Style and epoch (1982).

J244 Pearman, Hugh. Contemporary world architecture. London, Phaidon, 1998. 511p. il. (part col).

Beautifully illustrated anthology that "attempts no more than to condense thinking across thirteen broad categories of buildings."—*Introd.*

Contents: Visual arts: museums & galleries; Performance: opera houses, theatres & concert halls; Learning: schools, universities & libraries; Religion: places of worship; Consumerism: malls, shops & bars; Living: houses and apartments; Workplace: offices & business parks; Industry: factories & research centres; Leisure: theme parks, hotels & visitor centres; Transport: airports, stations & shipping terminals; Sport: stadia, gymnasia & pools; The civic realm: public space & structures; Towers: vertical cities.

Select bibliography, p.488–95. Index, p.496–509.

J245 Pehnt, Wolfgang. Expressionist architecture. Trans. by J. A. Underwood and Edith Küstner. N.Y., Praeger, [1973]. 231p. il.

Trans. of Die Architektur des Expressionismus, Stuttgart, Hatje, 1973; 2d ed., 1981.

Contents: Background (Politics and society; Beliefs and writings; Art and architecture); Development (Around 1910; Bruno Taut; Visionary architects; The early Bauhaus; Erich Mendelsohn; North German Expressionism; The architecture of Rudolf Steiner); Special concerns (New churches; Houses and tower blocks; The cinema); Parallels and sequels (Futurism; The school of Amsterdam; Expressionism and the New Architecture; Expressionism and the National Socialists).

Notes, p.210–18. Bibliography, p.219–26. Index, p.227–31.

J246 Peter, John. The oral history of modern architecture: interviews with the greatest architects of the twentieth century. N.Y., Abrams, 1994. 320p. il. + 1 computer disk.

From a project begun in the early 1950s and continued through the 1960s. Based on recordings of more than 70 architects and architectural engineers, ten of which are included in this book and the accompanying disc. Includes: F. L. Wright, Le Corbusier, L. Mies van der Rohe, W. Gropius, E. Saarinen, L. Kahn, P. Johnson, O. Niemeyer, J. L. Sert, and I. M. Pei.

Biographies, p.292–302. Bibliography, p.303–05. Time chart, p.306–07. Visitor's guide, p.308–12. Index, p.315–20.

J247 Portoghesi, Paolo. After modern architecture. Trans. by Meg Shore. N.Y., Rizzoli, 1982. xv, 150p. il. (part col.).

Trans. of Dopo l'architettura moderna. Roma, Bari, Laterza, 1980; several later Italian eds.

Contents: Foreword by Vincent Scully; (1) The trail of ashes; (2) The post-modern condition; (3) Architecture and the energy crisis; (4) Form follows fiasco; (5) The primitives of a new sensibility; (6) The star system and the crisis of the functionalist statute; (7) Italy in retreat; (8) The American situation; (9) The European horizon; (10) Conclusion.

Bibliography, p.149–50.

J248 ______. Postmodern, the architecture of the postindustrial society. Trans. by Ellen Shapiro. N.Y., Rizzoli, 1983. 153p. il. (part col.).

Trans. of Postmodern: l'architettura nella società post-industriale. Milano, Electa, 1982.

"This book is intended as an optimistic chronicle of the events of the past few years in international architecture."—*p.6.* Highlights the work of selected architects and sites.

J249 Postmodern visions: drawings, paintings, and models by contemporary architects. Ed. by Heinrich Klotz. Contrib. writers, Volker Fischer . . . [et al.] N.Y., Abbeville, 1985. 357p. il. (part col.)

Trans. by Yehuda Shapiro of Revision der Moderne: Postmoderne Architektur, 1960–1980. München, Prestel, 1984.

Based on the first exhibition at the Deutsches Architekturmuseum, Frankfurt (1984), incorporating many works acquired since its founding in 1979. Features designs by 37 European and American architects and firms.

Bibliography, p.353–54. Index, p.355–57.

J250 Risebero, Bill. Modern architecture and design: an alternative history. London, Herbert Pr., 1982. 256p. il., maps, plans, ports.

Accessible survey of modern architecture since the Industrial Revolution, for the general reader. Illustrated with line drawings.

Select bibliography, p.246–47. Index, p.248–56.

J251 Rowe, Colin. The architecture of good intentions: towards a possible retrospect. London, Academy, 1994. 144p. il.

Described by the author in his preface as "a long essay, in present form first offered at Cornell University as the Preston H. Thomas Lectures for 1982 . . . [and as] a Geistesgeschichte piece."

Contents: Epistemology; Eschatology; Iconography; Mechanism; Organism; Postscript.

Notes, p.134–40. Name index, p.142–44.

J252 Ruskin, John. The seven lamps of architecture. [Reprint.] N.Y., Dover, 1989. xii, 222p., il.

Repr. of the "new ed.," Sunnyside, Orpington, Kent, G. Allen, 1880. 1st ed., London, Smith, Elder, and Co., 1849. Numerous additional eds. publ. in the 1880s and early 1900s. Another reprint (London, Century, 1988), of an unspecified ed., includes a useful introd. by Andrew Saint.

Ruskin's observations on Gothic architecture—in chapters on Sacrifice, Truth, Power, Beauty, Life, Memory, and Obedience—were enormously popular for Victorian readers and have in recent years attracted renewed interest as documentation of 19th-century architectural taste.

J253 Rykwert, Joseph. The first moderns: the architects of the eighteenth century. Cambridge, Mass., MIT Pr., 1980. viii, 585p. il.

A thematic and philosophical study.

Contents: (1) Classic and neoclassic; (2) Positive and arbitrary; (3) The marvelous and the distant; (4) Universal architecture; (5) The pleasures of freedom; (6) Initiates to amateurs; (7) Pleasure and precision; (8) Neoclassical architecture; (9) Ephemeral splendors; (10) Truth stripped naked by philosophy.

Notes at ends of chapters. Bibliography, p.[507]–63. Index, p.[565]–85.

J254 Scruton, Roger. The classical vernacular: architectural principles in an age of nihilism. N.Y., St. Martin's, 1995. xviii, 158p. il.

A collection of 15 largely previously published essays and talks (most revised) from the past two decades, critical of modernism and post-modernism, that argue that the constants of architecture are aesthetic constants. The eight-page introd. discusses "our nature as organisms" and "our nature as rational beings."

Contents: (1) Reflections on a candlestick; (2) Architecture of the horizontal; (3) Vernacular architecture; (4) Public space and the classical vernacular; (5) Aesthetic education and design; (6) Building at a crossroads; (7) Architectural principles in an age of nihilism; (8) Alberti and the art of the appropriate; (9) Curtis Green at Chiswick; (10) Architecture and the Polis; (11) Adrian Stokes; (12) Buckminster Fuller; (13) David Watkin's morality and architecture; (14) Manfredo Tafuri's Marxism; (15) Art history and aesthetic judgement.

Bibliographical references. Index, p.155–58.

J255 Sharp, Dennis. Twentieth century architecture: a visual history. [New ed.] N.Y., Facts on File, 1991. 427p. il.

See GLAH 1:J139 for 1st ed.

In comparison with the 1st ed., gives greater prominence to vernacular, regional, and indigenous cultural views about architecture and the built environment. Material has been reorganized, in part "to reflect changed attitudes and values."—*Pref.*

Chronology, p.413–17. Index, p.421–27.

J256 Steele, James. Architecture today. London, Phaidon, 1997. 512p. col. il.

"This book aims to address the complex variety of issues that underlie contemporary architecture. . . . It introduces many new topics, such as ecological and populist architecture that are just beginning to emerge."—*Introd.* Focuses upon the 1940s to the present.

Contents: (1) The Modernist legacy; (2) European rationalism; (3) High-tech; (4) Minimalism; (5) The classical revival; (6) Post-modernism; (7) Deconstructivism; (8) Contemporary vernacular; (9) The new Expressionists; (10) Ecological architecture; (11) The new Moderns; (12) Populist architecture; (13) Megastructures; (14) The Los Angeles avant-garde; (15) Experimentation in Japan; (16) World cities.

Notes, p.488. Architects' biographies, p.489–99. Select bibliography, p.500–01. Chronology, p.502–03. Index, p.504–10.

J257 Tafuri, Manfredo. Architecture and utopia: design and capitalist development. Trans. by Barbara Luigia La Penta. Cambridge, Mass., MIT Pr., 1976. xi, 184p. il.

Trans. of Progetto e utopia. Roma, Bari, Laterza, 1973. A "reworking and sizeable enlargement of" an essay published in 1969 that addressed contemporary architectural ideology.—*Pref.*

Contents: (1) Reason's adventures: naturalism and the city in the century of the Enlightenment; (2) Form as regressive utopia; (3) Ideology and utopia; (4) The dialectic of the avant-garde; (5) "Radical" architecture and the city; (6) The crisis of utopia: Le Corbusier at Algiers; (7) Architecture and its double: semiology and formalism; (8) Problems in the form of a conclusion.

Bibliographical references.

J258 ———. The sphere and the labyrinth: avant-gardes and architecture from Piranesi to the 1970s. Trans. by Pellegrino d'Acierno and Robert Connolly. Cambridge, Mass., MIT Pr., 1987. 382p., il.

Trans. of La sfera e il labirinto: avanguardie e architettura da Piranesi agli anni '70. [Torino], Einaudi [1980] (Saggi, 620)

A theoretical work in which the "intention . . . has been to present, not a piece of history complete in itself, but rather an intermittent journey through a maze of tangled paths, one of the many possible 'provisional constructions.'"—*Introd.* The nine chapters (within three parts) include four appendixes with important pertinent texts.

Notes, p.[305]–06. Index, p.[367]–83.

J259 Theorizing a new agenda for architecture: an anthology of architectural theory 1965–1995. Ed. by Kate Nesbitt. N.Y., Princeton Architectural Pr., 1996. 606p. il

A collection of 51 previously published essays by architects and critics, including Robert Venturi, Peter Eisenman, Bernard Tschumi, Aldo Rossi, Tadao Ando, Anthony Vidler, Manfredo Tafuri, Juhani Pallasmaa, and Diana Agrest. Nesbitt views "architectural theory as a catalyst for change within the discipline, in both its academic and professional aspects."—*p.13.*

Contents: (1) Postmodernism; (2) Semiotics and structuralism; (3) Poststructuralism and deconstruction; (4) Historicism; (5) Typology and transformation; (6) Urban theory after modernism; (7) The school of Venice; (8) Political and ethical agendas; (9) Phenomenology; (10) Architecture, nature, and the constructed site; (11) Critical regionalism; (12) Tectonic expression; (13) Feminism, gender, and the problem of the body; (14) Contemporary definitions of the sublime.

Bibliography, p.585–90. Index, p.591–606.

J260 Vidler, Anthony. The architectural uncanny: essays in the modern unhomely. Cambridge, Mass., MIT Pr., 1992. xv, 257p. il.

"Intrigued by the unsettling qualities of much contemporary architecture. . . . I have been drawn to explore aspects of the spatial and architectural uncanny, as it has been categorized in literature, philosophy, psychology, and architecture from the beginning of the nineteenth century to the present."—*Pref.* The 15 chapters were previously published, 1987–1992.

Contents: (I) Houses; (II) Bodies; (III) Spaces.

Notes, p.[227]–47. Index, p.[251]–57.

J261 Watkin, David. Morality and architecture: the development of a theme in architectural history and theory from the Gothic revival to the modern movement. Oxford, Clarendon, 1977. viii, 126p. (Repr.: Chicago, Univ. of Chicago Pr., 1984)

Contents: (I) The theme in the nineteenth century: Pugin, Viollet-le-Duc; (II) The theme in the twentieth century: Lethaby, The Brave New World, Furneaux Jordan; (III) Pevsner: early writings, the historic mission, "historicism."

References, p.[117]–21. Index, p.[122]–26.

J262 Whittick, Arnold. European architecture in the twentieth century. 2d ed. [Aylesbury, Eng., Leonard Hill Books, 1974]. xiv, 706p. il.

See GLAH 1:J140 for original ed.

A broad survey by the author of the Encyclopedia of urban planning (GLAH 1:J33). Emphasizes topical coverage, in 46 chapters within five sections.

Contents: (I) Historical background and early years of the century to 1918; (II) Tradition, transition and change 1919–1941; (III) Functionalism, logic and light 1924–1942; (IV) Political determinism and classical monumentality 1930–1940; (V) Towards a better physical environment 1943–1970.

Bibliography, p.682–90. Index, p.691–706.

J263 Wigley, Mark. The architecture of deconstruction: Derrida's haunt. Cambridge, Mass., MIT Pr., 1993. xv, 278p.

On the recent discourse between philosophy and architecture inspired by the French philosopher. Earlier versions of portions of the text were published previously in periodicals.

Contents: (1) The translation of Deconstruction; (2) Unbuilding architecture; (3) The slippery art of space; (4) The domestication of the house; (5) Throwing up architecture; (6) Doing the twist; (7) Dislocating space.

Notes, p.[221]–62. References, p.[263]–71. Index, p.273–78.

J264 Zevi, Bruno. Linguaggi dell'architettura contemporanea. Milano, Etaslibri, 1993. (unpaged) il. (part col.) (Scienze del territorio)

In Italian and English. Highlights 100 buildings built between 1945 and 1990 by various architects in western countries.

Buildings index. Index of architects.

SEE ALSO: Texts and documents (GLAH 2:R103); Watkin, The rise of architectural history (GLAH 2:G89)

WESTERN COUNTRIES

Australia

J265 Jensen, Elfrida. Colonial architecture in South Australia: a definitive chronicle of development 1836–1890, and the social history of the times. Adelaide, Rigby, 1980. xi, 888p. il.

The most comprehensive work to date on colonial architecture and engineering developments in Australia, geographically encompassing the area from Darwin in the north to Port MacDonnell in the south. Straightforward chronological approach with more than 1,500 illustrations.

References, p.821–45. Index, p.847–85.

Canada

J266 Bergeron, Claude. Index des périodiques d'architecture canadiens, 1940–1980 = Canadian architectural periodicals index, 1940–1980. English trans. by Sylvia Bergeron. Québec, Presses de l'Université Laval, 1986. xiii, 518p.

A complete inventory of the contents of the nine Canadian architectural journals published during these years, inclusive. Presented in two sections: (1) Buildings and their architects, devoted to individual works of architecture which are arranged into twelve subject categories, supplemented by architect, building type, and place name indexes; (2) Miscellaneous subjects, "consists of a bibliography of articles on various aspects of the architectural profession, on the construction industry, and on construction materials and techniques in general, not related to a particular type of building."—*Foreword.*

Author index, p.[509]–18.

J267 Johnson, Patricia J. Index of Canadian architect and builder, 1888–1908. Ottawa, Society for the Study of Architecture in Canada, 1987. 156p.

Indexes the journal's contents through its entire publication history, other than editorials and advertisements, in a single-dictionary format. An excellent source for information on architecture, construction, and the engineering and building trades in Canada during the late 19th and early 20th centuries.

J268 Kalman, Harold D. History of Canadian architecture. N.Y., Oxford Univ. Pr., 1994. 2v. il., maps.

The first comprehensive study of the built environment of the many cultural groups found within the geographic boundaries of Canada, this history gives equal emphasis to the vernacular traditions as well "high" architecture. Both volumes contain an identical bibliography on the history of Canadian architecture and glossary of terms. Each vol. contains relevant notes for the text, an index to the buildings discussed in that vol., and a general index to the vol. Illustrated with high-quality black-and-white photographs and drawings.

Contents: Vol.1: (1) The first buildings; (2) New France; (3) British and American settlement on the Atlantic coast; (4) Classicism in upper and lower Canada; (5) Building for communications, defense, and commerce; (6) The return of the past: the Victorian revivals; (7) Early building on the prairies; (8) The settlement of the West coast. Vol.2: (9) The railway and the opening of the West; (10) Building the young dominion; (11) Domestic architecture; (12) Town planning; (13) The true North; (14) Architecture between the wars; (15) Modern architecture and beyond.

Notes, v.1, p.419–54, v.2, p.870–902. Bibliography, v.1, p.455, v.2, p.903. Glossary, v.1, p.456–59, v.2, p.904–07. Index of Canadian buildings, v.1, p.460–65, v.2, p.916–33.

J269 A union list of architectural records in Canadian public collections = Catalogue collectif de recherche documentaire sur l'architecture provenant de collections publiques canadiennes. Comp. by Portia Leggat. Montreal, Canadian Centre for Architecture, 1983. xxiii, 213p.

A useful first stop for research requiring original architectural records. Organized geographically, moving from easternmost provinces west, each entry provides address, telephone, and contact person information; notes on the scope of the collection and its special strengths; admissions policy; hours of operation; duplication processes available. Entries are in English or French, depending on the province surveyed.

Index to architects, p.189–201. Index to institutions, p.203–13.

France

Bibliography

J270 France. Archives nationales. Les sources de l'histoire de l'architecture religieuse aux Archives nationales, de la Revolution à la Separation, 1789–1905. Paris, Archives nationales, 1994. 196p. il., xvip. of plates.

Guide to archival materials dealing with religious architecture in the period 1789–1905 housed in the National Archives. Each chapter begins with an essay followed by the numbered list of files. Many entries offer detailed descriptions of the materials which range from correspondence to original drawings.

Contents: (1) Commissions et comités; (2) Édifices diocésains; (3) Édifices cultuels paroissiaux; (4) Lieux de culte particuliers; (5) Décor intérieur des églises; (6) Personnel.

Index, p.[167]–191.

J271 Institut français d'architecture. Archives d'architecture du XXe siècle. Liege, Mardaga, 1991– . (1)v. il. (part col.)

First vol. in a series documenting the archival holdings of the Institut, this covers 50 of more than 150 individual architectural collections. Entries consist of a biographical essay followed by a chronological outline of the individual's education, professional life, professional affiliations, and a bibliography. The majority of each entry is devoted to a descriptive listing of the archive's holdings arranged by date of project. Lastly, there are detailed cross references to other architects' files which contain related information. Illustrations are found throughout the entries.

List of the architects' files found in v.1 arranged by their file number, p.498. Name index, p.499–[502]. Geographic index, p.503–04. Paris street address index, p.505–[06]. Subject index, p.507–09. List of all the architects' files held at the Institute through January 1, 1991, p.510.

SEE ALSO: The Mark J. Millard architectural collection GLAH 2:J33).

Dictionaries and Encyclopedias

J272 Dugast, Anne, and Parizet, Isabelle. Dictionnaire par noms d'architectes des constructions élevées à Paris au XIXe et XXe siècles. Étab. sous la dir. de Michel Fleury. Paris, Service des travaux historiques, 1990– 4v. il. (Publications de la Sous-commission de recherches d'histoire municipale contemporaine, Ville de Paris, Commission des travaux historiques)

Authoritative biographical dictionary of Parisian architects of the 19th and 20th centuries.

Contents: (1) Notices 1 à 1340, Abadie à Cyr-Robert; (2) Notices 1341 à 2440, Dabernat à Guyran; (3) Notices 2441 à 3654, Hasser à Mutzig; (4) Notices 3655 à 4871, Nachon à Zwahlen.

Includes lists of abbreviations, bibliographies, name and topographical indexes.

Histories and Handbooks

General Works

J273 France. Archives nationales. Catalogue général des cartes, plans et dessins d'architecture, Série NN. Par Claude-France Rochat, avec la collab. de Michel Le Moël. Avant-propos par Jean Favier. Paris, Archives nationales. (Diffusé par la Documentation française, 1978.) 620p. plates, maps (part col.)

See GLAH 1:J149 for Série N.

Série NN contains primarily maps of Paris, but includes a smaller number of maps of other European cities, the United States, and world maps. Maps included date from before 1876.

List of manuscript maps, p.567–68. Index, p.571–612. Addendum, p.613–14. Table of contents (showing geographic breakdown of collection), p.617–20.

J274 France. Ministère de l'Éducation Nationale [Direction des Archives de France]. Catalogue général des cartes, plans et dessins d'architecture. Série N. Préface de Charles Braibant. Paris, 1958–74. 4v. il., plates, elevations.

See GLAH 1:J149 for previous vols. Includes indexes.

Selective contents: (4) Pays étrangers, by M. Le Moël and C.-F. Rochat (1974).

J275 Histoire de l'architecture française. Paris, Mengès, 1989–99. 3v. il. (part col.), facsims., plans, ports.

Exceptionally well-illustrated survey from the middle ages to the present, by three authorities. These titles are not cited individually elsewhere in this chapter.

Contents: (1) Erlande-Brandenburg, Alain. Histoire de l'architecture française: du Moyen Age à la Renaissance: IVe siècle début XVIe siècle (1995); (2) Pérouse de Montclos, Jean-Marie. Histoire de l'architecture française: de la Renaissance à la Révolution. Paris, Menges; Caisse nationale des monuments historiques et des sites (1989); (3) Loyer, François. De la Révolution à nos jours (1999).

Carolingian—Gothic

J276 Bony, Jean. French Gothic architecture of the 12th and 13th centuries. Berkeley, Univ. of California Pr., 1983. 623p. il., maps, plans. (California studies in the history of art, 20)

Important study which traces the development of Gothic style through nearly two centuries, illustrated by 449 excellent black-and-white photographs and numerous maps. It contributes major reinterpretations of the 12th-century phase of Gothic by focusing on lesser-known churches rather than only the predictable examples.

Notes, p.465–546. Selective bibliography, p.547–72. Index, p.573–623.

J277 Les Monuments de la France gothique. Collection dirigée par Anne Prache. Paris, Picard, 1987– . (7)v. il., plans.

Authoritative series documenting the religious and civic architecture of Gothic France, arranged by historic regions and further broken down by city and monument. Essays discuss the history and in some cases offer a detailed chronology of the restoration of the specific monuments. Good black-and-white photographs and excellent plans. Volumes inconsistently offer brief bibliographies either at the end of the essay or collected at the end of the vol. Some vols. have indexes.

Published to date: Bideault, Maryse and Lautier, Claudine. Ile-de-France gothique (2v., 1987–1988): (1) Les églises de la vallée de l'Oise et du Beauvaisis; (2) Les demeures seigneuriales. (v.2 by Jean Mesqui.); Burnand, Marie-Claire. La Lorraine gothique (1989); Gardelles, Jacques. Aquitaine gothique (1992); Blomme, Yves. Poitou gothique (1993); Andrault-Schmitt, Claude. Limousin gothique: les édifices religieux (1997).

Renaissance—Modern

J278 Bourget, Pierre. Les architectures baroques en France. Paris, Libr. Léonce Laget, 1993. 291p. il.

History of the Baroque period and Baroque influences into the 20th century. Illustrated, but lacks plans.

Bibliographie, p.281–82.

J279 Braham, Allan. The architecture of the French Enlightenment. Berkeley, Univ. of California Pr., 1980. 288p. il., maps.

Regarded as nearly definitive, in addition to documenting the architecture of pre-Revolutionary France, this study includes a wealth of information on the individuals involved, patrons as well as artists and thinkers. While it does not replace Louis Hautcoeur's Histoire de l'architecture classique en France (GLAH 1:J169), it incorporates more recent research. Numerous black-and-white illustrations, mainly plans, sections, and elevations of buildings discussed.

Notes to the text, p.262–78. General bibliography and list of abbreviations, p.279–82. Index, p.284–88.

J280 Egbert, Donald Drew. The Beaux-Arts tradition in French architecture. Illustrated by the Grands Prix de Rome. Ed. for publication by David Van Zanten. Tribute by Robert Venturi. Princeton, Princeton Univ. Pr., 1980. xxii, 217p. il., plates.

Comprised of two parts: a general history of the French academic tradition in architecture and a discussion of French academic principles and methods of design. The limited number of illustrations appear at the end of the vol. Most helpful are the appendixes: "Bibliographical and archival sources for the Grand Prix de Rome"; and "The Grand Prix Designs," which lists the year and title of the program, and names of the winners of the Grands Prix and other awards from 1702 through 1967.

Selected bibliography, p.203–11. Index, p.[213]–17.

J281 Jullian, René. Histoire de l'architecture en France de 1889 à nos jours: un siècle de modernité. Paris, Philippe Sers, 1984. 327p. il., plans.

A chronological survey of the last century discussing major stylistic movements from Style 1900 through the 1960s, including their proponents such as Guimard, Garnier, Perret, Le Corbusier, Mallet-Stevens, Lurçat, Roux-Spitz. Despite the title, little emphasis on architecture of the 1970s–1980s.

Index des noms cité, p.298–304. Index des bâtiments (Paris), p.304–09. Index des bâtiments (hors Paris), p.309–18. Bibliographie, p.319–23.

J282 Kalnein, Wend von. Architecture in France in the eighteenth century. Trans. from the German by David

Britt. New Haven, Yale Univ. Pr., 1995. 294p. il., maps (part col.) (Yale University Press pelican history of art)

Based on the architecture portions of W. Kalnein and M. Levey's Art and architecture of the eighteenth century in France (GLAH 1:I281).

Notes, p.[271]–82. Bibliography, p.[283]–87. Index, p.[288]–94.

J283 Lemoine, Bertrand. Architecture in France 1800–1900. Trans. from the French by Alexandra Bonfante-Warren. N.Y., Abrams, 1998. 200p. col. il.

Trans. of France du XIXe siècle. Paris, Martinière, 1993. German ed., Basel, Birkhäuser, 2000.

Important overview of 19th-century French architecture, organized thematically by building types.

Contents: The French tradition: churches and châteaux; Residential architecture: apartment buildings, villas, and town houses; Public architecture: government buildings, prisons, and hospitals; The education of the masses: museums, libraries, and schools; The pleasure palaces: theaters, circuses, spas, casinos, and hotels; The architecture of public space: monuments, street furniture, bandstands, and conservatories; The architecture of industry: factories, workers' housing, industrial buildings, and banks; Steam and speed: train stations; Temples of commerce: boutiques, shopping arcades, and department stores; The architecture of trade: open-air markets and covered market halls; Architecture as engineering: bridges, aqueducts, and viaducts.

Index, p.198–200. Bibliography, p.200.

J284 Lesnikowski, Wojciech G. The new French architecture. Introd. by Patrice Goulet. N.Y., Rizzoli, 1990. 223p. il. (part col.) [1]p. of plates.

Following an introductory essay, "From historicism to the new modernism," this book uses the work of 12 architects to demonstrate the range of design in the 1980s and 1990s. Illustrated with excellent photographs and many plans, each building is introduced with a brief statement.

Architects' biographies, p.222–23. No bibliography or index.

Germany and Austria

Early Christian—Gothic

J285 Meckseper, Cord. Kleine Kunstgeschichte der deutschen Stadt im Mittelalter. Darmstadt, Wissenschaftliche Buchgesellschaft, 1982. 306p. il., 160 plates.

Concise history of medieval German architecture discussed in two sections: the development of cities as influenced by the Celts, the Romans, etc., and the architecture of cities arranged primarily by building type. Plans and line drawings are interspersed in the text. Plates follow.

Literaturverzeichnis, p.[269]–80. Ortsverzeichnis, p.[281]–303.

J286 Ullmann, Ernst. Gotik: deutsche Baukunst 1200–1550. Leipzig, Seemann, 1994. 143p. il.

Basic history, mainly concerned with religious architecture. Exceptionally fine illustrations.

Zeittafel, p.138–40. Literaturhinweise, p.141–42. Ortsregister, p.143.

Renaissance—Modern

J287 Becker, Heidede. Geschichte der Architektur- und Städtebauwettbewerbe. Unter Mitarb. von Sabine Knott. Stuttgart, Kohlhammer, 1992. 345p. il., maps, plans. (Schriften des Deutschen Instituts für Urbanistik, Bd. 85)

"Discusses a number of key competitions in the fields of architecture, urban planning, and housing which shed light on the traditional problems and cul-de-sacs in competition procedures, but which also reveal promising experimental approaches."—*Summary.* Emphasis is on the period 1867 through the Third Reich. Appendixes 1–19 are facsimile copies of competition announcements and guidelines.

Summary [in English], p.13–15. Literatur, p.313–37. Personenregister, p.338–43. Ortsregister, p.344–45.

J288 Borsi, Franco, and Godoli, Ezio. Vienna 1900: architecture and design. N.Y., Rizzoli, 1986. 351p. il. (part col.)

Survey of architecture in the city the authors describe as "a great laboratory of experiments in form."—*Introd.* Chapters on Wagner, Olbrich, Hoffmann, Loos, the Wagner School, Wagner's followers, the Vienna school, and the Secession style. Reliance on period photographs means that some are muddy.

Chronology of buildings, arranged alphabetically by architect, p.305–30. Excellent bibliography, p.331–48. Index, p.349–51.

J289 Feldmeyer, Gerhard G. The new German architecture. Introd. by Manfred Sack. Essay by Casey C. M. Mathewson. [Trans. from the German by Mark Wilch.] N.Y., Rizzoli, 1993. 224p. il. (part col.)

Following an introductory essay, "From city planning to urban design: rebuilding Germany 1945–1992," this book uses the work of 24 architects to demonstrate the range of design in the 1980s and 1990s. Illustrated with excellent photographs and many plans, each building is introduced with a brief statement.

Architects' biographies, p.8–9. No bibliography or index.

J290 Hitchcock, Henry Russell. German Renaissance architecture. Princeton, Princeton Univ. Pr., 1981. xxxiv, 379p. il., plates.

First comprehensive English-language history of the period. "This book aims to provide a comprehensive account of architecture in Germany from the early influx of new Italian ideas in 1509 or 1510 to the outbreak of the Thirty Years' War more than a century later."—*Pref.*

Index, p.[361]–79.

J291 Klingensmith, Samuel John. The utility of splendor: ceremony, social life, and architecture at the court of

Bavaria, 1600–1800. Ed. for publication by Christian F. Otto and Mark Ashton. Chicago, Univ. of Chicago Pr., 1993. xx, 315p. il. (part col.), plans.

"A study of the enormous palaces of seventeenth- and eighteenth-century southern Germany as working buildings, structures whose . . . elaborately decorated rooms are here understood in new ways through the reconstruction of the private, social, and civic life that fostered them and filled them."—*Pref.*

Contents: (1) Introductions; (2) The Residenz in Munich; (3) The country houses; (4) Apartments and Säle: issues of program and plan; (5) Elements of everyday life; (6) State acts: diplomatic receptions and audiences. Appendixes.

Notes, p.[247]–99. Bibliography, p.[301]–08. Index, p.309–15. Plans, p.[317–26].

J292 Kräftner, Johann. Bauen in Österreich: die Fortführung einer grossen Tradition = Building in Austria: carrying on a great tradition. Text und Auswahl der Objekte von Johann Kräftner. Hrsg. von Traute Franke und Gerhart Langthaler. 289 Farbabbildungen nach Photographien von Georg Riha. Übers. in die englische Sprache, Günter Treffer. Wien, Brandstätter, 1983. 208p. il.

Comprised largely of color plates, this book covers Austrian architecture from the late 19th century to the present day. Exceptional photographs document interiors and exteriors of many different building types. A one-paragraph description accompanies the plates of each building. Useful for coverage of buildings outside Vienna.

Register = Index = Indexe [lists the architects and construction firms instrumental in the planning and realization of the constructions shown in the color plates, including restoration firms], p.200–08.

J293 Lane, Barbara Miller. Architecture and politics in Germany, 1918–1945. Cambridge, Mass., Harvard Univ. Pr., 1968. xv, 278p. il. (Repr.: 1985)

A study of the controversy over the "new" architecture of the Bauhaus, continuing through the years of the Weimar Republic, and the Nazi party's efforts to associate architecture with political objectives, ultimately leading to the government's efforts to establish control over the arts. Originally published in 1968, the paperback reprint contains a new preface which includes bibliographic notes on relevant publications and archival collections since 1968.

Selected bibliography, p.217–29. Notes, p.231–69. Index, p.271–78.

J294 Watkin, David, and Mellinghoff, Tilman. German architecture and the classical ideal. Cambridge, Mass., MIT Pr., 1987. 296p. il.

The first book in English to survey in depth German neoclassical architecture from 1740 to 1840. Part 1, "History, Style and Patronage," offers essays on the political and cultural background of Germany, as well as chapters on Schinkel, von Klenze, and the influence of French and English architecture. Part 2 is a gazetteer of neoclassical buildings in Germany. Well illustrated.

Bibliography, p.271–84. Index of places, p.287–91. Index of people, p.292–96.

J295 Zukowsky, John, ed. The many faces of modern architecture: building in Germany between the World Wars. With contrib. by Kennie Ann Laney-Lupton . . . [et al.] N.Y., Prestel (Distr. by te Neues, 1994). 256p. il., map.

Publishes "neglected contributions to the architecture of the interwar years in relation to better known German landmarks . . . [places] major sites within the broad context of architecture in the twenties and thirties, providing a generous survey of buildings in Germany from this era, particularly those with a modernist bent."—*Introd.* Excellent photographs.

Contents: (1) Berlin: capital of the modern movements; (2) "Das Neue Frankfurt"; (3) The West: Rhine and Ruhr; (4) Hamburg, Hanover, and Expressionist architecture in north Germany; (5) Stuttgart, Munich, and modernist masonry architecture; (6) The East: Silesia, Saxony, Thuringia, and Brandenburg.

Bibliographic notes within each chapter. Index of architects, artists, and designers, p.252–54. Index of places, p.255–56.

Great Britain and Ireland

Bibliography

J296 Archer, John. The literature of British domestic architecture, 1715–1842. Cambridge, Mass., MIT Pr., 1985. xxxvi, 1078p. il., plates.

The only bibliography devoted to the literature of British domestic architecture, it includes "only books and periodicals published in Great Britain and Ireland, first issues between 1715 and 1842, that contain original designs for habitations."—*Introd.* Scholarly essays precede the catalog of entries. Extensive annotations for each publication included.

Contents: (1) Architecture and the book trade; (2) Format and content; (3) Theory and design; (4) Principal entries. Appendixes: (A) Checklist of additional books by Crunden, Halfpenny, Langley, Nicholson, Pain, Richardson, Salmon and Swan; (B) Checklist of selected books showing domestic interiors; (C) Selected additional books concerning domestic architecture; (D) Addenda; (E) Short-title chronological list; (F) List of printers, publishers, and booksellers.

Index, p.[1061]–78.

J297 Hall, Sir Robert de Zouche, ed. A bibliography on vernacular architecture. Newton Abbot, David & Charles, 1972– . (3)v.

See GLAH 1:J177 for v.1; v.[2] originally called Vol.1, a supplement; v.[2] and 3 have publisher [York], Vernacular Architecture Group. Includes indexes.

Selective contents: [2] Current bibliography of vernacular architecture, 1970–1976, ed. by D. J. H. Michelmore; (3), Bibliography of vernacular architecture, 1977–1989, ed. by I. R. Pattison, D. S. Pattison & N. W. Alcock.

J298 Kamen, Ruth H. British and Irish architectural history: a bibliography and guide to sources of information. London, Architectural Pr., 1981. vi, 249p.

An essential tool with extensive annotations documenting publications through 1980. 870 entries were selected based on the author's experience in seeking information on architects, buildings, and architectural styles. Omits works on individual architects, specific buildings, and books of regional or local character (excepting London); instead instructs the user on methodology and location of information.

Contents: (1) How to find out: guides to the literature; (2) How to find out about architects and buildings: published sources; (3) How to find out about architects and buildings: unpublished sources, indexes and catalogues; (4) How to find out about architects and buildings: periodicals and periodical indexes; (5) Societies, institutions and organisations; (6) Sources of architectural photographs, slides and films; (7) British and Irish architectural history: a selective bibliography.

Index, p.225–49.

J299 McParland, Edward. A bibliography of Irish architectural history. [Dublin], Irish Historical Studies, 1989. p.[161]–212.

Reprinted from Irish historical studies, v.26, no.102 (Nov. 1988). "A list—covering items published between 1900 and 1986—of serious accounts of the history of important architectural projects undertaken in Ireland between the late seventeenth and early twentieth centuries. It is intended to be comprehensive in respect of monographs, collective works and articles in non-Irish periodicals, but in respect of Irish periodicals it is a supplement to Richard J. Hayes, Sources for the history of Irish civilisation: articles in Irish periodicals (9 vols., Boston, 1970)."—*Introd.* No annotations.

Subject index, p.199–212.

Dictionaries and Encyclopedias

J300 Colvin, Howard Montague. A biographical dictionary of British architects, 1600–1840. 3d ed. New Haven, Yale Univ. Pr., 1995. 1264p.

See GLAH 1:J179 for previous eds. (London, J. Murray)

New ed. of an indispensable dictionary. Essays on the building trades and the architectural profession. Adds more than 160 architects and 2,000 buildings to those found in previous eds. Also eliminates those individuals determined to have worked primarily outside this period or who are now deemed not to qualify as architects. Appendixes: (A) Some buildings erected before 1840 to the designs of Victorian architects not included in this dictionary; (B) Names included in previous editions of this dictionary but excluded from the second or third editions; (C) Public offices held by architects 1600–1840.

Includes bibliographical references. Index of persons, p.1157–88. Index of places, p.1189–1264.

J301 Curl, James Stevens. English architecture: an illustrated glossary. Drawings by John J. Sambrook. [2d rev. ed.] North Pomfret, Vt., David & Charles, 1986. 192p. il., plans.

1st ed. 1977. An essential work. "This book is intended to provide an introduction to the language that describes the national's built heritage so that the basic architectural elements can be identified."—*Pref.* Scots terms are included as many are encountered in the northern counties of England. Exceptional photographs and line drawings support the text.

Bibliography, p.189–91.

J302 Directory of British architects, 1834–1900. British Architectural Library, Royal Institute of British Architects. Comp. by Alison Felstead, Jonathan Franklin, and Leslie Pinfield. Foreword by Mark Girouard. N.Y., Mansell, 1993. xxvii, 1035p. il., ports.

A necessary starting point for research on the period. Focuses primarily on members of the RIBA, with more than 7,000 entries which include names and dates, addresses, education and training, qualifications, works and references (mostly to published obituaries, the Dictionary of National Biography, and RIBA files). Complements Colvin's Biographical dictionary of British architects, 1600–1840 (see GLAH 2:J300).

Includes a bibliography of additional sources, p.xix–xxii.

J303 Gray, A. Stuart. Edwardian architecture: a biographical dictionary. Photographs by Jean & Nicholas Breach. Drawings by Charlotte Halliday. Foreword by Nicholas Taylor. Iowa City, Univ. of Iowa Pr., 1986. 421p. il.

Comprised of 20 introductory sections and 348 biographical entries. Covering roughly 1900–1914, this work fills a gap left by the above-mentioned dictionaries. "Biased in favour of London as against the provinces, in favour of public buildings as against country houses, in favour of classicism as against Arts and Crafts."—*Introd.* Entries provide a biographical essay, list of major works, and citations for obituaries. Good black-and-white illustrations.

Index, p.397–421.

J304 Harvey, John Hooper. English mediaeval architects: a biographical dictionary down to 1550: including master masons, carpenters, carvers, building contractors, and others responsible for design. Rev. ed. With contrib. by Arthur Oswald. Gloucester, A. Sutton, 1984. lxii, 479p. plates, ports.

See GLAH 1:J199 for 1st ed.

16-p. supp. of additions and corrections pub. in 1987, Hulverstone Manor, Isle of Wight, Pinhorns.

J305 Loeber, Rolf. A biographical dictionary of architects in Ireland, 1600–1720. London, J. Murray, 1981. 127p.

A useful companion to Colvin's Biographical dictionary of British architects, 1600–1840 (see GLAH 2:J300). Entries on 107 individuals, nearly all of whom were craftsman-architects. For those with a sizable list of works the biographical essay is followed by a listing of the buildings by type with extensive notes regarding archival sources for further research.

Table of Irish royal works in the 17th century, p.[116]–[17]. Index of persons and places, p.118–27.

Histories and Handbooks

General Works

J306 Brown, R. J. Timber-framed buildings of England. London, R. Hale, 1986. 368p. il.

Documents the structural use of timber, focusing on surviving examples which span six centuries. Illustrated by excellent drawings and diagrams which offer a balance between historical and technical information.

Contents: (1) Construction and structural details; (2) Architectural features and details; (3) Churches and other ecclesiastical buildings; (4) Public and communal buildings; (5) Houses; (6) Farm buildings; (7) Industrial buildings; (8) Repair of timber-framed buildings.

Bibliography, p.357–59. Place index, p.[360]–66. General index, p.[367]–68.

J307 Brunskill, R. W. Illustrated handbook of vernacular architecture. 3d ed., rev. Boston, Faber and Faber, 1987. 256p. il.

1st ed., 1971. 2d ed., 1978.

"The most widely known and influential study of its type in the world . . . an excellent and amazingly condensed guide to the vernacular architecture of England and Wales."—*Review*, Vernacular architecture newsletter, v.33, no.7, autumn 1987. Excellent line drawings illustrate text. Appendix 1: How to study vernacular architecture, extensive, intensive and documentary; Appendix 2: Glossary notes.

Notes, references and recommendations for further reading, p.232–49. Index, p.250–56.

J308 The buildings of Britain. Alastair Service, gen. ed. London, Barrie & Jenkins, 1982– . (4)v. il.

Contents: (1) Airs, Malcolm. Tudor and Jacobean (1982); (2) Morrice, Richard. Stuart and Baroque (1982); (3) Service, Alistair. Anglo-Saxon and Norman (1982); (4) Watkin, David. Regency (1982).

Each vol. has bibliography and index.

J309 The buildings of Ireland. [Ed. adviser, Nikolaus Pevsner]. N.Y., Penguin Books, 1979– . (2)v. il., maps, plans.

Projected in 9v. Includes indexes.

Contents: (1) Rowan, Alistair. Northwest Ulster: the counties of Londonderry, Donegal, Fermanagh, and Tyrone (1979) (2) Casey, Christine and Rowan, Alistair. North Leinster: the counties of Longford, Louth, Meath, and Westmeath (1993).

J310 Clifton-Taylor, Alec. The pattern of English building. 4th ed. Ed. by Jack Simmons. London, Faber, 1987. 480p. il., 2 maps, 1 port.

See GLAH 1:J178 for 3d ed.

J311 Colvin, Howard M. The history of the King's works. London, H.M. Stationery Office, 1963–1982. 6v. il., plates (part col.), maps, plans, portfolio.

See GLAH 1:J180 for previously published vols. (1–3, 5–6).

Selective contents: (4) 1485–1660 (Part 2) by H. M. Colvin, D. R. Ransome, and John Summerson (1982).

J312 Craig, Maurice James. The architecture of Ireland: from the earliest times to 1880. London, Batsford, 1982. 358p. il., plans.

The best single book on the subject. Arranged chronologically, then by building type. Interiors are omitted entirely. Includes many plans.

References, p.[326]–38. [Selected] book list, p.[339]–43. Index, p.[344]–58.

J313 Durant, David N. The handbook of British architectural styles. Illustrations by N. S. Farnell. London, Barrie & Jenkins, 1992. 208p. il.

Pocket size guide divided into six sections: Romanesque era, Gothic era, Classical era, the Enlightenment, Victorian era, Modern era. Concise text gives a historical overview of each period, moves on to specific building types, describes typical features, and lists easily accessible buildings which exemplify the style. Sections end with biographical information on the most important architects working in the style. Illustrated by line drawings.

Bibliography, p.204–05. Index, p.206–08.

J314 Kidson, Peter; Murray, Peter; and Thompson, Paul. A history of English architecture. Rev. [2d] ed. Harmondsworth, Penguin, 1979. 394p. il.

See GLAH 1:J185 for 1st ed.

J315 London. County Council. Survey of London, issued by the Joint Publishing Committee representing the London County Council and the London Survey Committee. London, 1900– . (45)v. il., plates, plans.

See GLAH 1:J188 for original annotation. Publisher varies.

J316 Pevsner, Nikolaus. A compendium of Pevsner's Buildings of England on compact disc. Oxford, Oxford Univ. Pr., 1995. 1 computer disk. il. (Buildings of England)

"Provides an electronic index to the information contained in 42 volumes of the series [GLAH 1:J190]. The information contained in the four Greater London volumes is not included in the first release of the CD-ROM, as one of them has yet to be published."—*User guide.*

J317 ______, and Metcalf, Priscilla. The cathedrals of England. N.Y., Viking, 1985. 2v. il., maps.

Describes 62 major cathedrals dating from the Middle Ages to the 20th century. "Entries include a building chronology, recent bibliography, a detailed description of the architecture, and, where warranted, a discussion of the sculpture, painting, furnishings, and stained glass. Each section is illustrated by an excellent selection of well-reproduced photographs, plans and/or drawings."—*Review*, CHOICE, v.23, Dec. 1985, p.593.

Contents: (1) The cathedrals of England: Southern England; (2) The cathedrals of England: Midland, Eastern, and Northern England.

J318 Quiney, Anthony. The traditional buildings of England. London, Thames and Hudson, 1990. 224p. il. (part col.)

Focuses on everyday buildings of the past and their historical development. Gives a short history of England from the Conquest to the 19th century including social and economic reasons for the distribution of wealth and building types around the country. Links this to the distribution of building materials, and demonstrates a pattern of locally based building traditions that results. Exceptional photographs.

Glossary, p.217. Notes, p.218–19. Bibliography, p.219–21. Index, p.222–24.

J319 Watkin, David. English architecture: a concise history. N.Y., Oxford Univ. Pr., 1979. 216p. il.

Intended to expose "the high points of English creative genius as expressed in the noble art of architecture."—*Prelim. note.* Covers English architecture only from Anglo-Saxon to 20th century, omitting Scotland, Ireland, and Wales. Also omits architecture of industry, transport, or engineering as well as vernacular architecture.

Glossary, p.200–02. Bibliography, p.203–06. Index, p.208–16.

Early Christian—Gothic

J320 Bony, Jean. The English decorated style: Gothic architecture transformed, 1250–1350. Ithaca, N.Y., Cornell Univ. Pr., 1979. 315p. il. (The Wrightsman lectures, 10)

The first book-length English-language study of decorated-style architecture in England. Rather than adopting a chronological order for the material, Bony's "approach focuses on the elucidation of the formal processes involved in the style."—*Review*, Journal of the Society of Architectural Historians, v.39, Dec. 1980, p.318. The text is brief, supported by many black-and-white photographs.

Notes, p.71–92. Illustrations, p.[94]–[288.] List of illustrations, p.[289]–96. Bibliography, p.[297]–307. Index, p.[309]–15.

J321 Coldstream, Nicola. The decorated style, architecture and ornament 1240–1360. London, British Museum Pr., 1994. 208p. il.

Takes an opposing viewpoint to Bony (see preceding entry). Discusses the decorated style in a social and political context, emphasizing the influence of patronage. Rejects Bony's emphasis on space in favor of decoration as the principal characteristic.

Contents: Prologue: The decorated style; (1) Illuminated architecture; (2) Kingdom, land and people; (3) Mind and spirit; (4) The patrons; (5) Craftsmen and administrators; (6) Epilogue.

Genealogical tables linking patrons, p.193–200. Glossary of architectural and decorative terms, p.201. Bibliography, p.202–04. Index, p.205–08.

J322 Fernie, Eric. The architecture of the Anglo-Saxons. N.Y., Holmes & Meier, 1984. 192p. il., plans.

A concise and useful complement to Taylor's Anglo-Saxon architecture (see GLAH 1:J202) which focused almost exclusively on ecclesiastical buildings. Two chapters here are devoted to secular buildings, followed by nine chapters on ecclesiastical buildings. Many plans are included to illustrate those buildings no longer standing. Appendix of churches grouped by period.

Glossary, p.[179]–80. Notes, p.[181]–87. Bibliography, p.[188]. Index, p.[189]–92.

J323 Little, Bryan. Architecture in Norman Britain. London, Batsford, 1985. 191p. il., plans.

The only recent book to deal exclusively with Norman architecture in Britain. In addition to discussing the architectural history this book relates the buildings of Anglo-Norman Britain to historic events and liturgical practices of the time. Largely devoted to ecclesiastical architecture, although some coverage is given to castles, keeps, and manors. Appendix of "greater" churches.

Bibliography, p.183–84. Index, p.185–91.

J324 Platt, Colin. The architecture of medieval Britain: a social history. Photographs by Anthony Kersting. New Haven, Yale Univ. Pr., 1990. ix, 325p. il. (part col.)

Covers all of the British Isles from the Norman Conquest to the later 16th century examining the political and economic factors influencing architecture. Adopts a cynical attitude toward the role of faith in advancing architecture. Abundantly illustrated with excellent photographs.

Glossary, p.[296]–99. Notes, p.[301]–18. Index, p.[319]–25.

J325 Taylor, Harold McCarter, and Taylor, Joan. Anglo-Saxon architecture. Cambridge, [Eng.], Cambridge Univ. Pr., 1965–1978. 3v. il., maps, plans, plates.

See GLAH 1:J202 for v.1–2.

Selective contents: (3) by H. M. Taylor (1978).

Renaissance—Modern

J326 Crook, Joseph Mordaunt. The Greek revival: neoclassical attitudes in British architecture 1760–1870. Rev. ed. London, John Murray, 1995. xi, 204p. plates, map.

See GLAH 1:J207 for 1st ed.

Bibliography, p.165–[88], contains addenda for work published since 1972. Index, p.189–204.

J327 Cruikshank, Dan. A guide to the Georgian buildings of Britain & Ireland. N.Y., Rizzoli, 1986. 320p. il.

More than a guidebook, this is a history of British and Irish architecture in the period 1714–1830, organized largely by building type. Includes a gazetteer of all significant Georgian buildings (Great Britain, p.[180]–259; London, p.[260]–83; Ireland, p.[284]–99).

Bibliography, p.[300]–01. Glossary, p.[302]–03. Index of buildings and places, p.[304]–15. Index of architects and designers, p.315–20.

J328 Dunbar, John G. The architecture of Scotland. 2d rev. ed. London, Batsford, 1978. 209p. il., map, plans.

Rev. ed. of The historic architecture of Scotland (GLAH 1:J181). Text has been reorganized to proceed chronologically. Places greater emphasis on building materials and techniques than did the 1st ed.

Bibliography, p.198–99. Index, p.200–09.

J329 Fawcett, Richard. Scottish architecture: from the accession of the Stewarts to the Reformation, 1371–1560. Edinburgh, Edinburgh Univ. Pr., 1994. xxi, 386p. il. (Architectural history of Scotland)

Contents: Pt.1: From the late fourteenth to the early fifteenth century; (1) The resurgence of building activity. Pt.2: From the early fifteenth to the mid-sixteenth century; (2) The cathedral churches; (3) Monastic architecture; (4) The architecture of the friars; (5) Rural and academic collegiate churches; (6) The greater burgh churches; (7) Parish churches and chapels; (8) Castles and domestic architecture; (9) Artillery fortification; (10) The royal residences.

Bibliography, p.[366]–71. Index, p.372–86.

J330 Fenton, Alexander, and Walker, Bruce. The rural architecture of Scotland. Edinburgh, John Donald, 1981. xi, 242p. il.

"This is a good series of essays, full of measured and photographed examples of structural elements, farm layout and housing, and the changes wrought by agricultural technology, with a sample survey of farm buildings in Grampian Region."—*Review*, Journal of the Society of Architectural Historians, v.42, Dec. 1983, p.394.

Excellent bibliography, p.225–34. Index, p.235–42.

J331 Girouard, Mark. The Victorian country house. Rev. and enl. ed. New Haven, Yale Univ. Pr., 1979. vii, 467p. il. (part col.)

See GLAH 1:J210 for 1st ed.

Catalogue of country houses: England and Wales; Ireland; Scotland; Abroad.

Bibliographical notes on architects, p.436–43. Notes to the text, p.444–54. General index, p.455–63. Subject index, p.464–67.

J332 Harper, Roger H. Victorian architectural competitions: an index to British and Irish architectural competitions in The Builder, 1843–1900. Foreword by Sir John Summerson. London, Mansell. (Distr. by H.W. Wilson, 1983). xxxviii, 416p. il.

Indexes by place, architect's name, date, and building type more than 2,500 competitions as reported in The Builder from the date of the journal's first regular issue to 1900.

Selected bibliography, p.[xxvii]–xxxii.

J333 Howard, Deborah. Scottish architecture: Reformation to Restoration, 1560–1660. Edinburgh, Edinburgh Univ. Pr., 1995. xvi, 270p. il., plans. (Architectural history of Scotland)

"The first twenty years and the last twenty years will receive relatively little attention in this book, for both were too unsettled to allow as much ambitious architectural patronage as the middle years. . . . This book comprises a great variety of buildings, from the smallest salmon house to the most splendid royal palace."—*Introd.*

Contents: (1) Introduction; (2) The court; (3) The countryside; (4) The burghs; (5) The church; (6) Conclusion.

Notes, p.[221]–47. Bibliography, p.[248]–58. Index, p.[259]–70.

J334 Lubbock, Jules. The tyranny of taste: the politics of architecture and design in Britain 1550–1960. New Haven, Pub. for the Mellon Centre by Yale Univ. Pr., 1995. xv, 413p. il.

"The primary purpose of this book has been to present an historical reconstruction of a system of thought in which the design, manufacture and consumption of goods, architecture and town planning have been inextricably interlinked with issues of economic theory and policy, social policy and personal morality, from the Tudor period to that of the Welfare State, and to show how the 'Political Economy of Design' has shaped the physical environment of this country."—*p.366.*

Contents: (1) The consumer society; (2) The stable society; (3) The luxury debate; (4) Style and economics; (5) Good design; (6) Good modern design; (7) Conclusion, Plato's conundrum.

Notes, p.370–95. Index, p.396–412.

J335 McCarthy, Michael J. The origins of the Gothic revival. New Haven, Yale Univ. Pr., 1987. ix, 212p. il. (part col.)

Contents: (1) Literature of the revival; (2) Garden buildings in the Gothic style; (3) Horace Walpole and Strawberry Hill; (4) The domestic architecture of the Strawberry Hill architects; (5) The domestic architecture of Sanderson Miller and Sir Roger Newdigate; (6) Ecclesiastical architecture in the Gothic style; Appendix.

Notes, p.183–99. Bibliography, p.200–08. Index, p.209–12.

J336 One hundred and fifty years of architecture in Ireland: RIAI 1839–1989. [Ed. by John Graby]. Dublin, RIAI, 1989. 130p. il., facsim., plans, ports.

A series of essays on the history of Irish architectural design and the profession of architecture since the founding of the Royal Institute of the Architects of Ireland. Includes a brief history of nine major architectural firms, a list of past presidents of the RIAI, and RIAI medal winners.

Footnotes and appendixes, p.120–23. Index, p.124–29.

J337 Richardson, Ruth, and Thorne, Robert. The Builder: illustrations index, 1843–1883. London, The Builder Group, 1994. xiii, 832p. il., facsims., ports.

An index to more than 12,300 illustrations published in the most important British journal of architecture in the 19th century. Covers illustrations from the first regular issue through the resignation of George Godwin as editor in 1883, documenting changes in styles, building methods, and social problems as they relate to architecture. Each catalog entry lists the year of publication, page number, and type of illustration; title of illustration; names (plus roles); places; subjects; and observations and comments about the illustration and article it accompanied. Information can be found not only for the architect responsible, but also for the contractor, and often the draftsman or engraver of the plate. Two introductory essays precede the catalog and its six indexes.

Geographical index, p.457–501 (broken into London, Britain, and the world). Illustrations title index, p.503–32. Names index, p.533–609. Roles index, p.611–67. Styles index, p.669–78. Subjects index, p.679–831. List of subject headings, p.832.

J338 Rothery, Sean. Ireland and the new architecture, 1900–1940. Dublin, Lilliput Pr., 1991. xix, 281p. il.

The first general study of Irish architecture of the first half of this century, it contradicts the prevailing opinion that Ireland was an architectural backwater.

Contents: (1) New structures; (2) The influence of the Arts and Crafts; (3) Irish architectural journals; Education for architects; (4) The classical tradition lives on; (5) Writers and propagandists; (6) Patronage: The state and the church; (7) Architectural jazz; (8) The International style comes to Ireland; (9) Epilogue.

Notes, p.235–57. Select bibliography, p.259–68. Index, p.269–81.

J339 Service, Alastair. Edwardian architecture: a handbook to building design in Britain, 1890–1914. N.Y., Oxford Univ. Pr., 1977. 216p. il., plans.

"This book is the first concise study of the main, often conflicting, developments in British architecture between 1890 and 1914."—*Pref.* Divided into three parts: The end of the nineteenth century; Edwardian free design; and Edwardian classicism. Concludes with a list of the leading architects and some of their buildings, 1890–1914, which gives the briefest of biographical data plus buildings' names, dates, and addresses (p.197–213).

Index, p.213–16

J340 Service, Alastair, [ed.] Edwardian architecture and its origins. London, Architectural Pr., 1975. 504p. il., plans, ports.

A compilation of essays by many different authors on individual architects, many written over a period of 50 years for the Architectural review. Biographical essays are grouped chronologically by the architects' period of influence, each part being introduced by a brief overview written by Service.

Contents: (1) Pioneers of a free manner; (2) From Queen Anne towards a free style, 1875–1890; (3) Arts and Crafts architecture and the 1890s; (4) Scotland at the end of the century; (5) Church architecture; (6) The grand manner; (7) Edwardian free style; (8) Variations of the grand manner; (9) Conclusion: Goodhart-Rendel's Roll-Call. Principal architects of the late Victorian and Edwardian period.

Bibliographic notes follow most essays. Select bibliography, p.489–90. Index, p.491–98. Index to buildings illustrated, p.499–504.

J341 Stillman, Damie. English neo-classical architecture. London, Zwemmer (Distr. by Sotheby's, 1988). 2v. il. (part col.) (Studies in architecture, 26)

The first scholarly survey of the English version of this style. Organized first chronologically, and then by building type, it covers all aspects of English Neoclassicism from interiors to urban design. Fine illustrations.

Notes, v.2, p.525–600. Classified bibliography, v.2, p.601–26. Index, v.2, p.627–48.

J342 Summerson, Sir John N. Architecture in Britain, 1530 to 1830. Colour photography by A. F. Kersting. 9th ed. New Haven, Yale Univ. Pr., 1993. 588p. il. (part col.), maps. (Yale University Press pelican history of art, Z3)

See GLAH 1:J216 for 5th rev. ed. 6th rev. ed., 1977; 7th rev. ed, 1983; 8th rev. ed, 1991.

Notes, p.529–40. Bibliography, p.541–49. Publications since 1983: a narrative bibliography, p.550–53. List of illustrations, p.554–64. Index, p.565–88.

J343 Watkin, David. The English vision: the picturesque in architecture, landscape, and garden design. London, J. Murray, 1982. xi, 227p. il.

Integrates the study of architecture and landscape architecture with the belief that neither can be studied alone when dealing with picturesque influences. Covers topics from 18th-century landscape gardens to "picturesque" town planning in the 20th century. Two chapters on country houses form the bulk of the text.

Contents: (1) Early landscape gardens; (2) The Rococo and Chinoiserie phase; (3) The cult of the ruin; (4) Theory and practice in garden design: Capability Brown to J. C. Loudon; (5) The picturesque house: Vanbrugh to Soane; (6) The picturesque house: Salvin to Lutyens; (7) English influence abroad; (8) The picturesque in village and town.

Notes, p.201–04. Bibliography, p.204–16. Index, p.220–27.

Greece

J344 Greek traditional architecture. Ed. by Dimitri Philippides. [Trans. by David Hardy, Philip Ramp.] Athens, Melissa, 1983– . (2)v. il. (M library of art)

Projected to be complete in eight vols. The first two vols. examine the traditional architecture of four major island groups: the Eastern Aegean Islands, the Sporades, the Ionian Islands, and the Cyclades. Profusely illustrated with excellent color photographs and numerous drawings and plans.

Contents: (1) Eastern Aegean, Sporades-Ionian Islands; (2) Aegean, Cyclades.

Bibliography, v.2, p.306. Index of names and terms, v.1, p.307–13.

J345 Hetherington, Paul. Byzantine and medieval Greece: churches, castles, and art of the mainland and Peloponnese. London, J. Murray, 1991. xviii, 238p., il. (part col.), plates, maps, plans.

A guidebook to the most important Byzantine and medieval structures extant and easily accessible on the mainland and the Peleponnese. The islands have been omitted. Two essays precede the entries: An outline history of medieval Greece;

The architecture and art of medieval Greece. Entries describe the buildings found on site and their history, but most are illustrated only by a floor plan.

Glossary, p.[221]–24. Tables of Byzantine and medieval rulers, p.[225]–27. Main events in the history of medieval Greece, p.[228]–29. Bibliography, p.[230]–31. Index, p.[233]–38.

Italy

General Works

J346 Howard, Deborah. The architectural history of Venice. N.Y., Holmes & Meier, 1981. 263p. il., plans.

General survey tracing the architectural history of the city alone rather than the whole of the Veneto.

Notes, p.238–48. Bibliography, p.249–55. Index, p.256–63.

J347 Die Kirchen von Siena. Hrsg. von Peter Anselm Riedl und Max Seidel. Munchen, Bruckmann, 1985– . (2)v. il., plans.

An inventory of the churches of Siena, arranged alphabetically. For each it gives extensive information, including documentation, a summary of previous research, and bibliography. Projected publication of seven vols. Text in German, Italian, and Latin.

Contents: (1) Abbadia all'Arco-S. Biagio. T.1, Textband. T.2, Bildband. T.3, Planband; (2) Oratorio della Carita-S. Domenico. T.1, Textband (2v.). T.2, Bildband. T.3, Planband.

Each vol. contains a bibliography and index.

J348 Roma cristiana: collana diretta da Carlo Galassi Paluzzi. [Bologna], Cappelli, 1964–[75]. 18v. il. (part col.)

See GLAH 1:J222 for previously published vols.

Selective contents: (17) La Basilica di S. Pietro, [1975].

J349 Storia dell'architettura italiana. 2d ed. Milano, Electa, 1997– . (2)v. il. (part col.), plans.

Impressive historical survey; splendidly illustrated. Projected in nine vols. covering the 14th to the 20th century.

Selective contents: (2) Fiore, Francesco Paolo. Il Quattrocento (1998); (9) Dal Co, Francesco. Il secondo Novecento (1997).

SEE ALSO: Teague, Index to Italian architecture: a guide to key monuments and reproduction sources (GLAH 2:D47).

Early Christian—Gothic

J350 Bellafiore, Giuseppe. Architettura in Sicilia nelle età islamica e normanna (827–1194). Palermo, A. Lombardi, 1990. 366p. il. (La Civiltà siciliana, 1)

A history of Sicilian architecture over four centuries of Islamic and Norman rule. Essays precede the list of buildings discussed in detail, most of which are in or near present-day Palermo. Entries for buildings are organized by type.

Contents: (1) Il quadro storico; (2) La koiné fatimita; (3) Lo scenario territoriale e la cultura della città; (4) L'architettura palaziale urbana; (5) I giardini paradiso; (6) L'architettura religiosa; (7) L'universo decorativo; (8) Le opere.

Notes p.[165]–83. Nota bibliografica, p.[185]–92. Bibliografia, p.[193]–212. Glossario, p.223. Indice dei nomi, p.353–55. Indice dei luoghi e delle opere, p.357–65.

J351 Krautheimer, Richard. Rome, profile of a city, 312–1308. Princeton, Princeton Univ. Pr., 1980. 389p. il. maps.

Krautheimer strives "to outline a history of Rome during a thousand years through, rather than of, her monuments, and of changes in the map of the city."—*Introd.*

Contents: Pt.1, (1) Rome and Constantine; (2) The Christianization of Rome and the Romanization of Christianity; (3) The times of Gregory the Great; (4) Rome between East and West; (5) Renewal and renascence: the Carolingian age; (6) Realities, ideologies, and rhetoric; (7) The new rebirth of Rome: the twelfth century; (8) The thirteenth century: an epilogue. Pt.2, (9) The evidence; (10) The inheritance; (11) Growth of the Borgo; (12) The Abitato; (13) Houses, towers, and mansions; (14) The Disabitato and the Lateran.

Appendix: Chronological list of popes, p.[327]–28. Bibliographical note, p.[329]–30. Abbreviations, p.[331]–33. Notes to the text, p.[335]–72. Index of places and subjects, p.[373]–83. Index of people, p.[385]–89.

Renaissance—Modern

J352 Bellafiore, Giuseppe. Architettura in Sicilia (1415–1535). Palermo, Italia nostra, 1984. 331p. il., maps, plans.

A study of Sicilian architecture during the Renaissance period.

Contents: (I) Architettura e città; (II) La koiné aragonese; (III) La domus magnae; (IV) Logge mercantili, tocchi, opere edili civili; (V) Chiese ed edifici religiosi; (VI) Cantieri edili fabbricatori e marmorari; (VII) Tardogotico. Rinasita. Plateresco.

Note, p.[171]–99. Bibliografia, p.201–08. Indice degli artisti, p.323–24. Indice dei luoghi e delle opere, p.325–29.

J353 Burckhardt, Jacob. The architecture of the Italian Renaissance. Rev. and ed. by Peter Murray. Trans. by James Palmes. Chicago, Univ. of Chicago Pr., 1985. xxxv, 283p. il.

See GLAH 1:J123 for original German ed. Trans. of Die Geschichte der Renaissance, 6th ed. Esslingen a. N., Neff, 1920. Bibliography expands upon original citations, p.[xix]–xxix. A new introduction, a few new notes and corrections to previous errors have been added. Indexes and illustrations (lacking information on which reproductions are new and which are original to Burckhardt's 6th ed.).

J354 Etlin, Richard A. Modernism in Italian architecture, 1890–1940. Cambridge, Mass., MIT Pr., 1991. xxiii, 736p. il.

"This book is a study of the pluralistic and evolving notion of modernism in Italian architecture between 1890 and 1940."—*Introd.* A scholarly and complete account less suitable for general readers. Excellent coverage of the relationship between architecture and Fascism. Good complement to Tafuri's History of Italian architecture, 1944–1985 (see GLAH 2:J363).

Notes, p.[599]–678. Works cited, p.[679]–715. Index, p.[717]–36.

J355 Heydenreich, Ludwig H. Architecture in Italy, 1400–1500. Rev. by Paul Davies. New Haven, Yale Univ. Pr., 1995. 186p. il. (part col.), map, plans. (Yale University Press pelican history of art)

See GLAH 1:J240 for original publication.

Companion to Lotz, Architecture in Italy, 1500–1600 (see next entry). Heydenreich's original text has been retained in its entirety. New research has been incorporated into the text by means of asterisks which direct the reader to additional endnotes. These are used only when Heydenreich's text is incorrect or misleading.

Notes, p.[152]–69 Additional notes to the revised edition, p.[170]. Bibliography, p.[171]–76. Select bibliography of books published since 1974, p.[177]–80. Index, p.[181]–86.

J356 Lotz, Wolfgang. Architecture in Italy, 1500–1600. Rev. by Deborah Howard. New Haven, Yale Univ. Pr., 1995. viii, 205p. il. (part col.) (Yale University Press pelican history of art)

See GLAH 1:J240 for original publication.

Companion to Heydenreich, Architecture in Italy, 1400–1500 (see previous entry). Lotz's original text has been retained in its entirety. The same system of asterisks related to endnotes is used as that found in Heydenreich.

Notes, p.[173]–89. Additional notes to the revised edition, p.[190]. Bibliography, p.[191]–97. Select bibliography of books published since 1973, p.[198]–200. Index, p.[201]–05.

J357 Murray, Peter. The architecture of the Italian Renaissance. New and enl. ed. London, Thames & Hudson, 1969. 252p. il., maps, plans. ([The World of art library: architecture]) (Repr.: N.Y., Schocken Books, 1986)

See GLAH 1:J243 for 1st ed.

J358 Nicoletti, Manfredi. L'architettura liberty in Italia. Rome, Laterza, 1978. xii, 421p. il. (part col.)

A detailed history of Art Nouveau architecture which recognizes many lesser-known architects and buildings.

[Bibliografia], p.[387]–402. Indice dei nomi, p.[405]–17.

J359 Pommer, Richard. Eighteenth-century architecture in Piedmont: the open structures of Juvarra, Alfieri & Vittone. N.Y., New York Univ. Pr., 1967. xvii, 300p. il., plans.

The first attempt to place Piedmontese architecture of the period into its European context, it focuses on Juvarra, Alfieri and Vittone as the founder and most important followers of this new emphasis on openness in structures. Documents major buildings in great detail.

Contents: (1) Introduction; (2) The background; (3) Filippo Juvarra and the chapel at Venaria Reale; (4) The genesis of Sant'Andrea in Chieri; (5) The Duomo Nuovo in Turin; (6) The Palazzina di Stupinigi; (7) San Filippo Neri and the Carmine; (8) Benedetto Alfieri's SS. Giovanni e Remigio in Carignano; (9) On Bernardo Antonio Vittone; (10) Postscript. Appendixes: (1) Juvarra's sketchbooks; (2) Juvarra's projects of 1714–1715 for the Sacristy of St. Peter's; (3) Venaria Reale; (4) The parish church of Murisengo; (5) Sant'Andrea in Chieri; (6) Duomo Nuovo; (7) Stupinigi; (8) San Filippo Neri; (9) The Carmine; (10) Sant'Antonio in Chieri; (11) SS. Giovanni e Remigio in Carignano and Benedetto Alfieri; (12) Documents for Vittone's life and career; (13) Miscellaneous churches by Vittone.

Selected bibliography, p.286–92. Index, p.293–300.

J360 The Renaissance from Brunelleschi to Michelangelo: the representation of architecture. Ed. by Henry Millon and Vittorio Magnago Lampugnani. N.Y., Rizzoli, 1994. 731p. il. (part col.)

Catalog of the exhibition, Palazzo Grassi, Venice (1994). An essential scholarly work intended to "initiate a vast, nonspecialist public in the complexities and contradictions of Renaissance architecture, a phenomenon of uncertain origin with myriad paths of development and a somewhat elusive conclusion."—*Foreword.* Exceptional illustrations.

Contents: (1) Models in Renaissance architecture, by Henry A. Millon; (2) The relation of sculpture and architecture in the Renaissance, by Kathleen Weil-Garris Brandt; (3) Reflections on the early architectural drawings, by Christoph Luitpold Frommel; (4) Religious architecture in Renaissance Italy from Brunelleschi to Michelangelo, byArnaldo Bruschi; (5) Living all'antica: palaces and villas from Brunelleschi to Bramante, by Christoph Luitpold Frommel; (6) The Italian city, 1400–1600, by Nicholas Adams and Laurie Mussdorfer; (7) The panels in Urbino, Baltimore and Berlin reconsidered, by Richard Krautheimer; (8) The Renaissance of architecture, by Hubertus Günther; (9) Ordo, fondo et mensura: the criteria of architecture, by Oswald Mathias Ungers; (10) The regions of Italian Renaissance, James Ackerman; (11) The urban structure of Naples: utopia and reality, by Cesare De Seta; (12) The tale of two cities: Siena and Venice, by Carlo Bertelli; (13) St. Peter's: the early history, by Christoph Luitpold Frommel.

The works, p.[425]–678. Bibliography, p.681–715. Index of names, p.717–20. Index of works, p.721–28.

J361 Romanelli, Giandomenico. Venezia Ottocento: l'architettura, l'urbanistica. [Venezia], Albrizzi, [1988]. 524p. il. (part col.)

Thorough history of 19th-century architectural developments in Venice. Excellent illustrations.

Contents: (1) Tra Francia e Austria, 1797–1805; (2) Napoleone e il regno d'Italia, 1806–1814; (3) Il "Ritorno d'Astrea"; (4) Tra Quarantotto e Sessantasei; (5) Gli Italiani a Venezia; Appendixes.

Extensive endnotes with each chapter. Bibliografia, p.489–506. Indice dei nomi, p.509–14. Indice dei luoghi, p.515–24.

J362 ______. Venezia Ottocento: materiali per una storia architettonica e urbanistica della città nel secolo XIX. Roma, Officina, 1977. 622p. il., plates.

Substantial study of 19th-century Venetian architecture and urbanism.

Contents: (1) Tra Francia e Austria, 1797–1805; (2) Napoleone e il Regno d'Italia 1806–1814; (3) Il "ritorno d'Astrea"; (4) Tra Quarantotto e Sessantasei; (5) Gli Italiani a Venezia; Appendici.

Notes at ends of chapters. Bibliografia, p.[565]–602. Indice dei nomi, p.[603]–11. Indice dei luoghi, [612]–22.

J363 Tafuri, Manfredo. History of Italian architecture, 1944–1985. Trans. by Jessica Levine. Cambridge, Mass., MIT Pr., 1989. ix, 269p. il., plates.

Rev. ed. and trans. of Storia dell'architettura italiana, 1944–1985. Turin, Einaudi, 1986.

Contents: Pt.1: 1944–1979. (1) The years of reconstruction; (2) Aufklärung I: Adriano Olivetti and the Communitas of the intellect; (3) The myth of equilibrium: The Vanoni Plan and INA-Casa's second seven years; (4) Aufklärung II: The museum, history, and metaphor (1951–1967); (5) New crises and new strategies; (6) Two "masters": Carlo Scarpa and Giuseppe Samonà. Pt.2: 1980–1985, (7) The fragment and the city: Research and Exempla of the seventies; (8) Architecture as dialogue and architecture as "civil invective"; (9) The case of Aldo Rossi; (10) Rigorism and abstinence: Toward the 1980s; (11) Structural transformations and new experiences in planning; (12) The paradigms of pluralism; (13) Venice 1985: The Architecture Biennale; (14) "Gay Errancy": Hypermoderns (Postmoderns); (15) The threshold and the problem.

Notes, p.[203]–49. Bibliographical appendix, p.[251]–61. Index, p.[263]–69.

J364 ______. Venice and the Renaissance. Trans. by Jessica Levine. Cambridge, Mass., MIT Pr., 1989. xi, 296p. il., plates., maps.

Trans. of Venezia e il Rinascimento. Turin, Einaudi, 1985. A collection of seven essays in which Tafuri "dissects the relationship between the myth of Venice and its cinquecento reality, between an image of a putative ideal Renaissance city and the tortuous routes by which physical change was in fact wrought on the capital's fabric."—*Review*, Journal of the Society of Architectural Historians, v.50, Dec. 1991, p.457.

Notes, p.[197]–279. Glossary, p.[281]–83. Index, p.[285]–96.

J365 Varriano, John L. Italian Baroque and Rococo architecture. N.Y., Oxford Univ. Pr., 1986. 329p. il.

A good survey useful as an introduction to the history of Italian Baroque architecture.

Contents: (1) Introduction; (2) Precursors of the Roman Baroque: Vignola to Carlo Maderno; (3) Francesco Borromini; (4) Gianlorenzo Bernini; (5) Pietro da Cortona; (6) Other aspects of the Roman Baroque; (7) Rococo and academic classicism in eighteenth-century Rome; (8) Northern Italy in the seventeenth century; (9) Guarino Guarini; (10) Northern Italy in the eighteenth century; (11) Southern Italy.

Notes, p.295–308. Glossary, p.309–11.

J366 Wittkower, Rudolf. Architectural principles in the age of humanism. 4th ed. N.Y., St. Martin's Pr., 1988. 160p. il.

See GLAH 1:J248 for previous eds. With this ed. illustrations are integrated into the text.

Contents: (1) The centrally planned church and the Renaissance; (2) Alberti's approach to antiquity in architecture; (3) Principles of Palladio's architecture; (4) The problem of harmonic proportion in architecture; Appendixes: (1) Francesco Giorgi's Memorandum for S. Francesco della Vigna; (2) The problem of commensurability of ratios in the Renaissance; (3) Bibliographical notes on the theory of proportion; (4) Proportion in art and architecture: an amalgamation of previously unpublished lectures by Professor Wittkower.

Index, p.156–60.

Latin America

Bibliography

J367 Bibliografía iberoamericana de revistas de arquitectura y urbanismo. [Por] Ramón Gutiérrez, Marcelo Martín. Madrid, Instituto Español de Arquitectura; Consejo Académico Iberoamericano, 1993. 134p. il. (Ediciones de las Universidades de Alcala y Valladolid)

Bibliography of Latin American periodicals devoted to architecture and urbanism.

Contents: Bibliografía latinoamericana de revistas de arquitectura y urbanismo, by Ramón Gutiérrez . . . [et al.]; Bibliografía española de revistas de arquitectura y urbanismo, by Marcelo Martin . . . [et al.]

Referencias bibliográficas, p.131.

J368 Gutiérrez, Ramón, and Méndez, Patricia. Bibliografía de arquitectura y urbanismo en Iberoamérica, 1980–1993. Alcalá de Henares, Spain, Instituto Español de Arquitectura, Universidad de Alcalá y Valladolid; Buenos Aires, Centro de Documentación de Arquitectura Latinoamericana (CEDODAL), 1996. 76p.

Useful bibliography of recent literature on Latin American architecture and urbanism.

Contents: Arquitectura contemporanea; Arquitectura historica; Preservacion; Tecnologia; Urbanismo; Otros temas.

Indice de autores, p.9–22.

J369 Rivera de Figueroa, Carmen A. Architecture for the tropics: a bibliographical synthesis (from the beginnings to 1972): con una versión castellana resumida (Arquitectura para el trópica). Río Piedras, P.R., Editorial Universitaria, University of Puerto Rico, 1980. xi, 203p. il.

Bilingual (English-Spanish) bibliographical essay "developed to aid those architects who design for the tropics whether native to the region themselves or not."—*Introd.* Includes discussion of relevant materials on structures, techniques, design, sites, landscape, housing, and solar energy. A somewhat complex subject classification of all citations is appended as the third chapter.

Contents: (I) Man, climate and architecture; (II) Bibliography on architecture for the tropics: chronological development; (III) Architecture for the tropics: main aspects.

Abbreviations, p.147. Selected bibliographical references, p.149–50.

Dictionaries and Encyclopedias

J370 Pérez Calvo, Carlos E. Diccionario ilustrado de arquitectura: contiene más de 5.000 vocablos y 7.000 acepciones, voces técnicas y modismos, 400 ilustraciones y un vocabulario inglés-español con 1.600 palabras. [Rev. y complementado por Gustavo Perry Zubieta. Ilustrado por Ignacio Vargas Castro. Portada, C. Urquijo.] Bogotá, J. Plazas S., 1979. 231p. il.

Illustrated dictionary of architecture, including general terms relevant to contemporary and historical architecture. Appendix lists English-Spanish equivalents. Pen-and-ink drawings illustrate many entries.

Abreviaturas, p.[6]. Índice, p.[215]–31.

Histories and Handbooks

J371 Arango, Silvia. Historia de la arquitectura en Colombia. Bogotá, Centro Editorial y Facultad de Artes, Universidad Nacional de Colombia, 1990. 291p. il.

Survey of Colombian architecture from Precolumbian to 1985.

Contents: (I) Arquitectura indigena; (II) Arquitectura colonial; (III) El siglo XIX; (IV) Arquitectura republicana (1880–1930); (V) La transición (1930–1945); (VI) El movimiento moderno (1945–1970); (VII) Arquitectura actual (1970–1985).

Indice de nombres y lugares, p.279–86. Bibliografía, p.287–90.

J372 The architecture of Latin America. Ed. by Miguel Angel Roca. London, Academy (Distr. by National Book Network, 1995.) 141p. il. (part col.)

Features 19 architects from Argentina, Brazil, Chile, Colombia, Mexico, and Peru. Shows some of their designs.

Contents: Latin America, modernity and contemporaneity: notes from the south, by Miguel Angel Roca; Situated modernity: Argentinian architecture 1970–90, by Roberto Fernández; Brazilian architecture 1970–94, by Carlos Eduardo Días Comas; De Groote, Murtinho and Browne: three Chilean views on the contemporary architectural debate, by Fernando Pérez Oyarzun; New proposals in Colombian architecture, by Alberto Saldarriaga Roa; An approach to contemporary Mexican architecture, by Louise Noelle; An introduction to Peruvian architecture, by Gloria Camino de Broadbent.

Curricula vitae, p.[142]–[44] [short biographies of architects].

J373 Arquitectura colonial iberoamericana. Graziano Gasparini, coord. Autores, Eugenio Perez Montas . . . [et al.] Caracas, Venezuela, Armitano, 1997. 565p. il. (part col.)

Regional survey of Latin American colonial architecture. Each national essay by a single author.

Bibliografia, p.553–65.

J374 Arquitectura latinoamericana en el siglo XX. Ramón Gutiérrez, coord. Milan, Jaca Book; Barcelona, Lunwerg, 1998. 440p. il. (part col.), plans, ports.

Divided into three parts, the first two consisting of thematic essays, the third a dictionary of architects, institutions, and periodicals.

Contents: Textos preliminares. [Por] Eladio Dieste . . . [et al.]; Grandes voces. Red. de Ramón Gutiérrez, Graciela María Viñuales; Diccionario enciclopédico. Dir. por Ramón Gutiérrez.

Bibliografía general, p.89–94.

J375 La arquitectura mexicana del siglo XX. Coordinación y prólogo, Fernando González Gortázar. México, D.F., Consejo Nacional para la Cultura y las Artes, 1994. 339p. il. (part col.) (Cultura contemporánea de México)

Includes 50 essays on the history of architecture in Mexico during the 20th century. Some of the essays discuss the architects who shaped that history and their notable works. Well-illustrated in a large format.

Contents: (I) Las fiestas del centenario: recapitulaciones y vaticinios; (II) La búsqueda de una identidad; (III) El imperio de la razón; (IV) El futuro radiante: la ciudad universitaria; (V) Indagando las raíces; (VI) Las ciudades: el futuro y el olvido; (VII) Las nuevas tecnologías; (VIII) La crisis de la modernidad: un nuevo fin de siglo; Evolución de la crítica de la arquitectura en México: 1900–1990.

Bibliografía analítica, p.317–33. Indice onomástico, p.335–39.

J376 Carley, Rachel. Cuba: 400 years of architectural heritage. Photography by Andrea Brizzi. N.Y., Whitney Library of Design, 1997. 224p. col. il., maps.

"This book . . . is not only a celebration of an extraordinary timeline of history, but a documentation of what is here now but will likely disappear soon."—*Introd.* Informed survey from the precolonial era to the present.

Select bibliography, p.222–23. Index, p.224.

J377 Catálogo nacional, monumentos históricos inmuebles. [Mexico City], Secretaría de Educación Pública, Instituto Nacional de Antropología e Historia; Programa Cultural de las Fronteras, [1986]– . (13?)v. il., maps, plans.

All vols. are issued in co-publication with state governments.

Selective contents: Azcapotzalco, D.F.; Baja California; Baja California Sur; Chihuahua (2v.); Coahuila (4v.); Iztacalco, D.F.; Mexico (3v.); Querétaro (4v.); Tabasco; Tamaulipas (3v.); Tlalpan; Tlaxcala (3v.); Xochimilco.

Bibliographies included in each vol.

J378 Early, James. The colonial architecture of Mexico. Albuquerque, Univ. of New Mexico Pr., 1994. 221p. il. (part col.)

A synthetic work that provides an overview of the topic.

Contents: (I) Architecture for the Viceroyalty of New Spain; (II) Friars and Indians: the architecture of evangelism; (III) Towns and cities for the Spaniards; (IV) Baroque religious life and architecture I; (V) Popular or folk architecture; (VI) Eighteenth-century prosperity: domestic and civic architecture; (VII) Baroque religious architecture II; (VIII) Neo-classicism and beyond in New Spain and in Mexico.

Notes, p.205–06. Glossary, p.207–08. Bibliography, p.209–13. Index, p.215–21.

J379 Gutiérrez, Ramón. Arquitectura y urbanismo en Iberoamérica. [Madrid, Cátedra, 1983]. 776p. il. (Manuales arte Cátedra)

Classic, substantial survey from colonial times through contemporary period. Includes civil, military and domestic architecture, the profession of architecture, and urbanism.

Bibliografía general, p.715-[47]. Índice alfabético, p.749–76.

J380 Katzman, Israel. Arquitectura del siglo XIX en México. 2a ed. México, Trillas, 1993. 397p. il., maps, plans.

1st ed.: [México], Centro de Investigaciones Arquitectónicas, Univ. Nacional Autónoma de México, 1973.

Intended principally to summarize, classify, and quantify our knowledge of 19th-century Mexican architectural theory and practice. Includes a biographical section in dictionary arrangement of architects active in Mexico from 1790 to 1920.

Contents: (1) Influencias culturales; (2) La ciudad en el siglo xix; (3) Enseñanza de la arquitectura; (4) Transformación estética; (5) La teoria arquitectónica; (6) La construcción; (7) Arquitectos y constructores que ejercieron entre 1790 y 1920.

Índice onomástico, p.389–92. Índice analítico, p.393–97.

J381 Liernur, Jorge Francisco. America latina: architettura, gli ultimi vent'anni. Milano, Electa, 1990. 203p. il. (part col.) (Tendenze dell'architettura contemporanea, 3)

Multi-author survey of contemporary Latin American architecture, arranged by country, with chapters devoted to Argentina, Brazil, the Caribbean, Chile, Colombia, Mexico, Uruguay, and Venezuela.

Indice dei nomi, p.197–202.

J382 Markman, Sidney David. Architecture and urbanization of colonial Central America. Tempe, Ariz., Center for Latin American Studies, Arizona State Univ., 1993–95. 2v. il., maps.

"The archival documents cited in this book form a major segment of the corpus of primary sources relevant to research on colonial Central America."—*Introd.* Covers the period 1524 to 1821.

Contents: (1) Selected primary documentary and literary sources [arranges transcriptions of selected sources according to subject]; (2) A geographical gazetteer of primary documentary, literary and visual sources [lists alphabetically the 482 towns referred to in the sources].

Glossary, v.1, p.255–56. Bibliography, v.1, p.257–64, v.2, p.315–25. Index, v.1, p.265–82, v.2, p.326–42.

J383 Palm, Erwin Walter. Los monumentos arquitectónicos de la Española. 2a ed. ampliada. Santo Domingo, Editora de Santo Domingo, 1984. 1v. (various pagings) il. (Colección de cultura dominicana, 53)

See GLAH 1:J257 for 1st ed. (1955). Facsimile ed., with an epilog covering the period 1955–83 and updating the work with respect to historiography, urbanism, and theory.

J384 Yampolsky, Mariana. The traditional architecture of Mexico. Text by Chloë Sayer. N.Y., Thames and Hudson, 1993. 208p. il. (part col.), maps.

Popular treatment of Mexican vernacular architecture.

Contents: (1) Using colour; (2) Rural houses; (3) Public spaces; (4) The hacienda; (5) Town residences; (6) The uncommon touch.

Glossary, p.200–02. Bibliography, p.202–05. Index, p.205–08.

Low Countries

J385 Fanelli, Giovanni. Architettura moderna in Olanda 1900–1940. Firenze, Marchi & Bertolli, 1968. 371p. il. (Raccolta pisana di saggi e studi, 22)

Dutch ed. 1978. 'S-Gravenage, Staatsuitgeverij, 1978.

The only survey to date of this important period, it includes many lesser-known buildings. Many plans and drawings.

Includes a chronological bibliography (1850–1967), p.149–78. Biographies and list of major works for significant architects of the period, p.181–236. Plates, p.239–334. Abridged text in English, p.339–64. Index, p.365–71.

J386 Groenendijk, Paul, and Vollaard, Piet. Gids voor moderne architectuur in Nederland = Guide to modern architecture in the Netherlands. 5. geheel herziene en uitgebreide ed. Introd., Hans van Dijk. Photography, Piet Rook. Rotterdam, Uitgeverij 010, 1998. 372p. il.

1st ed., 1987. 2d ed., July 1987. 3d ed., 1989; 4th ed. 1992.

"A travel guide designed to help those interested in modern Dutch architecture to visit buildings and projects."—*Foreword.* Includes bilingual descriptions of nearly 500 buildings and urban projects, each with a recent photograph, information on the designer, dates of design and construction, address, and relevant literature. Modern here means design since Berlage, with the greatest emphasis on the most recent 40 years.

Place name index, p.340. Name index, p.345–60. Subject index, p.361–69. Bibliography, p.370–72.

J387 Kuyper, W. Dutch classicist architecture: a survey of Dutch architecture, gardens, and Anglo-Dutch architectural relations from 1625 to 1700. Delft, Delft Univ. Pr., 1980. xxx, 615p. il.

Contents: (1) Preludes to Classicism and seventeenth-century churches; (2) The architects of the Classicist period; (3) Country houses and gardens in Holland; (4) The Flat Style, 1670–1700; (5) Historicism; conclusions; contemporary sources.

Notes, p.229–326. Plates, p.327–592. Index, p.593–615.

J388 ______. The triumphant entry of Renaissance architecture into the Netherlands: the joyeuse entrée of Philip of Spain into Antwerp in 1549: Renaissance and Mannerist architecture in the Low Countries from 1530 to 1630. Alphen aan de Rijn, Canaletto, 1994. 2v. il., maps.

The first English-language survey of Netherlandish 16th-century architecture, this offers descriptions of many major monuments. Extensively illustrated with fine reproductions.

Contents: Vol.1 (Pt.1) The triumph of power, about 1535 to 1565; (Pt.2) Triumph of civic pride, about 1530 to 1570; (Pt.3) Artisan mannerism, about 1570 to 1630; Appendix 1: The "1543" lawsuit Jacob (James) van der Borch versus Willem (William) van Noort; Appendix 2: Schiappalari's Genoese Arch in perspective and some Mannerist works of the 1580s; Appendix 3: The Amsterdam public theatre of 1637; Vol.2: Plates.

Notes to text, v.1, p.329–89. Bibliographical annotations, v.1, p.391–95. Index, v.1, p.397–435.

J389 Puttemans, Pierre. Modern architecture in Belgium. Brussels, Marc Vokaer, 1976. 262p. il. (part col.), plates, plans.

Discusses many buildings not covered in other histories. Amply illustrated, including many plans.

Contents: (1) Neo-Classicism; (2) Historicism; (3) Towards functionalism; (4) Urban development in the nineteenth century; (5) Art Nouveau; (6) From Pompe and Hoffmann to the Cubists; (7) A time of certainties; (8) A time of stagnation; (9) After the war; (10) After 1968.

Notes, p.255–57. Bibliography, p.258. Index, p.259–62.

J390 Vandenbreeden, Jos, and Dierkens-Aubry, Françoise. The 19th century in Belgium: architecture and interior design. Photography, Christine Bastin and Jacques Evrard. [Tielt, Be], Lannoo, 1994. 240p. il. (part col.), plans.

Lavishly illustrated, this is not a comprehensive history but a selection of the most creative designs and most skillfully crafted buildings of the 19th century. Sections on Neo-classicism, Gothic Revival, eclecticism, Renaissance Revival, Art Nouveau, interior decoration, and sculpture as decoration. "A significant part of the book is dedicated to stylistic study and analysis."—*Foreword.*

Lacks an index. General bibliography, p.239–40.

New Zealand

J391 Brookes, Susan. Index to the Journal of the New Zealand Institute of Architects 1912–1980. [Wellington], School of Architecture, Victoria University of Wellington, [1982]. 125p. (Publication WP, 82–13) Supplements: 1981–1985, by Kathryn Bolland and Susan Brookes, [1987]; 1986–1990, by Julie Howarth and Kathryn Bolland, [1991]

A cumulative index with entries by architect, building type/subject, place, author.

J392 Shaw, Peter. New Zealand architecture: from Polynesian beginnings to 1990. Photographs by Robin Morrison. Auckland, Hodder & Stoughton, 1991. 216p. il. (part col.)

Cursory coverage of Maori architecture in first chapter. Heavy emphasis on domestic architecture in each period.

Contents: (1) Rauppo, timber and stone; (2) The birth of Antipodean Gothic; (3) Cottages, villas and country houses; (4) The architecture of prosperity; (5) Changing influences in domestic architecture; (6) The conservative solution; (7) Modern, Moderne, and Deco; (8) The search for the vernacular; (9) Architecture as individualism; (10) Experiment, debate and demolition.

Notes to text, p.199–201. Glossary, p.202–08. Select bibliography, p.209–12. Index of buildings and architects, p.213–16.

J393 Stacpoole, John. Colonial architecture in New Zealand. Wellington, Reed, 1976. 224p. il., facsims., plans, port.

Straightforward history covering roughly 1820s through early 1880s, excluding buildings developed by the Maori people.

Glossary, p.216–17. Bibliography, p.217–18. Index of people, p.219–21. General index, p.221–24.

Russia and Eastern Europe

General Works

J394 The architecture of historic Hungary. Ed. by Dora Wiebenson and József Sisa. Contrib. by Pál Lövei . . . [et al.] Cambridge, Mass., MIT Pr., 1998. xxviii, 328p. il. (part col.), plates., map.

"Comprehensive survey of Hungarian architecture from roman times to the present, the first to be published in English. . . . Both a study of the relationship between Hungary's own architecture and history, and an introduction to the larger field of Central European architecture."—*Foreword.* An important study.

[Bibliography], p.xxv–xxvii. Notes, p.[298]–307. Index, p.[310]–28.

J395 Boiadzhiev, Stefan K. Bulgarskata arkhitektura prez vekovete. Sofiia, Durzh. izd-vo "Tekhnika," 1982. 333p. il.

Written entirely in Cyrillic alphabet, for those who do not read Bulgarian this survey is useful for its many photographs and plans. Consists of four parts: (1) Medieval Bulgarian architecture, 7th to 16th century; (2) Architecture in the Bulgarian National Revival Period, 17th to 19th century; (3) Bulgarian architecture between 1878 and 1944; (4) Bulgarian architecture in the period of socialism. Extensive documentation of vernacular architecture.

English summary, p.332–[34].

J396 Brumfield, William Craft. A history of Russian architecture. N.Y., Cambridge Univ. Pr., 1993. 644p. il., maps.

Surveys the development of Russian architecture from the masonry churches of tenth-century Kievan Rus to the prefabricated built environments of the 1980s. Divided into four sections: (1) Early medieval architecture; (2) The Muscovite period; (3) The turn to Western forms; (4) The formation of modern Russian architecture. Adopts a more positive view of architecture of the Stalinist period than the author's Gold in azure (Boston, Godine, 1983). Exceptional photographs taken specifically for this text.

Appendix (Russian wooden architecture), p.501–26. Notes, p.527–611. Bibliography, p.612–31. Index, p.632–44.

J397 Buxton, David. The wooden churches of Eastern Europe: an introductory survey. N.Y., Cambridge Univ. Pr., 1982. 405p. il

The first English-language survey of blockwork churches—log construction on the horizontal principal—in Eastern Europe. Richly illustrated with drawings and photographs. Includes appendix on the log cabin in North America (p.[385]–86) and appendix on the vanished synagogues of Eastern Europe (p.[387]–94).

Bibliography, p.[395]–97. Index, p.[400]–05.

J398 Ionescu, Grigore. Arhitectura pe teritoriul României de-a lungul veacurilor. Bucarest, Editura Academiei Republicii Socialiste România, 1981. 711p. il. (part col.), plates.

Title on verso of title page in French and Russian: L'architecture sur le territoire de la Roumanie au long des siècles = Arkhitektura na territorii Rumynii na protiazhenie vekov.

Supplements the author's standard survey of Romanian architecture, available in French (see following entry).

Summary [in English], p.678–89. List of illustrations [in English], p.690–99. Indice selectiv de monumente si nume proprii, p.700–[12].

J399 ______. Histoire de l'architecture en Roumanie. De la préhistoire a nos jours. [Album. trad. par Radu Creteanu.] Bucarest, Éd. de l'Academie de la République Socialiste de Roumanie, 1972. 589p. with illus. (part col.), 3 leaves of maps. (Bibliotheca historica Romaniae. Monographies, 11)

Trans. of Istoria arhitecturii în Romînia. Bucarest, Editura Academiei Republicii Populare Romîne, 1963–65. 2v.

Standard survey documenting the many cultural influences on Romania's architecture. Amply illustrated with many fine line drawings and plans, good black-and-white photographs.

Bibliographie, p.565–73. Index, p.575–89.

Early Christian—Gothic

J400 Nickel, Heinrich L. Medieval architecture in Eastern Europe. Trans. by Alisa Jaffa. N.Y., Holmes & Meier, 1983. 209p. il., maps, plans.

Trans. of Östeuropäische Baukunst des Mittelalters. Köln, DuMont, 1981.

An introductory study for the general reader. "The book begins with a brief look at the legacy of Byzantium, examining the religious, political, and architectural background of the Byzantine Empire. This is followed by chapters on the architecture of the Balkans, covering Bulgaria, Serbia, and Romania; Kiev, including Vladimir-Suzdal'; Novgorod and Pskov; Moscow; and wooden architecture."—*Review*, Design book review, v.7, summer 1985, p.61. Buxton's The wooden churches of Eastern Europe (GLAH 2:J397) surpasses the final chapter of this book.

Bibliography, p.205–06. Index of place names, p.207–09.

Renaissance—Modern

J401 Åman, Anders. Architecture and ideology in Eastern Europe during the Stalin era: an aspect of Cold War history. N.Y., Architectural History Foundation, 1992. viii, 285p. il.

Trans. of Arkitektur och ideologi i stalintidens Östeuropa: ur det kall krigets historia. Stockholm, Carlssons i samarbete med Arkitekturmuseet, 1987.

An architectural history of the 1950s and Socialist Realism in East German, Poland, Czechoslovakia, Hungary, Romania, and Bulgaria. Does not include the Soviet Union except to establish a context for discussion of developments in other countries. Provides a basic ideological framework for understanding the use of art by the state.

Bibliographic essay, p.263–74. Index of names, p.[279]–81. Index of places, p.[283]–85.

J402 Avant-garde polonaise: urbanisme-architecture: 1918–1939 = Awangarda Polska: urbanistyka, architektura = The Polish avant-garde: architecture, town-planning. Conception, Olgierd Czerner, Hieronim Listowski. Contrib., François Wehrlin . . . [et al.] Paris, Éd. du Moniteur, 1981. 306p. il.

Trilingual catalog of the exhibition, École Speciale d'Architecture, Paris (1981). Four essays discuss the Polish artistic revolution and place it in the larger context of European developments in architecture.

List of Poland's participation in C.I.A.M. congresses and C.I.R.P.A.C. conferences, p.245–[54]. Biographies of noteworthy architects, p.255–89. Bibliography, p.292–[307].

J403 Brumfield, William Craft. The origins of modernism in Russian architecture. Berkeley, Univ. of California Pr., 1991. xxv, 343p. il., plates.

Comprehensive book on the radical changes in Russian architecture from the 1860s to 1917. Considers developments in both Moscow and St. Petersburg, style moderne and neoclassicist reactions against it. Chapter 2 focuses on Russian cultural and architectural journals of the period. Excellent illustrations.

Notes, p.297–321. Bibliography, p.323–27. Index, p.329–43.

J404 ———. Reshaping Russian architecture: Western technology, utopian dreams. N.Y., Cambridge Univ. Pr., 1990. xvii, 222p. il.

Through six essays by four contributors, this book documents the architectural transformation of imperial Russia into an industrialized Soviet empire.

Index, p.216–22.

J405 Cracraft, James. The Petrine revolution in Russian architecture. Chicago, Univ. of Chicago Pr., 1988. xxvi, 372p. il., map, plans, port.

"Recounts in detail how modern standards of architecture supplanted traditional building norms in Russia following a massive injection of European expertise and indicates how, in consequence, the modern Russian built world came into being."—*Pref.* Illustrations include many drawn by Peter the Great and foreign architects he invited to Russia.

Notes, p.337–56. Bibliography, p.357–64. Index, p.365–72.

J406 Eastern European modernism: architecture in Czechoslovakia, Hungary, and Poland between the wars. Ed. with introd. and essays by Wojciech G. Lesnikowski. Essays by Vladimir Slapeta . . . [et al.] N.Y., Rizzoli, 1996. 304p. il.

Welcome survey in English.

Contents: (1) Functionalism in Czechoslovakian, Hungarian, and Polish architecture from the European perspective, by Wojciech Lesnikowski; (2) Competing ideas in Czechoslovakian architecture, by Vladimir Slapeta; (3) Functionalism in Czechoslovakian architecture, by Vladimir Slapeta and Wojciech Lesnikowski; (4) Competing ideas in Hungarian architecture, by John Macsai; (5) Functionalism in Hungarian architecture, by Janos Bonta; (6) Competing ideas in Polish architecture, by Olgierd Czerner; (7) Functionalism in Polish architecture, by Wojciech Lesnikowski; (8) Holocaust and aftermath, by Wojciech Lesnikowski.

Authors' biographies, p.296–97. Select bibliography, p.298–301. Index, p.302–04.

J407 Feuer-Toth, Rozsa. Renaissance architecture in Hungary. Photographs by Kalman Konya. [Trans. by Ivan Feherdy.] Budapest, Magyar Helikon, 1981. 241p. il.

Chiefly illustrations. Brief essay discusses the early arrival of Renaissance style in Hungary (as compared to France and Germany) and its classicizing character. Plates include many architectural details; all have extensive descriptions.

Plates, p.[37–212]. Description of plates, p.[213]–25. Ground plans, p.[227–37]. Bibliography, p.[239–42]. List of place names, p.[243].

J408 Foltyn, Ladislav. Slowakische Architektur und die tschechische Avantgarde: 1918–1939. Dresden, Verlag der Kunst, 1991. 235p. il., plans.

Czech ed., Slovenská architekturá a ceská avantgarda 1918–1939. Bratislava, Vydavatel'stvo Spolku architektov Slovenska, 1993.

A chronological survey of a period in Slovak and Czech architecture which has been previously neglected. Excellent illustrations with many plans.

Anmerkungen, p.[224]–33. Personenregister, p.234–[36].

J409 Ikonnikov, Andrei Vladimirovich. Russian architecture of the Soviet period. Trans. by Lev Lyapin. Moscow, Raduga, 1988. 396p. il. (part col.), maps, plans.

Standard history, the first in English, covering 1917 through the early 1980s. "Offers to anyone who cannot read Russian exposure to the official view of Soviet architecture."—*Review*, Journal of the Society of Architectural Historians, v.44, Dec. 1980, p.462.

Contents: (1) Historical roots of Soviet Russian architecture; (2) Emergence of Soviet architecture (1917–1923); (3) Architecture in Russia during the years of reconstruction and socialist industrialization (1924–1932); (4) Russian architecture in the years before the Second World War (1933–1941); (5) The war years and post-war reconstruction (1941–1954); (6) Mass-scale housing construction, and the architecture of the late 1950s and the 1960s; (7) The quests of the 1970s and the early 1980s; (8) Conclusion.

Bibliography [in Cyrillic], p.396–[97].

J410 Khan-Magomedov, Selim O. Pioneers of Soviet architecture: the search for new solutions in the 1920s and 1930s. N.Y., Rizzoli, 1987. 618p. il.

Trans. of Pioniere der sowjetischen Architektur. Dresden, Verlag der Kunst, 1983.

The most comprehensive history of the period, it includes many buildings and projects previously unknown outside Russia. Divided into three sections: (1) Aesthetic problems of design; (2) Social tasks of architecture; (3) Masters and trends: biographies, statements, manifestos, the last of which gives information on architectural associations of the new direction. 1,544 illustrations support every aspect of the discussion.

Bibliography (p.602–10) is divided into publications in Russian, those in other languages, and a supplemental section for the English ed. Index of names, p.611–18.

J411 Kopp, Anatole. Constructivist architecture in the USSR. [Trans. from the French by Sheila de Vallée.] N.Y., St. Martin's, 1985. 160p. il.

Trans. of L'architecture de la periode Stalinienne. 2d ed. Grenoble, Presses Universitaires de Grenoble, 1985.

The first study of Stalinist architecture by a non-Soviet architectural historian. Traces the change from rich, experimental architecture of the Constructivist period to the mediocre, prescriptive designs of the 1950s. Concludes with interviews with architects and urban planners, both Soviet and Western, who worked in the U.S.S.R. during the period.

Bibliography, p.158. Index, p.159–60.

J412 Moravanszky, Akos. Competing visions: aesthetic invention and social imagination in Central European architecture, 1867–1918. Cambridge, Mass., MIT Pr., 1998. xv, 508p. il. (part col.)

Seeks to define the cultural characteristics of the architecture of the Austro-Hungarian Empire.

Contents: (1) Introduction: the identity of an imaginary region; (2) The city as political monument; (3) Antiquarian and individualist historicism; (4) Art nouveau: the will to style; (5) Imperial realism: the aesthetics of the Wagner circle; (6) The search for a national style; (7) The ornament: salvation or crime? (8) Folded facades: cubism and empathy; (9) Classicism as style, classicism as attitude; (10) The architecture of social reform.

Notes, p.445–74. Name index, p.481–88. Subject index, p.491–508.

J413 Quilici, Vieri. L'architettura del costruttivismo. Nuova ed. Roma, Laterza, 1978. xi, 330p. il., plates. (Universale Laterza, 440)

See GLAH 1:J268 for 1st ed.

Scandinavia

J414 Donnelly, Marian C. Architecture in the Scandinavian countries. Cambridge, Mass., MIT Pr., 1992. 401p. il., maps.

A valuable introduction to a large subject, this is "a comprehensive survey of the buildings by the architects as well as by the unknown builders of the vernacular in Scandinavia. About 400 structures dating from prehistory to the 1970s are described, with a black-and-white photograph for each adjacent to the text. This is a scholarly project of research, involving almost no criticism."—*Review*, CHOICE, v.29, May 1992, p.1382.

Appendix: Architects and Builders, p.[343]–47. Notes, p.[349–72]. Bibliography, p.[373]–91. Index, p.[393]–401.

J415 Faber, Tobias. A history of Danish architecture. [Trans. Frederic R. Stevenson]. [Copenhagen], Det Danske Selskab, 1978. 316p. il. (Denmark in print and pictures)

A basic survey of Danish architecture from prehistoric times to 1976.

Index, p.307–16.

J416 Hauglid, Roar. Norwegian stave churches. [English text by R. I. Christophersen.] Oslo, Dreyer, 1990. 119p. il.

See GLAH 1:J269 for original ed.

J417 Nikula, Riitta. Architecture and landscape: the building of Finland. [Trans. by Timothy Binham.] Helsinki, Otava, 1993. 159p. il.

A general introduction to the history of building in Finland, it disregards unbuilt plans. Coverage of 20th century architecture is compressed; readers will need to refer to Quantrill's Finnish architecture and the modernist tradition (GLAH 2:J422) for further information.

Selected bibliography, p.156–57. Name index, p.158. Place index, p.159.

J418 Norberg-Schulz, Christian. Modern Norwegian architecture. Oslo, Norwegian Univ. Pr. (Distr. by Oxford Univ. Pr., 1986). 159p. il.

Documents architectural developments from World War I to the 1980s. Attempts to inform readers about urban design and the full range of building types in contrast to most writing on Norwegian architecture which focuses on dwellings.

Contents: (1) The background; (2) National Romanticism; (3) Neoclassicism; (4) Competing trends in art; (5) Functionalism; (6) Urban dwelling; (7) The post-war years; (8) Optimism and belief in progress; (9) Stagnation and renewal; (10) Environmental crisis and need of place; (11) New Norwegian architecture.

Bibliography, p.155–56. Index of names, p.157–[60].

J419 ______. Nightlands: Nordic building. Trans. by Thomas McQuillan. Cambridge, MIT Pr., 1996. 230p. il. (part col.)

"This book is not a history of architecture. . . . Its aim, rather, is to examine what Nordic building truly is, and this is best achieved by contrasting it with its counterpart: the classical architecture of the South."—*Pref.* Focuses on building as it occurs in a local context rather than using a stylistic or chronological approach.

Notes, p.[199]–213. Bibliography, p.[215]–20. Index, p.[221]–30.

J420 ______. Scandinavie architecture 1965–1990. Paris, Moniteur, 1990. 184p. il. plans. (Tendances de l'architecture contemporaine)

A survey of recent architecture supported by fine color photographs and numerous plans. There is an introductory chapter followed by a chapter each on Denmark, Finland, Norway, and Sweden.

Index des noms et des oeuvres, p.182–83.

J421 Nordisk klassicism 1910–1930 = Nordic classicism, 1910–1930. [Ed., Simo Paavilainen]. Helsingfors, Finlands arkitekturmuseum, 1982. 180p. il. (part col.)

Italian trans., Classicismo nordico. Milan, Electa, 1988.

Bilingual catalog of the exhibition, Museum of Finnish Architecture, Helsinki (1982). Covers the neglected period between Art Nouveau and Functionalism. Essays on architecture in the respective countries are followed by entries for individual architects which illustrate several major projects. Numerous plans.

Contents: (1) Modern classicism in Norden, by Henrik O. Andersson; (2) Textures, by Carl Petersen; (3) Contrasts, by Carl Petersen; (4) Denmark, by Lisbet Balslev Jorgensen; (5) Finland, by Simo Paavilainen; (6) Norway, by Christian Norberg-Schulz; (7) Sweden, by Henrik O. Andersson; (8) The classical tradition and the European avant-garde: notes on France, Germany and Scandinavia 1912–37, by Kenneth Frampton.

Bibliography, p.176–79.

J422 Quantrill, Malcolm. Finnish architecture and the modernist tradition. N.Y., Chapman & Hall, 1995. xi, 242p. il. (part col.), plans.

"A more-or-less blow-by-blow account of how modernism came into being in Finland and how it made its mark on Finnish culture and life. . . . This book was conceived as the third part of a series on modern Finnish architecture, the first two being Alvar Aalto: A critical study (N.Y., Schocken, 1983) and Reima Pietilä: Architecture, context and modernism (N.Y., Rizzoli, 1985). In essence, the present volume was seen as providing the overall landscape of modern Finnish architecture against which the work of Aalto and Pietilä could be read."—*Pref.*

Contents: (1) Background and evolution; (2) The classicism of the 1920s; (3) Encounters with functionalism: 1927 to 1939; (4) The years of conflict and reconstruction; (5) A second Finnish renaissance; (6) The 1960s: standardization versus architectural standards; (7) Reima Pietilä: form follows approach; (8) After Aalto: form and formalism in the 1970s and 1980s; (9) Fin de siècle.

Selected bibliography, p.232–33. Index, p.238–42.

J423 Richards, James Maude. 800 years of Finnish architecture. Newton Abbot [Eng.], David & Charles, 1978. 191p. il., plates, plans, map.

Based on the author's Guide to Finnish architecture (1966, see GLAH 1:J275), this is a chronological treatment of the subject illustrated with more than 200 photographs.

Bibliography, p.188. Index, p.190–91.

J424 Sestoft, Jorgen, and Christiansen, Jorgen Hegner. Guide to Danish architecture. Copenhagen, Arkitektens Forlag, 1991–95. 2v. il., maps.

Arranged thematically; individual categories of building are divided into time segments of about a decade. Nearly 1,000 excellent illustrations.

Contents: (1) 1000–1960 (Contains an essay outlining Danish architecture, followed by the guide. Arranged chronologically, then thematically by building type as necessary. More than 850 excellent illustrations.) (2) 1960–1995 (Introductory essay "describes the changing architectural ideals of the post-war period, on the one hand, and the conditions for the creation of architecture that underwent dramatic changes in around 1960, on the other."—*Pref.*)

Place index, v.1, p.262–66, v.2, p.369–76. Name index, v.1, p.266–70, v.2, p.377–85. Index of categories, v.2, p.386–89. Includes a separate keyed map of buildings in Denmark.

J425 The work of architects: the Finnish Association of Architects, 1892–1992. Ed. by Pekka Korvenmaa. [Trans. by Juri Kokkonen.] Helsinki, Finnish Association of Architects, Finnish Building Centre, 1992. 320p. il.

Published on the occasion of the Association's centenary, this collection of essays covers the architecture of Finland from the early 1800s to the 1990s, providing an excellent history of the profession as well as the buildings of nearly 200 years. Includes chapters on female architects and on the history of the Architects' Club and the Finnish Association of Architects. Excellent illustrations.

Spain and Portugal

Bibliography

J426 Bonet Correa, Antonio. Bibliografia de arquitectura, ingenieria y urbanismo en España (1498–1880). Madrid, Turner Libros, 1980. 2v.

3,406 annotated entries covering the architectural writing of Spaniards and of foreigners writing about Spanish architecture. Organized by category of publication.

Indice onomastico, v.2, p.551–77. Indice geografico, v.2, p.578–88. Indice cronologico, v.2, p.589–95.

J427 Gutiérrez, Ramón. Bibliografia de arquitectura y urbanismo en Iberoamérica, 1980–1993. Alcalá de henares, Instituto Español de Arquitectura, Universidad de Alcalá y Valladolid, 1996. 76p.

Schematic bibliographical checklist.

Contents: Arquitectura contemporanea; Arquitectura historica; Preservacion; Tecnologia; Urbanismo; Otras temas.

Indice de autores, p.9–22.

J428 Montéquin, François-Auguste de. Muslim architecture of the Iberian Peninsula: eastern and western sources for Hispano-Islamic building arts. West Cornwall, Ct., Locust Hill Press, 1987. xv, 241p.

"The goal of this bibliographic compilation is to list works relevant to Hispano-Islamic architecture of all periods and regions written by Eastern and Western authors, from the early classical sources of historic times to the fourteenth century Anno Hegirae [1980/1981 Anno Domini]. The works gathered are not concerned solely with the arts of building although this is the major emphasis of the work. Also included in the compilation are materials from disciplines intimately related to architecture and without which the art of building cannot be fully understood, such as archaeology and art, cartography and geography, history, literature, botany and geology, ethnology, sociology, and various others, as well as those offering sources for research such as works concerned with archives, libraries, museums, and bibliographies."—*Introd.* The majority of entries are for 20th-century works. Citations appear in the language of origin. There are no annotations.

Master outline of the thematic index, p.173–87. Thematic index, p.189–234. Appendix to the thematic index, p.235–41.

J429 Reyes Pacios Lozano, Ana. Bibliografia de arquitectura y techumbres mudéjares, 1857–1991. [Teruel], Instituto de Estudios Turolenses, Excma. Diputación Provincial de Teruel, 1993. 450p. (Serie estudios mudéjares)

Substantial, classified bibliography.

Contents: (1) Obras de referencia; (2) Fuentes primarias.

Índices: de autores, p.347–62; de títulos, p.363–94; de materias, p.395–422; onomástico, p.423–26; de topónimos, p.427–36; de obras artísticas, p.437–50.

Histories and Handbooks

J430 Dodds, Jerrilynn Denise. Architecture and ideology in early medieval Spain. University Park, Pennsylvania State Univ. Pr., 1990. xiv, 174p. il., plates, map, plans.

A collection of essays encompassing the 6th through 10th centuries with the purpose of examining the ideological and social meanings that underlie architectural forms. Includes excellent coverage of many of the most well-known monuments, but is not intended to be a survey.

Notes, p.[117]–70. Index, p.[172]–74.

J431 Feduchi, Luis M. Spanish folk architecture. Barcelona, Ed. Blume, 1977– . (1)v. il. (New image collection)

Trans. of Itinerarios de arquitectura popular española. Barcelona, Blume, 1974– . (4)v. Largely photographic documentation of vernacular architecture arranged geographically. Each town has a brief description. Regions have a brief essay. Excellent photographs.

Selective contents: (1) The northern plateau (1977).

J432 Mackay, David. Modern architecture in Barcelona, 1854–1939. N.Y., Rizzoli, 1989. 119p. il.

"The four chapters of this book follow for convenience the orthodox classification of modern Catalan culture: the Renaixença of the nineteenth century, Modernisme bridging the two centuries, the Noucentisme of the dawning new century, the Rationalism of the Republican era."—*Introd.*

List of buildings mentioned in the text and their addresses, p.115–18. Bibliography, p.119.

J433 Zabalbeascoa, Anatxu. The new Spanish architecture. Introd. by Peter Buchanan. N.Y., Rizzoli, 1992. 222p. il. (part col.)

Following an introductory essay, "The journey to modernity," this book uses the work of 13 architects to demonstrate the range of design in the 1980s and 1990s. Illustrated with excellent photographs and many plans, each building is introduced with a brief statement.

Architects' biographies, p.10–11. No bibliography or index.

Turkey

J434 Altun, Ara. An outline of Turkish architecture in the Middle Ages. Trans. by Solmaz Turunc. Istanbul, Arkeoloji ve Sanat Yayinlari, 1990. vii, 249p. il., map.

For the general reader.

Contents: (I) Introduction; (II) Early Turkish-Islamic architecture and its influences outside Anatolia: (A) Architecture of the Karakhanid period; (B) Architecture of the Ghaznevid period; (C) Architecture of the Great Seljuks and its influences in Asia; (D) The architecture of Zengids and Azerbaidzhan Atabeks; (III) Anatolia: (A) Early Turkish architecture in Anatolia; (B) The architecture of the Anatolian Seljuks; (C) Architecture of the Emirates; (IV) The course of development in architectural types: (A) Mosques; (B) Medresses; (C) Funerary monuments; (D) Civil architecture; (V) On the sources.

Index, p.235–45. Appendix 1 (historical and geographical circles of Turkish architecture in the Middle Ages), p.247–49. Appendix 2 (map of Turkey), p.[250–51]. Appendix 3 (chronology of comparative Turkish architecture up to 1300), foldout.

J435 Kostof, Spiro. Caves of God: the monastic environment of Byzantine Cappadocia. Drawings by Malcolm C. Carpenter. Cambridge, Mass., MIT Pr., 1972. xviii, 296p. il.

"This book is about Christian Cappadocia, the land and its hidden monuments. . . . With minor exceptions it presents no unpublished buildings or paintings. Its purpose is twofold: to provide, for the interested layman, a readable introduction to the rockcut architecture of Cappadocia and its painted decoration; and for the student of Byzantine art, to present a critical review of the current state of scholarship on the subject and a reordering of its results."—*Pref.*

Glossary, p.[233]–35. Notes, p.[237]–59. Catalogue of known rockcut churches, arranged by period, p.[261]–76. Bibliographical note, p.[277]–85. Index, p.[287]–96.

J436 Mathews, Thomas F. The Byzantine churches of Istanbul: a photographic survey. University Park, Pennsylvania State Univ. Pr., 1976. xx, 405p. il.

"The purpose of this work is to present to the scholar or student of Byzantine architecture a reasonably complete photographic documentation of the churches of ancient Constantinople. This is not a history of Byzantine architecture in the capital, as desirable as that might be, but a visual record of the monuments on which such a history might be based."—*Introd.* Most photographs included have never been published before and most were taken expressly for this survey.

Index, p.403–05.

J437 Modern Turkish architecture. Ed. by Renata Holod and Ahmet Evin. [Philadelphia], Univ. of Pennsylvania Pr., 1984. vi, 192p. il., plan.

"This book is the first one in English to trace the development of . . . the rise of the architectural profession, and the transformation of the building industry in Turkey from the first decades of this century to the present day."—*Introd.*

Contents: (1) The social context of the development of architecture in Turkey; (2) The final years of the Ottoman Empire; (3) Finding a national idiom: the first national style; (4) To be modern: search for republican architecture; (5) The second period of Turkish national architecture; (6) International Style: liberalism in architecture; (7) Pluralism takes command: the Turkish architectural scene today; (8) To house the new citizens: housing policies and mass housing.

Herman Jansen's plan for Ankara, p.178–79. Index, p.180–83.

United States

Bibliography

J438 Cuthbert, John A.; Ward, Barry; and Keeler, Maggie. Vernacular architecture in America: a selective bibliography. Boston, Hall, 1985. xxi, 145p. il.

Focuses tightly on modern literature pertaining to architecture of the American folk tradition. Excludes: studies of gardening, farm implements, and general tools and crafts, broad anthropological and historical studies of American society, how-to manuals, 19th-century pattern books, histories of carpentry, and "popular urban vernacular architecture." Cites articles and books, with main entry by author. No annotations.

Comprehensive index, p.97–145.

J439 Doumato, Lamia. Architecture and women: a bibliography documenting women architects, landscape architects, designers, architectural critics and writers, and women in related fields working in the United States. N.Y., Garland, 1988. xvi, 269p. il., plates. (Garland reference library of the humanities, 886)

The most useful source for information on American women architects yet published. Begins by listing general sources arranged by publication type, then provides bibliographies on 128 individuals with entries divided into primary and secondary sources. Although substantial, it does not attempt to be comprehensive. Only occasional annotations.

Index, p.227–69.

J440 Goode, James M. Goode's bibliography: doctoral dissertations relating to American architectural history, 1897–1995. 2d ed. Washington, D.C., Goode, 1995. 198p.

1st ed. 1992.

"The principal criteria for inclusion in the list has been those studies dealing with the history of the built environment. Influenced by American Studies, [the list is expanded] to include not only buildings but related topics such as architectural sculpture, cemeteries, dams, the social history of buildings where they show how a building type was used, and terra cotta."—*Introd.* Also included are dissertations written before 1950 on the then-current issues concerning the built environment as they now have historical interest. Entries are arranged by date with a full citation and reference to the University Microfilms reproduction number.

Concludes with indexes of authors, p.125–55; degree granting institutions, p.156–64; and subjects, p.165–98.

J441 Marshall, H. American folk architecture: a selected bibliography. Washington, D.C., Library of Congress, 1981.

Less narrowly focused than Cuthbert's Vernacular architecture in America: a selective bibliography (GLAH 2:J438), this is divided into five categories: (1) Theory and general works; (2) Antecedents to American building; (3) Regional works; (4) Museums and historic preservation; (5) Field documentation. Cites articles and books. Native Americans have been almost completely neglected. No annotations. No index.

J442 Massey, James C.; Schwartz, Nancy B.; and Maxwell, Shirley. Historic American Buildings Survey/ Historic American Engineering Record: an annotated bibliography. [Washington, D.C.], HABS/HAER, National Park Service, U.S. Dept. of the Interior, 1992. x, 170p.

"The scope of this bibliography covers the years 1933 through 1991 and has been limited to publications issued by HABS/HAER, the National Park Service, and the Government Printing Office, those issued by HABS/HAER cooperators for HABS/HAER, and those in which HABS/HAER has substantially participated in preparing the publication. Not included are National Park Service park or regional publications using HABS/HAER records. . . . Substantive articles about the HABS/HAER and its history are included, however, generally favoring articles from journals over those found in newspapers and newsletters."—*Introd.* Entries are arranged by type of publication.

Index, p.157–70.

J443 Tubesing, Richard L. Architectural preservation and urban renovation: an annotated bibliography of United States congressional documents. N.Y., Garland, 1982. 650p. (Garland reference library of the humanities, 329)

Continuation of an earlier publication (see GLAH 1:J302a), this vol. cites all House and Senate bills, resolutions, and public laws concerning architectural preservation and urban renovation introduced by the 93rd, 94th, and 95th Congresses between 1973 and 1975. Improving upon the earlier vol., all citations are annotated. Information is organized by legislative body, then type of legislative action, and finally chronologically. The index provides access by names of specific sites and buildings, by building type, and by topics such as feasibility studies.

Directories

J444 Architectural records in Boston: a guide to architectural research in Boston, Cambridge and vicinity. Massachusetts Committee for the Preservation of Architectural Records, Inc. Nancy Carlson Schrock, project director and ed. N.Y., Garland, 1983. xxxviii, 286p. il. (Garland reference library of the humanities, 413)

Directory of archival sources for records, drawings, and photographs that collectively provide the developmental and documentary history of the built environment. An essential tool for historians and practitioners engaged in preservation work. Collections are divided into three types: architectural firms and businesses with pre-1970 records, repositories, and government agencies. Individual firm entries indicate the contact person, brief history of the practice, the type of records held. Entries for government agencies and repositories note the scope of the collection, holdings, as well as hours open and duplication options.

Glossary, p.xxxi–xxxv. Index, p.251–86.

J445 Architectural records in the San Francisco Bay Area. California Cooperative Preservation of Architectural Records. Waverly B. Lowell, project director and ed. Mary Hardy, surveyor. Lynn A. Downey, staff. N.Y., Garland, 1988. xvii, 350p. il., map, plans. (Garland reference library of the humanities, 799)

Companion to Schrock's Architectural records in Boston (see previous entry) with some improvements in format and level of detail. Individual firm entries indicate the contact person, brief history of the practice, the type of records held, and access policies. Includes a list of San Francisco architects in practice 1850–1910 and the history of their employment with Bay Area firms.

Select bibliography, p.19–22. Index, p.319–50.

J446 Landmark yellow pages: where to find all the names, addresses, facts, and figures you need. [2d ed.] National Trust for Historic Preservation. Pamela Dwight, gen. ed. Washington, D.C., Preservation Pr., 1993. ix, 395p. il.

The best single source for national and regional historic preservation information. Divided into three sections: (1) All about preservation; (2) Products and services; (3) The preservation network. Within each section information is arranged topically in a format that will assist novice researchers. The many references to relevant agencies and publications in each topical section increase its utility.

Index, p.391–95.

J447 Pro file: the official directory of the American Institute of Architects. Topeka, Kan., Archimedia, 1983– . Annual.

See GLAH 1:J328b for 1st ed.

Subtitle varies. Title of 10th ed. (1995): Profile, the directory of U.S. architectural design firms.

Dictionaries and Encyclopedias

J448 Carley, Rachel. The visual dictionary of American domestic architecture. Illustrated by Ray Skibinski and Ed Lam. N.Y., Holt, 1994. 272p. il.

An "illustrated reference guide to American building that defines terminology through the universal language of pictures, but also attempts to explain architectural types and styles within the framework of the social, historical, geographic, climactic, and ethnic influences that shaped them. . . . Beginning with the indigenous dwelling types of Native American groups and working up to the 1990s, styles and types are presented chronologically, grouped by chapters according to the names and periods by which they are generally recognized."—*Introd.* Concerned only with domestic architecture, it illustrates both high-style and vernacular buildings with exceptionally clear line drawings with architectural elements labeled. Brief descriptions introduce each entry which has an elevation and floor plan, and often interior details, provided.

Index, p.268–72.

J449 Harris, Cyril M. American architecture: an illustrated encyclopedia. N.Y., Norton, 1998. xi, 370p. il.

Illustrated with excellent line drawings, this source spans the full range of the built environment in America from precolonial times through the present. "In defining and illustrating all those terms that provide the basic language of American architecture, the intention is to provide readers not only with precise information about the various types of local dwellings, houses, civic and commercial buildings, and houses of worship illustrative of American architectural design, and the techniques and materials used in building them, but also to set this information in a context that recognizes the multiple influences which have shaped that design."—*Pref.* Entries contain historical as well as descriptive detail, covering construction materials and methods, decorative terms, technical processes, and practical devices.

J450 Lounsbury, Carl R., ed. An illustrated glossary of early southern architecture and landscape. Ed. assist. by Vanessa E. Patrick. Prepared at the Colonial Williamsburg Foundation. N.Y., Oxford Univ. Pr., 1994. xiv, 430p. il.

An exceptionally comprehensive source. "This work documents the transfer of English terminology to the southern mainland colonies in the 17th and 18th centuries and explores the subsequent growth of a regional vernacular through the early national period. The glossary defines and analyzes the various and sometimes changing meanings and usages of the South's building and landscape vocabulary. It is a compilation of nearly fifteen hundred words and terms known to have been in use from the 1610s through the 1820s in the region encompassing Delaware in the north, Georgia in the south, and the newly settled western regions of Kentucky and Tennessee."—*Pref.* Small, but high-quality black-and-white photographs and drawings support the text.

Bibliographical references, p.[417]–26.

J451 Packard, Robert T., and Korab, Balthazar. Encyclopedia of American architecture. 2d ed. N.Y., McGraw-Hill, 1995. xi, 724p. il. (part col.)

Rev. ed. of William Dudley Hunt, Jr.'s Encyclopedia of American architecture, N.Y., McGraw-Hill, 1980. "This book presents, in words and pictures, the vast breadth of American architecture. It is intended to be of interest and use to people who want to know about the culture and the environment in which they live, and how it came to be that way."—*Pref.* Nontechnical, intended for general readers. Specialized terms are defined where used. Entries are a mix of biographical and topical essays. Cross references appear at the end of essays as do occasional lists of suggested reading. Excellent color illustrations throughout.

Histories and Handbooks

J452 America preserved: a checklist of historic buildings, structures, and sites. 60th anniversary ed. Washington, D.C., Library of Congress, Cataloging Distr. Service, 1995. xxiv, 1152p. il.

Provides an easy way to identify and order copies of the measured drawings, large-format photographs and captions, and in many cases histories and field notes for 30,097 structures documented by the Historic American Buildings Survey and the Historic American Engineering Record from 1933 through 1993. Includes references to informal documentation contained in field records and cites full Library of Congress shelflist numbers to facilitate ordering of copies. The arrangement of entries follows the geographical organization used by the Library of Congress. The elements of an entry are: state, county, and city or nearest vicinity, structure or site name (record name), address, HABS or HAER

survey number, Library of Congress shelflist number, description of documentation on file, and location of documentation (within Library of Congress collections).
Index to county by city, p.1117–52.

J453 Bevitt, Emogene A. Second lives: a survey of architectural artifact collections in the United States. Washington, D.C., U.S. Dept. of the Interior, National Park Service, Preservation Assistance Division, for sale by the U.S. Gov. Print. Off., Supt. of Docs., 1994. x, 100p. il.
Concerned with collections holding three-dimensional parts of buildings salvaged for study, research, or display. Arranged in two parts: (Part 1) Listings by state. Entries are arranged alphabetically by city, and include information on address and contact persons, collection scope, dates of the collection materials, and a list of the types of artifacts, and the quantity of each type. (Part 2) Indexes. Offers access by type of artifact.

J454 Blumenson, John J. G. Identifying American architecture: a pictorial guide to styles and terms, 1600–1945. Foreword by Nikolaus Pevsner. With photos. from the Historic American Buildings Survey. 2d ed., rev. and enl. Nashville, American Association for State and Local History, 1981. viii, 118p. il.
"The purpose of this brief guide is to provide photographic illustrations of buildings, architecture details, elements, and forms to enable the user to make visual associations and to begin to recognize styles and elements."—*Pref.* Arranged by style, each example has a photograph, one-paragraph description, and list of characteristic features keyed to points on the photograph. The second half of the book comprises a pictorial glossary of terms.
Bibliography, p.117–18.

J455 Buildings of the United States. N.Y., Oxford Univ. Pr., 1993– . (6)v.
Sponsored by the Society of Architectural Historians, projected to be complete in 55v.
Contents: Hoagland, Alison K. Buildings of Alaska (1993); Gebhard, David, and Mansheim, Gerald. Buildings of Iowa (1993); Eckert, Kathryn Bishop. Buildings of Michigan (1993); Scott, Pamela, and Lee, Antoinette J. Buildings of the District of Columbia (1993); Noel, Thomas J. Buildings of Colorado (1997); Nicoletta, Julia. Buildings of Nevada (2000).
Includes bibliographical references and index.

J456 Carrott, Richard G. The Egyptian revival: its sources, monuments and meaning, 1808–1858. Berkeley, Univ. of California Pr., 1978. 221p. il.
The definitive work on an important movement in American architecture. It brings together a wealth of material from numerous widely scattered sources, many fairly inaccessible to most readers. It gives detailed attention to the European architectural background and to the iconography and meaning of the movement. Appendixes on specific monuments.
Bibliographic essay, p.193–205. Index, p.207–21.

J457 Catalog of national historic landmarks. Compiled by the History Division, National Park Service. Washington, D.C., U.S. Dept. of the Interior, 1987. iv, 290p.
Documents 1,811 properties designated as National Historic Landmarks through June 30, 1987. Intended to be published annually, but only 1987 was published. Entries are listed by state. Under each state heading, listings are in alphabetical order under the individual landmark names. Entries supply name of landmark, local address, city, county, historic date(s) and architect (if known), and a brief description of the landmark and its significance, followed by the date of its designation as a National Historic Landmark.

J458 Goode, James M. Addendum to American architectural drawings. [Philadelphia, s.n., 1977.] 102 leaves.
Addendum to American architectural drawings, compiled and ed. by George S. Koyl (1969; see GLAH 1:J322).

J459 Gottfried, Herbert, and Jennings, Jan. American vernacular design, 1870–1940: an illustrated glossary. N.Y., Van Nostrand Reinhold, 1985. xvii, 270p. il.
"Describes and illustrates the compositional elements and the design concepts that have underwritten much vernacular building."—*Pref.*
Contents: Elements [architectural elements]; Types [of building].
Bibliography, p.256–61. Index, p.262–70.

J460 Historic American buildings survey. The Historic American Buildings Survey. [microform.] Teaneck, N.J., Somerset House ([Washington, D.C.], Photoduplication Service, Library of Congress), 1980. 1,400 microfiches, il., maps.
Consists of 45,000 photographs with 35,000 pages of descriptive text, arranged by state and county, deposited in the Library of Congress, Prints and Photographs Division between 1933 and 1979.
______. 1st supplement. Historic American buildings survey. Part II [microform]. Alexandria, Va., Chadwyck-Healey, 1990–95. 2,729 microfiches, il.
Includes material received by the Library of Congress from 1980 through December 1988. Arranged by counties. Photographs and written historical and descriptive data prepared by the Historic American Buildings Survey, Office of Archeology and Historic Preservation, National Park Service.
Includes index.

J461 Historic America: buildings, structures, and sites. Recorded by the Historic American Buildings Survey and the Historic American Engineering Record. Checklist compiled by Alicia Stamm. Essays ed. by C. Ford Peatross. Washington, D.C., Library of Congress, 1983. xvi, 708p. il.
Sixteen illustrated essays serve as a guide to the use of the survey (see previous entry). The most useful portion of the book is the "Checklist of Buildings, Structures, and Sites" which notes 16,738 sites and structures recorded by HABS and HAER through 1981, p.287–680. This list renders the 1941 catalog and 1958 supplement obsolete.

Because the checklist entries are arranged by county, an index to counties by city names is provided, p.681–708.

J462 McAlester, Virginia, and McAlester, Lee. A field guide to American houses. N.Y., Knopf, 1984. xv, 525p. il.

The most complete field guide to American domestic architecture ever published. Arranged chronologically, each chapter treats one of the major architectural styles using photographs and drawings. Ample text supplements the illustrations, discussing the identifying features, principal subtypes, variants and details, and occurrence of each style. Introductory chapters on style, form, and structure, plus a pictorial key and pictorial glossary assist the novice.

Bibliography, p.501–10. Index, p.511–25.

J463 The National register of historic places, 1976. Washington, D.C., National Park Service. [For sale by the Supt. of Docs., U.S. Govt. Print. Off.], 1976. 2v. il.

1-vol. eds. published in 1969, 1974, are not entirely superseded by this two-vol. ed. as the descriptive information on properties differs from one ed. to another. "As the nation's official list of properties worthy of preservation, the National Register serves as a guide to assist Federal agencies and others in planning projects that might affect the environment."—*Foreword, v.2.*

Entries, organized alphabetically by state, county, then property name, offer the following data: city, property name, street address, date of construction and architect (historic sites and districts are dated by period of significance), descriptive statement including significance, ownership and accessibility to the public, survey designation (e.g., HABS or HAER). V.1 contains entries for the 9,500 properties listed through December 1974. V.2 completes the description of properties listed through 1976.

J464 National register of historic places, 1966 to 1994: cumulative list through January 1, 1994. Washington, D.C., National Park Service; Preservation Pr.; National Trust for Historic Preservation; National Conference of State Historic Preservation Officers, 1994. xxx, 923p. il., maps.

"This volume includes all the properties listed in the National Register of Historic Places between October 15, 1966 and December 31, 1993. It does not contain properties that have been determined to be eligible for the National Register but are not yet listed. Places are organized alphabetically by state, county, and property name. This volume also includes comprehensive lists of all State Historic Preservation Officers and Federal Preservation Officers."—*Introd.*

Lacks the descriptive text found in 1969, 1974, 1976 eds. of the National Register of Historic Places. Instead lists (in coded form): property name, address, town, date listed in the National Register, National Register criteria exceptions (if applicable), identification of National Park Service properties and National Historic Landmarks, the property's National Register Information Service computer reference number.

J465 Rifkind, Carole. A field guide to American architecture. N.Y., New American Library, 1980. xi, 322p. il.

"Included in this book are more than 450 line drawings which illustrate representative examples of American building up to about 1940. Because of their clarity and precision, these drawings are particularly revealing of how the builder's vocabulary . . . is used to fulfill function and convey meaning."—*Pref.* Nearly all drawings are from the Historic American Buildings Survey/Historic American Engineering Record. A small number of black-and-white photographs complement the drawings. The book is divided into four sections by building type: residential, ecclesiastical, civic and commercial, and utilitarian. Emphasis is on exteriors.

Recommended reading, p.313–17. Index, p.321–22.

J466 Scully, Vincent. American architecture and urbanism. New rev. ed. N.Y., Holt, 1988. 320p. il., plans.

See GLAH 1:J331 for 1st ed.

Adds a new chapter, "1988," and updates bibliography with publications since 1969. A note on method and bibliography, p.297–305.

J467 Smith, G. E. Kidder. The architecture of the United States. In assoc. with the Museum of Modern Art, New York. Introd. by Albert Bush-Brown . . . [et al.] Garden City, N.Y., Anchor Pr., 1981. 3v. il., maps.

Guidebook intended to "serve as a commentary on a cross section of each state's architectural resources from earliest times to the present. It is by no means an inventory of memorable works . . . but it will critically examine structures considered representative of major periods of development."—*Foreword.* Includes no private houses, correctional institutions, or mental institutions. Entries provide the address and date of the building, a paragraph of detailed description, and conclude with hours when the building is open to the public.

Contents: (1) New England and the Mid-Atlantic states; (2) The South and Midwest; (3) The Plains states and Far West.

Each vol. contains the same glossary (v.1, p.[727]–36) and a vol.-specific index (v.1, p.[737]–55; v.2, p.[723]–49; v.3, p.[793]–817).

J468 ———. Source book of American architecture: 500 notable buildings from the 10th century to the present. N.Y., Princeton Architectural Pr., 1996. 678p. il., maps.

Updated ed. of preceding entry, although it does not truly supersede it.

"The literature of American architecture: a general introduction," by Kazys Varnelis, p.637–43. Glossary, p.644–47. Regional lists of buildings, p.648–59. List of buildings by name, p.660–65. Architects and designers index, p.666–72. Building types index, p.673–78.

J469 Stern, Robert A. M.; Mellins, Thomas; and Fishman, David. New York 1880: architecture and urbanism in the gilded age. N.Y., Monacelli, 1999. 1164p. il.

Chronologically, the first of four landmark volumes on the architectural history of New York City. Traditional architectural history describing more than 875 buildings, monuments, gateways, esplanades, and bridges, with examples of all the major categories of urban architecture. Illustrated with period photographs; drawing heavily on published writing of architects, critics, urban planners, and city officials. Continued by: New York 1900: metropolitan architecture and urbanism, 1890–1915. N.Y., Rizzoli, 1983; New York 1930: architecture and urbanism between the two world wars. N.Y., Rizzoli, 1987; and New York 1960: architecture and urbanism between the second world war and the bicentennial. N.Y., Monacelli Pr., 1995. The 1900 and 1930 vols. have different sets of co-authors.

J470 Whiffen, Marcus. American architecture since 1780: a guide to the styles. Rev. ed. Cambridge, Mass., MIT Pr., 1992. xii, 326p. il.

See GLAH 1:J340 for 1st ed.

New sections have been added on Streamline Moderne, Late Modern, and Post-Modern styles. Bibliography has been removed.

J471 ———, and Koeper, Frederick. American architecture, 1607–1976. Cambridge, Mass., MIT Pr., 1981. xv, 495p. il.

Fine survey of architecture in the continental U.S., although not as comprehensive as Pierson and Jordy's multi-volume series American buildings and their architects (see GLAH 1:J319, GLAH 1:J320, GLAH 1:J328, GLAH 1:J328a). Not all buildings discussed are illustrated.

Notes, p.[435]–43. Sources of illustrations, p.[444]–56. Bibliography, p.[457]–67. Index, p.[469]–95.

J472 Wilson, William H. The City Beautiful movement. Baltimore, Johns Hopkins Univ. Pr., 1994. x, 365p. il. (Creating the North American landscape)

Focuses on the growth of the City Beautiful idea and its development into a cultural, aesthetic, political, and environmental movement using the examples of Chicago, Seattle, Kansas City, Dallas, and Denver.

Notes, p.307–50. Index, p.357–65.

J473 Wiseman, Carter. Shaping a nation: twentieth-century American architecture and its makers. N.Y., Norton, 1998. 412p. il. (part col.)

Readable, opinionated survey by a fine writer, attempting to "write a new draft of the history of American architecture up to the present day."—*Introd.*

Contents: Prologue: the themes take form; (1) The lure of the tall; (2) Domestic diversity; (3) Eclecticism and the uses of the past; (4) Modernism and the abstract tendency; (5) The romantic resistance; (6) The power of preservation; (7) The outbreak of the ordinary; (8) The "Whites," the "Grays," and Postmodernism; (9) High-rise, hard sell; (10) The flight from the real; (11) Refuge vs. community.

Index, p.389–412.

ASIAN COUNTRIES

China

J474 Ancient Chinese architecture. Compiled by [the] Chinese Academy of Architecture. [Project Eds., Qiao Yun, Sun Dazhang. Trans. by Wong Chi Kui, Chung Wah Nan.] Hong Kong, Joint Pub Co, 1982. 253p. chiefly il. (part col.)

Trans. of Chung-kuo ku chien chu. [Beijing], Chung-kuo chien chu kung yeh ch'u pan she, 1982.

Primarily a book of photographs of important ancient building sites as well as classical buildings still in existence. The brief text outlines the characteristics, history, and accomplishments of ancient Chinese architecture with special emphasis on technological advances.

J475 Liang, Ssu-ch'eng. A pictorial history of Chinese architecture: a study of the development of its structural system and the evolution of its types. Ed. by Wilma Fairbank. Cambridge, Mass., MIT Pr., [1984]. xxiv, 200p. il., plates

Written during World War II by the leader of the first generation of Chinese architectural historians, this was intended to be part of a larger history of Chinese art but the plan was never carried out. Published posthumously under the editorship of Wilma Fairbank.

The information is presented in five sections: "The Chinese structural system"; "Pre-Buddhist and cave-temple evidence of timber-framed architecture"; "Monumental timber-framed buildings"; "Buddhist pagodas"; and "Other masonry structures." The text and especially the drawings provide a brief survey of ancient Chinese architecture useful both as an introduction and for the specialist.

Glossary of technical terms, p.[189]–92. Guide to pronunciation, p.[193]. Bibliography, p.[195]–98. Index, p.[199]–[201].

J476 Liu, Laurence G. Chinese architecture. N.Y., Rizzoli, [1989]. 297p. il. (part col.)

Examines the meaning and symbolism of Chinese architecture, focusing on the cultural, philosophical, and religious influences and the life-style of the people. Chapters on historical background and characteristics of classical Chinese architecture are followed by chapters on building types.

Selected bibliography, p.281.

J477 Luo, Zhewen. Ancient pagodas in China. Beijing, Foreign Languages Pr., 1994. 331p. col. il., maps.

"Previously published in Chinese [as Su-chou ku tien yuan lin] by the Chinese Architecture and Building Press."—*verso of t.p.*

Beautifully presented volume on this important form of Chinese architecture. Primarily a work of color photographs accompanied by a brief, readable text on the development, uses, building materials, structures, and types of pagodas. Each pagoda is illustrated in color and described, providing a brief historical background of its building and style.

Contents: Part one: Theory and methods: (I) Introduction; (II) Layout; (III) Water; (IV) Rockeries; (V) Buildings; (VI) Flowers and trees; Part two: Chinese classical gardens.

Notes at end of chapters.

J478 Prip-Møller, Johannes. Chinese Buddhist monasteries: their plan and its function as a setting for Buddhist monastic life. [Reprint of 1937 ed.] Hong Kong,

Hong Kong Univ. Pr., 1982. 396p. il. (part col.), facsims., map, plans (part col.), ports.
See GLAH 1:J346 for original annotation. 3d impression of the original, with comparable quality photographs, line drawings, and plans. An announced reprint from the Univ. of Washington Pr., 1983, could not be traced.

J479 Steinhardt, Nancy Shatzman. Chinese imperial city planning. Honolulu, Univ. of Hawaii Pr., [1990]. xi, 228p., il.
Describes uniform elements and common architectural details found in Chinese royal cities of the last 4,000 years which created a powerful symbol for the ruler and an enduring tradition of Chinese imperial city planning.

"A convenient, brief summary of basic data about most of the major Chinese capitals from the early Bronze Age to modern times."—*Review*, Journal of the Society of Architectural Historians, v.51, 1992, p.87.

References, p.201–21.

J480 ______ . . . [et al.] Chinese traditional architecture. N.Y., China Institute in America, China House Gallery, [1984]. 168p. il., map, plans.
Catalog of the exhibition, China House Gallery (1984).

Includes a comprehensive survey of the development of architecture and building technologies in China and 11 essays by noted scholars on specific monuments or periods.

Bibliography, p.162–66.

J481 Yu, Zhouyun, comp. Palaces of the Forbidden City. Trans. by Ng Mau-Sang, Chan Sinwai, and Puwen Lee. N.Y., Viking Pr., 1984. 332p. il. (part col.), plans.
Trans. of Tzu Chin Ch'eng Kung Tien. Hong Kong, Shang wu yin shu kuan Hsiang-kang fen kuan, 1982; repr., 1988.

Yu Zhuoyun, a leading expert on Chinese architecture, senior engineer and vice-director of the Department of Ancient Architecture at the Palace Museum, worked with other departments within the Palace Museum to produce this lavishly illustrated work documenting the imperial palace complex. Built in the 1420s, the Forbidden City has the largest group of wooden structures extant in China. The photographs show interior and exterior views of the palaces, halls, buildings, pavillions, and gates. Architectural composition and decoration and services such as bridges and culverts, water and drainage, heating and lighting are described.

India, Nepal, Pakistan, Tibet

J482 Allen, Margaret Prosser. Ornament in Indian architecture. Newark, Univ. of Delaware Pr., 1991. 504p. il., map.
Consists mostly of black-and-white, full-page plates. "This [book's] primary aim is a visual presentation of some of India's architectural ornament."—*Pref.*

Contents: (1) Early Indian architecture; (2) The development of art and architecture during the Gupta Dynasty; (3) The development of the Indian temple; (4) Early South Indian architecture; (5) Post-Gupta and later architecture; (6) Late South Indian architecture; (7) Hindu shrines under Muslim rule; (8) Indo-Muslim architecture; (9) The Moghul period.

Notes, p.503–04.

J483 Architecture in Victorian and Edwardian India. Ed. by Christopher W. London. [Gen. ed. Pratapaditya Pal.] Bombay, Marg Publications, 1994. 148p. il. (part col.)
"Brings together a series of articles," by noted scholars, most "focused on an individual place or region."—*Pref.*

Contents: The formative period (circa 1856–1900): Sir J. J. School of Art and the Raj, by Partha Mitter; Orientalizing the Raj: Indo-Saracenic fantasies, by Giles H. R. Tillotson; Edwardian architects of Bombay: George Wittet and John Begg, by Christopher W. London; The splendour of Indo-Saracenic: the style Madras pioneered, by S. Muthiah; The courtly style: the remaking of Lucknow, by Rose Llewellyn-Jones; The later Mughals and Mughal successor states: architecture in Oudh, Murshidabad, and Rampur, by Catherine B. Asher; Little details of the long view: Victorian Cawnpore, by Zoë Yalland; A poet's vision: the houses of Rabindranath Tagore, by Andrew Robinson; The myth of the monuments: public commemorative statues, by Mary Ann Steggles.

J484 Asher, Catherine Ella Blanshard. Architecture of Mughal India. N.Y., Cambridge Univ. Pr., 1992. xxxi, 368p. il., maps. (The new Cambridge history of India, I, 4)
Seeks to summarize the state of research in this field, as well as "presenting a great deal of new material and also . . . providing a framework for understanding Mughal architecture."—*Pref.*

Contents: (1) Precedents for Mughal architecture; (2) The beginnings of Mughal architecture; (3) The age of Akbar; (4) Jahangir: an age of transition; (5) Shah Jahan and the crystallization of Mughal style; (6) Aurangzeb and the Islamization of the Mughal style; (7) Architecture and the struggle for authority under the later Mughals and their successor states.

List of abbreviations, p.xxiii. Glossary, p.xxv–xxix. Bibliographical essay, p.335–56. Index, p.357–68.

J485 Banerjee, N. R. Nepalese architecture. With a foreword by C. Sivaramamurti. Delhi, Agam, 1980. xxiii, 272p. il., plates.
Based mainly on inscriptional evidence. The result of researches conducted as Archaeological Adviser to the government of Nepal, 1966–1972.

Contents: (I) Introduction; (II) Geographical and cultural background; (III) Outlines of the history of Nepal; (IV) The Shahs; (V) The ensemble of architecture of Nepal in general; (VI) Main characteristics of the temple architecture of Nepal; (VII) Eduka (or terraced) and multiple-roofed temples of Nepal; (VIII) The preservation of architectural traditions in Nepal; (IX) The cultural relations between India and Nepal and their impact on Nepalese architecture.

Bibliography, p.241–52. Index, p.[253]–72.

J486 Bernier, Ronald M. Himalayan architecture. Madison, N.J., Fairleigh Dickinson Univ. Pr., 1997. 196p. il. (part col.), plates.

Argues for the existence of "a cohesive tradition of mountain aesthetic preferences from the foothills of Assam to the Northwest Frontier Province of Pakistan. The monuments treated here are animistic, Buddhist, Hindu, and Islamic. . . . The main focus is upon temples and mosques, although palaces and houses are treated as well."—*Introd.* Explores the impact of neighboring India and Tibet and of the Silk Route.

Contents: (1) Himalaya at a crossroads; (2) Assam and Nagaland in the Eastern Himalayan foothills; (3) Sikkim, Kalimpong, and Darjeeling: tradition and hill stations; (4) Palaces and monasteries of Bhutan; (5) Late and early arts of Nepal; (6) Building arts of Himachal Pradesh; (7) Survival arts of Ladakh; (8) Heritage of wooden arts in Kashmir; (9) Wooden arts of Northern Pakistan; Epilogue.

Notes, p.185–87. Bibliography, p.188–91. Index, p.192–96.

J487 Davies, Philip. Splendours of the Raj: British architecture in India, 1660 to 1947. London, Murray, 1985. 272p. il., maps, plans.

An important study of "an extraordinary historical episode" and its embodiment in buildings and memorials.

Contents: (1) Two tombs; (2) Madras: visions of antiquity; (3) Calcutta: power on silt; (4) Cantonment and residency; (5) Bungalows and hill stations; (6) The devil's wind; (7) Bombay: Urbs Prima in India; (8) Saracenic dreams; (9) New Delhi: the Rome of Hindostan; (10) Architectural reflections.

Glossary of terms, p.251–52. Biographical details of principal architects and engineers, p.253–57. Sources, p.258–60. Select bibliography, p.261–65. Index, p.266–72.

J488 Encyclopaedia of Indian temple architecture. Ed. by Michael W. Meister. Coord. by M. A. Dhaky. Philadelphia, American Institute of Indian Studies, Univ. of Pennsylvania Pr., 1983– . (2)v. in 12. il., maps, plans.

"Intended to help consolidate a generation of research, this Encyclopaedia particularly attempts to codify an appropriate technical terminology for Indian temple architecture, and to illustrate that terminology in chapters which survey the remains of temple architecture in India within a geographic and historical framework."—*Pref.* Some vols. ed. or co-ed. by M. A. Dhaky or Krishna Deva.

Contents: (1) South India. Pt.1: Lower Drāvidadēśa, 200 B.C.–A.D. 1324 (2v., text and plates); Pt.2: Upper Drāvidadēśa, A.D. 550–1075 (2v., text and plates); Pt.3: Upper Drāvidadēśa, A.D. 973–1326 (2v., text and plates); (2) North India. Pt.1: Foundations of North Indian style, 250 B.C.–A.D. 1100 (2v., text and plates); Pt.2: Period of early maturity, A.D. 700–900 (2v., text and plates); Pt.3: Beginnings of medieval idiom, A.D. 900–1000 (2v., text and plates).

J489 Evenson, Norma. The Indian metropolis, a view toward the west. New Haven, Yale Univ. Pr., 1989. ix, 294p. il. (part col.)

"I have attempted a broad survey of the architecture and planning of Bombay, Calcutta, Madras, and New Delhi from their inception until the present time," with a special focus on these cities as instruments of cultural change."—*Pref.*

Contents: (1) Three hybrid cities; (2) The architecture of empire; (3) The long debate; (4) Modern planning and the colonial city; (5) The modern movement; (6) The post-independence city; (7) The architecture of independence.

Notes, p.269–76. Selected bibliography, p.277–88. Index, p.289–92.

J490 Fischer, Klaus; Jansen, Michael; and Pieper, Jan. Architektur des indischen Subkontinents. Darmstadt, Wissenschaftliche Buchgesellschaft, 1987. viii, 264p. il.

Seeks to provide a comprehensive analysis of Indian architecture from prehistory through the 19th century. Includes helpful analytic drawings and many black-and-white plates.

Contents: (I) Einleitende Vorbemerkungen; (II) Grundelemente des indischen Umgangs mit Raum, Architektur, Stadt und Landschaft; (III) Bilden; (IV) Bauen; (V) Baugestalten; (VI) Chronologisch-geographischer Überblick.

Abkürzungsverzeichnis, p.243–44. Literaturverzeichnis, p.245–55. Glossar, p.257–60. Geographisches Register, p.262–64.

J491 Gaekwad, Fatesinhrao, Maharaja of Baroda. The palaces of India. With photos by Virginia Fass. N.Y., Vendome, 1980. 245p. il. (part col.)

Attempts to provide a "record in words and photographs" of the palaces of the princely states of India prior to Independence (1947).—*Foreword.* Arranged geographically. Many photographs.

Glossary, p.245.

J492 Grover, Satish. The architecture of India: Buddhist and Hindu. Ghaziabad, Vikas Pub. House, 1980. 231, [8]p. il.

"This book is intended to provide sufficient reading for the student of architecture to probe more detailed writings on the subject . . . to break down the cynicism of the practicing modern Indian architect to the country's architectural heritage."—*Pref.* Historical survey, by a practicing architect and architectural historian. Continued by following title.

Bibliography, p.[233]. Glossary, p.[235–36]. Index, p.[237–39].

J493 ———. The architecture of India: Islamic (727–1707 A.D.). New Delhi, Vikas Pub. House, 1981. xv, 224p. il.

Successor to the preceding title. "This volume covers the impact of resurgent Islamic thought, ideals, religion and philosophy on the ancient and established civilisation of the Hindus in India."—*Pref.*

Bibliography, p.223. Glossary, p.224. Index, p.[225]–[27].

J494 Gutschow, Niels. The Nepalese caitya: 1500 years of Buddhist votive architecture in the Kathmandu Valley. With drawings by Bijay Basukala and an essay by David Gellner. Stuttgart, Axel Menges, 1997.

328p. il., maps, plans (Lumbini International Research Institute. Monograph series, 1)
Substantial study of sacred architecture in Nepal, 6th–18th century, including 20th-century revivals, with a particular focus on typology. Richly illustrated with analytic drawings.
Bibliography, p.321–22. Index, p.323–28.

J495 Hardy, Adam. Indian temple architecture, form and transformation: the Karnata Dravida tradition, 7th to 13th centuries. Foreword by Kapila Vatsyayan. New Delhi, Indira Gandhi National Centre for the Arts, Abhinav Publications, 1995. xix, 614p. il., maps, plates.
"Evolves a conceptual base for examining the composition, the meaning, the formal values of the group of temples under investigation."—*Foreword.*
Select bibliography and list of abbreviations, p.382–86. Glossary, p.387–91. Index, p.[393]–96.

J496 Koch, Ebba. Mughal architecture: an outline of its history and development (1526–1858). München, Prestel (Distr. by te Neues, 1991).159p. il. (part col.), plans.
Outstanding survey of Mughal architecture in India, from Babur to Aurangzib and the Later Mughal Style.
Glossary, p.137–[42]. Select bibliography, p.143–55. Index, p.156–[60].

J497 Krishna, Deva. Temples of India. New Delhi, Aryan Books International, 1995. 2v. il.
Historical survey of Indian sacred architecture, intended for the scholar and general reader.
Contents: (1) Text; (2) Plates.
Reference glossary, v.1, p.261–73. Bibliography, v.1, p.275–77. Site and temple index, v.1, p.279–86.

J498 Merklinger, Elizabeth Schotten. Indian Islamic architecture: the Deccan 1374–1681. Warminster, Aris and Phillips Ltd, 1981. xiv, 146p. il., map, plans.
Preliminary description and analysis, intended to serve as the foundation for further study.
Glossary, p.viii–ix. Note on transliterature, Note on dating and abbreviations, p.x. Bibliography, p.xi–xiii.

J499 Metcalf, Thomas R. An imperial vision: Indian architecture and Britain's Raj. Berkeley, Univ. of California Pr., 1989. xiv, 302p. il. (part col.), plates.
"This work examines the relationship between culture and power as expressed in architecture during the heydey of European colonialism. It takes as its primary focus the British Raj in India."—*Pref.*
Contents: (1) Introduction; (2) The mastery of the past: the British and India's historic architecture; (3) Indo-Saracenic building under the Raj; (4) Princes, palaces, and Saracenic design; (5) Arts, crafts, and empire; (6) The classical revival; (7) New Delhi: the beginning of the end; (8) Conclusion.
Abbreviations, p.253. Notes, p.255–82. Glossary, p.283–86. Bibliography, p.287–92. Index, p.293–302.

J500 Michell, George. The Hindu temple: an introduction to its meaning and forms. N.Y., Harper and Row, 1977. 192p. il.
"This book is conceived as an introduction to . . . Hindu temple architecture."—*Pref*
Contents: Part one: The meaning of the temple: (1) The civilization of Hinduism; (2) The world of the gods; (3) The world of man; (4) The temple as a link between the gods and man; Part two: The forms of the temple: (5) The science of building; (6) Temple styles; (7) The temples of India; (8) The temples of South-East Asia; (9) The Hindu temple today.
Further reading, p.[185]–86. Indexes, p.[187]–92.

J501 ———. The royal palaces of India. Photographs by Antonio Martinelli. London, Thames and Hudson, 1994. 232p. il. (part col.)
"The present work . . . aims at the discovery of Indian royal architecture within a broad historical perspective."—*Pref. and ackn.*
Contents: (I) Courtly life and architecture: Divine power of kings; Defence and security; Formal reception; Royal worship; Privacy and pleasure; Essential services; (II) The buildings: historical and regional traditions: Palaces lost and imagined; Map; Early Muslim strongholds; Imperial Mughal capitals; Rajput forts; Citadels of the south; Princely residences; The palaces today.
Glossary of Indian terms, p.226. Bibliography, p.227–29. Index, p.229–32.

J502 Mumtaz, Kamil Khan. Architecture in Pakistan. Singapore, Concept Media, 1985. 206p. il., maps, plans.
"An overview from the earliest evidence of building activities to modern times."—*Pref.*
Contents: (1) Early communities; (2) Graeco-Indian; (3) Early Muslim; (4) Imperial Mughals; (5) The provinces; (6) British colonial; (7) Vernacular tradition; (8) Architecture after independence; Postscript: the Islamic debate.
Selected bibliography, p.198–99. Index, p.200–04. Glossary, p.205–06.

J503 Nagaraju, S. Buddhist architecture of western India, c. 250 B.C.– c. A.D. 300. With a foreword by M. N. Deshpande. Delhi, Agam Kala Prakashan, 1981 [i.e. 1980]. xxiv, 368, [59]p. il., map, plates.
"This work is primarily an attempt to reconstruct afresh the chronology and development of the 'Hinayana' phase of Buddhist rock-cut architecture of Western India."—*Pref.*
Contents: Part one: the background: (I) Introduction; (II) Geography and geology; (III) Historical background; Part two: aids to the reconstruction of chronology: (IV) Direct evidences for the reconstruction of chronology; (V) Palaeography; (VI) Architectural analysis; Part three: architectural development: (VII) Descriptive inventory and analysis of monuments and architectural development in different centres; (VIII) Summary and conclusions; Appendix.
Bibliography, p[347]–55. Index, p.[357]–68.

J504 Nath, R. History of Mughal architecture. New Delhi, Abhinav, 1982– . (3)v. il. (part col.), maps.

Vol.2 has imprint, Atlantic Highlands, N.J., Humanities Pr. To be complete in 5 vols.

Monumental history.

Contents: (1) [without special title]; (2) Akbar, 1556–1605 A.D.: the age of personality architecture; (3) The transitional phase of colour and design: Jehangir, 1605–1627 A.D.

Index in each vol.

J505 ______. History of Sultanate architecture. New Delhi, Abhinav Publications, 1978. xxvi, 121p. il., plates.

"This is [a] study of [the] evolution of the Sultanate Architecture . . . , its Techniques, Norms and Concepts . . . largely a descriptive catalogue of the monuments without reference to the historical background."—*Pref.*

List of abbreviations, p.[xiii]–xiv. Chronological tables (dynasty-wise), p.[xv]–xvi. List of monuments and sites (included in this study), p.[xvii]–xviii. Short bibliography, p.[115]–18. Index, p.[119]–21.

J506 ______. Mosque architecture: from Medina to Hindustan, 622–1654 A.D. Jaipur, Historical Research Documentation Programme, 1994. 104p. il.

"This is a simple and brief study of the architecture of 'mosque' as it evolved, through the ages."—*Pref.*

Abbreviations, p.[iii].

J507 The Penguin guide to the monuments of India. N.Y., Viking, 1989. 2v. il. (part col.)

Two excellent volumes, "intended as comprehensive handbooks to all the major monuments and sites."—*Pref.*

Contents: (1) Michell, George. Hindu, Buddhist, and Jain; (2) Davies, Philip. Islamic, Rajput, European.

Bibliography, v.2, p.599–600.

J508 Pereira, Jose. Elements of Indian architecture. Delhi, Motilal Banarsidass, 1987. 107p. il.

Studies the evolution of the Indian orders.

Contents: (1) The constituents of the Indian orders; (2) The orders of Indian architecture; (3) The evolution of the orders under Persian impact; (4) Hellenic civilization and India and its main cultural zones; (5) The evolution of the orders under the Hellenic impact; Postscript; Epilogue; Appendix: definitions of the five orders.

Notes, p.49–54. Index, p.105–07.

J509 Soundara Rajan, K.V. Cave temples of the Deccan. New Delhi, Archaeological Survey of India, 1981. xvi, 349p. il., plans, 145p. of plates.

"A survey of the whole series of the Brahmanical Cave Temples in the Deccan, carried out by the author on behalf of the Archaeological Survey of India . . . between 1964 and 1968."—*Pref.* An exhaustive survey covering the 6th to the 10th century A.D.

Select bibliography, p.331. Glossary of technical terms, p.332–38. Index, p.339–49.

J510 Srinivasan, P. R. The Indian temple, art and architecture. Mysore, Prasaranga, Univ. of Mysore, 1982. viii, 209, [1]p. il., plates.

By the former Chief Epigraphist to the Indian government.

Index, p.[201]–09. Select bibliography, p.[210].

J511 The Stupa: its religious, historical and architectural significance. Ed. by Anna Libera Dallapiccola in collab. with Stephanie Zingel-Avé Lallemant. Wiesbaden, Steiner, 1980. vii, 359p. il., plates. (Beiträge zur Südasienforschung, Bd. 55)

Proceedings of a wide-ranging seminar, South Asia Institute, University of Heidelberg (1978), devoted to the Buddhist stupa and its diffusion throughout India, Nepal, Tibet, and Southeast Asia.

Notes at ends of papers. Index of the works cited, p.329–43. Index of geographical names, persons, gods and monuments, p.344–51. List of photographs, p.352–59.

J512 Tadgell, Christopher. The history of architecture in India: from the dawn of civilization to the end of the Raj. London, Architecture, Design, and Technology Press, 1990. ix, 336p. il. (part col.)

An "introductory synthesis drawing together all the strands of India's architectural history in one volume, stressing continuity."—*Foreword.* From the 4th century B.C. to the 20th century.

Glossary, p.301–04. Bibliography and notes, p.305–28. Index, p.329–36.

J513 Tillotson, G. H. R. The Rajput palaces: the development of an architectural style, 1450–1750. New Haven, Yale Univ. Pr., 1987. vii, 224p.il. (part col.)

"The Rajput palaces are the surviving representatives of a now vanished civilization," built by the Rajput maharajas in their former state capitals, and "have by and large escaped serious study."—*Foreword.*

Contents: (1) General introduction; (2) Rajput and Mughal; (3) Chitor: in medias res; (4) Gwalior: the transformation of sources; (5) Orchha and Datia: experiments in symmetrical planning; (6) Amber and Udaipur: the developed theme; (7) Jaisalmer, Bikaner and Jodhpur: the desert; (8) Dungarpur, Bundi and Kota: the hills; (9) Jaipur city and palace: the call to order; (10) Dig and Bharatpur: Rajput mannerism; (11) Postscript: (1) Lesser and later palaces: developments after 1750; (2) The Rajput achievement.

Glossary, p.207–08. Notes, p.209–15. Bibliography, p.216–20. Index, p.221–24.

J514 ______. The tradition of Indian architecture: continuity, controversy and change since 1850. New Haven, Yale Univ. Pr., 1989. vii, 166p. il.

"A study of the changes in India's architectural tradition and in Indian taste that occurred in response to the influence of British architecture in India and the policies of British imperial rule."—*Pref.*

Notes, p.148–54. Bibliography, p.155–59. Index, p.160–66.

Japan

J515 Bognár, Botond. The new Japanese architecture. [Introd. by John Morris Dixon. Essays by Hajime Yatsuka and Lynne Breslin.] N.Y., Rizzoli, 1990. 222p. il. (part col.)

Presents a broad spectrum of important projects built during the 1980s, all of which reflect urban and cultural conditions in Japan.

Includes bibliographical references.

J516 Futagawa, Yukio, ed. Traditional Japanese houses. Text by Teiji Itoh. Trans. by Richard L. Gage. N.Y., Rizzoli, 1983. 356p. il. (part col.), map.

Trans. of Nihon no minka. Tokyo, Bijutsu Shuppansha, 1962.

Examines through superb photographs the traditional forms for Japanese houses. Beginning with the "minka" or folk house, residential buildings used by farmers, fishermen, merchants, tradesmen, and craftsmen built between 1185 and 1867, and continuing through houses built in the 19th and 20th centuries.

J517 A guide to Japanese architecture. [Tokyo], Shinkenchikusha (Distr. by The Japan Architect, [1984]). 251p. il., maps.

1st ed., 1971.

A photographic guide to the notable modern buildings and the famous architectural monuments in Japan. Organized geographically, entries include a miniature photograph along with building's name and location, architect, building area, floor area, and bibliographic citation.

Index by architecture, p.226–39. Index by architects, p.240–50.

J518 Kawashima, Chuji. Minka: traditional houses of rural Japan. Trans. by Lynne F. Riggs. N.Y., Kodansha, [1986]. 260p. il., maps.

Trans. and condensation of the 3-vol. set, Horobiyuku minka. Tokyo, Shufu to Seikatsusha, 1973.

Describes the traditional rural Japanese houses and the diverse styles which reflect the various climates and landscapes. Abundantly illustrated not only with photographs but also with plans and diagrams to demonstrate the details of structure and layout.

Contents: (1) Basic features; (2) Structure; (3) Styles.

Glossary, p.253–56. Index, p.257–60.

J519 Kidder, J. Edward. Japanese temples: sculpture, paintings, gardens and architecture. Photos by Tatsuzo Sato . . . [et al.] N.Y., Abrams, [1964]. 554p il. (part col.), maps, plans.

A substantial volume which combines analysis with numerous photographs. Begins in 593, when a great era of Buddhist construction began leading to a "long series of temples that have been the glory of Japanese architecture and the nucleus of Japanese religion and philosophy."—*p.13.*

Bibliography, p.549–54.

J520 Kurata, Bunsaku. Horyu-ji: Temple of the exalted law: early Buddhist art from Japan. Trans. by W. Chie Ishibashi. [N.Y.], Japan Society, [1981?]. 122, 44p. il. (part col.)

Catalog of the exhibition, Japan House Gallery (1981).

Documents the Buddhist images and treasures preserved at Horyuji, the temple founded in 607, and the usual starting point for anyone wishing to study Japanese art. The catalog also commemorated the 75th anniversary of the Japan Society and includes a 44p. supplement on Japanese art exhibitions in the U.S., 1893–1981.

Bibliography, p.115–17.

J521 Nishi, Kazuo, and Hozumi, Kazuo. What is Japanese architecture? Trans., adapted, and with an introd. by H. Mack Horton. N.Y., Kodansha, 1985. 144p. il.

Trans. of Nihon kenchiku no katachi. [Tokyo?], Shokokusha Pub. Co., [198?]

Introduces the forms, traditions, and monuments of Japanese architecture through chapters on worship, daily life, battle, and entertainment. Offers an overview of Japan's traditional building types to the end of the Edo period and a basic explanation of construction methods and terminology. Includes a list of addresses of "Sites mentioned in the text" and "Museums and other facilities of architectural interest" for travelers.

Bibliography, p.140–42.

Southeast Asia

J522 Aasen, Clarence. Architecture of Siam: a cultural history interpretation. N.Y., Oxford Univ. Pr., 1998. xix, 291p. il. (part col.)

Focuses on the "cultural and social functions of architecture . . . particularly in relation to groups that had confronted cultural and geographic displacements."—*Pref. and ackn.*

Contents: (1) Introduction; (2) Context and early cultural conjunctions, c.6000 BC–AD 500; (3) Constructing the local, c.AD 300–1300; (4) The essential Tai: transnational ethnic architecture, c.AD 500–1558; (5) The Ayuthayan kingdom: from state to empire, 1350–1767; (6) Architecture of modernism and nationalism, 1767–1932; (7) Outside the celestial domain: Chinese architecture in Siam; (8) Foreigners at the Siamese court; (9) Architecture of colonization, migration, and escape; (10) Architecture at the convergence of cultural differences.

Glossary, p.245–52. Bibliography, p.253–75. Index, p.276–91.

J523 Ancient capitals of Thailand. [By] Elizabeth Moore, Philip Stott, Suriyavudh Sukhasvasti. Photography by Michael Freeman. London, Thames and Hudson, 1996. 365p. il. (part col.), col. map.

"Combines descriptions of the geography, history, industrial base and art of these ancient sites with many superb photographs."—*Foreword.*

Contents: (1) Introduction: (2) The twin cities: Sukhothai and Si Satchanalai; (3) Sukhothai: the capital city; (4) Si Satchanalai: the city of the deputy king; (5) Kamphaeng Phet: strategic outpost for two kingdoms; (6) Phitsanulok: city of Phra Buddha Chinarat; (7) Ayutthaya: the golden city.

Glossary, p.354–56. Bibliography, p.357. Index, p.358–65.

J524 Angkor: cities and temples. [By] Claude Jacques. Photographs by Michael Freeman. [Trans., Tom White.] London, Thames and Hudson, 1997. 319p. col. il., maps, plans.
Trans. of Angkor: vision de palais divins. Paris, Éd. Hermé, 1997.
Beautifully produced overview of the history of the site and its successive temples.
Contents: (1) Khmer civilization; (2) The pre-Angkor period; (3) The first Angkor; (4) Moving the capital; (5) Angkor in the 11th century; (6) Suryavarman II and Angkor Wat; (7) Angkor Thom; (8) The 13th century and after.
Chronology, p.304–09. Glossary, p.310–13. Bibliography, p.314–15. Index, p.316–19.

J525 Chihara, Daigoro. Hindu-Buddhist architecture in Southeast Asia. Trans. by Rolf W. Giebel. N.Y., Brill, 1996. 278p. il. (Studies in Asian art and archaeology, 19).
The product of nearly 50 years of research.
Contents: Part one: The development of Hindu-Buddhist architecture; Part two: Legacies of the period of early Indianization; Part three: The golden age of Hindu-Buddhist architecture; Part four: Hindu-Buddhist architecture during the period of indigenization; Concluding remarks.
References, p.262–65. Index, p.267–78.

J526 Dawson, Barry, and Gillow, Jo. The traditional architecture of Indonesia. London, Thames and Hudson, 1994. 192p. il. (part col.), map.
Introductory survey.
Contents: (1) Materials and construction; (2) Sumatra, island of gold; (3) Java, Bali and Lombok, the teeming heartland; (4) Borneo and Sulawesi, home of tribes and ancestors; (5) The outer islands.
Glossary, p.186. Bibliography, p.188–89. Index, p.190–92.

J527 Naengnoi Suksri, M. R. Palaces of Bangkok: royal residences of the Chakri Dynasty. With photographs by Michael Freeman. London, Thames and Hudson, 1996. 368p. col. il.
"Covers the last 150 years of the absolute monarchy of Siam."—*Pref.*
Beautifully produced historical survey of the palaces.
Glossary, p.363. Bibliography, p.364. Index, p.365–68.

J528 Palaces of the gods: Khmer art and architecture in Thailand. [By] Smitthi Siribhadra, Elizabeth Moore. Photography, Michael Freeman. London, Thames and Hudson, 1997. 352p. il. (chiefly col.), col. maps.
Beautifully produced exploration of the religious significance of the Khmer temple complex.
Contents: (1) The Khmer civilisation; (2) The art of the Khmer; (3) The temples.
Itineraries, p.323–27. Plans of the temples, p.328–38. Notes on photography, p.339. Glossary, p.340–43. Bibliography, p.344. Index, p.345–49.

J529 Pichard, Pierre. Inventory of monuments at Pagan = Inventaire des monuments, Pagan. Paris, Unesco; Gartmore, Scotland, Kiscadale, 1992– . (6)v. il., maps, plans.
Chiefly in English, some text in French and Burmese.
"Comprehensive inventory of architectural riches on the site . . . richly illustrated description of the Pagan monuments."—*Pref.* To be complete in 9v.
Contents: (1) Monuments 1–255; (2) Monuments 256–552; (3) Monuments 553–818; (4) Monuments 819–1136; (5) Monuments 1137–1439; (6) Monuments 1440–1736.
Conventions and terminology, v.1, p.[29]–57. Each vol. has indexes.

J530 Riboud, Marc. Angkor: the serenity of Buddhism. Introd. by Jean Lacouture. With essays by Jean Boisselier and Marc Riboud. Photograph captions by Madeleine Giteau. [Trans. from the French by Ruth Sharman.] N.Y., Thames and Hudson, 1993. 159p. chiefly il.
Trans. of Angkor, sérénite bouddhique. Paris, Imprim. nationale éditions, 1992.
Consists largely of excellent black-and-white photographs.
Contents: A suspended tragedy, by Jean Lacouture; A Buddhist presence amidst the gods, by Jean Boisselier; Serenity, sensuality, by Marc Riboud; Captions to the photographs, by Madeleine Giteau (p.147–56); Afterword.

J531 Sumet Jumsai. Naga: cultural origins in Siam and the West Pacific. With contrib. by R. Buckminster Fuller. N.Y., Oxford Univ. Pr., 1988. xvi, 183p. il. (part col.), plates.
Seeks to elucidate abiding patterns in the culture and especially the built environment of Southeast Asia.
Contents: (1) Naga and rites; (2) Water-based civilization; (3) Amphibious architecture; (4) Land-based architecture; (5) Water towns; Epilogue.
Glossary, p.175–78. Select bibliography: p.179–81. Index, p.182–83.

AFRICA, OCEANIA, THE AMERICAS

Africa

J532 Blier, Suzanne Preston. The anatomy of architecture: ontology and metaphor in Batammaliba architectural expression. xx, 314p. 85 il., map. (RES monographs in anthropology and aesthetics)
Written by an eminent scholar, this book is about the meaning of architecture.
Contents: (1) Imagines Mundi: narrative, ritual, and architectural exemplars of cosmogony; (2) Architectural archetypes: reflections on housing in "Paradise"; (3) House temples: architecture for the gods; (4) Houses are human: architectural self-images; (5) At home: the complementarity of house, family, and tomb; (6) The power of architecture: politics, protections, and jurisprudence in house design and use; (7) "The Dance of Drums": notes on the architecture

and staging of funeral performances; Conclusions, architectural exegesis: on building ontology, metaphor, and multiplexity.

Bibliography, p.297–302. List of principal people interviewed, p.302–3. Index, p.305–14.

J533 Denyer, Susan. African traditional architecture: an historical and geographical perspective. Line drawings by Susan Denyer. Maps by Peter McClure. N.Y., Africana Pub., [1978]. xiv, 210p. 329il. maps.

A standard survey which illustrates hundreds of examples of architectural and building styles.

Contents: (1) Introduction; (2) Rural settlements; (3) States and towns; (4) Sacred, ceremonial and community buildings; (5) Defence; (6) The building process; (7) Decoration; (8) A taxonomy of house forms; (9) The distribution of styles; (10) The impact of modernization.

General bibliography, p.202–04. Index, p.205–10.

J534 Dmochowski, Zbigniew R. An introduction to Nigerian traditional architecture. [London], Ethnographica in assoc. with the National Commission for Museums and Monuments [Nigeria], 1990. 3v.

As the foundation for future studies of Nigerian architecture, this monumental survey revolves around three major cultural groups (Hausa, Yoruba, and Igbo) but also includes many other ethnic groups. The documentation consists of photographs and architectural drawings.

Contents: (1) Northern Nigeria; (2) South-West and Central Nigeria; (3) South-Eastern Nigeria: the Igbo-speaking people.

J535 Elleh, Nnamdi. African architecture: evolution and transformation. N.Y., McGraw-Hill, [1997]. 382p. il. (part col.), maps.

Lavishly illustrated with field and museum photographs, and drawings and diagrams. A comprehensive study of African architecture from antiquity to the the 20th century.

Contents: (1) Traditional African architecture; (2) Western architecture in Africa; (3) Islamic architecture in Africa; (4) The architecture of the kingdom of Morocco; (5) The architecture of Algeria, Tunisia, and Libya; (6) The architecture of Egypt; (7) Architecture of Djibouti, Ethiopia, Kenya, Somalia, and the Republic of Sudan; (8) The architecture of Burundi, Rwandi, Tanzania, and Uganda; (9) Architecture of the Congo Basin: Central African countries; (10) Architecture of Angola, Malawi, Mozambique, Madagascar, Mauritius, and Seychelles; (11) Architecture of Botswana, Namibia, Republic of Zambia, and Zimbabwe; (12) The architecture of the Republic of South Africa; (13) The architecture of Mauritania, Mali, Niger, and Chad; (14) The architecture of Gambia, Guinea Bissau, Guinea, and Senegal; (15) The architecture of Sierra Leone, Liberia, Cote d'Ivoire, and Burkina Fasso; (16) The architecture of Ghana, Benin Republic, Cameroon, Togo, Lao Tome; (17) The architecture of Nigeria; (18) Urbanism in Africa; (19) Urbanization in Africa; (20) Modern architecture: new towns as national development strategy for Africa. (21) Conclusion: developing the triple heritage architecture.

Glossary, p.355–58. Chronology, p.359–64. References, p.365–71. Index, p.373–82.

J536 Prussin, Labelle. African nomadic architecture: pace, place, and gender. With contrib. by Amina Adan . . . [et al.] [Foreword by Robert Farris Thompson.] Washington, Smithsonian Institution Pr., [1995]. xxii, 245p. il. 24 col. plates, maps.

Extensively illustrated with field photographs complemented by scholarly essays, this book is "surely one of the classics of twentieth-century architectural history."—*Foreword.*

Contents: (1) The tent in African history; (2) Environment and space; (3) The creative process; (4) The Hassaniya-speaking nomads: Tekna, Trarza, and Brakna, by Peter A. Andrews and excerpts from Odette Du Puigaudeau in translation; (5) The Tuareg: Kel Ahaggar and Kel Ferwan, based on excerpts from Johannes Nicolaisen and excerpts from Dominique Casajus in translation; (6) The Tubu: nomads in the Eastern Sahara; (7) Mahria tents: the woman's domain, by Uta Holter; (8) Rendille habitation, by Anders Grum; (9) Handicrafts of the Somali nomadic women, by Arlene Fullerton and Amina Adan; (10) The nomadic aesthetic.

Bibliography, p.223–32. Index, p.237–45.

J537 ______. Hatumere: Islamic design in West Africa. Berkeley, Univ. of California Pr., 1986. xxiii, 306p. il., col. plates, maps.

A landmark study. The Islamic design and concept of hatumere refers to amulets written in the form of squares and is emblematic of the built environment of the West African savanna.

Contents: (1) Introduction; (2) The physical environment; (3) The behavioral environment; (4) The conceptual environment; (5) The medieval age: West African empires; (6) The Manding diaspora: trade networks, integration, and urbanization; (7) The Fulbe diaspora: politics and sedentarization; (8) The Asante confederacy: Islam in the rain forest.

Bibliography, p.281–92. Index, p.295–306.

The Americas

J538 Gasparini, Graziano, and Margolies, Luise. Inca architecture. Trans. by Patricia J. Lyon. Bloomington, Indiana Univ. Pr., 1980. xv, 350p. il., map.

Trans. of Arquitectura Inka. Caracas, Centro de Investigaciones Históricas y Estéticas, Universidad Central de Venezuela, 1977.

Analysis of state and domestic architecture and construction technology in pre-contact Inca civilization. Includes photographs and line drawings. "A significant compilation, most of it based on the authors' fieldwork. . . . The photographs are superb."—*Annotation* for Arquitectura Inka in Handbook of Latin American studies, v.42, 1980.

Contents: (1) Technical and formal antecedents; (2) Urban settlements; (3) Domestic architecture; (4) The architecture of power; (5) Technical and aesthetic problems.

Notes, p.333–36. References, p.337–41. Glossary, p.342–43. Index, p.345–50.

J539 Marquina, Ignacio. Arquitectura prehispanica. [Facsimil de la 2. ed.] México, D.F., Instituto Nacional de Antropología e Historia, 1981. 2v. il., col. plates (part folded), maps, plans, tables. (Memorias del I.N.A.H., 1)

Facsimile reprint of GLAH 1:J365. Still the finest single source for the subject. Copiously illustrated with photographs and line drawings of architectural elements. The mediocre photographs of the original are poorly reproduced in the facsimile.

Index, v.2, p.[1006]–42.

J540 Morgan, William N. Ancient architecture of the Southwest. Austin, Univ. of Texas Pr., 1994. xx, 301p. il., plates, maps, plans.

"The volume analyzes and compares 132 ancient sites suggesting the breadth and variety of our architectural legacy in the Southwest."—*Introd.* Includes schematic plans of settlement dwellings.

Contents: Early settlement to A.D. 900; Regional developments, 900 to 1140; Unrest and adjustment, 1140–1300; Migration and consolidation, 1300 to 1540; Historic pueblos, 1540 to present.

Glossary, p.267–69; Pronouncing guide, p.271–72. Bibliography, p.273–86. Index, p.287–301.

J541 Nabokov, Peter, and Easton, Robert. Native American architecture. N.Y., Oxford Univ. Pr., 1989. 431p. il. (part col.), maps, plans.

"The combination of anecdotal, visual, and research material creates a thorough picture of major tribes and their architecture in nine regions of North America."—*Review*, American Indian culture and research journal, v.14, 1990, p.143.

Contents: (1) Wigwam and longhouse: Northeast and Great Lakes; (2) Mound, town and chickee: Southeast; (3) Earthlodge, grass house, and tipi: Great Plains; (4) Pit house and extended tipi: Plateau; (5) Winter house, iglu, and tent: Arctic; (6) Plank house: Northwest; (7) Wood, earth, and fiber: California; (8) Hogan, ki, and ramada: Southwest I; (9) Pueblo: Southwest II.

Annotated bibliography, p.[411]–20. Glossary, p.425. Index, p.426–31.

J542 Paternosto, César A. The stone and the thread: Andean roots of abstract art. Trans. by Esther Allen. Austin, Univ. of Texas Pr., 1996. xxi, 272p. il., map.

Trans. of: Piedra abstracta: la escultura inca, una visión contemporanea. Mexico, Buenos Aires, Fondo de Cultura Económica, 1989.

"As I will emphasize during the course of my exposition, it was weaving—the manipulation of thread—that became the structural matrix not only of the geometric designs but of the predominant orthogonal iconography of Andean arts. . . . I also hope to demonstrate how the working of the stone—in all its abstract stoniness—and the thread—unfolding its implicit geometric models—has created structural paradigms that still resonate in the art of the Americas."—*Introd.*

Notes, p.237–51. Works cited, p.253–62. Index, p.263–72.

J543 Scully, Vincent. Pueblo: mountain, village, dance. 2d ed. Chicago, Univ. of Chicago Pr., 1989. xvi, 412p. il.

See GLAH 1:J366 for original ed. Unchanged except for new pref. and 11p. "Postscript, 1988."

J544 Yampolsky, Mariana. The traditional architecture of Mexico. Text by Chloe Sayer. N.Y., Thames and Hudson, 1993. 208p. il. (part col.)

Accessible introduction.

Contents: (1) Using colour; (2) Rural houses; (3) Public spaces; (4) The hacienda; (5) Town residences; (6) The uncommon touch.

Glossary, p.200–02. Bibliography, p.202–05. Index, p.205–08.

LANDSCAPE DESIGN

Bibliography

J545 Garden literature: an index to periodical articles and book reviews, v.1, no.1– , Jan.–Mar. 1992– . Boston, Garden Literature Pr., 1992– . Two issues yearly.

Originally quarterly (1992–1993) with fourth quarter issue being the annual cumulation. Since 1994 the first issue is the "Sprout Issue," providing indexing to 10 major journals for the first half of the year. The second issue completely indexes 100 journals for the year.

J546 Making educated decisions: a landscape preservation bibliography. Ed. by Charles A. Birnbaum and Cheryl Wagner. Jean S. Jones, research assistant. Washington, D.C., National Park Service, Cultural Resources, Preservation Assistance Division, Historic Landscape Initiative, 1994. v, 160p. il.

"Prepared to guide the user in obtaining practical guidance to make educated decisions when researching, planning, managing, and undertaking project work in cultural landscape resources."—*Introd.* Contains more than 500 annotated citations for widely available English language publications with a predominant focus on landscape preservation philosophy, research, preservation planning, practice, treatment, management and maintenance, each evaluated for compatibility with the Secretary of the Interior's standards. Anticipated to be updated periodically.

Dictionaries and Encyclopedias

J547 The Oxford companion to gardens. Sir Geoffrey Jellicoe and Susan Jellicoe, consultant eds. Patrick Goode and Michael Lancaster, executive eds. N.Y., Oxford Univ. Pr., 1986. xiv, 635p. il., plans.

An indispensable work. "The first comprehensive reference work to deal with the art of garden design on a world-wide scale from the earliest records of civilization to the present day . . . primarily concerned with locating and describing gardens of all kinds . . . it touches upon influences such as geography, climate, and ethnic and social factors that have conditioned gardens of all ages. It includes brief biographies of the principal designers and of those patrons, such as the Medici family, who have often determined the course of landscape history."—*Pref.* Related entries are cross-referenced.

Selective bibliography is thematically arranged, p.[629]–35.

Histories and Handbooks

General Works

J548 Clifford, Derek. A history of garden design. Rev. ed. N.Y., Praeger, [1966]. 252p. il.

1st ed., Chatham, W., and Mackay, J. 1963.

"A synthetic view of the different ways in which men made gardens and an attempt to explore the reasons why they made them as they did."—*Pref.*

Contents: (1) Pliny and the Renaissance garden; (2) Islam and the gardens of Spain; (3) France; (4) The garden of Euphues; (5) The garden of suggestion; (6) The great revolution of taste; (7) Reassessment; (8) Humphry Repton; (9) The search for a style; (10) Tradition and the Americas; (11) The triumph of the wild improvers.

Appendixes of gardens by the most famous designers in history, p.222–38. Select bibliography, p.239–44. Index, p.245–52.

J549 Dumbarton Oaks colloquium on the history of landscape architecture. Washington, D.C., Dumbarton Oaks, 1971– . (18)v. il.

See GLAH 1:R24 for previous vols. A few of these titles are cited individually elsewhere in this chapter.

Selective contents: (4) MacDougall, Elisabeth B., and Ettinghausen, Richard, eds. The Islamic garden (1976); (5) MacDougall, Elisabeth B., ed. Fons sapientiae: Renaissance garden fountains (1977); (6) MacDougall, Elisabeth B., ed. John Claudius Loudon and the early nineteenth century in Great Britain (1980); (7) MacDougall, Elisabeth B., and Jashemski, Wilhelmina, eds. Ancient Roman gardens (1981); (8) McGuire, Diane Kostial, and Fern, Lois, eds. Beatrix Jones Farrand (1872–1959): fifty years of American landscape architecture (1982); (9) MacDougall, Elisabeth B., ed. Medieval gardens, (1986); (10) MacDougall, Elisabeth, B., ed. Ancient Roman villa gardens (1987); (11) MacDougall, Elisabeth B., ed. Nature's gardener (1989); (12) Hunt, John Dixon, ed. The Dutch garden in the seventeenth century, (1990); (13) Hunt, John Dixon, ed. Garden history: issues, approaches, methods, (1992); (14) Hunt, John Dixon, and Wolschke-Bulmahn, Joachim, eds. The vernacular garden, (1990); (15) O'Malley, Therese, and Treib, Marc, eds. Regional garden design in the United States, (1995); (16) Westcoat, James L., and Wolschke-Bulmahn, Joachim, eds. Mughal gardens: sources, places, representations, and prospects (1996); (17) O'Malley, Therese, and Wolschke-Bulmahn, Joachim, eds. John Evelyn's "Elysium Britannicum" and European gardening, (1998); (18) Wolschke-Bulmahn, Joachim, ed. Nature and ideology: natural garden design in the twentieth century, (1997).

J550 Jellicoe, Geoffrey, and Jellicoe, Susan. The landscape of man: shaping the environment from prehistory to the present day. 3d ed. N.Y., Thames and Hudson, 1995. 408p. il., maps, plans.

1st ed., N.Y., Viking, 1975; 2d rev. ed., N.Y., Thames and Hudson, 1987.

"This study is a concise global view of the designed landscape past and present, inclusive of all environment, from gardens to urban and regional landscape. Town-planning is included only when it is also landscape-planning. It is written objectively, as though the planet were seen from outer space, in which both hemispheres were equated. Part I runs from prehistory to AD 1700, a convenient date to make the change from the old world to the new, coinciding by chance with the death of the famous French landscape architect, André Le Nôtre; Part II runs from that date to the present day."—*Introd.* Extensively illustrated.

Bibliography, p.402–04. Index of people and places, p.405–08.

J551 Laurie, Michael. An introduction to landscape architecture. 2d ed. N.Y., Elsevier, 1986. xii, 248p. il.

1st ed. 1975.

A general overview of the field of landscape architecture and its component disciplines.

Bibliography, p.235–40.

J552 Newton, Norman T. Design on the land: the development of landscape architecture. Cambridge, Harvard Univ. Pr., 1971. xxiv, 714p., il., maps, plans.

Standard, scholarly history of the development of landscape architecture as an art and as a profession, from Egyptian temples through 20th-century urban open-space systems.

Bibliography, p.677–89. Index, p.703–14.

J553 Thacker, Christopher. The history of gardens. Berkeley, Univ. of California Pr., 1979. 288p. il.

A concise overview.

Contents: (1) The beginnings; (2) Persian and Islamic gardens; (3) Chinese gardens; (4) Japanese gardens; (5) Medieval gardens; (6) The Renaissance garden in Italy; (7) Jokes and puzzles; (8) The Renaissance garden in France and England; (9) The formal French garden; (10) Louis XIV and Versailles; (11) The development of the formal garden in Europe; (12) Leaping the fence; (13) The perfectly Arcadian farm; (14) The total landscape; (15) Gardens in the nineteenth century; (16) The modern garden.

Bibliography, p.281–84. Index, p.285–88

SEE ALSO: Gothein, M.L. A history of garden art (GLAH 1:J38).

Ancient—Medieval

J554 MacDougall, Elisabeth B., ed. Medieval gardens. Washington, D.C., Dumbarton Oaks, 1986. 278p. il., plates. (Dumbarton Oaks colloquium on the history of landscape architecture, 9)

Thirteen essays reconstruct medieval gardens through literary and visual sources and through documents and information on plants. Covers a vast chronological and geographical field, although northern Europe receives the most attention. Essays include bibliographical references. Some contain their own appendixes and bibliographies.

J555 Stokstad, Marilyn and Stannard, Jerry. Gardens of the Middle Ages. Lawrence, [Kan.], Spencer Museum of Art, Univ. of Kansas, 1983. 224p. il., plates (part col.).

Catalog of the exhibition, Spencer Museum of Art, Lawrence (1983). "We have looked on the garden as a work of art itself and, although the actual gardens are lost, we have tried to express the values and goals of the medieval patrons and artists."—*Pref.* Two essays, "Gardens in medieval art" and "Medieval gardens and their plants" are followed by color plates and catalogue entries.

Includes bibliographical references.

Islamic

J556 Brookes, John. Gardens of paradise: the history and design of the great Islamic gardens. N.Y., New Amsterdam, 1987. 240p. il. (part col.), map.

Contents: (1) The concept of the paradise garden; (2) Garden origins; (3) Muslim Spain; (4) Persia; (5) Mughal India; (6) North Africa, Egypt, Sicily and the Ottoman Empire; (7) Water and plants in the Islamic landscape; (8) The Islamic garden today and its future; (9) Notes on designing a garden in the Middle East.

Chronology of Islamic gardens, p.[231–34]. Select bibliography, p.235–36. Index, p.237–40.

J557 MacDougall, Elisabeth B., and Ettinghausen, Richard, eds. The Islamic garden. Washington, D.C., Dumbarton Oaks, 1976. 135p. il., plates. (Dumbarton Oaks colloquium on the history of landscape architecture, 4)

Five essays address Islamic gardens in Asia, Europe, and Africa from the 12th through the 19th centuries. Some essays contain appendixes.

Includes bibliographical references.

J558 Wilber, Donald N. Persian gardens and garden pavilions. 2d ed. Washington, D.C., Dumbarton Oaks, 1979. xiv, 104p. il., plates.

1st ed., Rutland, C. E. Tuttle, 1962; 2d ed. unchanged excepting the expanded bibliography, p.93–96. Plates follow text.

Contents: (1) Persian gardens and paradise; (2) Timurid gardens: from Tamerlane to Babur; (3) Imperial Isfahan in the Safavid Period; (4) Gardens along the Caspian: Safavid and later; (5) The royal gardens at Tehran; (6) Shiraz: home of gardens and poets; (7) Gardens north and south.

Renaissance—Modern

J559 Chadwick, George F. The park and the town: public landscape in the 19th and 20th centuries. N.Y., Praeger, 1966. 388p. il., plans.

Historical survey concerned with aesthetic and social implications of the development of public parks in western Europe and the United States.

Bibliography, p.[378]–83. Index, p.384–88.

J560 Cornish, Geoffrey S., and Whitten, Ronald E. The architects of golf: a survey of golf course design from its beginnings to the present, with an encyclopedic listing of golf course architects and their courses. Rev. and exp. ed. N.Y., HarperCollins, 1993. viii, 648p. il., ports.

Rev. ed. of The golf course, N.Y., Routledge Pr., 1981. The only book-length publication on the history of golf course design, an increasingly significant aspect of landscape design. Most useful for biographical information as it lacks plans. International in scope, but most heavily focused on American and British designers. After a history of design it offers profiles of course designers which document their work in detail, master list of golf courses cross-referenced to designers, glossary of terms, brief description of the evolution of course features, list of parallel developments in allied fields, list of course architects' associations, list of organizations and libraries.

Bibliography, p.635–40. Index, p.646–48.

J561 Laird, Mark. The formal garden: traditions of art and nature. N.Y., Thames and Hudson, 1992. 240p. il. (part col.), plans.

Survey which concentrates on the mainstream formal traditions of Italy, France, Germany, Holland, Great Britain, and the eastern United States, making the case that the differences between formal and natural gardens are often less clear than supposed. Excellent illustrations.

"Gazetteer of major formal gardens" offers description of gardens and information on public access, p.224–34. Glossary of planting terms, p.234. Bibliography, p.235–37. Index, p.239–40.

J562 Mosser, Monique, and Teyssot, Georges, eds. The architecture of Western gardens: a design history from the Renaissance to the present day. Cambridge, Mass., MIT Pr., 1991. 543p. il. (part col.)

Trans. of L'architettura dei giardini d'Occidente. Milano, Electa, 1990.

"This book is structured chronologically, but proceeds by a series of essays on specific subjects, intended not so much to provide the reader with any comprehensive catalogue of all the gardens laid out in the period under consideration as to demonstrate the wide range of research programmes currently being undertaken. . . . The aim of this book is . . . to provide an introduction to the architecture of the garden in Europe and the United States in recent times."—*Introd.* Heavily illustrated.

Contents: (1) The humanist garden: from allegory to Mannerism; (2) The straight line and the arabesque: from the Baroque garden to the classical park; (3) Picturesque, Arcadian, and sublime: the age of enlightenment; (4) The eclectic garden, and the town and city park; (5) Aspects of the contemporary garden: from the leisure park to artistic experimentation.

Bibliographical references appear at end of each essay. Index of people and places, p.532–43.

J563 Sirén, Osvald. China and gardens of Europe of the eighteenth century. N.Y., Ronald Pr., [1950]. xiv, 223p., 192p. of plates. il. (Repr.: Washington, D.C., Dumbarton Oaks, 1990.)

"This book . . . is still the most important, if also controversial, account of its subject, the widest and richest and best illustrated survey of what the French called in the late eighteenth century the jardin anglo-chinois."—*Introd.* Traces the general current of Chinese influence on the art of gardening in Europe, then describes its course in England, France, and Sweden. Given more recent disagreements with Sirén's views, readers today may find the fine plates more useful than the text.

Bibliography, p.215–19. Index, p.221–23.

J564 Treib, Marc, ed. Modern landscape architecture: a critical review. Cambridge, Mass., MIT Pr., 1993. 294p. il.

"This is the first book that deals exclusively with modernism and landscape architecture. It presents a history of the period (approximately 1920 to 1960), as well as some background so that the nonprofessional can understand the context of modernism, how it differed from its precedents and how it revolutionized design . . . gathers texts by landscape architects of the period . . . and by present day historians and critics evaluating the subject from the vantage point of time passed."—*Review*, Design book review, v.31, winter 1994, p.23.

Bibliographic notes follow chapters. Index, p.[290]–94.

Western Countries

Canada

J565 Baeyer, E. von. A preliminary bibliography for garden history in Canada. [Ottawa], National Historic Parks and Sites Branch, Parks Canada, Environment Canada, 1983. 24, 26p.

Limited to material on the history of designed (versus natural) gardens in Canada published before 1950, as well as contemporary literature on gardens existing before 1950. In addition to predictable topics such as garden ornaments, historic gardens, and periodicals, it includes the more unusual such as railway gardens, experimental farms, and northern gardens. A valuable substitute for the as-yet-unwritten comprehensive history of gardening in Canada.

France

J566 Imbert, Dorothée. The modernist garden in France. New Haven, Yale Univ. Pr., 1993. xv, 284p. il., plans.

The first book-length treatment of modernist landscape design in France from 1910 through the 1930s. Documents numerous private and public gardens no longer extant, including those of the 1925 Exposition Internationale des Arts Décoratifs et Industriels Modernes. Includes archival photographs and drawings made for this publication.

Contents: (1) Henri Duchène; Achille Duchène: a return to formalism; (2) J. C. N. Forestier: plants & planting; (3) Gardens at the Exposition; (4) Jardin régulier; jardin d'architecture; (5) André Vera; Paul Vera; Jean-Charles Moreux: modernity & tradition; (6) Pierre-Emile Legrain: garden design as applied art; (7) Gabriel Guévrékian: the modern paradise garden; (8) Le Corbusier: the landscape vs. the garden; (9) André Lurçat: the outdoor ensemble; (10) Epilogue.

Extensive endnotes, p.209–43. Comprehensive bibliography, p.247–63. Index, p.264–68.

J567 Wiebenson, Dora. The picturesque garden in France. Princeton, Princeton Univ. Pr., 1978. xviii, 137p. il., plates, maps.

The first book in English on this important 18th-century artistic manifestation. Possible origins of the picturesque garden in France are discussed along with French and English gardening theory, the various types of French picturesque gardens, and their relationship to urban planning.

Bibliography includes citations for specific gardens, p.[123]–32.

J568 Woodbridge, Kenneth. Princely gardens: the origins and development of the French formal style. London, Thames & Hudson, 1986. 320p. il.

"Surveys the history of French gardens from the Middle Ages through the early 20th century, focusing on the 16th and 17th centuries, on Italian influence, and on the development of what [Woodbridge] calls 'the formal style' . . . extremely useful as a reference text because its short and clearly marked subsections (together with a detailed index) allow the reader quickly to locate a particular theme or example."—*Review*, Journal of the Society of Architectural Historians, v.48, March 1989, p.90.

Notes to the text, p.292–99. Appendixes: A, "A list of plants used for ornamental purposes," p.300–05; B, "Four designs for figured gardens from the French version of Hypnerotomachia Poliphili," p.306; C, Chronology of French royalty and French and Italian garden construction, p.307. Glossary, p.308. Bibliography, p.309–14. Index, p.315–20.

Germany and Austria

J569 Hennebo, Dieter, and Hoffmann, Alfred. Geschichte der deutschen Gärtenkunst. Hamburg, Broschek, 1962–65. 3v. il., plans.

Indispensable scholarly work pub. in parts. No index.

Contents: (1) Gärten des Mittelalters (rev. ed. München, Artemis, 1987); (2) Der architektonische Gärten: Renaissance und Barock; (3) Der Landschaftsgärten.

Bibliographic notes at end of each vol.: v.1, p.187–96; v.2, p.401–31; v.3, p.295–303.

J570 Heyer, Hans-Rudolf. Historische Gärten der Schweiz: die Entwicklung von Mittelalter bis zur Gegenwart. Bern, Benteli, 1980. 272p. il. (part col.)

The first comprehensive, scholarly account of garden history in Switzerland. Well-illustrated, covering both public and private gardens from the Middle Ages to the present.

Literaturverzeichnis, p.268–70. Namen- und Ortsregister, p.271–72.

J571 Jellicoe, Geoffrey A. Baroque gardens of Austria. N.Y., Scribner's, 1993. 45p. il., map, plans.

Large-format history offers an introductory essay but relies largely on plates for documentation. Contains excellent plans of nine major gardens: Schloss Hellbrunn, Count Wallenstein's Garden, Belvedere Palace, Schwarzenberg Palace, Schonborn Palace, Schlosshof Palace, Mirabell Gardens, Abbey of St. Florian, and Schönbrunn Palace.

Bibliography, p.11. Chronological table of landscape developments in Italy, France and Austria, p.12.

Great Britain and Ireland

J572 Aldous, Tony, and Clouston, Brian. Landscape by design. London, Heinemann, 1979. xviii, 173p. il., plates, plans.

Written on the occasion of the 50th anniversary of the Institute of Landscape Architects, this book sketches the history of the landscape profession in the United Kingdom since 1929. The history is arranged by the type of client commissioning the work rather than the type of work itself, in the process discussing both private and public gardens, new towns, university campuses, government-owned forests, landscape as it relates to various transportation systems, industrial and corporate landscapes, the development of landscape education in the U.K., and British influence on landscape design in other countries. Sparsely illustrated.

Bibliography, p.160–64. Index, p.167–73.

J573 Coffin, David C. The English garden: meditation and memorial. Princeton, Princeton Univ. Pr., 1994. 304p. il.

The emphasis is on 17th- and 18th-century formal features and cultural responses to them. Explores the major built features of English gardens using manuscripts, letters, and diaries as well as better-known published works, many by women thereby correcting a long-standing misconception that women were not active in landscape design in the 17th and 18th century. The final chapter contains an annotated list of monuments and memorials.

Bibliographic notes, p.225–53. Index, p.255–70.

J574 Elliott, Brent. Victorian gardens. London, Batsford, 1986. 285p., plates, il.

"Especially good on the impact of inventions on Victorian gardening, the increasing professionalization of gardeners, advances in botany, the importance of colour effects, the growing interest in the history of gardening, and (not least) the gardens and gardeners to which and to whom William Robinson was indebted. . . . The most distinguished treatment of the subject."—*Review*, Journal of garden history, v.8, 1988, p.60–61.

Notes, p.[248]–68. Bibliography, p.[269]–71. Index, p.[274]–85.

J575 The English landscape garden. Ed. by John Dixon Hunt. N.Y., Garland, [1982]. 29v. il.

Important reprint series offering "examples of the important literature of the English landscape garden movement together with some earlier garden books."—*Series t.p.*

Contents: (1) Mountain, Dydymus (i.e., Thomas Hill).The gardeners labyrinth (London, 1594); (2) Markham, Gervase. The English husbandman (Books I and II) (London, 1613 and 1614); (3) Lawson, William. A new orchard and garden (London, 1618) bound with Marriott, John. Knots for gardens (London, 1625) bound with Austen, Ralph. A treatise of fruit-trees together with The spiritual use of an orchard (Oxford, 1653); (4) Caus, Isaac de. Wilton Garden (London, c1645) bound with Caus, Isaac de. New and rare inventions of water-works (London, 1659); (5) Worlidge, John. Systema Horti-culturae: or, The art of gardening (London, 1677); (6) de La Quintinie, Jean (trans. John Evelyn). The compleat gard'ner (London, 1693); (7) Nourse, Timothy. Campania Foelix (London, 1700); (8) Gentil, François (trans. George London and Henry Wise). The retir'd gard'ner (London, 1706; 2v.); (9) Laurence, John. Gardening improv'd (London, 1718); (10) Switzer, Stephen. Ichnographia Rustica: or, The nobleman, gentleman, and gardener's recreation (London, 1718; 3v.); (11) Langley, Batty. New principles of gardening (London, 1728); (12) Castell, Robert. The villas of the ancients illustrated (London, 1728); (13) Switzer, Stephen. An introduction to a general system of hydrostaticks and hydraulicks, philosophical and practical (London, 1729; 2v.); (14) Morris, Robert. An essay upon harmony as it relates chiefly to situation and building (London, 1739) bound with Trusler, John. Elements of modern gardening (London, 1784); (15) Serle, John. A plan of Mr. Pope's garden (London, 1745) bound with Gardens of Richmond, Kew, and environs (London, ?1730–1760); (16) The gardens at Stowe (London, 1732–1797); (17) Attiret, Jean Denis (trans. Joseph Spence). A particular account of the emperor of China's gardens near Pekin (London, 1752) bound with Shenstone, William. Unconnected thoughts on gardening and A description of the Leasowes (London, 1764) bound with Mason, George. An essay on design in gardening (London, 1768); (18) Walpole, Horace. The history of the modern taste in gardening (London, 1827) bound with Walpole, Horace. Journals of visits to country seats (Oxford, 1928); (19) Whately, Thomas. Observations on modern gardening (London, 1770); (20) Heely, Joseph. Letters on the beauties of Hagley, Envil, and the Leasowes (London, 1777); (21) Watts, William. The seats of the nobility and gentry in a collection of the most interesting and picturesque views (London, 1779); (22) Mason, William. The English garden (London, 1783); (23) Girardin, René Louis de (trans. Daniel Malthus). An essay on landscape (London, 1783) bound with A tour to Ermenonville (London, 1785); (24) Angus, William. The seats of nobility and gentry in Great Britain and Wales (London, 1787); (25) Mavor, William. New description of Blenheim (London, 1793); (26) Repton, Humphry. Fragments on the theory and practice of landscape gardening (London, 1816); (27) Johnson, George J. A history of English gardening, chronological, biographical, literary, and critical (London, 1829); (28) Loudon, J. C. An encyclopaedia of gardening (London, 1835;

2v.); (29) Loudon, J. C. The suburban gardener, and villa companion (London, 1838).

J576 Hunt, John Dixon. Garden and grove: the Italian Renaissance garden in the English imagination, 1600–1750. Princeton, Princeton Univ. Pr., 1986. 269p. il.

Divided into two sections: (1) Italy: The garden of the world; (2) England: The world of the garden. Describes the English experience of Italian gardens in the 17th and early 18th centuries and then charts how the English imagination realized these Italian ideas and images on native soil during the same period. Chapters on Elizabethan and Jacobean gardens offer much new information.

Bibliography, p.223–59. Index, p.261–68.

J577 ______, and Willis, Peter, eds. The genius of the place: the English landscape garden, 1620–1820. N.Y., Harper & Row, 1975. xx, 390p. il., plans, ports.

"This anthology and commentary on the English landscape garden is intended both for the general reader and for students in the visual arts."—*Pref.* Texts are taken from the original editions or manuscripts and presented with a minimum of editorial interference. The work of 57 authors is arranged in four parts: (1) Prelude: the seventeenth century and the reign of Queen Anne; (2) The early landscape garden; (3) The progress of gardening; (4) Picturesque taste and the garden.

Bibliography, p.381–82. Index, p.383–90.

J578 Jacques, David. Georgian gardens: the reign of nature. London, Batsford, 1983. 240p. il. (part col.), plates.

Covering the period 1733 to 1825 and restricted to English and Welsh gardens, this documents the natural style, chinoiserie and gothic revival, the picturesque style, and Regency gardens. Contains extensive information on lesser-known designers and gardens.

Notes, p.[207]–17. Bibliography, p.[218]–22. Index of names, p.[223]–34. Place index, p.[235]–40.

J579 Malins, Edward Greenway, and Bowe, Patrick. Irish gardens and demesnes from 1830. N.Y., Rizzoli, 1980. 190p. il. (part col.), plates.

Straightforward history from J. C. Loudon's writings, through imported influences of French and Italian Renaissance gardens, William Robinson and Gertrude Jekyll's designs, the introduction of exotic sub-tropical plants, to modern gardens of significant size. Illustrated with period photographs, plans, and engravings.

Notes, p.173–82. Bibliography, p.183–84. Index, p.187–90.

J580 McLean, Teresa. Medieval English gardens. London, Collins, 1981. 298p. il., plates.

"This book is about English gardens in the period between the Norman Conquest and the Renaissance. . . . The first four chapters deal with the location, ownership, purpose, layout, overall appearance, fashions and workmanship of English gardens, the last five with their contents and detailed appearance."—*Introd.*

Bibliography, p.273–83. Index, p.285–98.

J581 Ottewill, David. The Edwardian garden. New Haven, Yale Univ. Pr., 1989. x, 230p. il. (part col.), plans, ports.

The first comprehensive study of the Edwardian garden (covering roughly 1880–1920); integrates garden history with architectural history, concentrating on country houses. Lavishly illustrated with period photographs and drawings.

Notes, p.203–16. "Bibliography of principal sources," p.217–18. Gazetteer, p.219–24. Index, p.225–30.

J582 Strong, Roy, The Renaissance garden in England. London, Thames & Hudson, 1979. 240p. il.

The first book to reconstruct from visual and archival sources how England responded to the art form of the Renaissance garden. Concerned with the gardens of palaces and great houses from the reign of Henry VIII until the outbreak of the Civil War.

Extensive endnotes serve as bibliography, p.[224]–33. Index, p.237–40.

J583 Stuart, David. Georgian gardens. London, Hale, 1979. 256p. il., plans.

Covering the period 1730–1830, this addresses gardens in the broadest sense, from pleasure grounds to kitchen gardens and deer parks. Chapters are divided into four sections: introduction (documenting foreign influences); plants, gardeners and other elements; the gardens; mansions and demesnes. Numerous plans.

Includes a gazetteer of Georgian gardens, indicating those open to the public, p.201–46. Bibliography of contemporary sources, p.248–49. Bibliography of post-Georgian sources, p.250. Index, p.251–56.

J584 Tait, Alan Andrew. The landscape garden in Scotland, 1735–1835. Edinburgh, Edinburgh Univ. Pr., 1980. xi, 282p. il., plates.

The first book devoted to the history of gardens in Scotland of this period. Supplementary material is especially useful. Appendixes: (1) The text from Humphry Repton's Red Book for Valleyfield, c.1801; (2) The text of W. S. Gilpin's Improvements for Bowhill, c.1832; (3) List of landscape gardeners and their work in Scotland, c.1730–c.1840.

Location of sites discussed, p.260–63. Index, p.264–82.

J585 Triggs, H. Inigo. Formal gardens in England and Scotland: their planning and arrangement, architectural and ornamental features. Illustrated by seventy-two plates from drawings by the author and fifty-three reproduced from photographs by Charles Latham. [Reprint.] Woodbridge, Antique Collectors' Club, 1988. xxvi, 229p. il. (part col.)

Reprint of 1st U.S. ed. N.Y., Scribner, 1902. 1st ed (London, Batsford, 1902) published in 3 parts.

"Prepared chiefly with the object of showing, by means of a series of studies of some of the most complete and historical gardens now extant in [Britain], the principle involved in their planning and arrangement in relation to the house, which is an essential element in what it is the custom to call the Formal Garden."—*Pref.* A classic work most useful today for its drawings and period photographs, some of which have been supplemented by color plates of the same subject taken in 1988.

No bibliography or index.

J586 Turner, Tom. English garden design: history and styles since 1650. Woodbridge, Antique Collectors Club, 1986. 238p. il., plans.

Well-illustrated general history.

Contents: (1) English garden design: the background ideas; (2) 1650–1740: the Enclosed, French and Dutch styles; (3) 1714–1810: the Forest, Serpentine and Irregular styles; (4) 1794–1870: the Transition, Italian and mixed styles; (5) 1870–1985: the Arts and Crafts and Abstract styles; recent trends.

References and notes, p.228–33. Select bibliography, p.233. Index, p.234–38.

Italy

J587 Gromort, Georges. Jardins d'Italie; 148 planches donnant plus de 170 vues des villas de la Campagne romaine, de la Toscane et de la Haute-Italie, accompagnées de 25 plans, d'une préface et d'un texte explicatif. Paris, A. Vincent, 1922–31. 3v. il., plates, plans.

Brief text. Still useful, mainly for the plans and large-format photographs of the Renaissance gardens and villas.

J588 Lazzaro, Claudia. The Italian Renaissance garden: from the conventions of planting, design, and ornament to the grand gardens of sixteenth-century central Italy. Photographs by Ralph Lieberman. New Haven, Yale Univ. Pr., 1990. ix, 342p. il., plans.

A landmark study concerned primarily with establishing "a context for understanding gardens in the culture of the Renaissance, how they were conceptualized, the conventions of planting and design, and the ideas about nature that were given form in sculpted ornament . . . and to understand the grand surviving estates of the sixteenth century in central Italy—primarily Tuscany and Latium—within this context."—*Introd.* Briefly covers gardens in other areas of Italy, including Ferrara and Naples, the Veneto, Lombardy, Urbino, Parma, and Turin. Visual documentation is the best yet published, using contemporary views and original photographs of the gardens.

Appendixes offer supporting data: I, Common trees and plants in Italian Renaissance gardens; IIA, Chronology of the garden at Castello in the sixteenth century; IIB, Chronology of the Boboli Garden in the sixteenth century, III, Inventory of the Villa Lante at Bagnaia.

Notes (p.288–322) and bibliography (p.333–336) span primary and secondary sources of five centuries.

J589 Masson, Georgina. Italian gardens. N.Y., Abrams, 1961. 300p. plates, maps.

A classic work still relied on despite the publication of newer books covering narrower topics in Italian garden design. Includes chapters on gardens in the Veneto, the Marche, and Northern Italy. Heavily illustrated.

"Flowers grown in Italian gardens," p.279–88. Bibliography, p.293–96. Index of places, p.297–300.

J590 Platt, Charles A. Italian gardens. With an overview by Keith N. Morgan and additional plates by Charles A. Platt. Portland, Or., Timber Pr., 1993. 170p. il.

1st ed, N.Y., Harper, 1894.

The first illustrated publication in English on this topic, authored by the premier practitioner of the formal garden revival in America. "Consists of photograph, etchings, and drawings accompanied by 19 brief, impressionistic essays on Italian gardens. Platt freely admitted that the illustrations were more important than the text."—*p.103.*

Contents: (1) Italian gardens, by Charles A. Platt; (2) Al fresco: an overview of Charles A. Platt's Italian gardens, by Keith N. Morgan; (3) Additional plates, by Charles A. Platt.

Notes to overview, p.139–42. Index, p.167–70.

J591 Shepherd, J. C., and Jellicoe, Geoffrey A. Italian gardens of the Renaissance. N.Y., Princeton Architectural Pr., 1986. 26p. 92p. of plates. il., plans, map.

1st ed., London, E. Benn, 1925; student ed., London, A. Tiranti, 1953; library ed., N.Y., Architectural Book Club Co., 1966.

Published result of the authors' personal study of gardens in 1923. Gardens are documented by brief descriptions, renderings and sketches, and photographs. New ed. reproduces the 1st ed. with repagination and in a smaller format than the original.

J592 Triggs, H. Inigo. The art of garden design in Italy, illustrated by seventy-three photographic plates reproduced in collotype, twenty-seven plans and numerous sketches in the text taken from original surveys and plans specially made by the author and twenty-eight plates from photographs by Mrs. Aubrey Le Blond. N.Y., Longmans, Green, and Co., 1906. xii, 134p. il., 128 plates, plans.

Companion publication to Formal gardens in England and Scotland: their planning and arrangement, architectural and ornamental features (GLAH 2:J585). Very large-format source notable as the first to publish plans drawn to scale of some of the most important gardens in Italy. It attempts to include major gardens from throughout the country, but heaviest emphasis is on those found at villas near Florence and Rome. 39-page historical introd. gives an overview. Plans, descriptions, and period photographs of 31 gardens follow. Introd. contains footnotes.

Low Countries

J593 Hellerstedt, Kahren Jones. Gardens of earthly delight: sixteenth- and seventeenth-century Netherlandish gardens. Bloomington, Indiana Univ. Pr., 1986. 82p. il.

Catalog of the exhibition, Frick Art Museum, Pittsburgh (1986). Valuable "both for its detailed imagery and for its insistence upon the learned meanings of garden iconography."—*Review*, Journal of garden history, v.8, 1988, p.61.

Includes bibliographical references.

J594 Jong, Erik de. Natuur en kunst: Nederlandse tuin- en landscapsarchitectuur, 1650–1740. Amsterdam, Thoth, 1993. 259p. il., plans.

Examines Dutch gardens by determining which traditions shaped gardens in a country with a unique geography. "Based on the assumption that form, content and use cannot be separated, four main gardens are discussed, each created on the initiative of members of four different social groups."—*Summary.* Because none of the gardens survive, heavy use is made of archival material, topographical drawings, engravings and maps, descriptions in travel journals, country-house poems and other written documentation.

Endnotes follow each chapter. English summary, p.235–40. Bibliography, p.241–52. Indexes, p.253–[60].

Spain

J595 Casa Valdes, Teresa Ozores y Saavedra, marquesa de. Spanish gardens. [Trans. by Edward Tanner.] Woodbridge, Antique Collectors' Club, 1987. 299p. il. (part col.), plans.

Trans. of Jardines de España. Madrid, Aguilar, 1973.

Written "to describe as completely as possible the gardens that exist today in Spain and relate their history and the history of those that have disappeared."—*Introd.*

Contents: (1) Roman gardens in Spain; (2) The arrival of the Arabs; (3) Granada and its gardens; (4) The gardens of Seville; (5) Medieval and cloister gardens; (6) The gardens of the Renaissance; (7) The gardens during the Austrian Dynasty. Philip II to Philip IV; (8) The gardens of Aranjuez. Philip II to Philip IV. El Buen Retiro. La Quinta del Duque del Arco; (9) Aranjuez in the time of the Bourbons in the eighteenth century; (10) The gardens of La Granja; (11) History of Spanish botanical gardens and the botanical expeditions to the New World during the eighteenth century; (12) Galician "Pazos." The "Sones" of Mallorca. The "Cigarrales" of Toledo; (13) The Neoclassical style. Charles III and Charles IV. Aranjuez during the nineteenth century. The gardens of Campo del Moro; (14) Nineteenth and twentieth centuries. The romantic garden. Gaudí. Forestier and Neo-Arabism. Modern Gardens. The palm groves of Elché; (15) Present-day gardens in Spain.

Endnotes follow each chapter. General bibliography p.281–83. Index of persons, p.285–90. Index of places, p.291–97.

United States

Bibliography

J596 Pioneers of American landscape design: an annotated bibliography. Ed. by Charles A. Birnbaum and Lisa E. Crowder. Washington, D.C., U.S. Dept. of the Interior, National Park Service, Cultural Resources, Preservation Assistance Div., Historic Landscape Initiative, 1993. 142p. il.

Undertaken to fill the need for a single finding aid for researchers seeking information on those visionary practitioners who have had a significant impact on the designed American landscape. "This publication presents a representative cross section of 61 entries. For each there is a brief biographical profile, annotated period and modern sources, a concise statement on the location and contents of archival collections, and a likeness of the practitioner or an illustration of a related landscape project."—*Introd.*

J597 ______. 1st supplement. Pioneers of American landscape design II: an annotated bibliography. Ed. by Charles A. Birnbaum and Julie K. Fix. Washington, D.C., U.S. Dept. of the Interior, National Park Service, Cultural Resources, Preservation Assistance Div., Historic Landscape Initiative, 1995. 186p. il., maps.

Continuation of what is anticipated to be a long-term project with additional volumes appearing every few years.

Directories

J598 American Society of Landscape Architects. ASLA members' handbook. [Washington], D.C., American Soc. of Landscape Architects, 1978– .

Annual. Some issues provide only listings of members (individuals, private firms, and government agencies). Others give broader information. For instance, 1992 contents include information on the Society, its organization and activities; membership listings; chapters; accredited programs in landscape architecture and student chapters; related organizations; and licensure by states.

Dictionaries and Encyclopedias

J599 American landscape architecture: designers and places. [Ed. by William H. Tischler.] Washington, D.C., Preservation Pr., 1989. 244p. il., plans, ports.

"Profiled here are 21 landscape architects who have had a significant impact on how our country looks. These essays are paired with descriptions of 21 of our most important landscape types—all documenting the rich and varied American landscape heritage."—*Cover.* The only source for concise biographical data on several of these designers and the best starting point for American topics.

Bibliography, p.221–32. Index, p.234–44.

Histories and Handbooks

J600 Cranz, Galen. The politics of park design: a history of urban parks in America. Cambridge, Mass., MIT Pr., 1982. xiii, 347p. il.

"The first history of the first 130 years of the American park movement in one account, not restricted to one city, one region, or one period. . . . In keeping with social research methods, [it treats] three urban park systems—those of New York, Chicago, and San Francisco—as case studies. Together with occasional comparisons with other American towns and an overview of the urban park movement across the nation, they lead to generalization about the nature of the American park movement as a whole."—*Pref.*

Notes, p.[257]–99. Bibliography, including a methodological overview, p.[301]–39. Index, p.[341]–47.

J601 Cutler, Phoebe. The public landscape of the New Deal. New Haven, Yale Univ. Pr., 1985. xv, 182p. il., maps, plans.

History of changes in the American landscape resulting from the work of the Civilian Conservation Corps, Works Progress Administration, Tennessee Valley Authority, and the National Park Service during the period 1933–1942.

Appendix of recreation demonstration areas, p.157. Notes, p.159–66. Bibliography, p.167–73. Index, p.175–82.

J602 Griswold, Mac and Weller, Eleanor. The golden age of American gardens: proud owners, private estates, 1890–1940. N.Y., Abrams, 1991. 408p. il. (part col.), plans.

Well-illustrated history of significant private gardens, arranged geographically. In many cases reproduces color lantern slides from a nationwide set commissioned by the Garden Club of America just before World War I.

Notes, p.361–85. Appendix, "Catalogue of glass plate photographs in the collection of the Garden Club of America and the Archives of American Gardens/Slide Library of Notable Parks and Gardens," p.386–92. Index, p.393–407.

J603 McClelland, Linda Flint. Presenting nature: the historic landscape designs of the National Park Service, 1916 to 1942. Washington, D.C., National Park Service, Cultural Resources, Interagency Resources Division, National Register of Historic Places, 1993. vi, 314p. il., maps, plans.

This study defines and describes the characteristics of park landscapes, documenting the work of the Park Service in its earliest years and the more recent impact of such landscapes' addition to the National Register. Previously, emphasis had been almost exclusively on recognizing the structures designed for the parks while the larger park landscapes of which they are an integral part had been largely overlooked.

Contents: (1) Stewardship for a national park service; (2) Origins of a design ethic for national parks; (3) A policy and process for design, 1916 to 1927; (4) The work of the Western Field Office, 1927 to 1932; (5) A process for park planning; (6) A decade of expansion, 1933 to 1942; (7) A new deal for state parks, 1933 to 1942; Appendix A, Registering historic park landscapes in the National Register of Historic Places; Appendix B, Associated listings in the National Register of Historic Places.

Bibliography, p.295–303. Index, p.305–14.

J604 Walker, Peter, and Simo, Melanie. Invisible gardens: the search for modernism in the American landscape. Cambridge, Mass., MIT Pr., 1994. xvi, 365p. il. (part col.), plans.

"The main purpose of this book is to make visible the work of American landscape architects since World War II, that is, from about 1945, to the late 1970s."—*Introd.* Discusses at length the work of designers for whom the written record is sparse.

Notes, p.[320]–40. Bibliography, p.342–44. Index, p.[352]–65.

Asian Countries

General Works

J605 Rambach, Pierre, and Rambach, Suzanne. Gardens of longevity in China and Japan: the art of the stone raisers. [Trans. by André Marling.] N.Y., Rizzoli, [1987]. 231p. il. (part col.)

Trans. of Jardins de longévité. Genève, Skira, 1987.

A chosen mode of expression by creative artists in both China and Japan, stone-raising is a centuries-old tradition of providing stone compositions in a garden or courtyard environment. This work provides numerous examples of stone compositions depicted in art as well as in photographs of gardens and the accompanying text describes the relationship of the stones to philosophy, perception, and tradition.

Notes, p.212–14. List of gardens, p.215–16. Bibliography, p.217. Index, p.218–24. Index, p.225–30.

China

J606 Johnston, R. Stewart. Scholar gardens of China: a study and analysis of the spatial design of the Chinese private garden. Cambridge, Eng., Cambridge Univ. Pr., 1991. xix, 331p. il. (part col.), plans, map.

A study of the small private gardens belonging to the scholar-officials who created, in miniature, their own image of nature. Describes the garden as a device for contemplative study as well as for the enjoyment of nature, and discusses the garden's role in shaping the physical character of the Chinese city from the Song period (960–1279) to the early part of the Qing dynasty.

Contents: (1) The stone record; (2) The designers and builders of gardens; (3) Design concepts and techniques; (4) The Suzhou classical tradition; (5) Gardens of the city dweller; (6) The vernacular garden tradition.

Notes, p.316–23. Bibliography, p.324–25. Index, p.326–31.

J607 Liu, Dun-zhen. Chinese classical gardens of Suzhou. Trans. by Chen Lixian. English text ed. Joseph C. Wang. N.Y., McGraw-Hill, [1993]. iv, 459p. il.

Originally published as: Su-chou ku tien yüan lin. Beijing, Zhongguo jian zhu gong ye chu ban she, 1979. 2d ed. T'ai-pei, Shang lin chu ban she, min guo, 1985.

"A landmark book that makes accessible to a wider audience examples of gardens that flourished more than one thousand years ago, and explanations of the social and cultural contexts from which they grew."—*Review*, Design book review, v.31, winter 1994, p.36. A scholarly study of this southern China city's imperial gardens and parks and private gardens. Under the direction of Liu, a team of 14 researchers worked for more than 20 years producing meticulous measured drawings of 15 Suzhou gardens. Part 1 is organized according to design elements, e.g., layout, water, rockeries, buildings, flowers and trees, while part 2 discusses specific examples of classic gardens. All illustrations and plans are together, p.143–459, and comprise a large portion of the book.

J608 Qian, Yun, ed. Classical Chinese gardens. Hong Kong, Joint Publishing Co., [1984]. 240p. il. (part col.), plans.

Trans. of Chung-kuo yuan lin i shu. Hong Kong, Joing Pub. Co., 1982; 2d ed. T'ai-pei, Huang kuan ch'u pan she, 1988.

After introductory essays, this work functions as a guide to 36 Chinese gardens. The entries are grouped by type, e.g., imperial gardens, private gardens, natural scenic parks and temple gardens, and each entry includes photographs, commentary, and often a plan.

J609 Tsu, Frances Ya-sing. Landscape design in Chinese gardens. N.Y., McGraw-Hill, [1988]. xii, 244p. il., map, plans.

Aimed at architects, landscape architects, designers, this book emphasizes design principles through plans, illustrative photos, and diagrams of celebrated gardens. After providing historical background and comparisons of Chinese garden design with European and Japanese, concentrates on design components and on the design process.

Contents: Part one: Introduction: (1) General view; (2) Historical perspective; (3) Comparison of the Chinese and European garden; (4) Comparison of the Chinese and Japanese garden; (5) Classification of Chinese gardens; Part two: Components: (6) Hills and water; (7) Architecture; (8) Plant material; (9) Literature and art; Part three: Design process and essence; (10) Design process; (11) Creating spaciousness in a limited area; (12) Design for dynamic viewing: four seasons and five senses; Epilogue; Appendix 1: Plans of famous gardens; Appendix 2: Chronological table of Chinese Dynasties; Appendix 3: Names of Chinese gardens in English and in Chinese.

Bibliography, p.239. Index, p.241–44.

Japan

J610 Itoh, Teiji. The gardens of Japan. N.Y., Kodansha (Distr. by Harper and Row, [1984]). 228p. il. (part col.), maps.

A handsome presentation with many full-page color photographs of Japanese gardens and text by the architect, Teiji Itoh. Discusses design elements, e.g., stones, water, plants, as well as the various types of gardens, for example, residential, tea, temple. The last chapter is a selection of the author's favorite gardens, each with a photograph, comment and practical information for the visitor.

Bibliography, p.225. Index, p.226–27.

K. Sculpture

Books dealing with the history of sculpture, and essential books on sculptural techniques, are listed and described in this chapter.

GENERAL WORKS

K1 Avery, Charles. Fingerprints of the artist: European terra-cotta sculpture from the Arthur M. Sackler collections. Washington, D.C., Arthur M. Sackler Foundation; Cambridge, Mass., Fogg Art Museum (Distr. by Harvard University Press, 1981). 298p. il. (part col.)

Catalog of the exhibition, National Gallery of Art (U.S.) (1981), and other locations.

Includes biographical sketches of the artists and a full catalog entry for each work. Many illustrations printed in sepia tones. "A general criticism of the catalogue entries is that the information on provenance is unnecessarily scanty and uneven. . . . A more serious shortcoming is that some entries are a great deal less scholarly than others."—*Review*, Burlington magazine v.124, Dec. 1982, p. 765.

Contents: The Italian terra-cottas, 15th to 20th century, by Charles Avery; The French terra-cottas, 16th to 20th century, by Alastair Lang; The German, English, Netherlandish and Spanish terra-cottas, 16th to 19th century, by Charles Avery.

Alphabetical list of artists, p.283–84. Bibliography, p.285–89. Index, p.291–97.

K2 Bassett, Jane, and Fogelman, Peggy. Looking at European sculpture: a guide to technical terms. Los Angeles, J. Paul Getty Museum, 1997. 104p. il. (part col.)

Published in collaboration with the Victoria and Albert Museum (London).

Illustrated alphabetic dictionary of terms related to the production of sculpture. "The purpose of this book is to clarify the meanings and applications of terms related to European sculpture."—*Foreword*.

Selected bibliography, p.103.

K3 Bazin, Germain. A concise history of world sculpture. N.Y., Alpine, 1981. 317p. 553 col. il.

Survey for the beginning art student or amateur.

Contents: The origins; (I) Prehistoric art; (II) Development of sculpture in the Near and Middle East; (III) Greek and Roman sculpture; (IV) The twilight of sculpture in the West; (V) Primitive cultures; (VI) The Far East; (VII) The rebirth of sculpture in the West; (VIII) The Renaissance; (IX) Mannerism; (X) Baroque and classical; (XI) The nineteenth and twentieth centuries.

Index, p.313–17.

K4 Butler, Ruth. Western sculpture: definitions of man. Boston, New York Graphic Society, [1975]. 304p. il. (Repr.: N.Y., Icon, 1979)

A survey of the history of sculpture with emphasis on sociological context.

Contents: (1) The paragone; (2) The Mediterranean world; (3) The Christian west; (4) Renaissance sculpture; (5) The seventeenth and eighteenth centuries; (6) Neoclassicism and the nineteenth century; (7) Twentieth-century sculpture; (8) Epilogue.

Notes, p.283–92. Bibliographical essay, p.293–98. Index, p.299–303.

K5 Le corps en morceaux. Paris, Réunion des musées nationaux, 1990. 343p. il.

Catalog of the exhibition, Musée d'Orsay, Paris, and Kunsthalle Schirn, Frankfurt (1990). Essays focus on sculpture of body parts (e.g., torsos, heads, hands) rather than on full figures.

Contents: (1) Ex-voto, par Geneviève Bresc-Bautier; (2) Emblèmes, héraldique, symbolique: le fragment synecdoque, par Geneviève Bresc-Bautier; (3) Reliquaires, par Geneviève Bresc-Bautier; (4) Cires anatomiques, par Hélène Pinet; (5) Modèles d'atelier, par Hélène Pinet; (6) Antiques dérestaurés: les avatars d'un torse d'athlète au musée du Louvre: pugiliste ou discobole?, par Alain Pasquier; (7) Images de ruines, par Hélène Pinet; (8) Temps des prothèses avant l'âge de la restauration, par Geneviève Bresc-Bautier; (9) Michel-Ange, entre fragment et inachevé, par Jean-René Gaborit; (10) Copies d'antiques à la Villa Médicis, par Antoinette Le Normand-Romain; (11) Torse du Belvédère, par Antoinette Le Normand-Romain; (12) Torse de l'Illissos, par Antoinete Le Normand-Romain; (13) Homme qui marche, par Anne Pingeot; (14) Homme qui tombe, par Nicole Barbier; (15) Torses féminis: torses sculptées, par Antoinette Le

Normand-Romain; Torses photographiés, par Hélène Pinet; (16) Têtes coupées, par Anne Pingeot; (17) Mains: mains sculptées, par Anne Pingeot; Mains photographiées par Hélène Pinet; (18) Epaules, par Anne Pingeot; (19) Jambes et pieds, par Anne Pingeot; (20) Fragments tirés d'un ensemble 1: Rodin, le monument à Victor Hugo, par Anne Pingeot; (21) Reliefs, par Anne Pingeot; (22) Fragments tirés d'un ensemble 2: Bourdelle, le monument aux Morts de Montauban, par Antoinette Le Normand-Romain; (23) Vases où poussent les fragments, par Nicole Barbier; (24) Assemblages de Rodin, par Nicole Barbier; (25) Assembler ou couper?, par Antoinette Le Normand-Romain.

Rodin-fragments: synopsis du film, par Roland Schaer, p.259–63. Biographies des artistes suivies des notices de leurs oeuvres exposées, p.265–317. Bibliographie, p.319–32. Index (artistes, sujets, lieux, prêteurs), p.333–42.

K6 Finn, David. How to look at sculpture. N.Y., Abrams, 1989. 144p. il. (part col.)

Layman's guide to sculpture appreciation.

Contents: A different kind of reality; What makes a sculpture great?; Exquisite details; Naked beauty; The material truth—and beyond; Living with sculpture.

K7 Fusco, Peter. Summary catalogue of European sculpture in the J. Paul Getty Museum. Los Angeles, J. Paul Getty Museum, 1997. 79p. il.

Brief "distillation of the research, insights and informed opinions of numerous people . . . who have spent time at the Museum during the last thirteen years."—*Ackn.*

Contents: Catalogue of attributed works; Catalogue of unattributed works.

Subject index, p.77–78.

K8 Haskell, Francis, and Penny, Nicholas. Taste and the antique: the lure of classical sculpture, 1500–1900. New Haven, Yale Univ. Pr., 1981. 376p. 180 il.

Extensive historical essay and catalog of 95 key sculptures, mostly Roman copies of late Greek originals, that strongly influenced later Western taste, from the Renaissance on. "Performs a real and very much needed service in identifying, cataloguing and illustrating these forgotten classics of our past. The 95 photographs should be committed to memory, along with their various titles, by all students of Western art, and the book should be a work of constant reference for all historians of culture."—*Review*, Art history 5, no.1, March 1982, p.117.

Contents: (I) "A new Rome"; (II) The public and private collections of Rome; (III) Plaster casts and prints; (IV) Control and codification; (V) Casts and copies in the seventeenth-century courts; (VI) "Tout ce qu'il y a de beau en Italie"; (VII) Erudite interests; (VIII) Florence: the impact of the Tribuna; (IX) Museums in eighteenth-century Rome; (X) The new importance of Naples; (XI) The proliferation of casts and copies; (XII) New fashions in the copying of antiquities; (XIII) Reinterpretations of antiquities; (XIV) The last dispersals; (XV) Epilogue; Catalogue.

Notes to the text, p.125–31. Appendix, p.[342]–[43]. Bibliography, p.344–65. Index, p.366–75.

K9 Hibbard, Howard. Masterpieces of Western sculpture: from medieval to modern. N.Y., Harper and Row, [1977]. 239p. il. (some col.)

Brief history of sculpture with emphasis on masters and large mostly color photos of representative works.

Contents: The middle ages; Renaissance and mannerism; Baroque to romantic; From Rodin to the present.

Notes on the plates, p.209–38. Bibliography, p.239.

K10 Isabella Stewart Gardner Museum. Sculpture in the Isabella Stewart Gardner Museum. [By] Cornelius C. Vermeule, III . . . [et al.] Boston, Trustees [of the Museum], 1977. 188p. il.

"While it is not a collection of masterpieces, it does contain important works. . . . There are certain strengths in the collection which would be difficult to find in other American museums."—*Pref.*

Contents: (I) Classical; (II) Medieval; (III) Renaissance; (IV) Seventeenth to twentieth centuries; (V) Doubtful authenticity.

Bibliography, p.xi–xii. Checklist [of additional objects], p.173–80. List of agents, dealers and former owners, p.181. Index of artist, p.182–83. Index of locations, p.183–85. Index of subjects p.186–88.

K11 Ivory: an international history and illustrated survey. [By] Michael Vickers . . . [et al.] N.Y., Abrams, 1987. 352p. il. (part col.)

Text by 12 British decorative arts specialists.

Contents: The story of ivory; (1) Early civilizations; (2) Rome and the Eastern Empire; (3) Europe; (4) Africa; (5) The Near East, India; (6) The Far East, South-East Asia; (7) North America; (8) Central and South America; (9) Contemporary carvers.

Time chart, p.20. Glossary, p.330–39. Collecting ivory objects, p.340–[41]. Care and repair, p.342–43. Bibliography, p.344–45. Museums, p.346. Index, p.347–51.

K12 Liebieghaus. Nachantike grossplastische Bildwerke. Liebieghaus—Museum alter Plastik, Frankfurt am Main. Melsungen, Gutenberg, 1981– . (4)v. il. (Wissenschaftliche Kataloge)

Scholarly catalog under the general editorial supervision of Herbert Beck. Each vol. contains a concordance of inventory and catalog numbers, a bibliography, and a list of abbreviations.

Contents: (1) Zinke, Detlef. Italien, Frankreich, Spanien, Deutschland, 800–1380; (2) Maek-Gérard, Michael. Italien, Frankreich und Niederlande, 1380–1530/40; (3) Maek-Gérard, Michael. Die deutschsprachigen Länder, ca. 1380–1530/40; (4) Geese, Uwe. Italien, Niederlande, Deutschland, Österreich, Schweiz, Frankreich, 1540/50–1780.

K13 ———. Nachantike kleinplastische Bildwerke. Liebieghaus—Museum alter Plastik, Frankfurt am Main. Melsungen, Gutenberg, 1987–89. 3v. il. (Wissenschaftliche Kataloge)

Scholarly catalog under the general editorial supervision of Herbert Beck. Each vol. contains a concordance of inventory and catalog numbers, a bibliography, and a list of abbreviations.

Contents: (1) Schenkluhn, Wolfgang. Mittelalter, 11. Jahrhundert bis 1530/40 [Maasgebiet, Niederlande, England, Frankreich, Deutschland, Italien]; (2) Götz-Mohr, Brita von. Italien, Frankreich, Niederlande, 1500–1800; (3) Götz-Mohr, Brita von. Die deutschsprachigen Länder, 1500–1800.

K14 Mackay, James A. The dictionary of Western sculptors in bronze. Woodbridge, Suffolk, Antique Collectors' Club, 1977. 414p.

Provides brief biographical entries with birth and death dates when available, along with details of training, major influences, and some indication of the artist's style and thematic tendencies. Covers sculptors active from about the beginning of the 18th century until around 1960.

"The description 'Western' I have interpreted loosely to include sculptors working in Europe and the more Europeanised parts of the world, such as America and Australasia. Oriental sculptors are included in such cases where their training, environment and sculptural styles have been in the western idiom."—*Author's pref.*

Family trees, p.405–12. Select bibliography, p.413–14.

K15 Middeldorf, Ulrich Alexander. Sculptures from the Samuel H. Kress collection: European schools, XIV–XIX century. London, Phaidon (Distr. by Praeger, 1976). 305p. il.

Comprehensive catalog of the collection.

Bibliographical abbreviations, p.3. Indexes, by Anna Voris, p.[291]–305.

K16 Panofsky, Erwin. Tomb sculpture: four lectures on its changing aspects from ancient Egypt to Bernini. Ed. by H. W. Janson. [Reprint.] Foreword by Martin Warncke. N.Y., Abrams, 1992. 319p. plates.

See GLAH 1:K9 for original annotation.

K17 Penny, Nicholas. Catalogue of European sculpture in the Ashmolean Museum, 1540 to the present day. N.Y., Oxford Univ. Pr., 1992. 3v. il.

Each vol. is listed separately under its appropriate geographical classification.

"An extremely rich and varied collection of sculpture, much of it discussed in very detailed entries. When seen alongside the most comparable catalogue of sculpture— the admirable multi-volume work by various authors of the Liebieghaus Museum Frankfurt [GLAH 2:K12]—its production over a mere handful of years by a single author is without doubt a very remarkable achievement."—*Review*, Burlington magazine v.136, Dec. 1994, p.850.

Includes some metalwork, furniture, and objets d'art. In addition to catalog entries, each vol. contains essays, appendixes, a concordance, and an index of artists and craftsmen.

Contents: (1) Italian; (2) French and other European sculpture (excluding Italian and British); (3) British.

K18 Pyke, E. J. A biographical dictionary of wax modellers: supplement III. London, Pyke, 1986. xv, 12p. il. [8]p. of plates

Comprehensive work on wax modelers.

See GLAH 1:K11 for original annotation. Suppl., London, Pyke, 1981. Suppl. II, London, Pyke, 1983.

K19 Reynal's world history of great sculpture. N.Y., Reynal, in assoc. with Morrow, 1978–79. 6v. il. (part col.)

Each vol. focuses on a region or period. Most were originally published in Italian by Mondadori. Each has 191 pages and contains a bibliography and an index.

Contents: Michalowski, Kazimierz. Great sculpture of ancient Egypt (1978); Devambez, Pierre. Great sculpture of ancient Greece (1978); Gaborit, Jean René. Great Gothic sculpture (1978); Fagiolo dell'Arco, Maurizio. Great Baroque and Rococo sculpture (1978); Bernal, Ignacio. Great sculpture of ancient Mexico (1979); Nagahiro, Toshio; Yum, Eun Hyun; and Kuno, Takeshi. Great sculpture of the Far East (1979).

K20 Rogers, Leonard Robert. Relief sculpture. N.Y., Oxford Univ. Pr., 1974. 229p. il. (The appreciation of the arts, 8)

A survey of the history and properties of relief sculpture for the student or amateur.

Contents: (1) Introduction; (2) Space 1: between two and three dimensions; (3) Space 2: four approaches to space; (4) Form 1: form, contour, and background; (5) Form 2: varieties of form; (6) Line; (7) Light and form; (8) Some aspects of composition; (9) Coins and medals; (10) Relief decoration; (11) Relief in the twentieth century.

Index, p.227–29.

K21 Sculpture: from antiquity to the present. N.Y., Skira/Rizzoli, 1986–90. (v.1, Köln, Taschen, 1996) 4v. il (part col.) (Repr.: Köln, Taschen, 1996).

Ed.: Georges Duby and Jean-Luc Daval. Trans. of La sculpture: histoire d'un art. Geneva, Skira, 1986–91.

Lavishly illustrated history of western European sculpture. Each vol. contains valuable historical essays by European experts. Individual vols. are not listed separately elsewhere in this chapter.

Contents: (1) Bruneau, Philippe. Sculpture: the great art of antiquity from the eighth century BC to the fifth century AD (1996); (2) Duby, Georges. Sculpture: the great art of the Middle Ages from the fifth to the fifteenth century (1990); (3) Ceysson, Bernard. Sculpture: the great tradition of sculpture from the fifteenth to the eighteenth century (1987); (4) Le Normand-Romain, Antoinette. Sculpture: the adventure of modern sculpture in the nineteenth and twentieth centuries (1986).

K22 Suermondt-Ludwig-Museum Aachen. Europäische Bildwerk from Mittelalter zum Barock. [By] Ernst Günther Grimme, with the assist. of Renate Puvogel. Photos by Ann Münchow. Köln, DuMont, 1977. 140p. il. [131] leaves of plates. (Aachener Kunstblätter des Museumsvereins)

Catalog of the collection.

Erklärung von Fachausdrücken, p.138–39. Abgekürzt zitierte Literatur, p.140.

K23 Tardy. Les ivoires: évolution décorative du 1er siècle à nos jours par Tardy avec un abrégé d'iconographie chrétienne, avec le collab. de M. L'Abbé Bidault . . .

[et al.] Paris, Tardy, [1972–1977]. 2v. (Collection Tardy,126, 137)

See GLAH 1:K12 for earlier ed. Present ed. adds coverage of ancient Greek, Etruscan, Roman, and Egyptian ivories, and ivories carved in the polar regions, and expands treatment of ivory-carving in Africa, Islamic countries, and in south and east Asia.

Contents: (1) Europe et Byzance: sujets religieux; Europe et Byzance: sujets profanes; Les faux gothiques; Abrégé d'iconographie chrétienne; (2) Antiquitié; Islam; Inde et Asie du sud-est; Chine; Japon; Afrique noire; Régions polaires.

Ouvrages à consulter, v.1, p.[245]–47. Essai de muséographie pour l'Europe, v.1, p.[248]–53. Liste des ivoiriers connus, v.1, p.[255]–77. Table des illustrations, v.1, p.[279]–84. Table des objets, v.1, p.[285]–86. Sommaire, v.1, p.287.

K24 Tucker, William. The language of sculpture. [London], Thames and Hudson, [1974]. 174p. il. (New aspects of art)

Written from the perspective of a practicing sculptor. Expansion of a series of lectures given at the University of Leeds and subsequently published in Studio international. Treats mostly modern sculpture.

Contents: (1) Rodin; (2) Brancusi: the elements of sculpture; (3) Picasso: cubism and construction; (4) González; (5) The sculpture of Matisse; (6) The object; (7) Brancusi at Tîrgu Jiu; (8) Gravity.

Notes on the text, p.160–64. Index, p.171–74.

K25 United States. National Gallery of Art. Sculpture: an illustrated catalogue. Washington, D.C., The Gallery, 1994. 283p. il.

"This is the first summary catalogue dedicated exclusively to sculpture to be published by the National Gallery of Art. . . . In recent years, the sculpture collection has grown markedly in the areas of French and American sculpture, providing a balanced complement to the National Gallery's traditional areas of strength, particularly in works of the Italian Renaissance."—*Foreword.*

Donors to the sculpture collection, p.14–15. Notes to the reader [including abbreviations], p.16–17. Changes in attribution, titles, and nomenclature, p.239–47. Concordance of old and new accession numbers, p.249–65. Index of titles [including sitters' surnames], p.267–83.

K26 Victoria and Albert Museum, London. European sculpture in the Victoria and Albert Museum. Ed. by Paul Williamson. London, The Museum, 1996. 191p. il. (part col.)

Handbook rather than a full catalog.

"It should be stressed that this is . . . only a very selective sample of the great Collection at South Kensington."—*Foreword.*

Contents: The formation of the collection; Early Christian to Gothic (c.400–1400); Late Gothic and Renaissance; Mannerism and Baroque; From 1720 to 1920; the Cast Courts.

Bibliography, p.186–88. Index, p.189–91.

K27 Wittkower, Rudolf. Sculpture: processes and principles. London, Lane, 1977. 288p. il.

General history of sculpture based on lectures for undergraduates and the general public at the University of Cambridge. Emphasis on the masters and their techniques.

Contents: (1) Antiquity; (2) The middle ages: theoretical foundation; Chartres west; (3) The middle ages: Chartres, Rheims, Bamberg, Orvieto; (4) The Renaissance: Alberti, Gauricus, Leonardo; (5) Michelangelo; (6) Michelangelo, Cellini, Vasari; (7) Giovanni Bologna, Cellini; (8) Bernini; (9) Bernini, Bouchardon, Pigalle; (10) Falconet, Winckelmann, Canova, Schadow; (11) The nineteenth century: Rodin, Hildebrand; (12) The twentieth century.

Bibliography, p.[277]–80. Index, p.[285]–88.

TECHNIQUES

K28 Andrews, Oliver. Living materials: a sculptor's handbook. Berkeley, Univ. of California Pr., 1983. 348p. il.

"This manual . . . draws on many household methods of doing things, especially when they have proved to be most widely used and efficient."—*Foreword.*

Contents: (1) Living materials, living forms; (2) Clay; (3) Plaster building; (4) Mold-making and cold-casting; (5) Cement and concrete; (6) Stone carving; (7) Wood; (8) Plastics; (9) Metals; (10) Metal forming; (11) Welding; (12) Bronze casting by the lost-wax method; (13) Sand casting and shell casting; (14) New forms; (15) Planning a studio.

Index, p.[343]–[49].

K29 Baudry, Marie Therèse. La sculpture: méthode et vocabulaire. Avec la collab. de Dominique Bozo. Sous le contrôle scientifique de André Chastel, Jacques Thirion. Paris, Imprimerie nationale, 1978. 765p. il. (part col.) (Principes d'analyse scientifique) (Inventaire général des monuments et des richeses artistiques de la France)

Encyclopedic treatment of matters pertaining to sculpture. The first part contains descriptive essays related to how sculpture is created. The second part contains alphabetically arranged descriptive definitions related to specific techniques. The third section contains a bibliographic index and provides full bibliographic citations for works consulted and presents to the user a single alphabetic list of terms found in the "Vocabulaire" along with a list of synonyms, variants and terms no longer in use and refers to the equivalent form in the volume.

Contents: Première partie—Méthode: (I) Les auteurs, les gens de métier, les stades de la création; (II) Le modelage; (III) Le moulage; (IV) La technique de la taille; (V) La technique de la fonte et les autres techniques de mise en forme des métaux; (VI) Les techniques annexes, les traitements de surface, les teintures, les applications et les incrustations; (VII) Composition et traitement des formes. Deuxième partie— Vocabulaire: (I) Vocabulaire général; (II) Les auteurs, les gens de métier, et les stades de la création; (III) La technique du modelage; (IV) La technique du moulage; (V) Les outils et les matériaux du modelage et du moulage; (VI) La technique de la taille; (VII) Outils de la taille, matériaux, défauts et altérations spécifiques; (VIII) La technique de la fonte et les autres techniques de mise en forme des métaux; (IX) Outils de la fonte et du travail des métaux et des alliages. Matériaux, défauts et altérations spécifiques; (X) Outils usant les matériaux durs, polissage et abrasifs; (XI) Les revêtements. Les applications et les incrustations; (XII) Altérations de la forme des oeuvres et restaurations; (XIII) La composition. Troisième partie—Bibliographie table alphabétique.

Bibliographie, p.[707]–32. Table alphabétique des termes définis dans le vocabulaire, p.[735]–57.

K30 Clarke, Geoffrey, and Cornock, Stroud. A sculptor's manual. Rev. [corrected] ed. N.Y., Reinhold, 1970. 158p. il.

See GLAH 1:K13 for 1968 ed.

K31 Colinart, Sylvie; Drilhon, France; and Scherf, Guilhem. Sculptures en cire de l'ancienne Egypte à l'art abstrait. Paris, Éd. de la Réunion des musées nationaux, 1987. 465p. il. (Notes et documents des Musées de France, 18)

A comprehensive history of wax sculpture and review of techniques involved in its creation.

Contents: (I) Usage de la cire en sculpture, par Jean-René Gaborit; (II) Céroplastie médicale: art méconnu, par Nicholas Sainte Fare Garnot; (III) Étude scientifique des oeuvres, par France Drilhon et Sylvie Colinart; (IV) Matériaux constitutifs, par Sylvie Colinart; (V) Technologie et mise en forme, par France Drilhon and Anne Tassery-Lahmi; (VI) Conservation et restauration, par Didier Besnainou; (VII) Étude historique et technique des oeuvres; (VIII) Recensement des oeuvres conservées dans les collections nationales, par Guilhem Scherf et Marie Jeune avec la collab. de Christine Jausserand-Woringer.

Bibliographie, p.[441]–43. Glossaire, p.[445]–47. Index, p.[449]–58. Liste des oeuvres du chapitre VII suivant l'ordre du catalogue, p.[459]–61.

K32 Cutler, Anthony. The craft of ivory: sources, techniques, and uses in the Mediterranean World, A.D. 200–1400. Washington, D.C., Dumbarton Oaks, 1985. 58p. il.

A companion to Kurt Weitzmann's Catalogue of the Byzantine and early medieval antiquities in the Dumbarton Oaks collection, v.3, Ivories and steatites (Washington, D.C., Dumbarton Oaks, 1973).

Contents: (1) The nature of ivory; (2) The sources and availability of ivory; (3) Cutting and carving techniques; (4) The uses and image of ivory.

Bibliographical citations, p.55–56. List of abbreviated titles, p.56–58.

K33 Jackson, Harry. Lost wax bronze casting: a photographic essay on this antique and venerable art. [Reprint.] Foreword by John Walker. [Historical research by Richard Fremantle]. N.Y., Prentice Hall, 1986. 127p. il. (part col.)

See GLAH 1:K14 for original ed. Reprint of the 1972 ed., Flagstaff, Ariz., Northland.

K34 Lindquist, Mark. Sculpting wood: contemporary tools and techniques. Photography by Bill Byers. Worcester, Mass., Davis, 1986. 292p. il. (part col.)

"The book is for all students of woodworking and wood sculpture, whether they come from a technical or artistic background."—*Introd.*

Contents: (I) Wood for the sculpture; (1) Structure of wood; (2) Commercial harvesting of lumber; (3) Drying wood; (4) The forest—a source of material; (II) Basic tools and techniques; (5) The shop—basic power tools; (6) Preparing stock for use; (7) Beginning sculpture—learning to carve; (8) Using the band saw to create sculpture; (9) Finishing; (III) Harvesting and sculpting wood with the chain saw; (10) The chain saw; (11) Harvesting wood with the chain saw; (12) Chain saw carved vessels; (IV) Woodturning; (13) Woodturning tools; (14) Lathe safety and basic woodturning; (15) The development of the work; (16) Turning spalted wood; (17) Turning burls; (18) Turning vases.

Index, p.290–92.

K35 Marbres helleniques: de la carrière au chef d'oeuvre. [By] Doris Vanhove. Bruxelles, Crédit Communal, 1987. 191p. il. (part col.) maps

Catalog of the exhibition, Brussels (1987) organized by the Crédit Communal in collaboration with the Séminaire d'Archéologie grecque de l'Université de l'Etat à Gand. Discusses the origin, quarrying, and transportation of marble along with sculpture techniques.

Contents: Le marbre: la beauté née de la boue, par Paul De Paepe; Les carrières de marbre dans l'antiquité: techniques et organisation, par Tony Kozelj; Transport de pierres en Grèce ancienne: de la carrière au chantier, par Georges Raepsaet; Quelques considérations sur la genèse et l'évolution du temple grec, par Herman Mussche; Le temple de Poséidon au cap Sounion: evocation d'en chantier antique, par Doris Vanhove; La construction d'un temple grec: aspects administratifs, économiques, sociaux, par Herman Van Looy; Les techniques de la sculpture grecque sur marbre, par Olga Palagia; Enpreintes d'une pierre, par Luc Moens; Catalogue.

Petit lexique des termes techniques, p.188.

K36 Mills, John W. Encyclopedia of sculpture techniques. N.Y., Watson Guptill, 1990. 239p. il.

Alphabetical arrangement of articles on the methods and materials of sculpture. "This book is intended to help guide the novice sculptor towards a thorough knowledge of the practical aspects of his art."—*Introd.*

Bibliography, p.239.

K37 ——— The technique of casting for sculpture. [Rev. ed.] London, Batsford, 1990. 175p. il.

See GLAH 1:K15 for 1st ed. Expanded text.

Glossary, p.163–66. Suppliers, p.167–68. Index, p.171–75.

K38 Padovano, Anthony. The process of sculpture. Garden City, Doubleday, 1981. 331p. il.

A review of traditional and contemporary methods of sculpture.

Contents: (1) Clay sculpturing; (2) Wood carving and construction; (3) Stone carving; (4) Metal working; (5) Bronze casting; (6) Plastics.

Bibliography on plastics, sculpture and mold making, p.309–11. Books for further reading, p.[312]. Suppliers, p.[314]–18. Index, p.[323]–31.

K39 Penny, Nicholas. The materials of sculpture. New Haven, Yale Univ. Pr., 1993. 318p. il.

A materials-based examination of sculpture from many periods and places.

Contents: (1) The hardest stones; (2) Granite and porphyry; (3) White marbles and alabasters: part 1; (4) White marbles and alabasters: part 2; (5) The versatility of marble; (6) The traces of the tool; (7) Coloured marbles; (8) Schist, sandstone and limestone; (9) The structure and decoration of larger wooden sculpture; (10) Varieties of smaller wooden sculpture; (11) Ivory and horn; (12) Stamped and moulded clay; (13) Stucco and gesso; (14) Modelled clay; (15) Modelled wax; (16) Bronze and other copper alloys: part 1; (17) Bronze and other copper alloys: part 2; (18) Embossed and chased metal.

Notes, p.271–93; Glossary and indexes of materials, tools and techniques, p.294–313. Index of people and places, p.314–17.

K40 Rich, Jack C. The materials and methods of sculpture. [Reprint.] N.Y., Dover, 1988. 416p. il.

See GLAH 1:K16 for original annotation.

K41 ______ Sculpture in wood. [Reprint.] N.Y., Dover, 1992. 155p. il.

See GLAH 1:K17 for original annotation.

K42 Rockwell, Peter. The art of stoneworking: a reference guide. Cambridge, Mass., Cambridge Univ. Pr., 1993. 319p. il.

"My purpose was to help the reader to see a finished work in stone . . . as the product of a sequence of actions and tools: to look backward from the final product rather than forward from the raw materials."—*Introd.*

Line drawings throughout the text present vivid examples of how stone is quarried, moved to a site, lifted into place, and cut for architectural or sculptural purposes.

Contents: (1) Introduction; (2) Principles of stoneworking; (3) Stone; (4) Tools; (5) Tool drawings; (6) Methods; (7) Architectural process; (8) Sculptural process; (9) Design and process; (10) The project; (11) Quarrying; (12) Moving, transport and lifting; (13) Workshop organization; (14) Carving without quarrying and the reuse of stone; (15) The history of stoneworking technology; (16) Documentation I; (17) Documentation II; (18) Documentation of major monuments; (19) Computer documentation.

Photographs, p.254–91. Tables, p.292–98. References, p.299–308. Index, p.309–19.

K43 Schodek, Daniel L. Structure in sculpture. Cambridge, Mass., MIT Pr., 1993. 312p. il.

"This book deals with sculpture as a material construct. Drawing on straightforward physical principles of how sculptures stand and how material characteristics affect their shaping, the book illuminates the way principles are reflected in specific works."—*Introd.*

Contents: (1) The role of structure in sculpture: an overview; (2) Basic principles of balance and structural stability; (3) Shapes and elements; (4) Special structures; (5) Materials; (6) Observations; Appendix 1: Case study of Echo of the waves; Appendix 2: Additional notes on loading conditions; Appendix 3: Additional notes on designing structural elements in bending; Appendix 4: Advanced methods of structural analysis.

Index, p.[311]–12.

K44 Uhmann, Arnulf von. Bildhauer Technik des Spätmittelalters und der Frührenaissance. Darmstadt, Wissenschaftliche Buchgesellschaft, 1984. 154p. 52 plates.

Critical examination of late medieval and early renaissance sculpture techniques. Points out discrepancies between principles of theoretical treatises and empirically observed practice.

Abkürzungen und Literaturverzeichnis, p.143–54.

HISTORIES AND HANDBOOKS

Ancient

Egypt and Western Asia

K45 British Museum. Department of Western Asiatic Antiquities. Assyrian palace reliefs and their influence on the sculptures of Babylonia and Persia [Reprint with rev.] Text [by] Richard David Barnett. Photography by Werner Forman. [London], Trustees of the Museum, [1976]. 45p. [xx] plates, plan, maps.

See GLAH 1:K19 for original annotation. Shortened version, Assyrian palace reliefs in the British Museum, [London], British Museum, 1970; repr. with rev., 1976.

A description, with illustrations, of the important collection of Assyrian reliefs in the British Museum.

Notes, p.37–39. List of Assyrian kings whose sculptures appear in the Assyrian galleries, p.[40]. Short list of Assyrian sculptures in the Assyrian galleries, p.41–45.

K46 Getz-Preziosi, Pat. Sculptors of the Cyclades: individual and tradition in the third millennium B.C. Ann Arbor, Univ. of Michigan Pr., 1987. 254p. il. (part col.)

An investigation into the history and aesthetics of Cycladic sculpture that "aims at a much wider readership than the purely academic."—*Review*, Journal of hellenic studies v.109, 1989, p.258–9.

Contents: (1) The marble isles: an introduction to the early bronze age Cyclades; (2) The sculptural tradition; (3) Isolating the individual hand; (4) Three archaic sculptors; (5) Eight Classical sculptors; (6) Five late Classical sculptors; (7) Ending on a geographical note.

Abbreviations, p.143–44. Notes, p.145–51. Appendix 1: Checklists of figures attributed to sixteen sculptors, p.155–64. Appendix 2: Size range of works attributed to sixteen sculptors, p.165–[66]. Bibliography, p.167–71. Index, p.173–75. Plates, p.[179–244]. Notes on the plates, p.245–52.

K47 J. Paul Getty Museum. Metalwork from the Hellenized East: catalogue of the collections. [By] Michael Pfrommer. Malibu, The Museum, 1993. 244p. il. (part col.)

Records four separate collections, or "treasures," of mostly gold and silver vessels, jewelry, and horse trappings whose origins, though undocumented, are convincingly traced, via stylistic and iconographic analysis, to civilizations of the 2d- and 1st-century, B.C. Near East, whose decorative arts often displayed Hellenized tendencies.

"Since the material of all these treasures does not stem from regular excavations, our options in reaching final conclusions concerning the provenance and chronology are limited."—*p.2.*

Abbreviations, p.xi-xii. Profiles [of vessels], p.223–33. Index, p.235–43. Chart of flower types, p.244.

K48 James, T. G. H., and Davies, W. V. Egyptian sculpture. Cambridge, Mass., Harvard Univ. Pr., 1983. 72p. il. (part col.)

Provides both an introduction to the genre and a guide to the British Museum collection. Introductory chapters trace the history of the collection and the basic qualities peculiar to Egyptian sculpture. Remaining chapters describe the contents of the museum's various galleries.

Bibliography, p.69. Index to the collection numbers of the objects mentioned in the guide, p.70. Dynasties of Egypt with selected kings, p.71. Index, p.72.

K49 Matthiae, Paolo. L'arte degli Assiri: cultura e forma del relievo storico. Roma, Laterza, 1996. 255p. plates. (Storia e società)

Discusses relief sculpture as a narrative element in the history of Assyria. Some sites reconstructed based on evidence of fragments. Major themes related to the Assyrian pantheon, battles, and hunting expeditions fully discussed and related to the period during which reliefs were sculpted.

Contents: (I) Progetto, composizione e significato dei cicli narrativi nei palazzi di Kalkhu, di Dur Sharrukin e di Ninive; (II) Realtà storica e livelli di lettura nei relievi narrativi di Assurnasirpal II a Kalkhu; (III) Valore e gusto dell'arte di Assurnasirpal II nel Palazzo Nord-Ovest di Kalkhu; (IV) I rilievi del Palazzo Centrale di Kalkhu e le sperimentazioni spaziali di Tiglatpileser III; (V) Il classicismo sargonico di Dur Sharrukin tra tradizione arcaica e gusto innovativo; (VI) Programma figurativo e circolazione interna nel palazzo di Sargon II a Dur Sharrukin; (VII) Lo spazio architettonico e la rappresentazione dello spazio naturale da Sargon II a Sennacherib; (VIII) Spazio scenografico e miniaturismo plastico nella rivoluzione artistica di Sennacherib; (IX) L'arte de Assurbanipal a Ninive: recupero e superamento del codice tradizionale; (X) I rilievi venatori di Assurbanipal e il trionfo dello spazio astratto.

Bibliografia, p.[213]–32. Fonti delle illustrazioni e ringraziamenti, p.[233]–36. Indice dei nomi di persona di divinità e di popoli, p.[237]–38. Indice dei nomi di città, di stati, di templi, di regioni, di monti e di fiumi, p.[239]–44.

K50 Ortiz, George. In pursuit of the absolute art of the ancient world: the George Ortiz collection. Foreword by John Boardman. Berne, Benteli-Werd, 1996. 1v. (unpaged), col. il.

Catalog of the exhibition, State Hermitage Museum, St. Petersburg (1993), and other locations. Treats "ancient Greece, but . . . range[s] from prehistoric Mesopotamia, through the arts of the eastern steppes, to more recent works from Africa and Polynesia that are today classified as ethnographic."—*Foreword.*

Contents: Near East (Sumer, Bactria, Babylon, Elam, Khurvin, Levant, Ancient Anatolia); Egypt; Greek world (Neolithic, Cycladic, Minoan, Mycenaen, Cypriot); European bronze age, Greek World (Geometric, Geometric-Archaic, Archaic, Classical, Hellenistic, Gandhara); Sardinian; Etruscan; Iberian; Achaemenid; China; Eurasian Art ("Animal style"); Roman; Sassanian; Byzantine; Africa; America; Pacific (Polynesia, Micronesia).

Exhibitions archaeology. Exhibitions ethnography. Glossary archaeology. Glossary ethnography [unpaginated].

K51 Page, Anthea. Egyptian sculpture: archaic to Saite from the Petrie collection. With an introd. and trans. by Professor H. S. Smith. Warminster, Eng., Aris and Philips, [1976]. 124p. il.

Scholarly catalog of part of the Petrie Museum of Egyptian Antiquities at University College, London. The core of the collection was gathered by Sir W. M. Flinders Petrie in the late 19th and early 20th centuries. "The catalogue presents the statuary of stone and of wood representing human beings of the Dynastic period of Egypt's history."—*Pref.*

Objects published in previous catalogs of the collection are omitted.

Index of numbers [i.e., concordance], p.123. Index of names, p.124.

K52 Russmann, Edna R. Egyptian sculpture: Cairo and Luxor. Photographs by David Finn. Austin, Univ. of Texas Pr., 1989. 230p. col. il., maps.

"The text is not intended as an art history, or even a systematic analysis of Egyptian sculpture. It is a celebration of certain specific statues, and I have tried to describe what I find most attractive or intriguing in each."—*Author's pref.*

Contents: (1) The art of Egyptian sculpture; (2) The first great period; (3) The classic period; (4) Creation of an empire; (5) Revolution and aftermath; (6) Egypt the ancestor.

Bibliography, p.222–26. Index, p.227–30.

K53 Seidel, Matthias. Die königlichen Statuengruppen. Hildesheim, Gerstenberg, 1996– . (1)v. il. plates. (Hildesheimer ägyptologische Beiträge, 42)

A systematic study of royal statue groups, not statues of individuals.

Contents: (1) Die Denkmäler vom alten Reich bis zum Ende der 18. Dynastie.

K54 Spanel, Donald. Through ancient eyes: Egyptian portraiture. Birmingham, Birmingham Museum of Art, 1988. 159 p. il.

Catalog of the exhibition, Birmingham Museum of Art (1988). Thorough discussion of the nature of Egyptian portrait sculpture.

The kings of Egypt, p.135–39. Abbreviations, p.141–51. Select bibliography, p.153–56. Concordance, p.157–59.

K55 Spycket, Agnes. La statuaire du Proche-Orient ancien. Leiden, Brill, 1981. 474p. plates, map. (Handbuch der Orientalistik. Siebente Abteilung, Kunst und Archäologie; 1. Bd., Der alte Vordere Orient, 2. Abschnitt, Die Denkmäler, B. Vorderasien, Lfg. 2)

A comprehensive history of sculpture in the ancient Near East from its beginnings to the 6th century B.C.

Contents: (I) Des origines à l'apparition de l'écriture (ca. 8000–3200 av. J.-C.); (II) La période protohistorique (Fin Uruk-Jemdet Nasr: 3200–2900 env. av. J.-C,); (III) L'époque dynastique archaïque ou présargonique (2900–2350 env. av. J.-C.); (IV) La dynastie d'Akkad ou d'Agadé (2335–2150 av. J.-C.); (V) La fin du IIIe millénaire (2150–2000 av. J.-C.); (VI) Les premiers siècle du IIe millénaire (2000–1600 av. J.-C.); (VII) La second partie du IIe millénaire (1600–1000 av. J.-C.); (VIII) Le Ier millénaire jusqu'à la conquête du Proche-Orient par Alexandre le Grand (1000–333 av. J.-C.).

Bibliographie, p.[441]–49. Index, p.[450]–63. Index des statues par collections et par chapitres, p.[464]–74.

Classical World

General Works

K56 Ancient art from the V. G. Simkhovitch collection. Ed. by Wolf Rudolf and Adriana Calinescu. Bloomington, Indiana Univ. Art Museum, 1988. 198p. il.

Catalog of the exhibition, Indiana University Art Museum (1987). V. G. Simkhovitch, a scholar and teacher at Columbia University 1904–1944, was an avid collector who donated his treasures to Indiana University in 1963.

Contents: Stone sculpture [Cypriote, Greek, Roman]; Bronze and silver sculpture and metalwork [Greek, Etruscan and Italic, Roman, vessels]; Pottery; Terracotta; Varia, including non-classical.

Glossary, p.191–93. References cited in abbreviated form, p.194–97. Index of collections, p.198.

K57 Antike Plastik. Hrsg. im Auftrage des Deutschen Archäologischen Institutes von Walter-Herwig Schuchhardt. Berlin, Mann, 1962– . (21) Lfg. mounted il. plates, maps

See GLAH 1:K25 for previous installments. Lfg. XII–XX ed. by Felix Eckstein. Beginning Lfg. XXI ed. by Adolf Heinrich Borbein.

K58 Bartman, Elizabeth. Ancient sculptural copies in miniature. Leiden, Brill, 1992. 222p. il. plates. (Columbia studies in the classical tradition, 19)

Expansion of the author's dissertation.

"There can be no doubt that the author has produced a useful synthesis which displays considerable insight and sensitivity within a notoriously difficult area of scholarship."—*Review*, Burlington magazine v.135, Dec. 1993, p.830.

Contents: Part I: The miniature copy in context: (I) Definitions; (II) Statuary types and materials; (III) History and function. Part II: Case studies: (IV) Formal principles and techniques: the Resting Satyr; (V) Modern prejudices against the miniature: the Lateran Poseidon; (VI) The conceit of the small: the Heracles Epitrapezios. Appendices: (1) Herakles Epitrapezios and the Phoenicians; (2a) Comparative measurements of the large-scale replicas of the Resting Satyr; (2b) Comparative measurements of the large-scale heads of the Resting Satyr; (3) Comparative measurements of the small-scale replicas of the Resting Satyr; (4) Comparative measurements of replicas of the Lateran Poseidon; (5) Comparative measurements of replicas of the Herakles Epitrapezios.

Selected bibliography, p.[198]–203. Index of ancient passages cited, p.[209]. Museum index, p.[210]–17. Subject index, p.[218]–22.

K59 Bieber, Margarete. Ancient copies: contributions to the history of Greek and Roman art. N.Y., New York Univ. Pr., 1977. 302p. plates

Study of a large number of Greek and Roman statues in which the form of dress and the manner of draping costumes determines the sculpture to be authentic or a copy. Some chapters previously published in Proceedings of the American Philosophical Society (1959, 1962).

Contents: (1) Problems and research on copies (1889–1970); (2) The author's approach to the problem; (3) The importance of clothing in judging Roman copies; (4) Original and copy; (5) Addition of clothing and attributes; (6) Different reasons for denuding in Greek and Roman art; (7) Artemis and the Lares; (8) The fusing of parts of the same or of different dresses; (9) The shoulder-back mantle; (10) The right and wrong ways of draping the himation; (11) Roman men in Greek himation (Romani Palliati) and their female counterparts; (12) The copies of the Herculaneum women; (13) Portraits of Roman ladies as priestesses of Ceres and of empresses as Augustae or Divae; (14) Typical mistakes and mannerisms found on Roman copies; (15) An outline of the history of copying; (16) Late antique and early Christian copies.

List of abbreviations, xiii–xx. Bibliography, p.275–82. Museums and sites, p.283–95. Index, p.297–302.

K60 Bildkatalog der Skulpturen des Vatikanischen Museums. Berlin, de Gruyter, 1995– . (2)v. chiefly il.

Primarily a photographic record supplementing Walther Amelung's Die Sculpturen des Vanticanischen Museums. Berlin, Reimer, 1903–56. 4v.

Contents: (1) Museo Chiaramonti, von B. Andreae . . . [et al.] (3v.; 1995); (2) Museo Pio Clementino: cortile ottagono, von B. Andreae . . . [et al.] (1998).

K61 Boston. Museum of Fine Arts. Sculpture in stone: the Greek, Roman and Etruscan collections of the Museum of Fine Arts, Boston. [By] Mary B. Comstock and Cornelius C. Vermeule. Boston, Museum of Fine Arts, 1976. 296p. il.

"The purpose of this volume is to create a useful working reference, not a vast compendium of miscellaneous information."—*Introd.*

Contents: Cycladic; Archaic; Fifth century; Fourth century; Hellenistic; Greek portraits; Graeco-Roman, round; Graeco-Roman, relief; Roman portraits; Etruscan; Palmyrene; Cypriote; Post-Classical.

Bibliography, xvii–xx. Short title index; xxi–xxviii. Exhibition catalogues, xxix. Abbreviations, xxxi. Addenda to references accompanying the catalog entries, p.289. Index, p.291–94. Concordance, p.295–6.

K62 ———. Sculpture in stone and bronze: additions to the collections of Greek, Etruscan, and Roman art, 1971–1988, in the Museum of Fine Arts, Boston. Catalog [by] Cornelius C. Vermeule III. Bibliography [by] Mary B. Comstock. With contrib. by Ariel Herrmann . . . [et al.] Boston, The Museum, 1988. 132p. il.

Annotated catalog of the museum's acquisitions, 1971–88.

Contents: Sculpture in stone; Sculpture in bronze.

Short titles and abbreviations, p.10–17. Concordance, p.101. Index, p.103–05. Bibliography, p.106–28. Concordance for sculpture in stone, p.129–30. Concordance for Greek, Etruscan and Roman bronzes, p.131–32.

K63 La Collezione Boncompagni Ludovisi: Algardi, Bernini e la fortuna dell'antico. A cura di Antonio Giuliano. Venezia, Marsilio, [1992]. 256p. il. (part col.)

Catalog of the exhibition, Fondazione Memmo, Palazzo Ruspoli, Rome (1992). Discusses a collection of marble sculpture and its influence on later sculptors.

Contents: La Villa Ludovisi e la collezione di sculture, di Adele Anna Amadio; La fortuna dei marmi Ludovisi nel cinquecento e seicento, di Giulia Fusconi; La fortuna dei marmi Ludovisi nel settecento e ottocento, di Lucia Pirzio, Biroli Stefanelli; Catalogo delle opere; Apparati: Il mito della classicità e il restauro della sculture antiche nel XVII secolo a Roma, di Italo Faldi; Note sul restauro del marmi Ludovisi, di Maria Rita Sanzi Di Mino.

Appendix: Le "Osservationi della scoltura antica" di Orfeo Boselli, a cura di Adele Anna Amadio, p.235–42. Bibliografia, p.243–56.

K64 Glyptothek München. Katalog der Skulpturen. Hrsg. von Klaus Vierneisel. München, Beck, 1979– . (3)v. il.

Detailed catalog of a major collection of classical sculpture. Vols. published out of numerical sequence. Extensive annotations include detailed basic facts, list of possible replicas, dating, possible attributions, and bibliography.

Contents: (II) Klassische Skulpturen des 5. und 4. Jahrhunderts v. Chr., bearb. von Barbara Vierneisel-Schlörb; (III) Klassische Grabdenkmäler und Votivreliefs, bearb. von Barbara Vierneisel-Schlörb; (VI) Römische Idealplastik, bearb. von Michaela Fuchs. Projected volumes: (I) Archaische Skulpturen; (IV) Hellenistische Skulpturen; (V) Römische Portraits; (VII) Römische Reliefwerke; (VIII) Römische dekorative Marmorwerke.

Each vol. contains indices, bibliography and a concordance relating the new catalog numbers to the Furtwängler catalog of 1910.

K65 The Gods delight: the human figure in classical bronze. Organized by Arielle P. Kozloff and David Gordon Mitten. Sections by Suzannah Fabing . . . [et al.] Cleveland, Cleveland Museum of Art, 1988. 373p. il. (part col.)

Catalog of the exhibition, Cleveland Museum of Art (1988), and other locations. Lengthy annotations and notes related to condition, exhibition record, and publication citations accompany multiple views of each object.

Contents: Note on patina and surface decoration, by David Gordon Mitten; Greek bronzes, by Marion True; Etruscan bronzes, by Suzannah Fabing; Roman bronzes, by John J. Herrmann, Jr.

Abbreviated citations and bibliography, p.366–69. Glossary, p.370–73.

K66 Hanfmann, George M. A., and Ramage, Nancy H. Sculpture from Sardis: the finds through 1975. Cambridge, Mass., Harvard Univ. Pr., 1978. 322p. il. (Archaeological exploration of Sardis. Report, 2)

Description of a site in Turkey and catalog of the sculpture found there. Originally discovered in 1853, it contained important Lydian, Persian, Hellenistic, Roman, and Early Byzantine era architectural and free-standing sculpture.

Contents: (I) Scope of the work and character of the material; The sculpture of the prehistoric Lydian, and Persian periods: (II) An overview and appraisal; (III) Literary, epigraphic, and archaeological evidence; (IV) Catalogue; The sculpture of the Hellenistic, Roman, and early Byzantine periods: (V) Literary, epigraphic and archaeological evidence; (VI) Catalogue; Supplementary evidence for sculpture from Sardis: (VII) Sculpture from Sardis in European, Turkish, and American collections; (VIII) Sculpture from other sites in Lydia; (IX) Inscriptions of lost statues.

Appendix: The city goddess of Sardis on the base from Puteoli, p.[180]–81. Concordance of finds, p.[185]–88. Concordance of entry and text-page numbers, p.[189]–92. General index, p.[193]–203. Index of inscriptions, p.203.

K67 Harvard University. Art Museums. Stone sculptures: the Greek, Roman and Etruscan collections of the Harvard University Art Museums. [By] Cornelius C. Vermeule and Amy Brauer. Cambridge, Mass., Harvard Univ. Art Museums, 1990. 184p. il.

Detailed annotations and photographs of a collection of sculpture from the Classical world.

Contents: History of the collections; Note to the catalogue; Prehistoric and Archaic; Greek fifth and fourth centuries: originals and copies; Hellenistic: originals and copies; Roman Imperial: statuary and reliefs; Etruscan and Roman sarcophagi and urns; Roman portraits: republic to late antique; Roman-Egyptian and Syrian (Palmyrene) sepulchral reliefs; Post-Classical.

Bibliography, p.171–83. Concordance of acquisition numbers, p.184.

K68 Jenkins, Ian. Archaeologists and aesthetes in the Sculpture Galleries of the British Museum, 1800–1939. London, Trustees of the British Museum, 1992. 264p. il. (part col.) plans.

"Comprehensive account of the development of the sculpture collections of the British Museum. This book is a fine combination of first-rate scholarship and an engaging style."—*Review*, American journal of archaeology v.100, July 1996, p.633–34.

Contents: Part I: (1) "The triumph of excellence"; (2) The museum as a drawing school; (3) Light, colour and dirt; (4) The chain of art. Part II: (5) Arcadia in Bloomsbury: the Elgin and Phigaleian marbles; (6) The Townley gallery: Greece and Rome; (7) Lycian tombs and Assyrian palaces; (8) Charles Newton and the sculptures from Asia Minor. Part III: (9) The contest for Attica; (10) The chain is broken.

Notes, p.231–51. Chronology of principal events, p.252–53. Bibliography, p.254–60. Index, p.261–64.

K69 Mattusch, Carol C. Classical bronzes: the art and craft of Greek and Roman statuary. Ithaca, Cornell Univ. Pr., 1996. 241p. il.

Focuses on medium and technology, rather than style and iconography.

"A careful, erudite, richly informative treatment of Greek and Roman bronzes that forces a reevaluation of the very nature of the genre."—*Review*, American journal of archaeology v.101, July 1997, p.587–91.

Contents: (1) Art, market, and product; (2) Repeated images; (3) Portraits; (4) Bronzes of uncertain date; (5) A Greek bronze original?; (6) Torsos; (7) Tools of the trade.

Abbreviations, xv–xvii. Index, p.233–41.

K70 ______. The fire of Hephaistos: large classical bronzes from North American collections. With contrib. by Beryl Barr-Sharrar . . . [et al.] Cambridge, Mass., Harvard Univ. Art Museums, 1996. 359p. il. (part col.)

Catalog of the exhibition, Harvard University Art Museums (1996), and other locations.

"The detailed technical analysis of each piece represents a significant contribution to the study of ancient sculptural production and provides important and interesting insights into how the casting process might influence and affect the style and appearance of ancient bronzes."—*Review*, American journal of archaeology v.101, Oct. 1997, p.806–07.

Contents: The preferred medium: the many lives of classical bronzes, by Carol C. Mattusch; Color plates; Understanding, restoring, and conserving ancient bronzes with the aid of science, by Arthur Beale; The sculptor and the poet in classical art, by A. E. Raubitschek; Alexander the Great as patron of the arts, by Blanche R. Brown; The private use of small bronze sculpture, by Beryl Barr-Scharrar; Roman bronze statuary—beyond technology, by Brunilde Sismondo Ridgway; Honors to Romans: bronze portraits, by Andrew Oliver. Catalogue: (I) Introduction: Hephaistos: god of fire and of metals; (II) From the parts to the whole; (III) Forever young; (IV) Goddess or portrait of a woman?; (V) Men we think we ought to know.

General and bibliographic abbreviations, p.44–50. Technical abbreviations, p.179. General index, p.352–59.

K71 Paris. Musée National du Louvre. Département des antiquités orientales. Catalogue des antiquités de Chypre: sculptures. [By] Antoine Hermary. Avant-propos, Annie Caubet. Préf. Olivier Masson. Paris, Réunion des musées nationaux, 1989. 496p. il. (part col.) map.

Inventory-catalog of the collection. Includes a brief summary of the Vogüé, Waddington, Duthoit expedition to Cyprus in 1862, the Duthoit expedition of 1865, and subsequent expeditions and acquisitions.

Appendix: Sculptures "chypro-ioniennes," p.481–84. Références bibliographiques, p.485–87. Concordance des numéros d'inventaire avec ceux du catalogue, p.488–90. Concordance des numéros Vogüé avec les numéros d'inventaire, p.491. Provenance des objects, p.492–93. Liste des donateurs, p.494.

K72 Princeton University. Art Museum. Greek sculpture in the Art Museum, Princeton University: Greek originals, Roman copies and variants. [Ed.] by Brunilde S. Ridgway . . . [et al.] Princeton, N.J., The Museum, 1994. 131p. il. (part col.)

Annotated catalog of the collection with a note on its history.

Abbreviations, p.8. Index, p.127–30. Concordance, p.131.

K73 Ridgway, Brunilde Sismondo. Roman copies of Greek sculpture: the problem of the originals. Ann Arbor, Univ. of Michigan Pr., 1984. 111p. plates. (Thomas Spencer Jerome Lectures, 15th Ser.)

Questions the traditional view that Roman sculptors occupied themselves exclusively with the mechanical copying of Greek originals.

"The Jerome Lectures gave me the opportunity to try to reverse the familiar process: instead of looking at the Roman copies to reconstruct the Greek prototype behind them, why not attempt to locate the originals themselves, to determine their accessibility for copying?"—*Introd.*

Contents: (1) The Greek evidence; (2) The Roman evidence; (3) Defining copies and their problems; (4) The evidence of the Panhellenic sanctuaries; (5) Other Greek sanctuaries; (6) The evidence from the city of Athens and other sites; (7) Problems of definition and distribution; (8) Letting the "copies" speak for themselves.

Abbreviations, [ix]–xi.

K74 Schröder, Stephan F. Katalog der antiken Skulpturen des Museo del Prado in Madrid. Mainz am Rhein, Zabern, 1993– . (1)v. il. (part col.)

Complete catalog of classical sculpture sponsored by the Deutsches Archäologisches Institut, Madrid. First vol. includes a history of the collection by Pilar Léon.

Contents: (1) Die Porträts.

K75 Vermeule, Cornelius C. Greek and Roman sculpture in America: masterpieces in public collections in the United States and Canada. Berkeley, Univ. of California Pr.; Malibu, J. Paul Getty Museum, 1981. 406p. il. (part col.)

Illustrated inventory of 350 pieces from 81 collections in North America. Entries include location, physical description, and provenance, along with bibliographic references.

"Many a layman, high school teacher, or Latin student of twenty years ago will be surprised to find so many examples of Classical sculpture in their backyards."—*Review*, Journal of aesthetic education 21, winter 1987, p.158–60.

Contents: (I) Early Greek and archaic sculpture; (II) Classical sculpture of the fifth century, B.C.; (III) Classical sculpture of the early fourth century, B.C.; (IV) Cypriote sculpture; (V) Classical sculpture of the later fourth century, B.C.; (VI) Classical funerary sculpture; (VII) Hellenistic portraits; (VIII) Hellenistic sculpture; (IX) Archaistic and Neoattic sculpture; (X) Graeco-Roman sculpture; (XI) Roman sarcophagi; (XII) Other Roman sculpture; (XIII) Roman portraits; (XIV) Palmyrene funerary reliefs.

Glossary, p.390. Abbreviations, p. 391–93. Index of collections (by city), p.394–401. Index of personal names, p.402–03. Index of place names, p.403–04. Index of mythological names, p.405.

K76 Walker, Susan. Greek and Roman portraits. London, British Museum Pr., 1995. 112 p. il. (Classical Bookshelf)

History and functions of portrait sculpture in Greek and Roman antiquity. "This short book arises from a course of eight lectures on Greek and Roman portraits given to undergraduates at Cambridge University in 1992."—*Pref.*

Contents: (1) Introduction; (2) What is a portrait for?; (3) The beginnings of Greek portraiture; (4) Portraits of Greeks in the Roman world; (5) Greek portraits of rulers; (6) The imperial image of Augustus; (7) The Roman image; (8) Bearded and beardless men; (9) Dress; (10) Epilogue.

Further reading, p.[110]. Index, p.[111]–12.

Crete, Mycenae, and Greece

K77 Barron, John. An introduction to Greek sculpture. N.Y., Schocken, 1984. 176p. il.

"In this book I have sought to follow the development of full-scale Greek sculpture over a period of almost exactly five hundred years."—*Pref.*

Contents: (1) The early archaic period, c.660–580; (2) The middle archaic period, c.580–540; (3) The late archaic period, c.540–480; (4) The transitional period, c.480–450; (5) Classical idealism, c.450–380; (6) Fourth-century naturalism, c.380–300; (7) Hellenistic virtuosity, c.300–150.

Index, p.175–76.

K78 Bieber, Margarete. The sculpture of the Hellenistic age. [Reprint.] N.Y., Hacker, 1981. 259p. il. plates.

See GLAH 1:K39 for original annotation.

K79 Boardman, John. Greek sculpture: the archaic period: a handbook. N.Y., Thames and Hudson, 1991. 252p. il. (World of art)

1st ed., 1978.

Contains minor corrections and additions to the 1978 ed. along with 2 additional illustrations.

Surveys sculpture of the mainland, islands, and East Greeks from about 1000 B.C. to the early 5th century, B.C. "This is certainly the best introduction to the subject there is . . . a compact and astonishingly comprehensive survey, clearly and attractively presented."—*Review* by Martin Robertson, Burlington magazine v.121, Aug. 1979, p.527.

Contents: (1) Introduction; (2) The Dark Ages and Geometric period; (3) The Orientalizing styles; (4) Marble and the monumental; (5) The maturing Archaic styles; (6) The later Archaic styles; (7) Architectural sculpture; (8) Reliefs; (9) Animals and monsters; (10) Conclusions.

Abbreviations, p.241. Notes and bibliographies, p.242–44. Index of illustrations, p.248–49. Index of artists, p.250. General index, p.250–52.

K80 ———. Greek sculpture: the classical period: a handbook. N.Y., Thames and Hudson, 1985. 252p. il. (World of art)

Coverage limited to sculpture of the Greek homeland in the 5th century, B.C., not the western colonies. Sequel to the preceding entry. "The Classical Period is a book which will be essential reading for all students and a useful work of reference for more advanced scholars."—*Review*, Burlington magazine v.129, June 1987, p.400.

Contents: (1) Techniques and sources; (2) Early classical sculpture: introduction; (3) Early classical men and women: I; (4) Olympia: the temple of Zeus; (5) Early classical men and women: II; (6) Early classical relief sculpture; (7) Names and attributions; (8) Other copies of the early classical; (9) Classical sculpture and Athens: introduction; (10) The Parthenon; (11) Other Attic architectural sculpture; (12) Themes in Attic sculpture; (13) Other classical sculpture; (14) Other classical relief sculpture; (15) Names and attributions; (16) Other copies of the classical.

Abbreviations, p.241. Notes and bibliographies, p.242–47. Index of illustrations, p.248. Index of artists, p.249. General index, p.250–52

K81 ———. Greek sculpture: the late classical period. N.Y., Thames and Hudson, 1995. 248p. il. maps. (World of art)

"This volume is a sequel to the two on the Archaic and Classical periods of Greek sculpture. . . [GLAH 2:K79, GLAH 2:K80]. Its narrative ends more or less where R.R.R. Smith's Hellenistic sculpture [GLAH 2:K100] begins."—*Pref.*

Contents: (I) Late classical sculpture: (1) Introduction; (2) Architectural sculpture; (3) Names and attributions; (4) Gods and goddesses, men and women; (5) Portraiture; (6) Funerary sculpture; (7) Other reliefs; (II) The western Greeks: (8) Introduction; (9) Architectural sculpture; (10) Other sculpture; (III) Greek sculpture to east and south: (11) Anatolia; (12) The Levant and North Africa; (IV) Ancient and antique: (13) Collecting and collections.

Abbreviations, p.237. Notes and bibliographies, p.238–43. Index of illustrations, p.244. Index of ancient artists' names, p.245. General index, p.246–48.

K82 ———. The Parthenon and its sculptures. Photographs by David Finn. Austin, Univ. of Texas Pr., 1985. 256p. il. (part col.)

"Our method here has been . . . to let the building and its sculptures speak for themselves through photographs and the sympathetic imagination of the photographer's eyes."—*Pref.* "Its worth is enhanced by its emphasis on the historical, religious and iconographic context of the monument rather than on a merely art-historical description."—*Review*, Archaeology v.40, Mar./Apr. 1987, p.72–3.

Contents: The narrative (Celebration; Destruction; Conception; Creation; Completion); The plates (The pediments; The frieze; The metopes; Captions to the plates); The evidence: (1) The nature of our sources; (2) The later history of the Parthenon; (3) Athens and history; (4) The great Panathenaic festival; (5) The architecture; (6) The sculptures and cult statue; (7) The interpretation of the sculpture; (8) The Parthenon's role and significance, then and now.

Further reading, p.253–54. Index, p.255–56.

K83 Clairmont, Christoph W. Classical Attic tombstones. Kilchberg, Sw., Akanthvs, 1993– . (9)v. plates.

"The present work is meant to be a supplement to A Conze's Die attischen Grabreliefs [GLAH 1:K44]. . . . [In it] are gathered published and unpublished memorials which I could track down worldwide in addition to tombstones already known to Conze, irrespective of whether or not the originals have been seen by the present writer."—*Pref.*

Catalog entries include provenance, when available, and as complete a verbal description as possible.

Contents: Introductory volume; (I)–(IV) Catalogue; (V) Prosopography; (VI) Indexes; Plate volume; Supplementary volume.

Bibliography, Introductory volume, p.268–311.

K84 Fuchs, Werner. Die griechische Plastik. München, Beck, 1987– . (1)v. il.

Projected series of vols. on Greek sculpture. V.1 treats materials and techniques and geometric sculpture. Discussion of archaistic sculpture subdivide by region.

Contents: (I) Floren, Josef. Die geometrische und archaische Plastik (1987).

K85 Kleemann, Ilse. Frühe Bewegung. Untersuchungen zur archaischen Form bis zum Aufkommen der Ponderation in der greichischen Kunst. Mainz am Rhein, Zabern, 1984– . (1)v. il.

A discussion of the aesthetics and formal composition of Greek sculpture. Also includes remarks about sculptors' methods.

Contents: (1) Grundzüge der Anlage von Bewegung (2v., 1984).

K86 Moreno, Paolo. Scultura ellenistica. Rome, Libreria dello Stato, 1994. 2v. il. (part col.)

Major treatment of the history of Hellenistic sculpture from Alexander to Augustus throughout the Mediterranean world. Discusses individual pieces and groups similar works to arrive at stylistic conclusions. Also compares poses and themes of sculpture to works in other media.

Contents: Introduzione; Maniera classica (323–301): La libertà dell'artista; Autonomia e mimesi; Barocco ellenistico (301–168): La gloria dei regni; La città dei filosofi; Verità e bellezza; L'arte nella vita; Verità e allegoria; La vita nell'arte; Sublime metafisico; Luci e ombre; Tradizione e innovazione; Restaurazione romana (168–31): Rinascita del classico; Astrazione; Virtuosismo; Simbolismo; Verismo; Eclettismo.

Note, p.765–832. Abbreviazione, p.833–35. Bibliografia, p.837–904. Fotografie e disegni, p.905–09. Indici, p.911–69.

K87 Pfuhl, Ernst, and Möbius, Hans. Die ostgriechischen Grabreliefs, Mainz am Rhein, Zabern, 1977–79. 2v. in 4 il.

Catalog of reliefs from sepulchral monuments of the East Greeks. Entries are grouped by period and then typologically by activity or occupation of the subject. See reviews by Brunilde Sismondo Ridgway in American journal of archaeology 82, no.3, summer, 1978, p.414–15, and 84, no.4, Oct., 1980, p.543–44.

Contents: (I) Textband: Vorklassische und klassische Grabreliefs; Hellenistische und spätere Grabreliefs; Tafelband; (II) Textband: Hellenistische und spätere Grabreliefs [continued]; Tafelband.

Abkürzungen, v.I, p.[xvii]–xviii. Indices und Konkordanzen, v.II, p.[571]–612.

K88 Richter, Gisela Maria Augusta. The archaic gravestones of Attica. [Reprint.] Bedminster, Bristol, Bristol Classical Press, 1988. 184p. il.

See GLAH 1:K54 for original annotation.

K89 ______. Korai: archaic Greek maidens: a study of the development of the Kore type in Greek sculpture. [Reprint.] N.Y., Hacker Art Books, 1988. 327p. il.

See GLAH 1:K55 for original annotation.

K90 ______. Portraits of the Greeks. Abridged and rev. by R. R. R. Smith. Ithaca, N.Y., Cornell Univ. Pr., 1984. 256p. il.

See GLAH 1:K57 for original annotation.

Bibliography, p.[251]–52.

K91 Ridgway, Brunilde Sismondo. The archaic style in Greek sculpture. Princeton, N.J., Princeton Univ. Pr., 1977. 336p. plates.

"The present book attempts a formulation of questions meant to reopen old problems and to encourage further thinking. It is my hope that this work will be particularly helpful to students, to whom it is directed."—*Pref.*

Contents: (I) Defining archaic sculpture: (1) Problems of chronology, geography, and typology; (2) The problem of the origins: the Daedalic phase; (II) Sculptural types: (3) Kouroi and related male figures; (4) Korai and other female figures; (5) Seated, reclining and equestrian figures; (6) Funerary monuments, animals and monsters; (III) Architectural sculpture: (7) Pediments and akroteria; (8) Metopes; (9) Friezes; (IV) Sculptors and problems of style: (10) Sculptors and their workshops; (11) Archaizing; archaistic; Roman copies of archaic works.

Bibliographies following each chapter. List of photographic sources, ix–xi. List of abbreviations, xiii–xix. Index, p.323–36.

K92 ______. Fifth century styles in Greek sculpture. Princeton, N.J., Princeton Univ. Pr., 1981. 256p. plates.

"I have . . . conceived of my task as that of concentrating exclusively on sculpture . . . and of delving into complexities of style rather than of providing basic information. Thus not all fifth century monuments have been discussed, and those included are not all discussed to the same extent."—*Pref.*

Contents: (1) Greek sculpture in the fifth century; (2) Architectural sculpture: metopes; (3) Architectural sculpture: pediments and akroteria; (4) Architectural sculpture: friezes; (5) Greek originals: sculpture in the round; (6) Greek originals: reliefs; (7) The great masters; (8) Copies of fifth century works; (9) Echoes of fifth century styles in later periods—Roman creations; Appendixes.

Bibliographies follow each chapter. List of abbreviations, xiii–xv. Glossary, xvii–xix. Index, p.249–56.

K93 ———. Fourth-century styles in Greek sculpture. Madison, Univ. of Wisconsin Pr., 1997. 480p. il. plates (Wisconsin studies in classics)

Key survey in the history of sculpture before the Christian era. Based upon lectures and seminars delivered at institutions in the U.S. and Scotland.

Contents: (1) Greek sculpture in the fourth century; (2) Architectural sculpture on the mainland; (3) Architectural sculpture in the East (non-Greek); (4) Architectural sculpture in the East (Greek); (5) Original reliefs: funerary; (6) Original reliefs: votive, mythological, document; (7) The issue of the great masters; (8) Lysippos: a case study; (9) Random Harvest.

Bibliography, p.375–89. Selective index, p.391–400.

K94 ———. Hellenistic sculpture I. Madison, Univ. of Wisconsin Pr., 1990. (1)v. il. plates.

"Discusses a large number of works and adroitly presents the evidence, problems, and debates for each, while also offering numerous and often challenging theories of her own."—*Review* of v.1 by Mark D. Stansbury-O'Donnell, American journal of archaeology 95, July 1991, p.554–5.

Contents: (1) The styles of ca. 331–200 B.C. (1990).

K95 ———. Roman copies of Greek sculpture: the problem of the originals. Ann Arbor, Univ. of Michigan Pr., 1984. 111p. plates (Jerome Lectures, 15th ser.)

An analysis of the problem of Greek originals versus Roman copies of Greek sculpture.

"A long, hard look at the subject . . . that is both humane and engaging to the reader."—*Review* by Andrew Stewart, Journal of hellenic studies 105, 1985, p.232–3.

Contents: (1) The Greek evidence; (2) The Roman evidence; (3) Defining copies and their problems; (4) The evidence of the panhellenic sanctuaries; (5) Other Greek sanctuaries; (6) The evidence from the city of Athens and other sites; (7) Problems of definition and distribution; (8) Letting the "copies" speak for themselves.

Abbreviations, [ix]–xi.

K96 ———. The severe style in Greek sculpture. [Paperback reprint.] Princeton, N.J., Princeton Univ. Pr., 1979. 155, [67]p. plates.

See GLAH 1:K59 for original annotation.

K97 Rolley, Claude. Greek bronzes. Translated from the French by Roger Howell. Foreword by John Boardman. London, Sotheby's, 1986. 267p. il. (part col.) maps.

"For students and lovers of Greek art an arcane but rewarding subject is made intelligible."—*Foreword.*

Contents: (I) Bronze and bronzes: techniques and functions; (II) Apprenticeship and experience; (III) Greece of the city states: schools and local styles; (IV) Classicism—in the shadow of the masters; (V) The Hellenistic world: from kings to bourgeois; Epilogue: from Greece to Rome.

Catalogue, p.232–48. Glossary, p.249. A short chronological table, p.250–51. Bibliography, p.256–60. List of museums, p.261. Index of names, p.264–67.

K98 ———. La sculpture grècque. Paris, Picard, 1994– . (1)v. il. (part col.) maps. (Les manuels d'art et d'archéologie antiques)

Projected series on Greek sculpture. Also part of a grand scheme to create a series of vols. that treat early art and archeology for the benefit of university students and the interested general public.

Contents: (1) Des origines au milieu du Ve siècle (1994).

K99 Les sculptures grecques. Par Mariane Hamiaux, sous la dir. d'Alain Pasquier. Paris, Réunion des musées nationaux, 1992. 2v. il.

Catalog of Greek sculpture in the Département des antiquités grecques, étrusques et romaines, Musée du Louvre.

Contents: (1) Des origines à la fin du IVe siècle avant J.-C.; (2) La période hellénistique (IIIe–Ier siècles avant J.-C.).

Includes concordances, indexes, bibliographies.

K100 Smith, R. R. R. Hellenistic sculpture. N.Y., Thames and Hudson, 1991. 287p. il. (World of art)

Introduction summarizes key issues, including the context and function of Hellenistic sculptures, the relationship between patrons and sculptors, and the tension between surviving originals and copies. Two main sections survey Hellenistic sculpture by subject and by geographic area.

"A worthy complement to John Boardman's Greek Sculpture volumes [GLAH 2:K79, GLAH 2:K80] on the archaic and Classical periods. . . . Accessibility of its prose, its sound scholarship and ease of use make it a must for all students of ancient sculpture."—*Review*, American journal of archaeology v.96, July 1992, p.565–6.

Abbreviations, p.276. Notes and bibliography, p.277–82. Index of illustrations, p.284–85. Index, p.286–87.

K101 Spivey, Nigel Jonathan. Understanding Greek sculpture: ancient meanings, modern readings. N.Y., Thames and Hudson, 1996. 240p. il. map.

Focus on the material, placement, and purpose of Greek sculpture. Includes drawings that reconstruct sculpture and places it in an architectural context.

"Spivey's book is a readable, spirited one."—*Review*, American journal of archaeology v.101, July 1997, p.587–91.

Contents: (1) Introduction; (2) "The Greek revolution"; (3) Daedalus and the wings of Techne; (4) Sacred decoration; (5) Heroes apparent; (6) From Marathon to the Parthenon; (7) In search of Pheidias; (8) Revealing Aphrodite; (9) The patronage of kings; (10) Graecia Capta; Epilogue.

Sources and further reading, p.232–36. Index p.238–40.

K102 Stewart, Andrew F. Greek sculpture: an exploration. New Haven, Yale Univ. Pr., 1990. 2v. il.

"Though this book was begun as a successor to Gisela Richter's Sculpture and sculptors of the Greeks [GLAH 1:K58], it is emphatically neither a re-edition of that work, nor a comprehensive handbook to the art. . . . Instead, I have represented a personal selection of what I believe to be the most significant, interesting, and/or characteristic work of large-scale sculpture from the Dark Age to Augustus."—*Pref.*

Contents: V.1, Text. Introduction: sculpture in a Greek landscape; Part I: The sculptor's world: (1) Sources; (2) The sculptor's craft; (3) Functions; (4) The market; (5) Rewards; (6) Mimesis; (7) Personalities. Part II, The sculpture: (8) Forerunners (to ca. 600); (9) The road to maturity (ca. 600–ca. 540); (10) Ripe Archaic (ca. 550–ca. 500); (11) From Archaic to Classic (ca. 500–ca. 470); (12) Early Classic (ca. 480–ca. 450); (13) High Classic (ca. 450–ca. 430); (14) The Peloponnesian War and its legacy (ca. 430–ca. 360); (15) Late Classic (ca. 370–ca. 330); (16) The age of Alexander (ca. 340–ca. 310); (17) Early Hellenistic (ca. 320–ca. 220); (18) High Hellenistic (ca. 220–ca. 150); (19) Late Hellenistic (ca. 150–30). Part III, The sculptors: (20) The Archaic period; (21) The Early and High Classic periods; (22) In the wake of the great masters; (23) The fourth-century virtuosi; (24) The Hellenistic period. V.2, Plates; Appendix I, Extant Greek bronze statues; Appendix II: Extant originals by Greek sculptors mentioned in the literary sources; Appendix III: Absolute chronology of extant Greek sculpture; Appendix IV: Studying and photographing in museums.

Abbreviations, v.1, p.329. Museum catalogues and guides, v.1, p.331–32. References, v.1, p.333–48. Bibliography, v.1, p.349–65. Glossary of Greek and Latin words, v.1, p.367–68. Index, v.1, p.369–77.

K103 Todisco, Luigi. Scultura greca del IV secolo: maestri e scuole di statuaria tra classicità ed ellenismo. [Pref.] Mario Torelli. Milano, Longanesi, 1993. 507p. il. maps, plans. (Repertori fotografici, 8)

History of 4th-century Greek sculpture with an emphasis on masters and statues throughout the Mediterranean world. Photographic inventory includes museum numbers, provenance and bibliography where possible.

Contents: Introduzione alla storia della Grecità del IV secolo; (I) Statuaria; (II) Opere.

Bibliografia, p.[469]–95. Indici, p.[499]–506.

Etruria and Rome

K104 Brilliant, Richard. Visual narratives: storytelling in Etruscan and Roman art. Ithaca, N.Y., Cornell Univ. Pr., 1984. 200p. il.

Essays on relief sculpture as a narrative agent.

"This book is not a history of Roman narrative . . . but it is a stimulating series of essays providing valuable insights into Roman adaptations of Greek myths and the political uses of narrative art."—*Review*, Archaeology v.39, Sept./Oct. 1986, p.76.

Contents: Sight reading; (1) Etruscan cinerary urns: mythological excerpts in boxes; (2) Pendants and the mind's eye; (3) The Column of Trajan and its heirs: helical tales, ambiguous trails; (4) Mythological sarcophagi: proleptic visions.

Abbreviations, p.167–68. Notes, p.169–96. Index, p.197–200.

K105 Corpus signorum imperii romani = Corpus of sculpture of the Roman world. Oxford, Oxford Univ. Pr., 1967– . Many vols., plates.

A series undertaken by various scholarly academies and societies in places once occupied by the Roman Empire. Each group contributes one or more vols. to a comprehensive inventory of Roman imperial sculpture in its area. Participants to date include Austria, Germany, Great Britain (including Scotland and Wales), Hungary, Italy, Poland, Portugal, Switzerland, Tunisia.

K106 Fullerton, Mark D. The archaistic style in Roman statuary. Leiden, Brill, 1990. 215p. il. (Mnemosyne, biblioteca classica batava. Supplementum, 110)

Analysis of Roman statuary is presented to determine elements of style, chronology, development, regionalism, function, and iconography. Observations lead to the conclusion that formalism appealed to Roman taste.

Contents: (1) Archaistic statuary and the archaistic style; (2) Artemis/Diana; (3) Athena/Minerva; (4) Tyche/Fortuna; (5) Spes; (6) Dionysiac figures; (7) Apollo Citharoedus and Hermes Kriophoros; (8) Paraleipomena—anonymous and narrative figures; Conclusions.

Bibliography, p.[207]–10. Museum index, p.[211]–15.

K107 Haynes, Sybille. Etruscan bronzes. N.Y., Sotheby's Publications, 1985. 359p. il. (part col.)

Catalogue of bronzes, including household objects, votive statuettes, armor, and reliefs, from the British Museum and other European public collections.

Contents: Part one: (1) The country; (2) An outline of Etruscan history; (3) Bronzeworking techniques employed in antiquity; (4) Local traditions and styles; (5) Notes for collectors. Part two: [Catalog of] the bronzes.

List of abbreviations, p.325–34. Select bibliography, p.335–49. Glossary, p.351–52. Index, p.355–59.

K108 Inan, Jale, and Rosenbaum, Elisabeth. Roman and early Byzantine portrait sculpture in Asia Minor. [Reprint.] London, Published for the British Academy by the Oxford Univ. Pr., 1970. 244p. 187 plates.

See GLAH 1:K70 for original annotation.

K109 Kleiner, Diana E. E. Roman sculpture. New Haven, Yale Univ. Pr., 1992. 477p. il.

Survey of Roman sculpture from the Republican through Constantinian periods that takes special pains to elucidate the art's historical and social contexts. Includes significant coverage of monuments associated with plebeian, as well as patrician, patrons.

"A useful and accessible introductory text for the non-specialist and undergraduate reader, as well as being an excellent reference source for scholars."—*Review*, Apollo v.140, no.389, July 1994, p.59.

Contents: (I) The art of the Republic; (II) The age of Augustus and the birth of imperial art; (III) Art under the Julio-Claudians; (IV) The civil war of 68–69, the Flavian dynasty, and Nerva; (V) Art under Trajan and Hadrian; (VI) Antonine art: the beginning of late antiquity; (VII) The Severan dynasty; (VIII) The third century: a century of civil war; (IX) The Tetrarchy; (X) The Constantinian period.

Thematically organized bibliographies at the end of each chapter.

Abbreviations, p.[xi]–xii. Glossary of Greek and Latin terms, p.[465]–67. Index, p.[469]–77.

K110 Koch, Guntram. Roman funerary sculpture: catalog of the collections. Malibu, Calif., J. Paul Getty Museum, 1988. 128p. il.

Catalog of a collection of Roman sculpture related to sepulchral monuments. Entries include annotation, bibliography, and conservation assessment.

Contents: (I) Cinerary urns, Kline monument, and sarcophagi; (II) Grave reliefs and tomb altars; (III) Grave statues; (IV) Forgeries.

Abbreviations, p.xi–xii. Concordance, p.128.

K111 Kockel, Valentin. Porträtreliefs stadtrömischer Grabbauten: ein Beitrag zur Geschichte und zum Verständnis des spätrepublikanisch-frühkaiserzeitlichen Privatporträts. Mainz am Rhein, Zabern, 1993. 264p. 138p. of plates (Beiträge zur Erschliessung hellenistischer und kaiserzeitlicher Skulptur und Architektur, 12)

Attempts to establish typology of portrait sculpture based on such things as hair style and gestures. Bases for dating styles include inscriptions and materials. Evidence suggests that such sculptures are not necessarily real portraits but stylistic representations.

Contents: (I) Einleitung; (II) Gegenstand der Untersuchung; (III) Ikonographie der Reliefs; (IV) Grundlagen der Datierung; (V) Probleme von Ikonographie und Stil; (VI) Ergebnisse; Katalog.

Abkürzungsverzeichnis, p.xi. Abbildungsnachweise, p.237–38. Konkordanzen, p.239–40. Register, p.241–64.

K112 Landesmuseum Mainz. Römische Steindenkmäler: Mainz in Römischer zeit: Katalog zur Sammlung in der Steinhalle. Von Wolfgang Selzer. Unter Mitarb. von Karl-Viktor Decker und Anibal Do Paço. Mainz, Zabern, 1988. 267p. il. (part col.) (Katalogreihe zu den Abteilungen und Sammlungen, 1)

Description of the museum and its collection of stone monuments along with a history of the Roman occupation of the Mainz region.

Contents: Das Landesmuseum Mainz; Zur Geschichte der "Steinhalle"; Die Sammlung römischer Steindenkmäler; Mainz—von der Zeit des Augustus bis zum Ende der römischen Herrschaft; Zur Topographie des römischen Mainz; Römisches Militär in Mainz; Römische Kulte und Kultbauten in Mainz; Wichtige Denkmäler.

Literaturverzeichnis, p.108–10. Katalog, p.111–265. Plan der Steinhalle, p.266–67.

K113 Nerzic, Chantal. La sculpture en Gaule romaine. Paris, Errance, 1989. 343p. il. (Collection patrimoine)

Traces the development of sculpture in France from the 1st century B.C. to the 5th century A.D. both before and after the conquest of the Gauls by the Romans.

Contents: Les Gaulois avant la conquête romaine; Après la conquête romaine, heurts ou conpromissions; La fin du premier siècle: éléments de formation de l'art Gallo-Romain; Les monuments publics Gallo-Romaines au IIe siècle; L'art funéraire en Gaule; Première moitié du IIIe siècle, la continuité severienne; Le IIIe siècle et la rupture.

Bibliographie, p.331–35. Glossaire, p.336–40. Index, p.341–43.

K114 Rheinisches Landesmuseum Trier. Katalog der römischen Steindenkmäler des Rheinischen Landesmuseums Trier. Von Wolfgang Binsfeld, Karin Goethert-Polaschek und Lothar Schwinden. Mainz am Rhein, Zabern, 1988– . (1)v. plates, maps (fold.) (Trierer Grabungen und Forschungen, 12) (Corpus signorum imperii Romani. Deutschland, 4)

Catalog of the museum's Roman stone monuments and part of the German portion of Corpus signorum imperii romani (GLAH 2:K105).

Contents: (1) Götter- und Weihedenkmäler.

K115 Richardson, Emeline. Etruscan votive bronzes: geometric, orientalizing, archaic. Mainz am Rhein, Zabern, 1983. 2v. plates.

"I have tried to establish a trustworthy chronology, based on criteria that can be seen and evaluated by the interested reader, of the bronze votive figures made in Etruria in the seventh, sixth, and first half of the fifth centuries B.C. It is an attempt to produce a catalog comparable to Sir John Beazley's monumental studies of Attic vase paintings [GLAH 1:M55–57], and I hope that this work, like his, will prove to be useful not only in its own limited field, but for the study of ancient Mediterranean art in general."—*Pref.* See useful review, Art bulletin v.67, no.2, June, 1985, p.325–27.

Contents: Text vol.: (I) Geometric; (II) The orientalizing period; (III) The archaic period 1; (IV) The archaic period 2; (V) The archaic period 3. Plates vol.

Abbreviations, v.[1], p.[xv]–xxxvii. Indexes, v.[1], p.[365]–90.

K116 Strong, Donald Emrys. Roman imperial sculpture: an introduction to the commemorative and decorative sculpture of the Roman Empire down to the death of Constantine. [Reprint.] N.Y., Transatlantic Arts, 1971. vii, 104p. plates.

1st American ed. See GLAH 1:K74 for original annotation.

K117 Toynbee, Jocelyn M. C. Roman historical portraits. Ithaca, Cornell Univ. Pr., 1978. 208p. il. (Aspects of Greek and Roman life)

British ed., London, Thames and Hudson, 1978.

Catalog presents portraits found on coins and in sculpture which supply images of identifiable historical personages.

Contents: Part I: Republican and early Augustan notables; Part II: Foreign rulers (3rd century, B.C.–5th century).

Sources of illustrations, p.201. Index, p.201–08.

Early Christian—Byzantine

K118 Caillet, Jean-Pierre. L'antiquité classique, le haut moyen âge et Byzance au musée de Cluny. Paris, Réunion des musées nationaux, 1985. 269p. il. (part col.)

Catalog of important collection. Entries include provenance, physical description, and extensive commentary.

Contents: Sculpture et décoration monumentales: Reliefs figurés; éléments architecturaux et d'ornamentation non figurée; sarcophages; inscriptions funéraires; revêtements de sol; Petite sculpture: ivoire; schiste; pierres dures; Orfèvrerie et métallurgie: objets d'usage personnel et profane: éléments de parure vestimentaire; armes; objets utilitaires; Orfèvrerie et métallurgie: objets à destination votive ou liturgique: bronze; orfèvrerie et émaillerie.

Bibliographie, p.245–61. Tables de concordance, p.262–63. Modes d'entrée au musée, p.264. Index, p.265–69.

K119 ______, and Loose, Helmuth Nils. La vie d'éternité: la sculpture funéraire dans l'antiquité chrétienne. Paris, Cerf, 1990. 147p. il. (part col.)

Traces the development of the sepulchral monument in its various forms from its Greco-Roman origins in the 3d century through the 6th century.

Contents: Commanditaires; Production; Emploi; Message: L'héritage gréco-romain; L'Ancient Testament; Le Nouveau Testament; L'apostolat; Formes; Devenir; Épilogue .

Notes, p.125–33. Bibliographie, p.134–38. Index, p.139–46.

K120 Cutler, Anthony. The hand of the master: craftsmanship, ivory, and society in Byzantium (9th–11th centuries). Princeton, N.J., Princeton Univ. Pr., 1994. 293p. il.

Survey of ivory craftsmanship and use.

"The Hand of the master sets a standard for art historical writing about the middle ages: such a book can only be written after decades of handling artefacts and of treating each one as the principal source of information about itself."—*Review*, Burlington magazine v.137, Dec. 1995, p.851–2.

Contents: (I) The power of ivory; (II) Conditions of production; (III) Stages of production; (IV) The master in context; (V) Problems of classification and chronology; (VI) Ivory in Byzantine society.

Abbreviations, p.253. Frequently cited works, p.254–57. Notes, p.259–85. Glossary, p.286–87. Sources of illustrations, p.287. Index, p.288–93.

K121 Firatli, Nezih. La sculpture byzantine figurée au Musée archéologique d'Istanbul. Catalogue revue et présenté par C. Metzger, A. Pralong et J.-P. Sodini. Trad. turque par A. Arel. Paris, Librairie d'Amérique et d'Orient Adrien Maisonneuve, Jean Maisonneuve Successeur, 1990. 268p. plates. (Bibliothèque de l'Institut français d'études anatoliennes d'Istanbul, 30)

Documented catalog of Byzantine figural sculpture from an important Turkish museum. Entries include inventory numbers, provenance, physical description, comments, dating and references to the literature.

Contents: (I) Sculpture en ronde-bosse (nos 1–67); (II) Reliefs honorifiques et officiels (nos 68–78); (III) Sculpture funéraire (nos 79–115); (IV) Reliefs religieux et divers (nos 116–70); (V) Mobilier liturgique (nos 171–186); (VI) Architecture (nos 187–359); (VII) Ensembles de même provenance (nos 306–506); Addendum.

Tables de concordance, p.[217]–22. Traduction en Turc des commentaires, p.[223]–45. Index, p.[247]–64.

Carolingian—Gothic

K122 Cahn, Walter, and Seidel, Linda. Romanesque sculpture in American collections. N.Y., Franklin, 1979– . (2)v. il. (Publications of the International Center of Medieval Art, 1)

Project to catalog all the Romanesque sculpture in U.S. collections. Entries include full description, references to similar pieces in other collections, and bibliography.

Contents: (1) New England museums (1979); (2) New York and New Jersey, middle and south Atlantic states, the midwest, western and Pacific states (1999).

K123 Gillerman, Dorothy, ed. Gothic sculpture in America. N.Y., Garland, 1989– . (1)v. il. (Publications of the International Center of Medieval Art, 2)

Project to catalog all Gothic sculpture in U.S. public collections. Entries include lengthy annotations, provenance, and assessment by conservator.

Contents: (1) The New England museums (1989).

K124 Hearn, Millard Fillmore. Romanesque sculpture: the revival of monumental stone sculpture in the eleventh and twelfth centuries. Ithaca, N.Y., Cornell Univ. Pr., 1981. 240p. il.

"This book is an attempt to construct a systematic theory of the development of Romanesque sculpture, based on integration of several types of data and grounded in a unified method of classification."—*Introd.*

Contents: (1) From antiquity to the Romanesque revival; (2) The eleventh-century origins: capitals and relief slabs; (3) The crucial monuments (circa 1100): sanctuary sculpture; (4) The origin and development of architectural sculpture; (5) The great portals.

Selected bibliography, p.225–33. Index, p.235–40.

K125 Poeschke, Joachim. Die Skulptur des Mittelalters in Italien. Aufnahmen Albert Hirmer und Irmgard Ernstmeier-Hirmer. München, Hirmer, 1998–2000. 2v. il.

Splendid survey of medieval Italian sculpture, based on a special photographic campaign conducted in 1996–2000.

Contents: (1) Romanik; (2) Gotik.
Includes bibliographies and indexes.

K126 Porter, Arthur Kingsley. Romanesque sculpture of the pilgrimage roads. [Reprint.] N.Y., Hacker Art Books, 1985. 10v.
See GLAH 1:K92 for original annotation.

K127 Randall, Richard H., Jr. The golden age of ivory: Gothic carvings in North American collections. N.Y., Hudson Hills, 1993. 160p. il. (part col.)
Descriptive and illustrated inventory of ivory carvings in selected North American museums.
Contents: Religious ivories: sculpture; triptychs, and polyptychs; diptychs and plaques; Secular ivories; Italian ivories.
Bibliography, p.152–54. Index, p.155–60.

K128 Victoria and Albert Museum, London. Catalogue of Romanesque sculpture. [By] Paul Williamson. [London], Victoria and Albert Museum, 1983. 118p. il. (part col.)
Catalog of the collection arranged by country of origin.
"The principal aim of the present catalogue has been to introduce these sculptures for the first time into art-historical discussion."—*Foreword.*
Contents: France; Italy; England; Spain; Cyprus.
Abbreviations, p.[11]. Comparative illustrations, p.112–16. Numerical index, p.118

K129 ———. Northern Gothic sculpture 1200–1450. [By] Paul Williamson. Assisted by Peta Evelyn. [London], Victoria and Albert Museum, 1988. 211p. il. (part col.)
"This publication is not an exhaustive catalogue. . . . Instead it was the intention to produce a handbook . . . and to provide some background information at the beginning of the book so that the sculptures could be better understood."—*Foreword.*
Entries include provenance note and lengthy annotation as well as photographs of the backs of many free-standing figures.
Bibliography, p.201–09. Index of collectors and dealers, p.210. Concordance, p.211.

K130 Vöge, Wilhelm. Bildhauer des Mittelalters: gesammelte Studien. [Reprint.] Vorwort von Erwin Panofsky. Berlin, Mann, 1995. xxxi, 254p. il. port.
See GLAH 1:K93 for original annotation.

K131 Williamson, Paul. Gothic sculpture 1140–1300. New Haven, Yale Univ. Pr., 1995. 301p. il. (part col.) (Yale University Press pelican history of art)
Gothic sculpture in Western and northern Europe surveyed with authority and production quality typical of this series.
"In line with the new editorial policy for the Pelican History of Art series I have included both English and Italian Gothic sculpture, although the former was well treated in Lawrence Stone's Sculpture in Britain: the Middle Ages [GLAH 1:K145] and Italian sculpture after 1250 has been discussed in exemplary fashion in John White's Art and Architecture in Italy 1250–1400 [GLAH 1:I358]."—*Pref.*
Contents: Part One: The transition from Romanesque, and early Gothic: (1) France, c.1140–1230; (2) The Holy Roman Empire 1160–1240; (3) England 1160–1240; (4) Scandinavia 1170–1240; (5) Spain 1170–1230; (6) Italy 1180–1250; Part Two: Mature Gothic: (7) France 1230–1300; (8) The Holy Roman Empire 1240–1300; (9) England 1240–1300; (10) Scandinavia 1240–1300; (11) Spain 1230–1300; (12) Italy 1250–1300.
Glossary, p.[264]. Notes, p.[265]–91. Select bibliography, p.[292]–94. Index, p.[295]–301.

K132 ———. An introduction to medieval ivory carvings. Owings Mills, Md., Stemmer House, 1982. 47p. il. (part col.)
Brief but informative survey, well illustrated with examples from the Victoria and Albert Museum's collection.
Further reading, p.47.

Renaissance—Baroque

K133 Augustinermuseum, Freiburg. Bildwerk des Mittelalters und der Renaissance, 1100–1530: Auswahlkatalog. Bearb. von Detlef Zinke. München, Hirmer, 1995. 192p. il. (part col.)
Catalog of the exhibition, Augustiner Museum, Freiburg (1995). Although primarily German sculpture, the catalog includes works from neighboring German-speaking countries.
Contents: 1100–1300; 1300–1430; 1430–1480; 1480–1530; Skulpturen des Freiburger Münsters (1220–1300).
Verzeichnis der abgekürzt zitierten Literatur, p.189–90. Ikonographisches Verzeichnis, p.191. Verzeichnis nach Herkunftsorten, p.191. Konkordanz, p.192.

K134 Avery, Charles. Renaissance and Baroque bronzes in the Frick Art Museum. Pittsburgh, The Frick Art and Historical Center, 1993. 144p. il.
An annotated inventory of an important collection of statuettes.
Contents: Introduction: Bronzes in the collection of the Frick Art Museum; The bronze statuette in the Renaissance; Catalogue.
Biographies of sculptors represented, p.133–38. Bibliography, p.139–44.

K135 Bober, Phyllis Pray, and Rubinstein, Ruth. Renaissance artists and antique sculpture. With contrib. by Susan Woodford. Published with the assist. of the J. Paul Getty Trust. [Rev. ed.] London, Harvey Miller; N.Y., Oxford Univ. Pr., 1987. 522 p. il.
1st ed., 1986.
A catalog of classical figures, myths, and historical events depicted in ancient sculptural works that influenced artists and others in the Renaissance. Entries were selected from the "Census of antique works of art and architecture known to the Renaissance," which is available as a searchable database on the internet.

"This book is intended as a reference guide to the ancient monuments which served Renaissance artists as a visual reservoir of sculptural styles, iconographic types, and expressive poses from an admired past. Here one may find more than 200 ancient statues and reliefs, and may learn—from text and illustration—something of what can be known of their history in the Renaissance: when they were discovered, where and how they were displayed, how their subject matter was interpreted and which artists as well as antiquarians recorded them or otherwise profited by their presence."—*Pref.*

"Certainly one of the most useful art-historical reference books to have been published in recent decades."—*Review* by Nicholas Penny, Burlington magazine v.128, July 1986, p.510.

Abbreviations, p.25–29. Appendix I: Index of Renaissance artists and sketchbooks, p.451–70. Appendix II: Index of Renaissance collections, p.471–80. Bibliography, p.481–506. General index, p.507–22.

K136 Camins, Laura. Renaissance and Baroque bronzes from the Abbott Guggenheim collection. [San Francisco], The Fine Arts Museum of San Francisco, 1988. 150p. il.

"The contents of this collection . . . maps the cities traditionally thought to be the most important centers of bronze casting in Europe—Florence, Padua, Venice—each with its own discernible style."—*Introd.*

Abbreviated references, p.9–12.

K137 Cleveland Museum of Art. Renaissance bronzes from Ohio collections. [By] William D. Wixom. Cleveland, Cleveland Museum of Art, 1975. 184p. il. (part col.)

Catalog of the exhibition, Cleveland Museum of Art (1975).

"The scope of the . . . exhibition, while focused upon local collections, is broadly conceived representing Germany and the Netherlands as well as Italy and France. It encompasses plaquettes, medals and useful objects in addition to independent statuettes."—*Introd.*

Bibliography, p.172–84.

K138 Natur und Antike in der Renaissance. [Hrsg. des Katalogs und Ausstellungsleitung, H. Beck and P. C. Bol.] Frankfurt am Main, Liebieghaus, 1985. 600p. il. (part col.)

Catalog of the exhibition, Leibieghaus, Frankfurt am Main (1985). Essays discuss Renaissance bronze statuettes and reliefs as a reflection of classical forms, subjects, and taste. Catalog entries include substantive annotation and bibliography.

The catalog of this highly ambitious and comprehensive exhibition "not only provides us with a comprehensive study of bronzes as vehicles of classical revival but also attempts nothing less than a synoptic overview of the metaphorical uses of antique myth in Renaissance . . . a monument of major art-historical reinterpretation and reassessment of its subject."—*Review*, Art journal 46, no.2, summer 1987, p.134.

Contents: (I) Zur Technik des Bronzegusses in der Renaissance, von Dieter Blume; (II) Antike als Programm - Der Statuenhof des Belvedere im Vatikan, von Uwe Geese; (III) Die Umwertung der Antike: zur Rezeption des Marc Aurel in Mittelalter und Renaissance, von Norberto Gramaccini; (IV) Antike und Christentum, von Dieter Blume; (V) Mythos und Widerspruch, von Dieter Blume and Horst Bredekamp; (VI) Beseelte Natur und ländliche Idylle, von Dieter Blume; (VII) Das genaue Abbild der Natur: Riccios Tiere und die Theorie des Naturabgusses seit Cennini, von Norberto Gramaccini; (VIII) Antikisches Gebrauchsgerät-Weisheit und Magie in den Öllampen Riccios, von Heike Frosien-Leinz; (IX) Das Studiolo und seine Ausstattung, von Heike Frosien-Leinz; (X) Von der Kunstkammer zum bürgerlichen Wohnzimmer, von Herbert Beck; Katalog.

Bibliographie, p.591–98.

K139 Radcliffe, Anthony; Baker, Malcolm; and Maek-Gérard, Michael. The Thyssen-Bornemisza collection: Renaissance and later sculpture with works of art in bronze. Michael Maek-Gérard's text transl. from the German by E. F. N. Jephcott. London, Sotheby's, 1992. 437p. il. (part col.)

Annotated catalog of an important collection with essays by 3 scholars.

"The six preliminary essays . . . spring directly from the issues repeatedly discussed in the catalogue entries themselves. The whole volume should be compulsory reading for all serious students of the subject."—*Review* by Nicholas Penny, Burlington magazine v.136, Dec. 1994, p.849–50.

Contents: Originals, versions, multiples, copies and casts, by Malcolm Baker; The model and the marble in the Renaissance, by Anthony Radcliffe; Multiple reproduction in the fifteenth century: Florentine stucco Madonnas and the della Robbia workshop, by Anthony Radcliffe; Some versions and variants of the sculpture of Tilmann Riemenschneider, by Michael Maek-Gérard; The replication of sculpture in bronze, by Anthony Radcliffe; Terracotta and plaster multiples in eighteenth and early nineteenth-century France, by Malcolm Baker; Catalogue.

Bibliographical abbreviations, p.43–46. Concordance, p.[435]. Index of provenances, p.[437].

K140 Renaissance master bronzes from the collection of the Kunsthistorisches Museum, Vienna. [By] Manfred Leithe-Jasper. Washington, D.C., Scala in assoc. with Smithsonian Institution Traveling Exhibition Service (Distr. by Harper and Row, 1986). 304p. il (part col.)

Catalog of the exhibition, National Gallery of Art, Washington, D.C. (1986), and other locations. Entries include provenance, bibliography, and a lengthy annotation. Introduction discusses historical significance of the statuettes.

"The choice of works for this exhibition has been governed by the desire to provide a historical cross-section of a centuries-long collector's tradition, and also to exhibit bronze statuettes of which there are replicas, variants or counterparts in American collections."—*Author's ackn.*

Contents: Introduction, by Donald R. McClelland; On the nature of Renaissance bronzes, by Douglas Lewis; Renaissance bronzes and the Vienna collection, by Manfred Leithe-Jasper; The catalog.

Short list of books in English related to the exhibition, p.45. Biographies of the artists, p.279–83. List of inventories relevant to provenance of the bronzes, p.284–85. Bibliography, p.287–97. Index, p.298–304.

K141 Von allen Seiten schön: Bronzen der Renaissance und des Barock: Wilhelm von Bode zum 150. Geburtstag. Hrsg. von Volker Krahn. Heidelberg, Braus, 1995. 639 p. il. (part col.)

Catalog of the exhibition, Altes Museum, Berlin (1995–96). Festschrift for the founder of the Berlin museum's great collection of bronzes. Works included are primarily from the Staatliche Museen zu Berlin, Preussischer Kulturbesitz, but many from other museums and private collections are included. Entries include provenance, bibliography, and lengthy annotations.

Contents: [Introductory essays]: "Von allen Seiten schön" [and] "Ein ziemlich kühnes Unterfangen . . . " Wilhelm von Bode als Wegbereiter der Bronzenforschung, seine Erwerbungen für die Berliner Museen und seine Beziehungen zu Sammlern, von Volker Krahn; Aspekte der Porträtplastik in Bronze in der Renaissance, von Ulrich Becker; "Ars erit archetypus naturae," Zur Ikonologie der Bronze in der Renaissance, von Elisabeth Dalucas; "Del formare e del getto" Die Herstellung von Bronzestatuetten im 16. Jahrhundert, von Francesca Bewer; Katalog.

Kurzbiographien, p.620–28. Literaturverzeichnis, p.629–39.

Neoclassical—Modern

K142 Art Nouveau sculpture. [By] Alistair Duncan. N.Y., Rizzoli, 1978. 95p. il. (part col.)

Survey of the brief life of the small, sometimes erotic, objets d'art which graced parlors around the turn of the century. Primarily illustrations.

K143 Arwas, Victor. Art deco sculpture: chryselephantine statuettes of the twenties and thirties. N.Y., St. Martin's, 1992. 251p. il. (mostly col.)

Greatly expanded version of British ed., London, Academy, 1975, and rev. enl. ed, 1984, both published in the U.S. by St. Martin's.

Aimed at the collector and students. Describes materials and techniques employed in producing the once immensely popular sculpted figurines associated with the period. Includes foundry marks.

Contents: Art deco sculpture; Artists' biographies; Founders and editors.

K144 A century of modern sculpture: the Patsy and Raymond Nasher collection. Ed. by Steven A. Nash. N.Y., Rizzoli, 1987. 208p. il. (part col.)

Annotated catalog of the collection (Dallas, Texas) includes basic facts, description photo, markings, provenance, bibliography, and exhibitions.

Contents: Living with art, by Elizabeth Frank; Figures and phantoms: early modern figurative sculpture, by Steven A. Nash; Sculpture in the constructivist tradition, by Nan Rosenthal; Between apocalypses: after 1945, by Robert Rosenblum; Catalog, by Steven A. Nash.

Photo credits, p.207. Index, p. 208.

K145 Cooper, Jeremy. Nineteenth-century romantic bronzes: French, English, and American bronzes, 1830–1915. Boston, New York Graphic Society, 1975. 160p. il. (part col.)

Discussion of bronze figural sculpture in a romantic rather than a national context. "Sculptors who made a direct contribution to our subject . . . either worked primarily for bronze or sculpted marble with an eye to reproduction in bronze."—*Introd.*

Contents: (1) French sculpture from David d'Angers to Rodin; (2) The "new sculpture" in England; (3) American romantic bronzes; (4) French animalier bronzes.

Appendix: Market guide, p.156–57. Select bibliography, p.158. Index, p.159–60.

K146 The colour of sculpture, 1840–1910. [By] Andreas Blühm . . . [et al.] Amsterdam, Van Gogh Museum, 1996. 277p. il. (part col.)

Catalog of the exhibition, Van Gogh Museum, Amsterdam (1996), and other locations.

Contents: In living colour: a short history of colour and sculpture in the 19th century, by Andreas Blühm; Colour, sculpture, mimesis: a 19th-century debate, by Wolfgang Drost; Sculpture colouring and the industries of art in the 19th century, by Philip Ward-Jackson; Under the spell of Madame Tussaud: aspects of "high" and "low" in 19th-century polychromed sculpture, by Alison Yarrington; Art for the sake of the soul: polychrome sculpture and literary Symbolism, by Emmanuelle Héran; Painter-sculptors and polychromy in the evolution of modernism, by June Hargrove; Catalogue.

Notes, p.241–55. Select bibliography, p.257–70. Index, p.271–77.

K147 De Matisse à aujourd'hui: la sculpture du XXe siècle dans les collections des Musées et du Fonds Régional d'Art Contemporain du Nord-Pas-de-Calais. [Paris], Assoc. des Conservateurs des Musées du Nord-Pas-de-Calais, 1992. 300p. il. (part col.)

Catalog of the exhibition, Musée Matisse, Cateau-Cambrésis (1992), and other locations.

A look at European sculpture created in the 20th century, and the sequel to the Northwest French art museums' exhibition De Carpeaux à Matisse (1982).

Contents: Introduction, par Patrick Le Nouëne; L'arabesque dans la modernité Henri Matisse sculpteur, par Roger Benjamin; Du renouvellement à la continuité de la tradition, 1900–1950, par Patrick Le Nouëne; Quelques éléments à propos de l'histoire de la sculpture moderne en France, 1910–1937, par Patrick Le Nouëne; Situation de la sculpture en France après la deuxième guerre, 1944–1964, par Patrick Le Nouëne; Londres: und scène artistique, par Françoise Cohen; Objets et attitudes dans la sculpture occidentale des années soixante, par Marc Bormand.

Inventaire des collections par artiste, p.215–[76]. Répertoire des aritstes par musée, p.[277]–86. Ouvrages cités, p.289–95. Expositions citées, p.297–300.

K148 Elsen, Albert Edward. Modern European sculpture 1918–1945: unknown beings and other realities. N.Y., Braziller, 1979. 192p. il.

The effects of two wars, economic crises, and political turmoil discussed as possible influences upon sculptors which gave licence to greater self-expression.

Contents: (1) The figure in interwar modern sculpture; (2) Portraits and the evocative head; (3) The other realities of abstract sculpture; (4) Interwar relief sculpture; (5) Monuments and the monumental in modern interwar sculpture; (6) The sculptor's response to Fascism; Postscript: the artist as victim and villain.

Notes, p.158–65. Catalogue of the exhibition/biographies, p.171–88. Index, p.189–92.

K149 Forrest, Michael. World of art bronzes. West Chester, Pa., Schiffer, 1988. 493p. il. (part col.)

A general work primarily for the amateur and collector.

Contents: Introduction: The romantics; The animaliers; The Japanese influence; The American influence; The women artists; The frontier artists; The Victorians; Between the wars; The unusual, exotic and bizarre; A market guide. Biographies of the artists and founders.

Select bibliography, p.[487]–88. Index, p.[489]–93.

K150 Hammacher, Abraham Marie. Modern sculpture: tradition and innovation. N.Y., Abrams, 1988. 447p. il. (part col.)

Enl. ed. of Hammacher's The evolution of modern sculpture [GLAH 1:K103]. Expanded text includes developments after 1960.

Contents: (1) From Michelangelo to Rodin; (2) Rodin, Bourdelle, Maillol, and Rosso: their sources in earlier European art; (3) The painter-sculptors: their sources in archaic and primitive art; (4) Duchamp-Villon, Boccioni, and Brancusi; (5) The threshold of cubism; (6) Cubism in sculpture; (7) The complex world of the constructivists; (8) The struggle between archaism and abstraction: Arturo Martini; (9) The evolution of the younger sculptors between 1925 and 1940; (10) Sculpture from 1945 to 1960; (11) Space exploded—spaces explored: trails since 1960.

Notes, p. 435–36. Selected bibliography, p.437–40. Index, p.441–46.

K151 Hunisak, John M. Carvings, casts and replicas: nineteenth-century sculpture from Europe and America in New England collections. Middlebury, Vt., Middlebury College Museum of Art, 1994. 206p. il. (part col.)

Catalog of the exhibition, Middlebury College Museum of Art (1994).

"This highly readable volume will serve as a useful introduction to the field for a reader unfamiliar with nineteenth-century sculpture."—*Review*, Winterthur portfolio v.30, summer/autumn 1995, p.186–90.

Contents: New England's acquisition of nineteenth-century sculpture: a tale not told before, by Ruth Butler; Lenders to the exhibition; The catalogue.

Artists' biographies, p.172–99. Selected bibliography, p.200–05. Index of artists, p.206.

K152 Janson, H. W. 19th-century sculpture. N.Y., Abrams, 1985. 288p. il.

A comprehensive history of sculpture during the 19th century. An abridged version of the text appeared in 19th-century Art, by Robert Rosenblum and H. W. Janson [GLAH 2:I290].

Contents: (I) 1776–1815 (Introduction; England; Scandinavia; France, Canova; The early Thorvaldsen; Austria and Germany); (II) 1815–1848 (Introduction; The mature Thorvaldsen; England; The United States; Italy; Germany; France; The romantic theory of sculpture); (III) 1848–1870 (Introduction; France; Italy; England; The United States; Germany and Austria); (IV) 1870–1905 (Introduction; France; Italy; Belgium; Germany; England; The United States; Postscript: the fin de siècle).

Bibliography, p.[270]–79. Index, p.[280]–88.

K153 Kjellberg, Pierre. Bronzes of the 19th century: dictionary of sculptors. Translated by Kate D. Loftus, Alison Levie, and Leslie Bockol. Atglen, Pa., Schiffer, 1994. 684p. il. (part col.)

1st French ed., Les bronzes du XIXe siècle: dictionnaire des sculpteurs. Paris, Éd. de l'Amateur, 1987.

Alphabetical listings of brief biographical sketches, list of representative works, museums in which the works may be seen, and citations for sales in which the works appeared. A discussion of bronze casting precedes the dictionary. Some signatures or makers' marks, as well as founders' marks, reproduced in facsimile.

Contents: The magic of bronze; the birth of bronze; Dictionary of sculptors; Founders dictionary.

Bibliography, p.681–82.

K154 Krauss, Rosalind. Passages in modern sculpture. N.Y., Viking, 1977. 308p. il.

French ed., Passages: une histoire de la sculpture de Rodin à Smithson. Paris, Macula, 1977.

A critical, theoretical, and historical discussion of modern sculpture organized by general expressive concern of the artist.

Contents: (1) Narrative time: the question of the Gates of Hell; (2) Analytic space: futurism and constructivism; (3) Form and readymade: Duchamp and Brancusi; (4) A game plan: the terms of surrealism; (5) Tanktotem: welded images; (6) Mechanical ballets: light, motion, theater; (7) The double negative: a new syntax for sculpture.

Notes, p.289–98. Biography, p.299–302. Index, p.303–08.

K155 Lucie-Smith, Edward. Sculpture since 1945. N.Y., Universe, 1987. 160p. il. (part col.)

British ed., London, Phaidon, 1987.

A summary of post-World War II trends in sculpture, both national and international.

Contents: (1) The early modernists; (2) After the war: new and old traditions; (3) Post-war sculpture in Italy; (4) Post-war sculpture in Britain and France; (5) The American tradition; (6) David Smith and new American sculpture; (7) The revolution of the 1960s; (8) Pop, new realism and super realism; (9) Kinetic art; (10) Minimal art; (11) Conceptual art and land art; (12) Italian "arte povera" and British salvage art; (13) The pluralism of the 1970s; (14) Ethnography, archaeology and craft; (15) The return to figurative imagery.

Bibliography, p.154–56. Index, p.157–59.

K156 Merkel, Ursula. Das plastische Porträt im 19. und frühen 20. Jahrhundert: ein Beitrag zur Geschichte der Bildhauerei in Frankreich und Deutschland. Berlin, Akademie, 1995. 288p. il.

Chronological survey traces the stylistic and philosophical path of portrait sculptures in Germany and France from the 19th century to early modern times. Reference to the portrait tradition in both painting and sculpture point out basic differences between the two media. The basic techniques and materials are clearly described to allow the reader to judge what is innovative. References to the works of great sculptors, such as Canova, Houdon, Rodin, Maillol, and Barlach ground the theoretic aspects of the study to the reality of the product.

Contents: Einleitung; Grundlegende Aspekte zur Bildniskunst und Porträttheorie; Porträt and Bildhauerei; Entwicklungslinien der Porträtplastik vom Klassizismus bus zum Historismus und Naturalismus; Neue wege in der französischen Bildniskunst; Deutsche Porträtplastik im frühen 20. Jahrhundert; Avantgardistische Tendenzen in Frankreich; Zusammenfassung.

Includes a key to abbreviations; bibliography; list of detailed captions for plates; index by names and plates.

K157 Musée d'Orsay. Catalogue sommaire illustré des sculptures. Catalogue établi par Anne Pingeot, Antoinette Le Normand-Romain, et Laure de Margerie. Paris, Ministère de la Culture et de la Communication, Éd. de la Réunion des musées nationaux, 1986. 300p. il. (part col.)

Catalog of the museum's sculpture holdings arranged alphabetically by artist. Includes provenance information.

Contents: Formation de la collection; De la bonne utilisation du catalogue; Planches couleurs; catalogue illustré.

Liste extérieure, p.265–83. Index alphabétique, p.285–300.

K158 Nineteenth century French and Western European sculpture in bronze and other media. Ed. by Elizabeth Kashey, Robert Kashey. N.Y., Shepherd Gallery Associates, 1985. 312p. il. facs.

Catalog of the exhibition, Shepherd Gallery, New York (1985).

Appendix I: Obituary of Achille Collas, the inventor of réduction méchanique, by Albert Jacquemart; Appendix II: The founders of Barye's bronzes, by Joseph G. Reinis; Appendix III: Excerpts from a Barbedienne catalog; Appendix IV: Digest of works which appear both carved in stone and founded in metal with all relative dates of execution and exhibition as referred to in the Dictionnaire des sculpteurs de l'école français au dix-neuvième siècle [GLAH 1:K115], by Stanislas Lami, Paris, 1914, by Robert L. Allen; Appendix V: List of founders, editors, chiselers active in Western Europe during the nineteenth century.

General bibliography, p.306–10. Index of artists represented in the exhibition, p.311–12.

K159 Objectives: the new sculpture. Organized by Paul Schimmel. Essays by Kenneth Baker . . . [et al.] N.Y., Rizzoli, 1990. 192p. il. (part col.)

Catalog of the exhibition, Newport Harbor Art Museum, Newport Beach, Calif. (1990). Presents a detailed examination of work by eight artists who collectively represent an important strand of contemporary sculpture

Exhibition histories, p.176–[83]. Selected bibliography, p.184–[93].

K160 Qu'est-ce que la sculpture moderne? Paris, Centre Pompidou, 1986. 447p. il. (part col.)

Catalog of the exhibition, Paris, Centre Georges Pompidou, Musée national d'art moderne (1986). Entries arranged by style. Each section provided with a descriptive introduction. Includes seven essays by various authors and an anthology of historical writing related to art of the 20th century. Biographies of the artists represented include photos.

Contents: Catalogue; Liste des oeuvre exposées; Textes critiques (Échelle/monumentalité, modernisme/postmodernisme, la ruse de Brancusi), par Rosalind Krauss; Construire (l'historie de) la sculpture, par Benjamin H. D. Buchloh; Réponse à côté de la question "Qu'est-ce que la sculpture moderne?", par Thierry de Duve; La sculpture américaine: l'anti-tradition, par Barbara Rose; La nouvelle sculpture des années soixante, par Franz Meyer; Actualité de Robert Smithson, par Jean-Pierre Criqui; In situ, lieux et espaces de la sculpture contemporaine, par Jean-Marc Poinsot; Anthologie de texte historiques.

Biographie des artistes, p.393–400. Bibliographie sélective, p.441–44. Index des artistes exposés, p.445–47.

K161 Read, Herbert Edward. A concise history of modern sculpture. [Reprint.] N.Y., Thames and Hudson, 1987. (World of art)

See GLAH 1:K105 for original annotation. Rev. and enl. ed. 1968. Cover title: Modern sculpture, a concise history. Frequently published and trans.

K162 Rheims, Maurice. Nineteenth century sculpture. Translated by Robert E. Wolf. N.Y., Abrams, 1977. [433]p. il. (part col.)

Trans. of French ed., Paris, Arts et Métiers Graphiques, 1972 [GLAH 1:K106].

Survey of 19th-century European and American sculpture with emphasis on French works, especially important for French academic sculptors. Places works in political, social, and cultural context.

Contents: (1) Neoclassicism; (2) Romanticism; (3) David d'Angers; (4) Realism or positivist art; (5) Carpeaux; (6) Symbolism; (7) Pre-Raphaelites; art nouveau; (8) Art in fusion: Rodin and his disciples; (9) The eve of the twentieth century; expressionism; the return to the Greeks; (10) The world of work; (11) Historical and military subjects; (12) Sculpture in the streets; (13) Decorative sculpture; (14) Portraits; (15) Caricatures; (16) Animal sculpture; (17) Sculpture and religion; (18) Funerary art; (19) Sensualism; (20) Kitsch; (21) The unusual; the bizarre; (22) Precious materials.

Bibliography, p.417–18. Index, p.419–30.

K163 Rijksmuseum Kröller-Müller. Sculpture in the Rijksmuseum Kröller-Müller: catalog of the collection compiled and edited by Marianne Brouwer and Rieja Brouns. 5th Eng. ed. Amsterdam, Enschedé, 1992. 326p. il.

Scholarly catalog of an important collection.

Bibliography of exhibitions, p.[273]–326.

K164 Sculpture du XXe siècle: 1900–1945, tradition et ruptures. Saint-Paul, Fondation Maeght, 1981. 226p. il. (part col.)

Catalog of the exhibition, Fondation Maeght (1981). Arranged alphabetically by artist from Archipenko to Zadkine. Biographical sketches of artists include a photo of the sculptor and general description of the artist's works and specific commentary on the object in the collection.

Petit glossaire à l'usage du toucher, p.223–26.

K165 Senie, Harriet. Contemporary public sculpture: tradition, transformation, and controversy. N.Y., Oxford Univ. Pr., 1992. 276p. il.

"This book is not intended as an inclusive history of recent public sculpture. Rather it offers a conceptual overview and develops a typology that may serve as a basis for further study and critical discussion."—*Pref.*

Contents: (1) Memorials and monuments reconsidered; (2) Sculpture and architecture: a changing relationship; (3) The public sculpture revival of the 1960s: famous artists, modern styles; (4) Landscape into public sculpture: transplanting and transforming nature; (5) Sculpture with a function: crossing the high art—low art barrier; (6) The persistence of controversy: patronage and politics.

Notes, p.235–65. Index, p.267–76.

K166 Skulptur im 20. Jahrhundert. [Basel, s.n., 1984.] [Katalog:] Theodora Vischer. 234p. il. (part col.), plans (laid in).

Catalog of the exhibition, Basel (1980), curated by Ernst Beyeler, Reinhold Hohl, and Martin Schwander. Exhibition covers large outdoor sculpture; essays trace trends in 20th-century sculpture.

Contents: Tradition und Moderne im Menschenbild des 20. Jahrhunders, von Karina Türr; Der Primitivismus in der modernen Skulptur, von Alan G. Wilkinson; Kubistische Konstruktionen und "kubistische" Stilrichtungen, von Sarah Gossa; Henri Matisse, von Franz Meyer; Vom revolutionären zum idealistischen Konstruktivismus, von Willy Rotzler; Der Gegenstand und seine Verwandlung: das Objekt im Dada und Surrealismus, von Andreas Franzke; Von der Assoziation zur Kreation, von Joachem Heusinger v. Waldegg; Neuansätze der fünfziger Jahre: die neue Freiheit der Skulptur, von Laszlo Glozer; Der späte Picasso, von August Kaiser; Spiel mit der Wirklichkeit, von Werner Jehle; Gestaltwahrnehmung und Struktur, von Franz Meyer; Selbsterfahrung durch die Sinne, von Antje von Graevenitz; Der Reichtum des Elementaren, von Zdenek Felix; "Malerplastiker"—"Bildhauerplastiker": Aspekte der achtziger Jahre, von Martin Schwander, Theodora Vischer.

Bibliographies follow each chapter. Verzeichnis der ausgestellten Werke, p.218–33.

K167 Strachan, Walter John. Towards sculpture: drawings and maquettes from Rodin to Oldenburg. Boulder, Colo., Westview, 1976. 263p. il. (part col.)

British ed., Towards sculpture; maquettes and sketches from Rodin to Oldenburg. London, Thames and Hudson, 1976.

The history of twentieth-century sculpture outlined by tracing the development of individual works from conception to final product. Sketches and maquettes are described and illustrated to indicate the creative path some sculptors have taken.

Contents: (I) Introduction; (II) Rodin to Oldenburg [(1) Rodin: the watershed; (2) The relief and façade sculpture; (3) Sited sculpture and open-air monuments; (4) The torso and the nude; (5) Thematic and formal obsessions; (6) The hieratic and totemistic element; (7) Open forms and constructions; (8) Equestrian sculpture, animal, bird, fish; (9) The illusion of movement and the dance, drawings for mobiles; (10) Portrait head and statue, the head as form.]

Notes on the text, p.236. Biographical notes, p.237–50. Selected bibliography, p.251. Index, p.262–63.

K168 Türr, Karina. Farbe und Naturalismus in der Skulptur des 19. und 20. Jahrhunderts: Sculpturae vitam insufflat pictura. Mainz, Zabern, 1994. 297p. il. (part col.)

Examines the use of color in figurative sculpture in the 19th and 20th centuries.

"Türr's penetrating treatment of this period is complemented by an engrossing look at the aesthetic debates about polychromy; in particular the revival of interest in the coloured sculpture of the ancient Greeks."—*Review*, Burlington magazine v.137, Dec. 1995, p.854.

Contents: Entwicklungslinien farbiger Skulptur im 19. Jahrhundert; Die Diskussion um die Polychromie im 19. Jahrhundert; Zu den Quellen der Ablehnung farbiger Plastik; Aspekte des neuen Realismus in Malerei und Skulptur im 20. Jahrhundert; Immer noch: je mehr Natur, um so weniger Kunst?; Künstler und Werke; Vorwort zum Katalog; Katalog.

Verzeichnis der Abbildungen, p.284–91. Register, p.292–97.

K169 Waldman, Diane. Transformations in sculpture: four decades of American and European art. N.Y., Solomon R. Guggenheim Foundation, 1986. 272p. il. (part col.)

Catalog accompanying the seventh in the Guggenheim International Exhibition series.

"In this exhibition . . . I have chosen to single out and bring into perspective some of the most significant developments that have occurred in sculpture over the past four decades."—*Ackn.*

Chronology of exhibitions 1945–1985, p.240–50. Selected general bibliography, p.251–52. Artists' biographies, selected exhibitions and bibliographies, p.253–67. Index of artists in the catalogue, p.269.

WESTERN COUNTRIES

Australia

K170 Hedger, Michael. Public sculpture in Australia. Roseville East, NSW (Distr. by Craftsman House); United States, G+B Arts International, 1995. 132p. il (part col.)

Beautifully illustrated selective survey of major areas of Australian sculpture. Does not include funerary or ecclesiastical sculpture.

Contents: (1) Fountains; (2) War Memorials; (3) Commemorative sculpture; (4) Garden sculpture; (5) Architectural and corporate sculpture; (6) Gallery collections.

Bibliography, p.123–25. Index p.130–32.

K171 Sturgeon, Graeme. The development of Australian sculpture, 1788–1975. London, Thames and Hudson, 1978. 256p. il.

Well-illustrated, comprehensive survey of European sculptural traditions in Australia.

Contents: (1) In the beginning; (2) Early colonial 1831–1850; (3) Gold, growth and glory; (4) Early efforts; (5) Local boys make good; (6) The Academy triumphant; (7) Seeds of doubt 1923–1939; (8) Individuals, groups and great events 1939–1961; (9) Up, up and away 1961–1970; (10) Into the seventies: the New Sculpture. Appendix: Mildura Scupture Exhibitions: awards and selection panels.

Notes to the text p.238–46. Selected bibliography p.247–48. Index p.253–56.

Canada

K172 Porter, John R., and Bélisle, Jean. La sculpture ancienne au Québec: trois siècles d'art religieux et profane. Montréal, Ed. de l'Homme, 1986. 503p. il. (part col.), plates.

Substantial study of wood sculpture in Quebec.

Bibliographie, p.492–99.

K173 Swinton, George. Sculpture of the Inuit. 3d rev. ed. Toronto, McClelland and Stewart, 1999. 302p. il. (part col.)

1st ed. entitled Sculpture of the Eskimo, 1972; rev. and upd., 1982. Significantly revised 3d ed., with a new section "Changes 1971–1999."

A substantial study of Canadian Inuit art.

Contents: The varieties of Inuit sculpture; The sananguaq-art concept; (1) The environment; (2) Two principles of Inuit survival: adaptation and change; (3) Cultural patterns; (4) The development of prehistoric Inuit art; (5) The development of art in historic times; (6) The development of art since 1948/49; (7) Differences in culture and motivation; (8) Aesthetics: Inuit vs. Kablunait; (9) The new art form; (10) The place of Inuit art.

Catalogue of artists by area, p.145. A bibliography of Eskimo art, archaeology, and ethnography, p.288–95. General index, p.295–97. Index of artists, p.298–302.

France

K174 Bresc-Bautier, Geneviève. Sculptures des jardins du Louvre, du Carrousel et des Tuileries. Paris, Ministère de la culture, Éd. de la Réunion des musées nationaux, 1986. 2v. in 1. il. maps, plans. (Notes et documents des musées de France, 12)

Exhaustive inventory of sculpture in the gardens of the Louvre/Tuileries. V.1 offers historical background from 1564 through the early 1980s, along with biographical sketches of architects arranged chronologically by dates of activity. V.2 consists of an alphabetically arranged biographical dictionary of sculptors. Entries include biography, analysis of iconography, preparatory works, bibliographical references, and exhibitions. Classical works and copies (arranged by subject matter) and anonymous pieces comprise a separate section.

Les architects, les restaurateurs, v.1 p.[171]–78. Chronologie des oeuvres, v.1 p.[179]–91. Bibliographie, v.1, p.[193]–95. Index [to both vols.], v.1, p.[205]–16.

K175 Cabanot, Jean. Les débuts de la sculpture Romane dans le sud-ouest de la France. Paris, Picard, 1987. 291p. il., maps, plans.

Illustrated overview of the evolution of Romanesque sculpture in 11th-century France. Explores themes and motifs employed in various regions. Individual structures are documented with good quality illustrations, maps, plans, and bibliography.

Monographies, p.186–253. Notes, p. 255–82. Index des noms de lieux, p. 283–88. Tables des illustrations, p. 289–91.

K176 Clodion et la sculpture française de la fin du XVIIIe siècle. Sous le dir. de Guilhem Scherf. Paris, La documentation française, 1993. 594p. il., plans. (Louvre conférences et colloques)

Collection of papers presented at a colloquium on the sculptural works of Clodion and other prominent 18th-century French sculptors, Musée du Louvre (1992).

Index, p.567–91.

K177 Dictionnaire des sculpteurs français du moyen age. [Par] Michèle Beaulieu, Victor Beyer. Paris, Picard, 1992. 311p., il. map. (Bibliothèque de la Société Française d'Archéologie, 19)

This concise reference work provides biographical data, attributions, and bibliographical references on hundreds of medieval French sculptors. Arranged geographically with numerous cross-references.

Index des noms et surnoms, p.305–12.

K178 Germain Pilon et les sculpteurs françaises de la Renaissance. Sous la dir. de Geneviève Bresc-Bautier. Paris, La documentation française, 1993. 400p. il., plans. (Louvre conférences et colloques)

Collection of scholarly papers presented at a colloquium on the sculptural works of Pilon and other prominent French sculptors of the Renaissance, Musée du Louvre (1990).

Bibliographies, p.387–91. Index des noms propres, p.393–96. Index des oeuvres de Pilon (ou attribuées), p.397–98.

K179 Hargrove, June Ellen. The statues of Paris: an open air pantheon, the history of statues to great men. N.Y., Vendome, 1990. 382p., il., plates.
Richly illustrated study of French monumental sculpture from the Bourbon Monarchy to the post-World War II era.
Catalogue raisonné, p.341–55. Charts of subjects, p.375–76. Select bibliography, p.377–78.

K180 Janson, H. W. (Horst Woldemar). An iconographic index to Stanislas Lami's dictionnaire des sculpteurs de l'école française au dix-neuvieme siècle. N.Y., Garland, 1983. xi, 218p. (Garland reference library of the humanities, 364)
Alphabetical listing to entries in Stanislas Lami's classic reference work on 19th-century French sculptors (GLAH 1:K115). Items are arranged by original (French) titles as recorded in Lami.

K181 Kjellberg, Pierre. Les bronzes du XIXe siècle: dictionnaire des sculpteurs. Paris, Les Ed. de l'Amateur, 1987. 684p. il. (part col.)
Biographical dictionary of bronze sculptors active during the 19th century in France. Individual entries include biographical essay, inventory of works, museum collections, and auction sales citations. Most entries include one or more reproductions as well as signature specimen. A well-researched list provides important historical information on individual foundries.
Dictionnaire des fondeurs, p.653–[80]. Bibliographie sommaire, p.681–82.

K182 Lyman, Thomas W. French romanesque sculpture: an annotated bibliography. With Daniel Smartt. Boston, Hall, 1987. 450p. il. (Reference publication in art history)
Annotated bibliography of monographic and periodical literature on Romanesque sculpture in France. 2,173 entries divided into three sections: 1700–1900, 1900–1944, and 1945 onward.
Index, p.379–450.

K183 Martin, Michel. Les monuments equestres de Louis XIV: une grande entreprise de propagande monarchique. Paris, Picard, 1986. 239p. il., maps.
Well-illustrated analysis of the aesthetic and political dimensions of equestrian statuary produced under the reign of Louis XIV.
Contents: (1) La rencontre de l'art et de la politique; (2) Les premières ébauches d'un art de magnificence; (3) La politique monumentale de la monarchie glorieuse de Louis XIV; (4) Les projets inachevés; (5) L'hommage des courtisans.
Notes, p.219–30. Bibliographie, p.231–35.

K184 Musée National de Versailles. Les sculptures. [Par Simone Hoog]. Préf. de Jean-Pierre Babelon avec la collab. de Roland Bossard. Paris, Réunion des musées nationaux, 1993. (1)v. il., plans.
Catalog of sculptures arranged by subject matter/name of sitter. Most entries are illustrated, with dimensions, materials, inscription(s), dates of execution/commission, and other pertinent details.
Contents: (1) Le Musée.

K185 Musée d'Orsay. Catalogue sommaire illustré des sculptures. Paris, Ministère de la culture et de la communication, Éd. de la Réunion des musées nationaux, 1986. 300p. il (part col.)
Illustrated inventory of European sculpture in collections of the Musée d'Orsay. Individual entries include titles, materials, edition size for multiples, exhibition notes.
Liste extérieure, p.265–83. Index alphabétique, p.285–300.

K186 Normand-Romain, Antoinette le. Mémoire de marbre: la sculpture funéraire en France, 1804–1914. Photographies de Myriam Viallefont-Haas. Paris, Bibliothèque de la Ville de Paris, 1995. 447p. il., maps.
Well-illustrated and documented study of the development of French funerary sculpture in the 19th and early 20th century. Includes an overview of the advent of large urban cemeteries, surveys the religious and psychological meaning of funerary monuments as well as death itself in 20th-century French society.
Bibliographie p.391–401. Répertoire des tomes citées, p.402–33. Index des noms d'artistes et de défunts, p.437–46.

K187 Paris. Musée national du Louvre. Département des sculptures. Sculpture française. Par Françoise Baron, avec la collab. de Corinne Jankowiak et Christine Vivet. Paris, Réunion des musées nationaux, 1996– . (2)v. il.
Chronologically arranged catalog of French sculpture in the Louvre. Entries well documented, most illustrated, with copious bibliography.
Contents: (1) Le moyen age (1996); (2) Renaissance et temps modernes (1998).
Oeuvres écartées, v.1, p.278–80. Liste des dépôts, v.2, p.748–71. Bibliographie, v.1, p.281–84, v.2, p.772–78. Table de concordance entre les numéros de la description 1950 et les numéros d'inventaire, v.1, p.285–87. Table de concordance entre les numéros du catalogue de 1922, du supplément de 1933 et les numéros d'inventaire, v.1, p.288–90, v.2, p.779–800. Liste des numéros d'inventaire, v.1, p.291–97, v.2, p.801–15. Index, v.1, p.298–317, v.2, p.816–77.

K188 La sculpture flamboyant. Nonette, Créer, 1983– . (4)v. il., plates.
Beautifully illustrated treatment of "flamboyant" sculpture of the High Gothic in France.
Contents: (1) Les grands imagiers d'Occident (1983); (2) Champagne Lorraine (1991); (3) Normandie Ile-de-France (1992); (4) Bourgogne Franche-Comté.
Includes bibliographies and indexes.

K189 La sculpture française au XIXe siècle. Paris, Éd. de la Réunion des musées nationaux, 1986. xxviii, 471p. il.

Well researched, scholarly catalog of the exhibition, Galeries nationales du Grand Palais (1986).

Contents: (1) L'atelier du sculpteur; (2) Formation; (3) Techniques et matériaux; (4) Les commandes publiques politiques; (5) Les commandes publiques religieuses; (6) Mécanisme de choix et financement; (7) Urbanisme: le socle; (8) Sculpture mémoire; (9) La tradition classique; (10) L'esprit romantique; (11) Éclectisme; (12) Le réalisme; (13) Symbolisme et primitivisme.

Notes, p.407–28. Bibliographie, p.429–41. Expositions, p.442–45. Index, p.446–69.

K190 Souchal, François. French sculptors of the 17th and 18th centuries: the reign of Louis XIV: illustrated catalogue by François Souchal, with the collab. of Françoise de la Moureyre, Henriette Dumuis. Trans. from the French by Elsie Hill and George Hill. Oxford, Cassirer, 1977–93. 4v.

See GLAH 1:K119a for original annotation. An essential reference work on sculpture of the period. Profusely illustrated biographical dictionary includes information on individual works, variants, private and museum locations, replicas, etc. V.4 incorporates new research findings, additions, corrections, and supplement to earlier vols.

Contents: (1) A–F; (2) G–L; (3) M–Z; (4) Suppl.

K191 Stoddard, Whitney S. Sculptors of the west portals of Chartres Cathedral: their origins in Romanesque and their role in Chartrain sculpture including the west portals of Saint-Denis and Chartres. N.Y., Norton, 1987. xvii, 252p. il., map, plans.

Contains two books, including (reprinted in its entirety, but in a smaller format) The west portals of Saint-Denis and Chartres (Harvard Univ. Pr., 1952), and The sculptors of the west portals of Chartres Cathedral. The former title explores the sculpture of Saint-Denis, with particular reference to the façade ornamentation, columns, and heads. The second book, published here for the first time, explores in greater detail the west portals of Saint-Denis and Chartres, and the origins of the Chartres sculptors.

Measurements of the west portals of Chartres, p.237–38. Dijon, Saint-Benigne (W.S.S. with Ruth Pasquine), p.239–41. Chartres West to Burgundy—La Charité-sur-Loire, p.242–44. Selected bibliography since 1952, p.245–47. Index, 1952 and 1986, p.249–52.

K192 West, Alison. From Pigalle to Preault: neoclassicism and the sublime in French sculpture, 1760–1840. N.Y., Cambridge Univ. Pr., 1998. xi, 324p. il. (part col.)

Contents: (1) Of moral instruction; (2) Toward classicism and nudity in French sculpture; (3) The Goujon "revival" in France; (4) Rome; (5) Early neoclassicism in France; (6) French sculpture after 1789; (7) The sublime: gigantism, the persistence of illusion and the ugly; (8) Canova, Flaxman and the vicissitudes of the international style in France; (9) The Elgin marbles and the end of the international style in France.

Notes, p.251–304. Bibliography, p.305–17. Index, p.318–24.

Germany and Austria

K193 Baxandall, Michael. The limewood sculptors of Renaissance Germany, 1475–1525: images and circumstances. New Haven, Yale Univ. Pr., 1980. xx, 420p. il., maps, plates.

Pioneering monograph on the works of limestone sculptors active in pre-Reformation Germany, 1475 to 1525. Analyzes works by major sculptors of the period in their cultural and political setting.

"Notes on plates and sculptors" provides biographical data on artists, as well as selective bibliography on objects and their makers.

References, p.[217]–37. Select bibliography, p.239–42. Notes on plates and sculptors, p.[243]–317. Index, p.417–20.

K194 Budde, Rainer. Deutsche romanische Skulptur, 1050–1250. Aufnahmen, Albert Hirmer und Irmgard Ernstmeier Hirmer. München, Hirmer, 1979. 130, 303p. chiefly il. (part col.), map.

Descriptive catalog of ca. 300 works of German Romanesque sculpture.

Literaturverzeichnis, p.115–22. Register [places, persons, iconography], p.123–31.

K195 Deutsche Bildhauer, 1900–1945, entartet. Christian Tümpel (Hrsg.). In Zusammenarb. mit Dirk van Alphen . . . [et al.] Zwolle, Waanders, 1992. 264p. il. (part col.)

Catalog of the exhibition, Nijmeegs Museum Commanderie van Sint-Jan (1991–2), and other locations. Eight introductory essays on modern sculpture in Germany and its Nazi critics, followed by a scholarly catalog with reproductions.

Biographien, p.198–247. Bibliographie, p.248–57. Personenregister, p.258–61.

K196 Ethos und Pathos: die Berliner Bildhauerschule 1786–1914. Konzept und Leitung der Ausstellung, Peter Bloch, Sibylle Einholz, Jutta von Simson; Ausstellungsgestaltung, Roman Weyl. Berlin, Mann; Staatliche Museen Preussischer Kulturbesitz, 1990. 2v. il.

Published in conjunction with the exhibition, Staatliche Museen Preussischer Kulturbesitz, Berlin (1990).

Contents: (1) Beiträge, mit Kurzbiographien Berliner Bildhauer; (2) Ausstellungskatalog.

Verzeichnis der abgekürzten Literatur, v.1, p.377, v.2, p.407–9. Berliner Skulpturen des 19. Jahrhunderts: Bibliographie, v.1, p.379–98. Kurzbiographien Berliner Bildhauer, v.1, p.399–588. Personenregister, v.1, p.589–98, v.2, p.412–19.

K197 Gegen den Strom: Meisterwerke niederrheinischer Skulptur in Zeiten der Reformation 1500–1550. Hrsg. vom Suermondt-Ludwig-Museum Aachen.

Idee und Konzeption: Barbara Rommé. [Katalogred.: Sibylle Gross]. Berlin, Reimer, 1996. 387p. il. (part col.)

Catalog of the exhibition, Suermondt-Ludwig-Museum Aachen (1996–7). Wide-ranging, signed essays on the techniques, economics, and religious background of sculptural production in the period. 76 works reproduced, mostly in color, alongside scholarly catalog entries.

Abgekürzte Literatur, p.373–86.

K198 German Expressionist sculpture. Organized by Stephanie Barron. Los Angeles, Los Angeles County Museum of Art; Univ. of Chicago Pr., 1983. 224p. il. (part col.)

Catalog of an important exhibition, Los Angeles County Museum of Art and other locations (1983–84). Includes catalog entries for 150 sculptures.

Bibliography, p.213–18. Index, p.220–23.

K199 Hermann, Manfred. Kunst im Landkreis Sigmaringen: Plastik. Sigmaringen, Hohenzollerische Landesbank, Kreissparkasse Sigmaringen, 1986. 415p. il. (part col.)

Historical survey, Romanesque through modern, with full-page illustrations.

Includes bibliographical references. Verzeichnis der Kunstwerke, p.397–402. Verzeichnis der Künstler, p.403–06. Ortsverzeichnis, p.407–11.

K200 Liebmann, M. J. Die deutsche Plastik, 1350–1550. Leipzig, Seemann, 1982. 546p. il.

Trans. from Russian by Hans Störel.

Examination of German Renaissance sculpture, with particular focus upon the development of "national schools."

Contents: Allgemeine Probleme; Das Werden der nationalen Schule; Die Blütezeit der nationalen Schule; Die Dürerzeit.

Anmerkungen, p.495–533. Register, p.534–[47].

K201 Maué, Claudia. Die Bildwerke des 17. und 18. Jahrhunderts im Germanischen Nationalmuseum: Bestandskatalog. Mainz, Zabern, 1997– . (1)v. (Kataloge des Germanischen Nationalmuseums)

Collection catalog of German Baroque sculpture, planned in 3 vols.

Contents: (1) Franken.

Verzeichnis der abgekürzt zitierten Literatur, p.[245]–53. Konkordanzen, p.[254]–55. Register, p.[257]–69.

K202 Meisterwerke mittelalterlicher Skulptur. Hrsg. von Hartmut Krohm. Berlin, Reimer, 1996. 526p. il. (part col.), plates, plans.

Published to accompany the exhibition "Meisterwerke mittelalterlicher Skulptur—die Berliner Gipsabgusssammlung," Bode-Museum, Berlin (1996). Scholarly handbook and catalog of the collection of casts of medieval German sculpture in the Berliner Gipsabgusssammlung.

Contents: Die Sammlungen von Gipsabgüssen in Berlin; Studien an Originalen und in der Abgusssammlung; Der Strassburger Ecclesiameister; Der Naumburger Meister; Die Abgüsse der Skulpturensammlung und der Gipsformerei; Katalog einer Auswahl von Gipsabgüssen.

Literatur, p.516–25.

K203 Mensch, Figur, Raum: Werke deutscher Bildhauer des 20. Jahrhunderts. Hrsg. von den Staatlichen Museen zu Berlin, Nationalgalerie. Autoren der Textbeiträge, Peter H. Feist . . . [et al.] Berlin, Staatliche Museen zu Berlin, Nationalgalerie, [1988]. 296p. il. (part col.)

Catalog of the exhibition, Nationalgalerie (1988). Seven introductory essays, followed by an illustrated catalog.

Literaturhinweise, p.63–65. Zu den Künstlern: Biographien, Notate, Werke; alphabetisches Verzeichnis, p.81. Chronik—Internationale Plastik, p.258–84. Ausstellungsverzeichnis, p.285–95.

K204 Mittelrhein-Museum Koblenz. Die Skulpturen vom 12. bis 18. Jahrhundert. Bearb. von Gunther Fabian. Koblenz, Städtische-Museen Koblenz, Mittelrhein-Museum, 1993. 263p. il. (part col.) (Bestandskataloge des Mittelrhein-Museums Koblenz, Bd. 3)

Scholarly catalog of 103 works in the permanent collection.

Includes bibliographical references. Konkordanztabelle, p.259. Register, p.260–61.

K205 Niehr, Klaus. Die mitteldeutsche Skulptur der ersten Hälfte des 13. Jahrhunderts. Weinheim, VCH, Acta Humaniora, 1992. vi, 532p. il. (Artefact, Bd. 3)

Revision of the author's thesis (Universität Bonn,1987).

Long introductory survey. Scholarly topographical inventory-catalog with illustrations.

Abkürzungs- und Literaturverzeichnis, p.369–98. Register, p.399–409.

K206 Sculptures médiévales allemandes: conservation et restauration. Sous la dir. de Sophie Guillot de Suduiraut. Paris, Documentation française, 1993. 424p. il. (part col.), plates (Louvre conférences et colloques)

Proceedings of the conference, Musée du Louvre (1991) held in conjunction with the exhibition, "Sculptures allemandes de la fin du Moyen Age" (1991–2). Texts in French and German.

Includes bibliographical references. Index des noms propres, p.419–22.

K207 Les sculptures médiévales allemandes dans les collections belges. [Par] R. Didier, H. Krohm. Bruxelles, Société générale de banque, [1977]. lxviii, 240, [12]p. il. (part col.), plates.

Catalog of the Europalia exhibition (1977). Bilingual in French and Dutch.

Index des noms de lieux et des personnes, p.[241–42]. Bibliographie, p.[243–51].

K208 Smith, Jeffrey Chipps. German sculpture of the later Renaissance c. 1520–1580: art in an age of uncertainty. Princeton, Princeton Univ. Pr., 1994. xxi, 524p. il., map, plans.

Scholarly, well-documented analysis of mid-16th century sculpture in Germany. The impact of the Reformation on sculptural production in Germany is treated in depth.

Contents: (1) For our salvation: the role of religious art in Pre-Reformation Germany; (2) Art or idol? (3) The Impact of the Reformation on religious sculpture, c.1520–1555; (4) Religious sculpture after the Peace of Augsburg, 1555–1580; (5) In memoriam: epitaphs and simple tombs; (6) Commemorative series and complex tombs; (7) The renaissance fountain; (8) Sculpture and architecture; (9) Small collectible sculpture: a study in the history of taste; (10) The emergence of sculptural portraits; Conclusion.

"Biographical catalogue of selected sculptors" (biographical entries followed by lists of selected signed and/or documented works, major attributed works, and selective bibliography on 44 sculptors treated in the text), p.363–409. Summary bibliography, p.411–22. Notes, p.423–86. Index, p.489–515. Iconographic index, p.516–24.

Great Britain and Ireland

K209 Bailey, Richard N. England's earliest sculptors. Toronto, Pontifical Institute of Mediaeval Studies, 1996. xx, 155p., plates. (Publications of the dictionary of Old English, 5)

Overview of Anglo-Saxon stone sculpture, primarily 7th century A.D. Chapters are illustrated with line drawings of ornamental surface sculpture.

Bibliographical notes. p.125–29. Bibliography. p.130–47. Index, p.148–55.

K210 ______. Viking Age sculptures in Northern England. London, Collins, 1980. 288p., il.

Study of sculpture from the area that formed the pre-Viking kingdom of Northumbria. Examines historical background to the carvings as well as their political and cultural significance.

Contents: (1) Introduction; (2) The historical background; (3) Dating; (4) Sculpture in the Anglian and Viking periods: continuity and contrast; (5) Hogbacks; (6) Gods, heroes and Christians; (7) Christian monuments; (8) Regional groupings, village links and schools; (9) Sculpture and history: a wider perspective; (10) The sculptor at work.

Abbreviations of county names, p.xx. Sites to visit, p.263–66. Further reading, p.267–71. Bibliography, p.273–80. Index, p.281–88.

K211 Beattie, Susan. The New Sculpture. London, Published for the Paul Mellon Center for Studies in British Art by Yale Univ. Pr., 1983. 272p. il., plates.

Extensively illustrated in-depth analysis of the influences and ramifications of the New Sculpture and its aesthetic revolution. Divided into five principal sections: sculptors at school; architectural sculpture; sculpture for the art gallery; sculpture for the home; the monument.

Contents: (1) The shape of a renaissance; (2) The liberation of the clay-modelling class; (3) Early achievements; (4) The triumph of the collaborative ideal; (5) Consolidation and decline; (6) The search for a new aesthetic; (7) The cult of the statuette; (8) Public image, private dreams; (9) Retrenchment and eclipse.

Biographical notes, p.239–52. Notes to the text, p. 253–62. Select bibliography, p.263–64. Index, p.265–72.

K212 Blackwood, John . London's immortals: the complete outdoor commemorative statues. London, Savoy Pr., 1989. 380p. il (part color)

Comprehensive illustrated study of outdoor statues organized by categories of commemoration.

Contents: (1) Royalty; (2) Philanthropy and education; (3) The arts; (4) Science and medicine; (5) Politics; (6) The armed forces; (7) Exploration and religion; (8) Making of a bronze; (9) Vanished statues; (10) The present of the past; (11) Where to walk: maps; Appendix.

Sources and acknowledgments, p.371–76. Index p.377–78.

K213 British sculpture in the twentieth century. Ed. by Sandy Nairne and Nicholas Serota. [London], Whitechapel Art Gallery, 1981. 263p., il.

Catalog of the two-part exhibition, Whitechapel Art Gallery (1981–82). Covering eighty years and more than 300 works, this catalog is arranged on the basis of themes, with well-illustrated essays. Contains brief summaries of careers, exhibitions, and publications of more than 100 sculptors born between 1846 and 1945.

Contents: (I) The patronage and support of sculptors, by Dennis Farr; (II) Classical and decorative sculpture, by Ben Read; (III) Cubism and sculpture in England before the First World War, by Jane Beckett; (IV) War memorials, by Richard Francis; (V) The Primitive, objectivity and modernity: some issues in British sculpture in the 1920s, by John Glaves-Smith; (VI) Painting and sculpture in the 1920s, by Richard Shone; (VII) Overhead sculpture for the underground railway, by Richard Cork; (VIII) Sculpture and the new "New Movement," by Charles Harrison; (IX) The Surrealist object and Surrealist sculpture, by Anna Gruetzner; (X) Sculpture in the 1940s and 1950s: the form and the language, by John Glaves-Smith; (XI) Public sculpture in the 1950s, by Richard Calvocoressi; (XII) Constructivism after the Second World War, by Alastair Grieve; (XIII) New abstract sculpture and its sources, by Lynne Cooke; (XIV) Figurative sculpture since 1960, by Timothy Hyman; (XV) A rhetoric of silence: redefinitions of sculpture in the 1960s and 1970s, by Stuart Morgan; (XVI) Constructed sculpture, by Brendan Prendeville; (XVII) Symbols, presences and poetry, by Fenella Crichton.

Selected bibliography, p.236–47. Biographies, p.248–63.

K214 Cheetham, Francis W. English medieval alabasters: with a catalogue of the collection in the Victoria and Albert Museum. Oxford, Phaidon-Christie's, 1984. 360p. il. (part col).

Important contribution to the study of British medieval sculpture. Lengthy introduction treats altarpieces, devotional images, the export trade, and contemporary commercial value of alabaster carvings. Complete catalog of individual works in the museum, supplemented by bibliographical references. Appendixes on iconographical subjects (including the Saints, the life of the Virgin, the Passion of Christ), paint analysis, and English alabasters on the Continent.

Bibliography, p.339–47. Concordance [museum accession number to catalogue number], p.348–50. Museum collection containing English medieval alabasters, p.351–52. Index, p.353–60.

K215 Corpus of Anglo-Saxon stone sculpture. [Ed.] by Rosemary Cramp. N.Y., Published for the British Academy by the Oxford Univ. Pr., 1984– . (5)v. il. (part col.), maps.

Scholarly series on pre-Romanesque sculpture in England. Vols. organized by area containing catalog entries including present location, evidence for discovery, stone type, present condition, description, discussion, date, and references.

Contents: (1) General introduction. County Durham and Northumberland; (2) Cumberland, Westmorland, and Lanchashire North-of-the-Sands; (3) York and Eastern Yorkshire; (4) South-east England; (5) Lincolnshire.

K216 Darke, Jo. The monument guide to England and Wales: a national portrait in bronze and stone. Photography by Jorge Lewinski and Mayotte Magnus. London, Macdonald, 1991. 256p. il. (part col.), plates.

Illustrated guidebook of nationwide outdoor commemorative statues and memorials. Discusses their history and the individuals they commemorate. Organized geographically by county.

Contents: London; Southern counties; Wales; Central counties; Eastern counties; Northern counties.

Index, p.250–56.

K217 Harbison, Peter. Irish high crosses: with the figure sculptures explained. Drogheda, Boyne Valley Honey Company, 1994. 111p. il., maps.

Systematic survey of all Irish high crosses containing figure sculpture. Contains illustrations of entire crosses or drawings of the shafts outlining biblical scenes.

K218 Hill, Judith. Irish public sculpture: a history. Dublin, Four Courts Pr., 1998. 302p. il.

Valuable overview and census, arranged by period and location, concluding with contemporary public sculpture and its thematics.

Contents: (1) Pre-classical sculpture; (2) The classical tradition; (3) Nineteenth-century monuments; (4) Twentieth-century monuments; (5) New directions.

Notes, p.251–80. Bibliography, p.281–90. Index, p.295–302.

K219 Nairne, Sandy, and Serota, Nicholas, eds. British sculpture in the twentieth century. London, Whitechapel Art Gallery, 1981. 264p. il.

Published in conjunction with the exhibition, Whitechapel Art Gallery (1981–82), this survey identifies key issues, movements, and personalities instrumental in shaping of 20th-century British sculpture. Major chapters cover patronage and support of sculptors, war memorials, public sculpture, Cubism, Surrealism, Constructivism, and the resurgence of figurative sculpture in the 1960s.

Bibliography, p.236–47. Biographical sketches of "sculptors working in Britain, born between 1845 and 1945," p.248–63.

K220 Pre-Raphaelite sculpture: nature and imagination in British sculpture 1848–1914. Ed. by Benedict Read and Joanna Barnes. With contrib. by John Christian . . . [et al.] London, Henry Moore Foundation in assoc. with Lund Humphries, 1991. 176p. il. (part col.)

Catalog of the exhibition, Matthiesen Gallery, London (1991), containing eight essays on artists followed by catalog entries and a brief biographical summary. All 88 exhibit pieces are illustrated.

Contents: Introduction, by Benedict Read; Bernhard Smith: "The Missing Brother," by Juliet Peers; Thomas Woolner: PRB, RA, by Benedict Read; Beyond Captain Cook: Thomas Woolner and Australia, by Juliet Peers; Thomas Woolner and the image of Tennyson, by Leonee Ormond; Alexander Munro: Pre-Raphaelite Associate, by Katharine Macdonald; The sculpture of John Lucas Tupper: "The Extremest Edge of P.R.Bism," by Joanna Barnes and Alexander Kader; John Hancock: Pre-Raphaelite sculptor?, by Thomas Beaumont James; Burne-Jones and sculpture, by John Christian.

Catalogue and biographies p.92–168. Abbreviations and bibliography, p.168–72. List of lenders p.173. List of exhibits, p.175–76.

K221 Read, Benedict. Sculpture in Britain between the wars. London, The Fine Art Society, 1986. 157p., il.

Catalog of the exhibition, Fine Art Society (1986). Brief biographical accounts of 48 sculptors accompanied by full-page and half-page reproductions of their sculptural works and photographs of the artist.

General bibliography, p.22. References, p.23.

K222 ______. Victorian sculpture. New Haven, Published for Paul Mellon Centre for Studies in British Art by Yale Univ. Pr., 1982. 414p., il.

Major, well-researched study of sculpture in Britain, 1830–1914, intended to be the first comprehensive survey of the period. Covers more than 1,000 sculptures, more than half of them illustrated.

Contents: (I) The position of Victorian sculpture; (II) The life and the works; (III) Classes apart; (IV) The end of the century.

References, p.387–96. Bibliography, 397–403. Index, p.404–14.

K223 Strachan, Walter John. Open air sculpture in Britain: a comprehensive guide. London, Zwemmer; Tate Gallery, 1984. 279p. il.

Covers more than 550 three-dimensional works by primarily British modern sculptors. Organized by region. A small black-and-white photograph accompanies each entry.

Glossary of the main terms used in sculpture, p.245–56. Select bibliography, p.257–58. List of sculptors and their works and biographical notes, p.249–75.

K224 Virtue and vision: sculpture and Scotland, 1540–1990. Ed. by Fiona Pearson. [Edinburgh], National Galleries of Scotland, [1991]. 175p. il.

Published on the occasion of the exhibition, Royal Scottish Academy (1991). Twelve essays treating about 320 sculptures. Includes works produced in Scotland, sculpture by Scots working outside the country, and works commissioned and collected by Scots.

Contents: (I) Introduction, by Timothy Clifford; (II) Sculpture and Scotland 1540–1700, by David Howarth; (III) Scottish connoisseurship and the Grand Tour, by Basil Skinner; (IV) "Proper Ornaments for a Library or Grotto": London sculptors and their Scottish patrons in the eighteenth century, by Malcolm Baker; (V) Samuel Joseph and the sculpture of Felling, by Terry Friedman; (VI) Thomas Campbell and Laurence Macdonald: the Roman solution to the Scottish sculptor's dilemma, by Helen E. Smailes; (VII) Sir John Steell and the idea of a native school of sculpture, by Fiona Pearson; (VIII) The Scottish Medal, by J. D. Bateson; (IX) Nineteenth century sculpture in Glasgow, by Robin Lee Woodward; (X) Pittendrigh MacGillivray, by Robin Lee Woodward; (XI) The Scottish National War Memorial, by Ian Gow; (XII) The twentieth century, by Douglas Hall.

K225 Whinney, Margaret Dickens. Sculpture in Britain: 1530 to 1830. Second (integrated) ed. revised by John Physick. London, Penguin Books, 1988. 522p. il., maps. (Yale University Press pelican history of art)

See GLAH 1:K146 for previous eds. This ed. of the standard art historical survey contains new material added to the text as well as additional illustrations and maps.

Contents: (1) The sixteenth century; (2) The earlier seventeenth century; (3) Restoration sculpture and the Baroque: 1660–1714; (4) The Antique, the Baroque, and the Rococo: 1714–1760; (5) The first Royal Academicians; (6) Neo-Classicism; (7) The early nineteenth century.

List of the principal abbreviations, p.[426]. Notes, p.[427]–74. Bibliography, p.[475]–83. List of illustrations, p.[484]–92. Index, p.[493]–522.

Italy

K226 Abbate, Francesco. La scultura napoletana del Cinquecento. Roma, Donzelli, 1992. ix. 285p. il., plates. (Saggi arti e lettere)

Survey of 16th-century sculpture in Naples.

Contents: (I) La colonia lombarda; (II) Fiorentini e spagnoli a Napoli; (III) Giovanni da Nola: l'egemonia di una bottega.

Bibliografia, p.259–70. Indice delle illustrazioni, p.271–78. Indice dei nomi, p.279–85.

K227 Ames-Lewis, Francis. Tuscan marble carving, 1250–1350: sculpture and civic pride. Aldershot, Ashgate, 1997. xvii, 244p. il (part col.), plates, plans.

Surveys sculptural projects and architectural decoration with particular reference to Pisa, Siena, and Florence. Major and lesser-known individual artists are covered with emphasis on their work with marble.

Contents: (1) The civic context; (2) Materials, techniques and workshops; (3) Survival and reconstruction; (4) Pulpits; (5) Façades; (6) Funerary monuments; (7) Sculpture in the civic context.

Notes at the end of chapters. Select bibliography, p.226–33. Index, p.235–44.

K228 Bellonzi, Fortunato. Scultura figurativa italiana del XX secolo. Roma, De Luca, 1989. 167p. chiefly il.

Pictorial survey of 20th-century Italian sculpture, with introduction.

Indice degli scultori, p.167.

K229 Carli, Enzo. Gli scultori senesi. Milano, Electa [1981]. 250p. il. (part col.), plates.

Beautifully illustrated survey of 16th-century Sienese sculptors. Color and black-and-white plates include many excellent details of tomb sculpture, statuary, and bas-relief narrative scenes. The work of each sculptor is illustrated with from four to more than forty reproductions.

Biographical sketches of each artist include bibliographical references.

Indice dei nomi e dei luoghi, p.245–50.

K230 ———. La scultura italiana: da Wiligelmo al novecento. Milano, Martello, 1990. 584p. col. il.

Readable survey of Italian sculpture from the Middle Ages to the 20th century, by an authority. No scholarly apparatus.

K231 Ciardi, Roberto Paolo; Casini, Claudio; and Tomasi, Lucia Tongiorgi. Scultura a Pisa tra quattro e seicento. Pisa, Cassa di risparmio, 1987. 373p. il. plates.

Survey of Pisan sculpture, 15th–17th centuries.

Contents: Il quattrocento; Il cinquecento; Il rinnovamento dell'ornato scultoreo interno del duomo dal 1523 al 1545; Dalle cappelle dell'Annunziata e dell'Incoronata all'altare di San Ranieri nel Duomo di Pisa (1545–1592); La restaurazione del duomo negli interventi scultori del primo seicento; I monumenti sepolcrali cinquecenteschi nel composanto monumentali; la scultura bronzea.

Indice dei nomi, p.362–67. Indice delle illustrazione, p.368–72.

K232 Fittipaldi, Teodoro. Scultura napoletana del Settecento. Napoli, Liguori, 1980. 240p. il (part col.), plates. (Collona napoletana di studi e documenti in memoria del conte Giuseppe Matarazzo di Licosa, 1)

Illustrated catalog of nearly 600 works by 17th- and 18th-century sculptors in Naples. With a long introduction.

Bibliografia, p.230–40.

K233 Glass, Dorothy F. Italian Romanesque sculpture: an annotated bibliography. Boston, Hall, 1983. xxvi, 302p. il., plates, map. (Reference publications in art history)

Annotated bibliography of monographic and periodical literature on Romanesque sculpture in Italy. More than 1,000 entries divided into seventeen chapters, arranged by literary genre, sculptural genre, iconographic subjects, etc.

Author index, p.281–93. Analytical index to regions and sites, p.295–302.

K234 ______. Romanesque sculpture in Campania: patrons, programs and style. University Park, Pennsylvania State Univ. Pr., 1991. xix, 252p. il., plates, maps.

Contents: (1) Monte Cassino and its progeny; (2) Toward the Romanesque; (3) Salerno in the twelfth century; (4) A Campanian Romanesque school; (5) Before and after Frederick I; (6) The narrative programs; (7) The liturgical programs.

Selected bibliography, p.[225]–45. Index p.[247]–52.

K235 Imago lignea: sculture lignee nel Trentino dal XIII al XVI secolo. A cura di Enrico Castelnuovo. Testi di Marco Bellabarba . . . [et al.] Schede di Andrea Bacchi, Serenella Castri, Silvia Spada. Fotografie di Mario Ronchetti-Scala. Trento, Temi, 1989. 287p. il. (chiefly col.), 1 map. (Storia dell'arte e della cultura)

Lavishly illustrated survey of wood sculpture in the Trentino-Alto Adige region of Italy, 13th–16th century.

Bibliografia, p.279–83. Indice dei luoghi, p.284–86.

K236 Istituto statale d'arte (Florence, Italy). Gipsoteca. Il Medioevo nei calchi della Gipsoteca. A cura di Luisella Bernardini, Mila Mastrorocco, Fema Monaci Scaramucci, con la collab. di Massimo Becattini. Firenze, Cassa di risparmio; L'Istituto, 1993. clxxvii, 286p. il.

Catalog of an important collection of medieval plaster casts.

Fonti d'archivio, p.260–62. Sigle e abbreviazioni bibliografiche, p.263–78. Concordanze, p.279–86.

K237 ______. La scultura italiana dal XV al XX secolo nei calchi della Gipsoteca. A cura di Luisella Bernardini, Annarita Caputo Calloud, Mila Mastrorocco. Firenze, Cassa di risparmio; L'Istituto, 1989. xciii, 468p. il.

Survey of Italian sculpture, Renaissance to modern, based upon the important cast collection of the Gipsoteca, published in conjunction with a reorganization of the collection.

Contents: Saggi: La dotazione di calchi di opere rinascimentali nell'Accademia di Belle arti ed il centenario di Michelangelo (1784–1875); Memoria e progetto nei modelli decorativi proposti dall Scuola di Santa Croce: 1876–1907; Il calco e il committente novecentesco; Il tradimento del segno. Catalogo. Notizie relative a gessi e a formatori tratte dalle filze dell'Archivio dell'Accademia di Belle Arti di Firenze: Appendice documentaria a cura di Annarita Caputo Calloud.

Fonti d'archivio, p.421–25. Sigle e abbreviazioni bibliografiche, p.427–41. Concordanze, p.443–65. Nuove numerazioni, p.467–68.

K238 Italian renaissance sculpture in the time of Donatello: an exhibition to commemorate the 600th anniversary of Donatello's birth and the 100th anniversary of the Detroit Institute of Arts. Detroit, Detroit Institute of Arts, 1985. 268p. il. (part col.)

Italian ed. Donatello e i suoi. Milan, Mondadori, 1987.

Major catalog published to accompany the exhibition, Detroit Institute of Arts and other locations (1985–6). Signed catalog entries for 90 works of sculpture, by specialists.

Bibliography, p.247–67. Index of artists, p.268.

K239 Il Lauro e il bronzo: la scultura celebrativa in Italia, 1800–1900. A cura di Maurizio Corgnati, di Gianlorenzo Mellini e di Francesco Poli. [Torino, s.n., 1990.] 182p.

Catalog of the exhibition, Circolo Ufficiali, Torino (1990). Scholarly, illustrated catalog of monumental public sculpture in 19th-century Italy.

Note biografiche, p.151–73. Esposizioni, p.175–76. Bibliografia, p.177–80.

K240 Looking at Italian Renaissance sculpture. Sarah Blake McHam, ed. Cambridge, Mass., Cambridge Univ. Pr., 1998. xvi, 287p. il.

"Eleven essays by prominent scholars who analyze in depth certain problems and issues regarding Italian sculpture of the fifteenth and sixteenth centuries . . . primarily Tuscan and Roman."—*Introd.*

Contents: (1) The materials and techniques of Italian Renaissance sculpture, by G. M. Helms; (2) The revival of antiquity in early Renaissance sculpture, by H. W. Janson; (3) On the sources and meaning of the Renaissance portrait bust, by Irving Lavin; (4) Familiar objects: sculptural types in the collections of the early Medici, by John T. Paoletti; (5) Holy dolls: play and piety in Florence in the Quattrocento, by Christiane Klapisch-Zuber; (6) The virtue of littleness: small-scale sculptures of the Italian Renaissance, by Joy Kenseth; (7) Public sculpture in Renaissance Florence, by Sarah Blake McHam; (8) Looking at Renaissance sculpture with Vasari, by Paul Barolsky; (9) A week in the life of Michelangelo, by William E. Wallace; (10) Michelangelo: sculpture, sex and gender, by James M. Saslow; (11) Gendered nature and its representation in sixteenth-century garden sculpture, by Claudia Lazzaro.

Selected bibliography, p.275–78. Index, p.279–87.

K241 McHam, Sarah Blake. The chapel of St. Anthony at the Santo and the development of Venetian Renaissance sculpture. N.Y., Cambridge Univ. Pr., 1994. xvi, 432p. il. (part col.), plates.

"An analysis of the chapel's history provides a focused study of the development of Venetian Renaissance sculpture from the late fifteenth century until the end of the sixteenth century."—*Introd.*

Bibliography, p.249–63. Index, p.265–71.

K242 Montagu, Jennifer. Gold, silver, and bronze: metal sculpture of the Roman baroque. Princeton, Princeton Univ. Pr., 1996. xvii, 262p. il. (part col.), plates. (Bollingen series, XXXV, 39; The A. W. Mellon lectures in the fine arts, 1990)

Revised version of author's Andrew Mellon lecture. Rather than a survey of the period, this work examines specific small-scale metallic sculpture of 17th- and 18th-century Rome in detail.

Contents: (1) Introduction; (2) Roman bronzes around 1600; (3) Adoration of the host: tabernacles of the baroque; (4) The medal: Some drawings for the Hamerani; (5) Silver tribute from a prince to a grand duke: the "Piatti di San

Giovanni"; (6) Giardini and Giardoni: silversmiths and founders of the eighteenth century; (7) From Rome to Lisbon: The patronage of John V; Appendices: (A) The tabernacles of Jacopo del Duca; (I) The ciborium of Sta. Maria Maggiore; (II) The ciborium of Sta. Maria in Vallicella; (III) The tabernacle of the Cappella Aldobrandini in Bologna; (IV) The Virgin and Child for Lisbon; (V) The Virgin of the Immaculate Conception for Lisbon.

Notes, p.213–48. Bibliography, p.[249]–55. Index of names and locations, p.[256]–62.

K243 ______. Roman Baroque sculpture: the industry of art. New Haven, Yale Univ. Pr., 1989. xi. 244p. il., plates.

Well-researched and documented study of the unexplored area of art as an industry in baroque Rome. Includes material on training of sculptors, the role of the founders in the production of sculpture, etc.

Contents: (1) Beginnings; (2) From the quarry to the church; (3) Founders and sculptors; (4) The sculptor as executant; (5) The sculptor as designer; (6) The "boys"; (7) The influence on the baroque of classical antiquity; (8) Festivals and feasts.

Notes, p.198–220. Bibliography, p.228–36. Index of names and places, p.237–42. Index of subjects, p.243.

K244 Niveo de marmore: l'uso artistico del marmo di Carrara dall'XI al XV secolo. A cura di Enrico Castelnuovo. Genoa, Colombo, 1992. 370p. il. (part col.)

Published in conjunction with the exhibition, La Cittadella, Sarzana (1992).

Scholarly chronological survey of marble sculpture in Italy from the 11th through the 15th century. Essays by specialists.

Bibliografia generale, p.361–70.

K245 Olson, Roberta J. M. Italian Renaissance sculpture. N.Y., Thames and Hudson, 1992. 216p. il. (World of art)

Accessible, brief chronological survey of the subject.

Select bibliography, p.213–14. Index, p.215–16.

K246 Panzetta, Alfonso. Dizionario degli scultori Italiani dell'ottocento e del primo novecento. Milan, Allemandi, 1994. 3v. il. (Archivi dell'ottocento)

First published 1989 in 1 vol.

Very useful 3-vol., illustrated reference work providing biographical sketches of 19th-century Italian sculptors. Includes references to museums' holdings of individual works as well as published references.

Contents: (1) Dizionario; (2) Atlante illustrato delle opere; (3) Appendice rilevazione di mercato.

Vol.2 is comprised of reproductions, arranged alphabetically by sculptor. Individual entries include date, materials, dimensions, and location. Vol.3 (24p.) provides prices realized at auction.

Bibliografia, v.1, p.[291]–311.

K247 Pirovano, Carlo. Scultura italiana del Novecento. Contrib. di Rossana Bossaglia, Luciano Caramel, Ester Coen . . . [et al.] Milano, Banco Ambrosiano Veneto; Electa, 1991. 310p. il. (part col.)

Illustrated survey of 20th-century Italian sculpture. Most chapters explore major individual artists in depth. Includes some important letters and other primary source materials.

Nota bibliografica, p.305–06. Indice dei nomi, p.307–10.

K248 Poeschke, Joachim. Donatello and his world: sculpture of the Italian Renaissance. Photographs by Albert Hirmer and Irmgard Ernstmeier-Hirmer. Trans. From German by Russell Stockman. N.Y., Abrams, 1993. 496p. il.

Trans. of Die Skulptur der Renaissance in Italien, Bd.1. Donatello und seine Zeit. Munchen, Hirmer, 1990.

This overview of Italian Renaissance sculpture includes some very good photographic reproductions of major and minor works, along with many details. The "Documentation" section provides biographical entries on major and minor sculptors, complete with additional bibliographical references and analysis of individual works. Continued by the following title.

Bibliography, p.477–89. Index, p.490–95.

K249 ______. Michelangelo and his world: sculpture of the Italian Renaissance. Photographs by Albert Hirmer and Irmgard Ernstmeier-Hirmer. Trans. From the German by Russell Stockman. N.Y., Abrams, 1996. 272p., il. (part col.), maps, plates

Trans. of Die Skulptur der Renaissance in Italien, Bd.2. Michelangelo und seine Zeit. München, Hirmer, 1990.

See preceding entry for annotation.

Bibliography, p.236–57. Index, p.258–71.

K250 Pope-Hennessy, John Wyndham, Sir. An introduction to Italian sculpture. 4th ed. London, Phaidon, 1996. 3v. il., plates.

See GLAH 1:K164 for 1st and 2d eds. 3d ed. N.Y., Vintage, 1985. Revised version of classic study of the period, with bibliography updated through 1993.

Contents: (1) Italian Gothic sculpture; (2) Italian Renaissance sculpture; (3) Italian High Renaissance and Baroque sculpture.

K251 ______. The study and criticism of Italian sculpture. N.Y., Metropolitan Museum of Art; Princeton, Princeton Univ. Pr., 1980. 270p. il.

A classic collection of essays by the great authority originally presented as lectures.

Contents: Connoisseurship; The sixth centenary of Ghiberti; The Evangelist roundels in the Pazzi Chapel; The Medici Crucifixion of Donatello; Donatello and the bronze statuette; The Altman Madonna by Antonio Rossellino; Thoughts on Andrea della Robbia; The Italian plaquette; The forging of Italian Renaissance sculpture.

K252 Pratesi, Giovanni. Repertorio della scultura fiorentina del seicento e settecento. Consulenza scientifica di Ursula Schlegel e Sandro Bellesi. Biografie a cura di Silvia Blasio. Torino, Umberto Allemandi, 1993. 3v. il. (Archivi di arte antica)

Beautifully illustrated census of Florentine sculpture of the 17th and 18th centuries.

Contents: (1) Text; (2–3) Plates.

Biografie degli artisti, v.1, p.[33]–65. Indice topografico delle opere, v.1, p.[67]–110. Bibliografia citata, v.1, p.[111]–17. Tavola sinottica, v.1, p.[118–19].

K253 Scalini, Mario. L'arte italiana del bronzo, 1000–1700: toreutica monumentale dall'alto Medioevo al Barocco. Buste Arsizio, Bramanate, 1988. 361p. il. (part col.) (Arte e tecnica)

Brief chapters accompanied by many black-and-white plates, exploring the various uses of bronze in Italian architecture and sculpture from 1000 to 1700. Emphasis on major sculptors and their works.

Contents: Le grandi tappe della statuaria bronzea; Le porte bronzee; I complessi e gli arredi ecclesiastici; Il monumento equestre; Dalla lastra terragna al cenotafio dinastico; Il busto onorario e l'antico; Le artiglierie; Le fontane e l'arredo urbano; Le techniche; Le fonti [excerpts from selected literary sources].

Bibliografia, p.351–56. Indice dei nomi e dei luoghi, p.357–60.

K254 Schlegel, Ursula. Die italienischen Bildwerke des 17. und 18. Jahrhunderts in Stein, Holz, Ton, Wachs und Bronze mit Ausnahme der Plaketten und Medaillen. Berlin, Mann, 1978. xii, 198p. il., plates. (Bildwerke der Skulpturengalerie Berlin, Bd. 1)

Scholarly catalog of the Baroque collection.

Verzeichnis der Künstler, p.187–[90]. Verzeichnis der Orte, p.191–95. Vergleichendes Verzeichnis der Katalog- und Inventar-Nummern und der zur Zeit allgemein benutzten älteren Kataloge, p.196–[97]. Vergleichendes Verzeichnis von Inventar-Nummern und Katalog-Eintragungen, p.198–[99].

K255 La scultura a Genova e in Liguria. Genova, Cassa di risparmio di Genova e Imperia, 1987–1989. 3v. il. (part col.)

Monumental history of Genoese and Ligurian sculpture, beautifully illustrated.

Contents: (I) Dalle origini al Cinquecento; (II) Dal Seicento al primo Novecento; (III) Dalla prima guerra mondiale ad oggi.

Bibliografie, v.1, p.[395]–411, v.2, p.[491]–510. Indice dei nomi, dei luoghi e delle cose notevoli, v.1, p.[413]–27. Indice dei nomi e dei luoghi, v.2, p.[511]–22.

K256 La scultura: bozzetti in terracotta, piccoli marmi e altre sculture dal XIV al XX secolo. A cura di Giancarlo Gentilini e Carlo Sisi. Firenze, S.P.E.S., [1989]. 2v. il. (part col.) plates.

Catalog of the exhibition, Siena, Palazzo Chigi Saracini (1989). Well-documented entries, presented chronologically, include bibliographic references, textual analysis, and reproductions of sculptural works produced from the 14th through mid-20th centuries. Documentary appendixes.

Bibliografia, v.2, p.541–58.

K257 La scultura decorativa del primo Rinascimento. Roma, Viella, 1983. 216p. il., map, plans, plates.

Texts in English, French, German, or Italian. Proceedings of the first Convegno internazionale di studi, Pavia (1980). Essays on decorative and relief sculpture of the early Renaissance.

K258 Scultura del '600 a Roma. A cura di Andrea Bacchi, con la collab. di Susanna Zanuso. Milano, Longanesi, 1996. 862p. chiefly il. (Repertori fotografici, 10)

Alphabetically arranged, illustrated survey of 17th-century sculpture in Rome. Includes useful biographical sketches.

Indice degli artisti, p.7–8. Biografie, p.769–846. Bibliografia, p.847–60.

K259 Scultura italiana del XX secolo. Pres. di Luigi Testaferrata. Profili biografici di Giancarlo Caldini. Firenze, Casa editrice Il fiore, 1984. 285p. il.

Provides short (2–4p.) biographical sketches of 20th-century Italian sculptors, by different authors. Entries include numerous reproductions of individual works.

Indice degli artisti, p.283.

K260 Scultura nelle Marche. A cura di Pietro Zampetti. Testi di Luciano Arcangeli . . . [et al.] Firenze, Nardini, 1993 (1994 printing). 518p. il. (part col.)

Chronological survey of sculpture from the region, by various authors. Magnificently illustrated.

Bibliografia, p.499–510. Indice dei nomi, p.511–16.

K261 Scultura toscana del Novecento: Libero Andreotti . . . [et al.] A cura di Umberto Baldini. Firenze, Banca Toscana, 1980. 412p. il. (part col.)

Monographic survey of 20th-century Tuscan sculpture, organized alphabetically by artist (30 sculptors altogether).

Dati biografici essenziali, p.[401]–10.

K262 Vicario, Vincenzo. Gli scultori Italiani: dal Neoclassicismo al Liberty. 2d ed. (rev). Lodi, Pomerio, [1994]. 2v. il.

1st ed. in 1 vol. Lodi, Lodigraf, 1990.

Dictionary of biographical essays on Italian sculptors of the 18th and 19th centuries. Length of individual entries varies from very short (1 or 2 paragraphs) to long (20 pages or more). Entries include names of major works and monuments, with some illustrated in black and white.

K263 Wilk, Sarah Blake. Fifteenth-century central Italian sculpture: an annotated bibliography. Boston, Hall, 1986. xxvi, 401p. il. (Reference publication in art history)

Classified bibliography of published works focuses on "artists born in the provinces of Tuscany, Lazio, Umbria and the Marches." Topographical arrangement includes sections on general source material, collections of documents, literary sources, and individual monuments for each of the areas surveyed. Additional references to sites outside of central Italy, specific materials (other than stone), specialized commissions, and the lengthy section on individual sculptors make this an indispensable reference tool for the researcher of Italian art and related subjects.

Author index, p.355–66. Subject index, p. 367–401.

Latin America

K264 Calzadilla, Juan, and Briceño, Pedro. Escultura, escultores: un libro sobre la escultura en Venezuela. [Caracas], Maraven, [1977]. 233p. il. (part col.)
Survey of sculpture in Venezuela from colonial period to present. Includes biographical sketches of 79 sculptors active or influential in Venezuela.
Noticias biograficas, p.[214]–31. Bibliografia basica, p.232–33.

K265 Carvacho Herrera, Víctor. Historia de la escultura en Chile. Santiago de Chile, Bello, [1983]. 328p. il. (part col.)
Substantial history of Chilean sculpture from prehistory to the modern era.
Bibliografia, p.311–14. Indice de nombres, p.315–19.

K266 Kassner, Lily S. de. Diccionario de escultura mexicana del siglo XX. México, Univ. Nacional Autónoma de México, Coord. de Humanidades, 1983. 367p. il.
Brief entries on contemporary Mexican sculptors include biographical data and a list of exhibitions.

K267 Mesa, José de, and Gisbert, Teresa. Escultura virreinal en Bolivia. La Paz, Academia Nacional de Ciencias de Bolivia, 1972. 489p. il. (Publicación [de la] Academia Nacional de Ciencias de Bolivia, 29)
Survey of sculptors active in Bolivia during the colonial period, 16th–18th centuries. Includes transcriptions of four pertinent documents.
Bibliografía, p.477–83. Indice de artistas, p.487–90.

K268 Mexican monuments: strange encounters. Conceived and coord. by Helen Escobedo. Photographs by Paolo Gori. Essays by Nestor Garcia Canclini . . . [et al.] N.Y., Abbeville Press, 1989. 251p. chiefly il. (part col.)
Personal view of civic monuments and public sculpture conceived by a site-oriented sculptor, presented in photographs and essays.
Index, p.252.

K269 Moreno Villa, José. La escultura colonial mexicana. México, Fondo de Cultura Económica, 1986. 110p., il, plates. (Arte universal)
Reprint of original ed., [México,] El Colegio de México [1942]. A classic work on colonial Mexican sculpture, 16th–18th centuries.
Bibliografía, p.85–87. Índices: de lugares, p.97–98; de autores, p.99–101; de láminas, p.103–07.

K270 Rubiano Caballero, Germán. La escultura en América Latina (siglo xx). Bogotá, Univ. Nacional de Colombia, 1986. 118p. il., plates.
Ambitious yet brief survey of Latin American sculpture from the second half of the 19th century.
Contents: Mexico; Centroamerica; Las islas; Suramerica. Bibliographical references at ends of chapters.

K271 Sculpture of the Americas into the nineties. Washington, D.C., Museum of Modern Art of Latin America, 1990. 81p. il. (part col.)
Catalog of the exhibition, Museum of Modern Art of Latin America, Washington, D.C. (1990).

Low Countries

K272 Antwerp altarpieces: 15th–16th centuries. [Catalogue and essays ed. by Hans Nieuwdorp.] Antwerp, Museum voor Religieuze Kunst, 1993. 2v. il. (chiefly col.)
Texts in English, Dutch, and French. Catalog of the exhibition, Antwerp Cathedral (1993). "Highlights various aspects of Antwerp altarpiece art and its study and conservation."—*p.[9].*
Contents: (1) Catalogue; (2) Essays.
Register of Antwerp altarpieces, v.1, p.193–95. Index, v.1, p.197–98, v.2, p.171–74.

K273 Beelden in de late middeleeuwen en Renaissance = Late gothic and Renaissance sculpture in the Netherlands. [Reindert Falkenburg, Dulcia Meijers, Herman Roodenburg, . . . (et.al.), eds.] Zwolle, Waanders Uitgevers, 1994. 446p. il. maps, plans, plates. (Nederlands kunsthistorisch jaarboek, 45).
Collection of original essays, most in Dutch (with English summaries), surveys various aspects of late Gothic and Renaissance sculpture in the Netherlands. Heavily documented and illustrated, many of the essays address the issues of Protestant Reformation iconoclasm and the subsequent loss of sculptural works.
Notes at ends of chapters.

K274 Gérard, Jo. Histoire de la sculpture belge. Préf. de Léonard Dieleman. Bruxelles, J.M. Collet, [1988]. 125p. il. (1 col.)
Brief survey, with good black-and-white plates. No scholarly apparatus. Chapter one (The most European sculptors) is in English and offers an introduction to the subject.

K275 Jacobs, Lynn F. Early Netherlandish carved altarpieces, 1380–1550: medieval tastes and mass marketing. N.Y., Cambridge Univ. Pr., 1998. xv, 352p. il.
Careful study of some of the "most lavish and splendid examples of late medieval art" of which some 350 examples survive.—*Introd.* Focuses on production and distribution as evidence of late medieval taste.
Notes, p.259–327. References, p.329–41. Index, p.342–52.

K276 Laat-gotische beeldsnijkunst uit Limburg en grensland = Le Gothique tardif dans la sculpture du Limbourg et des pays frontières. Sint-Truiden [Belgium], Provinciaal Museum voor Religieuze Kunst, 1990–1992. 2v. il. (part col.)

Catalog of the important exhibition, Provinciaal Museum voor Religieuze Kunst, Sint-Truiden (1990), and other locations. Texts in Dutch, French, and German. V.1 is the exhibition catalog; v.2 is the proceedings of a related symposium, Hoepertingen, Sint-Truiden (1990).

Bibliografie, p.[IV.1]–IV.6. Indices, p.[IV.7]–IV.18.

K277 La sculpture au siècle de Rubens dans les Pays-Bas méridionaux et la principauté de Liège. S.l., s.n., 1977. 387p. il.

Catalog of the exhibition, Musée d'art ancien, Brussels (1977). Explores Baroque sculpture in the Low Countries.

Bibliographie, p.341–77 (includes general works as well as regional studies). Liste des expositions mentionnées, p.378–82. Liste des abréviations, p.383–86.

K278 La sculpture belge au 19ème siècle. Conception, coord. scientifique et choix des oeuvres exposées, Jacques van Lennep. Bruxelles, Générale de Banque, 1990. 2v. il., ports.

Contents: (1) Histoire: (I) Entre baroque et classicisme: a l'aube du 19e siècle, par Helena Bussers; (II) La sculpture sou le règne de Léopold Ier (1831–1865), par Jacques van Lennep; (III) La sculpture de 1865 à 1895, par Hugo Lettens; (IV) Académisme et mutations au tournant du siècle, par Bruno Fornari; Aspects: (V) Les monuments publics à Bruxelles et en Wallonie, par Richard Kerremans; (VI) Les monuments publics en Flandre, par Paul Verbraeken; (VII) La sculpture funéraire, par Ceclia Vandervelde; (VIII) La sculpture et la bourgeoisie, par Dorine Cardyn-Oomen; (IX) La représentation du travail dans la sculpture: autour de Constantin Meunier, par Pierre Baudson; (X) Les fonderies de bronze, par Pierre-Paul Dupont et Colette Huberty; (XI) L'enseignement de la sculpture, par Sophie Orloff; (2) Artistes et oeuvres [catalog with illustrated entries on individual artists, alphabetically arranged].

Abréviations utilisées, v.2, p.626. Index des sculpteurs cités, v.2, p.627–31. Bibliographie sommaire, v.2, p.633.

K279 Steyaert, John W. Late gothic sculpture: the Burgundian Netherlands. With the collab. of Monique Tahon-Vanroose, and contrib. by Wim Blockmans and Leon Smets. Ghent, Ludion Press (Distr. by Abrams, 1994). 352p. il., col. plates, maps.

Scholarly, beautifully illustrated catalog, published in conjunction with the exhibition, Museum voor Schone Kunsten, Ghent (1994). Attempts to tell "the story of the development of Late Gothic sculpture" in the Burgundian Netherlands.

Lenders to the exhibition, p.11. Bibliography, p.344–48. Index, p.349–51.

Russia and Eastern Europe

K280 Adamec, Ana. Hrvatsko kiparstvo na prijelazu stoljeća. Zagreb, Denona, 1999. 324p. il.

In Serbo-Croatian (Romanized). Study of modern Croatian sculpture.

Notes, p.319–24. Biography of the author, p.329.

K281 Gamulin, Grgo. Hrvatsko kiparstvo XIX. i XX. stoljeća. Zagreb, Naprijed, 1999. 454p. il. (part col.) (Povijest umjetnosti u hrvatskoj, 5)

Beautifully illustrated study of modern Croatian sculpture.

Bibliografija, p.433–40. Popis reprodukcija [list of illustrations, alphabetical by artist], p.441–49. Kazalo imena [index], p.450–54.

K282 Gosudarstvennaia Tret'iakovskaia Galeria. Skul'ptura i risunki skul'ptorov konsta XIX-nachala XX veka: katalog. Moskva, "Sovetskii khudozhnik," 1977. 637p. il.

Text in Russian. Catalog of the Tretyakov Gallery collection of modern Russian sculpture.

Includes bibliographical references and indexes.

K283 Gosudarstvennyi russki muzei (Leningrad). Skul'ptura, XVIII-nachalo XX veka: katalog = Sculpture, 18th to early 20th century: catalogue. [Otvetstvennyi red. L.P. Shaposhnikova.]. Leningrad, "Iskusstvo," Leningradskoe otd-nie, 1988. 318p. il.

In Russian. Introduction in Russian and English. Illustrated, scholarly catalog of the museum collection.

Abbreviations, p.15–[18]. Bibliographical references and indexes, p.308–[19].

K284 Kwiatkowska, Maria Irena. Rzezbiarze warszawscy XIX wieku. Warszawa, Wydawn. Nauk. PWN, 1995. 375p. il.

Survey of 19th-century sculpture in Warsaw. Mostly profiles of individual sculptors. Poorly illustrated.

Wykazy skrótów [abbreviations], 352. Indeks [index], p.353–69

K285 Monumental'naia i dekorativnaia skul'ptura Leningrada = Monumental and decorative sculpture of Leningard. [Sostaviteli E.V. Pliukhin, Abram Grigorevich Raskin.] Leningrad, Iskusstvo, 1991. 478p. il.

In Russian, with English summary and captions. Seeks "to show Leningrad's monumental and decorative sculpture in all its wealth and typological variety, including monuments, statues, busts, the decoration of buildings and triumphal arches, reliefs, ornaments and park and garden sculpture"—*p.95.* Includes an introductory history of outdoor sculpture in Leningrad.

[English summary], p.95–96. Index, p.476–[79].

K286 Muzeum Narodowe w Warszawie. Rzeźba polska XIX wieku od klasycyzmu do symbolizmu: katalog zbiorów. Warszawa, The Museum, 1993. 150p. il.

In Polish. Introduction in English. Catalog of 19th-century Polish sculpture in the collections of the National Museum, Warsaw.

Wykaz skrótów [abbreviations], p.10–11. No index.

K287 Narodni muzeum v Praze. Lapidarium of the National Museum Prague: guide to the permanent exhibition of Czech sculpture in stone of the 11th to 19th centuries in the pavilion of the Lapidarium in the Exhibition Grounds in Prague. Prague, ASCO PRAHA, 1993. 110p. col. il.

Contents: Characteristics of the collection; History of the collection; Technology of sculpture in stone; Catalogue.

Selected literature, p.108. Explanations of specialised terms, p.109–10.

K288 Pomerantsev, Nikolai Nikolaevitch. Russkaia dereviannaia skul'ptura = Russian wooden sculpture. Moskva, "Izobrazitelnoe iskusstvo," 1994. 324p. chiefly col. il., port.

1967 ed. Moskva, Sov. Khudozhnik, 1967.

In Russian, with English summary and bilingual captions. Illustrated overview. The result of decades of restoration work initiated by the author, a prominent historian of medieval Russian art.

Summary [English], p.323–24.

K289 Protić, Miodrag B. Skulptura XX veka. Beograd, [s.n.], 1982. 138p. col. il. (Umetnost na tlu Jugoslavije)

In Serbo-Croation (Romanized). Survey of 20th-century Yugoslav sculpture. Mostly color plates. Lacks scholarly apparatus.

K290 Rajna, György. Budapest köztéri szobrainak katalógusa. Budapest, Budapesti Városszépítyo Egyesület, 1989. 653p.

Substantial study of public monuments in Budapest.

Indexes, p.576–653.

K291 Schmidt, Igor' Maksmilianovich. Russkaia skul'ptura vtoroi poloviny XIX-nachala XX veka. Moskva, "Iskusstvo," 1989. 302p. il. (part col.)

"The first fundamental study of the history of Russian plastic art for over 70 years of its development—from the late 1830s to 1917."—*Summary*, p.303. Survey of pre-Soviet modern Russian sculpture.

Notes, p.272–90. Bibliography, p.291–93. Index, p.300–02. Summary [in English], p.303.

K292 Sovremennaia sovetskaia skul'ptura. [Avtory-sostaviteli N.M. Baburina, V.T. Sheveleva.] Moskva, "Sov. Khudozhnik," 1989. 279p. il. (part col.)

In Russian, with English summary. Survey of Soviet sculpture, 1960–1980.

Contemporary soviet sculpture [English summary], p.272. Catalogue, p.273–79.

K293 Tisucu godina hrvatskog kiparstva = Thousand years of Croatian sculpture. [Odgovorni urednik Ante Soric; urednik Igor Fiskovich.] Zagreb, Muzejsko Galerijski Centar, 1997. 373p. il. (part col.) (Znanstvena izdanja MGC, 4)

1st ed. 1991. In Serbo-Croatian (Romanized), with English summary. Originally published in conjunction with of the exhibition, Muzejsko Galerijski Centar, Zagreb (1997).

K294 Žitko, Sonja. Historizem v kiparstvu 19. stoletja na Slovenskem. Llubljana, Slovenska matica, 1989. 188p. il. (part col.)

Includes German and French summaries. Study of historicism in 19th-century Slovenian sculpture.

Notes, p.148–57. German summary, 165–70. French summary, p.171–76. Index, p.182–87.

Scandinavia

K295 Dänische Skulptur im 20. Jahrhundert. Ausstellung und Katalog, Renate Heidt. Übers. aus dem Dänischen, Georg Albrecht Mai, Renate Heidt. [Duisburg], Wilhelm-Lehmbruck-Museum der Stadt Duisburg, 1985. 134p. il.

Catalog of the exhibition, Wilhelm-Lehmbruck-Museum der Stadt Duisburg (1985), and other locations.

Biographische Daten, Ausstellungen, Literatur (Auswahl), p.113–30. Verzeichnis der ausgestellten Arbeiten, p.131–34.

K296 Nationalmuseum (Sweden). Nationalmuseum, Stockholm: illustrerad katalog över äldre svensk och utländsk skulptur = Illustrated catalogue of Swedish and European sculpture. Stockholm, The Museum, 1999. 431p. il.

The first and more substantial part of the catalog (p.[21]–253) is devoted to Swedish sculpture. Includes a brief history of the collection (in English).

Förklaringar till katalog, p.18–19. Abbreviated explanatory notes [in English], p.419. Nummerregister = numerical index, p.395–422. Register över omattribueringar = index of revised attributions, p.423–24. Register över avporträtterade = index of portrait subjects, p.425–31.

K297 Ny Carlsberg Glyptotek. Danish sculpture 1694–1889: catalogue. By Jens Peter Munk. [Copenhagen], Ny Carlsberg Glyptotek, 1995. 222p., il. (part col.)

"This volume is part of a series of catalogues of the collection in the Ny Carlsberg Glyptotek."—*t.p. verso.*

Bibliography, p.217. Concordance, p.219–22.

Spain and Portugal

K298 Agullo y Cobo, Mercedes. Documentos sobre escultores, entalladores y ensambladores de los siglos XVI al XVIII. Valladolid, Publicaciones del Departmento de Historia del Arte, 1978. 227p.

Scholarly compilation of documents organized chronologically within alphabetical listing of artists.

Indice onomástico, p.179–222. Indice topográfico, p.223–25. Indice iconográfico, p.227.

K299 Ara Gil, Clementia-Julia. Escultura Gótica en Valladolid y su provincia. Valladolid, Institucion Cultural Simancas, Exm. Diputación Provincial de Valladolid, 1977. 780p. il.

Scholarly work divided by century (from the 13th to the 16th) and further divided by type: La escultura funeraria, La imaginería, La escultura monumental, Los retablos, La talla ornamental en Madera. Accompanied by a large section of plates.

Contents: Introduccion; La Escultura de los siglos XIII y XIV; La Escultura de los dos primeros tercios del siglo XV;

La Escultura del ultimo tercio del siglo XV y de los primeros años del XVI.

Bibliografía, p.459. Indice, p.767–75. Indice general p.777–80.

K300 Barrio Loza, José Angel. Escultura romanista en La Rioja. [Madrid], Ministerio de Cultura, Dirección General de Bellas Artes, Archivos y Bibliotecas, Centro Nacional Información Artística y Arqueológica, [1981?]. 339p. il.

Overview of 16th-century sculpture followed by chapters devoted to workshops and artists in Logroño, Arnedo, Navarros, Sorianos. Each chapter contains plates.

Notas, p.284–98. Apéndice documental, 299–327. Indices, p.328–39.

K301 Buesa Conde, Domingo. La Virgen en el Reino de Aragón: imágenes y rostros medievales. Fotografías: José Antonio Duce. [Zaragoza], Ibercaja, [1994]. 461p. col. il.

Beautifully illustrated survey of Spanish Romanesque and Gothic polychrome sculpture representing the Virgin. Each unnumbered chapter is devoted to a specific region within the province of Aragon.

Contents: Los Valles del Viejo Aragón; El viejo Condado de Sobrarbe; Tierras de Ribagorza; Las Cinco Villas de Aragón; El reino de los Mallos; Las llanuras de Huesca; Las fronteras del Cinca; La gran llanura; La ciudad y el entorno de Zaragoza; Las tierras del río Ebro; Las Tierras del Moncayo; Los caminos del río Jalón; El Campo de Cariñena; La Comunidad de Daroca; Tierras del Bajo Aragón; La Depressión Ibérica; Las Tierras de Teruel; La Sierra de Albarracín; Tierras de Ganaderos; Nuestra Señora del Pilar.

Brief bibliographies at the end of each section. Bibliografía general, p.441–47. Indice de lugares, p.451–57.

K302 Calvo Serraller, F. Escultura Española-Actual: una generación para un fin de siglo. [Madrid?], Fundación Lugar, [1992]. 325p. il. (part col.)

This Spanish/English text is devoted to contemporary sculpture and includes a month-by-month chronology from 1980–1991 of exhibitions accompanied by excerpts of the shows.

Contents: (1) La escultura: de lo anti-moderno a lo posmoderno; (2) La actualidid: proceso de "impurificación"; (3) Es la escultura una expresión artística española?; (4) Panorámica tridimensional para el arte español de los chenta; (5) Antecedentes cirunstancialmente polémicos: los años setenta; (6) Las extravagantes sendas de extranjeros no identificados; (7) Dinámicas e interrogaciones de los ochenta; (8) Cuestiones regionales; (9) Cabos sueltos; (10) Espacialidad posmoderna y pédida de tiempo.

Cronología 1980–1991, p.127–216. Bibliografía, p.218–19. English texts, p.221–325.

K303 Cardesa García, María Teresa. La escultura del siglo XVI en Huesca. [Huesca], Instituto de Estudios Altoaragoneses, Diputación de Huesca, [1993] 2v. il. (Colección de estudios aragoneses, 36)

Scholarly work documenting artists and religious sculptural decoration in the capital of Alto Aragón. Based on the author's doctoral thesis (Univ. de Zaragosa, 1990).

Contents: (1): El ambiente histórico-artístico [Introducción; (2) Características generales; (3) Indice biográfico de los artistas que trabajaron en Huesca en el siglo XVI]; (4): Catálogo de Obras [Nota preliminar; Introducción; Obras documentadas; Obras sin documentar; Obras documentadas desaparecidas; Conclusiones].

Apéndice documental, v.1, p.271–370, v.2, p.217. Bibliografía, v.1, p.371–94, v.2, p.233–51.

K304 Chamoso Lamas, Manuel. Escultura funeraria en Galicia: Orense, Pontevedra, Lugo, La Coruña, Santiago de Compostela. Orense, Instituto de Estudios Orensanos "Padre Feijoo" de la Diputación Provincial, 1979. 657p. il. (part col.)

Divided by province, this work surveys funerary sculpture in the convents, churches, monasteries, chapels, museums, cemeteries of Galicia. Each work is accompanied by a photograph.

Bibliografía, p.637–38. Indice onomástico, p.639–50. Indice toponímico, p.651–57.

K305 Cortés Arrese, Miguel. El gótico en Teruel: la escultura monumental. Teruel, Instituto de Estudios Turolenses, 1985. 295p. il.

Detailed study of individual structures and their sculptural decoration in Teruel. Organized by century and type of sculpture: religious, funerary, civil.

Bibliografía, p.207–15. Indice de motivos representados, p.275–78. Indices, p.273–95.

K306 Dominguez Cubero, Jose. De la tradición al clasicismo pretridentino en la escultura jiennense. Jaen, Diputacion Provincial de Jaen, Instituto de Estudios Giennenses, 1995. 263p. il.

Study of Spanish renaissance and mannerist sculpture in this provincial capital.

Bibliografía, p.245–49. Apéndice documental, p.251–63. Indice general (unpaginated).

K307 Durliat, Marcel. La Sculpture romane de la route de Saint-Jacques: de Conques à Compostelle. Mont-de-Marsan, CEHAG, 1990. 508p. il.

In-depth, richly illustrated work examining the influences of southwestern France and Northern Spain on Romanesque sculptural decoration of the principal structures along the pilgrimage route.

Contents: Introduction; (I) Le Pélerinage à Saint-Jacques de Compostelle; (II) La mise en place du style; (III) Autour du "Maître de Jaca"; (IV) Le Temps des portails; (V) L'esprit d'un art.

Abbréviations, p.469–70. Notes, p.471–91. Index des noms de personnes et de lieux, p.492–500.

K308 Echeverría Goni, Pedro. Policromía del Renacimiento en Navarra. [Navarra], Govierno de Navarra, Departamento de Educacion, Cultura y Deporte, [1990]. 525p. il. (part col.) (Serie: Arte, 23)

In-depth study of renaissance polychrome sculpture including its evolution, religious context, esthetic, and technical aspects as well workshops and artists in Navarra.

Catálogo de modelos ornamentales, sus fuentes gráficas p.453–98. Glosario de términos, p.501–08. Bibliografía general y especializada, p.509–18. Indice de láminas, p.519–21. Indice de figuras y mapas, p. 522. Indice de cuadros, p.523. Indice toponímico de obras catalogadas, p.524–25.

K309 Escultura Catalana del segle XIX: del neoclassicisme al Realisme. [Barcelona], Fundacio Caixa de Catalunya, [1989]. 246p. il (part col.)

Catalog of the exhibition, Casa Llotja de Mar, Barcelona (1989). Discusses the history of the Renaixenca and Art Nouveau movement in Catalonia.

Contents: Introducció, Formació I producció; El fet religiós; L'impuls Oficial; El sector domèstic; L'expansió.

Biografies, p.183–91, Cronología comparada, p.194–99. Bibliografía, p.201. Versión española, p.205–25. English version, p.227–46.

K310 Estella Marcos, Margarita M. La escultura barroca de marfil en España: las escuelas europeas y las coloniales. Madrid, Consejo Superior de Investigaciones Científicas, Instituto Diego Velázquez, 1984. 2v. il.

This exhaustive work on ivory sculpture covers European and colonial schools. Each vol. contains: Los artistas españoles y las corrientes Europeas; La escultura en marfil Hispano-Filipina; La escultura en marfil Hispano-Americana; La escultura en marfil Luso-India.

Contents: (1) Texto y Laminas; (2) Catalogo.

Bibliografia, v.1, p.433–94. Indice de artistas, v.1, p.497–500. Indice de lugares, v.1, p.501–18. Indice iconográfico, v.1, p.519–22. Indice general, v.1, p.523–24.

K311 Fuentes Pérez, Gerardo. Canarias, el clasicismo en la escultura. Santa Cruz de Tenerife, Aula de Cultura de Tenerife, Cabildo de Tenerife, 1990. 484p. il., plates. (Publicaciones científicas. Arte e historia, 12)

In-depth study of neo-classical sculpture (c. 1750–1900) in the Canary Islands. Chapters devoted to 33 artists.

Contents: El proceso de la ilustracion en Canarias; Arte y academia en Canarias; Clasicismo en el escultor Canario; Autores y obras; Conclusiones.

Fuentes, p.473–82. Topónimos Canarios, p.483–84.

K312 Martín González, Juan José. Escultura barroca en España 1600–1770. Madrid, Cátedra, 1983. 628p. il.

A survey of Spanish Baroque sculpture organized by century and region.

Contents: (1) El siglo XVII: Castilla la Vieja y León; Andalucia: Sevilla; Andalucia: Granada; Canarias; Madrid; Otras regiones; (2) El Siglo XVIII.

Notas, p.535–86. Bibliografía, p.587–601. Indice, p.603–28.

K313 Museo Arquelógico Nacional. Catálogo de la escultura gótica. [Para] Ma. Angela Franco Mata. [2d ed.] Madrid, Ministerio de Cultura, Dirección General de Bellas Artes y Archivos, 1993. 286p. il.

Catalog of a major collection.

Contents: (I) Escultura exenta; (II) Escultura en relieve; (III) Escultura funeraria; (IV) Decoración arquitectónica; (V) Carpintería artística.

Bibliografía, p.253–71. Indice general, p.275–80. Indice de correspondencias, p.281–86.

K314 Parrado del Olmo, Jesús María. Los escultores seguidores de Berruguete en Palencia. Valladolid, Secretariado de Publicaciones, Universidad de Valladolid, Departmento de Historia del Arte, 1981. 488p. il.

Detailed study of the Alonso Berruguete school of Renaissance art. Abundantly illustrated.

Contents: (1) Rasgos generales; (2) Biografias, estilos y catalogos de obras; (3) Laminas.

Apéndice documental, p.385–456. Bibliografía, p.457–72. Indice de artistas, p.475. Indice geográfico, p.481. Indice general, p.485.

K315 Permanyer, L. Barcelona, open-air sculpture gallery. Photographs by Melba Levick. N.Y., Rizzoli, 1992. 299p. col. il.

Trans. of Barcelona, un museo de esculturas al aire. Barcelona, Poligrafía, 1991. French ed. Paris, Cercle d'art, 1992.

Surveys sculpture in twenty-seven of Barcelona's public squares and parks. Richly illustrated.

Index of sculptors and architects, p.299.

K316 Polo Sánchez, Julio J. Arte barroco en Cantabria: retablos e imaginería (1660–1790). [Santander], Universidad de Cantabria, Asamblea Regional de Cantabria, [1991]. 318p. il.

In-depth study of 17th- and 18th-century sculpture in Cantabria, including: romanista, pre-churrigueresco, churrigueresco, and rococo. Includes more than twenty altar-pieces and their sculptors.

Contents: (1) Consideraciones generales; (2) La escultura en Cantabria durante los siglos XVII y XVIII; (3) El barroco prechurrigueresco (c.1660–1700); (4). El barroco churrigueresco (c.1698–1745) y El roccocó (c.1745–1790); (5) Catálogo complementario.

Bibliografía, p.298–302. Indice de ilustraciones, p.303–07. Indice, p.308–18.

K317 Ramallo Asensio, Germán. Escultura barroca en Asturias. Oviedo, Instituto de Estudios Asturianos, Consejería de Educación y Cultura del Principado. 629p. il., plates.

General introduction to baroque sculpture in Asturias followed by chapters devoted to individual sculptors and their followers.

Apéndice complementario de artistas, p.525–48. Bibliografía, p.549–52. Catálogo complementario, p.553–611. Indices, p.615–29.

K318 Ramírez Martínez, José Manuel. Retablos mayores de La Rioja. Agoncillo, Labelgrafic, 1993. 394p. il.

Contents: (1) "Los artistas que les dieron vida en los siglos XVI, XVII y XVIII" [contains the sections: El mundo de los retablos, El foco artístico de Brines, Biografías]; (2) Las Obras [systematized by "Relación de retablos por orden cronológico"].

Bibliographical references throughout. Firmas de autores, p.367–94.

K319 ———. Los talleres barrocos de escultura en los límites de las provincias de Alava, Navarra y La Rioja. Logroño, Servicio de Cultura de la Excma. Diputación Provincial, 1981. 325p. il. map.
Compilation of documents relating to artists and their works.
Documentos, p.51–152. Arboles genealógicos, p.153–92.

K320 ———, and Ramírez Martínez, Jesús María. La escultura en la Rioja durante el Siglo XVII. Logroño, Comunidad Autónima de la Rioja, 1984. 317p. plates.
Scholarly presentation of 121 documents relating to sculptural work of the region.
Firmas, p.227–35. Gráficos y fotos, p.237–300. Indice de lugares, p.305–08. Indice de artistas, p.309–12. Indice documental, p.313–17.

K321 Real Academia de Bellas Artes de San Fernando. La escultura en la Real Academia de Bellas Artes de San Fernando: catálogo y estudio. Por Leticia Azcue Brea. [Madrid], Real Academia de Bellas Artes de San Fernando, 1994. 634p. il.
Systematic documentation of sculptural works arranged in chronological sections. Contains provenance and bibliographic information.
Contents: Introducción: Los escultores y la Real Academia; Ubicación de las colecciones y su conservación, con especial referencia a las colecciones escultóricas; Catálogo de la colección de Escultura del Museo de Real Academia de Bellas Artes de San Fernando; Análisis cualitativo y cuantitativo de la colección y valoración de su contenido. Esquema de trabajo; Catálogo sistemático ordenado cronológicamente; Fichas técnicas de las obras y documentación; Inventarios del Archivo y el Museo.
Bibliografía, p.605–21. Indice de escultores con obra en el museo, p.623–25. Temas tratados en el catálogo de escultura, p.627–31.

K322 Rincón García, Wilfredo. Un siglo de escultura en Zaragoza (1808–1908). Zaragoza, Caja de Ahorros de Zaragoza, Aragón y Rioja, [1984?]. 227p. il.
Three principal sections: Pervivencia del barroco y primeros escultores neoclásicos (1808–1851), Eclecticismo (1851–1890), and Realismo y modernismo (1890–1908). Entries on artists contain biographical information and a catalog of their works.
Bibliografía general y fuentes documentales, p.215–18. Indice onomástico, p.219–27.

K323 Spanish polychrome sculpture 1500–1800 in United States collections. Ed. by Suzanne L. Stratton. N.Y., Spanish Institute, 1993. 191p. il. (part col.)
Catalog of the exhibition, Spanish Institute (1993–94), and other locations. Full page illustrations accompany text on individual sculptures. An illustrated appendix includes a significant number of sculptures not exhibited.
Contents: Spanish polychrome sculpture and its critical misfortunes, by Gridley McKim-Smith; Painters, polychromy and the perfection of images, by Ronda Kasl; The sculpted retable in Spain, 1500–1750, by Judith Berg Sobré; Catalogue of the exhibition, by Samuel K. Heath.
Appendix, p.155. Bibliography, p.185. Glossary, p.190.

K324 Victoria and Albert Museum, London. Spanish sculpture: catalogue of the post-medieval Spanish sculpture in wood, terracotta, alabaster, marble, stone, lead and jet in the Victoria and Albert Museum. [By] Marjorie Trusted. London, The Museum, 1996. 172p. il. (part col.), plates, map.
Catalog of 86 works constituting "one of the most important single groups of Spanish sculpture outside Spain."—*Introd.* Divided geographically by region, and within those divisions chronologically.
Includes bibliographical references. Bibliography and bibliographical abbreviations, p.157–68. Index of artists, p.169. Index of subjects, p.170. Index of inventory numbers, p.171. Rejected attributions, p.172.

K325 Vila Jato, María Dolores. Escultura Manierista. Santiago de Compostela, Caixa de Ahorros Provincial de Ourense, 1983. 328p. il. (part col.), plates.
Survey of mannerist artists and their works.
Aparato critíco, p.283–311. Bibliografía, p.313–19. Siglas utilizadas, p.321. Indice, p.323–28.

Switzerland

K326 Felder, Peter. Barockplastik der Schweiz. Bern, Gesellschaft für schweizerische Kunstgeschichte; Basel, Wiese Verlag, 1988. 348p. il. (part col.) (Beiträge zur Kunstgeschichte der Schweiz, 6)
Scholarly study of Swiss sculpture, 1600–1800, including foreign sculptors active in Switzerland. Includes a biographical dictionary.
Meisterverzeichnis 1600–1800, p.199–317. Abkürzungsverzeichnis, p.318–21. Literaturverzeichnis, p.322–28. Register, p.329–47.

K327 Mötiers 1989: exposition suisse de sculpture = Schweizer Plastik Ausstellung = Esposizione svizzera di scultura. Une publication coord. par Jean-Pierre Brossard. La Chaux-de-Fonds, Editions d'En haut, 1989. 142p. il.
Text in French, German, and Italian. Catalog of the exhibition, Val-de-Travers (1985). Survey and catalog of works by 49 contemporary Swiss sculptors.

K328 Sculpture suisse en plein air, 1960–1991. Photographies couleur, Heinz Preisig. [Réalisation du catalogue, André Kuenzi et Annette Ferrari]. Martigny, Fondation Pierre Gianadda, [1991]. 140p. il. (part col.)
Catalog of the exhibition, Fondation Pierre Gianadda (1991). Photographic survey of works by contemporary Swiss sculptors.
Biographies, p.[93]–135.

United States

K329 Clark, Henry Nichols Blake. A marble quarry: the James H. Ricau collection of sculpture at the Chrysler

Museum of Art. With an essay by William H. Gerdts. N.Y., Hudson Hills Pr. in assoc. with the Chrysler Museum of Art (Distr. by National Book Network, 1997). 280p. il. (part col.), maps, plates.

Beautifully illustrated catalog of the collection of 19th-century American sculpture amassed by James H. Ricau. Arranged chronologically by sculptor's birth date, the catalog provides lengthy biographical essays. Descriptive entries for each work include provenance, exhibition history, bibliography, and locations of other versions.

Notes to the reader, p.37–38. Short references, p.269–71. Index, p.273–80.

K330 Connor, Janis C., and Rosenkranz, Joel. Rediscoveries in American sculpture: studio works, 1893–1939. Photographs by David Finn. Austin, Univ. of Texas Pr., 1989. viii, 208p. il. (part col.), plates.

Well-researched profiles of twenty little-known American sculptors working in the academic and figurative traditions and active between 1893 and 1939. Individual entries include portraits of the artists, black-and-white reproductions, one or more plates (often in color), and valuable references to published and unpublished materials.

Notes, p.186–88. Locations of works illustrated, p.191–94. Bibliography, p.195–200. Index, p.201–08.

K331 Craven, Wayne. Sculpture in America. [Rev. ed.] Newark, Univ. of Delaware Pr., 1984. xxi, 782p. il.

See GLAH 1:K197 for original ed. Revised ed. of a standard textbook on American sculpture. Includes information on works from the 17th century through 1970s.

Select bibliography, p.727–50. Index, p.751–82.

K332 Fine Arts Museums of San Francisco. American sculpture: the collection of the Fine Arts Museums of San Francisco. By Donald L. Stover. San Francisco, Fine Arts Museums of San Francisco, [1982?]. 95p. il.

Catalog of the exhibition, California Palace of the Legion of Honor (1982). Partial inventory of American sculpture held by the Fine Arts Museums. Individual entries, arranged by artist's birth date, include short biographical sketches and illustrations of works including titles, media, dates, markings, and donor information.

Checklist of the collection, p.81–93. Index of artists, p.94.

K333 Fort, Ilene Susan. The figure in American sculpture: a question of modernity. With contrib. by Mary L. Lenihan . . . [et al.] Los Angeles, Los Angeles Country Museum of Art in assoc. with Univ. of Washington Pr., 1995. [248]p. il. (part col.), plates.

Published in conjunction with the exhibition, Los Angeles County Museum of Art (1995), and other locations. Lengthy, illustrated catalog essays followed by short biographies of the artists in the exhibition.

Contents: The cult of Rodin and the birth of modernism in America, by Ilene Susan Fort; "Sculpture has never been thought a medium particularly feminine"; "Mere beauty no longer suffices": the response of genre sculpture; Primitivism, folk art and the exotic; Creating the new black image; Avant-garde or kitsch? modern and modernistic in American sculpture between the wars.

Artist biographies and exhibition checklist, p.[171]–236. Suggested readings, p.237–39. Lenders to the exhibition, p.243. Index, p.245–47.

K334 Kasson, Joy S. Marble queens and captives: women in nineteenth-century American sculpture. New Haven, Yale Univ. Pr., 1990. xviii, 293p. il.

Examines the subject matter of women in 19th-century American sculpture, with particular emphasis on public reception.

Contents: (1) Ideal sculpture: artists and patrons; (2) Viewing ideal sculpture: contexts and audiences; (3) Narratives of the female body: The Greek Slave; (4) Between two worlds: The White Captive; (5) Death and domesticity: Shipwrecked Mother and Child; (6) The problematics of female power: Zenobia; (7) Woman's other face: Eve and Pandora; (8) Domesticating the demonic: Medea; Conclusion: gender and power.

Notes, p.245–74. Selected bibliography, p.275–83. Index, p.285–93.

K335 Museum of Fine Arts, Boston. American figurative sculpture in the Museum of Fine Arts, Boston: catalogue. By Kathryn Greenthal, Paula M. Kozol, Jan Seidler Ramirez. Introd. essay by Jonathan L. Fairbanks. Boston, The Museum (Distr. by Northeastern Univ. Pr., 1986). xviii, 486p. il. (part col.) plates, ports.

Well-documented catalog of an important collection of 19th- and 20th-century American sculpture. Individual works are arranged chronologically by sculptor's birthdate. Anonymous works follow known artists' works. Lengthy biographical essays include extensive bibliography. Individual works' cataloging includes title, date(s), dimensions, provenance, and additional versions and their locations. An appendix provides information on certain works' metallic composition, foundry, etc.

Appendix: analysis of bronzes, [p.477]–82. Addenda, [p.483]. Index, [p.484]–86.

K336 The new sculpture, 1965–75: between geometry and gesture. Org. and ed. by Richard Armstrong and Richard Marshall. With essays by Richard Armstrong, John G. Hanhardt, Robert Pincus-Witten. N.Y., Whitney Museum of American Art, 1990. 355p. il (part col.)

Catalog of the exhibition, Whitney Museum of American Art (1990). Surveys ten years of avant-garde sculpture, along with some video and film works. Arranged chronologically, the main catalog includes illustrations and reprints of essays, journal articles and reviews of the period and/or works under consideration.

Selected exhibition history, p.332–45. Selected bibliography, p.346–51. Works in the exhibition, p.352–55.

K337 Ortiz, Glenn B. Dictionary of American sculptors: "18th century to the present." Poughkeepsie, Apollo, 1984. xxiii, 656p., plates.

Dictionary encyclopedia of American sculptors comprised of short sketches of more than 5,000 American artists. Entries include biographical data, major works and commissions, awards, museum collections, gallery representation, and some contact information for living sculptors.

K338 Pennsylvania Academy of the Fine Arts. Museum of American Art. American sculpture in the Museum of American Art of the Pennsylvania Academy of the Fine Arts. By Susan James-Gadzinski and Mary Mullen Cunningham. Eds.: Jacolyn A. Mott, Linda Bantel. Contrib.: Theresa Z. Esperdy . . . [et al.] Philadelphia, Museum of American Art of the Pennsylvania Academy of the Fine Arts, in assoc. with the University of Washington Press, Seattle, 1997. xvi, 351p. il. (part col.), plates.

Organized chronologically by sculptor's birth date, this illustrated inventory of American sculpture in the Academy's collections provides biographical sketches and object entries. The main catalog, which includes sculpture through 1950, includes dates, bronze casting information, dimensions, inscriptions, credit line (donor information) and accession number, exhibition history, "Ex collections" and related works. Later works, dated 1951 to 1995, are included (with illustrations) in a checklist.

Readers guide to the catalogue, p.xv–xvi. Appendix: Medals and cameos checklist, p.333–44. Selected bibliography, p.345. Index, p.346–51. Authors' index, p.351.

K339 Phillips, Lisa. The third dimension, sculpture of the New York school. N.Y., Whitney Museum of American Art, 1984. 110p. il. (part col.)

Catalog of the exhibition, Whitney Museum of American Art (1984), and other locations, devoted to postwar sculpture of the New York School (1945–65).

Chronology, p.98–102. Selected bibliography, p.103–06. Works in the exhibiton, p.107–09.

K340 Reynolds, Donald M. Masters of American sculpture: the figurative tradition from the American renaissance to the millennium. N.Y., Abbeville, 1993. [276]p. il. (part col.), plates.

Richly illustrated survey of figurative American sculpture, concentrates on public monuments but includes some statuary and medal design.

Contents: Introduction: the figurative tradition; (1) Beaux-arts symbiosis: architecture and the human figure; (2) A new perspective on the nature of public monuments; (3) Selected monuments to the great and the small; (4) Highlights of the equestrian monument in America; (5) Sentries, doughboys, and GI Joes; (6) Insights into the American portrait; (7) The art of the medal; (8) The first Americans remembered; (9) Everyday people doing everyday things; (10) Twentieth-century transfiguration.

Notes to the text, p.[257]–69. Index, p.[270]–75.

K341 Ricco, Roger; Maresca, Frank; and Weissman, Julia. American primitive: discoveries in folk sculpture. Photographs by Frank Maresca and Edward Shoffstall. N.Y., Knopf, 1988. x, 290p. il. (part col.), plates.

Encyclopedic overview of American folk and "outsider" sculpture, primarily of the 19th and early 20th centuries. Works from major collections illustrate thematic chapters.

Contents: (1) Figurative; (2) Utilitarian; (3) Portraiture and faces; (4) Weathervanes and whirligigs; (5) Articulated figures; (6) Decoys; (7) Carnival and entertainment; (8) Canes; (9) Animals; (10) Idiosyncratic and outsider art; (11) Religion and symbolism.

Notes, p.[285]–86. Bibliography, p.[287]–90.

K342 Rogers, Millard F. Sketches and bozzetti by American sculptors, 1880–1950. Cincinatti, Cincinatti Art Museum, 1987. 243p. il., ports.

Catalog of the exhibition, Cincinatti Art Museum (1987). Explores the three-dimensional sketch, or bozzetto, created by American sculptors from the 19th through mid-20th century. Includes an introductory discussion of techniques. The catalog is arranged alphabetically by artist's name and includes brief biographical sketches.

Contents: Sketch, bozzetto, model; Modelling: "sculpture . . . born in clay" The plaster cast; Sculptors and their works.

Bibliography, p.231–33. Index, p.235–43.

K343 Rubenstein, Charlotte Streifer. American women sculptors: a history of women working in three dimensions. Boston, Hall, 1990. xv, 639p., il.

Encyclopedic overview of monuments, decorative sculpture, and statuary by women artists of the United States. Chronologically arranged, chapters 3 through 11 provide short entries on sculptors of the period under consideration.

Contents: (1) The three-dimensional art of the early Native Americans; (2) Patience Wright: founding mother of American sculpture; (3) Pioneering American women sculptors: 1800–1875; (4) The gilded age: 1876–1905; (5) Fauns and fountains—traditional women sculptors: 1905–1929; (6) Women in the avant-garde: 1905–1929; (7) A new deal for sculpture: the 1930s; (8) The triumph of abstraction: 1940–1959; (9) High tech and hard edge: the 1960s; (10) Climbing Parnassus: the 1970s; (11) The 1980s and beyond.

Notes, p.575–603. Index, p.605–38.

K344 Sculpture inside outside. Introd. by Martin Friedman. Essays by Douglas Dreishpoon . . . [et al.] Profiles of artists, Peter W. Boswell, Donna Harkavy. N.Y., Rizzoli; Minneapolis, Walker Art Center, 1988. 288p. il. (part col.), plates.

Catalog of the exhibition, Walker Art Center (1988). Features the work of 17 contemporary sculptors. Lengthy catalog essays place the work of the sculptors within the tradition of American sculpture. Individual sculptors' profiles include biographical sketches, some color reproductions, as well as solo and group exhibition histories and selected bibliography.

Profiles of the artists, p.[73]–275. Lenders to the exhibition, p.277. Select bibliography, p.278–81. Index, p.282–86.

K345 Shapiro, Michael Edward. Bronze casting and American sculpture 1850–1900. Newark, Univ. of Delaware Pr., 1981. 207p. il. (American arts series)

Overview of the development of bronze casting in 19th-century America. Particularly valuable for its appendixes which detail costs associated with particular casting projects. Checklist of foundries active during the period include chronologies, major works cast, and markings.

Contents: (1) Introduction: sculptors and founders; (2) Casting at midcentury: Clark Mills and Henry Kirke Brown; (3) J. Q. A. Ward: selecting a foundry, choices of the 1870s and 1880s; (4) In France and America: Daniel Chester French and Augustus Saint-Gaudens, 1875–1900; (5) The development of lost-wax casting in America; Epilogue; Appendices.

Checklist of nineteenth-century American bronze foundries, p.165–76. Notes, p.177–93. Select bibliography, p.[194]–202. Index, p.203–07.

K346 Vanguard American sculpture: 1913–1939. [By] Joan M. Marter, Roberta K. Tarbell, Jeffrey Wechsler. New Brunswick, Rutgers Univ. Art Gallery, 1979. xi, 161p. il. (part col.), plates.

Catalog of the exhibition, Rutgers University Art Gallery (1979), and other locations. This well-researched catalog includes substantive, illustrated essays on the development of vanguard sculpture in America and its relation to trends in Europe from 1913–1939.

Contents: (1) Sculpture in America before the Armory Show: transition to modern; (2) Impact of vanguard exhibitions in Paris and New York, 1908–1929; (3) Early nonobjective sculpture by Americans; (4) Figurative interpretations of vanguard concepts; (5) Direct carving; (6) Dada, Surrealism and organic form; (7) Machine aesthetics and art deco; (8) Interaction of American sculptors with European modernists: Alexander Calder and Isamu Noguchi; (9) Developments in American sculpture during the 1930s; (10) Modern American sculpture at the New York World's Fair, 1939.

Notes at ends of chapters. Index, p.151–52. Lenders to the exhibition, p.153. Catalogue of the exhibition, p.154–59.

K347 Watson-Jones, Virginia. Contemporary American women sculptors. Phoenix, Oryx, 1986. x, 665p. il.

Important biographical dictionary. Includes, for each entry, artist's education, exhibition (group and solo) history, public and private collections, awards, media, additional art-related fields, bibliography, gallery affiliation, artist's statement, and mailing address.

Geographic index, p.658–60. Media index, p.661–64.

K348 Yale University. A checklist of American sculpture at Yale University. [By] Paula B. Freedman with assist. of Robin Jaffee Frank. Project photography by Marianne Bernstein. New Haven, Yale Univ. Art Gallery, 1992. 217p. il. (part col.)

Catalogue of 466 works by American sculptors, primarily of the 19th century. A brief introduction to the history of Yale's collection precedes the illustrated checklist. Individual entries, arranged alphabetically by sculptor's name, include basic biographical data, titles and dates of works, dimensions and inscriptions, information on bases and frames, and additional information. Works by unknown artists, arranged by century, follow the main catalog.

Notes to the reader, p.27. Accession number index, p.207–09. Title index, p.211–14. Donor index, p.215–16.

ASIAN COUNTRIES

Central Asia

K349 Bunker, Emma C. Ancient bronzes of the eastern Eurasian steppes from the Arthur M. Sackler collections. N.Y., Arthur M. Sackler Foundation (Distr. by Abrams, 1997). 401p.

Scholarly catalog of an important collection, which includes more than 500 artifacts.

Gazetteer, p.346–47. Bibliography, p.348–70. Concordance, p.371–74. Index, p.375–400.

China

K350 Ancient Chinese bronzes in the Arthur M. Sackler collections. Washington, D.C., Arthur M. Sackler Foundation (Distr. by Harvard Univ. Pr., 1987–1995). 3v. il. (part col.), maps.

A lavish set devoted to Chinese ritual bronze vessels which belonged to the late Dr. Arthur M. Sackler and are now the property of several American museums including the Metropolitan Museum of Art, the Princeton University Art Museum, the Sackler Collection at Harvard University, and the Sackler Gallery in Washington, D.C. Each vol. was prepared by a major scholar of the field, and each is distinguished by abundant illustrations, up-to-date archeological material, detailed descriptions, and extensive bibliographies.

Contents: (1) Bagley, Robert W. Shang ritual bronzes in the Arthur M. Sackler collections (1987); (2) Rawson, Jessica. Western Zhou bronzes from the Arthur M. Sackler collections (1990); (3) So, Jenny. Eastern Zhou ritual bronzes (1995).

K351 Art of the Houma Foundry = Hou-ma t'ao fan i shu / Shan-shi sheng k'ao ku yen chiu so. Princeton, Princeton Univ. Pr., 1996. viii, 523p. chiefly il., maps.

In English and Chinese.

"This book is a pictorial survey of two centuries of Chinese bronze decoration, as recorded in casting debris excavated from the largest ancient foundry site known anywhere in the world. . . . The heart of the book is the drawings and photographs of some 1160 pieces of foundry debris."—*Pref.* for English readers. Includes captions and an English summary. The text itself was prepared by the Institute of Archaeology of Shanxi Province, which excavated the foundry in the early 1960s.

K352 Caswell, James O. Written and unwritten: a new history of the Buddhist caves at Yungang. Vancouver, Univ. of British Columbia Pr., 1988. xv, 225p. il. (part col.), plates.

The caves, located in northern Shanxi Province and dating from the Northern Wei Dynasty of 1500 years ago, are major monuments which contain complex carvings and sculpture ranging from colossal Buddhas to small-scale pieces. This book offers alternative solutions to three issues: the history of the development of the caves, their patronage, and the reason(s) they were built.

Notes, p.127–92. Glossary, p.193–98. Bibliography, p.[199–216]. Index, p.217–25.

K353 Chinese ivories: from the Shang to the Qing: an exhibition. [London], The Oriental Ceramic Society (Distr. by Sotheby Publications, [1984]). 200p. il. (part col.)

Catalog of the exhibition, British Museum (1984). The first major publication on the subject of Chinese ivories. Describes and illustrates 2,283 of the finest pieces from public and private collections.

Bibliography, p.198–99.

K354 Fen, Chen Pei. Ancient Chinese bronzes in the Shanghai Museum. London, Scala (Distr. by Antique Collector's Club, 1995). 96p. il. (part col.)

One of the most comprehensive collections of ancient Chinese bronzes. Published in conjunction with the opening of the new Bronze Gallery, representing the first phase of construction of the new Shanghai Museum, this book includes information on the principal stages of bronze technology, discussions of casting techniques, and representative work from Chinese minorities.

Contents: The Shanghai Museum's "Hall of Ancient Chinese Bronzes"; The Xia Period: the emergence of Chinese bronzes; The Early and Middle Shang: the formative period; Late Shang to Early Western Zhou: a period of brilliance; Middle and Late Western Zhou and Early Spring and Autumn: a period of transition; Middle and Late Spring and Autumn and Warring States: a period of innovation; The collection.

K355 Loehr, Max. Relics of ancient China from the collection of Dr. Paul Singer. [Reprint.] N.Y., Arno, 1975. 170p. il. (part col.)

Reprint of GLAH 1:K209. The color reproductions have been replaced with black-and-white and the illustrations are on dull rather than glossy paper.

K356 Mowry, Robert D. China's renaissance in bronze: the Robert H. Clague collection of later Chinese bronzes, 1100–1900. Phoenix, Phoenix Art Museum, 1993. 256p. il. (part col.)

Catalog of the exhibition, Phoenix Art Museum (1993).

Bronze castings from the Song through the late Qing dynasty in this private collection are illustrated and described. A welcome addition to a neglected field.

Select bibliography, p.13–16.

K357 Munsterberg, Hugo. Chinese Buddhist bronzes. [Reprint.] N.Y., Hacker, 1988. 192p. il.

Reprint of GLAH 1:K214. Omits the colored frontispiece; other illustrations are not as sharp as in the original. Text and pagination unaltered.

K358 Paludan, Ann. The Chinese spirit road: the classical tradition of stone tomb statuary. New Haven, Yale Univ. Pr., [1991]. xiii, 290p. il. (part col.), map.

"The only book in which one can find lists of all imperial Chinese tombs, their locations, and a comparison of the statuary and plans of major imperial tombs or tomb clusters."—*Review*, Journal of the Society of Architectural Historians, v.51, June 1992, p.230. A pioneering study of non-Buddhist stone monumental sculptures lining the avenue of approach to an important tomb. Examples, representing a powerful and deep-seated tradition, date from 117 B.C. to the 1930s and come from all over China. Includes many fine photographs of statuary that is largely inaccessible. Appendixes deal with Shunling, a tomb in Shaanxi province, foreigners in the Northern Song Spirit Roads at Gongxian, and Ming tombs of a transitional period at Fengyang in Anhui province and Zuling in Jiangsu province.

Bibliography, p.271–80. Index, p.281–90.

K359 Powers, Martin J. Art and political expression in early China. New Haven, Yale Univ. Pr., [1991]. xiv, 438p. il.

Winner of the 1991 Joseph Levenson Prize from the Association of Asian Studies for books in pre-20th century Chinese studies.

Scholarly work concerned with the ways in which Chinese art and politics interact. Seeks to show, by means of a limited number of examples, how issues of political expression can be traced in Han pictorial art. Also discusses the two distinct traditions in Han dynasty art, stylized or ornamental and realistic or classical.

Notes, p.379–410. Glossary of Chinese characters, p.411–16. Bibliography, p.417–26. Index, p.427–38.

K360 Segalen, Victor. The great statuary of China. Trans. by Eleanor Levieux. Ed. by A. Joly-Segalen. Afterword by Vadime Elisseeff. Chicago, Univ. of Chicago Pr., 1978. 192p. il.

Trans. of Chine: la grande statuaire. Paris, Flammarion, 1972.

A study of Chinese stonework in its sculptural form, based on Segalen's trips to China in 1909, 1914, and 1917.

Index, p.189–92.

K361 Watson, William. Ancient Chinese bronzes. 2d ed. London, Faber and Faber, 1977. 128p. il., plates (part col.) (The arts of the east)

See GLAH 1:K220 for original annotation. "Reissued without change, apart from minor corrections."—*Pref. to second ed.*

Select bibliography, p.112–16. Notes, p.117–25. Index, p.126–28.

K362 Wu, Hung. The Wu Liang Shrine: the ideology of early Chinese pictorial art. Stanford, Stanford Univ. Pr., 1989. xxiii, 412p. il., plate.

Winner of the 1990 Joseph Levenson Prize from the Association of Asian Studies for books in pre-20th century Chinese studies.

Discusses the Wu Liang offering shrine of the Han dynasty, known primarily through sets of ink rubbings on paper made from the carved stones. Examines the Wu family cemetery, reviews previous scholarship for the site, and reconsiders the iconography of the carvings. In Part I, the author documents the shrine as an archeological relic, a work of art, and a cultural monument, and compares it to the Sistine Chapel and Chartres Cathedral as "an epic representation of human thought". Part II provides an interpretation of the decorative program of the shrine interior.

Bibliography of cited works, p.[371–92].

India, Nepal, Pakistan, Tibet

K363 Asher, Frederick M. The art of Eastern India, 300–800. Minneapolis, Univ. of Minnesota Pr., 1980. 143p., plates.

Careful, scholarly study of sculpture in Eastern India.

Contents: (1) Introduction; (2) The Gupta age; (3) Growth of the style (c.550–700); (4) Bridge to Pala art (c.700–800); (5) Concluding remarks.

Notes, p.107–23. Bibliography, p.127–36. Index, p.139–43.

K364 Bandyopadhyay, Bimal. Survey of Indian metal sculpture. Delhi, Sundeep Prakashan, 1987. xvi, 201p. il., plates.

"An efforts [sic] has been taken in the present work to make an asesthetic [sic] appraisal of the metal art of India."—*Pref.*

Contents: (1) Indian metal sculpture from the earliest period to the thirteenth century A.D.; (2) Iconographical study; (3) Some literary references on metal casting.

Glossary, p.[183]–88. Bibliography, p.[189]–93. Index, p.[195]–201.

K365 British Museum. A catalogue of the Gandhara sculpture in the British Museum. [By] W. Zwalf. London, British Museum Pr., 1996. 2v. il. (part col.), map.

Essential collection catalog.

Contents: (1) The name and the land; (2) The remains of Gandhara; (3) History of the collection; (4) Buddhism in Gandhara; (5) The stupa; (6) Statues and images; (7) Reliefs; (8) Some architectural elements; (9) Relics and reliquaries; (10) The art history; The catalogue.

Abbreviations, p.369–70. Bibliography, p.371–410. Concordance, p.411–13. Index 1: Institutional and individual owners, benefactors and agents, p.414–15. Index 2: Sites and other sources, p.416. Index 3: General index, p.417–23.

K366 Chandra, Pramod. The sculpture of India, 3000 B.C.–1300 A.D. Washington, D.C., National Gallery of Art, 1985. 224p. il. (part col.)

Catalog of the exhibition, National Gallery of Art (1985), inaugurating the Festival of India celebrations in the U.S. "A deliberate attempt has been made in this exhibition to give the viewer an impression of Indian sculpture as a whole."—*Introd.* Most illustrations are black-and-white.

Glossary, p.215–19. Bibliography, p.220–24.

K367 Czuma, Stanislaw J. Kushan sculpture: images from early India. With the assist. of Rekha Morris. Cleveland, Cleveland Museum of Art in coop. with Indiana Univ. Pr., 1985. xiv, 242p. il. (part col.)

Catalog of the exhibition, Cleveland Museum of Art (1985–86), and other locations. "This important phase of Indian art history has never been adequately explored."—*Foreword.*

Selected bibliography, p.233–41.

K368 Dehejia, Vidya. Art of the imperial Cholas. Columbia Univ. Pr., 1990. xviii, 148p. il. (The Polsky lectures in Indian and Southeast Asian art and archaeology)

"For a period of four hundred years, from the ninth to the thirteenth centuries, the Cholas were the dominant . . . force in south India and beyond. . . . The age produced dynamic royal personalities who shaped the artistic activity of the times; it is around these personalities that I have structured my chapters."—*Introd.* Brief introduction to the period.

Simplified genealogy of the Chola dynasty, p.127. Notes, p.129–33. Selected bibliography, p.135–37. Index, p.145–48.

K369 De Lippe, Aschwin. Indian medieval sculpture. N.Y., North-Holland Pub. Co. (Distr. by Elsevier-Holland, 1978). xxiii, 411p. il. (part col.)

"The present survey . . . concentrates on the post-Gupta and mediaeval periods. In addition, it uses as illustrations, almost exclusively, works of art that still are in situ. . . . It thus attempts to show . . . Indian sculpture in its proper aesthetic and religious framework and context."—*Pref.*

Bibliography, p.[401]–05. Glossary, p.[407]–08. Index, p.[409]–11.

K370 Desai, Devangana. Erotic sculpture of India: a socio-cultural study. 2d ed. New Delhi, Munshiram Manoharlal, 1985. xvi, 271p. il., maps, plates.

Based originally on the author's dissertation (Univ. of Bombay, 1970). 1st ed. New Delhi, Tata-McGraw Hill, 1975. The text is unchanged in this ed.; two photographs have been added.

"The book purports to be a study of practically the entire corpus of the empirical material of erotic motive and action and their significance . . . studied, first descriptively and then critically . . . the emphasis being on the period between A.D. 500 and 1400."—*Foreword.*

Contents: (I) Introduction; (II) Sexual representation in early art; (III) Sexual representation in the art of the period A.D. 500–900; (IV) Sexual representation in art of the period A.D. 900–1400; (V) Sexual representation in art—an analysis; (VI) Sex in religion: magico-religious beliefs and practices; (VII) Tantrism and erotic sculpture; (VIII) The Hindu temple in its social setting; (IX) Sex in society; (X) Eroticism in literary art; (XI) Conclusion.

Abbreviations, p.205–06. Notes, p.207–32. Glossary, p.233–37. Bibliography, p.238–51. Supplement to bibliography, p.252–53. List of drawings, p.254. List of photographs (with notes), p.255–62. Index, p.263–71.

K371 Gangoly, O. C. South Indian bronzes: a historical survey of south Indian sculpture with iconographical notes based on original sources. With an introd. note by J. G. Woodroffe. Rev. and enl. 2d ed. Calcutta, Nababharat Publishers, 1978. 23, 142p. il., plates.

1st ed. 1915.

New ed. of a pioneering work that "collected materials for the study of South Indian bronzes," attending closely to Sanskrit sources previously unpublished."—*Introd.*

Includes descriptive notes of the plates in Sanskrit (roman script) with English translation. Bibliography, p.[141]–42.

K372 Gods, guardians, and lovers: temple sculptures from North India A.D. 700–1200. Ed. by Vishakha N. Desai, Darielle Mason. N.Y., Asia Society Galleries in assoc. with Mapin Publishing, Ahmedabad, 1993. 288p. il. (part col.), map, plans.
Catalog of the exhibition, Asia Society Galleries (1993), and other locations.
Bibliography, p.280–287.

K373 Haque, Enamul. Bengal sculptures: Hindu iconography up to c. 1250 A.D. Dhaka, Bangladesh National Museum, 1992. 584p. il.
"The principal aim of this work is to study systematically the iconography of the Hindu sculptures of Bengal down to c. 1250 A.D. It is based on a corpus of extant specimens, the overwhelming majority of which are being noticed here for the first time."—*Introd.*
Abbreviation, p.14–17. Select bibliography, p.398–407. Index, p.567–84.

K374 Heeramaneck, Alice N. Masterpieces of Indian sculpture from the former collections of Nasli M. Heeramaneck. Introd. and descriptive catalogue by Alice N. Heeramaneck. [S.l.], Heeramaneck, 1979. [200]p. il. (part col.), map.
A tribute to a great collector, whose acquisitions have enriched many museums.
Bibliography, p.[63].

K375 Huntington, Susan L. The "Pala-Sena" schools of sculpture. Leiden, Brill, 1984. xxxiv, 296p. il., maps, plates. (Studies in South Asian culture, 10)
Originally presented as the author's PhD thesis (Univ. of California), devoted to the sculpture of Bihar and Bengal from the 8th–12th century.
"It seems to me that this new investigation of Paāla and Sena sculpture will constitute a landmark in Indian art studies."—*Ed. pref.*
Contents: (I) Introduction; (II) Origins and precedents; (III) Dated sculptures; (IV) Stone sculpture of Bihar; (V) Metal sculpture of Bihar; (VI) Stone sculpture of Bengal; (VII) Metal sculpture of Bengal; (VIII) Concluding remarks; Appendix of inscribed dated sculptures.
Abbreviations, p.xxxiii. Note on transliteration of Sanskrit words, p.xxxiv. Bibliography, p.[251]–79. Index, p.[280]–96.

K376 Indian bronze masterpieces, the great tradition: specially for the Festival of India. Consulting ed., Karl J. Khandalavala. Ed., Asha Rani Mathur. Assistant ed., Sonya Singh. New Delhi, Brijbasi Printers, 1988. 280p. chiefly col. il., map.
Multi-author survey of the subject.
Contents: (I) Early bronzes, by M. K. Dhavalikar; (II) Kushan bronzes from Chausa and Satavahana bronzes, by M. N. Deshpande; (III) The golden age of the Guptas, by Krishna Deva; (IV) The Buddha in bronze: Phophnar and Ramtek, by A. P. Jamkhedkar; (V) Jain bronzes from western India: Akota, Vasantagadh and Valabhi, by Umakant P. Shah; (VI) Bronzes from Karnataka and Andhra Pradesh, by B. V. Shetti; (VII) Bronzes of Kashmir, by Pratapaditya Pal; (VIII) Hill bronzes from the Chamba sarea, by Vishwa Chander Ohri; (IX) Eastern Indian bronzes: the Pala period; (X) South Indian bronzes, by R. Nagaswamy.

K377 Klimburg-Salter, Deborah E. Buddha in Indien: die frühindische Skulptur von König Asoka bis zur Guptazeit. Mit einem Aufsatz von Maurizio Taddei. Unter der Mitarb. von Eva Allinger . . . [et al.] Hrsg. von Wilfried Seipel. Milano, Skira; [Wien], Kunsthistorisches Museum Wien, 1995. 303p. il. (chiefly col.), maps.
Catalog of the exhibition, Kunsthistorisches Museum Wien (1995), devoted to early Buddhist sculpture from the 3d century B.C. to the 6th century A.D. Richly illustrated in color.
Objektbeschreibung, p.233–91. Literatur, p.293–301. Glossar, p.302–03.

K378 Living wood: sculptural traditions of southern India. Ed. by George Michell. Bombay, Marg Publications, 1992. 208p. il. (part col.)
Catalog of the exhibition, Whitechapel Art Gallery, London (1992), and other locations, devoted to the wooden sculpture of southern India.
Contents: Introduction, by George Michell; Vahanas: conveyers of the gods, by Joanne Punzo Waghorne; Chariot panels from Tamil Nadu, by George Michell; Doors and woodcrafts of Chittinad, by Deborah Thiagarajan; Christian altar figures, by George Michell; Carvings in Kerala temples, by George Michell; Bhuta figures of south Kanara, by Nima Poovaya-Smith; Exhibition catalogue, by George Michell.
Glossary of Indian names and terms, p.207–08.

K379 Mallebrein, Cornelia. Die anderen Götter: Volks- und Stammesbronzen aus Indien. Mit Beitr. von Heidrun Brückner . . . [et al.] Hrsg. von Gisela Völger. Köln, Braus, 1993. 559p. il. (part col.), maps.
Substantial, scholarly catalog of the exhibition, Rautenstrauch-Joest-Museum für Völkerkunde der Stadt Köln (1993–94), devoted to the anthropology and ethnography of bronze sculpture in India.
Die Metallanalyse der Volksbronzen, p.509–14. Sammlungen indischer Volks- und Stammesbronzen an europäischen Museen und Instituten, p.515–17. Autoren, p.518–20. Bibliographie Autorenteil, p.521–32. Bibliographie Katalogteil, p.533–42. Glossar, p.543–54. Index der Götternamen, p.555–57.

K380 ______. Skulpturen aus Indien, Bedeutung und Form: Sammlung Robert Gedon ergänzt durch Stücke aus Privatsammlungen und den Beständen des Staatlichen Museums für Völkerkunde, München. Einl., Gritli von Mitterwallner. München, Staatliches Museum für Völkerkunde, [1984]. 287p. il. (part col.), map, plates (1 folded).
Catalog of the exhibition, The Museum (1984), based on the Gedon collection, part of which was acquired by the mu-

seum in 1977; includes objects in several media from other private and public collections.

Contents: Steinbildkunst; Metallkunst; Elfenbeinkunst; Holzschnitzkunst; Anhang.

Erklärende Zeichentafeln, p.270–73. Glossar, p.274–78. Literatur, p.279–84. Index, p.285–87.

K381 Nehru, Lolita. Origins of the Gandharan style: a study of contributory influences. Delhi, Oxford Univ. Pr., 1989. xxii, 230p. il., maps.

Based on a "systematic analysis of the interaction between Gandharan sculpture and the various stylistic traditions upon which it drew."—*Foreword.*

Notes, p.107–29. Bibliography, p.130–39. Index, p.219–30.

K382 Newman, Richard. The stone sculpture of India: a study of the materials used by Indian sculptors from ca. 2nd century B.C. to the 16th century. Cambridge, Mass., Center for Conservation and Technical Studies, Harvard Univ. Art Museums, 1984. vi, 106p. il., charts, maps.

"The purposes of this study were three-fold: (1) to identify as precisely as possible the varieties of rocks used in these Indian sculptures, and to establish a consistent and geologically correct nomenclature for these rocks; (2) to discuss possible quarry sources for the sculptures based on a survey of the literature on Indian geology; (3) to determine the value of petrographic studies in establishing the provenance of Indian sculptures."—*Introd.*

References, p.104–06.

K383 Pal, Pratapaditya. Indian sculpture: a catalogue of the Los Angeles County Museum of Art collection. Los Angeles, Los Angeles County Museum of Art; Berkeley, Univ. of California Pr., 1986–88. 2v., il. (part col.)

Part of a series of scholarly catalogs of the Museum's distinguished Indian and Southeast Asian collections.

Contents: (1) Circa 500 B.C.–A.D. 700; (2) 700–1800.

Chronology, v.1, p.273–74. Bibliography, v.1, p.275–81, v.2, p.309–13. Index, v.1, p.283–87, v.2, p.315–19.

K384 Plaeschke, Herbert, and Plaeschke, Ingeborg. Frühe indische Plastik. Leipzig, Koehler und Amelang, 1988. 187p. il.

Survey of early Indian sculpture, 1st century B.C. through the 5th century A.D.

Literaturhinweise, p.177–79. Namen- und Sachverzeichnis, p.179–82.

K385 Poster, Amy G. From Indian earth: 4,000 years of terracotta art. Brooklyn, Brooklyn Museum, 1986. 208p. il. (part col.)

Catalog of the exhibition, Brooklyn Museum (1986), providing "a complete picture of terracotta art throughout India's history."—*Pref.*

Contents: Indian terracotta art: an overview, by Amy G. Poster; The social milieu of ancient Indian terracottas 600 B.C.–600 A.D., by Devangana Desai; Brick temples: origins and development, by Vidya Dehejia; Terracotta traditions in nineteenth- and twentieth-century India, by Stephen P. Huyler; Technical examination of terracottas, by Lambertus van Zelst.

Chronology, p.70. Selected bibliography, p.198–204. Index, p.204–08.

K386 Randhawa, Mohindar Singh, and Schreier Randhawa, Doris. Indian sculpture: the scene, themes, and legends. Bombay, Vakils, Feffer and Simons, 1985. xi, 368p. il.

"This book provides an introduction to the best specimens of Indian sculpture in stone."—*Pref.* Poor black-and-white plates, but a valuable survey.

Select bibliography, p.355–58. Index, p.359–68.

K387 Ray, Niharranjan; Khandalavala, Karl; and Gorakshkar, Sadashiv. Eastern Indian bronzes. New Delhi, Lalit Kala Akademi, 1986. 181p. il. (part col.), plates.

Large-format presentation, largely chronological in arrangement.

Descriptive notes, p.103–70. Select bibliography, p.171–77. Glossary, p.178–81.

K388 Reedy, Chandra L. Himalayan bronzes: technology, style, and choices. Newark, Univ. of Delaware Pr., 1997. 341p. il., maps.

"This book applies a new multidisciplinary approach to the study of 340 medieval-period Himalayan copper-based statues" and seeks to define the "technological style" of Himalayan bronzes, which complements their "visual style."—*Introd.*

Contents: (1) Introduction; (2) Geography, religion, and archaeology of the Himalayas; (3) Casting and decorating methods; (4) Metals; (5) Clay core materials; (6) Using technology to identify regional origins; (7) Final results: regional styles and iconography of Himalayan bronzes; (8) New approaches to interpreting works of art; Appendices.

Selected Sanskrit terms, p.304–06. Selected Tibetan terms, p.307. Selected technical terms, p.308–09. References cited, p.310–29. Index, p.330–37. Index of analyzed sculpture, p.338–41.

K389 Schroeder, Ulrich von. Indo-Tibetan bronzes. Hong Kong, Visual Dharma Publications (Distr. Nanda Distribution, 1981). 576p. il. (part col.), maps.

"This book, the result of a sixteen year study of Buddhist art, is the first full-length publication concerning the stylistic evolution of the image casting traditions of northern India, the Himalayas and Tibet, as well as those of China during the Ming and Qing Dynasties."—*p.11.* Monumental in format and substance, profusely illustrated.

Present locations of illustrated bronzes, p.558–60. Glossary, p.561–62. Bibliography, p.563–70. Index, p.571–76.

K390 Snead, Stella. Animals in four worlds: sculptures from India. With texts by Wendy Doniger and George Michell. Chicago, Univ. of Chicago Pr., 1989. ix, 199p. il.

"The title of this book refers to the perception of animals (more particularly, their representation in Indian sculpture) in nature, in the human world, in the divine world, and in the world of fantasy."—*p.3.* Consists largely of black-and-white photographs.

Contents: A note on dating; The four worlds, by Wendy Doniger; The sculptures, by George Michell; Plates, by Stella Snead.

Japan

K391 Bushell, Raymond. Netsuke masks. N.Y., Kodansha (Distr. by Harper and Row, 1985). 206p. il. (part col.)

The first book devoted entirely to netsuke masks. 400 color plates illustrate a broad range of masks in the Raymond Bushell collection. Establishes a classification scheme for the masks by the type of theatrical performance in which they appear, and identifies them by the characters they represent. Includes a list of signatures, inscriptions, kakihan, and masks.

Glossary, p.197–99. Selected bibliography, p.200–01. Index, p.202–06.

K392 Davey, Neil K. Netsuke: a comprehensive study based on the M. T. Hindson collection. Rev. ed. London, Sotheby, 1982. 566p. il. (part col.)

See GLAH 1:K229 for 1st ed.

"Revised edition with 296 new illustrations of which 182 are in full colour."—*T.p.* This ed. also features a preface that discusses changes in the auction market, the growing scholarly interest in the netsuke art form, and the revival of the form among artists in Japan and elsewhere, since the first ed.

Select bibliography, p.557.

K393 Harris, Victor. Netsuke: the Hull Grundy collection in the British Museum. London, British Museum, [1987]. 136p. il. (part col.), plates.

Catalog of the more than 600 objects from the 18th and 19th centuries in the important Hull Grundy collection of netsuke. The Introduction provides a useful overview of the art form by discussing use, history, subjects, materials, and artists. The catalog organizes the objects by the subject depicted (sections 1–10) and shape (sections 11–12), illustrates the pieces with small black-and-white photographs, and provides the name and technical data.

Bibliography, p.125. Index of artists' names, p.127–28. Index of subjects, p.129–31. Concordance, p.133–36.

K394 Lazarnick, George. Netsuke and Inro Artists, and how to read their signatures. Honolulu, Reed, 1982. 2v. 1376p. il. (part col.)

A comprehensive, well-arranged, exhaustively illustrated reference work with thousands of examples from museums, collectors, dealers, and auction houses. Noteworthy for the section on how to read signatures and inscriptions of the artists, and for the alphabetical listing of artists with examples of their work and their signatures.

Bibliography, p.1368–75.

K395 Nishikawa, Kyotaro, and Sano, Emily J. The great age of Japanese Buddhist sculpture, AD 600–1300. Fort Worth, Kimbell Art Museum, [1982]. 151p. il. (part col.)

Catalog of the exhibition at the Kimbell Art Museum (1982), and locations.

Marking the tenth anniversary of the Kimbell Museum, this exhibition of 36 items from active temples and major museum collections in Japan represents the history of Japanese Buddhist sculpture over a 700-year period. Examples were included to show how stylistic development was effected by changes in patronage and the evolution of Buddhist thought in Japan. An essay on Japanese Buddhist Sculpture by Nishikawa Kyōtarō is followed by the catalog with each object given a full-page color photograph, a complete description, bibliographic references, and record of exhibitions.

Selected bibliography, p.147. Index, p.148–51.

K396 Warner, Langdon. The craft of the Japanese sculptor. [Reprint.] N.Y., Hacker, 1976. 55p. il., plates.

See GLAH 1:K234 for original annotation. The photographic illustrations, particularly those with intricate detail, have lost a small degree of clarity in the reprint.

Southeast Asia

K397 Ancient Indonesian sculpture. Ed. by Marijke J. Klokke and Pauline Lunsingh Scheurleer. Leiden, KITLV Pr., 1994. 211p. il., maps (Verhandelingen van het Koninklijk Instituut voor Taal-, Land- en Volkenkunde, 165)

Papers from a symposium held in the Rijksmuseum, Amsterdam (1988).

Selective contents: Introduction, by Marijke J. Klokke and Pauline Lunsingh Scheurleer; "Rules" for change in the transfer of Indian art to Southeast Asia, by Robert L. Brown; Bronzes in the Amaravati style: their role in the writing of Southeast Asian history, by Sara Schastok; Some connections between metal images of Northeast India and Java, by Susan L. Huntington; Bronze images and their place in ancient Indonesian culture, by Pauline Lunsingh Scheurleer; An aspect of the Bodhisattva Avalokitesvara in ancient Indonesia, by Nandana Chutiwongs; The iconography of Borobudur revisited, by John C. Huntington; The so-called portrait statues in East Javanese art, by Marijke J. Klokke.

Spelling and abbreviations, p.vii. Glossary, p.[202–04]. Index, p.[205]–11.

K398 Boisselier, Jean. Trends in Khmer art. Ed. by Natasha Eilenberg. Trans. by Natasha Eilenberg and Melvin Elliott. Ithaca, N.Y., Southeast Asia Program, Cornell Univ., 1989. 118p. il. (Studies on Southeast Asia)

Rev. trans. of: Tendances de l'art khmèr. Paris, Presses universitaires de France, 1956; Japanese ed., 1984.

"The objective of this brief work is simply to present and describe twenty-four sculptures . . . representative of Khmer art . . . [from] the collections of the Phnom Penh National Museum."—*Introd.* By an outstanding scholar.

Glossary, p.[103]–15. Selected bibliography, p.[117]–18. The chronology, p.[119–24].

K399 Felten, Wolfgang, and Lerner, Martin. Thai and Cambodian sculpture from the 6th to the 14th centuries Photographs by Hugo Stiegler. London, P. Wilson Publishers, 1989. 253p. il. (part col.)

"This book presents sculpture dating from the sixth to the fourteenth centuries A.D. Previously unpublished, these works should help to broaden our knowledge of the history of art in Southeast Asia. They have been selected . . . for their artistic excellence and singularity."—*Foreword.*

Contents: Basic precepts; Introduction: towards an art history of Cambodia and Thailand; Stone sculptures; Bronze sculptures.

Notes to the introduction, p.245–47. Select bibliography, p.248–49. Chronological table: Cambodia, p.250, Thailand, p.251.

K400 Fontein, Jan. The sculpture of Indonesia. Washington, D.C., National Gallery of Art; N.Y., Abrams, 1990. 312p. il. (part col.), facsims., maps.

Catalog of the exhibition, National Gallery of Art (1990), and other locations, drawing on Indonesian collections as well as other Asian, European, and American collections.

Contents: Introduction: The sculpture of Indonesia, by Jan Fontein; Indonesian architecture of the classical period: a brief survey, by R. Soekmono; The making of Indonesian art, by Edi Sedyawati.

Glossary, p.301–02. Bibliography, p.303–11.

K401 Sculpture of Angkor and ancient Cambodia: millennium of glory. Washington, D.C., National Gallery of Art; N.Y., Thames and Hudson, 1997. xxxii, 381p. il. (part col.), col. maps.

Catalog of the exhibition, National Gallery of Art (1997), and other locations. "The aim of this exhibition has been to reunite the masterworks of two museums, the National Museum of Cambodia and the Musée Guimet in Paris, whose collections are for historical reasons complementary."—*Introd.*

Contents: History; Religion, epigraphy, and iconography; Architecture; Sculpture; Catalogue.

Glossary, p.357–63. Bibliography, p.365–71. Index, p.373–80.

K402 Woodward, Hiram W. The sacred sculpture of Thailand: the Alexander B. Griswold collection, the Walters Art Gallery. With contrib. by Donna K. Strahan . . . [et al.] Baltimore, the Gallery (Distr. by Univ. of Washington Pr., 1997). 326p. il. (part col.)

An account of Thai sculpture based on the most important collection outside Thailand.

Contents: (1) The Buddha image in Thailand; (2) Bronze casting in Thailand; (3) Dvaravati; (4) The period of Khmer domination; (5) The thirteenth century; (6) The rise and development of Sukhothai; (7) Ayutthaya in the fourteenth and fifteenth centuries; (8) Lan Na; (9) Ayutthaya, 1491–1767; Appendices.

Notes, p.288–305. Chronological chart, p.306–07. Glossary, p.310–13. Bibliography, p.314–20. Index, p.321–26.

AFRICA, OCEANIA, THE AMERICAS

General Works

K403 Collection Barbier-Mueller. Tribal sculpture: masterpieces from Africa, South East Asia and the Pacific in the Barbier-Mueller Museum. [By] Douglas Newton and Hermione Waterfield. Photographs by Pierre-Alain Ferrazzini. [N.Y.], Vendome Pr., [1995]. 346p. 295 col. il., maps.

A monumental and lavishly illustrated catalog of a major collection.

Contents: The story of a collection, by Jean Paul Barbier; The flat, the round and space, by Douglas Newton. The collection: Africa, by Hermione Waterfield, with Timothy Garrard and Zachary Kingdom; Indonesia, by Douglas Newton; Oceania, by Douglas Newton.

K404 Museo delle culture extraeuropee (Lugano, Switzerland). Culture extraeuropee: Collezione Serge e Graziella Brignoni = Extra-European cultures: The Serge and Graziella Brignoni Collection. Ed. by Claudio Gianinazzi, Christian Giordano. [Lugano], Edizioni Città di Lugano, [1989]. 366p. 541 il. (part col.), maps.

Text in Italian and English. A beautifully illustrated catalog that documents a significant collection of the sculptures of Africa, India, Oceania, and South-West Asia.

Contents: Extra-European cultures and Western imagery, problems and prospects of a museum (in statu nascendi), by Christian Giordano; Eclipse, prophylaxis and a certain continuity, by Ilario Rossi; The Brignoni donation: the significance behind the gesture, by Claudio Gianinazzi; Interview with Serge Brignoni "And then it starts all over again . . . , " by Elke-N. Kappus; Notes by an artist-collector, by Serge Brignoni.

Bibliographies, p.359–66.

Africa

K405 Afrikanische Skulptur: die Erfindung der Figur = African sculpture: the invention of the figure. Köln, Museum Ludwig, 1990. 260p. il. (part col.)

Text in German and English. Catalog of the exhibition, Museum Ludwig (1990), and other locations.

Beautifully illustrated, this book "concentrates on the inventiveness of African artists in the medium of sculpture, with works from twenty-eight tribes that lived south of the Sahara, from the west to the east coast of Africa."—*Pref.*

Contents: African sculpture at the Museum Ludwig, by Siegfried Gohr; Art or no art—that is the question, by Werner Schmalenbach; African art/art in Africa, by Miklós Szalay; The concept of style and its usefulness in the study of African figurative sculpture, by Bernard de Grunne; Comparisons, by Lucien Stéphan; The invention of the figure, by Kay Heymer; Catalogue of the exhibited works, by Kay Heymer; Mumuye, with a text by Jacques Kerchache.

Bibliography, p.257–60.

K406 Arnold, Marion I. Zimbabwean stone sculpture. Reprint of the 1981 ed. incorporating place-name changes and a new Postscript. Bulawayo, Louis Bolze, 1986. 234p. il., map.

1st ed. Bulawayo, Books of Zimbabwe, 1981. Based on the author's master's thesis, this book is the first major study of contemporary Zimbabwean stone sculpture. Includes a discussion of ancient stone sculpture.

Contents: (1) Stone sculpture from Great Zimbabwe; (2) The meaning of the Zimbabwe birds; (3) The twentieth-century Shona sculpture movement; (4) The interaction of form and content; (5) The human form; (6) Animal forms; (7) The supernatural.

Bibliography, p.169–81. Biographies of sculptors, p.182–228. Glossary of terms, p.229–30. Postscript, p.231–34.

K407 Bassani, Ezio, and Fagg, William B. Africa and the renaissance: art in ivory. Ed. by Susan Vogel, assisted by Carol Thompson. With an essay by Peter Mark. [N.Y.], Center for African Art and Prestel-Verlag, [1988]. 255p. il. (part col.)

Catalog of the exhibition, The Center for African Art (1988), and other locations. A well-illustrated catalogue raisonné and major treatise on Afro-Portuguese ivories.

Contents: Introduction: Africa and the renaissance, by Susan Vogel; European perceptions of Black Africans in the renaissance, by Peter Mark; (1) The legacy of the navigator; (2) The Afro-Portuguese ivories; (3) An art of stillness and beauty: the Sapi-Portuguese ivories, saltcellars, pyxes, spoons, forks and knife handles; (4) Sources for the Sapi-Portuguese ivories; (5) Sapi workshops and artists; (6) Conclusions on the Sapi-Portuguese ivories; (7) The Bini-Portuguese ivories: enter movement, the guild of ivory carvers; oliphants; salts; spoons; (8) The Bini-Portuguese artists; (9) A conjectural digression among the bronze casters; (10) A problematic Yoruba-Portuguese saltcellar; (11) The Afro-Portuguese apocrypha, an enigmatic Sapi-Portuguese oliphant, the Kongo oliphants, a unique Kongo knife case, Kongo geometric motifs, the mysterious fluted oliphants; (12) Conclusions on the Afro-Portuguese ivories.

Catalogue raisonné, p.224–50. Bibliography, p.251–54.

K408 Bastin, Marie-Louise. La sculpture Tshokwe. Trad. et adaptation en anglais, J. B. Donne. Meudon, Alain et Françoise Chaffin, [1982]. 291p. il. (part col.), map.

Extensively illustrated with text in French and English. This definitive work provides ethnographic data and iconographic and stylistic classification of the sculptural arts of the Chokwe.

Contents: Anthropology, geography, history; Material culture, social organization and religious beliefs; Art forms; Iconography and aesthetics; Stylistic variations; Related styles, influences.

Glossary, p.288–89. Bibliography, p.290–91.

K409 Biebuyck, Daniel P. La sculpture des Lega. Paris, Galerie Hélène and Philippe Leloup, [1994]. 205p. il. (part col.), map.

Text in English and French. Catalog of the exhibition, Galerie Hélène and Philippe Leloup, Paris (1994). The first major exhibition of Lega sculpture.

Contents: The Bwami association; The initiation objects; Lega artworks; The masks; The figurines.

Bibliography, p.202.

K410 Blier, Suzanne Preston. African vodun: art, psychology, and power. Chicago, Univ. of Chicago Pr., [1995]. xi, 476p. 163 il. (part col.), maps.

Profusely illustrated, this book is "an investigation of the psychological impact of certain West African objects on human behavior . . . a must for any art library collecting African art literature as well as for those concerned with the psychology of art."—*Review*, Art documentation, v.14, fall 1995, p.36.

Contents: (1) Vodun art, social history, and the slave trade; (2) Audiences, artists, and sculptural activators; (3) Design in desire: transference and the arts of Boci; (4) Bodies and being: anatomy, anamnesis, and representation; (5) The I and not-I in artistic expressions of the self; (6) Alchemy and art: matter, mind, and sculptural meaning; (7) Surface parergon and the arts of suturing; (8) The force of genre: sculptural tension and typology; (9) Power, art, and the mysteries of rule.

Appendix: Collections and stylistic features, p.355–59. Bibliography, p.433–61. Index, p.463–76.

K411 Bravmann, René A. Open frontiers: the mobility of art in Black Africa. Seattle, Published for the Henry Art Gallery by the Univ. of Washington Pr., [1973]. 95p. il. maps. (Index of art in the Pacific Northwest, no. 5)

Catalog of the exhibition, Henry Art Gallery, University of Washington (1973). Distinguished by the inclusion of field photographs and a scholarly text by an eminent scholar.

Contents: The Cercle de Bondoukou and west central Ghana; The Cameroonian grasslands.

Bibliography, p.93–95.

K412 Brett-Smith, Sarah C. The making of Bamana sculpture: creativity and gender. N.Y., Cambridge Univ. Pr., [1994]. xx, 352p. 60 il. maps. (RES monographs in anthropology and aesthetics)

Based on the author's research in West Africa. Focuses on understanding the artistic and creative process as practiced by Bamana sculptors.

Contents: (1) The Bamana universe; (2) The sculptor speaks with spirits: the other world; (3) The human world; (4) Trees and tools; (5) Carving and aesthetics; (6) Sacred secrets; (7) "The foundation of the world is with women."

Selected bibliography, p.338–41. Index, p.343–52.

K413 Chaffin, Alain, and Chaffin, Françoise. L'Art Kota: les figures de reliquaire. Trad. et adaptation en anglais, Carlos E. Garcia. Meudon, Alain and Françoise Chaffin, [1979?]. 348p. il. (part col.), map.

Text in French and English. Extensively illustrated. The authors present a stylistic classification of Kota funerary statuary.

Contents: (1) Geographical setting and human environment; (2) Exposition of the analytical method; (3) Morphological analysis and study of ornamentation; (4) Catalogue of Kota funerary figures; (5) Kota styles, the Ossyeba problem.

Bibliography, p.347–48.

K414 Detroit Institute of Arts. African masterworks in the Detroit Institute of Arts. Essays by Michael Kan and Roy Sieber. Text by David W. Penney, Mary Nooter Roberts, and Helen M. Shannon. Washington, D.C., Published for the Detroit Institute of Arts by the Smithsonian Institution Pr., [1995]. xi, 180p. il. (part col.), maps.

This catalog includes 88 of the museum's works representing the full range of major sub-Saharan sculptural traditions during the past three centuries.

Contents: An introduction to African art, by Roy Sieber; African art at the Detroit Institute of Arts, by Michael Kan; Western Sudan; Guinea coast; Cameroon and central highlands; Western Congo Basin and Ogowe River; Lower Congo and Kwango Basins; Eastern Congo Basin; East and South Africa.

Bibliography, p.169–75. Index, p.176–80.

K415 Dogon Statuary. [By] Hélène Leloup . . . [et al.] Trans. from the French by Brunhilde Biebuyck. Photography: Roger Asselbergs, Jerry L. Thompson. [Strasbourg], Daniele Amez, [1994]. 608p. il. (part col.), maps.

Trans. of Statuaire dogon. Strasbourg, D. Amez, 1994.

Lavishly illustrated, a major study of Dogon statuary.

Contents: Preface, by William Rubin; Dogon statuary, by Hélène Leloup; Richard Serra; Georg Baselitz.

Bibliography, p.583–602. Index, p.603–08.

K416 Ezra, Kate. A human ideal in African art: Bamana figurative sculpture. Washington, D.C., Published for the National Museum of African Art by the Smithsonian Institution Pr., 1986. 48p. il. map.

Catalog of the exhibition, National Museum of African Art (1986), and other locations. A valuable study of the ritual and social contexts of Bamana figurative sculptures.

References, p.45–46.

K417 Face of the spirits: masks from the Zaire Basin. Ed. by Frank Herreman and Constantijn Petridis. Photography, Dick Beaulieux. With contrib. by M.-L. Bastin . . . [et al.] [Gent, Snoeck-Ducaju and Zoon, 1993]. 261p. il. (part col.), maps.

Catalog of the exhibition, National Museum of African Art (1994), and other locations. Lavishly illustrated catalog with essays by noted scholars.

Contents: Face of the spirits, by Frank Herreman; Masks among the Kongo peoples, by Raoul Lehuard; An introduction to Nkanu and Mbeeko masks, by Alphonse Lema Gwete; Masks and masking among the Yaka, Suku, and related peoples, by Arthur P. Bourgeois; Pende mask styles, by Constanijn Petridis; The Akishi spirits of the Chokwe, by Marie-Louise Bastin; Material and formal aspects of copper masks from the Upper Kasai, by Rik Ceyssens; The practice of metal application to African masks, by Elze Bruyninx; Masks among the Kuba peoples, by Joseph Cornet; The Kifwebe masking phenomenon, by Dunja Hersak; South-East Zaire: masks of the Luba, Hemba and Tabwa, by François Neyt; Masks and initiation among the Lega cluster of peoples, by Daniel P. Biebuyck; The animal in us: the ubiquitous zoomorphic masking phenomenon of Eastern Zaire, by Marc Leo Felix; Mask styles and mask use in the north of Zaire, by Herman Burssens; Zairian masking in historical perspective, by Jan Vansina.

Bibliography, p.255–59.

K418 Felix, Marc Leo. Maniema. An essay on the distribution of the symbols and myths as depicted in the masks of Greater Maniema. [München, Fred Jahn, 1989]. 313p. il., [l] folded leaf of plates, maps.

Text in English and German. Within historical, social, and linguistic contexts, Felix provides a stylistic and symbolic typography of Maniema masks and plots these contexts geographically.

Contents: The importance of Maniema art history; From family to people; Chronology; The use of masks in Maniema; Belief systems and typology; Linguistic division of Maniema; Stylistic division of Maniema; Hypothesis; Central Maniema; Southern Maniema; Northern Maniema; Eastern Maniema.

Bibliography, p.311–13.

K419 ______. 100 peoples of Zaire and their sculpture: the handbook. Brussels, Zaire Basin Art History Research Foundation, 1987. xvi, 246p. il., maps.

Object oriented, this handbook covers the most significant ethnic groups in Zaire who have produced anthropomorphic sculpture. Topics covered for each ethnic group include sociopolitical organization, economy, history, religion, sculpture, and art style.

Glossary, p.213–15. Bibliography, p.217–22. Tentative clustering based on stylistic criteria, p.223–24. Index of alternative peoples names, p.225–45.

K420 For spirits and kings: African art from the Paul and Ruth Tishman Collection. Ed. by Susan Vogel. Trans. and additional research by Kate Ezra. Photographs by Jerry L. Thompson. N.Y., Metropolitan Museum of Art (Distr. by Abrams, [1981]). 256p. il. (part col.), maps.

All major sculptural traditions of Africa are illustrated in this catalog which documents one of the finest private collections of its kind in the United States.

Contents: The Western Sudan; The Guinea Coast; Nigeria; Equatorial Africa; Central Africa; Eastern and Southern Africa.

Glossary, p.244–45. Bibliography, p.245–52. Index, p.253–56.

K421 Griaule, Marcel. Masques Dogons. 4th ed. Paris, Institut d'Ethnologie, 1994. viii, 896p. 261 il. (part col.), 32p. of plates, map. (Travaux et Mémoires de l'Institut d'Ethnologie, 33)

1st ed. 1938; 2d ed. 1963; 3d ed. 1983. This seminal study covers Dogon mythology, rituals, and funerary ceremonies, as well as discussion of Dogon crafts, rock paintings, dance, and altars.

Contents: Livre 1: Les mythes: (1) Glose des mythes; (2) Texte en lingue du Sigui; (3) Les êtres mythiques personnels; (3) Principe mythique impersonnel; (4) Principe mythique impersonnel, le Nyama. Livre 2: Le Sigui: (1) A. Le rituel (Sanga), B. Notes sur le rituel de diverses régions; (2) Le matériel; (3) Les agents. Livre 3: Les funérailles: (1) Rituel général (Sanga); (2) Rituels spéciaux (Sanga). Livre 4: Le Dama: (1) A. Rituel de Sanga, B. Notes sur les rituels des régions voisines de Sanga; (2) A. Fabrication des masques, B. Les masques et leurs accessoires; (3) Les peintures rupestres; (4) Les danses. Livre 5: (1) Les autels du cult des masques; (2) Pratique et croyances diverses liées a l'institution des masques.

Lexique de la langue du Sigui, p.837–46. Tableau de l'usage rituel de la langue du Sigui, p.847–49. Table des masques, p.850–52. Table des rythmes et des danses, p.853–54. Table des animaux, p.855–57. Tables des plantes, p.858–59. Table des noms propres, p.860–61. Table des noms géographiques, p.862–66. Table analytique des matières, p.867–72. Table des objets cités, p.873–74. Table des films cinématographiques, p.875–76. Table des auteurs cités, p.877–78. Bibliographie, p.879–82.

K422 Hersak, Dunja. Songye masks and figure sculpture. London, Ethnographica, [1986]. ix, 189p. 133 il. (part col.), maps.

Major study of Zaïrian culture which includes classification of both masks and figures stylistically and according to formal qualities and coloration.

Contents: (1) Origin and structure of Songye chiefdoms; (2) Cosmology; (3) Witchcraft and sorcery; (4) The bwadi bwa kifwebe society; (5) The making and defining of masks; (6) Classification of Songye masks; (7) Figure sculpture and magic; (8) Characteristics of central Songye figures; (9) Summary; Appendix: Songs of the bwadi bwa kifwebe.

Selected bibliography, p.178–80. Glossary, p.182–86. Index, p.187–89.

K423 Holý, Ladislav. The art of Africa: masks and figures from eastern and southern Africa. Photographed by Dominique Darbois. London, Paul Hamlyn, 1967. 68p., 152p. of plates (part col.), map.

Amply illustrated with extensive notes on all plates, this work is an early classic on African sculpture.

Contents: The northern part of east Africa; Central east Africa; The southern part of east Africa; South Africa; The style of east and south African sculpture.

Bibliography, p.62–64.

K424 Horton, Robin. Kalabari sculpture. [Apapa], Department of Antiquities, Federal Republic of Nigeria, [1965]. 49p. 72p. il.

Standard work on the wooden sculptures and cult objects of the Kalabari-speaking peoples of Nigeria, and a selection of sculpture from other Ijo-speaking areas.

Contents: (1) An outline of Kalabari culture; (2) Sculpture and its uses; (3) Carving, criticism and the carver; (4) Meaning and form; (5) Summary and conclusions; Appendix I: Materials and tools; Appendix II: Kalabari and neighbouring styles; Appendix III: Kalabari sculpture and modern social change.

K425 Johnson, Barbara C. Four Dan sculptors. Continuity and change. [San Francisco], Fine Arts Museums of San Francisco (Distr. by the Univ. of Chicago Pr., [1986]). xvii, 102p. il. (part col.), map.

Catalog of the exhibition, Fine Arts Museums of San Francisco (1986–1987), and other locations. Perhaps the first exhibition and catalog to concentrate on four known sculptors—three carvers and one brasscaster from the Dan region of Liberia.

Contents: History, social organization, politics, and religion of the Dan people; Ritual, prestige, and decoration: the art forms of the Dan; Four sculptors—three generations; Continuity and change.

Bibliography, p.101–02.

K426 Krieger, Kurt. Ostafrikanische Plastik. Berlin, Museum für Völkerkunde, [1990]. 99p., 554 plates, map (Veröffentlichungen des Museums für Völkerkunde Berlin, Neue Folge, 50; Abteilung Afrika, 10)

Photo survey of sculpture from areas of East Africa extending from Sudan, Ethiopia, and Somalia in the north to Zambia, Malawi, and Mozambique in the south, and then into Madagascar. All works are from the Museum für Völkerkunde and were collected between 1877 and 1937.

Literatur, p.77–85. Stammes- und Ortsregister, p.87–88.

K427 Lehuard, Raoul. Art Bakongo. [Arnouville, France, Arts d'Afrique Noire, 1989–1993]. 3v. il. (part col.), maps (Arts d'Afrique noire, supplément au tome 55)

Extensively illustrated, this is a major corpus of art works collectively known as Kongo, or Lower Kongo, covering primarily figurative wooden sculptures in the first two vol. and in the third, masks.

Contents: (1–2) Les centres de style; (3) Les masques.

Index, v.3, p.864–866. Bibliographie, v.3, p.868–69.

K428 Mark, Peter. The wild bull and the sacred forest: form, meaning, and change in Senegambian initiation masks. N.Y., Cambridge Univ. Pr., [1992]. xv, 170p. 43 il., map.

This comprehensive study is focused on the horned initiation masks created in the Jola country in the Lower Casamance (Senegal). "It may serve as a model for understanding the way in which the process of Islamization has occurred, both elsewhere in Africa and in an earlier historical period."—*Foreword.*

Contents: (1) Introduction: method and subject; (2) Ethnographic background; (3) Bukut initiation; (4) History and provenance of the Ejumba mask; (5) Iconography of the horned mask; (6) Mandinka or Jola? art and culture as regional processes; (7) Islam and Casamance masking traditions; (8) Conclusion; Appendix.

Bibliography, p.161–66. Index, p.167–70.

K429 Perrois, Louis. Arts du Gabon: les arts plastiques du Bassin de l'Ogooué. [Arnouville-les-Gonesse, France, Arts d'Afrique Noire, 1979]. 290p. il. (part col.), plates, maps. (Arts d'Afrique noire, supplément au tome 20)

The arts of Gabon, largely those of the Fang, Kota, and Shogo, are extensively illustrated in this study.

Contents: (1) Le pays et les hommes: le bassin de l'Ogooué; (2) Les caractères de la sculpture traditionnelle; (3) Styles tribaux et styles régionaux; (4) L'art Fang; (5) L'art funéraire Kota: généralités et styles du nord; (6) Les styles du sud: Kota-Obamba et apparentés; (7) Les styles statuaires du Centre-Gabon; (8) Les masques du sud et de l'est du Gabon.

Bibliographie sommaire, p.289–90. Figures, cartes, p.291–[320].

K430 Rankin, Elizabeth Deane. Images of metal: post-war sculptures and assemblages in South Africa. Johannesburg, South Africa, Witwatersrand Univ. Pr., 1994. 206p. il.

Catalog of the exhibition, Standard Bank National Arts Festival, Grahamstown, South Africa (1994), and other locations.

Surveys the history and evolution of recent metal sculpture in South Africa examining the works of formally and informally trained sculptors.

Contents: Techniques and training; Art on the margins; Competitions and commissions.

Selected bibliography, p.198–200. Index of artists, p.201–206.

K431 ———. Images of wood: aspects of the history of sculpture in 20th-century South Africa. Johannesburg Art Gallery 1989. Biographies, Elizabeth Dell. Documentation of works, Julia Meintjes. [Johannesburg], Johannesburg Art Gallery, [1989]. 188p. il.

Catalog of the exhibition, Johannesburg Art Gallery (1989).

Catalog entries are arranged alphabetically by artist and provide a representative selection of sculptural traditions through the century.

Contents: (1) The early years: Indigenous beginnings; (2) Training opportunities in sculpture in South Africa; (3) Later developments in wood sculpture; (4) Aspects of contemporary sculpture.

Selected bibliography, p.184. Index, p.185–87.

K432 Tanzania: Meisterwerke Afrikanischer Skulptur = Sanaa za mabingwa wa Kiafrika. Hrsg. von Jens Jahn. Mit einl. Texten von Marc L. Felix and Maria Kecskési. Sowie Beitr. von Giselher Blesse . . . [et al.] München, Verlag Fred Jahn, 1994. 527p. il., map.

Text in German and Swahili. Catalog of the exhibition, Haus der Kulturen der Welt, Berlin (1994), and other locations. A lavishly illustrated catalog focusing primarily on figures and masks of Tanzania. "A significant addition to African art libraries, particularly those with a special interest in East Africa."—*Review*, African arts, v.28, no.3, summer 1995, p.90.

Contents: Einleitung, von Maria Kecskési; Eine kurze Geschichte von Tanzania, Wo kamen sie alle her?, von Marc L. Felix; Die traditionelle Skulptur Tanzanias, Ein Überblick, von Marc L. Felix; Traditionelle Skulptur aus Zentral-Osttanzania, von Enrico Castelli; Ton- und Holzskulpturen aus Nordost-Tanzania, von Georges Meurant; Die Bildhauerkunst der Nyamwezi, von Georges Meurant; Ostafrikanische hochlehnige Hocker: eine transkulturelle Tradition, von Nancy Ingram Nooter; Formenverwandtschaft: ästhetische Berührungspunkte zwischen Völkern West-Tanzanias und Südost-Zaires, von Allen F. Roberts; Annäherung an die Maskenschnitzerei Tanzanias, von Charles Meur; Der Südosten Tanzanias—die Kunst der Makonde und der Benachbarten Völker, von Giselher Blesse; Kunsthistorische Schlussbetrachtung, von Marc L. Felix.

Bibliographie, p.522–26.

K433 Thompson, Robert Farris, and Cornet, Joseph. The four moments of the sun: Kongo art in two worlds. Washington, D.C., National Gallery of Art, 1981. 256p. il., col. plates, map.

Catalog of the exhibition, National Gallery of Art (1981–1982). Richly illustrated with field photographs, "this became the first exhibition to focus upon the ancient and important funerary art of this African civilization, and at the same time to reveal the trans-oceanic significance of these images and their iconography."—*Foreword.*

Contents: (1) Kongo civilization and Kongo art; (2) The structure of recollection: the Kongo new world visual tradition; (3) Stone funerary sculpture; (4) Funerary terra cottas.

Bibliography, p.247–56.

K434 University of Pennsylvania. University Museum. African sculpture from the University Museum, University of Pennsylvania. [By] Allen Wardwell. Photography by Bobby Hansson. Philadelphia, Pa., Philadelphia Museum of Art (Distr. by the Univ. of Pennsylvania Pr., 1986). 151p. il. (part col.), maps.

Catalog of the exhibition, Philadelphia Museum of Art (1986–1987). A broad survey of the holdings of "one of the earliest important collections of African art in the United States."—*Foreword.*

Contents: African sculpture: criteria and methods of selection; History of the African collections of the University Museum, University of Pennsylvania.

Bibliographic abbreviations, p.146–50. Index of peoples, p.151.

K435 Vogel, Susan, and N'Diaye, Francine. African masterpieces from the Musée de l'Homme. Introd. by Jean Guiart. N.Y., Center for African Art, [1985]. 168p. il. (part col.), map.

Catalog of the exhibition, Center for African Art (1985). Well-illustrated catalog of a major African art collection which documents the inaugural exhibition of the Center for African Art.

Contents: Africa, the arts, and the Musée de l'Homme, by Jean Guiart; Catalogue, by Susan Vogel and Francine N'Diaye.

Selected bibliography, p.166–67. Index, p.168.

K436 West African masks and cultural systems. Ed. by Sidney L. Kasfir. Tervuren, Belgique, Musée Royal de l'Afrique Centrale, 1988. 252p. il., maps (Annales. Science humaines, 126)

Originally based on a symposium, this study contributes to the understanding of the masking phenomenon in African art and culture, with an emphasis on mask events in Nigeria, Sierra Leone, Liberia, and Gambia.

Contents: Introduction: masquerading as a cultural system, by the ed.; Igala masks: dynastic history and the face of the nation, by R. A. Sargent; The Gelede masked dance and Ketu society, by E. Babatunde; Anogiri: Okpella's masked festival heralds, by J. M. Borgetti; Celebrating male aggression: the Idoma Oglinye masquerade, by S. L. Kasfir; The Niger-Cross River hinterlands and their masks, by G. I. Jones; Ikem: the history of a masquerade in southeast Nigeria, by K. Nicklin and J. Salmons; Fighting fire with fire: the Mandinka Sengko mask, by P. Weil; Take it to the streets: urban Ode-Lay masquerades of Sierra Leone, by J. Nunley; Hearing is believing: acoustic masks and spirit manifestation, by E. Lifschitz; Masks and metaphysics: an empirical dilemma, by D. Napier; Cunning mysteries, by E. Tonkin.

Includes bibliographical references.

K437 Winter-Irving, Celia. Stone sculpture in Zimbabwe: context, content and form. Harare, Zimbabwe, Roblaw, [1991]. xviii, 210p., il.

"The stone sculpture in Zimbabwe, dating from 1956 . . . is easily the best-known manifestation of Southern African contemporary art."—*Introd.* Including background information on Great Zimbabwe and San rock art, this book provides a basic introduction to Zimbabwe's art and culture.

Contents: (1) The strength of its presence; (2) Unique artistic properties; (3) Cultural origins; (4) Frank McEwen and other early mentors; (5) The National Gallery of Zimbabwe; (6) Tengenenge; (7) The sculptors speak; (8) Visual culture in early history; (9) Visual arts since the nineteenth century; (10) Private patronage of the arts; (11) Government's policies foster art.

Bibliography, p.207. Index, p.208–10.

Oceania

K438 Cox, J. Halley. With William H. Davenport. Hawaiian sculpture. Rev. ed. Honolulu, Univ. of Hawaii Pr., [1988]. xxvi, 213p. il.

See GLAH 1:K257 for 1st ed.

Since publication of the first ed. which became an "instant 'classic' . . . new discoveries in the study of Hawaiian art have been made. . . . To bring the revised edition up-to-date Davenport has written a lengthy Introduction in which he discusses the research on Hawaiian art which has altered or added to our knowledge of the sculpture. Additional commentary for the catalog has been included, as well as new listings of extant objects. The revisions made by Davenport are valuable enough to make the book a must even for those who own the original."—*Review*, EthnoArts index, v.7, no.1, Jan.–March 1989, p.4.

Contents: Hawaiian sculpture; Catalog of extant pieces; Additions to catalog of extant pieces; Revisions to catalog of extant pieces.

Bibliography, p.207–10.

K439 Wardwell, Allen. The sculpture of Polynesia. [Chicago, The Art Institute, 1967]. 100p. 151 il. (part col.), map.

Catalog of the exhibition, Art Institute of Chicago (1967), and other locations. A standard introduction to the sculptural arts of Polynesia.

Contents: The sculpture of Polynesia; Western Polynesia/The Fiji Islands; Tonja and Samoa; Central Polynesia/The Cook Islands; The Society Islands/Tahiti; The Austral Islands; Mangareva and the Tuamotu Islands; The Marquesas Islands; The outlying Islands/Easter Island; The Hawaiian Islands; New Zealand.

Bibliography, p.98–99.

The Americas

K440 Baudez, Claude F. Maya sculpture of Copán: the iconography. Norman, Univ. of Oklahoma Pr., 1994. ix, 300p. il.

A catalog of the freestanding and architectural sculpture "including condition, dimensions, location, and archaeological history as well as the description and interpretation of motifs and glyphs incorporated in the sculpture."—*Review*, Latin American archaeology, v.7, 1996. Illustrated in many instances with complementary photographs and line drawings.

Contents: Introduction; Part 1. Analysis: (1) Freestanding monuments; (2) Architectural sculpture; Pt. 2. Synthesis: (3) The history of monumental art at Copán; (4) Religion and politics at Copán; Appendixes: Dedicatory dates of monuments analyzed in this study; Glyphic elements in Copán iconography.

References, p.[289]–96. Index, p.[297]–300.

K441 Fenton, William Nelson. The false faces of the Iroquois. Norman, Univ. of Oklahoma Pr., 1987. xxi, 522p. il., col. plates. (The Civilization of the American Indian series, 178)

An examination of the Iroquois Society of Faces maskmaking tradition. "The present work puts on record its paraphernalia, origin myths, beliefs, ceremonies, and cures, first for the native people themselves, second to enhance programs of interpretation and education in museums, and third to enlighten collectors of masks."—*p.501.*

Bibliography, p.509–16. Index, p.517–22.

K442 Fienup-Riordan, Ann. The living tradition of Yup'ik masks: Agayuliyararput, our way of making prayer. Trans. by Marie Meade. Photography by Barry McWayne. Seattle, Univ. of Washington Pr. in assoc. with the Anchorage Museum of History and Art and the Anchorage Museum Association, 1996. 320p. il. (part col.)

Published in conjunction with the exhibition, Anchorage Museum of History and Art (1996), and other locations. This monograph, prepared in close cooperation with the Yup'ik community, explores the rich tradition of maskmaking and mask performance among the Yup'ik of western Alaska, with emphasis on the accompanying storytelling; the history of performance, its supression and subsequent revival; and the 19th- and 20th-century museum collecting history of the masks.

Glossary, p.307. References, p.309–14. Index, p.315–20.

K443 Markman, Peter T., and Markman, Roberta H. Masks of the spirit: image and metaphor in Mesoamerica. With an introd. by Joseph Campbell. Berkeley, Univ. of California Pr., 1989. xxi, 254p. il. (part col.)

"Major, sweeping statement on the central importance of masks in Mesoamerican religion, shamanism, and ritual. . . . Whether or not their view of the nature and meaning of masks will stand, their book will long serve as a most valuable guide to the subject for Mesoamerican scholars."—*Review*, Handbook of Latin American studies, v.53, 1993. "Book is responsibly researched, but it has the predictable aura of mysticism."—*Review*, Handbook of Latin American studies, v.52, 1992.

Contents: Part 1: The metaphor of the mask in Pre-Columbian Mesoamerica: (1) The mask as the god; (2) The mask in ritual: metaphor in motion; (3) Coda 1: the mask as metaphor. Part 2: Metaphoric reflections of the cosmic order: (4) The shamanistic inner vision; (5) The temporal order; (6) The spatial order; (7) The mathematical order; (8) The life-force: source of all order; (9) Transformation: manifesting the life-force; (10) Coda 2: the mask as metaphor. Part 3: The metaphor of the mask after the conquest: (11) Syncretism: the structural effect of the conquest; (12) The Pre-Columbian survivals: the mask of the tigre; (13) The syncretic compromise: the Yaqui and Mayo pascola; (14) Today's masks.

Notes, p.207–23. Bibliography, p.225–43. Index, p.245–54.

K444 Robertson, Merle Greene. The sculpture of Palenque. Princeton, Princeton Univ. Pr., 1983– . (4)v. il. (part col., part folded)

A continuing series of monographs on the sculptural program of a principal Maya city. "The first four [volumes] will present all of the known sculpture of Palenque, both in stucco and in stone, and the fifth will be a summary, in collaboration with Donald Robertson."—*Foreword* to v.1. Combines black-and-white or color photographs with the author's detailed line drawings and interpretations. V.1 includes folded site map in pocket. "For thoroughness of detail, beauty of production, and breadth of discussion, this work is unique in Maya studies."—*Review*, Times literary supplement, Apr. 4, 1986. "The Sculpture of Palenque is thus easily the most comprehensive and usable pictorial record ever published by a single author on any archaeological site in the Americas."—*Review*, Art bulletin, v.70, 1988, p.360.

Contents: (1) The Temple of the Inscriptions; (2) The early buildings of the palace and the wall paintings; (3) The late buildings of the palace; (4) The Cross Group, the North Group, the Olvidado, and other pieces.

Each vol. includes bibliography and index.

L. Drawings

Works concerned with the history and technique of drawing are listed and described in this chapter.

GENERAL WORKS

L1 Ashwin, Clive. Encyclopaedia of drawing: materials, technique and style. Cincinnati, North Light, 1983. 264p. il. (part col.), plates.

British ed., London, Batsford, 1982.

Alphabetical arrangement of 200- to 2,000-word articles on all aspects of the art of drawing.

Index to artists, p.261–64.

L2 Baer, Curtis O. Landscape drawings. N.Y., Abrams, [1973]. 360p. il. (part col.)

"Published in association with the Drawing Society." Significant anthology of drawings devoted to the role of drawings in the history of landscape, seeking "to give an idea of the great variety of ways in which European art interpreted this one theme."—*Pref.*

Selected bibliography, p.357. Index of artists, p.359.

L3 Bjurström, Per. Dürer to Delacroix: great master drawings from Stockholm. With Ulf Cederlof and Borje Magnusson. Fort Worth, Kimbell Art Museum, 1985. 197p. il. (part col.)

Catalog of the exhibition of master drawings from the Nationalmusuem, Stockholm, National Gallery of Art, Washington, D.C. (1985–86), and other locations. "One of the most important drawing exhibitions ever to come to the U.S. . . . The Nationalmuseum ranks with the British Museum, Louvre, the Berlin State Museums, and the Albertina as one of the . . . greatest repositories of graphic arts in the world."—*Foreword* by J. Carter Brown . . . [et al.]

Bibliographic references and abbreviations, p.195–96. Index of artists, p.197.

L4 Il disegno. Dir. da Gianni Carlo Sciolla. [Torino], Istituto bancario San Paolo di Torino, 1991–94. 3v. in 4. il. (part col.)

Lavish Italian bank publication on the art of drawing, with a special focus on Italian collections.

Contents: (1) Forme, techniche, significati. Testi di Annamaria Petrioli Tofani . . . [et al.]; (2) I grandi collezionisti. Testi di Giulia Fusconi . . . [et al.]; (3) Le collezioni pubbliche italiane. A cura di Annamaria Petrioli Tofani . . . [et al.] (2v.).

L5 École nationale supérieure des beaux-arts (France). Renaissance et manièrisme dans les écoles du Nord: dessins des collections de l'École des beaux-arts. [Catalogue par Emmanuelle Brugerolles avec la collab. de David Guillet.] Paris, l'École, 1985. xxxvi, 266p. il. (part col.)

Scholarly catalog of the exhibition, the École (1985), and other locations. Includes essays on Renaissance and Mannerist drawings and on French taste in the drawings of Germany and the Low Countries.

Index des artistes, p.255. Index des museés et des collections, p.257. Table des concordances, p.259. Expositions, p.261–62. Bibliographie, p.263–[67].

L6 Eitner, Lorenz; Fryberger, Betsy G.; and Osborne, Carol M. Stanford University Museum of Art, the drawing collection. With contrib. by Dwight Miller and others. Stanford, Calif., Stanford University Museum of Art. (Distr. by Univ. of Washington Pr., 1993). 418p. il. (part col.)

Scholarly catalog of an exemplary university collection, formed with little money but a surpassing ability to identify bargains in the international art market.

References to exhibitions from the Stanford collection, p.[414]. Index of artists, p.[415]–18.

L7 Farr, Dennis, and Bradford, William. The Northern landscape: Flemish, Dutch and British drawings from the Courtauld Collections. London, Trefoil Books, 1986. 264p. il. (part col.)

Selection of drawings from an excellent collection, mostly watercolors, 16th–19th centuries.

Index, p.264.

L8 Fondation Custodia. The Netherlandish and German drawings of the XVth and XVIth centuries of the Frits Lugt collection. By Karel G. Boon. Paris, Institut néerlandais, 1992. 3v. il.

"The second publication of the intended series of catalogues raisonnés of all the different sections and aspects of the collection formed by Frits Lugt and his wife over some fifty years."—*Pref.* See GLAH 2:L104 for the catalog of Italian drawings.

Contents: (1) Text; (2) Addenda & indexes; (3) Plates.

Watermarks, v.2, p.83–111. Table of correspondence, v.2, p.113–17. Indexes: artists' names, v.2, p.121–30; previous owners, v.2, p.131–43; related works, v.2, p.144–53; subjects, v.2, p.154–58. Literature cited in abbreviated form, v.2, p.159–220. Exhibitions and exhibition-catalogues cited in abbreviated form, v.2, p.221–39.

L9 Graphische Sammlung Albertina. Beschreibender Katalog der Handzeichnungen in der Graphischen Sammlung Albertina. Wien, Schroll, 1926– . (9)v. il.

See GLAH 1:L18 for original annotation and previous vols. Vols. listed here published by the Albertina.

Contents: (7) Herrmann, Luke. Die englische Schule: Zeichnungen und Aquarelle britischer Künstler (1992); (8) Knab, Eckhart, and Widauer, Heinz. Die Zeichnungen der französischen Schule: von Clouet bis Le Brun (1993); (9) Gröning, Maren, and Sternath, Marie Luise. Die deutschen und schweizer Zeichnungen des späten 18. Jahrhunderts (1997).

L10 Hill, Edward. The language of drawing. Englewood Cliffs, Prentice-Hall, 1966. iv, 152p. il.

"Essentially . . . an attempt to define drawing. . . . The line of attack I have taken is neither historical nor technical . . . but, rather, conceptual" and based in personal experience as a draftsman and teacher.—*Pref.*

Contents: A definition; Drawing as seeing; The formmaker; Michelangelo's ark; Materials and miscellanea: a philosophy of craft; The pedagogical mirror; A new disposition.

Bibliography, p.146–52.

L11 J. Paul Getty Museum. European drawings: catalogue of the collections. [By] George R. Goldner, Lee Hendrix, Gloria Williams . . . [et al.] Malibu, Calif., Getty Museum, 1988– . (3)v. il. (part col.)

Scholarly catalog of an increasingly important collection. Vol.1 covers acquisitions from 1981–85, vol.2 the 144 drawings purchased 1986–89, vol.3 the last group acquired under the curatorship of George Goldner. Vol.4 will cover drawings acquired by his successor, Nicholas Turner, a co-author of vol.3.

Bibliographies and indexes in each vol.

L12 Jaffé, Michael. A great heritage: Renaissance & Baroque drawings from Chatsworth. Washington, D.C., National Gallery of Art (Distr. by Abrams, 1995). 240p. col. il.

Catalog of the exhibition, National Gallery of Art (1995), and other locations.

The most recent Chatsworth exhibition catalog and the most useful, but with a summary in the annotation of earlier traveling shows of Chatsworth drawings and their catalogs (1962–63, 1969–70, 1987–88, 1993–94), each of which contains different selections of drawings.

Select bibliography, p.233–36. Exhibitions, p.237. Exhibitions including loans from Chatsworth, p.238–39. Index of artists, p.240.

L13 Koschatzky, Walter. Die Kunst der Zeichnung: Technik, Geschichte, Meisterwerke. [Hrsg., Graphische Sammlung Albertina.] Salzburg, Residenz, 1977. 460p. il. (part col.)

Substantial survey of the techniques and history of drawing, by a prolific scholar.

Anmerkungen, p.447–49. Literaturverzeichnis, p.450–52. Auswahl zur Bibliographie der Handzeichnung, p.453–54. Register, p.455–60.

L14 Kunst des Sammelns: das Praunsche Kabinett. Meisterwerke von Dürer bis Carracci. [Katalog: Katrin Achilles-Syndram . . . (et al.)] Nürnberg, Germanisches Nationalmuseum, [1994]. 410p. il. (part col.) (Ausstellungskataloge des Germanischen Nationalmuseums Nürnberg)

Catalog of the exhibition, Germanisches Nationalmuseum Nurnberg (1994), of drawings from a great private collection.

Literatur, p.387–409. Künstlerverzeichnis, p.410.

L15 Kunstmuseum Düsseldorf. Facetten des Barock: Meisterzeichnungen von Gianlorenzo Bernini bis Anton Raphael Mengs aus dem Kunstmuseum Düsseldorf: Akademiesammlung. Katalog von Hein-Th. Schulze Altcappenberg und Susannah Cremer. Hrsg. von Hans Albert Peters. Düsseldorf, Das Museum, 1990. 295p. il. (part col.)

Catalog of the exhibition of Baroque drawings, Kunstmuseum Düsseldorf (1990).

Künstlerverzeichnis, p.[265]–82. Literaturverzeichnis, p.287–93.

L16 Lambert, Susan. Reading drawings: an introduction to looking at drawings. N.Y., Pantheon, 1984. 141, [2]p. il. (part col.)

Published on the occasion of the exhibition, Drawing Center, N.Y. (1984). "An earlier version of the text first issued to accompany the exhibition 'Drawing: Technique and Purpose' in London in 1981"—*T.p. verso.* Based on the collections of the Victoria and Albert Museum. A helpful introduction for the student and general reader.

Contents: Technique; Drawing as a discipline; Drawing as imagination; Drawing for utility.

Notes, p.142. Suggested reading, p.142. Index & concordance, p.143.

L17 Landscape drawings of 5 centuries, 1400–1900. [Evanston, Ill.], Mary and Leigh Block Gallery, Northwestern Univ., 1988. xii, 200p. il. (part col.)

Published to accompany the thematic exhibition of the same title, Mary and Leigh Block Gallery (1988).

Contents: Town and country: early landscape drawings, by Larry Silver; Topography and the imagination, modern landscape drawings, by Levi P. Smith III with the assist. of Martha Ward; Exhibition catalogue, by George Szabó.

Catalogue abbreviations and bibliography, p.198–99.

L18 Master drawings from the National Gallery of Canada. Washington, D.C., National Gallery of Art, 1988. 311p. il. (part col.)

Catalog of the exhibition showcasing the collections of the National Gallery of Canada, National Gallery of Art, Washington, D.C. (1988).

Bibliography, p.293–309. Index of artists, p.311.

L19 Mendelowitz, Daniel Marcus. Drawing. Stanford, Calif., Stanford Univ. Pr., 1980. xvi, 464p. il.

1st ed. 1967.

"This book has . . . been planned to extend horizons by surveying the art of drawing from a variety of viewpoints, both internal and external."—*Pref.*

Contents: (1) Introduction; (2) The history of drawing; (3) The art elements; (4) Drawing media; (5) Conclusion.

A selected bibliography, p.449–55. Index, p.456–64.

L20 Monnier, Geneviève. Drawing. [Introd. by] Jean Leymarie. [Text by] Geneviève Monnier, Bernice Rose. [Introd. and chapters 1–5 trans. from the French by Barbara Bray.] N.Y., Rizzoli, 1979. xx, 279p. il. (part col.) (History of an art)

Important general survey of the medium in a valuable series.

Contents: (1) Codices, model books, compilations; (2) Drawing and art theory; (3) The basic techniques of drawing; (4) Drawing and its purpose; (5) Drawing as a record of observation; (6) A view of drawing today.

Bibliography, p.254–65. Index of names and places, p.276–78.

L21 Museo del Prado. Catálogo de dibujos. Madrid, El Museo, 1972– . (4)v. il.

See GLAH 1:L74 for previous vols. and original annotation.

Contents: (1) Dibujos españñoles siglos XV–XVII; (2–3) Dibujos españñoles siglo XVIII; (6) Dibujos italianos del siglo XVII; (7) Dibujos italianos del siglo XVIII y del siglo XIX.

L22 Paris. Musée National du Louvre. Cabinet des dessins. Inventaire général des dessins des écoles du nord: écoles allemande, des Anciens Pays-Bas, flamande, hollandaise et suisse, XVe–XVIIIe siècles. Supplément aux inventaires publiés par Frits Lugt et Louis Demonts. Par Emmanuel Starcky. Paris, Ministère de la culture, de la communication, des grands travaux et du bicentenaire, Ed. de la Réunion des museés nationaux, 1988. 288p. il., ports.

Supplement to GLAH 1:L36, L69-71.

Index des artistes, p.255–57. Index des collectionneurs, p.256. Table de concordance, p.258–60. Ouvrages cités en abrégé, p.261–76. Expositions, p.277–81. Filigranes, p.283–88.

L23 Pierpont Morgan Library. From Mantegna to Picasso: drawings from the Thaw Collection at the Pierpont Morgan Library, New York. Catalogue by Cara Denison . . . [et al.] N.Y., Pierpont Morgan Library, 1996. xv, 247p. il. (part col.), ports.

Catalog of the exhibition, Royal Academy of Art (1996–97). An important private collection especially rich in landscape drawings.

Sources cited in abbreviated form, p.217–35. Index of artists, p.237.

L24 Pignatti, Terisio. Master drawings: from cave art to Picasso. Commentaries by Maria Agnese Chiari. N.Y., Abrams, 1982. 397p. il. (part col.)

Trans. of Il disegno: da altamira a Picasso. Milano, Mondadori,1981.

Three hundred master drawings. Surveys the entire field. By a great scholar of Italian art.

Bibliography, p.389–94. Index, p.395–97.

L25 Royalton-Kisch, Martin; Chapman, Hugo; and Coppel, Stephen. Old master drawings from the Malcolm Collection. London, British Museum Pr., 1996. 192p.

Stunning international collection of old master drawings from a collection acquired by the British Museum in 1895. Includes Italian, Spanish, French, German, and Netherlandish drawings.

Bibliography, p.191. Index of artists, p.192.

L26 The touch of the artist: master drawings from the Woodner collections. Ed. by Margaret Morgan Grasselli. Washington, D.C., National Gallery of Art (Distr. by Abrams, 1995). 412p. il. (part col.)

Catalog of the exhibition, National Gallery of Art, Washington, D.C. (1995–1996), of Italian drawings of the 14th–19th century from the distinguished collection of Ian Woodner.

References, p.395–410. Artist index, p.411.

TECHNIQUES

L27 Bicknell, Peter. Gilpin to Ruskin: drawing masters and their manuals, 1800–1860: exhibition sel. and catalogued by Peter Bicknell and Jane Munro. London, Christie's, 1987. 134, [4]p. il. (part col.)

Catalog of the exhibition, Fitzwilliam Museum, Cambridge (1987–88), and other locations. "In this exhibition are the illustrated manuals produced in England during the nineteenth century by a significant number of the leading landscape painters."—*Foreword.* Based largely on a single private collection.

Select bibliography, p.[135]. Index, p.[137]–[38].

L28 Chaet, Bernard. The art of drawing. 3d ed. N.Y., Holt, Rinehart and Winston, 1983. xi, 279p. ill. (part col.)

1st ed. 1970; 2d ed. 1978. "This third ed. . . . focuses on the latest developments in my drawing classes, which began at the Yale School of Art in 1951."—*Pref.*

Contents: (1) Directions; (2) The expressive means of drawing; (3) Composition; (4) Media and materials; (5) Landscape; (6) Forms from nature; (7) Interiors and objects; (8) Skulls; (9) Animals; (10) Introduction to the figure; (11) Individual projects; (12) Instrumentation; (13) Choices.

Index, p.267–78.

L29 Goldman, Paul. Looking at drawings: a guide to technical terms. [London], British Museum Publications, 1979. 16p. il. (part col.)
Slight handbook, alphabetically arranged (bistre-watermarks). An enhanced version of the text was merged into the author's Looking at prints, drawings, and watercolors (1988).

L30 Old master prints and drawings: a guide to preservation and conservation. By Carlo James . . . [et al.] Trans. and ed. by Marjorie B. Cohn. Amsterdam, Amsterdam Univ. Pr., 1997. 319p. il. (part col.)
Italian ed., Manuale per la conservazione e il restauro di disegni e stampe antichi. Firenze, Olschki, 1991.

A "clear and comprehensive guide."—*Pref.*

Contents: The material character of the work of art on paper: (I) Collectors and mountings; (II) Paper; (III) Drawing techniques; (IV) Print techniques; (V) Visual identification of graphic techniques and their supports; Preservation: (VI) The history of preservation of works of art on paper; (VII) Curatorial care today; (VIII) Technical problems in preservation; Conservation: (IX) The history of conservation; (X) Concerns of the curator and concerns of the conservator; Specific conservation techniques: (XI) The constituent materials of paper; (XII) Analytical methods; (XIII) Cleaning; (XIV) Removal of old mountings; (XV) Stain removal; (XVI) Bleaching; (XVII) Deacidification and alkaline reserve; (XVIII) Adhesives; (XIX) Consolidation and integration; (XX) Lining; (XXI) Integration of colors.

Selected bibliography, p.306–10. Reproduction references, p.311–12. Index, p.313–19.

L31 Rawson, Philip S. Drawing. 2d ed. Philadelphia, Univ. of Pennsylvania Pr., 1987. xiii, 322p. il.
1st ed., N.Y., Oxford Univ. Pr., 1969.

An attempt to put the study of drawing on a fresh critical footing by "writing . . . from the point of view of the maker of drawings" and substituting clear, unambiguous terminology for "cant terms of criticism which are so often uttered glibly without any explanation of what they mean."—*Pref.*

Contents: (1) The theoretical base; (2) Supports, materials, and implements; their significance; (3) Technical methods; (4) Rhythm and space; (5) The subject: its nature and function; (6) The different kinds of drawings.

Index, p.317–22.

WESTERN COUNTRIES

France

L32 Art Institute of Chicago. French drawings and sketchbooks of the nineteenth century. [By] Harold Joachim. Comp. by Sandra Haller Olsen. Chicago, Univ. of Chicago Pr., 1978–1979. 2v. & microfiche (19 sheets, all il. [part col.]) (Chicago visual library)
"This catalog is intended as a survey of drawings, watercolors, and pastels on paper in the Department of Prints and Drawings of the Art Institute of Chicago."—*Pref.* Reproduces the drawings on microfiche with an elaborate finding aid.

Bibliography, v.1, p.117–22, v.2, p.131–39.

L33 Bacou, Roseline. French landscape drawings and sketches of the eighteenth century: catalogue of a loan exhibition from the Louvre and other French museums at the Department of Prints and Drawings in the British Museum, 1977. London, British Museum Publications, 1977. 151p. il. (part col.)
Catalog of the exhibition, British Museum (1977), "one half of an exchange between the Louvre and the British Museum."—*Introd.*

Bibliography of works referred to in abbreviated form, p.16–18.

L34 Bjurström, Per. The art of drawing in France, 1400–1900: drawings from the National Museum, Stockholm. London, Sotheby's Publications (Distr. in the USA by Harper and Row, 1987). 223p. il. (part col.)
"Published in association with the Drawing Center, New York." Chronological survey of French drawings, based on the collections of the Nationalmuseum, Stockholm.

Bibliography, p.216–18. Index, p.220–23.

L35 Brachlianoff, Dominique. The real and the spiritual: nineteenth-century French drawings from the Musée des beaux-arts de Lyon. With an introd. by Philippe Durey. Trans. by Anne Bertrand. Ed. by DeCourcy E. McIntosh. Pittsburgh, Frick Art Museum, 1992. 188p. il. (part col.)
Catalog of the exhibition, Frick Art Museum, Pittsburgh (1992), and other locations.

Biographical notes, p.170–77. Books and articles, p.178–83. Exhibition catalogues, p.183–85. Artists in the exhibition, p.186.

L36 Da David a Bonnard: disegni francesi del XIX secolo dalla Biblioteca nazionale di Parigi. [By] Francois Fossier. Milano, Fabbri, 1990. 277p. il. (part col.)
In French and Italian. Catalog of the exhibition, Palazzo Vecchio, Florence (1990–91), of 19th-century French drawings from the Bibliothèque Nationale.

Bibliographie, p.267–69. Liste des artistes français du XIXe siècle, p.271–77.

L37 Dessins français du XVIIe siècle dans les collections publiques françaises. Paris, Ed. de la Réunion des musées nationaux, 1993. 323p. il. (part col.)
Catalog of the exhibition, Musée du Louvre (1993), with 161 drawings. Includes a historical sketch of 17th-century French drawings in provincial collections.

Bibliographie, p.310–17. Index des artistes exposés, p.318. Index des lieux de conservation, p.319. Index des dessins cités, p.320–23.

L38 Fogg Art Museum. David to Corot: French drawings in the Fogg Art Museum. [By] Agnes Mongan. Ed.

by Miriam Stewart. Cambridge, Mass., Harvard Univ. Pr., 1996. 306p.

Substantial scholarly catalog of 18th- and 19th-century French drawings from the Fogg collection.

Bibliography, p.295–301. Exhibitions, p.303–06.

L39 Goldfarb, Hilliard T. From Fontainebleau to the Louvre: French drawing from the seventeenth century. Cleveland, Cleveland Museum of Art in coop. with Indiana Univ. Pr., 1989. xvii, 214p. il.

Careful, scholarly study of the subject.

Biographical summaries of the artists, p.206–10. Index of artists mentioned, p.211–14.

L40 Lille (France). Musée des beaux-arts. Catalogue des dessins français du XVIIIe siècle: de Claude Gillot à Hubert Robert. Sophie Raux. Paris, Ed. de la Réunion des musées nationaux (Distr. by Seuil, 1995). 235p. il. (part col.)

Catalog of the collection of 18th-century French drawings.

Table de concordance, p.222–23. Artistes représenté dans la collection, p.224. Collectionneurs et marchands, p.225. Bibliographie, p.227–32. Expositions, p.233–35.

L41 Musée Carnavalet. La Revolution française, le Premier Empire: dessins du Musée Carnavalet. [Catalogue by Jean-Marie Brusson . . . (et al.)] Paris, Musées de la ville de Paris, 1983. 167p. il. (part col.)

Catalog of the exhibition of 18th-century French drawings, Musée Carnavalet, Paris (1982).

Index chronologique des événements illustrés par les oeuvres exposées, p.167–[68].

L42 Myers, Mary L. French architectural and ornament drawings of the eighteenth century. N.Y., Metropolitan Museum of Art (Distr. by Abrams, 1991). xxx, 224p. il. (part col.)

Excellent, scholarly catalog of the exhibition, Metropolitan Museum of Art (1991–92), of drawings owned by the Department of Prints and Photographs.

Works cited in abbreviated form, p.213–15. Abbreviation, p.215. Index, p.217–24.

L43 New York. Metropolitan Museum of Art. 15th–18th century French drawings in the Metropolitan Museum of Art. [By] Jacob Bean with the assist. of Lawrence Turcic. N.Y., Metropolitan Museum of Art, 1986. 325p. il.

Describes and reproduces all the drawings in the collection plausibly attributed to known artists of the period (358 drawings total).

Index of former collections, p.317–21. Concordance, p.322–23. Index of artists, p.324–25.

L44 Paris. Musée National du Louvre. Cabinet des dessins. Dessins français du XVIIIe siècle de Watteau à Lemoyne: 89e exposition du Cabinet des dessins. [Catalogue red. par Roseline Bacou . . . (et al.)] Paris, Ministère de la culture et de la communication, Ed. de la Réunion des musées nationaux, 1987. 127p. il.

Catalog of the exhibition of 18th-century French drawings, Musée du Louvre (1987).

Bibliographie, p.121–25. Index des artistes, p.126. Table de concordance, p.127.

L45 Pierpont Morgan Library. French master drawings from the Pierpont Morgan Library. [By] Cara Dufour Denison. N.Y., Pierpont Morgan Library, 1993. xx, 287p. il. (part col.)

Catalog of the exhibition, Musée du Louvre (1993), and other locations. 125 drawings from the Pierpont Morgan Library. Grouped by century.

Short title references, p.275–85. Index of artists, p.287.

L46 The Renaissance in France: drawings from the École des beaux-arts, Paris. Curator of the exhibition, Emmanuelle Brugerolles. Catalogue by Emmanuelle Brugerolles and David Guillet. [Trans. by Judith Schub]. Cambridge, Mass., Harvard Univ. Art Museums (Distr. by the Univ. of Washington Pr., 1995). xvi, 329p. il. (part col.)

Trans. of Dessin en France au XVIe siècle. Paris, ENSB-A, 1994.

Catalog of the major exhibition, École nationale supérieure des beaux-arts, Paris (1994), and other locations. "115 drawings and miniatures from a crucial century in the history of French art."—*p.viii.*

Index of artists, p.310–11. Index of museums and collections, p.312–14. Index of provenance, p.315. Table of concordance, p.316. Bibliography, p.317–26. Exhibitions, p.327–28.

L47 Roland Michel, Marianne. Le dessin français au XVIIIe siècle. Fribourg, Office du livre, 1987. 263p. il. (part col.)

Solid study of drawing in 18th-century France.

Contents: (I) Qu'est-ce que le dessin? (II) Techniques et médias; (III) L'enseignement du dessin-discours et praxis; (IV) Dessins et dessinateurs; (V) Fonctions du dessin; (VI) Quatre dessinateurs exemplaires; (VII) Usages et usagers: l'objet du dessin; (VIII) Le public des dessins.

Notes, p.254. Bibliographie sommaire, p.256–58. Index, p.259–62.

L48 Staatliche Kunsthalle Karlsruhe. Kupferstichkabinett. Die französischen Zeichnungen, 1570–1930: kritischer und erl. Katalog. Karlsruhe, Das Museum, 1983. 205p. il. (part col.)

Catalog of the exhibition, Staatliche Kunsthalle Karlsruhe (1983), documenting one of the most comprehensive collections of French drawings in Germany.

Künstlerverzeichnis, p.205.

L49 Städtische Galerie im Städelschen Kunstinstitut Frankfurt am Main. Französische Zeichnungen im Städelschen Kunstinstitut: 1550 bis 1800. Katalog und Ausstellung, Hildegard Bauereisen, Margret Stuffmann. Frankfurt am Main, Die Galerie, 1986. 194p. il. (part col.)

Catalog of the exhibition, Städtische Galerie im Städelschen Kunstinstitut, Frankfurt am Main (1987), of selected French drawings from a substantial collection.

Verzeichnis der Künstler, p.1.

Germany and Austria

L50 Deutsche Zeichnungen des 18. Jahrhunderts: zwischen Tradition und Aufklärung: eine Ausstellung aus den Beständen des Berliner Kupferstichkabinetts. Bearb. von Thomas W. Gaehtgens, Volker Manuth, Barbara Paul. Berlin, Mann, 1987. 177p. il. (part col.)

Catalog of the exhibition, Kupferstichkabinett, Berlin (1987), focusing on a neglected period, the 18th century.

Künstlerverzeichnis, p.176–77.

L51 Dickel, Hans. Deutsche Zeichenlehrbücher des Barock: eine Studie zur Geschichte der Künstlerausbildung. N.Y., Olms, 1987. ix, 415p. il. (Studien zur Kunstgeschichte, 48)

Revision of the author's thesis, Universität Hamburg, 1985. A significant study of instructional drawing manuals of the German Baroque.

Anmerkungen, p.279. Verzeichnis der bearbeiteten Zeichenlehrbücher und Vorlagenserien, p.390–96. Literaturverzeichnis, p.397–407. Verzeichnis der Abbildungnen, p.408–15.

L52 Dietrich-Boorsch, Dorothea. German drawings of the 60s. Exhibition and catalogue prepared by Dorothea Dietrich-Boorsch. New Haven, Yale Univ. Art Gallery, 1982. 91p. il.

Catalog of a significant exhibition, Yale University Art Gallery (1982), and other locations, focusing on "eleven artists from the two most vital art centers in Germany since World War II, Berlin and Düsseldorf."—*Foreword.*

Bibliography, p.12.

L53 German realist drawings of the 1920s = Deutsche realistische Zeichnungen der zwanziger Jahre. Ed. by Peter Nisbet. With essays by Hanne Bergius . . . [et al.] Cambridge, Mass., Harvard Univ. Art Museums, Busch-Reisinger Museums, 1986. x, 238p. il.

In English and German. Catalog of the exhibition, Guggenheim Museum, New York (1986), and other locations. Includes a series of essays on aspects of the subject (Neue Sachlichkeit, Berlin, Karlsruhe's contribution, Alexander Kanoldt, etc.).

Biographies and checklist, p.213–38.

L54 Goethezeit und Romantik: einhundert Meisterzeichnungen aus einer Privatsammlung. [Katalogbearb., Andreas Blühm, Gerhard Gerkens, C. J. Heinrich.] Lübeck, Graphische Werkstätten, 1990. 232p. il. (part col.)

Beautifully produced catalog of the exhibition of late 18th- and early 19th-century German drawings, Niedersächsische Landesgalerie Hannover (1990), and other locations.

Künstlerverzeichnis, p.232.

L55 Graphische Sammlung Albertina. Dessins germaniques de l'Albertina de Vienne. [Conception du catalogue, coord., José-Luis de Los Llanos]. Paris, Paris-Musée, 1991. 214p. il. (part col.)

Catalog of the exhibition of German drawings from the Albertina collection, Musée du Petit Palais (1991).

Liste des artistes, p.42–43. Ouvrages de référence, p.207. Expositions, p.208–10. Ouvrages et articles cités, p.211–14.

L56 Hamburger Kunsthalle. Kupferstichkabinett. Von Dürer bis Baselitz: Deutsche Zeichnungen aus dem Kupferstichkabinett der Hamburger Kunsthalle. [Konzeption und Auswahl: Werner Hofmann, Ekhard Schaar. Katalogbearb., Eckhard Schaar, Hanna Hohl, Matthias Eberle. Red. Eckhard Schaar, Hanna Hohl.] [Hamburg, Die Kunsthalle, 1989.] 292p. il. (part col.), plates.

Catalog of the exhibition, Hamburger Kunsthalle (1989), of 150 German drawings from this notable collection.

Biographien der Künstler, p.273–87. Bibliographie, p.289–92.

L57 Kunsthaus Zürich. Graphische Sammlung. Von Leibl bis Pechstein: deutsche Zeichnungen aus den Beständen der Graphischen Sammlung. [Bearb. von Annette Nolte-Jacobs]. Zürich, Kunsthaus Zürich, [1991?] 134p. il. (part col.)

Catalog of the exhibition, Graphisches Kabinett, Kunsthaus Zürich (1991). Slight but on an important period and collection.

Verzeichnis der zitierten Literatur, p.126–33. Publikationen, p.133.

L58 Nineteenth century German drawings from the Grand Duchy of Baden: lent by the Staatliche Kunsthalle Karlsruhe. Introd. and catalogue by Rudolf Theilmann. Trans. by Robert E. Lewis. Cincinnati, Cincinnati Art Museum, 1983. 105p. il., map.

Catalog of the exhibition, Cincinnati Art Museum (1983). Covers the years 1825–80.

Bibliography, p.52–53.

L59 Öffentliche Kunstsammlung Basel. Kupferstichkabinett. Zeichnungen deutscher Künstler des 19. Jahrhunderts aus dem Basler Kupferstichkabinett. [Bearb. von Eva Maria Krafft]. Basel, Das Kunstmuseum, 1982. 306p. il. (part col.), 117p. of plates.

Catalog of the exhibition of 19th-century German draftsmen, Kunstmuseum Basel (1982–83).

Bibliographie, p.293–301. Register, p.302–06.

L60 The Romantic spirit: German drawings, 1780–1850, from the Nationalgalerie (Staatliche Museen, Berlin) and the Kupferstich-Kabinett (Staatliche Kunstsammlungen, Dresden), German Democratic Republic. By Peter Betthausen . . . [et al.] Ed. by Gottfried Riemann and William W. Robinson with the assist. of Pamela T. Barr. N.Y., Pierpont Morgan Library; Oxford Univ. Pr., 1988. 275p. il. (part col.)

Catalog of the exhibition, Pierpont Morgan Library (1988–89). Includes background essays on the art of the period, including German draftsmen in Rome.

Chronology, p.13. Bibliography, p.266–74. Index of artists, p.275.

L61 Rowlands, John. Drawings by German artists and artists from German-speaking regions of Europe in the Department of Prints and Drawings in the British Museum: the fifteenth century, and sixteenth century by artists born before 1530. With assist. of Giulia Bartrum. London, British Museum Pr., 1993. 2v. il.

"This catalogue covers the main parts of the Department's collection of German drawings."—*Pref.*

Contents: (1) Catalogue; (2) Plates.

Bibliography, v.1, p.272–81. Concordances, v.1, p.282–89. Indexes (v.1): drawings and manuscripts in other collections, p.290–97; related works, other than prints, drawings and manuscripts, in other collections, p.298–303; former owners and agents, p.304–05; artists, p.306.

L62 Staatliche Graphische Sammlung München. Die deutschen Zeichnungen des 15. Jahrhunderts. Hrsg. von Tilman Falk. München, Staatliche Graphische Sammlung München, 1994. 32p. il. (part col.), plates.

Checklist of the more than 60 15th-century German drawings in the collection.

Includes bibliographical references.

L63 Staatliche Kunsthalle Karlsruhe. Kupferstichkabinett. Die deutschen Zeichnungen des 19. Jahrhunderts. Bearb. von Rudolf Theilmann, Edith Ammann. Karlsruhe, Müller, 1978. 2v. il.

Vol.2 prepared by Rudolf Theilmann.

Catalog of the collection of 19th-century German drawings.

Contents: (1) Text; (2) Abbildungen.

Bibliographie, v.1, p.9–11.Verzeichnis der Künstler, v.2, p.513–19.

L64 Staatsgalerie Stuttgart. Graphische Sammlung. Deutsche Landschaftszeichnungen des 18. Jahrhunderts aus der Graphischen Sammlung, Staatsgalerie Stuttgart. [Ausstellung und Katalog, Otto Pannewitz]. Stuttgart, Die Staatsgalerie, 1985. 149p. il.

Catalog of the exhibition, Staatsgalerie Stuttgart (1985). Surveys German Baroque drawing on the basis of a selection from the 1,500 sheets in this particularly comprehensive collection.

Literatur, p.146–47. Kataloge, p.148–49.

L65 Städtische Kunsthalle Mannheim. Die Zeichnungen und Aquarelle des 19. Jahrhunderts der Kunsthalle Mannheim. In sechs Banden hsg. von Manfred Fath. Weinheim, VCH, Acta Humaniora, 1988– . (6)v. il. (part col.)

Catalog of the collection of the Kunsthalle Mannheim. Vol.1–2 published by Akademie Verlag.

Contents: (1/2) Vom Klassizismus zur Spätromantik. Bearb. von Monika Schulte-Arndt (1997); (3) Caspar David Friedrich in seiner Zeit. Bearb. von Hans Dickel (1991); (4) Nazarenische Zeichenkunst. Bearb. von Pia Muller-Tamm (1993); (5) Ideal und Idyll. Bearb. von Walter Stephan Laux (1988); (6) Salon und Secession. Bearb. von Walter Stephan Laux (1989).

Includes bibliographies. Künstlerverzeichnis der Bände I–VI, v.1/2, p.377–79.

L66 Zeichnung in Deutschland: deutsche Zeichner 1540–1640. Katalog. [Einl.] Heinrich Geissler. [Katalogtexte, Heinrich Geissler . . . (et al.)] Stuttgart, Staatsgalerie, 1979–1980. 2v. il.

Catalog of the exhibition, Staatsgalerie Stuttgart (1979–80), and other locations, providing an overview of drawing in Renaissance Germany.

Bibliographie, v.2, p.235–37. Die Aufbewahrungsorte, v.2, p.239. Künstlerregister, v.2, p.241–47.

SEE ALSO: Fondation Custodia. The Netherlandish and German drawings of the XVth and XVIth centuries of the Frits Lugt collection (GLAH 2:L8); Paris. Musée National du Louvre. Cabinet des dessins. Inventaire général des dessins des écoles du nord: écoles allemande, des Anciens Pays-Bas, flamande, hollandaise et suisse, XVe–XVIIIe siècles (GLAH 2:L22).

Great Britain and Ireland

L67 British Museum. Pre-Raphaelite drawings in the British Museum. [By] J. A. Gere. London, British Museum Pr., 1994. 159p. il. (part col.)

Excellent catalog of an important collection. Includes an appendix providing a "complete list of works in the British Museum by artists included in the catalogue" (p.144–56).

List of artists, p.12. Bibliography and abbreviations, p.157–59.

L68 British sporting and animal drawings c.1500–1850: a catalogue. Comp. by Judy Egerton and Dudley Snelgrove. London, Tate Gallery, for the Yale Center for British Art, 1978. xv, 126p. il. (part col.), plates.

"Sport in art and books: the Paul Mellon Collection."—*T.p.* These drawings, reflecting the collector's love of fox-hunting and racing, constitute perhaps one third of the ca. 6,500 drawings in the Paul Mellon Collection.—*Pref.*

Bibliography, p.xv. Chronological table of artists, p.105–09. Index, p.113–26.

L69 India Office Library. British drawings in the India Office Library. [By] Mildred Archer. London, H.M.S.O., 1969–1994. 3v., plates. col. il.

Vol.3 published: London, The British Library. Vol.3, ed. by Patricia Kattenhorn, is "a supplementary catalogue of drawings acquired since 1969."—*Pref.* to v.3.

A major catalog. "The earliest drawings dates from 1756, the latest from 1931. As a whole therefore the collection, today numbering almost 11,000 drawings, constitutes at once a memorial and an illustrative record of the British connection with the East, and especially with India, through nearly two centuries."—*Pref.* to v.1.

Contents: (1) Amateur artists; (2) Official and professional artists; (3) [without special title].

Bibliography, v.2, p.643–62. Concordances, v.2, p.663–94. Index, v.2, p.695–712. Chronological table of artists, v.3, p.vii–xiii.

L70 National Portrait Gallery (Great Britain). Master drawings from the National Portrait Gallery, London: from Elizabeth I to Elizabeth II. By Malcolm Rogers. Alexandria, Va., Art Services International, 1993. 200p. il. (part col.)

Catalog of the exhibition organized and circulated by Art Services International to the Philbrook Museum of Art, Tulsa (1993), and other locations, presenting "no more than a taste of the collection which, as an assemblage of British portrait drawings, is unparalleled in the world."—*p.10.*

Select bibliography, p.198–200.

L71 Stainton, Lindsay, and White, Christopher. Drawing in England from Hilliard to Hogarth. London, British Museum Pubs., 1987. 255p. il. (part col.), ports. (part col.)

Catalog of the exhibition, British Museum (1987), and other locations, intended "to show the variety and quality of the work both of native English artists and of Continental artists in some way associated with England."—*Foreword.*

Select bibliography: works referred to in abbreviated form, p.252–54. Index of artists, p.255.

Italy

L72 Ames-Lewis, Francis. Drawing in early Renaissance Italy. New Haven, Yale Univ. Pr., 1981. xi, 196p. il.

"This book is intended to be no more than a 'primer' in early renaissance drawing. . . . I hope to cast fresh light on the role played by drawing in the development of renaissance art, and on the value of the study of drawing to our understanding of the early renaissance."—*Pref.* Focuses on the development of new types of drawing and drawing techniques in the quattrocento, and on changes in the use of drawings and resulting changes in artistic practice. A thoughtful study. "Greatly contributes to our understanding and appreciation of quattrocento drawings."—*Review*, Art bulletin, v.66, no.2, June 1984, p.337.

Contents: (I) Some general considerations; (II) Drawing surfaces; (III) Techniques; (IV) Model-books and sketchbooks; (V) Figure drawing; (VI) Compositional drawings; Epilogue: The quattrocento legacy.

Notes to the text, p.181–84. Bibliography, p.185–88. Glossary, p.189–91. Index, p.192–96.

L73 ———, and Wright, Joanne. Drawing in the Italian Renaissance workshop: an exhibition of early Renaissance drawings from collections in Great Britain. London, Victoria and Albert Museum, 1983. 328p. il. (part col.), ports.

Catalog of the exhibition, University Art Gallery, Nottingham (1983). Thoughtful introduction to the role of drawing in the Italian Renaissance workshop.

Contents: (I) Introduction to techniques; (II) Modelbooks and sketchbooks; (III) The draped figure; (IV) The nude figure; (V) Compositional drawings; (VI) Studies of heads.

Glossary, p.322–23. Biographies of artists, p.324–26. Select bibliography, p.[327]–28.

L74 Art Institute of Chicago. Italian drawings before 1600 in the Art Institute of Chicago: a catalogue of the collection. By Suzanne Folds McCullagh and Laura M. Giles. Chicago, The Art Institute, 1997. xl, 455p. il. (part col.)

Excellent, scholarly catalog of a significant collection.

Concordance, p.405–09. Bibliography, p.411–41. Index of artists, p.443–48. Index of previous owners, p.449–51. Index of related works, p.452–[56].

L75 ———. Italian drawings in the Art Institute of Chicago. [By] Harold Joachim and Suzanne Folds McCullagh. Chicago, Univ. of Chicago Pr., 1979. xvii, 202p. il.

The first of four projected vols. devoted to the collection of drawings owned by the Art Institute of Chicago. Intended as a selective catalog, highlighting the major acquisitions with thorough documentation and discussion of each piece and attempting to put them all in historical context.

Bibliography, p.191–99. Index of artists, p.201–02.

L76 ———. Italian drawings of the 15th, 16th, and 17th centuries. [By] Harold Joachim. Comp. by Suzanne Folds McCullagh and Sandra Haller Olsen. Chicago, Univ. of Chicago Pr., 1979. x, 191p. & microfiche (6 sheets) in pocket (Chicago visual library)

Reproduces the drawings on microfiche, with an elaborate finding aid.

Bibliography, p.173–85. Index, p.187–91.

L77 ———. Italian drawings of the 18th and 19th centuries and Spanish drawings of the 17th through 19th centuries. [By] Harold Joachim. Comp. by Suzanne Folds McCullagh and Sandra Haller Olsen. Chicago, Univ. of Chicago Pr., 1980. viii, 95p. & microfiche (3 sheets) in pocket (Chicago visual library)

"A survey of drawings, watercolors, and pastels on paper in the Department of Prints and Drawings of the Art Institute of Chicago."—*Pref.* Reproduces the drawings on microfiche.

Bibliography, p. 83–92. Index, p.93–95.

L78 Bellezze di Firenze: dessins florentins des XVIIe et XVIIIe siècles du Musée des beaux-arts de Lille. [Catalogue par Marco Chiarini. Trad. par Maria Caracciolo.] Paris, Réunion des musées nationaux, 1992. 215p. il. (part col.)

Catalog of the exhibition, Musée de l'Hospice Comtesse, Lille (1993), of 17th- and 18th-century French drawings from the Musées des beaux-arts de Lille.

Index des artistes, p.209. Bibliographie, p.211–12. Expositions, p.213.

L79 Biblioteca di disegni. Firenze, Alinari, 1976–1981. 29v. (chiefly col. il.)

Limited ed. of 1200 collotype facsimiles of Italian Renaissance and Baroque drawings selected from European and American public and private collections. Introds. and cataloging by noted drawings connoisseurs. Issued in portfolio.

Contents: (1) Maestri lombardi e lombardo-veneti del Rinascimento (introd. and cat. by Ugo Ruggeri); (2) Maestri lombardi del Seicento (introd. and cat. by Ugo Ruggeri); (3–4) Maestri Veneti del Quattrocentro (introd. and cat. by James Byam Shaw; appendix by Ulrich Middeldorf and Antonio Boschetto); (5–6) Maestri veneti del Cinquecento (introd. and cat. by W. R. Rearick); (7) Maestri veneti del Seicento (introd. and cat. by Nicola Ivanoff); (8–9) Maestri veneti del Settecento (introd. and cat. by James Byam Shaw); (10) Maestri genovesi dal Cinque al Settecento (introd. and cat. by Mary Newcome Schleier); (11) Maestri emiliani del Quattro e Cinquecento (introd. by Antonio Boschetto; cat. by Maria Grazia Vaccari); (12) Maestri emiliani del secondo Cinquecento (introd. and cat. by Sylvie Béguin and Mario Di Giampaolo); (13) Maestri emiliani del Sei e Settecento (introd. and cat. by Catherine Johnston); (14) Maestri senesi e marchigiani del Cinquecento (introd. and cat. by Françoise Viatte); (15) Maestri umbri del Quattro e Cinquecento (introd. by Konrad Oberhuber; cat. by Sylvia Ferino); (16) Maestri a Roma nel Cinquecento (introd. and cat. by Anthony Blunt); (17) Maestri toscani del Quattrocento [I] (introd. and cat. by Jeanne K. Cadogan); (18) Maestri toscani del Quattrocento [II] (with an anthology of critical writings from XVII to XX centuries by Ulrich Middeldorf and Antonio Boschetto; cat. by Maria Grazia Vaccari); (19) Maestri toscani del Quattro e primo Cinquecento (introd. and cat. by Luisa Vertova); (20) Maestri toscani del Cinquecento [I] (introd. by John Shearman; cat. by Caroline Coffey); (21) Maestri toscani del Cinquecento [II] (introd. by Anna Forlani Tempesti; cat. by Caroline Coffey); (22) Maestri toscani del Cinquecento [III] (introd. and cat. by Catherine Monbeig Goguel); (23) Maestri toscani del secondo Cinquecento (introd. by Luigi Grassi; cat. by Antonio Boschetto and Caroline Coffey); (24) Maestri del Sei e Settecento toscano (introd. and cat. by Anna Maria Petrioli Tofani); (25) Maestri romani del Sei e Settecento (introd. and cat. by Anthony Blunt); (26) Maestri napoletani del Sei e Settecento (introd. and cat. by Marina Causa Picone); (27) Maestri della caricatura (introd. by Fernando Tempesti; cat. by Laura Corti); (28) Maestri della decorazione e del teatro (introd. and cat. by Anna Maria Petrioli Tofani); [29] Indexes.

Bibliography in each vol. Index of names, v.[29], p.23–64. Index of places [i.e., collections], v.[29], p.65–74. Index of artists and their drawings, v.[29], p.75–121. Inventory numbers of drawings in public collections, v.[29], p.123–36. Iconographic index, v.[29], p.137–50.

L80 Bjurström, Per. Italian drawings: Venice, Brescia, Parma, Milan, Genoa. Stockholm, Nationalmuseum; LiberForlag, 1979. xxii, [210]p. il. (Drawings in Swedish public collections, 3)

See GLAH 1:L2 for previous vols. in this series. "The bulk of [the] contents come from Veneto."—*Foreword.*

Index, p.373–74. Concordance, p.375–76.

L81 British Museum. Dept. of Prints and Drawings. Italian drawings in the Department of Prints and Drawings in the British Museum. London, Published by the Trustees of the British Museum, 1950– . (6)v. in (11). il. plates.

See GLAH 1:L43 for original annotation and previous vols.

Contents: [8]–[9] Artists working in Rome, c1550 to c.1640. By J. A. Gere and Philip Pouncey, with the assist. of Rosalind Wood (2v.; 1983); [10]–[11] Roman Baroque drawings, c.1620 to c.1700. by Nicholas Turner, with the assist. of Rhoda Eitel-Porter (2v.; 1999).

Includes bibliographies, indexes, concordances.

L82 Cazort, Mimi, and Johnston, Catherine. Bolognese drawings in North American collections, 1500–1800. Ottawa, National Gallery of Canada, National Museums of Canada, 1982. 303p. il.

Surveys Bolognese drawings in North America.

Bibliography, p.291–301. Index of artists, p.303.

L83 Coleman, Robert Randolf. Renaissance drawings from the Ambrosiana. Catalog by Robert Randolf Coleman with contrib. by Giulio Bora . . . [et al.] Introd. by Robert R. Coleman and Louis Jordan. Org. by the Medieval Institute, University of Notre Dame. Sponsored by the Samuel H. Kress Foundation, 1984–1985. Notre Dame, Univ. of Notre Dame, 1984. 215p. il.

Catalog of the exhibition, National Gallery of Art, Washington, D.C. (1984), and other locations. A selection of Italian Renaissance drawings, with three German sheets.

Bibliography, p.205–13. Index of artists, p.215.

L84 Czére, Andrea. Disegni di artisti bolognesi nel Museo delle Belle Arti di Budapest. Bologna, Nuova Alfa, 1989. 180p. il. (part col.)

Catalog of the exhibition, San Giorgio in Poggiale (1989), of 83 drawings from the great Hungarian collection.

Indice degli artisti, p.9. Bibliografia, p.173–80.

L85 De Fiore, Gaspare. I modelli di disegno: nella bottega del Rinascimento. Con la pres. di Renato Guttuso. Milano, Fabbri, [1984]. 203p. il. (part col.)

Important study of the role of drawings in the transmission of workshop styles and the training of apprentices in the Italian Renaissance.

Indice, p.[205].

L86 Degenhart, Bernhard. Corpus der italienischen Zeichnungen, 1300–1450 [Bearb.:] Bernhard Degenhart [und] Annegrit Schmitt. Berlin, Mann, 1968– . (12)v. il.

See GLAH 1:L44 for original annotation and previous vols.

Magisterial corpus of Italian drawings of the early Renaissance. The standard work on the subject for years to come.

Contents: Teil 2, Bd.1–4: Venedig; Addenda zu Sud- und Mittelitalien (4v.; 1982); Teil 2, Bd.5–8: Venedig: Jacopo Bellini (4v.; 1990)

Includes bibliographies and indexes (including watermarks).

L87 Dessins bolonais et lombards de la collection Frits Lugt: écoles bolonaise, ferraraise, lombarde, emilienne, génoise et napolitaine, complétées par des lettres autographes. Paris; Florence, Fondation Custodia, 1988. xiv, 76p. il., plates. (Couverture, 25) (Istituto universitario olandese di storia dell'arte, 25)
Catalog of the exhibition of Italian drawings from the Lugt collection now belonging to the Institut néerlandais, Paris, held at the Institut (1988), and other locations.
Index, p.75–76.

L88 Dessins italiens du XVIIe siècle du Musée des Offices de Florence = Italian XVIIth-century drawings from the Uffizi Gallery in Florence. Montréal, Musée des beaux-arts de Montréal, 1986. 311p. il.
Text in French and English. Catalog of the exhibition, Musée des beaux-arts de Montréal (1986), of 80 17th-century Italian drawings from the Uffizi.
Bibliographie, p.306–10.

L89 I disegni di figura nell'Archivio storico dell' Accademia di San Luca. A cura di Angela Cipriani e Enrico Valeriani. Con un saggio di Olivier Michel. Roma, Quasar, 1988– . (3)v. il.
Catalog of figurative drawings from the collection, 17th–18th century, chronologically arranged.
Contents: (1) Concorsi e accademie del secolo XVII; (2) Concorsi e accademie del secolo XVIII (1702–1754); (3, pt. 1) Concorsi e accademie del secolo XVIII (1756–1795).
I concorsi del secolo XVII, v.1, p.195–96. Tabella delle concordanze, v.1, p.197. Indice dei temi, v.2, p.249–52. Indice degli artisti, v.2, p.241–47. Indice dei temi, v.3, p.211–13. Indice degli artisti, v.3, p.205–10.

L90 Disegni emiliani del Rinascimento. A cura di Mario di Giampaolo. Schede: Mario Di Giampaolo, Emilio Negro, Marco Tanzi. Biografie: Andrea Zezza. Coord. ed., Graziano Manni. Milano, Silvana, 1989. 317p. col. il.
Important study of Renaissance drawing in Emilia-Romagna.
Bibliografia, p.309–16. Indice degli artisti, p.317.

L91 Disegni emiliani dei secoli XVII–XVIII della Pinacoteca di Brera. [Mostra e catalogo a cura di Daniele Pescarmona.] Milano, Mazzotta, 1995. 239p. il.
Catalog of the exhibition, Pinacoteca di Brera, Milan (1995). Includes a series of essays on aspects of 17th–18th-century drawings from Emilia.
Bibliografia citata nelle schede, p.234–39.

L92 Disegni emiliani del Sei-Settecento: quadri da stanza e da altare. A cura di Daniele Benati. Introd. di Renato Roli. [Milano], Silvana, 1991. 325p. il. (chiefly col.)
17th–18th-century Emilian drawings related to paintings.
Bibliografia, p.313–25. Indice degli artisti, p.[326].

L93 Disegni genovesi dal Cinquecento al Settecento: giornate di studio (9–10 maggio 1989). Firenze, Ed. Medicea, 1992. 245p. il., map, plates.
At head of title: Kunsthistorisches Institut in Florenz. Proceedings of a symposium devoted to Genoese drawings, published in connection with the exhibition, Gabinetto dei disegni e delle stampe della Galleria degli Uffizi (1989).
Notes at ends of essays.

L94 Disegni lombardi del Cinque e Seicento: della Pinacoteca di Brera e dell' arcivescovado di Milano. [Mostra a cura di Daniele Pescarmona. Testi e schede di Luisa Arrigoni . . . (et al.)] Firenze, Cantini, 1986. 143p. il. (part col.)
Catalog of the exhibition, Pinacoteca di Brera, Milan (1986), of 16th–17th-century Lombard drawings from two principal Milanese collections.
Biografie degli artisti, p.125–32. Bibliografia, p.133–39.

L95 Disegni romani dal XVI al XVIII secolo. A cura di Simonetta Prosperi Valenti Rodinò. Roma, De Luca, 1995. 174p. il. (chiefly col.)
Catalog of the exhibition of drawings from Rome, Gabinetto delle stampe, Rome (1995). The collection of the Gabinetto delle stampe has rarely been exhibited. Includes an essay by the editor.
Filigrane, p.168–71. Bibliografia, p.172–73. Indice degli artisti, p.174.

L96 Disegni veneti della Collezione Lugt. Catalogo della mostra a cura di James Byam Shaw. Pres. di Rodolfo Pallucchini. Introd. di Carlos van Hasselt. Vicenza, N. Pozza, 1981. xix, 135p. il., plates. (Fondazione Giorgio Cini, Venice. Centro di cultura e civiltà. Istituto di storia dell'arte. Cataloghi di mostre, 44)
Catalog of the exhibition, Centro di cultura e civiltà, Vicenza (1981). A selection of Venetian drawings from the great collection of Frits Lugt.
Bibliografia, p.[99]–115. Esposizioni, p.117–23. Indice delle collezioni di provenienza dei disegni esposti, p.127–29. Indice degli artisti e dei luoghi, p.131–34.

L97 Il disegno fiorentino del tempo di Lorenzo il Magnifico. A cura di Annamaria Petrioli Tofani. [Cinisello Balsamo, Italy], Silvana, 1992. 311p. il. (part col.)
Catalog of the exhibition, organized by the Comitato nazionale per le celebrazioni del V centenario della morte di Lorenzo il Magnifico, Galleria degli Uffizi, Florence (1992).
Arranged by themes (models, figure studies, drapery studies, portraits, grotesques, compositional studies, cartoons, scientific drawings, landscape studies, architectural drawings, illustration and prints, Botticelli and Medici culture).
Biografie degli artisti, p.287–97. Bibliografia citata, p.298–306. Tavole delle concordanze, p.307–08. Indice degli artisti, p.309.

L98 Disegno italiano, 1908–1988 = Italienische Zeichnungen 1908–1988. [Katalog, Carlo Bertelli . . . (et al.) Red., Margret Stuffmann, Barbara Winter. Übers., Heide Rohrscheid, Annette Seemann]. Milano, Mazzotta, 1988. 236p. il. (part col.)
Text chiefly in German; some text in Italian. Catalog of the exhibition of 20th-century Italian drawings, Städtische Gal-

erie im Städelschen Kunstinstitut, Frankfurt am Main (1988), and other locations. Includes essays on the relationship between German and Italian art between 1912 and 1930 and on the avant-garde in Italy.

Kurzbiographien mit bibliographischen Hinweisen, p.211–30. Werkverzeichnis, p.231–36.

L99 Disegno italiano del Novecento. Contrib. di Giovanni Anzani, Fabio Benzi, Roberta Bernabei . . . [et al.] Milano, Electa, 1993. 349p. il. (part col.)

Anthology of studies of the role of drawing in 20th-century Italian art, with separate essays on Liberty, Futurism, Abstraction, Expressionism, Arte povera, etc.

Indice dei nomi, p.343–49.

L100 Disegno italiano fra le due guerre. [Catalogo a cura di Pier Giovanni Castagnoli, Paolo Fossati.] [Modena], Panini, [1983]. 399p. il., facsims.

Catalog of the exhibition of Italian drawing between the wars, Galleria Civica, Modena (1983).

Indice degli artisti e delle opere in catalogo, p.395–99.

L101 Dreyer, Peter. The famous Italian drawings in the Berlin Printroom. Italy, Riunione adriatica di sicurta, l'assicuratrice italiana, 1979. 275p. il. (part col.)

Trans. of Kupferstichkabinett Berlin: Italienische Zeichnungen. Stuttgart, Belser Verlag, 1979. "Edition of 400 copies not for sale."

Includes long (94p.) introduction, 60 black-and-white illustrations and 80 color plates, with catalog.

Notes, p.95–98. Bibliography, p.99–105.

L102 École nationale supérieure des beaux-arts (France). Les dessins venitiens des collections de l'École des beaux-arts. Paris, l'École, 1990. xiii, 257p. il.

Catalog of the exhibition of Venetian drawings, École nationale supérieure des beaux-arts (1990). Includes an essay on the taste of French collectors for Venetian drawings.

Index des artistes, p.241–42. Index des museés, p.243. Index des provenances, p.245. Table de concordance, p.247. Expositions, p.249–50. Bibliographie, p.251–56.

L103 Fondation Custodia. Dessins florentins et romains de la collection Frits Lugt: écoles florentine, siennoise, ombrienne et romaine completées par des lettres autographes. Paris, Institut néerlandais, 1984. xiv, 97p. il., 32p. of plates

Catalog of the exhibition of drawings from the collection of Frits Lugt, Institut néerlandais (1984).

Index des artistes, p.95–97.

L104 ______. The Italian drawings of the Frits Lugt collection. By James Byam Shaw. Paris, Institut néerlandais, 1983. 3v. il.

"The present catalogue . . . is the first of an intended series of catalogues raisonnés of all the different sections and aspects of the collection formed by Frits Lugt and his wife over some fifty years."—*Pref.* See GLAH 2:L8 for the catalog of Netherlandish and German drawings.

Contents: (1) Text; (2) Polidoro album; (3) Plates.

Watermarks, v.2, p.119–36. Table of correspondence, v.2, p.137–42. Indexes: artists' names, v.2, p.143–56; previous owners, v.2, p.157–68; related works, v.2, p.169–78; subjects, v.2, p.179. Literature cited in abbreviated form, v.2, p.189–239. Exhibitions and exhibition-related catalogues cited in abbreviated form, v.2, p.241–58.

L105 Gabinetto nazionale delle stampe. I grandi disegni italiani dal Gabinetto nazionale delle stampe di Roma. Testi e commenti di Maria Catelli Isola . . . [et al.] Milano, Silvana, [1981?] 275p. il. (part col.)

Includes long (97p.) introductory text, 63 black-and-white illustrations and 80 color plates, with catalog.

Note, p.98–101. Bibliografia, p.102–06.

L106 Gallerie dell'Accademia di Venezia. Catalogo dei disegni antichi. Coord. Giovanna Nepi Sciré e Francesco Valcanover. Milano, Electa, [1982–]. (15)v. il. (part col.)

Monumental catalog of a great collection, including a history of the collection itself (v.1).

Contents: (1) Storia della collezione dei disegni. Di Giovanna Nepi Sciré; (2) Disegni lombardi. Di Ugo Ruggeri; (4) Disegni del Figino. Di Annalisa Perissa Torrini; (6) Disegni emiliani. Di Mario Di Giampaolo; (7) Disegni umbri. Di Sylvia Ferino Pagden; (8) Disegni romani, toscani e napoletani. Di Simonetta Prosperi Valenti Rodinò; (9) Disegni di Giovan Battista Pittoni. Di Annalisa Perissa Torrini; (15) Disegni di Humbert de Superville. Di Annalisa Perissa Torrini.

Bibliographies and indexes in each vol.

L107 ______. Old master drawings from the Gallerie dell'Accademia Venice. [Ed. by Giovanna Nepi Sciré. Trans. into English by Brian Philips.] Milano, Electa, 1990. 119p. il. (part col.)

Solid catalog of a significant collection of Italian drawings. Includes a history of the collection.

Bibliography, p.116–19.

L108 I Grandi disegni italiani della Collezione Mariette al Louvre di Parigi. Testi e commenti di Roseline Bacou. Milano, Silvana, [1982?]. 277p. il. (part col.)

Trans. from the French.

Reproduces and describes the Italian drawings from the great collection of Pierre-Jean Mariette (1694–1774), now in the Louvre.

Elenco dei disegni italiani della collezione, p.247–62. Bibliografia, p.263–69. Indice della illustrazioni del testo, p.271–74. Indice delle tavole a colori, p.275–77.

L109 I Grandi disegni italiani delle collezioni dell' Ermitage di Leningrado. Testi e commenti di Irina Grigorieva, Asja Kantor-Gukovskja. Milano, Silvana, [1984?]. 259p. il. (part col.)

Trans. from the Russian. The Hermitage collection includes ca. 5,000 Italian drawings.

Bibliografia, p.249–51. Mostre, p.252–53. Indice delle illustrazioni nel testo, p.254–55. Indice delle tavole a colori, p.256–59.

L110 Graphische Sammlung Albertina. Die italienischen Zeichnungen der Albertina: Generalverzeichnis. [By] Veronika Birke, Janine Kertész. Wien, Böhlau, 1992– . (4)v. il. (Veröffentlichungen der Albertina, Bd. 33–35)

The standard, magisterial catalog of the great Viennese collection.

Contents: (1) Inv. 1–1200; (2) Inv. 1201–2400; (3) Inv. 2401–14325; (4) Inv. 14326–42255.

Includes bibliographies, concordances, lists of alternative attributions, indexes.

L111 Griswold, William, and Wolk-Simon, Linda. Sixteenth-century Italian drawings in New York collections. N.Y., Metropolitan Museum of Art, 1994. xii, 270p. il. (part col.)

Catalog of the exhibition, Metropolitan Museum of Art (1994), of 120 drawings. "The drawings in this exhibition are from three New York institutions—the Metropolitan Museum of Art, the Pierpont Morgan Library, and the Cooper-Hewitt Museum—as well as more than twenty private collections."—*Introd.* Arrangement by region.

References cited in abbreviated form, p.xii. Index of artists, p.269–70.

L112 Hessisches Landesmuseum Darmstadt. Genueser Zeichnungen des 16. bis 18. Jahrhunderts im Hessischen Landesmuseum Darmstadt. Mit einem Anhang: Genueser Zeichnungen in der Stiftung Kunsthaus Heylshof Worms. Hrsg. vom Hessischen Landesmuseum Darmstadt. [Red., Peter Märker und die Autoren.] Darmstadt, Hessisches Landesmuseum Darmstadt, 1990. 224p. il. (Kataloge des Hessischen Landesmuseums Darmstadt, 15)

Scholarly catalog of Genoese drawings in the collection.

Literaturverzeichnis, p.211–18. Künstlerregister, p.219. Konkordanzen, p.220–23.

L113 ______. Neapolitanische Barockzeichnungen in der Graphischen Sammlung des Hessischen Landesmuseums Darmstadt. Bearb. von Jan Simane. Darmstadt, Das Landesmuseum, 1994. 118p. il. (part col.)

Catalog of Neapolitan Baroque drawings in the collection, intended to address a growing interest in this field.

Includes bibliographical references. Abgekürzt zitierte Literatur, p.117–18.

L114 Jaffé, Michael. The Devonshire collection of Italian drawings. London, Phaidon, 1994. 4v. il. (part col.)

Magnificent catalog of a great private collection that consisted of perhaps 1,000 drawings, "approximately half the total number of drawings now traceable to the historic collection."—*Pref.*

Contents: (1) Tuscan and Umbrian schools; (2) Roman and Neapolitan school; (3) Bolognese and Emilian schools; (4) Venetian and North Italian schools.

Each vol. includes: Notes on collectors' marks, Select bibliography, List of exhibitions, Concordance, Index of artists, Index of works, General index.

L115 Loisel-Legrand, Catherine. Le dessin à Bologne, 1580–1620: la réforme des trois Carracci. Avec la collab. de Varena Forcione. Paris, Réunion des museés nationaux, 1994. 159p. il. (part col.)

Published on the occasion of the important exhibition of Bolognese drawings, Cabinet des dessins, Musée du Louvre (1994).

Table des ouvrages cités en abrégé, p.153–57. Index des collectionneurs, p.158. Expositions, p.159.

L116 Maiskaia, M. I. (Marina Ivanovna). I grandi disegni italiani del Museo Puskin di Mosca. Testi e commenti di Marina Maiskaja. [Trad. dal testo originale russo di Marussia Galmozzi Cremaschi.] Milano, Silvana, 1986. 262p. il. (part col.)

Includes long (75p.) introductory text, 60 black-and-white illustrations, 80 color plates, with catalog.

Note, p.76–77. Bibliografia, p.241–48.

L117 Musée des beaux-arts de Rennes. Disegno: les dessins italiens du Musée de Rennes: catalogue de l'exposition suivi d'un inventaire de la collection. [Coord. du catalogue, Patrick Ramade.] [Rennes], France, Le Musée, 1990. 253p. il. (part col.)

Catalog of the exhibition, Galleria Estense, Modena (1990), and other locations, with 91 catalog entries and color plates.

Inventaire des dessins italiens, p.197–239. Ouvrages cités en abrégé, p.243–47. Expositions cités en abrégé, p.248. Index des artistes exposés, p.249.

L118 Museum of Fine Arts, Boston. Italian drawings in the Museum of Fine Arts, Boston. By Hugh Macandrew. Boston, The Museum, 1983. 99p. il.

Scholarly catalog, "intended as the first volume of a complete catalogue of the museum's European drawings."—*Foreword.*

Concordance, p.97. Index of artists, p.97.

L119 Negri Arnoldi, Francesco, and Prosperi Valenti, Simonetta. Il disegno nella storia dell'arte italiana. Roma, La Nuova Italia scientifica, 1986. 319p. il. (Studi superiori NIS, 16)

Important manual providing an overview of the role of drawing in Italian artistic practice from a technical, formal, and critical perspective. Valuable classified bibliography of primary and secondary sources, including watermarks, collection inventories, exhibition catalogs, etc.

Contents: Parte prima: Il disegno dell'antichità: (1) Il disegno come technica, come pratica, come idea; (2) Le applicazioni del disegno e le tecniche derivate nel mondo antico e nel Medioevo; (3) Il disegno nel processo di rinnovamento dell'arte italiana; (4) I centri, le scuole, gli artisti; Parte seconda: Gli sviluppi del disegno dal Sei al Novecento: (5) Nuovi interessi e nuove problematiche nel disegno tra Sei e Settecento; (6) Il disegno nell'Otto e Novecento; (7) I centri, le scuole, gli artisti.

Glossario, p.297–300. Bibliografia generale, p.301–12. Indice dei nomi, p.313–19.

L120 New York. Metropolitan Museum of Art. Eighteenth century Italian drawings from the Robert Lehman

Collection of the Metropolitan Museum of Art. Introd. by Agnes Mongan. Catalogue by George Szabo. Org. and circulated by the International Exhibitions Foundation, Washington, D.C., 1983–1984. Washington, D.C., The Foundation, 1983. xi, 135p. il.

"The present exhibition makes it possible for us to become acquainted with the wide-ranging technical skills and the imaginative richness of Italian draftsmen of the eighteenth century."—*Introd.*

Bibliography, p.133–34.

L121 ______. Eighteenth century Italian drawings, from the Robert Lehman Collection: catalogue. By George Szabo. N.Y., The Museum, 1981. ca. 200p. il.

Catalog of 184 drawings from the great collection, reproduced in sepia. "The most extensive in the series intended to show all the drawings in the Robert Lehman Collection."—*Introd.*

Works abbreviated, [p.195–96].

L122 ______. 18th century Italian drawings in the Metropolitan Museum of Art. [By] Jacob Bean and William Griswold. N.Y., The Museum (Distr. by Abrams, 1990). 288p. il.

Describes and reproduces "all drawings in the collection that we feel may be plausibly attributed to known artists of the period."—*Pref.*

Index of former collections, p.283–85. Concordance, p.286–87. Index of artists, p.288.

L123 ______. 15th and 16th century Italian drawings in the Metropolitan Museum of Art. [By] Jacob Bean with the assist. of Lawrence Turčić. N.Y., The Museum, 1982. 330p. il.

Describes and reproduces "all the drawings in our collection that I feel can be plausibly attributed to known artists of the period."—*Pref.* Does not include the drawings in the Robert Lehman Collection. Includes an appendix listing 17th-century Italian drawings acquired since 1978.

Works cited in abbreviated form, p.9–13. Index of former owners, p.323–26. Concordance, p.327–28. Index of artists, p.329–30.

L124 ______. 17th century Italian drawings in the Metropolitan Museum of Art. [By] Jacob Bean. N.Y., The Museum (Distr. by Abrams, 1979). 299p. il.

Describes and reproduces "all drawings in the collection that I feel can be plausibly attributed to known artists of the period."—*Pref.*

Index of former owners, p.291–94. Concordance, p.295–97. Index of artists, p.298–99.

L125 Olson, Roberta J. M. Italian drawings, 1780–1890. N.Y., American Federation of Arts; Bloomington, Indiana Univ. Pr., 1980. 247p. il. (AFA exhibition, 80.2)

Catalog of the exhibition, National Gallery of Art, Washington, D.C. (1980), and other locations. "This exhibition is the first comprehensive, panoramic consideration of Italian nineteenth-century draftsmanship (or any art of the period) in the United States. [It] has two primary purposes, to define and to illuminate the multiple artistic trends operative between 1780 and 1890 in Italy and to present and to publish nineteenth-century Italian drawings in American collections (supplemented by important loans from several Italian museums)."—*Pref.*

Introductory essay of 22 pages is followed by plates and catalog entries (including descriptive and contextual information) for 102 drawings by 63 artists, each of whom is introduced with a few biographical paragraphs, along with two or three significant bibliographical citations.

Selected bibliography, p.241–44. Index, p.245.

L126 Olszewski, Edward J. The draftsman's eye: late Italian Renaissance schools and styles. With the assist. of Jane Glaubinger. Cleveland, Cleveland Museum of Art in coop. with the Indiana Univ. Pr., 1981. x, 177p. il.

Catalog of the exhibition, Cleveland Museum of Art (1979). "This study . . . provides an opportunity to introduce to the general public as well as to scholars a group of fine drawings never before shown together. The forty-seven Cleveland drawings are presented in the larger context of seventy-eight drawings borrowed from other American collections."—*Pref.* Arranged by region.

Bibliography, p.157–66. Provenance index, p.167–68. Index, p.169–77.

L127 Paris. Musée National du Louvre. Cabinet des Dessins. Inventaire général des dessins italiens. Paris. Éd. des Musées Nationaux, 1972– . (4)v. il.

See GLAH 1:L56 for original annotation and previous vols. Recent vols. published by the Réunion des musées nationaux.

Contents: (3) Viatte, Françoise. Dessins toscans XVIe–XVIIIe siècles ([1]v.; 1988–); (5) Cordellier, Dominique, and Py, Bernadette. Raphaël, son atelier, ses copistes (1992).

L128 Perez Sanchez, Alfonso E. I grandi disegni italiani nelle collezioni di Madrid. Milano, Silvana, [1978]. 264p. il.

Catalog of Italian drawings in Madrid collections.

Indice delle illustrazioni nel testo, p.257–60. Indice delle tavole a colori, p.261–64.

L129 Petrioli Tofani, Annamaria, and Smith, Graham. Sixteenth-century Tuscan drawings from the Uffizi. N.Y., Oxford Univ. Pr. in assoc. with the Detroit Institute of Arts, 1988. xix, 250p. col. il.

Catalog of the exhibition, Detroit Institute of Arts (1988–89). "The drawings of this exhibition are not only representative of the different types of drawings utilized in the sixteenth century, but they also illustrate the varied activities in which cinquecento artists engaged."—*Introd.*

Bibliography, p.231–46. Index, p.247–50.

L130 Pignatti, Terisio. Disegni antichi del Museo Correr di Venezia: catalogo. A cura di Terisio Pignatti. Vicenza, Pozza, 1980– . (5)v. il. (Fondazione Giorgio Cini, Venice. Centro di cultura e civiltà. Istituto di

storia dell'arte. Cataloghi di raccolte d'arte; nuova ser., 13, 15, 18, 20, 21)
Catalog of old master drawings in a distinguished collection.
Contents: (1) Aliense-Crosato; (2) Dall'Oglio-Fontebasso; (3) Galimberti-Guardi; (4) Guercino-Longhi; (5) Loth-Rubens.
Includes bibliographies, concordances, and indexes (names, places, titles).

L131 Rijksmuseum (Amsterdam, Netherlands). Italian drawings from the Rijksmuseum Amsterdam. Ed. by Bert W. Meijer. [Trans., Peter Spring]. Florence, Centro Di, 1995. 190p. il. (part col.) (Italia e i Paesi Bassi. Cataloghi, 4)
Catalog of the exhibition, Rijksmuseum, Amsterdam (1996), and other locations.
Bibliography, p.171–84. Exhibitions and exhibition catalogs, p.185–89. Index of artists, p.190.

L132 Roberts, Jane. Italian master drawings: Leonardo to Canaletto: from the British Royal Collection. London, Collins Harvill, 1987. [149]p. il. (part col.)
Catalog of the exhibition, National Gallery of Art, Washington, D.C. (1987), and other locations. A representative selection from the 30,000 old master and modern drawings at Windsor Castle, including "most of the great masters of Italian draughtsmanship."—*Foreword.*
List of works referred to in abbreviated form, p.20. Index of artists, p.149.

L133 Staatliche Museen zu Berlin—Preussischer Kulturbesitz. Kupferstichkabinett—Sammlung der Zeichnungen und Druckgraphik. Die italienischen Zeichnungen des 14. und 15. Jahrhunderts im Berliner Kupferstichkabinett: kritischer Katalog. [By] Hein-Th. Schulze Altcappenberg. Berlin, G & H Verlag, 1995. 339p. il. (part col.)
Critical catalog of the exhibition of selections from the Staatliche Museen zu Berlin's permanent collection (1995–96).
Künstlerregister (Bestandsverzeichnis), p.314–19. Konkordanz, p.320–25. Register der abweichender Zuschreibungen, p.326. Register der Vorbesitzer (Provenienzen), p.327. Bibliographie, p.328–39.

L134 Städtische Galerie im Städelschen Kunstinstitut Frankfurt am Main. Italienische Zeichnungen des 15. und 16. Jahrhunderts aus eigenen Beständen. Bearb. von Lutz S. Malke. Frankfurt am Main, Städel, 1980. 195p. il. (part col.)
Catalog of the exhibition, Städelsches Kunstinstitut und Städtische Galerie, Frankfurt am Main (1980), of selections from an outstanding collection of Italian drawings.
Abgekürzt zitierte Literatur, p.194.

L135 Szabo, George. Masterpieces of Italian drawing in the Robert Lehman Collection, the Metropolitan Museum of Art. N.Y., Hudson Hills Pr. (Distr. in the U.S. by Viking Penguin, 1983). xii, 243p. il. (part col.)
Catalog of 80 drawings from the great collection, many reproduced in color.
Bibliography for the introduction, p.73. Bibliography, p.237–43.

L136 Turner, Nicholas. Florentine drawings of the sixteenth century. London, British Museum Pubs., 1986. 272p. il. (part col.)
Catalog of the important exhibition, British Museum (1986).
List of works referred to in abbreviated form, p.267–69. Concordance, p.270–71. Index of artists, p.272.

L137 ______. Italian Baroque drawings. London, British Museum Pubs., 1980. 151p. il. (British Museum prints and drawings series)
"The collection of Italian Baroque drawings in the Department of Prints and Drawings of the British Museum . . . is unusually representative, including choice examples of most of the greatest artists of the period."—*Introd.* Brief introductory essay providing historical survey is followed by 65 plates illustrating the work of 42 artists, grouped geographically, with catalog information and commentary arranged on facing pages.
Contents: Roman drawings; Bolognese drawings; Florentine drawings; Genoese drawings; Venetian drawings; Neapolitan drawings.
List of works referred to in abbreviated form, p.150. Index of artists, p.151.

L138 ______. The study of Italian drawings: the contribution of Philip Pouncey. With an introd. by J. A. Gere. London, British Museum Pr., 1994. 127p. il.
"Catalogue of Italian drawings from the fifteenth to the eighteenth century, mostly from the British Museum," documenting the two decades Pouncey spent there cataloging the Italian drawings.—*Back cover.*
Bibliography, p.120–24. Concordances, p.126. Index of artists, p.127.

L139 Victoria and Albert Museum, London. Dept. of Prints and Drawings. Italian drawings. [By] Peter Ward-Jackson. London, HMSO, 1979–80. 2v. il.
Catalog of the collection.
Contents: (1) 14th–16th century; (2) 17th–18th century.
Bibliography, v.1, p.257–60, v.2, p.211–14. Includes concordances as well as indexes of artists, attributions, previous owners, locations of related works, selected subjects.

L140 Windsor Castle. Royal Library. The Italian drawings at Windsor Castle. London, Phaidon [1948]– . (12)v. in 14. il., plates.
See GLAH 1:L60 for original annotation and previous vols. in this essential series. Publisher varies. Complete illustrations of the drawings cataloged in this series have been published on microfilm: London, Mindata, 1982– . (Old master drawings in the Royal Library, Windsor)
Contents: Kurz, Otto. Bolognese drawings of the XVII & XVIII centuries in the collection of Her Majesty the Queen at Windsor Castle. With a new appendix to the catalogue by Henrietta McBurney (Bologna, Nuova Alfa Ed., 1988); Mahon, Denis. The drawings of Guercino in the collection of Her Majesty the Queen at Windsor Castle (N.Y., Cambridge

Univ. Pr., 1989); Parker, K. T. (Karl Theodore). The drawings of Antonio Canaletto in the collection of Her Majesty the Queen at Windsor Castle. With an appendix to the catalogue by Charlotte Crawley. (Bologna, Nuova Alfa Ed., 1990).

SEE ALSO: Sciolla, Il disegno (GLAH 2:L4); Museo del Prado. Catálogo de dibujos (GLAH 2:L21).

Latin America

L141 Recent Latin American drawings, 1969–1976: lines of vision. Essays by Barbara Duncan and Damián Bayón. Catalogue entries by Ana M. Casciero. Washington, D.C., International Exhibitions Foundation, 1977. 79p. il.

Exhibition organized and circulated by International Exhibitions Foundation, 1977–1978.

"A visual essay on contemporary Latin American drawing." Includes biographical information on the 100 artists represented in the exhibition, as well as an illustration for each work exhibited.

L142 Stofflet, Mary. Latin American drawings today. With essays by Shifra M. Goldman . . . [et al.] [San Diego], San Diego Museum of Art (Distr. by the Univ. of Washington Pr., 1991). 109p. il. (part col.)

Catalog of the exhibition, San Diego Museum of Art (1991), of contemporary Latin American drawing.

Bibliography, p.108–09.

Low Countries

L143 The Age of Bruegel: Netherlandish drawings in the sixteenth century. [By] John Oliver Hand . . . [et al.] Washington, D.C., National Gallery of Art, 1986. xii, 339p. il. (1 col.)

Catalog of the exhibition, National Gallery of Art (1986–87), and other locations, of 123 drawings. "The first major exhibition in the United States devoted solely to the achievement of sixteenth-century draftsmen of the Low Countries."—*Dir. foreword.*

Contents: The sixteenth century, by John Oliver Hand; Jan Gossaert and the new aesthetic, by J. Richard Judson; The functions of drawings in the Netherlands in the sixteenth century, by William W. Robinson and Martha Wolff; Catalogue; Note to the reader.

References cited, p.313–39.

L144 Bisanz-Prakken, Marian. Drawings from the Albertina: landscape in the age of Rembrandt. With a pref. by Konrad Oberhuber. 1st English ed., rev. Alexandria, Va., Art Services International, 1995. 212p. il.

Trans. of Landschaft im Jahrhundert Rembrandts: Niederlandische Zeichnungen des 17. Jahrhunderts aus der Graphischen Sammlung Albertina. Wien, Albertina, 1993.

Catalog of the exhibition, Drawing Center, New York (1995), and other locations.

References, p.201–11. Index of artists, p.212.

L145 Bolten, J. Method and practice: Dutch and Flemish drawing books, 1600–1750. Landau, Pfalz, PVA, 1985. 373p. il.

"The objective of this book is to provide information on Dutch and Flemish drawing books published between 1600 and 1750. . . . This study is the first on this subject."—*Foreword.* Describes the drawing books and seeks to place their contents in the context of art theory of the period. "Translated, expanded and partially revised version of a dissertation" completed in 1979.

Notes, p.285–327. Bibliography, p.335–58. Register of names, p.359–73.

L146 British Museum. Drawings by Rembrandt and his circle in the British Museum. [By] Martin Royalton-Kisch. London, British Museum Pr., 1992. 248p. il. (part col.)

Catalog of the exhibition, British Museum (1992).

Bibliography and abbreviations, p.230–38. Indexes: Related drawings in other collections, p.239–46; Former owners, p.246. Concordances: British Museum register numbers; Hind . . . and Benesch . . . , p.247–48.

L147 Catalogue of the Dutch and Flemish drawings in the Rijksprentenkabinet, Rijksmuseum, Amsterdam = Catalogus van de Nederlandse tekeningen in het Rijksmuseum te Amsterdam. 's-Gravenhage, Algemeene Landsdrukkerij, 1942– . (6)v. il. (part col.)

Publisher varies; title varies. Catalog of the principal collection.

Contents: (1) Henkel, Max Dilmar. Teekeningen van Rembrandt en zijn school (1942); (2) Boon, K. G. Netherlandish drawings of the fifteenth and sixteenth centuries (1978); (3) Schapelhouman, Marijn. Netherlandish drawings circa 1600 (1987); (4) Schatborn, Peter. Tekeningen van Rembrandt, zijn onbekende leerlingen en navolgers = Drawings by Rembrandt, his anonymous pupils and followers (1985); (5, pt.1–2) Kettering, Alison McNeil. Drawings from the Ter Borch Studio estate (2v.; 1988); (6) Dutch drawings of the seventeenth century in the Rijksmuseum, Amsterdam: artists born between 1580 and 1600 (2v.; 1998).

L148 Duparc, F. J. Landscape in perspective: drawings by Rembrandt and his contemporaries. Montreal, Montreal Museum of Fine Arts, 1988. 246p. il. (part col.), map.

Catalog of the exhibition, Arthur M. Sackler Museum, Harvard University (1988), and other locations. Valuable selection of Dutch landscape studies.

Exhibitions cited, p.234–38. Bibliography, p.239–43. Index of former owners, p.244–46.

L149 Hamburger Kunstshalle. Rembrandt und sein Jahrhundert: niederländische Zeichnungen in der Hamburger Kunsthalle. [Ausstellung und Katalog, Eckhard Schaar.] [Hamburg], Hamburger Kunsthalle; Heidelberg, Braus, [1994]. 196p. il. (part col.)

Catalog of the exhibition, Hamburger Kunsthalle (1994–95), of 130 drawings, held on the occasion of the 125th anniversary of the Kunsthalle.

Bibliographie, p.194–96.

L150 Hessisches Landesmuseum Darmstadt. Landschaftszeichnungen der Niederländer: 16. und 17. Jahrhundert aus der graphischen Sammlung des Hessischen Landesmuseums Darmstadt. Bearb. von Jan Simane und Peter Märker. Darmstadt, Das Landesmuseum, 1992. 191p. il. (part col.)

Catalog of the exhibition, Hessisches Landesmuseum Darmstadt (1992), documenting the collection of Dutch landscape drawings of the golden age.

Künstlerverzeichnis, p.189. Literatur, p.190–91.

L151 ———. Niederländische Zeichnungen 16. Jahrhundert im Hessischen Landesmuseum Darmstadt. Bearb. von Gisela Bergstrasser. Darmstadt, Roether, 1979. 206p. il. (part col.) (Kataloge des Hessischen Landesmuseums Darmstadt, 10)

"Erschienen als Beiheft zu Heft 18/19 der Zeitschrift Kunst in Hessen und am Mittelrhein." Catalog of 16th-century Netherlandish drawings in the collection.

Abkürzungen, p.10. Wasserzeichen, p.199–203. Konkordanz, p.205. Künstlerregister, p.206.

L152 Kassel. Staatliche Kunstsammlungen. Kupferstichkabinett. Niederländische Zeichnungen des 16. bis 18. Jahrhunderts. Bearb. von Lisa Oehler. Fridingen, Graf Klenau, 1979. 127p. il. (1 col.) (Kassel. Staatliche Kunstsammlungen. Kupferstichkabinett. Kataloge, 1)

Catalog of a significant, little-known collection.

Summary in English, p.10–12. Verzeichnis der Literatur-Abkürzungen, p.127.

L153 Pierpont Morgan Library. Rubens and Rembrandt in their century: Flemish and Dutch drawings of the seventeenth century from the Pierpont Morgan Library. [By] Felice Stampfle. N.Y., The Library; Oxford Univ. Pr., 1979. 298p. il.

"This volume contains one hundred thirty Flemish and Dutch drawings of the golden century. . . . This is the first survey from the Morgan Library of any of the European schools of draughtsmanship represented in its collection, with essays, full provenances, and bibliographical references for each of the drawings. It is published on the occasion of a series of exhibitions of these drawings in Paris, Antwerp, London, and New York."—*Foreword.* An exemplary catalog.

Index of artists, p.293. Index of former owners, p.294–98. Watermarks, p.[301]–[19].

L154 Staatliche Graphische Sammlung München. Niederlandische Zeichnungen des 16. Jahrhunderts in der Staatlichen Graphischen Sammlung München. [Katalog: Holm Bevers.] [München], Staatliche Graphische Sammlung München, [1989]. 219p. il. (part col.)

Catalog of the exhibition of 16th-century Netherlandish drawings, Staatliche Graphische Sammlung München (1989–90).

Includes bibliographical references.

L155 Vignau Wilberg-Schuurman, Thea. Das Land am Meer: holländische Landschaft im 17. Jahrhundert. München, Hirmer, 1993. 221p. il. (part col.)

Catalog of the exhibition, Staatliche Graphische Sammlung München (1993), and other locations. Catalog of a significant collection of Dutch landscape drawings of the golden age, organized thematically.

Abkürzungen, Photonachweis, p.208–09. Wasserzeichen, p.210–12. Bibliographie, p.213–18. Register, p.219–21.

L156 Wallraf-Richartz-Museum. Graphische Sammlung. Niederländische Zeichnungen vom 15. bis 19. Jahrhundert im Wallraf- Richartz-Museum Koln. Von Hella Robels. Köln, Das Museum, 1983. 279p. il. (part col.) (Kataloge des Wallraf-Richartz-Museums Graphische Sammlung, 1)

Catalog of a largely unpublished collection.

Verzeichnis der abgekürzt zitierten Literatur, p.271–73. Künstlerregister, p.274–75. Konkordanzliste, p.276–79.

L157 White, Christopher, and Crawley, Charlotte. The Dutch and Flemish drawings of the fifteenth to the early nineteenth centuries in the collection of Her Majesty the Queen at Windsor Castle. N.Y., Cambridge Univ. Pr., 1994. 548p. il.

Spine title: Dutch and Flemish drawings at Windsor Castle . . . . Supersedes earlier catalogs of the collection by Leo van Puyvelde: Flemish drawings . . . , London, Phaidon, 1942; Dutch drawings . . . , London, Phaidon, 1944.

"Superbly written, illustrated, indexed, and produced, the [present] catalogue is the culmination of many years of research and will be widely welcomed and used."—*Review*, Burlington magazine, v.138, March 1996, p.196.

Complete illustrations of the Dutch and Flemish drawings at Windsor Castle have been published on microfilm: Bath, Mindata, 1991, in the series, Old master drawings in the Royal Library, Windsor.

SEE ALSO: Fondation Custodia. The Netherlandish and German drawings of the XVth and XVIth centuries of the Frits Lugt collection (GLAH 2:L8); Paris. Musée National du Louvre. Cabinet des dessins. Inventaire général des dessins des écoles du nord: écoles allemande, des Anciens Pays-Bas, flamande, hollandaise et suisse, XVe–XVIIIe siècles (GLAH 2:L22).

Scandinavia

L158 Disegni di maestri danesi nel Museo nazionale di San Martino a Napoli. Catalogo a cura di Minna Heimburger. Firenze, Olschki, 1990. 173p. il., plates.

Catalog of a little-known collection of 19th-century Danish drawings.

Bibliografia, p.17. Indice degli artisti, p.169–70.

L159 Norregard-Nielsen, Hans Edvard. The golden age of Danish art: drawings from the Royal Museum of Fine Arts, Copenhagen. Alexandria, Va.: Art Services International, 1995. 255p. col. il.
Published as a companion to the exhibition of the same name, devoted to Danish drawings of the Romantic era, organized and circulated by Art Services International.
Select bibliography, p.252–53. Index, p.254–55.

Spain and Portugal

L160 Angulo Iñiguez, Diego. A corpus of Spanish drawings. By Diego Angulo & Alfonso E. Perez Sanchez. [Trans. from the Spanish by Nicholas Wyndham and Theodore Crombie.] Boston, New York Graphic Society, [1975]– . (4)v. plates.
See GLAH 1:L72 for previous vols. and original annotation.
Contents: (3) Seville, 1600–1650; (4) Valencia, 1600–1700.
Each vol. includes bibliographies and indexes of locations, themes, works of art, as well as a general index.

SEE ALSO: Art Institute of Chicago. Italian drawings of the 18th and 19th centuries and Spanish drawings of the 17th through 19th centuries (GLAH 2:L77); Museo del Prado. Catálogo de dibujos (GLAH 2:L21).

United States

L161 Adams, Henry, and Stenz, Margaret. American drawings and watercolors from the Kansas City Region. With Jan M. Marsh . . . [et al.] Kansas City, Mo., Nelson-Atkins Museum of Art, 1992. 495p. il. (part col.)
Catalog of the exhibition, Nelson-Atkins Museum of Art (1992).
Substantial, thematically arranged catalog that includes works from the Nelson-Atkins collection as well as works from the University of Kansas' Spencer Museum of Art.
American drawings and watercolors in the Nelson-Atkins Museum of Art, p.335–98. American drawings and watercolors in the Spencer Museum of Art, p.399–484. Index of artists, p.494–95.

L162 Carnegie Institute. Museum of Art. American drawings and watercolors in the Museum of Art, Carnegie Institute. Introd. by Henry Adams. Contrib. by Henry Adams . . . [et al.] Pittsburgh, The Museum (Distr. by the University of Pittsburgh Press, 1985). 314p. il. (part col.)
Catalog of a significant collection.
Includes bibliographical references throughout. Collection checklist, p.243–313. Index to artists: chapters 1–7, p.314.

L163 Corcoran Gallery of Art. American drawings, watercolors, pastels, and collages in the collection of the Corcoran Gallery of Art. By Linda Crocker Simmons. With the assist. of Adrianne J. Humphrey . . . [et al.] [Photographed by Robert Grove.] Washington, D.C., The Gallery, 1983. xii, 278p. il.
Illustrated checklist of this important collection.
Index of artists, p.271–76. Index of donors, p.277–78.

L164 Lee, Pamela M., and Mehring, Christine. "Drawing is another kind of language": recent American drawings from a New York private collection. With an essay by Dieter Schwarz and contrib. by Christian Schneegass, Julie Vicinus. Cambridge, Mass., Harvard University Art Museums; Stuttgart, Daco-Verlag Gunter Blase, 1997. 230p. il. (part col.)
Substantial, well-illustrated catalog of the exhibition of works from an anonymous private collection, Arthur M. Sackler Museum, Harvard University (1997–98), and other locations.
Index of artists, p.229.

L165 Munson-Williams-Proctor Institute. Life lines: American master drawings, 1788–1962 from the Munson-Williams-Proctor Institute. By Mary E. Murray, Paul D. Schweizer. With contrib. by Ross C. Anderson . . . [et al.] Utica, N.Y., Museum of Art, Munson-Williams-Proctor Institute, 1994. 160p. il. (part col.)
Catalog of the collection, published in conjunction with the exhibition (1994). 58 works are cataloged.
Index of artists, p.160.

L166 Wadsworth Atheneum. American drawings and watercolors from the Wadsworth Atheneum. By Judith A. Barter. With an introd. by Eugene R. Gaddis. N.Y., Hudson Hills in assoc. with the American Federation of Arts, 1987. 94p. il. (part col.)
A selection of works from the collection, mostly illustrations.
Bibliography, p.91–93. Index of artists, p.94.

L167 Whitney Museum of American Art. 20th-century drawings from the Whitney Museum of American Art. [Sel. by Paul Cummings.] N.Y., Whitney Museum of American Art, 1987. 176p. il. (part col.)
Catalog published to accompany the exhibition, Whitney Museum of American Art (1987). The collection embodies a recently developed collecting agenda, almost fifty percent of the works exhibited having been acquired since 1977.
Selected bibliography, p.168–76.

ASIAN COUNTRIES

India, Nepal, Pakistan, Tibet

L168 Welch, Stuart Cary. Indian drawings and painted sketches, 16th through 19th centuries. [N.Y.], Asia Society, 1976. 142p. il. (part col.)
Catalog of the exhibition, Asia House Gallery, New York (1976), the first significant exhibition of its kind.

Contents: Catalogue and plates: Folk and traditional art; Mughal art; British Indian art; Deccani art; Rajput art.
Selected bibliography, p.140–42.

L169 India Office Library. Company drawings in the India Office Library. [Catalogue by] Mildred Archer. London, Her Majesty's Stationery Office, 1972. 298p. 78 il. (4 col.)
"Lists and describes drawings made by Indians for British and other European patrons and clients. . . . The Library's collection [is] the largest and most comprehensive in the world, with some 2,750 drawings spanning the entire history of Company painting."—*Pref.*
Concordances, p.278–82. Indexes, p.283–98.

L170 Indian drawing. The exhibition chosen by Howard Hodgkin. Introd. by Terence McInerney. [London], Arts Council of Great Britain, 1983. ix, [1]p. il. (part col.), 52p. of plates.
Catalog of the exhibition, Hayward Gallery (1983), and other locations, of works from Howard Hodgkin's important collection.
Bibliography, p.[x]

AFRICA, OCEANIA, THE AMERICAS

The Americas

L171 Plains Indian drawings, 1865–1935: pages from a visual history. Ed. by Janet Catherine Berlo. N.Y., Abrams in assoc. with the American Federation of Arts and the Drawing Center, 1996. 240p. il. (part col.)
Catalog of the exhibition, The Drawing Center, New York (1996), and other locations.
A major study. Includes artists' statements.
Bibliography, p.224–31. About the contributors, p.232–33. Index, p.234–40.

M. Painting

Works concerning the history and technique of painting are listed and described in this chapter, in addition to significant collection catalogs. Entries for dictionaries, encyclopedias, and exhibition catalogs are listed with general literature, periods, or styles, and with specific countries or regions. Books on mosaics have been classified in this chapter. General collection catalogs are listed under Collections and Inventories; specialized collection catalogs will be found under the appropriate geographical or period headings.

COLLECTIONS AND INVENTORIES

M1 Akademie der Bildenden Künste in Wien. Gemäldegalerie. Gemäldegalerie der Akademie der Bildenden Künste in Wien: illustriertes Bestandsverzeichnis. Bearb. und Zusammenstell., Renate Trnek. Wien, Die Gemäldegalerie, 1989. 363p. chiefly il.

Illustrated handbook of the collection.

Verzeichnis des Gesamtbestandes einschliesslich aller Verluste und Abgänge in numerischer Abfolge der Inventarnummern und mit Angabe des Standortes, p.281–347. Alphabetisches Verzeichnis aller Künstlernamen, p.349–62. Verzeichnis der geänderten Zuschreibungen, p.[364–66].

M2 Alexander, J. J. G., and Temple, Elzbieta. Illuminated manuscripts in Oxford College libraries, the University Archives, and the Taylor Institution. N.Y., Clarendon Pr., 1985. xv, 142p. il., plates.

"Compiled as a complement to three catalogues [of the Bodleian Library collection] by Otto Pächt and J.J.G. Alexander published between 1966 and 1973" (see GLAH 1:M8).

Concordance of college shelf-marks, p.107–09. Index of other manuscripts and printed books cited, p.110–11. Dated or datable manuscripts, p.112. Index of texts and authors, p.113–15. Index of persons, mainly owners, p.118–24. Index of coats of arms, p.125. Index of mottoes, p.126. Index of places, p.127–29.

M3 Amsterdam. Rijksmuseum. All the paintings of the Rijksmuseum in Amsterdam, a completely illustrated catalogue. First supplement: 1976–91. By the Department of Paintings of the Rijksmuseum; Pieter J. J. van Thiel . . . [et al.] With a foreword by Henk W. Van Os, Director-General. Amsterdam, Rijksmuseum, 1992. 140p. il.

Supplements GLAH 1:M2. Includes "not only the new paintings that have entered the collection since 1976, but also a mass of data supplementing or correcting the entries in the complete catalogue."—*Foreword.*

Subject index, p.128–33. Index of provenances, p.133–34. New information on objects mentioned in the 1976 catalogue, p.135–57. Changed attributions, p.137–78.

M4 Art Institute of Chicago. French and British paintings from 1600 to 1800 in the Art Institute of Chicago: a catalogue of the collection. French entries by Susan Wise. Larry J. Feinberg, general ed. British entries by Malcolm Warner. Martha Wolff, general ed. With contrib. by Larry J. Feinberg and Martha Wolff. Chicago, Art Institute of Chicago in assoc. with Princeton Univ. Pr., 1996. xiii, 317p. il. (part col.)

Scholarly catalog of the collections.

Notes to the reader, xi. Bibliographical abbreviations, p.xii–xiii. List of previous owners, p.307–13. List of paintings by accession number, p.314–15. List of artists, p.316–17.

M5 Bayerische Staatsgemäldesammlungen. Gemäldekataloge. München, Bayerische, Staatsgemäldesammlungen, 1963– . (10)v. il.

Vols. [3, 5–7] have imprint: München, Hirmer.

Ongoing detailed catalog of the paintings in the Bavarian State Museums. Entries on each painting include extensive bibliographic references; each work is illustrated. Indexes by inventory number, personal name, and geographic place name.

Contents: (1) Spanische Meister. Bearb. von Halldor Soehner (2v., 1963); (2) Schack-Galerie. Bearb. von Eberhard Ruhmer (2v., 1969); (3) Nach-Barock und Klassizismus. Bearb. von Barbara Hardtwig [1978]; (5) Spätromantik und Realismus. Bearb. von Barbara Eschenburg [1984]; (6) Malerei der Gründerzeit. Bearb. von Horst Ludwig [1977]; (7) Impressionisten, Post-Impressionisten und Symbolisten, Ausländer Künstler. Bearb. von Gisela Hopp . . . [et al.] [1990]; (9) Venezianische Gemälde des 15. und 16. Jahrhunderts. Bearb. von Rolf Kultzen (2v., 1971); (10:1) Venezianische Gemälde des 17. Jahrhunderts. Bearb. von Rolf

Kultzen (1986); (10:2) Venezianische Gemälde des 18. Jahrhunderts. Bearb. von Rolf Kultzen und Matthias Reuss (1991); (14) Altdeutsche Gemälde, Köln und Nordwest-Deutschland. Bearb. von Gisela Goldberg und Gisela Scheffler (2v., 1972).

M6 Cambridge. Fitzwilliam Museum. Catalogue of paintings. Cambridge, Fitzwilliam Museum, 1960–77. 3v. il.

V.3 published by Cambridge Univ. Pr. for the Fitzwilliam Museum.

Detailed catalog of the Fitzwilliam collection; v.1 includes brief history of collection. Each painting entry includes biographical information on the artist, materials and dimensions of the work, physical description including notes on condition and provenance. Most are illustrated. Each vol. includes index of portraits, subjects and topography, index of previous owners and by catalog number.

Contents: (1) Gerson, Horst, and Goodison, J. W. Dutch and Flemish; Goodison, J. W., and Sutton, Denys. French, German, Spanish (1960); (2) Goodison, J. W., and Robertson, G. W. Italian schools (1967); (3) Goodison, J. W. British schools (1977).

M7 Corpus of illuminated manuscripts. Leuwen, Peeters, 1985– . (9)v. il.

Series of scholarly catalogs. Divided into two series: Low Countries and Oriental Series. Double numeration, one by general title (indicated here), another by sub-series.

Contents: (1) Cardon, Bert . . . [et al.] Typologische taferelen uit het leven van Jezus: a manuscript from the Gold Scrolls Group (Bruges, ca. 1440) in the Pierpont Morgan Library, New York, Ms. Morgan 649 (1985); (2–3) Oliver, Judith H. Gothic manuscript illumination in the Diocese of Liege (c. 1250–c. 1330) (1988); (4/5) Depuydt, Leo. Catalog of Coptic manuscripts in the Pierpont Morgan Library (1993); (6) Vlaamse miniaturen voor Van Eyck, ca. 1380–c. 1420: catalogus (1993); (7) Sed-Rajna, Gabrielle. Les manuscrits hébreux enluminés des bibliothèques de France (1994); (8) Flanders in a European perspective: manuscript illumination around 1400 in Flanders and abroad: international colloquium: papers (1995); (9) Cardon, Bert. Manuscripts of the Speculum humanae salvationis in the southern Netherlands, c. 1410–c. 1470 (1996).

M8 Detroit Institute of Arts. Flemish and German paintings of the 17th century. By Julius Samuel Held. Detroit, Detroit Institute of Arts, 1982. 143p. il. (part col.) (Detroit Institute of Arts. Collections of the Detroit Institute of Arts)

Planned to inaugurate a series of catalogs of the permanent collections.

Bibliography and exhibitions, p.129–34. Index of artists, p.135. Index of subject matter, p.137–38. Index of previous owners, p.139–42. Numerical index, p.143-[44].

M9 Euw, Anton von, and Plotzek, Joachim M. Die Handschriften der Sammlung Ludwig. Hrsg. vom Schnütgen-Museum der Stadt Köln. Köln, Das Museum, 1979–85. 4v. il. (part col.)

Sumptuous illustrated catalog of the great collection acquired by the J. Paul Getty Museum in 1983. Vol.3 is by Anton von Euw and Tarif al-Samman.

Includes bibliographical references and indexes.

M10 Gemäldegalerie Berlin: Gesamtverzeichnis. [Bearb. von Henning Bock . . . (et al.) Red., Rainald Grosshans.] Berlin, Staatliche Museen zu Berlin; Nicolai, [1996]. 638p. 2,902 il.

Earlier bilingual ed. publ. London, 1986.

This catalog provides an up-to-date accounting of paintings administered by the Stiftung Preussischer Kulturbesitz. Brief text entries on each work alphabetically arranged; thumbnail illustrations arranged in sections organized by geographic school.

Nummernverzeichnis des Gesamtbestandes, p.579–631. Literaturhinweise, p.635–38.

M11 Germanisches Nationalmuseum Nürnberg. Die Gemälde des 16. Jahrhunderts. Bearb. von Kurt Locher, unter Mitarb. von Carola Gries. Technologische Befunde, Anna Bartl und Magdalene Gartner. Ostfildern-Ruit, Hatje, 1997. 661p. il. (part col.)

Catalog of the permanent collection.

Verzeichnis der Themen, p.593–96. Verzeichnis der Personen, p.597–604. Verzeichnis der Gemälde nach Inventarnummern unter Angabe der Saitenzahl, p.605–07. Konkordanz der Inventarnummern der Bayerischen Staatsgemäldesammlungen und des Wittelsbacher Ausgleichsfonds mit denen des GNM, p.608. Verzeichnis der abgegebenen Gemälde, der zurückgegebenen Leihgaben und der zerstörten Gemälde, p.609–12. Bibliographie, p.613–61.

M12 Gosudarstvennyi Ermitazh (Russia). The Hermitage: catalogue of western European painting. Florence, Giunti, 1986– . (10)v. il.

V.11 published by Johnson Reprint/Harcourt Brace Jovanovich and Giunti. Published simultaneously in Russian and English. Issued out of sequence; to be complete in 16 volumes.

Detailed catalog of the Hermitage collection. Each vol. begins with an introduction to the Hermitage collections of the pertinent period, mentioning important collectors whose holdings are now among the museum's holdings. Each painting entry includes brief discussion of work, provenance, bibliography, and exhibition history. Unfortunately only black-and-white illustrations.

Contents: (1) Italian painting, 13th–16th centuries (1994); (2) Venetian painting, 14th–18th centuries (1992); (4) Spanish painting, 15th–19th centuries (1997); (5) Netherlandish painting, 15th and 16th centuries (1989); (10) French painting, 18th century (1986); (11) French painting, early and mid-19th century (1983); (12) French painting, mid-19th to 20th centuries (1991); (13) British painting 16th–19th centuries (1990); (14) German and Austrian painting, 15th to 18th centuries (1987); (15) German and Austrian painting, 19th and 20th centuries (1988).

M13 Gosudarstvennyi muzei izobrazitelnykh iskusstv imeni A. S. Pushkina. Katalog zhivopisi. [Obshchaia red. N. E. Danilova.] Moskva, Mazzotta, 1995. 775p. il. (part col.)

In English and Russian. Catalog of paintings in the State Pushkin Museum of Fine Arts.

Bibliography, p.736–50. Name index, p.751–60. General index, p.761–75.

M14 Houghton Library. Late medieval and renaissance illuminated manuscripts, 1350–1525, in the Houghton Library. [By] Roger S. Wieck. Cambridge, Mass., Dept. of Print. and Graphic Arts, Harvard College Library, 1983. xv, 190p. il.

Scholarly catalog of the collection.

Bibliography of frequently cited works, p.175. Index of authors and titles, p.176–79. Index of artists and scribes, p.180–81. Index of previous owners, p.182–85. Index by century and country, p.186–88. Index of cited manuscripts from other collections, p.189–90.

M15 Ingamells, John. The Wallace Collection catalogue of pictures. London, Trustees of the Wallace Collection, 1985–92. 4v. il. (part col.)

Extremely detailed catalog of the Wallace Collection; entries are arranged by geographic school, then alphabetically by artist, and include physical description, history, related drawings, and versions and provenance. Indexes by changed attribution, subject, previous owner, inventory number, and artist's name.

Contents: (1) British, German, Italian, Spanish (1985); (2) French nineteenth century (1986); (3) French before 1815 (1989); (4) Dutch and Flemish (1992).

M16 London. National Gallery. Catalogues. London, National Gallery, 1945– . il., atlases of plates.

See GLAH 1:M6 for earlier vols.

The latest vol. in this series is presented in more elaborate form, with color illustrations and more discursive text. The earlier exemplary catalogs were reissued; two are completely revised and the others reprinted with a list of new acquisitions appended.

Contents: Martin, Gregory. The Flemish School circa 1600–circa 1900 (1970, repr. 1986); Davies, Martin. The early Netherlandish school (1968, repr. 1987); Gould, Cecil. The sixteenth-century Italian schools (1975, repr. 1987); Davies, Martin. The early Italian schools: before 1400, rev. by Dillian Gordon (1988); MacLaren, Neil. The Spanish school, 2d. ed. rev. by Allan Braham (1970, repr. 1988); MacLaren, Neil. The Dutch School, 1600–1900, 2d ed. rev. and expanded by Christopher Brown (1991); Campbell, Lorne. The fifteenth-century Netherlandish schools (1998); Egerton, Judy. The British School (1998).

M17 ______. The National Gallery complete illustrated catalogue. Compiled by Christopher Baker and Tom Henry. London, National Gallery (Distr. by Yale Univ. Pr., [1995]). xxiv, 790p. il. (part col.) + computer disk.

Latest ed. of the 1-vol. catalog; concise entries include title, medium, size, brief commentary, provenance, and bibliography. Most illustrations are in color. The accompanying CD-ROM includes the same material on each painting but also provides details and full-size illustrations and allows searching by theme or keyword.

Bibliography, p.753–61. Index by inventory number, p.762–71. Detailed subject index, p.772–90.

M18 Madrid. Museo Nacional de Pintura y Escultura. Museo del Prado: inventario general de pinturas. Madrid, Museo del Prado, 1990– . (3)v. il.

Inventory of the Spanish national collection, including works on deposit in other locations. Paintings arranged by inventory number; each entry gives past and current attribution, inventory and catalog listings, size, and current location. Nearly all are illustrated.

Contents: (1) La Coleccion Real; (2) El Museo de la Trinidad (bienes desamortizados); (3) Nuevas adquisiciones (desde 1856).

Indexes are provided by artist's name, by location, and by broad iconographical theme. A concordance is provided to earlier inventories.

M19 Mauritshuis: illustrated general catalogue. [Compilation, Nicolette Sluijter-Seijffert with the assist. of Rieke van Leeuwen . . . (et al).] Amsterdam, Meulenhoff; The Hague, Mauritshuis, [1993]. 212p. il. 16 col. pl.

1st ed. publ. 1977. 2d ed. publ. as appendix to The Royal Picture Gallery "Mauritshuis." Amsterdam, Meulenhoff, 1985.

Includes brief illustrated entries for each painting in the collection. Organized alphabetically by artist with anonymous works following.

Appendix: Acquisitions 1985–93, p.192–97. Changed attributions, collaborators, p.198. Subject index, p.199–203. Inventory numbers, p.204–07. Key to abbreviated literature, p.208–12.

M20 National Gallery of Scotland. Italian and Spanish paintings in the National Gallery of Scotland. Catalogued by Hugh Brigstocke. 2d ed. Edinburgh, Trustees of the National Galleries of Scotland, 1993. 360p. il.

1st ed. 1978.

Scholarly catalog of a significant collection.

Numerical index of paintings in the permanent collection, p.211–12. List of attributions changed since the 1957 Catalogue, p.213. Pictures catalogued as Italian or Spanish in the 1957 Catalogue, p.214. List of attributions changed since the 1978 ed., p.214. Copies after Italian pictures, not included in the present Catalogue, p.215. Index of collectors, p.216–24.

M21 Netherlands. Rijksdienst Beeldende Kunst. Old master paintings: an illustrated summary catalogue. [Trans., Shirley van der Pols-Harris.] Zwolle, Waanders, 1992. 453p. il.

Summary catalog of a collection numbering 3,600 old master and 19th-century paintings and second only to the Rijksmuseum in Amsterdam among Dutch collections.

Subject index, p.425–37. Concordance, p.441–53.

M22 New York. Metropolitan Museum of Art. European paintings in the Metropolitan Museum of Art: by artists born in or before 1865: a summary catalogue. By Katharine Baetjer. N.Y., The Museum, 1980. 3v. il.

"This summary catalogue is intended to supply essential information on all of the paintings in the Museum by European artists born in or before 1865."—*Pref.* Superseded by the same author's 1995 "summary catalogue" (see following title).

Contents: (1) Catalogue; (2) Italian paintings, Florentine, XIII–XVII century; (3) Flemish paintings including Dutch XV–XVI century, and Portuguese XV–XVIII century.

Index, v.1, p.201–21.

M23 ______. European paintings in the Metropolitan Museum of Art by artists born before 1865: a summary catalogue. By Katharine Baetjer. Metropolitan Museum of Art (Distr. by Abrams, 1995). xiv, 527p. il.

Supersedes the 3-vol. catalog of the collection published in 1980 (see preceding title). "This catalogue is intended to supply essential information on all paintings, oil sketches, and finished pastels by European artists born before 1865 (not, as in the 1980 ed., in or before 1865) belonging to" the museum. Also includes entries for many paintings from anticipated bequests.—*Pref.* Organized chronologically and by national and regional school. Includes small, black-and-white illustrations.

Notes to the catalogue, p.xiv. Index of accession numbers, p.507–19. Index of artists, p.521–27.

M24 Paris. Bibliothèque nationale. Département des manuscrits, Centre de recherche sur les manuscrits enluminés. Manuscrits enluminés de la Bibliothèque nationale. Paris, Bibliothèque nationale, 1980– . (5)v. il. (part col.)

Ongoing catalog of the Western illuminated manuscripts. Entries for each manuscript include physical description, description of illuminations, provenance, and bibliographic references. Indexes include a concordance of ms. numbers, of cited manuscripts, authors, known artists, former owners, place names, and a detailed iconographic index.

Contents: Manuscrits enluminés d'origine italienne: (1) Avril, François, and Zaluska, Yolanta. VIe–XIIe siècles (1980); (2) Avril, François; Gousset, Marie-Thérèse; avec la collab. de Claudia Rabel. XIIIe siècles (1984); Avril, François . . . [et al.] Manuscrits enluminés de la péninsule ibérique (1982); Avril, François, and Stirneman, Patricia Danz. Manuscrits enluminés d'origine insulaire, VIIe–XXe siècle (1987); Avril, Francois, and Rabel, Claudia. Manuscrits enluminés d'origine germanique (1995).

M25 Paris. Musée National du Louvre. Catalogue sommaire illustré des peintures du Musée du Louvre. Par Arnauld de Lavergnée, Jacques Foucart, Nicole Reynaud. Paris, Ed. de la Réunion des musées nationaux, 1979–86. 5v., il.

V.3–5 have title: Catalogue sommaire illustré des peintures du Musée du Louvre et du Musée d'Orsay.

Complete catalog of Western painting. Brief alphabetical entries include inventory numbers, provenance, and bibliographic references. Anonymous works arranged by date. Most paintings illustrated with small black-and-white images. Appendixes include works on loan, changes of attribution, concordance of various inventory numbers, works on deposit at other institutions, index by provenance, index by format, and iconographical index.

Contents: (1) Écoles flamande et hollandaise; (2) Italie, Espagne, Allemagne, Grand Bretagne et divers; (3) École française A–K; (4) École française L–Z; (5) École française; Annexes et index.

M26 Philadelphia Museum of Art. Paintings from Europe and the Americas in the Philadelphia Museum of Art, a concise catalogue. [Philadelphia], Philadelphia Museum of Art; (Distr. by Univ. of Pennsylvania Pr., [1994]). xv, 548p. il.

Summary catalog of 3,921 paintings organized by national school, each one illustrated.

Indexes: artists, p.506–15; previous attributions, p.516–18; named sitters, p.519–22; donors, p.523–08; accession number, p.529–48.

M27 Pierpont Morgan Library. Masterpieces of medieval painting: the art of illumination. Ed. by William M. Voelke. Photographs by Charles V. Passela. [Chicago], Univ. of Chicago Pr., [1980]. xvii, 68p. 1,200 col. il. on 15 microfiche.

Catalog of the medieval illuminated manuscripts in the Morgan Library. Text volume is accompanied by new color illustrations of several pages in each manuscript, including details and some bindings.

Bibliographic note, p.xiv–xvi. Index of illuminators and scribes, p.65–66; of patrons and manuscripts, p.66–67; by century and country of origin, p.67–68.

M28 Rijksuniversiteit te Utrecht. Bibliotheek. Illuminated and decorated medieval manuscripts in the University Library, Utrecht: an illustrated catalogue. [By] Koert van der Horst. 's-Gravenhage, G. Schwartz; SDU, 1989. xiii, 75p. il. (part col.), 338p. of plates., facsims.

Scholarly catalog of the collection.

Concordance, p.50. Index of iconography, p.53–60. Index of Iconclass numbers, p.61–64. Index of artists, p.65. Index of scribes, p.65. Index of authors and texts, p.66–67. Index of origins, p.68. Index of provenances, p.69–70. Index of manuscripts cited, p.71. Literature cited, p.72–75.

M29 Schweers, Hans F. Gemälde in deutschen Museen: Katalog der ausgestellten und depotgelagerten Werke = Paintings in German museums: catalogue of exhibited works and depository holdings, 2. aktualisierte, erheblich erw. und verb. Ausg. München, Saur, 1994. 3v. in 10.

1st ed., 1981–82. 2v.

Voluminous guide to "nearly 110,000 paintings by approximately 18,000 painters from almost 420 museums and galleries" in Germany. Brief entries under each painter's name give painting title in German, date, medium, and size with an inventory number based on the museum's own catalog. Iconographic section provides access to paintings by broad theme (mythology, historical events, religious themes, etc.) The museum portion groups artists and their work under each museum.

Contents: (1) Künstler und ihre Werke (4v.); (2) Ikonographisches Verzeichnis (3v.); (3) Verzeichnis der Museen mit ihren Bildern (3v.)

M30 Solomon R. Guggenheim Museum, New York. The Guggenheim Museum collection: paintings, 1880–1945. By Angelica Zander Rudenstine. N.Y., The Museum, 1976. 2v. il. (part col.)

Exemplary collection catalog "intended primarily as a resource for scholars and students of nineteenth- and twentieth-century art."—*Introd.*

Chronological list of exhibitions organized by the Guggenheim Museum, p.700–21. Appendix—paintings 1800–1945: works acquired since 1970, p.722–24. Index, p.727–46.

M31 United States. National Gallery of Art. Collections of the National Gallery of Art: systematic catalog. Washington, D.C., The Gallery; N.Y., Oxford Univ. Pr., 1986– . (7)v. il. (part col.)

Systematic, illustrated catalog of the collections.

Contents: Hand, John Oliver, and Wolff, Martha. Early Netherlandish painting (1986); Brown, Jonathan, and Mann, Richard G. Spanish paintings of the fifteenth through nineteenth centuries (1990); Hayes, John. British paintings of the sixteenth through nineteenth centuries (1993); Oliver, John . . . [et al.] German paintings of the fifteenth through seventeenth centuries (1993); Miles, Ellen G. . . . [et al.] American paintings of the eighteenth century (1995); Kelly, Franklin . . . [et al.] American paintings of the nineteenth century (2v., 1996–98); De Grazia, Diane . . . [et al.] Italian paintings of the seventeenth and eighteenth centuries (1996).

M32 Vienna. Kunsthistorisches Museum Wien. Gemäldegalerie. Die Gemäldegalerie des Kunsthistorischen Museums in Wien: Verzeichnis der Gemälde. [Von] Sylvia Ferino Pagden. Wien, Brandstatter, 1991. 154p. il., 689p. of plates (Führer, 40)

Exemplary catalog of the great collection. Black-and-white reproductions and brief, scholarly catalog entries for ca. 2,300 of the most significant works in the collection.

Verzeichnis der zitierten Inventare und Kataloge, p.15–17. Verzeichnis der gekürzt zitierten Literatur, p.18–19. Verzeichnis der Gemälde, p.21–137. Geänderte Zuschreibungen gegenüber Verzeichnis 1973, p.138–39. Ikonographisches Register, p.140–54.

M33 Vienna. Nationalbibliothek. Die illuminierten Handschriften und Inkunabeln der Österreichischen Nationalbibliothek. (Fortsetzung des beschreibenden Verzeichnisses der illuminierten Handschriften in Wien). Hrsg. von Otto Pächt. Wien, Österreichischen Akademie der Wissenschaften, 1974– . (7)v. il. (part col.) (Österreichische Akademie der Wissenschaften. Philosophisch-Historische Klasse. Denkschriften, Bd. 118– .) (Veröffentlichungen der Kommission für Schrift- und Buchwesen des Mittelalters, Reihe 1)

See GLAH 1:M10 for earlier vols.

Ongoing series of catalogs of the illuminated manuscripts in the Austrian National Library. Detailed entries including bibliography; separate illustration vols.

Contents: (4) Duda, Dorothea. Islamische Handschriften I (2v., 1983); (5) Duda, Dorothea. Islamische Handschriften II (2v., 1992); (6) Pächt, Otto; Jenni, Ulrike; Thoss, Dagmar. Flämische Schule I (2v., 1983); (7) Pächt, Otto and Thoss, Dagmar. Flämische Schule II (2v., 1990); Fingernagel, Andreas, and Roland, Martin. Mitteleuropäische Schulen I (2v., 1997).

M34 Walters Art Gallery, Baltimore. Medieval and Renaissance manuscripts in the Walters Art Gallery. [By] Lilian M. C. Randall. Baltimore, Walters Art Gallery; Johns Hopkins Univ. Pr., 1989– . (3)v. il. (part col.)

Masterful catalog of the Western illuminated manuscripts in the Walters collection, to be completed in four vols. Each work is represented by a summary of the text, detailed descriptions of miniatures and decoration, notes on condition, history, and bibliography. General index, iconographic index, and index of incipits in each vol.

Contents: (1) France, 875–1420; (2) France, 1420–1540 (2v.); (3) Belgium, 1250–1530 (2v.).

M35 Wright, Christopher. The world's master paintings: from the early Renaissance to the present day: a comprehensive listing of works by 1,300 painters and a complete guide to their locations worldwide. London, Routledge, [1992]. 2v. 63p. of plates.

Selective guide to the location of paintings by primarily well-known artists in public collections. Painting listings, grouped by artist's name, are arranged by country and by century. A separate list of museum locations lists artists with the number of pictures in that collection. Title index is unfortunately organized by century. Selected bibliographic references listed under each artist and each museum.

PAINTERS

M36 Blättel, Harry. International dictionary miniature painters, porcelain painters, silhouettists = Internationales Lexikon Miniatur-Maler, Porzellan-maler, Silhouettisten = Dictionnaire international peintres miniaturistes, peintres sur porcelaine, silhouettistes. München, Arts and Antiques Edition Munich, [1992]. 1422p. il. (part col.)

Actually an index to other biographical reference works; entries include only dates and geographic region.

Contents: Miniatures: Short history and introduction; Explanations; Overview of systematization; Chronological tables; All miniature painters; Porcelain manufactories; Porcelain painters; Sèvres, Vienna and Meissen painters; Silhouettists; Enamelists.

Bibliography of artist reference works, p.139. Specialist literature, p.1392–1404. Authors, p.1405–12. Index of plates, p.1413–21.

M37 Schurr, Gerald, and Cabanne, Pierre. Dictionnaire des petits maîtres de la peinture: 1820–1920: Valeur de demain. Paris, Ed. de l'Amateur, 1996. 2v. il. (part col.)

Biographical dictionary of "minor" painters of the 19th and early 20th century.

Includes bibliographies and indexes.

M38 Witt Library. A checklist of painters, c1200–1994 represented in the Witt Library, Courtauld Institute of Art, London. 2d ed. London, Mansell; Chicago, Fitzroy Dearborn, 1995. xviii, 557p.

1st ed. A checklist of painters, c1200–1976, 1978.

Alphabetical list of the approximately 66,000 painters, draftsmen, and printmakers represented by reproductions of their work in the vast illustration collection known as the Witt Library (see GLAH 2:D66). Provides basic information, including name, life dates if known, and national school.

"However imperfect in ideal terms, the particular value of the Checklist has rested in the large numbers of artists it includes and in its wide range and coverage, which is Western- or European-inspired painting, drawing and engraving from c.1200 to the present day."—*Foreword to the 2d ed.*

An earlier checklist of the collection was compiled by Sir Robert Witt and privately published in 1920, followed by a supp. in 1925. For a checklist of British painters in the collection, see Checklist of British artists in the Witt Library, compiled by the Witt Computer Index (GLAH 2:M301).

Arrangement of illustrations in the Witt Library, p.[xii]. Bibliography of reference works and dictionaries, p.xiii–xviii.

TECHNIQUES

M39 Albers, Josef. Interaction of color. Interactive CD-ROM ed., Version 1.2 for the Macintosh. New Haven, Yale Univ. Pr., 1994. 1 computer disk, col., 4 3/4 in. + 1 computer installation disk (3 1/2 in.) + 1 guide (viii, 38p.).

See GLAH 1:M28 for 1963 ed.

CD-ROM version of the classic workbook on color relationships. Provides the same examples in automated form and allows the user to manipulate these to better understand how each contrast works.

M40 Artists' pigments, a handbook of their history and characteristics. Washington, D.C., National Gallery of Art, [1986–]. (3)v. il. (part col.)

V.2–3 published by Oxford Univ. Pr.

V.1 ed. by Robert L. Feller; v.2 ed. by Ashok Roy; v.3 ed. by Elisabeth West FitzHugh.

Benchmark series of technical studies "providing artists, conservators, scientists, and art historians with a contemporary, comprehensive publication on the history, analyses, properties, and occurrences of artists' pigments."—*Pref.*, v.2. Each of the chapters outlines terminology, sources, properties, notable examples, and bibliographic references for a specific pigment. V.2 incorporates articles originally published in Studies in conservation (GLAH 1:Q330).

M41 Binski, Paul. Painters. Toronto; Buffalo, Univ. of Toronto Pr., [1991]. 72p. 71 il. (part col.) (Medieval craftsmen)

A volume in the wonderful series of medieval technique books originally published by the British Museum, illustrated with examples from medieval manuscripts and other paintings.

Contents: (1) The painter; (2) The product; (3) The process.

Selected bibliography, p.71. Index, p.72.

M42 Callen, Anthea. Techniques of the impressionists. [Secaucus], Chartwell, [1982]. 192p. il. (part col.)

Well-illustrated, popular study of the Impressionists' painting techniques. Thirty paintings are analyzed in depth, using numerous color details as well as diagrams.

Chronology, p.182–85. Glossary, p.186–89. Bibliography, p.189. Index, p.190–01.

M43 Kay, Reed. The painter's guide to studio methods and materials. Englewood Cliffs, N.J., Prentice-Hall, 1983. xv, 288p. il.

1st ed. Garden City, Doubleday, 1972.

"The purpose of this book is to provide practicing artists and art students with information concerning the various painting media and to indicate some of the reasons that painters might choose one method or material over others."—*Pref.* The present ed. includes an expanded discussion of health and safety issues.

Contents: (1) Pigments; (2) Binders and diluents; (3) The oil technique; (4) Supports and grounds; (5) Water paints; (6) Tempera; (7) Casein; (8) Encaustic wax painting; (9) Cold wax techniques; (10) Fresco painting; (11) Synthetic resin paints; (12) Pastels; (13) Gilding; (14) Picture framing; (15) Photographic prints and color slides of paintings; (16) The studio; (17) Appendix: weights and measures, temperature scales, sources of supplies.

Bibliography, p.276–78. Index, p.279–88.

M44 Mayer, Ralph. The artist's handbook of materials and techniques. 5th ed., rev. and upd. by Steven Sheehan. [N.Y.], Viking, [1991]. xv, 761p. il.

See GLAH 1:M40 for 3d ed. 4th ed. called "1982 ed., revised and updated."

Remains a primary reference source on artists' techniques. New ed. includes an expanded list of approved pigments and revised guidelines on conservation and health hazards. Appendixes include glossary, formulas, and measures and suppliers.

Classified annotated bibliography, p.675–711. Index, p.713–61.

SEE ALSO: Gage, Color and culture (GLAH 2:I13); Kemp, The science of art (GLAH 2:I26); Mayer, The HarperCollins dictionary of art terms and techniques (GLAH 2:E17); Artists' pigments: a handbook of their history and characteristics (GLAH 2:T134).

HISTORIES AND HANDBOOKS

General Works

M45 Backhouse, Janet. The illuminated page: ten centuries of manuscript painting in the British Library. London, British Library; Toronto, Univ. of Toronto Pr., 1997. 240p. il.

"This book offers an anthology of reproductions in colour chosen from more than two hundred" manuscripts, selected from among "the largest and most comprehensive collections of western illuminated manuscripts in the world."—*Introd.* Manuscripts range from the 7th to the 17th century.

Contents: The early centuries; Romanesque Europe; Early Gothic manuscripts; Later Gothic manuscripts; International cross-currents around 1400; The prelude to printing; The later 15th century; Renaissance patrons; Postscript.

Further reading, p.238. Index of manuscripts, p.239–40.

M46 Greer, Germaine. The obstacle race: the fortunes of women painters and their work. N.Y., Farrar Straus Giroux, [1979]. 373p. il. 32 col. pl.

A by-now classic study that tries "to address the question of women's participation in the fine arts, not so much by repeating the legends which have grown up around single figures as by attempting to rejoin those freaks to the body of women from whom they have been separated and by placing these women in some sort of a social and cultural background."—*Introd.*

Contents: The obstacles: (1) Family; (2) Love; (3) The illusion of success; (4) Humiliation; (5) Dimension; (6) Primitivism; (7) The disappearing oeuvre: How they ran; (8) The cloister; (9) The Renaissance; (10) The magnificent exception; (11) The Bolognese phenomenon; (12) Still life and flower painting; (13) The portraitists; (14) The amateurs; (15) The age of academics; (16) The nineteenth century.

Index, p.361–73.

M47 Pittura in Europa. Milano, Electa, 1995– . (5)v. in 10. il.

Beautifully produced series devoted to the major European schools of painting. Each vol. by a specialist.

Contents: Pérez Sanchez, Alfonso E. La pittura spagnola (2v., 1995); Bott, Gerhard. La pittura tedesca (2v., 1996); Meijer, Bert W. La pittura nei Paesi Bassi (3v., 1997); Kitson, Michael, and Popescu, Grigore Arbore. La pittura inglese (1998); Rosenberg, Pierre. La Pittura francese (3v., 1999)

M48 Sterling, Charles. Still life painting, from antiquity to the twentieth century. 2d rev. ed. N.Y., Harper, [1981]. 325p. il.

See GLAH 1:M26 for earlier eds.

Corrected reprint with a new preface and additional bibliography, covering 1959–79. Remains one of the few studies of this genre as a whole.

M49 Stilleben in Europa [im Auftrage des Landschaftsverbandes Westfalen-Lippe und der Staatlichen Kunsthalle Baden-Baden. Hrsg. von Gerhard Langemeyer und Hans-Albert Peters.] [Münster, Landschaftsverband Westfalen-Lippe, 1979]. 619p. il. (part col.)

Catalog of the exhibition, Westfälisches Landesmuseum für Kunst und Kulturgeschichte (1979–80), and other locations, dealing primarily with 16th- and 17th-century still life, but including works from many European countries and a chapter on developments up to the 20th century.

Contents: (A) Das Stilleben im Zeitalter der Entdeckungen: Die Nähe und die Ferne, von Gerhard Langemeyer; Naturerscheinung, Bild-Erfinding und Ausführung: zur Arbeitsweise des Künstlers im 16. und 17. Jahrhundert, von Gisela Luther; Stilleben als Bilder der Sammelleidenschaft, von Gisela Luther; Arte et marte: durch Wissenschaft und Kriegskunst, von Géza Jászai; Weltdeutung: Allegorien und Symbole in Stilleben, von Christian Klemm; (B) Stilleben als Spiegel menschlichen Lebens: Das Stilleben als Attribut, von Gerhard Langemeyer; Trophäen des Krieges und der Jagd, von Christian Klemm und Claus Grimm; Wirtschafts- und sozialgeschichtliche Aspekte des Früchtestillebens, von Norbert Schneider; Das Blumenstilleben, von Norbert Schneider und Paul Pieper; Küchenstücke, Marktbilder, Fischstilleben, von Claus Grimm; Versicht and Zeremoniell: Zu den Stilleben von Sánchez-Cotán und van der Hamen, von Jutta Held; Fasten und Genuß: die angerichtete Tafel als Thema des Stillebens, von Joseph Lammers; Gemalte Schätze: Erinnerung an die Vergänglichkeit alles Irdischen wie Mittel zur Repräsentation, von Gerhard Bott; (C) Stilleben: Gemalte Gedanken zur Kunst und medium künstlerischer Erneuerungen: Das Buch im Stilleben: das Stilleben im Buch, von Jochen Becker; Innovation und Virtuosität, von Joseph Lammers; Stilleben und Avantgarde, von Ingo Bartsch.

Kurzbiographien, p.598–605. Verzeichnis der abgekürzt zitierten Literatur, p.607–14. Künstlerindex, p.615–18.

Ancient

General Works

M50 Bianchi Bandinelli, Ranuccio. La pittura antica. A cura di Filippo Carelli e Luisa Franchi dell'Orto. Roma, Riuniti, [1980]. x, 245p. il. (part col.), plates. (Biblioteca di storia antica, 11)

Collection of essays by an important scholar of classical art who has written widely on Roman, Etruscan, and Hellenistic subjects. Unfortunately printed on poor-quality paper with mediocre illustrations.

Contents: (1) Problemi generali; (2) Studi e note; (3) Problemi e tecniche della pittura antica.

Table of Greek painters working in Rome, p.228–31. Abbreviations, p.237–8. Index, p.239–45.

M51 Doxiadis, Euphrosyne. The mysterious Fayum portraits: faces from Ancient Egypt. Foreword by Dorothy J. Thompson. [N.Y.], Abrams, [1995]. 247p. il. (part col.), col. plates, maps.

Popular study of the funerary portraits from the Fayum region produced during the Greco-Roman period. Exceptional color illustrations and descriptions are arranged by the sites where the paintings were collected. The author is not a scholar but approaches these works as a painter in trying to make links between them and later Byzantine art.

Select bibliography, p.241–3. Index, p.244–6.

M52 Ancient faces: mummy portraits from Roman Egypt. [Ed. by] Susan Walker . . . [et al.] [London], pub. For the Trustees of the British Museum by British Museum Pr., [1997]. 224p. il. (part col.), map. (Catalogue of Roman portraits in the British Museum, IV)

Serves as exhibition catalog as well as collection catalog. Concise introduction to Greco-Roman portrait paintings. Six essays provide historical background.

Selective contents: Before the portraits: burial practices in Pharaonic Egypt, by John Taylor; Mummy portraits and Roman portraiture, by Susan Walker; The Fayum and its people, by R. S. Bagnall; Technique, by Euphrosyne C. Doxiadis; The discovery of the mummy portraits, by Morris Bierbrier; The conservation of the portraits and associated antiquities, by Gillian Roy.

Select bibliography, p.216–7. Glossary, p.217–18.

Egypt

M53 Harpur, Yvonne. Decoration in Egyptian tombs of the Old Kingdom: studies in orientation and scene content. Photographic reproductions by Paolo J. Scremin. London, KPI, [1987]. xiv, 596p. il. 145 plans, 218 figs., 29 pl. (Studies in Egyptology)

Detailed technical study of the arrangement of Old Kingdom tombs; effectively serves as a catalog of painted tomb decoration for this period.

Contents: (1) Location; (2) Kinship; (3) Chronology; (4) Entrance decoration; (5) Orientation; (6) The depiction of major and minor figures; (7) The development of scene content.

General abbreviations, p.558. Bibliography and publication abbreviations, p.559–71. Classified index, p.577–96.

M54 James, T. G. H. (Thomas Garnet Henry). Egyptian painting and drawing in the British Museum. Cambridge, Mass., Harvard Univ. Pr., 1986. 72p. il. (part col.)

First published London, British Museum Publications, 1985.

One of the British Museum's very useful brief introductions illustrated with works from their collection.

Contents: (1) Introduction; (2) The Egyptian artist, his materials and his techniques; (3) Mural painting; (4) Line drawing; (5) Illuminated papyri; (6) Other forms of painting.

Index, p.72.

M55 Wilkinson, Charles K. Egyptian wall paintings: the Metropolitan Museum of Art's collection of facsimiles. Catalogue compiled by Marsha Hill. N.Y., The Museum, [1983]. 165p. il. (part col.)

Catalog of 369 facsimiles of Egyptian tomb decoration produced by the Graphic Section of the Metropolitan Museum's Egyptian Expedition between 1907 and 1937. The original paintings, mostly from Thebes, are now scattered in a variety of collections. The author was one of those hired to make the copies, and his story provides insight into the excavating processes of the period.

Index of Theban tomb owners, p.163. Index of Theban tomb numbers, p.164. Index of monuments other than Theban tombs, p.165.

Classical World

Crete, Mycenae, Greece

M56 Amyx, Darrell A. Corinthian vase-painting of the Archaic period. Berkeley, Univ. of California Pr., [1988]. 3v. il. (part col.) 143 plates. (California studies in the history of art, 25)

The product of many years of research, this catalog updates the work of Humfry Payne in Necrocorinthia (1931) and is the definitive resource for vases from this region.

Contents: (1) Catalogue of Corinthian vases; (2) Commentary: the study of Corinthian vases; (3) Indexes, concordances, and plates.

Bibliography, v.2, p.ix–xviii. Index of collections, v.3, p.705–55. Index of painters and groups, v.3, p.757–62. General index, v.3, p.763–73. Concordances, v.3, p.775–96.

M57 Boardman, John. Athenian red figure vases, the classical period: a handbook. [N.Y.], Thames and Hudson, [1989]. 252p. 566 il. (World of art)

"Forms the sequel to his standard handbooks on Archaic Black Figure and Red Figure vase painting [GLAH 1:M60–61]. Like them, it offers a detailed survey of all the important painters and workshops."—*Cover text.*

Contents: (1) Introduction; (2) Early Classical; (3) Classical; (4) White ground and lekythoi; (5) Later Classical I; (6) Later Classical II; (7) The scenes; (8) Techniques, production and marketing; (9) Shapes and uses.

Notes and bibliography, p.242–44. Index of artists and groups, p.250–51. Index of mythological subjects, p.251–52. General index, p.252.

M58 ______. Early Greek vase painting, 11th to 6th centuries B.C.: a handbook. [N.Y.], Thames and Hudson, [1998.] 287p. 511 il. maps. (World of art)

Last in author's seminal series of introductory texts on Greek vases from the earliest periods.

Contents: (1) Introduction; (2) The protogeometric style; (3) The geometric style; (4) The orientalizing style; (5) East Greece: orientalizing and black figure; (6) The black figure styles; (7) Aftermath; (8) Early Greek vase painting, art and life.

Chronological chart, p.271. Notes and bibliographies, p.276–80. Index of collections, p.281–82. Index of figure subjects and decoration, p.283–84. General index, p.285–87.

M59 ______, and Cahn, Herbert A. Kerameus. Mainz, Zabern, [1974–]. (1) v. il. (Forschungen zur antiken Keramik, zweite Reihe)

See GLAH 1:M62 for earlier and other proposed vols.

Ongoing series of scholarly catalogs of the work of individual vase painters.

Contents: (3) Cook, R. M. Clazomenian sarcophagi (1981); (4) Böhr, Elke. Der Schaukelmaler (1982); (5) Hemelrijk, Jaap M. Caeretan hydriae (2v., 1984); (6) Lezzi-Hafter, Adrienne. Der Eretria-Maler: Werke und Weggefährten (2v., 1988); (7) Burow, Johannes. Der Antimenesmaler (1989); (8) Oakley, John Howard. The Phiale painter (1990); (9) Buitron-Oliver, Diana. Douris: a master-painter of Athenian red-figure vases (1995); (10) Kunisch, Norbert. Makron (2v., 1997); (11) Mommsen, Heide. Exekias, pt.1: Die Grabtafeln (1997).

M60 Carpenter, Thomas H.; Mannack, Thomas; and Mendonça, Melanie. Beazley addenda: additional references to ABV, ARV2 and Paralipomena. 2d ed. Oxford, publ. for the British Academy by Oxford Univ. Pr., 1989. li, 481p. port.

1st ed. 1982. See GLAH 1:M55–57 for original Beazley vols.

Latest additions to the Beazley vase catalogs, compiled by the staff of the Beazley Archive.

Abbreviations and bibliography, p.xxi–li. Index of museum collections, p.407–72. Index of artists, p.473–81.

M61 Cook, Robert Manuel. Greek painted pottery. 3d ed. N.Y., Routledge, [1997]. xxv, 375p. il.

See GLAH 1:M66 for previous eds. and original annotation.

Remains one of the principal references for Greek pottery in general. Text and bibliography have been revised and updated.

Index, p.257–75.

M62 Corpus vasorum antiquorum. Paris, Champion [etc.] 1922– . (many vols.) il., plates (part col.)

At head of title: Union Académique Internationale. Most issued in portfolio form. Imprint varies. See GLAH 1:M67 for fuller description.

International effort to catalog classical vases. Since 1978, series begun for Canada, Czechoslovakia, Hungary, Japan, New Zealand, Sweden.

M63 ______. Summary guide to Corpus vasorum antiquorum. Compiled by Thomas H. Carpenter at the Beazley Archive. Oxford, publ. for the British Academy by Oxford Univ.Pr., 1984. vi, 77p.

"Designed to assist the library-work of students of Attic figure-decorated pottery who may be confused by the differing numbering systems employed by the editors of CVA."—*Introd.* Index I lists fascicules alphabetically by country, Index II lists vase shapes and plate numbers, Index III indicates fascicules with a substantial selection of a given shape, and Index IV lists the principal non-Attic wares.

M64 Greek vases in the J. Paul Getty Museum. Malibu, Calif., The Museum, 1983– . (5)v. il. (Occasional papers on antiquities, 1–3, 5, 7)

Ongoing series of essays featuring the important and growing Greek vase collection of the Getty Museum. Detailed articles by important vase scholars each treating a specific vase, painter, or theme.

M65 Immerwahr, Sara Anderson. Aegean painting in the Bronze age. University Park, Penn. State Univ. Pr., [1990]. xxiv, 240p. il. (part col.), plates, maps, plans.

Thorough and detailed study of Aegean wall painting, beginning with the elaborate programs at Knossos; proposes chronology for Minoan, Cycladic, and Mycenaean painting.

Contents: (1) Orientation: Geography and chronology; (2) Techniques of painting; (3) The beginnings: Minoan pictorial art before the frescoes; (4) The first phase of Aegean wall painting; (5) Later Minoan painting and the formation of the Mycenaean style; (6) Mycenaean wall painting; (7) Epilogue: Non-palatial painting.

Catalogue of frescoes, p.169–204. Bibliography, p.223–30. Index, p.231–40.

M66 Moon, Warren G., and Berge, Louise. Greek vase-painting in Midwestern collections. [Chicago], Art Institute of Chicago, [1979]. xx, 231p. il. (part col.) 8 col. plates.

Catalog of the exhibition, Art Institute of Chicago (1979–80). Catalog of 127 vases from numerous Midwestern collections, many not included in Beazley. Catalog entries include bibliography, one or more details, discussion by a range of Classical art scholars.

Glossary, p.227. Index of collections, p.228–29. Index of shapes, p.230. Index of painters, potters, groups and classes, p.231.

M67 Noble, Joseph Veach. The techniques of painted Attic pottery. Rev. ed. [N.Y.], Thames and Hudson, [1988]. 216p. 263 il. 12 col. plates.

See GLAH 1:M68 for 1st ed.

Reprint with new preface, some bibliographic additions to the footnotes and two additional illustrations of this still useful text on the making of ancient pottery.

M68 Paris. Musée National du Louvre. Département des antiquités grecques, étrusques et romaines. Chefs-d'oeuvre de la céramique grecque dans les collections du Louvre. Par Martine Denoyelle. Introd. par Alain Pasquier. Paris, Réunion des musées nationaux, 1994. 199p. il. (part col.)

Judicious selection of masterpieces.

Notices bibliographiques, p.188–95. Lexique des formes, p.197. Index des numeros usuels, p.199.

M69 Robertson, Martin. The art of vase-painting in classical Athens. Cambridge, Cambridge Univ. Pr., [1992]. xii, 350p. il.

A history of red-figure vase painting, this book is the culmination of many years of study and publication. It is intended to complement and follow the tradition of Beazley's Development of Attic black-figure (1951; repr. 1986).

Contents: (1) The beginning of red-figure; (2) A time of ferment: the red-figure Pioneers and their contemporaries; (3) After the pioneers: red-figure mastery; the beginning of white-ground; (4) Archaic into Classical; (5) Early Classical; (6) High Classical; (7) Developments from the High Classical; (8) The later fifth century: developments into the fourth; (9) The fourth century.

Bibliography and abbreviations, p.324–32. Index, p.339–50.

M70 ———. Greek painting. [Reprint.] N.Y., Rizzoli, 1979. 193p. col. il., map.
Reprint of GLAH 1:M72.

M71 Trendall, Arthur Dale. The red-figured vases of Paestum. Rome, British School, 1987. xxxi, 452p. il., plates.
Thoroughly revised version of the author's Paestan pottery (1936). The third of his catalogs on the vases of Italy. "It attempts to classify as many as possible of the extant Paestan vases known to me and to indicate their place in the wider context of South Italian vase-painting."—*Pref.*

Contents: (1) Introduction and background; (2) The workshop of Asteas and Python; (3) Later Paestan.

Select bibliography, p.xxv–xxxi. Index of collections, p.394–422. Concordances, p.423–30. Classified subject index, 431–42.

M72 ———. Red figure vases of South Italy and Sicily: a handbook. [N.Y.], Thames and Hudson, [1989]. 288p. il. (World of art)
Summary study of this specialized region of vase painting, elsewhere cataloged in depth by the same author.

Contents: (1) General introduction; (2) The origin and development of red-figure vase-painting in south Italy and Sicily in the later 5th century B.C.; (3) Lucanian; (4) Apulian; (5) Campanian; (6) Paestan; (7) Sicilian; (8) Myth and reality.

Chronology, p.270–71. Abbreviations, p.272. Select bibliography, p.273–6. List of illustrations, p.277–83. Index of painters and groups, p.284–85. General index, p.285–87. Index of mythological subjects, p.287–88.

M73 ———, and Cambitoglu, Alexander. The red-figured vases of Apulia. Oxford, Clarendon, [1978–1982]. 3v. il. (Oxford monographs on classical archaeology)
Catalog of Apulian vases, an addition to the authors' efforts to document all the vases produced in the region of Magna Graecia.

Contents: (1:I) Early Apulian: The pioneers; (1:II) The development of the plain style; (1:III) The development of the ornate style; (2) Middle Apulian; (3) Late Apulian.

General bibliography, p.xli–xlv. Index to collections, p.1075–1219. Concordance with CVA and other publications, p.1220–68. Index to mythological scenes, p.1269–78. General index, p.1279–95. Index of painters, groups and sub-groups, p.1296–1301.

———. 1st suppl. London, 1983. xix, 252p. il. 40 leaves of plates. (Bulletin supplement, Univ. of London, Inst. of Classical Studies, no. 42)

———. 2d suppl. London, Univ. of London, Inst. of Classical Studies, 1991–92. 3v., il. (Bulletin supplement, Univ. of London, Inst. of Classical Studies; no. 60)
Catalogs more than 2000 new Apulian vases.

M74 Wehgartner, Irma. Attisch Weissgrundige Keramik: Maltechniken, Werkstätten, Formen,Verwendung. Mainz, Zabern, [1983]. xii, 238p. il. (part col.) 4, 54p. of plates. (Keramikforschungen, 5)
Study of a broad range of vase shapes on which white-ground decoration was used. The second section comprises a catalog of white-ground vases with outline decoration.

Verzeichnis der Gefässe nach Museen und Sammlungen, p.227–32. Verzeichnis der Vasenmaler, Töpfer und Werkstätten, p.233–34. Abbildungsverzeichnis, p.235–38.

Etruria and Rome

M75 La ceramica degli Etruschi: la pittura vascolare. A cura di Marina Martelli. Testi di Benedetta Adembri . . . [et al.] [Novara], Istituto Geografico De Agostino, [1987]. 344p. il. (part col.)
Essential survey of Etruscan vase painting, illustrated with beautiful color plates, summarizing recent research and providing an overview of the field.

Contents: La ceramica geometrica; La ceramica orientalizzante; La ceramica Etrusco-Corinzia; La ceramica a figure nere; La ceramica a figure rosse.

Bibliografia, p.332–41. Indice dei musei, p.342–43. Indice delle provenienze, p.343. Indice degli artisti, delle botteghe e dei gruppi, p.344.

M76 Etruscan painting, catalogue raisonné of Etruscan wall paintings. Stephan Steingräber, ed. English-lang. edition ed. by David Ridgway and Francesca R. Ridgway. Trans. from the German by Mary Blair and from the Italian by Brian Phillips. N.Y., Johnson Reprint, [1986]. 400p. 423 il. 198 col. plates, maps, plans.
"The aim of this new volume . . . is to produce as complete a documentation as possible of Etruscan tomb painting in both words and pictures. It is designed not only to satisfy academic needs but also to serve the legitimate interests of an ever growing wider public."—*Foreword.* With lavish new color photographs and essays by several Etruscan scholars, this is a major addition to the literature in English on Etruscan painting.

Contents: (1) The distribution of tomb painting in Etruria, by Stephan Steingräber; (2) Tarquinia: Topography, history and art, by Stephan Steingräber; (3) A historical survey of discoveries and research, by Francesco Roncalli; (4) Funerary architecture, by Stephan Steingräber; (5) Style, chronology and iconography, by Stephan Steingräber; (6) The historical, social, economic and religious background to Etruscan tomb painting, Francesco Roncalli; (7) Etruscan tomb painting and other types of Etruscan and Italic painting, by Francesco Roncalli; (8) Ancient painting in the Mediterranean basin, by Masanori Aoyagi; (9)Techniques and conservation of Etruscan painting, by Licia Vlad Borelli; (10) Plates; (11) Catalogue of Etruscan tomb paintings, by Stephan Steingräber.

Index of subjects, p.391–94. Concordances, p.394–96. Bibliography, p.397–99.

M77 Ling, Roger. Roman painting. N.Y., Cambridge Univ. Pr., [1991]. xii, 245p. il., col. plates, maps.

"The history of Roman painting is essentially a history of wall-painting."—*Introd.* This welcome study of Roman mural painting provides an overview of and summarizes recent research in the field.

Contents: (1) The antecedents; (2) The First Style; (3) The Second Style; (4) The Third Style; (5) The Fourth Style; (6) Mythological and historical paintings; (7) Other paintings; (8) The Pompeian style in the provinces; (9) Painting after Pompeii; (10) Technique; (11) Painters and patrons.

General bibliography, p.225–26. Bibliography for individual chapters, p.226–35. Index, p.241–45.

M78 Monumenti della pittura antica scoperti in Italia. Roma, Istituto poligrafico e Zecca dello Stato, Libreria dello Stato, 1937– . (22)v. il. (part col.)

See GLAH 1:M80 for description and earlier vols.

Contents: Sez. 1. Tarquinia: (6) Morandi, Allesandro. Le pitture della tomba del Cardinale (1983); Sez. 3. (C) Ostia: (5) Baccini Leotardi, Paola. Pitture con decorazioni vegetale dalle Terme (1978).

M79 La Peinture de Pompéi: témoinages de l'art romain dans la zone ensevelie par Vésuve en 79 ap. J.-C. Préf. de Georges Vallet. Textes de Alfonso De Franciscis . . . [et al.] [Paris], Hazan, [1993]. 2v. il. (part col.), col. plates, maps, plans.

V.1 also published in German as Pompejanische Wandmalerei (Stuttgart, Belser, 1980) and in Italian as La Pittura di Pompei (Milano, Jaca, 1991).

Substantive discussion of the mural paintings that remain in situ in the region of Pompeii. The first volume contains a variety of essays by prominent scholars and the lavish color plates; the second volume consists of a detailed, illustrated catalog of these paintings.

Contents: (1) "Il y avait une fois une ville," par Georges Vallet; La peinture à Pompéi, moments de la recherche et d'étude, par Alfonso De Franciscis; Signification de la peinture pompéienne, par Karl Schefold; Le Ier style, par Ann Laidlaw; Le IIe style, par Volker Michael Strocka; Le IIIe style, par Umberto Pappalardo; Le dernier style pompéien, par Giuseppina Cerulli Irelli; Représentations mythologiques dans la peinture pompéienne, par Erika Simon; Le paysage dans la peinture en Campanie, par Willem J. Th. Peters; Deux "genres" de la peinture pompéienne: la nature morte et la peinture de jardin, par Stefano de Caro; L'Art "populaire," par Fausto Zevi; Signification de la peinture pompéienne dans la peinture hellénistique et romaine, par Masanori Aoyagi. (2) Pompéi, Regio I; Regio II; Regio III; Regio IV; Regio V; Regio VI; Regio VII; Regio VIII; Regio IX, Sépultures; Pompéi, Villa dite des Mystères; Pompéi, pseudo-Villa Impériale; Herculanum; Oplontis; Stabies; Boscotrecase; Boscoreale. Appendices: Meyer-Graft, Reinhard. La technique des peintures murales romaines; Parise Badoni, Franca. Photographier à Pompéi. Le projet de l'Istituto per il catalogo e la documentazione; Strocka, Volker Michael. Le projets de documentation internationale de l'Institut allemand d'archéologie "Maisons de Pompéi."

Bibliographie, vol. 1, p.355–61. Index des noms, v.1, p.367–68. Index des lieux, v.1, p.369–70.

M80 Pompei: pitture e mosaici. Roma, Istituto della enciclopedia italiana, [1990–99]. 10v. il. (part col.), maps, plans.

Systematic and massive illustrated catalog of the wall paintings and mosaics in situ at Pompeii, reproducing photographs taken between 1977–80 by the Istituto Centrale per il Catalogo e la Documentazione. Each vol. treats one or more sectors; v.10 includes views of Pompeii in later European art.

Contents: (1) Regio I, pt.1 (1990); (2) Regio I, pt.2 (1990); (3) Regiones II-III-V (1991); (4) Regio VI, pt.1 (1993); (5) Regio VI, pt.2 (1994); (6) Regiones VI, pt.3, VII, pt.1 (1996); (7) Regio VII, pt.2 (1997); (8) Regio IX, pt.1 (1998); (9) Regio IX, pt.2 (1999); (10) La documentazione nell'opera di disegnatori e pittori dei secoli XVIII e XIX (1995).

Mosaics

M81 Boeselager, Dela von. Antike Mosaiken in Sizilien: Hellenismus und römische Kaiserzeit 3. Jahrhundert v. Chr.-3. Jahrhundert n. Chr. [Roma], Bretschneider, 1983. 220p. il. 67p. of plates, maps, plans. (Archaeologica, 40)

This study brings together recent scholarship on Sicilian mosaics of the Roman period; while not a complete catalog, works from many of the important sites are considered.

Contents: (1) Mosaiken der hellenistischen Zeit; (2) Schwarzweiss-Mosaiken des 1.-3.Jh. n. Chr.; (3) Polychrome Mosaiken des 2. und 3. Jh. n. Chr.; (4) Palermo, Haus A; (5) Ältere Erwähnungen von Mosaikfunden und im Text nicht eingehend behandelte Fragmente.

Konkordanz der wichtigsten Fundortnamen, p.213. Register, p.215–19.

M82 Borsook, Eve. Messages in mosaic: the royal programmes of Norman Sicily, 1130–1187. Oxford, Clarendon, 1990. xxiv, 112p., 118p. of plates, 8 col. plates (Clarendon studies in the history of art)

Well-illustrated investigation of the patronage of three Sicilian mosaic programs, using iconography and inscriptions as evidence of a coordinated scheme of decoration.

Contents: (1) The origins of the new monarchy and its style; (2) Cefalù: echoes of Jerusalem; (3) The Capella Palatina at Palermo; (4) Monreale: the legacy proclaimed.

Bibliography, p.87–101. Index, p.105–12.

M83 Corpus de mosaicos de España. Madrid, Instituto Espanol de Arqueología "Rodrigo Caro" del Consejo Superior de Investigaciones Científicas, 1978– . (10)v. il. (part col.), maps, plans.

Ongoing catalog of the Roman mosaics to be found at Spanish sites and museums. Each volume includes a discussion of regional considerations, plans of major sites, and bibliography.

Contents: (1) Blanco Freijeiro, Antonio. Mosaicos romanos de Mérida (1978); (2) Blanco Freijeiro, Antonio. Mosaicos romanos de Itálica (I) (1978); (3) Blázquez, José María. Mosaicos romanos de Córdoba, Jaén y Málaga (1981); (4) Blázquez, José María. Mosaicos romanos de Sevilla, Granada, Cádiz y Murcia (1982); (5) Blázquez, José María. Mosaicos romanos de la Real Academia de la Historia, Ciudad Real, Toledo, Madrid y Cuenca (1982); (6) Blázquez, José María, and Ortega, T. Mosaicos romanos de Soria (1983); (7) Blázquez, José María, and Mezquiriz, M. A. Mosaicos romanos de Navarra (1985); (8) Blázquez, José María . . . [et al.] Mosaicos romanos de Lérida y Albacete (1989); (9) Blázquez, José María . . . [et al.] Mosaicos romanos del Museo Arqueológico Nacional (1989); (10) Blázquez, José María . . . [et al.] Mosaicos romanos de Leon y Asturias (1993).

M84 Corpus des mosaïques de Tunisie. Margaret A. Alexander and Mongi Ennaifer, co-dir. Tunis, Institut national d'archéologie et d'arts, [1973–]. (7)v. il.

See GLAH 1:M87 for earlier vols.

Contents: (2) Region de Zaghouan, Atlas archéologique de la Tunisie, Feuille 35; fasc. 1: Alexander, Margaret A. . . . [et al.] Thuburbo Majus, les mosaïques de la région du Forum; fasc. 2: Ben Khader, Aicha Ben Abed . . . [et al.] Thuburbo Majus, les mosaïques de la region des Grands Thermes; fasc. 3: Ben Khader . . . [et al.] Thuburbo Majus, les mosaïques dans la region Ouest; fasc. 4: Alexander, Margaret A. Thurburbo Majus, les mosaïques de la region est mise à jour du catalogue de Thuburbo Majus et les environs. Les mosaïques de Ain Mziger, Bir Chana, Draa ben Jouder et Zaghouan.

M85 Daszewski, Wiktor Andrzej. Corpus of mosaics from Egypt I. Mainz, Zabern, 1985– . (1)v. il. (part col.) (Aegyptiaca Treverensia, 3)

First of a 2-vol. set cataloging mosaics found in Egypt; the second vol. will cover late Roman and Byzantine mosaics. Although not as numerous in Egypt as elsewhere in North Africa, the mosaics in Egypt are shown to have elements in common and distinct from others in the Roman Empire.

Contents: (1) Hellenistic and early Roman period (1985).

M86 Le Décor géometrique de la mosaïque romaine: répertoire graphique et descriptif des compositions linéaires et isotropes. Catherine Balmelle . . . [et al.] Dessins de Richard Prudhomme. Paris, Picard, 1985. 431p. il.

Compiled by members of the Association Internationale pour l'Étude de la Mosaïque Romaine, this vol. is a catalog of hundreds of decorative motifs used in Roman mosaics, including standardized terminology in English, French, German, Italian, and Spanish. Separate glossaries provide French equivalents for each language. Excellent pen-and-ink drawings illustrate each example; related motifs are illustrated on the same page to allow comparison.

Table des abréviations, p.407–10. Index, p.411–14. Lexique, p.415–27.

M87 Demus, Otto. Byzantine mosaic decoration: aspects of monumental art in Byzantium. [Reprint.] New Rochelle, Caratzas, 1976. xiii, 97p. il. 64p. of plates.

Originally published London, Paul, Trench, Trubner, 1948.

This essay remains a fundamental study of Byzantine mosaics.

Index, p.95–97.

M88 ———. The mosaics of San Marco in Venice. Chicago, Univ. of Chicago Pr., [1984]. 2v. in 4., il. (part col.)

The first detailed study of the medieval mosaics in San Marco, produced concurrently with a major campaign to photograph the entire interior. The author is the preeminent scholar of mosaics and his work on San Marco spans fifty years. V.1 covers the work of the 11th and 12th centuries; v.2 treats the 13th century. Each is accompanied by a separate vol. of plates, many of which are in magnificent color. Each vol. contains extensive bibliography and indexes of subjects, topography, names, and other topics.

M89 Dunbabin, Katherine M. D. The mosaics of Roman North Africa: studies in iconography and patronage. N.Y., Oxford Univ. Pr., 1978. xx, 303p. il. (part col.) 80p. of plates, maps. (Oxford monographs on classical archaeology)

"Although the opening and closing chapters deal with general aspects, and attempt to place African mosaics within the wider context of mosaic production in the rest of the Roman Empire, in the main part of the book I have concentrated on a study of the classes of subject-matter used on the figured mosaics."—*Pref.*

Selective bibliography, p.280–9. Indexes, p.292–300.

M90 ———. Mosaics of the Greek and Roman world. N.Y., Cambridge Univ. Pr., 2000. 357p. il. (part col.), plates, maps.

"Provides a comprehensive account of mosaics of the ancient world from the early pebble mosaics of Greece to the pavements of Christian churches in the east."—*Pub. note.*

Maps, p.331–38. Glossary of ornamental patterns, p.339–41. General glossary, p.342–43. Abbreviations and bibliography, p.344–47. Index of sites and monuments, p.348–52. General index, p.353–57.

M91 Kitzinger, Ernst. I mosaici del periodo normanno in Sicilia. Palermo, Accademia nazionale di scienze lettere e arti di Palermo, 1992– . (5)v. il. plates, plans.

Ongoing pictorial catalog of Norman mosaics, bringing together hundreds of photographs taken in three substantial campaigns in 1929, 1951, and 1954. Each fasc. includes a brief textual overview, a list of figures, and plans or elevations to indicate the placement of each section.

Contents: (1) La Capella Palatina di Palermo: i mosaici del Presbiterio (1992); (2) La Capella Palatina: i mosaici delle Navate (1993); (3) Il duomo di Monreale: i mosaici dell'abside, della solea e delle cappelle laterali (1994); (4) Il duomo di Monreale: i mosaici del transetto (1995); (5) Il duomo di Monreale: i mosaici dell navate (1996).

M92 Ling, Roger. Ancient mosaics. Princeton, Princeton Univ. Pr., 1998. 144p. 95 il. (part col.), map.

Well-illustrated introductory survey of Greek and Roman mosaics. "Ling traces chronologically and geographically the materials and techniques employed to decorate floors, and later walls and vaults and also addresses the functions and placement of mosaics, their diverse motifs, relations to work in other media, the aims of their patrons, and status of their creators."—*Review*, Bryn Mawr classical review, April 23, 1999.

Glossary, p.138–39. Select bibliography, p.140–41. Index p.142–44.

M93 Mosaici antichi in Italia. Roma, Istituto poligrafico e Zecca dello Stato, 1967– . (8)v. il. (part col.), maps, plans.

See GLAH 1:M92 for earlier vols.

Ongoing corpus of mosaics in Italy. Well-illustrated, with detailed plans and catalog entries.

Contents: Angiolillo, Simonetta. Sardinia (1981); Pisapia, Maria Stella. Regione 1, Stabiae (1989); Guidobaldi, Federico. Sectilia pavimenta di Villa Adriana (1994).

M94 Mosaics. General ed., Carlo Bertelli. [Written by] Xavier Barral i Altet . . . [et al.] N.Y., Gallery Books, [1989]. 360p., col. il.

Trans. of Il mosaico. Milan, Mondadori, 1988.

Pictorial survey of the uses of mosaic from classical times to the present; brief historical chapters are each followed by a selection of good quality illustrations.

Contents: Ancient mosaics, by Carlo Bertelli; The Christian world, by Per Jonas Nordhagen; Byzantine treasures, by Per Jonas Nordhagen; Mosaic vaults and floors in Islam and the West, Xavier Barral I Altet; Renaissance mosaics, by Carlo Bertelli; Mosaic in the eighteenth century, by Maria Grazia Branchetti; From traditional to modern styles, by Agnoldomenico Pica.

Bibliography, p.353–5. Index, p.356–60.

M95 Mosaics of Roman Africa: floor mosaics from Tunisia. [Par] Michèle Blanchard-Lemée . . . [et al.] Photographs by Gilles Mermet. Trans. from the French by Kenneth D. Whitehead. N.Y., Braziller, 1996. 296p. col. il., plans.

Trans. of Sols de l'Afrique romaine. Paris, Imprimerie nationale, 1995.

"Focus[es] . . . on the patrons of the mosaic artisans, the prominent people in the province and in its various cities who, individually and collectively, commissioned these floors."—*Introd.* While concentrating specifically on mosaics from Tunisia, this book presents stunning color illustrations, organized thematically.

Select bibliography, p.296. No index.

M96 Ovadiah, Asher. Geometric and floral patterns in ancient mosaics: a study of their origin in the mosaics from the classical period to the age of Augustus. Roma, Bretschneider, 1980. 205p. il., plates, map.

"The main concern of this work is . . . to study the origins of the geometric and floral patterns of mosaic pavements by seeking comparative material from the earlier arts."—*Introd.* Although this study synthesizes a broad range of mosaic pattern, its presentation is somewhat marred by inadequate illustrations. Note also that the plates are not directly referred to in the text. Abbreviations and bibliography, p.11–16. No index.

M97 ———, and Ovadiah, Ruth. Hellenistic, Roman and early Byzantine mosaic pavements in Israel. [Roma], Bretschneider, [1987]. 276p. il. (part col.), 192p. of plates. (Bibliotheca archaeologica, 6)

Serves as a sequel to the catalog by Michael Avi-Yonah, Mosaic pavements in Palestine (1933–35); this volume deals with mosaics discovered in the region between 1935 and 75. Organized by site. "The work is unfortunately incomplete in parts, as full details are not always given in the publications, and also because we were not in a position to examine the pavements for ourselves."—*Pref.*

Bibliography, p.189–99. Index of geometric motifs, p.201–08; floral motifs, p.208–10; figurative motifs, p.210–14; religious motifs, p.214–15.

M98 Piccirillo, Michele. The mosaics of Jordan. Ed. by Patricia M. Bikai and Thomas A. Dailey. Amman, Jordan, American Center of Oriental Research, [1993]. 383p. il. (part col.), map, plans. (American Center of Oriental Research Publications, 1)

Sumptuously illustrated survey of the mosaics found in Jordan, primarily made during the 5th through the 8th centuries A.D. Especially valuable for the juxtaposition of site views and plans with mosaics themselves.

Bibliography, p.367–74. Index, p.375–82. Index of mosaics, p.383.

M99 Recueil général des mosaïques de la Gaule. Paris, Centre national de la recherche scientifique, 1957– . (10)v. il., maps, plates (part col.), plans. (Supplément à Gallia, 10)

See GLAH 1:M95 for earlier vols.

Contents: (2) Province de Lyonnaise, fasc. 2: Stern, Henri, and Blanchard-Lemée, Michèle. Partie sud-est (1975); fasc. 3: Blanchard-Lemée, Michèle. Partie centrale (1977); fasc. 4: Blanchard-Lemée, Michèle. Partie occidentale (1991); fasc. 5: Darmon, Jean-Pierre. Partie nord-ouest (1994). (3) Province de Narbonnaise, fasc. 1: Lavagne, Henri. Partie centrale (1979); fasc. 2: Lancha, Janine. Vienne (1981). (4) Province d'Aquitaine, fasc. 1: Balmelle, Catherine. Partie méridionale (Piémont pyrénéen) (1980); fasc. 2, Balmelle, Catherine. Partie méridionale, suite (les pays gascons) (1987).

SEE ALSO: Wilpert, Die romische Mosaiken der kirchlichen Bauten vom IV.-XIII. Jahrhundert (GLAH 2:M114); Pompei: pitture e mosaici (GLAH 2:M80).

Early Christian—Byzantine

M100 Carr, Annemarie Weyl. Byzantine illumination, 1150–1250: the study of a provincial tradition. Chicago, Univ. of Chicago Pr., [1987]. xxxiv, 320p. il. 12 color microfiche. (Studies in medieval manuscript illumination) (Chicago visual library text-fiche series, 47)

Study and catalog of a group of more than 100 provincial Byzantine manuscripts exemplifying what the author calls "the decorative style," illustrated entirely on color microfiche. Catalog entries include detailed codicology, summary of illuminations and inscriptions, and bibliography.

"Works cited," p.292–313. Index of monuments, p.314–20.

M101 Cormack, Robin. Writing in gold: Byzantine society and its icons. N.Y., Oxford Univ. Pr., 1985. 270p. 100 il., map.

History of Byzantine art based primarily on contemporaneous texts. "I have chosen a series of texts and images which seem to me to offer a pattern through which it is possible to make sense of Byzantine art and culture."—*Pref.*

Contents: (1) The visible saint: St. Theodore of Sykeon; (2) The saint imagined: St. Demetrios of Thessaloniki; (3) Iconoclasm: the imposition of change; (4) After iconoclasm: the illusion of tradition; (5) Paradise sought: the imperial use of art; (6) Paradise gained: the private use of art.

Glossary, p.258–59. Bibliography, p.260–63. Index, p.267–70.

M102 Corpus der byzantinischen Miniaturenhandschriften. Hrsg. von Otto Demus. Red., Irmgard Hutter. Stuttgart, Hiersemann, 1977– . (4)v. in 8. il. (part col.) (Denkmäler der Buchkunst, Bd. 2–3, 5:1–2, 9:1–2)

See GLAH 1:M96 for original annotation.

Initial vols. of complete corpus of Byzantine manuscripts.

Contents: (1) Hutter, Irmgard. Oxford Bodleian Library I (1977); (2) Hutter, Irmgard. Oxford Bodleian Library II (1978); (3) Hutter, Irmgard. Oxford Bodleian Library III (2v., 1982); (4) Hutter, Irmgard. Oxford Christ Church (2v., 1993); (5) Hutter, Irmgard. Oxford College Libraries (2v., 1997).

M103 Cutler, Anthony. The aristocratic psalters in Byzantium. [Paris], Picard, [1984]. 253p. il. (Bibliothèque des cahiers archéologiques, 13)

Descriptive catalog of 58 Byzantine illuminated psalters; each entry contains a verbal description of each illumination as well as bibliography. The author intended a companion volume of analysis that has not yet appeared.

Bibliographic abbreviations, p.10–14. Index, p.121–23.

M104 Ethnike Bibliotheke. Catalogue of the illuminated Byzantine manuscripts of the Library of Greece. By Anna Marav-Chatzinicolaou, Christina Toufexi-Paschou. Athens, Publications Bureau of the Academy of Athens, 1978– . (2)v. il. (part col.).

Detailed catalog of 135 manuscripts (to date) from the National Library collection; a third vol. will deal with psalters and other Byzantine manuscripts. Particularly useful as these manuscripts have been scarcely published; the numerous color details will be particularly welcome. Each vol. includes bibliographic abbreviations and an index; manuscript entries contain descriptions of each folio, provenance, and bibliographic references.

Contents: (1) Manuscripts of New Testament texts 10th–12th century (1978); (2) Manuscripts of New Testament texts 13th–15th century (1985).

M105 The icon. [By] Kurt Weitzmann . . . [et al.] N.Y., Knopf, 1982. 419p. il. (chiefly col.)

Originally published as Le icone. Milan, Mondadori, 1981. French and German eds.

Lavishly illustrated and wide-ranging introductory survey of the history of icons.

Contents: (1) The icons of Constantinople, by Kurt Weitzmann; (2) The icons of Georgia, by Gainé Alibegasvili and Aneli Volskaya; (3) The icons of the Balkan peninsula and the Greek islands (1), by Manolis Chatzidakis and Gordana Babic; (4) The icons of the period of the Crusades, by Kurt Weitzmann; (5) The icons of Russia, by Mihail Alpatov; (6) The icons of the Balkan peninsula and the Greek islands (2), by Gordana Babic and Manolis Chatzidakis; (7) The post-Byzantine icons of Wallachia and Moldavia, by Teodora Voinescu.

Selected readings, p.413–15.

M106 Illuminierte Papyri, Pergamente und Papiere I. Hrsg. von Ulrike Horak. Wien, Holzhausen, [1992]. 2v. in 1. il. (part col.). (Pegasus Oriens, 1)

First volume of catalog of the illustrated Byzantine and Coptic papyrus collection in the Austrian National Library. Includes detailed entries on 67 fragments of manuscripts on papyrus, parchment, and paper. Useful for its summary list of 359 published fragments in other collections, with index of terms, p.262–78.

Abgekürzt zitierte Literatur, p.12–16. Weitere benützte Literatur, p.17–24. Sachindex zu den hier edierten Objekten, p.199–209. Allgemeiner Sachindex, p.210–22. Griechische und koptische Wörter, p.223. Verzeichnis zitierter Papyri, p.224–26.

M107 The illustrations in the manuscripts of the Septuagint. Ed. by Kurt Weitzmann, Herbert L. Kessler. Princeton, N.J., publ. for the Dept. of Art and Archaeology of Princeton Univ. by Princeton Univ. Pr., [1986–]. (2)v. (Princeton monographs in art and archaeology, 45).

The initial vols. of a long-awaited series originally proposed by Charles Rufus Morey at Princeton in the 1920s; six vols. were proposed, each to treat a separate category of Byzantine illustrations of books of the Old Testament.

Contents: (1) Weitzmann, Kurt, and Kessler, Herbert L. The Cotton Genesis: British Library Codex Cotton Otho B. VI (1986); (2) Weitzmann, Kurt, and Bernabò, Massimo. The Byzantine Octateuchs (1999).

M108 Lowden, John. Illuminated prophet books: a study of Byzantine manuscripts of the major and minor prophets. University Park, Penn. State Univ. Pr, [1988]. xvi, 128p. 92p. of plates (part col.)

Close study of small group of related manuscripts allows the author to "pose far-reaching questions about the nature of Byzantine manuscript painting."—*Review*, Speculum, v.66, 1991, p.437.

Notes, p.93–107. Catalogue of manuscripts, p.109–19. Ruling patterns, p.120–21. Descriptions of the prophets, p.122–23. Index, p.125–28.

M109 Talbot Rice, David, and Talbot Rice, Tamara. Icons and their dating: a comprehensive study of their chro-

nology and provenance. London, Thames and Hudson, [1974]. 192p. il., plates (part col.)
U.S. ed: Woodstock, N.Y., Overlook, 1974.

"The purpose of this book is to provide a framework for the chronology of icons by reproducing and analysing almost all those which can be dated with any degree of precision."—*Introd.* Presented in the form of a catalog, this book attempts to establish the outlines of the study of icons. Chapters on Byzantium, Yugoslavia, Bulgaria, Greece, Cyprus, and Russia include short histories of icons in these regions, followed by "Notes to the plates," individual comments on specific images. An appendix lists recorded icon painters; another lists more dated icons not discussed here.

Index, p.189–92.

M110 Velmans, Tania. La peinture murale byzantine à la fin du Moyen age. Paris, Klincksieck, 1977– . (1)v. il. maps. (Bibliothèque des cahiers archéologiques, 11)
The first of a proposed 2-vol. study of Byzantine mural painting; v.2, intended to discuss each monument more fully, has not appeared yet. Arranged in two sections: The first discusses the historical background of mural painting, the second contains a summary of each relevant church organized chronologically and geographically. Numerous illustrations, but references are only made to these from the overview section.

Bibliographie, p.259–76. Index des noms, p.279–85. Index des noms de lieux, p.286–92. Index iconographique, p.293–303. Index des noms d'auteurs modernes, p.304–10.

M111 Weitzmann, Kurt. Late antique and early Christian book illumination. N.Y., Braziller, [1977]. 126p. il. (chiefly col.)
Intended for the general reader, an overview of the early history of illuminated manuscripts with 48 color plates, each representing an important manuscript of the Early Christian period. Brief commentary on each plate. Very select bibliography, mostly out-of-date.

M112 ______, and Galivaris, George. The Monastery of Saint Catherine at Mount Sinai, the illuminated Greek manuscripts. Princeton, Princeton Univ. Pr., [1990–]. (1)v. il., plates (part col.)
Well-illustrated catalog of the manuscripts held at Saint Catherine, site of one of the oldest monastic libraries; the author has also published on its icons and its architecture. A second vol. is intended to cover the manuscripts of the 13th–15th centuries. Thorough entries for the manuscripts include descriptions of each illumination, notes on condition, a section on iconography and style and extensive bibliography. A general index, iconographic index, and an index of manuscripts are included.

Contents: (1) From the ninth to the twelfth century.

M113 ______, and Kessler, Herbert L. The frescoes of the Dura synagogue and Christian art. Washington, D.C., Dumbarton Oaks, [1990]. xiv, 202p. 202 il. (Dumbarton Oaks studies, 28)
Discussion of the origins and influence of the narrative structure of the Dura Europos synagogue frescoes in both Early Christian and Byzantine art. The authors see these paintings as a key link between Jewish and Christian art of the period.

Select bibliography, p.185–95. Index, p.197–202.

M114 Wilpert, Josef. Die romische Mosaiken der kirchlichen Bauten vom IV.-XIII. Jahrhundert. [Hrsg. von] Walter N. Schumacher. Freiburg im Breisgau, Herder, [1976]. 344p., 124 col. plates, part folded.
Partial reprint of the seminal work issued in 1916 as 2 vols. of a 4-vol. work: Die romischen Mosaiken und Malereien der kirchlichen Bauten vom IV. bis XIII. Jahrhundert (GLAH 1:M109). The original was particularly noted for its oversize, detailed color plates. This ed. attempts to replicate this quality; Schumacher has added descriptions of individual plates with updated bibliography; the number of illustrations has been slightly reduced.

Islamic

M115 Arthur M. Sackler Gallery (Smithsonian Institution). An annotated and illustrated checklist of the Vever Collection. [By] Glenn D. Lowry . . . [et al.] Contrib. by Elizabeth FitzHugh, Susan Nemazee, and Janet G. Snyder. Washington, D.C., Arthur M. Sackler Gallery; Seattle, Univ. of Wash. Pr., [1988]. 446p. il.
"The purpose of this checklist is to present in as clear and simple manner as possible the almost 500 works of art in the Vever Collection . . . acquired in 1986."—*Pref.* Preliminary catalog of this seminal collection; includes manuscripts, albums, individual paintings and drawings, calligraphy, and bookbindings. To be used in conjunction with the following title, which discusses the collector and provides color illustrations. Summary entries provide basic physical description, provenance, publication history, and notes.

Appendixes include a list of authors/manuscripts, p.388–89; artists, p.390; calligraphers, p.391; patrons, p.392; dates and geographic regions, p.393–94; seals, p.395–97; recent provenance, p.398–412; concordances, p.413–24; study of pigments, p.425–32; study of paper, p.433–40. Bibliographic abbreviations, p.441–46.

M116 ______. A jeweler's eye: Islamic arts of the book from the Vever Collection. [By] Glenn D. Lowry with Susan Nemazee. Washington, D.C., Arthur M. Sackler Gallery; Seattle, Univ. of Wash. Pr., [1988]. 240p. il. (chiefly col.), map, ports.
Collection of 76 color plates reproduced from manuscripts in the Vever collection, accompanied by a remembrance by his grandson and an overview of Vever's collections of both Western and Middle Eastern objects.

Chronology, p.221–4. Index, p.237–40.

M117 British Library. Dept. of Oriental Manuscripts and Printed Books. Miniatures from Persian manuscripts, a catalogue and subject index of paintings from Persia, India and Turkey in the British Library and the British Museum. [By] Norah M. Titley. [London], British Museum, [1977]. xii, 358p. 41 plates.
"This volume had its beginnings in response to a practical need—that of finding illustrations of a variety of subjects

both for research and for publication, from the large collection of Persian manuscripts in the British Library and British Museum."—*Pref.* Catalog of 404 manuscripts, arranged alphabetically by the author of the text; the bulk of each entry is an individual description of each miniature. The great value of this and the following work are the detailed subject and other indexes.

Author index, p.180–82; titles, p.183–85; artists, p.188–90; subjects, p.203–350. Classified bibliography, p.351–58.

M118 ______. Miniatures from Turkish manuscripts, a catalogue and subject index of paintings in the British Library and British Museum. [By] Norah M. Titley. [London], British Library, [1981]. 144p. il., 54 plates.

Catalog of the miniatures found in 72 manuscripts and related works.

Author index, p.74. Title index, p.75. Index of costume and emblems, p.77–78. Index of musical instruments, p.79. Index of occupations and ranks, p.80–82. Detailed subject index, p.85–139. Classified bibliography, p.140–44.

M119 Dickson, Martin Bernard. The Houghton Shahnameh, introd. and described by Martin Bernard Dickson and Stuart Cary Welch. Cambridge, publ. for the Fogg Art Museum by Harvard Univ. Pr., 1981. 2v. il., facsims. (part col.)

Deluxe full-size reproduction of all 258 miniatures, now scattered among numerous owners, from the most lavish and elaborate copy of this Persian epic. The first vol. provides an illustrated scholarly guide to the manuscript as well as discussion of each of the artists responsible for the miniatures. The second vol. contains the sepia-toned collotype reproductions, interspersed with narrative commentary, physical description including colors used, and notes on the illustrated inscription if present.

Bibliography, v.1, p.273–84. Index, v.1, p.285–93. Index of characters and places, v.2, p.543–55.

M120 A history of Turkish painting. [By] Gunsel Renda . . . [et al.] [Introd., Oleg Grabar]. [Genève], Palasar, [1987]. 444p. il. (chiefly col.)

Well-illustrated and thorough survey of Turkish painting of the last two centuries.

Contents: Traditional Turkish painting and the beginnings of western trends, by Gunsel Renda; Painting in Turkey in XIX and early XX century, by Turan Erol; Post-Second World War trends in Turkish painting, by Adnan Turani; The search for a new identity in Turkish painting, by Kaya Özsezgin; The art of the print in Turkey, by Mustafa Asher.

Index, p.440–44.

M121 India Office Library. Persian paintings in the India Office Library: a descriptive catalogue. [By] B. W. Robinson. [London], Sotheby, [1976]. xiii, 271p. il., 16 col. plates.

Summary catalog of the India Office collection of manuscripts and single leaves; entries include brief description and bibliography; the titles for each illumination are given.

Contents: The Mongol period; The Timurid period; The Safawid period; The Zand and Qajar periods.

Index of authors and texts, p.257–58. Index of painters and calligraphers, p.259. Index of subjects, p.260–68.

M122 James, David Lewis. Qur'ans of the Mamluks. N.Y., Thames and Hudson, [1988]. 270p. il. (part col.) map.

Beautifully illustrated study of the calligraphy and illumination of 14th-century korans, focusing on specific production centers and workshop practice. An appended catalog lists 76 dated examples (only some of which are covered in the text) with information on patronage, scribe and/or illuminator, and bibliography.

Contents: (1) Penmanship and painting in early Qur'ans; (2) The Bahri Mamluks; (3) Qur'ans in Cairo, 1304–30; (4) The imperial Qur'ans of Iraq; (5) The imperial Qur'ans of Iran; (6) Cairo and the beginning of the classic tradition; (7) Back to Baghdad; (8) Qur'ans of Sultan Sha'ban, 1363–76; (9) The century reviewed.

Glossary, p.259–60. Bibliography, p.261–65. Index, p.268–70.

M123 John Rylands Library. Persian paintings in the John Rylands Library: a descriptive catalogue. [By] B. W. Robinson. London, Sotheby, [1980]. 365p. il., 16 col. plates.

Well-illustrated summary catalog of the Rylands collection of manuscripts and single leaves; entries include brief description and bibliographic references. Titles for each illumination are given.

Indexes by author, painter or calligrapher, p.353; by subject, p.355–63.

M124 Lings, Martin. The Quranic art of calligraphy and illumination. Boulder, Colo., Shambhala, 1978. 242p. col. il. (Repr.: N.Y., Interlink, 1987)

First publ. in Great Britain by the World of Islam Festival Trust, 1976.

Beautifully illustrated overview of the styles of scripts and illumination used in Qur'ans.

Contents: (1) Kufic calligraphy; (2) Naskhi calligraphy; (3) The principles of Qur'an illumination; (4) The larger cursive calligraphy of the east; (5) Illumination under the Mamluks and the Mongols; (6) Illumination under the Timurids; (7) Illumination under the Ottomans and the Safavids; (8) Calligraphy and illumination in the Islamic west.

Index, p.240–41.

M125 New York. Pierpont Morgan Library. Islamic and Indian manuscripts and paintings in the Pierpont Morgan Library. By Barbara Schmitz. N.Y., Pierpont Morgan Library, 1997. xxii, 513p. il. (part col.)

The first catalog of the Morgan Library's holdings, which comprise more than 1,000 miniature paintings from the 13th to the 19th centuries and nearly 200 Qur'an leaves from the 9th to the 11th centuries. Many of these manuscripts and paintings, all of which are fully described, are reproduced here for the first time. Divided into six sections: Persian, Turkish, Arabic, Albums, Provincial Mughal, and Indian.

Bibliography, p.473–87. Indices of manuscripts in the Morgan Library (includes concordances, authors, titles, artists, calligraphers, dated manuscripts and leaves, bindings, and former owners), p.489–96. Iconographical index of miniatures and illustrations, p.497–513.

M126 New York Public Library. Islamic manuscripts in the New York Public Library. [By] Barbara Schmitz. With contrib. by Latif Khayyat, Svat Soucek, Massoud Pourfarrokh. N.Y., Oxford Univ. Pr., 1992. xxix, 439p. il. (part col.), plates.

Detailed catalog of the illuminated and textual Islamic manuscripts in the library's collections; each entry includes physical description, discussion, bibliographic notes, and provenance. Each illustration is listed with title and dimensions.

Contents: (1) Arabic illustrated manuscripts; (2) Persian illustrated manuscripts and lacquer bindings; (3) Illustrated manuscripts of the Late Mughal and provincial Indian schools; (4) Turkish illustrated manuscripts; (5) Manuscripts in Arabic; (6) Manuscripts in Persian and Urdu; (7) Manuscripts in Turkish.

Bibliography, p.383–94. Index of titles, p.395–99; of authors, p.400–03; of artists, p.404; of calligraphers, p.405–07; of former owners, p.408; subjects, p.409–24.

M127 Österreichische Nationalbibliothek. Islamische Handschriften. Wien, Verlag der Österreichischen Akademie der Wissenschaften, 1983– . (4)v. il. (part col.) (Die illumierten Handschriften und Inkunabeln der Österreichischen Nationalbibliothek, 4–[5])

Detailed scholarly catalogs of Islamic illuminated manuscripts and single miniatures. A third set will cover manuscripts in Turkish. Entries include detailed physical description including binding, decoration, colophon, type of calligraphy, provenance, and individual descriptions of illuminations, many of which are illustrated in the second vol.

Contents: (1) Duda, Dorothea. Persische Handschriften (2v., 1983); (2) ———. Die Handschriften in arabischer Sprache (2v., 1992).

Includes bibliography. Index of authors; titles; painters and calligraphers; patrons; iconographic themes.

M128 Pages of perfection: Islamic paintings and calligraphy from the Russian Academy of Sciences, St. Petersburg. Written by Yuri A. Petrosyan . . . [et al.] Essays by Marie Lukens Swietochowski and Stefano Carboni. [Lugano], ARCH Foundation, [1995]. 339p., col. il. maps.

Catalog of the exhibition, Musée du Petit Palais, Paris (1994–95), and other locations. Catalog also published in Italian, German, and French. This beautifully illustrated exhibition catalog documents 67 Islamic manuscripts from the Russian Institute of Oriental Studies. The ARCH Foundation supported the exhibition and provided funds for conservation. Four essays by Russian and American curators provide historical context; catalog entries were prepared by the Russian curators.

List of donors, p.321–27. Selected bibliography of Institute publications, p.332–35. Selected bibliography of primarily Russian publications, p.336–39.

M129 Soudavar, Abolala. Art of the Persian courts, selections from the Art and History Trust Collection. With a contrib. by Milo Cleveland Beach. N.Y., Rizzoli, [1992]. 423p. col. il.

Published in conjunction with the exhibition, Los Angeles County Museum of Art (1992). Written by the collector himself, this lavishly illustrated volume provides a useful introduction to the subject of Persian painting, using examples from a single collection.

Contents: (1) The Mongols; (2) Teymur; (3) The court of Soltan Hosayn Mirza Bayqara; (4) The Turkoman dynasties; (5) The Safavid synthesis; (6) Sixteenth-century painting; (7) Reza-e Abbasi and Esfahan painting; (8) Persian culture and Mughal India, by Milo Cleveland Beach; (9) European and Indian influences; (10) Eighteenth- and nineteenth-century Iran. Appendixes: Calligraphers copying masters; Persian as an administrative language; The Divine Glory.

Index, p.417–23.

M130 Titley, Norah M. Persian miniature painting and its influence on the art of Turkey and India: the British Library collections. Austin, Univ. of Texas Pr, [1984]. 272p. il. (part col.), map.

More than a guide to the British Library collections, this well-illustrated volume provides an accessible history of Persian painting, including comparison with examples from other repositories and highlighting its influences on the work of other cultures.

Contents: (1) Antecedents and invasions; (2) Development of the Persian miniature in the early fourteenth century; (3) Fourteenth-century painting at Tabriz and Baghdad: a reflection of the times; (4) The originality of fourteenth-century Shiraz painting and its influence abroad; (5) The brilliance of Herat as a centre under the patronage of the descendants of Timur, 1415–1447; (6) From the death of Shahrukh to Isma'il I, 1447–1500; (7) The early Safavid period, Tabriz and Bukhara; (8) Shiraz painting in the sixteenth century; (9) Qazvin, Mashhad and Herat: late sixteenth to early seventeenth century; (10) Shah 'Abbas the Great and his successors; (11) Ottoman Turkey; (12) The Sultanate period of India and the influence of Persian art, fifteenth to mid-sixteenth century; (13) Mughal India; (14) Methods and materials; (15) Literature.

Select bibliography, p.259–61. Index, p.267–72.

M131 Topkapi Sarayi Muzesi. The Topkapi Saray Museum: the albums and illustrated manuscripts. Trans., exp. and ed. by J. M. Rogers from the original Turkish by Filiz Cagman and Zeren Tanindi. Boston, Little Brown, [1986]. 280p. col. il, maps.

Composite of a Japanese ed. (Tokyo, Dentsu, 1980) and a Turkish ed. (Istanbul, Baskan, 1979).

Beautiful illustrated survey of manuscript illumination from one of the most important collections of Islamic art; issued as part of a multi-volume set on all aspects of the museum's collections. Each chapter provides a brief introduction, followed by a selection of illustrations with individual annotations.

Contents: (1) The Topkapi Saray Museum: the Library and its origins; (2) Scriptoria and studies: organization and methods; (3) Approval and disapproval of images in Islam; (4) Libraries in early Islam; (5) Secular illustration; (6) The

Mongols; (7) The Timurids and their rivals; (8) China, chinoiserie and Islam in the fifteenth century; (9) The Uzbeks and the Safavids: (10) The Ottomans: origins; (11) The Ottomans: the classical age; (12) Ottoman religious painting; (13) The seventeenth and eighteenth centuries and Westernization.

Selected bibliography, p.267. Index, p.277–80.

M132 Welch, Anthony, and Welch, Stuart Cary. Arts of the Islamic book: the collection of Prince Sadruddin Aga Khan. Ithaca, published for the Asia Society by Cornell Univ. Pr., [1982]. 240p. il. (part col.), plates.

Catalog of the exhibition, Asia Society (1982–83), and other locations. Highlights 80 objects from a seminal private collection of Islamic manuscripts; see the catalog of the collection for further information on individual works (GLAH 1:I180). Sections on Arab lands, Ottoman Turkey, Iran, and Iraq include a general introduction to each followed by annotations to individual illustrations.

SEE ALSO: Arts of the book in Central Asia (GLAH 2:N257); The Nasser D. Khalili Collection of Islamic Art (GLAH 2:I199).

Carolingian—Gothic

M133 Alexander, J. J. G. Medieval illuminators and their methods of work. New Haven, Yale Univ. Pr., 1992. vii, 214p. 247 il. (part col.)

Fundamental study of medieval painters' techniques and practices, based on the author's James P. R. Lyell Lectures in Bibliography at Oxford. Assimilates much previous scholarship on the topic. Copiously illustrated with examples from a wide range of source manuscripts.

Contents: (1) The medieval illuminator: sources of information; (2) Technical aspects of the illumination of a manuscript; (3) Programmes and instructions for illuminators; (4) Illuminators at work: The early Middle Ages; (5) Illuminators at work: The twelfth and thirteenth centuries; (6) Illuminators at work: The fourteenth and fifteenth centuries.

Bibliography, p.187–203. Index of manuscripts, p.204–08. Index of subjects, p.209–10. Index of names, p.211–14.

M134 Cahn, Walter. Romanesque Bible illumination. Ithaca, Cornell Univ. Pr., [1982]. 304p. 211 il. (part col.)

Well-illustrated survey of Bible illustration of the early medieval and Romanesque periods. Includes selective catalog of 150 11th- and 12th-century Bibles, including specific descriptions and bibliography.

Contents: (1) Ancient beginnings; (2) Bible illumination in Carolingian times; (3) Mozarabs, Anglo-Saxons and Ottonians; (4) The eleventh century; (5) Continuity and innovation; (6) Themes and variations; (7) The artists and their patrons.

Bibliography, p.295–97. Index, p.300–04.

M135 Calkins, Robert G. Illuminated books of the Middle Ages. Ithaca, Cornell Univ. Pr., [1983]. 341p. 182 plates (part col.)

"The purpose of this book . . . is to introduce various types of medieval illuminated manuscripts as coherent functional objects that were decorated and used in a particular way."—*Pref.* Survey of the most common types of liturgical and devotional medieval books, focusing on 15 key examples. Most useful for the researcher in need of a basic understanding of how these illuminated books were used.

Contents: (1) The insular gospel book; (2) The Carolingian bible; (3) The imperial gospel book; (4) The Ottonian evangelistary; (5) The mass book; (6) The psalter; (7) Books for the Divine Office; (8) The book of hours; (9) Other types of manuscripts.

Bibliography, p.324–34. Index, p.335–41.

M136 Carolingian painting. Introduction by Florentine Mütherich. Provenances and commentaries by Joachim E. Gaede. N.Y., Braziller, [1976]. 126p. il. (part col.)

Abbreviated survey of Carolingian manuscript painting with 48 individual illuminations annotated and described.

Select bibliography, p.23.

M137 Corpus vitrearum medii aevi. Pub. with the coop. of the Comité Internationale d'Histoire de l'Art [publisher varies], 1956– . il., plates (part mounted col.)

See GLAH 1:P434 for original annotation and previous vols.

Contents: ———. Belgique: (4) Bemden, Yvette vanden. Les vitraux de la première moitié du XVIe siècle conservés en Belgique: provinces de Liège, Luxembourg, Namur (1981); ———. Belgique. Série études: (1) Bemden, Yvette vanden, and Fontaine, Chantal. Cartons de vitraux du XVIIe siècle: la Cathedrale Saint-Michel, Bruxelles-Hodiamont, Arnout Balis (1994). ———. Deutschland: (1) Schwaben: (t.2) Becksmann, Rüdiger. Die mittelalterlichen Glasmalereien in Schwaben von 1350 bis 1530: ohne Ulm (1986); (t.3) Scholz, Hartmut. Die mittelalterlichen Glasmalereien in Ulm (1994); (2) Baden und Pfalz: (t.1) Becksmann, Rüdiger. Die mittelalterlichen Glasmalereien in Baden und der Pfalz: ohne Freiburg i. Br. (1979); (3) Hessen und Rheinhessen: (t.2) Hess, Daniel. Die mittelalterlichen Glasmalereien in Frankfurt und im Rhein-Main-Gebiet (1999); (4) Köln: (t.1) Rode, Herbert. Die mittelalterlichen Glasmalereien des Kölner Domes (1974); (7) Niedersachsen: (t.2) Becksmann, Rüdiger, and Korn, Dietrich. Die mittelalterlichen Glasmalereien in Lüneburg und den Heideklostern (1992); (13) Regensburg und Oberpfalz: (t.1) Fritzsche, Gabriela. Die mittelalterlichen Glasmalereien im Regensburger Dom (1987); (15) Erfurt: (t.1) Drachenberg, Erhard; Maercker, Karl-Joachim; and Schmidt, Christa. Die mittelalterliche Glasmalerei in den Ordenskirchen und im Angermuseum zu Erfurt (1976); (t.2) Drachenberg, Erhard. Die mittelalterliche Glasmalerei im Erfurter Dom (2v.; 1980–83); (16) Richter, Christa. Die mittelalterlichen Glasmalereien in Muhlhausen-Thuringen (1993); (18) Stendal: (t.1) Maercker, Karl-Joachim. Die mittelalterliche Glasmalerei in Stendaler Dom (1988); (t.2) Maercker, Karl-Joachim. Die mittelalterlichen Glasmalereien in der Stendaler Jakobikirche (1995). ———. Deutschland. Studien: (1) Scholz, Hartmut. Entwurf und Ausführung: Werkstattpraxis in der Nürnberger Glasmalerei der Dürerzeit (1991); (2) Bornschein, Falko . . . [et al.] Erfurt, Köln,

Oppenheim: Quellen und Studien zur Restaurierungsgeschichte mittelalterlicher Farbverglasungen (1996). ———. Espanya: (6–9) Catalunya: (1) Ainaud de Lasarte, Juan . . . [et al.] Els vitralls medievals de l'Esglesia de Santa Maria del Mar, a Barcelona (1985); (2) ———. Els vitralls de la Catedral de Girona (1987); (3) ———. Els Vitralls del monestir de Santes Creus i la Catedral de Tarragona (1992); (4) ———. Els vitralls de la Catedral de Barcelona i del Monestir de Pedralbes (1997). ———. France: (8) Département de Meurthe-et-Moselle: (1) Les vitraux de Saint-Nicolas-de-Port (1993); (9) Département du Bas-Rhin: (1) Beyer, Victor . . . [et al.] Les vitraux de la cathédrale Notre-Dame de Strasbourg (1986). ———. France. Série complementaire: (1) Les vitraux de Paris, de la région parisienne, de la Picardie et du Nord-Pas-de-Calais (1978); (2) Les vitraux du Centre et des Pays de la Loire (1981); (3) Les vitraux de Bourgogne, Franche-Comte, et Rhône-Alpes (1986); (4) Les vitraux de Champagne-Ardenne (1992); (5) Herold, Michel, Gatouillat, Françoise. Les vitraux de Lorraine et d'Alsace (1994). ———. France. Série "études": (2) Manhes, Colette. Les vitraux narratifs de la cathédrale de Chartres: étude iconographique (1993); (3) Grodecki, Louis. Études sur les vitraux de Suger a Saint-Denis (XIIe siècle) (1995). ———. Great Britain: (1) Newton, Peter A. The county of Oxford: a catalogue of medieval stained glass (1979); (2) Caviness, Madeline Harrison. The windows of Christ Church Cathedral, Canterbury (1981); (3) French, Thomas W., and O'Connor, David. York Minster: a catalogue of medieval stained glass (1987–). ———. Great Britain: Occasional papers: (2) Newton, Roy G. The deterioration and conservation of painted glass (2d ed., 1982); (3) Morgan, Nigel J. The medieval painted glass of Lincoln Cathedral (1983). ———. Great Britain: Summary catalogue: (1) Cole, William. A catalogue of Netherlandish and North European roundels in Britain (1993); (2) French, Thomas W. York Minster: the great east window (1995); (3) Hebgin-Barnes, Penny. The medieval stained glass of the county of Lincolnshire (1996); (4) Marks, Richard. The medieval stained glass of Northamptonshire (1998); (5) French, Thomas W. York Minster: the St William window (1999). ———. Italy: (4) La Lombardia: (1) Pirina, Caterina. Le vetrate del Duomo di Milano dai Visconti agli Sforza (1986). ———. Netherlands: (1, 3) The stained-glass windows in the Sint Janskerk at Gouda (1997–). ———. Österreich: (3) Bacher, Ernst. Die mittelalterlichen Glasgemälde in der Steiermark (1979) ———. Portugal: Barros, Carlos. O vitral em Portugal: seculos XV–XVI (1983). ———. Schweiz: (4) Kurmann-Schwarz, Brigitte. Die Glasmalereien des 15. bis 18. Jahrhunderts im Berner Münster (1998). ———. [Miscellaneous]: Corpus vitrearum, histoire et état actuel de l'entreprise internationale. Wien, Österreichische Akademie der Wissenschaften, 1982. Proceedings of various international colloquia related to the CVMA have also been published.

M138 De Hamel, Christopher. A history of illuminated manuscripts. 2d ed. rev., enl. and with new ill. [London, Phaidon, 1994]. 272p. 240 il. (chiefly col.)

1st ed. 1986.

Well-illustrated readable survey of medieval manuscripts, focusing less on the illustrations in isolation and more on the role of these books as a whole. "Gives the reader an excellent background knowledge from which to proceed to a more detailed consideration of their decoration."—*Review*, Burlington magazine, v.128, Nov. 1986, p.835.

Contents: (1) Books for missionaries; (2) Books for emperors; (3) Books for monks; (4) Books for students; (5) Books for aristocrats; (6) Books for everybody; (7) Books for priests; (8) Books for collectors.

Bibliographic notes, by chapter, p.258–63. Index of manuscripts, p.264–6. General index, p.267–72.

M139 Der Nersessian, Sirarpie. Miniature painting in the Armenian kingdom of Cilicia from the twelfth to the fourteenth century. Jointly prepared for publication with Sylvia Agemian. With an introd. by Annemarie Weyl Carr. Washington, D.C., Dumbarton Oaks, 1993. 2v. il., col. plates.

Posthumously published study of an important and distinctive group of Armenian manuscripts and their artists by one of the principal historians of Armenian art. Extensively illustrated.

Contents: (1) The twelfth century: Drazark, Hromkla and Skevra; (2) The thirteenth century; (3) The thirteenth century: the scriptorium of Grner and related manuscripts; (4) The thirteenth century: the royal and princely manuscripts; (5) The late thirteenth century to the fourteenth century and Sargis Pidsak; (6) Portraits.

Bibliography, v.1, p.177–86. General index, v.1, p.187–92. Index of manuscripts, v.1, p.192–96. Iconographic index, v.1, p.196–98.

M140 Dodwell, Charles Reginald. The pictorial arts of the West 800–1200. New Haven, Yale Univ. Pr., [1993]. 461p. il. (part col.), maps. (Yale University Press pelican history of art)

See GLAH 1:M130 for earlier version.

"This book is not an update of my earlier Painting in Europe: 800–1200 but—apart from some of the brief final chapter—is a new work incorporating wide areas of new research, relating the relevant arts to documentary sources, and now covering embroidery, mosaics, and stained glass as well as painting."—*Pref.* An important new survey, not only because of its scope, dealing with most of medieval Europe, but also for its inclusion of monumental painting and other related media.

Contents: (1) Eastern and western Christendom; (2) Embroidery: 800–1200; (3) Painting: 800–1200; (4) The Carolingian renaissance; (5) Painting in Ireland: 800–1170; (6) Anglo-Saxon Painting: 800–1200; (7) Painting in Germany and Austria: 900–1100; (8) Mosaics and painting in Italy and Sicily: 900–1200; (9) Painting in France and in Jerusalem; (10) Painting in Spain; (11) Painting in the Empire and Scandinavia; (12) Painting in England: 1100–1200; (13) Stained glass: 1100–1200; (14) Transitional.

Select classified bibliography, p.439–42. Index of iconography and of named artists and scribes, p.443–45. General index, p.449–61.

M141 Gutmann, Joseph. Hebrew manuscript painting. N.Y., Braziller, 1978. 118p. 19 il. 40 col. plates.

Well-illustrated brief survey of illumination in Hebrew manuscripts of the medieval and Renaissance periods. An introduction is followed by color reproductions with commentary on illuminations from 25 seminal manuscripts.

Selected bibliography, p.33–34.

M142 Kessler, Herbert L. The illustrated Bibles from Tours. Princeton, Princeton Univ. Pr., [1977]. xvii, 157p. il. (Studies in manuscript illumination, 7)

Seminal study of Carolingian illuminated manuscripts, characterized by single images created to illustrate each book of the Bible. Each chapter compares a single type of frontispiece with comparison to a wide range of pre-existing models.

Index, p.153–57.

M143 Köhler, Wilhelm Reinhold Walter, and Mütherich, Florentine. Die karolingischen Miniaturen, im Auftrage des Deutschen Vereins für Kunstwissenschaft. Berlin, Deutscher Verein für Kunstwissenschaft, 1958– . (6)v. il.

See GLAH 1:M133 for previous vols. and original annotation.

Ongoing catalog of Carolingian manuscripts; each vol. deals with a specific school. A text vol. accompanies each portfolio of large scale plates. Catalog entries consist of detailed description of each illumination and decorated initial in addition to extensive bibliography. Indexes by name or place and by iconographic theme.

Contents: (5) Die Hofschule Karls des Kahlen; (6) Die Schule von Reims: [pt.]1, Von den Anfängen bis zur Mitte des 9. Jahrhunderts.

M144 Mayr-Harting, Henry. Ottonian book illumination, an historical study. [London], Harvey Miller, [1991]. 2v. il., col. plates, maps.

Expanded version of the author's Slade Lectures, delivered in 1987. This is the first major study of a group of manuscripts primarily studied until now by German scholars. Its arrangement makes it less useful as an introductory survey, however, than as a series of essays on the topic of Ottonian manuscripts.

Contents: Vol.1: (1) The origins of Ottonian art; (2) Christ-centered art; (3) Religion and politics in Ottonian art; (4) The gospel book of Otto III and the Pericopes Book of Henry II; Vol.2: (1) The Bamberg apocalyptic manuscripts of c.1000; (2) The manuscripts of Egbert of Trier; (3) Cologne; (4) Fulda: saints and sacramentaries; (5) Corvey; (6) Some eleventh-century trends.

Detailed bibliography, chronological table, index of manuscripts, iconographic index, general index.

Notes to the text, v.1, p.213–30, v.2, p.231–48. Chronology, v.1, p.231–33. Abbreviations used in the bibliography, v.1, p.234. Bibliography, v.1, p.235–52 [replicated in v.2.] Index of iconography, v.1, p.257–58, v.2, p.279–80. Index of manuscripts, v.1, p.259–62, v.2, p.281–85. General index, v.1, p.263–70, v.2, p.286–94.

M145 Mazal, Otto. Buchkunst der Gotik. Graz, Akademische, 1975. 253p. il. (part col.) (Buchkunst im Wandel der Zeiten, 1)

General history of medieval bookmaking from the 13th–16th centuries including early printing and bookbinding, with sub-chapters on each European country. Primarily illustrated with works from the Austrian National Library.

Contents: (1) Die gotische Buchschriften; (2) Die gotische Buchmalerei; (3) Gotische Buchkunst in frühen Buchdruck; (4) Der gotische Bucheinband.

Bibliographie, p.211–20. [List of published facsimiles, p.220–23.] Register, p.225–48, Verzeichnis der zitierten Handschriften, p.249–54.

M146 ———. Buchkunst der Romanik. Graz, Akademische, 1978. 366p. il. (part col.) (Buchkunst in Wandel der Zeiten, 2)

Arranged similarly to the previous title, this vol. deals with roughly the 11th through the mid-12th centuries.

Contents: (1) Die romanische Buchschrift; (2) Der romanische Buchmalerei; (3) Der romanische Bucheinband.

Ausgewählte Bibliographie, p.317–28. Register, p.329–48. Verzeichnis der zitierten Handschriften, p.349–[67].

M147 Metzger, Thérèse, and Metzger, Mendel. Jewish life in the Middle Ages: illuminated Hebrew manuscripts of the thirteenth to the sixteenth centuries. N.Y., Alpine Fine Arts, [1982]. 316p. il. (part col.)

Transl. of La vie juive au moyen age. Fribourg, Office du Livre, [1982].

Generously illustrated study of medieval Jewish life as depicted in 259 illustrated Western European manuscripts from numerous repositories.

Contents: (1) The medieval Jew and the universe; (2) The Jewish quarter; (3) The house; (4) Costume; (5) The professional life of the Jewish community and its place in the medieval city; (6) Family life; (7) Religous life.

Summary catalogue of manuscripts mentioned, p.298–310. Select bibliography, p.311–13. Index to Hebrew manuscripts by type, p.315. Chronological index to manuscripts, p.316.

M148 Narkiss, Bezalel. Hebrew illuminated manuscripts in the British Isles: a catalogue raisonné. N.Y., Oxford Univ. Pr., 1982– . (1)v. in 2. il.

"The catalogue is planned to include four different areas of Hebrew illumination: (1) The Oriental schools of Egypt, Persia, Palestine, Yemen and North Africa; (2) The Sephardi schools of the Iberian Peninsula; (3) The Ashkenazi schools of France and Germany; and (4) The Italian schools."—*Pref.* to v.1.

Contents: (1) The Spanish and Portuguese manuscripts (2v.). No further vols. have appeared.

Includes bibliographies, glossaries, and indexes.

M149 Nordenfalk, Carl. Early medieval book illumination. [Reprint.] Geneva, Skira, [1988]. 145p. il., color plates.

Reprint of Early medieval painting from the 4th to the 11th century, pt.2, N.Y., Skira, 1957 (GLAH 1:M132).

Remains a useful pictorial summary of key manuscripts for those without access to the original ed.

M150 Pächt, Otto. Book illumination in the Middle Ages: an introduction. With a pref. by J. J. G. Alexander. [N.Y.], Oxford Univ. Pr., [1986]. 221p. il., color plates.

Trans. of Buchmalerei des Mittelalters, eine Einführung. München, Prestel, 1984.

Based on a series of lectures delivered in the late 1960s, these essays nonetheless provide an enduringly valid perspective on issues of manuscript illumination. "A magisterial book; the distillation of a lifetime's study of the field by one of the outstanding scholars of the history of medieval art."—*Review*, Apollo v.125, 1987, p.247.

Contents: (1) Pictorial decoration in the organic structure of the book; (2) The initial; (3) Bible illustration; (4) Didactic miniatures; (5) Illustration of the Apocalypse; (6) Illustration of the psalter; (7) The conflict of surface and space: an ongoing process.

Good selective bibliography, p.212. Bibliography of Pächt's work in the field, p.213–14. Index of manuscripts, p.216–18. General index, p.219–21.

M151 Sed-Rajna, Gabrielle. The Hebrew Bible in medieval illuminated manuscripts. [Trans. from the French by Josephine Bacon.] N.Y., Rizzoli, 1987. 173p. il. (part mounted col.)

Trans. of La bible hebraique. Fribourg, Office du Livre, [1987].

"The Hebrew Bible is first and foremost a selection of the most beautiful paintings and illustrations of biblical themes to be found in medieval Hebrew manuscripts."—*Introd.* Primarily valuable for its sumptuous illustrations, captioned with appropriate excerpts from the biblical text. Arranged by iconographical theme, with a general introduction to each.

Contents: Adam and Eve; Noah; Abraham, Isaac; Jacob; Joseph; Moses, Aaron; David; Solomon; The man of God; The woman of worth.

Select bibliography, p.165–77. Index, p.169–71.

M152 Treasures in heaven: Armenian illuminated manuscripts. Ed. by Thomas F. Mathews and Roger S. Wieck. N.Y., Pierpont Morgan Library; [Princeton], Princeton Univ. Pr., [1994]. xv, 229p. il., col. plates, maps.

Catalog of the exhibition, Pierpont Morgan Library (1994), and other locations.

Serves as a good introduction to the subject of Armenian manuscripts, which form a surprisingly cohesive whole in terms of both iconographical themes and production technique. The first half of the text provides detailed background information; the second half consists of a catalog of 88 manuscripts from an international group of repositories.

Contents: (1) The history of Armenia, by Nina G. Garsoïan; (2) The religion of Armenia, by Father Krikor H. Maksoudian; (3) The art of the Armenian manuscript, by Thomas F. Mathews; (4) The classic phase of Bagratid and Artsruni illumination, by Thomas F. Mathews; (5) Cilician manuscript illumination, by Helen C. Evans; (6) Armenian illumination under Georgian, Turkish and Mongol rule, by Alice Taylor; (7) The final centuries, by Helen C. Evans and Sylvie L. Merian; (8) The making of an Armenian manuscript, by Sylvie L. Merian, Thomas F. Mathews and Mary Virginia Orna.

Classified bibliography, p.213–16. General index, p.221–26. Index of manuscripts, p.226–27. Iconographic index, p.227–29.

Renaissance—Baroque

M153 The altarpiece in the Renaissance. Ed. by Peter Humfrey and Martin Kemp. N.Y., Cambridge Univ. Pr., [1990]. xiv, 274p. il. (1 col.)

Based on papers given at a conference of the Society for Renaissance Studies, London (1987). This collection of essays provides a range of approaches to the study of a specific painting type.

Contents: Introduction: The altarpiece in the Renaissance: a taxonomic approach, by Martin Kemp; (1) Some thoughts on writing a history of Sienese altarpieces, by H. W. Van Os; (2) The Renaissance altarpiece: a valid category? by Paul Hills; (3) The northern altarpiece as a cultural document, by Craig Harbison; (4) The Netherlandish carved altarpiece c. 1500: type and function, by Kim Woods; (5) Reform within the cult image: the German winged altarpiece before the Reformation, by Bernhard Decker; (6) Appropriation and application: the significance of the sources of Michael Pacher's altarpieces, by Mark Evans; (7) Fra Bartolomeo's Carondelet altarpiece and the theme of the "Virgo in nibibus" in the High Renaissance, by André Chastel; (8) "Divinità di cosa dipinta": pictorial structure and the legibility of the altarpiece, by David Rosand; (9) From cult images to the cult of images: the case of Raphael's altarpieces, by Sylvia Ferino Pagden; (10) Co-ordinated altarpieces in Renaissance Venice: the progress of an ideal, by Peter Humfrey; (11) The relationship of El Greco's altarpieces to the mass of the Roman rite, by David Davies; (12) The altarpiece in Catholic Europe: post-Tridentine transformations, by A. D. Wright.

Select bibliography, p.261–64. Index, p.265–73.

M154 Brown, Beverly Louise, and Wheelock, Arthur K. Masterworks from Munich: sixteenth- to eighteenth-century paintings from the Alte Pinakothek. Washington, D.C., National Gallery of Art, [1988]. 229p. il. (part col.)

Catalog of the exhibition, National Gallery of Art (1988), and other locations. This exhibition highlighted 62 paintings loaned by the Alte Pinakothek. Following a brief history of the institution, the bulk of the catalog provides commentary on each work including bibliographic references, accompanied by an illustration.

Index of artists, p.229.

M155 Campbell, Lorne. Renaissance portraits: European portrait-painting in the 14th, 15th and 16th centuries. New Haven, Yale Univ. Pr., 1990. xiii, 290p. il. (part col.)

Although not an exhaustive history, this survey of Renaissance portrait conventions is helpful for its excellent illustrations, its pan-European approach, and the author's insight into the technical problems of portrait painting for artists.

Contents: (1) Introduction; (2) Portrait types; (3) Poses; (4) Settings, clothes and attributes; (5) The sitters; (6) The painters; (7) Portrait method; (8) The functions and uses of portraits; (9) Italy and "the North."

Bibliography, p.275–83. Index, p.284–9.

M156 Castelfranchi Vegas, Liana. Italia e Fiandra nell pittura del Quattrocento. [Milano], Jaca, [1983]. 321p. il. (part col.), maps. (Le grandi stagioni)

French ed.: Flandre et Italie: primitifs flamands et renaissance italienne. Antwerp, Fonds Mercator, 1984.

Well-illustrated study of the impact of Flemish painting on Italian art, summarizing recent scholarship. Organized geographically, the book provides a useful overview of the topic.

Contents: (1) Masaccio e Van Eyck: due approcchi alla realtà; (2) 1440–1450: collezionismo, storiografia, viaggi; (3) La prima testa di ponte del fiammingo a Napoli. Antonello da Messina, pittore italiano e fiammingo; (4) Piero della Francesca e l'apice del gusto fiammingo a Urbino nel decennio 1465–75; (5) Il fiammingo nel Veneto e il suo ruolo nella pittura di Giovanni Bellini; (6) I fiamminghi a Firenze; (7) L'aria "ponentina" in Lombardia; (8) Italia e Fiandra tra la fine del Quattrocento e l'inizio del Cinquecento.

Bibliografia generale, p.293–99. Cataloghi delle principali esposizioni, p.300. Indice dei nome, p.301–4. Indice dei luoghi e delle opere, p.305–14. Indice delle illustrazioni, p.315–20. Tavola cronologica, p.321–25.

M157 Gagliardi, Jacques. La conquête de la peinture: l'Europe des ateliers du XIIIe au XVe siècle. [Paris], Flammarion, [1993]. 839p. il. (part col.)

Massive attempt to survey European painting from roughly 1200–1500. Focusing on individual artists and schools, the author attempts to depict the variety of forces active during this period. Lavishly illustrated with both familiar and many lesser-known works, this book is primarily of interest as a snapshot of painting in Italy and elsewhere during the Renaissance period.

Repères chronologiques, p.824–27. Bibliographie, p.828–38. Index des peintres, sculpteurs et architectes, p.838–39.

M158 Grössinger, Christa. North-European panel paintings, a catalogue of Netherlandish and German paintings before 1600 in English churches and colleges. [London], Harvey Miller, [1992]. 302p. il., col. plates.

Illustrated catalog of 76 panel paintings "still functioning in their ecclesiastical settings in England," useful primarily as a study of Netherlandish workshop production of the 15th century. Arranged alphabetically by location, each brief entry includes physical description, provenance, and comparison with possible models.

Brief biographies of artists, p.257–79. Handlist of panel paintings in English public collections, p.280–90. Bibliography, p.291–93. List of comparative works of art, p.295–98. General index, p.299–302.

M159 Hall, Marcia B. Color and meaning: practice and theory in Renaissance painting. Cambridge, Cambridge Univ. Pr., [1992]. xiv, 274p. il. (part col.)

Welcome overview of the theory and practice of color used in Renaissance painting, each chapter including both historical survey and analysis of specific pictures. Extensively illustrated, but the quality of the images is quite uneven.

Contents: Can we know what Renaissance color was?; The Cennini system; Alberti, Flemish technique and the introduction of oil; The modes of coloring in the Cinquecento; Mannerism and Counter-Reformation; Venice and the development of tonal painting.

Glossary, p.236–40. Bibliography, p.260–68. Index, p.269–74.

M160 London. National Gallery. Dürer to Veronese: sixteenth-century paintings in the National Gallery. [By] Jill Dunkerton . . . [et al.] New Haven, Yale Univ. Pr., 1999. xi, 317p. il. (chiefly col.), maps.

"Survey of European painting, written as a companion to Giotto to Dürer [see following title]" and based largely upon the National Gallery collections.—*Pref.*

Contents: Introduction: the new world and the old; (1) Power and imagery; (2) The altarpiece; (3) Private devotion; (4) Paintings for palaces; (5) Description and the ideal; (6) Preparing to paint; (7) Preparing the panel; (8) Paintings on panel; (9) Original developments; Conclusion: towards the Academy.

Chronology, p.x–xi. References, p.298–311. Index, p.312–16.

M161 ———. Giotto to Dürer: early Renaissance painting in the National Gallery. [By] Jill Dunkerton . . . [et al.] New Haven, Yale Univ. Pr., [1991]. 408p. il. (part col.), maps.

"Splendid in every way, Giotto to Dürer is beautifully produced, richly informative . . . essential reading for any student of painting between 1300 and 1520."—*Review*, Renaissance quarterly, v.47, no.3, autumn 1994, p.715–18. This survey brings together both northern and southern painting from the Gallery's collection and was published to coincide with the opening of the Sainsbury Wing and a major rehanging of the collection. The latest scientific evidence as well as scholarship is incorporated both into the general chapters as well as the commentaries on individual works.

Contents: (I) The uses of painting: (1) Christian worship and imagery; (2) Civic, dynastic and domestic art; (II) The making of paintings: (3) Craft and profession; (4) The workshop; (5) Techniques; (6) Conclusion: painting and the sister arts; (III) Paintings in the National Gallery: Plates with commentaries.

Chronology, p.16–17. Glossary, p.388–90. Classified bibliography, p.391–402. Index, p.403–07.

M162 Les manuscrits enluminés des comtes et ducs de Savoie: études publiées. Par Agostino Paravicini Bagliani. Introd. de Enrico Castelnuovo. [Torino], Allemandi, [1991]. 230p. 42 il., 64 col. plates.

Beautifully illustrated study of patronage of illuminated manuscripts by members of the House of Savoy. Illustrations, mostly color plates, provide ample evidence of the quality of manuscripts produced for these patrons, but are not directly linked to the text.

Contents: Portrait de trois princesses de Savoie (XVe–XVIe s.), par Marie Gabrielle, de Savoie; Les Heures d'Agnès de Savoie, par Giovanni Morello, Francesco Solinas; Les Heures de Blanche de Bourgogne, comtesse de Savoie, par Christopher de Hamel; Jean Bapteur et l'Apocalypse de l'Escorial, par Sheila Edmunds; Le missel de Félix V (Amédée VIII de Savoie), par Elisa Mongiano; Un livre d'heures du comte de Piémont, futur Duc Amédée IX de Savoie, par Clément Gardet; Bibliophilie savoyarde chez les Visconti, par Carlo Bertelli; Histoire archivistique d'un inventaire de l'ancienne Bibliothèque Ducale, par Isabella Massabò Ricci; Les images symboliques de Louise de Savoie dans ses manuscripts, par Anne-Marie Lecoq; Livres imprimés pour Louise de Savoie, par Mary Beth Winn; La bibliothèque de Marguerite d'Autriche, duchesse de Savoie, par Marguerite Debae; Le Cod. varia 84 de la Bibliothèque Royale de Turin, par Mauro della Valle; Catalogue des manuscrits savoyards, par Sheila Edmunds.

Bibliographie, p.225–30.

M163 McCorquodale, Charles. The Renaissance: European painting, 1400–1600. London, Studio, [1994]. 308p. 306 col. il., part fold.

Oversize, lavishly illustrated survey of Renaissance painting. Best used as a pictorial survey of the period, though the text and individual captions are informative as well.

Contents: (1) The historical background to the Renaissance; (2) Painting and drawing techniques in the Renaissance; (3) The rebirth of painting in Italy and the prelude to the Renaissance, 1250–1400; (4) Fifteenth-century Italian painting; (5) Fifteenth-century painting in the Netherlands; (6) The Renaissance of painting elsewhere in Europe; (7) The High Renaissance in Italy; (8) The later Renaissance and Mannerism in Italy; (9) Painting in Germany and the Netherlands in the sixteenth century; (10) The end of Mannerism and the dawn of the Baroque.

Bibliography, p.296–97. Index, p.304–08.

M164 Os, H. W. van. The art of devotion in the late Middle Ages in Europe, 1300–1500. [By] Henk van Os . . . [et al.] Trans. from the Dutch by Michael Hoyle. Princeton, Princeton Univ. Pr., [1994]. 192p. il. (part col.)

Catalog of the exhibition, Rijksmuseum, Amsterdam (1994–95).

Beautifully illustrated study of 44 European private devotional images, "a straightforward narrative aimed at the general public."—*Foreword.* Highly readable essays intended to illuminate the use of these objects in religious practice.

Contents: A treasury of stories; The culture of prayer; Devotional themes; New beginnings, by Henk van Os; The Antwerp-Baltimore polyptych: a portable altarpiece belonging to Philip the Bold, Duke of Burgundy, by Hans Nieuwdorp; The Rotterdam-Edinburgh diptych: Maria in sole and the devotion of the rosary, by Bernhard Ridderbos; Image and imagination in the medieval culture of prayer: a historical perspective, by Eugène Honée.

Catalogue, by Norbert Middelkoop, p.175–84. Bibliography, p.185–88. Summary index, p.191–92.

M165 Renaissance painting in manuscripts: treasures from the British Library. Ed. by Thomas Kren. Catalogue and essays by Janet Backhouse . . . [et al.] With an Introd. by D. H. Turner. N.Y., Hudson Hills, [1983]. xiv, 210p. il., col. plates, geneal. tables, maps.

Catalog of the exhibition, J. Paul Getty Museum (1983–1984), and other locations.

Introduction to miniature painting after the invention of printing featuring 24 illuminated manuscripts and one printed book of the 15th–16th centuries from the British Library collection. Each geographic section consists of an introduction followed by scholarly commentary on each manuscript, including physical description, provenance, and analysis.

Contents: Flemish manuscript illumination 1475–1550, by Thomas Kren; Italian manuscript illumination 1460–1560, by Mark Evans; French manuscript illumination 1450–1530, by Janet Backhouse.

Genealogical table of the ruling houses of Europe, p.193–95. Bibliography, p.196–204. Index, p.205–10.

M166 Ringbom, Sixten. Icon to narrative: the rise of the dramatic close-up in fifteenth-century devotional painting. 2d ed., rev. and augm. with a postscript 1983. [Doornspijk, The Netherlands], Davaco, [1984]. 241p. il.

Reprint of the 1965 ed. (GLAH 1:M148), corrected and with a new postscript, which briefly surveys subsequent literature.

Neoclassical—Modern

M167 Berko, P., Berko, V., and Cruysmans, Philippe. Peinture orientaliste: orientalist painting. Préf. de Philippe Roberts-Jones. [Trans. from French by Jonathan Fryer.] Bruxelles, Laconti, 1982. 143p. il. (part col.)

An illustrated survey in French and English of paintings by 19th-century European and American artists of the middle east and northern Africa, arranged by nationality of the artists. Lists major orientalist painters and includes biographical vignettes.

Contents: (1) France; (2) Italie; (3) Espagne, Portugal; (4) Grande Bretagne; (5) Belgique; (6) Pays Bas; (7) Danemark, Suède; (8) Suisse, Allemagne, Autriche; (9) Hongrie, Pologne, Russie, Tchecoslovaquie; (10) Grèce, Turquie; (11) Amérique.

M168 Clay, Jean. Romanticism. With a foreword by Robert Rosenblum. [Trans. by Daniel Wheeler and Craig Owen.] N.Y., Vendome, 1981. 320p. il. (part col.), plates (part col.)

1st ed., Le Romanticisme. Paris, Hachette, 1980.

An illustrated survey of European romantic painting from the late 18th to the late 19th century, based upon perceived transformations to the pictorial structure.

Contents: (1) The rediscovery of the picture surface; (2) The liberation of line; (3) The blurring of form; (4) The exploration of color; (5) Construction by assemblage.

Notes, p.314. Index of artists and their works, p.315–18. Full citations for figures 1–124, p.319.

M169 Daval, Jean-Luc. History of abstract painting. [Trans. by Jane Brenton.] Paris, Hazan, 1989. 214p. il. (part col.), ports.
French ed., Histoire de la peinture abstraite. Paris, Hazan, 1988.

An illustrated historical survey of international 20th-century non-representational painting. Includes useful biographical information about major abstract painters.

Contents: (1) The work of painting; (2) Pictorial realism; (3) Kandinsky and the invention of abstraction; (4) The Russians and the absence of the object; (5) Mondrian and denaturalization; (6) The abstractions of Dada; (7) From abstract art to concrete art; (8) The surrealist contribution; (9) Abstract expressionism; (10) Informal art; (11) Kinetic and spatial art; (12) Recent developments.

Biographies, by Diane Daval, p.153–201. Bibliography, p.211–[15].

M170 Eitner, Lorenz. An outline of 19th century European painting: from David through Cézanne. N.Y., Harper and Row, 1987–88. 2v. il. (IconEditions) (Repr.: 1992 [1v.])
General survey of 19th-century European painting that includes brief bibliographies at the end of certain sections. "Its focus is on the individual artist, as the embodiment of the ideas and artistic movements current in a particular society and period."—*Foreword.*

Contents: v.1 Text (1) Introduction; (2) David and his school; (3) Francisco José de Goya Lucientes, 1746–1828; (4) British neoclassicism and William Blake; (5) German romantics; (6) English landscape; (7) French romantics; (8) French landscape; (9) Realism; (10) Academic and Salon painters; (11) Edouard Manet, 1832–1883; (12) Edgar Degas, 1834–1917; (13) Impressionism; (14) Paul Cézanne, 1839–1906. v.2 Plates.

Index, v.1, p.443–56.

M171 Godfrey, Tony. The new image: painting in the 1980s. N.Y., Abbeville, 1986. 159p. il. (part col.), col. plates.
An international survey on postmodern or "new painting" from 1965 to the early 1980s as it emerged in Germany, Italy, the United States, Great Britain, and France.

Contents: (1) The Visigoths enter Rome; (2) Speaking German again; (3) Italian colour, poetry and skulls; (4) British painting at the crossroads; (5) The death of the school of Paris; (6) New York—when the worlds collide; (7) An icon of the twenty-first century.

Select bibliography, p.157. Index, p.158–59.

M172 Hook, Philip, and Poltimore, Mark. Popular 19th century painting: a dictionary of European genre painters. Woodbridge, Suffolk, Antique Collectors' Club, 1986. 632p. il. (part col.)
Thematic dictionary of 19th-century European genre painting, including the Middle East. In each subject section a brief introductory essay precedes an index of artists specializing in that genre with illustrations.

Select bibliography to text and further reading, p.616. Index of artists, p.616–31.

M173 Johnston, William R. The nineteenth-century paintings in the Walters Art Gallery. Baltimore, Trustees of the Walters Art Gallery, 1982. 208p. il. (part col.), ports.
Descriptive catalog of 268 paintings in the Walters Art Gallery, Baltimore. Entries for individual works include information about the artist, subject, provenance, condition, exhibition history, reproductions, and references to the literature.

Contents: (1) French paintings; (2) Belgian and Dutch paintings; (3) Scandinavian, central and east European paintings; (4) Spanish and Italian paintings; (5) British paintings.

Alphabetical index of artists, p.8. Abbreviations of bibliographic references, p.208.

M174 Kultermann, Udo. The new painting. [Rev. and upd. ed.] [Trans. by Wesley V. Blomster.] Boulder, Westview, 1977. 73,195p. il. (part col.), plates (part col.)
1st ed., Neue Formen des Bildes. Tubingen, Wasmuth, 1969; 2d ed. 1975.

An international selection of modern paintings from the 1950s through the 1970s, organized by subject and formal structural theme. "The chapters of this book do not designate a succession of styles and tendencies, but rather the juxtaposition of various expressions of the same source material as a sign of our multivalent culture."—*Pref.*

Chronological bibliography, p.67–73. Artists' biographies, p.149–93. Picture index, p.195.

M175 Malerei 1800 bis um 1900. Bearb. von Gabriele Howaldt. Hanau, Peters, 1979. 192p. il., plates (part col.) (Kataloge des Hessischen Landesmuseum, 7)
Descriptive catalog, arranged alphabetically by artist, of 130 19th-century European paintings in the Hessisches Landesmuseum, Darmstadt. Entries for individual works include critical notes, provenance, and references to the literature.

M176 McEvilley, Thomas. The exile's return: toward a redefinition of painting for the post-modern era. Cambridge, Cambridge Univ. Pr., 1993. xi, 231p. il.
Compilation of essays regarding the return to representational subjects in painting in the 1980s, concentrating on changes in abstractionism from 1965 to 1980. Analyzes various ways that artists formed by the modernist agenda "have redefined the practice of painting for a post-Modern age."—*Introd.*

Contents: (1) Introduction: painting's exile and return; (2) Seeking the primal through paint: the monochrome icon; (3) The opposite of emptiness; (4) Grey Geese Descending: the art of Agnes Martin; (5) Absence made visible: Robert Ryman's "Realist" painting; (6) The figure and what it says: reflections on iconography; (7) The case of Julian Schnabel: painting, modernism, and post-modernism in his oeuvre; (8) The work of "Georg Baselitz"?; (9) Carlo Maria Mariani's dialogue with history; (10) Pat Steir and the confrontation with history; (11) Flower power: trying to say the obvious about Sigmar Polke; (12) Ceci n'est pas un Bidlo? Rethinking quotational theory; (13) Frontal attack: the work of Leon Golub; (14) Now read this.

Notes, p.210–23. Index, p.225–31.

M177 Montreal Museum of Fine Arts. Lost paradise: symbolist Europe. [Organized by Pierre Théberge; chief curator Jean Clair.] Montreal, Montreal Museum of Fine Arts (Distr. by St. Martin's, 1995). 555p. il. (part col.), plates (part col.), ports.

French ed., Paradis perdus: l'Europe symboliste. Paris, Flammarion, 1995.

Catalog of the exhibition of 583 symbolist paintings, prints, drawings, books, photographs, sculpture, and pottery by late 19th and early 20th century European artists, Montreal Museum of Fine Arts (1995).

Contents: (1) The waning culture, by Guy Cogeval; (2) The self beyond recovery, by Jean Clair; (3) The homeland regained, by Gilles Genty; (4) The cycles of life, by Guy Cogeval; (5) New territories, by Gilles Genty; (6) Towards regeneration, by Constance Naubert-Riser.

List of works exhibited, p.507–28. Bibliography, 1984–1994, p.533–52.

M178 Norman, Geraldine. Biedermeier painting, 1815–1846: reality observed in genre, portrait and landscape. London, Thames and Hudson, 1987. 192p. il. (part col.), col. plates, ports.

City-by-city and artist-by-artist survey of early 19th-century German bourgeois genre painting known as the Biedermeier style, which spread to Austria, Denmark, and Italy.

"Biedermeier refers to a taste in furnishing, interior decoration, the fine arts and belles lettres evolved by the German middle classes . . . [during] the Metternich era, 1815–1848."—*Introd.*

Contents: (1) Vienna; (2) Berlin; (3) Copenhagen; (4) Munich; (5) Düsseldorf; (6) Dresden; (7) The Italian experience.

Bibliography, p.184–85. Index, p.190–92.

M179 Parsons, Thomas, and Gale, Iain. Post-impressionism: the rise of modern art. Foreword by Bernard Denvir. London, Studio, 1992. 424p. il. (part col.), col. plates (part fold.)

Sweeping survey of European post-impressionism that covers major painters, schools, styles, critics, and art historians. Large-scale folding plates include details.

Contents: Introduction: the naming of a movement; (1) Science and symbolism; (2) Three recluses; (3) The wild animals; (4) New geometrics; (5) Developments in Germany; (6) Towards abstraction; (7) Northern lights; (8) The English-speaking world; (9) Civilized carnage.

Chronology, p.400–07. Bibliography, p.408–10. Index, p.419–24.

M180 Roberts-Jones, Philippe. Beyond time and place: non-realist painting in the nineteenth century. Oxford, Oxford Univ. Pr., 1978. 228p. il. (part col.), plates (part col.)

An historical essay that postulates an alternate tradition in 19th-century painting of non-realist, intuitive mirroring of the artist's inner self. Covers Neoclassicism to Surrealism and discovers unfamiliar works.

Notes, p.193–96. Biographical notes, p.197–216. Bibliography, p.217–23. Index, p.224–27.

M181 Rosenblum, Robert. Modern painting and the northern romantic tradition: Friedrich to Rothko. N.Y., Harper and Row, 1988. 240p. il. (IconEditions)

1st ed. 1975; repr. with corr. 1983.

Argues for a direct line of succession from northern European romanticism to 20th-century avant-garde painting.

Contents: (1) Northern romanticism and the resurrection of God; (2) Romantic survival and revival in the late nineteenth century; (3) Romantic survival and revival in the twentieth century; (4) Transcendental abstraction.

Notes on the text, p.219–26. Index, p.237–40.

M182 Royal Academy of Arts. Great Britain. Post-impressionism: cross-currents in European painting. Ed. by John House and MaryAnne Stevens. N.Y., Harper and Row, 1979. 303p. il., col. plates.

Catalog of the exhibition of 428 Post-Impressionist paintings by approximately 170 European artists of varied nationalities, Royal Academy of Arts (1979). Notable for scholarly essays and critical notes on individual paintings.

Contents: (1) France: the legacy of impressionism in France. Innovation and consolidation in French painting, by John House and MaryAnne Stevens; (2) Germany, Norway and Switzerland: idealism and naturalism in painting, by Norman Rosenthal and Gillian Perry; (3) Great Britian and Ireland: two reactions to French painting in Britain, by Anna Gruetzner; (4) Italy: divisionism; its origins, its aims and its relationship to French post-impressionist painting, by Sandra Berresford; (5) The Low Countries: Belgian art; Les XX and the Libre Esthetique. Painting in Holland, by MaryAnne Stevens and Joop Joostens.

Chronology, p.280–97. Select bibliography, p.298–99. Index of artists, p.302.

M183 Ruhrberg, Karl. Die Malerei in Europa und Amerika, 1945–1960: die zweite Moderne. Köln, DuMont, 1992. 134p. il. (part col.), col. plates (DuMont's Bibliothek grosser Maler)

An illustrated survey of European and United States post-World War II painting that emphasizes major artists and styles.

Ausgewählte Literatur, p.131–33.

M184 Santini, Pier Carlo. Modern landscape painting. [Trans. by P. S. Falla.] London, Phaidon, 1972. 350p. il. (part col.)

1st ed., Il paesaggio nella pittura contemporanea. Venice, Electra, 1971.

An illustrated collection of landscape paintings by about 140 artists supplemented by excerpts from modern writers that relate to landscape, art, and architecture.

Contents: (1) Landscape in twentieth-century civilization and painting; (2) Literary extracts.

Biographies, p.291–338. Sources of literary extracts, p.339–41. List of collections, p.345–47. Index of artists and places, p.349–50.

M185 Schreiner, Ludwig. Die Gemälde des neunzehnten und zanzigsten Jahrhunderts in der Niedersächsischen Landesgalerie Hannover. Neu Bearb. und Erg. von Regine Timm. Hannover, Niedersächsisches Landesmuseum, 1990. 2v. il. (Kataloge der Niedersächischen Landesgalerie Hannover)

An illustrated catalog of 747 paintings from the 19th and 20th centuries primarily by European artists.

Contents: (1) Textband; (2) Bildband.

M186 Schurr, Gerald. 1820–1920, les petits maîtres de la peinture: valeur de demain. Paris, Eds. de l'Amateur, 1975–89. 7v. il. (part col.)

Encyclopedic history of lesser-known European painters from 1820 to 1920, arranged chronologically and thematically. Entries include brief biographical and critical information. Each vol. covers approximately 500 artists. Large format; lavish illustrations. A cumulative index of artists cited appears at the end of each vol. Illus. index at end of each vol.

Much of the data has been repackaged as a standard biographical dictionary as Dictionnaire des petits maîtres de la peinture: 1820–1920 (see GLAH 2:M37).

M187 Thornton, Lynne. The orientalists: painter-travellers. Courbevoie, Paris, ACR, 1994. 192p. col. il. (PocheCouleur)

French ed., Les orientalistes: peintres voyageurs, 1828–1908. Paris, ACR, 1983.

Illustrated handbook of about 60 19th-century European painter-travelers in Egypt, Syria, Lebanon, Palestine, North Africa, Spain, and Venice, arranged alphabetically by artist. Entries for individual artists include biographical and critical notes accompanied by color reproductions of representative paintings. "There was no school of Orientalist painting; the pictures were linked thematically rather than stylistically."—*Introd.*

Index, p.190–92.

M188 Weisberg, Gabriel P. Beyond impressionism: the naturalist impulse. N.Y., Abrams, 1992. 303p. il. (part col.)

Argues for an identifiable international naturalism in painting during the last quarter of the 19th century. Includes criticism and reproductions of paintings by provincial artists.

Contents: (1) The critical and literary worlds of naturalism; (2) The creation of a naturalist icon; (3) Naturalism in France: the great debate; (4) Rustic naturalism in England; (5) American naturalists in France; (6) Naturalism in central Europe: Hungary; (7) German naturalism; (8) Naturalism in the Low Countries; (9) Scandinavian naturalism.

Notes, p.279–89. Bibliography, p.290–94. Index, p.295–302.

M189 World impressionism: the international movement, 1860–1920. Ed. by Norma Broude. N.Y., Abrams, 1994. 424p. il. (part col.), col. plates.

1st ed. 1990.

An illustrated overview of impressionism's international manifestations and influences during the late 19th and early 20th centuries. "The essays have been arranged loosely in cultural and geographical clusters rather than in a chronological sequence. The first group of four deals with Impressionism in the English-speaking world; the second with Impressionism in countries whose native traditions influenced art in France during the Impressionist era; the third with Impressionism in a selection of countries in northern, central, and Eastern Europe and Russia."—*Pref.* Showcases works by lesser-known artists.

Contents: (1) A world in light: France and the international impressionist movement, 1860–1920, by Norma Broude; (2) Impressionism in the United States, by William H. Gerdts; (3) British impressionism: the magic and poetry of life around them, by Anna Gruetzner Robins; (4) Impressionism in Canada, by Dennis Reid; (5) The sunny south: Australian impressionism, by Virginia Spate; (6) The impressionist impulse in Japan and the far east, by J. Thomas Rimer; (7) Italian painting during the impressionist era, by Norma Broude; (8) The lure of impressionism in Spain and Latin America, by Eleanor Tufts; (9) Mussels and windmills: impressionism in Belgium and Holland, by Brooks Adams; (10) Nordic luminism and the Scandinavian recasting of impressionism, by Alessandra Comini; (11) Plein-air painting in Switzerland, by Hans A. Lüthy; (12) Impressionism in Austria and Germany, by Horst Uhr; (13) The impressionist vision in Russian and eastern Europe, by Alison Hilton.

Notes, p.407–15. Selected bibliography, p.416–19. Index, p.420–24.

WESTERN COUNTRIES

Australia

M190 Astbury, Leigh. Sunlight and shadow: Australian impressionist painters 1880–1900. General ed. Jennifer Phipps. Sydney, Bay, 1989. 232p. 159 col. plates.

Heavily illustrated historical overview of Australian impressionism. "The range of artistic subjects during the period is vast, encompassing the portrayal of the landscape in its many guises, the lives and activities of the people, the nationalistic ideals of society and its loftier cultural ambitions."—*Introd.*

Contents: (1) Painters and places; (2) The painting of modern life; (3) Seasons and moments; the new landscape; (4) Impressionism and the 9 by 5 exhibition; (5) "Sun-girdled queen": Sydney in the 1890s; (6) The shadows of impressionism; (7) Nature and the imagination; (8) National icons; (9) Federation and its aftermath.

References, p.216–19. Bibliography, p.220–22. List of plates, p.223–28. Index, p.229–32.

M191 Burn, Ian. National life and landscapes: Australian painting 1900–1940. Sydney, Bay, [1990]. 219p. 157 col. plates.

An historical and cultural survey of Australian painting in the first four decades of the 20th century. Discusses traditional practices of art and speculates about the general nature of the period and its imagery.

Contents: (1) A land of faded things; (2) The war to end all wars; (3) A pastoral new order; (4) Reflections in private spaces; (5) Tradition in modern life; (6) Cultures re-ordered.

References, p.206–10. Bibliography, p.211. List of plates, p.212–16. Index, p.217–19.

M192 Campbell, Jean. Australian watercolour painters: 1780 to the present day. Roseville, N.S.W., Australia, Craftsman House, 1989. 394p. il., col. plates.

1st ed. 1983.

Covers Australian watercolor painting from British antecedents in the early 19th century through the 1980s, with an emphasis on painters in the 20th century. Important for its breadth and biographical information. "The purpose of this book is to bring together the contribution of the watercolourists; to show the line of development and the diversified activities and trends that have fed the main stream of art in Australia, dwelling particularly on the outstanding exponents of this delightful medium with its distinctive, often indefinable qualities."—*Foreword.*

Contents: (1) Explorers, first fleeters, and convicts; (2) The colonists; (3) The 1850's, 1860's and 1870's; (4) The 1880's and 1890's: Victorian and New South Wales; (5) The 1880's and 1890's: the other states; (6) The twentieth century to 1914; (7) The artists of the first world war; (8) The boom of the 1920's; (9) The Australian Watercolour Institute; (10) Contemporary stirrings in Sydney; (11) The 1930's; (12) The Aranda watercolours; (13) The second world war; (14) The 1940's; (15) The 1950's and 1960's: Sydney and the abstract painters; (16) The 1950's and 1960's: developments in Victoria; (17) The 1950's and 1960's: developments in other states; (18) Watercolour painters in the 1970's; (19) Attitudes to watercolours in the 1970's and 1980's; (20) The 1980's.

List of abbreviations, p.275–76. Biographical listing of Australian watercolour painters, p.277–384. Members of the Australian Watercolour Institute (1923–89), p.385–86. Bibliography, p.387–90. Index of artists, p.391–94.

M193 Contemporary Australian painting. Ed. by Eileen Chanin. Roseville, N.S.W., Australia, Craftsman House, 1990. 192p. col. plates.

Reproduces and comments on paintings by 126 Australian painters active in the 1980s. "This look at painting in Australia today is a sketch for whoever is looking for an overview to the tapestry of activity of current Australian painting. It is a broad Introduction to Australian painting through the 1980s presented in short essays written by notable critics and curators."—*Introd.*

M194 Gleeson, James. Australian painters: colonial 1788–1880, impressionists 1881–1930, modern 1931–1970. General ed. John Henshaw. Sydney, Weldon, 1976. 392p. il. (part col.) 268 plates (part col.) (Repr.: 1985, 1990)

Comprehensive, heavily illustrated history of painting in Australia beginning with aboriginal painting and concentrating on the colonial through modern periods. Each major section includes an introduction, individual artist biographies and critical essays, selected bibliography, and works in public collections.

M195 Jones, Shar. Early painters of Australia, 1788–1880. General ed. Jennifer Phipps. Sydney, Bay, [1988]. 208p. 148 plates (part col.)

Thematic survey of early Australian painting: "The paintings and drawings in this book are a selection of those made in the colonies between 1788 and 1880. They have been chosen to present the broadest possible view of colonial art. Many are little known images by amateur artists, surveyors, genteel women, squatters and businessmen included to illustrate the rich diversity of our colonial visual heritage."—*Introd.*

Contents: Beginnings; Charting a continent; Celebrating colonial achievement; Towards a professional art establishment.

References, p.196. Books, articles and exhibition catalogues, p.202–04. Index, p.205–08.

M196 Quartermaine, Peter and Watkins, Jonathan. A pictorial history of Australian painting. London, Bison, 1989. 192p. il. (part col.), col. plates.

Sweeping history of Australian painting during its 200-plus years of European settlement in the context of Australia's cultural and social history. Features works by nearly 100 artists. Illustrated with numerous photographs and color plates.

Bibliography, p.191.

M197 Smith, Bernard. Australian painting, 1788–1990. With the three additional chapters on Australian painting since 1970 by Terry Smith. [3d ed.] N.Y., Oxford Univ. Pr., 1991. 592p. il. (part col.)

1st ed. 1962; 2d. ed. 1971.

Classic text, sweeping in scope and scholarship, by one of Australia's most distinguished art historians and critics. Terry Smith is head of the Department of Fine Arts, University of Sydney. "As in the first and second eds., the relationship between new influences from abroad and the changing political, social and artistic environments in Australia remains the central theme."—*Foreword.*

Contents: (1) The first artists, 1788–1824; (2) Artists on the pastoral frontier, 1821–51; (3) The late colonial artists, 1851–85; (4) Genesis, 1885–1914; (5) Exodus, 1881–1919; (6) Leviticus, 1913–32; (7) Contemporary art arrives, 1930–39; (8) Rebirth, 1939–50; (9) Figurative and non-figurative, 1950–60; (10) The art scene in the 1960s; (11) The expressive and symbolic styles of the 1960s; (12) Pop art and the traditional genres, 1960–70; (13) Colour painting, 1965–70; (14) A problematic practice, 1970–80; (15) From the desert: aboriginal painting, 1970–90; (16) Postmodern plurality, 1980–90.

A note on books and periodicals, p.565–67. Index, p.568–92.

Canada

M198 Beland, Mario. Painting in Quebec, 1820–1850. New views, new perspectives. Québec, Musée du Québec, 1992. 608p. il., 32 col. plates.

Monumental catalog to a traveling exhibition (1991–93) of nearly 300 Quebecois paintings from 1790–1860 drawn from more than 40 private and public collections. The exhibition marked the reopening of the expanded Musée de Quebec. "This publication is composed of two parts. The first one includes four essays on the fondamental [sic] questions raised by painting of the period from 1790 to 1860; the second, a catalogue of the exhibited works, is divided into three parts, respectively entitled Emergence, devoted to the 1790–1820 period; Affirmation, to the 1820–1850 period, and Perspectives, to the 1850–1860 period. For each of these periods, the artists are represented in alphabetical order and their works in chronological order."—*Notice to the reader.*

Contents: Introduction, by Mario Beland; The market for paintings: basic needs versus artistic taste, by John R. Porter; A look at likeness: portraiture in lower Canada, by Paul Bourassa; British landscape artists in Quebec: from documentary views to a poetic vision, by Didier Prioul; Yesterday's standard, today's fragment: element of esthetics in Quebec, 1820–1850, by Laurier Lacroix. Catalogue. The emergence, 1790–1820; The affirmation, 1820–1850; Perspectives, 1850–1860.

Index of names, p.577–87. Bibliography, p.589–605.

M199 Burnett, David. Masterpieces of Canadian art from the National Gallery of Canada. Foreword by Dr. Shirley L. Thomson. Edmonton, Hurtig, 1990. x, 230p. col. plates.

Survey of Canadian paintings largely drawn from the National Gallery of Canada's collections, highlighting works from 1789 to 1984. Each plate is accompanied by a critical text and a biographical note on the artist. In the author's words, "I sought a chronological balance—the larger number of examples from the modern period reflects the greater range and quantity of activity in comparison to earlier times. Second, my selection was based partly on the contribution that individual artists have made to art in Canada."—*Introd.*

Index, p.228–29.

M200 Edmonton Art Gallery. Modern painting in Canada: a survey of major movements in twentieth century Canadian art. An exhibition organized by The Edmonton Art Gallery as part of the cultural programme of the Commonwealth Games held in Edmonton, Alberta, 1978. [Text by Terry Fenton and Karen Wilkin.] Edmonton, Edmonton Art Gallery, 1978. 136p. 53 col. plates.

Exhibition catalog with brief essays "on the major movements and groups of painters which were influential in Canada during this period, particularly the ones which were instrumental, in some way, in establishing modern—or modernist—painting in this country."—*Introd.*

Contents: The Group of Seven; Montreal in the 1930s and the Contemporary Art Society; Two isolated modernists [David Milne and Emily Carr]; Montreal and the collective unconscious; New internationalism: abstraction in Montreal and Toronto; Western Canada and the Emma Lake workshops; Regionalism, populism, anti-Americanism.

Biography of artists, p.112–21. Selected bibliography, p.122–23. List of works, p.124–29. List of lenders, p.130.

M201 Reid, Dennis R. A concise history of Canadian painting. 2d ed. Toronto, Oxford Univ. Pr., 1988. xii, 418p. il., 36 col. plates.

See GLAH 1:M169 for 1st ed.

Standard reference and comprehensive account in 17 chapters of the history of Canadian painting from the French colonial period to 1980. "Readers familiar with the earlier [1973] version will find numerous changes, additions, some reinterpretations, and a few new names. The revisions and additions reflect the remarkable growth since 1973 in the study of the history of Canadian art."—*Introd.*

Index, p.401–18.

France

M202 Adams, Steven. The Barbizon school and the origins of impressionism. London, Phaidon, 1994. 240p. il. (part col.), col. plates, map, ports.

General introduction and history of the Barbizon painters with an emphasis on their influence on impressionism. "The aim of this book is to chart the often complex movement of landscape painting in the first half of the nineteenth century and to explain the role of Barbizon painting in the rural imagery in the 50 years that led up to the first Impressionist exhibition."—*Introd.*

Contents: (1) Landscape painting in restoration France, 1815–30; (2) Panoramas, parks and porcelain: nature and popular culture; (3) Landscape painting during the July monarchy; (4) Rural images and the 1848 Revolution; (5) Barbizon painting and impressionism.

Notes, p.227–30. Bibliography, p.236. Index, p.237–40.

M203 Les anneés romantiques: la peinture française de 1815 à 1850. [Commissariat gén., Isabelle Julia, Jean Lacambre, assist. de Sylvain Boyer.] Paris, Réunion des musées nationaux, 1995. 497p. il. (part col.), col. plates.

Catalog of the exhibition of 181 French romantic paintings by 110 artists, Musée des Beaux-Arts, Nantes (1995), and other locations.

Contents: (1) La peinture religieuse: art officiel et art sacré, par Georges Brunel; (2) Peintures commandées pour les églises de Paris de 1815 à 1850, par Georges Brunel; (3) Du "genre anecdotique" au "genre historique": une autre peinture d'histoire, par Marie-Claude Chaudonneret; (4) Versailles, les grandes commandes, par Claire Constans; (5) Delacroix et son temps, par Arlette Sérullaz; (6) Le salon de Paris de 1815 à 1850, par Claude Allemand-Cosneau; (7) Histoires d'esquisse, par Jean Lacambre; (8) L'étourdissement des paysages, par Isabelle Julia; (9) La fête de la narration, par Ariel Denis.

Biographies des artistes et notices des oeuvres, p.327–444. Répertoire des tableaux français peints entre 1815 et 1850, conservés dans les collections publiques de France, p.445–86. Ouvrages cités en abrégé, p.487–92. Principales expositions, p.493–96. Index des artistes représentés, p.497.

M204 Bajou, Thierry. Paintings at Versailles: XVIIIth century. Eng. trans. by Elizabeth Wiles-Portier. Paris,

Réunion des musées nationaux, 1998. 355p. il. (mostly col.)

"This is the first publication to contain colour reproductions of no fewer than one hundred and fifty XVIIIth century paintings at the Chateau de Versailles."—*Advertisement.* "In order to highlight stylistic trends in seventeenth-century painting, the structure of this book is based on the approximate chronology of the works."—*Introd.*

Bibliographical references, p.324–32. Exhibitions, p.333–34. Index of painters, p.335–53. Topographical index, p.353–[56].

M205 Bazin, Germain. L'univers impressionniste. 2d éd., revue et complétée. Paris, Somogy, 1982. 351p. il. (part col.), col. plates.

1st ed. L'époque impressionniste. Paris, Tisné, 1947.

Studious treatment of the French Impressionist world that traces its beginnings in Normandy in the 1850s to the founding of the Musée de l'Orangerie, Paris, in 1958.

Contents: Argument; (1) Genèse; (2) Argenteuil et Pontoise; (3) Epanouissement; (4) La tentation de la science; (5) De la nature au symbole; (6) Sorrow; (7) Le métier; (8) Resonances et survivances; (9) De par le monde; (10) Le sacré du printemps; (11) Posthume.

Notes, p.326–27. Table des illustrations, p.329–41. Bibliographie, p.342–46. Index, p.347–51.

M206 Bryson, Norman. Word and image: French painting of the ancien regime. N.Y., Cambridge Univ. Pr., 1981. xviii, 281p. il., facsims.

Engaging historical survey of narrative styles in 18th-century French painting from Le Brun to Ingres.

Contents: (1) Discourse, figure; (2) The legible body: Le Brun; (3) Watteau and reverie; (4) Transformations in rococo space; (5) Greuze and the pursuit of happiness; (6) Diderot and the word; (7) Diderot and the image; (8) 1785; Conclusion: style or sign?

Notes, p.254–69. List of societies affiliated to CINOA, p.270–71. Select bibliography, p.272–76. Index, p.277–81.

M207 Cahn, Walter. Romanesque manuscripts: the twelfth century. London, Harvey Miller, 1996. 2v. il. (part col.), plates (part col.), map (Survey of manuscripts illuminated in France)

Detailed, scholarly catalog of 152 major French illuminated manuscripts from the 12th century. Selections include Bibles, liturgical books, lives of the saints, canon law, and literary and historical writings. Catalog entries include a physical and content description of the manuscript, provenance, references to the literature, and exhibition history. "The aim of this volume is to present a descriptive overview of manuscripts illuminated in France during the twelfth century. As a practical matter, such an enterprise must be selective, and my catalogue entries document only the high points of a very large and, as yet, inadequately studied production. Major works have been included as a matter of course, but it has been my special concern to attempt to exemplify, as far as possible, the range and variety of this body of illumination."—*Pref.*

Contents: (1) Text and illustrations; (2) Catalogue.

List of manuscripts catalogued in volume two, v.1, p.38–40. Index of manuscripts, v.2, p.185–92. Types of book, v.2, p.193–94. Iconographical index, v.2, p.195–200. General index, v.2, p.201–09.

M208 Conisbee, Philip. Painting in eighteenth-century France. Ithaca, N.Y., Cornell Univ. Pr., 1981. 223p. il. (part col.), 15 col. plates.

Thematic survey of painting genres in France during the last two regimes of the ancien regime, focusing on the central importance of Paris to the rest of Europe.

Contents: (1) The artist's world; (2) Religious painting; (3) History painting; (4) Portraiture; (5) The minor genres; (6) Landscape.

Biographical notes, p.203–12. Select bibliography, p.215–16. Index, p.221–23.

M209 Crow, Thomas E. Painters and public life in eighteenth-century Paris. New Haven, Yale Univ. Pr., 1985. vi, 290p. il. (part col.), col. plates.

Illustrated history of 18th-century Parisian salons, with emphases on the transition from private audiences to public spaces for viewing paintings and on the emerging dynamics between painter, patron, academy, critic, and public viewer.

Contents: (1) A public space in the making; (2) Fêtes galantes and fêtes publiques; (3) The salon and the street; (4) Whose salon?; (5) Greuze and official art; (6) Painting and the politicians; (7) David and the salon.

Notes, p.259–77. Select bibliography, p.278–85. Index, p.287–90.

M210 Denvir, Bernard. Impressionism: the painters and the paintings. London, Studio, 1991. 424p. 393 col. plates (part fold.)

Well-documented and superbly illustrated folio edition of French impressionism that concentrates on its development, themes, and major painters.

Contents: (1) The birth of a revolution; (2) Early days; (3) A new realism; (4) Debates and discussions; (5) War and its aftermath; (6) A united front?; (7) The city versus the country; (8) The world of pleasure; (9) Doubts and dissensions; (10) The end of an epoch.

Chronology, p.401–14. Select bibliography, p.415. Index, p.421–24.

M211 Dictionnaire de la peinture française: la peinture en France du moyen âge à nos jours. [Conception éd., réalis. et sél. iconographique, Jean-Philippe Breuille. Documentation iconographique, Marianne Prost.] Paris, Larousse, 1989. 520p. col. il. (Essentiels).

Compilation of biographical notices of major French painters from the Middle Ages to the middle of the 20th century arranged alphabetically by artist's name. Entries range from a paragraph to several pages in length. Information for individual entries is extracted from Petite Larousse de la peinture and Dictionnaire de la peinture, published under the dir. of Michel Laclotte, director of the Louvre, assisted by Jean-Pierre Cuzin, conservator of the Paintings Department of the Louvre.

M212 Encyclopédie des Impressionnistes; des précurseurs aux héritiers. Sous la dir. de Dominique Spiess. Avec la participation de Dominique Buisson . . . [et al.] Lausanne, Edita, 1992. 382p. il. (part col.), col. plates.

Heavily illustrated encyclopedia that covers approximately 100 major and minor French Impressionist painters.

M213 Fare, Michel, and Fare, Fabrice. La vie silencieuse en France; la nature morte au XVIIIe siècle. Fribourg, Office du Livre, 1976. 438p. il., plates (30 col.).

Detailed, comprehensive examination of 18th-century French still life noted for its thorough research and illustrations.

Contents: Fastes et décors de la première moitié du dix-huitième siècle; Le retour à la réalité dans la seconde moitié du dix-huitième siècle; Les peintres provinçiaux; Conclusions.

Notes, p.409–19. Bibliographie, p.421–29. Table des illustrations, p.430–31. Table des artistes, p.432–35. Table des matières, p.437.

M214 Fine Arts Museums of San Francisco. French paintings 1500–1825. By Pierre Rosenberg [and] Marion C. Stewart with the assist. of Thierry Lefrancois. San Francisco, Fine Arts Museums of San Francisco, 1987. 373p. il. (part col.)

Descriptive, illustrated catalog of paintings by major French artists from 1500 to 1825 arranged by century and alphabetically by artist. Entries for individual works include critical notes, provenance, references to the literature, exhibitions history, subject, and iconography.

Contents: (1) History of the collections; (2) 16th century; (3) 17th century; (4) 18th century; (5) Reserve; (6) Paintings formerly considered French.

Exhibitions, p.351–54. References, p.356–64. Index of artists, p.366–72.

M215 ______. The new painting: Impressionism, 1874–1886. [By] Charles S. Moffett with contrib. by Richard R. Brettell . . . [et al.] 2d ed. Geneva, Burton (Distr. by Univ. of Washington Pr., 1986). 509p. il. (part col.)

1st ed., 1986.

Catalog accompanying the exhibition, Fine Arts Museums of San Francisco (1986), of 160 paintings included in the original eight Impressionist exhibitions in Paris. "The catalogue presents a detailed art-historical exegesis of each of the eight group shows, while the exhibition offers a unique opportunity to experience a large assemblage of works actually shown in the landmark exhibitions."—*Introd.* Emphasizes major figures and excerpts from contemporary 19th-century art criticism.

Appendix, p.[475]–84. Abbreviated references, p.485–89. Contemporary reviews, p.490–96. Bibliography, p.497–505. Index, p.506–09.

M216 ______. ______. Documentation. [By] Ruth Berson. San Francisco, The Museums (Distr. by Univ. of Washington Pr., 1996). 2v. il.

Documentary supplement to the exhibition catalog (see preceding title).

Contents: (1) Reviews; (2) Exhibited works.

Contributors to reviews, v.1, p.477–83. Lenders to the exhibition, v.2, p.285–94. Short references, v.2, p.295–97.

M217 Five hundred years of French painting: the Hermitage, Leningrad; the Pushkin Museum of Fine Arts, Moscow. Ed. by Liudmila Brylenko. [Trans. from the Russian by Yuri Pamfilov.] [Introd. article by Nadezhda Petrusevich.] Leningrad, Aurora, 1990. 2v. 283 col. plates.

Illustrated catalog of major French paintings held by the Hermitage and the Pushkin Museum of Fine Arts. An introductory essay describes the collections and their development. Entries for individual paintings include the artist's name, title of work, date, medium, size, and date acquired.

Contents: (1) 15th to 18th centuries; (2) 19th and 20th centuries.

Name index in each vol.

M218 Francastel, Pierre. Histoire de la peinture française. Avec la collab. de Galienne Francastel. Notices biographiques par Maurice Bex. Paris, Denöel, 1990. 475p. plates (part col.) (Médiations).

1st ed. 1955.

Chronological survey of French painting from the Middle Ages to Cubism, noteworthy for its coverage and lengthy biographical section.

Contents: Première partie: du moyen âge à la fin du XVIIIe siècle; Deuxième partie: du classicisme au cubisme.

Notice biographiques des peintres français du moyen âge à l'art moderne, p.335–468. Biographie [Pierre Francastel, 1900–70], p.469–70. Bibliographie, p.471–72. Table, p.473–75.

M219 Geneva (Switzerland). Musée d'art et d'histoire. Catalogue raisonné des peintures et pastels de l'école française, XVIe, XVIIe et XVIIIe siècles. [Par] Renée Loche. Genève, Slatkine, 1996. 533p. il. (part col.), ports.

Beautifully produced catalog of the collection of 131 French paintings and pastels, with an introductory history of the collection.

Catalogues et guides du Musée, p.491. Bibliographie des ouvrages cités, p.492–510. Expositions citées, p.511–15. Oeuvres par ordre croissant des numéros d'inventaire, p.516–18. Changements d'attributions, p.519–20. Titres, p.521–23. Anciennes collections, p.524–27. Noms d'artistes cités, p.528–30.

M220 Great paintings from the Barnes foundation: impressionist, post-impressionist, and early modern. [Essays by Richard J. Wattenmaker . . . (et al.)] N.Y., Knopf, in assoc. with Lincoln Univ. Pr., 1993. xvii, 318p. il. (part col.), col. plates.

Catalog of the exhibition, National Gallery of Art (1993), and other locations, of 19th- and 20th-century paintings by 15 artists from the reclusive Barnes collection in Merion, Pennsylvania. First-time color reproductions of selected works include details.

Contents: Dr. Albert C. Barnes and the Barnes foundation, by Richard J. Wattenmaker; Dr. Barnes in Paris, by Anne Distel.

Notes, p.297–313. Index of illustrations, p.315–17.

M221 Harambourg, Lydia. Dictionnaire des peintres paysagistes français au XIXe siècle. Neuchâtel, Ides et Calendes, 1985. 360p. il. (part col.), col. plates.

Comprehensive dictionary of major and minor 19th-century French landscape artists of all schools and genres (historical, pastoral, romantic, impressionist, etc.) arranged alphabetically by artist's name. Color plates include dimensions and provenance.

Contents: L'influence des voyages sur le développement de la peinture de paysage; Dictionnaire des peintres.

Bibliographie, ouvrages généraux, p.353–55. Bibliographie par artistes, p.355–60. Expositions, p.360.

M222 ———. L'école de Paris, 1945–1965: dictionnaire des peintres. Neuchâtel, Ides et Calendes, 1993. 526p. il. (part col.), col. plates.

Illustrated dictionary of School of Paris painters active between 1945 and 1965, arranged alphabetically by artist. Entries include a biographical and career sketch, major works, awards, exhibitions, publications, and references to the literature.

Index des peintres, p.517–21. Bibliographies, p.522–23. Expositions, p.523–24.

M223 Herbert, James D. Fauve painting: the making of cultural politics. New Haven, Yale Univ. Pr., 1992. 224p. 92 il. (part col.)

Extensively documented, analytical study of works by French Fauve painters from 1905 to 1910. "The paintings of the Fauves, I will argue, themselves performed the artistic reconciliation of tradition and innovation."—*Introd.*

Contents: Introduction: the dialogues of painting; (1) The north revisited, impressionism revised; (2) Mirroring the nude; (3) Painters and tourists in the classical landscape; (4) The golden age and the French national heritage; (5) Woman, Cézanne and Africa; Conclusion: figures of innovation and tradition.

Notes, p.184–212. Bibliography of cited sources, p.213–21. Index, p.222–24.

M224 Herbert, Robert L. Impressionism: art, leisure, and Parisian society. New Haven, Yale Univ. Pr., 1988. xix, 324p. il. (part col.), col. plates, map.

Topical overview of Impressionism that examines the representations of French social life and leisure activities in impressionist paintings from the 1860s to the mid-1880s. "I started with the pictures of the Impressionists then tried to answer the questions posed by the kinds of subjects that they preferred and the way they painted them."—*Pref.* Illustrations include numerous details.

Contents: (1) Paris transformed; (2) Impressionism and naturalism; (3) Café and café-concert; (4) Theater, opera, and dance; (5) Parks, racetracks, and gardens; (6) Suburban leisure; (7) At the seaside.

Notes, p.307–13. Bibliography, p.314–19. Index, p.320–24.

M225 The impressionists: a retrospective. Ed. by Martha Kapos. Southport, Conn., Hugh Lauter Levin [Distr. by Macmillan, 1991]. 380p. il. (part col.), plates (part col.) map.

Illustrated history of French Impressionism told largely through excerpts from correspondence and writings of major painters, writers, and critics, dating from 1865 to 1990.

Bibliographical index, p.10. Chronology, p.11–27.

M226 Kelder, Diane M. The great book of French impressionism. N.Y., Abbeville, 1980. 447p. il. (part col.), col. plates (part fold.) (Repr.: N.Y., Harrison [Distr. by Crown, 1984]; N.Y., Artabras, 1990.)

French trans., Paris, Bibliothèque des arts, 1986.

Spectacular, large-format view of French impressionism noted for its cogent text and magnificent color plates, including numerous details. Presents the lives and works of the forerunners of impressionism and the principal proponents as well as contemporary writings about the furor created by the new movement.

M227 Kostenevich, Albert. Hidden treasures revealed: impressionist masterpieces and other important French paintings preserved by the State Hermitage Museum, St. Petersburg. Ed. by James Leggo. St. Petersburg, Ministery of Culture of the Russian Federation; State Hermitage Museum (in assoc. with Abrams, 1995). 292p. il. (part col.), col. plates.

Catalog accompanying the exhibition of 74 French paintings dating from 1827 to 1927 by 23 masters, Hermitage (1995). Arranged by artist, information about each painting includes critical notes about the artist, subject, provenance, exhibition history, and references to the literature. Illustrations include details.

M228 Levêque, Jean-Jacques. Les années impressionnistes, 1870–1889. Paris, ACR, 1990. 660p. il. (part col.), col. plates, diagrs. maps, plans, ports. tables.

Sweeping year-by-year chronological survey of French Impressionism presented in vignettes of painters, themes, locations, and stylistic developments.

Index des oeuvres, p.656–59. Orientation bibliographique, p.660.

M229 Mérot, Alain. French painting in the seventeenth century. Trans. by Caroline Beamish. New Haven, Yale Univ. Pr., 1995. 324p. il. (part col.)

Trans. of La peinture française au XVIIe siècle. Paris, Gallimard/Electa, 1994.

Rigorously researched and superbly illustrated overview of 17th-century French painting. "The aim was to offer the reader or scholar of today a clear panorama, appropriately illustrated, which would take into account the recent contributions made by art historians and scholars from other disciplines, as well as the educational demands of the genre. . . . I have endeavoured to reconcile the chronological study of the main stylistic movements with the study of the different categories of painting."—*Foreword.*

Contents: (1) Space, time, styles; (2) Painters and their public; (3) The end of mannerism; (4) Reactions to mannerism; (5) Rome, Paris, Rome; (6) The founders of the academy; (7) Approaches to reality; (8) Portraiture; (9) Landscape; (10) Painters of still life and animals; (11) The two Apelles: Le Brun and Mignard; (12) From Louis XIV to the regency.

Bibliography, p.305–17. Index to names and works, p.318–23.

M230 Moffett, Charles S. Impressionist and post-impressionist paintings in the Metropolitan Museum of Art. N.Y., Metropolitan Museum of Art; Abrams, 1985. 255p. il. (part col.), col. plates.

Covers 126 paintings by 17 Impressionist and Post-Impressionist artists. Illustrations include details.

List of illustrations and selected bibliography, p.249.

M231 Montreal Museum of Fine Arts. Century of splendour: seventeenth-century French painting in French public collections. Paris, Réunion des musées nationaux, 1993. 400p. il (part col.). plates (part col.).

Catalog of the exhibition of 132 17th-century French paintings, Montreal Museum of Fine Arts (1993), and other locations.

Contents: Seventeenth-century French painting and art history: problems and methods; Catalogue; The end of mannerism; Caravaggism; Renewal; The classical ideal; The blossoming of a new era.

Bibliography, p.379–89. List of exhibitions cited, p.390–92. Lenders to the exhibition, p.393–95.

M232 Musée d'Orsay. Catalogue sommaire illustré des peintures. Ed. by Isabelle Compin . . . [et al.] Avec la collab. de Anne Distel . . . [et al.] Paris, Réunion des musées nationaux, 1990. 2v. il. (part col.), col. plates.

Illustrated catalog of approximately 2,500 paintings from 1848 to 1914 in the Musée d'Orsay, arranged alphabetically by artist. Concise entries for individual works include names and dates for the artist, title and date of the painting, provenance, exhibition history, and a small black-and-white reproduction.

Index des donateurs, v.2, p.512–17. Index des artistes par pays (à l'exception de la France), v.2, p.518. Bibliographie, v.2, p.519. Liste alphabetique des ouvrages cités en abrégé, v.2, p.520–21.

M233 Musée national de Versailles et des Trianons. Les peintures. Par Claire Constans. Pref. de Jean-Pierre Babelon. [Rev. ed.] Paris, Réunion des musées nationaux, 1995. 3v. il. (part col.)

1st ed., 1980. Vol.1–2 are the catalog, vol.3 a series of "annexes" (bibliography and indexes).

Bibliographie, p.1119–23. Cartons de tapisserie, p.1124. Artistes copiés, p.1125–32. Oeuvres de collaboration, p.1133–34. Commandes et ensembles décoratifs, p.1135–39. Collections de provenance, p.1140–60.

M234 Museum of Fine Arts, Boston. French paintings in the Museum of Fine Arts, Boston. By Eric M. Zafran. With the assist. of Katherine Rothkopf, and Sydney Resendez. Boston, The Museum, 1998– . (1)v. il. (part col.), ports.

"Of the various national schools within the European painting collection . . . the French school is by far the largest."—*Introd.*

Contents: (1) Artists born before 1790 (1998).

M235 New York. Metropolitan Museum of Art. France in the golden age: seventeenth-century French paintings in American collections. [By] Pierre Rosenberg. N.Y., Metropolitan Museum of Art, 1982. xix, 398p. il. (part col.)

French ed. La peinture française du XVIIe siècle dans les collections américaines. Paris, Réunion des musées nationaux, 1982.

Catalog of the exhibition, Metropolitan Museum of Art (1982), and other locations, of 124 French paintings. Notable for its extensive research of individual paintings.

Contents: (1) Principal political and artistic events of the seventeenth century, compiled by Claude Lesné; (2) Seventeenth-century French paintings; (3) Inventory of seventeenth-century French paintings in public collections in the United States; (4) Paintings granted to churches in the United States, by Elisabeth Foucart-Walter.

Index of inventory by city, p.378–79. Exhibitions, p.383–85. Bibliography, p.386–95.

M236 La peinture française. Sous la dir. de Jean-Louis Pradel. Paris, Dictionnaire Le Robert, 1983. 280p. il. (part col.), col. plates. ports.

Compilation of seven illustrated essays by prominent critics and scholars covering French painting from the Middle Ages to the late 19th century.

Contents: (1) Existe-t-il une peinture française? par Alain Jouffroy; (2) Le moyen âge et la renaissance, par Régis Labourdette; (3) La peinture française du XVIIe siècle: promenade dans un musée imaginaire, par Louis Martin; (4) Le VXIIIe siècle, par Renée Moll; (5) Le XIXe siècle: art et liberté, par Patrick Le Nouene; (6) L'Impressionnisme: entrée en scene du soleil, par Sophie Monneret; (7) Quelques aspects de l'art en France à partir de 1886, par Jean Clay.

Biographies des artistes, p.241–77. Bibliographie, p.277–78. Index, p.279–80.

M237 Perry, Gillian. Women artists and the Parisian avant-garde; modernism and "feminine" art, 1900 to the late 1920s. Manchester, Manchester Univ. Pr. (Distr. by St. Martin's, 1995). xi, 186p. il. 32 col. plates.

A history of painting by women in Paris in the early 20th century that concentrates on "some of the contradictions and shifts both in the work of these women artists and in the interests and allegiances of those contemporary critics who wrote about their painting."—*Introd.* Details the role of Berthe Weill in the early exhibition and promotion of the work of many femmes peintres.

Contents: (1) Professionalism, training and "the space of femininity"; (2) "In the wings of modern painting": women artists, the fauves and the cubists; (3) The art market and the school of Paris: marketing a "feminine style"; (4) Women painting women; (5) Postscript and conclusion; Appendix 1, biographical information on les femmes peintres; Appendix 2, Galerie Berthe Weill: exhibitions and artists shown, 1901–26; Appendix 3, extracts from Marevna Vorobëv, Life in two worlds.

Select bibliography, p.175–80. Index, p.181–86.

M238 The Post-impressionists: a retrospective. Ed. by Martha Kapos. [London], Hugh Lauter Levin (Distr. by Macmillan, 1993). 380p. il. (part col.) 119 col. plates (part fold.)

Sweeping, heavily illustrated overview of Post-Impressionism composed of excerpts from seminal critical and biographical writings, some translated into English for the first time. Texts date from 1879 to 1991.

Contents: Chronology; Impressionism and symbolism: symphonic form; The subjectivity of sensations; "Scientific" impressionism: the neo-impressionist reaction; The discovery of painting as an abstraction; The fragmentation of artistic movements; The artist's isolation; Symbolism and decadence; Redon: "suggestive art"; Gauguin: symbolism in painting; van Gogh: impressionism and expressionism; Cezanne: reading nature; The critics' reaction; Post-Impressionism defined; Matisse, Braque, and Bonnard; Twentieth-century views of post-impressionism.

Bibliographical index, p.10. Index, p.375–79.

M239 Silver, Kenneth E. Esprit de corps: the art of the Parisian avant-garde and the first world war, 1914–1925. Princeton, N.J., Princeton Univ. Pr., 1989. xxiv, 504p. il. (part col.), 8 col. plates.

Scholarly study of changes in the art of the Parisian avant-garde during the first world war and reconstruction. Examines French nationalist art, the distinction between combatant and civilian, the campaign against cubism and other avant-garde movements, the theory of an infiltration of French culture, the individual artist and his place in the collective war effort, the metaphor of construction and its meaning for France at this time, and the revision of attitudes to late 19th-century French art.

Contents: (1) "In the nightmare through which we are passing"; (2) The rewards of war; (3) Comme il faut; (4) Internecine warfare; (5) Fluctuat nec mergitur; (6) Blue horizons; (7) From analysis to synthesis; (8) Perchance to dream.

Notes, p.401–75. Bibliography, p.476–89. Index, p.491–504.

M240 Spate, Virginia. Orphism: the evolution of non-figurative painting in Paris, 1910–1914. Oxford, Oxford Univ. Pr., 1979. xxv, 409p. il.

Detailed, scholarly study of early French non-objective painters.

Contents: (1) The background to orphist painting; (2) The orphist painters.

Notes, p.345–65. Appendix, p.367–82. Bibliography, p.397–409.

M241 Sterling, Charles. La peinture médiévale à Paris, 1300–1500. Paris, Bibliothèque des Arts, 1987–90. 2v. il. (part col.), plates (part col.), maps.

Monumental survey of Parisian medieval illuminated manuscripts and paintings organized chronologically by artist. Includes descriptive notes that identify works and commentary on each illuminator and painter.

Table des illustrations, v.1, p.461–75, v.2, p.419–49. Bibliographie, v.1, p.477–90, v.2, p.451–71. Abréviations, v.1, p.491–97. Abréviations des deux tomes, v.2, p.472–79. Index des personnes, v.1, p.498–502. Index des sujets, v.1, p.503–505. Index des lieux, v.1, p.505–07. Index des manuscrits cités, v.1, p.508–11. Index tome 1, v.2, p.481–89. Index tome 2, v.2, p.491–99.

M242 Stuckey, Charles F. French painting. N.Y., Hugh Lauter Levin (Distr. by Macmillan, 1991). 320p. col. il.

Large-format, heavily illustrated overview of landmark French paintings by major artists beginning with the Limbourg Brothers in the 15th century. Emphasis on 19th- and 20th-century painting.

Contents: (1) An age of war and faith; (2) Courtly art from Italy; (3) French artists in Caravaggio's shadow; (4) French classicism and the academy; (5) Opera sets for love and sex: the rococo; (6) Morality as a middle-class value; (7) Immorality, morality, and revolution; (8) Art under Napoleon; (9) Full-blown romanticism; (10) Leaving Paris: from Barbizon to Ornans; (11) Real allegories; (12) Brushwork in the 1860s; (13) Landscape becomes modern; (14) Time and series in the 1870s; (15) Impressionist figure painting; (16) Beyond instantaneity; (17) Martyrs for modern art; (18) Art as escape from urban life; (19) The close of an era; (20) The wild beasts; (21) Picasso and early cubism; (22) Pure abstraction and pure fantasy; (23) Matisse's alternative to cubism; (24) Cubism and the machine style; (25) World War I, dada, and purism; (26) Surrealism and its affinities; (27) Old values and new threats; (28) World War II art; (29) Postwar abstract painting; (30) Objections to abstraction; (31) The end of painting since then.

Index, p.316–18.

M243 Tinterow, Gary, and Loyrette, Henri. Origins of impressionism. N.Y., Metropolitan Museum of Art (Distr. by Abrams, 1994). xvi, 486p. il. (part col.), col. plates.

Catalog of the exhibition, Metropolitan Museum of Art (1994–95), and other locations, of 193 paintings from the 1860s by 35 artists. Entries for major works include a facsimile, artist's biography, description, provenance, and bibliography. Exquisitely illustrated, including details.

Contents: (1) The salon of 1859, by Henri Loyrette; (2) History painting, by Henri Loyrette; (3) The realist landscape, by Gary Tinterow; (4) The nude, by Henri Loyrette; (5) Figures in a landscape, by Gary Tinterow; (6) Still life, by Henri Loyrette; (7) Portraits and figures, by Henri Loyrette; (8) The impressionist landscape, by Gary Tinterow; (9) Modern life, by Henri Loyrette.

Chronology of works in the catalogue, p.295–97. Chronology 1859–70, p.299–325. Abbreviated bibliographic references, p.468–73. Index, p.474–85.

M244 Wakefield, David. French eighteenth-century painting. London, Gordon Fraser, 1984. 185p. plates (part col.)

Revisionist treatment of 18th-century French painting, seeking balance to the rococo excesses expounded by the Goncourt Brothers by interweaving history, criticism, and social factors. Contends that French art of the 18th century is sensual and idealistic and that the notion of bon goût, accepted as a self-evident virtue in every educated observer, also implied the free expression of critical judgment.

Contents: (1) The opening of the century; (2) Watteau and the regency; (3) The decorative painters of the rococo; (4) The portrait; (5) Boucher and the reign of Madame de Pompadour; (6) The revival of history painting; (7) The still life and genre painting; (8) From pastoral to the sublime.

Notes, p.171–73. Location of main public collections, p.174–77. Bibliography, p.178–80. Index, p.181–85.

M245 Wright, Christopher. The French painters of the seventeenth century. Boston, Little, Brown, 1985. 288p. il. (part col.)

Study of 17th-century French painting in context of French history and culture, with the stated purpose of rescuing it from concentration on major artists and generalizations. "The purpose of this book is to give an account of the development of French painting in the seventeenth century, as far as can be deduced from the surviving pictures."—*Introd.*

Contents: (1) International mannerism and its effect in France, 1600–25; (2) Caravaggio and his French followers; (3) Painting in Paris, 1600–35; (4) French painters in Rome: the classical tradition; (5) Painting in Paris, 1635–60; (6) Painting under Louis XIV; Epilogue: The artists.

General bibliography, p.277–79. Index of locations, p.280–86. General index, p.287–88.

SEE ALSO: Hermitage catalogue of Western European painting (GLAH 2:M12).

Germany and Austria

M246 Baumgartl, Edgar; Lauterbach, Gabriele; and Otto, Kornelius. Maler in Franken: Leben und Werk von Künstlern aus fünf Jahrhunderten. Nürnberg, Spätlese, 1993. 320p. il. (part col.), maps, ports.

Dictionary of 109 major Franconian painters from the 14th to 20th centuries. Following an introduction about the history of painting and art in Franconia, the life and work of individual painters are presented chronologically. Each artist's entry notes locations of representative paintings and a bibliography.

Glossar, p.301–04. Abkürzungsverzeichnis, p.304. Allgemeine und abgekürzt zitierte Literatur, p.305. Personenregister, p.307–14. Ortsregister, p.314–19.

M247 Borsch-Supan, Helmut. Die deutsche Malerei von Anton Graff bis Hans von Marées, 1760–1870. München, Beck, 1988. 608p. il. (part col.), plates (part col.), ports.

Detailed, scholarly examination of major trends in German painting from 1760 to 1870, with an emphasis on individual painters. Particularly valuable for biographical information, bibliography, appendixes, and indexes.

Contents: Der Zustand der Malerei um 1763; Historienmaler vor 1800; Die Entwicklung der Landschaftsmalerei am Ende des 18. Jahrhunderts; Der Zustand der Malerei am Anfang des 19. Jahrhunderts; Die kunst und das Publikum; Die Gattungen der Malerei; Der Zustand der Malerei um 1830/40; Der Zustand der Malerei um 1860/70.

Verzeichnisse, p.488–514. Maler ausserhalb der Hauptzentren, p.514–94. Künstlerverzeichnis, p.595–609.

M248 Damus, Martin. Malerei der DDR: Funktionen der bildenden Kunst im Realen Sozialismus. Reinbek bei Hamburg, Rowohlt, 1991. 383p. il. (part col.)

Scholarly treatise on mid-20th century Social Realist painting in the former German Democratic Republic.

Contents: (1) "Auferstanden aus Ruinen und der Zukunft zugewandt"; (2) Diktatur des Proletariats und Sozialistischer Realismus; (4) Stanlinistische Entstalinisierung-Neubestimmung des Sozialistischen Realismus; (5) Kunst zwischen "sozialistischer Menschengemeinschaft" und industrieller Modernisierung; (6) Der "Reale Sozialismus"—Vielfalt der Kunst als Programm; (7) Götterdämmerung.

Literatur, p.368–70. Namenregister, p.373–79. Sachregister, p.380–83.

M249 Einem, Herbert von. Deutsche Malerei des Klassizismus und der Romantik: 1760 bis 1840. München, Beck, 1978. 252p. il. (part col.)

Well-documented, scholarly study of German classical and romantic painting from 1760 to the mid-19th century. Chapters on Protestant and Catholic Romanticism are particularly important.

Contents: (1) Der akademische Klassizismus, 1760 bis 1785; (2) Der reife Klassizismus, 1785 bis 1810; (3) Die Romantik, 1800 bis 1840; (4) Der protestantische Weg der Romantik; (5) Der katholische Weg der Romantik; (6) Die naturalistische Richtung; (7) Nachspiel von Klassizismus und Romantik, um 1840 bis 1870.

Anmerkungen zum Text, p.193–212. Literatur, p.213–14. Katalog der abgebildeten Werke, p.215–48. Personenverzeichnis, p.249–52.

M250 Elger, Dietmar. Expressionismus: eine deutsche Kunstrevolution. Hrsg. von Ingo F. Walther. Köln, Taschen, 1988. 260p. il. (part col.), col. plates.

Study of German expressionism that concentrates on major schools and individual artists.

Contents: Introduction; (1) Die "Brücke", eine Künstlergruppe; (2) Nörddeutscher Expressionismus; (3) "Der Blaue Reiter"; (4) Rheinischer Expressionismus; (5) Die Grotsstadt als Thema; (6) Expressionismus in Wien.

Biographien und Bibliographien, p.253–60.

M251 Fuchs, Heinrich. Die österreichische Bildnisminiatur von den Anfängen bis zur Gegenwart. Wien, Fuchs, 1981–82. 2v. il. (part col.)

An illustrated biographical dictionary of Austrian portrait miniaturists actively mainly in the 18th and 19th centuries, arranged alphabetically by painter. Entries range from a sentence to a page. Includes some signature facsimiles.

M252 ______. Die österreichischen Maler des 19. Jahrhunderts. Wien, Fuchs, 1972–74. 4v. il.
Comprehensive biographical dictionary of 19th-century-Austrian painters.
______. Ergänzungsband. Wien, Fuchs, 1978. 2v. il.
Contents: (1) A–K; (2) L–Z.

M253 ______. Die österreichischen Maler des 20. Jahrhunderts. Wien, H. Fuchs, 1985–86. 4v. il., plates, ports.
Comprehensive biographical dictionary of major 20th-century Austrian painters, including signatures and black-and-white plates reproducing their works. Individual entries range from a sentence to several pages.
______. Ergänzungsband. Wien, Fuchs, 1992. 2v. il.

M254 ______. Register: zu die österreichischen Maler des 19. Jahrhunderts; . . . Die österreichischen Maler der 20. Jahrhunderts; . . . Die österreichische Bildnisminiatur. Wien, H. Fuchs, 1988. 140p. port.
Provides detailed indexing of each of Fuchs's biographical dictionaries (see preceding entries).

M255 Geismeier, Willi. Die Malerei der deutschen Romantik. Stuttgart, Kohlhammer,
1984. 497p. il., 269 plates (part col.)
Scholarly treatment of 19th-century German Romantic painting from its origins to its influence on subsequent movements.
Contents: Romantische Reflexionen und Theorien über Geschichte, Gesellschaft, Kunst und Natur; Die frühromantischen Maler; Die nazarenischen Maler; Die Maler des romantischen Realismus und der Spätromantik.
Künstler- und Abbildungsverzeichnis, p.457–88. Literaturverzeichnis, p.489–92. Personenregister, p.493–97.

M256 Die Goldene Palette: Deutschland, Osterreich, Schweiz. 2. neubearb. Aufl. Hrsg. von Fritz Winzer. Braunschweig, Westermann, 1987. 432p. col. plates.
1st ed. 1968.
Historical survey of painting in Germany, Austria, and Switzerland beginning with examples from early illuminated manuscripts and ending with Georg Baselitz. A page of criticism accompanies each color plate.
Register, p.425–27.

M257 Hessisches Landesmuseum Darmstadt. Deutsche Malerei um 1260 bis 1550 im Hessischen Landesmuseum Darmstadt. Abbildungsteil: bearb. von Wolfgang Beeh. Darmstadt, Das Landesmuseum, 1990. 272p. il. (part col.), col. plates.
Descriptive catalog of German paintings from 1260 to 1550 in the Hessischen Landesmuseum. Each entry includes detail about the artist, work, provenance, references to the literature, and illustrations, including details.
Contents: (1) Mittelrhein und Hessen; (2) Köln und Niederrhein; (3) Niedersachsen, Westfalen, Nörddeutschland; (4) Oberrhein, Bodensee, Schwaben; (5) Franken, Sachsen (Bamberg, Nürnberg, Nördlingen).
Listen und Konkordanzen, p.263–72.

M258 Lammel, Gisold. Deutsche Malerei des Klassizismus. Leipzig, Seemann, 1986. 326p. il. (part col.).
Scholarly examination of German neoclassical painting in the 18th and 19th centuries.
Contents: Frühklassizismus: klassizistische Malerei in der Epoche des aufgeklärten Absolutismus 1760–1789; Reifer Klassizismus: klassizitische Malerei zur Zeit der grossen französischen Revolution und der Napoleonischen Kriege 1789–1815; Spätklassizismus: klassizistische Malerei zwischen Wiener Kongress und Reichsgründung 1815–1871.
Anhang, p.301–12. Literaturverzeichnis, p.312–15. Künstler-Register und Verzeichnis der Abbildungen, p.316–24.

M259 Lexikon der Dusseldorfer Malerschule: 1819–1918. Hrsg. vom Kunstmuseum Dusseldorf im Ehrenhof und von der Galerie Paffrath. Projektleit., Hans Paffrath. München, Bruckmann, 1997– . (2)v. il. (part col.)
Authoritative biographical dictionary of the Dusseldorf School of the 19th century.
Contents: (1) Abbema-Gurlit; (2) Haach-Murtfeldt.

M260 Lubbeke, Isolde. Early German painting, 1350–1550. General ed. Irene Martin. Trans. from the German by Margaret Thomas Will. London, Sotheby's, 1991. 431p. il. (part col.), plates (part col.), map.
An illustrated catalog of 91 paintings in the Thyssen-Bornemisza collection, Lugano.
Arranged alphabetically by artist, entries for individual works include critical notes about the painter, date of the work, subject, provenance, exhibition history, and references.
Artists' biographies, p.402–17. Index, p.421–31.

M261 Neidhardt, Hans Joachim. Deutsche Malerei des 19. Jahrhunderts. Leipzig, Seemann, 1990. 264p. il. (part col.)
Study of 19th-century German paintings held by museums in the former German Democratic Republic. Following introductory historical essays, 172 paintings dating from 1796 to 1904 are reproduced with commentary. Especially strong on German romanticism and late 19th-century realism.
Contents: (1) Umrisse der Epoche; (2) Deutsche Maler des 19. Jahrhunderts; (3) Eine Auswahl von Abbildungen mit Erläuterungen.
Literatur, p.249–51. Verzeichnis der Künstler und Abbildungen, p.252–64.

M262 Refigured painting: the German image, 1960–88. Ed. by Thomas Krens . . . [et al.] Munich, Prestel in assoc. with Solomon R. Guggenheim Museum, N.Y., 1989. 290p. il. (part col.), col. plates, ports.
Catalog of the exhibition, Guggenheim Museum (1989), and other locations, of 179 modern German figurative paintings by 41 artists held at five venues in Germany and the United States in 1989. Includes significant essays on new German painting and pressing aesthetic and cultural issues of the period.
Contents: (1) German painting: paradox and paradigm in late twentieth-century art, by Thomas Krens; (2) Blasphemy

on our side: fates of the figure in postwar German painting, by Joseph Thompson; (3) Meditations on A = B: romanticism and representation in new German painting, by Michael Govan; (4) Metaphors: positions in contemporary German painting, by Jürgen Schilling; (5) Abstraction and fiction, by Heinrich Klotz; (6) Double exposure—the golden shot? By one who set out to unlearn fear.

List of works, p.246–51. Biographies, selected exhibitions and selected bibliographies, p.252–85. General bibliography, p.286–89.

M263 Sabarsky, Serge. Malerei des deutschen Expressionismus. Hrsg. von Ralph Jentsch. Mit Beitr. von Hans Belting . . . [et al.] Stuttgart, Cantz, 1987. 415p. il., col. plates, ports.

Comprehensive overview of German Expressionism with contributions on individual major painters by various scholars. Begins with Die Brücke and Der Blaue Reiter and concludes with works in the early 1920s. Includes a chronology.

Contents: Die Brücke; Dokumentation zum Expressionismus; Biographien.

M264 Stärk, Beate. Contemporary painting in Germany. Roseville East, N.S.W., Craftsman House; G + B Arts International, 1994. vi, 253p. il. plates (part col.)

Illustrated survey of 48 contemporary German painters with reproductions of selected works from the 1980s and early 1990s, including artists working in the former German Democratic Republic. Arranged alphabetically by artist. A concise description of each artist's life and career is followed by illustrations of representative paintings. The Biographies section includes major career events, collections, and selected exhibitions.

Biographies, p.212–53.

M265 Vaughan, William. German romantic painting. 2d ed. New Haven, Conn., Yale Univ. Pr., 1994. v, 260p. il. 195 plates (32 col.), diagrs., maps, ports., tables.

1st. ed. 1980.

An introduction to 19th-century German romantic painting, tracing its cultural beginnings around 1800 and charting its course through mid-century. Rigorously researched and highly readable.

Contents: (1) The painter's Germany; (2) Classicism and expressionism; (3) Philipp Otto Runge; (4) Caspar David Friedrich; (5) Friedrich—the modern painter; (6) Friedrich's followers and imitators; (7) Naturalism and the naive; (8) The Nazarenes; (9) Legends and fairy-tales; (10) Art and propaganda; Epilogue.

Notes on the text, p.243–46. Select bibliography, p.247–51. Additional bibliography, p.252. Index, p.257–60.

M266 Vergo, Peter. Twentieth-century German painting. General ed. Irene Martin. London, Sotheby's, 1992. 386p. il. (part col.), plates (part col.)

Catalog of 106 20th-century German paintings by 32 artists in the Thyssen-Bornemisza collection of modern art. Arranged alphabetically by painter. Each entry includes descriptive information identifying the work, a note on condition, provenance, exhibition history, bibliographic references, and concise critical remarks. Vergo's introductory essay gives a brief history of the main groups represented in the collection and puts the works in perspective within historical movements.

Bibliography, p.377–81. Index of artists, p.385–86.

M267 Vogt, Paul. Geschichte der deutschen Malerei im 20. Jahrhundert. 3., erw. Aufl. Köln, DuMont, 1989. 478p. il. (part col.), col. plates. (DuMont Dokumente)

1st ed. 1972; 2d ed. 1976.

Comprehensive, illustrated history of 20th-century German painting from Impressionism to the 1960s, with emphasis on the Expressionist school and printmaking.

Contents: (I) Der Aufbruch der Jugend; (II) Das Jahrzehnt des Weltkrieges; (III) Die Malerei der zwanzinger Jahre; (IV) Die Malerei zwischen 1930 und 1945; (V) Deutsche Malerei nach 1945.

Ausgewählte Bibliographie, p.435–67. Namenverzeichnis, p.472–78.

M268 Zimmermann, Rainer. Expressiver Realismus: Malerei der verschollenen Generation. München, Hirmer, 1994. 480p. il. (part col.), plates (part col.)

An extensive, well-documented, and superbly illustrated historical and critical survey of German Expressionism. Critical essays are highlighted by vignettes on individual artists and representative works reproduced in plates.

Contents: (1) Geschichte; (2) Beispiele; (3) Biographien.

Verzeichnis der Abbildungen, p.465–69. Namenregister, p.471–80.

SEE ALSO: Bibliography of German expressionism: catalog of the Library of the Robert Gore Rifkind Center for German Expressionist Studies at the Los Angeles County Museum of Art (GLAH 2:A188); Collections of the National Gallery of Art: systematic catalogue (GLAH 2:M31); Hermitage catalogue of Western European painting (GLAH 2:M12).

Great Britain and Ireland

M269 Ackerman, Gerald M. Les orientalistes de l'école britannique. Courbevoie, Paris, ACR, 1991. 336p. il. (part col.), ports.

Survey of approximately 100 19th-century British artists who produced oil paintings and watercolors based on Middle Eastern landscapes, history, and peoples. Arranged alphabetically by artist, individual sections include a biographical and career sketch that emphasizes Middle Eastern subject matter, exoticism, and travel, accompanied by reproductions of representative works.

Contents: (1) Monographies illustrées; (2) Monographies non illustrées.

Orientalistes présumés, p.333. Bibliographie, p.333. Chronologie des voyages, p.333. Index des noms propres, p.334–36.

M270 Ayres, James. English naive painting, 1750–1900. Pref. by Andras Kalman. N.Y., Thames and Hudson, 1980. 168p. il. (part col.)

The first monograph devoted solely to English naive and folk painting, presented thematically.

Contents: Portraits of the people; Town life; Sports and pastimes; Rural life; Birds and beasts; The sea; Pictures without paint.

Bibliography, p.153. Chapter references, p.154–56. Index, p.165–68.

M271 Bendiner, Kenneth. An Introduction to Victorian painting. New Haven, Conn., Yale Univ. Pr., 1985. xv, 180p. il. 8 col. plates, ports.

This heavily contextual work concentrates on seven paintings marking the major decades of Queen Victoria's reign, covering genre painting and literary subjects, religious and history painting, portraiture, the nude, animal painting, and landscape.

Notes, p.149–65. Selected list of books and exhibition catalogues on Victorian art since 1960, p.167–73. Index, p.175–80.

M272 Billcliffe, Roger. The Glasgow boys: The Glasgow school of painting 1875–1895. Philadelphia, Univ. of Penn. Pr., 1986. 320p. il. (66 col.), map, ports.

Detailed, scholarly narrative of 15 Glaswegian naturalist landscape, figurative, and still-life painters active in the late 19th century who were the principals of the Glasgow School, known less formally as the Glasgow Boys.

Notes, p.305–12. Bibliography, p.313–15. Index, p.316–20.

M273 The British portrait 1660–1960. With an introd. essay by Sir Roy Strong and contrib. from Brian Allen . . . [et al.] Woodbridge, Suffolk, Antique Collectors' Club, 1991. 443p. il., 79 col. plates.

Collection of essays by various scholars arranged chronologically. Covers single portraits, family portraits, and special categories of British portraiture over three centuries. Well-illustrated and thorough.

Contents: The British obsession: an introduction to the British portrait, by Sir Roy Strong; (1) Lely to Kneller 1650–1723, by Richard Charlton-Jones; (2) The age of Hogarth 1720–1760, by Brian Allen; (3) The golden age 1700–1790, by Martin Postle; (4) The romantics 1790–1830, by John Wilson; (5) The Victorians 1830–1880, by Christopher Newall; (6) "Well-bred contortions" 1880–1918, by Kenneth McConkey; (7) The modern face 1918–1960, by Frances Spalding.

Select bibliography, p.422–30. Index, p.434–43.

M274 British sporting and animal paintings, 1655–1867: A catalogue compiled by Judy Egerton. London, Tate Gallery for the Yale Center for British Art, 1978. 382p. plates (part col.)

Selection of 400 British sporting and animal oil paintings by 111 artists from the 1,700 British paintings in the Paul Mellon Collection. Complete, descriptive catalog entries are arranged chronologically. Short biographies of artists are presented in order of their birth dates. "It is not an elitist selection: it includes all the sport and animal paintings c.1650–1850 which Paul Mellon has collected, and he chose each for its own appeal to him. The uneven quality of the paintings catalogued here accurately reflects the period's output. Stubbs' work stands out, as it does in any company."—*Pref.*

Bibliography, p.349–53. Index, p.354–82.

M275 Campbell, Julian. The Irish impressionists: Irish artists in France and Belgium, 1850–1914. Dublin, National Gallery of Ireland, 1984. 288p. il. plates (part col.), map, ports.

Catalog of the exhibition of 122 paintings by Irish impressionists shown at the National Gallery of Ireland.

Appendix 1: Lesser known Irish artists in France and Belgium, 1850–1914, not represented in this exhibition; Appendix 2: Works by Irish artists at the Paris Salon (Société des Beaux Arts), 1850–1914; Appendix 3: Irish students at the Académie Royale, Antwerp, 1867–1891. Bibliography, p.277–82. Index of lenders and catalogue numbers, p.282. Index, p.268–88.

M276 Cherry, Deborah. Painting women: Victorian women artists. London, Routledge, 1993. xvi, 275p. 47 plates. ports.

Landmark account of women artists active in the second half of the 19th century in Britain. Treats four central themes: production, representation, spectatorship, and significance. Part one, "Women Painting," examines the conditions in which women became and worked as artists. Part two, "Women Painting Women," concerns representatives of femininity in Victorian Britain.

Contents: Introduction: what is the difference, or why look at women's art?; (1) Family business; (2) Spinsters and friends; (3) An education in difference or an indifferent education? Art training for women; (4) Art institutions and the discourses of difference; (5) Professional and public identities; (6) Making a living; (7) Difference and domesticity; (8) Working women; (9) From towns to countryside and seaside; (10) Cultural collisions; Epilogue: in the foreground.

Checklist of artists, p.215–21. Appendices, p.222–25. Notes, p.225–65. Select bibliography, p.266–70. Index, p.271–75.

M277 Child, Dennis. Painters in the northern counties of England and Wales. Leeds, Dennis Child, 1994. x, 251p.

Includes brief biographical information on about 4,000 northern English painters, significant for its emphasis on Welsh artists. "The main purpose of this book is to provide a starting point for those searching out information about a painter. The period covered starts as far back as possible and comes up to those born around the 1930s. It gives a little about each artist, but only enough to start a searcher on the trail."—*Pref.* Counties covered include Cumbria, Northumbria, Durham, Cleveland, Lancashire, Yorkshire, Cheshire, Derbyshire, Lincolnshire, and Gwynedd and Clwyd in North Wales.

Select bibliography, p.250–51.

M278 Crookshank, Anne, and the Knight of Glin. The painters of Ireland, c.1660–1920. Foreword by James

White. 2d ed. London, Barrie and Jenkins, 1979. 304p. il., 65 col. plates, map, ports.
1st. ed. 1978.

Standard historical survey of Irish painting in 15 chapters covering Irish painting from the mid-17th to the early 20th century. "This work by Professor Anne Crookshank and the Knight of Glin is thus a pioneering one, and it will certainly prove of immense value to all of us who work in this area as well as being a standard work of reference for the future."—*Foreword.*

Notes, p.287–92. Bibliography, p.293–95. Appendix 1, "The Dublin society's drawing academy," p.296–97. Appendix 2, "The Metropolitan school of art, Dublin," p.298. Index, p.299–303.

M279 ———. The watercolours of Ireland: Works on paper in pencil, pastel and paint, c.1600–1914. N.Y., Abrams, 1995. 328p. il. (part col.)
Superbly illustrated, comprehensive chronological and thematic survey of Irish watercolors in 14 chapters, from the 17th century to 1914. Covers schools and movements as well as genre and subject painting, concentrating on artist biographies and connoisseurship.

Notes, p.286–95. Biographical dictionary, p.297–313. Bibliography, p.314–19. Index, p.320–28.

M280 Gaunt, William. Court painting in England from Tudor to Victorian times. London, Constable, 1980. viii, 226p. il. plates (part col.), ports.
Sweeping though undocumented survey of 400 years of English court painting, mostly portraiture, from Hans Holbein to the Victorian era.

A short bibliography, p.218. Index, p.219–26.

M281 Gillett, Paula. Worlds of art: painters in Victorian society. New Brunswick, N.J., Rutgers Univ. Pr., 1990. xiii, 299p. il. (part col.), 8 plates (part col.)
British ed., Glouscester, Sutton, 1990.

Examines from a variety of perspectives the ideas and values inherent in Victorian painting and its relation to society. "This study therefore has as its principal goal the broadening of our understanding of English social and cultural history to include the role of contemporary art and its creators."—*Foreword.*

Notes, p.243–82. Index, p.283–99.

M282 Glasgow girls: women in art and design 1880–1920. Ed. by Jude Burkhauser. Rev. ed. Edinburgh, Canongate, 1993. 263p. il. (part col.), ports.
Rev. and enl. ed. of the catalog to the exhibition, Mackintosh Museum, Glasgow School of Art (1988). "This book provides a comprehensive overview of the work of women artists and designers in Glasgow at the turn of the century. It is an investigation into their lives, their achievements and the historical circumstances in which they found themselves."—*Introd.*

Contents: (1) Second city of the empire: Glasgow 1880–1920; (2) The "new woman" in the arts; (3) The Glasgow style; (4) The designers; (5) The painters.

Notes, p.246–56. Bibliography and further reading, p.257–61. Index, p.262–63.

M283 Halsby, Julian. Scottish watercolours 1740–1940. London, Batsford, 1986. 312p. il. (part col.)
Covers watercolors by artists living and working in Scotland from the 1740s with the work of Robert Adams to 1940, an arbitrary date. Concentrates on Sir David Wilkie, Pre-Raphaelitism, the Glasgow school, art nouveau and symbolism, and the early 20th century.

Biographical dictionary of Scottish watercolour painters, p.245–89. Appendices, p.290–93. Notes, 294–97. Select bibliography, p.298–306. Index, p.307–12.

M284 ———, and Harris, Paul. The dictionary of Scottish painters 1600–1960. Edinburgh, Canongate, 1990. xxi, 236p. il. (part col.), ports.
Alphabetically arranged general reference work. "Our objectives are broadly as follows: to provide basic biographical information on all easel/studio painters working in oil, watercolour, pastel, pen and ink, etc. within Scotland during the period 1600 to 1960."—*Foreword.* The work of more than 300 painters is illustrated. Includes monograms and signatures for selected artists.

A guide to sources, p.x–xi.

M285 Handbook of modern British painting, 1900–1980. Ed. by Alan Windsor. Brookfield, Vt., Scholar, 1992. xii, 287p. il.
An alphabetical guide to approximately 1,400 20th-century British painters who had either finished their training by 1900 or had established themselves professionally by 1980. Brief entries include a biographical outline, characteristics of work, and suggestions for further reading.

M286 Hardie, William R. Scottish painting, 1837 to the present. Rev. and enl. 2d. ed. London, Studio Vista, 1990. 223p. 151 col. plates.
1st ed. 1976.

Comprehensive and well-illustrated overview of the last century-and-a-half of Scottish painting beginning in the year of Queen Victoria's accession and continuing to the late 1980s.

Contents: (1) Portraiture and landscape in Edinburgh; (2) High art; (3) Domestic and historical genre; (4) Pupils of Robert Scott Lauder in London; (5) William McTaggart and his contemporaries in Scotland; (6) The Glasgow school and some contemporaries; (7) Fin de siècle: a new art; (8) The colourists; (9) Between the wars; (10) Post-war painting in Edinburgh and Glasgow; (11) Contemporaries: abstraction and new figuration; (12) Coda.

Selected bibliography, p.217–19. Index, p.220–23.

M287 Lister, Raymond. British romantic painting. Cambridge, Eng., Cambridge Univ. Pr., 1989. 176p. 75 col. plates.
An historical essay on the development of romantic painting in Britain, 1750–1860, highlighting 75 paintings that show the diversity of styles and subjects. Each plate is accompanied by a biographical sketch, a commentary on the work, and on the artist's relations to peers.

Suggestions for further reading, p.176.

M288 Macmillan, Duncan. Painting in Scotland: the golden age. Oxford, Phaidon, 1986. 206p. il., 48 col. plates.
Catalog of the exhibition, Tate Gallery (1986), and other locations, of 207 paintings by 45 Scottish artists active from 1707 to 1843. Highlights painters of Edinburgh's "golden age" of the 18th to early 19th centuries.

Contents: (1) Artists and the union; (2) Empirical portraiture; (3) The epic style; (4) An Ossian's fancy and a Fingal's fire; (5) A vision of pastoral simplicity; (6) The portraiture of common sense; (7) The landscape painters; (8) Scenes of Scottish life and characters; (9) Artists and evangelicals.

Notes, p.187–91. Catalogue of exhibited works, p.192–98. Bibliography, p.199. List of lenders, p.200. Index, p.201–06.

M289 ______. Scottish art 1460–1990. Edinburgh, Mainstream, 1990. 432p. il. (part col.), plates (part col.)
Chronological survey of painting in Scotland from James III onwards, unequaled in breadth and scholarship. Particularly strong on the early periods.

Contents: (1) The emergence of a modern nation; (2) The Reformation; (3) A country without a court; (4) An age of transition; (5) A new art; (6) The good old bards; (7) The birth of Scottish landscape; (8) Portraits of the Enlightenment; (9) The poetry of common life; (10) Genre, history and religion; (11) Artists of the mid-nineteenth century; (12) The romantic landscape; (13) The high Victorians; (14) East and west; (15) The claims of decorative art; (16) The opening of the modern era; (17) The colourists; (18) The Scots renaissance; (19) The second world war and the post-war period; (20) The present day.

Abbreviations, p.409. Footnotes, p.409–12. Select bibliography, p.417–21. Index, p.422–32.

M290 McConkey, Kenneth. British impressionism. Oxford, Phaidon, 1989. 160p. 135 plates (part col.)
Critical survey of 45 British Impressionists. Brings attention to the dynamism of British art during the last decades of the 19th century and points out its derivations from the Paris ateliers.

Contents: (1) Difficulties of definition; (2) Figures and fields; (3) Secessionist societies—the "New English" and the "British artists"; (4) Impressionism in Britain; (5) "Seeds from a ruined garden"; (6) Exhibition-piece impressionism; (7) Impressionism: French or British?

Notes, p.152–55. Select bibliography, p.155. Biographical index, p.156–58. Index, p.159–60.

M291 ______. Impressionism in Britain. With an essay by Anna Gruetzner Robins. New Haven, Yale Univ. Pr., in assoc. with Barbican Art Gallery, 1995. 224p. il (part col.), plates (part col.)
Catalog of the exhibition, Barbican Art Gallery (1995), and other locations, that included 245 works by approximately 100 European (primarily British) painters. Essays describe the activities of French impressionists on their visits to Britain, explore the responses of British and Irish artists to the movements, and consider the dissemination of impressionist paintings through British dealers and collectors.

Contents: (1) Impressionism in Britain, by Kenneth McConkey; (2) The London impressionists at the Goupil Gallery, by Anna Gruetzner Robins; (3) Catalogue, by Kenneth McConkey with Ysanne Holt.

Endnotes, p.209–16. Bibliography, p.217–18. Index, p.219–22. List of lenders, p.223.

M292 Philadelphia Museum of Art. British painting in the Philadelphia Museum of Art from the seventeenth through the nineteenth century. By Richard Dorment. Ed. by Jane Iandola Watkins. Philadelphia, Philadelphia Museum of Art, 1986. xvii, 468p. il. (part col.), col. plates.
Catalog of 130 British paintings in the Philadelphia Museum of Art, primarily from the John H. McFadden collection, organized alphabetically by artist. A biographical introduction precedes detailed critical notes about attribution, subject, provenance, exhibition history, literature, and condition of each painting.

Bibliographical abbreviations, p.449–63. Index of titles, p.467–68.

M293 Rosenthal, Michael. British landscape painting. Ithaca, Cornell Univ. Pr., 1982. 191p. il., plates (part col.)
Detailed history of British landscape painting beginning with landscape depictions from the Luttrell Psalter of 1340 and ending with works from the early 1980s.

Contents: (1) The middle ages to the restoration; (2) Prospects and landscapes; (3) The expanding horizon; (4) Romanticism and reaction; (5) The Victorians and beyond.

Bibliography, p.185. Index, p.187–91.

M294 Rothenstein, Sir John. Modern English painters. [New ed.] London, Macdonald, 1984. 3v. 48 col. plates.
1st ed. 1952–74 (3v.); reprinted 1957 and 1962 (v.1–2) and 1974 (3v.). 1st rev. ed. 1976 (3v.).

3-vol. collection of erudite biographical and critical essays on 61 prominent English painters from Walter Richard Sickert to David Hockney. Each vol. includes a bibliography, list of location of art works mentioned, and index.

Contents: (1) Sickert to Lowry; (2) Nash to Bawden; (3) Hennell to Hockney.

M295 Stewart, Brian, and Cutten, Mervyn. The dictionary of portrait painters in Britain up to 1920. Woodbridge, Antique Collectors' Club, 1997. 502p. il. (part col.)
Biographical dictionary, with brief entries. Some museum locations cited, but no specific works mentioned.

Bibliography, p.12. Abbreviations, p.16.

M296 Tate Gallery, London. The Pre-Raphaelites. London, Tate Gallery; Penguin, 1984. 312p. il. (part col.), col. plates, ports. (Repr. with corrections: London, Tate, 1994.)
Catalog of a loan exhibition of 250 works by 29 Pre-Raphaelite artists, Tate Gallery (1984). Focuses chronologically on the Pre-Raphaelite Brotherhood from its founding

in 1848 to Rossetti's death in 1882. A final section is devoted to Pre-Raphaelite drawings and watercolors.

Contents: List of artists; Biographical notes.

M297 Waterhouse, Ellis Kirkham. The dictionary of British 18th century painters in oils and crayons. Woodbridge, Suffolk, Antique Collectors' Club, 1981. 443p. il., plates (part col.), frontis.

Biographical dictionary of British painters and foreign painters who visited England from 1700 to 1800. Entries range from one sentence to several pages and include bibliographic references.

Bibliography, p.436–39. Datable illustrations, p.440–42.

M298 ______. The dictionary of 16th and 17th century British painters. Woodbridge, Suffolk, Antique Collectors' Club, 1988. 308p. il., plates (part col.)

Standard, well-illustrated biographical reference to 16th- and 17th-century British painters arranged alphabetically by artist's name. Brief entries include the painter's birth and death dates, a biographical outline that mentions major works, and bibliographic references.

Bibliography, p.306–08.

M299 ______. Painting in Britain, 1530 to 1790. 5th ed. with an introduction by Michael Kitson. New Haven, Yale Univ. Pr., 1995. 394p. il. (part col.) ([Yale University Press] pelican history of art)

1st ed. 1953; 2d ed. 1962; 3d ed. 1969; 4th ed. 1978.

Concise survey of British painting from Holbein to the end of the 18th century by a leading authority.

Contents: (1) Painting under the Tudors; (2) Painting under the Stuarts, up to the revolution of 1688; (3) The age of Kneller and English baroque; (4) Hogarth and the precursors of the classical age; (5) The classical age.

Notes, p.337–50. Bibliography, p.351–58. Additional bibliography, p.359–71. Index, p.372–94.

M300 Williams, Andrew Gibbon, and Brown, Andrew. The bigger picture: a history of Scottish art. London, BBC, 1993. 224p. il. (part col.), diagrs., maps, ports.

General survey of Scottish art from the late 16th century to modern times, related to a BBC television program and "aimed at the many people both within Scotland and abroad who wish to discover and know more about Scottish painting, and thereby to obtain a general overview."—*Introd.*

Contents: (1) A true likeness; (2) Enlightened taste; (3) Victorian values; (4) Land of the mountain and the flood; (5) Modern movements; (6) Contemporary trends.

Further reading, p.218. Index, p.220–24.

M301 Witt Library. Checklist of British artists in the Witt Library, compiled by the Witt Computer Index. London, The Library, 1991. iv, 268p.

An alphabetical list of the approximately 14,000 British painters, draftsmen, and printmakers represented by reproductions of their work in the vast illustration collection known as the Witt Library (see GLAH 2:D66). Provides basic information: name, life dates, location of birth and death, professional associations, and some indication of the size of the artist's file of illustrations in the collection. The list was produced from the Witt Computer Index, a collaborative project of the Witt Library and the Getty Art History Information Program.

"Although the Witt Library covers all European and Western art, its coverage of British art is the most comprehensive. The British School is also the fastest growing and the most heavily consulted section of the Witt Library."— *Introd.*

For a checklist of all artists represented in the Witt Library through 1994, see A checklist of painters, c1200–1994 represented in the Witt Library, Courtauld Institute of Art, London (GLAH 2:M38).

Bibliography: (1) Biographical dictionaries, p.266–67; (2) Professional association lists, p.268.

M302 Wood, Christopher. The Pre-Raphaelites. N.Y., Viking, 1981. 160p. il. (part col.), col. plates.

An examination of the Pre-Raphaelite painters, close associates, and followers from 1848 to the end of the 19th century. The first part deals with the Pre-Raphaelite Brotherhood from 1848 to 1860; the second with Pre-Raphaelite landscape painters; and the third with the Aesthetic movement, represented in particular by Rossetti and Burne-Jones.

Bibliography, p.156. Index, p.157–60.

M303 ______. The dictionary of Victorian painters. 3d ed. [rev. and upd.] Research by Christopher Newall and Margaret Richardson. Woodbridge, Suffolk [Wappingers' Falls, N.Y.], Antique Collectors' Club, 1995. 2v. il. (part col.), col. plates. (Dictionary of British art)

1st ed. 1971; 2d ed. 1978.

The third ed. of this exhaustive survey features a revised and updated text as well as an enlarged collection of plates. Entries for individual painters include biographical information and bibliographical references. Arranged alphabetically by artist's last name. According to the author, "I think I can safely say that no other dictionary has such comprehensive bibliographies of Victorian artists."—*Introd.*

Contents: (1) Text [Research by Christopher Newall and Margaret Richardson]; (2) Historical survey and plates.

M304 Yale Center for British Art. A concise catalogue of paintings in the Yale Center for British Art. By Malcolm Cormack. New Haven, Yale Center for British Art, 1985. 271p. il.

Catalog of paintings in the permanent collection acquired before May 1985, the majority from the Paul Mellon collection. Arranged alphabetically by artist, entries for individual works include the medium, date, size, date acquired, and acquisition number.

SEE ALSO: Collections of the National Gallery of Art: systematic catalogue (GLAH 2:M31); Hermitage catalogue of Western European painting (GLAH 2:M12).

Greece

M305 Christou, Chrysanthos. Greek Painting, 1832–1922 [Reprint.] Athens, National Bank of Greece, 1994. 56p. 174 col. plates.

Reprint of 1981 ed. Helpful introductory text (49p.) precedes the selection of color reproductions.

Index of proper names, p.55–56.

M306 Ioannou, Andreas S. Greek painting, 19th century. English trans. by D. Dellagrammatika. Athens, Melissa, [1974]. 288p. col. il. (Fine arts library)

Introduction to a neglected period in the history of Greek painting

Notes, p.269. Index, p.278–83. Bibliography, p.284–85.

M307 Speteres, Tones P. Daskaloi tes Hellenikes zographikes tou 19ou kai 20ou aiona. Athena, Ekdoseis Kastaniote, 1982. 189p. il. (part col.), col. plates.

An examination of 19th- and 20th-century Greek painting.

Includes index.

Italy

General Works

M308 Baltimore Museum of Art. Italian paintings XIV–XVIIIth centuries from the collection of the Baltimore Museum of Art. Gertrude Rosenthal, ed. [Baltimore, The Museum, 1981]. 334p. il. (part col.)

Scholarly catalog of the collection, arranged by centuries, with brief essays on each painting.

Bibliographies and notes at ends of catalog entries. Index of artists, p.331–34.

M309 Carli, Enzo. La pittura italiana dal Medioevo al Novecento. Milano, Martello, 1987. 596p. col. il.

Intended to constitute "a first approach to Italian painting."—*Pub. note.* Handy survey by a distinguished specialist in Sienese painting. Without scholarly apparatus.

M310 Chastel, André. La pala, ou le retable italien des origines à 1500. Avec le concours de Christiane Lorgues-Lapouge. Préf. d'Enrico Castelnuovo. Paris, Levi, 1993. 300p. il. (part col.)

Posthumously published synthesis of years of research on the subject of the Italian altarpiece, by the great scholar of Italian painting. Catalog of 80 examples, with color illustrations.

Contents: Le problème de la pala; Origine de la pala; Histoire et typologie du retable italien; De la mosaïque à Titien; Conclusion.

Annexes: Mécènes et commandes, p.251–54. Fiches documentaires, p.[255–85]. Glossaire, p.287–[89]. Index des artistes, p.290–[97]. Bibliographie, p.299–[301].

M311 Chelazzi Dini, Giulietta; Angelini, Alessandro; and Sani, Bernardina. Sienese painting. N.Y., Abrams, 1998. 471p. il.

Trans. of Pittura senese. Milano, Motta, 1997.

Richly illustrated survey of Sienese painting from the 13th through the 17th century.

Contents: Sienese painting from 1250 to 1450, by Giulietta Chelazzi Dini; The second half of the fifteenth century, by Alessandro Angelini; The sixteenth and seventeenth centuries, by Bernardina Sani.

Notes at ends of chapters. Notes, p.458–59. Bibliography, p.462–67. Index of names, p.468–71.

M312 Crow, Sir Joseph Archer, and Cavalcaselle, Giovanni Battista. A new history of painting in Italy from the second to the sixteenth century. [Reprint.] N.Y., Garland, 1980. 3v. (Connoisseurship criticism and art history in the nineteenth century)

Repr. of original ed. 1864. For later eds. see GLAH 1:M294.

M313 Lavin, Marilyn. The place of narrative: mural decoration in Italian churches, 431–1600. Chicago, Univ. of Chicago Pr., 1990. xx, 406p. il. (part col.), plates.

Pioneering study of the disposition of narrative cycles of mural paintings within their architectural settings. An early attempt at creating a database in support of an art historical study.

Notes, p.293–371. Bibliography, p.373–94. Index, p.397–406.

M314 Martini, Egidio. Pittura veneta e altra italiana dal XV al XIX secolo. Rimini, Patacconi, 1992. 669p. il. (part col.)

Beautifully illustrated sampling of Italian painting, by region. Includes many previously unpublished works.

Contents: Scuola Veneta; Scuola Ferrarese ed Emiliani; Scuola Piemontese, Genovese e Lombarda; Scuola Toscana e Romana; Scuola Napoletana.

Cenni biografici sui pittori trattati, a cura di Carla Seno, p.621–51. Bibliografia citata, p.655–63. Indice delle tavole a colori e delle figure in bianco e nero inordine alfabetico per artista, p.667–69.

M315 Morelli, Giovanni. Della pittura italiana: studii [sic] storico-critici: le gallerie Borghese e Doria-Pamphili in Roma. A cura di Jaynie Anderson. Milano, Adelphi, 1991. 630p. il.

Trans. of Kunstkritische Studien über italienische Malerei. 1, Galerien Borghese und Doria Panfili in Rom. French ed., De la peinture italienne. Paris, Lagune, 1994.

New ed. of a pioneering study of Italian painting by the great connoisseur, based upon the Italian ed. of 1897. Includes new biographical material on Morelli.

Contents: La Galleria Borghese; La Galleria Doria-Pamphili; Cenni biografici intorno a Giovanni Morelli; Dietro lo pseudonimo.

Bibliography, p.[581]–605. Index, p.[609]–30.

M316 Museum of Fine Arts, Boston. Italian paintings in the Museum of Fine Arts Boston. Introd. by Eric Zafran. Boston, Museum of Fine Arts (Distr. by Northeastern Univ. Pr., 1994–). (1)v. il. (part col.).

Scholarly catalog of one of the richest American public collections of Italian painting.

Contents: (1) 13th–15th century.

M317 Nelson-Atkins Museum of Art. The collections of The Nelson-Atkins Museum of Art. Italian paintings,

1300–1800. By Eliot W. Rowlands. Kansas City, Mo., Nelson-Atkins Museum of Art in assoc. with the Univ. of Washington Pr., 1996. 487p. il. (part col.), map.

Scholarly catalog of the permanent collection, well-illustrated, with particular attention to iconography.

Notes to the catalogue and abbreviated sources, p.28–29. Index of proper names, p.473–81. Index of former collections, p.483–86.

M318 New York. Metropolitan Museum of Art. Italian paintings: a catalogue of the collection of the Metropolitan Museum of Art. [By] Federico Zeri. With the assist. of Elizabeth E. Gardner. N.Y., Metropolitan Museum of Art, 1971–86. 4v. il.

Continues the series begun with the Florentine and Venetian Schools (see GLAH 1:M300).

Contents: Sienese and Central Italian Schools (1980); North Italian School (1986).

M319 Paris. Musée National du Louvre. Département des peintures. École italienne, XVIIe siècle. Paris, Réunion des musées nationaux, 1996– . (1)v. il. (part col.), ports.

Catalog of the Baroque Italian paintings in the Louvre, intended to inaugurate a new systematic catalog of the paintings collection, a sequel to the Louvre's "catalogue sommaire" (GLAH 2:M25).

Contents: (1) Bologne.

M320 Pinacoteca di Brera. [La collezione della Pinacoteca]. Milano, Electa, 1988– . (4)v. il. (part col.) (Musei e gallerie di Milano)

Scholarly catalog of the great Brera collection of Italian paintings, under the scholarly coordination of Federico Zeri.

Contents: Scuole lombarda e piemontese, 1300–1535 (1988); Scuole lombarda, ligure e piemontese, 1535–1796 (1989); Scuola veneta (1990); Scuola emiliana (1991); Scuole dell'Italia centrale e meridionale (1992); Dipinti dell'Ottocento e del Novecento: collezioni dell'Accademia e della Pinacoteca (2v., 1993–94).

M321 La pittura in Emilia e in Romagna. Dir. ed., Carlo Pirovano. Milano, Electa, 1992–95. 2v. in 4. il. (part col.)

Commercial ed. of a work first pub. by Credito Romagnolo. Impressive survey of Lombard painting of the Renaissance, modeled upon the publisher's Pittura in Italia series (see following entry).

Contents: (1) Il Cinquecento (2v.); (2) Il Seicento (2v.)

M322 La pittura in Italia. Milano, Electa, 1986– . (8)v. in (18). il. (part col.)

An ambitious publishing enterprise, the "main ambition" of which "is that of reproducing the works of art in their precise topographical and chronological context." Each vol. is independently edited and consists of signed chapters followed by a lengthy biographical dictionary of artists. Splendidly illustrated.

Contents: L'altomedioevo; Il Duecento e il Trecento (2v.); Il Quattrocento (2v.); Il Cinquecento (2v.); Il Seicento (2v.); Il Settecento (2v.); L'Ottocento (2 v.); Il Novecento (3v. in 5).

M323 La pittura in Lombardia. Dir. ed., Valerio Terraroli. Milano, Electa, 1993– . (2)v. in (4). il. (part col.)

Impressive survey of Lombard painting of the Renaissance, modeled upon the publisher's Pittura in Italia series (see preceding entry). Each vol. is independently edited and consists of signed chapters followed by a lengthy biographical dictionary of artists. Splendidly illustrated.

Contents: (1) Il Trecento (3v.); (2) Il Quattrocento.

M324 Pittura murale in Italia. A cura di Mina Gregori. [Torino], Istituto Bancario San Paolo di Torino, 1995– . (3)v. in (5). il. (part col.)

Survey of mural painting in Italy from the 13th to the 18th century. Each chronological vol. arranged by region, with various authors.

Contents: (1) Dal tardo Duecento ai primi del Quattrocento; (2) pt.1 Il Quattrocento (2v.); (3) Il Seicento e il Settecento (2v.)

M325 La Pittura nel Veneto. Milano, Electa, 1989– . (4)v. in (8). il. (part col.)

Impressive survey of Lombard painting of the Renaissance, modeled upon the publisher's Pittura in Italia series (GLAH 2:M322). Each vol. is independently edited and consists of signed chapters followed by a lengthy biographical dictionary of artists. Splendidly illustrated.

Contents: Il Trecento (2v.); Il Quattrocento (2v., 1989); Il Cinquecento (2v.); Il Settecento (2v.)

M326 I Pittori bergamaschi dal XIII al XIX secolo: raccolta di studi a cura della Banca popolare di Bergamo. Bergamo, Poligrafiche Bolis, 1975– . (16)v. in (19). il.

Monumental, beautifully illustrated survey of painting in Bergamo. Extracts have been published separately, devoted to individual painters.

Contents: (1) Le origini; (2) Il Quattrocento; (3) Il Cinquecento (4v.); (4) Il Seicento (4v.); (5) Il Settecento (5v); (6) Ottocento (4v.)

M327 Repertori fotografici. Milano, Longanesi, 1982– . (8)v., plates.

Monumental photographic survey of Italian Baroque painting, by region. Most volumes consist of hundreds of full-page, black-and-white plates, with bibliographies and, in some cases, bio-bibliographies of artists.

Selective contents: (1) La pittura emiliana del '600 (1982); (2) La pittura del '700 a Roma (1983); (3) La pittura napoletana del '600 (1984); (4) La pittura lombarda del '600 (1985); (5) La pittura lombarda del '700 (1986); (6) La pittura neoclassica italiana (1987); (7) La pittura del '600 a Genova (1988); (9) La pittura bolognese del '700 (1994).

M328 United States. National Gallery of Art. Catalogue of the Italian paintings. By Fern Rusk Shapley. Washington, D.C., National Gallery of Art, 1979. 2v. il.

Updates Shapley's catalog of the Italian paintings in the Samuel Kress Collection (GLAH 1:M9), many of which have since passed into the National Gallery.

Contents: (1) Text; (2) Plates.

Subject index, v.1, p.549–56. Index of previous owners, v.1, p.556–73. Index of coats of arms and seals, v.1, p.573. Index of the location of related works, v.1, p.574–87. Numerical index, v.1, p.588–91.

M329 Vsevolozhskaya, Svetlana. Italian painting in the Hermitage, 13th to 18th century from the Hermitage Museum. N.Y., Abrams, 1981. 307p., il.

Trans. of Italianskaia zhivopis' trinadtsatogo—vosemnadtsatogo vekov. Leningrad, Aurora, 1981.

Collection of color plates, with scholarly catalog notes. See GLAH 2:M12 for the more specialized, scholarly volumes in the series The Hermitage catalogue of Western European painting.

Notes on the plates, p.263–304. Abbreviations, p.305. Index of artists, p.306–07.

M330 Walters Art Gallery. Italian paintings in the Walters Art Gallery. By Federico Zeri. With condition notes by Elisabeth C. G. Packard. Ed. by Ursula E. McCracken. Baltimore, Walters Art Gallery, 1976. 2v. il. (part col.), plates.

This distinguished collection, formed by Henry Walters between 1902 and 1931, offers "a balanced and uninterrupted survey of the history of Italian painting."—*Introd.*

Concordance, v.2, p.575–78. Appendix, v.2, p.579–80. Index of artists, v.1, p.301–12, v.2, p.581–92. Index of subjects, v.2, p.593–96. Index of locations, v.2, p.597–647.

M331 Zampetti, Pietro. Pittura nelle Marche. Firenze, Nardini, [1990]–1991. 4v. il. (part col.), chronological tables.

Vol.1: 2d ed., 1991.

Historical survey from the 15th to the 20th century. Many marvelous color plates.

Contents: (1) Dalle origini al primo rinascimento; (2) Dal rinascimento alla controriforma; (3) Dalla controriforma al barocco; (4) Dal barocco all'età moderna.

Bibliography, v.1, 475–89. Indexes, v.2, 491–510.

Early Christian—Gothic (excluding mosaics)

M332 London. National Gallery. The early Italian schools before 1400. By Martin Davies. Rev. by Dillian Gordon. London, National Gallery Publications, 1988. xv, 249p. il.

See GLAH 1:M6 for the 1st ed. The 2d ed. reflects recent scholarship both in the attributions and in the account of the condition of the paintings.

M333 Marques, Luiz C. La peinture du duecento en Italie centrale. Paris, Picard, 1987. 297p. il. (part col.).

"The fundamental ambition in these pages is to fill a lacuna in Italian Dugento studies by exploring the body of figurative facts that play an expressive role in the history of the period."—*Introd.* Handsomely produced, well illustrated.

Bibliography, p.263–79. Index, p.281–97.

Late Gothic—Renaissance

M334 Algeri, Giuliana, and De Floriani, Anna. La pittura in Liguria: il Quattrocento. [Genova], Tormena Editore, 1992. 558p. il. (part col.)

An important, scholarly study of 15th-century painting in Liguria.

Schede bio-bibliografiche, p.489–524. Bibliografia, p.525–42. Indice dei nomi di luogo e di persona, p.543–56.

M335 Armstrong, Lilian. Renaissance miniature painters and classical imagery: the Master of the Putti and his Venetian workshop. London, Philadelphia, Harvey Miller, 1981. viii, 223p. il., color plates, facs.

Pioneering study "principally concerned with the works of art produced by two Venetian miniaturists active in the 1470s and early 1480s. . . . [This] led into the relatively unexplored area of the confrontation of a new technology, printing, and an old art, that of painting in books."—*p.vii.*

Bibliography, p.139–48. Index, p.[210]–23.

M336 Art in the making: Italian painting before 1400. [By] David Bomford, Jill Dunkerton, Dillian Gordon . . . [et al.] With contrib. from Jo Kirby. London, National Gallery, 1989. x, 225p. il. (part col.).

Catalog of the exhibition, National Gallery, London (1989–90). Important examination of the materials and techniques of Italian painters of the early Renaissance. Part of a series of exhibitions focusing upon materials and techniques.

Glossary, p.207–09. Annotated bibliography [with an excursus on "Cenino Cenini and Fourteenth Century Technical Literature on Painting"], p.210–21. Index of painters and paintings, p.224–25.

M337 Art Institute of Chicago. Italian paintings before 1600 in the Art Institute of Chicago: a catalogue of the collection. By Christopher Lloyd. Contrib. by Margherita Andreotti, Larry J. Feinberg, and Martha Wolff. Martha Wolff, gen. ed. Chicago, Art Institute of Chicago in assoc. with Princeton Univ. Pr., 1993. xx, 312p. il. (part col.)

"This catalogue includes all the Italian paintings executed before 1600 in the collections of the Art Institute of Chicago, a group of close to one hundred paintings."—*Introd.* Exemplary catalog, arranged alphabetically by artist.

Bibliographical notes in catalog entries. Notes to the reader, p.xvii. Bibliographical abbreviations, p.xix–xx. List of previous owners, p.303–07. List of paintings by accession number, p.309–10. List of artists, p.311–12.

M338 Ashmolean Museum. A catalogue of the earlier Italian paintings in the Ashmolean Museum. Compiled by Christopher Lloyd. Oxford, Clarendon Pr., 1977. xxvii, 222p. il., plates.

"The present catalogue includes those paintings in the Ashmolean Museum painted by Italian artists born between the years 1260 and 1560. It therefore comprises paintings dating from between 1300 and 1600. There is also a small section devoted to the collection of icons."—*Pref.*

Abbreviations used in the text, p.[xi]–xii. Explanations, p.[xiii]–xiv. Index to religious subjects, p.[215]–17. Index to identifiable portraits, p.217. Index to profane subjects, p.217. Index of previous owners, p.[218]–21. Numerical index, p.221–22. List of artists represented in the collection, p.[223].

M339 Baxandall, Michael. Giotto and the orators: humanist observers of painting in Italy and the discovery of pictorial composition 1350–1450. Oxford, Clarendon, 1986. xii, 185p. il., 16p. of pls, 1 facs. (Oxford-Warburg studies)

Paperback ed. "with corrections." 1st ed. 1971.

Influential study "concerned with two related problems. . . . I have tried to identify a linguistic component in visual taste. . . . The second problem is the particular one of how the concept of pictorial 'composition' came to Alberti in 1435."—*Pref.*

Bibliography, p.178–80. Index, p.181–85.

M340 ______. Painting and experience in fifteenth-century Italy. 2d ed. N.Y., Oxford, Oxford Univ. Pr., 1982. 183p. il.

See GLAH 1:M317 for original ed. German ed., 1977; French ed., 1985. "The main change in this edition is that the original Italian or Latin of passages previously given only in English translation has been included."—*Pref.*

M341 Borsook, Eve. The mural painters of Tuscany: from Cimabue to Andrea del Sarto. 2d ed., rev. and enl. N.Y., Oxford Univ. Pr., 1980. 157p. il., plates. (Oxford studies in the history of art and architecture)

See GLAH 1:M324 for the original ed. of this standard overview of Italian mural painting of the Renaissance. For the 2d ed. the text was substantially rewritten, a few murals added, and many new photographs provided.

List of abbreviations, p.xv. Glossary, p.133–35. Bibliography of printed sources cited in the text, p.137–48. Index, p.149–57.

M342 Boschloo, Anton W. A., and Van der Sman, Gert Jan J., eds. Italian paintings from the sixteenth century in Dutch public collections. In collab. with Albert J. Elen and Elwin J. Hendrikse. Trans. from the Dutch by Mandy Sikkens. Florence, Centro Di, 1993. 166p. il. (part col.) (Italia e I paesi bassi, cataloghi, 2)

Important survey of the collecting of Italian painting in the Netherlands, based upon research initiated by Henk van Os in the 1960s.

Bibliography, p.154–64. List of artists, p.165. Locations of paintings, p.166.

M343 Boskovits, Miklos. Pittura fiorentina alla vigilia del Rinascimento, 1370–1400. Firenze, Edam, 1975. 856p. il. (part col.), plates.

Monumental study of early Italian Renaissance painting in Florence, by the great authority on Trecento painting.

Bibliografia, p.443–78. Indice dei nomi e dei luoghi, p.793–840. Indice delle illustrazioni, p.841–56.

M344 Brown, Patricia Fortini. Venetian narrative painting in the age of Carpaccio. New Haven, Yale Univ. Pr., 1988. 310p. il. (part col.)

Important study of the interplay of patronage and visual culture in the evolution of narrative style in Venetian Renaissance painting.

Glossary, p.[ix–x]. Bibliography, p.299–306. Index, p.307–10.

M345 Burckhardt, Jacob. The altarpiece in Renaissance Italy. Ed. and trans. by Peter Humfrey. N.Y., Cambridge Univ. Pr., 1988. 240p. il. (part col.)

Trans. of Das Altarbild, which appeared originally in the author's Beiträge zur Kunstgeschichte von Italien. Basel, Lendorff, 1898, and which "remains the best and most stimulating introduction" to the subject.—*Ed. introd.* This ed., unlike previous ones, is illustrated. Errors of fact have been noted in the annotations.

Notes, p.219–29. Select bibliography, p.231–32. Index of locations of works illustrated, p.233–35. Index, p.236–40.

M346 Carli, Enzo. La pittura senese del Trecento. Milano, Electa, 1981. 301p. il. (part col.)

Overview of 14th-century Sienese painting, many plates.

Note, p.257–66. Indice dei nomi e dei luoghi, p.267–76. French, English, German summaries, p.[277]–301.

M347 Chastel, André. A chronicle of Italian Renaissance painting. Trans. by Linda and Peter Murray. Ithaca, Cornell Univ. Pr., 1984. 294p. il. (part col.)

Trans. of Chronique de la peinture italienne à la Renaissance, 1280–1580. Fribourg, Office du Livre, 1983.

Survey by a great scholar, constructed around surviving documents.

Appendix of texts and documents, p.234–89. Index, p.290–94.

M348 Christiansen, Keith; Kanter, Laurance B.; and Strehlke, Carl Brandon. Painting in Renaissance Siena, 1420–1500. N.Y., Metropolitan Museum of Art (Distr. by Abrams, 1989). xiii, 386p. il. (part col.)

Catalog of the exhibition, Metropolitan Museum of Art (1988–89). The first major exhibition of Sienese painting outside Siena since the turn of the century. Focuses upon narrative painting in 15th-century Siena.

Selected bibliography, p.361–70. Index, p.371–84.

M349 Dunkelman, Martha Levine. Central Italian painting, 1400–1465: an annotated bibliography. Boston, Hall, 1986. xv, 351p. (Reference publication in art history)

"The intention of this book is to define . . . an essential corpus of those works that have made the most important scholarly contribution."—*Pref.* The emphasis is on the past forty years of scholarship. Organized by region.

Index of artists, p.329–35. Index of authors, editors and reviewers, p.337–51.

M350 Freedberg, Sydney Joseph. Painting in Italy, 1500–1600. 3d ed. New Haven, Yale Univ. Pr., 1993. 761p. il. (part col.) (Yale University Press pelican history of art)

See GLAH 1:M331 for original ed. of this standard work. Color illustrations have been added to this ed., along with updated bibliography and notes, and minor textual revisions.

List of the principal abbreviations used in the notes and bibliography, p.668. Notes, p.[669]–719. Bibliography, p.[720]–35. Index, p.[737]–61.

M351 Friedlaender, Walter F. Mannerism and anti-mannerism in Italian painting. N.Y., Columbia Univ. Pr., 1990. xxi, 89p. il., plates. (Interpretations in art)

Two classic essays, originally published in periodicals in 1925 and 1930, reissued as a book in 1957 and frequently reprinted. Helped define Mannerism as a period in the history and historiography of art.

Index, p.[85]–89.

M352 Garzelli, Annarosa. Miniatura fiorentina del Rinascimento, 1440–1525: un primo censimento. Firenze, Giunta Regionale Toscana, La Nuova Italia, 1985. 2v., il. (part col.)

Monumental, systematic study of Florentine miniature painting of the second half of the Quattrocento.

Contents: (I) Le immagini, gli autori, i destinatari, di A. Garzelli; New research on humanistic scribes in Florence, di A. de la Mare; (II) Illustrazioni.

Bibliografia [to Garzelli's corpus], v.1, p.[351]–91. Bibliography [to de la Mare's essay], v.1, p.[575]–91. Indice, v.2, p.ix–x.

M353 Gemäldegalerie Berlin. Frühe italienische Malerei: Gemäldegalerie Berlin, Katalog der Gemälde. Bearb. von Miklos Boskovits. Übers. aus dem Italienischen und redig. von Erich Schleier. Berlin, Staatliche Museen Preussischer Kulturbesitz, Mann, 1987. xiv, 417p. il. (part col.) (Gemäldegalerie Berlin, Katalog der Gemälde)

Catalog of one of the most important public collections outside Italy. First installment of a scholarly catalog of the entire collection of the paintings in the Gemäldegalerie.

Namensregister, p.189–93. Ortsregister, p.194–205. Ikonographisches Register, p.205–09. Verzeichnis der abgekürzt zitierten Literatur, p.213–15. Abkürzungen häufiger zitierter Zeitschriften, p.216. Konkordanz der Katalognummern, p.217–18.

M354 Gould, Cecil. An introduction to Italian Renaissance painting. London, Phaidon, 1957. 254p. il., col. plates.

Still one of the best brief introductions to the subject, by an authority.

Biographical index and list of illustrations, p.247–54.

M355 Hall, Marcia. After Raphael: painting in central Italy in the sixteenth century. N.Y., Cambridge Univ. Pr., 1999. xvi, 349p. il. (part col.), plates.

"I offer here a rethinking of what has been called Mannerist painting and of what followed and coincided with it."—*A note on style labels.*

Contents: (1) The High Renaissance; (2) The 1520s in Florence and Rome; (3) The diaspora of Roman style; (4) The Roman restoration; (5) The Counter-Reformation in Rome; (6) Ducal Florence; (7) The end of the century in Rome.

Notes, p.293–320. Bibliography, p.321–34. Index, p.337–49.

M356 Hills, Paul. The light of early Italian painting. New Haven, Yale Univ. Pr., 1987. 160p. il. (part col.).

"This book examines [the preoccupation with representing light] in the period 1250 to 1430."—*Pref.* An important study of the role and meaning of light and color in early Italian Renaissance painting.

Appendix: a list of treatises on colour and fragments of artists' handbooks, p.146–47. Notes to the text, p.148–58. Index, p.149–60.

M357 Humfrey, Peter. Painting in Renaissance Venice. New Haven, Yale Univ. Pr., 1995. vii, 320p. il. (part col.), map.

"This book is meant to be a brief introduction to painting in Venice (1440–1590) and is aimed primarily at the non-specialist."—*Foreword.* Good introductory survey by an authority.

Notes, p.268–76. Appendix of biographies, p.277–96. Bibliography, p.297–307. Index, p.308–19.

M358 Italian altarpieces 1250–1550: function and design. Ed. by Eve Borsook and Fiorella Superbi Gioffredi. N.Y., Oxford Univ. Pr., 1994. viii, 296p. il.

"This volume is the result of an international symposium held in June 1988 at the Harvard University Center for Italian Renaissance Studies at Villa I Tatti in Florence. . . . The essays in this volume . . . consider such diverse aspects of the Italian altarpiece as early ecclesiastical legislation, patronage, audience, structure, and artistic invention."—*Pref.* Solid summary of recent research, accomplishing for Italy what Humfrey and Kemp's The altarpiece in the Renaissance (GLAH 2:M153) does for Europe as a whole. Includes essays by Julian Gardner, Peter Humfrey, Patricia Rubin, Michelangelo Muraro, and others.

Bibliography, p.[269]–87. Index, p.[287]–96.

M359 Maginnis, Hayden B. J. Painting in the age of Giotto: a historical reevaluation. University Park, Pennsylvania State Univ. Pr., 1997. xviii, 217p. il. (part col.), plates.

"This book deals with the second of the three great revolutions in Western art to occur after antiquity. It examines the moment of transition between the Middle Ages and the Renaissance."—*Pref.* Thoughtful reassessment of a pivotal passage in the history of Italian art.

Selected bibliography, p.207–11. Index, p.213–17.

M360 Museum of Fine Arts, Houston. Italian paintings XIV–XVI centuries in the Museum of Fine Arts, Houston. By Carolyn C. Wilson. Houston, Rice University Press; The Museum, 1996. 416p. il. (part col.)

Catalog of the excellent Italian pre-Renaissance and Renaissance painting collection of the Museum of Fine Arts, Houston, which has as its core the private collection of Percy S. Straus. Organized by region.

Bibliographical abbreviations, p.9–11. Straus acquisition dates, p.410. Attributions by accession number, p.411–12.

Index of provenance by patrons, former owners, and locations, p.413–15.

M361 Offner, Richard. A critical and historical corpus of Florentine painting. By Richard Offner with Klara Steinweg. Continued under the dir. of Miklós Boskovits and Mina Gregori. Florence, Giunti Barbèra, 1984– . (8)v. il.

New ed., with additional material, notes, and bibliography. For original ed. see GLAH 1:M341. "Published under the auspices of the Istituto di storia dell'arte of the University of Florence, and with a grant from the Consiglio nazionale delle richerche, Rome."—*Section* 3, v.4, p.[5].

Selective contents: Section 1. (1) The origins of Florentine painting, 1100–1270. Section 3. Fourteenth century. (1) The school of the St. Cecilia Master; (2) Elder contemporaries of Bernardo Daddi; (3) The works of Bernardo Daddi; (4) Bernardo Daddi, his shop and following; (9) Painters of the miniaturist tendency. Section 4. (7) Pt.1: Tendencies of Gothic in Florence: Andrea Bonaiuti; Pt.2: Don Silvestro dei Gherarducci.

Includes bibliographical references and indexes.

M362 Os, H. W. van. Sienese altarpieces, 1215–1460: form, content, function. Trans. from the Italian by Michael Hoyle. Groningen, Egbert Forsten, 1984–90. 2v. il. (part col.) (Mediaevalia Groningana, fasc. 4, 9)

An important study by the authority on the subject.

Contents: (1) 1215–1344, with a contrib. by Kees van der Ploeg "On architectural and liturgical aspects of Siena cathedral in the Middle Ages"; (2) 1344–1460, with a contrib. by Gail Aronow, "A description of the altars in Siena."

Bibliography, v.1, p.157–60, v.2, p.243–51. Notes, v.2, p.239–42. General index, v.1, p.161–63, v.2, p.255–61.

M363 Painting and illumination in early Renaissance Florence, 1300–1450. N.Y., Metropolitan Museum of Art (Distr. by Abrams, 1994). x, 394p. il. (part col.)

Published in conjunction with the exhibition, Metropolitan Museum of Art (1994–95). "Surveys the accomplishments, in various media, of five generations of manuscript painters in Florence, from the contemporaries of Giotto . . . to Fra Angelico and his followers."—*Dir. foreword.* Beautifully produced.

Contents: The illuminators of early Renaissance Florence, by Laurence B. Kanter; The books of the Florentine illuminators, by Babara Drake Boehm; Fra Angelico studies, by Carl Brandon Strehlke; Painting and illumination in early Renaissance Florence, 1300–1450, by Barbara Drake Boehm . . . [et al.]

Bibliography, p.362–78. Index, p.379–93.

M364 Pietrangeli, Carlo. Paintings in the Vatican. Essays by Guido Cornini . . . [et al.] Trans. by Frank Dabell. Boston, Little, Brown, 1996. 605p. col. il.

Trans. of Dipinti del Vaticano. Udine, Magnus, 1996.

"This volume includes, in addition to the paintings in the Vatican Picture Gallery, those works in the Pontifical Apartments and the cycles of frescoes of the Apostolic Palace. . . . It is the first book to provide an overall survey of paintings in the Vatican."—*p.11.* Chronological survey by multiple authors.

Biographies of the artists, p.561–87. Bibliography, p.589–94. Index of artists' names, p.595–96. Index of works, p.597–604.

M365 Pignatti, Terisio. The golden century of Venetian painting. In collab. with Kenneth Donohue. Los Angeles, Los Angeles County Museum of Art, 1979. 173p. il. (part col.)

Catalog of the exhibition, Los Angeles County Museum of Art (1979–80). "A selection of paintings that offers . . . insight into the artistic personalities and forces that determined the evolution of Venetian painting from Giovanni Bellini . . . to the death of Tintoretto."—*Pref.*

Lenders to the exhibition, p.8. Collections, exhibitions, and literature, p.[153]–72.

M366 Röttgen, Steffi. Italian frescoes. Principal photography by Antonio Quattrone and Fabio Lensini. Trans. by Russell Stockman. N.Y. Abbeville, 1996–97. 2v. il. (part col.), col. maps, plans.

Trans. of Wandmalerei der Frührenaissance in Italien. München, Hirmer, 1996–97.

Lavish survey of Italian Renaissance fresco cycles, modeled upon Borsook's classic study of Tuscan mural cycles (GLAH 2:M341), but embracing all regions of Italy and addressed to general readers as well as scholars.

Contents: (1) The early Renaissance, 1400–1470; (2) The flowering of the Renaissance, 1470–1510.

Notes to the introduction, v.1, p.443–46. Bibliography, v.1, p.447–50, v.2, p.442–49. Chronicles of damage, restoration, and documentation, v.1, p.451–53, v.2, p.450–54. Legends, inscriptions, and quotations, v.1, p.454–58, v.2, p.455–64. Index of places, v.1, p.459–60, v.2, p.465–66. Index of names and subjects, v.1, p.461–64, v.2, p.467–70.

M367 Rosand, David. Painting in Cinquecento Venice: Titian, Veronese, Tintoretto. Rev. ed. New Haven, Yale Univ. Pr., 1982. 279p. il. (part col.), plates.

1st ed., 1982.

Standard work, contextualist in orientation and "concerned essentially with monumental public imagery, altarpieces and murals."—*Pref.*

Contents: (1) Introduction: The conditions of painting in Renaissance Venice; (2) Titian and the challenge of the altarpiece; (3) Titian's Presentation of the Virgin in the Temple and the Scuola della Carità; (4) Theater and structure in the art of Paolo Veronese; (5) Action and piety in Tintoretto's religious pictures; Appendix: Documents relating to the Scuola della Carità.

Notes, p.176–245. Bibliography, p.246–64. Index, p.265–79.

M368 Shearman, John K. G. The early Italian pictures in the collection of Her Majesty the Queen. N.Y., Cambridge Univ. Pr., 1983. xli, 452p. il., plates. (The pictures in the collection of Her Majesty the Queen)

Scholarly catalog of the 15th–16th century Italian paintings in the royal collection. Companion to Levey's catalog of the later Italian paintings (GLAH 2:M381).

Bibliography, p.xvii–xxxi. Abbreviations, p.xxxiii–xxxix. Index of provenances, p.425–26. General index, p.427–50. Classified subject index, p.450–52.

M369 Le Siècle de Titien: l'âge d'or de la peinture à Venise. Paris, Réunion des musées nationaux, 1993. 748p. il. (part col.).

Monumental catalog of the exhibition, Grand Palais, Paris (1993), devoted to High Renaissance painting in Venice.

Venise au XVIe siècle, p.693–96. Biographies, p.697–703. Bibliographie, p.705–44. Expositions citées en abrégé, p.745–[50]. Index des oeuvres exposées par nom d'artiste, p.[751]. Index des oeuvres exposées par lieu de conservation, p.[752]–[54].

M370 Smart, Alastair. The dawn of Italian painting, 1250–1400. Ithaca, Cornell Univ. Pr., 1978. viii, 152p. il. (part col.), plates.

"In the present book I have attempted to provide an introduction to the period . . . which will appeal both to students and to the general reader."—*Pref.* Solid, readable introductory survey.

Select bibliography, p.[141]–46. Index, p.[147]–52.

M371 Smyth, Craig Hugh. Mannerism and maniera. With an introduction by Elizabeth Cropper. 2d ed. Vienna, IRSA, 1992. 161p. il. (Bibliotheca artibus et historiae)

For original ed. see GLAH 1:M349.

Bibliography, p.136–145. Index: Introduction, p.150–52. Index: Mannerism and maniera, p.153–60.

M372 Thomas, Anabel. The painter's practice in Renaissance Tuscany. N.Y., Cambridge Univ. Pr., 1995. xix, 398p. il. (part col.), plates.

Lucid study of the concrete workshop setting of the Italian Renaissance painter in Tuscany, focusing upon the physical setting of the workshop, the production of workshop merchandise, and workshop style.

Notes, p.[314]–64. Bibliography, p.[365]–81. Index, p.[382]–98.

M373 Todini, Filippo. La pittura umbra: dal Duecento al primo Cinquecento. Milano, Longanesi, 1989. 2v. il. (part col.) (I Marmi, 151)

Photographic repertory of Umbrian painting from the 13th to the early 16th century, modeled on Berenson's "lists" (see GLAH 1:M319–322). Covers all artists of the period born or educated in Umbria and intended to provide the basis for a history of Umbrian painting.

Contents: (1) Testo e tavole a colori; (2) Illustrazioni.

Opere citate e di referimento, v.1, p.385–86. Indice dei luoghi, v.1, p.389–415.

M374 Voss, Hermann. Painting of the Late Renaissance in Rome and Florence. Rev. and trans. by Susanne Pelzel. San Francisco, Wofsy, 1997. 2v. il.

Trans. of GLAH 1:M351.

Contents: (1) From the High Renaissance to Mannerism 1520–1570; (2) The diffusion and transformation of Mannerism 1570–1600.

Bibliography, v.1, p.246–51. Index of names Volume I and Volume II, v.1, p.260–67. Index of places Volume I and Volume II, v.1, p.268–86. Bibliography and Indexes reprinted in v.2.

SEE ALSO: Hermitage catalogue of Western European paintings (GLAH 2:M12).

Baroque—Modern

M375 The age of Correggio and the Carracci: Emilian painting of the sixteenth and seventeenth centuries. Washington, D.C., National Gallery of Art, 1986. xxxi, 561p. il. (part col.), ports.

Catalog of the important exhibition, National Gallery of Art, Washington, D.C. (1986–87), and other locations, "the largest and most comprehensive exhibition ever held of Emilian painting in the centuries of its highest accomplishment."—*Foreword.*

References, p.543–61.

M376 Boime, Albert. The art of the Macchia and the Risorgimento: representing culture and nationalism in nineteenth-century Italy. Chicago, Univ. of Chicago Pr., 1993. xxi, 338p. il. (part col.), plates.

"My study explores the social and political foundations of Macchiaioli activity and the shared ideology that bound individuals from different regions and social classes into a coherent group."—*Introd.*

Contents: (1) (Re)constructing Italian nationalism; (2) Strategies of representation; (3) Macchiaiolismo versus Accademismo; (4) The Macchia and the Risorgimento; (5) The First Italian National Exhibition of 1861; (6) Patronage and reception of the Macchiaioli; (7) Religious and social themes; (8) Requiem for the Caffè Michelangiolo.

Notes, p.[307]–28. Index, p.[329]–38.

M377 Brejon de Lavergnée, Arnauld, and Volle, Nathalie. Musées de France: répertoire des peintures italiannes du XVIIe siècle. Paris, Éd. de la Réunion des musées nationaux, 1988. 511p. il. (part col.).

Catalog of the exhibition, Galeries nationales du Grand Palais (1989). Important survey of 17th-century Italian paintings in French collections. Alphabetical arrangement by artist.

Index par musées, p.477–90. Bibliographie, p.491–506. Catalogues et guides des musees cités, p.507–09.

M378 Broude, Norma. The Macchiaioli: Italian painters of the nineteenth century. New Haven, Yale Univ. Pr., 1987. xxiii, 324p. il. (part col.), plates.

Based on the author's dissertation (Columbia University). A pioneering attempt to redefine, document, and reevaluate the Macchiaioli.

Notes, p.284–310. Bibliography, p.311–19. Index, p.320–24.

M379 Cantelli, Giuseppe. Repertorio della pittura fiorentina del Seicento. Fiesole, OpusLibri, 1983. 158p. il., plates (Repertori, 1)

Corpus of black-and-white, full-page reproductions of Florentine paintings of the 17th century. Arranged alphabetically by artist.

Bibliografia generale, p.147–58.

M380 Haskell, Francis. Patrons and painters: a study in the relations between Italian art and society in the age of the Baroque. 2d rev. and enl. ed. New Haven, Yale Univ. Pr., 1980. xviii, 474p. il., plates.

See GLAH 1:M360 for original ed. The new ed. includes a Postscript to the Second Edition, in which the author responds to recent scholarship on the subject. Still the standard study.

M381 Levey, Michael. The later Italian pictures in the collection of Her Majesty the Queen. 2d ed. N.Y., Cambridge Univ. Pr., 1991. lxx, 396p. il. (The pictures in the collection of Her Majesty the Queen)

1st ed. 1964. "This catalogue deals with all the Italian paintings of the seventeenth and eighteenth centuries in the royal collection."—*Pref.* The 2d ed. takes into account recent scholarship. Companion to Shearman's catalog of the early Italian pictures (GLAH 2:M368).

Bibliography, p.xlix–lxiii. Abbreviations, p.lxv–lxviii. Index of previous owners, p.387–88. Index of subjects, p.389–93. Index of artists, p.394–96.

M382 ———. Painting in eighteenth-century Venice. 3d ed. New Haven, Yale Univ. Pr., 1994. xiii, 267p. il. (part col.)

See GLAH 1:M361 for original ed.; 2d ed. 1980. This ed. includes "a number of significant changes to the text."—*Foreword.*

Notes,, p.242–56. Bibliography, p.257–260. Index, p.261–66.

M383 London. National Gallery. The seventeenth and eighteenth century Italian schools. [Reprint.] By Michael Levey. London, National Gallery, 1986. 264p. (National Gallery catalogues)

Repr. of ed. cited in GLAH 1:M6.

M384 Martini, Egidio. La pittura del settecento veneto. Udine, Istituto per l'enciclopedia del Friuli Venezia Giulia, 1982. 746p. il. (part col.).

Complements the author's previous study of 18th-century Venetian painting (GLAH 1:M363), representing the culmination of 30 years of study of the subject. Reproduces many previously unpublished paintings.

Bibliografia citata, p.721–36. Indice dei nomi degli artisti, p.739–40. Indice dei luoghi, p.741–43. Indice delle illlustrazioni in ordine alfabetico per artista, p.745–46.

M385 National Gallery of Ireland. Later Italian paintings in the National Gallery of Ireland: the seventeenth, eighteenth and nineteenth centuries. By Michael Wynne. Dublin, National Gallery of Ireland, 1986. xvi, 147p. il., plates, ports.

Scholarly catalog of the collection.

Numerical index, p.132–35. Changes of attribution, p.136. Index of previous owners, p.137–39. Index of donors, p.140. Portrait index, p.141. Topographical index, p.142. Index of religious subjects, p.143–44. Index of identified saints and angels, p.145. Index of historical and mythological subjects, p.146. Bibliography of National Gallery of Ireland, catalogues of paintings, p.147.

M386 Olson, Roberta. Ottocento: romanticism and revolution in 19th-century Italian painting. Essays by Piero Dini . . . [et al.] Entries and biographies by Virginia Bertone . . . [et al.] N.Y, American Federation of Arts, 1992. 292p. il. (part col.)

Catalog of the exhibition, Walters Art Gallery (1992–93), and other locations. "The first comprehensive consideration of Italian 19th-century painting in the United States."—*Pref.*

Bibliography, p.282–289. Index of artists, p.291.

M387 Pallucchini, Rodolfo. La pittura veneziana del Seicento. [Venezia], Alfieri, [1981]. 2v. 1069p. il. (part col.) (Profili e saggi di arte veneta)

See GLAH 1:M365 for the author's companion study of the 18th century.

Contents: (1) Text; (2) Plates.

Abbreviazione dei titoli delle pubblicazioni periodiche, v.1, p.397–98. Repertorio bibliografico, v.1, p.399–425. Indice dei nomi e dei luoghi, v.2, p.1033–66.

M388 Pietrantonio, Vera Fortunati. Pittura bolognese del '500. Testi di Anna Maria Fioravanti Baraldi, Sylvie Béguin, Wanda Bergamini . . . [et al.] Bologna, Grafis, 1986 2v. il. (part col.)

Repertory of Bolognese painting of the 16th century, consisting mostly of biographical entries on 28 individual artists, by various authors, arranged chronologically to approximate a survey.

Bibliografia, v.2, p.871–73.

M389 Pittura in Lombardia: il medioevo e il rinascimento. [A cura di] Marco Carminati . . . [et al.] Milano, Electa, 1998. 247p. col. il., ports.

Beautifully illustrated overview of Lombard painting, intended for amateurs.

Lacks scholarly apparatus.

M390 Il primo '800 italiano: la pittura tra passato e futura. [Mostra e catalogo a cura di Renato Barilli.] Milano, Mazzotta, 1992. 297p. il. (part col.)

Catalog of the exhibition, Palazzo Reale, Milan (1992), devoted to Neoclassical and Romantic painting in early 19th-century Italy.

Dizionario biografico, p.251–81. Bibliografia, p.283–88. Catalogo delle opere, p.289–95. Indice alfabetico degli artisti, p.297

M391 Roli, Renato. Pittura bolognese, 1650–1800: dal Cignani ai Gandolfi. Bologna, Alfa, 1977. x, 740p. il. (part col.), plates.

Substantial survey of Bolognese painting, with many black-and-white illustrations.

Regesti biografici, bibliografia e cataloghi delle opere, p.221–300. Bibliografia generale, p.301–05. Indice dei nomi di persona e luogo, p.[307]–23. Indice alle tavole, p.[735]–38.

M392 Seicento: le siècle de Caravage dans les collections françaises. Paris, Éd. de la Réunion des musées nationaux, 1988. 424p. il. (part col.)
Catalog of the important exhibition, Galeries nationales du Grand Palais, Paris (1988–89), and other locations, of 17th-century Italian paintings from French collections.
Bibliographie, p.400–12. Catalogues et guides des musées cités, p.413–17. Liste des expositions cités, p.418–20.

M393 Sestieri, Giancarlo. Repertorio della pittura romana della fine del Seicento e del Settecento. Torino, Allemandi, 1994. 3v. il. (Archivi di arte antica)
Conceived not only as a comprehensive, illustrated corpus of Roman paintings of the late 17th and 18th century but as a complete work summarizing scholarship and serving as the point of departure for future studies. Biographical dictionary, with brief bibliographies. V.2–3 consist of full-page, black-and-white plates.
Bibliography, v.1, p.[189]–90.

M394 Voss, Hermann. Baroque painting in Rome. Rev. and trans. by Thomas Pelzel. San Francisco, Wofsy, 1997. 2v. il., plates.
Trans. of GLAH 1:M371.
Contents: (1) Caravaggio, Carracci, Domenichino and their followers 1585–1640; (2) The High and Late Baroque, Rococo and early Neoclassicism 1620–1790.
Note on the bibliography of Roman Baroque painting, v.1, p.181. Index of artists, v.1, p.182. Index of plates with locations, v.1, p.183–90. Index of plates by location, v.1, p.191–98. Bibliography and Indexes reprinted in v.2.

SEE ALSO: Art et les grandes civilisations (GLAH 2:I8); Repertori fotografici (GLAH 2:M327) Collections of the National Gallery of Art: systematic catalogue (GLAH 2:M31).

Latin America

M395 Bayón, Damián, and Pontual, Roberto. La peinture de l'Amérique latine au XXe siècle: identité et modernité. Paris, Mengès, 1990. 224p. il. (part col.)
Seeks to provide a solid survey of 20th-century Latin American painting.
Contents: Première partie: L'Amérique espagnole: avant-garde et résistances; Deuxième partie: Le Brésil: anthropophagie et construction.
Bibliographie, première partie, p.143–44. Bibliographie, deuxième partie, p.218–19. Index, p.220–23.

M396 Bento, Antonio. Brazilian painting: expressions of Brazilian art. N.Y., Alpine, 1984. 199p. col. il., col. maps.
In Portuguese and English. Cover title: Expressões da arte brasileira = Expressions of Brazilian art.
Introduction to Brazilian painting.
Contents: Indigenous objects; The baroque period; Art naïf; Landscape painting; Human figuration; Abstractions; Fantastic art; Tapestry; Short conclusion
Bibliography, p.191. Index of illustrations, p.192–98.

M397 Bienal Konex (2d, 1994: Buenos Aires, Argentina). 100 obras maestras: 100 pintores argentinos, 1810–1994. Buenos Aires, Gaglianone, 1994. 1v. (unpaged), col. il.
Catalog of the exhibition, Museo Nacional de Bellas Artes, Buenos Aires (1994). Selection of 100 key works of Argentine painting from 1810 to 1994. Each work is reproduced in splendid color and accompanied by a one-page critical and biographical essay written by one of eight art historians. A survey of Argentine painting through three epochs written by Mercedes Casanegra prefaces the chronologically arranged entries.
Indice cronológico de artistas. Bibliografía [unpaginated].

M398 Boulton, Alfredo. Historia de la pintura en Venezuela. 2a ed. Caracas, Armitano, 1972–75. 3v. il. (part col.), ports.
See GLAH 1:M375 for 1st ed. and original annotation.
Contents: (1) Epoca colonial; (2) Epoca nacional de Lovera a Reverón; (3) Epoca contemporánea.
Bibliografía, v.1, p.417–24. Indexes for each volume.

M399 Campofiorito, Quirino. História da pintura brasileira no século XIX. [Rio de Janeiro], Pinakotheke, 1983. 291p. il. (part col.) (Série Ouro, SO-3)
History of 19th-century Brazilian painting. Chapter six contains a series of 17 artist biographies.
Índice onomástico, p.277–87.

M400 Diccionario biográfico enciclopédico de la pintura mexicana = Biographic encyclopedic dictionary of Mexican painting. General ed., José Manuel Caballero-Barnard. México, Quinientos años, 1979– . (3)v. il. (part col.), ports.
Spanish and English parallel texts. Only v.1–3 of the subseries, Pintores contemporaneos, siglo XX have been published so far. Alphabetical arrangement; each entry includes a critique of the artist, a statement by the artist, and two illustrations, a portrait of the artist, and a representative work. Subseries on the colonial period, academic period, and the "modern epoch" are envisioned.

M401 Espejo, Beatriz. Historia de la pintura mexicana. Prólogos, Rufino Tamayo . . . [et al.] México, D.F., Comermex, Armonía, 1989. 3v. il. (part col.)
Monumental survey of Mexican painting in all media (codices, murals, panel painting, etc.). Many color plates.
Bibliografía general, v.3, p.[251–54].

M402 Galaz, Gaspar, and Ivelic, Milan. La pintura en Chile desde la colonia hasta 1981. Valparaíso, Univ. Católica de Valparaíso, 1981. 393p. il. (part col.), plates. (El Rescate)
Survey of Chilean painting from colonial times.
Bibliografia, p.391–93. Indice de nombres, p.[395]–[96]. Indice general, p.[397].

M403 García Saiz, María Concepcíon. La pintura colonial en el Museo de América. Madrid, Ministerio de Cultura, Dirección General del Patrimonio Artístico, Archivos y Museos, Patronato Nacional de Museos, 1980– . (2)v. il. (part col.)
Catalog of paintings in the Museo de América.
Contents: (1) La escuela mexicana; (2) Los enconchados. Bibliography and index of artists for each volume.

M404 Guzmán M., Virginia, and Mercader M., Yolanda. Bibliografía de códices, mapas y lienzos del México prehispánico y colonial. México, SEP, Instituto Nacional de Antropología e Historia, 1979. 2v. il. (Colección científica, 79. Fuentes para la historia)
Published in conjunction with an exhibition by the Biblioteca Nacional de Antropología e Historia, Mexico City (1979). More than 2,000 citations on native Mexican pictorial works, many produced during the colonial period. References are arranged according to the name of the painted manuscript to which they refer.
Indice de autor, v.2, p.441–69. Indice de ilustraciones, v.2, p.470.

M405 Juan, Adelaida de. Pintura cubana: temas y variaciones. México, D.F., Univ. Nacional Autónoma de México, 1980. 173p. il. (part col.), plates. (Instituto de Investigaciones Estéticas. Cuadernos de historia del arte, 15)
Collection of essays devoted to themes and episodes in the history of Cuban painting of the 19th and 20th centuries, from colonial times to the revolution.
Índice onomástico, p.171–73.

M406 Leite, José Roberto Teixeira. Dicionário crítico da pintura no Brasil. Ed., Raul Mendes Silva. Rio de Janeiro, Artlivre, 1988. 555p. il.
Dictionary of Brazilian painting. Includes artists, movements, and art terms in an alphabetical listing.
Índice remissivo, p.552–53.

M407 Messer, Thomas M. The emergent decade: Latin American painters and painting in the 1960's. Artists' profiles in text and pictures by Cornell Capa. [Ithaca, N.Y., Cornell Univ. Pr., 1966]. xv, 172p. il. (part col.) ports. (part col.)
"Prepared under the auspices of the Cornell University Latin American Year, 1965–1966, and the Solomon R. Guggenheim Museum." Discusses 33 contemporary painters from Brazil, Uruguay, Argentina, Chile, Peru, Colombia, Venezuela, and Mexico. Arranged by country.
Selected biographies, p.165–69. Bibliography, p.170–72.

M408 Modernidade: art brésilien du 20e siècle. [Paris], Ministère des affaires étrangères, Association française d'action artistique, 1987. 426p. il. (part col.), ports.
Catalog of the exhibition, Musée d'art moderne de la ville de Paris (1987–88), produced under the direction of Aracy Amaral and Marie-Odile Briot. Documents early critiques of the modernist movement in Brazil.
Entrée des artistes [index of artists], p.325–72. Temps de modernidade [chronology], p.373–405. Bibliographie générale, p.406–10. Documentation du Musée National d'Art Moderne, p.411–17.

M409 Pintura boliviana del siglo XX; Banco Hipotecario Nacional. Fernando Romero [textos escritos]. Pedro Querejazu [fotografías, edición y compilación]. La Paz, INBO, 1989. 317p. il. (part col.)
Analyzes contemporary Bolivian painting in six essays by recognized Latin American art critics. Many color plates. Appendixes include description of art education, techniques, bibliography (p.255–58), chronology, directory of painters, and selected quotes of the reviews of various artists.

M410 Pintura Latinoamericana: proyecto cultural, los colegios y el arte: breve panorama de la modernidad figurativa en la primera mitad del siglo XX. Textos, Aracy Amaral . . . [et al.] Buenos Aires, Banco Velox, [1999]. 413p. col. il.
Compilation of Latin American painting of the first half of the 20th century. Includes introductory essays on modernism and individual national traditions.
Biografías de artistas, p.369–95. Referencias de los autores de los textos, p.396. Índice de autores e ilustraciones, p.401–04.

M411 Robertson, Donald. Mexican manuscript painting of the early colonial period: the metropolitan schools. [Reprint.] Foreword by Elizabeth Hill Boone. Norman, Univ. of Oklahoma Pr., [1994]. xxii, 234p. il., plates, maps.
See GLAH 1:M382 for original annotation. "Still the best treatment of the corpus as a whole."—*Foreword.*
Bibliography, p.203–22.

M412 San Martín, María Laura. Breve historia de la pintura argentina contemporánea. Buenos Aires, Claridad, 1993. 389p. il. (Colección Breve historia)
Basic survey of Argentine painting of the 20th century. Covers developments in Buenos Aires and the provinces.
Nota bibliográfica, p.[349]–53. Índice de nombres, p.[355]–83.

M413 Sá Rego, Stella de, and Harrison, Marguerite Itamar. Modern Brazilian painting. 2d ed. Albuquerque, The Latin American Institute, Univ. of New Mexico, 1997. i, 63p. + slide list (22p.) (Brazilian curriculum guide specialized bibliography, series II)
1st ed., [1985?]
Short essay tracing history of Brazilian painting introduces an annotated bibliography arranged by broad chronological categories. List of image sources.

M414 Silva, Carlos. Historia de la pintura en Venezuela. [Venezuela?], Armitano, [1989]. (1)v. il. (part col.)
History of Venezuelan painting, with a biographical section in dictionary format. Includes list of illustrations, bibliographical references, and index. Complete with v.3 (v.1–2 never published).
Contents: (3) Modernismo y contemporaneidad.

M415 Toussaint, Manuel. Pintura colonial en México. Ed. de Xavier Moyssén. 3a ed. México, Univ. Nacional Autónoma de México, 1990. xix, 309p. il., plates (part col.)

See GLAH 1:M387 for 1st ed.; 2d ed., 1982.

Substantial survey of colonial painting in Mexico, 1521–1821, richly illustrated, mostly in black-and-white.

Apéndices de documentos, p.218–46. Bibliografía y abreviaturas, p.246. Notas, p.247–76. Bibliografía de la pintura colonial en México, p.277–78. Índice de nombres, p.295–306.

Low Countries

General Works

M416 Dictionnaire de la peinture flamande et hollandaise du moyen âge à nos jours. [Conception éd., réalis. et sél. iconographique Jean-Philippe Breuille.] Paris, Larousse, [1989]. 493p. col. il.

This standard biographical dictionary of Dutch and Flemish painting from the middle ages through today is the product of a collaboration of 25 historians. Illustrated with 220 color reproductions, it contains entries for 450 artists, movements, and historical locations, arranged alphabetically.

M417 Le dictionnaire des peintres belges du XIVe siècle à nos jours, depuis les premiers maîtres des anciens Pays-Bas méridionaux. Pref. de Elaine De Wilde. [Bruxelles], La renaissance du livre, [1995]. 3v. il. (part col.)

Beautifully illustrated, biographical dictionary covering 6300 Belgian painters from the 14th to the 20th century. Organized alphabetically by artist. Entries include bibliography and collection information.

Contents: (1) A–K; (2) L–Z; (3) Roberts-Jones, Philippe. Une histoire visuelle de la peinture en Belgique; plates.

Tableau chronologique, v.3, p.434–40. Tableau synoptique, v.3, p.441–60. Index, v.3, p.461–66.

M418 Flemish paintings in America: a survey of early Netherlandish and Flemish paintings in the public collections of North America. Sel. by Guy C. Bauman and Walter A. Liedtke with an introd. by Walter A. Liedtke. [Trans. by Ted Alkins and Linda Van Thielen.] [Antwerp], Fonds Mercator, [1992]. 383p. il. (part col.) (Flandria extra muros, 3)

Massive work presenting 502 paintings, 102 with individual essays by 19 leading experts in the field of Netherlandish art. "The intention was to survey Flemish paintings (dating from about 1400 to about 1700) in the collections of North America, which ultimately involved over a hundred city, state, national, private, and academic museums."—*Introd.* Arranged chronologically. Each work is illustrated, many with large color plates.

Bibliography, p.378–81. Index, p.382–83.

M419 Hendrick, Jacques. La peinture au pays de Liège, XVIe, XVIIe, et XVIIIe siècles. [Liège], Perron-Wahle, [1987]. 287p. il. (part col.), map, plans, ports.

Copiously illustrated survey of Belgian painters from the 16th to the 18th century. 249 works are arranged chronologically into separate chapters by century.

Post-scriptum, p.274. Notes, p.275–76. Bibliographie, p.277–83. Index des noms de peintres, p.283.

M420 The history of painting in Belgium from the 14th century tot [sic] the present day: from the earliest masters of the old southern Netherlands and the Principality of Liège to our contemporary artists. Introd. by Philippe Roberts-Jones. Bruxelles, La renaissance du livre, 1995. 530p. col. il.

Well-produced corpus of Belgian paintings, reproduced in color, with introductory text.

Painting in Belgium, synoptic tables, p.[491]–520. Bibliography, p.[521]–24. Index, p.525–[31].

M421 Kuznetsov, Yury, and Linnik, Irene. Dutch painting in Soviet museums. [Trans. by Yuri Nemetsky]. N.Y., Abrams, [1989]. 522p. il. (part col.)

Trans. of Gollandskaia zhivopis' v muzeiakh Sovetskogo Soiuza. Leningrad, Aurora, 1984.

Well-illustrated catalog of 322 paintings from 25 Russian museum collections. Entries are arranged chronologically by work, ranging from the 15th through the early 20th century.

Abbreviations, p.514–[21]. Index of artists, p.522–[23].

M422 London. National Gallery. Dutch school, 1600–1900. By Neil MacLaren. Rev. and exp. by Christopher Brown. London, National Gallery, [1991]. 2v. il. (National Gallery catalogues)

See GLAH 1:M6 for 1st ed.

Newly revised catalog of the National Gallery's collection of Dutch painting, with detailed entries on 433 works organized by name of artist or school. "I attempted to bring up to date the entries on all the paintings included in MacLaren's catalogue and have added entries for all the paintings acquired since then."—*Introd.* Exhaustive listings include provenance, references, alternate versions, exhibition history, with a short essay and illustration.

Contents: (1) Text and comparative plates; (2) Plates and signatures.

Glossary, v.1, p.507–08. List of paintings acquired since the 1960 edition of the catalogue, v.1, p.509. List of attributions changed since the 1960 edition of the catalogue, v.1, p.510–11. Index to religious subjects, v.1, p.514–15. Index to profane subjects, v.1, p.516–17. Index to portraits, v.1, p.518–19. Topographical index, v.1, p.520–21. Index of previous owners, v.1, p.522–42. Index by year of acquisition, v.1, p.543–49. Index by inventory number, v.1, p.550–54. Supplement, v.1, p.555–58. Comparative plates, v.1, p.559–677.

M423 New York. Metropolitan Museum of Art. Flemish paintings in the Metropolitan Museum of Art. [By] Walter A. Liedtke. [Foreword by Sir John Pope-Hennessy.] [N.Y.], Metropolitan Museum of Art, [1984]. 2v. il. (part col.)

"The two volumes of this catalogue encompass the seventeenth and eighteenth century Flemish paintings in the Metropolitan Museum of Art. The term 'Flemish' here, refers to the whole of the Southern, or Spanish Netherlands, and implies the very approximate dates of 1600 to 1800."—*Introd.*

V.1 includes a foreword by Sir John Pope-Hennessy, catalogue entries, and indexes, along with useful comparative illustrations. V.2 contains reproductions of the collection. The organization of both vols. is alphabetical by artist. Exhaustive entries include a scholarly essay, condition notes, signature data, bibliography, exhibition history, provenance, ex-collections, and credit line.

Comparative figures, v.1, p.281–328. Index of artists, by accession number, v.1, p.329–30. Index of collections, v.1, p.331–38. Index of names, v.1, p.339.

M424 Städtische Galerie im Städelschen Kunstinstitut Frankfurt am Main. Niederländische Gemälde vor 1800 im Städel. By Jochen Sander and Bodo Brinkmann. Frankfurt am Main, Blick in die Welt, [1995]. 82p. plates (part col.) (Kataloge der Gemälde im Städelschen Kunstinstitut, Frankfurt am Main, 1)

Catalog of the 189 Dutch and Flemish paintings from the 16th–18th centuries. Colored plates followed by detailed examinations of each work and extensive reference sources.

Inventarnummern und Konkordanz der Zuschreibungen, p.71–77. Provenienzen, p.78–80. Bildthemen, p.81–82.

Early Netherlandish

M425 Belting, Hans, and Kruse, Christiane. Die Erfindung des Gemäldes: das erste Jahrhundert der niederländischen Malerei. München, Hirmer, 1994. 301p. il. (part col.)

An important study of the meaning and role of "panel painting" and its emergence as an independent genre in early Netherlandish painting.

Contents: Die Erfindung des Gemäldes: Ästhetik und Weltbezug des neuen Staffeleibildes; Die grossen Altäre: Die Öffentlichkeit der Kunst im Wettbewerb der Maler; Die Tafeln (with documentation by Christiane Kruse).

Bibliographie, p.275–89. Tafelverzeichnis und Fotonachweis, p.293–95. Register: Sachregister, p.293–96. Namens- und Ortsregister, p.296–99.

M426 Briels, Jan. Peintres flamands en Hollande au début du siècle d'or, 1585–1630. [Trans. by Catherine Warnant . . . (et al.)] [Paris, Albin Michel, 1987]. 454p. il. (part col.)

Trans. of Vlaamse schilders in de Noordelijke Nederlanden in het begin van de Gouden Eeuw 1585–1630. Haarlem, Becht, 1987.

Richly illustrated in an oversize format, this massive catalog surveys the Golden age of Dutch and Flemish painting in ten chapters by genre or subject matter. A scholarly history that could easily be mistaken for a coffee-table book because of its beautiful design.

Notes, p.437–43. Bibliographie, p.444–51. Index des noms, p.452–54.

M427 Campbell, Lorne. The early Flemish pictures in the collection of Her Majesty the Queen. N.Y., Cambridge Univ. Pr., 1985. lxxii, 214p. il., plates. (Pictures in the Royal collection)

"The present catalogue deals with pictures in the royal collection by artists who worked in the southern provinces of the Low Countries during the fifteenth and sixteenth centuries."—*Pref.*

Bibliography, p.[li]–lxv. List of abbreviations, p.[lxvii]–lxx. Index of artists, p.209–11. Index of provenances, p.212. Classified subject index, p.213–14.

M428 Châtelet, Albert. Early Dutch painting: painting in the northern Netherlands in the fifteenth century. Trans. by Christopher Brown and Anthony Turner. Oxford, Phaidon, [1981]. 264p. il. (part col.) map.

Trans. of Les primitifs hollandais. Fribourg, Office du livre, 1980.

History of 15th-century Dutch panel painting, first published privately as Gerard de Saint Jean et la peinture dans les Pays-Bas du Nord au XVe siècle, Service de reproduction des theses of the University of Lille III, 1979 (3v.)

Contents: (1) The beginnings, the age of the counts of Holland and the House of Bavaria-Straubing; (2) Jan van Eyck in Holland; (3) The northern Netherlands from Philip the Good to Philip the Handsome (1428–1505); (4) The challenge of Flemish art, Guelders and the Haarlem school in the reign of Philip the Good; (5) Geertgen tot Saint Jans; (6) The workshops of Haarlem in the first third of the fifteenth century; (7) Workshops outside Haarlem, Delft, Leiden, Gouda, Utrecht; (8) The originality and the limitations of painting in the northern Netherlands.

Notes, p.181–88. Catalogue [of 15th century Northern Netherlandish painting], p.189–245. Bibliography, p.247–57. Index, p.259–64.

M429 Comblen-Sonkes, Micheline. Guide bibliographique de la peinture flamande du XVe siècle = Bibliografische gids van de Vlaamse schilderkunst van de XVe eeuw = Bibliographic guide for early Netherlandish painting. Bruxelles, Centre national de recherches "Primitifs flamands," 1984. xxiv, 149p.

Text in French, Dutch, English, and German. Intended as a "handy guide" to the literature on early Netherlandish painting. 1,051 entries, mostly of a general nature. Omits dissertations, provenance studies.

Contents: Généralités; Les oeuvres; Les grands musées; Les grandes expositions; Les peintres; Maîtres anonymes; Les oeuvres anonymes; Miscellanea.

Index, p.137–49.

M430 Eisler, Colin T. Early Netherlandish painting: the Thyssen Bornemisza collection. Gen. ed. Simon de Pury. London, Sotheby's, [1989]. 280p. il. (part col.)

One of the exemplary set of catalogs surveying the Thyssen Bornemisza collection. Written by a leading expert in the field and generously illustrated with color plates. Entries for the collection's 43 early Netherlandish paintings include provenance, exhibition history, and literature. "The catalogue entries follow a chronological sequence according to the date of the painting, although works by the same artist are grouped together."—*p.30.*

List of paintings, p.33. Artists' biographies, p.[269]–75. Index, p.276–80.

M431 The Flemish primitives: catalogue of early Netherlandish painting in the Royal Museums of Fine Arts of Belgium. [By] Cyriel Stroo . . . [et al.] Brussels, Brepols, 1996– . (2)v. il. (part col.)

A projected series of 5 vols. "covering the Museum's collection of 15th-century painting."—*Foreword* to v.2.

Contents: (1) The Master of Flemalle and Rogier van der Weyden groups; (2) The Dirk Bouts, Petrus Christus, Hans Memling and Hugo van der Goes groups.

Includes bibliographies and indexes.

M432 Friedländer, Max J. Von Van Eyck bis Bruegel: Studien zur Geschichte der niederländischen Malerei. [Neuausg. besorgt von Günter Busch.] [Frankfurt am Main], Fischer, [1986]. 364p. il. (part col.)

See GLAH 1:M406 for earlier eds. including the Eng. ed. (repr. Ithaca, Cornell Univ. Pr., 1981).

Written by the leading scholar in the field of Netherlandish art, this indispensable source has been kept in print since 1916.

Tafeln, p.179–336. Anmerkungen, p.337–43. Veränderte Standorte, p.344–48. Verzeichnis der Tafeln, p.349–59. Standortverzeichnis zu den Tafeln, p.360–63.

M433 Holländische Malerei in neuem Licht: Hendrick ter Brugghen und seine Zeitgenossen. Konzeption und Katalog: Albert Blankert und Leonard J. Slatkes. Beitr. von Marten Jan Bok . . . [et al.] Utrecht, Centraal Museum, [1986]. 374p. il. (part col.)

Catalog of the exhibition, Centraal Museum, Utrecht (1986–87), and other locations, devoted to the influence by Caravaggio on Dutch painting. Proceedings from a symposium held in conjunction with the exhibition published as Hendrick ter Brugghen und die Nachfolger Caravaggios in Holland, Braunschweig, Herzog Anton Ulrich-Museum, 1987. Catalog illustrates and examines 79 works with essays by 4 leading scholars.

Bibliographie, p.349–71.

M434 Lane, Barbara G. Flemish painting outside Bruges, 1400–1500: an annotated bibliography. Boston, Hall, [1986]. xxii, 260p. (Reference publication in art history)

An intentionally limited study of "Flemish painters other than Van Eyck, Christus, Memling, and their followers. . . . Only those painters included in volumes 2, 3, and 4 of Friedländer's Early Netherlandish Painting . . . will be found here."—*Introd.* "This volume begins by listing general studies of the field and then proceeds to specific investigations of the major artists concerned, with the entries on individual artists subdivided by topic. The final section on late fifteenth-century artists is arranged alphabetically by artist. Arrangement of the entries in each section is also alphabetical."—*Introd.*

Addenda, p.237–38. Index of authors, p.239–47. Index of artists and paintings, p.249–56. Index of subjects, p.257–60.

M435 Museum Boymans-van Beuningen. Van Eyck to Bruegel, 1400 to 1550. Rotterdam, Museum Boymans-van Beuningen, 1994. 408p. il. (part col.)

This exemplary catalog, loosely based on Max Friedländer's From Van Eyck to Bruegel (see GLAH 1:M406 and GLAH 2:M432), presents a detailed, scientific study of the Museum's collection of Dutch and Flemish paintings. Extensive entries for individual works by 67 artists, organized alphabetically by artist then chronologically by date, include provenance, exhibition history, literature, physical characteristics, dendrochronological examination, and infrared reflectography. Handsome color plates for each work.

No cumulative index.

M436 Philippot, Paul. La peinture dans les anciens Pays-Bas, XVe–XVIe siècles. Paris, Flammarion, 1994. 303p. il. (part col.) (Idées et recherches)

Trans. of Pittura fiamminga e Rinascimento italiano. Torino, Einaudi, 1970.

Beautifully illustrated survey of Netherlandish painting from the 15th and 16th centuries. Works are examined chronologically, in the context of other European influences.

Contents: (1) XVe siècle flamand et Quattrocento florentin; (2) Du Maître de Flémalle à Hugo van der Goes; (3) L'expressionnisme germanique; (4) La fin du XVe siècle, origines d'une nouvelle conception de l'image; (5) Le maniérisme gothique et la première Renaissance; (6) La crise de la culture figurative vers 1530–1540, Italianisme et tradition nationale; (7) Les provinces du Sud; (8) Les provinces du Nord; (9) La fin du XVIe siècle.

Épilogue, p.262–64. Notes, p.265–78. Notices biographiques et bibliographie, p.279–301. Index, p.302–[04].

M437 Les Primitifs flamands I. Corpus de la peinture des anciens Pays-Bas méridionaux au quinzième siècle. Anvers, De Sikkel, 1951– . (16)v. (Publications du Centre National de Recherches "Primitifs flamands")

See GLAH 1:M409 for earlier vols.

Continuation of an important series on 15th-century Flemish painting, including current technical methods and latest research. Each vol. arranged alphabetically by artist's name, with extensive bibliography, literature, and illustrations.

Contents: (1) Jannssens de Bisthoven, Alin. Musée communal des beaux-arts (Musée Groeninge) Bruges. Rev. and aug. with collab. by M. Baes-Dondeyne . . . [et al.] (1983); (14) Pierre Georgel. Musée des beaux-arts de Dijon (1985); (15) Comblen-Sonkes, Micheline. Les Musées de l'Institut de France, Musées Jacquemart-André et Marmottan à Paris, Musée Condé à Chantilly (1988); (16) Lievens-de Waegh, Marie-Léopoldine. Le Musée national d'art ancien et Le Musée national des carreaux de fäience de Lisbonne (1991).

M438 Les Primitifs flamands: II, Répertoire des peintures flamandes du quinzième siècle. Bruxelles, Centre national de recherches "Primitifs flamands," 1953– . (4)v. (Publications du Centre national de recherches "Primitifs flamands")

See GLAH 1:M410 for earlier vols.

Contents: (4) Vacková, Jarmila. Collections de Tchécoslovaquie (1985).

M439 Les Primitifs flamands et leur temps. Maryan Wynn Ainsworth . . . [et al.] Sous la dir. de Brigitte de Patoul et Roger Van Schoute. [Louvain-la-Neuve, Belgique], La renaissance du livre, [1994]. 656p. il. (part col.)

This history of medieval and Renaissance painting in Flanders brings together essays by 26 international scholars.

Contents: (1) Les Pays-Bay Bourguignons; (2) Le peintre et son métier; (3) La clientèle du peintre, l'iconographie; (4) Questions de style; (5) Les peintres et leurs oeuvres; (6) Le rayonnement des primitifs flamands.

Bibliographie commentée, p.626–47. Index des oeuvres citées, p.648–53. Index des illustrations, p.654–55.

M440 Ragghianti Collobi, Licia. Dipinti Fiamminghi in Italia 1420–1570. Bologna, Calderini, 1990. x, 318p. il. (part col.) (Musei d'Italia-Meraviglie d'Italia, 24)

Handy ready-reference to Netherlandish holdings in public collections throughout Italy. Lists 559 works, most illustrated, along with short entries. Organized chronologically with indexes to names, artists, and places.

Bibliografia, p.277–91. Indici, p.294–318.

M441 Städtische Galerie im Städelschen Kunstinstitut Frankfurt am Main. Niederländische Gemälde im Städel: 1400–1550. By Jochen Sander. Unter Mitarb. von Stephan Knobloch bei der gemäldetechnologischen Dokumentation. Mainz am Rhein, Zabern, [1993]. 497p. col. plates. (Kataloge der Gemälde im Städelschen Kunstinstitut, Frankfurt am Main, 2)

Catalog of the 29 early Dutch and Flemish paintings in Städelschen Kunstinstitut. Colored plates followed by detailed examinations of each work and extensive reference sources.

Dendrochronologische Untersuchungergebnisse, p.453–57. Konstruktion der Originalrahmen, p.458–66. Mehrfach Zitierte Literatur, p.467–68. Register, p.469. Verzeichnis der Personen, Orte und Werke, p.472–92. Verzeichnis der Bildthemen, p.493–96.

M442 Vienna. Kunsthistorisches Museum. La peinture flamande au Kunsthistorisches Museum de Vienne. By Arnour Balis . . . [et al.] [Anvers, Belgium], Fonds Mercator, [1987]. 301p. il. (part col.) (Flandria extra muros)

Major catalog of the Flemish painting collection of the Kunsthistorisches Museum, Vienna, with full essays as catalog entries, written by 12 scholars, illustrated with color plates. A second section repeats entry data for each work, along with a thumbnail reproduction, organized alphabetically for easy access.

Bibliographie, p.299. Index des peintres, p.300–01.

SEE ALSO: Collections of the National Gallery of Art: systematic catalogue (GLAH 2:M31).

Baroque—Modern

M443 Akademie der Bildenden Künste in Wien. Gemäldegalerie. Die holländischen Gemälde de 17. Jahrhunderts. [By] Renate Trnek. Wien, Böhlau, [1992]. xv, 556p. il. (part col.) (Kataloge der Gemäldegalerie der Akademie der Bildenden Künste, 1)

Complete inventory of the 17th-century Dutch painting collection at the Akademie de Bildenden Künste, Vienna. Exhaustive entries organized alphabetically by artist's name include illustrated essay, exhibition history, literature, provenance, signature data, and reproduction.

Addendum, p.450–52. Anhang, p.453–94. Besitzersiegel, p.495–98. Konkordanz der Zuschreibungsänderungen, p.499–504. Abkürzungsschlüssel, für Indices: Institutionen, Handbücher und Hauskataloge, p.505–06. Abgekürzt zitierte Literatur: nach Autoren, p.507–32. Ausstellungs- und Sammlungskataloge nach Orten, p.533–36. Ausstellungen in chronologischer Abfolge, p.537–40. Vergleichsabbildungen: nach Künstlern, p.541–47. Vergleichsabbildungen: nach Standorten, p.548–50. Themenübersicht, p.553–54. Künstlerverzeichnis, p.555–56.

M444 Alpers, Svetlana. The art of describing: Dutch art in the seventeenth century. [Chicago], Univ. of Chicago Pr., [1983]. xxvii, 273p. il. (part col.), plates.

The introduction states "this book is not intended as a survey of seventeenth century Dutch art," but rather as an investigation of 17th-century Dutch culture as it influences the painting of that period. Engaging essays are complimented with 177 illustrations.

Contents: (1) Constantijn Huygens and the new world; (2) "Ut pictura, ita visio": Kepler's model of the eye and the nature of picturing in the North; (3) "With a sincere hand and a faithful eye," the craft of representation; (4) The mapping impulse in Dutch art; (5) Looking at words: the representation of texts in Dutch art; (6) Epilogue: Vermeer and Rembrandt.

Notes, p.235–68. Index, p.269–73.

M445 Bernt, Walther. Die niederländischen Maler und Zeichner des 17. Jahrhunderts. München, Bruckmann, [1979–80]. 5v. il. (part col.)

V.1–3 are the 4th rev. ed. of Die niederlandischen Maler des 17. Jahrhunderts (see GLAH 1:M416 for previous eds.); v.4–5 are the 2d rev. ed. of Die niederlandischen Zeichner des 17. Jahrhunderts (see GLAH 1:L62 for previous eds.)

Issued together for the first time, these two pictorial dictionaries document and illustrate Dutch and Flemish paintings and drawings from the 17th century. Its nearly 2,000 entries include a short essay along with signature, reproduction, literature, and color plate.

Contents: (1) Achtschellinck-Heda; (2) Heem-Rombouts; (3) Romeyn-Zyl; Register; (4) Aken-Koninck; (5) Laer-Wyck; Register.

M446 Bordeaux (France). Musée des beaux-arts. L'or & l'ombre: catalogue critique et raisonné des peintures hollandaises du dix-septième et du dix-huitième siècles, conservées au Musée des Beaux-Arts de Bordeaux. Par Olivier Le Bihan. Avant-propos de Philippe Le Leyzour. Préf. de Jacques Foucart. [Bordeaux], Musée des beaux-arts de Bordeaux; [1990]. 459p. il., xxxiip. of col. plates.

Impressive collection catalog of the 17th- and 18th-century Dutch painting in the Musée des beaux-arts de Bordeaux. Contains scholarly essays on 111 paintings, arranged alphabetically by artist, along with information on copies and imitations.

Notices biographiques, p.409–17. Table de concordance, p.419–23. Bibliographie, p.425–42. Index général des notices du catalogue, p.443–59.

M447 Broos, B. P. J. De Rembrandt a Vermeer: les peintres hollandais au Mauritshuis de La Haye. La Haye, Fondation Johan Maurits van Nassau, [1986]. 395p. il. (part col.), ports.

Beautifully illustrated catalog of the exhibition, Galeries nationales du Grand Palais, Paris (1986), with scholarly texts by Hans Hoetink, Beatrijs Brenninkmeyer-de Rooij, and Jean Lacambre. Detailed entries for each of the exhibition's 57 works, arranged alphabetically by artist, include complete bibliography and provenance.

Notices historiques, p.91–105. Bibliographie abrégée, p.377–90.

M448 ______. Great Dutch paintings from America. With contrib. by Edwin Buijsen . . . [et al.] Final ed. by Rieke van Leeuwen. Exh. org. by Hans R. Hoetink. The Hague, Mauritshuis [Distr. by Waanders, 1990]. 561p. il. (part col.)

Catalog of the exhibition, Mauritshuis, The Hague (1990), and other locations. Includes 73 masterpieces of 17th-century Dutch painting from more than 40 museums and private collection in the United States. The catalog begins with five scholarly essays focusing on collectors and collecting patterns in the U.S., followed by catalog entries, organized alphabetically by artist's name. Each entry includes an illustrated essay along with provenance and bibliography.

Exhibitions of seventeenth-century Dutch art in American museums and public galleries, 1888–1991, p.494–98. Bibliography, p.499–541. Index, p.542–58.

M449 Brown, Christopher. Scenes of everyday life: Dutch genre painting of the seventeenth century. London, Faber and Faber, [1984]. 240p. il. (part col.)

The genesis of this study was the author's 1978 exhibition and catalog of Dutch genre paintings from the collection of the National Gallery, London. This book retains "the general arrangement of the catalogue—a lengthy introduction followed by short chapters on particular subjects treated by genre painters—and it inevitably uses some of the same examples."—*p.7.*

Notes, p.217–19. Biographies of the artists, p.220–33. Bibliography, p.234–36. Exhibition catalogues, p.237. Index, p.238–40.

M450 Chiarini, Marco. I dipinti olandesi del Seicento e del Settecento. Roma, Gallerie e musei statali di Firenze, 1989. xxiii, 671p. il. (part col.) (Cataloghi dei musei e gallerie d'Italia, nuova ser., n.1)

Well-illustrated, scholarly catalog surveying Dutch painting of the 16th and 17th centuries in the municipal galleries and museums of Florence. Organized alphabetically by artist, then chronologically by works. Each section begins with a biography of the artist, followed by an essay on each individual work, color plate, provenance, and bibliography.

Documenti manoscritti, p.651–52. Bibliografia, p.653–62. Mostre, p.663–64. Tavola delle concordanze, p.665–68. Cambi di attribuzione, p.669–70. Indice degli artisti, p.671–[72]. Indice generale, p.[673].

M451 Diaz Padron, Matias. El siglo de Rubens en el Museo del Prado: catalogo razonado de pintura flamenca del siglo XVII. Madrid, Museo del Prado, 1995. 3v. il. (part col.)

Sumptuous catalog of Flemish paintings of the golden age in the Prado.

Vol.3 comprises a bibliography and indexes.

M452 Flandre et Hollande au siècle d'or: chefs-d'oeuvre des musées de Rhône-Alpes. [France, Association Rhône-Alpes des Conservateurs, 1992]. 415p. il. (part col.)

Catalog of the exhibition, Musée des Beaux-Arts, Lyon (1992), and other locations. Brings together many of the strongest Netherlandish/Dutch holdings of French provincial museums. Scholarly essays by Jacques Foucart, Marie-Félicie Péres, and Gilles Chomer are followed by entries, arranged alphabetically by artist, on 146 works. Almost 400 additional paintings are given thumbnail illustrations and brief entries.

Répertoire, p.331–99. Bibliographie, p.402–[16]. Index des lieux de conservation, p.[418].

M453 Franits, Wayne, ed. Looking at seventeenth-century Dutch art: realism reconsidered. N.Y., Cambridge Univ. Pr., 1997. xviii, 274p. il.

Excellent collection of 14 essays "by prominent scholars that explore, through various approaches and perspectives, the significance of seventeenth-century Dutch art for its original audiences."—*Introd.* Admirable orientation to contemporary scholarship in the field.

Contents: (1) On the history of research concerning the interpretation of Dutch painting, by Konrad Renger; (2) A seventeenth-century theory of art: nature and practice, by J. A. Emmens; (3) Realism and seeming realism in seventeenth-century Dutch painting, by Eddy de Jongh; (4) Picturing Dutch culture, by Svetlana Alpers; (5) Tobacco, social deviance, and Dutch art in the seventeenth century, by Ivan Gaskell; (6) Didactic and disguised meanings? Several seventeenth-century texts on painting and the iconological approach to Dutch paintings of this period, by Eric J. Sluijter; (7) Dutch seventeenth-century genre painting: a reassessment of some current hypotheses, by Peter Hecht; (8) Ter Borch's ladies in satin, by Alison McNeil Kettering; (9) Style in Dutch art, by Walter Liedtke; (10) Naturalism as convention: subject, style, and artistic self-consciousness in Dutch landscape, by Lawrence O. Goedde; (11) Natural artifice and material values in Dutch still life, by Celeste Brusati; (12) The three-quarter length life-sized portrait in seventeenth-century Holland: the cultural functions of tranquilitas, by Ann Jensen Adams; (13) How to sit, stand, and walk: toward a historical anthropology of Dutch paintings and prints, by Herman Roodenburg; (14) The space of gender in seventeenth-century Dutch painting, by Elizabeth Alice Honig.

Notes, p.201–44. Bibliography, p.245–48. General bibliography, p.249–68. Index, p.269–74.

M454 Frère, Jean Claude. Early Flemish painting. Paris, Terrail, 1997. 206p. col. il.

Trans. of Les primitifs flamands. Paris, Terrail, 1996.

Accessible survey, without scholarly apparatus.

M455 Gaskell, Ivan. Seventeenth-century Dutch and Flemish painting: the Thyssen-Bornemisza collection. General ed. Simon de Pury. [London], Sotheby's, [1990]. 552p. il. (part col.)

One of the exemplary set of catalogs surveying the Thyssen Bornemisza collection. Written by a leading expert in the field and generously illustrated with color plates, entries for the collection's 128 17th-century paintings include provenance, exhibition history, and literature. "The entries are arranged in groups thematically and within each group more or less chronologically. This is in order to provide a text which is not simply a collection of discrete essays, but which exhibits some characteristics of a coherent account of several aspects of an art of the Netherlands during a long seventeenth century (c.1550–1740), incorporating a generous quantity of comparative material."—*p.37.*

Concordance, p.542. Index of dealers and former owners, p.543. Index, p.546–52.

M456 Gemälde der Rembrandt-Schüler. [Hrsg. von] Werner Sumowski. [Landau], Edition PVA, [1983]. 5v. il. (part col.)

Exhaustive survey of the artists of the Rembrandt School, his pupils, and his collaborators. Entries, with biography, complete inventory, and illustrations, are organized alphabetically in the first four vols. with references and sources filling out the set.

Contents: (1) J. A. Backer-A. van Dijck; (2) G. van den Eeckhout-I. de Joudreville; (3) B. Keil-J. Ovens; (4) Ch. Paudiss-Anonyme. Ortsregister; (5) Nachträge.

Ortsregister, p.3323–95. Ikonographisches Register, p.3396–495. Bibliographie, p.3496–514; (6) Einleitung-und Schlusswort, p.3517–85. Corrigenda und Addenda I–V, p.3586–88. Nachträge 2, p.3689–4144. Ortsregister, p.4145–58. Ikonographisches Register, p.4159–78. Bibliographie, p.4179–81. Künstlerverzeichnis I–VI, p.4182–84.

M457 Gerson, H. Ausbreitung und Nachwirkung der holländischen Malerei des 17. Jahrhunderts. [Reprint.] Eingel. und Erg. mit 90 neuen Abbildungen von B.W. Meijer. Amsterdam, B.M. Israël, 1983. xxi, 618p. 136p. of plates.

Reprint of the 1st. ed., Haarlem, De Erven F. Bohn, 1942.

Welcome reprinting of a major study of the influences of 17th-century Dutch painting around the world. A new introduction and 90 illustrations have been added to the previous text.

Contents: (1) Flandern; (2) Frankreich; (3) Italien; (4) Das Deutsche Reich; (5) Das 18. Jahrhundert; (6) Die Schweiz; (7) England; (8) Skandinavien and Osteuropa; (9) Russland; (10) Südosteuropa, das Mittelmeergebiet und die Pyrenäenhalbinsel; (11) Asien; (12) Afrika und Amerika.

Künstler, p.567–95. Sammler, p.599–603. Orte, p.607–11. Die Wichtigste, in abgekürzter form aufgeführte Literatur, p.611. Abbildungverzeichnis, p.613–18.

M458 Grössinger, Christa. North-European panel paintings: a catalogue of Netherlandish and German paintings before 1600 in English churches and colleges. N.Y., Oxford Univ. Pr., 1992. 302p. il. (part col.)

"The purpose of this book . . . is to bring together those North-European fifteenth- and sixteenth-century panel paintings, altarpieces, and fragments of altarpieces, still functioning in their ecclesiastical settings in England."—*Pref.*

Notes to the introduction, p.37–38. List of places catalogued, p.39. Biographies of artists, p.257–79. Hand-list of North-European panel paintings before 1600 in English public collections, p.280–90. Bibliography, p.291–93. List of comparative works of art, p.295–98. General index, p.299–302.

M459 Die Haager Schule: Meisterwerke der holländischen Malerei des 19. Jahrhunderts aus Haags Gemeentemuseum. Heidelberg, Braus, [1987]. 391p. il. (part col.)

Catalog of the exhibition, Kunsthalle Mannheim (1987), and other locations, of 19th-century Dutch painting. The book begins with three scholarly essays by John Sillevis, Hans Kraan, Roland Dorn followed by biographies of the exhibition's 17 painters. Entries for each of the 126 works are illustrated and arranged alphabetically by artist. Includes watercolor painting and some drawings.

Biographien, p.81–94. Dokumentation, p.359–84. Bibliographie, p.385–90.

M460 Haak, Bob. The golden age: Dutch painters of the seventeenth century. Trans. and ed. by Elizabeth Willems-Treeman. N.Y., Stewart, Tabori, and Chang, [1996]. 536p. il. (part col.), maps.

German ed., Das goldene Zeitalter der holländischen Malerei. Köln, DuMont, 1984.

Massive work detailing the history of 400 Dutch painters of the Golden age with more than 1,000 works illustrated. "The overall scheme is chronological, divided into four parts. Part 1 introduces the major developments with a discussion of their 16th-century antecedents, followed by a digression on the artists' social position, their patrons, and the categories of subject matter; part 2 covers the period from about 1580 to 1625 and introduces the round of Dutch art centers which I continue to pursue in the rest of the book as a valid way of tying things together. The years of greatest glory in Dutch painting are treated in parts 3 and 4, the first from 1625 to 1650, the second from 1650 to about 1680."—*Pref.*

Notes, p.505–11. Bibliography, p.512–24. Index of artists, p.525–35.

M461 Hairs, Marie-Louise. Flemish flower painters in the XVII century. Trans. by Eva Grzelak. [Bruxelles, Le-

febvre et Gillet, 1985]. 518p. il. (part col.) (Les peintres flamands du XVIIe siècle)
See GLAH 1:M422 for earlier eds.

Much expanded version of the author's study of 17th-century Flemish flower paintings. 103 artists are presented in this copiously illustrated oversize edition.

Contents: (1) The forerunners; (2) Jean Brueghel de Velous; (3) Daniel Seghers; (4) Other painters of flowers.

Notes, p.422–54. Catalogue, p.455–508. Table of color illustrations, p.509–11. Table of black and white illustrations, p.512–13. Index of artists, p.514–16.

M462 Kahr, Madlyn Millner. Dutch painting in the seventeenth century. 2d ed. [N.Y., HarperCollins, 1993]. xiv, 326p. il., map.
1st ed. N.Y., Harper and Row, 1978; repr. with corrections, 1982.

New ed. of a concise introduction to 17th-century Dutch painting. "I have revised and updated the text, notes, and bibliography for this second edition."—*Pref.*

Contents: (1) The birth of a nation; (2) Dutch culture and art; (3) Utrecht: from mannerism to Caravaggism; (4) Haarlem: strides toward naturalism; (5) Frans Hals and the portrait tradition; (6) Rembrandt; (7) The Rembrandt school; (8) Scenes of social life; (9) Still-life; (10) Landscape and seascape; (11) Architectural subjects: church interiors and town views; (12) Vermeer and the Delft school.

Notes, p.302–08. Selected bibliography, p.309–14. List of illustrations, p.315–20. Index, p.321–26.

M463 Larsen, Erik. Seventeenth century Flemish painting. Freren, Luca, 1985. 364p. il.
History of Flemish painting, concentrating on the artistic evolution of painting in the Southern Netherlands during the Golden century. The focus is on individual painters.

Critical bibliography, p.327–35. Collections of Flemish paintings of the period, p.336–40. Locations of paintings mentioned in this book, p.341–49. Index, p.358–64.

M464 Maere, J. de and Wabbes, M. Illustrated dictionary of 17th century Flemish painters. Ed. by Dr. Jennifer A. Martin. [Brussels], La renaissance du livre, [1994]. 3v. il. (part col.)
"Approximately 850 biographies of Flemish painters born between 1570 and 1670 form the main body of the text. . . . Each entry is followed by an essential bibliography and by a list of public collections that include works by the artist."—*p.7.* "This illustrated dictionary focuses on painters from the Southern Netherlands and from the principality of Liège, born between 1569 and 1670, whose stylistic aesthetic extends from late Mannerism to the Baroque. More than eight hundred painters are documented in this volume, which also makes mention of one hundred artists whose work is, as yet, unknown."—*p.15.*

List of abbreviations, v.1, p.19–21. Dictionary, v.1, p.23–443. Bibliography, v.1, p.445–48. Index of locations, v.1, p.449–506. Charts of stylistic influences, v.1, p.507–19. Chronological tables, v.1, p.520–36.

M465 Masters of light: Dutch painters in Utrecht during the Golden Age. [Ed. by] Joaneath A. Spicer with Lynn Federle Orr. With essays by Marten Jan Bok . . . [et al.] Baltimore, Walters Art Gallery; [San Francisco,] Fine Arts Museums of San Francisco (Distr. by Yale Univ. Pr., 1997). 480p. il. (part col.), maps.
Published in conjunction with the exhibition, Fine Arts Museums of San Francisco (1997). "The first exhibition in both America and Britain to highlight the unique achievements of the Utrecht school."—*Dir. foreword.*

Encyclopedic exploration of painting in Utrecht in the 17th century, treating patronage, religious and economic influences, the collecting of Utrecht school paintings. See also the slim companion volume: Brown, Christopher. Utrecht painters of the Dutch Golden Age. London, National Gallery Publications, 1997. 72p. il. (part col.)

Biographies, p.370–93. Notes, p.394–440. Short references, p.441–73. Index, p.474–79.

M466 Masters of seventeenth-century Dutch genre painting. Organized by Peter C. Sutton [with] Christopher Brown . . . [et al.] [Ed. by Jane Iandola Watkins.] [Philadelphia, Philadelphia Museum of Art, 1984]. lxxxviii, 397p. il. (part col.) plates.
Catalog of the exhibition, Philadelphia Museum of Art (1984), and other locations. Begins with two essay by Sutton, followed by color plates of the 127 works in the exhibition organized chronologically. Next are catalog entries arranged alphabetically by artist, with substantial essays by five scholars, along with additional illustrations, provenance, and literature.

Bibliography, p.363–93. Index of artists, p.397.

M467 National Gallery of Ireland. Later Flemish paintings in the National Gallery of Ireland: the seventeenth to nineteenth centuries. [By] David Oldfield. Dublin. National Gallery of Ireland, 1992. xvii, 194p. il., plates.
"To anyone unfamiliar with The National Gallery of Ireland, the number and quality of the later Flemish paintings may come as a pleasant surprise. . . . The strength of the collection is the . . . original paintings by the twenty-six . . . seventeenth-century painters from Antwerp other than Rubens, van Dyck, and Teniers."—*Introd.* Scholarly catalog of mostly 17th-century paintings.

Numerical index, p.164–66. Changes of attribution, p.167–68. Changes of title, p.169–70. The formation of the collection, p.171–72. Index of previous owners, p.173–75. Index of subjects, p.176–78. Index of dates, p.179–80. Bibliography, p.181–94.

M468 ______. Netherlandish fifteenth and sixteenth century paintings in the National Gallery of Ireland: a complete catalogue. [By] Christiaan Vogelaar. Dublin, The Gallery, 1987. xiv, 109p. il., plates, map.
The fourth title in a series of critical catalogs of the Old Master collections. "Describes a relatively small school consisting of no more than forty-six paintings . . . studied systematically."—*Foreword.*

Numerical index, p.95–96. Changes of attribution, p.97. Changes of title, p.98–99. Related works, p.100–102. Index of previous owners, p.103–04. Index of subjects, p.105–06.

The formation of the collection, p.107–08. Bibliography, p.109–[10].

M469 Philadelphia. Philadelphia Museum of Art. Northern European paintings in the Philadelphia Museum of Art: from the sixteenth through the nineteenth century. [By] Peter C. Sutton. Philadelphia, The Museum, 1990. xi, 400p. il. (part col.), ports.

"The Philadelphia Museum of Art's holdings of Northern European paintings are among the most extensive in the United States. Since it houses the John G. Johnson Collection (more than twelve hundred paintings) it is easily the largest repository of Dutch seventeenth-century painting (nearly three hundred works) in this country."—*Pref.* Catalogs only paintings in the permanent collection, with cross-references to the previously cataloged Johnson collection. Mostly black-and-white plates.

Includes bibliographical references. Bibliographical abbreviations, p.396–99.

M470 Repertory of Dutch and Flemish paintings in Italian public collections. [Ed. by Bert W. Meijer.] Florence, Centro Di, 1998– . (1)v. il. (part col.)

"The purpose of the project is . . . to make these paintings accessible by means of a scientifically ordered repertory. . . . The material will be divided over at least seven volumes, every volume including material of at least one, and sometimes more regions. . . . Entries have been limited to basic data."—*Introd.*

Contents: (1) Liguria.

Includes bibliographies and indexes.

M471 Slive, Seymour. Dutch painting, 1600–1800. New Haven, Yale Univ. Pr., 1995. 390p. il., plates (part col.) (Yale University Press pelican history of art)

Expanded and updated version of material originally published in the Pelican volume on Dutch art and architecture of the period (see GLAH 1:I388 for original annotation).

M472 Smeyers, Maurits. L'art de la miniature flamande du VIIIe au XVIe siècle. Trad. de Monique Verboomen. Tournai, Renaissance du livre, 1998. 528p. col. facsims.

Trans. of Vlaamse miniaturen van de 8ste tot het midden van de 16de eeuw. [Baarn], Tinion, 1998.

Survey of Flemish manuscript painting from the middle ages to the 16th century.

Bibliographie, p.505–16. Index des manuscrits, p.517–23. Index des miniatures, p.524–25. Liste des abréviations, p.526.

M473 Stechow, Wolfgang. Dutch landscape painting of the seventeenth century. 3d ed. [Reprint.] Oxford, Phaidon, 1981. x, 494p. il. (National Gallery of Art Kress Foundation studies in the history of European art, no.1)

Reprint of GLAH 1:M429, the standard study.

M474 Sutton, Peter C. The age of Rubens. With the collab. of Marjorie E. Wieseman and David Freedberg . . . [et al.] Boston, Museum of Fine Arts, [1993]. 630p. il. (part col.)

Well-illustrated catalog of the exhibition, Museum of Fine Arts, Boston (1993), and other locations. "The first international loan exhibition ever mounted in the United States to survey Flemish Baroque painting. . . . This catalog not only addresses the individual objects but also explores the historical context of the art."—*p.9.* Two introductory essays by Sutton are followed by essays on Rubens and his contemporaries. Catalog entries for 132 works are organized into 14 chapters by artists or by genre.

Bibliography, p.605–25. Index, p.626–30.

M475 ______. Dutch and Flemish seventeenth-century paintings: the Harold Samuel collection. Cambridge, Cambridge Univ. Pr., 1992, xii, 246p. [84]p. of col. plates.

Catalog of the exhibition, Barbican Art Gallery, London (1992), and other locations, of a private collection given that year to the Corporation of the City of London. "The Harold Samuel collection, comprising 84 seventeenth century Dutch and Flemish paintings, has been described as the finest private collection of such works to be formed in Britain this century."—*Introd.* Detailed entries are arranged alphabetically by artist and include provenance, exhibition history, literature, and condition report.

Bibliography, p.245–46.

M476 ______. Masters of 17th-century Dutch landscape painting. With contrib. by Albert Blankert . . . [et al.] Boston, Museum of Fine Arts, [1987]. xv, 563p. il. 123 col. plates.

Catalog of the exhibition, Rijksmuseum, Amsterdam (1987), and other locations, includes scholarly essays by Simon Schama, Josua Bruyn, and Alan Chong. 123 paintings by 57 artists are illustrated in color plates organized chronologically by work, followed by catalog entries arranged alphabetically by artist, including provenance, exhibition history, and literature.

Bibliography, p.538–61. Index of artists, p.563.

M477 Von Bruegel bis Rubens: das goldene Jahrhundert der flämischen Malerei. Hrsg. von Ekkehard Mai und Hans Vlieghe. Wien, Kunsthistorisches Museum, 1992. 646p. il. (part col.)

Catalog of the exhibition, Wallraf-Richartz-Museums, Köln (1992), and other locations, includes 21 essays on individual artists and schools by a international group of leading scholars in the field of Netherlandish art. A monumental study presenting more than 200 artists, with substantial sections on prints and drawings. Works are organized by genre or subject matter first, then alphabetically by artist.

Gemälde, p.259–480. Zeichnungen, p.481–556. Druckgraphik, p.557–612. Verzeichnis der abgekürzt zitierten Literatur, p.613–42. Verzeichnis der Leihgeber, p.643–44. Verzeichnis der Künstler, p.644–45.

M478 Valdivieso, Enrique. Pintura holandesa del siglo XVII en España. Valladolid, Universidad de Valladolid, 1973. 453p. plates.

Scholarly catalog of public and private Spanish collections of 17th-century Dutch paintings. Detailed entries, organized alphabetically by artist's name, include bibliographical references and provenance.

Contents: (1) Relaciones artisticas Hispano-Holandesas en el Siglo XVII; (2) La Pintura Holandesa en las colecciones españolas; (3) Obras y pintores representados en España; (4) Catalogo provisional de la pintura Holandesa del Siglo XVII en España; (5) Laminas.

Bibliografia, p.417–18. Inventarios de Colecciones Reales, p.419. Catálogos y guías de museos públicos, p.419. Catálogos y referencias de colecciones privadas, p.420. Catálogos de exposiciones efectoadas en España en las que figuran obras Holandesas, p.423. Obras generales y artículos, p.424. Indices, p.431–32. Indice de artistas, p.433–38. Indice de lugares, p.439–44. Indice iconográfico, p.445.

M479 Wright, Christopher. Dutch pictures in the collection of Her Majesty the Queen. Cambridge, Cambridge Univ. Pr., 1982. xcii, 344p. 250 plates, il. (The pictures in the collection of Her Majesty the Queen)

Divided chronologically into 3 sections: 16th, 17th, and 18th century. Short entries for 306 paintings are then arranged alphabetically by artist, followed by a section of black-and-white reproductions.

Bibliography, p.lxxiii–lxxxv. List of abbreviations, p.lxxxvii–xc. List of comparative illustrations, p.xci–xcii. Appendix, p.333–36. Index of subjects, p.337–38. Index of artists, p.338–42. Index of previous owners, p.342–44.

SEE ALSO: Collections of the National Gallery of Art: systematic catalogue (GLAH 2:M31).

New Zealand

M480 Brown, Gordon H., and Keith, Hamish. An introduction to New Zealand painting, 1839–1980. Rev. and enl. ed. Auckland, Collins, [1982]. 240p. il. (part col.)

1st ed., London, Collins, 1969.

"This book aims at simply being a general introduction to the subject."—*p.7.* "Except for the correction of errors in the original text, and amendments related to the ownership of paintings reproduced, the text remains unchanged up to page 157. [Remaining chapters] have been revised or extended to outline major developments since 1967. A general chapter has been added to extend the survey up to 1980."—*p.11.*

Contents: (1) The colonials; (2) Charles Heaphy; (3) William Fox; (4) Reverend John Kinder; (5) Arrivals and departures; (6) James McLachlan Nairn; (7) Petrus Van der Velden; (8) The search for a national identity; (9) Christopher Perkins; (10) The nineteen-forties; (11) Mountford Tosswill Woollaston; (12) Contemporary developments, 1947–1967; (13) Colin McCahon; (14) Patrick Hanly; (15) Painting in the seventies.

Sources, p.222–27. Index, p.228–40.

M481 Docking, Gil. Two hundred years of New Zealand painting. With additions by Michael Dunn covering 1970–90. Rev. ed. [Auckland], D. Batemen, [1990]. 248p. il. (part col.), ports.

See GLAH 1:M430 for 1st ed.

This revised ed. includes substantial new material updating the 1st ed., which covered up to 1971, including sections on neoexpressionism, recent abstractionists, new realism, Maori and Polynesian printing, and postmodernism, and a new bibliography of painting since 1970. The text concentrates on individual painters of the 19th and 20th centuries, divided chronologically into chapters under the broad headings: exploration, settlement, transition, and new impulses.

Notes, p.241–43. Bibliography, p.244. Index, p.245–48.

M482 Friedlander, Marti. Contemporary New Zealand painters. Photographs by Marti Friedlander. Text by Jim Barr and Mary Barr. Martinborough, N.Z., Taylor, 1980– . (1)v. il. (part col.)

"This is the first of two books about New Zealand painters in their environments. It is a record of the places in which they live, how they work and the way they see themselves and their paintings."—*p.7.* The works of 22 painters are illustrated in colorful, oversize plates, along with informal portraits of the artists and their homes. The first, and only published vol. to date, covers artists A–M.

Biographies, p.164–69. Sources, p.171–72. Index, p.173–74.

Russia and Eastern Europe

M483 Alpatov, Mikhail Vladimirovich. Drevnerusskaia ikonopis' = Early Russian icon painting. [Trans. by N. Johnstone.] Izd. 3. Moskva, "Iskusstvo," 1984. 330p. col. il.

See GLAH 1:M431 for earlier ed.

History of Russian and Byzantine icon painting from the 12th to the 17th century. Essays in Russian and English are followed by 203 color plates and bilingual entries arranged alphabetically by artist's name.

List of plates, p.325–[31].

M484 Benois, Alexandre. Istoriia russkoĭ zhivopisi v XIX veke. [Reprint.] Moskva, Izd-vo "Respublika," 1995. 446p. il. (part col.)

See GLAH 1:M432 for 1st ed.

Welcome reprint of a standard history of 19th-century Russian painting.

Notes, p.[420]–29. Bibliography, p.[430]–44. List of illustrations, p.445–[47].

M485 Bird, Alan. A history of Russian painting. Boston, Hall, [1987]. 303p. il., 16 col. plates, map.

Concise textbook history of Russian painting organized chronologically by movement.

Contents: (1) The development of the icon; (2) The establishment of Moscow as capital; the decline of icon painting; and the growth of secular art; (3) The triumphs of Russian painters in the eighteenth century; (4) The apotheosis of academic art; (5) Art outside the academy: Tropinin, Kiprensky, Venetsianov, and Fedotov; (6) The revolt against the academy and the growth of a self-consciously nationalist school; (7) "Fin-de-siècle" movements and reactions against the nationalist school; (8) Painting in ferment; (9) Primitivism and modernism before 1914; (10) 1914–1917: years of hectic modernism; (11) Art and revolution; (12) Malevich and Tatlin: the inability and unwillingness of artists to present a united front; (13) Proletarianism and the artist: the revival of easel painting; (14) Socialist realism; coercion of painters into disciplined organizations; Soviet art; (15) The thaw; freedom within the tenets of Socialist realism; dissidence among painters.

Notes, p.281–95. Bibliography, p.[296]–99. Index, p.300–03.

M486 Bowlt, John E., and Misler, Nicoletta. Twentieth-century Russian and East European painting: the Thyssen-Bornemisza collection. Gen. ed. Irene Martin. [London], Zwemmer (Distr. by Rizzoli, 1993). 329p. il. (part col.)

One in a series of comprehensive catalogs documenting one of the world's premier private art collections. "The catalogue of the twentieth-century Russian and Eastern European paintings in the Thyssen-Bornemisza Collection is written by two of the eminent scholars in the field. . . . Their three introductory essays put the works in context and are accompanied by a glossary of terms and acronyms for easy reference."—*p.[8]*. Exhaustive entries, arranged alphabetically by artist, describe 59 works by 34 artists and include provenance, exhibition history, literature, an essay, and large color plates.

Notes on the catalogue, p.44–45. List of works, p.46. Catalogue, p.48–299. Abbreviations, p.300. Glossary of terms and acronyms, p.302–05. Selected bibliography, p.306–10. Artists' biographies, p.311–21. Index, p.323.

M487 Bown, Matthew Cullerne. A dictionary of twentieth century Russian and Soviet painters, 1900–1980s. London, Izomar, [1998]. 372p. il.

"Intended for art historians, critics, art dealers, collectors, students and others with an interest in twentieth century Russian and Soviet art. . . . Provides a comprehensive roster of painters (approximately 13,000 names) . . . and offers concise biographical details."—*p.vii.*

M488 Derzhavnyi muzei ukrainskoho obrazotvorchoho mystetstva URSR. Spirit of Ukraine: 500 years of painting: selections from the State Museum of Ukrainian Art, Kiev. Winnipeg, Winnipeg Art Gallery, 1991. 333p. col. il.

Catalog of the exhibition, Winnipeg Art Gallery (1991), and other locations, celebrating the centenary of Ukrainian settlement in Canada. Text in both English and Ukrainian. Covers more than half a millenium of Ukrainian painting, arranged chronologically, with short essays on both the artists and the individual works.

Contents: (1) The development of Ukrainian painting, by Daria Zelska-Darewyck; (2) Ukrainian art of the 15th–18th centuries, by Larysa Chlenova; (3) The Ukrainian icon, by Sviatioslav Hordynsky; (4) Ukrainian art of the 19th–Early 20th century, by Iryna Horbachova; (5) The inconsequential in Ukrainian painting: in defense of Gerre, by Myroslava M. Mudrak; (6) The avant-garde in Ukraine, by Liudmyla Kovalska; (7) Ukrainian art and the twentieth century international avant-garde, by Gerald Needham; (8) Mykhailo Boichuk and his school, by Liudmyla Kovalska and Nelli Prystalenko; (9) The Boichuk School—theoretical underpinning, by Myroskav Shkandrij.

Editorial notes, p.332.

M489 Galeria de Arta Nationala (Romania). The National Gallery: Romanian painting in the collection of the Art Museum of the Socialist Republic of Romania. By Alexandru Cebuc. [Trans. from the Romanian by Ştephan Stoenescu and Thomas C. Carlson.] Bucharest, [Galeria de Arta Nationala,] 1984. 393p. il. (part col.)

Survey of 19th- and 20th-century Romanian painting in Romania's National Gallery. 268 works by 70 painters are presented in an oversize format with large color plates and brief entries for each painting.

Selected bibliography, p.73–[77].

M490 Gamulin, Grgo. Hrvatsko slikarstvo XIX. stoljeća. Zagreb, Naprijed, 1995. 407p. il. (part col.) (Povijest umjetnosti u Hrvatsko, sv.1)

In Serbo-Croatian (romanized). Beautifully illustrated survey of 19th-century Croatian painting. 165 artists are presented chronologically by movement. Taking advantage of large, color plates, this well-organized catalog is a helpful introduction to a group of seldom seen artists. See also the companion vol. on the 20th century (following title).

Kazalo imena [index], p.399–404.

M491 ———. Hrvatsko slikarstvo na prijelazu iz XIX. u XX. stoljeće. Zagreb, Naprijed, 1995. 381p. il. (part col.) (Povijest umjetnosti u Hrvatsko, sv.2)

Continues the preceding title, extending coverage into the 20th century.

Bibliografija, p.355–64. Kazalo imena [index], p.375–80.

M492 ———. Hrvatsko slikarstvo XX. stoljeća. Zagreb, Naprijed, 1987–88. 2v. il. (part col.) (Povijest umjetnosti u Hrvatsko, sv.3–4)

In Serbo-Croatian (romanized). Substantial survey of 20th-century Croatian painting.

Includes bibliographical references, v.1, p.526–38, v.2, p.579–88, and indexes.

M493 Gosudarstvennyi Ermitazh (Russia). Drevnerusskaia zhivopis' v sobranii Ermitazha = Early Russian painting in the Hermitage Collection. By A. Kostsova. Saint Petersburg, "Iskusstva," 1992. 486p. col. il.

Catalog of Medieval Russian painting from the collection of the Hermitage Museum, including icons, book miniatures, and ornaments from the 13th to the early 17th century. "Besides the usual information (title, the description of subject, dating, technique and dimensions, provenance, state of preservation, restorations, exhibitions, and bibliography) the catalog describes iconography with the features typical of different icons, and gives substantiation of dating and attribution, with references to relevant scholarly publications."—*p.479.*

Includes a useful summary and a list of illustrations in English. No general index or bibliography.

M494 Gosudarstvennaia Tret'iakovskaia Galereia. The Tretyakov Gallery, Moscow: Russian and Soviet painting. [Introd. and comp. by Lydia Iovleva. Trans. by Kristina Staros.] Leningrad, Aurora, [1986.] [343]p. il. (part col.)

Catalog of the painting collection the largest museum of Russian and Soviet art in Russia. "This volume presents the collection of paintings from the eleventh to the twentieth centuries, the most significant and interesting part of the museum."—*p.5.* 143 artists are discussed in sections organized chronologically by movement in a colorful, oversize format. Each chapter begins with an essay followed by reproductions, arranged alphabetically by artist.

Index of artists, p.[343].

M495 Jugoslovensko slikarstvo šeste decenije. Beograd, Muzej savremene umetnosti, 1980. 444p. il. (Jugoslovenska umetnost XX veka, 6)

Catalog of the exhibition, Muzej savremene umetnosti, Beograd (1980), presenting 440 paintings by 183 Yugoslavian artists from the tumultuous decade of the 1950s. 14 scholarly essays covering the years 1950–62, with French summaries.

Katalog, p.144–52. Dokumentacija, p.337–38. Pregled grupnih izložbi sa bibliografijom, p.418–34. Biografije i literatura o umetnicima, p.418–34. Resume, p.435–44.

M496 Kaufmann, Thomas DaCosta. The school of Prague: painting at the court of Rudolf II. Chicago, Univ. of Chicago Pr., [1988]. xix, 305p. il. (part col.), map.

Survey of 16th-century Czechoslovakian painting with information on the expatriate painters who were forced to leave under Rudolf II. This book is a "thoroughly revised version of my L'École de Prague: la peinture à la cour de Rodolphe II [Paris, Flammarion, 1985]."—*Pref.* Includes an introductory essay followed by a catalogue raisonné of paintings executed by the court artists.

Contents: (1) The Emperor and the arts; (2) The Emperor's artists; (3) The artist's tasks: genres of painting in Rudofine Prague; (4) Prague painting; modes of art and the modern style; (5) Painting at the court of Rudolf II and its place in the history of art.

Chronology, p.xi–xv. Notes, p.117–30. Bibliography, p.293–96. Index, p.297–304.

M497 Mansbach, Steven A. Standing in the tempest: painters of the Hungarian avant-garde 1908–1930. With contrib. by Richard V. West . . . [et al.] Santa Barbara, Santa Barbara Museum of Art; Cambridge, Mass., MIT Pr., 1991. 240p. il. (part col.)

Catalog of the exhibition, Santa Barbara Museum of Art (1991), and other locations, surveying Hungarian painting at the beginning of the 20th century. This beautifully designed catalog focuses on a revolutionary time in Hungary's history, placing important artistic achievements in an historical context. 168 works by 43 painters are illustrated.

Comparative chronology, p.187–211. Select bibliography, p.213–27. Checklist, p.228–38. Index, p.238–40.

M498 Masterworks of Russian painting from Soviet museums. [Sel. and introd. by Tatyana Ilyina. Trans. by Alexander Repyev.] Leningrad, Aurora Art, 1989. 295p. il. (part col.), ports.

Oversize catalog presenting the highlights of various Russian collections with selections by 78 painters. Each section, arranged chronologically, begins with an essay followed by entries for each artist and individual works. Large color plates and biographically essays enhance the research value of this work.

Contents: (1) The sources of the tradition: 11th to 17th century; (2) From Baroque to Romanticism: late 17th to early 19th century; (3) The age of Realism: 19th century; (4) The reappraisal of values: late 19th and early 20th centuries.

Bibliography, p.292–93. Literature, p.293–94. Index of painters, p.295.

M499 Nineteenth century Polish painting. [Catalog ed. by Agnieszka Morawińska.] N.Y., National Academy of Design, 1988. 180p. il. (part col.)

Introductory catalog of the exhibition, National Academy of Design (1988), prepared in conjunction with the National Museum in Warsaw, presenting 45 painters from 19th-century Poland. Organized chronologically by artist, catalog entries follow a brief essay Polish painting of the 19th century by Agnieszka Morawińska. Short biographies are given for each painter along with bibliographical references. Entries for each work include a brief statement and bibliography.

Index of Artists, p.21. Catalogue, p.23–172. Bibliography, p.173–78.

M500 La peinture roumaine 1800–1940. [Textes, Titus Hasdeu . . . (et al.)] [Anvers], Pandora, 1995. 256p. il. (part col.), maps.

Catalog of the exhibition, Hessenhuis, Anvers (1995), devoted to Romanian painting of the 19th and 20th centuries. Includes a series of essays on the subject.

Index biographique, p.242–52. Bibliographie générale, p.253.

M501 Pskov icons, 13th-16th centuries. [Introd. articles by Mikhail Alpatov and Irina Rodnikova. Cat. by Irina Rodnikova. Trans. by Anne Hansen Staros.] Leningrad, Aurora Art, [1991]. 318p. il. (part col.)

Major study of icon painting in the city of Pskov. Extensive catalog entries, arranged chronologically, include detailed color reproductions along with provenance, bibliography, exhibition history, and individual essays.

Contents: (1) The painting of Old Pskov, by Mikhail Alpatov; (2) The Pskov School of icon-painting, by Irina Rodnikova.

Catalogue, explanatory notes, p.290–315. Literature, list of abbreviations, p.316–17. Selected readings, p.317–18. List of exhibitions, p.319.

M502 Romanian painting. [Essays by] Vasile Drauţ . . . [et al.] [Rev. ed.] Trans. into English by Sylvia-May Oldfield Florescu and Florin Ionescu. Bucharest, Meridiane, 1977. 454p. il. (part col.)

1st ed. Bucharest, Meridiane, 1970. Trans. of Pictura românească în imagini, 1977. This ed. includes 600 illustrations, 315 in color.

Expanded version of a major study of Romanian painting, concentrating on the 19th and 20th centuries. "It has been revised and rearranged in the light of remarks and suggestions published in the press, and in keeping with changes which have occurred in the fields of research and creation themselves (this being notably the case of the final chapter). Departing from the formula reminiscent of an illustrated dictionary that was used in the first ed., the second has fewer illustrations."—*p.[8].*

Selected bibliography, p.441–[45]. Index of names and places, p.447–54.

M503 Rosiis'kyi zhyvopys v muzeiakh Ukraïny: al'bom = Russian painting in Ukrainan [sic] museums. [Avtory-uporiadnyky D. Kolesnykova, M. Faktorovych.] Kyïv, Vyd-vo Mystetstvo, 1986. 294p. col. il.

This study of Russian painting in Ukrainian museums, presented in a handsome, oversize format, begins with Old Russian icon paintings and ends with the 1960s. Large color plates are followed by catalog entries, arranged alphabetically by artist, including a thumb-nail reproduction as well as brief essay. Summaries and a list of illustrations in English enhance the volume's research value. A summary brochure in French accompanies some copies.

Summary in English, p.277–81.

M504 Russian avant-garde art: the George Costakis collection. [Gen. ed. Angelica Zander Rudenstine. Introd. by S. Frederick Starr.] [N.Y., Abrams, 1981.] 527p. il. (part col.)

Superb catalog published in conjunction with an exhibition, Solomon R. Guggenheim Museum (1981), of the Russian paintings once owned by George Costakis, now in the Tretyakov Gallery. This collection was assembled during Costakis' 30 years in Russia and the book documents his struggle collecting the paintings as well as difficulties leaving the collection to Russia. Includes a chronology of the visual arts alongside politics, literature, and the performing arts from 1894 to 1934.

Contents: (1) Collecting art of the avant-garde, by George Costakis; (2) The George Costakis collection: biographies, by Vasilii Rakitin, documentation, by Angelica Zander Rudenstine; (3) Chronology, by John E. Bowlt.

Index, p.520–27.

M505 Szabó, Júlia. Painting in nineteenth century Hungary. [Trans. by Ilona Patay.] [Budapest], Corvina, [1988]. 322p. il. (part col.)

Trans. of XIX. Század festészete Magyarországon. Budapest, Corvina, 1985.

This study of 19th-century Hungarian art begins with an essay, thoroughly indexed with references to the plates. "In the history of Hungarian art, the nineteenth century occupies a unique place, having been so far the most important epoch of all."—*p.7.* Entries are arranged chronologically and include short statements along with title, date, medium, size, and location. The biography section includes plate numbers and serves as an index.

A short bibliography, p.312–14. Artist biographies and plate references, p.314–22. Index of places outside present-day Hungary, p.[323].

M506 Two centuries of Hungarian painters, 1820–1970: a catalogue of the Nicolas M. Salgó collection. Washington, D.C., American Univ. Pr. (Distr. by National Book Network, 1991). 335p. il. (part col.)

Catalog of an important private American collection featuring 108 Hungarian painters of the 19th and 20th centuries. Organized chronologically, each artist receives a short biography, and each work is presented in large, color plates along with brief comments, provenance, and bibliography.

Selected bibliography, p.303–08. Index and biographies of the artists, p.309–35.

Scandinavia

M507 1880-årene i nordisk maleri. [Oslo], Nasjonalgalleriet, 1985. 311p. il. (part col.)

Beautifully illustrated catalog of the exhibition, Nasjonalgalleriet, Oslo (1985), and other locations. Foreign language versions published for each exhibition venue.

Prepared as the Scandinavian response to American scholar Kirk Varnedoe's exhibition Northern light (see GLAH 2:M519). Presents 126 works by artists who flourished in and around 1880. Entries are arranged alphabetically by artist, with an short essay, provenance, exhibition history, and literature history.

Contents: (1) Nordiskt 80-tal: verklighet, luft och ljus, by S. Ringbom; (2) Konstnärsrevolterna, by B. Lindwall; (3) Sosial tendens-kunst, by K. Berg and O. Thue; (4) Kunstnerkolonien på Skagen, by H. Westergaard.

Kalendarium, p.292–97. Bibliografi, utstillinger, p.298–300. Summary in English, p.301–310.

M508 Askeland, Jan. Norsk malerkunst: hovedlinjer gjennom 200 år. [Oslo], Cappelens, [1981]. 342p. il. (part col.)

Chronological textbook of Norwegian painting from the 18th–20th century. Treats individual artists by movement or school.

Contents: (1) 1700-Tallet; (2) 1800-Tallet; (3) 1900-Tallet.

Anvendt litteratur, p.329–[31]. Noter, p.333–38. Register, p.339–[43].

M509 Danske Kalkmalerier. Kobenhavn, Nationalmuseet, 1985–92. 8v. il. (part col.)

Survey of Medieval, Romanesque, and Renaissance Danish mural painting.

Contents: (1) Romansk tid 1080–1175; (2) Senromansk tid 1175–1275; (3) Tidling gotik, 1275–1375; (4) Gotik 1375–1475; (5) Sengotik 1475–1500; (6) Sengotik 1500–1536; (7) Efter reformationen, 1536–1700; (8) Registerbind.

Indexes in v.8: Indhold-bind 1–7, p.5–14. Forfattere, p.15–16. Landkort, p.17–37. Ordforklaringer, p.38–40. Registre, p.41–[62].

M510 Dreams of a summer night: Scandinavian painting at the turn of the century. Organized by the Nordic Council of Ministers and the Arts Council of Great Britain. [Catalog ed. and prod. by Leena Ahtola-Moorhouse, Carl Tomas Edam and Birgitta Schreiber.] [London], Arts Council of Great Britain, 1986. 328p. il. (part col.), map, ports.

Catalog of the exhibition, Hayward Gallery, London (1986), and other locations, presenting 38 artists from 5 countries. Foreign language versions published for each exhibition venue. "Artists are listed alphabetically and works by the same artist are listed in chronological order. The title of each work is given in English, as well as in the original language."—*p.63.*

Chronology, p.308–20. Selected bibliography, p.321–27.

M511 Gunnarsson, Torsten. Nordic landscape painting in the nineteenth century. Trans. by Nancy Adler. New Haven, Yale Univ. Pr., 1998. ix, 293p. il. (part col.)

"This book represents the first attempt to offer an overall view of the history of Nordic landscape painting in the nineteenth century."—*Foreword.* Arranged thematically, "according to the types of landscape that were predominant at different periods."

Notes, p.274–79. Select bibliography, p.280–87. Index, p.288–93.

M512 Monrad, Kasper. The golden age of Danish painting. Catalog by Kasper Monrad. Essays by Philip Conisbee . . . [et al.] N.Y., Hudson Hills Pr.; Los Angeles, Los Angeles County Museum of Art (Distr. by National Book Network, [1993]). 237p. il. (part col.)

Beautifully illustrated catalog of the exhibition, Los Angeles County Museum of Art (1993), and other locations, featuring 105 works by 17 Romantic Danish artists from the first half of the 19th century. The first large-scale exhibition of Danish paintings in the United States. Arranged alphabetically by artist, each entry begins with a biography followed by illustrations and catalog data.

Contents: (1) The Copenhagen school of painting, by Kasper Monrad; (2) "A small, poor country": Danish Society during the Golden Age, by Hans Vammen; (3) Bertel Thorvaldsens painting collection, by Bjarne Jørnaes; (4) Ordinariness and light: Danish painting of the Golden Age, by Philip Conisbee; (5) Catalogue, by Kasper Monrad.

Abbreviated references, p.223–32. Index, p.233–37.

M513 Nasjonalgalleriet (Norway). Norske malerier: katalog. [Redak., Marit Lange og Tone Skedsmo.] Oslo, Nasjonalgalleriet, 1992. 600p. il.

Comprehensive catalog of the Museum's Norwegian painting collection, arranged alphabetically by artist. Focuses on the works with minimal biographical material. Each painting illustrated by small black-and-white reproduction.

Fortegnelse etter inventarnummer, p.555–99.

M514 Norges malerkunst. [Redak., Knut Berg.] Oslo, Gyldendal norsk forlag, 1993. 2v. il. (part col.)

Concise, scholarly history of Norwegian painting from 1200 through the 1980s. Contains revised and updated chapters on works originally published in Norge kunsthistorie (7v.), 1981–1983 (see GLAH 2:I459). This well-illustrated vol. also contains a chapter on Norwegian printmaking.

Contents: (1) Fra middelalderen til 1900; (2) Vårt eget århundre.

Bibliografi, v.2, p.459–[69]. Register, v.2, p.471-[93].

M515 Ny Carlsberg Glyptotek. Danish painting of the golden age: catalogue. By Hans Edvard Nørregård-Nielsen. [Copenhagen], Ny Carlsberg Glyptotek, 1995. 305p. il. (part col.)

Trans. of Dansk guldalder maleri. Copenhagen, Glyptotek, 1995.

"This is part of a series of catalogues of the collection in the Ny Carlsberg Glyptotek."—*t.p. verso.* Small, beautifully illustrated catalog, organized alphabetically by artist, documenting 116 works by 21 Danish painters of the 19th century owned by the Museum.

Literature, p.301–03. Concordance, p.304–05.

M516 Scandinavian modernism: painting in Denmark, Finland, Iceland, Norway, and Sweden, 1910–1920. [Catalog prod. and ed. by Carl Tomas Edam, Nils-Göran Hökby, and Birgitta Schreiber.] [Trans. from Danish, Finish, Norwegian, and Swedish by Martha Gaber Abrahamsen. Trans. from French by David Macey. Trans. from Icelandic by Adalsteinn Ingólfsson.] Sweden, Nordic Council of Ministers, 1989. 262p. il. (part col.), ports.

Catalog of the exhibition, Göteborgs Konstmuseum, Gothenburg (1989), and other locations. A general survey of early 20th-century Scandinavian painting, covering 31 artists from 5 countries. "Artists are listed alphabetically and works by the same artist are listed in chronological order. The title of each work is given in English as well as the original language."—*p.71.*

Contents: (1) Scandinavian art seen from afar, by Serge Fauchereau; (2) The modernistic movement in Denmark, by Hanne Abildgäard; (3) The breakthrough in Finland, by Olli Valkonen; (4) The early years of Icelandic art, by Bera Nordag; (5) Norway's attitude towards modernism 1910–1920, by Trygve Nergäard; (6) Sweden and modernism: the art of the 1910s, by Folke Lalander.

Selected bibliography, p.254–60. Index to lenders, p.261.

M517 Schwartz, Alba. Skagen. [Reprint.] [Kobenhavn], Andersens, [1981]. 2v. il. (part col.), ports.

Originally published as Skagen: den svundne tid I sagn og billeder. Kobenhavn, Gyldendal, 1912 and Skagen: den nye tid, oplszelser og indtryk. Kobenhavn, Gyldendal, 1913.

Welcome reprinting of a personalized history of the painters and artists colony of Skagen, Denmark. Many interesting photographs, as well as examples of poetry and dialog of the period.

Contents: (1) Den svundne tid, I, sagn of billeder; (2) Den nye tid, I, oplevelser og indtryk.

Notes for both books at the end of v.2, p.[223].

M518 Varnedoe, Kirk. Northern light: Nordic art at the turn of the century. New Haven, Yale Univ. Pr., 1988. 285p. il. (part col.)

Monograph prepared by the curator after the close of the exhibition "Northern lights: realism and symbolism in Scandinavian painting, 1880–1910" (see following title), providing expanded coverage of the theme and several post-1900 artists. "In reshaping the exhibition catalog as a book . . . I have attempted to include several painters and paintings that were not present in the original version."—*p.7.* "The paintings are organized alphabetically by artist, with the artist's biography appearing just before his or her initial painting. . . . For the convenience of readers we have also provided a classification of the painters by country; as well as a chronological ordering of the paintings."—*p.11.*

Catalogue notes, p.11–12. Chronological list of paintings, p.38. Footnotes, p.277–78. Selected bibliography, p.279–85.

M519 ———. Northern lights: realism and symbolism in Scandinavian painting, 1880–1910. [N.Y.], Brooklyn Museum, [1982]. 240p. il. (part col.), map.

Scholarly catalog of the exhibition, Corcoran Gallery of Art, Washington, D.C. (1982), and other locations. Comprehensive look at turn-of-the-century Scandinavian art, seen for the first time in many American venues. Catalog presents 36 artists, organized alphabetically, with contributions from 17 international scholars.

Contents: (1) Nationalism, internationalism, and the progress of Scandinavian art, by Kirk Varnedoe; (2) Artistic revolution in Nordic countries, by Bo Lindwall; (3) Patronage and patrimony, by Tone Skedsmo; (4) George Brandes, cultural emissary, by Sven Møller Kristensen; (5) Art in Iceland at the turn of the century, by Selma Jónsdóttir; (6) The Scandinavian artists' colony in France, by Salme Sarajas-Korte; (7) Scandinavian painting and the French critics, by Emily Braun.

Selected bibliography, p.236–40. Index to lenders, p.240.

Spain and Portugal

M520 Ainaud de Lasarte, Joan. Catalan painting. [Trans. by Michael Heron.] N.Y., Rizzoli, 1990–92. 3v. col. il.

Trans. of La Pintura Catalana. Barcelona, Carroggio, 1989–91.

Scholarly work with coverage from Romanesque mural painting to contemporary Catalan painting. "The first volume dealing with Romanesque art took as its starting point the actual works, grouped for easier understanding although in a way that inevitably proved conventional. In the second, the artists' names were often fleshed out by biographical material, yet insight into their ideas and aims was not possible. In this third volume, however, alongside the works treated we shall hear the artists' own voice, as well as that of critics, commentators, and contemporary poets and prose writers."—*Introd.*

Contents: (1) The fascination of the romanesque; (2) From Gothic splendor to the Baroque; (3) From the nineteenth to the surprising twentieth century.

Each vol. includes bibliography.

M521 Barcelona (Spain). Museo de Arte Moderno. Catàleg de pintura segles XIX i XX: fons del Museu d'Art Modern. [Barcelona], Ajuntament de Barcelona, [1987]. 2v. il. (part col.)

Exhaustive catalog of the 19th- and 20th-century Spanish painting collection at the Museo de Arte Moderno, Barcelona. Entries, printed three to a page, are organized alphabetically by artist's name, then chronologically by works. Entries are brief but complete with thumb-nail illustrations of every work, most in black and white. Some entries include bibliographies and short observations.

Bibliografia, p.1131. Índex d'artistes, p.1132–36. Índex de procedéncies, p.1137–41.

M522 Brown, Jonathan. The golden age of painting in Spain. New Haven, Yale Univ. Pr., 1991. ix, 330p. il. (part col.)

Also published as La edad de oro de la pintura en España. Madrid, Nerea, 1991.

"In organizing the book, I have sought to maintain a balance between narrative and interpretation. The emphasis is on the careers of the major painters. . . . I have abandond a monographic approach—one chapter per major artist—and tried to show how they functioned within their microcultures."—*Introd.*

Contents: (1) The arrival of the Renaissance 1480–1560; (2) The revolution of Philip II; (3) El Greco; (4) Crosscurrents in Castile 1598–1621; (5) Nascent naturalism, Seville 1575–1625; (6) The dawn of a new Golden Age, Madrid 1620–1640; (7) The art of immediacy, Seville 1625–1640; (8) Jusepe de Ribera, a Spaniard in Italy; (9) Collectors and collections; (10) Painting in transition, Madrid 1640–1665; (11) Seville at mid-century 1640–1660; (12) The new era in Andalusia 1660–1700; (13) A grand finale.

Notes, p.315–18. Bibliography, p.319–23. Index, p.324–30.

M523 Cien años de pintura en España y Portugal (1830–1930). [Dir. de la obra, José Manuel Arnáiz . . . (et al.)] [Madrid] Antiguaria, [1988–1993]. 11v. il. (part col.)

Biographical dictionary of Spanish and Portugese painters flourishing from 1830 to 1930. Short entries include bibliographical notes. Many are illustrated.

Following v.1, separate indexes and bibliographies are found in most vols.

M524 De Greco à Picasso. [Catalog by Jose Manuel Pita Andrade and Julian Gallego.] Paris, Musée du Petit Palais, [1987]. 445p. col. il. (Cinq siècles d'art espagnol)

Catalog of the exhibition, Musée du Petit Palais, Paris (1987–88), presenting 155 works by 68 painters. Illustrated entries include exhibition history and bibliography.

Contents: (1) Un "siècle d'or" dans la peinture espagnole, par José Manuel Pita Andrade; (2) Le refus du classique, par Julián Gállego; (3) Catalogue: Le portrait de cour, Sánchez Coello; Le Greco et la peinture à Tolède; Ribalta, Ribera et la peinture à Valence; Velàzquez et son atelier; la peinture Madrilène; La peinture andalouse; Natures mortes "vanités" and peinture de fleurs au XVIIe siècle.

Expositions, p.427–29. Bibliographie, p.430–45.

M525 Dictionnaire de la peinture espagnole et portugaise du moyen âge à nos jours. Préf. d'Alfonso E. Pérez Sánchez. Paris, Larousse, [1989]. 319p. il. (part col.)
Biographical dictionary of Spanish and Portuguese painters since the middle ages with entries by 23 collaborating scholars. Well organized and easy to use. Includes more than 350 artists, illustrated with 120 color plates.

Extensive and useful bibliography, p.312–19, covering general works, exhibition catalogs, and major museum collection catalogs.

M526 Gaya Nuño, Juan Antonio. La pintura española del siglo XX. 2d ed. [Madrid], Ibérico Europea, [1972]. 440p., il. (part col.) (Colección arte contemporaneo)
See GLAH 1:M473 for earlier ed.

Chronological study of the major movements and painters in Spain from 1900 to 1970, concentrating on Picasso, Gris, and Miró. Published in an oversize format, copiously illustrated with large color plates.

Bibliografia, ordenada pr capítulos, p.[443–46]. Indice alfabetico de pintores, p.[447–50].

M527 Gudiol, Josep, and Alcolea i Blanch, Santiago. Pintura gótica catalana. [Barcelona], Poligrafa, [1986]. 494p. il. (part col.), plates
Extensive survey of nearly 700 Catalan paintings of the 14th and 15th centuries. Entries, organized chronologically, include biography and complete references. These are followed by 92 color plates and more than 1,000 black-and-white reproductions with convenient cross-references.

Contents: (1) Pintura lineal protogótica; (2) Pintura Italo-Gótica; (3) Pintura Gótica internacional; (4) La segunda mitad del siglo XV.

Apéndice, p.207–10. Illustraciones, p.211–464. Índices temáticos, p.465–85. Bibliografía, p.487–94.

M528 Historia de la pintura española. New ed. Madrid, Instituto Diego Velazquez, 1983– . (3)v. il., plates (Consejo superior de investigaciones cientificas)
See GLAH 1:M468 for earlier ed.

3 vols. of this ambitious series documenting the complete repertory of Spanish painting have been revised and reissued. Each well-illustrated vol. is organized alphabetically by artist with biography, inventory of works, and chronology.

Contents: (1) Angulo Iñiguez, Diego, and Pérez Sánchez, Alfonso E. Escuela madrileña del primer tercio del siglo XVII (1983); (3) Angulo Iñiguez, Diego, and Pérez Sánchez, Alfonso E. Escuela madrileña del segundo tercio del siglo XVII (1983); (4) Valdivieso, Enrique, and Serrera Contreras, Juan Miguel. Escuela sevillana del primer tercio de siglo XVII (1985).

Bibliographies, indexes in each vol.

M529 Jordan, William B., and Cherry, Peter. Spanish still life from Velázquez to Goya. London, National Gallery (Distr. by Yale Univ. Pr., [1995]). 224p. il. (part col.)
Catalog of the exhibition, National Gallery of Art, London (1995), and other locations. Beautifully illustrated study of Spanish still-life painting, organized chronologically, focusing on the individual painters' lives and works.

Notes, p.186–202. Bibliography, p.203–08. Index, p.220–24.

M530 Lafuente Ferrari, Enrique. Breve historia de la pintura española. Pres., Joan Sureda. Amplicación bibliográfica, Agustín Valle Garagorri. 5a ed. [Madrid], Akal, [1987]. 2v. il. (part col.) (Arte y estetica, 6–7)
See GLAH 1:M476 for earlier eds.

The 5th ed. of this popular, concise history of Spanish painting contains additional bibliography and text.

Bibliografie, p.537–56. Cuadros sinopticos de la historia de la pintura Española, p.559–607. Indexes, p.611–44. Apéndice, amplicación bibliografia, p.647–73. Apéndice al texto, p.675–81. Índice de illustraciones, p.683–701. Índice general, p.[702–04].

M531 Llompart, Gabriel. La pintura medieval mallorquina: su entorno cultural y su iconografia. Palma de Mallorca, [Luis Ripoll], 1977–1980. 4v. il. (Colección eura)
Thorough, scholarly survey of the medieval painting of Mallorca.

Contents: (1) La pintura medieval mallorquina; (2) La iconografía de la vida diaria: el trabajo; (3) Catálogo de las obras de la pintura medieval mallorquina, siglos XIII–XVI; (4) Documentación de archivo de la pintura medieval mallorquina, siglos XIII–XVI.

Each vol. includes cumulative indexes. Bibliography, v.1, p.18–39.

M532 Mallory, Nina A. El Greco to Murillo: Spanish painting in the Golden Age, 1556–1700. [N.Y.], HarperCollins, 1990. xx, 316p. il. (IconEditions)
Also published as Del Greco a Murillo: la pintura española del Siglo de Oro, 1556–1700. Madrid, Alianza Ed., 1991.

Concise history of Spanish painting of the 16th and 17th centuries.

Contents: (1) Spanish painting in the second half of the sixteenth century; (2) El Greco (1541–1614); (3) Early Baroque painting in Seville; (4) Early Baroque painting in Castile; (5) Jusepe de Ribera (1591–1652); (6) Francisco de Zurbarán (1598–1664); (7) Alonso Cano (1601–1667); (8) Diego de Silva y Velázquez (1599–1660); (9) The school of Madrid, I; (10) Baroque painting in Seville; (11) The school of Madrid, II.

Bibliography, p.295–304. Index, p.305–16.

M533 La pintura de historia del siglo XIX en España. [Dir. científica, José Luis Díez.] Madrid, Museo del Prado, [1992]. 493p. il. (part col.)
Beautifully illustrated catalog of the exhibition, Salas del antiguo Museo Español de Arte Contemporáneo, Madrid (1992–93), presenting 19th-century Spanish painting. A series of scholarly essays precede detailed catalog entries, arranged chronologically, for the exhibition's 52 works.

Contents: (1) Pintar la historia, by Alfonso E. Pérez Sánchez; (2) Los temas históricos en la pintura española del siglo XIX, by Carlos Reyero; (3) Evolución de la pintura española de historia en el siglo XIX, by José Luis Díez; (4) Apropiaciones y recreaciones de la pintura de historia, by Javier Pérez Rojas and José Luis Alcaide.

Bibliografía, p.470–78. Exposiciones, p.479.

M534 Schlunk, Helmut, and Berenguer, Magin. La pintura mural asturiana de los siglos IX y X. Trad. del alemán por María de los Angeles Vázquez de Parga. [Reprint.] Asturias, Principado de Asturias, Consejeria de educacion, [1991]. xxii, 188p. il. (part col.), plates, plans.

Reprint of GLAH 1:M482; an important study of pre-Romanesque mural painting and decoration in Asturias.

M535 Sullivan, Edward J., and Mallory, Nina A. Painting in Spain, 1650–1700, from North American collections. With a historical essay by J. H. Elliott. Princeton, Art Museum, Princeton Univ.; Princeton Univ. Pr., [1982]. xvi, 182p. il. (part col.)

Catalog of the exhibition, The Art Museum, Princeton University (1982), and other locations. Presents 47 works from collections throughout North America. "The catalogue is arranged in alphabetical order according to the artist's Spanish surname. Exhibition entries include medium, measurements, provenance when known, and literature."—*p.54.*

Contents: (1) The twilight of Hapsburg Spain, by J. H. Elliott; (2) Painting in Madrid 1650–1700, by Edward J. Sullivan; (3) Painting in Seville 1650–1700, by Nina A. Mallory.

Paintings in the exhibition, p.vii–ix. Comparative il., p.x–xii. Desiderata, p.165–74. Selected bibliography, p.175–82.

M536 Valdivieso, Enrique. Historia de la pintura sevillana: siglos XIII al XX. Textos de Enrique Valdivieso. Pról. Alfonso E. Pérez Sánchez. Sevilla, Ediciones Guadalquivir, 1986. 510p. col. il. (Repr.: 1992)

Beautifully illustrated history of painting in Seville from the 13th to 20th century. Organized chronologically, beginning with Gothic art, chapters for each century focus on the lives of individual artists.

Notas, p.485. Bibliografía, p.487–93. Indice de artistas, p.495–97. Indice iconografico, p.499–506. Indice general, p.509–10.

M537 Vision oder Wirklichkeit: die spanische Malerei der Neuzeit. [Hrsg.] Henrik Karge. [München], Klinkhardt and Biermann, [1991]. 352p. il. (part col.), ports.

Well-illustrated and scholarly text with chapters by 14 scholars covering the history of painters and paintings in 19th- and 20th-century Spain.

Literatur, p.342–44. Die Autoren, p.345. Register, p.346–51.

M538 Von Greco bis Goya: vier Jahrhunderte spanische Malerei. [München], Thiemig, [1982]. 317p. il. (part col.)

Catalog of the exhibition, Haus der Kunst München (1982), and other locations, covering 106 works from four centuries.

Contents: (1) Die spanische Malerei von El Greco bis Goya, von Alfonso Pérez Sánchez; (2) Geschichte der Sammlung spanischer Gemälde in der Alten Pinakothek, von Johann Georg Prinz von Hohenzollern; (3) Höfische Porträtmalerei Spaniens von Sánchez Coello bis Juan Carreño de Miranda in Österreich, von Friderike Klauner; (4) Geschichte der spanischen Sammlung im Museum der Bildenden Künste Budapest, von Eva Nyerges; (5) Der literarische und historische Hintergrund der spanischen Malerei, von Manuel Muñoz Cartés; (6) Farbtafeln; (7) Katalog.

Literaturverzeichnis, p.314–17.

SEE ALSO: Summa artis, historia general del arte (GLAH 2:I12); Collections of the National Gallery of Art: systematic catalogue (GLAH 2:M31).

Switzerland

M539 Billeter, Erika. La peinture suisse: cent chefs-d'œuvre provenant des musées suisses du XVe au XXe siècle. [Zurich], Silva, [1991]. 264p. il. (part col.)

First published in German as Schweizer Malerei. Bern, Benteli, 1990.

General introduction to Swiss painting. Covers 48 artists organized chronologically first by artist, then by works. Short biographies precede individual entries that include an essay and illustrations. A particularly useful index to Swiss museums, p.255–62, includes address and telephone numbers along with a general description of each collection.

Bibliographie, p.263. Index, p.264.

M540 Eggenberger, Christoph, and Eggenberger, Dorothee. Malerei des Mittelalters. [Zurich, Pro Helvetia; Disentis, Desertina, 1989]. vi, 305p. il. (part col.) (Ars helvetica, 5)

Beautifully illustrated and well-documented survey of early Swiss mural painting, covering the years 500–1500 and organized by region.

Contents: (1) Einleitung; (2) Von den römischen zu den bischöflichen Auftraggebern; (3) Kirchenprovinzen Mailand und Mainz-Patriarchat Aquileja; (4) Zillis; (5) Bodensee; (6) Zürich; (7) Königsfelden; (8) Oberrhein; (9) Bistümer Genf, Sitten, and Lausanne; (10) Eidgenössische Eigenentwicklungen vor und nach 1500; (11) Schluss.

Abkürzungen-Anmerkungen, p.287–300. Ortsregister, p.301–03.

M541 From Liotard to Le Corbusier: 200 years of Swiss painting, 1730–1930. With essays by Hans Ulrich Jost, Brandon Brame Fortune, and William Hauptman. Ed. by the Swiss Institute for Art Research on behalf of the Coordinating Commission for the Presence of Switzerland Abroad. Atlanta, High Museum of Art, [1988]. 191p. il. (part col.), ports.

Well illustrated catalog of the exhibition, High Museum of Art, Atlanta (1988). Surveys Swiss artists from 1730 to 1930. Biographical essays on each artist are followed by catalog entries and bibliographies.

Contents: (1) Nation, Politics, and Art, by Hans Ulrich Jost; (2) Painting in America and Switzerland, 1770–1870:

preliminaries for a comparative study, by Brandon Brame Fortune; (3) The Swiss artist and the European context: some notes on cross-cultural politics, by William Hauptman.

Catalogue, p.47–177. Biographies, p.178–89. Bibliography, p.190.

M542 Geneva (Switzerland). Musée d'art et d'histoire. Peintures et pastels de l'ancienne école genevoise, XVIIe–début XIXe siècle. By Danielle Buyssens. Genève, Musée d'art et d'histoire, 1988. 270p. il. (part col.), plates.

Catalog of the Swiss painting collection at the Musée d'art et d'histoire, Geneva. Difficult to use due to elaborate organization but exhaustive in scope. Entries, organized alphabetically by artist, include black and white thumbnail illustrations along with large color plates. Additional features such as chronology of the artist's life, complete exhibition history and bibliography add to the catalog's value.

Catalogues, p.215. Bibliographie, p.216–25. Expositions, p.226–32. Numéros d'inventaire, p.233–36. Noms propres liés à la provenance des oeuvres, p.237–43. Mode et chronologie d'entrée des oeuvres au Musée, p.244–47. Donateurs, p.248–49. Index iconographique, p.250–60. Musées et collections cités, p.261–62. Changements d'attribution, p.263. Copies, p.264. Noms d'artistes cités, p.265.

M543 Ich male für fromme Gemüter: zur religiösen Schweizer Malerei im 19. Jahrhundert. [Ausstellung, Martin Kunz.] [Luzern], Kunstmuseum Luzern, [1985]. 303p. il. (part col.) plates.

Exemplary catalog of the exhibition, Kunstmuseum Luzern (1985), focusing on religious iconography in 19th-century Swiss painting. Copiously illustrated and thoroughly researched essays are interspersed with catalog entries. No index.

Contents: (1) "Ich male für fromme Gemüter und nicht für Kritiker": Melchior Paul von Deschwanden als Kirchenmaler by Mathilde Tobler; Katalog 1; (2) Un und nach Deschwanden, von Benno Schubiger; Katalog 2; (3) Architektur als Bildträger: die Monumentalmalerei in der Deutschschweiz, von Benno Schubiger; Katalog 3; (4) Religion und Malerei in der Westschweiz: von der Helvetik zum Ersten Weltkrieg, von Dario Gamboni; Katalog 4; (5) Die Sakralmalerei des 19. Jahrhunderts im Tessin: ein Überblick, von Letizia Schubiger-Serandrei; Katalog 5; (6) Satire and Spott; Katalog 6; (7) Die "Beuroner kunstschule" und die Schweiz; Katalog 7; (8) Die Rezeption der frühchristlichen Kunst in der Schweiz im 19. Jahrhundert, von Harold Siebenmorgen; Katalog 8; (9) Symbolismus und Religion: Theologie und Kirche im 19. Jahrhundert, von Hans H. Hofstätter; Katalog.

Kurzbiografien, p.295–300.

Turkey

M544 Istanbul (Turkey). Kültür ışleri Daire Başkanlii. Greater Istanbul Municipality painting collection. [Ed. by Barika Goncu.] Istanbul, ıstanbul Büyükşehir Belediyesi Kültür ışleri Daire Başkanlii Yayinlari, 1991. 322p. col. il. (ıstanbul Büyükşehir Belediyesi Kültür ışleri Dairesi Başkanlii Yayinlari, 4)

Survey, with text in both English and Turkish, of the Turkish painting collection, Kültür ışleri Daire Başkanlii, Istanbul. Organized alphabetically by artist's name. Copiously illustrated entries include a brief biographical statement.

Footnotes, p.310–13. References, p.314. Greater Istanbul painting collection, p.315–20. Unsigned paintings, p.321.

M545 A history of Turkish painting. [Essays by Günsel Renda . . . (et al.)] [Genève], Palasar, 1987. 444p. 495 col. il. (Repr.: Seattle, Univ. of Washington Pr., 1988)

"May be considered as the first major publication on this subject in a foreign language."—*p.11.* This study of Turkish painting, in an oversize format with impressive color plates, concentrates on the late 19th and early 20th centuries. Organized chronologically, the book includes a small section on 20th-century Turkish prints.

Contents: (1) Traditional Turkish painting and the beginnings of Western trends, by Günsel Renda; (2) Painting in Turkey in XIX and early XXth century, by Turan Erol; (3) Post-second World War trends in Turkish Painting, by Adnan Turani; (4) The search for a new identity in Turkish painting, by Kaya Özsezgin; (5) The art of the print in Turkey, by Mustafa Asher.

Notes and sources, p.432–39. Index, p.440–44.

United States

General Works

M546 Abby Aldrich Rockefeller Folk Art Center. American folk paintings: paintings and drawings other than portraits from the Abby Aldrich Rockefeller Folk Art Center. Boston, Little, Brown, and Co.; Colonial Williamsburg Foundation, [1988]. xi, 449p. il. (part col.) (The Abby Aldrich Rockefeller Folk Art Center series, 2)

This catalog of the paintings of the preeminent American folk art collection, which contains more than 2,600 works, supplements their first vol. documenting portrait paintings (see following title). "The paintings and drawings in this catalogue are grouped primarily by subject matter. . . . Within each subject grouping in the catalog, works are divided into those whose artists are identified by name and those whose makers remain unknown by name."—*p.[12].* Detailed entries on 383 illustrated works include biographies, provenance, inscription and condition reports, and exhibition histories.

Short title list, p.432–37. Index, p.438–49.

M547 ———. American folk portraits: paintings and drawings from the Abby Aldrich Rockefeller Folk Art Center. [Gen. ed., Beatrix T. Rumford.] Boston, N.Y. Graphic Soc.; Colonial Williamsburg Foundation, [1981]. 295p. il. (part col.) (The Abby Aldrich Rockefeller Folk Art Center series, 1)

The first in a series of catalogs documenting 298 portrait paintings in this important collection of American folk art. "The portraits are organized in two groups: those by or attributed to known artists, and those by individuals whose identity is undetermined. The first section, known artists, is organized alphabetically by surname. . . . In the second section, likenesses by unidentified artists are arranged chronologically by date of execution."—*p.[36].* Detailed entries include biographies, provenance, inscription and condition reports, and exhibition histories.

Exhibition short title list, p.291–92. Publications short title list, p.293–95. Index, p.[296–304].

M548 American folk painters of three centuries. Ed. by Jean Lipman and Tom Armstrong. N.Y., Hudson Hills; Whitney Museum of American Art, [1980]. 233p. il. (part col.)

Well-illustrated catalog of the exhibition, Whitney Museum of American Art (1980), presenting the work of 37 indigenous, untrained American painters from the 18th, 19th and 20th centuries. "They are grouped by century according to the period of their major activity, and arranged alphabetically within each century. . . . The majority come from the eastern United States."—*p.8.* Essays by 22 scholars. Many of the texts are based on previously published books or articles.

Bibliographical references at end of chapters. Editors' bookshelf, p.225–26. Index, p.230–33.

M549 American painting: from the Colonial period to the present. Introd. by John Walker. Text by Jules David Prown and Barbara Rose. New upd. ed. [Geneva], Skira; N.Y., Rizzoli, [1977]. 277p. il. (part col.)

1st published in 2 vols., 1969; repr. 1980.

Rev. and reformatted ed. of two valuable studies presented conveniently in one vol. Tipped-in color plates in an oversize format add beauty to this standard history of American painting. Includes a new chapter on the 1970s and updated reference sources.

Contents: (1) Prown, Jules. From the beginnings to the Armory Show; (2) Rose, Barbara. The twentieth century.

Selected bibliography, p.255–264. List of color plates, p.265–70. General index, p.271–77.

M550 Black, Mary, and Lipman, Jean. American folk painting. [Reprint.] N.Y., Bramhall House (Distr. by Crown, [1987]). xxiv, 244p. il. (part col.)

Reprint (in oversize format) of GLAH 1:M491.

M551 Detroit Institute of Arts. American paintings in the Detroit Institute of Arts. Introd. by Nancy Rivard Shaw. Essays by Mary Black . . . [et al.] N.Y., Hudson Hills, 1991– . (2)v. il. (part col.)

Scholarly catalog of the collection. To be complete in three vols. Includes a brief history of the collection.

Contents: (1) Works by artists born before 1816; (2) Works by artists born 1816–1847.

Short references, v.1, p.273–92. Bibliography, v.2, p.309–28. Index of works by accession number, v.1, p.293–94, v.2, p.329–32. General index, v.1, p.295–303, v.2, p.333–40.

M552 Finch, Christopher. American watercolors. N.Y., Abbeville Pr., [1986]. 312p. il. (part col.)

Well-illustrated survey of the often ignored medium of watercolor painting. Covers works from 1564 through the 1970s, focusing on 31 individual artists in an opulent, oversize format. Organized chronologically with an emphasis on late 19th and early 20th century.

Notes, p.303–05. Selected bibliography, p.306–07. Index, p.308.

M553 Gerdts, William H. Art across America: two centuries of regional painting, 1710–1920. N.Y., Abbeville Pr., [1990]. 3v. il. (part col.) maps, ports.

An extensive survey of regional painters, organized geographically, including one work for each painter per region. "The purpose of this book is to expand the history of American painting beyond its traditional boundaries. The artists discussed in the pages that follow are professionals who worked outside the three cities—New York, Philadelphia, and Boston—that were the centers of the American art mainstream even after the 1920 end date of this study."—*p.7.* "This study is . . . limited to oil and watercolor painting, in sizes ranging from miniatures to panoramas."—*p.8.*

Contents: (1) New England, New York, the Mid-Atlantic; (2) The South, the Near Midwest; (3) The far Midwest, the Rocky Mountain West, the Southwest, the Pacific.

Notes, bibliography, and index in each vol.

M554 Lucie-Smith, Edward. American realism. N.Y., [Abrams, 1994]. 240p. il. (part col.)

16 varied sections discuss and display the finest and most influential work of different groups, schools, and periods since the Revolutionary war. Includes American impressionism, the Ashcan school, precisionism, American scene painting, urban realism, photorealism, and postmodern realism.

Bibliography, p.[232]–33. Index, p.234–39.

M555 New York. Metropolitan Museum of Art. American paintings in the Metropolitan Museum of Art. N.Y., Metropolitan Museum of Art; Princeton, Princeton Univ. Pr., [1980–1994]. 3v. il.

See GLAH 1:M505 for 1st ed. of v.1 (1965).

"The definitive and comprehensive publication of the museum's holdings in American paintings."—*Introd.* A monumental survey completely revised by editor Kathleen Luhrs in a new, larger format. Illustrated entries for each work, organized chronologically, include inscription and canvas stamp, related works, references, exhibitions, ex collections, accession number, and credit line.

Contents: (1) Caldwell, John, and Rodriguez, Oswaldo. A catalogue of works by artists born by 1815 (1994); (2) Spassky, Natalie. A catalogue of works by artists born between 1816 and 1845 (1985); (3) Burke, Doreen Bolger. A catalogue of works by artists born between 1846 and 1864 (1980).

Each vol. has two indexes: one for artists and titles of paintings and another for provenance. An alphabetical list of all artist represented in the three appears at the end of each vol.

M556 New York. New-York Historical Society. American landscape and genre paintings in the New-York Historical Society. Comp. by Richard J. Koke. Biographical entries by Elaine Andrews . . . [et al.] N.Y., New-York Historical Society; Boston, Hall, 1982. 3v. il.

Detailed inventory of the painting collection, excluding portraiture, at the New-York Historical Society acquired through 1978. Includes entries for more than 3,200 works. "Names of artists are listed in alphabetical order. . . . Following the biography, each numbered entry is listed in chronological sequence, with exact or approximate date, accompanied by pertinent information relative to medium, dimensions, inscriptions, stencils, printed labels, exhibition record, provenance and previous collections, publications and supporting documentation, references, and comment."—*Introd.*

Contents: (1) A–D; (2) E–M; (3) N–Y and unidentified artists.

Bibliography, v.3, p.377–409. Title index, v.3, p.411–38. Subject index, v.3, p.439–59.

M557 Picturing history: American painting, 1770–1930. Ed. by William Ayres. Chief contrib. Barbara J. Mitnick. Essays by Ann Uhry Abrams . . . [et al.] N.Y., Fraunces Tavern Museum; Rizzoli, [1993]. 256p. il. (part col.)

Catalog of the exhibition, I.B.M. Gallery of Science and Art, N.Y. (1993), and other locations. Surveys American history painting from its origins in the Revolutionary period through its decline with the advent of modernism. 11 essays by leading scholars annotated with 152 illustrations.

Notes, p.232–46. Bibliography, p.247–50. Index, p.251–56.

M558 Stebbins, Theodore E., Jr.; Troyen, Carol; and Fairbrother, Trevor J. A new world: masterpieces of American painting 1760–1910. With essays by Pierre Rosenberg and H. Barbara Weinberg. Boston, Museum of Fine Arts, 1983. 351p. il. (part col.), maps.

Catalog of the exhibition, Museum of Fine Arts, Boston (1983), and other locations. Presents 110 19th-century American paintings by 49 artists. Two general essays are followed by nine short, thematic sections illustrated with color plates. Catalog entries include a biography of the artist and selected readings, an essay on the individual work, provenance, exhibition history, and a black-and-white illustration.

Map of artists' locales, p.342. Selected bibliography, p.343–49. Index of artists and titles, p.350–51.

M559 Tanner, Clara Lee. Southwest Indian painting: a changing art. 2d ed. Tucson, Univ. of Arizona Pr., [1973]. xvii, 477p. il., map.

1st ed. 1954.

An examination of American Indian painting from prehistoric through the 1970s, including mural painting and decorative craft work. Chronological history documenting the work of 180 individual artists, emphasizing the 20th century.

Notes, p.449–52. Bibliography, p.453–58. Index, p.459–77.

M560 United States. National Gallery of Art. American paintings: an illustrated catalogue. Washington, [D.C.], National Gallery of Art, 1992. 545p. il.

1st ed. 1970.

"This is the third summary catalogue of American paintings in the National Gallery of Art that has been published each decade since 1970."—*p.9.* A fully illustrated inventory of almost 1400 works, this handbook also makes available in one vol. information derived from research for the partially completed systematic catalogue of the collection (see GLAH 2:M31).

Contents: (1) Paintings; (2) Paintings transferred to the National Portrait Gallery; (3) Paintings formerly considered American; (4) Concordance of old and new accession numbers.

Artist index, p.468–70. Title index, p.471–515. Tribal index, George Catlin, p.516–25. Subject index, p.526–45.

———. 1st supplement. Washington, D.C., National Gallery of Art, 1980.

M561 Weinberg, H. Barbara; Bolger, Doreen; and Curry, David Park. American impressionism and realism: the painting of modern life, 1885–1915. With the assist. of N. Mishoe Brennecke. N.Y., Metropolitan Museum of Art (Distr. by Abrams, 1994). xiii, 384p. il. (part col.)

Catalog of the exhibition, Metropolitan Museum of Art, N.Y. (1994), and other locations. "Brings together the appealing works of two generations of American painters and presents them from a fresh point of view."—*Introd.* Substantial scholarship combined with a beautifully illustrated catalog. Includes up-to-date biographies and bibliographies for 26 major American artists.

Notes, p.310–45. The painters, biographies, p.346–58. Selected bibliography, p.359–64. Works in the exhibition, p.365–67. Lenders to the exhibition, p.368. Index, p.369–83.

M562 Zellman, Michael David, comp. American art analog. N.Y., Chelsea House, 1986. 3v. il. (part col.)

Updated by the serial publication: Blue book, N.Y., Chelsea House, 1986, which ceased publication with v.2, 1987.

"Included are topical essays in the history of American art; summary biographies of more than 800 painters, many little-known and each represented with a color reproduction, and . . . figures and graphs that illustrate the market activity of paintings by these artists."—*Introd.*, v.1.

Contents: (1) Artists born from 1688–1842; (2) Artists born from 1842–1874; (3) Artists born from 1874–1930.

Glossary, bibliography, auction house list, and index are repeated in full at the end of each vol.

Colonial Period—19th Century

M563 American paradise, the world of the Hudson River School. Introd. by John K. Howat. N.Y., Metropolitan Museum of Art, [1987]. xvii, 347p. il. (part col.)

Catalog of the exhibition, Metropolitan Museum of Art, N.Y. (1987), in a heavily illustrated, oversize format. "Conceived as a presentation of the art of the Hudson River School and a summary of the most up-to-date scholarship on the School itself."—*Introd.* Entries for 84 paintings by 25 artists, arranged chronologically, include biography, bibliography, and a footnoted essay.

Contents: (1) A historiography of the Hudson River School, by Kevin J. Avery; (2) The exaltation of American landscape painting, by Oswaldo Rodriguez Roque; (3) A climate for landscape painters, by John K. Howat; (4) The Hudson River School in eclipse, by Doreen Bolger Burke and Catherine Hoover Voorsanger.

Essay notes, p.91–98. Short titles and abbreviations, p.331–36. Index, p.337–46.

M564 Craven, Wayne. Colonial American portraiture: the economic, religious, social, cultural, philosophical, scientific, and aesthetic foundations. Cambridge, Cambridge Univ. Pr., [1986]. xx, 459p. il.

Thorough examination of Colonial portraiture that approaches the paintings in the context of a broader, cultural history. 31 chapters are divided chronologically into 3 general periods: 1665–1680, 1680–1740, and 1740–1790.

Notes, p.406–36. Selected bibliography, p.437–50. Index, p.451–59.

M565 Detroit Institute of Arts. American paintings in the Detroit Institute of Arts. Introd. by Nancy Rivard Shaw. Essays by Mary Black . . . [et al.] N.Y., Hudson Hills Pr.; Detroit, Founders Society Detroit Institute of Arts, [1991–]. (1)v. il. (The collections of the Detroit Institute of Arts)

First part of a proposed 3-vol. survey of the Museum's American painting collection. Organized alphabetically by artist, entries include biography, inscriptions, provenance, exhibition history, references, and often, illustrations.

Contents: (1) Works by artists born before 1816.

Bibliography, p.309–28. Index of works by accession number, p.329–32. General index, p.333–40.

M566 Gerdts, William H. American impressionism. N.Y., Abbeville Pr., [1984]. 336p. il. (part col.)

Comprehensive survey by the leading expert in the field, presented in an oversize format with large, color plates.

Contents: (1) Prelude, to 1886; (2) Rising perceptions, 1886–1893; (3) The years of triumph, 1893–1898; (4) The impressionist establishment, 1989–1915.

Includes bibliographical references on 90 individual painters. Notes, p.309–18. Bibliography, p.321–31. Index, p.332–36.

M567 Johns, Elizabeth. American genre painting, the politics of everyday life. New Haven, Yale Univ. Pr., 1991. 288p. il. (part col.)

Highly original and persuasive history of antebellum genre painting in the United States. Paintings discussed in the context of a chronological social history.

Notes, p.205–43. Index, p.245–50.

M568 Little, Nina Fletcher. American decorative wall painting, 1700–1850. New enl. ed. N.Y., Dutton, [1989]. xx, 169p. il. (part col.), plates.

See GLAH 1:M503 for previous eds.

Substantially enlarged 3d ed. of an important study of the various techniques and styles of American wall painting, primarily in New England. "An added group of overmantels is included to bring the former list up to date, and Chapter 11 has been separately indexed for easier reference to the new materials and illustrations contained therein."—*Introd.* Also includes "a new chapter covering discoveries recorded since 1952."—*Introd.*

Contents: (1) Painted woodwork; (2) Painted plaster walls.

Biographical list of panel, chimney board and wall painters, p.150–53. Checklist of pictorial panels, p.154–58. Checklist of additional pictorial panels, p.159. Selective bibliography, p.160–62. Index, p.163–67. Index to chapter 11, p.168–69.

M569 Novak, Barbara. American painting of the nineteenth century: realism, idealism and the American experience. 2d ed. N.Y., Harper and Row, 1979. 350p. il.

See GLAH 1:M506 for 1st ed.

History of 19th-century painting, focusing on 14 individual painters. "My aim has been to provide an intermediary literature of intensive essays on some of the key figures."—*p.8.* "For this edition, I have made a few minor corrections in the text and have revised and updated the bibliography."—*p.10.*

Notes, p.289–318. Brief biographies of eighteenth- and nineteenth-century artists, p.319–34. Bibliography, p.335–39. Index, p.345–50.

M570 ______. Nineteenth-century American painting: the Thyssen-Bornemisza collection. [Catalogue ed. by Barbara Novak and Elizabeth Garrity Ellis. Entries by Elizabeth Garrity Ellis . . . (et al.) Gen. ed. Simon de Pury.] N.Y., Artabras, [1991]. 329p. il. (part col.), map, ports.

1st ed., London, Philip Wilson Pub. for Sotheby's, 1986, following an exhibition, American Masters: the Thyssen-Bornemisza Collection, which traveled from 1983 to 1986.

Scholarly treatment of more than 100 paintings owned by "the first European collector to focus his attention on 19th century American paintings."—*p.[7].* "The entries follow a chronological sequence but are sometimes grouped according to subject matter."—*p.45.* Each entry includes provenance, exhibition history, literature, and a short essay.

Biographies of the artists, p.313–24. Index, p.326–29.

SEE ALSO: Collections of the National Gallery of Art: systematic catalogue (GLAH 2:M31).

20th Century

M571 Abstract expressionism, the critical developments. Organized by Michael Auping. Essays by Michael Auping . . . [et al.] N.Y., Abrams; Buffalo, Albright-Knox Art Gallery, 1987. 302p. il. (part col.), port.

Catalog of the exhibition, Albright-Knox Art Gallery, Buffalo (1987), and other locations. Includes essays by seven scholars of American art, followed by the catalog of works in the exhibition, organized alphabetically by artist. Each entry is illustrated with color plates and portraits of the artists. An interview with Lawrence Alloway complements the historical essays.

Chronology, p.256–73. Artist's bibliographies and selected exhibitions, p.274–95. Index, p.296–301.

M572 Davidson, Abraham A. Early American modernist painting, 1910–1935. N.Y., Harper and Row, [1981]. viii, 324p. il., 8 col. plates.

Comprehensive study of "the period before American avant-garde painting assumed its position of international leadership."—*p.1.* Well-documented presentation of this brief but important movement in the United States along with its European influences.

Contents: (1) The Stieglitz group; (2) The Arensberg Circle; (3) Color painters; (4) Some early exhibitions, collectors, and galleries; (5) Precisionism; (6) The Independents.

Bibliography, p.[295]–304. List of illustrations, p.[305]–12. Index, p.[313]–24.

M573 Landauer, Susan. The San Francisco School of Abstract Expressionism. With an introd. by Dore Ashton. Laguna Beach, Laguna Art Museum; Berkeley, Univ. of Calif. Pr., [1996]. xxiii, 271p. il. (part col.), port.

Well-illustrated catalog of the exhibition, Laguna Art Museum (1996), and other locations, documenting the West Coast wing of the abstract expressionist movement. A scholarly study focusing on 54 painters but chronicling an entire era of artistic achievement.

Appendix 1, Artist biographies, p.177–93. Appendix 2: Group and joint exhibition history, 1940–1965, p.195–209. Notes, p.211–41. General bibliography, p.243–48. Selected bibliographies for individual artists, p.249–56. Index, p.257–71.

M574 Leja, Michael. Reframing abstract expressionism: subjectivity and painting in the 1940s. New Haven, Yale Univ. Pr., [1993]. viii, 392p. il.

Important, revisionist study treating the New York School of Art in the context of popular, American culture.

Contents: (1) The formation of an avant-garde in New York; (2) The mythmakers and the primitive: Gottlieb, Newman, Rothko and Still; (3) Jackson Pollock and the unconscious; (4) Narcissus in chaos, subjectivity, ideology, modern man and woman; (5) Pollock and Metaphor.

Notes, p.332–69. Bibliography, p.370–88. Index, p.389–92.

M575 Levin, Gail. Twentieth-century American painting: the Thyssen-Bornemisza collection. General ed. Simon de Pury. [London], Philip Wilson for Sotheby's, [1987]. 408p. il. (part col.)

One of a series of catalogs surveying the Thyssen Bornemisza collection. Arranged chronologically by period; includes detailed entries with provenance, literature, and exhibition history.

Contents: (1) Notes on the catalog; (2) List of paintings; (3) Early twentieth-century illustration; (4) The Eight and their followers; (5) Early modernists; (6) The 1930s, realism, magic realism, regionalism, and social realism; (7) Abstract expressionism and the New York School; (8) Representation in the 1940s and 1950s; (9) Legacy of dada and surrealism; (10) Pop art; (11) Minimal and reductivist art; (12) Recent representation.

Biographies of the artists, p.387–400. Bibliography, p.400–03. Index, p.404–08.

M576 Meisel, Louis K. Photo-Realism. Foreword by Gregory Battcock. Research and documentation by Helene Zucker Seeman. N.Y., Abrams, [1980]. 528p. il. (part col.), port.

"The purpose of this volume is to provide as complete a reference work as possible on the art of the Photo-Realists."—*p.7.* In an oversize format with huge color plates, this study includes separate chapters on 13 painters, each with an essay, portrait and illustrations, exhibition history, bibliography, and catalogue raisonné. Last section covers 15 painters peripherally involved with photo-realism.

Selected photo-realism exhibitions and bibliography, p.513–19. Index, p.520–27.

M577 ______. Photorealism since 1980. [N.Y.], Abrams, [1993]. 368p. il. (part col.)

Reproductions of works by 25 photorealist painters, supplementing the author's previous study (see preceding title). Includes brief biographical information followed by large, color plates.

Selected exhibitions, bibliographies, and biographies, p.358–64. Index, p.365–68.

M578 Polcari, Stephen. Abstract expressionism and the modern experience. Cambridge, Cambridge Univ. Pr., [1991]. xxiii, 408p. il. (part col.)

Copiously illustrated essays on 10 painters of the New York School of Art, focusing on their interaction with the intellectual life and culture in New York City at that period. "I have chosen to concentrate on the idea in one long chapter and to do monographic essays on the artists."—*Introd.*

Epilogue, p.367–69. Notes, p.371–95. Selected bibliography, p.397–401. Index, p.403–08.

M579 Rose, Barbara. American painting: the twentieth century. [New updated ed.] [Geneva], Skira; N.Y., Rizzoli, [1986]. 170p. col. il.

1st ed. 1969; new ed. 1977.

Popular introduction to 20th-century painting by a leading scholar in the field, heavily illustrated with color plates. Includes a new chapter on the 1980s and additional reference sources.

Contents: (1) The Armory Show and its aftermath; (2) The crisis of the thirties; (3) The New York School; (4) The sixties; (5) The seventies: American art comes of age; (6) Images of the eighties.

M580 Seitz, William C. Abstract expressionist painting in America. Washington, D.C., National Gallery of Art; Cambridge, Mass., Harvard Univ. Pr., 1983. xxii, 490p. il. (part col.) (The Ailsa Mellon Bruce studies in American art)

Begins with a foreword by Robert Motherwell, followed by eight chapters chronicling Abstract Expressionism. "The core of [this] book, chapters 2 through 6, is a detailed examination of what happens in each of his painters' works."—*Foreword.* Nearly 400 pages of illustrations focusing on six major American painters, organized alphabetically by name.

Motherwell's Chronology of abstract expressionism, p.168–70. Notes, p.171–82. Index of illustrations, p.471–74. Index, p.475–90.

M581 Ward, John L. American realist painting, 1945–1980. Ann Arbor, UMI Research Pr., [1989]. xiv, 431p. il. (Studies in the fine arts. The avant-garde, no.60)

Detailed study of realist painters often overshadowed by abstract expressionism.

Contents: (1) Postwar American painting, abstraction wins out; (2) The realist response to Abstract Expressionism; (3) The "new" realism; (4) Photo-realism.

Notes, p.[351]–89. Bibliography, p.[391]–420. Index, p.[421]–31.

ASIAN COUNTRIES

General Works

M582 Cahill, James. Lyric journey: poetic painting in China and Japan. Cambridge, Harvard University Pr., 1996. x, 251p. il. (The Edwin O. Reischauer Lectures, 1993)

Originally presented as lectures at Harvard University, the three chapters treat examples of poetic painting "In Southern Sung Hangchou," "In Late Ming Souchou," and "In Edo-Period Japan." Explores their common socioeconomic and literary contexts.

Notes, p.197–228. Bibliography, p.229–240. Glossary, p.241–44. Index, p.245–51.

M583 Pal, Pratapaditya. Buddhist book illumination. N.Y., Ravi Kumar, 1988. 339p. il. (part col.)

"This publication is limited and numbered to 500 copies only."—*t.p. verso.* "The present study . . . is the first to be dedicated exclusively to Buddhist manuscript illuminations."—*Pref.* Important study by an authority. Well-produced, on glossy paper.

Reference list, p.327–28. Bibliography, p.329–32. Index, p.334–39.

China

M584 Andrews, Julia. Painters and politics in the People's Republic of China, 1949–1979. Berkeley, Univ. of California Pr., [1994]. xv, 568p. il. (part col.)

Focusing on the bureaucratic context rather than individual artists, discusses the means by which cultural controls were asserted over art during these three decades in the PRC, the ways in which artists responded to the new system, and the works of art they produced.

Contents: (1) Revolutionaries and academics: the art of the republican period; (2) The reform of Chinese art, 1949–52; (3) From popularization to specialization; (4) The politicization of Guohua; (5) The Great Leap Forward and its aftermath: "More, faster, better, cheaper"; (6) The Cultural Revolution; (7) The transition to "artistic democracy," 1976–1979; Appendixes: (1) National Arts Administrators, 1949; (2) National Arts Administrators, 1960; (3) National Arts Administrators, 1979; (4) Oil painters in the soviet manner.

Notes, p.419–74. List of Chinese names and terms, p.475–96. Selected bibliography, p.497–520. Index, p.531–68.

M585 Barnhart, Richard M. Along the border of heaven: Sung and Yuan paintings from the C. C. Wang family collection. N.Y., Metropolitan Museum of Art, [1983]. 191p. il. (part col.)

Study of Chinese art, especially landscape and figure painting, from the 10th to the 14th centuries, based on the collection of Wang Chi-ch'ien, an extraordinary collector-connoisseur.

Index, p.187–91.

M586 ______. Painters of the great Ming: the Imperial Court and the Zhe school. Dallas, Dallas Museum of Art, [1993]. xvi, 360p. il. (part col.)

Catalog of the exhibition, Metropolitan Museum of Art (1993), and another location.

An important survey of the Zhe School and Academy painters, the professional painters of the Ming dynasty, from 1425 to 1525. Previously overlooked or misattributed, the works entered collections around the world and particularly influenced Japanese Muromachi period ink paintings.

List of figures, p.349–55. List of artists, p.356–57. Selected bibliography, p.358–60.

M587 ______. Peach blossom spring: gardens and flowers in Chinese paintings. N.Y., Metropolitan Museum of Art, [1983]. 143p. il. (part col.)

Catalog of the exhibition, Metropolitan Museum of Art (1983).

Study of the importance of gardens and the contemplation of nature in Chinese tradition. Includes examples of garden painting, often categorized as flower and bird painting, and explores their symbolic meaning.

Key to citations, p.126–27.

M588 Bickford, Maggie. Ink plum: the making of a Chinese scholar painting genre. N.Y., Cambridge Univ. Pr., 1996. xix, 295p. il., plates.

Study of the image of the flowering plum tracing the genre from its beginning in Northern Song through the Southern Song and Yuan dynasties. Interdisciplinary in approach with references to art historical, literary, cultural, and political activities.

Notes, p.218–59. Bibliography, p.260–71. Glossary/index, p.272–95.

M589 Cahill, James. Chinese painting. [Reprint.] N.Y., Skira/Rizzoli, 1985. 211p. col. il. (Treasures of Asia)

Reprint of GLAH 1:M523.

M590 ______. The compelling image: nature and style in seventeenth-century Chinese painting. Cambridge, Harvard Univ. Pr., 1982. 250p. il. (part col.), plates (Charles Eliot Norton Lectures, 1978–79)

Among the most important works on later Chinese painting to appear in any Western language, 1982 winner of the Charles Rufus Morey Award of the College Art Association of America. Based on two lectures delivered at Harvard in 1979, the book examines the "kinds of meaning that Chinese paintings (and especially landscape paintings) contain and the ways in which they convey those meanings."—*Pref.*

Essays devoted to eight landscape artists and one figure painter with excursions into the works and words of other artists and into other pertinent topics. Wide-ranging, with a wealth of ideas, arguments, interpretations, and explorations.

Notes, p.229–38. Index, p.243–50.

M591 ______. History of later Chinese painting, 1279–1950. N.Y., Weatherhill, 1976– . (3)v. il. (part col.), maps.

See GLAH 1:M526 for original annotation and previous vols.

Selective contents: (3) The distant mountains: Chinese painting of the late Ming dynasty, 1570–1644 (1982).

M592 ______. An index of early Chinese painters and paintings. Incorporating the work of Osvald Sirén and Ellen Johnston Laing. Berkeley, Univ. of California Pr., [1980–]. (1)v.

An index of all Chinese paintings, known to the author, by or attributed to artists active in the early periods. Organized by period, the artists' entries provide biographical information followed by lists of paintings grouped by collection or publication.

Contents: (1) T'ang, Sung, and Yüan. Two further vols. announced, on the Ming and Ch'ing periods.

M593 ______. The painter's practice; how artists lived and worked in traditional China. N.Y., Columbia Univ. Pr., [1994]. xi, 187p. il. (part col.) (Brampton lectures in America, 29)

Based on four lectures delivered at Columbia University (1991), this study of the Chinese artist's life and work spans the time period from the Six Dynasties to the late 19th century. In an attempt to establish the contexts of creation of Chinese painting, the book presents a fascinating account of the social and economic aspects of Chinese painting. It examines the varied ways in which the patron conveyed his wishes to the artist, the ways the artist was rewarded if he complied, and the dilemma of the artist with too many commissions and impatient clients.

Notes, p.[149]–67. Bibliography (works in English), p.[169]–75. Index, p.[181]–87.

M594 Chou, Ju-hsi, and Brown, Claudia. The elegant brush: Chinese painting under the Quianlong Emperor, 1735–1795. Phoenix, Phoenix Art Museum, 1985. 376p. il. (part col.)

Catalog of the exhibition, Phoenix Art Museum (1985), and other locations. Documents the art produced during the 18th-century reign of the Quianlong emperor. Includes 100 artists' biographies and commentaries on the works, which were borrowed from an impressive range of collections in Japan, France, and the U.S. Although packed with information and referenced with footnotes, the catalog lacks an index.

Selected bibliography, p.358–59.

M595 Chung-kuo ku taī shu hua t'u mu [= Group for the Authentication of Ancient Works of Chinese Painting and Calligraphy]. Chung-kuo ku taī shu hua chien ting tsu pien. [= Illustrated catalogue of selected works of ancient Chinese painting and calligraphy]. Beijing, The Cultural Relics Publishing House, 1986–1993. 12v.

Only the title pages, table of contents, preface, explanatory notes, and postscript are in English. All other text is Chinese.

"The task of the Group is to carry out comprehensive, systematic investigation and authentification in the country, as well as the compilation of catalogues, illustrated catalogues and special books."—*Pref.*

Approved by the Propaganda Department of the Central Committee of CPC in June 1983 and administered by the Administrative Bureau of Museums and Archeological Data, Ministry of Culture, the Group for the Authentication of Ancient Works of Chinese Painting and Calligraphy examined relevant collections in museums, cultural organizations, and private collections throughout China. Proceeding collection by collection, each vol. features more than 1,000 images and a descriptive appendix. Within each collection's list, the works are arranged chronologically by dynasty and by artists' dates. Includes signed and dated works, signed and undated works, and attributed works. Although not all authenticated works are illustrated, the appendix does include all authenticated works with a description of the format, material, color and size. An indication is also given if the authenticators were not unanimous in their opinion.

M596 Fong, Wen C. Beyond representation: Chinese painting and calligraphy, 8th–14th century. N.Y., Metropolitan Museum of Art; New Haven, Yale Univ. Pr., [1992]. xix, 549p. il. (part col.) (Princeton monographs in art and archaeology, 48)

"A history of early Chinese painting and calligraphy from the T'ang, Sung, and Yüan dynasties based on a selection of masterworks in the Douglas Dillon Galleries at the Metropolitan Museum of Art."—*Foreword.*

Intended not as a catalogue raisonné but as a historical narrative and as a companion to other volumes documenting the Museum's collections of Chinese painting and calligraphy. This luxurious volume illustrates all objects mentioned in the text.

Contents: (1) Of the human world: narrative representations; (2) Of nature and art: monumental landscape; (3) The art of the scholar-officials; (4) Sung imperial art; (5) Introspection and lyricism: Southern Sung painting; (6) Some Buddhist and Taoist themes; (7) The Yüan renaissance; (8) Revival and synthesis: Yüan literati painting.

Bibliography, p.503–14. Glossary-index, p.523–48.

M597 ______, . . . et al. Images of the mind: selections from the Edward L. Elliott Family and John B. Elliott collections of Chinese calligraphy and painting at the Art Museum, Princeton University. Princeton, Princeton Univ. Art Museum, [1984]. xvi, 504p. il. (part col.)

Catalog of the exhibition, Princeton University Art Museum (1984). The title is the English translation of the term by which the Chinese refer to calligraphy and painting and indicates the way the art work reflects the artist himself. Includes essays by Wen Fong and others and a catalog of 70 objects. All are illustrated, many in color, and information is provided on the date, form and medium, measurements, artists' seals, colophons, collectors' seals, artists' inscriptions and signature, and previous publication of the each work.

Selected bibliography, p.491–93. Index, p.494–504.

M598 Fu, Marilyn, and Fu, Shen. Studies in connoisseurship: Chinese paintings from the Arthur M. Sackler Collection in New York and Princeton. 3d ed. [Reprint.] Washington, D.C., Arthur M. Sackler Foundation, [1987]. xvi, 378p. il. (part col.), map.

See GLAH 1:M533 for original annotation and 1st ed; 2d rev. ed., 1976. Although called revised editions, these are unabridged reprints of the original.

M599 Gulik, Robert Hans van. Chinese pictorial art as viewed by the connoisseur. [Reprint.] N.Y., Hacker, 1981. xxxvii, 537p. il., plates.

Reprint of GLAH 1:M536.

M600 Ho, Wai-kam,. . . . et al. Eight dynasties of Chinese painting: the collections of the Nelson Gallery-Atkins Museum, Kansas City, and the Cleveland Museum of Art: with essays. Cleveland, Cleveland Museum of Art (Distr. by Indiana Univ. Pr., [1980]). lvi, 408p. il. (part col.), plates, maps.

Catalog of the exhibition, Cleveland Museum of Art (1980), and other locations. One of the early survey exhibitions of Chinese art in America from two great collections. Includes 282 works of art dating from 300 B.C. to 1850 A.D.

Contents: Chinese painting before 1100, by Laurence Sickman; Aspects of Chinese painting from 1100–1350, by Wai-kam Ho; Chinese painting from 1350 to 1650, by Sherman E. Lee; Continuity and change in Chinese painting from 1650 to 1850; Catalogue; Addendum.

Chronology of Dynastic China, p.xi. Emperors of Sung, Yüan, Ming, and Ch'ing, p.xii. Chronological list of artists, p.385–87. Bibliography, p.390–404. Index, p.405–08.

M601 Ku kung po wu yuan ts'ang Ch'ing tai Yang-chou hua chia tso p'in = Paintings by Yangzhou artists of the Qing dynasty from the Palace Museum. [Introd. essay by Mu Yiqin.] [Beijing], Ku Kung po wu yuan, 1984. 296p. il. (part col.), plates, maps.

Parallel text in Chinese and English. Catalog of the exhibition, Art Gallery, Institute of Chinese Studies, The Chinese University of Hong Kong (1984–5).

Includes 100 paintings from the Palace Museum collection, Beijing, by 18 representative artists active in the prosperous city of Yangzhou in the late 17th and the 18th centuries. The artists include those known as the "Eight Eccentrics" whose work, by deviating from the orthodox, created an original style independent of past traditions and current trends. Fully illustrated with color plates and numerous black-and-white details.

Select bibliography, p.294–96.

M602 Lim, Lucy. Contemporary Chinese painting: an exhibition from the People's Republic of China. San Francisco, Chinese Culture Foundation of San Francisco, [1983]. 191p., il (part col.), map.

Catalog of the exhibition, Chinese Culture Center of San Francisco (1983–84), and other locations. Prepared with the cooperation of the Chinese Artists Association of the People's Republic of China, this catalog introduces 36 painters and 66 works of art, mostly in the traditional Chinese ink-and-brush style, produced since 1949. Includes essays by James Cahill and Michael Sullivan as well as excerpts from Chinese essays on art.

Selected bibliography, p.187–88.

M603 Loehr, Max. The great painters of China. N.Y., Harper and Row, [1980]. viii, 336p. il. (part col.)

Concise survey of Chinese painting organized sequentially with little reference to historical or cultural background.

Contents: (1) The rise of pictorial art; (2) Figure painting of the Six Dynasties (221–589); (3) Figure painting of Sui (589–617) and T'ang (618–907); (4) Landscape painters of Sui and T'ang; (5) Landscape painters of the Five Dynasties (907–60); (6) Landscape painters of Northern Sung (960–1126); (7) Painters of Southern Sung (1127–1278); (8) Masters of the Yüan Period (1279–1367); (9) Masters of the Ming Period (1368–1644); (10) The Ch'ing or Manchu Period (1644–1911).

Bibliography, p.327–32. Index, p.333–36.

M604 Murck, Alfreda, and Fong, Wen C., eds. Words and images: Chinese poetry, calligraphy, and painting. N.Y., Metropolitan Museum of Art; Princeton, Princeton Univ. Pr., [1991]. xxii, 589p. il.

Papers presented at an international symposium, Metropolitan Museum of Art (1985), to commemorate the promised gift of John M. Crawford, Jr.'s collection of Chinese calligraphy and scholars' painting to the museum. 23 scholarly essays that explore the relationship between the "three perfections": Chinese poetry, calligraphy, and painting.

Chronology, p.xiii. Abbreviations, p.xiv. Index, p.537–89.

M605 Spiro, Audrey G. Contemplating the ancients: aesthetic and social issues in early Chinese portraiture. Berkeley, Univ. of California Pr., [1990]. xv, 259p. il.

"This book is about portraits that were not intended to be physical likenesses of their subjects and about why they look the way they do."—*Pref.*

The author's thesis is that many early portraits were character portraits rendering man's moral traits and made for the purpose of admiration, identification, and emulation. A good introduction to early portraiture as well as to the artistic and political culture of the Southern dynasties.

Notes, p.181–223. Glossary, p.225–30. Bibliography, p.231–45. Index, p.247–59.

M606 Sullivan, Michael. Chinese landscape painting: the Sui and T'ang dynasties. Berkeley, Univ. of California Pr., [1980]. xiv, 191p. il. (1 col.), map, plates.
Published as v.2 of GLAH 1:M551.

Contents: (I) Sui and T'ang: the historical and cultural background; (II) The painter in T'ang society; (III) T'ang aesthetics; (IV) The north-south dialectic in Chinese culture and painting; (V) Notes on the landscape painters of Sui and T'ang; (VI) Themes in Sui and T'ang landscape painting; (VII) Space, form, and technique in Sui and T'ang landscape painting; (VIII) Trees and plants: notes towards a repertory; (IX) Epilogue: the legacy of T'ang landscape painting.

A note on sources, p.161. Notes, p.163–77. Bibliography, p.178–84. Index, p.185–91.

M607 Suzuki, Kei. Chugoku kaigashi. Tokyo, Yoshikawa Kobunkan, [1981–1984]. 3 vols. in 8. il.
In Japanese. History of Chinese painting, by one of the most eminent scholars of the field. The work is organized chronologically by dynasty or period. Within each dynasty or period the information is grouped by topics such as landscape painting and then by individual artist. The black-and-white illustrations are collected together in each vol. with references to the plates in the text.

Each vol. includes end notes, an index, and a chronological table.

M608 ______. Chugoku kaigo sogo zuroku = Comprehensive illustrated catalogue of Chinese paintings. Tokyo, Univ. of Tokyo Pr., 1982–83. 5v.
Text in Japanese and English.

An extraordinary resource of illustrations of Chinese painting. This 5-vol. set consists of small black-and-white photographs of Chinese works of art inspected by the staff of the East Asian Art History and Archaeology Section of the Institute of Oriental Culture at the University of Tokyo between 1975 and 1983. The works are in public and private collections and primarily date before the 18th century. V.1–4 each feature a section of photographs and an index catalog of works organized by collection. The catalog includes an assigned number, attributed artist's name, name of work, attributed date, format, dimensions, collection number, and indication of the images taken by the research institute. V.5, the comprehensive index, has subject and artist indexes and a catalog in English of works organized by collection as well as by subject and artist. Continued by the following entry.

Contents: (1) American and Canadian collections; (2) Southeast Asian and European collections; (3) Japanese collections: museums; (4) Japanese collections: temples and individuals; (5) Indexes.

M609 ______. Chugoku kaigo sogo zuroku. Zokuhen = Comprehensive illustrated catalog of Chinese paintings. Second series. Tokyo, Tokyo Daigaku Toyo Bunka Kenkyujo, 1998– . (3)v.
Contents also in English. This planned 4-vol. ed. is a sequel to the 5-vol. ed. (1982–85) (see preceding entry).

Contents: (1) American and Canadian collections; (2) Asian and European collections; (3) Japanese collections.

M610 Three thousand years of Chinese painting. [By] Richard M. Barnhart, James Cahill, Wu Hung . . . [et al.] New Haven, Yale Univ. Pr., 1997. 402p. il. (part col.), map (The culture and civilization of China)
An important reassessment, written by a team of leading scholars.

Contents: Approaches to Chinese painting; The origins of Chinese painting; The Five Dynasties and the Song Period (907–1279); The Yüan Dynasty (1271–1368); The Ming Dynasty (1368–1644); The Qing Dynasty (1644–1911); Traditional Chinese painting in the twentieth century.

Notes, p.355–64. Glossary, p.365–70. Artists by period, p.371–84. Further readings, p.385–87. List of contributors, p.389. Index, p.391–402.

M611 Vinograd, Richard. Boundaries of the self: Chinese portraits, 1600–1900. N.Y., Cambridge Univ. Pr., 1992. xv, 191p. il. (part col.), plates.
Study of later Chinese portraiture where the "most attention is paid to informal portraits, often painted by nonspecialists with established art-historical identities, as opposed to ancestral or court portraits by anonymous professional portraitists."—*Introd.*

Topics include portraits of artists and self-portraits, the portrait and related issues of selfhood and identity, and the portrait as an event.

Selected bibliography, p.178–86.

M612 Yu, Fei-an. Chinese painting colors: studies of their preparation and application in traditional and modern times. Trans. by Jerome Silbergeld and Amy McNair. Seattle, Univ. of Washington Pr., [1988]. xiv, 93p., col. il., plates
Trans. of Chung-kuo hua yen se ti yen chiu. T'ai-pei, Hua cheng shu chü, min kuo, 1985.

Yu Feian (1889–1959) was a prominent painter of flowers and birds who originally published this work to fill a gap in the literature about the use of color in Chinese painting. An important resource, not only for the preparation of traditional colors and their derivations, but for practical information on methods and formulas. Chapter 1 discusses sources for pigments, both mineral and vegetable, the manner in which color is fixed to the ground, and the method by which paper and silk are sized. Chapter 2 provides a brief history of the use of color since neolithic times. Chapter 3 covers the use and preparation of ink. Chapters 4 and 5 provide more technical discussion of color.

Selected bibliography, p.84–86.

India, Nepal, Pakistan, Tibet

M613 Archer, Mildred. Company paintings: Indian paintings of the British period. Assisted by Graham Parlett. [London], Victoria and Albert Museum in assoc. with Mapin Publishing, 1992. 240p. il. (part col.) (Indian art series)

Catalog of Company paintings ("a special type of Indian painting which was produced for Europeans and was heavily influenced by European taste") in the Museum collection.

Contents: (1) South India; (2) Eastern and upper India; (3) Northern and western India; (4) Nepal, Burma, Sri Lanka, Malacca; (5) Other media.

Glossary, p.228–29. Bibliography, p.230–33. Concordance, p.234–35. Index, p.236–40.

M614 ———. India and British portraiture, 1770–1825. N.Y., Sotheby Parke Bernet (Distr. by Biblio Distribution Centre, 1979). 536p. il. (part col.)

"The purpose of the present study is to trace the careers of British portrait painters who worked in India during the years 1770 to 1825 and . . . to identify, attribute and date . . . examples of their work."—*Pref.* Substantial, scholarly study.

Bibliography: p.[477]–86. Index of sitters and oriental subjects, p.[523]–24. Index of British sitters and individual subjects, p.[525]–30. Index of artists, p.[531]–32. Index of engravers, p.[533].

M615 Bautze, Joachim K. Interaction of cultures: Indian and western painting, 1780–1910: the Ehrenfeld collection. Alexandria, Va., Art Services International, 1998. 378p. il. (part col.), col. maps.

Accompanied an exhibition organized and circulated by Art Services International, documenting the confrontation of Indian and western painting.

Contents: India and the west: the interaction of artists, by Joachim K. Bautze; The place of Company painting in Indian art, by J. P. Losty; The Indian artist as assimilator of western styles, by Toby Falk; The Raj, Indian artists, and western art, by Partha Mitter; Catalogue, by Joachim K. Bautze.

Index of artists, p.346–47. Glossary, p.348–52. Bibliography, p.353–72. Index, p.373–78.

M616 Beach, Milo Cleveland. The grand Mogul: imperial painting in India, 1600–1660. With contrib. by Stuart Cary Welch and Glenn D. Lowry. Williamstown, Mass., Sterling and Francine Clark Art Institute, 1978. 199p. il. (part col.), map, plates.

Catalog of the exhibition, Sterling and Francine Clark Art Institute (1978), and other locations. Focuses "on the central achievement of the Mughal school, the exploration of naturalism in the early seventeenth century."—*Foreword.*

Notes, p.183–86. Abbreviations, p.187. Genealogy, p.188–90. Bibliography, p.191–95. Index, p.196–99.

M617 ———. The imperial image: paintings for the Mughal court. Washington, D.C., Freer Gallery of Art, Smithsonian Institution, 1981. 237p. il. (part col.), map.

Catalog of the exhibition, Freer Gallery of Art (1981–82), based on the Freer's excellent collection. "Centers on paintings made under the patronage of the Mughal emperors of India and concentrates on the years 1560–1640."—*Pref. and ackn.*

Contents: Introduction; Catalogue: Pre-Mughal traditions; Mughal manuscripts; Mughal albums; Single paintings; Appendix: Major identified Imperial Akbar-Period manuscripts.

Key to abbreviated references, p.229–30. Selected bibliography, p.231–33. Index, p.234–37.

M618 ———. Mughal and Rajput painting. N.Y., Cambridge Univ. Pr., 1992. xxxii, 252p. il. (part col.) (The New Cambridge history of India, I, 3)

Seeks "to provide a continuous narrative" of a key period of Indian painting.

Contents: Introduction; (1) Painting in North India before 1540; (2) 1540–1580: painting at Muslim courts; (3) 1580–1600: the new imperial style and its impact; (4) 1600–1660: Mughal painting and the rise of local workshops; (5) 1660–1700: The growth of local styles; (6) 1700–1800: the dominance of Rajput painting; (7) 1800–1858: traditionalism and new influences; Appendix.

Bibliographical essay, p.240–47. Index, p.248–52.

M619 Brij Bhushan, Jamila. The world of Indian miniatures. Tokyo, Kodansha International (Distr., Harper and Row, 1979). 205p. il. (part col.)

"This book is intended for the non-specialist," outlining "the distinguishing features of the different schools, techniques and subject matter of Indian painting."—*Pref.*

Contents: (I) The tradition; (II) Materials and techniques; (III) The themes; (IV) The Schools.

Glossary, p.189–92. Bibliography, p.193–97. Index, p.199–205.

M620 Brooklyn Museum. Realms of heroism: Indian paintings at the Brooklyn Museum. [By] Amy G. Poster, with Sheila R. Canby, Pramod Chandra, and Joan M. Cummins. N.Y., Hudson Hills Pr. in assoc. with the Brooklyn Museum, 1994. 351p. il. (part col.), map.

Scholarly, lustrous catalog of an important collection.

Contents: Introduction, by Amy G. Poster; History of the collection, by Amy G. Poster; Catalogue: Pre-Mughal painting; Mughal painting; Deccani painting; Rajasthani painting; Punjab Hills; Other schools; Appendix: Indian drawings in The Brooklyn Museum, by Joan M. Cummins.

Bibliography, p.325–34. Glossary, p.335–41. Index, p.343–51.

M621 Chavan, Kamal. Maratha murals: late medieval painting of the Deccan, 1650–1850 A.D. New Delhi, B.R. Pub. Corp., 1983. x, 122p. il. (part col.), plates.

"I undertook an extensive survey of the Maratha homeland to examine the remains of murals and the results are presented in the following pages. . . . This thesis is the first scientific record of the murals extant today."—*Introd.* Regional survey.

Bibliography, p.[113]–18. Index, p.119–22.

M622 Chester Beatty Library. Mughal and other Indian paintings from the Chester Beatty Library. [By] Linda York Leach. London, Scorpion Cavendish, 1995. 2v. il. (part col.)

Monumental collection catalog.

Contents: Vol.1: (I) The paintings of Akbar's reign up to 1600; (II) Paintings from 1600 to 1615; (III) Imperial paintings from 1615 to 1658; (IV) Mughal paintings from 1658 to 1760; Vol.2: (V) Sub-imperial paintings from 1590 to 1750; (VI) Provincial Mughal paintings of the eighteenth century; (VII) Company-style paintings; (VIII) Late Mughal paintings from circa 1780 to 1860; (IX) Paintings of the Deccan and Kashmir; (X) Paintings of Rajasthan, Central and Western Asia; (XI) Miniatures from the Himalayan foothills.

Biographies of painters, v.2, p.1097–1118. Bibliography, v.2, p.1119–21. Concordance, v.2, p.1123–42. Index, v.2, p.1143–48.

M623 Cleveland Museum of Art. Indian miniature paintings and drawings. [By] Linda York Leach. Cleveland, Cleveland Museum of Art (Distr. by Indiana Univ. Pr., 1986). xvi, 324p. il. (part col.)

Scholarly catalog of one of the great collections.

Contents: (I) Early painting: Jain, Sultanate, and early Rajput schools; (II) Mughal painting from Akbar through Shah Jahan; (III) Subimperial, popular Mughal, and bazaar Mughal painting; (IV) Late imperial, provincial Mughal, Deccani, Kashmiri, and Company Style painting; (V) Rajasthani and central, eastern, and south Indian painting; (VI) Pahari painting.

Glossary, p.317–18. Select bibliography, p.319–24.

M624 Desai, Vishakha N. Life at court: art for India's rulers, 16th–19th centuries. With essays by B. N. Goswamy and Ainslie T. Embree. Boston, Museum of Fine Arts, 1985. xxiii, 162p. il. (part col.)

Catalog of the exhibition, the Museum (1985–86), and other locations. "Explores the interconnections between paintings made for Mughal, Rajput, and British rulers rather than approaching each of these types of painting individually."—*Pref. and ackn.*

Contents: (I) Rulers of India: 1500–1900, by Ainslie T. Embree; (II) Images of court life: 1500–1900, by Vishakha N. Desai; (III) Of devotées and elephant fights: some notes on the subject matter of Mughal and Rajput painting, by B. N. Goswamy; (IV) Catalogue; (V) Appendixes; (VI) Bibliography (p.159–161).

M625 Ehnbom, Daniel J. Indian miniatures: the Ehrenfeld collection. With essays by Robert Skelton and Pramod Chandra. N.Y., Hudson Hills Pr. in assoc. with the American Federation of Arts, (Distr. by Viking Penguin, 1985). 270p. il., col. plates, facsims.

Published in conjunction with American Federation of Arts exhibition 84–5, circulated September 1985–November 1987. The collection is unusually broad in its chronological and stylistic scope.

Bibliography, p.257–63. Index, p.265–70.

M626 The Emperors' album: images of Mughal India. [By] Stuart Cary Welch . . . [et al.] N.Y., Metropolitan Museum of Art (Distr. by Abrams, 1987). 318p. il. (part col.)

Published in conjunction with the exhibition, the Museum (1987). Examines and publishes for the first time a series of 41 leaves from the museum's 17th-century Kevorkian album.

Contents: Introduction, by Stuart Cary Welch; The calligraphy and poetry of the Kevorkian album, by Annemarie Schimmel; Decorative borders in Mughal albums, by Marie L. Swietochowski; The Kevorkian album; Appendix: comparative illustrations.

Chronology, p.296–306. Glossary, p.307. Bibliography, p.308–12. List of Kevorkian folios by accession number, p.313–15. Index, p.316–18.

M627 Ghosh, Deva Prasad. Mediaeval Indian painting: Eastern school, 13th century A.D. to modern times, including folk art. New Delhi, Sundeep, 1982. ix, 155p., plates (part col.)

"The pictorial records illustrated here . . . are mainly based on the Asutosh Museum Collections, the first University Museum in India," which the author built up from 1937 to 68.—*Pref.*

Contents: (I) Origins of the eastern trend of mediaeval Indian painting; (II) Pictorial style of the copper plate engravings of ancient Bengal and its influence in South East Asian art; (III) Mannerisms of eastern and western painting; (IV) Mediaeval Orissan painting; (V) Mediaeval Bengal painting; (VI) An illustrated Ramayana manuscript of Tulsidasa; (VII) Heritage of Indian pats; (VIII) Orissan pats and paintings—late mediaeval and modern; (IX) Bengal pats—late mediaeval and modern; (X) Kalighat school of painting—is it dead?; (XI) Tribal pats of Bengal and Bihar; (XII) Dasavatar playing cards of Visnupur and Orissa; (XIII) Technique of Orissan and Bengal pat painting; Conclusion; Appendices.

Bibliography, p.127–31. Index, p.133–40.

M628 Goswamy, B. N., and Fischer, Eberhard. Pahari masters: court painters of northern India. [Reprint.] Delhi, Oxford Univ. Pr., 1997. 391p. il. (part col.)

1st ed. Zürich, Artibus Asiae, 1992 (Supplementum, 38). Trans. of Pahari-Meister: höfische Malerei aus den Bergen Nord-Indiens. Zürich, Museum Rietberg, 1990.

"What is presented in these pages is neither a history of Pahari painting nor yet another study on the art of the northern hill-states. Fourteen masters, or groups very close to them, active over a period of nearly three hundred years, are presented here."—*p.5.*

Bibliography, p.388–90.

M629 ______, and Fischer, Eberhard. Wonders of a golden age: painting at the court of the great Mughals: Indian art of the 16th and 17th centuries from collections in Switzerland. Zürich, Museum Rietberg, 1987. 222p. col. il., ports.

Catalog of the exhibition, Museum Rietberg (1987), drawing on private and public Swiss collections and aiming to draw attention to "some of the dominant concerns of the Mughal painters."—*Authors' note.*

Contents: (1) Absorption; (2) Innovation and conservatism; (3) Virtuosity; (4) The imperial image; (5) Concern with the past; (6) Concern with the present; (7) Curiosity and observation; (8) Word and image; (9) Inward turning; (10) Chronological framework; (11) Changing times, new patrons.

Bibliography, p.218–21.

M630 Heeramaneck, Alice N. Masterpieces of Indian painting from the former collections of Nasli M. Heeramaneck. United States, Alice N. Heeramaneck (Distr. by Advent Books, 1984). viii, 263p., col. il., map.

Well-illustrated catalog of the excellent private collection of Rajput and Mughal painting donated to the Los Angeles County Museum of Art in 1969.

Notes, p.260. Bibliography, p.261–62.

M631 India Office Library. Indian miniatures in the India Office Library. [By] Toby Falk, Mildred Archer. London, Sotheby Parke Bernet; Delhi, Oxford Univ. Pr., 1981. 559p. il. (part col.), 16p. of plates.

Culmination of decades of effort.

Glossary, p.303–04. Concordances, p.324–32. Bibliography, p.333–38. Indices, p.339–51.

M632 Kramrisch, Stella. Painted delight: Indian paintings in Philadelphia collections. Philadelphia, Philadelphia Museum of Art, 1986. xxiii, 195p. il. (part col.)

Scholarly catalog of the exhibition, the Museum (1986), held in connection with the Festival of India.

Contents: Catalogue: Pre-Mughal painting; Mughal painting; Painting in the Deccan; Rajput painting in the plains; Rajput painting in the Panjab Hills; Folk painting.

Bibliography, p.191–95.

M633 ______. A survey of painting in the Deccan. [Reprint.] New Delhi, Oriental Reprint (Distr. by Munshiram Manoharlal Publishers, 1983). xiii, 234p. il., 24 leaves of plates (1 folded).

Reprint of original ed., London, India Society, 1937. Standard survey of Deccani painting.

Contents: (I) Ajanta; (II) Elura; (III) Vijayanagar; (IV) The last phase.

Notes, p.201–27. Index, p.231–34.

M634 Krishna, Chaitanya. A history of Indian painting. New Delhi, Abhinav Publications, 1976–1994. 5v. il.

Comprehensive history. The poor production quality improves by v.5.

Contents: (1) The mural tradition; (2) Manuscript, Moghul and Deccani traditions; (3) Rajasthani tradition; (4) Pahari traditions; (5) The modern period.

M635 Lahore. Central Museum. Catalogue of paintings in the Lahore Museum. Lahore, Lahore Museum, 1976– . (1)v. il.

Successor to Samarendranath Gupta's 1922 catalog of the collection.

Contents: (1) Mughal and Rajasthani schools.

M636 Miniatures de l'Inde impériale: les peintres de la cour d'Akbar, 1556–1605. [Catalogue réd. par Amina Okada.] Paris, Ministère de la culture, de la communication, des grands travaux et du bicentenaire, Eds. de la Réunion des musées nationaux, 1989. 220p. il. (part col.)

Catalog of the exhibition, Musée national des arts asiatiques Guimet (1989), based on private and public collections in France.

Contents: Akbar et l'Inde moghole; Les peintres de la cour d'Akbar; Les manuscrits akbariens; Les représentations de la faune et de la flore; L'art du portrait; Les gravures européenes et l'influence de l'Occident.

Notes at ends of chapters. Bibliographie, p.218–20.

M637 Nagpall, J. C. Mural paintings in India. Delhi, Gian Pub. House, 1988. ix [i.e., xiv], 230p. il., plates.

Summary record of Indian murals, by a former head of the preservation department of the Archaeological Survey of India. Poor quality paper and plates.

Bibliography, p.215–21. Index, p.228–30.

M638 National Gallery of Modern Art (New Delhi, India). Modern Indian paintings from the collection of the National Gallery of Modern Art, New Delhi. New Delhi, India, The Gallery, 1982. [69]p. il. (part col.)

Catalog of the exhibition, National Gallery of Modern Art (1982), of 50 paintings by contemporary 20th-century Indian artists.

Biographies [unpaginated, at back of vol.].

M639 Okada, Amina. Indian miniatures of the Mughal court. Trans. by Deke Dusinberre. N.Y., Abrams, 1992. 239p. il. (part col.), plates.

Focuses "primarily on the personal oeuvre of the finest court painters to the three most eminent emperors of the brilliant Mughal dynasty. . . . This book dwells, therefore, on the special relationship that existed between the emperor-patrons and the artists who painted an inspired and indulgent picture of imperial grandeur."—*Foreword.*

Manuscripts, p.226. Glossary, p.226. Bibliography, p.236–37. Index, p.238–39.

M640 Pal, Pratapaditya. The classical tradition in Rajput painting: from the Paul F. Walter Collection. [N.Y.], Pierpont Morgan Library, 1978. xii, 210p. il. (part col.)

Catalog of the exhibition, the Library (1978), and other locations, of approximately 80 paintings from an outstanding private collection. "Attempts to break fresh ground in the study of one kind of Indian painting, that of the Rajput school."—*Foreword.*

Bibliography, p.209–10.

M641 ______. Court paintings of India: 16th–19th centuries. N.Y., Navin Kumar, 1983. 334p. col. il.

"This book is about pictures . . . rendered between the sixteenth and nineteenth centuries in India, primarily for the courts of the Muslim and Hindu emperors and kings."—*Pref. and ackn.*

Notes, p.321. Bibliography, p.332. Index, p.333–34.

M642 ______. Indian painting: a catalogue of the Los Angeles County Museum of Art collection. Los Angeles, Los Angeles County Museum of Art (Distr. by Abrams, 1993–). (1)v. il. (part col.), map.

Scholarly, well-illustrated catalog of an important collection, to be complete in 2 vols. V.1 includes Buddhist and Jain manuscript illumination, illustrated books from the Sultanate period, and Mughal and Deccani painting and calligraphy from 1550 to 1700. V.2 will include the Rajput paintings as well as later Mughal and Company school works.

Contents: (1) 1000–1700.

M643 Rogers, J. M. Mughal miniatures. London, British Museum Pr., 1993. 128p. il. (part col.) (Eastern art series)

Lucid introduction, focusing upon illustrated manuscripts and albums.

Contents: (1) The Mughals and their empire; (2) Materials, techniques and workshop practices; (3) The beginnings of Mughal painting; (4) Painting at the court of Akbar; (5) Akbar's studio; (6) The imperial studio under Jahāngīr; (7) Painting under Shāh Jahān and Awrangzīb.

Further reading, p.124–25. Index, p.126–28.

M644 Rossi, Barbara. From the ocean of painting: India's popular paintings, 1589 to the present. With contrib. by Roy C. Craven, Jr. and Stuart Cary Welch. N.Y., Oxford Univ. Pr., 1998. xiv, 295p. il. (part col.), maps.

Seeks to elucidate "several forms of folk, tribal, and urban popular painting" that constitute a tradition distinct from more sophisticated traditions of painting.—*Pref.*

Contents: (1) Paintings from popular ritual tradition; (2) Paintings from popular iconic traditions; (3) Paintings from popular narrative traditions; (4) Paintings informed by sophisticated traditions; (5) Paintings on reverse glass; (6) Paintings serving didactic, divinatory, and other cultural functions; (7) Painting employed with other media in popular traditional artifacts.

Notes, p.231–54. Select bibliography, p.255–80. Index, p.283–95.

M645 Tuli, Neville. Indian contemporary painting. N.Y., Abrams, 1998. 478p. il. (part col.)

Originally published as: The flamed-mosaic. Middletown, N. J., Mapin Pub., 1997.

An appreciation of contemporary painting in India. Includes a survey of modern painting in India and conversations with 35 artists.

Biographical information, p.402–44. Bibliography, p.445–73. Index, p.474–78.

M646 Verma, Som Prakash. Mughal painters and their work: a biographical survey and catalogue. Delhi, Oxford Univ. Pr., 1994. xvi, 438p. il.

"Attempts to fill the lacuna in respect of painters of the Mughal School. . . . What is attempted here is systematic description and arrangement of their surviving work, together with whatever biographical information can be assembled about them. Painters of the later Mughal school of the eighteenth century have not been included."—*Introd.*

Bibliography, p.417–34. Indexes: Subject index, p.435–36. Index of portraits, p.437–38.

M647 Weber, Rolf. Porträts und historische Darstellungen in der Miniaturensammlung des Museums für Indische Kunst Berlin. Berlin, Das Museum, 1982. 624p. il. (part col.), [1] leaf of plates.

Detailed study of the museum's collection of 143 portrait miniatures (118 of them illustrated) and miniatures depicting historical subjects, with a catalog and full-page black-and-white reproductions.

Contents: (I) Grundlagen und Entwicklung des Porträts; (II) Das Problem der Ähnlichkeit; (III) Formen der Porträtdarstellung; (IV) Katalog; Appendices.

Index der porträtierten Personen, p.585–88. Abkürzungen, p.589. Bibliographie, p.591–619.

M648 Welch, Stuart Cary. Room for wonder: Indian painting during the British period, 1760–1880. N.Y., American Federation of Arts, 1978. 191p. il. (part col.)

Catalog of American Federation of Arts exhibition 78–1, circulated 1978–79. Introduction to a little-known period in Indian painting.

Chronology, p.179–87. Selected bibliography, p.188–91.

M649 Zebrowski, Mark. Deccani painting. Berkeley, Univ. of California Pr., 1983. 296p. il. (part col.)

"A surprisingly large proportion of the surviving masterpieces of Indian painting was produced for the mysterious sultans who ruled the Deccan, the vast plateau south of the Vindhya mountains, during the sixteenth and seventeenth centuries."—*Introd.* Detailed, scholarly study of the Deccani school of painting.

Bibliography, p.285–89. Index of artists, p.290. General index, p.291–96.

Japan

Bibliography

M650 Uyehara, Cecil H. Japanese calligraphy: a bibliographic study. Lanham, Md., Univ. Pr. of America, [1991]. viii, 364p.

An exhaustive and scholarly annotated bibliography of 672 works on Japanese calligraphy compiled from the collections at the Library of Congress and the Freer Gallery of Art. Citations are grouped into topical chapters, each introduced by an essay.

Contents: (I) Introduction and explanatory notes; (II) Calligraphy research; (III) Reference materials; (IV) Histories and commentaries; (V) Calligraphy collections; (VI) Calligraphy education and training; (VII) Implements; (VIII) Kao signatures; (IX) Calligraphic engravings; (X) Calligraphy and commercial art; (XI) Newspapers and periodicals.

Appendixes: Calligraphic styles, p.297. Chronological chart for China and Japan, p.298. Glossary, p.301–08. List of publishers, p.390–416. Author index, p.317–26. Index of titles, 327–42. Names/places in Kanji, p.343–63.

Histories and Handbooks

M651 Addiss, Stephen. The art of Zen: paintings and calligraphy by Japanese monks, 1600–1925. N.Y., Abrams, 1989. 223p. il. (part col.)

Documents works "created neither 'for art's sake' nor at the bidding of wealthy patrons, but rather to aid meditation and to lead toward enlightenment."—*Introd.*

Exemplifies, with its very readable text and delightful illustrations, the spontaneous, simple, and bold calligraphy and paintings of the Zen Buddhist monks who intended their art to reflect their inner lives.

Annotated bibliography, p.214–18.

M652 ______. Zenga and Nanga: paintings by Japanese monks and scholars, selections from the Kurt and Millie Gitter collection. New Orleans, New Orleans Museum of Art, 1976. 191p. il (part col.)

Catalog of the exhibition, New Orleans Museum of Art (1976), and other locations.

Traces the historical development of two schools of painting of the Tokugawa or Edo period (1615–1868) through the paintings and calligraphy of 22 Zenga artists and 33 Nanga painters.

Bibliography, p.189.

M653 Akiyama, Terukazu. Japanese painting. [Reprint.] Geneva, Skira, [1990]. 216p. col. il. (Treasures of Asia)

Reprint of GLAH 1:M566. The text is reproduced unabridged, but the table of contents has been moved to the front of the book. Minor loss of detail and some yellowing of the colors in the color illustrations.

M654 The arts of the Edo period: an international symposium. New Orleans, New Orleans Museum of Art, [1983?]. [205 leaves] il.

Nine of the papers delivered at the "International Symposium of the Arts of the Edo Period," New Orleans Museum of Art (1983), in conjunction with the exhibition "A Myriad of Autumn Leaves." Illustrated with photocopies of photographs.

M655 Clark, Timothy. Ukiyo-e paintings in the British Museum. Washington, D.C., Smithsonian Institution Pr., 1992. 256p. il. (part col.)

Catalog and study.

Contents: The study, collecting and forging of Ukiyo-e paintings; The paintings; Appendix: Fakes.

Alternative names of artists, p.250–51. Bibliography, p.241–50. Index, p.252–56.

M656 Conant, Ellen P.; Owyoung, Steven D.; and Rimer, J. Thomas. Nihonga: transcending the past: Japanese style painting 1868–1968. St. Louis, St. Louis Art Museum; [Tokyo], The Japan Foundation, 1995. 351p. il. (part col.)

Catalog of the exhibition, St. Louis Art Museum (1995).

An exhibition of 171 works of Nihonga or traditional Japanese-style painting from the Meiji, Taishō, and Shōwa eras. The works depict the times and characteristic themes as Japan opened to Western nations and assimilated their influence. The essays, which treat the various themes in a chronological order, are followed by the catalog,

Biographies, p.290–334. Notes to the reader, p.335. Bibliography, p.336–43. Index, p.344–50.

M657 Fister, Patricia. Japanese women artists, 1600–1900. Lawrence, Spencer Museum of Art, Univ. of Kansas, [1988]. 197p. il. (part col.)

Catalog of the exhibition, Spencer Museum of Art (1988), and another location.

Introduction to a subject neglected by Japanese and western scholars. Provides biographical information on women artists of the Edo period and elucidates their political, social, and economic context. Reproduces nearly 100 works of art.

Bibliography, p.184–91. Index, p.192–96.

M658 Kaigai ukiyoe shozai sakuin = Index of ukiyo-e in western collections. Kyoto, Kokusai Nihon Bunka Kenkyu Senta, 1996. 2v. (Kaigai Nihon Bijutsu Chosa Purojekuto hokoku = Report of Japanese art abroad research project, 6; Kokusai Nihon Bunka Kenkyu Senta Nichibunken sosho = International Research Center for Japanese Studies, Nichibunken Japanese Studies series, 11)

Vol.1 in Japanese, vol.2 in English.

Explanatory notes, v.2, p.4–5. Artist index, v.2, p.6–12.

M659 Murase, Miyeko. Emaki, narrative scrolls from Japan. [N.Y.], Asia Society, [1983]. 175p. il. (part col.)

Catalog of the exhibition, Asia Society (1983).

Emaki, narrative handscrolls combining pictures and text, constitute one of the most important parts of Japan's cultural heritage. The catalog documents the 34 scrolls from Japanese collections dating from mid-8th to the 20th century, which comprised the first exhibition on emaki ever shown outside Japan. The scrolls are organized into topical subdivisions: sacred texts; romantic tales; popular tales; portraits; biographies of celebrated priests; and histories of temples and shrines.

Selected bibliography, p.174–75.

M660 ______. Masterpieces of Japanese screen painting: the American collections. N.Y., Braziller, 1990. 232p. il., plates (part col.), (part folded).

Japanese ed. Tokyo, Iwanami Shoten, 1992.

"The works in this volume were created during the greatest eras of screen painting. . . . The works were chosen with an aim to represent the most important artists and schools of screen painting, and to provide a balanced overview of both the formats and techniques used and the wide range of subjects depicted in this magnificent art."—*Introd.*

A luxurious volume in a horizontal format, designed to accommodate reproductions of the 37 screens described and illustrated in the book. 13 gatefold reproductions allow side-by-side comparisons and careful examination of details.

Glossary, p.217–18. Biographies of the artists, p.219–22. Bibliography, p.223–24. Bibliographic references, p.225–28. Index of the artists, p.229. Index of the screens, p.230.

M661 ______. Tales of Japan: scrolls and prints from the New York Public Library. Oxford, Oxford Univ. Pr., 1986. xx, 267p. il. (part col.)

Catalog of the exhibition, New York Public Library (1986), and other locations.

Drawn from the Library's Special Collections department, this exhibit presents illustrated literary texts from printed books, handscrolls, and woodblock prints. Examples range from early Buddhist religious manuscripts of the 12th–14th century to scrolls and books of the 17th and 18th centuries including painters' accounts, manuals of veterinary medicine, and instructions on the art of flower arranging.

Contents: (I) Praise of the Buddha in words and images; (II) Heroes and heroines of classical literature; (III) Heroes and heroines of popular tales; (IV) Heroes and heroines of the stage; (V) Men and women of the real world; (VI) Keeping traditions alive; (VII) Scenes from the floating world.

Index, p.265–67.

M662 Rosenfield, John M., and ten Grotenhuis, Elizabeth. Journey of the three jewels: Japanese Buddhist paintings from Western collections. N.Y., Asia Society, [1979]. 203p. il. (part col.)

Catalog of the exhibition, Asia House Gallery (1979). Introduction to Japanese Buddhist painting.

Contents: (1) The Mahayana mainstream; (2) Esoteric Buddhist images; (3) Pure Land and popular Buddhist imagery; (4) Zen Buddhist paintings.

Glossary/index, p.193–200. Bibliography, p.201–03.

M663 Shimizu, Yoshiaki, and Rosenfield, John M. Masters of Japanese calligraphy 8th–19th century. N.Y., Asia Society Galleries; Japan House Gallery, [1984]. 340p. il., col. plates.

Catalog of the exhibition shown simultaneously at the Asia Society Galleries and Japan House Gallery (1984–85), and other locations.

Comprehensive exhibition of Japanese calligraphy dealing with the history, the writing systems and styles, and the schools of calligraphy.

Contents: (I) Buddhist texts; (II) Aristocratic scripts; (III) The Shōren-In tradition; (IV) The immortal poets; (V) Zen Buddhist masters; (VI) Masters of the tea ceremony; (VII) Renaissance in Kyoto; (VIII) The literati.

Chronology, p.325. Bibliography, p.326–27. Index, p.332–40.

Korea

M664 The fragrance of ink: Korean literati paintings of the Choson dynasty (1392–1910) from Korea Univ. Museum = Choson sidae sonbi ui mokhyang. Exhibition organized by the Korea Univ. Museum and Korea Studies Institute, Korea Univ. Circulated by the David and Alfred Smart Museum of Art, Univ. of Chicago. [Painting selection and catalog by Kwon Young-Pil, Byun Young-sup, Yi Song-mi.] Seoul, Korean Studies Institute, Korea Univ., 1996. 256p. il. (part col.), ports.

"The first-ever presentation in the United States of the traditional scholar painting of Korea's last dynasty, from one of the most important collections in Korea."—*Ackn.*

Contents: Plates: Landscapes; Figures in landscapes; Birds, animals, flowers, and insects; The "Four Gentlemen"; Essays; Catalog entries.

Selected bibliography, p.245. Contributors, p.255.

M665 Moes, Robert. Auspicious spirits: Korean folk paintings and related objects. Catalogue by Robert Moes. Washington, D.C., The Foundation, 1983. 199p. il. (part col.)

Catalog of the exhibition organized and circulated by the International Exhibitions Foundation and co-sponsored by the Korean Overseas Information Service (1983).

Contents: Introduction; Court paintings; Yangban paintings; Commoners' paintings; Religious folk paintings; Conclusion.

Explanatory notes to the text, p.12. Checklist of works in the exhibition, p.185–93. Selected bibliography, p.195. Topical index, p.197–99.

M666 Pratt, Keith L. Korean painting. N.Y., Oxford Univ. Pr., 1995. viii, 70p. il. (part col.), map.

Brief introduction.

Contents: (1) Korean painting in context; (2) The painter's world; (3) Human subjects; (4) Religious subjects; (5) Landscapes; (6) Flower and bird subjects; (7) Abstract art.

Glossary, p.63–64. Select bibliography, p.65–66. Index, p.67–70.

M667 Sorensen, Henrik Hjort. The iconography of Korean Buddhist painting. N.Y., Brill, 1989. 21p. il., 48p. of plates (Iconography of religions. Section XII, East and Central Asia, fasc. 9)

A selected bibliography is followed by essays, a catalog of illustrations, and plates. Includes many photographs of sculpture and paintings.

Selected bibliography, p.[ix].

M668 Traditional Korean painting: a lost art rediscovered. [By] Za-yong Zo (Cho Cha-yong), U Fan Lee (Lee U-ham). Trans. by John Bester. N.Y., Kodansha International, 1990. 176p. il., plates.

"Adapted from the original Japanese edition of Richúo no minga." Mostly devoted to color plates.

Contents: Yi-Dynasty painting and its categories, by U Fan Lee (Lee U-hwan); Yi-Dynasty painting and the concept of folk, by Za-yong Zo (Cho Cha-yong).

Southeast Asia

M669 Djelantik, A. A. M. Balinese paintings. 2d ed. N.Y., Oxford Univ. Pr., 1990. vii, 92p. il. (part col.), maps, 16p. of plates (Images of Asia)

1st ed. 1986.

"This book is an attempt by a Balinese to describe one of the most interesting branches of Balinese art—painting. . . . A concise account."—*Pref.*

Select bibliography p.89. Index, p.90–92.

M670 Gatellier, Marie. Peintures murales du Sri Lanka: école kandyenne, XVIIIe–XIXe siècles. Paris, École française d'Extrême-Orient, 1991. 2v. il. (part col.) (Publications de l'École française d'Extrême-Orient, 162)
Scholarly study, primarily iconographic, of Buddhist murals from Sri Lanka from the 18th to 19th century.
Contents: (1) Texte; (2) Planches.
Les castes a Sri Lanka, v.1, p.[245]–46. Liste alphabetique des principaux sanctuaires, v.1, p.[247]–48. Bibliographie, v.1, p.[249]–52. Index, v.1, p.[253]–59.

M671 Ginsburg, Henry. Thai manuscript painting. London, British Library, 1989. 112p. il. (part col.)
Lucid introduction.
Contents: (1) Cosmology; (2) Divination; (3) Elephants; (4) Ten Lives of the Buddha; (5) Phra Malai; (6) Genre scenes; (7) Notes on style; Appendix: List of illustrated Thai manuscripts in The British Library and other institutions.
Glossary, p.108–09. Bibliography, p.110–11. Index, p.112.

AFRICA, OCEANIA, THE AMERICAS

Africa

M672 Berman, Esmé. Painting in South Africa. [Johannesburg], Southern Book Publishers, [1993]. xxiv, 395p. 229 il., 99 col. pl.
Devoted primarily to white South African painting in the last years of the 20th century, this book presents "an outline of the sources, sequence and developments that have been significant, and a glimpse of the most prominent and influential careers and styles."—*Author's note.*
Contents: (1) Colonial culture and the great outdoors; (2) A link with the earliest Dutch settlers; (3) The landscape defined; (4) The subjective viewpoint; (5) The new group; (6) New South Africans; (7) Symbolism, fantasy and the mystique of Africa; (8) A unique indigenous tradition; (9) New media, new forms; (10) The landscape revisited; (11) The quest for identity; (12) What time is it?; (13) The shadow of humanity; (14) Traditions and transitions.
Glossary, p.379–87. Index, p.389–95.

M673 Bouttiaux-Ndiaye, Anne-Marie. Senegal behind glass: images of religious and daily life. München, Prestel in assoc. with the Royal Museum of Central Africa, Tervuren, [1994]. 167p. il., 150 col. pl., map.
Catalog of the exhibition, Hamburgisches Museum für Völkerkunde, Hamburg (1994), and other locations. The most comprehensive catalog to date on reverse-glass painting. Includes a thorough discussion of the history, techniques, themes, and style of Senegalese painting.
Contents: Senegalese reverse-glass painting; terminology and technique; origins and evolution; History of the Senegalese technique; Themes; Composition, style and technique; Professional training; The art market; Some leading artists; Other contemporary artists.
Bibliography, p.166–67.

M674 Garlake, Peter. The painted caves: an introduction to the prehistoric art of Zimbabwe. [Harare, Zimbabwe], Modus Publications, [1987]. iv, 100p. il. (part col.), plates.
Thorough introduction to 38 specific sites and includes essays on dating, techniques, conventions of the art, compositions, interpretation, and fourteen commonly depicted themes.
Contents: (1) The background to the paintings; (2) Interpretation and meaning; (3) Themes in the paintings; (4) Catalogue; (5) Directions to the sites.
Bibliography, p.96–97.

M675 Leakey, Mary D. Africa's vanishing art: the rock paintings of Tanzania. Garden City, N.Y., Doubleday, 1983. 128p. il. (part col.), map.
Extensively illustrated with color fieldwork illustrations. "A valuable record of an important area of African prehistoric art."—*Review*, African arts, v.18, August 1985, p.93.
Contents: (1) Introduction; (2) The paintings—their styles and subjects; (3) The Kolo sites; (4) The sites around Pahi; (5) Cheke and nearby sites; (6) Kisese, Kwa Mtea and Itololo; (7) Interpretations and implications.
Glossary, p.126. Bibliography, p.127. Index, p.127–28.

M676 Lhote, Henri. The search for the Tassili frescoes: the story of the prehistoric rock-paintings of the Sahara. Trans. from the French by Alan Houghton Brodrick. 2d ed. London [England], Hutchinson, [1973]. 236p. il. (part col.), col. maps (part folded), ports.
Trans. of À la découverte des fresques du Tassil. B. Arthaud, 1958; repr. 1988. This standard work on Tassili art includes extensive pictorial documentation about the ancient populations of the Sahara.
Contents: Saharan perspectives; Headed for the Tassili; The first survey at Tan-Zoumiatak; The cypresses of Tamrit; A herdman's culture; Jabbaren with its five thousand figures; The sanctuary of Aouanrhet; A Saharan summer; From one expedition to another; The new team at Ti-n-Tazarift; The great god of Sefar; The ancient route through the central Sahara; A dying people: the Tuareg of the Tassili; The fresco of twelve phases; Parachutes; Mission accomplished; Did we discover Atlantis?; Trial balance; The main art styles.
For further study, p.[237].

M677 Mercier, Jacques. Ethiopian magic scrolls. N.Y., Braziller, [1979]. 118p. 18 il., 40 col. plates.
Detailed examination of the talismanic art of ancient Ethiopian scrolls expounding on their meaning and symbolism, and commenting on colors, inscriptions, and motifs. The scrolls reproduced in the book primarily date from the 19th century.
Bibliography, p.34–35.

M678 Pittura Etiopica tradizionale. [Roma], Istituto Italo-Africano, [1989]. 165p. 90 col. il.

Text and plate documentation in Italian and English.

In a scholarly essay, Lanfranco Ricci discusses the stylistic chronology of the Ethiopian paintings, the progressive changes over the course of the 20th century brought about by Western influence, the Eritrea series, and individual artists. The plate documentation includes transcriptions and translations of artists' captions inscribed on the paintings in Gheez, Amharic, or Tigrinya.

Contents: The paintings: historical or assimilated subjects; Religious subjects; Various subjects; Appendix.

Index, p.165.

M679 60 ans de peinture au Zaïre. Joseph-Aurélien Cornet . . . [et al.] [Bruxelles], Les Editeurs d'Art Associés, [1989]. 212p. il. (part col.).

The standard survey of the history of modern painting in Zaïre.

Contents: (1) Précurseurs de la peinture moderne au Zaïre, par Joseph-Aurélien Cornet; (2) Pierre Romain-Desfossés, par Wim Toebosch; L'École de Lubumbashi, par Remi De Cnodder; (3) La peinture à Kinshasa, par Joseph-Aurélien Cornet.

Index des noms cités, p.207–209.

The Americas

M680 Bonavia, Duccio. Mural painting in ancient Peru. Trans. by Patricia J. Lyon. Bloomington, Indiana Univ. Pr., 1985. 224p. il. (part col.)

Rev. trans. of Ricchata quellccani: pinturas murales prehispánicas. Lima, Fondo del Libro del Banco Industrial del Perú, 1974.

"[A]ctually a completely restructured, enlarged, and updated version of the earlier book. . . . This volume is clearly the definitive work on ancient Peruvian murals."—*Review*, American antiquity, v.52, 1987, p.433. "This should be considered a basic text on prehispanic painting in Peru."—*Review*, Handbook of Latin American studies, v.50, 1990.

Appendix: Pigment analysis and comments, by Carlos Núñez Villavicencio, p.[199]–204. Notes, p.205–06. Bibliography, p.207–15. Index of persons and authors cited, p.219–21. Index of monuments, p.223–24.

M681 Brody, J. J. Anasazi and Pueblo painting. Albuquerque, Univ. of New Mexico Pr., 1991. xiv, 191p. il. (part col.), plates, maps.

Painting by the Anasazi and to a lesser extent their Pueblo descendants to 1900. Includes wall and rock painting, painting on pottery and on portable objects.

References, p.179–88. Index, p.189–91.

M682 Los códices mayas. Introd. y bibliografía por Thomas A. Lee, Jr. Tuxtla Gutiérrez, Mexico, Universidad Autónoma de Chiapas, 1985. 215p. col. il., map, facsims.

Brief descriptions accompany complete photofacsimile reproductions (reduced) of the Dresden, Madrid, Paris, and Grolier codices.

Extensive bibliography, p.177–213.

M683 Códices mexicanos. Graz, Austria, Akademische Druck- und Verlagsanstalt; Mexico City, Fondo de Cultura Económica, 1991– . (12)v. il. (part col.), col. facsims., maps.

Facsimile reprints of the principal Mexican pre- and post-Columbian manuscripts. Each boxed set includes a companion volume with description of the manuscript and its collection history; a discussion of the historical and cultural context of the manuscript; a page-by-page explanation of the manuscript; and a bibliography. While the design of the boxes is pretentious, the contents are nonetheless substantial. Many of the manuscripts were previously published in facsimile by Akademische Druck- und Verlagsanstalt in its Codices selecti series.

Contents: (1) Códice Vindobonensis Mexicanus I (1992); (2) Códice Zouche-Nuttall (1992); (3) Códice Borbónico (1991); (4) Códice Vaticano B.3773 (1993); (5) Códice Borgia (1993); (6) Códice Laud (1994); (7) Códice Fejérváry Mayer (1994); (8) Códice Cospi (1994); (9) Códices Egerton (1994); (10) Códice Vaticano A.3738 (1996); (11) Códice Ixtlilxóchitl (1996); (12) Códice Magliabechi (1996).

M684 Coe, Michael D., and Justin Kerr. The art of the Maya scribe. N.Y., Abrams, 1997. 240p. il. (part col.)

"We intend . . . to encompass all aspects of the script, wherever and on whatever it is found, above all during its apogee within the AD 250–900 span of the Classic period of Maya history."—*Pref.*

Contents: (1) The Maya universe; (2) The Maya script: its character and origins; (3) The world of the Maya scribes; (4) How the Maya wrote: surfaces, tools, and calligraphic techniques; (5) The Maya books; (6) The end of the calligraphic tradition.

Bibliography, p.233–34. Index, p.235–40.

M685 Feathered serpents and flowering trees: reconstructing the murals of Teotihuacan. Ed. by Kathleen Berrin. San Francisco, Fine Arts Museums of San Francisco, 1988. 238p. il. (part col.), map.

Describes the acquisition, conservation, and investigation of a bequest to the Fine Arts Museums of San Francisco of more than 70 mural fragments from Teotihuacán. Essays include bibliographies.

Contents: (1) An unexpected bequest and an ethical dilemma, by Thomas Seligman; (2) Reconstructing crumbling walls: a curator's history of the Wagner murals collection, by Kathleen Berrin; (3) A reinterpretation of Teotihuacan and its mural painting tradition, by Esther Pasztory; (4) Where do they all come from? The provenance of the Wagner murals from Teotihuacan, by René Millon; (5) A reexamination of the Teotihuacan tassel headdress insignia, by Clara Millon; (6) Catalogue of the Wagner murals collection; Appendix: Map of Teotihuacan; Construction and condition of the Wagner mural fragments, by Lesley Bone.

Index, p.234–38.

M686 Lester, Patrick D. The biographical directory of Native American painters. Tulsa, SIR Publications (Distr. by Univ. of Oklahoma Pr., 1995). xvii, 701p.

Updates Jeanne Snodgrass-King, American Indian painters. N.Y., Museum of the American Indian, Heye Foundation, 1968.

Directory of living and historical Native American painters in the United States and Canada. "The only criteria for inclusion in this directory are that the artist consider himself or herself to be Native American and be actively seeking a career as a painter."—*Pref.*

When available each entry has the following information: artist's name (and aliases); tribe(s); biographical information, including life dates and genealogy; narrative; residence; education; occupation; media; publications; illustrations; commissions; public collections; exhibits; awards; and honors. The narrative section includes paragraphs of human interest, many from the Snodgrass-King work.

Tribal index, p.647–63. Abbreviations, p.665–86. Bibliography, p.687–701.

M687 Miller, Mary Ellen. The murals of Bonampak. Princeton, Princeton Univ. Pr., 1986. xvii, 176p. il. (part col., part folded), plates.

Thorough investigation of the mural painting program at a Classic Maya settlement. Includes chapters on the hieroglyphic inscriptions in the murals and an appendix on the costumes depicted.

Bibliography, p.163–69. Index, p.171–76.

M688 Philbrook Museum of Art. Visions and voices: native American painting from the Philbrook Museum of Art. Ed. by Lydia L. Wyckoff. Tulsa, Philbrook Museum of Art (Distr. by Univ. of New Mexico Pr., 1996). 304p. il. (part col.)

Survey of 20th-century native American easel painting in the Philbrook Museum. More than 160 artists represented by illustrations of 484 paintings. Each entry has brief biographical data and in many cases artist's statement. Includes an essay, "A collective history of native American painting," by Lydia L. Wyckoff. In many instances provides the visual complement to Lester, Patrick D., The biographical directory of Native American painters. [GLAH 2:M686]

References cited, p.299–300. Index, p.301–04.

M689 La pintura mural prehispánica en México. Coordinadora, Beatriz de la Fuente. Mexico City, Universidad Nacional Autónoma de México, 1995– . (2)v. in 4. il. (part col.), maps, plans.

Exhaustive treatment of the discovery, technology, iconography, and conservation of the complete mural programs at Teotihuacán and Bonampak.

Contents: (1) Teotihuacán (2v.); (2) Area Maya Bonampak (2v.)

M690 Torrence, Gaylord. The American Indian parfleche: a tradition of abstract painting. Seattle, Univ. of Washington Pr. in assoc. with the Des Moines Art Center, 1994. 272p. il. (part col.), col. map.

Catalog of the exhibition, Des Moines Art Center (1994). "This publication . . . present[s] a comprehensive overview of the American Indian parfleche, a powerful tradition of abstract painting created by the women of more than forty tribal groups throughout the western half of North America during the eighteenth, nineteenth, and early twentieth centuries."—*Introd.* Includes chapters on techniques of painting and construction, forms and functions, and formal characteristics.

Bibliography, p.259–65. Index, p.269–72.

M691 Wyman, Leland C. Southwest Indian drypainting. Santa Fe, School of American Research; Albuquerque, Univ. of New Mexico Pr., 1983. xxiii, 320p. il. (part col.) (Southwest Indian art series)

"This work . . . presents readers with an understandable introduction to Navajo sand paintings and to the ephemeral religious art of other groups in the Southwest. . . . An excellent study that will be used as a standard reference for years to come."—*Review*, American Indian art magazine, v.10, summer 1985, p.3.

Contents: (1) Navajo drypainting; (2) Drypainting of the Apaches, Pueblos, Papagos, and California Indians; (3) Conclusion.

Notes, p.289–98. References, p.299–308. Supplementary bibliography, p.309–11. Index, 313–20.

N. Prints

This chapter includes works on the technique and history of prints. Book illustration, artists' books, and posters are treated more thoroughly here than in GLAH 1, but still not comprehensively. The arrangement is by form, followed by period or region.

BIBLIOGRAPHY

N1 Blas Benito, Javier. Bibliografia del arte grafico: grabado, litografia, serigrafia, historia, tecnicas, artistas. Madrid, Real Academia de Bellas Artes de San Fernando, 1994. 402p.

Substantial bibliography listing reference works, treatises, documentary sources, thematic studies, works devoted to specific types of prints, and works dealing with cataloging, conservation, collecting, and the print market.

N2 Ludman, Joan, and Mason, Lauris. Fine print references: a selected bibliography of print-related literature. Assist. by Carol Sirefman. Millwood, N.Y., Kraus, 1982. xv, 227p. (Print reference series)

"Deals with the published writings on prints [in 3,215 entries] . . . all possible references are cited on the history and technique of fine and historic prints."—*Note to the user.* Excludes photography, bookplates, posters, illustrations, and printed ephemera. Also excludes bibliography on individual artists and periodical literature. Topical arrangement.

Contents: (1) Collecting and connoisseurship; (2) History of printmaking: historical and critical works; pictorial surveys; (3) International, national and regional competitions and exhibitions; (4) Medium and technique: processes of printmaking; (5) Museum collections; (6) Private collections; (7) Reference works; (8) Society and club publications; (9) Topical prints: works grouped by subject matter

Author index, p.205–19. Museum and gallery index, p.221–27.

N3 Mason, Lauris; Ludman, Joan; and Krauss, Harriett P. Old master print references: a selected bibliography. White Plains, N.Y., Kraus, 1986. ix, 279p. (Print reference series)

More than 3,000 citations with an emphasis on catalogs—museum, dealer, and exhibition. Includes citations to journal articles. Some overlap with Print reference sources: A selected bibliography, 18th to 20th centuries (GLAH 1:N8). Arranged alphabetically by artist name, and then chronologically by year of publication.

N4 Riggs, Timothy A. Print Council Index to oeuvre-catalogs of prints by European and American artists. Under the sponsorship of the Print Council of America. Millwood, N.Y., Kraus, 1983. xlv, 834p.

An invaluable aid to print scholarship. "The PCI is for you if you need to know about the prints that a particular artist has made (or that have been made after his own designs) and want to find out if there is an oeuvre-catalog of his prints."—*Note to the User.* Arranged alphabetically by the name of the artist or publisher. Excludes catalogs published after 1972. A new ed. is in course of preparation.

Glossary of symbols and code words, p.xvii–xxi. List of abbreviations for frequently cited books and periodicals, p.xxiii–xxxv. Multi-artist catalogues not indexed, p.xxxvii–xli.

SEE ALSO: Print index: a guide to reproductions (GLAH 2:D46).

DIRECTORIES

N5 Contemporary graphic artists: a biographical, bibliographical, and critical guide to current illustrators, animators, cartoonists, designers, and other graphic artists. Maurice Horn, ed. Detroit, Gale, 1986– . (3)v. il. Biannual.

"CGA is a comprehensive new biographical, bibliographical, and critical guide that provides detailed information about the lives and accomplishments of graphic artists who have made a significant contribution to contemporary art. with more than 100 entries in each biannual volume, CGA includes biographies on a wide variety of graphic artists—illustrators, animators, cartoonists, designers, and other graphic artists whose work appears in books, newspapers, magazines, film, and other media."—*Pref.*

DICTIONARIES AND ENCYCLOPEDIAS

N6 New York Public Library. Print file [microform]. Alexandria, Va., Chadwyck-Healey, 1991– . 4,456 microfiche il. + index (3 microfiche) issued in looseleaf binder with [3]p. of introductory text.

A wide-ranging clippings and ephemera file on more than 15,000 printmakers, illustrators, and photographers. Surveys the history of Western printmaking from the 15th century to the present and Japanese printmaking from the 10th to the 20th centuries. The collection's particular strengths are American historical prints, 19th-century French and American prints, and an in-depth, representative collection of 20th-century American prints. The contents of each artist's file vary and may include exhibition brochures and small catalogs, gallery announcements, reviews, obituaries, magazine articles as well as reproduction and original prints. Much of the information found quickly in these files can only be traced elsewhere with difficulty, if at all. Most of the clippings have been sourced, further enhancing their value to scholars and researchers.

Index of 15,547 printmakers.

GENERAL WORKS

N7 Adhémar, Jean. La gravure, des origines à nos jours. Avec la partic. de Claude Roger-Marx et d'Eugène Rouir. Paris, Somogy, 1979. 319p. il. (part col.)

Readable historical survey by an authority.

Bibliographie, p.305–07. Index, p.309–19.

N8 Amsterdam. Rijksmuseum. Rijksprentenkabinet. Ornamentprenten in het Rijksprentenkabinet. [Van] Marijnke de Jong, Irene de Groot. Amsterdam, Het Kabinet; 's-Gravenhage, Staatsuitgeverij, 1988– . (1)v. il.

Scholarly catalog of a great collection of ornament prints. V.1 includes 15th- and 16th-century Dutch, German, Eastern European, French, and Italian prints.

Contents: (1) 15de and 16de eeuw.

N9 Bartsch, Adam von. The illustrated Bartsch. [Gen. ed.: Walter L. Strauss.] N.Y., Abaris, 1978– . (164)v. il.

See GLAH 1:N12 for a prepublication annotation of The illustrated Bartsch (TIB), and GLAH 1:N13 for the original Bartsch catalog, 21v., 1803–21. An important corpus of images that has resulted from an international project to supply illustrations for all of Bartsch's original entries and correct his errors of attribution and omission. The original idea was that, for each Bartsch volume, TIB would produce one volume of illustrations and one of commentary, in which misattributions would be corrected and prints, states, and other information unknown to Bartsch supplied. In practice, many of the original Bartsch volumes have needed more than two TIB volumes to illustrate and correct them; sometimes as many as eight have been required. Also, many volumes of additional material in such areas as 15th-century German book illustration and 19th-century French printmaking, which were not covered in the original Bartsch, have been added to TIB as "supplement" volumes. Particularly important among these is v.161–164, Richard S. Field, ed., German single-leaf woodcuts before 1500 (in progress), a project to illustrate and revise Wilhelm Ludwig Schreiber, Handbuch der Holz- und Metallschnitte des XV. Jahrhunderts, Leipzig. Hiersemann, 1826–30, 11v. (GLAH 1:N52).

In general, each of the TIB volumes in the illustration and commentary categories carries two numbers on the spine. The top one is its unique volume number in TIB; the bottom one represents the volumes in the original Bartsch that it illustrates or revises.

Because of inherent differences in printmakers' oeuvres, and a lack of editorial control over the series, standardization and consistency are not strong from volume to volume. Consequently, it is important in each case to read individual volume compilers' prefaces and keys to abbreviations when using TIB.

Some volumes have subject indexes. In addition, for iconographical indexing of some of the prints illustrated in TIB, using the Iconclass system, GLAH 2:F11, GLAH 2:F12, GLAH 2:F13.

N10 Bellini, Paolo. Storia dell'incisione moderna. Con un indice bio-bibliografico di 3000 artisti incisori. Bergamo, Minerva italica, 1985. 568p. il. (part col.)

Monumental survey of modern printmaking, 18th century to the present.

Indice bio-bibliografico di 3000 artisti incisori, p.[375]–526. Dizionario dei termini tecnici, p.529–38. Elenco dei principali Gabinetti di Stampe, p.539–43. Bibliografia, p.545–61.

N11 Beraldi, Henri. Les graveurs du XIXe siècle: guide de l'amateur d'estampe moderne. [Reprint.] Nogent-le-Roi, Lages, 1981. 12v.

Reprint of GLAH 1:N14.

N12 Bialler, Nancy Ann. Chiaroscuro woodcuts: Hendrick Goltzius (1558–1617) and his time. Amsterdam, Rijksmuseum; Ghent, Snoeck-Ducaju and Zoon, [1992]. 249p. (1 folded) il. (part col.)

Catalog of the exhibition, Rijksmuseum, Amsterdam (1992–93), and other locations. Covers more than 60 artists in addition to Goltzius. A "lucidly written and beautifully produced catalogue [which] is a wonderful complement and corrective to Walter Strauss [GLAH 1:N55]."—*Review*, Print quarterly, v.12, March 1995, p.80–81.

Notes at ends of chapters. Bibliography, p.238–41. List of figures and exhibited works, p.242–48. Index of artists and publishers, p.249.

N13 Bologna. Pinacoteca nazionale. Gabinetto delle stampe. Catalogo generale della raccolta di stampe antiche della Pinacoteca nazionale di Bologna, Gabinetto delle stampe. Bologna, Associazione per le arti Francesco Francia, 1973– . Many vols.

See GLAH 1:N16 for original entry. Continues to appear as announced, with slight changes in title and scope of individual vols.

N14 British Museum. Department of Prints and Drawings. Landmarks in print collecting: connoisseurs and donors at the British Museum since 1753. Ed. by Antony Griffiths. N.Y., Parnassus Foundation in assoc. with the Museum of Fine Arts, Houston, 1996. 304p. il. (part col.), plates, ports.

Published in conjunction with the exhibition, Museum of Fine Arts, Houston (1996), and other locations. "This exhibition and the accompanying catalogue present . . . an entirely new approach to print scholarship. Never before . . . has an exhibition been selected and organized around the collectors rather than the makers."—*Pref.* Structured around 10 collections, each profiled by a different specialist. Introduction by Antony Griffiths on the history of print collecting at the British Museum.

[Bibliography, p.18.] Glossary of printmaking terms, p.19. Notes to the catalogue, p.20. Index, p.302–04.

N15 Castleman, Riva. Printed art: a view of two decades. N.Y., Museum of Modern Art, 1980. 144p. il. (part col.)

Published in conjunction with the exhibition, Museum of Modern Art (1980). Devoted to the 1960s and 1970s, this title complements Wye, Thinking print . . . 1980–95 (GLAH 2:N44).

N16 ______. Prints of the twentieth century. Rev. and enl. ed. N.Y., Thames and Hudson, 1988. 240p. il. (part col.) (World of art)

Rev. ed. of GLAH 1:N19. Standard survey by an authority.

Contents: (1) Introduction: some nineteenth-century influences; (2) Expressionism in France and Germany up to World War I: Fauves, Die Brücke, Der Blaue Reiter; (3) Cubism and early abstract movements; (4) Postwar Expressionism and nonobjective art in Germany; (5) Dada and Surrealism; (6) Independent directions: the School of Paris and the revival of lithography; (7) Picasso after Cubism; (8) Between the wars: Mexico, the United States, Japan; (9) Printmaking after World War II: the persistence of Expressionism and Surrealism; (10) The flourishing of lithography in the U.S.A.: the prints of Pop Art; (11) Op, Kinetic, Concrete, and the Conceptual arts; (12) Pluralism and appropriation in Europe and America.

Notes on the text, p.227–28. Glossary of printmaking terms, p.229–30. Bibliography, p.230–36. Index, p.237–40.

N17 A census of fifteenth-century prints in public collections of the United States and Canada. Ed. by Richard S. Field, Louise S. Richards, and Alan Shestack. [Upd. and corr. ed.] New Haven, Yale University Art Gallery, 1995. [144]p.

1st ed. 1985. A slender but important reference work "published under the auspices of the Print Council of America."

Acronyms, institutions, and colleagues who helped, p.[7].

N18 Circa 1800: the beginnings of modern printmaking, 1775–1830. Rutgers, State Univ. of New Jersey, 1981. vi, 31p. il.

Catalog of the exhibition, Rutgers Univ. Art Gallery (1981), and other locations. Intended to be "an introduction to a vastly underrated period of printmaking history."—*Introd.* Essays by Phillip Dennis Cate and Jack Spector. Checklist includes European and British printmakers. Concentrates on original printmaking of the period.

Bibliography, p.32–34.

N19 Cohn, Marjorie B. A noble collection: the Spencer albums of old master prints. [Cambridge, Mass.], Fogg Art Museum, Harvard Univ. Art Museums, 1992. 365p. il.

Exemplary catalog of part of an important collection of old master prints originally assembled by the Mariettes and recently purchased by Harvard. Published in conjunction with the exhibition, Fogg Art Museum (1993), and other locations.

Index of artists in the exhibition, p.59. Bibliography, p.276–83. Description and checklist of the albums, p.[285]–305.

N20 Davis, Bruce. Mannerist prints: international style in the sixteenth century. Los Angeles, Los Angeles County Museum of Art, 1988. 336p. il. (part col.)

Catalog of the exhibition, Los Angeles County Museum of Art (1988), and other locations. Significant exhibition that surveyed French, Italian, and Netherlandish prints of this formative period, from the important collection of Mary Stansbury Ruiz.

Notes accompany catalog entries. Artists' biographies, p.325–31. Selected bibliography, p.332–34. Index of inventors, p.335.

N21 Donson, Theodore B. Prints and the print market: a handbook for buyers, collectors, and connoisseurs. N.Y., Crowell, 1977. xii, 493p. il.

Focuses upon "the difficult issues and choices that a person, whether a novice or a professional, will face in the marketplace."—*Foreword.* Topics covered include rarity, fakes and forgeries, connoisseurship, and the mechanisms of the print market. Explanatory and cautionary in nature. Appendixes include a bibliography of publications on prints by "familiar artists," a directory of print publishers in the U.S. and Great Britain, a directory of print conservators, print dealers, galleries, and booksellers, and a trilingual (English-French-German) lexicon. Dated, but still useful.

Bibliography, p.405–39. Index, p.[483]–93.

N22 Fioravanti, Giorgio. Il dizionario del grafico. Con la collab. di Ottorino Baseggio . . . [et al.] Bologna, Zanichelli, 1993. 503p. il. (part col.)

Substantial dictionary of the graphic arts.

Bibliografia, p.[499]–503.

N23 Gassier, Pierre. De Goya à Matisse: estampes de la Collection Jacques Doucet, Bibliothèque d'art et d'archéologie, Paris. Commissaire de l'exposition,

Pierre Gassier, en collab. avec Jean-Claude Romand. [Réalis. du catalogue, Pierre Gassier.] Martigny, Fondation Pierre Gianadda, 1992. 239p. il. (part col.)

Catalog of the exhibition, Fondation Pierre Gianadda, Martigny, Switzerland (1992), of a great private collection, amassed between 1911 and 1914 and subsequently donated to the Bibliothèque d'art et d'archéologie.

Orientation bibliographique, p.235.

N24 Goldman, Judith. The pop image: prints and multiples. With Ronny Cohen . . . [et al.] N.Y., Marlborough Graphics, 1994. 125p. il. (part col.)

Published on the occasion of the exhibition, Marlborough Gallery (1994). Detailed study of Pop printmaking activity between 1960 and 1971, with catalog of all significant work produced in that period.

Index of artists, p.107. Glossary of publishers and workshops, p.109–11. Selected sources on pop art, p.113–21. Select bibliography, p.122–23.

N25 Hults, Linda C. The print in the western world: an introductory history. Madison, Univ. of Wisconsin Pr., 1996. xx, 948p. il. (part col.)

A comprehensive survey of the history of printmaking in Western art, and an invaluable addition to the general literature on print history. Includes an introductory section on special issues relating to the history of printmaking—questions relating to value and originality, or the history of prints and the history of art.

Contents: (1) Early relief and intaglio techniques: northern printmakers before Dürer; (2) Dürer and other sixteenth-century northern artists; (3) Italian Renaissance prints; (4) Etching in the seventeenth century; (5) Reproductive printmaking and related developments from the later sixteenth through the eighteenth century; (6) Original etching and engraving in the eighteenth and early nineteenth centuries; (7) The print and socio-political reform: Hogarth and his heirs and Goya; (8) Lithography in the nineteenth century; (9) The nineteenth century: the etching revival and new technical approaches; (10) The German expressionists and related artists; (11) Picasso and other European printmakers to the 1940s; (12) American and Mexican printmaking to the mid-1940s; (13) Printmaking in Europe and America after World War II.

Notes and references at ends of chapters. Glossary, p.851–59. Select bibliography of print reference catalogs, p.860–62. Bibliographical note, p.863–71. Index, p.880–948.

N26 Hunnisett, Basil. Engraved on steel: the history of picture production using steel plates. Brookfield, Vt., Scolar, 1998. xvii, 387p. il. (part col.)

"The aim of the present work is to explore the study of steel engraving further in the wider context of its beginnings and its use outside the British Isles."—*Pref.*

Contents: Part one: (1) The prehistory of steel engraving; (2) The quest for the unforgeable document; (3) Mezzotints on steel; (4) British steel line engraving: books; (5) British steel line engraving: prints, maps, book plates; (6) Other intaglio prints on steel: paper, equipment; Part two: (7) German steel engraving; (8) French steel engraving; (9) Steel engraving in other European countries; (10) American steel engraving; (11) Twentieth-century steel engraving.

Sources, p.354–66. Index, p.367–87.

N27 Koschatzky, Walter, and Sotriffer, Kristian. Mit Nadel und Säure: fünfhundert Jahre Kunst der Radierung. Wien, Tusch, 1982. 262p. il.

Historical survey, mostly in the form of individual examples of prints with commentary.

Notes at ends of chapters. Alphabetisches Künstlerverzeichnis, p.6–7. Künstlerbiographien, p.234–48. Verzeichnis der Fachausdrücke, p.249–53. Alphabetisches Verzeichnis der . . . Oeuvre-Kataloge und Publikationen, p.258–59. Verzeichnis der Fachliteratur, p.260–61. Verzeichnis der Maler und ihre Nachstecher, p.262.

N28 Landau, David, and Parshall, Peter. The Renaissance print, 1470–1550. New Haven, Yale Univ. Pr., 1994. xii, 433p. il. plates.

An important synthetic treatment of a formative period in print history. The authors' approach "is broadly based, opening with the material and institutional circumstances surrounding print production, and then proceeding to examine workshop practices including technical and aesthetic experimentation undertaken by particular masters. Our eventual aim is to give a better approximation of the ways Renaissance prints were realized, distributed, acquired and eventually handled by their public."—*Pref.*

Contents: (I) Framing the Renaissance print; (II) Craft guilds, workshops, and supplies; (III) How prints became works of art: the first generation; (IV) From collaboration to reproduction in Italy; (V) The cultivation of the woodcut in the north; (VI) Artistic experiment and the collector's print; (VII) Epilogue. Appendix: Currencies, values, and wages.

Abbreviations, p.372. Notes to the text, p.373–414. Bibliography, 415–28. Index, p.429–33.

N29 Lithography: 200 years of art, history and technique. Domenico Porzio, gen. ed. With the collab. of Rosalba Tabanelli and Marcello Tabanelli. Essays by Jean Adhemar . . . [et al.] N.Y., Abrams, 1983. 280p. il. (part col.)

Well-illustrated summary of recent research on lithography. "It is the intention of this book to provide a profile both of the technical evolution of the medium and of the actual history of lithographic art."—*Pref.*

Contents: In praise of lithography, by Jean Adhémar; Invention and technical evolution, by Domenico Porzio; The artist and the printer, by Fernand Mourlot; The poster, by Alain Weill; Social comment and criticism, by Michel Melot; The illustrated book, by Jacqueline Armigneat; The discovery of the lithographic stone from the Complete course of lithography, by Aloys Senefelder.

Glossary, by Rosalba and Marcello Tabanelli, p.258–61. Biographies: essential information on artists of major importance, p.262–71. Bibliography, p.271. Index of illustrations, p.272–76. Index of names, p.276–79.

N30 Madrid (Spain). Museo Municipal. Gabinete de Estampas. Catálogo del Gabinete de Estampas del Mu-

seo Municipal de Madrid. [Madrid,] Ayuntamiento de Madrid, Concejalía de Cultura, 1985– . (2)v. in 4. il.
Contents: (1) Estampas españolas, grabado 1550–1820 (2v.); (2) Estampas extranjeras, grabado ca. 1513–1820 (2v.)

Relación de libros y colecciones de estampas, v.2, p.467–79. Bibliografía, v.2, p.481–82. Indices (onomastico, iconografico), v.2, p.483–501. Correspondencia entre el número de inventario de las estampas del Museo Municipal y el número de catálogo, p.503–09.

N31 Mayer, Rudolf. Gedruckte Kunst: Wesen, Wirkung, Wandel. Stuttgart, Hatje, 1984. 378p. il. (part col.)
A major work. Many brief, well-indexed essays on print techniques, themes, major figures, and the economics of print publication.

Contents: Vorgreifende Verfahren; Die frühe Druckerei in Ostasien; Der Hochdruck; Der Tiefdruck; Zweige des Tiefdrucks; Der Flachdruck; Peripheres Drucken; Farbendruck; Vom Handwerk zur Industrie; Der Verlag; Bild vom Bild; Fotografie und Fotomechanische Verfahren; Künstlergrafik; Künstlerisches Drucken—Druckerische Kunst in der Gegenwart; Nachwort.

Nomenklatur der Verfahren und Techniken, p.319–33. Literatur (Auswahl), p.335–41. Register, p.367–78.

N32 Milesi, Giorgio. Dizionario degli incisori. Saggio di bibliografia ragionata a cura di Paolo Bellini. [Bergamo], Minerva italica, [1989]. 362p. il.
Illustrated biographical dictionary of printmakers, with indication of principal media employed, iconographic subjects, and notable works, as well as characteristic artists' marks.

Saggio di bibliografia ragionata intorno ai più noti dizionari, repertori e cataloghi generali nella storia dell'incisione, di Paolo Bellini, p.5–13. Nozioni sulle tecniche più diffuse dell'arte a stampa, p.[15]–19. Bibliografia essenziale, p.[21]–37. Elenco degli artisti catalogati nello Hollstein, p.38–42.

N33 Museo del Prado. Museo del Prado: catálogo de estampas. [Por] Jesusa Vega. Madrid, Ministerio de Cultura, 1992. xviii, 506p. il.
Substantial catalog of a significant collection, recording a vast number of Spanish prints.

Abreviaturas, p.3. Referencias bibliograficas del catalogo, p.4. Indice onomastico, p.[447]–76. Bibliografia, p.[447]–95. Correspondencias numericas, p.[497]–506.

N34 Nelson-Atkins Museum of Art. The collections of the Nelson-Atkins Museum of Art. Prints, 1460–1995. By George L. McKenna. Kansas City, Mo., the Museum, in assoc. with the Univ. of Washington Pr., 1996. xv, 343p. il. (part col.)
Beautifully illustrated, scholarly catalog of a wide-ranging collection.

Notes on catalogue entries and abbreviations, p.xv. Note on catalogue lists, p.[244]. Catalogue lists, p.[245]–315. Bibliography, p.317–42. Index to catalogue numbers, p.343.

N35 The painterly print: monotypes from the seventeenth to the twentieth century. N.Y., Metropolitan Museum of Art, 1980. xiii, 261p. il. (part col.)
Catalog of the exhibition, Metropolitan Museum of Art (1980), and other locations. First exhibition surveying the history of the monotype (printed paintings or printed drawings), from the 17th to the 20th century. Includes historical essays by the authors of the catalog.

Notes at ends of essays. Bibliography, p.255–59. Index of artists, p.260–61.

N36 Das Phänomen Graphik: Holzschnitt, Radierung, Lithographie in Vergangenheit und Gegenwart. Mit Beitr. von Bernhard Holeczek, Walter Koschatzky, Wilhelm Weber u. eine Einf. von Ursula Weber. Hrsg. von Heinrich Lenhardt. Salzburg, Residenz, 1996. 215p. il. (part col.)
Beautifully illustrated, multi-author survey, arranged by printmaking medium, with chapters on woodcuts, engraving and etching, and lithography.

Literaturheinweise, p.210–12. Personenregister, p.213–14.

N37 Prints: history of an art. [By] Michel Melot, Antony Griffiths, Richard S. Field . . . [et al.] N.Y., Skira, 1981. 278p. il. (part col.)
French ed., Geneva, Skira, 1981. Spanish ed. Barcelona, Carroggio, 1981.

A standard monographic treatment of the history of prints and printmaking by leading scholars. Lavishly illustrated.

Contents: (I) The nature and role of the print, by Michel Melot; (II) The art and hand of the printmaker, by Antony Griffiths; (III) Contemporary trends, by Richard S. Field.

Notes, p.235–39. Glossary of technical terms, p.243–57. Bibliography, p.259–66. List of illustrations [by artist], p.267–75. Index of names and places, p.276–[79].

N38 Six centuries of master prints: treasures from the Herbert Greer French collection. Ed. by Kristin L. Spangenberg. With essays by David P. Becker . . . [et al.] Cincinnati, Cincinnati Art Museum, 1993. xv, 342p. il. (part col.)
Published on the occasion of the exhibition, Cincinnati Art Museum (1993). Scholarly, well-illustrated catalog of an important collection.

Herbert Greer French bibliography, p.330. Select bibliography, p.331–38. Index, p.338–42.

N39 Surrealist prints. Ed. by Gilbert Kaplan. Essays [by] Timothy Baum, Riva Castleman, and Robert Rainwater. Los Angeles, Grunwald Center for the Graphic Arts (Distr. by Abrams, 1997). 155p. il. (part col.)
Catalog of the exhibition, Armand Hammer Museum of Art and Cultural Center (1996–97). Rev. ed. of Visionary States: Surrealist prints from the Gilbert Kaplan collection (1996). "The first-ever survey of Surrealist prints."—*Introd.*

N40 Tallman, Susan. The contemporary print: from pre-pop to postmodern. London, Thames and Hudson, 1996. 304p. il. (part col.)

Major survey of the subject. "This book attempts to chart the forms and uses of the print over a period of some thirty-five years and two continents."—*Introd.*

Contents: (1) Painters and printers; (2) Johns and Rauschenberg; (3) Pop and print; (4) Multiplicity; (5) Material forms and social functions: 1960s into 1970s; (6) High tech and the human touch; (7) Uses of history; (8) The ethos of the edition.

Notes, p.242–49. Notes on the prints, p.250–61. Artists' biographies, p.262–82. Workshops and publishers, p.283–89. Bibliography, p.290–94. Glossary, p.295–99. Index, p.300–03.

N41 Wallen, Burr. The Cubist print. Catalogue by Burr Wallen and Donna Stein. Santa Barbara, Univ. Art Museum, Univ. of California, 1981. 219p. il. (part col.)

Published in conjunction with the exhibition, University Art Museum, Univ. of California, Santa Barbara (1982), and other locations. Extensive survey of an important category of 20th-century prints.

Catalogue, p.205–18. Glossary, p.219.

N42 Wax, Carol. The mezzotint: history and technique. N.Y., Abrams, 1990. 296p. il. (part col.)

A comprehensive monograph on a printmaking technique particularly influential in 18th- and early 19th-century Britain. Includes the early history of mezzotint, the status and business of mezzotint in England, the transition of mezzotint into steel plate in the 19th century, the rise of original mezzotinting, and mechanics of the mezzotint process.

List of suppliers, p.282. Selected bibliography, p.283–88. Index, p.289–95.

N43 Wend, Johannes. Ergänzungen zu den Oeuvreverzeichnissen der Druckgraphik. Leipzig, Zentralantiquariat der DDR, 1975– . (2)v. (Ergänzendes Handbuch zu den Oeuvreverzeichnissen der Druckgrafik, Bd.1,1)

See GLAH 1:N62 for previous ed.

Contents: (1) Das deutschsprachige Schrifttum; (2) Versteckte Oeuvreverzeichnisse der Druckgraphik.

N44 Wye, Deborah. Thinking print: books to billboards, 1980–95. N.Y., Museum of Modern Art (Distr. by Abrams, 1996). 160p. il. (part col.)

Published in conjunction with the exhibition, Museum of Modern Art (1996). Significant survey of recent developments. Complements Castleman's Printed art (GLAH 2:N15).

Checklist of the exhibition, p.124–34. Notes on the artists, p.135–48. Notes on the publishers, p.149–55. Selected bibliography, p.156–57. Index, p.157–59.

TECHNIQUES

N45 Gascoigne, Bamber. How to identify prints: a complete guide to manual and mechanical processes from woodcut to ink jet. N.Y., Thames and Hudson, 1986. 208p. il. (part col.)

A extremely useful handbook of print types and techniques. Covers, in three sections, "various types of [the] printed image," with a section on the tools and practicalities of print identification. Aided greatly by extensive illustrations of print types and processes, some in color.

N46 Goldman, Paul. Looking at prints: a guide to technical terms. [London, British Museum, 1981.] 16p. il.

A small but very useful visitor's pamphlet categorizing the major technical terms for printmaking with exemplary illustrations. Includes a brief introductory paragraph describing the types of printmaking. An enhanced version of the text was merged into Goldman's Looking at prints, drawings, and watercolors (1988).

N47 Griffiths, Antony. Prints and printmaking: an introduction to the history and techniques. 2d ed. Berkeley, Univ. of California Pr., 1996. 160p. il. (part col.)

1st ed. 1980.

A thorough introduction to the subject by the Keeper of the Print Room at the British Museum.

Catalogs of prints; books about printmaking and the history of prints, p.128–33. Abbreviations and lettering, p.134. Glossary, p.137–55. Index, p.157–60.

N48 Ivins, William Mills. How prints look: photographs with commentary. Rev. and exp. ed., rev. by Marjorie B. Cohn. Boston, Beacon, 1987. x, 188p. il.

New ed. of GLAH 1:N70. Standard guide.

N49 Ross, John; Romano, Clare; and Ross, Tim. The complete printmaker: techniques, traditions, innovations. Ed. and prod. by Roundtable Press. Rev. and exp. ed. N.Y., Free Press, 1990. viii, 352p. il. (part col.)

1st ed. 1972. Technical manual of printmaking processes.

Contents: (1) Relief prints; (2) Intaglio prints; (3) Collographs; (4) Screen prints; (5) Lithographs; (6) Dimensional prints; (7) Monotypes; (8) Photographic techniques; (9) Computers and the print; (10) Paper for prints; (11) Art of the book; (12) Business of prints; (13) Health hazards; (14) School printmaking; (15) Sources and charts.

Bibliography, p.344–46. Glossary, p.346–48. Index, p.349–52.

N50 Saff, Donald, and Sacilotto, Deli. Printmaking: history and process. N.Y., Holt, Rinehart and Winston, 1978. xii, 436p. il. (part col.)

"An attempt to bring together the most complete, accurate, and up-to-date information about all the various printmaking techniques. This book is planned for students of printmaking. . . . It will also serve as a basic resource book for the professional printmaker."—*Pref.*

Contents: (I) Relief; (II) Intaglio; (III) Lithography; (IV) Serigraphy; (V) Trends: processes/surfaces; Appendix A: The chemistry of etching; Appendix B: Steel facing; Appendix C: Presses.

List of suppliers, p.419–21. Bibliography, p.422–24. Glossary, p.425–30. Index, p.431–35.

WATERMARKS

N51 Briquet, Charles Moïse. Les filigranes. Dictionnaire historique des marques du papier des leur apparition vers 1282 jusqu'en 1600. [Reprint.] N.Y., Hacker, 1985. 4v.

Reprint of GLAH 1:N75.

N52 Churchill, William Algernon. Watermarks in paper in Holland, England, France, etc., in the XVII and XVIII centuries and their interconnection. [Reprint.] Nieuwkoop, De Graaf, 1990. 94, cdxxxii p. il., facsims.

Reprint of GLAH 1:N76.

N53 Gravell, Thomas L., and Miller, George. A catalogue of American watermarks, 1690–1835. N.Y., Garland, 1979. xxiii, 230p. (Garland reference library of the humanities, 151)

Standard catalog of U.S. watermarks. The Introduction offers a brief history of papermaking in America, with notes.

Bibliography, p.215–17. Proper name index, p.221–27. Subject index, p.229–30.

N54 ______. A catalogue of foreign watermarks found on paper used in America, 1700–1835. N.Y., Garland, 1983. xix, 286p. il. (Garland reference library of the humanities, 318)

Includes alphabetical listings of watermarks, American paper mills, and foreign paper makers distributing in America. Extensively illustrated.

Includes bibliographical references. Names and initials index, p.279–80. Subject index, p.281–86.

N55 Hauptstaatsarchiv Stuttgart. Die Wasserzeichenkartei Piccard im Hauptstaatsarchiv Stuttgart: Findbuch. Bearb. von Gerhard Piccard. Stuttgart, Kohlhammer, 1961– . (15)v. in 20. il.

Standard corpus of watermarks.

Bibliographical references throughout.

N56 Heawood, Edward. Watermarks, mainly of the 17th and 18th centuries. [Reprint.] Hilversum, Holland, Paper Publications Society, 1986. 154p., plates, port. (Monumenta chartae papyraceae historiam illustrantia, 1)

Reprint of GLAH 1:N77.

WESTERN COUNTRIES

Australia

N57 Art Gallery of New South Wales. Australian prints from the gallery's collection. [By] Hendrik Kolenberg and Anne Ryan. Sydney, Art Gallery of New South Wales, 1998. 164p. il. (part col.)

Published in conjunction with the exhibition, Art Gallery of New South Wales (1998–99). Beautifully produced selection of prints by more than 100 Australian artists, 18th–20th century.

Selected bibliography, p.163. Index of artists, p.164.

N58 Australian National Gallery. Australian prints: a souvenir book of Australian prints in the Australian National Gallery. [By] Roger Butler. Canberra, The Gallery, 1985. 55p. il. (part col.)

Cover title: Australian prints in the Australian National Gallery.

"The collection of Australian prints, posters and illustrated books in the Australian National Gallery is the most comprehensive in the country, comprising some twenty thousand works. The Gallery has concentrated on prints produced since 1880."—*[p.3].* A brief sampler.

N59 Carroll, Alison. Graven images in the promised land: a history of printmaking in South Australia, 1836–1981. Adelaide, Art Gallery of South Australia, 1981. 64p. il.

"This book is the first attempt at a comprehensive account of the medium from its earliest days in the 'Land of Promise.'"—*Foreword.* Historical essays, each followed by a brief catalog of prints from the Gallery collection.

Contents: (1) Propaganda and other devices: the colonial years; (2) The age of etching; (3) The relief print and the advent of modernism; (4) The last decades.

Notes at ends of essays.

N60 Grishin, Sasha. Australian printmaking in the 1990s: artist printmakers. [United States], G + B Arts International, 1997. 336p. il. (part col.)

"The present book sets out to present a balanced survey of printmaking in Australia in the period between 1990 and 1995."—*Ackn.* Beautifully illustrated biographical dictionary of contemporary Australian printmakers. Supplements Grishin's Contemporary Australian printmaking (see next entry).

Contents: Australian printmaking in the 1990s: some new beginnings; Profiles of Australian artist printmakers.

List of plates, p.334–35. Technical glossary, p.336

N61 ______. Contemporary Australian printmaking: an interpretative history. Roseville East, NWS, Craftsman House, 1994. 192p. il. (part col.)

"This book is the first comprehensive survey of recent artist-printmakers in Australia."—*Foreword.* Includes sections on migrant printmakers, training abroad, print workshops in Australian art schools, print prizes, and exhibitions. Supplemented by Grishin's Australian printmaking in the 1990s (see preceding title).

Endnotes, p.174–77. Bibliography, p.178–82. Technical glossary, p.189. Index of names, p.190–92.

N62 Masterpieces of Australian printmaking. Ed. by Josef Lebovic. [Comp. by Joseph Lebovic and Sandra Warner.] Paddington, Sydney, Australia, Josef Lebovic Gallery, 1987. 160p. il. (part col.)

Catalog of the exhibition, Lebovic Gallery (1987). "This exhibition surveys Australian printmaking from its tentative beginnings late in the nineteenth century, through a period of widespread popularity in the 1920s and 1930s, and culminates in the 1950s when the demand for decorative work was rekindled."—*Introd.* Catalog of 213 prints, arranged alphabetically by artist.

Bibliography, p.6. Index of artists, p.160.

Canada

N63 Allodi, Mary. Printmaking in Canada: the earliest views and portraits = Les débuts de l'estampe imprimée au Canada: vues et portraits. With contrib. from Peter Winkworth . . . [et al.] Toronto, Royal Ontario Museum, 1980. xxviii, 244p. il.

Comprehensive survey of early views and portraits printed in Canada up to 1850, especially separately issued (or single-sheet) prints intended for glazing and framing or for the print collector's portfolio. One of the few studies of pictorial printmaking in Canada.

Explanatory notes, p.xxvii. Abbreviations for institutions, p.xxviii. References, p.238–40. Selected readings, p.241–42. Index of artists, printmakers, and publishers, p.243–44.

N64 Art Gallery of Hamilton (Ontario). The Society of Canadian Painter-Etchers and Engravers in retrospect = La Société des Peintres-Graveurs Canadiens: vue rétrospective. Hamilton, The Gallery, 1981. 96p. il.

Text in English and French. Catalog of the exhibition, Art Gallery of Hamilton (1978), and other locations. "An exhibition selected from the Society's own archive collection of members' work which was bequeathed to the Art Gallery of Hamilton when the Society merged with the Canadian Society of Graphic Art to form the Print and Drawing Council of Canada in 1976."—*T.p. verso.*

Biographies, p.73–85. Chronology of principal exhibitions and important related activities, p.87–93. Checklist of artists represented in the archive collection of the CPE at the Art Gallery of Hamilton, p.95.

N65 Tovell, Rosemarie L. A new class of art: the artist's print in Canadian art, 1877–1920. Ottawa, National Gallery of Canada, 1996. 192p. il. (part col.), facsims., ports.

Catalog of the exhibition, National Gallery of Canada (1996), and other locations. "The current exhibition and its catalogue are the first to document from a Canadian perspective that momentous period in the nineteenth century when artists began to reclaim the print media as techniques for original artistic expression."—*Foreword.*

Contents: (1) Breaking the ground: the etching revival in Canada, 1880–1900; (2) In the mainstream: Canadians and the international print movement, 1877–1920; (3) Erecting the frame: the artist's print in Toronto, 1900–1917; (4) Completing the structure: the print movement becomes national, 1910–1920.

Explanation of technical terms, p.15–16. Endnotes, p.153–69. Works in the exhibition, p.171–79. Selected references, p.181–88. Index, p.189–92.

France

N66 Baas, Jacquelynn, and Field, Richard S. The artistic revival of the woodcut in France 1859–1900. Ann Arbor, Univ. of Michigan Museum of Art, 1984. 160p. il.

Catalog of the exhibition, University of Michigan Museum of Art (1984), featuring artistic uses of the woodcut revival in later 19th-century France. The essays include a period overview, discussions of techniques, and the French woodcut in the international context. Includes biographical essays on artists and extensive catalog entries.

Catalogues raisonnés and related sources, p.149–50. Selected bibliography, p.151–60.

N67 Bailly-Herzberg, Janine. Dictionnaire de l'estampe en France, 1830–1950. Pref. de Michel Melot. [Paris], Arts et metiers graphiques (Distr. by Flammarion, 1985). 384p. il.

Important reference work.

Abréviations, p.8. Quelques albums d'estampes, p.351–62. Associations et sociétés, p.363–72. Techniques, p.373–77. Index, p.379–84.

N68 Dictionnaire des éditeurs d'estampes à Paris sous l'Ancien Régime. Maxime Préaud, Pierre Casselle, Marianne Grivel . . . [et al.] Paris, Promodis, 1987. 334p.

Indispensable scholarly catalog of French print sellers and publishers from the 16th to the 18th century. Each entry contains references and notes.

Liste des abréviations, des ouvrages et des fonds de référence, p.[27]–29. Index des enseignes, p.[307]–09. Index des noms propres, p.[310]–34.

N69 Farwell, Beatrice. The charged image: French lithographic caricature, 1816–1848. Santa Barbara, Santa Barbara Museum of Art, 1989. 188p. il. (part col.)

Catalog of the exhibition, Santa Barbara Museum of Art (1989). Beautifully illustrated, scholarly catalog offering an overview of the first decades of French popular lithography, based upon the museum's collections.

Bibliography, p.187–88.

N70 ———. French popular lithographic imagery, 1815–1870 [microfiche]. Chicago, Univ. of Chicago Pr., 1981–97. 12v. (Chicago visual library text-fiche; no. 40, etc.)

"Selection of lithographs, drawn from the collections of the Bibliothèque nationale, Paris."—*Pref.* Accompanied by microfiche in pockets.

Contents: (1) Lithographs and literature; (2) Portraits and types; (3) Genre: urban and military; (4) The city; (5) The country; (6) Piety and the family; (7) Love and courtship; (8) Contemporary events and caricature; (9) Historicism and exoticism; (10) Tourism and travel; (11) Pinups and erotica; (12) Lithography in art and commerce.

N71 Fossier, François. Il fiore dell'impressionismo = La fleur de l'impressionnisme. Testo e schede a cura di

François Fossier. Con un testo introd. di Renato Barilli. Milano, Fabbri, 1990. 388p. il. (part col.)

Catalog of the exhibition, Centro Saint-Bernin, Aosta (1990), of prints from the Bibliothèque Nationale. Text in French and Italian. Long introductory texts, followed by a scholarly catalog of 105 prints, with full-page black-and-white reproductions.

Glossaire des termes techniques, p.381–84. Bibliographie sommaire, p.385.

N72 ______. La nébuleuse Nabie: les Nabis et l'art graphique. Paris, Bibliothèque nationale; Réunion des musées nationaux, 1993. 303p. il. (part col.)

Substantial study of the prints of the Nabis, based upon the collections of the Bibliothèque Nationale.

Contents: (I) Références et influences; (II) Les Cénacles; (III) Paysages intérierurs; (IV) Un graphiste entre la masse et le trait; (V) Des lissiers décorateurs; (VI) Des coloristes; (VII) Le livre nabi.

Bibliographie, p.289–92. Index des oeuvres, p.293–98. Index des noms cités, p.299–303.

N73 French caricature and the French Revolution, 1789–1799. Los Angeles, Grunwald Center for the Graphic Arts, Wight Art Gallery, University of California, Los Angeles (Distr. by the Univ. of Chicago Pr., 1988). 280p. il. (part col.)

French ed., Paris, Bibliothèque Nationale, 1985. Published in conjunction with the exhibition, Grunwald Center for the Graphic Arts (1988), and other locations.

Important scholarly catalog, "a first and invaluable compendium."—*Review*, Print collector's newsletter, v.20, May/June 1989, p.71.

Selected bibliography, p.275–80.

N74 The French Renaissance in prints from the Bibliothèque nationale de France. Ed. by Karen Jacobson. [Los Angeles], Grunwald Center for the Graphic Arts, Univ. of California, Los Angeles, 1994. 493p. il.

Catalog of the exhibition, Grunwald Center for the Graphic Arts (1994), and other locations. Scholarly catalog that seeks to redress "the relative neglect of sixteenth-century France [which] is out of all proportion to the historical importance and beauty of French art and the striking information it offers about a society very different [from either Italy or England]."—*Foreword.* Nine essays by leading experts in the field, followed by an extensive annotated catalog, beautifully illustrated.

Contents: Reflections on the School of Fontainebleau, by Georg Baselitz; Introduction, by Henri Zerner; Printmakers in sixteenth-century France, by Marianne Grivel; Stories beyond words, by Marie Madeleine Fontaine; The prints of the School of Fontainebleau, by Suzanne Boorsch; Courting the female subject, by Nancy J. Vickers; Of Marmites and martyrs: images and polemics in the wars of religion, by Philip Benedict; Portraiture as propaganda: printmaking during the reign of Henri IV, by Cynthia Burlingham; Renaissance ornament prints: the French contribution, by Peter Fuhring; Catalogue of the exhibition.

Biographies, p.265–79. Bibliography, p.481–92. Index of artists, p.493.

N75 The graphic arts and French society, 1871–1914. Ed. by Phillip Dennis Cate. New Brunswick, Rutgers Univ. Pr.; Jane Voorhees Zimmerli Art Museum, 1988. viii, 195p. il. (part col.), plates.

Studies how the print emerged as "the primary means to promote, criticize, or satirize social and political ideals, to record surroundings and events, and to advertise products."—*Introd.*

Contents: Paris seen through the artists' eyes, by Phillip Dennis Cate; Paris as a mecca of pleasure: women in fin-de-siècle France, by Ann Ilan-Alter; Between nature and symbol: French prints and illustrations at the turn of the century, by Jack Spector; The artist as illustrator in fin-de-siècle Paris, by Patricia Eckert Boyer.

Bibliography, p.185–87. Index, p.189–95.

N76 Garnier, Nicole. L'imagerie populaire française. Paris, Réunion des musées nationaux, 1990– . (2)v. il. (part col.)

Scholarly, well-illustrated catalog. A principal source for French popular prints from the late 18th century on.

Bibliographie, v.1, p.467–69, v.2, p.455–57. Expositions, v.1, p.470, v.2, p.458. Index iconographique, v.1, p.471–76, v.2, p.459–67. Index des noms de personnes et de lieux, v.1, p.477–81, v.2, p.468–69.

N77 Melot, Michel. Graphic arts of the pre-impressionists. Trans. by Robert Erich Wolf. N.Y., Abrams, 1980. 295p. chiefly il.

Trans. of Les grands graveurs. Paris, Art et métiers graphiques, 1978.

A monumental, though selective, oeuvre catalog of the printed works of the French Barbizon artists and others who constitute the so-called "pre-Impressionists." The scope of the catalog is intentionally more inclusive than previous treatments of the subject, in that it includes reproductive and commercial prints by or after the artists as well as "originals," and thus is more representative of the period of production. The catalog follows the numbering in Delteil (GLAH 1:N25), with the exception of Boudin, who was not included in Delteil's catalog.

Bibliography, p.25–27. Guide to the catalogues, p.256.

N78 ______. The Impressionist print. Trans. by Caroline Beamish. New Haven, Yale Univ. Pr., 1996. 296p. il. (part col.)

Trans. of L'estampe Impressioniste. Paris, Flammarion, 1994.

A comprehensive survey of the print production of artists associated with the French Impressionist movement and its immediate predecessors and successors. Melot argues that an understanding of this production is essential to an understanding of the production and reception of Impressionist art. A pendant volume to the author's Graphic art of the pre-impressionists (see preceding entry).

Notes, p.276–87. Bibliography, p.288–92. Index, p.293–96.

N79 Paris. Bibliothèque Nationale. Département des Estampes. Inventaire du fonds français. Paris, Bibliothèque Nationale, 1932– .

See GLAH 1:N86 for original annotation and previous vols.

Contents: Graveurs du XVIIe siècle, v.8 (Sébastien Leclerc)–12 (Jean Lepautre, pt.2), 17 (Claude Mellan), by Maxime Préaud. Inventaire du fonds français après 1800, v.15. Beginning with v.15 (letter M) has title: Inventaire du fonds français: Graveurs du XIXe siècle, and covers only the 19th century.

N80 Passeron, Roger. Impressionist prints. N.Y., Dutton, 1974. 222p. il. (part col.)

Trans. of La gravure Impressionniste: origines et rayonnement. Fribourg, Office du Livre, 1974.

Standard treatment of the subject.

Catalogue of the prints reproduced, p.[209–23].

N81 Reed, Sue Welsh. French prints from the age of the musketeers. With contrib. by Alvin L. Clark, Jr. . . . [et al.] Boston, Museum of Fine Arts, 1998. ix, 277p. il., facsims., ports.

Published in conjunction with the exhibition, Museum of Fine Arts, Boston, (1998–99), and other locations. "The first international exhibition to take as its subject printmaking in France from 1610–1660."—*Dir. pref.* Includes essays on printmaking and the print market in 17th-century France, followed by a catalog helpfully arranged by categories (genre subjects, current events, portraits, architecture and landscapes, religious subjects, allegories, ancient history, and mythology).

Biographies of the printmakers, by Sue Welsh Reed and Stephanie L. Stepanek, p.241–62. Bibliography, p.263–75. Index of printmakers, p.277.

N82 Regency to empire: French printmaking, 1715–1814. Organized by Victor I. Carlson, John W. Ittmann. Contrib. authors, David Becker . . . [et al.] [Baltimore], Baltimore Museum of Art, 1984. 371p. il. (part col.)

Catalog of the exhibition, Baltimore Museum of Art (1984–85), and other locations. Seeks to fill the gap "in our knowledge of Western printmaking . . . [in presenting] an area little studied despite the stature of many French artists of the period and the importance of their technical and aesthetic inventions."—*Foreword.* Includes essays on the painter-etcher, technical innovations in color printing, the portrait print, the illustrated book, design for ornament and architecture. Extensive catalog entries.

Artists' biographies, p.344–58. Glossary, p.359–60. Selected bibliography, p.361–67. Index, p.369.

Germany and Austria

N83 Bartrum, Giulia. German Renaissance prints, 1490–1550. London, British Museum Pr., 1995. 240p. il (part col.)

Catalog of the exhibition, British Museum (1995), and other locations. Serves as an extended checklist of the German Renaissance print holdings of the museum, and includes a brief history of the collection. One of the few available surveys of the topic.

Technical glossary, p.16. Notes to the catalogue, p.16. General bibliography, p.238. Index, p.239–40.

N84 Carey, Frances, and Griffiths, Antony. The print in Germany, 1880–1933: the age of expressionism: prints from the Department of Prints and Drawings in the British Museum. With a section of illustrated books from the British Library [by] David Paisey. N.Y., Harper and Row, 1984. 272p. il. (part col.), plates.

Catalog of the exhibition, British Museum (1984). The catalog contains more than 200 entries, 170 of which represent recent additions to the collections. Includes an essay on the printmaking techniques of the Brücke.

Bibliography, p.40. Supplementary bibliography [on illustrated books], p.236. Index of artists, p.272.

N85 Ereignis Karikaturen: Geschichte in Spottbildern, 1600–1930. [Hrsg. von Siegfried Kessemeister.] Münster, Lanschaftsverband Westfalen-Lippe, Westfälisches Landesmuseum für Kunst und Kulturgeschichte Münster, 1983. 384p. il. (part col.)

Catalog of the exhibition, Westfälisches Landesmuseum (1983), of historical caricatures from the 17th to the 20th century. Remarkable for its scholarship and its illustrations, an excellent catalog.

Bibliographical references in catalog entries. Biographisches Künstlerverzeichnis, p.374–80. Literaturverzeichnis, p.381–84.

N86 Fanelli, Giovanni. La linea viennese, grafica art nouveau. Firenze, Cantini, 1989. 338p. il. (part col.)

Important, beautifully illustrated study of Art Nouveau graphics in Vienna, by a specialist. Pays special attention to the wide range of media, including prints, book illustration, commercial art, ex libris design, postage stamps, etc.

Note, p.132–35. Bibliografia, p.137–41. Indice dei nomi, p.336–38.

N87 From a mighty fortress: prints, drawings, and books in the age of Luther, 1483–1546. [Ed. by] Christiane Andersson, Charles Talbot. [Detroit], Detroit Insitute of Arts, 1983. 411p. il.

Catalog of the exhibition, Detroit Institute of Arts (1983). An essential scholarly exhibition catalog devoted in part to German Renaissance print and book production. The exhibition draws from the collections of Kunstsammlungen der Veste Coburg and the Landesbibliothek Coberg in Germany. The works, "most of which have never before been seen outside Germany, were chosen not only for their artistic quality but also because they reflect so cogently the life of the period—its political realities, social mores, religious beliefs, and intellectual concerns."—*Foreword.* The critical catalog covers "Early German Drawings at Coburg," and "Prints and Illustrated Books at Coburg." Lengthy catalog entries, extensively illustrated.

Bibliography, p.294–410. Index of artists, p.411.

N88 Griffiths, Antony, and Carey, Frances. German printmaking in the age of Goethe. London, British Museum Pr., 1994. 240p. il.

Catalog of the exhibition, British Museum (1994), and other locations. "The present exhibition is the first ever held in Britain on German printmaking of the period of Goethe's life and this catalogue appears to be only the second survey of the subject published in any language other than German [the first being a small 1981 Goethe House (New York) pamphlet entitled Eden Revisited]."—*Pref.* Includes an historical introduction. The catalog entries are grouped around locations (e.g., Berlin, Vienna, Mannheim), themes (e.g., "Idylls," the "Nazarenes," "Romanticism"), or topics (such as "The Publishers of the 1790s").

Technical glossary, p.32. Books and periodicals cited in abbreviations, p.236. General bibliography, p.237–38. Index, p.239–40.

N89 Heller, Reinhold. Brücke: German expressionist prints from the Granvil and Marcia Specks collection. With contrib. by the participants in the seminar on German expressionism at the University of Chicago. Evanston, Il., Mary and Leigh Block Gallery, Northwestern Univ., 1988. x, 321p. il. (part col.)

Catalog of the exhibition, Block Gallery (1988), documenting an important private collection of prints related to German Expressionism and the Die Brücke movement of the early 20th century. Included are catalog entries for the leading artists associated with Die Brücke. Exhibition theme continued by Stark impressions (see following title).

Brücke: a bibliography, p.19–24. Notes to the reader, p.25–26.

N90 ______. Stark impressions: graphic production in Germany, 1918–1933. With contrib. by Erin Hogan . . . [et al.] Evanston, Il., Mary and Leigh Block Gallery, Northwestern Univ., 1994. 358p. il. (part col.)

Catalog of the exhibition, Block Gallery (1994). Substantial thematic sequel to Brücke (see preceding title) "broadened into a scholarly investigation into the broad spectrum of print production in Weimar Germany."—*Pref.* Includes an introductory essay on the period and the unique role of the print as an "instrument of salvation." The catalog entries are divided into six thematic sections: "War, Revolution, Counter-Revolution"; "The New Religion, the New Humanity"; "City, Town and Country"; "The Struggle for Existence"; "Women, Love and Sexuality"; and "Fantasy and Abstraction."

Bibliography of work catalogs for artists' prints, p.356–57.

N91 Hollstein, F. W. H. German etchings, engravings and woodcuts, ca. 1400–1700. Amsterdam, Herzberger, 1954– . (49)v. il. New series, Rotterdam, Sound and Vision Interactive, 1996– . (3)v. il.

See GLAH 1:N98 for original entry and previous vols. Publisher varies. A new series, entitled, The new Hollstein German engravings, etchings and woodcuts, 1400–1700, began in 1996, with various compilers and editors. It will include "a revision of the first ten volumes" of the original series.—*Editorial*, v.1.

Contents: (23) Erasmus Roy-Jakob Mayr; (24) Israhel van Mekenem; (25) Johan Ulrich Mayr to Matthaeus Merian the Elder; (26) Matthaeus Merian the Elder (cont'd); (26A) Matthaeus Merian the Elder (cont'd) to Matthaeus Merian the Younger; (27) P. Mertens to Johannes Meyer der Ältere; (28) Johannes Meyer der Jüngere to Johann Reinhard Mühl; (29) Johann Reinhard Mühl (cont'd) to Nickel Nehrlich the Elder; (30) Nickel Nehrlich the Younger to Michael Ostendorfer; (31) Michael Ostendorfer (cont'd) to Georg Pencz; (32) Johann Perfert to Johann Praetorius; (33) Michael Pregel to Johann Reisenleither; (34) Bartholomaeus Reiter to Gottfried Rogg; (35) Peter Rollos I to Christian Romstet; (36) Johann Ronzonius to Melchior Sachse; (37) J. M. Sacerer to Peter Salzburger; (38) Jacob von Sandrart; (39) Jacob von Sandrart (cont'd); (40) Joachim von Sandrart . . . Lorenz von Sandrart; (41) Susanna Maria von Sandrart; (42) Gordian Sanz to Hans Schäufelein; (43) Hans Schäufelein (cont'd); (44) Hans Schäufelein (cont'd) to Adolarius Schildknecht; (45) Johann Reinhold Schildknecht to Conrad Schnitt; (46) Johann Schnitzer to Lucas Schnitzer; (47) Erhard Schön; (48) Erhard Schön (cont'd); (49) Ludwig Schongauer to Martin Schongauer. New series: (1) Hans von Aachen; (2) Albrecht und Erhard Altdorfer; (3) Heinrich Aldegrever.

N92 Hütt, Wolfgang. Grafik in der DDR. Dresden, VEB Verlag der Kunst, 1979. 413p. il. (part col.)

Reproduces 360 prints from the former German Democratic Republic, with a suite of background essays.

Anmerkungen, p.363. Literaturhinweise, p.364–66. Biografien der Künstler, p.367–406. Verzeichnis der Abbildungen, p.407–[14].

N93 Kolb, Eberhard; Roters, Eberhard; and Schmied, Wieland. Kritische Grafik in der Weimarer Zeit. Stuttgart, Klett-Cotta, 1985. 226p. chiefly il. (part col.)

Complements Heller's Stark impressions (GLAH 2:N90). Scholarly study of polemical prints and caricatures in the Weimar Republic.

Biografien der Künstler, p.50–77.

N94 Pabst, Michael. Wiener Grafik um 1900. München, Silke Schreiber, 1984. 348p. il. (part col.)

Excellent, well-illustrated survey of Viennese graphic arts of the fin-de-siècle.

Anmerkungen, p.317–20. Künstlerbiographien, p.321–40. Literatur, p.341–44. Register, p.345–48.

N95 Reisenfeld, Robin. The German print portfolio, 1890–1930: serials for a private sphere. Introd. by Reinhold Heller. Ed. by Richard A. Born and Stephanie d'Alessandro. S.l., Philip Wilson in assoc. with the David and Alfred Smart Museum of Art, University of Chicago (Distr. by Rizzoli, 1992). 159p. il. (part col.), plates.

Catalog of the exhibition, Smart Museum of Art (1992), and other locations, examining "the print portfolio's central role in the modern graphic movement in Germany and Austria from 1890 to 1930," and based upon the museum's collections.

Select bibliography, p.[151]–55. Index, p.[157]–59.

N96 Schweiger, Werner J. Aufbruch und Erfüllung: Gebrauchsgraphik der Wiener Moderne, 1897–1918. Wien, Brandstatter, 1988. 224p. il. (part col.)

Wide-ranging survey of Viennese commercial art of the period, including calendars, calling cards, menus, theater programs, etc., with 835 illustrations.

Schlagwort- und Verweisregister, p.7–8. Literatur, p.218–21. Register, p.221–24.

N97 Sohn, Gerhart. Handbuch der Original-Graphik in deutschen Zeitschriften, Mappenwerken, Kunstbüchern und Katalogen (HDO), 1890–1933. Düsseldorf, Edition GS, 1989–1994. 7v. il.

Systematic catalog of original prints appearing in German periodicals, atlases, art books, and catalogs, 1890–1933, embracing ca. 5,000 prints in 200 publications.

Künstlerregister in each vol. Cumulative Registerband (Bd.7) includes a Literatur-Verzeichnis, p.33–36.

N98 The world in miniature: engravings by the German Little Masters, 1500–1550. Ed. by Stephen H. Goddard. Essays by Patricia A. Emison, Stephen H. Goddard, Janey L. Levy. Contrib. by Henry Fullenwider, Andrew Stevens. [Lawrence], Spencer Museum of Art, University of Kansas, 1988. 240p. il.

Catalog of the exhibition, Spencer Museum of Art (1988), and other locations, devoted to the neglected but important "second generation" of German printmakers. Thematically arranged, treating such subjects as allegory and antiquity, religious themes, mortality and sexuality, soldiers, peasants, and the secular world.

Biographical notes, p.220–25. Bibliography, p.226–35. Index of exhibited engravings, p.236. Index, p.237–40

SEE ALSO: Iconclass indexes: early German prints (GLAH 2:F12).

Great Britain and Ireland

N99 Alexander, David S., and Godfrey, Richard T. Painters and engraving: the reproductive print from Hogarth to Wilkie. New Haven, Yale Center for British Art, 1980. iv, 73p. il., plates.

Catalog of an important exhibition, Yale Center for British Art (1980), intended to bring attention to the often-neglected history of reproductive engraving in Britain. In addition to the catalog entries, mostly drawn from the rich holdings of the Yale Center, 13 short essays cover the history from the 1730s to the 1820s.

Entries include bibliographical references. Index of painters and engravers, p.72–73.

N100 Art Gallery of Ontario. Pictures for the parlor: the English reproductive print from 1775 to 1900. [By] Brenda D. Rix. Toronto, The Gallery, 1983. 88p. il.

Catalog of the exhibition, Art Gallery of Ontario (1983). "In this exhibition, the growing popularity of the reproductive print, its social context and artistic merits are explored within the boundaries imposed by [the museum's] Permanent Collection."—*Pref.* Entries divided into three sections on the 18th century, the early 19th century, and the Victorian period.

Principal catalogues raisonnés with abbreviations, p.86. Selected bibliography, p.87. Index of artists and titles, p.88.

N101 Bridson, Gavin D. R., and Wakeman, Geoffrey. Printmaking and picture printing: a bibliographical guide to artistic and industrial technique in Britain, 1750–1900. Williamsburg, Bookpress, 1984. 250p.

Extensive bibliography "concerned with the processes for preparing printed surfaces, and the means of printing from them, as practiced in Britain [in the 18th and 19th centuries]."—*Introd.* Divided into sections including works on printmaking and picture printing in general, and the major printing processes.

Periodicals consulted, p.211–15. Suggestions for a basic library, p.216–18. Index of processes, patent names, equipment and materials, p.221–33. Index of authors, contributors, editors and translators, p.234–50.

N102 British printmakers, 1855–1955: a century of printmaking from the Etching Revival to St. Ives. London, Garton, in assoc. with Scolar, 1992. x, 326p. il.

Collected essays "designed to be a resource of information about the developments of British printmaking which started in the middle of the nineteenth century and continued into the middle of the twentieth. . . . The dates . . . (1855–1955) are not chosen at random."—*Introd.*

Topics arranged by printing processes.

Includes bibliographical references. Artists' biographies, p.[1]–78.

N103 Calloway, Stephen. English prints for the collector. Woodstock, N.Y., Overlook Pr., 1981. 232p. il. (part col.)

Major survey of prints and print collecting in England.

Contents: (1) Early English printmaking; (2) Hollar and the English tradition; (3) The age of Hogarth; (4) The English Romantic tradition; (5) English landscape; (6) A new century; (7) Popular prints; (8) Nineteenth-century high art and the etching revival; (9) Fin-de-siècle to avant-garde; (10) The modern print; (11) Collecting and the care of prints.

Technical glossary, p.220–[22]. Bibliography, p.223–28. Index, p.230–32.

N104 Carey, Frances, and Griffiths, Antony. Avant-garde British printmaking, 1914–1960. With a contrib. by Stephen Coppel. London, British Museum, 1990. 240p. il.

Catalog of the exhibition, British Museum (1990). One of a series of exhibition catalogs, prepared by the Department of Prints and Drawings at the British Museum, on aspects of modern printmaking. The catalog concentrates on single-sheet prints, beginning with the Vorticists and ending with the late 1950s. Includes individual biographies and bibliographies for each artist. The examples are drawn from the extensive modern British print holdings of the department, the nucleus of which is the bequest of Campbell Dodgson, former Keeper. The introductory essay includes information on the print market and print collecting in the earlier 20th century in Britain.

General bibliography, p.238–39. Index of artists, p.240.

N105 Clayton, Timothy. The English print 1688–1802. New Haven, Published for the Paul Mellon Centre for Studies in British Art by Yale Univ. Pr., 1997. 337p. il. (part col.)

"A principal purpose of this book is to facilitate further study of prints in eighteenth-century England so that they can be rehabilitated in accounts of its cultural life."—*Pref.* Describes processes of publication and distribution of separately published prints, the structure of the trade, changing fashions in collecting, using and displaying prints, and the principal themes of the published output.

Notes, p.287–310. Bibliography, p.311–20. Index, p.321–37.

N106 Donald, Diana. The age of caricature: satirical prints in the reign of George III. New Haven, Published for the Paul Mellon Centre for Studies in British Art by Yale Univ. Pr., 1996. viii, 248p. il. (part col.)

Thematic essays attempting to address partially the need for "a general, critical study of caricature in the so-called 'golden age,' namely the later Georgian period."—*Pref.*

Contents: Introduction: The laughing audience; (1) "The miserable tribe of party etchers"; (2) Wit and emblem: the language of political prints; (3) "Struggles for happiness": the fashionable world; (4) The crowd in caricature: "A picture of England"; (5) "John Bull bother'd": the French Revolution and the Propaganda War of the 1790s; Epilogue: Peterloo and the end of the Georgian tradition in satire.

Notes, p.199–243. Index, p.244–48.

N107 Dyson, Anthony. Pictures to print: the nineteenth-century engraving trade. Williamsburg, Farrand Pr. (Distr. in North America by Book Press, 1984). xxx, 234p. il., facsims., plans, ports.

An invaluable resource on the business and trade practices of 19th-century English printers and engravers. Dyson draws his analysis largely from the records of the London firm of Dixon and Ross, included in an appended catalog.

Technical glossary, p.219–23. Bibliography, p.225–28. Index, p.229–34.

N108 Engen, Rodney K. Dictionary of Victorian engravers, print publishers and their works. Teaneck, N.J., Somerset House, 1979. 245p. il., plates.

Alphabetical lists of engravers, publishers, printers, and printsellers. Covers a long-neglected area of reproductive engraving history. The author "has built up a composite picture of nearly 1,000 major engravers, publishers, and their works on metal."—*Introd.* Draws largely from the Print Sellers Association catalogs from 1847 to 1912. Also draws from exhibition records of the Royal Academy, among other sources.

Books included in entries, p.[vii]. Periodicals included in entries, p.[viii]. Distinctions abbreviated, p.[ix]. Galleries abbreviated, p.[x].

N109 The English satirical print, 1600–1832. Teaneck, N.J., Chadwyck-Healey, 1986. (7)v. il.

Important series of monographs. Some vols. have Alexandria, Va., as place of publication. All vols. published 1986.

Contents: Brewer, John. The common people and politics, 1750–1790s; Dickinson, H. T. Caricatures and the Constitution, 1760–1832; Duffy, Michael. The Englishman and the foreigner; Langford, Paul. Walpole and the robinocracy; Miller, John. Religion in the popular prints, 1600–1832; Sharpe, J. A. Crime and the law in English satirical prints, 1600–1832; Thomas, Peter David Garner. The American Revolution.

N110 Friedman, Joan M. Color printing in England, 1486–1870. [New Haven], Yale Center for British Art, 1978. ix, 72p. il. (part col.)

Catalog of the exhibition, Yale Center for British Art (1978). An unsurpassed survey of the topic and an important source for the history of reproductive engraving. Enhanced by an excellent set of representative color plates.

Bibliography, p.67–68. Index, p.69–72.

N111 Garrett, Albert. A history of British wood engraving. Atlantic Highlands, N.J., Humanities Press, 1978. 407p. il.

"The purpose of this book is to show that there is now a British school of wood engraving with a common philosophical vision and a dominant aesthetic language to which many artists have made personal contributions."—*Introd.* Narrative survey through the 20th century, by a practitioner and former president of the Society of Wood Engravers.

Biographical notes, p.374–400. Index, p.401–07.

N112 Godfrey, Richard T. Printmaking in Britain: a general history from its beginnings to the present day. N.Y., New York Univ. Pr., 1978. 244p. il. (part col.)

A good, general survey of the field, with short biographies of major printmakers.

Notes, p.[134]–39. Technical glossary, p.[237]–39. Bibliography, p.[240]–41. Index, p.[242]–44.

N113 Hunnisett, Basil. An illustrated dictionary of British steel engravers. Brookfield, Vt., Gower, 1989. xix, 180p. il.

Expanded version of the author's A dictionary of British steel engravers. Leigh-on-Sea, Eng., F. Lewis, 1980. The authoritative dictionary.

List of portraits, p.ix. List of plates, p.xi. Notes on sources, p.xiii. List of sources, p.xv–xvi. Definitions, p.xvii. Select list of nineteenth century books consulted, p.173–80.

N114 ______. Steel-engraved book illustration in England. Boston, Godine, 1980. xvi, 263p. il.

Authoritative survey of the subject.

Contents: (1) Introducing the steel engraving; (2) Siderography and after; (3) Warren's steel plates; (4) The art of steel engraving; (5) The corporate life of the engravers; (6) Some steel engravers; (7) The artists; (8) The books; (9) Publishing and the publishers; (10) Plate printing and the printers; (11) Decline of the art; Appendix: "Engraved on steel" from All the year round, 27 October 1866.

Notes, p.217–39. Index, p.247–63.

N115 Lister, Raymond. Prints and printmaking: a dictionary and handbook of the art in nineteenth-century Britain. London, Methuen, 1984. 385p. il., plates.

A major dictionary of "engravers and others concerned in the production and distribution of prints in Great Britain during the nineteenth century."—*Table of contents*. Includes good survey chapters on the history of printmaking during this period.

Contents: (I) Introduction; (II) Printmaking at the beginning of the nineteenth century; (III) The impact of lithography; (IV) The spread of wood-engraving; (V) Technique and design in security printing; (VI) The age of steel engraving; (VII) The resurgence of etching; (VIII) Printmaking techniques; Dictionary.

General bibliography, p.100–05.

N116 Russell, Ronald. Guide to British topographical prints. North Pomfret, Vt., David and Charles, 1979. 224p. il.

"In this book we are concerned with the pictorial representation of such places as towns, districts, parts of the countryside and buildings by their setting."—*Introd.*

Contents: (1) Early etching, and line engravings on copper; (2) The Picturesque and the Turner print industry; (3) Aquatint and lithography; (4) Line engraving on steel; (5) Wood cutting and engraving; (6) Etching; (7) Methods; [Appendixes]: Books illustrated with prints; Painters and draughtsmen; Engravers, etchers and lithographers.

Select bibliography, p.217–18. Index, p.220–24.

Italy

N117 Da Carlevarijs ai Tiepolo: incisori veneti e friulani del Settecento. Catalogo della mostra a cura di Dario Succi. Saggio introd. di Giuseppe Maria Pilo. Premessa di Giandomenico Romanelli. Testi di Beatrice Di Colloredo Toppani . . . [et al.] Venezia, Albrizzi, 1983. 490p. il.

Catalog of the exhibition, Museo Correr, Venice (1983), and other locations, of 18th-century prints from the Veneto and Friuli. Annotated, scholarly catalog of more than 600 prints, with background essays.

Indice generale dei nomi, p.[492–508]. Indice degli autori citati nelle bibliografie, p.[509–12]. Indice degli autori dei repertori citati nelle schede delle opere, p.[513–14]. Indice dei prestatori, p.[514]. Indice, p.[515].

N118 Fuoco acqua cielo terra. A cura di Aurelio Rigoli e Annamaria Amitrano Savarese. Ricerca iconografica e catalogo di Clelia Alberici e Alberto Milano. Con la collab. red. di Barbara Cervetto. Vigevano, Diakronia; Centro internazionale di etnostoria, 1995. 821p. il. (part col.)

Monumental catalog of popular prints, mainly 18th–19th century. Treats such subjects as the four elements, the planets, geography, the seasons, love and marriage, satire and caricature, popular piety. Especially useful for its iconographic approach and illustrations grouped by themes.

Indice dei nomi, p.802–15. Scritti di Achille Bertarelli, p.816–18. Pubblicazioni di Francesco Novati riguardanti le stampe popolari, p.818. Bibliografia, p.819–21.

N119 Incisioni italiane del '600 nella raccolta d'arte Pagliara dell'Istituto Suor Orsola Benincasa di Napoli. A cura di Anna Caputi, Maria Teresa Penta. Milano, Mazzotta, 1987. 251p. il. (Stampe e disegni dell'Istituto Suor Orsola Benincasa, 1)

Important catalog of 16th-century Italian prints, arranged by region, then by artist.

Bibliographical references at the beginning of each regional section. Indice iconografico, p.245–46. Indice dei "pinxit" e "invenit," p.247. Indice delle tavole, p.249–50. Bibliografia generale, p.251.

N120 Karpinski, Caroline. Italian printmaking in the fifteenth and sixteenth centuries: an annotated bibliography. Boston, Hall, 1987. xxv, 305p. il. (Reference publication in art history)

Entries drawn mostly from the collections of the Library of Congress and the National Gallery of Art library. Introduction serves as a good overview of past and present scholarship on Italian Renaissance prints. Bibliography divided into 16 categories, including reference sources and general histories, foreign printmakers in Italy and Italian prints abroad, history of publishing and commerce, iconography, collections, etc.

Index of authors, p.275–87. Index of names, p.289–300. Index of subjects, p.301–05.

N121 Reed, Sue Welsh, and Wallace, Richard. Italian etchers of the Renaissance and Baroque. With contrib. by David Acton . . . [et al.] Boston, Museum of Fine Arts, 1989. xlvii, 302p. il., map.

Catalog of the exhibition, Museum of Fine Arts, Boston (1989), and other locations. "The first survey of the role of etching in Italy from about 1520 to 1700 . . . one of the few publications in English to present an overview of this important subject."—*Pref.*

Bibliography, p.289–300. Index of artists, p.301–02.

N122 Sopher, Marcus S. Seventeenth-century Italian prints. With the assist. of Claudia Lazzaro-Bruno. Stanford, Calif., Stanford Art Museum, Stanford University, 1978. 232p. il.

Catalog of the exhibition, Stanford Art Gallery (1978), documenting an important collection. "Attempts to provide a brief panorama of the development of the style and technique and the diversity of artistic character and subject matter evident in Italian printmaking during the period."—*Introd.*

Abbreviations, p.230–31. Selected bibliography, p.231. Index of artists, p.232.

SEE ALSO: Iconclass indexes: Italian prints (GLAH 2:F13).

Latin America

N123 Bermúdez, Jorge R. Gráfica e identidad nacional. México, D.F., Univ. Autónoma Metropolitana-Xochimilco, 1994. 204p. il.

Brief study of the evolution of a national identity in Mexican visual culture.

Contents: (I) El origen gráfico del Nuevo Mundo; (II) Carácter y desarollo de la imprenta americana; (III) El periodismo de la Ilustración Americana; (IV) Gráfica y nacionalidad; (V) La fotografía.

Bibliografía, p.199–202.

N124 Matrizes e gravuras brasileiras da colecção Guita e José E. Mindlin. Lisboa, Fundação Calouste Gulbenkian, Centro de Arte Moderna, 1993. 1v. (unpaged) il. (part col.)

Catalog of the exhibition, Fundação Calouste Gulbenkian, Centro de Arte Moderna, Lisbon (1993), of 195 prints by 34 Brazilian artists. Short essay by Lasar Segall on the history of Brazilian graphic arts.

N125 Tibol, Raquel. Gráficas y neográficas en México. México, D.F., Secretaría de Educación Pública, Univ. Nacional Autónoma de México, 1987. 302p. il. (Foro 2000)

History of the graphic arts in Mexico from the introduction of lithography in the 19th century to the present.

Advertencia de las fuentes, p.299–302.

Low Countries

N126 Ackley, Clifford S. Printmaking in the age of Rembrandt. Boston, Museum of Fine Arts, [1981]. xlviii, 316p. il. (part col.)

Authoritative catalog of the exhibition, Museum of Fine Arts, Boston (1981), widely cited in the art historical literature. Includes an important essay by William Robinson on collecting and connoisseurship in 17th-century Northern Europe.

Glossary, p.306–07. Abbreviated references used in the catalogue, p.308–15. Index of artists, p.316.

N127 Da Bruegel a Goltzius: specchio dell'antico e del nuovo mondo: incisioni fiamminghe e olandesi della seconda metà del Cinquecento dei Musei Civici di Padova. A cura di Caterina Limentani Virdis, Davide Banzato, Cinzia Butelli. Milano, Electa, 1994. 211p. il.

Catalog of the thematic exhibition, Museo Civico, Padua (1994), devoted to Flemish and Dutch Mannerist prints of the later 16th century.

Contents: Storie di santi, di eroi, di dei e di gente comune, di Caterina Limentani Virdis; Da Bruegel a Goltzius: stampe, temi e generi, di Davide Banzato; Biografie degli incisori, di Cinzia Butelli; Catalogo delle opere in mostra, schede di Cinzia Butelli.

Filigrane, p.206–07. Bibliografia, p.209–11.

N128 Freedberg, David. Dutch landscape prints of the seventeenth century. London, British Museum Publications, 1980. 79p. il., plates (British Museum prints and drawings series)

"The original intention of this book was simply to give some idea of the vast holdings of the British Museum in this field, but those holdings are so remarkable that it soon became apparent that more than enough material was available for a history of the genre."—*Foreword.*

Select bibliography, p.73–74. Alphabetical list of artists, p.75–76. List of museum registration numbers, p.77. Index, p.78–79.

N129 Goddard, Stephen H. Sets and series: prints from the Low Countries. [New Haven], Yale Univ. Art Gallery, [1984]. 39, [6]p. il.

An introductory catalog to the Gallery's collection. Intended to emphasize the phenomenon of "the complete set of prints" as a primary, historical classification scheme.

Bibliography, p.[41]–[45].

N130 Graphik der Niederlande, 1508–1617: Kupferstiche und Radierungen von Lucas van Leyden bis Hendrik Goltzius. [Katalogbehandlung: Konrad Renger, Cornelia Syre.] München, Staatliche Graphische Sammlung, 1979. 80p. il.

Catalog of the exhibition, Staatliche Graphische Sammlung, Munich (1979). Together with Graphik in Holland (see following title), constitutes a chronological survey of Netherlandish printmaking of the 16th and 17th centuries.

Anmerkungen, p.70–74. Abgekürzt zitierte Literatur, p.74–76. Register der Künstler und Verleger, p.77–78.

N131 Graphik in Holland: Esaias und Jan van de Velde, Rembrandt, Ostade und ihr Kreis: Radierung, Kupferstich, Schabkunst. [Katalogbearb.: Konrad Renger, Dorothea Schmidt.] München, Die Staatliche Graphische Sammlung, 1982. 167p. il.

Catalog of the exhibition, Neue Pinakothek, Munich (1982). Together with Graphik der Niederlande (see preceding title), constitutes a chronological survey of Netherlandish printmaking of the 16th and 17th centuries.

Anmerkungen, p.[150]–63. Abgekürzt zitierte Literatur, p.163–66. Register, p.167.

N132 Hollstein, F. W. H. Dutch and Flemish etchings, engravings, and woodcuts, ca. 1450–1700. Amsterdam, Hertzberger, 1949– . (54)v. il. New series, Roosendaal, Royal van Poll, 1993– . (9)v. il.

See GLAH 1:N126 for previous vols. and original annotation.

Contents: (21–22) Aegidius Sadeler to Raphael Sadeler II.; (23) Jan Saenredam to Roelandt Savery; (24) Salomon Savery to Gillis van Scheyndel; (25) Pieter Schenck; (26) François Schillemans to J. Seuler; (27) Christoffel van Sichem I to Herman Specht; (28) Louis Spirinx to M. Suys; (29) Samuel de Swaef to Jan Thesing; (31) Jan van der Vaart to Gerard Valck; (32) Petrus Valck to Esaias van de Valde; (33) Jan van de Valde II to Dirk Vellert; (34) Jan van de Valde II. Plates; (35) Adriaen van de Venne to Johannes

Verkolje I; (36) Claudius Vermeulen to Paulus Willemsz van Vianen; (37) David Vinck(e)boons to Hendrik Visjager; (38) Claes Jansz Visscher to Claes Claesz Visscher II [Nicolaes Visscher II]—Text; (39) Claes Jansz Visscher to Claes Claesz Visscher II [Nicolaes Visscher II]—Plates; (40) Cornelis de Visscher, Cornelis Visscher, Hendrick Jansz Visscher, Lambert Visscher; (41) Johannes [de] Visscher to Robert van Voerst; (42) Alexander Voet I to Anthonie de Vos; (43) Lucas Vorsterman I; (44) Maarten de Vos, text; (45) Maarten de Vos, plates, pt.1; (46) Maarten de Vos, plates, pt.2; (47) Vredeman de Vries, pt.1; (48) Vredeman de Vries, pt.2; (49) Cornelis de Vos to Aert van Waes; (50) Antoni Waterloo; (51) Isaac van Waesberge to Jean de Weert; (52) Nicolaus de Wees to Hendrick Winter; (53) Frederick de Wit to Lieven de Witte; (54) Gaspar Adriaensz. van Wittel to Moyses van Wtenbrouck. New series: (1) Maarten van Heemskerck, pt.1–2; (2) Hendrick Hondius; (3) Lucas van Leyden; (4) Gerard van Groeningen, pt.1–2; (5) The Van Doetecum family, pt.1–4; (6) Karel van Mander; (7) The Muller Dynasty, pt.1–3; (8) Cornelis Cort, pt.1–3; (9) The De Gheyn family, pt.1–2.

N133 Levesque, Catherine. Journey through landscape in seventeenth-century Holland: the Haarlem print series and Dutch identity. University Park, Pennsylvania State Univ. Pr., 1994. xxii, 169p. il., plates.

A study of some of the most important Dutch landscape print series of the so-called "Golden Age" of Dutch art. Draws on companion studies of Dutch culture and landscape painting for methodology, but concentrates specifically on prints as a principal vehicle of landscape iconography and public identity of place.

Contents: (1) The visual culture: prints and communication; (2) Pieter Bruegel's Large Landscapes and the sixteenth-century background; (3) Claes Jansz. Visscher's Pleasant Places; (4) Esaias van den Velde's Ten Landscapes; (5) Willem Buytewech's Various Small Landscapes; (6) Jan van de Velde's series of landscapes and ruins; Epilogue: Print culture and the interpretation of landscape.

Notes, p.[121]–56. Selected bibliography, p.[157]–63. Index, p.[165]–69.

N134 Maritime prints by the Dutch Masters. Sel., introd. and annot. by Irene de Groot and Robert Vorstman. Trans. from the Dutch by Michael Hoyle. London, Gordon Fraser, published in coop. with the printroom of the Rijksmuseum, Amsterdam, 1980. 284p. il. (part folded)

Illustrated, scholarly catalog of 250 maritime prints from the period 1560–1870.

Biographies, p.272–76. Literature, p.277–78. Glossary, p.279–81. Index, p.281–84.

N135 Orenstein, Nadine M. Hendrick Hondius and the business of prints in seventeenth-century Holland. Rotterdam, Sound and Vision Interactive, 1996. 246p. il. (Studies in prints and printmaking, 1)

Pioneering study of the print trade in 17th-century Holland.

Bibliography, p.219–37. Index, p.238–46.

N136 Riggs, Timothy. Graven images: the rise of professional printmakers in Antwerp and Haarlem, 1540–1640. Evanston, Il., Mary and Leigh Block Gallery, Northwestern Univ. (Distr. by Northwestern Univ. Pr., 1993). 203p. il., plates.

Catalog of the exhibition, Block Gallery (1993), and other locations. Examines influences and innovations among Northern European reproductive engravers at a critical juncture of the history of prints. Includes essays by Walter Melion, Timothy Riggs, and Larry Silver.

Notes at ends of chapters.

N137 Staatliche Museen Preussischer Kulturbesitz. Kupferstichkabinett. Manierismus in Holland um 1600: Kupferstiche, Holzschnitte und Zeichnungen aus dem Berliner Kupferstichkabinett. Bearb. von Hans Mielke. Berlin, Das Museum, 1979. 63p. il., plates

Catalog of the exhibition, Kupferstichkabinet, Berlin (1979), drawing exclusively upon the holdings of that collection. Scholarly catalog of 87 Dutch Mannerist prints.

Häufige Stichaufschriften, p.21. Verzeichnis der abgekürzt zitierten Literatur, p.62–63.

N138 Stone-Ferrier, Linda A. Dutch prints of daily life: mirrors of life or masks of morals? Essay and catalogue by Linda A. Stone-Ferrier. Lawrence, Kansas, Spencer Museum of Art, University of Kansas, 1983. xi, 231p. il.

Catalog of the exhibition, Spencer Museum of Art (1983), and other locations. Addresses the unresolved methodological challenge of interpreting quotidian imagery in Dutch prints.

Frequently cited sources, p.38–39. Works in the exhibition, p.40–41. Biographies, p.219–23. Selected bibliography, p.224–31.

SEE ALSO: Iconclass indexes: Dutch prints (GLAH 2:F11).

Russia and Eastern Europe

N139 La época heroica: obra gráfica de las vanguardias Rusa y Húngara, 1912–1925: las colecciones suizas. Valencià, Generalitat Valenciana, 1990. 222p. il. (part col.)

Catalog of the exhibition, IVAM Centre Julio González, Sevilla (1990), devoted to Russian and Hungarian avant-garde prints from the Cabinet des Estampes, Geneva.

Acontecimientos artísticos, literarios y políticos en Rusia y Hungría, 1910–1930: resumen cronológico, p.[215]–19. Bibliografía seleccionada, p.[221]–22.

N140 Goldscheider, Irena. Czechoslovak prints from 1900 to 1970. London, Published for the Trustees of the British Museum by British Museum Publications, 1986. 51p. il. 102 plates.

Catalog of the exhibition, British Museum (1986). Valuable as a rare study of the subject in English. Each chapter consists of biographical entries with selected catalog entries for each artist.

Contents: (1) The founding generation; (2) The Symbolists; (3) The Cubists and the Tvrdosíjní; (4) The "social trend"; (5) The Surrealists and Group 42; (6) The 1960s.

Technical glossary, p.49. Bibliography, p.50. Index of artists, p.51.

N141 Grafica russa 1917/1930: manifesti, stampe, libri da collezioni private russe. [Catalogo a cura di Renzo Federici. Con testi di Giovanni Spadolini . . . (et al.)] Firenze, Vallecchi; Centro culturale il Bisonte, 1990. 192p. il. (part col.)

Catalog of the exhibition, Palazzo Strozzi, Florence (1990), of Revolution-era prints from private Russian collections, offering a well-illustrated, chronological overview of production.

Catalogo dei volumi del Museo del Libro di Mosca, p.[181]–92.

N142 King, David, and Porter, Kathy. Images of revolution: graphic art from 1905 Russia. N.Y., Pantheon, 1983. 128p. chiefly il. (part col.)

Brief but valuable presentation of dissident graphic art from an earlier period than usually covered in treatments of Russian revolutionary artistic activity.

Bibliography, p.[128].

Spain and Portugal

N143 Gallego Gallego, Antonio. Historia del grabado en España. Madrid, Ediciones Cátedra, 1990. 542p. il. (Cuadernos arte Cátedra, 7)

1st ed. 1979.

A narrative history from the 15th to the 20th century. Sparsely illustrated.

Bibliografía sumaria, p.523–33. Siglas de revistas y publicaciones periódicas, p.534–36.

N144 Soares, Ernesto. Historia de gravura artistica em Portugal; os artistas e as suas obras. Nova ed. [Reprint.] Lisboa, Libraria Samcarlos, 1971. 2v. il.

Reprint of 1st ed., Lisboa, Gráfica Santelmo, 1940–41. 2v.

Major biographical dictionary of Portuguese printmakers and printmakers of all countries who worked in Portugal, with catalog entries for their prints.

Indicador onomástico e ideográfico, v.2, p.[IV]–XXXIV.

SEE ALSO: Catalogo del Gabinete de Estampas del Museo Municipal de Madrid (GLAH 2:N30); Museo del Prado. Catálogo de estampas (GLAH 2:N33); Summa artis (GLAH 2:I12).

United States

N145 Acton, David. A spectrum of innovation: color in American printmaking, 1890–1960. With contrib. by Clinton Adams, Karen F. Beall. Worcester, Mass., Worcester Art Museum; N.Y., Norton, 1990. 304p. col. il.

Catalog of the exhibition, Worcester Art Museum (1990). Selections from the graphic arts collection of the Worcester Art Museum, begun in 1901 and augmented by a major gift of color prints received in 1926. "The exhibition presents a selection of American color prints organized as a chronological survey [from the early nineteenth century to 1960]."—*Foreword.* Essays on print processes, richly illustrated.

Artists' biographies, p.248–92. Bibliography, p.293–303. [Index of] artists, p.304.

N146 Adams, Clinton. American lithographers, 1900–1960: the artists and their printers. Albuquerque, Univ. of New Mexico Pr., 1983. x, 228p. il. (part col.)

"This book is a history not of American lithography but of the artists and their printers."—*Pref.* An important chronological survey of the topic. Includes a "technical appendix."

Bibliography, p.209–16. Index, p.217–28.

N147 Bryce, Betty Kelly. American printmakers, 1946–1996: an index to reproductions and biocritical information. Lanham, Md., Scarecrow, 1999. xxxiv, 570p.

"This index brings together all the information on published visual images of American prints from 1946–1996 and the critical and biographical information on printmakers working during this period."—*Introd.* Designed to complement Williams, American printmakers, 1880–1945 (GLAH 2:N164).

Bibliography, p.[xv]–xxv. Abbreviations, p.[xxvii]. Printmaker index, p.[1]–270. Subject index, p.[271]–556. Author/title index, p.[557]–70.

N148 Castleman, Riva. American impressions: prints since Pollock. N.Y., Knopf, 1985. 195p. il. (part col.)

Solid survey of post-World War II American printmaking by an authority. Good illustrations.

Notes, p.185. Bibliography, p.187–89. Index, p.191–95.

N149 Field, Richard S., and Fine, Ruth E. A graphic muse: prints by contemporary American women. N.Y., Hudson Hills Press in assoc. with the Mount Holyoke College Art Museum, 1987. 163p. il. (part col.)

Published in conjunction with the exhibition, Mount Holyoke College Art Museum (1987). "Wide-ranging and solid. . . . The information here will give the book a place on the reference shelf for a long time to come."—*Review*, Print collectors newsletter, v.19, Jan.–Feb. 1989, p.236. Treats works by 24 printmakers.

Index, p.159–63.

N150 Henry Francis du Pont Winterthur Museum. Two centuries of prints in America, 1680–1880: a selective catalogue of the Winterthur Museum collection. [By] E. McSherry Fowble. Charlottesville, Published for the Henry Francis du Pont Winterthur Museum by the Univ. Pr. of Virginia, 1987. xiv, 543p. il., plates.

A lavish, oversize catalog of the extensive holdings of the Winterthur Museum and Library. Each of the almost 400 entries is accompanied by an illustration. Includes examples from both the display and the study collections. The catalog is divided into two main sections, "Prints for the American market" and "Prints produced in America," both subdivided by topical arrangement.

Concordance, p.536–38. Selected bibliography, p.539–40. Index of artists, printmakers, and printsellers, p.541–43.

N151 Johnson, Una E. American prints and printmakers: a chronicle of over 400 artists and their prints from 1900 to the present. Garden City, Doubleday, 1980. xviii, 266p. il. (part col.)

"A chronicle of twentieth-century American prints. . . . The present volume attempts to sketch the principal graphic developments in the United States during the past three quarters of this century, from 1900 to the late 1970s."—*Prol.*

Contents: (I) The early decades—1900 through the 1930s; (II) The 1940s and 1950s; (III) Prints by sculptors; (IV) Extensions of the printed image; (V) Graphic workshops; (VI) Ideas and images of the 1960s and 1970s; Epilogue.

Notes, p.252–54. Selected bibliography, p.255–59. Index, p.260–64.

N152 Kraeft, June, and Kraeft, Norman. Great American prints, 1900–1950: 138 lithographs, etchings, woodcuts. N.Y., Dover, 1984. xxi, 149p. chiefly il., plates.

Unusual survey of Realist prints, representing an atypical selection. "Our book focuses on the blossoming of . . . realism throughout the period 1900–1950."—*p.xiii.*

List of prints, p.ix–xi. Biographies of the artists, p.139–45. Selected bibliography, p.147–49.

N153 Marzio, Peter C. The democratic art: pictures for a 19th-century America: chromolithography, 1840–1900. Boston, Godine, in assoc. with the Amon Carter Museum of Western Art, 1979. xiv, 357p. il. (part col.)

"This book tells a simple story: from 1840 to 1900 original paintings were being reproduced lithographically in color and sold in America by the millions. These copies were called chromolithographs."—*Pref.* The standard work on chromolithography.

Notes, p.227–63. Bibliography, p.265–76. Index, p.345–57.

N154 Moser, Joann. Singular impressions: the monotype in America. Washington, D.C., Published for the National Museum of American Art by Smithsonian Institution Pr., 1997. x, 212p. il. (part col.)

Excellent survey, published in conjunction with the exhibition, National Museum of American Art (1997).

Contents: (1) American artists at home and abroad; (2) Color prints and printed sketches; (3) The emergence of the monotype; (4) The contemporary monotype phenomenon.

Notes, p.191–204. Selected bibliography, p.205–09. Index, p.211–12.

N155 New York. Museum of Modern Art. American prints, 1960–1985, in the collection of the Museum of Modern Art. N.Y., The Museum, 1986. xvi, 438p. il.

A collection catalog covering contemporary American prints in all media. The MOMA collection is designed to be expressive of "the most cogent artistic expressions of the time [and] the preponderance of works listed . . . are by artists who work primarily in other mediums, developing their unique voices before turning to printmaking."—*Pref.* Approximately 800 examples are inventoried. Excludes the study collection. Entries are alphabetical by artist. Description includes type of print (i.e., print, illustrated book, print-poster, multiple object, etc.).

Bibliography, p.xii–xvi.

N156 North American print conference. 1970– . (23?)v. il. Publisher varies. Annual conference, each devoted to a particular theme.

Selective contents: (1) Prints in and of America to 1850 (1970); (2) Boston prints and printmakers, 1670–1775 (1973); (3) American printmaking before 1876 (1975); (9) Prints of the American west (1983); (10) American portrait prints (1984); (11) Engravers and lithographers in 19th century Canada (1980); (14) The American illustrated book in the nineteenth century (1987); (17) Aspects of American printmaking, 1800–1950 (1988); (20) Prints and printmakers of Texas (1997); (23) Adirondack prints and printmakers (1998).

N157 Printmaking in America: collaborative prints and presses, 1960–1990. Trudy V. Hansen . . . [et al.] N.Y., Abrams in assoc. with Mary and Leigh Block Gallery, Northwestern Univ., 1995. 248p. il. (chiefly col.)

Catalog of the exhibition, Block Gallery (1995), and other locations.

Contents: Collaboration in American printmaking before 1960, by Joann Moser; Multiple visions: printers, artists, promoters, and patrons, by Trudy V. Hansen; Printmaking 1960 to 1990, by Barry Walker; Multiple purposes: collaboration and education in university and non-profit workshops, by David Mickenberg; Exhibition checklist.

Selected bibliography, p.220–42. Index, p.243–48.

N158 Proof positive: forty years of contemporary American printmaking at ULAE, 1957–1997. [Exhibition dir.: Jack Cowart. Guest co-curator: Sue Scott.] Washington, D.C., Corcoran Gallery of Art, 1997. 271p. il. (part col.)

Beautifully illustrated catalog of the exhibition, Corcoran Gallery of Art (1997), and other locations. Complements Sparks's catalog of the ULAE collection at the Art Institute of Chicago (GLAH 2:N160).

N159 Reilly, Bernard. American political prints, 1766–1876: a catalog of the collections in the Library of Congress. Boston, Hall, 1991. xxi, 638p. il.

Major scholarly catalog with most entries illustrated.

Selected bibliography, p.xix–xxi. Index to titles, p.617–23. Index to artists, printers, and publishers, p.625–28. Index to subjects, p.629–38.

N160 Sparks, Esther. Universal Limited Art Editions: a history and catalogue, the first twenty-five years. Chicago, Art Institute of Chicago; N.Y., Abrams, 1989. 551p. il. (part col.)

Catalog of the Art Institute of Chicago's comprehensive collection of the print publications of the ULAE, which played a leading role in reviving the interest of artists in printmaking. See also Proof positive (GLAH 2:N158).

Glossary, p.[529–32]. Bibliography, p.[533–42]. Index, p.[544–52].

N161 Stauffer, David McNeely; Fielding, Mantle; and Gage, Thomas Hovey. American engravers upon copper and steel. [Reprint.] New Castle, Del., Oak Knoll Books, 1994. 3v. il., facsims., ports.

Reprint (as a 3v. set) of GLAH 1:N137 and N142.

Contents: (1) Biographical sketches, illustrated; (2) Check-list of the works of the earlier engravers; (3) Biographical sketches and check lists of engravings: a supplement to David McNeely Stauffer's American engravers; An artist index to Stauffer's "American Engravers," by Thomas Hovey Gage [first pub. 1920].

N162 Thomson, Ellen Mazur. The origins of graphic design in America: 1870–1920. New Haven, Yale Univ. Pr., 1997. viii, 220p. il.

"This book examines the evolution of professional graphic design practice in the United States."—*Introd.* Elegant, readable study.

Contents: Introduction: making ideas visible; (1) Contexts and connections; (2) The trade journals; (3) Career transformations; (4) Professionalization; (5) The great divide; (6) Women in graphic design history; (7) At the end of the "mechanical revolution"; Appendix A: Periodicals of importance in American graphic design, 1852–1920; Appendix B: "New kind of print calls for new design."

Notes, p.191–214. Index, p.215–20.

N163 Watrous, James. American printmaking: a century of American printmaking, 1880–1980. Madison, Univ. of Wisconsin Pr., 1984. x, 334p. il. (part col.)

A useful survey of the American "peintre-graveur" over the course of a century. Of particular interest are chapters on later 20th-century print workshops and the print market, and national print exhibitions.

Notes, p.[311]–22. Selected references, p.[323]–25. Index, p.[327]–34.

N164 Williams, Lynn Barstis. American printmakers, 1880–1945: an index to reproductions and biocritical information. Metuchen, N.J., Scarecrow, 1993. xxxvi, 441p.

Coverage designed to be as broad as possible and to include as many printmakers of the period as could be identified. The index "deviates from common practice by not limiting general sources indexed to recent publications which are likely to be in print and thus easily accessible."—*Introd.* Entries include indexing for "biocritical" sources as well as reproductions of works. Supplemented by Bryce, American printmakers, 1946–1996 (GLAH 2:N147).

Bibliography, p.[xv]–xxxiii. Abbreviations, p.[xxxv]–xxxvi.

N165 Wilson, Raymond L. Index of American print exhibitions, 1882–1940. Metuchen, Scarecrow, 1988. xiii, 906p.

Covers the rich historical period of American original printmaking and exhibiting by aiming "to make available a reference to individual prints and printmakers represented at the annual salons of the leading societies."—*Pref.* Arranged by venue with an index of artists' names.

Index of artists, p.568–906.

N166 Wye, Deborah. Committed to print: social and political themes in recent American printed art. N.Y., Museum of Modern Art, 1988. 120p. il.

Catalog of the exhibition, Museum of Modern Art (1988). Arranged by themes, including race/cultures, gender, war/revolution, economics/class struggle, and the American dream. Embraces 108 artists from sixteen collections.

Contents: Government/leaders; Race/culture; Gender; Nuclear power/energy; War/revolution; Economics/class struggle/the American dream.

Chronology, 1960–1987, p.94–99. Notes on the artists, p.99–116. Bibliography, p.116–119. Index of artists, p.119–20.

ASIAN COUNTRIES

China

N167 Lust, John. Chinese popular prints. N.Y., Brill, 1996. vii, 352p., il. (part col.), map. (Handbuch der Orientalistik, Abt. 4, China, Bd. 11)

One of the first English-language treatments of Chinese woodblock prints. An excellent overview of this example of Chinese popular culture.

Contents: Introduction; (2) History; (3) Printmakers and printshops; (4) Society, symbolism and visual pun; (5) Categories of popular prints and their display; (6) Technical terms; Appendix 1: Guide to persons, symbols, puns, etc.; Appendix 2: Some images in the lore of the print.

Bibliography, p.[327]–36. Index, p.337–52.

Japan

Bibliography

N168 Abrams, Leslie E. The history and practice of Japanese printmaking: a selectively annotated bibliography of English language materials. Westport, Greenwood, 1984. xxii, 197p. (Art reference collection, 5)

A bibliography of more than 1,200 citations, many with annotations, for English-language books and articles on Japanese prints published between 1861 and 1980. After an introductory essay, the bibliographic citations are organized in topical chapters.

N169 Green, William, comp. Japanese woodblock prints: a bibliography of writings from 1822–1992, entirely or partly in English text. Leiden, Ukiyo-e Books, [1993]. 291p.

"Its purpose is to provide an extensive, authoritative, accurate, easily accessible . . . bibliographic guide of writings in English text on the subject of the Japanese Woodblock Print."—*Introd.*

Compiled by the founder of the Ukiyo-e Society of America, this work includes 6,114 citations dating from 1822 through 1992. Not annotated. Citations organized topically.

Histories and Handbooks

N170 British Museum. Japanese prints: 300 years of albums and books. [By] Jack Hillier and Lawrence Smith. London, British Museum Publications, 1980. 144p. il. (part col.)

Introduction, based on a catalog of Hillier's own collection, acquired by the British Museum in 1979.

Concordance, p.142. Glossary, p.142–43. Index of artists, p.143. Index of albums and books, p.143–44.

N171 Estampes japonaises: collections des Musées royaux d'art et d'histoire, Bruxelles = Ukiyoe hanga. Brussels, Europalia 89, Japan in Belgium, 1989. 214p. il., map.

Notable introduction to Japanese prints, based on Belgian collections.

Bibliographie, p.61. Liste des artistes et dessinateurs, p.217. Liste des titres des suites, p.219. Liste des éditeurs, p.221.

N172 Forrer, Matthi. Egoyomi and surinomo: their history and development. Uithoorn, Gieben, 1979. 148p. il.

A useful volume on these two forms of Japanese prints often overlooked by general histories of art. Egoyomi refers to a picture calendar while surinomo are privately produced prints meant to be distributed among friends. Includes an introductory essay and chapters on egoyomi and on surinomo.

List of artists, designers, engravers, printers, and publishers of egoyomi and surimono mainly of the Ukiyo school [with Japanese characters], p.39–84. Bibliography, p.87–89.

N173 Keyes, Roger S. The art of surinomo; privately published Japanese woodblock prints and books in the Chester Beatty Library, Dublin. London, Sotheby (Distr. by Harper and Row, 1985). 2v. il. (part col.)

Surinomo encompass miniature Japanese woodblock prints used to announce or commemorate certain events as well as publications that combine a picture with verse. Dating from the 18th and 19th centuries, they were often designed by amateurs, elaborately printed on special paper, and inscribed with a poem. This 2-vol. work has a foreword by Jack Hillier, an introductory essay on the art of surinomo by Roger Keyes, and an illustrated catalog of the renowned collection at the Beatty Library, the most comprehensive collection in Europe. The catalog is presented in three sections: Ukiyo-e artists (373 items); Books and albums (28 items); and Shijō artists (115 items).

Bibliography, v.2, p.523–27. Index of poets, v.2, p.528–55. General index, v.2, p.557–69.

N174 Lane, Richard. Images from the floating world: the Japanese print; including an illustrated dictionary of ukiyo-e. N.Y., Putnam, [1978]. 364p. il. (part col.) (Repr.: N.Y., Chartwell, 1978; N.Y., Dorset, 1982)

British ed., Oxford, Oxford Univ. Pr., 1978; German trans., Zürich, O. Füssli, 1978; French trans., Fribourg, Office du Livre, 1979.

Ukiyo-e prints flourished during the Edo period (1600–1868) and often depicted the vibrant, plebian life of Japan. This survey of the most popular art form in Japan provides a history of the genre and includes a 150-page illustrated dictionary with biographical, geographical, technique, and terminology entries.

Contents: (I) Early genre painting and the rise of Ukiyo-e; (II) The primitives and the first century of Ukiyo-e 1660–1765; (III) The golden age of the color print 1765–1810; (IV) Hokusai, Hiroshige and the Japanese landscape 1810–1880; Illustrated dictionary of Ukiyo-e.

Bibliography, p.356–60. Index, p.363–64.

N175 Meech-Pekarik, Julia. The world of the Meiji print: impressions of a new civilization. [Foreword by Edward Seidensticker.] N.Y., Weatherhill, 1986. xxi, 259p. il. (part col.), plates (part folded).

A study of the Japanese woodblock prints made during the span of years from 1860–1912 when Japan opened to Western trade and influence. Bright new pigments and a more realistic style of painting and shading reflect western influence while the subjects depicted provide insight into the Japanese culture of the time. Seldom exhibited in museums and undervalued by critics who have labeled the prints "garish" and "gaudy," this book fills a gap in the literature with scholarly text and fine reproductions.

Bibliography, p.243–49.

N176 Merritt, Helen. Modern Japanese woodblock prints: the early years. Honolulu, Univ. of Hawaii Pr., [1990]. x, 324p. il.

A topically organized study of woodblock prints produced in Japan between 1904 and 1957. In addition to describing the artists and the prints, the text examines the cultural, social, and intellectual background of the prints. The author makes the point that the Japanese viewed woodblock prints as commercial reproductions, unworthy of status as art. She also explains how the publisher/artist/artisan system works with the artist painting the image, the block carver carving the image, the printer producing the colored prints, and the publisher selling the work.

Notes, p.[293]–302. Glossary, p.[303]–06. Bibliography, p.[307]–12. Index, p.[313]–24.

N177 ———, and Yamada, Nanko. Guide to modern Japanese woodblock prints: 1900–1975. Honolulu, Univ. of Hawaii Pr., [1992]. x, 365p. il.

Conceived as a supplement to Modern Japanese woodblock prints: the early years (see preceding entry). Primarily a biographical dictionary of Japanese woodblock artists active between 1900 and the mid-1970s. Additional chapters on: the art schools, art organizations, and exhibitions in which print artists participated; small magazines; publishers, carvers and printers; seals and signatures used by the artists or publishers of a print; and a chronology of important events related to woodblock prints between 1900 and 1975.

Glossary, p.[357]–58. Bibliography, p.[359]–65.

N178 Michener, James A. The floating world. With commentary by Howard A. Link. Honolulu, Univ. of Hawaii Pr., 1983. xviii, 453p. il.

First published N.Y., Random House, 1954. A classic study of the ukiyo-e print by the Pulitzer-prize winning author.

Bibliography, p.429–40.

N179 Munsterberg, Hugo. The Japanese print: a historical guide. N.Y., Weatherhill, 1982. ix, 220p. il. (part col.)

"Intended to serve as an introduction to Japanese prints for the student of Japanese art or the beginning collector."—*Pref.*

A useful survey that begins with medieval Buddhist prints and concludes mid-20th century.

Selected bibliography, p.195–204.

N180 Narazaki, Muneshige, ed. Ukiyo-e masterpieces in European collections. N.Y., Kodansha, (Distr. by Harper and Row, [1988–1991]). 13v. il., plates (part col.) (part folded).

Text in Japanese, legends in English. Each vol. accompanied by English supplement laid in.

A significant set documenting the great European collections of Japanese prints.

Contents: (1) The British Museum I; (2) The British Museum II; (3) The British Museum III; (4) Victoria and Albert Museum I; (5) Victoria and Albert Museum II; (6) Musée Guimet I, Paris; (7) Musée Guimet II, Paris; (8) Bibliothèque Nationale, Paris; (9) Musées Royaux d'Art et d'Histoire, Brussels; (10) Museo d'Arte Orientale, Genoa I; (11) Museo d'Arte Orientale, Genoa II; (12) Museum für Ostasiatische Kunst, Berlin; (13) (Appendix) The Chester Beatty Library; Museum für Ostasiatische Kunst, Köln; Rijksmuseum Amsterdam.

N181 Smith, Lawrence. The Japanese print since 1900: old dreams and new visions. London, British Museum, [1983]. 144p. il. (part col.)

Written by the Keeper of Oriental Antiquities at the British Museum, a very readable introduction to Japanese graphic art in the 20th century as well as a catalog of the collection at the British Museum. More than 70 artists and 150 works from a previously neglected period.

Bibliography, p.144. Index, p.144.

N182 ______, ed. Ukiyo-e: images of unknown Japan. London, British Museum, [1988]. 184p. col. il.

Presents the British Museum's collection of prints, illustrated books, and albums of the Ukiyo-e school. Based on a selection of prints first exhibited Japan in 1985 and subsequently in Britain, the picture captions and artists' biographies were prepared by scholars from the Ukiyo-e Society for the Japanese version of the catalog. Smith added a new essay and glossary for this ed.

N183 Stewart, Basil. A guide to Japanese prints and their subject matter. [Reprint.] N.Y., Dover, 1979. xvi, 381p. il., plates.

Reprint of GLAH 1:N165. This reprint differs from the original by virtue of a change in title, a reduced format, and the substitution of black-and-white reproductions for the colored plates as well as changes in the grouping of the illustrations.

N184 Thompson, Sarah E., and Harootunian, Harry. Undercurrents in the floating world: censorship and Japanese prints. N.Y., Asia Society Gallery, [1991]. viii, 104p. il. (part col.)

Catalog of the exhibition, Asia Society Galleries (1991–92).

Assembled when the controversy over censorship and the National Endowment for the Arts raged, this exhibit focuses on Japanese woodblock prints of the 18th through the early 20th centuries and the hidden language of their imagery. The essays examine issues such as the relationship between politics and art, public morality, and the correct way to represent the past and present.

Bibliography, p.101–03.

ARTISTS' BOOKS

N185 Artists' books: a critical anthology and sourcebook. Ed. by Joan Lyons. Rochester, N.Y., Visual Studies Workshop Press (Distr. by Peregrine Smith Books, 1985). 269p. il.

"This anthology . . . is the first in-depth look [at the history and criticism of artists' books]. . . .The texts that follow, written by long-term participants and observers of the field, form a survey from which a much-needed critical discourse might evolve."—*Introd.*

Contents: A preface, by Dick Higgins; Plates: a visual preface; Book art, by Richard Kostelanetz; The new art of making books, by Ulises Carrión; The artist's book goes public, by Lucy R. Lippard; Conspicuous consumption: new artists' books, by Lucy R. Lippard; Words and images: artists' books as visual literature, by Shelley Rice; The page as alternative space: 1950 to 1969, by Barbara Moore and Jon Hendricks; Some contemporary artists and their books, by Clive Phillpot; The book stripped bare, by Susi R. Bloch; The artist as book printer: four short courses, by Betsy Davids and Jim Petrillo; Independent publishing in Mexico, by Felipe Ehrenberg, Magali Lara, and Javier Cadena; Photobookwords: the critical realist tradition, by Alex Sweetman; Systemic books by artists, by Robert C. Morgan.

Notes at ends of chapters. Artists' book collections, p.225–32. Bibliography of secondary sources, p.233–58. Index, p.259–66.

N186 Brall, Artur. Künstlerbücher, artists' books, book as art: Ausstellungen, Dokumentationen, Kataloge, Kritiken: eine Analyse. [Frankfurt am Main], Kretschmer and Grossmann, 1986. 176p. il.

An analysis of exhibitions, publications, and criticism devoted to artists' books. The bibliographical appendix is especially useful for its chronicle of exhibitions.

Anmerkungen, p.140–55. Bibliographischer Anhang, p.156–75.

N187 Bury, Stephen. Artists' books: the book as a work of art, 1963–1995. Brookfield, Vt., Scolar, 1995. xvi, 207p. il.

An overview of the history of contemporary artists' books, with a helpful bibliographical chronicle of the genre.

Contents: (1) The artist and the book format; (2) Towards a history of artists' books; (3) Mallarmé and Broodthaers; (4) Futurist books; (5) Fluxus books; (6) Minimalist and conceptual books; (7) Women and artists' books; Afterword: a note on collecting artists' books.

Notes at ends of chapters. Selective bibliography of artists' books 1963– , p.28–187. Chronology, p.188. Glossary, p.189. General bibliography, p.190–95. Index, p.196–207.

N188 Castleman, Riva. A century of artists' books. N.Y., Museum of Modern Art, 1994. 263p. il. (part col.)

Catalog of the exhibition, Museum of Modern Art (1994). The first major exhibition of artists' books from the collection of the Museum of Modern Art, the nucleus of which is the Bequest of Louis E. Stern. Includes an important, scholarly essay by Castleman.

Bibliography, p.246–55. Index, p.258–63.

N189 Drucker, Johanna. The century of artists' books. N.Y., Granary Books, 1995. xii, 377p. il.

"Provides an overview of the development of this artform by mapping a history of major areas of activity in artists' books over the last hundred years and offering a critical structure for looking at work in this field."—*p.vii.* An important monographic study by a prolific student and practitioner.

Contents: (1) The artist's book as idea and form; (2) Conceptualizing the book: precedents, poetics and philosophy; (3) Artists' books and the early 20th-century avant-garde; (4) The artist's book as a democratic multiple; (5) The artist's book as a rare and/or auratic object; (6) The codex and its variations; (7) Self-reflexivity in book form; (8) The book as a visual form; (9) Books as verbal exploration; (10) The book as sequence: narrative and non-narrative; (11) The artist's book as an agent of social change; (12) The book as conceptual space (performance and exhibition); (13) The book as document; (14) Metaphor and form: the artist's book in the 20th century.

Notes at ends of chapters. Index, p.365–77.

N190 Franklin Furnace (Archive). Franklin Furnace Archive artists book bibliography. N.Y., Franklin Furnace Archive, Inc., 1977–79. 3v. ([430] cards)

"Edition of 1100, unsigned, unnumbered." An annual that ceased with v.3 in 1979. Issued on notecards for interfiling. "As the books these cards describe go out of print, the FFAABB will remain a written record which includes statements by the artists themselves."—*Preliminary card.*

N191 Jentsch, Ralph. The artist and the book in twentieth-century Italy. With contrib. by Mirella Bentivoglio . . . [et al.] Turin, Allemandi, 1992. 341p. il. (part col.)

Published in conjunction with the exhibition, Museum of Modern Art (1992–93). "This catalog presents 549 artists' books with original prints as well as some book objects by more than 400 artists from the turn of the century up to today, all illustrated and fully described. In addition . . . there are more than 200 books listed. . . . Altogether, this publication, including a chapter on futurism, represents the most complete bibliography of artists and illustrated books in twentieth-century Italy to date."—*Introd.*

Bibliography, p.[329]–32. Index of names, p.333–41.

N192 Klima, Stefan. Artists books: a critical survey of the literature. N.Y., Granary Books, 1998. 109p.

"These essays are concerned with one conjectural part of the phenomenon of artists books: the body of literature representing a public debate which has endured for almost a quarter of a century."—*Introd.* A brief review of the literature on artists' books.

Contents: A beginning; Definition; Art as a book; Reading the book; Successes and/or failures; Bibliographic sources.

Bibliographical references. List of sources consulted, p.86–109.

N193 Lauf, Cornelia, and Phillpot, Clive. Artist/author: contemporary artists' books. N.Y., American Federation of Arts, 1998. 183p. il. (part col.)

Catalog of the exhibition, Weatherspoon Art Gallery, Greensboro, N.C. (1988), and other locations.

Contents: Books by artists and books as art, by Clive Phillpot; Cracked spines and slipped disks, by Cornelia Lauf; The artist's book and postmodernism, by Brian Wallis; Perplexed, by Renée Green; Interview with Martha Wilson (nos.72–93), by Thomas Padon; Itinerant texts (nos.94–105), by Jane Rolo; Artists' books: making literacy pay, by Glenn O'Brien.

Checklist of the exhibition, p.[154]–61. Artists' books publishers, p.[162]–[64]. Selected bibliography, p.[165]–[70].

N194 Smith, Keith A. Structure of the visual book. 3d ed. Rochester, N.Y., K.A. Smith Books, 1994. 238p. il.

1st ed. 1984; 2d ed. 1992.

An eccentric, small compendium of information and opinions, by a creator of artists' books, on "the potential of the book format."—*Pref.* Includes glossary and diagrams and emphasizes topics such as display, the relationship of pictures, movement (i.e., flip-books), structure, and composition. A useful adjunct to research on artists' books and their craftsmanship.

Bibliography, p.233–37.

N195 Strachan, Walter John. The artist and the book in France: the 20th century livre d'artiste. London, Owen, 1969. 368 il. (part col.), plates, facsims.

An important study, updated by the catalog of Strachan's own collection (see next entry). Chronological in approach, dealing mostly with the period 1900–1966. Includes chapters on technical aspects of the subject.

Notes, p.316–24. Catalogue raisonné, p.325–44. Glossary, p.345–49. Bibliography, p.350–53. Index, p.355–68.

N196 Taylor Institution. Le livre d'artiste: a catalogue of the W. J. Strachan gift to the Taylor Institution. Oxford, Ashmolean Museum; Taylor Institution, 1987. 92p. il. (part col.)

Updates Strachan's own The artist and the book in France (see preceding entry).

Author index, p.91–92.

N197 Victoria and Albert Museum, London. From Manet to Hockney: modern artists' illustrated books. Ed. by Carol Hogben and Rowan Watson. Introd. by Carol Hogben. [London], The Museum, 1985. 379p. il. (part col.)

An important selection of more than 150 of the most outstanding illustrated books in the National Art Library.

Select bibliography, p.376. Index of artists, p.377–78. Index of publishers, p.379.

SEE ALSO: JAB: the journal of artists' books (GLAH 2:Q217).

BOOK ILLUSTRATION

Dictionaries and Encyclopedias

N198 Fanelli, Giovanni, and Godoli, Ezio. Dizionario degli illustratori simbolisti e art nouveau. Firenze, Cantini, 1990. 2v. il. (part col).

Important reference work. Most entries are accompanied by a list of works illustrated and bibliographical references. Includes artists, architects, and other figures active as book illustrators. Covers all western countries.

Bibliografia, v.2, p.[295]–302.

N199 Lexikon der Buchkunst und Bibliophilie. Hrsg. von Karl Klaus Walther. N.Y., Saur, 1988. 386p. il. (part col.) (Repr.: 1995).

1st ed. Leipzig, Bibliographisches Institut, 1987.

A German-language dictionary of terms related to book illustration and bibliography. Entries include short bibliographies. Well-illustrated with good color plates. Accompanied by a combined key-word and name index.

Literaturverzeichnis, p.367. Register, p.369–86.

N200 Lexikon des gesamten Buchwesens: LGB2. Hrsg. Von Severin Corsten . . . [et al.] 2. völlig neu bearb. Aufl. Stuttgart, Hiersemann, 1987 [i.e. 1985]– . (4)v.

1st ed. in 4 v. titled Lexikon des Buchwesens, 1952–56.

General book arts encyclopedia with many entries on book illustration topics.

Contents: (1) A-Buch; (2) Buck-Foster; (3) Fotochemigrafische Verfahren-Institut für Buchmarkt-Forschung; (4) Institut für Buch- und Handschriftenrestaurierung-Lyser.

N201 Osterwalder, Marcus. Dictionnaire des illustrateurs. Paris, Hubschmid & Bouret, 1983– . (2)v. il.

Biographical dictionary of illustrators.

Contents: (2) 1800–1914: illustrateurs, caricaturistes et affichistes; (3) 1890–1945: XXe siècle, première generation, illustrateurs du monde entier nés avant 1885.

Includes bibliographies and indexes.

General Works

N202 Brenni, Vito Joseph. Book illustration and decoration: a guide to research. Westport, Greenwood, 1980. viii, 191p. (Art reference collection, 1)

"A selective [bibliography] that the student and researcher can use to find publications containing a wide range of information on the history and technique of book illustration and decoration and the many topics that relate to them."—*Pref.*

Contents: (1) Reference works; (2) Book decoration; (3) Manuals of illustration and other writings on technique; (4) History of methods of illustration; (5) History of book illustration from ancient times to the present day; (6) History of book illustration and decoration in the countries of the world; (7) Illustration and decoration in children's books; (8) Science and technology; (9) Medicine; (10) Music; (11) Geography and history.

Author index, p.[153]–82. Subject index, p.[183]–91.

N203 Buchillustrationen: eine Sammlung aus acht Jahrhunderten = Book illustrations: a collection from eight centuries. [Ed. by] Annemarie Verweyen. München, Bruckmann, 1989. 319p. chiefly il. (part col.) (Novum press)

In German and English. "This selection of more than 800 illustrations . . . has been classified according to generic theme: portraits, family scenes, professions, implements, human activities, religious motifs, architectural depictions, plants and animals, etc."—*Cover.* Useful as a picture resource.

Literaturverzeichnis, p.310–18. Verzeichnis der Künstlernamen, p.318–19.

N204 Fanelli, Giovanni. L'illustrazione Art nouveau. Roma, Laterza, 1989. 332p. il. (part col.), facsims. (part col.)

Substantial survey with nearly 800 illustrations.

Contents: (I) Edizioni per bibliofili versus editoria industriale; (II) La rilegatura e la copertina; (III) La carta da risguardi; (IV) Il frontespizio; (V) L'art nouveau e la tipografia; (VI) L'ornamento del libro; (VII) L'illustrazione; (VIII) Il libro per bambini.

Note, p.[301]–05. Bibliografia, p.[307]–22. Indice dei nomi, p.[325]–32.

N205 Fünf Jahrhunderte Buchillustration: Meisterwerke der Buchgraphik aus der Bibliothek Otto Schäfer. [Katalog und Ausstellung, Eduard Isphording unter Mitarb. von Manfred von Arnim. Literaturverzeichnis und Künstler-Register, Ursula Timann.] 2.

Aufl. 1988. [Nürnberg], Germanisches Nationalmuseum Nürnberg, 1987. xlviii, 188p. il. (part col.), plates (Ausstellungskataloge [Bayerische Staatsbibliothek], 42).

Catalog of the exhibition, Germanisches Nationalmuseum Nürnberg (1987), and other locations. Beautifully executed catalog of almost 200 of the best-known illustrated books, from 15th-century block books to contemporary livres d'artiste. Each title from this important private collection receives a one-page entry and an excellent illustration.

Verzeichnis der ausgestellten Bücher, p.[193–97]. Künstler-Register, p.[199–216]. Literaturverzeichnis, p.[217–20].

N206 Harthan, John P. The history of the illustrated book: the Western tradition. N.Y., Thames and Hudson, 1981. 288p. il. (part col.)

Standard, readable history of European book illustration.

Contents: (1) Manuscripts to the sixteenth century; (2) The birth of printing: fifteenth century; (3) The Renaissance: sixteenth century; (4) The Baroque: seventeenth century; (5) The Rococo: eighteenth century; (6) Romanticism and the mass market, 1800–1880; (7) The book beautiful and after, 1880–1980.

A note on techniques, p.282. Bibliographical note, p.283–84. Index, p.285–88.

N207 Houfe, Simon. Fin de siècle: the illustrators of the 'nineties. London, Barrie and Jenkins, 1992. 200p. il.

A significant study of an important decade in book illustration.

Contents: (1) From the "eighties to the nineties"; (2) A glance backwards; (3) The Arts and Crafts tradition; (4) American style; (5) Beardsley and his followers; (6) The Yellow Book and the magazines; (7) The broadsheet and poster style; (8) Children's books; (9) The illustrators of the "Georgian" school; (10) The end of an epoch.

Notes, p.191–93. Bibliography, p.195–96. Collections, p.196. Index, p.197–200.

N208 Hubert, Renée Riese. Surrealism and the book. Berkeley, Univ. of California Pr., 1988. xvii, 358p. il. (part col.), plates.

A scholarly study of Surrealist book illustration that attempts "not only to set up dialectical relationships between graphics and the written or printed word but also to situate and define the surrealist book in its various manifestations."—*Introd.*

Includes bibliographical references. Index, p.351–58.

N209 Lang, Lothar. Konstruktivismus und Buchkunst. Leipzig, Ed. Leipzig, 1990. 208p. il. (part col.)

International survey with splendid illustrations.

Literatur, p.203. Kataloge, p.204. Register, p.205–[09].

N210 ———. Surrealismus und Buchkunst. Leipzig, Ed. Leipzig, 1993. 215p. il. (part col.)

Well-illustrated survey of Surrealist book arts.

Contents: Annäherung und Überschau; Die Surrealisten als Illustratoren; Berührungen und Einflüsse; Dichter als Illustratoren; Malerbuch, Objektbuch und Fotobuch; Zeitschriften und Kataloge; Im kurzen Überblick; Der Surrealismus—eine Chronologie; Text zum Surrealismus.

Bibliographie, p.135–80. Register, p.209–15.

N211 Langer, Alfred. Jugendstil und Buchkunst. Leipzig, Edition Leipzig, 1994. 283p. il. (part col.), facsims.

Wide-ranging survey of Art Nouveau book arts throughout Europe. Arranged by country.

Anmerkungen, p.271–72. Ausgewählte Literatur, p.273–74. Register, p.275–83.

N212 Lewis, John Noel Claude. The 20th century book: its illustration and design. 2d ed. London, Herbert Pr., 1984. 271p. il.

1st ed. 1967.

Survey of the design and illustration of books in Britain and the United States in this century.

[Index], p.262–71.

N213 Libri cubisti. A cura di Donna Stein. Saggi di Enrico Crispolti, Alain Jouffroy e Ralph Jentsch. Firenze, La Casa Usher, 1988. 175p. il. (part col.)

Catalog of the exhibition, Palazzo Pubblico, Siena (1988).

Covers many more artists and titles, and is better illustrated, than the author's Cubist prints/cubist books (N.Y., Franklin Furnace, 1983).

Contents: I cubisti e il livre d'artiste, di Donna Stein; Qualche considerazione sul e dal libro illustrato cubista, di Enrico Crispolti; Sodalizi fra poeti e i pittori cubisti, di Alain Jouffroy; Il cubismo in Germania, di Ralph Jentsch.

Bibliografia essenziale, p.171–73. Indice degli illustratore delle opere in catalogo, p.174. Indice degli autore delle opere in catalogo, p.175.

N214 Livres d'art: histoire et techniques. Sous le dir. de Armand Israel. Assiste de Brigitte Waridel. Paris, Ed. des catalogues raisonnés, 1994. x, 213p. il.

Multi-author, handsomely-produced overview.

Contents: L'histoire du livre; La typographie; L'illustration; Le papier; Les encres d'imprimerie; La reliure d'art; L'emboîtage; La restauration et la conservation.

Notes at ends of chapters. Glossaire, p.203–13.

N215 Marantz, Sylvia S., and Marantz, Kenneth A. The art of children's picture books: a selective reference guide. 2d ed. N.Y., Garland, 1995. xx, 293p.

1st ed., 1988. Thorough, annotated bibliography with excellent indexes to artists, authors, and titles.

Contents: (I) History of children's picture books; (II) How a picture book is made; (III) Criticism of children's picture books, including their "use" with children; (IV) Artists anthologized; (V) Books, articles, and audiovisual materials on individual picture book artists; (VI) Guides and aids to further research; (VIII) Some collections and/or repositories of materials on picture books and their creators.

Index of artists, p.251–56. Index of authors, editors, and compilers, p.257–67. Index of titles, p.269–91.

N216 Melot, Michel. The art of illustration. [Trans. James Emmons.] N.Y., Skira/Rizzoli, 1984. 269p. il. (part col.)

Trans. of L'art de l'illustration. Geveva, Skira, 1984.

A lavishly produced, broad survey of the history of illustration since the Middle Ages. Includes sections on newspaper, periodical, and book illustration. By an authority on the graphic arts.

Books consulted and bibliographical guide, p.249–52. Index, p.265–69.

N217 Von Odysseus bis Felix Krull: Gestalten der Weltliteratur in der Buchillustration des 19. und 20. Jahrhunderts. [Red.: Ingeborg Becker, Klaus Popitz.] Berlin, Reimer, 1982. 395p. il. (part col.) (Veröffentlichung der Kunstbibliothek Berlin, 90)

Catalog of the exhibition, Kunstbibliothek Berlin (1982). An important thematic survey of 19th- and 20th-century book illustration. Brief essays by various authors.

Abgekürzte Literatur, p.383–84. Register der Autoren, p.385–86. Register der Illustratoren, p.387–95.

N218 Wakeman, Geoffrey. Graphic methods in book illustration. [Loughborough, Leicestershire], Plough Pr., 1981. 1 case, il. (part col.)

"The purpose of this book is to assist with the identification of prints used in book illustration."—*Introd.* Provides actual printed illustrations for the reader to practice connoisseurship, identification of techniques, etc. Contains introductory matter ([4] leaves within covers) and 18 numbered fascicles, each with an illustration, explanatory text, and one or more samples, mostly mounted detached leaves from older damaged and imperfect books.

Contents: Wood engraving; Etching; Copper engraving; Stipple engraving; Steel engraving; Aquatint; Mezzotint; Lithography, chalk style; Lithography, line style; Chromolithography; Colour printing (relief); Hand colouring; Photography; Woodburytype; Collotype; Photogravure; Photomechanical printing.

"Book list" [fasc. 1, p.3].

N219 ______. Victorian book illustration: the technical revolution. Detroit, Gale, 1973. 182p. il.

A history of Victorian book illustration from the standpoint of the technical advances made from the 1830s to the 1900s that permitted mass publishing and innovative printing processes. Singles out the invention of photography, electrotyping, and cross-line screening as the "three most important inventions in the printing of pictures."—*Introd.* Includes a useful appendix showing the "Frequency of use of different illustration methods 1850–1900."

Contents: (1) Introduction; (2) Before the Great Exhibition; (3) The Great Exhibition; (4) Wood engraving, 1850–1900; (5) The "Sixties"—the impact of photography; (6) Prelude to the photomechanical revolution; (7) The photomechanical revolution; (8) The 1890s; Appendix: Frequency of use of different illustration methods, 1850–1900.

List of works consulted, p.165–69. Notes, p.170–76. Index, p.177–82.

N220 Wendland, Henning. Die Buchillustration: von den Frühdrucken bis zur Gegenwart. Aarau, AT Verlag, 1987. 208p. chiefly il. (part col.)

Scholarly, well-produced survey.

Anmerkungen, p.202–04. Literaturverzeichnis, p.204–06. Sach- und Personenregister, p.207–08.

N221 Whalley, Joyce Irene, and Chester, Tessa Rose. A history of children's book illustration. London, Murray with the Victoria and Albert Museum, 1988. viii, 268p. il. (part col.), plates.

"The authors' aim in this work has been to look at both good and bad illustration in children's books from the beginning to the present day."—*Pref.* Impressive international scholarly survey, with coverage from the mid-17th century. "A remarkably complete and insightful history."—*Marantz*, The art of children's picture books (GLAH 2:N215).

Reproduction techniques of book illustration, p.245–48. Bibliography, p.249–52. Bibliographical notes to the illustrations, p.253–59. List of early publishers, p.261–62. General Index, p.263–68.

Western Countries

France

N222 L'Art d'illustration: französische Buchillustration des 19. Jahhunderts zwischen Prachtwerk und Billigbuch. [Ausstellung und Katalog, Ulrike Bodemann mit Beitr. von Silvia Friedrich-Rust, Horst Günther und Eckhard Schaar. Paul Raabe, Vorwort.] Wolfenbüttel, Herzog August Bibliothek, 1985. 219p. il. (part col.) (Ausstellungskataloge der Herzog August Bibliothek, 49)

Catalog of the exhibition, Herzog August Bibliothek (1985–86), including 228 19th-century French illustrated books, mostly from the Herzog August Bibliothek. Supplements Ray's monumental Art of the French illustrated book (GLAH 2:N224).

Contents: (I) Literarisches Vorspiel; (II) Zwischen Revolution und Restauration; (III) Die Revolutionierung der Buchgraphik; (IV) Romantische Bilderfreude; (V) Drei Buchillustratoren der Jahrhundertmitte; (VI) Populäre Gattungen; (VII) Nationale Themen in illustrierten Büchern; (VIII) Konservatives und Innovatives zur Zeit der III. Republik; (IX) Illustratorisches Nachspiel; (X) Literatur; (XI) Register.

Literatur, p.203–07. Autorenregister, p.208–09. Register der Zeichner, p.210–13. Register der Stecher, p.214–19.

N223 Chapon, François. Le peintre et le livre: l'âge d'or du livre illustré en France, 1870–1970. Paris, Flammarion, 1987. 319p. il. (part col.)

Substantial text, scholarly apparatus, valuable appendixes, in a coffee-table format.

Contents: Les précurseurs; Ambroise Vollard; Henry Kahnweiler; Des poètes et des peintres; Albert Skira; Aimé Maeght; Iliazd; Tériade; Pierre Lecuire; Louis Broder; Pierre André Benoit; Livre illustré instrument spirituel.

Description des principaux livres cités, p.277–304. Notes, p.305–15. Index, p.315–19.

N224 Ray, Gordon Norton. The art of the French illustrated book, 1700–1914. N.Y., Pierpont Morgan Library in assoc. with Dover, 1986. xxxii, 557p. il.

Originally pub. in 2v. N.Y., Pierpont Morgan Library; Ithaca, Cornell Univ. Pr., 1982.

Exemplary vol. in an important series by the Morgan Library on the art of the book. An essential compendium of references, scholarly entries, and short essays, including the author's appendix of "100 outstanding French illustrated books, 1700–1914."

Bibliography, p.533–42. Index of artists, p.543–47. Index of authors and titles, p.549–55. Index of binders, p.556. Index of provenances, p.557.

N225 Stewart, Philip. Engraven desire: eros, image and text in the French eighteenth century. Durham, Duke Univ. Pr., 1992. xiv, 380p. il.

Studies the "interrelation of text and image. . . . My purpose is to do justice to the power of the illustrative traditions as well as to the way they form, and are formed by, their relationship to literature."—*Pref.*

Notes, p.[339]–62. Bibliography, p.363–71. Index, p.[373]–80.

Germany and Austria

N226 Die Buchillustration in Deutschland, Österreich und der Schweiz seit 1945: ein Handbuch. Hrsg. von Wolfgang Tiessen, mit einem einl. Essay von Hans Adolf Halbey. [Neu-Isenburg], Verlag der Buchhandlung W. Tiessen [1968–]. 6v. illus.

Survey of post-World War II book illustration (1945–86) in Austria, Germany, and Switzerland. Full-page illustration and two-page spread (showing both illustration and text) from each of the approximately 500 titles covered.

Notes at end of Halbey's introduction.

N227 Die Deutsche Buchillustration in der ersten hälfte des XVI. Jahrhunderts. [Reprint.] Hrsg. von Max Geisberg. Doornspijk, Davaco, 1987. 2v. il. (part col.), facsims.

Originally published München, H. Schmidt, 1930–32.

Pioneering catalog of German book illustration in the early 16th century. Supplements the author's catalogs of German wood engraving of the period (GLAH 1:N95–96).

Contents: (1) Heft 1–5; (2) Heft 6–9.

N228 Eyssen, Jürgen. Buchkunst in Deutschland: vom Jugenstil zum Malerbuch: Buchgestalter, Handpressen, Verleger, Illustratoren. Hannover, Schlütersche, 1980. 245p. il. (part col.), facsims.

Good survey of 20th-century German book illustration, with many full-page illustrations of entire pages from the books.

Contents: Aufbruch um 1900; Buchgestalter; Die Handpressen; Verlegerpersönlichkeiten; Illustratoren; Entwicklung nach 1945.

Bibliographie, p.223–24. Anmerkungen, p.225–26. Auswahlbibliographie, p.227–35. Personen- und Sachregister, p.238–45.

N229 Jentsch, Ralph. Illustrierte Bücher des deutschen Expressionismus. [Übertrag. des Textes von Mario Verdone aus dem Italienischen, Renate Grasser]. Stuttgart, Cantz, [1989]. 399p. il. (part col.)

Catalog of the exhibition, Käthe Kollwitz-Museum Berlin (1989–90), and other locations. Full, scholarly treatment in a large format, with good illustrations.

Biographien, p.355–82. Bibliographie, p.383–92. Alphabetisches Namenverzeichnis, p.393–95. Sachregister, p.397–99.

N230 Die Kunst der Illustration: deutsche Buchillustration des 19. Jahrhunderts. [Ausstellung und Katalog, Regine Timm mit Beitr. von Ute Etzold . . . (et al.) Paul Raabe, Vorwort.] Weinheim, Acta Humaniora, VCH, 1986. 240p. il. (part col.) (Ausstellungskataloge der Herzog August Bibliothek, 54)

Substantial, scholarly catalog of the exhibition, Herzog August Bibliothek (1986–87), including 212 19th-century German illustrated books. Signed, thematic essays devoted to such topics as landscape, history, prose narratives, the natural sciences, etc., followed by related catalog entries.

Literatur, p.229–33. Künstlerregister, p.235–36. Autorenregister, p.237–38.

N231 Lang, Lothar. Expressionist book illustration in Germany, 1907–1927. Trans. by Janet Seligman. Boston, New York Graphic Society, 1976. 245p. il. (part col.)

Trans. of Expressionistische Buchillustration in Deutschland, 1907–1927. Leipzig, Ed. Leipzig, 1976. Aims "to describe German Expressionist illustration, to define it more exactly than has been done before and to list the works that have come to light."—*Foreword.*

Contents: (I) Expressionist illustration: characteristics, major works, chronology; (II) Trends in Expressionist illustration; (III) The masters of Expressionism; (IV) Writers as illustrators; (V) Excursus on Kubin, Barlach and Masereel; (VI) Periodicals; (VII) Publishers and series.

Illustrated works: a provisional bibliography, p.212–36. Works on Expressionism, p.237–39. Index, p.241–[46].

N232 Literatur und Zeiterlebnis im Spiegel der Buchillustration 1900–1945: Bücher aus der Sammlung v. Kritter: Illustration als Anregung zum Lesen: der Illustrator ein Partner des Autors: eine Dokumentation des Sammlerehepaares. [Red. Ulrich und Inge von Kritter.] Bad Homburg, Kritter, 1989. 338p. il. (part col.)

The first half of the 20th century reflected in book illustration, mostly German, as interpreted by two scholar-collectors.

Künstlerverzeichnis, p.317. Kurzbiographien alphabetisch, p.318–32. Autorenverzeichnis, p.333–35. Sekundärliteratur, p.336–37.

N233 Ries, Hans. Illustration und Illustratoren des Kinder- und Jugendbuchs im deutschsprachigen Raum 1871–1914: das Bildangebot der Wilhelminischen Zeit: Geschichte und Ästhetik der Original-Drucktechniken; internationales Lexikon der Illustratoren; Bibliogra-

phie ihrer Arbeiten in deutschsprachigen Büchern und Zeitschriften, auf Bilderbogen und Wandtafeln. [Hrsg. von Theodor Brüggemann.] Osnabruck, Wenner, 1992. 1067p.
Substantial, scholarly work: 400-page history followed by a biographical dictionary of illustrators with lists of their books.
Lexikon der Illustratoren mit Bibliographie, p.395–997. Literaturverzeichnis, p.998–1020. Titelregister, p.1021–29. Ortsregister, p.1030–31. Sachregister, p.1032–52. Personen- und Firmenregister, p.1053–65. Erläuterungen und Benutzungshinweise, p.1066–67. Abkürzungsverzeichnis, p.1067.

N234 Schweizer Bilderbuch-Illustratoren, 1900–1980: Lexikon = Dictionnaire des illustrateurs suisses de livres d'images, 1900–1980. Disentis, Desertina, 1983. 231p. il. (part col.)
Brief biographies, with many illustrations.
Hauptsächliche Quellen zur Biographie, p.XLVII. Eingesehene Bibliographien, p.XLVII. Häufig zitierte Nachschlagewerke, p.L. Abkürzungen, p.LI. Verzeichnis der Farbtafeln, p.171–72. Verzeichnis der Schwarzweiss-Abbildungen, p.173–217. Autorenregister, p.219–22. Verlagsregister, p.223–28. Chronologisches Register, p.229–31.

N235 Vom Jugendstil zum Bauhaus: deutsche Buchkunst 1895–1930. [Hrsg. von Joseph Lammers und Gerd Unverfehrt.] Münster, Landeschaftsverband Westfalen-Lippe: Westfälisches Landesmuseum für Kunst und Kulturgeschichte, 1981. 220p. il. (part col.)
Catalog of the exhibition, Westfälisches Landesmuseum für Kunst und Kulturgeschichte, Münster (1981), and other locations. Surveys book illustration, typography, and bookbinding.
Verzeichnis der abgekürzt zitierten Literatur, p.210–14. Register der Autoren, p.215–18. Register der Verlage, p.219–20. Im Katalog benutzte Fachausdrücke des Buchwesens, p.[220–24].

SEE ALSO: Wie das Photo ins Buch kam (GLAH 2:O8).

Great Britain and Ireland

N236 Casteras, Susan P. Pocket cathedrals: Pre-Raphaelite book illustration. With contrib. by Joel M. Hoffman . . . [et al.] New Haven, Yale Center for British Art, 1991. 112p. il.
Catalog of the exhibition, Yale Center for British Art (1991). Slender but valuable for its focus on an important circle. Six essays on individual illustrators, with an overview by the main author.
Checklist of the exhibition, p.[103]–12.

N237 De Mare, Eric Samuel. The Victorian woodblock illustrators. N.Y., Sandstone, 1981. 200p. il. (part col.)
U.K. ed. 1980.
Survey, more anecdotal than scholarly, but with excellent illustrations.
Contents: (1) Beginnings; (2) The craft; (3) The engravers; (4) Periodicals; (5) The Pre-Raphaelite group; (6) Some other artists; (7) Five eccentrics; (8) Five men of Punch; (9) The decade of colour; (10) Foreign relations; (11) Ends.
Bibliography, p.195–96. Index, p.197–200.

N238 Englische Buchkunst um 1900. Bearb. von Michaela Braesel. Hamburg, Museum für Kunst und Gewerbe, 1994. 222p. il., facsims.
Catalog of the exhibition, Museum für Kunst und Gewerbe, Hamburg (1994), of more than 100 books from the museum's distinguished collection.
Contents: Die englische Buchkunst im Museum für Kunst und Gewerbe; Zur Theorie der Illustration; Die englische Illustration um 1900; Katalog; Das "Private Press Movement"; Typographie, die Geschichte des Buches, Kalligraphie; Das illustrierte Buch um 1900; Kinderbücher; Englische Bucheinbände.
Glossar, p.203–06. Bibliographie, p.206–16. Index, p.216–22.

N239 Goldman, Paul. Victorian illustrated books, 1850–1870: the heydey of wood-engraving: the Robin de Beaumont collection. London, British Museum, 1994. 144p. il. (part col.)
Based upon Robin de Beaumont's collection of 366 books, "one of the most important collections of such material in the world" (*Pref.*), which was donated to the British Museum in 1992. "This book aims to provide a new introduction to the books, the periodicals, indeed the entire phenomenon which was Illustration of the Sixties."—*Introd.* Excellent survey of an important period in British and continental illustration.
Contents: Collector's progress, by Robin de Beaumont; (1) The literature; (2) The explosion in popular publishing; (3) Publishers, editors, engravers and entrepreneurs; (4) The readership: taste and reading habits; (5) The artists; (6) Foreign influences; (7) The history of criticism.
Notes, p.121–23. Select bibliography, p.124–25. Checklist of the de Beaumont Collection, p.126–42. Index, p.143–44.

N240 ———. Victorian illustration: the pre-Raphaelites, the Idyllic School, and the high Victorians. Brookfield, Vt., Scolar, 1996. xviii, 391p. il.
Aims to provide a comprehensive corpus of a substantial proportion of the wood-engraved book and magazine illustrations of the period generally referred to as "The Sixties." Largely devoted to lists and illustrations, but with careful bibliographical descriptions.
The illustrated magazines, p.264–69. Index of magazine illustrations, p.270–318. Index of illustrated books, p.319–65. Select bibliography, p.366–68. General index, p.381–91.

N241 Hammelmann, Hanns A. Book illustrators in eighteenth-century England. Ed. and completed by T. S. R. Boase. New Haven, Published for the Paul Mellon Centre for Studies in British Art (London) by Yale Univ. Pr., 1975. xiv, 120p. il., plates (Studies in British art)

Principally a brief biographical dictionary of 18th-century British book illustrators, assembled by Boase from posthumous notes. Valuable coverage of a period rarely treated.

Contents: Book illustration in the eighteenth century; Books illustrated in England in the eighteenth century by known artists; Plates unsigned by the designers.

Index of authors and titles, p.105–12. General index, p.113–20.

N242 Hodnett, Edward. Five centuries of English book illustration. Brookfield, Vt., Gower, 1987. 2 leaves, [4], 364, [2]p. il. (part col.), VI leaves of plates.

"The main aim of English Book Illustration is to present the first one-volume selective, comprehensive, and critical record of literary illustration in England during the five centuries since the introduction of printing."—*Introd.* Superior historical survey.

Contents: (I) A critical account of five centuries of literary illustration; (II) A selective catalog of illustrators and illustrated books.

Bibliography, p.357–60. Index, p.361–64.

N243 Horne, Alan J. The dictionary of 20th century British book illustrators. Woodbridge, Suffolk, Antique Collectors' Club, 1994. 456p. il. (part col.)

Conceived as a successor to Houfe, Dictionary of 19th century British book illustrators (see following title). Solid biographical dictionary, well-illustrated.

Bibliography, p.454–56. Abbreviations, p.456.

N244 Houfe, Simon. The dictionary of 19th century British book illustrators and caricaturists. Rev. ed. Woodbridge, Suffolk, Antique Collector's Club, 1996. 367p. il. (part col.)

1st ed. 1978, The dictionary of British book illustrators and caricaturists, 1800–1914; rev. ed. 1981. "This new edition has about 150 new names and many of the existing entries have been amended or updated to include new books, exhibitions or additional material."—*Introd.* The introductory chapters on the art of illustration have been dropped from this ed. Standard reference work.

Abbreviations used in the Dictionary, p.41–42. Monograms, p.360–61. Appendix A: Schools of illustration, p.362. Appendix B: Specialist illustration, p.363–64. Appendix C: Famous books and their illustrators, p.364–65. Bibliography, p.366–67.

N245 Peppin, Brigid, and Micklethwait, Lucy. Dictionary of British book illustrators: the twentieth century. London, Murray, 1983. 336p. il.

"This is the first reference book to attempt a comprehensive coverage of British book illustrators working in the twentieth century. The coverage is primarily of fiction and poetry illustrators, whose work was first published in Britain between 1900 and 1975."—*Foreword.* Standard reference work, with briefer biographies than Horne (GLAH 2:N243), lists of works illustrated and bibliographical references.

Abbreviations, references [unpaginated].

N246 Selborne, Joanna. British wood-engraved book illustration, 1904–1940: a break with tradition. Oxford, Clarendon Press, 1998. xxiii, 433p. il. (Clarendon studies in the history of art)

Based on the author's dissertation, Courtauld Institute of Art (1992). Comprehensive study of the subject.

Includes bibliographical references. Abbreviations, p.xxii–xxiii. Select bibliography, p.401–20. Index, p.421–33.

N247 Vries, Leonard de. A treasury of illustrated children's books: early nineteenth century classics from the Osborne collection. N.Y., Abbeville, 1989. 285p. col. il.

Beautifully illustrated, large-format anthology based on a remarkable collection.

Selected bibliography, p.284–85.

Italy

N248 Pallottino, Paola. Storia dell'illustrazione italiana: libri e periodici a figure dal XV al XX secolo. Bologna, Zanichelli, 1988. 374p. il. (part col.) (Arti grafiche e tipografiche)

Substantial history of Italian book and periodical illustration from the 15th to the mid-20th century, by an authority.

Bibliografia, p.[345]–55. Indice dei nomi e dei periodici, p.[357]–74.

Russia and Eastern Europe

N249 Compton, Susan P. The world backwards: Russian futurist books, 1912–16. London, British Library, 1978. 136p. il. (part col.), plates

"This study is mainly concerned with Russian futurist books published between 1912 and 1916 in Moscow and St Petersburg."—*Introd.* Useful survey of these rare titles, many from the British Library collection. Includes consideration of their influence on the development of avant-garde painting.

Notes, p.[117]–24. A list of futurist and related books arranged chronologically in order of appearance in Knizhnaya letopis', p.125–27. Select bibliography, p.129–30. Index of illustrations, p.[131]. Index, p.[133]–36.

N250 Wiercinska, Janina. Sztuka i Ksiazka. Wyd. 1-e. Warszawa, Pastwowe Wydawnictwo Naukowe, 1986. 222p. il. (part col.), plates, ports.

Attempts to relate Polish book illustration to that in other countries.

Przypisy [notes], p.164–[90]. Indeks nazwisk oraz tytuów Dzie literackich, ilustrowanych i plastycznych, p.191–[204]. Art and books: studies on book illustration in the 19th and 20th centuries [English summary], p.205–[13]. Spis tablic barwnych [bibliography], p.214–[23].

Spain

N251 García Vega, Blanca. El grabado del libro español: siglos XV, XVI, XVII: aportación a su estudio con

los fondos de las bibliotecas de Valladolid. Valladolid, Institución Cultural Simancas, Diputación Provincial de Valladolid, 1984. 2v. il.
Monograph on the illustration of early Spanish printed books, with a bibliography of more than 2,000 examples, arranged by city, then artist. Biographical information is provided for the artists; illustrations are fully described.
Libros consultados en las bibliotecas Vallisoletanas, v.2, p.391–430. Bibliografia, v.2, p.431–48. Indice onomastico, v.2, p.449–58.

Switzerland

SEE ALSO: Die Buchillustration in Deutschland, Österreich, und der Schweiz seit 1945 (GLAH 2:N226).

United States

N252 Bader, Barbara. American picturebooks from Noah's ark to the Beast within. N.Y., Macmillan, 1976. 615p. il.
Exhaustive survey of children's book illustration in America from the late 19th century. "Prodigious in scope, impressive in scholarship, yet a delightfully readable history."—*Marantz,* The art of children's picture books (GLAH 2:N215).
Notes, p.573–80. Bibliography, p.581–91. Index, p.592–605.

N253 Best, James J. American popular illustration: a reference guide. Westport, Greenwood, 1984. x, 171p. il.
A serviceable introduction to the field. "This book represents one person's efforts to determine the limits of what we know (and don't know) about American illustration."—*Pref.*
Contents: (1) A historical overview; (2) History and aesthetics of American illustration; (3) Major illustrated works: bibliographies and books; (4) The major illustrators; (5) The social and artistic context of illustration; (6) Illustration media; Appendix 1: Magazines and periodicals; Appendix 2: Research collections; Appendix 3: Bibliography of illustrated books.
Index, p.[163]–71.

N254 Delaware Art Museum. The American illustration collections of the Delaware Art Museum. [By] Rowland Elzea, Iris Snyder. Wilmington, The Museum, 1991. 248p. il. (part col.)
Catalog of one of the foremost American collections, which "covers some 140 years of American art history. . . . The main strength of the collection . . . [is] the period between 1880 . . . and 1930."—*p.7.*
Bibliographical listings [by artist], p.221–47.

N255 Innovators of American illustration. Ed. by Steven Heller. N.Y., Van Nostrand Reinhold, 1986. 224p. il. (part col.)
Includes 21 late-20th-century illustrators, with a useful interview with each. Provides coverage not readily available elsewhere.
Index, p.222–24.

N256 Meyer, Susan E. America's great illustrators. N.Y., Abrams, 1978. 311p. il. (part col.) (Repr.: N.Y., Galahad Books, 1982).
Important survey, focusing on the work of ten artists. Generous format, many illustrations.
Selected bibliography, p.305. Index, p.306–10.

Asian Countries

Central Asia

N257 The arts of the book in Central Asia, 14th–16th centuries. Gen ed., Basil Gray. Oleg Akimushkin . . . [et al.] Boulder, Colo., Shambhala Publications, 1979. xiv, 314p. il., map.
"This book is . . . unique in two respects: first in that it treats of all the arts of the manuscript from the copying to the binding; second that it represents the co-operation of scholars from East and West. . . . This volume presents . . . a fresh assessment of this classic period."—*Introd.*
Contents: (1) The arts of calligraphy, by Priscilla P. Soucek; (2) The art of illumination, by Oleg F. Akimushkin and Anatol A. Ivanov; (3) The art of bookbinding, by Oktay Aslanapa; (4) History of miniature painting, by Basil Gray . . . [et al.]; Appendix I: Literary sources for the history of the arts of the book in Central Asia; Appendix II: The Bakhshi in the 14th to 16th centuries.
Genealogy of the House of Timur, p.295. Glossary, p.296–97. Bibliography, p.301–07. Index of manuscripts, p.308–12. Index, p.313–14.

India, Nepal, Pakistan, Tibet

N258 Losty, Jeremiah P. The art of the book in India. London, British Library Reference Division Publications, 1982. 160p. il. (part col.), plates.
Catalog of the exhibition, British Library (1982).
Contents: (I) Early manuscript illumination; (II) Manuscript illumination during the Delhi sultanate; (III) The Imperial Library of the Great Mogul; (IV) Delhi and the Provinces, 1600–1850; (V) European influence on the manuscript tradition.
Select bibliography, p.156–60.

Japan

N259 Hillier, Jack. The art of the Japanese book. London, Sotheby (Distr. by Harper and Row, 1987). 2v. il., plates (part col.)
In 70 chapters, this collector/scholar of Japanese prints presents his lifetime study of Japanese printed books and albums illustrated with woodcut prints. This massive work deals with a limited number of books and artists with the intent of showing the most typical and impressive examples of the artistry of designers, artists, block-cutters, and printers

from the first books with artistic pretensions to 1951. 225 color plates and 691 black-and-white illustrations. The major work on this form of Japanese art.

Bibliography, p.1067–78. Index of Japanese artists named in the text, p.1079–1100. Index of Japanese illustrated books referred to in the text, p.1101–26.

N260 Japanese woodcut book illustrations. N.Y., Abaris, 1979–82. 3v. chiefly il.

Vol.3 never published. Ceased with vol.4. Compilers include Walter L. Strauss, Carol Bronze, Graham Hutt.

Contents: (1) Seventeenth century Monogatari fiction; (2) Tale of Genji; (4) Heike Monogatari.

Includes genealogical tables, bibliographies, glossaries, indexes, and chronologies.

Southeast Asia

N261 Bastin, John Sturgus, and Brommer, Bea. Nineteenth century prints and illustrated books of Indonesia with particular reference to the print collection of the Tropenmuseum, Amsterdam: a descriptive bibliography. Utrecht, Spectrum, 1979. 386p. il. (part col.)

Scholarly catalog of an important collection.

Abbreviations, p.[ix–x]. Notes, p.103–210. Artists, p.311–41. Bibliography, p.345–53. Collated books, p.357–67. Index, p.369–86.

N262 ———, and Rohatgi, Pauline. Prints of Southeast Asia in the India Office Library: the East India Company in Malaysia and Indonesia, 1786–1824. London, H.M.S.O., 1979. xxiii, 228p. il. (1 col.)

"The India Office Library's topographical prints of Malaysia and Indonesia described in this catalogue represent an almost complete collection of those which were published between 1786 and 1824."—*Pref.* Includes full-page black-and-white reproductions.

Contents: Malaysia: Prince of Wales Island and Malacca; Indonesia: Sumatra including Fort Marlborough Java and its dependencies.

Abbreviations, p.xv. Artists and engravers, p.199–216. Authors, p.217–20. Bibliography, p.221–24. Index, p.225–28.

POSTERS

N263 Building the collective: Soviet graphic design, 1917–1937: selections from the Merrill C. Berman Collection. Leah Dickerman, ed. N.Y., Princeton Architectural Pr., 1996. 186p. il. (part col.)

Published in conjunction with the exhibition, Miriam and Ira D. Wallach Art Gallery, Columbia University (1996). "One of the most comprehensive groups of Soviet posters and graphic works to be shown in the United States."—*Foreword.* Heavily illustrated, with full descriptions of posters from a major collection.

About the collection, p.165–66. Artist biographies, p.167–80. Select bibliography, p.181–83.

N264 Chelbi, Mustapha. L'affiche d'art en Europe. Pref. de Maurice Courtois. Paris. Ed. Van Wilder, 1989–91. 2v. il. (part col.)

163 full-page color reproductions; interviews with 54 contemporary poster artists.

Index des galeries, v.1, p.300, v.2, p.354. Index des artistes, v.1, p.301, v.2, p.355.

N265 Defining Russian graphic arts: from Diaghilev to Stalin, 1898–1934. Ed. by Alla Rosenfeld. New Brunswick, Rutgers Univ. Pr. and The Jane Voorhees Zimmerli Art Museum, Rutgers, the State University of New Jersey, 1999. xv, 219p. il. (part col.)

Catalog of the exhibition, Jane Voorhees Zimmerli Art Museum (1999). An important survey of the whole range of Russian graphic arts of the period.

Contents: The search for national identity in turn-of-the-century Russian graphic design, by Alla Rosenfeld; The graphic arts at the Academy of Fine Arts: a brief history, 1895–1935, by Ekaterina Grishina; Late nineteenth- and early twentieth-century cover designs from the collection of the research museum of the Russian Academy of Fine Arts, by Elena Litovchenko; Book and costume designs from the collection of the research museum of the Russian Academy of Fine Arts, 1900–1930, by Elena Pliusnina; The World of Art and other turn-of-the-century Russian art journals, 1989–1910, by Janet Kennedy; The World of Art group: book and poster design, by Alla Rosenfeld; A new aesthetic: word and image in Russian futurist books, by Nina Gurianova; The world turned upside down: Russian posters of the First World War, the Bolshevik Revolution, and the Civil War, by Alla Rosenfeld; "Modern icon," or "tool for mass propaganda"?: Russian debate on the poster, by Elena Barkhatova; Figuration versus abstraction in Soviet illustrated children's books, 1920–1930, by Alla Rosenfeld.

Glossary, p.199–200. Selected bibliography, by Edward Kasinec, p.201–08. A note on major printers and publishers, p.209–10. Index, p.213–19.

N266 Deutsches Historisches Museum. Kunst! Kommerz! Visionen!: deutsche Plakate, 1888–1933. [Hrsg. von Hellmut Rademacher, René Grohnert] Heidelberg, Braus, 1992. 292p. il. (part col.) (Bausteine)

Catalog of the exhibition, Deutsches Historisches Museum (1992). Covers German poster art from 1888 to 1933, drawn from the collections of the museum. Introductory essays cover the status of the poster between art and advertisement, the history of poster collecting in Germany and a survey of the collection of Hans Sachs (1881–1974). Also covers the history of literature on posters.

Synoptische Tabelle, p.280–91. Poster bibliography, p.292.

N267 Friese, Christiane. Plakatkunst, 1880–1935. Stuttgart, Klett-Cotta, 1994. 205p. col. il.

An introduction to the poster production of the Baden-Wurttemberg region in Germany during a rich period of the art form. Superbly illustrated in full color. Posters are arranged by topic (commercial, sports, publishers and newspapers, organizations, travel, exhibitions, etc.) Essays on the history of the commercial poster.

Biographien, p.199–203. Literaturverzeichnis, p.204–05.

N268 Henatsch, Martin. Die Entstehung des Plakates: eine rezeptionsästhetische Untersuchung. N.Y., Olms, 1994. 304p. il. (Studien zur Kunstgeschichte, 91)

Thorough study of the rise and reception of the modern poster.

Literaturverzeichnis, p.288–304.

N269 Heyman, Therese Thau. Posters American style. Washington, D.C., National Museum of American Art, Smithsonian Institution, in assoc. with Abrams, 1998. 191p. il.

Catalog of the exhibition, National Museum of American Art (1998).

"Brings together some of the great graphic images made in the United States over the past century."—*Foreword.*

Guide to postermaking terms, p.33. Biographies of postermakers, p.158–77. Bibliography, p.179–84. Chronological index, p.185–87. Index, p.188–91.

N270 Images of an era: the American poster, 1945–1975. Washington, D.C., National Collection of Fine Arts, 1975. 20, [11]p. il. (part col.), plates.

Catalog of the exhibition, National Collection of Fine Arts (1975). Documents an important period in the history of American poster art. Brief introductory essays grouped thematically.

Index [unpaginated] of artists, designers, and photographers.

N271 Landsberger, Stefan. Chinese propaganda posters: from revolution to modernization. Armonk, N.Y., M.E. Sharpe, 1995. 240p. il. (part col.)

"This study is devoted to one aspect of the communications practices of the People's Republic of China, namely, the visual or figurative propaganda that was produced between 1978 and 1987, and within the specific ideological framework of the Four Modernizations. The focus will be on the analysis of a body of some 1,000 posters."—*p.11.*

Contents: Traditional and modern propagation of behaviour in China; The propaganda poster during the Four Modernizations era; The future symbolized: propaganda posters of the Four Modernizations era; Epilogue.

Notes, p.213–18. Publication data of posters reproduced in this book, p.219–25. Bibliography (Chinese language sources), p.226–27. Bibliography (western language sources), p.228–35. Index, p.236–40.

N272 New York. Metropolitan Museum of Art. American art posters of the 1890s in the Metropolitan Museum of Art, including the Leonard A. Lauder collection. Catalogue by David W. Kiehl. Essays by Phillip Dennis Cate, Nancy Finlay, and David W. Kiehl. N.Y., The Museum, 1987. 199p. il.

Based upon the Metropolitan Museum's collections. Essays cover American art posters, and poster publishing in the 1890s, and the French poster, 1898–1900.

Notes on the artists, p.184–93. Bibliography, p.195–97.

N273 New York. Museum of Modern Art. The modern poster. [By] Stuart Wrede. N.Y., Museum of Modern Art, 1988. 263p. il. (part col.)

Catalog of the exhibition, Museum of Modern Art (1988), offering a comprehensive survey of poster art as represented in the museum's collection. The first such exhibition since 1968. Introductory survey essay by Wrede. Entries with full-color illustrations. Each poster is classified by category, for instance, theater poster, transportation poster, advertisement for a product, etc.

Bibliography, p.255–60. Index of illustrations, p.261–62.

N274 Pieske, Christa. Bilder für Jedermann: Wandbilddrucke 1840–1940. Mit einem Beitrag von Konrad Vanja. München, Keyser, 1988. 247p. il. (part col.), plates, facsims. (Schriften des Museums für Deutsche Volkskunde Berlin, 15)

Catalog of the exhibition, Museum für Deutsche Volkskunde SMPK, Berlin (1988), and other locations. Scholarly survey of German poster art, 1840–1940.

Anmerkungen, p.199–[206]. Literaturverzeichnis, p.207–[13]. Ausstellungen zum Wandbilddruck ab 1962, p.214–[15]. Verzeichnis von Kunstverlagen, p.216–[31]. Verzeichnis von Kunstverlagskatalogen, p.232–35. Sammlungen, p.241. Register, p.242–48.

N275 The power of the poster. Ed. by Margaret Timmers. London, V&A Publications, 1998. 252p. il. (part col.)

Collection of essays on the roles of posters in art, politics, commerce, and communication.

Contents: Part I: Pleasure and leisure: (1) Posters for performance, by Catherine Haill; (2) Posters for art's sake, by Dawn Ades; Part II: Protest and propaganda: (3) The propaganda poster, by David Crowley; (4) Four in focus, by Ruth Walton; Part III: Commerce and communication: (5) Commercial advertising, by Julia Bigham; (6) Selling the product, by John Hegarty; Epilogue, by Charles Newton.

Notes and bibliographies, p.243–49.

N276 Varona, Esperanza Bravo de. Posters of the Cuban diaspora: a bibliography. Albuquerque, SALALM Secretariat, General Library, Univ. of New Mexico, 1993. xiii, 116p. il. (Seminar on the Acquisition of Latin American Library Materials bibliography and reference series, 33)

In English and Spanish. Based on the collection in the Cuban Archives of the University of Miami Library.

Subject index, p.95–109. Artist index, p.111–16.

N277 Weill, Alain. The poster: a worldwide survey and history. Boston, Hall, 1985. 422p. il. (part col.)

Trans. of Affiche dans le monde. Paris, Somogy, 1984. Nouv. éd., rev. et augment., 1991.

A comprehensive history of posters. Includes historical essays and categories by period and nationality; some less-well-known subjects such as poster art in Japan between the wars. Well-illustrated and documented.

Biographical notes, p.375–99. Bibliography, p.400–05. List of illustrations (by artist), p.406–12. Index of names, p.413–22.

N278 White, Stephen. The Bolshevik poster. New Haven, Yale Univ. Pr., 1988. vii, 152p. il. (part col.)

An important, though selective, survey, including more than 100 examples drawn from both Soviet and non-Soviet collections. The author seeks to redress many misconceptions about the production and reception of poster art in the early Soviet Union, and covers both the sources and the legacy of the Bolshevik poster in Soviet life and art.

Notes, p.131–42. Note on sources, p.143. Bibliography, p.144–48. Index, p.150–52.

O. Photography

Titles selected for inclusion in this chapter treat the subject of photography from an art historical perspective. They include bibliographies, dictionaries, directories, histories, and technical handbooks. Monographs on individual photographers are not listed, although biography is covered in the section on photographers. The arrangement is by form, chronology, and country.

BIBLIOGRAPHY

O1 Barger, M. Susan. Bibliography of photographic processes in use before 1880: their materials, processing, and conservation. Rochester, N.Y., Graphic Arts Research Center, Rochester Institute of Technology, [1980]. 149p.

Concentrating on the pre-1880 English-language photographic journal literature, this annotated bibliography also contains references to select European, general scientific literature, and manuals of the period. Table of contents provides specific process access (e.g., "collodion, general," "wet collodion processes," "dry collodion processes," "collodion emulsion processes," "collodio-chloride printing out paper"). Citations include keywords, abstracts.

List of journals consulted, p.123. Non-English-language photographic periodicals cited, p.127. General and scientific journals cited, p.129. Author index, p.133–39. Keyword index, p.141–49.

O2 Dixon, Penelope. Photographers of the Farm Security Administration: an annotated bibliography, 1930–1980. N.Y., Garland, 1983. 265p. plates. (Garland reference library of the humanities, 373)

Annotated access to books and articles using FSA photographs, government publications, general or government-sponsored exhibitions, films, post-FSA publications, and interviews, for twelve selected FSA photographers and Roy Stryker, plus second section on materials pertaining to two or more of this group or the FSA in general. Individual photographer's sections include brief introductory essay and cross references to other individual photographer's sections.

Personal name index, p.259–65.

O3 Flukinger, Roy. Windows of light: a bibliography of the serials literature within the Gernsheim and Photography Collections of the Harry Ransom Humanities Research Center. [Austin], Harry Ransom Humanities Research Center, Univ. of Texas at Austin, [1994]. 411p. il., facs.

Originally published as The library chronicle of the Univ. of Texas at Austin, v.24, no.3/4, 1994.

Identifies serial holdings of the original Gernsheim collection, as well as the Center's own additions, providing title access to one of the major collections of 19th- and 20th-century photographic serial literature. Brief entries list author (when appropriate), serial title, holdings, and occasionally notes, some transcribed from the Gernsheim's original notes. Numerous illustrations of covers and page spreads. In two sections, alphabetically arranged by title, "Photography retrospective serials holdings," p.39–370, "all the retrospective runs and discontinued periodicals and annuals which are no longer current"; and "Current photography serials holdings through December 1993," p.371–410, "which records all serials presently being received at the Collection."

O4 Gernsheim, Helmut. Incunabula of British photographic literature: a bibliography of British photographic literature, 1839–75, and British books illustrated with original photographs. London, Scolar, 1984. 159p. il., facsims., ports.

Gernsheim's attempt at a catalogue raisonné contains 1,242 items. The term "original" in Part I refers to processes such as salt prints or albumen prints, etc., not permanent processes (autotype, woodburytype, etc.) or photomechanical printing processes (heliotype, etc.).

Each section is arranged chronologically, with photographs or facsimiles or illustrations of covers and title pages. Annotations often provide valuable commentary and edition information.

Contents: (I) British books illustrated with original photographs; Newspapers, periodicals and magazines illustrated with original photographs; (II) Bibliography of early British photographic literature, 1839–1875 [includes textbooks, pamphlets and distributors' catalogues]; (III) Photographic journals, almanacs and annuals; Non-photographic journals containing important source material on early photography; Important essays on photography [appearing in miscellaneous periodicals].

Some examples of the metaphorical use of the words heliography, photography and daguerreotype, p.147–48. Index to photographers, p.151–53. Index to authors and artists, p.155–59.

O5 Goldschmidt, Lucien, and Naef, Weston J. The truthful lens: a survey of the photographically illustrated book, 1844–1914. N.Y., Grolier Club, 1980. 241p. 172 plates.

Based on an earlier exhibition of 175 photographically illustrated books, Grolier Club (1974–75). Includes a selection from that exhibition as well as additional works, presenting 192 titles with images produced either via light-sensitive metal salts (albumen prints, palladium prints, etc.) or by photo-mechanical means (heliotype, gravure, etc.). Catalog entries are annotated, in some cases extensively. Naef's essay, "From illusion to truth and back again," provides a good introduction to the topic.

Title and name index, p.231–41.

O6 Hecht, Hermann. Pre-cinema history: an encyclopaedia and annotated bibliography of the moving image before 1896. Ed. by Ann Hecht. London, Bowker-Saur, in assoc. with the British Film Institute, 1993. xvi, 476p., plates.

With coverage of optical devices and the history of projection and visual entertainments, this title includes considerable material on early photographic process and developments in photography. Arranged chronologically from the beginning of the 16th century to 1986. Including monographs, periodical and newspaper articles, and patent specifications, the citations are extensively annotated. Material drawn from most European countries, especially Great Britain and Germany.

Personal name index, p.457–64. Subject index, p.465–76.

O7 Heidtmann, Frank. Bibliographie der Photographie: deutschsprachige Publikationen der Jahre 1839–1984: Technik, Theorie, Bild = Bibliography of German-language photographic publications, 1839–1984: technology, theory, visual. 2. verb. und erw. Ausg. München, Saur, 1989. 2v. (Schriftenreihe der Deutschen Gesellschaft für Photographie, Bd.3) (Veröffentlichungen des Instituts für Bibliothekswissenschaft und Bibliothekarausbildung der Freien Universität Berlin)

1st ed., Heidtmann, Frank; Bresemann, Hans-Joachim; and Krauss, Rolf H., Die deutsche Photoliteratur, 1839–1978: Theorie, Technik, Bildleistungen: eine systematische Bibliographie der selbstständigen deutschsprachigen Photoliteratur = German photographic literature, 1839–1978: theory, technology, visual: a classified bibliography of German-language photographic publications. München, Saur, 1980. (Schriftenreihe der Deutschen Gesellschaft für Photographie, Bd.1)

"This bibliography contains all the German-language literature (monographs and serials) published in Germany, Austria, Switzerland and abroad from 1839 . . . until the end of 1984. Non-German [language] photo literature published in the German-speaking area is excluded."—*Introd.* 24,347 titles included are classed in five major sections that are in turn sub-classed down three to five additional levels (e.g., B. Visual; B.3. Picture books and illustrated books; B.3.24. Geographical picture books and illustrated books; B.3.24.5. Europe, several countries; B.3.24.5.5. Germany as a whole). Bilingual throughout except for citations and index. No access to individual periodical articles.

Index of personal names, classification terms, title key words, p.777–886.

O8 ———. Wie das Photo ins Buch kam: der Weg zum photographisch illustrierten Buch anhand einer bibliographischen Skizze der frühen deutschen Publikationen mit Original-Photographien, Photolithographien, Lichtdrucken, Photogravuren, Autotypien und mit Illustrationen in weiteren photomechanischen Reproduktionsverfahren. Berlin, Berlin Verlag A. Spitz, 1984. 817p., [2], il., mounted col. port., mounted plates. (Schriftenreihe der Deutschen Gesellschaft fur Photographie, Bd. 2)

Essential source for study of early photographically illustrated books in German-speaking lands. Means of image reproduction includes both photo-mechanical (gravure, etc.) and prints produced via light-sensitive materials (albumen, etc.). Sections include extensive bibliography. Lacks cumulative index.

Selective contents: (2) Publikationen mit Photographien; (2.1) Skizze der Entwicklung, Annotationen; (2.2) Publikationen mit Photographien. Bibliographie; (2.3) Register für die Publikationen mit Photographien; (2.4) Photographien-Serien; (2.5) Publikationen mit Nicht-Silber-Kopierverfahren - Pigmentdruck [etc.]; (2.6) Publikationen mit Illustrationen nach Photographien; (2.7) Buch- und Publikationswesen im 19. Jahrhundert. (3) Die Photomechanischen Druckverfahren und ihre frühen Abbildungsleistungen; (3.1) Das Ätzen von Daguerreotypien; (3.2) Reliefabformungen. Sackgassen auf dem Wege zu ökonomischen photomechanischen Verfahren; (3.3) Flachdruckverhahren- Photolithographie [etc.]; (3.4) Photomechanische Farbendruckverfahren; (3.5) Hochdruckverfahren - Photozinkotypie [etc.]; (3.6) Tiefdruckverfahren - Heliographie [etc.]; (3.7) Raster-Kupfertiefdruck.

Bibliography of early German monographs and periodical titles on technical aspects of photographic reproduction, p.732–59. Publications after 1915, p.760–89. General bibliography, p.790–817. Four mounted plates (Rasterheliogravure, Autotypie, Photographie, and Lichtdruck).

O9 International Museum of Photography at George Eastman House, Rochester, N.Y. Library catalog of the International Museum of Photography at George Eastman House. Boston, Hall, 1982. 4v.

Catalog of the monographic holdings of the Museum's library, numbering more than 11,000 volumes at the date of the catalog's publication. In two sections, an author/title catalog (v.1–2) and a subject catalog (v.3–4).

O10 International photography index. Ed. by William S. Johnson. Boston, Hall, 1983–1984.

Continues: An Index to articles on photography. Rochester, N.Y., Visual Studies workshop, 1978–80, which covered the years 1977–78. Covers 1979–81.

With 1978, increases from 63 to 98 number of periodicals indexed. Author and Subject index refers back to subject heading section, since citations are not numbered. Subject headings include: By artist, By artist (group portfolio) . . . , By city or country . . . , collection, etc.

O11 Johnson, William. Nineteenth-century photography: an annotated bibliography, 1839–1879. Boston, Hall, 1990. 962p. [1] port.

Focuses less on technical and equipment literature than on photography as "a history of individuals engaged with a specific medium to communicate or persuade or express their understandings and feelings about their world."—*Introd.*

Selected bibliography of 19th-century literature in English. Contains "nearly twenty-one thousand references to books and periodical articles published from 1839 to the present about photography from 1839 to 1879." Drawn from a broad range of general interest as well as specialist photographic journals, books, manuals, and pamphlets. In two sections that do not duplicate citations, "References by Artist or Author" (lists citations by photographer when work cited is about a photographer) and "Special Topics," which lacks necessary specificity for good subject access: "Bibliography," "Prehistory," "History," "[History] By Country," "By Apparatus or Equipment," "By Application or Usage." Not all items annotated.

List of periodicals indexed, p.xii–xv. Index to authors, p.943–62 (for citations listed by photographer in "References by Artist or Author" section).

O12 Koelzer, Walter, ed. Bibliographie der Photo-und Film-Zeitschriften, 1840–1940 = Bibliography of photographic and cinematographic periodicals, 1840–1940 = Bibliographie des périodiques photo-cinéma, 1840–1940. Düsseldorf, Foto Brell, 1992. 406p. facsims.

"While publications in the U.K., Belgium, Germany, France, the United States and Russia have been treated extensively, publications of other countries such as those of Southeastern Europe, Spain, Portugal, and Latin America are represented in small numbers due to the lack of information hitherto obtainable."—*Foreword.*

Alphabetical title listing of more than 2,000 international periodicals with information on language, country of origin, publication dates, frequency, holding libraries (international), and sources consulted. Annotations are trilingual when included.

Periodicals indexed by country of origin, p.363–68. Personal and corporate name index, p.369–86. Sources consulted, p.387–90. Holding library symbols, p.391–406. "Select list of abbreviations used" issued as loose suppl.

O13 Lambrechts, Eric, and Salu, Luc. Photography and literature: an international bibliography of monographs. [N.Y.], Mansell, [1992]. 296p.

Provides access to "some 3,900 titles in about twenty languages" from 1839 to 1991. Works either combine verse/prose and photographs, are photographic works produced by writers or anthologies on photography by writers, explore relationships between photography and literature or artistic movements encompassing both, or contain photographs of writers or places memorable in fiction. Arranged in single alphabetical photographer/author index, with cross-references to editors, compilers, illustrators, etc.

Subject index, p.287–96.

O14 New York Public Library. Research Libraries. Photographica: a subject catalog of books on photography: includes books, pamphlets, and selected periodical articles on still photography and allied topics: drawn from the holdings of the Research Libraries of the New York Public Libraries, Astor, Lenox, and Tilden Foundations. Boston, Hall, 1984. 380p.

"Presents a unified subject bibliography of literature in books and periodicals on still photography and allied topics selected from card catalogs of The Research Libraries through December 1971 . . . no references will be found under personal or corporate names nor under titles or place names of any sort . . . nearly 8,000 entries are arranged alphabetically under approximately 120 subject headings."—*Pref.*

Includes titles not listed in either RLIN or OCLC bibliographic databases.

O15 Palmquist, Peter E. A bibliography of writings by and about women in photography, 1850–1990. 2d ed., rev. and enl. [Arcata, Calif., Palmquist, 1994]. 332p.

1st ed., 1990.

Chronological arrangement of 3,271 periodical citations with brief annotations from English-language sources. Absence of extensive subject index limits utility.

Selected bibliography: books and articles relating to women in photography globally, p.273–87. Index of women photographers, authors, p.289–321. Topical index, p.321–25. Index of male photographers, authors, p.325–32.

O16 Photographers: a sourcebook for historical research. Richard Rudisill . . . [et al.] [Ed. by Peter E. Palmquist.] Brownsville, Calif., Carl Mautz, 1991. 103p. il.

Combines a selection of six essays on "The experience of regional directory research" with Richard Rudisill's "Directories of photographers: an annotated world bibliography," p.[52]–101. Rudisill's annotated bibliography is truly international, providing access to a wide range of general, national, regional, and area-specific histories, directories, and bibliographies, and contains a section of "Works in progress" that includes the compiler's address.

Index of authors, p.99–101.

O17 Program for Art on Film, Direction des musées de France. Films and videos on photography. [N.Y., The Program, 1990]. 114p.

Contains 511 annotated entries, arranged alphabetically by title, from the Art on Film database of the Program for Art on Film. The Program is now affiliated with the Pratt Institute's School of Information and Library Science, Brooklyn, New York. Access to current database is through Pratt.

Subject index, p.85–95. Names index, p.97–103. Source index, p.105–14.

O18 Roosens, Laurent, and Salu, Luc. History of photography: a bibliography of books. London, N.Y., Mansell, [1989–]. (4)v.

Critically selective, yet broadly conceived, compilation of 25,902 entries drawn from books, exhibition catalogs, dissertations, essays, brochures, offprints, and trade literature on photography and related areas (silhouettes, optics, holography, etc.). Arranged in a single alphabetical index combining name with subject access (eg., bromoil printing process, kite photography, snapshots).

V.1 (1989) covers photographers born before 1914, v.2 (1994) photographers born before 1936, v.3 (1996) photographers born before 1950, and v.4 (1999) photographers born before 1962. Each vol. updates the coverage of the preceding ones. Headings are consistent from vol. to vol. with cumulative references for each entry.

O19 Sennett, Robert S. The nineteenth-century photographic press: a study guide. N.Y., Garland, 1987. 97p. (Garland reference library of the humanities, 6)

Handbook. Alphabetical list of 88 international journals published between 1840–1899 with selected citations from some titles and notes by the author. No attempt at comprehensiveness in either listing or indexing.

The nineteenth-century photographic press, p.5–11. Country of origin index, p.81–85. Author and subject index to citations, p.87–97.

O20 ———. Photography and photographers to 1900: an annotated bibliography. N.Y., Garland, 1985. 134p. (Garland reference library of the humanities, 594)

Selective monographic bibliography with brief annotations of 19th- and 20th-century literature on photographers and processes active before 1900. A handbook, not an attempt at comprehensive coverage.

Contents: General works; Early technical treatises; Early theoretical treatises; Monographs on photographers; Early views and topographic surveys.

Combined name and subject index, p.117–34.

O21 Wallis, Frank H. Photography of the nude: an annotated bibliography. Monroe, Conn., Source Publications, 1993. 168p.

"The focus is on photography of the nude, and not commentary on the nude. . . . Scholarly essays on photography of the nude are not included unless they contain visuals."—*Pref.* Photographs must have been published in order to be included.

Although the first section, arranged alphabetically by photographer, is far from comprehensive, and the later sections add little in terms of research value, this guide to published nude photographs serves as a useful initial research tool.

Contents: (I) Monographs, anthologies, and individual works; (II) The photographer's model; (III) Related articles; (IV) Reference works.

Glossary, p.151–52. Photographers in anthologies index, p.153–61. Model index, p.161–62. Special techniques, p.163–64. Subject areas, p.165–68.

DIRECTORIES

O22 Craig, John S. Craig's daguerreian registry. Comp. and ed. by John S. Craig. Torrington, Conn., Craig, 1994–1996. 3v.

Drawn primarily from U.S. city business directories, this directory aims to be the acknowledged reference guide to U.S. photographers and allied workers for the period 1839–1860.

V.1 (1994) provides name, location, occupation (daguerreotype, ambrotype, dealer, manufacturer, etc.), sex and race if known, and known dates, in table format for approximately 9,000 individuals. Data is presented alphabetically and then repeated in a geographical (state/city) listing. A third listing gives source notes alphabetically by photographer. V.2 and v.3 (1996) provide expanded information in paragraph format. V.3 contains an index by state only and a listing of sources.

Contents: (1) The overview; (2) Pioneers and progress, Abbott to Lytle; (3) Pioneers and progress, MacDonald to Zuky.

Bibliographic apparatus and indexes in each vol.

O23 European photography guide 6. Ed. by Peter Badge and Vladimir Birgus. [6th ed.] [Göttingen], European Photography [Distr. Distributed Art Publishers, 1997]. 249p.

1st ed., European photo galleries guide, [ed. by Harald Bessler], 1982.

Contents arranged by 31 individual countries, with the following sections where appropriate: Galleries and museums; Festivals and fairs; Magazines; Book publishers; Critics and journalists; Schools and workshops; Associations; Grants and awards; Video art.

Index by each of the above categories, p.227–49.

O24 Guide to Canadian photographic archives = Guide des archives photographiques canadiennes. Christopher Seifried, ed. Ottawa, Public Archives Canada. [Distr. by Canadian Govt. Publishing Centre, Supply and Services Canada, 1984]. 727p.

Provisional ed., 1979. Alain Clavet, coordinator.

"The 8,631 entries in the Guide represent collections reported by 139 participating archives up to 1982."—*Foreword.* Subject index uses Canadian Subject Headings and Library of Congress Subject Headings, as well as geographical, personal, and corporate names.

Repository index, p.[569]–600. Subject index, p.[601]–714. Photographer index, p.[715]–27.

O25 International photography: George Eastman House index to photographers, collections, and exhibitions. Andrew H. Eskind, ed. Greg Drake, Kirsti Ringger, Lynne Rumney, assoc. eds. N.Y., Hall, 1998. 3v.

Enl. and exp. version of Index to American photographic collections 3d enl. ed., 1996.

Essential reference work with collection and exhibition data on 78,881 photographers from 615 U.S. and foreign collections. Consistent with previous editions' format and institutional numbering scheme. The "Photographers" volume features an alphabetical listing and indicates collections that hold work and major exhibitions that included work. "Collections" volume gives address for collection and listing of photographers in that collection. "Exhibitions" volume arranged chronologically with location, dates, and list of photographers exhibited.

(1) Photographers; (2) Collections; (3) Exhibitions.

O26 Japanese photography guide. Ed. by Osam Hiraki and Maya Ishiwata. [Munich], Nazraeli Press, [1996]. 81p., map.

Contains more than 700 entries.

Contents: Agencies; Associations; Book publishers; Festivals/symposiums; Galleries; Grants/Awards; Museums; Periodicals; Photographers; Publicists/scholars/coordinators; Schools; Other contacts.

Index, p.77–81.

O27 National Photographic Record. Directory of British photographic collections. Compiled by John Wall. London, Heinemann, [1977]. 226p.

Guide to 1,582 private and public collections. Primary classification system by ten subject divisions (e.g., "Society and human relationships," "Arts and crafts"), but indexes provide additional access.

Subject index, p.179–201. Owner index, p.202–08. Location index, 209–12. Title of collection, p.213–18. Photographer index, p.219–24.

O28 Ochsner, Bjorn. Fotografer i og fra Danmark til og med år 1920 = Photographers in and from Denmark up to and including 1920. [Ballerup, Danmark], Bibliotekscentralens Forlag, 1986 (1985). 2v., plates.

Entries in Danish. Other texts, including a two-page introduction to early Danish photography, in Danish, English, German, and French. "The purpose of this book is first of all to assist with dating and location of Danish photographs until 1920 inclusive, comprising photographs taken in Denmark or by Danish photographers abroad."—*Pref.* Entries include, where possible: name, date and place of birth and death; parents or spouse; training or occupations; activities, exhibitions, etc.; specialities.

List of localities, p.[870]–917. Important amateurs, p.[918]–19. Photographers from abroad, p.[920]. Danish photographers known to have worked abroad, p.[921]–22. Danes emigrated as photographers, p.[923]. Photographers with books with tipped in plates, p.[924].

O29 Répertoire des collections photographiques en France, 1990. 6th ed. Paris, La Documentation française, 1990. 403p.

1,341 entries for personal and institutional collections. Each entry contains the address, contact person, description of the holding body, conditions of access, description of photographic techniques of the works in the collection, and a brief description of the collection.

Index des renvois, p.337–42. Index alphabétique thématique et géographique, p.347–403.

O30 Smithsonian Institution. Guide to photographic collections at the Smithsonian Institution. Diane Vogt O'Connor, [ed.] Washington, D.C., Smithsonian Institution Pr., 1989– . (4)v. plates.

Arranged by individual collection within the institution, with dates of photographs, collection origins note, physical description, subjects, arrangement, availability of finding aids, and restrictions.

Contents: (1) National Museum of American History (1989); (2) National Museum of Natural History, National Zoological Park, Smithsonian Astrophysical Observatory, Smithsonian Tropical Research Institute (1991); (3) Cooper-Hewitt Museum, Freer Gallery of Art, Hirshhorn Museum and Sculpture Garden, National Museum of African Art, National Museum of American Art, National Portrait Gallery, Arthur M. Sackler Gallery, Office of Horticulture (1992); (4) National Air and Space Museum (1995).

Creators index, forms and processes index, and subject index in each vol.

O31 USA photography guide 3. Ed. by Bill Jay with Pat Evans. [3d ed.] [Munich], Nazraeli Pr. [Distr. by DAP, 1999]. 158p.

Contents: Associations/Organizations; Book publishers; Critics/historians; Fellowships/grants/awards; Galleries; Museums/collections; Periodicals; Universities; Workshops.

Gallery index, p.153–55. Museum index, p.155–58.

O32 Voignier, J.-M. Répertoire des photographes de France au dix-neuvième siècle. [Chevilly-Larue], Le Pont de Pierre, 1993. 317p. il.

Access to brief biographical sketches for more than 8,000 French 19th-century photographers. Entries include birth, death, activity dates, residences, areas of activities, associations and collaborations, etc. Illustrated with photographer's name or studio cards.

Index départemental, p.[259]–317.

O33 Vous avez dit photographie?: guide des lieux et des activités de la photographie en France. [Paris], Documentation francaise, [1998]. 218 p. (Collection Photodoc)

1st ed., 1995.

Provides access to French museums, national and regional arts organizations, professional associations, prizes and awards, festivals, galleries, commissaires-priseurs, libraries, photographic journals, schools, and so on. Entries include full contact information with current internet addresses.

Photographes index links photographers to their galleries, p.185–92. Organismes par département, p.193–205. Organismes par nom, p.207–18.

DICTIONARIES AND ENCYCLOPEDIAS

O34 Auer, Michèle, and Auer, Michel. Photographers encyclopaedia International [computer file.] Neuchatel, Ides et Calendes, 1997. 1 computer disk, 1 booklet.

Considerably expanded version of Encyclopedie internationale des photographes de 1839 à nos jours = Photographers encyclopaedia international 1839 to the present. Hermance, Switzerland, Editions Camera Obscura, 1985; repr., 1990.

Data bank of photographers and other related artists and professionals, with a chronology of the history of photography, a lexicon of processes, biographies, exhibition lists, bibliographies and addresses for 3,135 people, less complete information for 3,000 others, and more than 5,900 images dating from the beginnings of photography. The database may be searched by a variety of selection criteria. May be run with either French or English interface. Guide booklet in French and English.

O35 Baldwin, Gordon. Looking at photographs: a guide to technical terms. [Malibu], Getty Museum, in assoc. with the British Museum Pr., [1991]. 88p. il. (part col.)

"As this book is intended for someone actually looking at photographs, the list of terms had been limited to those likely to appear on descriptive labels in exhibitions or in catalogue entries."—*Foreword.* Clear and concise definitions of technical, process, genre, and format terms, often illustrated, published in handbook format.

Selected technical and historical bibliography, p.87.

O36 Browne, Turner, and Partnow, Elaine. Macmillan biographical encyclopedia of photographic artists and innovators. N.Y., Macmillan, [1983]. 722p. 144 plates (part col.)

Besides basic biographical information on more than 2,000 photographers, each entry includes listings of publications, portfolios, collections, dealer or representative, and address. Produced through a combination of respondent questionnaires, informal advisors, and the efforts of the authors. "Dedication" and "visibility" were the two major criteria for inclusion (*Pref.*).

Museums, p.702. Photographic galleries, p.703–21.

O37 Contemporary photographers. Executive ed., Martin Marix Evans. Consultant ed., Amanda Hopkinson. Advisers, Andrey Baskakov . . . [et al.] 3d ed. N.Y., St. James Press, [1995]. 1234p. il. (Contemporary arts series)

"The addition of over 140 new entrants has necessitated the omission of many photographers listed in the previous edition. In order to maintain the contemporary relevance of the work, those entrants who died before 1 January 1975, those whom we are advised have not added significantly to their corpus of work since 1987 or whose achievements are not known to us have been excluded."—*Ed. note.* Each entry includes biography, individual exhibitions, selected group exhibitions, selected collections, bibliography of books and articles by and about the photographer, critical essay, and some entries include a statement by the photographer.

Nationality index, p.[1211]–19. Notes on advisers and contributors, p.[1221]–34.

O38 The Focal encyclopedia of photography. Ed. by Leslie Stroebel and Richard Zakia. 3d ed. Boston, Focal Pr., [1993]. 914p. il.

See GLAH 1:O8 for previous eds.

"This third edition updates material from the previous edition that is still relevant and includes numerous new topics related to changes and advances made in the broad field of photography during the intervening years."—*Pref.* Especially useful for technical definitions; biographical and historical entries are fairly brief. Twenty-four appendixes present additional technical information: conversion scales, film and paper reciprocity date, etc.

O39 Gilbert, George. The illustrated worldwide who's who of Jews in photography. N.Y., Gilbert, [1996]. 333p. il.

Brief biographies are organized by chapters based on chronological or topical divisions. Illustrations are only of photocopy quality.

Contents: (I) Nineteenth century photography by Jews; (II) Photojournalism; (III) News photography and the communication arts; (IV) Photography in the Holy Land - British Mandate - Israel; (V) In the studios and galleries; (VI) Jewish women in photography; (VII) Nobel Prize winners; (VIII) Associations established by Jewish photographers; (IX) Documenters of the Jewish culture; (X) Intellectualization of photography; (XI) Hitler and the American camera store.

Footnotes, p.311–13. Jews in photography, by Nachum T. Gidal, p.315–17. Bibliography, p.319–20. Jewish Pulitzer Prize winners, p.321–22. Names that changed, p.323–24. Index, p.327–33.

O40 International Center of Photography encyclopedia of photography. N.Y., Crown, [1984]. 607p. il., plates (part col.)

Comprehensive yet clearly written entries with see also references help to make even the most technical issues understandable. Good combination of historical, biographical, and technical coverage.

Biographical supplement of photographers, p.[576]–93. Photographic societies and associations, p.[594]–97. Bibliography, p.[600]–07.

O41 Mautz, Carl. Biographies of western photographers: a reference guide to photographers working in the 19th century American West. [Nevada City, Calif.], Mautz, 1997. 601p. il.

A significant expansion of the previously published Checklist of Western photographers, 3d ed., Brownsville, Calif., Folk Image Pub., 1986.

Combines in one vol. the efforts of several compilers of data on photographers in 27 Western states and Canada. Data varies from brief dates only to much fuller descriptions including names of businesses operated, addresses, and additional data gained from photographers' imprints and related research.

Selective contents: Photographers' imprints and information on antique photographs, by William C. Darrah; Dating early photographs by format and mount information, by Jeremy Rowe.

Index of photographers, p.527–93. Bibliography, p.595–99. Glossary, p.601.

O42 Nadeau, Luis. Encyclopedia of printing, photographic, and photomechanical processes: a comprehensive reference to reproduction technologies, containing invaluable information on over 1500 processes. [Fredericton, N.B., Canada, Nadeau, 1989–1990]. 2v. il.

Provides cross-referenced access to a wealth of historical and contemporary reproduction processes. Entries include relevant German term, brief discussion, footnotes, and bibliography. Footnotes of principle reproductive process entries usually cite where a specimen may be found.

Each vol. contains subject and name indexes, as well as a glossary of German terms. Only the v.2 subject index and German glossary cover both vols. List of principal reproductive processes, v.2, p.493–95. Glossary of common technical terms and abbreviations, v.2, p.497–500.

O43 Willis-Thomas, Deborah. Black photographers, 1840–1940: an illustrated bio-bibliography. N.Y., Garland, 1985. 141p. plates. (Garland reference library of the humanities, 401)

A selection of 65 "outstanding figures" arranged alphabetically in 4 chronological groupings, not an attempt at comprehensiveness. Entries vary from brief activity dates and location with reference citations to more extensive listings with biographical notes, principal subjects, bibliography, collections, etc. Numerous plates.

Glossary of photographic processes, p.xv–xviii. Bibliography, p.23–24. Plates, p.[27]–[136.] Name index, p.137. Geographical index, p.139–40. Index to photographic collections, p.141.

O44 ______. An illustrated bio-bibliography of Black photographers, 1940–1988. N.Y., Garland, 1989. 483p. plates. (Garland reference library of the humanities, 760)

Similar in format to preceding title. A selective alphabetical listing of major figures from the period, with entries ranging from brief activity dates and locations to more extensive listings with biographical notes, exhibition and collections listings, and bibliographies.

Plates, p.163–469. Bibliography, 475–78. Selected exhibitions 1969–1987, p.479–83.

PHOTOGRAPHERS

O45 Danziger, James, and Conrad, Barnaby. Interviews with master photographers. N.Y., Paddington Press. [Distr. by Grosset and Dunlap, 1977]. 175p., plates, ports.

Interviews with 8 major figures in photography, including Minor White, Cornell Capa, Yosuf Karsh, and Arnold Newman. Lacks index.

O46 Dialogue with photography. [By] Paul Hill and Thomas Cooper. Manchester, Cornerhouse Publications, 1994. 339, [9]p. ports.

First published N.Y., Farrar, Straus, and Giroux, 1979.

"The interviews in this book originally appeared in Camera magazine, Lucerne, Switzerland and were developed with the editorial counsel of Allan Porter." An essential collection of comprehensive interviews with 22 seminal figures.

Index, p.339–[48].

O47 Dugan, Thomas. Photography between covers: interviews with photo-bookmakers. Rochester, N.Y., Light Impressions, 1979. 220p., ports.

Fifteen interviews with contemporary photographers who contributed significantly to the development of the contemporary photographic picture book, including Nathan Lyons, Larry Clark, Duane Michals, and Bea Nettles. Lacks index.

O48 Edwards, Gary. International guide to nineteenth-century photographers and their works: based on catalogues of auction houses and dealers. Boston, Hall, 1988. 591p.

Good source for providing name confirmation of more than 5,000 19th-century photographers. Indicates if photographer's work was listed or illustrated in the more than 300 sales and dealer catalogs surveyed, most of which date from the 1970s and 1980s. Brief biographical and photographic practice information. Does not include prices.

O49 International Museum of Photography at George Eastman House, Rochester, New York. Masterpieces of photography: from the George Eastman House collections. By Robert A. Sobieszek. N.Y., Abbeville Pr., 1985. 466p. il., plates (part col.)

Arranged in four thematic and chronological sections, 200 works from the Museum's holdings present a pictorial overview of the medium. Each image is reproduced as a full-page plate and accompanied by a page of commentary, often with an additional illustration. Provides not only an introduction to the individual photographer but also to the photograph's context.

Bibliographic notes, p.422–40. Catalog of photographers, p.441–57. Index, p.459–66.

O50 Master photographers: the world's great photographers on their art and technique. Ed. by Pat Booth. London, Macmillan, [1983]. 200p. il.

16 interviews, mostly devoted to technical aspects of the photographers' work or to discussions of specific images.

Bibliography, p.197–98. Index, p.199–200.

O51 The photography book. [London, Phaidon, 1997]. 512p. chiefly il. (part col.)

Large-format publication provides a pictorial survey of the history of photography with works by 500 photographers. Each plate is accompanied by a very brief analysis written by Ian Jeffrey of that photographer's or photograph's significance.

Glossary of techniques and terms, p.504–06. Glossary of movements, groups, and genres, p.507–08. Directory of museums and galleries, p.509–10.

O52 Photography speaks: 66 photographers on their art. [Ed. by] Brooks Johnson. N.Y., Aperture, 1989. 141p., plates (part col.)

Briefly surveys 66 19th- and 20th-century photographers. Combines brief biographical commentary with a full-page plate and an excerpt by each photographer, some written specifically for this book. Works chosen from the Alice and Sol B. Frank Collection.

Bibliography, p.139–40. Index of photographers, p.141.

O53 Photography speaks II: from The Chrysler Museum collection: 70 photographers on their art. [Ed. by] Brooks Johnson. N.Y., Aperture; Norfolk, Chrysler Museum, 1995. 149p., plates (part col.)

Repeats format and expands coverage of Photography speaks (see preceding title). Works were chosen from the Chrysler Museum collection to complement the earlier vol.

Bibliography, p.147–48. Index of photographers, p.149.

O54 Visions and images: American photographers on photography. [By] Barbaralee Diamonstein. N.Y., Rizzoli, 1982. 191p. il.

Based on a series of interviews held at the New School for Social Research/Parsons School of Design. Interviews with 15 major photographers, including Horst P. Horst, Barbara Morgan, Frederick Sommer, and Garry Winogrand.

O55 Witkin, Lee D., and London, Barbara. The photograph collector's guide. Boston, N.Y. Graphic Society, 1979. 438p. il., 8 col. plates, ports.

Written with the collector in mind. Contains biographical profiles with sample signatures, information on photographic practices, and selected bibliography for 234 photographers. A separate listing provides names, dates, and locations for 1,000 daguerreotypists, and an additional listing gives names, dates, and locations for 6,000 additional 19th- and 20th-century photographers. Separate chapters are provided on collecting, care and restoration, and limited-edition portfolios (listed by photographer with contents described).

Photography chronology, p.[14]–27. Collector's glossary, p.[28]–45. Museums, galleries, auction houses, exhibition spaces, p.[389]–418. Bibliography, p.[419]–25. Index, p.427–38.

O56 World photographers reference series. Anne Hammond and Amy Rule, series eds. Robert G. Neville, exec. ed. Boston, Hall, 1992–95. 9v.

Outstanding series on major photographic figures. Each vol. is illustrated, contains selected essays and criticism, extensive bibliography, and chronology.

Contents: (1) Anne Hammond, ed. Frederick H. Evans (1992); (2) Amy Rule, ed. Imogen Cunningham (1992); (3) Mike Weaver, ed. Henry Fox Talbot (1992); (4) Amy Rule, ed. Carleton Watkins (1993); (5) Nigel Warburton, ed. Bill Brandt (1993); (6) William Buchanan, ed. J. Craig Annan (1994); (7) Sheryl Conkelton, ed. Frederick Sommer (1995); (8) Verna Posever Curtis and Jane Van Nimmen, eds. F. Holland Day (1995); (9) Ronald Gedrim, ed. Edward Steichen (1995).

TECHNIQUES

O57 Coe, Brian. Cameras: from daguerreotypes to instant pictures. N.Y., Crown Publishers, 1978. 232p. il., plates.

Provides thorough coverage of the development of the camera, with numerous illustrations and schematics. Chapters arranged by camera types, with additional chapters on lenses, shutters, exposure meters, and flash equipment.

Index, p.[233]–[40].

O58 ———, and Haworth-Booth, Mark. A guide to early photographic processes. [London], Victoria and Albert Museum, Hurtwood Pr., [1983]. 112p. il., 37 plates (part col.)

Useful for identifying photographic process types. The plates, which are accompanied by technical and descriptive commentary, are of suitable quality to convey reasonable sense of photographic processes.

Key to the identification of processes [flow chart], p.13–16. Illustrated glossary, p.17–28. Span of formats and processes [1840–1920 timeline], p.29. Selected bibliography, p.111–12.

O59 Coote, Jack H. The illustrated history of colour photography. [Surbiton, Surrey, England], Fountain Press, [1993]. 248p. il., plates (part col.)

Comprehensive explanations of the technological history of color photography, with numerous illustrations and schematics of equipment and techniques. Includes very brief explanation of digital imaging. Emphasis on developments in Great Britain.

Chronology, p.234–35. Bibliography, p.236–37. Literature and patent references, p.238–43. Index, p.244–47.

O60 Crawford, William. The keepers of light: a history and working guide to early photographic processes. Dobbs Ferry, N.Y., Morgan and Morgan, [1979]. 318p. il., plates (part col.)

Still a primary source for its joining of considerable technical data with the cultural properties of photography into a "syntax," following the model of William M. Ivins, Prints and visual communication (see GLAH 1:N35). This photographic syntax is presented along with a history of early processes in part I. Part II provides technical details on how these processes are performed.

Recommended reading, p.[307]–10. Sources of supply, p.[311]–14. Index, p.[315]–17.

O61 Farbe im Photo: die Geschichte der Farbphotographie von 1861 bis 1981. [Köln, Josef-Haubrich-Kunsthalle, 1981]. 304p. il. (part col.)

Catalog of the exhibition, Josef-Haubrich-Kunsthalle Köln (1981). Good examination of the development of color processes although German developments and illustrative material are emphasized. Chronologically divided into three areas of discussion: Pionierzeit (before 1900); Spezialistenzeit (1900–1936); Popularisierungszeit (after 1936). With 12 essays by Fritz Binder, Gert Koshofer, Rolf Sachsse, Klaus op ten Hötel, and Walter Boje.

Wichtige Daten aus der Geschichte der Farbphotographie, by Gert Koshofer, p.270–76. Glossar, by Gert Koshofer, p.277–81. Photographenbiographie, p.281–83. Verzeichnis der ausgestellten Objekte, p.284–302. Die Verfahren der Farbphotographie, by Gert Koshofer [endpapers].

O62 Lothrop, Eaton S. A century of cameras from the collection of the International Museum of Photography at George Eastman House. Rev. and exp. ed. Dobbs Ferry, N.Y., Morgan and Morgan, [1982]. 186p. il., 1 price guide.

See GLAH 1:O35 for 1st ed. and original annotation.

With an additional 21 cameras included, a total of 151 cameras are presented.

O63 Mitchell, William J. The reconfigured eye: visual truth in the post-photographic era. Cambridge, Mass., MIT Pr., 1992. 273p. il. (part col.)

Provides a detailed assessment of digital image manipulation techniques and their implications for the reportorial function of photography.

Contents: (1) Beginnings; (2) The nascent medium; (3) Intention and artifice; (4) Electronic tools; (5) Digital brush strokes; (6) Virtual cameras; (7) Synthetic shading; (8) Computer collage; (9) How to do things with pictures; (10) The shadows on the wall.

Notes, p.[227]–[54]. Selected readings, p.[255]–[68]. Index, p.[269]–73.

O64 Nadeau, Luis. History and practice of carbon processes. Trans. . . . by the author. [Fredericton, N.B., Canada, Nadeau, 1982]. 199p. il.

Presents history of carbon processes based on the discoveries of Alphonse Poitevin, including carbro, autotype, fresson, etc. While this vol. provides procedures for the contemporary application of carbon processes, it was later revised and published as two separate titles that significantly expanded this aspect, but with the loss of some of the historical data: Modern carbon printing: a practical guide to the ultimate in permanent photographic printing, monochrome carbon transfer and carbro, [2d ed.], [Fredericton, N.B., Canada, Nadeau, 1992]; Gum dichromate and other direct carbon processes, from Artigue to Zimmerman. [Fredericton, N.B., Canada, Nadeau, 1987.]

O65 ______. History and practice of oil and bromoil printing. [Fredericton, N.B., Nadeau, 1985]. 94p. il.

Although geared to the practitioner, the brief technical history and step-by-step explanations of the various processes and the equipment and chemicals required will be of interest to those researching non-silver processes. Handling of chemicals, conservation, restoration, and related issues are also discussed.

Bibliography, p.85–91. Index, p.93–94.

O66 ______. History and practice of platinum printing. 3d rev. ed. [Fredericton, N.B., Canada, Nadeau, 1994]. 192p. il.

Tipped-in specimen of a platinum/palladium print by Robert J. Steinberg.

Provides technological history of platinum process and thorough explanations of historical and contemporary approaches to platinum printing, from materials and equipment required to conservation of prints and handling and disposal of materials.

Chronology of platinum printing, p.141–42. Glossary, by William E. Briggs, p.159–67. Bibliography, sources, and suppliers, p.175–86. Index, p.187–92.

O67 Reilly, James M. Care and identification of 19th-century photographic prints. [Rochester, Eastman Kodak Company, 1986]. 116p. il. (part col.) (Kodak publication, no.G-2S)

Although intended as a preservation and restoration guide, this publication provides excellent explanations of early photographic and photo-mechanical processes. Specific instructions for identifying processes are aided by numerous enlarged details.

"Flowchart for identification guide" (1 folded leaf) inserted. Endnotes, p.111–13. Bibliography, p.114–15. Index, p.116.

O68 Wood, John. The art of the autochrome: the birth of color photography. Iowa City, Univ. of Iowa Pr., [1993]. 185p., 75 col. plates.

Discusses the autochrome era (1904–1920s) in the context of the various Secessionist movements, Symbolism, and societal inclinations. Extensive plate notes.

Bibliographic notes, p.[59]–68. Notes to the plates, p.[147]–64. Bibliography, p.[165]–85.

HISTORIES AND HANDBOOKS

General Works

O69 Ades, Dawn. Photomontage. Rev. and enl. ed. [London], Thames and Hudson, [1986]. 176p. 203 il. (World of art)

See GLAH 1:O57 for 1st ed.

With 32 additional illustrations, a revised text, and bibliography. Continues emphasis on photomontage of 1920s–30s.

Notes, p.162–64. Bibliography, p.172. Index, p.173–76.

O70 Anthropology and photography 1860–1920. Ed. by Elizabeth Edwards. New Haven, Yale Univ. Pr., 1992. 275p. 153 il.

Collection of five introductory essays on historical and theoretical perspectives (e.g., Photography: theories of realism and convention, by Terence Wright; The parallel histories of anthropology and photography, by Christopher Pinney), 20 case-study essays (e.g., Science visualized: E. H. Man in the Andaman Islands, by Elizabeth Edwards; Photography, power, and the Southern Nuba, by James C. Faris), and two concluding essays (e.g., A political primer on anthropology/photography, by James C. Faris).

Photographic techniques: an outline, p.264–67. Index, p.268–75.

O71 The art of photography, 1839–1989. Ed. by Mike Weaver. Photographs selected by Daniel Wolf with Mike Weaver and Norman Rosenthal. New Haven, Yale Univ. Pr., [1989]. 472p. 16 il., 462 plates (part col.)

Catalog of the exhibition, Museum of Fine Arts, Houston (1989), and other locations, celebrating photography's sesquicentennial. Not an attempt to produce a comprehensive history, but rather a roughly chronological grouping of 15 essential topics (e.g., "Early French masters," "Travel," "Pictorial effect," "Construction and appropriation"). Each section preceded by a brief essay (Robert Sobieszek, Peter Bunnell, Anne Tucker, et al.) and an excerpt from a text related to that pictorial grouping (Julia Margaret Cameron, Victor Burgin, et al.). Instead of one photograph each by a wide range of photographers, each grouping contains several works by a select number of photographers (88 photographers in all). All photographs from the exhibition are reproduced.

Chronology, p.4–6. Glossary, p.448–49. Biographies and checklist, p.450–71. Bibliography, p.472.

O72 Brothers, Caroline. War and photography: a cultural history. London, Routledge, [1996]. 277p. 29 il.

Using the Spanish Civil War as a case study, the text "seeks an understanding not of Spain but of the mind-set of 1930s Britain and France as it was expressed in the most public of images—in the news photographs of their daily and weekly press."—*Pref.*

Contents: (1) Photography, theory, history; (2) The Republican militiamen; (3) Insurgent soldiers and Moors; (4) Women-at-arms; (5) Semiology and the city at war; (6) The anthropology of civilian life; (7) Refugees and the limitations of documentary; (8) Casualties and the nature of photographic evidence; (9) If not about Spain . . . 1930s Britain and France; (10) Vietnam, the Falklands, the Gulf: photography in the age of the simulacral.

Notes, p.218–48. Bibliography, p.249–68. Index, p.269–77.

O73 The Camera at war: a history of war photography from 1848 to the present day. [Compiled by] Jorge Lewinski. N.Y., Simon and Schuster, [1978]. 240p. il., plates. (Repr.: N.Y., Simon and Schuster, 1980; London, Octopus, 1986).

Discusses war photography within context of political events, with accompanying analysis of how war photographs are taken, presented, and interpreted.

Contents: (1) Distant witness, 1848–1912; (2) Dispassionate observer, First World War-Spanish Civil War; (3) Enlisted combatant, Second World War; (4) Intimate companion, Korea-Northern Ireland; (5) Intense explorer, Vietnam; (Postscript) Civilians, children and women.

Bibliography, p.236–37. Index, p.238–40.

O74 Chevrier, Jean-François. Photo-Kunst: Arbeiten aus 150 Jahren: du XXème au XIXème siècle, aller et retour. Katalogtexte = textes, Ursula Zeller. Ulrike Gauss, Hrsg. = ed. [Stuttgart, Cantz, 1989]. 413p. 185 plates (part col.)

Text in German and French. Catalog for the sesquicentennial exhibition, Graphische Sammlung Staatsgalerie Stuttgart (1989). Provides interesting counterpoint to the U.S.-/U.K.-based sesquicentennial catalogs, Art of photography, 1839–1989 (GLAH 2:O71), On the art of fixing a shadow (GLAH 2:O92), Photography until now (GLAH 2:O99), with much greater emphasis on contemporary photographers. Extensive catalog texts with multiple works by contemporary figures.

Contents: Die Abenteuer der Tableau-Form in der Geschichte der Photographie = Les aventures de la forme tableau dans l'histoire de la photographie, by Jean-François Chevrier; (I) Coplans, Henson, Horsfield, Lafont, Wall; (II) 19. Jahrhundert und klassische Moderne = XIXème siècle et première moitié du XXème siècle; (III) 60er und 70er Jahre = Les années 60 et 70; (IV) Düsseldorf - Struth, Ruff, Gursky; Vancouver - Wallace, Lum, Douglas, Arden; Paris - Tosani, Milovanoff, Garnell, Faigenbaum.

Artists index, p.411–12.

O75 Coe, Brian, and Gates, Paul. The snapshot photograph: the rise of popular photography, 1888–1939. [London], Ash and Grant, [1977]. 144p. il., plates.

Illustrations drawn primarily from the Kodak Museum, London. Emphasis on snapshot photography in England to mid-1930s. Good coverage of technical issues, camera types, but lacking extensive analysis of the impact of photography on popular culture.

Glossary, p.136–37. Roll film sizes, p.138–39. Index, p.140–44. Bibliography, p.144.

O76 The contest of meaning: critical histories of photography. Ed. by Richard Bolton. Cambridge, MIT Pr., [1989]. 407p. il.

Postmodern criticism has campaigned for multiple "histories" vs. a "history" of photography. Monographic "history" volumes are increasingly being supplemented by edited collections of essays that question traditional assumptions and methods. Bolton's collection contains work by 14 pre-eminent contemporary critics, including Douglas Crimp, Abigail Solomon-Godeau, Carol Squiers, and Allan Sekula.

Index, p.392–406.

O77 Daval, Jean Luc. Photography, history of an art. [Trans. by R. F. M. Dexter.] N.Y., Skira/Rizzoli, [1982]. 269p. il. (part col.)

Trans. of Histoire d'un art, la photographie. Genève, Skira, 1982.

Instead of the usual chronologically arranged, technology related history, Daval links developments in photography to the socio-cultural milieu, with a special emphasis on related occurrences in the visual arts. Comprised of topical vignettes (e.g., "Photography for all," "The family album," "From ethnography to sociology") within larger chapters (e.g., "The popularizing of photography"). Emphasizes European photographers.

List of illustrations by artist's name, p.255–63. Index, p.265–69.

O78 Eisinger, Joel. Trace and transformation: American criticism of photography in the modernist period. Albuquerque, Univ. of New Mexico Pr., [1995]. 314p., il.

Straightforward examination of the development of photographic criticism in the United States. Good introduction to Sadakichi Hartmann, Alfred Stieglitz, Beaumont Newhall, Minor White, John Szarkowski, the Postmodern critics, and others.

Contents: (1) Pictorialism; (2) Straight photography; (3) Documentary photography; (4) Popular criticism; (5) Subjectivism; (6) An independent vision: Margery Mann; (7) Formalism; (Conclusion) Modernism and postmodernism.

Bibliographic notes, p.271–93. Bibliography, p.294–303. Index, p.304–14.

O79 Eyes of time: photojournalism in America. [Ed.] by Marianne Fulton. With contrib. by Estelle Jussim . . . [et al.] Boston, Little, Brown, [1988]. 326p. 369 il., 41 col. plates.

Catalog of the exhibition, International Museum of Photography at George Eastman House (1988), and other locations. Emphasis on United States, but coverage is international.

Contents: "Subjects of strange . . . and fearful interest": photojournalism from its beginnings in 1839, by William Stapp; "The tyranny of the pictorial": American photojournalism from 1880–1920, by Estelle Jussim; European visions: magazine photography in Europe between the wars, by Colin Osman and Sandra S. Phillips; Bearing witness: the 1930s to the 1950s, by Marianne Fulton; Changing focus: the 1950s to the 1980s, by Marianne Fulton.

Bibliographic notes, p.[276]–85. Bibliography, p.286–95. Biographies, p.296–317. Index, p.320–325.

O80 Gernsheim, Helmut. Creative photography: aesthetic trends, 1839–1960. N.Y., Dover, 1991. 258p. il., plates.

See GLAH 1:O26 for 1st ed.; repr.: N.Y., Bonanza, 1974.

"There was little that required change in this new edition, apart from small additions to the text here and there. . . . Creative Photography is not a history; I merely offer contemplative thoughts on the constantly changing ideals of aesthetic expression, often triggered by new technical inventions that extended the range of photography."—*Introd.*

Short biographies of photographers, p.230–47. Processes, p.248–51. Bibliography, p.251–54. Index, p.255–58.

O81 Glassman, Elizabeth, and Symmes, Marilyn. Cliché-verre, hand-drawn, light-printed: a survey of the medium from 1839 to the present. [Detroit], Detroit Institute of Arts, [1980]. 211p. il., plates (part col.)

Catalog of the exhibition, Detroit Institute of Arts (1980), and other locations. Excellent coverage of this unique photographic form presents the work of 82 practitioners, going beyond the usual examples of Corot and his Barbizon contemporaries in the 19th century, or Man Ray in the 20th. Extensive artists entries.

Survey of 19th-century clichés-verre in collections, p.177–201. Glossary, p.202–04. Bibliography, p.205–09. Index of artists, p.210.

O82 Hall-Duncan, Nancy. The history of fashion photography. N.Y., Alpine Book Co.; [Rochester,] International Museum of Photography, [1979]. 240p. il., plates (part col.)

Catalog of the exhibition, International Museum of Photography (1977), and other locations. Provides a running commentary from the mid-19th century to 1970s, emphasizing formal analysis of the photographs and related developments in art photography, fashion, and the role of women in society.

Biographies, p.224–31. Bibliography, p.232–34. Checklist, p.235–38. Index, p.239–40.

O83 Harrison, Martin. Appearances: fashion photography since 1945. London, Cape, [1991]. 312p. il., plates (part col.)

"Fashion photography demonstrably has a place in the analysis of the sign-language of dress, and a direct relationship with the diverse cultural codes reflected in the ways in which our bodies are presented, and represented."—*Chap.1.*

Extensively illustrated. Examines fashion photography within contemporary socio-cultural milieu. Includes analysis of fashion, fashion journals, and the role of the fashion editor and photographer.

Notes, p.308–10.

O84 Haworth-Booth, Mark. Photography, an independent art: photographs from the Victoria and Albert Museum, 1839–1996. London, V&A Publications, 1997. 208p. il. (part col.)

"This is a book about the art of photography. It is the first introduction to the Victoria and Albert Museum's Photography Collection, which is international and ranges from 1839 to the present day. . . . One hundred images have been selected from a total of some 300,000."—*Introd.*

Abbreviations and notes, p.203–05. Index, p.206–08.

O85 Henisch, Heinz K., and Henisch, Bridget A. The photographic experience, 1839–1914: images and attitudes. University Park, Penn., Pennsylvania State Univ. Pr., [1994]. 462p. il. (part col.)

Contains a wealth of vernacular historical anecdotes, images, and information. Supplemented by numerous non-photographic illustrations. Organized topically (e.g., "Family milestones," "Advertising and publicity," "Politics on a plate," "Photography and travel").

References and notes follow each chapter. Index, p.455–62.

O86 A history of photography: social and cultural perspectives. Ed. by Jean-Claude Lemagny and Andre Rouillé. Trans. by Janet Lloyd. N.Y., Cambridge Univ. Pr., [1987]. 288p. il. (part. col.)

Trans. of Histoire de la photographie. Paris, Bordas, 1986.

Chronological, but attempts in the essays to situate photography within socio-political contexts.

Chronology, p.259–67. Technical processes with chronology, p.269–74. Bibliography, p.275. Index, p.283–88.

O87 Kosinski, Dorothy M. The artist and the camera: Degas to Picasso. [Dallas], Dallas Museum of Art (Distr. by Yale University Press, [1999]). 335p. il. plates (part col.)

Catalog of the exhibition, San Francisco Museum of Modern Art (1999), and other locations. The combination of the four introductory essays and the contextual information provided within the 14 artist-specific essays creates a multi-faceted history of the role of photography in modern artistic production.

Checklist of the exhibition, p.310–22. Bibliography, p.323–26. Index, p.327–35.

O88 Lewinski, Jorge. The naked and the nude: a history of the nude in photographs, 1839 to the present. N.Y., Harmony Books, [1987]. 223p. il., plates (part col.)

Places discussion of the nude within the contexts of both the history of photography and social and moral attitudes. Includes both art photography and popular photography, yet steers clear of an open discussion, or illustration, of pornography.

Bibliography, p.[218]. Index, p.[220]–23.

O89 Maddow, Ben. Faces: a narrative history of the portrait in photography. Photographs comp. and ed. by Constance Sullivan. Boston, N.Y. Graphic Society, [1977]. 540p. plates.

Richly interpretive examination of photographic portraiture. Chronologically arranged, the narrative flows from the analysis of one photographer's work to the next. Numerous excerpts from photographers' writings.

Bibliography, p.532–35. Name index, p.536–40.

O90 A new history of photography. Ed. by Michel Frizot. Köln, Könemann, 1998. 775p. il. (part col.)

Trans. of Nouvelle histoire de la photographie. Paris, Bordas, 1994.

Magisterial survey composes a "history" by combining 41 topical essays by noted authors. Insets focused on a specific photograph/topic are included in each essay. Fourteen additional illustrated sections ("dossiers") enhance the text.

Illustrated glossary of photographic processes, by Anne Cartier-Bresson, p.755–57. Bibliography, by Fred and Elisabeth Pajerski, p.758–68. Name index, p.769–73.

O91 Newhall, Beaumont. The history of photography: from 1839 to the present. [Rev. 5th ed.] N.Y., Museum of Modern Art (Distr. by Bulfinch Pr., Little, Brown and Company, 1994). 319p. il. (part col.), ports. (part col.)

See GLAH 1:O36 for previous eds. and original annotation.

Fairly extensive revision with some new text and illustrations, revised bibliography, yet continues to follow same scheme of technological and aesthetic development. Expanded coverage of previously slighted topics (e.g., Dada and Surrealist photomontage). Final chapter "New directions" ceases with the mid-1960s.

Bibliography, p.307–12. Index, p.313–19.

O92 On the art of fixing a shadow: one hundred and fifty years of photography. [By] Sarah Greenough . . . [et al.] [Washington, D.C.], National Gallery of Art, [Chicago], Art Institute of Chicago, [1989]. 510p. il., 387 plates (part. col.)

Catalog of the exhibition celebrating photography's sesquicentennial, National Gallery of Art (1989), and other locations. Essays provide breadth and depth required to function as serviceable history. Escapes traditional emphasis on technological innovation.

Contents: (1) Inventing photography, 1839–1879, by Joel Snyder; (2) The curious contagion of the camera, 1880–1918, by Sarah Greenough; (3) Ephemeral truths, 1919–1945, by David Travis; (4) Beyond the photographic frame, 1946–1989, by Colin Westerbeck.

Checklist, p.467–82. Artists' bibliographies, p.483–95. Bibliography, p.497–99. Glossary, p.501–05. Index, p.507–10.

O93 Photographie/sculpture. Textes de Dominique Païni . . . [et al.] [Paris], Centre national de la photographie, [1991]. 157p. plates (part col.) (Photo copies, 16e)

Catalog of the exhibition, Palais de Tokyo (1991–1992). See also the proceedings of the related symposium: Sculpterphotographier, photographie-sculpture: actes du colloque organisé au Musée du Louvre par le service culturel les 22 et 23 novembre 1991. Sous la dir. de Michel Frizot et Dominique Païni. Paris, Musée du Louvre; Marval, 1993 (14 essays).

Contents: Photographie et sculpture, un bilan de proximité, by Dominique Païni and Michel Frizot; Un lexique et quelques remarques à l'usage commun du photographe et du sculpteur, by Michel Frizot; (1) L'Art de la lumière: créé par la lumière, le cliché sculptural, by Hubertus von Amelunxen; (2) Le musée idéal: les bibliothèques photographiques, by Hélène Pinet; La sculpture dans l'objectif, by Jean-René Gaborit; (3) Métaphore et mélancolie, by Françoise Ducros; (4) La photographie, un territoire de sculpteur. Photographie/sculpture: un terrritoire incertain, by Régis Durand.

O94 Pultz, John. The body and the lens: photography 1839 to the present. N.Y., Abrams, [1995]. 176p. 118 il. (part col.) (Perspectives)

"The emergence in recent years of postmodern and feminist thinking demands a reappraisal of how the body is represented in the visual arts."—*Introd.*

Contents: (1) The nineteenth century: realism and social control; (2) 1850–1918: gender and eroticism in pictorialist photography; (3) 1900–1940: heterosexuality and modernism; (4) 1930–1960: the body in society; (5) 1960–1975: the body, photography, and art in the era of Vietnam; (6) Photography since 1975: gender, politics, and the postmodern body.

Bibliography, p.170–71. Index, p.171–76.

O95 Robinson, Cervin, and Herschman, Joel. Architecture transformed: a history of the photography of buildings from 1839 to the present. N.Y., Architectural League of N.Y.; Cambridge, Mass., MIT, [1987]. 203p. 193 il., plates.

"The book advances two ideas. First, alternative manners of depicting buildings were apparent from the earliest days of photography and continue to this day; one formula stresses the factual component of pictures, and the other, their emotional content, both expressive devices. Second, photographers consciously capitalized on the significant interrelationship between any pair of subjects isolated in a picture in order to make critical statements."—*Introd.*

In four chronologically continuous chapters the authors present an interpretive survey, incorporating trends in photography, architecture, journalism, and photo-mechanical reproduction.

Biographical list of photographers, p.[188]–93. Bibliography, p.[194]–6. Index, p.197–203.

O96 Rosenblum, Naomi. A history of women photographers. Paris, Abbeville, 1994. 356p. 263 il., plates (part col.)

Provides extensive coverage of a topic that receives scant attention in most histories. The attempt to produce a comprehensive text does not allow in-depth discussion of individual photographers. Primarily U.S. and European photographers.

Notes, p.282–290. Biographies, by Jain Kelly, p.291–327. General and individual bibliographies, by Peter Palmquist, p.328–47. Index, p.348–56.

O97 ______. A world history of photography. Third ed. N.Y., Abbeville, [1997]. 695p. 819 il. (part col., some fold.), plates.

1st ed. 1984; rev. ed. 1989.

Broadest coverage currently available for pre-1839 to early-1990s. Extent of coverage does not allow thorough contextual development of specific topics or photographers. Provides more focused examination in three short technical histories ("Pre-photographic optical and chemical observations and early experiments in photography," "Materials, equipment, and processes," "Developments since 1910") and six primarily illustrated sections ("The Galerie Contemporaine—appearance and character in 19th-century portraiture," "The Western landscape—natural and fabricated," "A 19th-century forerunner of photojournalism—the execution of the Lincoln conspirators," "The origins of color in camera images," "Illuminating injustices: the camera and social issues," "The machine: icons of the industrial ethos"). Western/Eurocentric in photographers covered.

Notes, p.632–44. Time line, p.645–49. Glossary, p.650–54. Topical and photographer bibliography, p.655–70. Index, p.671–95.

O98 Sobieszek, Robert A. The art of persuasion: a history of advertising photography. N.Y., Abrams, [1988]. 208p. 36 il., 149 plates (part col.)

Published in conjunction with an exhibition, International Museum of Photography at George Eastman House (1988). Brief essays situate the illustrative material within the social fabric of the times.

Contents: Beginnings 1865–1921; Various modernisms 1922–36; Realism, fear, and color 1929–45; An American golden age 1945–65; Romance, coolness, and literacy 1966–86; Triumph of the image and new techniques 1980–87.

Notes follow each chapter. Biographies, by Jeanne W. Verhulst, p.192–99. Bibliography, p.200–05. Index, p.206–08.

O99 Szarkowski, John. Photography until now. N.Y., Museum of Modern Art. (Distr. by Bulfinch, [1989]). 343p. il., plates (part col.)

Catalog of the exhibition celebrating photography's sesquicentennial, Museum of Modern Art (1989), and other locations. Attempts to "sketch out a history of photographic pictures, organized according to patterns of technological change," where, besides the mechanical, optical, and chemical, technology is defined as also incorporating "methods of distribution of photographic imagery, economic restraints, and professional status."—*Introd.*

Contents: (1) Before photography; (2) The inventors; (3) The daguerreotype and the calotype; (4) Paper versus glass; (5) George Eastman and Alfred Stieglitz; (6) Photographs in ink; (7) After the magazines.

Bibliographic notes, p.298–311. Checklist, p.313–33. Name index, p.338–42.

O100 Tausk, Petr. A short history of press photography. Prague, International Organisation of Journalists, 1988. 232p. 206 plates (part col.)

Integration of economic, social, and technical information results in a reasonably good international survey of photojournalism.

Bibliography, p.226–30.

O101 Westerbeck, Colin, and Meyerowitz, Joel. Bystander: a history of street photography. Boston, Little, Brown, [1994]. 430p. il., plates (part col.)

Emphasis on intentional observation vs. casual snapshot. "The combination of this instrument, a camera, and this subject, the street, yields a type of picture that is idiosyncratic to photography in a way that formal portraits, pictorial landscapes, and other kinds of genre scenes are not."—*Introd.*

Contents: (1) Eugène Atget and the nineteenth century; (2) Cartier-Bresson and Europe in the twentieth century; (3) Walker Evans and America before the war; (4) Robert Frank and America since the war.

Interview between Westerbeck and Meyerowitz, p.373–403. Notes, p.[410]–12. Bibliography, p.[413]–22. Index, [423]–30.

SEE ALSO: Photography and architecture, 1839–1939 (GLAH 2:J99).

19th Century

O102 Barger, M. Susan, and White, William B. The daguerreotype: nineteenth-century technology and modern science. Washington, Smithsonian Institution Pr., [1991]. 252p. il., tables.

Primarily a technological history, with comprehensive explanations of equipment, chemistry, processing, and preservation issues. Essays include an examination of image making prior to 1839 and the use of the daguerreotype as scientific tool.

Bibliographic notes, p.219–42. Name index, p.243–45. Subject index, 246–52.

O103 Brettell, Richard R. Paper and light: the calotype in France and Great Britain, 1839–1870. Boston, Godine, 1984. 216p. 15 il., 141 plates (part col.)

Catalog of the exhibition, Museum of Fine Arts, Houston (1982), and other locations. Excellent introduction to the calotype with good integration of technical and aesthetic information.

Contents: The calotype and aesthetics in early photography, by Nancy Keeler; The calotype as print medium, by Richard R. Brettell, Nancy Keeler, Sydney Mallett Kilgore; The calotype and the photographic exhibition of the Society of Arts, London, 1852–1853, by Roy Flukinger; The photographers (in 5 topical sections).

Bibliography, p.207–15. Index of photographers, p.216.

O104 The daguerreotype: a sesquicentennial celebration. Ed. by John Wood. Iowa City, Univ. of Iowa Pr., [1989]. 141p. il., 100 plates.

Contents: Silence and slow time: an introduction to the Daguerreotype, by John Wood; Rembrandt perfected, by Ben Maddow; The genius of photography, by Janet E. Buerger; Mirror in the marketplace: American responses to the Daguerreotype, 1839–1851, by Alan Trachtenberg; Southworth and Hawes: the artists, by Matthew R. Isenburg; Southworth and Hawes: the studio collection, by Ken Appollo; Beard and Claudet: a further inquiry, by Roy Flukinger; Delicate and complicated operations: the scientific examination of the Daguerreotype, by M. Susan Barger; Heavy lightness, serious vanity: modern daguerreotype, by Grant B. Romer.

Annotated list of plates, p. 117–34. Annotated bibliography, p.137–41.

O105 Darrah, William Culp. Cartes de visite in nin[e]teenth century photography. Gettysburg, Penn., Darrah, [1981]. 221p. 448 il.

Comprehensive survey with extensive historical detail. Includes an illustrated subject section of 67 topics (e.g., advertising art; bridges; humor; montages, composite; sentimental; ships and shipping).

Bibliography, p.201–02. Index of photographers and publishers, p.203–10. Geographic index of photographers, p.211–18. Subject index, p.219–21.

O106 Galassi, Peter. Before photography: painting and the invention of photography. N.Y., Museum of Modern Art. (Distr. by N.Y. Graphic Society, Boston, [1981]). 151p. 37 il., plates (part col., some fold.)

Catalog of the exhibition held at the Museum of Modern Art (1981), and other locations. Brief essay accompanied by more extensive annotations in the checklist. "The object here is to show that photography was not a bastard left by science on the doorstep of art, but a legitimate child of the Western pictorial tradition."—*Essay.*

Illustrated and annotated checklist, p.[118]–45. Bibliography, p.146–49. Artists' index, p.151.

O107 Gernsheim, Helmut. The origins of photography. [London], Thames and Hudson, [1982]. 280p. 191 il. (part col.), plates, ports. (The history of photography, 1)

See GLAH 1:O28 for original annotation.

"The History of Photography by Helmut and Alison Gernsheim was first published in 1955 by the Oxford Univ. Pr., and republished in a new and enlarged edition in 1969 by Thames and Hudson. The first part of the History appears here in a revised third edition, with a new chapter, 'The origins of photography in Italy,' by Daniela Palazzoli."—*t.p. verso.*

Covers the pre-photographic era through the use of the calotype and other paper process, while Gernsheim's The rise of photography (see following entry) commences with the advent of the albumen and collodian processes. The final three sections of his History of photography ("The gelatine period," "Some applications of photography," "The evolution of colour photography," and "Photography and the printed page") have not been released in a new ed.

Text and organization essentially unchanged from relevant section of the author's History of photography, but with additional illustrations. Excellent source for historical data, photographers, technologies.

Notes, p.265–72. Biography [H. Gernsheim], p.273. Bibliography, p.274. Name index, p.276–80.

O108 ———. The rise of photography: 1850–1880, the age of collodion. [London], Thames and Hudson, [1988]. 285p. 236 il. (part col.), plates, ports (The history of photography, 2)

See GLAH 1:O28 for original publication and preceding entry for first part of this new ed. The second part of the author's History of Photography appears here in a revised third ed.

Commences with the introduction of the collodion process (c.1850) and continues through the development of dry plate processes. Text and organization essentially unchanged from original History, but with additional illustrations. Excellent source for historical data, photographers, technologies.

Notes, p.271–75. Biography [H. Gernsheim], p.276. Bibliography, p.277–79. Name index, p.281–85.

O109 Marien, Mary Warner. Photography and its critics: a cultural history, 1839–1900. [N.Y.], Cambridge Univ. Pr., [1997]. 222p. 68 il. (Cambridge perspectives on photography)

"Presents photography as an idea, shaped by social concerns and inherited concepts, and as a burgeoning visual practice. When photography is viewed as a multifaceted social idea, vested in the practice of but not limited to image making, the oft-made distinction between photographic document and photographic art can be transcended."—*Pref.* Consistently citing 19th-century sources as well as more modern critics, provides a "history of the idea of photography," revealing both the existence of diverse photographic practices and shifting notions of modernity.

Bibliographic notes, p.173–212. Bibliographic survey, p.213–17. Index, p.219–22.

O110 Schaaf, Larry J. Out of the shadows: Herschel, Talbot and the invention of photography. New Haven, Yale Univ. Pr., 1992. 188p. il. (part col.), plates.

"It will be argued that the weather, petty politics, mothers, and rheumatism had as much to do with the invention and progress of photography as did any physical or artistic concern. . . . The present study explores the relationship between Herschel and Talbot up until 1844."—*Prelude.*

Notes, p.162–85. Index, p.186–88.

O111 Schwarz, Heinrich. Art and photography: forerunners and influences: selected essays. Ed. by William E. Parker. Rochester, N.Y., Visual Studies Workshop Pr. (Distr. Gibbs M. Smith, 1984). 158p., 64 plates.

Posthumously published collection of seven essays by noted historian. Pioneering studies of the complex relationship between painting and photography.

Selective contents: Before 1839: symptoms and trends; Art and photography: forerunners and influences; Vermeer and the camera obscura; Daumier, Gill, and Nadar.

Bibliographic notes, p.146–57. Bibliography, p.158.

O112 Zannier, Italo. Le grand tour: in the photographs of travelers of 19th century = Dans les photographies des voyageurs du XIXe siècle = Nelle fotografie dei viaggiatori del XIX secolo. [Venezia], Canal and Stamperia, [1997]. 227p., il., plates (part col.) (I grandi libri)

Many of the iconic images of this period were produced to satisfy a growing hunger for travel and the experience of the exotic, whether in person or via photographic reproductions. Zannier's essay indicates the cultural context for the production of the images, and the Picture section follows the route of the Grand Tour.

Contents: Before photography, by Cesare de Seta; Photographers in places of the sun, by Italo Zannier; Pictures from the Alps to the Portofino, from Milan to Garda, from Verona to Venice, from Bologna to Pisa, from Rome to Tivoli, from Naples to Capri, from Taormina to Girgenti, from Athens to Rhodes, from Istanbul to Bosphorus, from Cairo to Jerusalem, from Algeria to the Alhambra.

Index of names, p.[229].

20th Century

O113 Das Fotogramm in der Kunst des 20. Jahrhunderts: die andere Seite der Bilder: Fotografie ohne Kamera. [Zusammengest. von] Floris M. Neusüss in Zusammenarb. mit Renate Heyne. Köln, DuMont, 1990. 499p. il., plates (part col.)

The most comprehensive coverage available on the topic, extensively illustrated. Numerous brief essays on a wide range of artists and topics.

Chronologie der Fotogramm-Veröffentlichungen in Zeitschriften Katalogen und Büchern, p.430–34. Texte zum Fotogramm, p.434–36. Künstler- und Autorenviten mit Bibliographie, p.437–81. Fotogramme-Arten, Verfahren, Techniken, p. 482–84. Glossar, p.484–85. Vervielfältigung von Fotogrammen (ein Widerspruch?), p.485–86. Portfolios, Alben, Mappen, p.487–89. Fotogrammausstellungen, p.490. Allgemeine Bibliographie, p.491–93. Künstler- und Autorenregister, p.498–99.

O114 Kempe, Erika; Kempe, Fritz; and Spielmann, Heinz. Die Kunst der Camera im Jugendstil. Frankfurt am Main, Umschau, 1986. 244p. 247 il. (part col.)

Texts and illustrations indicate the close relationship between photography and painting at the turn of the century, in a fashion similar to the standard treatments of Van Deren Coke (GLAH 1:M152) and Aaron Scharf (GLAH 1:I260).

Contents: (1) Photographische Avant-garde, von Fritz Kempe; (2) Kunsthistorische Kriterien der Photographie, von Heinz Spielmann.

Literatur-Verzeichnis, p.237–38. Biographie der Photographen, p.238–39. Verzeichnis der Abbildungen, p.240–44.

O115 Krauss, Rosalind E.; Livingston, Jane; and Ades, Dawn. L'amour fou: photography and Surrealism. Washington, D.C., Corcoran Gallery of Art, N.Y., Abbeville Pr. [1985]. 243p. 236 il., plates (part col.)

Catalog of the exhibition, Corcoran Gallery of Art (1985). Texts and extensive illustrations contribute to a critical and historical understanding of photography's special role within Surrealism.

Contents: (1) Photography in the service of surrealism, by Rosalind Krauss; (2) Corpus delicti, by Rosalind Krauss; (3) Man Ray and the Surrealist image, by Jane Livingston; (4) Photography and the Surrealist text, by Dawn Ades.

Artist biographies and bibliographies, compliled by Winifred Schiffman, p.[193]–237. Index, p.239–43.

O116 Photography after photography: memory and representation in the digital age. Ed. by Hubertus v. Amelunxen, Stefan Iglhaut, Florian Rotzer in collab. with Alexis Cassel and Nikolaus G. Schneider. [Amsterdam], G + B Arts, [1996]. 308p. il. plates (part col.)

Trans. of exhibition catalog, Fotografie nach der Fotografie. [Dresden], Verlag der Kunst, [1996].

With 14 brief essays, and works by 35 artists, this catalog reveals the numerous pictorial possibilities wrought by the digital revolution, which challenges existing notions of the photographic image, reproduction, digital appropriation, and realism.

Biographical information on the artists, p.290–303. Biographical information on the authors, p.304–05. Selected bibliography, p.306–07.

O117 Tausk, Petr. Photography in the 20th century. [Adapted by the author. Trans. by Veronica Talbot and J. David Beal.] London, Focal Pr., Focal/Hastings House, 1980. 344p. il.

Trans. of Geschichte der Fotografie im 20. Jahrhundert. Köln, DuMont, 1977.

Conventional technological and aesthetic history, with emphasis on European photographers, especially British and Czech.

SEE ALSO: Grundberg and Gauss, Photography and art: interactions since 1946 (GLAH 2:I260).

WESTERN COUNTRIES

Australia

O118 Davies, Alan, and Stanbury, Peter. The mechanical eye in Australia: photography 1841–1900. Melbourne, Oxford Univ. Pr., [1985]. 270p. il. plates.

Based on an earlier catalog and exhibition, The mechanical eye, a historical guide to Australian photography and photographers. Sydney, Macleay Museum, University of Sydney, 1977. The "Images of Australian photography" section combines 51 plates with a page providing information on the photographer(s) and numerous extracts from mostly contemporaneous sources. "Professional photographers to 1900 and amateur photographers to 1880" lists names, dates, and addresses for photographers, and is interspersed with ads, cartoons, and articles from the period.

Clues for dating photographs, p.111–15. Sources, p.259–64. Index, p.265–70.

O119 Holden, Robert. Photography in colonial Australia: the mechanical eye and the illustrated book. [Sydney], Hordern House, [1988]. 172p. il. plates.

Combines an essay on the introduction and development of photography in Australia and an examination of photographic genres with an extensively annotated bibliography of 130 works published in Australia in the 19th century with original albumen photographs.

References, p.165–66. Index of photographers, photographic studios, printers and publishers, p.167–69. General index, p.170–71.

O120 Newton, Gael. Shades of light: photography and Australia, 1839–1988. With essays by Helen Ennis and Chris Long and assist. from Isobel Crombie and Kate Davidson. Canberra, Australian National Gallery; Collins Australia, 1988. 218p. il. (part col.)

Catalog of the exhibition, National Gallery of Australia (1988). "Does not seek to tell the story of Australia in pictures, nor the history of photography as the successive arrival of a number of processes. Its nucleus is fine photographs and their makers, and the reasons behind the changing subject matter and physical appearance of photographs in different periods."—*Pref.*

O121 Willis, Anne-Marie. Picturing Australia: a history of photography. [North Ryde, NSW, Australia], Angus and Robertson, [1988]. 304p. il. plates.

"The aim is not to write a definitive account, but to begin to develop photographic history on different premises."—*Pref.* Examines a multiplicity of photographic practices, developing technologies, and the many functions of photography in Australian society to produce an account of photography's varied role in Australia.

Bibliography, p.280–95. Index, p.297–304.

Canada

O122 Greenhill, Ralph, and Birrell, Andrew. Canadian photography, 1839–1920. Toronto, Coach House Pr., [1979]. [184]p. 104 plates.

Substantial revision and expansion of Early photography in Canada (GLAH 1:O69). Well-illustrated historical survey of early Canadian photography.

Selected bibliography, p.[179]. Index, p.[180–84].

O123 Private realms of light: amateur photography in Canada, 1839–1940. Ed. by Lilly Koltun. [Markham, Ont.], Fitzhenry and Whiteside, [1984]. 335p. il. plates (part col.)

Catalog of an exhibition held at Public Archives Canada, Ottawa (1983), and other locations. With five essays by members of the National Photography Collection, this text serves as an excellent introduction to the growth of amateur photography in Canada, with extensively illustrated discussion of clubs, salons, exhibitions, and photographic processes and technology.

Biographies of photographers, p.304–28. Bibliography, p.329–32. Index, p.333–35.

SEE ALSO: Guide to Canadian photographic archives (GLAH 2:O24).

France

O124 Bouqueret, Christian. Des années folles aux années noires: la nouvelle vision photographique en France, 1920–1940. Paris, Marval, 1997. 285p. 269 il., plates (part col.)

Presents in four sections photographic practices at the beginning of the period under examination, the development of the modernist idiom in France, the spread of images via the press, journalism, and exhibitions, and an analysis of photographic activities within specific arenas (fashion, portraiture, the nude, reportage, etc.). Includes numerous illustrations of important books, magazines, and related ephemera. Text interspersed with focused inserts on individual topics.

Biographies, p.269–79. Bibliographie générale critique, p.280–81. Index, p.282–84.

O125 Buerger, Janet E. French daguerreotypes. Chicago, Univ. of Chicago Pr., [1989]. 256p. 268 il., 22 plates (col.)

Primarily a catalog of the Gabriel Cromer Collection in the International Museum of Photography at George Eastman House. In-depth account of early photographic practice and the role of the daguerreotype in French society.

Contemporary sources, p.139–49. French methods and materials for coloring Daguerreotypes, by Alice Swan, p.150–63. Bibliographic notes, p.177–91. Catalog of Eastman House Daguerreotypes and books illustrated with engravings from Daguerreotypes, p.193–250. Index, p.251–56.

O126 Jammes, Andre, and Janis, Eugenia Parry. The art of French calotype: with a critical dictionary of photographers, 1845–1870. Princeton, Princeton Univ. Pr., [1983]. 284p. 131 il., 69 plates.

Primarily an aesthetic history with consistent incorporation of technical advancements, personalities, and cultural imperatives. Includes extensive excerpts from accounts of the time. Biographical essays in the "Critical dictionary" (p.[129]–258) are often lengthy, with additional references to exhibitions, publications, and writings.

Bibliography, p.269–75. Index, p.277–84.

O127 Gouvion Saint-Cyr, Agnes de; Lemagny, Jean-Claude; and Sayag, Alain. Art or Nature: 20th century French photography. [N.Y.], Rizzoli, 1988. 176p. (part col.)

Catalog of the exhibition organized by the Barbican Art Gallery and the Association française d'action artistique and held at the Barbican Art Gallery (1988). Although the essays are very brief (Pictorialism, Rapportage I, Dada and Surrealism, Rapportage II, Contemporary photography) they do include references to important examples of photographic literature. The "Biographies" section provides additional information on the 39 photographers presented.

O128 [Marbot, Bernard]. After Daguerre: masterworks of French photography (1848–1900) from the Bibliothèque nationale. N.Y., Metropolitan Museum of Art, in assoc. with Berger-Levrault, Paris, [1980]. 187p. il. plates.

Catalog of the exhibition, Metropolitan Museum of Art (1980–81), and other locations. Published in France as Regards sur la photographie en France au XIXe siècle: 180 chefs-d'oeuvre du Département des estampes et de la photographie, Bibliothèque nationale, Paris, Berger-Levrault, 1980.

Brief essay by Weston Naef, "The beginnings of photography as art in France" (p.15–70), examines the continuing development of 19th-century photography in France after 1850 within technical, cultural, and political contexts. Bernard Marbot's annotated catalog section (p.[69]–171) adds considerable additional biographical and contextual information.

Selected bibliography, p.180–83.

O129 Thézy, Marie de. La photographie humaniste: 1930–1960, histoire d'un mouvement en France. Avec la collab. de Claude Nori. Paris, Contrejour, [1992]. 239p. il. plates.

Thorough examination of a photographic perspective that is considered to be uniquely French, a meeting of "modernité" and "réalisme poétique." Includes discussion of the role of illustrated magazines and monographs, salons and agencies, and presents a wide range of photographers beyond those popularly known.

Biographies et bibliographies, p.225–34. Revues et magazines, p.235. Index des personnes citées, p.236–38.

SEE ALSO: Répertoire des photographes de France au dixneuvième siècle (GLAH 2:O32).

Germany and Austria

O130 Benteler, Petra. Deutsche Fotografie nach 1945 = German photography after 1945. [Kassel, Fotoforum, 1979]. 228p. il.

Catalog of the exhibition, Kasseler Kunstverein (1979), and other locations. This selection of three works each by 50 photographers, including several who worked for magazines or in advertising, gives an overview of German photography in the post-war period. Each photographer's entry includes a brief bio-critical presentation.

Contents: Style critique of postwar photography in West Germany, by Wolfgang Kemp; German photography after 1945, by Petra Benteler.

Bibliografie, p.224–27. Index, p.228.

O131 German photography 1870–1970: power of a medium. Klaus Honnef, Rolf Sachsse and Karin Thomas (eds.) and Kunst- und Ausstellungshalle der Bundesrepublik Deutschland. With essays by Volker Albus, Hermann Glaser, Klaus Honnef . . . et al. [Trans., Pauline Cumbers, Ishbel Flett.] [Köln], DuMont, [1997]. 323p. il., 122 plates (part col.)

Catalog of the exhibition Deutsche Fotografie: Macht eines Mediums 1870–1970, Kunst- und Ausstellungshalle der Bundesrepublik Deutschland in Bonn (1997). Thirteen essays emphasize photography's political and social role as an instrument of the state or documentary tool, with discussions of photography in the Weimar Republic, the Third Reich, the German Democratic Republic and the Federal Republic of Germany. Plates expand coverage to more aesthetic realms.

Photographs in the exhibition, p.276–313. Biographical and bibliographic notes, p.315–21.

O132 Geschichte der Fotografie in Österreich. Bad Ischl, Verein zur Erarbeitung der Geschichte der Fotografie in Österreich, 1983. 2v. il. (part col.), ports.

Catalog of the exhibition, Museum des 20. Jahrhunderts, Vienna (1983–1985), and other locations.

V.1 (574p.) is an extensively illustrated history up to the early 1980s, including daguerreotypes, stereo views, travel and expedition photography, pictorialism, and propaganda photography. V.2 (220p.) contains discussion on techniques, amateur photography and photo salons, excerpts from critical writings of 1839 to 1940, and photographer's biographies (p.[93]–196).

Diverse publikationen österreichischer Autoren, v.2, p.197–98. Fotozeitschriften in Österreich, v.2, p.199–200. Zeitschriften Chronologie, v.2, p.201. Weitere Periodika, v.2, p.202. Bedeutende fotografische Ausstellungen in Österreich, v.2, p.203–08. Publikationen zur österreichischen Fotografiegeschichte, v.2, p.209. Namenregister, v.2, p.211–20.

O133 Hoerner, Ludwig. Das photographische Gewerbe in Deutschland 1839–1914. [Dusseldorf], GFW-Verlag, [1989]. 256p. il. (part col.)

With an emphasis on the "photographic trade" instead of photography as a fine art practice. The text and illustrations survey photography's role as both a recorder and vehicle of popular culture during the period. Emphasizes professional photographers, picture publishing houses, the carte-devisite, postcards, group portraits of professional associations and clubs, family portraits, theater portraits, etc.

Photographische Fachbetriebe in der Bundesrepublik Deutschland, p.236–45. Anmerkungen, p.246–49. Literaturverzeichnis, p.249–50.

O134 Kempe, Fritz. Daguerreotypie in Deutschland: vom Charme der frühen Fotografie. Seebruck am Chiemsee, Heering, 1979. 270p. il., plates (part col.) (Neue Fotothek)

Extensive coverage of early photographic activities and daguerreotypists in Germany. Organized by regions and major cities, with some chapters devoted to individual practitioners.

Literaturverzeichnis, p.261–64. Namenregister, p.267–68. Sachregister, p.269–70.

O135 Kuehn, Karl Gernot. Caught: the art of photography in the German Democratic Republic. Berkeley, Univ. of California Pr., [1997]. 305p. il.

Beginning with the "socialist formation period" of the 1940s to the 1970s. Readable text on the political parameters that defined appropriate photographic behavior in the GDR. The work of the late 1970s and 1980s reveals a growing artistic liberation that continued to be suppressed but could not be eradicated.

Notes, p.273–89. Bibliography, p.291–98. Index, p.299–305.

O136 Österreichische Fotografie seit 1945 aus den Beständen der Österreichischen Fotogalerie im Rahmen der Salzburger Landessammlungen Rupertinum. [Hrsg. von] Margit Zuckriegl. [Salzburg, Österreichische Fotogalerie im Rahmen der Salzburger Landessammlungen Rupertinum in zusammenarb. mit dem Bundesministerium fur Unterricht, Kunst und Sport: Ausg. für den Buchhandel im Universitätsverlag Anton Pustet, 1989]. 379p. il., plates (part col.)

Based on the collection of the Österreichische Fotogalerie. Zuckriegl's brief essay outlines the development of Austrian photography in the post-war era. The photographers section is extensive, with either biographical and bibliographic information or a short critical essay on each photographer, occasionally both.

O137 Peters, Ursula. Stilgeschichte der Fotografie in Deutschland: 1839–1900. Köln, DuMont, [1979]. 424p. il., plates.

Survey-like coverage from the camera obscura to the Jugendstil, touching on technical aspects, travel photography, portraiture and landscape, early relationship between photography and painting, and so on.

Anmerkungen, p.363–87. Literaturverzeichnis, p.389–415. Verzeichnis der im Text erwähnten, nicht abgebildeten Bildbeispiele, p.416–17. Namenverzeichnis, p.418–24.

O138 Photography at the Bauhaus. [Ed. for the Bauhaus-Archiv by Jeannine Fiedler.] Cambridge, MIT Press, 1990. 362p. il. (part col.)

Catalog of an exhibition of works from the Bauhaus-Archiv, Berlin (1990). German ed., Berlin, Das Archiv, Nishen, 1990; French ed., Paris, Carre, 1990.

With nine essays on "The masters" of the Bauhaus and six essays on "The topics" (typophoto, architecture and product photography, stage photography, etc.) this vol. provides excellent coverage of photography at the Bauhaus. Extensively illustrated with plates, all 435 works from the exhibition are reproduced in the Index of works, p.287–338.

Biographies, p.339–56. Bibliography, p.358–59. List of artists presented, p.361.

O139 Silber und Salz: zur Frühzeit der Photographie im deutschen Sprachraum, 1839–1860. Agfa Foto-Historama. Hrsg. von Bodo von Dewitz und Reinhard Matz. Köln, Braus, 1989. 696p. il., plates (part col.)

Catalog of the sesquicentennial exhibition, Josef-Haubrich-Kunsthalle, Cologne (1989), and other locations. With 24 essays this is the most extensive work on early photography in German-speaking lands.

Selective contents: Daguerre oder Talbot? Zur Konkurrenz der Verfahren im deutschen Sprachraum, von Bodo von Dewitz; Alexander von Humboldt: Förderer der frühen Photographie, von Hanno Beck; Trudpert Schneider and Söhne als Wanderphotographen durch Europa, von Leif Geiges and Reinhard Matz; Erotik der Rührung: zur stereoskopischen Akt-Daguerreotypie, von Otto Hochreiter; Der Verkauf photographischer Bilder in den frühen Jahren der Photographie, Beispiel: Köln, von Werner Neite.

Ausstellungskatalog, p.636–62. Glossar früher photographischer Techniken, p.664–68. Kurzbiographien der Photographen, p.670–78. English summaries, p.682–91. Personenregister, p.692–96.

Great Britain and Ireland

O140 Bartram, Michael. The Pre-Raphaelite camera: aspects of Victorian photography. Boston, Little Brown, [1985]. 200p. il., plates, ports.

British ed., London, Weidenfeld and Nicolson, 1985.

Rather than attempt to establish a strict corollary between the Pre-Raphaelite Brotherhood and early photographers, Bartram suggests that shared inclinations such as an interest in "truth to nature" and a certain romanticism of the era led to similar pictorial practices. Numerous examples from both painting and photography, especially from the 1850s to the early 1870s.

Biographical notes, p.[181]–92. List of paintings and drawings, p.[193]. Notes, p.[194]–96. Bibliography, p.[197]. Index, p.[198]–200.

O141 The golden age of British photography 1839–1900: photographs from the Victoria and Albert Museum, London, with selections from the Philadelphia Museum of Art . . . [et al.] Ed. and introd. by Mark Haworth-Booth. Philadelphia, Philadelphia Museum of Art, [1984]. 189p. il., plates, ports.

Catalog of the exhibition, Victoria and Albert Museum (1984), and other locations. A limited ed. portfolio of 300 copies, The golden age of British photography, with 16 hand-pulled photogravures, was also published in conjunction with the exhibition (N.Y., Silver Mountain Foundation, 1985).

Haworth-Booth's brief essays and biographical sketches profiling each section of the catalog are supplemented by an additional five essays, providing a good introductory text to this period.

References, p.189. Index, p.[190]–[91].

O142 Harker, Margaret F. The linked ring: the secession movement in photography in Britain, 1892–1910.

London, Heinemann, [1979]. 196p. il. (part col.), plates.
"This books aims to establish the importance of the Linked Ring in the development of the aesthetic of photography and recognition of the medium as an art in its own right."—*Introd.*

Contents: (1) The early years in photography; (2) The inter-action between photography and painting in the nineteenth century; (3) The search for photography's aesthetic; (4) The growth of societies and clubs; (5) The Robinson row; (6) The Secession movement in photography; (7) The Linked Ring Brotherhood; (8) The photographic salon; (9) The unlinking of the Ring; (10) The new realism.

Biographies, p.145–[66]. Principle processes, p.165–68. Notes, p.169–78. The roll of the Linked Ring, p.179–88. Plate index, p.189–94. Index, p.195–96.

O143 Stevenson, Sara. Light from the dark room: a celebration of Scottish photography: a Scottish-Canadian collaboration. With essays by Alison Morrison-Low . . . [et al.] Edinburgh, National Galleries of Scotland, 1995. 128p. il. (part col.), plates.
Catalog of the exhibition, Royal Scottish Academy, Edinburgh (1995).

Contents: Introduction: Scotland and photography, by Sara Stevenson; A new dimension: a context for photography before 1860, by Alison Morrison-Low and Allen Simpson; The continuum of realism: photography's beginnings, by Julie Lawson; Light from the dark room, by Sara Stevenson; Landscape in Scotland: photography and the poetics of place, by Ray McKenzie; Photography in Scotland: The human face, by Robin Gillanders; Scottish photography now: between the culture and the land, by James Lawson.

Notes and references, p.105–07. Catalog [with biographical notes], p.108–24. Select bibliography, p.125–27.

O144 ______, and Morrison-Low, A. D. Scottish photography: a bibliography, 1839–1989. Edinburgh, Salvia Books, 1990. 47p. il., plates.
While not intended to serve as a comprehensive bibliography on the topic, provides access to lesser-known photographers. Includes books and significant articles from 19th- and 20th-century literature. In a single alphabetical listing by photographer. Not annotated.

General works referring to Scottish photographers, p.37. Recommended works on the history and theory of photography, p.38. Name index, p.39–43. Photograph locations index, p.44–45. Technical terms index, p.46–47.

O145 Through the looking glass: photographic art in Britain 1945–1989. [Sel. by] Gerry Badger, John Benton-Harris. [London], Barbican Art Gallery. [Distr. by Lund Humphries, 1989]. 199p. il., plates (part col.)
Catalog of the exhibition, Barbican Art Gallery (1989), and another location.

Contents: Through the looking glass: photographic art in Britain, 1945–1989, by Gerry Badger; Newsreel, by Peter Turner; Taking issue: artists as photographers, by Sarah Kent; Post-war women's photography and independent imagery, by Val Williams; The foreignness of British photography, by Richard Ehrlich; Landscape: totality and the small time, by Ian Jeffrey.

Artists' biographies and list of works, p.[171]–99.

Italy

O146 Becchetti, Piero. Fotografi e fotografia in Italia, 1839–1880. [Roma], Quasar, 1978. 320p. il., plates
Combination of introductory essay on the period, directory-like listing of photographers by city, and plates. Entries in the directory section sometimes include only name and address, but generally provide more extensive biographical information, including examples of the photographers' studio cards.

Indice dei nomi, p.311–17. Indice delle tavole, p.318–19.

O147 Bertelli, Carlo. L'Immagine fotografica, 1845–1945. [Torino], Einaudi, [1979]. 2v. 676 plates. (Storia d'Italia. Annali, 2)
Integrates photographs from all venues, artistic, propaganda, portraits, etc. Bertelli's essay includes discussion of the introduction of various processes into Italy, salons and exhibitions, Futurism, both World Wars, and the rise of fascism. An appendix section reprints important Italian photographic texts from 1839–1941.

Plate section includes: (1) Il paesaggio fotografico; (2) Il Risorgimento; (3) Il catalogo dell'Italia unita; (4) Un paese moderno; (5) La grande guerra; (6) Vigilia e autoritratto di una dittatura; (7) Verso un linguaggio fotografico italiano; (8) Guerra e resistenza.

Appendice di testi e documenti, v.2, p.[199]–303. Indice dei fotografi, v.2, p.[305]–08.

O148 Fotografia italiana dell'Ottocento. [Milano], Electa; [Firenze], Alinari, [1979]. 193p. il., plates (part col.)
Catalog of the exhibition, Palazzo Pitti (1979). In addition to the catalog essays, a separate section presents a region-by-region history. Entries on the individual photographers are fairly extensive.

Contents: 1) Fotografia e storia, by Giulio Bollati; 2) La notizia dell'invenzione dello "specchio dotato di memoria" arriva in Italia, by Daniela Palazzoli; 3) L'età del collodio, by Marina Miraglia; 4) La massificazione della fotografia, by Italo Zannier.

Bibliografia, p.185–89. Indice dei nomi, p.[190]–93.

O149 Lista, Giovanni. Futurismo e fotografia. [Milano], Multhipla, [1979]. 355p., 326 plates (part col.) (Collana "Avanguardia")
Discusses and illustrates stylistic antecedents of Futurist photography and photography's relationships to the expression of Futurism in other media. Two appendixes contain checklists of five prominent Futurist photography exhibitions and 22 Futurist texts.

Indice degli autori, p.353–54.

O150 Valtorta, Roberta. Pagine di fotografia italiana, 1900–1998 = Pages of Italian photography, 1900–1998. [Milano], Charta, 1998. 214p. plates (part col.)

Catalog of the exhibition, Galleria Gottardo, Lugano, 1998. Not really a history proper, but a collection of photographers of the 20th century. Each photographer is represented by one work, which is accompanied on the facing page by a brief interpretive commentary on the photographer and the photograph.

List of works, p.209–14.

O151 Zannier, Italo. Storia della fotografia italiana. [Roma], Laterza, 1986. 423p., 289 plates (part col.) (Grandi opere)

Provides survey-like coverage of photography in Italy from the use of the camera obscura to the mid-1980s, including discussion of the Alinari, Futurism, Mussolini and fascism, and the "paparazzo."

Note, p.[387]–400. Bibliografia generale, p.[401]–02. Indici dei nomi, p.[403]–19.

Latin America

Bibliography

O152 Davidson, Martha. "Bibliography: photography of Latin America," in Latin American masses and minorities: their images and realities: papers of the thirtieth annual meeting of the Seminar on the Acquisition of Latin American Library Materials, Princeton University, Princeton, New Jersey, June 19–23, 1985. Ed. Dan C. Hazen. Madison, Wis., SALALM Secretariat, Univ. of Wisconsin-Madison, 1987, v.2, p.610–14.

Citations to 34 books and periodical articles.

O153 Gutiérrez, Ramón; Méndez, Patrícia; and Zúñiga, Solange. Bibliografia sobre história da fotografia na América Latina = Bibliografía sobre historia de la fotografía en la América Latina. Rio de Janeiro, FUNARTE; Buenos Aires, CEDODAL, 1997. 121p.

Important bibliography, indexed by author/title and by country/date.

Abreviaturas utilizadas, p.[iv].

Histories and Handbooks

O154 Billeter, Erika. A song to reality: Latin-American photography 1860–1993. [Barcelona], Lunwerg Editores. [Distr. by D.A.P., 1998]. 395p. il., plates (part col.)

Trans. of Canto a la realidad: fotografia latinoamericana, 1860–1993. Barcelona, Lunwerg, 1993.

Billeter's essay and selections present work that in her estimation reveals a uniquely Latin American cultural presence, social structures, and a photographers' "moral conception." Not designed to be encyclopedic, but a good overall survey.

Biographical summaries, p.381–91. Bibliography, p.393–94. General works, p.395.

O155 Carvalho, Maria Luiza Melo. Novas travessias: contemporary Brazilian photography. London, Verso, [1996]. 191p. il. (part col.)

Introductory essay situates contemporary photographic practice within the context of photographic modernism in Brazil. Plates introduced by excerpts from the 35 photographers included.

"Some of the photographic work featured here will be exhibited at The Photographers Gallery, London, in January-March, 1996."—*Ackn.*

Biographies, p.186–91.

O156 Coloquio latinoamericano de fotografía. Mexico, D.F., Consejo Mexicano de Fotografia, and others, 1981– . (3?)v.

See GLAH 1:O81, GLAH 1:O84 for first vol. of proceedings and related exhibition. Uncertain history; an important series, most colloquia accompanied by related exhibitions.

Selective contents: (2) Feito na América Latina (1987); (5) Libros sobre fotografía latinoamericana de 1978–1996 (1996).

O157 Debroise, Olivier. Fuga mexicana: un recorrido por la fotografia en Mexico. [Mexico, D.F., Consejo Nacional para la Cultura y las Artes, 1994]. 223p. il., plates. (Cultura contemporanea de Mexico)

Although arranged confusingly by musical terms such as "Oratoria" or "Tocato," the text integrates the role of photographers who visited Mexico, e.g., Claude Désiré Charnay, Teobert Maler, and Edward Weston with Mexican photographers, i.e., Lola and Manuel Álvarez Bravo, Graciela Iturbide, Agustín Víctor Casasola, and numerous lesser known or anonymous photographers. With coverage from the daguerreotype era through the modern.

Bibliografía, p.207–15. Índice onomástico, p.217–23.

O158 Facio, Sara. La fotografía en la Argentina: desde 1840 a nuestros dias. [Buenos Aires], La Azotea, [1995]. 123p. il., plates. (Coleccion Lo nuestro)

In Spanish and English. Succinctly surveys the highlights of Argentinian photography, including the introduction of the daguerreotype process, the Argentinian pictorialists, the growth of pictorial magazines, and significant groups such as the "Forum" group.

Bibliografía, p.121. Indice de nombres, p.121–22. Catalogo - Libros, p.123.

O159 Ferrez, Gilberto. Photography in Brazil, 1840–1900. Trans. by Stella de Sá Rego. Albuquerque, Univ. of New Mexico Pr., 1990. 243p. il., plates.

Trans. of Fotografía no Brasil, 1840–1900. Rio de Janeiro, Fundação Nacional de Arte, Fundação Nacional Pró-Memória, 1985. [2a. ed.]

Ferrez delineates his coverage geographically, with chapters on fourteen Brazilian states, plus one on the prominent photographer, Marc Ferrez.

Notes, p.[223]–27. Glossary of photographic terms, p.229–31. Glossary of Portugese terms, p.[233]. Bibliography, p.[235]–37. Index, p.[239]–43.

O160 Fotografie Lateinamerika von 1860 bis heute. [Konzept und Realis. von Ausstellung und Katalog: Erika Billeter]. Bern, Benteli, [1981]. 416p. il., plates, ports.

Catalog of the exhibition, Kunsthaus Zurich (1981). Trans. as Fotografia latinoamericana desde 1860 hasta nuestros (Madrid, El Viso, 1982) without most essays and with variations in photographers included.

While the eight essays are too limited to provide much more than brief historical context to this extensively illustrated catalog, this was the first major European exhibition of Latin American photography.

Biografien, p.[381]–99. Katalog, p.[402]–11. Zeittafel lateinamerikanischer Geschichte, p.412–13. Ausgewählte Literatur, p.415. Publikationen von oder zu einzelnen Fotografen, p.416.

O161 Gomez, Juan. La fotografía en la Argentina: su historia y evolucion en el siglo XIX, 1840–1899. [Buenos Aires, Abadia Editoria, 1986]. 180p. il., plates.

After a general presentation of photography's origins in Europe and early photographic processes, Gomez's text moves to the introduction of the daguerreotype in South America, tarjetas de visita (carte de visite) and related developments, extensively citing contemporaneous materials. Each page of the text is marked with the year(s) that page discusses, providing quick chronological access. The Chronologia is an alphabetical listing of photographers with dates and comments on their significant activities.

Chronologia, p.149–73. Bibliografia, p.175–78.

O162 Image and memory: Latin American photography, 1865–1992. Ed. by Wendy Watriss, Lois Zamora. Austin, Univ. of Texas Pr., 1998. 450p. il., plates (part col.)

In Spanish and English. Catalog published following a series of exhibitions at FotoFest, Houston (1992), and a later traveling exhibition.

While not intended as a comprehensive survey of a complex subject, provides good overall coverage of the works of 51 photographers and collections, with fifteen plate sections based on specific topics, e.g., "Guatemala: the colonial legacy: Religious photographs, 1880–1920."

Contents: Image and memory: photography from Latin America, 1866–1994, by Wendy Watriss; Photography in nineteenth-century Latin America: the European experience and the exotic experience, by Boris Kossoy; Crossover dreams: remarks on contemporary Latin American photography, by Fernando Castro; Quetzalcóatl's mirror: reflections on the photographic image in Latin America, by Lois Parkinson Zamora.

Bibliography, p.377–409. Artist biographies, p.411–32. Index, p.443–50.

O163 Levine, Robert M. Images of history: nineteenth and early twentieth century Latin American photographs as documents. Durham, Duke Univ. Pr., 1989. xi, 216p. il.

"This book examines how photography helped define the ways Latin Americans came to see themselves and the world. It focuses on the evolution of Latin American photography from its earliest origins in the late 1830s to the rise of mass communications . . . by the 1920s and 1930s."—*Introd.*

Contents: Part 1: Photography and society: (1) The Daguerreotype era; (2) Order and progress; Part 2: Photographs as evidence: (3) Reading photographs; (4) Posed worlds and alternate realities.

Notes, p.187–94. Glossary, p.195–96. Sources of the photographs, p.197–98. Bibliography, p.199–206. Index, p.207–16.

O164 McElroy, Keith. Early Peruvian photography: a critical case study. Ann Arbor, UMI Research Pr., [1985]. 192p., 69 plates. (Studies in photography, 7)

This revision of the author's thesis (Univ. of New Mexico, 1977) is one of the few studies of any size or depth on Peruvian photography.

Contents: (1) The daguerrean era; (2) The age of the carte-de-visite; (3) The business of photography.

Notes: p.[163]–83. Bibliography, p.[186]–88. Index, p.[189]–92.

O165 Nineteenth-century South America in photographs. [Comp. by] H. L. Hoffenberg. N.Y., Dover, 1982. vi, 152p. il. (Dover photography collections)

Comments on the history of photography in South America and identifies early photographers. Based on the compiler's collection of original vintage prints.

Contents: (1) Urban life; (2) Ports; (3) Transportation; (4) State and politics; (5) Military; (6) Leisure; (7) Rural life; (8) Indians; (9) Natural wonders.

List of photographers, p.152.

O166 La photographie contemporaine en Amérique latine. [Paris], Centre Georges Pompidou, Musée national d'art moderne, [1982]. 64p. chiefly il., ports.

Catalog of the exhibition, Centre Georges Pompidou, Musée National d'Arte Moderne (1982). Striking photographic reproductions and biographical data on 80 Latin American photographers.

Biographies, p.60–64.

O167 Serrano, Eduardo. Historia de la fotografía en Colombia. [Bogotá, Museo de Arte Moderno de Bogotá, 1983]. [2a ed.] 333p. il. (part col.), plates, ports.

Extensively illustrated and footnoted survey from the daguerreotype era to 1950.

Descripcion de tecnicas y procesos, p.313–15. Fotografos Colombianos 1840–1950, p.317–25. Indice, p.327–33.

Low Countries

O168 Abeels, G. Les pionniers de la photographie à Bruxelles. Zaltbommel, Bibliothèque européenne, 1977. 124p. il.

Important study of early photographers in Belgium.

Contents: (1) La vie quotidienne au XIXe siècle; (II) Les

photographes étrangers à Bruxelles; (III) Les précurseurs; (IV) Les calotypistes; (V) Les collodionistes; Conclusion.
Table des noms cités dans le texte, p.122–24.

O169 Antheunis, Georges; Deseyn, Guido; and van Gysegem, Marc. Focus op fotografie: fotografie te Gent van 1839 tot 1940. [Ghent], Museum voor Industriële Archeologie en Textiel; Gemeentekrediet, [1987]. 210p. il.
Catalog of the exhibition, Museum voor Industriële Archeologie en Textiel, Ghent (1987). The first 100 years of photography in Ghent.
Bibliografie, p.207–09.

O170 Coppens, Jan; Roosens, Laurent; and van Deuren, Karel. Door de enkele werking van het licht: introductie en integratie van de fotografie in Belgïe en Nederland, 1839–1869. Met een bijdr. van Frans Nooyens. Eindhoven, Gemeentekrediet, 1989. 303p. il.
Catalog of the exhibition, Museum voor Fotografie, Antwerp (1989), and other locations. On the diffusion of photography in Belgium and the Netherlands.
Personenregister, p.299–301.

O171 Directory of photographers in Belgium, 1839–1905. [By] Steven F. Joseph, Tristan Schwilden, Marie-Christine Claes. Antwerpen, C. de Vries-Brouwers, [1997]. 2v. il. (part col.)
Consists of 5,400 entries
Contents: (1) Text; (2) Album.
Place names in Belgium, v.1, p.23. Alphabetical index by locality 1839–1905, v.1, p.429–69. Chronological index by locality up to 1860, v.1, p.473–75. List of main sources, v.1, p.477–81. Bibliography, v.1, p.482–85.

O172 Fotografie in Nederland. 's-Gravenhage, Staatsuitgeverij, 1978– . (3)v. il. (part col.)
Survey of Dutch photography.
Contents: (1) 1839–1920; (2) 1920–1940; (3) 1940–1975.
Includes bibliographical references. List of photographers [in v.3 and insert] and index in each vol.

O173 De Fotografie in België 1940–1980 = La photographie belge 1940–1980 = Photography in Belgium 1940–1980. Deurne-Antwerpen, Afdeling Foto en Film, Het Sterckshof, Provinciaal Museum Voor kunstambachten, 1980. 155p. chiefly il. (part col.)
Published in conjunction with the exhibition, Provinciaal Museum Sterckshof (1980), offering a survey of modern Belgian photography.
Beknopte bibliografie, p.31.

O174 Vercheval, Georges. Pour une histoire de la photographie en Belgique: essais critiques, répertoire des photographes depuis 1839. Charleroi, Belgium, Musée de la Photographie, 1993. 472p. il. (part col.)
Text in French, Dutch and English. Catalog of the exhibition, Musée de la Photographie, Charleroi (1993).
Répertoire des institutions, p.379–81. Répertoire des photographes de 1839 à nos jours [biographical dictionary], p.383–463. Bibliographie générale, p.464–65. Index, p.469–71.

New Zealand

O175 Knight, Hardwicke. New Zealand photographers: a selection. Dunedin, N.Z., Allied Pr., 1981. [112]p. il.
"23 selected biographies illustrated with 96 photographs and a list of over 1,100 New Zealand photographers to 1900."—*T.p.*
List of New Zealand photographers to 1900 [unpaginated].

O176 Main, William, and Turner, John B. New Zealand photography from the 1840s to the present = Nga whakaahua o Aotearoa mai i 1840 ki naianei. Auckland, N.Z., PhotoForum, 1993. 88p. il. (part col.)
Anthology of 104 photographs by 84 New Zealand photographers.
Bibliography, p.86–87. Index, p.88.

Russia and Eastern Europe

O177 Ceská fotografie 90. let = Czech photography of the 1990s. [By] Vladimír Birgus . . . [et al.] [Prague], Kant [Distr. by D.A.P., 1998]. 205p. il. plates (part col.)
Catalog of the exhibition, Chicago Cultural Center (1999). Birgus's detailed 1990s chronology of events in Czech photography, his essay "Certainty and searching in contemporary Czech photography," and the photographers' biographical entries combine to deliver a good survey on contemporary trends.

O178 A Fenykep varazsa, 1839–1989 = The magic of photography, 1839–1989. [Ed. by Mihály Gera]. [Budapest], [Association of Hungarian Photographers], [Szabad Tér], [1989]. 415p. il., plates.
Combined catalog of 12 exhibitions covering 150 years of Hungarian photography. Organized by Budapest Art Weeks and the Association of Hungarian Photographers, 1989. In spite of somewhat problematic translations this collection of 16 brief essays, primarily by Hungarian writers, gives reasonable coverage of Hungarian photography from the daguerreotype era to the current day.

O179 Fotografija u Hrvatskoj, 1848–1951 = Photography in Croatia, 1848–1951. Ed. by Vladimir Malekovic. Photographs . . . sel. by Marija Tonkovic i Vladimir Malekovic. [Trans. by Sonia Wild Bicanic and Nikolina Jovanovic.] Zagreb, Muzej za umjetnost i obrt, 1994. 459p. il. (part col.)
Catalog of the exhibition, Muzej za umjetnost i obrt (1994). Fifteen essays mainly devoted to regions within Croatia. Explores the development of photography as both a uniqely Croatian experience and as one colored by Western influences. Good coverage of local clubs, salons, and the impact of exhibitions such as the appearance of the Deutsche Werkbund's "Film und Foto" in Zagreb in 1930.
Comparative chronology, p.401–22. Biographies and catalog, p.423–54. Index of photographers, p.455–59.

O180 Fotografija kod Srba 1839–1989 = Serbian photography 1839–1989. Exhibition and catalogue planned by Miodrag Djordjevic. Beograd, Srpska akademija nauka i umetnosti, 1991. 403p. il. (part col.) (Galerija srpske akademije nauki i umetnosti, 69)

Catalog of the exhibition, Galerija srpske akademije nauki i umetnosti (1991). With contributions by eighteen authors focusing on specific aspects of Serbian photography and extensive illustrations, the catalog provides a good survey of photography in Serbia. Text in Serbo-Croatian (Cyrillic) with English summaries; captions to photographs in Serbo-Croatian.

Selected bibliography, 1839–1989, p.159–85. Important dates in the history of Serbian photography, p.186–91.

O181 Fotografia polska, featuring original masterworks from public and private collections in Poland, 1839–1945, and a selection of avant-garde photography, film, and video from 1945 to the present. [N.Y., International Center of Photography, 1979] 49p. il. plates (part col.)

Catalog of the exhibition, International Center of Photography (1979). Revised version appeared as catalog of the exhibition La Photographie polonaise, 1900–1981, Centre Georges Pompidou (1981).

This small catalog provides a good assessment of the history of photographic practice in Poland.

Contents: A photographic heritage, by William Ewing; Notes on the history of Polish photography, by Jiuliusz Garztecki; Some notes on the pictorial movement, by Adam Sobota; Twentieth century experimentation, by Urszula Czartoryska; Polish press photography, by Jan Kosidowski.

Checklist of the exhibition issued separately.

O182 Photo manifesto: contemporary photography in the USSR. [By] [Joseph] Walker, [Christopher] Ursitti, [Paul] McGinniss . . . [et al.] N.Y., Stewart, Tabori and Chang, 1991. 231p. il., plates (part col.)

Presenting work by more than 50 photographers from the Moscow, Leningrad, Minsk, and other areas, the essays relate current photographic trends to both the tradition of Soviet photography and the break-up of the Soviet state.

Selective contents: Photo manifesto, by Walker, Ursitti, and McGinnis; Photography since the revolution, by Alexander Lavrentiev; Soviet artistic photography, by Valery Stigneev; A western view, by Grant Kester.

Index, p.226–31.

O183 Photography in Russia, 1840–1940. Ed. by David Elliott. [London], Thames and Hudson, [1992]. 256p. il. (part col.)

Catalog of the exhibition, Museum of Modern Art, Oxford (1992), and other locations.

Contents: The photograph in Russia: icon of a new age, by David Elliot; The first photographs in Russia, by Elena Barkhatova; Julius Fritzsche's report on the first photographs in Russia, [by Julius Fritzsche]; Early masters of Russian photography, by Tat'iana Saburova; Realism and document: photography as fact, by Elena Barkhatova; Pictorialism: photography as art, by Elena Barkhatova; Photo-dreams of the avant-garde, by Aleksandr Lavrentiev; The dilemma of the avant-garde: the new photography of the 1920s, by Klaus Honnef.

Chronology, p.79. Catalogue, p.225–52. Glossary, p.253–54. Bibliography, p.255–56.

O184 Shudakov, Grigory; Suslova, Olga; and Ukhtomskaya, Lilya. Pioneers of Soviet photography. [N.Y.], Thames and Hudson, [1983]. 255p. il., plates.

Trans. of Pionniers de la photographie russe sovietique. A later publication, 20 Sowjetische Photographen = 20 Soviet photographers = 20 photographes soviétiques = 20 Sowjet fotografen: 1917–1940 (Amsterdam, Fiolet and Draaijer Interfoto, 1990) contains the same text, but fewer illustrations.

Presentation of the work of 20 major photographers serves as a useful survey of the years 1917–1940. Shudakov's laudatory essay is supported by notes on the photographs.

Biographies, by Aleksandr Lavrentiev, p.249–52. Bibliography, p.253. Index, p.254–55.

O185 Tschechische Avantgarde-Fotografie, 1918–1948. Konzeption und Auswahl der Fotografien, Vladimír Birgus. [Stuttgart], Arnoldsche, 1999. 303p. il. plates (part col.)

Catalog of the exhibition, Staatliches Museum für Angewandte Kunst, Munich (1999). Ten essays provide analysis of Czechoslovakian photography and pictorialism, collage, abstract, and non-figurative tendencies, the Neue Sachlichkeit, advertising, Surrealism, social documentary photography, and book jacket design.

Chonologie der tschechischen Kunst 1918–1948, p.273–76. Chronologie der tschechischen Fotografie 1918–1948, p.277–82. Künstler-Biographien, p.283–96. Literatur, p.297–300. Register, p.301–03.

O186 Tschechoslowakische Fotografie der Gegenwart. Mit Beitr. von Vladimír Birgus und Reinhold Misselbeck. Köln, Museum Ludwig; Heidelberg, Ed. Braus, 1990. 168p. il. (part col.)

Catalog of the exhibition, Museum Ludwig (1990). Surveys Czech photography through 1990. Includes a helpful chronology of the period 1945–1990.

Biografien, p.162–68.

Scandinavia

O187 Friedman, Martin . . . [et. al.] The Frozen image: Scandinavian photography. Introd. essays by Martin Friedman. With contrib. by Henning Bender . . . [et al.] Minneapolis, Walker Art Center; N.Y., Abbeville, 1982. 207p. il. (part col.)

Catalog of the exhibition, Walker Art Center (1982), and other locations. An imporant assessment.

Contents: The endless vista; Beyond the arctic circle; Nomads and settlers; The early urbanists; Portraits; The painter's lens; The event; Scandinavia today.

Chronology, p.191–97. Bibliography, p.198. Photographers in the exhibition, p.199–201. Lenders to the exhibition, p.204–05.

O188 Kukkonen, Jukka; Vuorenmaa, Tuomo-Juhani; and Hinkka, Jorma. Valokuvan taide: Suomalainen valokuva 1842–1992. Helsinki, Suomalaisen Kirjillasuuden Seura, 1992. 478p. il. (part col.) (VB-valokuvakeskuksen julkaisuja, 2) (Suomalaisen kirjallisuuden seuran toimituksia, 559)
Added t.p. in English: Finnish photography, 1842–1992. Text in Finnish with an English translation by Michael Wynne-Ellis.
Substantial survey of Finnish photography over 150 years. Bibliography, p.431–35. Index, p.472–76.

O189 Nordberg, Kai, ed. Suomalainen valokuvataide, 1842–1986 = Finländsk fotokonst, 1842–1986 = Finnish photography, 1842–1986. Helsinki, Suomen valokuvataiteen museon säätïo, 1986. 182, [27]p. il. (Valokuvauksen vuosikirja, 1986)
Text in Finnish, Swedish, and English. Catalog of the exhibition, Helsingen taidehalli (1986), devoted to Finnish photography. Mostly plates.

O190 Sølv og salte: fotografi og forskning. Red. af Tove Hansen. København, Kongelige Bibliotek; Rhodos, 1990. 335p. il. (part col.)
Text in Danish, Swedish, and English; summaries in English.
Articles dealing with the founding of (mainly Danish) collections of photography, photographic history, and photography as an art form.
Noter samt oversaettelser af de fremmedsprogede artikler, se oversigt, p.270–320. Resumes, p.321–27. Forfatterpraesentationer, p.329. Register, p.331–35.

Spain and Portugal

O191 Congreso de Historia de la Fotografía Española (1st: 1986: Sevilla, Spain). Historia de la fotografía española, 1839–1986. Ed. prep. por Miguel Angel Yáñez Polo, Luis Ortiz Lara, José Manuel Holgado Brenes. Sevilla, Publicación de la Sociedad de Historia de la Fotografía Española, [1986]. 648p. il. (part col.)
Proceedings of the congress on the history of Spanish photography, Sevilla (1986). Accompanied by an exhibition and catalog, Historia de la fotografía española, 1839–1950.
Censo de autores cuyas obras fotograficas se exponen, con lugar y año basico de trabajo, p.9–18.

O192 Fontanella, Lee. La historia de la fotografía en España desde sus origenes hasta 1900. Madrid, El Viso, 1981. 288p. il. (part col.)
Overview of 20th-century Spanish photography.
Contents: (I) Antecedentes prefotográficos en España desde mediados del siglo XVIII; (II) La época del daguerrotipo; (III) Los métodos postdaguerrotípicos y la fotografía de Clifford; (IV) La fotografía de la reforma de la Puerta del Sol y la fotografía industrial y científica en décadas posteriores; (V) Manuel Castellano y su círclo fotográfico íntimo; Laurent y la comercialización de la fotografía; (VI) El retrato y sus diversas modalidades; (VII) Algunos fotógrafos y fotografías de provincias; Una mirada hacia el siglo XX; Apéndices [lists of 19th-century photographers in Spain, brief bibliography; notes].
Indice onomástico, p.284–[87].

O193 Mondéjar, Publio López. Las fuentes de la memoria. [Barcelona], [Lunwerg Editores], [1989–1996]. 3v. il., plates, ports. (part col.)
Impressive effort covering photography in Spain from the earliest days to the 1970s. Each well-illustrated vol. includes an extensive essay, a section of portraits and biography on the photographers presented, a comparative chronology citing events in photography, politics, and culture and society, and an index.
Contents: (1) Fotografía y sociedad en la España del siglo XIX (1989); (2) Fotografía y sociedad en España, 1900–1939 (1992); (3) Fotografía y sociedad en la España de Franco (1996).
Includes chronology and index in each vol.

O194 ———. Historia de la fotografía en España. Barcelona, Lunwerg Editores, 1997. 302p. il., facsims., ports.
Narrative history of Spanish photography, by an authority. Handsomely produced.
Notas, p.265–80. Glosario técnico, p.281–86. Bibliografía, p.287–89. Índice onomástico, p.291–302.

O195 Portuguese photography since 1854: Livro de Viagens. Ed. by M. Tereza Siza and Peter Weiermair. Texts by Jose Sarmento de Matos . . . [et al.] Kilchberg/Zurich, Switzerland, Edition Stemmle, 1998. 236p. chiefly il. (part col.)
Text in English; legends also in Portuguese. Accompanies the exhibition Livro de Viagens, Frankfurter Kunstverein (1997). "The constant factor is various interpretations of travel, some more introspective and/or conceptual, others more directly related to the situation of the Portuguese. . . . Contemporary photography has a substantial presence in this exhibition."—*p.[5].*
Biographies, p.215–36.

O196 The Spanish vision: contemporary art photography, 1970–1990 = La vision española: fotografia contemporanea de autor, 1970–1990. Sel. and catalogue by George L. Aguirre. N.Y., Spanish Institute, 1992. 212p. il. (part col.)
Catalog of the exhibition, Spanish Institute (1991). Useful survey of recent Spanish photographers.
Selected bibliography, p.29.

Switzerland

O197 Perret, René. Frappante Aehnlichkeit: Pioniere der Schweizer Photography: Bilder der Anfänge. Brugg, BEA + Poly-Verlags AG, 1991. 104p. il. (part col.)
"Sonderband zum 700 jährigen Jubiläum der Eidgenossenschaft." Photographs from the Swiss Photo Collection.
Anmerkungen, p.90. Glossar photographischer Techniken, p.91–92. Photographenverzeichnis, p.93–101. Bibliographie, p.102. Register, p.102–03.

O198 Photographie in der Schweiz von 1840 bis heute. [Gesamtred., Hugo Loetscher. Textred., George Sütterlin. Bildred., Walter Binder.] Bern, Benteli, 1992. 362p. il. (part col.) (Schweizer Photographie, 7)

Beautifully illustrated survey, superseding the exhibition catalog of the same title (1974), also ed. by Loetscher.

Contents: Die Anfänge; Das Porträt; Das Bildnis des Menschen im Wandel der Photographie; Reisephotographie; Natur und Umwelt; Das neue Sehen; Moment, Bewegung und Montage; Der Photojournalismus; Inszenierung und Experiment; Das jüngste Jahrzehnt; Anhang.

Phototechnische Fachausdrücke, p.292–95. Textanmerkungen, p.296–99. Namensverzeichnis, p.300–04. Herausgeber und Mitarbeiter, p.306–07. Schweizer Photographinnen und Photographen von A–Z, p.[309]–62.

United States

O199 America and the daguerreotype. Ed. by John Wood. Iowa City, Univ. of Iowa Pr., 1991. 273p. il., 100 plates (part col.)

Contents: The American portrait, by John Wood; The alternative aesthetic: the Langenheim Brothers and the introduction of the calotype in America, by Dolores A. Kilgo; Landscape in limbo, by John R. Stilgoe; Sex, death, and daguerreotypes, by David E. Stannard; The progress of civilization: the American occupational daguerreotype, by Brooks Johnson; Captured without resistance: a social view of the American militia, by John F. Graf; Silver plates on a golden shore, by Peter E. Palmquist; The contemporary daguerreotype, by Jeanne Verhulst.

Annotated list of plates, p.239–70. Bibliography, p.273.

O200 Amon Carter Museum of Western Art. Catalogue of the Amon Carter Museum photography collection. [Comp. by] Carol E. Roark, Paula Ann Stewart, and Mary Kennedy McCabe. Fort Worth, The Museum, 1993. xi, 703p. il.

"This publication is devoted to the most actively used exhibition prints, numbering almost 6,000 works by over 350 different photographers, and features acquisitions up to 1988. The works in this volume cover the broad scope of American photography, beginning with the medium's infancy."—*Introd.*

Bibliography, p.679–701.

O201 Bush, Alfred L., and Mitchell, Lee Clark. The photograph and the American Indian. Princeton, Princeton Univ. Pr., 1994. 334p., 311 plates. (part col.)

Primarily illustrated catalog of the exhibition, Princeton University (1985). "The photograph and the American Indian," by Lee Clark Mitchell, provides a succinct introduction to topic and related photographic and cultural issues.

Biographies of photographers, p.295–317. Bibliography, p.319–34.

O202 Carlebach, Michael L. The origins of photojournalism in America. Washington, D.C., Smithsonian Institution, [1992]. 194p. il., plates.

Primarily a technological and episodic survey covering the period 1839–1880. Well-illustrated with several examples of photographs and the engravings made from them.

Contents: (1) Daguerreotypes and the printed page; (2) Paper prints for the masses; (3) Photographs of war; (4) The West as photo opportunity; (5) Dry plates and halftones.

Glossary, p.[169]–70. Notes, p.171–83. Bibliography, 184–89. Index, p.191–94.

O203 Documenting America, 1935–1943. Ed. by Carl Fleischhauer and Beverly W. Brannan. Berkeley, Univ. of California Pr. in assoc. with the Library of Congress, 1988. 361p., plates.

All illustrations from the Farm Security Administration-Office of War Information Collection at the Library of Congress. Excellent introduction and analysis of the FSA-OWI projects.

Contents: The historian and the icon: photography and the history of the American people in the 1930s and 1940s, by Lawrence W. Levine; From image to story: reading the file, by Alan Trachtenberg; Photographic series [fifteen photographic series with brief explanatory essays].

The FSA-OWI collection, p.330–42. Bibliography, p.343–51. Photograph negative numbers, p.353–55. Index, p.357–61.

O204 Fleming, Paula Richardson, and Luskey, Judith. The North American Indians in early photographs. N.Y., Harper and Row, 1986. 256p., plates, map, ports. (Repr.: 1988; N.Y., Barnes and Noble, 1992)

Extensively illustrated overview of relations between Indians and whites during the 19th century, with an emphasis on the use of photography to record those interactions. More historical detail, less interpretation, than Bush and Mitchell, The photograph and the American Indian (GLAH 2:O201).

Timeline of American-Indian relations, p.10–11. Bibliography, p.248–53.

O205 Green, Jonathan. American photography: a critical history since 1945 to the present. Pictures sel. and sequenced by Jonathan Green and James Friedman. N.Y. Abrams, 1984. 247p. il. (part col.)

"In this book I have chosen to deal for the most part with the history the photographs themselves have made, not with the history or biographies of the photographers."—*p.10.*

Contents: (1) Photography and the American imagination; (2) Photography as popular culture: The Family of Man; (3) The search for a new vision; (4) Aperture in the Fifties: the word and the way; (5) The Americans: politics and alienation; (6) Surrogate reality; (7) Straight shooting in the Sixties; (8) The Sixties as subject; (9) The painter as photographer; (10) Photography as printmaking; (11) The new American frontier; (12) The new American Luminism; (13) Only a language experiment; (14) The political reconstruction of photography; (15) Scientific realism.

Selected bibliography, p.230–37. Index, p.243–47.

O206 Points of view, the stereograph in America: a cultural history. Ed. by Edward W. Earle. Rochester, Visual Studies Workshop Pr., 1979. 119p. il., plates (part col.)

Excellent interpretive cultural analysis of this popular photographic form.

Contents: Display as discourse, by Nathan Lyons; The stereograph in America: pictorial antecedents and cultural perspectives, by Edward W. Earle; Interpretive chronology: stereos, American history and popular culture 1850–1914; Stereographs: local, national and international art worlds, by Howard S. Becker; White Mountain stereographs and the development of a collective vision, by Thomas Southall; Pasteboard masks, the stereograph in American culture 1865–1910, by Harvey Green.

Bibliography, p.116–19.

O207 Rinhart, Floyd, and Rinhart, Marion. The American daguerreotype. Athens, Univ. of Georgia Pr., 1981. 446p. il., col. plates.

The standard scholarly survey, extensively illustrated and citing numerous contemporaneous sources. In two sections, the first a historical survey, the second devoted to topical studies (e.g., plates, apparatus, and processes; art influences; miniature cases).

Biographies, p.[379]–421. List of plate hallmarks, p.[423]–25. U.S. patent records, p.[426]–27. Bibliographic notes, p.[429]–38. Dictionary, p.[439.] Index, p.[441]–46.

O208 Stange, Maren. Symbols of ideal life: social documentary photography in America, 1890–1950. N.Y., Cambridge Univ. Pr., 1989. xvii, 190p. il.

Concerned with the dissemination of photographs as reform publicity.

Contents: (1) From sensation to science: documentary photography at the turn of the century; (2) The Pittsburgh survey: Lewis Hine and the establishment of documentary style; (3) "Symbols of ideal life": Tugwell, Stryker, and the FSA Photography Project; (4) In conclusion: Stryker, Steichen, and the search for "a good, honest photograph."

Notes, p.149–77. Index, p.179–90.

AFRICA, OCEANIA, THE AMERICAS

Africa

O209 Anthologie de la photographie africaine et de l'Océan Indien. [Par] Revue Noire. Sous la dir. de Pascal Martin Saint Léon. Avec N'Gone Fall . . . [et al.] Paris, Ed. Revue Noire, 1998. 432p. il.

Beautifully illustrated overview of photography in Africa.

Contents: Approches; Le premier âge; Les portraitistes; L'éveil d'un regard; Les agences officielles; Les images du réel; La recherche d'une esthétique; Océan indien; Diaspora.

Biographies des photographes, p.426–29. Bibliographie, p.430–31.

O210 In/sight: African photographers, 1940 to the present. [Curated by Clare Bell . . . (et al.)] N.Y., Guggenheim Museum (Distr. by Abrams, 1996). 275p. il., plates (part col.), ports.

Catalog of the exhibition, Guggenheim Museum (1996). With coverage of 30 African photographers.

Contents: Introduction, by Clare Bell; Colonial imaginary, tropes of disruption: history, culture, and representation in the works of African photographers, by Okwui Enwezor and Octavia Zaya; A critical presence: Drum magazine in context, by Okwui Enwezor; Photography and the substance of the image, by Olu Oguibe.

Bibliography, p.250. Artists' biographies, statements, and works in the exhibition, p.[253]–75.

ASIAN COUNTRIES

China

O211 Chung-kuo she ying i shu tso pin hsuan 1949–1989: selected works of the Chinese photographic art. Fuchou, Hai chao she ying i shu chu pan she, 1989. 286p. il. (part col.)

An anthology of Chinese photography, color and black-and-white. No commentary.

O212 Hu, Chih-ch'uan, and Ch'en, Shen. Chung-kuo tsao ch'i she ying tso p'in hsuan, 1840–1919 [= A collection of pictures of early-period Chinese photography, 1840–1919]. [Beijing], Chung-kuo she ying ch'u pan she, 1987. 16, 174p. il. (part col.)

Text (preface, tables of contents, legends) in Chinese and English.

An introductory essay is followed by about 200 photographs representing work by Chinese photographers, pictures taken in China by foreign photographers, and pictures taken by Chinese photographers while abroad. None of the photographers are identified although the works are captioned and presented in chronological order. Some photographs of historical events or personages are included but the emphasis of the book is on representing Chinese social life.

O213 Worswick, Clark, and Spence, Jonathan. Imperial China: photographs, 1850–1912: historical texts. [Reprint.] Canberra, Australian National Univ. Pr., 1980. 151p. il.

Reprint of GLAH 1:O110; reprint reissued simultaneously in Great Britain by Scolar Pr.

India, Nepal, Pakistan, Tibet

O214 Desmond, Ray. Victorian India in focus: a selection of early photographs from the collection in the India Office Library and Records. London, H.M.S.O., 1982. 100p. il.

"I have selected photographs which illustrate people, places and events and also some which, I hope, convey a feeling of the quality of life in India in Victorian times. . . . I have included a few Burmese photographs and one of Ceylon."—*Introd.* A photographic anthology, without commentary.

Contents: The Indian scene; Princes and peasants; Campaigns and conquests; Sahibs and memsahibs.

O215 Gutman, Judith Mara. Through Indian eyes. N.Y., Oxford Univ. Pr.; International Center of Photography, 1982. xii, 198p. il. (part col.)

Catalog of the exhibition, International Center of Photography (1982), and other locations, seeking to contextualize early photography in India. "Gutman's major theme is the use to which the non-Westernized, Indian, artist/photographer, has put an invention, the camera," in the late 19th and early 20th centuries.—*Pref.*

Contents: (1) Culture and photography; (2) Conceptual foundations; (3) Miniatures, perception, and form; (4) Who were the photographers?; (5) Painted photographs; (6) The many layers of culture.

Bibliography, p.189–94. Index, p.195–98.

O216 Thomas, G. History of photography, India, 1840–1980. [Hyderabad], Andhra Pradesh State Akademi of Photography, 1981. 87p. il., plates.

Attempts to map unexplored territory.

References and notes, p.[57]–74. Directory of books on India with genuine photographs, p.[65]–82. Index, p.[83]–87.

Japan

O217 Japan Photographers Association. A century of Japanese photography. N.Y., Pantheon Books, 1980. 385p. il. (part col.)

Trans. of Nihon Shashin Shi, 1840–1945. Tokyo, Heobon Sha, [1971].

The 17-page introduction by John W. Dower traces the history of Japanese photography from the 1850s through the mid-1940s. More than 500 photographs follow, each captioned with a title and date and, frequently, with the photographer's name. The work is organized into broad topics, e.g., commercial photography, art photography, records of war.

O218 Nihon shashin zenshū [= The complete history of Japanese photography]. Tokyo, Shogakkan, [1985–88]. 12v. il. (part col.)

Japanese text and illustration notes. Each vol. includes a brief English summary of the contents.

Covering the major periods, movements, trends and styles of photography in Japan, this 12-vol. set is the most comprehensive work to date on photography in Japan. Organized thematically, each vol. contains a scholarly essay on its topic and each is profusely illustrated.

Contents: (1) The origins of photography in Japan; (2) The heritage of art photography in Japan; (3) The modern photography movement in Japan; (4) War photography; (5) Figure and portrait; (6) Nude photography; (7) The pictured city; (8) Nature and landscape; (9) Culture and tradition; (10) Photojournalism; (11) Advertising photography; (12) New wave.

O219 Spielmann, Heinz. Die japanische Photographie: Geschichte, Themen, Strukturen. Köln, DuMont, [1984]. 264p. il. (part col.) (DuMont Foto, 5)

Four chapters on the history of Japanese photography from 1848 to 1982 are followed by chapters discussing topics depicted, and finally information about schools, associations, galleries and exhibitions, collections and museums, and biographies of 68 photographers.

P. Decorative and Applied Arts

This chapter is classified first by general works, then by the principal types of the decorative and applied arts. These sections are further classified, where expedient, into period and regional subdivisions. Costumes and textiles have been treated in particular depth in the belief that these related subjects are of special interest to the art historian; given the thematic overlap between the two subjects, cross-references have been kept to a minimum, the reader being urged to consult both sections in tandem.

BIBLIOGRAPHY

P1 American folk art: a guide to sources. Ed. by Simon J. Bronner. N.Y., Garland, 1984. xxxi, 313p. plates (Garland reference library of the humanities, 464)

Bibliography of folk art studies in America arranged by topic with annotations and introductory essays by specialist contributors. Introduction by the compiler traces the history of folk art scholarship from its origins to the present.

Contents: (A) Background and history; (B) Arts criticism and aesthetic philosophy; (C) Genres; (D) Biographies; (E) Region and locality; (F) Ethnicity and religion; (G) Afro-Americans; (H) Workers and trades; (I) Symbol, image, and theme; (J) Collectors and museums; (K) Educators and classrooms; (L) Films; (M) Topics on the horizon.

About the editor and contributors, p.xxix–xxxi. Author index, p.284–98. Subject index, p.[299]–313.

P2 Coulson, Anthony J. A bibliography of design in Britain 1851–1970. London, Design Council [Distr. by Heinemann, 1979]. 291p.

Broadly based introductory bibliography to "the more accessible works" in the field, including both contemporary and later writings on designers, exhibitions, competitions, and technological developments. Includes some periodical articles. No annotations, but brief explanatory introductions to each subject area.

Contents: (1) Table of important dates; (2) Fostering design; (3) Design and designers; (4) Areas of design activity; (5) Journals; (6) Bibliographies, indexes, abstracts, and catalogues; (7) Subject finder.

P3 De Winter, Patrick M. European decorative arts, 1400–1600: an annotated bibliography. Boston, Hall, 1988. xxxiv, 542p. (Reference publication in art history)

"In this volume have been gathered over twenty-two hundred annotated references to selected published material dealing with the various types of furnishings made for the church, the palace, and the home, as well as objects made for personal adornment, produced in Europe during the time that spans the late Gothic and Renaissance periods."—*Introd.* Authoritative, comprehensive, well-organized, fully annotated.

Author index, p.501–18. Subject index, p.519–35. Location index, p.537–43.

P4 Decorative arts and household furnishings in America, 1650–1920: an annotated bibliography. Ed. by Kenneth L. Ames and Gerald W. R. Ward. Winterthur, Del., Winterthur Museum [Distr. by the Univ. Pr. of Virginia, 1989]. 392p.

"Provides access and orientation to the study of household furnishings used in the United States from the seventeenth century to the early twentieth century. It is designed for use by the general public, collectors, college and university students, . . . the scholarly community, and librarians and other staff at a variety of cultural institutions."—*Introd.* Annotations and chapter introductions are by subject specialists. Introduction by Ames surveys state of current scholarship in the field.

Contents: (1) References and surveys; (2) Architecture; (3) Furniture; (4) Metals; (5) Ceramics and glass; (6) Textiles; (7) Timepieces; (8) Household activities and systems; (9) Artisans and culture.

Notes on contributors, p.359. Index, p.361–92.

P5 Design and applied arts index. v.1– Burwash, Eng., Design Documentation, 1988– . Updated quarterly.

Available in printed and CD-ROM eds. and via the internet. DAAI is an index of annotated references to articles found in more than 440 design and craft journals published between 1973 and the present; the majority of indexed articles are dated since 1987. Includes major and short articles, news items, book reviews, exhibitions, videos, conference reports, and obituary notices. Contains information on more than 40,000 designers, craftspeople, studios, workshops, and firms. Also includes four additional databases including an international directory of universities and colleges offering design and craft courses, an international directory of design and craft organizations, associations and societies, a directory of design and craft archives, and a directory of design and craft journals.

P6 Ehresman, Donald. Applied and decorative arts: a bibliographic guide. 2d ed. Englewood, Colo., Libraries Unlimited, 1993. xxxvii, 629p.

1st ed., 1977.

Annotated bibliography covering "those major works written in Western European languages and published in the past 100 years, and available in the major libraries of the United States For the second edition . . ., books published between 1975, the cut-off date for the first edition, and 1991, the cut-off date for the second edition have been surveyed, and 927 titles have been added. The literature published before 1975 has been reviewed afresh with the result that 349 titles have been added."—*Pref.* Arranged by media (general, ornament, folk art, arms and armor, ceramics, clocks, watches, automata, and scientific instruments, enamels, furniture, glass, ivory, jewelry, lacquer, medals and seals, metalwork, musical instruments, textiles, toys and dolls).

Author index, p.521–82. Subject index, p.583–629.

P7 Franklin, Linda Campbell. Antiques and collectibles: a bibliography of works in English, 16th century to 1976. Metuchen, N.J., Scarecrow, 1978. xxiii, 1091p.

Listing of more than 10,000 English-language references to books and catalogs documenting a wide range of topics, arranged by subject matter. Library locations provided for almost all pre-1925 imprints. No annotations; occasional contents notes. Geographic range of coverage is worldwide.

Bibliography, p.973–74. Subject index, p.975–1027. Author index, p.1028–91.

P8 Paris. Bibliothèque Forney. Catalogue matières: arts decoratifs, beaux-arts, métiers, et techniques. Paris, Société des Amis de la Bibliothèque Forney, 1970– . (3)v. in 7.

See GLAH 1:P5 for original annotation and first supplement.

Contents: Supplement: (2) L–Z (1980); Index alphabétique des auteurs (4v., 1982–83).

P9 Weisberg, Gabriel P., and Weisberg, Yvonne M. L. Japonisme: an annotated bibliography. Co-published with the International Center for Japonisme, The Jane Voorhees Zimmerli Art Museum, Rutgers University. N.Y., Garland, 1990. xxviii, 445p. il.

Well-annotated bibliography covering the history of Japanese art's influence on the arts of the west since the 1850s, in books, catalogs, articles, dissertations, and reviews.

Author index, p.405–13. Subject index, p.414–45.

DIRECTORIES

P10 Maloney, David J., Jr. Maloney's antiques and collectibles resource directory. 5th ed. Dubuque, Iowa, Antique Trader, 1999. xxiv, 856p. Biannual.

Originally published as Collector's information clearinghouse antiques & collectibles resource directory.

Valuable for collectors. Includes indexes.

DICTIONARIES AND ENCYCLOPEDIAS

P11 Arminjon, Catherine. Objets civils domestique: vocabulaire. Paris, Imprim. nationale, 1984. xxiii, 632p. il. (part col.) (Principes d'analyse scientifique)

Well-illustrated dictionary of everyday household objects, excluding furniture, used in France from ca.1400 to World War I, classified by function. Entries include synonyms and specific bibliographic references as appropriate. Illustrated with extant examples from French collections and period sources. A project of the Inventaire general des monuments et des richesses artistiques de la France (see GLAH 1:I280, GLAH 2:I314)

Contents: (I) L'alimentation; (II) La toilette; (III) Les soins medicaux domestiques; (IV) L'entretien de la maison; (V) L'entretien du linge; (VI) L'éclairage; (VII) L'âtre; (VIII) Le chauffage; (IX) Le decor; (X) Écrire; (XI) Fumer et priser; (XII) Les objets a ouvrage; (XIII) Les ensembles; (XIV) Les elements de structure.

Bibliographie, p.xv–xxiii. Index, p.606–25. Liste des provenances, p.626–29.

P12 Fleming, John, and Honour, Hugh. The Penguin dictionary of decorative arts. New ed. [N.Y.] Viking Penguin, [1990]. 934p. il., col. plates.

See GLAH 1:P16 for 1st ed.

Completely revised and expanded ed. of the essential dictionary of Western decorative arts, focusing chiefly on domestic furniture and furnishings. Selective entries for such non-Western arts as carpets and ceramics.

Bibliographical abbreviations, p.913–17. Ceramic marks, p.[919]–27. Hall-marks on silver, p.[929]–31. Makers' marks on silver and pewter, p.[933]–[35].

P13 Haslam, Malcolm. Marks and monograms: the decorative arts, 1880–1960. Rev. and enl. ed. London, Collins and Brown, 1995. 448p. il.

1st ed., Marks and monograms of the modern movement, 1875–1930. N.Y., Scribner, 1977.

Marks, monograms, and signatures of artists, designers, and manufacturers in the applied arts. Arrangement is by medium, and then by country and alphabetically by name.

Contents: Ceramics; Glass; Metalwork and Jewelry; Graphics; Furniture and textiles.

Index, p.412–48.

P14 Prather-Moses, Alice Irma. The international dictionary of women workers in the decorative arts: a historical survey from the distant past to the early decades of the twentieth century. Metuchen, N.J., Scarecrow, 1981. xvii, 200p.

Succinct biographical entries for women craftspersons and entrepreneurs.

Sources consulted, p.xi–xvii. Index of subjects, p.181–200 [lists biographies by type of product or by company, in the case of ceramics decorators].

P15 Savage, George. Dictionary of 19th century antiques and later objets d'art. N.Y., Putnam, 1979. xi, 401p. il., col. plates.

Includes "discussion of styles, materials, processes, manufacturers, designers, and artists, and deals with those subjects most likely to be of interest to the collector."—*Pref.* Major emphasis is on 19th-century England but entries cover European and American material as well. Appendix I: English and Scottish silver marks. Appendix II: British Registry marks. Appendix III: Art forgery in the 19th century.

Bibliography, p.390–401.

HISTORIES AND HANDBOOKS

P16 Ball, Victoria Kloss. Architecture and interior design: a basic history through the 17th century. N.Y., Wiley, [1980]. xiii, 448p. il., col. plates.

Broad survey of domestic interiors and furnishings from prehistory through 17th-century England, with emphasis on stylistic interrelationships. Reflects author's long experience in academic interior design instruction. Continued by the following title.

General references, p. 411–18. Notes, p.419–22. Index, p.423–48.

P17 ———. Architecture and interior design: Europe and America from the colonial era to today. N.Y., Wiley, [1980]. xvii, 442p. il., col. plates.

Continuation of the preceding title, with similar emphasis. Primary focus is on the domestic setting in England, France, Italy, and the United States.

General references, p.399–409. Notes, p.411–15. Index, p.417–42.

P18 British Museum. Catalogue of the Waddesdon Bequest in the British Museum. [By] Hugh Tait. London, British Museum Publications, 1986– . (3)v.

Projected 5-vol. scholarly catalog of Baron Ferdinand de Rothschild's collection of Renaissance courtly objects.

Contents: (1) The jewels; (2) The silver plate; (3) The curiosities.

P19 The Country Life antiques handbook: G. Bernard Hughes, Therle Hughes, Judith Banister . . . [et al.] [Twickenham], Country Life Books [Distr. by Hamlyn, 1986]. 832p. il., col. plates.

Comprehensive survey of antiques aimed at the beginning collector. Articles by experts are confined to British examples, with the exception of glass, which covers all periods and cultures. Illustrated primarily with line drawings and diagrams.

Contents: Furniture; Clocks; Silver; China; Glass; Small collectibles. Appendices: List of clockmakers; Some useful dates; Weights and measures; the Patent Office Design Registry.

Bibliography, p.794–800. Index, p.801–32.

P20 Dirsztay, Patricia. Church furnishings: a NADFAS guide. London, Routledge and Kegan Paul, 1978. [ix], 246p. il.

Useful, well-illustrated visual guide and glossary to church architecture and decorative elements in Britain, compiled under the auspices of the National Association of Decorative and Fine Arts Societies. Especially helpful for symbolism, heraldry and decorative elements. Includes furniture, textiles, metalwork, and architecture; widely applicable to secular decorative art as well. Many line drawings and diagrams keyed to text.

Index, p.238–46.

P21 Gombrich, E. H. The sense of order: a study in the psychology of decorative art. Ithaca, Cornell Univ. Pr., [1979]. xi, 410p. il. (part col.), plates (The Wrightsman Lectures)

Magisterial series of essays on the decorative elements of pictorial art in all cultures, by a distinguished art historian.

Notes, p.[307]–23. Full titles of books cited, p.389–90. Index, p.[401]–11.

P22 J. Paul Getty Museum. Decorative arts: an illustrated summary catalogue of the collections of the J. Paul Getty Museum. [By] Charissa Bremer-David . . . [et al.] [Rev. and exp. ed.] Malibu, The Museum, 1993. 308p.

1st ed. 1986 titled Decorative arts: a handbook of the collections of the J. Paul Getty Museum. Includes many objects added since 1984 to a collection known for its rich holdings in European decorative arts. Objects are grouped by country of origin and then chronologically, with supporting information on materials, provenance, and bibliography. While most entries are for objects originating in continental Europe, includes chapters devoted to English and to Asian arts.

Index of makers, p.290–95. Index of previous owners, p.296–308.

P23 The James A. de Rothschild Collection at Waddesdon Manor. Fribourg, Office du Livre for the National Trust. 1967– . (9)v. il., plates (some fold., part col.)

See GLAH 1:P19 for original annotation and previous vols.

Contents: (8) Charleston, R. J. and Archer, Michael. Glass and stained glass (1977); (9) Marcheix, Madeleine, and Charleston, R. J. Limoges and other painted enamels (1977); (10) Verlet, Pierre. The Savonnerie: its history; The Waddesdon Collection (1982); (11) Pons, Bruno. Waddesdon manor, architecture and panelling (1996)

P24 London. Victoria and Albert Museum. Pattern and design: designs for the decorative arts, 1480–1980: with an index to designers' drawings in the Victoria and Albert Museum. Ed. by Susan Lambert. [London], The Museum, [1983]. xi, 196p. il. (part col.)

Catalog of the exhibition, Victoria and Albert Museum (1983). Serves also as an extensive index to the Museum's collection of design drawings. Fields covered in the collection include architecture, ceramics, fans, furniture, gardens, interior design, jewelry, metalwork, ornament, sculpture, stained glass, textiles, theater, and transport. Individual entries on renderings illustrated are by museum staff.

Contents: (1) Drawn and printed source material; (2) The adaptation of designs to different materials and styles; (3) Drawings and prints as sources of information; (4) The Museum's collections as a grammar of design.

Indexes to designers' drawings in the Victoria and Albert Museum, p.145–96.

P25 Materials and techniques in the decorative arts: an illustrated dictionary. Ed. by Lucy Trench. [Chicago], Univ. of Chicago Pr., [2000]. ix, 572p. il., 18 col. plates.

Comprehensive dictionary by specialist contributors focusing on English-language terminology for processes and materials used to create decorative arts objects of all cultures through the end of the 20th century. Cross-referenced throughout text.

Bibliography, p.[558]–69.

P26 McCorquodale, Charles. History of the interior. N.Y., Vendome [Distr. by Viking, 1983]. 224p. il. (part col.)

British ed., The history of interior decoration. London, John Calmann and Cooper, 1983.

Survey of the interior from the classical world to the 20th century, aimed at a general audience.

Glossary, p.220–21. Bibliography, p.221–22. Index, p.223–24.

P27 Museum Boymans-van Beuningen, Rotterdam. Afdeling Kunstnijverheid en Vormgeving = Department of Applied Arts and Design. Kunstnijverheid Middeleeuwen en Renaissance = Decorative art Middle Ages and Renaissance. Amsterdam, De Bataafsche Leeuw, 1994. 319p. il. (part col).

In Dutch and English. Fully illustrated catalog of a portion of the Museum's permanent collection of applied arts, arranged by period and by type of object. Artifacts are primarily European and represent a range of household furnishings and everyday objects.

Contents: A brief history of the Department of Decorative Art and Design; Middle Ages (ca.1000–ca.1500); Renaissance, South Europe; Renaissance, North-West Europe.

P28 Smithsonian Institution. Finders' guide to decorative arts in the Smithsonian Institution. [By] Christine Minter-Dowd. Washington, D.C., Smithsonian Institution, 1984. 213p. il.

Succinct guide to decorative arts holdings of 50 divisions and collections of the Smithsonian Museum, including archeological, technological, and ethnological artifacts. Catalog is arranged by office or collection. Descriptions are primarily in essay form, and include bibliographical references and information on access and finding aids.

Index, p.145–73. Location guide to artists, designers, makers, manufacturers, production centers, and retailers [in the eight major decorative arts collections of the Smithsonian], p.175–213.

SEE ALSO: Collections of the National Gallery of Art, systematic catalogue (GLAH 2:M31).

ISLAMIC

P29 Rogers, J. M. Islamic art and design, 1500–1700. [London], British Museum, [1983]. 167p. il. (part col.), map.

Catalog of the exhibition, British Museum (1983). Covers Islamic painting and decorative arts of the Mughal, Safavid, and Ottoman Empires. Includes general interpretive essays and entries for 213 individual objects.

P30 Tulips, arabesques, and turbans: decorative arts from the Ottoman Empire. Ed. by Yanni Petsopoulos. N.Y., Abbeville, 1982. 224p. il. (part col.), map.

Published in conjunction with the exhibition, Leighton House, London (1982).

Contents: Introduction: the Ottoman style; The Ottoman milieu, by Godfrey Goodwin; Metalwork: silver and gold, by Julian Raby, Copper, brass and steel, by James Allan; Ceramics, by John Carswell; Textiles, by Walter Denny; Calligraphy-Husni-i-Hat, by Heath Lowry; Painting, by Ernst Grube.

Analysis of Ottoman metalwork, by A. M. Pollard, p.217. Footnotes, p.218–21. Bibliography, p.221–23. Index, p.224.

RENAISSANCE—MODERN

P31 Art and design in Europe and America, 1800–1900. Introd. by Simon Jervis. N.Y., Dutton, [1987]. 224p. il. (part col.)

Commemorates the opening of a gallery at the Victoria and Albert Museum, devoted to a survey of 19th-century Western decorative arts. "Represents an anthology of the gallery, a handbook to its contents, and an episodic survey of nineteenth-century art and design in Europe and America."—*Foreword.* Introductory essay discusses related English examples. Chronologically arranged entries for 100 objects selected from the gallery's holdings, by museum staff, include illustrations and bibliographical references.

Bibliography, p.220–21. Index, p.222–24.

P32 Bayley, Stephen, Garner, Philippe, and Sudjic, Deyan. Twentieth-century style and design. N.Y., Van Nostrand Reinhold, [1986]. 320p. il. (part col.)

Well-illustrated survey aimed at a general audience. Narrative texts cover architecture and urban design, decorative arts, and industrial design separately within successive time periods from 1900 to the present. Includes biographies of major figures.

Select biographies, p.298–305. Select bibliography, p.306–07. Index, p.308–19.

P33 British Museum. Decorative arts, 1850–1950: a catalogue of the British Museum Collection. [By] Judy Rudoe. [London], British Museum Pr., [1991]. 312p. il., 26 col. plates.

Thorough, well-documented catalog of the Museum's collection of more than 300 pieces of metalwork, ceramics, and glass from Britain, Europe, and America produced between 1850 and 1950. Arrangement is by designer or manufacturer.

Designers and companies with entries in the catalogue, p.11–12. Bibliography, p.134–42. List of comparative illustrations, p.289–90. Index of marks, monograms and signatures, p.291–303. Concordance of register and catalogue numbers, p.304–06. Index of contemporary exhibitions, p.307. Index, p.308–12.

P34 Callen, Anthea. Women artists of the arts and crafts movement, 1870–1914. N.Y., Pantheon, [1979]. [viii], 232p. il.

British ed. titled Angel in the studio: women in the arts and crafts movement 1870–1914. London, Architectural Pr., 1979.

"This book hopes to provide . . . a broader knowledge of the real nature of the Arts and Crafts movement while throwing new light on the social and economic circumstances of middle-class women workers at the turn of the nineteenth century."—*Pref.*

Contents: Introduction: class structure and the Arts and Crafts elite; Design education for women; Ceramics; Embroidery and needlework; Lacemaking; Jewellery and metalwork; Woodcarving, furniture and interior design; Handprinting, book-binding and illustration; Conclusion: Feminism, art and political conflict; Appendix I: Biographical notes on selected craftswomen; Appendix II: A comparative note on women's wages.

Select bibliography, p.228–29. Index, p.230–32.

P35 Calloway, Stephen. Twentieth century decoration, 1900–1980. N.Y., Rizzoli, 1988. 407p. il. (part col.)

Thorough, authoritative examination of the many aspects of 20th-century interior decoration in England, Europe, and the United States, by a curator and design historian. More than 500 contemporary prints, photographs, and paintings of interiors, with commentaries on each.

Contents: Introduction: Taste, fashion, and the way rooms change; Before 1900: The legacies of the past; 1900–1920: The avant-garde and the revival of period styles; 1920–1930: The lure of antiques and the modern style; 1930–1945: Pleasing decay and the all-white room; 1945–1960: Austerity and the new look; 1960–1980: Alternative lifestyles and reflecting success; 1980–1988: The cult of design and the new ornamentalism.

Index, p.403–08.

P36 Cumming, Elizabeth, and Kaplan, Wendy. The arts and crafts movement. [N.Y.], Thames and Hudson, [1991]. 216p. il. (part col.) (World of art).

Useful one-vol. survey of the arts and crafts movement in England, America, and Europe by two experts in the field.

Contents: (1) Sources and early ideals; (2) Architecture in Britain; (3) Studios, education and industry; (4) Regionalism in American architecture; (5) Arts and Crafts production in America; (6) The Arts and Crafts Movement on the continent; Postscript.

Select bibliography, p.208–11. List of illustrations, p.212–14. Index, p.215–16.

P37 Egyptomania: Egypt in western art, 1730–1930. [Par Jean-Marcel Humbert, Michael Pantazzi, Christiane Ziegler.] Paris, Réunion des Musées Nationaux; Ottawa, National Gallery of Canada, [1994]. 607p. il. (part col.)

Catalog of the exhibition, Musée du Louvre (1994), and other locations. Essays discuss Egyptomania from antiquity to the 20th century. Catalog illustrates almost 400 objects, principally 18th- and 19th-century, in many media. An appendix lists previous exhibits on this and relevant subjects.

Bibliography, p.583–96. Index of persons, p.601–06.

P38 The Encyclopedia of decorative arts, 1890–1940. Ed. by Philippe Garner. N.Y., Van Nostrand Reinhold, [1979]. 320p. il. (part col).

"The aim of this encyclopedia has been to cover the entire period in detail from the dual viewpoints of style and theory and of actual production."—*Introd.* Heavily illustrated narrative texts by specialists in each area. Topical organization.

Contents: (I) Styles and influences in the decorative arts: Art Nouveau, Art Deco, Modernism, Surrealism and Neo-Baroque, Revivalism, Industrial design; (II) Designs and designers: France, United Kingdom, United States, Germany and Austria, Belgium, The Netherlands, Scandinavia, Italy and Spain, Eastern Europe; (III) The background to the decorative arts: The great exhibitions, photography and the cinema, painting and the decorative arts, literature and the decorative arts.

Major craftsmen and designers, 1890–1940, p.306–09. Select bibliography, p.310–12. Glossary, p.313. Index, p.314–19.

P39 Fahr-Becker, Gabriele. Wiener Werkstaette 1903–1932. Köln, Taschen, 1994. 244p. il. (part col.)

Handsome survey of the furniture, glass, ceramics, silver and metalwork, jewelry, and fashion produced by this movement.

Biographien, p.222–37. Chronologie, p.238–39. Anmerkungen, p.240. Ausgewählte Bibliographie, p.241.

P40 Gere, Charlotte. Nineteenth-century decoration: the art of the interior. N.Y., Abrams, [1989]. 408p. il. (part col.)

Well-illustrated survey of the elite and middle-class interior in Britain, Europe, and America from 1800 to 1900, based on contemporary paintings, photographs, and design documents.

The working library of a nineteenth-century architect and designer: James O'Byrne, p.389–95. Biographical index of artists, designers, decorators, and architects, including their principal societies and firms, p.396–401. Index, p.404–08.

P41 ______, and Whiteway, Michael. Nineteenth-century design from Pugin to Mackintosh. [N.Y.], Abrams, [1994]. 312p. il.(part col.)

Heavily illustrated examination of 19th-century design and designers in social and cultural context, with particular emphasis on innovative design in Great Britain. Appendix of more than 100 biographies of principal designers and histories of major manufacturers.

Contents: (1) Reformed Gothic and engineering; (2) The Art Movement; (3) New beginnings and the Arts and Crafts Movement; Appendix of architects, designers and manufacturers.

Select bibliography, p.299–302. Index, p.306–12.

P42 ______. Nineteenth century interiors: an album of watercolors. Ed. by Joseph Focarino. [N.Y.], Thames and Hudson, [1992]. 167p. il. (part col.)

Catalog of the exhibition, Frick Collection (N.Y.) (1992). Includes views of 19th-century English and European interiors. Covers a range of countries and dwelling types. An excellent visual documentation of the period.

Select bibliography, p.167. Index of artists represented, p.167.

P43 The history of decorative arts. Pref. by Jacques Thuillier. Ed. by Alain Gruber. With the collab. of Margherita Azzi-Visentini . . . [et al.] N.Y., Abbeville, 1994– . (2)v. il. (part col.)

French ed., L'art decoratif en Europe. Paris, Citadelles and Mazenod, 1992–94. 3v.

Massive, well-illustrated 3-vol. survey of European decorative arts from the Renaissance through Art Nouveau, with contributions by a team of scholars.

Contents: (1) The Renaissance and Mannerism in Europe (1994); (2) Classicism and the Baroque in Europe (1996).

P44 Klein, Dan, and Bishop, Margaret. Decorative art, 1880–1980. Oxford, Phaidon/Christie's, [1986]. 263p. il. (part col.) (Christie's pictorial histories)

Largely pictorial treatment aimed at collectors and the general public, based on objects auctioned by Christie's in the 1980s. Includes prices realized.

Price list, p.[252]–56. Index, p.[257]–63.

P45 Miller, R. Craig. Modern design in the Metropolitan Museum of Art (1890–1990). Photographs by Mark Darley. N.Y., Metropolitan Museum of Art; Abrams, 1990. xiii, 312p. il. (part col.)

Sumptuous catalog of 125 representative examples of glass, ceramics, metalwork, lighting, furniture, costume, and related arts chosen from the collection of the Metropolitan Museum of Art, and accompanied by essays on the development of these arts and the formation of the Museum's holdings. Appendix A: Selected exhibitions held at the Metropolitan Museum of Art including modern design and architecture. Appendix B: Credits for chapter openings.

Index, p.309–12.

P46 Smith, Charles Saumarez. Eighteenth-century decoration: design and the domestic interior in England. London, Weidenfeld and Nicolson, 1993. 407p. il. (part col.), plates.

Important, richly illustrated study of the domestic visual environment as represented in period sources.

Notes, p.383–93. Bibliography, p.394–97. Index, p.398–407.

P47 Thornton, Peter. Authentic decor: the domestic interior, 1620–1920. [N.Y.], Viking, [1984]. 408p. il. (part col.)

Major contribution to the history of the interior, by a preeminent scholar, entirely illustrated from period sources. Wide-ranging, informative, international in scope, enjoyable to read; destined to be a standard reference for many years to come.

Index, p.398–408.

P48 ______. Form and decoration: innovation in the decorative arts, 1470–1870. London, Weidenfeld and Nicolson, 1998. 216p. il. (part col.), map.

"This book is a straightforward account of how style developed in the decorative arts between 1470 and 1870. It is primarily written for students of design history."—*Introd.* A regional and historical survey, focusing on the key international capitals.

Index, p.212–16.

P49 ______. The Italian renaissance interior, 1400–1600. N.Y., Abrams, 1991. 407p. il. (part col.)

Important study by a leading scholar, illustrated from period sources.

Contents: (1) The architectural shell and its embellishment; (2) Furnishings; (3) Architectural planning; (4) Creating the interior.

Inventories, p.363–65. Abbreviated titles, p.367. Notes, p.368–97. Index, p.398–407.

P50 ______. Seventeenth-century interior decoration in England, France and Holland. New Haven, Published for the Paul Mellon Centre for Studies in British Art by Yale Univ. Pr., 1978. xii, 427p. il.

Important survey by a leading scholar.

Contents: (I) France and aristocratic fashion; (II) The spread of the French ideal; (III) The architectural framework; (IV) The upholsterer's task; (V) The upholsterer's materials; (VI) The upholsterer's furnishings; (VII) Beds, cloths of estate and couches; (VIII) Upholstered seat-furniture; (IX) Tables and cup-boards; (X) Other furniture and decorative features; (XI) Lighting; (XII) Specific rooms and their decoration.

Abbreviations, p.330–35. Notes to the text, p.336–99. Notes to the plates, p.400–14. Index, p.415–27.

P51 The triumph of humanism: a visual survey of the decorative arts of the Renaissance. Introd. by D. Graeme Keith. With contrib. by Charles Avery. . . [et al.] [San Francisco, The Fine Arts Museums, 1977]. 95p. il. (part col.)

Catalog of the exhibition, Fine Arts Museums of San Francisco (1977–78). Covers northern and southern Europe, with chapters by specialists in their respective fields.

Contents: The patronage of the Medici; Small bronzes; Goldsmiths' work and jewelry; Renaissance arms and armor; Renaissance timepieces; Ceramics and glass; Furniture and woodcarving; Gold-tooled bookbindings of the Renaissance.

Catalogue of the exhibition, p.81–95. Selected bibliography, p.95.

P52 Weismann, Elizabeth Wilder. Americas: the decorative arts in Latin America in the era of the Revolution. Washington, D.C., Published for the Renwick Gallery of the National Collection of Fine Arts by the Smithsonian Institution Pr., 1976. 80p. il. (part col.)

Catalog of the exhibition, Renwick Gallery (1976–77). The narrative cites documentary sources valuable for art historical research in ironwork, weaving, ceramics, goldwork, silverwork, jewelry, costume, cabinetry, and woodwork during the colonial period. Document sources and locations of collections in Latin America and the United States also given. No footnotes, index, or bibliography.

P53 Wichmann, Siegfried. Japonisme: the Japanese influence on western art in the 19th and 20th centuries. N.Y., Harmony Books,1981. 432p. il. (part col.)

German ed., Japonismus: Ostasien-Europa: Begegnungen in der Kunst des 19. und 20. Jahrhundert. Herrsching, Schuler, 1980.

The standard history of Japonisme in art, architecture, and the decorative arts in the 19th and 20th centuries, with discussions and illustrations of typical Japanese forms and motifs and their use in Eastern and Western art and art objects.

Contents: (1) Representative objects; (2) Birds, beasts and flowers; (3) Objects from Eastern life; (4) Artistic devices; (5) Symbols, themes, and aspirations; (6) Ceramics and glass; (7) House and garden; (8) Calligraphy.

Select bibliography, p.417–19. Artists' biographies, p.420–26. Index, p.427–32.

ASIAN COUNTRIES

China

P54 The great treasury of Chinese fine arts. Beijing, Cultural Relics Publishing House (Distr. by China International Book Trading Comp., 1988–). (4)v. chiefly il. (part col.)

Trans of. Chung-kuo mei shu chu'an chi. Beijing, Wen wu chu pan she, 1985–1989. 59v.

English ed. appearing in sections corresponding to those of the original ed.: Shu fa chuan k'o pien = Calligraphy, seals, & inscriptions (7v.); Tiao su pien = Sculpture including cave sculpture and early stone carving (13v.); Chien chu I shu pien = Architecture (6v.); Kung I mei shu pien = Arts and crafts (12v.); Hui hua pien = Painting and printmaking (21v.)

Selective contents: Painting: (2) Paintings of the Sui, T'ang and Five dynasties; Sculpture: (2) Sculpture of the Qin and Han dynasties; Arts and crafts: (4) Bronzes; (6) Printing dyeing weaving and embroidery.

P55 Lynn, Pan. True to form, a celebration of the art of the Chinese craftsman. N.Y., Weatherhill, 1996. 148p. col. il.

Well-illustrated in color; makes a consistent distinction between art for and by the lettered and the unlettered.

Contents: Living; Instruments of office; Pleasures of leisure; Daily round; Tools of the trade; Pastimes.

India, Nepal, Pakistan, Tibet

P56 Barnard, Nicholas. Arts and crafts of India. Photographs by Robyn Beeche. London, Conran Octopus, 1993. 192p., col. il.

Well-illustrated "introduction to the life and work of the craftsmen and women of today's India."—*Foreword.*

Contents: Foundations and inspirations; Wood and stone; Paint; Metalwork; Jewellery and decorative metalwork; Textiles; Pottery; A miscellany of crafts.

Glossary, p.[188]–89. Index, p.[190]–91. Select bibliography, p.192.

P57 Cooper, Ilay, and Gillow, John. Arts and crafts of India. Photographs by Barry Dawson. N.Y., Thames and Hudson, 1996. 160p. il. (part col.), map.

Introductory survey.

Contents: (I) Clay, lacquer and glass; (II) Stone and wood; (III) Bronze, brass and iron; (IV) Jewelry, gold and silver; (V) Silk, satin and cotton; (VI) Miniatures to papier-mâché; (VII) A craft miscellany; Collecting Indian arts and crafts.

Glossary, p.157–58. Bibliography, p.158–59. Index, p.159–60.

P58 Garde, Anne. Maharajas' palaces: European style in imperial India. Photographs, Anne Garde. Text, Sylvie Raulet. Foreword, Laure Vernière. [Trans. from French by Judith Hayward.] London, P. Wilson, 1997. 295p. il. (part col.)

Trans. of Salon indien. Paris, Hazan, 1996.

Significant survey of "European taste" in the decoration of maharajas' palaces, arranged by location.

Glossary, p.292. Bibliography, p.293.

Japan

P59 Smith, Lawrence, and Harris, Victor. Japanese decorative arts from the 17th to the 19th centuries. London, British Museum, [1982]. 128p. il. (part col.), plates.

A study of the objects of use made by craftsmen/artisans between 1600 and 1900, attempting to place them in the wider context of Japanese traditional material culture. All examples are from the British Museum's collection.

Contents: (1) Introduction; (2) Metalwork; (3) Sculpture and decorative carving; (4) Lacquer; (5) Ceramics; (6) Postscript—textiles and the hidden artefacts of Japan.

Bibliography, p.126. Japanese historical periods, p.127. Index of Japanese terms, p.127–28.

P60 The traditional crafts of Japan. Editorial supervisors: Inumaru Tadashi and Yoshida Mitsukuni. Technical advisor: Japan Traditional Craft Center. Tokyo, Diamond, 1992. 8v. il., plates (part col.), maps + 8 videos.

The "aim in producing these books has been to use the highest techniques in order to transmit faithfully not only visual beauty, but also feel and functionality of each item, while supplying information about the history, origins, methods of production and special characteristics of each."—*Foreword.* The set represents all 171 crafts that have been designated as Traditional Craft Industries as well as 37 additional crafts that await nomination.

Contents: (1–2) Textiles; (3) Ceramics; (4) Lacquerwork; (5) Wood and bamboo; (6) Metal and stone; (7) Paper and dolls; (8) Writing utensils and household Buddhist altars. Videos: (1) Weaving: Hishijin textiles; (2) Dyeing: Kyoto Yuzen; (3) Ceramics: Shingaraki ware; (4) Lacquer: Wajima ware; (5) Woodworking: Kyoto joinery; (6) Metalworking: Sakai forged blades; (7) Papermaking: Echizen paper; (8) Brushes and sumi ink: Nara writing utensils.

Southeast Asia

P61 Capistrano-Baker, Florina H. Art of island Southeast Asia: the Fred and Rita Richman Collection in the Metropolitan Museum of Art. With an introd. by Paul Michael Taylor. N.Y., Metropolitan Museum of Art, 1994. 155p. il. (part col.), map.

Beautifully illustrated catalog of the exhibition, the Museum (1994). Includes an introductory essay on the subject.

Glossary, p.148–49. References cited, p.150–55.

P62 Fraser-Lu, Sylvia. Burmese crafts: past and present. N.Y., Oxford Univ. Pr., 1994. xiv, 371p. il. (part col.), maps.

Substantial introduction to the "scope and beauty of Burmese traditional crafts."—*Pref.*

Contents: (1) Introduction; (2) The temple and pagoda arts of brick, stone, stucco, and tempera; (3) Wood and ivory; (4) Bronze, iron, and associated metals; (5) Precious metals and jewellery; (6) Ceramics: pottery and plaques; (7) Lacquer; (8) Textiles and costume; (9) Palm and bamboo; (10) Conclusion; Appendix.

Glossary, p.323–37. Bibliography, p.338–58. Index, p.359–71.

P63 Richter, Anne. Arts and crafts of Indonesia. Special photography by John Storey. London, Thames and Hudson, 1993. 160p. il. (part col.), map.

An introduction.

Contents: Jewelry and metalwork; Ceramics; Wood, bone, horn and stone; Textiles and beading; Ephemera from paradise; Masks and puppets; Collecting Indonesian arts and crafts.

Map and glossary, p.154–56. Bibliography, p.157–58. Index, p.159–60.

P64 Warren, William, and Invernizzi Tettoni, Luca. Arts and crafts of Thailand. Consultant: Chaiwut Tulayadham. London, Thames and Hudson, 1994. 160p. il. (part col.), map.

Introduction to the subject.

Contents: (I) Introduction; (II) Crafts as symbols of status; (III) Ceremonial crafts; (IV) The crafts of village life; (V) Textiles; (VI) Architectural woodcarving; (VII) Theatre and other diversions; (VIII) Tradition continued: contemporary Thai crafts.

Glossary, p.156–58. Bibliography, p.158. Index, p.160.

BASKETRY

Africa, Oceania, The Americas

The Americas

P65 Porter, Frank W. Native American basketry: an annotated bibliography. N.Y., Greenwood Pr., 1988. 249p. (Art reference collection, 10)

More than 1,100 entries on prehistoric and historic native American basketry, organized into chapters by culture region. Introduction includes brief historiography of Indian basketry and selected references.

Author index, p.[225]–37. Subject index, p.[239]–49.

P66 Whiteford, Andrew Hunter. Southwest Indian baskets: their history and their makers. Santa Fe, School of American Research (Distr. by Univ. of Washington Pr., 1988). 219p. il. (part col.), 14 plates.

"In this book I have tried to summarize . . . [previous scholars'] observations and interpretations . . . and to develop a synthesis which will facilitate our understanding of basket typology and of the many factors which have affected the development of basketmaking among the Indians of the Southwest."—*Pref.*

Contents: (1) The ancestry of Southwestern baskets; (2) The Southern Paiutes; (3) The Navajos; (4) The Apaches; (5) The Yuman-Pai tribes; (6) The Piman peoples; (7) The Pueblos; (8) The state of the art and its future; Appendix: the School of American Research collection of Southwestern Indian baskets.

References, p.206–14. Index, p.215–19.

ORNAMENT

Dictionaries and Encyclopedias

P67 Lewis, Philippa, and Darley, Gillian. Dictionary of ornament. N.Y., Pantheon, [1986]. 319p. il.

"A survey of ornament, pattern, and motifs in the applied arts and architecture. The coverage is mainly of European and North American buildings and objects from the Renaissance to the present day with reference, where relevant, to ancient and oriental sources and precedents."—*p.[7]*. Illustrations are both line and photograph, and include a visual key at beginning of vol. Cross-indexed.

References, p.[17]–[18].

Histories and Handbooks

P68 Byrne, Janet S. Renaissance ornament prints and drawings. N.Y., Metropolitan Museum of Art, [1981]. 143p. il.

Published in connection with the exhibition, Metropolitan Museum of Art (1981–1982).

Heavily illustrated account of the spread of ornamental design in the 16th century by means of prints and drawings. Includes an introductory essay on these sources, their creation, and their use, and serves as an accessible, compact introduction to the genre.

Index of artists illustrated, p.143.

P69 Fuhring, Peter. Design into art: drawings for architecture and ornament: The Lodewijk Houthakker Collection. [London, Philip Wilson (Distr. by Harper, 1989)]. 2v. il. (part col.)

Sumptuous catalog of a major collection of drawings, principally European, for ornament, architecture, and ephemeral constructions for spectacle, the theater, and events from the 16th to the 20th century. Introductory essays on the authorship, methods, and purposes of these drawings. Comprehensive, meticulous, and handsome. A major source of information on ornament and its associated arts.

Contents: Vol.I: (I) Drawings for ornament; (II) Drawings for the decorative arts; Vol.II: (III) Drawings for architecture, gardens, and fountains; (IV) Drawings for the theatre and events; (V) Drawings for sculpture, machines and miscellaneous objects.

Bibliography, p.767–76. Index of names, p.779–86. Subject index, p.787–91.

P70 Snodin, Michael, and Howard, Maurice. Ornament: a social history since 1450. New Haven, Yale Univ. Pr., 1996. 232p. il. (part col.)

Well written, accessible history of ornament in Western culture from the Renaissance to the present day, with a chapter on the role of exotic cultures in the formation of design. Many illustrations are drawn from the collections of the Victoria and Albert Museum.

General bibliography, p.218–26. Index, p.227–31.

P71 Wilson, Eva. Ornament, 8,000 years: an illustrated handbook of motifs. [N.Y.], Abrams, [1994]. 208p. il.

Handbook of basic ornamental design, appropriate for general audiences, arranged by motif, with examples drawn from all cultures. Illustrated with line drawings.

Selected sources, p.202–04. Index, p.205–08.

Asian Countries

China

P72 Chung-kuo wen shih [= Chinese decorative design]. Fu jen ta chih p'ing fu chuang hsűeh hsi hui. T'aipei, Nan tien shu chű, [1987]. 4v. il. (part col.)

Text in Chinese and English.

Based on Fu Jen University Textile Department's Chinese design archive of 4,000 traditional Chinese decorative designs drawn from art objects such as pottery, porcelain, bronze, jade, lacquer, gold and silver, textiles, paintings, sculptures, architecture, etc. The designs are organized according to a classification scheme of 17 categories and each illustration is captioned with the main decorative theme, the source object, location, and historical period. Includes "General editor's preface" in v.1 only.

Bibliography, v.4, p.457–59. Index, v.4, p.461.

P73 Rawson, Jessica. Chinese ornament: the lotus and the dragon. London, British Museum, [1984]. 240p. il. (part col.), plates, maps.

Catalog of the exhibition, British Museum (1984).

The author, Deputy Keeper of Oriental Antiquities in the British Museum, addresses the question, "what are the sources of flower and animal designs that are widely displayed in Chinese art and especially on Chinese porcelains?"—*Pref.* A lavishly illustrated work that includes Chinese examples of objects with flower and animal motifs from the 4th through the 16th centuries as well as objects from other cultures, e.g., Greek, Turkish, Persian, which may have influenced or been influenced by Chinese art.

Bibliography, p.228–31.

COSTUME

Bibliography

P74 Colas, René. Bibliographie générale du costume et de la mode: description des suites, recueils, séries, revues et livres français et étrangers relatifs au costume civil, militaire et religieux, aux modes, aux coiffures et aux divers accessoires de l'habillement, avec une table méthodique et un index alphabétique. [Reprint.] Mansfield, Conn., Maurizio Martino, [1994]. viii, 1411, 69p.

See GLAH 1:P75 for original annotation.

P75 Kesler, Jackson. Theatrical costume: a guide to information sources. Detroit, Gale, 1979. x, 308p. (Performing arts information guide series, 6) (Gale information guide library)

Broad-based annotated bibliography, the principal purpose of which "is to provide for costume designers, primarily, a practical, utilitarian listing, mostly of English-title books in the field in more recent years."—*Pref.* Focus is on publications from 1957, thus partially updating Monro's and Cook's Costume index (see GLAH 1:P78). Cross references.

Contents: (1) Reference works; (2) Theatrical costume; (3) Historical costume; (4) Accoutrements and special categories; (5) Theatrical and historical movement and dance; (6) Manners, modes and customs; (7) Selected illustrated social history; (8) Costume design; (9) Ornamentation and symbols; (10) Costume construction techniques and pattern sources; (11) Textile history and conservation; (12) Textile decoration: dyeing, painting and printing; (13) Fashion designers and the fashion world; (14) Theory and psychology of fashion and costume.

Author index, p.261–75. Title index, p.277–99. Subject index, p.301–08.

P76 Letexier, Gérard. Mode et costume civil: collections de la Bibliothèque Forney: bibliographie. Paris, Bibliothèque Forney, 1992. 255p. il.

Catalog of the holdings of this important Parisian library in the field of fashion. This publication builds on previous publications that listed the Library's fashion periodical holdings (see GLAH 2:P78). The present bibliography, comprising approximately 3,000 entries, covers books, periodicals, periodical articles, exhibition and collection catalogues, reviews and published collections of images. The emphasis is on civilian dress, with military and religious dress excluded from consideration. Most of the bibliography is unannotated, although some entries do include minimal bibliographical annotations if the work is an update or adaptation of an earlier work.

Contents: (1) Ouvrages de references; (2) Histoire du costume; (3) Types particuliers de vêtements; (4) Haute-couture; (5) Accessoires et matériaux; (6) Iconographie; (7) Regards sur la mode.

Index des auteurs, p.221–38. Index des créateurs, p.239–44. Index des périodiques, p.245–52.

P77 Mode, Tracht, Kostüm: Sammlung Eva Larrass, Darmstadt. 3. erw. Aufl. des Kataloges: Bücher, Zeitschriften, Druckgraphik. Hrsg. von Otto Weber. [Ober-Ramstadt, Verein für Heimatgeschichte, 1988]. vii, 259p. il.

Published on the occasion of the exhibition "Festtagskleidung - Werktagskleidung," Museum Ober-Ramstadt (1988). All aspects of European holiday, leisure, working dress and accessories, as well as more fashionable dress forms are covered, and close attention is paid to the socio-cultural and artistic context. The focus is on German-language bibliographic resources although sources in other Western languages are also included. Unannotated. More than 2,000 titles are listed.

Contents: (A) Allgemeine Kultur- und Socialgeschichte als Grundlage von Tracht und Mode; (B) Kunstgeschichte und Kunstsammlung als Quellen der Kostümkunde; (C) Theorie der Kleidung und der Mode; (D) Geschichte der Mode und des Kostüms; (E) Volkstrachten; (F) Kinderkleidung; (G) Standestrachten, Berufs- und Arbeitskleidung; (H) Militärische Trachten; (J) Festkleidung und Maskenkostume; (K) Einzelteile und Beiwerk der Kleidung; (L) Schmuck; (M) Haar- und Barttrachten, Hygiene und Kosmetik; (N) Wohnung und Garten; (O) Wappen und Fahnen, Orden und Auszeichnungen; (P) Kunsthandwerk und -gewerbe; (R) Textilkunst, -gewerbe und -industrie; (S) Bildung und Wissenschaft; (T) Theater, Musik, Tanz, Film, Zirkus, Varieté; (U) Sport und Reisen; (V) Spiel und Spielzeug, Puppenkleidung; (W) Essen, Trinken, Rauchen; (X) Kleiderordnungen und Etikette; (Y) Satiren und Karikaturen; (Z) Zeitschriften und Almanache.

Zeittafel der Modezeitschriften, p.232–34. Verfasser-Register, p.235–59.

P78 Modes et textiles 1785–1985: 200 ans de périodiques à la Bibliothèque Forney. Paris, Société des Amis de la Bibliothèque Forney, 1987. 87p. il.

1st ed., Périodiques de mode, 1785–1980, 1982.

Publishes the fashion periodical holdings of the Bibliothèque Forney.

Contents: (I) Liste chronologique des périodiques de mode; (II) Liste thématique: mode et textile.

P79 Prichard, Susan Perez. Film costume: an annotated bibliography. Metuchen, N.J., Scarecrow, 1981. xiii, 563p.

Alphabetically arranged (by author) "annotated bibliography to almost 4,000 books and periodical articles on costume design in the film industry."—*Foreword.* Publications of the period 1920s–1970s are the primary focus. An introduction discusses the bibliography's scope, and provides a brief survey of the literature on the history of dress in film.

Subject index, p.438–563.

P80 Seligman, Kevin L. Cutting for all: the sartorial arts, related crafts, and the commercial paper pattern: a bibliographic reference guide for designers, technicians, and historians. Carbondale, Southern Illinois Univ. Pr., 1996. xv, 351p. il.

Partially annotated, chronologically arranged compilation of source materials covering the subject of flat pattern and draping methods, and commercial paper pattern companies. The objective is to enable researchers and designers to understand and/or recreate historically accurate cuts of clothing for every culture and period covered. Each chapter or section opens with a brief introduction to the period or specific subject area, followed by a bibliographical listing for that topic; books, journal articles and catalogs are included, with the main focus on American and English sources.

Contents: (1) History of the development of the publication of books, professional journals, and the emergence of the paper pattern industry; (2) Chronological listings; (3) Professional journals; (4) Journal articles; (5) Costume and dance; (6) Dolls; (7) Folk and national dress; (8) Footwear; (9) Millinery; (10) Wigmaking and hair; (11) Commercial pattern companies, periodicals, and catalogs; Appendix: Pattern companies, publishers, and publications.

Notes, p.40–43. Bibliography, p.44–46. Introduction to indexes, p.309. Author index, p.311–22. Title index, p.323–44. Subject index, p.345–50. Chronological index, p.351.

Directories

P81 Lambert, Eleanor. World of fashion: people, places, resources. N.Y., Bowker, 1976. 361p.

Reference volume containing information about the designers, manufacturing centers, geographic resources, principal exports, training institutes, collections and other resources available to researchers of modern dress in each part of the world. Organized geographically, the contribution of each country to modern dress is summarized, and its fashion and trade organizations, schools, museums, awards and periodicals are also listed. Each country also includes sections on "Fashion designers and firms" and on "Fashion influentials."

Contents: Africa; Asia; Europe; The Americas; Hall of fame; Appendix: Coty Award winners [for their contribution to world fashion], 1943–75.

Bibliography, p.345–49. Name index, p.351–61.

P82 McDowell, Colin. McDowell's directory of twentieth century fashion. Rev. ed. N.Y., Prentice Hall, 1988. 320p. il. (part col.), ports.

1st ed., Englewood Cliffs, N.J., Prentice Hall, 1985; 2d, rev. ed., London, Muller, 1987.

Introductory chapters provide an overview of the history of fashion and its function in society. The alphabetically arranged directory of fashion designers makes up the second part of this vol., followed by another alphabetically organized directory of image makers not themselves designers.

Contents: Clothes as a weapon; Fashion and the arts; Creating the line; From Salon to street; The first couturier; The Directory.

Autobiographies, p.293. Fashion education, p.294–95. Fashion organizations, p.296–97. Fashion awards, p.298–305. Glossary, p.306–17. Index, p.318–19.

Dictionaries and Encyclopedias

P83 Baclawski, Karen. The guide to historic costume. N.Y., Drama Book, 1995. 240p. il., ports.

Dictionary encyclopedia of the components of fashionable and everyday dress represented in British public collections. Professional and military uniforms, ethnographic and folk dress are excluded, but foreign-made dress worn by the British is covered. Each entry is divided into two sections. The first section defines and describes the named item and traces its development. The second section lists some surviving examples, providing their museum locations.

Glossary, p.232. Museums [from which the works described in the catalog entries are taken], p.233. Bibliography, p.240.

P84 Bildwörterbuch der Kleidung und Rüstung: vom Alten Orient bis zum ausgehenden Mittelalter. Hrsg. von Harry Kühnel. Stuttgart, Kröner, [1992]. lxxxi, 334p. il. (Kröners Taschenausgabe, Bd. 453)

Introductory essays by various authors, followed by the dictionary of dress terms relevant to the periods covered.

Contents: Die griechische Kleidung, by Friedrich Brein; Die römische Kleidung, by Erwin Pochmarski; Die Kleidung im byzantinischen Reich, by Karoline Czerwenka-Papadopoulos; Kleidung und Gesellschaft im Mittelalter, by Harry Kühnel; Die Kriegsrüstung im europäischen Mittelalter, by Peter Krenn.

Bibliographical references follow each introductory essay. Auswahlbibliographie, p.308–31.

P85 Calasibetta, Charlotte Mankey. Fairchild's dictionary of fashion. 2d ed. N.Y., Fairchild Publications, 1988. 749p. il.

See GLAH 1:P87 for original annotation.

P86 Cassin-Scott. Jack. The illustrated encyclopaedia of costume and fashion 1550–1920. N.Y., Blandford Pr., 1986. 160p. col. il.

1st ed., 1971.

"The aim of this book is to highlight those points of fashion which express changes in style over a period of nearly four centuries."—*Introd.* A brief introduction provides a short historical overview. The remainder of the work comprises a series of chronologically arranged near full-page colored drawings by the author, based on portrait paintings or fashion prints from each period discussed, and are accompanied by brief analytical commentaries. Focus is on Western high-end fashion.

Glossary, p.6–7. Index, p.159–60.

P87 ———. The illustrated encyclopaedia of costume and fashion: from 1066 to the present. Rev. and exp. ed. London, Studio Vista, 1997. 192p. col. il.

1st ed., 1971.

180 near full-page colored drawings by the author, based on period sources. Divided into 16 sections. The organization and part of the contents duplicate the author's The illustrated encyclopaedia of costume and fashion 1550–1920 (see preceding entry).

Glossary, p.8–9. Index, p.191–92.

P88 Colangeli, Oronzo. Dizionario della moda e del costume. Galatina, Salentina, 1986. 571p. il.

Dictionary of more than 10,000 current terms relating to dress, accessories, textiles and embroidery. Italian-language terms predominate, although since many foreign terms (especially English, French, and German) have been adopted into Italian usage, these too are listed. Definitions are brief, and examples of use in context are provided.

P89 The complete footwear dictionary. Comp. and ed. by William A. Rossi. Malabar, Fl., Krieger, 1994. vii, 171p. il.

Alphabetically organized guide to the terminology of footwear fashion, retailing, and industry. Approximately 4,000 items and definitions are discussed. Appendix I: Origin of footwear-related words; Appendix II: English words with foot or shoe origins.

P90 Costume language: a dictionary of dress terms. Comp. and il. by Stephanie Curtis Davies. Malvern [U.K.], Cressrelles, 1994. 183p. il.

This posthumously published dictionary provides succinct descriptions and definitions for approximately 2,500 dress types and styles. Includes entries on historically important figures in the world of dress. Appendixes: Couturiers, designers and couture houses; Costume collections.

Exhibitions of ancient civilisations, p.182. Bibliography, p.177–78.

P91 Guillemard, Colette. Les mots du costume. Paris, Belin, 1991. 349p. il. (Collection Le français retrouve, 24)

Investigation into the origin and evolution of dress terminology. Covers not only French-language terms, but also words imported from abroad, or used by specific groups. Accessories and fabric types are also considered. Each chapter focuses on a specific theme; relevant terms within the chapter are arranged alphabetically. Illustrations are taken mostly from early fashion prints and posters.

Contents: (I) Costumes, vêtements et habits; (II) Le corps du sujet; (III) Des piedes . . .; (IV) . . . À la tête; (V) Le linge de corps; (VI) Ornements et accessoires; (VII) Les mots de la couturière; (VIII) Les matériaux de nos vêtements.

Index, p.333–47. Bibliographie, p.348–49.

P92 Leloir, Maurice. Dictionnaire du costume et de ses accessoires, des armes et des étoffes, des origines à nos jours. 2d ed. Paris, Grund, [1961]. 390p. il., ports.

See GLAH 1:P93 for original annotation.

P93 Loschek, Ingrid. Reclams Mode- und Kostümlexikon. 3. rev. und erw. Aufl. Stuttgart, Reclam, [1994]. 551p. il. (part col.)

1st ed., 1987; 2d ed., 1988.

Series of chronologically arranged chapters briefly discussing dress and textile history of specific periods, beginning with the early cultures of southern Europe, the Mediterranean, Mesopotamia and Asia, and the Prehistoric period in North and Central Europe, and ending with a global perspective on the 20th century. Particular attention is paid to the relationship between fashion and society. A dictionary-format listing of more than 2,000 terms and their definitions follows. European couturiers, designers and design companies, from the 18th century to the present are separately listed, as are sources of fashion images from the 16th century on.

Literaturhinweise, p.525–[52].

P94 Petrascheck-Heim, Ingeborg. Die Sprache der Kleidung: Wesen und Wandel von Tracht, Mode, Kostüm und Uniform. 2., neubearb. Aufl. [Baltmannsweiler], Schneider, [1988]. viii, 137p. il., 77 plates.

1st ed., Wien, Notring der Wissenschaftlichen Verbände Österreichs, 1966.

Rather than aiming to provide a history of dress, investigates the social, cultural, and psychological forces underlying fashion and dress choices. This theoretical approach is applied to European folk dress and uniforms as well as to more fashionable dress forms. All illustrations are extensively annotated.

Contents: (I) Die Tracht; (II) Die Mode; (III) Die Bedeutung des Reizes für die Mode; (IV) Die Bedeutung der Form in Tracht und Kleider-Mode; (V) Die praktische Ausführung der Kleider Mode; (VI) Die europäische Volkstracht; (VII) Das Kostüm in Beziehung zu Tracht und Mode; (VIII) Die Uniform in Beziehung zu Tracht und Mode; (IX) Anregungen zur wissenschaftlichen Bearbeitung von Tracht und Mode.

Bildbeschreibungen, p.106–23. Anmerkungen, p.124–29. Literaturverzeichnis, p.130–34. Sachregister, p.136–37.

P95 Racinet, Albert Charles Auguste. The historical encyclopedia of costume. Introd. by Dr. Aileen Ribeiro. N.Y., Facts on File, 1988. 320p. col. il.

See GLAH 1:P99 for original French ed.

This ed. has numerous revisions, deletions, and modifications to Racinet's original. For example, many of the plates in Racinet's original work included plates on furniture and ornaments, and these have been eliminated from the present ed. Parts of the text have also been reorganized to follow a more straightforward chronology. European dress is the principal focus of this publication; countries that were part of France's colonial history (China, India, North Africa), as well as Japan, are also considered.

The introduction by Ribeiro, which sets Racinet's original work in its historical and publishing context, precedes a selection of Racinet's descriptions and approximately 150 of his original plates.

Contents: (1) The ancient world; (2) 19th century antique civilizations; (3) Europe from Byzantium to the 1800s; (4) Traditional costumes of the 1880s.

Index, p.314–20.

P96 Stegemeyer, Anne. Who's who in fashion. 3d ed. N.Y., Fairchild Publications, 1996. xi, 300p. il. (part col.), ports.

1st ed., 1980; 2d ed., 1988.

Wide-ranging biographical dictionary based on Who's who in fashion, by Josephine Ellis Watkins (N.Y., Office of Community Resources, Fashion Institute of Technology, 1972). Covering greater and lesser fashion designers, information sources include questionnaires, press clippings, and personal interviews. The emphasis is on 20th-century personalities although historically important figures are included. Also included is "a selection of the many newcomers who promise to become the establishment of the future."—*Pref.* A final section, "The stylemakers," covers influential figures in the fashion world who were not themselves designers.

Contents: Appendix: Council of Fashion Designers of America (CFDA) Awards; Coty American Fashion Critics' Awards; Nieman Marcus Awards.

Bibliography, p.285–92. Index of designers, p.293–94. Index, p.295–300.

P97 Stevens Cox, J. An illustrated dictionary of hairdressing & wigmaking. Containing words, terms and phrases (current and obsolete) dialectical, foreign, and technical, used in Britain and America pertaining to the crafts of hairdressing and wigmaking: also words derived from these crafts having a wider use. Rev. ed. N.Y., Drama Book, 1984. 312p. il.

1st ed., Philadelphia, G.S. MacManus, 1966.

Extensively illustrated, extremely comprehensive, alphabetically organized dictionary. "The aim of the present work is to list and describe not only the literary, vernacular and technical craft words of the 20th century, but also archaic, dialectal and obsolete words, their uses and meanings. Words of foreign origin that are and were habitually used in the hairdressing craft in Britain to describe processes or coiffures are also noticed. The compilation is based on English and foreign printed and manuscript sources."—*Introd.* Many of the illustrations are taken from 18th–20th century fashion plates and journals. Cross references.

Bibliography, p.171–81.

P98 Who's who in fashion: a biographical encyclopedia of the international red series containing some 6,000 biographies of living prominent personalities in the fields of fashion, beauty, and jewellery . . . [et al.] Ed. by Karl Strute and Theodore Doelken. Zurich, Who's who, the international red series Verlag, 1982. 1v.

Planned as a 3-vol. publication comprising biographies of approximately 6,000 significant people in the international fashion, beauty, and jewelry worlds. Although intended to be triennial, no later issues were published.

Table of abbreviations, p.ix–xi. Index of names, p.600–45. Appendices: Intellectual life [professional libraries, documentation centers, museums, trade fairs and exhibitions, arranged by country], p.648–750; Economic life [famous companies, manufacturers, producers, wholesalers and retailers of fashionable clothing, including shoes and hats], p.751–906.

P99 Wilcox, Ruth Turner. The dictionary of costume. [Reprint.] London, Batsford, 1992. 406p. il.

U.S. ed., N.Y., Scribner, 1987. See GLAH 1:P102 for original annotation.

P100 Yarwood, Doreen. The encyclopedia of world costume. N.Y., Scribner, 1978. 471p. il. (part col.) (Repr.: N.Y., Bonanza, 1986)

Wide-ranging dictionary encyclopedia of the history and development of garment types. The publication covers dress from most parts of the world although the emphasis is on areas of greatest relevance to the English-speaking world. Military and ecclesiastical dress are excluded. Most of the many illustrations are artists' impressions of the garments described.

Sources of information on costume [museum collections in the U.K.], p.453–54. Bibliography, p.454–59. Index, p.461–71.

SEE ALSO: Dictionnaire de la mode au XXe siècle (GLAH 2:P157).

Histories and Handbooks

General Works

P101 Arnold, Janet. A handbook of costume. [Reprint.] N.Y., Phillips, 1980. 336p. il.

See GLAH 1:P82 for original annotation.

P102 Batterberry, Michael, and Batterberry, Ariane. [Reprint.] Fashion: the mirror of history. N.Y., Greenwich House, 1982. 400p. il. (part col.), ports. (part col.)

1st ed., Mirror, mirror: a social history of fashion, N.Y., Holt, Rinehart and Winston, 1977.

Chronological survey of dress and accessories from the period of the Ancient Near East to the 20th century. Focus is on the history of Western dress traditions although other cultures are explored. The many illustrations include illuminated manuscripts, wall paintings and mosaics, vase paintings, portrait paintings and photographs, and surviving examples of dress and accessory items.

Bibliography, p.392–93. Index, p.396–400.

P103 Bell, Quentin. On human finery. Rev. ed. London, Allison and Busby, 1992. 199p. il.

See GLAH 1:P83 for original publication (1947, 1976) and annotation. French trans., Mode et société: essai sur la sociologie du vêtement, Paris, Presses Universitaires de France, 1992.

P104 Boucher, François. 20,000 years of fashion: the history of costume and personal adornment. [Exp. ed.] N.Y., Abrams, 1987. 459p. il. (part col.)

See GLAH 1:P85 for original publication (1967?) and annotation.

P105 Bruhn, Wolfgang, and Tilke, Max. A pictorial history of costume: a survey of costume of all periods and peoples from antiquity to modern times including national costume in Europe and non-European countries. [Reprint.] N.Y., Arch Cape, 1988. 200p. il. (part col.)

See GLAH 1:P86 for original annotation (with author's surname misspelled as "Brun").

P106 Corson, Richard. Fashions in hair: the first five thousand years. London, Owen, 1995. 719p. il., 173 plates

1st ed., N.Y., Hastings House, 1965; rev. ed., 1977; 4th impression with rev. suppl, 1980.

Surveys the history of hair styles. Organized chronologically, each chapter contains a brief historical overview, and includes extracts of commentary from that period, where available. The latter part of each chapter comprises a series of line drawings, accompanied by a page of factual data.

Sources, p.696–704. Index, p.705–19.

P107 Cunnington, C. Willett, and Cunnington, Phillis. The history of underclothes. N.Y., Dover, 1992. 266p. il.

1st ed., London, M. Joseph, 1951; rev ed., by A. D. and Valerie Mansfield, London, Faber, 1981.

Chronological survey of men's, women's, and children's underwear and nightwear, from the medieval period to 1950. An introductory chapter discusses basic concepts, for example materials, construction, and methods of fastening. Subsequent chapters are organized chronologically and follow a uniform format. Each chapter opens with a brief summary of the dress tendencies of the period, and is completed by a series of annotations arranged according to clothing type. Line drawings illustrate the text.

Bibliography, p.259–60. Appendix, p.261–62. Index, p.263–66.

P108 Davenport, Millia. The book of costume. [Reprint.] N.Y., Crown, 1976. 2v. in 1. 958p. il.
See GLAH 1:P88 for original annotation.

P109 De Marly, Diana. Fashion for men: an illustrated history. N.Y., Holmes and Meier, 1985. 166p. il., ports.
Chronologically arranged general survey of aristocratic and upper class male dress of the Western European tradition, from the Middle Ages to the 1980s. Emphasis is on British fashion, although the dress of medieval and Revolutionary France, and 20th-century U.S. dress are also covered. Principal sources of information include manuscript illumination, effigies, and portrait painting.

Notes, p.153–58. Glossary, p.159. Bibliography, p.160–62. Index, p.163–66.

P110 Die Frisur: eine Kulturgeschichte der Haarmode von der Antike bis zur Gegenwart: veranschaulicht an Kunstobjekten der Sammlung Schwarzkopf und internationaler Museen. Hrsg. von Maria Jedding-Gesterling [und] Georg Brutscher. Mit Beiträgen von Rolf Hurschmann . . . [et al.] München, Callway, 1990, 269p. il. (part col.)
Extensively illustrated catalog published to accompany the exhibition "Die Frisur: Haarmode aus vier Jahrtausenden," Museum für Kunst und Gewerbe, Hamburg (1990). Ten essays provide a historical survey of hair styles from ancient times to the 20th century.

Contents: Antike, by Rolf Hurschmann; Germanen und frühes Mittelalter, by Rolf Hurschmann; Spätes Mittelalter, by Renate Scholz; Renaissance, by Renate Scholz; Barock, by Maria Jedding-Gesterling; Régence, Rokoko und Louis XVI, by Maria Jedding-Gesterling; Französische Revolution, Directoire und Empire, by Hanna Plutat-Zeiner; Biedermeier, by Ingrid Baireuther; Historismus, by Hanna Plutat-Zeiner; Zur Technik der Frisurgestaltung, by Georg Brutscher.

Anmerkungenn, p.247–50. Literatur, p.251–54. Register, p.255–62.

P111 Giorgetti, Cristina. Manuale di storia del costume e della moda. [Firenze], Cantini, [1990]. 478p. il. (part col.), ports. (part col.), maps.
Well-researched chronological survey of dress from ca. 31,000 B.C. to the 1980s. Particularly interesting for its juxtapositions among the illustrations.

Bibliografia, p.463–75.

P112 Gorsline, Douglas. A history of fashion: a visual survey of costume from ancient times. N.Y., Viking, 1953. iii, 266p. il. (Repr.: London, Batsford, 1993)
1st British ed. titled What people wore. London, Batsford, 1953.

Brief introductory essays on each historical and geographical sub-section are accompanied by numerous drawings by the author. Especially useful for its section on American dress.

Contents: (I) Costume of the ancient world; (II) European costume; (III) American costume.

Bibliography: "Costume of the ancient world" and "European costume," p.249–53. Bibliography: "American costume," p.254–56. Sources for "Costume of the ancient world" and "European costume," p.257–63. Sources for "American costume," p.264–66.

P113 History of dress series. General ed., Dr. Aileen Ribeiro. [Atlantic Highlands], Humanities Pr., [1980]–81. 2v.
Extensively illustrated.

Contents: (1) Scott, Margaret. Late Gothic Europe, 1400–1500 (1980); (2) Herald, Jacqueline. Renaissance dress in Italy 1400–1500 (1981).

Notes, bibliographies and indexes in each vol.

P114 Laver, James, and de la Haye, Amy. Costume and fashion: a concise history. Concluding chapter by Amy de la Haye. Rev., exp. & upd. ed. N.Y., Thames and Hudson, 1995. 296p. il. (part col.), ports. (World of art)
See GLAH 1:P92 for original publication (1969) titled A concise history of costume and fashion.

P115 Marangoni, Giorgio. Evoluzione storica e stilistica della moda. Nuova ed. Milano, SMC [Stil, Moda, Costume], 1987–89. 3v. il. (part col.)
Chronological survey amply illustrated with line drawings based on original examples of dress and accessories. Chapters and chapter-parts open with introductory texts that include cross-references to the illustrations. The illustrations that follow have explanatory captions itemizing the pieces shown and explaining relevant terminology. Chapters end with brief historical summaries and dress analyses. The focus is on fashionable dress of the Western European upper classes, although some ancient civilizations in other parts of the world are also included.

Contents: (1) Dalle antiche civiltà mediterranee al Rinascimento; (2) Dal secolo diciasettesimo alla conquista della Luna; (3) Il novecento: dal Liberty alla computer-art.

Bibliografia, v.I, p.305–308; v.II, p.305–308; v.III, p.341–44. Indice dei nomi, dei luoghi e dei personaggi citati, v.I, p.309–16; v.II, p.309–16; v.III, p.345–50.

P116 Payne, Blanche; Winakor, Geitel; and Farrell-Beck, Jane. The history of costume: from ancient Mesopotamia through the twentieth century. 2d ed. N.Y., Harper Collins, 1992. ix, 659p. il., maps.
See GLAH 1:P96 for original publication (1965) and annotation.

P117 Peacock, John. The chronicle of western fashion: from ancient times to the present day. N.Y., Abrams, 1991. 224p. il. (part col.)
British ed. titled The chronicle of western costume: from the ancient world to the late twentieth century. London, Thames and Hudson, 1991.

Survey comprising eight sections beginning with one on the ancient civilizations and ending with 1980. Provides a "visual chronology of the mainstream development of Western costume."—*Pref.* Focus on upper- and middle-class dress; ethnic and national dress and their derivatives are excluded from consideration. Organized chronologically, each section comprises a series of colored drawings by the author and is used to illustrate the principal features of the period's fashion trends. Brief annotations at the end of each section, detailing color, fabrics, foundation garments, and regional or national variations, provide background information to the visual repertoire.

Illustrated glossary of terms, p.213–23. Bibliography, p.224.

P118 Ribeiro, Aileen. Dress and morality. N.Y., Holmes and Meier, 1986. 192p. il., ports.

Examines the relationship between dress styles and the dictates of social mores. This chronological survey begins with the Classical Greek period and ends with the 1980s.

Contents: (1) Body and soul; (2) Vile bodies; (3) The world, the flesh and the devil; (4) The ship of fools; (5) Rags of sin, robes of shame, and provocations of lust; (6) The vanity of human wishes; (7) The great divide; (8) Dress and disorder.

Notes, p.172–85. Bibliography, p.186. Index, p.187–92.

P119 Rubens, Alfred. A history of Jewish costume. Rev. and enl. ed. London, Owen, 1981. xviii, 221p. il. (part col.), ports.

See GLAH 1:P100 for original publication (1967; repr. 1973) and annotation.

P120 Tarrant, Naomi E. A. The development of costume. N.Y., National Museums of Scotland in conjunction with Routledge, 1994. xv, 176p. il., ports. (The heritage: care—preservation—management)

Based on work done for a new installation at Edinburgh's National Museums of Scotland. Focus is on the structure and construction of western European dress and its interaction with culture and technology. The first part discusses the theme of the installation and attempts to investigate "the hidden social codes which lie behind dress." Part two deals with the practicalities of achieving this objective at the Museum. Numerous illustrations, including diagrams of the cut of clothes, paintings, manuscript illuminations, photographs, sculpture, advertisements from the period covered, and surviving examples of dress.

Bibliography, p.169–72. Index, p.173–76.

P121 Thiel, Erika. Geschichte des Kostüms: die europäische Mode von den Anfängen bis zur Gegenwart. 6. stark erw. und neu gestalt. Aufl. Wilhelmshaven, Heinrichshofen, 1985. 463p. il. (part col.), 60 col. plates.

1st ed., Berlin, Henschelverlag Kunst und Gesellschaft, 1963; frequently reissued.

Thorough history of European dress, chronologically organized, covering the Stone Age era through the early 1960s. Extensively illustrated, with reproductions of portrait paintings, fashion prints, vase paintings, loom and weave structures.

Schriftum, p.443–46. Sachregister, p.447–56. Personenregister, p.457–60.

P122 Tilke, Max. Costume patterns and designs: a survey of costume patterns and designs of all periods from antiquity to modern times. N.Y., Praeger, [1957]. 49p. il. (part col.) 128 plates (chiefly col.) (Repr.: N.Y., Rizzoli, 1990)

Trans. of Kostümschnitte und Gewandformen. Tübingen, Wasmuth, 1956.

"Posthumous publication of a volume planned by Tilke as a supplement to A Pictorial history of costume, edited by himself in collab. with Wolfgang Bruhn."—*Introd.* (see GLAH 1:P86 for original annotation). As with the earlier work, coverage is worldwide and the arrangement is chronological, ranging from antiquity to the 19th century. The plates receive descriptive captions (ed. by Bruhn). These plates, based on Tilke's earlier publications (particularly his Costume of the Far East and Costumes of Eastern Europe), were revised and reorganized by him for this new publication. The excellent illustrations include accessories and details of cut and construction.

P123 Tortora, Phyllis G., and Eubank, Keith. Survey of historic costume: a history of western dress. 3d ed. N.Y., Fairchild, 1998. 556p. il. (part col.)

1st ed., 1989; 2d ed., 1994.

Textbook "intended for use as a basic text for readers who desire an overview of the history of costume in the West."—*Pref.* Covers the period ca. 3,000 B.C. to 1990, arranged chronologically. Each chapter provides a brief summary of the major historical developments pertaining to the period, with a discussion of influential technological and social changes. Focus is on western dress and accessories, but includes cross-cultural influences. Individual chapters examine the elements of men's, women's, and children's dress.

Notes and selected readings at ends of chapters. Bibliography, p.536–42. Index, p.543–56.

Ancient

P124 Bieber, Margarete. Griechische Kleidung. [Reprint.] Berlin, de Gruyter, 1977. 100p. il., 64 leaves of plates.

See GLAH 1:P104 for original annotation.

P125 Bonfante, Larissa. Etruscan dress. Baltimore, Johns Hopkins Univ. Pr., 1975. ix, 243p. il.

Individual chapters discuss fabric and patterns, as well as specific clothing types, accessories, and hairstyles. Foreign influences and local styles are also examined. 164 illustrations accompanied by detailed captions follow the main text.

Contents: (1) Fabrics and patterns; (2) Perizoma and belts; (3) Chiton and tunic; (4) Mantles; (5) Shoes; (6) Hats, hairstyles, and beards; (7) Foreign influences and local styles; Appendix I: Strange costumes and special problems; Appendix II: Vocabulary.

Chronological table of Greek and Etruscan dress, p.7–10. Notes, p.105–54. Bibliography and abbreviations, p.213–30. Index, p.233–43.

P126 Goette, Hans Rupprecht. Studien zu Römischen Togadarstellungen. Mainz am Rhein, von Zabern, [1989]. x, 207p. il. (part col.), 94p. of plates. (Beiträge zur Erschliessung hellenistischer und kaiserzeitlicher Skulptur und Architektur, Bd. 10)

In-depth scholarly study of the representation of toga styles of the last years of the Roman Republic through the period of the Roman Empire. The first comprehensive survey of the subject. An important reference resource for the dating of sculpture and for iconographical study.

Bibliographical references throughout the text. Abkürzungsverzeichnis, p.ix–x. Listen zur Typologie und Chronologie der Toga-Darstellungen, p.106–175. Index der antiken Schriftquellen und Inschriften, p.176–77. Index wichtiger Begriffe und Personennamen, p.178–83. Index der Denkmäler nach ihrem Aufbewahrungsort, p.184–202.

P127 Losfield, Georges. Essai sur le costume grec. Pref. de François Charmouz. Paris, De Boccard, 1991. 415p. il.

Philological analysis of ancient Greek dress primarily based on contemporary literary sources. Weaving techniques are also examined.

Contents: (I) Connaissance du vêtement grec; (II) Généralités vestimentaires; (III) Le vêtement de l'homme; (IV) Le vêtement de la femme; (V) Vêtements divers.

Index des 336 termes et expressions grecs relatifs aux vêtements et aux métiers de l'habillement rencontrés dans l'ouvrage, p.327–39. Index bibliographique: (I) Textes antiques consultés et cités, p.340–69; (II) Textes médiévaux et modernes consultés et cités, p.370–99. Table analytique des matières, p.401–11.

P128 Morrow, Katherine Dohan. Greek footwear and the dating of sculpture. [Madison], Univ. of Wisconsin Pr., [1985]. xxx, 231p. il. (Wisconsin studies in classics)

Documents variations in Greek footwear, using the resulting documentation as a tool to establish a relative chronology for sculpture. Analysis is confined to footwear appearing on Greek original sculpture. Roman copies or adaptations of Greek originals are generally omitted from the analysis, as are vase paintings.

Contents: (1) Foot and leg vases; (2) The archaic period; (3) The severe period; (4) The classical period: fifth century; (5) The classical period: fourth century; (6) the Hellenistic period; (7) Footwear forms and the chronology and interpretation of sculpture; Appendix 1: Figures [analyzing the stages of development of sandal shapes and styles]; Appendix 2: Footwear on Roman copies; Appendix 3: Classical Greek footwear terms.

Notes, p.185–216. Selected bibliography, p.217–18. Index, p.219–30.

P129 Pekridou-Gorecki, Anastasia. Mode im antiken Griechenland: textile Fertigung und Kleidung. München, Beck, [1989]. 159p. il. (Beck's archäologische Bibliothek)

Describes the stages of manufacture, preparation, and care of textiles, as well as the confection of clothing in the ancient world. Most illustrations are taken from contemporary vase paintings or textiles.

Contents: (I) Herstellung der Stoffe; (II) Walken und Reinigung der Gewebe; (III) Färben der Gewebe; (IV) Herstellung der Kleider; (V) Pflege und Aufbewahrung der Stoffe und Kleider; (VI) Grundformen der weiblichen und männlichen Kleidung; (VII) Kleider im Kult; (VIII) Luxus; (IX) Kleidung und Gesellschaft.

Anmerkungen, p.138–54. Sachregister, p.158–59.

P130 Roche-Bérnard, Geneviève, and Ferdière, Alain. Costumes et textiles en Gaule Romaine. [Paris], Errance, [1993]. 175p. il. (Collection des Hesperides)

In-depth scholarly study of textiles and dress in Roman Gaul.

Contents: (I) Le vêtement des enfants et des femmes; (II) Le costume masculin; (III) Vêtements de travail et de chasse. Les accessoires du vêtement; (IV) Les matières premières; (V) La mise en oeuvre des matières premières; (VI) Le tissage; (VII) La teinture; (VIII) Finitions, entretien. Les foulons; (IX) Fabrication et commercialisation des textiles; Annexes: Presence du textile avant la conquête romaine; Principales sources documentaires.

Glossaire, p.157–64. Bibliographie, p.165–75.

P131 Vogelsang-Eastwood, Gillian. Pharaonic Egyptian clothing. N.Y., Brill, 1993. xxii, 195p. il., map. (Studies in textile and costume history, 2)

Guide to the clothing types worn in ancient Egypt, and investigation into how ancient Egyptian clothes were made. Based on surviving textile fragments rather than on tomb paintings, and its focus is on items from non-royal contexts. The period covered extends from the Late Predynastic to the 26th dynasty.

Contents: (1) Introd.; (2) Loincloths; (3) Aprons; (4) Kilts and skirts; (5) Sashes and straps; (6) The Archaic wraparound; (7) Dresses; (8) Bag-tunics; (9) Shawls and cloaks; (10) Headgear; (11) Conclusions.

Glossary, p.xvii–xxii. List of abbreviations used in the text, p.xxiii. Bibliography, p.185–91. Index of personal names with a reference to the tombs mentioned in the text, p.193–94. Index of geographical names, p.195.

P132 The world of Roman costume. Ed. by Judith Lynn Sebesta and Larissa Bonfante. [Madison], Univ. of Wisconsin Pr., [1994]. xviii, 272p. il. (Wisconsin studies in classics)

Collection of scholarly papers originally presented at the seminar "The religious, social and political significance of Roman dress," American Academy in Rome (1988). Explores dress styles worn in Rome and in other parts of the Roman Empire. Individual dress components, such as the toga, jewelry, and footwear are examined, and the symbolism of clothes and their colors is also discussed.

Contents: (1) The toga: from national to ceremonial costume, by Shelley Stone; (2) Symbolism in the costume of the Roman woman, by Judith Lynn Sebesta; (3) The costume of the Roman bride, by Laetitia La Follette; (4) Tunica ralla, tunica spissa: the colors and textiles of Roman costume, by Judith Lynn Sebesta; (5) Jewelry as a symbol of status in the Roman Empire, by Ann M. Stout; (6) Roman footwear, by

Norma Goldman; (7) Cicero as evidence for attitudes to dress in the Late Republic, by Julia Heskel; (8) De habitu vestis: clothing in the Aeneid, by Henry Bender; (9) The social, religious, and political aspects of costume in Josephus, by Douglas R. Edwards; (10) Graeco-Roman dress in Syro-Mesopotamia, by Bernard Goldman; (11) Costume in Roman Palestine: Archaeological remains and the evidence from the Mishnah, by Lucille A. Roussin; (12) Costume as geographic indicator: barbarians and prisoners on cuirassed statue breastplates, by Richard A. Gergel; (13) Reconstructing Roman clothing, by Norma Goldman.

Bibliographical references follow each essay. Glossary, p.241–48. Bibliography, p.249–61. Index, p.263–72.

P133 Zoffili, Ermanno. Costume e cultura dell'antico Egitto: da Narmer a Cleopatra. A c. di Peter A. Clayton. Pref. di Silvio Curto. Milano, Fabbri, [1991]. 255p. il. (chiefly col.), maps, ports. (chiefly col.)

German trans., Berlin, Propyläen, 1992.

Splendidly illustrated (with excellent color photographs and beautifully drawn and colored sketches), in-depth investigation into the dress and accessories of the Egyptians from the Pre-Dynastic period to the end of the Ptolemaic-Roman period. Textual and visual analyses are provided not only of clothing, its construction, and how it was worn, but also of hairstyles, beards, wigs, head-gear, make-up, shoes, and jewelry. Dress at all social levels is examined, as are foreign influences.

Contents: Il canoni proporzionali Il potere assoluto; La bellezza femminile; Il concetto della visione.

Bibliografia, p.254–55.

Early Christian—Gothic

P134 Braun, Joseph S. J. Die liturgische Gewandung im Occident und Orient; nach Ursprung und Entwicklung, Verwendung und Symbolik. Freiburg im Breisgau, Herder, 1907. xxiv, 797p. il. (Repr.: Darmstadt, Wissenschaftliche Buchgesellschaft, 1964)

Important and thorough early dictionary of liturgical vestments, omitted from GLAH 1. Definitions cover French, English, German, and Italian terminology.

Contents: (I) Die liturgischen Untergewänder: (1) Der Amikt; (2) Der Fanone; (3) Die Albe; (4) Das Cingulum; (5) Das Subcinctorium; (6) Rochett und Superpelliceum; (II) Die liturgischen Obergewänder: (1) Die Kasel; (2) Dalmatik und Tunicella; (3) Das Pluviale; (III) Die liturgischen Bekleidungsstücke der Hände, der Füsse und des Kopfes: (1) Die Pontifikalhandschuhe; (2) Die pontifikale Fussbekleidung; (3) Die Mitra; (4) Tiara, Pileolus, Birett; (IV) Die Insignien: (1) Der Manipel; (2) Die Stola; (3) Das Pallium; (4) Das Rationale; (V) Symbolik, Farbe und Segnung der liturgischen Gewänder; (2) Die liturgischen Farben; (3) Segnung der liturgischen Gewänder; Die liturgische Gewandung in ihrer Gesamtentwicklung.

Bibliographical references throughout the text. Verzeichnis der häufiger benutzten mittelalterlichen Werke, p.xvii. Verzeichnis bemerkenswerter für die Arbeit benutzter Inventare, p.xviii–xxii. Verzeichnis der besprochenen alten Gewänder, p.787–89. Übersicht über die dem Werk zu Grunde liegenden Monumentalen und schriftlichen Quellen, p.789–93. Sachregister, p.793–97.

P135 Brüggen, Elke. Kleidung und Mode in der höfischen Epik des 12. und 13. Jahrhunderts. Heidelberg, Winter, 1989. 327p. il., 295 plates (Beihefte zum Euphorion, H. 23)

Scholarly study based on the author's doctoral thesis (Universität Köln, 1986/87) of 12th- through early 14th-century aristocratic dress and textiles as revealed in the texts and illuminations of German courtly romances. The excellent collection of comparative illustrations includes not only illuminated manuscripts, but also seals, sculpture, monumental effigies and reliefs, wall paintings, and jewelry, with most examples drawn from the French and German schools. Particularly important for its analysis of medieval German clothing terminology, discussed not only in the final chapter, but also in an extensive glossary.

Bibliographical references throughout the text. Glossar, p.202–93. Literaturverzeichnis, p.294–314. Abkürzungs- und Siglen-verzeichnis, p.315–17.

P136 Bruhn, Jutta-Annette. Coins and costume in Late Antiquity. Washington, D.C., Dumbarton Oaks Research Library and Collection, 1993. 68p. il., map (Dumbarton Oaks Byzantine collection publications, 9)

Concise discussion focusing on the use of coins and medallions in Roman and Late Antique jewelry and the impact on costume in general. The origins of this custom during the early Roman Empire period are examined, as is the tradition's subsequent development. The primary focus is on the Late Antique period. A catalog of 15 items (all illustrated) follows the general discussion.

Notes, p.54–61. Glossary, p.62–63. Bibliography, p.64–65.

P137 Demay, Germain. Le costume au Moyen age d'après les sceaux. Repr. en fac-similé de l'edition de 1880, avec une étude d'introduction, de nouveaux compléments illustrés et une table onomastique par Jean-Bernard de Vaivre. [Paris], Berger-Levrault, 1978. il. 496p. il. (part col.)

1st ed., Paris, Dumoulin, 1880.

Reprint, with a new introduction, of a ground-breaking early history of medieval costume using seals as the primary source of visual information. Areas of particular focus include royal, military, ecclesiastical, and female dress. The reprint lacks the original edition's color plates.

Contents: Costume royal ou de majesté; Vêtement féminin; Habillement chevaleresque; Type héraldique; Vêtement de chasse; Maires et échevins; Type naval; Vêtement sacerdotal; Les trois personnes divines; Les anges; La vierge et les saintes.

Table onomastique, p.[xxxi]–xlv. Table alphabetique des matières, p.[485]–90. Table analytique, p.[491]–96.

P138 Egan, Geoff, and Pritchard, Frances. Dress accessories, c.1150–c.1450. With contrib. by Justine Bayley . . . [et al.] Principal illustrators, Susan Mitford and

Nick Griffiths. London, HMSO, [1991]. xi, 410p. il. (part col.), maps (Museum of London. Medieval finds from excavations in London, 3)
Collection of essays by various authors examining accessories discovered during excavations. The many illustrations include photographs of the objects found and drawings based on excavated items; images of (mostly) effigies showing accessory items being worn are also included.

Bibliography, p.402–10.

P139 Grew, Francis, and Neegaard, Margrethe de. Shoes and pattens. Illus. By Susan Mitford. London, HMSO, [1988]. vi, 145p. il., map (Museum of London. Medieval finds from excavations in London, 2)
"Medieval shoes, boots and pattens, being made of leather or wood, are rarely preserved on sites, and their appearance is normally inferred from such sources as manuscript illustration, monumental effigies and brasses, or contemporary writings. The recovery of well over a thousand examples, many of them complete and in almost perfect condition, is thus an achievement of great significance."—*Introd.* The many illustrations include photographs of excavated shoes, and drawings showing their construction.

Contents: Shoes from London sites, 1100–1450; Shoemaking and cobbling; Pattens; Sizes and wear patterns: social inferences; Shoes in art and literature.

Recording methods, archive and conventions used in the report, p.7–8. Glossary, p.123–25. Appendix I: The excavations, p.131–36. Appendix II: Conservation, by Katharine Starling, p.137–39. Bibliography, p.140–42. Summaries in French and German, p.143–45.

P140 Houston, Mary Galway. Medieval costume in England and France: the 13th, 14th, and 15th centuries. N.Y., Dover, 1996. 228p. il.
See GLAH 1:P108 for original annotation.

"Unabridged and slightly altered republication of the work first published . . . in 1939. In [this] edition, the original color plates appear in black and white within the text and are reproduced in color on the covers."—*Bibliographical note.*

P141 Innemee, Karel C. Ecclesiastical dress in the medieval Near East. N.Y., Brill, 1992. x, 300p. il., 64p. of plates (Studies in textile and costume history, 1)
Scholarly text investigating Nubian, Coptic, Syrian, Byzantine, and Armenian liturgical and/or monastic vestments, with an emphasis on the first category. Wall paintings and manuscript illustrations and texts are the primary sources of information.

Contents: (1) History of the research, state of research and questions; (2) Liturgical vestments in eastern churches other than Nubian; (3) Monastic vestments in eastern churches other than Nubian; (4) An iconographical analysis of vestments depicted on Nubian wall-paintings; (5) An iconological analysis of vestments depicted on Nubian wall-paintings; Appendix: Catalogue of Nubian mural paintings.

Bibliographical references throughout the text. Bibliography, p.217–25. Indices: Proper names, p.293–95; Geographical names, p.295; Ecclesiastical vestments [Armenian; Byzantine, Greek and Russian; Coptic; Latin; Nubian; Syrian], p.295–99; General index, p.299.

P142 Piltz, Elisabeth. Le costume officiel des dignitaires byzantins à l'époque Paléologue. Uppsala, [Uppsala Univ.], 1994. 172p. il., 73 plates (Acta Universitatis Upsaliensis. Figura Nova Series, 26. Uppsala studies in the history of art)
Examines differences in rank, as exemplified by variations in dress and insignia, throughout the Byzantine Empire. The function of dress distinctions in the consolidation of Byzantine imperial power is also discussed.

Contents: (I) Introduction; (II) Insignes dans le traité de Pseudo-Kodinos; (II.1) La première classe des dignitaires; (II.2) La seconde classe des dignitaires; (II.3) La troisième class des dignitaires; (III) Les insignes byzxantins; (III.1) Titulature, offices et distinctions de classes; (III.1.1) Distinction des deux classes des archontes; (III.1.2) Autre distinction des deux classes des archontes; (IV) Le symbolisme des insignes; (V) Conclusion.

Bibliographie, p.81–87. Appendice, p.88–93. Index, p.94–99.

P143 Piponnier, Francoise, and Mane, Perrine. Dress in the Middle Ages. Trans. by Caroline Beamish. New Haven, Yale Univ. Pr., 1997. vii, 167p. il.
Trans. of Se vêtir au Moyen Age. Paris, Birò, 1995.

Discusses dress in medieval Western Europe from the Carolingian period on.

Contents: (1) Sources and applications; (2) materials; (3) The acquisition of clothing; (4) The history of working-class clothing; (5) Kings and warriors: the ruling classes and their fashions; (6) The diffusion and regulation of fashion; (7) The cycles of life; (8) Clothes as identification markers; (9) Beyond society's limits.

Bibliography, p.157–63. Glossary, p.164–67.

P144 Le vêtement: histoire, archéologie et symbolique vestimentaires au Moyen Age. Paris, Léopard d'or, 1989. 332p. il. (Cahiers du Léopard d'or, 1)
Collection of scholarly essays, focusing on issues surrounding medieval dress.

Contents: Historiographie du vêtement, by Odile Blanc; Le symbolism vestimentaire du dépouillement chez saint Martin de Tours à travers l'image et l'imaginaire médiévaux, by Pierre Bureau; Les robes de rêve: robes de roi, robes de fée, robes de fleurs, robes du ciel, by Alice Planche; Emergence du vêtement de travail à travers l'iconographie médiévale, by Perrine Mane; Du drapeau à la cotte: vêtir l'enfant au Moyen Age (XIIIe–XVe s.), by Danièle Alexandre-Bidon; Les livrées de textiles et de fourrures à la fin du Moyen Age: l'exemple de la cour du roi Edouard Ier Plantagenêt, by Frédérique Lachaud: Signes de hiérarchie sociale à la fin du Moyen Age d'après les vêtements: méthodes et recherches, by Christian de Mérindol; Une révolution dans le costume masculin au XIVe siècle, by Françoise Piponnier; Vêtement féminin, vêtement masculin à la fin du Moyen Age: le point de vue des moralistes, by Odile Blanc; Le costume français, miroir de la sensibilité (1350–1500), by Michèle Beaulieu; De la tunique d'Adam au manteau d'Elie, by François Garnier. Du symbole au vêtement: fonction et signification de la couleur dans la culture courtoise de la Pologne médiévale, by Malgorzata Wilska.

Bibliographical refernces follow each essay.

SEE ALSO: Bildwörterbuch der Kleidung und Rüstung: vom Alten Orient bis zum ausgehenden Mittelalter (GLAH 2:P84); History of dress series, v.1: Scott, M. Late Gothic Europe, 1400–1500 (GLAH 2:P113).

Islamic

Dictionaries and Encyclopedias

P145 Dozy, R. P. A. Dictionnaire détaillé des noms des vêtements chez les Arabes: ouvrage couronné et publié par la troisième classe de l'Institut Royale des Pays-Bas. Beirut, Librairie du Liban, [1969?]. viii, 444p.

1st ed., Amsterdam, Muller, 1845.

Pioneering dictionary of Islamic dress terminology is based on research into the manuscript sources of the different Arabic-speaking countries (Africa, Arabia, Persia, Syria, etc.). Most of the manuscripts date from the medieval period and were surveyed in libraries of the Low Countries, and especially that at Leiden.

An introductory historical survey precedes the dictionary, which is ordered following the Arabic. Each entry includes an extensive discussion of the term, the sources where it is to be found, and the parts of the Islamic world where the particular dress item is/was worn. Where possible, French and/or non-French language equivalents also are given.

Liste des mots arabes et autres expliqués dans les notes, p.439–44. Liste des mots appartenant aux langues européennes et dont cet ouvrage fait connaître la signification ou l'étymologie, p.445.

Histories and Handbooks

P146 Besançenot, Jean. Costumes of Morocco. Pref. by James Bynon. Trans. by Caroline Stone. N.Y., Kegan Paul International (Distr. by Routledge, Chapman and Hall, 1990). 204p. il., 60 col. plates, map.

Trans. of Costumes du Maroc. Paris, Horizons de France, 1942; 2d ed., Aix-en-Provence, Edisud, 1988.

The original publication was a luxury ed. of only 300 copies. This later ed. has updated texts, where appropriate, but the original hand-colored illustrations have been kept. Examines the derivatives of the ancient draped costume, worn throughout the Mediterranean world. Sketches delineate the various stages in the history of the draping process, and provide specific male and female examples of dress, accessories, and jewelry.

The plates are divided among the different groups that live (or lived) in Morocco. Descriptive essays include historical surveys of culture and society in Morocco.

Contents: The townspeople; The Chaouïa; The peoples of northern Morocco; The mountain tribes of central Morocco; The Chleuh; The Saharan tribes practising long-range nomadism; The urban Jews; The Jewish communities of southern Morocco.

P147 Les costumes traditionnels féminins de Tunisie: ouvrage collectif réalisé par le Centre des Arts et Traditions Populaires. [Contrib. by] Alya Bayram . . . [et al.] [Tunis], Maison Tunisienne de l'Édition, [1988]. 282p. il. (chiefly col.), 68 col. plates, map.

Study of traditional Tunisian female costume, based on a group research project conducted 1965–70. Illustrations, consisting of line and colored drawings based on the model of Besançenot's Costumes of Morocco (GLAH 2:P146), are extensively annotated.

Glossaire, p.255-[77]. Bibliographie, p.[278]–[82].

P148 Languages of dress in the Middle East. Ed. by Nancy Lindisfarne-Tapper and Bruce Ingham. [London], Curzon in assoc. with the Centre of Near and Middle Eastern Studies, SOAS, [1997]. 196p. il.

Collection of essays examining the "complex relation between clothing practices and natural languages in the Middle East."—*Pref.* Approaches drawn from social anthropology, history, ethnology, and linguistics.

Contents: (1) Approaches to the study of dress in the Middle East, by Nancy Lindisfarne-Tapper and Bruce Ingham; (2) Men's dress in the Arabian peninsula: historical and present perspectives, by Bruce Ingham; (3) Changing the habits of a lifetime: the adaptation of Hejazi dress to the new social order, by Mai Yamani; (4) The dress of the Shahsevan tribespeople of Iranian Azerbaijan, by Nancy Lindisfarne-Tapper; (5) Felt capes and masks of the Caucasus, by Robert Chenciner; (6) Male dress in the Caucasus, with special reference to Abkhazia and Georgia, by George Hewitt and Zaira Khiba; (7) Fashions and styles: Maltese women's headdress, by Dionisius Agius; (8) The Burza face cover: an aspect of dress in Southeastern Arabia, by Dawn Chatty; (9) Faith and fashion in Turkey, by John Norton; (10) Politics of dress: the dress reform laws of 1920–1930s Iran, by Patricia L. Baker.

Bibliographical references at ends of essays. Index, p.193–96.

P149 Majda, Tadeusz, and Mrozowska, Alina. Tureckie stroje i sceny rodzajowe: z kolekcji Króla Stanisława Augusta: katalog rysunkòw = Costumes et moeurs turques de la collection du roi Stanislas Auguste: catalogue de dessins. Warszawa, Wydawnictwa Uniwersytetu Warszawskiego, 1991. 448p. il., 256 plates (Prace Biblioteki Uniwersyteckiej w Warszawie = Acta bibliothecae universatis varsoviensis, XI)

Catalog of drawings formerly in the collection of the last King of Poland, Stanislas Augustus Poniatowski, and now in the Drawings Collection at the University of Warsaw Library. These drawings illustrate late-18th-century court and everyday dress of the different groups living under the Ottoman Empire, especially those in Istanbul; they also provide information concerning the furnishing of interiors. Groups represented include Armenians, Arabs, Ciliciens, (Western) Europeans, Greeks, Jews, and the various echelons of Turkish society.

The drawings are divided into the following categories: the Sultan's court, and various court officials; officers of state; ecclesiastical dress; the military; civil servants; miscellaneous; and buildings and monuments. A full catalog entry is provided for each drawing; titles are translated into French.

Resume [in French], p.163–68. Skróty bibliograficzne, p.169. Indeks nazw polskich, p.171–76. Indeks nazw francuskich, p.177–82. Indeks nazw tureckich, p.183–90.

P150 Mayer, L. A. Mamluk costume: a survey. Geneva, Kundig, 1952. 120p. 20 plates.

Building on Dozy's fundamental research (see GLAH 2:P145), attempts to connect the literary terms analyzed by Dozy to visual equivalents. With Mamluk costume in Egypt and Syria, 1250–1517, as the principal focus, this was the first 20th-century attempt to survey an area of Islamic dress.

An introductory essay reviews bibliographical sources such as Arab chronicles, manuals for government officials, illuminated manuscripts, and bronze objects. European travel accounts are also discussed. A separate section analyzes the importance of early Italian paintings as a visual resource since (as the author notes) few actual costume pieces have survived.

Contents: The caliph; The sultan; The military aristocracy; Arms and armour; The ecclesiastics; Robes of honour; Christians, Jews and Samaritans; Women; Appendix I: The Qumash; Appendix II [bibliographical references].

Bibliographical references throughout the text. Bibliography, p.83–111. Index, p.112–19.

P151 Ross, Heather Colyer. The art of Arabian costume: a Saudi Arabian profile. 4th ed. Studio City, Calif., Empire Publishing Service/Players Pr., 1994. 188p. il. (chiefly col., maps.

1st ed., London, Kegan Paul, 1981; French trans., Clarens-Montreux, Arabesque, 1989.

Contents: The historical background; Influence; Traditional Arabian costume; People of the Arabian Peninsula; Regional styles; Body ornament; Arts and crafts; Appendix 1: Embroidery stitches; Appendix 2: Bedouin dress embroidery; Appendix 3: Care of textiles.

Bibliography, p.158–59. Glossary of Arabic words, p.160–79. List of technical terms, p.180–86. Index, p.187–88.

P152 Scarce, Jennifer M. Women's costume of the Near and Middle East. London, Unwin Hyman, 1987. 192p. il.

Surveys the range of female dress worn throughout the Ottoman Empire, and documents its cultural and economic diversity. Many of the clothing items illustrated are in the collection of the Royal Museum of Scotland, Edinburgh.

Contents: (1) The arrival and establishment of the Ottomans; (2) The Ottoman inheritance—Byzantium; (3) The Ottoman inheritance: Central Asia; (4) The Ottomans at home: mainly Istanbul; (5) The Ottomans abroad: South-East Europe; (6) The Ottomans abroad: the Arab world; (7) Close and distant neighbours: Persia and Afghanistan.

Notes, p.184–88. Select bibliography, p.189–192.

P153 Silks for the sultans: Ottoman imperial garments from Topkapi Palace. Photography and concept [by] Ahmet Ertug. Essays by Patricia L. Baker, Hülya Tezcan, and Jennifer Wearden. [Istanbul], Ertug and Kocabiyik, 1996. 250p. col. il.

Outstandingly illustrated, superbly produced. Based on approximately 5,000 garments in the collection of the Topkapi Palace Museum, this publication illustrates some of the most beautiful and impressive Ottoman period silk kaftans and other dress items worn by the sultans and (male) members of their families. Each garment is illustrated complete, usually back as well as front. Large-scale photographs show details of motifs, weave structure, and additional workmanship (e.g., embroidery). A brief descriptive entry accompanies each set of photographs. Reproductions of illuminated manuscripts and early costume books, showing kaftans in use, are also included. The plates are divided into sections based on motif, fabric type and origin, and method of decoration; a chronological order is followed within these sections.

Contents: The Imperial robe collection at Topkapi Palace Museum, by Hülye Tezcan; Textile patterns on royal Ottoman kaftans, by Patricia L. Baker; The technical skill of Ottoman craftsmen, by Jennifer Wearden.

Bibliography, p.249–50.

P154 Stillman, Yedida Kalfon. Palestinian costume and jewelry. Albuquerque, Univ. of New Mexico Pr., 1979. xv, 135p. il. (part col.)

Catalog of the collection belonging to the Museum of International Folk Art, Museum of New Mexico, Santa Fe. Includes a broader study of Palestinian dress and its relationship to Middle Eastern costume in general.

Contents: (1) An introduction to the region; (2) Men's clothing; (3) Women's clothing; (4) Jewelry; (5) Middle Eastern embroidery, including "A sampler of traditional motifs."

Glossary, p.113–19. Notes, p.120–29. Bibliography, p.130–38.

P155 The Topkapi Saray Museum: costumes, embroideries and other textiles. Trans., exp. and ed. by J. M. Rogers from the original Turkish by Hülye Tezcan and Selma Delibas. Boston, Little, Brown, 1986. 216p. col. il.

Beautifully illustrated selection of clothing and textiles from the wardrobes of sultans, members of the royal family, and court officials. Approximately 2,500 pieces have survived, primarily items of male attire. Inscribed woven silks, including tomb-covers and banners, have also survived. Following a number of brief introductory essays, 121 items are described and illustrated in the catalog (which comprises 85 items of dress and 25 embroideries).

Contents: (I) Costume: (1) The collection of Sultan's and other Ottoman costumes and embroideries in the Topkapi Saray and their history; (2) Silk textiles: geography and types; (3) Dyes and dyestuffs; (4) The silk industry: organization; (5) Garments: fashion, style and pattern; (6) Some sources for the history of Ottoman textiles; (7) Hierarchies and rank; (8) Wool and mohair; (9) The Ottoman fur trade;

(II) Embroideries: Turkish embroideries: historical documentation.

Bibliographical references (which have been expanded upon by the present ed.) follow each chapter. Bibliographical note, p.211. Index, p.215–16.

P156 Weir, Shelagh. Palestinian costume. Austin, Univ. of Texas Pr., in coop. with British Museum Publications, 1989. 288p. il. (chiefly col.), maps.

Handsomely illustrated in-depth examination of the history of Palestinian costume in Israel, the Occupied Territories, and Jordan. The many illustrations include 19th- and early 20th-century photographs and paintings documenting costume, as well as photographs of pieces in public and private collections (primarily the Museum of Mankind, London).

Contents: (1) Materials and merchants; (2) Men's costume; (3) Women's costume: body garments; (4) Women's costume: head wear and jewellery; (5) Changing fashions in Beit Dajan; (6) Wedding rituals in Beit Dajan.

Notes, p.279–81. Arabic transcriptions of songs, p.282. Select bibliography, p.283–84. Index and glossary, p.285–88.

Renaissance—Modern

Dictionaries and Encyclopedias

P157 Dictionnaire de la mode au XXe siècle. Collectif sous la dir. de Bruno Remaury. Paris, Regard, 1994. 592p. il. (part col.)

Comprehensive, extensively illustrated dictionary encyclopedia. International in scope, its approximately 2,500 entries examine all aspects of 20th-century fashion and the fashion industry: production, creation, diffusion, and advertising. Fields covered include: accessories, artistic directors, associations, authors, boutiques, clothing types, costumiers, couturiers, creaters, fabrics, fibers, fashion journals, fashion schools, fashion trends, financing, hairdressers, hatmakers, illustrators, industrial groups, jewelry makers and jewelers, journalists, machinery, make-up artists, managers, models, modistes, museum collections, perfumers, photography, the ready-to-wear industry, shoe makers and designers, stylists, tailors, and trademarks.

Bibliographie, p.589–92.

P158 The fashion book. London, Phaidon, 1998. 512p. il. (part col.)

"Spanning 150 years . . . [this] is an A–Z guide to 500 clothes and accessory designers, photographers, models and those iconic individuals who instigated or symbolize a whole fashion movement."—[*Introd.*] Each entry comprises one page—mostly an illus. showing work typical of the individual's oeuvre/style. A brief caption, providing very basic biographical and design information, accompanies each image.

Glossary of movements, genres and technical terms, p.504–08. Directory of museums and galleries, p.509–10.

P159 Martin, Richard. The St. James fashion encyclopedia: a survey of style from 1945 to the present. [Rev. ed.] Detroit, Visible Ink Pr., 1997. x, 438p. il.

1st ed., Contemporary fashion, N.Y., St. James Pr., 1995.

Alphabetical listing of more than 200 late-20th-century clothing designers, and fashion and design houses, with an emphasis on U.S. names. High-end fashion as well as avant-garde and mass-market individuals and groups are included. Excluded from consideration are stylists, fashion models, and photographers. Each entry opens with a brief history and/or biography, including exhibitions and awards. Publications by and/or about the subject follow; significant statements or comments on fashion made by individuals are also included. The main body of each entry comprises a (generally chronological) survey of the subject's work.

Fashion chronology, p.ix–x. Appendix: Brief entries, p.423–32. Nationality index, p.433–34.

P160 O'Hara, Georgina. The encyclopedia of fashion. Introd. by Carrie Donovan. N.Y., Abrams, 1986. 272p. il. (part col.)

Dictionary encyclopedia focusing on the five major fashion capitals of the 19th and 20th centuries: London, Milan, New York, Paris, and Rome. Topics covered: clothes, the elements of clothing and clothing manufacture, accessories and fabrics; designers, manufacturers, personalities and trend-setters; and journalists, editors, artists, and illustrators (including those working in the film industry). Illustrations are taken from 19th- and 20th-century fashion magazines.

Bibliography, p.269–72.

P161 Schoeffler, O.E., and Gale, William. Esquire's encyclopedia of 20th century men's fashions. N.Y., McGraw-Hill, 1973. x, 709p. il. (part col.), ports.

Thematically organized encyclopedia detailing "every item of apparel worn by the American man of this century while exploring the society of which his clothes are a reflection."—*Introd.* Fifty chapters survey not only clothing types (most notably the suit), but also hairstyles, accessories (for example luggage), fibers and fabrics, manufacturing processes, and fashion colors. Most of the numerous illustrations are taken from 20th-century fashion magazines.

Glossary, p.644–98. Index, p.690–709.

Histories and Handbooks

P162 Chenoune, Farid. A history of men's fashion. Trans. from the French by Deke Dusinberre. Pref. by Richard Martin. Paris, Flammarion, 1993. 336p. il. (part col.), ports. (part col.)

Trans. of Des modes et des hommes: deux siècles d'élégance masculine. Paris, Flammarion, 1993.

Extensively illustrated, in-depth study of 18th–20th century men's dress in the Western world. The numerous illustrations include contemporary paintings, fashion plates, designer sketches, caricatures, tailors' patterns, and photographs. Cross-cultural influences (such as Anglomania and Orientalism) are examined, as are trend-setters in the fashion world.

Contents: (I) Dress coat and frock coat: 1760–1850. (II) Overcoat and morning coat: 1850–1914. (III) Lounge suit and business suit. (IV) Pin stripes and black leather: 1940–1990.

Notes, p.319–29. Bibliography, p.330. Index, p.331–35.

P163 Costume accessories series. Ed. by Aileen Ribeiro. N.Y., Distr. by Drama Book Publishers, 1982–85. 9v.
Series of concise publications, each focusing on an area of dress accessory, 1600 to the present. The Western European tradition is given primary consideration although non-Western influences are also taken into account. Each vol. is arranged chronologically. Endnotes, a glossary, a bibliography, and a list of museums to visit are also common to all the vols.

Contents: Foster, Vanda. Bags and purses (1982); Alexander, Hélène. Fans (1984); Cumming, Valerie. Gloves (1982); Clark, Fiona. Hats (1982); Scarisbrick, Diana. Jewellery (1984); Mackrell, Alice. Shawls, stoles and scarves (1986); Swann, June. Shoes (1982); Farrell, Jeremy. Socks and stockings (1992); Farrell, Jeremy. Umbrellas and parasols (1985).

P164 An elegant art: fashion and fantasy in the eighteenth century: Los Angeles County Museum of Art collection of costumes and textiles. Organized and ed. by Edward Maeder. Essays by Edward Maeder . . . [et al.] Los Angeles, Los Angeles County Museum of Art; Abrams, 1983. 255p. il. (part col.)
Catalog published in conjunction with the exhibition, Los Angeles County Museum of Art (1983). Three main trends of the 18th century—Enlightenment, Revolution and Classicism—and their manifestation through contemporary fashion are surveyed. The catalog comprises 72 items, all of them illustrated with black-and-white and/or color photographs and with detailed accompanying descriptions.

Contents: The elegant art of dress, by Edward Maeder; The elegant art of movement, by Alicia M. Annas; The elegant art of woven silk, by Natalie Rothstein; The elegant art of embroidery, by Nikki Scheuer; The elegant art of lace, by Anne Ratzki-Kraatz; The elegant art of tapestry, by Anna G. Bennett; The elegant art of fancy dress, by Aileen Ribeiro; Appendix: Costume and textile conservation.

Bibliographical references appear at ends of chapters. Selected glossary: Eighteenth century costume and textile terms, p.221–48. Bibliographies, p.249–54.

P165 Ewing, Elizabeth. History of twentieth century fashion. 3d ed., rev and upd. by Alice Mackrell. Lanham, Md., Barnes & Noble Books, 1992. xi, 300p. il. (part col.)
See GLAH 1:P111 for 1st ed. (1974) and original annotation; rev. ed. 1986.

The 3d ed. includes a concluding chapter on fashion from the mid-1980s to the early 1990s.

Index, p.299–300.

P166 Hart, Avril, and North, Susan. Historical fashion in detail: the 17th and 18th centuries. Photographs by Richard Davis. Drawings by Leonie Davis. London, V&A Publications, 1998. 223p. il. (part col.)
Anthology of photographs of objects in the Victoria and Albert Museum's collection of historical dress, with technical commentary, "offering a lively survey of fashionable patterns, fabrics and colours."—*Introd.*

Contents: Stitching, seams, quilting and cording; Gathers, pleats and looped drapery; Collars, cuffs, and pockets; Buttons; Trimmings; Applied decoration; Slashing, pinking and stamping; Knitting, lace and openwork; Stomachers; Gloves and shoes.

Glossary, p.220–22. Selected further reading, p.223.

P167 Holland, Vyvyan Beresford. Hand coloured fashion plates, 1770 to 1899. [Reprint.] London, Batsford, 1988. 192p. il. (part col.)
See GLAH 1:P112 for original annotation.

P168 Hollander, Anne. Seeing through clothes. N.Y., Viking Pr., 1978. xvi, 504p. il. (Repr.: Berkeley, Univ. of California Pr., 1993)
Examines the relationship between clothes portrayed in works of art and clothes worn in real life, arguing that clothes should be seen and studied in the same way that paintings are seen and studied. Each chapter "explores the idea that in civilized Western life the clothed figure looks more persuasive and comprehensible in art than it does in reality."—*Pref.* The contribution that Western dress plays in forming the image of the self is an important theme.

Contents: (I) Drapery; (II) Nudity; (III) Undress; (IV) Costume; (V) Dress; (VI) Mirrors.

Notes, p.469–78. Bibliography, p.479–84. Index, p.485–504.

P169 Milbank, Caroline Rennolds. Couture: the great designers. N.Y., Stewart, Tabori and Chang, 1985. 430p. il. (part col.), ports. (part col.)
An introductory chapter provides a brief overview of the history of couture. "In the seven chapters that follow, designers and couturiers [are] grouped in categories according to how their clothes look."—*Introd.* Each couturier is presented individually. The many illustrations are taken from designer sketches, fashion shows, film, and contemporary fashion journals.

Contents: The founders; The artists; The purists; The entertainers; The extravagants; The architects; The realists.

Bibliography, p.416–18. Index of designers, p.419–29.

P170 Mulvagh, Jane. Vogue history of 20th century fashion. With a foreword by Valerie D. Mendes. London, Viking, 1988. vii, 410p. il. (chiefly col.), ports. (part col.)
Profusely illustrated survey of designers, craftspeople, models, photographers, illustrators, journalists, and fashion pundits. Divided chronologically into eight stylistic periods, a succession of year-by-year analyses is provided. Attention is paid not only to national stylistic characteristics, but also to international connections. Accessories are an important component of this survey, as are interviews with fashion designers.

Index, p.404–09.

P171 Newton, Stella Mary. Health, art, and reason: dress reformers of the nineteenth century. London, John Murray, 1974. 192p. il., 66 plates.
Traces the history of the women's dress reform movement in the U.S. and (primarily) in Britain from the 1850s on.

Contents: (1) Women with views: (2) Pre-Raphaelite clothing; (3) Grecian fillets; (4) The strong-minded woman; (5) The early 'eighties; (6) Sanitarians and woolleners; (7) New attitudes to reform; (8) The attack on tubes; (9) Socialist gowns.

Appendixes, p.169–71. Notes, p.172–79. Bibliography, p.180–83. Index, p.185–92.

P172 Peacock, John. Men's fashion: the complete sourcebook. With over 1000 color illustrations. N.Y., Thames and Hudson, 1996. 216p. il.

Chronological review of the development of men's fashion in the Western tradition from the 1790s to the late 20th century. While focusing on clothes worn by members of the upper classes, the later period also covers street style fashions. Divided into illustrative sections comprising colored drawings by the author, each covering an approximate decade. Within these sections clothes are grouped into headings relevant to the period covered, and captions at the end of these sections provide annotations concerning color, cut, and fashion details.

Chart of the development of men's fashion, p.202–08. Concise biographies of designers, tailors and outfitters, p.209–14.

P173 ———. 20th-century fashion: the complete sourcebook. With a pref. by Christian Lacroix. 1100 detailed original drawings in color. N.Y., Thames and Hudson, 1993. 240p. il. (chiefly col.)

Decade-by-decade survey of women's clothing and accessories, 1900–1990. Each decade primarily consists of a series of colored drawings by the author, followed by brief notes about the items featured. The decade's illustrations begin with impressions of fashions by leading couturiers and designers, followed by sections on underwear, leisure wear, day wear, evening wear, bridal wear, and accessories.

Chart of the development of 20th-century fashion, p.226–31. Concise biographies of couturiers and designers, p.232–39. Sources for 20th-century fashion, p.239–40.

P174 Reineking von Bock, Gisela. 200 Jahre Mode: Kleider vom Rokoko bis heute. Köln, Museum für Angewandte Kunst Köln,, 1991. 239p. chiefly il. (part col.), ports. (part col.) (Kataloge des Museums für Angewandte Kunst Köln, Bd. XII)

Chronologically arranged catalog of dress items in the museum's permanent collection. While there is an obvious emphasis on foreign fashions, the publication is useful for its inclusion of German designers within this broader context.

P175 Ribeiro, Aileen. The art of dress: fashion in England and France, 1750 to 1820. New Haven, Yale Univ. Pr., 1995. 257p. il. (part col.), ports. (part col.)

Lavishly illustrated, important, and wide-ranging scholarly discussion of the relationship of politics, painting, dress (including fancy dress), and portraiture, and of the relationship between France and England as revealed in fashion and its portrayal.

Contents: Introduction: truth and history: the meaning of dress in art, 1750–1820; (1) The fabric of society: fashion from 1750 to 1789; (2) Painters of modern life: fashion from 1789 to 1820; (3) The stuff of heroes: historical themes in dress and art in France; (4) Remembrance of things past: image and reality in fancy dress in England.

Notes, p.237–45. Select bibliography, p.246–48. Index, p.249–57.

P176 ———. Dress in eighteenth-century Europe, 1715–1789. London, Batsford, [1984]. 220p. il., 5 col. plates.

While the pre-eminence of French fashion throughout much of the 18th century is acknowledged, dress in other European countries (particularly England, Germany, and Italy), and including Turkish influences on Eastern Europe, is also examined. Includes such topics as the part played by dress in society, the fashion trade and consumerism, the impact of the rococo style, etiquette, and fancy dress.

Contents: (I) 1715–1740: the dominance of France; (II) Getting and spending; (III) Wider Europe; (IV) 1740–1770: the triumph of the rococo; (V) Dress and etiquette; (VI) 1770–1789: frivolity and freedom; (VII) Fantasy and fancy dress; Appendix A: European currencies in the 18th century; Appendix B: A chronology of significant events in politics and culture, 1713–1789.

Notes, p.189–201. Glossary, p.205–06. Bibliography, p.207–12. Index, p.213–16.

P177 Steele, Valerie. Fashion and eroticism: ideals of feminine beauty from the Victorian era to the Jazz age. N.Y., Oxford Univ. Pr., 1985. 327p. il.

Important scholarly study examining the notion that the underlying message conveyed by clothing and fashion is one of eroticism. Covers the 1820s–1920s, with a focus on the period 1860–1914. Countries of principal interest are England and France, with some reference to the U.S. and Germany. The social focus is on the urban upper and middle classes although some urban working class dress is also examined.

Contents: (1) The fig leaf: explanations of clothing and fashion; (2) Fashion and eroticism: the psychoanalytic approach; (3) A new theory of fashion: sexual beauty and the ideal self; (4) Victorian fashion; (5) Victorian sexuality; (6) The Victorian ideal of feminine beauty; (7) Artificial beauty, or the morality of dress and adornment; (8) The revolt against fashion: dress reform and aesthetic costume; (9) The corset controversy; (10) The attractions of underclothes; (11) the changing ideal of feminine beauty; Appendix [The corset and the "tight-lacing" correspondence].

Notes, p.253–86. Bibliography, p.287–316. Index, p.317–27.

P178 Turnau, Irene. European occupational dress from the fourteenth to the eighteenth century. Trans. by Izabela Szymanska. Warsaw, Institute of Archaeology and Ethnology, Polish Academy of Sciences, 1994. 202p. il. (The library of Polish ethnography, no. 49)

Scholarly examination of non-courtly, non-aristocratic dress, focusing on clothes used for work, and for professional activities. "This book discusses comfortable garments which made physical labour possible and did not hinder any kind of activity."—*Chapter I.* The geographical range includes Armenia, Finland, Russia, Provence, Poland, Denmark, and Slovakia. Illustrations are taken from paintings, seals, engravings, and illuminated manuscripts of the period.

Contents: (I) Occupational or everyday dress? (II) Everyday peasant dress; (III) Working clothes in craft and trade; (IV) Dangerous professions; (V) The professional clothes of the intelligentsia; (VI) Dress of servants; (VII) Working disguises of beggars and strolling players; (VIII) Conclusions.

Bibliography, p.184–89.

P179 Vinken, Barbara. Mode nach der Mode: Kleid und Geist am Ende des 20. Jahrhunderts. Frankfurt am Main, Fischer, 1993. 169p. il. (Zeitschriften)

Survey of 20th-century fashion, unusual for its strong emphasis on the relationships among fashion, society, and film.

Literatur, p.168–69.

P180 Wilcox, Claire, and Mendes, Valerie. Modern fashion in detail. Photography by Richard Davis. Line drawings by Leonie Davis. Woodstock, Overlook, 1991. 143p. il. (part col.)

Focuses on the decorative elements of 20th-century high fashion, for example, details of fabric, construction, and trimming. Close-up full-page color photographs of each item, together with a line drawing of the complete piece and an adjoining description of the specific features, enable researchers to appreciate the intricate skills of high fashion. Drawing on the vast dress collections of the Victoria and Albert Museum, some stunning examples of more than 40 designers' works are presented.

Contents: Seams; Gathers, tucks and pleats; Collars, cuffs and pockets; Buttons; Bows; Beads and sequins; Applied decoration.

List of designers, p.6–7. Glossary, p.141–42. Selected reading, p.143.

P181 Wilson, Elizabeth. Adorned in dreams: fashion and modernity. Berkeley, Univ. of California Pr., 1985. 290p. il.

Wide-ranging volume investigating the social, economic, political, psychological, and above all aesthetic functions of modern Western dress. The relationship that binds fashion to modernity is also a particular focus.

Contents: (1) Introduction; (2) The history of fashion; (3) Explaining it away; (4) The fashion industry; (5) Fashion and eroticism; (6) Gender and identity; (7) Fashion and city life; (8) Fashion and popular culture; (9) Oppositional dress; (10) Utopian dress and dress reform; (11) Feminism and fashion.

References, p.248–66. Bibliography, p.267–76. Index, p.277–90.

P182 Yarwood, Doreen. Fashion in the Western world 1500–1900. N.Y., Drama Book, 1992. 176p. il. (part col.), 42 col. plates.

Presents the elements of fashionable dress in the modern Western world. Organized chronologically, with each chapter concentrating on the principal dress and accessory trends of several decades. The numerous accompanying illustrations comprise either period paintings or prints, or (primarily) drawings by the author based on paintings and fashion magazine illustrations as well as surviving original objects.

Glossary, p.165–69. Bibliography, p.170–71. Index, p.172–76.

P183 Zavaroni, Adolfo. La natura abbigliata: discorsi sull'abbigliamento femminile del XIX e XX secolo. [Reggio Emilia], Libreria Nuova Rinascita, 1985. 407p. il. (part col.)

Published to accompany the "event," "Sex-appeal dall'Ottocento al Novecento," held in conjunction with the 1985 Festa dell'Unità at Reggio Emilia, Italy. Six chapters discuss the evolution of women's dress and the dress code in the context of significant sociological and political events during the 19th and 20th centuries. Considerable space is devoted to such issues as the body, the sexual revolution, the women's liberation movement, and the importance of new technologies in the development of standards of hygiene and in clothing manufacture, particularly in the area of undergarment production. Many of the illustrations are taken from 19th- and 20th-century fashion journals and trade catalogs.

Bibliografia, p.399–407.

Western Countries

Australia

P184 Fletcher, Marion. Costume in Australia, 1788–1901. N.Y., Oxford Univ. Pr., [1984]. 208p. il. (part col.), ports. (part col.)

Decade-by-decade survey, discussing the characteristics of Australian dress that distinguished it from its British counterpart. Illustrations comprise primarily portrait paintings and photographs, and fashion journal images.

Glossary of fabric and costume terms, p.191–94. Notes, p.195–200. Bibliography, p.201–02. Recommended reading, p.203. Index, p.204–08.

France

Dictionaries and Encyclopedias

P185 Pellegrin, Nicole. Les vêtements de la liberté: abécédaire des pratiques vestimentaires en France de 1780 à 1800. Postface [by] Daniel Roche. Aix-en-Provence, Alinea, 1989. 208p. il. (part col.), col. plates. (Collection "Femmes et révolution") (Librairie du bicentenaire de la Révolution française)

Excellent dictionary encyclopedia surveying the socio-historic implications of dress during the French Revolutionary period. Thorough and wide-ranging entries cover dress types, gestures, fashion and social concepts, fashion figures, regional dress, social distinctions as revealed by dress, members of the fashion industry, and professional types.

Apparences révolutionaire ou révolution des apparences, by Daniel Roche, p.193–201. Notes, p.202. Bibliographie, p.203–07.

Histories and Handbooks

P186 Age of Napoleon: costume from revolution to empire 1789–1815. Katell le Bourhis, general ed. Essays by Charles Otto Zieseniss . . . [et al.] N.Y., Metropolitan Museum of Art; Abrams, 1989. 270p. il. (part col.), ports. (part col.)

Published in conjunction with the exhibition, Costume Institute, Metropolitan Museum of Art (1989–1990). Essays examine the role of dress (including uniforms), textiles, and jewelry in French culture, and their impact on contemporary European and American fashion. Napoleon's use of artistic commissions to enhance his political standing is also discussed.

Contents: (1) Costume in the age of Napoleon, by Philippe Séguy; (2) Jewels of the Empire, by Clare Le Corbellier; (3) Joseph Cardinal Fesch and the liturgical vestments of Lyon, by Pierre Arizzoli-Clémentel; (4) Silk from Lyon during the Empire, by Jean Coural and Chantal Gastinel-Coural; (5) Uniforms in the Napoleonic era, by Raoul Brunon; (6) The Emperor's wardrobe, by Colombe Samoyault-Verlet; (7) American women and French fashion, by Michele Meyer; Appendix: A selected list of Parisian luxury boutiques and suppliers.

Genealogy, p.14–16. Chronology, p.17–22. Source notes, p.238–45. Glossary, p.246–53. Index, p.265–70.

P187 Barthes, Roland. The fashion system. Trans. by Matthew Ward and Richard Howard. N.Y., Hill and Wang, [1983]. 303p.

Trans of Système de la mode. Paris, Seuil, 1967.

"The object of this inquiry is the structural analysis of women's clothing as currently described by Fashion magazines; its method was originally inspired by the general science of signs postulated by Saussure under the name semiology."—*Foreword.* One of the first experiments in semiotic analysis as applied to mass culture.

Contents: (1) Written clothing; (2) The relation of meaning; (3) Between things and words; (4) The endless garment; (5) The signifying unit; (6) Confusions and extensions; (7) The assertion of species; (8) Inventory of genera; (9) Variants of existence; (10) Variants of relation; (11) The system; (12) The syntagm; (13) The semantic units; (14) Combinations and neutralizations; (15) The vestimentary sign; (16) The analysis of the rhetorical system; (17) Rhetoric of the signifier: the poetics of clothing; (18) Rhetoric of the signified: the world of fashion; (19) Rhetoric of the sign: the reason of fashion; (20) Economy of the system; Appendixes: (1) History and diachrony of fashion; (2) Fashion photography.

P188 Beaulieu, Michele, and Baylé, Jeanne. Le costume en Bourgogne: de Philippe le Hardi à la mort de Charles le Téméraire (1364–1477). Paris, Presses Univ. de France, 1956. 220p. il., 24 plates, map.

In-depth scholarly study of 14th–15th century Burgundian dress, omitted from GLAH 1. The plates are complemented by many drawings detailing parts of clothing, especially of military dress.

Contents: (I) Les matières premières; (II) Les fournisseurs des ducs; (III) Le costume masculin; (IV) Le costume féminin; (V) Les accessoires du costume; (V) Le costume populaire; (VII) Les costumes spéciaux; (VIII) Le costume militaire.

Bibliographical references throughout the text. Sources et bibliographie, p.1–15. Index, p.189–209.

P189 Coleman, Elizabeth Ann. The opulent era: fashions of Worth, Doucet and Pingat. Brooklyn, Brooklyn Museum (Distr. by Thames and Hudson, 1989). 208p. il. (part col.), ports.

Catalog accompanying the exhibition, Brooklyn Museum (1989–1990). The Museum's extensive holdings in the field are heavily drawn upon, although pieces from other collections are also included. Of particular interest are the many paintings and photographs of clients wearing clothes similar or identical to the pieces on display; full-page color photographs of surviving ensembles are provided.

Contents: (1) The House of Worth; (2) the House of Doucet; (3) The House of Pingat.

Appendix: Worth labels, p.107–11. Notes, p.201–06. Bibliography, p.207.

P190 Delpierre, Madeleine. Dress in France in the eighteenth century. Trans. by Caroline Beamish. New Haven, Yale Univ. Pr., 1997. 208p. il., ports.

Trans. of Se vêtir au XVIIIe siècle. Paris, Birò, 1996.

"In this book the history of French costume is considered from a social, economic and literary point of view, as well as from an aesthetic one."—*Pref.* Posthumously published survey of 18th-century French male, female and children's attire.

Contents: (1) Clothing and fashion; (2) Underwear; (3) Accessories; (4) Fabrics and their decoration; (5) French fashion and fashion in Europe and the East; (6) Clothes for special occasions; (7) Etiquette and uniforms; (8) The world of elegance; (9) Clothes for the working-class; (10) Fashion and current events; (11) Dress, politics and ideology; (12) Clothing and accessories, craft and trades; (13) The price of elegance; (14) The dissemination of fashion; (15) Fashion and literature.

Notes, p.152–57. General bibliography, p.158–59. Glossary, p.164–66.

P191 De Marly, Diana. Louis XIV and Versailles. N.Y., Holmes and Meier, 1987. 143p. il. (part col.), ports. (Costume and civilization)

A history of the life and times of Louis XIV with an emphasis on the court and aristocratic dress at significant events during Louis' reign.

Contents: (1) The French impact 1660–1680; (2) The textile war; (3) Court dress and masquerades; (4) Fashion 1680–1700; (5) Conclusion 1700–1715.

Chronology [1589–1722], p.[9–10]. Glossary of terms not explained in the text, p.131. Notes, p.132–34. Appendix I: Money, p.135. Appendix II: The Royal Wardrobe, p.136–37. Bibliography, p.138–39. Index, p.141–43.

P192 Deslandres, Yvonne, and Müller, Florence. Histoire de la mode au XXe siècle. Paris, Somogy, 1986. 404p. il. (part col.), ports. (part col.)

Apart from an introduction covering the broader, international context (for example the emancipation of women, the emergence of the couturier icon, and the contribution of the media), deals primarily with French dress from 1900 to the 1980s. Chronologically organized, six specific periods are identified, and designers, dress, and accessories are treated for each. The many illustrations include photographs of significant events, street action, and runway shows; 19th- and 20th-century fashion journal plates; and 19th-century photographs.

Couturiers et créateurs au XXe siècle, p.353–88. Dates et événements remarquables, p.389–95. Index des noms cités, p.396–401.

P193 Enlart, Camille. Le costume. Paris, Picard, 1916. xxix, 614p. il. (Manuel d'archéologie française depuis les temps merovingiens jusqu' à la Renaissance, t. 3)

In-depth, highly detailed study of the history of male and female costume in France from the Merovingian and Carolingian periods to the reign of Henri IV, omitted from GLAH 1. Illustrations comprise line drawings based on surviving pieces relevant to the period covered. There are also black-and-white photographs of prints, sculpture, and illuminated manuscripts.

Contents: (I) Le vêtement; (II) La coiffure; (III) Accessoires du costume; (IV) Costumes spéciaux et insignes.

Bibliographical references throughout the text. Bibliographie critique, p.XXI–XXIX. Index alphabétique, chronologique et raisonné, p.533–607.

P194 Gaudriault, Raymond. Répertoire de la gravure de mode français des origines à 1815. [Paris], Promodis, 1988. 309p. il.

Inventory of 17th-, 18th-, and early 19th-century French fashion plates. The detailed catalog is arranged chronologically, beginning with Louis XIII's reign and ending with the Directoire, Consulat, and Empire periods. The author has surveyed the major archival, library, and print collections in France (for example, the Archives Nationales, and the Cabinet des Éstampes at the Bibliothèque Nationale), estimating that approximately 3,500 fashion plates by major and minor artists have survived.

Bibliographie, p.297–300. Index p.301–05.

P195 Lebas, Catherine, and Jacques, Annie. La coiffure en France du Moyen Age à nos jours. Paris, Delmas International, 1979. 358p. il. (part col.), ports. (part col.)

In-depth study of 14th- to 20th-century hair dressing, hair styles, and hair accessories in France. Three chapters provide a wide-ranging history of the hairdresser's role, the evolution of the profession, and the history of hairdressing techniques. Numerous illustrations, from manuscript illuminations, paintings, engravings, fashion magazines, and advertisements are included.

Tableau récapitulif de l'évolution du métier, p.350–51. Bibliographie, p.353–56. Index des coiffeurs cités, p.357.

P196 Martin, Richard. Fashion and Surrealism. N.Y., Rizzoli, 1987. 238p. il. (part col.), ports. (part col.)

Traces fashion's "persistent preoccupation with Surrealism and Surrealism's fascination with fashion."—*Introd.* Examines the beginnings of the Surrealist movement and its interaction with fashion, and follows Surrealism's impact on 20th-century art, dress, and the representation of the (usually female) body. Excellently illustrated. Works by Surrealist artists and the fashion designers with whom they were connected are shown and discussed, as well as pieces by later Surrealist-influenced designers.

Contents: Metaphor and metamorphosis; Bodies and parts; Displacements and illusions; Natural and unnatural worlds; Doyenne and dandy; Surrealism and the world of fashion.

Index, p.237–39.

P197 Mille ans de costume français: 950–1950. Thionville, G. Klopp, 1991. 245p. il. (chiefly col.)

Thematically arranged survey vol. containing essays by various authors examining upper, middle, and (where possible) working class dress and accessories. Military, ceremonial and regional dress are also considered. A conclusion examines post-1950 dress. Visual resources include illuminated manuscripts, paintings, and portraits, 19th- and 20th-century photographs, surviving examples, and 20th-century artists' renditions.

Contents: (I) La vêture, by Sylvie Legrand, Perrine Mare and Françoise Piponnier; (II) La Parrure, by Anne Margerie and Monique Poulenc, with Renée Davray-Piekolek and Valérie Guillaume; (III) Revêtire-travestire, by Marie-Claude Groshens, with Yves Bardon; Conclusion, by Sylvie Legrand.

Bibliographie, p.235–36.

P198 Perrot, Philippe. Fashioning the bourgeoisie: a history of clothing in the nineteenth century. Trans. by Richard Bienvenu. Princeton, N.J., Princeton Univ. Pr., 1994. 273p. il.

Trans. of Les dessus et les dessous de la bourgeoisie: une histoire du vêtement au XIX siècle. Paris, Fayard, 1981.

Revised English-language ed., the product of collaboration and revision between author and translator. "Describes the early manifestations, stages, and consequences of [the 19th century's] dual trend toward differentiation and similarity. To understand contemporary dress we must study the nineteenth century, the century that pushed to the fore the individual and the anonymous crowd, dandyism and uniformity, distinctiveness and conformism."—*Pref.* Emphasis is on bourgeois clothing, examining the so-called "trivial" components of dress: underpants, petticoats, neckties, shawls, corsets, and socks. Focuses on the Second Empire period, and examines 19th-century etiquette manuals and novels as indicators of the social meaning of dress.

Contents: (I) Toward a history of appearances; (II) Clothing's old and new regimes; (III) The vestimentary landscape of the nineteenth century; (IV) Traditional trades and the rise of ready-made clothing; (V) The department store and the spread of bourgeois clothing; (VI) New pretensions, new distinctions; (VII) The imperatives of propriety; (VIII) Derivations from the norm; (IX) Invisible clothing; (X) The circulation of fashions.

Notes, p.193–251. Bibliography, p.253–66. Index, p.268–73.

P199 ———. Le travail des apparences: le corps féminin, XVIIIe–XIXe siècle. [Paris], Seuil, [1991]. 280p. il. (Points. Histoire, H141)
1st ed., Le travail des apparences: ou les transformations du corps féminin, XVIIIe–XIXe siècle, Paris, Seuil, 1984.

Documents the transformation of French society through changing notions about how the female body should appear and be represented. Covering the 17th through the 20th centuries, but with a focus on the 18th century. Views the female body as a social, cultural, and historic product. Interesting for its analysis of technological developments (for example, advances in water engineering and the mechanization of cosmetics production techniques), and scientific developments (such as new ideas about diet and hygiene), and their impact on changing notions about dress and the eroticization of the female body.

Contents: (I) Le retour de l'eau; (II) La vérité des masques; (III) La grâce des chairs; (IV) Le chiffre des apparences; (V) La vague hygiéniste; (VI) Le simulacre du naturel; (VII) Le corps immolé.

Notes, p.211–277.

P200 Ribeiro, Aileen. Fashion in the French Revolution. N.Y., Holmes and Meier, 1988. il. (part col.), 159p. of plates, ports. (part col.)
Chronological examination of the relationship between politics, fashion, and society, focusing on the Revolution and Diréctoire periods. Illustrations taken from portraiture, fashion plates, and pattern and sample books of the period.

Contents: (1) The waiting years; (2) Politics and fashion 1789–1794; (3) Brave new world: people and state, 1789–1794; (4) Decline and fall: Thermidor and Directory 1794–1799; Appendix: The Revolutionary calendar.

Chronological table, 1789–1799, p.15–18. Notes, p.143–53. Select bibliography, p.155–56. Index, p.157–59.

P201 Roche, Daniel. The culture of clothing: dress and fashion in the "Ancien régime." Trans. by Jean Birrel. [N.Y.], Cambridge Univ. Pr., [1994]. 537p. il. (Past and present publications)
Trans. of La culture des apparences. Paris, Fayard, 1989.

Based on the premise that one of the major themes of Enlightenment thinking was the debate about appearance and morality as reflected by dress. Both a history of clothing and a history of clothing's production, commodification, trade, consumption, and theft. Draws extensively on archival sources (especially inventories) to investigate the function and importance of different types of dress for members of different social strata.

Contents: (1) Towards a history of clothing; (2) The economy of wardrobes; (3) Producing, selling and stealing: the distribution of appearances; (4) Truth and the mask.

Bibliographical references throughout the text. Index, p.521–37.

P202 Steele, Valerie. Paris fashion: a cultural history. N.Y., Oxford Univ. Pr., 1988. 317p. il.
In-depth study by a leading scholar in the field. Focuses on late 18th–19th century fashion and the context in which Parisian clothes were worn.

Contents: (1) Mode and meaning in the capital of style; (2) The picture of Paris; (3) The Revolution: liberty, equality, and antiquity; (4) Parisian types; (5) The Black Prince of elegance; (6) Art and fashion; (7) Fashionable rendez-vous; (8) Le high life; (9) Le five o'clock tea; (10) Proust's world of fashion; (11) Fashion revolution; (12) Haute couture in the twentieth century.

Notes, p.287–301. Selected bibliography, p.303–10. Index, p.311–17.

P203 Viollet le Duc, Emmanuel. Encyclopédie médiéval d'après Viollet le Duc. [Reprint.] 2v. Realisée par Georges Bernage. Mise en pages de Marc Le Carpentier. Bayeux, France, Heimdal, 1978–80.
Several recent reprints. See GLAH 1:P45 for original annotation.

SEE ALSO: Crowfoot, Pritchard, and Staniland, Textiles and clothing c.1150–c.1450. (GLAH 2:P851); Ribeiro, The art of dress: fashion in England and France, 1750 to 1820 (GLAH 2:P175).

Germany and Austria

P204 Biegler-Sander, Heidede. Die Kostümsammlung der Familie von Bassermann-Jordan als Beispiel für die zeitgenössische bürgerliche Mode von 1760–1870. [Speyer, Pfalzischen Gesellschaft zur Förderung der Wissenschaften, 1990]. xi, 199p. il., 70p. of plates, ports. (Veröffentlichung der Pfälzischen Gesellschaft zur Förderung der Wissenschaften in Speyer, Bd. 84)
Catalog of the Von Bassermann-Jordan family collection of clothing and accessories, spanning five generations (1760–1870) and housed at the Historisches Museum der Pfalz. Male, female, and children's attire are examined, as well as dress appropriate to different occasions. Particularly useful features of the catalog are the cutting patterns of many of the items on display; and portraits of the Von Bassermann-Jordan family, or contemporaries, wearing clothes similar or identical to those documented. Most of the extant pieces are also illustrated with black-and-white photographs.

Contents: (1) Die Kostümstücke der Von-Bassermann-Jordan-Sammlung und ihre Träger; (2) Darstellung grundlegender Gestaltungselemente der Kostüme; (3) Vergleichende Darstellungen der Kostüme.

Literaturverzeichnis, p.184–87. Anhang: Stammbaum der Familie von Bassermann-Jordan, p.190. Vokabular der Textiltechniken, p.191–95.

P205 Buxbaum, Gerda. Mode aus Wien, 1815–1938. [Salzburg], Residenz, [1986]. 427p. il. (part col.), 283 col. plates, ports. (part col.)
In-depth examination of the nature and history of Viennese 19th- and early 20th-century dress. Includes upper-, middle-, and lower-class dress. The many illustrations include fashion prints and photographs, and porcelain figurines.

Contents: "Wiener Mode"—Fiktion oder Realität?; Was ist Mode? Zur theorie des Phänomens Mode; "Wiener

Mode"—Quellen vor 1815; Modeübersicht 1815–1938; Die Laufstege der Wiener Mode; Modesalons—Strukturwandell. Klientel und Werbemethoden; Kunst und Mode—die Darstellung von Mode in der bildenden Kunst; Wienerinnen in exponierter gesellschaftlicher Position als Galionsfiguren der Mode; Tracht und Mode.

Anmerkungen, p.348–56. Wiener Modeschöpfer, Modehäuser, Schneider, Friseure, Putzmacher und andere Modeschaffende, p.359–79. Bibliographie der Wiener Modezeitschriften, p.380–93. Verzeichnis der Mode- und Gesellschaftsphotographen, p.394–96. Fachausdrücke, p.397–406. Literaturverzeichnis, p.407–15. Bildnachweis, p.416–23. Personenregister, p.424–27.

P206 Hansen, Traude. Wiener Werkstätte Mode: Stoffe, Schmuck, Accessoires. Unter Mitarb. von Gino Wimmer. Wien, Brandstätter, 1984. 208p. il. (part col.), ports.

Using archival sources, provides an extensive survey of the Austrian dress reform movement and the Wiener Werkstätte's influence on clothing, jewelry, and other accessories. The designs of most of the men and women involved with the Werkstätte are examined. Numerous fashion drawings by members of the movement are included, as are photographs of members wearing the Werkstätte clothes.

Contents: Vom Reformkleid zur Kunstmode; Mode der Wiener Werkstätte: die Vorgeschichte; WW—auf dem Weg zur Haute Couture; Eduard Josef Wimmer-Wisgril und sein Werk; Die Modekünstler der Wiener Werkstätte; Schmuck und Accessoires; Wiener Werkstätte—Mode im Spiegel der Zeit.

Anmerkungen, p.201–02. Künstlerbiographien, p.203–06. Quellen- und Literaturverzeichnis, p.206. Register, p.207–08.

P207 Tracht in Österreich: Geschichte und Gegenwart. Hrsg. von Franz C. Lipp . . . [et al.] Beitr. von Eva Bakos . . . [et al.] Wien, Brandstätter, 1984. 263p. il. (part col.), ports. (part col.)

Survey with a strong geographical focus. 31 essays by various authors examine historical and regional dress, dress for specific occasions (including military dress), haute couture, and folk dress. The primary emphasis of this vol. is regional dress, although its interaction with fashionable dress is also examined. The many illustrations include contemporary and historical paintings, prints, portraits, photographs, and colored drawings.

Glossar, [by] Ingeborg Petrascheck-Heim, p.254–56. Anmerkungen und Literatur, p.257–63.

SEE ALSO: Brüggen, Kleidung und Mode in der höfischen Epik des 12. und 13. Jahrhunderts (GLAH 2:P135); Reineking von Bock, 200 Jahre Mode: Kleider vom Rokoko bis heute (GLAH 2:P174).

Great Britain and Ireland

Dictionaries and Encyclopedias

P208 Cunnington, Cecil Willett, and Beard, Charles. A dictionary of English costume. [Reprint.] London, A and C. Black, 1976. vi, 284p. il.

See GLAH 1:P121 for original annotation.

Histories and Handbooks

P209 Arnold, Janet. Patterns of fashion. [Reprint.] N.Y., Drama Book, 1995. 2v. il.

1st ed., London, Wace, 1964–66; corr. ed., 1972; 2d ed., London, Macmillan, 1977.

Pioneering texts on pattern cutting and garment construction and guide to designing period costumes. Drawing upon letters, magazines, and books of the period, the author gives a brief history of pattern cutting, dressmaking, and tailoring. Studies of individual clothes and undergarments, all illustrated with annotated drawings, focus on details of construction; scaled and annotated patterns are also provided. All pieces used have been dated from contemporary prints, portraits, fabrics, fashion plates, and/or photographs. Reference is made to English and French examples now in British collections, although the emphasis is on dress worn in Great Britain. A final section deals with metric conversions.

Contents: (1) Englishwomen's dresses and their construction c. 1660–1860; (2) Englishwomen's dresses and their construction c. 1860–1940.

List of selected books, in both vols.

P210 ______. Patterns of fashion: the cut and construction of clothes for men and women c1560–1620. London, Macmillan, 1985. 128p. il., ports. (Repr.: N.Y., Drama Book, 1995)

"This is the first book in a series on the cut and construction of clothes for both men and women, covering periods of varying length between the Middle Ages and the twentieth century, related to portraits and other visual sources."—*Introd.* Expands upon the author's Patterns of fashion (see preceding entry), which focused on female dress only. Provides a practical guide to cutting period costumes as well as a text and many illustrations that place the pattern in context. Patterns have been taken from original garments, and illustrations of stitching, fabric types, and trimmings are included.

Measurements and metric conversions, p.124–25. Using the patterns for full-scale work, p.126. Table of measurements, p.127. Select bibliography, p.127–28.

P211 Ashelford, Jane. The art of dress: clothes and society 1500–1914. Special photography by Andreas von Einsiedel. London, National Trust (Distr. by Abrams, 1996). 320p. il. (part col.), ports. (part col.)

Comprehensive, chronologically organized survey of 400 years of dress and accessories in Britain. Focus is on adult court, aristocratic, and upper-class dress as represented in the collections of the British National Trust. The many illustrations include magnificent portrait paintings and photographs of British sitters wearing significant items of dress. Illustrations of surviving clothing are taken from the National Trust's dress collections at Killerton House (Devon), Springhill (Northern Ireland), and Snowshill Manor (Gloucestershire).

Contents: (1) Gorgeous attyre 1500–1603; (2) Careless romance 1603–1660; (3) Wigs and drapery 1660–1720; (4) Uniformly elegant 1720–1780; (5) Perfect cut and fit 1780–1850; (6) Tyranny of fashion 1850–1914; (7) Swaddling to sailor's suits; children's clothes; (8) Dress suitable to their station: clothes for servants.

Notes, p.304–13. Select bibliography, p.314. Index, p.315–20.

P212 Bradfield, Nancy. Costume in detail: women's dress 1730–1930. [Reprint.] Boston, Plays, Inc., 1983. ix, 391p. il.

1st ed., Toronto, Harrap, published under the author's former name, Nancy Sayer; 2d ed., 1981.

Chronologically organized study of the dress and accessories of the upper and middle classes. Each chapter opens with an essay describing the dress of the period, accompanied by numerous line drawings by the author; these drawings are based on surviving pieces and on period paintings and prints showing the dress items in use. The primary visual sources include dressed tomb effigies, paintings, and prints. Particular attention is paid to the contents of two collections, the Charles Wade Collection at Snowshill Manor (Gloucestershire), and nearby Chastleton House.

Appendix: Further detailed studies, 1806, 1814 and 1913, p.371–80. Cycling in the 1890s, p.381–83. Books consulted, p.384–85. Index, p.386–91.

P213 Breward, Christopher. The culture of fashion: a new history of fashionable dress. Picture research, Jane Audas. N.Y., Manchester Univ. Pr. (Distr. by St. Martin's, 1994). xii, 244p. il. (part col.) (Studies in design and material culture)

"The author moves through six centuries of fashion with the explicit aim of exposing the meanings behind the garments which people wore. He reveals the extent to which clothing moves beyond its role as a screen for the body to become a gathering of information and symbols for the communal consumption."—*General ed. foreword.* Integrating approaches from the disciplines of art history, design history, and cultural studies, and structured chronologically, each chapter focuses on issues specific to the period. Reference is primarily to English dress (15th–20th century), although the impact of foreign influences is also discussed.

Contents: (1) Medieval period: fashioning the body; (2) Renaissance: the rhetoric of power; (3) Seventeenth century: clothing and crisis; (4) Eighteenth century: clothing and commerce; (5) Nineteenth century: fashion and modernity; (6) Early twentieth century: clothing the masses; (7) Late twentieth century: catwalk and street style.

Bibliographical references at ends of chapters. Select bibliography, p.237–41. Index, p.242–44.

P214 Buck, Anne. Clothes and the child: a handbook of children's dress in England 1500–1900. Rev. ed. N.Y., Holmes and Meier, 1996. 271p. il. (part col.), 6 col. plates.

1st ed., 1965.

Examines the dress of infants, children, and young adults, and how they were represented in portraiture. Focus tends to be on the dress of the wealthier classes, since more evidence has survived in that area. All garment, undergarment, and accessory types are considered. Illustrations include portrait paintings, photographs and sculpture (including effigies), patterns, and surviving examples of dress.

Contents: (1) Infancy; (2) Childhood; (3) Growing up.

References, p.253–56. Glossary, p.257–63. Select bibliography, p.264. Children's costume collections, p.264. Index, p.266–71.

P215 ______. Dress in eighteenth-century England. N.Y., Holmes and Meier, [1979]. 240p. il. (part col.), col. plates, ports.

Contents: (I) Crown and court; (II) People of fashion; (III) The gentry; (IV) Servants; (V) The common people; (VI) Buying and making clothes; (VII) Fabrics and wearers; (VIII) Dress and society.

Notes, p.211–24. Glossary, p.225–27. Bibliography, p.229–40. Index, p.233–40.

P216 ______. Victorian costume and costume accessories. 2d ed. Bedford, Bean, 1984. 224p. il.

See GLAH 1:P115 for original publication (1961) and annotation.

P217 Byrde, Penelope. Nineteenth-century fashion. London, Batsford, 1992. 192p. il. (part col.), 8 plates, ports. (part col.)

Traces the evolution of British dress styles from the late Neo-Classical Georgian period to the late Victorian era. Illustrations taken primarily from period fashion prints, or portrait drawings, paintings, and photographs.

Contents: (1) Classical inspiration: women's dress 1800–1825; (2) The romantic spirit: women's dress 1825–1850; (3) Prosperity and expansion: women's dress 1850–1875; (4) Fin de siècle: women's dress 1875–1900; (5) Sense and sobriety: men's dress 1800–1900; (6) Status, time and place: the etiquette of dress I; (7) Luxurious profession: making and buying clothes; (8) Occasions, leisure and pleasure: the etiquette of dress II.

Notes, p.175–81. Glossary, p.182–86. Bibliography, p.185–86. Index, p.187–92.

P218 Cunnington, Cecil Willett, and Cunnington, Phillis. Handbook of English mediaeval costume. 2d repr. with corr. London, Faber and Faber, 1973. 210p. il. (part col.), col. plates.

See GLAH 1:P120 for original annotation.

P219 Cunnington, Phillis, and Lucas, Catherine. Occupational costume in England from the eleventh century to 1914. [Reprint.] London, Black, 1976. 427p. il.

See GLAH 1:P122 for original annotation.

P220 ______, and Mansfield, Alan. English costume for sports and outdoor recreation: from the sixteenth to the nineteenth centuries. [Reprint.] N.Y., Barnes and Noble, [1970]. 388p. il. (part col.), ports. (part col.)

See GLAH 1:P123 for original annotation.

P221 Dunbar, John Telfer. Costume of Scotland. London, Batsford, 1981. 212p. il.

Investigates the origins of the national dress of Scotland. Discusses the "Romantic and nationalist attempts to provide an extensive ancestry for the clan-related kilt and for tartans."—*Introd.*

Contents: (1) Shirts, mantles and plaids; (2) The trews; (3) The proscription and repeal; (4) The kilt; (5) George IV and Queen Victoria; (6) The tartan; (7) The ladies of Scotland; (8) Scottish tweed; (9) The Scottish bonnet; (10) Fisher folk; (11) Medieval Highland warriors; (12) Scottish military uniform; (13) The Royal Company of Archers; (14) Highland arms.

Bibliography, p.207–08. Index, p.209–12.

P222 Dunlevy, Mairead. Dress in Ireland. N.Y., Holmes and Meier, 1989. 192p. il. (part col.), ports. (part col.)

Chronological survey of dress and textiles in Ireland ranging from those found in Bronze Age bog burials to the year 1910. Each chapter is further subdivided into dress, textile, and/or accessory types, according to the specifics of the period under review. Dress of different social levels is examined, and English influences are also discussed. Many of the illustrations are taken from manuscript illuminations and sculpture for the medieval period, and from fashion plates and photography for the 19th and 20th centuries.

Notes, p.178–86. Select glossary, p.187–89. Index, p.190–92.

P223 Ginsburg, Madeleine. Victorian dress in photographs. [Reprint.] N.Y., Holmes and Meier, 1988. 192p. il.

1st ed., London, Batsford, 1982.

Collection of photographs "chosen to illustrate the range of clothing and the sequence of fashion changes in Britain throughout the Victorian era."—*Introd.*

Contents: Clothes in camera; Ladies' dress; Children's dress; Men's dress; Occupational and regional dress; Appendix: Quotations from contemporary sources: Ladies' dress from the 1840s; The 1850s and early 1860s; 1865–1879; Late 1870s–1890s; Children's dress; Men's dress.

Bibliography, p.188–89. Index, p.189–92.

P224 The inventory of King Henry VIII: Society of Antiquaries MS 129 and British Library MS Harley 1419. Ed. by David Starkey. Transcribed by Philip Ward, asst. ed. Indexed by Alasdair Hawkyard. London, Harvey Miller for the Society, 1998– . (1)v. (Reports of the Research Committee of the Society of Antiquaries of London, n. 56)

Transcript and analysis of the inventory of Henry VIII's possessions taken on this death in 1547, to be completed in 3v. A large portion of this inventory comprised items of dress, furnishings, jewelry, furs, embroideries, and ecclesiastical vestments.

P225 A lady of fashion: Barbara Johnson's album of styles and fabrics. Ed. by Natalie Rothstein. N.Y., Thames and Hudson, 1987. 208p. il. (part col.), ports.

Beautifully produced publication documenting the scrapbook of numerous textile samples (1746–1823) and correspondence of Barbara Johnson (1738–1825), together with the clothing account book (1738–48) of George Thomson (1717–81?). Related archival materials permit the placing of album and account book and textiles in their full historical and social context. The many illustrations reproduce the samples, annotations, accounts (which are also fully transcribed), and contemporary fashion engravings from the original documents.

Contents: (1) Introduction: the family and the album, by Natalie Rothstein; (2) Barbara Johnson and fashion, by Madeleine Ginsburg; Textiles in the album, by Natalie Rothstein; The fashion engravings, by Anne Buck; Topographical and other prints, by Jean Hamilton.

Bibliographical references at ends of chapters. Notes on the Album, p.145–46. Appendices: (1) George Thomson: in search of the man, by Natalie Rothstein, p.147–48; (2) The clothing accounts of George Thomson, by Avril Hart, p.149–53; (3) George Thomson's trips to the theatre, by James Fowler, p.154–56; (4) Transcription of the accounts, by Natalie Rothstein, p.157–201; (5) Notes on the accounts, by Natalie Rothstein, p.202–03. Glossary, p.204–05. Index, p.206–08.

P226 Mayo, Janet. A history of ecclesiastical dress. N.Y., Holmes and Meier, 1984. 192p. il. (part col.), 6 col. plates, ports. (part col.)

Opens with a chronological introduction covering the Early Christian period up to the 1980s. Subsequent chapters provide a more extended chronological survey from the 6th century on, focusing on the British Isles. Eastern Orthodox vestments are dealt with only briefly.

Notes to the text, p.179–84. Bibliography, p.185–186. Index, p.187–92.

P227 Owen-Crocker, Gale R. Dress in Anglo-Saxon England. With line drawings by Christine Wetherell. Wolfboro, N.H., Manchester Univ. Pr., 1986. xi, 241p. il.

Scholarly work that examines most aspects of dress—including textile production—in England from the 5th century to 1066. Female and male dress are treated separately. Costume accessories, especially jewelry and other forms of metalwork, are also covered. Aims to differentiate Anglo-Saxon dress from that of the later Middle Ages, and from medieval dress in the rest of Western Europe. Draws on evidence provided by manuscript illuminations, archeological excavations, and literary sources. Appendix: Old English garment names.

Abbreviations in the notes and the bibliography, p.209. Notes, p.211–25. Bibliography, p.227–34. Index, p.235–41.

P228 Peacock, John. Costume 1066–1966. N.Y., Thames and Hudson, 1986. 128p. il. (chiefly col.)

Chronologically arranged volume documenting changes in male and female dress from 1066. While the starting point is the dress of the kings and queens of England, cross-national connections mean that the trends depicted reflect those of the rest of Europe. Each section represents a reign. A series of briefly annotated drawings by the author illustrate dress and accessory features for the period.

Further reading, p.127–28.

P229 Queen Elizabeth's wardrobe unlock'd: the inventories of the Wardrobe of Robes prepared in July 1600: edited from Stowe MS 557 in the British Library, MS LR 2/121 in the Public Record Office, London, and MS V.b.72 in the Folger Shakespeare Library, Washington, D.C.. Ed. and with a commentary by Janet Arnold. Leeds, Maney, 1988. xvi, 376p. il. (part col.), plates, ports. (part col.), maps.

Impressive volume building on the author's earlier publication, Lost from Her Majesties back (Costume Society extra series, no. 7, 1980), a transcription of the Day Book of the Wardrobe of the Robes, 1561–85. The extensive archival records documenting Queen Elizabeth I of England's equally extensive wardrobe provide "a unique source for the study of dress during the second half of the sixteenth century."—*Introd.* Inventories made in 1600 of the Queen's clothes (listing approximately 2,000 items) are transcribed in full.

Bibliographical references at ends of chapters. Bibliography, p.ix–xi. Index I: Miscellaneous subjects including paintings, persons, places and events, p.351–58. Index II: Clothing, textiles, jewels, motifs, colours, techniques, and articles for the toilet, p.359–76.

P230 Rose, Clare. Children's clothes since 1750. N.Y., Drama Book, 1989. 160p. il. (part col.)

Chronological examination of children's dress, 1750–1985, and related notions of childhood. Babies, girls, and boys are considered in separate sections for each period. Although focused on Great Britain, U.S. influences are of obvious relevance to the later chapters.

Notes, p.153–55. Glossary, p.156–57. Select bibliography, p.158. Index, p.159–60.

P231 Sichel, Marion. Costume reference. Boston, Plays, Inc., 1977–78. 10v. il. (part col.) (Repr.: Boston, Plays, Inc., 1983)

Covers male, female, and children's dress, accessories, and beauty aids of all classes, where available. Each vol. provides historical overviews for the period's dress. The many line drawings are accompanied by descriptive captions.

Contents: (1) Roman Britain and the Middle Ages; (2) Tudors and Elizabethans; (3) Jacobean, Stuart and Restoration; (4) The eighteenth century; (5) The Regency; (6) The Victorians; (7) The Edwardians; (8) 1918–1939; (9) 1939–1950; (10) 1950 to the present day.

Glossary, bibliography and index in all vols.

P232 A visual history of costume. N.Y., Drama Book, 1983–1986. 6v. il.

One-vol. abridgement: Aileen Ribeiro and Valerie Cumming, The visual history of costume, London, Batsford, 1989.

Series of survey volumes primarily dealing with dress in England, including foreign influences when their impact on England was particularly significant. Each vol. is divided into two parts. Each vol. comprises a brief introductory essay, in which a chronological survey is provided and sources are discussed, followed by a series of illustrations relative to the period. Contemporary paintings and prints, as well as modern line drawings, are the visual source materials, accompanied by extensive captions.

Contents: (1) Scott, Margaret. The fourteenth & fifteenth centuries (1986); (2) Ashelford, Jane. The sixteenth century (1983); (3) Cumming, Valerie. The seventeenth century (1984); (4) Ribeiro, Aileen. The eighteenth century (1983); (5) Foster, Vanda. The nineteenth century (1984); (6) Byrde, Penelope. The twentieth century (1986).

Select bibliographies, and glossaries functioning as select indexes in all vols.

SEE ALSO: Arnold, A handbook of costume (GLAH 2:P101); Ribeiro, The art of dress: fashion in England and France, 1750 to 1820 (GLAH 2:P175).

Italy

Dictionaries and Encyclopedias

P233 Vitali, Achille. La moda a Venezia attraverso i secoli: lessico ragionato. Pref., Doretta Davanzo Poli. Venezia, Filippi, 1992. 473p. il.

Dictionary, with thoroughly researched entries. Not all terms discussed are Venetian, but all are terms known to have been used in Venice to describe aspects of dress, textiles, and accessories worn in Venice. Focus is on the period up to the Napoleonic conquest of Venice, when the impact of customs and vocabularies ultimately caused Venetian terms to decline in usage. Most illustrations are taken from Venetian paintings or prints of the of the period.

Contents: Appendice: Tabella dei colori più in uso.

Bibliographical references at ends of chapters. Bibliografia, p.469–72.

Histories and Handbooks

P234 Il costume al tempo di Pico e Lorenzo il Magnifico. A cura di Aurora Fiorentini Capitani, Vittorio Erlindo, [e] Stefania Ricci. Milano, Charta, 1994. 98p. il. (chiefly col.)

1st ed., Il costume al tempo di Lorenzo il Magnifico: Prato e il suo territorio, Milano, Charta, 1992.

Collection of essays published in conjunction with the exhibition, Palazzo Municipale, Mirandola (1994), and with the international conference commemorating the 500th anniversary of the death of the Renaissance philosopher Pico della Mirandola (d. 1494). The first version of this exhibition Museo Communale, Prato (1992), and catalog was on the occasion of the 500th anniversary of the death of Lorenzo de' Medici. Most of the illustrations of textile and dress details are taken from 15th-century frescoes and illuminated manuscripts. Examples of surviving textile fragments are also illustrated.

Contents: Arti e mestieri a Prato nel Quattrocento, di Aurora Fiorentini Capitani and Stefania Ricci; La lavorazione del panno nella Prato del XIV e XV secolo, di Patrizia Bagani, Marco De Liguori; I tessuti del contrado fiorentino nel scolo XV, di Rosaria Bonito Fanelli; Considerazioni sull'abbigliamento del Quattrocento in Toscana, di Aurora Fiorentini Capitani and Stefania Ricci; Fogge, ornamenti e tecniche: qualche appunto sulla storia materiale dell'abito nel Quattrocento, di Ornella Morelli.

Bibliographical references follow each essay. [Notes], p.94–96. Bibliografia, p.97–98.

P235 Il costume nell'età del Rinascimento. A cura di Dora Liscia Bemporad. [Firenze], Edifir, [1998]. 387p. il. (part col.), plates.

Wide-ranging papers from an international conference.

Bibliographical references follow each essay. Bibliografia, p.365–87.

P236 Crispolti, Enrico. Il Futurismo e la moda: Balla e gli altri. Venezia, Marsilio, 1986. 151p. il. (part col.), ports.

Overview of Futurism in its avant-garde artistic and fashion milieu. Part II, comprising 277 catalog entries (all illustrated) surveys the components of Futurist dress: textiles, male and female attire, and theatrical dress. Also covers some Russian Constructivist and Bauhaus parallels, as well as work by the Delaunays. Portrait photographs, Futurist paintings, and Futurist theater designs are reproduced.

Bibliographical references throughout the text.

P237 Italian fashion. N.Y., Rizzoli, 1987. 2v. il. (part col.)

"The two volumes of this work should be seen as an attempt to reflect the complexity of problems that the Italian 'fashion system' has had to deal with in the last few decades."—*Introd.* Discusses the emergence of Italian fashion as an independent entity, and seeks to define what sets it apart from French, English, and U.S. equivalents. Numerous color photographs of pieces presented at fashion shows form a significant part of this volume. Includes many catalog entries for individual pieces. Biographical notes for designers and clothing manufacturers of relevance appear at the end of each chapter.

Contents: (1) The origins of high fashion and knitwear. A cura di Gloria Bianchino . . . [et al.] Contributi di Paolo Barbaro . . . [et al.]; (2) From anti-fashion to stylism. A cura di Grazietta Butazzi e Alessandra Mottola Molfino. Contributi di Niccoletta Bocca . . . [et al.]

Bibliography, v.2, p.298. Index, v.1, p.297–300, v.2, p.299–301.

P238 Levi Pisetzky, Rosita. Il costume e la moda nella società italiana. Introd. di Grazietta Butazzi. Torino, Einaudi, 1995. 385p. il. (Einaudi tascabili. Saggi, 269)

1st ed., 1974.

Classic text by one of this century's leading costume historians, re-issued with a new introd. by another leading historian of dress.

Contents: (1) Le forme della moda: Introduzione, by Grazietta Butazzi; (I) Abbigliamento e costume; (II) Il colore; (III) I tessuti; (2) Il costume nella storia: (I) Il costume romano dall'età reppubblicana all'apogeo dell'impero; (II) Il costume nell'alto medioevo; (III) I grandi secoli della civiltà italiana; (IV) Gli inizi e l'avento della moda francese.

Bibliographical references throughout the introductory text.

P239 Il Libro del sarto della Fondazione Querini Stampalia di Venezia. Saggi di Fritz Saxl . . . [et al.] Ferrara, ISR; Modena, Panini, [1987]. 72p. il. (part col.), 161plates, ports. (Istituto di Studi Rinascimentali, Ferrara. Testi)

Beautifully reproduced facsimile ed. of the so-called Libro del sarto, the first book on tailoring known to have survived and now in the collection of the Querini Stampalia Foundation, Venice. Reprints a pioneering study by Fritz Saxl (1936). The other essays provide a critical analysis of Saxl's study, a codicological analysis of the text, and discussions of the dress and textile imagery in the book.

The many illustrations comprise drawings and colored sketches of the tailor's entire range of activities; not only are clothes and their construction patterns shown, but also sketches for tents, riding gear and armor (for horse and rider), flags, banners and emblems, miscellaneous architectural and decorative motifs, and figure studies.

Contents: Introduzione a un libro senza nome, by Alessandra Mottola Molfino; Il "Libro del sarto" e i paradigmi del moderno, by Paolo Getrevi; Costumi e teste della nobiltà milanese negli anni della dominazione spagnola, by Fritz Saxl; La moda nel "Libro del sarto," by Doretta Davanzo Poli; Parole e cifre: le annotazioni nel "Libro del sarto," by Alessandra Schiavon.

P240 Moda alla corte dei Medici: gli abiti restaurati di Cosimo, Eleonora e don Garzia. Firenze, Centro Di, 1993. 107p. il. (part col.), ports.

Publication accompanying the exhibition, Palazzo Pitti, Forence (1993) of the burial clothes of Duke Cosimo Medici (d. 1574), his wife Eleonora di Toledo (d. 1562), and son don Garcia (d. 1562). These clothes were removed when the Medici tombs were reopened in 1947, following which some were lost. The exhibition provided the occasion to study, conserve, and display those that remained.

Contents: Tra storia e leggenda: cronaca di vita medicea, by Stefania Ricci; La moda alla corte di Cosimo I de' Medici, by Giovanna Lazzi; L'amore del lusso e la necessità della modestia: Eleonora fra sete e oro, by Roberta Orsi Landini; Cut and construction, by Janet Arnold; Recupero e restauro, by Mary Westerman Bulgarella.

Bibliographical references at ends of essays. Bibliografia, p.105–06. Documenti e manoscritti, p.107.

SEE ALSO: History of dress series, v. 2: Herald, Renaissance dress in Italy 1400–1500. (GLAH 2:P113).

Latin America

P241 Sayer, Chloë. Mexican textiles. Repr. with corr. London, British Museum Publications, 1990. [240]p. il. (part col.)

Originally published as Mexican costume (London, British Museum Publications, 1985) and Costumes of Mexico (Austin, Univ. of Texas Pr., 1985).

Survey of Mexican costume, from Precolumbian to modern.

Contents: (I) Costume before the Conquest; (II) The post-Conquest heritage; (III) Twentieth-century Mexico.

Glossary, p.235. Bibliography, p.236–38. Index, p.238–40.

Low Countries

P242 Kostuum verzamelingen in beweging: twaalf studies over kostuumverzamelingen in Nederland & inventarisatie van het kostuumbezit in Nederlandse openbare collecties. [Ed. by H. M. A. Breuklink-Peeze . . . et al.] [Zwolle], Nederlandse Kostuumvereniging voor Mode en Streekdracht, 1995. 196p. il.
Collection of scholarly essays on costume collections in the Netherlands. Covers ecclesiastical collections, the Rijksmuseum, the Fries Museum, the Centraal Museum, Utrecht, the Nederlands Openluchtmuseum, the Nederlands Kostuummuseum/Kabinet, the Haags Gemeentemuseum, the Museum Beeckesteijn, and other collections.

Noten, p.151–62. Inleiding bij de beschrijving van het kostuumbezit in Nederlandse openbare collecties, by Carin Schnitger, p.163. Inventarisatie van het kostuumbezit in Nederlandse openbare collecties, by Andrea Kroon, p.164–90. Index, p.191–95. Informatie addressen, p.196.

Russia and Eastern Europe

P243 The art of costume in Russia: 18th to early 20th century: The Hermitage. Rev. ed. Leningrad, Aurora, 1979. 319p. il. (chiefly col.) ports. (chiefly col.)
1st ed., 1979; French rev. and enl. trans., Le costume en Russie: XVIIIe–début du XXe siècle, Leningrad, Aurora, 1983.

"This book presents a selection of some of the best and most representative examples of eighteenth- to early twentieth-century costume . . . at the Hermitage."—*Introd.* The collection includes the wardrobe of Peter the Great. The introductory text describes the nature and history of the collection, in which areas of focus are court, aristocratic, and military dress, as well as that of the merchant classes and a vast number of accessories.

Magnificently illustrated, the vol. publishes numerous full-page color photographs of dress and accessory items in the collection, as well as period portrait paintings. Close-up photographs show some extraordinary textile patterns and weave structures. All plates are accompanied by detailed captions.

Notes on the text, p.34–35. Selected bibliography, p.312–13. Fashion houses, their owners, and their labels, p.314–19.

P244 Ceská móda 1780–1870: od valciku po tango. [Praha], Umeleckoprumyslové Muzeum v Praze, 1989. 108p. il. (part col.), ports.
Catalog of the exhibition, Museum of Decorative Arts, Prague (1989), which drew on the museum's permanent collections. Chronological in approach, 264 items are featured. Specific topics examined include the influence of foreign fashions, especially through French, German, and Viennese journals; the function of the textile industry and textile trade on a national level; the importance of national and international exhibitions for promoting Bohemian manufactures; and accessories. The many illustrations are drawn primarily from items in the Museum's collection as well as fashion magazine plates; a number of views of textile sellers' and dressmakers' interiors are also included.

Viber y literatury, p.86. Resumé: Fashion in Bohemia, 1780–1870: from the Viennese waltz to the tango, p.106–07.

P245 Gutkowska-Rychlewska, Maria. Historia ubiorów. Wroclaw, Zaklad Narodowy imienia Ossolinskich Wydawnictwo, 1968. 961p. il. viii col. plates, ports.
Surveys the history of dress and dress accessories in Poland. Discusses the kinds of information obtained from archeological, visual, and archival sources in Poland. Chronological in approach, with male and female attire discussed in separate chapters for the later periods. While information concerning dress of the upper classes dominates the volume, regional and military dress are also examined, as is the impact of foreign fashions. Extensively illustrated with some 900 photographs, line drawings, and diagrams of the cut of some dress items.

Bibliographical references follow each chapter. [Table of illustrations, with annotations concerning dress elements: in Polish], p.877–924; [in French], p.925–60. Slownik nazw ubiorów, tkanin i akcessoriów ubioru [Glossary], p.860–76. Le costume polonais: résumé, p.847–59.

P246 History of Ukrainian costume: from the Scythian period to the late 17th century. Melbourne, Bayda Books, 1986. 62p. il.
"Deals with the costumes worn during three distinct periods in Ukrainian history: the Scythian period, the times of ancient Rus' [10th–13th centuries] and the Cossack era [15th–17th centuries]."—*Introd.* Accessories, especially head gear, hairstyles, and footwear, are also examined, and the later period's dress is surveyed along differing social and regional lines.

Bibliography, p.61–62.

P247 In the Russian style. Ed. by Jacqueline Onassis. With the coop. of the Metropolitan Museum of Art. Introd. by Audrey Kennett. Designed by Bryan Holme. N.Y., Viking Pr., 1976. 184p. il. (part col.)
Extensively illustrated study of 18th- and 19th-century court, aristocratic, military, bourgeois, and regional dress, arranged chronologically. Examines fashions in dress and other luxury items.

Bibliography, p.183.

P248 Nicolescu, Corina. Istoria costumului de curte în ţările Române: secolele XIV–XVIII. Bucuresti, Ştiinţifică, 1970. 308p. il. (part col.), 224 plates, ports. (part col.)
"The best Romanian dress history."—*Review*, Textile history, v.22, no.1, spring 1991, p.65, n.31). Thorough and comprehensive survey of 14th- through 18th-century Romanian court dress. The numerous illustrations include surviving dress and textile fragments, and testify to the rich Romanian pictorial and textile traditions documenting dress.

Part I deals with weaving and textiles. Part II discusses court and aristocratic dress. A catalog of 173 items follows, all accompanied by full descriptive entries.

Histoire du costume de cour dans les pays roumains (XIVe–XVIIIe siècles): résumé, p.287–88. [Summary in Russian], p.289–91. Bibliographical references throughout the text. Bibliografie, p.293–306.

P249 Patrik, Arakel N. Armenian national costumes: from ancient times to our days. 2d ed. Erevan, Sovetakan Grogh, 1983. 199p. il. (part col.) 91 plates (part col.), map.

Surveys Armenian costume from ancient historical times up to the first quarter of the 20th century. Includes male and female, military, aristocratic, and some folk dress and accessories. Sources of the illustrations include illuminated manuscripts, seals, paintings, and photographs of surviving items. Extensively illustrated, with captions in Armenian, Russian, and English.

Summaries in Russian and English, p.14–16.

P250 Strizhenova, Tatiana. Soviet costume and textiles 1917–1945. [Paris], Flammarion, 1991. 311p. il. (part col.), ports. (part col.)

Profusely illustrated, reproductions include textile, costume and theater designs, portrait paintings and photographs, fashion sketches, and posters and stills from Soviet theater and film. Many works illustrated are by Russian Constructivist artists.

Contents: The history of early Soviet clothing design; The October Revolution and the new art; Stereotypes and the new symbolism; The Red Army uniform; The first steps; The attitude toward "fashion" in the early 1920s; The revival of the garment industry; Nadezhda Lamanova; Soviet costume at the 1925 International exhibition of decorative and industrial arts in Paris; Constructivist design; Clothing design in the late 1920s; Clothing of the 1930s—problems of an industrial standard; Creation of the Moscow House of Clothing Design—designers of the 1930s; Clothing during world War II (1941–1945).

Bibliographical references throughout the text. Publications [English-language texts of official reports and artists' statements concerning Soviet dress], p.304–11.

P251 Zaletova, Lidya . . . [et al.] Revolutionary costume: Soviet clothing and textiles of the 1920s. N.Y., Rizzoli, 1989. 193p. il. (chiefly col.), ports. (part col.)

Trans. of L'abito della rivoluzione. Venezia, Marsilio, 1987; British ed., Costume revolution: textiles, clothing and costume of the Soviet Union in the twenties. London, Trefoil, 1987.

Extensively illustrated vol. accompanying the exhibition, Venice (1987). Essays by various authors cover early Soviet-period textiles and dress. Particular areas of focus are workers' and theatrical dress, as well as sportswear.

Selective contents: Textiles and Soviet fashion in the twenties, by Tatiana Strizenova; Manufacturing dreams: textile design in revolutionary Russia, by John E. Bowlt; When fashion returned to costume, by Fabio Ciofi degli Atti; The science of dressing from the industrial workshop: the Russian Academy of Artistic Science and Costume—a summary, by Nicoletta Misleri; The VkhUtemas and the Bauhaus: a common story?, by Franco Panizi; Manifestoes and articles [an anthology of contemporary documentary sources in translation].

Bibliographical references follow each essay. Biographies, p.187–91. Glossary, p.192–93.

Scandinavia

P252 Danske dragte. [Copenhagen], Nationalmuseet; Arnold Busck, 1979– . (5)v.

Series of in-depth studies of specific aspects or periods of dress history in Denmark. Vols. are generally divided into two parts, the first comprising an historical survey of the dress and accessories of the period or subject area, the second consisting of a catalog of surviving pieces, mostly in Copenhagen's Nationalmuseet. Catalog entries in each vol. are in Danish and English, with English summaries for the main text. Illustrations include period portraits and photographs, surviving examples of dress in Danish collections, and cutting patterns. All vols. have glossaries, bibliographies, and indexes.

Contents: Andersen, Ellen. Moden I 1700-arene (1977); Bech, Viben, and Andersen, Ellen. Kostumer og modedragter fra del Kgl. Teaters herregarderobe (1979); Andersen, Ellen. Moden 1790–1840 (1986); Bech, Viben. Moden 1840–1890 (1989); Cock-Clausen, Ingenbord. Moden 1890–1920 (1994).

P253 Dräkthistoria, folkdräkter, uniformer: bibliografisk hjälpreda. Sammanställd av Mats Rehnberg. [Stockholm, Institutet for Folklivsforskning, 1981]. 74p.

Unannotated, thematically organized bibliography of costume covering primarily Swedish publications, with some other Scandinavian references.

Contents: Dräkthistoria, allmän; Förhistorisk och medeltida dräkt; Kvinnodräkt; Mansdräkt; Barndräkt; Prästdräkt; Bröllopsdräkt; Sorgdräkt; Huvudbonad; Skodon; Handskar och vantar; Smycken; uniformer; Frisyr; Folkdräkter, allmänt; Folkdräkter, flera landskap; Folkdräkter, landskapsvis; Folkdräktsrörelsen.

P254 Kopisto, Sirkka. Muodin vuosikymmenet: 1810–1910: Suomen kansallismuseo = Dress and fashion: 1810–1910: National Museum of Finland. Helsinki, Museovirasto = National Board of Antiquities, [1991]. 176p. il. (part col.)

Chronological survey of fashionable dress in Finland from the Empire period to the Belle Epoque, as reflected in the collections of the National Museum of Finland. The majority of pieces were made for women, although where available some male attire is included; military dress is excluded. Extensively illustrated, with captions in English and Finnish. Illustrations of surviving items are supplemented by portraits and photographs from the picture archives of the National Board of Antiquities. The impact of foreign fashions and fashion journals on Finland is also discussed.

Viitteet, p.169. Kirjallisuus/Bibliography, p.169. Asiahakemisto, p.170–71. Henkilöhakemisto, p.172. English summary, p.173–76.

P255 Pylkkänen, Riitta. Säätyläisnaisten pukeutuminen Suomessa 1700-luvulla = Dress of gentlewomen in Finland in the 18th century. Helsinki, [Suomen Muinaismuistoyhdistyks], 1982. 515p. il. (part col.), 9 col. pl., maps, ports. (part col.), map (Suomen muinaismuistoyhdistyksen aikakauskirja finska fornminnesföreningens tidskrift, 84)

Extremely thorough scholarly study of 18th- and early 19th-century dress, textiles, and their use and re-use in Finland. Following an introductory section placing the country and its fashions in their historical and geopolitical context, the survey comprises a chronological analysis of Finnish fashions from the late baroque to the neo-classical period. Individual chapters also focus on specific accessories, most notably fans, headgear, and footwear. Clothing construction, including that of undergarments, is also examined. The importance of foreign influences forms a significant part of the discussion. With more than 450 illustrations, the majority of which are of 18th-century Finnish portrait paintings, drawings, caricatures, and textile fragments, this is a key reference work documenting textiles and dress in Finland.

Huomautukset ja lähdeviitteet, p.394–454. Lahde ja kirjallisuusleuttelo, p.496–509. English summary, p.510–15.

Spain and Portugal

P256 Alcega, Juan de. Tailor's pattern book, 1589: facsimile. With trans. by Jean Pain and Cecilia Bainton. Introd. and notes by J. L. Nevinson. Carlton, Bedford [U.K.], Ruth Bean, 1979. [89], 66p. il.

Facsimile and translation of the 2d ed. of Alcega's Libro de geometria, pratica, y traça [Book on the practice of tailoring: measuring and marking out] (Madrid, 1589), now in the collection of the Victoria and Albert Museum. Also included is one folding leaf from Madrid's Biblioteca Nacional copy, missing from that of the Victoria & Albert.

Bibliographical references throughout the translated text. List of patterns, p.6–8. Bibliographical note, p.8. References, p.12. Note on the translation, p.13–14. Glossary, p.61–62. Main notes, p.63–65. Select bibliography, p.66.

P257 Anderson, Ruth Matilda. Hispanic costume 1480–1530. N.Y., Hispanic Society of America, 1979. x, 293p. il. (part col.) (Hispanic notes and monographs, essays, studies and brief biographies. Peninsular series)

Scholarly study of mostly upper-class dress, dress accessories, and hair styles worn on the Iberian Peninsular. The impact of Islamic influences is considered. Each section comprises an historical survey of the fashionable dress (royal, aristocratic, ceremonial, and military) of the period, followed by a series of catalog entries detailing relevant individual garment types. Extensively illustrated with more than 500 small images, with reproductions arranged in groups focusing on individual dress components within a broader chronological development; many details have been taken from prints and paintings of the period.

Contents: (I) Men and their dress occasions; (II) Men's dress; (III) Women and their dress occasions; (IV) Women's dress.

Notes, p.251–64. References, p.265–69. Index, p.273–93.

P258 Bernis, Carmen. Indumentaria española en tiempos de Carlos V. Madrid, Instituto Diego Velazquez, del Consejo Superior de Investigaciones Cientificas, 1962. 114p. 231 plates. (Artes y artistas)

By important costume historian. Documents Spanish dress from the period 1500–58. A wide array of illustrative material, each plate extensively annotated.

Contents: Importancia del vestido en la sociedad española del renacimiento; Moda nacional y moda europea; Trajes regionales.

Obras y documentos citados, p.111–14.

P259 Bernis Madrazo, Carmen. Indumentaria medieval española. Madrid, Instituto Diego Velazquez, del Consejo Superior de Investigaciones Cientificias, 1956. 87p. il., 48 plates. (Artes y artistas)

Beginning with the period immediately following the collapse of the Roman Empire, provides a chronological survey of the development of dress and accessory styles in medieval Spain. Each chapter includes a historical overview of the period, followed by a series of definitions and discussions, in semi-dictionary format, of a list of dress types specific to the period. 184 illustrations follow. Mostly taken from Spanish paintings and sculpture of the period, and amply discussed in notes.

Bibliografia, p.55. Notes, p.59–85. Indice de terminos, p.86–87.

P260 ———. Trajes y modas en la España de los Reyes Catolicos. Madrid, Instituto Diego Velazquez, del Consejo Superior de Investigaciones Cientificas, 1978–79. 2v. il. (part col.), plates (Artes y artistas)

The first part of each vol. comprises a discussion of court and aristocratic dress during the second half of the 15th and the first decades of the 16th century. Considerable attention is paid to archival and literary sources. The impact of Arabic, French, and Italian costume on Spanish styles as well as the influence of late 16th-century Spanish court dress on the rest of Europe is examined. The second part of each vol. comprises an extensively annotated catalog of images in which noteworthy examples of Spanish attire are portrayed; paintings, illuminated manuscripts and sculpture are the primary sources.

Contents: (1) Las mujeres; (2) Los hombres.

Obras y documento citados v.I, p.65–59, v.II, p.137–50. Relación de las obras citadas como referencia en el capítulo Los cambios de la moda, v.II, p.49–52. Glosario, v.II, p.53–136.

P261 L'Evêque. Portuguese costumes. Londres 1814. Ediçao fac-similada do exemplar da Biblioteca Nacional. Introd. de Maring de Albuquerque. Lisboa, Inapa, 1993. [n.p.] 50 col. plates. (Coleçao historia da cultura portuguesa)

1st ed., Portuguese costumes: with a description of the manners and usages of the country. London, Colnaghi, 1814.

Full-page colored illustrations of individuals from all stations of religious and secular, urban, pastoral, and regional life in late 18th–early 19th-century Portugal. Each illustration, and the one–two page description that accompanies it, shows one or two representatives of a specific group engaged in activities representative of that group and wearing the dress that distinguishes it. Local characteristics as well as the impact of foreign fashions (particularly on the upper classes) are included in the survey. The descriptions note each group's place in Portuguese society and discuss the special features of the dress its members wear.

P262 A moda em Portugal através da imprensa 1807–1991. Lisboa, Biblioteca Nacional, 1991. 257p. il. (part col.) (Biblioteca Nacional. Catalogo 35)

Extensively illustrated catalog published in conjunction with the exhibition, Biblioteca Nacional, Lisbon (1991), covering 19th- and 20th-century fashionable dress in Portugal, and documenting the library's collections of fashion journals, prints, and engravings from this period. Women's fashionable dress, accessories, and hairstyles are the principal focus of this vol., although men's attire is briefly examined. A brief historical introduction and three essays by different authors describe the trends and influences operating in Portugal following the introduction of that country's first fashion journal, the Correio das modas, in 1807. Followed by several sections containing articles reproduced from fashion journals of the period (primarily 1807–1929). The catalog that follows also serves as a guide to the fashion prints and literature available for this period.

Contents: (1) Jornais e revistas de moda; (2) Artigos e colunas sobre moda; (3) Adenda; (4) Iconografia; (5) Trajos e acessórios.

Indice de publicaçoes periódicas, p.249–54.

United States

P263 Copeland, Peter F. Working dress in Colonial and Revolutionary America. Westport, Greenwood, [1977]. xv, 223p. il., ports. (Contributions in American history, 58)

Covers the century 1710–1810, when mass-produced clothing was not yet available. Although evidence regarding the dress of wealthier Americans has survived for this period, few sources indicate what members of the working classes wore. Following an introduction to the topic, subsequent chapters investigate the dress of specific categories of worker; much of the clothing is inferred by reference to European sources. Elements of the textile and clothing trade are also discussed.

Contents: (1) Seafarers and fishermen; (2) Farmers and rural workers; (3) Craftsmen and urban workers; (4) Tradesmen and peddlers; (5) Frontiersmen and pioneers; (6) Transportation workers; (7) Public servants; (8) Soldiers and militia men; (9) Professionals; (10) House servants; (11) Indentured servants and slaves; (12) Criminals; (13) National groupings.

Glossary, p.199–207. Bibliography, p.209–10. Index, p.213–23.

P264 De Marly, Diana. Dress in North America. N.Y., Holmes and Meier, 1990– . (1)v. il., col. plates, ports. (part col.)

Historical survey of the development of dress styles and their relationship to social conditions in the U.S. and Canada. Dress traditions of the English, French, and Native American inhabitants of the continent are examined. To date, only vol. one has been published.

Contents: (1) The New World, 1492–1800 (1990).

P265 Earle, Alice (Morse). Two centuries of costume in America, 1620–1820. [Reprint.] Williamstown, Corner House, 1974. 2v. xx, 824p. il. (Corner House Publishers social science reprints)

See GLAH 1:P128 for original annotation.

P266 Hall, Lee. Common threads: a parade of American clothing. Boston, Little, Brown, 1992. ix, 324p. il.

Chronological survey of the dress of all classes and cultures in North America from 1492 to the 1980s. Focuses on the impact of historical and societal developments on clothing. Of special interest are the 19th- and early 20th-century photographs documenting the interrelationships between social conditions and dress.

Contents: (1) In the beginning . . .; (2) The seventeenth century: Mixing cultures; (3) Birth of a country: the eighteenth century; (4) Overview: 1800–1899; (5) Manufacturing and the work force: industrialization and clothing; (6) Communication and the cult of womanhood; (7) The sewing machine and the paper-pattern empires; (8) Dress reform; (9) Masters and slaves: Southern hierarchy and clothing; (10) Western frontier; (11) Levi's; (12) Conspicuous consumption and self-consciousness; (13) overview: the twentieth century; (14) Clothing for the ages; (15) The roaring twenties: dress reform redux; (16) Sports; (17) Gender and clothing: identity, self, and society; (18) College styles; (19) Consumerism and communication; (20) Diversity and uniformity; (21) Superstars: the new aristocracy.

Notes, p.304–08. Bibliography, p.309–14. Index, p.315–23.

P267 Leese, Elizabeth. Costume design in the movies: an illustrated guide to the work of 157 great designers. Rev. ed. N.Y., Dover, 1991. 171p. il. (part col.), ports.

1st ed., London, BCW, 1966; 1st U.S. ed., N.Y., Frederick Ungar, 1977.

Dictionary encyclopedia of the film industry's dress designers. Entries for each designer include a list of films on which the designer worked. The present ed. has extended these film credit listings up to 1987. An introductory chapter, by Barbara A. Schreier, discuses the evolution of the fashion newsreel into fashion design for feature films. The many illustrations have been taken from the films discussed, or from designers' fashion sketches.

Index, p.132–57. Supplementary index, p.158–62. Appendix: Oscar nominations, p.163–68. BAFTA nominations, p.169–70.

P268 Men and women: dressing the part. Ed. by Claudia Brush Kidwell and Valerie Steele. Washington, D.C., Smithsonian Institution Pr., [1989]. 188p. il. (part col.), 27 col. plates.

Produced to accompany the exhibition, National Museum of American History, Washington, D.C. (1989). Examines the interaction between gender identity and dress, with an emphasis on Western fashion and its significance for U.S. society.

Contents: Introduction, by Barbara A. Schreier; Appearance and identity, by Valerie Steele; The children's department, by Jo B. Paoletti and Carol L. Kregloh; Clothing and sexuality, by Valerie Steele; Dressing for work, by Valerie Steele; Sporting wear, by Barbara A. Schreier; Gender symbols or fashionable details?, by Claudia Brush Kidwell; Challenging gender symbols, by Shelley Foote; Conclusion, by Jo B. Paoletti and Claudia Brush Kidwell.

Notes, p.162–73. Index, p.185–88.

P269 Milbank, Caroline Rennolds. New York fashion: the evolution of American style. N.Y., Abrams, 1989. 304p. il. (part col.)

Lavishly illustrated chronological survey ranging from the beginning of the 19th century to the 1980s. From the 1940s on, each chapter comprises an analysis of each decade's fashions, together with a series of alphabetically arranged catalog entries describing individual dress designers' activities for that period.

Bibliography, p.296–97. Index, p.298–302.

P270 Oliver, Valerie Burnham. Costume/clothing/fashion: information access: sources and techniques. [United States], Costume Society of America, Region I, 1993. vi, 101p.

Partially annotated bibliography of books, articles, and essays, designed to complement the author's Fashion and costume in American popular culture (see following entry). Approximately 450 entries cover all aspects of the history of dress (including the social sciences), fashion, and the fashion business; each section also includes suggestions for additional avenues of research.

Contents: Guides to the literature; Encyclopedias; Dictionaries; Directories; Bibliographies; Bibliographic indexing and abstracting services; Visual sources; Primary sources; [Computer] networks.

Author index, p.87–89. Keyword subject/selected title index, p.91–99. Abbreviations/acronyms, p.100–01.

P271 ———. Fashion and costume in American popular culture: a reference guide. Westport, Greenwood, [1996]. xii, 279p. (American popular culture)

Bibliography, primarily devoted to monographic literature; includes some masters' and Ph.D. theses. Omits the business aspects of the fashion industry, fashion illustration and photography, fashion merchandising, and military and Native American dress. Each chapter or section comprises an introductory essay surveying the literature. Bibliographical listings follow.

Contents: (1) Guides to the literature; (2) Encyclopedias; (3) Histories of fashion and costume in the United States; (4) Specific clothing and accessories; (5) Psychological, sociological and cultural aspects; (6) Dictionaries; (7) Specialized bibliographies; (8) Indexing and abstracting services; (9) Media; (10) Research centers; (11) Costume museums and collections; (12) Professional organizations and related conference proceedings; (13) Periodicals; Appendix: Clothing and accessory terms used in OCLC/WorldCat database, July 6, 1995 (sorted for books, serials, and media, in English).

Notes, p.241–46. Author index, p.247–60. Subject index, p.261–79.

P272 Owen, Bobbi. Costume design on Broadway: designers and their credits, 1915–1985. N.Y., Greenwood, 1987. xv, 254p. il., 100 plates (Bibliographies and indexes in the performing arts, 5)

Brief introductory essay on the changing role of costume design for the stage, followed by an alphabetical listing of more than 1,000 Broadway costume designers and the productions they worked on. Much of this information has been compiled from playbills and theater yearbooks, thus creating a very useful reference resource.

Contents: Appendix 1: Tony Award; Appendix 2: Maharam Award; Appendix 3: Donaldson Award.

Index of plays, p.183–254.

P273 Severa, Joan L. Dressed for the photographer: ordinary Americans and fashion, 1840–1900. Kent, Kent State Univ. Pr., 1995. xxii, 592p. il.

Explores "the problem of how ordinary Americans [of the 19th century] handled the often conflicting dictates of fashion, hard work and economy in their clothing choices."—*Pref.* The interrelationship between the history of portrait photography and the history of dress forms an integral part of the discussion. Each chapter considers a decade and comprises an introductory essay followed by approximately 30–50 extensively annotated photographs. Focus is on women's dress, since greater evidence has survived in this category; but men's and children's attire are also considered where photographs exist. Where available, photographs of people from different ethnic backgrounds are also discussed.

Glossary, p.541–48. Bibliography, p.555–66. Index, p.567–92.

P274 Worrell, Estelle Ansley. Children's costume in America 1607–1910. N.Y., Scribner, 1980. 216p. il. (part col.), 8 col. plates.

Based on the premise that studying children's costume can provide insights into a society's attitude towards its young. The focus is on children's clothes of the upper and middle classes, and the organization is chronological. The author also discusses the impact of foreign fashions, sports, and new technologies (such as the invention of rubber and synthetic fabrics) in the area of children's dress and accessories. Line drawings by the author comprise the vol.'s visual repertoire.

SEE ALSO: Gorsline, A history of fashion (GLAH 2:P112).

Asian Countries

China

P275 Ethnic costumes and clothing decorations from China. Hong Kong, Hai Feng, [1986?]. 336p. il. (part col.), map.

The customs, religious rites, geographical and climatic conditions, and artistic traditions of China's 56 nationalities are reflected in their costumes and accessories. Ethnic costumes, with their bright colors, exquisite workmanship, and unique styles, are depicted in the 700 drawings and photos and described in the brief accompanying text.

P276 5000 years of Chinese costumes. Text: Zhou Xun and Gao Chunming. Ed.: The Chinese Costumes Research Group of the Shanghai School of Traditional Operas. San Francisco, China Books and Periodicals, [1987]. 256p. il. (part col.), ports.

Trans. of Chung-kuo fu shih wu chīen nien. Hong Kong, Shang wu yin shu kuan Hsiang-kang fen kuan; Shang-hai, Hsüüeh lin ch'u pan she, 1984.

Basic reference source for the colorful and artistic styles of costume throughout Chinese history. The authors present vivid renderings of garments and accessories, based on descriptions from historical records and depictions in art.

Bibliography, p.252–53. Index of illustrations, p.254–56.

P277 Garrett, Valery M. Chinese clothing: an illustrated guide. Hong Kong, Oxford Univ. Pr., 1994. xiv, 224p. il. (part col.)

Until the 20th century, the Chinese used costume and adornment to identify the wearer's rank and function in society. The author, who has worked in fashion design in Hong Kong and was instrumental in the formation and cataloging of the Chinese costume collection at the Hong Kong Museum of History, traces the development of Chinese dress and accessories from the Ming dynasty to the present day. Useful resource for social history as well as costume history.

Contents: (I) The Ming dynasty (1368–1644); (II) The Qing dynasty (1644–1911); (III) The twentieth century (after 1912); (IV) Military uniforms and dress for special occasions; (V) Children's wear; (VI) Minority dress; (VII) Materials; Afterword.

Glossary, p.[212]–14. Select bibliography, p.215. Index, p.[219]–24.

P278 Wilson, Verity. Chinese dress. [London], Victoria and Albert Museum, [1986]. 135p. il. (part col.), map (Far Eastern series)

An introduction, not a complete history of Chinese costume, based on examples from the Victoria and Albert Museum's collection of official and court dresses, and other dress styles primarily from the Qing Dynasty (1644–1911). Also includes information about cultural phenomena such as jewelry, hairstyles, and make-up and about fabric, tailoring, embroidery, and dating of garments. Intended for both the general public as well as scholars in the field. A useful contribution with a readable text and superb illustrations.

Bibliography, p.131. Index, p.132–35.

India, Nepal, Pakistan, Tibet

P279 Maheswari, C. S. Uma. Dress and jewellery of women, Satavahana to Kakatiya. Madras, New Era Publications, 1995.130p. il.

Brief study of the social roles of female dress and ornament in India. Sparsely illustrated, with poor photographs and line drawings

Contents: (1) Introduction; (2) Political background; (3) Dress and jewellery of women as depicted in epigraphy and literature; (4) Dress and jewellery depicted in sculptures; (5) Conclusion.

Bibliography, p.125–27. Select index, p.128–30.

P280 Mohapatra, Ramesh Prasad. Fashion styles of ancient India: a study of Kalinga from earliest times to sixteenth century A.D. Delhi, B.R. Publishing Corp., 1992. 2v. in 1. il.

"The present book envisages a study of Orissa's coiffures and costumes from the first century to the end of the fifteenth and sixteenth century on the basis of archaeological evidences and literary corroborations."—*Pref.* Posthumously published. Poor black-and-white illustrations; line drawings.

Bibliography, p.[81]–83. Index, p.[85]–89. Glossary of terms, p.[91]–100.

P281 Sulochana Ayyar. Costumes and ornaments as depicted in the sculptures of Gwalior Museum. Delhi, India, Mittal Publications, 1987. xii, 199p. il., map, 31p. of plates.

Historical overview, based largely on the collections of the Central Archaeological Museum, Gwalior.

Bibliography, p.177–84. Index, p.185–94.

Japan

P282 Buisson, Sylvie, and Buisson, Dominique. Kimono: art traditionnel du Japon. [Lausanne], Edita, [1983]. 271p. il. (part col.)

Introduction to this Japanese icon including a history, the making and decorating of the cloth, the variety of uses in theater, ceremonies, and as traditional costume, the accessories worn with the kimono, and interpretations of the kimono form by contemporary Japanese fashion designers.

Bibliography, p.270.

P283 Dalby, Liza Crihfield. Kimono: fashioning culture. New Haven, Yale Univ. Pr., [1993]. xi, 384p. il.

Uses the subject of the kimono to explore Japanese culture through one of its most characteristic manifestations. A result of the author's research on geisha for her doctoral dissertation in anthropology. Primarily a discussion of the contemporary kimono, although some historical background is provided.

Notes to the text, p.337–49. Notes to the illustrations, p.350–58. Bibliography, p.359–67. Index and glossary, p.369–84.

P284 Gluckman, Dale Carolyn, and Tadeka, Sharon Sadako. When art became fashion: kosode in Edo-pe-

riod Japan. Los Angeles, Los Angeles County Museum of Art; N.Y., Weatherhill, 1992. 351p. il. (part col.), map.
Catalog of the exhibition, Los Angeles County Museum of Art (1992–93).

The kosode, a garment similar to the modern kimono, was worn by both men and women during the Edo period in Japan and remains an evocative symbol of traditional cultural values. This catalog, through essays by both Japanese and American scholars, analyzes the aesthetic and cultural context of the kosode making this work not simply a book about Japanese clothing but truly a work concerning Japanese art and culture. An appendix provides a quick visual record of the changes in the placement of design motifs on kosode from the 16th–19th centuries.

Glossary, p.332–39. Bibliography, p.340–45. Index, p.346–50.

P285 Kennedy, Alan. Japanese costume: history and tradition. Paris, Biro (Distr. by Rizzoli, 1990). 153p. il. (part col.)
Beautifully illustrated introduction to costumes from three spheres of Japanese life: the ruling class, represented by the kimonos of the very wealthy or highly placed; the theater, represented by the theater costumes from Nō actors; and Buddhism, represented by the mantles of the Buddhist clergy.

Glossary, p.[155]. Selected bibliography, p.[156]. Index of costume styles and types, p.[157].

P286 Stinchecum, Amanda Mayer. Kosode, 16th–19th century textiles from the Nomura collection. N.Y., Japan Society, [1984]. 234p. il. (part col.), port.
Catalog of the exhibition, Japan House Gallery (1984).

Assembled by Shōjirō Nomura and now housed in the National Museum of Japanese History, this collection of 156 complete robes and 100 robe fragments mounted on screens from the 16th–19th centuries is recognized as one of the finest and most extensive. In addition to a chapter on the collector, the catalog includes an essay on Kosode techniques and design, a chapter on dyes and pigments written by Monica Bethe, and appendixes discussing technical aspects of the textiles.

Footnotes, p.200–18. Glossary, p.220–22. Bibliography, p.224–27. Index, p.230–34.

Africa, Oceania, The Americas

General Works

P287 Marks of civilization: artistic transformations of the human body. Ed. by Arnold Rubin. Los Angeles, Museum of Cultural History, UCLA, [1988]. 279p. il. (part col.), maps.
Based on a symposium titled "Art of the Body," UCLA (1983). Includes scholarly essays and extensive illustration.

Contents: Introduction: Africa, by Arnold Rubin; Tattoo in ancient Egypt, by Robert S. Bianchi; Significance of differences in the male and female personal art of the Southeast Nuba, by James Faris; Tabwa tegumentary inscription, by Allen F. Roberts; Ga'anda scarification: a model for art and identity, by Marla C. Berns; Beauty and scarification amongst the Tiv, by Paul Bohannan; Beauty and being: aesthetics and ontology in Yoruba body art, by Henry John Drewal; Baule scarification: the mark of civilization, by Susan Vogel; Introduction: Asia, by Arnold Rubin; Historical and cultural dimensions of the tattoo in Japan, by Donald McCallum; The spiritual significance of Newar tattoos, by Jehanne Teilhet-Fisk; Tattoo trends in Gujarat, by Arnold Rubin; Introduction, Oceania, by Arnold Rubin; Hawaiian tattoo: a conjunction of genealogy and aesthetics, by Adrienne Kaeppler; Contexts of Maori Moko by Peter Gathercole; Introduction: Native America, by Arnold Rubin; Labrets and tattooing in native Alaska, by Joy Gritton; Women, marriage, mouths and feasting: the symbolism of Tlingit Labrets, by Aldona Jonaitis; Introduction, Contempoary Euro-America, by Arnold Rubin; The variable context of Chicano tattooing, by Alan Govenar; Drill and frill: client choice, client typologies, and interactional control in commercial tattooing settings, by Clinton R. Sanders; The tattoo renaissance, by Arnold Rubin.

Bibliography, p.265–76.

Africa

P288 African dress II: a select and annotated bibliography. [By] Ila M. Pokornowski . . . [et al.] East Lansing, Mich., African Studies Center, Michigan State Univ., [1985]. x, 316p. map.
See GLAH 1:P135 for first vol. (1969).

A partially annotated bibliography of 1,260 citations, intended as a supplement to the first vol.

Contents: The study of African dress, by Otto Charles Thieme and Joanne Bubolz Eicher; Resource materials for the study of African dress, by Otto Charles Thieme; User's guide; Africa: general; North Africa: general; West Africa: general; Central Africa: general; South central Africa: general; East Africa: general; Southern Africa: general.

Author index, p.267–316.

P289 Carey, Margaret. Beads and beadwork of east and south Africa. [Princes Risborough, UK, Shire, 1986]. 64p. 43 il. map. (Shire ethnography, 3)
Authoritative and well-researched, this work discusses beads as personal adornment and as decoration on objects of use in east Africa (particularly Kenya and Tanzania) and in southern Africa (particularly among the Ndebele, Xhosa, and Zulu).

Contents: (1) Introduction; (2) Beads; (3) East and central Africa; (4) Southern Africa and Madagascar; (5) Museums to visit; (6) Further reading (p.63).

Index, p.64.

P290 ______. Beads and beadwork of West and central Africa. [Princes Risborough, UK, Shire, 1991]. 56p. 45 il. map. (Shire ethnography, 21)
Well-researched and carefully documented text that treats the history of the bead trade, and the making and uses of beads. Can serve as an identification guide.

Contents: (1) Introduction; (2) Bead types; (3) Senegal, the Sahel and Ghana; (4) Nigeria; (5) The Bight of Biafra to Gabon; (6) Zaire and Angola; (7) Museums; (8) Further reading (p.54–55).

Index, p.56.

P291 Morris, Jean. Speaking with beads: Zulu arts from Southern Africa. Text by Eleanor Preston-Whyte. [N.Y.], Thames and Hudson, [1994]. [96]p. il. (part col.), map.

Extensively illustrated with color photographs taken in Southern Africa. Documents the techniques and styles of beadwork as well as the context within which beads are worn.

Contents: (1) Voices from the past; (2) Speaking with beads; (3) Speaking of meaning; (4) Speaking of religion; (5) Speaking of fashion and art; (6) Speaking of tradition and nationalism.

Bibliography, p.[95]. Beadwork suppliers, p.[96].

P292 Spring, Christopher. African arms and armour. Washington, D.C., Smithsonian Institution Pr., [1993]. 144p. 134 il., 30 col. plates, map.

Amply illustrated with field photographs, surveys both the aesthetic and social characteristics of African weapons and armor.

Contents: (1) Arab and Berber, North Africa and the Sahara; (1) Knights of the Savanna, Warfare in Sudanic Africa; (3) The forest kingdoms of West Africa; (4) The shining mystery, Throwing knives of Africa; (5) Royal blacksmiths, The Kuba kingdom and the Congo Basin; (6) The Horn of Africa; (7) Cattle and conflict, East African pastoralists and their neighbours; (8) Mfecane, the Zulu and the Nguni diaspora in southern Africa.

Bibliography, p.139–40. Index, p.142–44.

The Americas

P293 Oakes, Jill, and Riewe, Rick. Our boots: an Inuit women's art. N.Y., Thames and Hudson, 1995. 224p. il. (part col.), maps.

Attractive, comprehensive, and sensitive treatment of a vital Inuit material culture and the society that surrounds its production. "The tools, materials, and construction techniques employed to produce skin footwear are covered in Chapters 1 through 3. Chapters 4 through 11 present the eight general Canadian cultural groups and include regional overviews of the physical and human geography, as well as summaries of past and present clothing styles, to provide an environmental, social, cultural, and historical setting for the descriptions of footwear."—*Pref.* Includes appendixes of the scientific names of animals and glossary.

Reference list, p.209–13. Index, p.215–24.

P294 Paterek, Josephine. Encyclopedia of American Indian costume. Denver, ABC-CLIO, 1994. xiv, 516p. il.

Entries for specific North American Indian groups arranged within 10 chapters arranged by culture. "The following categories of dress are discussed for each group (with some variation): Men's Basic Dress; Women's Basic Dress; Footwear; Outer Wear; Hair Styles; Headgear; Accessories; Jewelry; Armor; Special Costumes; Garment Decoration; Face and Body Embellishment; and Transitional Dress."—*Introd.* Entries are illustrated with historic photographs or Western depictions and object photographs of selected costume types and each includes a select bibliography.

Appendixes: Clothing arts of the American Indians, p.431–59; Glossary, p.461–71. Bibliography, p.473–85. Index, p.493–516.

FURNITURE

Dictionaries and Encyclopedias

P295 Edwards, Clive. Encyclopedia of furniture materials, trades and techniques. [Brookfield, Vt.], Ashgate, [2000]. vii, [2], 254p. il, 24 col. plates.

Dictionary focusing on the materials and processes of furniture-making "limited principally to British and American furniture and furnishings of the period 1500–2000, with diversions to other periods and countries as required."—*Introd.* Includes references to textiles used in upholstery. Some entries accompanied by bibliographical references and some by quotations from period sources.

Bibliography, p.[247]–54.

P296 Gloag, John. A complete dictionary of furniture. Rev. and upd. by Clive Edwards. Woodstock, N.Y., [1991]. 828p. il., charts.

Originally published as A short dictionary of furniture. London, 1952; rev. and enl. ed., London, 1969.

New ed. of a standard dictionary of furniture and furnishings made and used in England since 1100 A.D. and in North America since the mid-17th century. Terms new to the dictionary are included in an appendix by Edwards.

Contents: (I) The description of furniture; (II) The design of furniture; (III) Dictionary of names and terms; (IV) Furniture makers in Britain and America; (V) Books and periodicals on furniture and design; (VI) Periods, types, materials, and craftsmen from 1100 to 1950. Appendix by Clive Edwards.

Histories and Handbooks

P297 Brunt, Andrew. Phaidon guide to furniture. Oxford, Phaidon, [1978]. 256p. il. (part col.)

Compact handbook to furniture of all cultures from ancient times to the present. Introductory section on techniques is followed by country-by-country surveys by time period.

Makers and designers, p.243–49. Glossary, p.250–53. Index, p.255–56.

P298 Duncan, Alastair. Art nouveau furniture. N.Y., Clarkson Potter (Distr. by Crown, [1982]). 192p. il. (part col.)

Authoritative history of British and European Art Nouveau furniture with emphasis on the master designers who created the style. Includes a brief discussion of woods, marquetry, and mounts. Useful bibliographies of contemporary criticism of the work of individual designers in the periodical literature.

Bibliography, p.185. Designers' bibliographies, p.186–90. Index, p.191–92.

P299 Mang, Karl. History of modern furniture. Trans. by John William Gabriel. N.Y., Abrams, [1979]. 185p. il.

First published as Geschichte des modernen Möbels. Stuttgart, Hatje, 1978.

Concise 1-vol. history of furniture design in the 19th and 20th centuries with particular emphasis on European designers.

Contents: (1) Anonymous furniture in the nineteenth century-harbingers of the machine aesthetic; (2) The theories of William Morris and the challenge of industry; (3) From De Stijl to the International Style; (4) Scandinavian furniture-from anonymity to world renown; (5) Furniture design after World War II.

Includes bibliographical references. Bibliography, p.179–180. Index, p.181–83.

P300 Miller, Judith, and Miller, Martin. The antiques directory: Furniture. Chief consultant ed.: John Bly. American consultants: Lita Solis-Cohen, Kelvyn Grant Lilley. Boston, Hall, 1985. 639p. il. (part col.)

Consists principally of illustrations of more than 7,000 pieces of furniture, arranged by country and by furniture form, with particular emphasis on American, British, and French examples. Includes section on Oriental furniture. Brief information is given for each piece. Useful primarily for basic identification and comparison. Includes price codes.

Glossary, p.625–32 (includes chart of periods and styles). Index, p.633–39.

P301 Ostergard, Derek, ed. Bent wood and metal furniture: 1850–1946. Text by Alessandro Alvera, Graham Dry, Robert Keil. . . [et al.] [N.Y.], American Federation of Arts, [1987]. xvi, 366p. il.

Published in conjunction with an exhibition organized by the American Federation of Arts.

"The first comprehensive examination of furnishings made from materials that have been bent"—*p.xi*. Although discussing pre-industrial origins of these forms, principal emphasis is on the 19th and 20th centuries. Includes interpretive essays and catalog of the exhibition.

Appendix: Bent-wood furniture manufacturers, 1849–1914, by Graham Dry. Glossary, p.343–45. Bibliography, p.347–59. Index, p.361–65.

P302 Page, Marian. Furniture designed by architects. N.Y., Whitney Library of Design/Watson-Guptill, [1979]. 224p. il.

Succinct and readable discussion of furniture designed by 26 notable American, English and European architects from the 18th to the mid-20th centuries.

Selected bibliography, p.218–20. Index, p.221–24.

P303 Philp, Peter, and Walkling, Gillian. Field guide to antique furniture. Advisory ed.: John Bly. [Boston], Houghton Mifflin, 1992. 336p. il. (part col.)

Handy quick-reference guide to European, English, and New World furniture by type, with succinct information on materials, construction, decoration, and finish, and on fakes and altered pieces. Especially useful for beginning collectors.

Glossary, p.329–31. Prices, p.332–33. Index, p.334–36.

P304 Pile, John F. Furniture: modern + postmodern, design + technology. 2d ed. N.Y., Wiley, [1900]. xii, 312p. il. (part col.), tables.

1st ed. 1979.

Introduction to the history, design process, and manufacturing technology of today's mass-manufactured furniture from the viewpoint of a design professional. Appendix 1: Standard and recommended dimensions and seating profiles; Appendix 2: Problems of design piracy and design protection, design credit, and attribution; Appendix 3: Safety considerations.

Bibliography, p.303–06. Index, p.307–12.

P305 Stimpson, Miriam F. Modern furniture classics. N.Y., Whitney Library of Design, 1997. 208p. il.

Presents "the largest collection of modern furniture classics ever assembled in one vol.—not only chairs and stools, but tables, sofas, lounges, chests, and wall units."—*Pref.* A useful quick-reference source.

Contents: The beginning of modernism; Arts and crafts movement; Early modernism in the United States; Art nouveau; Vienna Secession, Wiener Werkstätte, Deutscher Werkbund; Modernism in Holland; Art deco; The 1930s; Postwar Scandinavia; Postwar America; Postwar Italy; Postwar Germany, France, England, Brazil, Mexico; The 1970s; The 1980s.

Directories, p.188–94. Selected bibliography, p.195–96. Index, p.197–203.

P306 Victoria and Albert Museum. Western furniture: 1350 to the present day in the Victoria and Albert Museum, London. Ed. by Christopher Wilk. London, Philip Wilson in assoc. with the Victoria and Albert Museum, 1996. 231p. il. (part col.)

Catalog, with full-page color plates, of 100 examples from the collection.

Note to the text, p.24. Index, p.226–30. Index of museum numbers, p.231.

P307 Wallace Collection. Catalogue of furniture, by Peter Hughes. London, 1996. 3v. il. (part col.)

Supersedes Francis Watson's pioneering catalog of the great collection (1956). Concludes the series of catalogs of the Wallace Collection documenting the furniture, paintings, and porcelain. Includes concordances with the Watson catalog.

Contents: (I) Gothic and renaissance style; Carved furniture; Lacquer furniture; Barometers and clocks; (II) Boulle furniture; Veneered furniture; (III) Gilt bronze; Miscellaneous; Appendices.

Abbreviations, v.3, p.1577–78. Abbreviations of published and unpublished works, v.3, p.1578–1604. Glossary, v.3, p.1604–21. Index of proper names, v.3, p.1622–67.

P308 World furniture. Ed. by Noel Riley. Foreword by Kenneth L. Ames. N.Y., Mayflower, 1980. 320p. il. (part col.)

Well-illustrated 1-vol. history of furniture from the ancient world to the 20th century, most suitable for a general audience.

Guide to museums and collections, p.312–13. Glossary, p.314–15. Index, p.316–20.

Western Countries

Australia

P309 Fahy, Kevin; . . . [et al.] Nineteenth-century Australian furniture. Chippendale, NSW, David Ell Press, 1986. 624p. il. (part col.), ports.

Substantial survey.

Contents: Nomenclature of Australian furniture timbers; New South Wales; Queensland; South Australia; Tasmania; Victoria; Western Australia; Styles and sources; Labels, stamps, stencils and inscriptions.

Directory of cabinet, chair and furniture makers, p.529–612. Index, p.617–24.

Canada

P310 Living in style: fine furniture in Victorian Quebec. General ed., John R. Porter. Montreal, Montreal Museum of Fine Arts, [1993]. 537p., il., col. plates, maps, plans, tables.

Published to accompany the exhibition, Montreal Museum of Fine Arts (1993), and other locations.

Exhibit and catalog focus on domestic furnishings, made in Quebec, and situate them within the usages of society and household ritual, with considerable use of contemporary documentation and pictorial evidence. A chapter is devoted to the furniture makers and their methods. "The vocabulary of domestic furniture" (p.487–509), defines English and French terminology for furniture forms and decoration.

Select bibliography p.513–19. List of art works presented in the exhibition, p.521. Index of names, p.522–27.

P311 Pain, Howard. The heritage of country furniture: a study in the survival of formal and vernacular styles from the United States, Britain and Europe found in Upper Canada, 1780–1900. Foreword by Dean A. Fales, Jr. Introd. by William Kilbourne. N.Y., Van Nostrand Reinhold, [1978]. 548p. il. (part col.), col. fold. maps.

Extensive pictorial documentation of Ontario furniture, based on almost 1500 illustrated examples, with commentary on each piece by a recognized authority in this field. Chapters devoted to the contributions of Germanic, Polish, and French-Canadian cabinetmakers as well as those of English and Loyalist origins.

Notes on the text, p.519–20. Technical notes on the plates, p.521–39. Glossary of terms, p.540–41. Bibliography, p.544. Index, p.545–48.

P312 Webster, Donald Blake. English-Canadian furniture of the Georgian period. Foreword by Charles F. Hummel. Toronto, McGraw-Hill Ryerson, [1979]. 232p. il. (part col.)

Focuses on formal furniture in the English tradition made in Canada to about 1830. Attention is paid to similarities and differences between Canadian and American furniture of the same period. A pioneering and valuable work.

Bibliography, p.227–29. Index, p.230–32.

France

Bibliography

P313 Viaux, Jacqueline. Bibliographie du meuble (mobilier civil francais). Paris, Société des Amis de la Bibliothèque Forney, 1966. 589p.

See GLAH 1:P153 for original annotation.

———. Bibliographie du meuble (mobilier civil francais): Supplement 1965–1985. Paris, Bibliothèque Forney, 1988.

———. Bibliographie du meuble. Second supplement 1985–1990 et complements: mobilier civil français. Paris, Bibliothèque Forney, 1998. 252p.

Dictionaries and Encyclopedias

P314 Pradère, Alexandre. French furniture makers: the art of the ébéniste from Louis XIV to the Revolution. Trans. by Perran Wood. Malibu, Getty Museum, [1989]. 442p. il. (part col.)

Well-documented biographical dictionary of more than 60 of the most prominent ébénistes, or cabinet-makers, working in 18th-century Paris. In addition to general bibliography, each personal entry has specific bibliography.

Glossary of woods, p.431. Glossary of French terms, p.433–34. The stamp, p.435. List of identified ebenistes of the 17th and 18th centuries, p.436–37. Bibliography, p.438. Index of principal names of persons, p.440–41. Index of principal place-names, p.441.

P315 Reyniès, Nicole de. Le mobilier domestique: vocabulaire typologique. Paris, Imprimerie nationale, 1987. 2v. il. (part col.)

Detailed, heavily illustrated dictionary of French furniture terminology, from the middle ages to the 20th century, arranged by function, and under function by form, structure, or other determining factor. Each term is extensively documented. Illustrated by extant examples of furniture and period prints, paintings, and book illustrations. Introductions explain terminology and method. Table of contents in each vol. serves as guide to arrangement of furniture types and sub-types.

Bibliographie, v.II, p.1177–90. Index: Elements constituifs, Termes typologiques, Lieux de conservation, Meubles estampilles, Auteurs des peintures, dessins, et estampes, v.II, p.1191–1220.

Histories and Handbooks

P316 Boccador, Jacqueline. Le mobilier français du Moyen Age à la Renaissance. [Saint Just en Chaussée], Ed. d'Art Monelle Hayot, [1988]. 342p. il. (part col.), genealogical chart.

Extensive, well-illustrated study of French furniture from 1200 to 1590, principally based on extant examples.

Contents: (1) Le Moyen Age (1200–1490); (2) Le première Renaissance française (1490–1530); (3) La seconde Renaissance française (1530–1590); (4) Conclusion: Tresors du Moyen Age et de la Renaissance: Émaux, ferronnerie, dinanderie, faience.

Index, p.323–32. Bibliographie selective, p.333–38. Textes et divers (Index of illustrations from books), p.339. Notes, p.340–41.

P317 Duncan, Alastair. Art Deco furniture: the French designers. N.Y., Holt, 1984. 192p. il. (part col.)

Includes biographies of 85 "furniture designers who embraced either the Art Deco or modernist styles, or both, and whose furniture was made between 1910 and the mid-1930s."—*p.11.*

Contents: Art Deco and modernism; The U.A.M.; The scope of the book; The 1920s/30s furniture designers; Furniture materials; The Paris department stores; The 1925 Exposition; Contemporary collectors; Ocean liners; Biographies of designers; Appendix.

Bibliography, p.189. Index, p.191–92.

P318 Fligny, Laurence. Le mobilier en Picardie, 1200–1700. Publié avec le concours du Centre national des Lettres. [Paris], Picard, [1990]. 358p. il. (part col.), chart, maps.

Exemplary study of furniture in Picardy, a region of northwestern France, from the middle ages through the 17th century. Attempts to distinguish the specific characteristics of Picard furniture, and links extent examples to surviving architectural woodwork of the same period. Projected as first of a series of studies of French regional furniture.

Includes bibliographical references. Répertoire: mobilier picard accessible dans les eglises, musées et chateaux ouverts au public, p.345–50. Lexique, p.351–54. Bibliographie, p.355–57.

P319 Furniture collections in the Louvre. Pref. by Baron Edmond de Rothschild. Photographs: Jean-Yves and Nicolas Dubois. [Dijon], Editions Faton, [1993]. 2v., col. il.

Thorough, well-illustrated catalog of a notable collection of fine French furniture from the medieval period through the 19th century, with emphasis on the work of individual craftsmen. Includes a history of the collection, which includes French royal furniture. Authors are curators of furniture at the Louvre.

Contents: (I) Middle ages, Renaissance, 17th–18th centuries (ébénisterie), 19th century, by Daniel Alcouffe, Anne Dion-Tenenbaum, Amaury Lefebure; (II) Chairs and consoles (menuiserie), 17th and 18th centuries, by Bill G. B. Pallot.

Bibliography, v.I, p.347–49, v.II, p.202–03. Index of proper names, v.I, p.350–52, v.II, p.204–07. Table of catalogue entries, v.I, p.353, v.II, p.209. Biographies of menuisiers en sièges (chair-makers) whose work is represented in the Louvre, v.II, p.185–209.

P320 Kjellberg, Pierre. Le meuble français et européene du moyen age à nos jours. [Paris], Les Eds. de l'Amateur, [1991]. 591p. il. (part col.)

Massive, extensively illustrated history of French furniture from the middle ages to the mid-20th century, including its relationship to that of other European countries. A chapter summarizes regional furniture characteristics.

Le mobilier français dans les musées, p.5. Index des artistes, artisans, designers, fabricants et éditeurs, p.587–90. Index des termes specifiques au mobilier, p.591.

P321 Ledoux-Lebard, Denise. Les ébénistes du XIXe siècle, 1795–1889: leurs oeuvres et leurs marques. [Paris]. Les Eds. de l'Amateur, [1984]. 699p. il.

See GLAH 1:P159 for previous ed.

Revised and greatly expanded ed. of the standard, monumental dictionary of French 19th-century cabinetmakers, now including more than 4800 names.

Bibliographie, p.690–99.

P322 Pallot, Bill G. B. The art of the chair in eighteenth-century France. Pref. by Svend Eriksen. Foreword by Theodore Dell and by Karl Lagerfeld. [Courbevoie], ACR-Gismondi, [1989]. 332p. il. (principally col.), plan.

Trans. of L'art du siège au XVIIIe siècle en France. Paris, Gismondi, 1987.

Masterful, detailed examination of the French 18th-century chair and its makers by an acknowledged authority. Biographical section includes reproductions of each chair-maker's stamp.

Contents: (1) Chair making in the eighteenth century; (2) The effect of the principal stylistic movements on chair design; (3) A singular case history: Nicolas Huertaut, master joiner and master carver (1720–1771); (4) Techniques in chair making; (5) Selected biographies of French chair makers (1730–1775); (6) Sources and documents

Notes, p.324. Bibliography, p.325–27. Index, p.328–31.

P323 Thirion, Jacques. Le mobilier du Moyen Age et da la Renaissance en France. Pref. de Daniel Alcouffe. Dijon, Ed. Faton, 1998. 279p. il. (part col.)

Important survey of medieval and renaissance French furniture, by a specialist.

Contents: Le Moyen Age: Les données techniques; Le décor I: les ornements; Le décor II: par catégories de meubles; Le premièr Renaissance: une nouvelle parure; Les catégories de meubles; La seconde Renaissance: La métamorphose du meuble; Les catégories de meubles; Le décor I: les ornements; Le décor II: les sujets; Annexes.

Bibliographie, p.262–69. Index, p.270–279.

P324 Verlet, Pierre. French furniture of the eighteenth century. Trans. by Penelope Hunter-Stiebel. Charlottesville, Univ. Pr. of Virginia, [1991]. xv, 256p. il., plates (part col.)

Originally published as Les meubles français du XVIIIe siècle. Paris, 1954 (see GLAH 1:P168). This trans. from second, rev. ed. (1983).

Verlet was acknowledged as the expert on pre-Revolutionary French furniture.

This translation summarizes that knowledge, covering everything from working methods to stylistic development to fakes and documentation to the evolution of prices from the 18th century to the present. Illustrates makers' stamps, and lists ébénistes (cabinetmakers) and menuisiers (chairmakers).

Contents: (1) Structures; (2) Menuiserie furniture; (3) Ebenisterie furniture; (4) Collections and collectors.

Bibliography, p.227–36. Index, p.237–56.

P325 ______. Le mobilier royal français. Paris, Picard, 1990–92. 4v. il. (part col.)

Series examining extant examples of French royal furniture, now in both public and private collections, by a renowned furniture historian. For previous eds. of some of these vols. see GLAH 1:P166, GLAH 1:P169.

Contents: (1) Meubles de la couronne conservés en France (2d ed., 1992); (2) Meubles de la couronne conservés en France, avec une étude sur le garde-meuble de la couronne (2d ed., 1990); (3) Meubles de la couronne conservés en Angleterre et aux États-Unis (1991) [first published as French royal furniture: an historical survey followed by a study of forty pieces preserved in Great Britain and the United States, London, Barrie and Rockliffe, (1963)]; (4) Meubles de la couronne conservés en Europe et aux États-Unis. [Paris], Picard (1990).

SEE ALSO: The Frick Collection: an illustrated catalogue. v.V, Furniture, Italian and French; v.VI, Furniture and gilt bronzes, French (GLAH 2:I1).

Germany and Austria

P326 Behal, Vera J. Möbel des Jugendstils: Sammlung des Österreichischen Museum für angewandte Kunst, Wien. München, Prestel, 1981. München, Prestel, 1981. 358p. il. (part col.)

Catalog of an important collection, preceded by a series of essays on the pedagogical programs of the Österreichisches Museum für Kunst und Industrie.

Abkürzungsverzeichnis, p.352–53. Bibliographie, p.354–56. Namen- und Ortsregister, p.357–[59].

P327 Jervis, Simon. Furniture of about 1900 from Austria and Hungary in the Victoria and Albert Museum. [London], Victoria & Albert Museum, [1986]. 93p. il.

Catalog of 32 pieces of Viennese furniture produced during a fifteen year period around 1900, and now in the Victoria and Albert Museum. Each entry includes materials, dimensions, bibliography, and supporting material.

Contents: (1) Introduction; (2) Catalogue; (3) Designers and makers; (4) Concordance of museum and catalogue numbers.

Index, p.91–93.

P328 Katalog der Möbelsammlung des Münchner Stadtmuseums. [By] Hans Ottomeyer . . . [et al.] [München], Prestel, [1988–93]. (3)v. il., col. plates.

Series of five vols. planned to catalog the notable collection of the Stadtmuseum in Munich. Detailed entries include provenance, dimensions, materials, exhibition history, and bibliography for each piece.

Contents: Möbel des Neoklassizismus und der Neuen Sachlichkeit (1993); Zopf- und Biedermeiermöbel (1991); Jugendstilmöbel (1988).

P329 Wilkie, Angus. Biedermeier. N.Y., Abbeville, [1987]. 216p. il. (part col.)

Readable, well-illustrated introduction to the Biedermeier interior (1815–1848), with particular attention to furniture, by a collector and dealer. Illustrations include contemporary design drawings and interior views.

Contents: 1) Domestic life and the Viennese interior; 2) Biedermeier design; 3) Centers of production; 4) Furniture categories; 5) Decorative objects; 6) Painting; Conclusion.

Notes, p.209–10. Bibliography, p.211–13. Index, p.214–16.

Great Britain and Ireland

Dictionaries and Encyclopedias

P330 Bamford, Francis. A dictionary of Edinburgh wrights and furniture makers, 1660–1840. [London], Furniture History Society, 1983. [vii], 137p., 92 plates.

Published simultaneously as Furniture History, v.XIX, 1983.

Detailed, authoritative dictionary of all known makers active in Edinburgh from the later 17th to the mid-19th centuries, based on extensive archival research, and illustrated by extant examples of their work. An extensive introduction discusses the development of the furniture trade. Entries include transcriptions from contemporary references.

Glossary, p.[137].

P331 Beard, Geoffrey, and Gilbert, Christopher, ed. Dictionary of English furniture makers, 1660–1840. Assistant eds., Brian Austen . . . [et al.] [London], Furniture History Society and W.S. Maney and Son Ltd., [1986]. [xix], 1046p., 43 plates.

An essential reference for the study of furniture makers of any nationality active in England during the time period covered, this is a monument of meticulous scholarship. "Editors' explanation" discusses sources, abbreviations, and commissioned articles (on figures of particular importance).

Supplemented by: Evans, Angela, ed. Index to the Dictionary of English furniture makers, 1660–1840. [London], Furniture History Society, [1990]. [v], 166p.; 30,000 entries arranged in a single sequence of names and places. Excludes references to craftsmen entered under their own names in the Dictionary. Includes a separate "Supplement of 'C' and 'F': surnames omitted from English city and town entries, due to a computer sorting error."

Index of tradesmen and apprentices, p.1017–46.

P332 Edwards, Ralph. The dictionary of English furniture: from the middle ages to the later Georgian period, by Percy Macquoid and Ralph Edwards. Rev. and enl. by Ralph Edwards. [Woodbridge], Barra Books, [1983]. 3v. il., col. plates.

See GLAH 1:P187 and GLAH 1:P177 for previous and condensed eds.

Latest ed. of the indispensable dictionary for English furniture studies, emphasizing fine rather than vernacular styles. Entries include furniture forms, materials, makers, and accessories such as lighting devices. Extensively illustrated.

P333 Gilbert, Christopher. Pictorial dictionary of marked London furniture, 1700–1840. [London and Leeds], Furniture History Society in assoc. with W. S. Maney and Son Ltd., [1996]. 480p. il.

"A pictorial record of all known marked items made by London furniture makers between 1700 and 1840."—*flyer.* Based on trade labels, name-stamps, and signatures in extant pieces. Entries for 335 makers; extensively illustrated.

P334 Pictorial dictionary of British 19th century furniture design. Introd. by Edward Joy. [Woodbridge, Antique Collectors' Club, 1977]. xlvii, 585p. il. (An Antique Collectors' Club research project)

"This Dictionary is planned to show the complete range of Victorian furniture in illustrations drawn from contemporary sources."—*p.ix.* Monumental compendium of "some 5,000" illustrations from design books and catalogs, grouped by furniture form. All pieces are dated and identified by designer or manufacturer. Useful preliminary chapter discusses each designer or firm and their publications.

Contents: (1) Key dates in 19th century British furniture history; (2) Contemporary sources quoted in the dictionary; (3) The designers and design books; (4) Contents to pictorial dictionary; (5) Pictorial dictionary.

P335 White, Elizabeth, comp. Pictorial dictionary of British 18th century furniture design: the printed sources. [Woodbridge], Antique Collectors' Club, [1990]. 503p. il.

Extensive anthology of approximately 3,000 "engraved designs for furniture published in England during the eighteenth century."—*p.11.* The compiler claims to present nearly all such material available to the 18th-century consumer, although not every plate from each source is illustrated. Preliminary chapter furnishes brief biographies of designers included.

Contents: (I) The purpose of the designs; (II) The development of furniture design books in eighteenth century England; (III) English furniture design in the eighteenth century: a brief outline; (IV) Books from which plates are reproduced in this work; (V) Notes on the designers whose work is reproduced in this work; (VI) The arrangement of the plates: (I) Upholstery work and other seat furniture; (II) Cabinet work; (III) Carvers' work; (IV) Miscellaneous items; (V) Interior elevations and room plans. Appendix: The Weale Re-strikes, c.1833–1858. Modern reprints of Eighteenth century design books.

Selective bibliography of modern works, p.494–97. Index, p.499–503.

Histories and Handbooks

P336 Agius, Pauline. British furniture, 1880–1915. [Woodbridge], Antique Collectors' Club, [1978]. 195p. il., chart.

Survey of furniture design and designers from the later Victorian period to the early 20th century. Brief "Postscript" surveys furniture from 1915 to 1940. Chapter on furniture trade includes information on mechanization, provincial furniture-making centers, and a list of major manufacturing firms operating during this period. Numerous illustrations include period sources.

Contents: (1) The scene 1880–1915 and its prehistory; (2) Continuing Victorian forms; (3) Fashionable reproduction furniture 1880–1915; (4) Original designs and Art Furniture; (5) Progressive furniture c.1885–1910; (6) Woods, finishes and some fashions and innovations; (7) Exact copies and fakes; (8) The furniture trade 1880–1915; Postscript 1915–40.

"A partial bibliography," p.186–90. Index, p.191–95.

P337 Beard, Geoffrey. The National Trust book of English furniture. [N.Y.], Viking in assoc. with the National Trust, [1985]. 295p. il.

Readable introduction to the history of English furniture, based on the furnishings of properties of the National Trust. Includes vernacular and garden furniture.

Contents: Part one: The trade: 1) The craftsmen and workshops; 2) Methods and techniques; 3) The commission; 4) Decorative styles. Part two: The furniture: 5) For crown and country; 6) For gentlemen; 7) For the servants; 8) Out of doors; Appendix 1: Woods in common use; Appendix 2: A list of cabinet-makers and designers

Includes bibliographical references. Bibliography, p.270–73. Glossary of terms, p.274–83. Index, p.284–95.

P338 ———. The National Trust book of the English house interior. N.Y., Viking in assoc. with the National Trust, 1990. 308p. il.

Reliable survey of the English house interior, from the Middle Ages to the eve of World War I, based on the houses administered by the National Trust.

Contents: (1) Medieval patterns; (2) Tudor symmetry; (3) 'Solidity, conveniency and ornament': the seventeenth century; (4) The spirit of building, 1700–1760; (5) Visions and revivals, p.1760–1830; (6) Convenient, spacious or snug, 1830–1914.

Notes on the text, p.275–86. Glossary, p.287–93. Bibliography, p.294–97. Personal names index, p.298–302. General index, p.303–08.

P339 ———, and Goodison, Judith. English furniture, 1500–1840. Oxford, Phaidon-Christie's, [1987]. 302p. il. (part col.) (Christie's pictorial histories)

A pictorial survey of English furniture, based on pieces sold at auction. Arranged by period and under period, by form. Images drawn primarily from Christie's archives.

Glossary of terms, p.279–83. Bibliography, p.285–86. Price list (sale prices realized for objects illustrated), p.287–93. Index, p.295–302.

P340 Carruthers, Annette, and Greenstead, Mary. Good citizen's furniture: the Arts and Crafts collections at Cheltenham. [Cheltenham], Cheltenham Art Gallery and Museums in assoc. with Lund Humphries, [1994]. 168p. il. (part col.)

Catalog of a notable collection of Arts and Crafts furniture, arranged chronologically by designer or firm, preceded by interpretive introductory essays. Includes the work of several contemporary designers working in the Arts and Crafts tradition. Illustrations include period photographs of interiors, furniture workshops, and clients.

Contents: 1) "Good citizen's furniture"; 2) The Arts and Crafts movement in the Cotswolds; 3) Arts and Crafts at Cheltenham; 4) The catalogue.

Bibliography, p.161–63. Index, 166–68.

P341 Chinnery, Victor. Oak furniture: the British tradition: a history of early furniture in the British Isles and New England. [Woodbridge], Antique Collectors' Club, [1979]. 579p. il., col. plates, map.

The basic book on the subject, covering oak furniture made in the British Isles from the medieval period through the mid-18th century, and in New England to 1720. Well documented, heavily illustrated with extant examples.

Contents: (1) Time and place—the historical context; (2) Makers and methods—the practical context; (3) Form and language—the functional types and nomenclature; (4) The Stylistic themes—a decorative and regional chronology; Appendix I: Extracts from A description of England by William Harrison; Appendix II: Extracts from An academie or store house of armory & blazon, by Randle Holme; Appendix III: The life of Humphrey Beckham of Salisbury; Appendix IV: Selections from the probate inventories of provincial woodworkers; Appendix V: Distribution of population in the British Isles, 1662; Appendix VI: The public and private collector.

Bibliography, p.570–71. Index, p.575–78.

P342 Collard, Frances. Regency furniture. [Woodbridge], Antique Collectors' Club, [1985]. 346p. il. (part col.) (Repr.: 2000).

The standard, authoritative source on furniture produced between 1790 and 1840. Illustrations include period interior views and plates from design sources. A chapter is devoted to the Regency Revival of the late 19th and early 20th centuries, and one to upholstery materials and methods.

Appendix: Prominent Regency craftsmen and designers, p.330–34. Bibliography, p.335–37. Index, p.338–46.

P343 Cotton, Bernard D. The English regional chair. [Woodbridge], Antique Collectors' Club, [1990]. 511p. il. (part col.), charts, maps.

Masterful, detailed study of English regional chairs, based on extensive fieldwork and archival research. Organized by region. Illustrations include period design sources and photographs as well as hundreds of examples of chair design. Although confined to one furniture type, this study, by the pioneer in this field, is important for the consideration of English vernacular furniture in general.

Index: Regional chair makers and turners 1700–1900 [by region], p.440–509. Bibliography, p.510–11.

P344 Gilbert, Christopher. English vernacular furniture, 1750–1900. Pub. for the Paul Mellon Centre for Studies in British Art. New Haven and London, Yale, 1991. viii, 294p. il. (part col.)

An authoritative study by a major furniture historian that considers institutional and commercial as well as domestic furnishings; especially important for its coverage of ordinary furniture seldom discussed by scholars. Based on extensive documentary and field research, and illustrated with period paintings, graphics, and photographs as well as furniture pieces.

Bibliography of provincial price books, p.257–58. The Bolton Supplement to the London Book of Cabinet Piece Prices (1802), p.259–63. The Wycombe Chairmakers' List of Prices (1872), p.264–66. Glossary, p.267–69. Bibliography, p.277–82. Indes, p.283–94.

P345 ______. Furniture at Temple Newsam House and Lotherton Hall: a catalogue of the Leeds Collection. In two volumes. [Leeds], Pub. jointly by the National Art-Collections Fund and the Leeds Art Collections Fund, 1978. 2v. il. (part col.)

Catalog of an important furniture collection housed in two country house museums now maintained by the city of Leeds. Detailed entries are by furniture form, and include such furnishings as chandeliers. Separate sections catalog several groups of signed 19th-century furniture, ormolu, papier-mâché, and some vernacular furnishings, as well as continental, South African, Peruvian, and Far Eastern pieces.

Contents: Introduction: The formation of the collection; (1) English furniture; (2) Continental furniture; (3) Colonial and Oriental furniture; (4) Documentary material; manuscript designs; The Pratt Collection of furniture trade catalogues and ephemera.

Index, p.[513]–22.

P346 ______. The life and work of Thomas Chippendale. N.Y., Macmillan, [1978]. 2v. il., plan, plates (part col.)

The definitive work on this influential 18th-century cabinetmaker, including extensive reproduction of documentary sources.

Contents: Vol.I: (I) Chippendale's life and business; (II) Chippendale's furniture designs; (III) Chippendale's patrons and furniture; Vol.II: Furniture illustrations

Glossary of terms used by Chippendale, v.1, p.302–09. Bibliography, v.1, p.310–15. Index, v.1, p.316–29. Furniture illustrations classified under house of origin, v.2, p.[vi].

P347 Joy, Edward T. English furniture, 1800–1851. London, Sotheby Parke Bernet in assoc. with Ward Lock, [1977]. 318p. il. (part col.)

Comprehensive, well-illustrated history of English furniture of the first half of the 19th century, by a well-known furniture historian. Includes a discussion of the export trade in British furniture during this period. Illustrations include period photographs and plates from design books, trade literature, and other contemporary sources.

Contents: (1) The Regency; (2) The Grecian, Egyptian and Chinese tastes; (3) The historic revivals; (4) The Royal furniture-makers; (5) Interiors; (6) Patent furniture; (7) The structure of the furniture industry; (8) Materials and methods; (9) The Great Exhibition, 1851.

References, p.297–307. Index, p.311–18.

P348 Kinmonth, Claudia. Irish country furniture, 1700–1950. New Haven, Yale Univ. Pr., 1993. x, 249p. il. (part col.), map.

Authoritative, well-illustrated account of Irish vernacular furniture, with attention to its setting in Irish history and culture, and based on extensive fieldwork. Separate chapters are devoted to each furniture type. Introduction includes discussion of vernacular architecture, furniture materials, craftsmen, and painted furniture.

Small furnishings, p.195–202. Gazetteer (of museums with Irish vernacular furniture in their collections), p.203. Glossary of terminology, p.205–07. Bibliographic note, p.208. Index, p.242–49.

P349 Tracy, Charles. English medieval furniture and woodwork. London, Victoria and Albert Museum, 1988. 216p. il. (part col.)

"The strength of the collection undoubtedly lies in the fragments of ecclesiastical woodwork. . . . This catalogue succeeds and replaces" the previous collection catalog of 1923 (rev. 1929)—*Introd.*

Contents: (I) Ecclesiastical; (II) Domestic.

Collation of Museum numbers and catalogue entries, p.206–07. Abbreviations and select bibliography, p.208–15. Index of places, p.216.

Italy

P350 Cera, Maurizio. Il mobile italiano: dal XVI al XIX secolo: gli stili, le forme, il mercato. [Milan], Longanesi, [1983]. 293p. il.

A photographic survey, by form, of Italian furniture from the Renaissance to the 19th century; useful as a visual resource. Based on examples sold at auction in Italy and includes prices realized.

P351 Chiarugi, Simone. Botteghe di mobilieri in Toscana. Florence, Studio per Edizioni Scelte, 1994. 2v. il. (part col.)

Extensive, well-documented history of furniture and its makers in Tuscany during the later 18th and the 19th centuries, illustrated from period documents and extant examples. V.1 discusses the trade and its products, with a consideration of fakes and copies. V.2 is principally devoted to biographical entries on furniture craftsmen.

Bibliografia, v.2, p.567–91. Indice dei nomi, v.2, p.593–609.

P352 Colle, Enrico. Il mobile di Palazzo Pitti. Florence, Centri Di/Allemandi, 1992. 2v. il.

Scholarly catalog with inventory and documents.

Contents: (1) Il primo periodo lorenese 1737–1799; (2) Il secondo periodo lorenese 1800–1846.

Bibliografia, v.1, p.253–55, v.2, p.286–87.

P353 Massinelli, Anna Maria. Il mobile toscano. [Milan], Electa, [1993]. 225p. il. (part col.)

Well-illustrated history of furniture made in Tuscany from 1200 to 1800; includes some early 19th-century examples.

Repertorio degli artefici, p.209–17. Bibliografia, p.218–25.

Latin America

P354 Bomchil, Sara, and Carreño, Virginia. El mueble colonial de las Américas y su circunstancia histórica. Buenos Aires, Sudamericana, 1987. 919p. il., plates.

Substantial historical survey of western hemisphere colonial furniture, including brief essays on Asian and Renaissance influences. Covers all countries of South and Central America, as well as Mexico, Cuba, Puerto Rico, the United States, and Canada. Illustrated principally with line drawings.

Glossaries at ends of some chapters. Bibliografía general, p.899. Bibliografías regionales, p.900–08.

Low Countries

P355 Baarsen, Reiner. Nederlandse Meubelen, 1600–1800 = Dutch furniture, 1600–1800: Rijksmuseum Amsterdam. Amsterdam, Rijksmuseum, in assoc. with Waanders, Zwolle, [1993]. 143p. col. il. (Aspecten van de verzameling beeldhouwkunst en kunstnijverheid = Aspects of the collection, sculpture and decorative arts, 4)

In Dutch and English. Selection of 67 pieces from the fine collection of Dutch furniture in the Rijksmuseum, with commentary by the leading specialist in this field.

Verkort geciteerde literatuur = Literature referred to in the text, p.142–43.

P356 Voorst tot Voorst, J. M. W. van. Meubels in Nederland, 1840–1900. Lochem, De Tijdstroom, 1979. 2v. il., chart.

Survey of 19th-century Dutch furniture by furniture form. Illustrations include contemporary photographic views of interiors and a comparative timeline of Dutch, French, and English styles during this period.

Register van deel I en II: A. Meubelmakers, magazijnhouders etc.; B. Meubels, v.2, p.111–12.

Russia and Eastern Europe

P357 Chenevière, Antoine. Russian furniture: the golden age, 1780–1840. Research advisor: Emmanuel Ducamp. N.Y., Vendome [Distr. Rizzoli, 1988]. 312p. il. (part col.), ports.

Readable, well-illustrated survey of Russian furniture of the later 18th and early 19th centuries. Includes discussion of Western influences and special chapters on Tula steel and hardstone furniture.

Biographical details—architects, other artists, cabinetmakers, carvers, carpenters, joiners and gilders, workers in hard stones, p.287–95. Description of the Palace of Pavlosk, p.296–301. Bibliography, p.304–08. Index, p.309–12.

Scandinavia

P358 Steensberg, Axel, and Lerche, Grith. Danske bondemobler = Danish peasant furniture. [Copenhagen], Arnold Busck, [1989]. 2v. il. (part col.), maps on endpapers, plans.

4th, enl. ed. of a standard work first published in 1949. In Danish and English.

Contents: (I) Danish peasant furniture: Introduction, definition and origins, sources of peasant wealth, impact and response, placing of furniture inside the farm, permanence and mobility; Tables and benches; Chairs; Bedsteads; Chests; Traveling boxes, chests, and small cases; (II) Conservation of painted furniture; Techniques of wood and stone imitation and use of stencils; Press cupboards, dressers, and wardrobes; Chests of drawers and bureau-cabinets; Shelves; Mirrors and pictures; Clocks, clock-and watch-cases.

Ordforklaringer [Glossary, in Danish only], v.2, p.211–13. Handvaerkernavne = Names of craftsmen, v.2, p.214. Museumsnavne = Names of museums, v.2, p.215. Litteratur = Literature, v.2, p.216–17.

Spain and Portugal

P359 Aguilo Alonso, Maria Paz. El mueble en Espana - siglos XVI–XVII. Madrid, Antiquaria, 1993. 472p. il. (part col.)

Provides a historical and typological analysis of Spanish furniture of the 16th and 17th centuries, followed by a scholarly, illustrated catalog of examples.

Glosario, p.420–25. Documentos, p.426–41. Inventarios utilizados, p.442–46. Bibliografía, p.447–68. Abreviaturas utilizadas p.469.

United States

Dictionaries and Encyclopedias

P360 Hageman, Jane Sikes. Ohio furniture makers. [Cincinnati, Hageman, 1984–1989]. 2v. il. (part col.), col. maps.

Vol.2 co-author: Edward M. Hageman.

Thoroughly researched biographical dictionary of known furniture makers in Ohio from the beginning of settlement to the mid-19th century. V.1 concerns southern Ohio, V.2, northern Ohio.

Contents: (1) 1790 to 1845; (2) 1790 to 1860.

P361 Ketchum, William C., Jr. American cabinetmakers: marked American furniture, 1640–1940. William C. Ketchum, Jr., with the Museum of American Folk Art. N.Y., Crown, [1995]. x, 404p. il.

Biographical directory of more than 1,600 furniture craftsmen whose signatures, brands, or marks have been identified. Each entry has at least one bibliographical reference; some, but not all, reproduce the marks themselves. While a useful source, researchers should be aware that there are omissions, and should use in conjunction with other directories for more complete coverage.

Initials as marks, p.383. Unidentified intitials, p.385. Sources, p.387–89. Index, p.393–404.

P362 Robinson, Charles A. Vermont cabinetmakers and chairmakers before 1855: a checklist. Introd. by Philip Zea. Ed. by Kenneth Joel Zogry. [Shelburne], Shelburne Museum, [1994]. 126p. il. (part col.), map.

Meticulous checklist, based on extensive research in primary sources. Index includes listings of craftsmen recorded as living in each town cited.

Contents: (1) Craftsmen and culture: an introduction to Vermont furniture making, by Philip Zea; (2) Checklist of craftsmen; (3) Index to checklist, arranged by town.

P363 Semowich, Charles J., comp. American furniture craftsmen working prior to 1920: an annotated bibliography. Westport, Greenwood, [1984]. xi, 381p. (Art reference collection, 7)

An essential source for research on this subject. The only general bibliography devoted to the subject. Includes references to periodical articles, primary sources, and trade catalogs. Each entry is briefly annotated.

Contents: (1) Works about individual craftsmen; (2) Works about groups of craftsmen; (3) General works; (4) Trade catalogues.

American furniture periodicals, p.233–34. Manuscript collections, p.235–39. Craftsmen—biographical index, p.[241]–75. Author-title index, p.[276]–360. Subject index, p.[361]–81.

Histories and Handbooks

P364 American antiques from Israel Sack Collection. [Washington, D.C.], Highland House, [1969–]. (9)v. il. (part col.), ports.

Series of bound vols. of sales brochures issued from 1957 to the present by Israel Sack, for decades one of the leading firms dealing in fine American furniture. Vol.VIII includes an overview of the history of the firm; later vols. each include essays on topics of interest to collectors. All pieces are briefly described; those now in public collections are so identified. An important visual reference to American furniture of high quality. Each vol. is separately indexed; index to the series in vol.IX.

P365 Baltimore Museum of Art. American furniture, 1680–1880, from the collection of the Baltimore Museum of Art. William Voss Elder and Jayne E. Stokes, with the assist. of Lu Bartlett . . . [et al.] [Baltimore, Baltimore Museum of Art, 1987]. 183p. il. (part col.)

Catalog of an important collection of American furniture, especially strong in pieces made in Baltimore and Annapolis, major early centers of cabinetmaking.

Contents: Catalogue: Seating furniture, case furniture, desks, clocks, tables, miscellaneous.

Exhibitions and references, p.181–83.

P366 Barquist, David L. American tables and looking glasses: in the Mabel Brady Garvan and other collections at Yale University. Essays by Elisabeth Donaghy Garrett and Gerald W. R. Ward. Photographs by Charles Uht. New Haven, Yale Univ. Art Gallery, 1992. 424p. il. (part col.)

Volume in a series of catalogs of Yale University's notable collection of American furniture, founded on the donation by Francis P. Garvan and enriched over the succeeding years. Tables are cataloged by form, looking glasses by date. Includes discussion of fakes and altered pieces and diagrams illustrating terminology relating to these furniture forms.

Contents: Preface by Patricia E. Kane; The intersections of life: tables and their social role, by Gerald W. R. Ward; Looking glasses in America, 1700–1850, by Elisabeth Donaghy Garrett; Catalogue: Tables; Looking glasses; Study collection Appendices: (A). Diagrams of terminology; (B) Woods; (C) Donors to the collection; (D) Dealers patronized by Francis P. Garvan; (E) Bibliographical abbreviations; (F) Concordance of art gallery accession numbers and catalogue numbers.

Index, p.412–22.

P367 Bivins, John, Jr. The furniture of coastal North Carolina, 1700–1820. Winston-Salem, Museum of Early Southern Decorative Arts (Distr. Univ. of North Carolina Pr., [1988]). xiii, 562p. il., maps. (The Frank L. Horton series)

Extensive, meticulous consideration of the furniture of a region lacking in large urban centers and influenced by both British and local vernacular forms, by an authority in the decorative arts of the South. First of a series planned by MESDA to document these arts, long neglected by scholars.

Coastal North Carolina cabinetmakers, 1700–1820, p.449–513. Locations of coastal North Carolina artisans in the furniture trades. The formation of North Carolina counties, 1700–1850. Notes, p.527–33. Bibliography, p.535–42. Index, p.543–62.

P368 Butler, Joseph T. Field guide to American furniture. By Joseph T. Butler in collab. with Kathleen Eagen Johnson. Illus. by Ray Skibinski. N.Y., Facts on File, [1985]. 399p. il.

"By using a systematic visual approach, this book chronologically traces the evolution of style in American antique furniture from the 17th century through the early 20th century."—*p.5.* Through more than 1,700 line drawings based on actual pieces, arranged by furniture form, the book allows readers to compare and contrast furniture by style and by period. An introductory chapter summarizes furniture history. Especially useful for the non-specialist.

Contents: Anatomy of furniture; (1) History of American furniture; (2) Field guide to American antique furniture.

Sources of furniture illustrated, p.364–65. Outstanding collections of American furniture, p.366. Selected bibliography, p.367–68. Glossary, p.369–78. Index, p.379–99.

P369 Darling, Sharon. Chicago furniture: art, craft, and industry, 1833–1983. [Chicago], Chicago Historical Society in assoc. with Norton, [1984]. xi, 416p. il., 4 leaves of col. pl.

Definitive study of Chicago furniture by the curator of decorative arts at the Chicago Historical Society, based on a catalog of the society's furniture collections, and accompanying an exhibition. Includes illustrations from contemporary sources of interiors, showrooms, advertising, and workmen.

Contents: (I) Introduction; (II) Furniture "For the million," 1873–1917; (III) Art furniture, 1873–1917; (IV) Modernism to Mies, 1918–1983; Epilogue; Appendix: Other Chicago designers and manufacturers.

Sources, p.401–06. Index, p.407–16.

P370 Evans, Nancy Goyne. American Windsor chairs. N.Y., Hudson Hills in assoc. with Winterthur, [1996]. 744p. il. (part col.), maps, ports.

Monumental, long-awaited study, detailed and authoritative. Arranged by region. Illustrations include chairmakers' labels and brands and contemporary genre scenes and advertisements. Checklist of makers includes 2,400 names.

Contents: (1) Background history and overview; (2) Regional studies: Products and producers; Summary.

American Windsor craftsmen, 1745–1850, p.681–717. Glossary, p.719–24. Select bibliography, p.725–33. Index, p.735–44.

P371 Fabian, Monroe H. The Pennsylvania-German decorated chest. N.Y., Main Street-Universe, [1978]. 230p. il. (part col.)

Comprehensive study of a notable and distinctive regional furniture form. Extensively illustrated.

Contents: (1) The European background; (2) The chest in Pennsylvania; (3) Cabinetmaking and woods; (4) Construction; (5) Hardware; (6) Surface decoration; (7) Paint; (8) Decoration and decorators; (9) Outside Pennsylvania.

Selected bibliography, p.222–25. Index, p.226–30.

P372 Fairbanks, Jonathan, and Bates, Elizabeth Bidwell. American furniture, 1620 to the present. N.Y., Marek, [1981]. xii, 561p. il., ports. (part col.)

Comprehensive, fully illustrated history of furniture in America, with attention to regional and vernacular examples and to the work of contemporary artist-craftsmen.

Glossary, p.527–36. Bibliography, by Wendell Garrett and Alison Eckardt, p.537–52. Index, p.553–61.

P373 Fitzgerald, Oscar P. Four centuries of American furniture. Radnor, Chilton, 1995. 400p. il.

Rev. ed. of: Three centuries of American furniture. Englewood Cliffs, Prentice-Hall, 1982.

Thorough, comprehensive survey of American furniture history from the 17th century to the present, with a useful bibliography arranged by chapter. A basic, standard reference source, accessible to non-specialists. Illustrations are black and white.

Contents: (1) The Jacobean period: joiners and cabinetmakers in the new world; (2) William and Mary: the years of transition; (3) Queen Anne: the line of beauty; (4) The Chippendale style; (5) Furniture of the Federal period; (6) American Empire; (7) The country cabinetmaker; (8) Southern furniture; (9) Furniture of the folk: Shaker and Pennsylvania German; (10) Victorian furniture: the gothic and rococo revivals; (11) Victorian furniture: the renaissance revival; (12) The Eastlake and other revivals; (13) The American mission: 1900–1915; (14) Traditional revivals for a conservative public; (15) Modern furniture, 1920–1941: is it here to stay?; (16) America takes the lead: 1950s and 1960s modern; (17) Post-modernism: avant-garde furniture since 1975.

Bibliography, p.368–82. Index., p.383–401.

P374 Flanigan, J. Michael. American furniture from the Kaufman Collection. Introd. essays: Wendy A. Cooper, Morrison H. Heckscher, Gregory R. Weidman. Washington, D.C., National Gallery of Art, [1986]. 263p. il. (part col.)

"Selections from the collection of George M. and Linda H. Kaufman and the Kaufman Americana Foundation"—*p.[4].* Published in conjunction with the exhibition of furniture from a private collection notable for its quality, National Gallery of Art (1986). Extended entries accompany excellent photographs of each piece.

Contents: American furniture styles in the colonial period, by Morrison H. Heckscher; Furniture from the colonial period; The neoclassical style in New England and New York, 1785–1840, by Wendy A. Cooper; The neoclassical style in Philadelphia and the South, 1785–1840, by Gregory A. Weidman; Furniture from the Federal and Empire periods.

Bibliography and abbreviated titles, p.244–48. Comparative details, p.249–51. Unupholstered frames, p.252–55. [Pictorial] Glossary, p.256–59. General index, p.260–61.

P375 Forman, Benno M. American seating furniture 1630–1730: an interpretive catalogue. N.Y., Norton, [1988]. xxv, 397p. il., port., tables. (A Winterthur book)

Exemplary catalog of seating furniture at Winterthur Museum, by a noted furniture historian. Includes stimulating essays on connoisseurship of furniture, on woods and woodworking craftsmen, and on each chair type. Detailed entries on each individual piece.

Contents: (1) Connoisseurship and furniture history; (2) The woods used in American furniture; (3) Seventeenth-century woodworking craftsmen and their crafts; (4) The catalogue: Seating furniture made by turners; Seating furniture made by joiners; Cromwellian-style upholstered chairs and couches; Cane chairs and couches; Carved topp'd, plain topp'd, and crook'd back leather chairs; Easy chairs and low chairs; Appendix 1: The 1708 inventory of Charles Plumley, Philadelphia joiner; Appendix 2: The art of caning: "The Fourth Section" from Roubo's Menuisier.

Bibliography, p.381–87. Concordance: guide to the Winterthur objects illustrated, p.389. Index, p.391–97.

P376 Gilborn, Craig. Adirondack furniture and the rustic tradition. N.Y., Abrams, [1987]. 349p. il. (part col.), ports.

History of rustic furniture made for vacation homes in the Adirondack Mountains of New York, from the 19th century to the present day, as well as certain other furniture types characteristic of these settings. Illustrations include period photographs of interiors and of craftsmen.

Contents: (1) The background: Rustic taste in England and America; (2) An Adirondack aesthetic: from shanty to great camp; (3) Adirondack tree furniture; (4) Cottage and bungalow furniture; (5) From old-time rustic workers to contemporary craftsmen.

Rustic furniture makers in the Adirondacks, p.317–27. Bibliography, p.335–39. Index, p.[341]–49.

P377 Gusler, Wallace B. Furniture of Williamsburg and Eastern Virginia, 1710–1790. Richmond, Virginia Museum, [1979]. xiii, 194p. il. (part col.)

Published in conjunction with the exhibition, Virginia Museum (1979), of early Virginia furniture, with emphasis on the work of known cabinetmakers' shops in Williamsburg. Author is curator of furniture at Colonial Williamsburg.

Contents: (I) The furniture of Williamsburg; (II) Furniture from other areas of eastern Virginia; Appendix: The appraisement of the personal estate of Major Edmund Dickenson decd, taken this 28th July 1778.

References cited, p.184–85. Index, p.186–91. Index of illustrations, p.191–94.

P378 Hanks, David A. Innovative furniture in America from 1800 to the present. Introd. by Russell Lynes. With essays by Rodris Roth and Page Talbott. N.Y., Horizon Press, [1981].

Catalog of a traveling exhibition organized by the Smithsonian Institution, which examined furniture design in terms of "technological changes, new materials, approaches to comfort, and concerns for portability, multiple functions, efficiency, and cost"—*p.[17].* Covers such materials as wicker, cast iron, and bentwood, and discusses patent furniture and prominent designers. The essential work on the subject.

Index to illustrations [by furniture type], p.[9]–10. Objects in the exhibition of Innovative Furniture in America, p.189. Designers and manufacturers of objects in the exhibition (chronologically arranged), p.190. Index, p.197–99.

P379 Hewitt, Benjamin A. The work of many hands: Card tables in Federal America, 1790–1820. Benjamin A. Hewitt, Patricia A. Kane, Gerald W. R. Ward. [Foreword by Alan Shestack]. New Haven, Yale Univ. Art Gallery, 1982. 198p. il. (part col.), charts.

Detailed analysis of a specific furniture form, based on many years of computer analysis of known examples by the author-collector, and published to accompany an exhibition of these tables. Essays place these forms in their social setting and discuss their design-book sources. An important contribution to furniture studies, detailed and stimulating for its demonstration of the many ways in which furniture can be studied.

Contents: (1) Preface, by Benjamin A. Hewitt; (2) "Avarice and conviviality": card playing in Federal America, by

Gerald W. R. Ward; (3) Design books and price books for American Federal-period card tables, by Patricia E. Kane; (4) Regional characteristics of American Federal–period card tables, by Benjamin A. Hewitt; (5) A regional survey of American Federal–period card tables: selections from the study, by Benjamin A. Hewitt with the assistance of Barbara McLean Ward.

List of tables included in the study, p.178–83. List of patterned inlays and the tables in which they appear, p.184–85. List of pictorial inlays and the tables on which they appear, p.186. Charts I–XVI, p.187–95. Index of cabinetmakers and other craftsmen, p.197–98.

P380 Hurst, Ronald L., and Prown, Jonathan. Southern furniture 1680–1830: the Colonial Williamsburg Collection. Williamsburg, The Colonial Williamsburg Foundation in assoc. with Abrams, [1997]. 640p. il. (some col.), maps. (Williamsburg decorative arts series)

Comprehensive consideration of Southern furniture based on the collections of Colonial Williamsburg; originally accompanied an exhibition of the same title. Detailed individual entries are accompanied by bibliographies and provenance. Extensive introductory essays discuss aspects of Southern life and material culture. Authors were curators at Colonial Williamsburg.

Contents: (1) Foreword, by Graham Hood; (2) Preface, by Ronald L. Hurst; (3) Acknowledgements. The People and the places; (4) The Chesapeake, by Ronald L. Hurst. (5) The Low Country, by J. Thomas Savage. (6) The Backcountry, by Jonathan Prown. (7) Note to the reader. The Furniture: (8) Seating furniture (9) Tables (10) Case furniture (11) Other forms.

Short title list, p.615–16. Bibliography, p.617–23. Index, p.624–39.

P381 Jobe, Brock, ed. Portsmouth furniture: masterworks from the New Hampshire seacoast. With contrib. by Diane Carlsberg Ehrenpreis . . . [et al.] Photographs by David Bohl. [Boston], Society for the Preservation of New England Antiquities (Distr. by Univ. Pr. of New England, [1993]). 454p. il. (part col.), 14 col. plates, maps, ports.

Definitive study of furniture produced in this important early urban center from the 17th century through 1840, with contributions by a number of furniture historians. Primarily based on (but not limited to) a survey of the Portsmouth holdings of the Society for the Preservation of New England Antiquities.

Contents: (1) "That little world, Portsmouth" by James L. Garvin; (2) Furniture making in eighteenth century Portsmouth, by Brock Jobe; (3) Portsmouth furniture making, 1798–1837, by Johanna McBrien; (4) Reader's note; (5) Catalogue: Case furniture; Tables; Seating furniture; Beds; Looking glasses and picture frames; Appendix A: Furniture makers and allied craftsmen, by Kevin Shupe; Appendix B: Portsmouth branded furniture, by Kevin Nicholson

Institutions consulted, p.439–40. Bibliography, p.441–47. Index, p.448–54.

P382 ———, and Kaye, Myrna. New England furniture: the colonial era: selections from the Society for the Preservation of New England Antiquities. With the assist. of Philip Zea. Photography by Richard Cheek. Boston, Houghton Mifflin, 1984. [xviii], 494p. il., 12 col. plates, charts.

Detailed, authoritative catalog of an important collection of New England furniture of the 17th and 18th centuries, housed in the numerous properties of the society. Extensive introductory essays on rural and urban craftsmen and design and on construction methods and materials make this catalog widely applicable to the study of New England furniture in general. Useful bibliographical essay accompanies listings.

Bibliography, p.466–79. Collections and institutions, p.480–81. Index, p.[482]–94.

P383 Kane, Patricia E. 300 years of American seating furniture: chairs and beds from the Mabel Brady Garvan and other collections at Yale University. [Introd. by Charles Montgomery]. Boston, New York Graphic Society; Little, Brown, [1976]. 319p. il., 14 col. plates, ports.

Volume in a series of interpretive catalogs to the Yale University Art Gallery's collection of American arts. Includes 298 entries for objects made from the 17th through the mid-20th century. Each entry includes a detailed physical description, provenance, bibliographical references, and commentary.

Concordance, p.[308]–09. Index, p.[310]–19.

P384 Kassay, John. The book of American Windsor furniture: styles and technologies. With measured drawings by the author. Amherst, Univ. of Massachusetts Pr., 1998. viii, 195p. il.

A careful analysis of American windsor chairs, settees, cradles, stools, candlestands, and tables.

Notes, p.193–94. Bibliography, p.195.

P385 Kirk, John T. American furniture and the British tradition to 1830: the dependence and independence of American craftsmen, the sources of American furniture design and construction in British and Continental practices, the tradition of painted furniture in Europe and America, the emergence of an American aesthetic. New York, Knopf, 1982. xiv, [4], 398p. il. (part col.), map, ports.

Detailed study, by a major scholar, of American furniture in a world context, emphasizing in particular the relationship with British furniture of the same period. The author aims to distinguish the key characteristics of American furniture through extended examination of similarities and differences with that of Britain.

Map of England using old county designations, p.xv. Reigns of the English monarchs, p.xvii. Indexes (List of English pieces, organized by county or region; List of Irish or possibly Irish pieces; Dated furniture and related pieces; General index), p.391–97.

P386 Metropolitan Museum of Art. American furniture in the Metropolitan Museum of Art. N.Y., Metropolitan

Museum, Random House, [1985–]. (1)v. il. (part col.), ports.

Series planned to cover the Metropolitan Museum's American furniture collection. Each cataloged entry is analyzed in detail. Extensive section of photographs of furniture details emphasizes regional stylistic differences.

Contents: (II) Heckscher, Morrison H. Late Colonial period: The Queen Anne and Chippendale styles.

P387 Monkhouse, Christopher P., and Michie, Thomas S. American furniture in Pendleton House. With the assist. of John M. Carpenter. Providence, Rhode Island School of Design, 1986. 228p. il. (part col.), plans, ports.

Catalog of an important collection of American furniture, published in conjunction with the exhibition "Cabinetmakers and collectors: Colonial furniture and and its revival in Rhode Island," RISD (1986), by two curators at the Rhode Island School of Design.

Extensive introductory essay examines Charles Pendleton and collecting in the 19th century, and discusses the Colonial Revival and its impact on attitudes toward early American furniture.

Bibliography, p.223–28.

P388 Moses, Michael. Master craftsmen of Newport: the Townsends and Goddards. Cosponsored by Israel Sack, Inc. [Tenafly, N.J., MMI Americana Pr., 1984.] xii, 361p. il. (part col.)

Thorough examination of the furniture of the two dominant families of furniture craftsmen in 18th-century Rhode Island, considered to have created some of the finest furniture of their period. A study unlikely to be superseded for many years.

Contents: (1) Introduction; (2) John Townsend; (3) Authenticating John Townsend's furniture; (4) John Goddard; (5) Authenticating John Goddard's furniture; (6) Other Townsends and Goddards; (7) Authenticating the furniture of other Townsends and Goddards; (8) Other improtant [sic] pieces.

Bibliography, p.359–61.

P389 Naeve, Milo M. Identifying American furniture: a pictorial guide to styles and terms, Colonial to contemporary. [3d ed., rev. and exp.] N.Y., Norton, [1998]. xi, 108p. il.

1st ed. 1981; 2d ed. 1989.

Compact, heavily illustrated brief guide to the major elements that distinguish American furniture styles, from the 17th century to the present. Extensive classified bibliography.

Further reading, p.85–100. Index, p.101–08.

P390 Richards, Nancy E., and Evans, Nancy Goyne. New England furniture at Winterthur: Queen Anne and Chippendale periods. With Wendy A. Cooper and Michael S. Podmaniczky. Research assist. by Clare G. Noyes. Winterthur, Winterthur Museum (Distr. by Univ. Pr. of New England, 1997). xix, 514p. il.

Scholarly catalog of one of the most important collections.

Short-title bibliography, p.497–500. Index, p.501–14.

P391 Rieman, Timothy D., and Burks, Jean M. The complete book of Shaker furniture. N.Y., Abrams, [1993]. 400p. il. (part col.), ports.

Wide-ranging, authoritative survey of the history of Shaker furniture by two authorities in the field. After an introduction to the history of Shakers and their design and technological methods, furniture is discussed by community, supported by a wealth of illustrations, including period photographs and trade catalog illustrations.

Selected bibliography, p.376–82. Glossary of Shaker terms, p.383–84. Glossary of technical terms, p.385–90. Index, p.[391]–400.

P392 Rodriguez Roque, Oswaldo. American furniture at Chipstone. With a foreword by Stanley Stone. [Madison], Univ. of Wisconsin Pr., [1984]. xl, 439p. il. (part col.)

Detailed, informative catalog of 199 pieces from one of the most notable private collections of American furniture, Chipstone, now a museum. Includes a charming introduction by the collector, whose affection for his furniture is very evident.

Contents: (1) "Life begins at fifty," by Stanley Stone; (2) Style in American furniture, 1650–1820; (3) Short title index (of bibliographical references); (4) Color illustrations; (5) Case furniture; (6) Clocks; (7) Seating furniture; (8) Looking glasses; (9) Tables and stands; (10) Unusual and specialized furniture; (11) Beds; (12) Fire screens.

General index, p.427–37. Index of former owners, p.438–39.

P393 Santore, Charles. The Windsor style in America. Ed. by Thomas M. Voss. Photographs by Bill Holland. Philadelphia, Running Press, [1981–1987]. 2v. il., col. plates.

Readable, heavily illustrated survey of American Windsor furniture based on extant examples, and arranged by form. Explanatory diagrams of Windsor chairs on end-papers.

Contents: (I) A pictorial survey of the history and regional characteristics of the most popular furniture form of eighteenth-century America, 1730–1830; (II) A continuing pictorial study of the history and regional characteristics of the most popular furniture form of eighteenth-century America, 1730–1840.

The construction of Windsor chairs, v.1, p.197–98. The re-creation of Thomas Jefferson's swivel Windsor, v.1, p.199–200. The brands of Ebenezer Tracy, v.1, p.201. A checklist of Windsor makers, v.1, p.202–10, v.2, p.241–69. Notes, v.1, p.211–12, v.2, p.[270]. Index, v.1, p.213–15, v.2, p.[271]–76. Brands and labels: The maker's mark, v.2, p.239–40.

P394 Smith, Nancy A. Old furniture: understanding the craftsman's art. 2d, rev. ed. Drawings by Glenna Lang. Photographs by Richard Cheek. N.Y., Dover, [1991]. 186p. il.

"This Dover edition, first published in 1991, is a revised and enlarged republication of the work originally published by the Bobbs-Merrill Company, Indianapolis, 1975 (corrected printing published by Little, Brown, and Company, Boston, 1976)." For the Dover ed. the author has updated the text and written an entirely new chapter (Chapter 14, "Upholstery").—*T.p. verso.*

A clear and readable introduction to the construction techniques, materials, and subsequent history of furniture made before the age of mass production, useful to readers on many levels and made even more useful by well-chosen illustrations.

Contents: (I) Furniture-making techniques; (II) What happens to furniture in time.

Glossary, p.173–79. Selected bibliography, p.180. Index, p.181–86.

P395 Ward, Gerald W. R. American case furniture in the Mabel Brady Garvan and other collections at Yale University. Photographs by Charles Uht. New Haven, Yale Univ. Art Gallery, [1988]. xv, 483p. il., col. plates.

Volume in a series of catalogs of the notable collections of American furniture at Yale. An indispensable reference for historians of American furniture for the periods covered. Detailed, well-documented catalog of 233 chests, boxes, cupboards, desks, cabinets, secretaries, and other related furniture forms ranging in date from the 17th to the mid-20th century. The bulk of these fall before 1850. Each entry is meticulously described and documented. Individual bibliographies accompany each entry.

Concordance, p.471–72. Index, p.473–83.

P396 Weidman, Gregory R. Furniture in Maryland, 1740–1940: the collection of the Maryland Historical Society. Baltimore, Maryland Historical Society, [1984]. 342p. il., col. plates.

Catalog of 259 pieces of furniture made or used in Maryland or associated with a major event or figure in that state's history, with emphasis on the history of each piece as well as on its design and construction. Valuable checklist of Maryland furniture craftsmen.

Short title list, p.20–23. Checklist of Maryland furniture craftsmen, p.263–328. Selected bibliography, p.330–31. Index, p.333–42.

Asian Countries

China

P397 Beurdeley, Michel. Chinese furniture. Trans. by Katherine Watson. N.Y., Kodansha, 1979. 199p. il. (part col.)

An introductory survey written by a French dealer. Organized in three parts: Chinese furniture before the Ming dynasty; the art of living in China; and Chinese furniture from the Ming period (1368–1644) to the 19th century. Includes lacquer furnishings from temples, palaces, and aristocratic houses as well as hardwood furniture.

Winning bids at public sales in Paris, London, and New York, p.187–89. Glossary [with Chinese characters], p.190–95. Dynasty marks, p.196. Bibliography, p.197–98.

P398 Clunas, Craig. Chinese furniture. Photography by Ian Thomas. London, Bamboo, 1988. 119p. il. (part col.) (Far Eastern series)

Using examples from the Victoria and Albert Museum's collection, this book emphasizes how Chinese furniture was used to convey social status and taste. "The reader will therefore find less about the timbers and types of joints involved in the manufacture of furniture . . . than about what type of object could acceptably stand where at what periods."—*Introd.*

Includes sections on seat furniture, tables and platforms, the Chinese cabinetmaker's tools, and tradional Chinese furniture in the modern world. Extensive footnotes with references to literary sources as well as to articles on art.

P399 Ecke, Gustav. Chinese domestic furniture in photographs and measured drawings. [Reprint.] N.Y., Dover, 1986. lx, 161p. il.

Reprint of GLAH 1:P228. A publisher's note explains technical improvements in format and presentation, including addition of page numbers to the table of contents, translation of the original Chinese colophon, etc.

P400 Tien, Chia-ching. Classic Chinese furniture of the Qing dynasty. Trans. by Lark E. Mason, Jr., and Juliet Yung-Yi Chou. London, Philip Wilson, 1996. 307p. chiefly il. (some col.)

Trans. of Ching tai chia chu. Xianggang, San lian shu dian (Xianggang) you xian gong si, 1995.

"This book is the first scholarly publication of Qing dynasty furniture."—*Foreword.*

P401 Wang, Shixiang. Classical Chinese furniture: Ming and early Qing dynasties. Trans. by Sarah Handler and the author. San Francisco, China Books and Periodicals, 1986. 327p. il. (part col.) (Repr.: Chicago, ArtMedia Resources, 1991).

Trans. of Ming shu jiaju zhen shang. Beijing, Wen wu ch'u pan she; Hsin hua shu tien Pei-ching fa hsing so fa hsing; Hong Kong, San lien shu tien Hsiang-kang fen tien, 1985.

A study of the materials, methods of construction, types of pieces and variations in style of Chinese furniture by an author who devoted more than 40 years of intense research to the subject and who is recognized as China's foremost furniture historian. The English text provides a description of the historical evolution of the main types of hardwood furniture, illustrated by examples from Chinese collections never before documented. Noteworthy for the range of domestic furniture included, e.g., stools, chairs, tables, beds, shelves, cabinets, and for the detail drawings that show the structural integrity of the joinery. The definitive reference work on the subject.

Bibliography, p.322–23.

P402 ———. Connoisseurship of Chinese furniture: Ming and early Qing dynasties. Trans. by Wang Shixiang, Lark E. Mason, Jr., and others. Illustrated by Yuan Quanyu. [Chicago], Art Media Resources, 1990. 2v. il., plates.

Trans. of Ming shi jiaju yanjiu. Hong Kong, Joint Publishing, 1989.

Divided into text and plate vols., this set is the standard reference tool for the study of Chinese furniture. The author is renowned for his research that included visiting master cabinet-makers, photographing, collecting, and drawing furniture in private collections, and taking apart pieces in his own collection to understand the construction. In addition to the introductory chapter on Ming and early Qing furniture, the author discusses the types and forms of furniture, construction and joinery, decoration, materials, and problems of dating and alterations. Includes a glossary of terms providing a clear and precise language for describing the objects.

Glossary, v.1, p.205–06. Index, v.1, p.210–26.

Japan

P403 Koizumi, Kazuko. Traditional Japanese furniture. Trans. by Alfred Birnbaum. N.Y., Kodansha, 1986. 223p. il. (part col.) map. (Repr.: 1995)

Trans. of Wakagu. Tokyo, Shogakkan, [1977].

A broad overview of Japanese furniture types from the Edo period (1600–1868) into the Meiji era (1868–1912) illustrated with numerous reproductions. Chapters on the history, aesthetics, and techniques of hand-worked Japanese furniture. The author's focus on the development and types of furniture styles, the social significance of furniture, and technical information make this the most comprehensive work in English on the subject.

Index, p.222–23.

Africa, Oceania, The Americas

Africa

P404 African seats. Ed. by Sandro Bocola. Munich, Prestel, [1995]. 200p. il. (part col.), maps.

First published in German on the occasion of the exhibition Afrikanische Sitze, Vitra Design Museum, Weil am Rhein (1994), and other locations.

The first "extensive, if not exhaustive, survey of aspects of a material culture that is even now approaching extinction. The objects . . . come exclusively from sub-Saharan Africa, and date mostly from the first half of this century."—*Introd.*

Contents: Through Western eyes, by Sandro Bocola; Concerning African objects, by Lorenz Homberger and Piet Meyer; African furniture between tradition and colonization, by Roy Sieber; Early evidence of African seats, by Ezio Bassani; The small grandfather chairs of the Gere, by Hans Himmelheber; Asante stools; Plates with introductory texts by Lorenz Homberger; Sudanese Savannah and Coast of Guinea; Cameroon; Central Africa; East and southern Africa; Catalogue, by Andrea Knecht Oti-Amoako.

Bibliography, p.196–99.

P405 Baraitser, Michael, and Obholzer, Anton. Town furniture of the Cape. Cape Town, Struik, [1987]. 224p. il., col. plates, port.

Comprehensive history of South African furniture in the European tradition, produced principally during the 18th and 19th centuries, with attention to characteristic styles and woods of the area.

Further reading, p.223. Index, p.224.

P406 Sieber, Roy. African furniture and household objects. Bloomington, Indiana Univ. Pr., in assoc. with the American Federation of Arts, [1980]. 279p. il. (part col.), maps.

Catalog of the exhibition, Indianapolis Museum of Art (1980), and other locations.

Generously illustrated, this catalog surveys the utilitarian arts of Africa bringing together an enormous amount of heretofore scattered information on the everyday objects of traditional life in Africa: cooking and farming implements; containers of all kinds; and furniture.

Contents: House and compound; Artisans; Implements; Furniture; Containers.

Bibliography, p.269–76.

CLOCKS AND WATCHES

Dictionaries and Encyclopedias

P407 Smith, Alan, ed. The Country Life international dictionary of clocks. N.Y., Putnam, [1979]. 351p. il. (part col.)

Comprehensive, useful dictionary of all aspects of clocks and clockmaking, with contributions by specialists.

Contents: (I) The history and styles of clocks; (II) The mechanical parts of clocks; (III) Tools, materials, and workshop methods; (IV) International clock making, with a selection of important makers; (V) Sundials and astronomical instruments.

Contributors, p.7–8. Bibliography, p.339–42. Index., p.[343]–51.

Histories and Handbooks

P408 Britten, Frederick James. Watch and clockmaker's handbook, dictionary and guide. 11th ed. [Reprint of 1915 ed.] Woodbridge, Antique Collectors' Club, 2000. 499p. il.

Reprint of a classic dictionary.

P409 ______. Britten's old clocks and watches and their makers. 9th ed. rev. and enl. by Cecil Clutton, with a list of 25,000 makers rev. and extended to 1875. . . . London, Methuen in assoc. with Spon, 1982. xxvii, 700p. il. (part col.), facsims., plates (Repr.: London, Bloomsbury Books, 1990)

Reprint of a classic dictionary; many previous eds. and reprints.

Glossary of technical terms, p.663–74. Select bibliography, p.675–81. Index, p.683–700.

P410 Bruton, Eric. The history of clocks and watches. N.Y., Rizzoli, [1979]. 288p. il. (part col.), ports.

Heavily illustrated world history of clocks, watches, and related instruments, aimed at a general readership. Illustrations include very early depictions of time-keeping.

Glossary, p.274–77. Bibliography, p.278–80. Index, p.281–87.

P411 Good, Richard. Victorian clocks. London, British Museum Pr., 1996. 207p. il. (part col.)

Authoritative, readable survey illustrated with examples from the British Museum collections.

Bibliography, p.[200]–02. Index of clockmakers, p.203–04. General index, p.[205]–07.

P412 Landes, David S. Revolution in time: clocks and the making of the modern world. Cambridge, Mass., Harvard Univ., Pr., 1983. xvii, 482p., 32 plates (part col.), map, tables.

Readable, stimulating exploration of the invention and development of the mechanical clock in Renaissance Europe and its subsequent effect on human history, concluding with appearance of the quartz watch in our own century.

Notes, p.390–466. Index, p.469–82.

P413 Shaffer, Douglas. Clocks. [N.Y.], Cooper-Hewitt Museum, [1980]. 127p. il. (part col.) (The Smithsonian illustrated library of antiques).

Compact general history of clocks of the world, most suitable for the non-specialist. Includes a chapter on watches.

Glossary, p.122–24. Reading and reference, p.124. Some public collections of clocks and watches, p.125. Index, p.126–27.

P414 Shenton, Alan. Pocket watches: 19th and 20th century. [Woodbridge], Antique Collectors' Club, [1995]. 431p. il., col. plates, ports.

Wide-ranging, well-illustrated survey of pocket watches of the world, arranged by type and by country of origin, and based on illustrations of extant examples. Aimed primarily at an audience of collectors. Illustrations include period advertising matter.

Index, p.427–31.

Western Countries

Canada

P415 Langdon, John E. Clock and watchmakers and allied workers in Canada, 1700 to 1900. Toronto, Anson-Cartwright, 1976. xix, 195p.

Alphabetical listing of clock and watchmakers and jewelers in Canada, culled from advertisements, directories, and other documents. Entries include name, profession, place, date of citation, and source of information.

Geographical index, p.181–95.

France

P416 Edey, Winthrop. French clocks in North American collections. N.Y., The Frick Collection, 1982. 104p. il.

Compact book produced to accompany the exhibition, Frick Collection (1982–83), centering on several 18th-century clocks in the Frick collection, supplemented by examples from other public and private sources. A brief but lucid and informative introduction is followed by informed commentary on the examples illustrated.

Bibliography, p.23.

P417 Hughes, Richard. French eighteenth-century clocks and barometers in the Wallace Collection. London, Trustees of the Collection, 1994. 103p. il. (part col.)

"The clocks and barometers in this book were nearly all acquired by Richard Seymour-Conway (1800–70), 4th Marquess of Hertford . . . the principal benefactor behind the formation of the Wallace Collection."—*Foreword.*

Contents: Clock cases in eighteenth-century France; Clock movements and barometers in eighteenth-century France; The clocks and barometers.

Glossary, p.98–99. Bibliography, p.100. Index of names and places, p.101–03.

P418 Musée de la Renaissance. Catalogue de l'horlogerie, et des instruments de precision du début du XVIe au milieu du XVIIe siècle. [Par] Adolphe Chapiro, Chantal Meslin-Perrier, Anthony Turner. Paris, Éd. de la Réunion du Musées Nationaux, 1989. 141p. il.

Catalog of early clocks, watches, and time-keeping instruments in the French national collection. Includes sundials and astrolabes.

Bibliography, p.134–35. Expositions, p.135. Table de concordance, p.136. Liste des facteurs ayant signé les objets de ce catalogue, p.137. Index général, p.138–39.

Germany and Austria

P419 Maurice, Klaus, and Mayr, Otto. The clockwork universe: German clocks and automata, 1550–1650. Washington, D.C., Smithsonian Institution (Distr. by Neale Watson, 1980). ix, 321p. il. (part col.), ports., tables.

German-language ed., Die Welt aus Uhr. München, Deutscher Kunstverlag, 1980.

Catalog of the exhibition, Smithsonian Institution (1980–81), and other locations, produced jointly by that institution and by the Bayerisches Nationalmuseum, Munich. Extended examination of the development and production of mechanical clocks in Renaissance Germany, and a consideration of the various meanings of timekeeping in the society of the period. Includes contributions from many scholars. Introductory essays are followed by a catalog of the objects included in the exhibition.

Glossary, p.310–17. Index of names, p.318–21.

Great Britain and Ireland

P420 Dawson, Percy G., Drover, C. B., and Parkes, D. W. Early English clocks: a discussion of domestic clocks up to the beginning of the eighteenth century. [Woodbridge], Antique Collectors' Club, [1982]. 550p. il. (part col.)

Detailed examination of early English clocks by three specialists, and particularly useful for the informed reader. The illustrations include many excellent views of clock mechanisms.

Bibliography, p.544–45. Makers' index, p.546–47. Subject index, p.548–50.

P421 Loomes, Brian. Complete British clocks. Newton Abbott, David & Charles, [1978]. 256p. il.

Readable, authoritative history of British clocks and their makers in the 17th and 18th centuries. Includes a chapter of advice to the collector and a listing of some of the best-known London clockmakers.

Glossary, p.231–49. Recommended reading, p.251–52. Index, p.255–56.

P422 ______. Painted dial clocks. [Woodbridge], Antique Collectors' Club, [1994]. 280p. il. (part col.), chart.

A much enlarged and rewritten version of the author's previous books on white dial clocks, this extensive survey of painted clock faces and associated clock cases includes a chapter on American dials and one on care and handling. Chapter Four, "Names and identification," lists recorded British dial makers.

Longcase clock dial features, p.276. Longcase clock case features, p.277. Index, p.278–80.

P423 Robinson, Tom. The longcase clock. [Woodbridge], Antique Collectors' Club, [1981]. 467p. il. (part col.)

Detailed history of the development of the longcase, or "grandfather" clock in England, from the mid-17th to the end of the 18th century. Includes a chapter on repair, restoration, and fakes.

Glossary, p.441–56. Conversion table: Imperial to metric measurements, p.457. Bibliography, p.458–60. Makers' index, p.463–64. Subject Index, p.465–67.

United States

P424 Ball, Robert W. D. American shelf and wall clocks: a pictorial history for collectors. Atglen, Penn., Schiffer, [1992]. 272p. il. (part col.)

Primarily a pictorial survey of more than 2,000 shelf and wall clocks, principally of the 19th century. Includes a listing of American clockmakers and a separate "Value guide" laid in.

Selected bibliography, p.272.

P425 Schorsch, Anita. The Warner collector's guide to American clocks. N.Y., Warner, [1981]. 256p. il., col. plates (Warner collectors's guides)

A compact field guide to American clocks geared to the nonspecialist, illustrated with numerous examples. Includes price range for each example, now useful chiefly for comparative purposes.

Selected bibliography, p.252–53. Index, p.254–56.

P426 Zea, Philip, and Cheney, Robert C. Clock making in New England, 1725–1825: an interpretation of the Old Sturbridge Village Collection. Caroline F. Sloat, ed. Photography by Thomas Neill. Sturbridge, Old Sturbridge Village, 1992. 173, [2]p. il., col. plates.

Discussion of clocks made in New England between 1725 and 1825, based on the Old Sturbridge Village collection. Includes chapters on the practice of clockmaking, on the Willard family, and on fakes, reproductions, and repaired pieces.

Technical data on the Old Sturbridge Village collection, p.157–70. Glossary, p.171–73.

Asian Countries

China

P427 Needham, Joseph; Ling, Wang; and De Solla Price, Derek J. Heavenly clockwork: the great astrological clocks of medieval China. 2d ed. with suppl. N.Y., Cambridge Univ. Pr., 1986. xvi, 266p. il. (Antiquarian Horological Society monograph, 1)

1st ed. 1960.

Traces "the history of the Chinese tradition," examining the relationship to Islam and Europe

Chronological table, p.x–xi. Notes and conventions, p.xii–xiv. Supplement, p.206–15. Bibliography to supplement, p.216–18. General bibliography, p.219–28. Tables of Chinese characters, p.229–42. Index, p.243–66.

Japan

P428 Brandes, Wilhelm. Alte japanische Uhren: ein handbuch für Sammler und Liebhaber. München, Klinkhardt und Biermann, 1984. vi, 195p. il. (part col), plates (1 folded)

Begins with an essay on Chinese and Japanese astronomy followed by examples of Japanese clocks and watches.

Literaturverzeichnis, p.[191]. Personen- und Sachregister, p.193–[96].

P429 Kojima, Kenji. Meiji no tokei. Tokyo, Azekura Shobo, 1988. 354p. il., plates.

Compact study of clocks of the Meiji period.

Includes bibliography and index.

POTTERY AND PORCELAIN

Bibliography

P430 Campbell, James Edward. Pottery and ceramics: a guide to information sources. Detroit, Gale, [1978]. xi, 241p. (Art and architecture information guide series, 7)

Comprehensive annotated bibliography of works, primarily in English, of all periods and countries, covering every aspect of ceramics. Some periodical articles are included, as are lists of ceramics periodicals and societies.

Author index, p.207–16. Title index, p.217–30. Subject index, p.231–41.

Dictionaries and Encyclopedias

P431 Cameron, Elisabeth. Encyclopedia of pottery and porcelain: the 19th and 20th centuries. London, Faber, 1986. 366, [18]p. il., col. plates.

An important resource for information on ceramics of the world produced between 1800 and 1960. The more than 2,500 entries include firms, potters, designers, and terminology for forms and processes especially characteristic of this period. Entries include cross-references and bibliographic references.

Reference abbreviations, p.[369]–[79].

P432 Cohen, David Harris, and Hess, Catherine. Looking at European ceramics: a guide to technical terms. [Mailbu], Getty Museum in assoc. with British Museum Pr., [1993]. 91p. il. (part col.)

"The aim of this book is to assist the [museum] visitor by providing brief definitions of the terms most commonly used by artists and art historians when discussing the manufacture of European ceramics."—*p.5.* Compact, readable, handsomely illustrated, an attractive introduction to its subject.

Selected bibliography, p.91.

P433 Cushion, J. P. and Honey, W. B. Handbook of pottery and porcelain marks. 4th ed., rev. and exp. London, Faber, 1980. vii, 272p. il., maps.

Rev. ed. of GLAH 1:P265.

Expanded ed. of an essential reference work on pottery and porcelain marks of the world. Includes many added 19th- and 20th-century marks, decorators' signatures, and British design registry tables. Arrangement is alphabetical by country and by town.

The use of marks on pottery and porcelain, p.3–5. Index, p.244–72.

P434 Danckert, Ludwig. Handbuch des europäischen Porzellans. Stark erw. und umfassend bearb. Neuausg. München, Prestel, 1992. 980p. il.

1st ed., 1954; 2d ed., 1967; 3d ed., 1974; 4th ed., 1978; 5th ed. 1988; English ed. titled Directory of European porcelain: marks, makers and factories. London, N.A.G. Press, 1981; repr. 1995; French ed., Fribourg, Office du livre, 1980.

Latest ed. of this substantial dictionary of European porcelain; includes marks.

Literatur, p.971–80.

P435 Fournier, Robert. Illustrated dictionary of pottery form. Drawings by Sheila Fournier. N.Y., Van Nostrand Reinhold, [1981]. xiii, 257p. il.

The author, a potter, has produced a dictionary of pottery forms past and present, emphasizing shape and function as defining characteristics. Examples cited are from many cultures and historical periods, though primary emphasis is on hand-made, rather than machine-made, forms. Illustrations include line drawings and photographs.

Booklist, p.ix–xii.

P436 Kovel, Ralph, and Kovel, Terry. Kovel's new dictionary of marks. N.Y., Crown, [1986]. xii, 290p. il.

The authors, well-known and prolific writers on antiques and collectibles, here identify more than 3,500 marks on 19th- and 20th-century American, European, and Oriental pottery and porcelain. A companion to their earlier Dictionary of Marks-Pottery and Porcelain (1953), which compiled a similar listing for marks of the 17th, 18th, and early 19th centuries. Marks are listed by use of objects (such as animals) or by use of letters. An accessible, useful resource.

The vocabulary of marks, p. 229–35. Dating systems used by specific factories, p.236–55. Additional tips for dating pottery and porcelain, p.256–57. Pottery and porcelain "family trees," p.257–66. Marks used by many factories, p.266–68. Fakes and forgeries, p.269–71. Selected reading, p.272–77. Index, p.278–90.

P437 Penkala, Maria. European pottery: a handbook for the collector. 5816 marks on majolica, faience and stoneware. [3d ed.] Schiedam, The Netherlands, Interbook International, 1980. 472p. il., plates (part col.)

1st ed., 1968; 2d ed., rev. 1969.

Handbook reproducing pottery marks and sometimes brief histories of "all known European factories," arranged by country. When known, names of potters are listed under factory histories.

Bibliography, p.459–62. Index to persons and factories, p.463–72.

P438 Savage, George, and Newman, Harold. An illustrated dictionary of ceramics: defining 3,054 terms relating to wares, materials, processes, styles, patterns, and shapes from antiquity to the present day. With an introductory list of the principal European factories and their marks, compiled by John Cushion. [London], Thames and Hudson, [1985]. 320p. il.

Rev. ed. of GLAH 1:P277.

Most recent ed. of a standard dictionary of terminology relating to ceramics, including those relating to form, function, processes, materials, and decoration. Includes some foreign-language terms. Geographical coverage is worldwide. Well cross-indexed. No bibliography.

Principal European factories and their marks, p.[7]–[18].

P439 Zühlsdorff, Dieter. Keramik-Marken Lexikon: Porzellan und Keramik Report. 1885–1935 Europa (Festland). [Stuttgart], Arnoldsche, [1994]. 753p. il., ports.

Massive German-language dictionary of marks, makers, and factories in late 19th-century and early 20th-century Europe. Includes brief English-language explanation for users. Marks are arranged in alphabetical or pictorial order. While this vol. may be challenging to use for many readers, it contains a wealth of information on its subject.

Contents: (1) Marken-Abbildungen. (2) Künstler-Biographen. (3) Firmen-Dokumentationen, Fachschulen; (4) Anhang: Technisches Glossar; Ausstellungen.

Ausstellungen, p.672–85. Bibliographie, p.687–97. Index, p.699–753.

Histories and Handbooks

P440 Atterbury, Paul, ed. The history of porcelain. N.Y., Morrow, 1982. 256p. il. (part col.)

The history of porcelain, from its origins in China to mass-produced and studio wares of the 20th century, is traced in a series of essays by well-known specialists, forming a comprehensive, readable history of the subject. Includes a chapter on forgeries.

Glossary, p.240–43. Bibliography, p.244–47. Index [249]–56.

P441 Battie, David, ed. Sotheby's concise encyclopedia of porcelain. Boston, Little, Brown, [1990]. 208p., col. il., map.

Series of essays by experts on the history of porcelain from its discovery to the 20th century, constituting a readable, reliable general introduction to the subject.

Contents: (1) The discovery of porcelain; (2) Qing Imperial porcelain; (3) Chinese export porcelain; (4) Japanese porcelain; (5) Early continental porcelain; (6) Early English porcelain; (7) English and Welsh porcelain, 1780 to 1820; (8) Continental porcelain 1780 to 1930; (9) Later British and American porcelain; (10) Fakes and forgeries

Select bibliography, p.193. Glossary, p.194–98. Summary of factories and biographies, p.199–202. [Map of] Kiln sites in China; Chinese dynasties and periods, p.203. Index, p.204–07.

P442 Caiger-Smith, Alan. Lustre pottery: technique, tradition, and innovation in Islam and the Western world. London and Boston, Faber, 1985. 246p. il., col. plates.

"Attempts to bring together . . . three inseparable facets of the lustre tradition, its historical setting, its practical technology, and its symbolism."—*Author's pref.*

Contents: (1) Iraq: the first lustred pottery; (2) Early figurative lustre of Iraq; (3) Egyptian lustre of the Fatimid period; (4) Syrian lustre; (5) Moorish lustre of Andalucía; (7) Hispano-Moresque lustre; (8) Lustre in Italy: Deruta and Gubbio; (9) Revival; (10) Post-revival; (11) Alchemy and symbol; (12) The technique of reduced-pigment lustre; (13) Old technical methods; (14) The science of lustre: questions and answers.

Table of analyses of lustre sherds, p.236. Bibliography, p.[237]–41. Index, p.[242]–46.

P443 Fay-Halle, Antoinette, and Mundt, Barbara. Porcelain of the nineteenth century. N.Y., Rizzoli, [1983]. 302p. il. (part col.), map.

Trans. of: La porcelain européene au XIX siècle. Fribourg, Office du Livre, 1983.

Heavily illustrated general survey of the development of porcelain in Europe and Britain from 1800 to Art Nouveau. Arranged by country and by factory.

Contents: (I) The techniques of nineteenth-century porcelain; (II) 1800–1830: The triumph of painting; (III) 1830–1850: From art institute to industrial manufactory; (IV) 1850–1880: Historismus; (V) Eclecticism and Art Mouveau Conclusion.

Catalogue of porcelain marks, p.278–87. [Map of] Nineteenth-century porcelain factories, p.288–89. Bibliography, p.290–95. Index, p.297–302.

P444 Kingery, W. David, and Vandiver, Pamela B. Ceramic masterpieces: art, structure, and technology. N.Y., Free Pr., [1986]. xxv, 339p. il., 24 col. plates, tables.

Detailed, scholarly examination of ceramic technology, using ten masterpieces from varied cultures as examples. Challenging reading for the non-specialist.

Contents: (I) Introduction; (II) Ceramic masterpieces; (III) Ceramic technology; (IV) Studying ceramic objects.

Some special terminology, p.315–24. Index, p.325–39.

P445 McCready, Karen. Art deco and modernist ceramics. Introd. by Garth Clark. [London], Thames and Hudson, [1995]. 192p. il., col. plates.

Well-illustrated survey of world ceramics produced between the two World Wars, both hand-crafted and factory-made. Particularly useful for 201 color plates of representative objects and for extensive section of biographical and historical sketches of factories and individual ceramists.

Contents: (1) Introduction: a survey of ceramic art and design, 1919–1939, by Garth Clark; (2) The plates; (3) An A–Z of ceramists, designers, and factories.

Glossary, p.187–88. Bibliography, p.189–91. Index, p.192.

P446 Meister, Peter Wilhelm, and Reber, Horst. European porcelain of the 18th century. Trans. by Ewald Osers, Ithaca, Cornell Univ. Pr., [1983]. 320p. il. (part col.), maps, tables.

First published as Europäisches Porzellan. Stuttgart, Belser, 1980.

The authors, experts in Chinese and Japanese and in European porcelain respectively, examine the development of 18th-century continental porcelain with attention to the influence upon it of Eastern wares. Includes discussion of the history of porcelain collecting and of forgeries.

Contents: (1) The term porcelain and its use on the seventeenth and eighteenth centuries; (2) Chinese porcelain and the West; (3) Manufactories as porcelain centres of European porcelain; (4) Porcelain manufactories as artistic centres; (5) Artists and artisans; (6) History of porcelain style in the eighteenth century; (7) Porcelain as an article of use in the eighteenth century; (8) Iconography of European porcelain in the eighteenth century; (9) Important customers and patrons of porcelain in the eighteenth century; (10) Eighteenth-century porcelain in the nineteenth and twentieth centuries.

Bibliography, p.297–304. Maps and chronological tables, p.[305]–14. Index, p.315–18.

P447 Morley-Fletcher, Hugo, and Roger McIlroy. Christie's pictorial history of European pottery. Englewood Cliffs, Prentice-Hall, [1984]. 319p. il. (part col.), maps.

Primarily pictorial survey of the development of pottery in Europe and England between 1400 and 1820, especially suitable as a visual introduction to the subject for the beginning collector. Based on objects sold by Christie's in recent years, and includes their auction prices. Arrangement is by country and by period.

Glossary, p.306. Further reading, p.307. Price list, p.308–16. Index, p.317–19.

P448 Robacker, Earl F., and Robacker, Ada F. Spatterware and sponge: hardy perennials of ceramics. South Brunswick, Barnes, [1978]. 167p. il., col. plates, map.

The only general history and survey of wares from all countries and periods with spattered and sponged decoration, informative for both collectors and researchers. Chapter on sources lists known makers by country. Also includes explanation of registry marks and a glossary (p.154–56).

Annotated bibliography, p.159–62. Index, p.163–67.

Western Countries

Australia

P449 Ioannou, Noris. Ceramics in South Australia 1836–1986, from folk to studio pottery. [Netley, South Australia], Wakefield Pr., [1986]. xiii, 386p. il., ports. (part col.), maps.

Comprehensive, well-illustrated history of South Australian pottery, produced by makers working in both the English and the Germanic traditions, from the colony's settlement to the present day.

Includes bibliographical references. Appendix: Marks with notes on identification for collectors, p.357–61. Abbreviations, p.362. Select bibliography and further reading, p.375. Index, p.376–86.

Canada

P450 Collard, Elizabeth. Nineteenth-century pottery and porcelain in Canada. 2d ed. Montreal, McGill-Queen's University Press, 1984. xx, 477p. il., facsims., ports.

1st ed., 1967.

Surveys both wares made in Canada and imported wares.

Contents: The tide of imports: toils and hazards; How pottery and porcelain were sold; The earthenwares; The porcelains; Printed earthenware with Canadian views and emblems; Canadians compete; Appendix A: Concerning marks; Appendix B: A checklist of nineteenth-century Canadian potters; Addenda.

Notes, p.443–66. Index, p.467–77.

France

P451 Dawson, Aileen. A catalogue of French porcelain in the British Museum. [London], British Museum Pr., [1994]. xviii, 429p. il., 42 col. plates, maps.

Authoritative catalog of 301 pieces of French porcelain from more than 40 factories in the Museum's collections, which were assembled with emphasis on signed and dated pieces. Entries, by factory, are detailed and include individual bibliographical references and illustrations of marks.

Contents: Soft-paste factories; Hard-paste factories; Hard-paste factories in Paris; Unidentified factories.

Scientific analysis, p.xiii. French porcelain: a technical discussion, p.xiv. Donors, p.xvi. Explanation of the catalogue, p.xvii. Map of French factories, p.xviii. Addendum: Porcelains in Franks Catalogue, 1896, now reattributed to non-French factories, p.404–07. Concordance of catalogue and register numbers, p. 408–09. Selected bibliography, p.410–20. Exhibition catalogues, p.421–22. Index, p.423–29.

P452 Eriksen, Svend, and de Bellaigue, Geoffrey. Sèvres porcelain: Vincennes and Sèvres, 1740–1800. Danish text trans. by R. J. Charleston. London, Boston, Faber, [1987]. 379p. il., col. plates. (Faber monographs on pottery and porcelain)

Definitive history of the Sèvres factory to 1800 by two acknowledged authorities, based on new archival research. Includes detailed commentary on almost two hundred individual objects from many collections, and reproductions of painter's and gilder's marks.

Contents: (I) The early years; (II) The later period; (III) Marks and forgeries; (IV) The plates.

Bibliography, p.359–64. Index, p.365–79.

P453 Paris. Musée du Louvre. Département des Objets d'art. Catalogue des porcelaines françaises I: [Paris], Réunion des musées nationaux, [1992]. 314p. il. (part col.)

Catalog of porcelain objects in the collections of the Louvre. Detailed and authoritative, including introductory essays on each factory. Vol.1 is devoted to factories other than Vincennes-Sèvres, for which a second vol. is planned.

Contents: (1) by Plinval de Guillebon, Régine de Chantilly, Mennecy, Saint-Cloud, Boissette, Bordeaux, Limoges, Niderviller, Paris, Valenciennes (1992).

P454 Plinval de Guillebon, Régine de. Faience et porcelaine de Paris, XVIIIe–XIXe siècles. Pref. de Jacques Chirac. [Dijon], Faton, [1995]. 475p. il. (chiefly col.), ports.

Handsomely illustrated history of pottery and porcelain produced in Paris and its neighboring region in the 18th and 19th centuries, by a well-known historian of ceramics.

Contents: (1) La Faience à Paris au XVIIIe siècle; (2) La porcelaine à Paris au XVIIIe siècle; (3) Les changements economiques au XIXe siècle; (4) La faience à Paris au XIXe siècle; (5) La porcelaine à Paris au XIXe siècle.

Conclusion, p.416–18. Répertoire des marques, p.421–43. Notes, p.445–53. Glossaire, p.454–55. Bibliographie, p.456–62. Index, p.464–75.

P455 Saint-Porchaire ceramics. Ed. by Daphne Barbour and Shelley Sturman. Washington, D.C., National Gallery of Art (Distr. Univ. Pr. of New England, [1996]). 160p. il. (part col.), graphs, tables. (Studies in the history of art, 52) (Monograph series, II)

Ten papers resulting from an international conservation-curatorial colloquy sponsored by the Center for Advanced Study in the Visual Arts, focusing on this group of striking and enigmatic French Renaissance ceramics.

Select bibliography, p.157–58. Contributors, p.159–60.

Germany and Austria

Dictionaries and Encyclopedias

P456 Röntgen, Robert E. Marks on German, Bohemian, and Austrian porcelain, 1710 to the present. Exton, Penn., Schiffer, [1981]. 636p. il.

Authoritative guide to marks on porcelain produced in the Germanic countries, in German and English. Arrangement is by symbol or by initial letters. Includes chapters on manufacturers and factories (by location), and on confusing or misleading marks. Indispensable for those working with this material.

Index of names, p.585–607. Bibliography, p.609–19. List of motifs and symbols appearing in marks, p.620–27. Appendix (addenda), p.629–36.

Histories and Handbooks

P457 Kaufmann, Gerhard. North German folk pottery of the 17th to the 20th centuries. Catalogue by Gerhard Kaufmann. [Richmond], International Exhibits Foundation, [1979]. 145p. il. (part col.), maps.

Catalog of a traveling exhibition of earthenware from Northern Germany, assembled from several German museum collections. Includes both ornamental and functional wares in a variety of forms, principally produced during the 18th and 19th centuries. An informative introductory chapter discusses purpose, materials, and methods of the creation of these ceramics.

Selected bibliography, p.145.

P458 Syz, Hans; Miller, Jefferson, II; and Ruckert, Rainer. Catalogue of the Hans Syz collection, Volume I: Meissen porcelain and Hausmalerei. Washington, D.C., Smithsonian Institution, 1979. 607p. il. (part col.)

First (and to date, only) vol. in a projected 4-vol. catalog of a notable collection of continental and related ceramics now housed at the Smithsonian Institution. This vol., devoted principally to Meissen porcelain and Böttger stoneware, furnishes a comprehensive survey of the output of the Meissen factory from its beginning in 1710 to the 1760s.

Marks, p.591–94. Bibliography, p.595–603. Concordance, p.605–07.

P459 Walcha, Otto. Meissen porcelain. Photographs by Ulrich Frewel and Klaus G. Beyer. Ed. by Helmut Reibig. N.Y., Putnam, [1981]. 516p. il., 259 plates (part col.)

Originally published as Meissner Porzellan. Dresden, Verlag der Kunst, 1973.

Comprehensive, well-illustrated history of Meissen porcelain from its 18th-century beginnings to the mid-20th century, by the former curator of the Meissen archives. Includes a visual chronology of the development of Meissen illustrated by characteristic pieces arranged by period.

Chronology of the Meissen porcelain factory, p.459–61. Museums with significant collections of old Meissen porcelain, p.462. A chronological survey of forms and decorations of Meissen ware, p.463–98. Meissen marks, p.499–501. Glossary, p.502–03. Bibliography, p.504–09. Index of names, p.510–16.

Great Britain and Ireland

Dictionaries and Encyclopedias

P460 Atterbury, Paul, and Batkin, Maureen. The dictionary of Minton. Historical introd. by Terence A. Lockett. [Woodbridge], Antique Collectors' Club, [1990]. 370p. il. (part col.), charts, ports.

Comprehensive dictionary of the Minton company's wares, artists, and decorators from its founding in the 18th century to the present, based on research in the Minton archives.

Contents: (1) Dictionary of Minton Wares; (2) Biographies of Minton artists, designers, and decorators; Appendixes: (1) Marks and dating; (2) Majolica catalogue, 1880s; (3) The 1884 illustrated catalogue of shapes; (4) Secessionist ware catalogue, 1902; (5) Photographs from factory promotional booklet, c.1933.

Select Minton bibliography, p.367–68.

P461 Bergesen, Victoria. Encyclopedia of British art pottery, 1870–1920. Ed., with a foreword, by Geoffrey A. Godden. London, Barrie and Jenkins, [1991]. 304p. il., 40 col. plates.

Dictionary of the designers, decorators, and companies producing art pottery wares in Britain during the later 19th and early 20th centuries, ranging from individual artist potters to mass manufacturers. Each entry includes description of marks, bibliographical references, and lists of decorators and artists when known. Brief introductory essay discusses these ceramics and their production.

Bibliography, p.296–300. Index, p.301–04.

P462 Branyan, Lawrence; French, Neal; and Sandon, John. Worcester blue and white porcelain, 1751–1790: an illustrated encyclopedia of the patterns. London, Barrie and Jenkins, [1981]. 367p. il., charts.

Encyclopedia of the majority of patterns produced at the Worcester factory from its foundation to 1790, utilizing evidence unearthed during recent excavations at the factory site as an aid in dating. Includes both painted and early transfer-printed designs. Each entry includes name, date, marks, shapes, and other relevant commentary.

Contents: (1) A brief view of Worcester blue and white wares; (2) How blue and white porcelain was made; (3) An introduction to the Worcester patterns; (4) The patterns: I. The painted patterns; II. The printed patterns; III. The border patterns.

Bibliography, p.364. Index of patterns, p.365–67.

P463 Coysh, A. W. and Henrywood, R. K. The dictionary of blue and white printed pottery 1780–1880. [Woodbridge], Antique Collectors' Club, [1982, 1989]. 2v. il. (part col.), maps.

Detailed dictionary of marks, pattern names, designers, factories, and other information relating to British blue-and-white transfer-printed pottery during the height of its popularity. Vol.2 includes information newly come to light and some post-1880 wares. An essential reference for research on this subject.

Index of potters' initial marks printed or impressed on wares, v.1, p.414–16. Source books known to have been used by makers of blue and white printed earthenwares, v.1, p.417. Maps of the Ganges and Jumna Valley and the Two Sicilies, v.1, p.418. Bibliography, v.1, p.419–20, v.2, p.239. Unattributed patterns, v.2, p.220–36. Initial marks, v.2, p.237. Source books, v.2, p.238.

P464 Godden, Geoffrey A. Encyclopaedia of British porcelain manufacturers. London, Barrie and Jenkins, [1988]. 855p. il., 25 col. plates.

Comprehensive compilation in dictionary form of information on all known British porcelain manufacturers from the 1740s to the present, by a major authority. Includes discussions of manufacturing methods, marks and patterns, and lists of manufacturers by decades. Bibliography includes contents of each vol. of the English Porcelain Club and English Ceramic Circle. An indispensable reference for its field.

Contents: (I) China or porcelain: the basic types of body; (II) A general guide to makers' marks and pattern numbers; (III) Check list of British porcelain manufacturers, 1740–1840; (IV) British porcelain manufacturers (an alphabetical list); (V) List of identifying initials.

Bibliography, p.831–38. Index, p.839–53.

P465 Reilly, Robin. Wedgwood: the new illustrated dictionary. [Woodbridge], Antique Collectors' Club, [1995]. 515p. il. (part col.), genealogical chart, ports.

Updated ed. of a comprehensive dictionary of Wedgwood wares by a leading scholar of the firm and its history. Includes designers, patterns, forms, processes, and materials, and covers period from the founding of the firm to 1986.

Wedgwood chronology, p.501–02. Wedgwood trade marks, p.503–06. Registry marks, p.507. Pattern number prefixes, p.508. The Wedgwoods of Etruria, p.[509–10]. Bibliography, p.511–15.

P466 Sandon, John. The dictionary of Worcester porcelain. [Woodbridge], Antique Collectors' Club, [1993]– . (1)v. il. (part col.)

Comprehensive dictionary of patterns, shapes, forms, designers, decorators, and other information on this important factory during its first century. Includes information based on recent archeological explorations of the early factory site. V.1, the only vol. published to date, is introduced by an extensive essay on the history of the firm.

Contents: 1751–1851 (1993).

Histories and Handbooks

P467 Adams, Elizabeth. Chelsea porcelain. London, Barrie and Jenkins, [1987]. 224p. il., 16 col. plates.

Comprehensive account of the history and wares produced by this important 18th-century factory, including a chapter on fakes, forgeries, and collecting, and appendixes on marks and museum collections.

Bibliography, p.212–17. Index, p.218–24.

P468 ———, and Redstone, David. Bow porcelain. [Rev. and exp. ed.] London, Faber, [1991]. xiv, 257p. il., 16 col. plates, map. (Faber monographs on pottery and porcelain)

Rev. and expanded 2d ed. of London, 1981.

New ed. of the standard account of this 18th-century London porcelain factory, incorporating recently discovered archival materials.

Bibliography, p.[243]–47. Index, p.[243]–51.

P469 Archer, Michael. Delftware: the tin-glazed earthenware of the British Isles: a catalogue of the collection in the Victoria and Albert Museum. London, HMSO, in assoc. with the Museum, 1997. xv, 642p. il. (part col.), plates.

Catalog of the finest collection in the world. Includes essays on social history, manufacture, distribution, and influences on shape and decoration.

Concordance of Museum and catalogue numbers, p.593–602. Bibliography and abbreviations, p.603–21. Index, p.623–42.

P470 Atterbury, Paul. The Parian phenomenon: a survey of Victorian parian porcelain statuary and busts. Ed. by Paul Atterbury with contrib. from Maureen Batkin . . . [et al.] Shepton Beauchamp, Somerset, R. Dennis, 1989. 268p. il. (part col.)

"The major part of this book comprises the lists of Parian made by the four most important manufacturers, Minton, Copeland, Wedgwood and Worcester."—*p.[5].* Richly illustrated in black-and-white, with line drawings.

Biographies of Parian sculptors and modellers, p.260–64. Biographies of Parian subjects, p.264–67. Marks on Parian, p.268.

P471 Austin, John C. British delft at Williamsburg. Williamsburg, Colonial Williamsburg, in assoc. with Jonathan Horne, London, [1994]. 299p. il., col. plates. (Williamsburg decorative arts series)

Catalog of the outstanding collection of 727 pieces of British Delftware in the collections of Colonial Williamsburg, important not only for its depth and breadth but for the light it sheds on ownership of these ceramics by Williamsburg residents. Wares are arranged by function.

Contents: (1) Introduction; (2) English delft from Williamsburg's archaeological contexts, by Robert Hunter; (3) Catalog conventions; (4) Selected examples (Color plates); (5) The catalogue.

Short title list, p.13. Index, p.[292]–99.

P472 Batkin, Maureen. Wedgwood ceramics 1846–1959: a new appraisal. London, Richard Dennis, [1982]. 244p. il. (part col.), ports.

History of Wedgwood ceramics from the mid-19th through the mid-20th centuries, a period generally overlooked in many considerations of this firm. "The aim of this book is to introduce the Wedgwood collector to the wares of this period."—*p.9.* Extensively illustrated. Section on marks includes useful information on dating and a list of the firm's proprietors.

Marks, p.227–31. Alphabetical list of selected artists, designers, modellers, painters and gilders associated with Wedgwood, p.232–41. Selected bibliography, p.242–44.

P473 Battie, David. David Battie's guide to understanding 19th and 20th century British porcelain: including fakes, techniques, and prices. [Woodbridge], Antique Collectors' Club, [1994]. 320p. il. (part col.)

Updated ed. of Price guide to 19th and 20th century British porcelain (1975, 1979). An extensive pictorial survey, aimed at collectors, and arranged by functional form.

Fakes and forgeries, p.299–308. Damage, p.309. Techniques, p.310–16. 19th century British & Irish porcelain factories, p.317. Bibliography, p.318. Factory index, p.319–20.

P474 Birmingham Museum of Art. The Dwight and Lucille Beeson Wedgwood collection at the Birmingham Museum of Art, Birmingham, Alabama. [By] Elizabeth Bryding Adams. Birmingham, Birmingham Museum, [1992]. 400p. il., ports. (part col.)

Meticulous catalog of a major collection of Wedgwood ceramics of the 18th and 19th centuries, based on extensive research. Introductory essays discuss Wedgwood's various wares and their development, with special attention to printed design sources for decoration.

Bibliography, p.385–89. Index, p.390–400.

P475 Bradshaw, Peter. Derby porcelain figures, 1750–1848. London, Faber, [1990]. xxvii, 484p., 19 col. plates. (Faber monographs on pottery and porcelain)

Detailed, authoritative catalog of more than 750 known Derby figures, already regarded as essential for research on this subject.

Appendix A: Sculptors, modellers and craftsmen, 1770–96, p.443–61. Appendix B: Modellers and other craftsmen, 1796–1848, p.462–65. Bibliography, p.466–69. Index, p.470–84.

P476 ______. Eighteenth-century English porcelain figures, 1745–1795. [Woodbridge], Antique Collectors' Club, [1981]. 327p. il., col. plates.

Definitive, well-illustrated history of figures made by all of the 18th-century English porcelain manufactories. Appendixes list all known figures with references to sources of illustration and further information, and a discussion of Commedia dell'arte as represented in this form. An essential resource for the subject.

Bibliography, p.319. Index, p.320–27.

P477 Britton, Frank. English delftware in the Bristol collection. Foreword by Arnold Wilson. Pref. by Michael Archer. [London], Sotheby, [1982]. 335p. il., col. plates, tables.

Detailed catalog of the major collection of Delftware held by the City of Bristol Museum and Art Gallery, forming a comprehensive survey of these wares. Catalog incorporates considerable new research and includes discussions of ownership and print sources. Introductory essays discuss Delftware as a form and the evolution of the Bristol collection.

Chronological table of delftware factories, p.12. Underrim markings, p.[309]–17. Shapes of plates and dishes, p.[321]. Correlation between museum numbers and catalogue numbers, p.[323]–27. Report of the Institute of Geological Sciences on the cause of pink-coloration, p.[329]–30. A select bibliography, p.[331]–32. Index, p.[333]–35.

P478 Clark, Garth. The potter's art: a complete history of pottery in Britain. [London, Phaidon, 1995]. 239p. il. (part col.), ports.

Readable, handsomely illustrated history of British pottery from its earliest beginnings to the present day, aimed at the general reader.

Contents: (1) The peasant potter; (2) The industrial potter; (3) The artist-potter; (4) The studio potter.

Selected bibliography, p.224–28. Selected chronology, p.229–31. Glossary, p.232–33. Index, p.234–37.

P479 Cox, Alwyn, and Cox, Angela. Rockingham pottery and porcelain, 1745–1842. London, Faber, [1983]. 262p. il., 10 col. plates, genealogical chart, map. (Faber monographs on pottery and porcelain)

Thorough account of this factory (originally named Swinton) and its wares, based on new documentary and scientific research. Includes a chapter on the artists and other workpeople and one on the factory's marks.

Bibliography, p.[253]–54. Index, p.[255]–62.

P480 Degenhart, Richard K. Belleek: the complete collector's guide and illustrated reference. 2d ed. Radnor, Penn., Wallace-Homestead, [1993]. xii, 244p. il., col. plates, ports.

1st ed., Huntington, N.Y., Portfolio Pr., 1978.

The standard work on this Irish porcelain, first manufactured in the mid-19th century and still in production. While valuable for collectors, also an important source for researchers. Includes a "Value guide" laid in.

Contents: (1) Belleek: A history of the pottery and its ware; (2) Belleek: a gallery of old and current ware.

The 1904 catalogue, p.179–202. The 1928 catalogue, p.203–13. Bibliography, p.215. Current Belleek parian ware, p.217–20. Old Belleek parian ware and earthenware, p.221–38. Index, p.239–44.

P481 Edwards, Diana. Black basalt: Wedgwood and contemporary manufacturers. [Woodbridge], Antique Collectors' Club, [1994]. 334p. il., col. plates.

Comprehensive history of these distinctive black wares, developed by Wedgwood in imitation of the antique. The author discusses the work of other manufacturers and attempts to assist in identification of their work.

Egyptian black prices from Staffordshire potters price fixing agreements: notes by George L. Miller, August 1991, p.299–303. Assorted recipes for Egyptian black, p.304–06. Bibliography, p.307–14. Index, p.327–34.

P482 Emmerson, Robin. British teapots and tea drinking. London, HMSO Books, 1992. 330p. il., 24p. of plates.

"Illustrated from the Twining Teapot Gallery, Norwich Castle Museum," the "greatest collection of British pottery and porcelain teapots in the world."—*Introd.* Introductory chapters on tea-drinking, tea ceremony, and the trade, followed by a catalog of selected examples.

Select bibliography, p.315–24. Index, p.327–30.

P483 Godden, Geoffrey A. Eighteenth-century English porcelain: a selection from the Godden Reference Collection. London, Granada, [1985]. xiii, 426p. il., col. plates.

Godden, a well-known scholar, dealer, and teacher of ceramic history, presents a selection from a collection built to illustrate characteristic wares of the principal English 18th-century porcelain factories. He also discusses fakes and other situations that collectors face, based on his many years of experience. A very personal collecting history, concluding with a tribute to his antique dealer father, and immensely enjoyable to read.

Selected bibliography, p.[418]–[21]. Index, p.[423]–26.

P484 ———. Godden's guide to English porcelain. Radnor, Penn., Wallace-Homestead, [1992]. 223p. il. (part col.)

First published in Great Britain by Hart-Davis, MacGibbon, 1978.

Readable narrative history of English porcelain, its makers, and methods, by a noted authority. Aimed at the nonspecialist or beginning collector, considerable attention is given to practical advice on collecting, by one who knows. An excellent introduction to a vast field.

Appendix: Registered designs, p.213–14. Select bibliography and associations, p.215–19. Index, p.220–23.

P485 ———. Lowestoft porcelains. [2d ed., rev. and exp.] [Woodbridge], Antique Collectors' Club, [1985]. 261p. il., col. plates.

1st ed. titled The illustrated guide to Lowestoft porcelains. London, Herbert Jenkins, 1969.

Updated ed. of the standard work on this 18th-century English porcelain, incorporating much new research, by an acknowledged authority. Useful bibliographical essay.

Dated Lowestoft porcelains, p.219–36. Sale records, p.237–52. Fakes and false attributions, p.253–55. Bibliography, p.256–59. Index, p.260–61.

P486 ———, ed. and main author. Staffordshire porcelain. London, Granada, [1983]. xiv, 593p. il., col. plates.

Massive compilation of essays by Godden, and twelve specialist authors, on the known Staffordshire porcelain manufacturers, concentrating primarily on the pre-1851 period. Includes an extensive bibliography, a chapter on working and living conditions of potters in the 19th century, and a chronology. An immensely helpful resource for study of this subject.

Chronology, p.xi–xiv. The Staffordshire Potteries, p.352–364. Check-list of Staffordshire porcelain manufacturers, p.[366]–505. The design registration systems, p.[507]–35. Pattern numbers as a help to identification, p.[537]–44. Sources of information, p.[546]–54. A problem group of porcelains, p.[556]–69. Specialist contributors, p.[571]–73. Brief notes on: The Gladstone Pottery Museum, The City Museum and Art Gallery, Stoke-on-Trent, The Northern Ceramic Society, The Godden Reference Collection, p.[575]–77. Index, p.[583]–93.

P487 ———, and Gibson, Michael. Collecting lustreware. London, Barrie & Jenkins, [1991]. 384p. il., plates (part col.)

Comprehensive history of 19th-century British lustre pottery and porcelain, valuable for both collectors and researchers. Includes a chapter on hints for the collector.

Technique and lustre recipes, p.352–66. Platinum in the decoration of porcelain and pottery, by Dr. L. B. Hunt, p.367–73. Bibliography, p.374–78. Index, p.379–84.

P488 Grant, Alison. North Devon pottery: the seventeenth century. [Exeter], Univ. of Exeter, 1983. xvi, 156p. il., plates (part col.), maps, genealogical charts, tables.

Expansion of the author's Ph.D. thesis (University of Exeter).

Account, incorporating considerable archeological evidence, of pottery manufactured in North Devon and its export to Ireland and to the American colonies and the West Indies. Includes chapters on methods of manufacture, on marketing, and on the coastal trade in these wares.

North Devon pottery types, p.136–37. Museums holding important collections of North Devon pottery, p.138–39. Notes on initialed wares, p.140–42. Bibliography, p.143–50. Index, p.151–56.

P489 Halfpenny, Pat. English earthenware figures 1740–1840. [Woodbridge], Antique Collectors' Club, [1991]. 346p. il. (part col.)

The first book in many years on these appealing ceramic figures, produced for the popular market. The author discusses techniques of production and includes a chapter on fakes, forgeries, and reproductions.

Documentary evidence relating to figure production, p.314–27. Impressed numerals on figures, p.327–36. Bibliography, p.337–39. Museums and galleries with figure collections, p.340. Index, p.341–46.

P490 Jones, A. E. (Jimmy), and Joseph, Sir Leslie. Swansea porcelain shapes and decoration. Cowbridge, D. Brown and Sons, 1988. xiv, 274p. il. (part col.), plans.

Comprehensive, detailed study of the work of the well-known Welsh porcelain factory, with chapters on the decorators, shapes, decoration, and marks, by two recognized collector-experts.

Glossary, p.261–67. Bibliography, p.269–70. Index, p.271–74.

P491 Lewis, Griselda. A collector's history of English pottery. [5th rev. ed.] [Woodbridge], Antique Collectors' Club, [1999]. 383p. il. (part col.)

First published 1969, London, Studio Vista; 2d ed., London Barrie & Jenkins, 1977; 3d ed., rev. and enl., Woodbridge, Antique Collectors' Club, 1985; 4th ed. 1987.

Wide-ranging, heavily illustrated general history of pottery in England from its earliest beginnings to the studio and factory-made pottery of the 20th century. A standard, authoritative work. In addition to general bibliography, each chapter concludes with specialized suggestions for further reading.

Bibliography, p.368–74. Index of subjects from museum collections, p.375. Index, p.376–83.

P492 Northern Ceramic Society. Creamware and pearlware: the fifth exhibition from the Northern Ceramic Society. [Eds., T. A. Lockett and P. A. Halfpenny. Stoke-on-Trent, Stoke on Trent City Museum and Art Gallery, 1986]. 106p. il. 4 col. plates.

Catalog of an important exhibition of these wares, with essays by a number of specialist contributors. Includes concise explanations of techniques and printed sources of decoration.

Contents: (1). The technical characteristics of creamware and pearl-glazed earthenware, by G. W. Elliott; (2) Early creamware to 1770, by P. A. Halfpenny; (3) Techniques of transfer-printing on cream coloured earthenware, by P. Holdway; (4) On-glaze transfer-printing on creamware: the first fifty years, by N. Stretton; (5) Later black printing in Staffordshire, by E. M. Hampson; (6) Named and dated creamware and pearlware, by S. N. W. Bidgood; (7) The later creamwares and pearlwares, by T. A. Lockett; (8) Problems of attribution, by T. A. Lockett.

Bibliography, p.59–62. Catalogue, by P. A. Halfpenny, p.63–106.

P493 Oswald, Adrian. English brown stoneware, 1670–1900, by Adrian Oswald in collab. with R. J. C. Hildyard and R. G. Hughes. [London], Faber, [1982]. 308p. il., col. plates, charts. (Faber monographs on pottery and porcelain)

The authoritative history of these wares, with particular emphasis on utilitarian wares. "Figures I–XII" (p.274–297) illustrate the variations in shape and decoration of brown stoneware, drawn from extant examples. Thorough coverage of all known potters and manufactories.

Scotland, p.[223]–42. Dated hunting mugs, p.[243]–55. Dated Derbyshire pieces, p.[256]–73. Short bibliography, p.[298]–300. Index, p.[301]–08.

P494 Reilly, Robin. Wedgwood. [N.Y.], Stockton Pr., [1989]. 2v. il., ports., 302 col. plates, charts, genealogical charts.

First published London, Macmillan, 1989.

Monumental history of the work of the Wedgwood firm from its beginnings to the present day, and unlikely to be soon supplanted. An essential resource for extended research on Wedgwood.

Josiah Wedgwood's code, v.1, p.686–87. Sadler and Green, v.1, p.688–90. Engine-turning, v.1, p.691–93. Josiah Wedgwood's 'Price book of workmanship', v.1, p.694–95. Production processes, v.2, p.644–50. Wedgwood trademarks, v.2, p.651–57. The 2 February 1805 mark, v.2, p.658–59. The Wedgwoods of Etruria, v.2, p.660–663. Cameos and intaglios 1773–1795, v.2, p.664–79. Portrait medallions: Antique subjects, v.2, p.680–82. Portrait medallions, modern subjects 1771–1967, v.2, p.683–726. Tablets, placques and medallions 1769–1795, v.2, p.727–48. Busts 1774–1967, v.2, p.[749]–53. Figures 1769–1795, v.2, p.754–57. Bibliography, v.2, p.[783]–90. Index, v.2, p.791–823.

P495 Sandon, John. The Phillips guide to English porcelain of the 18th and 19th centuries. London, Merehurst, [1989]. 160p. il. (part col.)

Concise, readable history of this subject, aimed at beginning collectors and the general reader, by a well-known expert.

A list of the most important English porcelain factories in the eighteenth and nineteenth centuries, p.147–51. Marks, p.152–53. Glossary, p.154–57. Index, p.158–60.

P496 Towner, Donald. Creamware. London, Faber, [1978]. 240p. il. (part col.) (Faber monographs on pottery and porcelain)

Rev. ed. of English cream-coloured earthenware. London, Faber, 1957.

The standard, essential work on this subject, by the acknowledged authority on creamware.

P497 Walton, Peter. Creamware and other English pottery at Temple Newsam House, Leeds: A catalogue of the Leeds collection. [Bradford, Manningham, 1976]. xi, 293p. il., col. plates, port.

Catalog of more than 1,000 pieces of English pottery, chiefly of the later 18th and early 19th centuries, housed in the Leeds City art museums. Creamware and the pottery produced in Leeds itself are particular strengths of the collection.

Contents: Introduction: The formation of the Leeds collection; (1) English pottery from about 1650 to 1750; (2) Creamware; (3) Fine stonewares; Details: Terminals and handles, knobs, miscellaneous, Leeds pottery marks.

Select bibliography, p.281–84. Index, p.285–93.

P498 Williams, Petra. Staffordshire romantic transfer patterns: cup plates and early Victorian china. Jeffersontown, Kent, Fountain House East, 1978–1986. 2v., il., map, port.

Co-author of vol.II: Marguerite R. Weber.

Exhaustive visual dictionary of transfer patterns on Staffordshire pottery, principally dating from c.1835 to c.1855. Arrangement is by subject category. Vol.II was issued to include newly identified patterns.

A selection of backstamps, v,1, p.[737]–[44]. Patterns which could not be located or photographed, v.1, p. 745. Bibliography, v.1, p.747, v.2, p.690. Glossary, v.1, p.748–49. Index, v.1, p.751–57. Index of patterns, v.2, p.691–95.

P499 Williams-Wood, Cyril. English transfer-printed pottery and porcelain: a history of over-glaze printing. London, Faber, [1981]. 249p. il., 8 col. plates. (Faber monographs on pottery and porcelain)

History of the development of the transfer-printing process in England in the mid-18th century, the techniques involved, its makers, and their wares.

Glossary of colour terms used p.[235]–39. Bibliography, p.[240]–43. Index, p.[244]–49.

Italy

P500 Watson, Wendy M. Italian Renaissance maiolica from the William A.Clark collection: The Corcoran Gallery of Art and the Mount Holyoke College Art Museum. [London], Scala, [1986]. 192p. il. (part col.), map.

Catalog of a traveling exhibition organized by the Corcoran Gallery of Art and the Mount Holyoke College Art Museum, based on an outstanding collection assembled by William Andrews Clark and now housed at the Corcoran. 70 objects, arranged by city of origin, are illustrated and thoroughly discussed.

Checklist of additional works in the William A. Clark collection, p.176–86. Shapes, p.187. Bibliography, p.188–89. Index, p.190–91.

P501 Wilson, Timothy. Ceramic art of the Italian Renaissance. With the collab. of Patricia Collins, and an essay by Hugo Blake. Austin, Univ. of Texas Pr. in collab. with British Museum Pub., [1987]. 192p. il., 24 col. plates, map.

Catalog of the exhibition centering on the British Museum collection of Renaissance maiolica, or painted tin-glazed earthenware. While directed toward the non-specialist public, entries are informative and include specific bibliographical entries. Later chapters discuss the pottery's diffusion abroad, its survival in later centuries, and forgeries.

Contents: Introduction: Maiolica and the Italian Renaissance; Technique; Archaeology and maiolica, by Hugo Blake; The British Museum collection; Museum collections of maiolica. The catalogue.

Glossary, p.179. Bibliography of works cited, p.180–87. Index, p.188–91.

SEE ALSO: Rasmussen, The Robert Lehman collection, X: Italian majolica (GLAH 2:I4).

Latin America

P502 Litto, Gertrude. South American folk pottery. Studio photography by Robert Emerson Willis. Illus. by Frank Litto. N.Y., Watson-Guptill, 1976. 223p. il. (part col.)

Combines a travel account with a "serious examination of ceramic design, technique, and practices."—*Foreword.*

Contents: Peru; Bolivia; Chile; Ecuador; Colombia; Venezuela; Oriente Selva Vaupes.

Pottery areas data chart, p.218–20. Bibliography, p.221. Glossary/index, p.221–24.

Low Countries

P503 Dam, Jan Daniel van. Gedateerd Delfts aardewerk = Dated Dutch Delftware. Zwolle, Waanders [for the] Rijksmuseum Amsterdam, [1991]. [152]p., col. il.

Book illustrating and discussing dated examples of Dutch delftware from the Rijksmuseum's collection, in sequence by date from 1630 to 1804, an arrangement that provides discussion of the development, stylistic change, and eventual decline of these ceramics. In Dutch and English.

P504 Fourest, H.-P. Delftware: faience production at Delft. Trans. by Katherine Watson. N.Y., Rizzoli, [1980]. 201p. il. (part col.)

Trans. of La faience de Delft. Fribourg, Office du Livre, 1980.

Well-illustrated general history of Delft faience from its beginnings to the end of the 18th century, including a description of materials and methods of production.

Factory marks, p.187–94. Bibliography, p.195–96.

P505 Lunsingh Scheurleer, D. F. Delft: Niederländische Fayence. Aus dem Niederländischen ubertr. von Claudia List-Freytag und Christian Zinsser. München, Klinkhardt und Biermann, [1984]. 379p. il. (part col.)

Thorough examination of Delftware by a well-known scholar. Extensive bibliography.

Literatur, p.345–60. Begrifss- und Namenslauterungen, p.361–63. Register, p.364–70. Markentafel, p.[371]–79.

P506 Philadelphia Museum of Art. Dutch tiles in the Philadelphia Museum of Art. Essays by Jan Daniel van Dam and Pieter Jan Tichelaar. Catalogue by Ella Schaap with Robert L. H. Chambers, Marjorie Lee Hendrix, and Joan Pierpoline. Technical notes by Andrew Lins. [Philadelphia], Philadelphia Museum of Art, 1984. 229p. il. (part col.), charts, map.

Catalog of the exhibition, Philadelphia Museum of Art (1984). Many of the tiles are from the collection of Francis P. Garvan. Complete data on each tile. Catalog arrangement is by subject.

Selective contents: A survey of Dutch tiles, by Jan Daniel van Dam; The production of tiles, by Pieter Jan Tichelaar; An essay on conservation and restoration, by Andrew Lins.

P507 Scholten, Frits T. Dutch majolica & Delftware, 1550–1700: the Edwin van Drecht collection, exhibited at the Paleis Lange Voorhout Museum, The Hague. [Pref. by Michael Archer. Foreword by Edwin van Drecht.] 263p. il. (part col.)

In Dutch and English. Book accompanying the exhibition, The Museum (1993–94). Catalog of an important collection of early Dutch majolica and Delftware, including informative introductory essays describing the origin, techniques, and sources of decoration of these wares.

Russia and Eastern Europe

P508 Lobanov-Rostovsky, Nina. Revolutionary ceramics: Soviet porcelain, 1917–1927. London, Studio Vista, 1990. 160p. il. (part col.), ports.

Well-illustrated survey of the porcelains produced in Russia during the first ten years following the Revolution: Avant-garde, inspired by Russian folk arts, or overtly propagandistic.

Chronology, p.142. Biographies of the designers, p.143–47. Artists and other signatures, p.148–53. Initials and monograms, p.154–55. Monograms of unidentified artists, p.155. Factory marks, p.156. The symbols on propaganda porcelain and their meaning, p.157. Bibliography, p.158. Index, p.159–60.

Scandinavia

P509 Opie, Jennifer Hawkins. Scandinavia: ceramics and glass in the twentieth century. N.Y., Rizzoli, [1989]. 183p. il. (part col.), map. (The collections of the Victoria and Albert Museum)

Published in conjunction with the exhibition, Victoria & Albert Museum (1989–90).

Survey of 20th-century ceramics and glass in Norway, Sweden, Denmark, and Finland, based on the Victoria and Albert Museum's collections. Introductory essay for each country is followed by catalog entries for objects.

Biographies and factory histories, p.149–79. Concordance, p.180–81. Index, p.182–83.

Spain and Portugal

P510 Lister, Florence C., and Lister, Robert. Andalusian ceramics in Spain and New Spain: a cultural register from the Third century B.C. to 1700. Tucson, Univ. of Arizona Pr., [1987]. xxv, 411, [1]p. il., maps, tables.

History of the development of pottery in southern Spain, with attention to the contributions of Muslim potters, and its diffusion in Morocco, the Canary Islands, the Indies, and Mexico, or New Spain. Based on extended archeological and documentary research. Includes a chapter devoted to the work routines and daily lives of the potters themselves.

Notable seventeenth-century paintings by Sevillian masters depicting local ceramics, p.[307]–09. Sixteenth-century Spanish shipping records containing references to ceramics and architectural terra cottas, p.[311]–18. Glossary, p.[353]–62. Bibliography, p.[363]–95. Index, p.[396]–411.

P511 Metropolitan Museum of Art. Portugal and porcelain. N.Y., Metropolitan Museum of Art, 1984. 89p. il., 1 map.

Published in conjunction with the exhibition, Metropolitan Museum of Art (1984), organized in collaboration with the Museu Nacional de Arte Antiga (Lisbon) and presenting "the continuum of Portugal's experience of porcelain, from the early sixteenth century . . . to the mid-1930s."—*Foreword.*

P512 Ray, Anthony. Spanish pottery 1248–1898: with a catalogue of the collection in the Victoria and Albert Museum. Catalogue photographs by Pip Barnard. London, V&A Publications, 2000. xiii, 418p. il. (part col.), map.

A concise history of Spanish pottery as well as a catalog of an important collection.

Contents: The pottery of medieval Spain; Sixteenth-century pottery; Seventeenth- and eighteenth-century pottery; Nineteenth-century pottery; Tiles; Modern imitations.

Glossary, p.401. Select bibliography, p.402–08. Concordance of museum and catalogue numbers, p.409–10. Index, p.411–18.

Switzerland

P513 Messerli Bolliger, Barbara E. Keramik in der Schweiz: von den Anfängen bis heute. Zürich, Verlag Neue Zürcher Zeitung, 1993. 186p. il. (part col.)

Economical survey of Swiss ceramics from antiquity to the present.

Anmerkungen, p.178–83. Register, p.184–86.

United States

Bibliography

P514 Strong, Susan R. History of American ceramics: an annotated bibliography. Metuchen, N.J., Scarecrow, 1983. xxii, 184p.

Annotated bibliography of "books (or portions of books), pamphlets, exhibition catalogues, trade catalogs, theses, and dissertations published before 1983" on American ceramics from the colonial period to 1966. Excludes periodical articles and material on clay resources and ceramic technology. Arrangement is by subject.

Author index, p.151–[58]. Title index, p.157–[73]. Subject index, p.174–84.

P515 Weidner, Ruth Irwin, comp. American ceramics before 1930: a bibliography. Westport, Greenwood, [1982]. xx, [281]p., chart. (Art reference collection, 2)

Bibliography of materials published in America through December 1980 relating to American pottery and porcelain made before 1930, with primary emphasis on decorative ceramics. Includes periodical articles. Arrangement is by type of source.

Contents: (A) Books and pamphlets; (B) Conference proceedings and chapters from books; (C) Catalogs of exhibitions, collections, and sales; (D) Theses and dissertations; (E) Federal, state, and municipal publications; (F) Trade publications; (G) Periodical articles.

Guide to selected American clayworking, ceramics, china painting, and crockery journals before 1930, p.216–21. Author index, p.223–37. Subject index, p.239–79.

Dictionaries and Encyclopedias

P516 DeBolt, C. Gerald. The dictionary of American pottery marks: whiteware and porcelain. Rutland, Tuttle, [1988]. [v], 153p. il.

Illustrated dictionary of marks on American porcelain and whitewares to ca. 1930. Includes discussions of fakes, some British marks, and distinguishing characteristics of American marks. A useful resource for collectors.

Bibliography, p.115. Index, p.117–53.

P517 Derwich, Jenny B., and Latos, Dr. Mary. Dictionary guide to United States pottery and porcelain (19th and 20th century) (with 96 full-color photographs). Franklin, Mich., Jenstan Research in United States Pottery and Porcelain; Bloomfield Hills, Mich., Research in American Ceramics, [1984]. 276p., col. il.

Dictionary of American potters and manufacturers, especially helpful for collectors and for information on obscure makers and firms.

Bibliography, p.258–59.

P518 Evans, Paul. Art pottery of the United States: an encyclopedia of producers and their marks, together with a directory of studio potters working in the United States through 1960. 2d ed., rev. and enlarged. N.Y., Feingold & Lewis, [1987]. [6], 445p. il., col. plates, ports.

Updated ed. of the standard work on American art pottery, first published in 1974.

Authoritative, well-documented resource on American art potteries, arranged by name of firm or maker. Includes studio pottery of the 20th century.

Geographical listing of art potteries, p.405–06. Vital statistics of significant art pottery figures, p.406–07. Expositions involving art pottery of the United States, p.407. Bibliography of principal reference works cited in the text, p.407–08. Substantive changes made in original text, p.408. A directory of studio potters working in the United States through 1960, compiled from lists of entrants in the Robineau Memorial/National Ceramic Exhibitions and from other sources as noted, p.409–35. Index, p.436–44.

P519 Lehner, Lois. Lehner's encyclopedia of U.S. marks on pottery, porcelain and clay. [Paducah], Collector Books, [1988]. 634p. il.

Dictionary of "over 1,900 companies, potters, potteries with more than 8,000 marks, logos, symbols, etc. divided about equally among the old folk potters, studio potters, dinnerware manufacturers, selling agencies or distributors, decorative or art pottery, decorators, decorating companies and decorative tile."—*p.4.* Coverage extends to the late 20th century.

Definitions, p.533–34. Companies listed by location, p.535–53. Miscellaneous lists of various types of manufacturers, p.554–71. Railroad letters and symbols, p.572–[75]. Syracuse National winners, p.576–81. Electrical porcelain insulator markings, p.581–87. Bibliography, p.588–600. Index, p.601–34.

Histories and Handbooks

P520 American ceramics: the collection of the Everson Museum of Art. Ed. by Barbara Perry. Syracuse, Everson Museum; N.Y., Rizzoli, [1989]. 400p. il. (part col.)

A survey of the outstanding holdings of the Everson Museum, long known for its excellence in this field, with essays by specialist contributors. Reflects the strength of the Museum's 20th-century objects, and especially valuable for that coverage.

Contents: Ancient American ceramics, by Barbara Perry; American ceramics 1700–1880: Part I, Early pottery and porcelain, by William C. Ketchum, Jr.; Part II, Early potters of Syracuse and Onondaga County, by Richard G. Case; Art pottery 188–1920, by Ulysses G. Dietz; American ceramics 1920–1950, by Barbara Perry; American ceramics since 1950, by Garth Clark.

Contributors, p.343. Bibliography, compiled by Rosemary Romano, p.384–97. Index, p.398–400.

P521 Branin, M. Lelyn. The early potters and potteries of Maine. Middletown, Conn., Wesleyan Univ. Pr., [1978]. xvii, 262p., 34p. of illus., 2p. map, tables.

Thoroughly researched town-by-town account of potteries in Maine from their late-18th-century origins to the end of the 19th century, with emphasis on utilitarian wares. Valuable appendixes on mills and kilns, marks, prices, potters, pottery owners, and manufacturers.

Index, p.[250]–62.

P522 ———. The early makers of handcrafted earthenware and stoneware in southern New Jersey. Rutherford, Fairleigh Dickinson Univ. Pr., [1988]. 266p. il., maps, plans.

Comprehensive account of southern New Jersey potteries in the 18th and 19th centuries, based on extensive archival research. Valuable appendixes on manufacturing statistics, local records, business practices, prices, inventories, pottery facilities.

Suggested readings, p.256. Index, p.257–66.

P523 Broderick, Warren F., and Bouck, William. Pottery works: potteries of New York State's Capital District and Upper Hudson region. Madison, N.J., Fairleigh Dickinson Univ. Pr., [1995]. 285p. il., maps.

History of earthenware and stoneware potteries in New York's Albany, Rensselaer, Saratoga, and Washington counties from their origins to the early 20th century, based on extensive archival research. Arrangement is by locality. Appendixes on marks, etc.

Bibliography, p.271–73. Index, p.274–85.

P524 Bruhn, Thomas P. American decorative tiles, 1870–1930. Exhibition and catalogue by Thomas P. Bruhn. Storrs, Conn., William Benton Museum of Art, 1979. 48p. il.

Concise but informative catalog for an exhibition of American decorative tiles, arranged alphabetically by maker or factory, with an introduction placing these wares in context. Catalog entries include bibliographical references.

Bibliography, p.14.

P525 Burrison, John A. Brothers in clay: the story of Georgia folk pottery. Athens, Univ. of Georgia Pr., [1983]. xviii, 326p. il., 12 col. plates, ports., map.

Comprehensive history of Georgia pottery from the 18th century to the present day. Includes descriptions of the business and technologies of potting, a statewide survey of potters and potteries by location, and interviews with present-day craftsmen.

Respondents, p.[301]–03. Selected bibliography, p.[305]–07. Checklist and index of Georgia folk potters, p.[309]–21. General index, p.[323]–26.

P526 Clark, Garth. American ceramics, 1876 to the present. [Rev. ed.] N.Y., Abbeville, [1987]. 351p. il. (part col.), ports.

Rev. ed. of A century of ceramics in the United States, 1878–1978. N.Y., Dutton in assoc. with the Everson Museum of Art, 1979.

Updated and expanded version of this noted ceramics historian's overview of American ceramics from the Centennial to the 1980s. Especially valuable for its coverage of recent work and for its many biographical sketches, extensive bibliography, and excellent illustrations. Arrangement is by decade.

Chronology, p.241–44. Selected exhibitions, p.245–50. Biographies, p.251–311. Index to bibliography, p.312–24. Bibliography, p.325–41. Index, p.342–51.

P527 Comstock, Harold Eugene. The pottery of the Shenandoah Valley region. Chapel Hill, Univ. of North Carolina Pr., [1994]. 538p. il. (part col.), maps (The Frank L. Horton series)

Comprehensive study of the pottery of this western Virginia area by a long-time collector, valuable for collectors and historians alike. Includes detailed discussions of the potters, their shops, and their working methods.

Contents: (I) The setting; (II) The Shenandoah Valley pottery trade; (III) The pottery; (IV) The potters.

Pottery scales, inventories, and price lists used by Shenadoah Valley potters, p.503–14. Glossary, p.515–17. Bibliography, p.519–21. Index, p.523–38.

P528 Cunningham, Jo. The collector's encyclopedia of American dinnerware. Paducah, Collector Books, [1982]. 319p. il. (part col.)

Selective encyclopedia of the major manufacturers of mass-produced whitewares in American during the 19th and 20th centuries and their most popular patterns. Illustrations include marks and period advertising matter. Includes illustrated discussion of "How dinnerware is made" (p.10–16), and on advertising pieces. Listing is by company name. "Price guide to the Collector's Encyclopedia of American Dinnerware: Value guide 4189" laid in.

Glossary, p.312–16. Index, p.317–19.

P529 Darling, Sharon. Chicago ceramics and glass: an illustrated history from 1871 to 1933. Artifacts photographed by Walter W. Krutz. Chicago, Chicago Hist. Soc., 1979. xiii, 221p. il., (part col.), ports.

Detailed, informative book accompanying the loan exhibition, Chicago Historical Society (1979–80). Provides information on many manufacturers and individual artisans working in Chicago during a period of great creativity in these arts.

Contents: (1) Decorative arts: Introduction to decorative arts; Handpainted china; Art pottery; Cut and engraved glass; (2) Architectural arts: Introduction to architectural arts; Stained and ornamental glass; Architectural terra cotta.

Other shops and craftworkers, p.205–09. Sources, p.211–13. Index, p.215–21.

P530 Denker, Ellen, and Denker, Bert. The Main Street pocket guide to North American pottery and porcelain. Pittstown, N.J., Main Street, [1985]. 256p. il., 50 col. plates.

Originally pub. as The Warner collector's guide to North American pottery and porcelain. N.Y., Warner Books, 1981.

Compact, well-illustrated collectors' field guide to American and Canadian ceramics, from early utilitarian pottery to 20th-century mass-produced dinnerwares, arranged by type of ware.

Selected bibliography, p.250–51. Index, p.252–56.

P531 Detweiler, Susan Gray. George Washington's chinaware. With prologue and epilogue by Christine Meadows. N.Y., Abrams, [1982]. 244p. il. (part col.), genealogical charts. (A Barra Foundation/Mount Vernon Ladies' Association book)

Through examination of this exceedingly well-documented collection of ceramics, the authors illuminate not only George Washington's own private life and personal tastes in household furnishings but the preferences and usages of other well-to-do 18th-century Americans as well. Also discusses commerce, foodways, and social conventions of the period.

The documents, p.[199]–221. Bibliography, p.[222]–30. Brief Custis family genealogy, p.[233]. Brief Washington family genealogy, p.[234]–[35]. Index, p.[236]–44.

P532 Frelinghuysen, Alice Cooney. American porcelain, 1770–1920. N.Y., Metropolitan Museum of Art (Distr. by Abrams, [1989]). xv, 320p. il. (part col.)

Published in conjunction with the exhibition, Metropolitan Museum of Art (1989).

Substantial publication documenting a major exhibition of American porcelain and serving as a history of this form as it developed in this country, from its 18th-century beginnings to the work of 20th-century art potters.

Bibliography, p.303–09. Index, p.310–19.

P533 Greer, Georgeanna Herman. American stonewares: the art and craft of utilitarian potters. Exton, Penn., Schiffer, 1981. 286p. il.

Survey of American utilitarian stoneware, with a focus on European origins.

Some general keys for stoneware identification, p.263–64. Glossary of ceramic terms, p.265–68. An annotated bibliography for American stonewares, p.269–75. Bibliography, p.277–80. Index, p.281–86.

P534 Henzke, Lucile. Art pottery of America. Rev. 3d ed. Exton, Penn., Schiffer, 1999. 368p. il. (part col.) (A Schiffer book for collectors)
1st ed. titled American art pottery. Camden, T. Nelson, 1970; 2d ed. under the present title, Exton, Schiffer,1982.
"A chronology of events from the beginning to the time the potteries closed their doors."—*Introd.* Presented alphabetically by name of pottery.
Bibliography, p.361. Index of lines and patterns, p.362–64. Index of pottery locations, p.364. General index, p.364–68.

P535 Ketchum, William C., Jr. Potters and potteries of New York State, 1650–1900. 2d ed. [Syracuse], Syracuse Univ. Pr., [1987]. x, 626p. il.
Rev. ed. of Early potters and potteries of New York State. N.Y., Funk & Wagnalls, 1970.
Comprehensive history and survey by region of utilitarian potters working in New York State through the end of the 19th century. Introductory essays discuss forms, methods, and materials. Listing of potters transcribes but does not illustrate marks.
A list of New York potters and their marks, p.453–509. Potters working in New York State, seventeenth to twentieth centuries, p.511–80. Bibliography, p.581–608. Index, p.609–26.

P536 Lehner, Lois. Complete book of American kitchen and dinner wares. [Des Moines, Wallace-Homestead, 1980]. 240p. il., port.
History of "the companies that follow the mechanization of the dinnerware and kitchenware industry"—*p.8.* Emphasis is on mass-produced tablewares of the 20th century, or whiteware, listed by name of company. Excludes hand-thrown pottery and art pottery. Illustrates marks, but does not list detailed pattern information.
Chronology of whiteware production developments, p.9–10. A few definitions, p.11–13. Understanding practices of the potteries, p.16–17. A note about cookie jars, p.18. Various aspects of the pottery industry, p.19. List of shapes, decorations, lines, and type of ware, p.201–17. Further suggested reading, p.218–19. Bibliography, p.220–28. Index of factories, p.229–39. About the author, p.240.

P537 ———. Ohio pottery and glass marks and manufacturers. Des Moines, Wallace-Homestead, [1978]. 113p. il.
Alphabetical listing of all known pottery and glass makers and manufacturers working in Ohio to the present day. Includes illustrations of marks and in some cases decorators' marks. Arrangement is by location.
Alphabetical listing of factories, p.4–12. Index of hard to identify marks, p.103–08. Bibliography of books, p.109–10. Centennial and special publications, p.111. Company history furnished by the companies, p.111. Magazines and periodicals, p.112–13.

P538 Montgomery Museum of Art. The traditional pottery of Alabama. Montgomery, Montgomery Museum of Art, 1983. 70p. il. (part col.)
Catalog of the exhibition, Montgomery Museum of Art (1983), documenting "the growth and history of Alabama pottery from its inception . . . through the traditional potters of today."
Selected bibliography, p.47–48.

P539 Myers, Susan H. Handcraft to industry: Philadelphia ceramics in the first half of the nineteenth century. Washington, D.C., Smithsonian Institution Pr., 1980. iii, 117p. il., map (Smithsonian studies in history and technology, no. 48).
History of the production of pottery in Philadelphia from the War of 1812 to mid-century, with emphasis on the economic and technological changes that transformed the industry during this period.
Checklist of Philadelphia potters, 1800–1850, p.50–90. Census statistics on manufactures, p.91–96. Potters' inventories, p.97–104. References, p.111–17.

P540 Sweezy, Nancy. Raised in clay: the Southern pottery tradition. Washington, D.C., Smithsonian Institution Pr., 1984. 280p. il. (part col.)
Published in conjunction with the exhibition, Smithsonian Institution (1984), and other locations. Survey of Southern potters.
Bibliography, by Stuart C. Schwartz, p.273–80.

P541 Whisker, James Biser. Pennsylvania potters, 1660–1900. Lewiston, Edwin Mellen Pr., [1993]. 330p.
Alphabetical listing of potters and pottery manufacturers working in Pennsylvania to 1900, based on extensive archival research, including city directory, census and tax records.
Bibliography, p.[305]–30.

P542 Zug, Charles G., III. Turners and burners: the folk potters of North Carolina. Chapel Hill, Univ. of North Carolina Pr., [1986]. xxi, 450p. il., 20 col. plates, map, genealogical charts, ports. (The Fred W. Morrison series in Southern culture)
Comprehensive, thorough account of folk potters and their wares in North Carolina from their beginnings to the present day, based on archival research and interviews with today's traditional potters.
Contents: (1) History; (2) Technology; (3) Culture.
Bibliography, p.[429]–34. Index of North Carolina potters, p.[435]–47. General index, p.[448]–50.

Asian Countries

China

P543 Beurdeley, Cecile, and Beurdeley, Michel. A connoisseur's guide to Chinese ceramics. Trans. by Katherine Watson. [Drawings by Danica Peter.] [Reprint.] N.Y., Alpine Fine Arts Collection, [1984]. 317p. il. (part col.)
Reprint of GLAH 1:P359. Printed in Hong Kong, lacking the glossy paper used in the original ed. (printed in Switzerland).

P544 The ceramics of China: the Yangshao culture, the Song dynasty. Compiled by Yang Gen, Zhang Xiqiu, Shao Wengu. Beijing, Science Pr.; London, Methuen Pr., 1985. vi, 179p. col. il.

Traces the early history of ceramics in China from the neolithic age through the Song dynasty (960–1279). In addition to full color images of objects and an introductory text, the book includes several useful tables of technical information such as chemical compositions and kiln characteristics.

P545 Curtis, Julia B. Chinese porcelains of the seventeenth century: landscapes, scholars' motifs and narratives. With an essay by Stephen Little. N.Y., China Institute Gallery, China Institute [Distr. by Univ. of Washington Pr., 1995]. 168p. il. (part col.)

Summary in Chinese. Catalog of the exhibition, China Institute Gallery (1995).

Discusses the porcelains made at Jingdezhen between 1630 and 1700, which reflect, through iconography and decorative style, the profound economic and social transformations occuring in 17th-century China. Through essays and a catalog of the objects, the book explores the themes of landscapes, scholar-official and scholars' motifs, and scholars' narratives.

Select bibliography, p.163–65.

P546 Garnsey, Wanda, with Rewi Alley. China: ancient kilns and modern ceramics; a guide to the potteries. Canberra, Australian National Univ. Pr., 1983. xiii, 144p., il. (part col.), maps.

After an introductory essay, the book is organized geographically, providing a guide to potteries in 16 Chinese provinces. Intended as "an illustrated book giving a general description of Chinese ceramics, which is interesting to the layman and yet informative enough for those who are practicing potters."—*Pref.*

Bibliography, p.137–38.

P547 Gompertz, G. St. G. M. Chinese celadon wares. 2d ed., rev. and exp. and reset. London, Faber and Faber, 1980. 216p. il. (part col.), plates. (Faber monographs on pottery and porcelain)

See GLAH 1:P363 for original annotation.

P548 Gray, Basil. Sung porcelain and stoneware. London, Faber and Faber, [1984]. 205p. il. (part col.), plates, map. (Faber monographs on pottery and porcelain)

Incorporates archeological discoveries made since the author's Early Chinese pottery and porcelain (GLAH 1:P364).

Basic guide to the porcelain and stoneware produced during the period from the 10th to the end of the 13th century. Kiln sites and techniques are discussed as well as artistic, historic, and social context.

Bibliography, p.196–99. Index, p.200–05.

P549 In pursuit of the dragon: traditions and transitions in Ming ceramics: an exhibition from the Idemitsu Museum of Arts. Seattle, Seattle Art Museum, [1988]. 160p. il. (part col.)

Catalog of the exhibition, Seattle Art Museum (1988), and other locations. "Traces the development of ceramic styles from the Yuan to the Ming dynasties and documents the full flowering of Ming ceramics production."—*Foreword.*

With the dragon occurring in many of the objects as the main or secondary decorative motif, the title reflects that this catalog is also an iconographic study of the mythical beast through artists' interpretations during several periods and ceramic styles.

Selective contents: Advances in Jingdezhen research, by Tadanori Yuba; Fourteenth century and early Ming blue and white porcelain, by John Ayers; Polychrome wares of the Ming dynasty, by Henry Trubner.

Suggested reading, p.160.

P550 Jenyns, Soame. Ming pottery and porcelain. 2d ed. London, Faber, 1988. xviii, 237p. il. (part col.) (Faber monographs on pottery and porcelain)

See GLAH 1:P370 for original annotation. The 2d ed. includes a Foreword by Margaret Medley, and Introduction by William Watson, and additional color plates. Minor errors have been corrected, some substitute illustrations included, and the bibliography revised and updated.

P551 Jorg, Christiaan J. A. Chinese ceramics in the collection of the Rijksmuseum, Amsterdam: the Ming and Qing dynasties. London, Philip Wilson, 1997. 352p. il. (part col.)

Scholarly catalog of an important collection.

Bibliography, p.331–44. Index, p.345–52.

P552 Kerr, Rose. Chinese ceramics, porcelains of the Qing dynasty 1644–1911. Photography by Ian Thomas. [London], Victoria and Albert Museum, [1986]. 142p. il. (part col.), map. (Far Eastern series)

Using examples from the Victoria and Albert Museum's collection, this study serves as an introduction to Qing ceramics with a focus on pieces made for use in China. Discusses the porcelain center of Jingdezhen in southern China, the marks on Qing dynasty porcelain, and the decorative programs typical for objects made through both high-fired and low-fired techniques. Generously illustrated with a readable discussion of the historical, technical, and aesthetic aspects.

Select bibliography, p.136.

P553 Krahl, Regina. Chinese ceramics from the Meiyintang collection. London, Azimuth, 1994. 2v. col. il., maps.

"The Meiyintang collection consists mainly of Chinese ceramics and was assembled over a period of some forty years. . . . The first volume of this catalogue contains mainly earthenwares and stonewares from the Neolithic period to the Song dynasty . . . the second porcelains from the Yuan . . . to the Qing dynasty. Although the two volumes belong together, they are conceived as individual books, each with its own working bibliography."—*Pref.*

Bibliography, v.1, p.338–43; v.2, p.316–19.

P554 Kuwayama, George, ed. New perspectives on the art of ceramics in China. Los Angeles, Far Eastern Council, Los Angeles County Museum of Art, [Distr. by the Univ. of Hawaii Pr., 1992]. 156p. il.

Seven selected papers from a symposium, Los Angeles Country Museum of Art (1989), in conjunction with the exhibitions "Imperial Taste: Chinese Ceramics from the Percival David Foundation" and "In Pursuit of the Dragon: Traditions and Transitions in Ming Ceramics."

Notes at ends of papers.

P555 Li, He. Chinese ceramics: a new comprehensive survey from the Asian Art Museum of San Francisco. N.Y., Thames and Hudson, 1996. 352p. il. (part col.), maps.

U.K. ed. titled: Chinese ceramics: the new standard guide.

"The purpose of this book—based as it is on the comprehensive collection of Chinese ceramics in the Asian Art Museum of San Francisco—is to serve the general reader, the educator, the connoisseur, and the scholarly researcher."—*Introd.*

Contents: (I) The Neolithic Period to the Five Dynasties; (II) The Liao-Song-Jin-Yuan Periods (10th–14th centuries); (III) The Ming Dynasty (1368–1644); (IV) The Qing dynasty to the Republic (1644–early 20th century).

Chronology of China, p.334. Glossary, p.335–38. Bibliography, p.339–40. Museums with major collections of Chinese ceramics, p.341. List of Chinese characters, p.342–45. Index, p.346–52.

P556 Liu, Liang-yu. Ch'ing official and popular wares: a survey of Chinese ceramics = Chung-kuo li tai t'ao tz'u chien shang. T'ai-pei, Aries Gemini Publishing Ltd., 1991–92. 5v. col. il., maps.

Text in English. List of plates also in Chinese.

Contents: (1) Early wares: prehistoric to tenth century; (2) Sung wares; (3) Liao, Hsi-Hsia, Chin and Yuan wares; (4) Ming official wares; (5) Ch'ing official and popular wares.

Includes bibliographical references in Chinese.

P557 Lo, K. S. The stonewares of Yixing: from the Ming period to the present day. With an index of potters, artistic collaborators and collectors comp. by Lai Suk Lee and Ip Wing Chi. N.Y., Sotheby's; Hong Kong, Hong Kong Univ. Pr., [1986]. 287p. il. (part col.), maps.

A study of the Yixing teapots that "have played an important part in Chinese social and cultural life in general, and in that of the scholar class in particular, over the past five hundred years."—*Pref.* Written by a collector, this scholarly work includes information on craftsmen, patrons, styles, and the production, decoration, and function of the objects.

Notes on the text, p.255–57. Bibliography, p.258–59. Chronology of dynasties and reigns, p.260. Index of potters, artistic collaborators and collectors, p.261. General index, p.283–87.

P558 London University. Percival David Foundation of Chinese Art. Illustrated catalogue of [ceramics] in the Percival David Foundation of Chinese art. Rev. ed. London, The Foundation, 1991– . (1)v.

See GLAH 1:P373 for original annotation. The thorough revision of the text and illustrations was prepared by Rosemary E. Scott, and includes new work on identifying and translating the seals and inscriptions on a number of pieces. The revision uses the pinyin rather than Wade-Giles romanization of Chinese characters, with even the title altered. The bibliography has been expanded, the images integrated into the text, and color illustrations added.

Contents: (2) Ch'ing enamelled wares, by Lady David (1991).

P559 Medley, Margaret. The Chinese potter: a practical history of Chinese ceramics. 3d ed. Oxford, Phaidon, 1989. 288p. il. (part col.), plates.

See GLAH 1:P375 for original annotation and 1st ed.; 2d ed. 1982.

P560 ______. T'ang pottery and porcelain. London, Faber, 1981. 151p. il., plates, map. (Faber monographs on pottery and porcelain)

A useful early study produced before extensive archeological work was available for this important period. Introduces the change from earthenware to stoneware, the voluptuous shapes, the realistic depictions in tomb figures, and the bright coloring typical of the lead-glazed wares.

Contents: (1) Introduction; (2) The lead-glazed and unglazed earthenwares; (3) Lead-glazed and unglazed earthenware figures; (4) Northern high-fired wares; (5) Southern wares; (6) Yüeh wares; (7) Laio wares.

Select bibliography, p.[145]–46. Index, p.147–51.

P561 Mowry, Robert D. Hare's fur, tortoiseshell, and partridge feathers: Chinese brown-and black-glazed ceramics, 400–1400. With contrib. by Eugene Farrell and Nicole Coolidge Rousmaniere. Cambridge, Harvard Univ. Art Museums, [1996]. 280p., il. (part col.), map.

Catalog of the exhibition, Sackler Museum (1995–6), and other locations.

Introduces China's dark-glazed ceramics and trace their evolution from the 5th to the 15th century. The text indicates that, although largely ignored in Ming and Qing China, the dark-glazed wares were admired by the Japanese where they were associated with the tea ceremony and served as models for tea ceramics.

Selected bibliography, p.272–79.

P562 Vainker, S. J. Chinese pottery and porcelain: from prehistory to the present. London, British Museum Pr., 1991. 240p. il. (part col.), maps.

A historical survey of Chinese stoneware, porcelain, and religious sculpture from neolithic to modern time using examples from the Museum's collection. Includes appendices on clays, glazes, kilns, and firing.

Bibliography, p.228–32. Index, p.233–40.

P563 Valenstein, Suzanne G. A handbook of Chinese ceramics. Rev. and enl. ed. N.Y., Metropolitan Museum of Art (Distr. by Abrams, [1989]). xxvii, 331p. il. (part col.), plates.

See GLAH 1:P378 for original annotation. The 2d ed., partially rewritten and much-enlarged, includes such additions as an index, more illustrations, and new information derived from recent archeological investigations.

P564 Watson, William. Pre-Tang ceramics of China: Chinese pottery from 4000 BC to 600 AD. Boston, Faber and Faber, [1991]. 237p. il. (part col.), maps. (Faber monographs on pottery and porcelain)

Traces the history of Chinese pottery from its earliest appearance until the eve of the T'ang dynasty with a concentration on the shapes and ornament of vessels. "The information used in this book comes almost entirely from excavation reports and other studies made by Chinese scholars."—*Pref.* Organized by regional zones.

Bibliography, p.231–32. Index, p.233–37.

Japan

P565 Baekeland, Frederick, and Moes, Robert. Modern Japanese ceramics in American collections. N.Y., Japan Society, 1993. 206p. il. (part col.)

Catalog of the exhibition, Japan Society Gallery and other locations (1993–94). The objects in the exhibition are described as traditional glaze styles, Chinese-influenced, nontraditional functional, or ceramic sculpture.

Contents: Modern Japanese studio ceramics and their development, by Frederick Baekeland; Classical traditions of modern Japanese ceramics, by Robert Moes; Japanese ceramics: forms, functions and methods of production, by Frederick Baekeland; Modern Japanese studio ceramics in Great Britain and their representation in the Victoria and Albert Museum, by Robert Faulkner; Japanese public collections of modern ceramics and their direction: from a museum curator's viewpoint, by Kazunobu Nakanodô; Modern Japanese studio ceramics in Germany, by Masako Shono-Sladek; and Western influences on modern Japanese ceramics: a potter's point of view, by Gerd Knäpper.

Museums in the United States with contemporary Japanese art by potters, p.192. Potters in exhibition represented in museums in the United States, p.192–93. Select bibliography, p.194–98. Index, p.200–06.

P566 Collections Baur: Japanese ceramics. By John Ayers. Geneve, Collections Baur, [1982]. [184]p. il. (part col.)

Introductory essay in English and French.

The essay, by the former Keeper at the Victoria and Albert Museum, provides both a history of this portion of the Alfred Baur collection and a general introduction to Japanese ceramics. The bulk of the book is a catalog of the 133 items in the collection, mainly an assemblage of wares dating from the 17th–19th centuries. Each piece is photographed, described, and often compared to pieces in other collections.

P567 Cort, Louise Allison. Seto and Mino ceramics. Washington, D.C., Freer Gallery of Art, Smithsonian Institution, 1992. 254p. il., col. plates, maps. (Japanese collections in the Freer Gallery of Art)

An introductory essay on the ceramic centers of Seto and Mino and the collecting practices of the Freer Collection is followed by the catalog of 126 pieces from the Freer. The catalog is arranged chronologically, with works ranging from the 7th century through the Meiji period. Each piece is illustrated, and the accompanying text describes the ware, the clay body, glaze, and decoration.

Bibliography, p. 230–32. Concordance of catalogue and accession numbers, p.248–50. Index, p.251–54.

P568 Famous ceramics of Japan. Tokyo, Kodansha, 1981–84. 12v. il. col. plates, maps.

Issued originally in Japanese as the series Nihon no Yakimono, conceived by the ceramic historian and potter Koyama Fujimio (1900–1975), and published in 26 vols. by Kodansha between 1975–77.

The English-language version consists of tall, slender volumes, each treating a ceramic center in Japan describing the history and characteristics, the kilns, distinctive glazes, and decorations. Each tome consists of a short introductory text, an abundance of colored plates, plate notes, and maps.

Contents: (1) Imaizumi, Motosuke. Nabeshima (1981); (2) Kozuru, Gen. Agano and Takatori (1981); (3–4) Mizuo, Hiroshi. Folk kilns (1981); (5) Nagatake, Takeshi. Kakiemon (1981); (6) Nagatake, Takeshi. Imari (1982); (7) Sawada, Yoshihary. Tokoname (1982); (8) Murayama, Takeshi. Oribe (1982); (9) Nakazato, Taroemon. Karatsu (1983); (10) Furukawa, Shosaku. Kiseo and Setoguro (1983); (11) Kawano, Ryosuke. Hagi (1983); (12) Kuroda, Ryoji. Shino (1984).

P569 Jenyns, Soame. Japanese porcelain. London, Faber and Faber, 1965. xiii, 351p. plates, map (Faber monographs on pottery and porcelain) (Repr.: 1979).

"First full-length study of the subject in English."—*Foreword.*

Now the standard study for the topic. Describes the various porcelain types, the export trade, and the influence of Chinese porcelain. Plates are grouped together at the end of the text.

Bibliography, p. 321–23.

P570 Kenrick, Douglas. Jomon of Japan: the world's oldest pottery. Routledge, Chapman and Hall, 1995. xviii, 144p., il. (part col.), maps.

Using carbon-14 methods, Jomon pottery has been dated from 10,000 to 300 B.C. thus justifying the subtitle of this book. After an initial discussion of scientific dating and the phases of the Jomon period, the text describes pottery techniques, styles, and decoration. Nicely illustrated.

End notes, p.64–71. Bibliography, 72–74. Index, p.142–44.

P571 Klein, Adalbert. A connoisseur's guide to Japanese ceramics. Trans. by Katherine Watson. London, Alpine Fine Arts Collection, [1987]. 275p. il. (part col.), maps.

Trans. of Japanische Keramik von de Jomon-Zeit bis zur Gegenwart. Fribourg, Office du Livre, 1984.

Traces the history of Japanese ceramics from Jomon culture (5th millennium B.C.) to the 20th century along with chapters on tea ceremony vessels, legends, style, and techniques. Includes earthenware, stoneware, and porcelain by potters, sculptors, and designers.

Notes, p.251–56. Selected bibliography, p.257–60. Chronological table, p.261. Names and dates of reigning emperors starting in 1501, p.262. Marks, p.262. Glossary, p.263–64. Index, p.271–74.

P572 Wilson, Richard L. Inside Japanese ceramics: a primer of materials, techniques and traditions. N.Y., Weatherhill, 1995. 190p. il. (part col.), plates, map.

Intended to span the gap between historical and ethnographical accounts of Japanese ceramics, this book provides an English-language introduction to the tools, materials, and techniques of Japanese ceramics. Photographs detail step-by-step processes.

Contents: Of craft and life; Setting up; Forming; Decoration; Glazes; Kilns and firing; Five traditional approaches; Japanese methods and western potters.

Works consulted, p.183–84. Index, p.185–89.

Southeast Asia

P573 Art Gallery of South Australia. South-east Asian ceramics: Thai, Vietnamese, and Khmer: from the collection of the Art Gallery of South Australia. [By] Dick Richards. Photography by Clayton Glen. N.Y., Oxford Univ. Pr., 1995. xiv, 196p. il. (part col.), map. (The Asia collection)

A record of more than 300 pieces from the collection, which is "strongest in its Thai holdings, followed by Vietnamese and then Khmer."—*Pref.*

Contents: (1) Introduction; (2) Thailand; (3) Vietnam; (4) Cambodia; (5) Epilogue; The wares.

Select bibliography, p.185–191. Index, p.192–96.

P574 Guy, John S. Oriental trade ceramics in South-East Asia, ninth to sixteenth centuries: with a catalogue of Chinese, Vietnamese and Thai wares in Australian collections. N.Y., Oxford University Press, 1986. xiv, 161p. il. (part col.) (Oxford in Asia studies in ceramics)

Rev. and exp. version of a publication published in conjunction with the exhibition, National Gallery of Victoria, Australia (1980), titled Oriental trade ceramics in Southeast Asia, 10th to 16th century.

Comparative chronology, p.142. Glossary, p.143–44. Select bibliography, p.145–59. Index, p.160–61.

P575 Harrisson, Barbara. Later ceramics in South-East Asia. N.Y., Oxford Univ. Pr., 1995. xxii, 116p. il. (part col.), maps, plates. (Oxford in Asia studies in ceramics)

"The present text describes ceramics from the sixteenth century to the twentieth, most of which are former heirlooms."—*Introd.* Successor vol. to Guy, Oriental trade ceramics in South-East Asia (GLAH 2:P574).

Contents: (1) The Swatow style: favourite in South-East Asia, 1550–1650; (2) The wares of Jingdezhen: trend-setter world-wide, 1550–1700; (3) Wares of special character, 1550–1750; (4) Chinese porcelain: splendid and plain, 1700–1930; (5) Painted and printed wares, 1700–1930; (6) The colour of the present, 1860–1960; Epilogue; Appendix.

Bibliography, p.106–13. Index, p.114–16.

P576 Stevenson, John, and Guy, John. Vietnamese ceramics: a separate tradition. With contrib. by Louise Allison Cort . . . [et al.] [Chicago,] Art Media Resources, with Avery Pr., 1997. 422p. il. (part col.)

A collection of essays that seeks to "define more precisely the nature of Vietnam's relationship with China: the shared aspects and those unique to Vietnam."—*p.11.*

Contents: (1) Vietnamese ceramics and cultural identity, by John Guy; (2) The evolution of Vietnamese ceramics, by John Stevenson; (3) Vietnamese ceramics in international trade, by John Guy; (4) Vietnamese ceramics in Japanese contexts, by Louise Allison Cort; (5) Kilns of Northern Vietnam, by Morimoto Asako; (6) From prehistory to Han, by Philippe Truong; (7) Ivory-glazed wares of Ly and Tran, by John Stevenson; (8) Vietnamese celadons and their relationship to the celadons of Southern China, by Peter Lam; (9) Vietnamese blue-and-white and related wares, by Regina Krahl; (10) Ceramics used in a Buddhist context, by Trian Nguyen; Appendix 1: Limepots, by Philippe Truong; Appendix 2: Bleu du Hue, by Philippe Truong; Appendix 3: Toward a chronology: dated and datable Vietnamese ceramics, by Nguyen Dinh Chien and John Guy.

Bibliography, p.410–16. Index, p.417–22.

Africa, Oceania, The Americas

Africa

P577 Barley, Nigel. Smashing pots: feats of clay from Africa. [London], British Museum Pr., [1994]. 168p. il. (part col.)

An informative resource book with excellent color plates covering pottery forms and types from Morocco to South Africa.

Contents: (1) The techniques of potting; (2) Potters and the earth; (3) Male and female in the making of pots; (4) The role of pots; (5) Vessels of spirit; (6) Pots as instruments of harmony; (7) Decoration and innovation; (8) Motifs, motivation and motives; (9) New pots for old; (10) Postscript: pots as feats of clay.

Bibliography, p.161–65. Index, p.166–68.

P578 Berns, Marla C., and Hudson, Barbara Rubin. The essential gourd: art and history in northeastern Nigeria. Los Angeles, Museum of Cultural History, UCLA [1986]. 190p. 38 col. plates. 151 il., maps.

Catalog of the exhibition, Wight Art Gallery, UCLA (1986), and other locations.

The standard survey on the history, uses, techniques, designs, meaning of gourd decorations, and their relationship to other artistic traditions.

Contents: (1) Introduction; (2) An ethnography of gourd use; (3) An ethnography of gourd decoration; (4) The Ga'anda; (5) Decorated gourds and history; (6) Gourds and modern change; Appendix, Word lists by language family.

Bibliography, p.186–90.

P579 Chappel, T. J. H. Decorated gourds in north-eastern Nigeria. [London], Ethnographica, 1977. 222p. il. (part col.), map.

In this part of Africa, "decorated gourds may be classified as a major graphic system."—*Introd.* Research was conducted for the Nigerian Federal Department of Antiquities.

Contents: (1) The area and its peoples; (2) The gourd and its uses; (3) Decorative techniques and designs; (4) Gourd designs and their meanings; (5) Carving as an individual activity; (6) Carving as a social and cultural activity; (7) The appreciation of decorated gourds; (8) Gourd-carving and modern change; Appendix A: Carving exercises; Appendix B: The aesthetic appreciation of decorated gourds.

Bibliography, p.216–18. Index, p.220–22.

P580 Stössel, Arnulf. Nupe Kakanda Basa-Nge. [Gefässkeramik aus Zentral-Nigeria]. Wissenschaftliche Bearb. und Text, Arnulf Stössel. [Malcolm Leybourne (Übersetz.)]. München, Galerie Biedermann, 1981. 96p. il., map.

Text in German and English. Catalog of the exhibition, Galerie Biedermann, Munich (1981), and other locations.

A crucial work on northern Nigerian pottery.

Contents: Country, language, ethnography; History and monarchy; Pottery and the position of the woman in society; Technique; The clay vessel in the narrative; Clay vessels in the ritual and in magical-religious practices; (1) Stelelike vessels; (2) Vessels with shell-shaped opening; (3) Ovoid vessels with broad opening; (4) Ovoid vessels with neck; (5) Spherical vessels with rim; (6) Spherical vessels without rim; (7) Appendix A; (8) Appendix B: The problem of teriomorphic decoration.

Literatur, p.96.

Oceania

P581 May, Patricia, and Tuckson, Margaret. The traditional pottery of Papua New Guinea. Sydney, Bay Books, [1982]. 378p. il. (part col.), 12 maps.

"This is a dramatic and monumental study of pottery industries in Papua New Guinea. The determination to be comprehensive is amply demonstrated. . . . This is both a scholar's and a professional's book. . . . It is awesome in its length and detail, but the superlative photographs make it a treat even for casual inspection."—*Review*, African arts, v.18, no.1, Nov. 1984, p.87.

Includes one chapter on clay and techniques. Arranged by province. Appendixes on terminology and clay analysis.

Glossary, p.353–56. Bibliography, p.357–62. Sources of and acknowledgements for photographs, 363–66. Index, p.367–78.

The Americas

P582 Brody, J. J. Mimbres painted pottery. Santa Fe, School of American Research (Distr. by Univ. of New Mexico Pr., 1977). xxiii, 253p. il., col. plates. (Southwest Indian arts series)

Comprehensive technical and iconographic examination of an example of prehistoric Southwestern "climax ware, a type of pottery on which a certain set of visual ideals and values was pushed to its ultimate limits."—*Introd.* Additional chapters on the physical and human geography of the Mimbres region. Appendix includes collection data on the 196 illustrated examples.

Notes, p.237–41. References, p.243–49. Index, p.251–53.

P583 Dillingham, Rick. Acoma and Laguna pottery. With Melinda Elliott. Ed. by Joan Kathryn O'Donnell. Santa Fe, School of American Research (Distr. by Univ. of Washington Pr., 1992). xii, 241p. il. (part col.)

An exploration of pottery production in two Pueblo communities based on the collections of the Indian Arts Research Center of the School of American Research in Santa Fe. Appendixes include lists of potters active at Acoma, Laguna, and nearby villages in 1910 and 1991; "Signs of commercial origin in pottery"; and a catalog of the School of American Research collection.

References, p.232–35. Index, p.237–41.

P584 Donnan, Christopher B. Ceramics of ancient Peru. Los Angeles, Fowler Museum of Cultural History, UCLA, 1992. 128p. il. (part col.), col. maps.

Published in conjunction with the exhibition, Fowler Museum of Cultural History, UCLA (1992). While neither the most exhaustive nor lavishly illustrated examination of the topic, nevertheless a succinct, comprehensive, and authoritative handbook. Includes chapters on ceramic technology and ceramic tradition.

Bibliography, p.125–26.

P585 Kerr, Justin. The Maya vase book: a corpus of rollout photographs of Maya vases. N.Y., Kerr Associates, 1989– . (5)v. il. (part col.)

V.2 available on CD-ROM.

Chiefly a visual survey of Maya incised and painted vases using the author's circumferential photographic technique. Each vol. includes 3–5 essays on topics in hieroglyphic decipherment and vase iconography. Issued in spiral binding.

Contents: Essays published to date: (1) The history of the study of Maya vase painting, by Mary Ellen Miller; A brief note on the name of the vision serpent, by Linda Schele; Hieroglyphics on Maya vessels, by David Stuart; The Hero Twins: myth and image, by Michael D. Coe; (2) The primary standard sequence in Chocolá style ceramics, by Nikolai Grube; The God N/step set in the primary standard sequence, by Barbara MacLeod; Notes on the Maya vision quest through enema, by Brian Stross and Justin Kerr; (3) Lord Smoke Squirrel's cacao cup: the archaeological context and sociohistorical significance of the Buenavista "Jauncy vase," by Stephen D. Houston, David Stuart, and Karl Taube; Painted ladies: costumes for women on Tepeu ceramics, by Dicey Taylor; A name glyph for Classic Maya dwarfs, by Stephen D. Houston; (4) The birth vase: natal imagery in ancient Maya myth and ritual, by Karl Taube; A census of Xibalba: a complete inventory of way characters on Maya ceramics, by Nikolai Grube and Werner Nahm; (5) The painted king list: a commentary on codex-style dynastic vases, by Simon Martin; Where the wayob live: a further examination of Classic Maya supernaturals, by Inga Calvin;

Rebirth and resurrection in Maize God iconography, by Michel Quenon and Genevieve Le Fort. Essays generally include a bibliography.

P586 Peckham, Stewart. From this earth: the ancient art of Pueblo pottery. Photographs by Mary Peck. Santa Fe, Museum of New Mexico Pr., 1990. xi, 169p. il. (part col.), maps (part col.)

A typological study of archeological and, less comprehensively, historical Pueblo pottery based on the collections of the Museum of New Mexico's Museum of Indian Arts and Culture and Laboratory of Anthropology in Santa Fe. An appendix includes data on individual objects in the collection.

Glossary, p.156–61. Selected bibliography, p.162–65. Index, p.166–69.

P587 Reents-Budet, Dorie. Painting the Maya universe: royal ceramics of the Classic Period. With contrib. by Joseph W. Ball . . . [et al.] Photographs by Justin Kerr. Durham, Duke Univ. Pr., 1994. xx, 381p. col. il.

Catalog of the exhibition, Duke University Museum of Art (1994), and other locations. A stylistic analysis of vase painting styles in the Classic Period, supplemented by a catalog of 95 objects.

Contents: (1) Classic Maya pottery painting; (2) Classic Maya pottery painters; (3) Functions of Classic Period painted pottery; (4) The art of calligraphy: image and meaning, by Barbara MacLeod and Dorie Reents-Budet; (5) Painting styles, workshop locations and pottery production, by Dorie Reents-Budet, Ronald Bishop, and Barbara MacLeod; (6) Pictorial themes of Classic Maya pottery; (7) Collecting Pre-Columbian art and preserving the archaeological record; Catalog, by Virginia Fields; Appendix: Type: variety analysis and masterworks of Classic Maya polychrome pottery, by Joseph Ball.

References, p.366–73. Index, p.374–76.

GLASS

Bibliography

P588 Corning Museum of Glass. The history and art of glass: index of periodical articles, 1956–1979. Comp. by Louise K. Bush and Paul N. Perrot. Ed. by Gail P. Bardhan. Boston, Hall, 1982. vii, 876p.

Comprehensive index of articles, conference proceedings, and chapters in annuals and yearbooks concerning the art, conservation, and technology of glass. Based on the annual checklists published in the Journal of glass studies. Includes "substantive" book reviews. Excludes contemporary technological and scientific literature. Majority of entries concern the history of glass and are principally arranged by country, with separate sections for modern glass and stained glass.

[Author] index, p.729–876.

P589 ———. The history and art of glass: index of periodical articles, 1980–1982. Comp. by Louise K. Bush. Ed. by Gail P. Bardhan. Boston, Hall, 1984. xii, [1], 298p.

Supplement to preceding entry, including articles from 1980–1982, with a few citations to earlier material. Compiled from the annual checklist appearing in the Journal of glass studies, v.23–25, 1980–1982.

Author index, p.241–98.

Directories

P590 Corning Museum of Glass and The American National Commitee for the History of Glass. Glass collections in museums in the United States and Canada. Corning, [The Corning Museum of Glass, 1982]. 224p. il.

Compact guide to glass collections arranged alphabetically by city. Entries include hours, admission information, and a brief description of the size, period and geographical area of coverage, and highlights of each collection. Separate entries for Canada contributed by Peter Kaellgren, Royal Ontario Museum.

Index: United States: museum or collection, p.216–21. United States: state and city, p.222–23. Canada: museum and/or collection; Province and city, p.224.

P591 Who's who in contemporary glass art: a comprehensive world guide to glass: artists, craftsmen, designers. 1st ed. 1993/1994– . Munich, Waldrich, 1993– .

"Comprehensive documentation of international contemporary glass art. Withover 1,500 entries, the present volume offers an international overview of . . . the use of glass by artists, craftsmen and designers from over 55 countries."—*Pref.* Includes native country index, residence index, lists of abbreviations.

Dictionaries and Encyclopedias

P592 Bray, Charles. Dictionary of glass: materials and techniques. Philadelphia, Univ. of Pennsylvania Pr., 1995. 240p. il. (part col.)

"Intended to be a source of reference for individuals operating in small glass workshops and studios, and teachers and students. It concentrates on the fundamentals . . . on the materials, processes and techniques relating to glassmaking."—*Pref.*

Bibliography, p.227. Journals, periodicals, etc., p.228. Suppliers of materials and equipment, p.229–32. Museums and galleries, p.233–37. Schools and colleges offering courses in glass, p.238–40.

P593 Hartmann, Carolus. Glasmarken Lexikon, 1600–1945: Signaturen, Fabrik- und Handelsmarken: Europa und Nordamerika. Stuttgart, Arnoldsche, 1997. 1006p. il.

Texts in German, French, English, and Japanese. Substantial dictionary of glass marks. "The main objective . . . was . . .

to give collectors and dealers as well as all connoisseurs and lovers of glass more assurance in identifying and dating their glass."—*Pref.*

Künstler- und Firmenbiographien, p.498–890. Abkürzungsverzeichnis, p.892–93. Sachwortverzeichnis, p.895–99. Technisches Glossar, p.901–11. Ortsverzeichnis, p.913–15. Bibliographie, p.947–70. Register, p.973–1006.

P594 Jones, Olive, and Sullivan, Catherine. The Parks Canada glass glossary: for the description of containers, tableware, flat glass, and closures. With contrib. by George L. Miller . . . [et al.] [Ottawa], Parks Canada, 1985. 184p. il. (Studies in archaeology, architecture and history)

Simultaneously published in French as Glossaire du verre de Parcs Canada. [Ottawa], Direction des lieux et des parcs historiques nationaux, Parcs Canada, 1985.

Well-illustrated dictionary of glass form, technology, and dating methods devised for the classification and cataloging of 18th- and 19th-century artifacts from France, Britain, and the United States from sites excavated by Parks Canada. A useful resource not only for those dealing with glass collections but more widely for researchers in glass history of the period, especially objects in common use.

Bibliography, p.173–78. Index, p.179–84.

P595 Pullin, Anne Geffken. Glass signatures, trademarks and trade names, from the seventeenth through the twentieth century. [Lombard, Ill., Wallace-Homestead, 1986]. 368p. il., port.

Compilation of signatures, marks, and selected trade names found on glassware, with reduced size reproductions of actual marks in most cases and brief information on maker or factory, arranged in strict alphabetical order. Scope is international. Omits "most" bottle marks. Illustrated with line drawings.

Contents: (1) Introduction: How to use this book; Sources of reference; (2) How to look at glass; (3) Index of signatures, trademarks, and trade names.

Glossary: translations of selected foreign words, p.353. Benchmark dates, technical and historical, p.354–57. Bibliography, p.358–60. Index, p.361–68.

P596 Whitehouse, David, comp. Glass: a pocket dictionary of terms commonly used to describe glass and glassmaking. Corning, Corning Museum of Glass, [1983]. 88p. il. (chiefly col.)

Useful compact dictionary of terms dealing with glassware and the processes and tools used in making it, aimed at students and collectors. Compiled by the director of the Corning Museum of Glass and illustrated with objects from Corning's collections.

Descriptions of illustrated objects, p.86–87.

Histories and Handbooks

P597 Arwas, Victor. Glass: Art nouveau to Art deco. 2d rev. ed. N.Y., Rizzoli, 1995. 384p. il. (part col.)

Dictionary of makers, alphabetically arranged.

Bibliography, p.250–54. Index, p.255–56.

P598 Charleston, Robert J. Masterpieces of glass: a world history from the Corning Museum of Glass. N.Y., Abrams, [1980]. 239p., col. il. (A Corning Museum of Glass monograph)

Handsomely illustrated history of glass from the Egyptian Eighteenth Dynasty B.C. to the mid-20th century, in the form of essays and illustrations of 102 objects from the Corning Museum collection, preceded by a brief introductory essay. Accessible, especially suitable for non-specialist readers.

Glossary, p.223–28. Bibliography, p.229–32. Index, p.233–39.

P599 Goldstein, Sidney M.; Rakow, Leonard S.; and Rakow, Juliette K. Cameo glass: masterpieces from 2000 years of glassmaking. Corning, N.Y., Corning Museum of Glass, [1982]. 140p. il. (part col.)

Catalog accompanying the exhibition, Corning Museum of Glass (1982), emphasizing the creation of the form in the Roman period, its survival in the Chinese and Islamic glassblowing traditions, and its revival in the West in the 19th century.

Glossary, p.130–31. Bibliography with shortened titles, p.132–34. Index, p.135–40.

P600 The history of glass. General eds., Dan Klein and Ward Lloyd. Foreword by Robert Charleston. London, Orbis, [1984]. 288p. il. (part col.)

Comprehensive, well-illustrated narrative history of glassmaking from its origins to the present day, in the form of chronologically arranged essays by specialists in each period. A readable and attractive overview for the interested student or beginning collector.

Glossary, p.272–74. Bibliography, p.275–76. Index, p.277–87.

P601 Hollister, Paul M. The encyclopedia of glass paperweights. [Reprint.] Santa Cruz, Calif., Paperweight Pr., 1986. vi, 312p. il. (part col.), plates.

Originally published N.Y., C.N. Potter, 1969.

Primarily concerned with paperweights of the Classic period (mid-19th century).

Contents: (I) Paperweight genesis; (II) The individual makers; (III) Examination of paperweights.

Bibliography, p.290–98. Glossary, p.299–304. Some museums having glass paperweights, p.305. Index, p.307–12.

P602 ———, and Lanmon, Dwight P. Paperweights: "flowers which clothe the meadows." Corning, Corning Museum of Glass, [1978]. 167p. il. (part col.)

A special exhibition, The Corning Museum of Glass, April 29–October 21, 1978.

Catalog of 306 19th-century European and American paperweights considered to embody the "greatest technological achievements of the paperweight makers."—*p.8.* Introductory essay by Hollister discusses this art, and is followed by catalog arranged by country and by factory, when known. Includes extensive section of color illustrations.

Glossary, p.166. A short bibliography, p.167.

P603 Klesse, Brigitte, and Mayr, Hans. European glass from 1500–1800: the Ernesto Wolf collection. [Vienna], Kremayr and Scheriau, [1987]. 151, [440]p. il. (part col.)

Massive, well-illustrated catalog of the highlights of an important collection of European glass, focusing on decorated glass of the Renaissance and Baroque eras. Extensive introductory essays consider the principal forms included, with special attention to contemporary graphic sources of decorative motifs found on these artifacts.

Bibliography, p.137–47. Auction catalogs (arranged chronologically), p.149.

P604 Mehlman, Felice. Phaidon guide to glass. Oxford, Phaidon, [1982]. 256p. il. (part col.)

Compact history of glass and guide to commonly found glass forms by function. Includes chapters on "popular decorative styles of the 19th and early 20th centuries" and on collecting, with remarks on fakes.

Bibliography, p.246–47. Glossary, p.248–51. Index, p.252–56.

P605 Merrill, Nancy O. A concise history of glass, represented in the Chrysler Museum glass collection. [Norfolk], Chrysler Museum, 1989. 227p. il. (part col.)

Heavily illustrated volume featuring highlights of the important collection of glass formed by Walter P. Chrysler Jr. and now housed in the Chrysler Museum. Includes ancient and European glass, but emphasizes 19th- and 20th-century examples, particularly American. Serves as a good visual survey of the period.

Catalogue information, p.[185]–223. Bibliography, p.225–27.

P606 Phillips, Phoebe. The encyclopedia of glass. [Reprint.] N.Y., Crescent Books, 1987. 320p. il. (part col.), 2 maps.

Originally published, London, Heinemann, 1981; U.S. ed., N.Y., Crown, 1981.

"Designed to show the enormous range and the unique qualities of glass."—*Introd.*

Contents: (1) History by period and region; (2) Techniques.

Glossary, p.286–95. Glass museums, p.296–97. Glass periodicals, p.298–314. Index, p.315–20.

P607 Ritsema van Eck, Pieter C., and Zijlstra-Zweens, Henrica. Glass in the Rijksmuseum. Zwolle, Waanders, 1993–1995. 2v., il. (part col.) (Catalogues of the applied arts in the Rijksmuseum Amsterdam, ed. by R. J. Baarsen; v.2 –I, 2-II)

Author of v.2: Pieter C. Ritsema van Eck.

Catalog of the glass collections of the Rijksmuseum Amsterdam, which is particularly rich in Dutch glass and in Venetian and other European glassware. V.2 concentrates on Dutch and related German and Bohemian engraved glass of the 16th through the 19th centuries, v.1 on other European glass through the 20th century and on non-European objects. Entries include physical description, provenance, and bibliographical references for each object. Includes photographs of marks.

Abbreviations, v.1, p.375. Bibliography, v.1, p.375–82, v.2, p.473–78. Glossary, v.1, p.383–85. Verklarende woordenlijst, v.1, p.385–87. Concordance, inventory numbers-catalogue numbers, v.1, p.388–90, v.2, p.479–81. Signatures, v.1, p.392–93. Biographies of the engravers discussed in the catalogue, v.2, p.468–72. Index of engravings, v.2, p.482–93. Index of provenances, v.2, p.494–95.

P608 Saldern, Axel von. Glass 500 B.C. to A.D. 1900: the Hans Cohn collection, Los Angeles, Cal. Mainz, Philipp von Zabern, [1980]. 288p. il., 39 col. plates.

Published to accompany the exhibition, UCLA (1981), and other locations. Parallel texts in German and English.

Well-illustrated catalog of a collection whose strengths include ancient, Islamic, and European glass of the 17th and 18th centuries. Informative introductions to each section discuss glassmaking methods characteristic of the period.

Contents: (1) Pre-Roman and Roman glass; (2) Sassanian and Islamic glass; (3) European glass.

Bibliography, p.284–88.

P609 Sotheby's concise encyclopedia of glass. General eds., David Battie, Simon Cottle. Boston, Little, Brown, [1991]. 208p. il. (part col.)

Not an encyclopedia, but a well-illustrated general survey of glass history from pre-Roman times through the 20th century, in the form of essays on each period by specialist contributors. A good introduction to the subject for the general reader or beginning collector. Includes a chapter on fakes and forgeries.

Select bibliography, p.193. Care and conservation, p.194. Paperweights and cane, p.195. Glossary, p.196–200. Glasshouses and biographies, p.201–03. Index, p.204–08.

P610 Spillman, Jane Shadel. American and European pressed glass in the Corning Museum of Glass. Corning, The Corning Museum of Glass, 1981. 404p. il., 16 col. plates. (Corning Museum of Glass catalog series)

Illustrated catalog of more than 1500 pressed glass objects, preceded by a brief introduction to this important 19th-century process, which was perfected in the United States. Objects are arranged by type, date, and decoration. Entries include physical description, provenance and literature as appropriate, and references to similar pieces. Especially valuable for its visual coverage of a great range of glass pieces.

List of references cited, p.11. Index, p.400–04.

P611 Tait, Hugh, ed. Glass: 5,000 years. N.Y., Abrams, 1991. 256p. il. (part col.)

Ambitious survey of the history of glass, with multiple authors.

Contents: Introduction, by Hugh Tait; (1) Before the invention of glassblowing, by Veronica Tatton-Brown and Carol Andrews; (2) The Roman Empire, by Veronica Tatton-Brown; (3) Early medieval Europe AD 400–1066, by Veronica Tatton-Brown; (4) The Islamic lands and China, by

Ralph Pinder-Wilson; (5) Europe from the Middle Ages to the Industrial Revolution, by Hugh Tait; (6) Europe and America 1800–1940, by Paul Hollister; Epilogue, by Hugh Tait.

Techniques of glassmaking and decoration, by William Gudenrath, p.213–41. Glossary, p.242–47. Further reading, p.248–49. Illustration credits and museum accession numbers, p.250–51. Index, p.252–56.

P612 Vose, Ruth Hurst. Glass. Drawings by C. R. Evans. London, Connoisseur, 1975. 222p. il., 8 col. plates. (The Connoisseur illustrated guides)

Authoritative history of glassmaking technology through a chronological survey of the evolution and techniques of each process. Well illustrated with line drawings of actual objects exemplifying the processes discussed.

Contents: (1) Techniques before blowing; (2) Blowing and moulding; (3) Coloured glass; (4) Clear colourless glass; (5) Adding: the glass-maker's skill; (6) Adding: the skill of the decorator; (7) The techniques of taking away; (8) Later techniques.

Select bibliography, p.213–15. Index, p.216–22.

P613 Zerwick, Chloe. A short history of glass. Corning, The Corning Museum of Glass, [1980]. 95p. il. (part col.), map.

Concise history of glass of the world from pre-Roman times to the present, based on the Corning Museum's collections. Serves also as an introduction to these major collections, and summarizes the museum's first thirty years of collecting.

Bibliography, p.94. Object index, p.94–95.

Asian Countries

China

P614 Brown, Claudia, and Rabiner, Donald. Clear as crystal, red as flame: later Chinese glass. N.Y., China House Gallery, China Institute in America, 1990. 103p. col. il.

Catalog of the exhibition, China House Gallery (1990).

More than 60 examples from North American collections illustrating the technical development and stylistic experimentation in Qing dynasty glass.

Japan

P615 Kindai Nihon no garasu kogei: Meiji shoki kara gendai made = Modern Japanese glass: early Meiji to present. [Tokyo], Tokyo Koruitsu Kindai Bijutsikan, [1982]. [172]p. il. (part col.)

Text in Japanese and English. Catalog of the exhibition, National Museum of Modern Art, Tokyo (1982).

The catalog includes work by artists who developed and fostered modern Japanese glass such as Takijirō Iwaki and Magoichi Shimada, vividly colored glass of the Meiji and Taishō periods, and works by major post-war artists active today. An introductory essay by Kazunobu Nakanodō on modern Japanese glass is followed by 170 labeled color plates reproducing the objects, and biographies for 17 of the artists.

ENAMELS

Dictionaries and Encyclopedias

P616 Speel, Erika. Dictionary of enameling. [Brookfield, Vermont], Ashgate, [1998]. xvi, 152p. il., ports., 100 col. plates.

Comprehensive, heavily illustrated dictionary of enamel forms, processes, and major creative figures. Entries include cross-references and individual bibliographies. Range of coverage is universal, from earliest appearance of the form to the present and through all cultures.

Asian Countries

China

P617 Brinker, Helmut, and Lutz, Albert. Chinese cloisonné; the Pierre Uldry collection. Trans. by Susanna Swoboda. N.Y., Asia Society Galleries, 1989. 144p. il. (part col.), plates.

Trans. of Chinesisches Cloisonné: Die Sammlung Pierre Uldry. Zürich, Museum Rietberg, 1985.

A scholarly study of Chinese enamels that first appeared as a catalog for the exhibition, Rietberg Museum, Zurich (1985). The Pierre Uldry collection "contains pieces from all important periods of cloisonné; reveals every major technical aspect of the craft; and offers in form and color, in artistic quality and perfection, as well as in the state of preservation of its items, the ultimate achievement in collecting."—*Authors' pref.*

After a long introductory section, the chapters provide a background of eight chronologically organized essays relating directly to the collection with individual pieces referred to and discussed.

Complete catalogue of pieces and their marks. Glossary of decorative motifs on cloisonné. Bibliography (unpaginated).

Japan

P618 Coben, Lawrence A., and Ferster, Dorothy C. Japanese cloisonné: history, technique, and appreciation. N.Y., Weatherhill, 1982. xii, 323p. il. (part col.)

The book is divided into six parts describing the authors' thesis and methodology and including a chronological history and a collectors' guide. Attention has been paid to the technical and commercial aspects of cloisonné as well as the aesthetics. Illustrations are included for pieces in public and private collections as well as historic photographs of pieces that no longer exist.

Bibliography, p.301–08.

METALWORK

Dictionaries and Encyclopedias

P619 Brett, Vanessa. The Sotheby's directory of silver: 1600–1940. [London, Philip Wilson for] Sotheby's [Distr. in the U.S. by Harper, 1986]. 432p. il., genealogical charts.

Primarily a visual encyclopedia of European and North American silver, drawn from examples sold by Sotheby's between 1920 and 1984. Especially valuable for the great number of pieces and makers illustrated. Arrangement is by country and by maker or mark.

Family trees of Augsburg goldsmiths, p.[416]–21. Currency conversion and bullion price tables, p.[422]. Bibliography, p.423–[24]. Index of objects, p.425–27. Index of goldsmiths, including assay masters, designers, retailers and engravers, p.[428]–30. Index of heraldry and inscriptions, p.431–32.

P620 Clayton, Michael. The collector's dictionary of the silver and gold of Great Britain and North America. Woodbridge, Antique Collectors' Club, 1985. 481p. il. (part col.)

First published, N.Y., World Pub. Co., 1971.

Adequately illustrated, mostly in black-and-white.

Bibliography, p.472–80.

P621 Divis, Jan. Guide to gold marks of the world. [London, Promotional Reprint Co. for Fraser Stewart, 1994]. 246p. il.

Originally published Prague, Aventinum, 1978.

World dictionary of marks found on gold, platinum, and palladium. Introductory essays discuss these metals and their alloys, and relevant goldsmithing techniques. Arrangement of marks is by subject.

Glossary of alloys of gold, platinum and their imitations, p.23–27. Conversion tables, p.37–38. Selected bibliography, p.239. Index of cities and countries, p.240–46.

P622 Newman, Harold. An illustrated dictionary of silverware: 2,373 entries relating to British and North American wares, decorative techniques and styles, and leading designers and makers, principally from c.1500 to the present. [London], Thames and Hudson, [1987]. [367]p. il., 16 col. plates.

Standard, comprehensive dictionary of British, Canadian, United States, and modern Mexican silverware in all its aspects, excluding jewelry, small personal articles, and scientific instruments. Some entries include bibliographical references. An essential source.

Histories and Handbooks

General Works

P623 Hernmarck, Carl. The art of the European silversmith, 1430–1830. London, Sotheby Parke Bernet, [1977]. 2v. il.

Magisterial history of European secular and ecclesiastical silver by a major scholar, likely to remain a major source for many years. Emphasis is on cultural, stylistic, and functional aspects of silverwork. Includes a chapter on decoration and its techniques. V.2 is devoted to more than 1,000 photographs of individual objects keyed to the text.

Bibliography, v.1, p.[376]–87. Index of goldsmiths, artists and craftsmen, v.1, p.[391]–99. Index of museums and collections, v.1, p.[400]–02. General index, v.1, p.[403]–11.

P624 The history of silver. General ed.: Claude Blair. N.Y. Ballantine, [1987]. 256p. il. (part col.)

Well-illustrated history of silver in the West from the ancient world to the 20th century, in the form of chapters on each period contributed by well-known silver scholars. Forms a compact, intelligent one-vol. introduction to the subject for interested non-specialists.

The craft of the silversmith, by Claude Blair, p.225–32. The metals: hallmarking and methods of assay, by John Hughes. p.233–40. Notes, p.241–42. Bibliography, p.243–45. Glossary, p.246–48. Index, p.249–56.

P625 Muller, Hannelore. The Thyssen-Bornemisza Collection: European silver. Trans. from the German by P. S. Falla and Anna Somers Cocks. General ed., Simon de Pury. [N.Y.], Vendome, [Distr. by Rizzoli, 1989]. 311p. il. (part col.)

Well-documented catalog of an important assemblage of English and European luxury silver objects, preceded by a history of the collection and a discussion of the major types of objects represented. Each entry includes detailed physical description, provenance, design sources, bibliography, and a consideration of the object's place in the social history of its period.

Biographical notes on goldsmiths, p.[296]–300. Abbreviated bibliography of often cited works, p.[301]. Bibliography of works directly connected with goldsmithing, p.[301]–03. Index of marks, p.[304]–07. General index, p.[308]–11.

P626 Schroder, Timothy. The Gilbert Collection of gold and silver. [Los Angeles], Los Angeles County Museum of Art, [1988]. 688p. il. (part col.)

Massive catalog of a major collection of British, European, American, and Indian silver and gold ranging from the 15th to the 19th centuries. Principal concentration is on English and continental 16th- and 17th-century silverwork and English work of the 18th and early 19th centuries. Each piece is extensively described and its design sources, maker, and history discussed in detail.

Goldsmiths' biographies, p.650–66. Glossary, p.667–71. Bibliography and exhibitions, p.672–82. Index, p.683–87.

Ancient

P627 Silver for the Gods: 800 years of Greek and Roman silver. Catalogue by Andrew Oliver, Jr. Exhibition organized by Kurt T. Luckner. [Toledo], Toledo Museum of Art, [1977]. 175p. il., maps.

Catalog of a loan exhibition, Toledo Museum of Art (1977), and other locations.

"The primary goal of this exhibition is to provide a balanced view of the range and development of ancient silver during the eight centuries from Classical Greece, about 500 B.C. to the late Roman Empire, about 320 A.D."—*p.7.* All 119 objects in the exhibit are thoroughly described and illustrated.

Entries include individual bibliographical citations.

Early Christian—Gothic

P628 "The work of angels": masterpieces of Celtic metalwork, 6th–9th centuries AD. Ed. by Susan Youngs. With contrib. by Paul T. Craddock . . . [et al.] Austin, Univ. of Texas Pr. in coop. with British Museum Pubs., [1989]. 223p. il., 40 col. plates, map.

Book published to accompany the exhibition, British Museum (1989), devoted to Celtic metalwork of Ireland and the Celtic kingdoms of Britain. Includes both secular and ecclesiastical objects of many kinds. A chapter is devoted to metalworking techniques and tools.

Glossary, p.214–15. Bibliography, p.216–22.

Islamic

P629 Atil, Esin; Chase, W. T.; and Jett, Paul. Islamic metalwork in the Freer Gallery of Art. Washington, D.C., Freer Gallery of Art, 1985. 273p. il., graphs, maps, tables.

Published to accompany the exhibition, Freer Gallery (1985–1986).

Detailed consideration of 38 metal objects from the Freer permanent collection, in relation to Islamic metalwork traditions. Entries for each piece include discussion of design, construction, composition, and makers, when known. Particularly suitable for the informed researcher.

Sources, p.233–56. Notes concerning the X-ray fluorescence analysis, p.257–64. Names of articts, names of patrons, names of later owners, dated pieces, p.265. [Islamic metalwork from the Freer Collection excluded from the catalogue]. p.266–68. List of objects in the Freer Gallery of Art by order of accession numbers, p.269–70. List of objects in other collections used as reference illustrations, p.271–73.

P630 Kurkman, Garo. Ottoman silver marks. Istanbul, [Mathusalem], 1996. 293p. il. (part col.)

Compilation of Ottoman makers' marks and assay office marks, accompanied by a discussion of the creation of Ottoman silverwork. The first such compendium, important for scholars and collectors alike. Extensive section of color illustrations of silver objects and their marks.

Contents: (1) Tugra and silvermarks; (2) Makers' marks; (3) Assay offices; (4) Silver ware; Appendix: Documents; Ottoman sultans and their reigns; List of silversmiths; List of goldsmiths; List of silversmiths in the register of the Bostancibasi, 1230–1815; List of silversmiths, goldsmiths, gilders, engravers, craftsmen who did studded jewel work, gold thread makers, silver sheet makers and makers of undecorated gold or silver ware who paid tax to the Armenian Patriarchate in 1872.

Bibliography, p.290. Index, p.291–93.

Renaissance—Baroque

P631 The art of the European goldsmith: silver from the Schroder collection. Introd. and catalogue by Timothy B. Schroder. Essay by J. F. Hayward. [N.Y.], American Federation of Arts, [1983]. 208p. il., col. plates.

Catalog of a traveling exhibition of objects from a notable private collection of English and European silver, particularly strong in work of the 16th and 17th centuries. Each piece is illustrated and discussed in detail. Introductory essays introduce the craft and its makers and the history of the formation of the collection.

[Works in the collection not included in the exhibition], p.[187]–97. Marks, p.[199]–203. Bibliography, p.[205]–08.

Neoclassical—Modern

P632 Clayton, Michael. Christie's pictorial history of English and American silver. Oxford, Phaidon-Christie's, [1985]. 319p. il. (part col.)

A heavily illustrated history of silver from the Elizabethan through the Victorian periods, drawn from examples sold by Christie's during the twenty years preceding this volume's publication, and aimed primarily at an audience of collectors. Prices and dates sold are provided for each piece illustrated.

Further reading, p.[305]–[06]. Price list, p.[307]–12. Index, p.[313]–19.

P633 Gruber, Alain. Silverware. N.Y., Rizzoli, [1982]. 305p. il. (part col.)

French language ed.: L'Argenterie de maison du XVIe au XIXe siècle. Fribourg, Office du Livre, 1982.

History of household silver in Europe from the Renaissance to the 19th century, by a respected scholar. After a discussion of table setting and etiquette, text is devoted to a detailed examination of the typology of silver objects by function. Very well illustrated with period views of silver in its domestic settings and of individual pieces.

Hallmarks of towns where the objects illustrated in this volume were made, p.287–90. Bibliography, p.291–97. Index, p.298–303.

P634 Krekel-Aalberse, Annelies. Art nouveau and Art deco silver. N.Y., Abrams, [1989]. 272p. il., 25 col. plates.

History of European, British, and American silver from 1880 to 1940, by country. Includes valuable appendixes of marks and biographical sketches of makers.

Contents: Introduction: Silver and the modern movement, 1880–1940; (1) Great Britain; (2) France; (3) Belgium; (4) United States; (5) Germany; (6) The Netherlands; (7) Austria; (8) Scandinavia, Finland, and Russia.

Biographies, p.251–61. Silvermarks, 1880–1940, p.261–63. Makers' marks, p.264–69. Bibliography, p.269–70. Index, p.271–72.

P635 Langford, Joel. Silver: a practical guide to collecting silverware and identifying hallmarks. [Secaucus], Chartwell, [1991]. 128p. il. (part col.)

Compact, approachable introduction to British and American silver and to Sheffield plate for the novice collector. Explanations are clear and well-illustrated.

Contents: (1) Silver standards and hallmarking; (2) Old Sheffield Plate/fused plate; (3) Condition and quality; (4) Styles, 1700–1930; (5) Care and cleaning.

Glossary of terms, p.6–11. Index, p.126–27. Selected bibliography, p.128.

P636 Minneapolis Institute of Arts. English and American silver in the collection of the Minneapolis Institute of Arts, by Francis J. Puig, Judith Banister, Gerald W. R. Ward . . . [et al.] Minneapolis, Minneapolis Institute of Arts, 1989. vi, 312p. il. (part col.)

Scholarly catalog of one of the finest collections in the country, ranging from the 15th century to the present.

Bibliography, p.306–08. Exhibitions, p.309. Index of silversmiths, p.310–11. Index of donors, p.312.

P637 Silver of a new era: international highlights of precious metalware from 1880 to 1940. [Exhibition organized and catalogue ed. by: Mrs. A. Krekel-Aalberse, Dr. J. R. ter Molen, Dr. R. J. Willink. Rotterdam, Museum Boymans-van Beuningen (Distr. by Univ. of Washington Pr., 1992)]. 264p. il. (part col.)

Heavily illustrated book produced to accompany the exhibition of modern silver by English and European makers, Museum Boymans-van Beuningen (1992). Arranged by country, with brief introductory essays by specialists in each area, and many illustrations of individual objects.

Contents: Introduction, by Jooset Willink; Great Britain, by Eric Turner; France, by Evelyne Posseme; Belgium, by L. Daenens; Netherlands, by Annelies Krekel-Aalberse; Germany, by Dr. R. Joppien; Austria, by Dr. Elisabeth Schmuttermeier; Scandinavia, by Helene Dahlback-Lutteman.

Bibliography, p.258–59. Index, p.260–63.

P638 Sotheby's concise encyclopedia of silver. General ed., Charles Truman. London, Conran Octopus, [1993]. 208p., col. il.

World history of silver from Mesopotamia to the 20th century. Intended for a general audience, with chapters contributed by various specialists. Includes a chapter on fakes and forgeries.

The contributors, p.8–9. Select bibliography, p.193. Hallmarks and standards, p.194–95. Glossary, p.196–99. Biographies [of makers], p.200–03. Index, p.204–07.

P639 Truman, Charles. The Gilbert Collection of gold boxes. [Los Angeles], Los Angeles County Museum of Art [Distr. by Abrams, 1991]. 431p. il. (part col.)

Catalog of an important collection of English and European snuffboxes, arranged by country, and preceded by an essay on the design and manufacture of these objects. Entries provide extensive information on each box, including illustrations of makers' marks and individual bibliographical references.

Bibliography, p.424–27. Index, p.428–31.

Western Countries

Australia

P640 Hawkins, John Bernard. Nineteenth-century Australian silver. Woodbridge, Antique Collectors' Club, 1990. 2v. il. (part col.)

Thorough, scholarly survey, by region.

Bibliography, v.2, p.332–35. Index of silversmiths, v.2, p.337–38. Index of silversmiths' marks, v.2, p.339–68. Index, v.2, p.369–72.

Canada

P641 The covenant chain: Indian ceremonial and trade silver. The covenant chain by N. Jaye Frederickson. Catalogue of the exhibition by Sandra Gibb. A traveling exhibition of the National Museum of Man. Ottawa, National Museums of Canada, [1980]. 168p. il. (part col.), ports.

Simultaneously published in French as La chaine d'alliance. Ottawa, Musées nationaux du Canada, 1980.

Exhibition of silver produced by Canadian, English, and European silversmiths as diplomatic gifts and trade goods during the fur trade of the late 18th and early 19th centuries. Later copied by Iroquois silversmiths, including those of the present day. Examines the use and status of these objects in the context of cultural interaction of the period.

Bibliography, p.163–64. Index, p.167–68.

P642 Detroit Institute of Arts. Quebec and related silver at the Detroit Institute of Arts. By Ross Allan C. Fox. Detroit, Wayne State Univ. Pr. for the Founders Society, Detroit Institute of Arts, 1978. 174, [2]p. il., charts.

Catalog of the important collection of French Canadian silver held by the Detroit Institute of Arts, by a specialist in the field. Arrangement is by maker. Entries are extensive and detailed.

Silver inventories, p.151–52. Elemental analysis, p.153–66. Glossary, p.167–69. Index, p.171–74.

P643 Fox, Ross Allan C. Presentation pieces and trophies from the Henry Birks collection of Canadian silver.

Ottawa, National Gallery of Canada, 1985. x, 123p. il. (part col.), tables.

Catalog accompanying an exhibition of a portion of the Birks Collection, focusing principally on presentation pieces of the 19th century. Includes "all those commemorative pieces donated by a benefactor for presentation to individuals in honor of some outstanding achievement"—*p.vii*, and discusses the social context of their creation.

Some notes on silversmiths' marks, p.93–105. The Hendery and Leslie silver factory in 1894, p.107–09. List of works in the exhibition: Canadian presentation pieces from the Henry Birks Collection, p.111–14. Selected bibliography, p.115. Index, p.116–23.

France

Dictionaries and Encyclopedias

P644 Dictionnaire des poinçons de l'orfèvrerie provinciale française. Genève, Droz, 1976– . (4)v. il., plates.

Series devoted to provincial gold and silvermarks.

Contents: (1) Brault-Lerch, Solange. Les orfèvres de Franche-Comté et de la Principauté de Montbéliard du Moyen Age au 19e siècle (1976); (2) Verlet-Réaubourg, Nicole. Les orfèvres du ressort de la monnaie de Bourges (1977); (3) Godefroy, Gisèle, and Girard, Raymond. Les orfèvres du Dauphiné: du Moyen Age au XIXe siècle: répertoires biographiques, poinçons, oeuvres (1985); (4) Brault-Lerch, Solange. Les orfèvres de Troyes en Champagne (1986).

Bibliographies and indexes in each vol.

P645 Dictionnaire des poinçons de l'orfèvrerie française. Paris, Imprimerie nationale, 1989– . (9)v. il, maps, plans, plates. (Inventaire général des monuments et des richesses artistiques de la France. Cahiers de l'Inventaire)

Series devoted to French gold and silvermarks. Publisher varies.

Contents: Muel, Francis . . . [et al.] Orfèvrerie nantaise (1989); Arminjon, Catherine. Dictionnaire des poinçons de fabricants d'ouvrages d'or et d'argent de Paris et de la Seine (1991–); Chalabi, Maryannick, and Jazé-Charvolin, Marie-Reine. Poinçons des fabricants d'ouvrages d'or et d'argent: dictionnaire des poinçons de l'orfèvrerie française: Lyon 1798–1940 (1993); Castel, Yves P. Les orfèvres de basse Bretagne (1994); Cartier, Nicole. Les orfèvres de Douai (1995); Jacob, Monique. Les orfèvres d'Anjou et du bas Maine (1998); Chassey, Arnaud de. Les orfèvres de Bourgogne (1999); Chalabi, Maryannick. L'orfèvrerie de Lyon et de Trévoux du XVe au XXe siècle (2000).

Bibliographies and indexes in each vol.

P646 Ris-Paquot, Oscar Edmond. Dictionnaire des poinçons, symboles, signes figuratifs, marques et monogrammes des orfèvres français et étrangers. [Reprint of 1890 ed.] N.Y., Garland, 1978.

Reprint of a standard work.

Contents: (1) Statuts et privilèges du corps des marchands orfèvres et joualliers de la ville de Paris; (2) Armorial de la corporation des orfèvres de France; (3) Tableau explicatif des poinçons et de leur apposition sur l'argenterie . . . [etc.]; (4) Dictionnaire des noms des gardes de l'orfèvrerie de Paris depuis 1337 jusqu'en 1710; (5) Dictionnaire des noms des fermiers généraux, contrôleurs, maîtres des monnaies, orfèvres, villes dont les poinçons, symboles, etc., sont contenu dans l'ouvrage.

Histories and Handbooks

P647 Bimbenet-Privat, Michele. Les orfèvres parisiens de la Renaissance, 1506–1620. Paris, Commission des travaux historiques de la ville de Paris, 1992. 691p. il. (part col.)

Beautifully produced study, based on the author's thesis (École des Chartes, 1982).

Contents: Étude historique; Catalogue d'oeuvres conservées; Dictionnaire des orfèvres; Textes édités en annexes; Gardes et lettres-dates de 1507 a 1644.

Abréviations, p.12. Principales sources, p.13–14. Orientation bibliographique, p.15–23. Index des noms des orfèvres figurant au catalogue des objets, p.655. Index des objets figurant au catalogue, p.657. Index des poinçons des maîtres insculpés entre 1507 et 1620, p.659–76. Index des noms de personnes et de lieux cités dans l'étude historique, p.677–89.

P648 Carré, Louis. Guide de l'amateur d'orfèvrerie française. Nouvelle ed., avec une introd. par Maurice Bouvier-Ajam et une bibliographie. [Paris], De Nobele, 1990. 281, [13]p. il., 24 plates.

Reprint of the 1974 ed. of the standard guide to French gold and silvermarks. For previous English-language ed., see GLAH 1:P485. Bibliography covers material to 1974.

Contents: Première partie: Les poinçons de l'orfèvrerie française du XIIIe siècle à la fin du XVIIIe siècle. Deuxième partie: Les poinçons de l'orfèvrerie française depuis la loi du 19 Brumaire An VI jusqu'à nos jours.

Bibliographie, p.[269]–81.

P649 Cassan, Claude Gerard. Les orfèvres de la Normandie du XVIe au XIXe siècles et leurs poinçons. Paris, De Nobele, 1980. 276p. il.

Regional biographical dictionary of goldsmiths and silversmiths of the ancien regime, with marks illustrated.

P650 Clarke de Dromantin, Jean, and Clarke de Dromantin, Jacques. Les orfèvres de Bordeaux et la marque du roy. Suresnes, Eds. du Puygiron, [1987]. [566]p. il., charts, genealogical tables.

Exhaustive history of silversmithing in Bordeaux, focusing on makers and their marks. Well-documented and based on extensive archival research. Whenever possible, marks and silver objects are illustrated. An invaluable resource for the specialist in this subject.

Contents: (I) La communaute des orfèvres de Bordeaux; (II) Les poinçons; (III) Le droit de marque, aspect juridique et fiscal; (IV) Devolution des baux de la ferme de la marque de Paris à la généralité de Guyenne; (V) Répertoire des maitres orfèvres.

Tables: Orfèvrerie du XVIe siècle, p.474–77. Contrats d'apprentissage, p.478–481. Emplacement des poinçons, p.482–84. Inventaires, p.485–86. Instruction, sur la regie des droits de Marque, p.487–93. Erreurs ou imprecisions, p.494–97. Poinçons non identifiés et cas particuliers, p.498–99. Bibliographie, p.500–02. Liste alphabetique des orfèvres de Bordeaux et de la généralité, p.504–18. Liste alphabetique des poinçons, p.519–28. Répertoire chronologique de pièces d'orfèvrerie de la généralité de Bordeaux, p.529–39. Répertoire général des poinçons, p.540–57. Index des illustrations, p.558–60. Index des noms cités, p.561–64. Tables des matières, p.[565–67].

P651 Haug, Hans. L'orfèvrerie de Strasbourg dans les collections publiques francaises. Paris, Eds. des musées nationaux, 1978. [225]p. il. (Inventaire des collections publiques françaises, 22)
History of silversmithing in Strasbourg from the 15th through the 19th centuries as seen through objects on view in public collections. Arrangement is by period and by silversmith. Includes an illustrated section on silvermarks.
Quatre tables d'insculpation des orfèvres, de 1567–1612/1691–1751, p.[37–42]. Bibliographie, p.[43–44].

P652 Helft, Jacques. Nouveaux poinçons, suivis de recherches techniques et historiques sur l'orfèvrerie sous l'ancien régime. Paris, Berger-Levrault, 1980. 418p. il.
Careful study of a recently discovered cache of hallmarks, elucidating their role in the daily life of the ancien regime. No bibliography or index.

P653 Lightbown, R. W. French silver. London, HMSO, [1978]. x, 117p. il. (Victoria and Albert Museum catalogues)
Catalog of religious and secular French goldsmith's work of the 12th through the 19th centuries in the Victoria and Albert Museum collections, with particular strength in early pieces. Each object is thoroughly described and well illustrated. Arrangement is chronological.
Short bibliography of French goldsmith's work, p.[viii]–ix. Abbreviations, p.[x]. Index of places of origin, p.116. Index of names of makers, p.116. Index of unidentified makers' marks, p.117. Concordance of museum and catalogue numbers, p.117.

P654 Mabille, Gerard. Orfèvrerie française des XVIe, XVIIe, XVIIIe siècles: catalogue raisonné des collections du Musée des Arts Décoratifs et du Musée Nissim de Camondo. [Paris], Musée des Arts Décoratifs (Distr. by Flammarion, [1984]). 237, [2]p. il.
Catalog of a major collection of French silver, arranged by locality and by silversmith. Entries are detailed and extensive, and include scientific analysis of metals.
Table de concordance, p.230–31. Sources et bibliographie, p.232–33. Liste des expositions, p.233. Index: noms de personnes; Collectionneurs et donateurs, p.234–35.

P655 Taburet-Delahaye, Elisabeth. L'orfèvrerie gothique au Musée du Cluny: XIIIe–debut XVe siècle. Paris, Eds. de la Réunion des musées nationaux, 1989. 294p. il. (part col.)
Scholarly catalog, with black-and-white plates.
Contents: Orvèfrerie religieuse; Orfèvrerie profane; Annexes.
Bibliographie, p.270–71. Tables de concordance, p.282–85. Index, p.286–92.

Germany and Austria

Dictionaries and Encyclopedias

P656 Neuwirth, Waltraud. Lexikon Wiener Gold- und Silberschmiede und ihre Punzen, 1867–1922. Vienna, Neuwirth, 1976. 2v. il. (part col.)
Texts in German and English. Dictionary of Viennese gold- and silversmiths and their hallmarks.
Verzeichnis der entwerfender Künstler, v.1, p.361–63, v.2, p.373–74.

Histories and Handbooks

P657 Silber und Gold: Augsburger Goldschmiedekunst für die Hofe Europas. Hrsg. von Reinhold Baumstark und Helmut Seling. Katalog von Lorenz Seelig. Mit Beitr. von Ulli Arnold . . . [et al.] München, Hirmer, [1994]. 613, lxxivp. il., ports. (part col.)
Catalog of the exhibition, Bayerisches Nationalmuseum (1994).
Extensive, detailed, and beautifully illustrated treatment of the work of Augsburg gold- and silversmiths of the 17th and 18th centuries, with contributions by many specialists. Emphasis is on rare and unusual objects of the highest quality. Includes interpretive essays, marks, and biographical entries.
Markentafeln, p.i–vii. Biographien der Augsburger Goldschmiede, p.viii–xxix. Glossar zu Erläuterung der Fachbegriffe, p.xxx–xxxvi. Abkürzungen, p.xxxvii. Abgekürzt zitierte Literatur, p.xxxviii–lx. Register, p.lxi–lxxiii.

P658 Spies, Gerd. Braunschweiger Goldschmiede. München, Klinkhardt und Biermann, 1996. 3v. il. (part col.), ports., fold. charts, genealogical chart.
Massive, detailed history of goldsmiths and their work in Brunswick from the medieval period through the 19th century. Includes detailed information on all known workers with individual bibliographical references.
Contents: (1) Geschichte; (2) Werke; (3) Meister und Marken; Anhang: Privileg von 1231; Gildeordnung vom 30. November 1562; Gildeordnung vom 15. April 1701.
Abkürzungen, p.226. Literaturauswahl, p.227–38. Register, p.241–43.

Great Britain and Ireland

Dictionaries and Encyclopedias

P659 Culme, John. The directory of gold and silversmiths, jewellers and allied traders 1838–1914, from the

London Assay Office Registers. [Woodbridge], Antique Collectors' Club, [1987]. 2v. il., ports.
Massive compendium of information on 19th-century British precious metalworkers with marks registered at Goldsmiths' Hall. Succeeds Grimwade, which covers the preceding period. First vol. consists of biographical and historical entries for individuals and firms, based on extensive archival evidence. Second vol. reproduces 15,000 marks. An essential reference for the period.

Contents: (1) Introduction; Attitudes to old plate, 1750–1900; Trades; The biographies; (2) The marks.

Abbreviations, v.1, p.xvi–xv. Index to the biographies, v.2, p.345–91.

P660 De Giovanni, Andrea. Sheffield and Birmingham Victorian electroplaters book of marks. [Milan, EMI, 1991]. 138p. il. (EMI manuali teccnici, 01)
Compact alphabetical compendium of the marks on 19th-century English electroplate, preceded by a brief discussion of the process. All marks are illustrated by photographs.

Index of manufacturers, p.125–28. References, p.129. Index, p.130. The author, p.131. Table of "Diamond" registry marks, p.136–37.

P661 Fallon, John P. Marks of London goldsmiths and silversmiths, 1837–1914. London, Barrie and Jenkins, [1992]. 390p. il.
Successor to GLAH 1:P503 (covering 1697–1837). Compact handbook of historical entries and marks for some 200 of the better-known London metalworking firms, illustrating more than 1,300 of these firms' marks. Based on the registers of the Goldsmiths' Company.

Index of makers' marks, p.331–90.

P662 Grimwade, Arthur G. London goldsmiths, 1697–1837: their marks and lives: from the original registers at Goldsmith's Hall and other sources. 3d ed. rev. and enl. London, Faber, 1990. vii, 773p. il., plates.
1st ed., 1976. 2d ed., 1982. The new ed. includes "further corrections and additions to both marks and biographical sections."—*Note to the third ed.* Separate sections devoted to marks and a biographical dictionary. No bibliography or index.

P663 Jackson's silver and gold marks of England, Scotland, and Ireland. Ed. by Ian Pickford. Woodbridge, Antique Collectors' Club, 1989. 766p. il.
For earlier ed., see GLAH 1:P507.

P664 The silversmiths of Birmingham and their marks, 1750–1980. General ed., Kenneth Crisp Jones. Contribs., Judith Banister . . . [et al.] London, N.A.G. Press, [1981]. 416p. il., ports., 43 col. plates.
History of silversmithing in Birmingham from the 18th century to the present day, with essays on aspects of the trade and more than 2,400 makers' marks from the Birmingham Assay Office registry.

Contents: (I) The history of Birmingham's silversmiths; (II) The organization of management and labour; (III) Major Birmingham silversmiths, bullion dealers and companies of the 20th century; (IV) The makers' marks; (V) Glossary, decorative terms and techniques.

Bibliography, p.400–01. General index, p.403–08. Index of makers' marks, p.409–16.

Histories and Handbooks

P665 Bennett, Douglas. Collecting Irish silver, 1637–1900. [London], Souvenir Press, [1984]. 228p. il., 20 col. plates.
Compact, authoritative history of silver in Ireland, equally useful for collector or researcher. Includes extensive lists of makers and marks for Dublin, Cork, Limerick, and the provinces, and an illustrated discussion of hall-marks on Irish silver.

Comparative tables of weights, p.224–25. Bibliography, p.226. Index, p.227–28.

P666 Culme, John. Nineteenth-century silver. [London], Country Life, [1977]. 232p. il., col. plates.
Comprehensive history of the silver industry in 19th-century England, with attention to issues of technology and labor as well as those of style and merchandising.

Contents: (1) The industry; (2) The trade: styles and retailers; (3) The exhibitions: showmen and craftsmen.

Sources, p.225–26. Index, p.227–32.

P667 Glanville, Philippa. Silver in England. [Winchester, Mass., Allen and Unwin, 1987]. xii, 366p. il., 4 col. plates. (English decorative arts)
Readable, authoritative general history of silver in England from the medieval period to the present day, by a major scholar of the craft.

Contents: (I) History; (II) Craft, company and customers; (III) Design and ornament; (IV) Silver and society.

Bibliography, p.338–55. Index, p.356–66.

P668 ______. Silver in Tudor and early Stuart England: a social history and catalogue of the national collection, 1480–1660. [London], Victoria and Albert, [1990]. 528p. il. (part col.), ports.
Extensive, detailed catalog of Tudor and Stuart liturgical and secular silver in the Victoria and Albert Museum, accompanied by essays placing these objects in their social, historical, and economic settings. Many illustrations, including contemporary paintings showing silver in use.

Contents: (I) The social context; (II) Function and ornament; (III) The catalogue.

Bibliography, p.[506]–14. Concordance, p.[515]. Index, p.[516]–28.

P669 Lomax, James. British silver at Temple Newsam and Lotherton Hall: A catalogue of the Leeds Collection. [Leeds], Leeds Art Collections Fund and W.S. Maney, [1992]. xv, 191p. il., 4 col. plates.
Catalog of an important collection of British silver dating from the early 17th century to the early 20th, the property of the city of Leeds and housed at its two country house museums. Objects are arranged chronologically by function

and described in detailed entries. Includes an introductory history of the formation of the collection.

Contents: (1) Church silver; (2) Presentation silver; (3) Silver for drinking; (4) Silver for dining; (5) Silver for the drawing room; (6) Silver about the house; (7) Silver for the bedroom and for personal use; (8) Vinaigrettes and small boxes; (9) Fakes, forgeries, etc.

Abbreviations [of works cited], p.[xiii]–xv. Appendix: Leeds silver, p.[183]–86. Index, p.[187]–91.

P670 Oman, Charles. English engraved silver, 1150 to 1900. London, Faber, [1978]. 158p. il.

Detailed consideration of engraved silver by an acknowledged expert: the standard work on this subject.

Catalogue of the works attributed to the Engraver P over M, p.141–46. Apprenticeships of engravers, p.147–53. Short bibliography, p.154. Index, p.155–58.

P671 Pickford, Ian. Silver flatware: English, Irish and Scottish 1660–1980. [Woodbridge], Antique Collectors' Club, [1983]. 231p. il., genealogical charts, ports.

Comprehensive discussion of silver flatware, aimed at collectors, but useful also for researchers. Includes the history of the development of table services, an extensive section on pattern identification, and one on serving pieces.

Select bibliography, p.221–22. Indexes, p.223–31.

P672 Schroder, Timothy. The National Trust book of English domestic silver, 1500–1900. [Harmondsworth], Viking in assoc. with the National Trust, [1988]. xii, 338p. il.

Readable narrative history of silver in England, with considerable emphasis on the social, economic, and technological influences that shaped its development, while not neglecting developments in style and design. Useful biographical appendix covers the more prominent silversmiths, and includes illustrations of their marks.

Biographical appendix, p.289–305. Suggested further reading, p.319. Glossary, p.321–26. General index, p.327–32. Index of goldsmiths and manufacturers, p.333–35. Index of collections, p.337–38.

Italy

P673 Donati, Ugo. I marchi dell'argenteria Italiana: oltre 100 marchi territoriali e di garanzia dal XIII secolo a oggi. [Novara], De Agostini, [1993]. 264p. il., port.

Dictionary of Italian provincial and territorial silver marks, arranged by motif.

Tabelle delle once dei denari e dei bajocchi rapportati al millesimo, p.249–50. Glossario, p.251–54. Bibliografia, p.255–57. Indice dei nomi, p.258–59. Indice dei luoghi, p.260–62.

Latin America

P674 Esteras Martin, Cristina. Marcas de plateria hispanoamericana: siglos XVI–XX. [Madrid], Ed. Tuero, 1992. l, 197, [2]p. il. (part col.) (Coleccion investigacion y critica)

Dictionary, by country, of the marks of Mexican, Central American, and South American silversmiths. As appropriate, includes makers' marks, town or city marks, assay marks, and taxation marks. All marks are illustrated. Introductory essay discusses Latin American silverwork.

Cronologia de los plateros, p.179–82. Abreviaturas, p.183–84. Bibliografia, p.185–89. Indice onomastico, p.191–94. Indice geografico, p.195–97. Sumario, p.[199].

P675 Fernández, Alejandro; Munoa, Rafael; and Rabasco, Jorge. Enciclopedia de la plata española y virreinal americana. Prólogo de José Manuel Cruz Valdovinos. 2a ed., corr. y aum. Madrid, A. Fernández, R. Munoa, J. Rabasco (Distr., 1985). xiv, 591p. il.

1st ed., Madrid, Asociación Española de Joyeros, Plateros y Relojeros, 1984. Suplemento, 1985.

Encyclopedia of hallmarks, silversmiths, and their work. Covers colonial Latin America to the 20th century.

Bibliography, p.545–62.

P676 Ribera, Adolfo Luis, and Schenone, Hector H. Plateria Sudamericana de los siglos XVII–XX. Munich, Hirmer, [1981]. 454p. il., 40 col. plates.

Comprehensive, well-illustrated history of Latin American secular and church silver from the Colonial period to the present, including discussions of mining and metallurgy.

Contents: (1) La extraccion de la plata ye la metalurgia colonial; (2) La orfebreria colonial; (3) La orfebreria Argentina del siglo XIX; (4) Catalogo.

Glosario, p.103–08. Notas, p.109–14. Bibliografia, p.115–20. Apuntes para un diccionario de orfebres rioplatenses (siglos XVI–XIX), p.[385]–451.

Low Countries

Dictionaries and Encyclopedias

P677 Citroen, Karel. Dutch goldsmiths' and silversmiths' marks and names prior to 1812: a descriptive and critical repertory. Leiden, Primavera Pr., 1993. 283p. il.

Dictionary of the marks and/or names of "all those goldsmiths and silversmiths . . . that were active in this country prior to the founding of the Kingdom of the Netherlands."—*p.*7. Includes 6,350 marks used by 5,000 craftsmen and 5,500 names of craftsmen whose marks are unrecorded.

Contents: (I) The maker's mark; (II) Silversmiths without recorded marks; (III) Town marks; (IV) Date letters; (V) Sources and works of reference.

Glossary: English-Dutch-French-German, p.234–39. Dutch-English, p.240–42. French-English, p.243–45. German-English, p.246–48. Index to names in chapter I, p.249–83.

P678 Meestertekens van Nederlandse Goud- und Zilversmeden = Makers' marks of Dutch gold- and silversmiths. [3d ed.]. 's-Gravenhage, Staatsuitgeverij, 1981. 2v. il.

Text in Dutch and English. 3d ed. of a standard dictionary of Dutch gold and silver marks used between 1814 and 1963. For the preceding ed., see GLAH 1:P524; for its successor publication, see the following entry.

Contents: (1) 1814–1963; (2) 1963–1980.

P679 Nederlandse verantwoordelijkheidstekens sinds 1797 = Netherlands' responsibility marks since 1797 . . . a review of the Dutch makers' marks, importers' marks, assay office identification marks, assayers' marks and trade assayers' marks for gold, silver and platinum since the introduction of the Law of the 19th Brumaire year 6 (9–11–1797). Ed. 1995. [Gouda, Waarborg Platina, Goud en Zilver N.V., 1995]. 1v. (various paginations). il., map.

Massive compilation of Dutch and Belgian silvermarks from 1797 to the present, designed to succeed and replace Meestertekens van Nederlandse goud- en zilversmeden (GLAH 1:P524 and the preceding entry). Includes historical introduction and explanation of the ordinances affecting hallmarking from 1797 to the present.

P680 Stuyck, R. Belgische zilvermerken = poinçons d'argenterie Belges. Antwerp, Erasme, 1984. 314p. il.

In Dutch and French. Dictionary of Belgian hallmarks.

Register = index, p.105–06. Jaar- of dekenaatsletters = lettres décanales annales, p.307–12. Bibliografie = bibliographie, p.313–14.

Histories and Handbooks

P681 Marechal, Dominique. Chefs d'oeuvre de l'orfèvrerie brugeoise. [Bruges, Stichting Kunstboek, 1993]. 455p. il. (part col.)

Catalog of a major exhibition of religious and secular silver and goldwork made in Bruges during the 17th and 18th centuries, Bruges, Musées Memling and Brangwyn (1993). All objects are illustrated in color; illustrations include an extensive section of marks. Preliminary essays discuss the history of precious metalworking in Bruges, its clientele, and its practitioners and their working methods.

Catalogue des poinçons, p.384–406. Registre des orfèvres, p.407–08. Registre des objets, p.409–10. Registre des lieux de conservation de des prêteurs, p.411–12. Les conseils d'administration du metier des orfèvres et argentiers, 1363–1794, p.413–33. Indexe, p.433–38. Section documentaire, p.439. Bibliographie, p.441–45. Liste des expositions, p.447–48.

P682 Nederlands zilver, 1580–1830 = Dutch silver, 1580–1830. Red. = ed. by A. L. den Blaauwen. s'Gravenhage, Staatsuitgeverij, 1979. l, 390p. il., map, ports.

In Dutch and English. Catalog of the exhibition, Rijksmuseum, Amsterdam (1979–80), and other locations, of Dutch silver from the late 16th to the early 19th centuries, with much attention to regional and local styles.

Contents: Dutch silver 1580–1830, by J. Verbeek; Silver, silversmiths and silver marks, by J. H. Leopold; Catalogue. Biographies of silversmiths included in this catalogue, p.350–69. Glossary, compiled by J. Verbeek, p.370–73. Bibliography of Dutch silver (up to c.1830), compiled by A. L. den Blaauwen, p.374–85. Index of personal names, p.386–89. Index of towns where the objects were made, p.389.

P683 L'orfèvrerie civile ancienne du pays de Liège. [Liège, Musée de l'art wallon, 1991]. 327, [1]p. il., plan, port.

Catalog of an exhibition, Musée de l'art wallon, Liege (1991), of secular gold and silverwork produced in the province of Liège, Belgium, in the 17th and 18th centuries.

Contents: L'orfèvrerie civile ancienne de la cite de Liège, par Pierre Colman; Table d'interpretation des lettres annales; Poinçons corporatifs; Répertoire general des poinçons d'orfèvres liègeois, par Pierre Colman and Luc Engen; Bibliographie; Catalogue Liège, par Luc Engen; L'orfèvrerie civile ancienne des "bonnes villes" de la principaute de Liège, par Jean-Jacques van Ormelingen; Catalogue "bonnes villes," par Luc Engen and Jean-Jacques van Ormelingen.

Abbreviations, p.314. Abstracts (in Dutch, English, and German), p.316–19. Index, p.321–23. Plan de la vitrine centrale, p.324–25.

Malta

P684 Bologna, Alaine Apap. The silver of Malta. [Lija, Malta], MAG, 1995. 271p. il. (part col.)

While produced as a catalog to accompany an exhibition on Maltese silver sponsored by the Fondazzjoni Patrimonju Malti, this vol. serves as a history and guide to the craft from the 16th century to the present. Includes many color illustrations of silverwork, object of vertu and filigree, and an illustrated listing of makers' marks.

Glossary, p.14. Bibliography, p.247. Makers' marks, in alphabetical order, p.248–69. Other marks, p.270–271.

P685 Farrugia, Jimmy. Antique Maltese domestic silver. [Valletta], Said, [1992]. xx, 347p. il. (part col., 1 fold.), port.

Comprehensive, well-illustrated history of silversmithing and silverwork in Malta from the 16th century to the present. Includes list of known goldsmiths and silversmiths and reproductions of assay and makers' marks, and a chapter on jewelry.

Maltese and metric equivalent measures of weight of gold and silver (1640–1982), p.294–95. Documents, p.297–316. Bibliography, p.319–21. Index, p.325–47.

Russia and Eastern Europe

P686 Baroque splendor: the art of the Hungarian goldsmith. By Istvan Fodor, Katalin Foldi-Dozsa, Ibolya Gerelyes . . . [et al.] N.Y., Bard Graduate Center, [1994]. 227p. il., ports. (part col.)

Catalog of an exhibition held at the Bard Graduate Center (1994).

While devoting primary attention to the work of Hungarian precious metalworkers of the 17th and 18th centuries, this well-illustrated catalog also discusses architecture, portraiture, arms and armor, and architecture of the period.

Biographies and makers' marks, p.217–21. Bibliography, p.223–27.

P687 Musée du Petit Palais, Paris. Splendeurs de Russie: mille ans d'orfèvrerie. [Paris, Paris-Musées, 1993]. 288p. il., part col.

Well-illustrated catalog of a loan exhibition of Russian silver, enamel, and goldwork from the 10th century to the beginning of the 20th century, lent by various Russian museums. Catalog includes essays by a team of Russian and French specialists in the various periods and materials.

Glossaire, p.279–81. Bibliographie du catalogue, p.283–85. Bibliographie indicative, p.285–86.

P688 Paulson, Paul L. Guide to Russian silver hallmarks. [Washington, D.C., Paulson, 1976]. xxxi, [1], 34, [1]p. il.

Compact but informative introduction to Russian assayers' marks and hallmarks, with an introductory essay on their use and illustrated lists of silversmiths and their marks and the assayers' marks of Russian cities.

Bibliography, p.xxxix.

P689 Solodkoff, Alexander von. Russian gold and silverwork, 17th–19th century. N.Y., Rizzoli, [1981]. 238p. il. (part col.)

History of metalworking in Russia during the previous three centuries, with emphasis on forms and usages that distinguish this work from that of other countries. Detailed but accessible for the non-specialist.

Contents: Organization of the goldsmith's trade in Russia; Styles and influences in the goldsmith's art in Russia; Material, techniques, and typical objects; Marks on Russian gold and silver objects; Centres of gold and silverwork; Important masters, workshops and firms.

Lists of masters, p.206–20. Russian town marks, p.221–22. Index of marks and signatures, p.223–30. Select bibliography, p.231–33. Index, p.234–37.

Scandinavia

P690 Holmquist, Kersti. Svenskt silversmide: Guld- och silverstämplar, 1850–1912. Stockholm, Nordiska Museet, 1995. 350p., col. il.

In Swedish. Summary in English.

Companion vol. to the same publisher's Guld- och silverstämplar i Sverige, 1520–1850 (see GLAH 1:P531). Comprehensive listing of the marks of silversmiths, goldsmiths, and jewelers working in Sweden 1850–1912. Arrangement is by town and under town, chronologically. All marks are illustrated. Many entries include individual bibliographical references. English-language summary discusses the background of the volume and its predecessors, the laws and practices of hallmarking in Sweden, and important archival sources.

Register over stads- och andra ortssamplar, p.311–37. Tryckta källor [bibliography], p.338–40. Förkortningar [abbreviations], p.342. Inventarieforteckning [inventory numbers], p.343. Person- och företagsregister, p.344–50.

P691 Lightbown, R. W. Catalogue of Scandinavian and Baltic silver. N.Y., Alpine, [1984]. 255p. il.

Catalog of the Victoria and Albert Museum's collection of silverwork from the Scandinavian and Baltic countries. Introductory essays discuss the history of the collections and characterstic styles and types of work produced in these countries, followed by detailed entries for each object. An accessible and useful English-language introduction to the subject.

Selected bibliography of Scandinavian and Baltic silver, p.[24]–28. Index of makers and artists, p.[252]–53. Numerical concordance, p.[254]–55.

Spain and Portugal

P692 Fernández, Alejandro; Munoa, Rafael; and Rabasco, Jorge. Enciclopedia de la Plata española y Virreinal americana. Publicada con los auspicios de la Asociacion Espanola de Joyeros, Plateros, y Relojeros, y de la Federacion de Anticuarios y Almonedistas. Prologo de Jose Manual Cruz Valdovinos. Madrid, Edicion de los autores, 1984. xiii, [3], 566, [1]p. il., maps.

Comprehensive illustrated history of mining, metalworking, and silversmithing in Spain and Spanish America. Includes illustrations of marks and lists of known silversmiths in these areas.

Bibliografia unificada de la Plateria, espanola y virreinal, p.537–[53]. Indice tematico, p.554–62.

SEE ALSO: Esteras Martin, Marcas de plateria hispanoamericana (GLAH 2:P674).

Switzerland

P693 Gruber, Alain. Weltliches Silber: Katalog der Sammlung des Schweizerischen Landesmuseum Zurich. Unter der Mitarb. von Anna Rapp. Zurich, Berichthaus, [1977]. 344p. il. (part col.)

Catalog of the collection of silverware at the Swiss National Museum, Zurich, which includes objects from the 14th through the early 20th centuries. With its many illustrations, individual entries, and reproductions of hallmarks, this catalog serves as a chronological guide to the development of silverwork in Switzerland.

Zusammenfassungen-resume-riassunto-summary, p.325–28. Konkordanztabelle, p.329–32. Bibliographie, p.333–35. Meister-, Namen-, und Ortsregister, p.337–43. Register der datieren Werke, p.344.

United States

Dictionaries and Encyclopedias

P694 Belden, Louise Conway. Marks of American silversmiths in the Ineson-Bissell Collection. [Winterthur],

Winterthur Museum [and] the Univ. Pr. of Virginia, [1980]. ix, 505, [1]p. il., port.

Illustrated guide to more than 1700 American silversmiths' marks, found on objects made between 1670 and 1870, and housed in a collection at the Winterthur Museum. All marks are reproduced photographically. Directory and other bibliographical references and notes are furnished for each mark. Arrangement is by last name of silversmith. Includes a useful introductory essay on identification of marks.

An illustrated glossary of spoon terms, p.[467]–[88]. References, p.[489]–505.

P695 Ensko, Stephen Guernsey Cook. American silversmiths and their marks IV. A rev. and enlarged ed. comp. by Dorothea Ensko Wyle. Foreword by Alice Winchester. Boston, Godine, [1989, c1988]. xiii, [478]p. il., maps.

For previous ed., see GLAH 1:P537. "This final, revised edition is a compilation of the 1915 book written by my grandfather, Robert Ensko, and the 1927, 1937, 1948 books written by my father, Stephen Guernsey Cook Ensko."—*p.[v].*

A standard reference for marks and names of American silversmiths, now issued in one vol., and still an important source for research in this area. Bibliography revised as of 1969. Marks are illustrated by drawings.

Locations of silversmiths' shops, by Helen Burr Smith, p.365–81. Maps showing locations of silversmiths in New York 1660–1750, New York 1750–1800, Boston 1650–1800, and Philadelphia 1695–1800, p.[383]–91. Bibliography, p.393–99. Facsimile pages from the four previous Ensko books, p.401–77.

P696 Green, Robert Alan. Marks of American silversmiths, revised (1650–1900). Illustrated with 300 original photographs and 4000 drawings of marks of silversmiths, jewelers, watchmakers, clockmakers and vendors. Key West, Green, [1984]. x, 267p. il.

Compact, handy compilation of hallmarks, trademarks, and associated information of particular use to collectors. Reproduces drawings of marks found in standard references as well as photographs of marks taken by the author.

General index, p.209–67.

P697 Kovel, Ralph, and Kovel, Terry. Kovels' American silver marks. N.Y., Crown, [1989]. x, 421p. il.

"Portions of this book originally appeared in [the authors'] A directory of American silver, pewter and silver plate, 1961."—*p.[iv].*

Principally a listing of American silvermarks, 1650 to the present, arranged by name. Brief entries include working dates, locations, and bibliographical references. Not all marks are illustrated, but does include year marks for prominent firms. Illustrations also include guides to dating spoons and creamers by shape. Authors are well known for their many works aimed at an audience of collectors and researchers.

Bibliography, p.418–21.

P698 Rainwater, Dorothy T. Encyclopedia of American silver manufacturers. 3d ed., rev.. West Chester, Schiffer, [1986]. vi, 266p. il.

1st ed. titled American silver manufacturers, 1966; 2d ed., 1975 under the present title.

Most recent ed. of the standard, indispensable reference for the names and marks of the manufacturers and distributors of American silver and silverplate from the 19th century to the present. Entries usually include drawings or photographs of marks, location, and brief history of the firm.

Unascribed marks, p.234–36. Alphabetical listing of trade names, p.238–44. Key to unlettered marks, p.245–52. Glossary, p.254–58. Silverplate specifications, p.259. Table of equivalents, p.260. Bibliography, p.261–66.

Histories and Handbooks

P699 Elegant plate: three centuries of precious metals in New York City. Ed. by Deborah Dependahl Waters. Essays by Kristan H. McKinsey, Gerald W. R. Ward, and Deborah Dependahl Waters. Catalogue entries by Deborah Dependahl Waters. [N.Y.], Museum of the City of New York (Distr. by Univ. Pr. of New England, [2000]). 2v. il., 16 col. plates.

Exhaustive catalog of the collection of silver and gold objects at the Museum of the City of New York, created from the last years of the 17th century into the 20th. Detailed individual entries for each piece are preceded by interpretive essays by specialist silver historians, allowing the work to serve as a history of silver objects and their makers in New York City.

Glossary and frequently cited references, p.86–89. Notes to the reader, p.96. Index of makers and firms, p.612–15. Index of owners, presenters, and selected events, p.616–19.

P700 Fennimore, Donald L. Silver and pewter. With photographs by Rosmarie Hausherr. N.Y., Knopf, [1984]. 478, [2]p. il. (part col.) (Knopf collectors' guides to American antiques)

Compact field guide to American silver and pewter from the 17th century to the present, with objects arranged by function. Especially informative for the collector.

Contents: (1) Introduction; (2) Silver and silver plate; (3) Pewter.

Caring for your collection, p.420–21. Flatware patterns, p.422–24. Glossary, p.[425]–[29]. Illustrated guide to American makers and marks [whose work is featured in this book], p.430–[49]. Price guide, p.450–[64]. Bibliography, p.466–[69]. Silver and silver plate index, p.470–[75]. Pewter index, p.476–78.

P701 Johnston, Phillip M. Catalogue of American silver: the Cleveland Museum of Art. [Introd. by Henry H. Hawley]. Made possible by the Luce Foundation. Cleveland, Cleveland Museum of Art [and the] Indiana Univ. Pr., [1994]. xxiii, 180p. il.

Detailed, well-documented catalog of an important collection of American silver, originally formed by the pioneer Boston collector Hollis French. Catalog incorporates the results of newly developed scientific testing of metals and includes discussion of fakes and forgeries discovered during catalog research.

Notes on metal analyses, by Bruce Christman, p.xiv–xvii. Abbreviations, p.xix–xxiii. Index of silversmiths, p.177–78. Index of accession numbers, p.179–80.

P702 Quimby, Ian. American silver at Winterthur. Winterthur, Winterthur Museum [and] Charlottesville, Univ. of Virginia Pr., 1995. xvii, 490p. il.

Substantial, scholarly catalog illustrated in black-and-white, with a valuable set of introductory essays.

Contents: On the nature and use of silver; Silver and material culture; The question of authorship Style in American silver; Building a collection; Scientific analysis of silver; Notes on the catalogue; The catalogue: New England, New York, Pennsylvania and the South; Appendix: Analysis of hollowware by wall thickness.

Bibliography, p.487–90.

P703 Venable, Charles L. Silver in America, 1840–1940: a century of splendor. Tom Jenkins, lead photographer. Biographical entries by D. Albert Soeffing. [Dallas], Dallas Museum of Art (Distr. Abrams, [1994]). 365p. il. (part col.)

Published to accompany the exhibition, Dallas Museum of Art (1994), and other locations.

Thorough, well-illustrated history of the American silver industry during the second half of the 19th century and first half of the 20th, with considerable attention to technological developments, labor organization and working methods, and economic trends, as well as to design influences. Very useful section of biographical sketches of leading figures and firms.

References, p.301–11. Glossary, p.312–13. Biographies of selected silver producers and retailers, p.314–24. Exhibition checklist and list of illustrations, p.325–54. Index, p.355–65.

P704 Warren, David; Howe, Katherine S.; and Brown, Michael K. Marks of achievement: four centuries of American presentation silver. With an introd. by Gerald W. R. Ward. Houston, Museum of Fine Arts in assoc. with Abrams, [1987]. 207p. il. (part col.)

Catalog of the exhibition, the Museum (1987), of three centuries of American presentation silver, given to commemorate personal, civic, and national events of importance. Handsomely illustrated and carefully researched, this vol. discusses silver objects that by their very nature are of high quality and exceptional design, forming a landmark history of exceptional silverwork.

Bibliography, p.194–200. Index, p.201–07.

P705 Yale University Art Gallery. Silver in American life: selections from the Mabel Brady Garvan and other collections at Yale University. Ed. by Barbara McLean Ward and Gerald W. R. Ward. An exhibition organized by the Yale University Art Gallery and the American Federation of Arts. [N.Y., American Federation of Arts, 1979]. xiii, 193p. il. (part col.)

Publication accompanying a traveling exhibition sponsored by the American Federation of Arts and based on the collections of silver at the Yale University Art Gallery.

Comprehensive, wide-ranging examination of the many aspects of silver and its uses in America over three centuries.

Contents: (1) Six themes in American silver: "A mineral of that excellent nature": the qualities of silver as a metal, by William A. Lanford; "You shall not crucify man on a cross of gold": silver and money in America, by John P. Burnham; "The most genteel of any in the mechanic way": the American silversmith, by Barbara McLean Ward; "From the shop to the manufactory": silver and industry, 1800–1970, by Stephen K. Victor; "An handsome cupboard of plate": the role of silver in American life, by Gerald W. R. Ward; "As good as sterling": art in American silver, by Martha Gandy Fales; (2) Silver in American life: catalogue of the exhibition, by Barbara McLean Ward, Gerald W. R. Ward, and Kevin L. Stayton; (3) Silver: its sources and uses; (4) Coins and medals; (5) Traditional craft practices; (6) Mass production and craft revival; (7) Silver and society; (8) A gallery of American silver.

Selected bibliography, p.190–92. Index, p.193.

Asian Countries

General Works

P706 Roth, H. Ling. Oriental silverwork: Malay and Chinese. [Reprint.] Kuala Lumpur, Oxford Univ. Pr., 1993. xxviii, 300p. il., maps. (Oxford in Asia hardback reprints)

Reprint of GLAH 1:P545.

China

P707 White, Julia M., and Bunker, Emma C. Adornment for eternity; status and rank in Chinese ornament. With contrib. by Chen Peifen. Denver, Denver Art Museum; Woods, [1994]. 214p. il. (part col.), map.

Text in English and Chinese. Catalog of the exhibition, Denver Art Museum (1994), and other locations.

Includes introductory essays and descriptions of 113 items of personal adornment, e.g., jewelry, mirrors, belthooks, from the Mengdiexuan Collection. The objects, primarily metalwork from the 6th century B.C. to the Qing dynasty, are described not only as works of art but also as indicators of status and rank in ancient Chinese society.

Bibliography, p.[206]–14.

India, Nepal, Pakistan, Tibet

P708 Stronge, Susan. Bidri ware: inlaid metalwork from India. [London,] Victoria and Albert Museum, 1985. 96p. il. (part col.)

Based on the Museum's collection of 19th-century wares.

Contents: The technique; Origins of bidri; Uses of bidri; Catalogue.

Bibliography, p.92–93. Glossary and abbreviations, p.94. Index of museum numbers, p.95.

P709 Wilkinson, Wynyard R. T. The makers of Indian colonial silver: a register of European goldsmiths, silversmiths, jewellers, watchmakers and clockmakers in India and their marks, 1760–1860. London, Wilkinson, 1987. xxii, 230p. il., maps, ports., genealogical charts.

Compendium of the marks of European workers in precious metals in India, based on extensive archival research, by the recognized expert in this field. Some marks and silver objects are illustrated.

Index of makers marks to be found in the text, p.222. Index to objects illustrated in the text, p.223. Ships mentioned in the register, p.223. Cross-reference index to makers with their own entries in the register, p.224–26. Main index, p.227–29.

P710 Yule, Paul. Metalwork of the bronze age in India. München, Beck, 1985. xii, 127p. il., 108p. of plates (Prähistorische Bronzefunde. Abteilung XX, Bd. 8)

"No other area of Indian archaeology is so controversial, yet so inadequately documented as the non-Harappan of the second millennium B.C. Justification for yet another treatment . . . lies in the appearance of a new and dramatically more representative material, the systematic compilation, study and publication of which results in basic changes in our understanding."—*Foreword.*

General abbreviations, p.114. Abbreviations used in the references, p.115. Select bibliography, p.116–23. General index, p.124. Index of museums and collections, p.125. Index of findspots, p.126–27. Index of artifacts by type, p.128.

Japan

P711 Harris, Victor, and Ogasawara, Nobuo. Swords of the Samurai. London, British Museum, [1990]. 175p. il. (part col.)

Catalog of the exhibition, British Museum (1990).

Discusses the technical excellence and artistry of the swords, using examples from the 9th century onwards held in Japanese collections. The essays also examine the role of the samurai class in Japanese history, the sword as part of the Imperial regalia, and the relationship of the sword to Zen Buddhism. Swords, sword blades, sword guards, and representations of swords in Japanese painting and prints are all included in the catalog.

Bibliography, p.169. Glossary, p.[172]–75. Index of makers, p.175.

P712 Ogasawara, Nobuo. Sword guards and fittings from Japan: the collection of the Museum of Decorative Art, Copenhagen: bequest of Dr. Hugo Halberstadt. N.Y., Kodansha, 1983. 2v., il. (part col.)

Text in English and Japanese.

Although this set presents the collection of sword guards and fittings in the Museum of Decorative Arts, the critical commentary and plate descriptions were written by the curator of the Arms and Armor Department at the Tokyo National Museum. Each vol. has an introductory essay but the bulk of the presentation is devoted to photographs of the more than 1,500 individual pieces in the collection. Each piece is fully labeled, with many detail photographs.

Africa, Oceania, The Americas

Africa

P713 Garrard, Timothy F. Akan weights and the gold trade. [London], Longman, [1980]. xix, 393p. 61 il., maps. (Legon history series)

The standard study of the goldweights of the Akan that provides information about gold producers and artisans, metal-casting technology, and the gold trade as well as the daily life of the Akan peoples of Ghana and the Ivory coast.

Contents: (1) The origins of the Akan gold trade; (2) Gold in the Akan states; (3) The Guinea trade; (4) The art of the goldsmith; (5) Gold production and export, 1400–1900; (6) Goldweights in Akan society; (7) Evolution of the Akan weight-system; (8) Akan weight-names; (9) The dating of Akan goldweights; (10) Goldweight production: a numerical estimate; Appendix I: Units of weight and weight-ranges; Appendix II: Traditional sterling values of goldweights; Appendix III: Weight-lists from individual informants; Appendix IV: Published weight-lists, 1852–1973; Appendix V: Glossary (p.357–63).

Bibliography, p.364–74. Index, p.375–93.

P714 Herbert, Eugenia W. Iron, gender, and power: rituals of transformation in African societies. Bloomington, Indiana Univ. Pr., 1993. xii, 277p., 47 il., maps.

A classic work on the arts and material culture of Sub-Saharan Africa.

Contents: Part 1: Those who play with Fire: African metallurgy as epic drama, (1) The actors and the artifacts; (2) Rituals of transformation and procreation; (3) Rituals of transformation: exclusions and taboos; (4) The smith and the forge; (5) Ironmaking and belief. Part 2: Symmetries and asymmetries: power and fertility, (6) Le Roi-Forgeron; (7) Of forests and furnaces, anvils and antelopes; (8) Potters and pots. Conclusion: Anthropomorphism and the genderization of power; Appendix: Reconstructions of iron smelting in Africa.

Bibliography, p.241–70. Index, p.271–77.

P715 ______. Red gold of Africa: copper in precolonial history and culture. [Madison], Univ. of Wisconsin Pr., [1984]. 413p. 40 il., col. plates, maps.

A comprehensive and scholarly study of the role of copper in African society.

Contents: Part 1: Copper resources and copper metallurgy in precolonial Africa, (1) "Ancient workings" in sub-Saharan Africa; (2) The smith as Nganga: ritual, social, and political aspects of copperworking; (3) "Mangeurs de cuivre": mining and smelting; (4) Smithing, drawing, casting, and alloying. Part 2: The copper trade, (5) Gold for copper: the copper trade before the period of European discoveries; (6) Manillas, Neptunes, rods, and wire: the maritime trade from the discoveries to c. 1800; (7) The copper economy in the nineteenth century. Part 3: Copper in traditional society; (8) Copper as a medium of exchange; (9) Copper as a medium of art; (10) Copper as a medium of power; (11) Shango and Nommo: copper and the language of materials.

Bibliography, p.373–91. Index, p.393–413.

P716 McNaughton, Patrick R. The Mande blacksmiths: knowledge, power, and art in West Africa. Bloomington, Indiana Univ. Pr., [1988]. xxiv, 241p. 77 il., col. plates, maps. (Traditional arts of Africa)

This scholarly study is about the art, beliefs, and rituals of the Bamana (Bambara), a Mande-speaking people, living in Mali, West Africa. "Recommended for all academic libraries building African art collections, as are other titles in the 'Traditional Arts of Africa' series."—*Review*, Art documentation, v.7, no.4, winter 1988, p.172.

Contents: (1) Blacksmiths in Mande society; (2) The Mande smiths as craftsmen; (3) Smiths and the shape of civilized space; (4) The blacksmiths' sculpture; (5) The Mande smiths as men of means.

Bibliography, p.217–35. Index, p.237–41.

P717 Westerdijk, H. Ijzerwerk van Centraal-Afrika: een systematische indeling van mensen, sabels en bijlen, met een overzicht van oorlogsen statiesperen, pijlen, geldmiddelen en muziekinstrumenten, voorafgegaan door een inleiding over de smid en zijn werk. Rotterdam, Museum voor Land- en Volkenkunde, 1975. 154p. il., plates, maps.

The standard introduction to African weapons and includes numerous drawings depicting the forms and styles of these artifacts.

Contents: (1) Komst van het ijzer in Afrika; (2) Ijzerwinning; (3) De smid, zijn werk en zijn gereedschappen; (4) Benoeming van messen, sabels en bijlen; (5) Overzicht van oorlogs- en statieperen; (6) Overzicht van de pijlen; (7) Ijzergeld; (8) Musiekinstrumenten; (9) Overige ijzerprodukten.

Bibliografie, p.152–54.

The Americas

P718 Jones, Julie. The art of Precolumbian gold: the Jan Mitchell collection. Curator, Julie Jones. Color photography, Justin Kerr. N.Y., Metropolitan Museum of Art, 1985. 248p. il., maps.

Catalog of the exhibition, Metropolitan Museum of Art (1985). Six authored essays and a catalog focus on Costa Rica, Panama, Colombia, and northern Peru.

Contents: The Old World and the gold of the New, by Priscilla Muller; Symbolism of gold in Costa Rica and its archaeological perspective, by Michael Snarskis; The goldwork of Panama: an iconographic and chronological perspective, by Richard Cooke and Warwick Bray; Cultural patterns in the Prehispanic goldwork of Colombia, by Clemencia Plazas and Ana María Falchetti; Behind the gold mask: the Sicán gold artifacts from Batán Grande, Peru by Paloma Carcedo Muro and Izumi Shimada; Ancient American metallurgy: five hundred years of study, by Warwick Bray; Catalogue, by Julie Jones and Heidi King.

Bibliography, p.243–48.

MEDALS

Dictionaries and Encyclopedias

P719 Forrer, Leonard. Biographical dictionary of medallists; coin-, gem-, and seal-engravers, mint masters, etc., ancient and modern, with references to their works, B.C. 500–A.D. 1900. Maastricht, A.G. Van der Duussen, [1980]. 8v. il.

For previous ed., see GLAH 1:P562. Facsimile reprint of the standard dictionary of medallists, originally published London, Spink, 1902–1930, and still indispensable for research in this field.

Histories and Handbooks

P720 Elvehjem Museum of Art. Catalogue of the Vernon Hall Collection of European medals. Madison, Elvehjem Museum, University of Wisconsin, 1978. 100p. il., ports.

Catalog of a collection of European medals of the 15th through the early 19th centuries. Includes an informative introduction that discusses history, fabrication, and connoisseurship of medals, and a useful bibliographical essay.

Concordance with other works, p.88–90. Index of inscriptions, p.90–95. Translations into English of typical inscriptions of medals in the collection, p.95–97. Index of artists, p.98. Index of persons, gods, and personifications, p.99–100.

P721 Jones, Mark. The art of the medal. [London], British Museum, [1979]. 192p. il., 8 col. plates.

Well-illustrated international history of medallic art from its origins to the 20th century by a well-known authority, with particular attention to the work of individual medallists.

Index, p.188–91. Bibliography, p.191–92.

P722 Julian, R. W. Medals of the United States Mint: the first century, 1792–1892. Ed. by N. Neil Harris. [El Cajon, Calif.], Token and Medal Society, [1977]. xlvii, 424p. il. ports.

Thorough and meticulous catalogue, by type, of all medals struck by the United States Mint during its first century. Includes illustrations and detailed descriptions of each medal, and lists and numbers of medals manufactured by year.

General history, p.xviii–xxx. Coverage of this catalog, p.xxxi–xliii. Bibliography, p.xliv–xlvii. Appendix: Directors of the Mint; Specific gravity; Conversion tables; Mintage records, p.[373]–417. Index of artists, p.418–19. Index of medals, p.420–24.

P723 The medal in America: Coinage of the Americas Conference at the American Numismatic Society,

New York, September 26–27, 1987. Ed. by Alan M. Stahl. [N.Y., American Numismatic Society, 1988]. xi, 247p. il., tables.
Papers from a conference on the American medal, on topics ranging from Indian peace medals to American women medalists, by specialists in this art. Includes a history of the Society of Medalists, by Joseph Veach Noble.

P724 Norris, Andrea S., and Weber, Ingrid. Medals and plaquettes from the Molinari Collection at Bowdoin College. With an introd. to the Medals Catalogue by Graham Pollard. Brunswick, Maine, [Bowdoin College], 1976. xi, 292p. il.
Catalog of an important collection of European medals of the Renaissance through the 19th century, with concentration of those of France and Italy. Catalog entries include detailed descriptions and illustrations for each example, and include separate bibliographies for medals and for plaquettes.

Contents: (1) Historical note; (2) Catalogue of the exhibition of medals: Introduction, Bibliography, Catalogue, by Andrea S. Norris; Graham Pollard, collaborator; (3) Catalogue of the exhibition of plaquettes: Introduction, Bibliography, Catalogue, by Ingrid Weber; David P. Becker, editorial assistant; (4) Illustrations.

Index to the medals catalogue, p.277–90. Index to the plaquettes catalogue, p.291–92.

P725 One hundred years of American medallic art, 1845–1945: the John E. Marqusee Collection. Catalogue by Susan Luftschein. Ithaca, Herbert F. Johnson Museum of Art, Cornell Univ., [1995]. xxvi, 98p. il.
Catalog accompanying the exhibition, the Museum (1995), of a notable collection of American medals, forming a useful survey of this art. Arrangement is by medalist. Includes a preface by the collector discussing the formation of the collection, an introductory essay, and biographical sketches of medalists represented.

Frequently cited sources, p.83–85. Selected medals organized by categories, p.87–88. Selected medalist biographies, p.89–96. Index to catalogue, p.97–98.

GEMS AND JEWELRY

Bibliography

P726 Klein, Christine De Bow. Jewelry history: a core bibliography in support of preservation. Washington, D.C., Commission on Preservation and Access, 1992. [51]p., charts.
"This bibliography is a compilation of suggestions from . . . nine jewelry historians who are knowledgeable experts in their fields, one subject expert librarian's bibliography, and 11 bibliographies . . . from notable jewelry historians' books."—*p.[19].* Bibliography identifies 284 core titles that should be the focus of preservation efforts, and discusses the holdings of six especially rich library collections. Entries include variant editions, OCLC record numbers, and reprint information.

Dictionaries and Encyclopedias

P727 Newman, Harold. An illustrated dictionary of jewelry: 2,530 entries, including definitions of jewels, gemstones, materials, processes, and styles, and entries on principal designers and makers, from antiquity to the present day: 685 illustrations, 16 in colour. [N.Y.], Thames and Hudson, [1981]. 354, [1]p., 16 col. plates.
Wide-ranging, authoritative dictionary of jewelry in all cultures. Excludes watches, decorative accessories such as snuff-boxes, and objects of vertu. A basic resource for jewelry studies.

Histories and Handbooks

P728 Bury, Shirley. Jewellery, 1789–1910: the international era. [Woodbridge], Antique Collectors' Club, [1991]. 2v. il. (part col.), ports.
Well-documented, thorough history of jewelry by an expert in this field, covering design, fabrication, and jewelry in its cultural context. Illustrations include design drawings, contemporary portraits, and surviving examples of characteristic pieces.

Contents: (I) 1798–1861; (II)1862–1910.

Registry marks, v.2, p.789–91. A chronology of the Hanoverian claim to the Crown jewels, v.2, p.792–98. Currencies and exchange rates, v.2, p.798–809. Bibliography, v.2, p.811–28. Index, v.2, p.829–62.

P729 Duncan, Alastair. The Paris salons, 1895–1914. [Woodbridge], Antique Collectors Club, [1994]. 2v. il. (part col.)
Primarily pictorial compendium of the work of jewelers exhibited at the four major Paris Salons from the early Art Nouveau period to the outbreak of World War I. Arrangement is by designer. Informative introductory essay in v.1 discusses the Salons and the work of the major designers, primarily French, exhibiting in them.

Contents: (I) Jewellery: the designers, A–K; (II) Jewellery: the designers, L–Z.

Index of jewellery designers, v.2, p.285–305.

P730 Hackenbroch, Yvonne. Renaissance jewellery. [London], Sotheby Parke Bernet; Munich, Beck, published in assoc. with the Metropolitan Museum, [1979]. xv, 424p. il., 45 col. plates, ports.
Comprehensive account of jewelry in Italy, France, Germany, The Netherlands, England, Portugal, and Spain from the mid-15th century in Italy to the early 17th century, arranged by country. Illustrations include design documents, contemporary portraits, and examples from many collections. constituting a major resource for this topic.

Bibliography, p.379–84. Documents (by country), p.385–411. Index, p.413–24.

P731 Kunstgewerbemuseum der Stadt Köln. Schmuck. Anna Beatriz Chadour and Rüdiger Joppien. Köln, Kunstgewerbemuseum, 1985. 2v. il., col. plates, ports. (Kataloge des Kunstgewerbes Museums Köln, Bd. X)

Detailed catalog of the extensive jewelry collection of the Kunstgewerbemuseum, Cologne, Germany, which includes work from many countries. Each entry includes individual bibliographical references, dimensions, materials, and commentary. Illustrations include marks and supporting design documentation. There is an extensive section of makers' biographies.

Contents: (I) Hals-, Ohr-, Arm- und Gewandschmuck; (II) Fingerringe.

Konkordanz der Inventar- und Katalognummern, v.1, p.593–97, v.2, p.237–39. Künstlerbiographien und Geschichte der Manufakturen, v.2, p.241–319. Literaturverzeichnis, v.2, p.321–73.

P732 Phillips, Clare. Jewelry, from antiquity to the present. [N.Y.], Thames and Hudson, [1996]. 224p. il. (part col.) (World of Art)

Readable and well-illustrated introduction to the history of jewelry for the non-specialist.

Bibliography, p.217–19. Index, p.221–24.

P733 Tait, Hugh, ed. Jewelry: 7000 years: an international history and illustrated survey from the collections of the British Museum. [N.Y.], Abradale, [1991]. 255p. il. (part col.)

Originally published N.Y., Abrams, 1987.

Wide-ranging, heavily illustrated volume based on an exhibition of the jewelry holdings of the British Museum, with essays by many specialists. Constitutes an accessible introduction to this art for the general reader, as well as to the Museum's holdings.

The contributors, p.[6]. Select glossary, p.241. Further reading, p.244. References for the illustrations, p.245–50. Bibliography, p.251. Index, p.252–55.

Western Countries

Great Britain and Ireland

P734 Gere, Charlotte, and Munn, Geoffrey C. Artists' jewelry: Pre-Raphaelite to Arts and Crafts. [Woodbridge], Antique Collectors' Club, [1989]. 244p. il., ports. (part col.)

Consideration of jewelry primarily designed by and for 19th-century English artists, their friends, and families, with discussion of the cultural context for these pieces. Well-illustrated with design documents, contemporary portraits, and surviving pieces.

Bibliography, p.240. Index: p.241–44.

P735 Scarisbrick, Diana. Jewellery in Britain, 1066–1837: a documentary, social, literary and artistic survey. Norwich, Michael Russell, 1994. xxiii, 431p. il. (part col.), ports.

"Detailed over-view of the complex history of jewellery in Britain."—*Foreword.* First study in 75 years, and the most thorough, with a focus on the social context.

Source notes, p.369–97. Bibliography and abbreviated references, p.398–414. Index, p.415–31.

Russia and Eastern Europe

P736 Habsburg-Lothringen, Géza von. Fabergé. With essays by Christopher Forbes . . . [et al.] Geneva, Habsburg, Feldman (Distr. Faber and Faber, 1987). 359p. il. (part col.), ports., genealogical chart.

Revised ed. of a catalog of the exhibition, Hypo Kulturstiftung, Munich (1986–87).

Thorough, detailed survey of the life and work of Carl Peter Fabergé, with essays by the major Fabergé scholars. Includes essays on techniques, hallmarks, design influences, competitors, and the history of collecting Fabergé jewelry and objets d'art. Exhibition included objects from numerous public and private collections.

Glossary, p.348–50. Bibliography, p.351–53. Index, p.354–59.

P737 McCanless, Christel L. Fabergé and his works: an annotated bibliography of the first century of his art. Metuchen, N.J., Scarecrow, 1994. viii, 408p. il., plates.

Contents: History of the project; Major sources consulted; Chronology of the House of Fabergé; Genealogy chart of the Fabergé family; Explanatory notes; Annotated bibliography.

Index, p.367–408.

United States

P738 Fales, Martha Gandy. Jewelry in America, 1600–1900. [Woodbridge], Antique Collectors' Club, [1995]. 447p. il., ports. (part col.)

Substantial survey, from Colonial times to 1900.

Bibliography, p.425–36. Index, p.437–47.

P739 Rainwater, Dorothy T. American jewelry manufacturers. West Chester, Schiffer, [1988]. 296p. il.

Dictionary of American jewelry makers and manufacturers and their marks from the 18th to the early 20th century, arranged by name. Includes essays on the historical background of jewelry manufacturing in America and on methods of manufacture.

Trade names, p.265–72. Glossary, p.[273]–80. Manufacturing jewelers listed in city directories: Boston, New York, Philadelphia, Providence. Bibliography, p.[287]–88.

Asian Countries

India, Nepal, Pakistan, Tibet

P740 Brij Bhushan, Jamila. Masterpieces of Indian jewellery. Bombay, Taraporevala, 1979. viii, 54p. il., plates.

Chronological overview, with thematic chapters devoted to the craft of the goldsmith, hints for the collector. Black-and-white photographs.

List of ornaments of ancient and modern India, p.45–49. Books for further reading, p.51–54.

P741 Chandra, Rai Govind. Indo-Greek jewellery. New Delhi, Abhinav Publications, 1979. 136p. il., plates.

Seeks "to disentangle the Hellenic Greek and the Indian forms of jewellery and to study the various forms which developed out of the contact of these two great peoples."—*Pref.*

Contents: (1) The Greeks and the Indians; (2) Indian jewellery prior to the advent of the Greeks; (3) The Greek jewellery; (4) Indo-Greek jewellery; (5) The ornaments; (6) Manufacturing processes.

Selected bibliography, p.119–23. Index, p.125–29.

P742 Höpfner, Gerd, and Haase, Gesine. Metallschmuck aus Indien. Berlin, Museum für Völkerkunde, 1978. 91p. il. (4 col.), map, plates. (Veröffentlichungen des Museums für Völkerkunde Berlin. Abteilung Südasien, 2; Veröffentlichungen des Museums für Völkerkunde Berlin, n.F., 35)

Publicizes one of the lesser-known but very significant collections of the Museum für Völkerkunde.

Literatur, p.25.

P743 The jewels of India. Ed. by Susan Stronge. Bombay, Marg Publications, 1995. 136p. il. (part col.)

Survey, beautifully illustrated in color.

Contents: Early jewellery of Bengal: the Shunga period, by Zulekha Haque; The sacred and the secular: jewellery in Buddhist sculpture in the northern Kushan realm, by Carolyn Woodford Schimst; Jewellery in the temples of Karnataka, by Choodamani Nanda Gopal; Jewels and gems in Goa from the sixteenth to the eighteenth century, by Nuno Vassallo e Silva; The royal jewels of Tirumala Nayaka of Madurai (1623–1659), by Jean-François Hurpré; Jewels for the Stadholder, by Pauline Lunsingh Scheurleer; Indian Jewellery and the great exhibitions, by Susan Stronge; Swami jewellery: cross-cultural ornaments, by Oppi Untracht.

Glossary of selected terms, p.133–34. Index, p.135–36.

P744 Latif, Momin. Bijoux Moghols = Mogols juwelen = Mughal jewels. Prés. par la Société générale de banque, Bruxelles]. Bruxelles, La Société, [1982]. 212p. il. (part col.), maps, ports.

Catalog of the exhibition, Musées Royaux d'art et d'histoire, Brussels (1982). In French, Dutch, and English. Survey with detailed illustrations in color and black-and-white.

Contents: The Mughal emperors; Jewellery in India; Enamel in Indian jewellery; Craftsmen, tools and techniques; Medallions and portraits: Shast and Jharoka; India and the renaissance; Jewels and miniatures [i.e., plates].

Bibliography, p.209–11.

P745 Stronge, Susan; Smith, Nima; and Harle, J. C. A golden treasury: jewellery from the Indian subcontinent. Rizzoli in assoc. with the Victoria and Albert Museum and Grantha Corp., 1988. 144p. il. (part col.) (Indian art series)

Catalog of the exhibition, Cartwright Hall, Bradford Art Galleries and Museums (1988), and other locations.

Contents: Jewellery in Indian sculpture, by James Harle; Jewellery in the Mughal period, by Susan Stronge; The darker side of gold, by Nima Smith.

Abbreviations, p.[8]. Glossary, p.138–39. Bibliography, p.140–41. Index, p.142–44.

P746 Untracht, Oppi. Traditional jewelry of India. N.Y., Abrams, 1997. N.Y., Abrams, 1997. 430p. il. (part col.)

Wide-ranging historical survey.

Contents: (1) Origins: early ornament; (2) Formulating the Indian jewelry tradition; (3) Indian jewelry typology: from head to toe; (4) Gold and silver: makers' means, users' obsessions; (5) Gemstones; (6) The Mughal jewelry tradition; (7) Euro-Indian and Indo-European jewelry: a cross-cultural exchange; Epilogue.

Traditional Indian jewelers' tools and vernacular terms, p.408–09. Bibliography, p.410. Index, p.418.

P747 Weihreter, Hans. Schmuck aus dem Himalaja. Graz, Akademische Druck- u. Verlagsanstalt, 1988. 302p. il. (part col.), [1] leaf of plates.

Scholarly study of the religious and anthropological significance of jewelry in the Himalayan provinces.

Literaturverzeichnis, p.151–52. Geographischer Index, p.153. Glossar, 155–58.

Africa, Oceania, The Americas

Africa

P748 Camps-Fabrer, Henriette. Bijoux Berbéres d'Algérie: Grande Kabylie-Aurés. Dessins: Yvette Assié. La Calade, Aix-en-Provence, Édisud, [1990]. 143p. il. (part col.)

The author, an authority on Berber jewelry, presents a comprehensive exposition of the craft of jewelry making, the origins and evolution of the techniques, and primary types.

Contents: Le travail du bijoutier; Les bijoux; Évolution et origine des bijoux Kabyles et Aurasiens.

Lexique des termes berbéres, p.137–8. Bibliographie, p.139–43.

The Americas

P749 Jernigan, E. Wesley. Jewelry of the prehistoric Southwest. Santa Fe, School of American Research, 1978. xii, 260p. il. (part col.), plates, maps. (Southwest Indian arts series)

Analysis of the small craft production of pre-contact Southwest Indians based on material from documented excavations.

Contents: (1) Introduction; (2) A new world: early man in the Southwest; (3) The Hohokam: masters of shell; (4) The Mogollon and the mixed traditions: bone pins and stone animals; (5) The Anasazi: blue turquoise and black jet; (6) Prehistoric jewelry craft: time and sandstone; (7) Mining, materials, and trade: picks, packs, and Mesoamerica; (8) Jewelry without fire: conclusion.

References, p.247–56. Index, p.257–60.

RUGS AND CARPETS

Bibliography

P750 Textile Museum. Arthur D. Jenkins Library. Rug and textile arts: a periodical index, 1890–1982. Boston, Hall, 1983. xiii, 472p.

"This catalog represents the selective indexing of textile and rug articles found in more than 300 periodical titles."—*p.vi.* Reflects the Museum's interest in ethnographic and non-Western textiles and in Oriental rugs, but includes Western examples as well. From 1930, concentration is on periodicals not included in the Art Index, and thus supplements that index's coverage. Entries are in catalog card form, divided into author and subject/title sections.

Periodicals indexed by the Arthur D. Jenkins Library, p.vii–xiii.

Histories and Handbooks

P751 Faraday, Cornelia Bateman. European and American carpets and rugs. [Reprint.] [Woodbridge], Antique Collector's Club, [1990]. 484p. il. (part col.), 112 col. plates.

Reprint of a standard survey first published Grand Rapids, Mich., Dean-Hicks, 1929. New introd. to this ed. by Ian Bennett.

History of rugs and carpets in Europe and America, both hand-woven and machine-made, with a chapter on technique. Bibliography has been updated.

Bibliography, p.475–79. Text index, p.481–84.

P752 Sherrill, Sarah. Carpets and rugs of Europe and America. N.Y., Abbeville, 1996. 463p. il. (part col.)

Regional survey, well-illustrated.

Contents: (1) Origins and oriental influences; (2) Spain and Portugal; (3) France; (4) Belgium; (5) Great Britain; (6) United States; (7) Lesser-known rug traditions; (8) Progressive design, mid-19th century to the present.

Notes, p.396–433. Bibliography, p.396–446. Index, 447–63.

Western Countries

United States

P753 Kopp, Joel and Kopp, Kate. American hooked and sewn rugs: folk art underfoot. N.Y., Dutton, 1975. 128p. il. (part col.)

General history of hooked and sewn rugs in America, with emphasis on "those rugs we consider to be folk art."

Contents: Bed rugs; Yarn-sewn rugs; Shirred rugs; Embroidered and braided rugs; Hooked rugs-Part I: Nineteenth-century Shaker rugs; Hooked rugs-Part II: Twentieth-century Grenfell rugs; Illustrations of techniques; Cleaning, storage and display.

Selected bibliography, p.128.

P754 Von Rosenstiel, Helene. American rugs and carpets: from the seventeenth century to modern times. N.Y., Morrow, [1978]. 192p. il. (part col.)

Well-illustrated general history of floor coverings of all kinds, including linoleum, matting, and floorcloths, and of floor treatments such as stenciling.

Ingrain pattern chronology, p.174–[77]. Glossary, p.[178]–83. Bibliography, p.[184]–87. Index, p.[190]–92.

Asian Countries

Bibliography

P755 O'Bannon, George W. Oriental rugs: a bibliography. Metuchen, N.J., Scarecrow Pr., [1994]. ix, 744p. il.

Intended as a comprehensive bibliography of oriental rug literature, 1877–1992. Oriental rugs are defined as those from Islamic countries as well as from some non-Islamic areas such as China, Tibet, Eastern Europe, and Spain. In addition to books on carpets, the bibliography includes references for Islamic arts and textiles and for books on caring for rugs.

Dictionaries and Encyclopedias

P756 Denny, Walter B. Sotheby's guide to Oriental carpets. Illustrations by Norma Jean Jourdenais. N.Y., Simon and Schuster, [1994]. 203p. il., 48 plates (part col.), map.

Compact, informative introduction to Oriental carpets and their collecting for the general reader, by a well-known specialist. Carpets are discussed by region. Includes discussions of care and display, major public collections, and increasing one's knowledge of the field, and a useful chapter on "What to read about Oriental rugs and carpets." An excellent first book on this subject.

Glossary, p.191–94. Index, p.195–203.

P757 Eiland, Murray L. Chinese and exotic rugs. Boston, New York Graphic Society, [1979]. [x], 246p. il., maps, 48 col. plates.

Detailed consideration of the rugs of China, Tibet, Mongolia, Turkestan, India, North Africa, and the Balkans, by a leading scholar and collector, with much attention to methods of weaving and dyeing.

Laboratory identification of dyes, p.[225]–26. Use of the microscope, p.227–28. Silk weighting, p.229. Pile carpet findings in Eastern Turkestan, p.230–33. Glossary, p.234. Index, p.[241]–46.

P758 Neff, Ivan C., and Maggs, Carol V. Dictionary of Oriental rugs: with a monograph on identification by weave. N.Y., Van Nostrand Reinhold, 1979, [1977]. 238p. col. plates, fold. map.
An introduction to the meaning of rug names and an essay on weave patterns is followed by the dictionary that defines places, terms, and techniques important to understanding oriental rugs. Includes numerous color illustrations of rugs with detailed views to show the weave patterns.
Bibliography, p.148–51.

P759 Stone, Peter F. The Oriental rug lexicon. Seattle, University of Washington Pr., 1997. xvi, 267p. il. (part col.), map.
"This Lexicon includes definitions and explanations for names and terms referring to: pile rugs and flatweaves of the Near East, North Africa, continental Asia, Europe and the United States; geographic locations and ethnic groups noted for their rugs and weavings; functional weavings of tribal and nomadic origin; the rug trade and the rug-weaving craft and industry; designs, motifs and symbols of pile rugs and flatweaves; rug and textile structures; specific rugs of historical significance."—*Introd.*
Bibliography, p.261–65.

P760 Thompson, Jon. Oriental carpets: from the tents, cottages, and workshops of Asia. N.Y., Dutton, [1988]. 176p. il. (chiefly col.), maps.
"Under the title Carpet Magic, this book was first published in the U.K. in association with the Barbican Art Gallery, London, 1983."—*t.p. verso.*
Handsomely illustrated survey of Oriental carpets in the context of their makers—tribal, cottage industry, workshop and court. Accessible and informative introduction to this art for the general reader and beginning collector.
Notes for buyers and sellers, p.158–62. Glossary, p.162–68. [Maps], p.[170]–[73]. Further reading, p.174–75.

Histories and Handbooks

General Works

P761 Bode, Wilhelm von, and Kühnel, Ernst. Antique rugs from the Near East. 4th rev. ed. Trans. by Charles Grant Ellis. Ithaca, Cornell Univ. Pr., 1984. 187p. il. (part col.), plates.
See GLAH 1:P617 for previous eds. and original annotation.

P762 Eiland, Murray L. Oriental rugs: a new comprehensive guide. 3d ed. Boston, Little, Brown, [1981]. 294p. il. (part col.), plates.
See GLAH 1:P620 for original annotation; rev. ed., 1976, with many new color plates and some textual changes. The 3d ed. is a thorough revision. The technical aspects of rug weaving are described in greater detail, the chapter on Turkoman has been substantially revised, and a new section on non-Turkoman rugs of Central Asia has been added.

P763 Ford, P. R. J. Oriental carpet design: a guide to traditional motifs, patterns, and symbols. London, Thames and Hudson, [1989]. 352p. il. (part col.), maps.
Intended not as a survey but rather a handbook of basic rug styles available for purchase.
Contents: (I) Introduction; (II) Border Designs; (III) Universal Designs; (IV) Geometric Designs; (V) Floral Designs.
Select bibliography, p.342. Index of carpet origins illustrated, p. 348. Index, p.349–52.

Central Asia

P764 Gans-Ruedin, E. Caucasian carpets. Photographs by Micheline Hilber. Drawings by Ronald Sautebin. N.Y., Rizzoli, 1986. 369p. il. (part col.)
"Our chief intention is to gather together a representative selection of fine specimens woven at the end of the nineteenth and the beginning of the twentieth centuries, and which are still to be found on the market."—*Pref.* Employs the classification used by dealers.
Glossary, p.362–64. Bibliography, p.365–66. Index, p.367–69.

P765 Schurmann, Ulrich. Caucasian rugs: a detailed presentation of the art of carpet weaving in the various districts of the Caucasus during the 18th and 19th century. [Reprint.] Poolesville, Md., Old 99 Associates, 1990. 359p. il. (part col.)
Reprint of GLAH 1:P628, with color reproductions nearly as clear as those in the original.

China

P766 Gans-Ruedin, E. Chinese carpets. Photos by Leo Hilber. London, Allen and Unwin, [1981]. 200p. il. (part col.), maps.
Trans. of Tapis de Chine. Fribourg, Office du Livre, 1981.
Short essays on the history of Chinese carpets and on the characteristics of Chinese carpets are followed by a classification of carpets by regions. Several examples are provided for each region.
Glossary, p.192–95. Bibliography, p.196–98. Index, p.199–200.

P767 Larsson, Lennart. Carpets from China, Xinjiang and Tibet. Boston, Shambala (Distr. by Random House, 1989). 142p. il. (part col.) map.
Trans. of Mattor från Kina, Sinkiang och Tibet. 1st English ed. London, Bamboo Publishing, 1988.
"The intention of this book is to describe the historical, geographical and artistic background to the Chinese carpet. In addition, it aims to give as complete a picture as possible of the Chinese carpet and its relatives from Xinjiang, Tibet and Nepal (carpets from the latter country being woven by Tibetan refugees). Basically it is a picture which will enable the reader to recognize and learn about older as well as the newer examples."—*Introd.*
Glossary, p.137. Bibliography, p.138–39. Index, p.140–41.

P768 Rostov, Charles I., and Guanyan, Jia. Chinese carpets. N.Y., Abrams, 1983. 223p. il. (part col.), maps.
Contents: (1) History; (2) Symbols and symbolism; (3) Weaving methods and techniques; (4) Materials; (5) Identification and dating; Appendix I: The Chinese classics; Appendix II: Chinese measurements; Appendix III: Chinese calendars; Appendix IV: A note on Pinyin; Appendix V: Time chart.

Bibliography, p.222. Index, p.223–24.

TAPESTRIES

General Works

P769 Adelson, Candace J. European tapestry in the Minneapolis Institute of Arts. [Minneapolis], Minneapolis Institute of Arts (Distr. Abrams, [1994]). xvii, 476p. il. (part col.), port.
Massive, well-researched catalog of a rich collection of tapestry of the 15th–18th century, constituting a major resource for the study of this art, especially for the advanced researcher.

Contents: Introduction to the collection; About European tapestry; Catalogue: Technical note; Flanders and France; Germany and Holland; Italy; Norway and other lands.

Works and exhibitions cited, p.433–48. Index, p.449–76.

P770 Bennett, Anna Gray. Five centuries of tapestry from the Fine Arts Museums of San Francisco. Rev. ed. San Francisco, Fine Arts Museums of San Francisco; Chronicle Books, 1992. xii, 329p. il. (part col.)
1st ed., 1976. The new ed. includes tapestries acquired since 1976 and other revisions.

Scholarly catalog of an important collection.

Bibliography, p.322–25. Index, p.326–29.

P771 The book of tapestry: history and technique, by Pierre Verlet . . . [et al.] N.Y., Vendome (Distr. Viking, [1978]). 229, [1]p. il. (part col.)
Originally published as La tapisserie histoire et technique du XVIe au XXe siècle. Lausanne, Edita, 1965, 1977.

History of tapestry and its makers from the Gothic period to the 20th century, by a team of scholars. Chapter on technique includes a glossary and many illustrations, both period and contemporary.

Contents: Preface, by Joseph Jobe; Gothic tapestry, by Pierre Verlet; Classical tapestry, by Michel Florisoone; Contemporary tapestry, by Adolf Hoffmeister; The weaver's art, by François Tabard.

Bibliography, p.226–27. Principal historical figures mentioned in this book, p.228–29.

P772 Phillips, Barty. Tapestry. [London, Phaidon, 1994]. 240p. il. (chiefly col.)
Handsomely produced world history of tapestry for the general reader. Illustrations include contemporary interior scenes demonstrating use of tapestry in interiors.

Contents: (1) Medieval and Gothic; (2) The age of princes; (3) Competition and diversity; (4) The search for a new identity; (5) The modern tapestry; (6) Contemporary masters; (7) Tribal tapestry weaves.

Buying and caring for tapestries, p.222–25. Tapestry collections, p.226–29. Bibliography, p.230–32. Glossary, p.233–36. Index, p.237–40.

P773 Standen, Edith Appleton. European post-medieval tapestries and related hangings in the Metropolitan Museum of Art. N.Y., Metropolitan Museum, [1985]. 2v., il. (part col.)
Detailed, well-illustrated catalog of the Metropolitan Museum's large and varied collection by a major scholar. Entries are extensive and include bibliographical references. A major resource for the serious researcher.

Contents: (I) The Netherlands: Sixteenth, seventeenth, and eighteenth centuries; France: Sixteenth and early seventeenth centuries; France: The Gobelins; (II) France: Beauvais; France: Aubusson; France: Savonnerie manufactory and seventeenth-century embroideries; England and Ireland; Other countries.

Frequently cited sources, v.1, p.12. Concordance of accession and catalogue numbers, v.2, p.821–22. Index, v.2, p.823–48.

TEXTILES

Bibliography

P774 Bibliography. Published in Textile Society of America newsletter, v.8, no.2, summer 1995– . Washington, D.C., The Textile Museum, 1995– .
"This bibliographic issue of the Textile Society of America Newsletter is a joint endeavor of the Society and the Textile Museum in Washington, D.C. The citations include new titles catalogued in the Arthur D. Jenkins Library of the Museum as well as late arrivals. . . . The compilation and editing of the bibliography is the work of Mary Mallia Samms, Librarian at the Textile Museum."—*Introd.* The annual listing now takes up the greater part of each summer issue of the TSA newsletter.

Covers articles and books, reflecting the textile collections of the Textile Museum itself: primarily the history and techniques of ancient and ethnographic textiles and rugs. Within that scope, textiles, dress, embroidery, weaving, tapestries, rugs, and designers are covered.

P775 Bibliographica textilia historiae: towards a general bibliography on the history of textiles. Based on the Library and Archives of the Center for Social Research on Old Textiles [CSROT]. Over 5,000 works published since the fifteenth century on textiles as art, craft, technology, industry and commerce. Including archaeological, ethnographic, religious (Islamic, Christian, Buddhist), secular, decorative, folk textile—Asia, Europe, the Americas, Oceania, Africa—

prehistoric, ancient, medieval, Renaissance, Baroque, rococo—woven silk, wool, linen, cotton, velvet, printed textiles, embroidery, lace, carpets, dyeing, tapestry, costume, and related subjects. Most with collations; many with descriptions; some with illustrations. . . . Ed. by Seth Siegelaub. N.Y., International General, 1997. 415p. il.

Seeks to situate the history of textiles "within the broader history of economic, social and cultural life, work and technological change."—*Introd.* More comprehensive than might be expected from a bibliography focusing on the subject of textiles. Coverage is similarly broad in terms of textile type, textile and fiber technology, geographic region, historical period, and dates of publication (1468–late 20th century). Drawn primarily from the research collections of the Center for Social Research on Old Textiles, now housed in Amsterdam. Ca. 5,000 alphabetically arranged author-title entries, approximately 3,000 of which are accompanied by annotations of varying length and detail. The subject-oriented listing is considerably shorter.

Contents: (I) Introduction: notes towards a critical history of the literature of textiles; (II) Bibliographica textilia historiae: the alphabetical author-title entries; (III) Basic works on the history of textiles; a classification by subject and country; (IV) Appendix: abbreviations, bibliographic references, addenda.

Abbreviations, p.411. Bibliographic references frequently cited, p.412. Addenda [additional works or information acquired during the course of the final preparation of this work], p.413–15.

P776 Bibliographie. [Comp. by Monique King] Published in Bulletin du CIETA. Nr. 2, 1955– . Lyons (France), Centre International d'Étude des Textiles Anciens, 1955– .

Variant titles: Bulletin du Centre International d'Étude des Textiles Anciens; Bulletin de Liaison du Centre International d'Étude des Textiles Anciens.

Annual publication covering books and periodical articles on all aspects of the history and conservation of historic textiles and dress. Major reference tool. All entries receive a full bibliographic citation, plus a brief annotation. The first bibliographical compilation was prepared by Edith Standen.

Contents: Afrique, Amérique/Africa, America; Broderie/Embroidery; Commerce, Industrie, Techniques/Trade, Industry, Techniques; Costume et mode/Costume and fashion; Dentelles imprimés, Tricot/lace, printed textiles, knitting; Divers/Various; Moyen-Orient, Extrême-Orient/Middle East, Far East; Musées et collections/Museums and collections; Tapis, tapisseries/Carpets, tapestries; Tissus tissés/Woven textiles.

P777 Bibliography of theses and dissertations on ethnic textiles and dress. Comp. by Catherine Cerny, Suzanne Baizerman, and Joanne B. Eicher. Monument, Colo., International Textile and Apparel Association, 1993. iii, 60p. (ITAA special publication, 6)

Comprehensive bibliography of 795 mostly U.S. masters' theses and doctoral dissertations on ethnic textiles. The introduction defines the terms "ethnic," "textiles," and "dress," and discusses research resources.

Contents: Geographic index; Author index.

Bibliographical references follow each introductory section. Bibliographic sources, p.4–7.

P778 Niessen, Sandra A., comp. Textile network bibliography. [Canada?, s.n., 1990?]. 86p. on [43] leaves.

Covers books, journal articles, symposia, exhibition catalogs, and Festschriften. Approximately 500 references are listed.

Contents: (I) [North] America; Central America; South America; South Asia; S.E. Asia; East Asia; Africa; Middle East; Europe; Scandinavia; (II) General; Technique and structure; Dye; Loom; Basketry; Archaeology; Ethnography, Economy, History; Costume; Folk textiles; Art; Design; Method and theory; Conservation; Collections; Reviews.

P779 Ron, Moshe. Bibliotheca tinctoria: annotated catalogue of the Sidney M. Edelstein collection in the history of bleaching, dyeing, finishing and spot removing. Jerusalem, Jewish National and University Library, 1991. 507p. il., facsims.

1st ed., Catalog of the Sidney M. Edelstein collection of the history of chemistry, dyeing, and technology. Jerusalem, Jewish National and University Library Pr., 1981.

Catalog of a formerly private collection now held at the Jewish National and University Library, Jerusalem, and a major bibliographic resource for the subject. The fully annotated catalog lists approximately 1,220 books, manuscripts, and periodicals on all aspects of textile dyeing and printing, with a focus on chemical treatises and the history of chemical technology. Publication dates range from the 16th to the 20th century: translations and/or transcriptions of much earlier works (for example, of Ancient Egyptian papyri) are also included. Illustrations are facsimiles of title pages from some of the incunables in the collection.

Bibliography, p.457. Name index, p.461–72. Title index, p.473–96. Subject index, p.497–507.

P780 Wilson, Sadye Tune, and Jackson, Ruth Davidson. Textile arts index 1950–1987: selected weaving, spinning, dyeing, knitting, fiber periodicals. Nashville, Tungstede, 1988. 1006p.

Periodical index focusing on 16 journals covering contemporary textiles. Postings in periodicals about events, calendars, directories, exhibition schedules, product and equipment reviews, and new items are not covered.

Contents: Subject index; Author index.

SEE ALSO: O'Bannon, Oriental rugs: a bibliography (GLAH 2:P755); Textile Museum. Arthur D. Jenkins Library. Rug and textile arts: a periodical index, 1890–1982 (GLAH 2:P750).

Directories

P781 Directory of textile collections in the United States and Canada. [Comp. by the Handweavers Guild of America Textile Collections Committee . . . (et al.)] [Ed. by Jenna Tedrick Kuttruff.] [Bloomfield, Conn.], Handweavers Guild of America, 1991. 70p.

Alphabetical listing by state/province, then by city, of approximately 500 collections housing textiles. Each collection receives a brief description of the textiles collected.

P782 The network: an international directory of textile scholars. [Salem, Mass.], Textile Society of America, 1991. 85p.

Alphabetical listing. Each scholar's research interests are described.

Contents: East and Central Asia; Southeast Asia; South Asia; West Asia and North Africa; Europe; SubSaharan Africa; North America; Mesoamerica; South America; Oceania; General; Weaving methods, tools and equipment; Nonwoven methods, tools and equipment; Color; Stitchery; Fibers; Clothing and accessories; Interiors; Graphics; Meanings of textiles; Political economy of textiles.

P783 Textile, costume and doll collections: in the United States and Canada. Ed. by Pieter Bach. Lopez, Wash., R.L. Shep, 1981. 69p. il.

Divided into three sections (textiles, costume and dolls), arranged alphabetically by state and city. For museums with all three types of collection, the entry is repeated. Numerous smaller, less well-known collections are included. Descriptions of collections' contents are provided.

SEE ALSO: Quilt collections: a directory for the United States and Canada (GLAH 2:P912).

Dictionaries and Encyclopedias

P784 Burnham, Dorothy K. Warp and weft: a dictionary of textile terms. Adapted and exp. from the Vocabulary of technical terms, 1964, with permission of the Centre International d'Étude des Textiles Anciens. Diagrams by Dorothy K. Burnham. N.Y., Scribner, 1981. xiv, 216p. il.

Building on the multi-lingual textile glossaries produced under the auspices of CIETA, the Centre International d'Étude des Textiles Anciens (see GLAH 2:P785), organized according to weave characteristics. For most of the approximately 550 English-language entries, corresponding weaving terms in French, German, Italian, Portuguese, Spanish, and Swedish are provided. Especially strong in its definitions of silks and silk weaving techniques. Its many diagrams and photographs facilitate identification and comparison.

Table of weaves, p.193–98. Specialized French terms, p.199–201. Notes, p.203–07. Literature cited, p.209–16.

P785 Centre Internationale d'Étude des Textiles Anciens. Fabrics: a vocabulary of technical terms: English, French, Italian, Spanish. 2d ed. Lyons, France, C.I.E.T.A., [1964]. v, 62p.

1st. ed., in English, French and Italian, 1959; German ed., Vokabular der Textiltechniken deutsch: englisch, französisch, italienisch, spanisch, schwedische = Terminologie textile en lange allemande, tissus: allemande, anglaise, franz., ital., espagn., suédois, Lyons, CIETA, 1971; Scandinavian ed., Nordisk textilteknisk terminologi, Oslo, Tanum, 1974.

The origins of this vocabulary lie in the decision to compile an inventory of surviving ancient textiles throughout the world. In order to do this an internationally recognized vocabulary for the standard description of these textiles was needed. This multi-lingual vocabulary was carried out under the auspices of CIETA; all involved were leading textile scholars in their respective fields.

The 1964 vocabulary is an English-based listing. That is, terms are listed in English, with French, Italian, and Spanish equivalent terms listed below. An English-language definition of that term is provided.

Addenda, p.60–62.

P786 Cyrus-Zetterström, Ulla. Textile terminology: Chinese - English - French - Swedish = Terminologie textile: Chinois - Anglais - Français - Suédois = Textil terminologi: Kinesisk - Engelsk - Fransk - Svensk. The Chinese text is written in collab. with Associate Professor Xu Guoha, Vice Director of Nantong Textile Museum. Borås, Centraltryckeriet Ake Svenson AB, 1995. 119p. il. (part col.)

"This terminology is intended as an aid to textile researchers and translators in China and in the Western countries, and aims to further the exchange of ideas about old textiles in both the East and the West."—*Pref.* Covers terms for pre-industrial woven fabrics, textile fibers, textile-related tools, and resist-dyed fabrics. 383 terms are provided under 277 headings. English, French, and Swedish terms are also given where equivalents exist. Color plates, magnified black-and-white photographs, and diagrams.

Measure words, p.102–03. Chronology, p.104–06. Chinese index, p.107–11. English index, p.112–14. French index, p.115–16. Swedish index, p.117.

P787 Emery, Irene. The primary structures of fabrics: an illustrated classification. [Rev. ed.] N.Y., Watson-Guptill/Whitney Library of Design; Washington, D.C., Textile Museum, 1994. xxvi, 339p. il.

1st ed., Washington, D.C., Textile Museum, 1966.

Pioneering study providing a "detailed and systematic investigation of the essential characteristics of ancient and primitive fabrics."—*Foreword.* Laid the groundwork for establishing a consistently used English-language vocabulary and resolving confusion over the appropriate terms needed to describe textiles and their structures. Terms and definitions are mostly accompanied by diagrams of weave structures to aid terminological identification.

Contents: (1) Components of fabric structures; (2) Classification of the structures of fabrics; (3) Structures accessory to fabrics.

Sources of information [not updated in the new ed.], p.259–308. Index, p.309–39.

P788 Encyclopedia of textiles: an illustrated and authoritative source book on textiles, presenting a complete and practical coverage of the entire field—its history and origins, its art and design, its natural and man-made fibers, its manufacturing and finishing processes, color and dyes, textile printing, specialty end uses; plus a comprehensive dictionary of textile terms. By the editors of American fabrics and fashions magazine. 3d ed. Englewood Cliffs, Prentice-Hall, 1980. 636p. il. ports.

1st ed., AF Encyclopedia of textiles, 1960; 2d ed., 1972.

Comprehensive encyclopedia of all categories of woven and nonwoven textiles, fibers, textile technology and textile history. Especially useful for its documentation of the increasingly rapid development of textile fiber and production technologies, particularly since 1945. The many diagrams and photographs are especially interesting for their illustration of textile manufacturing processes, and of manmade fibers.

Contents: Manmade fibers; Cotton; Wool; Specialty fibers; Silk; Bast and other plant fibers; Chronological history; Inventors and their inventions; Origins of fabric names; Masterpieces of textile design; Peruvian textiles; Textiles in the New World; Spinning; Weaving; Knitting; Lace-making; Ribbon-making; Nonwoven fabrics & felts; The finishing processes; Color and the human being; Dyes and dyeing processes; Printing of textiles; Curtains & draperies; Sheets & quilts; Rugs & carpets; Industrial fabrics.

Dictionary of textile terms, p.512–601.

P789 Fairchild's dictionary of textiles. Ed. by Phyllis G. Tortora. Consulting ed., Robert S. Merkel. 7th ed. N.Y., Fairchild, [1996]. xx, 662p. il.

1st ed., prepared by Louis Harmouth, 1915; 2d ed., 1920; 3d ed., 1924; 4th ed., prepared by Stephen Marks, 1959; 5th ed., 1967; 6th ed., ed. by Isabel B. Wingate, 1979.

Basic reference tool for those working in the textile industry as well as for textile historians. Substantially updated with each ed., many recent technological advances are documented. Organized alphabetically, the scope comprises textile fibers, yarns and fabric, textile structure and construction, and dyeing and finishing.

Contents: Appendix: Multinational and North American trade, professional and educational organizations related to the textile industry.

References, p.659–62.

P790 Hardingham, Martin. The illustrated dictionary of fabrics. London, Studio Vista, 1978. 159p. il.

Covers textiles and fibers.

Contents: Wool; Cotton; Silk; Other plant fibers; Manmade fibers; Textile terms; Obsolete fabrics.

Glossary of obsolete fabrics, p.152. Bibliography, p.154. Index, p.158–59.

P791 Hardouin-Fugier, Elisabeth; Berthod, Bernard; and Chavent-Fusaro, Martine. Les étoffes: dictionnaire historique. Avec la participation de Florence Charpentier-Klein. Dessins de Camille Deprez. [Paris], Éditions de l'Amateur, [1994]. 419p. col. il.

Beautifully illustrated volume comprising a considerable amount of in-depth research into the history, manufacture, and function of hundreds of textile types. An extremely comprehensive dictionary comprises the greater part of this volume, preceded by several scholarly essays. The excellent illustrations include dress items, textiles and textile designs, weave and fiber twist diagrams, history and genre paintings, and fashion photographs showing specific fabric types in use; sample and pattern books are also illustrated.

Contents: Ou chercher les noms d'étoffes?; Noms d'étoffes; Un guide pour explorer le Dictionnaire historique des étoffes; Choix et conventions du dictionnaire.

Actes royaux concernant le textile du XVe au XVIIIe siècle, p.50–54. List des ouvrages citées en abrégé, p.55–57. Index topographique, p.413–16.

P792 Humphries, Mary. Fabric glossary. Upper Saddle River, N.J., Prentice Hall, 1996. viii, 291p. il.

Seeks "to illustrate all stages of fabric make-up: fibers typically used, characteristics of yarn and fabric construction, plus the effect of finishing procedures, including coloring by dyeing and printing."—*Pref.* All fabrics discussed are accompanied by small black-and-white close-up photographs.

Contents: (1) Overview; (2) Fabric files [glossary].

References and resources, p.281–82. Index, p.283–91.

P793 Jerde, Judith. Encyclopedia of textiles. N.Y., Facts on File, [1992]. ix, 260p. il. (part col.)

Dictionary encyclopedia covering "fabric types, methods of production and construction, technical terms and prominent individuals in the history of textiles."—*Pref.* Emphasis is on 20th-century textiles and textile manufacture. The numerous illustrations include full- or half-page details of weave structures and fibers.

Bibliography, p.255–57. Subject index, p.259–60.

P794 Seiler-Baldinger, Annemarie. Textiles: a classification of techniques. Washington, D.C., Smithsonian Institution Pr., 1994. xvi, 256p. il. (part col.)

Trans. of "Systematik der textilen Techniken," in Basler Beiträge zur Ethnologie, v. 32, 1991.

Based on the pioneering work by Kristen and Alfred Buhler-Oppenheim, Grundlagen zur Systematik der gesamten textilen Techniken (Denkschriften der Sweizerischen naturforschenden Gesellschaft, v.LXXVIII, Pt.2, Zurich, 1948). Extremely thorough basic reference work. Focuses on a classification of textile terminology for textile production processes and techniques, rather than on the resultant textile structures. Clearly formulated diagrams provide visual explanations to the terms discussed, and excellent color photographs (mostly of ethnographic objects) show some of the more distinctive results of specific weave types. Alternative vocabulary for each term is also provided, in English and other languages.

Contents: The techniques of element production; The techniques of fabric production; The techniques of fabric ornamentation.; The techniques of fabric processing (joining of fabrics); Appendix: Structures and possible ways of production and identification.

References, p.156–72. Bibliography, p.173–236; Index [English, French, German, Italian, Portuguese, Spanish, and Scandinavian languages], p.237–56.

P795 Textile terms and definitions. Comp. by the Textile Institute Textile Terms and Definitions Committee. Ed. by M. C. Tubbs, and P. N. Daniels. 10th ed., rev. and enl. [Manchester, UK], The Textile Institute, [1995]. ix, 401p. il., tables.

1st ed., 1954; 2d ed., rev. and enl., 1955; 3d ed., rev. and enl., 1957; 4th ed., rev. and enl., 1960; 5th ed., rev. and enl., 1963; 6th ed., rev. and enl., 1970; 7th ed., rev. and enl., 1975; 8th ed., rev., and enl., 1986; 9th ed., rev. and enl., 1991.

Comprehensive compendium of textile terms in the English language, including North American terminology. Terms relating to the utilization and making up of textiles are excluded. Many photographs, macrophotographs, and diagrams aid in identifying weave, fiber and knotting structures, and chemical composition.

Contents: Textile terms and definitions; Systems for yarn number or count; SI units and conversion factors; Classification of textile fibres.

Notes, p.vii–viii. Abbreviations and symbols, p.ix.

Histories and Handbooks

General Works

P796 Anquetil, Jacques. Silk. With the collab. of Pascale Ballesteros for the history of fashion. Photography by Marc Walter. N.Y., Flammarion, [1996]. 200p. col. il.

Sumptuously illustrated vol. comprising many images of silk textiles in use as furnishing or dress items, as well as details of weaves.

Contents: The origins of silk weaving; Silk weaving in Europe: Renaissance Italy; The silk industry in Tours and Lyon; The China trade; The golden age of silk; Change and continuity; Luxury and technology. The silk revival: The tradition of fine silk

Bibliography, p.197. Glossary, p.198. Index, p.199.

P797 Balfour-Paul, Jenny. Indigo. [London], British Museum Pr., [1998]. 264p. il. (chiefly col.)

Beautifully illustrated volume presenting a considerable body of research on the history of the indigo trade and indigo dyeing practices, worldwide. Includes many photographs of traditional dyers from a variety of countries and cultures.

Contents: (1) Introduction: the myth and the magic; (2) From Antiquity to the Middle Ages; (3) Indigo's heyday, the downfall of woad and salvation by denim; (4) Indigo plants and the making of their dye; (5) Blue nails: indigo dyeing worldwide; (6) The variety of decorative techniques; (7) "For richer, for poorer": textiles prestigious and popular; (8) Blue art; (9) "In sickness and in health": blue beards, blue bodies; (10) Into the future; Appendix: Chemical formulae.

Notes, p.235–51. Select bibliography, p.252–57. Glossary, p.258. Index, p.261–64.

P798 Blum, Dilys E. The fine art of textiles: the collections of the Philadelphia Museum of Art. Color photography by Lynn Rosenthal. Philadelphia, Philadelphia Museum of Art, 1997. 208p. il. (chiefly col.)

Documents the history and range of the Philadelphia Museum's textile collections, reproducing approximately 400 pieces. Organized geographically, then by textile type. Tapestries and carpets are excluded from the survey.

Contents: Europe and the Americas; The Mediterranean and Middle East; India; Southeast Asia; China; Japan; Twentieth-century international design.

Glossary, p.204–06. Bibliography, p.207–08.

P799 Collezione Antonio Ratti. [various imprints], 1992– . (6)v. il. (chiefly col.)

Catalogs of the Antonio Ratti textile collection (Como, Italy) comprising approximately 3,000 individual pieces and 1,550 sample books. Individual vols. are published in English and Italian in limited editions, and document specific sections of the collection. All are magnificently illustrated, including many large photographs showing details of pattern and weave structure. One or more descriptive essays are followed by a catalog of relevant items in the collection.

Contents: (1) Buss, Chiara. Silk gold and silver: eighteenth century textiles (Milano, Fabbri, 1992); (2) Qibti: the Coptic textiles of the Antonio Ratti collection, ed. by Anna Maria Donadoni Roveri. Introductory and scientific texts by Franca Angonoa Gilardi ([Milano], Fabbri, 1992); (3) Peter, Irmgard. Cravattes ([Como], Ratti, 1994); (4) Levi-Strauss, Monique. Il cachmire: Indian and European shawls ([Como], Ratti, 1995); (5) Buss, Chiara. Velvets ([Como], Ratti, 1996); (6) Silk and colour, ed. by Chiara Buss (Milano, Grafiche Mazzucchelli, 1997).

Glossaries and bibliographical references are provided for all vols.

P800 Devoti, Donata. Il tessuto in Europa. Milano, Bramante, 1993. [Rev. ed.] 271p. il. (part col.) (Arti e tecniche)

1st ed., L'arte del tessuto in Europa, 1974.

Important scholarly survey focusing on the history of textiles in Western Europe. Organized chronologically, the survey ranges from the 11th to the 20th century. A catalog comprising 240 items makes up the second part of the text. Each item is illustrated with a large color reproduction, accompanied by a detailed catalog entry. The numerous illustrations include diagrams of weave/pattern structures.

Notizie dei luoghi e delle fabbriche, p.233–42. Notizie delle collezioni pubbliche e private, p.243–47. Vocabolario dei termini tecnici, p.249–55. Bibliografia, p.257–61. Nota bibliografica dei disegni e camponari, p.261. Indice dei luoghi di conservazione, p.265. Indice dei luoghi di fabbricazione, p.267. Indice dei nomi, p.269–71.

P801 Geijer, Agnes. A history of textile art. [Reprint, with corrections.] London, Pasold Research Fund in assoc. with Sotheby Parke Bernet (Distr. by Biblio Distribution Center, 1982). xi, 317p. il., plates, maps.

Rev. trans. of Ur textilkonstens historia. Lund, Gleerup, 1972; 1st English-language ed., London, Pasold Research Fund in assoc. with Sotheby Parke Bernet, 1979.

Wide-ranging history of the development of weaving. North and South American textiles are excluded from the discussion, as are (generally) textiles later than the 18th century. Considerable attention throughout is paid to Scandinavian textiles.

Contents: (I) Materials; (II) Weaving implements; (III) Woven fabrics and weaving techniques; (IV) Development of plain weaving; (V) Individually patterned weaves; (VI) Mechanical patterning; (VII) Silk weaving in Asia; (VIII) Silk weaving in Europe; (IX) Silk weaving in Scandinavia; (X) Linen damask and other table linen; (XI) Knotted pile fabrics and other fleecy textiles; (XII) Dyeing, textile printing and pattern dyeing; (XIII) Miscellaneous textile techniques; (XIV) The textile trade with the Orient; (XV) Textiles and textile crafts in the Scandinavian countries; (XVI) When and how textiles have been preserved—and should be preserved.

Notes, p.276–88. Bibliography, p.290–305. Index, p.310–17.

P802 Higgins, J. P. P. Cloth of gold: a history of metallised textiles. London, Lurex, [1993]. 112p.

Traces the history of metallised textiles from ancient Chinese times, and their diffusion via the Silk Road throughout the Mediterranean and the West. Coverage extends to the 20th century, with attention paid to the increasing use of non-precious metals to create the metallic look. Important areas of focus are the history of trade and technology, and the impact of metallics on 20th–century fashion.

Contents: (1) Oriental, Classical and Islamic precious textiles; (2) Romanesque and Gothic precious texts; (3) Renaissance and Baroque metallised textiles; (4) English and French work 1485–1815; (5) The impact of trade and industrialisation; (6) Metallics in haute couture; (7) Lurex the high technology metallised textile; (8) Lurex in modern and post-modern fashion.

Bibliography, p.111–12.

P803 King, Monique, and King, Donald. European textiles in the Keir collection: 400 BC to 1800 AD. Boston, Faber, 1990. vi, 311p. il. (part col.) (Keir collection, 6)

Documents a vast textile collection assembled by Edmund de Unger. "A selection of the most interesting and representative pieces, illustrating the evolution of design and technique in European textiles from antiquity to the eighteenth century."—*Introd.* The range of the Keir collections is so comprehensive that the catalog can serve as a general history of textiles. Arranged chronologically, each chapter begins with an introductory essay discussing the predominant styles and techniques of the period, followed by detailed catalog entries. Italian textiles are strongly represented, with French and Spanish also figuring prominently. Some Northern European textiles, as well as a few Asian and North African textiles, are included here for comparative purposes.

Glossary, p.295–300. Appendix: Museums with textile collections referred to in the catalogue, p.301. Bibliographical references, p.303–05. Index, p.307–11.

P804 Markowsky, Barbara. Europäische Seidengewebe des 13.-18. Jahrhunderts. Köln, Kunstgewerbemuseum der Stadt Köln, 1976. 463p. il. (chiefly col.) (Kataloge des Kunstgewerbemuseums Köln, Bd. VIII)

Important catalog of a significant collection of European woven silks.All items are illustrated with small black-and-white and/or larger color reproductions.

Contents: Die Entstehung der Sammlung: Die Geschichte der europäischen Seidenweberei; Die kunstgeschichtliche Entwicklung der europäischen Seidenweberei; Organisationsformen der Seidenweberei; Handwerker und Künstler; Zur Verwendung von Seidengeweben; Katalog.

Vokabular der Textiltechniken, p.99–113. Abgekürzt zitierte Literatur, p.445–54. Ortsregister und Verzeichnis abgekürzt zitierter Museen und Sammlungen, p.461–63.

P805 Nylander, Jane C. Fabrics for historic buildings: a guide to selecting reproduction fabrics. 4th ed., rev. Washington, D.C., Preservation Pr., 1990. 303p. il.

1st ed., 1977; 2d ed., 1980; 3d ed., 1983.

"This book is intended to help people with limited fabric experience select and order documentary reproduction fabrics that are suitable for furnishing historic properties."—*Introd.* Catalog of fabrics used in the United States from the colonial period to the 20th century.

Contents: 1700 to 1790: a dependence on imported fabrics; 1790 to 1815: changing tastes and technology; 1815 to 1840: technological advances and complex designs; 1840 to 1870: increasing diversity in furnishing fabrics; 1870 to 1900: new influences and variety; The twentieth century: innovation and tradition; Modern textiles: continuing a tradition; Appendix: Suppliers; Glossary; Bibliography; Sources of information.

P806 Pasold studies in textile history. [various imprints], 1981– . (10)v. il.

Important series covering the history of textiles and dress. All vols. are by leading scholars in their respective fields.

Contents: (1) Chapman, S. D., and Chassagne, S. European textile printers in the eighteenth century: a study of Peel and Oberkampf (London, Heinemann Educational Books, [1981]); (2) Cloth and clothing in medieval Europe: essays in memory of Professor E. M. Carus-Wilson, ed. by N. B. Harte and K. G. Ponting (London, Heinemann Educational; [Edington], Pasold Research Fund, 1983); (3) Jenkins, D. T., and Ponting, K. G. The British wool textile industry, 1770–1914 (Brookfield, Vt., Scolar Pr., 1987); (4) Bridbury, A. R. Medieval English clothmaking: an economic survey (London, Heinemann Educational, 1982); (5) Evans, Nesta. The East Anglian linen industry: rural industry and local economy, 1500–1850 (Brookfield, Vt., Gower, 1985); (6) Honeyman, Katrina, and Goodman, Jordan. Technology and enterprise: Isaac Holden and the mechanisation of woolcombing in France, 1848–1914 (Brookfield, Vt., Gower, 1986); (7) Newton, Stella Mary. The dress of the Venetians, 1495–1525 (Brookfield, Vt., Scolar Pr., 1987); (8) Singleton, John. Lancashire on the scrapheap: the cotton industry, 1945–1970 (N.Y., Oxford Univ. Pr., 1991); (9) Lemire, Beverly. Fashion's favourite: the cotton trade and the consumer in Britain, 1660–1800 (N.Y., Oxford Univ. Pr., 1991); (10) The new draperies in the Low Countries and England, 1300–1800, ed. by N. B. Harte (N.Y., Oxford Univ. Pr., 1997).

P807 Scott, Philippa. The book of silk. [London], Thames and Hudson, [1993]. 256p. il. (part col.)

Beautifully illustrated chronological survey of the history of silk textiles and dress.

Contents: (1) Origins: China and Japan; (2) Central Asia and the Silk Road; (3) India's woven winds; (4) The ancient world, Egypt and Byzantium; (5) The tide of Islam; (6) Mongols, Mamluks, Ottomans; (7) The Persian flowering; (8) Silk weaving comes to Europe; (9) French style; (10) Western highlights; (11) Silk in the modern world.

Compendium of information: Terms and techniques, p.234–42. Collecting, p.243–44. Care and conservation, p.244–45. Museums and collections, p.246–48. Publications, p.248–51. Index, p.253–55.

P808 Textile history: readings. [Ed. by] Anna M. Creekmore and Ila M. Pokornowski. [Washington, D.C.], Univ. Pr. of America, [1982]. viii, 332p. il.

Previously published articles and excerpts illustrating the history of textiles, textile technology, and the textile trade, from ancient Egyptian times to 1914. Focuses primarily on western textiles, and on textiles or textile technologies produced by other groups that had a significant impact on western textile history. Textiles produced for industrial purposes, as interior furnishings, and non-woven fabrics are not considered.

Contents: (I) Ancient Egypt, the Near East, and the Eastern Mediterranean; (II) Greco-Roman World; (III) Oriental and later Mid Eastern influences; (IV) Revival of commercial life; (V) Commercial expansion; (VI) New World; (VII) Industrial revolution..

References follow each part. General references, p.330–32.

P809 Textiles, 5,000 years: an international history and illustrated survey. Ed. by Jennifer Harris. [N.Y.], Abrams, [1993]. 320p. il. (chiefly col.), maps.

Comprehensive, extensively illustrated survey with contributions by leading textile scholars in their respective fields.

Contents: (I) A survey of textile techniques, by Jennifer Harris; (II) A survey of world textiles: the ancient world: (1) Introduction, by Joan Allgrove McDowell; (2) The Mediterranean, by Joan Allgrove McDowell; (3) Central and northern Europe, by John-Peter Wild; (4) Sassanian textiles, by Joan Allgrove McDowell; (5) Early Islamic textiles, by Joan Allgrove McDowell; (6) Byzantine silks, by Anna Muthesius; (7) Safavid Iran (1499–1722), by Joan Allgrove McDowell; (8) The Ottoman Empire, by Joan Allgrove McDowell; (9) Central Asian textiles, by Jennifer Wearden; (10) Palestinian embroidery, by Shelagh Weir; (11) [India and Pakistan]: Historical development and trade, by Margaret Hall; (12) Tribal textiles, by Margaret Hall; (13) Carpets of the Middle and Far East, by Patricia L. Baker; (14) China, by Verity Wilson; (15) Japan, by Susan-Marie Best; (16) South-East Asia, by Sylvia Fraser-Lu; (17) Sicilian silks, by Anna Muthesius; (18) Italian silks (1300–1500), by Lisa Monnas; (19) Italian silks (1500–1900), by Jacqueline Herald; (20) Spanish silks, by Jacqueline Herald; (21) French silks (1650–1800), by Lesley Miller; (22) Figured linen damasks, by Jacqueline Herald; (23) Tapestry, by Thomas Campbell; (24) Embroidery, by Santina M. Levey; (25) Lace, by Santina M. Levey; (26) Printed textiles, by Jennifer Harris; (27) Eastern Europe, by Jennifer Wearden; (28) Greece, the Greek Islands and Albania, by Roderick R. Taylor; (29) Colonial North America (1700–1790s), by Mary Schoeser; (30) Native North America, by Colin Taylor and Betty Taylor; (31) Latin America, by Chloë Sayer and Penny Bateman; (32) North Africa, by Caroline Stone; (33) Sub-Saharan Africa and the offshore islands, by John Mack.

Further reading and sources cited, p.306–11. Glossary, p.312–14. Index, p.317–20.

P810 Thomas, Michel; Mainguy, Christine; and Pommier, Sophie. Textile art. N.Y., Rizzoli, 1985. 279p. il. (part col.)

Trans. of Histoire d'un art: l'art textile. Geneva, Skira, 1985.

Extensively illustrated survey of the history of textiles and textile design. Textiles discussed range in date from ca. 8,000 B.C. to the late 20th century. Particular consideration is given to 20th-century textile arts and their relationship with the so-called fine arts. Many of the illustrations show examples of textile arts made from non-traditional materials.

Contents: (I) World centers of textile art; (II) The primacy of tapestry in the West; (III) The revival of textile art; (IV) Perspectives.

Bibliography, p.259–63. Index of names, p.274–79.

P811 Wilckens, Leonie von. Die textilen Kunste: von der Spätantike bis um 1500. München, Beck, [1991]. 427p. il. (part col.)

In-depth, scholarly examination of the history of textiles (including tapestries), textile weaving, and embroidery techniques. Extensively illustrated, an excellent overview of extant early medieval textile types.

Contents: (I) Gewebe bis zum 7. Jahrhundert; (II) Seidengewebe des 7. Bis 13. Jahrhunderts; (III) Gewebe und Borten, u.a. mit Gold- und Baumwollfäden; (IV) Seidengewebe vom 13. Jahrhundert bis um 1500; (V) Gemusterte Leinen und Mischgewebe; (VI) Gemusterte Gewebe durch Färben und Aufdrücken; (VIII) Die Bildwirkerei; (IX) Sonstige textile Techniken

Anhang: Abkürzungsverzeichnis, p.340. Abgekürzt zitierte Literatur, p.341. Anmerkungen, p.342–80. Glossar, p.381–86. Ausgewählte Literatur, p.387–405. Geographisches Register, p.407–13. Personen- und Sachregister, p.414–25.

P812 Wilson, Kax. A history of textiles. Boulder, Colo., Westview Pr., [1979]. xxi, 357p. il. 130 plates.

"The purpose of this book is . . . to serve as a text for college classes and to aid textile history researchers."—*Pref.*

Contents: (1) Some relationships; (2) Spinning and raw materials; (3) Fabric construction; (4) Finish and color for textiles; (5) Patterned textiles; (6) The medieval textile industry in Southern Europe; (7) Textiles of the Far East; (8) Textiles in Northern Europe; (9) Textiles and independence in colonial America; (10) Industrialization and textiles in nineteenth century America; (11) Fabrics of the American Southwest; (12) Fabrics of South and Middle America.

Notes and bibliographical references at ends of chapters. Glossary, p.345–48. Index, p.349–57.

Ancient

P813 Barber, E. J. W. Prehistoric textiles: the development of cloth in the Neolithic and Bronze Ages: with special reference to the Aegean. [Princeton], Princeton Univ. Pr., [1991]. xxix, 471p. il. (part col.), 4p. of plates, maps.

Pioneering work reviewing the information provided by archeological textiles and textile fragments within the context of paleobiological and linguistic studies, and discussing the ways this information can be used to draw conclusions about prehistoric societies, for example, to provide evidence for cross-cultural connections. Wide-ranging geographically and chronologically. Detailed technical analyses are provided, and the function and significance of weaving by women is also discussed.

Bibliography, p.397–430. Index, p.431–71.

P814 Germer, Renate. Die Textilfärberei und die Verwendung gefärbter Textilien im alten Ägypten. Wiesbaden, Harrassowitz, 1992. x, 149p. il. (part col.) (Ägyptologische Abhandlungen, Bd. 53)

Scholarly study, mostly in German but with some sections (primarily extracts from excavation reports) in English and French. Hieroglyphics and contemporary images are discussed, and the chemical analyses of excavated finds are surveyed for evidence of the fibers, weave structures, and in particular dyes. Line drawings, based primarily on wall-paintings, illustrate the intricacies, function, and symbolism of color in Egyptian dress.

Literaturangaben, p.143–49.

P815 Hald, Margrethe. Ancient Danish textiles from bogs and burials: a comparative study of costume and Iron Age textiles. [2d ed.] [Copenhagen], National Museum of Denmark, [1980]. 398p. il. (part col.) (Publications of the National Museum. Archaeological-historical series, XXI)

1st ed., Olddanske tekstiler, 1950; supplemented by "Olddanske tekstiler: fund fra 1947–1955," in Aarborger for Nordisk oldkyndighed og historie, 1955.

Scholarly analysis of cloth fragments recovered from grave sites in peat bogs across Northern Europe. Extensively illustrated, the publication includes photographs of textile fragments showing their construction, and diagrams of weave structures.

Bibliographical references follow each chapter. Literature, p.394–98.

P816 Hall, Rosalind M. Egyptian textiles. [Aylesbury, Shire, 1986]. 72p. il., map. (Shire Egyptology, 4)

Succinct introduction to all aspects of dynastic Egyptian textiles and dress. The numerous illustrations include scenes from Egyptian wall paintings where the dress is especially distinctive, as well as textiles and dress items found during excavations.

Contents: (1) The archeological importance of textiles; (2) Woven fabrics and dyeing; (3) Spinning and weaving; (4) Representations of costume; (5) Garments for life and death; (6) Tutankhamun's wardrobe; (7) The Egyptian laundry; (8) Sewing and darning; (9) Dress and rank in ancient Egypt.

Chronology, p.5–6. Museums to visit, p.68–69. Index, p.71–72.

P817 Hooft, Ph. P. M. van 't . . . [et al.] Pharaonic and early medieval Egyptian textiles. Leiden, Rijksmuseum van Oudheden, 1994. xviii, 198p. il., 39 plates, tables. (Collections of the National Museum of Antiquities at Leiden, VIII)

Scholarly examination and catalog of the early textiles collection at the National Museum of Antiquities at Leiden (The Netherlands). Part of the collection was also shown in the 1993–95 traveling exhibition, "De kleren van de farao" (Clothing of the pharaohs), which opened at Leiden.

Contents: (I) The Pharaonic textiles, by E. H. C. van Rooij and G. M. Vogelsang-Eastwood; (II) The early medieval Egyptian textiles, by Ph. P. M. van't Hooft and G. M. Vogelsang-Eastwood.

Glossary, p.ix–xiii. Indices: (I) General, p.196–97. (II) Names of persons, p.198.

P818 Masurel, Hubert. Tissus et tisserands du premier Age du Fer. Saint-Germaine-en-Laye, Société des Amis du Musée des Antiquités Nationales et du Château de Saint-Germain-en-Laye, 1990. 303p. il., 8 col. plates. (Antiquités nationales. Mémoire, 1)

Scholarly, technical analysis of the textile contents of the so-called tombe d'Apremont, located in the region of Haute-Saône, in eastern France. The contents of this burial site, dating from 600 B.C., are compared with those of several other approximately contemporary European sites.

Bibliographie, p.296–97.

P819 Mayer-Thurman, Christa C., and Williams, Bruce. Ancient textiles from Nubia: Meroitic, X-Group, and Christian fabrics from Ballana and Qustul. Chicago, Art Institute of Chicago, 1979. 148p. il. (part col.), maps.

Scholarly catalog of the exhibition, Art Institute of Chicago (1979). The 187 textiles exhibited were retrieved during archeological salvage operations prior to the flooding of the area behind the Aswan Dam and date from the period 100–600 A.D. All exhibited pieces are illustrated with excellent black-and-white and/or color photographs, and detailed catalog entries are provided for each item.

Bibliographical references at ends of chapters.

P820 Petzel, Florence Eloise. Textiles of ancient Mesopotamia, Persia and Egypt. [Corvallis, Or.?], F. E. Petzel, 1987. xii, [iv], 226p.

Covering the period 4,000–300 B.C., this vol. "traces the early development of textile fibers, yarn and fabric constructions, dyeing, and finishing, decorative media and textile designs in Mesopotamia, Persia and Egypt. Attention is also given to textiles for specific uses. Textile characteristics are considered in relation to factors such as the nature of the region and the people, astrology, religious beliefs, economic and social systems, and foreign influences."—*Pref.* The three regions (Mesopotamia, Persia, Egypt) are considered separately, with uniform subdivisions for each.

Notes on Mesopotamian chronology, p.xii–[xvi]. Bibliography [Mesopotamia], p.72–80, [Persia], p.123–39, [Egypt], 215–26. Glossary: Egypt, p.214–15.

Early Christian—Byzantine

P821 Baginski, Alisa, and Tidhar, Amalia. Textiles from Egypt, 4th–13th centuries C.E. [Jerusalem], L.A. Mayer Memorial Institute for Islamic Art, 1980. 176p. il. (part col.), IV col. plates.

Catalog of the exhibition, Mayer Institute (1980) of Coptic textiles and dress. 272 catalog entries provide technical analyses, weaving details, and comparisons with published items from other collections. All pieces are illustrated.

Bibliographical references follow the Introduction. Technical information, p.19–23. Glossary, p.24–33. Bibliography and abbreviations, p.174–76.

P822 Ierusalimskaja, Anna A. Die Gräber der Moščevaja Balka: frühmittelalterliche Funde an der Nordkaukasischen Seidenstrasse. Hrsg. vom Bayerischen Nationalmuseum München, und von der Staatliche Ermitage Sankt Petersburg. München, Maris, 1996. 338p. il., 88 plates (part col.)

Documents the finds from an important archeological grave site located on the northernmost route of the Silk Road. Finds include textiles and clothing from many regions along the route, including the Byzantine empire, Syria, Sogdiana, and China.

Abkürzungen und Bibliographie, p.327–38.

P823 Der Lebenskreis der Kopten: Dokumente, Textilien, Funde, Ausgrabungen. Zusammengest. von Helmut Buschhausen, Ulrike Horak, Hermann Harrauer. Unter Mitarb. von Monika Hasitzka . . . [et al.] Wien, Hollinek, 1995. xx, 308p. il., 71 col. plates. (Mitteilungen aus der Papyrussammlung der Österreichischen Nationalbibliothek. Papyrus Erzherzog Rainer. Neue Serie, XXV. Folge)

Scholarly catalog of the exhibition, Österreichischen Nationalbibliothek, Vienna (1995). 331 textiles, papyri, parchments, ostraka, and other objects from the massive Papyrus Collection of the Austrian National Library. The numerous inscriptions are discussed, and some of the papyri include designs or sketches relating to textiles. All items receive a detailed catalog entry, and are excellently photographed.

Bibliographical references throughout the text. Abgekürzte Literatur, p.297–99. Sachindex, p.301–08.

P824 Lorquin, Alexandra. Les tissus coptes au Musée National du Moyen Age, Thermes de Cluny: catalogue des étoffes égyptiennes de lin et de laine de l'Antiquité tardive aux premiers siècles de l'Islam. Paris, Réunion des Musées Nationaux, 1992. 395p. il. (part col.), map.

Catalog of an important collection. 173 Coptic, Islamic, and tiraz textiles, all of them illustrated and accompanied by detailed entries, are described.

Contents: (I) Origine et histoire de la collection; (II) Typologie des pièces; (III) Aperçu technique; (IV) Iconographie; (V) Catalogue.

Chronologie sommaire, p.9. Annexes: Index chronologique, p.364. Index thématique, p.365–69. Lexique des termes techniques, p.372–77. Abréviations bibliographiques, p.378–93.

P825 Martiniani-Reber, Marielle. Lyon, Musée Historique des Tissus: soieries sassanides, coptes et byzantines: Ve–XIe siècles. Paris, Ministère de la Culture et de la Communication, Réunion des Musées Nationaux, 1986. 129p. il. (part col.) (Inventaire des collections publiques françaises, 30)

Catalog of 109 pieces, each with a detailed entry and accompanied by a black-and-white photograph.

Contents: Le Musée Historique des Tissus; Rappel chronologique; Utilisation et techniques des tissus étudiés; Catalogue.

Bibliographical references at ends of chapters. Lexique des principaux termes techniques utilisés dans les notices, p.19–21. Publications citées en abrégé, p.22–23.

P826 ______. Textiles et mode sassanides: les tissus orientaux conservés au département des Antiquités égyptiennes, Musée du Louvre. Avec la participation de Dominique Bénazeth. Préf. de Christiane Ziegler. [Paris], Réunion des Musées Nationaux, [1997]. 155p. il. (part col.) (Inventaire des collections publiques françaises, 39)

Catalog of this important collection of Sassanian textiles, mostly excavated at Antinoë (Antinoopolis), Egypt.

Contents: Les tissus sassanides; Restauration des étoffes; Histoire de la collection; Catalogue; Vêtements et fragments de vêtements; Tissus d'ameublement; Fragments de vêtements avec tapisserie.

Bibliographical references follow the Introduction. Bibliographie, p.143–46. Vocabulaire technique, p.147–50. Index, p.151.

P827 ______. Tissus coptes. Avec la collab. de Claude Ritschard, Georgette Cornu, and Barbara Raster. Geneva, Musée d'Art et d'Histoire, [1991]. 2v. il., map.

Excellent catalog of an important collection.

Contents: (I) L'Égypte copte: cadre historique, by Marielle Martiniani-Reber; Historique de la collection, collectionneurs et lieux de provenance des tissus, by Marielle Martiniani-Reber; Fonction des étoffes de la collection, by Marielle Martiniani-Reber; Le décor des tapisseries coptes: permanence de l'ancienne Egypte?, by Claude Ritschard; Les tisserands coptes après la conquête islamique, by Georgette Cornu; Technique des tissus coptes, by Marielle Martiniani-Reber; Catalogue: tissus, by Marielle Martiniani-Reber; Catalogue: instruments de filage, tissage et couture, by Marielle Martiniani-Reber and Claude Ritschard; (II) Catalogue: tissus; Catalogue: instruments de filage, tissage et couture.

Tableau chronologique, p.10. Vocabulaire technique, p.35. Orientation bibliographique, p.112–13. Indexes in both vols.

P828 Muthesius, Anna. Byzantine silk weaving, AD 400–AD 1200. Ed. by Ewald Kislinger and Johannes Koder. Vienna, Fassbaender, 1995. xxviii, 260p. il. (part col), map.

Based on a survey of more than 1,000 Eastern Mediterranean silks in Western ecclesiastical collections. Reproductions are of poor quality.

Contents: (1) Production of the raw material; (2) Introduction to hand drawlooms; (3) Introduction to Byzantine dyes; (4) The datable Byzantine lion and elephant silks with woven inscriptions, and their relationship to some similarly patterned uninscribed silks; (5) Paired main warp twills with lion, eagle and griffin motifs; (6) The London Charioteer silk (Victoria and Albert Museum T. 762–1892) and some related pieces; (7) Falke's so-called "Alexandrian" group of silks and some related pieces; (8) Three more groups of single main warp twills; (9) Monochrome patterned silks of the tenth to twelfth centuries; (10) Byzantine influence on Central Asian silk weaving: the Ram silk at Huy and related silks of the seventh to tenth centuries; (11) An imperial Byzantine tapestry weave silk and the Bullock silk of St. Servatius, Maastricht; (12) Byzantine and other Eastern Mediterranean tabby weave, tabby weave with extra pattern weft, and damask weave silks of the fourth to the twelfth centuries; (13) Silk production in southern Italy and in Sicily; (14) The uses of silks in the West; (15) Western silk patrons; Appendix 1: Weaving types; Appendix 2: List by location; Appendix 3: Main catalogue: silk numbers M1 to M120; Appendix 4: Handlist: silk numbers M 121–1391.

Bibliographical references at ends of chapters. Bibliography, p.xii–xxviii. Index, p.245–54.

P829 Rutschowscaya, Marie-Hélène. Coptic fabrics. [Paris], Birò, [1990]. 159p. il. (chiefly col.), map.

Trans. of Tissu coptes. Paris, Birò, 1990.

Examines the style, decoration, trade, and production of Coptic textiles and dress. Generously illustrated with examples primarily from French public collections. Surviving Coptic dress, illuminated manuscripts, and weave structure analyses also form part of the visual repertoire.

Contents: Historical outline; From burial clothes . . .; A discovery becomes fashion; Making cloth; The textile economy; The history of decorated fabrics; The problems of chronology in Coptic fabrics; Use of fabrics; Stylistic evolution of Coptic fabrics; Pharaonic vestiges; Greco-Roman influences; Oriental influences; Christian iconography.

Important dates, p.11. The development of collections, p.149–50. Some examples of decoration, p.151. Glossary, p.152–53. Index, p.154–55. Bibliography, p.156–59.

P830 Stauffer, Annemarie. Spätantike und koptische Wirkereien: Untersuchungen zur ikonographischen Tradition in spätantiken und frühmittelalterlichen Textilwerkstätten. N.Y., Lang, [1992]. 297p. il.

A cornerstone in late antique textile studies, based on the author's doctoral dissertation (Universität Bern, 1990). Examines technique, iconography, and chronology, as well as textiles from Egypt under the Roman Empire and after the Arab invasions. Catalog of 99 works discussed in the text, with detailed entries.

Contents: Mysterienglauben, östliche Heilslehren, Magie und Christentum; Textilhandwerk in Ägypten; Dekorationsschemata; Das Wirken; Spätantike Periode; Wirkereien von der Spätantike bis zur Arabischen Invasion; Wirkereien nach der Arabischen Invasion; Katalog.

Bibliographical references throughout. Verzeichnis der abgekürzt zitierten Literatur, p.280–94.

P831 ______. Textiles d'Égypte de la collection Bouvier: antiquité tardive, période copte, premiers temps de l'Islam. = Textilien aus Ägypten aus der Sammlung Bouvier: Spätantike, Koptische und frühislamische Gewebe. Avec une contrib. de = Mit einem Beitr. von Andreas Schmidt-Colinet. Fribourg, Musée d'Art et d'Histoire; Bern, Benteli, [1991]. 231p. il. (part col.)

Published to accompany the exhibition, Musée d'Art et d'Histoire, Fribourg (1991–92). All 116 items in the catalog are illustrated with excellent reproductions and accompanied by detailed entries.

Contents: Textiles d'Egypte; Le collectionneur Maurice Bouvier; Production locale et importations; Les deux carrés entrelacés: de la signification d'un ornement géometrique, by Andreas Schmidt-Colinet; Le jardin aux arbres: de l'origine et de la signification des tentures "à motifs d'arbres" de l'Antiquité tardive.

Bibliographical references at ends of chapters. Liste des ouvrages cités en abrégé, p.230–31.

P832 ______. Textiles of late antiquity. Entries by Marsha Hill, Helen C. Evans, and Daniel Walker. N.Y., Metropolitan Museum of Art, [1995]. 48p. il. (chiefly col.), map.

Published in conjunction with the exhibition, Metropolitan Museum of Art (1995–1996). This essay, by a leading scholar in the field, accompanies a group of important Coptic pieces, all illustrated with good color reproductions.

Bibliographical references follow the essay.

P833 Trilling, James. The Roman heritage: textiles from Egypt and the eastern Mediterranean 300 to 600 AD. [Special issue of the] Textile Museum journal, v.21 [also given as v.20]. Washington, D.C., Textile Museum, 1982. 112p. il. (part col.)

Catalog of the exhibition (Textile Museum, Washington, D.C. (1982)) focusing on the textile art of the late Roman period. 117 pieces in the museums's collection are included. The first piece in the catalog was (to date) the largest Late Roman tapestry extant.

Bibliography, p.111–12.

SEE ALSO: Hooft, Pharaonic and early medieval Egyptian textiles (GLAH 2:P817); Mayer-Thurman and Williams, Ancient textiles from Nubia (GLAH 2:P819).

Islamic

P834 Baker, Patricia L. Islamic textiles. [London], British Museum Pr., [1995]. 192p. il. (part col.), map.

Focuses on religious and secular work produced in Egypt, Syria, Anatolia, and Iran. Rugs and carpets are excluded. The many illustrations are taken not only from textiles themselves, but also from illuminated manuscripts, paintings, and photographs.

Contents: (1) Textiles, trade routes and society; (2) Early Islamic period I: textiles as tribute; (3) Early Islamic period II: textiles at court; (4) Mamluk textiles; (5) Ottoman opulence; (6) Safavid splendour; (7) Textiles of Qajar Iran; (8) Eighteenth- and nineteenth-century Ottoman fabrics; (9) The contemporary world.

Bibliography, p.181–86. Index, p.189–92.

P835 Balfour-Paul, Jenny. Indigo in the Arab world. [Richmond, England], Curzon Pr., [1997]. 283p. il., 14 plates (part col.), maps.

Drawing on eye-witness accounts and merchants' records, this extremely thorough and readable survey documents the significance of indigo from antiquity through the early 20th century.

Contents: (1) Historical background; (2) Indigo in the great age of Islam; (3) Post-Mamluk trade in indigo and Ottoman influences; (4) Agricultural production; (5) The organization of the indigo dyeing industry; (6) Raw materials and techniques of dyeing; (7) Indigo in textiles; (8) Substance or colour? The versatility of indigo.

Notes, p.175–245. Bibliography, p.246–67. Glossary, p.268–70. Chemical formulae, p.271–72. Index, p.273–83.

P836 Bier, Carol. The Persian velvets at Rosenborg. With a contrib. by Mogens Bencard. Copenhagen, [De Danske Kongers Kronologiske Samling and Dadema Trading Aps], 1995. 111p. il. (part col.), map, ports.

"The Persian Velvets at Rosenborg Palace in Copenhagen comprise the largest and most important corpus of Safavid velvets in the world."—*p.7.* Scholarly study of the 61 examples in the collection, including some significant fragments dating from the early 17th century.

Glossary of pattern and textile types, p.97–100. Analytical bibliography, p.101–09.

P837 Cornu, Georgette. Tissus islamiques de la collection Pfister. Avec la collab. de Odile Valansot et Hélène Meyer. Città del Vaticano, Biblioteca Apostolica Vaticana, 1992. xix, 655p. il. (part col.), maps. (Documenti e riproduzioni, 4)

Scholarly inventory-catalog of the collection of the approximately 250 Islamic textile fragments assembled by the textile colorist and scholar, Jean Jost Rodolphe Pfister (1867–1955), now housed at the Vatican Library. The chronological range is from the proto/ancient Islamic period (8th–10th centuries) to the 15th and 16th centuries. Woven and printed textiles are included, as well as tiraz embroideries and ikats. Primarily from Egypt, examples from other parts of the Islamic world are also part of the collection. All pieces are extensively described, and reproduced in excellent-quality photographs.

Lexique générale, p.428–32. Lexique technique des termes de tissage et de tapisserie, p.433–36. Notice sur les antiquaires, p.437. Chronologie des califes abbassides et fatimides et des princes toulounides et des ikhshidites, p.438–39.

P838 Early Islamic textiles. Ed. by Clive Rogers. Contribs.: Hero Granger-Taylor . . . [et al.] Brighton, Rogers and Padmore, 1983. 47p. il. (part col.), 10 col. plates, map.

Collection of short essays providing a useful introduction to Islamic textiles and dress. The majority of items considered come from Egypt. All items illustrated are accompanied by detailed captions.

Contents: Textile techniques of the Near East at the time of the Arab conquest; The construction of tunics, by Hero Granger-Taylor; Some aspects of the Octagon, by Simon Crosby; Early Islam: an historical background, by Clive Rogers; The tiraz issue, by Clive Rogers; The influence of Persian textile motifs, by Clive Rogers; Cotton and silk in the early Islamic world, by Hero Granger-Taylor; Textiles from Quseir al-Qadim, by Gillian Eastwood.

Bibliographical references follow each essay. Bibliography, p.47.

P839 Geijer, Agnes. Oriental textiles in Sweden. Copenhagen, Rosenkilde and Bagger, 1951. 139p. il. 104 plates (part col.)

Important volume documenting the number and significance of Chinese, Persian, and Turkish, medieval and later, ecclesiastical, and secular textiles to have survived in Sweden. The catalog comprises 169 examples, all illustrated.

Contents: (I) A review of Sweden's intercourse with the East; (II) Documentary evidence about the use of oriental textiles; (III) Silk woven fabrics; (IV) Embroideries; (V) Carpets; Catalogue; Appendix: Extract from Johan Philipp Kilburger: Kurzer Unterricht von dem russichen Handel wie selbige, mit aus- und eingehenden Waaren 1674 durch ganz Russland getrieben worden ist.

Bibliographical references throughout the text. Index of specimens treated, p.131–32. Index of personal names, p.132–33. Bibliography, p.135–39.

P840 Islamische Textilkunst des Mittelalters: aktuelle Probleme. Beitr. von Muhammad 'Abbās Muhammad Salīm . . . [et al.] Riggisberg [Switzerland], Abegg-Stiftung, 1997. 219p. il. (part col.) (Riggisberger Berichte, 5)

Collection of papers from an interdisciplinary conference held in conjunction with the exhibition, Wirkereien und Gewebe aus der Welt des Islam, Abegg-Stiftung (1993), and with the simultaneous publication of the Abegg-Stiftung's first collection catalog, Mittelalterliche Textilien I: Ägypten, Persien, Mesopotamien, Spanien und Nordafrika (see GLAH 2:P843). Illustrations include diagrams of weave structures and patterns, as well as details of surviving textiles.

Literaturnachweis, p.209–17.

P841 Lombard, Maurice. Les textiles dans le monde musulman du VIIe au XIIe siècle. N.Y., Mouton, 1978. 316p. il., maps. (Études d'économie médiévale, III) (Civilisations et sociétés, 61)

Posthumously published. "M. Lombard is the first historian to show the leading part played by the Musulmann world in the diffusion of the production of different kinds of textile fabrics and in the development of techniques."—*Review*, Textile history, v.11, [1980], p.225. Important scholarly study tracing the development of the primary fibers (wool, linen, cotton, and silk) in the countries surrounding the Mediterranean and primarily those of the Islamic tradition; special attention is paid to the Egyptian Delta region, and to Spain.

Contents: (I) Les progrès de deux textiles anciens: la laine et le lin; (II) L'avènement de deux textiles nouveaux: le coton et la soie; (III) Les textiles secondaires ou rares; (IV) Les teintures et les produits nécessaires a la préparations des étoffes; (V) Un exemple de centre textile: le delta égyptien; (VI) Volume et qualité de la production textile; (VII) Travail et techniques.

Bibliographical references throughout the text. Bibliographie, p.259–79. Index géographique et historique, p.281–311.

P842 Neumann, Reingard, and Murza, Gerhard. Persische Seiden: die Gewebekunst der Safawiden und ihrer Nachfolger. Leipzig, Seeman, 1988. 335p. il. (part col.)

Extended essay on the history and development of Persian silks, followed by a catalog comprising 354 items, all of which are illustrated. Most of the silks belong to four German collections: the Museum für Kunstgewerbe, Berlin-Kopenick; the Museum für Volkerkunde, Leipzig; the Museum für Kunsthandwerk der Staatlichen Kunstsammlungen Dresden; and the Museum des Kunsthandwerks (Grassi-Museum), Leipzig.

Anmerkungen, p.324–29. Literaturverzeichnis, p.329–32. Abkürzungen, p.332. Namensregister - geographisches Register, p.333. Nachweis der nicht im Katalog enthaltenen Abbildungen, p.334. Verzeichnis der im Katalog enthaltenen Inventarnummern, p.334–35.

P843 Otavsky, Karel, and Muhammad Salim, Muhammad 'Abbas. Mittelalterliche Textilien. I. Ägypten, Persien und Mesopotamien, Spanien und Nordafrika. Unter Mitarb. von Cordula M. Kessler. Riggisberg [Switzerland], Abegg-Stiftung Riggisberg, 1995. 302p. il. (part col.) (Die Textilsammlung der Abegg-Stiftung, Bd. 1)

Catalog of an important collection. The extensive catalog entries, for 182 pieces, are complemented by excellent black-and-white and/or color photographs, together with technical analyses.

Contents: (I) Textilien mit gewirktem und gesticktem Dekor aus Ägypten; (II) Gewebe aus Ägypten, Persien und Mesopotamien, Spanien und Nordafrika; (III) Gefälschte persische Textilien im Stile des 10.-12. Jahrhunderts.

Glossar, by Cordula M. Kessler, p.279–85. Register: Historische Personen, Sammler und Kunsthändler Orte, Sammlungen oder Kunstwerke nach Orten, p.286–89. Literaturnachweis, p.291–302.

P844 Serjeant, R. B. Islamic textiles: material for a history up to the Mongol conquest. Beirut, Librairie du Liban, [1972]. 263p., maps.

Collection of seminal articles originally published in Ars islamica, v.IX–XVI (1942–51). Arranged by region.

Bibliographical references throughout the text. Indexes: (1) Arabic and Persian terms not relating to textiles, p.223–28. (2) Place names, p.228–41. (3) Technical terms, p.242–63.

P845 Spring, Christopher, and Hudson, Julie. North African textiles. [London], British Museum Pr., [1995]. 144p. il. (chiefly col.), maps.

Survey of the textiles and dress of the Islamic, Christian, and Jewish traditions primarily in the Magreb region of North Africa. Includes contemporary and urban textiles.

Contents: (1) The threads of North African history; (2) Food of the loom; (3) Patterns of life; (4) Display and modesty: textiles for marriage; (5) Textiles of town and country; (6) Beyond the loom: non-woven designs and techniques; (7) Secular and sacred: the textiles of Ethiopia; (8) Continuity and change.

Bibliography, p.140–41. Glossary, p.142. Index, p.143–44.

P846 Tissus d'Égypte: témoins du monde arabe, VIIIe–XVe siècles: collection Bouvier. Thonon-les Bains, Albaron, 1993. 347p. il. (part col.), maps.

Published to accompany the traveling exhibition, Musée d'Art et d'Histoire, Geneva (1993), and other locations. The catalog comprises 215 splendidly illustrated pieces. Items date from the Islamic, Fayyum, Fatimid, and Mamluk periods and include early examples of complex knitting techniques. Each item receives a detailed catalog entry.

Contents: Textiles islamiques de la collection Bouvier, par Marielle Martiniani-Reber; Antiquaires et collectionneurs, par Marielle Martiniani-Reber; Textiles islamiques: études en laboratoire, par Anne Rinuy and Thérèse Flury; Conservation et restuaration des textiles, par Barbara Raster; Les tissus dans le monde arabo-islamique oriental jusqu'à l'époque mamluke, par Georgette Cornu; Le mobilier textile au moyen age chez les Arabes, tentures, nattes et tapis, par Joëlle Lemaistre; Figuration et abstraction dans les décors islamiques, par Claude Ritschard.

Lexique des termes techniques, by Marielle Martiniani-Reber, p.328–30. Lexique général, by Georgette Cornu, p.331–35. Cartes, by Georgette Cornu, p.336–37. Evolution des styles épigraphiques, by Georgette Cornu, p.338–39. Chronologie des dynasties, by Georgette Cornu, p.340. Bibliographie et abréviations, p.341–45. Translittération, p.346. Index, p.347.

P847 Vogelsang-Eastwood, G. M. Resist dyed textiles from Quseir al-Qadim, Egypt. Paris, A.E.D.T.A., 1990. 123p. il. (part col.), 5 col plates, maps.

Discussion of inter-cultural connections among India, China, and the Arabian peninsula as demonstrated by surviving medieval textile fragments. The catalog comprises 69 excellently photographed fragments.

Contents: Quseir al-Qadim; The medieval Indo-Egyptian trade in resist dyed textiles; Resist and block printed textiles from known archaeological sites; The cloth and its preparation; The dyes and mordants; Block printing; Direct block printing; Block printing and hand painting; Tritik and bandhan; Catalogue.

Bibliography, p. 27–30.

P848 A wealth of silk and velvet: Ottoman fabrics and embroideries. Ed. by Christian Erber. With contrib. by Gisela Helmecke . . . [et al.] Trans. by Michaela Nierhaus. [Bremen], Temmen, [1993]. 288p. il. (part col.)

Trans. of Reich an Samt und Seide: osmanische Gewebe und Stickereien. Bremen, Temmen,1993.

Fully illustrated catalog of the exhibition, Altona Museum, Hamburg (1993), occasioned by the 7th International Conference on Oriental Carpets, Hamburg.

Contents: The Ottomans: a world power between the Orient and the Occident, by Martina Einhorn; Floral style and çintamani: aspects of Ottoman ornamental style, by Reingard Neumann; Workshop and harem: textile crafts in the Ottoman empire: The fabric, by Reingard Neumann; The embroidery, by Gisela Helmecke; Gold fabric and silk embroidery: Trends in Ottoman fabric making, by Reingard Neumann; Ottoman fabrics in German museums and private collections, by Reingard Neumann; Characteristics of Ottoman court embroidery, by Gisela Helmecke; Ottoman court embroideries in German museums and private collections, by Gisela Helmecke; Oriental textiles in central European collections, by Birgitt Borkopp; Documentation [catalog]: The fabrics, by Reingard Neumann and Ulrike Reichert;

Bibliographical references follow each chapter. The Ottoman sultans, 1290–1924, p.9. Technical glossary for the textile analyses, by Ulrike Reichert, Gisela Helmecke, p.280. Bibliography, p.281–85.

P849 Woven from the soul, spun from the heart: textile arts of Safavid and Qajar Iran, 16th–19th centuries. Ed. by Carol Bier. Washington, D.C., Textile Museum, 1987. xvi, 336p. il (part col.), maps, ports.

Catalog of a traveling exhibition, Textile Museum (1987), and other locations, based on the holdings of the Textile Museum, "one of the largest, culturally most significant, and representative collections of Persian textile arts in the world."—*Introd.* The occasion was "the first comprehensive exhibition and catalogue of sixteenth- through nineteenth-century textile arts in Iran, presented within their historical context and political, socio-economic and cultural setting."—*Foreword.* Carpets as well as other textile types are included. A collection of scholarly essays precedes a catalog of 107 items. Illustrations include diagrams of weave structures, photographs of textile workers, manuscript illuminations and sketches, and photographs of people wearing the clothes and in spaces containing carpets and other textiles.

Contents: Textiles and society, by Carol Bier; Image and metaphor: textiles in Persian poetry, by Jerome W. Clinton; Sericulture and silk: production, trade, and export under Shah Abbas, by Linda K. Steinmann; Economy and society: fibers, fabrics, factories, by Willem Floor; Vesture and dress: fashion, function, and impact, by Jennifer M. Scarce; Pattern and weaves: Safavid lampas and velvet, by Milton Sonday; Visual and written sources: dating eighteenth-century silks, by Layla S. Diba; Court and commerce: carpets of Safavid Iran, by Carol Bier; Production and trade: the Persian carpet industry, by Leonard M. Helfgott; City and country: Rural textile production in Northeastern Iran, by Mary Martin; Catalogue of the exhibition, by Carol Bier, Mary Anderson McWilliams, John Wertime, and Mary Martin.

Bibliographical references throughout the text and at ends of essays. Transliteration, p.xvi. Chronology, p.xvi. Glossary, p.325–27. Bibliography, p.328–36.

SEE ALSO: Étoffes merveilleuses, v.3: Tissus de l'Orient, de l'Italie et de l'Espagne (GLAH 2:P871); Gervers, The influence of Ottoman Turkish textiles and costume in Eastern Europe (GLAH 2:P900); Lorquin, Les tissus coptes au Musée National du Moyen Age—Thermes de Cluny (GLAH 2:P824); The Topkapi Saray Museum: costumes, embroideries and other textiles (GLAH 2:P155).

Romanesque—Gothic

P850 Branting, Agnes, and Lindblom, Andreas. Medeltida vävnader och broderier i Sverige. [Reprint.] [Lund, Signum, 1997]. 2v. in 1.

1st ed., Uppsala and Stockholm, Almqvist & Wiksells, 1928; English trans., Medieval embroideries and textiles in Sweden, Uppsala, Almqvist & Wiksells, 1943.

Important survey of Swedish and non-Swedish textiles and embroideries found in Swedish collections. V.1 examines textiles by type: doubleweaves; wool, linen, silk, gold, and silver thread embroidery; and beadwork. V2 provides a chronological survey of Swedish embroidery and weavings from the Romanesque to the Gothic periods, with additional chapters on Florentine and other foreign textiles extant in Sweden (mostly in church treasuries). Many fine illustrations.

Contents: (1) Svenska arbeten; (2) Utländska arbeten.

Bibliographical references throughout the text. Förklaring på några viktigare tekniska termer, v.1, p.xxv. Vid litteraturhänvisningar använda förkortningar, v.1, p.xxv. Literatur efter 1929, v.1, p.[xi–xii]. Register över I del I och del II omnämnda textilier, v.2, p.xxiii–xxix.

P851 Crowfoot, Elisabeth; Pritchard, Frances; and Staniland, Kay. Textiles and clothing c.1150–c.1450. Photography by Edwin Baker. Illustrations by Christina Unwin. London, HMSO, [1992]. x, 223p. il. (part col.) (Medieval finds from excavations in London. Museum of London, 4)

Based on the results of archeological investigations conducted at various sites in London during the 1970s and 1980s. All items described are now in the collection of the Museum of London.

Contents: The excavations, by Alan Vince; Techniques used in textile production; Wool textiles; Goathair textiles; Linen textiles; Silk textiles; Mixed cloths; Narrow wares; Sewing techniques and tailoring.

Appendix: The dyes, by Penelope Walton, p.199–201. Concordance, p.202–11. Glossary, p.212–14. Bibliography, p.215–23.

P852 Durian-Rees, Saskia. Meisterwerke mittelalterlicher Textilkunst aus dem Bayerischen Nationalmuseum: Auswahlkatalog. München, Schnell & Steiner, 1986. 192p. il. (part col.)

Introduction to this important collection of medieval textiles at the Bayerisches Nationalmuseum, Munich. The catalog of 71 items is a selection from the wide-ranging medieval holdings. All objects are illustrated.

Bibliographical references follow the introductory essay. Glossar zu den Paramenten und Gewebetechniken, p.185–88. Verwendete und abgekürzt zitierte Literatur, p.189–92.

P853 Fils renoués: trésors textiles du moyen âge en Languedoc-Roussillon. Carcassonne, [France], Musée des Beaux-Arts de Carcassonne, [1993]. 166p. il. (part col.)

Catalog published in conjunction with the exhibition, Musée des Beaux-Arts de Carcassonne (1993). Most of the textiles and items of clothing discussed originated in countries of the Mediterranean basin (Egypt, Sicily, Spain), and their survival is due primarily to their association with the cult of relics. Relevant archival documents are also discussed. All items are illustrated with full-page color photographs, as well as color enlargements of details. Diagrams of weave structures and black-and-white photographs of fiber fragments also accompany detailed texts analyzing and describing the pieces.

Notes, p.148–51. Lexique des principaux termes techniques utilisés dans les notices, p.152–53. Bibliographie, p.154–56. Analyse des colorants, p.158–65. Les filés métalliques, p.166.

P854 Franzén, Anne Marie, and Nockert, Margareta. Bonderna från Skog och Överhogdal: och andra medeltilda väggbeklädnader. Stockholm, Kungl. Vitterhets Historie och Antikvitets Akademien, 1992. 131p. il. (part col.)

Studies a group of hangings from the churches of Skog and Överhogdal, both located in Sweden. The various weaving techniques used for Scandinavian wall hangings are an important feature of the volume, and the differences in technique between the earlier (pre-1300) and later (1300–1500) medieval periods are described. Explores geographic distribution, regional variations in terminology, and iconography in relationship to Nordic mythology and history. Literary and archival sources are also discussed in the attempt to determine these textiles' functions.

Contents: Materialets strukture; Materialets funktion; Katalog.

Ordförklaringar, p.111–12. Summary, p.113–25. Litteraturförteckning, p.127–28.

P855 Jorgensen, Lise Bender. North European textiles until AD 1000. Aarhus, Aarhus Univ. Pr., 1992. 285p. il., maps.

Most of the textile types discussed come from burial sites excavated across northern Europe. They date from the Late Mesolithic period to the beginnings of the High Middle Ages (more than 5,000 years).

Contents: (I) Introduction; (II) Gt. Britain and Ireland; (III) The Netherlands; (IV) Germany; (V) Poland; (VI) Finland; (VII) Comparative material in Central and South Europe; Catalogue of textile finds; Appendix A: Table of textiles from Anglo-Saxon cemeteries, by Elisabeth Crowfoot; Appendix B: Scandinavia.

Summary in Danish, p.162–78. Notes, p.179–80. Bibliography, p.181–96. Site lists for distribution maps, p.265–75. Index, p.283–85.

P856 Schmedding, Brigitta. Mittelalterliche Textilien in Kirchen und Klöstern der Schweiz: Katalog. Bern, Stampfli, 1978. 325p. il. (part col.) (Schriften der Abegg-Stiftung Bern, Bd. 3)

Catalog of approximately 300 mostly woven textiles, a number of embroideries, and several items of secular clothing as well as religious vestments. All are housed, or are known to have been housed, in Swiss ecclesiastical collections. Most of the fragments originate from Byzantium, Central Asia, the Near and Middle East, other countries surrounding the Mediterranean, and Northern Europe. Each catalog entry includes a technical description, one or more photographs of the fragment, and an extended discussion attempting to place the piece in the context of other documented examples.

Zusammenfassungen (deutsch, französisch, englisch, italienisch), p.313–16. Worterklärungen, p.317–19. Orts- und Namensregister, p.320–22. Sachregister, p.323.

P857 Stauffer, Annemarie. Die mittelalterlichen Textilien von St. Servatius in Maastricht. [Riggisberg, Switzerland], Abegg-Stiftung Riggisberg, [1991]. 236p. il., 16 col. plates. (Schriften der Abegg-Stiftung Riggisberg, Bd. VIII)

Catalog of 158 large and small pieces, including purses, reliquary holders, liturgical items, and items of clothing, all of which belonged to the treasury of the church of St. Servatius in Maastricht. An introductory text describes the historical context, the shroud of St. Servatius and the origins of the church's textile treasury, and the vicissitudes of this treasury in the 19th and 20th centuries. All items, which range in date from the Late Antique to the 15th century, are illustrated and documented by thorough catalog entries.

Bibliographie, p.226–33. Register, p.234–36.

P858 Stof uit de kist: de middeleeuwse textielschat uit de Abdij van Sint-Truiden. Leuven, Peeters, 1991. 406p. il. (part col.), map.

Inventories and discusses this important collection of 13th- and 14th-century textile fragments, originally housed in the reliquaries of the Abbey of Sint-Truiden. All pieces are extensively analyzed, with detailed weave structure diagrams.

Bibliographical references follow each essay. English-language summaries follow each essay. Meetalige lijst van technische termen [glossary of textile terms in Dutch, English, French, and German]. p.395–97. Lijst van verkort geciteerde bibliografie, p.398–402.

SEE ALSO: Wilckens, Die textilen Kunste von der Spätantike bis um 1500 (GLAH 2:P811).

Renaissance—Modern

P859 Cavallo, Adolph S. Textiles: Isabella Stewart Gardner Museum. Boston, Trustees of the Isabella Stewart Gardner Museum, 1986. [v], 223p. il. (part col.), ports. (part col.)

Catalog of tapestries, furnishings and upholstery pieces, ecclesiastical dress items, needlework and embroideries, lace, textile samples and fragments, and kimonos. 261 entries, most illustrated.

Frequently cited sources, p.[iv]. City and weavers' marks: tapestries, p.216.

P860 Devoti, Donata; Guandalini, Gabriella; and Bazzani, Elisabetta. La collezione Gandini del Museo Civico di Modena: i tessuti del XVIII e XIX secolo. [Bologna], Nuova Alfa, [1985]. 458p. il. (part col.), plan.

Collection of scholarly essays and an inventory-catalog of the 18th- and 19th-century textile samples and fragments (including embroideries and lace) assembled by the 19th-century collector, Count Luigi Alberto Gandini. The entire collection is now housed at the Museo Civico di Storia e Arte Medievale e Moderna at Modena, Italy, and comprises mostly Western European pieces, dating from the Middle Ages to the later 19th century. 514 Italian or French items are described and partly illustrated. Includes transcripts of archival documents (letters, prints) relating to the textile samples, and photographs of the original installation of the collection following its donation to the Museum in 1884.

Bibliografia, p.433–48. Tavole di raffronto, p.451–55. Indice delle tipologie tecniche, p.457–58.

P861 Meller, Susan, and Elffers, Joost. Textile designs: two hundred years of European and American patterns for printed fabrics organized by motif, style, color, layout, and period. Ed. consultant, David Frankl. Photographs by Ted Croner. N.Y., Abrams, 1991. 464p. col. il.

Lavishly illustrated "catalogue of images on printed cloth."—*Pref.* Most of the designs are taken from the Design Library and the Design Loft, a collection begun in 1972 by Susan and Herbert Meller. Designs from 19th- and early 20th-century swatch and pattern books are among the patterns presented. The focus is on textiles used in everyday life rather than the more high fashion textiles that tend to feature in museum collections.

Organization based on the collection's in-house classification system, by motif rather than by date or geographical origin. Each section comprises a variety of patterns and designs (some full-page), together with a brief introductory text. All illustrations are briefly annotated, and for most examples dates and country of origin are identified.

Contents: Floral; Geometric; Conversational; Ethnic; Art movements; Period styles.

Explanation of terms. p.10–12. Bibliography, p.444–45. Index, p.446–49. Table of contents and brief introduction, in French, p.450–52; in German, p.453–55; in Italian, p.456–58; in Spanish, p.459–61; in Japanese, p.462–64.

P862 Pitoiset, Gilles. Toiles imprimées, XVIIIe–XIXe siècles: Bibliothèque Forney: catalogue. Paris, Société des Amis de la Bibliothèque Forney, 1982. 143p. il. (part col.), 8 col. plates, ports.

Catalog of 338 printed textiles in the collections of the Bibliothèque Forney. All items are illustrated, and brief inventory data is provided.

Bibliographie, p.143–44.

P863 Prinet, Marguerite. Le damas de lin historié du XVIe au XIXe siècle: ouvrage de haute-lice. Suivi d'une analyse technique de Gabriel Vial. Berne, Fondation Abegg; Fribourg, Office du Livre, 1982. 340p. il. (part col.) (Publications de la Fondation Abegg, Berne, t. V)

Comprehensive vol. describing the linen fiber and linen textiles, collections of linen, and conservation issues.

Contents: (1) Histoire du lin damassé: (I) L'invention du damas de lin historié; (II) Diffusion des manufactures de damas de lin en Europe du XVIe au XVIIIe siècle; (III) La France: les manufactures; (IV) Les français, amateurs de beau linge; (V) La mécanisation au XIXe siècle; (2) L'originalité artistique du damas de lin: (I) La disposition des motifs; (II) Les thèmes, evolution du style ou variation du goût; (III) Les sources d'inspiration; (IV) Les problèmes d'attribution.

Summary (traduction en anglais), p.273–75. Lexique, p.284–85. Catalogue des pièces identifiées, p.287–304. Autre linge connu, p.305–06. Bibliographie, p.307–12. Pièces annexes, p.313–19. Analyse technique d'un damas, par Gabriel Vial, p.321–31. Index, p.337–40.

P864 Schoeser, Mary, and Rufey, Celia. English and American textiles: from 1790 to the present. N.Y., Thames and Hudson, 1989. 256p. il. (chiefly col.)

"Beginning with the 1790s, this book examines furnishing fabrics and their use in Britain and the United States up to the present day."—*Introd.* Organized chronologically, covering period revivals as well as new styles. Attempts to trace the development, design, manufacture, and distribution of such fabrics, and numerous illustrations are provided for comparative purposes.

Notes, p.244–47. Further reading, p.247–50. Index, p.253–56.

SEE ALSO: La collezione Gandini: tessuti dal XVII al XIX secolo (GLAH 2:P888).

Western Countries

Canada

P865 Burnham, Dorothy K. The comfortable arts: traditional spinning and weaving in Canada. Ottawa, National Gallery of Canada, 1981. xvii, 238p. il.

French-language ed., L'art des étoffes: le filage et le tissage traditionnels au Canada. Ottawa, Galerie Nationale du Canada, 1981.

Catalog of the exhibition, National Gallery of Canada (1981), outlining the range of textile traditions across Canada. A brief essay provides an introduction to basic weaving traditions and techniques. The catalog of 162 pieces follows.

Contents: (1) Textile traditions of the Native Peoples; (2) Braiding of the Native Peoples and the French; (3) French traditions; (4) Loyalist traditions; (5) Scottish, Irish, English traditions; (6) German traditions; (7) Multi-cultural traditions in Western Canada.

Footnotes, p.234–36. Bibliography, p.237–38.

P866 Burnham, Harold B., and Burnham, Dorothy K. "Keep me warm one night:" early handweaving in eastern Canada. [Toronto, Univ. of Toronto Pr., in coop. with the Royal Ontario Museum, 1972]. xix, 387p. il., map.

Important scholarly study exploring the tradition of handweaving in Eastern Canada, 1800–1900. Extensively illustrated, the vol. is the result of a documentation project begun during the 1940s. 378 cataloged coverlets are presented.

Contents: (1) The background; (2) Tools and equipment; (3) The basic weaves, tabby twill, and simple patterns; (4) Costume; (5) Carpets, blankets, linens; (6) An introduction to coverlets; (7) Two-shaft coverlets; (8) Overshot coverlets; (9) "Summer and winter" coverlets; (10) Multiple-shaft coverlets; (11) Twill diaper diaper coverlets; (12) Doublecloth coverlets; (13) Jacquard coverlets; Appendix [list of Royal Ontario Museum accessions to which reference is made].

Select bibliography, p.379–80. Index, p.385–87.

P867 McKendry, Ruth. Traditional quilts and bedcoverings. Photographs by Blake McKendry. Foreword by William E. Taylor, Jr. N.Y., Van Nostrand Reinhold, 1979. 240p. il. (part col.), map, ports.

Canadian ed. titled Quilts and other bed coverings in the Canadian tradition. Toronto, Van Nostrand Reinhold, 1979.

Examines the various types of bedding and bed paraphernalia made and used in Ontario in the 19th century. 441 quilts are discussed and/or illustrated.

Contents: (1) Immigrants and imports: the Loyalists and after; (2) Making cloth at home; (3) The bedstead; (4) Bead furniture; (5) The feather bed; (6) Blankets, sheets and pillowcases; (7) Quilts, counterpanes and coverlets; (8) The fabrics used in making quilts; (9) Sets, borders and batts; (10) Quilt names; (11) Symbolism in quilts; (12) Dates, origins and styles.

Notes, p.226–28. Glossary of terms, p.229–30. Bibliography, p.233–34. Index, p.235–40.

SEE ALSO: Quilt collections: a directory for the United States and Canada (GLAH 2:P912); Textile, costume and doll collections: in the United States and Canada (GLAH 2:P783).

France

P868 Brédif, Josette. Printed French fabrics: Toiles de Jouy. N.Y., Rizzoli, 1989. 184p. il. (part col.), ports. (part col.)

Based on a trans. of Toiles de Jouy. Paris, Birò, 1989; British ed. titled Classic printed textiles from France, 1760–1843: toiles de Jouy. London, Thames and Hudson, 1989.

Handsome, in-depth history of the printed cottons produced at the Oberkampf factory at Jouy-en-Josas, 1758–1843. Particular attention is paid to the manufacturing processes, and especially to fabric printing techniques. The many illustrations show original textile designs and surviving textiles, as well as the factory and manufacturing procedures.

Bibliographical references at ends of chapters. Bibliography, p.178–79. Index, p.180–84.

P869 Chefs d'oeuvre du Musée de l'Impression sur Étoffes, Mulhouse. Publication dir. par Jacqueline Thomé Jacqué. Avec la collab. de Véronique de Bruignac. Red. responsable, Takahiko Sano. Tokyo, Gakken, 1978. 3v. il. (chiefly col.)

Text in French and Japanese.

Gloriously illustrated survey of printed textiles, based on the collections of the Musée de l'Impression sur Étoffes at Mulhouse, France. More than 700 pieces are discussed and illustrated, generally with full-page color reproductions.

Contents: (I) Imprimés français I; (II) Imprimés français II, européens et orientaux; (III) Dessins, empreintes et papiers peints.

Lexique, v. II, p.xxii–xxiv. Bibliographie, v. II, p.246–47.

P870 Coural, Jean. Paris, Mobilier National: Soieries Empire. Avec la collab. de Chantal Gastinet-Coural et Muriel Müntz de Raïssac. Paris, Réunion des Musées Nationaux, 1990. 586p. il. (Inventaire des collections publiques françaises, 25)

Comprehensive catalog of the silks produced by the Mobilier National for palaces and government buildings during the Empire period. The silk manufactories were revived by order of Napoleon Bonaparte and their output was used to refurbish the numerous buildings whose contents had been destroyed during the French Revolution. Most of this vol. comprises a catalog of 135 surviving silks and silk designs from the period. All items are illustrated and accompanied by detailed catalog entries.

Contents: Brocarts; Velours; Gros de Tours et satins; Damas; Damas économiques: cannetillés, moires et gourgourans; La réglementation des commandes de soieries; Marques et étiquettes.

Sources manuscrites, p.25–26. Liste des inventaires des châteaux et palais impériaux, royaux, nationaux, p.27. Ouvrages cités en abrégé, p.28–29. Lexique des principaux termes techniques utilisés dans les notices, p.30–34. Index: Changements d'attribution de soieries reproduites dans les deux volumes de Dumonthier: I: 1909, II: 1914, p.475–78. Identifications de soieries reproduites sans attribution dans les deux volumes de Dumonthier: I: 1909, II: 1914, p.479–80. Tableau chronologique des achats et commandes, p.481–83. Fabricants, p.484. Marchands d'étoffe de soie, p.485. Lieux de destinations, achats et commandes, p.486–88. Utilisations des Soieries: classement chronologique, p.489–547. Table de concordance des anciens inventaires et du nouveau catalogue, p.548–56. Index des noms propres, p.577–86.

P871 Étoffes merveilleuses du Musée Historique des Tissus, Lyon. Publication dir. par Jean-Michel Tuchscherer. Red. responsable, Takahiko Sano. [Tokyo], Gakken, 1976. 3v. il. (chiefly col.)

Text in French and Japanese.

Sumptuous survey of this museum's renowned collection of historic textiles. Technical analyses for all pieces reproduced are provided. More than 600 textile pieces are illustrated.

Contents: (1) Soieries françaises du XVIIe et du XVIIIe siècle; (2) Soieries françaises du XIXe et du XXe siècle; (3) Tissus de l'Orient, de l'Italie et de l'Espagne.

Technique de tissage, et lexique, by Gabriel Vial, v.3, p.xix–xxvii.

P872 French textiles from the Middle Ages through the Second Empire. Ed. by Marianne Carlano and Larry Salmon. Essays by Jean-Michel Tuchscherer . . . [et al.] Hartford, Conn., Wadsworth Atheneum, 1985. 197p. il. (part col.), ports.

Collection of essays published to accompany the exhibition, Wadsworth Athenaeum (1985).

Contents: Woven textiles, by Jean-Michel Tuchscherer; The art of silk, by Jean-Michel Tuchscherer; Embroidery, by Marianne Carlano; The lace industry, by Anne Kraatz; Printed textiles, by Jacqueline Jacqué.

Bibliographical references at ends of essays. Glossary and bibliography for technical terms, by Larry Salmon, p.173–80. Bibliography, p.183–96.

P873 J. Paul Getty Museum. French tapestries and textiles in the J. Paul Getty Museum. [By] Charissa Bremer-David. Los Angeles, The Museum, 1997. xiii, 187p. il. (part col., folded).

"Offers readers the first opportunity to study the Museum's entire collection of French textiles."—*Foreword.* Catalog of a noteworthy collection comprising a "representative survey of the French royal manufactories that operated from about 1660 until the period of the Revolution."—*Introd.*

Contents: Gobelins manufactory; Beauvais manufactory; Savonnerie manufactory; Needlework hangings.

Index, p.183–87.

P874 Schoeser, Mary, and Dejardin, Kathleen. French textiles: from 1760 to the present. [London], L. King, [1991]. 224p. il. (chiefly col.)

Surveys the history of French furnishing textiles. Particular attention is paid to their use in American and British interiors. The many illustrations include surviving fabrics, textile designs, furniture, and views of interiors.

Notes, p.212–18. Selected museums with collections of French furnishing textiles, p.219. Selected reading, p.220–21. Index, p.222–23. Subject index, p.224.

P875 Toiles de Nantes, des XVIIIe et XIXe siècles. [Mulhouse], Musée de l'Impression sur Étoffes, [1978]. 159p. il. (part col.), maps.

Catalog of the exhibition Musée de l'Impression sur Étoffes (1977–78). 129 items, comprising printed textiles and printing plates, with detailed entries as well as half- or full-page illustrations.

Liste chronologique des Toiles de Nantes, 1786–1835, p.156. Bibliographical references follow the introductory essays. Bibliographie, p.157–58.

SEE ALSO: Bremer-David, The J. Paul Getty Museum French tapestries and textiles: catalogue of the collections (GLAH 2:P873).

Germany and Austria

P876 Völker, Angela. Biedermeierstoffe: die Sammlungen des MAK—Österreichisches Museum für Angewandte Kunst, Wien, und des Technischen Museums Wien. Mitarb. Ruperta Pichler. N.Y., Prestel, [1996]. 143p. il. (chiefly col.)

Traces the development of the Biedermeier textile industry, and the history of the major textile collections that originated under the Hapsburgs. From these collections a total of 20,000 samples have been cataloged in recent years. Selected pieces are reviewed in the present publication, accompanied by excellent illustrations of pattern book pages, Biedermeier interiors, fashion prints, and surviving dress items.

Contents: Zur Entstehungsgeschichte der Textilsammlung des Polytechnischen Instituts Wien: Material und Quellen; Die Stoffmustersammlungen des Wiener Fabrikanten Paul Mestrozi und des Badener Ärztes Anton Rollelt; Die Entwicklung der Textilindustrie in der ersten Hälfte des 19. Jahrhunderts; Die Entwicklung der Biedermeierlichen Textilindustrie in der habsburgischen Monarchie; Fabrikanten und Fabriken; Das Musterzeichnen; Zusammenfassender Katalog.

Anmerkungen, p.112–16. Glossar, p.135–38. Verzeichnis der abgekürzt zitieirten Literatur, p.139–41. Fabrikantenliste, p.142–44.

P877 ______. Textiles of the Wiener Werkstätte, 1910–1932. With the collab. of Ruperta Pichler. N.Y., Rizzoli, [1994]. 256p. il. (chiefly col.)

Trans. and adapted from Stoffe der Wiener Werkstätte, 1910–1932. Wien, Brandstätter, 1990.

Lavishly illustrated scholarly study based primarily on the archives and textile collections of the Wiener Werkstätte, now housed at the Österreichisches Museum für Angewandte Kunst, Vienna. The illustrations show not only the original textiles and/or designs, but also their use in dress or furnishings of the period.

Contents: The Wiener Werkstätte: an outline of its background history and archival and other evidence of its artistic and business activities; Questions of dating and the sequence of pattern names and numbers; A new interest: fabric designs before the establishment of the Wiener Werkstätte's own textile department; The beginnings of the Wiener Werkstätte's own textile department; Style and forms of the early period; Wiener Werkstätte textiles in the War years, 1914–1918; The twenties; Forms and locations of production; Examples of use; Sales policy and customers; The most significant artists; Wiener Werkstätte fabrics: international resonances; Catalogue of artists and patterns.

Biographies of artists, p.246–47. Concordance of pattern names and designers, p.248–53. Bibliographical sources, p.254–56.

P878 Weltge, Sigrid Wortmann. Women's work: textile art from the Bauhaus. San Francisco, Chronicle Books, [1993]. 208p. il. (part col.)

British ed. titled Bauhaus textiles: women artists and the Weaving Workshop. London, Thames and Hudson, 1993.

In-depth study of the Bauhaus's Weaving Workshop, first in Weimar and then in Dessau. "This book is neither a catalog raisonné nor a compilation of weave data. Instead, it pays tribute to members of the Bauhaus whose names are not known to a larger public."—*Introd.*

Contents: (1) Beginnings; (2) The gender issue; (3) Gunta Stölz; (4) The Weaving Workshop and Johannes Itten; (6)

Georg Much and the 1923 Bauhaus exhibition; (7) Dessau: a new direction; (8) From craft to industry.

Notes, p.193–97. Bibliography, p.197–98. Chronology, p.199–200. Biographies, p.201–06. Index, p.206–08.

P879 Wilckens, Leonie von. Geschichte der deutschen Textilkunst: vom späten Mittelalter bis in die Gegenwart. München, Beck, 1997. 291p. il. (part col.), ports.

The first modern general reference work on the history of German textiles and dress, 15th century through 1980. The excellent photographs include surviving pieces, textiles in paintings, and textiles used in interior decoration..

Exkurs: Sammeln und Erforschen von Textilien: ein Überblick, p.233–37. Abkürzungen, p.240. Anmerkungen, p.241–56. Glossar, p.257–63. Künstlerverzeichnis, p.263–67. Bibliographie, p.267–74. Geographisches Register, p.276–79. Personen- und Sachregister, p.280–90.

Great Britain and Ireland

P880 Beard, Geoffrey. Upholsterers and interior furnishing in England, 1530–1840. New Haven, Yale Univ. Pr. for the Bard Graduate Center for Studies in the Decorative Arts, 1997. 346p. il. (part col.), ports. (part col.)

Important scholarly text presenting much previously unpublished information. The visual repertoire comprises portraits and prints of the period showing interiors and furnishings, as well as individual furniture items and their construction.

Contents: (I) The arte or misterie of upholdrs; (II) Tudor opulence; (III) For court and country 1603–1660; (IV) "Solidity, conveniency and ornament"; (V) The upholstered room 1702–1760; (VI) Visions and revivals 1760–1790; (VII) Fluctuations in taste 1791–1840; Appendix A: A selection of inventories 1509–1818. Appendix B: Extracts from R. Campbell's The London Tradesman (1848).

Bibliographical references throughout the text. Glossary, p.317–28. Bibliographical references and abbreviations, p.329–37. Index, p.338–46.

P881 British textile design in the Victoria and Albert Museum. Directed by Donald King. With the collab. of Santina Levey and Natalie Rothstein. Executive ed., Takahito Sano. 3v. Tokyo, Gakken, 1980. il. (chiefly col.)

Text in English and Japanese.

Magnificently illustrated luxury edition covering the textile collections of the Victoria and Albert Museum in London, "probably the largest and most comprehensive in existence."—*Introd.* For a reformatted ed. aimed at a broader market, with somewhat poorer illustrations and a slightly different text, see The Victoria and Albert Museum's textile collection. N.Y., Canopy, 1992–99. 7v.

Contents: Vol.I: The Middle Ages to Rococo (1200–1750): (I) Embroidery of the Middle Ages, by Donald King; (II) Embroidery and other textiles, Renaissance to Rococo, by Santina Levey; (III) Woven and printed textiles to 1750, by Natalie Rothstein; Vol.II: Rococo to Victorian (1750–1850): (I) Woven textiles, 1750–1850, by Natalie Rothstein; (II) Printed textiles, 1750–1850, by Wendy Hefford; (III) Embroidery, 1750–1850, by Santina Levey; (IV) Shawls and other textiles, by Natalie Rothstein and Wendy Hefford; Vol.III: Victorian to Modern (1850–1940): (I) Victorian and Art Nouveau textiles, by Linda Parry; (II) Twentieth century textiles, by Valerie Mendes.

Bibliographical references follow each essay. Each vol. contains a glossary, brief individual biographies of key figures, and/or notes on firms and designers.

P882 Clabburn, Pamela. The National Trust book of furnishing textiles. [N.Y.], Viking in assoc. with The National Trust, [England], [1987]. [272]p. il., map, port.

"This book is an attempt to explain what fabrics the upholsterer had at his disposal from the late middle ages onwards, and how he used them in the service of his clients."—*Introd.* Most of the textiles described and discussed appear in National Trust properties in England; not all of them are of English origin, but all have existed in an English context for many years.

Contents: (I) A history of furnishings; (II) The furnishings: (5) The upholsterer; (6) Wall hangings; (7) Beds; (8) Household linen; (9) The furnishing of windows; (10) Seat furniture; (11) Case covers; (12) Miscellaneous furnishings; (13) Carpets and floor coverings; (14) Techniques.

Glossary of upholstery fabrics and terms, p.238–56. Bibliography, p.259–66. Index, p.267–72.

P883 Levey, Santina M. Elizabethan treasures: the Hardwick Hall textiles. London, The National Trust; N.Y., (Distr. by Abrams, 1998). 112p. il. (chiefly col.)

British ed. titled An Elizabethan inheritance: the Hardwick Hall textiles. London, National Trust, 1998.

Provides an overview of the collections of England's most important repository of 16th- and 17th-century textiles.

Contents: (1) Before the building of the New Hall; (2) Hardwick New Hall and the 1601 inventory; (3) Embroidery, needlework and other techniques; (4) The seventeenth and eighteenth centuries; (5) The 6th Duke and beyond.

Notes, p.105–07. Bibliography, p.108–09. Appendix, p.109. Glossary, p.110. Index, p.111–12.

P884 Parry, Linda. Textiles of the Arts and Crafts movement. N.Y., Thames and Hudson, 1988. 160p. il. (chiefly col.), 120 col. plates, ports.

Extensively illustrated study of the artists involved and the textiles displayed in London by the Arts and Crafts Exhibition Society, 1888–1916.

Contents: (1) The artistic and industrial background; (2) The evolution of a style; (3) Textiles in the Arts and Crafts exhibitions; manufacturers, shops; (4) Designers, Catalogue of designers, craftsmen, institutions and firms involved in textile production during the period.

Notes, p.154–55. Bibliography, p.156. Index, p.158–60.

P885 Rothstein, Natalie. Silk designs of the eighteenth century in the collection of the Victoria and Albert Museum, London: with a complete catalogue. Boston, Little, Brown, 1990. 351p. il. (chiefly col.)

In-depth analysis of the Museum's 18th- and early 19th-century pattern books, designs and samples, particularly those from the Warner Archive and Vanners Silks collections. Most of the designs are by the British silk designers, Christopher Baudouin, Joseph Dandridge, Anna Maria Garthwaite, and James Leman; a few from the Lyon-based firm Galy Gallien are also discussed. Following brief introductory essays on the history of 18th-century silk design, the designs and surviving silks are divided into chronological sections, 1700–1826. Most of the vol. comprises a catalog of the Museum's pieces.

Technical glossary, p.283–300. Biographical index [of individuals known to have worked in the 18th-century British textile industry], p.300–44. Bibliography, p.345. General index, p.349–51.

Italy

P886 Bonito Fanelli, Rosalia. Five centuries of Italian textiles: 1300–1800: a selection from the Museo del Tessuto, Prato: catalogue of the traveling exhibition. Prato, Cassa di Risparmi e Depositi di Prato, 1981. 349p. il. (part col.)

Catalog accompanying a traveling exhibition of 100 textile fragments belonging to the Museo del Tessuto, Istituto Tullio Buzzi, Prato. Chronologically organized, then arranged in thematic and typological sections, each grouping is preceded by an introductory commentary including historical information, notes on design and pattern structure, and references from archival sources. Each textile is illustrated in color. Similar design examples in the other decorative arts and related textiles appearing in paintings and sculpture of the period are also reproduced.

Technical data concerning the 100 exhibited textiles, p.331–40. Glossary of technical textile terms, p.343–44. Bibliography, p.347–49.

P887 Bussagli, Mario. La seta in Italia. [Roma], Editalia, [1986]. 303p. il. (part col.)

Lavishly illustrated history of silk textiles and dress in Italy. Particular emphasis is paid to the East-West connection, beginning with the transfer of silk production techniques from China to Italy. Central Asian, Persian, Byzantine, and Islamic influences are also discussed.

Contents: La via della seta; Il commercio cinese; La seta in Occidente; I motivi decorativi e le loro migrazioni; La seta nell'Italia medioevale; Il problema delle sete di Cangrande della Scala: La seta nella pittura italiana del sec. XIV; Importanza della seta nell'economia e nella moda: le leggi suntuarie; La seta nella crisi rinascimentale e la crisi della seta nel 1700; La seta, la moda e l'arte; Trattato dell'arte della seta, di Anonimo fiorentino del sec. XV.

Bibliografia, p.235–36, 239.

P888 La collezione Gandini del Museo Civico di Modena: tessuti dal XVII al XIX secolo. A cura di Donata Devoti and Marta Cuoghi Costantini. Modena, Panini, 1993. 269p. il. (part col.), ports. (part col.)

Second catalog of this important collection of textile samples and fragments, now housed at the Museo Civico di Storia e Arte Medievale e Moderna, at Modena. In this vol., the vast majority of textiles discussed are of Italian origin, with a small percentage originating in France. Laces, ribbons, galloons, and tassels are omitted. The catalog comprises 545 items, all of which receive a detailed entry and an illustration. Photographs of some of the textiles in their original installation are also provided.

Contents: Crisi e riconversione delle manifatture seriche italiane nel Seicento, by Domenica Digilio; Il tessile nella decorazione degli interni del XVII secolo, by Iolanda Silvestri; Continuità e innovazione nei tessuti d'abbigliamento del Seicento, by Elisabetta Bazzani.

Bibliographical references at ends of essays. Bibliografia, p.257–61. Indice delle tipologie tecniche, p.265–66. Tavole di raffronto, p.267–69.

P889 Davanzo Poli, Doretta, and Moronato, Stefania. Le stoffe dei veneziani. Venezia, Albrizzi, 1994. 180p. il. (part col.) (Venetiae)

Scholarly survey of the history of Venetian textiles from the Byzantine period to the early 19th century. The high-quality reproductions illustrate surviving textiles and dress, pattern books, and historic interiors and collections.

Note, p.161–69. Bibliografia citata, p.173–76. Glossario, p.177–80.

P890 Mazzaoui, Maureen Fennell. The Italian cotton industry in the later Middle Ages 1100–1600. N.Y., Cambridge Univ. Pr., 1981. 250p. il.

Scholarly study examining the significance and extension of the cotton industry within the urban economy of the later Middle Ages.

Contents: (I) The role of cotton; (II) The organization of the North-Italian industry; (III) The growth of cotton manufacture north of the Alps; Appendices: (I) Costs of production for cotton yarn in Milan in the early 16th century; (II) The products of the Italian cotton industry.

Notes, p.168–226. Select bibliography, p.227–43. Index, p.244–50.

P891 Le stoffe di Cangrande: ritrovamenti e ricerche sul '300 veronese. A cura di Licisco Magagnato. Saggi critici e schede di Licisco Magagnato . . . [et al.] [Firenze], Alinari, [1983]. 298, [22]p. il. (part col.), map, ports.

Published on the occasion of the exhibition, Castelvecchio, Verona (1983). Studies of textiles in 14th-century Verona; includes technical studies.

Alcune precisazioni sui filati d'oro e d'argento impiegati nella tessitura, p.[307]. Glossario, p.[308–15]. Bibliografia generale, p.[316–20].

P892 Tessuti nel Veneto: Venezia e la Terraferma. A c. di Giuliana Ericani e Paola Frattaroli. [Verona], Banca Popolare di Verona, [1993]. xvi, 570p. il. (chiefly col.), map.

Scholarly essays on the history of textiles and the textile industry in Venice and its mainland territories from medieval times to the 18th century. Includes a scholarly catalog of 176 surviving pieces (mostly liturgical vestments). The many illustrations draw upon archival sources and pattern books, and include illuminated manuscripts and paintings showing the textiles in context.

Bibliographical references throughout the text. Bibliografia, a cura di Denise Modonesi, p.533–50. Glossario, di Michele Cortelazzo, Adriana Da Rin, e Paola Frattaroli, p.551–54. Indice dei nomi e dei luoghi, a c. di Franco Didonè e Denise Modonesi, p.555–70.

P893 Tietzel, Brigitte. Italienische Seidengewebe des 13., 14. und 15. Jahrhunderts. Köln, Deutsches Textilmuseum Krefeld, 1984. 480p. il. (part col.) (Kataloge des Deutschen Textilmuseums Krefeld, Bd. I)

Scholarly catalog of 161 items from the important textile collection at the Deutsches Textilmuseum, Krefeld. Catalog entries are extremely detailed, including weaving analyses, bibliographical references, a list of comparable pieces and where they are located, and a small illustration; comparative illustrations with items from other collections are also occasionally provided.

Bibliographical references throughout the introduction. Literaturverzeichnis, p.465–76.

P894 Torino sul filo della seta. A cura di Giuseppe Bracco. Con i contributi di Giuseppe Bracco . . . [et al.] Torino, Archivio Storico della Città di Torino, 1992. 345p. il. (part col.), maps, ports., tables.

Forms part of an (untraced) series of publications intended to reveal the wealth of Torinese archival documents. The scholarly essays cover the history of silk textiles and the silk industry in Turin from the Renaissance to the 20th century. The numerous illustrations are taken from archival and early published sources, prints (including fashion plates), architectural drawings, maps, and photographs of surviving textile-related buildings.

Bibliographical references throughout the text. Indice dei nomi di persona, p.337–44.

SEE ALSO: Devoti, Guandalini, and Bazzani, La collezione Gandini del Museo Civico di Modena (GLAH 2:P860).

Latin America

P895 Anderson, Marilyn. Guatemalan textiles today. N.Y., Watson-Guptill, 1978. 200p. il. (part col.)

Well-illustrated overview of the subject, exploring the social and economic as well as the esthetic aspects of woven garments, both traditional and contemporary. Specific techniques and tools are illustrated with photographs and line drawings.

Contents: Weaving in Highland Guatemala; Materials of weaving; Backstrap-loom weaving; Treadle-loom weaving; Stitchery and other techniques.

Glossary, p.[194]–96. Annotated bibliography, p.197–98. Index, p.199–200.

P896 Cáurio, Rita. Artêxtil no Brasil: viagem pelo mundo da tapeçaria = Textilart in Brazil: a journey through the world of tapestry. [Rio de Janeiro], Cáurio, 1985. 304p. il. (part col.)

Survey of tapestry-making and textile art in Brazil. English summaries for each chapter. Appendix defines textile art terms. Chronology from 1942 to 1985 of textile-art-related events in Brazil. Bibliography of 127 items and name index.

Bibliography, p.293–94. Index of names, p.295–302.

Low Countries

P897 Sits: Oost-West relaties in textiel. Red. Ebeltje Hartkamp-Jonxis. Zwolle, Waanders, [1987]. 216p. il. (part col.), ports, maps.

Published in conjunction with the exhibition, Rijksmuseum voor Volkskunde (1987), and other locations. "Sits" is the Old-Dutch term for the English word "chintz." Highlights the role of the Dutch East India Company in promoting the diffusion of chintz fabrics in Europe. Includes a catalog of 155 surviving chintz pieces in European public collections.

Bibliographical references at ends of essays. Bibliografie, p.212–15.

P898 Stone-Ferrier, Linda A. Images of textiles: the weave of seventeenth-century Dutch art and society. Ann Arbor, UMI Research Pr., [1985]. 285p. il., ports.

Based on the author's Ph.D. dissertation (Univ. of California, Berkeley, 1980) exploring the "relationship between images of textile manufacture, images of textiles, and the society which produced these images as well as the cloth goods themselves."—*Introd.* Uses 17th-century Dutch paintings, prints and drawings to examine the primary aspects of cloth production such as weaving, spinning, winding, lace-making, and embroidery.

Contents: (1) A Leiden painter's Leiden textile workers; (2) Haarlem painters; Haarlem weavers; (3) Depictions of female handwork: the tangle of virtue and folly; (4) Ruisdael's and Rembrandt's Haarlem linen-bleaching fields; (5) Fijnschilders' paintings à la mode.

Notes, p.233–73. Bibliography, p.275–82. Index, p.283–85.

Russia and Eastern Europe

P899 Domonkos, Otto. Blaudruckhandwerk in Ungarn. [Budapest], Corvina, [1981]. 124p. il. (part col.), 85, XXXVII plates, ports. (part col.), maps.

Trans. of A magyarországi kékfestés. Budapest, Corvina, 1981.

Synthesis of previously published books and articles discussing the history and technology of Hungarian indigo-printed textiles. Detailed information is given about guilds and important early industrial manufacturers engaged in cloth printing. Archival sources are also examined. Generously illustrated with examples of blue cloth types, wooden printing blocks, and paintings and photographs showing the production process.

Anmerkungen, p.92–104. Archivquellen, p.105. Literaturverzeichnis, p.106–08. Gewährsleute, p.109–10. Verzeichnis der Ortsnamen, p.123–24.

P900 Gervers, Veronika. The influence of Ottoman Turkish textiles and costume in Eastern Europe, with particular reference to Hungary. Toronto, Royal Ontario Museum, 1982. xv, 168p. il. (part col.) (History, technology, and art. Monograph, 4)

Based on a paper read at the symposium "Islam and the Balkans," organized in connection with the World of Islam Festival, Royal Scottish Museum, Edinburgh (1976). Textiles in the countries of Eastern Europe that at one time or another were under Turkish rule are considered. Most of the many illustrations are of objects in the collections of the Royal Ontario Museum.

Contents: Trade; Garments; Embroidery; Carpets; Appendix 1: A chronological outline of the rise and decline of the Ottoman Turkish empire in central and eastern Europe; Appendix 2: Rulers of the House of Osman; Appendix 3: Rulers of Hungary and Transylvania; Appendix 4: A select bibliography for the political, social, and economic history of European Turkey; Appendix 5: Turks and Hungarians: editions of 16th to 18th century sources from Hungary and Transylvania; Appendix 6: Turkish and oriental fabrics used in Hungary and Turkey from the 15th through the 18th century.

Glossary, p.65–66. Literature cited, p.67–80.

P901 Taraian, Z. R. Naboika v Armeni. Erevan, Armenian Academy of Science, Institute of the Arts; Izd-vo AN Armianskoi SSR, 1978. 131p. il. (part col.), 27 plates (part col.)

Text in Russian, with parts in Armenian.

The first survey of the ancient tradition of Armenian textile printing. Beginning with the medieval period, this vol. surveys the history and techniques of textile dyes and printing in Armenia. Of particular interest is the large collection of Armenian printed textiles that survived as manuscript covers in Matenadaran, Erevan, and the printed altar curtains used in all Armenian churches.

[Bibliography], p.127–31.

P902 Yasinskaia, I. Revolutionary textile design: Russia in the 1920s and 1930s. Introd. by John E. Bowlt. N.Y., Viking Pr., [1983]. 106p. il. (chiefly col.) (A Studio book)

British ed. titled Soviet textile design of revolutionary period. London, Thames and Hudson, 1983.

The introductory text describes the relationship between art and revolution, and in particular the impact of the Constructivists on textile design. The fully illustrated catalog, which comprises most of the vol., shows the cotton prints produced by mills in Moscow and its environs.

Notes, p.6.

Scandinavia

P903 Becker, John . . . [et al.] Damask og drejl: daekketøjets historie i Danmark. [Copenhagen], Borgen, [1989]. 303p. il. (part col.), port.

"This book is the result of a nation-wide registration of Danish privately and publicly owned household linen carried out in the period 1965–74."—*Summary.* Essays on the history and sociology of table linen. Emphasis is on Danish textiles, with reference to the wider European context. Many illustrations, taken from archival records, surviving pieces, advertisements, factory scenes, and weavers with their looms.

Bibliographical references follow each essay. Summary—Damask and twill, p.271–78. Zuzammenfassung—Damast und Drell, p.279–85. Forkortelser, p.288. Indeks, p.289–99. Litteratur, p.301–03.

P904 Hansen, Viveka. Swedish textile art: traditional marriage weavings from Scania: the Khalili collection. [London], Nour Foundation, [1996]. 248p. col. il., maps. (The Khalili collection of textile art, 1)

Rev. and updated trans. of Textila kuber och Blixtar. [Sweden], Institutet för Kulturfoskring, 1992. Lavishly illustrated with many full-page color reproductions, loosely based on the Swedish ed.

Contents: The international appeal of Swedish textile art, by Michael Franses; Traditional marriage weavings from Scania, by Viveka Hansen; Structural analyses of the textiles in the Khalili collection, by Alex Couchman.

Notes to the text, p.240–43. Works cited, p.244–45. Glossary, p.246. Index, p.247–48.

P905 Jørgensen, Lise Bender. Forhistoriske textiler i Skandinavien: Prehistoric Scandinavian textiles. København, [Kongelige Nordiske Oldskriftselskab], 1986. 390p. il., maps. (Nordiske fortidsminder, Serie B, Bd. 9)

Text in Danish and English.

Detailed, scholarly survey of textile production techniques from the Bronze Age to the Viking period. Focuses on textile fragments found with grave-found metal artifacts (thus aiding dating), primarily excavated in Denmark but also in Sweden, Norway, and Germany. The main text is followed by a catalog of Bronze Age through Viking Age textiles in Denmark. Extensively illustrated, with details of the fragments' weave structures, as well as maps showing the locations of finds are of particular interest.

Contents: (I) Introduction; (II) Bronze Age textiles; (III) Pre-Roman Iron Age textiles; (IV) Roman Iron Age textiles; (V) Migration period textiles; (VI) Merovingian period textiles; (VII) Viking Age textiles; (VIII) The development of textiles from the Early Bronze Age to the Viking Age; (IX) Comparative material in North and Central Europa.

Notes, p.362–66. Bibliography, p.367–75.

P906 Martin, Edna, and Sydhoff, Beate. Svensk textilkonst = Swedish textile art. The Swedish text is trans. into English by William Barrett. Stockholm, LiberFörlag, [1979]. 151p. il.

Focuses on Swedish textile art since 1945.

Contents: Swedish textile art prior to 1945; Textile art: material and techniques; The new textile art; Textile art in public environments; Areas of textile art; Free experiment.

Bibliography, p.144–45. Index, p.146–51.

P907 1700-tals textil: Anders Berchs samling i Nordiska Museet = 18th century textiles: the Anders Berch collection at the Nordiska Museet. Ed. by Elisabet Stavenow-Hidemark. Stockholm, Nordiska Museet, [1990]. 280p. il. (chiefly col.), port., maps.

Text in English and Swedish.

Excellent introduction to, and catalog of, the collection of textile samples formed by Anders Berch (1711–74). His collection, including 1,672 woven fabrics and lace from Europe, India, and China, was acquired by the Nordiska Museet in 1876. The samples are arranged mostly in pattern books, or on loose-leaf pages, and are accompanied by notes describing their origins, manufacturers, and technical details, written in 18th-century handwriting. Numerous high-quality reproductions.

Bibliographical references at ends of essays, and of each appendix. Noter till katalogen/Notes to the catalogue, p.246–61. Enheter för mått- vikt- och mynt, använda i Berchska samlingen/Units of measure and weight and monetary units used in the Berch collection, p.275. Bibliography, p.277–79. Register/Index, p.279–81.

SEE ALSO: Geijer, A history of textile art (GLAH 2:P801); Franzén and Nockert, Bonaderna från Skog och Överhogdal (GLAH 2:P854).

Spain and Portugal

P908 Herrero Carretero, Concha. Museo de Telas Medievales, Monasterio de Santa María la Real de Huelgas. Madrid, Patrimonio Nacional, [1988]. 134p. il. (chiefly col.)

Founded at Burgos in 1187 by Alfonso VIII of Castile and his wife Eleonora of England, the Monasterio de Santa María la Real de Huelgas subsequently functioned as a pantheon of the Castilian royal family. This vol. provides a catalog of the mortuary textiles and garments in or with which members of the royal family were buried. These date primarily from the 12th and 13th centuries and range in origin from Sassanian to African and Coptic. Amply accompanied by detailed photographs, the catalog entries are preceded by an introductory essay in which manuscript illuminations are also discussed for comparative purposes.

Terminos textiles, p.127–28. Informes y bibliografia, p.131–34.

P909 Morral i Romeu, Eulàlia, and Segura i Mas, Antoni. La seda en España: leyenda, poder y realidad. Fotografías Xavier Catalan. [Barcelona], Lunwerg, [1991]. 159p. col. il., map

Technical and historical analysis of silk, silk manufacture, silk textiles, and dress in Spain. The second part of this publication consists of a catalog of 240 items dating from the 5th to the 20th century. The excellent reproductions include photographs of silks and silk velvets in 15th-century paintings, sample and pattern books, and of the elements of silk production.

[Glosario], p.157–59. [Bibliografia], p.159.

P910 Navarro Espinach, German. El despegue de la industria sedera en la Valencia del siglo XV. Valencia, Generalitat Valenciana, Consell Valencia de Cultura, 1992. 156p. il. (part col.)

In-depth, historical survey of the silk industry in Valencia during the 15th century, using notary documents, regulations of the silk workers' associations, as well as personal papers and inventories. The illustrations primarily show silk-working tools and some of the buildings constructed by the silk workers.

United States

Bibliography

P911 Gordon, Beverly. Domestic American textiles: a bibliographic sourcebook. Ambridge, Center for the History of American Needlework, 1978. 217p.

Annotated bibliography of "those fiber constructions that were (and are) made in the North American home for personal and decorative use. It does not refer to the textiles of the native Americans." Also generally excluded are printed textiles, costume, and basketry. Publications up to 1977 are listed: 574 books and articles, and 70 catalogs.

Index, p.161–76.

Directories

P912 Quilt collections: a directory for the United States and Canada. Comp. by Lisa Turner Oshins. With state commentaries by Barbara S. Bockman. Washington, D.C., Acropolis Books, 1987. 255p. il. (part col.), ports.

Directory based on a survey conducted by the American Folklife Center (1985–87), designed to locate and describe public quilt-resource collections in N. America; more than 25,000 quilts were documented. The directory provides listings of where these quilts can be seen and studied, and lists the locations of other resources (patterns and instructions, diaries, journals, letters, oral histories, photographs, illustrations, paintings, advertisements, and film).

The listing is divided between the U.S. and Canada. Each country is subdivided by state (U.S.) or province (Canada), prefaced by a brief quilt-related commentary for the region. Many of the photographs of quilts in use are taken from the Farm Security Administration Collection, housed at the Library of Congress.

Contents: (I) U.S.; (II) Canada; Appendix 1: Quilt documentation projects in the United States and Canada; Appendix 2: Selected listing of regional, national, and international quilt associations; Appendix 3: Conservation.

Quilts in collections questionnaire, p.224–26. Glossary, p.232–35. Selected filmography, p.237–38. Selected bibliography, p.239–43. List of participating institutions, p.244–55.

Dictionaries and Encyclopedias

P913 A checklist of American coverlet weavers. Comp. for the Abby Aldrich Rockefeller Folk Art Center by

John W. Heisey. Ed. and exp. by Gail C. Andrews and Donald R. Walters. Williamsburg, Colonial Williamsburg Foundation (Distr. by the Univ. Pr. of Virginia, [1978]). x, 149p. il. (part col.), plates, map.

Listing of 942 professional weavers active in America, primarily during the second and third quarters of the 19th century. 2,500 coverlets were surveyed for the project.

Trademarks, p.125–29. Where to see coverlets [list of the most important public and private collections of coverlets in the U.S., Canada, and England], p.131–33. Glossary, p.135–38. Bibliography, p.139–42. Geographical index, p.143–49.

P914 Encyclopedia of pieced quilt patterns. Comp. by Barbara Brackman. Paducah, Ky., American Quilter's Society, 1993. 551p. il.

1st, loose-leaf ed., 1984.

The "most complete index to published names for American quilt design."—*Pref.* Surveys the history of quilt pattern publication in North America from 1835 and analyzes pattern name categories. Sale and distribution methods are also discussed, and a brief bibliographical history is provided. Extensively illustrated, black-and-white line drawings accompany each pattern entry.

Key for locating patterns, p.16–19. References, p.520–27. Alphabetical indexes, p.528–51.

P915 Khin, Yvonne M. The collector's dictionary of quilt names & patterns. Drawings by the author and color photographs by Glen San Lwin. Washington, D.C., Acropolis Books, 1980. 489p. il. (Repr.: N.Y., Portland House, 1988)

Dictionary catalog of more than 2,400 quilt patterns documented as used for traditional American quilts (Hawaiian quilts not included), organized according to geometric type. All patterns are illustrated with a black-and-white line drawing analyzing the design. Commentary includes alternative names for the pattern, the first company to publish the pattern, and names of quilt designers where available.

Some helpful publications, p.17–18. Helpful quilting terms, p.29–30. Index, p.455–89.

P916 Montgomery, Florence M. Textiles in America 1650–1870: a dictionary based on original documents, prints and paintings, commercial records, American merchants' papers, shopkeepers' advertisements, and pattern books with original swatches of cloth. N.Y., Norton, [1984]. xviii, 412p. il. (part col.), col. plates, ports. (A Winterthur/Barra book)

"A landmark in textile studies."—*Review*, Textile history, v.16, no.1, Spring 1985, p.116. In-depth survey based upon extensive surviving archival evidence documenting the textile trade in colonial North America. The many illustrations include swatches and samplers, as well as designs for furniture, upholstery and interiors.

Contents: Furnishing practices in England and America; Bed hangings; Window curtains; Upholstery; Textiles for the period room in America; Dictionary.

Bibliographical references at ends of chapters. Bibliography, p.379–412.

Histories and Handbooks

P917 Affleck, Diane L. Fagan. Just new from the mills: printed cottons in America: late nineteenth and early twentieth centuries from the collection of the Museum of American Textile History. North Andover, Museum of American Textile History, 1987. 108p. il. (part col.)

Documents this extensive collection of printed textiles from factories in New England and Pennsylvania. Includes several hundred thousand parts of sample books and salesman's sheets produced by early American manufacturers. The numerous fully annotated illustrations of surviving textile samples provide examples of textile manufacturing design and practice of early industrial America.

Contents: Technology; Marketing; Design and fashion; Prints; Print Works: Allen Print Works; Arnold Print Works; Clyde Bleachery and Print Works; Cocheco Manufacturing Company; Eddystone Manufacturing Company; Hamilton Manufacturing Company; Manchester Mills; Merrimack Manufacturing Company; Windsor Print Works Company.

Bibliography, p.99–107.

P918 America's glorious quilts. Ed. by Dennis Duke and Deborah Harding. N.Y., H.L. Levin (Distr. by Macmillan, 1987). 320p. col. il. (Repr.: N.Y., Park Lane, 1989)

Collection of essays on different types of quilt; distinctions are drawn according to region, period, and original recipient. Numerous large, high-quality illustrations complement the text.

Contents: An American tradition, by Laura Fisher; Quilts: America's folklore, by Deborah Harding; Quilts: the art of the Amish, by Phyllis Haders; Hawaiian quilts, by Lee S. Wild; Quilts: crazy memories, by Virginia Gunn; Baby, crib and doll quilts, by Pat Long and Dennis Duke; Quilts at an exhibition, by Donna Wilder; Contemporary quilts, by Luella Doss; A quilt-collector's primer, by Celia Y. Oliver; Living with quilts, by Phyllis George Brown.

Bibliography, p.315–17. Index, p.318–20.

P919 Bishop, Robert Charles; Secord, William; and Weissman, Judith Reiter. Quilts, coverlets, rugs and samplers. William C. Ketcham, series consultant. N.Y., Knopf, 1982. 476p. il. (part col.) (The Knopf collectors' guides to American antiques)

Illustrated introductory handbook of quilt, coverlet, rug, and sampler types, comprising a visual index of these textiles, grouped according to their design and pattern. Every photographic example is accompanied by a discussion of the type, placing it within the broader American context.

Quilt pattern guide, p.430–35. Quilting stitches guide, p.436–39. Coverlet pattern guide, p.440–43. Sampler and needlework stitches guide, p.444–46. Bibliography, p.447–48. Antiques publications, p.449–50. Glossary, p.451–54. Price guide, p.455–72. Index, p.474–77.

P920 Dee, Anne Patterson. Quilter's sourcebook: the super guide to quilts, quilters, & quilting. [Lombard, Ill., Wallace-Homestead, 1987.] 200p. il.

Practical guide to acquiring, making, looking at, and learning about quilts and quiltmaking, with each chapter organized as a series of catalog entries.

Contents: (1) Mail-order sources for patterns, supplies, and publications; (2) Quilt and quilt-oriented shops; (3) Handmade quilts and related gift items; (4) Guilds, groups, and associations; (5) Workshops, lectures, and professional quilters; (6) Museums with permanent quilt collections; (7) Books, publications, and periodicals (p.151–78).

Index, p.179–99.

P921 Gordon, Beverly. Shaker textile arts. Hanover, Univ. Pr. of New England, 1980. xiv, 329p. il. (part col.), chart.

Comprehensive study of the textiles produced by the Shakers. The numerous illustrations include early photographs of members of Shaker communities, their dress, interiors, and the textile and clothing items they made and sold.

Contents: (1) Who the Shakers were; (2) The textiles overall; (3) Production of textiles; (4) Household textiles; (5) Clothing accessories; (6) Fancywork; Appendixes: (I) Location of Shaker communities; (II) Government and organization of the Hancock community, and the Church family; (III) Weaving patterns; (IV) Recipes and instructions; (V) Items purchased in the Enfield, Connecticut, Fancy goods store, 1910.

Notes, p.283–90. References, p.291–99. Glossary, p.305–14. Index, p.315–29.

P922 Kiracofe, Roderick. The American quilt: a history of cloth and comfort 1750–1950. Text with Mary Elizabeth Johnson. Photographs by Sharon Risedorph. Design by Adrian Stark. N.Y., Clarkson Potter, 1993. xiii, 290p. col. il.

Lavishly illustrated historical survey of quilt making in America and of the fabrics used to make them.

Dating antique quilts, p.249–55. Investigating a quilt, p.256–58. Owning an antique quilt, p.259–64. Where to see America's quilts, p.256–70. Where to buy quilts, p.271–75. Notes, p.276. Bibliography, p.283–86. Index, p.287–90.

P923 Orlofsky, Patsy, and Orlofsky, Myron. Quilts in America. N.Y., McGraw-Hill, 1974. 368p. il. (part col.) (Repr.: N.Y., Abbeville Pr., [1992])

The reprint is greatly improved in the quality of its color reproductions. More than 300 examples of quilts are illustrated.

Contents: (1) The history of quilts in America; (2) The quilt; (3) Quilting; (4) Tools and equipment; (5) Stencilled, all-white, and embroidered quilt tops; (6) The whole-cloth quilted spread; (7) Types of quilts; (8) Patterns and pattern names; (9) Signing and initialing; (10) The age of the quilt; (11) Care.

Bibliographical references throughout the text. Bibliography, p.358–62. Index, p.363–68.

P924 Peck, Amelia. American quilts and coverlets in the Metropolitan Museum of Art. N.Y., Metropolitan Museum of Art; Dutton Studio Books, 1990. 262p. il. (part col.), ports.

Catalog of an important collection of 199 pieces acquired by the Museum since 1910. Although providing examples of most types of bed coverings, the collection is strongest in East Coast examples. The first part discusses 71 particularly important pieces in the collection and is arranged according to construction typology. The second part comprises a catalog of the collection. All items in this section are illustrated with excellent color reproductions.

Bibliography, p.253–56. Index, p.257–62.

P925 Safford, Carlton L., and Bishop, Robert. America's quilts and coverlets. [Reprint.] N.Y., Bonanza Books, 1985. 313p. il. (part col.)

See GLAH 1:P678 for original annotation.

P926 Warren, Elizabeth V., and Eisenstat, Sharon L. Glorious American quilts: the quilt collection of the Museum of American Folk Art. N.Y., Penguin Studio; Museum of American Folk Art, 1996. xi, 203p. il. (chiefly col.)

Complete catalog of the museum's collection. Most pieces are illustrated with excellent color photographs, accompanied by smaller black-and-white photographs.

Contents: (1) Whole-cloth quilts; (2) Chintz quilts; (3) Signature quilts; (4) Appliqué quilts; (5) Pieced quilts; (6) Log-cabin quilts; (7) Show-quilts; (8) Revival quilts; (9) Amish quilts; (10) African-American quilts; (11) Contemporary quilts.

Glossary, p.150–51. Notes, p.152–56. Catalogue of quilts, p.157–94. Bibliography, p.195–97. Index, p.199–203.

P927 Wilson, Sadye Tune, and Kennedy, Doris Finch. Of coverlets: the legacies, the weavers. Introd. by Else Regensteiner. Photography by Sadye Tune Wilson. Nashville, Tenn., Tungstede, 1983. 494p. il. (part col.), ports.

Based on a documentation project conducted in 1978–83 by the Tennessee Textile History Project, designed to "investigate the status of early handwoven textiles in Tennessee and to preserve written and photographic records of the extant textile legacies and their weavers."—*p.15.* 1,000 coverlets, counterpanes, blankets, sheets, and ticking were recorded, including details concerning fibers, patterns, names of weavers and owners. Many of the items are 19th-century; a few date from the 18th century. A catalog of the items recorded takes up most of the vol. Each item is illustrated and is accompanied by a detailed technical caption.

Contents: Catalog; Appendix A: Comparative index of coverlet drafts by motif class and page number; Appendix B: Illustrated cross-reference index to coverlet pattern names; Appendix C: Index of documented textiles by owner name.

Bibliography, p.469–70. Index, p.473–93.

SEE ALSO: Schoeser and Rufey, English and American textiles: from 1790 to the present (GLAH 2:P864).

Asian Countries

General Works

P928 Pattern and loom; a practical study of the development of weaving techniques in China, Western Asia and Europe. By John Becker. With the collab. of Donald B. Wagner. Copenhagen, Rhodos, [1987]. Text and suppl. 316p. il. (part col.); suppl. 80p. il. (part col.)

"The book has two objectives: 1) A detailed practical account of the weaving of preserved ancient textiles and a technical classification of the main types. This will be of importance for textile scholars and textile conservators. 2) An inspiration for students and weavers today, who will be able to find new possibilities from practical descriptions of older techniques."—*Pref.*

The culmination of 20 years of weaving experiments by John Becker at his textile workshop in Denmark, this book is mainly for the advanced professional weaver and the knowledgeable textile historian or conservator. The five sections of the book are concerned with the patterned weaves of Han China, early western Asia, the Mediterranean regions, and Tang China, and weaving implements. Each chapter within a section reviews the surviving textile material, quotes the literature, and provides some brief historical information. The work serves as a handbook of ancient weaving with a rich body of illustrations.

Central Asia

P929 Harvey, Janet. Traditional textiles of central Asia. London, Thames and Hudson, 1996. 160p. il. (part col.), maps.

Describes "the wide range of the region's textiles, from the historical fabrics to the unique and exquisite objects . . . to the products of more modern design and technology."—*Pref.*

Contents: (1) The history and motifs; (2) The materials and dyes; (3) Felts, weavings and dress; (4) Applied decoration.

Glossary, p.153–56. Further reading, p.157. Museums and galleries, p.158. Index, p.159–60.

India, Nepal, Pakistan, Tibet

P930 Gabriel, Hannelore. Jewelry of Nepal. London, Thomas E. Hudson, 1999. xiv, 209. il. (part col.), map.

A valuable survey of a neglected subject.

Contents: (1) The land, religion, and the function of jewelry; (2) A history of jewelry in Nepal; (3) Symbolism; (4) Materials; (5) The Newar; (6) The Tibeto-Burman middle hills group; (7) The Tibeto-Nepalese; (8) The Indo-Nepalese; (9) The Tharu; (10) Ritual jewelry of the shamans; (11) Jewelry makers; Tips for the collector.

Notes, p.199–200. Bibliography, p.201–[03]. Index, p.204–[10].

P931 Gillow, John, and Barnard, Nicolas. Traditional Indian textiles. N.Y., Thames and Hudson, 1991. 160p. il. (part col.), map.

Introductory survey.

Contents: (1) The history of textile production; (2) The materials; (3) The techniques of textile decoration; (4) The west; (5) The north; (6) The east and the south; (7) Guide to further information: Bibliography, Museums and galleries with collections of Indian textiles, Glossary (p.153–56).

Index, p.158–60.

P932 Textile arts of India: Kokyo Hatanaka collection. San Francisco, Chronicle Books, 1996. 344p. col. il., map.

Devoted largely to color plates, grouped in thematic chapters. Includes a foreword by the collector.

Contents: (I) Painted and block-printed cloths, cloths decorated with gold and silver leaf; (II) Roller-printed cloths, tie-dyed cloths; (III) Woven cloths and embroideries; History of Indian textiles, by Zahid Sardar; Afterword.

Bibliography, p.343.

P933 The woven silks of India. Ed. by Jasleen Dhamija. Bombay, Marg Publications, 1995. 156p. il. (part col.)

Multi-author survey, with many color illustrations.

Contents: A group of early silks: the tree motif, by Steven Cohen; Vaishnavite silks: the figured textiles of Assam, by Rosemary Crill; Mughal silks: the Metropolitan Museum collection, by Daniel Walker; Baluchari textiles: pictorial brocades, by Eva-Maria Rakob; Paithani weaves, by Jasleen Dhamija; Kanchivani: the saris of Kanchipuram, by Rathi Vinay Jha; Benares brocades: varying themes, by Yashodhara Agrawal; Ashavali saris of Ahmedabad: revival of a technique, by Radhika Lalbhai; India and Europe:the trade in embroideries, by Valérie Berinstain; India and West Africa: transformation of velvets, by Joanne B. Eicher and Barbara Sumberg.

Glossary, p.155–56.

Japan

P934 Beyond the Tanabata Bridge: traditional Japanese textiles. Ed. by William Jay Rathbun. N.Y., Thames and Hudson in assoc. with the Seattle Museum, 1993. 197p. il. (part col.), map.

Published in conjunction with the exhibition, Textile Museum, Washington, D.C. (1993), and other locations. Includes an overview of Japanese folk textiles (by several authors) and a catalog of the collection in the Seattle Museum.

Index, p.[198]–[99].

P935 Ito, Toshiko. Tsujigahana, the flower of Japanese textile art. Trans. by Monica Bethe. Tokyo, Kodansha (Distr. by Harper and Row, 1981). 202p. il. (part col.) (Repr.: 1985).

Trans. of Tsujigahanazome. Tokyo, Kodansha, 1981.

Tsujigahana is a technique combining tie-dying, hand-painting, and embroidery. This book discusses its history, techniques, and esthetics.

Contents: (1) The genesis, flowering, and fading of Tsujigahana; (2) Tie dyeing; (3) Tie dyeing and painting; (4) Tie dyeing with painting and gold- or silver-leaf imprint; (5) Tie dyeing with embroidery, gold- or silver-leaf imprint, and painting; (6) Defining tsujigahana; Appendix.
Index, p.201–02.

P936 Matsumoto, Kaneo. Jōdai-gire: 7th and 8th century textiles in Japan from the Shōshō-in and Hōryū-ji. Kyoto, Shikosha, 1984. 251p. il. (part col.), maps.
Text in Japanese and English.
Because ancient textiles such as the ones described here are rarely seen on display, the photographs and annotations in this catalog are especially useful for scholars of Japanese culture and of textiles. 136 color plates followed by a scholarly text describing materials, techniques, and styles.
Bibliography, p.251.

P937 Nihon Sens'i Ishō Sentā. Textile designs of Japan. Rev. ed. Tokyo, Kodansha, 1980. 3v., plates (part col.)
See GLAH 1:P681 for original annotation. A reissue of this important set with slightly revised vol. titles.
Contents: (1) Free-style designs; (2) Geometric designs; (3) Okinawan, Ainu, and foreign designs.

P938 Yang, Sunny, and Narasin, Rochelle M. Textile art of Japan. Tokyo, Shufunotomo/Japan Publications (Distr. by Farrar, Straus and Giroux, 1989). 144p. col. il., map.
A basic introduction to the history, motifs, and techniques used to create Japanese fabrics.
Contents: (1) The history of the kimono; (2) The history of the obi; (3) Dyed textiles; (4) Woven textiles; (5) Needlework and applied decoration; (6) Contemporary creations.
Museums and galleries, p.138–39. Bibliography, p.140–41. Sources [for purchasing contemporary and antique Japanese textiles], p.142. Index, p.143–44.

Southeast Asia

P939 Conway, Susan. Thai textiles. Bangkok, Asia Books, 1992. 192p. il. (part col.)
Includes a discussion of weaving legends, the significance of textiles in religious and animist ceremonies, historic costume, textile production from the cultivation of raw materials to weaving techniques, regional variations in weaving patterns, and their connection with ethnic identity. Well-illustrated, with many photographs by the author.
Contents: (1) Introduction; (2) Textiles, religion and society; (3) Silk and cotton production; (4) Looms and weaving techniques; (5) Thai costumes; (6) Ceremonial and household textiles; (7) Textiles of north Thailand; (9) Textiles of central and south Thailand; (10) Conclusion.
Bibliography, p.186–87. Glossary, p.188–89. Index, p.190–92.

P940 Fraser-Lu, Sylvia. Handwoven textiles of South-East Asia. N.Y., Oxford Univ. Pr., 1988. xix, 229p. il. (part col.), plates.
A book whose "primary purpose is to make known to the general public the beauty and scope of South-East Asian handwoven textiles, both past and present."—*Pref.* Provides a general historical overview and describes materials, equipment, weaving techniques, and the use of textiles, with a regional survey.
Contents: (I) A general introduction to weaving; (II) A survey of textiles by country.
Bibliography, p.215–22. Index, p.223–29.

P941 Gillow, John. Traditional Indonesian textiles. Photographs by Barry Dawson. London, Thames and Hudson, 1992. 160p. il. (part col.), map.
Introductory survey.
Contents: (1) The textile history of Indonesia; (2) Yarns, looms and dyes; (3) The decorative craft of Batik; (4) A world of pattern; (5) The art of embellishment; A textiles guide to the islands.
Glossary, p.153–54. Further reading, p.155. Museums and galleries with collections of Indonesian textiles, p.156. Index, p.158–60.

P942 Hauser-Schäublin, Brigitta; Nabholz-Kartaschoff, Marie-Louise; and Ramseyer, Urs. Textiles in Bali. [English trans., Dennis Q. Stephenson.] Berkeley, Periplus, 1991. xv, 143p. col. il.
Trans of Textilien in Bali. Berlin, Reimer, 1991.
"Concerned pre-eminently with the manufacture, use and significance of various textiles which reflect the island's great cultural richness and diversity. . . . The collection of the Basel Museum of Ethnography forms the material basis for this book."—*Pref.* Richly illustrated in color, and arranged by textile categories.
Contents: (1) The universe arrayed: textiles in Bali I; (2) Endek: Ikat production in transition; (3) Songkèt: golden threads, caste and privilege; (4) Perada: gilded garments for humans, gods and temples; (5) Bebali: borderlines between the sacred and the profane; (6) Keling: archaic cloths from Nusa Penida; (7) Polèng: the dualism of black and white; (8) Cepuk: sacred textiles from Bali and Nusa Pentida; (9) Geringsing: magical protection and communal identity.
Glossary, p.136–37. Bibliography, p.138–39. Index, p.140–43.

P943 Khan Majlis, Brigitte. Indonesische Textilien: Wege zu Göttern und Ahnen, Bestandskatalog der Museen in Nordrhein-Westfalen. Köln, Wienand, 1984. 373p. il. (part col.), plates. (Ethnologica [Cologne, Germany], n.F., Bd. 10)
Catalog of the exhibition, Rautenstrauch-Joest-Museum für Völkerkunde, Cologne (1984), and other locations, including a scholarly catalog of the regional collections.
Glossar, p.360–65. Bibliography, p.366–73.

P944 Maxwell, Robyn J. Textiles of Southeast Asia: tradition, trade, and transformation. N.Y., Oxford Univ. Pr., 1990. 432p. il. (part col.)
Substantial, broadly conceived survey, seeking to appreciate both geographic and cultural diversity and common theme. Richly illustrated.

Contents: (1) An introduction to Southeast Asian textile history; (2) The foundations; (3) Indian impressions; (4) Chinese themes; (5) Islamic conversions; (6) European incursions; (7) The changing role of textiles in Southeast Asia: conclusions.

Notes, p.408–15. Glossary of technical terms, p.416–19. Bibliography, p.419–25. Index, p.426–32.

P945 Selvanayagam, Grace Inpam. Songket: Malaysia's woven treasure. N.Y., Oxford Univ. Pr., 1990. xxii, 204p. il. (part col.)

A study of "the richest and most complex of all Malaysian art crafts," originally presented as the author's thesis (MA, University of Malaya, 1982) under title Kain sungkit patterns in peninsular Malaysia.

Select bibliography, p.199–201. Index, p.202–04.

P946 Solyom, Bronwen, and Solyom, Garrett. Fabric traditions of Indonesia. Pullman, Wash., Washington State Univ. Pr.; Museum of Art, Washington State Univ., 1984. vii, 60p. il. (part col.)

Intended to provide "an introduction to many aspects of the culture of Indonesia . . . [and] to add in a modest way to the scholarship on Indonesian textiles."—*Foreword.*

Contents: The traditions and their beginnings; Bark-cloth; Mats and plaitwork traditions; Beads and shells: echoes of an ancient trade; Warp stripes and warp ikat; Exotic silks and international trade; Of ships and trees: cotton supplementary weft traditions; Cloth painting and batik traditions; Traditional techniques: puzzles and innovations; A selection of ceremonial skirts.

Notes, p.54–56. Glossary, p.57–59.

P947 To speak with cloth: studies in Indonesian textiles. Mattiebelle Gittinger, ed. Los Angeles, Museum of Cultural History, Univ. of California, 1989. 256p. il. (part col.), maps.

An anthology of studies that "assess textiles and their role in discrete micro-environments of Indonesia."—*Pref.* Essays address the role of gender, regional textile types and decorative means, and batik issues.

Glossary, p.240–41. Bibliography, p.242–52. Contributors, p.253–54.

P948 Weaving patterns of life: Indonesian textile symposium 1991. Marie-Louise Nabholz-Kartaschoff, Ruth Barnes and David J. Stuart-Fox, eds. Basel, Museum of Ethnography, 1993. 460p. il.

Wide-ranging papers from the symposium, Basel (1991).

Contents: Topic 1: Textiles in archaeology and history; Topic 2: Iconography; Topic 3: Function and meaning; Topic 4: Techniques and their interpretation.

List of authors, p.359–60.

Africa, Oceania, The Americas

Africa

P949 Adler, Peter, and Barnard, Nicholas. African majesty: the textile art of the Ashanti and Ewe. [N.Y.], Thames and Hudson, [1992]. 192p. il., 131 col. plates., maps.

A beautifully illustrated book of West African strip-weaving with descriptions of the origin of this fiber art, weaving techniques, and raw material composition.

Contents: (1) Strip-weaving in West Africa; (2) Ashanti and Ewe—a history; (3) The Ashanti cloth; (4) The Ewe cloth; (5) The looms and materials.

Further reading, p.188. Glossary, p.189. Index, p.190–92.

P950 Lamb, Venice, and Holmes, Judy. Nigerian weaving. Roxford, [England], H. A. and V. M. Lamb, 1980. 276p. 424 il. (part col.)

Profusely illustrated, this definitive work is grouped by loom type (horizontal and vertical) and arranged by ethnic group.

Contents: Part one: the horizontal loom, by Venice Lamb: (1) The Yoruba; (2) The Nupe and some of their neighbors; (3) Hausaland; (4) Borno and Adamawa; (5) The Jukun, the Tiv and the Angas. Part two: the vertical loom, by Judy Holmes: (6) The woman's vertical loom; (7) The Yoruba; (8) The Nupe, the northern Igbira and associated peoples; (9) Okene and its neighbours; (10) The Ibo-speaking weavers; (11) Northern Nigeria; (12) Vertical looms used by men, by Venice Lamb and Judy Holmes.

Bibliography, p.271–73. Index, p.274–76.

P951 ———, and Lamb, Alastair. Au Cameroun weaving—tissage. Hertingfordbury, French trans. of the English text by Cathy Martin. Hertfordshire, Roxford, 1981. 192p. 278 il. (part col.), map.

Abundantly illustrated with field photographs, this study traces the history of Cameroon through its weaving and provides a systematic survey of the major categories of indigenous weaving. Text in English and French.

Contents: (1) Ndop cloth; (2) The narrow strip horizontal treadle loom; (3) Ground looms and vertical looms; (4) Raphia weaving; (5) Old styles and new textiles.

Select bibliography, p.192.

P952 Mack, John. Malagasy textiles. Princes Risborough, Aylesbury, Bucks, Shire Publications, 1989. 60p. 36 il. map. (Shire ethnography, 14)

Survey of the rich variety of textile traditions of Madagascar including information about the materials, techniques, and elaborate patterns.

Contents: (1) Introduction; (2) Raw materials; (3) Weavers and looms; (4) Decorative techniques; (5) The significance of textiles; (6) Museums; (7) Further reading (p.57).

Index, p.58–60.

P953 Picton, John. The art of African textiles: technology, tradition and lurex. [With] Rayda Becker . . . [et al.] London, Barbican Art Gallery, Lund Humphries Publishers, [1995]. 140p. il. (part col.), maps.

Catalog of the exhibition, Barbican Art Gallery (1995). Extensively illustrated, this catalog documents a major exhibition that broadly examined African textile design, primarily in the 20th century.

Contents: Technology, tradition and lurex: the art of textiles in Africa, by John Picton; The tapestries of Thiés: woven images of negritude, by Elizabeth Harney; Bogolan: from symbolic material to national emblem, by Pauline Duponchel; Aspects of embroidery in Africa, by David Heathcote; Textile markets in Nigeria: a diary, by Pat Oyelola; Textile design in Ghana: extracts from a report, by Atta Kwami; The Kanga: an example of East African textile design, by Julia Hilger; Weaving in Madagascar, by Simon Peers; Clothing and identity in southern Africa, by Rayda Becker; Southern African textiles today: design, industry and collective enterprise, by Jackie Guille.

Bibliography, p.130–31. Glossary, p.132.

P954 ______, and Mack, John. African textiles. [2d ed.] N.Y., Harper and Row, [1989]. 208p. il. (part col.), maps.

1st ed, 1979. Drawn primarily from collections in the British Museum, this major study examines the dynamic and changing nature of African textile traditions.

Contents: (1) Introduction; (2) The raw materials; (3) The loom; (4) The single-heddle loom; (5) The double-heddle loom; (6) Weaving in Madagascar; (7) Pattern dyeing; (8) Drawn, painted, printed and stencilled patterns; (9) Appliqué and related techniques; (10) Embroidery.

Bibliography, p.202–5. Index, p.206–8.

P955 Polakoff, Claire. Into indigo: African textiles and dyeing techniques. N.Y., Anchor Books, Anchor Pr./Doubleday, 1980. xiii, 269p. 129 il., col. plates, map.

A basic overview of West African textile design focusing on the techniques, symbolism, and social use of textiles.

Contents: (1) American interest in African textiles; (2) African fabrics; (3) The art of tie and dye in Africa; (4) Wax and paste resist patterning—"batik"; (5) The hand-printed Adinkra cloth of Ghana; (6) Bokolanfini—the mud cloth of Mali; (7) Korhogo cloth of Ivory Coast; (8) Traditions/transitions: working with African textiles today; Appendix: Indigo—the legend and technique.

Glossary, p.239–42. Bibliography, p.243–53. Index, p.259–69.

P956 Reswick, Irmtraud. Traditional textiles of Tunisia and related North African weavings. Pref. by Jay D. Frierman. Los Angeles, Craft and Folk Art Museum (Distr. by the Univ. of Washington Pr., [1985]). xvii, 242p. 80 il. 35 col. plates, maps. (Folk art monographs, 1)

The standard study of Tunisian textiles that includes extensive technical descriptions of the techniques and technology of weaving and looms.

Contents: (1) Introduction; (2) Raw materials used in textile arts; (3) The preparation of the fiber; (4) The loom; (5) Flat-woven decorated textiles: use, motifs and colors; (6) Carpets; (7) Algerian carpets and flat-woven decorated textiles; (8) Moroccan carpets and flat-woven decorated textiles; (9) Libyan textiles and carpets; (10) Conclusion; Appendix.

Glossary, p.209–24. Bibliography, p.225–31. Index, p.233–42.

P957 Schaedler, Karl-Ferdinand. Weaving in Africa, south of the Sahara. [München], Panterra, [1987]. 487p. il. (part col.), maps.

Issued by the publisher simultaneously in German as Die Weberei in Afrika südlich der Sahara and in French as Le tissage en Afrique. A major synthesis of the research about the weaving technologies and traditions in sub-Saharan Africa. Profusely illustrated with contemporary and historical photographs and line drawings.

Contents: Weaving technology in Africa south of the Sahara; Individual weaving peoples and their products—use and marketing; The African weaver as a craftsman, his identity, training and economic position; The treadle loom and the origins of weaving in Africa south of the Sahara.

Bibliography, p.465–81. Index, p.482–86.

P958 Spring, Christopher, and Hudson, Julie. North African textiles. Washington, D.C., Smithsonian Institution Pr., [1995]. 143p. il. (part col.), map.

Illustrated with numerous color photographs, this book surveys the textile tradition of North Africa describing the techniques and materials as well as the social contexts of cloth and costume.

Contents: (1) The threads of North African history; (2) Food of the loom; (3) The patterns of life; (4) Display and modesty; (5) Textiles of town and country; (6) Beyond the loom; (7) Secular and sacred; (8) Continuity and change.

Bibliography, p.140–41. Glossary, p.141–42. Index, p.143–[44].

P959 Stone, Caroline. The embroideries of North Africa. Burnt Mill, Harlow, Essex, Longman Group Ltd., 1985. 218p. il. (part col.), map.

Generously illustrated in color and with numerous diagrams of motifs and stitches, this book surveys the main urban styles of indigenous embroidery of Morocco, the urban and village needlework of Tunisia, and includes limited information on Algerian and Turkish embroideries.

Contents: The embroideries of Morocco; The embroideries of Algeria; The embroideries of Tunisia; Turkish embroideries in North Africa; Stitches and applications.

Glossary, p.204–209. Bibliography, p.211–15. Index, p.216–18.

Oceania

P960 Pendergrast, Mick. Feathers and fibre. A survey of traditional and contemporary Maori craft. Photographs by John Martin and Alex Wilson. Auckland, N.Z., Penguin, 1984. 237p. 280 il. (part col.)

Catalog of the exhibition, Rotorua Art Gallery (New Zealand) (1984?).

Primarily composed of plates, this book surveys the development of Maori fibre craft over a 150-year period with an emphasis on plaited works ranging from clothing to basketry.

Glossary, p.235–37.

The Americas

P961 The Junius B. Bird Pre-Columbian Textile Conference: May 19th and 20th, 1973. Ed. by Ann Pollard

Rowe and Elizabeth P. Benson. Washington, D.C., Textile Museum and Dumbarton Oaks, 1979. 278p. il.

Fifteen papers on Pre-Columbian Andean textiles and textile technology, with one essay on Mesoamerica.

Includes bibliographies.

P962 The Junius B. Bird Conference on Andean textiles: April 7th and 8th, 1984. Ed. by Ann Pollard Rowe. Washington, D.C., Textile Museum, 1986. 381p. il.

Nineteen papers, 12 on archeological textiles of the Andes and 7 on ethnological textiles of Peru and Bolivia.

Includes bibliographies.

P963 Kent, Kate Peck. Prehistoric textiles of the Southwest. Santa Fe, School of American Research; Albuquerque, Univ. of New Mexico Pr., 1983. 315p. il. (part col.), maps. (Southwest Indian arts series)

An examination of "the history, technology, and cultural significance of prehistoric southwestern textiles"—*Foreword.* "[The author] has synthesized the bulk of textile evidence available to date on her subject matter and presents it in an organized and detailed manner, with appropriate visual material including technical drawings which she rendered, fine black and white photographs and excellent color plates."—*Review*, Museum anthropology, v.8, no.1, Jan. 1984, p.20.

Contents: (1) The search for clues: reconstructing prehistoric textile arts; (2) The preparation of fibers and dyes; (3) Nonloom single element fabrics; (4) Nonloom warp-weft weaves; (5) Loom-woven fabrics; (6) Textile design; (7) Form and function; (8) Regional and temporal traditions; Appendix: the location, age, and textile-related contents of sites mentioned in the text.

Glossary, p.295–300. Bibliography, p.301–10. Index, p.311–15.

P964 Schevill, Margot Blum. Maya textiles of Guatemala: the Gustavus A. Eisen collection. 1902, the Hearst Museum of Anthropology, the University of California at Berkeley. With a historical essay by Christopher H. Lutz. Austin, Univ. of Texas Pr., 1993. xiii, 295p. il. (part col.), maps.

Illustrates a rich collection of 222 19th-century Maya textiles and textile-related objects, most of them never previously published. Includes appendix on the classification of textiles in the collection by function and type.

Contents: (1) The communicative nature of cloth; (2) The Eisen Guatemalan textile collection; (3) Gustavus A. Eisen: 1847–1940; (4) The late nineteenth-century Guatemalan Maya in historical context: past and future research, by Christopher H. Lutz; (5) Textile production; (6) The Eisen Guatemalan textile catalogue; Appendixes: Classification of textiles and textile-related objects in the Eisen collection by function and type; The "Cofradia" of the Indians of Guatemala by Gustav Eisen, 1903.

Notes, p.251–70. Glossary of weaving technology, p.271–72. Bibliography, p.273–85. Figure index, p.287–88. Catalogue index, p.289–90. Subject index, p.291–95.

EMBROIDERY AND NEEDLEWORK

Asian Countries

General Works

P965 Chung, Young Yang. The art of oriental embroidery: history, aesthetics, and techniques. N.Y., Scribner's, 1983, [1979]. 183p. il. (part col.), plates.

Outlines the history of embroidery in China, Japan, and Korea and explains the techniques used in each country. A popular treatment of the subject intended for both the scholar and the craftsman with illustrations of particular stitch techniques as well as examples of robes, accessories, scrolls, screens, and banners.

Contents: (1) The foundations of oriental silk embroidery; (2) Home accessories; (3) The Chinese dragon robe; (4) The Japanese kimono; (5) The Korean bridal robe; (6) Costume accessories; (7) Scrolls, screens, and banners; (8) Oriental embroidery design; Appendix: Design symbolism.

Bibliography, p.175–78. Index, p.179–83.

China

P966 Mailey, Jean. Embroidery of Imperial China. N.Y., China House Gallery, China Institute in America, [1978]. 55p. il.

Catalog of the exhibition, China House Gallery (1978).

A small but important study of Chinese embroidery and its relationship to Chinese life. The essay discusses examples from the Shang dynasty through current practice.

Selected bibliography, p.53.

IVORY AND SCRIMSHAW

General Works

P967 Burack, Benjamin. Ivory and its uses. Rutland, Tuttle, [1984]. 240p. il. (part col.)

A complete history of ivory and articles made from it, by a long-time collector. Classified listing of the many uses of ivory is especially useful.

Contents: Part one: History, art, and craft; (I) Historical development; (II) Sources of ivory; (III) Ivory substitutes; (IV) Cutting and carving; (V) Coloration of ivory; (VI) Care and cleaning; (VII) Testing for ivory; Part two: The uses of ivory.

Museum collections, p.205–08. Notes, p.209–23. Bibliography, p.225–28. Index, p.229–40.

P968 Frank, Stuart M. Dictionary of scrimshaw artists. With contrib. by Joshua Basseches . . . [et al.], and a foreword by Norman Flayderman. Mystic, Mystic Seaport Museum, 1991. 198, [1]p. il.

Dictionary of all known scrimshaw artists through the early 20th century, based on extensive archival research, with introductory essays on the origin and fabrication of scrimshaw.

Anonymous pictorial masters, p.155–62. "Questioned" scrimshaw from the Calhoun Collection, p.[163]–65. Scrimshaw on the floating-factory ships and shore stations, p.[167]–70. Glossary of specialized terms, p.[171]–78. Bibliography, p.[179]–185. Taxonomic and geographical index, p.186–91. Index of vessels mentioned in the text, p.[192]–98. The author and contributing editors, p.[199]. Addenda: Index of public repositories laid in.

P969 Ivory: an international history and illustrated survey. [Contrib.: Michael Vickers, Peter Lasko, Pamela Tudor-Craig . . . (et al.)] N.Y., Abrams, [1987]. 352p. il. (part col.)

Well-illustrated world history of ivory for a non-specialist audience, with texts by experts in each period.

Glossary, p.330–39. Collecting ivory objects, p.340. Care and repair, p.342–43. Bibliography, p.344–45. Museums, p.346. Index, p.347–51.

P970 Randall, Richard H., Jr. Masterpieces of ivory from the Walters Art Gallery. With texts by Diana Buitron . . . [et al.] N.Y., Hudson Hills in assoc. with the Walters Art Gallery, [1985]. 338p. il., 280 col. plates.

Catalog of a notable collection of ivories of worldwide scope. Arranged by period, with introductory essays for each chapter. Individual entries are detailed and include bibliographical references.

Concordance, p.325–26. Bibliography, p.327–29. Index, p.331–38.

JADE

General Works

P971 Jade. Consult. ed., Roger Keverne. N.Y., Lorenz Books, 1995. 376p. il. (part col.)

"Our intention . . . is to . . . combine in a single work the most authoritative contemporary jade research . . . with the best illustrations that modern technology can produce."—*Introd.* A multi-author, regional survey. Includes chapters offering "advice for buyers and collectors" as well as a chapter on jade collections.

Glossaries, p.353–55. A jade bibliography, p.356–67. Notes, p.368–70. Index, p.371–75.

Asian Countries

China

Bibliography

P972 Born, Gerald M., comp. Chinese jade: an annotated bibliography. Chicago, Celadon Pr., 1982. 431p. il. (part col.)

More than 800 annotated citations for English-language books, articles, and films published or produced between 1880–1981 on the topic of Chinese jade. Chinese jade is defined by the compiler as "objects that have been worked, shaped or carved in nephrite or jadeite by a Chinese craftsman regardless of his regional or ethnic origin."

Contents: Introduction; The literature of Chinese jade: Sources in Chinese; Sources in English; Bibliography; Addendum.

Abbreviations, p.362. Title index, p.363–81. Index, p.383–431.

Histories and Handbooks

P973 Chinese jade from the neolithic to the Qing. By Jessica Rawson. With the assist. of Carol Michaelson. Photography by John Williams and David Gowers. London, British Museum Pr., [1995]. 462p. il. (part col.), maps.

Catalog of the exhibition, British Museum (1995).

The collection of Sir Joseph Hotung, which covers the full span of Chinese jade carving from the neolithic period to the Qing dynasty and includes more than 300 pieces, is documented in this catalog. The essay sets the jades in their archeological, social, and intellectual context and attempts to establish a dating system.

Bibliography, p.[424]–50. Chronological table, p.[451]. Index, p.452–63.

P974 Laufer, Berthold. Jade: its history and symbolism in China. [Reprint.] N.Y., Dover, 1989. xiv, 370p. il., plates.

Reprint of GLAH 1:P712. Dover produced a reprint of the 1912 ed., under the original title, in 1974, then another in 1989, using an alternate title. In this ed. all of the plates have been reduced in size slightly, and the original 6 color plates are now black-and-white.

P975 Watt, James C. Y. Chinese jades from Han to Ch'ing. N.Y., Asia Society, [1980]. 235, [1]p. il. (part col.)

Catalog of the exhibition, Asia House Gallery (1980), the first show at the Gallery devoted to the subject. After an introductory essay that covers the history, dating, and stylistic issues, the objects are presented with extensive notes about each piece.

Contents: The Stone; Animals; Birds and Fishes; Figures; The Scholar's Desk; Vessels; Plaques and Personal Ornaments.

List of Chinese names and terms, p.225–30. Selected bibliography, p.231. Other works cited in the text, p.233–[36].

LACQUER

Asian Countries

General Works

P976 Lee, Yu-kuan. Oriental lacquer art. N.Y., Weatherhill, [1971]. 394p. il. (part col.), map.

Standard study of lacquerware by a collector-dealer with photographs and descriptions of 264 objects from public and private collections. Discusses the materials, techniques, identification, and dating of lacquerware, before presenting the plates and commentaries.

Bibliography, p.360–61.

P977 Watt, James C. Y., and Ford, Barbara Brennan. East Asian lacquer: the Florence and Herbert Irving collection. N.Y., Metropolitan Museum of Art (Distr. by Abrams, [1991]). xi, 388p. il. (part col.), map.

Catalog of the exhibition, Metropolitan Museum of Art (1992).

Documents a collection promised to the museum, and "presents a systematic study and informed interpretation of the unique art form that is lacquer."—*Foreword.* The objects date from the 12th century to the present day and include examples from Japan, China, Korea, and the Ryukyu Islands. After the introductory essay, the 178 pieces are organized by country of origin with each photographed and described.

Contents: China, by James C. Y. Watt; Japan, by Barbara Brennan Ford; Korea, by James C. Y. Watt; Ryukyu Islands, by James C. Y. Watt.

Appendix of marks, p.372–75. Glossary, p.376–78. Bibliography, p.379–82. Index, p.383–88.

China

P978 Clifford, Derek. Chinese carved lacquer. London, Bamboo, 1992. 160p. il. (part col.)

A well-illustrated introduction that concentrates on objects from the 9th century to today in which the decoration has been carved into a lacquer body.

Select bibliography, p.158–60.

P979 Garner, Harry. Chinese lacquer. London, Faber, 1979. 285p. il. (part col.), plates. (Arts of the East)

Written at a time when excavations in China were uncovering new examples of ancient lacquers, this book considers no finds after 1974. This scholarly study primarily considers laquerwares from the Yüan dynasty onward.

Bibliography, p. 275–80. Index, p.281–85.

Japan

P980 Collections Baur: Japanese lacquer (selected pieces). By Pierre F. Schneeberger. Trans. by K. Watson. Geneve, Collections Baur, 1984. 193p., il. (part col.), folded plate.

This is the 9th vol. in the general catalog of the Baur Collection. Discusses 171 objects including writing boxes, tea caddies, incense boxes, and medicine boxes or inrō dating from the 17th to early 20th century. Each piece is fully described and photographed. A short biography (p.183–84), list of artists, and images of the signatures on the lacquer follow the catalog of objects.

P981 Japanese lacquer art: modern masterpieces. Ed. by the National Museum of Modern Art, Tokyo. Trans. by Richard L. Gage. N.Y., Weatherhill, 1982. 299p. col. plates.

Trans. of Kindai Nihon no Shitsugei. Tokyo, Do Bijutsukan, 1979.

Originally published in 1981 and based on the catalog of the exhibition, National Museum of Modern Art, Tokyo in 1979 and the Kyoto National Museum in 1980.

This large-format book is beautifully illustrated with more than 200 color photographs of objects and numerous color images of the technical processes and materials. Includes 38 artists with examples of their work, commentary on each piece, and biographical notes.

P982 Okada, Barbra Teri. Symbol and substance in Japanese lacquer: early lacquer boxes from the collection of Elaine Ehrenkranz. N.Y., Weatherhill, (1995). 191p. il. (part col.)

Illustrated introductory essay on lacquer production and lacquer art. Sets the context for examining the 55 examples of pre-19th-century Japanese lacquer boxes in the Elaine Ehrenkranz Collection. Full-color illustrations and descriptions that include comments on the provenance, construction, decoration, and connoisseurship for each piece makes the collection catalog especially useful.

Notes, p.174–76. Provenance of selected boxes from the collection, p.177. Chemical analysis, p.178. Glossary, p.179–82. Bibliography, p.183–86. Index, p.187–91.

WALLPAPER

General Works

P983 Oman, Charles C., and Hamilton, Jean. Wallpapers: an international history and illustrated survey from the Victoria and Albert Museum. Bibliography by E. A. Entwisle. London, Sotheby in assoc. with the Victoria and Albert Museum, [1982]. 486p. il. (part col.)

Authoritative, heavily illustrated survey of wallpaper history in the form of a catalog of the extensive collections of the Victoria and Albert Museum. Includes historical essay by Charles Oman first published in 1929 in the Museum's first listing of its holdings, supplemented by Hamilton's essay on more recent acquisitions. Catalog is arranged in three sections: Anonymous papers and designs; Pattern books; and Designers. Very extensive classified bibliography.

Bibliography, p.457–466. General index, p.467–75. Index of titles and pictorial subjects, p.477–86.

P984 The Papered wall: history, pattern, technique. Ed. by Lesley Hoskins. [N.Y.], Abrams, [1994]. 256p. il. (part col.)

Well-illustrated history of wallpaper from the 15th to the 20th centuries, in the form of essays by specialists in each area.

Contents: (1) Manifold beginnings: Single-sheet papers, by Geert Wisse; (2) Flocks, florals, and fancies: English manufacture 1680–1830, by Anthony Wells-Cole; (3) The

China trade: Oriental painted panels, by Gill Saunders; (4) Luxury perfected: the ascendancy of French wallpaper, 1770–1870, by Bernard Jacque; (5) Arabesques and allegories: French decorative panels, by Veronique de Bruignac; (6) Wide horizons: French scenic papers, by Odile Nouvel-Kammerer; (7) An ocean apart: imports and the beginning of American manufacture, by Richard C. Nylander; (8) The English response: mechanization and design reform, by Joanna Banham; (9) Proliferation: Late 19th-century papers, markets and manufacturers, by Christine Woods, Joanne Kosuda Warner, and Bernard Jacque; (10) Unsteady progress: From the turn of the century to the Second World War, by Sabine Thummler and Mark Turner; (11) Post-war promise: pattern and technology up to 1970, by Joanne Kosuda Warner and Lesley Hoskins; (12) Off the shelf: design and consumer trends since 1970, by Mary Schoeser. Postscript: the rescue and care of wallpapers, by Sarah Mansell.

Bibliography, p.248–50. Glossary, p.250–51. Wallpaper reference collections open to the public, p.251–52. Additional sources of information, p.252. Suppliers of historic patterns, p.252–53. Index, p.254–56.

P985 Teynac, Francoise; Nolot, Pierre; and Vivien, Jean-Denis. Wallpaper: a history. Foreword by David Hicks. N.Y., Rizzoli, [1982]. 251p. il. (part col.)

First published as Le monde du papier peint. Paris, Berger-Levrault, 1981.

Well-illustrated narrative history of wallpaper from its beginnings to the present, suitable for a general audience. Includes a chapter briefly discussing manufacturing techniques.

Bibliography, p.235–38. Index of names, p.241–51.

Western Countries

France

P986 Jacque, Bernard. Le papier peint: decor d'illusion. Avec la collab. d'Odile Nouvel-Kammerer. [Barembach], Eds. Jean-Pierre Gyss, [1987]. 35, ix, [2]p. il., 68 leaves of col. plates.

Primarily a pictorial survey of French wallpaper based on examples from the Musée du Papier Peint de Rixheim, of which Jacque is curator. Introductory essays consider design and manufacturing techniques. Especially valuable for its many color illustrations.

Bibliographie sommaire, p.[xi].

P987 Nouvel, Odile. Wall-papers of France 1800–1850: a contribution to the study of the decorative arts. With an introd. by Jean-Pierre Seguin. Trans. by Margaret Timmers. N.Y., Rizzoli, [1981]. [132]p., col. il.

Text in English, French, and German.

Based on research for the exhibition, Musée des Arts Décoratifs, Paris (1967). Attempts to establish a typology of French wallpaper design. Following a concise introduction to the craft and its methods of fabrication, 600 examples of wallpapers are illustrated, classified by design elements, and furnishing a comprehensive overview of wallpapers of the period.

Index: Factories; Designers or engravers, p.[132].

P988 Papiers peints panoramiques. Sous la dir. d'Odile Nouvel-Kammerer. [Paris], Musée des Arts Décoratifs/Flammarion, [1990]. 335p. il. (part col., part fold.), map, chart.

Comprehensive, detailed consideration of French panoramic wallpapers, published in conjunction with the exhibition, Musée des Arts Décoratifs, Paris (1990–1991). Includes essays by a group of scholars and a catalogue raisonné of all known patterns, arranged by subject.

Includes bibliographical references. Bibliographie, p.331. Index, p.332–35.

United States

P989 Lynn, Catherine M. Wallpaper in America from the seventeenth century to World War I. With a foreword by Charles van Ravenswaay. N.Y., Norton, [1980]. 533p. il. (part col.), ports. (A Barra Foundation/Cooper-Hewitt Museum book)

The standard work on wallpaper made, or imported for use, in America. Basing her work on the extensive collections of the Cooper-Hewitt Museum and other institutions and historic houses, the author discusses the papers themselves, their use, and their social and cultural context. An essential resource for the study of the American interior.

Colors commonly used in eighteenth- and early nineteenth-century wallpaper manufacture, p.[485]–86. Checklist of American manufacturers in business before 1845, p.[487]–89. Wallpaper reference collections, p.[490]. Sources, p.[491]. Index, p.[518]–32.

P990 Nylander, Richard; Redmond, Elizabeth; and Penny J. Sander. Wallpaper in New England: selections from the Society for the Preservation of New England Antiquities. With essays by Abbott Lowell Cummings and Karen A. Guffey. Boston, Society for the Preservation of New England Antiquities, 1986. ix, 283p. il. (part col.)

Catalog of a notable and extensive collection of wallpapers, the majority of which are documented to specific buildings, and range from mid-18th century English imports to reproduction papers of the 20th century. In addition to the papers themselves, illustrations include invoices, trade cards, and period photographs of papered interiors. Because of the scope of the collection, this vol. can serve as a widely useful general resource for paper history.

Contents: Part one: Essays: (I) The use and manufacture of wallpaper in New England, 1700–1820, by Abbott Lowell Cummings; (II) From paper stainer to manufacturer: J.F. Bumstead and Co., manufacturers and importers of paper hangings, by Karen A. Guffey; Part two: Catalogue.

Bibliography, p.275–76. Description of SPNEA, p.277. Index, p.278–83.

P991 ———. Wallpapers for historic buildings: a guide to selecting reproduction wallpapers. 2d ed. [Washington, D.C.], Preservation Pr., [1992]. 263p. il. (part col.)

1st ed., 1983.

While the primary purpose of this handbook is to guide curators and owners of historic houses in the selection of appropriate reproduction wallpapers, the concise and informed discussions of each period's typical paper designs are valuable for any researcher needing such information in summary form. Includes extensive and specific information on papers currently available.

Contents: (1) 1700 to 1780: The English influence; (2) 1840 to 1870: Revival styles and machine printing; (3) 1870 to 1910: Stylized designs for the late Victorian era.

Suppliers, p.251–53. Glossary, p.254–55. Bibliography, p.256–61. Sources of information, p.262–63.

Q. Periodicals

This chapter presents a wide variety of significant new and established art periodicals. Periodicals are defined as numbered and regularly issued publications, unique in their frequency, appearance, and contents. Series, even those that are issued regularly, are dealt with in the next chapter.

Periodicals have been chosen based on their scholarly content, lasting research value, availability, use of summaries or abstracts in English or other romance language (for foreign publications), and incorporation in the major periodical indexes. Subjects include art, architecture, photography, design, decorative arts, and, to some extent, archeology. Coverage is international in scope. Interdisciplinary and historical journals are included when their coverage of art is considered substantial. While most journals began publication sometime between 1977 (the cutoff date of GLAH 1) and 1997, several older periodical titles not in GLAH 1 have been included if they were determined to be particularly noteworthy.

The beginning of this chapter ("Part 1") includes those GLAH 1 titles that ceased publication or continued under a new title. GLAH 1 titles that either began a new series, underwent a change in publisher, or were suspended for any length of time, have been given a new entry in GLAH 2, and are referenced in Part 1 under the old title. An effort was made to cite only the most recent information regarding title, place of publication, publisher, and distributor in the periodical entries. Information about internet availability is selective, and does not include addresses.

Local and regional art journals, art, design, and architecture school journals, as well as conservation-related periodicals are selectively covered. Museum publications are also judiciously included and incorporate only those that began publication after 1977. Mention should be made of two excellent bibliographical sources for serials that round out many of the areas only selectively dealt with here: Doris Robinson, Fine arts periodicals: an international directory of the visual arts (N.Y., Peri Pr., 1991) and Frances Gretes' Directory of international periodicals and newsletters on the built environment (2d ed., N.Y., Van Nostrand Reinhold, 1992).

Omitted from this list are: most professional publications, society newsletters, art newspapers, magazines for hobbyists, technical journals, as well as fashion, art education, art therapy and other subjects peripheral to the study of art history.

Indexes, with abbreviations:

A.D.P.: Art/Design/Photo
Acad.Search: Academic Search Elite (EBSCOhost) electronic database
Am.H.&L.: America: history and life
Am.Hum.ind.: American humanities index
Anth.ind.: Anthropological index
Anth.lit.: Anthropological literature
Arch.per.ind.: Architectural periodicals index
Art full: Art full text (Wilson) electronic database (1997–)
Art index: Art index / abstracts, paper and (Wilson) electronic database (1984– , as an electronic database; 1994– , with added abstracts)
Art Ar.Te.Abs.: Art and archaeology technical abstracts
ARTbib.curr.: ARTbibliographies current titles
ARTbib.mod.: ARTbibliographies modern
ArtHum.: Arts & humanities citation index (Institute for Scientific Information) electronic database
Article1st: ArticleFirst (OCLC) electronic database
Avery: Avery index to architectural periodicals
BHA: Bibliography of the history of art / Bibliographie d'histoire de l'art
B.H.I.: British humanities index
Biog.ind.: Biography index
Bk.rev.ind.: Book review index
Br.tech.ind.: British technology index
Can.ind.: Canadian index
Can.per.ind.: Canadian periodicals index
Clo.T.A.ind.: Clothing and textile arts index
Contents1st: ContentsFirst (OCLC) electronic database
Curr.Cont.A&H.: Current Contents: arts & humanities (Institute for Scientific Information) electronic database
Curr.Cont.Connect: Current contents connect (Institute for Scientific Information) electronic database
Des.&Ap.A.ind.: Design and applied arts index
Des. int. ind.: Designers international index
Dyabola: Dyabola
EBSCO Master.: EBSCO MasterFILE FullTEXT electronic database
ECO: Electronic collections online (OCLC) database
Ethno: Ethnoarts index
Exp.Acad.: Expanded Academic ASAP (The Gale Group) electronic database

Francis: FRANCIS (Institut de l'information scientifique et technique du Centre national de la recherche scientifique, Paris) electronic database
Gard.lit.: Garden literature: an index to periodical articles & book reviews
HAPI: Hispanic American periodicals index
Hist.abs.: Historical abstracts
Hum.ind.: Humanities index
Ibidem: Ibidem: Bibliographie zur Gegenwarts Kunst. Auswertung Internationaler Kunstzeitschriften und Tageszeitungen
I.B.Z.: Internationale Bibliographie der Zeitschriftenliteratur aus allen Gebieten des Wissens
Ind.hist.pres.per.: Index to historic preservation periodicals
Ind.legal per.: Index to legal periodicals
Int.photo.ind.: International photography index
Ind.art.Jewish.st.: Index of articles on Jewish studies
Legal jour.ind.: Legal journals index
LISA: Library & information science abstracts
Lib.lit.: Library literature
Legal res.ind.: Legal resource index
MLA: Modern language association bibliography
PerAbs: Periodical abstracts (University Microfilm International) electronic database
PerCont.ind.: Periodicals contents index (Chadwyck-Healey) electronic database
Photohi.: Photohistorica: literary index of the European Society for the History of Photography
Proquest: Proquest 5000 (Bell & Howell) electronic database
Rép.d'art: Répertoire d'art et d'archéologie
Repère: Repère: index analytique d'articles de périodiques de langue française
RILA: International repertory of the literature of art
RILM: RILM (Répertoire international de littérature musicale) abstracts of music
Rug text.arts: Rug and textile arts: a periodical index
Uncover: UnCover (CARL Corporation) electronic database
WilsonSelect: H.W. Wilson Select full-text electronic database

PART 1
CEASED TITLES, TITLE CHANGES, AND NEW SERIES TITLES

Q1 AARP: art and archaeology research papers [GLAH 1:Q1] (London), 1972–84. Continued by Environmental design: journal of the Islamic Environmental Design Research Centre (Como), 1, 1985– . (See GLAH 2:Q175).

Q2 ARIS: art research in Scandinavia [GLAH 1:Q2] (Lund, Sweden), v.1, 1969–78/79– ; becomes a series with nova ser., nr. 1, 1982, dealing with individual subjects (nova. ser., no.4, 1989 last vol. published).

Q3 ARLIS/NA newsletter [GLAH 1:Q4] (Tucson, Ariz.), v.1–9, no.6, Nov. 1972–Dec. 1981. Superseded by Art documentation, v.1, Feb.1982– . (See GLAH 2:Q101).

Q4 Albertina Studien: Jahresschrift der Graphischen Sammlung Albertina [GLAH 1:Q11] (Wien), Bd. 1–5/6, 1963–68. Ceased publication.

Q5 Alte und moderne Kunst [GLAH 1:Q12] (Wien), Jahrg.1–30, 1956–85. Ceased publication.

Q6 American Institute of Architects (A.I.A.) journal [GLAH 1:Q17] (Wash., D.C.), v.1–72, no.6, Jan. 1944–June 1983. Continued by: Architecture: the A.I.A. journal, v.72, no.7–v.85, no.12, July 1983–Dec. 1996; disaffiliated from the A.I.A. to become Architecture with v.86, no.1, Jan. 1997. (See GLAH 2:Q92).

Q7 Architects' yearbook [GLAH 1:Q37] (London), v.1–14, 1945–74. Ceased publication.

Q8 Arkhitektura SSSR [GLAH 1:Q55] (Moskva), 1933–48, 1951–no.4 (July/Aug. 1991). Ceased publication.

Q9 Art and artists [GLAH 1:Q61] (London), no.1–243, Apr. 1966–Dec. 1986. Absorbed by: The Artist (London) with v.102, issue 672, no.2, Feb. 1987.

Q10 Art international [GLAH 1:Q69] (Lugano, Switzerland), v.1–27, 1956–84. Ceased publication. Continued by Art International (Paris) no.1–14, autumn 1987–spring/summer 1991. (See GLAH 2:Q104).

Q11 The Art quarterly [GLAH 1:Q75] (N.Y.), v.1–37, winter 1938–spring 1975; new ser. v.1–2, no.2, autumn 1977–spring 1979. Ceased publication.

Q12 Artes de México [GLAH 1:Q85] (México), no.1–201/202, Oct./Nov. 1953–Abr./Mayo 1976; continued by Artes de México, nueva epoca, no.1, otoño 1988. (See GLAH 2:Q113).

Q13 Arts and architecture [GLAH 1:Q93] (Los Angeles), v.61, no.2–v.84, no.7/8, Feb. 1944–July/August 1967. Continued by Arts and architecture; new ser., v.1–6, no.4, fall 1981–1987/1988. (See GLAH 2:Q118).

Q14 Arts in society [GLAH 1:Q96] (Madison, Wis.), v.1–13, no.2, Jan. 1958–summer/fall 1976. Ceased publication.

Q15 Arts magazine [GLAH 1:Q98] (N.Y.), v.1–66, no.8, Nov. 1926–Apr. 1992. Ceased publication.

Q16 Artscanada [GLAH 1:Q99] (Toronto), v.1–24, n.248/249, Oct./Nov. 1943–Nov. 1982. Ceased publication. Continued by: Canadian art, 1984– . (See GLAH 2:Q141).

Q17 Biblical archaeologist [GLAH 1:Q107] (Cambridge), changed title to Near Eastern archaeology with v.61, no.1, March 1998.

Q18 La Biennale di Venezia [GLAH 1:Q108] (Venezia), [anno] 1–21 (no. 1–67/68), 1950–71. Ceased publication.

Q19 British Museum yearbook [GLAH 1:Q113] (London), v.1–4, 1976–80. Ceased publication.

Q20 Cahiers de la céramique, du verre et des arts du feu [GLAH 1:Q126] (Sèvres), n.1–59, 1955–77. Ceased publication.

Q21 Cahiers de l'art médiéval [GLAH 1:Q126] (Strasbourg), v.1–6, fasc.1, 1947–71/73. Ceased publication.

Q22 Centro Internazionale di Studi d'Architettura Andrea Palladio, bollettino [GLAH 1:Q131] (Vicenza), 1–24, 1959–82–87. Ceased publication.

Q23 Commentari [GLAH 1:Q134] (Roma), anno 1–28, no.4, 1950–77. Ceased publication. Continued by Commentari d'arte: rivista di critica e storia dell'arte, anno 1, 1995– . (See GLAH 2:Q150).

Q24 The Connoisseur [GLAH 1:Q138] (London), v.1–222, no.961, Dec.1901–Feb.1992. Ceased publication.

Q25 Copenhagen. Statens Museum for Kunst. Kunstmuseets årsskrift [GLAH 1:Q139] (København), 1–71, 1914–93. Ceased publication. Continued by Statens museum for kunst journal, v.1, 1997– (See GLAH 2:Q319).

Q26 La Critica d'arte [GLAH 1:Q144] (Firenze) v.1–8, ott. 1935–50; n.s. no.1, genn. 1954– . The journal is now up to series seven (See GLAH 2:Q157).

Q27 Dansk brugskunst: tidsskrift for kunsthåndvaerk og design [GLAH 1:Q145] (København), arg.41–43, 1968/69–72. Superseded by: B.I.D.; brugskunst og industriel design, (København), with v.44, 1973.

Q28 Dekorativnoe iskusstvo SSSR [GLAH 1:Q147] (Moskva), 1957–no.1, 1991– . Begins a new series in 1991 (See GLAH 2:Q163).

Q29 Derrière le miroir [GLAH 1:Q148] (Paris), n.1–253, Dec. 1946–Dec.1982. Continued by: Repères, Paris, Galerie Maeght, 1982– (See GLAH 2:Q299).

Q30 Design quarterly [GLAH 1:Q149] (Minneapolis), no.1–169, 1946–summer 1996. Ceased publication.

Q31 Deutsche Kunst und Denkmalpflege [GLAH 1:Q150] (Berlin), v.10–35, 1899–1933; n.F., 1–15, no. 7/8, 1934–42; Jahrg. 10–51, 1952–93. Continued by: Denkmalpflege, Jahrg.52, 1994– . (See GLAH 2:Q165).

Q32 Dresden. Staatliche Kunstsammlungen. Jahrbuch [GLAH 1:Q162], 1959–1970/71. Continued by Staatliche Kunstsammlungen Dresden, Beiträge und Berichte der Staatliche Kunstsammlungen Dresden, 1972–75, followed by Jahrbuch der Staatliche Kunstsammlungen Dresden, 1976/77– (See GLAH 2:Q218).

Q33 Gentsche bijdragen tot de kunstgeschiedenis [GLAH 1:Q175] (Antwerp) deel 1–26, 1934–1981/84. Changed to Gentse bijdragen tot de kunstgeschiedenis en de oudheidkunde, with deel 27, 1988. Title varies slightly.

Q34 Graz. Austria. Universität. Kunsthistorisches Institut. Jahrbuch, Bd.1–12, 1965–77 (GLAH 1:Q180]. Continued by Kunsthistorisches Jahrbuch Graz, with Bd. 13, 1978. (See GLAH 2:Q238).

Q35 Historic preservation [GLAH 1:Q182] (Wash., D.C.), v.4–48, no.3, spring 1952–May/June 1996. Continued by Preservation with v.48, no.4, July/August 1996.

Q36 Indian Society of Oriental Art Journal, [GLAH 1:Q185] (Calcutta), v.1–19; June 1933–1952/53; n.s. (v.1)–10; 1965/66–1978/79. Ceased publication.

Q37 L'information d'histoire de l'art [GLAH 1:Q186] (Paris), année 1–20, 1955/56–75. Ceased publication.

Q38 Istituto Nazionale di Archeologia e Storia dell'Arte, Rome. Rivista [GLAH 1:Q192] (Roma) , anno 1–9, 1929–42; nuova ser., anno 1–24, 1952–77. Continues with 3.ser., anno 1, 1978– . (See GLAH 2:Q305).

Q39 Jahrbuch der Hamburger Kunstsammlungen [GLAH 1:Q196] (Hamburg), Band.1–25, 1948–1980. Continued in two parts: 1.Idea: Jahrbuch der Hamburger Kunsthalle, neue Folge, Bd.1–10. München, Prestel, 1982–91, followed by Im Blickfeld, 1, 1994 - (See GLAH 2:Q207); 2. Jahrbuch des Museums für Kunst und Gewerbe Hamburg, neue Folge, Bd.1, 1982– . (See GLAH 2:Q219).

Q40 Kobijutsu: quarterly review of the fine arts [GLAH 1:Q210] (Tokyo), no.1–105, Jan. 1963–Feb. 1993. Ceased publication.

Q41 Kunst des Orients [GLAH 1:Q214] (Wiesbaden), Bd.1–12, 1950–1978/79. Ceased publication.

Q42 Die Kunst und das schöne Heim: Monatsschrift für Malerei, Plastik, Graphik, Architektur und Wohn Kultur [GLAH 1:Q215] (München), title varies,

Jahrg.47–96, Heft 3, Apr. 1949–Marz 1984. Ceased publication. Continued in Apr. 1984 (to 9/88) by Die Kunst [München: 1984], assuming its numbering. Absorbed by: Pan (Offenburg), 1992/4, then continued as Pan Spezial, 1–3, 1992 (See GLAH 2:Q273).

Q43 Das Kunstwerk: eine Zeitschrift über alle Gebiete der bildenden Kunst [GLAH 1:Q220] (Stuttgart), Jahrg. 1–44, no.4, Aug.1946–Dec.1991. Ceased publication.

Q44 Marsyas studies in the history of art [GLAH 1:Q233] (N.Y.), v.1–22, 1941–83/85. Ceased publication.

Q45 Les Monuments historiques de la France [GLAH 1:Q241] (Paris), v.1–4, 1936–39; nouv. sér., v.1–17, 1955–71; 1972–no.1, 1977; continued by:Monuments historiques: mh, no.101–106, 1977–Dec. 1979; Monuments historiques, no.107–202, 1980–Mai/Juin 1996. Ceased publication.

Q46 Museum [GLAH 1:Q245] (Paris and N.Y., UNESCO), v.1–44, no.4 (July 1948–92). Continued by: Museum international, with v.45, no.1, (= no.177), 1993, published for UNESCO by Blackwell, 1993– .

Q47 Oppositions: a journal for ideas and criticism in architecture [GLAH 1:Q262] (Cambridge, Mass.), n.1–26; Sept. 1973–spring 1984. Ceased publication.

Q48 Palladio; rivista di storia dell'architettura [GLAH 1:Q270] (Roma) anno 1–5, 1937–41; nuova ser., anno 1–24, 1951–77; terza ser. v.25–28, 1978–79; anno 3, 1980. Initiates a new series with anno 1 (giugno 1988). (See GLAH 2:Q272).

Q49 Pantheon: Internationale Zeitschrift fur Kunst/international art journal [GLAH 1:Q272] (München), Jahrg.1–37, 1928–79. Continued by Bruckmanns Pantheon, with Jahrg. 38, heft 3, Juli/Sept. 1980. With v.43, becomes a hardcover annual.

Q50 Paris. Musée National du Louvre. Laboratoire de Recherche des Musées de France. Annales [GLAH 1:Q274] (Paris), 1970–82. Ceased publication.

Q51 The Prairie school review [GLAH 1:Q278] (Palos Park, Ill.), v.1–13, no.4, 1964–76. Ceased publication.

Q52 Print collector: il conoscitore di stampe [GLAH 1:Q279] (Milano), n.1–14, Mar./Apr. 1973–Sept./Oct. 1975. Merged with: Quaderni del conoscitore di stampe to form: Conoscitore di stampe, nos.29–60; Nov./Dec. 1975–83.

Q53 Print collector's newsletter [GLAH 1:280] (N.Y.), v.1–27, no.2, Mar./Apr.1970–May/June 1996. Ceased publication. Continued by On paper: the journal of prints, drawings and photography, v.1–2, Sept./Oct. 1996–July/August 1998, then Art on paper, v.3, 1998– . (See GLAH 2:Q107).

Q54 Print review [GLAH 1:Q282] (N.Y.), no.1–20, 1973–85. Ceased publication.

Q55 Progressive architecture [GLAH 1:Q283] (Stamford, Conn.), v.26, no.10–v.76, no.12, Oct. 1945–Dec.1995. Ceased publication.

Q56 La Revue du Louvre et des musées de France [GLAH 1:Q301] (Paris), t.11, no.1–t.40, no.6, 1961–90, continued by Revue du Louvre: la revue des musées de France with 41. annee, 1, mars 1991.

Q57 Rivista d'arte [GLAH 1:Q303] (Firenze), anno 1–36, 1903–1961/1962. Ser.4, anno 37, 1984– . Suspended after anno 44, 1992. (See GLAH 2:Q304).

Q58 Roma. Università. Istituto di Storia dell'Architettura. Quaderni [GLAH 1:Q306] (Roma), n.1–73/78, 1953–66. Continued as a new series with nuova ser. fasc/1–10 (1983/87). (See GLAH 2:Q290).

Q59 Römisches Jahrbuch für Kunstgeschichte [GLAH 1:Q308] (Tübingen), Bd.1–23/24; 1937–88. Continued by: Römisches Jahrbuch der Bibliotheca Hertziana, with Bd.25, 1989.

Q60 Royal Institute of British Architects. London. Journal. [GLAH 1:Q310] (London). 3d series. v.1–67, no.6, 1894–Apr. 1960. Continued by RIBA journal, v.67, no.7–v.93, no.3, May 1960–Mar. 1986; followed by The Architect: journal of the Royal Institute of British Architects, v.93, no.4–v.95, no.10 (Apr.1986–Oct. 1987); then by Journal (Royal Institute of British Architects), v.95, no.11–v.100, no.8 (Nov. 1987–Aug. 1993), and finally by RIBA journal, with v.100, no.9, Sept. 1993.

Q61 Schweizerisches Institut für Kunstwissenschaft. Jahrbuch [GLAH 1:Q313] (Zürich), v.1–23/24, 1963–88. Ceased publication.

Q62 Società Piemontese di Archeologia e di Belle Arti, Bollettino [GLAH 1:Q318] (Torino), anno 1–19, no.2. 1917–35; nuova ser., anno 1–20, 1947–66. Begins new series with anno 35, 1981 (See GLAH 2:Q131).

Q63 Studio international [GLAH 1:Q331] (London), v.1–201, no.1020, Apr. 1893–July 1988. Ceased publication.

Q64 Victoria and Albert Museum yearbook [GLAH 1:Q340] (London), v.1–4, 1969–74. Ceased publication.

Q65 XXe siècle [GLAH 1:Q341] (Paris), année 1–2, no.1, mars 1938–39. Continued by XXe siècle: cahiers d'art, nuov. ser., n.1–59; juin 1951–sept. 1985. Ceased publication.

Q66 Werk/Archithese [GLAH 1:Q348] (St. Gallen), v.64–66, 1977–79 [v.1–60, 1914–73 as Das Werk; v.61–63, 1973–76 as Werk/oeuvre]. Split into: Werk, Bauen + Wohnen (Zurich, 1980-) (See GLAH 2:Q347) and Archithese (Niederteufen, 1980–) (See GLAH 2:Q94).

Q67 Zodiac: revue internationale d'architecture contemporaine [GLAH 1:Q356] (Milano), v.1–22; 1957–73; 1. semestre (1989)– . New series. Milan; Alfieri (See GLAH 2:Q354).

PART 2
NEW TITLES

Q68 A–IA. Sovremennoe russkoe iskusstvo = A–JA. Contemporary Russian art, 1–7, 1979–86. Elancourt, France, B. Karmashov. Semiannual.
Large-format English and Russian contemporary art journal specializing in dissident art and expatriate Russian artists living abroad. Serves to acquaint Russian artists with others working in mixed media, painting, sculpture, photography, and performance arts, and to provide a forum for Russian writers to express their artistic viewpoints. Contemporary Russian artists are reviewed with occasional articles on modern movement artists.

Q69 A + U: Architecture & urbanism, v.1, 1971– . Tokyo, A + U Publishing. Monthly.
Alternative title: Kenchiku to Toshi. Stunning Japanese and English bilingual journal featuring contemporary architects and architectural projects. Monographic in scope, with detailed coverage of major architects and contemporary themes. Glossy, full-page color plates. Supplemental issues called Extra edition (begun in 1977) and Special issues (begun in 1993), focus on modern and contemporary architects and their projects. Text in Japanese with English summaries. Occasional yearly indexes. Arch.per.ind.; Art index (1986–); Avery; Biog.ind.; Curr.Cont.A&H.; Curr.Cont.Connect.

Q70 AA Files: annals of the Architectural Association School of Architecture, v.1, winter 1981/82– . London, Architectural Association. Semiannual, 1981–83; three issues a year, 1984– .
Continues: AA Quarterly. v.1–13, no.4, winter 1968/69–July/Dec. 1982. Scholarly and sophisticated publication of the Architectural Association in London by distinguished architects and architectural historians, providing a forum for its many activities, including lectures, seminars, exhibitions, and juried shows. Articles cover architectural history, contemporary architecture, city planning, and theory. Also included are discussions, signed book and exhibition reviews. Index no.1–22, (1981–91). Arch.per.ind.; Art index (1998–); ARTbib.mod.; Avery; BHA; Francis; RILA; Uncover.

Q71 AAM: Archives d'architecture moderne, no. 11–40, juillet 1977–mai 1990. Bruxelles, Archives d'architecture moderne. Quarterly.
Continues: Bulletin d'information mensuel: Archives d'architecture moderne, no.1–8, oct.1975–mai 1976; then, Bulletin d'information mensuel, no.9–10, déc. 1976–avril 1977. Nicely realized journal devoted to modern European architecture, its theory and criticism, as well as the conservation of architectural documents. Issues are thematic. Book reviews. In French and English. Arch.per.ind.; Avery; BHA.

Q72 AFT: semestrale dell'Archivio fotografico toscano, anno 1, maggio 1985– . Prato, Italy, Gli Archivio. Semiannual.
House organ of the Tuscan Photographic Archive in Prato, presenting the history, theory, and methodology of photography, as well as its preservation, collections, and conservation methods. Includes signed book reviews. In Italian, with short summaries in English. Table of contents to 1–19 (1985–94) in: History of photography, v.20, no.1, spring 1986, p.69–72. BHA.

Q73 AICARC: bulletin of the Archives & Documentation Centers for Modern & Contemporary Art, v.10, no.18 (1) 1983– (no.2/1994 last published). Zurich, International Association of Art Critics (IAAC/AICA) with the assist. of UNESCO. Semiannual.
Continues: AICARC bulletin (Lund, Sweden), no.1–17, 1974–82. Society bulletin of the International Association of Art Critics, documenting both the contemporary art scene in which their annual conference takes place, as well as archives and documentation centers for modern and contemporary art worldwide. Issues are thematic and have covered documentation centers in Greece, Latin America, Russia, as well as the current state of contemporary art in such countries as Belgium and Austria. Authors are prominent art critics, historians, and librarians. Articles in English or French. ARTbib.mod.; BHA; Francis; Ibidem.

Q74 Abitare, no.1–147,1960–luglio/agosto 1976; nuova serie, no.148, sett. 1976– . Milano, Abitare. Ten issues a year.
International, glossy journal of contemporary architecture, interior and industrial design, housing, building, furniture design, gardens, lighting, and the latest in design accessories. Book, exhibition and magazine reviews, competitions, and award information, as well as design guide supplements and yearly indexes. Published in Italian and English with resumes in French, Spanish, and Dutch. Beginning in 1977, supplements accompany some issues. Separately published annual indexes beginning in 1981. Arch.per.ind.; Art index (1984–); ARTbib.mod.; Avery; Clo.T.A.ind.; Des.&Ap.A.ind.

Q75 Abstract, 1987/88–. N.Y., Graduate School of Architecture, Planning and Preservation, Columbia Univ. Annual.
Monographic annual on architecture, providing a summary of student and faculty work of the past year. Essays are organized around an exhibition of student projects. Avery.

Q76 Achademia Leonardi Vinci: journal of Leonardo studies & bibliography of Vinciana, v.1–10, 1988–97. Firenze, Giunti. Annual.

Ed.: Carlo Pedretti.

Variant title: ALV journal. Scholarly, impressive yearbook from the Armand Hammer Center for Leonardo Studies at UCLA. Befitting the subject, the journal is beautifully produced, in large format, on laid paper, with fine color plates in the back of each vol. Articles, bibliographies, and archival reports are written by leading international scholars. Articles published in English, French, German, or Italian. "A bibliophile's delight."—*Review* by Max Marmor, Renaissance quarterly, v.47, no.3, autumn 1993, p.721–23. Art Ar.Te.Abs.; Avery; BHA; Francis.

Q77 Affiche, no.1–16, 1992–96. Arnhem, The Netherlands, Wabnitz Ed. Quarterly.

Highly visual international journal devoted to the poster, with articles on its design and history, as well as poster designers, and museums and galleries devoted to poster art. Exhibition reviews and auctions. Early issues in Dutch and English; later ones in English only. Color illustrations. ARTbib.mod.; Des.&Ap.A.ind.

Q78 Afterimage: the journal of media arts and cultural criticism, v.1, 1972– . Rochester, N.Y., Visual Studies Workshop. Ten issues a year, 1972–95; bimonthly, 1995– .

Also available on microfilm: Ann Arbor, UMI.

Significant tabloid publication on photography, independent film, video and computer media, with articles, interviews, conference reports, notices of NEA grants to visual arts organizations, job announcements, exhibition calendars, and book reviews. Annual indexes in first issue of following year. Acad.Search; Art full; Art index (1984–); ARTbib.mod.; Article1st; BHA; Bk.rev.ind.; Contents1st; Exp.Acad.; Ibidem; Int.photo.ind.; PerAbs; ContentsIndx; Photohi.; Proquest; RILA; WilsonSelect.

Q79 American art. v.5, no.1–2, winter/spring 1991– . N.Y., Oxford Univ. Pr. in assoc. with the National Museum of American Art, Smithsonian Institution, Wash., D.C. Quarterly. Publisher varies.

Exec. Dir.: Elizabeth Broun.

Also available on microfilm: Ann Arbor, UMI.

Continues: Smithsonian studies in American art, v.1–4, 1987–90, and has undergone significant changes in format and intent since then. "While the fine arts are still the journal's primary focus, its scope has been expanded to include all aspects of the cultural history of this country."—*Review*, Art documentation, v.12, no.1, spring 1993, p.36. Scholarly articles on the arts in America from colonial to the contemporary period, not specifically limited to the Smithsonian Institution's holdings. The journal offers an interdisciplinary and broadly based approach to American art. Annual index to the complete run. Acad.Search; Am.H.&L; Art index (1994–); ARTbib.mod.; BHA; EBSCO Master; Francis; Hist.abs.; Hum.ind.; Per.Abs.; Proquest; Uncover.

Q80 American ceramic circle journal, v.6, 1988– . N.Y., American Ceramic Circle. Annual.

Formerly: American ceramic circle bulletin, no.1–5, 1970/71–1986. Scholarly publication covering the spectrum in ceramic studies. International in scope, with articles on pottery, porcelain, patronage, and collecting. Some vols. have distinctive titles. BHA; Rép.d'art.

Q81 American furniture, v.1, 1993– . Milwaukee, Chipstone Fdn. (Distr. by Univ. Pr. of New England). Annual.

Scholarly journal dedicated to American furniture made or used in the Americas from the 17th century to the present, covering conservation, connoisseurship, historic techniques, and artisans work. Also includes signed book reviews, indexes, and records extensive bibliographies in back of books, and catalogs published on furniture. Art index (1998–); BHA.

Q82 American Indian art magazine, v.2, no.3, summer 1977– . Scottsdale, Mary G. Hamilton. Quarterly. Publisher varies.

Continues: American Indian art, v.1–2, no.2, autumn 1975–spring 1977. Lavishly illustrated journal documenting, in a sensitive and intelligent way, both the traditional and contemporary art forms of Native Americans, including painting, carving, beadwork, textiles, basketry, jewelry, and metalwork. Contains lengthy signed book and exhibition reviews as well as calendar of events and auction information. Index v.1–12 (1977–87) in v.13, no.1 (winter 1987). Am.H.&L.; Anth.ind.; Art index (1984–); ARTbib.curr.; ARTbib.mod.; Article1st; Clo.T.A.ind.; Contents1st; Francis; Hist.abs.; Per.ContentsIndx.; RILM; Rug text.arts; Uncover.

Q83 Anales del Instituto de Investigaciones Estéticas, 1, 1937– . México, Universidad Nacional Autónomia de México. Irregular to 1994; semiannual, 1995– .

Significant journal on Mexican art. Vast coverage given to well- and lesser-known Mexican artists, architecture, book arts; providing extensive articles and archival documentation when needed. Occasional coverage of non-Mexican artists, as well as the other arts, including Mexican literature, theatre, dance, and music. A section on exhibition catalogs, issuing from Mexican museums and galleries, appeared from 1938 to 1972. Black-and-white and color plates, indexes, signed book reviews, calendar of events and activities of the Institute for the year. Supplements accompany some vols. Mainly in Spanish; lately, occasional articles in English. Am.H.&L.; HAPI; Hist.abs.

———. Índice general, núms. 1–70 (1937–1997). México, Universidad Nacional Autónomia de México, 1998. 135p.

Q84 Ancient Mesoamerica, v.1, 1990– . Cambridge, Mass., Cambridge Univ. Pr. Semiannual.

"The first journal devoted exclusively to Pre-Columbian archaeology, art history, and ethnohistory in the Mesoamerican region [with] reports emerging from the numerous archaeological excavations and surveys currently taking place in the region."—*Advert.* Scholarly and well-presented, it gathers together several diverse fields of study. Primarily in English, with contributions in Spanish (with English summaries). Anth.ind.; Anth.lit.; Article1st; Contents1st; HAPI; Uncover.

Q85 Andon: Bulletin of the Society for Japanese Arts and Crafts/Vereniging voor Japanse Kunst, no.1, 1981– . The Hague, The Society. Quarterly. Subtitle varies.
Short, scholarly articles covering traditional Japanese arts and crafts. Issues tend to be thematic, and include: Ukiyo-e, Japanese prints, print collectors, netsuke, ceramics, lacquer, the decorative arts, and the Japanese influence on foreign artists and architects. BHA.

Q86 Annales d'histoire de l'art et d'archéologie: publication annuelle de la Section d'histoire de l'art et d'archéologie de l'Université libre de Bruxelles, 1, 1979– . Bruxelles, l'Université. Annual.
Small format journal serving as a forum for articles by students and faculty of the school on all aspects of art, architecture, archeology. Includes a section in back called "Chronique," offering lists of doctoral and master recipients from the Section d'histoire de l'art et d'archéologie, as well as publications and activities of members of the school and signed book reviews. Illustrated with black-and-white and color illustrations. In French, occasional English. BHA; Dyabola; RILA; RILM.

Q87 Annali (Fondazione Roberto Longhi) / Fondazione di studi di storia dell'arte Roberto Longhi. 1, 1984– . Pisa, Pacini. Irregular.
Hardcover vols. on research conducted by scholars at the Fondazione who have visited since its founding in 1971. Areas covered include Italian art history and patrimony, frescoes, and architecture, from the 1400s to the 1800s. Included in back are full-page black-and-white plates, a list of scholars, their papers, and when these articles appeared in Paragone (see GLAH 1:Q273), from 1971 to 1984. In Italian (occasional French). BHA; Dyabola.

Q88 Antiek: Tijdschrift voor liefhebbers en kenners van oude kunst en kunstnijverheid. Jaarg.1–31, nr.10, juni/juli 1966–mei 1997. Lochem, The Netherlands, De Tijdstroom. Ten issues a year.
"A journal for amateurs and connoisseurs of old art and decorative arts" (subtitle). Articles cover pottery, metalwork, textiles, architecture, sculpture, and painting, with regular sections on sales auctions, as well as signed book and exhibition reviews and art dealers fairs. In Dutch, with English summaries. Art Ar.Te.Abs.; ARTbib.curr.; ARTbib.mod.; BHA; RILA.

Q89 Antologia di belle arti, N.1–20, Mar. 1977–83; nuova serie, N.21/22, 1984– . Torino, Allemandi. Quarterly (slightly irregular; many numbers combined). Publisher varies.
Ed. by Federico Zeri and Alvar González-Palacios.

Suspended publication 1982–83. Scholarly, hardcover journal of connoisseurship, in Italian, English, and French. Later vols. are thematic, and have covered neoclassicism and sculpture, mainly over several issues. Well-illustrated. Avery; BHA; Francis; Rép.d'art; RILA.

Q90 Archaeological review from Cambridge, v.2, no.1, spring 1983– . Cambridge, Eng., Cambridge Univ., Dept. of Archaeology. Semiannual.
Continues: Archaeological reviews from Cambridge, v.1, no.1–2, July 1981–Jan. 1982. Thematic journal serving as a platform for the publication of all types of research related to archeology, particularly research in progress and analyses of theoretical aspects of the discipline. Also includes signed book reviews. Produced by graduate students in the Department. Anth.lit.; BHA; Francis.

Q91 Architectural design: A.D., v.38, no.5, May 1968– . London, Academy Ed.. (Distr. by VCH Pub. Inc., Deerfield Beach, Fla.). Monthly, 1968–80; bimonthly, 1981–. Publisher varies.
Ed.: Andreas Papadakis.

Variant title: AD. Continues: Architectural design and construction, 1930–36; Architectural record of design and construction, 1937; Architectural design and construction; 1938–46; Architectural design, 1947–1968. Valuable forum for contemporary theory of architecture and art. Issues are thematic and guest edited; articles are well-illustrated, with an international viewpoint. Areas covered include commercial and residential architecture, interior design, and furniture. Some issues are monographic in scope. In 1977, a regular feature titled "A.D. profile" (beginning in 1985, "Architectural design profile") was begun. Focusing on contemporary architects, issues, and trends, it forms part of the regular issues of the journal, as well as being available separately. Each profile is numbered, often guest-edited, and thematic in scope, with essays on individual architects and trends in contemporary architecture. Other features include signed book reviews, design awards, calendar of events, books received, conferences, as well as occasional supplements and special issues. Book reviews; indexes. A French-language edition of A.D. was begun in 1980. Arch.per.ind.; Art index (1984–); ArtHum.; Article1st; Avery; Brit.tech.ind.; Clo.T.A.ind.; Contents1st; Curr.Cont.A.&H.; Curr.Cont.Connect; Uncover.

Q92 Architecture, v.86, no.1, Jan. 1997– . N.Y., BPI Communications. Monthly.
Also available on microfilm: Ann Arbor, UMI.

Continues: American Institute of Architects (A.I.A. journal (Wash., D.C.), v.1–72, no.6, Jan. 1944–June 1983; Architecture: the A.I.A. journal, v.72, no.7–85, no.12, July 1983–Dec. 1996. Absorbed Architectural technology in Oct. 1986 (See Part 1 and GLAH 1:Q17).

Newly independent journal of architecture, recently disassociated from the American Institute of Architects. Now with a redesigned look, it continues the vol. numbering of its previous title. Inspired by the defunct Progressive architecture (see Part 1), also owned by BPI Communications, Architecture will present the winners of the Progressive Architecture Awards, and offer in-depth reporting on practice, technology, education, and design. Serves as an unofficial voice for the profession. Earlier vols. included annual indexes. Acad.Search; Arch.per.ind.; Art index (1984–); Article1st; Avery; Contents1st; Curr.Cont.A&H; Curr.Cont.Connect; Exp.Acad.; Gard.lit.; PerCont.ind.; Proquest; Uncover.

Q93 Architettura, storia e documenti: rivista semestrale di storia dell'architettura del Centro di studi storico-archivistici per la storia dell'arte e dell'architettura medioevale e moderna. no.1–1/2, 1985–90. Venezia, Marsilio. Semiannual.
Journal of architectural history, particularly the Italian Renaissance and Baroque periods, focusing primarily on the historiography of architecture and the documentation of its archival records. In Italian, with short English summaries, signed book reviews. Arch.per.ind.; Avery.

Q94 Archithese, 1–80, 1980– . Niederteufen, Switzerland, Niggli. Bimonthly.
Continues, in part: Werk/Archithese [GLAH 1:Q348] (St. Gallen), v.64–66, 1977–79 [v.1–60, 1914–73 as Das Werk; v.61–63, 1973–76 as Werk/oeuvre]. Split into: Werk, Bauen + Wohnen (Zurich, 1980–), itself is a merger in 1980 of Werk and Bauen + Wohnen, and Archithese (See Part 1 and GLAH 2:Q347). Issues for 1980– , also called 10. Jahrg.– . A French version with same title published in Lausanne (no.2–20, 1971–76). Issued by the Verband Freierwerbender Schweizer Architekten. Offers pragmatic articles and timely information for the practicing architect. Each issue has a distinctive title. In German. Arch.per.ind.; ARTbib.mod.; Art index (1984–); Avery.

Q95 Architronic: the electronic journal of architecture, v.1–8, no.1, Dec. 1992–Jan. 1999. Kent, Ohio, Kent State Univ., School of Architecture and Environmental Design. Three issues a year with irregular supplements.
Electronic journal on architecture available on the internet. Architronic covers a broad spectrum of topics within architecture and serves as a platform for the discussion of scholarly and critical issues as well as encouraging the computerized exchange of ideas within the architectural community. Includes articles, conference reports, signed book reviews, and notices. "The overall quality of the contributions and the apparent efforts of the editorial board to expand the range of scholarly discussion make Architronic a useful addition to the field."—*Review*, Art documentation, v.13, no.1, spring 1994, p.42. Since 1994, issues include an annual listing of books taken from the SAH (Society of Architectural Historians) newsletter booklist. Avery.

Q96 Art & antiques, v.3, no.1–v.6, no.6, Jan./Feb. 1980–Sept./Oct. 1983; Premier issue Mar. 1984– . Mt. Morris, Ill., Trans World Publications. Bimonthly, 1978–83; Ten issues a year, 1984– . Publisher varies.
Also available on microfilm: Ann Arbor, UMI.
Suspended Nov. 1983–Feb. 1984.
Continues: American art & antiques, v.1–2, July/Aug.1978–Nov./Dec. 1979. Incorporates: Antique monthly in 1994. Authoritative and inviting journal on the art of collecting, geared to the educated general public. Includes information on where to buy art works and on collectors and decorating, with essays by well-known writers and excellent photographs. Signed exhibition and book reviews. Am.H&L; Art Ar.Te.Abs.; Art index (1986–); ARTbib.mod.; Article1st; Avery; BHA; Clo.T.A.ind.; Contents1st; Francis; Hist.abs.; Hum.ind.; Ind.hist.pres.per.; RILM; Uncover.

Q97 Art & design, v.1–12, Feb. 1985–Dec. 1997. London, AD Ed. Ltd. Monthly, 1985–86; bimonthly, 1987–97.
Ed.: Andreas Papadakis.
Glossy international art journal, created to complement its sister publication, Architectural design (see GLAH 2:Q91). Well-illustrated, with broad coverage given to architecture, design, urbanism, graphic design, furniture, music, fashion, and food. After v.2, the journal becomes bimonthly and thematic in coverage. Recent issues have covered Latin American art, art from Eastern Europe, installation art, photography, and the visual arts. Also included are exhibition and gallery listings, sales information, signed book and exhibition reviews, and symposia. Each issue contains an original artist's lithograph. "This magazine has great appeal for keeping readers abreast of art world happenings."—*Review*, Art documentation, v.5, no.2, summer 1986, p.93. Related to Art & design profile (See GLAH 2:R8). Arch.per.ind.; Art index (1994–96); Article1st; Avery; BHA; Contents1st; Des.&Ap.A.ind.; Des.int.ind.; Uncover.

Q98 Art, antiquity and law, v.1, Feb. 1996– . The Hague, Kluwer Law International; Leicester, Institute of Art and Law. Quarterly.
International journal of cultural property, copyright, forgery of antiquities, art thefts, return of indigenous artifacts, and other issues and important rulings related to art and law. Articles are by legal experts and art dealers from throughout the world. Published jointly by Kluwer Law International and the Institute of Art and Law in Leicester. Includes book reviews. Legal jour.ind.

Q99 Art bulletin of Nationalmuseum Stockholm, v.1/2, 1994/95– . Stockholm, Nationalmuseum. Annual.
Continues: Nationalmuseum bulletin, v.1–18, 1977–94. Museum bulletin highlighting the collections of painting, sculpture, prints, decorative and book arts, and reports on the extensive restoration and rebuilding of the museum. Mainly in English, occasionally French or Swedish. Art index (1998–); ARTbib.mod.; BHA; Clo.T.A.ind.; Francis; RILA.

Q100 Art criticism, v.1, spring 1979– . Stony Brook, Dept. of Art, State Univ. of New York at Stony Brook. Quarterly, 1979; Three issues a year, 1985/86–1989/90; semiannual, 1990/91– .
Eds: Lawrence Alloway and Donald B. Kuspit. Suspended 1982–84.
Serious, small-format journal that encourages the practice and writing of art criticism. Articles (approximately seven per issue) are unillustrated and written by art historians on subjects of their own choosing, although modern art predominates. Art index (1998–); ARTbib.mod.; ArtHum.; Article1st; Avery; BHA; Contents1st; Curr.Cont.A&H; Curr.Cont.Connect; Clo.T.A. ind.; Francis; RILA; Uncover.

Q101 Art documentation: bulletin of the Art Libraries Society of North America, v.1, spring 1982– . Raleigh, N.C., Art Libraries Society of North America (AR-

LIS/NA). Quarterly, 1982–95; semiannual, 1996– . Place of publication varies.
Also available on microfilm: Ann Arbor, UMI.

Continues: ARLIS/NA newsletter, v.1–9, no.6, Nov. 1972–Dec. 1981 (see GLAH 1:Q4). Professional journal of the Art Libraries Society of North America (ARLIS/NA), serving art librarians, visual resource curators, and library science students. Began as a newsletter of timely information, reflecting the concerns of its members and the objectives of the society, developing over time into a refereed journal of noteworthy articles, mainly written by society members. The journal was later augmented by a newsletter, ARLIS/NA update. Art documentation articles cover such subjects as authority control, copyright, cataloging, image technology, on-line database searching, library management, and security. Regular features have included conference proceedings, government documents, publications received (for later review), and extensive, signed book reviews, many of these columns now appearing on the society's website. Annual indexes located in first issue of each vol. after 1987. A.D.P.; ARTbib.mod.; Article1st; BHA; Contents1st; Des.&Ap.A. ind.; Des.int.ind.; Francis; LISA; Lib.lit.; Uncover.

______. Cumulative index, v.1–6 (1982–87), compiled by Lynette Korenic. Tucson, The Society, 1988. 44p.

Q102 Art history: journal of the Association of Art Historians, v.1, Mar. 1978– . Oxford and Boston, Blackwell. Quarterly, 1978–98; Five issues a year, 1999– . Publisher, place of publication varies.
Eds.: Marcia Pointon and Paul Binski.

Also available on microfilm: Ann Arbor, UMI.

Well-respected and scholarly English language publication of the Association of Art Historians, a U.K.-based organization founded in 1974 to promote art history locally and internationally. The journal offers a platform for original ideas and personal opinion on all aspects of art history, including architecture, design history, photography, and non-Western art. Current plans call for a special issue to be published once a year, both as a number of the journal and as a part of a series published by Blackwell titled Art history book. Includes extensive book reviews, and conference reports. Annual indexes in last issue of each year. Index to first 11 vols. in v.12, no.2 1989; annual thereafter. Also available on the internet by subscription. Acad.Search; Am.H&L; Arch.per.ind.; Art index (1986–); ARTbib.curr.; ARTbib.mod.; ArtHum.; Article1st; Avery; BHA; B.H.I.; Biog.ind.; Contents1st; Curr.Cont.A&H; Curr.Cont.Connect Clo.T.A.ind.; Des.&Ap.A.ind.; Des.int.ind.; Dyabola; EBSCO Master; ECO; Exp.Acad.; Francis; Hist.abs.; Hum.ind.; I.B.Z.; PerAbs; Rép.d'art; RILA; RILM; Uncover.

Q103 Art in America: annual guide to galleries, museums, artists, Aug. 1982– . N.Y., Neal-Schuman; Marion, Ohio, Art in America, Inc., Annual (appearing as August issue of Art in America).
1982 issue appeared as a separate publication, published by Neal/Schuman. Useful directory to the contemporary art scene drawn from information received each year via questionnaire from more than 2,100 institutions in the United States. Helpful for locating museum addresses, information on the latest exhibits, and whether a catalog to an exhibition was produced. Information is presented alphabetically by state, then city. Indexes to artists, galleries, and museums. Art index; Article1st; BHA; Contents1st; EBSCO Master; PerAbs.; Uncover.

Q104 Art international, no.1–14, autumn 1987–spring/summer 1991. Paris, Archive Pr. Quarterly.
Also available on microfilm: Ann Arbor, UMI.

Continues: Art international (Lugano, Switzerland), v.1–27; 1956–84 (See Part 1 and GLAH 1:Q69), a periodical of the same title published between 1956 and 1984 by ed. Michael Peppiatt. The journal continued for a few more years under the editorship of James Fitzsimmons, who maintained its coverage of international contemporary art and its criticism, expanding it to include interviews and contributions from artists as well as art critics. A.D.P.; ARTbib.curr.; ARTbib.mod.; ArtHum.; Art index (1984–91); Avery; Ibidem; PerCont.ind.; Rép.d'art; RILA; Uncover.

Q105 Art New Zealand, no.1, Aug./Sept.1976– . Auckland, Art Magazine Press. Bimonthly, 1976–77; quarterly, 1977– . Publisher varies.
Filling a gap created by the demise of Art in New Zealand at the end of the 1940s, this national art magazine presents thoughtful and intelligent articles on modern and contemporary New Zealand art, Maori art, photography, folk art, collections, as well as on theater and cinema. Publishes accounts of the annual Sydney Biennale. Book reviews, indexes. ARTbib.curr.; ARTbib.mod.; BHA; Des.&Ap.A.ind.; RILM; Uncover.

Q106 Art nexus: the nexus between Latin America and the rest of the world, no.1, mayo 1991– . Bogotà, Colombia, Arte en Colombia. (Distr. by Howard Karno Books, Valley Center, Calif., and Total Circulation Services, Hackensack, N.J.). Quarterly. Subtitle varies.
Continues: Arte en Colombia (Edición internacional), no.1–46, 1976–91. Beginning with no.5– , issues carry also numbering for Arte en Colombia no.51– . Considered one of the most significant art journals in Latin America, covering contemporary art, architecture, film, and photography. Since 1991, it has developed from the national art magazine of Colombia into one that covers all Latin America. Also available in Spanish under title, Arte en Columbia. Articles in English are translated from Spanish. Book and exhibition reviews. Art full; Art index (1994–); ARTbib.curr.; ARTbib.mod.; BHA; Biog.ind.; Francis; HAPI :WilsonSelect.

Q107 Art on paper, v.3, no.1, Sept./Oct. 1998– . N.Y., Fanning Pub. Co. Bimonthly.
Publisher and Ed.-in-Chief: Gabriella B. Fanning.

Continues Print collector's newsletter, v.1–27, no.2, Mar./Apr.1970–May/June 1996 (See Part 1 and GLAH 1:Q280); On paper: the journal of prints, drawings and photography, v.1–2, Sept./Oct. 1996–July/Aug. 1998. Finely printed journal expanding the scope of Print collector's newsletter, to include all works on paper, including photography. Ca. seven short articles per issue by well-known scholars and critics cover both contemporary graphic artists and the old masters; critical essays; collections, information on printmakers, photographers, makers of artists' books; with interviews, reviews of prints and multiples, and signed book reviews, artists books, and auction sales. Extensive calendar of events. A supplemental publication titled Hands on paper was begun in November 1997, dealing with issues of digitization. It has since been superseded (in April 1998) by Artbyte, a substantial publication on the digital arts. Art index; ARTbib.curr.; ARTbib.mod.; BHA.

Q108 Art reference services quarterly: ARSQ, v.1, fall 1991– . Binghamton, N.Y., Haworth Pr. Quarterly (lately irregular).

Also available on microfilm: Ann Arbor, UMI.

Ed.: Tinsley E. Silcox.

Refereed journal on a wide variety of practical and theoretical issues concerning art reference services, bibliographic control, and computer applications and service needs associated with architectural and visual arts libraries. Articles are by respected art librarians and visual resource curators. "Has the potential to be a valuable source for a fairly wide range of art information professionals."—*Review*, Art documentation, v.12, no.3, fall 1993, p.139. Includes signed book reviews and references to reviews in other journals. Art Ar.Te.Abs.; BHA; Des.&Ap.A.ind.; LISA; Uncover.

Q109 Arte documento: rivista di storia e tutela dei beni culturali, 1, 1980– . Monfalcone, Italy, Edizioni della Laguna. Annual. Place of publication, publisher varies.

Lavish annual on the patrimony and conservation treatment of art objects in Italy, published in assoc. with the art history department at the Univ. of Udine. Covers all the arts: painting, sculpture, graphics, urban planning, mainly from Medieval to Baroque periods. Scholarly articles in Italian, French, and English, with English summaries. Color plates. Special issues have been published, including one on Titian (in 1992). Occasional supplementary issues titled Libri extra. BHA; Francis.

Q110 Arte medievale: periodico internazionale di critica dell'arte medievale, n.1–2, 1983–85; 2. ser., anno.2, n.1, 1987– . Roma, Istituto della Enciclopedia Italiana. (Distr. by Licosa, Florence). Semiannual. Publisher varies.

Ed.: Angiola Maria Romanini.

Scholarly journal written by an international circle of medievalists covering all aspects of medieval art, including manuscripts, architecture, and painting. Articles in English, French, German and Italian, with summaries in English and Italian. Profusely illustrated. Signed book and exhibition reviews, conference reports, and notices of articles appearing in other art historical journals. Avery; BHA; Dyabola; Ind.art.Jewish.st.; RILM.

Q111 Arte tessile: rivista-annuario del Centro italiano per lo studio della storia del tessuto, N.1, febbr. 1990- (N.4, 1993 last published). Firenze, Edifir. Annual.

Lavish, scholarly journal on the history of textile manufacturing and fabrics, including embroidery, tapestries, liturgical vestments, and theatrical costumes. Published by C.I.S.S.T., which was founded in 1979 to unite scholars and students and to save and study textiles. Articles cover a variety of topics, from a study of jeans to processional costumes of the 18th century. Bibliographies of fashion and costume are included. Articles in Italian with English summaries in back. Book reviews, news, and exhibition events. BHA; Francis.

Q112 Artefactum, Nr.1–53, Dec. 1983/Jan. 1984–autumn 1994. Antwerpen, Belgium, Artefactum. Bimonthly, 1983–86; five issues a year, 1987–92; quarterly, 1993–94.

Journal of contemporary art in Europe serving as a forum for new works of art, with short articles, essays, exhibition reviews, calendar of events, as well as signed book reviews. A regular feature called "Catalogus", on issues related to the publishing of exhibition catalogs, as well as a selective list of them, appeared regularly from nrs. 1 to 24. Articles in French, English, Dutch or German. Index to 1988–93 (nrs. 25–49) in nr.50, 1993/94. Art index (1994); ARTbib.curr.; ARTbib.mod.; BHA; Francis; RILA; RILM.

Q113 Artes de México, nueva epoca, no.1, otoño 1988– . México, D.F., Artes de México y del Mundo, S.A. Quarterly.

Suspended June 1976–1987.

Continues: Artes de México, no.1–201/202, Oct./Nov. 1953–abr./mayo 1976. (See Part 1 and GLAH 1:Q85). Highly visual journal on Mexican art and architecture from prehistory to modern times with articles by leaders in the field. With this new series, there is more emphasis on modern art, film, and photography. Thematic in coverage and in a larger format than previously, with full-page color illustrations. American edition contains English summaries. Book lists. Anth.ind.; Art index (1994–); ARTbib.mod.; ArtHum.; BHA; HAPI (1970–); RILM.

———. Index: Indice de la revista Artes de México, 1a. época, números 1–60, 1953–1965, edited by Elsa Barberena Blásquez. México, Universidad Nacional Autónoma de México, 1982. 301p.

Q114 Artext, no.68, February–April 2000– . Los Angeles, Foundation for International Art Criticism. Quarterly. Place of publication, publisher, frequency varies.

Continues: Art/text, no. 56–67, Feb.–Apr.1997–Nov. 1999/ Jan. 2000; Art & text, no. 1–55, autumn 1981–Oct. 1996. Variant title: A & T. Quality journal of contemporary art, photography, video, film, and performance art scene, mainly in the galleries, with another section on gallery exhibits worldwide. Emphasis is on Australia from where the journal is co-published, but good coverage given to other countries as well. Extensive exhibition reviews. Occasional special issues. Art full; Art index (1994–); ARTbib.mod.; BHA; Francis; Uncover; WilsonSelect.

Q115 Artibus et historiae: an art anthology, N.1, 1980– . Krakow, IRSA. (Distr. by Polnische Buchhandlung,

Vienna). Semiannual. Place of publication, subtitle varies.
Ed.: Josef Grabski.

Interdisciplinary, scholarly, lavishly produced hardcover journal published by the International Institute for Art Historical Research (IRSA) located in Venice. The journal presents unique approaches to analyzing western art history, combining it with such fields as philosophy, psychology, literature, and sociology. Articles cover a variety of topics within art history, including photography, cinema, and film, and are written by an international group of scholars. In English, French, German, and Italian, with summaries in English. Index to numbers 1 to 26 (1980–92) in number 27. Related to the series title, Bibliotheca Artibus et historiae (See GLAH 2:R18). Art index (1994–); ARTbib.mod.; Avery; BHA; Francis; I.B.Z.; Rép.df; RILA; RILM.

Q116 Artista: critica dell'arte in Toscana, 1, 1989– . Firenze, Le Lettere. (Distr. by Licosa, Florence). Annual.
Scholarly hardcover annual on the art of Tuscany. Covers all periods of Florentine painting, architecture photography, video, and theater; works housed in Florentine churches and palaces, as well as artists influenced by Florence and Tuscany. In Italian. BHA; Francis.

Q117 Artpress, no.1, déc.1972/jan. 1973– . Paris, Art Press. Eleven issues a year (slightly irregular). Publisher varies.
Variant title: Art press. Continues: Art press, no.1–22, déc. 1972/jan. 1973–jan./fév. 1976; Art press international (Paris, EUROPROM), nouv. sér., no.1–33, été 1976–nov. 1979. Upbeat journal on the contemporary European art scene, covering art, architecture, cinema, music, theater, video, and dance. Important for its thought-provoking articles and critical exchange of ideas, unhampered by commercial dictates. Includes interviews, articles, critical signed reviews of books and new art periodicals, and extensive exhibition calendars. In the mid-1980s, unnumbered issues called Art press spécial were published on thematic topics (i.e., dance, design, theater). Starting in Nov. 1992, the journal becomes bilingual, French and English. Table of contents of latest issue available on the internet. A.D.P.; Art index (1994–); ARTbib.curr.; ARTbib.mod.; BHA; Francis; Ibidem; Rép.d'art.

Q118 Arts & architecture, new ser., v.1–4, no.2, fall 1981–May/July 1985. Los Angeles, Arts and Architecture. Quarterly, 1981–85.
Also available on microfilm: Ann Arbor, UMI.

Suspended Sept. 1967–summer 1981.

Continues: Arts & architecture, v. 61, no.2–84, no. 7/8, Feb. 1944–July/Aug. 1967 (See Part 1, and GLAH 1:Q93 for prior publication history). Substantial art journal, shaped early on by publisher and ed. John Entenza. The new series continues its focus on West Coast architecture, with case studies of houses, calendar of events, film and signed book reviews, and product information. Arch.per.ind.; Art index; Avery.

Q119 Arts & the Islamic world, no.1, winter 1982/83– . London, Islamic Arts Fdn. by New Century. Quarterly.
Nicely realized journal, exploring all areas of Islamic arts, including painting, calligraphy, architecture, metalwork, decorative arts, numismatics, etc. Especially concerned with art in the context of culture and nature. Since no.33, special thematic hardbound issues have appeared on one theme or country. Includes reports and signed book reviews and occasional supplementary material. Art full; Art index (1994-); ARTbib.mod.; Avery; Uncover; WilsonSelect.

Q120 Arts d'Afrique noire, 1, printemps 1972– . Arnouville, France, Raoul Lehuard. Quarterly. Publisher, place of publication vary.
Contemporary art journal from Francophone Africa for the free expression of art. Considered a French language counterpart to African arts. Areas cover the art and cultural movements of Africa, traditional arts, collections, and museums. Exhibition and book reviews, and art sales news are included. Publishes separate cumulative index to numbers 1–57 in no.57 (spring 1986). In French, occasionally English. Table of contents available on the internet. Anth.lit.; Art full; Art index (1984–); ARTbib.mod.; Francis; PerCont.ind.

Q121 Arts of Asia, v.1, Jan./Feb. 1971– . Kowloon, Hong Kong, Arts of Asia Publications. Bimonthly.
Patriarchal journal of Asian art, written for the collector and investor of Asian art, directed from the beginning by Ms. Tuyet Nguyet. Covers all East and South East Asian countries, including Indonesia, Japan, Philippines, India, and Nepal. Exhaustive coverage of a range of media, including pottery, enamels, bronze, textiles, and architecture. Also features articles, book and exhibition reviews, and sales information. Index to years 1971–90 in v.21 (Jan./Feb. 1991); indexes also compiled every three years. Nicely produced, on high-quality paper. Arch.Per.ind.; Art Ar.Te.Abs.; Art index (1984–); ARTbib.curr.; ARTbib.mod.; ArtHum. Article1st; Avery; Clo.T.A.ind.; Contents1st; Curr.Cont.A&H.; Curr.Cont.Connect; Ind.art.Jewish.st.; IRAP; RILM; Rug text.arts; Uncover.

Q122 Artscribe, no.72–90, Nov./Dec. 1988–Feb./Mar. 1992. London, Artscribe Ltd. Bimonthly.
Continues: Artscribe, no.1–54, Jan./Feb.1976–Sept./Oct. 1985; Artscribe international, no.55–71, Dec./Jan. 1985/86–Sept./Oct.1988. Glossy British journal of contemporary art in the United Kingdom, as well as in Europe, and more recently in the United States. Critical analysis of contemporary art, including photography, performance art, and printmaking, with interviews, debates, and news. Includes exhibition reviews, calendar of events, exhibition information. ARTbib.curr.; ARTbib.mod.; Des.&Ap.A.ind.; RILA.

Q123 Asian art & culture / Arthur M. Sackler Gallery, Smithsonian Institution, v.7, no.1–9, no.3, winter 1994–fall 1996. N.Y., Oxford Univ. Pr. Quarterly, 1987–93; three times a year, 1994–96.
Also available on microfilm: Ann Arbor, UMI.

Continues: Asian Art. v.1–6, no.4, fall/winter 1987/88–fall 1993. Thematic journal on the arts of Asia (China, Japan,

Korea, Cambodia, Vietnam, India, Indonesia), taking as its basis the exhibition program at the Sackler Gallery, consistently attentive to religion, culture, and social practices. Issues cover a range of subjects, including painting, sculpture, decorative arts, folk traditions, textiles, poetry, performing arts, gardens, and art collecting. Continued in 1997 by series titled Asian art & culture (unnumbered). Art index; ARTbib.mod.; ArtHum.; Article1st; Avery; Contents1st; Curr.Cont.A&H; Curr.Cont.Connect; Clo.T.A.ind.; Francis; RILM; Uncover.

Q124 Assemblage: a critical journal of architecture and design culture, no.1, Oct. 1986– . Cambridge, Mass., MIT Pr. Three issues a year.
Also available on microfilm: Ann Arbor, UMI.

Reflective journal focusing on the relationship between architectural theory and design. Articles averaging six per issue, are written by leading architectural critics and theorists from a variety of disciplines, including architecture, art history, philosophy, literary theory and politics. Arch.per.ind.; Art full; Art index (1998–); ARTbib.mod.; Avery; BHA; Francis; Ind.art.Jewish.st.; MLA; Uncover.

Q125 Athanor, v.1, 1981– . Tallahassee Fla., Dept. of Art History, Florida State Univ. Annual.
Graduate school publication offering a forum for the exchange of various points of view and presentations on art history and recent research. Some articles originate from papers presented at an annual symposium in the history of art held at the school. Black-and-white plates. ARTbib.mod.; BHA; Clo.T.A.ind.; Francis; RILA.

Q126 Australian journal of art / Art Association of Australia, v.1, 1978– . Brisbane, Qld., Australia, The Association, c/o Art History Dept. Univ. of Queensland, St. Lucia, Brisbane, Qld., Australia. Annual. Publisher, place of publication vary.
Small-format annual publication of the Art Association of Australia. Not restricted to Australians or matters pertaining to Australian art. Provides a vehicle for publishing articles on broad spectrum of topics. ARTbib.mod.; BHA; Clo.T.A.ind.; Francis; RILA.

Q127 Avant garde: journal of theory & criticism in architecture & the arts, no.1–6, 1988–93. Denver, Univ. of Colorado, School of Architecture & Planning. Biannual.
Small-format school publication created to provoke discussion between readers on issues related to architecture and design. Essays on contemporary architects and designers and their works. BHA.

Q128 Block, no.1–15, 1979–spring 1989. East Barnet, Hertfordshire, Eng., Middlesex Polytechnic. Irregular.
Critical essays and long articles on the politics, economics, and ideologies of the arts in societies, including material culture, feminist views, and mass media. Published by the Arts Council of Great Britain. ARTbib.mod.; Des.&Ap.A.ind.; RILA.

Q129 Boletin del Museo Chileno de Arte Precolombino, no.1, 1986– . Santiago de Chile, El Museo. Annual.
Bulletin created to promote the museum that was established in 1981, and to investigate areas concerning history, life, and art of the Americas before the arrival of Europeans. Articles on Pre-Columbian art and related themes. Black-and-white plates. Anth.ind.; Anth.lit.

Q130 Boletin del Museo del Prado, T. 1, no.1, enero-abr.1980– . Madrid, El Museo. Three issues a year.
Journal providing information on the museum's activities and articles related to its collections, written by the museum's curators. Also contains notices of recent acquisitions, restorations. Art Ar.Te.Abs.; ARTbib.mod.; BHA; Rép.d'art; RILA.

Q131 Bollettino della Società Piemontese di Archeologia e Belle Arti. Nuova ser., anno 35, 1981– . Torino, Società Piemontese di Archeologia e Belle Arti. Quarterly.
Suspended 1936–46; 1967–80.

Continues: anno 1–19, no.2. 1917–35; nuova ser., anno 1–20, 1947–66. Begins new series with anno 35, 1981 (See Part 1 and GLAH 1:Q318). Scholarly journal of Piedmontese art and architecture. BHA; Dyabola; Francis; Rép.d'art.

Q132 Bulletin of the Asia Institute, new ser., v.1, 1987– . Bloomfield Hills, Mich., The Institute. Annual. Place of publication varies.
Began in 1931 as Bulletin of the American Institute for Persian Art & Archaeology; continued through the war years as Bulletin of the American Institute for Iranian Art & Archaeology; to become the Bulletin of the Asia Institute of Pahlavi Univ. in 1969.—*Introd.*, new ser. v.1. Hardcover multilingual (English, French, German, Spanish) scholarly journal on art, archeology, and culture of Western and Central Asia from the second millennium B.C. through the mid-Islamic period. Features little-known collections of artifacts and summaries of archeological activities. Later vols. have distinct titles. Signed book reviews and indexes. Table of contents of recent vols. available on the internet. Avery; BHA; Curr.Cont.Connect; Dyabola; Francis.

Q133 C: international contemporary art, issue 34, summer 1992– . Toronto, C Magazine. (Distr. by Total Circulation Services, Hackensack, N.J.). Quarterly. Subtitle varies.
Also available on microfilm: Toronto, Micromedia.

Continues: Impressions, Mar. 1970–winter/spring 1983; C: a visual critical art magazine, then C, no. 1–33, winter 1983/84–spring 1992. Journal of contemporary art, criticism and experimentation, with special emphasis on the Canadian art scene, particularly in the cities of Toronto, Québec City, Vancouver, and Montréal, as well as New York City and beyond. Well-designed, with interesting typeface. Exhibition reviews. Contents of latest issue available on the internet. Art index (1998–); ARTbib.mod.; BHA; Can.ind.; Can.per.ind.

Q134 Cahiers de la photographie, no.1, 1981– (suspended with no.31, 1992). LaPlume, France, Association de critique contemporaine en photographie. Quarterly.

Critical photography journal with black-and-white plates. Each issue has a distinct title and is devoted to a particular theme or individual photographer. ARTbib.mod.; BHA; Int.photo.ind.

Q135 Les cahiers de la recherche architecturale et urbaine, No. 1, mai 1999– . Paris, Éditions du patrimoine. Quarterly.

Continues: Les cahiers de la recherche architecturale, no.1–42/43, déc. 1977–98. Scholarly serial of architecture, city planning, anthropology, ethnology, sociology, and space design. Issues are thematic in nature, frequently having a central theme, such as neighborhoods, houses and villas, Asian cities, and city ports. Some thematic issues called "Supplements." Index to 1977–93. Arch.per.ind.; Avery; BHA; Francis.

Q136 Cahiers du CCI, no.1–6, 1986–89. Paris, Ed. du Centre Pompidou / Centre de Création Industrielle (CCI). Irregular.

Thematic journal directed by Francois Burkhardt, Director of the CCI, reflecting the Center's interests as well as those of the Georges Pompidou Museum, including design, architecture, urbanism, and new technologies. Issues have individual titles. Includes occasional special numbers called Numero special. Art Ar.Te.Abs.; ARTbib.mod.; RILA.

Q137 Cahiers du Musée National d'Art Moderne, n.1, juil.–sept. 1979– . Paris, Ed. du Centre Georges Pompidou. Semiannual (slightly irregular), 1979–86; quarterly (some issues combined), 1987– .

Inviting publication based on the museum's collection, with articles studying, re-evaluating, and exploring new perspectives and ideas. Issues are monographic and thematic, covering 20th-century modern art movements and media. Some issues also serve as catalogs of exhibitions, and include poetry, symposiums held at the museum, and new museum acquisitions. Includes occasional special numbers titled, Hors-serie/archives. Art Ar.Te.Abs.; Art index (1987–); ARTbib.mod.; ArtHum.; Avery; BHA; Francis; RILA.

Q138 Cambridge archaeological journal, v.1, Apr. 1991– . Cambridge, Eng., Cambridge Univ. Pr. for the McDonald Institute for Archaeological Research, Univ. of Cambridge. Semiannual.

Scholarly, exhaustive articles covering all periods of archeology, with an emphasis on the art and culture of early societies. One article per issue is based on a lecture given at The McDonald Institute for Archaeological Research, Univ. of Cambridge (founded 1990), on psychological aspects of human behavior. Signed book reviews. Anth.lit.; Anth.ind.; Art Ar.Te.Abs.; ArtHum.; Avery; Curr.Cont.A&H; Curr.Cont.Connect; Dyabola; Uncover.

Q139 Camera Austria international, 36, 1991– . Graz, Austria, M. Willmann. (Distr. by Distributed Arts Publishers: DAP). Quarterly.

Continues: Camera Austria: Zeitschrift für Fotografie, 1–35, 1980–90. Dynamic contemporary photography journal, featuring photo essays/interviews on international contemporary photographers. Focus is on Austria. Includes signed exhibition and book reviews, symposium reports, calendar of events. Occasional indexes. Bilingual, German and English. Full-color plates. Summaries of latest issue available on the internet. ARTbib.mod.; Ibidem.

Q140 Camerawork: a journal of photographic arts, v.19, no.1, spring 1992– . San Francisco, San Francisco Camerawork Inc. Semiannual.

Continues Newsletter, San Francisco Camerawork newsletter (San Francisco Camerawork), v.1–10, no.2, 1974–June 1983; San Francisco camerawork quarterly, v.10, no.3–v.11, no.2, autumn 1983–summer 1984; Sf camerawork quarterly, v.2 [i.e., 11], no.3–v.18, no.3/4, fall 1984–summer/fall 1991. Quality photographic journal of essays and images by the San Francisco Camerawork, a nationally recognized nonprofit artist organization, whose purpose is to encourage discussion and deliberation on contemporary photography. Signed book reviews. Art index (1998–); ARTbib.mod.

Q141 Canadian art. v.1, fall 1984– . Toronto, Canadian Art Fdn. in assoc. with Key Publishers. Quarterly. Publisher varies.

Also available on microfiche: Toronto, Micromedia.

Formed by the merger of Artscanada (Toronto, 1967–82) (See Part 1 and GLAH 1:Q99) and Artmagazine (Toronto, 1974–83). Glossy, popular journal of contemporary arts in Canada, similar to Artnews, covering the latest in art, film, video, performance art, and architecture. Includes articles, profiles of emerging and established artists, signed exhibition and book reviews, and news of events. Art index (1994–); ARTbib.mod.; BHA; Can.ind.; Can.per.ind.; Francis.

Q142 Center: a journal for architecture in America, v.1, 1985– . Austin, Center for the Study of American Architecture, School of Architecture, Univ. of Texas at Austin. Annual.

Publication of the Center, focusing on contemporary American architecture and city planning, particularly in the central states. Thematic in coverage, individually titled, and monographic in nature, with intelligently written articles and case studies showing how architecture can best serve the needs of the community, written by leading critics and architects, some associated with the Center. Arch.per.ind.; Avery.

Q143 The Chicago architectural journal, v.1–8, 1981–89. Chicago, Chicago Architectural Club. Annual.

Annual society publication chronicling activities and member projects held at the prestigious Chicago Architectural Club, founded in the 1880s. Coverage focuses primarily on Chicago and the Midwest, and articles are based on lectures held at the Club. Index to works and projects by members in v.3. Avery, Br.tech.ind.

Q144 Church monuments: journal of the Church Monuments Society, v.1, part 1, June 1985– . Pinner, Middlesex, Eng., The Society. Annual.

Supersedes: International Society for the Study of Church Monuments Bulletin. Published with grant money from the Paul Mellon Centre for the Study of British Art, this small-format publication is devoted to church decoration, iconography, ornament, funerary sculpture, and monuments. Focus is on Great Britain, with the occasional article on continental influences. "The material awaiting art historians in English churches is almost proverbially rich and neglected and the new Journal provides good opportunities for publication."—*Review*, Burlington magazine, v.128, July 1986, p.513. Arch.per.ind.; Avery; BHA; Clo.T.A.ind.; Francis.

Q145 The classicist: annual of the Institute for the Study of Classical Architecture, no.1, 1994/95– . N.Y., the Institute. (Distr. by Transaction Publishers, Rutgers Univ., Piscataway, N.J.). Annual.

Society journal devoted exclusively to artistic and architectural classicism, with essays on architectural theory, education, urbanism, and practical information on building, as well as a section on related arts. Features include portfolios highlighting works by architects, signed book reviews, and bibliographies of recommended titles. The society, established at the New York Academy of Art, was founded to foster educational programs on traditional building. Aimed at both the professional and lay reader. Avery.

Q146 Cleveland studies in the history of art, v.1, 1996– . Cleveland, Cleveland Museum of Art. Annual.

Continues: Bulletin of the Cleveland Museum of Art, v.1–81, no.10, 1914–Dec.1994. "Publishes scholarly articles and shorter notes that are the result of original research on the collections and related issues. Fosters research on works in the museum's collections. When appropriate, articles treating relevant related subjects will be entertained for publication."—*Advert.* BHA; Francis.

Q147 Colóquio: artes; Revista trimestral de artes visuals, musica e bailado, 2.ser., año 13, no.1, marco 1971–38, no.111, out.–dez. 1996. Lisbon, Portugal, Fundação Calouste Gulbenkian. Five issues a year.

Formerly: Colóquio: revista de arte e letras., 1–61, 1959–70. Superseded by Colóquio: artes and Colóquio: letras.

Multilingual (Portuguese, Spanish, Italian, occasional English/French summaries) journal of art criticism, covering ancient to contemporary art, music, performance, film, theater, photography, and video in Portugal. Listings of cultural activities in Portugal. ARTbib.curr.; ArtHum.; BHA; Curr.Cont.A.&H.; Curr.Cont.Connect; Francis; Ibidem; RILA.

Q148 Columbia: VLA journal of law & the arts, v.10, no.1, summer 1985– . N.Y., Columbia Univ. School of Law and Volunteer Lawyers for the Arts. Quarterly

Also available on microfilm: Buffalo, William S. Hein.

Continues: Art & the law, v. 1–6, no.4, Dec. 1974–81; Columbia journal of art and the law, v.7–9, 1983–85. Quarterly journal of law and the arts, entertainment, communications, and intellectual property, with well-researched articles on such issues as copyright law, fair use, stolen art, fine art liability, and government funding, written by lawyers and professors of law. News related to the Volunteer Lawyers for the Arts, as well as signed book reviews and indexes. Each issue is entirely student-edited. Ind.legal per; Legal res.ind. (1985–); Uncover.

Q149 Columbia documents of architecture and theory: D, v.1, 1992– . N.Y., Columbia Univ. Grad. School of Architecture, Planning and Preservation. (Distr. by Distributed Art Publishers: D.A.P.). Semiannual.

Ed.: Bernard Tschumi.

Architecture school publication offering essays, theoretical discussions, symposium reports, on architecture and urban planning, by leading faculty and outside architects. Avery.

Q150 Commentari d'arte: rivista di critica e storia dell'arte, anno 1, maggio-agosto 1995– . Roma, De Luca. (Distr. by Casalini Libri, Fiesole). Quarterly.

Dir.: Alessandro Marabottini.

Continues: Commentari (See Part 1 and GLAH 1:Q134). Serious, scholarly publication, following in the illustrious footsteps of the older journal, Commentari, edited by the famed art historian Mario Salmi, which ceased publication in 1977. According to the publisher, the new series continues the original Commentari, by covering similar material, only now with a new ed., staff, and updated format. Its mandate is to present methodology as it relates to the study and understanding of Italian artistic patrimony, from medieval to contemporary times, in the form of articles, essays, and research in progress. Includes signed book reviews. BHA; Francis.

Q151 Composición arquitectónica: art & architecture, no.1–10, Oct. 1988–93. Bilbao, Spain, Instituto de Arte y Humanidades, Fundación Faustino Obregozo. Three issues a year.

Independent Spanish, Basque and English journal "contributing to the debate concerning architecture and art from point of view of the specific cultural environment."—*Introd.* Past issues have been devoted to outstanding architects of many nations. "An interesting mix of articles."—*Review*, Art documentation, v.9, no. 2, summer 1990, p.115–16. Bilingual, Spanish and English. Color photographs, plans. Arch.per.ind.; Avery.

Q152 Computers & the history of art, v.1, part 1, 1990– . Chur, N.Y., Harwood Academic Pub. Bimonthly.

Continues: CHArt newsletter, History of Art Dept., Univ. College, Univ. of London, no.1–10, autumn 1985–spring 1989. An international journal published in assoc. with CHArt (Computers and the History of Art), a British society founded in 1989 by art historians and other scholars for the advancement of computers in the history of art. The society supports an annual conference, this scholarly journal, and awards, and has issued a book of the same title. Articles cover new methodologies, the creation of image databases, the development of software, as well as conference proceedings, indexes, and book and software reviews. Latest issue and membership information available on the internet. Art index; BHA; Francis.

Q153 Construction history: journal of the Construction History Group, v.1, 1986– . Ascot, Berks, Eng., Chartered Institute of Building. Annual.

Continues: Construction science. Journal of the history of construction and building industries, particularly in Great Britain, investigating such areas as the study of building firms, civil engineering, surveying history, building materials, carpentry, housing, suspension bridges, and structures. "A significant resource in the expanding field of building preservation."—*Review*, Art documentation, v.7, no.1, spring 1988, p.37–38. Signed book reviews, abstracts of periodical literature. Arch.per.ind.; BHA; Francis.

Q154 Controspazio: rivista bimestrale di architettura e urbanistica dell'EDIS-Calabria, anno I–XVI, n.4, giugno 1969–ott.–dic.1985; nuova serie, anno XIX, no.1, July/August 1988– . Roma, Gangemi. Monthly, 1969–1977. Bimonthly. Publisher, place of publication vary.

Journal of architecture and urban planning directed by Paolo Portoghesi, with theoretical and research articles on international architects and projects. Occasional special issues, such as one devoted to Futurism and its manifestos (1971). With v.19 a new series is initiated, which includes a change in format and the addition of English abstracts. Also includes book reviews, and notices of journal articles from European, U.S., and Japanese architecture journals. Cumulative indexes. Avery.

Q155 The Cornell journal of architecture, v.1, 1981– . Ithaca, N.Y., Cornell Univ., Dept. of Architecture. (Distr. by Distributed Art Publishers: D.A.P.). Irregular.

Articles by practitioners and theorists on a broad range of topics, from urban planning to computer technology. Earlier issues covered undergraduate studio projects, competitions, and theses. Illustrated with plans, 3-D renderings, and other images. Avery.

Q156 Craft history, no.1–2, Oct.1988–Apr. 1989. Bath, Eng., Combined Arts. Quarterly.

Oct. 1988 issue reprinted with revisions and corrections, Nov. 1988.

Short-lived, small-format decorative arts journal, which began with an interesting mandate: to research the history and development of British craft history in the late-19th and 20th centuries. Long research articles touch on issues of morality, women's roles, religion, politics, and class, and are written by British craft historians and scholars. Articles cover such subjects as the documents of Craft Revival, the celebration of the Centenary of the Arts & Crafts Exhibition Society, and the murals of the Arts & Crafts movement. "Offers a scholarly perspective to the various craft disciplines."—*Review*, Art documentation, v.9, no.1, spring 1990, p.26. Signed book and exhibition reviews. Avery; Des.&Ap.A.ind.Art ind.

Q157 Critica d'arte, ser. 8, anno 62, no.1, marzo 1999– . Firenze, Casa Ed. La Lettere. (Distr. by Licosa, Florence). Quarterly, 1984– (slightly irregular, some issues combined).

Subtitle, publisher, and frequency vary.

Two supplementary issues of Critica d'arte africana published in 1984 and 1985.

Continues: La Critica d'arte (See Part 1 and GLAH 1:Q144). Well-respected Italian art history journal that has successfully maintained its scholarly appearance and contents, despite many changes in publishers and series, as well as with the passing of its director and founder, Carlo Ludovico Ragghianti, in 1987. Published under the direction of the Università Internazionale dell'Arte di Firenze, Critica d'arte offers quality Italian scholarship for all periods of art history and criticism. ARTbib.mod.; ArtHum.; Avery; BHA; Francis; RILA.

Q158 El Croquis de arquitectura y de diseño, ano 1, spring 1982– . Madrid, El Croquis. (Distr. by Philip Galgiani, N.Y.). Quarterly, 1982–84; bimonthly (slightly irregular), 1985– .

Incorporates La Revista de la Nueva Arquitectura in 1986. Large, glossy journal devoted to contemporary architecture, design and construction, publishing information on recent works, and extensive interviews. Amply illustrated and monographic in nature, later issues are in both Spanish and English, focusing on international contemporary architects. Includes occasional supplementary monographs. Summaries of past issues available on the internet. Arch.per.ind.; Avery.

Q159 Cuadernos de arquitectura mesoamericana, no.1, feb. 1984– . México, D.F., División de Estudios de Posgrado, Facultad de Arquitectura, Universidad Nacional Autónoma de México (UNAM). Three issues a year.

Scholarly treatment given to Mesoamerican, monumental, and funerary architecture and urban planning. Issues have covered laws governing patrimony and protection of cultural properties in Mexico and Central America, and bibliographies of pre-Hispanic archeology and architecture. Some articles in English. Black-and-white illustrations. Anth.lit.; Anth.ind.; Arch.per.ind.; Avery.

Q160 The Daguerreian annual, 1991– . Pittsburgh, the Daguerreian Society. Annual. Place of publication varies.

Official yearbook of the Daguerreian Society focusing on daguerreotypes, covering both the prehistory of photography as well as daguerreotypes today and modern conservation procedures. Articles written mostly by members, are short (about 3–4 pages each) and numerous (about 30 in each vol.), and offer original biographical research. Also included are reprints of several 19th-century journal articles on photography. Appendices include biographies and indexes to names in articles. ARTbib.mod.; BHA; Curr.Cont.Connect; Francis.

Q161 Daidalos, Architektur, Kunst, Kulture, 1, 15 Sept. 1981– . Basel, G & B Arts International. Quarterly.

Place of publication, publisher, subtitle vary.

Also published in English as: Daidalos, architecture, art, culture, beginning 69/70, December 1998/January 1999– . Distinguished and refined journal of architecture, from classical period to present, with scholarly articles written by leading architects, historians. and critics. Thematic in scope, the focus is on Western Europe, with an interdisciplinary approach to art, architecture, and culture. Index to issues 1–20 found in no.15 (1986), and to nos.21–40 in no.42 (1991). ARTbib. curr.; Arch.per.ind.; Avery; BHA; RILA.

Q162 Damaszener Mitteilungen / Deutsches Archaölogisches Institut, Station Damaskus, Bd. 1, 1983– . Mainz-am-Rhein. Irregular.

Scholarly hardcover publication from the recently established Syrian branch (1981) of the D.A.I. Like the earlier important publications of this organization (see GLAH 1:Q152ff), provides an outlet to report and publish regional archeological discoveries. Articles in German, French, or English. Plates, folded maps in back of each vol. BHA; Dyabola; Francis; Rép.d'art.

Q163 Dekorativnoe iskusstvo - Dialog istorii i. kultury, no.1–12, 1994– . Moskva, Izdatel'stvo DI-DIK. (Distr. by Victor Kamkin, Rockville, MD). Monthly (lately irregular).

Alternatively known as: DI, DIK. Formed by the 1994 merger of Dialog istorii I Kultury and Dekorativnoe iskusstvo, which was formerly (until no.1, 1991) Dekorativnoe iskusstvo SSSR (See Part 1 and GLAH 1:Q147), then Dekorativnoe iskusstvo: uchrediteli SKH SSSR, 1991, 2– . Change of title with 1991, no.3 issue to: DI: Zhurnal Dekorativnoe iskusstvo. Issues are also numbered consecutively. Two issues numbered no.1–2, 1997. Journal of Russian art history and theory, with articles on painting, sculpture, and decorative arts. Text in Russian, summaries in English. ARTbib.mod.

Q164 Delineavit et sculpsit, nr.1, Aug. 1989– . Leiden, Vrienden van het Prentenkabinet der Rijksuniversiteit te Leiden. Two to three issues a year.

Journal of Dutch prints and drawings produced prior to 1850. Some issues serve as catalogs to exhibits in Dutch museums. Dutch articles have English summaries, with the occasional article in English. Separate index insert to numbers 1–10 (augustus 1989–juni 1993). BHA; Francis.

Q165 Die Denkmalpflege. 52. Jahrg., heft 1, 1994– . München, Deutscher Kunstverlag, for the Vereinigung der Landesdenkmalpfleger in der Bundesrepublik Deutschland. Semmiannual.

Continues Deutsche Kunst und Denkmalpflege 1952–93 (See Part 1 and GLAH 1:Q150). German art publication, which under its new title expands its scope to include discussions not only of the art, architecture, and monuments of lower Saxony, but all of Germany, and with increased emphasis on conservation. Arch.per.ind.; Art Ar.Te.Abs.; ARTbib.mod.; ArtHum.; Avery; BHA; Curr.Cont.A.&H; Curr.Cont.Connect; RILA.

Q166 Design book review: DBR, 1, 1983– . San Francisco, California College of Arts and Crafts. Quarterly. Place of publication, publisher vary.

Invaluable journal specializing in reviews of recently published design and architecture books. Each issue contains long, well-illustrated essays on recent publications, mainly on design, architecture, decorative arts, interior design, landscape, city planning, and the graphic arts, by design professionals and specialists. Issues are thematic, and besides reviews, include essays on various design issues, interviews, and symposia. "An important addition to art bibliography."—*Review*, Art documentation, v.2, no.6, Dec. 1983, p.207. Annual index. Art index (1994–); ARTbib.mod.; Avery; BHA; Bk.rev.ind.; Des.&Ap.A.ind.; Francis; RILA; Uncover.

Q167 Design issues: a journal of history, theory and criticism, v.1, spring 1984– . Pittsburgh, Carnegie Mellon Univ.. (Distr. by MIT Pr.). Semiannual, 1984–85; three issues a year (slightly irregular), 1994– . Subtitle varies.

Eds.: Victor Margolin, Dennis Doordan, and Richard Buchanan.

Also available on microfilm: Ann Arbor, UMI.

Academic journal that takes a critical look at the history, theory, and criticism of design. Some issues are thematic and guest edited, and articles are written by leaders in the field. Long associated with the School of Art and Design of the Univ. of Illinois at Chicago (from 1984 to 1993), it is now published by Carnegie Mellon Univ. Included is a feature titled "document," which analyzes records and other material of interest to designers. The journal is "intended to acquaint faculty, students, and designers with the historical perspectives, theoretical propositions, and critical assumptions of their profession."—*Review*, Art documentation, v.5, no.1, spring 1986, p.33. Includes signed book reviews. Acad.Search; Art full; Art index (1994-); ARTbib.mod.; ArtHum.; Avery; BHA; Curr.Cont.A.&H.; Curr.ont.Connect; Des.&Ap.A.ind.; Des.int.ind.; MLA; Uncover.

Q168 DoubleTake, v.1, summer 1995– . Durham, Center for Documentary Studies, Duke Univ. Semiannual, 1995; quarterly, 1996– .

Powerful journal of photography and literature, "presenting those who rarely make their way into pages of contemporary magazines."—*Introd.* Combines fiction, poetry, and photography. Includes information about events at the Center, and signed book reviews. ARTbib.mod.

Q169 Drawing: the international review published by the Drawing Society, v.1–20, no. 2, May/June 1979–winter 1998/99. N.Y., The Society. Bimonthly.

Coverage includes all aspects of drawing, from the Old Masters to contemporary drawing, as well as connoisseurship, conservation, architectural drawings, and pedagogy. Also included are signed book, CD-ROM, and exhibition reviews, interviews, museum acquisitions, collection information, and auction previews. A.D.P.; Art Ar.Te.Abs.; Art full; Art index (1986–); ARTbib.curr.; ARTbib.mod.; Article1st; Avery; BHA; Biog.ind.; Contents1st; Francis; Ibidem; RILA; Uncover; WilsonSelect.

Q170 Eastern art report: fortnightly survey of the arts of the Middle East, South Asia, China & Japan, v.1, Mar.

1–15, 1989– . London, Centre for Near East, Asia and Africa Research (NEAR), Eastern Art Publishing. Semimonthly, 1989–90; bimonthly, 1990/91– . Subtitle varies.

Timely publication on art treasures, decorative arts, and cultural institutions in this area of the world. Combines scholarly articles on the visual arts, both tradition and modern, with interviews, art and sales events, signed book and exhibition reviews. Index to back issues available on the internet and in v.4, no.2. ARTbib.mod.

Q171 L'Ecrit voir / Collectif pour l'histoire de l'art, no.1–12, mai 1982–89/90. Paris, Le Collectif. Semiannual. Subtitle varies.

Publication created entirely by students at the Sorbonne, covering all periods of art history. Thematic issues have featured lists of masters theses and dissertations in art history by students in Paris universities from 1971 to 1984, and festschriften. Includes colloquia. Rép.d'art.

Q172 Eidos: rivista di cultura, anno 1–11, ott.1987–dic.1992. Asolo, Italy, Asolo Arti. Semiannual.

Erudite publication covering the fine arts from ancient to modern. Articles are in Italian, occasionally translated from English to Italian. Cinema and music also covered, as are exhibition and book reviews. Index to 1987–1990 and 1990–92 included in issue numbers 6 and 11 respectively. Avery; BHA; Francis.

Q173 Emblematica: an interdisciplinary journal for emblem studies, v.1, spring 1986– . N.Y., AMS Pr. Semiannual.

Interdisciplinary journal serving as a forum for researchers working in the field of emblem studies. Includes articles, essays, research reports, and bibliographies, as well as theses, works in progress, conference reports, signed book reviews, and other notices. BHA; Francis; MLA.

Q174 Emigre: non-stop design: the magazine that ignores boundaries, no.1, 1982– . Berkeley, Emigre Graphics. Quarterly. Subtitle varies.

Influential journal of graphic design, offering typographic experiments and new approaches to graphic design. Unique in both size (varying from issue to issue) and layout. Visually challenging and controversial publication, focusing on specific design topics, and offering the latest in computer typesetting and type designs, with painting, drawing, and poetry. The magazine has had "a far-reaching influence; the echoes of Emigre style are everywhere."—*Review*, I.D. 41, May/June 1994, p.32–33. A monograph tracing ten years of its publication has been published: Èmigré: Graphic design into the visual realm. (N.Y., Van Nostrand Reinhold, 1993). Summaries of past issues available on the internet. Art index (1998–); ARTbib.mod.; Des.&Ap.A.ind.; MLA.

Q175 Environmental design: journal of the Islamic Environmental Design Research Centre, 1, 1985– . Como, Environmental Design. (Distr. By Licosa, Florence). Irregular. Publisher varies.

Ed.: Attilio Petruccioli.

Variant titles: A.A.R.P. Environmental design; Journal of the Islamic Environmental Design Research Centre. Continues AARP art and archaeology research papers, no.1–20/21, June 1972–84 (See Part 1). Thematic publication that studies design in the urban context, emphasizing the mission of the Centre, which is to "promote research and studies in the field of architecture and town planning in the countries of the Islamic world . . . integrating various specialists to the problems of environmental analysis . . . establishing a rapport and exchange of technical knowledge with other major institutes engaged in similar studies."—*Introd.* Monographic issues have distinctive titles, such as "Water & architecture" and "Urban morphogenesis." Arch.per.ind.; Avery; Uncover.

Q176 Espace sculpture: revue trimestrielle du Conseil de la sculpture du Québec, v.1, hiver. 1982– . Montréal, Le Centre de Diffusion 3D. Quarterly.

International journal of contemporary sculpture covering a broad range of topics. Articles, interviews, and special issues examine individual sculptors, installations, public art, with extensive exhibition reviews. Bilingual French/English. Table of contents of latest issue available on the internet. ARTbib.mod.; BHA; Can.ind.; Can.per.ind.; Repère.

Q177 Eupalino: cultura della città e della casa / city & house culture, N.1–11/12, inverno 1983/84–89/90. Roma. "L'Erma" di Bretschneider. Irregular.

Dir.: Paolo Portoghesi.

Large-format journal of architectural theory, interior design, and city planning, ed. by Paolo Portoghesi and reflecting his vision. Strives to link postmodern architecture to history and culture. In English and Italian. Avery; Des.&Ap.A.ind.

Q178 European photography, v.1, Jan./Feb./Mar. 1980– . Göttingen, Germany, A. Müller-Pohle. (Distr. by Abrams and Distributed Arts Publishers: DAP). Quarterly.

Absorbed: Print letter. Beautifully produced journal focusing on contemporary photography by artists living and working in Europe. In addition to portfolios of major and emerging European photographers, the journal includes information on the latest trends, projects, signed book and exhibition reviews, book lists, festivals, calendar of events, guide to photography in various European cities. Large, full-page color plates. Biannual index. Bilingual, German and English. Art full; Art index (1994–); ARTbib.curr.; ARTbib.mod.; Ibidem; Int.photo.ind.; Photohi.; WilsonSelect.

Q179 FMR: the magazine of Franco Maria Ricci, Engl. ed., no.1, June 1984– . N.Y., Franco Maria Ricci International. Ten issues a year (some combined), 1984–85; bimonthly, 1985–.

Glossy, large-format journal covering a wide variety of art historical topics, well-known for its astonishingly beautiful full-page color illustrations. Articles by art historians and literary figures, many of them Italian. Extensive listing of museum exhibitions. Index to numbers 1 to 100 available separately (Milan, F.M. Ricci, 1994, 263p.). Unnumbered supplements accompany some issues. "Modeled after the highly successful Italian edition which began publication in 1982."—*Review*, Art documentation, v.5, no.2, summer 1986, p.93. Also available in French, Italian, Spanish, and German editions. Art index (1994–); ARTbib.mod.; Avery; Des.&Ap.A.ind; Des.int.ind.; Dyabola; RILM; Uncover.

Q180 The feminist art journal, v.1–6, no.2, Apr. 1972–summer 1977. Brooklyn, N.Y., Feminist Art Journal Inc. Quarterly (slightly irregular).

Also available on microfilm: Ann Arbor, UMI.

A landmark journal for feminist art. The journal's mission: "to carry women artists' voices throughout world; to enhance status of women in all the arts; to discuss and illustrate their work and to expose all institutions and personages who exploit or discriminate against artists."—*Introd.* Articles and announcements cover art, music, dance, film, and theater. The journal "recorded the formative years of the women artists' movement, especially as it developed on the East Coast, and reflected the ambiguities and conflicts of that early period."—*Review*, Woman's art journal 2, no.2, fall/winter 1982, p.19–24. Exhibition reviews. A.D.P.; Clo.T.A.ind.

Q181 Folk art, v.17, no.3, fall 1992– . N.Y., Museum of American Folk Art. Quarterly (varies slightly, some issues combined).

Continues: The Clarion, v.1–17, no.2, winter 1971–summer 1992. Museum publication written by curators, scholars, and collectors, with articles on collectors, recent exhibitions, information on the museum and on American folk art, including crafts, painting, prints and drawings, furniture, weaving, pottery, quilts, samplers. Signed book reviews, news of collections, and members. Some issues are thematic, topics having included the history of the museum and collecting folk art. Heavily illustrated with ads. Art index; ARTbib.curr.; ARTbib.mod.; BHA; Biog.ind.; Clo.T.A.ind.; Francis; RILA; Uncover.

Q182 Fotogeschichte: Beiträge zur Geschichte und Ästhetik der Fotografie, Jahrg..1, 1981– . Frankfurt-am-Main, T. Starl. Semiannual, 1981; quarterly, 1982– . Publisher varies.

Finely produced journal on the history of photography, particularly in Germany. Scholarly articles have included wartime photography, tourism, and collections in museums in Berlin. Exhibition reviews. Separate index to 1981–90 published by Jonas Verlag, Marburg. Lately the index is published annually in the journal. In German, with separate inserts of English and French summaries. ARTbib.mod.; BHA; I.B.Z.; Dyabola; Francis; Ibidem; Int.photo.ind.

Q183 Fotologia: quaderno di storia della fotografia, 1, giugno 1984– . Ferrara, Italy, Belborgo. Irregular. Publisher varies.

Official organ of the Fratelli Alinari, Museo di storia della fotografia.

Ed.: Italo Zannier.

Scholarly publication on the history of photography, particularly Italian photography, edited by one of Italy's best known photo historians. With articles on collections, museums, and lately, visual technologies, as well as exhibition and signed book reviews. The journal serves as the bulletin for the Alinari Museum of the History of Photography, in Florence. Also includes reprints of articles appearing in 19th-century photography journals. List of contents to nos.1–15 (1984–92) published in History of photography 20, no.1, spring, 1996, p.65–68. ARTbib.mod.; BHA; Francis; Int.photo.ind.

Q184 Frieze: contemporary art and culture. issue 1, 1991– . London, Frieze. Bimonthly.

Energetic journal of contemporary art, music, film, and mass media. Well-written, short articles on the latest art forms emanating from Great Britain, Europe, North and South America, and Japan, with a slight British preference. Typographically interesting, on quality paper, with sharp color illustrations. Premiere issue featured a limited edition print. Interviews, exhibition and gallery reviews. ARTbib.mod.; Des.&Ap.A.ind.

Q185 Fuse magazine, v.11, no.4, winter 1987/88– . Toronto, Arton's Pub. Five issues a year.

Also available on microfiche: Toronto, Micromedia.

Continues: Centerfold, v.1–4, no.1, Aug. 1976–Nov. 1979; Fuse, v.4, no.2–11, no.3, Jan. 1980–fall 1987. Activist magazine focusing on the international arts culture (art, theater, music, multimedia, video and performance art, film), particularly that which exists outside of major museums and galleries, while touching on social and cultural issues of race, censorship, violence, and sexual politics. Extensive coverage of Canadian art, including critical essays, interviews, art projects, video and exhibition reviews, annual indexes. ARTbib.mod.; Can.per.ind.; Uncover.

Q186 GA: Global architecture, 1, 1970– . Tokyo, A.D.A. Edita. Irregular.

One of the oldest monographic serials issuing from Japan and devoted to individual architects from around the world. Each vol. has a distinctive title, and analyzes in detail one or two projects by a recognized architect, accompanied by critical analysis by a well-known architectural critic or historian. Includes stunning full-page black-and-white and color plates and line drawings. The intention is to create an encyclopedia of modern architecture. Accompanied by this journal is Global architecture detail (1976–77), with line drawings taken from some of the issues of Global architecture, as well as GA architect (1982–), a monographic serial exploring individual architects or firms, and GA Japan: environmental design (1992–), consisting of full-page illustrations of architectural projects in Japan. In English and Japanese. Arch.per.ind.; Art index (1994–); Avery.

Q187 GA document, no.1, summer 1980– . Tokyo, A.D.A. Edita. Two to three issues (slightly irregular), 1980–89; quarterly (slightly irregular), 1990– .

Ed.: Yukio Futagawa.

Large-format serial documenting the latest architectural works from around the world, with striking black-and-white and color full-page plates. International scholars provide critical analyses. Also publishes GA document: Special issue

(1980–), an occasional monographic publication, each vol. having a distinctive title, and GA document extra (1995–), a new series devoted to the latest works of individual architects. "Effectively combines the visual strength of Global architecture with the depth of commentary found in some of GA's monographic works."—*Review*, Art documentation, 6, no.1, spring 1987, p.41–42. In English and Japanese. Arch.per.ind.; Art index (1985–); Avery.

Q188 GA houses, 1, 1976– . Tokyo, A.D.A. Edita. Irregular.

Each issue chronicles a variety of contemporary homes worldwide by outstanding new and established architects. An occasional supplement called GA houses special (1985–), provides monographic coverage. In Japanese and English. Arch.per.ind.; Avery.

Q189 Garden history: the journal of the Garden History Society. v.1, 1972– . London, The Society. Quarterly, 1972–80; semiannual, 1981– .

Formerly Occasional paper: Garden History Society newsletter. Society publication that contextualizes the history of garden design and horticulture as well as issues of conservation and preservation. Articles emphasize gardens in the United Kingdom, Ireland, and Australia. Index to garden literature taken from 19th-century periodicals (in v.4). Bibliographies, signed book reviews. Arch.per.ind.; Art Ar.Te.Abs.; Avery; BHA; Br.tech.ind.; Francis; Gard.lit.; RILA.

Q190 Die Gartenkunst, Jahrg.1, 1989– . Worms-am-Rhein, Germany, Wernersche Verlagsgesellschaft. Semiannual.

Notable scholarly journal on the history of landscape architecture, horticulture and garden design in Germany and surrounding countries, from the 17th to 19th centuries. Extensive bibliographies, signed book reviews, color plates. In German, occasional article in English. Avery; BHA; Francis.

Q191 Genders, 1, spring 1988– . Austin, Univ. of Texas Pr. in cooperation with the Univ. of Colorado at Boulder. Three issues a year.

Also available on microfilm: Ann Arbor, UMI.

Ceased publishing paper copies with number 26, 1997; currently available on the internet beginning with number 27, 1998. Scholarly journal on sexuality and gender in art, literature, film, media, and history, and relating gender to historical and economical contexts. Two or more articles per issue concern art. Issues are thematic and guest edited. Am.H.&L.; Am.Hum.ind.; ARTbib mod.; ArtHum.; BHA; Exp.Acad.; Francis; Hist.abs.; MLA; PerAbs; Uncover.

Q192 Georgian Group journal, (1), 1991– . London, The Group. Annual.

Continues : Report & journal of the Georgian Group, 1–5, 1986–90. Purpose of journal is to "save Georgian buildings, monuments, parks and gardens from destruction, to stimulate knowledge of Georgian architecture and to promote appreciation of products of the classical tradition in England, from Inigo Jones to present."—*Introd.* Well-researched and illustrated. Arch.per.ind.; Avery; BHA; Uncover.

Q193 Grafica d'arte: rivista di storia dell'incisione antica e moderna e storia del disegno, no.1, genn./mar. 1990– . Milano, Grafica d'arte. Quarterly.

"Instrument for the understanding and appreciation of graphic arts, from ancient to contemporary graphic design and its techniques."—*Introd.* Covers all the graphic arts, including silography, linoleum, acquafort, etc. Articles on collections, with catalog entries, news on sales, as well as signed book and exhibition reviews. In Italian. BHA; Francis.

Q194 Hafnia: Copenhagen papers in the history of art, no.1–11, 1970–88. Copenhagen, Institute of Art History, Univ. of Copenhagen. (Distr. by Rosenkilde og Bagger Forlag, Copenhagen). Biennial, 1970–78; annual, 1979–81; biennial, 1983–87 (slightly irregular).

Scholarly journal with long articles on a variety of topics in art history, written in English, French, or German, most by Danish art historians. 1976 vol. contains articles issuing from the 23d International Congress on Art History, held in Granada in Sept. 1975. ARTbib.mod.; Avery; BHA; Clo.T.A.ind.; Francis; Rép. d'art; RILA.

Q195 Hali: the international magazine of antique carpet and textile art, v.1, spring 1978– . London, Oguz Pr.; Philadelphia, HALI Publications. Bimonthly. Subtitle varies.

Glossy, highly visual and profusely illustrated journal covering all aspects of oriental rugs and occasionally textiles from the Middle East (primarily Turkey and Persia), Europe, Africa, and India. Articles are substantial. Issues also include collection reports, conference reports, sales, exhibition and book reviews. Contributions are both scholarly and commercial. Articles in German or English, those in German having an English summary. "Presents an unprejudiced attitude toward all Oriental textiles, antique and modern."—*Review*, ARLIS/NA newsletter, v.7, no.4/5, summer 1979, p.105–06. Also publishes occasional annual issues with distinctive titles. Art Ar.Te.Abs.; Art index (1994–); ARTbib.curr.; ARTbib.mod.; ArtHum.; Clo.T.A.ind.; Rug text.arts.

———. Index to v.1–11, issues 1–48 (1978–89), 1990. 76p.

———. Index to issues 1–84. (1978–95), 1997. 240p.

Q196 Hand papermaking, v.1, spring 1986– . Washington, D.C., Hand Papermaking Inc. Semiannual. Place of publication varies.

Oversized journal devoted to Eastern and Western techniques of papermaking, published by the non-profit organization of the same name. Intended for those working in the field as well as those who appreciate handmade papers. Includes articles, profiles of paper makers, signed book and exhibition reviews, and a handmade paper sample in each issue. Index to vols.1–7, 1986–92. Also publishes a separately produced quarterly newsletter. Art index (1998–).

Q197 The Harvard architecture review, v.1–10, 1980–98. Cambridge, Mass., MIT Pr. Annual.

Architecture school journal published by students and faculty of the Harvard Graduate School of Design, each issue devoted to a single theme. Articles discuss architectural theory and history and city planning. Also includes symposiums, book reviews. ArtHum.; Art index (1986–93); Avery; BHA; Br.tech.ind.; PerCont.ind.; Uncover.

Q198 Harvard design magazine, winter/spring 1997– . Cambridge, Mass., Harvard University Graduate School of Design. Three issues a year.

Continues: HGSD news, v.1–11, no.5, 1973–83; GSD news, v.12, no.1, Sept./Oct. 1983–fall 1996. Large-format publication on architecture, landscape architecture, urban design, and planning. Articles are thematic and written by practicing architects and faculty. Includes signed book reviews. Avery; Des.Ap.A.ind. (1999–).

Q199 Harvard University Art Museums bulletin, v.1, fall 1992– . Cambridge, Mass., Harvard Univ. Art Museums. Three issues a year.

Continues: Harvard Univ. Art Museums newsletter, v.1–v.2, no.1, spring 1984–spring 1985.

Monographic serial, well-researched and wide-ranging; not limited to objects in the Harvard museum collections. Occasional significant thematic issues on a range of topics (Dutch prints, Greek terracottas, art conservation). With annual reports for the year. Art index (1998–); BHA; Dyabola.

Q200 Hephaistos: kritische Zeitschrift zur Theorie und Praxis der Archäologie und angrenzender Wissenschaften, 1, 1979– . Bad Bramstedt, Germany, Moreland. Irregular. Place of publication, publisher vary.

Scholarly journal, promoting different approaches to the study of classical antiquities, classical art, and archeology. Articles mostly in German, occasional article in English, Italian, and French, with summaries in English. "The writing is consistently clear, straight-forward, and intelligent."—*Review*, Art documentation, v.8, no.3, May 1980, p.90. Works in progress, projects, signed book reviews. Avery; BHA; Dyabola; Rép.d'art.

Q201 Heresies: a feminist publication on art & politics, v.1–7, no.3 (1–27), Jan. 1977–93. N.Y., Heresies Collective. Quarterly, 1977–84; semiannual, 1985–93.

Stimulating activist publication written and published by a collective of feminist writers, poets, and artists, who disband after each issue is produced, resulting in a different viewpoint each time. The journal offers a feminist perspective on topics related to contemporary art, literature, dance, film, and politics. Issues are thematic and include bibliographies. Art index; ARTbib.mod.; Biog.ind.; Clo.T.A.ind.; EBSCO Master; PerCont.ind.; Uncover.

Q202 High performance: a publication of Art in the Public Interest, v.1–20, no.2–76, Feb.1978–summer 1997. Los Angeles, Astro Artz. Quarterly. Subtitle, place of publication and publisher vary.

Also available on microfilm: Ann Arbor, UMI.

Journal of performance art, as well as theater, dance, video, installation art, which chronicles the fleeting nature of these art events. Substantial signed reviews, and regular columns on artist books, film, new music, calendar of events, etc. Though recently defunct, the organization Art in the Public Interest still maintains a website where many articles from past issues are archived. "Through its feature articles, it provides a compendium of the who and what of performance art."—*Review*, Art documentation, v.6, no.2, Summer 1987, p.93. Artist index to years 1978–87 in v.11, no.1–2 (spring/summer 1988). Art index; ARTbib.curr.; ARTbib.mod.; Ibidem; Uncover.

Q203 Histoire de l'art : bulletin d'information de l'Institut National d'Histoire de l'Art, publie en collaboration avec l'Association des Professeurs d'Archeologie et d'Histoire de l'Art des Universités, N.1/2, juin 1988– . Paris, Ed. C.D.U.-S.E.D.E.S. Three issues a year, 1988–1996; biannual, 1996– .

House organ of the Institut National d'Histoire de l'Art and later the APAHAU, with scholarly articles covering all fields of art history, mainly by French art historians. Issues are thematic, and include articles, essays, and an indispensable section in the back called "Informations," covering legislative concerns, conference reports, prizes, book lists, notices of new periodicals, and listings of master's and Ph.D. degrees awarded in France in art history, organized by subject area and subdivided by city/district in France. With English summaries. ARTbib.mod.; Avery; BHA; Francis.

Q204 Historic preservation forum: the journal of the National Trust for Historic Preservation, v.5, no.1, Jan.–Feb. 1991– . Washington, D.C., National Trust for Historic Preservation. Quarterly.

Continues: Preservation forum, v.1–4, no.3, fall 1987–fall 1990. Slim publication on historic preservation issues, property rights, etc., published as part of membership to the National Trust for Historic Preservation (together with Forum newsletter, Preservation news and Historic preservation). Includes position papers, addresses, news, etc. Avery; Uncover.

Q205 Hoogsteder mercury, no.11–13/14, summer 1990–92. Doornspijk, The Netherlands, Davaco. Irregular. Publisher varies.

Ed.: Albert Blankert.

Continues: Hoogsteder Naumann mercury, no.1–10, 1985–89. Named after the god Mercury, the Galerie Hoogsteder BV in s'Gravenhage, and Hoogsteder Naumann Mercury Ltd in New York. Presents newly discovered paintings and original iconographic interpretations of Northern European art. Articles are written in English, by established art historians. In December 1996, a new journal titled Hoogsteder journal was initiated by the Dutch art gallery Hoogsteder & Hoogsteder, dedicated to Dutch and Flemish paintings, and written primarily for collectors and the art market. BHA; Rép.d'art. Also available on microfilm: Ann Arbor, UMI.

Q206 ID, v. 31, no.5, Sept./Oct. 1984– . N.Y., Design Publications. Bimonthly. Subtitle varies.

Continues: Industrial design, v.1–25, Feb.1954–78; Industrial design magazine: ID, v.26–30, no.4, Jan./Feb. 1979–July/Aug. 1983; Industrial design: I.D., v.30, no.5–v.31, no.4, Sept./Oct.1983–July/Aug. 1984; since July/Aug. 1992, called ID: the international design magazine. Authoritative and readable journal aimed at both the designer and layperson, with short articles on graphic design, design history, product design, profiles on designers, news, signed book reviews, and product information. Annual index. The July/Aug. issue consists of the Annual design review, which examines winners of competitions, and the December issue is the Annual design sourcebook, a buyer's guide to designer needs. Awards, calendars, resource listings. Arch.per.ind.; Art index; Avery; Biog.ind.; Des.&Ap.A.Ind.; Proquest; Uncover.

Q207 Im Blickfeld: Jahrbuch der Hamburger Kunsthalle, 1, 1994– . Hamburg, Christians. Annual.

Continues: Idea: Jahrbuch der Hamburger Kunsthalle, neue Folge, Bd.1–10, 1982–91 (München, Prestel). Continues, in part, Jahrbuch der Hamburger Kunstsammlungen, Bd. 1–25, 1948–80 (See Part 1 and GLAH 1:Q196). Publication of the Hamburger Kunsthalle, a decorative arts museum with collections of modern and contemporary art, Arts & Crafts, photography, textiles, and graphic design. While a companion publication, Jahrbuch des Museums für Kunst und Gewerbe Hamburg (1982– , see GLAH 2:Q219), concentrates on annual museum activities, Im Blickfeld presents extensive scholarly articles, many presented in symposiums at the museum. Includes lists of new acquisitions. BHA.

Q208 Information design journal, 1979– . London, Information Design Journal Ltd. Three issues a year.

Journal of graphic arts and typography. Presents articles and case-study papers on various interdisciplinary issues. Signed book reviews. ARTbib.mod.; Des.&Ap.Arts; Uncover.

Q209 INKS: cartoon and comic arts studies, v.1–4, no.3, Feb. 1994–Nov.1997. Columbus, Ohio, Ohio State Univ. Three issues a year.

Also available on microfilm: Ann Arbor, UMI.

"[The journal's purpose] is to advance the knowledge of cartooning through meticulous research focusing on American and western European work of the nineteenth and twentieth centuries."—*Advert.* Ed. at the Ohio State Univ. Cartoon, Graphic and Photographic Art Research Library, the largest repository of cartoon-related material in the USA. Scholarly and international coverage of comic art studies. Articles give a broad and diverse overview and provide original scholarship and historical evaluation. Writers have included art historians, literary critics, sociologists and economists, political scientists, and educators. "Presents a broad spectrum of cartoon and comic art studies in an attractive format."—*Review*, Art documentation, v.13, no.3, fall 1994, p.154–55. Includes signed book, exhibition and video reviews. ARTbib.mod.; BHA; DesAp.A.ind.; MLA.

Q210 International journal of cultural property, v.1, 1992– . N.Y., de Gruyter. Semiannual.

Published for the International Cultural Property Society, this interdisciplinary journal covers all aspects of cultural property including law, ethics, economics, and exportation of art. Created to foster better international understanding of cultural property policies. Scholarly articles cover a wide spectrum of disciplines. Annual index. Available on the internet by subscription. Anth.lit.; ARTbib.mod.; BHA; Uncover.

Q211 International review of African American art, v.6, no.1, 1984– . Hampton, Va., Hampton Univ. Museum. Quarterly. Place of publication, publisher vary.

Continues: Black art, an international quarterly (Jamaica, N.Y., Black Art, Ltd.), v.1–5, no.4, fall 1976–84. Founded by noted artist and art historian, Samella S. Lewis, and dedicated to the understanding and exploration of art of the international Black world, particularly African American art and culture and its African influences. Issues are thematic, with interviews and profiles, feature articles, collectors news, and exhibition news. Well-illustrated. Summary of latest issue available on the internet. Am.H.&.L.; Art full; Art index (1994–); ARTbib.mod.; ArtHum.; Article1st; Avery; BHA; Clo.T.A.ind.; Contents1st; Curr.Cont.A.&H.; Curr.Cont.Connect; Exp.Acad.; Francis; PerAbs.; Proquest; Uncover.

———. Guide to Black art: an international quarterly and the International review of African American art. Index, to v.1–10 (1976–93), compiled by Karen C. Costa. Hampton, Va., Hampton Univ. Museum, 1993. 71p.

Q212 Inuit art quarterly, v.1, spring 1986– . Balderson, Ontario, Kingait Pr. Quarterly.

Unique journal on the arts of the Polar areas. Covers both traditional forms of art, including painting, printmaking, wall hangings, carvings, metalwork, textiles, and newer forms, such as video and electronic art. Articles feature artists, collectors, and curators. Beautifully produced and sensitive to the various ethnic groups, the journal includes artist profiles, signed book and exhibition reviews, news of publications, exhibitions, new acquisitions, ads. Of interest to collectors and curators, critics, librarians, and teachers. Includes annual indexes. Table of contents of current issue available on the internet. Anth.ind.; Art index (1994–); ARTbib.mod; Biog.ind.

Q213 Irish arts review yearbook, v.8, 1991/92– . Dublin, Ireland, State Apartments. Annual.

Continues: Irish arts review, v.1–4, no.4, spring 1984–winter 1987; The GPA Irish arts review yearbook, v.5–7, 1988–90/91. Authoritative annual that began as a quarterly. Art of all periods and media (painting, sculpture, architecture, metalwork, design, book arts), museum highlights, interviews, and new acquisitions, written by curatorial staff and faculty of museums and universities. Includes signed book and exhibition reviews. Art full; Art index (1998–); ARTbib.mod.; Avery; BHA; Des.&Ap.A.ind.; Francis; RILA; RILM.

Q214 Iskusstvoznanie: zhurnal po istorii i teorii iskusstva, 1, 1998– . Moskva, RAN, Institut iskusstvoznaniia. Quarterly, some issues combined.

Continues: Voprosy iskusstvoznaniia: zhurnal Mezhdunarodnoi assotsiatsii iskusstvovedov = Inquiries in art history: a Russian quarterly journal of art and architectural history, 1993–97. Russian art historical journal providing one of the few outlets for scholarly publishing in art history in Russia. Exhaustive in coverage and without illustration. Articles have covered the art and architecture of Russia, particularly the Russian avant garde, with occasional articles on western artists. In Russian, sometimes with English summaries. BHA.

Q215 Islamic art, v.1, 1981– (last published: v.4, 1991). N.Y., Islamic Art Fnd. (Distr. by Oxford Univ. Pr.). Irregular.

Eds.: Ernst Grube and Eleanor Sims.

Modelled after the defunct Ars Islamica (see GLAH 1:Q57), this extensive annual is dedicated to the art and culture of the Muslim world. First vol. is a report of papers read at colloquia on art and archeology in Asia. Other vols. cover architecture, painting, decorative arts, early Ottoman bindings, and Byzantine manuscripts. Avery; Clo.T.A.ind.

Q216 The Israel Museum journal, v.1, spring 1982– . Jerusalem, The Museum. Annual.

Continues, in part: The Israel Museum news. 1965– . Museum annual published primarily for benefit of the Friends of Museum, offering well-researched articles on Jewish art. Topics cover archeology, Israel and European art, numismatics, Judaica, prints and drawings, photography, design, architecture, etc. New acquisitions, news events. Anth.ind.; ARTbib.mod.; Avery; BHA; Clo.T.A.ind.; Dyabola; Francis; Ind.art.Jewish.st.; RILA; Rug text.arts.

Q217 JAB: the journal of artists' books, v.1, spring 1994– . N.Y., Brad Freeman, Interplanetary Productions. Semiannual.

Variant title: Journal of artists' books. Independent publication providing a "forum for serious and lively debate about artists books and the contents within them."—*Introd.* Short articles, interviews, news items, reviews, on quality paper; interesting graphics. Art index (1997–).

Q218 Jahrbuch der Staatliche Kunstsammlungen Dresden, 1976/77– . Dresden, Staatliche Kunstsammlungen Dresden. Annual.

Continues: Dresden. Staatliche Kunstsammlungen. Jahrbuch, 1959–1970/71, followed by Staatliche Kunstsammlungen Dresden, Beitrage und Berichte der Staatliche Kunstsammlungen Dresden, 1972–75 (See GLAH 1:Q162). Devoted to artworks in the museums in Dresden. Avery; BHA; Francis; Rép.d'art.

Q219 Jahrbuch des Museums für Kunst und Gewerbe Hamburg, neue Folge, Bd.1, 1982– (Bd.14, 1995 last issue published). Hamburg, Museum für Kunst und Gewerbe. Annual.

Continues, in part: Jahrbuch der Hamburger Kunstsammlungen, Bd. 1–25, 1948–80 (See Part 1 and GLAH 1:Q196). Hardcover scholarly museum annual published for the Museum, whose collections include arts and crafts from antiquity to the 20th century, modern and contemporary art, Asiatic art, photography, graphics, and textile design. Includes articles, new acquisitions, and museum events. BHA; Francis.

Q220 Jahrbuch des Zentralinstituts für Kunstgeschichte, Bd. 1–5/6, 1985–1989/90. München, Beck. Annual.

Short-lived, scholarly publication by the Zentralinstitut für Kunstgeschichte in Munich, covering all aspects of the traditional arts, including painting, sculpture, architecture, and book arts. Clothbound and substantial, each vol. primarily in German, with English abstracts. ARTbib. mod.; Avery; Clo.T.A.ind.; Rép. d'art; RILA.

Q221 The Japan architect: international edition of Shinkenchiku, v.34, no.1–403/404, Jan./Feb.1959–Nov./Dec. 1990; 1, 1991– . Tokyo, Shinkenchiku-Sha. Bimonthly, 1959; monthly, 1959–90; quarterly, 1991– .

Other title: JA, July 1965– . Continues: Sinkentiku, v.33, no.2–12, Feb.–Dec. 1959 (title varies: Shinkenchiku). International edition begins with v.31, no.6 of the Japanese edition; identical contents. Beginning with Jan./Feb. 1959, called The Japan architect. Glossy journal of contemporary architecture, featuring mainly Japanese architects and firms, with large, color plates. One issue per year devoted to winners of competitions sponsored by the publishers. In Japanese and English beginning 1991, each issue also having a distinctive title. Annual indexes. Arch.per.ind.; Art index (1984–); ArtHum.; Avery; Curr.Cont.A.&H.; Uncover.

Q222 Jewellery studies, v.1, 1983/84– . London, Society of Jewellery Historians. Annual.

Scholarly society journal covering the field of jewelry and metal work, from ancient to modern times. Circa nine articles are included per annual issue, and covering topics as wide-ranging as Phoenician earrings to Jewish marriage rings. Section of reviews on recent publications covers both general and technical publications, as well as exhibition catalogs. Art Ar.Te.Abs.; BHA; Dyabola; Francis.

Q223 Jewish art, v.12/13, 1986/87– . Jerusalem, The Center for Jewish Art, the Hebrew Univ. of Jerusalem. Annual.

Continues: Journal of Jewish art, v.1–11, 1974–85. Hardcover annual presenting scholarly articles on Jewish art, archeology, and artifacts, in English, as well as book reviews, calendar of events, and lists of current publications. Art index; ARTbib. mod.; ArtHum.; Avery; BHA; Clo.T.A.ind.; Curr.Cont.A.&H.; Dyabola; Francis; Ind.art.Jewish.st.; Rép. d'art; RILA; RILM.

Q224 Jong Holland: tijdschrift voor beeldende kunst en vormgeving na 1850/journal for art and design after 1850, v.1, 1985– . The Hague, Stichting Jong Holland. Bimonthly. Subtitle varies.

Complements the journal Oud Holland (GLAH 1:Q268), by covering Dutch art, architecture, and design after 1850. Articles by a team of Dutch art historians. Mainly in Dutch, with English summaries; occasional issue or article in English (e.g., Art after Guernica in 1991). Signed book reviews. Index to vols.1–5, then annual indexes afterwards. Arch.per.ind.; ARTbib.curr.; ARTbib.mod.; BHA; RILA.

Q225 Journal of contemporary art, v.1, spring 1988– (suspended with v.7, no.2, 1995). N.Y., Journal of Contemporary Art. Semiannual. Publisher varies.

Candid interviews and conversations with contemporary artists, photographers, and filmmakers form the basis of this small-format journal. Cumulative indexes. Future plans by the publisher are to transform the publication into an online journal, with more features and regular updates. Art index (1994–96); BHA; Uncover.

Q226 Journal of decorative & propaganda arts, no.1, spring 1986– . Miami Beach, The Wolfsonian Foundation of Decorative and Propaganda Arts. Quarterly, 1986–90; annual, 1992– .

None published in 1991. Fascinating, scholarly publication for the study of decorative arts, design objects, images, and propaganda arts from 1875 to 1945. Past topics have focused on national themes, and have included issues on Italian, Russian/Soviet, Yugoslav, Swiss, Brazilian, and Dutch design; current issues offer more general coverage. Lavish illustrations complement well-researched articles and interviews with prominent designers, by an international group of scholars. "Should be of interest to a varied audience of scholars, curators, educators, and collectors as well as those with interests in design and architecture."—*Review*, Art documentation, v.6, no.1, spring 1987, p.42. Art index (1998–); ARTbib. mod.; Avery; BHA; Clo.T.A.ind.; Des.&Ap.A.ind.; Francis; RILA; Uncover.

Q227 Journal of design history, v.1, 1988– . Oxford, Oxford Univ. Pr. Quarterly.

Also available in microfilm: Ann Arbor, UMI.

Significant academic, refereed journal of the Design History Society. Aims to be a forum for new research exploring the whole range of design history, including industrial and decorative design, textiles, interior design, as well as the history of arts and crafts and applied arts. Interdisciplinary in approach and international in scope, it includes articles, book reviews, conference reports, and information on archives and collections. Some issues thematic. Am.H.&L.; Art index (1994–); ARTbib. mod.; Avery; BHA; Biog.ind.; Clo.T.A.ind.; Des.&Ap.A.ind.; Des.int.ind.; Francis; Hist.abs.; Uncover.

Q228 Journal of philosophy and the visual arts: JPVA, no.1, 1989– . London, Academy Group Ltd. Irregular.

Ed.: Andrew Benjamin.

Monographic glossy publication on philosophy and aesthetics and its relationship to modern art and architecture. Each issue has distinctive title, such as The Body (no.4); Abstraction, (no.5), and Complexity, (no.6). Essays by well-known contemporary philosophers and critics, as well as architects and artists. Full-color illustrations. ARTbib.mod.; BHA; Francis.

Q229 Journal of pre-Raphaelite studies, new series, v.1, spring 1992– . Toronto, Strong College, York Univ. Semiannual. Place of publication, publisher varies.

Continues: The pre-Raphaelite review, v.1–3, no.2, Nov.1977–May 1980; The journal of pre-Raphaelite studies, v.1–7, no.2, Nov.1980–May 1987; Journal of pre-Raphaelite and aesthetic studies, v.1–2, no.2, fall 1987–fall 1989. Dedicated to arts and crafts and literature of the pre-Raphaelite movement. Extensive coverage given to major figures of the period. Written by scholars of English literature and art history. Cumulative index for 1977–87 in v.1, no.1 (1987). Signed book reviews. Finely produced. Table of contents of last three issues available on the internet. Am.Hum.ind.; ARTbib. mod.; ArtHum.; BHA; Curr.Cont.A.&H.; Francis; MLA; PerCont.ind.; Rép.d'art; RILA; Uncover.

Q230 Journal of Roman archeology, v.1, 1988– . Journal of Roman Archeology, Portsmouth, R.I. Annual. Place of publication, publisher varies.

Variant title: JRA. Academic journal concerned with archeology of ancient Italy and the Roman world from 700 B.C. to 700 A.D. Topics cover excavations, antiquities, and archeology, with articles in all languages. Signed book reviews. In English, French, German, and Italian. Latest issue and table of contents of older vols. available on the internet. Art index (1994–); Dyabola; Ind.art.Jewish.st.

Q231 Journal of the history of collections, v.1, 1989– . Oxford, Oxford Univ. Pr. Semiannual.

Engrossing, scholarly journal for the study of collecting and patronage in the broadest sense. Explores the social, ethnological, artistic, and political basis for collecting during all periods. "In a real sense, a new discipline of enquiry has been formed."—*Review*, Antiquity, v.65, Dec. 1991, p.1004–06. Also includes conference reports, news events, and signed book and exhibition reviews. Am.H.&L.; Anth.ind.; Art index (1994–); BHA; Clo.T.A.ind.; Francis; Hist.abs.

Q232 Journal of the Museum of Fine Arts, Boston, v.1–6, 1989–94. Boston, The Museum. (Distr. by Northeastern Univ. Pr.) Annual.

Scholarly articles on objects acquired in the collection, by curators from various departments of the museum. Art index (1994); BHA.

Q233 Kalías, año 1, feb. 1989– . Valencia, Spain, Generalitat Valenciana. Conselleria de Cultura, Educació i Ciencia, IVAM Centre Julio González. (Distr. by Harrassowitz, Wiesbaden). Semiannual.

Museum publication of modern Spanish and European art movements issuing from Valencia's contemporary art museum, IVAM, Instituto Valenciano de Arte Moderno, established from the estate of the Catalan artist Julio González. Exhibition notices and signed book reviews. In Spanish. ARTbib. mod.; BHA.

Q234 Katalog: journal of photography & video, v.1, Oct. 1988– . Odense, Denmark, Museet for Fotokunst. Quarterly. Subtitle varies.

Scholarly, elegant publication of the Museet for Fotokunst established in 1987 in order to exhibit contemporary Danish and international photographers. Its central focus is the museum's exhibitions program. Serves as a forum for essays, interviews, and debates on emerging and established photographers. Also includes book, exhibition, and gallery reviews, calendar of events, and annual indexes. In large format, with excellent layout and color illustrations. Text in Danish and English. Beginning in 2000, issues also available on the internet. ARTbib. mod.; BHA; Francis.

Q235 Kritische Berichte: Zeitschrift für Kunst-und Kulturgeschichte, Jahrg.1, 1973– . Frankfurt-am-Main, Jonas Verlag. Subtitle varies. Bimonthly, 1973–81; quarterly, 1982– (some issues combined). Place of publication, publisher, subtitle varies.

Small-format journal of art criticism and aesthetics by the Ulmer Verein für Kunstwissenschaft (1973–75; then Ulmer Verein, Verband für Kunst-und Kulturwissenschaften from 1975 onwards), an association for art and culture. The role of the journal is to examine the interrelationships between art history and socio-political systems, as well as urban renewal, conservation, museum work, and the politics of media. Book reviews; separate index to years 1973–92. Mostly in German, occasional article in English. ARTbib. mod.; Avery; BHA; Francis; Ibidem; Rép.d'art; RILA.

______Kritische Berichte . . . [etc.] Index, 1973–92, compiled by Annette Schmiedel. Marburg, Jonas Verlag, 1994.

Q236 Kunst og kultur: Norwegian journal for pictorial art, architecture & handicrafts, 1, 1910– . Oslo, Scandinavian Univ. Pr. in assoc. with the Oslo National Gallery. Quarterly. Publisher varies.

Well-established journal of Norwegian and Scandinavian art, important for its coverage of contemporary art, architecture, and crafts, with the occasional article on major European artists. Last issue of year contains book reviews. Index to v.1–50, 1910–1967 issued as v.54, no.4, 1971; annual indices begin in 1982. Text in Norwegian, summaries in English. Table of contents of last two vols. available on the internet. ARTbib. curr.; ARTbib. mod.; BHA; Francis; RILA.

Q237 Kunstforum international: Die aktuelle Zeitschrift für alle Bereiche der bildenden Kunst, Jahrg.1, März/Apr.1973– . Ruppichteroth, Germany, Kunstforum International. Monthly, 1983–85; bimonthly, 1985–92; five issues a year, 1992–95; quarterly, 1996– .

Small-format, voluminous journal offering an exhaustive view of contemporary art, particularly in Germany, as well as the rest of Europe. Includes feature articles, essays, project reviews, and interviews with leading contemporary artists, as well as extensive exhibition reviews. Covers all forms of modern art, including architecture, photography and video arts. Some issues have been thematic. Artists index in back of each issue. Art index (1994–); ARTbib.curr.; ARTbib.mod.; Avery; BHA; I.B.Z.; Int.photo,ind.; RILA.

Q238 Kunsthistorisches Jahrbuch Graz, Universität Graz, Institut fur Kunstgeschichte. Graz, Austria, Akademische Druck und Verlagsanstalt, Jahrg. 13, 1978– . Annual (slightly irregular).

Continues: Graz, Austria. Universität. Kunsthistorisches Institut. Jahrbuch, v.1–12, 1965–77 (See GLAH 1:Q180). Hardbound, scholarly publication of the Institute of Art History at the Univ. of Graz. Well-illustrated articles. Changes format with v.34 (1987), increasing in size and becoming thematic. Later vols. have covered such subjects as: Nature and art; International Gothic style in Eastern Europe, and Baroque art. Avery; BHA; Francis; Rép.d'art; RILA.

Q239 Labyrinthos, studi e ricerche sulle arti nei secoli XVIII e XIX, N.1/2, gennaio/giugno-luglio/dicembre 1982– . Firenze, Vallecchi. (Distr. by Licosa, Florence). Semiannual (some issues combined). Subtitle varies. Publisher, subtitle varies.

Ed.: Gian Lorenzo Mellini.

Scholarly publication covering art, architecture, literature, and history of the 18th and 19th centuries in Italy. Archival reports, unpublished manuscripts, and articles on little-known Italian artists characterize this journal, the only one devoted to this period of Italian art. Articles in English, French, German, or Italian. Arch.per.ind.; ARTbib. mod.; Avery, BHA; Francis; Rép.d'art; RILA.

Q240 Landscape architecture, v.1, Oct. 1910– . Washington, D.C., American Society of Landscape Architects. Quarterly, 1910–75; bimonthly, 1976–1984; monthly, 1985– . Place of publication varies.

Official journal of the American Society of Landscape Architects, covering all aspects of landscape architecture, landscape planning, design, development, and construction. Includes biographies of important landscape architects. Illustrated, with bibliographies, annual indexes, extensive, signed book review section, awards, products and buyers guides, coming events section for academic and professional meetings. Directory & buyer's guide (1997–). Index to last two years of the journal available on the internet. Arch.per.ind.; Art index (1984–); ARTbib. mod.; ArtHum.; Article1st; Avery; Biog.ind.; Contents1st; Curr.Cont.A.&H.; Gard.lit.; Uncover.

______. Compiled index to v.1–20 (Oct. 1910–July 1930), Boston, Landscape Architecture Pub. Co., 1930. 55p.

______. Index to Landscape architecture magazine, 1910 to 1982, compiled by Bruce K. Ferguson. Mesa, Ariz., PDA, 1982. 312p.

______. Landscape architecture magazine cumulative index 1910–1987. Mesa, Ariz., PDA, 1988. 311p.

Q241 Landscape design, no.93, Feb. 1971– . Surrey, Eng., Landscape Design Trust. Quarterly. Publisher varies.

Continues: Journal of the Institute of Landscape Architects, no.1–92, Aug. 1941–Nov. 1970. Journal of landscaping, gardens, land design, new techniques, and management problems with particular emphasis on Great Britain and Ireland. Well-researched articles often accompanied by bibliographies. Also included are annual indexes, book reviews, calendar of events, plans, charts, annual indices. Arch.per.ind.; Art index (1998–); Article1st; Avery; Br.tech.ind.; Contents1st.; Uncover.

Q242 Landscape journal: design, planning and management of the land, v.1, spring 1982– . Madison, Wis., Univ. of Wisconsin Pr. Semiannual.

Also available on microfilm: Ann Arbor, UMI.

Scholarly journal of landscape architecture ed. at the Dept. of Landscape Architecture, Univ. of Wisconsin–Madison, in cooperation with the Council of Educators in Landscape Architecture. Aimed at both the practicing landscape designer and academics, offers research papers, project reports, and theoretical essays. Illustrated, with annual index and signed book reviews. Arch.per.ind.; Art index (1998–); Article1st; Avery; BHA; Contents1st; Francis; Gard.lit.; Ind.hist.pres.per.; Uncover.

Q243 Landscape research, v.2, no.1, winter 1976– . Cambridge, Mass., Carfax Pub. Co. Three issues a year. Place of publication, publisher varies.
Also available in microfilm: Ann Arbor, UMI.

Formerly: Landscape research news, v.1, no.1–12, Aug. 1968–summer 1976. Membership journal of the Landscape Research Group Ltd. International and interdisciplinary journal of land use research and the environment. Audience comprises architects, town planners, ecologists, economists, and geographers. Includes exhibition and book reviews, bibliographies. Author and subject index for vols. 1–16 (1968–91). The society also publishes Landscape news extra (no.1, winter 1988–), a supplement that includes news, events, and conference reports. Art Ar.Te.Abs.; Article1st; BHA; Contents1st.; Francis; Uncover.

Q244 Latin American antiquity: a journal of the Society for American Archeology, v.1, Mar. 1990– . Wash., D.C., The Society. Quarterly.
Also available in microfilm: Ann Arbor, UMI.

Scholarly journal of archaeology, prehistory, and ethnohistory of the Indians of Mesoamerica, Central, and South America. Promotes communication between English, and Spanish-speaking archaeologists working in Latin America. Articles by Latin American scholars, as well as reports, signed book reviews, indexes. "Published by the Society for American Archeology as a companion to its longstanding journal American antiquity."—*Review*, Antiquity, v.66, Mar. 1992, p.269–270. In Spanish and English. Table of contents of all issues available on the internet. Acad. Search; Anth.ind.; Anth.lit.; ArtHum.; Curr.Cont.A&H.; Curr.Cont.Connect; EBSCO Master; HAPI; Uncover.

Q245 Latin American art, v.1–6, no.1, spring 1989–94. Scottsdale, Ariz., Latin American Art Inc. Quarterly.
Well-written, illustrated journal, covering mainly modern and contemporary art (painting, sculpture, architecture, photography drawings, textiles, and graphics) in Latin America. Occasional articles on Pre-Columbian and colonial art, as well as on those artists influenced by Latin America. In addition to articles and interviews, there are reports from Latin America, auction information, and signed exhibition, and book reviews. Spanish summaries. Table of contents of issues available on the internet. Art index; ARTbib.mod.; BHA; Francis; HAPI; RILM; Uncover.

Q246 Luna córnea, Núm.1, invierno 1992/93– . México, D.F, Consejo Nacional para la Cultura y las Artes, invierno. (Distr. by Distributed Arts Publishers: DAP). Quarterly.
Mexico's premier photography journal, covering its rich photographic heritage as well as those of other countries. Issues include photo essays by leading photographers, profiles of photographers both living and deceased, and articles examining time periods and movements. Some issues thematic. In Spanish with English abstracts. Summaries of past issues available on the internet. ARTbib.mod.

Q247 M/E/A/N/I/N/G, no.1–19/20, Dec. 1986–May 1996. N.Y., M/E/A/N/I/N/G. Semiannual.
Artist-run journal addressing issues in contemporary art and serving as a forum for practicing artists engaged with critical issues. Contains articles, interviews, statements, writings, essays, and book reviews, written by artists, writers, poets, and critics. Conceived as an alternative to mainstream art journals. "The writing is accessible, intelligent, articulate, and sometimes visionary."—*Review*, New art examiner, v.17, no.3, Mar. 1990, p.57–58. Index to numbers 1–20 in no.19/20. ARTbib.mod.; Ibidem.

Q248 The medal, no.1, 1982– . London, British Art Medal Society. Semiannual.
Impressive, beautifully produced, scholarly society publication covering ancient to contemporary medal crafts, important medalists, coins, metallic art, and metalwork. Published by the British Art Medal Trust, in assoc. with the Fédération Internationale de la Médaille, to encourage and support the practice and study of medallic art. Articles mainly in English, occasionally in French and German, with English summaries. Separate index inserts to numbers 1–10, 1982–86; 11–20, 1987–91; 21–30, 1992–97. News and signed book reviews. ARTbib.mod.; BHA; Francis; RILA.

Q249 Mediamatic, v.1–9, no.4/v.10, no. 1, May 1986–fall 1999. Groningen, The Netherlands, Stichting Mediamatic. (Distr. by Bernard De Boer, Nutley, N.J.). Quarterly, 1986–99; Three computer disks per vol.
V.1, no.1, May 1986 preceded by v.0, no.0, Dec. 1985.

International, bilingual (Dutch/English) journal on electronic media, video and computer art, and related art, as well as hardware design. Currently published both on the internet and on computer disk. Issues have unique titles and include theoretical articles, historical overviews, technical essays, and interviews with artists. Issues are visually striking, with interesting typography, and also include book and video reviews, and a calendar of events. ARTbib. mod.; Clo.T.A.ind.; Ibidem; RILA.

Q250 Mimar: architecture in development, no.1–43, July/Sept. 1981–June 1992. Singapore, Concept Media. Quarterly.
Mimar, meaning master builder or architect, provides coverage of contemporary architecture, building, and design in Asia, Africa, the Middle East, the Far East, and Latin America. Created to foster communication and lively debate in developing countries. Some issues have been thematic and have included topics such as the mosques of Mali, winners of the Aga Khan Award for Architecture, and low-income housing in Jordan. "Mimar leads the field in its high-quality presentation of heretofore neglected works."—*Review*, Art documentation, v.5, no.2, summer 1986, p.93. Signed book and exhibition reviews, annual conferences, news, and excellent color reproductions. Arch.per.ind.; Art index; Avery; BHA; Biog.ind.; Clo.T.A.ind.; Francis; Uncover.

Q251 Minerva: the international review of ancient art and archaeology, v.1, Jan. 1990– . London, Aurora Publications. Ten issues a year, 1990; bimonthly, 1991– .
Continues: Popular archaeology, v.1–7, no.7, July 1979–Oct./Nov. 1986; Archaeology today, v.8–9, no.4, Feb. 1987–

Apr. 1988. Glossy, attractive, controversial journal of ancient art, antiquities, and archaeology, focusing on objects that have been newly acquired or have recently surfaced. Popular handling of ancient art and archaeology with regular departments discussing questions of stolen objects, new discoveries, auction results, as well as signed book and exhibition reviews. The journal aims to contribute to the effort to eliminate the illegal trade in stolen cultural property. Heavily illustrated with dealer and trade ads. BHA; Dyabola; Francis; Uncover.

Q252 Modern painters: a quarterly journal of the fine arts, v.1, spring 1988– . London, Fine Art Journals Ltd. Quarterly. Publisher varies.

Candid, outspoken, and readable art journal, devoted mainly to British painters and sculptors, from Victorian times to contemporary art. Well-known art critics, artists, and authors, such as Hilton Kramer, Anthony Caro, and Germaine Greer, examine aspects of modern British art. "A new magazine on modern British art with a strongly held point of view."—*Review*, Burlington magazine, v.130, April 1988, p.267. Signed book and exhibition reviews, calendar of events. Acad.Search; Art index (1994–); ARTbib. curr.; ARTbib. mod.; BHA; B.H.I.; Biog.ind.; Des.&Ap.A.ind.; Des.int.ind.; Francis.

Q253 Modernism/modernity, v.1, Jan. 1994– . Baltimore, Johns Hopkins Univ. Pr. Three issues a year.

Absorbing interdisciplinary, scholarly journal covering the effects of modernism on history, literature, social theory, and the arts during the first half of this century, with particular emphasis on European modern movements. Thus far, thematic issues have covered modernity as it relates to such areas as racism, Italian futurism, culture, and anarchism. Signed book reviews. Available on the internet by subscription. Am.H.&.L.; Am.Hum.ind.; Art index (1998–); ARTbib. mod.; ArtHum.; BHA; ECO; Curr.Cont.Connect; Hist.abs.; MLA; Uncover.

Q254 Le Moniteur architecture AMC. no.1, mai 1989– . Paris, Groupe Moniteur. Ten issues a year.

Continues: AMC, no.1 nouvelle serie- 23/24, mai 1983–dec 1988/jan. 1989; preceded by: Architecture, mouvement, continuité: bulletin de la Société des architectes diplômés par le gouvernement, no.1–54/55, nov. 1967–juin/sept. 1981 (other title: AMC déc. 1979–81). Numbers 1–12 also called 161–172 in continuation of: Bulletin mensuel d'informations de la Société des mensuel diplomés par le gouvernement, (Paris, 1951–67), which it supersedes. Tabloid-size society publication, with conference reports and proceedings, and other professional information. International in scope, with numerous articles on city planning, architecture, and design. Also publishes two special issues, one on architectural projects in France and Europe, and the other on completed projects for the year. Arch.per.ind.; Avery; BHA; Des.&Ap.A.ind.

Q255 Muqarnas: an annual on the visual culture of the Islamic world, v.1, 1983– . Leiden, The Netherlands, Brill. Annual. Publisher, subtitle vary.

Ed.: Oleg Grabar, then Gulru Necipoglu.

Sponsored by the Aga Khan Program for Islamic Architecture at Harvard Univ. and MIT. Scholarly, exhaustive treatment given to all phases and aspects of Islamic art and architecture, decorative arts, metalwork, and textiles, both historical and contemporary, with contributions by specialists in the field. Some vols. thematic. The journal is related to the hardcover series titled, Studies in Islamic art and architecture ("Supplements to Muqarnas"). (See GLAH 2:R95). Cumulative index, v.1–10 in v.10. Arch.per.ind.; Avery; Francis.

Q256 Muse, v.1, spring 1983– . Ottawa, Canadian Museums Association/Association des Musées Canadiens. Quarterly.

Also available in microfiche: Toronto, Micromedia.

Continues: Canadian Museums Association bulletin, v.1–14, 1940–63; CMA gazette, v.1–7, no.6, Nov. 1966–Mar./Apr. 1974 ; Gazette (Canadian Museums Association), v.8–15, winter 1975–fall 1982; Journal of the CMA, 1972–83.

Well-respected quarterly journal of the Canadian Museums Association, presenting research and commentary related to museum practices. While mainly devoted to Canadian museums, there is some coverage of American museums. Special issues have included design in Canada; museums and indigenous peoples; the 150th anniversary of the invention of photography and museum trusteeship."A highly respected periodical focusing on major themes and issues facing the Canadian museum community."—*Review*, Museum, v.42, no. 4, 1990, p.217–218. Bilingual, English, and French. Book and exhibition reviews, bibliographies. Am.H.&L.; Art Ar.Te.Abs.; ARTbib. mod.; BHA; Can.ind.; Can.per.ind.; Hist.abs.

Q257 Museum international, v.45, no.1, (= no.177), 1993– . Oxford, published for UNESCO by Blackwell. Quarterly.

Continues: Museum (Paris & N.Y., UNESCO), v.1–44, no.4 (July 1948–92) (see Part 1 and GLAH 1:Q245). Continues its focus on museums and collections from around the world; museum education, management, and other aspects of museology. Includes information on disaster planning and professional concerns. French and Spanish editions are published in Paris, an Arabic edition in Cairo, and a Russian edition in Moscow. Earlier title included index to vols.34–44, 1984–92 in v.45, no.3. Available on the internet by subscription. Arch.per.ind.; Art index; ArtHum.; Avery; Curr.Cont.Connect; Des.&Ap.A.ind.; Dyabola; ECO; IBZ; Uncover.

Q258 Museum management & curatorship, v.9, no.1, Mar. 1990– . Oxford, Elsevier Science Scientific Ltd. Quarterly. Publisher varies.

Continues: International journal of museum management and curatorship, v.1–8, no.4, Mar. 1982–Dec. 1989. Authoritative, scholarly journal on issues facing museums today, offering a forum for exchange of information on the administration, preservation, care, and presentation of museum collections. Written by and for the museum field, including curators, museum administrators, conservators, and designers. Bibliographies, annual indexes. Available on the internet by subscription. Arch.per.ind.; Art.Ar.Te.Abs.; Art index; ARTbib.mod.; Avery; BHA; Clo.T.A.ind.; RILA; RILM.

Q259 The museum studies journal, v.1–3, no.2, spring 1983–spring/summer 1988. San Francisco, Center for Museum Studies, John F. Kennedy Univ. Semiannual.

Academic journal aimed at museum professionals with practical information and techniques on such issues as museum administration, marketing, computerizing collections, and technology. Articles by museum administrators, curators, and researchers at various institutions across the country. Includes a useful bibliography on museum studies articles dating back to 1918. Arch.per.ind.; Art index; ARTbib.mod.; BHA; Uncover.

Q260 Museums journal, Nr.1, Aug. 1987– . Berlin, Museumspädagogischer Dienst. Quarterly. Publisher varies.

Absorbed: Staatliche Museen Preussischer Kulturbesitz. Berliner Museen. Beautifully produced and well-researched journal examining in detail exhibitions taking place in major museums in Berlin and Potsdam. The journal serves as a permanent record of these exhibitions, with articles written mainly by directors and curators of museums. Some museums covered include the Akademie der Künste, Bauhaus-Archiv, Museum für Gestaltung, and the Die Brücke Museum. 19th- and 20th-century art predominate, as well as graphic arts, photography, and film. Calendar of events. In German. Summaries of last several vols. available on the internet. BHA; Francis; RILM.

Q261 NKA: journal of contemporary African art, issue 1, fall/winter 1994– . Ithaca, The Mario Einaudi Center for international Studies & the Africana Studies and Research Center, Cornell University. Semiannual.

Published since 1995 in conjunction with the Africana Studies and Research Center, Cornell University. Sophisticated and graphically well-designed journal exploring new perspectives in contemporary African art. Thought-provoking and intelligent articles cover such issues as self-identification, race, and gender, as well as profiles on Africa's leading contemporary artists, written by theorists, scholars, and artists. Includes exhibition reviews, poetry, and short stories. Table of contents of issues available on the internet. ARTbib. Mod.

Q262 National Gallery, London. Technical bulletin, v.1–13, 1977–89; n.s. v.14, 1993– . London, National Gallery Publications Ltd. (Distr. by Yale Univ. Pr.) Annual.

Published by the National Gallery in London and presenting the latest in conservation and restoration techniques being carried out at the museum. Articles by curators, conservators, restorers, and art historians. Particular attention given to technical analysis, cleaning, and restoration efforts on paintings and other objects in the museum. Color plates, tables, and diagrams. Art Ar.Te.Abs.; BHA; Francis; RILA.

Q263 New art examiner: independent voice of the visual arts, v.12, no.10, summer 1985– . Chicago, Chicago New Art Association. Eleven issues a year (varies slightly).

Merger of: The new art examiner Midwest ed, v.1–7, no.10, Oct. 1973–July 1980, and East Coast ed., which began in 1980 and continued its numbering. Subtitled "the independent voice of the visual arts," NAE is committed to presenting diverse points of view on all aspects of artistic practice in the United States. Published in Chicago with a network of regional editors throughout the country, the journal covers a variety of issues, from government funding of the arts, to the thought processes that go into the creation of art, to the underlying agendas of major exhibitions. Other features include information on employment opportunities and noteworthy periodical and exhibition reviews. Full text of latest issue and table of contents of older vols. available on the internet. "The NAE's unique combination of interests has made it one of the most provocative art magazines."—*Review*, Art documentation, v.6, no.4, winter 1987, p.166 A.D.P.; Art full; Art index (1986–); ARTbib. curr.; ARTbib. mod.; Article1st; Avery; BHA; Biog.ind.; Clo.T.A.ind.; Contents1st; Francis; Int.photo.ind.; MLA; Rép.d'art; RILA; RILM; WilsonSelect.

Q264 Nineteenth century, v.1, Jan. 1975– . Philadelphia, Victorian Society of America, Quarterly, 1975–84; semiannual, 1990– . Publisher varies.

Also available on microfilm: Ann Arbor, UMI.

Absorbed: Classic America, in 1990. Suspended 1985–1989. Resumed publishing with v.10, no.1, spring 1990. Society journal for the study of the cultural and social history of the Victorian period in the United States from 1790 to 1917, particularly art and architecture. Typical articles include such subjects as Victorian resorts and hotels and Victorian furniture. Some issues thematic. Also includes conference reports and signed book reviews. Index to vols.1 to 9 in v.9, no.1–2, spring 1984. Am.H.&L.; Art index (1984–); ARTbib.curr.; ArtHum.; Avery; BHA; Clo.T.A.ind.; Curr.Cont.A.&H.; Gard.lit.; Hist.abs.; Ind.hist.pres.per.

Q265 Nuovi studi: rivista di arte antica e moderna, anno 1, 1996– . Trento, Italy, Temi. Semiannual.

Scholarly journal founded by a group of young Italian art historians. Articles include new discoveries and attributions concerning both well-known and unfamiliar Italian artists of the Renaissance through Neoclassical periods. Excellent black-and-white plates in the back of each vol. In Italian, occasionally in English or French. BHA.

Q266 OPD restauro: rivista dell'Opificio delle pietre dure e laboratori di restauro di Firenze, nuova ser., 1, 1989– . Firenze, Centro Di. Annual. Subtitled, publisher vary.

Continues: OPD restauro: quaderni dell'Opificio delle pietre dure e laboratori di restauro di Firenze, 1–3, 1986–88. Scholarly treatment given to articles on the conservation and restoration of art works from this well-known conservation laboratory in Florence. Notes, news events, activities of the Opificio. Mainly in Italian. Includes supplementary vols. Avery; BHA; Ibidem.

Q267 October, v.1, spring 1976– . N.Y., Institute for Architecture and Urban Studies; Cambridge, Mass., MIT Pr. (Distr. by J. Reitman, N.Y.). Quarterly.
Also available on microfilm: Ann Arbor, UMI.
Individualistic opinion magazine of art criticism and theory, founded by critic Rosalind Krauss and former editors of Artforum, and sponsored by the Institute for Architecture and Urban Studies (IAUS) in New York. Focuses on the structural and social interrelationships between various contemporary arts, such as painting, sculpture, photography, music, film, dance, performance art, theater, and literature. Credited with bringing "Marxist and structuralist theory into foreground of contemporary criticism."—*Introd.* Takes its title from Eisenstadt's film that celebrates the tenth anniversary of the revolution. Occasional special issues. Index to nos.1–50, 1976–89 in v.16 (summer 1992), then yearly. Two anthologies have been published: October: the first decade, 1976–1987 (Cambridge, Mass., MIT Pr., 1987), and October: the second decade, 1986–1996. (Cambridge, Mass., MIT Pr., 1997). Table of contents of last five years available on the internet. Acad.Search; Art full; Art Ar.Te.Abs.; Art index (1986–); ARTbib. curr.; ARTbib. mod.; ArtHum.; Article1st; Avery; BHA; Br.tech.ind..; Clo.T.A.ind.; Contents1st; Curr.Cont.A.&H.; Curr.Cont.Connect; Francis; Ibidem; Int.photo.ind.; MLA; RILA; Uncover.

Q268 Orientations, v.1, Jan. 1970– . Hong Kong, Orientations Magazine Ltd. Eleven issues a year (slightly irregular).
Subtitled: "the monthly magazine for collectors & connoisseurs of Asian art," this collector-oriented journal has become more scholarly over the years. Examines fine art and craft in Asia (ceramics, decorative arts, painting, sculpture, architecture, and archaeology), with at least one article on the textile or ceramic arts of China, Japan, or Korea. Occasional critical work on the political analysis of art, ancient to contemporary, drawing on the social history, cultural studies, and linguistics. Also includes bibliographies, sales and auction information, long book and exhibition reviews, reports from various cities worldwide, book reviews, and calendar of events related to Asian art worldwide. Some issues thematic. Numerous ads. Cumulative index for 1970–1989, then yearly. Summaries of principal articles of last few years available on the internet. Art Ar.Te.Abs.; Art index (1998–); ARTbib.curr.; ARTbib.mod.; Article1st; Clo.T.A.ind.; Contents1st; Francis; Rug text.arts; Uncover.

Q269 Oxford art journal, v.1, Oct. 1978– . Oxford, Oxford Univ. Pr. Semiannual.
Also available on microfilm: Ann Arbor, UMI.
Issues for 1978–79 (no.1–3) lack vol. numbering but constitute v.1–2. Scholarly, non-traditional art history journal, with a British slant. Issues contain long research articles drawing on social history, politics, cultural studies, language, and linguistics. Covers all periods and geographic areas of art history. Extensive, signed book and exhibition reviews. Some issues thematic. Table of contents and summaries of last few issues available on the internet. Am.H&L.; Art index (1985–); ARTbib.mod.; ArtHum.; Article1st; Avery; BHA; B.H.I.; Biog.ind.; Clo.T.A.ind.; Contents1st; Curr.Cont.Connect; Des.&Ap.A.ind.; Des.int.ind.; Francis; Hist.abs.; PerCont.ind.; RILA; Uncover.

Q270 Oxford journal of archaeology, v.1, Mar. 1982– . Oxford, Blackwell. Three issues a year.
Also available on microfilm: Ann Arbor, UMI.
Scholarly English language journal of archaeology from Paleolithic to Roman periods in the Mediterranean, Europe, and British Isles. Subject areas covered include architecture, numismatics, metalwork, ancient art, and antiquities. Notes of excavations, annual indexes. Available on the internet by subscription. Anth.lit.; Art Ar.Te.Abs.; ArtHum.; Article1st; Avery; BHA; Contents1st; Curr.Cont.Connect; Dyabola; ECO; Francis; RILA; Uncover.

Q271 Pacific arts, no.1 & 2, 1990– . Honolulu, Pacific Arts Association, c/o Metropolitan Museum of Art, Dept. AAOA. Semiannual (some issues combined).
Continues: Pacific Art newsletter (PAN), no.1–7, June 1975–June 1978; Pacific Arts newsletter (PAN), no.8–29, Jan. 1979–89.
Journal of the Pacific Arts Association, an international organization whose aim is to study the arts of all of Oceania, including Pacific rim countries. Subject areas mainly concern those collections and museums with holdings in Oceanic art. Articles are numerous and are written by university professors, ethnologists, artists, and museum curators. Includes signed reviews of Oceanic art books. The association also publishes a Newsletter (no.1, 1993–). Anth.lit.; Anth.ind.; ARTbib.mod.; RILM.

Q272 Palladio: rivista di storia dell'architettura, nuova ser. anno 1–2, giugno 1988– . Roma, Istituto Poligrafico e Zecca dello Stato. (Distr. by Casalini Libri, Fiesole). Semiannual. Publisher varies.
Continues: Palladio; rivista di storia dell'architettura anno 1–5, 1937–41; nuova ser., anno 1–24, 1951–77; terza ser. v.25–28, 1978–79, anno 3, 1980 (See GLAH 1:Q270). Publication suspended 1981–87. A notable Italian journal of architectural history that began publication before the second World War. Returned after a six-year hiatus in a thoroughly revised and expanded edition. The journal strives for diversity in its topics, using different approaches and providing discussions on architectural history, urban landscape, and planning. Signed book reviews. Summaries in English, French, German, and Spanish. Cumulative index, 1937–91. Art index; Avery; BHA; Dyabola; Francis.

Q273 Pan Spezial, 1–4, 1992. Offenburg, Germany, Burda GmbH. Quarterly.
Continues: Die Kunst und das schöne Heim: Monatsschrift für Malerei, Plastik, Graphik, Architektur, und Wohn Kultur, Jahrg.47–96, Heft 3, Apr. 1949–Marz 1984 (See Part 1 and GLAH 1:Q215); Die Kunst, Apr. 1984–Sept. 1988; Absorbed by Pan, 1992/4. Shortlived, glossy journal of contemporary European art. Thematic in content, issues covered include: Impressionism, Documenta IX, and Art in Cologne. Color illustrations. In German. ARTbib.mod.

Q274 Parachute, 1, Oct./Dec. 1975– . Montréal, Ed. Parachute. Quarterly.

Also available on microfiche: Toronto, Micromedia.

Premier journal for Canadian contemporary art and art criticism, ed. since its inception by two art critics, Chantal Pontbriand and France Morin. Its main purpose is to make contemporary art in Québec and Canada known to the outside world. Contains articles, interviews, an opinionated debate section, news on the contemporary local, national and international art scene, and exhibition and book reviews (including new art journals). Attractively designed in large format. Bilingual French/English. Art full; Art index (1998–); ARTbib.curr.; ARTbib.mod.; BHA; Can.ind.; Can.per.ind.; Francis; Ibidem; Int.photo.ind.; Repère; RILA; Uncover.

Q275 Parkett, no.1, 1984– . New York and Zürich, Parkett Verlag. (Distr. by Distributed Art Publishers: DAP). Quarterly (slightly irregular).

Luxurious, monographic journal of European and American contemporary art. Each issue (called "collaborations") examines, through interviews and essays, one or two important artists and is written with their assistance. Substantial in size, and beautifully produced on heavy paper, the journal is issued in a regular and deluxe edition. The latter includes a signed original art work by one of the artists featured, the former a reproduction of that same art work. Also includes exhibition reviews. Amply illustrated with full-page color plates. Bilingual text in German and English. "Parkett's deluxe presentation is clearly intended to intrigue and entertain."—*Review*, New art examiner, v.14, no.9, May 1987, p.17–18. Index to 1984–94 in issue no.40/41. Art index (1994–); ARTbib.mod.; BHA; Francis; Ibidem.

Q276 La part de l'oeil, no.1, 1985– . Bruxelles, Presses de l'Academie royale des beaux-arts de Bruxelles. Annual.

Substantial journal exploring the role of perception in art and its relationship with painting, poetry, film, and psychoanalysis. Written by a group of international art critics and scholars, issues are thematic in scope. In French. Black-and-white illustrations. ARTbib.mod.; BHA; Francis; RILA.

Q277 Perspektief: quarterly photography magazine, Nr.1–49, 1980–spring 1995. Rotterdam, Stichting Perspektief. Bimonthly, 1980–81; quarterly, 1981– . Subtitle varies.

Bilingual Dutch/English (since July 1982) thematic contemporary journal of photography and the visual arts. Serves as a platform for the Perspektief Foundation, begun in 1980 as an artists' initiative and evolving into a center offering exhibitions, workshops, and lectures by and about emerging international photographers, as well as new developments in photography. Also includes portfolios, signed book and exhibition reviews, calendar of events, bibliographies, indexes, as well as a regular feature titled Fotodok, an index to current issues of thirty-five international photography periodicals. ARTbib.mod.

Q278 Phoebus: a journal of art history, 1, 1978– (latest published: 7, 1995). Tempe, College of Fine Arts, Arizona State Univ. Irregular.

Art history school publication produced by the Art History faculty of the college. Small format. Concerned mainly with art in Arizona collections. But subjects cover all areas. Later issues have been thematic. Includes papers from symposia held at the school. Last published issue on native art in colonial Latin America. BHA; Francis; RILA.

Q279 Photographic collector, v.1–5, no.3, spring 1980–85. London, Bishopsgate Pr. Quarterly.

Absorbed Photographs, a collectors newsletter. "Serves as a forum for connoisseurship, and a marketplace for antique and collectible photography which is bought, sold or traded for the purpose of being enjoyed."—*Introd.* Subject areas concern only pre-WWII subjects. Int.photo.ind.; Photohi.

——— Michael Pritchard, The photographic collector: a cumulated index: 1980–1985. Bushley, England, ALLM Books, 1988. 24p.

Q280 Photographies, no.1–8, printemps, 1983–sept. 1985; número hors-série, mars 1986. Paris, Association française pour la diffusion de la photographie. Quarterly.

Well-respected and stylish international journal of contemporary photography, published under the auspices of the Bibliothèque nationale and the Direction du Patrimoine. International in scope. Portfolios of individual photographers focus a particular theme. Other articles feature the photography collection holdings at the Bibliothèque nationale, the Musée national d'art moderne and the Musée d'Orsay. Includes exhibition review and technical information on cameras. English summaries. ARTbib.mod.

Q281 Places: a forum of environmental design, v.1, fall 1983– . Berkeley, Univ. of Calif.; Brooklyn, N.Y., Center for Environmental Design, Pratt Institute; Design Hist. Fdn. (Distr. by Eastern News Inst., N.Y.). Quarterly, 1983–93; three issues a year, 1994– . Subtitle, publisher varies.

Also available in microfilm: Ann Arbor: UMI.

Alternative publication on architecture and planning, exploring how places are designed, built, used, and maintained. Topics covered include civic space, parks, work and community spaces, gardens, and environmental aspects. Broadly interpreted to allow for discussion and debate. Critiques of design competitions, book reviews. "Visually appealing and the articles . . . are refreshingly free of jargon."—*Review*, Art documentation 5, no.4, winter 1986, p.183. Arch.per. ind.; Art abst; Art index (1994–); ArtHum.; Article1st; Avery, Contents1st; Curr.Cont.A.&H.; Curr.Cont.Connect; Des.&Ap.A.ind.; Gard.lit.; Ind.hist.pres.per.; Uncover; WilsonSelect.

Q282 Polish art studies, Polska Akademia Nauk, Instytut Sztuki, v.1–14, 1979–92. Wrocaw, Polish Academy of Sciences, Institute of Fine Art / Zaklad Narodowy im. Ossolinskich. Annual.

Scholarly journal presenting Polish art, architectural history and photography. Articles are translated into English or French. Signed book reviews. Am.H&L.; ARTbib.mod.; Avery; Hist.abs.; RILA.

Q283 Pratt journal of architecture, v.1–3, 1986–92. New York, School of Architecture, Pratt Institute. Biennial.

Thematic architecture school publication whose large monographic issues look at architecture and its relationship to other subjects (art, philosophy, etc.). Essays written by both students and faculty at the school as well as outside architects and architectural historians. Includes Pratt faculty and student projects. Elegantly presented with interesting typography. Avery.

Q284 The Princeton architectural journal, v.4, 1992. Princeton, N.J., Princeton Architectural Pr. for the School of Architecture, Princeton Univ. Irregular.

Continues: The Princeton journal: thematic studies in architecture, v.1–3, 1983–88.

Independent architecture school journal produced by students of the School of Architecture. Vols. have distinct titles, such as "ritual" (v.1); "landscape" (v.2); "canon" (v.3); and "fetish" (v.4), which are related to projects and articles by faculty, students, and alumni. Also includes interviews. Arch.per.ind.; Avery.

Q285 Print quarterly, v.1, Mar. 1984– . London, Print Quarterly Publications. Quarterly.

Considered by many to be one of the best scholarly journals devoted to prints and printmaking in Western Europe and the United States, from the 15th century to the present. Long articles, notices, and notes are written by scholars and museum curators. From 1984–87, published in assoc. with the J. Paul Getty Trust. Well-illustrated. Extensive exhibition and signed book reviews. Am.H.&L.; Art Ar.Te.Abs.; Art index (1994–); ARTbib.curr.; ARTbib.mod.; ArtHum.; Article1st; Avery; BHA; Biog.ind.; Curr.Cont.A.&H.; Clo.T.A.ind.; Contents1st; Francis; Hist.abs.; RILA; Uncover.

———. The Print quarterly index, vols. I–X, 1984–1993, compiled by Felix Pollak. London, Print Quarterly Publications, (1995). 166p.

Q286 Process: architecture, no.1–134, Aug. 1977–Mar. 1998. Tokyo, Prot Galaxy. Irregular.

International journal of contemporary architecture, well-illustrated, with plans and layouts. The journal's goal is to take readers through the entire design process, from the first presentation to completion. Issues are thematic and cover architects, architectural firms, housing, and landscapes. Publishes occasional special issues. Publishes occasional supplements. In Japanese and English. Arch.per.ind.; Art index (1994–); Avery; Uncover.

Q287 Prospettiva: rivista di storia dell'arte antica e moderna, n.1, apr. 1975– . Firenze, Centro Di. (Distr. by Centro Di, Florence). Quarterly.

Established Italian art history journal of ancient through modern art, in the tradition of Critica d'arte and L'Arte, with contributions by well-known Italian scholars. Published under the auspices of the Univ. of Siena, in assoc. with the Regione Toscana, a special section of the journal being devoted to cultural heritage news and events in Tuscany. Occasional special issues (e.g. festschriften). Exhibition reviews, news, recent acquisitions at the Uffizi, restorations, cumulative indexes. Profusely illustrated. ArtHum.; Avery; BHA; Curr.Cont.A.&H.; Curr.Cont.Connect; Francis; RILA.

Q288 Psychoanalytic perspectives on art: PPA, v.1–3, 1985–88. Hillsdale, N.J., Analytic Pr. (Distr. by Lawrence Erlbaum Associates, Mahwah, N.J.). Annual.

Ed.: Mary Mathews Gedo.

Short-lived, hard-covered annual focusing on the psychoanalytic meaning of the work of art, including style and iconography. Subjects covered are subdivided according to aesthetics, art theory, portraiture, and sculpture. Signed book reviews. "It holds out to the reader a promise of an erudite and rigorous discourse."—*Review*, Artweek, v.18, Dec. 12, 1987, p.9. Rép.d'art.

Q289 Public art review, v.1, winter/spring 1989– . Minneapolis, Forecast Public Artworks. Semiannual.

Valuable journal devoted to the field of public art. Created by Forecast Public Artworks to help audiences learn more about the field and to make public art more accessible. Types of public art covered include environmental and performance arts, murals and graffiti art, collaborations, festivals, sculpture gardens, memorials, and temporary projects. Articles, opinions, essays, and interviews written by experts in the field. Past issues have focused on multiculturalism, historic places, percent-for-art programs, first-amendment issues, and public art as it relates to the waterfront. Separate inserts included inside issue. Also includes information about competitions, book and project reviews. Art full; Art index (1994–); ARTbib.mod.; Uncover; WilsonSelect.

Q290 Quaderni dell'Istituto di storia dell'architettura/Facoltà di architettura, Università di Roma, nuova ser. fasc.1–10, 1983/87– . Roma, Bonsignori. Irregular. Publisher varies.

Continues: Roma. Università. Istituto di Storia dell'Architettura, quaderni no.1–73/78, 1953–66.

(See Part 1 and GLAH 1:Q306). Scholarly hardcover on architectural history, issuing from the Università degli studi di Roma "La Sapienza," Dipartimento di storia dell'architettura, restauro e conservazione dei beni architettonici. Areas covered range from medieval to 19th-century architecture, by noted scholars in the field. Lately vols. have been thematic in scope (e.g., fasc. 25–30 on St. Peter's). In Italian, occasional article in English, German, or Spanish. Arch.per.ind.; Avery; BHA; Dyabola; Francis.

Q291 Quaderni di Palazzo Te, anno 1–4, n.8, luglio/dec. 1984-genn./giugno 1988; nuova serie, anno 1, luglio/dic. 1994– . Milano, Electa. Place of publisher and publisher varies. Semiannual, 1984–88; Irregular, 1994– .

None published 1989–93.

Scholarly publication by the Centro Internazionale di Arte e Cultura di Palazzo Te, devoted to the description and history of Palazzo Te and the art of Mantua. Covers Mannerist art and architecture across disciplines (figurative arts, literature, history, religion, music, theater) as well as methodologies. Occasional translations of important authors' works originally appearing in another language. Fine color plates. In Italian or French. Avery; BHA; Dyabola; Francis.

Q292 Quaerendo: a quarterly journal from the Low Countries devoted to manuscripts and printed books, v.1, Jan. 1971– . Leiden, Brill. Quarterly.

Scholarly, academic journal created to fill gap created by demise of Het Boek, a Belgian/Dutch journal that ceased in 1967, covering the history of the book, early printing and printing presses, typography, libraries and humanism, early bookbindings. Articles mainly in English, occasionally in French and German, with English summaries. Also includes Dutch book auction sales, signed book reviews, and bibliographies. Cumulative indexes (latest is v.1–26, 1971–96), as well as annual ones. Am.H.&L.; BHA; Francis; I.B.Z.; Ind.art.Jewish.st.; Rép.d'art; RILA.

Q293 48/14, la revue du Musée d'Orsay, n.1, sept. 1995– . Paris, Ed. de la Réunion des musées nationaux. Semiannual.

Continues: Quarante-huite/quatorze: conférences du Musée d'Orsay, n.1–7, 1989–94. Annual.

Dir.: Henri Loyrette.

Handsome bi-annual publication of the Musée d'Orsay, focusing on the museum's collection for the period 1848 to 1914. Short, illustrated pieces on exhibitions and lectures held in the museum or at the Grand Palais are followed by longer articles, written by curators and art historians on topics related to painting, architecture, design, music, dance, literature, and philosophy. New acquisitions are included. Earlier vols. serve as records of conferences held at the museum. BHA.

Q294 Rassegna: quarterly of themes in architecture, anno 1, dic. 1979– . Bologna, Compositori. Quarterly. Subtitle, publisher varies.

Ed.: Vittorio Gregotti.

Elegantly presented, international journal of contemporary architecture, design, and technology, in style similar to Domus. Each issue presents a monographic study on mainly European design, architectural projects, town-planning, furniture, and individual architects. Currently published in separate English and Italian editions. Index to no.1–49 in issue 50, June 1992. Summary of contents of latest issue available on the internet. Arch.per.ind.; Avery; BHA; Des.&Ap.A.ind.; Dyabola; PerCont.ind.; RILA.

Q295 Raw vision: international journal of intuitive and visionary art, v.1, spring 1989– . N.Y., Raw Vision Ltd. (Distr. by Distributed Art Publishers: DAP). Semiannual.

Captivating journal dedicated to the examination and criticism of outsider art, self-taught art, naive art, art brut, and contemporary folk art, issued in collaboration with Outsider Archive, London. Inspired by the writings of Jean Dubuffet, founder of the Art Brut concept, which embraces all forms of art coming from basic creative urges. Engaging illustrations complement articles on artists worldwide, written by an international group of writers, researchers, and curators. Occasional article in French. Book reviews. Art index (1998–); Artbib.mod.; BHA; Francis; Ibidem; Uncover.

Q296 Reales sitios: revista del Patrimonio Nacional, año1, jul. 1964– . Madrid, Patrimonio Nacional Palacio Real de Madrid. Quarterly.

Journal of historic buildings, urban planning, and art and architectural patrimony of Spain. Also covers decorative arts, cinema, theater, and music. Some issues thematic. Color illustrations. In Spanish. Avery; BHA; Dyabola; Francis; RILA.

______. Indices de la revista Reales sitios, 1964–1986. Madrid, Patrimonio Nacional, n.d., 88p.

______. Indice, Reales sitios 1964–1992. Madrid, Patrimonio Nacional, 1994. 170p.

Q297 La recherche photographique, no.1–20, automne 1986–printemps 1997. Paris, Paris Audovisuel: Presses universitaires de Vincennes, Université de Paris VIII. Semiannual.

University publication, co-produced by the Maison Européenne de la photographie by Paris Audovisuel, and the Université de Paris, VII, to promote and stimulate discussions on the historical and aesthetic aspects of photography. Thematic issues have included "the family" (no.8); "Japan" (no.9); and "Europe 1970–1990" (no.13), which marks the beginning of its bilingual (French/English) status. Beautifully produced, full-page illustrations on heavy stock. Includes interviews, book reviews, listings, bibliographies. ARTbib.mod.; Photo.

Q298 Religion and the arts, a journal from Boston College, v.1, fall 1996– . Boston & Leiden, Brill. Quarterly. Place of publication, publisher varies.

Interdisciplinary, refereed journal exploring religious and spiritual expression in the visual, verbal, and performing arts, including literary criticism, religion, art, and architecture. About half the journal devoted to art-related issues. Written by scholars and theologians. Also includes book reviews, announcements of conferences and exhibitions, and lists of books received. Color and black-and-white illustrations. Preview of contents available on the internet. BHA.

Q299 Repères: cahiers d'art contemporain. no.1, 1982– . Paris, Galerie Lelong. Irregular.

Gallery name varies: Galerie Maeght; Galerie Maeght Lelong, lately Galerie Lelong.

Less lavish continuation of Derrière le miroir, n.1–253, Dec. 1946–Dec. 1982 (see Part 1 and GLAH 1:Q148) in the form of an exhibition catalog series on individual artists. Each issue has distinctive title and is devoted to a contemporary artist. Good color plates and signed text but, unlike Derrière le miroir, does not include original lithographs or indexes. ARTbib.mod.

Q300 Representations, n.1, Feb. 1983– . Berkeley, Univ. of California Pr. Quarterly.

Also available in microfilm: Ann Arbor, UMI.

Interdisciplinary journal founded by scholars from the Univ. of California at Berkeley, examining areas of "representation" in our society, particularly the way in which institutions and structures portray themselves in language, art, and culture. Authors are psychologists, philosophers, art historians, and literary critics. Special issues have focused on sexuality in the 19th century. Publishes indices at irregular intervals. Table of contents of past five years and author index available on the internet. Am.H.&L.; Am.Hum.ind.; ARTbib.mod.; ArtHum.; Article1st; BHA; Contents1st; Curr.Cont.A.&H.; Exp.Acad.; Francis; Ind.art.Jewish.st.; MLA; RILA; Uncover.

Q301 Res: anthropology and aesthetics, no.1, spring 1981– . Cambridge, Mass., Peabody Museum of Archaeology and Ethnology, Harvard Univ. (Distr. by Univ. of Penn. Museum Publications). Semiannual. Publisher, distributor vary.

Scholarly, interdisciplinary journal of "primitive" and non-Western art. Published by The Getty Center for the History of Art and the Humanities from 1981 to 1995, with the Peabody Museum of Archeology and Ethnology, Harvard Univ., in collaboration with the Laboratoire d'ethnologie et de sociologie comparative, Université de Paris X, Nanterre. Serves as a forum for exploring anthropology and aesthetic and cultural objects originating from all cultures and societies, both ancient, archaic and modern. Res unites an international group of art historians, philosophers, critics, linguists, and architects. Articles in English or French. Well-illustrated, includes book reviews. Anth.ind.; Anth.lit.; Art index (1994–); ARTbib.mod.; Avery; BHA; Clo.T.A.ind.; Francis.

Q302 Revue des archéologues et historiens d'art de Louvain, 1, 1968– . Louvain, Belgium, Institut supérieur d'archéologie et d'histoire de l'art, Université catholique de Louvain. Annual.

Small-format school publication on art history and archaeology, written predominantly by its students and faculty. Includes reports by recipients of doctorates and master's degrees from the school, as well as book reviews. Publishes occasional supplements. Articles in French, English, or Spanish. Art Ar.Te.Abs.; Avery; BHA; Dyabola; Rép.d'art; RILA.

Q303 Revue noire: art contemporain africain / African contemporary art, no.1, printemps 1991– . Paris, Revue Noire. (Distr. by Speedimpex, Long Island City, N.Y. and Distributed Art Publishers: DAP). Three issues a year, 1991; quarterly, 1992– .

Engrossing, oversize journal of African contemporary arts (painting, sculpture, dance, music, design, theater, literature), mainly of Black Africa and its diaspora. The focus is on the impetus behind the artist's artwork, not on art criticism. Thematic issues have covered arts of Mozambique, Mali, Benin, and AIDS and African artists. Also includes interviews, exhibition reviews of African artists residing around the world, calendar of events, indexes. Audio CDs accompany some issues. Text in French and English. Also publishes Revue Noire collection soleil, a series featuring photographers whose work is of or about the African continent. Art index (1998–).

Q304 Rivista d'arte, ser.4, anno 37, 1984– . Firenze, Olschki. Annual.

Continues: Rivista d'arte (Firenze) (See Part 1 for publication history and GLAH 1:Q303).

Suspended after anno 44, 1992.

Dir.: Ugo Procacci.

Continues in the scholarly tradition of the earlier series, by documenting the history of art and archival studies in Tuscany. Many articles originate from research conducted at the Istituto di Storia dell'Arte at the Università di Firenze. Includes name and place indexes. Art Ar.Te.Abs.; ARTbib.mod..; BHA; Francis; Hist.abs.; Hum.ind.; IBZ; PerCont.ind.; Rép.d'art; RILA.

Q305 Rivista dell'Istituto nazionale di archeologia e storia dell'arte, 3.ser., anno 1, 1978– . Roma, "L'Erma"di Bretschneider. Annual.

Continues: Istituto Nazionale di Archeologia e Storia dell'Arte, Rome. Rivista, anno 1–9, 1929–42; nuova ser., anno 1–24, 1952–76/77. (See Part 1 and GLAH 1:Q192).

Suspended 1943–51.

Continues to cover Italian art and archaeology, iconography, architecture, and painting. Includes indexes. In 1997, a separately published monographic series called "Supplementi" was initiated. In Italian. Avery; BHA; Dyabola; Francis; IBZ; Rép.d'art.

Q306 Rivista di archeologia, anno 1, fasc.1–2, 1977– . Roma, Giorgio Bretschneider. Semiannual, 1977; annual, 1978– .

Learned and handsomely produced hardcover journal of classical archaeology from an art historical perspective. Circa nine articles and fourteen book reviews per issue cover such subjects as pottery, sarcophagi, excavations, and scrolls. Includes reports from the sites. Articles in Italian, English, or German. Black-and-white plates in back of issue. Avery; Dyabola; RILA.

Q307 Rivista di storia della miniatura, no.1/2, 1996/97– . Firenze, Centro Di. Annual.

Continues: Miniatura: arte dell'illustrazione e decorazione dell libro, nos.1–5/6, 1993/96.

Beautifully produced society publication on medieval and Renaissance illuminated manuscripts and books, artistic production, botanical illustration, and ornamentation issued by the Società Internazionale di Studi di Storia della Miniatura. Profusely illustrated. Signed exhibition and book reviews. In Italian with English abstracts. BHA.

Q308 Rivista di studi pompeiani, v.1, 1987– . Roma, "L'Erma" di Bretschneider. Irregular.

Continues: Cronache Pompeiane, 1975–79; Pompeii, Herculaneum, Stabiae, v.1, 1983. Related to: Rivista di studi pompeiani (Napoli), 1934–46. House organ of the Associazione Internazionale Amici di Pompei, dedicated to furthering scholarly research on Pompeii, Herculaneum, and Stabiae. The journal is divided into two parts: articles in Italian (occasionally in English and German) on matters related to excavations, urban planning, and architecture; and association information on the excavation and restoration activities of the Soprintendenza Archeologica di Pompeii. Signed book reviews, color plates, with overlays. Summaries of contents of issues available on the internet. Avery; Dyabola.

Q309 The Rutgers art review, v.1, 1980– . New Brunswick, Students of the Graduate Program in Art History at Rutgers Univ. Annual.

Distinguished art history school journal, with contributions from graduate students from America and abroad. Articles and shorter research notes cover all facets and periods of art history and art criticism, including interdisciplinary approaches to art, literature, philosophy, feminist, and social sciences. Early vols. featured an in-depth interview with a prominent art historian. Index to vols.I–V in v.5, spring 1984. Amer.H.&L.; ARTbib.mod.; Avery; BHA; Francis; Hist.abs.; RILA.

Q310 Scandinavian journal of design history, v.1, 1991– . Copenhagen, Rhodos International Science and Art Pub. Irregular.

Independent journal conceived by its ed. Mirjam Gelfer (formerly ed. of Hafnia), and sponsored by The Danish Museum of Decorative Art in Copenhagen. Articles on all periods of Scandinavian design, furniture, art objects, arts and crafts, industrial and theater design, and interiors. Published in English to reach a more international readership. Signed book reviews of Scandinavian and non-Scandinavian publications; color plates. Amer.H.&L.; Art index (1998–); ARTbib.mod.; BHA; Des.&Ap.A.ind.; Francis; Hist.abs.

Q311 Sculpture, (v.6, no.2), Mar./Apr. 1987– . Chicago, International Sculpture Center. Bimonthly, 1987–1997; ten issues a year, 1997– .

Continues National Sculpture Center bulletin (Lawrence, Kan.) to 1977; International Sculpture Center bulletin, no.18, fall 1977–1981; Sculptors international, v.1–4, no.1, 1982–85; International sculpture, v.4, no.2–6, (no.1), Apr./May 1985–Jan./Feb. 1987. Absorbed Maquette in Jan. 1996. Membership journal of the International Sculpture Center in Chicago (formerly located in Washington, D.C.). An informative publication for the practicing sculptor, as well as collectors, directors, and the interested public. Articles are both practical and historical, and special issues have covered installation, the human form, and public art. Interviews, calendar of events, book and exhibition reviews. Modified version of latest issue and earlier ones available on the internet. Art Ar.Te.Abs.; Art index (1994–); ARTbib.mod.; Avery; BHA; Hist.abs.; Ibidem; Uncover.

Q312 The sculpture journal, v.1, 1997– . London, Public Monuments and Sculpture Association. (Distr. by Getty Trust Pubns., Los Angeles). Annual.

Scholarly annual of the Public Monuments and Sculpture Association, established in 1991 to promote and protect public monuments and sculptures in the U.K. Articles and approaches are diverse, and cover a range of topics from medieval to modern: such as European sculpture, garden sculpture, sculpture in museums. New attributions and workshop practices, patronage, collecting, and conservation also covered. BHA; Francis.

Q313 See: a journal of visual culture, premier issues, autumn 1994; v.1–2, no.3, 1995–96. Carmel, Calif., Friends of Photography. Quarterly.

Continues: Untitled, no.1–58, 1972–94.

Ed.: Andy Grundberg.

Sleek journal of the Friends of Photography, San Francisco, directed by former New York Times photo critic Andy Grundberg, who has set its tone and direction. Explores the impact of lens-based images on contemporary visual culture. Includes short photographic essays on contemporary culture, mass media, literature, and poetry. Beautifully produced portfolios of photographs and color illustrations complement articles. "Truly an extraordinary journal, which is attempting through its glossy, upbeat format and powerful images, graphics, and writing, to break new ground in an analysis of our visually-oriented society."—*Review*, Art documentation, v.16, no.1, 1997. p.43–44. Includes signed book and exhibition reviews. Art index (1998–); ARTbib.mod.

Q314 Sèvres: revue de la Société des amis du Musée national de céramique, n.1 1992– . Sèvres, France, La Société. Annual.

Distinctive society journal written for both the scholar and collector of French ceramics, particularly those manufactured in Vincennes and Sèvres. Circa eight articles per issue, including acquisitions by the museum for the year, news of the museum, bibliographies, and calendar of events. Color illustrations. In French. BHA.

Q315 Skala: Nordisk magasin for arkitektur og design, 1. Arg., nr.1–30, Apr. 1985–94. København, Henning Larsens Tegnestue. Bimonthly.

Tabloid journal of contemporary Nordic design and architecture. Interviews. In Danish and English. Index to no.1–30, 1985–94, in no.30. Avery; BHA; RILA.

Q316 Source: notes in the history of art, v.1, fall 1981– . N.Y., Ars Brevis. Quarterly.

Small-format, scholarly publication, on art and archaeology of all periods. Articles are concise (2,000 words), in keeping with strict 32-page format, and written by prominent art historians. The focus is on new discoveries and original research, with occasional thematic issues. ARTbib.curr.; ARTbib.mod..; ArtHum.; Article1st; Avery; BHA; Contents1st; Clo.T.A.ind.; Curr.Cont.A.&H.; Curr.Cont.Connect; Ind.art.Jewish.st.; RILA; RILM; Uncover.

Q317 Spazio e società / Space & society: rivista internazionale di architettura e urbanistica, n.s. 1, genn.1978. Rimini, Maggioli. Quarterly. Publisher, subtitle varies.

Ed.: Giancarlo De Carlo.

Continues Spazio e società : Espaces et société, 1976. Issues for Mar. 1982 to Dec. 1983 published with MIT Press. International journal of architecture and environmental design, and the relationship between "space and society." Theoretical articles, profiles on architects, commentary on projects and buildings, city planning, gardens and parks, environments. Also includes information on education, competitions. In Italian and English. Indexes for nos.1–36

(1978–86) and nos.37–72 (1987–95). Also has initiated a series titled Quaderni di spazio e società = Space & society, in 1998. Arch.per.ind.; ArtHum.; Avery

———. Index, nos.1–36, 1978–1986. Firenze, SAGEP. 86p.

Q318 Sponsored research in the history of art, v.1–13, 1983–93/94. Wash., D.C., Center for Advanced Study in the Visual Arts. National Gallery of Art. Annual.

Continues, in part: Research reports, history of art, (1), 1980/81; Center research reports & records of activity, 2–11, 1981/82–90/91; Center for Advanced Study in the Visual Arts, Center record of activities and research reports, 12, 1991/92– . Provides annual report of fellowships in art history awarded by public and private granting institutions, foundations, museums, and government agencies, both in the U.S., Canada, and recently, internationally. Using information provided by the agencies, each entry includes the recipient's name and institution, title of work, type of project, and year. A five-year cumulative vol. appeared in v.5. Available on the internet by subscription through the Canadian Heritage Information Network.

Q319 Statens museum for kunst journal, v.1, 1997– . Copenhagen, The Museum. Annual.

Continues: Copenhagen. Statens Museum for Kunst, Kunstmuseets årsskrift (København), 1–71, 1914–93 (See Part 1 and GLAH 1:Q139). Beautifully presented annual by the Statens Museum for Kunst, a leading institution of art historical research in Denmark. In a smaller format than its earlier version, Kunstmuseets årsskrift, its focus is now broader, with articles written mainly by curators from the museum. Now published entirely in English, in order to reach a more international audience. BHA; Francis.

Q320 Storia della città: rivista internazionale di storia urbana e territoriale, anno [1]–15 (no.1–54/56), sett.1976–apr./dic.1990. Milano, Electa. Semiannual, 1976–82; quarterly, 1983–90. Occasional double or triple numbers issued. Subtitle varies.

Ed. Enrico Guidoni.

Scholarly international journal of city and town history, issuing from the Istituti di storia dell'architettura e di Fondamenti dell'architettura dell'Università di Roma. After no.25, becomes hardcover with thematic issues. Articles are published in language of author (Italian, German, French, or English) with summaries in English, French, and German appearing at end of each issue. Separate index to nos.1–50, 1976–1989. AATA; Avery; BHA; Francis; Rép; RILA.

Q321 Studi di storia dell'arte, 1, mar.1990– . Todi, Italy, Ediart. (Distr. by Centro Di, Florence). Annual.

Scholarly hardcover presenting articles mainly on Italian Renaissance art, discussing principally lesser known and regional artists. Articles mainly in Italian, occasionally in English. Name and place indexes. Avery; BHA; Francis.

Q322 Studies in iconography, v.1, 1975– . Tempe, Ariz., Arizona State Univ. Annual. Place of publication varies depending on ed.

V.14–16 dated irregularly.

Scholarly articles on issues related to the literary and pictorial uses of iconography in art and literature, covering all periods of history. Began publication at Northern Kentucky State College to complement acquisitions to the Emile Mâle Collection. Signed book review section. Illustrated. Art full; Art index (1998–); ARTbib.mod.; ArtHum.; Avery; BHA; Curr.Cont.A.&H.; Clo.T.A.ind.; Francis; MLA; Rép.d'art; RILA.

Q323 Studies in the decorative arts, v.1, fall 1993– . N.Y., Bard Graduate Center for Studies in the Decorative Arts. Semiannual.

Interdisciplinary journal of the Bard Graduate School established to provide a forum for the examination of all aspects of decorative arts as documents of material culture. Covers all cultures and periods, relating the decorative arts to other disciplines, such as sociology, politics, and cultural history. The journal has a distinguished board of editorial advisors. "The scholarship is sound and well supported with generous notes at the end of each article."—*Review*, Art documentation, v.13, no.1, spring 1994, p.42–43. Book reviews. Am.H.&L.; Art index (1998–); ARTbib.mod.; Avery; BHA; Des.&Ap.A.ind.; Francis; Hist.abs.

Q324 Studies in the history of gardens & designed landscapes, v.18, no.1, Jan.–Mar. 1998– . Washington, D.C., Taylor & Francis. Quarterly.

Ed. John Dixon Hunt.

Also available on microfilm: Ann Arbor, UMI.

Continues: Journal of garden history, v.1–17, no.4, Jan./Mar. 1981–Oct./Dec. 1997. Scholarly, refereed journal, international in scope, filling a need for presenting research in English on gardens from around the world. With this title change, the journal continues its familiar format and interdisciplinary approach to garden history, with well-researched articles covering social and economic history, restoration of gardens, botany, and horticulture. Special issues are guest edited. Also includes signed book and exhibition reviews, indexes, and color illustrations. Amer.H.&L.; Arch.per.ind.; Art index; ARTbib.mod.; ArtHum.; Avery; BHA; B.H.I.; Biog.ind.; Curr.Cont.A.&H.; Curr.Cont.Connect; Clo.T.A.ind.; Francis; Gard.lit.; Hist.abs.; MLA; RILA; Uncover.

Q325 Tableau: fine arts magazine / Tijdschrift voor beeldende kunst, 1ste. jaarg., oct./nov. 1978– . Haastrecht, The Netherlands, Tableau Fine Arts Magazine. Bimonthly. Subtitle, place of publication varies.

Distinguished, well-illustrated. The leading fine arts journal in Holland. Articles cover the Old Masters through contemporary art, with reports of exhibitions both in The Netherlands and abroad, auction news, and calendar of events. In Dutch with abridged English translations. Index to 1978–94 in Jahrg. 17, nr.4, februari 1995. ARTbib.mod.; Avery; BHA; Francis.

Q326 I Tatti studies: essays in the renaissance, v.1, 1985– . Florence, Villa I Tatti, The Harvard Univ., Center for Italian Renaissance Studies. (Distr. by Olschki, Florence). Biennial.

Subjects include history, art history, economics, music, and literature. Articles in English, French, German, or Italian. ARTbib.mod.; BHA; Francis; Hist.abs.; RILA.

Q327 Technology & conservation: magazine of art, architecture, and antiquities, v.1, spring 1976– . Somerville, Mass., Technology Organization. Quarterly. Some issues combined. Subtitle, place of publication vary.

V.1 (1976) called Archaeology today; v.10 had only one issue (spring 1989).

Practical journal for the conservator and those interested in the conservation, preservation, and restoration of art, textiles, architecture, and antiquities, as well as issues of fire safety, disaster planning, and theft. Book reviews, calendar of events, index. Arch.per.ind.; Art Ar.Te.Abs.; Art index (1985–); Avery; Clo.T.A.ind.; RILA; Uncover.

Q328 Tema celeste: rivista d'arte contemporanea, anno 1, nov. 1983– . Siracusa, Italy, Prisma. (Distr. by Speedimpex, Long Island City, N.Y.). Three issues a year. Subtitle varies.

Journal of international contemporary art, important for its coverage of Italian artists. Founded by curator/critic Demetrio Paparoni, shaped by his particular vision, with articles, interviews, essays, book and exhibition reviews. In English and Italian. ARTbib.mod.; BHA; Ibidem; Francis.

Q329 Ten.8, n.1–36, Feb. 1979–spring 1990; v.2, no.1–3, spring 1991–spring 1992. Birmingham, Eng., Sidelines. Quarterly, 1979–89; annual, 1990; semiannual, 1991–92.

British photography magazine examining socio-political issues, media art, and journalism. High-quality reproductions. Issues are thematic. Interviews, book reviews. ARTbib.mod.; BHA; Francis; Int.photo.ind.; RILM.

Q330 Third text: Third World perspectives on contemporary art & culture, no.1, autumn 1987–. London, Kala Pr. (Distr. by Bernard DeBoer, Nutley, N.J.). Quarterly.

Continues: Black phoenix., no.1–3, winter 1978–spring 1979.

Intelligent, international publication examining art, architecture, politics, and literature of developing countries and its relationship to art of the West, with articles and interviews with artists and academics. Special issues have included one on cultural identity (in Dutch and English), and another on the art of Africa. Well-illustrated. "It aims to promote wider discussion and a deeper understanding of the work of Third World and black artists than can be provided from an exclusively Eurocentric or 'Western' viewpoint."—*Review*, Art libraries journal, v.13, no.3, 1988, p.20–21. Annotated index of past issues available on the internet. Art index (1994–); ARTbib.mod.; BHA; Francis; Uncover.

Q331 Threshold: journal of the School of Architecture, the Univ. of Illinois at Chicago, v.1–5/6, 1982–(1991). N.Y., Rizzoli. Annual.

Architecture school publication serving as a forum for publishing work by students and faculty. Issues are thematic, mainly focusing on Chicago architecture, and include essays, interviews. Avery.

Q332 TRANS> arts.cultures.media, v.1, Nov. 1995– . N.Y., Passim, Inc. (Distr. by Distributed Art Publishers: DAP). Three issues a year.

Original, graphically interesting, modern art journal published in Spanish, French, Portuguese, and English, utilizing electronic technology to explore art and cultural criticism in the Americas. An interactive feature of the journal found on the internet is meant to foster the exchange of information; some exchanges are reprinted in the journal. Articles, interviews, essays, and exhibition reviews cover the world of contemporary art, in the Americas primarily. "The writing reflects sound scholarship."—*Review*, Art documentation, v.16, no.1, 1997, p.33–34. ARTbib.mod.; Des.&Ap.A.ind.

Q333 Turner studies: his art and epoch 1775–1851, v.1–11, no.2, 1981–winter 1991. London, Mallord Pr. in assoc. with the Tate Gallery. Semiannual.

Unique, well-illustrated journal on the English artist J. M. W. Turner and his time. Scholarly articles by experts in the field cover the entire range of his career and influences and include correspondence, papers of symposiums on Turner held at Clore Gallery, sales records, reprints of older material as well as signed book and exhibition reviews and calendar of events. V.11, no.2 includes index to v.1–11. RILA; Uncover.

Q334 20/1: twentieth-century art & culture, v.1, no.1–2, fall 1989–spring 1990. Chicago, School of Art & Design, College of Architecture, Art & Urban Planning, the Univ. of Illinois at Chicago. Semiannual. Subtitle varies.

Short-lived, well-designed, and significant small-format journal providing new perspectives on the history, theory, and criticism of the arts in the 20th century. Second issue devoted to architecture. Signed book reviews. Avery.

Q335 Twentieth century architecture, no.1, summer 1994– . London, The Twentieth Century Society. Biennial.

Continues: Thirties Society journal, no.1–7, 1982–91. Thematic, slim, society publication focusing on buildings in Great Britain since World War I. Includes articles and lists of published houses, churches, and other buildings in the U.K. Arch.per.ind.; Avery; BHA; Francis.

Q336 UIA international architect, issues 1–8, 1983–85. London, International Architect Pub. Inc. Irregular. Subtitle, publisher varies.

Continues: International architect, v.1–2, no.9, 1979–82. Large-format journal of the Union Internationale des Architectes, examining the architecture of a particular location, culture, or time. Thematic issues have covered: Australian architecture (1983), Malaysian architecture (1984), and South African architecture (1985). Articles in English with summaries in German, Italian, French, and Spanish. "Provides extended coverage of current developments in ordinary architecture on an international basis."—*Review*, Art documentation, v.5, no.3, fall 1986, p.139–140. ARTbib.mod.; Avery.

Q337 Umbrella, v.1, Jan. 1978– . Santa Monica, Umbrella Associates. Bimonthly (Slightly irregular) 1978–84; semiannual, 1985– . Place of publication varies.
Ed.: Judith A. Hoffberg.

Absorbing, timely newsletter on contemporary and experimental art and artists, mail art, names in the news, conservation and preservation issues and activities in the book arts world. Extensive book and exhibition reviews, information on new periodicals and artists' publications. For art historians, librarians, artists, and anyone who wants to keep current in these areas. Summary of latest issue available on the internet. ARTbib.mod.; Int.photo.ind.

Q338 Urbi: arts, histoire, ethnologie des villes, 1–11, sept. 1979–été 1989. Liege, Mardaga. Quarterly.
Scholarly publication on city and urban planning, garden history, military architecture, and engineering issuing from the Centre de recherche d'urbanisme and the Ecole d'Architecture de Paris-Conflans. Occasional thematic issue; e.g., military architecture in XI, 1989. In French with English abstracts. Arch.per.ind.

Q339 V & A album / Victoria and Albert Museum, 1–6, summer 1982–spring 1987. London, Templegate Pub. in assoc. with the Friends of the V & A, Annual, 1982–87; quarterly (slightly irregular) 1988–89.
Yearbook of the museum with numerous short articles written for the general reader by V & A scholars and curators, on art works in the museum, recent acquisitions, and activities in the museum. Subjects covered include the decorative arts, such as jewelry, rugs, and furniture. Heavily illustrated with ads. Avery; BHA.

Q340 VRA bulletin, v.16, no.1, spring 1989– . Columbus, Ohio State Univ. Quarterly. Place of publication, publisher vary.
Also known as Visual Resources Association bulletin, 1989–90, then VRA, Visual Resources Association bulletin, 1990–92. Continues: Mid-America College Art Association, slides & photographs newsletter, v.1–6, 1974–79; followed by International bulletin for photographic documentation of the visual arts, v.7–15, 1980–88. Society publication of the Visual Resources Association. Members comprise visual resource curators, art librarians, and all those who administer image collections and deal with issues of cataloging, processing, storing, and projecting images, as well as purchasing equipment. Starting as a slim newsletter of society information and professional news, the bulletin has developed into a substantial publication of international importance, which since 1994 publishes three or more articles per issue. These range in subject matter from digital image technology, to visual collections, to cataloging and copyright issues. One issue per year is devoted to conference papers and reports. Annual index and cumulative indexes every five years. Articles printed in the bulletin are available on the internet. Related to VRA special bulletin (see GLAH 2:R105).

Q341 Venezia arti: bollettino del Dipartimento di Storia e Critica delle Arti dell'Università di Venezia, 1, 1987– . Roma, Viella. Annual.
Beautifully illustrated, learned annual on all aspects of Venetian art and culture, with articles in Italian, and occasionally in French or English. Topics cover art, antiquities, architecture, film, and music. With exhibition reviews, congress papers, reports of restorations and inventories, book reviews, and information on the department. Avery; BHA; Dyabola; Francis; RILA.

Q342 Venezia cinquecento: studi di storia dell'arte e della cultura, anno 1, genn./giugno 1991– . Roma, Bulzoni. Semiannual.
Scholarly, small-format monographic journal focusing on the Venetian school of painters in the 16th century. Contributors are well-known scholars in the field. Issued by the Università degli studi di Roma "La Sapienza," Istituto di storia dell'arte. In Italian, with an occasional article in English and French. Black-and-white illustrations. BHA; Francis.

Q343 Vie des arts, no.1, janvier/février 1956– . Montréal, Societé La Vie des arts. Bimonthly, 1956–57; quarterly, 1957– .
One of the oldest surviving Canadian art journals concentrating mainly on the art of French-speaking Québec, as well as national and international art. Well-written articles cover mainly established contemporary artists and collections in Canadian museums and elsewhere, as well as art history, architecture, and museology. Includes reviews of exhibitions in Canada, North America, and Europe, as well as signed book reviews and indexes. In French or English. Art index (1998–); ARTbib.curr.; ARTbib.mod.; Can.ind.; Can.per.ind.; Int.photo.ind.; Rép.d'art; Repère.

Q344 View, v.1–8, no.2, April 1978–winter 1993. Oakland, Point Publications. Ten issues a year, 1978–80; bimonthly, 1980–93.
Provides excellent interviews with contemporary artists, one per issue, most of them printmakers associated with Crown Point Pr. ARTbib.mod.; BHA; Ibidem.

Q345 Visible religion / Institute of Religious Iconography, State Univ. Groningen, The Netherlands, 1–7, 1982–90. Leiden, Brill. Irregular.
Scholarly journal devoted to religious iconography of all traditions and cultures. Vols. are thematic with distinct titles, past issues have covered: popular religion, approaches to iconology and genres in visual representations. Articles in language of author, mainly English, French, or German. Anth.ind.; ARTbib.mod.; Clo.T.A.ind.; Dyabola.

Q346 Visual resources: an international journal of documentation, v.1, spring 1980– . Chur, Switzerland, Gordon & Breach - Harwood Acad. (Distr. by International Publishers Distributors, Newark, N.J.). Three issues a year, 1980–82; quarterly, 1983, 1986– . Subtitle, publisher and place of publication varies.
None published Sept. 1983–spring 1986.
Eds.: Helene E. Roberts and Christine L. Sundt.

Scholarly publication which provides an international forum for the study and documentation of visual materials.

Sponsored by the Visual Resources Association since 1986. Articles broadly cover the field of image documentation, including acquisition, access, organization, and preservation, utilizing the latest technology while promoting an appreciation for the field. Thematic issues, many of them guest edited by leaders in the field, have covered: Iconclass; electronic visual imaging in the museum; categories for the description of works of art; copyright; fair use issues; and papers presented at Visual Resource Association conferences and joint meetings. "Appeals to a wide audience interested in the use of images."—*Review*, Art documentation, v.6, no.3, fall 1987, p.138–139. Includes lengthy, signed book reviews, news items, and annual indexes. Arch.per.ind.; Art index (1994–); ARTbib.mod.; BHA; Clo.T.A.ind.; Francis; Rép.d'art; RILA; Uncover.

Q347 Werk, Bauen + Wohnen, 34. Jahrg., 1980– . St. Gallen, Bund Schweizer Architekten. Ten issues a year. Place of publication, publisher varies.

Continues, in part: Werk/Archithese [GLAH 1:Q348] (St. Gallen), v.64–66, 1977–79 [v.1–60, 1914–73 as Das Werk; v.61–63, 1973–76 as Werk/oeuvre]. Split into: Werk, Bauen + Wohnen (Zurich, 1980–), which itself is a merger in 1980 of Werk and Bauen + Wohnen, and Archithese (See Part 1 and GLAH 2:Q94). Vols. for 1980– called 67./34/ Jahrg. Continuing the numbering of Werk-Archithese and Bauen und Wohnen. Vols. for 1980–81 published in Zürich. Official journal of the Bund Schweizer Architekten and aimed at the practicing architect, each issue has a distinctive title. In German, French, and English. Occasional annual indexes. Arch.per.ind.; Art index (1984–); Avery; RILA.

Q348 WhiteWalls: a journal of language and art, v.1 Mar. 1978– . Chicago, WhiteWalls. Semiannual (slightly irregular) 1978–83; three issues a year, 1984–93; semiannual, 1994– . Subtitle varies.

A journal of experimentation, using essays, poetry, and critical writings by artists to explore the relationship between language and images. Some of these undertakings have included word and image projects, conceptual art, criticism, performance, film, video, and installations. Showcases artists who may have limited opportunities to exhibit their work, and includes emerging and established artists from Chicago and beyond. The journal also sponsors performances, lectures, and exhibitions by artists. Ed. until 1990 by artist and critic Buzz Spector, whom many consider to be the journal's "guiding force [who kept] the publication alive with unflagging devotion."—*Review*, New art examiner, v.14, no.5, Feb. 1987, p.19–20, 45. ARTbib.mod.

Q349 Woman's art journal. v.1, spring/summer 1980– . Laverlock, Pa., Woman's Art Inc. Semiannual. Place of publication, publisher varies.

Ed.: Elsa Honing Fine.

Also available in microfilm: Ann Arbor, UMI.

Revisionist scholarly journal documenting women in the visual arts. Launched in 1980, it filled a void left by the demise of Feminist art journal (GLAH 2:Q180) and Womanart (N.Y., 1976–78). Articles, mostly by recognized feminist art critics and art historians, cover American, European, Latin American, and Caribbean women artists, particularly those who are lesser known. Some issues thematic. Signed book reviews. Index to vols. 1–13 in v.13 (fall/winter 1992/93). Art full; Art index (1985–); ARTbib.curr.; ARTbib.mod.; ArtHum.; Article1st; Avery; BHA; Contents1st; Curr.Cont.A.&H.; Clo.T.A.ind.; Des.&Ap.A.ind.; Francis; Ibidem; PerCont.ind.; RILA; Uncover; WilsonSelect.

Q350 Women artists news book review, (1, 1993)– . N.Y., Midmarch Arts Pr. Annual.

Continues: Women artists newsletter, v.1–3, no.6, Apr. 1975–Dec. 1977; Women artists news, v.3, no.7–v.17, Jan. 1978–92. Issues for 1993– called also v.18, in continuation of numbering of Women artists news. Numbering begins with v.2, 1994. Began as a voice and advocate for women artists, increasing their visibility and covering all the visual arts. Includes articles reviews, interviews, and most importantly, biographical information on women artists, often lesser known. Lately issues concentrate solely on book reviews on women artists and their social environment. Art full; Art index (1986–); ARTbib.mod.; BHA; RILA; WilsonSelect.

Q351 Word & image: a journal of verbal/visual inquiry, v.1, Jan.–Mar.1985– . Bristol, Pa., Taylor & Francis. Quarterly. Place of publication varies.

Ed.: John Dixon Hunt.

Refined and scholarly journal focusing on the relationship between words and visual images in the humanities, with reference to iconography, linguistics, anthropology, semiotics, and the history of art. Most issues are on a single theme, with one issue per year being of a general nature. Special issues have included "poems on pictures" (v.2); "African art and literature," and "book illustration" (v.3). Some issues are guest-edited. Articles sometimes derive from papers given at conferences and colloquia on images, and are in language of author. "Though the scope of this journal is broad and far-reaching, the actual content is highly specialized and esoteric."—*Review*, Art documentation, v.5, no.1, spring 1986, p.33. Includes signed book reviews. Index to vols. 1 to 8 (in v.8), yearly thereafter. Amer.H.&L. (1985–95); Art index (1994–); ARTbib.curr.; ARTbib.mod.; ArtHum.; Article1st; BHA; Clo.T.A.ind.; Contents1st; Curr.Cont.A.&H.; Francis; Hist.abs.; MLA; RILA; RILM; Uncover.

Q352 The world of tribal arts = Le monde de l'art tribal, Engl. ed., v.1, Mar. 1994– . San Francisco, Tribarts Ltd. Quarterly.

Beautifully illustrated journal focusing on the culture, history, ethnography, and traditional arts of tribal peoples worldwide, for both the specialist and enthusiast. Popular treatment given to wide range of subjects such as Indonesian textiles, African crafts, Pre-Columbian ceramics, by leading authorities. Includes book reviews, auction news, calendar of events, copious ads. Issued also in a French edition. Preview of current issue available on the internet. "No other publication strives to be quite so global."—*Review*, Art documentation, v.16, no.1, 1997, p.33–34. Table of contents of past issues available on the internet. Art index (1998–); Ethno.; Uncover.

Q353 Xenia antiqua, v.1, 1992– . Roma, "L'Erma" di Bretschneider. Irregular.

Continues: Xenia (Roma, De Luca), no.1–22, 1981–91 and supplement: Quaderni di Xenia (1–10, 1981–91). Hardcover Italian journal of Greek and Roman antiquity, presenting original research and archival reports. Beautifully produced, with color plates. Articles in Italian, occasionally in English, French, and German. Also accompanying this title is a supplementary annual series (also published by "L'Erma" di Bretschneider) called Xenia antiqua, monografie, offering more thematic studies on ancient art and its influences on later periods. Summaries of contents of past vols. available on the internet. Avery; BHA; Dyabola; Francis; RILA.

Q354 Zodiac: international architecture magazine, bilingual ed., nuova serie 1, 1989–. Milano, Abitare Segesta. (Distr. by Watson Guptill Publications). Semiannual.

Ed.: Guido Cannella.

Continues: Zodiac: revue internationale d'architecture contemporaine (Milano), v.1–22; 1957–73 (See Part 1 and GLAH 1:Q356). V.1–5 issued in two eds., English and Italian; with v.6, a single bilingual Italian/English edition. New series of a most distinguished Italian architecture journal, founded by Adriano Olivetti. The new series continues this tradition of presenting the latest in architectural projects, urban planning, and design. Contains theoretical essays, studies on new buildings, and interviews with international architects. New publisher, editor, and numbering. Contents of no.1–15 in issue 16. Cumulative table of contents of issues in back of each issue. Arch.per.ind.; Avery.

R. Series

This chapter concerns series, that is, monographic titles issuing from the same publisher and related to each other either in subject matter or theme and having, in addition to their own individual title, a uniform title related to the group as a whole. The series titles included in this chapter were chosen with the art research library in mind, but make no pretense of being comprehensive.

Subjects covered are similar to Chapter Q, Periodicals, and include: art, architecture, photography, design, decorative arts, and archeology. Series were chosen without limitation as to country, time period, or language, the main criteria for inclusion being scholarship and lasting research value. Reprint series are included. While the majority of the series included herewith began after 1977 (the cut-off date of GLAH 1), as with the Periodicals chapter, those pre-1977 series not included in GLAH 1 which were considered especially noteworthy have been included. The editorial decision has been made not to repeat series titles that appeared in GLAH 1, either to record new volumes or to make any other updates. The scale of this chapter precluded this.

Excluded from this chapter are series that are tightly coordinated in terms of subject or artistic medium. For example, series focusing upon a particular medium (architecture, photography, sculpture) may be found under the appropriate particular subject chapters. Also excluded from this chapter are those series of an encyclopedic nature, covering a span of time and issued in a systematic fashion; these series titles can be found elsewhere in GLAH 2 under their appropriate subject, especially in Chapter I, Histories and Handbooks. Exceptions to this are series covering subjects that have no designated chapters in GLAH 2 (i.e., Islamic art, archeology, modern art). Exhibition and collection series published by museums and art galleries are selectively included. Many monographs cited in this chapter are also listed individually elsewhere in this book.

With some exceptions (clearly indicated in the text), *all* monographic titles within a given series are listed below their common series title. In this respect we have deviated from GLAH 1, which recorded only representative monographic titles appearing in series, and in the interest of legibility we have departed in this chapter from some of the stylistic norms employed elsewhere in this volume. Selective contents are listed, however, where the scope of the series goes beyond the history of art; in such instances, only volumes treating art historical topics are listed here. In those instances when a numbered volume could not be verified, that number was eliminated from the sequence of numbered titles. Series that began numbering their volumes and then dropped this device with subsequent volumes will have their numbered titles listed first followed by the unnumbered volumes, with the latter in publication year order. Numbered titles that belong together but are numerically apart have been listed together for economy sake [e.g.: (17, 35) William Lloyd MacDonald, The architecture of the Roman Empire, rev. ed. 2v., 1982–86 (Yale studies in the history of art)].

R1 Acta humaniora: Schriften zur Kunstwissenschaft. Berlin, Akademie, 1989– .

Scholarly, exhaustively researched hardcovered series on art, architecture, and related humanities disciplines. Most vols. originally presented as the authors' dissertations. Color and black-and-white plates, bibliographies, indexes.

Contents: Gisela Gramaccini, Jean-Guillaume Moitte (1746–1810): Leben und Werk, 2v., 1993; Barbara Gretenkord, Künstler der Kolonialzeit in Lateinamerika: ein Lexikon, 1993; Julius Ritter von Schlosser, Tote Blicke: Geschichte der Porträtbildnerei in Wachs: ein Versuch, 1993; Hermann Ulrich Asemissen, Malerei als Thema der Malerei, 1994; Hubert Locher, Raffael und das Altarbild der Renaissance: die "Pala Baglioni" als Kunstwerk im sakralen Kontext, 1994; Claudia Nordhoff, Jakob Philipp Hackert, 1737–1807: Verzeichnis seiner Werke, 2v., 1994; Peter Johannes Schneemann, Geschichte als Vorbild: die Modelle der französischen Historienmalerei 1747–1789, 1994; Dorothee Hansen, Das Bild des Ordenslehrers und die Allegorie des Wissens: ein gemaltes Programm der Augustiner, 1995; Jürgen Krüger, Rom und Jerusalem: Kirchenbauvorstellungen der Hohenzollern im 19. Jahrhundert, 1995; Ursula Merkel, Das plastische Porträt im 19. und frühen 20. Jahrhundert: ein Beitrag zur Geschichte der Bildhauerei in Frankreich und Deutschland, 1995; Christoph Danelzik-Brüggemann, Ereignisse und Bilder: Bildpublizistik und politische Kultur in Deutschland zur Zeit der französischen Revolution, 1996; Ulrike Ilg, Das Wiltondiptychon: Stil und Ikonographie, 1996; Mechthild Modersohn, Natura als Göttin im Mittelalter: Ikonographische Studien zu Darstellungen der personifizierten Natur, 1997; Philine Helas, Lebende Bilder in der italienischen Festkultur des 15. Jahrhunderts, 1999.

R2 The aesthetic movement & the Arts & Crafts movement, 1–38. N.Y., Garland, 1977–78.

Ed.: Peter Stansky and Rodney Shewan.

A series that focuses on two of the most important artistic developments of the second half of the 19th century in Victorian Britain. 48 of the period's most important books are reprinted in 38v. Amply illustrated.

Contents: (1) John Ruskin, The nature of gothic: a chapter from the Stones of Venice (1892), 1977; (2) Christopher Dresser, Unity in variety (1859), 1978; (3) Christopher Dresser, The development of ornamental art in the International Exhibition (1862), 1977; (4) Christopher Dresser, The art of decorative design (1862), 1977; (5) Christopher Dresser, Japan, its architecture, art and art manufactures (1882), 1977; (6) Oscar Wilde, Essays and lectures (1908), 1978; (7) Rational Dress Association, Catalogue of exhibits, (1883), bound with, Rational Dress Society, Gazette (1888–89), 1978; (8) Moncure Daniel Conway, Travels in South Kensington (1882), 1977; (9) Lucy Crane, Art and the formation of taste (1882), 1977; (10) Walter Crane, The bases of design (1898), 1977. Art at home series; (11) William John Loftie, A plea for art in the house, bound with: Rhoda and Agnes Garrett, Suggestions for house decoration, Margaret Oliphant, Dress, and John Hullah, Music in the house, (1876–78), 1978; (12) M. J. Loftie, The dining room, bound with: Lucy Orrinsmith, The drawing room, and Lady Barker, The bedroom and the boudoir (1876–78), 1978; (13) Mary Smith Lockwood and Elizabeth Glaister, Art embroidery (1878), 1978; (14) Edward William Gordon, Art, furniture, bound with: Artistic conservatories (1880), 1977. Sylvia's home help series; (15) Artistic homes, or how to furnish with taste (1881), 1978; (16) Mary Eliza Joy Haweis, The art of beauty, (1878), bound with: The art of dress (1879), 1978; (17) Mary Eliza Joy Haweis, The art of decoration (1889), 1977; (18) Lewis Forman Day, Instances of accessory art (1880), 1978. Textbooks of ornamental design; (19) Lewis Forman Day, Everyday art (1882), 1977; (20) Lewis Forman Day, The anatomy of pattern (1887), 1977; (21) Lewis Forman Day, The planning of ornament (1887), 1977; (22) Lewis Forman Day, The application of ornament (1888), 1977; (23) Lewis Forman Day, Nature in ornament (1892), 1977; (24) Lewis Forman Day, Art in needlework (1900), 1977; (25) Marianne Margaret Compton Cust Alford, Viscountess, Needlework as art (1886), 1978; (26) Christopher Dresser, Modern ornamentation (1886), 1978; (27) Charles Robert Ashbee, A few chapters in workshop reconstruction and citizenship (1894), bound with: An endeavour towards the teaching of John Ruskin and William Morris (1901), 1978; (28) Charles Robert Ashbee, Craftsmanship in competitive industry (1908), 1977; (29) Charles Robert Ashbee, Should we stop teaching art (1911), 1978; (30) T. J. Cobden-Sanderson, Ecce Mundus, industrial ideals, the book beautiful, (1902), bound with, The Arts and Crafts movement (1905), 1977; (31) Walter Crane, Ideals in art (1905), 1979; (32) Charles Robert Ashbee, Manual of the Guild and School of Handicraft (1892), 1978; (33) John Dando Sedding, Art and handicraft (1893), 1977; (34) Arts and Crafts Exhibition Society, Arts and crafts essays (1893), 1977; (35) Art and life: the building and decoration of cities (1897), 1978; (36) Ernest Gimson, his life and work (1924), 1978; (37) A. H. Mackmurdo, ed., Selwyn Image letters (1932), 1977; (38) Thomas Howarth, Charles Rennie Mackintosh and the modern movement (1932), 1977.

R3 Allard Pierson series, 1– . Amsterdam, Allard Pierson Museum, 1980– .

Ed.: H. A. G. Brijder.

Distinguished series on ancient vase painting and pottery issuing from the Allard Pierson Museum, an archeological collection forming part of the University of Amsterdam, whose holdings include objects from Egypt, the Ancient Near East, Cyprus, and the Greek and Roman worlds, 4000 B.C. to 1000 A.D. Occasional vols. consist of proceedings of conferences on classical archeology held at the museum.

Contents: (1) Gertrud Schneider-Hermann, Red-figured Lucanian and Apulian Nestorides and their ancestors, 1980; (2) D. C. Steures, Monte Finocchito revisited; part 1: the evidence, 1980; (3) J. H. Crouwel, Chariots and other means of land transport in Bronze Age Greece, 1981; (4) H. A. G. Brijder, Siana cups I and Komast cups, parts 1 & 2, 1983; (5) H. A. G. Brijder, ed., Ancient Greek and related pottery: Proccedings of the International Vase Symposium Amsterdam, 1984; (6) H.A.G. Brijder . . . [et al.], eds., Enthousiasmos: essays on Greek and related pottery presented to Jaap M. Hemerlrijk, 1986; (7) C. W. Neeft, Protocorinthian Subgeometric Aryballoi, 1987; (8) H. A. G. Brijder, Siana cups II: the Heidelberg Painter, parts 1 & 2, 1991; (9) J. H. Crouwel, Chariots and other wheeled vehicles in Iron Age Greece, 1993; (10) Pieter Heesen, The Jacques L. Theodor collection of Attic black figure vases, 1995; (11) Vincent Tosto, The black-figure pottery signed Nikosthenespoiesen, 2v., 1999.

R4 The American arts series. Newark, Del., Univ. of Delaware Pr., 1985– .

Authoritative, lavishly illustrated unnumbered series on various topics in American art.

Contents: Lewis I. Sharp, John Quincy Adams Ward, dean of American sculpture, 1985; Michael Edward Shapiro, Bronze casting and American sculpture, 1850–1900, 1985; Ila Weiss, Poetic landscape: the art and experience of Sanford R. Gifford, 1987; Milo M. Naeve, John Lewis Krimmel: an artist in Federal America, 1987; Joseph S. Czestochowski, Arthur B. Davies: a catalogue raisonné of the prints, 1987; Ann Lee Morgan, ed., Dear Stieglitz, dear Dove, 1988; Ellwood Parry, The art of Thomas Cole: ambition and imagination, 1988; Charles Marion Russell, Charles Russell, 1989; Louise Minks, Hudson River school, 1989; Richard P. Wunder, Hiram Powers: Vermont sculptor, 1805–1873, 2v., 1989–91; John Sloan's oil paintings: a catalogue raisonné, compiled by Rowland Elzea, 2v., 1991; Michael Conforti, ed., The portrait in eighteenth-century America, 1993; Michael Conforti, ed., Minnesota 1900: art and life on the upper Mississippi, 1890–1915, 1994; Mary Mullen Cunningham, Heinz Warneke, 1895–1983: a sculptor first and last, 1994; Thomas P. Somma, The apotheosis of democracy, 1908–1916: the pediment for the House wing of the United States Capitol, 1995; Betsy Fahlman, John Ferguson Weir: the labor of art, 1997; Frederick C. Moffatt, Errant bronzes: George Grey Barnard's statues of Abraham Lincoln, 1998.

R5 Archaeologica, 1– . Roma, Giorgio di Bretschneider, 1975– .

Scholarly series on the archeology, art, architecture, and antiquities of ancient Greece and Rome. Handsomely produced, with black-and-white plates included in each vol. In Italian, German, French, or English.

Selective contents: (1) Mauro Cristofani, Statue-cinerario chiusine di età classica, 1975; (2) Maria Pia Rossignani, La decorazione architettonica romana in Parma, 1975; (3) Bianca Maria Felletti Maj, La tradizione italica nell'arte romana, v.1– , 1977– ; (7) Gabriele Foerst, Die Gravierungen der pränestinischen Cisten, 1978; (8) Sylvia Diebner, Aesernia-Venafrum: Untersuchungen zu den römischen Steindenkmälern zweier Landstädte Mittelitaliens, 2v., 1979; (9) Stephan Steingräber, Etruskische Möbel, 1979; (10) Bianca Candida, Altari e cippi nel Museo nazionale romano, 1979; (11) Gabriella Capecchi; Lucia Lepore; and Vincenzo Saladino, eds., La Villa del Poggio Imperiale, 1979; (12) Gabriella Capecchi . . . [et al.], eds., Palazzo Peruzzi, Palazzo Rinuccini, 1980; (13) Giampiero Pianu, Ceramiche etrusche a figure rosse, 1980; (14) Hugo Meyer, Medeia und die Peliaden: eine attische Novelle und ihre Entstehung: ein Versuch zur Sagenforschung auf archäologischer Grundlage, 1980; (16) Lucrezia Campus, Ceramica attica a figure nere: piccoli vasi e vasi plastici, 1981; (17) Hetty Joyce, The decoration of walls, ceilings, and floors in Italy in the second and third centuries A.D., 1981; (18) Renate Thomas, Athletenstatuetten der Spätarchaik und des strengen Stils, 1981; (19) Kora Neuser, Anemoi: Studien zur Darstellung der Winde und Windgottheiten in der Antike, 1982; (20) Jocelyn Penny Small, Studies related to the Theban cycle on late Etruscan urns, 1981; (21) Giampero Pianu, Ceramiche etrusche sovradipinte, 1982; (23) Adriana Travaglini, Inventario dei rinvenimenti monetali del Salento: problemi di circolazione, 1982; (24) Rudolf H. W. Stichel, Die römische Kaiserstatue am Ausgang der Antike: Untersuchungen zum plastischen Kaiserporträt seit Valentinian I. (364–375 v. Chr.), 1982; (25) Nevio Degrassi, Lo Zeus stilita di Ugento, 1981; (27) John Peter Oleson, The sources of innovation in later Etruscan tomb design (ca. 350–100 B.C.), 1982; (28) Eugene Joseph Dwyer, Pompeian domestic sculpture: a study of five Pompeian houses and their contents, 1982; (29) Joachim von Freeden, Oikia Kyrrestou: Studien zum sogenannten Turm der Winde in Athen, 1983; (30) Diana E. E. Kleiner, The monument of Philoppapos in Athens, 1983; (32) Carlo Tronchetti, Ceramica attica a figure nere: grandi vasi, anfore, pelikai, crateri, 1983; (33) Elena Pierro, Ceramica "ionica" non figurata e coppe attiche figure nere, 1984; (34) Ursula Finster-Hotz, Der Bauschmuck des Athenatempels von Assos: Studien zur Ikonographie, 1984; (35) Götz Lahusen, Untersuchungen zur Ehrenstatue in Rom: literarische und epigraphische Zeugnisse, 1983; (36) Alois Riegl, Late Roman art industry, trans. from the Viennese and ed. by Rolf Winkes, 1985; (37) Hans G. Frenz, Römische Grabreliefs in Mittel- und Suditalien, 1985; (38) Grete Stefani, Terrecotte figurate, 1984; (39) Heidi Hänlein-Schäfer, Veneratio Augusti: eine Studie zu den Tempeln des ersten römischen Kaisers, 1985; (40) Dela von Boeselager, Antike Mosaiken in Sizilien: Hellenismus und römische Kaiserzeit, 3. Jahrhundert v. Chr.-3 Jahrhundert n. Chr., 1983; (42) Sabina Brodbeck-Jucker, Mykenische Funde von Kephallenia im Archäologischen Museum Neuchâtel, 1986; (45) Luca Bianchi, Le stele funerarie della Dacia: un'espressione di arte romana periferica, 1985; (46) David Parrish, Season mosaics of Roman North Africa, 1984; (48) Lea Cumino, La collezione Mieli nel Museo Archeologico di Siena, 1986; (49) Maria Grazia Marzi Costagli and Luisa Tamagno Perna, eds., Studi di antichità in onore di Guglielmo Maetzke, 3v., 1984; (50) Giovanni Camporeale, La caccia in Etruria, 1984; (51) Paolo Emilio Pecorella, La cultura preistorica di lasos in Caria, 1984; (52) Fred S. Kleiner, The Arch of Nero in Rome: a study of the Roman honorary arch before and under Nero, 1985; (53–54,99) Hierapolis: scavi e ricerche, 1985–91; (56) John Herrmann, The Ionic capital in late antique Rome, 1988; (57) Anne Laidow, The first style in Pompeii: painting and architecture, 1985; (59) Monika Boosen, Etruskische Meeresmischwesen: Untersuchungen zu Typologie und Bedeutung, 1986; (61) Esther Giraud . . . [et al.], eds., Colloque sur les problèmes de l'image dans le monde méditerranéen classique (1982), 1985; (62) Diana E. E. Kleiner, Roman imperial funerary altars with portraits, 1987; (64) Felice Gino Lo Porto, La collezione cipriota del Museo di Antichità di Torino, 1986; (65) Stefano Bruni, I lastroni a scala, 1986; (66) Fernanda Pompili, ed., Studi sulla ceramica laconica, 1986; (67) Sylvia Diebner. Reperti funerari in Umbria a sinistra del Tevere: I sec. a.C.-I sec/ d.C., 1986; (71) Cornelius C. Vermeule, The cult images of imperial Rome, 1987; (72) Birgitte Ginge, Ceramiche etrusche a figure nere, 1988; (75) Helen Nagy, Votive terracottas from the "Vignaccia," Cerveteri, in the Lowie Museum of Anthropology, 1988; (76) Jenifer Neils, The youthful deeds of Theseus, 1987; (77) Stephan F. Schröder, Römische Bacchusbilder in der Tradition des Apollon Lykeios: Studien zur Bildformulierung und Bildbedeutung in späthellenistisch-römischer Zeit, 1989; (79) Armando Cherici, Ceramica etrusca dela Collezione Poggiali di Firenze, 1988; (80) Maria Cecilia D'Ercole, La stipe votiva del Belvedere a Lucera, 1990; (81) Marina Cipriani, S. Nicola di Albanella: scavo di un santuario campestre nel territorio di Poseidonia-Paest um, 1989; (82) Frances Dodds Van Keuren, The frieze from the Hera I Temple at Foce del Sele, 1989; (83) Studia tarquiniensia, 1988; (86) Maria Reho-Bumbalova, La ceramica attica a figure nere e rosse nella Tracia bulgara, 1990; (87) Marga Weber, Baldachine und Statuenschreine, 1990; (88) Francesca Baffi Guardata and Rita Dolce, Archeologia della Mesopotamia: l'età cassita e medio-assira, 1990; (92) Sergio Rinaldi Tufi, Militari Romani sul Reno: l'iconografia degli "stehende Soldaten" nelle stele funerarie del I secolo d.C., 1988; (95) Francesco Tomasello, Acquedotto romano e la necropoli presso l'istmo, 1991; (96) Ingrid E. M. Edlund-Berry, The seated and standing statue akroteria from Poggio Civitate (Murlo), 1992; (97) Mario Denti, Ellenismo e romanizzazione nella X regio: la scultura delle elites locali dall'età repubblicana ai Giulio-Claudi, 1991; (99) Giorgio Bejor, Le statue, 1991; (101) Giovannangelo Camporeale, La collezione C.A.: impasti e buccheri, v.1– , 1991– ; (102) Maria Grazia Maioli, La stipe di villa e i culti degli antichi veneti, 1992; (103) Anne Weis, The hanging Marsyas and its copies: Roman innovations in a Hellenistic sculptural tradition, 1992; (104) John Griffiths Pedley, The Sanctuary of Santa

Venera of Paestum, v.1– , 1993– ; (106) Luigi Donati, La Casa dell'Impluvium: architettura etrusca a Roselle, 1994; (107) Antonella Pautasso, Il deposito votivo presso la porta nord a Vulci, 1994; (108) Maria Donatella Gentili, I sarcofagi etruschi in terracotta di età recente, 1994; (111) Gemma Sena Chiesa and Maria Paola Lavizzari Pedrazzini, Angera Romana: scavi nell'abitato, 1980–1986, 2v., 1995; (114) Maria Paola Bini, Gianluca Carmella and Sandra Buccioli, eds., I bronzi etruschi e romani, 2v., 1996; (115) Giandomenico Spinola, Le sculture nel Palazzo Albertoni Spinola a Roma e le collezioni Paluzzi ed Altieri, 1995; (121) Luigi Todisco, La scultura romana di Venosa e il suo reimpiego, 1996; (123) Raffaella Bonifacio, Ritratti romani da Pompei, 1997; (124) Paola Baldassarri, Sebastoi sotéri: edilizia monumentale ad Atene durante il saeculum Augustum, 1998.

R6 Ars Neerlandica: studies in the history of art of the Low Countries 1–2. Kortrijk, Belgium, Van Ghemmert, 1979–80.

Short-lived but scholarly series on Dutch iconography and iconology. Two vols. (one double) were published, each a substantial, original contribution. Both include ample bibliographies and indexes and are profusely illustrated with excellent color and black-and-white plates.

Contents: (1) James H. Marrow, Passion iconography in northern European art of the late Middle Ages and early Renaissance, 1979; (2) Herwig Guratzsch, Die Auferweckung des Lazarus in der niederländischen Kunst von 1400 bis 1700: Ikonographie und Ikonologie, 2v., 1980.

R7 Art and architecture information guide series, 1–14. Detroit, Gale, 1974–80.

Ed.: Sydney Starr Keaveney.

This series forms part of the Gale information guide library, which broadly covers areas in the social sciences, humanities, and current affairs. The vols. in this series follow a familiar format and begin with general reference sources, including dictionaries, encyclopedias, and indexes, moving into more specific types of resources, including research collections housing materials in that particular area.

Contents: (1) Sydney Starr Keaveney, American painting: a guide to information sources, 1974; (2) Mary Buckley, Color theory: a guide to information sources, 1975; (3) Lawrence Wodehouse, American architects from the Civil War to the First World War: a guide to information sources, 1976; (4) Lawrence Wodehouse, American architects from the First World War to the present: a guide to information sources, 1977; (5) Janis Ekdahl, American sculpture: a guide to information sources, 1977; (6) Clarence Bunch, Art education: a guide to information sources, 1978; (7) James E. Campbell, Pottery and ceramics: a guide to information sources, 1978; (8) Lawrence Wodehouse, British architects, 1840–1976: a guide to information sources, 1978; (9) Ann-Marie Cutul, Twentieth-century European painting: a guide to information sources, 1980; (10) Darlene A. Brady, Stained glass: a guide to information sources, 1980; (11) Lamia Doumato, American drawing: a guide to information sources, 1979; (12) Lawrence Wodehouse, Indigenous architecture worldwide: a guide to information sources, 1980; (13) Arnold L. Markowitz, Historic preservation: a guide to information sources, 1980; (14) David M. Sokol, American decorative arts and Old World influences: a guide to information sources, 1980.

R8 Art & design profile, 1–57. N.Y., St. Martin's, 1985–97.

Ed.: Andreas C. Papadakis.

Attractive, well-illustrated series, utilizing a familiar format and covering contemporary art movements and artists. Issues are published as part of the periodical, Art & design (see GLAH 2:Q97), while maintaining their own unique numbering. Each profile offers a thematic study on issues related to contemporary art, with articles, interviews, and signed book and exhibition reviews. Most issues are ed. by Andreas C. Papadakis, and guest edited by others, as noted.

Contents: (1) 20th century British art, 1987; (2) The post-modern object, 1987; (3) Abstract art: the rediscovery of the spiritual, 1987; (4) Post avant-garde paintings in the eighties, 1987; (5) British and American art: the uneasy dialectic, 1987; (6) Sculpture today, 1987; (7) David Hockney, 1988; (8) The new modernism: deconstructivist tendencies in art, 1988; (9) Classical sensibility in contemporary painting & sculpture, 1988; (10) Art in the age of pluralism, 1988; (11) British art now, 1988; (12) The new romantics, 1988; (13) Italian art now and the southern European tradition, 1989; (14) 40 under 40: the new generation in Britain, 1989; (15) Malevich, 1989; (16) New York new art, 1989; (17) German art now, 1989; (18) Aspects of modern art, 1989; (19) New art international, 1990; (20) Art and the tectonic, 1990; (21) Louwrien Wijers and Johan Pijnappel, eds., Art meets science and spirituality, 1990; (22) New museology, 1991; (23) Christopher Martin, ed., The ruralists, 1991; (24) Pop art, 1992; (24, sic) Marking the city boundaries: Groningen, 1992; (25, sic) Andrew Benjamin, ed., Contemporary painting, 1992; (27) Patrick Caulfield: paintings 1963–1992, 1992; (28) Johan Pijnappel, ed., Fluxus today and yesterday, 1993; (29) Victor Arwas, ed., The great Russian utopia, 1993; (30) Andrew Benjamin, ed., Installation art, 1993; (31) Johan Pijnappel, ed., World wide video, 1993; (32) Time and tide: The Tyne International Exhibition of contemporary art, 1993; (33) Clare Farrow, ed., Parallel structures: art, dance, and music in the 20th century, 1993; (34) Clare Farrow, ed., A. Reinhardt, J. Kosuth, F. Gonzalez-Torres: Symptoms of interference: conditions of possibility, 1994; (35) Paul Crowther, ed., New art from Eastern Europe: identity and conflict, 1994; (36) Art and the natural environment, 1994; (37) Oriana Baddeley, ed., New art from Latin America: expanding the continent, 1994; (38) Performance art into the 90s, 1994; (39) Johan Pijnappel, ed., Art and technology, 1994; (40) Paul Crowther, ed., The contemporary sublime: sensibilities of transcendence and shock, 1995; (41) British art: defining the 90s, 1995; (42) Philip Peters, ed., The ideal place, 1995; (43) Nikos Papastergiadis, ed., Art and cultural difference: hybrids and clusters, 1995; (44) John Strathatos, ed., Photography in the visual arts, 1995; (45) Nicholas Zurbrugg, ed., The multimedia text, 1995; (46) Amanda Crabtree, ed., Public art, 1996; (47) Michael Petry, ed., Abstract eroticism: touch me, 1996; (48) David Moos, ed., Painting in the age of artificial intelligence, 1996; (49) Art and film, 1996; (50) John Strathatos, ed., Art and the city: a dream of urbanity, 1996; (51) David A. Greene, ed., Art and the home, 1996; (52) Curating: the contemporary art museum and beyond, 1997; (53) Art and animation, 1997; (54) A thing of beauty is . . . , 1997; (55) Sculpture, 1997; (56) Sci-Fi aesthetics, 1997; (57) Art & the garden: travels in the continental mindscape, 1997.

R9 The art experience in late nineteenth century America, 1–24. N.Y., Garland, 1976–77.

Ed.: H. Barbara Weinberg.

Important collection of primary sources in the field of late 19th-century American art, many biographical or autobiographical, published in 33v. All illustrations are reproduced.

Contents: (1) Barbara Weinberg, ed., A landscape book, by American artists and American authors: sixteen engravings on steel, from paintings by Cole, Church, Cropsey, Durand, Gignoux, Kensett, Miller, Richards, Smillie, Talbot, Weir (1868), 1976; (2) James Jackson Jarves, Art thoughts: the experiences and observations of an American amateur in Europe (1869), 1976; (3) The masterpieces of the Centennial International Exhibition, 3v.: 1. Edward Strahan, Fine art, 2. Walter Smith, Industrial art, 3. Joseph M. Wilson, History, mechanics, science (1876–78), 1977; (4) Samuel Greene Wheeler Benjamin, Contemporary art in Europe (1877), 1976; (5) William J. Clark, Jr., Great American sculptures (1878), 1977; (6) Samuel Greene Wheeler Benjamin, Our American artists, and Our American artists, second series (1879 and 1881), 1977; (7) Earl Shinn, The art treasures of America, 3v. (1879–82), 1977; (8) Samuel Greene Wheeler Benjamin, Art in America: a critical and historical sketch (1880), 1976; (9) George William Sheldon, Hours with art and artists (1882), 1978; (10) Sylvester Rosa Koehler, The United States art directory and year-book, 2v. (1882–84), 1976; (11) Book of American figure painters (1886), 1977; (12) Sylvester Rosa Koehler, American etchings, and American art (1886), 1978; (13) Alfred Trumble, Representative works of contemporary American artists (1887), 1978; (14) Frank Torrey Robinson, Living New England artists (1888), 1977; (15) Clarence Cook, Art and artists of our time, 3v. (1888), 1978; (16) George William Sheldon, Recent ideals of American art (1888–90), 1977; (17) Walter Montgomery, ed., American art and American art collections, 2v. (1889), 1978; (18) Thomas Ball, My threescore years and ten: an autobiography (2d ed., 1891), 1977; (19) John Charles Van Dyke, ed., Modern French masters (1896), 1976; (20) Benjamin Champney, Sixty years' memories of art and artists (1900), 1977; (21) John La Farge and August F. Jaccaci, eds, Noteworthy paintings in American private collections, 2v. (1907), 1979; (22) Will Hicok Low, A painter's progress, being a partial survey along the pathway of art in America and Europe . . . (1910), 1977; (23) Homer Saint-Gaudens, ed., The reminiscences of Augustus Saint-Gaudens (1913), 1976; (24) Edward Simmons, From seven to seventy: memories of a painter and a Yankee (1913), 1977.

R10 Art history series, 1–6. Washington, D.C., Decatur House Pr., 1977–83.

Each vol. written by a prominent scholar and devoted mostly to Italian painting and the influence of ancient art on later periods. Vols. are well illustrated, with bibliographies and indexes.

Contents: (1) Frank R. DiFederico, Francesco Trevisani, eighteenth-century painter in Rome: catalogue raisonné, 1977; (2) Otto Brendel, The visible idea: interpretations of classical art, 1980; (3) Elizabeth Basye Gilmore Holt, The triumph of art for the public: the emerging role of exhibitions and critics, 1980; (4) Anthony M. Clark, Studies in Roman eighteenth century painting, 1981; (5) Hugo Buchthal, Art of the Mediterranean world, A.D. 100 to 1400, 1983; (6) Millard Meiss, Francesco Traini, 1983.

R11 Art reference collection, 1– . Westport, Conn., Greenwood, 1980– .

Authoritative, exhaustive series of annotated bibliographies, a must for most art library reference collections. Some vols. are self-contained indexes to reproductions, such as Print index and Index to Italian architecture.

Contents: (1) Vito Joseph Brenni, Book illustration and decoration: a guide to research, 1980; (2) Ruth Irwin Weidner, American ceramics before 1930: a bibliography, 1982; (3) James A. Findlay, Modern Latin American art: a bibliography, 1983; (4) Pamela Jeffcott Parry and Kathe Chipman, Print index: a guide to reproductions, 1983; (5) Leslie E. Abrams, The history and practice of Japanese printmaking: a selectively annotated bibliography of English language materials, 1984; (6) Susan P. Besemer and Christopher Crosman, From museums, galleries and studios: a guide to artists on film and tape, 1984; (7) Charles J. Semowich, American furniture craftsmen working prior to 1920: an annotated bibliography, 1984; (8) Edward R. Hagemann, German and Austrian Expressionism in the United States, 1900–1939: chronology and bibliography, 1985; (9) Jeanne Somers, Index to The dolphin and The fleuron, 1986; (10) Frank W. Porter III, Native American basketry: an annotated bibliography, 1988; (11) Eugene C. Burt, Serials guide to ethnoart: a guide to serial publications on visual arts of Africa, Oceania, and the Americas, 1990; (12) Edward H. Teague, World architecture index: a guide to illustrations, 1991; (13) Edward H. Teague, Index to Italian architecture: a guide to key monuments and reproduction sources, 1992; (14) R. Scott Harnsberger, compiler, Ten Precisionist artists: annotated bibliographies, 1992; (15) Ellen Mazur Thomson, American graphic design: a guide to the literature, 1992; (16) John Gray, Action art: a bibliography of artists' performance from Futurism to Fluxus and beyond, 1993; (17) Russell T. Clement, compiler, Les Fauves: a sourcebook, 1994; (18) Martha Kriesel, American women photographers: a selected and annotated bibliography, 1999; (19) Margaret Culbertson, American house designs: an index to popular and trade periodicals, 1850–1915, 1994; (20) Russell T. Clement, Four French symbolists: a sourcebook on Pierre Puvis de Chavannes, Gustave Moreau, Odilon Redon, and Maurice Denis, 1996; (21) Cecilia Puerto, Latin American women artists, Kahlo and look who else: a selective, annotated bibliography, 1996; (22) Donald Langmead, Dutch modernism: architectural resources in the English language, 1996; (23) Russell T. Clement, Neo-impressionist painters: a sourcebook on Georges Seurat, Camille Pissarro, Paul Signac . . . , 1999.

R12 Arte e archeologia, studi e documenti, 1– . Firenze, Olschki, 1972– .

Learned, elegantly presented series on the archeology and art of Italy. In large format, with color and black-and-white plates.

Contents: (1) Roberto Patrucco, Lo sport nella Grecia antica, 1972; (2) Lorenzo Gori Montanelli, La tradizione architettonica toscana, 1971; (3) Victor F. Denaro, The goldsmiths of Malta and their marks, 1972; (4) Giulio Schmiedt, Il livello antico del mar Tirreno: testimonianze dei resti archeologici, 1972; (5–7, 11, 24) Mario Bernocchi, Le monete della Repubblica, 5v., 1974–85; (8) Angelo Lipinsky, Oro, argento, gemme e smalti: tecnologia delle arti dalle origini alla fine del medioevo, 3000 a.C.–1500 d.C., 1975; (9) Nelida Caffarello, ed., Archaeologica: scritti in onore di Aldo Neppi Modona, 1975; (10) Mirella Levi D'Ancona, The garden of the Renaissance: botanical symbolism in Italian painting, 1977; (12–18) Giuseppe Tomassetti, La campagna romana: antica, medioevale e moderna, 7v., 1979–80; (19, 22, 23) Natale Rauty and Guido Vannini, L'antico Palazzo dei Vescovi a Pistoia, 3v., 1981–87; (20) Mirella Levi D'Ancona, Botticelli's Primavera: a botanical interpretation including astrology, alchemy, and the Medici, 1983; (21) Pietro C. Marani, L'architettura fortificata negli studi di Leonardo da Vinci: con il catalogo completo dei disegni, 1984; (25) Amelio Fara, Leonardo a Piombino e l'idea della città moderna tra quattro e cinquecento, 1999.

R13 Arte Hispalense, 1– . Sevilla, Spain, Publiaciones de la Excma. Diputacion Provincial de Sevilla, 1972– .
Small, uniform series covering little-known Sevillian artists, architects, sculptors, periods and movements. Vols. written by art professors, many associated with the University of Sevilla. Extensive bibliographies and color plates in each vol. Earlier vols. have been reissued.

Selective contents: (21) Lorenzo Abad Casal, Pinturas romanas en la Provincia de Sevilla, 1979; (22) Alfredo José Morales, La Capilla Real de Sevilla, 1979; (28) Manuel Rodríguez-Buzón Calle, La Colegiata de Osuna, (1982); (35) Teodoro Falcón Márquez, La Torre del Oro, 1983; (36) Alfredo José Morales, La sacristía mayor de la Catedral de Sevilla, 1984; (37) Aurora León, Los fondos de arquitectura en la pintura barroca sevillana, 1984; (39) José Fernández López, La pintura de historia en Sevilla en el siglo XIX, 1985; (47) María José del Castillo Utrilla, El Convento de San Francisco, Casa Grande de Sevilla, 1988; (53) Aurora León, Iconografia y fiesta durante el lustro real, 1729–1733, 1990; (67) Alberto Morales Chacón, Escultura funeraria del renacimento en Sevilla, 1996; (68) Ana Valseca Castillo, De las torres parroquiales de Écija en el siglo XVIII, 1996.

R14 Beiträge zur Kunstgeschichte, 1– . Witterschlick-Bonn, Germany, Wehle, 1989– .
Scholarly series devoted to German art and architecture. Some vols. are published as revised theses. Each vol. includes bibliographies.

Contents: (1) Angelika Rusche, Der Sockel: typologische und ikonographische Studien am Beispiel von Personendenkmälern der Berliner Bildhauerschule, 1989; (2) Maria Adele Coutts-Dohrenbusch, Untersuchungen zu Ikonographie und Gestaltung der Antwerpener Gemäldeepithaphien im 16. und 17. Jh., 1989; (3) Thomas Meurer, Die Eisenbahn in der deutschen Kunst: die künstlerische Rezeption der Technik im 19. und frühen 20. Jahrhundert, 1989; (4) Frithjof Detlev Paul Hampel, Schinkels Möbelwerk und seine Voraussetzungen, 1989; (5) Ulrike Surmann, Studien zur ottonischen Elfenbeinplastik in Metz und Trier: Nordenfalks Sakramentar- und Evangeliargruppe, 1990; (6) Maria Linsmann, Schriftähnliche Zeichen und Strukturen in der Kunst des 20. Jahrhunderts, 1991; (7) Margret Ribbert, Untersuchungen zu den Elfenbeinarbeiten der Älteren Metzer Gruppe, 1992; (8) Ines Wagemann, Der Architekt Bruno Möhring, 1863–1929, 1992; (9) Claus Pfingsten, Aspekte zum fotografischen Werk Albert Renger-Patzschs, 1992; (10) Rolf Berger, Die Peterskirche auf dem Petersberg zu Erfurt: eine Studie zur Hirsauer Baukunst, 1994; (11) Ulrich Appel, Satire als Zeitdokument: der Zeichner Erich Schilling (1995); (12) Rolf Berger, Hirsauer Baukunst: ihre Grundlagen; Geschichte und Bedeutung, Bd. 1– , 1995– ; (13) Thomas Dann, Georg Ludwig Laves (1785–1864): das Möbelwerk, 1996.

R15 Beiträge zur Kunstgeschichte des Mittelalters und der Renaissance, Band 1– . Münster, Rhema. 1995– .
Scholarly softcover German series on Medieval and Renaissance art, with black-and-white plates in back of each vol. Well researched, most vols. derived from the authors' dissertations.

Contents: (1) Martina Harms, Matteo Civitali: Bildhauer der Frührenaissance in Lucca, 1995; (2) Mortiz Woelk, Benedetto Antelami: die Werke in Parma und Fidenza, 1995; (3) Michaela Kalusok, Tabernakel und Statue: die Figurennische in der italienischen Kunst des Mittelalters und der Renaissance, 1996; (4) Candida Syndikus, Leon Battista Alberti: das Bauornament, 1996; (5) Thomas Weigel, Das Reliefsäulen des Hauptaltarciboriums von San Marco in Venedig: Studien zu einer spätantiken Werkgruppe, 1997; (6) Hildegard Sahler, San Claudio al Chienti und die romanischen Kirchen des Vierstützentyps in den Marken, 1996; (7) Hans Thümmler, Zur Architektur und Skuptur des Mittelalters: gesammelte Aufsätze, 1998; (8) Johannes Myssok, Bildhauerische Konzeption und plastisches Modell in der Renaissance, 1999.

R16 Beiträge zur Kunstwissenschaft, 1– . München, Scaneg, 1984– .
Vol. one published by Klein, München. Scholarly, exhaustively researched German series on art and architecture. Most vols. originally presented as the author's thesis. Bibliographies with black-and-white plates in back of vols.

Contents: (1) Karlheinz Hemmeter, Studien zu Reliefs von Thorvaldsen: Auftraggeber, Künstler, Werkgenese: Idea und Ausführung, 1984; (2) Christine Goetz, Studien zum Thema "Arbeit" im Werk von Constantin Meunier und Vincent van Gogh, 1984; (3) Sabine Poeschel, Studien zur Ikonographie der Erdteile in der Kunst des 16.–18. Jahrhunderts, 1985; (4) Ulrich Willmes, Studien zur Scuola di San Rocco in Venedig, 1985; (5) Richard Lukas Freytag, Die autonome Theotokosdarstellung der frühen Jahrhunderte, 2v., 1985; (6) Ingeborg Pohlen, Untersuchungen zur Reproduktionsgraphik der Rubenswerkstatt, 1985; (7) Ita Heinze-Mühleib, Erich Mendelsohn, Bauten und Projekte in Palastina (1934–

1941), 1986; (8) Christine Winkler, Die Maske des Bösen: groteske Physiognomie als Gegenbild des Heiligen und Vollkommenen in der Kunst des 15. und 16. Jahrhundert, 1986; (9) Annette Menke, Funktion und Gestalt von Beamten-und Kauengebauden auf Steinkohlenzechen 1850–1930: dargestellt an ausgewählten Beispielen der Harpener Bergbau-Aktiengesellschaft: ein Beitrag zur Industriearchäologie, 1986; (10) Ulrich Luckhardt, Lyonel Feininger: die Karikaturen und das zeichnerische Frühwerk: der Weg der Selbstfindung zum unabhängigen Künstler, mit einem Exkurs zu den Karikaturen von Emil Nolde und George Grosz, 1987; (11) Sonja Anna Meseure, Architektur der Antwerpener Börse und der europäische Börsenbau im 19. Jahrhundert, 1987; (12) Petra Wichmann, Die Campi Venedigs: entwicklungsgeschichtliche Untersuchungen zu den venezianischen Kirch-und Quartiersplätzen, 1987; (13) Klemens Klemmer, Jacob Koerfer (1875–1930): ein Architekt zwischen Tradition und Moderne, 1987; (14) Ulrike Looft-Gaude, Glasmalerei um 1900: musivische Verglasungen im deutschsprachigen Raum zwischen 1895 und 1918, 1987; (15) Georg Baumgartner, Schloss Hohenschwangau: eine Untersuchung zum Schlossbau der Romantik, 1987; (16) Irene Helmreich-Schoeller, Die Toskanazimmer der Würzburger Residenz: ein Beitrag zur Raumkunst des Empire in Deutschland, 1987; (17) Barbara Rietzsch, Künstliche Grotten des 16. und 17. Jahrbunderts: Formen der Gestaltung von Aussenbau und Innenraum an Beispielen in Italien, Frankreich und Deutschland, 1987; (18) Gabriele Schickel, Neugotischer Kirchenbau in München: Vergleichende Studien zu Architektur und Ausstattung der Kirchen Maria-Hilf in der Au und Heilig-Kreuz in Giesing, 1987; (19) Martina Schmitz, Album cover: Geschichte und Ästhetik einer Schallplattenverpackung in den USA nach 1940: Designer, Stile, Inhalte, 1987; (20) Volker Krahn, Bartolomeo Bellano: Studien zur Paduaner Plastik des Quattrocento, 1988; (21) Suzanne Schrader, Architektur der barocken Hoftheater in Deutschland, 1988; (22) Detlef Lorenz, Gustav Adolf Closs: Leben und Werk des Malers, Illustrators und Reklamenkunstlers mit einem Exkurs über das Reklame-Sammelbilderwesen, 1988; (23) Martin Sonnabend, Antoine-Louis Barye (1795–1875): Studien zum plastischen Werk, 1988; (24) Helge Siefert, Themen aus Homers Ilias in der fränzosischen Kunst (1750–1831), 1988; (25) Barbara Edle von Germersheim, Unternehmervillen der Kaiserzeit (1871–1914): Zitate traditionaller Architektur durch Träger des industriellen Fortschritts, 1988; (26) Ursula Wolf, Die Parabel vom reichen Prasser und armen Lazarus in der mittelalterlichen Buchmalerei, 1989; (27) Dietrich von Frank, Die "Maison de plaisance": ihre Entwicklung in Frankfriech und Rezeption in Deutschland, dargestellt an ausgewählten Beispielen, 1989; (28) Gabriela Dressel, Strukturen mittelalterlicher Mirakelerzählungen in Bildern: ausgewählte Beispiele der französischen Glasmalerei des 13. Jahrhunderts, 1993; (29) Günter Kolb, Otto Wagner und die Wiener Stadtbahn, 2v., 1989; (30) Ilse Dolinschek, Die Bildhauerwerke in der Austellungen der Wiener Sezession von 1898–1910, 1989; (31) Martin Mannewitz, Stift Admont: Untersuchungen zu Entwicklungsgeschichte, Ausstattung und Ikonographie der Klosteranlage, 1989; (32) Manfred Jauslin, Die gescheiterte Kulturrevolution: Perspektiven religiös-romantischer Kunstbewegung vor der Folie der Avantgarde, 1989; (33) Hermann Diruf, Paläste Venedigs vor 1500: Baugeschichtliche Untersuchungen zur venezianischen Palastarchitketur im 15. Jahrhundert, 1990; (34) Suzanne Rother, Beckmann als Landschaftsmaler, 1990; (35) Ulrich Coenen, Die spätgotischen Werkmeisterbücher in Deutschland: Untersuchung und Edition der Lehrschriften für Entwurf und Ausführung von Sakralbauten, 1990; (36) Johanne Stahl, Graffiti: zwischen Alltag und Ästhetik, 1990; (37) Bruno Kauhsen, Omphalos: zum Mittelpunktsgedanken in Architektur und Städtebau dargestellt an ausgewählten Beispielen, 1990; (38) Christiane Kaszubowski-Manych, Studien zu venezianischen Kaminen der Renaissance, 1991; (39) Brigitte Selden, Das dualistische Prinzip: zur Typologie abstrakter Formensprache in der angewandten Kunst, dargestellt am Beispiel der Wiener Werkstätte, des Artel und der Prager Kunstwerkstätten, 1991; (40) Roland Krischel, Jacopo Tintorettos "Sklavenwunder," 1991; (41) Sabine Fischer, Zwischen Tradition und Moderne: der Bildhauer Walter Schelenz (1903–1087): eine monographische Studie mit Werkkatalog, 1991; (42) Dagmar Nowitzki, Hans und Wassili Luckhardt: das architektonische Werk, 1992; (43) Marianne Vogel, Zwischen Wort und Bild: das schriftliche Werk Paul Klees und die Rolle der Sprache in seinem Denken und in seiner Kunst, 1992; (44) Martin Riehl, Vers une architecture: das moderne Bauprogramm des Le Corbusier, 1992; (45) Andrea El-Danasouri, Kunststoff und Mull: das Material bei Naum Gabo und Kurt Schwitters, 1992; (46) Bernhard Klein, Die physiokratische Verlandschaftung der Stadt um 1800: Städtebau und Stadtauflösung in der Realität von Freiburg i.B. sowie in der Utopia des französischen Revolutionsarchitekten Ledoux, 1993; (47) Kristine Scherer, Martin Schwarz: ein Maler in Rothenburg o.T. um 1500, 1992; (48) Ursula Tjaden, Das grafische Werk von Helios Gómez: eine Untersuchung zur politisch-engagierten Kunst Spaniens in den 20er/30er Jahren, 1993; (49) Regina Hanemann, Johann Lorenz Fink: Fürstbischöflicher Hofwerkmeister und Hofarchitekt in Bamberg, 1993; (50) Matthias Klein, Münchner Goldschmiedegewerbe von 1800–1860: Meister, Marken, Materialien, 1993; (51) Almuth Heidegger, Georg Wilhelm Issel (1785–1870): Monographie und Werkkatalog eines Landschaftsmalers des 19. Jahrhunderts, 1993; (52) Joanna Waltraud Kunstmann, Emanuel von Seidl (1856–1919): die Villen und Landhäuser, 1993 ; (53) Bernd M. Mayer, Johann Rudolf Bys (1662–1738): Studien zu Leben und Werk, 1994; (54) Shai-Shu Tzeng, Imitation und Originalität des Ornamentdesigns: Studien zur Entwicklung der kunstgewerblichen Musterbücher von 1750 bis 1900 in Frankreich, Deutschland, und besonders England, 1994; (55) Sylvia Jäkel-Scheglmann, Zum Lobe der Frauen: Untersuchungen zum Bild der Frau in der niederländischen Genremalerei des 17. Jahrhunderts, 1994; (56) Reinhard Wegner, Nach Albions Stränden: die Bedeutung Englands fur die Architektur des Klassizismus und der Romantik in Preussen, 1994; (57) Brigitte Monstadt, Judas beim Abendmahl: Figurenkonstellation und Bedeutung in Darstellungen von Giotto bis Andrea del Sarto, 1995; (58) Gotthard Kiessling, Der Herrschaftsstand: Aspekte repräsentativer Gestaltung im evangelischen Kirchenbau, 1995; (59) Sabine Scunk-Heller, Die Darstellung des ungläubigen Thomas in der Italienischen Kunst bis um 1500 unter Berücksichtigung der lukanischen Ostentatio Vulnerum, 1995; (60) Andrea Pophanken, Graf Schack als Kunstsammler: private Kunstförderung in München (1857–1874), 1995; (61) Lydia Kessel, Festarchitketur in Turin zwischen 1713 und 1773: Repräsentationsformen in einem jungen Königtum, 1995; (62) Beate von Mickwitz, Streit um die Kunst: über das Spannungsreiche Verhältnis von Kunst, Öffentlichkeit und Recht: Fallsstudien aus dem 19. und 20. Jahrhundert mit dem Schwerpunkt, 1996; (63) Folkhard Cremer, Die St. Nikolaus- und Heiligblut-Kirche zu Wilsnack (1383–1552): eine Einordnung ihrer Bauformen in die Kirchenarchitektur zwischen Verden und Chorin, Doberan und Meissen im Spiegel bischöflicher und landesherrlicher Auseindersetzungen, 2v., 1996; (64) Anke Charlotte Held, Georg Philipp Rugendes (1666–1742): Gemälde und Zeichnungen, 1996; (65) Franz Hofmann, Der Freskenzyklus des Neuen Testaments in der Collegiata von San Gimignano: ein herausragendes Beispiel italienischer Wandmalerei zur Mitte des Trecento, 1996; (66) Johannes Franz Hallinger, Das Ende der Chinoiserie: die Auflösung eines Phänomens der Kunst in der Zeit der Aufklärung, 1996; (67) Dietmar Popp, Duccio und die Antike: Studien zur Antikenvorstellung und zur Antikenrezeption in der Sieneser Malerei am Anfang des 14. Jahrhunderts, 1996; (68) Achim Gnann, Polidoro da Caravaggio (um 1499–1543): die römischen Innendekorationen, 1997; (69) Ulrich Reisser, Physiognomik und Ausdruckstheorie der Renaissance: der Einfluss charakterologischer Lehren auf Kunst und Kunsttheorie des 15. und 16. Jahrhunderts, 1997; (70) Petra Schmied-Hartmann, Die Dekoration von Palladios Villa Poiana, 1997; (71) Helmut Möhring, Die Tegernseer Altarretabel des Gabriel Angler und die Münchener Malerei von 1430–1450, 1997; (72) Evamarie Blattner, Holzschnittfolgen zu den Metamorphosen des Ovid: Venedig 1497 und Mainz 1545, 1996; (73) Carolin Bohlmann, Tintorettos Maltechnik: zur Dialektik von Theorie und Praxis, 1998; (74) Gudrun Dauner, Neri da Rimini und die rimineser Miniaturmalerei des frühen Trecento, 1998; (75) Barbara Spahn, Piero Manzoni (1933–1963): seine Herausforderung der Grenze von Kunst und Leben, 1999; (76) Jeannette Susanne Stoschek, Das Caffeaus Papst Benedikts XIV. in den Gärten des Quirinal, 1999.

R17 Bibliotheca archaeologica, 1– . Roma, "L'Erma" di Bretschneider, 1980– .

Scholarly hardcover archeology series. Beautifully produced, with full-page plates, folded plans, maps. Vols. mainly in Italian; occasionally in English, German, and Spanish, as well as multilingual texts.

Contents: (1) Maurizio Harari, Il "Gruppo Clusium" della ceramografia etrusca, 1980; (2) Alessandro Morandi, Epigrafia italica, 1982; (3–4) Sandro Stucchi, Divagazioni archaeologiche, 2v., 1981; (5) Renato Arena and Maria Bonghi Jovino, eds., Ricerche a Pompei: l'insula 5 della Regio VI dalle origini al 79 d.C., 1984; (6) Ruth Ovadiah, Hellenistic, Roman and early Byzantine mosaic pavements in Israel, 1987; (7) Sandro De Maria, Gli archi onorari di Roma e dell'Italia romana, 1988; (8) Patrizio Pensabene, Il teatro romano di Ferento: architettura e decorazione scultorea, 1989; (9) Marina De Franceschini, Villa Adriana: mosaici, pavimenti, edifici, 1991; (10) Goritsa Team, eds., A Greek city of the fourth century B.C., 1992; (11–12) László Török, Coptic antiquities, 2v., 1993; (13) Marisa Bonamici, Orvieto: la necropoli di Cannicella (1977), 1994; (14) Vincenzo Tusa, I sarcofagi romani in Sicilia, 2d ed., 1995; (15) László Török, Hellenistic and Roman terracottas from Egypt, 1995; (16) Maria Stella Busana, Oderzo: forma urbis: saggio di topografia antica, 1996; (17) Shirley Jean Schwarz, Greek vases in the National Museum of Natural History, Smithsonian Institution, Washington, D.C., 1996; (18) Alessandro Naso, Architetture dipinte: decorazioni parietali non figurate nelle tombe e camera dell'Etruria meridionale: VII–V sec. A.C., 1996; (19) László Barkóczi, Antike Gläser, 1996; (20) Janine Lancha, Mosaïque et culture dans l'occident romain (Ier–IVe s.), 1997; (21) Fabrizio Mori, The great civilisations of the ancient Sahara: neolithisation and the earliest evidence of anthropomorphic religions, 1998; (22) Lorenzo Bianchi, Case e torri medioevali a Roma . . . 1. Documentazione, storia e sopravvivenza di edifici medioevali nel tessuto urbano di Roma, 1998– ; (23) David Soren and Noelle Soren, eds., A Roman villa and a late Roman infant cemetery: excavation at Poggio Gramignano, Lugnano in Teverina, 1999; (24) Eugenia Equini Schneider, ed., Elaiussa Sebaste I: campagne di scavo, 1995–1997, 1999; (25) José Luis De La Barrera, La decoración arquitectónica de los foros de Augusta Emerita, 1999; (26) Lorenzo Bianchi, Roma: il Monte di Santo Spirito tra Gianicolo e Vaticano: storia e topografia dall' antichità classica all'epoca moderna, 1999; (27) Lucrezia Spera, Il paesaggio suburbano di Roma dall'antichità al medioevo: il comprensorio tra le vie Latina e Ardeatina dalle mura Aureliane al III miglio, 1999.

R18 Bibliotheca Artibus et Historiae. Vienna, Irsa, 1990– . Authoritative and scholarly series authored by respected art historians. Each vol. comprises a collection of essays covering a broad range of art historical topics related to the author's area of expertise. Occasionally a vol. is a reprint of an earlier book or set of articles or lectures by the author. In original language of publication.

Contents: Jan Bialostocki, The message of images, studies in the history of art, 1988; Creighton E. Gilbert, L'arte del quattrocento nelle testimonianze coeve, 1988; Rachel Wischnitzer, From Dura to Rembrandt, studies in the history of art, 1990; Seymour Howard, Antiquity restored, essays on the afterlife of the antique, 1990; Jozef Grabski, ed., Opus sacrum: catalogue of the exhibition from the collection of Barbara Piasecka Johnson, 1990; Moshe Barasch, Imago hominis, studies in the language of art, 1991, 1972; Patrik Reuterswärd, The visible and invisible in art, studies in the history of art, 1991; Philipp P. Fehl, Decorum and wit: the poetry of Venetian painting, essays in the history of the classical tradition, 1992; Craig Hugh Smyth, Mannerism and maniera, 2d rev. ed., 1992; Dieter Wuttke, Auf Warburgs Spüren: Renaissancephilologie als Kulturwissenschaft, 1992.

R19 Bibliothèque des écoles françaises d'Athènes et de Rome, ser.1, fasc. 1– . Rome, École Française de Rome, 1876– . (Distr. by E. de Broccard, Paris). Publisher varies.

Fundamental series on Greek and Roman antiquity, covering art and archeology as well as church history, economics, agriculture, and language.

Selective contents: (244) Jean-Paul Morel, Céramique campanienne: les formes, 1981; (246) Jean-Marie Dentzer, Le motif du banquet couché dans le Proche-Orient et le monde grec du VII e du IVe siècle avant J.-C., 1982; (250) Francis Croissant, Les protomés féminines archaïques: recherches sur les représentations du visage dans la plastique grecque de 550 à 480 av. J.-C., 1983; (254) J.-M. Spieser, Thessalonique et ses monuments du IVe au VIe siècle: contribution a l'étude d'une ville paléochrétienne, 1984; (257) Françoise-Hélène Massa-Pairault, Recherches sur l'art et l'artisanat étrusco-italiques à l'époque hellénistique, 1985; (269) Mary-Anne Zagdoun, La sculpture archaïsante dans l'art hellénistique et dans l'art romain du haut-empire, 2v., 1989; (274) Agnèes Rouveret, Histoire et imaginaire de la peinture ancienne: Ve siècle av. J.-C.-1er siècle ap. J.-C., 1989; (278) Marie-Christine Hellmann, Recherches sur le vocabulaire de l'architecture grecque, d'après les inscriptions de Délos, 1992; (279) Jérôme Baschet, Les justices de l'au-delà: les réprésentations de l'enfer en France et en Italie, XIIe–XVe siècle, 1993; (280) Christian Michel, Charles-Nicolas Cochin et l'art des lumières, 1993; (285) Gilles Sauron, Quis deum?: l'expression plastique des idéologies politiques et religieuses à Rome à la fin de la République et au début du principat, 1994; (287) Colette Vallat, Rome et ses borgates (1960–1980): des marques urbaines à la ville diffuse, 1995; (293) François Fossier, Les dessins du fonds Robert de Cotte de la Bibliothèque nationale de France: architecture et décor, 1997; (301) Catherine Brice, Monumentalité publique et politique à Rome: le Vittoriano, 1998; (303) Manuel Royo, Domus imperatoriae: topographie, formation et imaginaire des palais impériaux du Palatin: 2. siècle av. J.C.-1er siècle ap. J.C., 1999.

R20 Bio-bibliographies in art and architecture, 1– . Westport, Conn., Greenwood, 1991– .

Solidly researched reference tools providing bibliographical (primary and secondary sources) and biographical information for some of the most important European artists and architects of the early 20th century. Covers all aspects of the artist's life, and includes published and unpublished manuscripts, catalogue raisonnés, monographs, articles, exhibition catalogs, films, videos, and other media, etc. Vols. include names and places indexes.

Contents: (1) Russell T. Clement, Paul Gauguin: a bio-bibliography, 1991; (2) Russell T. Clement, Henri Matisse: a bio-bibliography, 1993; (3) Russell T. Clement, Georges Braque: a bio-bibliography, 1994; (4) Donald Langmead, Willem Marinus Dudok, a Dutch modernist: a bio-bibliography, 1996; (5) Donald Langmead, J. J. P. Oud and the international style: a bio-bibliography, 1999.

R21 Bulletin of the Institute of Classical Studies, supplement, 63– . London, Univ. of London, Institute of Classical Studies, 1996– .

Continues Bulletin supplement (Univ. of London. Institute of Classical Studies), nos.2–62, 1956–95 and Bulletin (Univ. of London. Institute of Classical Studies), Supplementary papers. Scholarly series issuing from the Institute on all aspects of ancient studies, including civilization, literature, mythology, religion, drama, history, philology as well as art and architecture.

Selective contents: (10) Terence Bruce Mitford, Studies in the signaries of south-western Cyprus, 1961; (19) Arthur Dale Trendall, Phlyax vases, 1967; (26, 31, 41) Arthur Dale Trendall, The red-figured vases of Lucania, Campania and Sicily: supplement, 3v., 1970–83; (27) Axel Seeberg, Corinthian komos vases, 1971; (34) Gertrud Schneider-Herrmann, Apulian red-figured paterae with flat or knobbed handles, 1977; (42) Arthur Dale Trendall and Alexander Cambitoglou, First supplement to the red-figured vases of Apulia, 1983; (44) Rosalinde Kearsley, The pendent semi-circle skyphos: a study of its development and chronology and an examination of it as evidence for Euboean activity at Al Mina, 1989; (59) Olga Krzyszkowska, Ivory and related materials: an illustrated guide, 1990; (60) Arthur Dale Trendall, Second supplement to The red-figured vases of Apulia, 3v., 1991–92; (62) Lori-Ann Touchette, The dancing maenad reliefs: continuity and change in Roman copies, 1995.

R22 California studies in the history of art, discovery series, 1– . Berkeley, Univ. of California Pr., 1988– .

Scholarly series that examines in detail the symbolic and biblical significance of specific artworks and religious buildings. Related to California studies in the history of art (see GLAH 1:R19).

Contents: (1) Ruth Mellinkoff, The devil at Isenheim: reflections of popular belief in Grunewald's altarpiece, 1988; (2) Walter Williams Horn, The forgotten hermitage of Skellig Michael, 1990; (3) Edwin Hall, The Arnolfini betrothal: medieval marriage and the enigma of Van Eyck's double portrait, 1994; (4) Panny Howell Jolly, Made in God's image?: Eve and Adam in the Genesis mosaics at San Marco, Venice, 1997; (5) Bernadine Barnes, Michelangelo's "Last Judgment," the Renaissance response, 1998; (6) William L. Pressly, The French Revolution as blasphemy: Johan Zoffany's paintings of the Massacre at Paris, August 10, 1792, 1999; (7) Elise Goodman, The portraits of Madame de Pompadour: celebrating the Femme Savante, 2000; (8) Richard Brilliant, My Laocoön: alternative claims in the interpretation of artworks, 2000.

R23 Cambridge monographs on American artists. N.Y., Cambridge Univ. Pr., 1989– .

General ed.: David M. Sokol.

Scholarly series giving full monographic coverage to select American artists.

Contents: Russell Paul J. Staiti, Samuel F. B. Morse, 1989; Anthony F. Janson, Worthington Whittredge, 1989; Jeffrey Hayes, Oscar Bluemner, 1991; Sally Webster, William Morris Hunt, 1991; Joan M. Marter, Alexander Calder, 1992.

R24 Cambridge studies in American visual culture. N.Y., Cambridge Univ. Pr., 1995– .

Newly created series that "provides a forum for works on aspects of American art that implement methods drawn from related disciplines in the humanities, including literature, postmodern cultural studies, gender studies, and 'new history.'"—*Introd.* Black-and-white plates, bibliographies, indexes.

Contents: Jonathan Harris, Federal art and national culture: the politics of identity in New Deal America, 1995; David Bjelajac, Washington Allston, secret societies, and the alchemy of Anglo-American painting, 1997; Albert Boime, The unveiling of the national icons: a plea for patriotic iconoclasm in a nationalist era, 1998; David Craven, Abstract expressionism as cultural critique: dissent during the McCarthy period, 1999; Melissa Dabakis, Visualizing labor in American sculpture: monuments, manliness and the work ethic, 1990–1935, 1999.

R25 Cambridge studies in new art history and criticism. N.Y., Cambridge Univ. Pr., 1988– .

General ed.: Norman Bryson.

From 1988–91, titled Cambridge new art history and criticism. "This series provides a forum for studies that represent new approaches to the stud of the visual arts. The works cover a range of subjects, including artists, genres, periods, themes, styles, and movements. They are distinguished by their methods of inquiry, whether interdisciplinary or related to developments in literary theory, anthropology, or social history. The series also aims to publish translations of a selection of European material that has heretofore been unavailable to an English-speaking readership."—*Introd.* to Deborah J. Haynes, Bakhtin and the visual arts (1995).

Contents: Norman Bryson, ed., Calligram: essays in new art history from France, 1988; Michael Camille, The gothic idol: ideology and image making in medieval art, 1989; Stephen Bann, The true vine: on visual representation and the western tradition, 1989; Whitney Davis, The canonical tradition in ancient Egyptian art, 1990; Marcia R. Pointon, Naked authority: the body in western painting 1830–1908, 1990; Mieke Bal, Reading "Rembrandt": beyond the word-image opposition: the Northrop Frye lectures in literary theory, 1991; Mark A. Cheetham, The rhetoric of purity: essentialist theory and the advent of abstract painting, 1991; Peter J. Holliday, Narrative and event in ancient art, 1993; Carol Duncan, The aesthetics of power: essays in the critical art history, 1993; Peter Brunette and David Wills, eds., Deconstruction and the visual arts: art, media, architecture, 1994; Amelia Jones, Postmodernism and the en-gendering of Marcel Duchamp, 1994; Simon Goldhill and Robin Osborne, eds., Art and text in ancient Greek culture, 1994; Jas Elsner, Art and the Roman viewer: the transformation of art from the Pagan world to Christianity, 1995; Deborah J. Haynes, Bakhtin and the visual arts, 1995; Jean Louis Schefer and Paul Smith, eds., The enigmatic body: essays on the arts, 1995; Jeremy Gilbert-Rolfe, Beyond piety: critical essays on the visual arts, 1986–1993, 1995; Timon Screech, The western scientific gaze and popular imagery in later Edo Japan: the lens within the heart, 1996; Natalie Boymel Kampen, Sexuality in ancient art: Near East, Egypt, Greece, and Italy, 1996; Jas Elsner, Art and text in Roman culture, 1996; Peter Duro, ed., The rhetoric of the frame: essays on the boundaries of the artwork, 1996; Paolo Berdini, The religious art of Jacopo Bassano: painting as visual exegesis, 1997; Paul Duro, The academy and the limits of painting in seventeenth-century France, 1997; Wolfgang Kemp, The narratives of Gothic stained glass, 1997; Jill M. Ricketts, Visualizing Boccaccio: studies on illustrations of The Decameron, from Giotto to Pasolini, 1997; Victor Ieronim Stoichita, The self-aware image: an insight into early modern meta-painting, 1997; Cristelle Louise Baskins, Cassone painting, humanism, and gender in early modern Italy, 1998; Suzanne Lewis, The rhetoric of power in the Bayeux Tapestry, 1999; Lisa Saltzman, Anselm Kiefer and art afer Auschwitz, 1999.

R26 Cambridge studies in the history of art. N.Y., Cambridge Univ. Pr., 1986– .

Ed.: Francis Haskell and Nicholas Penny.

Unnumbered series of "carefully selected original monographs and more general publications, aimed primarily at art historians, students and scholars, representing a broad range of topics from all branches of art history, and demonstrating a wide variety of approaches and methods."—*Introd.*, first vol.

Contents: C. Parsons and Martha Ward, A bibliography of Salon criticism in Second Empire Paris, 1986; Moshe Barasch, Giotto and the language of gesture, 1987; Janet Southorn, Power and display in the seventeenth century: the arts and their patrons in Modena and Ferrara, 1988; Richard G. Mann, El Greco and his patrons: three major projects, 1989; John Sweetman, The oriental obsession: Islamic inspiration in British and American art and architecture 1500–1920, 1989; Peter Stupples, Pavel Kuznetsov: his life and art, 1989; Dwight C. Miller, Marcantonio Franceschini and the Liechtensteins, 1991; Neil McWilliam, ed., A bibliography of Salon criticism in Paris from the Ancien Régime to the Restoration, 1699–1827, 1991; Neil McWilliam, A bibliography of Salon criticism in Paris from the July Monarchy to the Second Republic, 1831–1851, 1991; Philip Sohm, Pittoresco: Marco Boschini: his critics and their critiques of painterly brushwork in seventeenth- and eighteenth-century Italy, 1992; Philip Rylands, Palma Vecchio, 1992; Klaus Berger, Japonisme in western painting from Whistler to Matisse, 1992; Anne Thorold, Letters of Lucien to Camille Pissarro, 1883–1903, 1993; Marie Busco, Sir Richard Westmacott, sculptor, 1995; Richard Eldridge, Beyond representation: philosophy and poetic imagination, 1996; Charles E. Cohen, The art of Giovanni da Pordenone: between dialect and language, 1996.

R27 Chicago visual library text-fiche series, 1– . Chicago, Univ. of Chicago Pr., 1976– .

Title formerly: Chicago visual library. A publishing program of the University of Chicago Press, to reproduce the major collections of the world's most important museums, in an inexpensive, highly visual format. With few exceptions, vols. are unavailable in any other format. Called "text-fiches," each title contains artworks on microfiche and commentary in an accompanying book with annotated catalog entries connected to the artwork on the fiche, and a bibliography.

Contents: (1–2) James Henry Breasted, The 1905–1907 Breasted Expeditions to Egypt and the Sudan, 2v., 1976; (3) Oriental Institute, Perspolis and ancient Iran, 1976; (4) Sue Allen, Victorian bookbindings, 1976; (5) John Kennardh

White, Pottery techniques of native North America, 1976; (6) Cheney Cowles Memorial Museum, Cornhusk bags of the Plateau Indians, 1976; (7) Dumbarton Oaks collections, Pre-Columbian art, 1976; (8) Phillips Collection, A collection in the making, 1976; (9) International Museum of Photography, British masters of the albumen print, 1976; (10) Baltimore Museum of Art, American prints, 1870–1950, 1976; (11) National Collection of Fine Arts, American art in the Barbizon mood, 1976; (12) Commonwealth Institute, The arts of the Hausa, 1977; (13) Isabelle Stewart Gardner Museum, A selection of paintings, drawings and watercolors, 1976; (14) Whitney Museum of American Art, Selections from the permanent collection, 1977; (15) Art Institute of Chicago, French drawings of the sixteenth and seventeenth centuries, 1977; (16) Birmingham Museums and Art Gallery, Pre-Rephaelite drawings: Dante Gabriel Rossetti, 1977; (17) Hispanic Society of America, Rugs of Spain and Morocco, 1977; (18) Art Institute of Chicago, French drawings and sketchbooks of the eighteenth century, 1977; (19) James Henry Breasted, The 1919/20 Breasted Expedition to the Near East: a photographic study, 1977; (20) Corning Museum of Glass, A survey of glassmaking from ancient Egypt to the present, 1977; (21) National Collection of Fine Arts, Academy: the academic tradition in American art, 1978; (22) Lewis Wickes Hine, Lewis Wickes Hine's interpretive photography: the six early projects, 1978; (23) Library of Congress, Charles Fenderich: lithographer of American statesmen, 1978; (24) Courtauld Institute of Art, The painting collections of the Courtauld Institute of Art, 1979; (25–26) Art Institute of Chicago, French drawings and sketchbooks of the nineteenth century, 2v., 1978–79; (27) Dumbarton Oaks collections, Byzantine art, 1979; (28) Nationalmuseum Stockholm, Drawings of Johan Tobias Sergel, 1979; (29) Hirshhorn Museum and Sculpture Garden, The Thomas Eakins collection of the Hirshhorn Museum and Sculpture Garden, 1979; (30) Joseph S. Czestochowski, The works of Arthur B. Davies, 1979; (31) Art Institute of Chicago, Italian drawings of the 15th, 16th, and 17th centuries, 1979; (32) Art Institute of Chicago, Italian drawings of the 18th and 19th centuries and Spanish drawings of the 17th through 19th centuries, 1980; (33) John Christian, The Oxford Union murals, 1981; (34) Daryl R. Rubenstein, Max Weber: a catalogue raisonné of his graphic work, 1980; (35) Art Institute of Chicago, Twentieth-century European paintings, 1980; (36) Oriental Institute, Ptolemais Cyrenaica, 1980; (37) Pierpont Morgan Library, Masterpieces of medieval painting: the art of illumination, 1981; [40, 44, 48–49, 51, 52, 53, 55, 57] Beatrice Farwell, French popular lithographic imagery, 1815–1870, v.1– , 1981– ; (41) Carney E. S. Gavin, The image of the East: nineteenth century Near Eastern photographs by Bonfils: from the collections of the Harvard Semitic Museum, 1982; (42) Otto Demus, The medieval mosaics of San Marco, Venice: a color archive, 1986; (43) Philadelphia Museum of Art and the Henry Francis du Pont Winterthur Museum, Pennsylvania German art 1683–1850, 1984; (45) Oleg Grabar, The illustrations of the Maqamat, 1984; (46) National Museum of American Art, Portrait miniatures in the National Museum of American Art, 1984; (47) Annemarie Weyl Carr, Byzantine illumination 1150–1250: the study of a provincial tradition, 1987; (50) Arthur Ewart Popham, Old master drawings at Holkham Hall, 1986; (54) Nancy Paterson Sevcenko, Illustrated manuscripts of the Metaphrastian menologion, 1990.

R28 The Clarendon studies in the history of art. N.Y., Oxford Univ. Pr., 1989– .

General ed.: Dennis Farr.

Scholarly series devoted to the art and architecture of Western Europe, from the Middle Ages to present day, presenting the results of recent research in an attractive format.

Contents: William L. Barcham, The religious paintings of Giambattista Tiepolo: piety and tradition in eigtheenth-century Venice, 1989; John Bold, John Webb architectural theory and practice in the seventeenth century, 1989; Eve Borsook, Messages in mosaic: the Royal programmes of Norman Sicily 1130–1187, 1990; Linda Gertner Zatlin, Aubrey Beardsley and Victorian sexual politics, 1990; Gale Barbara Murray, Toulouse Lautrec: the formative years 1878–1891, 1991; Colin Cunningham, Alfred Waterhouse 1830–1905: biography of a practice, 1992; Julian Gardner, The tomb and the tiara: curial tomb sculpture in Rome and Avignon in the later Middle Ages, 1992; Kathryn Horste, Cloister design and monastic reform in Toulouse: the romanesque sculpture of La Daurade, 1992; George Knox, Giambattista Piazzetta, 1682–1754, 1992; Eric Fernie, An architectural history of Norwich Cathedral, 1993; Perri Lee Roberts, Masolino da Panicale, 1993; Timothy Mitchell, Art and science in German landscape painting 1770–1840, 1993; George Knox, Antonio Pellegrini 1675–1741, 1995; Sanda Miller, Constantin Brancusi: a survey of his work, 1995; Louise Campbell, Coventry Cathedral art and architecture in post-war Britain, 1996; Liz James, Light and colour in Byzantine art, 1996; Lisa A. Reilly, An architectural history of Peterborough Cathedral, 1997; Joanna Selborne, British wood-engraved book illustration, 1904–1940: a break with tradition, 1997; Anat Tcherikover, High Romanesque sculpture in the Duchy of Aquitaine c.1090–1140, 1997; Thomas Martin, Alessandro Vittoria and the portrait bust in Renaissance Venice: remodelling antiquity, 1998; Joanna Selborne, British wood-engraved book illustration, 1904–1940: a break with tradition, 1998.

R29 The Classical America series in art and architecture. N.Y., Norton, 1977– . Place of publication and publisher vary.

Ed.: Henry Hope Reed and H. Stafford Bryant Jr.

Scholarly, society publication of Classical America, an organization that encourages the classical tradition in the arts of the United States. Some vols. are derived from earlier published works. Plans call for other noteworthy titles to be reprinted.

Contents: William R. Ware, The American Vignola (1905–06), 1977; Geoffrey Scott, The architecture of humanism: a study in the history of taste (1914), 1974; Kenyon Cox, The classic point of view (1911), 1980; Edith Wharton and Ogden Codman Jr., The decoration of houses (1902), 1998, 1997; William A. Coles, ed., Classical America IV (1959), 1977; Hector d'Espouy, Fragments from Greek and Roman architecture: the Classical America edition of Hector d'Espouy's plates, 1981; McKim, Mead & White, Monograph of the work of McKim Mead & White 1879–1915, student's ed., 1981; Herbert Small, The Library of Congress, its architecture and decoration (1901), 1982; Albert Edward Richardson, Monumental classic architecture in Great Britain and Ireland (1914), 1982; Paul Marie Letarouilly, Letarouilly on Renaissance Rome, the students edition of Paul Letarouilly's Edifices de Rome moderne and Le Vatican et la basilique de Saint-Pierre, 1984; Henry Hope Reed, The New York Public Library: its architecture and decoration, 1986; Pierce Rice, Man as hero: the human figure in western art, 1987; Kenyon Cox, What is painting? Winslow Homer and other essays, 1988.

R30 The Collector's series. Roma, Bozzi, 1976– .

Scholarly series on late Renaissance and Italian Baroque art. Each vol. includes bibliographies and indexes. In Italian.

Contents: Andrea Busiri Vici, Andrea Locatelli e il paesaggio romano del settecento, 1976; A. Busiri Vici, Trittico paesistico romano del '700: Paolo Anesi, Paolo Monaldi, Alessio De Marchis, 1976; Luigi Salerno, Pittori di paesaggio del seicento a Roma / Landscape painters of the seventeenth century in Rome, 3v., 1977; Giuliano Briganti, I bamboccianti: pittori della vita quotidiana a Roma nel seicento, 1983.

R31 Colloquies on art and archaeology in Asia. London, Percival David Foundation of Chinese Art, School of Oriental and African Studies, Univ. of London, 1970– .

Contents: (1) Watson, William, ed. Pottery and metalwork in T'ang China: their chronology and external relation (1971). 2d ed. 1976; (2) Watson, William, ed. Mahayanist art after A.D. 900 (1971); (3) Watson, William, ed. The westward influence of the Chinese arts from the 14th to the 18th century. 1973; (4) Watson, William, ed. The art of Iran and Anatolia from the 11th to the 13th century AD (1975); (5) Medley, Margaret, ed. Chinese painting and the decorative style (1976); (6) Watson, William. Artistic personality and decorative style in Japanese art (1977); (7) Denwood, Philip, ed. Arts of the Eurasian steppelands (1978); (8) Medley, Margaret, ed. Decorative techniques and styles in Asian ceramics (1979); (9) Watson, William. ed. Landscape style in Asia (1980); (10) Grube, Ernst J., and Sims, Eleanor, eds. Between China and Iran: paintings from four Istanbul albums. 1985; (11) Watson, William, ed. Lacquerwork in Asia and beyond (1982); (12) Picton, John, ed. Earthenware in Asia and Africa (1984); (13) Unable to trace; (14) Scott, Rosemary E. and Hutt, Graham, eds. Style in the East Asian tradition (1987); (15) Whitfield, Roderick, ed. The problem of meaning in early Chinese ritual bronzes (1993); (16) Scott, Rosemary E., ed. The porcelains of Jingdezhen (1993); (17) Scott, Rosemary, and Guy, John, eds. South East Asia and China: art, interaction and commerce (1995).

R32 Columbia studies on art, 1– . N.Y., Columbia Univ. Pr., 1989– .

Irregularly published, scholarly series. Several of the vols. are catalogs to accompany exhibitions at the Wallach Art Gallery at Columbia University.

Contents: (1) Vidya Dehejia, Impossible picturesqueness: Edward Lear's Indian watercolours, 1873–1875, 1989; (2) Janis A. Tomlinson, Graphic evolutions: the print series of Francisco Goya, 1989; (3) Jackie Kestenbaum, ed., Emerging Japanese architects of the 1990s, 1991; (4) Eugenie Tsai, Robert Smithson unearthed: drawings, collages, writings, 1991.

R33 Connoisseurship, criticism and art history in the nineteenth century, 1–23. N.Y., Garland, 1978–79.

Series of facsimile reprints of 23 of the most important art historical works written by some of the foremost historians and critics of the time. In 30v. Titles were selected by Sydney J. Freedberg.

Contents: (1) Charles Baudelaire, The painter of modern life and other essays, (1964), 1978; (2) Charles Baudelaire, Eugène Delacroix, his life and work (1863), 1979; (3) Jakob Christoph Burckhardt, An art guide to painting in Italy (1918), 1979; (4) Jakob Christoph Burckhardt, Recollections of Rubens (1949), 1978; (5) Michel Eugène Chevreul, The principles of harmony and contrast of colours (1839), 1980; (6) Joseph Archer Crowe and G. B. Cavalcaselle, The early Flemish painters (1872), 1978; (7) Joseph Archer Crowe and G.B. Cavalcaselle, A new history of painting in Italy, 3v. (1864–66), 1980; (8) Joseph Archer Crowe and G.B. Cavalcaselle, Titian, his life and times, 2v. (1877), 1978; (9) Eugène Delacroix, The journals of Eugène Delacroix, trans. by Lucy Norton (1847), 1979; (10) Henry Fuseli, The lectures of Henry Fuseli (1831), 1979; (11) Adolf von Hildebrand, The problem of form in painting and sculpture (1932), 1978; (12) William Morris, Hopes and fears for art (1917), 1978; (13) William Morris, Architecture, industry, and wealth (1883–84), 1978; (14) William Young Ottley, An inquiry into the origin and early history of engraving, 2v. (1816), 1978; (15) William Young Ottley, The Italian school of design (1823), 1980; (16) Johann David Passavant, Tour of a German artist in England, 2v., (1836), 1978; (17) Johann David Passavant, Raphael of Urbino and his father Giovanni Santi (1872), 1978; (18) A.C. Quatremère de Quincy, An essay on the nature, the end, and the means of imitation in the fine arts (1823), 1979; (19) A.C. Quatremère de Quincy, History of the life and works of Raffaello (1824), 1979; (20) John Ruskin, The stones of Venice, 3v. (1851–53), 1979; (21) John Ruskin, Lectures on architecture and painting (1853), 1978; (22) John Ruskin, Lectures on art (1870), 1978; (23) John Ruskin, The art of England lectures given in Oxford (1884), 1979.

R34 Contemporary American art critics, 1– . Ann Arbor, UMI Research Pr. 1984– .

Ed.: Donald Burton Kuspit.

Series on art criticism, written by distinguished art historians and critics of contemporary art. Some of the more noteworthy titles are being reprinted.

Contents: (1) Lawrence Alloway, Network: art and the complex present, 1984; (2) Donald Burton Kuspit, The critic is artist: the intentionality of art, 1996, 1984; (3) Joseph Masheck, Historical present: essays of the 1970s, 1984; (4) Robert Pincus-Witten, Eye to eye: twenty years of art criticism, 1984; (5) Dennis Adrian, Sight out of mind: essays and criticism on art, 1985; (6) Peter Howard Selz, Art in a turbulent era, 1985; (7) Nicolas Calas, Transfigurations, art critical essays, on the modern period, 1985; (8) Dore Ashton, Out of the whirlwind: three decades of arts commentary, 1987; (9) Peter Plagens, Moonlight blues: an artist's art criticism, 1995, 1986; (10) Arlene Raven, Crossing over: feminism and art of social concern, 1988; (11) Michael D. Hall, Stereoscopic perspective: reflections on American fine and folk art, 1988.

R35 Contemporary artists and their critics. N.Y., Cambridge Univ. Pr., 1993– .

Wide-ranging topics in contemporary art and architecture by leading art historians and critics in the field.

Contents: Joseph Masheck, Building-art: modern architecture under cultural construction, 1993; Thomas McEvilley, The exile's return: toward a redefinition of painting for the postmodern era, 1993; Donald Burton Kuspit, Signs of psyche in modern and postmodern art, 1993; Mary Mathews Gedo, Looking at art from the inside out: the psychoiconographic approach to modern art, 1994; Robert C. Morgan, Art into ideas: essays on conceptual art, 1996; Eleanor Heartney, Critical condition: American culture at the crossroads, 1997; Barry Schwabsky, The widening circle: consequences of modernism in contemporary art, 1997; Peter Howard Selz, Beyond the mainstream: essays on modern and contemporary art, 1997; Jack J. Spector, Surrealist art and writing, 1919–1939: the gold of time, 1997; Matthew Biro, Anselm Kiefer and the philosophy of Martin Heidegger, 1998.

R36 Contemporary arts series. N.Y., St. Martin's; Chicago, St. James, 1977– . Publisher varies.

Ed.: Colin Naylor.

Each vol. provides detailed biographical information on hundreds of the world's greatest artists, architects, photographers and designers. An invaluable resource for artist information, including exhibitions, collections, dealers' names and addresses, bibliographies, as well as an essay of evaluation.

Contents: Joann Cerrito, ed., Contemporary artists, 4th ed., 1996; Colin Naylor, ed., Contemporary photographers, 3d ed., 1995; International contemporary arts directory, 1985; Ann Lee Morgan and Colin Naylor, eds., Contemporary architects, 3d ed., 1994; Colin Naylor, ed., Contemporary designers, 3d ed., 1997; Colin Naylor, ed., Contemporary masterworks, 1991; Richard Martin, ed., Contemporary fashion, 1995.

R37 Contributions to the study of art and architecture, 1– . Westport, Conn., Greenwood, 1992– .

Wide-ranging topics within art and architecture. Each vol. includes bibliographies and indexes.

Contents: (1) Joan Jeffri, ed., The Craftsperson speaks: artists in varied media discuss their crafts, 1992; (2) Joan Jeffri, ed., The painter speaks: artists discuss their experiences and careers, 1993; (3) Leslie Ross, Text, image, message: saints in medieval manuscript illustrations, 1994; (4) Joseph D. Masheck, Van Gogh 100, 1996; (5) F. Graeme Chalmers, Women in the nineteenth-century art world: schools of art and design for women in London and Philadelphia, 1998.

R38 Critical voices in art, theory & culture. G&B Arts International.

Ed.: Saul Ostrow.

"A library of contemporary theory on the cutting edge of modernist and postmodern thought . . . by authorities of international prominence in art history, art criticism, philosophy, and the theoretical study of technology, architecture, and music/dance/film/theater."—*Advert.* Each hardcover vol. presents original or previously published essays by well-known theorists.

Contents: Thomas McEvilley, Capacity: history, the world, and the self in contemporary art and criticism, 1996; Stephen Melville and Jeremy Gilbert-Rolfe, Seams: art as a philosophical context, 1996; Arthur C. Danto, ed., The wake of art: criticism, philosophy and the ends of taste, 1998; Moira Roth and Jonathan D. Katz, Difference/indifference: musings on postmodernsm, Marcel Duchamp and John Cage, 1998; Richard and Susan King Roth, eds., Beauty is nowhere: ethical issues in art and design, 1998.

R39 Current debates in art history, 1–3. Binghamton, N.Y., State Univ. of New York at Binghamton, 1989–91.

Proceedings of an annual symposium held by the Dept. of Art and Art History of the State University of New York at Binghamton. Includes bibliographical references.

Contents: (1) John Tagg, The cultural politics of "postmodernism," 1989; (2) never completed; (3) Anthony D. King, ed., Culture, globalization and the world-system: contemporary conditions for the representation of identity, 1991.

R40 Documentary sources in contemporary art, 1– . Cambridge, Mass., MIT Pr. and N.Y., New Museum of Contemporary Art, 1984– .

Series ed.: Marcia Tucker.

Contemporary art series presenting essays, interviews, and discussions by today's foremost artists. Co-published by the Museum of Contemporary Art in Soho, the series is dedicated to exhibiting recent work by living artists, and was edited at one time by the museum's now-former director, Marcia Tucker. Some vols. have been reprinted.

Contents: (1) Brian Wallis, ed., Art after modernism: rethinking representation, 1984; (2) Brian Wallis, ed., Blasted allegories: an anthology of writings by contemporary artists, 1987; (3) Russell Ferguson, ed., Discourses: conversations in postmodern art and culture, 1990; (4) Russell Ferguson, ed., Out there: marginalization and contemporary cultures, 1990; (5) Ella Shohat, Talking visions: multicultural feminism in a transnational age, 1998.

R41 Documenting the image, 1– . Langhorne, Pa., Gordon & Breach, 1994– . Place of publication varies.

Ed.: Helene E. Roberts and J. Brent Maddox.

Scholarly series offering theoretical discussions, essays as well as reference information on visual and photographic documentation. Includes annotated bibliographies.

Contents: (1) Roelof van Straten, An introduction to iconography: symbols, allusions and meaning in the visual arts, rev. English ed., 1994; (2) Helene E. Roberts, Art history through the camera's lens, 1995; (3) Donald Martin Reynolds, "Remove Not the Ancient Landmark": public monuments and moral values, 1996; (4) Anthony J. Hamber, "A Higher Branch of the Art": photographing the fine arts in England, 1839–1880, 1996; (5) William Craft Brumfield, Landmarks of Russian architecture: a photographic survey, 1997; (6) Régine Thiriez, Barbarian lens: western photographers of the Qianlong emperor's European palaces, 1998.

R42 Dumbarton Oaks studies, 1– . Washington, D.C., Dumbarton Oaks Center for Byzantine Studies (Distr. by J.J. Augustin, Locust Valley, N.Y., 1950–).

Distinguished series from the Dumbarton Oaks Center for Byzantine Studies, covering a wide range of topics related to the Byzantine Empire.

Selective contents: (2) George Maxim Anossov Hanfmann, The Season sarcophagus in Dumbarton Oaks, 1951; (5) Jozsef Deer, The dynastic porphyry tombs of the Norman period in Sicily, 1959; (6) Otto Demus, The Church of San Marco in Venice: history, architecture, sculpture, 1960; (7) Erica Cruikshank Dodd, Byzantine silver stamps, 1961; (8) Cyril A. Mango, Materials for the study of the mosaics of St. Sophia at Istanbul, 1962; (10) Paul Julius Alexander, The oracle of Baalbek: the Tiburtine sibyl in Greek dress, 1967; (12) Michael F. Hendy, Coinage and money in the Byzantine Empire 1081–1261, 1969; (14) Arthur H. S. Megaw and E. J. W. Hawkins, The Church of the Panagia Kanakaria at Lythrankomi in Cyprus: its mosaics and frescoes, 1977; (15) Hans Belting, The mosaics and frescoes of St. Mary Pammakaristos (Fethiye Camii) at Istanbul, 1978; (16) Hugo Buchthal, Patronage in the thirteenth-century Constantinople: an atelier of late Byzantine book illumination and calligraphy, 1978; (20) Anthony Bryer, The Byzantine monuments and topography of the Pontos, 1985; (22) Ann Wharton, Tokali Kilise: tenth-century metropolitan art in Byzantine Cappadocia, 1986; (23) Robert W. Edwards, The fortifications of Armenian Cilicia, 1987; (25) Robert G. Ousterhout, The architecture of the Kariye Camii in Istanbul, 1987; (27) Ernst Kitzinger, The mosaics of St. Mary's of the Admiral in Palermo, 1990; (28) Kurt Weitzmann, The frescoes of the Dura synagogue and Christian art, 1990; (29) Thomas F. Mathews and Avedis K. Sanjian, Armenian gospel iconography: the tradition of the Glajor Gospel, 1991; (31) Sirarpie Der Nersessian, Miniature painting in the Armenian Kingdom of Cilicia from the twelfth to the fourteenth century, 2v., 1993.

R43 Essays in art and culture. London, Reaktion Books, 1989– .

Scholarly series providing original research and fresh appraisals by well-known art historians. Earlier vols. were first published in the United States by Harvard Univ. Press. Color and black-and-white plates, bibliographies, and footnotes.

Contents: Roger Cardinal, The landscape vision of Paul Nash, 1989; Norman Bryson, Looking at the overlooked: four essays on still life painting, 1990; David Brett, C. R. Mackintosh, the poetics of workmanship, 1991; Richard Brillant, Portraiture, 1991; Karen Lucic, Charles Sheeler and the cult of the machine, 1991; Ernst van Alphen, Francis Bacon and the loss of self, 1992; Michael Camille, Image on the edge: the margins of medieval art, 1992; Joseph Hillis Miller, Illustration, 1992; David H. T. Scott, Paul Delvaux: surrealizing the nude, 1992; Fred Orton, Figuring Jasper Johns, 1994; Francette Pacteau, The symptom of beauty, 1994; James Henry Rubin, Manet's silence and the poetics of bouquets, 1994; Martin Warnke, Political landscape: the art history of nature, 1994; Victor Ieronim Stoichita, Visionary experience in the golden age of Spanish art, 1995; Wu Hung, The double screen: medium and representation in Chinese painting, 1966; Robin Cormack, Painting the soul: icons, death masks, and shrouds, 1997; David Pascoe, Peter Greenaway: museums and moving images, 1997; Victor Ieronim Stoichita, A short history of the shadow, 1997; Lindsay Blair, Joseph Cornell's Vision of Spiritual Order, 1998; Sergiusz Michalski, Public monuments: art in political bondage, 1870–1997, 1998; Martin Pawley, Terminal architecture, 1998; Victor Ieronim Stoichita, Goya: the last carnival, 1999.

R44 Estudios de arte y estética, 1– . México, Instituto de Investigaciones Estéticas, Universidad Nacional Autónoma de México, 1958– .

Exhaustively researched series on all facets of Mexican art. Some vols. contain papers from colloquia sponsored by the Institute. Small format, with black-and-white plates in back. In Spanish.

Contents: (1) Jean M. Rivière, El arte y la estética del budismo, 1958; (2) Johann Joachim Winkelmann, De la belleza en el arte clásico: selección de estudios y cartas, 1959; (3) Justino Fernández, Coatlicue: Estética del arte indígena antiguo, 2d ed., 1959; (4) Justino Fernández, El retablo de la reyes. Estética del arte de la Nueva España, 1959; (5) Justino Fernández, El hombre: estética del arte moderno y contemporáneo, 1962; (6) Samuel Ramos, Estudios de estética: biografía, recopilacion y clasificacion de Juan Hernández Luna, 1963; (7) Jean M. Rivière, El arte zen, 1963; (8) Francisco de la Maza, Cartas barrocas desde Castilla y Andalucía, 1963; (9) Justino Fernández, Miguel Angel: de su alma, 1964; (10) Francisco de la Maza, Antinoo, el último dios del mundo clásico, 1966; (11) Manuel González Galván, De Guatamala a Nicaragua: diario del viaje de un estudiante de arte, 1968; (12) Justino Fernández, Estética del arte mexicano: Coatlicue. El retablo de los reyes. El hombre, 2d ed., 1990; (13) Pedro José Márquez, Sobre lo bello en general: Dos monumentos de arquitectura mexicana: Tajín y Xochicalco, 1972; (14) La dicotomia entre arte culto y arte popular: Coloquio Internacional de Zacatecas, 1979; (15) La dispersíon del manierismo, 1980; (16) La iconografía en el arte contemporáneo, 1982; (17) El arte efimero en el mundo hispánico, 1983; (18) Las Academias de arte, 1985; (19) La ciudad: concepto y obra, 1987; (20) Los estudios sobre el arte mexicano: examen y prospectiva, 1986; (21) Ramón Xirau, Ciudades, 1985; (22) Dúrdica Šégota, Valores plásticos del arte Mexica, 1995; (23) never published; (24) Joseph A. Baird, Los retablos del siglio XVIII en el sur de España, Portugal y México, 1987; (25) El nacionalismo y el arte mexicano/IX Coloquio de Historia del Arte, 1986; (26) Iconología y sociedad: arte colonial hispanoamericano, 1987; (27) Rubén Bonifaz Nuño, Imagen de Tláloc: hipótesis iconográfica y textual, 1986; (28) Simpatías y diferencias: relaciones del arte mexicano con el de América Latina, 1988; (29) Elia Espinosa, Jean Cocteau, el ojo entre la norma y el deseo, 1988; (30) Historia, leyendas y mitos de México: su expresión en el arte, 1988; (31) Juan Antonio Ortega y Medina, Imagen y carácter de J. J. Winckelmann: cartas y testimonios, 1992; (32) 1492, dos mundos: paralelismo y convergencias, 1991; (33) Tiempo y arte, 1991; (34) Encuentros y desencuentros en las artes 1994; (35) Los discursos sobre el arte, 1995; (36) El arte y la vida cotidiana, 1995; (37) Arte, historia e identidad en América: visiones comparativas, 3 v., 1994; (38) Arte y violencia, 1995; (39) Historia del arte y juicio crítico, 1998; (40) La Catedral de México: problemática, restauración y conservación, 1997; (41) Especulacíon y patrimonio, 1997; (42) Temas y problemas, 1997; (43) Arte y espacio, 1997; (44) La sociedad civil frente al patrimonio cultural, 1997; (45) Patrimonio y turismo, 1998; (46) Patrocinio, colección, y circulación de las artes, 1997; (47) Estudios sobre arte: sesenta años del Instituto de Investigaciones Estéticas, 1998; (48) not yet published; (49) La abolición del arte, 1998.

R45 Frankfurter Fundamente der Kunstgeschichte, Bd.1– . Frankfurt-am-Main, Germany, Kunstgeschichtliches Institut der Johann Wolfgang Goethe-Universität, 1982– .

Learned series, with contributions by students and professors at the Institute.

Contents: (1) Gerhard Eimer, Zur Dialektik des Glaubens bei Caspar David Friedrich, 1982; (2) Gerhard Eimer, Quellen zur Politischen Ikonographie der Romantik: Steins Turmbau in Nassau, 1987; (3) Roger M. Gorenflo, Die Mittelalterliche Baugeschichte der ehemaligen Abteikirche Amorbach, 1983; (4) Silvia Maria Busch, Graltempelidee und Industrialisierung: St. Nikolaus zu Arenberg: eine Wallfahrtsanlage du Katholischen Spätromantik im Rheinland (1845–1892), 1984; (5) Ilona Oltuski, Kunst und Ideologie des Bezalels in Jerusalem: ein Versuch zur jüdischen Identitätsfindung, 1987; (6) Gudrun Radler, Die Schreinmadonna "Vierge Ouvrante": von den bernhardinischen Anfängen bis zur Frauenmystik im Deutschordensland: mit beschreibendem Katalog, 1990; (7) Jürgen Schwarz, Bildannoncen aus der Jahrhundertwende: Studien zur künstlerischen Reklamegestaltung in Deutschland zwischen 1896 und 1914, 1990; (8) Gerhard Eimer, ed., Van Gogh Indices: Analytischer Schlüssel für die Schriften des Künstlers, 1992; (9) Gabriele Wolff, Zwischen Tradition und Neubeginn: zur Geschichte der Denkmalpflege in der 1. Hälfte des 19. Jahrhunderts: geistesgeschichtliche Grundlagen in den deutschsprachigen Gebieten, 1992; (10) Ariane Grigoteit, Joseph Beuys: Wasserfarbe auf Papier (1936–1984/85), 2v., 1992; (11) Kerstin Appelshäuser, Die öffentliche Grünanlage im Städtebau Napoleons in Italien als politische Aussage, 1994; (12) Jürgen Schwarz, Architektur und Kommerz: Studien zur Deutschen Kauf- und Warenhausarchitektur vor dem Ersten Weltkrieg am Beispiel der Frankfurter Zeil, 1995; (13) not yet published; (14) Hasso von Haldenwang, Christian Haldenwang, Kupferstecher (1770–1831), 1997; (15) Jacqueline Kempfer, Das Amt des Architetto del Popolo Romano: die Geschichte einer Institution unter besonderer Berücksichtigung von Carlo Rainaldi, 1997.

R46 Franklin D. Murphy lectures, 1– . Lawrence, Kan., Helen F. Spencer Museum of Art, Univ. of Kansas, 1983– .

"The Murphy lectureship in art began as the inspired idea of Dr. Franklin D. Murphy, a devoted educator, connoisseur, and lover of the arts . . . who arranged for the establishment of a generous endowment at the University of Kansas which allows the University to bring a figure of international stature in art or art history to the campus each year."—*Introd.* Slim, scholarly series whose vols. are based on lectures held at the museum. Vols. are well-illustrated and include bibliographies and footnotes.

Contents: (1) Pierre Rosenberg, Chardin: new thoughts, 1983; (2) not yet published; (3) Nai Heia, Jade and silk of Han China, 1983; (4) not yet published; (5) Robert G. Calkins, Programs of Medieval illumination, 1984; (6) not yet published; (7) Nobuo Tsuji, Playfulness in Japanese art, 1986; (8) David Rosand, The meaning of the mark: Leonardo and Titian, 1988; (9) James Francis Cahill, Three alternative histories of Chinese painting, 1988; (10) William Vaughan, Art and the natural world in 19th-century Britain: three essays, 1990; (11) Walter S. Gibson, Pieter Bruegel the Elder: two studies, 1991; (12) Thomas Lawton, A time of transition: two collectors of Chinese art, 1991; (13) not yet published; (14) never published; (15,16) not yet published; (17) Karal Ann Marling, Civil rights in Oz: images of Kansas in American popular art, 1997.

R47 Garland publications in the fine arts. N.Y., Garland, 1991–94.

Richly illustrated, exhaustive, and well-researched vols. on a variety of modern art topics.

Contents: Fereshteh Daftari, The influence of Persian art on Gauguin, Matisse, and Kandinsky, 1991; Geraldine Wojno Kiefer, Alfred Stieglitz: scientist, photographer, and avatar of modernism 1880–1913, 1991; Beth S. Gersh-Nešic, The early criticism of André Salmon, 1991; A. Dierdre Robson, Prestige, profit, and pleasure: the market for modern art in New York in the 1940s and 1950s, 1994.

R48 Getty Museum studies on art. Malibu, Calif., J. Paul Getty Museum, 1988– .

"This series seeks to introduce individual works or small groups of closely related works in the Museum's collections to a broad public. Each monograph includes a close discussion of its subject as well as a detailed analysis of the broader context in which the work was created, considering relevant historical, cultural and chronological issues."—*Advert.*

Contents: Louise Lippincott, Edvard Munch: Starry Night, 1988; Louise Lippincott, Lawrence Alma Tadema: Spring, 1991; Mark Haworth-Booth, Camille Silvy: River Scene, France, 1992; Richard Thomson, Edgar Degas: Waiting, 1995; Anne W. Lowenthal, Joachim Wtewael: Mars and Venus Surprised by Vulcan, 1995; Christopher White, Anthony van Dyck: Thomas Howard, The Earl of Arundel, 1995; Gordon Baldwin, Roger Fenton: Pasha and Bayadère, 1996; John Webb, Jan Steen: The Drawing Lesson, 1996; Dawson William Carr, Andrea Mantegna: The Adoration of the Magi, 1997; Elizabeth Cropper, Pontormo: Portrait of a Halberdier, 1997; John House, Pierre-Auguste Renoir: La

Promenade, 1997; Dorothy Johnson, Jacques-Louis David: The Farewell of Telemachus and Eucharis, 1997; Carol C. Mattusch, The Victorious Youth, 1997; Colin B. Bailey, Jean-Baptiste Greuze: The Laundress, 1999.

R49 Gothenburg studies in art and architecture, 1– . Göteborg, Sweden, Acta Universitatis Gothoburgensis, 1978– .

Subseries of Acta Universitatis Gothoburgensis. Irregularly published Swedish art series offering studies by members of the Department of Art of the University of Gothenburg.

Contents: (1) Ingvar Bergstrom, Interpretationes selectae, 1978; (2) Andre Krauss, Vincent van Gogh: studies in the social aspects of his work, 1983; (3) Maj-Brit Wadell, Evangelicae historiae imagines: Entstehungsgeschichte und Vorlagen, 1985; (4) Yvonne Eriksson, Tactile pictures: pictorial representations for the blind, 1784–1940, 1998; (5) Eva Nodin, Estetisk pluralism och disciplinerande struktur: om barnkolonier och architektur i Italien under fascismens tid, 1999.

R50 Grunwald Center studies, 1–6, 1980–85. Los Angeles, Univ. of California, Los Angeles, Grunwald Center for the Graphic Arts. Annual.

Monographic series issuing from the Grunwald Center for the Graphic Arts at UCLA, consisting of exhibition catalogs from the Center's shows, with a section on acquisitions for the year.

Contents: (1) Lucinda H. Gedeon, Graphic art of Henri Matisse, 1980; (2) Burr Wallen, Picasso and printmaking, 1981; (3) Franklin D. Murphy: a study in patronage, (1982); (4) Early twentieth century German prints in the collection of the Grunwald Center for the Graphic Arts, 1983; (5) Lucinda H. Gedeon; Gordon Fuglie; and James Smalls, Tamarind, from Los Angeles to Albuquerque, 1985; (6) Celebrating two decades in photography: recent work by UCLA/MFA recipients, 1985.

R51 Hagop Kevorkian series on Near Eastern art and civilization. N.Y., NYU Pr., 1977–.

Beautifully produced, high-quality series on Islamic art and culture. Issued by the Hagop Kevorkian Center for Middle Eastern Studies of New York University, where the "Kevorkian lectures," which have inspired some of the vols., are held.

Contents: Dietrich Wildung, Egyptian saints: deification in Pharaonic Egypt, 1977; Heinz Gaube, Iranian cities, 1979; Annemarie Schimmel, Calligraphy and Islamic culture, 1984; Andre Raymond, The great Arab cities in the 16th–18th centuries: an introduction, 1984; Avraham Negev, Nabatean archaeology today, 1986; J. Christoph Burgel, The feather of Simurgh: the "licit magic" of the arts in medieval Islam, 1988; Oleg Grabar, The great mosque of Isfahan, 1990; Basil William Robinson, Fifteenth century Persian paintings: problems and issues, 1991; Zdzislaw Zygulski, Ottoman art in the service of the empire, 1992; Michael Meinecke, Patterns of stylistic change in Islamic architecture: local traditions versus migrating artists, 1996.

R52 Hesperia supplement, 1– . Princeton, N.J., American School of Classical Studies at Athens, 1937– . Place of publication, publisher varies.

Vols. inspired by research being undertaken at the excavations in Athens. Related to the periodical, Hesperia (see GLAH 1:Q181).

Selective contents: (2) Rodney Stuart Young, Late geometric graves and a seventh century well in the Agora, 1939; (3) Gorham Phillips Stevens, The setting of the Periclean Parthenon, 1940; (4) Homer A. Thompson, The Tholos of Athens and its predecessors, 1940; (7, 10) Gladys R. Davidson and Dorothy Burr Thompson, Small objects from the Pnyx, 2v., 1943–56; (15); Stephen V. Tracy, The lettering of an Athenian mason, 1975; (16) Merle K. Langdon, A sanctuary of Zeus on Mount Hymettos, 1976; (19) Studies in Attic epigraphy, history, and topography presented to Eugene Vanderpool, 1982; (20) Studies in Athenian architecture, sculpture, and topography: presented to Homer A. Thompson, 1982; (22) Elizabeth J. Walters, Attic grave reliefs that represent women in the dress of Isis, 1988; (23) Claireve Grandjouan, Hellenistic relief molds from the Athenian Agora, 1989; (24) Jeffrey S. Soles, The prepalatial cemeteries at Mochlos and Gournia and the house tombs of Bronze Age Crete, 1992; (25) Susan I. Rotroff and John H. Oakley, Debris from a public dining place in the Athenian Agora, 1992; (26) Ira S. Mark, The sanctuary of Athena Nike in Athens: architectural stages and chronology, 1993; (27) Proceedings of the International Conference on Greek Architectural Terracottas of the Classical and Hellenistic Periods: Dec. 12–15, 1991, 1994; (28) Darrell Arlynn Amyx, Studies in archaic corinthian vase painting, 1996.

R53 Interpretations in art. N.Y., Columbia Univ. Pr., 1990– .

Small-format, scholarly series. Some vols. are reissues of important early 20th-century essays with modern interpretations by art historians. Each vol. includes bibliographical references and indexes.

Contents: Walter F. Friedlaender, Mannerism and anti-mannerism in Italian painting (1957), 1990; Rainer Crone, Paul Klee: legends of the sign, 1991; Johanna Drucker, Theorizing modernism: visual art and the critical tradition, 1994; Norris Kelly Smith, Here I stand: perspective from another point of view, 1994; Mary Ann Caws, Robert Motherwell: what art holds, 1996.

R54 Issues and debates. Santa Monica, Calif., Getty Center for the History of Art and the Humanities, 1991– .

Ed.: Julia Bloomfield, Kurt W. Forster, Thomas F. Reese.

Beautifully produced, refined collections of essays on variety of art historical topics by the Getty Center Publication Programs.

Contents: David Freedberg and Jan de Vries, eds., Art in history, history in art: studies in seventeenth-century Dutch culture, 1991; Thomas W. Gaehtgens and Heinz Ickstadt, eds., American icons: transatlantic perspectives on eighteenth- and nineteenth-century American art, 1992; Harry Francis Mallgrave, ed., Otto Wagner: reflections on the raiment of modernity, 1993; Luisa Ciammitti, Steven F. Ostrow, and Salvatore Settis, eds., Dosso's fate: painting and court culture in Renaissance Italy, 1998; Robert C. Post, ed., Censorship and silencing: practices of cultural regulation, 1998; Alexandre Kostka and Irving Wohlfarth, eds., Nietzsche and "an architecture of our minds," 1999; Michael S. Roth and Charles G. Salas, eds. Disturbing remains: memory, history, and crisis in the twentieth century, 2000.

R55 Journal of Roman studies monographs, 1– . London, Society for the Promotion of Roman Studies, 1982– .
Scholarly archeology series, related to Journal of Roman studies (see GLAH 1:Q209), offering more extensive studies on Roman art and civilization.

Contents: (1) Joyce Marie Reynolds, Aphrodisias and Rome: documents from the excavation of the theatre at Aphrodisias conducted by Professor Kenan T. Erim, together with some related texts, 1982; (2) John Bryan Ward-Perkins and Kathleen Mary Kenyon, eds., Excavations at Sabratha, 1948–1951, 1986; (3) M.S. Spurr, Arable cultivation in Roman Italy, c.200 B.C.–c. A.D. 100, 1986; (4) Christopher William Machell Cox, Monuments from the Aezanitis, 1988; (5) Charlotte Roueché, Aphrodisias in late antiquity: the late Roman and Byzantine inscriptions including texts from the excavations at Aphrodisias conducted by Kenan T. Erim, 1989; (6) Charlotte Roueché, Performers and partisans at Aphrodisias in the Roman and late Roman periods: a study based on inscriptions from the current excavations at Aphrodisias in Caria, 1993; (7) Christopher William Machell Cox, Monumenta Asiae Minoris antiqua: Monuments from the Upper Tembris Valley, Cotiaeum, Cadi, Synaus, Ancyra, and Tiberiopolis, 1993; (8) Andrew Graham Poulter, Nicopolis ad Istrum: a Roman, late Roman and early Byzantine city: excavations, 1985–1992, 1995.

R56 Kunst, Geschichte und Theorie, Bd. 1– . Essen, Germany, Blaue Eule, 1985– .
Scholarly series with bibliographies on a variety of topics. Some vols. derive from the authors' theses. In German.

Contents: (1) Arthur Engelbert, Die Linie in der Zeichnung: Klee, Pollock, Twombly, 1985; (2) Lieselotte Kugler, Studien zur Malerei und Architektur von Pietro Berrettini da Cortona: Versuch einer Gattungs-übergreifenden Analyse zum Illusionismus im römischen Barock, 1985; (3) Ulrich Wilmes, Rosso Fiorentino und der Manierismus: ein Beitrag zur Entwicklung der Tafelmalerei im 16. Jahrhundert, 1985; (4) Hans-Günter Golinski, Kurt Weinhold (1896–1965): sinnbildschaffende Malerei des 20. Jahrhunderts in Deutschland, 1985; (5) Kunibert Bering, Kunst und Staatsmetaphysik des Hochmittelalters in Italien: Zentren der Bau- und Bildpropaganda in der Zeit Friedrichs II, 1986; (6) Kunibert Bering, Die Rolle der Kunst in der Philosophie Ludwig Wittgensteins: Impulse für die Kunstgeschichte?, 1986; (7) Anja Thomas-Netik, Gerhard Richter: mögliche Aspekte eines postmodernen Bewusstseins, 1986; (8) Michael Henning, Die Tafelbilder Bartholomaus Sprangers (1546–1611): höfische Malerei zwischen "Manierismus" und "Barock," 1987; (9) Alarich Rooch, Stifterbilder in Flandern und Brabant: stadtbürgerliche Selbstdarstellung in der sakralen Malerei des 15. Jahrhunderts, 1988; (10) Kunibert Bering, Herrschaftsbewusstsein und Herrschaftszeichen: zur Rezeption staufischer Architekturformen in der Baupropaganda des 13. und 14. Jahrhunderts, 1988; (11) Angelika Engbring-Strysch, Die Madeleine-Kirche in Paris: Enstehungsgeschichte, Rezeption, architekturtheoretische Debatte, 1989; (12) Ralf-Peter Seippel, Architektur und Interpretation: Methoden und Ansätze der Kunstgeschichte in ihrer Bedeutung für die Architekturinterpretation, 1989; (13) Gerhard Graulich, Die leibliche Selbsterfahrung des Rezipienten: ein Thema transmodernen Kunstwollens, 1989; (14) Hans-Jürgen Schwalm, Individuum und Gruppe: Gruppenbilder des 20 Jahrhunderts, 1990; (15) Kunibert Bering, Fragwürdigkeiten der Postmoderne: Decodierung aktueller Tendenzen in der Architektur, 1989; (16) Cornelia Bering, Wille Schenk (1901–1981), Existenzkunst im Spannungsfeld von Welt und Ich: ein Beitrag zur Kunst der verschollenen Generation in Deutschland, 1990; (17) Kornelia Imesch Oehry, Die Kirchen der Franziskanerobservanten in der Lombardei, im Piemont und im Tessen und ihre "Letterwande": Architektur und Dekoration, 1991; (18) Dorothee Lehmann, Das Sichtbare der Wirklichkeiten: die Realisierung der Kunst aus ästhetischer Erfahrung: John Dewey, Paul Cézanne, Mark Rothko, 1991; (19) Dagmar Regina Täube, Monochrome gemalte Plastik: Entwicklung, Verbreitung und Bedeutung eines Phänomens niederländischer Malerei der Gotik, 1991; (20) Petra Römer-Westarp, Kunst im Stadtbild: das Spannungsfeld Werk-Auftraggeber am Beispiel von Schulen und Unternehmen in Köln, 1992; (21) Annette Lobbenmeier, Raum und Unendlichkeit: die Perspektive als Bedeutungsträger in Florentiner Bildprogrammen des Quattrocento, 1995.

R57 Landmarks in art history. Ithaca, Cornell Univ. Pr.; Oxford, Phaidon, 1980– .
Vols. also called, "A Phaidon book."

Handsome, sturdy reprint series of seminal works in art history, incorporating minor corrections from subsequent reprints. Many vols. originally published by Phaidon Press, then issued in paperback by Cornell Univ. Pr.

Contents: Henri Focillon, The art of the west in the Middle Ages (1963), 3d ed., 2v., 1980; Heinrich Wölfflin, Classic art: an introduction to the Italian Renaissance (1952), 5th ed., 1994, (1952); Bernard Berenson, The Italian painters of the Renaissance (1952), 3d ed., 1980; John Ruskin, The lamp of beauty: writings on art (1959), 2d ed., 1980; Charles Robert Leslie, Memoirs of the life of John Constable: composed chiefly of his letters (1951), 2d ed., 1980; Jakob Rosenberg, Rembrandt, life and work (1968), 4th ed., 1980; Eugène Delacroix, The journal of Eugène Delacroix: a selection (1951), 1989 rev. ed., 2d ed., 1980; Wolfgang Stechow, Dutch landscape painting of the seventeenth century (1968), 3d ed., 1981; Charles Baudelaire, Art in Paris, 1845–1862: salons and other exhibitions (1965), 2d ed., 1981; Edmond de Goncourt, French eighteenth-century painters: Watteau, Boucher, Chardin, La Tour, Greuze, Fragonard (1948), 2d ed., 1981; Jacob Burckhardt, The civilization of the Renaissance in Italy: an essay (1955), 2d ed., 1981; Max J. Friedländer, From Van Eyck to Bruegel (1969), 3d ed., 1981; Eugène Fromentin, The masters of past time: Dutch and Flemish painting from Van Eyck to Rembrandt (1948),

2d ed., 1981; Richard Redgrave, A century of British painters (1947), 2d ed., 1981.

R58 Leids kunsthistorisch jaarboek, 1– . Barn, The Netherlands, De Prom; London, Archetype, 1981– . Publisher varies.

Extensive Dutch series by work of faculty and students at the University of Leiden's History of Art department, on the arts of Northern Europe. In Dutch, German, or English.

Contents: (1) Rudolf II and his court, 1982; (2) Art in Denmark 1600–1650, 1984; (3) J. J. Terwen, Bouwen in Nederland: vijfentwintig opstellen over nederlandse architectuur, 1985; (4) Achttiende-eeuwse kunst in de Nederlanden, 1987; (5–6) Anton W. A. Boschloo, ed., Academies of art between Renaissance and Romanticism, 1989; (7) M. H. Wurzner, Aspecten van het interbellum: beeldende kunst, film, fotografie, cultuurfilosofie en literatuur in de periode tussen de twee wereldoorlogen, 1990; (8) H. Blasse-Hegeman ed., Nederlandse portretten: bijdragen over de portetkunst in de Nederlanden uit de zestiende, zeventiende en achttiende eeuw, 1990; (9) J. Bolten, ed., Het Leidse Prentenkabinet: de geschiedenis van de verzamelingen, 1994; (10) Voor Nederland bewaard: de verzamelingen van het Koninklijk Oudheidkundig Genootschap in het Rijksmuseum, 1995; (11) Erma Hermens, ed., Looking through paintings: the study of painting techniques and materials in support of art historical research, 1998.

R59 The Library of American art. N.Y., Abrams, in assoc. with the National Museum of American Art, Smithsonian Institution, 1987– .

Large-format series jointly sponsored by the National Museum of American Art and Harry N. Abrams. Monographs by leading scholars in the field, cover painting, sculpture, and the decorative arts. Each monograph includes bibliographical references and indexes.

Contents: Richard B. K. McLanathan, Gilbert Stuart, 1986; John Walker, James McNeill Whistler, 1987; Robert Carleton Hobbs, Edward Hopper, 1987; William Kloss, Samuel F. B. Morse, 1988; Diane Waldman, Willem de Kooning, 1988; James K. Ballinger, Frederic Remington, 1989; Peter H. Hassrick, Charles M. Russell, 1989; Nicolai Cikovsky, Winslow Homer, 1990; Charles C. Eldredge, Georgia O'Keeffe, 1991; Alastair Duncan, Louis Comfort Tiffany, 1992; Nancy Mowll Mathews, Mary Cassatt, 1992; Michael Edward Shapiro, George Caleb Bingham, 1993; Nicolai Cikovsky, George Inness, 1993; Richard J. Wattenmaker, Maurice Prendergast, 1994; Trevor Fairbrother, John Singer Sargent, 1994; Bruce Robertson, Marsden Hartley, 1995; Barbara Dayer Gallati, William Merritt Chase, 1995; Patricia Hills, Stuart Davis, 1996; Ella M. Foshay, John James Audubon, 1997; Karal Ann Marling, Norman Rockwell, 1997.

R60 Lund studies in art history, v.1– . Lund, Sweden, Lund Univ. Pr., 1988– .

Scholarly art publication. Vols. cover a range of subjects, from aspects of conservation in urban India to the 20th century. Text in English, French, or Swedish.

Contents: (1) Viviane Renaud, Les chromos: consommation et reception de la peinture a l'huile de serie, 1988; (2) Anna Lena Lindberg, Konstpedagogikens dilemma, 1988; (3) Sune Rudnert, I historiemalarens verkstad: Carl Gustav Hellqvist, liv och verk, 1991; (4) Sven Nilsson, ed., Aspects of conservation in urban India, 1995.

R61 Making & meaning. London, National Gallery Publications (Distr. by Yale Univ. Pr., 1993–).

Distinguished exhibition series from the National Gallery in London, highlighting best-loved works, and placing them in their historical, technical, and scientific context. Large color plates, bibliographies, and indexes in each vol.

Contents: Dillian Gordon, The Wilton Diptych, 1993; Michael Hirst and Jill Dunkerton, The young Michelangelo: the artist in Rome, 1496–1501, 1994; Judy Egerton, Turner, The Fighting Temeraire, 1995; Christopher Brown, Ruben's landscapes, 1996; Susan Folster; Ashok Roy; and Martin Wyld, Holbein's Ambassadors, 1997.

R62 Manuskripte zur Kunstwissenschaft in der Wernerschen Verlagsgellschaft, 1– . Worms, Wernersche Verlags, 1984– .

Exhaustively researched softcover German series on art, architecture, book arts, and its relationship to culture and aesthetics. Vols. derive mainly from the authors' dissertations. Includes black-and-white plates in the back, with bibliographies.

Contents: (1) Ingeborg Bähr, Saint Denis und seine Vita im Spiegel der Bildüberlieferung der französischen Kunst des Mittelalters, 1984; (2) August Rave, Christiformitas: Studien zur franziskanischen Ikonographie des florentiner Trecento am Beispiel des ehemaligen Sakristeischrankzyklus von Taddeo Gaddi in Santa Croce, 1984; (3) Anette Kruszynski, Der Ganymed-Mythos in Emblematik und mythographischer Literatur des 16. Jahrhunderts, 1985; (4) Fabian Stein, Charles Le Brun: la tenture de l'Histoire du Roy, 1985; (5) Norbert Suhr, Christian Lotsch, Philipp Veit und Eduard von Steinle: zur Künstlerkarikatur des 19. Jahrhunderts, 1985; (6) Michael Viktor Schwarz, Höfische Skulptur im 14. Jahrbundert: Entwicklungsphasen und Vermittlingswege im Vorfeld des Weichen Stils, 2v., 1986; (7) Christine Stephan, Ein byzantinisches Bildensemble: die Mosäiken und Fresken der Apostelkirche zu Thessaloniki, 1986; (8) Elsbeth Wiemann, Der Mythos von Niobe und ihren Kindern: Studien zur Darstellung und Rezeption, 1986; (9) Dieter Griesbach, Illustrationen zur deutschsprachigen Lyrik von der Romantik bis zum Expressionismus: eine Untersuchung uber das Verhältnis von Wort und Bild, 1986; (10) Wiltrud Heber, Die Arbeiten des Nicolas de Pigage in den ehemals kurpfälzischen Residenzen Mannheim und Schwetzingen, 2v., 1986; (11) Eva-Andrea Wendebourg, Westminster Abbey als königliche Grablege zwischen 1250 und 1400, 1986; (12) Corinna Höper, Bartolomeo Passarotti, 1529–1592, 2v., 1987; (13) Sonja Brink, Mercurius Mediceus: Studien zur panegyrischen Verwendung der Merkurgestalt im Florenz des 16. Jahrhunderts, 1987; (14) Frank Zöllner, Vitruvs Proportionsfigur: quellenkritische Studien zur Kunstliteratur im 15. und 16. Jahrhundert, 1987; (15) Sabine Hansen, Die Loggia della Mercanzia in Siena, 1987; (16) Ulrike Hanschke, Die flämische Waldlandschaft: Anfänge und Entwicklungen im 16. und 17. Jahrhundert, 1988; (18) Friedrich Polleross, Das sakrale Identifikationsporträt: ein höfischer Bildtypus vom 13. bis zum 20. Jahrhundert, 1988; (19) Jürgen Fabian, Der Dom zu Eichstätt, 1989; (20) Brigitte Schoch-Joswig, Da flamt die gräuliche Bastille: die französische Revolution im Spiegel der deutschen Bildpropaganda (1798 [sic]–1799), 1989; (21) Wolfgang Illert, Das Treppenhaus im deutschen Klassizismus, 1988; (21, i.e., 17) Norbert Jopek, Studien zur Deutschen Alabasterplastik des 15. Jahrhunderts, 1988; (22) Ina Conzen-Meairs, Edgar Allen Poe und die bildende Kunst des Symbolismus, 1989; (23) Ellen Hermann-Atorino, Francesco Brizio: Bologna (ca.1574–1623), 1989; (24) Walter Stephan Laux, Waldemar Rösler: eine Studie zur Kunst der Berliner Sezession, 1989; (25) Dorthe, Nebedahl, Die schönsten Antiken Roms: Studien zur Rezeption antiker Bildhauerwerke im römischen Seicento, 1990; (26) Harald Knobling, Studien zum zeichnerischen Werk Ernst Barlachs: 1892–1912, 1989; (27) Sabine Komm, Heiligengrabmäler des 11. und 12. Jahrhunderts in Frankreich: Untersuchung zu Typologie und Grabverehrung, 1990; (28) Sigrid Randa, Alexander Koch: Publizist und Verleger in Darmstadt: Reformen der Kunst und des Lebens um 1900, 1990; (29) Kirsten Ahrens, Hyacinthe Rigauds Staatporträt Ludwigs XIV: typologische und ikonologische Untersuchung zur politischen Aussage des Bildnisses von 1701, 1990; (30) Felicitas Buch, Studien zur Preussischen Denkmalpflege am Beispiel konservatorischer Arbeiten Ferdinand von Quasts, 1990; (31) Eduard Sebald, Die Baugeschichte der Stifkirche St. Marien in Wetzlar, 1990; (32) René Hirner-Schüssele, Von der Anschauung zur Formerfindung: Studien zu Willi Baumeisters Theorie moderner Kunst, 1990; (33) Barbara Streider, Johann Zick (1702–1762): Die Fresken und Deckengemälde, 1990; (34) Bärbel Manitz, Wand, Wölbung und Rotunde: Themen und Leitmotive in Balthasar Neumanns kurvierter Sakralarchitektur, 2v., 1992; (35) Petra Sevrugian, Der Rossano-Codex und die Sinope-Fragmente: Miniatruen und Theologie, 1990; (36) Ines Kehl, Vittore Carpaccios Ursulalegendezklus der Scuola di Sant'Orsola in Venedig: eine venezianische Illusion, 1992; (37) Frank Martin, Die Apsisverglasung der Oberkirche von S. Francesco in Assisi: ihre Entstehung und Stellung innerhalb der Oberkirchenausstattung, 1993; (38) Ute Esbach, Die Ludwigsburger Schlosskapelle: eine evangelische Hofkirche des Barock: Studien zu ihrer Gestalt und Rekonstruktion ihres theologischen Programms, 1991; (39) Anne-Marie Kassay-Friedländer, Die Bildhauer Christoph Voll, 1897–1939, 1994; (40) Doris Fischer, Die St. Paulinuskirche in Trier: Studien zu Architektur, Bau- und Planungsgechichte, 1994; (41) Dorothee Kemper, SS. Niccolò e Cataldo in Lecce: als ein Ausgangspunkt für die Entwicklung mittelalterlicher Bauplastik in Apulien und der Basilicata, 1994; (42) Hans-Rudolf Meier, Die normannischen Königspaläste in Palermo: Studien zur hochmittelalterlichen Residenzbaukunst, 1994; (43) Bettina Paust, Studien zur Barocken Menagerie im deutschsprachigen Raum, 1996; (44) Jan Kneher, Edvard Munch in seinen Austellungen zwischen 1892 und 1912: eine Dokumentation der Ausstellungen und Studie zur Rezeptionsgeschichte von Munchs Kunst, 1994; (45) Carla Th. Mueller, Giovanni Battista Tiepolos Fresken im ehemaligen Patriarchenpalast zu Udine, 1995; (46) Ulrike Koenen, Das "Konstantinskreuz" im Lateran und die Rezeption frühchristlicher Genesiszyklen im 12. und 13. Jahrhundert, 1995; (47) Claudia Hartmann, Das Schloss Marly: eine mythologische Kartause: Form und Funktion der Retraite Ludwigs XIV, 1995; (48) Dagmar Walden-Awodu, "Geburt" und "Tod": Max Beckmann im Amsterdamer Exil: eine Untersuchung zur Entstehungsgeschichte seines Spätwerks, 1995; (49) Petra Tiegel-Hertfelder, " Historie war sein Fach": Mythologie und Geschichte im Werk Johann Heinrich Tischbeins d.A. (1722–1789), 1996; (50) Axel Christoph Gampp, Die Peripherie als Zentrum: Strategien des Städtebaus im römischen Umland 1600–1730: die Beispiele Ariccia, Genzano und Zagarolo, 1996; (51) Christiane Dessauer-Reiners, Das Rhythmische bei Paul Klee: eine Studie zum genetischen Bildverfahren, 1996; (52) Iris Grötecke, Die Bild des Jüngsten Gerichts: die ikonographischen Konventionen in Italien und ihre politische Aktualisierung in Florenz, 1997; (53) Ute Germund, Konstruktion und Dekoration als Gestaltungssprinzipien im Spätgotischen Kirchenbau, 1997; (54) Peter Keller, Die Wiege des Christuskindes, 1998.

R63 Materialien zur Kunst- und Kulturgeschichte in Nord- und Westdeutschland, 1– . Marburg, Germany, Jonas, 1991– .

Regional series covering the arts and architecture of North and Western Germany. Some vols. derive from the author's dissertations. Others gather papers presented at symposia.

Selective contents: (5) Baudekoration als Bildungsanspruch, 1993; (6) Karin Tebbe, "Uns und unseren Nachkommen zu Ruhm und Ehre": Kunstwerke im Weserraum und ihre Auftraggeber, 1992; (11) Sigrun Brunsiek, Auf dem Weg der alten Kunst: der "altdeutsche Stil" in der Buchillustration des 19 Jahrhunderts, 1994; (12) Georg Ulrich Grossmann; Petra Krutisch; and Holger Reimers, eds., 500 Jahre Garantie: auf den Spuren alter Bautechniken, 1994; (13) Thorsten Albrecht, Die Hämelschenburg: ein Beispiel adliger Schlossbaukunst des späten 16. und frühen 17. Jahrhunderts im Weserraum, 1995; (14) Otmar Plassmann, Die Zeichnungen Heinrich Aldegrevers, 1994; (15) Claudia Horbas, Möbel der Renaissance im Weserraum, 1994; (16) Heiner Borggrefe, Die Residenz Bückeburg: Architekturgestaltung im frühneuzeitlichen Fürstenstaat, 1994 (17) Dorothea Heppe, Das Schloss der Landgrafen von Hessen in Kassel von 1557 bis 1811, 1995; (18) Karin Tebbe, Epitaphien in der Grafschaft Schaumburg: die Visualisierung der politischen Ordnung im Kirchenraum, 1996; (19) Michael Sprenger, Bürgerhäuser und Adelshöfe in Rinteln: bau- und sozialgeschichtiche Untersuchungen zu frühneuzeitlichen Hausformen im mittleren Weserraum, 1995; (21) Rathäuser im Spätmittelalter und in der frühen Neuzeit . . . in Zusammenarbeit mit der Stadt Höxter vom 17. bis zum 20. November 1994 in Höxter, 1997; (22) . . . zur Zierde und Schmuck angelegt . . .: Beiträge zur frühneuzeitlichen Garten- und Schlossbaukunst, 1996; (23) Birgit Kümmel, Der Ikonoklast als Kunstliebhaber: Studien zu Landgraf Moritz von Hessen-Kassel (1592–1627), 1996; (25) Weserrenaissance-Museum Schloss Brake. Symposion (7th: 1995), Der Adel in der Stadt des Mittelalters und der frühen Neuzeit, 1996.

R64 Modern arts criticism, 1–4. Detroit, Gale, 1981–94. Annual.

"A biographical and critical guide to painters, sculptors, photographers, and architects from the beginning of the modern era to the present." Includes bibliographies and indexes. Ceased with vol.4, 1994.

R65 Modern masters series, 1– . N.Y., Abbeville, 1983– .
Attractive, uniformly designed paperbound series by Abbeville of artists of the postwar era, each vol. containing circa 128 pages of text and 100 pages of illustrations, chronology, annotated bibliography, lists of exhibitions and collections, index, and artist statements.

Contents: (1) Lawrence Alloway, Roy Lichtenstein, 1983; (2) Harry F. Gaugh, Willem de Kooning, 1983; (3) Elizabeth Frank, Jackson Pollock, 1983; (4) Carter Ratcliff, Andy Warhol, 1983; (5) Phyllis Tuchman, George Segal, 1983; (6) Karen Wilkin, David Smith, 1984; (7) Richard Francis, Jasper Johns, 1984; (8) Melvin P. Lader, Arshile Gorky, 1985; (9) Hugh Davies and Sally Yard, Francis Bacon, 1986; (10) Cynthia Goodman, Hans Hofmann, 1986; (11) Robert Storr, Philip Guston, 1986; (12) Eric Shanes, Constantin Brancusi, 1989; (13) Andrew Kagan, Marc Chagall, 1989; (14) Karen Wilken, Georges Braque, 1991; (15) Robert Carleton Hobbs, Lee Krasner, 1993; (16) Bruce Altshuler, Isamu Noguchi, 1994; (17) Peter Clothier, David Hockney, 1995; (18) Jean E. Feinberg, Jim Dine, 1995; (19) Peter Selz, Max Beckman, 1996.

R66 Monografie della Scuola archeologica di Atene e delle missioni italiane in Oriente, 1– . Padova, Bottega d'Erasmo: A. Ausilio, 1964– . Publisher, place of publication vary.
Scholarly hardcover archeology series. Interdisciplinary in subject matter.

Contents: (1–2) Luigi Bernabò Brea, Poliochni città preistorica nell'isola di Lemnos, 2v., 1964–76; (3) Antonino Di Vita, ed., Gortina 1, 1988; (4) Luigi Polacco, Il teatro di Dioniso Eleutereo ad Atene, 1990; (5) Morella Massa, La ceramica elenistica con decorazione a rilievo della bottega di Efestia, 1992; (7) Antonino Di Vita and Archer Martin, eds., Gortina 2: Pretorio: il materiale degli scavi Colini: 1970–1977, 1997; (8) Ilaria Romeo, Gortina 3: le sculture, 1998; (9) Pietro Militello, Haghia Triada I: gli affreschi, 1998.

R67 Monumenta Graeca et Romana, 1– . Leiden & N.Y., Brill, 1963– , 1977– .
Ed.: Herman F. Mussche.

Slim, well-illustrated, and documented English language series on Greek and Roman art, sculpture, and architecture. Vols. include bibliographies and indexes.

Contents: (1) José Dörig, Onatas of Aegina, 1977; (2) Herman F. Mussche, ed., Greek architecture, 2v., 1963–68: 1. Religious architecture, 2. Civil and military architecture; (3) Olga Palagia, Euphranor, 1980; (4) Spyros E. Iakovidis, Late Helladic citadels on mainland Greece, 1983; (5) Claude Rolley, Greek minor arts, (1)v., 1967: 1. The bronzes; (6) José Dörig, The Olympia Master and his collaborators, 1987; (7) Olga Palagia, The pediments of the Parthenon, 1993, 2d unrev. ed., 1998; (8) Doris Vanhove, Roman marble quarries in southern Euboea and the associated road systems, 1996.

R68 Movements in the arts, 1–2. Westport, Conn., Greenwood, 1985–86.
Promising but shortlived series on modern art periods.

Contents: (1) Stanley Trachtenberg, ed., The postmodern moment: a handbook of contemporary innovation in the arts, 1985; (2) Larry McCaffery, ed., Postmodern fiction: a bio-bibliographical guide, 1986.

R69 Münchener archäologische Studien, Bd.1–8. Munich, Germany, Fink, 1970–87.
Slim, small format, well-researched series on Greek and Roman art. Many vols. are revisions of dissertations. Some vols. published out of chronological sequence. In German.

Contents: (1) Stefan Hiller, Bellerophon: ein griechischer Mythos in der römischen Kunst, 1970; (2) Hugo Meyer, Der weisse und der rote Marsyas: eine kopienkritische Untersuchung, 1987; (3) Florens Felten, Thanatos- und Kleophonmaler: weissgründige und rotfigurige Vasenmalerei der Parthenonzeit, 1971; (4) Hugo Meyer, Kunst und Geschichte: vier Untersuchungen zur Antiken Historienkunst, 1983; (5) Berthold Fellmann, Die antiken Darstellungen des Polyphemabenteuers, 1972; (6) Wassiliki Felten, Attische Unterweltsdarstellungen des VI. und V. Jh. v. Chr., 1975; (7) Siegrid Düll, Die Götterkulte Nordmakedoniens in römischer Zeit, 1977; (8) Christoph Schwingenstein, Die Figurenausstattung des griechischen Theatergebäudes, 1977.

R70 Neue Berner Schriften zur Kunst, 1– . Frankfurt, Peter Lang, 1996– .
Scholarly German hardcover series on art and aesthetics issuing from the Institut für Kunstgeschichte der Universität Bern. Vols. derive from conference reports, revisions of dissertations, and original research. Indexes, bibliographies.

Contents: (1) Volker Hoffmann and Hans Peter Autenieth, eds., Denkmalpflege heute, 1996; (2) Norberto Gramaccini, Theorie der französischen Drukgraphik im 18. Jahrbundert: eine Quellenanthologie, 1997; (3) Die Hagia Sophia in Istanbul, 1997; (4) Pascal Griener and Peter J. Schneemann, eds., Images de l'artiste / Künstlerbilder, 1998; (5) Keiko Suzuki, Bildgewordene Visionen oder Visionserzählungen: vergleichende Studie über die Visionsdarstellungen in der Rupertsberger "Scivias"-Handschrift und im Luccheser "Liber divinorum operum": Codex der Hildegard von Bingen, 1998; (6) Sabine Schlütter, Gaspare Fossatis Restaurierung der Hagia Sophia in Istanbul, 1847–49, 1999.

R71 New Directions in American art. Washington, D.C., Smithsonian Institution Pr., 1985– .
Scholarly, elegant series, many vols. extensions of doctoral dissertations. Beautifully produced on heavy stock with fine illustrations.

Contents: Ann Uhry Abrams, The valiant hero: Benjamin West and grand-style history painting, 1985; M. Sue Kendall, Rethinking regionalism: John Stuart Curry and the Kansas mural controversy, 1986; Franklin Kelly, Frederic Edwin Church and the national landscape, 1988; John Michael Vlach, Plain painters making sense of American folk art, 1988; David Bjelajac, Millennial desire and the apocalyptic vision of Washington Allston, 1988; Katherine Emma Manthorne, Tropical Renaissance: North American artists exploring Latin America, 1839–1879, 1989; Barbara Melosh, Engendering culture: manhood and womanhood in New Deal public art and theater, 1991; Albert Boime, The magisterial gaze: manifest destiny and American landscape painting, c.1830–1865, 1991; Joni Louise Kinsey, Thomas Moran and the surveying of the American West, 1992.

R72 La nuit des temps, 1– . Paris, Zodiaque, 1954– .
Scholarly French series on Romanesque architecture and art in Europe. Divided according to feudal regions of Europe, each vol. serves as an inventory of churches and other structures in that area, with plans, elevations, maps, diagrams, and colored illustrations and indexes. Beautifully presented and illustrated. Covers mainly architecture, sculpture, and reliquaries, with commentary on stained glass and mosaics. Many earlier vols. have been revised or reprinted, and several were originally published as special issues of the journal, Zodiaque. Some vols. originally published in English and Italian. Summaries in English and German.

Contents: (1) Raymond Oursel, Bourgogne romane (1954) 8th ed., 1986; (2) Bernard Craplet, Auvergne romane (1955), 6th ed., 1992; (3) Dom Jean-Marie Berland, Val-de-Loire roman (1956), rev. ed., 3d ed., 1980; (4) André Varagnac . . . [et al.], L'art gaulois (1956), 2d ed., 1964; (5) Yvonne Labande-Mailfert, Poitou roman (1957), 2d ed., 1962; (6) Odilon Aymard, Touraine romane (1957), 3d ed., 1977; (7) Marcel Durliat, Roussillon roman (1958), rev. ed., 4th ed., 1986; (8) P. Bouffard . . . [et al.], Suisse romane (1958), rev. ed., 3d ed., 1996; (9) Pierre Herbecourt, Anjou roman (1959), rev. ed., 2d ed., 1987; (10) Marguerite Vidal . . . [et al.], Quercy roman (1959), 2d ed., 1969; (11) Jean Maury . . . [et al.], Limousin roman (1960), 3d ed., 1990; (12–13) Jean Ainaud de Lasarte and Éduouard Junyent, Catalogne romane (1960), 2v., rev. ed., 3d ed.,1994; (14) Charles Daras, Angoumois roman, 1961; (15) Olivier Beigbeder and Raymond Oursel, Forez-Velay roman (1962), 2d ed., 1981; (16 & 34) Anselme Dimier and Jean Porcher, L'art cistercien (1962–71), 2v., 3d ed., 1982; (17) Georges Guillard . . . [et al.], Rouergue roman (1963), rev. ed., 3d ed., 1990; (18–20) Françoise Henry, L'art Irlandais, 3v., 1963–64; (21) Paul Deschamps, Terre sainte romane, 1990, (1964); (22) Robert Will and Hans Haug, Alsace romane, 3e éd. 1982, (1965); (23–24) Luis-María de Lojendio and Abundio Rodríguez, Castille romane, 2v., 1966; (25, 41) Lucien Musset, Normandie romane (1967–74), 3d ed., 1987; (26) Luis-María de Lojendio, Navarre romane, 1967; (27) Jean Secret, Périgord roman (1968), 2d ed., 1979; (28–29) Peter Anker and Aron Andersson, L'art scandinave, 2v. 1968–69; (30) Marcel Durliat and Victor Allègre, Pyrénées romanes (1969), 2d ed., 1978; (31) Pierre Dubourg-Noves, Guyenne romane, 1969; (32) Jean Favière and Jacques de Bascher, Berry roman (1970), 2d ed., 1976; (33) François Eygun, Saintonge romane (1970), 2d ed., 1979; (35) Angel Canellas-López and Angel San Vicente, Aragon roman, 1971; (36) Antonio Viñayo González, Leon roman, 1972; (37) Geneviève Moracchini-Mazel, Corse romane, 1972; (38 & 47) Jacques Fontaine, L'art préroman hispanique, 2v., 1973–77; (39) Manuel Chamoso Lamas . . . [et al.], Galice romane, 1973; (40 & 46) Jean-Maurice Rouquette and Guy Barroul, Provence romane (1974–77), 2v., 2d ed., 1980–81; (42) Raymond Oursel, Haut-Poitou roman (1975), 2d ed., 1984; (43) Jacques Lugand . . . [et al.], Languedoc roman (le Languedoc méditerranéen) (1975), 2d ed., 1985; (44) Michel Dillange, Vendée romane, 1976; (45) Jean Dupont, Nivernais-Bourbonnais roman, 1976; (48) Sandro Chierici, Lombardie romane, 1978; (49) Marcel Durliat, Haut-Languedoc roman, 1978; (50) Jean Cabanot, Gascogne romane, 1978; (51) Sandro Chierici and Duilio Citi, Piémont-Ligurie roman, 1979; (52) René Tournier . . . [et al.], Franche-Comté romane—Bresse romane, 1979; (53) Adriano Prandi . . . [et al.], Ombrie romane, 1980; (54) Jacques Thirion, Alpes romanes, 1980; (55) H. Collin . . . [et al.], Champagne romane, 1981; (56) Mario D'Onofrio and Valentino Pace, Campanie romane, 1981; (57) Renato Stopani, Toscane romane, 1982; (58) Louise-Marie Tillet, Bretagne romane, 1982; (59 & 69) Lucien Musset, Angleterre romane, 2v., 1983–88; (60) Anne Prache, Île-de-France romane, 1983; (61) Hans-Günter Marschall and Rainer Slotta, Lorraine romane, 1984; (62) Sergio Stocchi, Émilie romane (Plaine du Pô), 1984; (63) France Sharratt and Rainer Sharratt, Écosse romane, 1985; (64) Marcel Deyres, Maine roman, 1985; (65) Giovannella Cassata, Sicile romane, 1986; (66–67) Gerhard N. Graf, Portugal roman, 2v., 1986–87; (68) Pina Belli D'Elia, Pouilles romanes, 1987; (70) Chiara Garzya Romano, Calabre et Basilicate romanes, 1988; (71) Xavier Barral i Altet, Belgique romane et Grand-Duché de Luxembourg, 1989; (72) Renata Serra, Sardaigne romane, 1989; (73) Raymond Oursel, Lyonnais, Dombes, Bugey et Savoie romans, 1990; (74) Paolo Favole, Abruzzes Molise romans, 1990; (75) Robert de Saint Jean, Vivarais Gévaudan romans, 1991; (76) Gianna Suitner Nicolini, Vénétie romane, 1991; (77) Guy Barruol, Dauphiné roman, 1992; (78) Enrico Parlato and Serena Romano, Rome et Latium romans, 1992; (79) Dethard von Winterfeld, Palatinat roman, 1993; (80) Paolo Favole, Marches romanes, 1993; (81) Ada van Deijk, Pays-Bas romans, 1994; (82) Hervé Oursel, Nord roman: Flandre, Artois, Picardie, Laonnois, 1994; (83) Richard Strobel, Bavière romane, 1995; (84) Raymond Oursel, Terres de Bourgogne, 1995; (85) Walter Wulf, Saxe romane, 1996; (86) Jean-Claude Fau, Terres de Rouergue, 1996; (87) José Javier Lopez de Ocarisz, Pas Basque roman, 1997; Uwe Lobbedey, Westphalie romane, 1999.

R73 Occasional papers (Art Libraries Society of North America), 1– . Place varies, 1982– . Irregular.
Society series reflecting concerns and research tools needed by art librarians. Vols. are written by leaders in the field.

Contents: (1) AACR2 goes public, 1982; (2) Standards for art libraries and fine arts slide collections, 1983; (3) Current issues in fine arts visual resources collections, 1984; (4) Christine Bunting, ed., Reference tools for fine arts visual resources collections, 1984; (5) Sheila M. Klos and Christine M. Smith, eds., Historical bibliography of art museum serials from the United States and Canada, 1987; (6) Karen Muller, ed., Authority Control Symposium: papers presented during the 14th annual ARLIS/NA Conference, New York, Feb. 10, 1986, 1987; (7) Patricia J. Barnett and Amy E. Tucker, eds., Procedural guide to automating an art library, 1987; (8) Lyn Korenic and Clayton Kirking, Grant development for large and small libraries, 1990; (9) Beryl K. Smith, Space planning for the art library, 1991; (10) Toni Peterson, ed., Art & architecture thesaurus sourcebook, 1996; (11) ARLIS/NA Staffing Standards Task Force, Staffing standards for art libraries and visual collections, 1996; (12) Ann Baird Whiteside; Pamela Born; and Adeane Alpert Bregman, eds., Collection development policies for libraries & visual collections in the arts, 1999.

R74 Occasional papers (Princeton University. Department of Art and Archaeology. Index of Christian art), 1– . Princeton, Princeton Univ. Pr., 1992– .

Occasional series consisting of papers issuing from colloquia sponsored by the Index of Christian Art.

Contents: (1) Brendan Cassidy, ed., The Ruthwell cross, 1992; (2) Brendan Cassidy, ed., Iconography at the crossroads, 1993; (3) Colum Hourihane, Image and belief: studies in celebration of the eightieth anniversary of the Index of Christian Art, 1999.

R75 Oculi: studies in the arts of the Low Countries 14–15th centuries, 1– . Amsterdam, Benjamins/Forsten, 1987– .

Scholarly series offering well-illustrated studies in the arts of the Low Countries, from the 14–15th century to the present.

Contents: (1) Rob Ruurs, Saenredam, the art of perspective, 1987; (2) Reindert Leonard Falkenburg, Joachim Patinir: landscape as an image of the pilgrimage of life, 1988; (3) Tsukasa Kodera, Vincent van Gogh: Christianity versus nature, 1990; (4) Elise Goodman, Rubens: The Garden of Love as "Conversatie à la mode," 1992; (5) Reindert Leonard Falkenburg, The fruit of devotion: mysticism and the imagery of love in Flemish paintings of the Virgin and Child, 1450–1550, 1994; (6) Cornelia Homburg, The copy turns original: Vincent van Gogh and a new approach to traditional art practice, 1996; (7) Paul Huys Janssen, Jan van Bijlert (1597/98–1671), catalogue raisonné, 1998.

R76 Outstanding theses from the Courtauld Institute of Art. N.Y., Garland, 1984–86.

Scholarly theses from one of the major art historical institutions outside of the United States. Vols. cover mainly English art of all periods.

Contents: Francis Ames-Lewis, Library and manuscripts of Piero di Cosimo de' Medici, 1984; Mary Beal, A study of Richard Symonds: his Italian notebooks and their relevance to seventeenth century-painting techniques, 1984; Lindsay Errington, Social and religious themes in English art, 1840–1860, 1984; Tessa Garton, Early romanesque sculpture in Apulia, 1984; Richard Marks, The stained glass of the Collegiate Church of the Holy Trinity, Tattershall (Lincs.), 1984; John Philip McAleer, The Romanesque church facade in Britain, 1984; Amanda Simpson, The connections between English and Bohemian painting during the second half of the fourteenth century, 1984; Catherine W. Morley, John Ruskin: late work 1870–1890, the Museum and Guild of St. George: an educational experiment, 1984; John Osborne, Early mediaeval wall-paintings in the lower church of San Clemente, Rome, 1984; Aileen Ribeiro, The dress worn at masquerades in England, 1730 to 1790, and its relation to fancy dress in portraiture, 1984; Amanda Simpson, The connection between English and Bohemian painting during the second half of the fourteenth century, 1984; Helen Smith, Decorative painting in the domestic interior in England and Wales, c.1850–1890, 1984; Sarah Symmons, Flaxman and Europe : the outline illustrations and their influence, 1984; Alan G. Wilkinson, The drawings of Henry Moore, 1984; Charlotte Yeldham, Women artists in nineteenth century France and England: their art education, exhibition opportunities and membership of exhibiting societies and academies, with an assessment of the subject matter of their work and summary biographies, 2v., 1984; Elizabeth Parker McLachlan, The Scriptorium of Bury St. Edmunds in the twelfth century, 1986.

R77 Oxford monographs on classical archaeology, 1– . Oxford: Oxford Univ. Pr., 1947– .

Ed.: Martin Robertson, John Boardman, J. J. Coulton . . . [et al.].

Scholarly archeology series, exhaustively researched, with black-and-white plates. Most vols. were originally presented as the authors' theses, predominantly from Oxford University.

Contents: (1) John Davidson Beazley, Etruscan vase-painting, 1947; (2) Vincent Robin d'Arba Desborough, Protogeometric pottery, 1952; (3) Paul Jacobsthal, Greek pins and their connexions with Europe and Asia, 1956; (4) Semni Karouzou, The Amasis painter, 1956; (5) Dietrich F. Von Bothmer, Amazons in Greek art, 1957; William Llewellyn Brown, The Etruscan lion, 1960; Lilian Hamilton Jeffery, The local scripts of archaic Greece: a study of the origin of the Greek alphabet and its development from the eighth to the fifth centuries B.C., 1961; H. W. Catling, Cypriot bronzework in the Mycenaean world, 1964; Varvara Philippake, The Attic stamnos, 1967; Arthur Dale Trendall, The red-figured vases of Lucania, Campania and Sicily, 2v., 1967; Dorothy Burr Thompson, Ptolemaic oinochoai and portraits in faience: aspects of the ruler-cult, 1973; Keith Branigan, Aegean metalwork of the Early and Middle Bronze Age, 1974; Donna C. Kurtz, Athenian white lekythoi: patterns and painters, 1975; J. J. Coulton, The architectural development of the Greek stoa, 1976; Katherine Dunbabin, The mosaics of Roman North Africa: studies in iconography and patronage, 1978; Arthur Dale Trendall, The red-figured vases of Apulia, 3v., 1978–82; Donna C. Kurtz, The Berlin painter, 1983; Thomas H. Carpenter, Dionysian imagery in archaic Greek art; its development in black-figure vase painting, 1986; Lucilla Burn, The Meidias painter, 1987; Nigel Jonathan Spivey, The Micali Painter and his followers, 1987; R. R. R. Smith, Hellenistic royal portraits, 1988; Henry R. Immerwahr, Attic script: a survey, 1990; Karim W. Arafat, Classical Zeus: a study in art and literature, 1990; Veronique Dasen, Dwarfs in ancient Egypt and Greece, 1993; Nancy A. Winter, Greek architectural terracottas: from the prehistoric through to the archaic period, 1993; A. T. Reyes, Archaic Cyprus: a study of the textual and archaeological evidence, 1994; Diane Harris, The treasures of the Parthenon and Erechtheion, 1995; Carol L. Lawton, Attic document reliefs: art and politics in ancient Athens, 1995; A. T. Fear, Rome and Baetica: urbanization in southern Spain c.50 BC–

AD 150, 1996; Janet Huskinson, Roman children's sarcophagi: their decoration and its social significance, 1996; Christopher John Smith, Early Rome and Latium: economy and society c.1000 to 400 B.C., 1996; Zofia Archibald, The Odrysian kingdom of Thrace: Orpheus unmasked, 1997; Thomas H. Carpenter, Dionysian imagery in fifth-century Athens, 1997; Anthony McNicoll, Hellenistic fortifications from the Aegean to the Euphrates, 1997; Janet Huskinson, Roman children's sarcophagi: their decoration and social significance, 1996; Zofia Archibald, The Odrysian kingdom of Thrace: Orpheus unmasked, 1998; Dimitris Plantzos, Hellenistic engraved gems, 1999.

R78 Oxford studies in Islamic art, 1– . Oxford, Oxford Univ. Pr., 1985– .

Occasional series dedicated to the art and architecture of the Muslim world, all periods and places, diverse media, and methodologies. Serves as a vehicle for publishing studies and conference proceedings too long for a scholarly journal and too short for trade publication.

Contents: (1) Julian Raby, ed., The art of Syria and the Jazira, 1100–1250, 1985; (2) Abbas Daneshvari, Animal symbolism in Warqa wa Gulshah, 1986; (3) Pots & pans: a colloquium on precious metals and ceramics in the Muslim, Chinese and Graeco-Roman worlds, Oxford, 1985, 1986; (4) James W. Allan and Caroline Roberts, eds., Syria and Iran: three studies in medieval ceramics, 1987; (5) Simon Digby, The mother-of-pearl overlay furniture of Gujarat: a sixteenth- and seventeenth-century Indian handicraft and its markets in the Islamic East and Europe, 1987; (6) Robert W. Hamilton, Walid and his friends: an Umayyad tragedy, 1988; (7) Jonathan M. Bloom, Minaret, symbol of Islam, 1989; (8) George Michell, Firuzabad: palace city of the Deccan, 1992; (9) Julian Raby and Jeremy Johns, eds., Bayt al-Maqdis: 'Abd al-Malik's Jerusalem, pt.1, 1992; (10) James W. Allan, ed., Islamic art in the Ashmolean Museum, 2v., 1995; (11) Raya Shani, A monumental manifestation of the Shi'ite faith in late twelfth-century Iran: the case of the Gunbad-i 'Alawyan, Hamadan, 1996; (12) The court of the Il-khans, 1290–1340: the Barakat Trust Conference on Islamic Art and History, St. John's College, Oxford, Saturday, 28 May 1994, 1996; (13) Selma M. S. Al-Radi, The "Amiriya in Rada": the history and restoration of a sixteenth-century madrasa in the Yemen, 1997; (14) Chase Robinson, ed., A medieval Islamic city reconsidered: an interdisciplinary approach to Samarra, 1998.

R79 Oxford-Warburg studies. Oxford, Clarendon Pr., 1963– .

General ed.: Denys Hay and J. B. Trapp.

Scholarly series on intellectual and cultural history with particular emphasis on classical antiquity. Sponsored jointly by the Warburg Institute of the University of London and the Clarendon Press.

Contents: Ann Coffin Hanson, Jacopo della Quercia's Fonte Gaia, 1965; L. D. Ettlinger, The Sistine Chapel before Michelangelo: religious imagery and papal primacy, 1965; Michael Baxandall, Giotto and the orators: humanist observers of painting in Italy and the discovery of pictorial composition, 1350–1450, 1971; Michael Podro, The manifold in perception: theories of art from Kant to Hildebrand, 1972; Marcia B. Hall, Renovation and Counter-Reformation: Vasari and Duke Cosimo in Sta. Maria Novella and Sta. Croce, 1565–1577, 1979; Nicolai Rubenstein, The Palazzo Vecchio, 1298–1532: government, architecture, and imagery in the Civic Palace of the Florentine republic, 1995.

R80 Papers in art history, 1– . University Park, Pa., The Pennsylvania State Univ. Pr., 1984– .

"Each volume of the series had its origin in a lecture series held annually at Penn State, sponsored by the Department of Art History and the Institute for the Arts and Humanistic Studies."—*Advert.*

Contents: (1) Hellmut Hager and Susan Scott Munshower, eds., Projects and monuments in the period of the Roman Baroque, 1984; (2) Hellmut Hager and Susan Scott Munshower, eds., Light of the eternal city: observations and discoveries in the art and architecture of Rome, 1987; (3) Roland E. Fleischer and Susan Scott Munshower, eds., The age of Rembrandt: studies in seventeenth-century Dutch paintings, 1988; (4) George Mauner . . . [et al.], eds., Paris: center of artistic enlightenment, 1988; (5) Craig Zabel and Susan Scott Munshower, eds., American public architecture: European roots and native expressions, 1989; (6) Barbara Wisch and Susan Scott Munshower, eds., "All the world's a stage . . ." art and pageantry in the Renaissance and Baroque, 2v., 1990; (7) Jeanne Chenault Porter and Susan Scott Munshower, eds., Parthenope's splendor: art of the golden age of Naples, 1993; (8) Henry A. Millon and Susan Scott Munshower, eds., An architectural progress in the Renaissance and Baroque: sojurns in and out of Italy: essays in architectural history presented to Hellmut Hager on his 65th birthday, 2v., 1992; (9) Susan C. Scott, ed., The art of interpreting, 1995; (10) Mary Louise Krumrine and Susan Scott Munshower, eds., Art and the Native American, perceptions, reality and influences, 1997; (11) Roland Fleischer and Susan C. Scott, eds., Rembrandt, Rubens, and the art of their time: recent perspectives, 1997; (12) Carolyn Smyth and Susan C. Scott, eds., From Milan to Venice: the Renaissance art of northern Italy, 1998; (13) Elizabeth Bradford Smith and Susan C. Scott, eds., The fortune of medieval art in America, 1999.

R81 Persian art series, 1– . Costa Mesa, Calif., Mazda, 1981– . Publisher varies.

Distinguished series that is part of a larger entity titled Bibliotheca Persica, published in assoc. with the Center for Iranian Studies, Columbia University, and covering the art, history, literature, and culture of Iran.

Contents: (1) Richard Ettinghausen and Ehsan Yarshater, eds., Highlights of Persian art, 1979; (2) Linda Komaroff, The golden disk of heaven: metalwork of Timurid Iran, 1992.

R82 Princeton essays on the arts, 1– . Princeton, Princeton Univ. Pr., 1975– .

"A series of short-length books in the fine arts and aesthetics, and includes interdisciplinary essays as well as original contributions in a single field. Works draw in substance upon the visual arts, music, literature, drama, film, etc. Volumes published both in hardback and paperback editions."—*Introd.*, v.14.

Contents: (1) Guy Sircello, A new theory of beauty, 1975; (2) Rab Hatfield, Botticelli's Uffizi "Adoration": a study in pictorial content, 1976; (3) Rensselaer Wright Lee, Names on trees: Ariosto into art, 1976; (5) Robert Fagles, I, Vincent: poems from the pictures of Van Gogh, 1978; (6) Jonathan Brown, Images and ideas in seventeenth-century Spanish painting, 1978; (7) Walter Cahn, Masterpieces: chapters on the history of an idea, 1979; (8) Roger Scruton, The aesthetics of architecture, 1979; (10) James Henry Rubin, Realism and social vision in Courbet & Proudhon, 1980; (11) Mary Ann Caws, The eye in the text: essays on perception, mannerist to modern, 1981; (12) Egbert Haverkamp-Begemann, Rembrandt: The Nightwatch, 1982; (13) Morris Eaves, William Blake's theory of art, 1982; (14) John V. Fleming, From Bonaventure to Bellini: an essay in Franciscan exegesis, 1982; (16) John N. King, Tudor royal iconography: literature and art in an age of religious crisis, 1989; (17) Conrad Rudolph, Artistic change at St-Denis: Abbot Suger's program and the early twelfth century controversy over art, 1990; (18) Andree Hayum, The Isenheim altarpiece: God's medicine and the painter's vision, 1st pbk. printing, with corrections, 1993 (1989); Pamela Askew, Caravaggio's Death of the Virgin, 1990; Thomas DaCosta Kaufmann, The mastery of nature: aspects of art, science, and humanism in the Renaissance, 1993.

R83 The Princeton series in nineteenth century art, culture, and society. Princeton, Princeton Univ. Pr., 1993– .

Ed.: Jacques de Caso and Petra ten-Doesschate Chu.

Covers the period from the American and French Revolutions to the end of the 19th century. European art has been the major focus.

Contents: Katherine Fischer Taylor, In the theater of criminal justice: the Palais de Justice in Second Empire Paris, 1993; Dorothy Johnson, Jacques Louis David: art in metamorphosis, 1993; Petra ten-Doesschate Chu and Gabriel P. Weisberg, eds., The popularization of images: visual culture under the July Monarchy, 1994; Albert Boime, Art and the French commune: imagining Paris after war and revolution, 1995; Michele Hannoosh, Painting and the Journal of Eugène Delacroix, 1995; Bradford R. Collins, ed., 12 views of Manet's Bar, 1996; John Davis, The landscape of belief: encountering the Holy Land in nineteenth-century American art and culture, 1996; Marc J. Gotlieb, The plight of emulation: Ernest Meissonier and French Salon painting, 1996.

R84 RES monographs in anthropology and aesthetics. N.Y., Cambridge Univ. Pr., 1987– .

"Like the journal from which it takes its name, it will provide a point of encounter for contributions from very diverse sources, to the study of what anthropologists once called material culture . . . to the anthropology of art. Broad in scope and eclectic in range of subjects covered."—*Pref.* Each vol. includes substantial bibliographies.

Contents: Suzanne Preston Blier, The anatomy of architecture: ontology and metaphor in Batammaliba architectural expression, 1987; Gottfried Semper, The four elements of architecture and other writings, trans. by Harry Mallgrave and Wolfgang Herrmann, 1989; Peter Mark, The wild bull and the sacred forest: form, meaning and change in Senegambian initiation masks, 1992; David Leatherbarrow, The roots of architectural invention: site, enclosure, materials, 1993; Kathlyn Maurean Liscomb, Learning from Mount Hua: a Chinese physician's illustrated travel record and painting theory, 1993; Mark Franko, Dance as text: ideologies of the baroque body, 1993; Sarah C. Brett-Smith, The making of Bamana sculpture: creativity and gender, 1994; Debra Hassig, Medieval bestiaries: text, image, ideology, 1995; Arthur G. Miller, The painted tombs of Oaxaca, Mexico: living with the dead, 1995; Haim N. Finkelstein, Salvador Dali's art and writing 1927–1942: the metamorphoses of Narcissus, 1996.

R85 Saecula spiritalia, 1– . Baden-Baden, V. Koerner, 1980– .

Ed.: Dieter Wuttke.

Scholarly interdisciplinary hardcover series on iconography and emblem studies. Some vols. are edited collections of essays by well-known art historians. Black-and-white illustrations. Publishes occasional supplements.

Selective contents: (1) Dieter Wuttke, ed., Aby Warburg, 1866–1929, Augewählte Schriften und Würdigungen, 1980; (7) Jan Bialostocki, Dürer and his critics 1500–1997: chapters in the history of ideas including a collection of texts, 1986; (17) Egon Verheyen, ed., William S. Heckscher, Art and literature: studies in relationship, 1985; (24) Michael Bath, The image of the stag: iconographic themes in Western art, 1992; (29, 30) Dieter Wuttke, Dazwischen: Kulturwissenschaft auf Warburgs Spuren, 2v., 1996; (31) Suzanne De Ponte, Ereignis und Wahrnehmung: eine interdisziplinare Untersuchung zu den Events der Künstlergruppe Gang Art, 1996; (33) Werner Müller, Von deutscher Sondergotik: Architekturphotographie, Computergraphik, Deutung, 1997; (36) Emblematic perceptions: essays in honor of William S. Heckscher on the occasion of his 90th birthday, 1997.

R86 Schriften des Warburg-Archivs im kunstgeschichtlichen Seminar der Universität Hamburg, 1– . Weinheim, Germany, VCH, 1991– .

Scholarly series dealing with the work of German art historian Aby Warburg (1866–1929) and his successors. Some vols. are documentary in nature, others publish the proceedings of conferences held at the University of Hamburg.

Contents: (1) Horst Bredekamp . . . [et al.], eds., Aby Warburg: Akten des internationalen Symposions, Hamburg 1990, 1991; (2) Michael Diers, Warburg aus Briefen: Kommentare zu den Kopierbüchern der Jahre 1905–1918, 1991; (3) Erwin Panofsky: Beiträge des Symposions, Hamburg 1992, 1994; (4) Volker Breidecker, ed., Siegfried Kracauer, Erwin Panofsky, Briefwechsel 1941–1966: mit einem Anhang: Siegfried Kracauer "Under the spell of the living Warburg tradition," 1996.

R87 Schriften zur Bildenden Kunst = Papers on art = Scritti dell'arte 1– . Frankfurt-am-Main, P. Lang, 1995– .

V.1–4 published as, Monographien zur bildenden Kunst = Monographs on art = Monografie dell'arte. Exhaustively researched, scholarly series, with some vols. originally presented as the author's thesis. Mainly in German with English summaries.

Contents: (1) Sigrid Dirkmann, Carl Philipp Fohr (1795–1818): Studien zu den Landschaften, 1993; (2) Michael Herrmann, John von Wicht, 1888–1970: the way to abstraction, 1995; (3) Monika von Wild, George Augustus Wallis (1761–1847): englischer Landschaftsmaler: Monographie und Oeuvrekatalog, 1996; (4) Eva-Bettina Krems, Raffaels "Marienkronung" im Vatikan, 1996; (5) Petra S. Kuhner, Gustav Bauernfeind: Gemälde und Aquarelle, 1995; (6) Klaudia Murmann D'Amico, Deckendekorationen emilianischer Sakralbauten von 1530 bis 1630; (7) Damian Dombrowski, Giuliano Finelli: Bildhauer zwischen Neapel und Rom, 1997; (8) Markus Heinzelmann, Die Landschaftsmalerei der neuen Sachlichkeit und ihre Rezeption zur Zeit des Nationalsozialismus, 1998.

R88 Schriftenreihe der Kommission für Niedersächsische Bau- und Kunstgeschichte bei der Braunschweigischen Wissenschaftlichen Gesellschaft, Bd. 1– . Berlin. Akademie Verlag, 1983– . Publisher, place of publication vary.

Scholarly German series on regional architecture and sculpture. Each vol. consists of the published papers of a symposium organized by the Kommission.

Contents: (1) Martin Gosebruch, Vom oberrheinisch-sächsischen Weg der Kathedralgotik nach Deutschland, 1983; (2) Martin Gosebruch, ed., Der Braunschweiger Burglöwe, 1985; (3) Bernwardinische Kunst, 1988; (4) Helmarshausen und das Evangeliar Heinrichs des Löwen, 1992; (5) Der Magdeburger Dom, 1989; (6) Goslar: Bergstadt, Kaiserstadt in Geschichte und Kunst, 1993; (7) Ernst Ullmann, ed., Halberstadt, Studien zu Dom und Liebfrauenkirche: Königtum und Kirche als Kulturträger im östlichen Harzorland-Halberstadt, 1997.

R89 Selected studies in the history of art. London, Pindar, 1977– .

Series whose aim is to make available previously published articles and papers published by leading authorities on the history of art grouped around a common theme or the art of a particular period. Each vol. gathers together related studies published over a number of years by one author, with additions, such as a new preface, index, and notes. Recent vols. unnumbered.

Selective contents: (9) Ralph H. Pinder-Wilson, Studies in Islamic art, 1985; (14–15) George Henderson, Studies in English Bible illustration, 2v., 1985; (36) Michael Herity, Studies in the layout, buildings and art in stone of early Irish monasteries, 1995; Jean Ebersolt, Constantinople byzantine et les voyageurs du Levant, 1985; Thomas Alan Sinclair, Eastern Turkey: an architectural and archaeological survey, 4v., 1987–90; John Gordon Davies, Medieval Armenian art and architecture: the Church of the Holy Cross, Aght'amar, 1991; Edward B. Garrison, Studies in the history of medieval Italian painting, 4v., 1993; Eric Fernie, Romanesque architecture: design, meaning and metrology, 1995; Doula Mouriki, Studies in late Byzantine painting, 1995; Anna Muthesius, Studies in Byzantine and Islamic silk weaving, 1995; William Watson, Studies in Chinese archaeology and art, 2v., 1995; Charles Reginald Dodwell, Aspects of art of the eleventh and twelfth centuries, 1996; Iohannis Spatharakis, Studies in byzantine manuscript illumination and iconography, 1996.

R90 Studi e documenti di architettura, n.1–10. Firenze, Teorema, 1972–83; nuova serie, no.11– , June 1983– . Firenze, Alinea. Publisher varies. Irregular.

Supersedes: Università degli Studi di Firenze. Istituto di Composizione Architettonica. Quaderni. Numbers 1–(2) issued by the Istituto di composizione architettonica I-II della Facoltà di architettura di Firenze. Scholarly series of Italian architecture and urban planning. Each issue on a different theme. Occasional parallel texts in English/Italian.

Contents: (1) Omaggio ad Alberti, 1972; (2) no unique title, 1973; (3, 7) Domenico Taddei, Piazze di Toscana, 2v., 1973–78; (4) Giancarlo Cataldi, Il territorio della Piana di Gioia Tauro, 1975; (5) Paolo Maretto, Edificazioni tardosettecentesche nella Calabria meridionale, 1975; (6) Alessandro Gambuti . . . [et al.], Vasari architetto: rilevamenti e note, 1977; (7) Piazze di Toscana, 2v., 1973–78; (8) 2000 anni di Vitruvio, 1978; (9–10) Luigi Vagnetti, De naturali et artificiali perspectiva: bibliografia ragionata, delle fonti teoriche e delle ricerche di storia della prospettiva: contributo alla formazione della conoscenza di un'idea razionale nei sviluppi da Euclide a Gaspard Mong e, 1979; (11) Omaggio a L.(uigi) Vagnetti, 1983; (12) Saverio Muratori, Saverio Muratori: architetto (1910–1973): il pensiero e l'opera = The thought and the work, 1984; (13) Giancarlo Cataldi, ed., All'origine dell'abitare: mostra itinerante, 1986; (14) Paolo Maretto . . . [et al.], Edilizia seriale pianificata in Italia, 1500–1600, 1987; (15) Giancarlo Cataldi, ed., Le ragioni dell'abitare: mostra itinerante = Les raisons de l'habiter: exposition itinéraire, 1988; (16) Emma Mandelli, Palazzo del Rinascimento dal rilievo al confronto, 1989; (17) Saverio Muratori, Da Schinkel ad Asplund: lezioni di architettura moderna: 1959–1960, 1990; (18) Renato Bollati, L'organismo architettonico: metodo grafico di lettura, 1990; (19) Saverio Muratori, Antologia critica degli scritti di Saverio Muratori, 1991; (20) Mario Gallarati, Architettura a scala urbana = Urban scale architecture, 1994.

R91 Studi e testi di storia e critica dell'arte, 1–18. Napoli, Società editrice napoletana, 1975–84.

Scholarly series focusing primarily on the art of Italy, specifically its southern regioun. Includes bibliographies and black-and-white plates.

Contents: (1) Raffaele Mormone, Critica e arti figurative dal positivismo alla semiologia, 1975; (2) Mario Rotili, L'arte del Cinquecento nel Regno di Napoli, 1976; (3) Mario Alberto Pavone, Paolo De Majo: pittura e devozione a Napoli nel secolo dei lumi, 1977; (4) Mario Rotili, L'arte a Napoli dal VI al XIII secolo, 1978; (5) Franco Strazzullo, ed., La Real Cappella del Tesoro di S. Gennaro: documenti inediti, 1978; (6) Salvatore Abita . . . [et al.], eds., Le arti figurative a Napoli nel settecento: (documenti e ricerche), 1979; (7) Rosario Assunto, Infinita contemplazione, gusto e filosofia dell'Europa barocca, 1979; (8) Carl Arnold Willemsen, I castelli di Federico II nell'Italia meridionale, 1979; (9)

Paul Signac, Da Delacroix al neoimpressionismo, trans. by Raffaele Mormone, 1979; (10) Marialuisa Angiolillo, Leonardo, feste e teatri, 1979; (11) Gérard Labrot, Baroni in città: residenze e comportamenti dell'aristocrazia napoletana, 1530–1734, 1979; (12) Alfonso Gambardella, Architettura e committenza nello stato pontificio tra barocco e rococò, 1979; (13) Stefano Romano, L'arte organaria a Napoli: dalle origini al secolo XIX, 2v., 1980–90, [v.2 pub. by Arte Tipografica]; (14) Maria Raffaela Pessolano, Il Palazzo d'Angri: un opera napoletana fra tardobarocco e neoclassicismo, 1980; (15) Mario Rotili, Filippo Raguzzini nel terzo centenario della nascita: precisazioni, aggiunte e prospettive di studio, 1982; (16) Giovanni Fallani, Da Giotto a De Chirico, 1983; (17) Annamaria Negro Spina, Giulio Parigi e gli incisori della sua cerchia, 1983; (17, sic) Andrea Mariani, Scrittura e figurazione nell'Ottocento americano: da Horatio Greenough a Elihu Vedder, 1984; (18) Luigi R. Cielo, La cattedrale normanna di Alife, 1984.

R92 Studien zur Kunst und Kulturgeschichte, Bd.1– . Marburg, Germany, Jonas, 1985– .

Well-researched, small-format series on various issues in art, architecture, and iconography, from medieval to contemporary periods. Some vols. are revisions of authors' theses. In German.

Contents: (1) Hans-Werner Schmidt, Die Förderung des vaterländischen Geschichtsbildes durch die Verbindung für historische Kunst, 1854–1933, 1985; (2) Hans Lange, Vom Tribunal zum Tempel: zur Architektur und Geschichte deutscher Hoftheater zwischen Vormärz und Restauration, 1985; (3) Horst Scholz, Brouwer invenit: druckgraphische Reproduktionen des 17.–19. Jahrhunderts nach Gemälden und Zeichnungen Adriaen Brouwers, 1985; (4) Klaus Jan Philipp, Pfarrkirchen: Funktion, Motivation, Architetur: eine Studie am Beispiel der Pfarrkirchen der schwäbischen Reichsstädte im Spätmittelalter, 1987; (5) Wolfgang Kersten, Paul Klee: Zerstörung, der Konstruktion zuliebe?, 1987; (6) Elisabeth Epe, Die Gemäldesammlungen des Ferdinando de Medici, Erbprinz von Toskana (1663–1713), 1990; (7) Christiane Keim, Städtebau in der Krise des Absolutismus: die Stadtplanungsprogramme der hessischen Residenzstädte: Kassel, Darmstadt und Wiesbaden zwischen 1760 und 1840, 1990; (8) Michael Hütt, ed., Unglücklich das Land, das Helden nötig hat: Leiden und Sterben in den Kriegsdenkmälern des Ersten und Zweiten Weltkrieges, 1990; (9) Cordula Bischoff, Strategien barocker Bildpropaganda: Aneignung und Verfremdung der heiligen Elisabeth von Thüringen, 1990; (10) Suzanne Grötz, Sabbioneta: die Selbstinszenierung eines Herrschers, 1993; (11) Richard Hüttel, Spiegelungen einer Ruine: Leonardos Abendmahl im 19. und 20. Jahrhundert, 1994; (12) Jutta Karpf, Strukturanalyse der mittelalterlichen Bilderzählung: ein Beitrag zur kunsthistorischen Erzählforschung, 1994; (13) Ingeborg Deborre, Palladios teatro olimpico in Vicenza: die Inszenierung einer lokalen Aristokratie unter venezianischer Herrschaft, 1996; (14) Ingrid Sedlacek, Die Neuf Preuses: Heldinnen des Spätmittelalters, 1997; (15) Matthias Staschull, Industrielle Revolution im Königspark: Architekturverkleidungen "Technischer" Parkgebäude des. 19. Jahrhunderts in Potsdam am Beispiel von Ludwig Persius' Dampfmaschinenhaus für den Park von Sanssouci, 1999.

R93 Studies in Baroque art history, 1–5. Ann Arbor, UMI Research Pr., 1982.

Ed.: Ann Sutherland Harris.

Well-respected series by scholars in the field.

Contents: (1) Charles Scribner III, The Triumph of the Eucharist: tapestries designed by Rubens, 1982; (2) Susan Saward, The golden age of Marie de' Medici, 1982; (3) Christine Skeeles Schloss, Travel, trade, and temptation: the Dutch Italianate harbor scene, 1640–1680, 1982; (4) Deborah Marrow, The art patronage of Maria de'Medici, 1982; (5) David Wilton Steadman, Abraham van Diepenbeeck: seventeenth century Flemish painter, 1982.

R94 Studies in design and material culture. Manchester and N.Y., Manchester Univ. Pr., 1992– . (Distr. in U.S. by St. Martin's)

Ed.: Paul Greenhalgh.

"These books will largely be concerned with the major genres of architectural ornament, ceramics, furniture, glass, graphics, jewelry, metal-working, textiles, product and interior design and will cover painting and sculpture to provide a context for these other genres."—*Introd.* Erudite and engaging British series on design history, with black-and-white and color plates, indexes.

Contents: David Crowley, National style and nation-state: design in Poland from the vernacular revival to the international style, 1992; Paul Greenhalgh, Quotations and sources on design and the decorative arts, 1993; Clive Edwards, Victorian furniture: technology and design, 1993; Helen C. Long, The Edwardian house: the middle-class home in Britain, 1880–1914, 1993; Ray Batchelor, Henry Ford, mass production, modernism, and design, 1994; Ray Crozier, Manufactured pleasures: psychological responses to design, 1994; Clive Edwards, 20th century furniture: materials, manufacture, and markets, 1994; John E. Findling, Chicago's great world's fairs, 1994; Christopher Breward, The culture of fashion: a new history of fashionable dress, 1995; Clive Edwards, Eighteenth-century furniture, 1996; Paul Jobling, Graphic design: reproduction and representation since 1800, 1996; The culture of craft: status and future, 1997; Pioneers of modern craft: 12 essays profiling key figures in the history of 20th century craft, 1997; Gregory Votolato, American design in the twentieth century: personality and performance, 1998; Christopher Breward, The hidden consumer: masculinities, fashion and city life 1860–1914, 1999; Amy de la Haye and Elizabeth Wilson, eds., Defining dress: dress as object, meaning, and identity, 1999; Elizabeth McKellar, The birth of modern London: the development and design of the city 1660–1720, 1999; Sarah Richards, Eighteenth-century ceramics: products for a civilised society, 1999.

R95 Studies in Islamic art and architecture, 1– . N.Y., Brill, 1987– .

Variant title: Muqarnas. Supplement.

Exhaustively researched vols. on Islamic architecture, art, and culture, each one with extensive notes, bibliographies, and illustrations. Related to the journal, Muqarnas (see GLAH 2:Q255).

Contents: (1) Cafer Efendi, Risale-i mi'mariyye: an early-seventeenth century Ottoman treatise on architecture: facsimile with translation and notes, 1987; (2) Mehrdad Shokoohy, Bhadresvar: the oldest Islamic monuments in India, 1988; (3) Doris Behrrens-Abouseif, Islamic architecture in Cairo: an introduction, 2d impression 1992, (1989); (4) Eva Baer, Ayyubid metalwork with Christian images, 1988; (5) Sheila Blair, ed., The monumental inscriptions from early Islamic Iran and Transoxiana, 1992; (6) Lisa Golombek and Maria Subtelny, eds., Timurid art and culture: Iran and Central Asia in the fifteenth century, 1992; (7) Attilio Petruccioli, ed., Gardens in the time of the great Muslim empires: theory and design, 1997; (8) Hafiz Hüseyin al-Ayvansarayî, The garden of the mosques: Hafiz Hüseyin al-Ayvansarayî's guide to the Muslim monuments of Ottoman Istanbul, trans. by Howard Crane, 1999.

R96 Studies in modern art, 1– . N.Y., Museum of Modern Art (Distr. by Abrams, 1991-). Annual.

Ed.: John Elderfield.

"Publishing vehicle for the Research and Scholarly Publications Program of The Museum of Modern Art, New York . . . [whose] goal . . . is to foster and sustain the study of the Museum's unparalleled collection of works of art and archival material . . . focus[ing] on the Museum's own holdings, this series serves a wider purpose, with each issue addressing a different topic of general interest to students of modern art. . . . Essays by both Museum of Modern Art staff members and outside scholars."—*Advert.*

Contents: James Leggio and Susan Weiley, eds., American art of the 1960s, 1991; (2) John Elderfield, ed., Essays on assemblage, 1992 ; (3) William Stanley Rubin . . . [et al.], eds., Les Demoiselles d'Avignon, 1994; (4) John Szarkowski, The Museum of Modern Art at mid-century: at home and abroad, 1994; (5) John Elderfield, ed., The Museum of Modern Art at mid-century: continuity and change, 1995; (6) Philip Johnson and the Museum of Modern Art, 1998; (7) Imagining the future of the Museum of Modern Art, 1998.

R97 Studies in Netherlandish art and cultural history, 1– . Waanders, Zwolle, 1997– .

Promising hardcover series on Netherlandish art and civilization, with one vol. published thus far, based on the author's doctoral thesis, with excellent color and black-and-white plates.

Contents: Mariët Westermann, The amusements of Jan Steen: comic painting in the 17th century, 1997.

R98 Studies in prints and printmaking, v.1– . Rotterdam, Sound & Vision Interactive, 1996– .

Finely bound series of scholarly works on prints and printmaking, based on the authors' dissertations. Exhaustively researched, with bibliographies, indexes, and color plates.

Contents: (1) Nadine Orenstein, Hendrick Hondius and the business of prints in 17th century Holland, 1996; (2) Jan van der Stock, Printing images in Antwerp: the introduction of printmaking in a city: 15th century to 1585, trans. by Beverley Jackson, 1998.

R99 Studies in Renaissance art history, 1–3. Ann Arbor, UMI Research Pr., 1983–84.

Short-lived scholarly series on Renaissance art by scholars in the field.

Contents: (1) Sheila Ffolliott, Civic sculpture in the Renaissance: Montorsoli's fountains at Messina, 1984; (2) Lynn Frier Kaufmann, The noble savage: satyrs and satyr families in Renaissance art, 1984; (3) Burr Wallen, Jan van Hemessen: an Antwerp painter between reform and counter-reform, 1983.

R100 Studies in the fine arts: art theory, 1– . Ann Arbor, UMI, 1981– .

Ed.: Donald B. Kuspit.

One of a suite of titles issuing from the larger UMI Studies in the fine arts series. This particular title presents outstanding vols. on art theory by scholars in the field.

Contents: (1) Stewart Buettner, American art theory, 1945–1970, 1981; (2) William G. Plank, Sartre and surrealism, 1981; (3) William Ivor Fowkes, A Hegelian account of contemporary art, 1981; (4) Eugenio Fernández Granell, Picasso's Guernica: the end of a Spanish era, 1981; (5) Geoffrey F. De Sylva, John Ruskin's Modern Painters I and II: a phenomenological analysis, 1981; (6) Leatrice Mendelsohn, Paragoni: Benedetto Varchi's Due lezzioni and cinquecento art theory, 1982; (7) Clive Ashwin, Drawing and education in German-speaking Europe, 1800–1900, 1981; (8) Judith Wechsler, The interpretation of Cézanne, 1981; (9) Amy Cohen Simowitz, Theory of art in the Encyclopédie, 1983; (10) Misook Song, Art theories of Charles Blanc, 1813–1882, 1984; (11) Miriam R. Levin, Republican art and ideology in late nineteenth century France, 1986; (12) Bernard Schultz, Art and anatomy in Renaissance Italy, 1985; (13) Jo Anna Isaak, The ruin of representation in modernist art and texts, 1986; (14) Matthew Rohn, Visual dynamics in Jackson Pollock's abstractions, 1987; (15) Kent William Hooper, Ernest Barlach's literary and visual art: the issue of multiple talent, 1987.

R101 Studies in the fine arts: the avant-garde, 1– . Ann Arbor, UMI Research Pr., 1980–89.

Ed.: Stephen C. Foster.

Established series of outstanding vols. exploring 19th- and 20th-century art movements by scholars in the field.

Contents: (1) Whitney Chadwick, Myth in surrealist paintings, 1929–1939, 1980; (2) Charlotte Cummings Douglas, Swans of other worlds: Kazimir Malevich and the origins of abstraction in Russia, 1980; (3) Haim N. Finkelstein, Surrealism and the crisis of the object, 1979; (4) Allan Carl Greenberg, Artists and revolution: Dada and the Bauhaus, 1917–1925, 1979; (5) Hannah Lucille Hedrick, Theo van Doesburg, propagandist and practitioner of the Avant-garde, 1980; (6) Steven A. Mansbach, Visions of totality: Laszlo Moholy Nagy, Theo van Doesburg and El Lissitzky, 1980; (7) Annabelle Melzer, Latest rage the big drum: Dada and surrealist performance, 1980; (8) Christiana J. Taylor, Futurism: politics, painting, and performance, 1979; (9) Harriett Ann Watts, Chance, a perspective on Dada, 1980; (10) David G. Zinder, The surrealist connection: an approach to a surrealist aesthetic of theatre, 1980; (11) Brigid S. Barton,

Otto Dix and Die neue Sachlichkeit 1918–1925, 1981; (12) Linda F. McGreevy, The life and works of Otto Dix: German critical realist, 1981; (13) Catherine C. Bock-Weiss, Henri Matisse and neo-impressionism 1898–1908, 1981; (14) Susan Barnes Robinson, Giacomo Balla, divisionism and futurism 1871–1912, 1981; (15) Kestutis Paul Zygas, Form follows form: source imagery of constructivist architecture, 1917–1925, 1981; (16) Beeke Sell Tower, Klee and Kandinsky in Munich and at the Bauhaus, 1981; (17) Susan L. Ball, Ozenfant and purism, the evolution of a style 1915–1930, 1981; (18) David W. Seaman, Concrete poetry in France, 1981; (19) Thomas Kush, Wyndham Lewis's pictorial integer, 1981; (20) Ruth L. Bohan, The Société Anonyme's Brooklyn Exhibition: Katherine Dreier and modernism in America, 1982; (21) Sherry A. Buckberrough, Robert Delaunay: the discovery of simultaneity, 1982; (22) Andrew DeShong, The theatrical designs of George Grosz, 1982; (23) R. L. Held, Endless innovations: Frederick Kiesler's theory and scenic design, 1982; (24) Eugene Anthony Santomasso, Origins and aims of German expressionist architecture: an essay into the expressionist frame of mind in Germany, especially as typified in the work of Rudolf Steiner, 1985; (25) Roy F. Allen, Literary life in German expressionism and the Berlin circles, 1983; (26) Annette Cox, Art-as-politics: the abstract expressionist avant-garde and society, 1982; (27) Reidar Dittmann, Eros and psyche: Strindberg and Munch in the 1890s, 1982; (28) Jeffrey W. Howe, The symbolist art of Fernand Khnopff, 1982; (29) Robert James Bantens, Eugène Carrière: his work and his influence, 1983; (30) Wendy Slatkin, Aristide Maillol in the 1890s, 1982; (31) Jehanne Teilhet-Fisk, Paradise reviewed: an interpretation of Gauguin's Polynesian symbolism, 1983; (32) Sharon L. Hirsh, Hodler's symbolist themes, 1983; (33) Julius Kaplan, The art of Gustave Moreau: theory style and content, 1982; (34) Novelene Ross, Manet's Bar at the Folies-Bergère and the myths of popular illustration, 1982; (35) Aline Isdebsky-Pritchard, The art of Mikhail Vrubel (1856–1910), 1982; (36) Elisa Evett, The critical reception of Japanese art in late nineteenth century Europe, 1982; (37) Caroline Boyle-Turner, Paul Serusier, 1983; (38) Joseph Garrett Glover, The Cubist theatre, 1983; (39) Ileana B. Leavens, From "291" to Zurich: the birth of Dada, 1983; (40) Craig E. Adcock, Marcel Duchamp's notes from the Large glass: an n-dimensional analysis, 1983; (41) Jane Block, Les XX and Belgian avant-gardism, 1868–1894, 1984; (42) Timothy Edward O'Connor, Politics of Soviet culture: Anatolii Lunacharskii, 1983; (43) Sally Banes, Democracy's body: Judson Dance Theater, 1962–1964, 1983; (44) Jonathan David Fineberg, Kandinsky in Paris, 1906–1907, 1984; (45) Katia Samaltanos-Stenström, Apollinaire, catalyst for primitivism, Picabia, and Duchamp, 1984; (46) Roberta Bernstein, Jasper Johns' paintings and sculptures, 1954–1974: "the changing focus of the eye," 1985; (47) Jeanne Siegel, Artwords: discourses on the 60s and 70s, 1985; (48) Stephen C. Foster, ed., Dada/dimensions, 1985; (49) Sherrye Cohn, Arthur Dove: nature as symbol, 1985; (50) Myroslava Mudrak, The New Generation and artistic modernism in the Ukraine, 1986; (51) Marilyn R. Brown, Gypsies and other bohemians: the myth of the artist in nineteenth-century France, 1985; (52) William Steven Bradley, Emil Nolde and German expressionism: a prophet in his own land, 1986; (53) Merrill Schleier, The skyscraper in American art, 1890–1931, 1986; (54) Patrick S. Smith, Andy Warhol's art and films, 1986; (55) Timothy O. Benson, Raoul Hausmann and Berlin Dada, 1987; (56) Robert Saltonstall Mattison, Robert Motherwell: the formative years, 1987; (57) Stephen C. Foster, ed., "Event" arts and art events, 1988; (58) Gwen Finkel Chanzit, Herbert Bayer and modernist design in America, 1987; (59) Patrick S. Smith, ed., Warhol: conversations about the artist, 1988; (60) John Lawrence Ward, American realist painting, 1945–1980, 1989; (61) Dorothy M. Kosinski, Orpheus in nineteenth century symbolism, 1989; (62) Elizabeth Hutton Turner, American artists in Paris, 1919–1929, 1988; (63) John Francis Moffitt, Occultism in avant-garde art: the case of Joseph Beuys, 1988; (64) Margot Lovejoy, Postmodern currents: art and artists in the age of electronic media, 1989; (65) Margherita Andreotti, The early sculpture of Jean Arp, 1989; (66) Ann Eden Gibson, Issues in abstract expressionism: the artist-run periodicals, 1990; (67) Elizabeth M. Legge, Max Ernst: the psychoanalytic sources, 1989; (68) Tricia Henry, Break all rules!: punk rock and the making of a style, 1989.

R102 Studies in the fine arts: criticism, 1– . Ann Arbor, UMI Research Pr., 1980– .

Well-known series of outstanding vols. by scholars in the field focusing on art criticism and its connection to reception history (the history of appreciation and criticism).

Contents: (1) David A. Flanary, Champfleury, the realist writer as art critic, 1980; (2) Stephen C. Foster, The critics of abstract expressionism, 1980; (3) Arlene Rita Olson, Art critics and the avant-garde, New York, 1900–1913, 1980; (4) Lynne L. Gelber, In/stability: the shape and space of Claudel's art criticism, 1980; (5) Lynn Gamwell, Cubist criticism, 1980; (6) Joan Ungersma Halperin, Félix Fénéon and the language of art criticism, 1980; (7) Lee McKay Johnson, The metaphor of painting: essays on Baudelaire, Ruskin, Proust, and Pater, 1980; (8) Jacqueline Victoria Falkenheim, Roger Fry and the beginnings of formalist art criticism, 1980; (9) Reinhild Janzen, Albrecht Altdorfer: four centuries of criticism, 1980; (10) Carol M. Zemel, The formation of a legend: van Gogh criticism, 1890–1920, 1980; (11) Harry E. Buckley, Guillaume Apollinaire as an art critic, 1981; (12) Therese Dolan Stamm, Gavarni and the critics, 1981; (13) Melinda A. Lorenz, George L. K. Morris, artist and critic, 1982; (14) Ian J. Lochhead, The spectator and the landscape in the art criticism of Diderot and his contemporaries, 1982; (15) Sandra Lee Underwood, Charles H. Caffin, a voice for modernism, 1897–1918, 1983; (16) Martin Pops, Vermeer: consciousness and the chamber of being, 1984; (17) Susan Noyes Platt, Modernism in the 1920s: interpretations of modern art in New York from expressionism to constructivism, 1985; (18) Patricia Townley Mathews, Aurier's symbolist art criticism and theory, 1986; (19) Annette Kahn, J.-K. Huysmans: novelist, poet and art critic, 1987; (20) Beverly Hamilton Twitchell, Cézanne and formalism in Bloomsbury, 1987; (21) Roger Benjamin, Matisse's "Notes of a painter": criticism, theory, and context, 1891–1908, 1987; (22) Robert Pincus-Witten, Postminimalism into maximalism: American art, 1966–1986, 1987; (23)

Carol Anne Runyon Mahsun, Pop art and the critics, 1987; (24) Jeanne Siegel, ed., Artwords 2: discourse on the early 80s, 1988; (25) Lawrence Wayne Markert, Arthur Symons: critic of the seven arts, 1988; (26) never published; (27) Arlene Raven . . . [et al.], eds., Feminist art criticism: an anthology, 1988; (28) Donald Burton Kuspit, The new subjectivism: art in the 1980s, 1988; (29) Carol Anne Runyon Mahsun, ed., Pop art: the critical dialogue, 1989; (30) Barbara Buhler Lynes, O'Keeffe, Stieglitz and the critics, 1916–1929, 1989; (31) Katherine Hoffman, ed., Collage: critical views, 1989; (32) Arlene Raven, ed., Art in the public interest, 1989; (33) never published; (34) Frances Colpitt, Minimal art: the critical perspective, 1990.

R103 Texts & documents. Santa Monica, Calif., Getty Center for the History of Art and the Humanities (Distr. by Univ. of Chicago Pr., 1988–).

Scholarly, unnumbered documentary series published by The Getty Center Publication Programs. "Offers to the student of art, architecture, and aesthetics neglected, forgotten, or unavailable writings in English translation."—*Advert.* Makes available for the first time in English many classics of modern art literature. Includes introductions and commentaries.

Contents: Otto Wagner, Modern architecture: a guidebook for his students to this field of art, trans. by Harry Francis Mallgrave, 1988; Heinrich Hübsch . . . [et al.], In what style should we build?: the German debate on architectural style, trans. by Wolfgang Herrmann, 1992; Nicolas Le Camus de Mézières, The genius of architecture, or, The analogy of that art with our sensations, trans. by David Britt, 1992; Claude Perrault, Ordonnance for the five kinds of columns after the method of the ancients, trans. by Indra Kagis McEwen, 1993; Friedrich Gilly, Friedrich Gilly: Essays on architecture, 1796–1799, trans. by David Britt, 1994; Hermann Muthesius, Style-architecture and building-art, trans. by Stanford Anderson, 1994; Robert Vischer . . . [et al.], eds., Empathy, form, and space: problems in German aesthetics, 1873–1893, trans. by Harry Francis Mallgrave and Eleftherios Ikonomou, 1994; Sigfried Giedion, Building in France, building in iron, building in ferroconcrete, trans. by J. Duncan Berry, 1995; Hendrik Petrus Berlage, Hendrik Petrus Berlage: thoughts on style, 1886–1909, trans. by Iain Boyd Whyte and Wim de Wit, 1996; Adolf Behne, The modern functional building, trans. by Michael Robinson, 1996; Alois Riegl, The group portraiture of Holland, trans. by Evelyn M. Kain, 1999; Aby Warburg, The renewal of pagan antiquity: contributions to the cultural history of the European Renaissance, trans. by David Britt, 1999; Walter Curt Behrendt, The victory of the new building style, trans. by Harry Francis Mallgrave, 2000; Jean-Louis Durand, Précis of the Lectures on architecture with Graphic portion of the lectures on architecture, introd. by Antoine Picon, 2000; Karel Teige, Modern architecture in Czechoslovakia and other writings, introd. by Jean-Louis Cohen, 2000.

R104 Trierer Winckelmannsprogramme, Heft 1/2– . Mainz-am-Rhein, Germany, Zabern, 1981– .

Scholarly German series devoted to classical archeology, particularly sculpture.

Contents: (1/2) Erika Simon, Die Götter am Trajansbogen zu Benevent, 1981; (3) Klaus Parlasca, Syrische Grabreliefs hellenistischer und römischer Zeit: Fundgruppen und Probleme, 1982; (4) Henning Wrede, Der Antikengarten der del Bufalo bei der Fontana Trevi, 1983; (5) Bernd Harald Krause, Iuppiter Optimus Maximus Saturnus: ein Beitrag zur ikonographischen Darstellung Saturns, 1984; (6) Franz Georg Maier, Alt-Paphos auf Cypern: Ausgrabungen zur Geschichte von Stadt und Heiligtum 1966–1984, 1985; (7) Nikolaus Himmelmann, Antike Götter im Mittelalter, 1986; (8) Bernard Andreae, Plinius und der Laokoon, 1987; (9) Paul Zanker, Pompeji: Stadtbilder als Spiegel von Gesellschaft und Herrschaftsform, 1988; (10) Annalis Leibundgut, Künstlerische Form und konservative Tendenzen nach Perikles: ein Stilpluralismus im 5. Jahrhundert v. Chr.?, 1991; (11) Jean Charles Balty, Porträt und Gesellschaft in der römischen Welt, 1993; (12) Michael Pfrommer, Göttliche Fürsten in Boscoreale: der Festsaal in der Villa des P. Fannius Synistor, 1993; (13) Marianne Bergmann, Der Koloss Neros, die Domus Aurea und der Mentalitätswandel im Rom der frühen Kaiserzeit, 1994; (14) Wolf-Dieter Heilmeyer, Das Reiterreleif Giustiniani in Berlin, 1996; (15) François Baratte, Silbergeschirr, Kultur und Luxus in her römischen Gesellschaft, 1999; (16) Michael J. Vickers, Skeuomorphismus oder die Kunst, aus wenig viel zu machen, 1999.

R105 VRA special bulletin, 1– . Austin, Visual Resources Association, 1987– . Place of publication varies.

Special bulletins to accompany journal, VRA bulletin (see GLAH 2:Q340). Written by leading visual resource curators, topics are timely and cover such areas as copyright issues, cataloging standards, technology, equipment, and supplies.

Contents: (1) Anne-Marie S. Logan ed., British artists authority list from the Yale Center for British Art, Photograph Archive, 1987; (2) Nancy S. Schuller, Standard abbreviations for image descriptions for use in fine arts visual resources collections, 1988; (3) Christine L. Sundt, Conservation practices for slides and photograph collections, 1989; (4) Eleanor Mannikka, Selected topics in cataloging Asian art, 1989; (5) Jonny Prins, Source list for illustrations in Gardner's Art through the ages, 1994; (6) Nancy S. Schuller . . . [et al.], Iconographic contents and diagrams for descriptive cataloging of complex works of art, forthcoming; (7) Lise J. Hawkos, ed., Disaster planning for visual resources collections, 1994; (8) Art & Architecture Thesaurus Project, Directory of AAT Users, 1995; (9) Astrid R. Otey, Visual Resources Association computer users directory, 1996; (10) Mary M. Lampe, ed., Guide to rights and reproduction at American art museums, 1996; (11) Jenny Rodda and Christa Blackwood, eds., Guide to copy photography for visual resources professionals, new ed., 1996; (12) Colum Hourihane, Subject classification for visual collections: an inventory of some of the principal systems applied to content description in images, 1999.

R106 Villa I Tatti series, 1– . Firenze, Olschki, 1972– . Publisher varies.

Scholarly series emanating from the Villa I Tatti in Florence, owned by Harvard University's Center for Italian Renaissance Studies. Each vol. consists of essays on the Renaissance written by distinguished historians and art historians.

Selective contents: (3) Charles Gates Dempsey, Annibale Carracci and the beginnings of Baroque style, 1977; (4) James H. Beck, Masaccio, the documents, 1978; (5) Florence and Venice, comparisons and relations: acts of two conferences at Villa I Tatti in 1976–1977, 2v., 1979–80; (7) Renaissance studies in honor of Craig Hugh Smyth, 1985; (8) Diane Finiello Zervas, The Parte Guelfa, Brunelleschi & Donatello, 1988; (9) Eve Borsook and Fiorella Superbi Gioffredi, eds., Tecnica e stile: esempi di pittura murale del Rinascimento italiano, 2v., 1986; (10) Robert W. Gaston, ed., Pirro Ligorio, Artist and antiquarian, 1988; (11) Florence and Milan: comparisons and relations, acts of two conferences at Villa I Tatti in 1982–1984, 2v., 1989; (12) John Wyndham Pope-Hennessy, Sir, On artists and art historians, selected book reviews of John Pope-Hennessy, 1994; (14) Suzanne B. Butters, The triumph of Vulcan: sculptors' tools, porphyry, and the prince in ducal Florence, 1996.

R107 Villa Spelman colloquia, 1– . Bologna, Nuova Alfa; Baltimore (Distr. By Johns Hopkins Univ. Pr., 1989–).

Erudite series based upon the annual colloquium at the Villa Spelman in Florence, Italy.

Contents: (1) William Tronzo, ed., Italian church decoration of the Middle Ages and early Renaissance: functions, forms and regional traditions, Florence, 1989; (2) Giovanna Perini, ed., Gli scritti dei Carracci: Ludovico, Annibale, Agostino, Antonio, Giovanni Antonio, 1990; (3) Elizabeth Cropper . . . [et al.], eds., Documentary culture: Florence and Rome from Grand-Duke Ferdinand I to Pope Alexander VII, 1992; (4) Elizabeth Cropper, ed., Florentine drawing at the time of Lorenzo the Magnificent: papers from a colloquium held at the Villa Spelman, Florence, 1992, 1994; (5) Charles Dempsey, ed., Quattrocento Adriatico: fifteenth-century art of the Adriatic Rim, 1996; (6) Herbert L. Kessler, Gerhard Wolf, eds., The Holy face and the paradox of representation, 1998.

R108 Vintage contemporary artists. N.Y., Vintage, 1987–88.

Monographs on contemporary artists, mainly in the form of interviews with artists who made their mark in the 1980s.

Contents: David Salle, Salle [an interview with David Salle by Peter Schjeldahl], 1987; Robert Rauschenberg, Rauschenberg [an interview with Robert Rauschenberg by Barbara Rose], 1987; Eric Fischl, Fischl [an interview with Eric Fischl by Donald Kuspit], 1987; Francesco Clemente, Clemente [an interview with Francesco Clemente by Rainer Crone and Georgia Marsh], 1987; Louise Bourgeois, Bourgeois [an interview with Louise Bourgeois by Donald Kuspit], 1988; Donald Sultan, Sultan [an interview with Donald Sultan by Barbara Rose], 1988.

R109 Yale publications in the history of art, v.1– . New Haven, Yale Univ. Pr., 1939– .

V.1–12 titled Yale historical publications. History of art. Academic series covering all periods of art and architecture by leading scholars in their fields, published under the direction of the Department of the History of Art at Yale University. Some earlier vols. have been reprinted.

Contents: Charles Seymour Jr., Notre Dame of Noyon in the twelfth century: a study in the early development of Gothic architecture, 1939; (2) Elizabeth Lawrence Mendell, Romanesque sculpture in Saintonge, 1940; (3) Sumner McKnight Crosby, The abbey of St. Denis, 475–1122 (1942), 1979; (4) Henri Focillon, The life of forms in art, 1942; (5) George Kubler, Mexican architecture of the sixteenth century (1948), 2v., 1972; (6) Anthony N. B. Garvan, Architecture and town planning in colonial Connecticut (1951), 1982; (7) George Heard Hamilton, Manet and his critics (1954), 1986; (8) J. Leroy-Davidson, The Lotus Sutra in Chinese art: a study in Buddhist art to the year 1000, 1954; (9) Henry Russell Hitchcock, Early Victorian architecture in Britain (1954), 2v., 1973; (10) Vincent Joseph Scully, The shingle style: architectural theory and design from Richardson to the origins of Wright (1955), 1971; (11) Carroll L. M. Meeks, The railroad station: an architectural history, 1956; (12) Donald Robertson, Mexican manuscript painting of the early colonial period: the Metropolitan schools, 1959; (13) Marcel Röthlisberger, Claude Lorrain: the paintings, 2v., 1961; (14) William R. Crelly, The painting of Simon Vouet (1962), 1987; (15) Louis Grodecki, Bibliographie Henri Focillon, 1963; (16) Filarete, Antonio Averlino, known as, Treatise on architecture; being the treatise by Antonio di Piero Averlino, known as Filarete (1965), 2v., 1985; (17, 35) William L. MacDonald, The architecture of the Roman Empire: an introductory study (1965), 2v., 1982–86; (18) Spiro Kostof, The Orthodox Baptistry of Ravenna, 1979, (1965); (19) George L. Hersey, Alfonso II and the artistic renewal of Naples, 1485–1495, 1969; (20) Vincent Joseph Scully, The shingle style and the stick style: architectural theory and design from Richardson to the origins of Wright, 1991, (1971), first pub. in 1955 under title: The shingle style (see no.10); (21) Sumner McKnight Crosby, The apostle bas-relief at Saint-Denis, 1972; (22) Kermit Swiler Champa, Studies in early Impressionism, 1988, (1973); (23) Charles Seymour, Jacopo della Quercia sculptor, 1990, (1973); (24) George L. Hersey, The Aragonese arch at Naples, 1443–1475, 1973; (25) Jerry Jordan Pollitt, The ancient view of Greek art: criticism, history, and terminology, 1991, (1974); (26) Theodore E. Stebbins, The life and works of Martin Johnson Heade, 1975; (27) Judith Colton, The Parnasse françois: Titon du Tillet and the origins of the monument to genius, 1992, (1979); (28) David Cast, The Calumny of Apelles: a study in the humanist tradition, 1981; (29) Marilyn Aronberg Lavin, Piero della Francesca's Baptism of Christ, 1981; (30) George Kubler, Studies in ancient American and European art: the collected essays of George Kubler, 1985; (31) Elizabeth Anne McCauley, A. A. E. Disdéri and the carte de visite portrait photograph, 1985; (32) David M. Lubin, Act of portrayal: Eakins, Sargent, James, 1985; (33) Caroline Astrid Bruzelius, The 13th-century church of St-Denis, 1985; (34) Sylvia Ardyn Boone, Radiance from the waters: ideals of feminine beauty in Mende art, 1986; (36) Charles B. McClendon, The imperial abbey of Farfa: architectural currents of the early Middle Ages, 1987; (37) Sumner McKnight Crosby, The Royal Abbey of Saint Denis: from its beginnnings to the death of Suger, 475–1151: album and drawings, 1987; (38) Melanie Louis Simo, Loudon and the landscape: from country seat to metropolis, 1783–1843,

1988; (39) Anna C. Chave, Mark Rothko: subjects in abstraction, 1989; Jeffrey F. Hamburger, The Rothschild canticles: art and mysticism in Flanders and the Rhineland circa 1300, 1990; George Kubler, Esthetic recognition of ancient Amerindian art, 1991; Nancy J. Troy, Modernism and the decorative arts in France: Art Nouveau to Le Corbusier, 1991; Diane E. E. Kleiner, Roman sculpture, 1992; Molly Nesbit, Atget's seven albums, 1992; Anna C. Chave, Constantin Brancusi: shifting the bases of art, 1993; Marcia Ann Kupfer, Romanesque wall painting in central France: the politics of narrative, 1993; Christine Poggi, In defiance of painting: Cubism, Futurism and the invention of collage, 1993; Jonathan Edman Weinberg, Speaking for vice: homosexuality in the art of Charles Demuth, Marsden Hartley, and the first American avant-garde, 1993; Elizabeth Anne McCauley, Industrial madness: commercial photography in Paris, 1848–1871, 1994; David M. Lubin, Picturing a nation: art and social change in nineteenth-century America, 1994; Esther da Costa Meyer, The work of Antonio Saint'Elia: retreat into the future, 1995; Alexander Nemerov, Frederic Remington and turn-of-the-century America, 1995; Carol Oakman, Ingres's eroticized bodies: retracing the serpentine line, 1995; Romy Golan, Modernity and nostalgia: art and politics in France between the wars, 1995; Elizabeth A. Honig, Painting and the market in early modern Antwerp, 1998; Jodi Hauptman, Joseph Cornell, stargazing in the cinema, 1999.

S. Patronage and Collecting

Literature examining the history and critical context of art patronage and collecting has increased dramatically during the last twenty years. Together with studies addressing the history and social role of museums, these investigations comprise an area not specifically represented in GLAH 1. Titles selected for inclusion here favor recent publications with sound research apparatus such as bibliographies, notes, indices, and chronologies as well as substantial bibliographic coverage of important works published before 1900. Inventories of collections have been excluded, except where they appear together with substantial historical surveys and analysis. Studies on single individuals, courts, or cities have been limited to topics of major importance. Works on practical museology and contemporary issues of governmental support for the arts have been excluded.

BIBLIOGRAPHY

S1 Art and the development of taste, collecting & connoisseurship. Introd. by Charles Ryskamp. N.Y., Ursus Rare Books, [1993?]. 1v. (unpaginated), il.

Catalog compiled by Ursus Books to accompany an exhibition and sale held to benefit the Frick Collection. The catalog contains chiefly books as well as some prints and drawings documenting "the evolution of taste and connoisseurship in the formation of European and American collections, both public and private."—*Introd.* The first section contains 238 fully annotated entries for rare and historic materials; the second section contains 515 briefly annotated entries for reference works covering a wide range of topics concerning the history of collecting, collections, and connoisseurship.

S2 From Wunderkammer to museum. Oxford, Diana Parikian in assoc. with Bernard Quaritch, 1984. 82p.

Fully annotated antiquarian book catalog including an introductory essay and 75 entries for works focusing on the early "cabinet of curiosities" published from the 16th to 19th centuries. Entries contain references to modern publications. Numerous early collection catalogs are included.

Index of authors, compilers of catalogues, and owners of collections, p.82

S3 Gardner, Elizabeth E. A bibliographical repertory of Italian private collections. Ed. by Chiara Ceschi with the assist. of Katharine Baetjer. Vicenza, Neri Pozza, 1998– . (1)v.

First volume of extraordinarily detailed survey of sources for the history of collecting in Italy. Arranged by collector name, entries provide biographical information, collection and sale details, references to inventories, and other primary sources and bibliographical notes. The bibliography is divided into sections for manuscripts, published books and articles, exhibition catalogs, and sales records. Future vols. in preparation.

Bibliography, p.277–403. Index, p.407–39.

S4 Murray, David. Museums, their history and their use: with a bibliography and list of museums in the United Kingdom. Glasgow, James MacLehose, 1904. 3v.

An extensive bibliography of early publications on museum collections and their history in Europe, Great Britain, Scandinavia, North and South America, and Russia. Entries arranged by collection name, location, and subject. Essays in the first vol. selectively survey the history of collectors, collecting, and the formation of museums in Europe and Great Britain.

Contents: Vol.1: (I) Introductory; (II) The Renaissance: the collecting of objects of ancient art; (III) The progress of science: collections of natural objects; (IV) Early museum catalogues; (V) The use of the term museum; (VI) Some old exhibits; (VII) Some early museums; (VIII) Later museums; (IX) The beginnings of the British Museum; (X) Special collections; (XI) Scottish collectors and Scottish museums; (XII) Museums as shows; (XIII) Dispersion of museums; (XIV) Non-scientific character of early museums; (XV) Arrangement of old museums; (XVI) The modern museum; Archaeological museums; (XVII) Glasgow museums. The museums of Hamburg, Bremen and Lübeck; (XVIII) The use of museums. Appendices: The Leyden catalogue of 1591; List of museums in the United Kingdom. Vols.2–3: Bibliography: (I) Literature of museums: bibliography of bibliographies; (II) Museography; (III) The collection, preparation and preservation; the registration and exhibition of specimens; (IV) Catalogues and other works relating to particular museums; (V) Travels and general literature.

Index, v.1, p.313–39.

GENERAL WORKS

S5 L'age d'or du mécénat (1598–1661): actes du colloque international CNRS (mars 1983), Le mécénat en Europe, et particulièrement en France avant Colbert. Paris, Ed. de C.N.R.S., 1985. 440p.

40 diverse papers from an international colloquium sponsored by the Centre National de la Recherche Scientifique devoted to examining the role of arts patronage in France during the ancien regime. Though of uneven quality these "contributions purvey a quantity of new information and help make this vol. an indispensable repository of facts on early seventeenth-century patrons and their proteges."—*Review*, Journal of modern history, v.59, Sept. 1987, p.555. Covers architecture, the decorative arts, literature, and theater, as well as painting, sculpture, and graphic arts.

Selective contents: (1) Les mécènes; (2) Les protégés des mécènes: fidèles, clients, fournisseurs; La condition sociale des écrivans, des artistes, des savants; (3) Les thèmes et les oeuvres.

Notes at ends of essays.

S6 The age of the marvelous. Ed. by Joy Kenseth. Hanover, N.H., Hood Museum of Art, Dartmouth College (Distr. by the Univ. of Chicago Pr., 1991). 485p. il. (part col.), plates.

Published in conjunction with the exhibition, Hood Museum of Art (1991), and other locations. While frequently emphasizing the "scientific" nature of collecting in the 16th and 17th centuries, this ambitious and successful catalog also focuses on the role of art in early collections. Nine essays precede detailed, well-documented entries for 225 objects. The extensive bibliography is strong in works published before 1775 as well as modern literature.

Contents: The age of the marvelous: an introduction, by Joy Kenseth; The aesthetics of the marvelous: the wondrous work of art in a wondrous world, by James V. Mirollo; "A world of wonders in one closet shut," by Joy Kenseth; Strange new worlds: mapping the heavens and the earth's great extent, by James A. Welu; Remarkable humans and singular beasts, by William B. Ashworth, Jr.; A paradise of plants: exotica, rarities, and botanical fantasies, by Elisabeth B. Macdougall; Love, monsters, movement, and machines: the marvelous in theaters, festivals, and gardens, by Mark S. Weil; Trompe-l'oeil painting: visual deception or natural truths?, by Arthur K. Wheelock, Jr.; "A time fertile in miracles": miraculous events in and through art, by Zirka Zaremba Filipczak.

Bibliography, p.459–79. Index, p.480–85.

S7 Alsop, Joseph. The rare art traditions: the history of art collecting and its linked phenomena wherever these have appeared. N.Y., Harper & Row, 1982. xxiii, 691p. il., plates. (The A. W. Mellon lectures in the fine arts, 1978) (Bollingen series XXXV, no.27)

Eclectic survey that analyzes art collecting as a social habit from its documented beginnings through the 17th century. Each chapter is based on an historical incident, individual, or object. A good companion to more conventional overviews of the history of collecting. Includes Asian and Middle Eastern topics. The bibliography is strong in 19th century and earlier works.

Selective contents: (I) The altered Apollo; (II) Art for use; (III) Art collecting; (IV) The Litmus test; (V) The Siamese twins; (VI) The other by-products of art; (VII) "The Greek miracle"; (VIII) The pattern repeats; (IX) The pattern vanishes—and returns; (X) Art collecting revives; (XI) The role of Cosimo; (XII) The role of Lorenzo; (XIII) The climax in the west; (XIV) The seventeenth century.

Notes, p.[477]–613. Bibliography, p.[615]–65. Index, p.[667]–91.

S8 L'anticomanie: la collection d'antiquités aux 18e et 19e siècle. Textes rassemblés par Annie-France Laurens et Krzysztof Pomian. Paris, École des hautes études en sciences sociales, 1992. 351p. il. (Civilisations et sociétés, 86)

25 papers presented at an international colloquium held in Montpellier (1988) examining the role of "rediscovered" antiquities in individual collecting and the formation of museums in western Europe.

Selective contents: Introduction, par Francis Haskell; (I) Les collections et les collectionneurs; (II) Entre l'Italie et la France: autour du commerce d'art et d'antiquitiés; (III) De la collection au musée; (IV) Archéologie classique, archéologie nationale; (V) Les antiquités et les arts.

Includes bibliographical references.

S9 Art and business: an international perspective on sponsorship. Ed. by Rosanne Martorella. Westport, Conn., Praeger, 1996. xiv, 268p. il.

20 essays in the form of case studies cover topics of international corporate patronage and sponsorship in the fine and performing arts since the 1960s. Thoroughly researched and documented with analyzed statistical data throughout. Useful for anyone investigating the impact of corporate influence on artists and the arts. The bibliography is especially strong on newspaper and periodical literature references.

Contents: (1) Art and business: an international approach on sponsorship, by Rosanne Martorella; (2) Corporate patronage of the arts in the United States: a review of the research, by Rosanne Martorella; (3) Corporate involvement in the arts and the reproduction of power in Canada, by Gerald S. Kenyon; (4) Business support to the arts and culture in Argentina, by Rodolfo S. Gonçebate and Margo E. Hajduk; (5) Business and culture in Brazil, by José Carlos Durand; (6) Business support for the arts in Europe and CEREC, by Ann Vanhaeverbeke; (7) Corporate collectors of contemporary art in Britain, by Chin-tao Wu; (8) Art sponsorship by the Austrian business sector, by Brigitte Kössner; (9) The role of foundations in support of the arts in Germany, by Virginia Glasmacher and Count Rupert Strachwitz; (10) Emerging corporate arts support: Potsdam, Eastern Germany, by Völker Kirchberg; (11) Sponsorship and patronage in Italy: some regional cases, by Stefano Piperno; (12) Art patronage among banks in Italy, by Patrizia Zambianchi; (13) Art support as corporate responsibility in the postindustrial city of Rotterdam, the Netherlands, by Erik Hitters; (14) Modern enterprise and the arts: sponsorship as a metamechanism of culture in Greece, by George Halaris and

George Plios; (15) Art audiences and art funding: contemporary relationships between art and business in Australia, by Annette Van den Bosch; (16) Japan's corporate support of the arts: synopsis of the 1992 survey, by ACSA (Kigyo Mecenat Kyogikai); (17) Art and cultural policy in Japan, by Kenichi Kawasaki; (18) Japanese corporate collectors: a social and industrial elite, by Rosanne Martorella; (19) Monet for money? Museum exhibitions and role of corporate sponsorship, by Victoria D. Alexander; (20) The rise and fall of the impresario, by Patricia Adkins Chiti; (21) Positive rationales for corporate arts support, by Roland Kushner.

Notes at ends of chapters. Bibliography, p.[247]–59. Index, p.[261]–64.

S10 Bazin, Germain. The museum age. Trans. from the French by Jane van Nuis Cahill. N.Y., Universe Books, 1967. [303]p. il. (part col.), facsims., plans.

Trans. of Le temps des musées. [Brussels], Desoer, [1967].

One of the earlier general works to appear on the history of private collections and the formation of museums. Covers collecting patterns in Europe from antiquity to the 20th century. Includes a chapter on the United States. Suitable for the general reader. Minimal notes, no bibliography.

Contents: (I) Prelude; (II) Interlude; (III) Renaissance; (IV) Mannerism; (V) Royal art; (VI) Museographia; (VII) The cabinet and the gallery; (VIII) The age of enlightenment; (IX) Revolutions; (X) The museum age; (XI) The new world; (XII) Present and future.

Index, p.281–89.

S11 Brown, Jonathan. Kings and connoisseurs: collecting art in seventeenth-century Europe. Princeton, Princeton Univ. Pr., [1995]. 264p. col. il. (The A. W. Mellon lectures in the fine arts, 1994) (Bollingen series, XXXV, no.43)

Readable narrative covering the most important events, together with historical background, in the formation and transfer of royal and aristocratic collections during the 17th century. Special attention is given to the painting and sculpture acquired by Charles I and the Spanish royal collections. Thoroughly and instructively illustrated.

Contents: (I) Charles I and the Whitehall group; (II) The sale of the century; (III) "The greatest amateur of paintings among the princes of the world"; (IV) "Amator artis pictoriae": Archduke Leopold William and picture collecting in Flanders; (V) Reasons of state; (VI) The prestige of painting; Postscript: Where have all the old masters gone? An essay on the market for old pictures, 1700–1995.

Notes, p.254–56. Bibliography, p.257–60. Index, p.261–64.

S12 The Courts of Europe: politics, patronage, and royalty 1400–1800. Ed. by A. G. Dickens. London, Thames and Hudson, 1977. 335p. il. (part col.) (Repr.: N.Y., Greenwich House [Distr. by Crown Publishers, 1984])

Introductory survey covering collecting activities in the major courts of Europe from the end of the Middle Ages through the 18th century. Emphasizes the political, social, and geographical context for each collection discussed. Well illustrated.

Contents: (1) Monarchy and cultural revival, by A. G. Dickens; (2) The courtier, by Sydney Anglo; (3) The golden age of Burgundy, by C. A. J. Armstrong; (4) Lorenzo de'Medici, by E. B. Fryde; (5) Francis I, by R. J. Knecht; (6) The Austrian Hapsburgs, by R. J. W. Evans; (7) The Tudors, by Neville Williams; (8) Philip IV of Spain, by John H. Elliott; (9) Charles I of England, by Peter W. Thomas; (10) Urban VIII, by Judith A. Hook; (11) Louis XIV, by Ragnhild Hatton; (12) Peter the Great, by M. S. Anderson; (13) Maria Theresa, by E. Wangermann; (14) Louis XV, by J. H. Shennan.

Bibliography, p.328–31. Index, p.332–35.

S13 The cultures of collecting. Ed. by John Elsner and Roger Cardinal. Cambridge, [Mass.], Harvard Univ. Pr., 1994. viii, 312p. il.

Selection of essays by established scholars. Attempts a "bricolage of theoretical, descriptive and historical papers whose collective ambition is not to invoke canons and confirm taste, but to lay bare a phenomenon at once psychological and social, one that not only has its less than obvious material history, but also a continuing contemporary presence."—*Introd.*

Contents: (1) The system of collecting, by Jean Baudrillard; (2) "Unless you do these crazy things . . .": an interview with Robert Opie; (3) Identity parades, by John Windsor; (4) Collecting and collage-making: the case of Kurt Schwitters, by Roger Cardinal; (5) Telling objects: a narrative perspective on collecting, by Mieke Bal; (6) Licensed curiosity: Cook's Pacific voyages, by Nicholas Thomas; (7) From treasury to museum: the collections of Austrian Habsburgs, by Thomas DaCosta Kaufmann; (8) A collector's model of desire: the house and museum of Sir John Soane, by John Elsner; (9) Cabinets of transgression: Renaissance collections and the incorporation of the New World, by Anthony Alan Shelton; (10) Death and life, in that order, in the works of Charles Willson Peale by Susan Stewart; (11) "Mille etre": Freud and collecting, by John Forrester; (12) Collecting Paris, by Naomi Schor.

References, p.[275]–302. Select bibliography, p.[303]–04. Index, p.[305]–12.

S14 Documents for the history of collecting. Published periodically in Burlington Magazine v.128– . (1986–)

Series of more than 25 articles devoted to inventories of paintings and other documents for the history of collecting.

S15 Documents for the history of collecting. [Publisher varies], 1992– . (3)v. in 4. il., plates, maps, ports.

Important series of inventories of outstanding 17th- and 18th-century collections, coordinated by the Provenance Index of the Getty Research Institute.

Contents: Italian inventories: (1) Labrot, Gérard. Collections of paintings in Naples, 1600–1780 (N.Y., Saur, 1992); (2) Safarik, Eduard A. Collezione dei dipinti Colonna: inventari 1611–1795 = The Colonna collection of paintings: inventories 1611–1795 (New Providence, Saur, 1996) (31 unpublished inventories); Spanish inventories: Burke, Marcus B., and Cherry, Peter. Collections of paintings in Madrid

1601–1755 (2v., 1996) (140 inventories from Madrid archives).

S16 From court Jews to the Rothschilds: art, patronage, and power, 1600–1800. Ed. by Vivian B. Mann and Richard I. Cohen. Munich, Prestel-Verlag, 1996. 251p. il. (part col.)

Collection of essays and catalog published in conjunction with the exhibition held at the Jewish Museum, New York (1996–97) examining the influence of Jews in European court patronage and collecting. Provides additional historical background for the role of Jews in court life in Islamic countries and Christian Spain until the 15th century. Catalog contains 271 in-depth entries with bibliographic references. Covers architecture and works of art. Many useful illustrations.

Contents: Court Jews before the Hofjuden, by Yosef Kaplan; Court Jews in economics and politics, by Michael Graetz; Riches and Dangers: Glickl bas Judah Leib on court Jews, by Natalie Zemon Davis; The Case of Alexander David of Braunschweig, by Ralf Busch; The despised queen of Berlin Jewry, or the life and times of Esther Liebmann, by Deborah Hertz; The last of the court Jews: Mayer Amschel Rothschild and his sons, by Fritz Backhaus; Melding worlds: court Jews and the arts of the baroque, by Richard I. Cohen and Vivian B. Mann.

Footnotes to the essays, p.124–31. Selected bibliography, p.248–49. Index of proper names and places, p.250–51.

S17 Haskell, Francis. Rediscoveries in art: some aspects of taste, fashion, and collecting in England and France. Rev. repr. Ithaca, Cornell Univ. Pr., 1980. 234p. il. (The Wrightsman lectures, no.7)

1st ed., 1976.

Though chiefly an exploration of aesthetics from the late 18th to the late 19th centuries, this work includes substantial discussion of art dealers, connoisseurs, collectors, and critical reaction during the period. Retains the accessible style of a lecture series. Together with useful notes and bibliography it serves as a good introduction to the topic. This ed. contains corrections, updated references, and some additional evidence in support of the author's arguments.

Notes, p.[181]–213. Books and articles consulted, p.[214]–25. Index, p.[230]–34.

S18 Holst, Niels von. Creators, collectors and connoisseurs: the anatomy of artistic taste from antiquity to the present day. Introd. by Herbert Read. Trans. by Brian Battershaw. N.Y., Putnam's, 1967. 400p. il. (part col.)

Trans. and rev. ed. of Künstler, Sammler, Publikum. [Darmstadt], Luchterhand, [1960].

Textbook-like survey of the development of the aesthetics of collecting and the history of "taste," suitable for the general or special interest reader. The notes, bibliography, and index as well as an expanded text are unique features of the English translation.

Selective contents: The theme; (1) Antiquity to the middle ages; (2) The fifteenth and sixteenth centuries; (3) The age of the baroque; (4) The age of enlightenment; (5) The nineteenth century; (6) From "fin de siècle" to modern times.

Notes on the text, p.368–80. Bibliography, p.381–85. Index, p.394–400.

S19 Jacobson, Marjory. Art and business: new strategies for corporate collecting. [London], Thames and Hudson, 1993. 224p. il. (part col.)

Selection of case studies of contemporary corporate patronage and sponsorship programs in the United States, Germany, France, Italy, and Japan. Each project is documented in a separate section that includes a narrative description, history, interviews, notes, and ample, high-quality color and black-and-white photographs. A lively introduction to a topic on which relatively little has been published in monographic form.

Contents: (1) Introduction: redefining art in business; (2) Maecenas, mécénat, Mäzenatentum: the new breed of business patron; (3) The pantheon: fruits of professional commitment; (4) The new museums of the magnates: purpose and performance; (5) The corporate Kunsthallen: exhibitions and their influence; (6) Collaborations: joint ventures for public places; (7) Beyond the sculpture gardens of the tycoons: art out of doors; (8) Not just another canvas on the wall: character and quality in art at the office; (9) Entrepreneurship and culture: expanding the company benefits package; (10) Launching an art program: a practical guide.

Notes, p.207–16. Select bibliography, p.217–20. Index, p.222–24.

S20 Koch, Georg Friedrich. Die Kunstausstellung: ihre Geschichte von den Anfängen bis zum Ausgang des 18. Jahrhunderts. Berlin, de Gruyter, 1967. vii, 324p. il., plates.

A scholarly examination of the evolution of the exhibition of art works in western Europe from antiquity to the 19th century. The substantial bibliography is strong in 19th- and early 20th-century literature.

Selective contents: (I) Zur Begriffsbestimmung; (II) Vor- und Frühformen der Kunstausstellung; (III) Die Verkaufsausstellung des 15. bis 17. Jahrhunderts; (IV) Die Anfänge der autonomen Ausstellungsformen in Italien; (V) Die Académie Royale de Peinture et Sculpture und das Ausstellungsleben während des 17. und 18. Jahrhunderts in Paris; (VI) Die Ausbreitung des akademischen Ausstellungswesens während des 18. Jahrhunderts in Europa; (VII) Der Übergang zum 19. Jahrhundert.

Includes bibliographical references. Literaturverzeichnis, p.[277]–97. Register, p.[298]–317.

S21 Levey, Michael. Painting at court. N.Y., New York Univ. Pr., 1971. 229p. il. (part col.) (The Wrightsman lectures, no.5)

Engaging survey of royal and papal patronage from the 14th to the 19th century based on a series of lectures given at the Metropolitan Museum of Art in 1968. A good introduction for the general reader.

Contents: (1) The court of heaven; (2) Courts of earth; (3) Propaganda for the prince; (4) The courtier-artist; (5) A hero to his painters; (6) At home at court.

Notes, p.217–21. Index of persons, p.227–[229].

S22 Macrocosmos in Microcosmo: die Welt in der Stube: zur Geschichte des Sammelns 1450–1800. Hrsg. von Andreas Grote. Opladen, Leske + Budrich, 1994. 966p. il. (Berliner Schriften zur Museumskunde, Bd.10)

42 essays, papers, and lectures presented at the Institüt für Museumskunde in Berlin, 1990, at an international conference held to explore the nature of collecting in historical and social contexts. Though a number of the essays treat the scientific and ethnographic aspects of early collections, the role of art collecting is emphasized throughout. Includes a list of contributors, with addresses. Each paper is followed by scholarly notes and references.

Selective contents: (I) Annäherungen: Das Sammeln der Erkenntnis, von Reinhard Brandt; Die besondern Eigenschaften der "Kunstkammer," von Arthur MacGregor; Sammlungen—eine historische Typologie, von Krzysztof Pomian; (II) Die Zeit von 1450 bis 1630: Das Sammeln und die "ars memorie," von Lina Bolzoni; Die Sammlung—Nutzbarmachung und Funktion, von Giuseppe Olmi; Die Medici. Ikonographische Propädeutik zu einer fürstlichen Sammlung, von Andreas Grote; Kunstkammern der Spätrenaissance zwischen Kuriosität und Wissenschaft, von Brigitte Hoppel; Eine private fürstliche Kunstkammer: Rosenberg 1718/Gottorf 1694, von Mogens Bencard; Die Sammlung des Kardinals Alessandro Farnese (1530–1589) als Stellvertreterin für das antike Rom, von Christina Riebesell; Zur Stellung des sakralen Bildes in der neuzeitlichen Kunstsammlung, Die "Blumenkranzmadonna" in den "Cabinets d'Amateurs," von Victor I. Stoichita; (III) Die Zeit von 1630 bis 1750: Neue Meisterschaft einer neuen Kultur - Forschung und Sammeltätigkeit im Rom der Barberini, von Francesco Solinas; "Mundus combinatus" und "ars combinatoria" als geistesgeschichtlicher Hintergrund des Museum Kircherianum in Rom, von Thomas Leinkauf; Philipp Hainhofer - Seine Kunstkammer und seine Kunstschranke, von Hans-Olof Boström; Das Linck'sche Naturalien- und Kunstkabinett aus Leipzig jetzt in Waldenburg (Sachsen), von Harry Beyrich; Sammlungsgegenstände aus Natur und Technik: der Kunstkammer des Ernst I. von Sachsen-Gotha-Altenberg (1640–1675), von Wolfgang Zimmerman; (IV) Die Zeit von 1750 bis 1800: Die Kunstkammer der Bürgerbibliothek in der Wasserkirche in Zürich. Eine Fallstudie zur Gelehrten Gesellschaft als Sammlerin, von Christine Barraud Wiener and Peter Jezler; Museen im Zeichen der Französischen Revolution: vom evolutionären zur revolutionären Museum; Von der fürstlichen Sammlung zum öffentlichen Museum, von Cornelius Steckner; Zur Geschichte des deutschen Kunstmuseums, von James J. Sheehan; Wegwerfgesellschaft und Bewahrungskultur, von Odo Marquand.

Literaturverzeichnis, p.[921]–33. Personenregister, p.[934]–61.

S23 Molfino, Alessandra Mottola. Il libro dei musei. Torino, Allemandi, 1991. 271p. il (Archivi del collezionismo)

An overview of European museums from their inception to the contemporary period including architectural analyses of the buildings that house them. The author explores the thesis that the art museum is a "'documento globale' (Gesamtkunstwerk) della storia della società."—*Chap.1.* Many good quality illustrations, both black-and-white and color.

Contents: (1) La forma museo; (2) I musei della ragione; (3) I musei della colpa; (4) Collezionismo e musei; (5) Museo "opera chiusa"; (6) Museologia vs museografia; (7) Il museo prossimo venturo; (8) Musei Americani vs musei Europei; (9) I nuovi musei.

Includes bibliographical references and bibliographies at ends of chapters. Indice dei nomi, p.[263]–67. Indice dei luoghi, p.[268]–70.

S24 The origins of museums: the cabinet of curiosities in sixteenth- and seventeenth-century Europe. Ed. by Oliver Impey and Arthur MacGregor. Oxford, Clarendon, 1985. xiii, 335p. il., plates. (Repr. 1986, 1987).

One of the first and best publications to gather together scholarly investigations into the history of early collections throughout Europe. Contains 33 papers presented at a symposium honoring the tercentenary of the Ashmolean Museum. A key work for anyone beginning research on this subject.

Selective contents: (1) Science - Honour - Metaphor: Italian cabinets of the sixteenth and seventeenth centuries, by Giuseppe Olmi; (3) Towards a history of collecting in Milan in the late Renaissance and Baroque periods, by Antonio Aimi, Vicenzo de Michele, and Alessandro Morandotti; (4) The collection of Archduke Ferdinand II at Schloss Ambras: its purpose, composition, and evolution, by Elisabeth Scheicher; (5) The Hapsburg collections in Vienna during the seventeenth century, by Rudolf Distelberger; (6) The collection of Rudolf II at Prague: cabinet of curiosities or scientific museum?, by Eliška Fučíková; (7) "His majesty's cabinet" and Peter I's Kunstkammer, by Oleg Neverov; (8) The Basle cabinets of art and curiosities in the sixteenth and seventeenth centuries, by Hans Christoph Ackermann; (9) Elector Augustus's Kunstkammer: an analysis of the inventory of 1587, by Joachim Menzhausen; (10) The Munich Kunstkammer, 1565–1807, by Lorenz Seelig; (11) Philipp Hainhofer and Gustavus Adolphus's Kunstschrank in Uppsala, by Hans-Olof Boström; (12) The Kunstkammer of the Hessian Landgraves in Kassel, by Franz Adrian Dreier; (13) The Brandenburg Kunstkammer in Berlin, by Christian Theuerkauff; (14) Early Dutch cabinets of curiosities, by Th.H. Lunsingh Scheurleer; (16) From the royal Kunstkammer to the modern museums of Copenhagen, by Bente Gundestrup; (17) Some notes on Spanish Baroque collectors, by Ronald Lightbown; (18) The cabinet of curiosities in seventeenth century Britain, by Arthur MacGregor; (20) Some cabinets of curiosities in European academic institutions, by William Schupbach; (23) "Curiosities to adorn cabinets and gardens," by John Dixon Hunt; (26) Greek and Roman antiquities in the seventeenth century, by Michael Vickers; (29) African material in early collections, by Ezio Bassani and Malcolm McLeod; (30) Exotica from Islam, by Julian Raby; (31) The early China trade, by John Ayers; (32) Japan: trade and collecting in seventeenth-century Europe, by Oliver Impey; (33) Indian art and artefacts in early European collecting, by Roger Skelton.

Notes at ends of chapters. Bibliography, p.[281]–312. Index, p.[313]–35.

S25 Patronage in the Renaissance. Ed. by Guy Fitch Lytle and Stephen Orgel. Princeton, Princeton Univ. Pr., 1981. xiv, 389p. il. (Folger Institute essays)

Collection of papers given at a Folger Institute Symposium (1977) together with other contributions on related topics. Coverage of English patronage extends to the court of Charles I.

Selective contents: (1) Patronage in the Renaissance: an exploratory approach, by Werner L. Gundersheimer; (2) Court patronage and government policy: the Jacobean dilemma, by Linda Levy Peck; (3) Corruption and the moral boundaries of patronage in the Renaissance, by Robert Harding; (4) Religion and the lay patron in Reformation England, by Guy Fitch Lytle; (5) Henry VII and the origins of Tudor patronage, by Gordon Kipling; (6) The political failure of Stuart cultural patronage, by Malcolm Smuts; (12) Artists, patrons, and advisors in the Italian Renaissance, by Charles Hope; (13) The birth of "artistic license": the dissatisfied patron in the early Renaissance, by H. W. Janson; (14) Patterns of preference; patronage of sixteenth-century architects by the Venetian patriciate, by Douglas Lewis.

Bibliographic note, p.381–82. Index, p. 383–89.

S26 Pomian, Krzysztof. Collectors and curiosities: Paris and Venice, 1500–1800. Trans. by Elizabeth Wiles-Portier. [Cambridge, Eng.], Polity Pr., 1990. 348p.

Trans. of Collectionneurs, amateurs et curieux. Paris, Gallimard, 1987. Also published in Italian as Collezionisti, amatori e curiosi: Parigi-Venezia, XVI–XVIII sécolo. Milano, Saggiatore, 1989.

A collection of previously published essays on the history and meaning of collecting. In this, as well as his other works, the author "has made a convincing case for the proposition that we need a history of collecting that is quite distinct, in its analytic and methodological terms, from the history of art."—*Review*, Art bulletin, v.73, no.4, Dec. 1991, p.688.

Selective contents: (1) The collection between the visible and the invisible; (2) The age of curiosity; (3) Collections in Venetia in the heyday of curiosity; (4) Medals/shells = Erudition/philosophy; (5) Dealers, connoisseurs and enthusiasts in eighteenth century Paris; (6) Maffei and Caylus; (7) Collectors, naturalists and antiquarians in the Venetian Republic of the eighteenth century; (8) Private collections, public museums.

Notes, p.[276]–333. Index, p.[334]–48.

S27 Sachs, Hannelore. Sammler und Mäzene: zur Entwicklung des Kunstsammelns von der Antike bis zur Gegenwart. Leipzig, Koehler & Amelang, [1971]. [198]p. il.

An early survey of the rise of art as a commodity and patterns of collecting from antiquity to the 20th century. The bibliography is very strong in early 20th-century literature on collecting and patronage.

Selective contents: Einleitung; Antike und Mittelalter; Die italienische Renaissance; Erste deutsche Kunstsammler; Fürstliche Kunstkammern; Das Zeitalter des Absolutismus; Künstler als Sammler; Kunstfreunde der Goethezeit; Kunstkäufe der Grossbourgeoisie um die Jahrhundertwende; Das Geschäft mit der Kunst—die Liebe zur Kunst.

Literatur, p.181–87. Register, p.192–[98].

S28 Scarpa Sonino, Annalisa. Cabinet d'amateur: le grandi collezioni d'arte nei dipinti dal XVII al XIX sécolo. Milano, Berenice, 1992. 175p. il. (part col.) (Il mondo delle forme)

Scholarly study and catalog of historical and imaginary "painting cabinets," as depicted in the works of artists such as Teniers the Younger and Frans Francken II. The catalog contains a biographical essay on each artist and a thorough analysis of each painting included. Published in large-format and very well-illustrated.

Includes bibliographical references. Bibliografia, p.167–73.

S29 Schlosser, Julius, Ritter von. Die Kunst- und Wunderkammern der Spätrenaissance: ein Beitrag zur Geschichte des Sammelwesens. 2. durch. und verm. Ausg. Braunschweig, Klinkhardt & Biermann, 1978. vii, 268p. il.

1st ed.: Leipzig, Klinkhardt & Biermann, 1908 (Monographien des Kunstgewerbes, n.F. XI) Also published in Italian as Raccolte d'arte e di meraviglie del tardo Rinascimento. Firenze, Sansoni, 1974.

A classic early work examining Renaissance collecting patterns and the content of collections. Begins with an historical overview of collecting in western Europe and continues with descriptions of individual collectors emphasizing the members of the Hapsburg royal family and related collections. The last chapter surveys collecting phenomena in Italy, France, England, and the Netherlands. The 2d ed. includes Schlosser's own additions and corrections, as well as the publisher's updated bibliography, index, additions and revisions, and newly produced illustrations.

Selective contents: Vorgeschichte der Kunst- und Wunderkammern; Die Kunst- und Wunderkammern; Die kirchlichen Kunst- und Wunderkammern; Fernere Entwicklung des Sammelwesens.

Anmerkungen, p.242–54. Literaturverzeichnis, p.255–59. Namen- und Sachregister, p.261–68.

S30 Studies in the fine arts: art patronage. Ann Arbor, UMI Research Pr., 1983– . 6v. il.

Series of monographs on aspects of art patronage, most based on dissertations.

Contents: (1) Severini, Lois. The architecture of finance: early Wall Street (1983); (2) Weisz, Jean S. Pittura e misericordia: the oratory of S. Giovanni Decollato in Rome (1984); (3) Muller, Sheila D. Charity in the Dutch Republic: pictures of rich and poor for charitable institutions (1985); (4) Stone-Ferrier, Linda A. Images of textiles: the weave of seventeenth-century Dutch art and society (1985); (5) never published; (6) King, Lyndel Saunders. The industrialization of taste: Victorian England and the Art Union of London (1985).

S31 Taylor, Francis Henry. The taste of angels, a history of art collecting from Rameses to Napoleon. Boston,

Little, Brown, 1948. xxx, 661p. il. (part col.), plates, geneal., tables.

Italian ed.: Artisti, principi e mercanti; storia del collezionismo da Ramsete a Napoleone. [Turin], Einaudi, 1954.

One of the first general works written in English, still useful for an initial approach to the subject. Taylor's style is readable, the amount of material covered is impressive, and many important early published sources are mentioned in the text and included in the bibliography. Three appendices contain short essays on monetary values, ancient collections in Egypt, and a translation of an extract from Sansovino's Venetia, città nobilissima e singolare (1581). Minimally illustrated.

Bibliography, p.[619]–40. Index, p.[643]–61.

S32 Thurn, Hans Peter. Der Kunsthändler: Wandlungen eines Berufes. München, Hirmer, 1994. 296p. il., facsims., ports.

History of the profession of art dealing from antiquity to the present. Includes discussion of historic and modern trends in the art market.

Contents: Hermes und seine ersten Kollegen; Vom Wanderhändeler zum Hofleiferanten; Die bürgerliche Kunsthandel entsteht; Kunstverkauf als ästhetische Aufklärung; Ein Beruf gewinnt Kontur; Krisen, Technik, neue Märkte; Im Kampf für die junge Kunst; Modernisierung und Politisierung; Zwischen Anpassung und Widerstand; Der amerikanische Weg zum Markt; Kunsthandel im "Wiederaufbau"; Staatskommerz oder Messekunst?; Handel aus Passion und Profession.

Anmerkungen, p.259–75. Literatur, p.276–85. Personenregister, p.286–96.

S33 Verzamelen: van rariteitenkabinet tot kunstmuseum. Ed. by Ellinoor Bergvelt . . . [et al.] Heerlen, Gaade Houten for Open Universiteit, 1993. 491p. il., 144 col. plates.

17 substantial essays by Dutch and international scholars focus on collectors and collections in the Germanic countries of northern Europe with an emphasis on how early collections evolved to the modern notion of the art museum. Very well illustrated throughout. The table of contents is translated in Journal of the history of collections, v.6, no.2, 1994, p.225.

Selective contents: De vorstelijke Kunst- und Wunderkammer in de zestiende en zeventiende eeuw: (1) De vorstelijke Kunst- und Wunderkammer, van Elisabeth Scheicher; (2) Twee vorstelijke verzamelingen: van Ferdinand II en Rudolf II, van Elisabeth Scheicher; (3) Samuel Quicchebergs "Inscriptiones": de encyclopedische verzameling als hulpmiddel voor de wetenschap, van Dirk Jacob Jansen. Verzamelingen in Italie en de Nederlanden: (4) Italiaanse verzamelingen van de late middeleeuwen tot de zeventiende eeuw, van Giuseppe Olmi; (5) Noordnederlandse verzamelingen in de zeventiende eeuw, van Rudolf van Gelder; (6) Galerij en kabinet, vorst en burger. Schilderijencollecties in de Nederlanden, van Jaap van der Veen; (7) Institutionele verzamelingen in de tijd van de wetenschappelijke revolutie (1600–1750), van K. van Berkel; (11) Verzamelingen van oudheden van 1750 tot heden, van Daniela Gallo; De negentiende eeuw; (12) Het Alte Museum te Berlin. Wijzigingen in het museumconcept omstreeks 1800, van Elsa van Wezel; (13) Tussen geschiedenis en kunst. Nederlandse nationale kunstmusea in de negentiende eeuw, van Ellinoor Bergvelt; (14) Kunstnijverheidsmusea, van Jet Pijzel-Dommisse. De twintigste eeuw; (15) Stichters en schenkers. Particuliere verzamelaars en openbare kunstmusea in Europa en de Verenigde Staten, van Bram Kempers; (16) De herinrichting van Duitse musea in de Weimarrepubliek, van Monika Flacke; (17) Presentatie na 1945. De museale opstelling als demonstratie van een standpunt, van Fieke Konijn.

Gebruikte literatuur, p.469–79. Register: personen en zaken, p.480–87, galerijen, musea et tentoonstellingsruimten per plaats, p.487–89. Over de auteurs, p.490.

S34 Warnke, Martin. The court artist: on the ancestry of the modern artist. Trans. by David McLintock. N.Y., Cambridge Univ. Pr., 1993. xx, 299p.

Trans. of Hofkünstler: zur Vorgeschichte des modernen Kunstlers. Köln, Dumont, 1985.

In this vol. the author, building on nearly twenty years of research and publication, "attempts to describe the ways in which art and artists were received at the courts of western Europe from early modern times and argues that these contacts were ultimately responsible for the fact that we look upon art as a higher spiritual or intellectual faculty."—*Introd.*

Contents: Part 1: The artist between city and court: (1) Stages of mutual influence, the beginnings of organized court art and their consequences, the divorce between the civic and courtly spheres, Italian courts and city republics around 1400, the theoretical dimension, the appointment of Renaissance artists to positions at court, continued tension between city and court; (2) Artistic agents, city administrators, merchants, humanists, artists, applications for court appointments, initiatives emanating from the courts. Part 2: Artists at court: (3) The position of artists at court, admission to the court family, forms of remuneration: securing a livelihood, forms of remuneration: regular salaries, the work of art without price, The conferment of titles, list of artists granted titles up to 1800; (4) Offices and functions, public building projects: the artistic director, public monuments: the court sculptor, artistic relations between the courts: the court painter, the court portrait: the "counterfeiter," art and artists in the prince's private domain. A look back in anger: dependence and freedom at court.

Includes bibliographical references. Bibliography, p.261–83. Index, p.287–99.

S35 Women and art in early modern Europe: patrons, collectors, and connoisseurs. Ed. by Cynthia Lawrence. University Park, Pa. State Univ. Pr., 1997. viii, 263p. il.

Twelve papers selected from the Temple University symposium, Matronage: women as patrons and collectors of art, 1300–1800 (1990). These studies reflect "the larger impulse in the field of art history to recover the history of women's involvement with art. While there has been considerable interest in female artists during the past two decades, there has not been a commensurate expression about the important contributions that women have made to artistic culture as patrons, collectors, or connoisseurs."—*Introd.* Scholarly notes and references throughout.

Contents: Jeanne d'Evreux as a founder of chapels: patronage and public piety, by Carla Lord; Margaret of Austria's funerary complex at Brou: conjugal love, political ambition, or personal glory?, by Alexandra Carpino; A Ferrarese lady and a Mantuan Marchesa: the art and antiquities collections of Isabella d'Este Gonzaga (1474–1539), by Clifford M. Brown; An instance of feminine patronage in the Medici court of sixteenth century Florence: the chapel of Eleonora da Toledo in the Palazzo Vecchio, by Carolyn Smith; The ideal queenly patron of the Renaissance: Catherine de' Medici defining herself or defined by others?, by Sheila ffolliot; Wife in the English country house: gender and meaning of style in early modern England, by Alice T. Friedman; Imagining images of powerful women: Maria de' Medici's patronage of art and architecture, by Geraldine A. Johnson; Spiritual philanthropists: women as convent patrons in seicento Rome, by Marilyn R. Dunn; An eighteenth-century English Artemesia: Sarah Churchill and the invention of the Blenheim Memorials, by Kathleen Szpila; Jeanne-Baptiste d'Albert de Luynes, Comtesse de Verrue (1670–1736), by Cynthia Lawrence and Magdalena Kasman; The extinction and survival of the Medici: Anna Maria Luisa de' Medici and the family pact of 1737, by Elena Ciletti; An unmarried woman: Mary Edwards, William Hogarth, and a case of eighteenth century British patronage, by Nadia Tscherny.

Selected bibliograpy, p.[255]–259.

S36 Wunderkammer des Abendlandes: Museum und Sammlung im Spiegel der Zeit. Bonn, Kunst- und Ausstellungshalle der Bundesrepublik Deutschland, 1994. 224p. il. (part col.)

Catalog published to accompany a major exhibition, Kunst- und Ausstellungshalle der Bundesrepublik Deutschland, Bonn (1994). Explores the "cabinet of curiosities" as the precursor to the modern museum in the western world. Eight chapters survey the typology of historical "cabinets" and 13 essays cover specific facets of collecting and types of objects. Good quality color illustrations.

Selective contents: (IX) Das Museum: die Quintessenz Europas, von Krzysztof Pomian; (X) Einen eigenwillige Idee für eine neue Art, Vorführungen zu gestalten, von G. W. von Leibniz; (XI) Der kuriose, der klassifizierende und der biologische Blick, von J. E. Kristensen; (XII) Kunst-und Wunderkammern: Konturen eines unvollendbaren Projektes, von Hans Holländer; (XIII) Schloss Skokloster - ein Gedächtnistheater, von Arne Losman; (XIV) Opfer für einen Sammler, von Sverker Sörlin; (XV) Das goldene Zeitalter der Museen, von Jørgen Jensen; (XVI) Sir John Soane's Museum: das Interieur als Welttheater, von Carsten Thau; (XVII) Drei Thesen über die Welt im ethnographischen Museum, von Inger Sjørslev; (XVIII) Trines Locke und die Laube oder: Das imaginäre Museum auf neuen Abenteueren, von Frederik Stjernfelt; (XIX) Der Tanzplatz der Dinge, von Arnfinn Bø-Rygg; (XX) Museum und Enzyklopädie, von Walter Grasskamp; (XXI) Von der Liebe zu den Dingen, von Marie-Louise von Plessen.

Notes at ends of chapters. Literatur, p.206–07. Allgemeine Literatur, p.208–22.

SEE ALSO: Journal of the history of collections (GLAH 2:Q231).

WESTERN COUNTRIES

France

S37 Berger, Robert W. A royal passion: Louis XIV as patron of architecture. N.Y., Cambridge Univ. Pr., 1994. xix, 204p. il., maps, plans, ports.

In-depth, accessible survey of the royal architecture of Louis XIV and his extensive role as a patron of building. Arranged chronologically by project. Black-and-white illustrations include many plans and contemporary engravings.

Contents: (1) Introduction; (2) The Regency (1643–1661); (3) The early years of personal rule: the King and Colbert (1661–1671); (4) The Louvre and Tuileries; (5) A building for the sciences: the Observatoire; (6) Versailles - I (1661–1677); (7) Paris - I; (8) A palace for a mistress: the Chateau of Clagny and the rise of Jules Hardouin-Mansart; (9) The Invalides; (10) Versailles - II (1678–1715); (11) Marly; (12) Paris - II; (13) Vauban and the architecture of war; (14) Le Roi-Architecte; (15) Absolutism and architecture; (16) Epilogue: the old King in triumph and sorrow.

Glossary, p.194–95. Bibliographical guide, p.196–200. Index, p.201–04.

S38 Lord, Carla. Royal French patronage of art in the fourteenth century: an annotated bibliography. Boston, Hall, 1985. xxiv, 215p. (Reference publication in art history)

Fully annotated bibliography that brings together primary archival sources as well as published documents from the 17th century to 1980, with addenda covering 1981–1984. Includes references to periodical literature and multi-author works. Divided into sections on history and documentation, sites and monuments, and French monarchs. Each section is well-organized, containing numerous detailed subdivisions.

Author index, p.197–205. Subject index, p.207–15.

S39 Schnapper, Antoine. Collections et collectionneurs dans la France du XVIIe siècle. Paris, Flammarion, 1988–1994. 2v. il. (Art, histoire, société)

Thorough study of the types of objects collected in France before the Enlightenment and their meanings and values, with a particular interest in the differences between art and "curiosities." "The fascination and importance of Schnapper's book lies in its demonstration that distinctions of this kind are particularly difficult to make in the seventeenth century. Schnapper should not be missed by anyone interested in the new frontiers being opened by studies of collecting."—*Review*, New York review of books, v.39, no.3, Jan.

30, 1992, p.29. Illustrations, though black-and-white, are of good quality and complementary to the text.

Selective contents: Vol.I: Le géant, la licorne et la tulipe: Histoire et histoire naturelle: (I) La pierre d'aigle et la rose de Jéricho; (II) Du colibri aux géants; (III) Bijoux savants; (IV) Curieux d'histoire et d'histoire naturelle; (V) Histoire et histoire naturelle. Vol. II: Curieux du Grand Siècle: oeuvres d'art: (I) Les oeuvres; (II) Le tableau et son prix; (III) Les marchands; (IV) Au temps du Marie de Médicis et de Richelieu; (V) La génération de 1630; (VI) Curieux ministres; (VII) Clients et amateurs de Poussin (1635–1665); (VIII) Curieux de papier; (IX) Les débuts de la collection de Louis XIV; (X) Le cabinet du roi à Paris (1660–1681); (XI) Louis XIV à Versailles; (XII) Princes et ministres; (XIII) Gens de la cour et de la ville.

Bibliographie, v.1, p.315–51, v.2, p.429–61. Index, v.1, p.401–11, v.2, p.561–71.

SEE ALSO: L'age d'or du mécénat (1598–1661) (GLAH 2:S5); Meiss, French painting in the time of Jean De Berry (GLAH 1:M182–184).

Germany and Austria

S40 Calov, Gudrun. Museen und Sammler des 19. Jahrhunderts in Deutschland. Berlin, De Gruyter, [1969]. 196p. il., ports. (Museumskunde, Bd.38, Heft 1–3)

Detailed and well-documented history of the development of private collections and museums in Germany. Includes substantial background on 18th-century precedents.

Selective contents: (I) Die Entwicklung des Kunstsammelns in der Epoche der Aufklärung und der französischen Revolution: (1) Die Entwicklung des Kunstsammelns in England und Frankreich; (2) Vorstufen in Deutschland; (3) Die Kunstsammlungen und Kunstkabinette in den Städten von der 2. Hälfte des 18. Jh. bis zum Beginn des 19. Jh.; (4) Die Situationen der Kunstsammlungen in Deutschland zur Zeit der französischen Besetzung und der Befreiungskriege; (II) Das Interesse an exotischen Objekten, ethnographische Gegenstände in der Kabinetten; (III) Die Wiederentdeckung der "altdeutschen" Kunst: (1) Die Galerie der Bruder Sulpiz und Melchoir Boisserée; (2) "Altdeutsches" Kunstgut in den rheinischen Sammlungen; (3) "Altdeutsche" Sammelmode im 18. Jh.; (4) Die Beziehungen der Brüder Boisserée zu anderen Sammlern; (5) Glasmalerei und Glasgemäldesammlungen; (6) Skulpturen und kunsthandwerkliche kirchliche Gebrauchsgegenstände; (IV) Die Wiederentdeckung der frühen italienischen Malerei; (V) Neue Antikenbegeisterung in den ersten Jahrzehnten des 19. Jh.: (1) Die Vermittlertätigkeit der Künstler, Gelehrten und Diplomaten; (2) Private Antikensammlungen; (3) Einige Bemerkungen zu Sammlungen von Gemmen und Gemmenabdrücken; (VI) Die universale Sammlung: (1) Kulturgeschichtliche Altertümer und Steindenkmale; (2) Goethes Sammlungen; (3) P. Ch. W. Beuth; (4) Vermächtnisse und Stiftungen von Sammlungen, die das Kunstgut verschiedener Epochen beinhalten; (VII) Die nationalen Bestrebungen in Deutschland: (1) Museumsgründungen als Provinzialmuseen mit nationalem Charakter; (2) Die nationalen Bestrebungen in den Nachbarländern; (3) Das Germanische National Museum in Nürnberg; (4) Die Grundung von Geschichts- und Altetumsverein; (5) Die Kulturgeschichtlichen- und Provinzialmuseen; (6) Die Entstehung der Kunstvereine; (7) Die Nationalgalerie in Berlin; (VIII) Die Sammlungen zeitgenössicher Malerei; (IX) Die Kunstgewerblichen Sammlungen; (X) Tendenzen im Sammlertum.

Literaturverzeichnis, p.176–93. Register, p.194–96.

S41 Friedrich der Grosse, Sammler und Mäzen. Hrsg. von Johann Georg Prinz von Hohenzollern. Mit Beitr. von Johan Georg Prinz von Hohenzollern . . . [et al.] München, Hirmer, 1992. 423p. il. (part col.), geneal. tables, music, plans, ports.

Catalog of the exhibition, Kunsthalle der Hypokulturstiftung, Munich (1992–93). Beautifully produced catalog comprised of two introductory essays describing Frederick the Great's collecting and patronage in the context of German princely traditions followed by detailed catalog entries for 212 objects arranged by media. Each medium is introduced by a shorter descriptive essay.

Selective contents: Fürstliches Sammeln, von Johann Georg Prinz von Hohenzollern; Friedrich der Grosse und Kurbayern, von Hubert Glaser; Architektur, von Hans-Joachim Giersberg; Skulpturen, von Huberta Heres; Gemälde und Miniaturen, von Helmut Börsch-Supan; Prunk-Tabatièren, von Winfried Baer; Silber - Porzellan, von Winfried Baer and Christiane Keisch; Möbel, von Jutta Nicht; Bibliothek - Musik von Hans-Joachim Giersberg and Wolfgang Goldhan; Stöcke - Waffen - Uniform, von Winfried Baer; Medaillen und Münzen, von Johann Georg Prinz von Hohenzollern; Nachleben, von Martin Schawe.

Literatur, p.410–16. Zeittafel, p.417–21. Stammbaum des preussischen Königshauses, p.422–23.

S42 Heres, Gerald. Dresdener Kunstsammlungen im 18. Jahrhundert. Leipzig, Seemann, 1991. 227p. il. (part col.), plans, ports.

Traces the evolution of royal collections in Dresden from princely cabinets to museums, including the design and construction of exhibition buildings and spaces. Very good illustrations including many ground plans. "This thoroughly researched book will remain a valuable scholars' handbook for years to come."—*Review*, Journal of the history of collections, v.4, no.1, 1992, p.147.

Selective contents: August der Starke und der Aufbau der Dresdener Sammlungen, 1694–1733; Stagnation und Reorganisation: die Dresdener Sammlungen unter August III, 1733–1763; Die Dresdener Sammlungen im Zeitalter der Aufklärung und des Klassizismus, 1763–1794.

Anmerkungen, p.209–21. Literaturverzeichnis, p.222–25. Register, p.226–27.

S43 Sammler, Stifter und Museen: Kunstforderung in Deutschland im 19. und 20. Jahrhundert. Köln, Bohlau, 1993. 337p. il., facsims., ports.

Collection of scholarly essays on personal and corporate collecting patterns and patronage in Germany. Published as the proceedings of a joint symposium, "Kunst als Geschichte," held at the Werner-Reimers-Stiftung, Bad Homburg, and the Institute for Avanced Studies, Princeton (1990–91).

Contents: Mäzene, Sammler und Museen—Problematisches zur Einleitung, von Ekkehard Mai and Peter Paret; Sammlertum, Mäzenatentum und staatliche Kunstförderung in Geschichte und Gegenwart—aus verfassungsrechtlicher Sicht, von Frank Fechner; Sammler und Sammlungen in der frühen Neuzeit, von Hans-Ulrich Thamer; "Wallrafs Chaos" (Goethe)—Städels Stiftung, von Ekkehard Mai; Privatvergnügen oder Staatsaufgabe? Monarchisches Sammeln und Museum, 1800–1914, von Wolfgang Hardtwig; Die Einbürgerung der Kunst: Korporative Kunstförderung im 19. Jahrhundert von Walter Grasskamp; Graf Adolf Friedrich von Schack und seine Galerie: Anmerkungen zur Münchner Sammlungsgeschichte, von Andrea Pophanken; Der deutsche Kunstmarkt, 1840–1923: Integration, Veränderung, Wachstum, von Robin Lenman; Wilhelm Bode und seine Sammler, von Thomas W. Gaehtgens; Bemerkungen zu den Thema: Jüdische Kunstsammler, Stifter, und Kunsthändler, von Peter Paret; Kunst für Alle: Das Volk als Förderer der Kunst von Beth Irwin Lewis; Alfred Lichtwark und die "Gymnastik der Sammeltätigkeit," von Henrike Junge; Museen und die Zeitgenössische Kunst in der Weimarer Republik, von Vernon L. Lidtke; Eduard Arnhold, Mäzen und Freund des Kunstreferats der Kulturabteilung des Auswärtigen Amts im Kaiserrich und in der Weimarer Republik, von Kurt Duwell; Das Pseudomäzenatentum Adolf Hitlers, von Winfried Nerdiger; "Bausteine" für die Museen nach 1945: Die Sammlungen Haubrich—Sprengel—Reemtsma, von Ingrid Severin; Künstler als Mäzene: Zwei Beispiele privaten Stiftertums zwischen Vergangenheitspflege und Zukunftssicherung, von Peter Springer.

Ausgewählte und abgekürzt zitierte Literatur, p.[321]–32. Kurzbiographie der Autoren, p.[333]–37.

S44 Trevor-Roper, Hugh. Princes and artists: patronage and ideology at four Hapsburg courts, 1517–1633. N.Y., Thames and Hudson, 1991. 159p. il.

1st ed. N.Y., Harper and Row, 1976.

Originally a series of lectures, this study focuses on the Hapsburgs' devotion to the arts. Examines the influence of historical and ideological crises on patronage and the impact of Hapsburgian patronage on successive courts. This ed. contains a revised preface.

Contents: (1) Charles V and the failure of humanism; (2) Philip II and the anti-Reformation; (3) Rudolf II in Prague; (4) The Archdukes and Rubens.

Bibliographical notes, p.153–56. Notes on the text, p.156–58. Index, p.159–[160].

Great Britain and Ireland

S45 Art and patronage in the Caroline courts: essays in honor of Sir Oliver Millar. Ed. by David Howarth. [Cambridge, Eng.], Cambridge Univ. Pr., [1993]. xvii, 303p. il.

Collection of studies, chiefly by British scholars, published to honor Sir Oliver Millar, Surveyor Emeritus of the Queen's Pictures. Draws its theme from Millar's lifelong interest in Stuart culture and 17th-century English art. Focuses on painting, especially portraiture, but includes sculpture, and architecture. Modestly illustrated.

Contents: (1) Van Dyck and George Gage, by Susan Barnes; (2) Patrons and collectors of Dutch painting in Britain during the reign of William and Mary, by Christopher Brown; (3) Foreigners at court: Holbein, Van Dyck and the Painter-Stainers Company, by Susan Foister; (4) The etchings of John Evelyn, by Anthony Griffiths; (5) The politics of Inigo Jones, by David Howarth; (6) The Standard Bearer: Van Dyck's portrayal of Sir Edmund Verney, by Michael Jaffé; (7) Sir Peter Lely and Sir Ralph Bankes, by Alastair Laing; (8) Isaac Besnier, sculptor to Charles I and his work for court patrons, c1624–1634, by Ronald Lightbown; (9) Laudian literature and the interpretation of Caroline churches in London, by John Newman; (10) Clarendon and the art of prose portraiture in the age of Charles II, by Richard Ollard; (11) The great picture of Lady Anne Clifford, by Graham Parry; (12) "Golden houses for shadows": some portraits of Thomas Killigrew and his family, by Malcolm Rogers; (13) Sir Godfrey Kneller as painter of histories and portraits historiés, by J. Douglas Stewart; (14) Mayerne and his manuscript, by Hugh Trevor-Roper.

Notes at ends of chapters. Index, p.294–303.

S46 Art and patronage in the English Romanesque. Ed. by Sarah Macready and F. H. Thompson. London, Society of Antiquaries of London (Distr. by Thames and Hudson, 1986). viii, 184p. il. (Occasional paper, new series, no.8)

Papers from two symposia held to coincide with the exhibition "English Romanesque art, 1066–1200" (1984) (See GLAH 2:I352).

Contents: Sculpture in stone in the English Romanesque art exhibition, by George Zarnecki; Niello in England in the twelfth century, by Neil Stratford; Seals as evidence for metalworking in England in the later twelfth century, by T. A. Heslop; English Romanesque book illumination: changes in the field, 1974–1984, by C. M. Kauffmann; Who designed the Eadwine Psalter?, by Margaret Gibson; The "Old Conventual Church" at Ely: a false trail in Romanesque studies?, by Thomas Cocke; The Bishop's Chapel at Hereford: the roles of patron and craftsman, by Richard Gem; The role of musicians at court in twelfth century Britain, by Laurence Wright; Wealth and artistic patronage at twelfth century St. Albans, by Brian Golding; Bestiaries: an aspect of medieval patronage, by Xenia Muratova; Intellectuality and splendour: Thomas Becket as a patron of the arts, by Ursula Nilgren; Henry of Blois as a patron of sculpture, by George Zarnecki.

Notes at ends of chapters. General index, p.173–84.

S47 Herrmann, Frank, comp. The English as collectors: a documentary sourcebook. Sel., introd., and annot. . . . by Frank Herrmann. New Castle, Del., Oak Knoll, 1999. 461p. il.

1st ed., The English as collectors: a documentary chrestomathy. London, Chatto and Windus, 1972.

Selection of excerpts from primary sources that illuminate the history of collecting in England from Charles I to the present. Prefaced by a substantial introduction outlining the emergence of the individual collector and developing patterns that influenced art patronage and the art market. Contains a useful list of catalogs of early English collections. The new ed. provides an updated introduction. Few illustrations.

Select, annotated bibliography, p. 418–36. Index, p.437–61.

S48 The History of the King's works. General ed., H. M. Colvin. London, H. M. Stationary Office, 1963–1982. 6v. il. plans, plates.

See GLAH 1:J180 for earlier vols. (published out of sequence).

Contents: (IV) 1485–1660 by H. M Colvin . . . [et al.], 1982.

S49 Holloway, James. Patrons and painters: art in Scotland, 1650–1760. [Edinburgh], Scottish National Portrait Gallery, 1989. 152p. il. (part col.)

Published to accompany the exhibition, Scottish National Portrait Gallery (1989). Accessible study of the patronage activities of several major families in Scotland in historical and cultural contexts. Includes the work of many lesser known artists.

Contents: David Scougal, Jacob de Wet, John Michael Wright and the patronage of the Royal House of Stewart; Sir John de Medina, William Gouw Ferguson, John Scougal and the patronage of the Earls of Leven and Melville; William Aikman, James Norie and the patronage of John, 2nd Duke of Argyll; Richard Waitt, John Smibert and the patronage of Clan Grant; John Alexander, William Mosman and the patronage of the Duffs and Gordons; Academies, societies, and the patronage of the City of Edinburgh; Allan Ramsay and the patronage of John 3rd Earl of Bute.

Notes, p.139. Artist biographies [with suggestions for further reading], p.140–50. Select bibliography, p.150. Index, p.[151].

S50 The late King's goods: collections, possessions and patronage of Charles I in the light of the Commonwealth Sale Inventories. Ed. by Arthur MacGregor. London, Alistair McAlpine; Oxford Univ. Pr., 1989. 432p. il. (part col.), facsims., ports.

Essays by noted art historians describing and analyzing the royal collections of Charles I. Each essay corresponds to numbered entries in the inventories compiled for the sale of Charles' collections and personal effects. Scholarly notes follow each chapter. Well illustrated.

Contents: (1) The King's goods and the Commonwealth Sale. Materials and context, by Arthur MacGregor; (2) Charles I and the tradition of European princely collecting, by Ronald Lightbown; (3) Charles I, sculpture and sculptors, by David Howarth; (4) The limnings, drawings and prints in Charles I's collection, by Jane Roberts; (5) Charles I's collection of pictures, by Francis Haskell; (6) Charles I and the art of the goldsmith, by Ronald Lightbown; (7) The King's regalia, insignia and jewellery, by Ronald Lightbown; (8) "Shadows, not substantial things." Furniture in the Commonwealth Inventories, by Simon Jervis; (9) Textile furnishings, by Donald King; (10) "Great vanity and excesse in apparell": some clothing and furs of Tudor and Stuart royalty, by Valerie Cumming; (11) Arms, armour, and militaria, by A. V. B. Norman; (12) The household below the stairs: officers and equipment of the Stuart court, by Arthur MacGregor; (13) Horological, mathematical and musical instruments: science and music at the court of Charles I, by Penelope Gouk; (14) The King's disport. "Sports, games, and pastimes of the early Stuarts," by Arthur MacGregor.

Notes at ends of chapters. Index, p.423–32.

S51 The treasure houses of Britain: five hundred years of private patronage and art collecting. Ed. by Gervase Jackson-Stops. Washington, D.C., National Gallery of Art; New Haven, Yale Univ. Pr., 1985. 680p. il. (part col.)

Richly illustrated catalog of the exhibition, National Gallery, Washington (1985–86). Organized chronologically, the catalog begins with a group of historical essays by scholars noted for their work in patronage and collecting studies. Covers the development of patronage in Britain from the 16th century to the present and emphasizes the role of the "private house" in the formation of collections. Contains 589 detailed entries with references for both fine and decorative arts. Excellent bibliography.

Selective contents: Temples of the arts, by Gervase Jackson-Stops; The power house, by Mark Girouard; Portraiture and the country house, by Oliver Millar; The Englishman in Italy, by Brinsley Ford; The British as collectors, by Francis Haskell; The backward look, by John Cornforth; The last hundred years, by Marcus Binney and Gervase Jackson-Stops.

Bibliography, p.664–73. Index to sitters, artists, and locations, p.677–79.

Italy

S52 Art and production in the world of the Caesars by T. J. Cornell . . . [et al.]. Milan, Olivetti, 1987. 52p. il., maps.

Published to honor cultural relations between Italy and Britain and in conjunction with the exhibition, Glass of the Caesars, this slender vol. is a useful introduction for the general reader to arts patronage during the Roman Empire.

Contents: (1) The Roman Empire and the Roman emperors, by J. A. North; (2) Artists and patrons, by T. J. Cornell; (3) Tableware for Trimalchio, by M. H. Crawford.

Suggestions for further readings, p.45–46. Maps, p.48–49. Roman emperors, p.51–52.

S53 Builders and humanists: the Renaissance popes as patrons of the arts. Houston, Univ. of St. Thomas Art Dept., 1966. 363p., il., facsims., plans, plates, ports.

Published to accompany an exhibition of drawings, engravings, and books chronicling the patronage of the Renaissance papacy, University of St. Thomas (1966). Spans the pontifcate of Nicholas V (1447–55) to Clement IX (1667–69). Contains an introductory essay useful for the general reader and a catalog of annotated entries for 309 items including architectural projects, paintings, drawings, sculpture, objects, medals, coins, seals, and engravings.

Includes bibliographical references. Index, p.347–53.

S54 Burckhardt, Jacob. Die Sammler, in Beiträge zur Kunstgeschichte von Italien: Das Altarbild-Das Porträt in der Malerei-Die Sammler. Berlin, Deutsche Verlags-Anstalt Stuttgart, 1930. xv, 496p (Gesamtausgabe, hrsg. von Heinrich Wölfflin, Bd.12).

A classic discussion; several eds. For an English trans. of the chapter in the same book devoted to the altarpiece, see GLAH 2:M345.

S55 Chevallier, Raymond. L'artiste, le collectionneur & le faussaire: pour une sociologie de l'art romain. Paris, Colin, 1991. 354p.

Survey covering the production and collecting of artistic works during the pre-Roman and Roman period. Emphasizes political, social, and economic contexts. Many references to primary source materials.

Selective contents: (1) Avant Rome, l'Orient; (2) Rapts d'oeuvres d'art; (3) Artistes et ateliers; (4) Le marché de l'art à Rome; (5) Les lieux de collections; (6) La réflexion sur l'art. Ensiegnement artistique et critique d'art en Grèce et à Rome; (7) Le "Centre du pouvoir"; (8) L'Italie: quelques exemples; (9) La situation des provinces: quelques exemples.

Lexique, p.317–26. Bibliographie générale, p.327–54.

S56 Collezioni di antichità a Venezia, nei secoli della Repubblica (dai libri e documenti della Biblioteca Marciana). Catalogo a cura di Marino Zorzi . . . [et al.] Roma, Istituto Poligrafico e Zecca dello Stato, 1988. 219p. il. (part col.), plates, facsims.

Published to accompany the exhibition, Biblioteca Marciana (1988). The catalog includes manuscripts, books, and works of art arranged chronologically by individuals and families of collectors. An essay on illustrated collection catalogs comprises the rest of the vol. Useful for identifying early Venetian collections and related primary source material.

Elenco dei manoscritti citati in forma abbreviata, p.[183]. Elenco dei manoscritti Marciani citati, p.[185]. Elenco delle opere a stampa citate, p.[187]–215. Elenco dei collezionisti, p.[217].

S57 De Benedictis, Cristina. Per la storia del collezionismo italiano: fonti e documenti. Firenze, Ponte alle Grazie, c1991. 358p. il., plates. (Theatrum mundi)

Systematic examination of collecting in Italy from the 14th to the 18th century. The first section is comprised of an extended historical essay; the second, larger section consists of extracts from significant primary source documents. Modestly illustrated.

Selective contents: Per la storia del collezionismo italiano: Metodo e limiti della museologia; Le prime testimonianze dal Medioevo al Preumanesimo; Firenze e il gusto dei Medici nel Quattrocento; Le botteghe degli artisti; Gli studiolo; La corrispondenza di Isabella d'Este Gonzaga; Roma e il recupero dell'antico; Le collezioni fiorentine e gli Ufizzi nel Cinquecento; Antico e moderno nelle raccolte di Padova, Verona, e Venezia; Gallerie e quadrerie nobiliari; Musei ideali e gallerie poetiche; Sui criteri di disposizione, decorazione e arredo degli spazi interni e sulle modalità di allestimento dei dipinti e dei disegni; Virtuosi, dilettanti e conoscitori; Dalla meraviglia al metodo: Wunderkammern e raccolte scientifiche; La fortuna dei primitivi; Dalla collezione al museo pubblico.

Bibliografia, p.[319]–41. Indice dei nomi, p.[345]–58.

S58 I Farnese: arte e collezionismo. A cura di Lucia Fornari Schianchi, Nicola Spinosa. Milano, Electa, 1995. 2v. il. (part col.)

Massive, beautifully produced catalog published to accompany the exhibition, Palazzo Ducale di Colorno, Parma (1995), and other locations. The catalog vol. consists of twelve essays on the history of the Farnese family and examines selected areas of their collecting interests together with 292 detailed entries for objects ranging from the fine arts to militaria. The second vol., Studi, contains 21 essays on aspects of Farnese patronage and collecting activities. The catalog vol. includes a list of Farnese inventories. Essays in both vols. are followed by scholarly notes. Well-illustrated.

Inventari, v.1, p.493–95. Bibliografia, v.1, p.496–527. Indice degli artisti e delle opere, v.1, p.528–33.

S59 Goldberg, Edward L. Patterns in late Medici art patronage. Princeton, Princeton Univ. Pr., 1983. xiii, 425p. il., plates.

Scholarly exploration of the patronage roles of Cardinal Prince Leopoldo and Cosimo III in the late 17th century. Goldberg's contribution "is an unusual and valuable one. This is not just because it contains a mass of previously unpublished documents . . . but because it deliberately sets out to dismantle the conventional account of Medici activity."—*Review*, Art history, v.7, no.3, Sept. 1984, p.380. Extensive notes contain numerous references to primary source material.

Contents: (I) Methods and motives; (II) Bologna: the Cospi-Ranuzzi and the Sirani; (III) Venice: Paolo del Sera; (IV) Rome: The Medici and the Falconieri; (V) Ottavio Falconiere and the antiquity market; (VI) The Medici and foreigners: Monsù Louis Vouet; (VII) Paolo Falconieri, Ciro Ferri, and the Academy of the Grand Duke of Tuscany; (VIII) Vicente Victoria and the Tuscan Academy; (IX) Paolo Falconiere, Cirro Ferri and the early patronage of Cosimo III; (X) Ercole Ferrata, Innocent XI, and the "Venus de' Medici."

Notes, p.252–409. Bibliography, p.411–15. Index, p.417–25.

S60 Goldthwaite, Richard A. Wealth and the demand for art in Italy, 1300–1600. Baltimore, Johns Hopkins Univ. Pr., 1993. 266p.

Addresses questions raised by the dramatic increase in the demand for and production of art and architecture during the Renaissance and examines how new styles quickly penetrated Italian material culture during this period. Uses various models of consumption to demonstrate how material culture was generated. Footnotes and references throughout.

Selective contents: The economic background: The level of wealth, the structure of wealth, decline and conclusion; The demand for religious art: The consumption model, variables of consumer behavior, the material culture of the

Church and incipient consumerism; Demand in the secular world: Italy and tradition consumption habits, urban foundations of new consumption habits, the culture of consumption, consumption and the generation of culture.
Index, p.257–66.

S61 Haskell, Francis. Patrons and painters: a study in the relations between Italian art and society in the age of the Baroque. Rev. and enl. ed. New Haven, Yale Univ. Pr., 1980. xviii, 474p. il., plates.
See GLAH 1:M360 for original annotation. The revised ed. contains corrections throughout, a new introduction, and a postscript, arranged by chapter, comprising the author's commentary on the relevance of materials published since the first ed. The bibliography has also been updated.

Contents: Part I: Rome: (1) The mechanics of seventeenth century patronage; (2) Pope Urban VIII and his entourage; (3) The religious orders; (4) The private patrons; (5) The wider public; (6) The decline of Roman patronage. Part II: Dispersal: (7) The intervention of Europe; (8) The provincial scene. Part III: Venice: (9) State, nobility, and church; (10) Foreign influences; (11) The foreign residents; (12) The Enlightenment; (13) Publishers and connoisseurs; (14) Francesco Algarotti; (15) A new direction; (16) Dealers and petits bourgeois; (17) The last patrons; Appendices; Postscript.
Bibliography, p.[411]–441. Index, p.443–74.

S62 Hochmann, Michel. Peintres et commanditaires à Venise (1540–1628). Roma, École française de Rome, 1992. 441p. il. plates. (Collection de l'école française de Rome, 155)
Examines the complex relationships between 16th-century painters and the diverse individuals and organizations such as patricians, confraternities, scuole, churches, and religious orders who became their patrons. With "his preference for an empirical approach to patronage . . . Hochmann has provided a valuable and stimulating survey of an important phase in Italian renaissance patronage."—*Review*, Burlington magazine, v.135, Sept. 1993, p.639. Modestly illustrated.

Selective contents: Le peinture: (I) Le prix de tableaux; (II) Le peintre dans la société vénitienne du seizième siècle; (III) L'atelier et la corporation des peintres. Peintres et lettres: (I) Le lettré, intermédiare et impresario; (II) Le lettré, théoricien et critique d'art; (III) Le lettré, conseiller iconographique du peintre; Le particuliers: (I) Le gôut pour la peinture; (II) Les cittadini; (III) Les patriciens; Églises, ordres religieux et Confreries: (I) Le réglementation de l'Église et la théorie de l'art; (II) Églises et couvents; (III) Les confréries.
Pièces justificatives, p.[349]–66. Sources, p.[367]–68. Ouvrages cités, p.[367]–83. Index, p.[389]–408.

S63 Hollingsworth, Mary. Patronage in Renaissance Italy from 1400 to the early sixteenth century. London, John Murray, [1994]. xi, 372p. il., geneal.
Investigates patronage beyond the traditional centers of the Italian Renaissance including such cities as Urbino, Ferrara, and Naples. This book "provides a synthesis of the current state of knowledge about renaissance patronage, is full of interesting facts which are coherently and clearly employed and it is written with a pithy no-nonsense style."—*Review*, Apollo, v.140, Aug. 1994, p.75. Covers architecture as well as fine arts. The bibliography is especially strong on periodical literature and the appendices contain genealogical charts.
Notes, p.[316]–39. Bibliography, p.[340]–57. Appendices, p.[358]–62. Index, p.[361]–72.

S64 ———. Patronage in sixteenth-century Italy. London, John Murray, 1996. 452p. il.
Building on the author's earlier vol. (see preceding entry), this study "examines sixteenth-century patrons, the impact of political and religious change on their motivation, how they acquired their wealth, why they spent so much on art, what factors governed their choice of themes and styles, their complex relationships with artists, agents and advisers, and the extent to which they controlled the final appearance of their projects."—*Introd.* The appendices consist of lists of popes, doges, and genealogical charts.

Contents: Part one: Rome: (1) Rome: Christianity in crisis; (2) In princely style: the papal court in early sixteenth-century Rome; (3) Magnificence and reform I: the popes, 1534–1559; (4) Magnificence and reform II: the papal court, 1534–1559; (5) Roma resurgens; (6) Reformation and counter-reformation; (7) Piety and power: the papal court in late sixteenth-century Rome. Part two: Venice: (8) Venice: the new Rome; (9) The image of the state; (10) Piety and prestige: the scuole; (11) Tradition and innovation. Part three: The courts: (12) The battle for control: Power and dynasty in the Italian courts; (13) Florence: the return of the Medici; (14) Florence: a ducal court; (15) The Farnese; (16) The Gonzaga; (17) Kings, emperors and Italian art.
Notes, p.[323]–80. Bibliography, p.[381]–427. Appendices, p.[428]–435. Index, p.[438]–452.

S65 Kempers, Bram. Painting, power, and patronage: the rise of the professional artist in the Italian Renaissance. Trans. from the Dutch by Beverley Jackson. N.Y., Penguin, 1992. xiv, 401p. il., map.
Trans. of Kunst, macht en macenaat: het beroep van schilder in sociale verhoudingen, 1250–1600. Amstersdam, Arbeiderspers, 1987.

A detailed survey of the emergence of the professional artist from the late medieval period through the 19th century in central Italy. Both the structure of this vol. and the analysis it presents are grounded in broad sociological, historical, and religious contexts. Few illustrations.

Selective contents: (I) Mendicant orders: (1) Popes, cardinals, friars; (2) A new system of panel paintings; (3) A far-flung and diversified network of patrons; (II) The Republic of Sienna [sic]: (1) The formation and structure of a city-state; (2) The cathedral; (3) The town hall, seat of power, seat of patronage; (4) The profession of painting; (III) Florentine families: (1) The professionalization of painters in Florence; (2) Patronage, commissions and negotiations; (3) Sacred images and social history; (4) Civilization and state formation; (IV) The courts of Urbino, Rome and Florence: (1) Federico da Montefeltro, knight, scholar and patron of art; (2) The pope as a statesman and patron; (3) Cosimo I and Vasari, excellence in government and in art; (V) Social contexts to the present day: (1) Italy, 1200–1600, a first Renaissance; (2) Looking forward, 1600–1900; (3) The twentieth century, art in flux.

Notes, p.[318]–72. Sources and literature, p.[373]–89. Index, p.[391]–401.

S66 Patronage, art, and society in Renaissance Italy. Ed. by F. W. Kent and Patricia Simons, with J. C. Eade. Canberra, Humanities Research Centre Australia; N.Y., Oxford Univ. Pr., 1987. x, 331p. il., plates.

Papers contributed by 17 scholars to a conference held in Melbourne (1983). Artistic activity in Florence is emphasized together with the themes of patronage and society and patronage and the artist. "This richly informative and wide-ranging book offers an excellent introduction to the present study of patronage in renaissance Italy and the problems that study has to face."—*Review*, Burlington magazine, v.130, Sept. 1988, p.707. Scholarly notes and references throughout. Sparsely illustrated.

Contents: (1) Renaissance patronage: an introductory essay, by F. W. Kent and Patricia Simons; (2) Taking patronage seriously: Mediterranean values and Renaissance society, by Ronald Weissman; (3) Friendship and patronage in Renaissance Europe, by Guy Fitch Lytle; (4) The dynamic power in Cosimo de' Medici's Florence, by Dale Kent; (5) Ties of neighbourhood and patronage in Quattrocento Florence, by F. W. Kent; (6) Neighbourhood government in Malatesta Cesena, by Ian Robertson; (7) Liturgy and patronage in San Lorenzo, Florence, 1350–1650, by Robert Gaston; (8) The Medici and the Savonarolans, 1512–1527: the limitations of personal government and of the Medicean patronage system, by Lorenzo Polizzotto; (9) The empire of things: consumer demand in Renaissance Italy, by Richard Goldthwaite; (10) Patronage in the circle of the Carrara family: Padua, 1337–1405, by Margaret Plant; (11) Palla Strozzi's patronage and pre-Medicean Florence, by Heather Gregory; (12) Patronage in the Tornaquinci Chapel, Santa Maria Novella, Florence, by Patricia Simons; (13) The priority of the architect: Alberti on architects and patrons, by John Oppel; (14) Patronage and diplomacy: the north Italian residences of Emperor Charles V, by William Eisler; (15) Patterns of patronage: Antonio da Sangallo the Younger and the setta of sculptors, by Till Verellen; (16) Patronage and the production of history: the case of Quattrocento Milan, by Gary Ianziti; (17) Marx and the study of patronage in the Renaissance, by Margaret Rose.

Index, p.[321]–31.

S67 Siena, Florence, and Padua: art, society, and religion, 1280–1400. Ed. by Diana Norman. New Haven, Yale Univ. Pr. in assoc. with the Open University, 1995. 2v.

Beautifully produced volumes offer interpretive essays and "case studies" influenced by Jacob Burckhardt's thematic approach to the study of Renaissance art. A variety of media and different types of patronage relationships are examined. Each vol. contains extensive bibliography of primary and secondary sources. Copiously illustrated throughout.

Contents: Vol.I: (1) The three cities compared: patrons, politics and art, by Diana Norman; (2) City, contado and beyond: artistic practice, by Diana Norman; (3) Duccio: the recovery of a reputation, by Diana Norman; (4) Giotto and the "rise of painting," by Charles Harrison; (5) The arts of carving and casting, by Catherine King; (6) The building trades and design methods, by Tim Benton; (7) "The glorious deeds of the Commune": civic patronage of art, by Diana Norman; (8) "Splendid models and examples from the past": Carrara patonage of art, by Diana Norman; (9) Change and continuity; art and religion after the Black Death, by Diana Norman; (10) Astrology, antiquity and empiricism: art and learning, by Diana Norman; (11) The Trecento: new ideas, new evidence, by Catherine King. Vol.II: (1) The three cities compared: urbanism, by Tim Benton; (2) For the honour and beauty of the city: the design of town halls, by Colin Cunningham; (3) "A noble panel": Duccio's Maestà, by Diana Norman; (4) The Arena Chapel: patronage and authorship, by Charles Harrison; (5) Effigies: human and divine, by Catherine King; (6) The design of Siena and Florence Duomos, by Tim Benton; (7) "Love justice, you who judge the earth": the paintings of the Sala dei Nove in the Palazzo Pubblico, Siena, by Diana Norman; (8) Those who pay, those who pray and those who paint: two funerary chapels, by Diana Norman; (9) "Hail most saintly Lady": change and continuity in Marian altarpieces, by Diana Norman; (10) The art of knowledge: two artistic schemes in Florence, by Diana Norman; (11) Women as patrons: nuns, widows and rulers, by Catherine King.

Notes, v.1, p.[234]–45, v.2, p.[267]–78. Bibliography, v.1, p.246–50, v.2, p.[279]–82. Index, v.1, p.[251]–60, v.2, p.[283]–90.

S68 Southorn, Janet. Power and display in the seventeenth century: the arts and their patrons in Modena and Ferrara. N.Y., Cambridge Univ. Pr., 1988. xiii, 200p. il. (part col.), plates.

Accessible scholarly study of religious and secular patronage of architecture and the fine arts. This "careful and learned book . . . explores the intriguing—and indeed much neglected—issue of artistic patronage and production in the eastern regions of the Po Valley after the fall of the Duchy of Ferrara in 1597."—*Review*, Renaissance quarterly, v.43, no.1, spring 1990, p.187. A substantial portion of this work focuses on the activities of the Este family. Modestly illustrated.

Contents: Part I: The Este in Modena (1598–1658): (1) Reactions; (2) Restoring the ancient splendour; (3) Ways and means. Part II: The Bentivoglio (1598–1660): (4) Patrons, agents and entrepeneurs. Part III: The papal state of Ferrara (1598–1660): (5) The state of the faith; (6) The papal legation; (7) The Ferrarese nobility.

Notes, p.151–81. Select bibliography; p.182–88. Index, p.189–200.

S69 Wackernagel, Martin. The world of the Florentine Renaissance artist: projects, and patrons, workshop and art market. Trans. by Alison Luchs. Princeton, Princeton Univ. Pr., 1981. 447p.

Trans. of Der Lebensraum des Künstlers in der florentinischen Renaissance: Aufgaben und Auftraggeber, Werkstatt und Kunstmarkt. Leipzig, Seeman, [1938].

Pioneering study of artistic production and patronage within "the whole complex of economic-material, social and cultural circumstances and pre-conditions which in any way affected the existence and activity of the artist."—*Trans. introd.* A valuable analysis with extensive, scholarly footnotes throughout and substantial bibliography, both updated by Luchs.

Contents: (1) Great projects and work on them from 1420 to 1530; (2) Sculptural commissions; (3) Painting commissions; (4) Artistic participation in the staging of public festivities and spectacles; (5) The city government and the guilds; (6) Private patronage in the early and mid-Quattrocento; (7) Lorenzo Magnifico, Piero di Lorenzo, and Lorenzo di Pierfrancesco de' Medici; (8) Patrons from the Medici circle in Florence and the Netherlands: the Sassetti, Portinari, Tornabuoni, Filippo Strozzi and others; (9) Patrons of the High Renaissance and the extra-Florentine commissioners and collectors; (10) The general attitude toward art: the public and the artist; (11) The artist class; its numerical strength, professional organization, and occupational divisions; (12) Studios and their working procedures; (13) Business practices in the workshop and art market; (14) The artists.

Author's bibliography, p.[371]–76. Translator's bibliography, p.[377]–403. Index, p.[405]–47.

SEE ALSO: Baxandall, Painting and experience in fifteenth century Italy (GLAH 2:M340); Documents for the history of collecting (GLAH 2:S15).

Low Countries

S70 De wereld binnen handbereik: nederlandse kunst- en rariteitenverzamelingen, 1585–1735. Amsterdam, Amsterdams Historisch Museum, [1992]. 2v. il.

Major catalog produced to accompany the exhibition, Amsterdams Historisch Museum (1992). The essay and catalog vols., both well illustrated, explore the social context of art and ethnography collectors and collecting, the libraries of collectors, and the patterns and reactions of visitors to collections. The essay vol. includes two appendixes describing the collections of 89 individuals in Amsterdam and a list of collectors elsewhere in the Netherlands. A separate English translation of the catalog entries was published simultaneously under the title, Distant worlds made tangible: art and curiosities, Dutch collections 1585–1735.

Selective contents: De wererld binnen handbereik, van Roelof van Gelder; De wereld ontsloten, van Leo Noordegraaf and Thera Wijsenbeek-Olthuis; Met grote moeite en losten, van Jaap van der Veen; Kunst en rariteiten in het Hollandse interieur, van C. Willemijn Fock; Schatkamers van geleerdheid, van C. L. Heesakkers; Uitzonderlijke verzamelingen, van Henk Th. van Veen; Kiefhebbers, handelaren en kunstenaars, van Jaap van der Veen; Wankelend wereldbeeld, van Jan van der Waals; Exotische rariteiten, van Jan van der Waals; Citaten uit het boek der natur, van K. van Berkel; Schelpenverzamelingen, van H. E. Coomans; Met boek en plaat, van Jan van der Waals; Dit klain Vertrek bevat een Weereld vol gewoel, van Jaap van der Veen; Leifhebbers en geleerde luiden, van Roelef van Gelder.

Noten, v.1, p.293–312. Lijst van gebruikte manuscripten, v.1, p.339. Literatuur, v.1, p.340–60. Register, v.1, p.361–68. Lijst van gebruikte literatuur, v.2, p.193–209. Register, v.2, p.210.

S71 Floerke, Hanns. Studien zur niederländischen Kunst- und Kulturgeschichte: die Formen des Kunsthandels, das Atelier und die Sammler in den Niederlanden vom 15.–18. Jahrhundert. [Reprint.] [Soest, Davaco, 1972]. viii, 231p. il., plates.

1st ed., München, Muller, 1905.

An early, detailed study of collecting, art dealing, and the general market for artistic production in the Netherlands. Contains "the most important information that had been gathered until the time of his writing about the art market, dealers, exhibits, prices, studio practice, and guild regulations, both in the southern and northern Netherlands . . . still a useful starting point for almost any conceivable research on the subjects he covered."—J. Montias, Art bulletin, v.72, no.3, Sept. 1990, p.361.

Contents: (1) Der Markt- und Strassenhandel mit Kunstwerken; (2) Bilder als Zahlungsmittel; (3) Weitere Formen des Kunsthandels; (4) Austellungen; (5) Der niederländische Aussenhandel mit Kunstwerken; (6) Die Kunsthändler; (7) Das Atelier; (8) Die Sammler: Preisverhältnisse.

Benützte Literatur, p.[v]–viii. Anmerkungen, p.[183]–218. Register, p.[219]–31.

S72 Montias, John Michael. Le marché de l'art aux Pays-Bas, XVe–XVIIe siècles. Paris, Flammarion, 1996. 191p. il., plates. (Art, histoire, société)

Focusing on painting and sculpture, the author has structured this study as a critique of existing socio-economic theories of the sale and collecting of art in the Netherlands from the middle ages through the Renaissance. Concentrates on a small group of major collectors. Minimally illustrated.

Contents: (I) À la recherche du passé; (II) Moyen âge et renaissance; (III) L'analyse de la demande: les collections en Hollande au XVIIe siècle; (IV) Du côté de l'offre; (IV Annexe) Compagnons et apprentis dans la guilde de Haarlem; (V) Contacts direct et intermédiaires.

Bibliographie, p.183–87. Index de noms cités, p.188–91.

S73 North, Michael. Art and commerce in the Dutch Golden Age. Trans. by Catherine Hill. New Haven, Yale Univ. Pr., 1997. 164p. il.

Trans. of Kunst und Kommerz im Goldenen Zeitalter: zur Socialgeschichte der niederländischen Malerei des 17. Jahrhunderts. Koln, Böhlau, 1992.

A readable introduction to the complexities of artistic production in 17th-century Holland, "this study investigates the developments that took place in economic, social and artistic areas, as well as the way these areas interacted."—*Introd.*

Contents: (I) Historical interpretations of Dutch painting; (II) The Dutch economy; (III) Dutch society; (IV) Artists' origins and their social status; (V) Patronage and the art market; (VI) Collections and collectors; (VII) Conclusion.

Notes, p.[139]–49. Bibliography, p.[150]–59. Index of Netherlandish artists, p.[160]–62.

SEE ALSO: Duverger, Antwerpse kunstinventarissen uit de zeventiende eeuw (GLAH 2:H94); Verzamelen: van rariteitenkabinet tot kunstmuseum (GLAH 2:S33).

Russia and Eastern Europe

S74 Burrus, Christina. Art collectors of Russia: the private treasures revealed. Trans. from the French by Ros Schwartz and Sue Rose. London, Tauris Park, 1994. 249p. col. il., ports.

Trans. of Collectionneurs russes: d'une revolution à l'autre. Paris, Chene, 1992.

General, well-illustrated volume covering 13 major private collections assembled in Russia in the 19th and 20th centuries. Includes numerous photographs documenting the collections in their original surroundings.

Contents: Schukin, Morozov, Kostakis, the precursors; Salomon A. Schuster's collection, the spirit of St. Petersburg; Valantina Golod's collection, a miniature palace; Vladimir I. Paleev's collection, a heritage preserved; Dimitri S. Varchavsky's collections, guided by sensuality; Igor G. Sanovich's collection, a cabinet of curiosities; Valeri Dudakov's collection, a curator's dream; Yuri Weitsman's collection, in the footsteps of Catherine the Great; Abraham F. Chudnovsky's collection, a marriage of art and science; Mikhail Perchenko's collection, a contemporary boyar; The Moscow Bank collection, the western mirage.

Biographies of Russian artists, p.243–47. Index, p.248–49. Chronology, p.[250]–[53].

S75 Prag um 1600: Kunst und Kultur am Höfe Rudolfs II. [Übers. der Texte von R. J. W. Evans and Joaneath Spicer aus dem Englischen, Petra Kruse]. Freren, Luca-Verlag, 1988. 2v.

Catalog of an extensive exhibition, Villa Hugel, Essen (1988), and other locations. 14 essays by international scholars, a comprehensive catalog of 825 fully documented entries for objects related to the patronage of Rudolf II, and surveys of historical and artistic events. Also contains numerous charts, plans, genealogies, and chronologies in support of the essays that explore the historical, political, and social context of Rudolf's court. Contributors to the essay vol. "understand that the emergence of a magnet for creative talent in Prague, as a result of the ambitions and predilections of an emperor who was one of the most versatile and avid patrons in European history, offers remarkable opportunities for investigating the interactions between the arts, politics, and society."—*Review*, Journal of interdisciplinary history, v.20, no.3, Winter 1990, p.440. Very well illustrated throughout.

Selective contents: Rudolf II: Prag und Europa um 1600, von R. J. W. Evans; Zur Einführung: die Kunst am Hofe Rudolfs II.—eine rudolfinische Kunst? von Lars Olof Larsson; Kaiser Rudolf II. in Prag: Persönlichkeit und imperialer Anspruch, von Herbert Haupt; Späthumanismus und Manierismus im Kreise Kaiser Rudolfs II., von Erich Trunz; Mythologische Themen am Hofe Rudolfs II. des Kaisers, von Görel Cavalli-Bjorkman; Die Architektur unter Rudolf II., gezeigt am Beispiel der Prager Berg, von Ivan Muchka; Bildhauerkunst und Plastik am Hofe Rudolfs II., von Lars Olof Larsson; Die Malerei am Hofe Rudolfs II., von Eliška Fučíková; Zeichnung und Druckgraphik, von Teréz Gerszi; Die Kunstkammerstücke, von Rudolf Distelberger; Medaillen, Münzen und Wachsbossierungen am Hofe Rudolfs II., von Rudolf-Alexander Schütte; Die Prager Judenstadt zur Zeit der rudolfinischen Renaissance, von Vladimír Sadek.

Verzeichnis der abgekürzt zitierten Literatur, v.1, p.610–20, v.2, p.306–14. Künstlerverzeichnis, v.1, p.623–24, v.2, p.319–20. Inventare und Sammlungs Kataloge, v.2, p.315.

S76 Rudolf II and Prague: the court and the city. Ed. by Eliŝska Fuçíková . . . [et al.] N.Y., Thames and Hudson, 1997. ix, 792p. il. (part col.)

In English and Czech. Published in conjunction with the exhibition, Rudolf II and Prague, the imperial court and residential city as the cultural and spiritual heart of Central Europe, Prague (1997).

Monumental, multi-authored survey of court culture, collecting, and the art patronage of Rudolf II in 17th-century Prague. V.2 offers Czech versions of the essays published in English in v.1.

Includes bibliographical references. Exhibitions, p.773–75. Literature, p.776–89. Index, p.790–92.

SEE ALSO: Balogh, Die Anfänge der Renaissance in Ungarn: Matthias Corvinus und die Kunst (GLAH 2:I434); Kaufmann, Court, cloister and city: the art and culture of Central Europe, 1450–1800 (GLAH 2:I444); Kaufmann, The school of Prague: painting at the court of Rudolf II. (GLAH 2:M496).

Scandinavia

S77 Christian IV and Europe: the 19th annual exhibition of the Council of Europe. [Copenhagen], Foundation for the Christian IV Year 1988, 1988. 607p. il. (part col.), facsims., plans, ports.

Catalog of a series of exhibitions held in conjunction with the celebration of the Christian IV Year, 1988. Short essays preface catalog entries for more than 1900 objects including architecture, painting, and decorative arts produced during the reign of Christian IV of Denmark, (1588–1648). Provides a useful survey in English of the formation of Danish royal collections.

Contents: Frederiksborg. Christian IV: the fortunes and fate of a King; Kronborg. Christian IV: patron of the arts: The visual and performing arts at the Danish Court, 1588–1648, tapestries, Christian IV and music, Christian IV and drama; Rosenborg. Treasures of Christian IV; Nationalmuseet. Christian IV: the enterprising King; Den klg. Kobberstiksamling. Rubens' cantoor, selected drawings by Willem Panneels; Statens Museum for Kunst. The age of Christian IV, art centres and artists in northern Europe; Tøjhusmuseet. Christian IV: defender of crown and faith; Rundetårn/Trinitatis kirke. "Things in heaven and earth": science and learning during the reign of Christian IV; Koldinghus. Christian IV and his architecture; Aarhus Kunstmuseum. Christian IV, the image of posterity.

Bibliography, p.590–605

S78 Gundestrup, Bente. Det Kongelige danske Kunstkammer 1737 = The Royal Danish Kunstkammer 1737. [Copenhagen], Nationalmuseet, 1991. 2v.
Though primarily an inventory catalog recreating an early 18th-century royal Kunstkammer collection, v.I contains a useful introductory essay in English. The catalog vol. contains a remarkable array of objects that convey the eclectic quality of early collections. Very well illustrated, with a bibliography strong in primary sources. No index.

Litteratur op kilder, v.2, p.455–60.

Spain and Portugal

S79 Checa Cremades, Fernando. Felipe II, mecenas de las artes. 2d ed. Madrid, Nerea, 1993. 514p. il. (part col.), plans.
1st ed., 1992.

Survey of royal patronage of arts and architecture during the reign of Philip II (1556–1598). Includes extensive examination of the planning and construction of the palace and monastery of Escorial. Contains chapters on the historical, political and religious contexts that influenced artistic programs. "Checa's great achievement is to have interpreted the documentation, reviewed published research and redressed the imbalance caused by excessive concentration on Philip's religious interests."—*Review*, Burlington magazine, v.135, Sept. 1993, p.641. Small illustrations are chiefly black-and-white.

Guia de personas reales, p.465–66. Notas, p.469–93. Bibliografia, p.495–507. Indice de nombres, p.509–14.

S80 Moran, Miguel J., and Checa, Fernando. El coleccionismo en Espana: de la camera de meravillas a la galleria de pinturas. Madrid, Catedra, 1985. 306p. il. (Ensayos arte)
Acknowledging a debt to Schlosser (GLAH 2:S29), the authors have prepared a detailed study of collecting in Spain from the late medieval period through the 17th century. As the title indicates, the chief focus of their analyses is the transition from the cabinet of curiosities to painting collections. Notes and references throughout. Few illustrations. No index.

Contents: (I) Los origenes medievales; (II) El siglo XV: colecciones, tesoros, riquezas; (III) Los tesoros en la primera mitad del siglo XVI y los bienes de Carlos V; (IV) Carlos V y el planteamiento de un nuevo sentido de la colección regia de pinturas; (V) El contexto europeo de Felipe II; (VI) Colecciones y organización del saber. La biblioteca de Felipe II; (VII) Las colecciones de Felipe II; (VIII) La fascinación de América; (IX) Eruditos y arqueólogos: el jardin como marco de la colección; (X) Coleccionistas del siglo XVI; (XI) Relicarios y camarines: la Contrarreforma y el coleccionismo fantástico; (XII) Entre la cámara de maravillas y la galeria de pinturas; (XIII) El culto al objecto y las colecciones a principios el siglo XVII; (XIV) Las colecciones de Felipe III; (XV) El gusto por la pintura en la primera mitad del siglo XVII; (XVI) Las colecciones de Felipe IV; (XVII) Las colecciones de la nobleza.

S81 Reyes y mecenas; los Reyes Catolicós, Maximiliano I y los incios de la casa de Austria en España. [Milano], Electa, 1992. 626p. il. (chiefly col.), maps.
Catalog of the exhibition, Museo Santa Cruz, Toledo (1992). Examines Renaissance patronage and artistic activities in 15th- and 16th-century Spain under the rule of Maximillian I and in the courts of Spanish kings and nobles between 1475 and 1515. Detailed, well-illustrated catalog entries describe 269 objects representing all media.

Selective contents: Poder y piedad: patronos y mecenas en la introducción del Renacimiento en España, por Fernando Checa; Arquitectura y magnificencia en la España de los Reyes Catolicós, por Rosario Díez del Corral; El proyecto político de los Reyes Católicos, por Miguel Ángel Ladero; Príncipes y humanistas en los comienzos del Renacimiento español, por Francisco Rico; España en la era de las exploraciones: una encrucijada de culturas artísticas, por Jonathan Brown; El arte de los Países Bajos en la España de los Reyes Católicos, por Joaquín Yarza; La pintura del primer Renacimiento en la Corona de Aragón, por Ximo Company; Italia, los italianos y la introduccíon de Renacimiento en Andalucía, por Alfredo J. Morales; Impresores y libros en el origen del Renacimiento en España, por Jesus Vega; Maximiliano y el arte, por Karl Schütz; La doble boda de 1496/97. Planeamiento, ejecucíon y consecuencias dinásticas, por Alfred Kohler.

Los artistas de la época, p.527–78. Los artistas de Maximiliano, p.579–81. Bibliografía del arte en tiempos de los reyes católicos, p.583–619. Bibliografía del arte en torno a Maximiliano, p.621–26.

SEE ALSO: Bottineau, L'Art de cour dans l'Espagne des lumières, 1746–1808 (GLAH 2:I471); Documents for the history of collecting (GLAH 2:S15).

Switzerland

S82 Das Amerbach-Kabinett. Basel, Öffentliche Kunstsammlung Basel, 1991. 5v. (Sammeln in der Renaissance)
Published to accompany an exhibition, Öffentliche Kunstsammlung Basel (1991), marking the 400th anniversary of Basilius Amerbach's death. These beautifully illustrated volumes reconstruct the entire extant collection from several museums in detailed catalog entries and numerous scholarly essays befitting the importance of the Amerbach family in the history of the Kunstkammern. The first four vols. contains several introductory essays, catalog entries, and bibliography. The fifth vol. contains substantial essays with scholarly notes and references throughout together with the text of original documents.

Contents: (I) Die Gemälde; (II) Die Zeichnungen; (III) Die Basler Goldschmiederisse; (IV) Die Objekte im Historischen Museum Basel; (V) Beiträge zu Basilius Amerbach.

Turkey

S83 Islamic art and patronage: treasures from Kuwait. Ed. by Esin Atil. N.Y., Rizzoli, 1990. 313p. il. (part col.), map.

Catalog of the loan exhibition from the al-Sabah Collection, Walters Art Gallery, Baltimore (1990–91). Covers architecture and the fine and decorative arts and contains substantial introductory essays by well-known art historians. "The exhibition was conceived to concentrate on objects that reflect the development of the artistic traditions in the world of Islam, represent diverse periods and regions, and highlight unique techniques and styles, united by the theme of patronage."—*Pref.* Well-illustrated with many color plates.

Selective contents: An introduction to the al-Sabah Collection, by Marilyn Jenkins; Patronage in Islamic art, by Oleg Grabar; Early Islam: emerging patterns (622–1050), by Estelle Whelan; The classical period (1050–1250), by Jonathan M. Bloom; The post-classical period (1250–1500), by Sheila S. Blair; Late Islam: the age of empires (1500–1800), by Walter B. Denny.

Notes, p.300–05. Dynastic table, p.306–07. Suggested readings, p.309–10. Index, p.311–13.

United States

S84 Brody, J. J. Indian painters & white patrons. Albuquerque, Univ. of New Mexico Pr., [1971]. xvii, 238p. il. (part col.), maps.

Reinterpretation of modern American Indian painting, examining mutual influences and interactions between Native Americans and white patrons and collectors. Seeks to balance opposing views of Native American painting as an indigenous form or the result of colonial subjugation. Includes a chapter on pre-20th century Indian painting. The appendix contains a roster of significant modern American Indian painters. Modestly illustrated.

Notes on sources, p.214–22. Selective bibliography, p.223–29. Index, p.230–38.

S85 Burt, Nathaniel. Palaces for the people: a social history of the American art museum. Boston, Little, Brown, 1977. 446p. il. plates.

Accessible general history of American art museums and the development and growth of individual collections, both major and lesser-known, across America. Includes biographical material on 19th-century collectors and background anecdotal material on individuals who supported the formation of public collections. Few illustrations.

Books and acknowledgements, p.423–32. Index, p.433–46.

S86 Constable, William George. Art collecting in the United States of America; an outline of a history. London, Nelson, [1964]. xi, 210p., 36 plates.

Follows, roughly chronologically, the major periods of European painting from medieval to modern and includes chapters on the Far East and works on paper. Useful for background on the development of major private collections that later became part of American museums including the collections of Duncan Phillips, Samuel Kress, William Corcoran, and Chester Dale.

Note, p.xi. Index, p.197–210.

S87 Miller, Lillian B. Patrons and patriotism: the encouragement of the fine arts in the United States, 1790–1860. Chicago, Univ. of Chicago Pr., [1966]. 335p. il.

In-depth and well-documented study of how Americans sought to define and foster the role of artistic achievement in public and private forums. Includes a section on early government-sponsored arts initiatives and institutions.

Contents: (1) The nationalist apologia; (2) The apologia continued: Emerson, Ruskin, Norton; (3) Building the Capitol; (4) Painting and politics; (5) Sculpture, politics, and the taste of politicians; (6) Decorations for Capitol extension; (7) The artists' protest; (8) New York sets the pattern: The American Academy of Fine Arts; (9) Philadelphia: The Pennsylvania Academy of Fine Arts; (10) Boston: The Athenaeum Gallery; (11) Charleston: The southern experience; (12) Baltimore: art in a border city; (13) American collections; (14) The American Art-Union; (15) Art in the West; (16) Art and nationality.

Notes, p.233–95. Bibliography, p.299–315. Index, p.317–35.

S88 Robson, A. Deirdre. Prestige, profit, and pleasure: the market for modern art in N.Y. in the 1940s and 1950s. N.Y., Garland, 1995. xiv, 375p. il. (Garland publications in the fine arts)

An analysis of the role of museums, collectors, dealers, and galleries in the emergence and subsequent demand for the work of artists of the New York School. Includes some background material on the 1930s. Based on the author's dissertation. A readable, well-documented account.

Selective contents: (I) Prologue: Birth of the support system, New York—the art market before 1930; (II) The players: Museums: Preliminary histories; The ultimate purpose will be to acquire, to help people enjoy, understand, and use the visual arts of our time—museums as tastemakers; Dealers: Innovation- or audience-oriented dealers; Invention- or artist-oriented dealers; Collectors: On-guard collectors; Avant-Garde collectors; Action on Fifty-Seventh Street; (III) Epilogue: The New York art market circa 1960; Appendices: Tables; locations of galleries; auction sales.

Notes, p.305–54. Selected bibliography, p.355–67. Index, p.369–75.

S89 Saarinen, Aline B. The proud possessors: the lives, times and tastes of some adventurous American art collectors. N.Y., Random House, [1958]. xxiv, 423p. il.

Published in numerous eds.

Written by the wife of architect Eero Saarinen and friend of Bernard Berenson, this conversational work combines accounts of personalities and the intricacies of art collecting among socially and politically powerful Americans from the 1880s to the 1950s.

Contents: Provincial princess: Mrs. Potter Palmer; C'est mon plaisir: Isabella Stewart Gardner; The grandiose gesture: J. Pierpont Morgan; Gamesmanship: John G. Johnson; Tea and champagne: Charles Lang Freer; The last word: The Henry O. Havemeyers; American in Paris: Gertrude, Leo, and Sarah Stein; Patron: John Quinn; Propagandist: Katherine Sophie Dreier; The quiet world: Edward Wales Root; Little man in big hurry: Jospeh H. Hirshhorn; Americana: Electra Havemeyer Webb; Cowboys and Indians: Thomas Gilcrease; Apassionata of the avant-garde: Peggy Guggenheim; The one luxury: The Rockefellers.

Sources and obligations, p.[397]–414. Index, p.[415]–23.

ASIAN COUNTRIES

S90 American collectors of Asian art. Ed. by Pratapaditya Pal. Bombay, Marg Publications, 1986. 224p. il. (part col.), ports.

Well-illustrated biographies of ten major American collectors. Useful for an understanding of the patterns of collecting Asian art and the formation of several important American museum collections such as the Freer Gallery and the Asian Art Museum of San Francisco. Notes follow each chapter. No bibliography or index.

Contents: Charles Lang Freer (1856–1919), by Robert E. Fisher; Avery Brundage (1887–1975), by Clarence F. Shangraw; John D. Rockefeller, 3rd (1906–1975), by Robert L. Brown; Nasli M. Heeramaneck (1902–1971), by Nancy Thomas; Edwin Binney, 3rd (1925–1986), by Thomas W. Lentz, Jr.; Norton Simon (1907–), by Pratapaditya Pal; Samuel Eilenberg (1913–), by Shehbaz H. Safrani; The Zimmerman Family Collection, by Valrae Reynolds; John Gilmore Ford (1934–), by Eva Ray; Paul F. Walter (1935–), by Vidya Dehejia.

S91 Artists and patrons: some social and economic aspects of Chinese paintings. Co-eds., James Cahill, Wai-Kam Ho. Contrib., Claudia Brown . . . [et al.] Lawrence, Dept. of Art History, Univ. of Kansas; Kansas City, Nelson-Atkins Museum of Art (Distr. by Univ. of Washington Pr., 1989). 248p. il.

Essays published from the Workshop on Chinese Painting held at the Nelson-Atkins Museum of Art (1980) in conjunction with the exhibition, Eight dynasties of Chinese painting: the collections of the Nelson-Atkins museum of Art and the Cleveland Museum of Art (see GLAH 2:M600). A collaborative effort between established and younger scholars, this volume represents one of the earliest works in English to explore, in detail, the role of patronage amidst "aesthetic appreciation, stylistic analysis, connoisseurship, documentation, iconographical study and literary treatment . . . in the broader context of Chinese culture."—*Pref.*

Contents: Types of artist-patron transactions in Chinese painting, by James Cahill; Sung Kao-tsung as artist and patron: the theme of dynastic revival by Julia Murray; Aspects of painting and patronage at the Mongol Court, 1260-1368, by Marsha Smith Weidner; A-er-hsi-p'u and his painting collection, by Marshall Wu; Reassessment of painters and paintings at the early Ch'ing Court by Daphne Lange Rosenzweig; Guests at Jade Mountain: aspects of patronage in fourteenth century K'un-shan, by David Sensabaugh; Some aspects of late Yüan patronage in Suchou, by Claudia Brown; The formation of the family collection of Huang Tz'u and Huang Lin, by Steven D. Owyoung; Wen Chia and Suchou literati, by Alice R. M. Hyland; Hsiang Yüan-pien and Suchou artists, by Kwan S. Wong; Patronage in Anhui during the Wan-li period, by Sewall Oertling II; Huichou merchants as art patrons in the late sixteenth and early seventeenth centuries, by Jason Chi-sheng Kuo; Chou Liang-kung and his Tu-hua-lu painters, by Hongnam Kim; Yün Shou-p'ing and his patrons, by Ginger Tong; Merchant patronage of the eighteenth century Yangchou painting, by Ginger Cheng-chi Hsu; Art patronage of Shanghai in the nineteenth century, by Stella Yu Lee.

Notes at ends of chapters. Index, p.[232]–48.

S92 Beurdeley, Michel. The Chinese collector through the centuries, from the Han to the 20th century. [Trans. by Diana Imber]. Rutland, Vt., Tuttle, [1966]. 286p. il. (part col.), fold. col. map.

Trans. of L'amateur chinois des Han au 20e siecle. Fribourg, Office du Livre, [1966].

An introduction for the general reader to connoisseurship and patronage from a Chinese perspective up to the early period of collecting Chinese art by westerners. Includes a catalog of 184 objects with brief descriptions intended to further illustrate the range of artistic styles and expression from the neolithic period to the end of the 19th century. Well-illustrated.

Contents: In search of the past; The soul of a dragon; Royal taste at the T'ang court; Yang Kuei-fei, a romantic character; Li Lung-mien: a Sung archaeologist; Mi Fu, connoisseur and collector; The scholar's table; Li Ch'ing-chao's tragic flight to save her collection; Strange and rare stones; Chia Ssû-tao, an unusual collector; The Yüan Dynasty or the Mongol occupation; The Ming court; Chang Ying-wên, art historian; The tribulations of Hsiang Yûan-pien's album; South of the Yangtze-kiang; Li-Yu; The Imperial Palaces; The Forbidden City; The Yüan Ming Yüan; Ch'ien-lung, maecenas and collector; The Imperial workshops; Prime Minister Ho-k'un; The Chinese conoisseur and the West; The antiques market on the eve of the revolution.

Bibliography, p.263–67. Map of China, p.270–71. Chronology, p.274–82. Index, p.283–[87].

S93 Clunas, Craig. Superfluous things: material culture and social status in early modern China. Cambridge, Polity, 1991. vii, 219p. il., plates.

A study examining the perception of objects based on the author's analysis of material culture dating from the Ming Dynasty and the surviving literature of connoisseurship of the 16th and 17th centuries. This work "is an enormously suggestive book, leading the reader off in a variety of interesting directions—to consideration of the nature of authorship in the Ming, the relations between craftsmen and patrons, comparative uses of the past, and the techniques of art dealership and forgery, to mention just a few."—Social history, v.18, no.3, Oct., 1993, p.395. Two appendixes list the editors of Treatise on superfluous things and selected prices for works of art and antique artifacts c.1560–1620.

Contents: (1) Books about things: The literature of Ming Connoisseurship; (2) Ideas about things: themes in Ming connoisseurship literature; (3) Words about things: the language of Ming connoisseurship; (4) Things of the past: uses of the antique in Ming material culture; (5) Things in motion: Ming luxury objects as commodities; (6) Anxieties about things: consumption and class in Ming China.

Notes, p.[182]–96. Bibliography of primary sources, p.[197]–98. Bibliography of secondary sources, p.[199]–209. Index, p.[210]–19.

S94 Cohen, Warren I. East Asian art and American culture: a study in international relations. N.Y., Columbia Univ. Pr., 1992. xxi, 264p. il.

Combines analysis of collectors and collecting with Asian art history. Includes background chapters on Asian history and culture. Traces early collecting patterns in America and the growth of museum collections. "Cohen's volume will be most useful for those in need of an introduction to the history of East Asian art collections in America. Beginning collectors and students will find it stimulating and probably be encouraged to run down some of Cohen's references, especially now-neglected early publications and reviews."—Journal of the American Oriental Society, v.114, no.2, 1994, p.330.

Contents: (1) Art and American understanding of East Asian culture, 1784–1900; (2) The golden age of East Asian art collecting in America, 1893–1919; (3) Professionalism in America, Chaos in China: John Lodge and Langdon Warner; (4) War, depression, opportunity; (5) The fortunes of war: America's East Asia; (6) The East Asian art historians.

Notes, p.[207]–33. Bibliography, p.235–52. Index, p.253–64.

S95 Jessup, Helen Ibbitson. Court arts of Indonesia. N.Y., The Asia Society Galleries in assoc. with Abrams, 1990. 288p. il. (part col.), maps.

Catalog of the exhibition, Asia Society (1990–1992), and other locations. The first comprehensive examination of court patronage and the arts in Indonesia. Four richly illustrated essays emphasize the most important provinces of the Indonesian archipelago: Java, Sumatra, Kalimantan, Sulawesi, Bali, Nusa Tenggara, and Maluku. The catalog contains 157 objects in all media.

Contents: (I) From the mountain to the sea: Myth, legend, and literature in the origin and legitimacy of Princes; (II) Warriors, traders, and the celestially grand king: Establishing and maintaining princely power; (III) Princely pavilions: Architecture as an index to court and society; (IV) Pomp and circumstance: The court as center of ritual and patronage.

Chronology, p.267–68. Glossary, p.269. Notes, p.270–74. Bibliography, p.275–80. Index, p.281–88.

S96 The powers of art: patronage in Indian culture. Ed. by Barbara Stoler Miller. N.Y., Oxford Univ. Pr., 1992. x, 338p. il., plates.

Drawn from papers presented at the multi-disciplinary conference, Patronage in Indian Culture (1985). 13 of the 19 essays in this volume address aspects of Indian art and architecture.

Selective contents: (I) Patronage and community, by Romila Thapar; Collective and popular bases of early Buddhist patronage: sacred monuments, 100 BC–AD 250, by Vidya Dehejia; Female patronage in Indian Buddhism, by Janis D. Willis; A dynasty of patrons: the representation of Gupta Royalty in coins and literature, by Barbara Stoler Miller; Before the fall: pride and piety at Ajanta, by Walter M. Spink; The patronage of the Lakshmana Temple at Khajuraho, by Devangana Desai; (II) Royal architecture and imperial style at Vijayanagara, by George Mitchell; (III) Mughal sub-imperial patronage: the architecture of Rāja Mān Singh, by Catherine Singer; Jahāngīr's Jahāngīr-Nāma, by Milo C. Beach; The painter Nainsukh and his patron Blawant Singh, by B. N. Goswamy; (IV) Status and patronage of artist during British rule in India (c.1850–1900), by Partha Mitter; Transformation of objects into artifacts, antiquities and art in nineteenth-century India, by Bernard S. Cohn.

Notes at ends of chapters. Index, p.330–38.

S97 Royal patrons and great temple art. Ed. by Vidya Dehejia. Bombay, Marg, 1988.144p. il. (part col.)

An introduction to the cultural and religious context for patronage of temple art and architecture in the Buddhist, Jain, and Hindu traditions. Plentiful illustrations throughout though image quality is uneven.

Contents: Patron, artist and temple: an introduction, by Vidya Dehejia; Munificent monarch and a superior sculptor: eighth century Chamba, by Pratapaditya Pal; Inspired patron of Himalayan art: eighth century Kashmir, by Robert E. Fisher; Innovative emperor and his personal chapel: eighth century Kanchipuram, by R. Nagaswamy; Two Chalukya queens and their commemorative temples: eighth century Pattadakal, by Carol Radcliffe Bolon; Kalachuri Monarch and his circular shrine of the Yoginis: tenth century Bheraghat, by Vidya Dehejia; Lord of Kalajara and his shrine of Emerald Linga: eleventh century Khajuraho, by Devangana Desai; Scholar-emperor and a funerary temple: eleventh century Bhojpur, by Kirit Mankodi; A military general and his temple by the lake: thirteenth century Palampet, by Shebaz H. Safrani; Ganga Monarch and a monumental Sun Temple: thirteenth century Orissa, by Thomas E. Donaldson.

Notes at ends of chapters.

T. Cultural Heritage

A distinctive feature of the 20th century is the frequency with which movable and non-movable material products of our cultural heritage are dispersed or destroyed. A parallel trend has been the attempt to impede such dispersal and destruction, either through practical preservation techniques (conservation), or through policies and legislation aimed at establishing standards for the administration and protection of, and commerce in, cultural property at local, national, or international levels. This field is in a state of bibliographic flux: it is a relatively new area of investigation; scientific research encourages an ongoing evolution in preservation training and practice; and in the law and policy arena, case law and intergovernmental/political shifts propel changes in attitudes and governance.

The objective of this chapter is to map this bibliographically complex and expanding terrain. Given the parameters of this guide, the focus will be on interdisciplinary rather than on purely scientific or legal texts. The following subject areas are not specifically treated: art law (as opposed to cultural heritage legislation), case law, intellectual property law, museology, and performing arts law.

With the exception of those topics that have a longer history of study and research (e.g., fakes and forgeries, paintings conservation), most publications cited are recent and, where possible and appropriate, in English. While for the purposes of structural consistency with the rest of this volume the efforts of individual countries (or cultures) feature prominently, an attempt has been made to underscore the supranational characteristics of protection and preservation, not only because preservation practices are (or should be) universal, but also because many of the issues addressed transcend political boundaries. Judicious cross-references within this chapter will be helpful in identifying these overriding themes.

While GLAH 2 departs from its predecessor in devoting a separate chapter to Cultural Heritage, various titles listed throughout GLAH 1 are pertinent to this chapter. We have not attempted to draw attention to those titles through cross-references here but refer the interested reader to GLAH 1 and its index.

This chapter is divided into two parts: Preservation, followed by Preservation Law, Policy, and Ethics.

PART 1 PRESERVATION

BIBLIOGRAPHY

T1 A bibliography on historical organization practices. Ed. by Frederick L. Rath and Merrilyn Rogers O'Connell. Nashville, American Association for State and Local History, [1975–84]. 6v.

Useful collection of partially annotated bibliographies covering journal articles and monographs essential for an understanding of the foundations of the modern conservation movement. Covers books and journal articles. Although somewhat outdated, the bibliographies are useful for the thoughtful organization of subject-areas into sub-categories that accurately describe each field.

Contents: (1) Historic preservation; (2) Care and conservation of collections; (3) Interpretation; (4) Documentation of collections; (5) Administration; (6) Research.

Index in all vols.

T2 Collections care: a basic reference shelflist. Based on the Collections Care Information Service, a project of the National Institute for the Conservation of Cultural Property. Supported by the Institute of Museum Services and The Bay Foundation. Ed. by Amparo R. de Torres. Washington, D.C., National Institute for the Conservation of Cultural Property, 1990. 183p.

Unannotated bibliography comprising references to books and individual essays in books, conference papers, government reports, and journal articles. The period 1954–1990 is covered.

Contents: Basic collections care; Architectural conservation; Collections management law, ethics and policies; Collections storage; Emergency preparedness and response; Environmental control: illumination; Environmental control: pest management; Environmental control: pollution; Environmental control: temperature and relative humidity; Exhibitions and packing for shipment; Informatics of documentation; Safety and health.

T3 The conservation of cultural property: a basic reference shelflist. Ed. by James Bernstein. Washington,

D.C., National Institute for the Conservation of Cultural Property, [1985]. 45p.
Contents: General conservation readings and references; Conservation periodicals and journals; Conservation bibliographies; Education and training; Written and photographic documentation; Conservation safety; History and technology of materials; Conservation safety; History and technology of materials; Conservation science; Analysis and authenticity; Museum environment, security, and care of collections; Archaeology/ethnography; Stone and masonry; Architecture and building materials; Metals; Glass and ceramic; Wood and furniture; Fibers and textiles; Paper, parchment, books, library and archive materials; Leather; paintings and paint; Photographic materials; Miscellaneous; A partial list of conservation publications suppliers; Organizations listed by initials.

T4 Kahn, M. M., and Kumar, Devendra. Conservation: a selective bibliography. 2d ed. Lucknow [India], National Research Laboratory for Conservation of Cultural Property, 1994. 56p.
1st ed., 1987.
Unannotated bibliography covering books and journal articles.
Contents: (A) Causes of deterioration; (B) Materials used in conservation; (C) Conservation: general; (D) Scientific analysis in conservation; (E) Metals; (F) Stone; (G) Ceramics, terracotta & glass; (H) Coins and medals; (I) Wood and wooden furniture; (J) Textiles; (K) Paper, archives and library materials; (L) Manuscripts in paper, palm leaves and birch bark; (M) Paintings; (N) Paints, dyes, pigments and varnish; (O) Photographic and audiovisual materials; (P) Leather and skin; (Q) Bones and ivory; (R) Architecture, monuments and building materials; (S) Archaeological materials; (T) Ethnological materials; natural history materials; (U) Miscellaneous materials; (V) Miscellaneous materials; Appendix I: Journals relating to conservation.
Author index, p.51–55.

T5 Krist, Gabriela . . . [et al.] Bibliography: theses, dissertations, research reports in conservation: a preliminary report. [2d ed.] Rome, ICCROM, 1990. vii, 282p.
1st ed., Budapest, ICOM Committee for Conservation, 1987. 282p.
"Covers 3,500 titles from 74 training institutions in 20 countries."—*Pref.*
Contents: List of titles; List of authors; List of institutions.

SEE ALSO: Art and archaeology technical abstracts (GLAH 2:A2).

DIRECTORIES

T6 1985 directory, National Trust member organizations. Washington, D.C., National Trust for Historic Preservation, 1985. 75p.
"Organized regionally, according to the geographic jurisdictions of the National Trust regional offices. Information about each regional office precedes each section and member organizations are then listed alphabetically by state, city and organization name."
Contents: Mid-Atlantic region; Midwest region; Mountains/Plains region; Texas/New Mexico; Northeast region; Southern region; Western region; Foreign countries.

T7 American Institute for Conservation of Historic & Artistic Works. Directory. Washington, D.C., AIC., 1982(?)– .
Previously variously titled either AIC directory or Membership directory.
Important annual reference resource for conservation practitioners and administrators. Provides regional, national, and international information concerning members, committees, related organizations, suppliers and services, conservation terminology, code of ethics, bylaws, funding agencies, and training programs.

T8 Conservation sourcebook. The Conservation Unit, Museums & Galleries commission. [Rev. ed.] London, HMSO, 1991. 122p.
1st ed. titled Conservation sourcebook for conservators, craftsmen, and those who have historic objects in their care. London, Crafts Advisory Committee, 1979.
"Information on organisations of relevance to the conservation of artefacts and buildings."—*Introd.*
Contents: Directory of organisations; Appendix 1: International conservation organisations; Appendix 2: Full-time training courses in conservation.
Subject index, p.111–22.

T9 Heritage directory = Le répertoire du patrimoine. [Ottawa], Heritage Canada Foundation, [1974]–(1998).
In English and French.
Also available on the internet through the Canadian Heritage Information Network (CHIN).
Lists more than 600 Canadian national, provincial, and municipal organizations, government departments and agencies, as well as a selected list of foreign and international groups that are engaged in heritage activities. Extremely clearly presented.
Contents: (1) National associations; (2) Federal government departments; (3) Federal government agencies; (4) The Canadian ministry; (5) Provincial and territorial associations; (6) Provincial and territorial government departments; (7) Provincial and territorial ministers of natural and cultural sites; (8) Municipal heritage organizations; (9) Major museums; (10) University and college programs; (11) Community foundations; (12) Foreign and international organizations; Selected subject index.

T10 International directory of training in conservation of cultural property. Comp. by Cynthia Rockwell. In collab. with Kim Dalinka . . . [et al.] Printed as a joint venture with the Getty Conservation Institute. [5th ed.] Rome, ICCROM, 1994. viii, 167p.
1st ed., 1975. 4th ed., International index on training in conservation of cultural property = Répertoire international des institutions donnant une formation pour la conservation des biens culturels. Marina del Rey, Getty Conservation Institute, 1987.

"Designed to provide information on a wide variety of training opportunities at different levels and in various fields of conservation and restoration worldwide. The different types of programs include specialized multiyear courses leading to a degree, short-term courses for specialists, as well as conservation courses offered within programs leading to degrees in other fields."—*Pref.*

Contents: How to use the directory; Course listings.

Subject index, p.157–64. Country codes, p.167.

DICTIONARIES AND ENCYCLOPEDIAS

T11 Clydesdale, Amanda. Chemicals in conservation: a guide to possible hazards and safe use. 2d ed. [Edinburgh], Scottish Society for Conservation and Restoration, [1990]. [43]p.

Alphabetical listing of chemicals used in conservation, with descriptions.

Glossary, p.15–17. Bibliography, p.18–19. Index, p.20–43.

T12 A glossary of terms useful in conservation: with a supplement on reporting the condition of antiquities. Comp. by Elizabeth Phillimore. Ottawa, Canadian Museums Association, 1976. 45p.

Dictionary-format series of definitions, specifically covering the following fields: ceramics, enameling, general terms, glass, metals, miscellaneous materials, paintings, textiles, wood, and furniture.

Reporting the condition of antiquities, p.35–45. A glossary of terms useful in conservation: with a supplement on reporting the condition of antiquities.

T13 Savage, George. The art and antique restorers' handbook: a dictionary of materials and processes used in the restoration & preservation of all kinds of works of art. [Rev. ed.] N.Y., Praeger, [1967]. 142p.

Useful compilation, with some definitions long as four pages of text.

Bibliography, p.133. Index, p.135–42.

HISTORIES AND HANDBOOKS

T14 Adhesives and consolidants: preprints of the contributions to the Paris congress, 2–8 September 1984. Ed. by N. S. Brommelle . . . [et al.] London, International Institute for Conservation of Historic and Artistic Works, [1984]. 222p. il., tables.

Extremely useful resource. 47 contributions by leading practitioners and researchers in the field. Synthetic and natural adhesives, and their changing uses for a variety of media, are considered.

Bibliographical references follow most papers.

T15 American Institute for the Conservation of Historic and Artistic Works (AIC). Code of ethics and guidelines for practice of the American Institute for Conservation of Historic and Artistic Works. Washington, D.C., AIC, 1964– .

1st formulation, "The Murray Pease report . . . report of the Murray Pease Committee: I.I.C. American standards of practice and professional relations for conservators," in Studies in conservation, v.9, pt.3 Aug. 1964, p.116–21. 2d formulation and 1st individual ed., [New York, IIC-American Group, 1968] titled The Murray Pease report. Code of ethics for art conservators. 3d formulation (Washington, D.C., AIC, 1985) titled Code of ethics. Standards of practice. Most recent revision in AIC news, Nov. 1999: 6. Reprinted annually in the American Institute for Conservation of Historic & Artistic Works Directory (GLAH 2:T7).

The primary purpose of this code remains "to provide accepted criteria against which a specific procedure or operation can be measured when a question as to its adequacy has been raised."—*Studies in conservation*, v.9, pt.3, p.116. Continually reevaluated and revised by the AIC membership and the AIC's Ethics and Standards Committee.

T16 The art of the conservator. Ed. by Andrew Oddy. Washington, D.C., Smithsonian Institution Pr., 1992. 192p. il. (part col.)

Collection of essays aiming to elucidate for a broad audience what the museum world means by the term "conservation." For this reason "outstanding artefacts of international importance conserved using a wide range of materials and numerous scientific techniques of investigation" (*Introd.*), and themselves made of a variety of different materials, are presented. Excellent illustrations.

Bibliographical references follow each essay. Index, p.190–92.

T17 Arte e restauro. Fiesole [Florence], Nardini, 1978– .

Series of monographs on the theory and method of art restoration.

Contents: Baldini, Umberto. Teoria del restauro e unità di metodologia (1978–81); Casazza, Ornella. Il restauro pittorico nell'unità di metodologia (1st ed. not part of series; 6th ed., 1999); Matteini, Mauro, and Moles, Arcangelo; Scienza e restauro: metodi d'indagine (1986; 4th ed., 1993); Parronchi, Alessandro. Botticelli fra Dante e Petrarca (1985); Monticolo, Roberto. Meccanismi dell'opera d'arte: da un corso di disegno per il restauro (1987); Matteini, Mauro, and Moles, Arcangelo. La chimica nel restauro: I materiali dell'arte pittorica (1989); Il restauro del legno. A cura di Gennaro Tampone (1989–90); Brachert, Thomas. La patina nel restauro delle opere d'arte (1990); Althöfer, Heinz. Il restauro delle opere d'arte moderne e contemporanee (1991?); Conservare l'arte contemporanea. A cura di Lidia Righi (1992); Giannini, Cristina. Lessico del restauro: storia tecniche strumenti (1992); Lippi, Gabriella. Le professioni del restauro: formazione e competenze (1992); Archeologia: recupero e conservazione. A cura di Luisa Masetti Bitelli (1993); Fabbri, Bruno, and Ravanelli Guidotti, Carmen. Il restauro della ceramica (1993); Montagna, Giovanni. I pigmenti: prontuario per l'arte e il restauro (1993); Restauro di strumenti e materiali: scienza, musica, etnografia. A cura di Luisa Masetti Bitelli (1993); Scicolone, Giovanna. Il restauro dei dipinti contemporanei (1993); Arte contemporanea, conservazione e restauro: contributi al Colloquio sul restauro dell'arte moderna e contemporanea. A cura di Sergio Angelucci (1994); Caneva, Giulia . . . [et al.] La biologia nel restauro (1994; 2d ed., 1997); Conservazione dei dipinti su tavola. A cura di Luca Uzielli e Ornella Casazza (1994); Corallini, Americo, and Bertuzzi, Valeria. Il restauro delle vetrate (1994); Ambiente, città e museo: orientamenti per la conservazione e valorizzazione dei beni culturali. A cura di Gabriella Lippi (1995); Colombo, Luciano. I colori degli antichi (1995); Fazi, Benedetta, and Vittorini, Benedetta. Nuove tecniche di foderatura: le tele vaticane di Pietro da Cortona ad Urbino (1995); Mehra, V. Raj. Foderatura a freddo (1995?); Organi storici delle Marche: gli srumenti restaurati, 1974–1992. A cura di Paolo Peretti (1995); Palazzi, Sergio. Colorimetria: La scienza del colore nell'arte e nella tecnica (1995); Caneva, Giulia . . . [et al.] Il controllo del degrado biologico: i biocidi nel restauro dei materiali lapidei (1996); Ordoñez, Cristina . . . et al. Il mobile: conservazione e il restauro (1996); Pertegato, Francesco. Il restauro degli arazzi (1996); Althöfer, Heinz. La radiologia per il restauro delle opere d'arte moderne e contemporanee (1997); Teatri storici: dal restauro allo spettacolo. A cura di Lidia Bortolotti e Luisa Masetti Bitelli (1997); Aerobiologia e beni culturali. A cura di Paolo Mandrioli and Giulia Caneva (1998); Catalano, Maria Ida. Brandi e il restauro: percorsi del pensiero: con lettere inedite dal carteggio fra Cesare Brandi e Enrico Vallecchi (1998); Fancelli, Paolo. Il restauro dei monumenti (1998).

T18 Arte e restauro/Strumenti. Fiesole [Florence], Nardini, 1991– .

Distinct from preceding entry. Volume numeration inconsistently applied by publisher.

Contents: Massa, Vincenzo, and Scicolone, Giovanna C. Le vernici per il restauro: i leganti (1991); Liotta, Giovanni. Gli insetti e i danni del legno: problemi di restauro (1991); Copedè, Maurizio. La carta e il suo degrado (1991); Berger, Gustav A. La foderatura; Cristoferi, Elena. Gli avori: problemi di restauro (1992); Jacob, Michael G. Il dagherrotipo a colori: tecniche e conservazione (1992); Pertegato, Francesco. I tessili: degrado e restauro (1993); Dipinti su tela: metodologie d'indagine per i supporti cellulosici. A cura di Giovanna Scicolone (1993); Guglielmino, Giorgio. Le opere d'arte trafugate: legislazione e normativa internazionale (1997); Palazzi, Sergio. Analisi chimica per l'arte e il restauro: principi, tecniche, applicazioni (1997).

T19 Bail, Stephen. Larger & working objects: a guide to their preservation and care. Ed. by Peter Winsor. [London, Museums and Galleries Commission, 1997.] 71p. il.

Establishes "practical and realistic standards that preservation groups and small museums" specializing in large, working objects can follow.

Contents: (1) Acquiring and building the collection; (2) Care and conservation; (3) Making, keeping and using records: recommended relative humidity and temperature conditions for archives storage; (4) Access, loans and research; (5) To work, or not to work?: preserving the intangible; (6) Understanding and controlling the environment in which the collection is housed; (7) Damage, dust, dirt and pests; (8) Trains and boats and planes: some specialist aspects of care; (9) Is your collection safe?; (10) Security; (11) Doom and disaster: planning for the worst; Appendix: useful information.

Important references, p.62–66. Useful addresses, p.67–71.

T20 Brandi, Cesare. Il restauro: teoria e pratica 1939–1986. A cura di Michele Cordaro. [Roma], Editori Riuniti, [1994]. 337p. 9 plates.

Collection of Brandi's writings on conservation theory and practice, key to the development of conservation as a recognized discipline. The essays, grouped thematically, range from discussions of individual art works and the conservation work carried out on them, to specific conservation methods, to broader issues of urban development, and to more general reflections on the nature of conservation.

Contents: La definizione teorica del restauro; L'esperienza concreta del restauro; Cronaca e critica dei restauri: Urbanistica; L'archeologia e il rudere; Il restauro architettonico; Inquinamento e restauro delle facciate; Rifacimenti e aggiunte; La pulitura e la patina dei dipinti; Il restauro preventivo.

Bibliographical references follow the Introd. Note del curatore, p.299–315. Bibliografia degli scritti di Brandi sul restauro, p.317–26. Indice dei nomi, p.327–32. Indice dei luoghi notevoli, p.333–37.

T21 ______. Teoria del restauro. [Torino], Einaudi, [1977]. 154p.

1st ed., Roma, Edizioni di storia e letteratura, 1963. The first ed. also included a bibliography of Brandi's publications, a brief biography, and 40 plates illustrating his arguments.

Pioneering publication on conservation methodology, based on lectures delivered by Brandi at the Istituto Centrale di Restauro, founded by him in 1939, and directed by him 1939–1961. Brandi advocated that the objective of conservation should not be to return a work to its original aspect ("restoration"). Rather, he argued, any missing parts of a work of art should undergo only minimal intervention, thus reducing the risk of misinterpreting the artist's original intentions. Brandi also rejected the then-widespread practice in conservation of eliminating subsequent additions or modifications that made up part of the object's history, and instead argued for their retention in the conserved item. Brandi's ideas became an integral part of conservation theory and practice in Italy, spreading rapidly to other countries. In 1972 Brandi's theories were incorporated into the Carta del restauro.

T22 Burroughs, Alan. Art criticism from a laboratory. Boston, Little, Brown, 1938. xv, 277p. il., ports.

Early text on the application of scientific investigation to art, art history, and conservation.

Contents: (1) The aesthetic background; (2) The tools of criticism; (3) Testing the tools; (4) Applying the tools of science; (5) Forgeries; (6) Copies and imitations; (7) Artists at work; (8) The development of an artist: Nicolas Maes; (9) Titian and Giorgione; (10) A Flemish art factory; (11) Two problems in the Rembrandtesque; (12) The problem of the Van Eycks; (13) The reality of Robert Campin; Appendixes A–D.

Index, p.271–77.

T23 Butterworth-Heinemann series in conservation and museology. Boston, Butterworth-Heinemann, 1982– . Formerly titled Butterworths series in conservation and museology. Important series of monographs on conservation and museology.

Contents: Agrawal, Om Prakesh. Conservation of manuscripts and painting of South-east Asia (1984); Mora, Paolo; Mora, Laura; and Philippot, Paul. Conservation of wall paintings (1984); Kuhn, H. Conservation and restoration of works of art and antiquities (1986); Stolow, Nathan. Conservation and exhibitions: packing, transport, storage and environmental consideration (1986); Thomson, Garry. The museum environment (2d ed., 1986); Conservation of library and archive materials and the graphic arts. Ed. by Guy Petherbridge (1987); Conservation of marine archaeological objects, Ed. by Colin Pearson (1987); Conservation of building and decorative stone. Ed. by John Ashurst and Francis G. Dimes (1990, 1998); Horie, C. V. Materials for conservation: organic consolidants, adhesives and coatings (2d ed., 1992); Landi, Sheila. The textile conservator's manual (2d ed., 1992); Buys, Susan, and Oakley, Victoria. Conservation and restoration of ceramics (1994); Mills, John S., and White, Raymond. The organic chemistry of museum objects (2d ed., 1994); The care and conservation of palaeontological materials. Ed. by Chris Collins (1995); Newton, Roy, and Davison, Sandra. Conservation of glass (rev ed., 1996); Radiography of cultural material. Ed. by Janet Lang and Andrew Middleton (1997); Chemical principles of textile conservation. Ed. by Agnes Timar-Balazsy and Dinah Eastop (1998); Historic floors; their history and conservation. Ed. by Jane Fawcett (1998); Timar-Balazsy, Agnes, and Eastop, Dinah. Chemical principles of textile conservation (1998); Jokilehto, Jukka. A history of architectural conservation (1999); Warren, John. Conservation of brick (1999); Warren, John. Conservation of earth structures (1999).

T24 Care of collections. Ed. by Simon Knell. N.Y., Routledge, [1994]. 282p. il., charts, diags., tables. (Leicester readers in museum studies)

Collection of previously published essays chosen to "provide information of practical use to the student of collections management."—*Pref.*

Contents: (1) The ethics of conservation, by Jonathan Ashley-Smith; (2) Cleaning and meaning: The ravished image reviewed, by Gerry Hedley; (3) Solvent abuse, by Michael Daley; (4) Working exhibits and the destruction of evidence in the Science Museum, by Peter R. Mann; (5) The role of the scholar-curator in conservation, by Peter Cannon-Brookes; (6) Do objects have a finite lifetime?, by Susan M. Bradley; (7) Audits of care: a framework for collections condition surveys, by Suzanne Keene; (8) Preventive conservation, by the Getty Conservation Institute; (9) Paintings: the (show) case for passive climate control, by Emil Bosshard; (10) Silica gel and related RH buffering materials, conditioning and regeneration techniques, by Nathan Stolow; (11) Conservation in the computer age, by Richard Hall; (12) Museums tune in to radio, by Graham Martin and David Ford; (13) Fresh-air climate conditioning at the Arthur M. Sackler Museum, by Michael Williams; (14) Light and environmental measurement and control in National Trust houses, by Sarah Staniforth; (15) The Clore Gallery for the Turner collection at the Tate Gallery: lighting strategy and practice, by Peter Wilson; (16) Construction materials for storage and exhibition, by Ann Brooke Craddock; (17) Indoor air pollution: effects on cultural and historic materials, by Norbert S. Baer and Paul N. Banks; (18) Managing museum space, by U. Vincent Wilcox; (19) Museum collections storage, by John D. Hilberry and Susan K. Weinberg; (20) Here's what to consider in selecting high-density storage, by Abigail Terrones; (21) A policy for collections access, by Jeanette A. Richoux, Jill Serota-Braden and Nancy Demyttenaere; (22) Visible storage for the small museum, by Paul C. Thistle; (23) Curator's closet, by Carrie Rebora; (24) Rules for handling works of art, by Eric B. Rowlison; (25) Rentokil bubble: results of test, by R. M. Entwistle and J. Pearson; (26) Carpet beetle: a pilot study in detection and control, by Lynda Hillyer and Valerie Blyth; (27) Pest control in museums: the use of chemicals and associated health problems, by Martyn J. Linnie; (28) Experiencing loss, by Barclay G. Jones; (29) Museum disaster preparedness planning, by John E. Hunter; (30) Emergency treatment of materials, by M. S. Upton and C. Pearson; (31) Protecting museums from threat of fire, by H. L. Lein.

Bibliographical references follow each essay. Further reading, p.280. Index, p.281–82.

T25 Caring for your collections. The National Committee to Save America's Cultural Collections, Arthur W. Schultz, Chairman. Foreword by Arthur W. Schultz. Introd. by the Honorable Robert McCormick Adams. N.Y., Abrams, [1992]. 216p.

Collection of essays designed to provide practical and authoritative information for individual collectors on the best ways to preserve the objects they own.

Contents: The mortality of things, by Joyce Hill Stoner; Creating and maintaining the right environment, by Steven Weintraub; Paintings, by William R. Leisher; Works of art on paper, by Margaret Holben Ellis; Library and archival collections, by Doris A. Hamburg; Photographs, by Debbie Hess Norris; Furniture, by Brian Considine; Textiles, by Sara J. Wolf; Decorative arts, by Met Craft; Metal objects, by Terry Drayman-Weisser; Stone objects, by George Segan Wheeler; Musical instruments, by J. Scott Odell; Ethnographic materials, by Carolyn L. Rose; Security for cultural objects in the home, by Wilbur Faulk; The increasing value of art and historical artifacts; Authenticating your collections, by Richard Newman; Appraising and insuring your collections, by Huntington T. Block; Donating your collections, by Leonard L. Silverstein; Obtaining professional conservation services, by Shelley G. Sturman.

Conservation resources, p.[202]. Further reading, p.[203]–07. Index, p.211–16.

T26 Conservatie en restauratie van moderne en actuele kunst: een interdisciplinair gebeuren. Wetenschappelijke coördinatie, Claire Van Damme. [Gent], CoReModAc [Studiecentrum voor Conservatie en Restauratie van Moderne en Actuele Kunst, Rijksuniversiteit Gent], [1992]. 236p. il. (part col.)

In Flemish, French, and German. Papers by internationally recognized experts, originally presented at a conference (Gent, 1990).

Selective bibliografie, by P. Vandepitte, p.227–36.

T27 Conservation concerns: a guide for collectors and curators. Ed. by Konstanze Bachmann. Washington, D.C., Smithsonian Institution Pr., [1992]. ix, 149p. il., tables.

Based on a series of conservation bulletins produced under the aegis of the Cooper-Hewitt Museum, New York. The intention is "to make the basic concepts of preservation and conservation readily accessible to everyone caring for collections, especially those who lack the resources and trained personnel that usually are available to larger public collections."—*Introd.*

Contents: Principles of storage, by Konstanze Bachmann and Rebecca Anne Rushfield; Emergency planning, by Mary Ballard; Control of temperature and humidity in small collections, by Ann Brooke Craddock; Storage of works on paper, by Marjorie Shelley; Warning signs: when works on paper require conservation, by Marjorie Shelley; Storage and care of photographs, by Klaus B. Hendriks; Warning signs: when photographs need conservation, by Klaus B. Hendriks; The preservation and storage of sound recordings, by Klaus B. Hendriks; Painting storage: a basic guideline, by Kenneth S. Moser; When is it time to call a paintings conservator?, by Charles von Nostitz; Storage of historic fabrics and costumes, by Christine Giuntini; Textile conservation, by Patsy Orlofsky; Warning signs: when textiles need conservation, by Lucy A. Commoner; Storage of stone, ceramic, glass, and metal, by Lynda A. Zycheman; The care and conservation of metal artifacts, by Elayne Grossbard; Furniture conservation, by Susan Klim; Upholstery conservation, by Kathryn Gill; Preserving ethnographic objects, by Carolyn L. Rose; Care of folk art: the decorative surface, by Valerie Reich Hunt; Composite objects: materials and storage conditions, by Valerie Reich Hunt; Appendix: Conservation suppliers; Conservation centres; Conservation and collections care training.

Reading list, p.141–49.

T28 Conservation monograph series. London, Archetype, 1993– . 3v.

Contents: Electronic environmental monitoring in museums. Ed. by Robert Child (1993); Conservation of geological collections. Ed. by R. E. Child (1994); Pinniger, David. Insect pests in museums (3d ed., 1994).

T29 The conservation of cultural property: with special reference to tropical conditions. Prepared in co-operation with the International Centre for the Study of the Preservation and Restoration of Cultural Property, Rome, Italy. [Paris], Unesco, [1968]. 341p. il., maps, tables. (Museums and monuments, XI) (Repr.: Paris, Unesco, 1979)

"The primary aim of this manual is to meet the needs of institutions in the tropical regions of the world."—*Foreword.* Basic guide to the conservation requisites for governments, policy makers, and practitioners in these countries.

Contents: (1) The significance of cultural property, by Hiroshi Daifuku; (2) Climate and microclimate, by Paul Coremans; (3) Combating moulds, by Roger Heim . . . [et al.]; (4) Identification and control of insect pests, by J. J. H. Swent-Ivany; (5) Organization of a national service for the preservation of cultural property, by Paul Coremans; (6A) Equipping the laboratory: basic equipment and processes by H. W. M. Hodges; (6B) Equipping the laboratory: an example of Unesco's programme to aid countries in the tropical regions of the world, by H. Daifuku; (7) Moulding, casting and electrotyping, by B. A. F. Nimmo and A. G. Prescott; (8) Pottery and glass, by I. Gedye; (9) Preservation of entomological materials in the tropics, by J. L. Gressit; (10A) Monuments: problems in the preservation of monuments, by H. J. Plenderleith; (10B) Monuments: examples of problems encountered in the field, by Paul Coremans; (10C) Examples of the preservation of monuments in India, by T. R. Gairola; (11) The conservation of urban sites, by R. M. F. de Andrade; (12) The conservation of wall paintings, by Paul Philippot and Paolo Mora; (13) The conservation research: conservation and restoration of easel paintings, by William Boustead; (14) The conservation of stone, by R. V. Sneyers and P. J. de Henau; (15) The conservation of metals in the tropics, by H. J. Plenderleith and G. Toracca; (16) The conservation of textiles, by E. R. Beecher; (17) The conservation of leather, wood, bone, ivory and archival materials, by A. E. Werner; (18) Lighting, air-conditioning, exhibition, storage, handling and packing, by N. S. Brommelle; Appendix: Synthetic materials used in the conservation of cultural property.

Bibliographical references throughout the text, and following each essay. Index of trade names, p.329–31. Index of producers, p.332–35. Subject index, p.337–41.

T30 Conservation of the Iberian and Latin American cultural heritage: preprints of the contributions to the Madrid congress, 9–12 September 1992. Ed. by H. W. M. Hodges . . . [et al.] London, International Institute for Conservation of Historic and Artistic Works, [1992]. 183p. il., 26 col. plates, diags., tables.

38 papers on specific case histories as well as broader conservation research issues. A range of media is discussed.

Bibliographical references follow each paper.

T31 Conservation research: Washington, D.C., National Gallery of Art, 1993– . (Studies in the history of art, 41, 42, 51, 57; Monograph series, 2)

Intermittently issued series reporting on the research and technical studies pursued by the National Gallery of Art's conservation division.

Contents: (41) [Without special title]; (42) Studies of fifteenth- to nineteenth-century tapestry. Ed. by Lotus Stack (1993); (51) Conservation research 1995 (1995); (57) Conservation research 1996/1997 (1997).

Bibliographical references follow each paper.

T32 The conservator as art historian: papers given at a UKIC Wall paintings section conference on 20 June

1992 at Abingdon, Oxfordshire. Ed. by Anna Hulbert . . . [et al.] London, United Kingdom Institute for Conservation of Historic and Artistic Works of Art, 1993. 44p. il.

"The aim of these transactions is to form a starting point for the collection of historical information encountered during conservation work, both for the benefit of art historians . . . and for the encouragement of awareness in conservators with regard to the usefulness of their professional examination."—*Pref.* The focus is on paintings and architectural polychromy.

Contents: Glastonbury Abbey: The Lady Chapel doors and their dating in the light of the 1986 conservation programme, by Jerry Sampson; Exeter Cathedral: exterior polychromy, by Eddie Sinclair; The recovery of the Jesse Tree sequence of panels in St Helen's, Abingdon, and workshop notes, by Anna Hulbert; Examination and analysis prior to the restoration of a 14th century stained glass window, by Stephen Jones; Recent discoveries in Cormac's Chapel, Cashel, Co Tipperary, Eire, by Mark Perry.

Bibliographical references follow each paper. List of churches with recorded wall paintings, by E. Clive Rouse, p.36. Bibliography of publications and theses on wall paintings, p.37–40. An interim list of publications by conservators and historians on discoveries and observations make in English buildings, p.41–44.

T33 Conservazione del patrimonio culturale: ricerche interdisciplinari. Roma, Accademia nazionale dei Lincei, 1994– .

Focused monographs on the conservation of cultural properties.

Contents: (1) [without special title]; (2) [without special title]; (3) La diffusione in Italia delle metodologie scientifiche per lo studio e la conservazione delle opere d'arte; (4) Marabelli, Maurizio. Conservazione e restauro dei metalli d'arte.

T34 La conservazione e il restauro oggi. Firenze, Nardini, 1992– .

Monographs on current trends in conservation and restoration.

Contents: (1) Le professioni del restauro: formazione e competenze. A cura di Gabriella Lippi (1992); (2) Conservare l'arte contemporanea. A cura di Lidia Righi (1992); (3) Archeologia: recupero e conservazione. A cura di Luisa Masetti Bitelli (1993); (4) Restauro di strumenti e materiali: scienza musica etnografia. A cura di Luisa Masetti Bitelli (1993).

T35 Ex fabrica: cultura, storia e tecniche della conservazione. Milano, F. Angelo, 1984– .

Scholarly monographic series focusing on the preservation of Italy's architectural heritage. Includes several bibliographically complex sub-series on, for example, the history, techniques, and economics of preservation in Italy.

T36 GCI scientific program reports. Pasadena; Marina del Rey, Calif., Environmental Quality Laboratory, California Institute of Technology; Getty Conservation Institute, 1988– .

Series of specialist papers by conservation research scientists.

Contents: Cass, Glen R. Protection of works of art from photochemical smog (1988); Energy conservation and climate control in museums. . . . Prepared by Ayres Ezer Lau Consulting engineers (1988); Koestler, Robert J. Assessment of the susceptibility to biodeterioration of selected polymers and resins (1988); Standard operating protocol: analysis of aldehydes, ketones and carboxylic acids using HPLC. Prepared by Cecily M. Druzik and Amy Taketomo (1988); Annotated bibliography of sulfur flouride. [Comp. by Mary T. Baker . . . (et al.)] (1989); Hisham, Mohamed W.M., and Grosjean, Daniel. Air pollution in Southern California museums (1989); Preusser, Frank. Development of a prototype sealed storage and display case (1989); Preusser, Frank, and Druzik, James R. Environmental research at the Getty Conservation Institute: background, recent findings and goals, 1984–1989 (1989); Abgabian, M. S. . . . [et al.] Evaluation of seismic mitigation measures for art objects (1990); Schilling, Michael R. Analysis of polymeric and composite materials using thermogravimetry (1990); Williams, Edwin L., and Grosjean, Daniel. Exposure of deacidified paper to ambient levels of SO2 and N02 (1990); Nazaroff, William . . . [et al.] Protection of works of art from soiling due to airborne particulates (1992); Reedy, Terry J., and Reedy, Chandra L. Principles of experimental design for art conservation research (1992); Rust, Michael K., and Kennedy, Janice M. The feasibility of using modified atmospheres to control insect pests in museums (1993); Research abstracts of the scientific program. Ed. by James R. Druzik (3d ed., 1994); Tolles, E. Leroy . . . [et al.] Survey of damage to historic adobe buildings after the January 1994 Northridge earthquake (1996).

T37 Gilardoni, Arturo . . . [et al.] X-rays in art = Raggi X nell'arte. 2d ed. Mandello Lario (Lecco, Italy), Gilardoni, 1994. 342p. il. (part col.), col. ports., tables.

1st ed., 1977. Text in English and Italian.

Describes "the role played by x-rays in the interpretation of paintings, ceramics, stamps and antique pieces."—*Foreword.* The numerous illustrations are accompanied by detailed captions describing technical details.

Glossary, p.301–10. Analytic-alphabetical index, p.317–21. Bibliography, p.323–36.

T38 The heritage: care-preservation-management. Ed. by Andrew Wheatcroft. N.Y., Routledge, 1991– .

Series primarily dealing with museological topics, but with some titles specifically on conservation.

Selective contents: Alfrey, Judith, and Putnam, Tim. The industrial heritage: managing resources and uses (1992); Walsh, Kevin. The representation of the past: museums and heritage in the post-modern world (1992); Science for conservators: conservation science teaching series 3v. (2d ed., 1992); Strike, James. Architecture in conservation: managing developments at historic sites (1994).

T39 Historic preservation in foreign countries. Ed. by Robert E. Stipe. Washington, D.C., ICOMOS, 1982–84.

Contents: (1) Dale, Antony. France, Great Britain, Ireland, The Netherlands, and Denmark; (2) Will, Margaret T. West Germany, Switzerland and Austria.

T40 Historical and philosophical issues in the conservation of cultural heritage. Ed. by Nicholas Stanley Price, M. Kirby Talley Jr., and Alessandra Melucco Vaccaro. Los Angeles, Getty Conservation Institute, [1996]. xvii, 500p. il. (part col.), ports. (part col.) (Readings in conservation, 1)

"The main aim of this volume has been to compile a number of writings that have proved to be influential in the development of thinking about the conservation of cultural heritage. . . . The present volume of readings presents texts and commentary relevant to the appreciation and conservation of all works of art."—*Pref.* Thoughtful selection of key texts, of which all foreign-language items are provided in English translation.

Contents: (I) The eye's caress: looking, appreciation, and connoisseurship: (1) The lamp of memory, I, by John Ruskin; (2) Aesthetics and history in the visual arts, by Bernard Berenson; (3) Art, by Clive Bell; (4) Looking at pictures, by Kenneth Clark; (5) The history of art as a humanistic discipline, by Erwin Panofsky; (6) The modern cult of monuments: its essence and its development, by Alois Riegl; (7) Principles of art history, by Heinrich Wölfflin; (8) Italian painters of the Renaissance, by Bernard Berenson; (9) Conversations with Berenson, by Umberto Morra; (10) Fundamental laws of sculpture, by John Ruskin; (11) From light into paint, by E. H. Gombrich; (12) Of Turnerian mystery: secondly, willful, by John Ruskin; (13) Rudiments of connoisseurship, by Bernard Berenson; (14) On art and connoisseurship, by Max J. Friedländer; (15) Connoisseurship, by John Pope-Hennessy ; (16) The nature of Gothic, by John Ruskin; (II) The original intent of the artists: (17) Art in transition, by Albert Albano; (18) Crimes against the Cubists, by John Richardson; (19) The autonomy of restoration: ethical considerations in relation to artistic concepts, by Ernst van de Wetering; (III) The emergence of modern conservation theory: (20) That mighty sculptor, Time, by Marguerite Yourcenar; (21) Restoration from the perspective of the humanities, by Paul Philippot; (22) Theory of restoration, I, by Cesare Brandi; (23) The integration of the image: problems in the restoration of monuments, by Giovanni Carbonara; (24) Knowing how to "question" the object before restoring it, by Albert France-Lanord; (25) Introduction to archaeological conservation, by Marie Berducou; (IV) Historical perspective: (26) Historic preservation: philosophy, criteria, guidelines, I, by Paul Philippot; (27) Degradation, conservation, and restoration of works of art: historical overview, by R. H. Marijnissen; (28) Further materials for a history of conservation, by Sheldon Keck; (29) The surgery of memory: ancient sculpture and historical restorations, by Orietta Rossi Pinelli; (V) Restoration and anti-restoration: (30) Restoration, by Eugène-Emmanuel Viollet-le-Duc; (31) Manifesto of the Society for the Protection of Ancient Buildings, by William Morris; (32) The Lamp of memory, II, by John Ruskin; (VI) Reintegration of losses: (33) On restorations, by Max J. Friedländer; (34) The problem of the integration of lacunae in the restoration of paintings, by Albert Philippot and Paul Philippot; (35) Theory of restoration, II, by Cesare Brandi; (36) Problems of presentation, by Paolo Mora, Laura Mora, and Paul Philippot; (37) Theory of restoration and methodological unity, by Umberto Baldini; (38) Historic preservation: philosophy, criteria, guidelines, II, by Paul Philippot; (VII) The idea of patina: (39) The idea of patina and the cleaning of paintings, by Paul Philippot; (40) Theory of restoration, III, by Cesare Brandi; (41) The cleaning of pictures in relation to patina, varnish, and glazes, by Cesare Brandi; (42) A review of the history and practice of patination, by Phoebe Dent Weil; (43) The surface of objects and museum style, by Ernst van de Wetering; (VIII) The role of science and technology: (44) Scientific research and the restoration of paintings, by Paul Coremans; (45) The scientist's role in historic preservation with particular reference to stone conservation, by Giorgio Torraca; (46) The science and art of conservation of cultural property, by Giovanni Urbani.

Annotated bibliography, p.451–71. Index, p.486–500.

T41 ICCROM technical notes = Notes techniques de l'ICCROM. Rome, International Centre for the Study of the Preservation and the Restoration of Cultural Property, 1972– .

Focused series of technical monographs.

Contents: Foramitti, Hans. Mesures de sécurité et d'urgence pour la protection des biens culturels (1972); Gazzola, Pietro. The past in the future (2d ed., 1975); Marasovic, Tomislav. Methodological proceedings for the protection and revitalization of historic sites (experiences of Split) (1975); Stambolov, T., and Van Asperen de Boer, J. R. J. The deterioration and conservation of porous building materials in monuments (1976); Massari, Giovanni. Humidity in monuments (2d ed., 1977); Torraca, Giorgio. Solubilité et solvants utilisés pour la conservation des biens culturels (1980); Torraca, Giorgio. Solubilidad y disolventes en los problemas de conservación (1981); De Angelis d'Ossat, Guglielmo. Guide to the methodical study of monuments and causes of their deterioration (2d ed., 1982); Torraca, Giorgio. Solubility and solvents for conservation problems (3d, rev. ed., 1984); Gallo, Fausta. Biological factors in deterioration of paper (1985); Masschelein-Kleiner, Liliane. Ancient binding media, varnishes and adhesives (1985); Torraca, Giorgio. Matériaux de construction poreux (1986); Torraca, Giorgio. Porous building materials: materials science for architectural conservation (3d ed., 1988).

T42 International Centre for the Study of the Preservation and the Restoration of Cultural Property. Works and publications. Rome, ICCROM; or Paris, Eyrolles, 1960–1978.

Focused series of technical monographs.

Contents: (1) International inventory of the museum laboratories and restoration workshops (1960); (2) Conservation of mural paintings in different countries: reports on the general situation (1960); (3) Climatologie et conservation dans les musées = Climatology and conservation in museums (1960); (4) [Untraced]; (5) Synthetic materials used in the conservation of cultural property (1963); (6) Plenderleith, Harold James. La conservation des antiquités et des oeuvres d'art (Eyrolles, 1966); (7) Iniguez Herrero, Jaime. Alteration des calcaires et des grès utilisées dans la construction (Paris, Eyrolles, 1967); (8) Problems of conservation in museums (Eyrolles, 1969); (9) Foramitti, Hans. Mésures de securité et d'urgence pour la protection des biens culturels (1972); (9; sic) Flieder, Françoise. La conservation des documents graphiques (Eyrolles, 1969); (10) Massari, Giovanni. Bâtiments humides et insalubres: pratique de leur assainissement (Eyrolles, 1971); (11) Muhlethaler, Bruno. Conservation of waterlogged wood and wet leather (Paris, Eyrolles, 1973); (12) Torraca, Giorgio. Solubility and solvents for conservation problems (2d ed., 1978); (13) Marasovic, Tomislav. Methodological proceedings for the protection and revitalization of historic sites (experiences of Split) (1975); (14) Bachmann, Karl-Werner. La conservation durant les expositions temporaires = Conservation during temporary exhibitions (1975); (15) Gazzola, Pietro. The past in the future (1975); (16) Stambolov, T., and Asperen de Boer, J. R. J. van. The deterioration and conservation of porous buiding materials in monuments: a review of the literature (2d ed., 1976); (17) [Untraced]; (18) Torraca, Giorgio. Porous building materials: materials science for architectural conservation (2d, rev. ed., 1982).

T43 Keene, Susan. Managing conservation in museums. Boston, Butterworth-Heinemann, [1996]. vii, 265p. il., tables.

"Sets out to open the box labelled 'management' and see what is in it that conservators could use."—*Pref.* Emphasizes the need not only for conservators to acquire information, but also for them to use it judiciously with the aim of achieving greater influence in the organizations.

Contents: (1) Introduction; (2) Museums and collections; (3) Management and information; (4) Management tools: quantitative planning; (5) Management tools: options and priorities; (6) A systems view; (7) The preservation system; (8) Information for preservation (9) Collections condition; (10) Directions and strategies; (11) Planning and monitoring work; (12) Computerizing conservation information; (13) Future, present, past.

Bibliographical references at the end of each chapter. Index, p.257–65.

T44 Laser cleaning in conservation: an introduction. Ed. by Martin Cooper. [Boston], Butterworth-Heinemann, [1998]. [8], 98p. il., 6 col. plates, charts, diags., tables.

Series devoted to various applications of laser technology.

Bibliographical references follow each chapter. Glossary, p.93–95. Index, p.97–98.

T45 Macarrón Miguel, Ana M. Historia de la conservación y la restauración: desde la Antigüedad hasta finales del siglo XIX. [Madrid], Tecnos, [1995]. 189p. il. (part col.)

Discusses the history of conservation and restoration, with reference to the prevailing aesthetics, philosophies, religious ideas, politics and ideologies, and scientific and technical advances of each period. From the time of ancient Greece to the 19th century, attitudes to conservation as well as examples of conservation procedures are examined. The primary focus is architecture, painting, and sculpture, although issues surrounding archeological excavations (e.g., trade and collecting) are also addressed.

Bibliografía, p.185–88.

T46 Manual of curatorship: a guide to museum practice. [Ed. by] John M. A. Thompson . . . [et al.] 2d ed. [Boston, Butterworth-Heinemann, 1992]. xvii, 756p. il.

"Comprehensive reference work for museum professionals involved in the diversity of activities which characterize museums in the 1990s."—*Pref.* Includes extensive coverage of conservation method and practice.

Contents: Conservation: Introduction, by Peter N. Lowell; Documenting collections, by Sheila M. Stone; Conservation documentation, by Michael Corfield; Control and measurement of the environment, by Sarah Staniforth; Buildings, environment and artefacts, by Trevor Skempton; Conservation and storage: archival paper, by Michael Bottomley; Conservation and storage: prints, drawings and water-colours, by Jane McAusland; Conservation and storage: easel paintings, by David Bomford and James Dimond; Conservation and storage: photographic materials, by Anne Fleming and Elizabeth Martin; Conservation and storage: textiles, by Jean M. Glover; Conservation and storage: leather objects, by C. V. Horie; Conservation and storage: wood, by John Kitchin; Conservation and storage: ceramics, by Christine Daintith; Conservation and storage: stone, by Jennifer K. Dinsmore; Conservation and storage: metals, by Hazel Newey; Conservation and storage: machinery, by John Hallam; Conservation and storage: archaeological material, by Elizabeth Pye; Conservation and storage: geological material, by Francis M. P. Howie; Conservation and storage: zoological collections, by Geoffrey Stansfield; Object handling, by Gwyn Miles; Storage systems, by James Tate and Theo Skinner; Conservation aspects of storage and display, by Susan M. Bradley; Pest control in museums, by Richard Dennis; Scientific examination of artefacts, by Andrew Oddy; Disaster planning, by Sue Cackett.

Bibliographical references follow each essay.

T47 Marijnissen, R. H., and Kockaert, L. Dialoog met het geschonden beeld na 250 jaar restaureren. [Antwerpen], Mercatorfonds, [1995]. 275p. il. (part col.), col. plates, ports. (part col.) (Bibliotheek van de Vrienden van het Mercatorfonds, 4)

Clearly presented and excellently illustrated. Wide-ranging in media examined, the focus is on Flemish and Netherlandish art.

Contents: Hoe werd er vroeger gerestaureerd?; De levensloop van een kunstwerk; De oorspronkelijke toestand; Restauratie en webenschap; De duurzaamheid van moderne en hedendaagse kunst; Proeve van methode; De deontologie van het vak; De scholing; Bij wijze van besluit.

Bibliographical references throughout. Bibliographie, p.273–74.

T48 The National Trust manual of housekeeping. Comp. by Hermione Sandwith and Sheila Stainton. [Rev.

ed.] N.Y., Viking in assoc. with the National Trust, 1991. 351p. il., ports.

1st ed, London, A. Lane in assoc. with the National Trust, 1984.

Useful general manual originally compiled for the "historic buildings representatives and house staff of the National Trust."—*Foreword.*

Contents: (1) The right environment; (2) Books and documents; (3) Ceramics; (4) Clocks and watches; (5) Floors; (6) Furniture; (7) Glass; (8) Metalwork; (9) Musical instruments; (10) Natural history collections; (11) Pests, moulds and insects; (12) Photographs; (13) Pictures; (14) Stone, including marble and alabaster; (15) Textiles; (16) Walls, ceilings and windows; (17) Miscellaneous; Appendices: (1) Methods and protection against light; (2) Special equipment and protection; (3) The housemaids' cupboard; (4) Suppliers of equipment and materials; (5) Suppliers' addresses.

Index, p.339–51.

T49 Preventive conservation: practice, theory and research. Ed. by Ashok Roy and Perry Smith. Preprints of the contributions to the Ottawa congress, 12–16 September 1994. London, International Institute for Conservation of Historic and Artistic Works, [1994]. 244p. il. (part col.), 9 col. plates, plans, tables.

Papers covering an important aspect of conservation practice. Includes various case studies.

Bibliographical references follow each paper. French abstracts, p.238–44.

T50 Quaderni di studi e restauri del Museo Poldi Pezzoli. v.1– . [various imprints], 1995– .

Series documenting conservation work carried out on works in this important collection. The museum has held an early leadership position in Italian art preservation.

Bibliographical references and/or notes follow each essay. Bibliografia ragionata in each vol.

T51 Reclams Handbuch der künstlerischen Techniken. Stuttgart, Reclam, 1984– .

The individual vols. in this series constitute significant contributions, by practising conservators, to the literature of their respective fields.

Contents: (1) Kuhn, Harmann . . . [et al.] Farbmittel, Buchmalerei, Tafel- und Leinwandmalerei (1984); (2) Knoepfli, Albert. Wandmalerei, Mosaik (1990); (3) Weiss, Gustav. Glas, Keramik und Porzellan, Mobel, Intarsie und Rahmen, Lackkunst, Leder (1986).

Bibliographies in all vols.

T52 Research in conservation. Marina del Rey, Calif., Getty Conservation Institute, 1988– .

Series presenting the most recent conservation-related research in a condensed, clearly explained format. Recent vols. are unnumbered.

Contents: (1) Reedy, Terry J., and Reedy, Chandra L. Statistical analysis in art conservation research (1988); (2) Selwitz, Charles M. Cellulose nitrate in conservation (1988); (3) Feller, Robert L., and Wilt, M. Evaluation of cellulose ethers for conservation (1990); (4) Feller, Robert L. Accelerated aging: photochemical and thermal aspects (1994); (5) Cass, Glen R. . . . [et al.] Protection of works of art from atmospheric ozone (1989); (6) Nazaroff, William W. . . . [et al.] Airborne particles in museums (1993); (7) Selwitz, Charles. Epoxy resins in stone conservation (1992); Price, C.A. Stone conservation: an overview of current research (1996); Oxygen-free museum cases. Ed. by Shin Maekawa. (1998); Selwitz, Charles, and Maekawa, Shin. Gases in the control of museum insect pests (1998).

Bibliographical references follow most texts. Indexes.

T53 Restauratoren Taschenbuch. Hrsg. Ulrike Besch. München, Callwey, 1995– . il.

Extremely useful, biennial handbook for conservators. Focus is on educational resources. Each vol. concludes with a group of essays on issues of the moment in such areas as law and (most recently) the internet.

Contents: Ausbildung; Schulen; Stipendien; Schulen und Handwerk; Diplomarbeiten; Fortbildung; Grundsatzpapiere; Restauratorenverbände; Naturwissenschaftliche Institute; Stiftungen; Preise; Forschung; Museumsorganisation; Schlösserverwaltungen; Archivämter; Öffentliche Einrichtungen; Denkmalpflege; Datenbanken, bibliographische Informationen; Online; Internationale Fachmessen; Fachzeitschriften; Fachverlage; Fotografie; Zentrale Restaurierungswerkstätten; Wer liefert? Quellen A–Z; Aktuelle Themen: Basiswissen; Betriebswirtschaft; Recht; Versicherung; Giftstoffe; Restaurierungswerkstätten im Ausland.

Fachlexikon (deutsch-englisch—englisch-deutsch), p.244–71.

T54 Restaurierung und Museumstechnik. v.1–v.(12). Weimar, Museum für Ur- und Frühgeschichte Thuringens, 1976– .

Series of focused monographs on restoration techniques in museums.

Contents: (1) Stambolov, T. Korrosion und Konservierung metallener Altertümer und Kunstgegenstände (1976); (2) Ersfeld, Joachim. Formen und Giessen (1977; 2d ed., 1982); (3) Hücke, Joachim. Chemikalien und Rezepte (1981; 3d ed., 1985); (4) Bleck, Rolf-Dieter. Chromatographische Analysenmethoden (1981); (5) Bleck, Rolf-Dieter. Pflege und Erhaltung von Kunst- und Kulturgut, v.1 (1984); (6) Pasch, Astrid. Rekonstruktion einer Goldblechscheibenfibel (1985); (7) Farke, Heidemarie. Archäologische Fasern, Geflechte, Gewebe (1986); (8–9) Stambolov, T. . . . [et al.] Korrosion und Konservierung von Kunst- und . . . (1987); (10) Bleck, Rolf-Dieter. Stoffdatenblätter für Restauratoren (1990); (11) Bleck, Rolf-Dieter. Pflege und Erhaltung von Kunst- und Kulturgut [vol.2] (1992); (12) Keiler, John-Albrecht. Bergung und Präparation pleistozäner Wirbeltierreste unter Berucksichtigung des Fossilmaterials der Komplexfundstelle Untermassfeld/Sudthuringen (Stuttgart, Theiss, 1995).

T55 Restoration: Is it acceptable? Ed. by Andrew Oddy. [London, British Museum], Department of Conservation, 1994. 169p. il. (part col.), plates (part col.) (Occasional paper, 99)

Papers from a conference intended "to explore attitudes to restoration."—*Foreword.*

Contents: Restoring what wasn't there: reconsideration of the eighteenth-century restorations to the Lansdowne Herakles in the collection of the J. Paul Getty Museum, by Jerry Podany; Objects as systems: a new challenge for conservation, by Suzanne Keene; Clocks and watches, a re-appraisal?, by Francis Brodie; Changing taste in the restoration of paintings, by David Bomford; Restoration of art on paper in the West: a consideration of changing attitudes and values, by Joanna Kosek; Is wall painting restoration, a representation of the original or a reflection of contemporary fashion? An Austrian perspective, by Heinz Leitner and Stephen Paine; Conservation and restoration of miniatures: past and present, by L. E. Fleming; Restoration: acceptable to whom?, by Tiamat Molina and Marie Pincemin; Gilt-wood restoration: When is it acceptable?, by Colin Jenner; A constant approach to a mixed collection, by Jonathan Ashley-Smith; The care of rugs and carpets: the case for textile conservators, by Sharon Manitta; Restoration or conservation, issues for textile conservators: a textile conservation perspective, by Mary Brooks . . . [et al.]; The treatment of an upright grand pianoforte, c. 1808, by Timothy Hayes; The restoration of vehicles for use in research, exhibition, and demonstration, by Peter Mann; Putting things in context: the ethics of working collections, by Bob Child; Filling lacunae in Florentine mosaic and tessera mosaic: reflections and proposals, by Anna Maria Giusti; The armourer's craft: restoration or conservation, by David Edge; Filling and painting of ceramics for exhibition in the British Museum, by Sandra Smith.

Notes and bibliographical references follow each paper.

T56 Saving the twentieth century: the conservation of modern materials = Sauvegarder le XXe siècle: la conservation des matériaux modernes. Proceedings of a conference symposium '91—Saving the twentieth century, Ottawa, Canada 15 to 20 September 1991. Organized by the Canadian Conservation Institute, Communications Canada. Ed. by David W. Grattan. Ottawa, Canadian Conservation Institute, 1993. 440p. il., diags., tables.

Texts in English or French with summaries in English or French, as appropriate.

36 papers addressing the particular issues involved in the conservation of recently created and often complex objects. Types of materials considered include "synthetic materials, complex electronic circuitry, sophisticated alloys, and many new types of coatings."—*Introd.*

Contents: (1) Modern materials in collections; (2) Conservation policies and plans; (3) History of technology; (4) Processes of deterioration; (5) Case studies and specific problems with material; (6) Testing and development of conservation processes; (7) Methods of analysis and identification.

Bibliographical references follow each paper.

T57 Shelley, Marjorie. The care and handling of art objects: practices in the Metropolitan Museum of Art. Contrib. by members of the curatorial and conservation departments of the Metropolitan Museum of Art. Illus. by Helmut Nickel. Rev. ed. N.Y., Metropolitan Museum of Art (Distr. Abrams, 1992). 102p. il., tables.

1st ed., 1987.

"Practical guide to the care and handling of objects in the Museum's collection. It is addressed to all who are responsible for the well-being of the collection or who are permitted access to works of art. While in no way a primer of conservation techniques, it describes the fundamental principles that underlie current Museum practice."—*Pref.*

Contents: Part I: (1) Three-dimensional objects; (2) Musical instruments; (3) Paintings; (4) Works on paper and books; (5) Far Eastern works of art on silk and paper; (6) Textiles; (7) Costumes; Part II: (1) Lighting; (2) Relative humidity and temperature; (3) Photography; (4) Environment and the deterioration of art objects; (5) Museum loans.

Selected glossary, p.84–97. Suggested reading, p.98–100.

T58 Standards in the museum. London, Museum and Galleries Commission, 1992.

Contents: (I) Care of archaeological collections; (II) Care of biological collections; (III) Care of geological collections; (IV) Care of larger and working objects; (V) Care of musical instruments; (VI) Touring exhibitions; (VII) Care of photographic collections; (VIII) Care of costume and textile collections.

T59 Studies and documents on the cultural heritage = Études et documents sur le patrimoine culturel. Paris, Unesco, 1983–88.

Series of focused monographs.

Contents: (1) Preservation and presentation of rock art; (2) The protection of monuments and sites against atmospheric pollution; (3) Méthode d'analyse morphologique des tissus urbains traditionnels; (4) Basic museum bibliography; (5) Markov, V. B.; Mironyuk, G. I.; and Yavtushenko, I. G. Holography and its applications in museum work; (6) Emergency measures and damage assessment after an earthquake; (7) Conservation of rock art; (8) Norton, Ruth E. Storage and display of textiles for museums in South Asia; (9) Vernacular architecture and its conservation: annotated bibliography; (10) Moutsopoulos, Nikolaos K. L'architecture vernaculaire dans les Balkans; (11) Soubeyran, Muriel Taylor. Architecture vernaculaire au Sultanat d'Oman; (12) Van der Meerschen, Michel. Les medinas maghrebines; (13) Rock art in the Sahara: methodology and management; (14) Basic museum bibliography; (15) Conservation des sites et du mobilier archéologiques: principes et methodes; (16) Lazzarini, Lorenzo, and Pieper, Richard, eds. The deterioration and conservation of stone: notes from the international Venetian courses on stone restoration.

T60 Technical studies in the arts, archaeology, and architecture. [various imprints], 1982.

Contents: Feilden, Bernard M. Conservation of historic buildings (Boston, Butterworth-Heinemann, 1982); Harley, R. D. Artists' pigments c. 1600–1835: a study in English documentary sources (2d ed., Boston, Butterworth Scientific, 1982).

T61 Thornes, Robin. Protecting cultural objects through international documentation standards: a preliminary survey. [Malibu, Calif.], Getty Art History Information Program, [1995]. [4], 51p. col. il.
Overview of the threats to the world's cultural objects (e.g., pillage of archeological sites, illegal export, theft, military conflict, neglect). Reviews the response of the international community. Stresses the importance of documentation in the protection of cultural resources. Useful selected bibliography includes recent newspaper articles.

Contents: The threats to the world's cultural objects; The response of the international community; The importance of documentation in the protection of cultural objects; Networked access to information; The need for documentation standards; The value of core information; The objectives of this project; The survey; The organizations; Use of information technology; Visual documentation; Condition information; Candidate core categories; Appendix A: Responding organizations and initiatives; Appendix B: Results of the survey of condition reporting documentation.

Notes, p.39–41. Selected Bibliography, p.43–51.

T62 United Kingdom Institute for Conservation of Historic and Artistic Works. Occasional papers. Ed. by Katharine Starling. London, UKIC, 1980– .
Series of focused studies.

Contents: (1) Conservation, archaeology and museums. Ed. by Suzanne Keene (1980); (2) Microscopy in archaeological conservation. Ed. by Michael Corfield and Kate Foley (1982); (3) Lead and tin: studies in conservation and technology. Ed. by Gwyn Miles and Sarah Pollard (1985); (4) Corrosion inhibitors in conservation. Ed. Suzanne Keene (1985); (5) Archaeological bone, antler and ivory. Ed. by Katharine Starling and David Watkinson (1987); (6) Restoration of early musical instruments. Ed. by Christina Huntley and Katharine Starling; (7) From pinheads to hanging bowls: the identification, deterioration and conservation of applied enamel and glass decoration on archaeological artefacts. Ed. by Louise Bacon and Barry Knight (1987); (8) Evidence preserved in corrosion products: new fields in artefact studies. Ed. by Robert Janaway and Brian Scott (1989); (9) Conservation of stained glass. Ed. by Linda Cannon (1989); (10) Archaeological textiles. Ed. by Sonia O'Connor and Mary Brooks (1990); (11) Glass and enamel conservation. Ed. by Christine Daintith (1992); (12) Archaeological conservation: training and employment. Ed. by Robert White (1992).

Bibliographies in all vols.

T63 Wie haltbar ist Videokunst? Beiträge zur Konservierung und Restaurierung audiovisiueller Kunstwerke: Symposium im Kunstmuseum Wolfsburg = How durable is videoart? Contributions to preservation and restauration of the audiovisual works of art: symposium at the Kunstmuseum Wolfsburg, 25. November 1995. [Wolfsburg, Kunstmuseum Wolfsburg, 1997.] 114p. il.
"Since artists' videos and video installations have now become a regular feature in almost all public art collections, the question of how to preserve this medium is becoming more and more urgent."—*Foreword.* Papers address issues of relevance to art historians, media experts, technicians, restorers, legal experts, and philosophers. Of particular interest, given this highly reproducible medium, is the question of authenticity.

Contents: The technology of analogue and digital media, by Manfred Müller; The conservator's struggle with the volatile medium of video, by Rudolf Frieling; Video art: [how original video art is], by Wulf Herzogenrath; Problems in the restoration of film and video, by Harald Brandes; On the gradual disappearance of the Original, by Erich Gantzert-Castrillo; Media art between reproducibility and progressive interactivity, by Axel Wirths; Copyright and the integrity of the work in video art, by Jullia Meuser; Authenticity in the fine arts (to the present day), by Hans Ulrich Reck; An interview with the artist: Nam June Paik.

Further information on the subject, p.109.

ARCHEOLOGY
(including ethnographic objects)

T64 Archaeological wood: properties, chemistry, and preservation. Developed from a symposium sponsored by the Cellulose, Paper, and Textile Division at the 196th national meeting of the American Chemical Society, Los Angeles, California, September 25–30, 1988. Ed. by Roger M. Rowell and R. James Barbour. Washington, D.C., American Chemical Society, 1990. xii, 472p. il., ports., tables. (Advances in chemistry, 225)
Emphasizes the need to understand more fully the mechanisms of wood degradation in order to provide a more scientific basis for its conservation.

Bibliographical references follow each paper. Author index, p.453. Affiliation index, p.453. Subject index, p.454–72.

T65 Bibliography of works on the conservation of ethnographic materials. Comp. by Ruth Norton and Sue Walson. Sydney, ICOM, Committee for Conservation, Working Group on Ethnographic Materials, 1987. 119p.
"Includes references to conservation case histories, research reports and information on the handling, storage, display, and transport of ethnographic objects as well as on education and training and the development of ethnographic conservation as a speciality within the conservation profession. It does not specifically include references on the behaviour of materials or on the technology of manufacture of ethnographic objects, nor does it include references on materials and techniques which are used in other fields of conservation."—*Introd.*

T66 La conservation en archéologie: méthodes et pratique de la conservation-restauration des vestiges archéologiques. Coordonné par Marie Cl. Berducou. Textes de J. P. Adam . . . [et al.] Illustrations de M. Symphorien. Préf. De J. P. Sodini. Paris, Masson, 1990. xii, 469p. il.

Collection of essays on the principle aspects of archeological objects conservation, aimed especially at conservation students.

Contents: (I) Introduction à la conservation en archéologie, by M. Berducou; (II) Intervention sur le terrain: le mobilier, by F. Chavignier; (III) La céramique archéologique, by M. Berducou; (IV) Le verre, by M. Bailly; (V) Les métaux archéologiques, by R. Bertholon and C. Relier; (VI) Les matériaux organiques, by S. de La Baume; (VII) Les mosaïques de pavement, by F. Chantriaux-Vicard; (VIII) Les enduits peints antiques, by L. Krougly and R. Nunes Pedroso; (IX) Restauration architecturale et préservation des sites archéologiques, by J. P. Adam and A. Bossoutrot; (X) La conservation à long terme des objets archéologiques, by D. Guillemard; (XI) Gérer le matériel archéologique , by N. Meyer; Annexe: Liste alphabétique des fournisseurs; Liste des fournitures; Aides-mémoires.

Bibliographie, p.437–60. Index alphabétique des matières, p.461–69.

T67 The conservation of archaeological sites in the Mediterranean region: an international conference organized by the Getty Conservation Institute and the J. Paul Getty Museum, 6–12 May 1995. Ed. by Marta de la Torre. Los Angeles, Getty Conservation Institute, 1997. 164p. il. (part col.), 3 col. plates, charts, maps, plans, tables.

French trans., La conservation des sites archéologiques dans la région méditerranéenne. Los Angeles, Getty Conservation institute, 1997.

Papers from a meeting "of senior government officials and other specialists in the areas of culture, archaeology, and tourism" the purpose of which "was to promote the protection of the archaeological heritage through coordinated management of its appropriate uses—research, education, and tourism."—*Pref.*

Contents: Conclusions of the conference participants; The archaeological heritage in the Mediterranean region, by Marta de la Torre and Margaret Mac Lean; A planning model for the management of archaeological sites, by Sharon Sullivan; Management considerations at a Mediterranean site: Akrotiri, Thera, by Christos Doumas; Reconstruction of ancient buildings, by Hartwig Schmidt; The presentation of archaeological sites, by Renée Sivan; The Roman villa at Piazza Armerina, Sicily, by Nicholas Stanley-Price; Knossos, by John K. Papadopoulos; Ephesus, by Martha Demas; Appendix A: Summary of charters dealing with the archaeological heritage.

Bibliographical references follow each paper.

T68 Conservation on archaeological excavations: with particular reference to the Mediterranean area. Ed. by N. P. Stanley Price. 2d ed. Rome, ICCROM, 1995. xiii, 152p. il.

1st ed., 1984. Italian trans., Roma, Centro di conservazione archeologica, 1986. Spanish trans., Madrid, Ministerio de Cultura, 1990.

Collection of papers from a conference (Cyprus, 1983). "There were two main aims of the conference: to review responsibilities for conservation, making particular reference to the 1956 UNESCO Recommendation on International Principles applicable to Archaeological Excavations; and to discuss the basic principles of conservation on excavations."—*Foreword.*

Contents: Excavation and conservation, by Nicholas Stanley Price; The role of the objects conservator in field archaeology, by Kate Foley; Object interred, object disinterred, by Gaël de Guichen; First aid treatment for excavated finds, by Catherine Sease; Packaging and storage of freshly excavated artefacts from archaeological sites, by UKIC - Archaeology Section; On-site storage of finds, by Giovanni Scichilone; The site record and publication, by John Coles; Protection and presentation of excavated structures, by John H. Stubbs; Conservation of excavated intonaco, stucco and mosaics, by Paolo Mora; Protection and conservation of excavated structures of mudbrick, by Alejandro Alva Balderrama and Giacomo Chiari; Planning and executing anastylosis of stone buildings, by Dieter Mertens; Conservation on excavations and the 1956 Unesco Recommendation, by Nicholas Stanley Price; Appendix I: The Unesco Recommendation on International principles applicable to archaeological excavations.

Additional references, p.151–52.

T69 Cronyn, J. M.The elements of archaeological conservation: with particular reference to the Mediterranean area. [N.Y.], Routledge, [1990]. xx, 326p. il.

Intended "for those other than professional conservators who are involved in the understanding and care of excavated materials whether excavators, finds specialists, archaeometrists, museum curators, collectors, or administrators."—*Pref.* Extremely clear and detailed exposition, covering agents of deterioration and preservation, general techniques of conservation, siliceous and related materials, metals, and organic materials.

Archaeological conservation: a guide to organizations, training, and literature, p.296–97. References, p.298–311. Bibliography, p.312–16. Index, p.317–26.

T70 Dorrell, Peter G. Photography in archaeology and conservation. 2d ed. [Cambridge], Cambridge Univ. Pr., [1994]. 266p. il., figs., tables. (Cambridge manuals in archaeology)

1st ed., 1989.

"This book is based on courses in archaeological and conservation photography given to students at the Institute of Archaeology, University College London."—*Pref.*

Contents: (1) The early days of archaeological photography; (2) Basic principles and practice; (3) Equipment; (4) Lighting by flash; (5) Photographic materials, processing and printing; (6) Architecture and standing monuments; (7) Survey photography; (8) Site photography; (9) Principles of object photography; (10) Principles of close-up photography; (11) Ultra-violet and infra-red photography; (12) Photographing finds; (13) Flat copy; (14) Preparation of material for publication; (15) The future.

References, p.257–60. Index, p.261–66.

T71 Florian, Mary-Lou E; Kronkright, Dale Paul; and Norton, Ruth E. The conservation of artifacts made from plant materials. [Marina del Rey, Calif., Getty Conservation Institute, 1990] xiii, 332p. il.

"Objects made from plant materials comprise a large portion of the ethnographic material in collections around the world. Conservation of such perishable artifacts is especially problematic when they are housed in climates different from those in which they were collected."—*Pref.* Intended more as an "informal reference source for practicing conservators rather than as a textbook," this vol. presents class notes used for a Getty Conservation Institute course on this topic.

Glossary, p.309–14. Index, p.315–32.

T72 Gaudel, Paul. Bibliographie der archäologischen Konservierungstechnik. 2, erw. Ausg. Berlin, Hessling, 1969. 374p. (Berliner Jahrbuch für Vor- und Frühgeschichte. Ergänzungsbände, Bd. 2)

1st ed., [Berlin, 1960].

Extremely thorough, annotated bibliography of 1,803 titles in European languages, including Hungarian and Polish. Lists books and journal articles, with an emphasis on the latter. Publications on all kinds are media, and on a wide variety of conservation issues are discussed. Especially useful is the coverage of 19th- and early 20th-century conservation literature. Organized by categories (conservation of various materials, materials and tools, copies and reconstructions, exhibition procedures, the training and status of technical staff in museums).

Personenregister, p.331–40. Firmen- und Hersteller-Register, p.341–42. Sachregister, p.343–68. Markennamen-Register, p.369–71. Topographisches Register der Fundorte, p.372–74.

T73 In situ archaeological conservation: proceedings of meetings, April 6–13, 1986, Mexico. Miguel Angel Corzo, conference coord. Henry W. M. Hodges, senior ed. [Mexico City], Instituto Nacional de Antropologia e Historia de Mexico; [Marina del Rey], Getty Conservation Institute, [1987]. 206p. il., 28 col. plates

Spanish ed., Conservación arqueologica in situ. [Mexico City], Instituto Nacional de Antropologia e Historia de Mexico, 1993.

Collection of papers focusing on the problems of archeological site conservation.

Contents: Preventive measures during excavation and site protection: a review of the ICCROM/University of Ghent conference, November 1985, by N. P. Stanley Price; (I) The sites and the contexts; (II) Materials; (III) Three case studies in Mexico.

Bibliographical references follow most papers.

T74 Materials issues in art and archaeology. v.1– . Pittsburgh, Materials Research Society, 1988– . (Materials Research Society symposium proceedings)

Series of conference proceedings organized with the aim of promoting "a dialogue between those who examine the materials science underlying ancient artifacts and those who develop the materials science and technology underlying modern ones."—*Pref.* Intended to help conservators understand more about deterioration processes, and use new technologies in their work with ancient artefacts.

T75 Répertoire des organismes de gestion du patrimoine archéologique = Directory of archaeological heritage management organizations. Montréal, ICOMOS, 1995. 205, 5, 4, [1]p.

1st ed., 1986.

Lists 521 organizations. Information concerning each organization includes the following: "Function, type of organization, and field of activity."—*Explanation of headings.*

Contents: Country index; Organizations index; The organizations; The Charter for the Protection and Management of the Archaeological Heritage; Directory registration form.

T76 Robinson, S. First aid for underwater finds. [2d, enl. and upd. ed.] [London], Archetype, [1998]. 128p. il. (part col.) 34 col. plates.

1st ed., First aid for marine finds, London, National Maritime Museum, 1981.

"Intended to supplement texts on the theory, practice and techniques of archaeology underwater. . . . It is a response to the need for immediate and practical advice on the preservation of finds . . . until the advice of a qualified conservator can be sought."—*Pref.*

Glossary, p.119–22. Bibliography, p.123–24. Index, p.125–28.

T77 Sease, Catherine. A conservation manual for the field archaeologist. 3d ed. Los Angeles, Institute of Archaeology, Univ. of California, 1994. v, 114p. il. (Archeological research tools, 4)

1st ed., Los Angeles, Institute of Archaeology, University of California, Los Angeles, 1987; 2d ed., 1992.

"This book . . . provides excavators with the techniques necessary to safeguard and protect artifacts from the moment they are unearthed until they are fully treated in a properly equipped conservation laboratory by professional conservators."—*Introd.*

Contents: (1) Important points; (2) Safety; (3) Supplies and materials; (4) General treatment techniques; (5) Specific materials and treatments; Appendix I: Making impressions; Appendix II: Making up solutions; Appendix III: Sources of conservation supplies; Appendix IV: Organizations and publications.

Bibliography, p.111–12. Index, p.113–14.

T78 Symposium 86: the care and preservation of ethnological materials: proceedings = L'entretien et la sauvegarde des matériaux ethnologiques: actes. Ed. by R. Barclay . . . [et al.] [Ottawa?], Canadian Conservation Institute, [1986?], 272p. il. (part col.).

Text in English; abstracts in French.

Collection of 35 papers with a particular focus on the developing countries.

Contents: Packing and shipping; Feathers; Skin and leather; Conservation in the cultural context; Glass and ceramics; Investigation and analysis; Bark and fibrous materials; Wood; Maori buildings; Museum reports; Appendix 1 [poster sessions]; Appendix 2: Workshop sessions.

ARCHITECTURE

T79 The Acropolis restoration: the CCAM interventions. Ed. by Richard Economakis. London, Academy Editions, [1994]. 224p. il. (chiefly col.)

Superbly illustrated overview of the conservation work sponsored by the Committee for the Conservation of the Acropolis Monuments, 1975–94.

Restoration work on the Acropolis (1975–94), p.12–15. The architecture of the Athenian Acropolis: terminology, p.16–19.

T80 All about old buildings: the whole preservation catalog. Ed. by Diane Maddex. Washington, D.C., Preservation Pr., 1985. 433p. il., ports.

Reference work showing "what to look for, where to go, who to see . . . [including] excerpts from listed sources and quotations from a variety of observers in addition to organizations to contact, books to read, articles to consult, illustrations of examples and outlines of preservation steps."—*Pref.*

Contents: (1) Fugitive places; (2) Preservation; (3) Looking at the built environment; (4) Form and function; (5) Preservationists; (6) Protecting the past; (7) Taking action; (8) Building roots; (9) Rehabilitation and restoration; (10) Adaptive use; (11) Historic sites; (12) Neighborhoods; (13) Main streets; (14) Paying for preservation; (15) Education.

Bookstores and publishers, p.427–28. Index of subjects, p.431–33.

T81 Andrew, Christopher; Maureen Young; and Tonge, Kenneth. Stone cleaning: a guide for practitioners. [Aberdeen], Historic Scotland and the Robert Gordon University, [1994]. 122p. il., 5 color plates.

Useful, clearly written overview.

Contents: (1) Sandstone; (2) The soiling of building facades; (3) Stone cleaning aesthetics; (4) Physical cleaning methods; (5) Chemical cleaning methods; (6) Testing methodology; (7) Health and safety; (8) Planning.

References, p.121–22.

T82 Architectural ceramics: their history, manufacture and conservation: a joint symposium of English Heritage and the United Kingdom Institute for Conservation, 22–25 September 1994. [Ed. by Jeanne Marie Teutonico]. London, James & James, 1996. 134p. viii, il. (part col.)

Presents papers reflecting the current research trends and practices in British architectural ceramics conservation, particularly terracotta and faience.

Bibliographical references follow each essay.

T83 Architectural heritage documentation centres in Europe: directory = Centres de documentation du patrimoine architectural en Europe: répertoire. Strasbourg, Council of Europe, 1990– .

Inventory of approximately 200 specialist documentation center, libraries, and institutes in 26 countries. Each country receives a brief general overview, discussing the historic, legal, and administrative framework. Listings for relevant centers in that country follow, with each center's focus of interest very thoroughly delineated.

T84 Ashurst, John, and Ashurst, Nicola. Practical building conservation. N.Y., Halsted Pr., 1988. 5v. il. (English heritage technical handbook)

Broad-based series aimed at architects, surveyors, building contractors, and private owners.

Contents: (1) Stone masonry; (2) Brick, terra cotta and earth; (3) Mortars, plasters and renders; (4) Metals; (5) Wood, glass and resins.

Bibliographical references follow each chapter.

T85 Ashurst, Nicola. Cleaning historic buildings. [London], Donhead, [1994]. 2v. il.

Contents: (1) Substrates, soiling and investigations; (2) Cleaning materials and processes.

Bibliography, v.1, p.231–38, v.2, p.241–48. Index, v.1, p.239–48, v.2, p.249–58.

T86 Das Baudenkmal: zu Denkmalschutz und Denkmalpflege = Le monument historique: termes concernant la protection et la conservation des monuments historiques = The historic monument: terminology connected with the protection and the preservation of historic monuments. Mit deutschem, französischem und englischem Index. Tübingen, Niemeyer, 1981. 326p. il. (Glossarium artis, Bd. 8)

Detailed listings of architectural, construction, and preservation terms. While the dictionary is trilingual, definitions are in German only.

Contents: (1) Die Denkmäler = Les monuments = The monuments; (2) Allgemeine Begriffe der Denkmalpflege = Termes généraux concernant la conservation des monuments historiques = Terminology connected with the preservation of historic monuments; (3) Wertkategorien und Wertbegriffe = Catégories et termes de valeur = Categories and judgements of value; (4) Das Inventar = L'inventaire = The survey; (5) Bewertungskriterien = Critères de classification/Criteria of judgement; Annexes: (1) Fangblätter; (2) Stichworthilfen für die Inventarisation; (3) Punktwertung (Bewertungsrichtlinien für Baudenkmäler); (4) Internationale Klassifizierung.

Bibliography, p.201–38. Author index, p.244–49. Index of German terms, p.250–87. Index of French terms, p.288–304. Index of English terms, p.305–321.

T87 Bercé, Françoise, and Foucart, Bruno. Viollet-le-Duc: architect, artist, master of historic preservation. With contrib. by Jean-Jacques Aillagon . . . [et al.] Washington, D.C., Trust for Museum Exhibitions, 1988. 100p. il. (part col.), map.

Survey of the architectural restoration activities of "one of the founders of historic restoration and preservation as we know it today . . . [and] whose theories and their impact extended far beyond his place and time."—*From the Trust for Museum Exhibitions.*

Contents: Viollet-le-Duc and his theories of restoration; A selection of historic monuments restored by Viollet-le-Duc; Viollet-le-Duc as a contemporary architect and designer.

Footnotes, p.93–94. Biographical note, by Geneviève Viollet-le-Duc, p.95. Chronology, p.96–97. Bibliography, p.98–100.

T88 Bibliographie sur la preservation, la restoration et la rehabilitation des architectures de terre = Bibliography on the preservation, restoration and rehabilitation of earthen architecture. [Comp. by Pascal Odul . . . (et al.)] [Rome], CRATerre/EAG/ICCROM, 1993. xix, 136p.

Unannotated bibliography covering books, articles, conferences proceedings, and papers. Publications are listed, according to language.

Contents: The GAIA bibliography; Deutsch; English; Espagnol; Français; Italiano; Other languages.

T89 Building maintenance and preservation: a guide for design and management. Ed. by Edward D. Mills. 2d ed. [enl. and upd.] [Boston], Butterworth-Heinemann, 1994. 309p. il.

1st ed., 1980.

Collection of essays emphasizing the relevance of maintenance considerations at the design stage as well as the need for such maintenance throughout the life of the building. Includes information on the maintenance of modern buildings, the rehabilitation and reuse of existing buildings, and on the latest applicable U.K. and European Union legislation.

Contents: (1) Design and building maintenance, by Edward D. Mills; (2) The economics of maintenance, by J. T. William; (3) Energy utilization, audits and management, by W. T. Bordass and J. W. Field; (4) Thermal standards, methods and problems, by Norman Sheppard and Sylvester Bone; (5) Building materials and their maintenance, by Alastair Gardner; (6) Services design and maintenance, by David M. Lush; (7) The maintenance and design of security systems, by David M. Lush; (8) Maintenance of the building structure and fabric, by Alan Blanc; (9) The spaces between and around buildings, by Hugh Clamp; (10) Conservation: the maintenance of older buildings, by John Earl; (11) The conservation of modern buildings, by John Allan; (12) Safety and security in accessibility for maintenance, by E. Geoffrey Lovejoy; (13) Maintenance policy, programming and information feedback, by Douglas L. Warner; (14) Fire safety and means of escape, by Margaret Law; (15) Rehabilitation and re-use of existing buildings, by Alan Johnson; (16) Euro legislation, by Richard Dyton; (17) Statutory inspections and spare parts, by E. Geoffrey Lovejoy; (18) Maintenance manuals and their use, by Jacob Blacker; (19) Directory of organizations, by Pauline Borland.

Bibliography, p.298–303. Index, p.304–09.

T90 Butcher-Younghans, Sherry. Historic house museums: a practical handbook for their care, preservation, and management. N.Y., Oxford Univ. Pr., 1993. vi, 269p. il.

Curatorial manual "intended for those managers, curators, and directors . . . who undertake historic house management with the difficulties and limitations inherent to the small, low-budget museum."—*Introd.* Covers governance, personnel, collections storage and exhibition, preservation, security.

Bibliographical references follow each chapter. References, p.243–62. Index, p.263–69.

T91 Concerning buildings: studies in honour of Sir Bernard Feilden. Ed. by Stephen Marks. [Boston], Butterworth-Heinemann, 1996. 319p. il., port.

"This collection of essays explains how during the last thirty years, in a reaction against the continuing devastation Britain has developed a system for protecting historic buildings more comprehensive than in any other country." The festschrift is in honor of Bernard Feilden, "one of the few architects of his generation to specialize in historic buildings, pioneering the use of modern technology and showing how new elements could be designed in an unmistakably contemporary idiom yet fit the existing context."—*Foreword.*

Contents: (1) A tribute to Sir Bernard, by Patrick Nuttgens; (2) The conservation of buildings in Britain since the Second World War, by Matthew Saunders; (3) Principles and problems, ethics and aesthetics, by John Warren; (4) International standards, principles and charters of conservation, by Jukka Jokilehto; (5) Protecting the world's cultural heritage, by Henry Cleere; (6) The education of a conservation architect: past, present and future, by Derek Linstrum; (7) Assessment and recording: a practitioner's view, by Jo Cox; (8) Using and re-using buildings, by Sherban Cantacuzino; (9) Glorious repair, or the "British way of making good," by James Simpson; (10) Understanding historic structures, by David Teomans; (11) Art history, architectural history and archaeology, by Richard Morrice; (12) Historic landscapes and gardens and their conservation, by Peter Goodchild; (13) Financing conservation, by David McLaughlin; (14) A bibliography of the writings of Sir Bernard Feilden, by Keith Parker.

Index, p.303–19.

T92 La conservation de la pierre monumentale en France. Coord. par Jacques Philippon . . . [et al.] [Paris], Presses du CNRS, [1992]. 269p. il. (part col.) (Conservation du patrimoine)

"The intention of this book is to present the state of the art of the use and conservation of natural stone in monuments in France. It consists of four parts, three dealing with stone as a building material and the fourth describing 14 case studies." The essay by A. Blanc and C. Lorenz, "a marvellous survey of the quarries from which the stones used in monuments are or were extracted," is "a major reference work for everybody who has to deal with French stone."—*Review*, Studies in conservation, v.39, 1994, p.142–43.

Echelle stratigraphique internationale, p.255–56. Glossaire, p.257–60. Bibliographie et notes, p.261–66.

T93 Conservation of monuments in the Mediterranean basin = La conservazione dei monumenti nel bacino del Mediterraneo = La conservation des monuments dans le bassin mediterranéen. 1st– . [various imprints], 1990– . il., col. plates, diags., maps, plans, tables.

Important conference series examining the conservation needs of buildings, monuments, and sculptures in all countries bordering the Mediterranean Sea.

Bibliographical references follow most papers.

T94 Conservation of stone and other materials: proceedings of the international RILEM/UNESCO congress:

Conservation of stone and other materials: research - industry - media, held at UNESCO headquarters, Paris, with the cooperation of ICCROM, EUREKA/ EUROCARE, ICOM, ICOMOS, and the Getty Conservation Institute, Paris, June 29–July 1, 1993. Ed. by M.-J. Thiel. N.Y., Spon, [1993]. 892p. il., tables.

Collection of 106 papers, important for the many and varied, and up-to-date perspectives presented, "economic, political, geographic, climatic, and psychological."—*Pref.* Contributions vary from general or specific technical studies, to case histories from many countries

Contents: (I) Causes of disorders and diagnosis: (1) Pollution and chemical effects; (2) Physical effects; (3) Biological effects; (4) Petrography; (II) Prevention and treatments: (5) The role of structure; (6) Prevention and treatments.

Bibliographical references follow each paper. Abstracts of French papers in English, p.869–82. Author index, p.883–85. Subject index, p.886–92.

T95 The conservation of twentieth century historic buildings: proceedings of a conference held at the Institute of Advanced Architectural Studies, the University of York, 4–6 May 1993. Ed. by Peter Burman . . . [et al.] 1996. 130p. il.

Contents: Conservation and creativity, by Alan Powers; The listing of post-1945 buildings, by Diane Kay; "Doon the water" and other Scottish experiences, by Ingval Maxwell; Restoring the pioneers, by John Allan; Britain's youngest listed building, by Bob Kindred; The conservation of twentieth century buildings in Cambridge, by John Preston; The repair of Die Hütte, Freiburg, by Leo Schmidt; Urbanism and ideology during the 1950s in East and West Berlin, by Gabi Dolff-Bonekämper; Modern architecture restored: the role of DOCOMOMO, by Christopher Dean; Modern architecture improved: the role of the Royal Fine Art Commission, by Sherban Cantacuzino; The conservation and repair of the Architecture of Jože Plečnik, by Aleksandra Gersak; Learning from Vignola: the adaptation of Lutyens' Britannic House, 1987–90, by Peter Inskip; The conservation of twentieth century churches and Cathedrals, by Tim Ellis; The corrosion of sheet metal on walls and roofs, by William Allen; Architectural paint research: two twentieth century case studies, by Helen Hughes; Contemporary conservation methodology and modern architecture: the Rose Seidler House, Sydney; Buckingham Court, Magdalene College, Cambridge, by Rob Dunton; Port Sunlight: continuity and change, by Michael Shippobottom; The conservation of twentieth century social housing, by Hilary Chambers; Cataloguing the past for the future: the historic 20th century building products database, by Thomas C. Jester; Listing: kiss of death or a new lease of life, by Andrew Derbyshire; Appendix 1: Listed buildings post-1939; Appendix 2: Résumé; Appendix 3: Zusammenfassung; Appendix 4: Resumen.

Bibliographical references follow each paper.

T96 La cultura del restauro: teorie e fondatori. A cura di Stella Casiello. Venezia, Marsilio, 1996. 411p. (Polis) (Saggi Marsilio)

Collection of historiographic essays exploring the contribution of key English, French, German, and Italian theorists and practitioners (biographical profiles provided) to present architectural conservation practices. The function of architectural conservation in archeology is also discussed.

Note biografiche, p.373–404. Indice dei nomi, p.405–411.

T97 Denkmalpflege: deutsche Texte aus drei Jahrhunderten. Hrsg. von Norbert Huse. München, Beck, 1984. 256p. il.

Collection of texts central to the historiographic understanding of the theory and practice of architectural preservation as it developed in Germany, Austria, and Central Europe during the 19th and early 20th centuries. Approximately 50 extracts from key texts, arranged thematically and chronologically, are grouped into eight chapters. Each group of extracts is preceded by a brief introductory essay.

Contents: Italienische Präludeien; Vorstufen und Voraussetzungen; Nationaldenkmäler; Karl Friedrich Schinkel; Restaurieren oder Konservieren?; Denkmalwerte: Alois Riegl und Georg Dehio; Denkmalpflege und Heimatschutz; Denkmalpflege und Wiederaufbau; Probleme von Heute.

Anmerkungen, p.245–48. Ausgewählte Literatur, p.249–56.

T98 Denslagen, Wim. Architectural restoration in Western Europe: controversy and continuity. Amsterdam, Architectura & Natura Pr., 1994.

Trans. of Omstreden herstel: kritiek op het restaureren van monumenten: een thema uit de architectuurgeschiedenis van Engeland, Frankrijk, Duitsland en Nederland (1779–1953). 's-Gravenhage, Staatsuitgeverij, 1987.

Important, in-depth examination of a formerly widespread restoration technique: reconstruction, discussing the resultant controversies and misconceptions. Each chapter reviews several case histories of national significance, including England, France, the German-speaking countries, the Netherlands; as well as restoration principles in the modern world.

Selected bibliography, p.267–78. Notes, p.279–313. Index, p.315–19.

T99 Dictionary of building preservation. Ed. by Ward Bucher. Christine Madrid, illustration ed. N.Y., Wiley, [1996]. 560p. il.

Intended "first, to clarify the specialized terms used in the preservation field in the United States and Canada; and second, to allow a recorder to fully describe a historic resource."—*Introd.*

Bibliography, p.555–60.

T100 European directory of training centres in heritage skills and crafts. [Strasbourg], Council of Europe, [1995]. 308p.

Lists 190 training establishments in 23 countries. Clearly presented, the directory focuses on institutions specializing in conservation of the architectural heritage. Each country listing begins with a brief national conservation overview. This is followed by a detailed entry for each training institute.

Index by country, p.239–43. Index by field of activity, p.245–304. Index by centre, p.305–08.

T101 Feilden, Bernard, and Jokilehto, Jukka. Management guidelines for world cultural heritage sites. Rome, ICCROM, 1993. vii, 122p.
Manual for managers of cultural heritage sites as designated under the 1972 Convention concerning the Protection of the World Cultural and Natural Heritage.
Contents: (1) Summary of the guiding principles; (2) General policy of the convention; (3) Evaluation for conservation; (4) Management of world heritage sites; (5) Management by resource projects; (6) Maintenance programme; (7) Staffing and personnel services; (8) Treatments and authenticity; (9) Urban planning and world heritage towns; (10) Visitors to world heritage sites; Appendix A: The Venice Charter; Appendix B: Unesco conventions and recommendations; Appendix C: List of world cultural heritage sites.
Bibliographical references throughout the text. References, p.107–09.

T102 The future of the past: attitudes to conservation 1174–1974. Ed. by Jane Fawcett. [Contrib. by] Nikolaus Pevsner . . . [et al.] N.Y., Watson-Guptill, [1976]. 160p. il.
Collection of classic texts arising from an exhibition organized by the Victorian Society (London, Central School of Art and Design, 1970–71). The essays discuss the changing cultural and legal attitudes towards historic buildings from the 16th through the 20th centuries in the U.S. and (primarily) in Great Britain.
Contents: (I) The law's delays: conservationist legislation in the British Isles, by Nicholas Boulting; (II) Scrape and anti-scrape, by Nikolaus Pevsner; (III) A preservationist's progress, by John Betjeman; (IV) What should we preserve?, by Osbert Lancaster; (V) A restoration tragedy: cathedrals in the eighteenth and nineteenth centuries, by Jane Fawcett; (VI) Living with the past: Victorian alterations to country houses, by Mark Girouard; (VII) Conservation in America: national character as revealed by preservation, by Robin Winks; (VIII) Old sites and new buildings: the architect's point of view, by Hugh Casson.
Notes on the text, p.153–58. Index, p.159–60.

T103 A glossary of historic masonry deterioration problems and preservation treatments. Comp. by Anne E. Grimmer. [Washington, D.C.], Dept. of the Interior, National Park Service, Preservation Assistance Division, 1984. iii, 65p. il.
Vocabulary originating in the work of the Census of treated historic masonry buildings and its desire to establish a universally recognized set of technical terms.
Contents: (1) Deterioration problems; (2) Preservation treatments.
Selected reading list, p.64–65.

T104 Guide to recording historic buildings. Boston, Butterworth Architecture, 1990. 80p. il.
Produced under the auspices of ICOMOS. Addresses the need for recording historic buildings and their modifications, as well as the principle methods that should be used.
"The purpose of this book is to discuss why and when buildings ought to be recorded, the techniques that exist for doing it, who may be the best people to undertake it, and the actual procedures that may conveniently be followed."—*Introd.* Introducing the various types of recording, examples are taken from English buildings and building features.

T105 Historic building facades: the manual for maintenance and rehabilitation. Ed. by William G. Foulks. [Rev. ed.] N.Y., Wiley, 1997. xiv, 203p. il.
1st ed., ed. by Robert E. Meadows. N.Y., New York Landmarks Conservancy Technical Preservation Services Center, 1986.
"Presents an approach to analyzing problems of and prescribing solutions for the façades of old buildings for building owners and professionals who have limited experience working with historic buildings. . . . [It] is not concerned exclusively with landmark buildings, which are protected against indiscriminate stripping and repair, but with all buildings that affect the appearance of historic urban communities."—*Pref.*
Bibliographical references follow each chapter. Selected bibliography, p.191–93. Index, p.195–203.

T106 Index to historic preservation periodicals. National Trust for Historic Preservation Library of the University of Maryland, College Park. General ed., Hye Yun Choe. Indexers, Hope Headley . . . [et al.] Boston, Mass., Hall, 1988. xiv, 354p.
1st supplement, 1992.
"Compilation of the monthly listing of articles and ephemera that, since 1979, have been issued by the Library of the National Trust for Historic Preservation. . . . The periodicals examined comprise those issued by international, national, regional, state, and local historic preservation organizations. Popular and scholarly serials that include material bearing on the historic preservation movement are considered as well . . . [as are] selected pamphlets, clippings and brochures."—*Pref.* Partially annotated, more than 6,000 entries, listed alphabetically by subject. The supplement covers the period 1987–90, and includes a thesaurus of subject and geographic headings with cross-references.

T107 International congress on deterioration and conservation of stone, 1st– . [various imprints], [1979]– .
Formerly known as International symposium on deterioration of building stones. Standard resource for architectural and sculptural conservationists.

T108 Madsen, S. T. Restoration and anti-restoration: a study of English restoration philosophy. Oslo, Universitetsforlag, [1976]. 164p. il., 18 plates.
"This study is concerned with the origin of the ideas of restoration in England, but even more with the reaction against different forms of restoration."—*Pref.* Important text examining the conservation debate provoked by the restoration of ecclesiastical buildings in 19th-century Britain. The origins and etymology of the term "restoration" are also discussed.
Bibliographical references throughout the text. Bibliography, p.147–56. Index, p.157–62.

T109 Marconi, Paolo. Il restauro e l'architetto: teoria e pratica in due secoli di dibattito. Venezia, Marsilio, 1993. viii, 236p. il. (part col.), 121 plates (part col.) (Polis)
History of architectural conservation, covering classical through modern buildings. Differing conservation approaches, drawing upon case histories all over Europe, are discussed. The text gives an indication as to how polemical the conservation debate can become in Italy.
Bibliographical references throughout the text. Indice dei nomi, p.229–33. Indice dei luoghi, p.235–36.

T110 Markowitz, Arnold L. Historic preservation: a guide to information sources. Detroit, Gale Research, 1980. xv, 279p. (Art and architecture information guide series, 13) (Gale information guide library)
Wide-ranging, annotated bibliography of "books, pamphlets and other separate publications, including entire periodical issues devoted to historic preservation or closely related themes. With a very few exceptions, individual periodical articles and individual contributions to collected works have not been included."—*Introd.* Most of the literature cited is in English.
Contents: (1) General reference works; (2) Historical and current overviews; (3) Financial, legal, and planning aspects; (4) Description and documentation; (5) Guidebooks; (6) Districts, ensembles, neighborhoods, and towns; (7) The physical fabric: materials and technology; (8) Renovation, restoration, and re-use of existing buildings; (9) Interpretation of history through buildings, objects, and sites; (10) Related disciplines and specialized preservation areas; (12) Losses; (13) Periodicals; (14) A checklist of historic American buildings; Appendix: Developing the historic preservation library; Select list.
Author index, p.205–13. Organization index, p.215–23. Title index, p.225–45. Subject index, p.247–79.

T111 Massey, James C. Readings in historic preservation: an annotated bibliography to the key books and periodicals. Washington, D.C., National Preservation Institute, 1986. 38p.
Useful introduction to the field, albeit covering books published only up to the end of 1985. The focus is on "definitive and comprehensive works, and some key technical volumes."—*Introd.* Partially annotated.
Contents: (I) Architectural history: basic references; (II) General historic preservation topics; (III) Historic districts and design guidelines; (IV) Restoration, rehabilitation and development of historic buildings; (V) Historic preservation law, real estate and taxation; (VI) Surveys and documentation; (VII) Style and building guides; (VIII) Gardens and rural areas; (IX) Historic sites archeology; (X) Historic interiors and furnishings; (XI) Urban planning; (XII) Reference books; (XIII) Periodicals; (XIV) Book lists and book catalogs.
Includes author index, p.33–37.

T112 Materiali lapidei: problemi relativi allo studio del degrado e della conservazione. Ed. by Agostino Bureca, Maris Laurenzi Tabasso, and Giorgio Palandri. Roma, Libreria dello Stato, 1987. il. (part col.), plans. 2v. (Bollettino d'Arte. Supplemento al n.41)
Collection of 26 essays discussing stone conservation techniques (for buildings, monuments, and their sculptures), in the process documenting the decaying state of much of Italy's built cultural patrimony. Particularly disturbing is the photo-reportage of the degradation suffered by some of Italy's most important monuments, in part caused by atmospheric pollution.
Bibliographical references follow each essay.

T113 Nelson, Carl L. Protecting the past from natural disasters. Washington, D.C., Preservation Pr., 1991. 192p. il.
"This book challenges Americans, particularly preservationists and public officials, to begin now to protect our heritage before the next—inevitable—natural disaster strikes. . . . [It] outlines the process by which all players can prepare for and weather disasters."—*Pref.* The vol. takes as its starting point two 1989 disasters, Hurricane Hugo and the Loma Prieta earthquake.
Where to get help, p.172–81. Further reading, p.182–84. Sources, p.185–88. Index, p.189–92.

T114 Powys, A. R. Repair of ancient buildings: with a new introd. and additional notes. London, S.P.A.B., 1995. xiv, 213p. il.
1st ed., London, Dent, 1929; repr., 1981.
Based on the conservation philosophy of the Society for the Protection of Ancient Buildings, termed "conservative repair. . . . The basic idea is that ancient fabric should be disturbed as little as possible, the patina of age left on unscraped surfaces, and history not falsified by moving buildings to other sites or completing unfinished portions."—*Introd.*
Contents: (1) General advice to those in charge of ancient buildings; (2) The survey of an ancient building; (3) Temporary supports, scaffolding, and protection from damage during work; (4) The disposal of rain-water; (5) Masonry, brickwork, and walls generally; (6) The repair of ancient timber roofs and other works of fine carpentry; (7) Roof coverings; (8) Church bells and bell-hanging; (9) The repair of window glazing; (10) Ceilings; (11) Joinery; (12) The protection of wall paintings; Appendix I: Notes on the heating of ancient churches; Appendix II: Notes on the use of electricity in ancient churches.
Glossary, p.200–05. Index, p.206–08. Notes of the text, p.209–13.

T115 Preservation yellow pages: the complete information source for homeowners, communities, and professionals. Rev. ed. Ed. by Julie Zagars. Washington, D.C.: National Trust for Historic Preservation; N.Y., Wiley, 1997. 277p. il., tables.
1st version titled The brown book: a directory of preservation information (Washington, D.C., Preservation Press, 1983); 2d version titled Landmark yellow pages; 2d ed., 1993.
Excellent resource, issued to mark the 40th anniversary of the establishment of the U.S.'s National Trust for Historic Preservation. Provides names, addresses, facts, and figures on the preservation movement in the U.S., and about 5,000 individuals and organizations are listed.

Contents: (I) How to use this book; Why preserve? Preservation primer; (2) Preservation topics: Overview; Architectural styles; National Register of Historic Places; Secretary of the Interior's standards for rehabilitation; Historic rehabilitation tax credit; Introduction to historic preservation law; Degree programs in historic preservation; Glossary; Resources and readings; Chronology: preservation in America; (3) Preservation partners: Overview; National Park Service; National Trust for Historic Preservation; Advisory Council on Historic Preservation; Federal programs; National and regional organizations; International programs; (4) Preservation phone book: state and local contacts.

Index, 271–77.

T116 The restoration and conservation of Islamic monuments in Egypt. Ed. by Jere L. Bacharach. [Cairo], The American Univ. in Cairo Pr., [1995]. 194p. il.

Collection of conference papers by art historians, engineers and architects (Cairo, June 1993). The conference addressed problems relating to the preservation of Islamic monuments in Egypt, with particular regard to Cairo.

Bibliographical references follow some papers. Index, p.191–94.

T117 Riegl, Alois. Il culto moderno dei monumenti: il suo carattere e il suoi inizi. Introd. e note di Sandro Scarrocchia. Trad. dal tedesco di Renate Trost e Sandro Scarrocchia. Bologna, Nuova Alfa, 1985. 76p. (Rapporti, 50)

Italian trans. of Riegl's Der moderne Denkmalkultus: sein Wesen und seine Entstehung. Wien, Braumulter, 1903.

Useful introduction to Riegl's classic work on historic monuments preservation, situating it within a broader context.

Contents: (I) Posizione del Denkmalkultus nell'opera di Riegl e nella storia dell'arte, di Sandro Scarrocchia; (II) Periodi della cultura di tutela: trasformazione del concetto di monumento, di Sandro Scarrocchia; (III) Riegl - Dehio - Dvořák - Clemen: il contributo degli storici dell'arte alla moderna cultura di tutela, di Sandro Scarrocchia; (IV) Attualità del pensiero di Riegl per una politica dei beni culturali; Il culto moderno dei monumenti: il suo carattere e i suoi inizi, di Alois Riegl.

Bibliografia, p.20–23. Note alla traduzione, p.75–76.

T118 ______. Kunstwerk oder Denkmal? Alois Riegls Schriften zur Denkmalpflege. Hrsg. Ernst Bacher. Wien, Böhlau, [1995]. 239p. il. (Studien zu Denkmalschutz und Denkmalpflege, Bd. 15)

Introduces and reprints Riegl's most influential writings. Riegl was the first modern author to write on the cultural significance of artistic and historic monuments, on the notion of "heritage values", and on conservation theory.

Contents: (I) Wesen und Entstehung des modernen Denkmalkultur; (II) Das Denkmalschutzgesetz; (III) Bestimmungen zur Durchführung des Denkmalschutzgesetzes.

Bibliographical references throughout. Ausgewählte, weiterführende Literatur zu Alois Riegl und die Denkmalpflege, p.235–39.

T119 Smith, John F. A critical bibliography of building conservation: historic towns, buildings, their furnishings and fittings. London, Mansell, 1978. xxv, 207p.

Annotated bibliography covering all aspects of the built environment.

Contents: (I) History, philosophy and attitudes to conservation; (II) Legislation; (III) Towns and villages; (IV) Buildings: (A) History of building construction; (B) Building types; (C) General problems of repair and conservation; (D) The fabric: analysis and agents of deterioration; (E) The fabric: structural elements: history and conservation; (F) Furnishings and fittings: history and conservation; (G) Installations: history and conservation; (H) Materials: history of use and conservation (I) Special requirements, precautions and problems; (V) Historic gardens and landscapes; (VI) Tourism; (VII) Archaeology in conservation; (VIII) The organisation of conservation; (IX) Conservation abroad; (X) Bibliographies, directories and dictionaries of conservation, and advisory and grant giving bodies.

Place index, p.191–95. Author index, p.197–207.

T120 Structure and style: conserving 20th century buildings. Ed. by Michael Stratton. N.Y., Spon, 1996. x, 230p. il.

Essays on aspects of the conservation of modern buildings.

Contents: Towards a philosophy for conserving twentieth century buildings, by Peter Burman; A case for reforming architectural values, by Andrew Saint; The non-domestic building stock of England and Wales, by Philip Steadman; Beyond the fringe, by Kenneth Powell; Making the recent past fit for the future, by David Jenkin and John Worthington; Concrete and steel in twentieth century construction, by Bill Addisi; The relationship between building structure and architectural expression, by Peter Ross; Clad is bad?, by Michael Stratton; Quality, longevity, and listing, by Robert Thorne; Conserving carbuncles: dilemmas of conservation in practice, by Susan Macdonald.

T121 Twentieth-century building materials: history and conservation. Ed. by Thomas C. Jester, National Park Service. [N.Y., McGraw-Hill, 1995.] 352p. il., col. plates.

"Explores the history of many of the materials used to build modern America . . . intended to sound a call for more investigation into the deterioration and conservation of twentieth-century materials."—*Pref.* 37 essays, and one photographic reportage discuss and document the principal materials used in 20th-century building construction.

Contents: Metals; Concrete; Wood and plastics; Masonry; Glass; Flooring; Roofing, siding, and walls.

Notes, p.278–324. Bibliography, p.325–32. Sources for research, p.333–43. Index, p.344–52.

T122 United States Department of the Interior. National Park Service. The National Register of historic places, 1966 to 1994: cumulative list through January 1, 1994. Washington, D.C.: National Park Service [1994]. xxx, 923p. il., maps.

See GLAH 1:J334 for original annotation.

T123 Weaver, Martin E. Conserving buildings: guide to techniques and materials. With F. G. Matero. Rev. ed. N.Y., Wiley, 1997. xiv, 270p. il., diags.

1st ed., 1993.

"A magnificent achievement which can be read from cover to cover for sheer interest and certainly ought to be bought for reference."—*Review*, Studies in conservation, v.39, 1994, p.215. Comprehensive, clearly written treatment of the subject with excellent illustrations.

Contents: (1) Introduction; (2) Investigating old buildings; (3) The study of building materials; (4) Restoring and repairing old wooden structures; (5) Restoring stonework; (6) Architectural ceramics; (7) Cementitious materials; (8) Cleaning masonry; (9) Architectural metalwork; (10) Paints and coatings, by Frank G. Matero; (11) Architectural glass; (12) Foundations and footings; (13) restoring slate roofing; (14) Synthetic resins, polymers, and preservation; (15) Historic wallpapers.

Bibliographical references follow each chapter. Index, p.265–70.

T124 Wihr, Rolf. Fussböden: Stein, Mosaik, Keramik, Estrich: Geschichte, Herstellung, Restaurierung. [München], Callwey, [1985]. 283p. il. (part col.), 20 plates (part col.)

Comprehensive survey of the history, structure and techniques, and conservation practices of floors. Extensively illustrated, largely with examples in Italy.

Anmerkungen, p.275–77. Literaturverzeichnis, p.277–78. Register, p.281–83.

T125 ______. Restaurierung von Steindenkmalern: ein Handbuch für Restauratoren, Architekten, Steinbildhauer und Denkmalpfleger. [2. überarb. Aufl.] München, Callwey, [1980]. 236p. il. (part col.), tables.

Comprehensive discussion of the history, science, and practice in the conservation of stone structures and objects. The focus is primarily, but not exclusively, on the conservation of German monuments.

Verwendete und empfohlene Literatur, p.225–31. Anmerkungen, p.232–33. Register, p.234–35.

T126 Zuzanek, Jiri; Luscot, Brenda; and Nordley Beglo, Jo. Heritage preservation: tradition and diversity: an annotated bibliography. Waterloo, Ontario, Otium, 1996. 343p.

Partially annotated. Focuses on Canadian historic buildings and sites. Covers "books, journal articles, conference proceedings, government documents and other reports."—*Pref.*

Contents: (I) Significance of the past: history and theory of heritage preservation; (II) Our vanishing heritage: issues, controversies and advocacy; (III) Protecting built heritage: legislation and policies; (IV) Heritage preservation and urban planning; (V) Saving old buildings, streetscapes and neighbourhoods: the magnificent obsession; (VI) Tradition and diversity: ethnic and regional variations in Canada's built heritage; (VII) Places and landmarks: the images of the past; (VIII) Economics of heritage perservation; (IX) Management and interpretation of heritage resources; (X) Practical guides to heritage restoration; (XI) Heritage documentation, inventorization and research; (XII) Historic architecture: styles and techniques; (XIII) Heritage bibliographies and directories; (XIV) Selected scholarly, professional, and general circulation periodicals covering heritage preservation issues.

Author index, p.316–35. Location index, p.336–43.

SEE ALSO: Storia dell'arte italiana, pt.3, Situazioni momenti indagini, v.3, Conservazione, falso, restauro (GLAH 2:I383).

SCULPTURE

T127 From marble to chocolate: the conservation of modern sculpture. Ed. by Jackie Heuman. London, Archetype, [1995]. 172p. il. (part col.), ports.

Collection of papers falling "broadly into three categories. The first includes studies of artists from the mid-nineteenth century. . . . A second section highlights current scientific research projects concerned with modern materials. . . . The final category focuses on the use of modern materials by twentieth century sculptors, both living and dead."—*Introd.*

T128 Naudé, Virginia N., and Wharton, Glenn. Guide to the maintenance of outdoor sculpture. [Washington, D.C.], American Institute for Conservation of Historic and Artistic Works, [1993]. vi, 62p, il.

"The intent of this guide is to present a model for developing maintenance programs for outdoor sculpture. It was written for public art administrators, registrars, curators, museum directors, conservators, and others involved in the care of outdoor sculpture."—*Introd.* Essential references resource.

Contents: (1) Maintaining outdoor sculpture; (2) Whose job is it?; (3) Surveying the collection; (4) The long-range maintenance plan; (5) The maintenance program; (6) Materials used in outdoor sculpture; (7) Contracting maintenance activities.

Resources, p.56–58.

T129 Sculpture conservation: preservation or interference? Ed. by Phillip Lindley. [Brookfield, Vt.], Scolar Pr., [1997]. xxxii, 208p. il. (part col.), plates (part col.)

"The field of sculpture conservation has long been a contentious one."—*Introd.* Collection of essays reviewing the debate on past and present methods and techniques of sculpture conservation. The function of institutions in conservation practice and the legal position of restorers is also discussed.

Contents: (1) Cathedrals in England: the statutory context for conservation, by R. Gem; (2) Sculpture conservation in England and Wales: an architect's view, by M. B. Caroe; (3) The bureaucratic tendency: polemic reflections on the control of conservation work, with reference to the Romanesque frieze at Lincoln Cathedral, by J. Baily; (4) The historic monuments of France and their fate: Who makes the decisions?, by I. Pallot-Frossard; (5) Conservation: a direct route to the protection and study of monuments, by R. Nardi; (6) Sculpture in active service, by J. Farnsworth; (7) Preservation or desecration? The legal position of the restorer, by R. Fry; (8) A standard for care: the role of English heritage in the provision of conservation expertise, by K. Foley; (9)

Sculpture conservation: treatment or reinterpretation, by J. Larson; (10) An assessment of the "Lime Method" of conservation of exterior limestone sculpture, by N. Duran; (11) Treatment and protection of public monumental stone sculpture in Britain: the role of the sculpture conservator, by J. Porter; (12) Perspectives on the repatination of outdoor bronze sculptures, by J. Heuman; (13) The monument to George Home, 1st Earl of Dunbar, by Maximilian Colt, c. 1611, in Dunbar Parish Church, by K. Taylor; (14) Vasari's theory on the origins of oil painting and its influence on cleaning methods: the ruined polychromy of the early thirteenth century crucifix from Haug, Norway, by K. Kollandsrud; (15) Problems in the cleaning of polychromed wood sculpture, by B. Schleicher; (16) Pietro Torrigiano's tomb of Dr Yonge in the Public Record Office: conservation discoveries and decisions, by C. Galvin and P. Lindley; (17) A view of sculpture conservation in Finland, by L. Wikström; (18) Variations in the surface of stone owing to the presence of organic and inorganic substances, by A. Parronchi; (19) The display and conservation of sculpture at Petworth, by T. Proudfoot and C. Rowell; (20) Some observations and reflections on the restoration of antique sculpture in the eighteenth century, by B. Vaughan.

Bibliographical references throughout the text.

T130 La scultura in terracotta: tecniche e conservazione. A cura di Maria Grazia Vaccari. [Firenze], Centro Di, [1996]. 401p. il. (part col.), col. plates, tables.

Collection of 28 essays on the conservation of terra-cotta sculpture in Italy. The works themselves are not necessarily of Italian origin. Historical as well as technical aspects are discussed. The last section, comprising case histories, is the largest.

Contents: Materiali e tecnologie; Metodi di indagine; Processi di alterazione; Studi e interventi.

Bibliographical references follow each essay. Bibliografia, p.375–401.

T131 Strangstad, Lynette. A graveyard preservation primer. Walnut Creek, Calif., Altamira Pr., [1995]. xii, 126p. il. (American Association for State and Local History book series)

1st ed., Nashville, Tenn., American Association for State and Local History in cooperation with the Association for Gravestone Studies, 1988.

"Intended specifically for nonprofessionals involved in small to mid-sized projects who are having difficulty in getting started because of the lack of staff or resources."

Contents: (1) Assessing the problem; (2) Organizational concerns; (3) Collecting data; (4) Remedies; Appendix A: Sample gravestone rubbing regulations; Appendix B: Sample cemetery survey forms; Appendix C: Consultants, contractors, conservators, and carvers; Appendix D: Sample cemetery legislation.

Glossary, p.109–12. Sources of additional information, p.113–121. Index, p.123–26.

T132 Sturman, Shelley; Unruh, Julie; and Spande, Helen. Maintenance of outdoor sculpture: an annotated bibliography. [Washington, D.C., National Institute for the Conservation of Cultural Property, 1996.] 70p.

Annotated bibliography "originally prepared for the pre-session of the annual meeting of the American Institute for Conservation of Historic & Artistic Works (Buffalo, N.Y., 1992), titled Maintenance of outdoor sculpture: whose job is it?."—[*Pref.*] This updated version was produced under the auspices of the Save Outdoor Sculpture! (S.O.S.) organization. "The primary audience remains professionals in the conservation field, though a number of sources cited are particularly relevant for arts managers, curators, custodians and artists."—[*Pref.*] Lists more than 400 citations. Books, journal articles, conference proceedings, and papers are covered.

Contents: (1) General; (2) Acid rain; (3) Metal; (4) Corrosion; (5) Coatings; (6) Stone; (7) Wood.

PAINTING

T133 Art in transit: studies in the transport of paintings. Ed. by Marion F. Mecklenburg. Organizing institutions: Canadian Conservation Institute of Communications Canada; Conservation Analytical Laboratory of the Smithsonian Institution; National Gallery of Art; Tate Gallery. International conference on the packing and transportation of paintings, September 9, 10, and 11, 1991, London. Washington, D.C., National Gallery of Art, [1991]. 372p. il., charts, tables.

Collection of papers presenting the current state of research into the science, technology, practices, and philosophies relating to the transport of paintings.

Selected bibliography, by Michael R. Skalka, p.359–72.

T134 Artists' pigments: a handbook of their history and characteristics. (3v.) Washington, D.C., National Gallery of Art, 1986– . il. (part col.), ports. (part col.)

V.1 ed. by Robert L. Feller; v.2 ed. by Ashok Roy; v.3 ed. by Elisabeth West FitzHugh.

Essential, comprehensive reference resource on pigments used in the creation of works of art. Covers natural and manmade pigments. Extensively illustrated. Many of the individual essays are based on a series of articles published in Studies in conservation, with the addition of new material.

Bibliographical references follow each essay. References and an index in all vols.

T135 Conservation and restoration of pictorial art. Ed. by Norman Brommelle and Perry Smith. Boston, Butterworths, [1976]. xv, 270p., il., col. plate, diags.

"The chapters of this book consist substantially of papers presented at a Congress in Lisbon of the International Institute for Conservation of Historic and Artistic Works in October 1972 on Conservation of paintings and the graphic arts."—*Pref.* 35 excellent, wide-ranging papers discussing Western and non-Western conservation practices in a variety of media.

Contents: Painting methods and materials; Identification of paint media; Practical painting restoration; Varnishes; Solvent action; Technology of adhesives; Works of art on paper and parchment; Japanese paintings and methods.

Bibliographical references follow most papers. Painting methods and materials: a brief survey of published work from 1961 to 1972, by Joyce Plesters. Index, p.263–70.

T136 The conservation of wall paintings: proceedings of a symposium organized by the Courtauld Institute of Art and the Getty Conservation Institute, London, July 13–16, 1987. Ed. by Sharon Cather. [Marina del Rey, Calif.], Getty Conservation Institute, 1991. 148p. il. 56 col. plates.

Papers addressing the issues of diagnosis, documentation, and monitoring of the condition of wall paintings. The rationale behind the conference was a focus on interdisciplinary approaches. The vol. also constitutes a useful overview and comparison of some of the world's most important wall painting conservation projects of the late 20th century. Excellent color illustrations.

Contents: Scientific and technical examination of the tomb of Queen Nefertari at Thebes, by Frank Preusser; Preliminary research for the conservation of the Brancacci Chapel, Florence, by Ornella Casazza and Sabino Giovannoni; Pretreatment examination and documentation: the wall paintings of Schloss Seehof, Bamberg, by Karl Ludwig Dasser; The role of the architectural fabric in the preservation of wall paintings, by Claus Arendt; The conservation in situ of the Romanesque wall paintings of Lambach, by Ivo Hammer; The frescoes of Michelangelo on the vault of the Sistine Chapel: conservation methodology, problems, and results, by Fabrizio Mancinelli; The frescoes of Michelangelo on the vault of the Sistine Chapel: original technique and conservation, by Gianluigi Colalucci; Conservation of central Asian wall painting fragments from the Stein collection in the British Museum, by S. B. Hanna and J. K. Dinsmore; Destruction and restoration of Campanian mural paintings in the eighteenth and nineteenth centuries, by Eric M. Moormann; Monitoring wall paintings affected by soluble salts, by Andreas Arnold and Konrad Zehnder; In review: an assessment of Florentine methods of wall painting conservation based on the use of mineral treatments, by Mauro Matteini.

Bibliographical references follow each paper.

T137 Conti, Alessandro. Manuale di restauro. A cura di Marina Romiti Conti. [Torino], Einaudi, [1996]. 399p. il. (Biblioteca studio, 30)

Key text by an important theorist on conservation practice. Posthumously published.

Contents: (I) Inizio; (II) Premess; (III) Normative e orientamenti; (IV) Documentazione; (V) Arte e scienza; (VI) Il restauratore; (VII) L'affresco; (VIII) Tecniche; (IX) Foderature e intelaiature; (X) Sinopie e puliture; (XI) Ancora sulle puliture: pigmenti, arte contemporanea, affreschi; (XII) Puliture della scultura, policromie e problemi di presentazione; (XIII) Ridipinture; (XIV) Integrazioni: metodi di intervento I; (XV) Integrazioni: metodi di intervento II; (XVI) La vernice; (XVII) Ancora sulle vernici, il metodo Pettenkofer, il problema delle luci.

Bibliographical references throughout the text. Bibliografia, p.331–74. Indice degli argomenti, dei concetti e delle tecniche, p.375–86. Indice dei nomi, p.387–99.

T138 ———. Storia del restauro e della conservazione delle opere d'arte. [Milano], Electa, [1998]. 383p. il. (part col.) (Saggistica universale illustrata, 2) 1st ed., Milano, Electa, 1973.

Important history of conservation traditions and practices in Italy by a leading scholar of the field.

Contents: (I) Verso il restauro; (II) La conservazione delle opere d'arte nel Cinquecento; (III) Alcuni tradizioni locali in Italia; (IV) I quadri da galleria; (V) Restauri settecenteschi in Italia e in Francia; (VI) Venezia e Pietro Edwards; (VII) Tra Settecento e Ottocento; (VIII) Il restauro fra accademia e romanticismo; (IX) Il restauro nell'Italia Unita.

The first ed. included an important introductory essay, "Problemi di lettura e problemi di conservazione," by Roberto Longhi.

Note, p.329–60. Bibliografia, p.361–66. Indice dei nomi, p.367–74. Indice dei luoghi e delle opere, p.375–82.

T139 Lambert, David. Conserving Australian rock art: a manual for site managers. Ed. by Graeme K. Ward. Canberra, Aboriginal Studies Pr., 1989. 102p. il. (part col.), 35 pl. (part col.) (Australian Institute of Aboriginal Studies. Institute report series)

Manual detailing methods and techniques for conserving rock paintings and drawings (pictographs), and rock engravings (petroglyphs). It is directed specifically at "site managers who have received on-site training in conservation methods."—*Introd.*

Contents: (1) The impact of surface water; (2) Salt deterioration; (3) Soil and vegetation; (4) Microflora; (5) Animals; (6) Managing sites to reduce visitor impact; (7) Site vandalism and visitor impact; (8) Specialised techniques; Appendix 1: Some materials used in conservation; Appendix 2: Sample analytical techniques; Appendix 3: The Burra Charter.

References, p.63–67. Index, p.79–82.

T140 Looking through paintings: the study of painting techniques and materials in support of art historical research. Ed. by Erma Hermens. Associate eds. Annemiek Ouwerkerk and Nicola Costaras. Baarn (The Netherlands), de Prom, 1998. 519p. il. (part col.), col. plates, ports. (part col.) (Leids kunsthistorisch jaarboek, 11)

"The papers in this volume circle around an area of study that has become known informally as 'technical art history' . . . a wide-ranging, inclusive evocation of the making of art and the means by which we throw light on the process."—*Pref.* Included in this approach is the examination of old painting manuals and descriptions.

Contents: Some reflections upon the impact of scientific examination on art historical research, by J. R. J. van Asperen de Boer; Design, technique and execution: the dichotomy between theory and craft in nineteenth-century British instruction manuals on oil painting, by Leslie Carlyle; Taking a closer look: art historians, restorers and scientists, by John Leighton; Colour words in the High Middle Ages, by John Gage; White and golden tin foil in applied relief decoration 1240–1530, by Josephine A. Darrah; Links with Schongauer in three Early Netherlandish paintings in the National Gallery, by Rachel Billinge; Painters' methods to prevent colour changes described in sixteenth to early eighteenth century sources on oil painting techniques, by

Margriet van Eikema Hommes; Thoughts on the use of the green glaze called "copper-resinate" and its colour-changes, by Renate Woudhuysen-Keller and Paul Woudhuysen; The intriguing changes through restoration of a newly discovered painting by Cornelis Cornelisz. van Haarlem, by Annetje Boersma and Jeroen Giltaij; The glow in late sixteenth and seventeenth century Dutch painting, by Paul Taylor; The Antwerp brand on paintings on panel, by Jøgen Wadum; Meaning and development of the ground-layer in seventeenth century painting, by Nico van Hout; Johannes Verspronck: The technique of a seventeenth century Haarlem portraitist, by Ella Hendriks; The Pekstok papers: lake pigments, prisons and paint-mills, by Erma Hermens and Arie Wallert; Aspects of drawing and painting in seventeenth century Spanish treatises, by Zahira Veliz; French painting technique in the seventeenth and early eighteenth centuries and De la Fontaine's Academie de la Peinture (Paris 1679), by Ann Massing; Two still-life paintings by Jan van Huysum: an examination of painting technique in relation to documentary and technical evidence, by Joris Dik and Arie Wallert; Holman Hunt on himself: textual evidence in aid of technical analysis, by Melissa R. Katz; Posing, reposing and decomposing: life-size lay figures, living models and artists' colourmen in nineteenth century London, by Sally Woodcock; The Hafkenscheid collection, by Ineke Pey; Artistic craftsmanship in the age of impatience, by Cor Blok.

Bibliographical references follow each essay.

T141 Manual on the conservation of paintings. [London], Archetype, [1997]. 296p. il.

Trans. of Manuel de la conservation et restauration des tableaux, Paris, International Institute of Intellectual Cooperation, 1939. 1st English ed., 1940.

"It could be said that the first international congress [for the study of scientific methods for the examination and preservation of works of art], in Rome in 1930 and the resulting Manual marked the beginning of modern conservation-restoration since, for the first time, renowned international restorers, historians and scientists combined their knowlege in one handbook."—*Cover verso of the 1997 ed.* Deals with easel paintings only.

Contents: (1) Conservation: (I) General principles applying to the conservation of paintings in museums; (II) Methods of investigation applied to the examination of pictures; (III) The surroundings; (IV) The action of light on paintings; (V) Effects of candle smokes and certain methods of heating; (VI) Reactions of the constituent parts of paintings to humidity and temperature changes; (VII) Heating and air conditions; (VIII) Local protective and precautionary measures; (IX) Protection against fire; (X) Transport and packing of paintings; (2) Restoration: (XI) General principles concerning the restoration of paintings; (XII) Maladies and treatment of the varnish layer; (XIII) Maladies and treatment of the paint layer; (XIV) Maladies and treatment of the ground; (XV) Maladies and treatment of canvas; (XVI) Other supports; Appendices: Practical recommendations.

Bibliographical references follow each paper. Bibliography of studies published in the review Mouseion on the conservation and restoration of paintings, p.263–70. Table of colours, p.273–91. Index, p.293–96.

T142 Das 19. Jahrhundert und die Restaurierung: Beiträge zur Malerei, Maltechnik und Konservierung. Hrsg. Heinz Althöfer. München, Callwey, 1987. 397p. il. (part col.)

Text primarily in German. Some essays in English or French.

47 essays by various authors, divided into five sections, focus on the interaction of art history, art education, materials and techniques, and restoration concepts during the 19th century. Some of the essays are conservation case histories.

Contents: Kunstgeschichte und Restaurierung; Künstler und Schulen; Maltechnik und Restaurierung; Restaurierung im 19. Jahrhundert; Kunststoffe als neues Material.

Bibliographie zur Maltechnik und Restaurierungsgeschichte im 19. Jahrhundert (Auswahl), von Sabine Euler-Künsemüller, p.347–56. Anmerkungen, p.357–82. Personen-, Orts- und Sachregister, p.383–96.

T143 Nicolaus, Knut. The restauration of paintings. Ed. by Christine Westphal. [Cologne], Könemann, [1998]. 422p. col. il., tables.

"An attempt to summarize the current state of knowledge and to present it in a 'popular scientific' manner, and additionally to refine the use of restoration terminology and offer new terms for debate."—*Foreword.* In-depth exposition of the complexities of late 20th-century paintings conservation, and the high level of training that conservators must possess. Includes numerous excellent illustrations, including many before-and-after sequences, and images showing the damage resulting from inexpert practices.

Contents: Wooden supports; Textile supports; The paint layer; Varnish.

Bibliographical references follow some essays. Bibliographical references follow each chapter. Documentation, p.372–82. Notes, p.383. Glossary, p.384–91. Bibliography, p.392–406. Index, p.408–22.

T144 Perusini, Giuseppina. Il restauro dei dipinti e delle sculture lignee: storia, teorie e tecniche. [Udine], Del Bianco, [1989]. 303p.

Previous ed., Introduzione al restauro: storia, teorie e tecniche (1985).

Useful overview of the history and theory of conservation in the fields of paintings and wooden sculpture.

Contents: (1) Storia del restauro; Allegato A: Carta del restauro 1972; Allegato B: Carta 1987 della conservazione e del restauro degli oggetti d'arte e di cultura; (2) Teoria del restauro; (3) Il "restauro preventivo"; (4) Scienza e conservazione; (5) Fattori di deterioramento; (6) La pittura murale; (7) Dipinti su tela, tavola e sculture lignee; (8) Cenni sugli antichi materiali pittorici.

Bibliographical references throughout the text. Bibliografia, p.291–98.

T145 Petit, Jean, and Valot, Henri. Glossaire des peintures et vernis, des substances naturelles et des materieux synthetiques. Paris, Section française de l'institut international de conservation, [1991]. ix, 127p. il.

Alphabetical listing of paint and varnish terminology. Each entry comprises a definition, followed by one or more commentaries.

T146 Le pitture murali: tecniche, problemi, conservazione. A cura di Cristina Danti, Mauro Matteini, Arcangelo Moles. [Firenze], Centro Di, [1990]. 371p. il. (part col.), plans.

Comprehensive survey of current wall painting conservation research, methods, and practices in Italy, primarily originating in the conservation studios of the Opificio delle Pietre Dure, Florence. Includes an overview of a period that began with the view that complete detachment of wall paintings ("stacchi") was the only way to restore them, to a more integrated, in situ approach. The numerous case histories of work undertaken 1950s–1980s are of interest not only to conservators, but also to art historians.

Il restauro delle pitture murali nella letteratura italiana e straniera: 1975–1989, di Anna Mieli Pacifici, p.329–71.

T147 Restaurierte Gemälde: die Restauriertwerkstätte de Gemäldegalerie des Kunsthistorischen Museums, 1986–1996. [Milano], Skira, [1996]. 211p. il. (chiefly col.), ports. (chiefly col.)

Catalog of the exhibition, Vienna, Kunsthistorisches Museum (1996–1997) illustrating conservation work carried out on 43 of the museum's paintings. Excellently produced, part of the vol.'s interest lies in the fact that museum and catalog include some of the world's most famous paintings. Each catalog entry comprises a conservation history for the painting and many high-quality photographs illustrating conservation details.

T148 Ruhemann, Helmut. The cleaning of paintings: problems and potentialities. [Reprint.] N.Y., Hacker, 1982.

See GLAH 1:M44 for original annotation.

Particularly significant for its extensive, annotated bibliography, by Joyce Plesters, on the history of conservation, p. 262–481.

SEE ALSO: Mayer, Artist's handbook of materials and techniques (GLAH 2:M44); Mayer, The HarperCollins dictionary of art terms and techniques (GLAH 2:E17).

WORKS ON PAPER (except photographs)

T149 Chantry, J. M. H. A bibliographical guide to some useful articles for the paper conservator: to be found in periodical journals and conference preprints held in the Library of the Institute of Paper Conservation. Finstock [England], [The Institute], 1993. 189p.

Alphabetical listing by title.

Contents: (I) Bibliography; (II) Title index; (III) Subject index.

T150 Clapp, Anne F. Curatorial care of works of art on paper: basic procedures for paper preservation. [3d, rev. ed.] N.Y., Lyons & Burford, 1987. x, 191p. il.

1st ed., N.Y., Lyons & Burford, 1973. 2d, rev. ed., Oberlin, Ohio, [Intervention Conservation Association], 1974; 3d, rev. ed., Oberlin, Ohio, Intermuseum Laboratory, 1978.

"Designed to aid the conservation technician, private or institutional, in caring for works of art on paper. Only basic problems and procedures are discussed; techniques of advanced restoration are omitted because all major treatment should be submitted to a trained, qualified conservator working in a well-equipped laboratory. . . . The person this book especially addresses is he whose business it is to care for paper objects, yet who has not had the advantage of years of training under a conservator or of education in a conservation program."—*Introd.*

Notes, p.172–80. Bibliography, p.181–86. Index, p.187–91.

T151 Ehrenberg, Ralph E. Archives and manuscripts: maps and architectural drawings. Chicago, Society of American Archivists, 1982. 64p. il. (SAA basic manual series)

Generalist text whose underlying theme is the preservation of the cartographic and architectural heritage.

Contents: (1) Accession and appraisal; (2) Arrangement; (3) Description; (4) Conservation; (5) Storage; (6) Reference and access.

Bibliographical references throughout. Glossary, p.56–57. Selected bibliography, p.62–64.

T152 Ellis, Margaret Holben. The care of prints and drawings. Walnut Creek, Calif., AltaMira Pr., 1995. 253p. il.

1st ed., Nashville, AASLH Pr., 1987.

"The purpose of this book is to give practical, straightforward advice to those responsible for the care of prints and drawings, works of art traditionally made on paper or . . . on parchment."—*Introd.*

Bibliographical references follow each chapter. An annotated bibliography, p.243–46. Index, p.247–53.

T153 James, Carlo . . . [et al.] Old master prints and drawings: a guide to preservation and conservation. Trans. and ed. by Marjorie B. Cohn. [Amsterdam], Amsterdam Univ. Pr., [1997]. 319p. il.

Trans. of Manuale per la conservazione e il restauro di disegni e stampe antichi. Firenze, Olschki, 1991.

Comprehensive examination of the history and techniques of conservation of drawings and prints beginning with the introduction of paper to Europe in 1150 and ending with the mid-19th century. "Essential reading for all students, teachers and practitioners in the conservation of Old Master drawings and prints."—*Review*, Studies in conservation, v.38, 1993, p.136–37.

Contents: (I) Collectors and mountings; (II) Paper; (III) Drawing techniques; (IV) Print techniques; (V) Visual identification of graphic techniques and their supports; (VI) The history of preservation of works of art on paper; (VII) Curatorial care today; (VIII) Technical problems in preservation; (IX) The history of conservation; (X) Concerns of the curator and concerns of the conservator; (XI) The constituent materials of paper; (XII) Analytical methods; (XIII) Cleaning; (XIV) Removal of old mountings and lining; (XV) Stain removal; (XVI) Bleaching; (XVII) Deacidification and alkaline reserve; (XVIII) Adhesives; (XIX) Consolidation and integration; (XX) Lining; (XXI) Integration of colors.

Bibliographical references throughout the text. Selected bibliography, p.306–10. Index, p.313–19.

T154 Koyano, Masako. Japanese scroll paintings: a handbook of mounting techniques. [Washington, D.C.], Foundation of the American Institute for Conservation, 1979. 112p. il., plates.

"Deals with the craft of mounting and remounting hanging scrolls as practised by Japanese mounters," and introduces "conservators . . . to the ideas and methods of the oriental painting restorer."—*Introd.* Clearly written and with many illustrations.

Notes, p.95–105. Index, p.107–111.

PHOTOGRAPHY

T155 Conservation of photographic materials: a basic reading list = La conservation des documents photographiques: liste d'ouvrages de référence de base. Comp. by Klaus B. Hendriks and Anne Whitehurst. [Ottawa], National Archives of Canada, [1988]. vi, 32p.

Text in English and French.

Unannotated bibliography covering books and journal articles.

Contents: (I) History of photography; (II) Basic photography technology; (III) Structure and properties of photographic materials; (IV) Identification and dating of photographic records; (V) Conservation of photographic materials; (VI) Duplication and copying; (VII) Processing of black-and-white films and papers; (VIII) Colour photographic materials; (IX) Conservation treatments; (X) Organization of photographs; (XI) Publications by the American National Standards Institute (ANSI) on the preservation and storage of photographic materials.

Index, p.29–32.

T156 Hendriks, Klaus B. . . . [et al.] Fundamentals of photograph conservation: a study guide. [Toronto], Lugus, [1991]. viii, 560p. il. (chiefly col.), diags., tables.

"The purpose of the present study guide is to summarize laboratory experiments and their theoretical foundations that are helpful in introducing interested students to practical work in the field of photograph conservation."—*Foreword.*

Contents: (1) Photograph conservation training program; (2) Darkroom and laboratory equipment and procedures; (3) Light-sensitive materials: theory, structure, and deterioration mechanisms; (4) Black-and-white processing; (5) Historical photographic processes; (6) Duplication and copying; (7) Paper conservation treatments as applied to photographs: a review; (8) Chemical treatments; (9) Preservation, storage, and display of photographs; (10) Tests for image stability and suitability of conservation materials; (11) Condition reports, treatment proposals, and collection preservation surveys.

Bibliographical references follow each chapter. Bibliography, p.507–36. Index, p.537–60.

T157 Keefe, Laurence E., and Inch, Dennis. The life of a photograph: archival processing, matting, framing, and storage. 2d ed. Boston, Focal Pr., [1990]. xi, 384p. il., tables.

Contents: (1) Processing black and white prints for permanence; (2) Processing film for permanence; (3) Flattening prints; (4) Techniques for conservation mounting; (5) Dry mounting; (6) Mat board; (7) Hand cutting conservation mats; (8) Decorative mats; (9) Metal frames; (10) Clip and passe-partout frames; (11) Wood frames; (12) Choice, cutting, and handling of glazing materials; (13) Planning an exhibition of framed prints; (14) Copying, duplicating, and video as tools for photographic conservation; (15) Storage of prints; (16) Storage of film; (17) Caring for color; (18) Family photographs; (19) Nineteenth-century photographs; (20) Inspecting and reframing old prints; Appendix A: Suppliers; Appendix B: How to order framing and conservation supplies through the mail; Appendix C: Plastics used for photographic enclosures.

Glossary, p.370–71. Bibliography, p.372–73. Index, p.375–84.

T158 Rempel, Siegfried. The care of photographs. N.Y., N. Lyons, 1987. 184p. il.

Focuses on preservation conservation techniques, and also "includes many of the concepts employed by professionals in photographic preservation."—*Introd.*

Contents: (1) Photographic processes; (2) Examining and handling photographs; (3) Deterioration of photographs; (4) Cleaning and stabilizing photographs; (5) Environments for photographic materials; (6) Housing photographs; (7) Conservation services.

Suppliers, p.167–69. Bibliography, p.171–78. Index, p.179–84.

T159 Ritzenthaler, Mary . . . [et al.] Archives & manuscripts: administration of photographic collections. Chicago, Society of American Archivists, 1984. 171p. il. (SAA basic manual series)

"This manual is directed toward archivists, manuscript curators, librarians, picture specialists, and others who work with historical photographs. Its primary focus is on photographs that have documentary value as historical resource materials for research, publication, and exhibition."—*Introd.*

Contents: (1) Photographs in archival collections, by Margery S. Long; (2) History of photographic process, Gerald J. Munoff; (3) Appraisal and collecting policies, by Margery S. Long; (4) Arrangement and description, by Gerald J. Munoff; (5) Preservation of photographic materials, by Mary Lynn Ritzenthaler; Legal issues, by Mary Lynn Ritzenthaler; Managing a photographic copy service, by Mary Lynn Ritzenthaler.

Glossary, p.153–55. Bibliography, p.156–59. Appendix C: Supplies for the care and storage of photographic materials, p.160–63. Funding sources for photographic collections, p.164. Index, p.165–71.

T160 Weinstein, Robert A., and Booth, Larry. Collection, use, and care of historical photographs. Nashville, American Association for State and Local History, [1977]. 222p. il.

Contains "common-sense suggestions, basic information, and explanations that any nontechnical person can employ."—*Pref.* A collections care guide aimed at the curator or collector, rather than a manual for the conservator.

Contents: (1) Historical photographs: definitions and descriptions; (2) Uses for historical photographs; (3) Thoughts about collecting historical photographs; (4) A case study in collecting photographs; (5) Preservation of photographic materials; (6) Restoration of photographic materials; (7) Modern photographic processes; Appendix A: Where do we turn for help?; Appendix B: George Eastman House list.

Suggested reading, p.211–15. Index, p.217–22.

T161 Wilhelm, Henry Gilmer. The permanence and care of color photographs: traditional and digital color prints, color negatives, slides, and motion pictures. With contrib. author Carol Brower. Grinnell, Iowa, Preservation Pub. Co., [1993]. ix, 744p. il. (part col.)

Includes consideration of digital images.

Contents: (1) Traditional and digital color prints, color negatives, and color slides: Which products last longest?; (2) Accelerated tests for measuring light fading, dark fading, and yellowish stain formation in color prints and films; (3) Light fading stability of displayed color prints; (4) The effects of print lacquers, plastic laminates, 3M photogard, and UV-absorbing plastic filter; (5) Dark fading and yellowish staining of color prints, transparencies, and negatives; (6) Projector-caused fading of 35mm color slides; (7) Monitoring the long-term fading and staining of color photographs in museum and archive collections; (8) Color print fading and the professional portrait and wedding photographer; what to do about a troubling situation; (9) The permanent preservation of color motion pictures; (10) The extraordinarily stable technicolor dye-imbibition: motion picture color print process (1932–1978); (11) Print mounting adhesives and techniques, tapes, rubber stamps, pencils, inks, and spotting methods for color and B&W prints; (12) The handling, presentation, and conservation matting of photographs, by Carol Brower; (13) Composition, pH, testing, and light fading stability of mount boards and other paper products used with photographs, by Carol Brower and Henry Wilhelm; (14) Envelopes and sleeves for films and prints; (15) Framing materials, storage boxes, portfolio cases, albums, cabinets, and shelves; (16) The storage environment for photographs: relative humidity, temperature, air pollution, dust, and the prevention of fungus; (17) Display and illumination of color and black-and-white prints; (18) Handling and preservation of color slide collections; (19) Frost-free refrigerators for storing color and black-and-white films and prints; (20) Large-scale, humidity-controlled cold storage facilities for the permanent preservation of B&W and color films, prints and motion pictures.

Bibliographical references follow each chapter. Index, p.727–44.

SEE ALSO: Bibliography of photographic processes in use before 1880 (GLAH 2:O1); Reilly, Care and identification of 19th-century photographic prints (GLAH 2:O67).

DECORATIVE ARTS

Furniture (including wood)

T162 Bonner, Kevin Jan. Furniture restoration and repair for beginners: practical crafts series. [Lewes, U.K.], Guild of Master Craftsmen, [1994] 192p. il. (chiefly col.), diags., col. port.

Useful introduction for the amateur, accompanied by excellent illustrations. The emphasis is on repair rather than on conservation.

Contents: (1) About wood; (2) What to restore; (3) Safety; (4) Workspace, tools and materials; (5) Identifying finishes; (6) Stripping; (7) Antiquikstrip; (8) Repairing finishes; (9) Repairing structural damage; (10) Fixing odds and ends; (11) Veneers; (12) Fillers; (13) Stains; (14) Waxes; (15) Oil finishes; (16) French polishing for the absolute beginner; (17) French polishing with a brush; (18) Polyurethane varnish; (19) Modern mass-production lacquers; (20) Water-based varnishes; (21) Ebonizing; (22) Painted finishes; (23) Distressing and patina.

Glossary, p.187. Index, p.190

T163 Buchanan, George. The illustrated handbook of furniture restoration. N.Y., Harper and Row, [1985]. 239p. il. (part col.), col. plates.

Lucid and straightforward text, accompanied by numerous explanatory illustrations.

Contents: (1) The workshop; (2) Wood and its identification; (3) Preparing for work; (4) Safety; (5) Tools; (6) Joints; (7) Dismantling furniture; (8) Common faults and their remedies; (9) Gluing and fastening; (10) Frame furniture; (11) Carving; (12) Carcass furniture; (13) Veneering; (14) Chairs; (15) Woodturning; (16) Steaming and laminating timber; (17) Finishing: Minor work; (18) Finishing: major work; (19) Upholstery.

Bibliography, p.236. Index, p.237–39.

T164 Conservation of wood in painting and the decorative arts: preprints of the contributions to the Oxford congress, 17–23 September 1978. Ed. by Norman S. Brommelle . . . [et al.] London, International Institute for Conservation of Historic and Artistic Works, [1978]. viii, 198p. il., charts, tables.

42 papers by internationally recognized theorists and/or practitioners examining aspects of "the deterioration and conservation of wood in painting and the decorative arts, together with its background theory, with a sidelong glance at recent developments in the reinforcement as distinct from replacement of fixed wooden structures."—*Introd.* Some of the papers are case histories of specific objects and/or treatments.

Contents: Wood technology; Biological attack; Furniture; Wood in architecture; Wood sculpture; Panel paintings: technical studies; Panel paintings: treatment.

Bibliographical references follow each paper. English abstracts, p.xiii–xviii. French abstracts, p.xix–xxv.

T165 Germond, François. L'ébéniste restaurateur. [Paris], A. Colin, [1992]. 173p. il. (Arts d'interieurs)

Clearly outlined text, with many explanatory sketches and diagrams.

Contents: Être restaurateur; La documentation; Les causes de dégradation; La consolidation des bois; L'outillage; Les colles; Les patines, les matériaux; La restauration du meuble massif; La remise en état des bois massifs; Les tourillons;

Les tiroirs; Les entures; La restauration des sièges; La restauration des meubles plagués; La marqueterie Boulle; La chimie et les finitions; Les décors et accessoires métalliques; La serrurerie; Le propriétaire du meuble et l'ébéniste-restaurateur.

Glossaire, p.168–70. Bibliographie, p.172.

T166 Gilded wood: conservation and history. Madison, Conn., Sound View Pr., 1991. 428p. il. (part col.), 37 col. plates, tables.

"This volume is an outgrowth of the October 1988 Gilding conservation symposium, held at the Philadelphia Museum of Art."—*T.p. verso.* Presents a substantial body of work by an international group of art historians, conservators and conservation scientists, and curators. Papers cover aspects of connoisseurship, research, and conservation treatment. Excellent illustrations of objects undergoing conservation.

Bibliographical references follow each paper. Index, p.419–28.

T167 McGiffen, Robert F. Furniture care and conservation. Rev., 3d ed. Foreword by Caroline K. Keck. Nashville, Tenn., American Association for State and Local History Pr., [1992]. 235p. il.

1st ed., 1983; 2d ed., 1989.

Contents: (1) Restoration and conservation; (2) Environment and its effects on wooden artifacts; (3) Furniture examination techniques; (4) Cleaning dirty furniture; (5) Wooden elements: repair and replacement; (6) Metal elements and metal leaf: repair and replacement; (7) Surface and finish: care and repair; (8) Good housekeeping for artifacts; (9) Moving and storing furniture and artifacts; (10) Insects and other pests: some things to do about them; (11) Health hazards and safety practices; (12) Proper furniture conservation: finding a laboratory and a conservator; Appendix 1: AIC code of ethics and standards of practice; Appendix 2: Conservators: a listing; Appendix 3: Training programs in conservation: Appendix 4: Sample forms for conservation work; Appendix 5: Partial list of regional conservation centers, associations, and guilds; Appendix 6: Materials and suppliers.

Bibliographical references follow each chapter. Notes, p.218–20. Glossary, p.221–26. Bibliography, p.227–28. Index, p.231–35.

T168 The structural conservation of panel paintings: proceedings of a symposium at the J. Paul Getty Museum, 24–28 April 1995. Ed. by Kathleen Dardes and Andrea Rothe. Los Angeles, Getty Conservation Institute, [1998]. 565p. il. (part col.), tables.

"The purpose of the symposium was to document the techniques, both traditional and contemporary, of panel stabilization."—*Foreword.* Comprises 31 papers.

Contents: (I) Wood science and technology; (II) History of panel-making techniques; (III) History of the structural conservation of panel paintings; (IV) Current approaches to the structural conservation of panel paintings.

Bibliographical references follow each paper.

T169 Taylor, V. J. The manual of furniture restoration: the complete manual, 17th–20th century. [Newton Abbot, U.K.], David and Charles, [1994]. 224p. il., diags.

1st ed. (1992) titled Repairing and restoring furniture.

Extremely clear and thorough guide. "Deals with three kinds of woodwork, namely reviving, repairing and restoring furniture."—*Introd.* Many excellent explanatory drawings.

Contents: (1) The tools you will need; (2) Accessories you can make for yourself; (3) Dismantling and preparation; (4) Repairs to cabinets; (5) Repairs to chairs; (6) Repairs to tables, drawers, and drawer framing; (7) Upholstery repairs; (8) Repairing mouldings and beadings; (9) Repairs to veneers and bandings; (10) Stains, polishes, and traditional finishes; (11) Special finishes and effects; (12) Associated materials and techniques; (13) Historical guide to decoration and fittings; Appendices: Miscellaneous technical information.

Bibliography, p.221. Index, p.222–24.

Clocks and Watches

T170 Clock cleaning and repairing. Ed. by Bernard E. Jones. 6th ed. London, Cassell, [1978]. 176p. il.

1st ed., London, Cassell, 1917; subsequent, bibliographically obscure, eds. 1954, 1967.

Discusses all aspects of the subject.

Index, p.174–76.

T171 De Carle, Donald. Practical clock repairing. Illustrations by E. A. Ayres. 3d ed. London, N.A.G. Pr., [1969]. 319p. il., charts, tables.

1st published serially in Horological journal, 1943–1945; 1st ed., 1946. 2d, rev. ed., 1964. Italian trans., Milano, Hoepli, 1948. Spanish trans. Barcelona, J. Montesó, 1950.

Extremely thorough textbook, surveying all aspects of the subject.

Index, p.315–19.

T172 Jendritzki, H. La réparation des pendules anciennes. Lausanne, Scriptar, [1987]. 138p. il., diags.

Contains extremely useful and clear discussions, excellent diagrams with lengthy captions, and many photographs of tools and equipment.

Outillage, p.124–38.

Pottery and Porcelain, Glass, Stained Glass, and Mosaics

T173 Acton, Lesley, and McAuley, Paul. Repairing pottery and porcelain: a practical guide. [N.Y.], Lyons and Burford, [1996]. 112p. il. (part col.), tables.

"This book aims to guide the student, the amateur and the professional restorer through each and every stage of restoration . . . and to provide practical information on every aspect of the ceramic repair process."—*Introd.*

Contents: (1) Tools and materials; (2) Examination and identification; (3) Cleaning; (4) Bonding; (5) Filling, modelling and moulding; (6) Retouching; (7) Four case studies; Appendix: Glossary of materials; Manufacturers and sup-

pliers in the UK; Manufacturers and suppliers in the USA; Conservation advice and further study; Client-conservator agreement; Suggested further reading.
Index, p.111–12.

T174 André, Jean-Michel. The restorer's handbook of ceramics and glass. N.Y., Van Nostrand Reinhold, [1976]. 129p. il. (part col.)
Trans. of Restauration de la céramique et du verre. Fribourg, Office du Livre, 1976.
Contents: (I) Cleaning; (II) Gluing; (III) Filling; (IV) Retouching; (V) Glass.
Technical notes, p.122–25. Bibliography, p.127. Index, p.128–29.

T175 Glass, ceramics and related materials: interim meeting of the ICOM-CC Working Group, September 13–16, 1998, Vantaa, Finland. Ed. by Alice B. Paterakis. Vantaa, EVTEK-Institute of Arts and Design, 1998. 204p. il., diags., tables.
26 papers, mostly comprising case histories, recent research and teaching developments, and conservation ethics.
Contents: Glass; Ceramics; Training.
Bibliographical references follow each paper.

T176 Mosaics = Mosaïque = Mosaicos. Rome, ICCROM for the International Committee for the Conservation of Mosaics [and various other imprints], 1978– .
Series of vols. profiling in situ mosaic conservation projects.

T177 Newton, R. G. The deterioration and conservation of painted glass: a critical bibliography. [2d ed.] N.Y., Published for the British Academy by Oxford Univ. Pr., 1982. xxxii, 103p. (Corpus vitrearum medii aevi. Great Britain. Occasional papers, II)
1st ed., 1974.
"This bibliography is intended to be of use to conservators and restorers of painted window glass (commonly known as 'stained glass') and to research scientists working close to those fields. . . . The abstracts are selective in the sense that only the relevant parts of a paper have been abstracted."—*Introd.*
Contents: (1) History of manufacture of medieval window glass, how to characterise it, and how to make windows from it; (2) The causes of weathering (corrosion) of glass; (3) Ethics of conservation and restoration; (4) Cleaning painted glass; (5) Conservation (or holding together what already exists); (6) Restoration (or trying to make the window what it was like in the beginning); (7) Preservation (or trying to stop the window getting any worse); (8) Bibliographies; Abstracts.

T178 Sloan, Julie L. Conservation of stained glass in America: a manual for studios and caretakers. [Wilmington, Del.], Art in Architecture Pr., [1995]. 225p. il.
Presents the state of stained glass conservation research and practice in late 20th-century America. Intended for conservators, craftspeople, and owners of stained glass.
Contents: (1) Definition of terms; (2) Conservation philosophy; (3) The technical history of stained glass and restoration; (4) Condition analysis and contracting; (5) Glass; (6) Cames, putty and structure; (7) Glass paint; (8) Cleaning; (9) Documentation; (10) Protective glazing.
Bibliographical references throughout the text. Bibliography, p.i–vii. Index, p.i–vi.

T179 Wihr, Rolf. Restaurieren von Keramic und Glas: Entwicklung - Erhaltung - Nachbildung. München, Callwey, [1977]. 275p.
Thorough handbook on the restoration of ceramics and glass.
Bezugsquellen und Materialhinweise, p.267–68. Literaturverzeichnis, p.269–74.

Metalwork

T180 Ancient and historic metals: conservation and scientific research: proceedings of a symposium organized by the J. Paul Getty Museum and the Getty Conservation Institute, November 1991. Ed. by David A. Scott, Jerry Podany, and Brian B. Considine. [Marina del Rey, Calif.], Getty Conservation Institute, 1994. xii, 304p. il. (part col.), map, tables.
Conference papers reflecting the wide-ranging interests of "conservators, conservation scientists, curators, and museum staff with an interest in the technology, history, structure, and corrosion of ancient and historic metalwork."—*Pref.*
Contents: The monument of Marcus Aurelius: research and conservation, by Maurizio Marabelli; Restoration of the monument of Marcus Aurelius: facts and comments, by Paola Fiorentino; Bronze objects from lake sites: from patina to "biography," by François Schweizer; The royal art of Benin: surfaces, past and present, by Janet L. Schrenk; Considerations in the cleaning of ancient Chinese bronze vessels, by Jane Bassett and W. T. Chase; Tomography of ancient bronzes, by Stephen D. Bonadies; Chinese bronzes: casting, finishing, patination, and corrosion, by W. T. Chase; The corrosion of bronze monuments in polluted urban sites: a report on the stability of copper mineral species at different pH levels, by Andrew Lins and Tracy Power; The technology of medieval jewellery, by Jack Ogden; Gold foil, strip, and wire in the Iron Age of Southern Africa, by Andrew Oddy; Conservation of architectural metalwork: historical approaches to the surface treatment of iron, by Frank G. Matero; Techniques of mercury gilding in the eighteenth century, by Martin Chapman; Production and restoration of nineteenth-century zinc sculpture in Denmark, by Knud Holm; Real-time survival rates for treatments of archaeological iron, by Suzanne Keene; Conservation of corroded metals: a study of ships' fastenings from the wreck of HMS Sirius (1790), by Ian Donald Macleod; The conservation of outdoor zinc sculpture, by Carol A. Grissom.
Bibliographical references follow each paper.

T181 A bibliography of books on corrosion and protection of metals. Comp. by Eric Jackson. 3d ed. [London], Institution of Corrosion Science and Technology, 1988. v, 125p.
1st ed., Sheffield [U.K.], Sheffield Polytechnic, Dept. of Metallurgy, 1972.

Guide to mostly English-language publications (with some important foreign-language texts) since 1940. Journal literature is excluded.

Contents: (1) Electrochemistry; (2) Corrosion; (3) Protection against corrosion; (4) Corrosion testing, monitoring and experimentation.

Author index, p.55–125.

T182 Conservation of metal statuary and architectural decoration in open-air exposure = Conservation des oeuvres d'art et decorations en metal exposées en plein air: symposium, Paris, 6–8.X.1986. Rome, ICCROM, 1987. vi, 297p. il.

Collection of case studies.

Bibliographical references follow each paper. Bibliographie, p.297.

T183 Metal plating and patination. Ed. by Susan La Niece and Paul Craddock. Boston, Butterworth-Heinemann, 1993. x, 305p. il., col. plates.

"The papers in the volume underline the importance of integrating the knowledge and experience of scientists, conservators and art historians."—*Pref.* They explore the diversity and history of plating and surface treatments, their identification, and types of damage and corrosion. The attribution of present appearances to recent restoration, alteration, or total invention are also extensively discussed.

Index, p.301–05.

T184 Metals in America's historic buildings: uses and preservation treatments. [Rev. ed.] Washington, D.C., U.S. Dept. of the Interior, National Park Service, Cultural Resources, Preservation Assistance, 1992. v, 167p. il.

1st ed., Washington, U.S. Dept. of the Interior, Heritage Conservation and Recreation Service, Technical Preservation Services Division, 1980.

Designed "to promote an awareness of metals in the buildings and monuments of the United States, and to make recommendations for the preservation and repair of such metals. This report was developed for use by owners, architects, and building managers who are responsible for the preservation and maintenance of America's architectural heritage."—*Foreword.*

Contents: (I) A historical survey of metals, by Margot Gayle and David W. Look; (II) Deterioration and methods of preserving metals, by John G. Waite.

Gems and Jewelry

T185 Catello, Corrado. Argenti antichi: tecnologia, restauro, conservazione: rifacimenti e falsificazioni. [Sorrento], F. Di Mauro, [1994]. 155p. il.

Focuses on Italian craftsmanship, and on the conservation of pieces primarily from churches in Naples and the surrounding area.

Note, p.93–97.

T186 Il restauro delle oreficerie: aggiornamenti = Goldware: restoration updates. Ed. by Loretta Dolcini. Milano, Museo Bagatti Valsecchi, 1996. 73p. il., ports, tables. (Appunti del Museo Bagatti Valsecchi)

"The essays collected in this volume provide a synopsis of the training seminar on goldwork restoration organised by the Museo Bagatti Valsecchi of Milan in 1996."—*Foreword.*

Contents: The restoration of goldwork: an introduction to method, by Loretta Dolcini; Copper - silver - gold: compositions and alloys, by Mauro Mattteini; The diagnosis and scientific analysis of metals and goldwork, by Giancarlo Lanterna; Appendix: Basic metalworking techniques, ed. by Giorgio Pieri; Appendix: Non-metallic materials in goldwork, ed. by Giovanni Burgalassi.

Textiles

T187 Conservation and restoration of textiles: international conference, Como 1980 = Conservazione e restauro dei tessili: convegno internazionale, Como 1980. Ed. by Francesco Pertegato. Milano, C.I.S.S.T., Sezione Lombarda, [1982]. 285p. il., charts, tables.

In English and Italian.

Major international conference organized by the Centro Italiano per lo Studio della Storia del Tessuto, presenting 47 papers. Particularly useful for the wide variety of textile/dress types discussed.

Contents: (1) Textile conservation: environment control; (2) Textile conservation: cleaning; (3) Textile conservation: restoration; (4) Profile of a modern textile conservation and restoration center; (5) Case histories.

Bibliographical references follow most papers. Author index, p.[14–16].

T188 Directory of hand stitches used in textile conservation. Researched by the Study Group on Threads and Stitching Techniques. Comp. by Martha Winslow Grimm. Illus. by Rachel Paar. N.Y., Textile Conservation Group, Inc., 1993. 46p. il.

Extremely useful resource. "The purpose of this stitch directory is to provide a record of hand stitches in use by conservators today as well as their possible applications and a standardization of the terminology. The directory is meant to be a reference for conservators and educators working in the field of textile conservation."—*Introd.* Each stitch description is divided into four sections: Directions; Comments; Possible uses; a diagram of the stitch being worked.

List of references, p.45–46.

T189 Flury-Lemberg, Mechthild. Textile conservation and research: a documentation of the textile department on the occasion of the twentieth anniversary of the Abegg Foundation. [Bern], Abegg-Stiftung, 1988. 532p. il. (chiefly col.), folding il. (Schriften der Abegg-Stiftung Riggisberg, Bd. VII)

Trans. of Textilkonservierung im Dienste der Forschung: ein Dokumentarbericht der Textilabteilung zum zwanzigjahrigenbesten der Abegg-Stiftung. Bern, Abegg-Stiftung, 1988.

Based on conservation work carried out at the Abegg Foundation, Riggisberg, at the Historical Museum, Berne. Not intended as a training manual. The 95 pieces worked on at Riggisberg include items from the Abegg's own outstanding textile collection as well as items from other important collections. Ancient through modern textiles are covered, as are Western and non-Western pieces. Excellent photographic documentation.

Contents: (I) Methods of textile conservation: (1) Preliminary examination and documentation; (2) Cleaning; (3) Conservation with needle and thread; (4) Conservation under glass; (5) Experience with conservation using plastics; (6) Storage and display; (II) Examples of conservation work [case histories]: (1) Tapestries; (2) Flags; (3) Embroidery; (4) Liturgical and secular garments; (5) Burial finds; (6) Textile relics; (7) Water finds; (8) Textile prints; (9) Problems of reconstruction; (10) Etruscan linen book; (11) Reconstruction of antique wall hangings; (12) Reconstruction of patterns; (13) Reconstruction of garments; (III) Technical catalogue [information about the objects conserved in II].

Abbreviated bibliographical references, p.509–15. General index, p.518–32.

T190 ———, and Illek, Gisela. Spuren kostbarer Gewebe. Mit Beitr. von Barbara Matuella . . . [et al.] Riggisberg, Abegg Stiftung, 1995. 260p. il. (part col.) (Riggisberger Berichte, 3)

Discusses the conservation of Late Antique, medieval and early Renaissance textiles at the Abegg Foundation, primarily through a series of case histories. Extensively illustrated with excellent reproductions. Not all of the pieces are in the collections of the Foundation.

Technischer Kataloge, p.223–35. Literaturverzeichnis, p.256–58.

T191 International perspectives on textile conservation: papers from the ICOM-CC Textiles Working Group meetings, Amsterdam 13–14 October 1994 and Budapest 11–15 September 1995. Ed. by Ágnes Tímár-Balázsy and Dinah Eastop. [London], Archetype, [1998]. 169p. il.

37 papers collectively describe the state of textile conservation worldwide at the end of the 20th century.

Contents: Man-made materials and textile conservation; "So many countries, so many customs": different approaches to textile conservation.

Bibliographical references follow each paper.

T192 Textile conservation. Ed. by Jentina E. Leene. London, Butterworths, [1972]. 275p. il. (part col.)

Important pioneering publication on textile conservation, comprising essays by leading conservators from Europe and North America.

Contents: (1) Introduction; (2) Textiles, by Jentina E. Leene; (3) Natural dyestuffs, by Johanna M. Diehl; (4) Principles of fragile textile cleaning, by James W. Rice; (5) Bleaching, by Jentina E. Leene; (6) Textile pests and their control, by H. J. Hueck; (7) Textiles in the museum environment, by Garry Thomson; (8) Storage and display, by Anne Buck; (9) The equipment of a textile conservation workroom, by Sheila B. Landi; (10) Restoration and conservation, by Johan Lodewijks; (11) Tapestries, by Johanna M. Diehl and F. Visser; (12) Carpets, by Dora Heinz; (13) Flags and banners, by Johan Lodewijks; (14) White linen damasks, by C.A. Burgers; (15) Historic costumes, by Gudrun Ekstrand; (16) Uniforms, by P. M. Mader and J. G. Kerkhoven; (17) Lace, Maria José Taxinha; (18) Beadwork, by K. S. Finch; (19) Gloves, by K. S. Finch; (20) Ethnographical textile collections, by A. C. van der Leeden; (21) Ethnographical featherwork, by Harold J. Gowers; (22) Some new techniques for archaeological textiles, by Hanna Jedrzejeweska; (23) Leather objects, by John W. Waterer.

Bibliographical references follow each essay. Index, p.267–75.

T193 Textile conservation symposium in honor of Pat Reeves, 1 February 1986. Ed. by Catherine C. McLean, Patricia Connell. Los Angeles, Conservation Center, Los Angeles County Museum of Art, [1986]. 82p. il. (part col.), port.

Collection of papers particularly significant for their focus on the conservation of non-Western textiles.

Bibliographical references follow some papers.

Lacquer

T194 International symposium on the conservation and restoration of cultural property: conservation of urushi objects: November 10–12, 1993. Tokyo, Tokyo National Research Institute of Cultural Properties, [1995]. viii, 337p. il.

16 papers on urushi conservation practices in Asian, European, and North American collections.

Bibliographical references follow each paper.

T195 Urushi: proceedings of the Urushi Study Group, June 10–27. 1985, Tokyo. Ed. by N. S. Bromelle and Perry Smith. [Marina del Rey, Calif.], Getty Conservation Institute, [1988]. xi, 258p. col. il. (part col.), map.

Wide-ranging collection of 27 papers, the result of "an effort to stimulate an interdisciplinary discussion and approach to the conservation of this ancient and contemporary art form."—*Prol.*

Contents: History; Conservation and techniques; Science.

Leather

T196 Conservation of leather in transport collections: papers given at a UKIC Production. Ed., Julie Marsden and Victoria Todd. London, United Kingdom Institute for Conservation, 1991. 36p.

Papers presented at a United Kingdom Institute for Conservation symposium.

T197 Hallebeek, Pieter . . . [et al.], eds. The conservation of leathercraft and related objects: interim symposium at the Victoria and Albert Museum, London, 24–25 June, 1992. [London, ICOM Committee for Conservation, 1992.] 63p. il., ports.

21 papers on leather conservation research and case histories. A variety of object-types are considered, including

bookbindings, banners, clothing, furniture, and archeological objects.

Bibliographical references follow each paper.

T198 Leather: its composition and changes with time. Ed. by Christopher Calnan and Betty Haines. [Northampton, U.K.], Leather Conservation Centre, [1991]. 90p. il.

Edited proceedings of the first conference held by the Leather Conservation Center, August 1986, Nene College, Northampton. "An excellent source-book for students, conservators and scientists."—*Review*, Studies in conservation, v.37, 1992, p.281.

Contents: (I) The composition of skin and leather: (1) Skin structure and leather properties, by B. M. Haines; (2) The structure of collagen, by B. M. Haines; (3) The principles of tanning, by R. L. Sykes; (4) A history of leather processing from the medieval to the present time, by R. S. Thomson; (5) Vegetable tannins, by J. C. Bickley; (6) Mineral, alum, aldehyde and oil tannage, by B. M. Haines; (7) Lubricants, by A. W. Landmann; (8) Surface coatings and finishes, by R. S. Thomson; (II) The deterioration of skin and leather: (9) Ageing of vegetable tanned leather in response to variations in climatic conditions, by C.N. Calnan; (10a) Taxidermy treatments and their effect on tensile properties of skin, by P. Hanacziwskyj . . . et al.; (10b) Effects of taxidermy treatments on DSC behaviour of deer skin collage, by P. Hanacziwskyj . . . et al.; (11) Some aspects of the photochemistry of fibrous proteins, by D. M. Lewis; (12) Natural ageing of leather in libraries, by B. M. Haines; (13) Acidic deterioration of vegetable tanned leather, by Claire Chahine; (14) Deterioration under accelerated acidic ageing conditions, by B. M. Haines.

Bibliographical references follow each chapter.

T199 Waterer, John W. A guide to the conservation and restoration of objects made wholly or in part of leather. London, Bell, 1972. x, 60p., 15 plates.

Abbreviated ed. titled John Waterer's guide to leather conservation and restoration. Northampton, Museum of Leathercraft, 1986.

"The purpose of this publication is . . . to act as a guide for those museum directors and conservators who have in their charge objects of any kind in the making of which leather played an important part."—*Introd.*

Contents: The conservation and restoration of objects made wholly or in part of leather; The treatment of old leather; Physical restoration; Appendix I: Products used in restoring and conserving leather; Appendix II: The PIRA test; Appendix III: Glossary of leather terms.

Select bibliography, p.59–60.

T200 Young, Laura. Bookbinding and conservation by hand: a working guide. [Rev. ed.] Illustrations by Sidonie Coryn. Photographs by John Hurt Whitehead III. With rev. by Jerilyn Glen Davis. New Castle, Del., Oak Knoll Books, 1995. xiii, 273p. il., diags.

1st ed., N.Y., Bowker, 1981.

"Designed as a working guide in the field of hand bookbinding and book conservation. It is intended as a practical manual for teachers and their students; as an instruction guide to be followed by the beginner attempting to learn binding on his or her own; and as a ready reference for experienced binders, book collectors, book dealers, and librarians."—*Pref.*

Bibliography, p.259–62. Index, p.263–73.

PART 2
PRESERVATION LAW, POLICY, AND ETHICS

BIBLIOGRAPHY

T201 Bibliography. Published annually in Spoils of war: international newsletter. Nr. 0, 05.07.1995– . Magdeburg, Koordinierungsstelle der Länder fur die Rückführung von Kulturgütern, [1995]– .

Comprehensive, annotated listing of recent publications covering the impact of World War II on current ownership issues relating to cultural property.

Contents: (1) Books and articles on general aspects; (2) Books and articles on specific countries.

T202 Faking it: an international bibliography of art and literary forgeries, 1949–1986. Comp. by James Koobatian. Washington, D.C., Special Libraries Association, 1987, x, 240p.

Updates and expands upon Reisner's bibliography, which covered the period 1848–1948 (see GLAH 1:A193). Although largely unannotated, provides references to abstracts for the publications covered that appeared in major international indexes, as well as to Reisner. Books, parts of books, and periodical articles are covered. Newspaper articles are not included.

Contents: Philosophical [issues]; Paintings; Drawings; Sculpture; Ceramics; Hallmarks; Antiquities; Inscriptions; Coins; Medallions; Arms and armor; Brass; Bronze; Pewter; Silver; Goldsmithing; Minerals, gems and jewelry; Glass; Ivory and bone; Scrimshaw; Icons; Antiques; Woodcraft; Ethnographic arts; Prints; Photography; Maps; Postage stamps; Diptychs; Tapestry; Mosaics; Miniatures; Netsuke; Cameos; Bookplates and bookbindings; Music and musical instruments; Scientific instruments; Postcards; Papier-mâché; Sale stamps and certificates of authenticity; Media; Computer art; Technical [the scientific examination of works of art]; Architecture; Patents; Literary [literary forgeries]. Law; Chronological list of some exhibitions and exhibition catalogs of fakes and forgeries; Exhibition reviews.

Author index, p.229–40.

T203 Heritage law bibliography [computer file]. Compiled by Patrick O'Keefe and Lyndel Prott. 1992– . [Hull, Quebec], Canadian Heritage Information Network, 1992– . Updated annually.

Available online through CHIN. Not available in print form, although many of the publications cited appear in the bibliographies of Prott's and O'Keefe's numerous publications, specifically their Law and the cultural heritage series (see

GLAH 2:T276). Contains references to books, journal articles, law reports, conference proceedings, essays, national legislations, international treaties, and other types of government documents pertaining to legal and administrative issues concerning the cultural and natural heritage. Most of the publications included are in English and range in date from the late 1960s to the present.

T204 Houdek, Frank G., comp. and ed. Protection of cultural property and archaeological resources: a comprehensive bibliography of law-related materials: international law bibliography. N.Y., Oceana Publications, 1988. vii, 122p. (Collection of bibliographic and research resources)

Important annotated bibliography. Coverage is confined to English-language publications, and attention is focused on the U.S. Many of the references, however, are of global relevance. The cut-off date is 1987.

Contents: (1) Books and documents: (I) Books; (II) U.S. government documents; (III) Bibliographies; (2) Periodical articles: (I) Movable cultural property: (A) International protection efforts; (B) American protection efforts; (C) Protection efforts of other nations; (D) Law of treasure trove; (E) Protection efforts of non-governmental organizations; (II) Nonmovable cultural property: archaeological resources; (III) Underwater cultural property; (IV) Law review symposia; (V) Case notes; (3) Legislation: (I) International agreements; (II) International legislation and recommendations; (III) National legislation: (A) U.S.: (1) Federal; (2) State; (B) Other nations.

T205 Safeguarding our cultural heritage: a bibliography on the protection of museums, works of art, monuments, archives and libraries in time of war. Comp. by Nelson R. Burr. Washington, D.C., Library of Congress, Reference Department, General Reference and Bibliography Division, 1952. x, 117p.

Comprehensive annotated listing, with a particular focus on publications covering the Spanish Civil War, and World War II and its aftermath (in Europe and Asia). Most of the literature cited is in English. Covers books, articles, and government papers and circulars. Many of the titles listed are also concerned with practical preservation and the precautionary measures necessary for the safekeeping of the cultural heritage during wartime.

Contents: Archives; Film records; International conventions; Libraries; Museums, works of art, and monuments; Packing and transportation; Salvage of damaged records; War damage insurance.

Author index, p.113–17.

T206 Winson, Gail. Art and the law: bibliographic sources. St. Paul, Minn., West, 1989. 16p.

Unannotated bibliography covering books, articles, and newsletters.

Contents: Art as an investment; Artists' contracts; Artists' rights; Berne Convention; Bibliographies; Copyright; Forgeries, fakes, and frauds; Free speech issues; International movement of art; Legislation; Moral rights; Museums; Prints; Resale proceeds right; Taxation; Theft; Underwater archaeology; Valuation.

T207 ______. Art and the law: international law bibliography. N.Y., Oceana, 1990. viii, 141p. (Collection of bibliographic and research resources)

Upd. and exp. ed. of "Visual arts and the law: a bibliography, Parts I and II," in Hastings communications and entertainment law journal, v.10, 1988, p.885–919.

Partially annotated bibliography covering books, selected U.S. documents, Legal Institute Program materials, and articles.

Contents: Abandoned shipwrecks; Aid to the arts; Archaeological resources; Architecture; Art as an investment: Artists' contracts; Artists' handbooks; Artists' rights; Auctions; Berne convention; Bibliographies; Consignment; Copyright; Cultural policy; Cultural property; Estate planning; Federal aid to the arts; Forgeries, fakes, and frauds; Free speech issues; Helsinki Accords; International movement of art; Legislation; Moral rights; Museums; Nonprofit organizations; Prints; Public art; Resale proceeds right; Taxation; Theft; UNESCO Conventions; Valuation; War treasures; Work for hire.

Author index, p.123–41.

DICTIONARIES AND ENCYCLOPEDIAS

T208 DuBoff, Leonard. The art business encyclopedia. N.Y., Allworth, [1994]. 320p.

Extremely useful dictionary encyclopedia (from "Accountant" to "Zoning") of the most common terms used in the art world, including terms from the art, business, finance, legal, and planning professions.

Bibliography of printed references, p.303–04. Index, p.315–20.

HISTORIES AND HANDBOOKS

T209 Adams, Laurie. Art on trial: from Whistler to Rothko. N.Y., Walker, 1976. xix, 236p. il.

Examines the best-known court cases of the art world. Where possible, the material on each trial has been taken from original court transcripts, excerpts of which are included in the text.

Notes, p.225–29. Index, p.231–36.

T210 Adams, Robert. The lost museum: glimpses of vanished originals. N.Y., Viking, 1980. 255p. il. (A studio book)

Explores the various reasons for the destruction or disappearance of works of art over the centuries. Discusses Western as well as non-Western art. The many illustrations include reproductions of, or copies after, works no longer in existence.

Contents: (1) Ancient civilizations; (2) The Middle Ages; (3) The Renaissance; (4) The making and breaking of collections; (5) World War II: (6) Freaks and failures of survival.

Index, p.249–53.

T211 Alexandrov, Emile. Le pacte Roerich et la protection internationale des institutions et des valeurs culturelles. [Sofia], Sofia-Presse, 1974. 26p.

Documents the early contribution that Nikolaï Constantinovitch Roerich (1874–1947) made to the protection of cultural property through international legal measures. "The Roerich Pact," signed in 1935 at Washington, D.C., by representatives of the governments of North, Central, and South America, was the first international convention designed specifically to protect cultural property in time of military conflict. Discusses the historical and legal background to the pact.

Includes bibliographical references.

T212 Antiquities: trade or betrayed: legal, ethical and conservation issues. Ed. by Kathryn Walker Tubb. [London], Archetype in conjunction with UKIC Archaeology Section, 1995. 363p. il. (part col.), 36 col. plates.

Collection of essays illustrating the differing opinions on trading in antiquities. Mostly case studies.

Notes at ends of essays.

T213 Approaches to the archaeological heritage: a comparative study of world cultural resources management systems. Ed. by Henry Cleere. N.Y., Cambridge Univ. Pr., [1984]. 138p. il., charts., maps. (New directions in archaeology)

Series of essays exploring the laws and administrations used in various countries to govern their ancient monuments, sites, and antiquities.

Contents: (1) Value and meaning in cultural resources, by William D. Lipe; (2) Czechoslovakia, by Milan Princ; (3) Denmark, by Kristian Kristiansen; (4) Federal Republic of Germany, by Joachim Reichstein; (5) France, by Alain Schnapp; (6) Great Britain, by Henry Cleere; (7) India, by B. K. Thapar; (8) Italy, by Bruno d'Agostino; (9) Japan, by Migaku Tanaka; (10) Mexico, by José Luis Lorenzo; (11) Nigeria, by Nwanna Nzewunwa; (12) Peru, by Duccio Bonavia; (13) United States of America, by Charles R. McGimsey III and Hester A. Davis; (14) World cultural resource management: problems and perspectives, by Henry Cleere.

Notes at ends of essays. Index, p.132–38.

T214 Archaeological ethics: readings from Archaeology magazine. Ed. by K. D. Vitelli. Walnut Creek, Calif., AltaMira Pr., [1996]. 272p., map.

Anthology reprinting notable essays on the whole range of ethical issues in archeology.

Notes at ends of essays. Bibliography, p.266–72.

T215 Archaeological heritage: current trends in its legal protection. Athens, Sakkoulas, 1995. 235p. (Institute of Hellenic constitutional history and constitutional law, Studies, 5)

Proceedings of an international conference, Athens (1992).

Contents: (1) The definition of the archaeological heritage, by Lyndel Prott; (2) Protection of the archaeological heritage under the United States Constitution, by James Nafziger; (3) Protection of the archaeological heritage: the role of criminal law, by Patrick O'Keefe; (4) Archaeological heritage: the Greek experience, by Nikos Zias; (5) Is there a conflict between constitutional and international law protection of archaeological heritage?, by Theodora Antoniou; (6) The constitutional foundations of memory and aesthetics, by Eleni Trova; (7) International regulations and internal measures of protection of the archaeological heritage, by Emmanuel Roukounas; (8) The "New World Order" and archaeological heritage: Can the one protect the other?, by Sharon Williams; (9) Protection of under-water cultural heritage, by Anastasia Strati; (10) Civil protection of cultural property, by George Koumantos; (11) The drafts of Uni-Droit and of the E. C. Directive: A parallel set-back?, by Spyridon Vrellis; (12) Archaeological heritage: the view of the private possessor (The recovery of an archaeological object—the search for the enrichment), by Ioannis Karakostas; (13) The protection of archaeological property and the internal market, by Harry Post; (14) The idea of a common European cultural heritage, in the perspective of the abolition of internal frontiers, by Dafni Voudouri.

Includes bibliographical references.

T216 Archaeological heritage management in the modern world. Ed. by Henry Cleere. Boston, Unwin Hyman, [1989]. 318p. il., maps., plans, tables. (One world archaeology, 9)

Papers mostly resulting from an international congress, Southampton (1986). The majority of these papers address legislation issues pertaining to archeological excavation in specific countries or regions.

Notes at ends of essays. Index, p.309–18.

T217 Archival legislation 1981–1994 = Législation archivistique 1981–1994. [By the] International Council on Archives. New Providence, Saur, 1995–96. 2v. (Archivum, v.XL–XLI)

1st ed., 1963.

Legislation pertaining to the national archives of 115 states. Includes information about supranational and international organizations. For each country a national report is prepared by an archives law specialist of that state. Contributions in English, French, German, Italian, Portuguese, and Spanish.

Contents: (1) Albania-Kenya; (2) Latvia-Zimbabwe.

T218 Bator, Paul. The international trade in art. Chicago, Univ. of Chicago Pr., 1983. vii, 108p. (Repr.: Chicago, Univ. of Chicago Pr., 1998.)

1st ed. "An essay on the international trade in art" in Stanford law review, v.34, no.2 (January 1982).

Important essay describing the 1970 Convention on the Means of Prohibiting and Preventing the Illicit Import, Export and Transfer of Ownership of Cultural Property. The author argues that total art export embargos are not only impossible to enforce but also encourage the illicit market rather than eliminate it.

Includes bibliographical references.

T219 Bildersturm: die Zerstörung des Kunstwerks. Hrsg. von Martin Warnke. [Frankfurt am Main], Fischer, [1988]. 179p. il. 14 plates. (Fischer Wissenschaft)

1st ed., München, Hanser, 1973 (Kunstwissenschaftliche Untersuchungen, 1)

Collection of essays surveying art mutilation from antiquity to the 20th century.

Contents: Bilderstürme, von Martin Warnke; Bilderstürme und Bilderfeindlichkeit in der Antike, von Dieter Metzler; Der byzantinische Bilderstreit, von Bazon Brock; Renaissancekultur als "Hölle": Savonarolas Verbrennungen der Eitelkeiten, von Horst Bredekamp; Durchgebrochene Geschichte: Die Bilderstürme der Wiedertäufer in Munster 1534/1535, von Martin Warnke; Von der Gewalt gegen Kunst zur Gewalt der Kunst: die Stellungnahmen von Schiller und Kleist zum Bildersturm, von Martin Warnke; Säkularisation als verwerteter "Bildersturm": zum Prozess der Aneignung der Kunst durch die bürgerliche Gesellschaft, von Berthold Hinz; "National sozialistischer Bildersturm": Funktion eines Begriffs, von Marcel Struwe.

Anmerkungen, p.141–79.

T220 Bodkin, Thomas. Dismembered masterpieces: a plea for their reconstruction by international action. London, Collins, 1945. 47p. il., 76 plates.

Historical survey of the looting, vandalism, and/or dismemberment of composite art works. Includes a series of case histories, discussing specific art works and individuals. The illustrations comprise the individual components of dismembered works, the multiple locations of which are listed.

Index, p.44–47.

T221 Brown, G. Baldwin. The care of ancient monuments: an account of the legislative and other measures adopted in European countries for protecting ancient monuments and objects and scenes of natural beauty, and for preserving the aspect of historical cities. Cambridge, Cambridge Univ. Pr., 1905. 260p.

Key early 20th-century text on the practices of historic preservation worldwide. Addressing most of the issues that were to become important during the latter part of the 20th century, the focus is on historic buildings and ancient monuments, with consideration of archeological objects and sites, and other objects of historical and artistic interest. Essential resource on early cultural property protection.

Contents: (1) The significance and history of the care of monuments; (2) The meaning of the term "monument"; (3) The limit of age for monuments; (4) The different kinds of monuments; (5) Why should monuments be preserved?; (6) Quis custodiet ipsos custodes? The function of public opinion; (7) Means for the preservation of monuments, A: Private societies and publications; (8) Means for the preservation of monuments, B: Official and semi-official agencies, museums; (9) Means for the preservation of monuments, C: Legislation, national and local; (10) Restoration and anti-restoration; (11) "Classement," inventorization, and official publications; (12) Superintendence of excavations and disposal of "finds": treasure-trove; (13) Prohibition of sale or exportation; (14) Expropriation or compulsory purchase; (I) France; (II) Germany; (III) Italy; (IV) Great Britain and Ireland; (V) The Austrian empire; (VI) Belgium, Holland, and Switzerland; (VII) Denmark, Norway, and Sweden; (VIII) Russia and Finland; (IX) Spain and Portugal; (X) Greece and Turkey; (XI) The Danubian provinces; (XII) India, Egypt, Algeria, Tunis; Appendix: A note on the care of monuments in the United States.

Bibliographical references at the beginning of each chapter. General bibliography, p.xiii. Index, p.249–60.

T222 Burnham, Bonnie. The art crisis. N.Y., St. Martin's Pr., [1975?]. 256p.

By a pioneering author in the field. Aims "to show how the various elements of art collecting and marketing—both legal and illegal—contribute to the crisis of . . . theft, pillage, speculation and over-valuation."—*Introd.*

Contents: (1) Stolen art; (2) The antiquities crisis; (3) The art boom.

Notes, p.245–48. Index, p.249–56.

T223 Carmilly-Weinberger, Mosche. Fear of art: censorship and freedom of expression in art. N.Y., Bowker, 1986. xiii, 249p. il.

"Study of how the 'fear of art' . . . has caused those in power, whether religious or political, to censor art and artists or to use certain types of art as propaganda tools."—*Pref.* Ranges from the 2d century B.C. to the present.

Contents: (1) Religious attitudes and art; (2) Government, politics and the role of art; (3) Modern art movements; (4) Is it art or erotica? (5) Art destruction by the artist.

Bibliography, p.215–34. Index, p.235–49.

T224 Carducci, Guido. La restitution internationale des biens culturels et des objets d'art volés ou illicitement exportés: droit commun, Directive CEE, Conventions de l'Unseco et d'Unidroit. Préf. De Paul Lagarde. [Paris], L.G.D.J., [1997]. 493p. (Droit des affaires)

Useful text collecting and analyzing the various international legal instruments that can be used to effect restitution.

Includes bibliographical references. Index alphabetique, p.483–86.

T225 Censorship and silencing practices of cultural regulation. Ed. by Robert C. Post. Los Angeles, Getty Research Institute, 1998. 344p. il. (Issues and debates series)

"This volume . . . evolved from a symposium titled 'Censorship and Silencing: Practices of Cultural Regulation' . . . Getty Research Institute for the History of Art and the Humanities, 15–16 December 1995, in collaboration with the American Academy of Arts and Sciences and the Humanities Research Institute of the University of California."—*t.p. verso.* A wide-ranging anthology of papers delivered at symposia held over the course of several months in 1994 and 1995. Part I inquires "into the specific dynamics of explicit legal control of speech through criminal and civil sanctions. In Part II we investigate other forms of state regulation of speech, ranging from subsidies to property rights. And in Part III we examine justifications for state interventions to regulate private power that constrains expression."—*p.5.*

Contents: (I) Censorship: the repressive state; (II) Discourse: the tutelary state; (III) Silencing: the egalitarian state.
Notes at ends of essays. Biographical notes on the authors, p.333–34. Index, p.335–44.

T226 Chamberlin, Russell. Loot! the heritage of plunder. N.Y., Facts on File, [1983]. 248p. il., col. plates.
Reviews, through a chronologically arranged series of case histories, the debate over the propriety of one nation holding cultural property created within another. Examines not only the removal of treasures during warfare, but also elginisme—"the retention by richer nations of the cultural property of poorer nations—usually obtained under duress."—*Introd.*
Contents: (1) The marbles of Greece; (2) The plundering of Egypt; (3) The gold of Ashanti; (4) The stone of Scone; (5) The crown of St. Stephen; (6) Napoleon Bonaparte; (7) Adolf Hitler; (8) City of blood; (9) The corporate memory; (10) Whose heritage?
Bibliography, p.236–39. Index, p.246–48.

T227 Clapp, Jane. Art censorship: a chronology of proscribed and prescribed art. Metuchen, N.J., Scarecrow, 1972. xii, 582p. il., 1 col. plate.
"Brings together from scattered sources a record of suppression, restriction and restraint of visual communication in the plastic . . . and the decorative arts."—*Pref.* Photography and film are excluded. Events are presented in a chronology of censored art, beginning with 3400–2900 B.C. (Egyptian art), and ending with May 1971 (the U.S. Supreme Court's reinstatement of the ban on "importation of obscene materials into the country for commercial use"—*Chronology*).
Bibliographical sources, p.385–423. Index, p.425–82.

T228 Conklin, John E. Art crime. Westport, Conn., Praeger, [1994]. 322p.
Investigates the various crimes involving art and the art world.
Contents: (1) The value of art; (2) Fakes and forgeries; (3) Fraud; (4) Art theft: opportunities and motives; (5) The social organization of art theft; (6) The distribution of stolen art; (7) Vandalism; (8) Curbing art crime.
Bibliography, p.285–99. Index, p.301–22.

T229 Conventions and recommendations of Unesco concerning the protection of the cultural heritage. Repr. and upd. [Paris], Unesco, [1985]. 239p.
1st ed., 1983; French trans., Paris, Unesco, 1985.
Full texts of 14 international cultural property conventions and recommendations drawn up by or enacted under the auspices of Unesco, 1954–1980.
Contents: (A) Conventions; (B) Recommendations.

T230 Demandt, Alexander. Vandalismus: Gewalt gegen Kultur. [Berlin], Siedler, 1997. 319p. il.
Comprehensive treatment of the history of vandalism from antiquity to the 1990s. Includes a fascinating chronology of key events.
Includes bibliographical references. Kalendar, p.277–93. Literatur, p.294–97. Register, p.298–319.

T231 DuBoff, Leonard D. Art law in a nutshell. 2d ed. St. Paul, Minn., West, 1993. xxix, 350p. il. (Nutshell series)
1st ed., 1984; CD-ROM ed. 1995.
Guide for artists, collectors, financial planners, government agencies, and members of the legal profession. Focuses on the U.S., but coverage extends to international considerations, where appropriate.
Contents: (1) Art: the customs definition; (II) Art: international movement; (III) Art: the victim of war; (IV) Art as investment; (V) Auctions; (VI) Authentication; (VII) Insurance; (VIII) Tax problems: collectors and dealers; (IX) The working artist; (X) Aid to the arts; (XI) Tax problems: artists; (XII) Copyright; (XIII) Trademark; (XIV) Moral and economic rights; (XV) Freedom of expression; (XVI) Museums.
Table of cases, p.xix–xxix. Index, p.331–50.

T232 ———, and Caplan, Sally Holt. The deskbook of art law. 2d ed. [Dobbs Ferry], Oceana Publications, 1993– . (2)v.
1st ed., 1977.
Standard textbook, comprising a series of "booklets," some of which have different release dates and different collaborating authors. Coverage is wide-ranging and the topics discussed are treated in considerable depth.
Contents: (A) Art: the customs definition; (B) International movement of art; (C) Theft; (D) Art: the victim of war; (E) The preservation of art; (F) Protest art; (G) Censorship: obscenity & pornography; (H) Other censorship problems; (I) Aid to the arts; (J) Art as an investment; (K) Authentication; (L) Insurance; (M) Auctions; (N) Tax problems: collectors & dealers; (O) Tax problems: artists; (P) Copyright; (Q) Trademark; (R) The working artist; (S) Moral & economic rights; (T) The museum organization; (U) Internal museum problems; Appendices 1–28 [full texts and extracts of relevant laws, agreements and codes of ethics].
V.2 includes 58-p. index booklet.

T233 Ethical considerations and cultural property. Ed. by Patty Gerstenblith: Special issue [of] International journal of cultural property, v.7, no.1, Oxford, Oxford Univ. Pr., 1998. 301p.
Wide-ranging anthology of papers by key participants in the field. In addition to the papers and documents listed below, includes several case studies.
Selective contents: Thinking in terms of law and morality, by Kent Greenawalt; Cultural property ethics, by John Henry Merryman; Codes of ethics: form and function in cultural heritage management, by Patrick J. O'Keefe; United States cultural property legislation: observations of a combatant, by Clemency Chase Coggins; When data become people: archaeological ethics, reburial, and the past as public heritage, by Lawrence J. Zimmerman; The ethics of archaeology, subsistence digging, and artifact looting in Latin America: point, muted counterpoint, by David Matsuda; Codes of ethics for conservation, by Catherine Sease; The ethics of art dealing, by Peter Marks; Ethics, the antiquities trade, and archaeology, by James Ede; The ethics of collecting, by Elizabeth A. Sackler; Museums and ethics: long

history, new developments, by Elisabeth des Portes; Architectural heritage: the paradox of its current state of risk, by Bonnie Burnham; Documents: a selection of ethics codes: Archaeological Institute of America; College Art Association; Confédération Internationale des Négociants en Oeuvres d'Art; International Council on Monuments and Sites—Australia—Charter for the conservation of Places of Cultural Significance (Burra Charter); ICOMOS—Charter on the Protection and Management of the Underwater Cultural Heritage; International Council of Museums; Principles for Partnership in Cross-Cultural Human Sciences Research with a particular View to Archaeology (Rüschlikon Principles); Society for American Archaeology; United Kingdom for the Conservation of Historic and Artistic Works.

T234 Ethics and the arts: an anthology. Ed. by David E. W. Fenner. N.Y., Garland, 1995. vii, 323p. (Garland reference library of social science, 993) (Garland studies in applied ethics, 5)

Contents: Art and censorship, by Richard Serra; Protected space: politics, censorship and the arts, by Mary Devereaux; Aesthetic censorship: censoring art for art's sake, by Richard Shusterman; Art and inauthenticity, by W. E. Kennick; Forging issues from forged art, by L. B. Cebik; No dance is a fake, by Kenton Harris; Why artworks have no right to have rights, by Francis Sparshott; A defense of colorization, by James O. Young; Worldmaking: property rights in artistic creations, by Peter H. Karlen; Can government funding of the arts be justified theoretically?, by Noël Carroll; Not with my tax money: the problem of justifying government subsidies, by Joel Feinberg; Should the government subsidize the arts?, by Ernest van den Haag; The politics of culture: art in a free society, by Gordon Grahan; Serious problems, serious values: are there aesthetic dilemmas?, by Marcia Muelder Eaton; Taste and the moral sense, by Marcia Cavell; The inter-relationship of moral and aesthetic excellence, by Ron Tontekoe and Jamie Crooks.

Notes at ends of essays.

T235 Ethics and values in archaeology. Ed. by Ernestene L. Green. N.Y., The Free Pr., [1984]. xii, 301p.

Wide-ranging collection of essays on the impact of the world of government, business and academia on archeology and archeologists, their ethics, values, and responsibilities. Essays focus on the U.S. context.

References, p.273–90. Index, p.291–301.

T236 The ethics of collecting cultural property: Whose culture? Whose property? Ed. by Phyllis Mauch Messenger. Albuquerque, Univ. of New Mexico Pr., [1989]. xxvi, 266p. il.

"The purpose of this volume is to present a range of perspectives on issues relating to the ownership and preservation of the artifacts of past cultures."—*Pref.* Wide-ranging, with many case studies.

Index, p.257–66.

T237 Études en droit de l'art = Studies in art law. Zürich, Schulthess, 1992– .

With the exception of (to date) two vols., this series comprises vols. primarily based on international conferences organized by the Centre du Droit de l'Art, Geneva. Each vol. deals with a specific ethical or legal aspect of the movable cultural property debate.

Bibliographical references in all vols. Texts or compendia of relevant legislation in most vols.

T238 Fake? The art of deception. Ed. by Mark Jones. With Paul Craddock and Nicholas Barker. London, British Museum, 1990. 312p. il. (part col.)

Important catalog accompanying the exhibition, British Museum (1990). Drawing largely on the British Museum's own collections, individual texts explore the relationship of fakes and forgeries to copies and reproductions. More than 600 artifacts whose authenticity has come into question since the museum acquired them are documented. Essays examine the roots of faking. All catalog entries include detailed technical and stylistic analyses, and most items are illustrated.

Contents: Introduction: Why fakes?, by Mark Jones; Forging the past, by David Lowenthal; Textual forgery, by Nicholas Barker; Catalogue: (1) What is a fake? (2) Rewriting history; (3) The limits of belief: religion, magic, myth and science; (4) Faking in the East; (5) Faking in Europe from the Renaissance to the 18th century; (6) The 19th century: the great age of faking; (7) Faking in the 20th century; (8) The art and craft of faking: copying, embellishing and transforming, ed. by Paul Craddock; (9) The scientific detection of fakes and forgeries, ed. by Paul Craddock and Sheridan Bowman; (10) The limits of expertise.

Further reading, p.308–09. Index, p.310–12.

T239 Feldman, Franklin, and Weil, Stephen E. Art law: rights and liabilities of creators and collectors. With the collab. of Susan Duke Biederman. Boston, Little, Brown, 1986. xiii, 524p.

1st ed., 1986. Successor to Art works: law, policy, practice. N.Y., Practising Law Institute, 1974.

Contents: (1) The artist's right of expression; (2) Reproduction rights; (3) Relationships with art dealers; (4) Commissioned works; (5) Moral right; (6) Resale rights; (7) Other legislation protective of artists; (8) The artist's estate; (9) Private sales; (10) Public sales; (11) Claims by third parties; (12) Claims against third parties; (13) Charitable contributions; (14) Art as a "collectible" asset.

Includes tables of cases and statutes, bibliographies, and indexes.

———. Supplement 1988.

———. Supplement 1993. Prepared by Susan Duke Biederman.

T240 Fleming, Stuart J. Authenticity in art: the scientific detection of forgery. Foreword by Professor S. A. Goudsmit. N.Y., Crane, Russack, [1976]. 164p. il.

Discusses the methodology and incorporation of scientific analyses into the detection of art forgeries.

Contents: (1) Introduction; (2) Paintings; (3) Ceramics; (4) Metals; Appendix [further examples].

Bibliography, p.155–57. Index, p.159–64.

T241 The forger's art: forgery and the philosophy of art. Ed. by Denis Dutton. Berkeley, Univ. of California Pr., 1983. x, 276p. il.

Collection of essays examining the nature of the authentic, its place in aesthetic history, and its impact on the viewer. Examines "why forged paintings must be considered inferior to originals, when 'nobody can tell the difference'"—*Pref.*

Contents: Han van Meegeren fecit, by Hope B. Werness; What is wrong with a forgery?, by Leonard B. Meyer; Art and authenticity, by Nelson Goodman; Originals, copies, and aesthetic value, by Jack W. Meiland; The aesthetic status of forgeries, by Mark Sagoff; Art, forgery and authenticity, by Joseph Margolis; Artistic crimes, by Denis Dutton; Is, Madame? Nay, it seems!, by Michael Wreen; Notes on forgery, by Monroe C. Beardsley; On duplication, by Rudolf Arnheim; The disappointed art lover, by Francis Sparshott.

Includes bibliographical references. Bibliography, p.265–72. Index, p.273–76.

T242 Gamboni, Dario. The destruction of art: iconoclasm and vandalism since the French Revolution. New Haven, Yale Univ. Pr., 1997. 416p. il.

Wide-ranging examination of 19th- and 20th-century art destruction, with an emphasis on the post-World War II period. International in scope. Focuses on Europe, the former Soviet Union, and the U.S.

Contents: (1) Theories and methods; (2) A historical outline; (3) The fall of the "Communist monuments"; (4) Political iconoclasm in democratic societies; (5) Outside the First World; (6) Iconoclasm and multiplication; (7) Free art and the "free world"; (8) Legal abuse; (9) The degradation of art in public places; (10) Museums and pathology; (11) Embellishing vandalism; (12) Reformations of church art; (13) Modern art and iconoclasm; (14) Mistaking art for refuse; (15) Disqualification and heritage.

References, p.337–93. Bibliography, p.394–404. Index, p.405–16.

T243 ______. Un iconoclasme moderne: théorie et pratiques contemporaines du vandalism artistique. Zurich, Institut Suisse pour l'Étude de l'Art, 1983. 118p. il.

Survey of vandalism against 20th-century art. Includes a detailed analysis of vandalism at the 1980 Exposition suisse de sculpture de Bienne.

Includes bibliographical references.

T244 Geary, Patrick J. Furta sacra: thefts of relics in the central Middle Ages. Rev. ed. Princeton, Princeton Univ. Pr., [1990]. xvi, 219p.

Documents examples of cultural property theft in the form of removal of Christian relics from their former places of veneration to locations better able to pay for them. Examines the activities and organization of relic forgers, thieves, and merchants across Europe and the function of relics in the medieval power structure.

Contents: (1) Relics and saints in the Central Middle Ages; (2) The cult of relics in Carolingian Europe; (3) The professionals; (4) Monastic thefts; (5) Urban thefts; (6) Justifications; Appendix A: Critique of texts; Appendix B: Handlist of relic thefts.

Bibliography, p.191–217. Index, p.219–27.

T245 Greenfield, Jeannette. The return of cultural treasures. 2d ed. [N.Y.], Cambridge Univ. Pr., [1996]. xviii, 351p. il., maps.

1st ed., 1989.

Important, pioneering, and wide-ranging volume covering recent controversies involving the restitution of artistic, paleontological, and ethnographic objects.

Contents: (1) The Icelandic manuscripts; (2) The Elgin marbles debate; (3) British and other European approaches; (4) Some British cases; (5) American and Canadian approaches; (6) International and regional regulation; (7) Art theft and the art market; (8) Russia and the former Soviet Union; (9) The Hebrew manuscripts; (10) The return of cultural treasures: some conclusions.

Bibliography, p.334–49. Index, p.350–51.

T246 Harvey, Brian W., and Meisel, Franklin. Auctions law and practice. 2d ed. Oxford, Oxford Univ. Pr., 1995. 401p.

1st ed., London, Butterworths, 1985.

Exhaustive, standard reference work on auction law and practice with specific reference to the U.K. The international context is a necessary component, however, due to the U.K.'s membership in the European Union as well as its central place in the international auction world.

Contents: (1) The evolution and economics of auction sales; (2) Auctioneers: restrictions on trading; (3) Capacity and authority; (4) The rights of an auctioneer; (5) Duties and liabilities of the auctioneer; (6) Conditions of sale affecting buyers and bidders; (7) Export licensing; (8) Criminal practices at auctions and their consequences; (9) Sales of land by auction or tender; (10) Vehicle auctions and specialised auctions of other property; (11) Sales by vendors in special positions; (12) Value Added Tax; Appendix 1: Conditions of sale; Appendix 2: Statutory and other material: selected extracts; Appendix 3: Rules of procedure: selected extracts; Appendix 4: Title in cases of theft of goods in the UK; . . . [etc.].

Includes bibliographical references. Table of statutes, p.xv–xxi. Table of cases, p.xxiii–xxxv. Table of statutory instruments, p.xxxvii–xxxviii. Index, p.395–401.

T247 An illustrated inventory of famous dismembered works of art: European painting: with a section on dismembered tombs in France. Paris, Unesco, 1974. 221p. il.

Contributions from European art specialists, invited by Unesco "to describe some famous works of art which have been dismembered in their own countries, give an account of the circumstances in which this was done, and state what measures have been or could be taken in order to restore these works to their original unity." Intended to "facilitate the identification of fragments and increase the chances of reconstituting the originals."—*Pref.* Contributions are divided into brief essays on individual art works. These essays (respectively on Italian, Flemish, French, Spanish, German, and Russian painting, illuminated manuscripts, and tombs) give present locations of the component parts, all of which are illustrated.

Bibliographical references follow each essay.

T248 Information on the implementation of the Convention for the Protection of Cultural Property in the Event of Armed Conflict, The Hague 1954: 1995 reports. Paris, Unesco, 1995. 48p.
French and Spanish eds.

The latest in a collection of reports documenting the adoption of the 1954 Hague Convention, covering the period 1990–September 1995. Unesco's activities with respect to the conflicts between Iraq and Kuwait, between Armenia and Azerbaijan, and in the former Yugoslavia are also discussed. National reports differ considerably in their detail and length; the best provide extensive administrative, legal, military, and technical information.

T249 International protection of works of art and historic monuments. [By F. Charles De Visscher.] [Reprint.] [Washington, D.C.], Dept. of State. Office of Public Affairs. Division of Publications, [1949], p.821–72. (Department of State publication 3590. International information and cultural series, 8)
Trans. of pioneering texts by Belgian jurist Charles De Visscher, resuscitated as nations recognized the need for stronger guarantees to safeguard cultural resources under international law.

Contents: (I) Historic monuments and works of art in time of war and in the treaties of peace; (II) The protection of national artistic and historic possessions: the need for international regulation; Appendix A: Texts of a draft international convention and a draft international declaration for the protection of monuments and works of art in time of war; Appendix B: Texts of draft international conventions for the protection of national collections of art and history.

Includes bibliographical references.

T250 International sales of works of art = La vente internationale d'oeuvres d'art. N.Y., ICC Publishing; Boston, Kluwer Law and Taxation Publishers, 1988– . (5)v. (ICC publication, 436, 477, 484, 513, 532)
Papers from a series of conferences organized by the Institute of International Business Law and Practice, part of the International Chamber of Commerce based at Geneva, Switzerland; participants at these conferences are leading figures from importing and exporting countries. All vols. in the series comprise general and national reports by regional experts that review international, national, and regional legislation of relevance to the topic of each conference. Texts of relevant international agreements are also included.

Contents: (1) International sales of works of art (1988); (2) International sales of works of art (1990); (3) International art trade and law (1991); (4) Legal aspects of international art trade (1993); (5) Legal aspects of international trade in art (1996).

T251 Italia, Salvatore. I beni culturali in Italia e in Europa. [Rev. & exp. ed.] [Udine], Del Bianco, [1999]. 606p., forms, tables.
First published in 1988 as two independent vols. under the titles: L'amministrazione dei beni culturali and La tutela dei beni culturali nell'ambito internazionale.

Extremely thorough analysis of all aspects of the legal mechanisms for protecting and preserving cultural property in Italy and Europe. Includes texts of relevant legislation, with introductory expositions. International bodies are also discussed.

Bibliographical references throughout.

T252 Kowalski, Wojciech W. Art treasures and war: a study on the restitution of looted cultural property, pursuant to public international law. Ed. by Tim Schadla-Hall. [Leicester, England, Institute of Art and Law, 1998.] 173p.
Discusses reparations in the post-Cold War context with particular reference to Austrian, German, and international law, and as applied to the Polish context.

Contents: (I) The concept of restitution in international law; (II) The restitution of works of art and the development of restitution as a rule of custom in international law; (III) Works of art and restitution law: World War II, its aftermath and subsequent developments; Annexes 1–10.

Includes bibliographical references. Bibliography, p.161–70. Table of international treaties and conventions, p.171. Index, p.172–73.

T253 Kurz, Otto. Fakes: a handbook for collectors and students. 2d rev. and enl. ed. N.Y., Dover, 1967. 348p. il.
1st ed., New Haven, Yale Univ. Pr., 1948; Italian trans., Vicenza, Neri Pozza, 1961.

Important early text on the subject.

Contents: (I) Painting; (II) Classical paintings and mosaics; (III) Illuminated manuscripts; (IV) Drawings; (V) Prints; (VI) Stone sculpture; (VII) Terra-cotta; (VIII) Sculpture in wood; (IX) Ivory carvings; (X) Bronze sculpture; (XI) Chinese bronzes; (XII) Goldsmiths' work; (XIII) Pottery and porcelain; (XIV) Glass; (XV) Furniture; (XVI) Tapestries; (XVII) Bookbindings; (XVIII) Fakes without models; An early Dürer forgery; Dutch forgers of the 18th century; German medieval frescoes; Han van Meegeren; The female heads from Centuripe; Early forgeries of classical sculptures; Etruscan terra-cotta figures; Teutonic jewellery from the migration period; Early Chinese ceramics.

Includes bibliographical references. Index, p.343–48.

T254 Lerner, Ralph E., and Bresler, Judith. Art law: the guide for collectors, investors, dealers, and artists. 2d ed. N.Y., Practicing Law Institute, [1998]. 2v.
1st ed., 1989; upd., 1992.

Intended to "illuminate the law in an accessible way to enable investors, collectors, dealers, artists, appraisers, critics, scholars, [and] practicing lawyers . . . to understand and proceed with the business of art."—*Pref.* Substantially updated and expanded edition covering legal issues of the art world in an extremely broad sense. Jurisdictional coverage is also broad: while the focus is on New York State law and practice, other U.S. states' laws, U.S. federal laws, and foreign and international laws are also taken into consideration. Each chapter concludes with texts of relevant legislations or examples of agreements.

Contents: (1) Artist-dealer relations; (2) Private sales; (3) Theft, forgery, authenticity, and statutes of limitations; (4) Auctions; (5) Prints and sculpture multiples; (6) Commissioned works; (7) Expert opinions and liabilities; (8) International trade; (9) First Amendment rights; (10) Copyrights; (11) Moral rights; (12) Resale rights; (13) The collection as investment property; (14) Tax and estate planning for collectors; (15) Tax and estate planning for artists; (16) Museums; (17) The emerging technologies; Statutory appendix.

Table of authorities, p.TA1–44. Index, p.Ind.1–44.

T255 Lowenthal, David. The past is a foreign country. N.Y., Cambridge Univ. Pr., 1985. xxvii, 489p. il.

A wide-ranging examination, by an important scholar in the field, of individual and societal attitudes to the tangible past, focusing in particular on the interaction of cultural amnesia with its polar opposite, preservation mania, pervasive nostalgia, and the manipulation of history.

Contents: (I) Wanting the past (Nostalgia); (II) Knowing the past; (III) Changing the past.

Bibliography and citation index, p.413–70. General index, p.471–89.

T256 ______. Possessed by the past: the heritage crusade and the spoils of history. [N.Y.], Free Pr., [1996]. xiii, 338p.

British ed. titled The heritage crusade and the spoils of history. London, Viking, 1997.

Examines the 1980s–1990s cult of heritage. Discusses the relationship between heritage and history, and heritage and preservation, as well as the related practice of "heritage fabrication."

Contents: (1) Heritage ascendant; (2) Personal legacies; (3) Collective legacies; (4) Heritage assailed; (5) The purpose and practice of history; (6) The purpose of heritage; (7) The practice of heritage; (8) Being first; (9) Being innate; (10) Rivalry and restitution.

References, p.251–91. Select bibliography and citation index, p.292–314. Index, p.314–38.

T257 Material culture in flux: law and policy of repatriation of cultural property: special issue [of the] University of British Columbia law review, 1995. 345p. il.

Comprises papers delivered at a wide-ranging conference, University of British Columbia (1994).

Notes at ends of papers.

T258 Merryman, John Henry, and Elsen, Albert E. Law, ethics, and the visual arts. 3d ed. Boston, Kluwer Law International, 1998. xxxii, 1032p. il.

1st (temporary) ed., 1975; looseleaf ed., N.Y., Matthew Bender, 1979; 2d ed., Philadelphia, Univ. of Pennsylvania Pr., 1987.

A pioneering and essential reference work, by a law scholar and an art historian, initially designed as a textbook for art history and law school students. "Describes how law and ethics apply to the people and institutions in the Art world."—*Introd.* Broad coverage. Each chapter is organized around a specific theme. Includes extracts from relevant case histories, court decisions, and outlines of the questions raised by such cases, scholarly discussions, and newspaper reports.

Contents: (1) Plunder, reparations and destruction; (2) The illicit international trade in art: Who owns the past? (3) The artist's rights in the work of art; (4) Artistic freedom; (5) The artist's life; (6) The collector; (7) Museums.

Includes bibliographical references. Tables of readings, p.xxiii–xxxvi. Table of cases, p.xxvii–xxxii. Index, p.1021–32.

T259 Meyer, Karl E. The plundered past: the traffic in art treasures. Rev. ed. [N.Y.], Penguin, [1977]. 303p. il.

1st ed., 1973. German trans., Zug [Switzerland], Sven Erik Bergh in der Europabuch AG, 1977.

Pioneering survey of the scope and nature of the illicit trade in artistic, historical, and archeological artifacts. Focuses on antiquities from archeological sites (frequently illegally excavated), especially those originating in Central and South America. Associated museum acquisition practices are also examined.

Contents: (1) After Cortés; (2) Sailing from Byzantium; (3) See Italy quickly; (4) The sherd trade; (5) Whose past? Appendix A: Some major thefts [list of major art thefts, 1911–75]. Appendix B: Table of national protective laws.

Notes, p.259–66. Bibliography, p.267–90. Index, p.291–303.

T260 Museum ethics. Ed. by Gary Edson. N.Y., Routledge, [1997]. xxiii, 282p. (The heritage: care—preservation—management)

"Conceived primarily to assist people working in museums, including trustees and volunteers, to understand the importance of ethics as a guidance concept."—*Introd.* Explores ethics in relation to: cultural identity, indigenous peoples, training, museology, the environment, collecting, conservation, exhibitions, and public programs.

References, p.256–66. Glossary, p.267–71. Bibliography, p.272–76. Index, p.277–82.

T261 Nationalism and archaeology in Europe. Ed. by Margarita Díaz-Andreu and Timothy Champion. [London], UCL [University College London] Press, [1996]. 314p.

Aims "to analyze the influence of the political doctrine of nationalism and the structure of the nation-states on the appearance and institutionalization of archaeology, and on its later development."—*Introd.* After an introduction by Margarita Díaz-Andreu, surveys the topic by nation.

Notes at ends of essays. Index, p.301–14.

T262 Nationalism, politics, and the practice of archaeology. Ed. by Philip L. Kohl and Clare Fawcett. [N.Y.], Cambridge Univ. Pr., [1995]. xi, 329p., maps.

Collection of essays investigating the manipulation of archeological data in the service of the state, and the role of archeologists in the construction of national identities. Introductory "theoretical considerations" by the ed. are followed by discussions of Spanish nationalism, Nazi ideology, Soviet and Russian archeology, Chinese archeology, etc.

Notes at ends of essays. Bibliography, p.280–317. Index, p.318–29.

T263 Noblecourt, A. Protection of cultural property in the event of armed conflict. Trans. From the author's original French text of August, 1956. [Paris], Unesco, [1958]. xix, 346, 60p. il., 137 plates, charts, maps, plans, tables. (Museums and monuments, VIII)

1st ed., Lavachery, Henri A., and Noblecourt, A., Les techniques de protection des biens culturels en cas de conflit arme. [Paris], Unesco, [1954].

A detailed, technically oriented practical manual on what to do with cultural property before, during, and after military conflict, and in light of the 1954 Hague Convention for the Protection of Cultural Property in the Event of Armed Conflict. Aims to create a link between curators and those concerned with military defense. Many photographs of the precautions taken against, as well as the results of, World War II bombardments of cultural property.

Bibliography, p.343–46.

T264 O'Keefe, Patrick J. Trade in antiquities: reducing destruction and theft. [Paris], Unesco, [1997]. x, 134p.

By a leading legal scholar in the field. Discusses issues of theft from legitimate collections, the undocumented destruction of sites and monuments, and the arguments for increasing and restricting the flow of antiquities.

Bibliographical references throughout. Selected bibliography, p.106–12.

T265 One hundred missing objects. Paris, ICOM, 1993– . (2)v. il. (part col.)

French ed. titled Cent objets disparus.

Series documenting the impact of vandalism and theft by traffickers in archeological objects. Each vol. covers a particularly badly affected region or individual monument.

Contents: Looting in Africa (1994); Looting in Angkor (1997).

T266 Palmer, N. E. Art loans. Specialist contributors Lionel Bently . . . [et al.] Boston, Kluwer and International Bar Association, [1997]. 607p. port. (International Bar Association series)

Indispensable volume for curators and registrars discussing, in great depth, the law, practice, and ethics of art lending. Covers the legal doctrines that bear on art loans, the standard terms of lending and borrowing, and the attitudes of museum officials and others to the interaction of law and practice in the field.

Includes bibliographical references. List of respondent institutions, p.xv–xviii. Table of cases, p.xxv–xxxix. Table of statutes, p.xli–lii. Index, p.591–607.

T267 Patrimoine, temps, espace: patrimoine en place, patrimone déplacé. Sous la presidence de Francois Furet. [Paris, Fayard; Caisse nationale des monuments historiques et des sites, Ed. du patrimoine, (1997)]. 437p. il. (part col.) (Actes des Entretiens du patrimoine)

Papers from a conference, Paris (1996), by leading scholars discussing the history of cultural heritage protection in Europe, with an emphasis on France. Also includes the texts of round table discussions and commentaries from the conference. Excellent introduction to many aspects of the cultural heritage debate.

Includes bibliographical references.

T268 Paul, Eberhard. Gefälschte Antike von der Renaissance bis zur Gegenwart. Wien, Schroll, 1981. 283p. il.

A useful historical overview. 38 sub-sections, many of them case histories, discuss various types and manifestations of the fake, as well as specific forgers.

Contents: (I) Antikenfälschungen der Renaissance: (II) Antikenfälschungen des Barocks; (III) Antikenfälschungen des Klassizismus; (IV) Antikenfälschungen des Neubarocks; (V) Antikenfälschungen der Neuzeit.

Anmerkungen, p.267–74. Erläuterungen von Namen und Begriffen, p.274.

T269 Petzet, Michael. Grundsätze der Denkmalpflege = Principles of monument conservation . . .: Charta von Venedig (1964): Charta von Florenz (1981): Charta von Washington (1987): Charta von Lausanne (1989. . . . [München], ICOMOS, [German National Committee], 1992. 68p.

Text in German, English, and French.

Presents texts of the principal charters and agreements covering the conservation of monuments and sites.

Contents: Principles of monument conservation; International Charter for the Conservation and Restoration of Monuments and Sites; Charter of the Preservation of Historic Gardens; Charter for the Conservation of Historic Towns and Urban Areas; Charter for the Protection and Management of the Archaeological Heritage.

T270 The protection of cultural property: handbook of national legislations. Compiled by Bonnie Burnham. [Paris], International Council of Museums, [1974]. 203p.

Pioneering volume providing national legislative texts governing the discovery, ownership, circulation, and sale of movable cultural property. Alphabetical by country (Afghanistan-Zambia). Abstracts of national legislations are provided in English.

Useful addresses, p.159–73. International resolutions and conventions, p.174–200. Bibliography, p.201–03.

T271 The protection of movable cultural property: collection of legislative texts. [Paris], Unesco, 1985–1988. 26v.

Collection of legislative texts elaborating on The protection of movable cultural property: compendium of legislative texts (see preceding title). Publishes the "legislative texts governing the protection of movable cultural property in a series of booklets, each presenting the laws and regulations of one country."—*Pref.* Covers 26 countries omitted from the previous vol.

T272 The protection of movable cultural property: compendium of legislative texts. [Paris], Unesco, [1984]. 2v.

Trans. of La protection du patrimoine culturel mobilier: recueil de textes législatifs. Paris, Unesco, 1979–81.

Intended for "museum curators, art dealers, antique dealers, private collectors, protection, customs and police services . . . with a view to fostering international cooperation in the prevention and repression of offences concerning movable cultural property."—*Pref.* Extracts of relevant legislation are provided for each country covered. Alphabetical by country (Algeria-Uganda).

Includes bibliographical references.

T273 Protection or plunder: safeguarding the future of our cultural heritage. Ed. by Lyndel V. Prott and James Specht. Canberra, Australian Government Publishing Service, [1989]. 129p.

Papers of the UNESCO regional seminar on the Movable Cultural Property Convention, Brisbane, Australia (1986). Contains reports on national protection measures in the region.

Notes at ends of some papers. List of UNESCO conventions and recommendations on the protection of cultural property, p.115. Convention on the Means of Prohibiting and Preventing the Illicit Import, Export and Transfer of Ownership of Cultural Property [1970]: [full text and] List of States having deposited an instrument of ratification, acceptance or accession as of 31 December 1987, p.116–25. Select bibliography, p.126–27. Addresses, p.128–29.

T274 Prott, Lyndel V. Commentary on the Unidroit Convention 1995. [Leicester, England, Institute of Art and Law, 1997.] viii, 145p.

Detailed commentary on the 1995 Unidroit Convention on Stolen and Illegally Exported Cultural Objects by a leading scholar of cultural property law. "The Convention applies to claims of an international character for: (a) the restitution of stolen cultural objects; (b) the return of . . . illegally exported cultural objects."—*Article 1.* Each chapter is devoted to one of the ten articles that make up the Convention, including the context of the discussions behind each provision. The full text of this Convention is provided, as are texts of related conventions, case notes, and other documents.

Includes bibliographical references. Table of cases, p.vi. Select bibliography, p.90.

T275 ———, and O'Keefe, P. J. Handbook of national regulations concerning the export of cultural property. [Paris], Unesco, [1988]. xiii, 239p.

"This handbook has been prepared in response to the need expressed for a quick reference guide on rules governing the export of cultural property. It is designed to provide indications to customs officials, museum curators, art and antique dealers and private collectors of works of art, antiques, and archaeological objects, as well as others concerned with the movement and acquisition of cultural property, on the objects which are subject to export control under national laws."—*Pref.* At the end of each national section is a list of those international agreements to which the country in question is party. Alphabetical by country (Afghanistan–Zimbabwe).

T276 ———. Law and the cultural heritage. Foreword by Henry Cleere. Publisher varies, 1984– . (2)v.

Important series by two of the leading scholars. In-depth, multi-disciplinary comparison of national and international legislation and case law dealing with cultural property. Designed as a reference tool for people with or without formal legal training, covers laws from more than 300 national and local jurisdictions, and international agreements. Five vols. projected.

Contents: (1) Discovery and excavation; (2) Creation and preservation [forthcoming]; (3) Movement; (4) Monuments and sites [forthcoming]; (5) Principles [forthcoming].

Extensive bibliographies in all vols.

T277 Recovery of stolen art: a collection of essays. Ed. by Norman Palmer. [London, Kluwer Law, 1998]. xviii, 262p.

Useful collection of essays intended "to identify and explain the increasing body of specialist law and practice dedicated to the restitution or retrieval of misapplied art."—*Introd.* International in scope, contributions are clearly written for the non-legal user.

Includes bibliographical references. Table of cases, p.vii–xiv. Table of statutes, p.xv–xvi. Index, p.261–62.

T278 Rembrandt/not Rembrandt in the Metropolitan Museum of Art: aspects of connoisseurship. N.Y., Metropolitan Museum (Distr. by Abrams, 1995). 2v.

Published in conjunction with the pioneering exhibition, Metropolitan Museum of Art (1995–96), whose stated purpose was to demystify for the public the kind of research that art historians and conservators undertake in the attempt to establish artists' authorship and the authenticity of works attributed to them.

Contents: (I) Sonnenberg, Hubertus von. Paintings: problems and issues; (II) Liedtke, Walter . . . [et al.] Paintings, drawings and prints: art historical perspectives.

Glossary, v.1, p.136–38. Selected bibliography, v.1, p.139–46, v.2, p.246–57. Index, v.1, p.147–48, v.2, p.258–61.

T279 Rieth, A. Archaeological fakes. Trans. Diana Imber. N.Y., Praeger, [1970]. 183p. il.

Trans. of Vorzeit gefälscht. Tübingen, Wasmuth, 1967.

Focuses on the manufacture and identification of prehistoric fakes. A "short survey" introduces a suite of case studies.

Bibliography, p.181–83.

T280 Savage, George. Forgeries, fakes and reproductions: a handbook for collectors. [Reprint.] London, White Lion, [1976]. xii, 341p. il., 38 plates, ports.

1st ed., London, Barrie and Rockliff, 1963; 1st U.S. ed, N.Y., Praeger, 1964.

"This book discusses the making of forgeries, fakes, replicas, reproductions, and deceptive copies in a way which is intended to help the collector avoid them."—*Pref.* Useful for the variety of media considered.

Includes bibliographical references. Bibliography [partially annotated], p.324–34. Index, p.335–41.

T281 The spoils of war: World War II and its aftermath: the loss, reappearance, and recovery of cultural property. Ed. by Elizabeth Simpson. [N.Y.], Abrams, in assoc. with The Bard Graduate Center for Studies in the Decorative Arts, [1997]. 336p. il. (part col.), 25 col. plates, ports. (part col.)

Based on the papers delivered at an important symposium, Bard Graduate Center for Studies in the Decorative Arts (1995), which focused international attention on the subject. Papers by art historians, museum curators, government officials, and law specialists from eastern and western Europe and North America as well as from countries of the former USSR. The many illustrations include archival photographs documenting the removal, recovery, destruction, and/or conservation of some of the works discussed.

Terms and abbreviations, p.312–14. Selected bibliography, p.315–19. Index, p.326–35.

T282 Strati, Anastasia. The protection of the underwater cultural heritage: an emerging objective of the contemporary law of the sea. Boston, Nijhoff, [1995]. 479p. (Publications on ocean development, 23)

Comprehensive and scholarly study examining the impact of technological developments of relevance to marine archeology. Discusses the need not only for national laws but also for international agreements to regulate activities involving underwater cultural property.

Bibliographical references follow each chapter. Bibliography, p.375–435. Table of cases, p.435–48. Table of treaties, p.449–58. Table of national legislation, p.459–73. Index, p.475–79.

T283 Suspended license: censorship and the visual arts. Ed. by Elizabeth C. Childs. Seattle, Univ. of Washington Pr., [1997]. vii, 413p. il., ports.

Contents: The censorship of images in Reformation Germany, 1520–1560, by Christiane Andersson; Aretino, the public, and the censorship of Michelangelo's Last judgement, by Bernadine Barnes; Veronese and the Inquisition: the geopolitical context, by Paul H. D. Kaplan; Goya and the censors, by Janis A. Tomlinson; The body impolitic: censorship and the caricature of Honoré Daumier, by Elizabeth C. Childs; Manet's Maximilian: censorship and the Salon, by John House; "Chambers of horrors of art" and "degenerate art": on censorship in the visual arts in Nazi Germany, by Christoph Zuschlag; Seeing red: the Dallas Museum in the McCarthy era, by Francine Carraro; Censorship and controversy in the career of Edward Kienholz, by Gerald Silk; Art censorship in Socialist China: a do-it-yourself system, by Jerome Silbergeld; David Wojnarowicz: a portrait of the artist as x-ray technician, by Peter F. Spooner; The trials of Robert Mapplethorpe, by Steven C. Dubin.

Notes at ends of essays. Index, p.395–415.

T284 Tietze, Hans. Genuine and false: copies imitations forgeries. N.Y., Chanticleer Pr., [1948]. 80p. il. (part col.)

Brief but important early essay on the nature, function, and impact of art forgeries. The illustrations and their accompanying commentaries illustrate prominent examples of initially successful forgeries, subsequently detected.

Contents: Forgeries were made at all times; The counterfeiter's weapons; The expert's counter-measures; The forger's triumph; The forger's unmasking and condemnation.

T285 Toman, Jirì. The protection of cultural property in the event of armed conflict: commentary on the Convention for the Protection of Cultural Property in the Event of Armed Conflict and its Protocol, signed on 14 May 1954 in The Hague, and on other instruments of international law concerning such protection. [Brookfield, Vt.], Dartmouth Pub. Co., [1996]. xvi, 525p. il.

Trans. of La protection des biens culturels en cas de conflit armé. Paris, Unesco, 1994.

The most comprehensive commentary on the 1954 Convention (whose text is provided in full) to date, including an exhaustive survey of earlier and later related international negotiations and agreements.

Select bibliography, p.495–512. Index, p.513–25.

T286 Why fakes matter: essays on problems of authenticity. Ed. by Mark Jones. London, British Museum Pr., 1992. 198p. il.

Collection of essays based on papers originating at a symposium held in conjunction with the exhibition Fake? The art of deception (see GLAH 2:T238). Much of the discussion concerns works exhibited in the concurrent exhibition, as well as the wider significance of forgery.

Contents: (1) Coin faking in the Renaissance, by Andrew Burnett; (2) The faking of gems in the eighteenth century, by Judy Rudoe; (3) Clytie—a false woman?, by Susan Walker; (4) The restoration of classical sculpture in the eighteenth century and the problem of authenticity, by Gerard Vaughan; (5) Fakes, intention, proofs and impulsion to know: the case for Cavaceppi and clones, by Seymour Howard; (6) A short history of the patination of bronze, by P. T. Craddock; (7) "La vraye histoire de Troye la grant": truth and romance in the late medieval story of Troy in literature and art, by Scot McKendrick; (8) "The marvellous boy": Chatterton manuscripts in the British Library, by Sally Brown; (9) Instruments of torture, by A. R. E. North; (10) Samuel Pratt and armour faking, by K. N. Watts; (11) Renaissance stoneware from the Rhineland: continuing problems of authentification, by David R. M.Gaimster; (12) Reinhold Vasters: goldsmith, restorer and prolific faker, by Hugh Tait; (13) "Vive le vol": Louis Marcy, anarchist and faker, by Marian Campbell and Claude Blair; (14) Connoisseurs and aficionados: the real and the fake in Ming China (1368–1644), by Craig Clunas; (15) Peiresc and new attitudes to authenticity in the seventeenth century, by David Jaffé; (16) The importance of provenance: rehabilitated fakes, by Clive Wainwright; (17) Authenticity? The dogma of self delusion, by David Lowenthal.

Bibliographical references follow each essay. Index, p.195–98.

T287 Williams, Sharon A. The international and national protection of movable cultural property: a comparative study. Dobbs Ferry, Oceana, 1978. 302p.

Scholarly, pioneering study providing a comprehensive overview of the subject.

Contents: (1) International law and cultural property in perspective; (2) International protection of cultural property in the event of armed conflict at the present time; (3) International protection of cultural property in time of peace; (4) Domestic protection of cultural property rendered by international agreements and recommendations; Appendices I–VIII [texts of relevant national and international regulations and agreements]

Table of cases, p.296–98. Index, p.299–302.

SEE ALSO: The future of the past: attitudes to conservation 1174–1974 (GLAH 2:T102) Hewison, The heritage industry: Britain in a climate of decline (GLAH 2:T313).

WESTERN COUNTRIES

Australia

T288 Conserving the national estate: a bibliography of national estate studies. Canberra, Australian Government Printing Service, 1991. 217p. (Australian Heritage Commission bibliography series, no. 5)

1st ed., 1988.

Comprehensive annotated bibliography of 1,284 titles, with each broad chapter heading sub-divided into numerous more specific categories.

Contents: General; Natural and cultural conservation management; Historic environment; Aboriginal environment; Natural environment.

Subject index, p.189–96. Author index, p.197–210. Locality index, p.211–17.

T289 Ley, John F. Australia's protection of movable cultural heritage: report on the ministerial review of the Protection of Movable Cultural Heritage Act 1986 and regulations. Canberra, Australian Govt. Publishing Service, 1991. xiv, 160p.

Thorough examination of Australian movable cultural property regulation in the international context.

Glossary, p.xi–xiv.

SEE ALSO: Protection or plunder: safeguarding the future of our cultural heritage (GLAH 2:T273).

Canada

T290 Theft of cultural property in Canada = Vol de biens culturels au Canada. Ottawa, Interpol, 1988. 223p. il.

1st ed., 1984.

"Reference manual for the quick verification of works of art and artifacts of doubtful provenance. It is especially addressed to national police departments, art organizations, museums, galleries, auction houses, insurance companies and to all other groups that are in contact with the art market or involved in the detection and prevention of art crime." Information on approximately 900 missing objects is provided. Each object listed receives a brief catalog entry and a photograph, where available.

Contents: Fine arts—Beaux-arts; Decorative arts—Arts décoratifs; Native arts—Arts autochtones; Oriental art—Art oriental; Antiquities—Antiquités; Miscellaneous—Divers; Seizure—Saisie.

Index = Sommaire, p.iii–xi.

SEE ALSO: The heritage directory (GLAH 2:T9); Répertoire des organismes de gestion du patrimoine archéologique = Directory of archaeological heritage management organizations (GLAH 2:T75).

France

T291 Bastien, Hervé. Droit des archives. Préf. Alain Erlande-Brandenburg. Paris, Direction des Archives de France, 1996. 192p.

Useful account of French legislation regulating archival collections and their administration; also discusses the history of French archives regulation.

Bibliographie générale, p.10–12. Table chronologique des textes cités, p.161–74. Table chronologique de la jurisprudence citée, p.174–79. Index matières, p.181–86.

T292 Bercé, Françoise. Les premiers travaux de la Commission des Monuments Historiques 1837–1848: procés-verbaux et relevés d'architectes. Préf. de Jean Hubert. Paris, A. et J. Picard, 1979. 452p. il., 177 plates. (Bibliothèque de la sauvegarde de l'art français)

Exhaustive study of the role played by 19th-century Parisian and provincial learned societies in the protection, preservation, and saving of France's architectural heritage.

Contents: La Commission des Monuments historiques de 1837 à 1848; Procès-verbaux de la Commission, 1838–1848; Relevés d'architectes; Annexe: les enquêtes de 1810 à 1837.

Bibliographie, p.425–26. Index des noms de lieux, p.427–36. Index des noms de personnes, p.437–41. Index des rerum, p.443.

T293 Beurdeley, Michel. La France à l'encan 1789–1799: exode des objets d'art sous la Révolution. Préf. Maurice Rheims. [Paris], Tallandier, [1981]. 232p. il. (part col.)

Documents the impact of the French Revolution on art works in France, including the destruction and dispersion of private collections, the most significant sales and auctions, and the establishment of the future Musée du Louvre.

Annexes, p.216–18. Bibliographie sélective, p.220–25. Index, p.226–31.

T294 Chatelain, Françoise; Pattyn, Christian; and Chatelain, Jean. Oeuvres d'art et objets de collection en droit français. 3d. ed. Paris, Berger-Levrault, 1997. 236p.

1st ed., by Jean Chatelain, 1984; 2d, rev. ed., by Jean Chatelain and Françoise Chatelain, 1990.

An introduction discusses definitions of the terms culture and cultural property. The main text is divided into two parts, the first dealing with general aspects of cultural heritage protection, and the second focusing on the art market.

Contents: (I) La protection du patrimoine culturel: (1) Le domaine public mobilier; (2) Le classement des oeuvres d'art et objets de collection; (3) Le régime des fouilles; (4) L'exportation des oeuvres d'art; (5) La fiscalité des oeuvres d'art et objets de collection. (II) Le marché de l'art: (1) L'authenticité des oeuvres d'art; (2) Les ventes aux enchères publiques; (3) La propriété artistique; (4) Les traffics illicites; (5) L'assurance des oeuvres d'art.

Notes at ends of chapters. Bibliographie, p.231–34. Index, p.235–36.

T295 Gould, Cecil. Trophy of conquest: the Musée Napoléon and the creation of the Louvre. London, Faber, [1965]. 151p. il.

Discusses the establishment of the Louvre as a publicly accessible collection in 1793, following the French Revolution. Documents the growth of its collections, principally following Napoleon's triumphs across Europe, and the accumulation of art works as war booty.

Bibliography, p.136–41. Index, p.143–51.

T296 Liste des immeubles protégés au titre de la législations sur les monuments historiques et sur les sites au cours de l'année. . . . Ministère d'État, Affaires Culturelles, Direction de l'Architecture. [1979–]. 94v.

Preceded by Liste des immeubles classés parmi les monuments historiques, à la data du 31 déc., 1942. Paris, Imprimerie Nationale, 1943; continued by Inventaire supplémentaire des monuments historiques à la date du 31 déc. 1942. Updated by Liste des immeubles protégés au titre des législations sur les monuments historiques et sur les sites.

Vast, intermittently issued series, comprising various related series and sub-series, listing historic buildings and sites in France subject to protection under French law. Each listing is divided according to département. Entries give each building's or site's name and location and a brief description, and note which elements of the property are covered by the listing (for example, whether the interior, exterior, or both are covered; whether gardens are included; or which sections of land are included in the measure).

T297 Protection du patrimoine historique et esthétique de la France (textes législatifs et réglementaires). [Paris, Direction des journaux officiels], 1991. 664p.

Collection providing the full text of laws, circulars, decrees, codes, and other regulations governing the protection of cultural property in France.

Contents: (1) Patrimoine immobilier: (I) Monuments historiques; (II) Protection des monuments naturels et des sites; (III) Zones de protection du patrimoine architectural et urbain; (IV) Secteurs sauvegardés; (V) Archéologie; (VI) Environnement: (VII) Publicité, enseignes et préenseignes; (VIII) Patrimoine et urbanisme; (2) Patrimoine mobilier: (I) Oeuvres d'art; (II) Archives; (3) Recherches et études patrimoniales: (I) Inventaire général des monuments et richesses artistiques de la France; (II) Ethnologie; (4) Règles de maîtrise d'ouvrage et de maîtrise d'oeuvre concernant le patrimoine immobilier: (I) Règles particulières de maîtrise d'ouvrage en matière de monuments historiques classés; (II) Règles de maîtrise d'oeuvre; (5) Subventions et fiscalité: (I) Subventions; (II) Fiscalité.

Sommaire chronologique, p.xv–xxvii.

T298 Réau, Louis. Histoire du vandalisme: les monuments détruits de l'art francais. Ed. augm. par by Michel Fleury and Guy-Michel Leproux. 2v. in 1. Paris, R. Laffont, 1994. 1190p. il. (Bouguins)

1st ed. in 2v. Paris, Hachette, 1959.

Scholarly, pioneering, and in-depth investigation, focusing on architectural monuments and sites. A supplementary introduction, the last chapter, as well as many of the appendices, are new to this edition, with coverage extended to the 1990s. Numerous photographs have been added to this last section, illustrating the changing face of the French urban environment in the late 20th century.

Contents: (I) Le vandalisme avant 1789; (II) La révolution et l'empire; (III) Le vandalisme moderne (1814–1914); Le vandalisme contemporain (1914–1958); Complément: La Cinquième République.

Notes at ends of chapters. Répertoire chronologique des monuments detruits ou mutilés, p.1069–85. Répertoire topographique des monuments detruits ou mutilés, p.1086–94. Répertoire des différents catégories de monuments, p.1095–1101. Le pilori des vandales, p.1102–04. Le palmarès des défenseurs de l'art français, p.1105–06. Tableau d'honneur de quelques défenseurs du patrimoine, p.1107–09. Le vandalisme exemplaire de la Banque de France, p.1110–15. Charte de Venise, p.1116–18. Décret relatif à la Commission supérieure des monuments historiques, p.1119–26. Un exemple de vandalisme municipal, p.1127–29. Le patrimoine architectural et l'ingénierie culturelle, p.1130–37. Darwinisme patrimonial, p.1138–43. Compétence territoriale des architectes en chefs des monuments historiques, p.1144–47. Liste des Ministre de la Culture depuis 1958, p.1148–49. Index des noms de personnes, p.1153–58. Index des noms de lieux, p.1159–70.

T299 Souchal, François. Le vandalisme de la Révolution. Paris, Nouvelles Éditions Latines, [1993]. 309p.

Important, wide-ranging history of art vandalism during the French Revolution.

Bibliographie, p.294–96. Index, p.297–309.

T300 Wescher, Paul. I furti d'arte: Napoleone e la nascita del Louvre. Trad. Flavio Cuniberto. Torino, Einaudi, 1988. xix, 200p. il., plates, ports. (Saggi, 715)

Trans. of Kunstraub unter Napoleon. Berlin, Mann, 1976.

Posthumously published, in-depth historical study. The principal focus is on Napoleon's "acquisitions" through his various military campaigns.

Indicazioni bibliografiche, p.159–67. Elenco delle opere trafugate, p.169–200.

SEE ALSO: Kostenevich, Hidden treasures revealed (GLAH 2:T352); Patrimoine, temps, espace (GLAH 2:T267) Quatremère de Quincy, Lettres à Miranda sur le déplacement des monuments de l'art de l'Italie (GLAH 2:T328).

Germany and Austria

T301 Barron, Stephanie. Exiles + emigrés: the flight of European artists from Hitler. With Sabine Eckmann. Contrib. by Matthew Affron . . . [et al.] Los Angeles, Los Angeles County Museum of Art; N.Y., Abrams, 1997. 432p. il. (part col.), ports. (part col.)

German trans., München, Prestel, 1997.

Published in conjunction with the exhibition, Los Angeles County Museum of Art (1997). Covering the period 1933–45, this volume "seeks to chart not only the course of the exiles' journeys within Europe and to the United States but also their activities in exile, the characteristics of the work they produced, and the nature of the responses they faced in their host countries."—*Foreword*. The numerous high-quality reproductions include many documentary photographs.

Chronology, p.386–400. Selected bibliography, p.408–17. Index, p.424–29.

T302 Braun, Johann. Kunstprozesse von Menzel bis Beuys: 13 Fälle aus dem Privatrecht. München, Beck, 1995. 212p.

Sophisticated survey revealing legal controversies in the German art world. Cases involved Adolf Menzel, Lovis Corinth, Joseph Beuys, etc.

Includes bibliographical references. Personen- und Sachregister, p.211–12.

T303 Dokumentation der Verluste: Staatliche Museen zu Berlin—Preussischer Kulturbesitz. Berlin, Die Museen, 1995– . (1)v. il., ports.

Catalog of art works lost from the Berlin Museums during World War II. All pieces receive a brief catalog entry and are accompanied by a small photograph.

Contents: (1) Gemäldegalerie. Bearb. von Rainer Michaelis.

T304 Feliciano, Hector. The lost museum: the Nazi conspiracy to steal the world's greatest works of art. [Rev. trans.] [N.Y.], Basic Books, [1997]. 278p. il.

Rev. trans. of Le musée disparu: enquête sur le pillage des oeuvres d'art en France par les Nazis. Paris, Austral, 1995.

Focuses on the appropriation of works of art belonging to French Jewish collectors and dealers following the German invasion of France in 1940. Draws on previously unavailable, or unresearched, documentation. The collaboration of art dealers (frequently French and Swiss) in the dispersal of works from these collections is discussed, as is the fate of these art works after the end of World War II.

Notes, p.257–65. Index, p.267–78.

T305 Internationaler Kulturgüterschutz und deutsche Frage: völkerrechtliche Probleme der Auslagerung, Zerstreuung und Rückführung deutscher Kulturgüter nach dem Zweiten Weltkrieg. Hrsg. Wilfried Fiedler. Berlin, Mann, [1991]. 332p. (Forschungsergebnisse der Studiengruppe für Politik und Völkerrecht in Verbindung mit der Kulturstiftung der deutschen Vertrieben, Bd. 7)

In-depth review of the laws pertaining to the impact of World War II on the ownership and dispersal of German cultural property. Includes an extended discussion of the historical development (18th–20th centuries) of cultural property law as a sub-set of the laws regarding armed conflict, and of the restitution/reparations debate.

Bibliographie zum internationalen Kulturgüterschutz, p.211–42. Zusammenfassung = Summary = Résumé, p.303–28. Stichwortverzeichnis, p.329–32.

T306 Kleeberg, Rudolf, and Eberl, Wolfgang. Kulturgüter in Privatbesitz: Handbuch für das Denkmal- und Steuerrecht. Heidelberg, Recht und Wirtschaft, [1990]. 389p. (Bücher des Betriebs-Beraters)

Detailed commentary on the laws and regulations covering the rights and responsibilities in Germany of owners of movable and non-movable cultural property. Also discusses related areas of Germany's tax laws. Briefly considers the international fiscal environment with regard to cultural property.

Literaturverzeichnis, p.28–36. Übersicht über die Denkmalschutzgesetze, p.375–76. Verzeichnis der obersten Denkmalschutzbehörden, p.377. Verzeichnis der Denkmalämter, p.378–80. Sachregister, p.381–89.

T307 Kulturgutschutz in Deutschland: ein Kommentar. Bearb. von Norbert Bernsdorff und Andreas Kleine-Tebbe. Köln, Heymanns, [1996]. 224p.

Discusses German laws applicable to the protection of movable cultural property. Regional, federal, and European Union regulations are reviewed. Of particular interest is the commentary on the 1995 federal law concerning the protection of German cultural property against export, and the discussion of the European Union's position on art market regulation.

Contents: (A) Gesetz zum Schutz deutschen Kulturgutes gegen Abwanderung (KgSchG); (B) Landesrechtliche Verordnungen zum Kulturgutschutzgesetz; (C) Die Denkmalschutzgesetze der Länder; (D) Das europäische Gemeinschaftsrecht.

Schriftum, p.213–18. Sachregister, p.219–24.

T308 Nicholas, Lynn H. The Rape of Europa: the fate of Europe's treasures in the Third Reich and the Second World War. N.Y., Knopf, 1994. x, 498p. il.

German trans., München, Kindler, 1995; Spanish trans, Barcelona, Destino, 1996.

Pioneering publication marking the beginnings of a renewed interest in the fate of European-owned art works during World War II. Traces the vast quantity of cultural property that was confiscated, transported, stolen, sold, dismembered, or destroyed as the Nazi regime sought to control Europe and the Soviet Union not only politically but also culturally. Draws upon extensive archival research, as well as interviews with participants in the post-War salvage operations.

Notes, p.445–65. Bibliography, p.467–75. Index, p.477–98.

T309 Petropoulos, Jonathan. Art as politics in the Third Reich. Chapel Hill, Univ. of North Carolina Pr., [1996]. xviii, 439p. il.

Originally presented as the author's doctoral thesis (Harvard University, 1990). Of particular interest are the outlines of individual Nazi leader's collections, and their acquisition methods.

Contents: (1) The establishment of the National Socialist cultural bureaucracy, 1933–1936; (2) Degenerate art and state interventionism, 1936–1938; (3) From confiscation to aryanization: the radicalization of cultural policy, 1938–1939; (4) Art and avarice abroad: the advent of Nazi plundering in Poland, the Baltic States, and South Tyrol, 1939–1940; (5) Occupation and exploitation, 1940–1943; (6) The contraction of the cultural bureaucracy, 1943–1945; (7) An overview of the leaders' collections and methods of acquisition; (8) Art collecting as a reflection of the National Socialist leaders' worldviews; (9) Art collecting and interpersonal relations among the National Socialist elite; (10) Art collecting, luxury, and the National Socialist elite's conception of status.

Glossary of key figures, p.317–21. Notes, p.323–83. Bibliography, p.385–415. Index, p.417–39.

T310 Verlorene Werke der Malerei in Deutschland in der Zeit von 1939 bis 1945: zerstörte und verschollene Gemälde aus Museen und Galerien. Bearb. von Marianne Bernhard. Beratende Mitarb. Kurt Marin. Hrsg. von Klaus Pogner. München, F.A. Ackermann, [1965]. 231p., 225 plates.

Catalog of the many paintings in German collections destroyed or lost during World War II. The listing is arranged alphabetically by location, and then by collection. Illustrations divided according to school. The number of works illustrated (225) is far smaller than the listed works (many of which had not been photographed); the illustrations are good, mostly large, black-and-white photographs.

Contents: (I) Altdeutsche Malerei: Deutsche Malerei, 17.–20. Jahrhundert; (II) Altniederländische Malerei; (III) Vlämische und Holländische Malerei; (IV) Italienische Malerei; (V) Spanische Malerei; (VI) Französische Malerei, 15.–18. Jahrhundert; (VII) Französische Malerei, 19. Jahrhundert.

Literaturverzeichnis mit Abkürzungen, p.186. Register, p.189–232.

Great Britain and Ireland

T311 Carman, John. Valuing ancient things: archaeology and law. N.Y., Leicester Univ. Pr., [1996]. x, 246p.

Historical survey of English law as it relates to archeology. Omits Wales, Scotland, and Northern Ireland.

References, p.228–41. Index, p.242–46.

T312 The destruction of the country house: 1875–1975. [By Roy Strong . . . (et al.)] London, Thames and Hudson, 1974. 192p. il.

Published in conjunction with the exhibition, Victoria and Albert Museum (1973). The 26 contributions discuss the heritage role of the country house, primarily in England, Scotland, and Wales, but also in the U.S. Both book and exhibition marked a significant turning point in the fortunes of the country house. All the illustrations in this book show buildings that by 1973 no longer existed. In addition to the chapters listed here, there is a series of profiles of individual country houses.

Selective contents: The country house in our heritage, by James Lees-Milne; Gone to ground, by John Harris; The tale in Scotland, by Colin McWilliam; The picture collection, by Sir Oliver Millar; The library, by A. N. L. Munby; The park, by Marcus Binney; The garden, by Miles Hadfield; The muniment room, by Roger Ellis; America: the country house as museum, by Christopher Monkhouse; The economics of the country house, by Donald Insall; The house and the estate, by Sir Michael Culme-Seymour; Saving the contents, by Peter Thornton; The preservation societies, by Nikolaus Boulting; The Historic Buildings Council, by I. M. Glennie; The National Trust, by Robin Fedden; Country houses and the law, by Nicholas Cooper; The future of the country house, by Marcus Binney; County lists of houses destroyed, in England, Scotland and Wales, by Peter Reid.

T313 Hewison, Robert. The heritage industry: Britain in a climate of decline. [London], Methuen, [1987]. 160p. il.

Excoriates what the author sees as Britain's obsession with the past, and its consequent focus on the manufacture of heritage, "a commodity which nobody seems able to define."—*Introd.*

Contents: (1) Living in a museum; (2) The climate of decline; (3) Brideshead re-revisited; (4) The heritage industry; (5) The politics of patronage; (6) A future for the past.

Notes, p.147–52. Index, p.153–60.

T314 Merrill, Linda. A pot of paint: aesthetics on trial in Whistler v Ruskin. Washington, D.C., Smithsonian Institution Pr. in collaboration with the Freer Gallery of Art, Smithsonian Institution, 1992. xv, 419p. il. (part col.)

Although the official transcript of the art world's possibly most famous court case has not survived, the author attempts to reconstruct the trial by piecing together surviving reports.

Notes, p.323–404. Select bibliography, p.405–07. Index, p.409–19.

T315 Preserving the past: the rise of heritage in modern Britain. Ed. by Michael Hunter. [Stroud, U.K.], Sutton, [1996]. 224p. il.

Collection of essays examining the history and development of historic preservation in Great Britain.

Contents: (1) Introduction: the fitful rise of British preservation, by Michael Hunter; (2) The first conservation militants: William Morris and the Society for the Protection of Ancient Buildings, by Chris Miele; (3) Protecting the monuments: archaeological legislation from the 1882 Act to PPG 16, by Timothy Champion; (4) London government: a record of custodianship, by John Earl; (5) The art of keeping one jump ahead: conservation societies in the twentieth century, by Gavin Stamp; (6) Nationalising the country house, by Peter Mandler; (7) How listing happened, by Andrew Saint; (8) From comprehensive development to conservation areas, by Sophie Andreae; (9) Open-air and industrial museums: windows on to a lost world or graveyards for unloved buildings?, by Michael Stratton; Appendix: key events in the history of preservation in Britain.

Bibliographical essay, p.177–90. Notes, p.196–212. Index, p.213–24.

T316 Pugh-Smith, John, and Samuels, John. Archaeology in law. With contrib. from Richard Harwood and James Rouse. London, Sweet & Maxwell, 1996. xli, 378p.

"The purpose of this book is to set out clearly the scheme of current archaeological legislation and government . . . and to discuss its implications within the planning system."—*Introd.* English law is the primary focus, although reference is also made to Wales and, to a lesser extent, other parts of the U.K.

Contents: (1) Introduction; (2) Historical background; (3) The organisation of British archaeology; (4) Ancient Monuments and Archaeological Areas Act; (5) Other forms of legal protection and guidance; (6) Development controls; (7) Fiscal considerations; Appendices A–R [Texts of/extracts from planning policy documents, regulations, and specifications].

[Tables of cases and legal provisions], p.xv–xli. Index, p.359–78.

T317 Report of the Committee Concerned with the Outflow of Works of Art. Dublin, Stationery Office, 1985. xii, 43p.

Prompted by a concern that "the State is not in a position to exercise any effective control over the export of works of art and other valuable heritage material."—*Introd.*

Contents: (1) The present situation concerning the outflow of works of art; (2) Value Added Tax on works of art; (3) Incentives to encourage the retention of works of art and assets to the heritage, in the State; Appendix A: The Documents and Pictures (Regulation of Export) Acts, 1945; Appendix B: List of submissions received and persons consulted; Appendix C: Important sales in recent years which have resulted in the dispersal of collections and in significant works of art and other heritage material leaving the country.

T318 Richards, Ruth. Conservation planning: a guide to planning legislation concerning our architectural heritage. Foreword by Dame Judi Dench. [London, Planning Aid], 1990. 44p.

Booklet outlining the laws and procedures of the British planning system.

Contents: (1) Foreword; (2) Planning framework; (3) Listed buildings; (4) Planning control and listed buildings; (5) Repairs to listed buildings; (6) Conservation areas; (7) Planning controls in conservation areas; (8) Archaeology; (9) Ancient monuments; (10) Crown exemption; (11) Ecclesiastical exemption; (12) Trees; (13) Advertisement control; (14) Grants; Appendix A: Useful organizations (p.39–42); Appendix B: Further reading (p.43).

T319 Ross, Michael. Planning and the heritage: policy and procedures. 2d ed. N.Y., Spon, 1996. 189p. il., chart.

1st ed., London, Chapman Hall, 1991.

Comprehensive review of current legislation, policy, and procedures relating to the preservation of architecturally and/or historically significant buildings and sites. Focuses on the British system of "listed buildings," "conservation areas," and "ancient monuments." Ten chapters examine the origins of the system and its significance for architects, developers, planners, and conservationists. Discusses conservation and heritage philosophy. Appendixes contain the criteria for listing and a list of addresses.

Bibliography, p.182–83. Index, p.185–88.

T320 Strong, Roy. Lost treasures of Britain. N.Y., Viking, 1990. 232p. il. (part col.), plates, ports. (part col.)

Extended essay ranging from the English Reformation period to the 1834 Westminster Palace fire. The author discusses the widely held view in Britain that "what is old is de facto worthy of preservation," and questions Britain's "fixation with the past" and its potentially negative impact on modern creativity.—*Introd.* The excellent illustrations include many no longer extant buildings and art works.

Contents: (1) The destruction of shrines and relics; (2) The dissolution of the monasteries; (3) The reformation of images; (4) The dispersal of libraries; (5) The sale of the royal jewels and the plate; (6) The purging of cathedrals and churches; (7) The fate of the royal palaces; (8) The destruction of the crown jewels; (9) The Great Fire of London; (10) The demolition of Nonsuch Palace; (11) The burning of Whitehall Palace; (12) Three famous Holbeins lost; (13) The end of Wilton's gardens; (14) Somerset House destroyed; (15) The fall of Fonthill; (16) Westminster in flames.

Select bibliography, p.225–28. Index, p.229–32.

T321 Suddards, Roger W., and Hargreaves, Jane M. Listed buildings: the law and practice of historic buildings, ancient monuments, and conservation areas. With contributions by David Hicken and Chris Allen. Foreword by Sir Desmond Heap. 3d ed. London, Sweet & Maxwell, 1996. xli, 502p. il.

1st ed., 1982; 2d, rev. ed., 1988.

Aims "to present in one book a comprehensive statement of the law and the practice relating to historic buildings, be they listed, in a conservation area, or ancient monuments."—*Pref.* English law is the primary focus, although reference is also made to laws regulating Scotland and Wales.

Contents: (1) Introduction; (2) Listing; (3) Conservation areas; (4) Listed building consent: the criteria for consent to demolish, alter and extend; (5) Listed buildings: the mechanics of control; (6) Problem operations and features: the nuts and bolts of listed building and conservation area control; (7) "Problem buildings": redundancy, neglect and disrepair; (8) Ancient monuments and archaeology; (9) Value Added Tax ("VAT"); (10) Churches; (11) Rights of entry; (12) Grant and loan facilities; (13) Public rights: buildings, conservation areas and ancient monuments; Appendix A: Planning policy guidance: planning and the historic environment; Appendix B: Directions from circular 8/87.

Table of cases, p.xv–xix. Table of statutes, p.xxi–xxix; Table of statutory instruments, p.xxxi–xxxiii. Table of circulars, p.xxxv–xxxvi. Planning policy guidance notes, p.xxxix–xli.

T322 Treasures for the nation: conserving our heritage. Ed. by Suzannah Gough. [London], British Museum Publications for the National Heritage Memorial Fund, 1988. 176p. il. (part col.), ports. (part col.)

Catalog of the exhibition, British Museum (1988–89), commemorating the preservation accomplishments of the National Heritage Memorial Fund.

Contents: The national heritage: the development of an idea since 1870, by John Cornforth; The albatross and the phoenix: the fate of great houses, by Marcus Binney; The National Heritage Memorial Fund: a continuing role, by Brian Lang; The memorial aspect, by Alan Borg; The Fund and the church, by Claude Blair; Archaeology and treasure trove, by I. H. Longworth; Museums and the heritage, by D. M. Wilson; Portraits of nature, by Fred Holliday; The landscape park and garden, by Christopher Thacker; Music and literature, by Brian Moriss; The country house, by Brian Lang; Explorers and travellers, by Ann Savours; The industrial past, by David Sekers; Movies, piers and postcards, by C. Chapman.

Index, p.175–76.

SEE ALSO: Harvey and Meisel, Auctions law and practice (GLAH 2:T246).

Italy

T323 Alibrandi, Tommaso, and Ferri, Piergiorgio. I beni culturali e ambientali. Collab. di Ilaria Alibrandi. 3d, rev. ed. Milano, Giuffre, 1995. xi, 774p. (Commentario di legislazione amministrativa)

1st ed., 1978; 2d ed., 1985.

Thorough review of the Italian legal framework for the protection and preservation of cultural and environmental property in Italy. The historical survey is also very useful.

Includes bibliographical references. Indice analitico, p.763–74.

T324 ______. Il diritto dei beni culturali: la protezione del patrimonio storico-artistico. [Reprint.] Rome, Nuova Italia Scientifica, 1997. 182p. (Beni culturali, 5)

Useful introduction to cultural property protection in Italy.

Bibliografia essentiale, p.179–80. Indice cronologico dei principali provvedimenti legislativi, p.181–82.

T325 Carugno, G. N. . . . [et al.] Codice dei beni culturali: annotato con la giurisprudenza. Milano, Giuffrè, 1994. xiv, 1106p.

The first complete compilation of cultural property legislation in force in Italy. Includes the full texts of relevant international, national, and regional legal instruments, together with commentaries. Includes relevant parts of the new Concordat (with the Vatican State) governing cultural property, as well as regulations originating with the European Union.

Indice analitico, p.1053–68. Indice chronologico, p.1069–77. Indice sistematico, p.1079–1106.

T326 Emiliani, Andrea. Leggi, bandi e provvedimenti per la tutela dei beni artistici e culturali negli antichi stati italiani, 1571–1860. [2d ed.] Introd. di Andrea Emiliani. Pref. di Elio Garzillo. Postfazione di Giulio Volpe. [Bologna], Nuova Alfa, 1996. 331p. (Rapporti, 73)

1st ed., Bologna, Alfa, 1978.

Compilation of the regulations governing cultural property in Italy's individual states prior to political unification.

Contents: Legge, bandi e provvedimenti, 1571–1860; Provincie Toscane; Provincie Romane; Provincie Venete e Lombarde; Provincie Meridionali; Provincie dell'Emilia; Provincie Piemontesi; Relazione di Giovanni Rosadi sul disegno D.D.L.; "Per le antichità e le belle arti"; La parabola della tutela artistic italiana da Carlo Fea a Giovanni Rosadi, by Giulio Volpe.

Indice dei provvedimenti, p.287–90. Indice tematico, p.291–317. Indice dei luoghi, p.319–20. Indice dei nomi, p.321–23. Indice delle istituzioni, p.325. Indice dei mestieri, p.327–28. Indice dei materiali e degli oggetti, p.329–31.

T327 Hartt, Frederick. Florentine art under fire. Princeton, Princeton Univ. Pr., 1949. 148p. il., maps.

Documents the damage to, and removal of, art works in Florence and Tuscany during World War II.

Contents: (I) Introduction; (II) Siena and its province; (III) The pictures of Florence; (IV) The salvation of Florence; (V) Salvage in and around Florence; (VI) More Florentine pictures; (VII) Salvage in Pisa and Arezzo; (VIII) The return of the Florentine art treasures; Appendix I: Intact monuments; Appendix II: Damaged monuments and their repairs; Appendix III: Monuments totally destroyed; Appendix IV: Destroyed works of art; Appendix V: Walled-up pictures.

T328 Quatremère de Quincy, M. Lettres à Miranda sur le déplacement des monuments de l'art de l'Italie. Introd. et notes par Édouard Pommier. [Paris], Macula, [1989]. 146p.

1st ed., Lettres sur le préjudice qu'occasionneraient aux arts et à la science, le déplacement des monuments de l'art de l'Italie. Paris, Desenne, 1796.

Publication, with an extensive commentary, of the seven letters written by Antoine-Crysostome Quatremère de Quincy (1755–1849) in 1796, important for their early criticism of Napoleon's art-removing policies as he swept through Europe. The letters were especially critical of Napoleon's Italian campaign. The ed.'s introd. sets the text in its historical and political context, discusses the recipient of the letters, the cosmopolitan Francisco de Miranda (1756–1816), and reviews the Lettres' publishing history.

Notes, p.69–83.

T329 Segni del passato regole del presente: bibliografia ragionata sulla normativa per I beni ambientali e architettonici. A cura di Silvia Belforte. Testi di Carlotta Battistoni . . . [et al.] Schede bibliografiche di Carlotta Battistoni . . . [et al.] [Firenze], Alinea, [1993]. 280p.

Clearly organized and extensively annotated bibliography covering the preservation of the architectural environment. While the focus is the Italian legislative system, relevant references from non-Italian, non-legal literature are also included.

Contents: (1) Segni del passato, regole del presente, di Danilo Riva; (2) Aspetti e caratteri della norma per i beni ambientali e architettonici, di Silvia Belforte; (3) Beni culturali: cultura, tutela, società e norma, di Paolo Cornaglia; (4) Le politche: intenzionalità nella normativa per i beni ambientali e architettonici, di Silvia Belforte; (5) Manualistica, di Silvia Belforte; (6) Bibliografia generale; (7) Documenti internazionali per la protezione del patrimonio culturale e carte del restauro, di Carlotta Batttoni; (8) Leggi e norme italiane per la tutela dei beni ambientali e architettonici, di Silvia Tonin.

Notes at ends of chapters. Indice degli autori, p.275–77.

T330 Speroni, Mario. La tutela dei beni culturali negli stati preunitari. Milano, Giuffre, 1988– . (1)v. (Collana degli annali della Facoltà di Giurisprudenza della Università di Genova, 59)

Important historical survey of legislative attitudes to cultural property protection and preservation in Italy prior to political unification.

Contents: (1) L'età delle riforme.

T331 Treasures untraced: an inventory of the Italian art treasures lost during the Second World War. Roma, Istituto Poligrafico e Zecca dello Stato, 1995. 339p. il.

Trans. of L'opera da ritrovare: repertorio del patrimonio artistico italiano disperso all'epoca della seconda guerra mondiale. Roma, Istituto Poligrafico e Zecca dello Stato, 1995.

Lists works destroyed and/or removed from Italian museums, churches, public institutions, and private collections by German forces. All items receive a brief entry describing the history of the object and its movement during World War II. Includes small photographs, where available, and the objects' present locations (if known).

Bibliography, p.321–26. Index of artists' names and working contexts, p.329–35. Index of places of origin and location of works, p.336–39.

Latin America

T332 Coelho, Olinio Gomes P. Do patrimonio cultural. Rio de Janeiro, Coelho, 1992. 182p. il.

Discusses cultural property protection in Brazil. Provides the texts of international and Brazilian agreements and recommendations, and of national, regional, and local Brazilian legislation. The illustrations show examples of significant Brazilian architecture either in a state of abandon, in the process of demolition, or otherwise under threat.

Bibliography, p.71–78.

T333 Díaz Berrio, Salvador. Conservación del patrimonio cultural en México. [Córdoba], Instituto Nacional de Antropologia e Historia, [1990]. 436p. il., maps. (Colección textos basicos y manuales)

In-depth historical survey of cultural property preservation measures in Mexico, as well as a history of the loss of Mexican cultural property. Organizations engaged in protecting the cultural heritage in Mexico are discussed, as is relevant Mexican legislation.

Notes at ends of chapters I–III. Cuadros e tablas comparativos, p.375–90. Bibliografía, p.427–36.

T334 Harvey, Edwin R. Legislación cultural andina: ordenamiento selectivo. Bogota, Convenio "Andres Bello," 1981–1982. 8v.

Compilation of legislation pertaining to cultural affairs and cultural property enacted by the signatory countries to the so-called "Andres Bello Convention." Following an introductory vol., each vol. is devoted to one country. Includes introductions and full texts of 520 relevant legislative enactments. Wide-ranging. Designed as a reference tool for artists, the media, lawyers, cultural administrators, legislators, and politicians.

Contents: (I) Introducción general; (II) Legislación cultural de Bolivia; (III) Legislación cultural de Colombia; (IV) Legislación cultural de Chile; (V) Legislación cultural de Ecuador; (VI) Legislación cultural de Panama; (VII) Legislación cultural de Peru; (VIII) Legislación cultural de Venezuela.

T335 Illicit traffic of cultural property in Latin America = Le trafic illicite des biens culturels en Amérique latine. [Paris], ICOM, 1996. 203p.

Publishes the proceedings of a workshop on illicit traffic in cultural property, Cuenca, Ecuador (1995). Contributions by representatives from each country of the region.

Contents: (I) Argentina, Belize, Bolivia, Brazil, Chile, Colombia, Cuba, Dominican Republic, Ecuador, El Salvador, Guatemala, Honduras, Mexico, Nicaragua, Panama, Paraguay, Peru, Surinam, Uruguay, Venezuela; (II) ICOM, Unesco, Interpol; (III) Recommendations: Declaration of Cuenca; Working group reports from the private Cuenca workshops.

T336 Legislación dominicana sobre museos y protección del patrimonio cultural, 1870–1977. Recopilación [by] Pina P. Plinio. Santo Domingo, Museo del Hombre Dominicano, 1978. 136p. (Catalogos y memorias, no.5)

Comprises the texts of 50 laws, decrees, and other regulations governing cultural property protection in the Dominican Republic.

T337 El patrimonio nacional de México. Coord., Enrique Florescano. [2d ed.] México, Consejo Nacional para la Cultura y las Artes, [1997]–(1997). 2v. (Biblioteca mexicana. Serie historia y antropologia, v.1–2)

1st ed. titled El patrimonio cultural de México. México, Consejo Nacional para la Cultura y las Artes, 1993.

Surveys the cultural properties of Mexico, including archeological sites, architecture and urbanism, maps, etc. Includes a suite of introductory essays.

Contents: El patrimonio nacional: valores, usos, estudio y difusión, por Enrique Florescano; Nuestro patrimonio cultural: un laberinto de significados, por Guillermo Bonfil Batalla; El patrimonio cultural de México y la construcción imaginaria de lo nacional, por Néstor García Canclini; Hacia una nueva política cultural, por Rafael Tovar y de Teresa; La creaciòn del Museo Nacional de Antropología, por Enrique Florescano; El patrimonio arqueológico: conceptos y usos, por Jaime Litvak and Sandra L. López Varela; El patrimonio arquitectónico y urbano (de 1521 a 1900), por

Sonia Lombardo de Ruiz; Historias de papel: los archivos de México, por Clara García Ayluardo; La cartografía como patrimonio cultural, por Miguel León Portilla.

Notes at ends of most essays.

T338 Peruvian antiquities: a manual for United States Customs. [Ed. by Mary Livingston Azoy.] [Washington, D.C., Organization of American States, Department of Cultural Affairs, 1983]. [x], 74p. il. (part col.) (Repr.: 1985)

Guide arising out of the Agreement between the United States of America and the Republic of Peru for the Recovery and Return of Stolen Archaeological, Historical and Cultural Properties (Lima, 1981). Illustrates and discusses the primary types of Peruvian cultural property that were/are illegally exported so that U.S. customs officials might more easily identify them.

Brief essays by various authors discuss issues surrounding the precolonial, prehispanic, and colonial cultural heritage of Peru and its illegal removal from that country.

Notes at ends of some essays. Peruvian cultural chronology, p.[x]. 1981. Agreement between the United States of America and the Republic of Peru for the Recovery and Return of Stolen Archaeological, Historical and Cultural Properties [Lima Agreement], p.67–68. Catalog of selected Peruvian artefacts, p.69–72. Additional reading, p.73.

T339 Recopilación de leyes para la protección del patrimonio arqueológico nacional. [San Juan], Instituto de Cultura Puertorriqueña, 1991. 47p.

Provides an introduction to, and the full texts of, the three major laws governing Puerto Rican archeological objects and sites.

T340 Schávelzon, Daniel. La conservación del patrimonio cultural en America Latina: restauración de edificios prehispánicos en Mesoamérica: 1750–1980. Buenos Aires, Univ. de Buenos Aires, Facultad de Arquitectura, Diseño y Urbanismo; Instituto de Arte Americano e Investigiaciones Esteticas "Mario J. Buschiazzo," [1990]. 270p. il.

Based on the author's doctoral thesis (UNAM, Facultad de Arquitectura, 1984), this important publication surveys the history of, and theory behind, the preservation movement in Central America, setting it within its political, economic, and social framework. Focuses on theft and outright destruction of cultural property. The emphasis is on pre-colonial archeological sites (including early excavation reports); case histories drawn from Belize, Guatemala, Honduras, and Mexico. The author seeks to demonstrate that the conservation of the cultural heritage is a deeply political fact in the preservation of cultural identities.

Notas, p.235–55. Bibliografía, p.257–70.

T341 ———. El expolio del arte en la Argentina: robos y tráfico ilegal de obras de arte. Buenos Aires, Editorial Sudamericana, [1993]. 161, [30]p. il.

Argentina was until recently the only country in Latin America not to have a national law in place protecting the country's cultural patrimony. Individual chapters address problematic sectors of the Argentine cultural property situation.

Notas (referencias a la bibliografía), p.[171–74]. Bibliografía, p.[175–89].

SEE ALSO: Meyer, The plundered past: the traffic in art treasures (GLAH 2:T259).

Low Countries

T342 Archaeological heritage management in the Netherlands: fifty years State Service for Archaeological Investigations. Ed. by W. J. H. Willems . . . [et al.] [Assen], Van Gorcum, 1997. 359p. il., maps.

Collection of 15 scholarly essays documenting changes in Dutch archeology, especially in light of the 1992 European Convention of Valletta and the revised Dutch Monuments Act (1988).

Notes at ends of essays.

T343 Marijnissen, Roger H. Paintings: genuine, fraud, fake: modern methods of examining paintings. Brussels, Elsevier, 1985. 415p. il. (part col.)

In-depth investigation of the complexities of ascertaining authenticity. Confined to Flemish and Dutch painting, examples are taken primarily from public collections. Many extensively annotated photographs, including macro-photographs, x-rays, etc. Extracts from reports of court cases surrounding the "restoration" of art works, dating as far back as the 15th century.

Contents: The certificate; True or false?; The scientific approach; Essay in method; The preliminary examination; The physical examination; Non-physical investigation; The synthesis of the investigation; Technical equipment: applications.

Bibliography, p.399–408. Index, p.409–13.

Middle East

T344 Abstracts of the papers for the conference on the preservation of architectural heritage of Islamic cities. [Saudi Arabia], Arab Towns Organization, Arab Urban Development Institute], [1985–1988].

Collection of 80 papers and reports given at a conference held at Istanbul (1985). The objective of this conference was to define the common cultural characteristics of the Islamic city, especially through its architecture. Papers range in subject from legislative and administrative to historic considerations and include case studies of specific sites as well as the impact of tourism and 20th-century urban structural change. All published papers are in English.

T345 Khater, A. Le régime juridique des fouilles des antiquités en Égypte. Le Caire, L'Institut Français d'Archéologie Orientale, 1960. 337p. (Recherches d'archéologie, de philologie et d'histore, t.XII)

Scholarly, in-depth survey of Egyptian legislation regulating archeological excavations and objects. Covers the period since 1835, the year the first regulation designed to protect archeological objects was enacted.

Table des matières, p.333–37.

T346 Lost heritage: antiquities stolen from Iraq's regional museums. [various imprints], 1992– . (3)v.
Series documenting the toll on cultural property in Iraq during the 1992 Gulf War. Each fascicule is compiled by a different group of researchers, and includes a catalog of stolen items, together with illustrations. Data are taken from a master list produced by the Iraqi Department of Antiquities.

Russia and Eastern Europe

T347 Akinsha, Konstantin, and Kozlov, Grigorii. Beautiful loot: the Soviet plunder of Europe's art treasures. With Sylvia Hochfield. N.Y., Random House, 1995. 301p.
British ed. titled Stolen treasure: the hunt for the world's lost masterpieces. London, Weidenfeld and Nicolson, 1995; German trans., München, Deutscher Taschenbuch, 1995.

Documents the more than 2.5 million art objects, books, and archival documents confiscated by the Soviet forces from the defeated Germans at the end of World War II. Divided into four parts, comprising 32 case histories concerning individual works or groups of works removed from Germany.

Principal persons referred to in the text, p.261–67. Notes, p.269–86. Bibliography, p.287–92. Index, p.293–301.

T348 Bieńkowska, Barbara. Losses of Polish libraries during World War II. Warsaw, Ministry of Culture and Art, Bureau of the Government Plenipotentiary for the Polish Cultural Heritage Abroad, 1994. 142p. il., maps (Polish cultural heritage, series A: Losses of Polish culture)
A "shortened version of the Report on Polish library losses in World War II prepared by the Bureau of the Government Plenipotentiary for Polish Heritage Abroad."—*Introd.* (See Straty bibliotek w czasie II wojny światowej w granicach Polski z 1945 roku: wstępny raport o stanie wiedzy [= Library losses during World War II within Poland's boundaries of 1945: preliminary report on the state of information], Warsaw, 1994.)

Footnotes, p.65–74. Tables 1–20, p.75–116. Calendar of major events, p.117–123. Bibliography, p.124–29. Name index, p.130–32. Library index, p.133–42.

T349 Cultural heritage of Croatia in the war 1991/1992. Ed. by Radovan Ivancevic. Texts by Igor Fiskovic . . . [et al.] Photographs Kresimir Tadic . . . [et al.] Zagreb, Hrvatska sveucilisna naklada, 1993. 304p. il., 9 col. plates, maps. (Croatia in the war, 4)
Reviews losses inflicted on Croatian cultural properties during World War II.

Contents: (I) The cultural heritage of Croatia; (II) War damage inflicted on the cultural heritage in Croatia [listings by region, and by institution].

T350 Issues of historical preservation in Central Europe and Russia: conference proceedings. Ed. by Jodi Koehn. Washington, D.C., Kennan Institute for Advanced Russian Studies, [1994]. vi, 80p. (Kennan Institute for Advanced Russian Studies, Occasional paper, no.259)
Transcript of panel sessions at the conference "Historical preservation: issues confronting Eastern Europe and Russia," Radziejowice, Poland (1994). Examines the issues facing historic preservation programs in the former socialist world, the impact of state, public, and private financing on preservation, and the increase in decay, theft, and insensitive reuse of these countries' cultural property.

Contents: (I) Maintaining a sense of national heritage; (II) Defining a sense of place; (III) Multiple cultures, multiple heritage; (IV) Issues facing Novgorod and Iaroslavl; (V) Preservation pluralism: managing conflicting interests.

T351 King, David. The commissar vanishes: the falsification of photographs and art in Stalin's Russia. Pref. by Stephen F. Cohen. Photographs from the David King collection. N.Y., Metropolitan Books, 1997. 191p. il. (part col.), ports. (part col.)
Documents five decades of official falsification of history through the manipulation of "documentary" photographs and "history" paintings under the Stalin regime, 1929–53. Numerous images, and groups of images illustrating first and subsequent printings, are accompanied by brief captions.

Bibliography, p.190. Index, p.190–91.

T352 Kostenevich, Albert. Hidden treasures revealed: Impressionist masterpieces and other important French paintings preserved by the State Hermitage Museum, St. Petersburg. Moscow, Ministry of Culture of the Russian Federation; St. Petersburg, State Hermitage Museum; in assoc. with N.Y., Abrams, 1995. 292p. il. (chiefly col.)
French trans., Paris, Martinière, 1995; German trans., München, Kindler, 1995; Italian trans., Milano, Leonardo, 1995.

Ground-breaking catalog of the exhibition, State Hermitage Museum (1995) of French paintings, 1827–1927, from German collections, clandestinely stored at the Hermitage since the end of World War II. Each painting is reproduced in a full-page color plate, accompanied by smaller black-and-white comparative photographs and an extensive catalog entry.

T353 The "Sacco di Budapest" and depredation of Hungary, 1938–1949: works of art missing from Hungary as a result of the Second World War: looted, smuggled, captured, lost and destroyed art works, books and archival documents: preliminary and provisional catalogue: includes archives photographs and document from Hungarian public archives, as well as from libraries, museums and private collections. Comp. by Láslo Mravik. Budapest, Hungarian National Gallery, 1998. 468p. il., ports.
Documents the "especially tragic consequences" (*Introd.*) of World War II for Hungarian art, destroyed, or looted first by the Germans and then by Soviet troops. The provisional catalog of these works "constitutes official proof that research is being pursued in Hungary into art works and cultural trea-

sures removed from the country in tempestuous times or taken abroad in some other unlawful manner."—*Pref.* Includes selected documents of the period relating to the dispersal of public and private collections. Illustrations of missing art works and interiors in which they were displayed, and of collection inventories.

Important auctions, p.22–24. Important exhibitions up to 1945, p.25–29. A history of Hungarian art collections, 15th–20th centuries: selected literature and other references, p.30–55. Index of more important place-names, p.65.

T354 Varshavsky, Sergei, and Rest, Boris. The ordeal of the Hermitage: the siege of Leningrad, 1941–1944. [Trans. from the Russian.] N.Y., Abrams, [1985]. 270p. il. (part col.), 388 plates (part col.)

Based on contemporary accounts (such as the Nurenburg trial archives). Documents the efforts of the Hermitage staff and others during World War II to save this priceless collection; and the restoration work on the museum and its collections during the years following. Accompanied by a fascinating collection of contemporary photographs of the city's wartime devastation, and of the recovered splendors of the Hermitage and other major buildings in the area.

Spain and Portugal

T355 Alvarez Alvarez, José Luis. Sociedad, estado y patrimonio cultural. Madrid, Espasa Calpe, 1992. 344p. (Espasa universidad, 27)

In-depth, scholarly study of cultural property protection, primarily in Spain but also with reference to the international context.

T356 Alvarez Lopera, Jose. La politica de bienes culturales del gobierno republicano durante la guerra civil española. [Madrid, Direccion General de Bellas Artes, Archivos y Bibliotecas, Centro Nacional de Informacion Artistica, Arqueologica y Etnologica, 1982]. 2v. il., 71 plates.

Based on the author's doctoral thesis (University of Granada, Spain, 1980). Thorough history of the measures undertaken by the Republican government to protect cultural property in Spain during the Civil War.

Includes bibliographical references. Bibliografia, v.2, p.143–71.

T357 Benítez, Félix de Lugo y Guillén. El patrimonio cultural español (aspectos jurídicos, administrativos y fiscales; incentivos en la ley de fundaciones). 2d ed. Granada, Comares, 1995. xxxi, 740p. il.

1st ed., 1988.

Wide-ranging survey of administrative, fiscal, and legislative aspects of Spanish cultural property management. Includes ecclesiastical properties, archeological sites, ethnographic materials, archives, libraries, and museums.

Includes bibliographical references.

T358 Mapa del patrimonio historico inmeuble. [Madrid], Ministerio de Cultura, [1995– .] (1)v.

Comprehensive inventory of the sites of cultural and historic interest in Spain. Approximately 13,000 sites/locations are listed in v.1. Covers monuments, historic gardens, historic centers, archeological sites, and castles. Organized by region, then by municipality; each location receives a brief descriptive entry.

T359 Patrimonio histórico artístico. Madrid, Boletin Oficial del Estado, 1989. 529p. (Colección textos legales, 76)

Collection of the laws, decrees, and other regulations, 1866–1987, governing the protection of cultural property in Spain. Includes the complete text of each provision. Opens with the most important piece of Spanish legislation in the field, the Ley 16/1985, de 25 de junio, del Patrimonio Historico Español, which defines the parameters for all other legislation in the field.

Contents: Museos; Archivos; Bibliotecas; Patrimonio nacional; Regimen del suelo y ordenación urbana; Expropriación forzosa; Normas tributarias; Normas organicas; Acuerdos internacionales; Comunidades autónomas.

Tabla cronologica de disposiciones, p.453–92. Indice analitico, p.493–529.

T360 Querol, M. Ángeles, and Martinez Diaz, Belén. La gestión del patrimonio arqueológico en España. [Madrid], Alianza, [1996]. 438p. il.

Thorough survey of archeological heritage management in Spain. Includes the administration of archeological objects and sites, on the national and regional levels, and professional ethics.

Bibliografía, p.423–33. Directorio de los organismos gestores del patrimonio arqueológico, p.435–37. Directorio de los colegios y asociaciones profesionales de arqueología, p.438.

Switzerland

T361 Schweizerisches Inventar der Kulturgüter von nationaler und regionaler Bedeutung: Kulturgüterschutzverzeichnis gemäss Haager Abkommen vom 14. Mai 1954 für den Schutz von Kulturgut bei bewaffneten Konflikten = Inventaire suisse des biens culturels d'importance nationale et régionale; inventaire de la protection des biens culturels selon la Convention de La Haye du 14 mai 1954 pour la protection des biens culturels en cas de conflit armé = Inventario svizzero dei beni culturali d'importanza nazionale e regionale: inventario dei beni culturali secondo la Convenzione dell'Aia del 14 maggio 1954 per la protezione dei beni culturali in caso di conflitto armato. [Berne?], Eidgenössisches Justiz- und Polizeidepartement, Bundesamt für Zivilschutz, 1995. 527p.

1st ed., 1988.

Listing of mostly non-movable cultural property of national or regional significance in Switzerland. Although drawn up as a result of Switzerland's having signed the 1954 Hague Convention for the Protection of Cultural Property in the Event of Armed Conflict, this listing is of relevance in a much wider context, and each edition reflects the Swiss growing awareness of the significance of cultural heritage held within its borders.

The listing is in alphabetical order by canton, then by commune. For each commune heritage items of national and regional significance are identified separately. Geographical coordinates for each item are also given.

Gemeindeverzeichnis = Liste des communes = Elenco dei comuni, p.17–31.

United States

T362 American Indian cultural resources: a preservation handbook. Rev. by Gladine G. Ritter. 2d, rev. ed. Salem, Ore., Commission on Indian Services, 1991. xi, 293, [1]p. il., maps.

1st ed. (1985) by Kathy Gorospe.

Compiled primarily as a guide for American Indian tribes in Oregon to aid in protecting their cultural resources. Also of use to archeologists, law enforcement officials, and local, state, or federal cultural resource administrators and museum officials. Texts of major federal and state (Oregon) antiquities laws are provided and analyzed. Includes discussion of issues and resources in the first six parts of the vol. Part VII, the largest section, contains copies of most of the state and federal statutes presented in the handbook.

Part VI, Sources of other information, p.66–68.

T363 American Indian sacred objects, skeletal remains, repatriation and reburial: a resource guide, 1994. [Comp. by Rayna Green and Nancy Mari Mitchell.] [Washington, D.C.], American Indian Program, National Museum of American History, Smithsonian Institution, 1990. 60p.

Unannotated bibliography covering books, journal articles, conference proceedings, and government documents.

Contents: General bibliography; International federal, tribal, state, judicial and institutional legislation, policy, rules, regulations, memoranda; Films; Periodical publications of organizations which deal regularly with related issues.

T364 Art and the public sphere. Ed. by W. J. T. Mitchell. Chicago, Univ. of Chicago Pr., 1992. 268p. il., 2 folding col. plates.

"Controversies over public support and reception of the arts have become a staple of the mass media in the late twentieth century."—*Introd.* Many of the essays in this vol. originated in the context of a symposium, "Art and public spaces: daring to dream," organized for Sculpture Chicago by John Hallmark Neff in 1989, and were published in various issues of the journal Critical inquiry.

Includes bibliographical references. Index, p.262–68.

T365 Art in the public interest. Ed. with an introd. by Arlene Raven. Ann Arbor, UMI. Research Pr., 1989. 373p. il.

Notable collection of essays commenting on the definition of, and reaction to, late 20th-century new art forms in U.S. public spaces. Many of the contributions had previously appeared elsewhere, although some of them have been revised for this publication.

Notes at ends of essays. Bibliography, compiled by Judy Collischan van Wagner, p.351–65. Index, p.367–73.

T366 Brancusi contre États-Unis: un procès historique, 1928. Préf. Margit Rowell. Postface et fortune critique par André Paleologue. Trad. Jocelyne de Pass. [Paris], Birò, 1995. 144p.

Proceedings from the 1928 court case held in New York, arising from the refusal of American customs officials to exempt a Brancusi sculpture, Bird in Space, from import tax on the grounds that the piece was not a work of art but, rather, metal.

T367 Critical issues in public art: content, context and controversy. Ed. by Harriet F. Senie and Sally Webster. [N.Y.], IconEditions, [1992]. 315p. il.

Papers from a College Art Association panel (N.Y., 1990). "Since its inception, issues surrounding [public art's] appropriate form and placement, as well as its funding, have made public art an object of controversy more often than consensus or celebration."—*Introd.* All essays focus on the U.S. context.

Bibliographical references follow each essay. Index, p.309–14.

T368 Culture wars: documents from the recent controversies in the arts. Ed. by Richard Bolton. N.Y., New Pr., 1992. xviii, 363p. il.

Compilation of newspaper and journal articles, statements made before Congress, and press releases surrounding the intellectual and political debate over freedom of expression and government funding for the arts. Covers the late 1980s–early 1990s. The position of the National Endowment for the Arts, its leadership and its congressional authorization, is also examined.

Chronology [major cases of censorship and controversy in American culture, 1962–1990], by Debra Singer and Philip Brookman, p.331–63.

T369 Darraby, Jessica L. Art, artifact & architecture law. [Deerfield, Ill.], Clark Boardman Callaghan, [1995–]. (looseleaf)

"Provides a thorough treatment of legal issues, gives hands-on advice, and examines the policies and laws of the visual arts, which encompasses art, photography, artifacts, antiques, antiquities, and architecture. . . . Directed toward legal practitioners as well as other professionals in the field of visual arts, including auctioneers, appraisers, preservationists, and curators."—*[Release cover]*. Coverage consists of U.S. federal and state law, 1970s to the present; international conventions are included only where they have been adopted into the U.S. legal framework.

Contents: (1) Fundamentals of art law; (2) Trade practices overview; (3) Valuation and appraisal; (4) Uniform Commercial Code; (5) Auction; (6) International trade; (7) Copyright; (8) Trademark and unfair competition; (9) Artists' rights; (10) Display and exhibition: constitutional precepts; (11) Art fraud; (12) Multiples; (13) Archaeology and artifacts; (14) Historic preservation and conservation; Appendices: 1–21.

Bibliography I: Art law: a selected bibliography, Release #2, 11/97: p.Bib.I: 1–66. Bibliography II: Artists' reference: a selected bibliography, Release #1, 9/96, p.Bib.II: 1–29. Table of cases, Release #2, 11/97, p.TC - 1–26. Index, Release #2, 11/97, p.Ind. - 1–104.

T370 The destruction of Tilted arc: documents. Ed. by Clara Weyergraf-Serra and Martha Buskirk. Introd. by Richard Serra. Cambridge, Mass., MIT Pr., [1991]. xi, 287p. il.

"A version of the present work was published as Richard Serra's Tilted arc, ed. Clara Weyergraf-Serra and Martha Buskirk (Eindhoven, Van Abbemuseum, 1988)."—*T.p. verso.* Richard Serra's introduction was previously published as "'Tilted arc' destroyed," in Art in America, May 1989. Comprises the documentation pertaining to the 1979 commissioning, 1980 installation, subsequent court litigation, and 1989 removal of Richard Serra's site-specific Tilted Arc installation from Federal Plaza, New York. Each part of this book is preceded by an essay setting the documentation in context.

Chronology, p.1–2. Notes, p.273–80. Index, p.283–87.

T371 Doss, Erika Lee. Spirit poles and flying pigs: public art and cultural democracy in American communities. Washington, D.C., Smithsonian Institution Pr., 1995. x, 278p. il.

"This is not a general survey of public art. Rather [it] focuses on six public art episodes . . . . This book considers why public art has become the focus of heated debate."—*Pref.*

Contents: Prologue: Public art in Little Tokyo; (1) Contemporary public art controversy; (2) Public spirit and spirit poles; (3) Public art in the corporate sphere; (4) Sculptures from strip mines; (5) Raising community consciousness with public art; (6) Public art and flying pigs; Epilogue.

Notes, p.251–74. Index, p.275–78.

T372 Federal historic preservation laws. Rev. ed. Washington, D.C., U.S. Department of the Interior, National Park Service, Cultural Resources Programs, 1993. 92p.

1st ed., comp. by Sara K. Blumenthal, 1989.

Brings together the major federal historic preservation laws applicable to historic structures and archeological sites throughout the U.S.

Contents: Laws governing national historic preservation programs; Laws governing national historic landmarks; Laws governing the Federal Archaeology Program; Laws governing federal preservation tax incentives; Other major federal historic preservation laws. Appendix: Implementing federal regulations and guidelines.

T373 Heins, Marjorie. Sex, sin, and blasphemy: a guide to America's censorship wars. N.Y., New Pr. (Distr. by Norton, 1993). xii, 210p.

Focuses on art and politics in the late 20th-century U.S.

Contents: (1) "Obscenity": the First Amendment's second-class citizen; (2) Movies: censoring the dream factory; (3) Censorship by suggestion: the problem of government threats; (4) "The Devil's music": the oddity of warning labels on art; (5) Getting naked: censorship of nudity in art, theater, and dance; (6) "The taxpayers' money": the question of government funding; (7) The dreaded "P" word: pornography; (8) Blasphemy, subversiveness, and other sins.

Notes, p.193–201. A few suggestions for further reading, p.203–04. Index, p.205–10.

T374 Hutt, Sherry; Jones, Elwood W.; and McAllister, Martin F. Archaeological resource protection. [Washington, D.C.], Preservation Pr., [1992]. 179p.

"This book presents an overview of the importance of protecting archeological materials on federal and Indian lands in the United States."—*Foreword.* Its purpose "is to provide a concise overview of the Archaeological Resources Protection Act (ARPA) of 1979, its regulations, and subsequent amendments of both."—*Pref.*

Contents: (1) Overview of the Archeological Resource Protection problem; (2) The Archaeological Resources Protection Act of 1979, related laws and regulations: (3) Archeological crime scene investigation; (4) Damage assessment in archeological violation cases; (5) ARPA and the courts: case presentation. Appendixes A–H.

Glossary, p.156–67. Notes, p.172. Bibliography, p.174–75. Index, p.176–79.

T375 King, Thomas F. Cultural resource laws and practice: an introductory guide. Walnut Creek, Calif., AltaMira Pr., [1998]. xi, 303p. il. (Heritage resources management series, 1)

Designed for use in university programs in historic preservation, cultural resource management, and related areas. Provides information on the historical, scientific, technical, legal, administrative, procedural, and public exhibit aspects of heritage resources management.

Bibliography, p.249–55. Regulations cited, p.257–58. Some useful world wide web sites, p.259–60. Index, p.295–301.

T376 Mending the circle: a Native American repatriation guide: understanding and implementing NAGPRA and the official Smithsonian and other repatriation policies. N.Y., American Indian Ritual Object Repatriation Foundation, [1996]. 167p. il., ports.

"This publication is intended to guide all concerned with matters of repatriation through the maze of pertinent law, policies and procedures."—*Introd.*

Contents: (I) NAGPRA; (II) The Smithsonian Institution; (III) Museum and on-site considerations; (IV) The private sector; (V) Personal viewpoints.

Bibliographical references follow each section. Appendices A–U, p.97–167.

T377 Murtagh, William J. Keeping time: the history and theory of preservation in America. Rev. ed. N.Y., Wiley, 1997. 246p. il., port.

1st ed., N.Y., Sterling, 1988.

"The book's primary purpose is to discuss the subject of historic preservation, the various forms it takes, and something about its background in order to understand what it is and how it has evolved."—*Pref.*

Contents: (1) The language of preservation; (2) The preservation movement and the private citizen before World War II; (3) The preservation movement and the National Trust for Historic Preservation; (4) Government and the preservation movement; (5) Government and preservaton since World War II; (6) The historic room and house museum; (7) Outdoor museums; (8) Historic districts; (9) Rehabilitation and adaptive use; (10) Landscape preservation; (11) Rural and small town preservation; (12) Archaeology; (13) Preservation in practice; Epilogue: And what of the future?; Appendix A: Selected federal legislation; Appendix B: The national register's criteria for evaluation; Appendix C: The Secretary of the Interior's standards for rehabilitation and guidelines for rehabilitating historic buildings.

Chronology, p.205–12. Glossary, p.213–17. Bibliography, p.218–25. Index, p.230–37.

T378 Price, H. Marcus. Disputing the dead: U.S. law on aboriginal remains and grave goods. Columbia, Univ. of Missouri Pr., 1991. 136p.

Reviews the "issues involved in the controversy surrounding the appropriate disposition of prehistoric aboriginal remains and grave goods."—*Introd.* Reviews general, federal, and state law. Includes federal policies and implementing government bodies, particularly in the context of the 1990 Native American Graves Protection and Repatriation Act. Lists related cases.

Works cited, p.127–36.

T379 Protecting the past. Ed. by George S. Smith [and] John E. Ehrenhard. Boca Raton, CRC Pr., [1991]. 314p.

Collection of essays illustrating "examples of efforts to fight looting; and descriptions of organizations, legal, and informational tools that can be used in [the] fight to protect the nation's archaeological resources."—*Pref.*

Notes at ends of essays. Index, p.303–14.

T380 Tabah, Agnes. Native American collections and repatriation. Ed. by Sara Dubberly. Washington, D.C., American Association of Museums, 1993. 188p. (Technical Information Services forum: occasional papers on museum issues and standards)

Reviews those portions of the 1990 Native American Graves Protection and Repatriation Act (NAGPRA) that directly affect federally funded museums. Documentation includes reprinted informational material designed to help museums understand their rights and responsibilities under the Act.

Contents: (I) Native American Graves Protection and Repatriation Act: opportunities and challenges; (II) Collections management of Native American materials; (III) Resources.

Includes bibliographical references. Readings, p.19–139. Sample documents, p.140–88.

T381 United States Conference of Mayors, Special Committee on Historic Preservation. With heritage so rich: National Trust for Historic Preservation. [By] Albert Rains, Chairman, and Laurance G. Henderson, Director. New introd. by Charles B. Hosmer, Jr. [Rev. reprint.] Washington, D.C., Preservation Pr., 1983. 229p. il.

1st ed., With heritage so rich: a report. N.Y., Random House, [1966].

Seminal publication whose content—and the public support it aroused—contributed to the enactment of landmark legislation, the National Historic Preservation Act of 1966. The present edition reprints the complete text of the Act, with relevant amendments up to 1996. Numerous photographs, illustrating buildings that have been successfully preserved since 1966 are also included in this edition.

T382 Zuni and the courts: a struggle for sovereign land rights. Ed. by E. Richard Hart. [Lawrence, Kan.], Univ. Pr. of Kansas, [1995]. xxi, 337p. il. (Development of western resources)

24 essays documenting the efforts made by and on behalf of the New Mexico-based Zuni tribe during three court cases aimed at establishing and protecting the tribe's land claims and access rights.

Notes at ends of chapters. Index, p.327–37. CD-ROM [containing full texts of the expert depositions submitted on behalf of the tribe].

SEE ALSO: Material culture in flux: law and policy of repatriation of cultural property (GLAH 2:T257); Theft of cultural property in Canada (GLAH 2:T290).

ASIAN COUNTRIES

T383 Biswas, Sachindra Sekhar. Protecting the cultural heritage: national legislations and international conventions. New Delhi, Aryan Books International, 1999. X, 263p. il., plates.

Compendium of Indian art and antiquities legislation since 1878.

Contents: (I) National legislations; (II) International conventions.

Index, p.[261]–63.

T384 Cultural heritage in Asia and the Pacific: conservation and policy. Organized by the U.S. Committee of the International Council on Monuments and sites for the U.S. Information Agency, with the cooperation of the Getty Conservation Institute. Ed. by Margaret G. H. Mac Lean. Marina del Rey, Calif., Getty Conservation Institute, 1993. 117p. il.

Proceedings of a symposium, Honolulu, Hawaii (1991).

Contents: The impact of policy on cultural heritage protection, by Lyndel V. Prott; Conservation policy delivery, by Sharon Sullivan; Legal and policy issues in the protection of cultural heritage in South Asia and the Pacific, by Cathy Lynne Costin; Issues that affect cultural property, specifically objects, in South Asia and the Pacific, by Colin Pearson; Building for conservation: appropriate design for environmental control in the tropics, by Steve King; Appendix: Disasters and extreme events.

References, p.96–98. The plenary session: summary of the discussion, p.105–07. Resources guide [institutions and organizations], p.107–12.

T385 Fragile traditions: Indonesian art in jeopardy. Ed. by Paul M. Taylor. Honolulu, Univ. of Hawaii Pr., [1994]. 171p. il., map.
Collection of essays examining the loss of cultural heritage in Indonesia. Such losses are seen as deriving from the increase in international art collecting, tourism, neglect, theft, insufficient legal controls, and the impact of western cultural standards on indigenous art forms.
Notes at ends of essays. Index, p.167–71.

T386 Le Goff, Michèle. Protection et gestion des sites patrimoniaux au Japon. Sous la dir. de Jean-Michel Agnus. [Paris], Ministère de la Culture et de la Communication, Dir. de l'Administration Générale et de l'Environnement Culturel, Département des Etudes et de la Prospective, 1988. 115 leaves. il.
Presents Japanese legislation in the field of cultural property protection as among the world's most restrictive. Describes the interaction of national, regional, and local administrations, and the impact of tourism and urban expansion on Japanese sites (especially Kyoto).

T387 Murphy, J. David. Plunder and preservation: cultural property law and practice in the People's Republic of China. N.Y., Oxford Univ. Pr., 1995. xvi, 205p. il., map.
Comprehensive survey of China's cultural property law and practice. Focuses on the depredation of cultural property in China due to (for example) tomb-robbing and smuggling. Helpful chronological tables of Chinese historical periods and statutory legislation in the People's Republic of China.
Index, p.201–05.

T388 Nabi Khan, Ahmad. Archaeology in Pakistan: administration, legislation and control. [Karachi], Ministry of Culture, Sports and Tourism, Department of Archaeology & Museums, [1990?]. 60p.
Analyzes the administration of cultural property in Pakistan, including legislation and control, the role of the Department of Archaeology, the conservation of archeological sites and historic monuments, the establishment and maintenance of museums, research and publication, and finances.
[Bibliography], p.56–58.

T389 Pal, H. Bisham. The plunder of art. [New Delhi], Abhinav, [1992]. 176p. il. (part col.)
Focuses on the depredations of Indian temple architecture and sculpture, and the theft of paintings and illuminated manuscripts from Indian temple and museum collections.
Index, p.175–76.

T390 Protection or plunder: safeguarding the future of our cultural heritage: Papers of the UNESCO regional seminar on the Movable Cultural Property Convention, Brisbane, Australia, 1986. Ed. by Lyndel V. Prott and James Specht. Canberra, Australian Government Publishing Service, [1989]. 129p.
Contains reports on national protection measures in the Pacific region (Australia, Burma, Fiji, Indonesia, Japan, Korea, Malaysia, New Zealand, Papua New Guinea, Solomon Islands, Thailand, et al.), including the work of UNESCO.
Bibliographical references follow some of the papers. List of UNESCO conventions and recommendations on the protection of cultural property, p.115. Convention on the Means of Prohibiting and Preventing the Illicit Import, Export and Transfer of Ownership of Cultural Property [1970]: [full text and] List of States having deposited an instrument of ratification, acceptance or accession as of 31 December 1987, p.116–25. Select bibliography, p.126–27. Addresses, p.128–29.

T391 Sarkar, H. Museums and protection of monuments and antiquities in India. Delhi, Sundeep Prakashan, 1981. vi, 227p. il., [12] plates, map.
Outlines the history of the museum in India from the 18th century to the present. Covers Indian museums' problems in protecting their cultural property as well as the legislative measures enacted to bolster their attempts to do so. Omits individual states' legislations.
Index, p.213–27.

SEE ALSO: One hundred missing objects (GLAH 2:T265).

AFRICA, OCEANIA, THE AMERICAS

Africa

T392 Illicit traffic of cultural property in Africa. [Paris], ICOM, 1995. 263p.
"Papers presented by the participants in the workshops held in 1993 in Tanzania, and in 1994 in Mali. These workshops, which were organized jointly by ICOM and UNESCO, brought together African museum professionals, as well as customs and police officials."—*Pref.* A series of national reports. Brief entries providing a useful overview of the historical background, the problems encountered, and the measures enacted on this continent.

T393 Plundering Africa's past. Ed. by Peter R. Schmidt and Roderick J. McIntosh. Bloomington, Indiana Univ. Pr., [1996]. xiii, 280p. il. (Carter lecture series)
Important collection of essays documenting the depredation and degradation of Sub-Saharan Africa's cultural heritage from the colonial period up to the present. Includes, in addition to the essays listed here, essays on specific African nations.
Selective contents: The African past endangered, by Peter R. Schmidt and Roderick J. McIntosh; The human right to a cultural heritage: African applications, by Peter R. Schmidt; Saving the heritage: UNESCO's action against illicit traffic in Africa, by Lyndel V. Prott; Just say shame: excising the rot of cultural genocide, by Roderick J. McIntosh; A view inside the illicit trade in African antiquities, by Michel Brent; U.S. efforts in the protection of cultural property: implementation of the 1970 UNESCO Convention, by Maria Papageorge Kouroupas; A conservation dilemma over

African royal art in Cameroon, by Paul Nchoji Nkwi; Past as prologues: empowering Africa's cultural institutions, by Henry John Drewal; Coping with collapse in the 1990s: West African museums, universities, and national patrimonies, by Merrick Posnansky; How accurate are interpretations of African objects in Western museums?, by Francis B. Musonda;

Notes at ends of essays. List of states party to the 1970 UNESCO Convention, p.261. Index, p.266–80.

SEE ALSO: One hundred missing objects (GLAH 2:T265).

Oceania

T394 Charola, A. Elena. Easter Island: the heritage and its conservation. [N.Y.], World Monuments Fund, [1994] 68p. il. (part col), maps. (Future of the past, I)

Documents efforts undertaken to protect and preserve the cultural artefacts of this remote island, especially its renowned colossal statues and sanctuaries. Excellent color photographs.

Glossary, p.65. Bibliography, p.66–67. Easter Island's key sites, p.68.

SEE ALSO: Cultural heritage in Asia and the Pacific (GLAH 2:T384).

Index

The space following the particles "de," "der," "di," "la," and "le" in surnames is disregarded in alphabetizing.

B

C

D

E

F

I

P

S

U

V

W